RECLAIMING
HISTORY

RECLAIMING HISTORY

THE ASSASSINATION OF PRESIDENT JOHN F. KENNEDY

VINCENT BUGLIOSI

W. W. NORTON & COMPANY   NEW YORK   ·   LONDON

For information about permission to reproduce selections from this book, write to Permissions,
W. W. Norton & Company, Inc.,
500 Fifth Avenue, New York, NY 10110

Manufacturing by R. R. Donnelley, Willard Division

Library of Congress Cataloging-in-Publication Data

Bugliosi, Vincent.
Reclaiming history : the assassination of President John F. Kennedy / Vincent Bugliosi. — 1st ed.
p. cm.
Includes bibliographical references and index.
ISBN 978-0-393-04525-3 (hardcover)
1. Kennedy, John F. (John Fitzgerald), 1917–1963—Assassination. 2. Oswald, Lee Harvey.
3. Conspiracies—United States. I. Title.
E842.9.B84 2007
973.922092—dc22
2007001545

W. W. Norton & Company, Inc.
500 Fifth Avenue, New York, N.Y. 10110
www.wwnorton.com

W. W. Norton & Company Ltd.
Castle House, 75/76 Wells Street, W1T 3QT

1 2 3 4 5 6 7 8 9 0

To the historical record, knowing that nothing in the present can exist without the paternity of history, and hence, the latter is sacred, and should never be tampered with or defiled by untruths.

Contents

Introduction

At approximately 12:30 p.m. on November 22, 1963, while President John F. Kennedy, the most powerful man in the free world, rode in his presidential limousine slowly past the Texas School Book Depository Building and down Elm Street in Dallas, Texas, three shots rang out from the southeasternmost window on the sixth floor of the building. One of the bullets struck the president in the upper right part of his back and exited the front of his throat, another entered the right rear of his head, exiting and shattering the right side of his head. While the presidential limousine screeched away to Parkland Memorial Hospital, where he was pronounced dead shortly thereafter, John F. Kennedy, his life blood gushing from his body, lay mortally wounded on his wife Jacqueline's lap. The assassin had succeeded in brutally cutting down, at the age of forty-six, the thirty-fifth president of these United States, a man whose wit, charm, and intelligence had captivated a world audience. The assassin's bullets had also extinguished a flame of hope for millions of Americans who saw in the youthful president at least the promise of excellence in national life.

As the years have shown, Kennedy's assassination immediately transformed him into a mythical, larger-than-life figure whose hold on the nation's imagination resonates to this very day. "The image of Kennedy is not based on what he accomplished, but on his promise, the hope he held out," said historian Stephen Ambrose in 1993.[1] Years earlier, *New York Times* columnist James Reston wrote similarly that "what was killed in Dallas was not only the President but the promise. The heart of the Kennedy legend is what might have been. All this is apparent in the faces of the people who come daily to his grave on the Arlington Hill."[2] In 1993, Ambrose added, "There's a very strong sense that if he had not died, we would not have suffered the 30 years of nightmare that followed—the race riots, the white backlash, assassinations, Vietnam, Watergate, Iran-Contra."[3] While this is, of course, speculative, what is not is JFK's legacy of rekindling the notion that public service is a noble calling. If it is any barometer of the sense of hope and promise that Kennedy inspired in the American people, the ever-decreasing trust by Americans in their government down through the years started with the Kennedy assassination and the subsequent erroneously perceived notion—fostered by conspiracy theorists—that the government concealed the full truth about the assassination from them. Trust in our leaders in Washington to do what is right for the people plummeted from 76 percent around the time of the assassination to a low of 19 percent three decades later.[4] "There's such a gulf in history between the day before and the day after Kennedy's assassination," says historian Howard Jones of the University of Alabama. "It's as if we passed through a hundred years in a day."[5] In 2004, a national poll showed that trust in our government to do what's right was only at 36 percent.[6]

Since Kennedy's death, the nation has not seen, in any of his successors, his cosmopolitan intellectualism or the oratorical eloquence with which he sought to lead the nation by the power of his words. What also is beyond dispute was the way Kennedy, the first president born in the twentieth century, inspired the young of his generation by his youthful vigor and the bold, fresh initiatives of his New Frontier, such as his Peace Corps, civil rights bills, and pledge to put a man on the moon. Idealism was in the air, and the nation's capital had never seen such an invasion of young people who wanted to change the world for the better. The most accurate indicator of Kennedy's popularity among the nation's youth at the time is a 2003 Gallup Poll of people of various age groups as to whom they regarded as our greatest president. In the fifty-to-sixty-four-year age group, those who were young during Kennedy's presidency, Kennedy ranked number one among all presidents. Among all age groups he ranked number two, behind only Lincoln.[7]

Undoubtedly, two other factors have burnished and enlarged the Kennedy aura. He was among the most attractive and naturally charismatic public figures the nation has seen. And the Choate- and Harvard-educated son of privilege* and wealth ignored the wishes of his powerful father and a medical condition that could easily have exempted him from combat and became a World War II hero. Kennedy historian Richard Reeves writes that JFK had a "range of illnesses" that commenced as a child. "He could never have passed a real military physical examination, so he used the riches and influence of his father, Joseph P. Kennedy, to become a naval officer. The old man persuaded friends in the military to accept a certificate of good health, a false one, from a family doctor . . . [JFK's] executive officer, Leonard Thom, wrote home that Kennedy was the only man in the Navy who faked good health."[8] After seeing extensive combat in the Japanese theater, not long after midnight on August 2, 1943, in the Solomon Islands in the South Pacific, the twenty-five-year-old navy lieutenant personally rescued one of the crew members of the patrol torpedo boat (PT 109)[†] he commanded when it was cut in half and sunk by the Japanese destroyer *Amagiri*, by swimming four hours to the nearest island towing the man by attaching a strap from the man's life jacket to his teeth. In a typical example of Kennedy's well-known laconic wit, when he was once asked how he became a war hero, he responded with his famous understated smile, "It was involuntary. They sank my boat."

Kennedy's magic started with the people (particularly, as indicated, the young, to whom the words of his inaugural address seemed to be aimed), as evidenced by the fact that

---

*As is well known, John Fitzgerald Kennedy, the second of nine children of Joseph and Rose Kennedy, was born into great wealth, and the family's domiciles reflected it. The Kennedys summered at their six-acre compound containing three homes in Hyannis Port, Massachusetts, on Cape Cod off the waters of Nantucket Sound, and vacationed in the winter at their Palm Beach, Florida, mansion off the Atlantic Ocean. Even the clan's main sports reflected plutocracy—tennis, boating, swimming, and, oh yes, *touch* football.

†PT boats were known to be "dangerous beyond the call of duty" (Blair and Blair, *Search for JFK*, p.158).

although he had won the presidency with only 49.7 percent of the popular vote, a Harris Poll right after his inaugural showed his approval rating jumping up to an incredible 92 percent. Though his rating would soon return to the atmosphere, the speech, considered by many one of the finest inaugural addresses in the nation's history, demonstrated that Kennedy was no ordinary politician. It wasn't just the words of the speech ("Ask not what your country can do for you—ask what you can do for your country"; "Let the word go forth from this time and place to friend and foe alike, that the torch has been passed to a new generation of Americans—born in this century, tempered by war, disciplined by a hard and bitter peace [cold war], proud of our ancient heritage"), but the dramatic way in which he uttered them on this memorably bright day, a day, author Thurston Clarke wrote, where the cold winter air turned his breath into white clouds, the words appearing to be going forth into the exhilarating air. "God, I'd like to be able to do what that boy did there," his political opponent Barry Goldwater said. The power in Kennedy's delivery of the words had to be helped by the fact that apart from the "Ask not" clause, the words were written by him and told his own story.[9]

In writing this book about the assassination, I inevitably got into, though tangentially, the man, John F. Kennedy. Governor John Connally's wife, who herself was married to a handsome and dynamic man, wrote that "I thought I knew what 'charisma' meant before I met Jack Kennedy, but our young President gave the word a new definition."[10] But there was more to the man than mere charisma, an indelible element to his personality that lassoed the attention of the onlooker. When Kennedy died, the worldwide mourning that his death induced was unprecedented. Perhaps the most impressive testament of what Kennedy possessed was the way his death was greeted by the tens of millions of people behind the Iron Curtain during the very height of the cold war. The masses behind the curtain were *only* fed Soviet propaganda, the level of censorship being virtually complete, isolating the people within from the outside world. Yet when Kennedy died, the evidence is overwhelming that millions of Soviet citizens and those in the Soviet Bloc satellite countries in Eastern Europe took his death almost as hard as we in America did, these adversary countries being immediately swept up in national mourning and tears. Under the prevailing censorship, how much could the people of these nations have possibly been exposed to Kennedy, the tiniest snippet of his person or his words reaching them during his three years in power? In addition to the youthful vigor and indefinable charisma that he projected, my sense is that these masses, who heard so few of his words, and could understand none of them, picked up in the sound of his voice and the inherent decency and sincerity in his always pleasant face and smile, that he was different, and it was these additional critical components that enabled the essence of the man, from just a glance, to pierce the curtain of iron that had descended upon these countries and to touch the hearts of its citizens. How else, for instance, can one explain what Nobel Prize–winning novelist John Steinbeck witnessed in Warsaw when news of Kennedy's assassination reached the Polish capital? Steinbeck had been on a cultural tour of Iron Curtain countries at the time, and he said that the "great sorrow" he saw among the Polish people over Kennedy's death "was the most fantastic thing I ever saw. I've never seen anything like it. The Poles said they'd never seen its like either, *for anyone*."[11]*

---

*People spoke of JFK's "irresistible charm," it was well known that he was not vindictive toward his political opponents, and unlike his brother Bobby, he had few, if any, bitter enemies. Except for segregationists, the militant right, and some in big business, from what I have read people liked John F. Kennedy. As *Look* magazine observed, "Even his political opponents liked and respected him" (Attwood, "In Memory of John F. Kennedy," p.12).

Political author Thomas Powers cannot be accused of hyperbole when he observes that Kennedy's assassination "was probably the greatest single traumatic event in American history."[12] Years later, it remains a festering wound on the nation's psyche. Though Powers made his remark several years ago, its truth continues to this day. As we will see in the next section of this book, there is little comparison between the nation's response to Kennedy's death and its response to the World Trade Center catastrophe on September 11, 2001, even though the response to the latter was enormous. Just two indications among many of the difference. On the day of Kennedy's assassination and for three consecutive days thereafter, all three national television networks suspended all of their commercial shows and advertising. And while only a relatively small number of books have been written about 9-11, far more books continue to be written to this very day, over forty years later, about Kennedy's assassination. How could one death cause greater personal anguish to more people than three thousand deaths? The World Trade Center victims were known only to their loved ones, entirely unknown to the rest of the country. But the dazzling First Couple of JFK and Jackie, and their two children, Caroline and John-John, were perceived by many as the closest to royalty this nation had ever seen. Nearly all Americans felt they knew JFK intimately, his charm and wit regularly lighting up the television screen at home. This is why polls showed that millions of Americans took his assassination like a "death in the family." Some, even more deeply than the death of their parents, because, as Kennedy confidant Ted Sorenson observed, the latter often represented a "loss of the past," while Kennedy's death was to them an "incalculable loss of the future."[13] It was written that "never in the land did so many, out of a feeling of personal identification with a dead leader," mourn his death.[14]

It is believed that more words have been written about the assassination than any other single, one-day event in world history. Close to one thousand books have been written. So why the need for this book, which can only add to an already overwhelming surfeit of literature on the case? The answer is that over 95 percent of the books on the case happen to be pro-conspiracy and anti–Warren Commission, so certainly there is a need for far more books on the other side to give a much better balance to the debate. But more importantly, although there have been hundreds of books on the assassination, no book has even attempted to be a comprehensive and fair evaluation of the *entire* case, including all of the major conspiracy theories.

On the issue of fairness, the more I studied the assassination and the writings of the conspiracy theorists and Warren Commission critics, the more I became disturbed with them. Though they accused the bipartisan Warren Commission of bias, distorting the evidence, and deliberately suppressing the truth from the American people, I found that for the most part it was they, not the Warren Commission, who were guilty of these very same things. I haven't read all of the pro-conspiracy books. I don't know anyone who has. I have, however, read all the major ones, and a goodly number of minor ones. And with a few notable exceptions, when the vast majority of these conspiracy authors are confronted with evidence that is incompatible with their fanciful theories, to one degree or another their modus operandi is to do one of two things—twist, warp, and distort the evidence, or simply ignore it—both of which are designed to deceive their readers. Waiting for the conspiracy theorists to tell the truth is a little like leaving the front-porch light on for Jimmy Hoffa.

Ninety-nine percent of the conspiracy community are not, of course, writers and authors. These conspiracy "buffs" (as they are frequently called) are obsessed with the assassination, have formed networks among their peers, and actually attend conspiracy-oriented conventions around the country. Though most of them are as kooky as a three-dollar bill in their beliefs and paranoia about the assassination, it is my sense that their motivations are patriotic and that they are sincere in their misguided and uninformed conclusions. I cannot say that about the conspiracy authors. Unlike the buffs—virtually none of whom have a copy of the forty official volumes on the case—the authors possess and work with these volumes. Yet the majority of them knowingly mislead their readers by lies, omissions, and deliberately distorting the official record. I realize this is an astonishing charge I am making. Unfortunately, it happens to be the truth. In any other field, such as the scientific or literary disciplines, even a fraction of these lies, distortions, and omissions by a member would cause the author to be ostracized professionally by his colleagues and peers. But in the conspiracy community of the Kennedy assassination, where one's peers have turned their mothers' pictures against the wall and are telling even bigger lies themselves, and where the American public is unaware of these lies, not only is this type of deception routinely accepted by most members of the community, but the perpetrators are treated as celebrities who lecture for handsome fees and sign autographs at conventions of Warren Commission critics and conspiracy theorists.

When the Warren Commission released its 888-page, 296,000-word report on September 24, 1964, a national poll showed that only a minority of Americans (31.6 percent) rejected the conclusion of the Commission that Oswald had acted alone.[15] But through their torrent of books, radio and TV talk shows, movies, college lectures, and so on, over the years the shrill voice of the conspiracy theorists finally penetrated the consciousness of the American people and actually succeeded in discrediting the Warren Commission Report[*] and convincing the overwhelming majority of Americans that Oswald either was a part of a high-level conspiracy or was just a patsy framed by some exotic and elaborate group of conspirators ranging from anti-Castro Cuban exiles to organized crime working in league with U.S. intelligence. Although I had commenced my work on the case with a completely open mind, I found there was absolutely no substance to their charges and that they have performed a flagrant disservice to the American public. Dissent is what makes this country the great nation that it is, but this was not responsible dissent. This was wanton and reckless disregard for the facts of the case.

Throughout the years, national polls have consistently shown that the percentage of Americans who believe that there was a conspiracy in the assassination usually fluctuates from 70 to 80 percent, down to 10 to 20 percent for those who believe only one person was involved, with about 5 to 15 percent having no opinion. The most recent Gallup Poll, conducted on November 10–12, 2003, shows that a remarkable 75 percent of the American public reject the findings of the Warren Commission and believe there was a conspiracy in the assassination. Only 19 percent believe the assassin acted alone, with 6 percent having no opinion.[†] It is the ambitious objective of this work to turn the per-

---

[*]Officially called the *Report of the President's Commission on the Assassination of President John F. Kennedy*.

[†]Contrary to popular belief, the Warren Commission didn't quite say there was no conspiracy in the assassination. The commissioners wrote, "The Commission has found *no evidence* that either Lee Harvey Oswald or Jack Ruby was part of any conspiracy, domestic or foreign, to assassinate President Kennedy . . . Because of the difficulty of proving negatives to a certainty the possibility of others being involved with either Oswald or Ruby cannot be rejected categorically, but if there is any such evidence it has been beyond the reach of all

centages around in the debate. If I can even come close to doing so I will feel I have achieved something meaningful. Such an objective, after all, is not misplaced when the Kennedy assassination is perhaps the most important murder case ever, arguably altering the course of American as well as world history.

It should be added that the millions of Americans who have been hoodwinked into buying into the conspiracy illusion don't believe that Oswald conspired with some other lowly malcontent like himself to assassinate the president. Instead, though most don't clearly articulate the thought in their mind, they believe that Oswald was merely the triggerman for organized crime, a foreign nation, or conspirators who walked the highest corridors of power in our nation's capital—people or groups who eliminated Kennedy because his policies were antithetical to their interests. Such a belief, gestating for decades in the nation's marrow, obviously has to have had a deleterious effect on the way Americans view those who lead them and determine their destiny. Indeed, Jefferson Morley, former Washington editor of the *Nation*, observes that Kennedy's assassination has been "a kind of national Rorschach test of the American political psyche. What Americans think about the Kennedy assassination reveals what they think about their government."[16]

Nineteenth-century French statesman and author Alexis de Tocqueville noted a characteristic of the American body politic that he felt boded well for America: its capacity for self-correction. But in the Kennedy assassination, we'll soon be approaching the half-century mark, and the substantial majority of Americans still erroneously believe that their thirty-fifth president was murdered as a result of a high-level conspiracy.

My professional interest in the Kennedy assassination dates back to March of 1986 when I was approached by a British production company, London Weekend Television (LWT), to "prosecute" Lee Harvey Oswald as the alleged assassin of President Kennedy in a proposed twenty-one-hour television trial to be shown in England and several other countries, including the United States. I immediately had misgivings. Up to then, I had consistently turned down offers to appear on television in artificial courtroom settings. But when I heard more of what LWT was contemplating, my misgivings quickly dissolved. Although this could not be the real trial of Oswald, inasmuch as he was dead, LWT, working with a large budget, had conceived and was putting together the closest thing to a real trial of Oswald that there would likely ever be, the trial in London being the only "prosecution" of Oswald ever conducted with the real witnesses in the Kennedy assassination. Through painstaking and dogged effort, LWT had managed to locate and persuade most of these original key lay witnesses, many of whom had refused to even talk to the media for years, to testify in the television trial of Oswald. There would be absolutely no script whatsoever (Mark Redhead, the LWT producer for the project, said to me, "I assure you, there will be no script. The script will be your yellow pad, which I've been told you have a love affair with"), and no actors would be used. Lucius Bun-

---

the investigative agencies and resources of the United States and has not come to the attention of this Commission" (WR, pp.21–22).

Note: Throughout this book emphasis by italics in quotations has been added by the author unless otherwise indicated.

ton, a highly respected U.S. district judge for the Western District of Texas, would preside over the trial. And a real jury, selected from the jury rolls of the Dallas federal district court, each having served on a federal jury in Dallas in 1985,[17] was to be impaneled to hear the case, completely free to vote whichever way the jurors pleased on the issue of whether Oswald was guilty or not guilty.* Gerry Spence, about whom the great trial lawyer Edward Bennett Williams once said, "If I ever got in trouble, I'd want Gerry Spence to defend me," and who had emerged as the leading criminal defense lawyer in America, had been selected to oppose me and represent Oswald.

Nothing like this had ever been done before on television (re-creations of real trials invariably being with scripts and actors), and LWT had ambitiously started at the top of the hill with the Kennedy assassination. Originally, the trial was to be held in Dallas, but fearful of the media circus it felt sure the trial would inevitably create, LWT quietly jetted everyone to England for a trial in a London courtroom that was an exact replica of a Dallas federal courtroom.

The historical importance of the trial was immediately apparent to Spence and me. Unlike their appearances before the Warren Commission and the House Select Committee on Assassinations (HSCA), where they testified in a non-adversarial context and were not cross-examined, the key witnesses in the assassination would now be exposed to cross-examination—the greatest legal engine ever invented, one legal scholar wrote, for the discovery of the truth. And as a London paper later wrote, "Witnesses who had thought they were in for an anxiety free, all-expense paid trip to London reeled out of the witness box after being subjected to sustained barrages of cross-examination."[18]

I proceeded to set aside everything I was doing, and seven days a week immersed myself completely in the prosecution of the case, virtually insulating myself from the outside world. For close to five months, I averaged between 100 and 120 hours per week, my only break being when I would visit my elderly parents for two hours each week. The reason for this effort was simply that the task was monumental. The Warren Commission in 1964 and the HSCA, which reinvestigated the assassination for over two years in the late 1970s, had wrestled with the complexities of the case, trying to come to grips with its seemingly endless issues.

In preparing for the trial in the average murder case, even a complex one, for the most part all a prosecutor has to look at, in terms of reading, are the police reports, coroner's report, witness statements, and the transcript of the preliminary hearing. And the only person raising issues against him is the defense attorney. But here, in preparing for trial, I was dealing with the forty massive official volumes of small print on the case (the twenty-six volumes of the Warren Commission plus the one-volume Warren Report, which summarizes the Commission's findings, and the twelve volumes of the HSCA together with the one-volume HSCA Report, which likewise is a summary of the HSCA findings) and the hundreds of issues raised by countless Warren Commission critics and conspiracy

---

*Even the court reporter was a real one, from the federal Eastern District of Virginia. Eagerly anticipating the trial, Judge Bunton told the media, "If Oswald had been tried, any judge would have wanted to do it. It's going to be just as true to life as they can get it—with the real witnesses and a real jury flown in from Dallas. It's going to record a lot of what would have developed if, in fact, Lee Harvey Oswald had come to trial." Bunton explained that the trial would take some liberties with history. "It will be tried in federal court as opposed to state court. At the time that President Kennedy was killed, it was not a federal offense to kill the president. Since that time the law has been changed." (United Press International, July 17, 1986) The case was tried under the Federal Rules of Criminal Procedure.

theorists in their articles and books. Plus, all the new material gathered by the LWT staff, a very competent and dedicated group of people ably led by producer Mark Redhead and executive director Richard Drewett. Redhead actually traveled to several countries working on the case. LWT's two chief researchers for the docu-trial were Kerry Platman and Richard L. Tomlinson, each of whom did an excellent, highly professional job.

With both the Warren Commission and the Select Committee, the areas of inquiry had been compartmentalized, separate groups of lawyers being assigned to work on specific parts of the case only—for example, the identity of President Kennedy's assassin, the basic facts of the assassination, Lee Harvey Oswald's background, Jack Ruby's killing of Oswald, possible conspiratorial relationships, and so on. But working alone, I had to know as much of the entire case as possible. And having the burden of proving Oswald's guilt beyond a reasonable doubt, I could not afford to say to myself, "Well, this is only a television trial. I'll just ignore this issue." If I had been so cavalier, I knew the issue I ignored could be utilized by the defense to raise a reasonable doubt in the jury's mind. After all, the issue was no longer whether or not Oswald murdered Kennedy, one of the two main issues the Warren Commission dealt with. The issue now was different. Even if the jury ultimately came to believe from the evidence that Oswald murdered the president, would they believe it *beyond a reasonable doubt*? Because if they didn't, the verdict would still have to be not guilty. As in any criminal case, the defense in London never had any legal burden to prove Oswald's innocence or even to present a coherent or plausible alternative account of what happened. To prevent a conviction, it was enough for Spence to plant a reasonable doubt in the minds of one or more jurors. Playing on this reality, Spence would later tell the London jury, "There is only one truth in this case, and this is that nobody knows the truth."

During my examination of the evidence in preparation for the trial, I found that virtually every piece of evidence against Oswald maddeningly had some small but explainable problem with it. However, two things became obvious to me: One was that Oswald, an emotionally unhinged political malcontent who hated America, was as guilty as sin. Based on the Himalayan mountain of uncontroverted evidence against Oswald, anyone who could believe he was innocent would probably also believe someone claiming to have heard a cow speaking the Spanish language. Secondly, there was not one speck of *credible* evidence that Oswald was framed or that he was a hit man for others in a conspiracy to murder the president. I meticulously examined every major conspiracy theory that had thus far been adduced, and although there were a few (a precious few) that at first blush seemed plausible, upon sober scrutiny they did complete violence to all conventional notions of logic and common sense. Though there are some notable exceptions, by and large the persistent ranting of the Warren Commission critics, some of whom were screaming the word *conspiracy* before the fatal bullet had even come to rest, came to remind me, as H. L. Mencken said in a different context, of dogs barking idiotically through endless nights.

The hard-core conspiracy theorists believe not only that there was a massive conspiracy to kill the president, but that the Warren Commission learned about this conspiracy, and, as pawns of the U.S. government, entered into a new conspiracy to cover it up. "The Warren Commission engaged in a cover-up of the truth and issued a report that misrepresented or distorted almost every relevant fact about the crime," Howard Roffman writes in his book, *Presumed Guilty*.[19] Gerald D. McKnight, a professor of history, no less, writes that the Warren Commission members were "men intent on deceiving the nation." Just in the area of the president's autopsy alone, he says, "the Commission sanctioned perjury, connived at the destruction of the best evidence, boycotted key witnesses, and deliberately and knowingly suppressed material medical records and legal documents."[20] There were "two conspiracies," conspiracy theorist Jim Marrs confidently asserts. "One was the conspiracy to kill the president. The second conspiracy was the conspiracy to cover up the first conspiracy," the second conspiracy being committed by "officials high within the U.S. government to hide the truth from the American public."

One of the first purveyors of this silliness was New Orleans district attorney Jim Garrison. During his investigation of Clay Shaw for the president's murder, he said that "the United States government—meaning the present administration, Lyndon Johnson's administration—is obstructing the investigation . . . It has concealed the true facts, to be blunt about it, to protect the individuals involved in the assassination of John Kennedy."[21] The promotional literature for conspiracy theorist Carl Oglesby's 1992 book, *Who Killed JFK?*, likewise reflects this commonly held belief of the conspiracy community, which it accepts as a mosaic truth: "In this clear, readable book, prominent assassination researcher Carl Oglesby proves that JFK must have been killed by a conspiracy, not a lone gunman. Even scarier, he knows that the U.S. government has been, *and still is* covering up that conspiracy." If we're to believe Oglesby, our current federal government (as well as all previous ones since 1963) is engaged in a conspiracy to cover up the truth in the assassination.

Apparently, then, such distinguished Americans as Chief Justice Earl Warren, Senators John Sherman Cooper and Richard B. Russell, Representatives Gerald Ford and Hale Boggs, former CIA director Allen Dulles and former president of the World Bank John J. McCloy (the members of the Warren Commission), as well as the Commission's general counsel, J. Lee Rankin, a former solicitor general of the United States, and fourteen prominent members of the American Bar (assistant counsels to the Commission), people of impeccable honor and reputation, got together in some smoky backroom and *all* of them agreed, for some ungodly reason, to do the most dishonorable deed imaginable—give organized crime, the CIA, the military-industrial complex, or whoever was behind the assassination, a free pass in the murder of the president of the United States. And in the process, not only risk destroying everything they had worked for—their reputation and legacy to their families—but expose themselves to prosecution for the crime of accessory after the fact to murder. Ask yourself this: would Earl Warren, for instance, risk being remembered as the chief justice of the United States Supreme Court who was an accessory after the fact to the murder of this nation's president, one who disgraced himself, his country, and the highest court in the land? The mere asking of the question demonstrates the absurdity of the thought. As political columnist Charles Krauthammer put it, it is preposterous to believe that "Earl Warren, a liberal so principled that he would not countenance the conviction of one Ernesto Miranda [of *Miranda v. Arizona* fame] on the grounds that police had neglected to read him his rights, was an accessory to a fascist coup d'etat."[22] Indeed, why would any of the members of the Warren Commission and their staff stake their good reputation on a report they prepared which they knew to be fraudulent?[*]

And if the conspiracy to kill Kennedy was as obvious as conspiracy theorists want us to believe, how then could the Warren Commission members have had any confidence

---

[*]It is an anomaly that Earl Warren, someone who one would think would be viewed like Caesar's wife among all sensible people, would be attacked and his integrity impugned by those from all areas of the political spectrum, even by many on the political left, who heretofore had sung his praises for the progressive direction he had taken the court in the area of civil rights. Apparently the Kennedy assassination trumped everything.

that the conspiracy's existence would not have surfaced in the future? Moreover, if we adopt the cover-up theory, did all seven Commission members, on their own, decide to suppress the truth? Or was there a ringleader or architect of the cover-up, like Warren? If the latter, how was he able to get the other six members (and, necessarily, a significant number of the Commission's assistant counsels and staff) to go along with his nefarious scheme? Indeed, not knowing what their response might be, wouldn't he have been deathly afraid to even approach them with such a monumentally base and criminal proposal? The whole notion is too ridiculous to even contemplate. Adding a touch of humor to it all, as Commission member Gerald Ford said, "The thought that Earl Warren and I would conspire on anything is preposterous."[23]

A concomitant fact that's obvious but never mentioned is that if the Warren Commission covered up for those it knew to be responsible for the assassination, it would necessarily also be guilty of falsely accusing Oswald and framing him for Kennedy's murder. But would any sane individual actually believe this?

Don't these conspiracy theorists know what all sensible adults have learned from their own personal lives? That it's almost impossible to keep a secret? Even a small one? Yet here, with not one, but two massive conspiracies, not one word, one syllable, has leaked out in over forty years. As I told the jury in London, "I'll agree that three people can keep a secret. But only if two are dead." Making the proposition of containing a secret in the Kennedy case even more implausible than it already is, anyone with knowledge of a Kennedy conspiracy who came forward could expect to receive very large sums of money from the media. And if we're to believe the conspiracy theorists, not only were the multitudinous conspirators so incredibly efficient that they never once did anything wrong that revealed, even remotely, their existence, but not one of them has become disgruntled and wants to strike a bargain with the authorities (most likely immunity from prosecution for his testimony against the others), no ex-wife or mistress has decided to get even by talking, and not one of the members of the conspiracy or the cover-up has wanted to clear his conscience on his deathbed.

The point should be made that even if a sense of honor and duty were not the primary motivating factors in the Warren Commission's work, simple self-interest would naturally have induced its members not to try to cover up the existence of a conspiracy if, in fact, they found one. As Commission assistant counsel David Slawson, whose area of responsibility, along with William T. Coleman Jr., was to determine if there was a conspiracy, told me, "We were all motivated to find something unexpected, such as other gunmen or a hidden conspiracy. *It would have made us heroes.* But these hopes gradually disappeared as the evidence that it was just Oswald rolled in."[24] (Kenneth Klein, assistant deputy chief counsel for the later HSCA, said essentially the same thing in his article, "Facts Knit the Single Bullet Theory": "Since the validity of the Warren Commission's finding that Lee Harvey Oswald was the lone assassin rested firmly on the validity of the single-bullet theory, the staff members of the Select Committee would have been thrilled to have disproved it. To have done so would surely have led to fame and fortune. Only one thing prevented us from doing so, the evidence.—Goodby fame. Goodby fortune.")[25]* Slawson, by the way, a Harvard Law School graduate who just recently retired

---

*And naturally, this motivation to uncover a conspiracy, if there was one, applies equally well to the media. As CBS television news anchor Dan Rather has said, "If I could prove Oswald didn't do it or Oswald didn't act alone, it would be the greatest accomplishment of my career" (*USA Today*, February 4, 1992).

as a professor of law at the University of Southern California, not only was a supporter of Jack Kennedy when he ran for president in 1960, but got to know him and worked on his campaign, his Denver law office actually allowing him to spend a substantial portion of his time working for Kennedy instead of for the firm. That's one more reason why the position of conspiracy theorists—that someone like Slawson would deliberately turn a blind eye to the existence of a conspiracy—is absurd on its face.

As Warren Commission staff member Richard M. Mosk, a lifelong Democrat, said, "I was a young private sector lawyer, just out of the military, and I certainly had no incentive to cover up anything. Indeed, my father, Stanley Mosk, then California attorney general, was instrumental in running President Kennedy's 1960 campaign in California and was close to the Kennedy family."[26]

In his memoirs, Chief Justice Earl Warren, after pointing out that his commission uncovered "no facts upon which to hypothesize a conspiracy," and that separate investigations by the FBI, Central Intelligence Agency, Secret Service, and Departments of State and Defense could not find "any evidence of conspiracy," wrote, "To say now that these [agencies], as well as the Commission, suppressed, neglected to unearth, or overlooked evidence of a conspiracy would be an indictment of the entire government of the United States. It would mean the whole structure was absolutely corrupt from top to bottom, not one person of high or low rank willing to come forward to expose the villainy, in spite of the fact that the entire country bitterly mourned the death of its young President."[27]*

The late CBS news commentator Eric Sevareid, commenting on the members of the Warren Commission being men of unblemished reputation and high national standing, observed eloquently, "The deepest allegiance of men like Chief Justice Warren, or John McCloy, does not lie with any president, political party, or current cause—it lies with history, their name and place in history. That is all they live for in their later years. If they knowingly suppressed or distorted decisive evidence about such an event as a presidential murder, their descendants would bear accursed names forever. The notion they would do such a thing is idiotic."[28]

Yet the conspiracy theorists are convinced that even before the Warren Commission, the whole purpose of President Lyndon Johnson establishing it was to whitewash what really happened, either because he was complicit himself or because he was fearful that if it came out that Russia or Cuba was behind the assassination, it might precipitate a nuclear war. But this ignores the fact that the Warren Commission (five of whose members were Republican, unlikely candidates to cover up anything, much less a murder, for a Democratic president) wasn't even LBJ's idea. As far as is known, Yale Law School's Walt Rostow first suggested it to LBJ's press secretary, Bill Moyers, in a telephone conversation on the morning of November 24, 1963, the day after the assassination. ("My suggestion is that a presidential commission be appointed of very distinguished citizens in the very near future. Bipartisan and above politics," Rostow told Moyers.) Almost concurrently, the *Washington Post*, lobbied by LBJ's own Justice Department (particularly Deputy Attorney General Nicholas Katzenbach), let it be known to the White House that it favored the idea also.

---

*"In their exploitation of a national tragedy, [the conspiracy theorists] have impugned the character and motives of hundreds of reluctant participants in that disaster. By plain inference they have indicted scores of public servants, from the lowliest cop on the beat in Dallas to the Chief Justice of the United States, for malfeasance bordering on treason" (Roberts, *Truth about the Assassination*, p. 120).

LBJ, in fact, was originally strongly opposed to the idea, saying it was "very bad" and the inquiry into the assassination should be a "state matter" handled by the attorney general of the state of Texas with only the assistance of the FBI. "[We can't] start invading local jurisdictions," he said before he was eventually persuaded by some members of his staff, cabinet, and Congress that a presidential commission would be the most appropriate and effective way to investigate the assassination. LBJ was so opposed to the idea that he called FBI Director J. Edgar Hoover on the morning of November 25, asking Hoover to use "any influence you got with the *Post*" to discourage it from pushing the appointment of a presidential commission in its editorials. Hoover responded, "I don't have much influence with the *Post* because I frankly don't read it. I view it like the *Daily Worker* [a Communist publication]."[29]

Conspiracy theorists can find little comfort in the finding of the HSCA that President Kennedy "was probably assassinated as a result of a conspiracy."[30] Nowhere did the HSCA conclude that any of the groups frequently mentioned by the theorists, such as the CIA, FBI, Secret Service, organized crime, Cuban government, anti-Castro Cuban exiles, and so on, were involved in any conspiracy to kill the president. To the contrary, the select committee specifically concluded just the opposite, that they were "not involved."[31] For example, the HSCA said, "Based on the Committee's entire investigation, it concluded that the Secret Service, FBI, and CIA were not involved in the assassination."[32] The sole basis for the HSCA's conclusion that there was a conspiracy was its contested and far less-than-unanimous belief that in addition to the three shots it determined that Oswald fired from the Book Depository Building (two of which, it concluded, struck the president), there was a "high probability" that a fourth shot, which it said did not hit the president,[33] was fired from the grassy knoll. If such were actually the case, a conclusion of conspiracy would be compelled—unless one drew the unrealistic inference that two people, acting totally independently of each other, just happened to try and kill the president at the same place and moment in time.

The basis for this fourth-shot conclusion was an acoustical analysis of a police Dictabelt recording from Dallas police headquarters containing sounds, the HSCA believed, from a police motorcycle in Dealey Plaza whose radio transmitting switch was stuck in the "on" position. HSCA acoustic experts thought that the sounds heard on the tape were probably those of four gunshots. However, as is discussed in considerable depth in an endnote, this fourth-shot conclusion has been completely discredited and proved to be in error by subsequent analyses of the Dictabelt. In 1982, twelve of the most prominent experts in ballistic acoustics in the country were commissioned by the National Research Council to reexamine the Dictabelt. The panel found "conclusively" from other concurrent and identifiable background noise on the Dictabelt that the sound which the HSCA experts believed to be a fourth shot actually occurred "about one minute after the assassination," when the presidential limousine was long gone down Stemmons Freeway on its way to Parkland Memorial Hospital. In fact, knowing I could rebut it, Gerry Spence did not even bother to introduce the fourth-shot Dictabelt evidence at the trial in London.

When one removes the Dictabelt "fourth shot" from the HSCA findings, all that is really left is the HSCA's conclusion that Oswald killed Kennedy, and the fact that the committee found no evidence of any person or group having conspired with Oswald, the identical findings of the Warren Commission. But the conspiracy theorists are in even worse shape with the HSCA findings than with those of the Warren Commission. Their tired allegation that the Warren Commission, because of a bias or under instructions going in, suppressed evidence of a conspiracy, obviously cannot be applied to the HSCA, which concluded (erroneously, we now know) that there *was* a conspiracy. Indeed, to *support* its conclusion of a conspiracy and establish its credibility, any bias the HSCA might have had would have been in the opposite direction—to look for and reveal evidence of a conspiracy, not suppress it.

What kept me up working until three o'clock every morning in my study preparing for the London trial was the knowledge that this would be the first real opportunity for a national television audience to see why the Warren Commission ultimately concluded that Oswald was responsible for the assassination of John F. Kennedy.* Other than the massive media coverage of the assassination back in 1963 and early 1964, previously, in books and on television, all that the public had heard in depth was the persistent and jackhammer message of the conspiracy theorists and Warren Commission critics. By and large, then, all that the vast majority of the public had heard, as of 1986, was the conclusion of the Warren Commission, not the basis for that conclusion. True, the basis for the Commission's conclusion was available, but how many Americans had purchased the twenty-seven volumes put out by the Warren Commission? This realization impelled me to make sure I was as prepared at the trial as I could possibly be.

I organized and prepared the prosecution of Oswald in the same way I had done with the many other murder cases I had prosecuted in my career at the Los Angeles County district attorney's office, among other things interviewing my witnesses to the point where several told me they were more prepared than when they had testified before the Warren Commission. And through my interviews, a few new pieces of damaging circumstantial evidence against Oswald surfaced.

The defense was also hard at work. I learned that Spence had two lawyers in his Jackson Hole, Wyoming, law firm working full-time on the case assisting him, and near the end LWT dispatched its chief researcher on the case, who had a doctoral degree in history, to Spence's home to live and work with him there for three weeks. Spence said, "I worked as hard in preparation for this trial as if I had defended Lee Harvey Oswald in the flesh."[34]

Indeed, anyone watching the trial on television could tell from Spence's and my intensity that we were very serious. It was the same with the jury. Jack S. Morgan, who had just finished sitting on a Dallas federal jury a few weeks before LWT called him to sit on the London jury, became the foreman of the jury in London. As he says, "All of us jurors in London felt a strong responsibility to reach the correct decision as to Oswald's guilt or innocence. We gave our best in our discussions and balloting, just as we would have had Oswald been tried in Texas before us. The whole concept of this court case was presented to us in such a way that the judge, lawyers and jurors considered it a real trial. It was the only one that Mr. Oswald would get, so we needed to be accurate in sifting through the facts to determine the truth."[35]

The trial in London had all the earmarks and reality of an actual trial. The courtroom was packed, the witnesses were sworn to testify to the truth, and there was a real judge and jury listening intently to their testimony and observing their demeanor on the wit-

---

*Just as the U.S. government, if it had prosecuted Oswald in real life, would not have charged him with conspiring with anyone to kill Kennedy (since the government did not believe he did), the jury in London only dealt with the issue of whether Oswald was guilty or not guilty of murdering Kennedy. However, the issue of conspiracy unavoidably permeated the entire trial. (See later discussion.)

ness stand. Although Oswald, the defendant, was of course not present and could not testify, it has to be noted that he was not present at the Warren Commission hearings either, and at the hearings he had no real lawyer representing his interests or cross-examining witnesses who testified against him, as he did in London with Spence. I might add that even if Oswald had been alive and prosecuted, he, like so many defendants in criminal trials, might very well have elected not to take the stand and subject himself to cross-examination. For example, Jack Ruby never testified at his trial.

Although Oswald's widow, Marina, declined to testify, I can't think of one *absolutely critical* witness I would have needed—were Oswald alive and I had prosecuted him—whom I did not have at the London trial. (When you have witnesses like the lady at whose home Oswald spent the night before the assassination with his wife, and who testified to Oswald's storing the murder weapon on the garage floor of her home; the witness who drove Oswald to work on the morning of the assassination and saw Oswald carry a large bag into the Texas School Book Depository Building, Oswald's place of employment; the witness who was watching the presidential motorcade from a window right below where Oswald was firing his rifle at Kennedy and actually heard the cartridge casings from Oswald's Mannlicher-Carcano rifle falling to the floor directly above him; a witness who saw Oswald shoot and kill Dallas police officer J. D. Tippit just forty-five minutes after the assassination; expert witnesses from the HSCA, as well as one from the Warren Commission, who conclusively tied Oswald to the assassination by fingerprint, handwriting, photographic, neutron activation, and firearm analyses; and so on, you know you're dealing with the real thing.) I simply would have called, in some areas, *more* witnesses to establish the same thing—for example, more witnesses than the ones I called to place Oswald at the Tippit murder scene.

The trial in London took place on July 23, 24, and 25, 1986. After the jury was out deliberating for six hours, they returned, on July 26, with a verdict of guilty, convicting Oswald of the murder of John F. Kennedy.[*] Obviously, were it not for my participation in this docu-trial of Oswald, which *Time* magazine said was "as close to a real trial as the accused killer of John F. Kennedy will probably ever get,"[36] this book would never have been written.

Before I go on, I'd like to relate an incident I feel may strike home with many readers of this book. Back in early 1992, a few months after the strongly pro-conspiracy movie *JFK* came out, I was speaking to around six hundred lawyers at a trial lawyers' convention on the East Coast. My subject was "Tactics and Techniques in the Trial of a Criminal Case," not the Kennedy assassination, but during the question-and-answer period that followed, the assassination came up, and I could tell from the rhetorical nature of the questions that the questioners believed there was a conspiracy in the assassination.

I asked for a show of hands as to how many did not accept the findings of the Warren Commission. A forest of hands went up, easily 85 to 90 percent of the audience. So I said to them, "What if I could prove to you in one minute or less that although you are all intelligent people you are not thinking intelligently about the Kennedy case?" I could sense an immediate stirring in the audience. My challenge sounded ridiculous. How could I *prove* in one minute or less that close to six hundred lawyers were not

---

[*]A condensed version of the trial was shown in England and several major European countries as well as Australia, and also to a very large national audience on Showtime here in the states on November 21 and 22, 1986.

thinking intelligently? A voice from my right front shouted out, "We don't think you can do it." I responded, "Okay, start looking at your watches." With the clock ticking, I asked for another show of hands as to those who had seen the recent movie *JFK* or at any time in the past had ever read any book or magazine article propounding the conspiracy theory or otherwise rejecting the findings of the Warren Commission. Again, a great number of hands went up—about the same, it seemed to me, as the previous hand count. I proceeded to tell the group that I didn't need a show of hands for my next point. "I'm sure you will all agree," I said, "that before you form an intelligent opinion on a matter in dispute you should hear both sides of the issue. As the old West Virginia mountaineer said, 'No matter how thin I make my pancakes they always have two sides.' With that in mind, how many of you have read the Warren Report?" It was embarrassing. Only a few people raised their hands. In less than a minute (one member of the audience later told me it was forty-seven seconds) I had proved my point. The overwhelming majority in the audience had formed an opinion rejecting the findings of the Warren Commission without bothering to read the Commission's report. And mind you, I hadn't even asked them how many had read the twenty-six volumes of the Warren Commission, just the single-volume Warren Report.

Well over a hundred million Americans reject the findings of the Warren Commission, whose report at least ninety-nine out of a hundred have never read.

If Oswald's guilt as the lone assassin is as obvious as I suggest, why, one may logically ask, the need for this extraordinarily long book? Make no mistake about it. The Kennedy assassination, per se, is not a complicated case. I've personally prosecuted several murder cases where the evidence against the accused was far more circumstantial and less robust than the case against Oswald. Apart from the fact that there is no audio on the famous Zapruder film (the film of the assassination by amateur photographer Abraham Zapruder, which, if reference is made only to it, would prevent one from knowing, with certainty, the number, timing, and sequence of the shots fired), the case against Oswald himself is overwhelming and relatively routine.* Earl Warren himself said, "As district attorney of a large metropolitan county [Oakland, California] for years . . . I have no hesitation in saying that had it not been for the prominence of the victim, the case against Oswald could have been tried in two or three days with little likelihood of any but one result."[37]

The allegation of conspiracy introduces an element of complexity into the case

---

*Throughout this book I will be referring to Oswald as Kennedy's killer, and conspiracy theorists, as well as legal purists, have maintained for years that the only proper way to refer to Oswald is "alleged assassin," on the rationale that under our system of justice in America, a suspect or defendant is presumed to be innocent until a jury finds him guilty in a court of law. But this invests a power and legitimacy to a verdict of guilty or not guilty that it does not have. A verdict of not guilty, for instance, cannot change the reality of whether or not the defendant committed the crime. That reality was established the moment of the crime, and nothing that happened thereafter can ever change it. If a courtroom verdict could, then if the defendant actually robbed a bank, but the three witnesses who saw him do it were unavailable to testify against him at the trial (e.g., the defendant's associates had either killed them or threatened them into not testifying), his subsequent not-guilty verdict means he didn't really rob the bank. In other words, the jury verdict succeeded in doing something that God can't even do—change the past. Likewise, if someone did not rob a bank, but in a case of mistaken identity he was found guilty, the new reality is that he actually did rob the bank. To those who have challenged my calling Oswald guilty throughout the years by saying he was never found to be guilty in a court of law, I've responded that "under that theory, Adolf Hitler never committed any crimes, Jack the Ripper never committed any crimes, and the only crime Al Capone ever committed was income tax evasion."

because it is inherently more difficult to prove a negative than a positive, and this complexity is compounded by the fact that Oswald was a deeply troubled person and a restless Marxist who traveled to Russia and Mexico. But the complexity is only superficial. As will be shown in this book, upon scrutiny the various conspiracy theories turn out to be weightless and embarrassingly devoid of substance. Again, then, if the case is not complex, why such a massive tome? The answer is that a tenacious, indefatigable, and, in many cases, fraudulent group of Warren Commission critics and conspiracy theorists have succeeded in transforming a case very simple and obvious at its core—Oswald killed Kennedy and acted alone—into its present form of the most complex murder case, *by far*, in world history.

Refusing to accept the plain truth, and dedicating their existence for over forty years to convincing the American public of the truth of their own charges, the critics have journeyed to the outer margins of their imaginations. Along the way, they have split hairs and then proceeded to split the split hairs, drawn far-fetched and wholly unreasonable inferences from known facts, and literally invented bogus facts from the grist of rumor and speculation. With over eighteen thousand pages of small print in the twenty-seven Warren Commission volumes alone, and many millions of pages of FBI and CIA documents, any researcher worth his salt can find a sentence here or there to support any ludicrous conspiracy theory he might have. And that, of course, is precisely what the conspiracy community has done. To give the critics their day in court (which they never give to the Warren Commission and the HSCA), and thus effectively rebut their allegations, does regrettably and unavoidably take a great many pages. For instance, it takes only one sentence to make the argument that organized crime had Kennedy killed to get his brother, Attorney General Robert Kennedy, off its back, but it takes a great many pages to demonstrate the invalidity of that charge.

There are several reasons, over and above Jack Ruby's supposedly "silencing" Oswald and a general distrust of government and governmental agencies, which was only intensified by the Vietnam War and the Watergate scandal, why the majority of Americans have embraced the conspiracy theory and rejected the findings of the Warren Commission. One is that people inevitably find conspiracies fascinating and intriguing, and hence subconsciously are more receptive to conspiratorial hypotheses. As author John Sparrow points out, "Those who attack the Warren Report enjoy an advantage over its defenders: they have a more exciting story to tell. The man in the street likes to hear that something sinister has been going on, particularly in high places."[38] And, of course, we know that humans, for whatever reason, love mysteries (which, to most, the JFK assassination has become), whether fictional or real, more than they do open-and-shut cases. For example, who killed JR? Who is Deep Throat? (Now answered.) Are there really UFOs? We all know about the considerable popularity of murder mysteries in novels and on the screen. Tom Stone, who teaches a course on the Kennedy assassination at Southern Methodist University, says that "by the late 90's I had come to believe that Oswald was probably the only shooter. But I found I was taking the fun out of the assassination for my students."[39] Stories of conspiracy, then, are simply more appealing to Americans than that of a gunman acting alone. And when one prefers an idea, one is obviously more apt to accept its legitimacy, even in the face of contrary evidence.

Secondly, a wide-ranging conspiracy, in a strange way, gives more meaning not only to the president's death but to his life. That powerful national interests killed Kennedy because he was taking the nation in a direction they opposed emphasizes the importance of his life and death more than the belief that a lone nut killed him for no reason other than dementia. Abraham Lincoln scholar Reed Turner says, "Somehow it is more satisfying to believe that a president died as the victim of a cause than at the hands of a deranged gunman."[40] Even Jacqueline Kennedy was moved to say that her husband "didn't even have the satisfaction of being killed for civil rights. It had to be some silly little communist. It even robs his death of meaning."[41] In the unconscious desire of many to make a secular saint out of the fallen president, the notion of martyrdom was inevitable. But a martyr is not one who dies at the hands of a demented non-entity. Only powerful forces who viewed Kennedy's reign as antithetical to their goals would do.

And thirdly, in a related vein, there's the instinctive notion that a king cannot be struck down by a peasant. Many Americans found it hard to accept that President Kennedy, the most powerful man in the free world—someone they perceived to occupy a position akin to a king—could be eliminated in a matter of seconds by someone whom they considered a nobody. On a visceral level, they couldn't grasp the enormous incongruity of it all. To strike down a king, as it were, something more elaborate and powerful just had to be involved—"It's preposterous on the face of it to believe that a mousy little guy with a $12.95 rifle could bring down the leader of the free world."[42] But of course this type of visceral reasoning has no foundation in logic. The lowliest human can pull a trigger just as effectively as someone of power and importance. And bullets are very democratic. They permit anyone to fire them through the barrel of a gun, and they injure or kill whomever they hit. There have been three assassinations of American presidents other than Kennedy (Lincoln, 1865; Garfield, 1881; McKinley, 1901) and six attempted assassinations (Jackson, 1835; FDR [president-elect], 1933; Truman, 1950; Ford, 1975 [twice]; and Reagan, 1981). With the exception of Lincoln's murder and the attempt on Truman's life (both of which, particularly in Truman's case, were very limited conspiracies in their scope), all were believed to be carried out by lone gunmen—demented assailants, acting alone.

But the above reasons are only ancillary to the principal reason why I believe the conspiracy theorists have been successful in persuading the American public that their charges are true. To paraphrase Joseph Goebbels, the propaganda minister of Hitler's Third Reich, if you push something at people long enough, eventually they're going to start buying it, particularly when they haven't been exposed to any contrary view. And for over forty years, almost all that the American people have heard has been the incessant and all-pervasive voice of the conspiracy theorists. (The evidence that supports this view of mine is the previously stated fact that when the Warren Commission first came out with its findings, the majority of Americans *did* accept its conclusion of Oswald's guilt and no conspiracy.) Oliver Stone's widely seen but factually impoverished movie in 1991, *JFK*, only augmented for millions of Americans all the misconceptions and myths about the case. Then, too, there's the reality that you only know if someone is lying to you if you know what the truth is. If you don't know, and you make the assumption that the author of a book, for instance, is honorable and has a duty to the reader and history to be truthful, you accept what he says as being factual, and hence are misled. It has nothing to do with intelligence. Einstein may have had an IQ in the stratosphere, but if he didn't know anything about chess and a purported expert on chess told him a lie about the game, Einstein would likely accept it. To know whether authors or film producers like Stone are telling the truth, you'd have to have on hand the Warren Commission and HSCA volumes so you could check out the accuracy of everything they say. But the Warren Report and its supporting volumes, for instance, cost around a thousand dollars today (originally, around four dollars for the report and seventy-six dollars for the twenty-six volumes), and very few Americans have them. In fact, even most libraries don't. Only 2,500 sets of the volumes were printed by the Government Printing Office, 1,340 of which went to selected libraries.[43] And the HSCA volumes are almost impossible to find anywhere.

So those peddling misinformation about the Kennedy assassination have been able to get by with their blatant lies, omissions, distortions, and simply erroneous statements because their readers aren't in a position to dispute the veracity of their assertions. A few examples among countless others: When conspiracy theorists and critics of the Warren Commission allege, as we've all heard them do a hundred times, that no one, not even a professional shooter, has ever been able to duplicate what Oswald did on the day of the assassination,[*] that is, get off three rounds at three separate distances with the accuracy the Warren Commission says Oswald had (two out of three hits) in the limited amount of time he had, how would any reader who didn't have volume 3 of the Warren Commission know that this is a false assertion? On page 446 of volume 3 we learn that way back in 1964, one "Specialist Miller" of the U.S. Army, using Oswald's own Mannlicher-Carcano rifle, not only duplicated what Oswald did, but improved on Oswald's time. In fact, many marksmen, including the firearms expert from Wisconsin whom I used at the London trial, have done better than Oswald did.

When Jim Garrison says in his book, *On the Trail of the Assassins*,[44] that Lee Harvey Oswald "was a notoriously poor shot" with "an abysmal marksmanship record in the Marines," unknowledgeable readers would probably accept this if they didn't have volume 11 of the Warren Commission. U.S. Marine Corps Major Eugene D. Anderson testified that Marine Corps records show that on December 21, 1956, Oswald fired a 212 on the range with his M-1 rifle, making him a sharpshooter.[45][†]

When conspiracy theorist Walt Brown tells the readers of his book, *Treachery in Dallas*,[46] what most theorists say, that Oswald's Mannlicher-Carcano rifle was a "piece of junk" that "lacked accuracy," how would a reader know that although it wasn't the best of rifles, Ronald Simmons, the chief of the Infantry Weapons Evaluation Branch of the Department of the Army, said that after test-firing Oswald's rifle forty-seven times, he found it was "quite accurate"; indeed, he said, as accurate as "the M-14" rifle, the rifle used by the American military at the time?[47]

The conspiracy theorists are so outrageously brazen that they tell lies not just about verifiable, documentary evidence, but about clear, photographic evidence, knowing that only one out of a thousand of their readers, if that, is in possession of the subject photographs. Robert Groden (the leading photographic expert for the conspiracy proponents who was the photographic adviser for Oliver Stone's movie *JFK*) draws a diagram on

---

[*]For example, prominent conspiracy theorist Anthony Summers says, "No professional marksman was able to achieve [what Oswald did] in subsequent tests" (Summers and Summers, "Ghosts of November," p.98); see also Henry Hurt's book, *Reasonable Doubt*, page 8: "The United States government . . . has never conducted a test in which Oswald's shooting ability has been matched. The country's top experts can work the ancient Mannlicher-Carcano rifle bolt with sufficient speed. Those experts can hit a similarly moving target. But no official expert has ever been able to do both at the same time. That feat belongs to Oswald alone— a man of questionable shooting skills."

[†]Even on May 6, 1959, when Oswald was about to leave the Marine Corps, and hence, wouldn't have had any incentive to fire well, he fired a 191, qualifying him as a "marksman" with the M-1 rifle.

page 24 of his book *High Treason* of Governor Connally seated *directly in front* of President Kennedy in the presidential limousine and postulates the "remarkable path" a bullet coming from behind Kennedy, and traveling from right to left, would have to take to hit Connally—after passing straight through Kennedy's body, making a right turn and then a left one in midair, which, the buffs chortle, bullets "don't even do in cartoons." What average reader would be in a position to dispute this seemingly common-sense, geometric assault on the Warren Commission's single-bullet theory? (The theory is a sine qua non to the Commission's conclusion that there was only one gunman, and the same bullet that hit Connally had previously hit Kennedy.) But, of course, if you start out with an erroneous premise, whatever flows from it makes a lot of sense. The only problem is that it's wrong. The indisputable fact here—which all people who have studied the assassination know—is that Connally was *not* seated directly in front of Kennedy, but to his left front. Though President Kennedy was seated on the extreme right in the backseat of the limousine, Connally was in a jump seat situated a half foot from the right door.[48] Moreover, at the time Connally was hit, the Zapruder film, unlike Groden's diagram, shows he was turned to his right.[49] Additionally, the jump seat was three inches lower than the backseat.[50] Therefore, because of the alignment of Connally's body vis-à-vis Kennedy's, it was virtually inevitable that a bullet traveling on a downward trajectory and passing on a straight line through soft tissue in Kennedy's body (as both the Warren Commission and HSCA concluded) would go on to strike Connally where it did.[51] But again, how would average lay readers know that Groden had deliberately altered reality to mislead them? (Groden declined a request by the defense to testify at the trial in London and thus avoided being cross-examined.)

I am unaware of any other major event in world history which has been shrouded in so much intentional misinformation as has the assassination of JFK. Nor am I aware of any event that has given rise to such an extraordinarily large number of far-fetched and conflicting theories. For starters, if organized crime was behind the assassination, as many believe, wouldn't that necessarily mean that all the many books claiming the CIA (or Castro or the KGB, and so on) was responsible were wrong? And vice versa? Unless one wants to believe, as Hollywood producer Oliver Stone apparently does, that they were *all* involved. I mean, were we to believe Mr. Stone, even bitter enemies like the KGB and the CIA got together on this one. Indeed, at one time or another in Mr. Stone's cinematic reverie, he had the following groups and individuals acting suspiciously and/or conspiratorially: the Dallas Police Department, FBI, Secret Service, Vice President Lyndon B. Johnson, CIA, KGB, Fidel Castro, anti-Castro Cuban exiles, organized crime, and the military-industrial complex. Apparently nobody wanted President Kennedy alive. But where did all these people meet to hatch this conspiracy? Madison Square Garden?

The Warren Commission has been attacked for decades by the critics for conducting a highly biased investigation of the assassination. Yes, the Commission was biased against Oswald, but only *after* it became obvious to any sensible, reasonable person that he had murdered Kennedy. Actually, that fact was clearly evident within hours of the assassination. Among other things, law enforcement learned that the apparent murder weapon, a 6.5-millimeter Mannlicher-Carcano rifle found on the sixth floor of the Book Depository Building—later confirmed to be the murder weapon by firearm tests—had been traced back to Oswald; that forty-five minutes after the assassination Oswald murdered Dallas police officer J. D. Tippit, and shortly thereafter tried to shoot his arresting officer; and that during his interrogation he told one provable lie after another—such as claiming he never owned a rifle—showing an unmistakable consciousness of guilt. With evidence like this *already* in existence against Oswald on the very first day that the Warren Commission started its work on the case, how could the Commission possibly not start out with at least the working hypothesis of Oswald's guilt? And of course, all of the evidence that the Commission gathered thereafter only served to confirm this original hypothesis.

One of the most common arguments made by critics of the Warren Commission—even by those few who do not impute dishonorable motives to the Commission members—is that it was acting under intense political and societal pressure to reach a conclusion in the case and that it was very rushed in its investigation. This is one reason why, they say, the Commission reached an erroneous conclusion. But this is invalid criticism. The Commission had nine months, far more than enough time to reach a conclusion that was obvious to nearly everyone involved in the investigation within days—that a nut had killed Kennedy, and he had himself been killed by another nut, with the possibility of a conspiracy being highly implausible. If the president weren't the victim, a normal investigation of a murder with the same set of facts and circumstances as this one could be wrapped up by any competent major city police department in a few weeks, with the prosecution being a rather short one. The Warren Commission, in addition to having one hundred times the investigative manpower and resources of a local police department, took, as indicated, nine months. As Warren Commission member John McCloy said, "The conclusions [we reached] weren't rushed at all . . . [They were] arrived at in our own good time."[52]

It should be noted that the completely natural and almost humanly unavoidable bias of the Warren Commission against Oswald, as one piece of evidence after another kept pointing ineluctably to his guilt, did not prevent it from conducting an extremely thorough, almost microscopic investigation of the assassination.* Nor did it militate against its being willing to examine, even seek out, any evidence that would controvert this bias. As David Belin, assistant counsel for the Warren Commission, said about himself and his colleague Joseph Ball (the two Warren Commission lawyers whose job was to answer the sole question of who killed President Kennedy, not other, related areas of inquiry), "Ball and I were always looking for something that might shed new light on the assassination. Could it be that Oswald was not the assassin? Could it be that if Oswald was the assassin, one or more people were involved? Could it be that Oswald merely aided the assassin, or that he unwittingly aided someone else?"[53]

Though the Warren Commission perhaps should have considered the possibility of a conspiracy more than it did, contrary to popular belief it did conduct a fairly extensive probe into the issue of whether or not any person or group was behind Oswald's act. Apart from a great number of references to the possibility of a conspiracy in the multiple volumes of the Commission, and many sections in the Warren Report itself that, by defini-

---

*However, once evidence made the hypothesis of guilt unavoidable, just as unavoidable was the unconscious partiality toward any piece of evidence, or interpretation of evidence, that supported the hypothesis. This was the one weakness of the Warren Commission, but short of a surgical operation on human nature, I know of no way to avoid such a problem. Fortunately, because the evidence of Oswald's guilt was so complete and overwhelming, and there simply was no evidence that he acted in concert with others, this weakness of the Warren Commission, which is inherent in any and all investigative bodies, had no negative impact on the Commission's findings. Only if there were substantive evidence of Oswald's innocence or substantive evidence of his complicity with others in the assassination, one or both of which the Commission ignored or did not examine objectively, would there be cause to question seriously the validity of the Commission's conclusions.

tion, inferentially dealt with the issue (e.g., discussion about grassy knoll witnesses), the report contains a 131-page chapter (by far the longest chapter in the report) dealing exclusively with the issue of conspiracy. The Commission asserted that it "has investigated each rumor and allegation linking Oswald to a conspiracy which has come to its attention, regardless of source."[54] Indeed, one very long June 1964 document, titled "Oswald's Foreign Activities: Summary of Evidence Which Might Be Said to Show That There Was Foreign Involvement in the Assassination of President Kennedy," wasn't even included in the Warren Commission volumes. The authors of the document (a memorandum from Assistant Counsels W. David Slawson and William Coleman to the Warren Commission) noted that "*one of the basic purposes* of the [Warren] Commission's investigation of the assassination of President Kennedy is to determine whether it was due in whole or in part to a foreign conspiracy," and concluded that "there was no foreign involvement" in Kennedy's murder.[55]

One of the key pieces of documentary evidence that conspiracy theorists cite as proof that the Warren Commission *only* had an interest in presenting a case against Oswald, and had no interest in ascertaining whether there was a conspiracy, is a January 11, 1964, "Memorandum for Members of the Commission" from Commission chairman Earl Warren in which he sets forth a "tentative outline" that was prepared, he said, by Warren Commission general counsel J. Lee Rankin to aid in "organizing the evaluation of the investigative materials received by the Commission." Since by January 11, a month and a half after the assassination, it was very obvious that Oswald had killed Kennedy, subdivision II of the memorandum was titled "Lee Harvey Oswald as the Assassin of President Kennedy." Under this subdivision were subheadings like "Brief Identification of Oswald [Dallas resident, employee of Texas School Book Depository, etc.]"; "Movements [of Oswald] on November 22, 1963, Prior to Assassination"; "Entry into Depository"; "Movements after Assassination until Murder of Tippit"; and so on. I respectfully ask, what other way was there for "organizing the evaluation of the investigative materials" when the investigative materials (i.e., evidence) all dealt, of necessity (since the evidence that had already been gathered all pointed to Oswald as the killer of Kennedy), with Oswald? To give Oswald an alias? Or mention some third party who was *not* identified in the investigative materials as the chief suspect? Moreover, the Warren Commission critics don't mention that Warren, to allow for the fact that the investigation might take the Commission in different directions, wrote, "As the staff reviews the [investigative] materials, the outline will certainly undergo substantial revision." Perhaps most importantly, what the critics usually fail to mention is that subdivision II H reads, "Evidence Implicating Others in Assassination or Suggesting Accomplices."

Even if the evidence up to January 11, 1964, the date of the subject memorandum, had not pointed only to Oswald, and even if there was no reference to a possible conspiracy in the tentative outline, the best way to judge the work of the Warren Commission on this point is not by what the Commission wrote or said, but by what it did. (One of my favorite sayings is "Your conduct speaks so loudly I can't hear a word you are saying.") And we will see that the Commission's conduct throughout the investigation clearly shows that its members only had *one* objective, to discover the truth of what happened.

In addition to the aforementioned long chapter on conspiracy, many sections of the Warren Report deal with the conspiracy issue. For instance, in the thirty-one-page appendix XII to the report, the Commission responds to 126 speculations and rumors, some dealing expressly with the allegation of conspiracy, most dealing in one way or the other with the allegation. Appendix XIV deals with Oswald's finances in great detail, showing he was not in possession of money from an unknown source. And certainly the long biography of Jack Ruby and an analysis of the polygraph test he took,[56] in many places expressly, and in virtually all places at least implicitly, address themselves to the conspiracy issue.

It has to be noted that after the FBI became the chief investigative agency of the Warren Commission, no fair and sensible person could ever accuse the bureau of conducting a superficial investigation. It was exceedingly thorough. As Tom Bethell, who was in charge of the research for New Orleans district attorney Jim Garrison's investigation and prosecution of Clay Shaw for the assassination of President Kennedy, has written, "Garrison's investigators were quietly impressed by the speed and thoroughness of the FBI's inquiry . . . It turned out that the FBI, far from having done a poor job, had very thoroughly interviewed anyone and everyone with the most tangential relationship to the assassination."[57]

Just two examples, among so many, of the FBI investigating the issue of conspiracy, examples that no book pushing the conspiracy theory would ever dream of mentioning. The enigmatic fellow with a checkered history who sat next to Oswald on the bus that transported Oswald to Mexico in September 1963, an extremely peripheral figure, was the subject of an investigation into his identity and background that remarkably generated ninety-nine pages in an FBI report.[58] Also, the FBI obtained not only all records of toll calls made by Jack Ruby, but also those of his three brothers and four sisters, and twelve other persons known to have been in close contact with Ruby between September 26 (when it was reported in the newspapers for the first time that Kennedy would be in Dallas on November 22) and November 22, 1963.[59] This had nothing directly to do with Oswald killing Kennedy, and everything to do with a possible conspiracy.

The Warren Commission critics who do not believe that the Commission covered up the assassination allege instead that the Commission conducted a very superficial, incompetent investigation of the assassination. But in my opinion, the Warren Commission's investigation has to be considered the most comprehensive investigation of a crime in history. Even leading Warren Commission critic Harold Weisberg acknowledges that the Commission "checked into almost every breath [Oswald] drew."[60] Very few people are more critical than I. And I expect incompetence wherever I turn, always pleasantly surprised to find its absence. Competence, of course, is all relative, and I find the Warren Commission operated at an appreciably higher level of competence than any investigative body I know of. It is my firm belief that anyone who feels the Warren Commission did not do a good job investigating the murder of Kennedy has never been a part of a murder investigation.

Of one thing I am certain. The Commission's conclusions have held up remarkably well against all assaults on their validity. This is true not only of its basic conclusions, but also of its finer points. For example, with all the technological advances in photographic enhancement to which the Zapruder film of the assassination has been exposed, the very latest interpretation by most of the experts on precisely when the first of two shots hit the president (the only one in controversy, the second shot being the visible head shot)— somewhere between frames 210 and 225—just happens to coincide with what the Warren Commission concluded[61] way back in 1964.

With respect to the depth of the Warren Commission inquiry, there are hundreds of thousands of pages of investigative reports and documents on its investigation that are *in addition* to the twenty-seven published volumes of the Commission. These volumes consist of the 888-page, single-volume Warren Report; 8,082 pages of testimony in small print in volumes 1 through 15; and 9,833 pages of documents and exhibits in volumes 16 through 26. They all add up to 18,803 pages and close to 10.4 million words, almost all of which consist of substance, not fluff, as Warren Commission critics would want the public to believe.* The commission or its staff took direct testimony, affidavits, or statements from 552 witnesses,† more than ten times, for instance, the number of witnesses called before the Joint Congressional Committee that investigated, in 1945–1946, the attack on Pearl Harbor. The FBI alone (there were also companion investigations of the assassination by other agencies) conducted an unprecedented 25,000 interviews as the investigative arm of the Warren Commission, and submitted 2,300 separate reports. Eighty additional FBI agents were ordered into the Dallas area alone, and a great many more agents around the country worked on various parts of the case. A total of 3,154 items of evidence were introduced before the Commission in its investigation of the assassination.

As author Relman Morin observed, "Never in history was a crime probed as intensely, and never in history was the inquiry itself subjected to such intense scrutiny."[62] Speaking later, as the district attorney of Philadelphia, former Warren Commission assistant counsel Arlen Specter said that "I have never seen the resources devoted to the determination of the truth as were the resources of the United States of America devoted in this case . . . There has been no equal of this kind of inquiry, anywhere."[63]‡ A "monumental work" and "an outstanding achievement," Lord Devlin, former justice of England's High Court, Kings Bench Division, averred.[64] As *Newsweek*'s White House correspondent Charles Roberts put it back in 1967, the Warren Commission "interrogated strip-teasers and senators, street urchins and psychiatrists . . . It explored more theories, tracked down more leads, and listened to more rambling witnesses, expert and illiterate, than any body of its kind in history."[65] Paul L. Freese, in the *New York University Law Review*, wrote, "The Commission is without

---

*Whenever I hear someone say the Warren Commission investigation was superficial, I immediately know that the person has never read or worked with the twenty-seven volumes of the Commission, and is just parroting hearsay from some other person who also hasn't read or worked with them.

One of the deficiencies of the Warren Report and its supporting volumes is that although there are two separate name indexes, there is no subject index. In 1966, Sylvia Meagher eliminated that problem with her *Subject Index to the Warren Report and Hearings and Exhibits*, an absolutely invaluable reference work for anyone studying the assassination. In 1980, in collaboration with Gary Owens, she published her *Master Index to the J.F.K. Assassination Investigations*, which is a name and subject index to the Warren Report and volumes as well as the HSCA Report and volumes.

†Ninety-four witnesses gave testimony before members of the Warren Commission. An additional 395 were questioned under oath by members of the Commission's legal staff, 61 gave affidavits, and 2 gave statements. (WR, p.xiii) As *Time* magazine said, "That is surely not a record of investigators refusing to listen to witnesses who might disturb their eventual conclusion" ("Who Killed J.F.K.? Just One Assassin," p.32). Nearly all of the ninety-four witnesses gave their testimony at the closely guarded headquarters of the Commission in Washington's Veterans of Foreign Wars Building. Some of the additional 395 were also flown in to give their depositions before Warren Commission assistant counsels, although most depositions of witnesses were taken outside Washington, D.C. (See Warren Commission volumes 1–15; Telephone interview of Richard Mosk by the author on September 8, 2005; closely guarded: "Warren Commission Report," *Time*, p.48)

‡And the case will continue to be investigated and examined and analyzed for years and years to come. Indeed, in testimony before the Warren Commission, Richard Helms, the CIA's head of covert operations, said, "I assume the case will never be closed" (5 H 124). And FBI Director J. Edgar Hoover told the Commission, "So far as the FBI is concerned, the case will be continued in an open classification for all time" (5 H 100).

rival in its display of investigative energy. It gathered a prodigious amount of evidence."[66] And yet, as conspiracy author Walt Brown accurately points out, "The Warren Commission . . . became the most vilified fact-finding body ever assembled in the United States of America."[67]

But very little of the vilification is warranted. Although the Warren Commission appears to have fudged on some small points here and there—unfortunately, not uncommon for law enforcement—overall it did a very thorough and exemplary investigative job. Apart from the commissioners' natural inclination to conduct themselves honorably, one reason why the Warren Commission (as opposed to the individual authors, investigators, and conspiracy theorists who followed) was fair and objective is that it was essentially forced to be so. The Commission and its lawyers and investigators consisted of a considerable number of people, many of whom were very familiar with the case, and hence, even if a member of this group was duplicitous and dishonorable enough to want to deceive the American public, he would have known he simply couldn't do this because his colleagues would be in a position to question immediately the fabrication or distortion he wrote, or the important fact he curiously omitted.

What follows is a typical example of what I'm referring to, a September 14, 1964 (ten days before the Warren Report was published), memorandum from Warren Commission assistant counsel Wesley Liebeler to fellow assistant counsel Howard Willens regarding, Liebeler writes, the galley proofs of "that portion of chapter VI [of the prospective Warren Report] dealing with conspiracy beginning with 'Investigation of Other Activities.'" These are but a few excerpts from many more points in the memorandum: "We have not conducted sufficient investigation to state that there is no evidence that FPCC [Fair Play for Cuba Committee] and ACLU [American Civil Liberties Union] were aware that they were authorized to receive mail at P. O. Box 6225, or that mail was ever addressed to them there." "We cannot say that all of Oswald's transactions in connection with firearms were undertaken under an assumed name, only his known transactions." "The last sentence in that paragraph [first full paragraph on page 259] is not supported by the TV films we got from CBS. It should be deleted." "Whiteworth and Hunter do not now say Oswald drove down the street, and only Mrs. Whiteworth said so before." "I know of no evidence that Ryder and Greener talked on the 24th." "The paragraph about the psychiatrist is quite unfair. It states that Odio 'came forward' with her story, whereas she did not come forward at all and was quite reluctant to get involved at all." "Why do we fail to mention the Cuban or Mexican that one of the Western Union employees said was with the man Hambian thought was Oswald?"[68] And so on. Liebeler wrote a similar memorandum on September 6, 1964, with respect to perceived inaccuracies and overstatements in chapter IV ("The Assassin") of the pending report.[69] Such was the methodology used by the members of the Warren Commission and its staff in their effort to arrive at the truth in the assassination of John F. Kennedy. Yes, as in virtually all involved criminal cases (and here there were three separate and distinct murders to deal with—the murders of JFK, Officer J. D. Tippit, and Lee Harvey Oswald), there were unresolved questions and areas of speculation, but as Liebeler testified before the HSCA on November 8, 1977,

> As to the *basic facts* of the assassination relating to questions of the President's wounds, source of the shots and identity of the assassin, the physical evidence alone shows without doubt that Oswald was the assassin and that he fired from the sixth

floor of the school book depository. The Commission pursued to the extent that it could all plausible leads suggesting the involvement of persons other than Oswald and it could not establish any facts that would seriously suggest the existence of a conspiracy to assassinate the President.

The staff was highly motivated and competent with no inclination or motive not to pursue the issues to the truth. The work of the staff of the Commission was not perfect. [But] when compared to the criticisms that have been made of our work or compared to the product of other human institutions, and not to some ideal of perfection, we might ask ourselves, or you might ask yourselves whether you would have been likely to have done better at the time, and when thought of in that way and when compared to those standards I think the Commission's work will pass muster very well.

As I have said, I have never doubted the nature of the conclusions of the report and I do not doubt them now. In spite of what has happened since the publication of the report I think that eventually it will stand the test of time.[70]

It is quite interesting to note that if, as the conspiracy theorists maintain, the Warren Commission only presented evidence in its volumes that supported its conclusions, and deliberately suppressed information that did not, why is it that *the source* the conspiracy theorists cite for upwards of 95 percent of their arguments is some document, affidavit, or testimony contained—for all the world to see—*within* the Warren Commission volumes? Some suppression. One example among a great many others. The Warren Commission critics and conspiracy theorists allege, of course, that the fatal shots came from the grassy knoll, not the Book Depository Building where Oswald was, and they claim further that the Warren Commission knows this but suppressed evidence pointing to this fact. Yet the Commission called and took testimony from many witnesses who said it was their belief (proved to be incorrect by the weight of all the other evidence) that the shots came from the grassy knoll. Again, some suppression. Warren Commission critic David Lifton, a committed grassy-knoll-theory devotee, speaks enthusiastically in his book, *Best Evidence*, of reading an article in the March 1965 issue of *Minority of One* in which the testimony of many of these witnesses is set forth. He refers to the article— which he says supported his position that the shots came from the knoll, not the Book Depository Building as the Warren Commission claimed—as being "something of a classic." He then adds, perhaps unaware of the irony, that the article was "based *entirely* on information from the twenty-six volumes" of the Warren Commission.[71] Conspiracy author Michael E. Eddowes writes, "When the Warren Report and its 26 supporting volumes of testimony and exhibits became available, my several assistants and I began to study them . . . The basis of my study has always been the contents of the volumes of testimony and exhibits, from which my assistants and I were able finally to assemble evidence disclosing the truth."[72] The critics of the Warren Commission should ask themselves whether publishing evidence damaging to one's own position is the mark of an honest and honorable person or group, or the opposite.

"It is the very thoroughness of the Warren Commission that has caused its problems," the late Pierre Salinger noted. "It listened patiently to everyone, no matter how credible or incredible the testimony. It then appended all this testimony to its report, providing an opportunity to anyone with a typewriter and a lot of time on his hands to write a book on the subject."[73]

A tactic used by authors of virtually every single book I've ever read that propounds a conspiracy theory is to attack an agency as being part of a conspiracy in the Kennedy assassination, but when this same agency comes up with something favorable to the author's position, the author will cite that same agency as credible support for his argument. This tactic is neither subtle nor logical, yet that is precisely what almost *all* the conspiracy theorists do, seeking to pick and choose and have it both ways. Just one example among hundreds: Referring to a threatening note that Oswald delivered to the FBI office in Dallas less than two weeks before the assassination, which was subsequently destroyed, Mark Lane, the granddaddy of all conspiracy theorists, writes in the introduction to his book *Rush to Judgment*, "An obvious and reasonable explanation as to why [the note] was destroyed is that it contained material prejudicial to the FBI . . . [It] was but one of the illegal police actions to silence [Oswald]. The ultimate action was to murder him."[74]

Pretty serious allegations against the FBI, right? But then Lane, without even blushing, turns to the FBI for support whenever an FBI finding is helpful to his position. In other words, the FBI, though per Lane apparently complicit in the assassination as well as the murder of Oswald, is suddenly imbued with honor and integrity and is out there working diligently to discover the truth in the assassination. He writes later in his book, "If it is accurate, the December 9 FBI report provides proof that the [Warren] Commission explanation of the throat wound is inaccurate . . . Hoover would not presume to summarize the 'medical examination of the President's body' . . . unless the autopsy report had been studied carefully." And later, to support his position that Oswald was not Kennedy's assassin, he writes, "After the FBI had examined the rifle, a letter from Hoover reported: 'It is noted that at the time of firing these tests, the telescopic sight [on Oswald's rifle] could not be properly aligned with the target since the sight reached the limit of its adjustment before reaching accurate alignment.'"[75]

Finally, there is another need for this book. Amid the blizzard of defective and misleading anti–Warren Commission and pro-conspiracy books, there have only been two books of prominence on the other side in the last twenty years: first, *Conspiracy of One* by Jim Moore in 1991, and the much more well-known *Case Closed* by Gerald Posner in 1993. Both books (particularly *Case Closed*, which was well received by the mainstream press) have been valuable contributions to JFK assassination literature, and I agree with their two principal conclusions, namely, that Oswald killed Kennedy and acted alone. (I disagree 100 percent with Posner's conclusion that organized crime may have intended to kill Kennedy, but Oswald "beat the Mafia to it.") But what a disappointment it was to me when, after years and years of pro-conspiracy books, these two books finally came out on the other side and I saw the authors engaging in many of the same unfortunate tactics as the Warren Commission critics.

Just a very few examples among many to illustrate the often misleading writing of Moore and Posner. Earlene Roberts was the manager of the rooming house Oswald lived in at the time of the assassination. In his book, Moore refers to her testimony that Oswald arrived back at the rooming house shortly after the assassination, was in a big hurry, and left minutes thereafter. But Moore, who reasons well in his book, completely ignores the most potentially important part of her testimony, that she heard the honk of a car, glanced out the window, and saw, she claims, a Dallas police car in front of the rooming house just before Oswald left—information which, if true, clearly goes in the direction of a conspiracy. If you're being fair and objective, and the issue is whether Oswald was involved with anyone in the assassination, how is it possible to omit information like this? Let's take Sylvia Odio. Odio is the seemingly credible witness who testified before the Warren Commission that one evening in late September 1963 (less than two months before the assassination), Lee Harvey Oswald, in the company of two anti-Castro Cuban men, appeared at her door in Dallas seeking funds for the anti-Castro cause. The next day, one of the three called her and told her that Oswald said Kennedy should have been assassinated after the Bay of Pigs, and that killing Kennedy would be "easy to do." Anti-conspiracy theorists, of course, don't want there to be any evidence that Oswald was seen in the company of unknown men before the assassination, particularly with men who may have had a motive to kill Kennedy (such as anti-Castro Cubans angry at JFK over his lack of support at the Bay of Pigs), and Moore, remarkably, writes off Odio, a very important witness, with just one sentence.[76]

Posner is even worse, writing what can only be characterized as a distortion and misrepresentation of Odio's testimony. In his book he dismisses the accuracy of her identification of Oswald as being the man at her door by quoting highly selective testimony of Odio's, including this testimony of Odio's when shown a photo of Oswald by Warren Commission counsel: "I think this man was the one in my apartment. I am not too sure of that picture. *He didn't look like this.*"[77] Sounds like the man at the door might not have been Oswald, right? That's because Posner omits what Odio said immediately thereafter (on the same line of the transcript) to explain why Oswald did not look like he did in the photo: "He was smiling that day. He was more smiling than in this picture." But much more importantly by far, Posner doesn't tell his readers about other photos (even television footage) of Oswald that Odio was shown where she positively identified him as the man at the door. Although Posner expressly tells his readers that "Odio could not positively identify [Oswald] when shown photos during her Warren Commission testimony," this is simply and categorically not true. When Odio was asked whether one photograph of Oswald depicted "the man who was in your apartment," she jocularly stated, "If it is not, it is his twin." When asked, "When did you first become aware of the fact that this man who had been at your apartment was the man who had been arrested in connection with the assassination?" she replied, "It was immediately."

Question: "As soon as you saw his picture?"

"Immediately, I was so sure."

Summing up her testimony after Warren Commission counsel asked her, "Do you have any doubts in your mind after looking at these pictures that the man who was in your apartment was Lee Harvey Oswald?" she replied, "I don't have any doubts."[78] Because this testimony of Odio's goes in the direction of contradicting Posner's position that the visitor at the door "was not Oswald" and his larger position of no conspiracy, none of it can be found in *Case Closed*, and hence, the unsuspecting reader can merrily proceed to the next page, not troubled at all by a very, very troubling witness (Odio).

One of the favorites of the conspiracy theorists is Rose Cherami. In fact, Oliver Stone started his movie *JFK* with her story. Cherami (true name, Melba Christine Marcades) was a prostitute and heroin addict who was found lying on the road near Eunice, Louisiana, on the evening of November 20, 1963, two days before the assassination. She said she had been pushed out of a moving car. Bruised and disoriented, she was taken to the nearby Louisiana State Hospital in Jackson, Louisiana, where she reportedly told the attending physician that President Kennedy was going to be killed during his forthcoming trip to Dallas. Now let's go to Posner. Dismissing Cherami, he writes, "Doctor Victor Weiss, a treating physician, told investigators that he did not hear her say anything about the assassination *until* November 25th [three days after the assassination]." Posner is clearly implying here that Weiss was in Cherami's presence *before* the assassination and she never said a word about the president going to be killed. It was only *after* the assassination that she said anything to him. In fact, Posner later says that Cherami "made up her story" not just after the assassination, but "*after* Ruby had shot Oswald."[79] But when we look at Posner's own citation for this (HSCA volume 10, page 200), we find something quite different: "Doctor Victor Weiss verified that he was employed as a resident physician at the hospital in 1963. He recalled that on Monday, November 25, 1963, he was asked by another physician, Dr. Bowers, to see a patient who had been committed November 20 or 21. Dr. Bowers allegedly told Weiss that the patient, Rose Cherami, had stated *before* the assassination that President Kennedy was going to be killed." So, directly contrary to what Posner suggested to his readers, not only hadn't Weiss seen Cherami before the assassination, but at least reportedly, Cherami had indeed said before the assassination that Kennedy was going to be killed. Cherami can be responsibly dealt with, but certainly not in the way it is done in *Case Closed*.

If these examples were isolated, they perhaps would not be worth mentioning, although each one clearly reflects the state of mind and proclivity of the author. But Posner does this type of thing too much to be ignored. The problem with the writings of Posner and the conspiracy theorists is that, as I indicated earlier, unless the reader has all the volumes of the Warren Commission and those of the HSCA to refer to, which perhaps only one out of ten thousand readers would have, how can one possibly know whether what they are reading is true, half-true, or false? In former *Wall Street Journal* reporter Jonathan Kwitny's long review of Posner's book, *Case Closed*, for the *Los Angeles Times* on November 7, 1993, he writes that Posner "does not sink as low as his slimiest predecessors on the case (Jim Garrison, Oliver Stone and Mark Lane); he doesn't knowingly present concoctions as fact. But he does lie down with such predecessor assassination-book writers as Anthony Summers, Jim Marrs and Edward J. Epstein, in that he presents only the evidence that supports the case he's trying to build, framing this evidence in a way that misleads readers who aren't aware that there's more to the story."[*] Kwitny's review would have been more accurate if he had said that Posner "frequently" presents only the evidence that . . . But it's a shame that Posner, in his book (which was written in only two years, a remarkably short period for such an immense undertaking), engaged too often in the tactics of the conspiracy theorists, because despite his omissions and distortions he managed to write an impressive work. If his book had been more comprehensive, particularly in the vast area of conspiracy, and, more importantly, had more credibility, the enormous conspiracy community would not have had the ammunition that they have used against him.

I can assure the conspiracy theorists who have very effectively savaged Posner in their books that they're going to have a much, much more difficult time with me. As a trial lawyer in front of a jury and an author of true-crime books, credibility has always meant

---

[*]Obviously, it is those most familiar with the facts of the case who have the most problems with Posner's scholarship. G. Robert Blakey, the chief counsel for the HSCA, wrote, "Like [Mark] Lane, Posner often distorts the evidence by selective citation and by striking omissions. Although Posner is not as disdainful of the truth as Lane, his book is a mirror image of Lane's 'Rush to Judgment'" (*Washington Post*, National Weekly Edition, November 15–21, 1993, p.23).

everything to me. My only master and my only mistress are the facts and objectivity. I have no others. The theorists may not agree with my conclusions, but in this work on the assassination I intend to set forth all of their main arguments, and the way they, not I, want them to be set forth, before I seek to demonstrate their invalidity. I will not *knowingly* omit or distort anything. However, with literally millions of pages of documents on this case, there are undoubtedly references in some of them that conspiracy theorists feel are supportive of a particular point of theirs, but that I simply never came across.

Some may say it is petty, perhaps even improper, to criticize others in writing a book about the case. I don't agree. The Kennedy assassination is a historical event. And when anyone purporting to write the history of the event fabricates, distorts, or misleads about the facts of the case, it is not only advisable but incumbent upon those who subsequently write about the event to point out these lies and distortions. If they do not, the lies themselves will harden in the future into "facts" and millions will be misled. This is precisely what has already happened in this case. After all, if future writers don't correct the errors and distortions of their predecessors, then who will? If they don't have the responsibility to do this, then who does? Therefore, if those who follow me find that in writing this book I myself have taken liberties with the truth, I would expect them to bring this to the attention of their readers.

Another defect I shall studiously avoid in this book—one that characterizes so many authors of books on the assassination—is to falsely suggest to the reader that what he or she is reading is new information that the author has mined from his research. For instance, the reader of *Case Closed* can only come, *from the context*, to one conclusion about the section on Failure Analysis Associates' computer reconstruction of the shooting in Dealey Plaza, and the section debunking all the supposedly mysterious deaths of people associated with the assassination: that the author, Posner, worked with Failure Analysis on its reconstruction and/or commissioned Failure Analysis's work, and that the author, in his research, had discovered that there were no mysterious deaths associated with the assassination. But Failure Analysis, a leading engineering and scientific consulting firm with offices worldwide, was commissioned to do its work not by Posner, but by the American Bar Association for a mock trial on the assassination the association conducted in San Francisco at its annual convention in 1992.[*] Roger McCarthy, president and CEO of Failure Analysis Associates who testified as an expert witness at the trial in San Francisco, told me that Posner "didn't have anything to do" with their project, and they weren't even aware he was in the process of writing a book at the time. What particularly troubled McCarthy was that "Posner only presented in his book the prosecution side of our presentation in San Francisco, completely omitting what we presented for the defense, which was important enough to help bring about a hung jury."[80]

---

[*]I was asked by Chicago lawyer Michael Stiegel, representing the litigation section of the American Bar Association (ABA), to prosecute the case, but declined, because unlike the docu-trial in London, none of the actual Warren Commission witnesses testified. The witnesses were actors and employees of Failure Analysis. Further, the length of the trial was only five hours, not nearly enough time to get into the case. Prominent American trial lawyers represented each side of the case, including John W. Keker for the prosecution and David Boies for the defense. The August 10, 1992, ABA trial resulted in a hung jury, seven for conviction, five for acquittal. The only other serious mock (an oxymoron?) trial of Oswald I know of in addition to the London and ABA trials was on April 1, 1967, at Yale Law School. The six-hour trial used Yale law students as lawyers and witnesses, though medical testimony was given by some doctors. The jury of educators, theologians, executives, and housewives couldn't reach a verdict, and deadlocked at six for conviction, six for acquittal. (*New York Times*, April 2, 1967, pp.1, 37)

Similarly, way back in 1977, sixteen years before the publication of *Case Closed*, the HSCA thoroughly investigated the entire "mysterious deaths" allegation and wrote of its extensive research and findings discrediting the allegation in volume 4, pages 454–467, of the HSCA's report to Congress. Yet Posner does not tell his readers this in his book. Show me one reader out of a hundred who read *Case Closed* who didn't think that the author was sowing new ground in his section on mysterious deaths.[81] These tactics of authors of books on the assassination remind one of Oscar Levant's observation about Leonard Bernstein: "Leonard Bernstein has been disclosing musical secrets that have been well known for over 400 years." Many competent and hard-working people have labored diligently in the investigative vineyards of the Kennedy assassination case throughout the years, and this book will pay homage to their work and findings.

Another, though more benign, feature of the constantly evolving literature on the assassination is the erroneous assertion or implication in book after book that they contain accounts of the assassination from new and previously unknown witnesses, or new revelations from known witnesses. Even the very prestigious *Journal of the American Medical Association* (*JAMA*) descended to this type of tabloid rhetoric by announcing in a press release that JFK's autopsy doctors "broke their 29 year silence" on the case in *JAMA*'s May 27, 1992, published interview with two of the doctors. *JAMA*'s obvious intent was for the mass media to headline their stories with the "silence" hook, which they in fact did. To the public, the phrase "breaking one's silence" can only mean that the person has never written or spoken about the subject before. But testifying for the public record before the Warren Commission, as the autopsy doctors did, and signing their name to an autopsy report that is published for the world to see, would hardly qualify as "silence." And they were certainly under no obligation to reiterate their position. *JAMA*'s press release also neglected to mention the fact that two of the three autopsy doctors (James J. Humes and Pierre A. Finck), in 1978, testified before the HSCA—again for public consumption—and the third (J. Thornton Boswell) was interviewed by the House Select Committee staff. And Humes, the main autopsy surgeon, gave an interview on his findings to Dan Rather on national television in June of 1967. I only mention the *JAMA* deception to point out that if there is misleading sensationalism about this case from the likes of *JAMA*, one can imagine why it's only downhill from there.

Because this is the most investigated case in world history, any witness (unless someone credible eventually gives testimony of the alleged conspiracy) who has not come forward by now is immediately suspect. Likewise with a known witness who suddenly comes forward with new and vital information. The incontrovertible fact is that the FBI, Secret Service, Warren Commission, and HSCA, as well as police, authors, journalists, historians, private investigators, and an army of ferocious amateur sleuths, have worn the evidentiary terrain in this case all the way through to China. Virtually every important witness has testified under oath, some several times. All important witnesses and almost all of the very peripheral, unimportant ones have already been interviewed. Therefore, as indicated, absent a member of one of the innumerable alleged conspiracies coming forward, the only likely remaining revelations about the case are in the area of new interpretations and analyses of existing evidence. This is not to suggest that these necessarily reduced possibilities render additional inquiry insignificant. Further analytical examination of the case can serve to either strengthen or weaken the official position on the issues of Oswald's guilt and conspiracy, which is of no small moment. As suggested earlier, we are, after all, dealing with the most consequential murder in American, perhaps world, history. To the argument that unless one can reveal some new, critical evidence about the assassination, there's no need to write another book about it, I would respond with the question, why write a book analyzing the New Testament, inasmuch as two thousand years later no one is about to come up with any new evidence on the life of Jesus? Indeed, no one has come up with anything new for two thousand years. Even the Dead Sea Scrolls, discovered in Jordan in 1947 by Bedouin shepherds, are mostly pre-Christian in origin. Yet scholarly books interpreting the New Testament are written every year.* And in terms of volume, there's infinitely less to interpret in the four short Gospels, for example, than in all the vast literature and evidence surrounding the assassination. Reinterpretation of the evidence in the Kennedy assassination will be a never-ending process, and interpretation and analysis are the very heart of this book.

The supreme irony about the Kennedy assassination is that although belief in a conspiracy knows no ideological or political boundaries, most conspiracy theorists I have met look up to Kennedy and his legacy, and many revere him. How very odd, then, that so many of them have virtually dedicated their lives to exonerating the man who killed their hero. To counter the incontrovertible evidence pointing to the guilt of the person who cold-bloodedly murdered Kennedy, they come up with extraordinary and often ludicrous arguments. They defend Oswald with a protective passion normally reserved only for one's immediate family. Indeed, in their mind, everyone (*any* person or group will do, for them) other than Oswald is responsible for Kennedy's death. Obviously, the primary motivation of the conspiracy theorists is not to defend Oswald but to attack the Warren Commission, but in the process they go completely overboard in defending Lee Harvey Oswald the person.

But the very best testament to the validity of the Warren Commission's findings is that after an unrelenting, close to forty-five-year effort, the Commission's fiercest critics have not been able to produce *any new credible evidence* that would in any way justify a different conclusion.

No Warren Commission critic is more venerated by the conspiracy community than the late, legendary Harold Weisberg. Nor has any been remotely as prolific; Weisberg wrote an astonishing eight books on the case. By common consensus, Weisberg did more research on the assassination and accumulated more documents pertaining to the assassination (sixty file cabinets containing a quarter of a million pages as a result of a great many Freedom of Information Act [FOIA] requests and thirteen separate FOIA lawsuits)[82] than any other human. His farm home in Frederick, Maryland, was a mecca to which nearly all serious conspiracy theorists eventually visited to pay homage and browse through his voluminous Kennedy-assassination basement library. As his friend and fellow researcher James Tague said, "Harold spent over 35 years, often seven days a week, in his quest for the truth in the assassination of President John F. Kennedy."[83] Always believing there was a massive federal effort to "whitewash" (the title of his first book on the assassination in 1965) the facts of Kennedy's murder for the American public, and to prevent researchers like himself from finding out what really happened, Weisberg writes on the last page (page 404) of his third book on the assassination (*Oswald in New Orleans*)

---

*There's even, since 1985, a "Jesus Seminar" of seventy-five prominent New Testament scholars with advanced theological degrees who analyze, write about, debate, and eventually cast their vote for one of four levels of authenticity (ranging from "Jesus definitely said or did it," to "Jesus didn't say or do it") that each feels a particular Gospel passage has.

that for the first time he saw "the shadow of a happy ending." Till the end, he still believed that there was a conspiracy in the assassination, but candidly acknowledged to me in 1999, after devoting much of his life to the case, that "much as it looks like Oswald was some kind of agent for somebody, *I have not found a shred of evidence to support it*, and he never had an extra penny, so he had no loot from being an agent."[84]

The vast conspiracy community, which disbelieves everything in the Warren Report except the page numbers, should (but won't) be influenced in their thinking by such a dramatic admission from their most esteemed titan,[*] one who relentlessly, obsessively and, as opposed to most of his peers, honestly put every aspect of the case under a microscope for almost four decades. Instead of spending literally thousands of their hours "seeing" traces, hints, and ephemeral shadows of a conspiracy from plain and unambiguous conduct and events, they should realize, as painful as it may be to them, that sometimes things are exactly as they appear to be, and nothing more. Even Sigmund Freud—celebrated for his ability to find the hidden meaning of dreams—noted that sometimes a cigar is just a cigar.

Not the smallest speck of evidence has ever surfaced that any of the conspiracy community's favorite groups (CIA, mob, etc.) was involved, in any way, in the assassination. Not only the Warren Commission, but the HSCA came to the same conclusion. Moreover, the idea itself overtaxes credulity. The very thought of CIA officials sitting around a conference table at their Langley, Virginia, headquarters, or the heads of the Mafia families gathering at a summit meeting in the Adirondacks, or the captains of industry, like the presidents of General Motors, IBM, Lockheed, and so on, meeting clandestinely with America's top military leaders (Oliver Stone's "military-industrial complex") to actually plot the murder of the president of the United States, is much too far-fetched and preposterous on its face for even a Robert Ludlum novel. But conspiracy theorists, as suspicious as a cat in a new home, find occurrences and events everywhere that feed their suspicions and their already strong predilection to believe that the official version is wrong. However, as *Newsweek* magazine pointed out, "If *any* moment in history were to be scrutinized with the obsessiveness focused on 12:30 p.m., November 22, 1963, you could come up with weird coincidences, hidden connections, terrifying portents."[85]

To create something out of nothing requires considerable powers of imagination, and the conspiracy theorists have indeed soared on the wings of their dreams, wishes, and fantasies. As writer Joe Patoski says, "They have accepted all supposed evidence that sup-

---

[*]Just two examples among many of the high esteem with which Weisberg is held in the conspiracy community: The aforementioned Robert Groden, the author of several conspiracy books, said before Weisberg's death that "there is no man living today who knows more about the work of the Warren Commission and the FBI on the assassination, or whose writings on the case have so successfully withstood all challenges to their accuracy, than Harold Weisberg" (1996 reply brief by Groden in the U.S. Court of Appeals for the Second Circuit, p.11, *Robert Groden v. Random House, The New York Times, and Gerald Posner*, Docket 94-9100). Walt Brown, one of today's leading conspiracy theorists, has written books on the assassination and publishes the foremost monthly magazine for conspiracy devotees, *JFK/Deep Politics Quarterly*. Speaking of Weisberg's death on February 21, 2002, Brown wrote that Weisberg was the "dean" of all Warren Commission critics and his "mentor." He added that "everyone who ever had even a passing interest in the concept of conspiracy owes a massive debt of gratitude to Harold . . . He was a living history of the documentation of the most significant event of the 20th Century." (*JFK/Deep Politics Quarterly*, April 2002, pp.18, 21) Weisberg's power and reach in the conspiracy community were such that fellow Warren Commission critic and conspiracy theorist Harrison E. Livingstone, himself a prolific and noteworthy writer in the conspiracy genre, but one who resented Weisberg's fame and adulation, said that for years and years, "if he [Weisberg] damned something, it was lost. If he praised something, which was rare, then it or the person became an object of worship" (Livingstone, *Radical Right and the Murder of John F. Kennedy*, p.505).

ports their thesis, no matter how shaky, and ignored all evidence that undermines it, no matter how certain." Any district attorney or police detective in the country will tell you that contrary to literature and the big screen—where murder cases are eventually all wrapped up neatly—in virtually every criminal case with any complexity to it at all, there are unexplained discrepancies, unanswered questions, things that don't quite fit. And if these cases were put under the high-powered microscope the Kennedy assassination was, there would be even more. That's true because of the nature of life. Things don't happen in life with mathematical precision and in apple-pie order. As Walter Cronkite put it in a June 27, 1967, CBS special on the assassination, "Only in fiction do we find all the loose ends neatly tied. Real life is not all that tidy."[86]

Law enforcement veterans will also tell you that because of the fallibility of human beings, it is routine, for instance, for five witnesses to observe the same robbery yet give five different physical descriptions of the robber, and for even their own experts to make errors (in forensic analysis of blood, hair, fingerprints, etc.) that are caught and proved to be errors by other experts. Ignoring these realities, the almost unwavering modus operandi of the conspiracy theorists in this case has been to focus only on the inevitable discrepancies and inconsistencies arising out of the statements and work of hundreds upon hundreds of people, as if the discrepancies themselves prove a conspiracy, never bothering to tell their readers, number one, what they believe precisely did happen, and number two, what solid and irrefutable evidence they have to prove it. I mean, do discrepancies and inconsistencies add up to life as we know it, or to conspiracy, as the theorists would want us to believe?

The conspiracy community regularly seizes on one slip of the tongue, misunderstanding, or slight discrepancy to defeat twenty pieces of solid evidence; accepts one witness of theirs, even if he or she is a provable nut, as being far more credible than ten normal witnesses on the other side; treats rumors, even questions, as the equivalent of proof; leaps from the most minuscule of discoveries to the grandest of conclusions; and insists, as the late lawyer Louis Nizer once observed, that the failure to explain everything perfectly negates all that is explained.

All humans make mistakes. But there is no room or allowance in the fevered world of conspiracy theorists for mistakes, human errors, anomalies, or plain incompetence, though the latter, from the highest levels on down, is endemic in our society. Every single piece of evidence that isn't 100 percent consistent with all the other evidence pointing toward Oswald's guilt and the absence of a conspiracy is by itself proof of Oswald's innocence and the existence of a conspiracy. There is also no such thing for these people as a coincidence. With both feet planted firmly in the air, the conspiracy theorists have created a cottage industry that thrives to this very day, and whose hallmark, with noted exceptions, has been absurdity and silliness. Believe it or not, a conspiracy theory that was floating around in the conspiracy community for a time was that the assassin of JFK was really the Secret Service agent driving the presidential limousine, who turned around in his seat (while his fellow agent in the passenger seat leaned over and steered the car for him) and shot Kennedy at point-blank range. Despite the absurdity of their allegations and the total lack of evidence to support their charges, the conspiracy theorists have not only convinced the vast majority of Americans that the Warren Commission was wrong, but have succeeded in convincing virtually all Americans that there will never be a satisfactory resolution of this case. *Indeed, this is even the belief of those who agree that Oswald killed Kennedy and he acted alone.* One example of this latter group is Dan Rather, who says that people will be talking about the assassination "a hundred years from now, a thousand years from now, in somewhat the same way people discuss 'The Iliad.' Different people read Homer's description of the wars and come to different conclusions, and so shall it be with much about Kennedy's death."[87] Author Bob Katz seconds Rather when he states what has become the conventional wisdom: "The truth in this case lies buried forever. The unsolved murder of the twentieth century has entered the realm of myth."[88]

But I don't believe for one moment that the truth in this case has been buried forever or that there *has* to be substantial questions about this case for thousands of years to come. If I did, I would never have started working on this book, which has consumed so many years of my life. I firmly believe that the evidence in this case enables all sensible people who look at it to be completely satisfied as to exactly what happened.

I want to assure the readers of this book that I commenced my investigation of this case with an open mind. But after being exposed to the evidence, I have become satisfied beyond *all* doubt that Lee Harvey Oswald killed President Kennedy, and beyond all *reasonable* doubt that he acted alone. I am very confident that the overwhelming majority of objective readers of this book will end up feeling the same way.

As one gets further into this book and starts to learn more about Oswald, it will become increasingly obvious that if any group such as the CIA or organized crime had wanted to kill the president, the unreliable and unpredictable loner and loser Lee Harvey Oswald would have been the last man on earth whom it would have entrusted with such a monumental undertaking.

Any reader of this book has to be struck by three things, one of which is its abnormal length.* In defense of its length, in addition to the point I made previously that conspiracy theorists have transformed Kennedy's murder into the most complex murder case ever, I would remind the reader that more words have been written about Kennedy's assassination than any other single, one-day event in history. Obviously, more words have been written about Christ, but not about his life and death, since so very little is known. Instead, they have been written mostly about the ramifications of his life and death and their profound influence on history. The scope and breadth of issues flowing from the Kennedy assassination are so enormous that typically authors write entire books on just one aspect of the case alone, such as organized crime, or the CIA, or Castro, or Jack Ruby, or Oswald's guilt or innocence in Kennedy's murder, or the murder of Officer Tippit, or the prosecution of Clay Shaw in New Orleans for Kennedy's murder, or the mind of Lee Harvey Oswald, or the Warren Commission, et cetera, et cetera.

When looked upon in the above light, and with my objective being to compress the essence of the vast and limitless words and literature on the assassination into one single volume, one could possibly say about the seemingly inordinate length of this book, "Is that all you have to say, Mr. Bugliosi?" On the other hand, I suspect that at some point in their reading of this book, many other readers will say to themselves, "Why does he [yours truly] keep piling one argument upon another to prove his point? He's already made it twelve ways from Sunday, so why go on?" To those readers I say that the Warren Commission also made its point, and well, over forty years ago, yet today the overwhelming majority of

---

*Indeed, if this book (including endnotes) had been printed in an average-size font and with pages of normal length and width, at 1,535,791 words, and with a typical book length of 400 pages, and 300 words per page, this work would translate into around thirteen volumes.

Americans do not accept its conclusion that Oswald acted alone, a great number not even believing he killed Kennedy. Hence, the overkill in this book is historically necessary.

What about the companion CD-ROM of endnotes numbering 954 pages? With forty official volumes, 933 books, and literally hundreds of millions of other words written in newspapers and magazines about the most important murder case in our history, one of my very biggest tasks for you, the reader, was to separate the wheat from the chaff out of the virtually endless allegations, controversies, and issues surrounding the case. I believe I have done this, and it is this wheat, as it were, that constitutes this very long book.* The endnotes are for the following people: those lay readers who want to know more about a matter in the main text; conspiracy theorists and serious, longtime students of the assassination; and scholars and future historians. To put the material presently in the endnotes into the main body of the text would have substantially slowed down and interrupted the flow of the narrative and interfered with the average reader's enjoyment of the book. And if the truth be told, and the reader promises not to tell, I had a big inducement to put whatever I could in an endnote. Since the book is already uncommonly long, and therefore heavy, whatever I could put in an endnote helped enable me to put out a book that wasn't prohibitively long and unmanageable.

Readers might be interested to know that I commenced my work on this book following the London trial in 1986. So I have been working on this book for twenty-one years. Most of the early years were devoted to research, reading, and writing, not interviewing witnesses to fill in the holes, which I did do much of to supplement my continuing reading, writing, and research in later years.

Finally, I believe readers will also be struck by the incredibly rich cast of diverse characters who people the Kennedy assassination saga, characters who would rival those in the most inspired of fiction, including that of Shakespeare. I don't read fiction but I've been told that most prominent novelists really only have four or five characters who keep reemerging, in different clothing, in their various stories, whereas Shakespeare allegedly had more than twenty disparate characters. I can assure the readers of this book that within its pages they will meet many extremely fascinating people in addition to President Kennedy himself and his wife, Jackie, not the least of which, you will find, are Lee Harvey Oswald and Jack Ruby. J. Edgar Hoover, Lyndon Johnson, Fidel Castro, and Che Guevara are among the many others.† Conspiracy author Paris Flammonde said it well when he observed that the dramatic personalities in the Kennedy case were among "the most extraordinary ever to stride, slink, and flee across the stage of greater human events . . . , and like the pageant of characters" in "Lawrence Durrell's *Alexandria Quartet*, almost all enter as enigmas and most are hardly more understandable when they depart."[89] Longtime JFK assassination researcher Bill Drenas connects these characters with the unbe-

---

*At some point, of course, my writing on this case had to come to an end. Since the production and lead time for this outsized book was several months, and advance copies were scheduled to be sent out to reviewers on March 1, 2007, that point was in early November of 2006, when the book was in final galley form and my editor informed me that no further writing by me about new allegations being made in the case would be possible, only corrections to the galleys, or a very short insert here or there for clarification or other necessary purposes. So I was unable to respond to any book or other publication on this case that was published after early November of 2006.

†One character, for example, and there are many others, is so interesting that when Warren Commission counsel called him to testify about his relationship to Oswald, counsel became so captivated by the man and his story that counsel just listened to him, even telling the witness at one point, when the witness, on his own, started talking about Oswald, "I want to get to that," but "first" he wanted to hear more of the man's background—that part of the witness's testimony consuming over twenty pages of small print in a Commission volume.

lievable twists and turns in this story when he says, "If you sat down and tried to write something that was this interesting about a presidential assassination, you couldn't do it. It's the most fascinating story ever told. That's why people will never stop talking about this case."[90]

Though the president's murder happened in Dallas, Texas, the long journey you the reader are about to embark on will take you to many other places—New Orleans's colorful and steamy French Quarter, a hotel room in Moscow, the beaches of the Bay of Pigs in Cuba, and the roiling waters of the Gulf of Tonkin off North Vietnam; from a mob hangout in Chicago to the little town of Stanley, North Dakota; a park bench in Central Park and bullring in Mexico City to the anti-Castro–laden streets of Miami's Little Havana; and so on. Though a good portion of the subject matter will be complex, sometimes even arcane, I hope I will have infused even these areas with enough interesting and understandable narrative to keep your interest throughout this very long and circuitous journey.

Vincent Bugliosi
January 2007
Los Angeles, California

BOOK ONE

Matters of Fact

What Happened

Four Days in November

Author's Note: All times noted throughout this chapter are derived, when possible, from reliable sources (e.g., Dallas police radio recordings, television videotapes with times on screen). When not, times are inferred from the unfolding events and the totality of witness statements. This methodology is necessary because the time estimates given by, for instance, a single witness would often change every time the witness was interviewed and nearly always be in conflict with those given by other witnesses. All of this, of course, is normal and to be expected. I believe the following chronology to be the most accurate reconstruction to date. Throughout this chronology, the times, unless stated otherwise, are those of Central Standard Time.

Friday, November 22, 1963

6:30 a.m.

Marina Oswald awakens in the dark. This late in November the sun doesn't rise until seven, even as far south as Irving, Texas. The young Russian woman, born Marina Nikolaevna Prusakova, is still tired from an uneasy night. She and her American husband, Lee, argued the night before, not as intensely as usual, but unpleasantly enough, particularly as they hadn't seen each other for nearly two weeks. And their newborn, Rachel, awoke twice, as babies will.

Lee usually woke up before the alarm went off, but this morning he didn't, sleeping through the sound, and Marina awakened him about ten minutes later. In the other bedroom Marina's friend Ruth Paine, the owner of the house, is still asleep with her kids.[1]

Lee has changed a lot in the two and a half years since Marina first met him at a dance at the Palace of Culture in Minsk, the capital city of the Soviet province of Byelorussia. She was only nineteen then, he was twenty-one and just a few months out of the U.S. Marines. Marina thought him to be very well dressed in his gray suit, white shirt, and white tie.[2] When she found out later that he was an American defector to the Soviet Union, it only increased her attraction to him. She still finds him good looking, in some ways even more so since he has been losing weight and some of the babyish plumpness of cheek that made him look a bit like a chipmunk. At five foot nine inches and less than 150 pounds, Lee is rather small of build. But he's wiry, and his hands and arms are unusually strong. He is hardening into a man, and Marina is still Lee's woman, despite his crazy imagination. Honestly, some of his ideas would make the cat laugh. He told her not long ago that in twenty years he would be the "prime minister."

The lingering squabble from the night before is nothing out of the ordinary. They have been bickering from the first day of their marriage, and Lee isn't above hitting her when he loses his temper. They quarrel when they live together, they quarrel when they live apart. Marina has plenty of reason to want to live apart, but now he wants her to come back to live with him. He wants to take an apartment near his job, in Dallas, so they can all be together again—quite a turnaround from the pressure he had been putting on her to return to the Soviet Union, unless he is just trying to manipulate her again for some hidden reason of his own. Marina can never be quite sure. She knows she will eventually have to go back to him—she can't presume upon the hospitality of Ruth much longer— but she isn't ready yet. She is particularly outraged that Lee has been living in Dallas under an assumed name—more of his foolishness. She doesn't even know where in Dallas—some cheap furnished room somewhere, she supposes—and it was more or less an accident that she found out about the phony name at all.

Lee didn't come out to Irving last weekend. He didn't call her either. Perhaps he was angry because she had asked him not to come. Ruth, an intellectually inclined Quaker, was having a birthday party for her daughter on Saturday, her estranged husband Michael would be there, and Marina felt Lee's presence would be an intrusion on what ought to be a family day.

Then on Sunday, baby June, their two-year-old, was playing with the telephone dial, and Marina, perhaps feeling a little guilty, impulsively asked Ruth to call Lee. After seventeen months in the United States, Marina still doesn't speak English, so she had Ruth call for her. The man who answered the phone told Ruth that no one by the name of Lee Oswald lived at that number. Neither she nor Ruth knew that he was living there under an assumed name, and when he finally did call on Monday, Marina let him know she was furious that he was up to his childish tricks again. He got very angry and ordered her to remove his name and phone number from Ruth's address book. She said she wouldn't, and they argued about it. He claimed he did it because he didn't want the landlady to know his real name. She might, he said, read in the paper that he had defected to Russia. He told her he also didn't want the FBI to know where he lived because his contacts with the bureau were unpleasant. He never did tell her what name he had registered under at the rooming house.[3]

She is further aggravated by the fact that Lee came out to Irving last night—Thursday—instead of Friday, in violation of their understanding with Ruth. Lee is allowed to come out on Friday evening and stay over the weekend, but this week he'd come out a day early, which he had never done before, claiming he'd gotten "lonesome for my girls." But he wanted more, begging her to come live with him again, in Dallas, with their two girls.[4]

For all his faults, Lee loves the children. Last night he played with them out on the lawn in the gathering dusk—Ruth's children, the neighbors' kids, and his and Marina's own toddler, June. He loved that. They were still out on the lawn and it was nearly dark when he asked Marina for the third and last time to come back to him. He even agreed to buy her a washing machine, an unusual gesture for Lee, who was always so close with the little money he had. Marina nearly did give in. If he'd waited until Friday evening, she might have said yes. The truth of the matter is, despite their sorry marriage, he's all she's got. Even the warm friendship and support of Ruth, who only speaks sufficiently serviceable Russian to teach it part-time at a private high school and is delighted to have Marina around the house to pick up better Russian from her, doesn't make up for Lee's absence. But she isn't ready to give in yet. For once, she enjoys having the upper hand, however slight.

Lee didn't sleep well last night, although he'd turned in at ten o'clock, an hour earlier than usual. She could tell he was very upset when he retired for the evening and wasn't really asleep when she crept into bed after a late, hot bath. Around three in the morning she rested her foot on his leg, but he shoved her foot away hard. "My, he's in a mean mood," she thinks, believing he's angry at her for not coming back to him right away. She senses he may not have slept at all until about five o'clock in the morning.[5]

His mood has changed since last night, as it so often does. He seems upset rather than angry. Marina, at the mercy of his moods, knows the difference well. He is quiet and calm. He doesn't ask her to come to live with him in Dallas anymore.

As Lee finishes dressing, he comes over to the bed.

"Have you bought those shoes you were going to get?" he asks.

"No, I haven't had time," Marina answers.

"You must get those shoes, Mama," Lee tells her, then adds, "Don't get up, I'll get breakfast myself."

It was an odd comment for him to make, since there was little danger that she would. Lee rarely ate breakfast, it was usually just a cup of instant coffee, which he had this morning, and she certainly had never fixed him anything before. Why would he say that? she wondered.[6]

Before he leaves the bedroom, Lee kisses the children, as he always does, then walks to the bedroom door. He stops and returns to the side of the bed. He has always kissed his wife good-bye and Marina assumes he will do so now. But this time, she only hears his voice.

"I've left some money on the bureau," he says in his odd, if fluent, Russian. "Take it and buy everything you and Junie and Rachel need."

In the dark he has left $170 in bills, and something else—his wedding ring, quietly placed in a little china teacup that had belonged to Marina's grandmother. She won't find it until later that day.

"Bye-bye," he says, then turns and goes out the door.

Marina is surprised at her husband's sudden and unexpected kindness. She knows his $1.25-an-hour job doesn't really allow for a lot of new shoes, much less everything she and the children need. He certainly had never said such a thing before. But she is used to his erratic behavior, and it doesn't keep her from drifting back to sleep.[7]

7:21 a.m.

Linnie Mae Randle fixes a lunch at the kitchen counter for her nineteen-year-old brother, Wesley Frazier, to take to work. She sees a man crossing Westbrook Street. She doesn't recognize him at first but realizes he is heading to where her brother's automobile is parked in the carport.

"Who was that?" Linnie Mae's mother asks from the breakfast table, having caught a glimpse of him as he looked in the kitchen window.

"That's Lee," Wesley says.

He looks at the clock. It's late. Wesley likes to leave the house by 7:20 for the fifteen-mile drive into Dallas, even if that means getting there a few minutes early. He finishes off his coffee and jumps up from the table, where he has been having breakfast with his mom and his sister's kids, and hurries to get his lunch and a jacket. It is a gray, cold, miserable morning, and he will probably need that jacket.[8]

Linnie Mae, at the back door, watches Lee go over to Wesley's beat-up '59 Chevy four-door, open the right rear door—the sticky one with the broken window—and lay the package he's carrying on the backseat. She doesn't pay much attention to the light brown paper package. It's a couple of feet long, and wider at the bottom than at the top, where he carries it in the fashion soldiers call "trail arms."[9]

It isn't so surprising that she didn't recognize Lee, even though in a way she was responsible for getting him his job. She has only caught a couple glimpses of him when he came by to ride into work with Wesley. Linnie Mae knows that he is the husband of that Russian girl who has been staying with Ruth Paine, a neighbor who lives up the street from her. He came up in a conversation one afternoon at another neighbor's house. In early October, just about the time Marina's baby was due, Ruth and Marina were there drinking coffee. They were talking about Marina's husband being out of work at the worst possible time. Linnie Mae told them about the job Wesley had just found at the Texas School Book Depository, a private company at 411 Elm Street near downtown Dallas that warehoused and shipped school textbooks for various publishers. She thought there might be another vacancy there,[10] so Ruth called the Depository and was told to have Lee come on in for an interview.[11]

Linnie Mae doesn't have a lot of time to think about Marina's husband, although she realizes vaguely that it is out of the ordinary for him to be out in Irving on a Friday morning. She's heard about the odd arrangement where he lives in Dallas and only visits his wife and kids on the weekend. She was surprised to see him coming back with Wesley the night before when she was on her way to the store. Wesley told her Lee had come in a day early to get some curtain rods or something.[12]

Wesley is relieved when the old Chevy finally fires up. It has been raining off and on all night and the battery is really weak. He notices that Lee doesn't have a lunch bag with him, something he has always had before on trips back into Dallas.[13]

"Where's your lunch?" Wesley asks.

"I'm going to buy it today," Lee replies.

Wesley figures Lee will get something from the catering truck that comes around the warehouse at ten o'clock. A lot of the boys do that.[14] As Wesley backs the car out, he glances over his right shoulder and notices a brown paper package on the rear seat.

"What's the package, Lee?" he asks.

"Curtain rods," Oswald says.

"Oh, yeah," Wesley nods, shifting into forward. "You said you were going to go get them last night."[15]

Lee doesn't have a lot to say. He rarely does. Lee is one of those guys who just doesn't talk very much. Wesley, on the other hand, feels it's important to make friends. That's why he introduced himself to Lee when Lee came on the job in mid-October.

"We're glad to have you," he had told Lee. Wesley, a self-described country boy from

Huntsville, Texas, had only been on the job four or five weeks himself, but he felt like a veteran. He already knew that Lee's wife was living up the street from him, so he told Lee, "Any time you want to go, just let me know."[16]

Lee told him he had an apartment in Dallas and wouldn't be going home every night like most men do. He said he didn't drive either. That's when he asked Wesley if he could ride out with him "on Friday afternoon on weekends and come back on Monday morning," and Wesley said that would be just fine with him.

Wesley knows Lee's wife is from Russia but doesn't think anything about that. Lee said something about being in Russia, Germany, and France, and Wesley figured he had been in the service or something. Wesley doesn't know much more than that. Come to think of it, he doesn't even know Lee's last name.[17]

Back in Dallas, nightclub operator Jack Ruby is still asleep. Jack's day starts when most people are thinking about going home from work. Today he will get up around ten to get his ad into the offices of the *Dallas Morning News*, but that's early for him. Jack's Carousel Club, on Commerce Street halfway between the county jail and the police station, stays open until two every morning, even though the curious Texas liquor laws require customers to stop drinking at a quarter past midnight. This is kind of a pain in the behind, but Jack is scrupulous about keeping drinks off the table after hours. He runs a clean joint, which everyone knows. Even that vice-squad dick Gilmore has never cited him, and, as one of Jack's girls says, Gilmore would cite his own mother.

Dallas is a "dry" town, meaning that hard liquor cannot be sold in a public bar. So Jack's profit is in beer and champagne. His beer is the cheapest money can buy, and it is served in a glass with a bottom that works like a lens to magnify the modest quantity inside. His bartender also sells "setups," nonalcoholic beverages to which the customer may add his own liquor from the bottle he brought to the club in a paper bag, which is legal but not very profitable. The real dough is in champagne. Jack sells his champagne, which costs him $1.60 a bottle, for $17.50, and the waitress usually gets the change from a twenty as a tip. The champagne girls get $2.50 for each bottle they persuade their customers to buy. There are over a dozen of Jack's girls—waitresses, champagne and cigarette girls, and strippers. The strippers work under the American Guild of Variety Artists (AGVA) contract, but the others live on their tips and the commissions on the champagne.[18]

The champagne or cocktail girls are called B-girls, companions to the male customers to induce them to buy drinks, but Jack is proud of them. They aren't hookers. He's hell on any girl he suspects of making dates with the customers. His girls have class. He really cares about that. So what if most of his customers think his B-girls are hookers and keep buying Jack's rotgut champagne for them, while the girls keep pouring the stuff into bar towels and ice buckets to avoid drinking it. They are provided with "spit glasses," frosted tumblers ostensibly filled with ice water, really just ice, that they use to spit the champagne in their mouth into. Jack doesn't want the girls to drink any more than they absolutely have to. He doesn't like drunks any more than hookers. Jack's girls are a major preoccupation. He is always flying off the handle at them, browbeating, bullying, firing them. Diana Hunter, a veteran, reckons Jack has fired her two hundred times. But he's good to them too, always there with a bit of cash or even a pint of blood when they're really in trouble. They scream back at him when he loses his temper and turns cruel and mean, but they also know that a short time later he will have forgotten all about it. The girls love Jack in some odd way. Jack is a mensch.[19]

Jack Ruby lives in a low-rent district south of downtown, Oak Cliff. Though he is a neat dresser and his personal hygiene is high—taking two or three showers a day—he lives in an apartment full of litter, dirty clothes, unread newspapers, unwashed glasses—an apartment as implacably disordered, out of control, and marginal as his life.[20] Jack has troubles. His rock-and-roll joint out on Oak Lawn in North Dallas, the Vegas Club, which his sister Eva runs for him, is in trouble. With Eva out sick, he has to get the kid, Larry Crafard, to look after things out there, but who knows how long that's going to last— Crafard is a drifter. He was working as a roustabout with Bob Craven's carny show, "How Hollywood Makes Movies," until it folded in Dallas last month. Jack lets Larry sleep in the room down at the Carousel and gives him a buck or two for his meals at the Eat Well Café in return for doing odd jobs around the Carousel. So who knows how long Larry will last? Larry's a good kid, but no way is he going to get back together with that ballsy wife of his, and Jack knows he won't be around Dallas long.[21]

Not only is Eva sick, but Little Lynn is too—that's one of his strippers, out the whole damned weekend, probably. Drank too much champagne and passed out over at Nichols Brothers garage, but wouldn't let Jack drive her to the hospital.[22] He'll probably have to send her a couple of bucks, wire it to her over in Fort Worth. She's most likely pregnant, and that salesman boyfriend of hers is out of work because his car broke down.[23]

Jack has his own problems. Like recently with the stripper Jada? He goes to all sorts of trouble and expense to bring her up from New Orleans because she's supposed to be such a class act, and he's paying her way over scale, and then she gets out of line, starts doing front bumps and other kinds of things that could get his club shut down in a place like Dallas, and Jack has to douse the lights when it gets too raunchy. Jack screams at Jada and, she says, threatens her. Her agent calls the cops, and Jada files a "threats warrant" for Jack's arrest. At the peace-bond hearing, Jada tells the judge that Jack was trying to get out of paying her on the rest of her contract by threatening to cut up her wardrobe if she gives him trouble. Her wardrobe, she says, is worth $40,000. Jack's own arresting officer tells Jada, "Young lady, how in the world could you have $40,000 worth of G strings because that's all I've ever seen you in?"[24] And where's Jack going to get the dough to pay if old Judge Richberg ends up giving him a stiff fine when he's way behind on the union welfare payments for his dancers?[25]—particularly with the feds after him for delinquent income taxes,[26] and the competition, the Weinstein brothers, beating him to death with their fake "amateur nights" at Abe's Colony Club and the Theatre Lounge? They have pros there pretending to be housewives and working for ten or fifteen bucks a show,[27] way under scale, and you can't get the AGVA to do anything about it, probably because someone's paying them off or something. Jack spends his whole time trying to get the AGVA off the dime and start protecting its artists the way it should, but that bunch is so crooked they'd cheat God. In the meantime, Jack has just paid the rent on the Carousel, five hundred bucks, by certified check,[28] so he can breathe easy for another little while anyway. People go and tell you show biz is the life, but listen to Jack. Jack knows—it's tough, really tough.

Jack's favorite dachshund, Sheba, snuffs and begins to snore, but Jack sleeps on. Jack really loves Sheba. He tells some people she's his wife. Sheba is always with Jack, goes everywhere with him, even sleeps in his bed. The four dachshunds he's now keeping in a room off the kitchen at his club (he's had as many as ten dogs at a time) he calls his children. He gets really pissed off if you take that as a joke, tilting his head in a menacing way.[29]

7:30 a.m.

In Fort Worth's dowdy, brown-brick Texas Hotel, George Thomas enters the small foyer of suite 850 and raps lightly on the door of the master bedroom. He hears a stirring beyond the door and then the word "okay," a communication from the president that the First Lady had not slept in her husband's bedroom that night. If she had, like at the White House, the president's response would have been a cough if he didn't want to disturb her in her slumber.

"Mr. President," the portly black valet calls gently, then pushes the door open and steps across the threshold.

"It's raining," Thomas says.

A voice, with a distinctive Boston accent, groans from under the covers, "That's too bad."[30]

President John F. Kennedy throws back the comforter and swings his legs over the side of the bed, planting his feet on the icy floor. His first appearance of the day is out of doors, and later, several motorcades are planned—useless for vote-getting if the president and his wife have to be driven past sodden, disgruntled crowds, hidden beneath the limousine's plastic bubble top. While the president showers, Thomas lays out his clothes—a blue-gray, two-button suit, a dark blue tie, and a white shirt with narrow gray stripes.[31]

If, for a few moments in this blandly impersonal hotel room, he seems like just another American head of a household getting up to go to work, that's an illusion, for Jack Kennedy is the chief executive of the most powerful government on earth, the commander of its most powerful military machine, the most powerful man alive. Even the impression that this nondescript eighth-floor suite* in Fort Worth is far from the White House is an illusion. The White House is there, in the hotel with him, in the suite, never beyond the sound of Jack Kennedy's voice. To make sure that none of the far-flung people and agencies of the American government are out of range of that voice, an elite group of Signal Corps technicians from the White House Communications Agency travels ahead of the president to install a jungle of special telephone circuits, relays, and networks that are tied back to the key switchboard in the east basement of the executive mansion, and Jack Kennedy is never allowed to be more than five minutes away from that network.

Many of his enormous entourage are already awake and waiting for him to emerge from the shower. Some who watched through the night, like the nine Secret Service agents of the White House detail† on the twelve-to-eight shift, will sleep only after passing their responsibilities on to the next shift. John F. Kennedy's presidency is in fact a collection of special teams that never sleep, teams with code names: an S team for communications, a D team for the Secret Service, a W team for the president's staff, a V team for the vice president's staff. The L team is the president and his family—Jack is Lancer, Jackie is Lace, their children Lyric and Lark, and they all live in the Crown (or Castle), a code name for the White House. There are political advisers, medical men, the military, sec-

---

*It was not the most expensive and plush suite in the hotel. That was the Will Rogers Suite on the thirteenth floor, normally going for $100 a night, but rejected by the Secret Service because there was more than one access to it. So LBJ and Lady Bird stayed in that suite. (Gun, *Red Roses from Texas*, p.24)

†Twenty-eight Secret Service agents accompanied the president on his trip to Texas (HSCA Report, p.228).

retarial pools, and a luggage crew, and every individual has a precisely worked-out itinerary and schedule specifying his transportation, accommodations, and duties for every
moment of the three-day trip through Texas.[32]

A peculiarly inconspicuous but nonetheless vivid symbol of the president's power is
Warrant Officer Ira D. Gearhart, the man with the "satchel," or the "football." The football is a locked metal suitcase jammed with thirty pounds of codes and equipment that
Kennedy can use to launch America's nuclear strike force. In the event of a missile attack
on America or Europe the president will have only fifteen minutes to make up his mind
on how to respond. Kennedy's military aides will actually operate the equipment, but it
is Gearhart's lugubrious duty to be there with the football—and to remember the combination of the lock—if Kennedy decides to push the button. Gearhart, known to the
president's staff as "The Bagman," is never far from the president.[33]

7:52 a.m.
In Dallas, the drizzle from a gray sky has stopped by the time Wesley Frazier and Lee
Oswald exit Stemmons Freeway. The Pacific cold front that rolled in from New Mexico
last night is moving faster than predicted and is already on the way out of central Texas,
taking its scattered thundershowers with it. The air behind it is cold, but it looks as though
the day will turn fair after all.[34]

Wesley circles around up Record Street to McKinney and down to the wire-fenced
parking lot reserved for employees at the corner of Munger and Broadway, across the
street from the Texas School Book Depository Warehouse. It's about a twelve-hundred-
foot walk back to the Depository's rear door, but they'll be able to get there for the workday, which starts at 8:00 a.m. and ends at 4:45 p.m., with a forty-five-minute lunch period
starting at noon.[35]*

Lee gets out, takes his package from the backseat, and starts toward the rear of the
Depository Building. Wesley stays in the car for a minute or so to rev the engine so his car
battery will have a good charge when they quit work. Trains are switching back and forth
in the train yards off to the west. Lee waits for him at the end of the cyclone fence, and
Wesley notices that Lee is carrying the long, paper package in his right hand.[36] When Wesley cuts the engine and gets out, Lee starts off toward the Depository again. As Wesley
begins to follow, Oswald quickens his pace, keeping an ever-increasing distance between
them. It's the first time that Lee has walked ahead of him; usually they walk together.[37]

Wesley doesn't bother to catch up. They've got plenty of time and he likes to watch the
switch engines shunting freight cars around the yards. He stops to watch some guys welding a section of track. You have to be careful crossing the tracks here, because you never
know when a string of boxcars might be bearing down on you. Wesley steps over the rusty
rails, avoiding the puddles, and spots Lee, fifty feet ahead, still carrying the package, as he
goes in the back door of the Depository, the one near the Houston Street loading dock. By
the time Wesley gets there, Lee is nowhere in sight. Wesley goes downstairs, hangs up his
coat, puts up his lunch, and goes to work filling orders for schoolbooks.[38]

---

*The Texas School Book Depository Company had two buildings: an administrative office and storage
area at 411 Elm Street (at Houston), and a warehouse four blocks north at 1917 North Houston (between
Munger and McKinney). Parking lot 1, designated for "employees and publishers," was located across the
street from the warehouse (Frazier parked there). Parking lots 2 ("company officials and customers") and 3
("publishers and managers") were located on the west side of the Depository Building.

8:00 a.m.

In a Fort Worth hotel bathroom, the president can hear the murmur of the crowd awaiting him eight floors below as he drags a razor across his face. In the mirror he looks good. He has to. Americans want their president to be the picture of robust health. They will never know how much it costs him to give them that image. Although muscular and well developed, the president has been bedeviled all his life by an endless series of debilitating illnesses, starting in his early childhood when he had all the traditional childhood illnesses, including scarlet fever, as well as high fevers and allergies. "Jack was sick all the time," a boyhood friend would say. He was thirty before the doctors figured out that most of his health problems stemmed from Addison's disease, an extremely grave disorder of the adrenal glands that weakens the immune system, leaving the victim unable to fight off infection. The first crisis occurred on a trip to England in 1947. The British doctor who first diagnosed the disease in Kennedy gave him a year to live. He was taken off the ship that brought him home, the *Queen Mary*, on a stretcher, so near death that he had to be given the Catholic Church's sacrament of extreme unction—the last rites.[39]

Even though the disease has been brought under control by a relatively new (1939) hormone derived from the adrenal gland, cortisone, the hormone causes odd fat deposits, such as a slight upper-back "buffalo hump" and full cheeks, both of which the president exhibited, and he is forced to keep himself well tanned to hide its typical brownish discoloration of the skin. His frequent bouts of fever are explained away as recurrences of the malaria he caught during the war. In fact, he is extremely prone to infection and takes various medications, including painkillers, every day—including some that had never been prescribed by his White House doctors[40] and might earn anyone else a stretch in jail.

The most painful of his multiple disabilities is his back, which never ceases tormenting him and even causes him to use crutches or a cane in private.[41] One of his shoes has a quarter-inch riser in it, he wears a stiff, six-inch-wide elastic corset to immobilize his lower back, and he sleeps on a special bedboard of thick plywood with a five-inch horsehair pad. Two of these Spartan devices follow him wherever he goes. By 1954, Kennedy's back pain "had become almost unbearable. X-rays showed that the 5th lumbar vertebra had collapsed, most likely the consequence of the corticosteroids he was taking for the Addison's disease. He could not bend down to pull a sock on his left foot and he had to climb and descend stairs moving sideways."[42] In 1954, he again was given the last rites when he fell into a coma after a risky operation to fuse the deteriorating vertebrae—with no better than a fifty-fifty chance of surviving. Because of his condition, the family has stashed small quantities of deoxycorticosterone acetate, or DOCA, the powerful corticoid drug that might save his life in the event of another crisis, in safe deposit boxes all over America.[43] His brother Robert, the attorney general, is one of the few who knows that Jack spends half the hours of his life in pain.*

---

*Presidential historian Robert Dallek, the first scholar to examine Kennedy's medical records on file at the Kennedy presidential library in Boston, reported in 2002 that Kennedy had nine previously undisclosed hospital stays between 1955 and 1957 and took a substantial amount of medication during his presidency on a daily basis. Included on the list were painkillers for his back, steroids for his Addison's disease, antispasmodics for his colitis, antibiotics for urinary-tract infections, antihistamines for allergies, and, on at least one occasion, an antipsychotic for a severe mood change that Mrs. Kennedy believed was brought on by the antihistamines. According to Dallek, three doctors were treating Kennedy, including the famous "Dr. Feelgood," Max Jacobson, who was giving him amphetamine shots during his first summit with Soviet premier Nikita Khrushchev. Although Dallek suggested that Kennedy and his advisers had recklessly deceived the public by not telling voters in 1960 just how sick he really was, Ted Sorenson, one of Kennedy's closest advis-

The president finishes shaving and begins the arduous task of wrapping himself firmly in his back brace.[44] As he slips on his shirt, he decides to have a look at the crowd in the parking lot eight floors below. He can't see them from where he is, so he tiptoes into his wife's bedroom.

"Gosh, look at the crowd!" he beams.

About five thousand people are down there, hemmed in by two loan companies, two bus stations, a garage, a theater, and mounted police in rain-wet yellow slickers. The politician in him is pleased. It looks like a great crowd, mostly working men—Texas senator Ralph Yarborough's constituency—tough men who don't mind a bit of rain, with a few secretaries from nearby office buildings. They had begun to gather about two hours before dawn to see and hear the president. He appreciates every opportunity to show himself to ordinary people. He needs every one of their votes. He tells Jackie he'll see her later at breakfast in the hotel, where he is meeting with the Fort Worth Chamber of Commerce. In the meantime she can catch another hour of sleep.[45]

Jackie is still recovering from the death of their infant son Patrick, who died just forty hours after his birth in August. Only those close to the First Family know how devastating the loss was for both of them. Jack had wept hard, and in his grief had put his arms around the small white casket at the grave site. Jackie didn't leave the hospital until four days after the funeral, and her emotional convalescence was long. Once, when Jack was comforting her, she told him, "There's just one thing I couldn't stand—if I ever lost you."[46]

Jackie has tried hard to put the trauma of that sorrowful event behind her, and even though she has never campaigned with him before, the dark-haired beauty with a European elegance who disdains the vulgarity of politics can muster a practical gesture on occasion, and she volunteered to make this trip to Texas. To everyone's delight, she actually seems to be enjoying herself, prompting the president to ask her if she would like to accompany him on a forthcoming trip to the West Coast, and she said yes. After leaving the White House the previous morning, the president and Jackie had flown to San Antonio, where Vice President Johnson and his wife, Lady Bird, joined the presidential party, and the president had dedicated new research facilities at the U.S. Air Force School of Aerospace Medicine. The four had then flown to Houston in the late afternoon for a testimonial dinner that evening for U.S. Representative Albert Thomas. (There had been motorcades through both San Antonio and Houston.) They arrived in Fort Worth after 11:00 p.m., leaving very little time to sleep and get ready for another vigorous day that would end that night with a fund-raising dinner in Austin. Then back to Washington, D.C., on Saturday morning in time for their son John-John's third birthday on Monday.[47] Jack is grateful to Jackie for accompanying him on the trip and being

---

ers, and reporter Hugh Sidey, who followed Kennedy from 1957 to 1963, denied that the president's medication kept him from performing his duties. Both reported that the president never faltered during the grueling 1960 presidential campaign, one that left them, and everyone else, absolutely exhausted. Sidey wrote that the newly released medical records were indisputable, "but they don't give the whole picture and do leave the impression that Kennedy was little more than a chemical shell ready to self-destruct. I have my doubts. John Kennedy was a strong, determined President partly handicapped by a weakened body. But he was never an invalid." In 1970, long before Dallek's revelations, Kennedy's two closest assistants, Kenneth P. O'Donnell and David F. Powers, wrote of Kennedy's "tireless energy and stamina which wore out everybody following him on an average eight-hour day of campaigning." (Lawrence K. Altman and Todd S. Purdom, "In J.F.K. File, Hidden Illness, Pain and Pills," *New York Times*, November 17, 2002, pp.1, 28; see also Dallek, *Unfinished Life*, pp.213, 262, 398–399, 471; Lacayo, "How Sick Was J.F.K.?" pp.46–47; Sidey, "When It Counted, He Never Faltered," pp.46–47; Peggy Noonan, "Camelot on Painkillers," *Wall Street Journal*, November 22, 2002, p.A12; O'Donnell and Powers with McCarthy, *Johnny, We Hardly Knew Ye*, p.116)

such a trooper. He knows her presence is an enormous plus, but doesn't want to put her under any more strain than absolutely necessary. He slips out of her bedroom and quietly pulls the door shut.

The president, who loves a good cigar from time to time, reaches a friend, James Chambers Jr., on the phone. "Can you get me some Macanudo cigars?" Kennedy asks. "They don't have any over here in Forth Worth." Chambers, president of the *Dallas Times Herald*, is delighted to hear from the president and answers, "Sure." "Well, get me about a half a dozen." "Fine," Chambers says. He goes to the United Cigar store in Dallas and gets the president six expensive Macanudo cigars. He'll give them to the president at the luncheon scheduled that day at the Trade Mart.[48] The president finishes a light breakfast consisting of coffee and a roll, and is knotting his tie and fastening it with the obligatory PT 109 tie clip when David F. Powers, one of his closest friends and confidants, enters the suite. The president lets him know how thrilled he is over the crowd awaiting him below, speaks of the great crowds in San Antonio and Houston yesterday, and the brilliant reception accorded Jackie, who is turning into the star of the whole show. It seems that most of the crowds have come to see her rather than the president.[49]

8:30 a.m.

Brigadier General Godfrey McHugh, Kennedy's air force aide, comes into the president's suite with the CIA situation report on Saigon, Cyprus, and Korea, which the president looks over. He also scans the leading metropolitan dailies.[50]

The news for November 22, 1963, is pretty light: a Labour victory in a British by-election; a Soviet note complaining about American convoys to Berlin; the death of the "Birdman of Alcatraz" at the age of seventy-three; the trial of Jimmy Hoffa in Nashville—brother Bobby's doing; and the removal of a portrait of the president from an American Legion Post wall in Abilene because he is "controversial." The crucial news—for a president all too aware that his trip to the South to shore up support for next year's election, and how he is received in Texas, represent the real beginning of the campaign for his reelection—is the squabble in the Texas Democratic Party between its conservative and liberal wings.

An editorial in the *Chicago Sun-Times* confirms his instinct about the value on this matter of the enthusiastic reception Jackie has received thus far on the Texas trip: "Some Texans, in taking account of the tangled Texas political situation, have begun to think that Mrs. Jacqueline Kennedy may turn the balance and win her husband this state's electoral vote." Other papers are less reassuring. The front-page headline stories in the *Dallas Morning News* hammer the point home: "Storm of Political Controversy Swirls around Kennedy on Visit"; "Yarborough Snubs LBJ"; and "President's Visit Seen Widening State Democratic Split."[51] But one of the main purposes behind the Texas trip was to narrow this split, bridge the gap between the two factions, which would help not only the Democratic Party in Texas, but, with a united front, Kennedy's own reelection effort in the state.[52]*

---

*The *Dallas Morning News*, Texas's largest circulation daily at the time, with a readership of over a quarter of a million, was no friend of JFK's, its editorials consistently being anti-Kennedy because of the right-wing inclination of its publisher, E. M. "Ted" Dealey. Indeed, in a White House meeting in the autumn of 1961 between Kennedy and a contingent of Texas media leaders, Dealey bluntly told JFK, "You and your administration are weak sisters," adding that the country needed "a man on horseback to lead the nation, and many people in Texas and the Southwest think that you are riding Caroline's tricycle." (Aynesworth with Michaud, *JFK: Breaking the News*, pp.6–7)

In recent days and weeks, although Dallas's morning paper has been carrying plenty in its front pages about the widening chasm in the state's Democratic Party, the paper's emphasis this morning in its lead editorial is simple, extending a welcoming hand to the young president as he arrives in a city, it says, "with a substantial Republican representation."[53] The previous day, former vice president Richard Nixon, in town for a bottler's convention, urged Dallas residents to give President and Mrs. Kennedy "a courteous reception."[54] United States Attorney Barefoot Sanders says he is investigating whether certain scurrilous leaflets—apparently mugshots of Kennedy captioned "Wanted For Treason,"[55] five thousand of which appeared on the streets the previous day and that morning—violate federal laws. Dallas police chief Jesse E. Curry says anybody caught distributing them will be arrested for littering,[56] and in a press conference on Wednesday, November 20, says that "nothing must occur that is disrespectful or degrading to the President of the United States. He is entitled to the highest respect, and the law enforcement agencies of this area are going to do everything possible to insure that no untoward incident" takes place. "We will take immediate action if any suspicious conduct is observed, and we also urge all good citizens to be alert for such conduct . . . Citizens themselves may take preventative action if it becomes obvious that someone is planning to commit an act harmful or degrading to the president . . . I am sure that all but a handful of our citizens will cordially welcome the president of the United States to Dallas." Curry said 350 Dallas policemen, about a third of the force, would be assigned to the Kennedy guard detail, and this would be supplemented by forty state police and fifteen Dallas deputy sheriffs. Police officials said it was the largest security detail ever assembled in Dallas.[57]*

The businessmen of Dallas, not natural Kennedy supporters, have nonetheless made it clear to Curry that they want his eleven-hundred-man force to do everything possible to ensure that there be no incidents, however trivial, during the presidential visit. A front-page article in the *Dallas Morning News* of November 17, 1963, was captioned "Incident-Free Day Urged for JFK Visit," and quoted Dallas leaders such as the president of the Dallas Chamber of Commerce and the county Republican chairman asking Dallas citizens to put aside politics and accord the president of the United States a very warm and hospitable welcome. Dallas, a notorious hotbed for right-wing conservatives, simply couldn't afford any repetition of last month's Stevenson incident. What happened to UN Ambassador Adlai Stevenson in Dallas shocked America and gave Dallas a black eye. On October 24, UN Day, after speaking optimistically about world peace through the United Nations to an audience of five thousand people, Stevenson was jeered by a mob of unruly demonstrators, hit in the head with an anti-UN picket sign carried by a woman, and spat upon as he left Dallas's municipal auditorium and was being escorted to his limousine.[58] The following day, one hundred Dallas civic and business leaders sent a telegram to Stevenson apologizing profusely and saying the city was "outraged and abjectly ashamed of the disgraceful discourtesies you suffered at the hands of a small group of extremists."[59] Mayor Earle Cabell lashed out at the "right wing fanatics" responsible for the Stevenson incident, saying these

---

*Ultimately, 447 Dallas police officers were used on specific assignments associated with the president's visit, 178 of them assigned to the motorcade route. The biggest assignment (one would think inappropriately from a priority standpoint) was to the Trade Mart, where 63 were assigned to work the parking area outside and 150 under the command of a deputy chief were to provide security inside. (King Exhibit No. 5, 20 H 464)

"so-called patriots" were "not conservatives" but "radicals" who had become "a cancer in the body politic."[60]

And it's not just the lunatic right-wing fringe that was capable of the Stevenson kind of incident. Back in 1960, then-senator Lyndon Johnson (years before his civil rights legislation, when few perceived him as liberal) and his wife Lady Bird had been spat upon at Dallas's Adolphus hotel—and the Johnsons were Texans. Some members of Kennedy's staff opposed his visiting Dallas, being the cauldron of conservatism it was, and indeed the state itself, much of Texas not being favorably disposed to the president. And Stevenson, as well as Byron Skelton, the National Democratic committeeman from Texas, urged Kennedy not to make the trip. From 1961 to 1962, the Secret Service had recorded thirty-four threats on the president's life from Texas.[61]

Kennedy overlooks another article about Nixon in the same paper—"Nixon Predicts JFK May Drop Johnson."* Jack Kennedy, though elected by a mere handful of votes over Nixon in 1960 (Kennedy's margin of victory was one-tenth of 1 percent, receiving 34,221,355 votes to Nixon's 34,109,398), has nevertheless been popular with most Americans from the beginning of his administration. His approval rating soared to 83 percent in April 1961, ironically in the wake of his biggest failure, the abortive invasion of Cuba at the Bay of Pigs. By now, though, three years after his election, it has slumped to 59 percent. Just last month, in October, *Newsweek* estimated that Kennedy's pro-black position on the civil rights issue had cost him 3.5 million votes and reported that no Democratic president had ever been so disliked in the South. In Georgia the marquee of a movie theater showing the film *PT 109* read, "See how the Japs almost got Kennedy."[62] Indeed, less than two months earlier, the chairman of the Georgia Democratic Party had persuaded JFK to cancel a speech in Atlanta because of the political climate in his state resulting from JFK's pending civil rights bill.[63] However, Kennedy did include Florida on the trip that took him to Dallas, since Florida had gone Republican in 1960.[64] The South, overwhelmingly Democratic in presidential elections since the Reconstruction era following the Civil War, was more conservative than any other region of the country. But the long-standing distrust by southerners for the Republican Party (northern Republicans were largely responsible for Reconstruction, which brought the former Confederate states back into the United States and was unpopular in the South) was showing signs everywhere of melting away.

Kennedy can ill afford to lose those southern votes to Barry Goldwater, the conservative senator from Arizona who appears to have a lock on the Republican nomination for president. Texas voted for Kennedy over Nixon in 1960 by a mere 46,233 votes out of more than two million cast (he lost in Dallas, the only large American city to vote for Nixon over Kennedy), mostly owing to Lyndon Johnson's presence on the ticket. Texas, being conservative, had voted for Eisenhower in 1952 and 1956.[65] Texas's senior senator, Ralph Yarborough, also accounted for a lot of votes by appealing to the state's dwindling, old-style liberals and unionists. Texas, three years later, now looks weak for the Kennedy ticket, and it is Kennedy's own suggestion and desire to come to Texas to raise money and to try to appeal to the business community (which was suspicious of him) and the

---

*In the spring of 1964, Robert Kennedy stated, "There was no plan to dump Lyndon Johnson. It didn't make any sense . . . And there was never any discussion about dropping him." The president himself told a close confidant in October 1963 that the idea of dumping Johnson was "preposterous on the face of it. We've got to carry Texas in '64, and maybe Georgia." (Schlesinger, *Robert Kennedy and His Times*, p.605)

conservative wing of the Democratic Party, thereby enhancing his political fortunes there.[66] He couldn't have a better forum to appeal to that group than at the luncheon that noon. The Dallas Citizens Council, an informal organization of the leading businessmen of Dallas which had been a "behind-the-scenes force in Dallas affairs" for years, was the main sponsor of the luncheon.[67] Governor Connally tells his wife and others, "Nellie, if the people of Texas can just get a look at him, up close, I know they will vote for him."[68]

However, Johnson, Connally (Johnson's conservative protégé and ally), and the liberal Yarborough are at each other's throats, hacking the Democratic Party right down the middle. If they and their factions cannot be reconciled soon, or at least made to look as though they are, the Democrats could lose all twenty-five of the state's electoral votes in the 1964 election, an unthinkable disaster.

Kennedy, angered by the story which suggests that his visit is widening the split in the state's party, grabs the phone to call Kenneth P. O'Donnell, one of his principal political advisers and the one responsible for all the arrangements of the Texas trip. O'Donnell, whose official title is appointments secretary, is Kennedy's political right hand, troubleshooter, devil's advocate, and, per White House press secretary Pierre Salinger, "the most powerful member" of the president's staff.[69] Another member, Dave Powers, has been with Kennedy the longest, ever since he emerged from Boston's Eleventh District to back young Jack's first campaign for the Senate in 1946, one of several young World War II veterans who helped shape the "new generation" rhetoric that Kennedy continues to employ into the 1960s.[70] O'Donnell and Larry O'Brien are of more recent vintage, dating from the 1952 senatorial campaign which saw the creation of the "Kennedy machine." O'Donnell, one of Bobby's classmates and friends at Harvard, where he captained the football team, has a reputation for cool, ruthless efficiency that rivals Bobby's own, and Jack means to employ it now.[71]

Kennedy has had enough of the childish antics of Connally, Yarborough, and Johnson. For weeks, ever since the Texas trip was first suggested, the three of them have been arm wrestling each other for the symbolic trappings of political power, freezing each other out of seats at ceremonial dinners, refusing each other places in the Texas trip motorcades, and bending the president's itinerary to suit their own agendas and to humiliate their rivals. None of this has gone unnoticed by the Texas papers, which are watching and reporting on the day-to-day ups and downs of the embattled Yarborough: "Yarborough Seating Pondered"; "Yarborough Gets JFK Table Spot"; "Yarborough Invited to Travel with JFK"; "Demo Factions to Be Pacified, Salinger Says"; "New Fuss Erupts over JFK Tickets."[72]

Kennedy may indeed have widened the rift between Johnson and Yarborough when he acceded to Johnson's demand for half of Yarborough's senatorial patronage—the right to select judges, postmasters, and other presidential appointments in Texas—but the quarrel has to end now, before it brings the Texas party down with it. Kennedy orders O'Donnell to tell Yarborough to get in the vice president's limousine today. O'Donnell and O'Brien have to make it clear to the senator that he no longer has any choice.

"You tell him," Kennedy barks at O'Donnell, "it's ride with Lyndon or walk."[73]

8:50 a.m.
The president starts down to the parking lot, meeting Fort Worth congressman Jim Wright and his party in the corridor. He speaks briefly to his Secret Service bodyguards who fall in behind him, pauses for a word with an elderly woman in a wheelchair, and

graciously offers to be introduced to some Dallas friends of his personal secretary, Evelyn Lincoln.

As the president moves toward the parking lot, his entourage snowballs. He picks up Vice President Johnson, Governor Connally, Senator Yarborough, several congressmen, and Raymond Buck, president of the Fort Worth Chamber of Commerce. Bill Greer, his veteran Secret Service driver, dashes up with the president's raincoat—it's drizzling again—but Kennedy shrugs it off. He walks out under the marquee that reads "Welcome, Mr. President" and "Welcome to Fort Worth, where the West begins,"[74] and around to the parking lot to mount the flatbed truck awaiting him there.[75]

After a brief introduction by the vice president, Jack Kennedy steps to the microphone to address the crowd that has waited in the rain for three and a half hours to see him. "There are no faint hearts in Fort Worth!" he says gaily to the crowd, which manages a cheer in spite of the drizzle. "Mrs. Kennedy is [still] organizing herself. It takes her a little longer"—the crowd breaks into laughter as the president grins broadly—"but, of course, she looks better than we do when she does it."[76]

Upstairs in her bedroom, Jackie hears her husband's voice booming over the public address system. She is glad it is still raining. She hopes the Plexiglas bubble top will be on the presidential limousine for the noon motorcade in Dallas. Then her hair won't get mussed in the open car. She sits at her dressing table and looks into the mirror. She looks tired.

"Oh, God," she moans to an attendant, "one day's campaigning can age a person thirty years."[77]

9:10 a.m.

Bolstered by the enthusiastic Fort Worth crowds, the president reenters the hotel and climbs aboard the elevator to take him to the next event on the schedule, a formal breakfast. However, in the elevator, Acting Press Secretary Malcolm Kilduff* persuades Kennedy to make a slight detour. Kilduff has read the newspapers and shares the president's political concerns. To improve the situation, he has convinced Governor Connally to hold a press conference and thought that the president might want to discuss it with the governor first. The president agrees and is escorted to the Longhorn Room, down the mezzanine from the Grand Ballroom, where hundreds of breakfast guests await his presence.

Kennedy reviews the governor's prepared statement and finds it rather bland and meaningless. Nevertheless, the president endorses it and returns to the hallway, where he runs into Senator Yarborough and bluntly tells him to ride in the vice president's car. When the senator starts to object, the president lets him have it.

"For Christ's sake cut it out, Ralph," he snaps. Yarborough responds that he *had* ridden to the hotel with Johnson. Kennedy shook his head. It wasn't good enough. He had no intention of being thwarted by evasions.

The president turns and makes his way into the kitchen of the Grand Ballroom, leaving the chastised senator to lick his wounds. For a moment, the entourage stands wedged between a corridor of stainless-steel sinks and gigantic pots and pans. Kennedy looks over his shoulder. One member is missing.

---

*Kilduff was the acting press secretary in the absence of Pierre Salinger, who was en route to Hawaii at the time of the assassination.

"Where's Mrs. Kennedy?" he asks a nearby Secret Service agent. "Call Mr. Hill. I want her to come down to the breakfast."

The guests in the Grand Ballroom are on their tiptoes, straining their necks in the direction of the kitchen entrance. Amid a spattering of applause, Governor Connally, Vice President Johnson, Senator Yarborough, and other dignitaries file into the ballroom. As they stand at attention at the head table, the band breaks into the familiar "Hail to the Chief," and a smiling John F. Kennedy strolls into the ballroom. Now the cheers are loud and sustained, although many present must be disappointed that the First Lady is not with him.[78]

Upstairs, Jackie Kennedy is putting the finishing touches to her outfit, a navy blue blouse and matching purse and a rose pink suit with a navy collar and matching pink pillbox hat. The president wants her to be elegant in Dallas and she means to be, although it does take time. She wavers over two pairs of white gloves, one short and one long. She decides the short ones are more restrained, and holds up her wrists while her attendant buttons them for her. She has become so preoccupied with the idea of going to Dallas that she forgets all about the breakfast reception downstairs. When the elevator arrives at the mezzanine floor, she is confused.

"Aren't we leaving?" she asks Secret Service agent Clint Hill, who accompanies her on the ride down.

"No, you're going to a breakfast," he says.[79]

9:20 a.m.

In the Grand Ballroom, the anticipation that the First Lady may appear is tremendous. The crowd has been keeping an eye on the kitchen entrance throughout breakfast and the subsequent performance by the Texas Boys Choir. When toastmaster Raymond Buck spots Agent Hill peering from the kitchen entrance, he steps to the microphone at the head table and introduces the First Lady like a ringmaster: "And now—an event I know you have all been waiting for!" Buck sweeps his arm toward the kitchen door as Clint Hill leads Mrs. Kennedy into the ballroom. Two thousand businessmen and their wives leap to their feet and cheer enthusiastically. The First Lady spots her husband smiling from behind the head table and is drawn toward him through the cheers and smiles of a generous crowd. As the spontaneous response dies down, the president is introduced and steps to the microphone.

"Two years ago I introduced myself in Paris as the man who had accompanied Mrs. Kennedy to Paris," he says. "I'm getting somewhat that same sensation as I travel around Texas."*

The crowd cheers wildly as the president grins.

"Nobody wonders what Lyndon and I wear—"

A wave of laughter sweeps again over the crowd. The president is hitting all the right notes and the guests are loving every minute of it.[80]

After what one reporter described as a "ripsnorting political speech"† by the presi-

---

*The president's exaggeration was not great. Jacqueline Kennedy, traveling abroad to thirteen countries, alone or with the president, and speaking fluent French, Spanish, and Italian as she went, "soon carved for herself a niche of fame" independent of JFK. Described by many as beautiful, cultured, and imperious, "she drew crowds by the thousands and became a good-will ambassador for America on her own." (Associated Press, November 26, 1963)

†Kennedy had unquestionably become an effective politician, but unlike most in his chosen profession,

dent, in which he emphasized national defense,[*] the president of the Fort Worth Chamber of Commerce provides a jovial moment when he presents the President and First Lady with parting gifts. "Mr. President, we couldn't let you leave Fort Worth without providing you with some protection against the rain," he says, and offers the president a ten-gallon hat. The audience shouts for him to put it on. Jack, who dreaded the idea of looking ridiculous, has always managed to avoid putting on a cowboy hat, sombrero, or Indian headdress. He grins and dodges the gesture, responding, "I'll put it on in the White House on Monday. If you'll come up there you'll have a chance to see it then."[81]

9:45 a.m.

Lee Harvey Oswald ostensibly continues to go about his work. His job is to pick up orders for schoolbooks on the first floor, fix them to his clipboard, take one of the two big freight elevators at the back of the Depository Building up to the sixth floor, search out the requested books from the thousands of titles stored there, take them back down in the elevator to the order desk on the first floor for eventual shipping, and pick up the next lot of orders. He's a human conveyor belt, not particularly distinguishable from the fourteen other "order fillers," or stock boys in the warehouse crew.[82] But this particular morning, only one order was known to have been worked on by Oswald.[83]

The Texas School Book Depository Company is, in spite of the official ring to its name, private, with no connection to the state of Texas. The seven-story building, which has been occupied by the company since January of 1962, is an old, rust-colored brick structure at the corner of Elm and Houston, not the original building at this location. That building, erected in 1883, was home to the Southern Rock Island Plow Company. In 1901, the building was struck by lightning and almost burned to the ground. It was rebuilt that same year to look identical to the previous structure, only the new building had seven stories instead of five.[84][†]

In view of the enormous number of titles handled by the company, the stock boys tend to specialize. Since starting work at the Depository, Lee has been focusing on the books of Scott, Foresman & Company, some of which are kept on the first floor, which is handy to the shipping department, with the vast majority up on the sixth floor. The women in the office write orders and drop them down a sort of dumbwaiter to the men below, who carry them to a little table by the checking stand and sort them out by publisher and location. If there aren't enough orders for Scott, Foresman & Company to keep him busy, Lee will fill orders for one of the smaller publishers, like Gregg Publishing Company, but that doesn't happen often.[85]

---

he wasn't inordinately ambitious, was famous for never taking himself too seriously, and once said that he only started in politics "because Joe died. [Joseph P. Kennedy Jr., JFK's older brother, was the one of the four sons of Joe Sr. who was being groomed for high political office; he and his copilot died during the Second World War when their plane, laden with explosives to be dropped on a German bomb-launching base in France, exploded in midair over the English Channel on August 12, 1944.] If something happened to me tomorrow, my brother Bobby would run for my seat in the Senate. And if Bobby died, Teddy would take over for him." (*New York Times*, November 23, 1963, p.13)

[*]The president received a long, standing ovation when he referred to the controversial TFX jet fighter, built at the General Dynamics plant in Fort Worth, as a powerful force for freedom (*Dallas Morning News*, November 23, 1963, p.11).

[†]For years prior to its occupancy by the Texas School Book Depository Company, when it became known as the Texas School Book Depository Building after its principal occupant, the building was known as the Sexton Building, and many old-timers continued to call it that for years thereafter.

Most of the people working in the Depository Building this day are not aware of Oswald, he goes about his work so unobtrusively. Lee's boss, Roy S. Truly, did happen to notice him earlier in the morning.

"Good morning, Lee."

"Good morning, sir," Lee answered.

Truly likes that, the word "sir," one which a lot of the other stock boys don't use. Truly is pleased with Lee, who is "quiet and well-mannered, a nice young fellow." The job is only temporary, but when he hired him, Truly assumed that Lee was just out of the Marines—Lee had mentioned no other employment history—and the young man certainly needed work, with his second child due shortly after he took the job. In fact, the baby was born at Dallas's Parkland Memorial Hospital just five days later. Mr. Truly remembers that well, because Lee asked for and got a few days' grace in filling out his withholding tax deduction form, which allowed him to claim the new dependent. Truly occasionally asked about the baby, and Lee would respond with a big smile, but that was about the extent of any conversation he'd ever had with him. Lee is a loner, working day after day on his own, taking the orders up, bringing the books down, keeping to himself, but that's fine with Roy Truly.[86]

One of the few other employees in the Depository who even notices Lee this morning is the order checker, James Jarman Jr. It's "Junior" Jarman's job to make sure the books brought down to the first floor by the order fillers match those on the order forms. He saw that Lee was already at work when he came in that morning around eight, and later had occasion to send him back upstairs to correct a botched order.[87]

It's between 9:30 and 10:00 a.m. when Jarman sees Lee at one of the windows between two of the long book bins on the first floor. Outside, people are already beginning to gather on the corner of Elm and Houston and Lee asks Jarman why. Jarman tells Lee they're picking spots to watch the presidential motorcade, which is supposed to pass right by the building this afternoon.

"Do you know which way he's coming?" Lee asks.

Junior explains that the motorcade will be coming down Main, turning right onto Houston, then left onto Elm, passing right under their windows.

"Oh, I see," Lee says, and walks off.[88]

10:15 a.m.

The president and his wife don't make it back to suite 850 until after ten o'clock, but find they have nearly an hour before the flight to Dallas. Kennedy takes time to call former vice president John Nance Garner to wish him a happy ninety-fifth birthday while Jackie spends a moment looking around the suite. She discovers something they were all too busy to notice until now, that the paintings aren't the usual by-the-yard hotel-room art, but real paintings—a Monet, a Picasso, a Van Gogh, a dozen others, and some bronzes, all borrowed from the local museum for the pleasure of America's First Couple. From a specially prepared catalog they find the name of the woman who made it all possible, Ruth Carter Johnson. The First Couple telephone Mrs. Johnson, the wife of a newspaper executive, and thank her for her kindness. Mrs. Johnson is both flabbergasted and touched by the graciousness of the gesture, one she will never forget.[89]

Ken O'Donnell shows the president what is at best a disrespectful advertisement in the *Dallas Morning News*. It's a full-page ad draped with a funeral black border, and headlined "WELCOME MR. KENNEDY TO DALLAS." Placed by the "American Fact-

Finding Committee," chaired by one Bernard Weissman, the ad, with twelve questions for Kennedy, rapidly moves from inane innuendo—"WHY has Gus Hall, head of the U.S. Communist Party, praised almost every one of your policies and announced the party will endorse and support your re-election in 1964?"—to outright accusation of treason—"WHY has the Foreign Policy of the United States degenerated to the point that the C.I.A. is arranging coups and having staunch Anti-Communist Allies of the U.S. bloodily exterminated?"[90]

"Can you imagine a paper doing a thing like that?" Jack says to O'Donnell, and then, making light of it to Jackie, who is sickened by the hate behind the ad, he adds, "Oh, we're heading into nut country today."[91]

Of course, Jack Kennedy knows that the presidency is a vulnerable position, just as every chief of state is aware of the special hazards he faces, but he simply refuses to accept the notion that an American president can't go into any American city. He prowls the room restlessly.[92]

"It would not be a very difficult job to shoot the president of the United States," he says to nobody in particular. "All you'd have to do is get up in a high building with a high-powered rifle with a telescopic sight, and there's nothing anybody could do."[93]

10:30 a.m.

The motorcade that will take the presidential party to Fort Worth's Carswell Air Force Base—long lines of limousines, cars, and press vehicles stacked three abreast—is clogging Eighth Street. O'Donnell and O'Brien are lying in wait outside the hotel, determined to make sure Senator Yarborough gets into the car with the vice president, as the president has ordered.[94] They are relieved to see that the drizzle is finally clearing, and O'Brien even hopes for what he likes to call "Kennedy weather."

Vice President Johnson and his wife, Lady Bird, emerge from the Texas Hotel to a smattering of applause. O'Brien escorts them to the waiting convertible, with a grumpy Yarborough walking closely behind. The political orchestration pays off. When the motorcade finally pulls out just after eleven o'clock for the short drive to Carswell, a bit behind schedule, Senator Yarborough and the vice president are seen smiling and riding together by the media. Although neither man may be happy about the close contact, the needs of the Democratic Party have been served.[95]

11:00 a.m.

It usually takes Jack Ruby a good while to get going in the morning. For one thing, he is really meticulous about his physical appearance. In addition to his morning shower and shave, he takes care to dress in a good suit, tie, and hat. He tries to keep in shape too, exercising every day at the YMCA and working out with weights he keeps both at his office and in his apartment. Keeping up his appearance is a daily struggle. He worries about creeping baldness and his weight. He is five foot eight (five foot nine inches by some accounts), weighs 175 pounds, and is brawny in the arms and shoulders. He is always dieting, usually with the help of pills.[96]

It is around eleven before Ruby gets to the offices of the *Dallas Morning News* at the corner of Houston and Young streets.[97] The building is only five blocks from the Texas School Book Depository.[98] Since there are no high buildings on the west side of Houston, one can actually see the Depository Building from the northwest corner windows of the advertising department's second floor.[99]

The morning visit to the *News* is a regular Friday event for Jack, one he looks forward to. He takes particular pains composing the weekend ads in the classified-ad office of the *News* for his two clubs, because the weekend is "very lucrative," and Jack has a way of making his ads, as he says in his strange way of talking, "where they have a way of selling the product I am producing or putting on the show." It's not always easy to figure out what Jack is saying. "It's been a lovely, precarious evening," he might say, or, to an attractive woman, "You make me feel very irascible." A favorite expression is "In lieu of the situation, let's do this."[100]

On his way to the elevator in the lobby, he spots a *News* employee he's always friendly with and has recently dated, Gladys Craddock, who works in the classified-ad department on the first floor, and cheerily shouts out to her across the lobby, "Hi, the president is going to be here today."[101] He gets a quick breakfast in the building's cafeteria on the second floor[102]—part of his Friday routine.

Jack then saunters over to the advertising and promotion department, also on the second floor. He could walk around the department blindfolded. He knows its big bullpen for the ad-space salesmen, and the cubicles along the sides for the executives. He knows every employee, and he knows the routine: how to leave his ad copy in the box if John Newnam (not Newman), his designated salesman, isn't there and how to get help if he needs it in preparing his ad.

Newnam isn't there today. This morning a lot of the twenty-six ad salesmen are adjusting their schedules to take in the presidential motorcade when it cuts through the downtown on Main Street a few blocks away.[103]

The fact that Newnam isn't there is no problem for Jack. It gives him time to go up to Tony Zoppi's office on the third floor of the building.[104] Zoppi, the paper's nightclub editor, is one of Jack's preoccupations. He has known Zoppi for a dozen years—Zoppi will never forget being introduced to the audience in one of Ruby's clubs, the night they first met, and hearing Ruby explain how "superfluous" it was to have Tony Zoppi there.[105] Ruby is always trying to get Zoppi to mention his clubs in his daily column or his television show. That's worth far more than any amount of advertising, and what's more, it's free, while the ads have to be paid for in cash. At least Jack's ads do. His credit with the *News*, in spite of the fact that he's a steady customer, is not terrific. In fact, it's nonexistent.

Zoppi isn't there either—someone tells Jack he's in New Orleans for a couple of days—but Jack sees the brochure he left for Zoppi a few days before about the emcee at the Carousel, Bill DeMar. Jack is annoyed with Zoppi, who promised him a story, which amounted to a "build" of one or two lines. Picking up the brochure, Jack meanders back to Newnam's desk to work up the copy for his weekend ads when Don Campbell turns up to distract him.

Campbell is not just another ad-space salesman, but a friend and a colleague, so to speak. Campbell operates and manages the Stork Club, a supper club out on Oak Lawn across from another club called the Village, and they often talk shop. Jack particularly wants to apologize for the other evening, when Campbell came over to Jack and his friend, Ralph Paul, as they were having dinner at the Egyptian Lounge to invite them to come along with him to the nearby Castaway Club. Jack, still seething over the way the Castaway Club had once pirated his whole band from the Vegas, turned down the invitation, and now wants to be sure Campbell's feelings weren't hurt.

Jack has a lot on his mind: his troubles with Jada, the crazy stripper from New Orleans who's going to get him closed down if she doesn't clean up her act; the struggle to keep his two clubs afloat. Campbell has known Jack for three or four years, and it's not the first time he has heard Jack's complaints about the lousy business they are in, running nightclubs. Jack moans about the fights he gets into with what he regards as undesirable customers, "characters" or "punks," as he calls them. Fortunately, Jack is, he tells Campbell, a very capable fighter. Also, anytime he is fixing to have trouble with someone, he gets a gun and keeps it on his person.

Neither Campbell nor Ruby mentions the presidential motorcade, which will be passing within four blocks of the *News* building in a few minutes. When Campbell goes off to see another client about 12:25, Jack is still sitting at Newnam's desk, working on his ad copy.[106]

11:25 a.m.
The flight from Carswell Air Force Base in Fort Worth to Love Field, Dallas's airport, is just thirty miles and takes but thirteen minutes. The presidential party could easily have driven the distance in half an hour, but presidential aide Ken O'Donnell vetoed that. It would cut out the welcome at the airport for the president and Jackie, and O'Donnell knows that the airport arrival, with the inevitable cameras recording the enthusiasm of the crowd, is as important to modern political campaigns as all those whistlestop appearances on the rear platform of the cross-country train were to Harry Truman's astonishing upset victory in 1948.

Short as the flight is, O'Donnell and the president use the fleeting minutes to put the squeeze, as O'Donnell puts it, on Governor Connally, who is aligned with LBJ against Yarborough in the state's Democratic bloodletting. The president motions at Texas congressman Albert Thomas from the doorway of his cabin and asks him to "give Kenny a hand with Connally." Thomas is glad to oblige, and the governor begins to wilt under their pressure.

Senator Yarborough was particularly incensed about a deadly slight Governor Connally had in store for him—after selling $11,200 in tickets to tomorrow night's dinner in Austin, there was no place for his wife. Worse, he hadn't been invited to the Connally's formal reception for the Kennedys.[107]

"It was my wife who didn't want the senator at the reception, not me," Connally tells O'Donnell and Thomas, taking advantage of Nellie's temporary absence. "She said she wouldn't let that man in her house, and when your wife says something like that, what can you do?"

At a strategic moment O'Donnell nudges the governor and the senator into the president's cabin, and watches his boss expertly wield the overwhelming Kennedy charm to solve the problem in three minutes. The governor finds himself agreeing not only to invite Senator Yarborough to the reception at the Governor's Mansion, but to seat him at the head table for the dinner.

The president, who has already changed suits once that morning, excuses himself to change his shirt. The governor mutters to the smug O'Donnell, "How can anyone say no to that man?"

"So we land in Dallas with everybody on the plane in love with each other and the sun shining brightly," O'Donnell thinks. The day is looking up.[108]

11:40 a.m.
Air Force One, code-named Angel, touches down at Love Field, just north of downtown

Dallas, and rolls across the puddled tarmac to the red and green terminal building.[109]* The last U.S. Weather Bureau temperature reading at Love Field, at 10:55 a.m., was fifty-seven degrees. But by the next reading, at 11:55, sixteen minutes after the president arrived, it had risen to sixty-three degrees.[110] The president is pleased at his first glimpse of the waiting crowd from the plane's window. He says to O'Donnell, "This trip is turning out to be terrific. Here we are in Dallas, and it looks like everything in Texas is going to be fine for us."[111]

The stage directions for the airport welcome call for the vice president's plane to land ahead of the president's by a minute or two, enough time to allow Johnson and his wife to position themselves to greet President and Mrs. Kennedy at the foot of the ramp, as though they hadn't just left them a quarter hour earlier in Fort Worth.[112]

Aura, though a reality, cannot be adequately described. It just is. And JFK's aura was legendary. Reporting live for radio KBOX in Dallas, reporter Ron Jenkins waits for the door to Air Force One to open. When it does, no one emerges for several moments. "And then all of a sudden President Kennedy appeared," he would later recall. "And he had a way of doing this like no one I had ever seen before. And it was a presence bigger than life. I never knew how tall the man was, or anything else, but he looked about 7 feet tall when he came out of that door all by himself."[113] Unwittingly, Jenkins's words contained their own validation. He was so struck by Kennedy he had forgotten that Jackie Kennedy, someone few overlooked, had emerged from the plane door ahead of the president.

Texas governor John Connally and his wife, Nellie, followed Kennedy and Jackie down the stairs of Air Force One in the dazzling sunlight. "We were two couples in the prime of our lives," Nellie Connally recalled. "We were two women, so proud of the men we loved . . . That day, November 22, 1963, the autumn air was filled with anticipation."[114]

11:45 a.m.
Police Chief Jesse Curry, waiting in the open door of the motorcade's lead car, checks on communications with Deputy Police Chief George L. Lumpkin. A few minor problems are solved.

"Ervay Street is completely blocked with pedestrians and is completely out of control," Sergeant Campbell informs Inspector J. H. Sawyer.

"I've got two reserves I'm bringing down now," Sawyer says.

"I have two 3-wheels [a three-wheel police motorcycle] with me," Campbell adds, "and we still can't get the pedestrians off of Ervay, so Ervay is completely closed."

"Ten-four [radio jargon for "acknowledged"]. I'm on my way."

Captain J. M. Souter asks the dispatcher for a progress report. The dispatcher contacts the driver of the pilot car, Deputy Chief Lumpkin, who is assigned to drive over the

---

*The $8.6 million Boeing 707 jet, tail number SAM26000, was delivered to the air force on October 10, 1962. Though not the first Air Force One, it is the first jet aircraft designed specifically for presidents, JFK being the first one to make extensive use of a jet for presidential travel. (James Sawa, "JFK Air Force One: Conspiracy or Not," self-published, 2004) When JFK first saw the new Air Force One, he exclaimed, "It's magnificent! I'll take it." President Gerald Ford would later say, "When they fly you on Air Force One, you know you're the president." (TerHorst and Albertazzie, *Flying White House*, p.13)

motorcade route a quarter of a mile ahead of the main body of the procession in an effort to spot and avert any potential trouble.

"Are they moving yet?" the dispatcher asks him.

"No," Lumpkin replies.

"Have not started yet," the dispatcher relays to Captain Souter.[115]*

Bill Greer, the president's Irish-born driver and, at age fifty-four, the oldest man in the Secret Service's White House detail, will drive the waiting presidential limousine—a 1961 Lincoln Continental convertible built at Ford Motor Company's Wixom, Michigan, plant and customized to rigid Secret Service specifications for the president by the Hess & Eisenhardt Company in Cincinnati. The car was leased to the White House in June of 1961. To the Secret Service it is known as SS-100-X.[116] Weighing about seventy-five hundred pounds with its special build and heavy armor, and being a full twenty-one feet eight inches long, it is a big chore to deliver it to every place the president intends to be—which is why they didn't have it in Fort Worth. A government C-130 cargo plane—the kind they fly tanks around in—brought it from Washington, D.C., down to San Antonio. From San Antonio they flew it down to Dallas, skipping the president's stop in Houston and overnight stay in Fort Worth.[117]

In addition to the armor, the car is fitted with jump seats behind the front seat, effectively making the car comfortable for seven passengers and allowing the president to accommodate guests without having them obscure the crowds' view of him on the slightly higher backseat. There is also an electrical system, operable by the president himself provided the top is down, to raise that seat and its footrest by as much as eight inches from their normal positions.[118] Over the back of the front seat, a sort of roll bar, fitted with handholds, allows the president to ride standing up for certain occasions. On the back bumper, on each side of the elegant spare-tire housing at the rear of the car's trunk, are two steps, each large enough to permit a Secret Service agent to ride there while holding on to the special handgrip fitted to the trunk. Dashboard-controlled, retractable running boards run along each side of the limousine and can accommodate additional agents, but unlike prior presidents who had agents riding on the side running boards of their limousines, Kennedy does not want this, and these side running boards are never used. It is also possible to bolt a bubble top—six panels of clear plastic kept in the trunk— to the frame, with a black canvas-type cover that buttons over the top of the plastic. Neither plastic nor canvas are bulletproof, or even bullet resistant, just protection from the weather.[119]

Today, the car is without the bubble top. Kennedy never wanted it when the weather was clear. This morning in Fort Worth, Ken O'Donnell told Secret Service agent Roy Kellerman that with the weather breaking, there would be no need for the bubble top. Kellerman passed the word on to the Secret Service's advance man in Dallas, Winston G. Lawson.[120]

---

*Variations in transcripts of both channels 1 (regular) and 2 (presidential motorcade) of the Dallas police radio transmissions are common. In 1982, the National Academy of Science's Committee on Ballistic Acoustics (NAS-CBA) created a new recording of the channel 2 radio traffic at the time of the assassination directly from the original Gray Audograph disk. This recording proved to be the best to date, avoiding many of the skips and repeats inherent in previous recordings. Throughout this book, the most complete versions of channel 1 and 2 radio traffic conversations, primarily from the recordings themselves, are utilized.

11:47 a.m.

Some of the stock boys in the Texas School Book Depository Building are laying new flooring up on the sixth floor. The schoolbook business is a little slow this late in the year, and rather than lay the boys off entirely, Bill Shelley, a Depository manager, put them to work resurfacing the upper floors, where most of the books are stored.* Half a dozen of them are at it—Bill Shelley himself, Bonnie Ray Williams, Charles Givens, Danny Arce, Billy Lovelady, and occasionally Harold Norman, when he has time to give them a hand.

The work is pretty straightforward. They have to move the heavy cartons of books from one side of the floor to the other, then back, as they lay new flooring over the old planks. It took them about three weeks to do the fifth floor, and they're just starting in on the sixth, moving as many cartons as they can from the west side of the open floor over to the east. Given the number of books they have to move, they aren't very far along. They're still working on the first section, on the westernmost portion of the sixth floor.[121]

At one point, Bonnie Ray Williams thought he saw Lee Oswald, though he is not sure, messing around with some cartons near the easternmost freight elevator on the sixth floor, during the half hour before noon. He didn't pay much attention though. Oswald is always messing around, kicking and shoving cartons around.[122]

The warehouse crew usually knocks off about five minutes before noon to give themselves time to wash up for lunch, but today, anxious to see the president, they quit a little earlier. In high spirits, the young men commandeer both of the big freight elevators for a mock race to the bottom. Bonnie Ray, Billy, Danny, and Charlie all pile into the east elevator and head for the bottom. The rest of them take the west elevator. It isn't really much of a race. The east elevator is faster, and they all know it.[123]

Charlie Givens notices Lee Oswald in front of the elevator shaft on the fifth floor as they flash past on their way to the ground floor.[124]

"Guys!" Oswald calls after them. "How about an elevator?"

Givens tosses his head back as the freight elevator plunges down.

"Come on, boy!" Givens calls out, suggesting Oswald come down to the bottom floor too, though apparently not on their moving elevator.

"Close the gate on the elevator," Oswald shouts down the shaft, "and send the elevator back up."[125] Oswald means the west elevator. The east elevator has to be manned, but the west one can be summoned from any floor if its gate is closed.[126] When they get to the first floor, however, no one bothers with Oswald's request.

Out at Ruth Paine's house in Irving, Marina Oswald, who still hasn't dressed for the day, watches television alone. Ruth has left to run some errands. Marina doesn't understand much of what the announcers are saying, but the live images speak for themselves.[127] She sits on the edge of the couch and watches as Air Force One taxies up close to the reception line at Dallas Love Field. Crewmen run under the wings and throw down the chock-blocks as the jet comes to a halt and the engines wind down. A ramp is pushed up to the back entrance of the jet as the door is propped open. The excited crowd watches the back door, giggling with anticipation. Suddenly, Jackie's pink suit comes into view.

---

*The Depository had previously been occupied by a wholesale grocery company engaged in supplying restaurants and institutions, and during the time it occupied the building, the floors became oil-soaked and this oil was damaging the books that were now being stacked on the floor (CD 205, p.135).

"There is Mrs. Kennedy and the crowd yells," the TV announcer says, a smile in his voice, "and the President of the United States. And I can see his suntan all the way from here!" The President and First Lady descend the ramp and shake hands with the official welcoming party, one of whom, the Dallas mayor's wife, Mrs. Earle Cabell, presents Mrs. Kennedy with a brilliant bouquet of red roses.* The sunshine is blinding, the weather absolutely beautiful. They look like Mr. and Mrs. America.[128]

Robert Donovan, Washington bureau chief of the *Los Angeles Times*, thinks to himself that if Hollywood had tried to cast a president and his wife, it could never have dreamed up John F. Kennedy and Jacqueline Kennedy. They were just two beautiful, glamorous people, and were receiving a screaming reception. (He would later add that "there was never a point in the public life of the Kennedys, in a way, that was as high as that moment in Dallas.")[129]

Marina can see the presidential party making its way toward the cars. Suddenly, the President and First Lady turn toward the cheering crowds hugging the fence line.

"The press is standing up high, getting a lot of shots of this!" the television announcer says excitedly. "This is great for the people and makes the eggshells even thinner for the Secret Service whose job it is to guard the man."

Secret Service agent Roy Kellerman, the assistant special agent in charge of the White House detail for this trip to Texas, slips up close to the fence, scrutinizing every hand that reaches over toward the president. The happy and loudly exuberant crowd, perhaps two thousand strong,[130] is tightly packed behind the fence at gate 28. The president can't seem to soak up enough of their warmth. He moves along the fence line, his image growing larger on local television screens as he nears the pool camera setups. The eager, out-stretched hands reach for him. Jackie follows closely behind, radiant and gay, her beauty enhanced by the bouquet of red roses.[131]

"And here they come, right down toward us!" the TV announcer gushes. "I can see Mrs. Kennedy, and they're going to come right on down and shake hands with *everybody*. Mrs. Kennedy gave a lovely wave and a smile that time. There's the president shaking hands with the people. He's waving at a lot of people. Smiling. Secret Service men all around. Boy, this is *something*!"[132]

But there is palpable tension at Love Field too. Those on the scene are all too aware of the discordant placards among the signs of welcome. "IN 1964, GOLDWATER AND FREEDOM"; "YANKEE GO HOME"; "YOU'RE A TRAITOR." Liz Carpenter, Jackie's assistant, thought some of them were the ugliest she had ever seen.[133]

Roy Kellerman follows the president by inches, ready, like the other nearby agents, to use his body as a human shield. Any contact with the public is a nightmare for the Secret Service, but the agents also know that it is the lifeblood of electioneering. So far, they have been unable to persuade Jack Kennedy to be more cautious on these occasions.[134]†

---

*Jackie would later recall that three times on the Texas trip "we were greeted with bouquets of the yellow roses of Texas. Only in Dallas they gave me red roses. I remember thinking: How funny—red roses for me" (Gun, *Red Roses from Texas*, unnumbered p.5).

†The president's personal style causes the Secret Service deep concern. Not only does he travel more frequently than any previous president, but he relishes contact with crowds of well-wishers. The problem is compounded by the fact that Kennedy is not receptive to many of the measures designed to protect him, treating the danger of assault philosophically. (HSCA Report, p.228)

Bill Greer, noticing how far down the fence the president is getting, drives the armored Lincoln at a crawl alongside him. Other Secret Service men are trying to get everyone to take his or her place in the long line of vehicles strung out along the fence behind the president's car. The radio networks are alive with reports, queries, and advisories. Security men strung out for miles along the route all the way to the Trade Mart know from their radios that the president is on the ground, that the next forty-five minutes, as the motorcade threads its way across the city, will require their utmost alertness and preparedness.

The president and Mrs. Kennedy finally step toward the presidential limousine, where Governor Connally and his wife wait, standing just in front of the jump seats. *Newsweek* White House correspondent Charles Roberts manages to get in a quick question to Jackie: "How do you like campaigning?" "It's wonderful, it's wonderful," she says, sounding as if she almost means it.[135] The president places his hand in the small of Mrs. Kennedy's back and helps her into the backseat first. She moves to the left side as the president steps in and takes his seat on the right. Mrs. Kennedy places the bouquet of red roses on the seat between her and the president. The governor and his wife fold the jump seats back and sit down, the governor in front of the president, and Nellie in front of Mrs. Kennedy. Secret Service agent Roy Kellerman takes his position in the front passenger seat next to the driver, Special Agent Bill Greer.

Television cameras zoom in on the limousine as the president and Mrs. Kennedy continue waving to the cheering crowds.

"The party is now leaving Love Field," the announcer tells television viewers. "And of course thousands will be on hand for that motorcade now, which will be [through] downtown Dallas, down Cedar Springs to Harwood, and on Harwood it will turn on Main, from which point it will go all the way down to the courthouse area, which is the end of Main, it'll turn on Houston Street to Elm, under the Triple Underpass, out to the Mart, where the president talks at approximately one o'clock, which will also be carried live right here on most of these channels. And then we'll be back here, as we told you, at about two-fifteen for the president's departure."[136]

11:55 a.m.
The motorcade finally gets underway on its scheduled nine-and-one-half-mile journey to the Trade Mart, driving right through an opening in a section of the Love Field fence that Special Agent Forrest Sorrels has had removed. Sorrels has been working on the presidential visit since November 4, when Special Agent-in-Charge Gerry Behn of the White House detail alerted him to the likelihood of the visit, and he is reasonably sure that the arrangements they've made are satisfactory under the circumstances.[137] An advance car, driven by Dallas police captain Perdue D. Lawrence, head of the Traffic Division, is already a half mile out in front of the motorcade watching for any potential problems.

First through the opening in the fence is the so-called pilot car, a white Ford sedan driven by Deputy Chief Lumpkin, who scouts the route a quarter of a mile ahead, on the lookout for motor vehicle accidents, fires, obstructions, or any other problem necessitating a last-instant change of route or procedure. Along for the ride are two Dallas homicide detectives, B. L. Senkel and F. M. Turner, and Lieutenant Colonel George Whitmeyer, commander of the local Army Intelligence reserve unit.[138] Three two-wheel Dallas police motorcycle officers under the command of Sergeant S. Q. Bellah are next, followed by five two-wheel motorcycle officers under the command of Sergeant Stavis Ellis. The "lead car," an unmarked white Ford police sedan driven by Dallas police chief

Jesse Curry, follows a short distance behind. Accompanying Curry are Secret Service agents Lawson and Sorrels, and Dallas sheriff Bill Decker.

Five car lengths back, and the third car in the motorcade, is the presidential limousine with four motorcycle escorts, two on each side, flanking the rear bumper. Although, as indicated, the president's car is equipped to allow Secret Service agents to ride on the running boards or rear bumper steps, no agents are there this day. Kennedy is weary of seeing bodyguards hovering behind him every time he turns to see the crowds.[139]

Less than a car length behind is the Secret Service follow-up car, a black 1955 four-door modified Cadillac convertible touring car—"Halfback" to the agents—with Agent Sam Kinney at the wheel. Emory Roberts, the car's commander, is at his side. Agent Clint Hill is standing on the left running board, Agent Bill McIntyre right behind him. Agent John Ready stands on the right running board, Agent Paul Landis behind him. President Kennedy's close friends and advisers, Dave Powers and Ken O'Donnell, are seated in the right and left jump seats. Agent George Hickey sits in the left rear seat, Agent Glen Bennett on the right. Between them is an AR-15 .223 caliber automatic rifle, capable of blowing a man's head off.

Two and a half car lengths behind Halfback is the vice presidential limousine, a light-blue 1961 Lincoln convertible carrying the vice president and Mrs. Johnson, Senator Yarborough, Secret Service agent Rufus Youngblood, and the driver.

Immediately behind the vice president is another Secret Service follow-up car, a yellow Ford Mercury four-door hardtop nicknamed "Varsity." Driven by Texas Ranger Hurchel Jacks, the car contains vice presidential aide Cliff Carter and three Secret Service agents. Dallas mayor Earle Cabell and his wife ride in the next vehicle, a white Ford Mercury convertible, along with Congressman Ray Roberts.

The national press pool car, a blue-gray Chevrolet sedan on loan from the telephone company, complete with driver, follow through the fence opening next. Assistant Press Secretary Malcolm Kilduff and United Press International (UPI) correspondent Merriman Smith occupy the front seat, with Smith in the middle, next to the radiophone mounted on the transmission hump under the dashboard. Jack Bell of the Associated Press (AP), Robert Baskin of the *Dallas Morning News*, and Bob Clark of the American Broadcasting Company (ABC) are in the backseat.

The rest of the motorcade follows: two camera cars carrying local motion and still photographers; two Dallas police motorcycle escorts (H. B. McLain and Marrion L. Baker); a third camera car; three cars full of congressmen; a VIP staff car carrying a governor's aide and the military and air force aides to the president; two more motorcycle escorts (J. W. Courson and C. A. Haygood); a White House press bus; a local press car with four *Dallas Morning News* reporters; a second White House press bus; two more Dallas police motorcycle escorts (R. Smart and B. J. Dale); a Chevrolet sedan carrying the president's physician, Admiral George G. Burkley, and the president's personal secretary, Evelyn Lincoln; a 1957 black Ford hardtop carrying two representatives from Western Union; a white 1964 Chevrolet Impala containing White House Signal Corps officer Art Bales and Army Warrant Officer Ira Gearhart ("Bagman"); a 1964 white-top, dark-body Chevrolet Impala; a third White House bus carrying staff and members of the Democratic Party; a 1963 black-and-white Ford police car; and at the rear, a solo three-wheel Dallas police motorcycle escort.[140]

In a long procession the motorcycles and cars turn left out of Love Field onto Mockingbird Lane, then almost immediately southeast onto Lemmon Avenue, heading for downtown. There aren't many people along this first long straightaway down Lemmon Avenue, which is flanked by those low, nondescript structures characteristic of the light industry near airports. Clumps of people, mostly workers from the factories, have gathered to watch the procession flash past, but there are long barren stretches too. Mostly, the road looks much like any avenue through a suburban industrial park in the middle of an ordinary workday.

Jackie, squinting in the bright sunshine, looks forward to the looming Cotton Belt overpass—cleared of onlookers by police orders—for the fleeting moment of shade it will provide. She tries to put on her sunglasses, but the president asks her not to—the people have come to see her, and the dark glasses might make her look distant and aloof. She keeps them in her lap, though, and sneaks them on for a moment or two whenever there is no one along the road to see.[141]

12:00 p.m.

At the Book Depository, some of the stock boys wade into their lunches in the small, first-floor employee's lounge, which the architects designated as the recreation room and which employees call the "domino room," after their favorite pastime, while others eat while standing in front of the building. Charlie Givens discovers he left his cigarettes in the pocket of his jacket up on the sixth floor. The thirty-eight-year-old navy veteran goes back up on the elevator. The sixth floor appears deserted as he crosses the wide space they cleared for the new flooring, but when he gets back to the elevator with the cigarettes and prepares to go down, he is startled to see Lee Oswald, whom he had seen a few minutes earlier on the fifth floor, now on the sixth floor, walking along the east aisle, away from the southeast corner of the room, clipboard in hand.

"Boy, are you going downstairs?" Givens calls out. "It's near lunchtime."

"No, sir," Oswald replies. Oddly, he again asks for the west elevator gate to be closed when Givens gets back downstairs.

"Okay," Givens shrugs.[142]

When he returns to the first floor on the east elevator, he turns to close the west elevator gate, as Oswald requested, but finds it missing—it's up on some other floor.[143] After eating lunch in front of the building, he joins Harold Norman and James Jarman inside at a first-floor window looking onto Elm Street, but after a bit they decide to go outside for the motorcade. Later, Norman and Jarman change their minds and go back in to watch from the fifth floor, while Givens walks over to the corner of Main and Record to watch the motorcade with a couple of friends.[144]

12:06 p.m.

At the corner of Lemmon and Lomo Alto Drive, the president's eye catches a group of children with a large placard: "MR. PRESIDENT, PLEASE STOP AND SHAKE OUR HANDS."

"Let's stop here, Bill," Kennedy calls to the driver.

The car is immediately mobbed by the squealing, ecstatic kids. People as far as a block away start to run toward the car. When he realizes that the president has stopped, Chief Curry stops the lead car and begins to back up. The motorcycle escorts in front of him wheel around and head back toward the limousine. It's all Secret Service agent Kellerman and the men from the follow-up car can do to restore some order and get the motorcade moving again.

A few blocks farther on, the president stops again, this time for a bunch of little children and a nun—an irresistible temptation for America's first Catholic president. The nervous agents don't interfere, partly out of tact and partly because they are satisfied with their progress so far. They still have every chance of getting to the Trade Mart in good time.[145]

At the Book Depository Building, Bonnie Ray Williams had picked up his lunch in the domino room on the first floor, gotten a Dr. Pepper from the soda machine, and taken the east elevator back up to the sixth floor, expecting to find some of the other guys up there. Billy Lovelady said he was going to watch the motorcade from there, and Bonnie had more or less agreed with Danny Arce that they would too—but he doesn't see anyone on the sixth floor when he gets there.

Bonnie settles down anyway, in front of the third double-window from the southeast corner overlooking Elm Street, to eat his lunch—a piece of chicken on the bone, two slices of bread, and a bag of Fritos. No one else shows up. After a while he gets up and perches on a "two-wheeler," one of the hand trucks they use to buck the heavy boxes of books around. It's dead quiet up here, nothing moving but specks of dust in the air. To his right he can see the west wall, because that's where they cleared the books out to resurface the floor. His view to the left is blocked by the unusually high piles of boxes the workers moved there in preparation for the reflooring job. It's so quiet he can hear the pigeons on the roof above and someone moving around on the floor below—someone walking, then moving a window. He hears the traffic and growing murmur of the crowd in the street below. It's finally clear that no one else is coming up to watch from the sixth floor. He finishes off his Dr. Pepper, puts the chicken bones back in the paper sack, leaves the bottle and sack there, and goes back to the elevator to see who's on the floor below.[146]

12:12 p.m.
Howard L. Brennan, a forty-four-year-old steamfitter, watches the crowd gathering outside the windows as he finishes his lunch in the cafeteria at the corner of Record and Main streets. Brennan could join the crowd right there on Main Street, but folks are already jostling for position, and he reckons he'll walk back toward the railroad yards near Elm and Houston, where he's been working on a pipeline for Wallace and Beard Construction for the past seven weeks.[147]

12:15 p.m.
Arnold Rowland and his wife Barbara find a place to watch the motorcade on the sidewalk in front of the Criminal Courts Building on Houston Street, near the west entrance to Sheriff Decker's office. The young couple are still students at Dallas's Adamson High School, but both got off early today and came downtown to shop for a while before Arnold goes to his job at the Pizza Inn on West Davis Avenue.[148]

A hundred yards to the west the Rowlands can see policemen on the railroad bridge over the Triple Underpass and another two-dozen or so uniformed officers in the streets around the plaza. Arnold and Barbara remember the nasty incidents involving Adlai Stevenson and Lyndon Johnson not too long ago and understand that security will be tight for the motorcade.[149] Arnold knows the building on the next corner very well— several times he has been to the Texas School Book Depository to get books, including a physics notebook he bought there two or three weeks ago.[150] He and his wife take note of a number of people looking out the windows of the building, including a black man hanging out of one of the southeast corner windows.[151]

A nearby police radio squawks out the progress of the motorcade.

"What's the location?" Inspector J. H. Sawyer asks.

"Now turning onto Cedar Springs Road off of Turtle Creek," the dispatcher informs him.

"Ten-four," Sawyer replies.[152]

Arnold Rowland can tell from the conversation that the motorcade is about two miles away now.[153] As he continues to scan the upper floors of the Depository, Rowland would later say he spotted a man holding a high-powered rifle at port arms (across his chest) in the window at the west end of the sixth floor. That's some distance away, but Arnold knows his way around guns, and he can tell by the relative proportion of the scope to the rifle that it's a heavy piece, no .22 caliber. Though the rifleman is a couple of feet back in the shadows, Arnold, whose eyesight is better than 20/20,[154] sees him very clearly, a slender man in his early thirties, with a light complexion and either well-combed or close-cut dark hair, wearing a light-colored, open-collared shirt over a T-shirt.[155]

"Hey, you want to see a Secret Service man?" he asks his wife Barbara.

"Where?" she asks, staring intently at a commotion developing across the street.

"In the building there," Arnold says, pointing back up at the Depository. His wife, however, is paying no attention and instead directs him to look across the street at a couple of police officers assisting a young black man who's having some sort of epileptic fit. By the time Arnold gets his wife's attention and points out the open window, the man with the rifle has disappeared.

"What did he look like?" she asks, disappointed to have missed him.

Arnold describes the man and how he was holding a rifle with a scope.

"Oh," she sighs, "I wish I could have seen him. He's probably in another part of the building now, watching people."

Her attention returns back to the action across the street, where an ambulance arrives to take the epileptic to Parkland Hospital. Although Arnold continues to scan the upper floors of the Depository every thirty seconds or so, hoping to catch another glimpse of the man he assumes is a Secret Service agent so that he can point him out to his wife, he doesn't see the rifleman again. Nor, to his later regret, does he bother to mention what he saw to a nearby police officer.[156]

Bonnie Ray Williams steps off the elevator onto the fifth floor of the Depository. He discovers Harold Norman and James "Junior" Jarman there.[157] With seven big double-windows across the Elm Street face of the building, there's plenty of room for the three of them to watch the motorcade. Harold squats at the window in the southeast corner, and Bonnie Ray joins him there, taking the second window of the pair. Junior kneels at the second double-window, leaning over the low sill. If they lean out far enough, they can talk to each other outside. The view is terrific, since from their perch they can see south to the corner of Houston and Main and beyond, as well as all the way west down the curving sweep of Elm to the Triple Underpass, with nothing in their line of sight but the thick foliage clustered on the branches of an oak tree[158] nearly right below them along the north side of Elm. Except for that oak, they will get a pretty good view of the motorcade from the moment it turns off Main Street until it disappears into the shadow of the underpass leading to the Stemmons Freeway.[159]

12:20 p.m.
In the pilot car, Deputy Chief Lumpkin rolls closer to the downtown area. As each block passes, the skyline of Dallas grows taller and larger and the crowds increase in size. Already, police officers are finding it nearly impossible to keep people back onto the sidewalks and behind the barricades.

"Need some motorcycles—just to kinda keep the crowd over to Harwood and Ross," Chief Lumpkin warns Curry over the radio. "They're kinda getting out into the street here."

"We've got 'em," Curry answers.

"[Unit] One [Curry], are you approaching Ross?" the dispatcher asks.

"Just approaching at this time," Curry says over the roar of the crowd.[160]

Governor Connally had feared some ugly incident occurring in this most conservative of cities. But these fears have fallen away as the people are friendly, waving, smiling. And it is plain the president is enjoying himself.[161]

12:21 p.m.
Charles F. Brehm is very pleased with his position for the motorcade, on the northwest corner of Main and Houston. Compared to the throngs on Main Street, there are relatively few people here, and a better chance that his son will get a clear view of the president. Joe is five years old. He doesn't really understand the significance of it now, but his father feels he is old enough to remember seeing John F. Kennedy and his wife for the rest of his life. It's a story he will be able to tell his own grandchildren one day. The position has another advantage. If the motorcade is moving slowly enough, Brehm may be able to run diagonally across the adjacent plaza to Elm Street for a second bite of the cherry. Little Joe is too big to carry for long, but not too big for a quick sprint down the grassy slope to Elm.[162]

12:22 p.m.
Deputy Chief Lumpkin turns the pilot car right off Harwood onto Main Street and gets his first good look at the crowds awaiting the motorcade. "Crowd on Main Street's in real good shape," he tells Chief Curry over the police radio. "They've got 'em back off on the curb."

"Good shape," Curry says, barely audible over the shrieks and screams of the cheering crowds. "We're just about to cross Live Oak."

"Ten-four," Lumpkin replies.[163]

At Live Oak Street, two and a half blocks from Main, where the high buildings of downtown turn the streets into deep canyons, the motorcade plunges into an avalanche of roaring cheers from people standing eight and ten deep and hanging out the windows high above. Curry's men are helpless against the press of the crowd, which closes in, narrowing the passage for the cars and forcing Greer to drop his speed from twenty miles an hour to fifteen, to ten.

"There's certainly nothing wrong with this crowd," O'Donnell says to Powers, beside him on the jump seat of the Secret Service follow-up car. The steady roar from the crowd is deafening. It is by far the happiest and most enthusiastic crowd they've seen in Texas. They also see the faces of the president and his wife in the car immediately ahead when they turn to wave to the swarms of people pushing past the police barricades into the street. The president seems thrilled by the unexpected warmth of the welcome, and O'Donnell is pleased to note that Jackie is following his last-minute instruction to keep turned toward her own side of the street, to make sure that the crowds on both sides get at least a glimpse of one or the other of the country's most famous couple.[164]

12:23 p.m.

Seven minutes from Dealey Plaza, the crowds on Main are the heaviest. This is the mouth of the bottle. Ahead lies a twelve-block-long forest of humanity nestled between the tall buildings and eight skyscrapers of downtown Dallas. Fifteen hundred yards of screaming, whistling, cheering pandemonium. The throngs of people on both sides of the street are so heavy they threaten to choke it off entirely.

Governor Connally thinks it looks like about a quarter of a million people have turned out to greet the Kennedys in Dallas, an enormous crowd for a city with a population of around three-quarters of a million in 1963.[165]* Connally's estimate of the crowd is almost assuredly overblown, but by all accounts, it's the largest and friendliest crowd so far on Kennedy's Texas trip. And the crowd is certainly more than Captain Perdue Lawrence expected. As the Dallas police officer in charge of crowd control for the day, he began to realize early on that things are a bit out of hand. The Dallas police simply don't have enough men, barricades, or rope to handle this kind of reception.[166]

Secret Service agent Greer slows the presidential limousine to a crawl as the crowds press in. The motorcycle escorts find their handlebars bumping people standing out in the street.

"Escort, drop back," Curry commands. "Have to go at a real slow speed now."[167]

A teenage boy dashes from the crowd, camera in hand, and chases after the limousine. Running between the motorcycle escorts on the right and the president's car, the boy raises the camera to his eye. Before he can get a picture off, a Secret Service agent jumps from the follow-up car, overtakes the boy, and throws him back into the crowd, causing people to tumble to the ground.[168] Chief Curry can see that the lead motorcycle escorts are too far ahead, allowing the crowd to close in behind them.

"Hold up escort," Curry orders, then a moment later, "Okay. Okay, move along."[169]

The reception is phenomenal. The First Lady lifts her white-gloved hand and flutters her fingers at the faces on her left, evoking a nearly hysterical "Jackiiieee!" from the crowd. The president is working the right side of the street with equal results. It is the crowning moment of the parade.[170]

Howard Brennan's hunch was right—he does indeed find a great spot, at the corner of Houston and Elm, right across the street from the Book Depository. He even has a seat, a low, ornamental wall curving around the end of the long reflecting pool—or "lagoon," as Dallas folk call it—along the west side of Houston Street. His aluminum hardhat shields his head from the sun, and he reckons he will have, in a couple of minutes, a good view of the First Family.

His eyes rove over the swelling crowd. There's quite a bunch on the steps of the Depos-

---

*According to U.S. Census records, the population of the city of Dallas was 679,684 in 1960. In 1970, it had increased to 844,401.

itory Building across the street, and more people turning up every moment. If the crowd gets too thick he can always stand up on top of the low wall to see well over their heads. He notices quite a few people in the windows of the Texas School Book Depository, in particular three black men on the fifth floor near the southeasternmost side of the building, leaning way out of their windows to chatter to each other, and a fellow just above them on the sixth floor, who for a moment sits sideways on the low windowsill.[171] It strikes Brennan as odd that this guy is alone, while almost everyone else is with someone. The man in the sixth-floor window seems to be in his own little world, unsmiling, calm, with no trace of excitement. Brennan, who is farsighted, has especially good vision at a distance, and sees him very clearly.

12:25 p.m.

It took Abraham Zapruder a while to find the right spot. At the urging of his secretary, the fifty-eight-year-old Dallas dressmaker, a bespectacled, balding man wearing his trademark fedora and bowtie, had returned home earlier in the morning and retrieved his new 8-millimeter Bell & Howell movie camera. At first he thought he would use the telephoto lens to shoot pictures from his office in the Dal-Tex Building, across the street from the Texas School Book Depository, but after he came back to the office he realized his office window was too far away. So, he and Marilyn Sitzman, his receptionist, went down into the plaza. He tried standing on a narrow abutment along the north side of Elm, but it was too narrow and he was afraid that he'd lose his balance trying to shoot pictures from there. A bit farther down Elm Street he found the perfect spot—a larger, square abutment about four feet high at the west end of the ornamental pergola. The perch would place him right in the middle of that stretch of Elm, and high enough to give him a pretty clear view of the motorcade from the corner of Houston and Elm on his left, down to the Triple Underpass on his right. There is even enough room for Marilyn to stand behind him on the abutment and help steady him if he gets dizzy looking through the telescopic lens.[172]

As the limousine proceeds down Main between Ervay and Akard, all eyes in the car instinctively turn to the left to see the giant display windows of Neiman Marcus, the pride of Dallas and, indeed, the premier luxury retail store in the world. As elegant and expensive a shopper as Jackie is, nothing in New York City, London, and Paris, her normal shopping grounds, quite compares to it. The store caters not only to the oil zillionaires of Texas but to those with very deep pockets everywhere. They tell the story about the oil magnate who approached the store's owner, Stanley Marcus, one day before Christmas and said, "I'll buy all the window-displays as they stand. Just shift the lot to my ranch, around my wife's window—it's my Christmas present to her."[173]

12:26 p.m.

FBI special agent James P. Hosty Jr., the man responsible for monitoring right-wing political activists in Dallas, watches the motorcade rumble past from the corner of Field Street, about halfway down Main. Hosty is really pleased to see the tumultuous welcome. As a Kennedy Democrat he doesn't like the radical rightist atmosphere of the city at all, but it's clear that Dallas has turned out for the president with real enthusiasm. As soon as the motorcade passes, he crosses the street to a restaurant to get some lunch.[174]

Senator Yarborough, riding two cars behind the presidential limousine, is astonished at the enthusiasm of the crowds on the sidewalks. But the people looking out the windows on the floors high above the street are a different story. The senator doesn't see a single smile there, and he imagines that some of those faces express sheer dislike. As the motorcade approaches Dealey Plaza* at the end of Main Street, and he sees the open area sloping down to the Trinity River beyond, he starts to feel relief about leaving the high-rise buildings behind. "What if," he wonders uneasily, "someone throws a flowerpot down on top of Mrs. Kennedy or the president?"[175]

There is a lot of good-natured grumbling in the Chevrolet convertible to which Bob Jackson has been assigned. The twenty-nine-year-old *Dallas Times Herald* staff photographer sits on the top of the backseat and wrestles with one of his two cameras, trying to rewind and unload the film he shot at Love Field and during the motorcade procession so he can toss it to the *Times Herald* staffer who will be waiting for it at the corner of Main and Houston. He and the others—Jim Underwood of KRLD-TV; Tom Dillard, chief photographer for the *Dallas Morning News*; and a couple of newsreel guys from WFAA, the *Dallas Morning News*'s radio station, and Channel 11—figure they might as well be in the next county. They are *eight* cars behind the president. They know because they counted. That far back, their chance of getting a lens on anything worth printing or broadcasting is just about nil. Even from his perch on the rear deck, Jackson catches only occasional glimpses of the president's limousine. He hopes things will be better at the Trade Mart.[176]

12:28 p.m.
"Crossing Lamar Street," Chief Curry says into the lead car's radio microphone.

"Ah, ten-four, [Unit] One [Curry]" the dispatcher replies. "Is there a pretty good crowd there?"

"Big crowd, yes," Curry replies.

The dispatcher knows there must be. He can hear the squeals of delight in the background of the chief's transmission. Deputy Chief Lumpkin cuts in, "Uh, notify Captain Souter . . . [of] the location of the convoy now."

"Fifteen, car two [Souter]," the dispatcher calls. "On Main, probably just past Lamar."

"Just crossing Market Street," Curry says, updating the motorcade's progress.

"Now at Market, car two [Souter]," the dispatcher quickly repeats.[177]

The president is now just two blocks from the open sky of Dealey Plaza.

On the southwest corner of Elm and Houston, directly across the street from the Book Depository, Ronald Fischer, a young auditor for Dallas County, and Bob Edwards, a util-

---

*Dealey Plaza is a three-acre, well-manicured patch of land with concrete pergolas and peristyles, reflecting pools, and some office buildings. It is called "The Front Door of Dallas" and was named in 1935 after George Bannerman Dealey, a Dallas civic leader and the founder of the city's main paper, the *Dallas Morning News*. The plaza is in the form of a triangle, with three main thoroughfares, Main Street in the middle having east and westbound lanes, and flanked by Elm to the north having only westbound lanes, and Commerce to the south with only eastbound lanes. The three arteries converge at a triple underpass built in 1936 beneath the Union Terminal Railroad overpass at the southwestern tip of the plaza. (CE 877,17 H 897–898) The site of the Texas School Book Depository Building at the northwest corner of Houston and Elm in the plaza was originally owned by John Neely Bryan, the founder of Dallas.

ity clerk from the same office, wait at the curb for the motorcade. Edwards notices a white man, on the thin side, among the boxes at the sixth-floor southeast corner window of the Depository Building. "Hey, look at that guy in the window," Edwards says, poking Fischer. "He looks like he's uncomfortable."[178]

He does look uncomfortable, Fischer thinks, when he spots the man in the window, a slender man with brown hair in his early twenties, casually dressed. Oddly enough, even though the motorcade is likely to appear at any moment now, this guy isn't watching out for it. Instead of looking south toward the corner of Main and Houston like most of the crowd, he's staring west toward the Triple Underpass, or maybe even beyond to the Trinity River. He is curiously still too, not moving his head or anything else. He appears to be kneeling or sitting on something, literally boxed in by the high wall of boxes behind him. Edwards laughs, wondering who the guy is hiding from. Fischer goes on watching him for a while, but never sees a movement. The man seems "transfixed." It's very strange.[179]

On the southeast corner of Houston and Elm, diagonally across the street from the Book Depository Building, young James Crawford, a deputy district clerk in the Records Building, anxiously awaits the motorcade with his friend and coworker Mary Ann Mitchell. They had left their office on Houston Street just a few minutes earlier but had no trouble getting a good position along the parade route.[180]

A sudden jolt of excitement hits the crowd. The pilot car driven by Deputy Chief Lumpkin, its red lights flashing, sweeps around the corner off Main onto Houston Street. They can hear the crowd near Main and Houston begin to break into applause, screams, and whistles. The presidential limousine can't be more than a minute away now.

12:29 p.m.

Five lead motorcycles round the corner from Main onto Houston followed by the white 1963 Ford sedan driven by Chief Curry, its red front grill lights pulsating rhythmically. Suddenly, the presidential limousine bursts into view, the two flags mounted on its front fenders fluttering majestically in the breeze. The crowd in Dealey Plaza breaks into spontaneous applause. As the limousine makes the slow right turn onto Houston Street and heads north, Mrs. Kennedy reaches up and steadies her bright pink hat against the strong wind that whips across the open grass of the Plaza. Two motorcycle escorts flank each rear fender, with the Secret Service follow-up car and its jumble of agents following only a few feet behind them.

The crowds lining both sides of Houston Street cheer wildly. Nellie Connally is overwhelmed by the unexpected response of the people of Dallas. She turns and beams brightly at the president.

"Mr. President," she says, as the president leans toward her, "they can't make you believe now that there are not some in Dallas who love you and appreciate you, can they?"

The president leans back, waves, and flashes the famous Kennedy smile at the passing faces.

"No, they sure can't," he grins.[181]

The limousine moves slowly up Houston toward the large brick Texas School Book Depository Building looming over them just ahead, and to the left. Mrs. Kennedy, looking to her left across the reflecting pools onto Elm Street, can see that the pilot car of the motorcade is heading toward an underpass and thinks how cool the shade will feel after basking in the warm rays of the Texas sun.[182] As the first three of the five lead motorcycles round the corner at Elm and Houston, Abraham Zapruder begins filming.

After a few seconds, he stops his home movie camera and waits until the president comes into view.[183] Chief Curry, right behind the three motorcycle escorts, swings the lead car left off Houston, through the hairpin turn, and onto the gently curving downslope of Elm Street.

"Approaching the Triple Underpass," Curry tells the dispatcher.

"Ten-four, [Unit] One [Curry]," the dispatcher responds.[184]

Secret Service agent Winston Lawson, in Chief Curry's car, contacts the agents waiting at the Trade Mart.

"Five minutes away," he says into his radio.[185]

Charles Brehm, with little Joe in his arms, runs down the lawn of Dealey Plaza from Houston to Elm, and arrives well before the presidential limousine. He puts Joe down and tells him to get ready to wave to the president. There's hardly anyone that far down Elm, and he and his five-year-old boy have a completely unobstructed view as Chief Curry's lead car sweeps past them—the presidential limousine just beginning the turn onto Elm.[186] It is sunny and the temperature is sixty-five degrees.[187]

While the NBC television affiliate covered the president's appearance in Fort Worth that morning and the CBS and ABC affiliates covered the president's landing at Love Field, no live TV cameras are even remotely close to Dealey Plaza, and there is also no live radio coverage of the motorcade in the plaza.

As noted earlier, President Kennedy had requested that Secret Service agents not ride on the two steps built into the rear bumper of the presidential limousine, but Clint Hill, the Secret Service agent riding on the left running board of the follow-up vehicle just five feet behind had disregarded this request for four separate but brief moments since the motorcade left Love Field when he felt the situation created an increased danger, all of which happened on Main Street, where the crowds were the greatest. (Since Mrs. Kennedy was Hill's primary responsibility this day, he got on the left rear step.) On at least one of the four occasions, when the limousine stopped for the president to shake hands with people alongside the road, Secret Service agent John Ready, Hill's counterpart riding on the right running board of the follow-up car, had left the running board and gotten on the rear step on the president's side of his limousine.[188] But the crowds are lighter now and neither Hill nor Ready see any need to stand on the two rear steps of the presidential limousine.

12:29:45 p.m.

The glistening, dark blue limousine carrying the president of the United States—license plate number GG300 under District of Columbia registry—approaches the Texas School Book Depository Building. Cheers from the crowd ripple across the plaza as the president's limousine commences its turn onto Elm Street.

Bonnie Ray Williams, Harold Norman, and James Jarman, the three black stock boys seen by people on the street below, have a perfect view of the president from their fifth-floor Depository perch. Sunlight glints run down the length of the chrome trim as the presidential limousine completes its turn onto Elm Street, straightens out, and passes directly below their window. Bonnie Ray and Harold can see the president brushing his chestnut hair back from his face.[189]

Zapruder points his camera at the approaching limousine and again presses the camera's release button, which sends film shuttling through the camera with a soft, whirling sound. The clock on the Hertz sign high atop the Texas School Book Depository rolls over to twelve-thirty.[190]

12:30 p.m.

First Shot—:00.0 seconds BANG!—The loud crack is quickly swallowed up by the sound of sputtering motorcycles. The three stock boys in the Depository think it's a firearm salute for the president, or maybe, Bonnie Ray Williams thinks, it's a motorcycle backfire. The thought that it could be anything more serious is beyond their imagination.[191]

Virgie Rachley, a young bookkeeper for the Texas School Book Depository, watching from the curb in front of the Depository, is startled to see sparks fly off the pavement in the far left lane, right behind the presidential limousine. She thinks it's a firecracker thrown by some boys who are fixing to get in a lot of trouble.[192]

Secret Service agent Paul Landis, riding on the right running board of the Secret Service follow-up car, knows immediately what the sound is—the report of a high-powered rifle coming from over his right shoulder. Landis snaps his head back toward the Depository. Nothing. He begins scanning the crowd but doesn't see anything unusual.

"What was it?" Agent John Ready says. "A firecracker?"

"I don't know," Landis answers, beginning to doubt his own senses. "I don't see any smoke." Landis now starts to wonder whether it was a blowout and glances at the tires on the right side of the presidential limousine. The one he can see, the right front, seems all right. The doubts unnerve him and he draws his gun.[193]

Secret Service agent Rufus W. Youngblood, riding in the front seat of the vice president's car, isn't sure what the sound is either—some kind of explosive noise. Vice President Johnson is equally puzzled. Youngblood quickly surveys the crowd, then the Secret Service follow-up car ahead of him, and notices the agents aboard making "unnatural movements." Fear suddenly consumes him. In a flash, Youngblood turns and hits the vice president on the right shoulder, shoving him down into the backseat. "Get down!" he shouts.[194]*

Governor Connally knows *exactly* what the sound is—the report of a high-powered rifle. An avid hunter all his life, Connally knows it isn't a firecracker or a blowout or anything else. It's a rifle shot. He turns and looks over his right shoulder, in the direction of the sound. Faces in the crowd blur past, but he sees nothing out of the ordinary. There is only one horrific thought that crosses his mind—this is an assassination attempt. In despair, thinking that such a beautiful day and warm reception are about to end in tragedy, Connally blurts out, "Oh no, no, no!"[195]

Mrs. Kennedy, who is looking to her left, mistakes the sound for a motorcycle backfire. Suddenly, however, she hears the governor's exclamation of "Oh no, no, no" and turns to her right, toward him.[196] Nellie Connally is turning too, startled by the loud frightening noise that emanates from somewhere to her right.[197]

Motorcycle escort Marrion L. Baker is seven cars back behind the presidential limousine, having just turned north onto Houston, and knows exactly what the sound is too. He just came back from deer hunting, where he heard the firing of a lot of high-powered rifles. He sees a great number of pigeons flying around the top of the Texas Book Depository Building and suspects a sniper is firing from the roof. Baker instinctively revs his Harley-Davidson, rumbles past the faltering motorcade press cars, and races toward the building two hundred feet in front of him.[198]

Twenty-year-old high school dropout James R. Worrell Jr. is standing right in front of the Book Depository, his back to the building from watching the motorcade come up Houston. When he hears the first shot, Worrell throws his head back, looks straight up,

---

*There is no evidence that the two Secret Service agents in the president's limousine, Greer and Kellerman, were as alert as Youngblood and directed the president to get down.

and sees six inches of gun barrel with the forepart of the stock sticking out a window high overhead on the southeasternmost side of the building.[199]

Across the street, ninth-grader Amos Euins thinks it's a car backfire and begins looking around, then up. He spots a pipelike object sticking out of the southeasternmost window of the sixth floor.[200]

A few feet away, Howard Brennan sits on the low stone wall of the reflecting pool. He thinks it's the backfire of a motorcycle, or a firecracker thrown from the Depository. Those around him must be thinking the same thing, because there's no immediate reaction by the crowd. He looks up. The man he saw earlier in the sixth-floor window is aiming a rifle straight down Elm Street toward the presidential limousine. Brennan sees him from the waist up with awful clarity, the rifle braced against his right shoulder as he leans against the left window jamb. The gunman's motions are deliberate and without panic. After a few seconds, he fires again.[201]

Second Shot—:03.5 seconds BANG!—The report is so loud inside the fifth floor of the Texas School Book Depository Building that the windows rattle, and loose plaster and dirt fall from the ceiling onto Bonnie Ray Williams's hair.[202]

The car is very close to Charles Brehm and his son, maybe twenty feet away, so they can see the president's face very well when the shot rings out. The president stiffens perceptibly, and his hands swoop toward his throat. "My God," Brehm thinks, "he's been shot."[203]

Secret Service agent Glen Bennett, sitting in the right rear seat of the follow-up car, is looking right at the president when the second shot hits him, he estimates, "about four inches down from the right shoulder."[204] "He's hit!" Bennett shouts, and reaches for the Colt AR-15 assault rifle on the seat, but Agent George Hickey has already got it. Hickey cocks the rifle and spins toward the right rear, from where the shots appear to have come. Bennett draws his own side arm but there is nothing to shoot at.[205] Special Agent Clint Hill leaps off the running board of the follow-up car and dashes toward the president's limousine.[206] Special Agent Roy Kellerman, riding in the front passenger seat of the president's limousine, turns back to his right, the direction from which he hears the firecracker-like pop. He believes he hears the president say, "My God, I am hit!"[207]* Kellerman sees the president's elbows have flown up higher than his shoulders, hands lower, fists clenched. He immediately turns his body back to the front and turns to his left to look into the backseats, where he sees Connally in clear distress.[208]

Unable to see the president over his right shoulder, and deeply concerned for his safety, Governor Connally is in the middle of a turn to look back over his left shoulder into the backseat, to see if Kennedy has been hit, when he feels a hard blow to the right side of his own back, like a doubled-up fist. Driven down into the seat by the shot, Connally spins back to his right, a gaping, sucking wound in his chest drenching his shirt with blood.

"My God," he cries out, "they're going to kill us all!"[209]

His wife, Nellie, reaches out and pulls her wounded husband down into her arms and out of what she believes is the line of fire. She puts her head down over his head and doesn't look up.[210]

---

*Kellerman is the only one in the car who heard this remark. In 1964 he testified that he spoke often with the president during the three years he served him, and would not have mistaken the presidents's Boston accent (2 H 75). But it's unlikely the president *could* have spoken after the bullet penetrated his throat.

Mrs. Kennedy turns toward her husband, who has a strange, quizzical look on his face—almost like he has a slight headache.[211]

Greer had thought the sound of the first shot was a backfire from one of the police motorcycles accompanying the motorcade, but when he heard the second loud sound, he glances over his right shoulder, momentarily slowing the car down, and sees Governor Connally in the process of slumping down. He turns back facing the front again, but knows something is very wrong now. At the same time, his partner, Kellerman, yells at him, "Let's get out of here. We're hit."[212]*

In the vice president's car, Agent Youngblood vaults over the front seat and sits on top of the crouched-down figure of the six-foot four-inch Lyndon Johnson as Mrs. Johnson and Senator Yarborough collapse toward the vice president. There is no doubt in Youngblood's mind what the sound is now—gunshots![213]

Abraham Zapruder hears the shot. The thought flashes in his mind, as he sees the president jerk and slump to his left against Jackie, that it's a joke, the president clowning around like people sometimes do when they hear a shot, "Oh, he got me." But even his confused mind is already telling him that the president of the United States does not make jokes like this.[214]

Across the street, Mary Moorman and her friend, schoolteacher Jean Hill, watch as the president's limousine glides toward them, curiously unaware that shots have already been fired. Mary knows she will have only one chance to get a picture of the president with her Polaroid camera, which takes about ten seconds to recycle, and fears he will be looking away from her, to his right, at people on the north side of Elm street. As the limousine draws closer, Jean thinks that President and Mrs. Kennedy are looking down at something in the seat. She calls out to the president so Mary can get a good snapshot, "Hey, we want to take your picture!"[215]

From the moment he looked up after the first shot, James Worrell hasn't taken his eyes off the barrel of the rifle sticking out the window, and when he sees it fire again he sees a little flame and smoke coming out of the barrel. There is a lot of commotion, people screaming and saying, "Duck." Frightened, he turns and starts to run toward Houston, just feet away, intending to run to the back of the building, which he feels is the safest place.[216]

Amos Euins scuttles for cover behind a bench near the reflecting pool. From there he can see that the pipelike object sticking out of the southeasternmost window of the sixth floor of the Depository is a rifle. He can see a good portion of it, from the trigger housing to the front sight. The fifteen-year-old can't take his eyes off the rifleman as he again takes aim.[217]

Third Shot—:08.4 seconds BANG!—A final shot rings out. Howard Brennan, who is also looking directly at the gunman as he fires, turns quickly to his left to see if it hit, but his view of the president's car is blocked by part of the concrete peristyle.[218]

---

*Back at Love Field, where Air Force One pilot Colonel James B. Swindal is listening to the radio chatter of the Secret Service agents in the motorcade (the plane's communication center was linked with the White House Communications Agency's temporary signal board in the Sheraton Dallas Hotel, which in turn was linked to the Secret Service radio frequency), he hears two loud shouts over the radio frequency around 12:30 that he recognizes as the voice of Roy Kellerman. Then he hears a third sharp cry from Kellerman: "*Dagger* cover *Volunteer*," the code names, respectively, for Rufus Youngblood, the chief Secret Service agent in LBJ's limousine, and Vice President Johnson. But the radio immediately becomes a "babel of screeching voices. Then it fell silent." (TerHorst and Albertazzie, *Flying White House*, pp.199, 210–211)

Zapruder's view, on the other hand, is clear and unobstructed. He pans his camera with the limousine as it rolls inexorably on down the long slope, the angle changing from three-quarter frontal to near broadside. As it draws abreast of him and only a few yards away, he hears a shot and sees, through the viewfinder, to his horror, the right side of the president's head explode.[219] His receptionist, Ms. Sitzman, sees the president's "brains come out, you know, his head opening . . . between the eye and the ear." It must have been a "terrible shot," she says, "because it exploded his head, more or less."[220]

Mrs. Kennedy is six inches from her husband's face when the bullet strikes, driving pieces of his skull into the air. His limp body bounces off the back of the seat and topples onto her shoulder in one horrifying, violent motion. She cries out, "Oh, no, no no. Oh my God, they have shot my husband. I love you, Jack."[221]

Just as Agent Clint Hill's hand reaches for the handhold on the trunk of the limousine, he hears the sound of a fired bullet smacking into a hard object.[222] In the front seat, Special Agent Roy Kellerman feels a sickening shower of brain matter blow into the air above his head and hears Mrs. Kennedy shout, "What are they doing to you?"[223]

From the follow-up car, Agent Paul Landis hears a muffled exploding sound—like shooting a bullet into a five-gallon can of water or a melon. He sees pieces of flesh and blood flying through the air and thinks, "My God, the president could not possibly be alive after being hit like that." He is not certain from which direction this shot came, but senses it came from the president's right front.[224]

Governor Connally, grievously wounded, is nonetheless still conscious at the moment of the head shot and knows all too well that the president has been hit. He and his wife are even more horrified to hear Jackie, somewhere behind them, saying, "They've killed my husband. I have his brains in my hand."[225]

At the same time that Kellerman yelled to Greer they were hit and to take off, Kellerman had grabbed the microphone used to access the Secret Service radio network linking the cars of the motorcade.

"Lawson, this is Kellerman," he shouts into the mike. "We're hit. Get us to the hospital immediately!"[226] But as he's starting to talk to Lawson and before Greer accelerates, a third shot rings out. Greer stomps on the gas pedal and the massive limousine lunges forward.[227]

Agent John Ready, who had jumped off the running board of the Secret Service follow-up car when the limousine had slowed and had started to run across the asphalt for the president's car, doesn't make it in time as the limousine speeds up, and Special Agent Emory Roberts orders Agent Ready back to the follow-up car.[228] As soon as he's aboard, Halfback's driver, Agent Sam Kinney, hits the accelerator and releases the car's siren as they shoot after the presidential limousine.[229]

Clint Hill, his hand grasping the trunk handhold, loses his footing, but jumps onto the back of the car just as it lurches forward.[230] Mrs. Kennedy has already climbed out of the backseat and is crawling toward him.* Hill senses that she is probably reaching for something coming off the right rear bumper of the car. He thinks he sees something come off the back of the car too, but he cannot be sure.[231] Hill pushes the First Lady back into

---

*Mrs. Kennedy would later have no recollection of crawling on the trunk of the car. Looking at still frames from the Zapruder film while working with author William Manchester, she said they brought nothing back to her. It was as though she were looking at photographs of another woman. (Manchester, *Death of a President*, p.161 footnote)

the seat. "My God, they have shot his head off," she cries. Hill climbs toward her, clinging to the trunk as the limousine picks up more speed.

An instant after the head shot, Mary Moorman, on the grass fifteen feet away near the south curb of Elm Street, snaps a picture of the presidential limousine passing by. She quickly falls to the ground and tugs on Jean Hill's slacks, shouting, "Get down, they're shooting." Despite her pleas, Jean Hill is too stunned to move and just stands there for a moment, transfixed, before she slumps to the grass.[232]

A few feet away, Charles Brehm instinctively throws himself on his young son, covering him with his body. Brehm, a former army staff sergeant, knows about gunfire. Nineteen years before, at Brest in Normandy, not long after D-day, a German bullet went through his chest and blew his elbow joint apart. Now, despite his desperate hopes, he is positive that the president was also hit.[233]

"They've killed him, they've killed him!" Abraham Zapruder cries, his finger frozen on the movie camera's button. He pans to his right, following the presidential limousine as it lunges toward the Triple Underpass. Only after it disappears into the shadows of the underpass does Zapruder release the switch.[234]

Before James Worrell makes the left turn to start running north on Houston, he pivots and looks back over his shoulder before the window with the rifle in it is out of sight and sees the rifle fire a third time. Crossing Houston he runs north nearly a block along the east side of the Depository, stopping finally at the corner of Pacific to catch his breath. All he can think of is the sight of that gun barrel firing over his head.[235]

Across from the Depository, Howard Brennan dives off the stone wall. Caught up in the confusion and hysteria around him, he half expects bullets to start flying from every direction. His eyes swing back to the sixth-floor window. He watches as the gunman pulls the rifle back from the window as though drawing it back to his side. The gunman pauses another second as though to assure himself that he hit his mark, and then he disappears.[236]

Press photographer Bob Jackson, twenty-nine, saw the gun being withdrawn from the window too. All the press guys in Jackson's car (James R. Underwood, Thomas Dillard, Jimmy Darnell, and Malcolm O. Couch) were still laughing at a reporter chasing a canister of film across the street when the gunfire had broken out. Jackson had tossed it to him, as scheduled, at Main and Houston but it got caught in a strong gust of wind and started bouncing away from its pursuer. The press car was halfway up the block toward Elm when its occupants heard the first shot. Dillard told his companions that it sounded like a firecracker, but the words were barely out of his mouth when they heard the other two shots and realized it was gunfire. Jackson looked straight ahead at the Book Depository. He noticed two black men in the southeast corner window of the fifth floor leaning out to look up to the floor above. Jackson followed their gaze and saw the better part of a rifle barrel and stock being withdrawn, rather slowly, back out of sight behind the right edge of the window.

"There's the gun!" Jackson shouts.

"Where?" the others ask.

"It came from that window!" he says, pointing at the southeast corner window of the sixth floor.[237]

WFAA-TV cameraman Malcolm Couch, hearing Jackson, catches a one-second glimpse of "about a foot of a rifle" barrel being brought back "into the window" on the "far right" of "the sixth or seventh floor." He snatches his camera up from his lap and starts shooting the window, but there's nothing more to be seen there, just stacks of cartons.

The press car rounds the corner onto Elm, and Couch finds his camera's viewfinder filled with people running in all directions. Dillard, Underwood, and Darnell jump out at the corner, leaving Couch and Jackson to wonder whether they should follow them or stay with the motorcade.[238]

James Crawford had thought the first loud sound he heard to be a backfire of a car, but he quickly realized that the quality of the cars in the motorcade would not be the type to have backfires. Then he heard the second sound and began to look around, thinking someone was firing firecrackers. As the report from the third shot sounded, he looked up and saw a very quick, indistinct movement in the southeasternmost window on the sixth floor of the Book Depository Building. It was a profile, somewhat from the waist up, of something light colored, perhaps caused by the reflection of the sun, and what came to his mind automatically was that it was a person having moved out of the window. He also saw boxes stacked up behind the window. Crawford turned to his friend Mary Ann Mitchell, and pointing to the window, tells her, "If those were shots, they came from that window," but she is unable to see anything. Neither Crawford nor Mitchell saw or was aware of the president being hit and they soon returned to their office to listen to the radio to learn what had taken place.[239]

Aftermath Agent Bill Greer pulls the president's car to the right as he charges the lead car, overtaking it in the cool darkness of the underpass. Chief Curry accelerates the lead car to catch them. As the two cars emerge into the sunlight on the west side of the underpass, Agent Clint Hill, spread over the trunk of the president's car, looks into the backseat. The sight sickens him. The president's head is covered in blood, a portion blasted away. Hill can see a chunk with hair on it lying on the seat next to him. There is blood everywhere. Hill looks forward to the jump seats and notices Governor Connally's chest covered in blood. Only then does he realize that the governor, too, has been shot. But for Hill, the heart-wrenching scene is in the backseat, where Mrs. Kennedy is cradling the president's head, whimpering over and over, "Jack, Jack, what have they done to you?"[240]

Hill looks back to his left rear toward the lead car they are passing and yells as loud as he can, "To the hospital, to the hospital!"[241]

The Secret Service follow-up car rockets out of the shadow of the underpass. From the right running board, Agent Paul Landis looks toward the president's limousine just ahead. He can see Clint Hill lying across the back of the trunk. Hill looks back toward Landis, shakes his head back and forth, and gives a thumbs-down sign with his hand.[242] In the follow-up car's front seat, Agent Emory Roberts picks up the car radio.

"Halfback to Lawson," Roberts hollers, "the president has been hit. Get us to the nearest hospital!"

The Secret Service men in the follow-up car turn back to the vice president's car trailing a half block behind them and begin waving frantically, motioning the driver to close the gap. Roberts looks over at Agent William McIntyre, who's clinging to the follow-up car's left running board, the wind whistling through his hair.

"They got him! They got him!" Roberts shouts. "You and Bennett take over Johnson as soon as we stop!"

Roberts eyes Agent Hickey as he waves the AR-15 assault rifle aimlessly.

"Be careful with that!" he warns.[243]

Dallas police officers James M. Chaney and Douglas L. Jackson, the two motorcycle officers who had been flanking the right rear of the president's limousine, catch up with

Chief Curry's lead car as they accelerate up the entrance ramp leading to Stemmons Freeway.[244]

"What happened?" Curry calls out.

"Shots have been fired," Chaney shouts.

"Has the president's party been hit?" Curry asks.

"I'm sure they have," Chaney confirms, as Curry grabs the radio microphone.[245]

"We're going to the hospital!" Chief Curry shouts frantically into his radio transmitter. "Parkland Hospital.* Have them standby. Get men on top of that there over—underpass. See what happened up there. Go up to the overpass. Have Parkland stand by."[246] But Officer J. W. Foster, who was *on* the overpass at the time of the shooting, is convinced the shots came from the Book Depository Building, and indeed, he sees some officers running toward the building. He immediately gets off the overpass and runs toward the building, where he will assist in blocking it off.[247]

Officer Marrion L. Baker, who had been pretty sure the shots came from the roof of the Book Depository, wheels his motorcycle to a stop at the curb in front of the building. Quickly dismounting, Baker looks to his left and notices people lying on the grass in Dealey Plaza, others rushing to grab their children. A woman near him is screaming, "Oh they shot that man, they shot that man!"[248] He turns and runs toward the front steps of the Depository, pushing his way through the spectators crowding the entranceway.[249]

Roy Truly, the building superintendent, sees Baker coming and immediately understands that the young motorcycle officer is looking for a way to the roof. Truly follows him up the front steps, through the glass front doors, and into the vestibule, where he finds Baker asking people in the lobby where the stairs are.

"I'm the building manager," Truly tells him.

"Where is the stairway?" Baker asks.

"This way," Truly says, pushing his way through another set of double-doors. Officer Baker is right on his heels and bumps into Truly's back when they start to cut through a little swinging door at the call counter. A bolt has slid out of place and keeps the door from opening. Truly frantically fumbles with the latch, pushes the door wide, and plunges diagonally toward the freight elevators at the back of the building, Officer Baker in hot pursuit.[250]

The chaos and confusion in the plaza is indescribable. The remainder of cars, motorcycles, and buses that make up the motorcade bunch up at the corner of Elm and Houston, then speed away toward the underpass. People are running every which way. Some who aren't running lie on the ground in fear. A motorcycle policeman, seeing some people on the ground pointing to the railroad yards, lets his bike fall at the north curb of Elm just east of the Fort Worth road sign and dashes up the grassy slope toward the yards.[251] Several police officers and a number of civilians run toward the area of the grassy knoll and retaining wall.[252]

The three stock boys on the fifth floor of the Depository peer down at the confusion unfolding below them. With the last shot still ringing in his ears, James Jarman jumps up and moves toward Bonnie Ray Williams and Harold Norman.

---

*Parkland Memorial Hospital, a ten-story county hospital about four miles from Dealey Plaza, was the largest and best hospital in Dallas County, a distinction it holds to this very day. Taking its name from the wooded parkland it sat on, the hospital opened on May 19, 1894. The present Parkland Hospital, on a new site, was dedicated on October 3, 1954.

"That's no backfire," Jarman says. "Someone's shooting at the president."

"No bullshit!" Bonnie Ray says rising to his feet, still in disbelief.[253]

"I think it came from above us," Norman says. "I'm sure of it." Jarman and Williams agree.[254]

The three stock boys run toward the west side of the building where Jarman yanks a window open so they can see what's going on below. Jarman can see police officers and people running across the railroad tracks to the west of the building, the area behind the pergola, and the police "searching the boxcar yard and the passenger train."[255]

It doesn't take long for Jarman to also see the plaster dust in Bonnie's hair.

"That shot probably did come from above us," Jarman concedes.

"I *know* it did," Norman answers excitedly. "I could hear the action of the bolt and the cartridges hitting the floor."[256] Norman is very familiar with the sound of the bolt being pushed backward and forward because he has fired a bolt-action rifle before.[257]

12:31 p.m.

In the lead car, Sheriff Decker takes the radio microphone from Chief Curry and identifies himself to the police dispatcher.

"Go ahead, Dallas One [Decker]," the dispatcher replies crisply. Decker blurts back instructions over the wail of police sirens.

"Have Station Five [call sign for the sheriff's radio dispatch room] move all men available out of my department," Decker says, "back into the railroad yards there in an effort to try to determine just what and where it happened down there, and hold everything secure until the homicide and other investigators can get there."

"Ten-four, Dallas One. Station Five will be notified," the dispatcher says.[258]

By now the motorcade is flying at top speed* along Stemmons Freeway, all sirens screaming, past the stunned and puzzled onlookers scattered along both sides of the freeway to see the president. Curiously, the motorcade is still on its planned route, although now, when the cars turn off Stemmons onto Industrial Boulevard, they will pass their original destination, the Trade Mart, and go straight to Parkland Memorial.† In the backseat throughout the ride to the hospital, Jackie Kennedy cradles the president's head in her lap, bending over him and saying, "Jack, Jack, Jack. Can you hear me? I love you Jack." As she would later recall, "I kept holding the top of his head down, trying to keep his brains in . . . but I knew he was dead."[259]

At police headquarters, the dispatcher asks Chief Curry for any information he can give him.

"Looks like the president's been hit," Curry shoots back. "Have Parkland stand by."

"Ten-four. Parkland has been notified."[260]

Bob Jackson doesn't know what happened, or where the press car is going now, or why, only that it is following the rest of the motorcade toward Stemmons Freeway at a high

---

*Later estimates of the speed vary. Two of the motorcycle escorts gave estimates of the speed on Stemmons Freeway ranging from 80 to 90 mph (Savage, *JFK First Day Evidence*, p.364; Sneed, *No More Silence*, pp.129, 156). Dallas police radio recordings (NAS-CBA DPD tapes, C2, 12:34 p.m.) indicate approximately four minutes were required to cover the four-mile ride to Parkland, which computes to an average speed of 60 mph over the entire route, which accounts for the slowing down of the limousine once it got off the Stemmons Freeway onto Industrial and then Harry Hines Boulevard.

†Not all pass the Trade Mart. The first press bus in the motorcade, unaware the president has been shot, proceeds to the Trade Mart, where the bus passengers soon learn he's been shot and is at Parkland Hospital (Semple, *Four Days in November*, pp.591–592).

speed. He is still holding his empty camera in his lap. The other one, which is loaded, is still strapped around his neck.[261] It all happened so fast he didn't get a single photograph. If he had only gotten a picture of the rifle barrel in the window, he undoubtedly would have won the Pulitzer Prize for the best news photograph of the year.[*]

Journalist Merriman Smith is sitting beside the driver of the press pool car, which puts him in control of the car's only radio telephone. He grabs it and calls the Dallas bureau of United Press International and tells the bureau operator, "Three shots were fired at President Kennedy's motorcade in downtown Dallas." He goes on talking as the press car shoots forward, trying to catch up with the rapidly vanishing motorcade. He has little to add to his one-liner, except to say that there are "no casualties" to report, but the longer he can keep the phone out of the hands of Associated Press reporter Jack Bell, sitting directly behind him in the center of the backseat, the bigger his "beat" of the rival wire service. On an event as big as this, getting the story even a couple of minutes ahead of the competition is a coup. Smith, stalling, asks the bureau operator to read back his dictation. Bell is beside himself, but Smith claims that nearby, overhead electric wires could have caused interference and he has to be sure his news bureau got the story. Bell, by now furious, tries to grab the phone. Smith, hanging onto it, crouches under the dash, while Bell flails at him. When Bell finally gets the phone, it goes dead in his hands.[262]

Deputy Sheriff E. R. "Buddy" Walthers and dozens of sheriff deputies are sprinting across the lawn in Dealey Plaza. They were out on the sidewalk on Main Street, in front of the Dallas County Criminal Courts Building, when they heard what sounded like shots. Some run toward the Book Depository Building, but Walthers and others, like Deputy Sheriff Eugene Boone, dash across Houston Street and run toward the grassy knoll area, Walthers going over the stockade fence, Boone the concrete retaining wall, into the train yards and parking area to the rear to search for the gunman.[263]

Roy Truly and Officer Baker arrive at the back of the Depository, having crossed the first-floor shipping area, and find that neither freight elevator is there. Truly looks up the shaft and sees that both elevators appear to be on the fifth floor. He punches a nearby button, trying to summon the west elevator. A bell rings, but nothing happens—the elevator gate has been left open on the fifth floor.

"Turn loose the elevator!" he shouts up the shaft. He punches the button and hollers again. Nothing.

"Let's take the stairs!" Baker says, impatiently.

"Okay," Truly replies, and in a wink, spins and bolts up the northwest stairwell.[264]

Baker draws his service pistol and races up behind him. Truly is already pounding up the flight of stairs leading to the third floor when Baker reaches the second-floor landing. Just as the officer leaves the stairway and steps out onto the second floor, his eyes sweep across the area to his right through the window of the second-floor door, and he catches a glimpse of a man inside, walking away from him. Baker opens the door and runs through the doorway, then sees the man more clearly through a little window in the door

---

[*]Jackson redeemed himself two days later when he took a Pulitzer Prize–winning photograph of the murder of Lee Harvey Oswald by nightclub owner Jack Ruby.

to a vestibule that leads to a lunchroom. The man, twenty feet away, continues to walk away from Baker inside the lunchroom. Baker opens the vestibule door and walks through the vestibule about five feet to the door frame of the lunchroom. Leveling his gun waist-high at the man, he commands, "Come here."[265]

The man turns and walks back to within three feet of the officer. He appears calm, expressionless.[266]

Meanwhile, Roy Truly, who realizes that the officer is no longer following him, comes back down the stairs to the second floor, hears voices in the lunchroom, and steps into the vestibule behind Baker. He sees that the officer has drawn a gun on Lee Oswald, one of his employees. Oswald doesn't seem to be excited, overly afraid, or anything. He might be a bit startled, like Truly might have been if someone had confronted him with a gun, but otherwise Oswald's expression doesn't change one bit.[267]

"Do you know this man?" Baker asks, turning slightly to look at Truly over his left shoulder.

"Yes," the building superintendent says, "he works here."[268]

Officer Baker doesn't waste another second. He doesn't even bother to look back at Oswald. He brushes past Truly, makes his way back to the stairwell, and continues toward the roof, the building superintendent close behind him.[269]

Thomas P. Alyea, a camera-reporter for WFAA-TV in Dallas, is stopped (with his partner, Ray John) at the traffic light located at Commerce and Houston streets listening to Dallas police radio as well as the WFAA commercial radio. He hears a voice (Chief Curry) over the police radio instructing officers to go to Parkland Hospital. He has no reason to associate this with President Kennedy, but twenty seconds or so later he hears newsman John Allen over the commercial radio announce that shots had been fired at the president. Alyea immediately grabs Ray John's fully loaded camera and three extra cans of film, gets out of the car, and runs toward the intersection of Houston and Elm, filming the emerging, chaotic scene along the way. He notices several people pointing toward the upper floors of the Depository Building and runs inside along with a number of others who appear to be plainclothes detectives. Right behind him is *Dallas Morning News* reporter Kent Biffle. Biffle with his pencil and pad and Alyea with his camera would end up being the only two newsmen in the building during the period after the shooting. While Alyea starts filming, and Biffle recording on his notepad, the police search for the assassin on the various floors of the building.[270]

Newsman Robert MacNeil, of later *MacNeil/Lehrer News Hour* fame, far down the motorcade in the first press bus, is jolted out of a half sleep by the sound of a shot, but he isn't sure. Working on three and a half hours of shut-eye, a light breakfast, and then an unwise Bloody Mary on the flight to Dallas from Fort Worth, he has been finding it hard to stay awake. MacNeil was only recently made the number-two man on NBC's White House detail covering the president's Texas trip because Sandy Vanocur chose to accompany most of the cabinet on a mission to the Far East.

From his seat in the bus he has only been catching glimpses of the president's limousine seven cars ahead, and when he hears two more very distinct explosions, he knows they are shots, and he shouts out, "Stop the bus! Stop the bus!"

The driver opens the door as he turns the corner onto Elm Street, and MacNeil jumps out. People are down on the grass on both sides of the street, covering their children, and the air is filled with screaming. The sun is so bright it makes his eyes ache. Seeing some people run toward the far end of the grassy slope right next to the railroad overpass, MacNeil dashes after them—they may be chasing the sniper. But he really can't imagine that the president was hit. It must be some right-wing nut making some kind of crazy demonstration.

MacNeil climbs up on the bottom ledge of the concrete railroad bridge alongside many other spectators and looks over the top with them. He sees nothing of significance except police searching the area and realizes he had better find a telephone, fast.

He runs back and into the first building he comes to, the Texas School Book Depository, running into a young man in shirtsleeves coming out whom he would later come to believe may have been Oswald. He asks for a phone. The young man points inside to a man talking on a phone near a pillar. "Better ask him," he says.

Inside, MacNeil asks another young man, who steers him to another phone in an office, four of its five lines occupied. Mercifully, he gets through to the radio news desk in New York, but, infuriatingly, is asked to wait. He screams into the phone until Jim Holton comes on the line. "This is MacNeil in Dallas. Someone shot at the president."

Holton switches on a tape recorder and MacNeil records all he knows so far: "Shots were fired as President Kennedy's motorcade passed through downtown Dallas. People screamed and lay down on the grass as three shots rang out. Police chased an unknown gunman up a grassy hill. It is *not* known if the shots were directed at the president. This is Robert MacNeil, NBC News in Dallas."

Outside again, MacNeil rushes over to a policeman listening to the radio on a motorcycle. "Was he hit?"

"Yeah. Hit in the head. They're taking him to Parkland Hospital."

MacNeil dashes out into the street, dodging the police cars whose wailing sirens are pulling up from all directions, bouncing over curbs, flowerbeds, and lawn. Not a taxi in sight. Traffic is beginning to jam. He sprints across Dealey Plaza to Main Street and leaps out in front of the first car that comes along.

"This is a terrible emergency," he tells the driver. "The president's been shot. I'll give you five dollars to take me to Parkland Hospital."

The driver, about thirty, not too swift, smiles and says, "Okay." The car is filled with packages that look like cake boxes. "Yeah, I heard something about that on the radio a couple of minutes ago," he says.

"Where's the radio?"

"I put it in the backseat."

MacNeil grabs the little transistor and holds it out the window to clear the antenna. They are already bogging down in the rapidly jamming traffic. He begs the driver to speed, take risks, run red lights, anything—MacNeil will pay the fines. All the police cars are headed in the opposite direction, back toward the Texas School Book Depository.[271]

12:32 p.m.
Mrs. Robert A. Reid, a clerical supervisor, had been watching the motorcade from in front of the Book Depository Building. Right after the shots were fired she runs into the building and is returning to her desk in the big central office space on the second floor of the Depository as Oswald cuts through the office from the lunchroom, a full bottle of Coke in hand.

"The president has been shot," she tells him as he walks past her, "but maybe they didn't hit him."

Oswald mumbles something in reply, but what it was does not register with her. She feels it is a little strange for a stock boy to be up in the office at that time. Indeed, the only time she had seen Oswald in the office before is when he needed change, presumably to get a drink from the soda machine in the lunchroom. But this time, Oswald already has a Coke. She takes off her jacket and scarf as Oswald heads toward the stairs leading to the front entrance of the building.[272]

Baker and Truly round the stairwell on the fifth floor and discover one of the freight elevators. They take it to the top floor—the seventh—then climb one more flight of stairs to come out, through a little penthouse over the stairhead, onto the roof. Officer Baker trots over to the west side of the roof and immediately realizes the parapet, five feet high, is too high to look or shoot over. He has to stand on tiptoes to even see the street and the railroad yards below. He starts to check the huge Hertz sign atop the Depository roof, but after climbing ten feet up the ladder attached to it, Baker rules that out too—there's nothing to hold onto up there.[273]

The motorcade rockets along Stemmons Freeway, the president's car right on the tail of motorcycle escorts Stavis Ellis, Jim Chaney, and B. J. Martin. They know if they lose control of their motorbikes, they'll be run down by the four-ton monster behind them. They try to put some distance between themselves and the president's car but each time they accelerate and look back, limousine driver Bill Greer has increased his speed and closed the gap.[274]

Secret Service agent Rufus Youngblood is still crouching in the backseat of the vice president's car, trying to shout to Johnson over the roar of the wind and wailing sirens.

"When we get to the hospital," he hollers, "I want you and Mrs. Johnson to stick with me and the other agents as close as you can. We don't know the extent of the emergency in the president's car, but it may be necessary for you to be acting president. We are going into the hospital and we aren't gonna stop for anything or anybody. Do you understand? We will separate from the other party the moment we stop!"

"Okay, pardner," Johnson says.[275]

From his vantage point next to Mrs. Johnson, Senator Yarborough can see Clint Hill, sprawled over the back of the speeding presidential limousine, beating his fist on the trunk, his face contorted by grief, anguish, and despair. Whatever has happened, Yarborough knows it is serious.[276]

There is little movement in the president's car. The governor lapses into unconsciousness, believing, as he closes his eyes, that he is dying. So does his wife. Nellie puts her lips to his ear and whispers, "It's going to be alright, be still," though she can scarcely believe it herself. For a moment, she thinks he is dead. Then, his hand trembles slightly. She can only hold on tighter.

Behind them, they hear the muted sobs of the First Lady, "He's dead—they've killed him—oh Jack, oh Jack, I love you." There is a pause, then, in shock, she begins again.[277]

The motorcade exits the freeway onto the service road, barely slowing to make the right turn onto Industrial Boulevard, where the entrance to the Trade Mart is located. Sergeant Striegel and some other officers are there trying to flag them down, unaware that there's been a shooting. Striegel steps into the street and waves frantically for them to stop as the lead motorcycles accelerate and blast past him at a frightening speed for a surface street.[278]

The motorcade fast approaches Harry Hines Boulevard, where they'll have to navigate a forty-five-degree left turn toward Parkland Hospital. Just before Harry Hines, the road rises sharply to cross a railroad grade. The motorcycle escorts are familiar with the turn, but limousine driver Bill Greer is not, and he pushes the president's car faster, moving dangerously close to the motor jockeys. With the limousine's front grill barking at their heels, the police escorts hit the rise wide open, go airborne, and nearly lose control as they slam to earth in the middle of the boulevard, thirty feet away. On contact, the Harley-Davidson motorcycles bank hard into the left turn, sparks kicking up from their footstands dragging across the pavement. The president's car is right behind them, hitting the rise with a *Whump!*, then into the turn on squealing tires. Greer is doing all he can to handle the careening limousine, which bumps J. W. Courson's motorcycle briefly into the curb.[279] The men frantically pull out of the turn and accelerate toward the emergency entrance of Parkland Hospital three-quarters of a mile up the road. It's a wonder they haven't wrecked yet.

12:34 p.m.

Just four minutes after the shooting, United Press International, getting the story from the Dallas office after its reporter, Merriman Smith, called it in from the radiophone on the dashboard of the White House press pool car in the motorcade, flashes the news, "Three shots were fired at President Kennedy's motorcade today in downtown Dallas," to its vast network of subscribers—newspapers, radio and television stations, and business offices all over the world. It is the first word to the outside world of what has happened in Dallas.[280]

As word of the shooting starts to spread throughout the land into every city and town, and every hamlet with a phone, radio, or TV set, people everywhere are physically staggered and stricken by the news. Groups of people gather everywhere, even around parked automobiles waiting for the next news bulletin over the car radio. Telephone switchboards light up like never before. The news spreads quickly across the Atlantic and Pacific oceans and the whole civilized world becomes "one enormous emergency room."[281]

12:35 p.m.

In Dealey Plaza, motorcycle officers and squad cars are swarming the Book Depository Building.[282] In the railroad yard, Deputy Sheriff Buddy Walthers encounters many police and spectators rummaging around, many beginning to doubt whether shots had been fired at all.

"Well, they sounded like rifle shots to me," Walthers tells the other officers. Walthers is familiar with the freight yards, having chased a couple of escapees from the county jail over here before, and knows that there's nowhere to hide. It's a wide-open river-bottom area as far as anyone can go, and he quickly begins to question whether anyone would be foolhardy enough to shoot from back here. Deputy Walthers walks back down the grassy slope to Elm Street and begins checking around a sewer cover off the south curb, where it appears that a bullet has chugged through the turf.[283]

Nearby, Dallas police motorcycle officer B. W. Hargis has located an eyewitness to the shooting, grabs his radio, and contacts the dispatcher.

"A passerby standing under the Texas School Book Depository stated that the shots came from that building," Hargis tells him.[284] This is the first police broadcast pinpointing the Book Depository as the source of the shots, but it will not be the last.

The reports are coming in fast now. The next one is from Officer C. A. Haygood.

"I just talked to a guy up here at the scene of this, where these shots were fired at, and he said that he was sitting here close to it, and . . . he thought they came from the Texas School Book Depository Building here, with that Hertz rental sign on top."

"Ten-four," the dispatcher says. "Get his name, address and phone number, and all the information you can. 12:35 p.m."[285]

12:36 p.m.

Sergeant D. V. Harkness, standing at the west end of the Elm Street extension, is asking for witnesses when young Amos Euins walks up, points to the Depository, and tells him he saw a man shooting from that building.[286] Harkness puts Euins on his three-wheel motorcycle and shuttles him to the front door of the Depository.[287] Harkness asks Euins which window he saw the man firing from. The teenage boy tells him it was the eastern-most window of the floor "under the ledge"[288]—which makes it the sixth floor.

"It was a colored man," Euins says excitedly, "he was leaning out of the window and he had a rifle."[289]

Sergeant Harkness grabs the radio on his motorcycle and notifies headquarters, "I have a witness that says it came from the *fifth* floor of the Texas . . . ah . . . Depository Bookstore at Houston and Elm. I have him with me now. I'm gonna seal off the building."[290]*

As Harkness hangs up the radio mike, Inspector J. Herbert Sawyer, a twenty-three-year veteran of the Dallas Police Force, pulls his car to the curb in front of the Depository. For the last few minutes, the forty-seven-year-old plainclothes officer has been working his way toward the shooting scene from Main and Akard, where he had been in charge of crowd control.[291] Sawyer jumps from the car, and Harkness tells him that he's got a witness who says that shots were fired from the fifth floor of the Depository.[292]

"The building is sealed off," Harkness tells him. "There are officers all around the building."[293] The inspector grabs two officers. "Come with me," he says, and heads for the front door, intent on going to the fifth floor to check out Euins's story. Meanwhile, Harkness puts Euins in the back of Sawyer's car and tells him to stay put until someone can get a statement from him.[294]

Howard Brennan, standing across the street from the Depository, watches as the officers seem to be directing their search to the west side of the Book Depository Building and down Houston Street. He runs across the street toward Officer W. E. Barnett, who is at the front of the building.

"Get me someone in charge," Brennan tells Barnett, who had just come from searching the north and east sides of the Depository Building. "You're searching in the wrong direction. The man is definitely in this building. I was across the street there and I saw the man in the window with a rifle."

"Which window?" Barnett asks.

---

*Harkness testified that Euins told him, "It was under the ledge," which referred to the sixth floor (6 H 313). Photographs of the building show a decorative ledge separating the sixth and seventh floors. Harkness further testified that "it was my error in a hasty count of the floors" (6 H 313) that led to his broadcast reference to the "fifth floor." Harkness's error is understandable in light of the fact that in 1963 the Depository's first-floor windows were covered with decorative masonry. Persons unfamiliar with the building could easily mistake the second floor for the first, third for the second, and so on—making the sixth floor appear as if it were the fifth floor. This is apparently what Harkness did during these initial confusing moments.

"One window from the top," Brennan says, pointing to the southeasternmost window on the sixth floor of the Depository Building.[295]

When Sawyer returns to the street after his cursory search found nothing, he takes two patrolmen and stations them at the front door to the Depository Building with instructions not to let anyone in or out.[296]

James R. Underwood, the assistant news director of KRLD-TV and radio, who had been riding in the motorcade and bailed out at the sound of the shots, approaches the squad car where Amos Euins sits in the backseat.

"Did you see someone with a rifle?" Underwood asks.

"Yes, sir," the fifteen-year-old boy answers.

"Were they white or black?"

"It was a colored man," Euins says.

"Are you sure it was a colored man?" Underwood presses.

"Yes, sir," Euins replies.[297]*

At Parkland Hospital, the presidential limousine pulls up abruptly at the emergency entrance. Secret Service agent Roy Kellerman leaps from the car and opens the back door. Not a gurney or a hospital orderly is in sight. Almost by the time it took the Dallas police to notify Parkland of the president's imminent arrival, the limousine was already at the back entrance.[298] The Secret Service follow-up car skids to a stop and a half-dozen agents tumble out.

"Go get us two stretchers on wheels!" Kellerman yells to them.[299]

The governor, lying face up in his wife's lap, begins to regain consciousness.

"Governor, don't worry," Kellerman says, "everything is going to be all right."

Special Agent Winston Lawson is the first into the building. He spots two gurneys at the end of a long corridor being pushed toward him. He dashes down and helps Nurse Diana Bowron and an orderly, Joe Richards, race them back to the entrance.[300]

Dave Powers and Ken O'Donnell jump from the follow-up car and bound toward the Lincoln. Powers hears Secret Service agent Emory Roberts shouting at him to stop, but he ignores him. When Powers reaches the side of the limousine, he half expects to hear the familiar voice say, "I'm all right." He and Jack Kennedy have been through so much. He finds his friend in Jackie's arms, his eyes open, and for a moment thinks he's conscious.

"Oh, my God! Mr. President, what did they do?"

Jackie looks up at him and shakes her head, "Dave, he's dead."

Suddenly, he realizes that the open eyes are in a fixed, vacant stare—the left eye bulging from its socket. Powers breaks down in tears.

Ken O'Donnell can only turn away.[301]

The vice president's car pulls up and agents hustle Lyndon Johnson, seen lightly rubbing his arm,† into the safety of the building. Senator Yarborough hears one of the Secret Service agents refer to Johnson as the "president," and he knows that John Kennedy must

---

*Later that afternoon, Euins told the Dallas County Sheriff's Department in a sworn and signed statement that the shooter "was a white man" (CE 367, 16 H 963).

†The gesture, witnessed by a spectator, became the basis for an early report that Johnson had been wounded or suffered a heart attack (Associated Press wire copy, November 22, 1963, 1:18 p.m.; Manchester, *Death of a President*, p.169).

be dead. He runs over to the president's limousine and sees Mrs. Kennedy there in the backseat covered in blood, her head bowed.

"They murdered my husband," she moans.

Ralph Yarborough is devastated. It is the most tragic sight of his life.[302]

Emory Roberts opens the left rear door of the limousine. He sees the First Lady covering the president's body with hers and tells her they have to get the president out of the limousine, but she doesn't move. "Mrs. Kennedy, you've got to get out," an unidentified Secret Service agent shouts imploringly.

"There's no need," she replies faintly.

Roberts lifts her elbow for a close look at the president, then drops it.

"You stay with Kennedy, I'm going to Johnson," Roberts says to Kellerman, undoubtedly aware of the cruelly insensitive mechanical transfer of power.[303]

Nellie Connally grows agitated at the men fussing over the president. To her the situation is clear. The president is dead. She saw the gore; no one could live through that. Everyone is fretting over a dead man instead of helping her husband.[304] The governor, conscious enough to realize that his jump seat is blocking access to the president in the backseat, tries to get out, then collapses in pain.

"My God, it hurts," he groans.[305] A gurney rolls up to the side of the car.[306] A Dallas police motorcycle officer and two Secret Service agents lift Connally's body onto the stretcher.[307] Hospital attendants push him quickly inside as Mrs. Connally stumbles after them.

Roy Kellerman folds the jump seats out of the way, as agents turn their attention to the president. Agent Paul Landis grabs Mrs. Kennedy by the shoulders and tries to help her up, but she resists, "No, I want to stay with him!"[308]

It is the most pitiful sight. The First Lady refuses to budge, crooning softly as she huddles over the mess in her lap. Agent Clint Hill mounts the rear bumper behind her and touches her gently on her trembling shoulders.

"Please, Mrs. Kennedy," he says tenderly.

Everyone around her is quiet. Seconds pass. Her moans are barely audible.

"Please," Hill mumbles again. "We must get the president to a doctor."

"I'm not going to let him go," she finally manages to say.

"We've got to take him in," Hill pleads.

"No, Mr. Hill. You *know* he's dead," she answers. "Let me alone."

Now, Hill thinks he realizes why Jackie isn't moving. She doesn't want everyone around to see the horror she is cradling. He quickly removes his suit coat and covers the president's head and upper chest with it to shield the horror from photographers, and Jackie releases her husband as a second gurney is pushed closer to the side of the limousine. Several agents pull the president toward them, struggling to lift the lifeless body onto the stretcher. The stretcher is quickly wheeled into the emergency entrance, a flock of people running alongside of it. Mrs. Kennedy is one of them; Jackie's hat and the red roses she'd been given at Love Field heaped on top of the president's body.[309]*

---

*There was one red rose from the bouquet that did not make it into the hospital. Stavis Ellis, one of the Dallas police cyclists who had led the close-tailing presidential limousine to Parkland is among the large crowd of people who have swarmed around the emergency area in back of the hospital. After President Kennedy's body and Connally have been removed from the limousine he can't resist the temptation to look inside the car. He sees several puddles of blood on the rear seat and floorboard. Right in the middle of one of the puddles lay a beautiful red rose. Years later he would recall, "I never forgot that. I can still see it, that red rose in that blood." (Sneed, *No More Silence*, p.147)

The national press pool car and several other motorcade vehicles left behind in Dealey Plaza begin to arrive at the hospital. Doors fly open and UPI correspondent Merriman Smith runs up and grabs Clint Hill.

"How is he?" Smith asks.

Hill curses, then says, "He's dead."

The reporter dashes into the hospital, bursts into the emergency room's cashier's cage, and snatches a telephone. "How do I get outside?" he demands.

"Dial nine," she stutters.

He calls the local UPI office.

"Kennedy has been seriously wounded—perhaps, fatally," Smith tells them.[310]

12:38 p.m.

The emergency room* is sheer bedlam. Roy Kellerman, moving as quickly as he can, enters a doctor's office and asks the medic there, "Can I use either one of these phones to get outside?"

"Yes, just pick one up."

Kellerman calls Gerald Behn, chief of the Secret Service White House detail, in Washington. "Gerry, . . . the president and the governor have been shot. We're in the emergency room of Parkland Memorial Hospital. Mark down the time."

Kellerman notes it as 12:38, Behn as 12:41 p.m.[311] Officially, the president is logged into the hospital register at 12:38 p.m. as "No.24740, Kennedy, John F."[312]

12:39 p.m.

Dallas police are quickly mobilizing in Dealey Plaza. More reports are coming in, each focusing on the building commanding the northwest corner of Elm and Houston.

"Get some men up here to cover this building, this Texas School Book Depository." Officer Clyde A. Haygood radioes in. "It is believed these shots came from [there]."[313]

Officer E. D. Brewer cuts in with another report: "We have a man here that saw [a gunman] pull a weapon back through the window off the second floor† on the southeast corner of that Depository building."[314]

C̲ecil McWatters, an eighteen-year veteran bus driver for the Dallas Transit Company, has been driving the Marsalis-Munger route for about two years now, zigzagging diagonally across the city from the Lakewood Addition out in the northeast to Oak Cliff in the southwest, and back again. There's only a handful of people in the forty-four-passenger bus as

---

*Inside the emergency area at Parkland were four emergency rooms, Trauma Rooms One, Two, Three, and Four. They were located on what was called the ground floor, not the first floor, at Parkland Hospital. Kennedy was immediately taken to Trauma Room One. (3 H 358–359, WCT Dr. Charles James Carrico) Above the ground floor were floors one through ten. The operating rooms were on the second floor. Though Governor Connally, who was taken to Trauma Room Two, was eventually brought up to an operating room on the second floor, Kennedy never left Trauma Room One. The entire emergency area at Parkland has since been reconstructed, and the Trauma Room One that Kennedy was brought into is no longer in existence. (Telephone interview of representative of Parkland's Corporate Communication section by author on January 21, 2004)

†Photographs show this second-floor window to be closed at the time of the shooting. Brewer no doubt meant the sixth-floor sniper's nest window, which would have been at the southeast corner, *second floor down from the roof.*

he heads west on Elm in downtown Dallas, but McWatters more or less expects that, since so many folks went into town earlier for the presidential motorcade.[315]

While at a complete stop in traffic on Elm at Murphy (just before Griffin), which is seven blocks east of the Depository, a man bangs on the door and McWatters lets him board, collecting the twenty-three-cent fare, even though, as indicated, he is not at a bus stop. The man takes the second seat back, on the right. From that seat he will be passing right by the scene of the assassination.[316]

Mary E. Bledsoe is sitting right next to the front door of the bus. She turns her face away as the man gets on, hoping he doesn't recognize her. It's Lee Oswald and there is just something about him that she has never liked. Mary's been divorced for a good many years, but she's managed to scrape by and raise her two boys on a little money her doctor father had left her and by renting out two or three of the four bedrooms in her house on North Marsalis. Back in October she had rented a room to Oswald for seven dollars a week, then five days later asked him to leave the premises. He was always fussing with someone over the phone looking for a job. And she didn't like his big-shot attitude or the fact that while using the telephone once she heard him talking in a foreign language. She told a lady friend of hers, "I don't like anybody talking in a foreign language."[317]

His appearance now—a hole in the right elbow of his brown shirt, which is "undone," his trousers "all ragged" in the waist area, and a "bad" look on his "distorted" face— reaffirms her opinion of him. He passes right in front of her and sits somewhere behind her.[318]

12:40 p.m.
Harry McCormick, a veteran police reporter at the *Dallas Morning News*, pulls into Dealey Plaza and jumps from his car, which is filled with fellow newsmen. They were scheduled to cover the president's luncheon at the Trade Mart, but after hearing of the shooting they immediately raced to the scene of the crime. One of the first people McCormick encounters is Abraham Zapruder, who is highly agitated, almost weeping.

"I saw it all through my camera," Zapruder half sobs to himself.

"What happened?" McCormick asks.

"I got it all on film," Zapruder replies. "There were three shots. Two hit the president and the other Governor Connally. I know the president is dead. His head seemed to fly to pieces when he was hit the second time."

McCormick knows that if Zapruder really did capture the assassination on film, it could be the most important film in history.

"The Secret Service will want to see those films," McCormick says. "Where are you going?" Zapruder tells him that he's going back to his office, across the street from the Book Depository. Thinking fast, McCormick assumes the authority of an officer.

"Go ahead," he tells Zapruder. "I'll find Forrest Sorrels, head of the Secret Service here, and we'll be back to talk with you."

McCormick didn't have a clue where he was going to find Sorrels, whom he had known personally for many years, but he knew he'd have to find him fast, before his competition found out about Zapruder's film.[319]

Zapruder stumbles back to his office in a state of shock, muttering, "They killed him, they killed him." At his office, Zapruder calls his twenty-six-year-old son, Henry, a government lawyer. "The president is dead," he says. Henry suggests his father is wrong, that he had just heard over the radio the president was wounded and on his way to the hospital. "No," the elder Zapruder says, "he's dead," explaining he had seen the president's head exploding through the lens of his camera.[320]

James Tague, who had witnessed the shooting from the mouth of the Triple Underpass, walks up to plainclothes deputy sheriff Buddy Walthers, combing the grass near the south curb of Elm Street.

"Are you looking to see where some bullets may have struck?" Tague asks.

"Yes," Walthers replies, barely paying attention.

"I was standing right there where my car is parked," Tague says, pointing to where Commerce meets the underpass, "when those shots happened. Well, you know, now I recall something stung me on the face while I was standing down there."[321]

Walthers looks up.

"Yes, you have blood there on your cheek," he says, rising to his feet.

Tague reaches up and wipes his fingers through a few drops of blood.

"Where were you standing?" Walthers asks.

"Right down here," Tague says, leading him toward a concrete strip that runs between Commerce and Main Street just east of the Triple Underpass.[322]

Twenty-three feet from the east face of the underpass,[323] along the south curb of Main Street, Walthers spots a mark on the top of the curb. It is quite obvious to both of them that the fresh gash was made by a bullet, and from the angle of the mark, it came from the direction of the Texas School Book Depository.[324]

Across America, housewives are following the fortunes of the characters of *As the World Turns*, the CBS network's popular soap opera. Actress Helen Wagner turns to fellow actor Santos Ortega and says, "And I gave it a great deal of thought, Grandpa." Suddenly, the program is cut off, replaced by a blank screen with the words "CBS NEWS" and in larger, white type, the single word "BULLETIN." Over it comes the sound of the network's leading newscaster, Walter Cronkite, his voice charged with emotion.[*]

"Here is a bulletin from CBS News. In Dallas, Texas, three shots were fired at President Kennedy's motorcade, in downtown Dallas. The first reports say President Kennedy has been seriously wounded by this shooting."

Cronkite fumbles momentarily with a fresh sheet of wire copy handed to him.

"More details just arrived," he says, scanning it quickly. "These details about the same as previously. President Kennedy shot today just as his motorcade left downtown Dallas. Mrs. Kennedy jumped up and grabbed Mr. Kennedy. She called, 'Oh no!' The motorcade sped on. United Press International reports that the wounds perhaps could be fatal."

The network suddenly returns to *As the World Turns*, the actors, working live in their New York studio, unaware of the interruption. Shocked viewers who switch to ABC or

---

[*]At the time, CBS did not have the capability of putting a commentator on camera immediately. "It took nearly twenty minutes to set up the cameras so Cronkite's voice could be joined by his face, and because of that experience, CBS would later install a 'flash studio' to enable visual, as well as audio, bulletins to be transmitted immediately." (Gates, *Air Time*, p.3)

NBC are treated to similar bulletins, equally terse, equally alarming. All three networks will soon cancel all programming and commercials for coverage of the event in Dallas.[325]

At Parkland Hospital, thirty-four-year-old Dr. Malcolm O. Perry is enjoying a quiet lunch with Dr. Ronald C. Jones in the main dining room. They hear Dr. George Shires being paged.

Perry knows that Shires, chief of the emergency surgical service at the hospital, was actually delivering a paper to a medical conference in Galveston that morning and may not be back yet. When Shires is paged a second time, Perry asks Jones to pick up the page to see if it's a matter on which they might be of some assistance.

Jones rushes back to their table to report that the president has been shot and is being brought to emergency, not knowing the president had already arrived by the time he received the message from the hospital operator. The two surgeons bolt from the dining room and, too rushed to wait for the elevator, gallop down the flight of stairs to the emergency room.[326]

12:41 p.m.

Out in Irving, Marina Oswald and Ruth Paine, who has returned from her errands, are taking care of some household chores. When Ruth goes into the kitchen to fix lunch for them, Marina retires to her bedroom to get dressed. She hears a sudden, loud, puzzling commotion from the television set in the living room, but makes no sense of it—until Ruth appears in the doorway, ashen. Someone shot at the president.

They run to the living room and stare at the television, waiting for it to tell them something, anything. There are no images of the event, nothing but a news announcer who seems to be at a loss too, obviously marking time until some real information comes in, and it's clear that he knows little more than they do. Ruth is crying as she translates the essential information—President Kennedy's been taken to Parkland Hospital. Marina knows Parkland—she had baby Rachel there just a month ago.

Lunch is forgotten. No one feels like it now. Ruth lights some candles, and lets her little girl light one. Marina, who knows that her friend takes her Quaker religion very seriously, asks, "Is that a way of praying?"

"Yes, it is," Ruth says, "just my own way."

Marina goes to her room and cries.[327]

Dr. Charles Carrico is standing in Trauma Room One, a narrow room with gray-tiled walls and a cream-colored ceiling, when the president is wheeled in on an emergency cart. Carrico is only twenty-eight and still doing his residency in surgery, but he has already seen nearly two hundred gunshot wounds at Parkland Hospital.[328] He rapidly assesses the president's condition—his color is "blue white, ashen," an indication of failing blood circulation; his respiration is slow, agonal (death throes), and spasmodic, with no coordination; there are no voluntary movements at all; his eyes are open and staring, with no reaction to light, his pupils dilated; and there is no palpable pulse. With the assistance of Drs. Don T. Curtis and Martin G. White and Nurse Diana Bowron, Dr. Carrico opens the president's suit coat and shirt and puts his ear to the president's chest. He listens for a few seconds and detects a faint heartbeat. Other nurses arrive and continue to remove

Kennedy's clothing. Carrico slips his hands under the president's midsection and runs them up his back past his back brace.[*] He can feel blood and debris, but no wounds. He looks briefly at the president's head wound—a gaping hole, oozing with blood and shredded scalp and brain tissue—then turns his attention to restoring the president's breathing and circulation.[329]

Carrico orders Drs. Curtis and White to do a cutdown on the president's right ankle—a small incision to lay bare a large vein into which they can insert polyethylene catheters

---

[*]After eliciting from Carrico and other Parkland doctors that the president was wearing a back brace, nowhere did Warren Commission counsel go on to ask the doctors just what they did with the famous brace, although one could assume they would have removed it at some point. One doctor testified he saw it "lying loose" (6 H 66, WCT Dr. Gene Coleman Akin), though another said he "pushed up the brace" to feel the president's femoral pulse (3 H 368, WCT Dr. Malcolm O. Perry), suggesting it wasn't removed. In less-than-clear testimony, Secret Service agent William Greer suggested that the brace was among the items of the president's belongings he was given in two shopping bags by a Parkland nurse when the body was ready for removal (2 H 125), but this wouldn't tell us when, if at all, it was removed by the Parkland doctors *during* their effort to save his life. Almost thirty years later, Dr. Marion T. "Pepper" Jenkins, one of the Parkland doctors, said the president "must have had really severe back pain judging by the size of the back brace *we cut off*. [Again, not when, though the natural assumption would be at the beginning of the effort to save the president. But Dr. Paul Peters, who arrived at least five minutes after the president entered Trauma Room One, said the brace was still on, and he only refers to his removing "an elastic bandage wrapped around his pelvis," but says nothing about removing the back brace (6 H 70).] He was tightly laced into this brace with wide Ace bandages making figure-of-eight loops around his trunk and thighs" (Breo, "JFK's Death, Part II," p.2805). A Parkland doctor described it as a "corset-type" brace with "stays . . . and buckles" (3 H 359, WCT Dr. Charles James Carrico).

Dr. John Lattimer, who studied the assassination for years, researched the entire brace issue and concluded it may have been responsible for Kennedy's death. He writes that Kennedy had "bound himself firmly in a rather wide corset, with metal stays and a stiff plastic pad over the sacral area, which was tightly laced to his body. The corset was then bound even more firmly to his torso and hips by a six-inch-wide knitted elastic bandage, which he had wrapped in a figure eight between his legs and around his waist, over large thick pads, to encase himself tightly . . . He apparently adopted this type of tight binding as a consequence of the painful loosening of his joints around the sacroiliac area, probably a result of his long-continued cortisone therapy." The result? When he and Connally were hit by the same bullet, the "corset prevented him from crumpling down out of the line of fire, as Governor Connally did. Because the president remained upright, with his head exposed, Oswald was able to draw a careful bead on the back of his head." (Lattimer, *Kennedy and Lincoln*, p.171; Lattimer, "Additional Data on the Shooting of President Kennedy," p.1546)

Since the first bullet that struck Kennedy passed through soft tissue and did not penetrate any organ of the body, it was the opinion of Dr. Perry, Kennedy's chief attending surgeon, that "barring the advent of complications, this wound was tolerable, and I think he would have survived it" (3 H 372). Writer James Reston Jr. captioned his article on this issue, "That 'Damned Girdle': The Hidden Factor That Might Have Killed Kennedy" (*Los Angeles Times*, November 22, 2004, p.B9). If this is true, the Japanese destroyer that sunk Kennedy's PT boat in World War II and killed two of his crewmates, only injuring Kennedy's already fragile back when he was hurled backwards onto the deck (Leaming, *Jack Kennedy*, p.139; O'Donnell and Powers with McCarthy, *Johnny, We Hardly Knew Ye*, p.48), finally claimed Kennedy as its third victim twenty years later.

If there is no certainty as to the role the president's back brace played in his death, there is something closer to certainty that caused his death and which he himself was responsible for. As indicated earlier, President Kennedy did not want Secret Service agents riding on the steps attached to the right and left rear bumper of the presidential limousine. Gerald A. Behn, special agent in charge of the White House Secret Service detail, said that shortly after assuming his job in late 1961, President Kennedy had told him this. No fewer than five Secret Service agents gave statements to the Warren Commission that it was common knowledge among the White House detail that this was Kennedy's desire, which he reiterated twice in the summer of 1963, once in Rome on July 2, 1963, the other time in Tampa, Florida, just four days before the assassination. Kennedy's desire was not etched in stone, and since the Secret Service has the right to do whatever is necessary to protect the president, in Tampa, on November 18, Special Agent Donald Lawton was standing on the right rear step, Special Agent Charles Zboril on the left rear. Kennedy told Special Agent Floyd Boring, who was seated in the right front seat of the limousine, to have the two agents return to the follow-up car. When the limousine slowed through downtown Tampa about three minutes later, the two agents dismounted. (CE 1025, 18 H 805–809; "Kennedy Barred Car-Step Guards," *New York Times*, November 24, 1964, pp.1, 33)

The likelihood is high that if Kennedy had not been opposed to Secret Service agents riding on the back of his car—the agent standing on the *right rear* step would have blocked Oswald's sight on Kennedy's head.

through which fluid, medicine, and blood can be administered to maintain the body's circulatory system.[330] The president is losing so much blood that the trauma room is already awash with it. Meanwhile, Carrico inserts a plastic endotracheal tube down the president's throat into the trachea (windpipe) in order to create an adequate air passage. He notices a small ragged tear to the right of the larynx (voice box) and ragged tissue below, indicating tracheal injury. Carrico steers the plastic tube deep into the throat and begins connecting the cuff inflator (a latex cuff designed to prevent air leakage) to a respiratory machine.[331]

Just then, Drs. Perry and Jones arrive. Perry sheds his dark blue glen-plaid jacket and wristwatch in the corner, and takes charge.[332] Dr. Charles Baxter, another thirty-four-year-old assistant professor of surgery at the school, and director of the emergency room at Parkland, arrives around the same time, having made a dead run from the school as fast as he could when he heard the news.[333]* The trauma room is now filled with law enforcement officers and several members of the president's party. Supervising nurse Doris Nelson has already arrived and is struggling to clear them from the room.[334]

Dr. Perry steps over toward the ambulance gurney where the president is lying under the hot glare of an overhead lamp, a sheet over his lower extremities and trunk. He is surprised to find the president a bigger man than he thought, and is momentarily awed by the thought, "Here is the most important man in the world." Perry quickly notes the deep blue color of his face and the short, jerky contractions of his chest and diaphragm as he struggles to draw a breath.[335]

12:43 p.m. (1:43 p.m. EST)

Robert Kennedy, the nation's attorney general, had been in a good, even bouncy mood this morning. He called a meeting in his office with U.S. attorneys from around the country to report to him on his war against organized crime in their respective districts. As was his style, he loosened his tie, and with his suit coat hanging over a nearby chair, rolled up his shirt sleeves and got down to work with his associates. The news he received was encouraging. The mob was on the run. Breaking for lunch he got into his car with the U.S. attorney for the Southern District of New York, Robert Morgenthau, and Morgenthau's chief deputy, Silvio Mollo, and drove to his Hickory Hill home in a Virginia suburb of Washington, D.C. It was an unseasonably warm day for November 22, and the men and RFK's wife, Ethel, took their lunch of clam chowder and tuna-fish sandwiches at an outdoor patio. When a pool-side extension phone rings nearby, Ethel leaves the table to answer it.

"It's J. Edgar Hoover," she says, holding the phone out toward her husband.

He knows something extraordinary has happened; Hoover never calls him, and certainly not at home. It is an open secret that there is no love lost between Hoover and RFK. Hoover had never been in a position before of having an attorney general who was closer to the president than he was, and he resented this. Also, RFK's strong offensive against organized crime was, in effect, a slap in the face to Hoover in that it implied that the FBI had not been the gangbusters everyone had been brought up to think they were. RFK rises and crosses over to take the phone, "Hello?"

Morgenthau sees one of the workmen painting the new wing of the house spin and race toward them, clutching a transistor radio. He's shouting something unintelligible.

---

*Per the Warren Report, "As the President's limousine sped toward the hospital, 12 doctors rushed to the emergency area." The report named the twelve (four surgeons, one neurologist, four anesthesiologists, one urological surgeon, one oral surgeon, and one heart specialist), but omitted at least two doctors, Dr. Carrico and Dr. Charles Crenshaw. (WR, p.53)

"I have news for you," Hoover says formally. "The president's been shot. It's believed to be fatal. I'll call you back when I find out more."

Bobby Kennedy turns away, his hand to his mouth. There is a look of shock and horror on his face. Ethel rushes to his side. For a few seconds he can't speak. Then, he forces the words out: "Jack's been shot. It may be fatal."[336]

On the other side of Washington, the U.S. Senate press liaison officer, Richard Riedel, darts onto the Senate floor and gives the message of the president's shooting to the first senator he encounters, S. L. Holland of Florida. He repeats the message to Senator Wayne Morse and then spots Senator Edward Kennedy on the dais, presiding over the chamber in a desultory debate over a bill on federal library services. He immediately rushes to the young senator.

"The most terrible thing has happened!" Riedel exclaims.

The senator, who is signing correspondence, looks up.

"What is it?"

"Your brother, the president," Riedel says. "He's been shot."

Ted Kennedy gasps.

"No!" he says. "How do you know?"

"It's on the ticker. Just came in on the ticker."

Senator Kennedy quickly gathers up his papers and runs from the chamber. He knows he must get his sister Eunice and fly immediately to Hyannis Port to be with his mother and father. When Majority Leader Mike Mansfield learns the news, he is too overcome with grief to make a motion for adjournment.[337]

With the Senate in recess, senators and reporters rush to the "marble room," the lobby behind the Senate chamber where UPI and AP printers ("tickers") are slowly delivering the tragic and unfolding story on paper. A young CBS reporter, Roger Mudd, sees Richard B. Russell, the conservative, states-rights senator from Georgia who opposed civil rights legislation, bent over the cabinet enclosing the UPI ticker, reading the Teletype out loud to the crowd around him as tears are streaming down his face.[338]

A̲t Parkland Hospital in Trauma Room Two, across the hall from the president, Dr. Robert R. Shaw attends to Governor Connally. Shaw, chief of thoracic surgery at Parkland, saw the motorcade fly past the intersection of Harry Hines and Industrial boulevards as he drove back to Parkland from Children's Hospital. Continuing on to the medical school,* where he expected to have lunch, he heard the news of the shooting on his car radio. At the medical school, he overheard a student telling three others that the president was dead on arrival at Parkland.

"You're kidding, aren't you?" one of the three asked.

"No, I'm not. I saw him. And Governor Connally has been shot through the chest."

Shaw sprinted over to the hospital's emergency room, where he found the governor being attended by three doctors. Now, Connally complains of difficulty breathing due to a deep pain in the right side of his chest. He has apparently been conscious, except for brief moments, since the shooting. Shaw notes that the team has already put a tight occlu-

---

*The medical school, so often referred to in assassination literature, is the University of Texas Southwestern Medical School located right next door to Parkland Hospital. In fact, the first floors are connected by a long corridor. The two institutions are separately owned and governed but have an extremely close relationship, Parkland being the "teaching hospital" for the medical school. In fact, many of the doctors on the Parkland staff are professors at the school, and most of the school's graduates do their residency at Parkland.

sive dressing over the large sucking wound in the chest, and a rubber tube, connected to a water seal bottle, between the second and third ribs—an attempt to expand the collapsed right lung. Shaw steps outside for a moment to relay to Nellie Connally that a sample of the governor's blood has been sent for cross-matching, and that a regular operating room two floors above has been alerted. A few minutes later, the team transports the governor upstairs by elevator.[339]

Across the hall, in Trauma Room One, Dr. Perry orchestrates the treatment of the president. Dr. Carrico finishes hooking up the respirator and flips the switch, pumping air into the president's lungs. Carrico listens briefly to the president's chest. His breathing is better, but still inadequate. Air is leaking from the small hole in the throat.[340] Dr. Perry examines the chest briefly but can see no wound. He pushes up the body brace on the president's left side to feel for his femoral pulse.* There is none. Perry can see that the president is still struggling to breathe, despite the endotracheal tube Dr. Carrico inserted in his throat. Perry knows that a more effective air passage must be made immediately. He asks someone to bring him a tracheotomy tray as he snaps on a pair of surgical gloves, but finds there is already one there. Perry gestures toward a small hole in the throat. "Did you start a tracheotomy?" he asks Carrico.

"No," Carrico replies, shaking his head. "That's a wound." Carrico had previously observed foamy blood oozing, with each attempt at respiration, from a small, fairly round wound in the front of the president's throat just below and to the right of the Adam's apple.[341]

Commencing a tracheotomy (incision into the windpipe), Dr. Perry grabs a scalpel and makes a quick, large incision directly through the hole in the throat.[342]†

Other doctors are now arriving en masse. Dr. William Kemp Clark, the hospital's senior neurosurgeon, pushes his way in and helps to withdraw Dr. Carrico's endotracheal tube as Dr. Perry is about to insert a plastic tracheotomy tube directly into the windpipe.[343] Drs. Charles R. Baxter and Robert N. McClelland, both general surgeons, along with urologist Dr. Paul C. Peters, assist Perry in inserting the tracheotomy tube, while Dr. Marion T. Jenkins, professor and chairman of Parkland's Department of Anesthesiology, and his assistant, Dr. Adolph H. Giesecke Jr., hook up the tube to an anesthesia machine, which they had brought down from the Anesthesia Department on the second floor in order to better control the president's circulation.[344]

Perry asks Dr. Peters to make an incision in the chest and insert a tube to drain any blood or air that might be accumulating in the right side of the chest cavity.[345] Meanwhile, Dr. Ronald C. Jones inserts a chest tube into the left side of the chest, then, along with several other doctors (including surgery interns and residents Drs. Don T. Curtis, Kenneth E. Salyer, Martin C. White, and Charles A. Crenshaw),[346] makes additional cutdowns on the president's right and left arms and legs in order to quickly infuse blood and fluids into the circulatory system.[347] The pace is very quick and intense. Dr. Clark works his way around closer to the president's massive head wound. He exchanges a desperate glance with Perry. Both know there is no chance of saving the president. They are only going through the motions.[348]

Admiral George Burkley, the president's personal physician, rushes into the room and immediately sees that the president's condition is hopeless and death is certain. Whatever life might still exist in the motionless body on the gurney will be impossible to sustain no matter what the Parkland doctors do. He sees that the surgical team is working to supply

---

*The femoral artery is the main artery of the thigh and can be felt in the pelvic area.
†The bullet wound happened to be located in the precise place where a tracheotomy is normally performed.

type O RH-negative blood. He informs them that Kennedy's type is O RH-positive[349]*
and asks Dr. Peters to administer steroids to the president, essential because of the president's adrenal deficiency, which leaves his body unable to cope with stress and trauma. He hands over three 100-milligram vials of Solu-Cortef, muttering, "Either intravenously or intramuscularly."[350] Burkley knows there is really no need for it, but knows also that they have to do everything they can.[351]

The president's personal physician steps out into the corridor, where Mrs. Kennedy is sitting on a folding chair, dazed. Afraid that her husband's death is imminent, she wants to go into the operating room.

"I'm going in there," she murmurs.

Doris Nelson, the strong-muscled supervising nurse with plenty of starch in her collar, hears her and bars the door, the policy of the hospital, as with most hospitals, being not to allow relatives into an operating room.

"You can't come in here," she says sharply, setting her rubber-soled shoes against the frame of the door.

"I'm coming in, and I'm staying," Mrs. Kennedy says and pushes. The nurse, considerably stronger, pushes back. Jackie Kennedy always used to bow to medical advice. She was young, and the doctors, she thought, always knew best. When she heard her husband calling her after his back operation in 1954, she tried to go to him, but no one would admit her and she backed off. Then, after the operation, when a specialist's treatments began to fail, they talked her out of bringing in a consultant. The president subsequently suffered through four months of intense pain. She vowed then and there not to allow doctors and nurses to intimidate her.

"I'm *going* to get in that room," she whispers fiercely to the nurse blocking the door.

The commotion attracts Admiral Burkley, who suggests that Mrs. Kennedy take a sedative.

"I want to be in there when he dies," she tells him, and she refuses the sedation,[352] wanting, it seems, to soak up as much pain as she can. To cheat pain at a moment like this, when her husband has suffered the most horrible wounds and was near death, would have diminished her and what they had meant to each other.

The admiral nods understandingly.

"It's her right, it's her prerogative," he says as he leads her past the nurse, who mistakenly believes he is a Secret Service agent.

Looking shell-shocked, Mrs. Kennedy aimlessly circles the hospital gurney where technicians work feverishly on her husband's body. Her hands are cupped in front of her, as if cradling something. As she passes Dr. Jenkins, she nudges him with her elbow and hands him what she has been nursing—a large chunk of brain tissue. Jenkins quickly gives it to a nearby nurse.[353] The president's physician ushers Mrs. Kennedy into a corner of the trauma room, now overflowing with people. She rests her cheek on Admiral Burkley's shoulder, then drops briefly to the floor, closes her eyes and prays.[354]

The McWatters bus carrying Lee Oswald rumbles west on Elm Street, the smell of diesel exhaust permeating the floorboards. Between Poydras and Lamar, the driver pumps the air brakes as the bus rolls up behind traffic that is stalled for four blocks from the assas-

---

*The Parkland doctors chose type O RH-negative blood because it is safe to give to anyone, regardless of his or her type, as it causes no adverse reaction.

sination scene. From the looks of it, they won't be going anywhere soon. A man climbs out of a car stopped in front of the bus, and walks back. McWatters pulls the lever next to him and the front doors hiss open.

"I heard over my car radio that the president has been shot," the man says.

The passengers are astonished. Some don't believe it.

The woman across from Mrs. Bledsoe realizes in panic that the bus may not move for a very long time, and she has to catch a train at Union Station, four blocks away. She decides to walk, even if it means lugging her suitcase all that way. She asks McWatters if she can have a transfer so she can get back on the bus if it breaks free from traffic, and McWatters is happy to oblige.

Oswald gets up and asks McWatters for a transfer too, following the woman off the bus. He walks right past his former landlady again, and this time Mary Bledsoe thinks he might have recognized her. In any event, she is happy enough to see the last of him.[355]

The area around the entrance to the Depository is quickly growing chaotic. Dealey Plaza witnesses are offering various bits of information. Inspector Sawyer knows he will need help to handle the situation, and reaches for his car radio.

"We need more manpower down here at this Texas School Book Depository," he says and instructs the dispatcher to have some squad cars pick up the officers stationed along the motorcade route and bring them down to the Depository.[356]

Officer E. W. Barnett, with Howard Brennan in tow, tells Sawyer that he has an eyewitness who saw the gunman.

"What did you see?" Sawyer asks Brennan.

The steelworker gives him a description of the man in the window and the inspector mashes the button on his car radio again: "The wanted person in this is a slender white male about thirty. Five foot ten. A hundred and sixty-five. And carrying a—what looked like—a 30-30 or some type of Winchester."

"It was a rifle?" the dispatcher asks.

"A rifle, yes," Sawyer replies.

"Any clothing description?"

"The current witness can't remember that," Sawyer says.[357]

The dispatcher immediately throws a switch in the radio room that allows him to broadcast simultaneously on both channels of the Dallas police radio, effectively reaching every officer in the city. "Attention all squads. Attention all squads. The suspect in the shooting at Elm and Houston is reported to be an unknown white male, approximately thirty. Slender build, height five feet, ten inches. Weight one hundred sixty-five pounds. Reported to be armed with what is thought to be a thirty caliber rifle." The dispatcher repeats the message, adding, "No further description or information at this time. 12:45 [p.m.] KKB-364, Dallas."[358]*

12:45 p.m.

In Irving, Marina is hanging up clothes in the backyard when Ruth comes out and joins her with the latest news: "They're reporting that the shots were fired from the Texas School Book Depository."

---

* "KKB-364" is the radio call sign of the Dallas police radio station.

Marina's heart drops. She thinks about the rifle she knows that Lee has stored in Ruth Paine's garage, about the last time he used it—a few months earlier in trying to murder Dallas John Birch Society figure Major General Edwin Walker—and whether that might have been the real reason he came out to the house last night. She hopes that Ruth can't see the fear in her face.

As soon as she can do it inconspicuously, Marina slips into the garage. She knows exactly where the rifle is, wrapped in a green and brown wool blanket, near the garage door, by some suitcases. She saw the blanket there in early October and unwrapped it then and found the rifle inside. Is it still there? When she gets inside the garage, she sees the familiar bundle laying in the same place it had been before, and feels a great weight lift from her shoulders.

"Thank God," she thinks.[359]

William Whaley, a squat, burr-haired former navy gunner who won a Navy Cross during the battle of Iwo Jima, pulls his cab up to the cabstand at the Greyhound bus station on the northwest corner of Jackson and Lamar, four blocks south of Elm Street, and realizes that he's out of cigarettes. He's about to go inside the terminal to get a pack when he sees a fare walking toward him down Lamar Street.[360]

"May I have the cab?" the man asks.

"You sure can," Whaley says. "Get in."

To Whaley, Lee Oswald looks like a wino who has been off his bottle for about two days, like he's been sleeping in his clothes, although he isn't actually dirty or nervous or anything.[361] Oswald gets in the front, which is allowed in Dallas, and Whaley's got nothing against it. A second later an elderly woman pokes her head in the passenger's window and asks if she can get in his cab.

"There'll be a cab behind me in a few moments that you can take," Whaley tells her, and he vaguely recalls that Oswald may have told the woman something similar.[362] As he pulls the 1961 Checker sedan out into Lamar and turns west into Jackson, he asks his fare where he wants to go.

"Five hundred North Beckley."

Police cars, their sirens wailing, are crisscrossing everywhere.

"I wonder what the hell is the uproar," Whaley muses, but Oswald doesn't answer and Whaley figures he's one of those people who doesn't like to talk, which is fine with him.[363]

Whaley, who has been driving cabs for thirty-seven years, notices Oswald's silver ID bracelet. He always takes note of watchbands and identification bracelets because he makes them himself, and this one is unusual. Most of them are made with chain links, not stretch bands, like this one.[364] They drive in silence, turning left at the first corner, Austin, and then onto Wood. They catch the light at Lamar and Jackson and several others as they move smartly through traffic down to Houston, the street they call the "old viaduct," which is the fastest way to Oak Cliff.[365]

Dallas police radio dispatcher Murray J. Jackson can see from the callboard in front of him that many of the patrolmen assigned to the Oak Cliff area (south of the Trinity River, which separates it from downtown Dallas, and before the emergence of North Dallas in later years, perhaps the biggest area of Dallas) have gone downtown to help in the assassination investigation.[366] He knows that if an emergency such as an armed robbery or a major accident occurs in that area, there might not be anyone to respond quickly to the call. He decides to pull two of the outermost patrol units in Oak Cliff closer to central Oak Cliff just in case something comes up. Units 78 and 87 (radio call numbers for Dallas Police Districts 78 and 87)* get the call—J. D. Tippit and Ronald C. Nelson.[367]

"[Units] 87 and 78, move into central Oak Cliff area," Jackson orders, basically giving Tippit and Nelson a blank check to move at will within the roughly five or six police districts that could be considered as Oak Cliff.

Tippit, cruising his beat alone in south Oak Cliff on the 7:00 a.m. to 3:00 p.m. day shift, lifts the radio microphone first.

"I'm at Kiest and Bonnieview," Tippit replies.

But Nelson shoots back, "[Unit] 87's going north on Marsalis, [at] R. L. Thornton."[368]

Dispatcher Jackson knows from Nelson's location that he is already on his way downtown to join other units. He decides to let him go. Tippit can handle anything that might come up, he figures. Jackson has known "J. D."† for eleven years and in that time they've become close friends. In fact, it was Tippit who originally got Jackson interested in police work. In 1952, Murray was a high school graduate working at a Mobil filling station where Tippit and his partner used to stop occasionally. Tippit was his image of a hero, and through J. D.'s encouragement, Jackson was successful at joining the force. After a promotion to patrolman, Jackson and Tippit were partnered for eight months and the bond between the two men strengthened.

One night in the early 1960s, Jackson was working temporarily with new partner Bill Johnson when they arrested seven teenagers for being drunk and disorderly. En route to the Oak Cliff substation, the teenagers decided they didn't want to go to jail and a fight broke out in the squad car. Jackson put out a call for assistance and J. D. was the first to arrive.

"Thanks, partner," Jackson told him, "you saved my life."

The humor of the situation wasn't lost on Tippit, who joked and chided Jackson, "I turn you loose one time and I got to come down here and save your life." Of course, Jackson's life wasn't really in any danger. It was just Tippit's way of kidding his former police apprentice.

It was with this incident in mind that Jackson called on Tippit to help him out again, this time by covering an area outside his own assigned district.[369]

But it obviously wasn't necessary for Jackson to have this prior relationship with Tippit to get him to go into central Oak Cliff. Tippit was on duty and had to go wherever assigned. Moreover, Tippit was not the type of officer to complain about much, being easy to get along with. Not overly ambitious, and with only a tenth-grade educa-

---

*The city of Dallas was broken down into eighty-six police districts. Each day was broken down into three eight-hour shifts ("platoons"). Most districts only had one patrolman assigned to it, although "hot districts" (those with a higher incidence of crime) had two. The number "78" was Tippit's radio call number because it was the police district, number 78, he was assigned to.(Eighty-six districts: "Dallas Police Department Squad Districts as of January 1, 1960," DMA, box 7, folder 10, item 3; Telephone interview of Jim Bowles by author on March 25, 2004)

†The author of the only book on the Tippit murder case wrote that "the initials [J. D.] he was known by didn't have any particular meaning. To everyone he was just J. D." Tippit's brother, Wayne, told the author that reports that his brother's initials stood for "Jefferson Davis" were incorrect. (Myers, *With Malice*, pp.28, 588 note 20) However, at least as to the first initial, a fellow officer who worked with Tippit for a while referred to him as John (Sneed, *No More Silence*, p.463).

tion, he wasn't "sharp enough," as one Dallas detective who knew Tippit said, to pass department promotional exams. However, the shy officer loved his job and seemed more than satisfied to remain a patrolman, resigned to his inability to advance because of his limited education. Well liked by his fellow officers, his immediate supervisor on the force, Sergeant Calvin B. Owens, described Tippit as a "good officer" who used "good common sense." A Dallas police officer, Donald Flusche, said that Tippit and he "worked together in West Dallas. He was really a good and decent man . . . He was pretty much a country boy . . . He was kind of bashful, thought a little slow, moved a little slow, but there was nothing dishonest about him."[370] Seldom talking about politics, Tippit, age thirty-nine, had voted for John F. Kennedy in the 1960 presidential election. On this day, Tippit had come home to have lunch with his wife, Marie, around 11:30 a.m., hurried through his food, and reported back for duty by 11:50 with a "78 clear" transmission from his car radio to the police dispatcher.[371]

12:50 p.m.

Forrest Sorrels, the agent in charge of the Dallas Secret Service office, arrives at the side of the Texas School Book Depository and walks to the same backdoor used by Frazier and Oswald that morning.[372] There is a black employee on the loading dock who doesn't seem to realize what's happened.

"Did you see anyone run out the back?" Sorrels asks him, as he approaches.

"No, sir," the man replies.

"Did you see anyone leave the back way?" Sorrels probes.

"No, sir," the man says again.[373]

The agent proceeds to the first floor by the rear loading-dock door, and to his surprise there's nobody in law enforcement there to challenge him.

"Where is the manager here?" he asks upon entering the building.

Someone directs him to Roy Truly. Sorrels pulls out his Secret Service credentials.

"I want to get a stenographer," he tells him, "and we would like to have you put down the names and addresses of every employee in the building."[374] Sorrels has not yet learned that shots have been fired from the building. He simply wants to establish the identity of everyone present at the time of the shooting so that they can be interviewed later.[375] Sorrels heads for the front of the building, pushes open the glass front doors, and steps out onto the concrete landing, "Is there anyone here that saw anything?"

"That man over there," a voice calls out, pointing to Howard Brennan standing nearby.

Sorrels bounds down the steps and identifies himself to the construction worker. "What did you see?" he asks.

Brennan tells him what happened and how he glanced up at the building and saw the man take deliberate aim and fire the third shot. "He just pulled the rifle back in and moved away from the window, just as unconcerned as could be," Brennan says.

After Brennan gives him a description of the gunman, Sorrels asks him if he thought he could identify him and Brennan says, "Yes, I think I can."

"Did anyone else see it?" Sorrels asks Brennan, who points out Amos Euins.

Sorrels questions the boy and learns that Euins also saw the gunman for a few brief seconds, but now Euins isn't sure if the man he saw was white or black. Asked if he, too, thought he could identify the man if he saw him again, Euins says, "No, I couldn't."[376]

Eventually, Sorrels escorts the two eyewitnesses over to the sheriff's office across the street to give a statement.[377]

12:52 p.m.

"This will do fine," Oswald tells the cabdriver. William Whaley pulls over to the curb at the northwest corner of Neely and North Beckley, which is the 700, not the 500 block Oswald had first requested, but it's all the same to Whaley.[378] The meter on the six-minute trip has just clicked over to ninety-five cents, about two and a half miles. Oswald gives Whaley a buck, gets out, and crosses the street in front of the cab, and that's the last Whaley sees of him. A big tipper.[379]

When he finally gets around to entering the trip in the passenger manifest required by the Dallas authorities, he writes it up as 12:30 to 12:45 p.m. Nobody at the cab company really cares about exact time, so when he gets a chance Whaley just marks it to the nearest quarter-hour or so.[380]

12:53 p.m. (1:53 p.m. EST)

All three networks headquartered in New York are gearing up for exclusive coverage of the shooting in Dallas for what will turn out to be over three consecutive days. A representative network is NBC, which, at 1:53 p.m. EST, cancels all regular programs to devote all of its time and resources to the unfolding events in Dallas. This will continue until 1:17 a.m. Tuesday morning, November 26.[381]

12:54 p.m.

Police dispatcher Murray Jackson checks in with patrol Unit 78—Officer J. D. Tippit.

"You are in the Oak Cliff area, are you not?" Jackson asks.

"Lancaster and Eighth," Tippit responds affirmatively.

"You will be at large for any emergency that comes in," Murray says.

"Ten-four," J. D. replies.[382]

The patrolman cruises north on Lancaster. He's a long way from his roots in Red River County. Born and raised south of Clarksville, Texas, J. D. Tippit grew up during the Great Depression on the family farm, where electricity and running water were only dreams. The Tippits were sharecroppers, renting farmland to raise cotton. The work was hard and the tools of the day primitive. J. D., the oldest of five brothers and two sisters, spent many days behind a mule team and plow. He grew to become a crack horseman and although outsiders found him quiet and reserved, his family knew him as fun-loving. As World War II entered its last bloody year in Europe, J. D. joined the U.S. Army, volunteering to become a member of the elite paratroopers. In 1945, he landed in France as an ammo bearer with the Seventeenth Airborne Division as it fought its way through the Rhine Valley. Like many men, the war made deep impressions on him and he returned with a renewed sense of duty and honor. Tippit's background was similar to that of many other officers on the force who came from small Texas towns with names like Athens, Palestine, and Ferris. Not a lot of academics, many not quite making it through high school. A lot of military service, which is good—guys who knew something about discipline and teamwork and were comfortable with firearms and uniforms.

In December 1946, at the age of twenty-two, J. D. married his high school sweetheart, Marie Frances Gasaway, age eighteen. They briefly moved to Dallas to find work after the war, but soon returned to Red River County, where they hoped to farm and raise a family. Nature's wrath took its toll on J. D.'s dreams of farming, and in July 1952 he joined the Dallas Police Department to feed his growing family. At $250 a month, Tippit soon found himself moonlighting to make ends meet. In early 1961, J. D. took a part-time job as a security guard from 10:00 p.m. until 2:00 a.m. every Friday and Saturday night at Austin's Barbeque in Oak Cliff, a popular teen hangout, and every Sunday afternoon at the Stevens Theater located in a shopping center. Tippit enjoys the free time he spends with his family—enjoying his three young children, taking dance lessons with his wife, listening to the music of Bob Wills and the Texas Playboys, or horsing around with his boyhood pal and brother-in-law, Jack Christopher.

In fact, J. D. has plans to see Jack and his family tonight. Earlier this morning, J. D. stopped at his sister's house on the way to work and got a ticket to the South Oak Cliff High School football game, where his niece, Linda, will be performing with the Golden Debs cheerleading squad. As he's done on Friday nights past, he'll have to beat it over to Austin's Barbeque before the game gets out and a good part of the grandstand shows up. It'll be another busy Friday night keeping the high school rowdies in line at Austin's.[383]

12:57 p.m.

In a second-floor operating room at Parkland, an anesthesiologist rapidly evaluates Connally's condition and starts to put the governor under for an operation that will last well over three hours.[384]

Dr. Robert Shaw and Dr. Charles F. Gregory, chief of orthopedic surgery, enter the operating room, where Connally lies ready for surgery. Dr. Shaw removes the temporary dressing and inspects Connally's chest wounds. After three years with the U.S. Army Medical Corps in the European Theater of Operations, Shaw is no stranger to bullet wounds.[385]

The surgeons place an endotracheal tube into the pharynx and trachea to control the governor's breathing, then roll him over to inspect the entrance wound just behind his right armpit, a roughly elliptical puncture with relatively clean-cut edges. Turning to the large and ragged exit wound below the right nipple, Shaw excises its edges, and then carries the incision back along the right side of the governor's chest and finds that about four inches of the fifth rib have been shattered and carried away from what appears to have been a glancing strike by the bullet. Several small fragments of the rib are still hanging to bits of partly detached tissue from the rib's lining. An X-ray reveals no metallic fragments left behind by the bullet in the area of the ribs. There's a lot of damage to the right lung, which is engorged with blood and rib fragments. It will have to be closed and sutured, along with the muscles surrounding the rib cage, but the diaphragm is uninjured, and the wounds are far from fatal. The governor has also sustained wounds on both sides of his right wrist and a superficial wound in his left thigh. X-rays reveal a shattering of the radius bone just above the right wrist and the presence of a number of small metallic fragments. There's several hours of work to do, but it's clear to the surgeons that Governor Connally will survive his injuries.[386]

12:58 p.m.

An unmarked squad car pulls up to the front of the Book Depository, and Police Captain Will Fritz, Detectives Sims and Boyd, and Sheriff Bill Decker climb out. An officer in front of the building tells them that the man who did the shooting is believed to be still in the building. Several officers take out their shotguns and follow Fritz and his men as they enter the Depository. They quickly locate an elevator and go up to the second floor, where they see several officers already there. They continue up, finding officers already stationed on the third and fourth floors.

This particular elevator only goes to the fourth floor, so Fritz and his men exit the elevator and cross over to the freight elevators near the northwest corner of the building, and take one up to the fifth floor. They make a hurried search along the front and west side windows, then, joined by some other officers, go up to the sixth floor. A few officers get off on the sixth, and Fritz, Sims, and Boyd continue up to the seventh floor and start to search along the front windows.[387]

Father James Thompson drives into Parkland in the black Ford Galaxie belonging to Holy Trinity Church. Parkland is only three miles from the church, but the traffic is brutal. Even though he took a "secret route" taking advantage of back streets, he and Father Oscar Huber found themselves held up by what seemed like endless traffic delays. Both of them are worried because they know that the last rites of the Catholic Church, to be valid, must be administered to the dying before the soul has left the body. Father Huber, like many parish priests, takes a liberal view of that—to his way of thinking, there can be quite a long time between what the doctors call clinical death and the eventual flight of the soul, but that's no reason to dally. As they pull up, Father Thompson tells Father Huber to jump out of the car and hurry into the hospital while he finds a place to park.[388]

Father Huber saw Jack Kennedy, it seems to him, only minutes ago. He knew that the president's motorcade would pass within three blocks of Holy Trinity, and when he rose at five this morning in his room at the rectory, he resolved to go down to see it. He was disappointed that he couldn't interest any of the other priests in the project.

"Well, I'm going," he told them. "I'm seventy years old and I've never seen a president. I'll be danged if I'm going to miss this chance."

Huber, a short, stocky man, had to leap up and down to see over the heads of the dense crowd, but managed to get a glimpse of Kennedy, who turned and seemed to look right at him. Now he hurries to the emergency entrance to give the last rites to this once-vibrant man. The significance of his arrival is not lost on anyone.

"This is it," Congressman Henry Gonzalez thinks as he sees Huber arrive at the hospital. Malcolm Kilduff, the president's acting press secretary, whispers to Congressman Albert Thomas, "It looks like he's gone."[389]

In Oak Cliff, at 1026 North Beckley, Earlene Roberts tugs at the "rabbit ear" antennas trying to get a clear picture on the television set when the young man she knows as "O. H. Lee" enters, walking unusually fast, in shirt sleeves.

"You sure are in a hurry," the housekeeper says, but he goes straight to his room without saying a word.[390]

That isn't so strange. Since renting the room in mid-October, "O. H. Lee" has hardly said two words to anyone. Once, Mrs. Roberts said "good afternoon" to him and he just gave her a dirty look and walked right past her. At night, if one of the other boarders had the television on in the living room, he might stand behind the couch for a couple of minutes, but then he'd go to his room and shut the door without a word. For the most part, "O. H. Lee" has kept to himself, which is why Mrs. Roberts doesn't really know anything about him, least of all the fact that his real name is Lee Harvey Oswald.[391]

Oswald is in his room just long enough to get his revolver and his jacket. He comes out of his room, zipping up his jacket, and rushes out.[392] Mrs. Roberts glances out the window a moment later and notices Lee standing at the curbside near a bus stop in front of the rooming house. That's the last she sees of him.[393] He apparently doesn't wait to board any bus since there is no record of anyone seeing him on a bus after one o'clock, and if he had boarded a bus in front of his home, it would take him in a direction away from where we know he was next seen.

1:00 p.m.

At Parkland Hospital, Dr. Kemp Clark feels the carotid artery in the president's neck for a pulse. There is none. Clark asks that a cardiotachyscope (a cardiac monitor that measures heartbeat) be connected to the president's body, and starts external heart massage,[394] an unsophisticated physical procedure practiced by physicians from the sixteenth century, even before they understood anything about the circulation of blood in the body.

The anesthesiologists, Drs. Jenkins and Giesecke, now report a carotid pulse in the neck, and Dr. Jones reports a pulse in the femoral artery in the leg. After a few moments, Dr. Perry takes over for Dr. Clark, who is in an awkward physical position to continue the rigorous cardiac massage.[395]

"Somebody get me a stool," Dr. Perry commands. A stool is slid near the table and Perry stands on it to get better leverage as he works the livid white flesh beneath his palms. Drs. Jenkins and Clark watch the cardiotachyscope. The green dot suddenly darts across the screen trailing a perfectly smooth line of fluorescence, without the tiniest squiggle of cardiac activity.[396] Dr. Clark shakes his head sadly, "It's too late, Mac." Perry slowly raises himself up from the body, steps down off the stool, and walks numbly away. Dr. Jenkins reaches down from the head of the cart and pulls a white sheet up over the president's face as Dr. Clark turns to Mrs. Kennedy.

"Your husband has sustained a fatal wound," he says solemnly.

Her lips move silently, forming the words, "I *know*."

It is one o'clock and it's all over. The thirty-fifth president of the United States is dead.[397]*

As the senior neurosurgeon, Dr. Clark will sign the death certificate, and the cause is so obviously the massive damage to the right side of the brain.[398] It is what they call a four-plus injury,[†] which no one survives, even with the five-star effort they made. Clark knows what Carrico and the others knew from the outset—medically, the president was alive when he entered Parkland Hospital, but from a practical standpoint he was DOA, dead on arrival.[399] As *New York Times* White House correspondent Tom Wicker, who was in Dealey Plaza at the time of the shooting, put it, Kennedy probably died way back on Elm Street a half hour earlier. He "probably was killed instantly. His body, as a physical mechanism, however, continued to flicker an occasional pulse and heartbeat."[400]

Dr. Jenkins starts disconnecting the multitude of monitoring leads running to the life-

---

*The Parkland doctors had worked on the president in the emergency room for forty-two minutes before he expired. (See also *New York Times*, November 23, 1963, p.2)

Dr. Charles Baxter, one of the many surgeons attempting to save the president, would later recall, "As soon as we realized we had nothing medical to do, we all backed off from the man with a reverence that one has for one's president. And we did not continue to be doctors from that point on. We became citizens again, and there were probably more tears shed in that room than in the surrounding hundred miles" ("Surgeon Who Operated on JFK in Dallas Dies," Associated Press, March 12, 2005).

†In emergency medicine, injuries are described as one-plus, two-plus, et cetera. A four-plus injury is a worst-case scenario.

less body and removing the intravenous lines. Admiral Burkley begins to weep openly. Mrs. Kennedy moves toward the hospital cart where her husband lies, and Jenkins retreats quietly to a corner of the room. Looking pale and remote, she leans down and kisses the president through the sheet on the foot, leg, thigh, abdomen, chest, and finally on the partly covered face.[401]

Father Oscar Huber enters the room out of breath and walks directly to Jackie Kennedy. He whispers his sympathies, draws back a sheet that is covering the president's face, pulls the purple and white stoll over his shoulders, wets his right thumb with holy oil and administers in Latin the last rites of the Catholic Church, the sacrament of extreme unction, including the anointing of a cross with his thumb over the president's forehead. Because the president was dead, a "short form" of absolution was given, and in a few minutes he finishes and steps back.

"Is that *all?*" Admiral Burkley blurts out, offended at the brevity of the ceremony. The death of a president deserves more, he thought. "Can't you say some prayers for the dead?"

Father Huber quickly obliges with a recitation of the Lord's Prayer and a Hail Mary, joined by the widow and Admiral Burkley, while the nurses who are cleaning up the appalling mess in the room remain still, their heads bowed. Father Thompson, having parked the car outside, steps in just as they are finishing.

Mrs. Kennedy turns and walks back out into the corridor, slumping into the folding chair just outside the door. The two priests follow.

"I am shocked," Father Huber says to her, his body beginning to tremble. "I want to extend my sympathy and that of my parishioners."

"Thank you for taking care of the president," she whispers. "Please pray for him."

"I am convinced that his soul had not left his body," he assures her. "This was a valid last sacrament."

Mrs. Kennedy's head drops down as she struggles to keep from fainting. Father Thompson signals a passing nurse.

"Do you want a doctor?" Father Huber asks Mrs. Kennedy.

"Oh, no," she mumbles. The nurse brings her a cold towel anyway. The First Lady presses it to her forehead and leans over until the spell passes.[402]

Across the hall from Trauma Room One, the two priests confer briefly. What will they say to the horde of reporters outside as they leave? It's clearly not their role to make any statement at all. In fact, as they head for the exit a Secret Service agent warns Huber, "Father, you don't know anything about this."

Just as they feared, they are besieged in the parking lot by the news media. Father Thompson refuses to give his name, but Father Huber is unable to remain silent.

"Is he dead?" Hugh Sidey of *Time* magazine asks.

"He's dead all right," Huber answers.[403]

1:05 p.m. (2:05 p.m. EST)

At his Virginia home, Robert Kennedy is in an upstairs bedroom with his wife, Ethel, preparing to leave for Dallas. The White House extension phone rings and he practically dives for it. It's Captain Taz Shepard, the president's naval aide, with news from Parkland.

"Oh, he's dead!" Bobby cries out in anguish.

"Those poor children," Ethel says in tears.

The attorney general stares out the window.

"He had the most wonderful life," he finally manages to say.

Bobby Kennedy descends the stairs and pokes his head into the living room where Robert Morgenthau and several others are watching television coverage.

"He died," Kennedy says in a low voice and walks toward the pool, where the extension phone has rung. It's J. Edgar Hoover again. He informs the attorney general, in a cold and unsympathetic manner characteristic of the FBI director, that the president is in "very, very critical condition." Bobby Kennedy listens politely, then says, "It may interest you to know that my brother is dead."[404]

RFK is plunged into a staggering gloom and depression by his brother's murder, one from which his intimates said he never recovered. For months thereafter, a biographer wrote, he "seemed devoured by grief. He literally shrank, until he appeared wasted and gaunt. His clothes no longer fit, especially his brother's old clothes—an old blue topcoat, a tuxedo, and a leather bomber jacket with the presidential seal—which he insisted on wearing and which hung on his narrowing frame. To close friend John Seigenthaler, he appeared to be in physical pain, like a man with a toothache or on a rack. Even walking seemed too difficult for him, though he walked for hours, brooding and alone . . . On many winter nights he arose before dawn and drove, too fast, in his Ford Galaxie convertible with the top down, sometimes to see his brother's grave." That is why it is all the more remarkable that within an hour of his brother's death, and in the trancelike midst of his dark abyss, the protective concern over his dead brother's well-manicured image enables him to extricate himself enough to call JFK's national security adviser, McGeorge Bundy, over at the White House. He instructs Bundy to immediately change the locks on his brother's personal files in the event that Lyndon Johnson decides to comb through them, and transport them to the offices of the national security staff located in the Old Executive Office Building, with a round-the-clock guard. And though he has no jurisdiction over the Secret Service, he has them dismantle and remove the secret taping system his brother had installed in the Oval Office and Cabinet Room.[405]

1:06 p.m.

It doesn't take long for Captain Fritz, Detectives Sims and Boyd, and other police officers to assure themselves that there's no one hiding on the seventh floor of the Book Depository and no sign that anyone fired at the president from there. The whole floor is one big open space with a few stacks of books here and there, some shelves, and not much else. A storage room in the southeast corner yields nothing but a collection of forgotten desks, chairs, and other office space odds and ends. The windows facing Elm Street are still closed, as they were at the time of the shooting.[406]

On the sixth floor below, Dallas police officers and deputy sheriffs are systematically searching the entire floor—from the cleared space on the west side, where the new flooring is going down, toward the stacks of boxes that have been piled into rows on the east side.

Deputy Luke Mooney is near the southeastern corner of the floor when he whistles loudly and hollers to his fellow officers.[407] He's inside the sniper's nest, a roughly rectangular screen of boxes stacked around the southeasternmost window. Anybody sitting or crouching behind them would be completely hidden from anyone else on the floor. Two more cartons on top of each other are right in front of the window. A third box lies closer to the window, resting in a canted position on the windowsill. In the corner, a long, handmade, brown paper bag is bunched up. On the floor, at the baseboard beneath the window, are three spent cartridge casings—"hulls," as they call them in Texas.

Dallas police sergeant Gerald L. Hill walks over to an adjacent window, sticks his head out and yells down to the street for the crime lab, but fears that no one can hear him over the sirens and crackling police radios. He starts down himself to report the find and meets Captain Fritz and Detectives Sims and Boyd at the freight elevator on the sixth floor. They had heard Mooney's and Hill's shouts through the cracks in the floorboards and came down to investigate. Hill tells them he's going down to the street to make sure the officers know where to send the crime-lab boys.[408]

Fritz, Sims, and Boyd work their way across the sixth floor over to the southeast corner window, where Deputy Mooney stands and other officers begin to congregate. Mooney tells Captain Fritz that everything is just as he found it. Fritz orders Detectives Sims and Boyd to stand guard and don't let anyone touch anything until the crime lab can get there, then Fritz turns to the officers present and instructs them to turn the sixth floor upside down. If there's a weapon here somewhere, he means to find it.[409]

1:07 p.m.
At the New York Stock Exchange, news of the president's shooting has brought about a wave of selling that reaches panic proportions, and the Dow Jones Industrial Average plummets 21.16 points.[410]

1:08 p.m.
Officer J. D. Tippit, probably traveling south on Beckley or southeast on Crawford in the general direction of Jefferson Boulevard in central Oak Cliff, spots Oswald walking on the right side of the street in front of him and sees that he vaguely fits the physical description of the suspect in the Kennedy assassination that he heard over the police radio in his squad car, it having been broadcast over channel 1 at 12:45 p.m., 12:48 p.m., and again at 12:55 p.m.[411] Slowly tailing Oswald from behind, he tried to call the radio dispatcher for a further description of the suspect. "Seventy-eight" (Tippit's call number, the police district he is assigned to), he says into his radio microphone, but he is not acknowledged by the dispatcher. Seconds later, he calls in "seventy-eight" again, but once again is not acknowledged by the dispatcher, he assumes because of the heavy radio traffic due to the assassination, and he continues to slow-tail Oswald.[412]*

---

*The few minutes leading up to Tippit's murder were only known to Tippit and Oswald. (Witnesses to the murder were only aware of the previous minute, not minutes.) So we have to infer what happened from what little we do know. Looking at the map in the photo section, we know that to get to Tenth and Patton, where Tippit was murdered, Oswald had to have at least started out by going south on Beckley. We also know that the last time we heard from Tippit was at 1:08 p.m. when he called the channel 1 police dispatcher twice to communicate but was never acknowledged. Since this time is so close to the time of his death, in February of 2004 I called the person I felt would be most qualified to confirm or dispel my suspicion that the 1:08 p.m. transmission by Tippit was related to his death, Dallas sheriff Jim Bowles, a fifty-three-year member of Dallas law enforcement—thirty years with the Dallas Police Department, twenty-three with the Dallas sheriff's office, the last eleven as sheriff. Responding to my amazement over his fifty-three years in law enforcement, Bowles said, "Most police officers have starved to death [on their low pay] by that time." Just as important as Bowles's long experience in law enforcement is the fact that he was a Dallas police radio dispatcher supervisor in November of 1963. (Because of his father's stroke, Bowles was off duty on the day of the assassination.) Indeed, it was Bowles who transcribed the recordings on the police radio tapes for the Warren Commission. "Oh, I don't think there's too much question the two 1:08 transmissions from Tippit pertained to Oswald," Bowles said. I asked Bowles when would the 1:08 transmissions have likely been made, shortly before the murder or earlier? "Most likely earlier, when Tippit first saw Oswald walking like the devil possessed, probably back on Beckley or Crawford, and he just slow-tailed him to Tenth." (Confirmation of Bowles's analysis that Tippit was slowly following Oswald comes from witness William Scoggins, who said that when he saw Tippit's car cross the intersection

1:10 p.m.

At Parkland Hospital, Ken O'Donnell, acting as a stoic messenger between Trauma Room One and Lyndon Johnson, enters the vice president's cubicle in Minor Medicine.

"He's gone," O'Donnell says.

The vice president finds the whole thing hard to believe. A few hours ago he was having breakfast with John Kennedy; he was alive, strong, and vigorous. Now, he is dead.[413] Mrs. Johnson turns to her husband, her eyes filled with anger and sorrow, her voice choked with emotion. "*I must* go see Mrs. Kennedy and Nellie," she says.

Johnson nods and wishes to go with her. Agent Youngblood, however, refuses to let him leave the ward.[414] Agent Emory Roberts and Congressman Jack Brooks escort Lady Bird Johnson to the hall outside Trauma Room One, where Mrs. Kennedy stands, "quiet as a shadow," as Lady Bird later remembered. Mrs. Johnson always thought of the president's wife as a woman insulated, protected, and is now struck by the realization that in this moment she is terribly alone. "I don't think I ever saw anyone so much alone in my life," she would later recall. She goes to Jackie, puts her arm around her, and says, crying, "Jackie, I wish to God there was something I could do." But there is nothing she can do and eventually she slips away.

On the second floor of the hospital, Lady Bird greets her close friend of a quarter century, Nellie Connally. They hug each other tightly, both giving in to tears.

"Nellie, he's going to be all right."

"He *is*, Bird," Nellie says. "He's going to be all right."

Mrs. Connally's eyes well up and Jack Brooks, sensing they're about to spill over, hands her his handkerchief.

"Oh, he'll be out there deer hunting at ninety," he quips.

She dabs her eyes and smiles.[415]

In the corridors below, the Kennedy staff stands numb and stricken. No one seems to be in charge or knows what to do.

Mac Kilduff seeks out Ken O'Donnell.

"This is a terrible time to have to approach you on this," Kilduff says, "but the world has got to know that President Kennedy is dead."

O'Donnell looks at him, incredulous. "Don't they know it already?"

It seems like Kilduff's been carrying the burden of the death for a hundred years.

---

of Tenth and Patton, Tippit was traveling "not more than ten or twelve miles an hour" behind where Oswald was walking on Tenth [3 H 324]. And Helen Markham also noticed that the police car was "going real slow . . . real slow" [3 H 307].) I asked Bowles, "Tippit wouldn't have pulled his squad car over to the curb next to Oswald shortly after spotting him, and was calling in at 1:08 to let the dispatcher know he was leaving his patrol car [and radio, since in 1963 the Dallas Police never had walkie talkies] to approach Oswald?" Bowles, who worked for ten years in the Dallas police radio dispatcher's office, said, "Possible, but that wouldn't be the norm for an officer under these circumstances, particularly Tippit. I knew Tippit. He was a slow, cautious, deliberate guy. The norm would have been for him to call in for a further description of the suspect from the dispatcher. But not being acknowledged, after following Oswald for a few minutes he pulled over to see what this person [Oswald] is up to." "You don't think Tippit had enough PC [not as in *probable cause* for an arrest, but still used as a loose way of referring to a reasonable suspicion of criminal activity justifying a police officer to stop a pedestrian or driver of a car for questioning] to stop Oswald because Oswald vaguely fit the general description of the suspect sent out over police radio?" "Possibly," Bowles said, "but his PC was probably the description coupled with some overt behavior by Oswald like walking too fast, looking over his shoulder, walking in some erratic, jerky way. Remember, Oswald had just killed the president. He probably wasn't walking in a normal, casual way and a police officer would pick up on this more than someone else would." (Telephone interview of Dallas sheriff Jim Bowles by author on February 23, 2004)

"No, I haven't told them," Kilduff says.

"Well, you're going to have to make the announcement," O'Donnell replies. He thought about the new order of things a moment, then added, "Go ahead, but you'd better check it with Johnson."

An agent leads Kilduff through the maze of cubicles in Minor Medicine until they round a corner and Mac spots Lyndon Johnson sitting on an ambulance cart, head down, legs dangling. Kilduff swallows hard, "Mr. President . . ."

Johnson's head snaps up sharply. It's the first time Lyndon Johnson has been addressed that way; the first time he *knows* he is the thirty-sixth president of the United States.

Kilduff proceeds to ask Johnson if he can announce President's Kennedy's death. Johnson nods yes, then says, "No. Wait. We don't know whether it's a Communist conspiracy or not. I'd better get out of here and back to the plane." Kilduff and Johnson agree that he will not announce Kennedy's death until after Johnson leaves the hospital.[416]

Ken O'Donnell enters the ward and finds Johnson, frightened and nervous, conferring with the Secret Service agents. Emory Roberts, the ranking agent in the room, jumps up when O'Donnell comes in: "What'll we do, Kenny, what'll we do?"

"You'd better get the hell out of here," O'Donnell replies, "and get back to Washington right away. Take Air Force One."[*]

"Don't you think it might be safer if we moved the plane to Carswell Air Force Base and took off from there?" Johnson asks.

O'Donnell doesn't like it. It would take time to get one of the jets from nearby Love Field to the air force base, and the thirty-five-mile drive from Dallas to Carswell would be risky. He suggests that Johnson should head to Love Field and take off for Washington as soon as he gets there.

"How about Mrs. Kennedy?" Johnson asks.

"She will not leave the hospital without the president," O'Donnell says.

There is no doubt about which president he is referring to. Afraid that the public might view his departure as deserting the Kennedys, Johnson digs his heels in.

"I don't want to leave Mrs. Kennedy like this," he says.

O'Donnell tells Johnson that he will stay behind with Mrs. Kennedy until the president's body is ready to be moved to the airport.

---

[*]The Kennedy loyalists felt it was in the worst of taste for President Johnson to take the former president's plane back to Washington instead of flying back on Air Force Two, the plane he had come to Texas in. And indeed, when Warren Commission counsel asked O'Donnell if, after he informed LBJ that the president had died, there was "any discussion about his taking the presidential plane, AF-1, as opposed to AF-2?" O'Donnell replied, "There was not" (7 H 451). And he reiterated this in his book (O'Donnell and Powers with McCarthy, *Johnny, We Hardly Knew Ye*, p.40). But one wonders if O'Donnell found it convenient to deny the conversation when he thereafter heard the sentiments of his associates about Johnson flying on Air Force One. President Johnson told the Warren Commission that after O'Donnell informed him that Kennedy had died, O'Donnell "said that we should return to Washington and that we should take the president's plane" (5 H 563). And Secret Service agent Rufus Youngblood, special agent in charge of the vice presidential detail for the Texas trip, testified before the Warren Commission that "O'Donnell told us to go ahead and take Air Force One. I believe this is mainly because Air Force One has better communications equipment and so forth than the other planes [Air Force Two and the cargo plane]" (2 H 152–153). *U.S. News & World Report* sought to confirm this and was told by a former White House official that, at the time, the three jet planes in the presidential fleet were being "regeared for communications of a classified nature. Naturally, the first plane to be re-equipped was AF-1. Most of the new gear had been installed in AF-1. The other two jet planes had not been completed" ("Fateful Two Hours without a President," p.73).

Another reason to believe LBJ and Youngblood on this point is that the weight of the evidence (see later text) is that LBJ was very sensitive to the feelings of the entire Kennedy camp following the assassination.

"You take good care of that fine lady," Johnson says.[417*]

Secret Service agents are already arranging for a couple of unmarked police cars to spirit Johnson and his party away to Love Field. The agents at the airfield have taken extraordinary measures to secure the area around the two presidential planes, directing local police and airport people to clear all the buildings, hangars, and warehouses of both employees and civilians. It seems bizarre to prepare such a departure for the president of the United States, in his own country, but the fact is, none of them know where the assassin or assassins are, or what they plan to do next.[418†]

William W. Scoggins, a forty-nine-year-old cabdriver, eats a sandwich in his taxi and ponders the shooting of the president. He's just dropped a fare from the airport, and after a brief stop at the Gentleman's Club, a domino parlor and lunch spot on Patton (on the other side of the street from where Scoggins parked his car, about a half a block south in the direction of Jefferson Boulevard), to watch coverage of the assassination on TV, he returns to his parking spot at the corner of Tenth and Patton. The area is a "scruffy, working-class residential neighborhood of aging frame houses" about four miles from Dealey Plaza. He's only been there a few seconds when he notices Dallas police car number 10—J. D. Tippit's squad car—crossing left to right a few yards in front of him as it prowls very slowly eastbound on Tenth Street. Scoggins takes another bite of his sandwich and swigs a Coke.[419]

A woman stands on the corner diagonally across from Scoggins, waiting for traffic to clear so she can cross the street. A pair of work shoes in her hand, Helen Markham, forty-seven, is on her way to catch the 1:15 p.m. bus at the next corner (the corner of Patton and Jefferson), the same one she takes every day to the Eatwell Restaurant on Main Street downtown, where she works as a waitress.[420] She sees "this police car slowly cross [the intersection] and sorta ease up alongside the man."[421]

---

*O'Donnell thought that he had convinced Johnson to depart immediately upon his arrival at Love Field; however, Johnson wasn't about to fly back to the capital alone, with a dead president and a grieving widow on a following plane. He agreed to return to Love Field but was determined to wait for Mrs. Kennedy and the president's body before departing for Washington. (5 H 563, WC statement of President Lyndon Baines Johnson; O'Donnell and Powers with McCarthy, *Johnny, We Hardly Knew Ye*, p.34; Bishop, *Day Kennedy Was Shot*, pp.193–194; Telephone interview of Assistant Special Agent-in-Charge Lem Johns by author on June 28, 2005)

†Although the FBI and other members of law enforcement first suspected that the nation's right wing was behind the assassination, Warren Commission chronicler and assassination researcher Max Holland writes, "For officials whose instincts were honed by national-security considerations, the Soviet-American rivalry loomed over what had happened and dictated what immediately needed to be done. The overwhelming instant reaction among these officials was to suspect a grab for power, a foreign, Communist-limited conspiracy aimed at overthrowing the U.S. government. The assassination might be the first in a concerted series of attacks on U.S. leaders as the prelude to an all-out attack . . . When Major General Chester Clifton, JFK's military aide, arrived at Parkland Hospital, he immediately called the National Military Command Center and then switched to the White House Situational Room to find out if there was any intelligence about a plot to overthrow the government. The Defense Department subsequently issued a flash warning to every U.S. military base in the world and ordered additional strategic bombers into the air. General Maxwell Taylor [chairman of the Joint Chiefs of Staff] issued a special alert to all troops in the Washington [D.C.] area, while John McCone, director of Central Intelligence, asked the Watch Committee to convene immediately at the Pentagon. The committee, an interdepartmental group organized to prevent future Pearl Harbors, consisted of the government's best experts on surprise military attacks" (Holland, "Key to the Warren Report," pp.52, 54).

1:11 p.m.

Scoggins watches the police car stop around 120 feet down Tenth Street to his right, and it is then that he also notices a man in a light-colored jacket standing on the sidewalk. The man walks over toward the police car, passing out of Scoggins's sight behind some shrubs.[422] Markham has an unobstructed view and sees the man go over to the squad car, lean over, and place his arms on the ledge of the open front window on the passenger side. She observes him "talking to the officer through the open window" and assumes it is a friendly conversation.[423]

Jack Ray Tatum, a twenty-five-year-old medical photographer for Baylor University Medical Center, turns onto Tenth Street from Denver and heads west in his red Ford Galaxie. Tatum's boss has given him an afternoon off and he's been spending it running errands and buying a watch and ring for his wife, on a lay-a-way, at Gordon's Jewelers on Jefferson. Approaching Patton, he sees a squad car driving east on Tenth Street and a young white male "was also walking east, the same direction the squad car was going." When the squad car pulls over to the curb, he sees the man approaching the squad car on the passenger side. As Tatum drives past, he can see the police officer in the front seat leaning over toward the man, whose hands are crammed into the pockets of his light-gray zipper jacket. He gets the impression they are talking. Tatum wonders why the cop has stopped him.[424]*

Domingo Benavides is in his pickup truck a half-dozen car lengths behind Tatum. The mechanic from Dootch Motors is pretty annoyed with himself. He was on his way to the auto parts store at Marsalis and Tenth to get a carburetor and was damned near there when it dawned on him that he'd forgotten the part number. He's heading back west on Tenth Street when he sees the police car ahead on the left.[425] (See photo section for diagram of Tippit murder scene with location of Tippit's car, Oswald, and witnesses.)

1:12 p.m.

Just after Tatum passes the squad car, Helen Markham watches the driver's door open and the police officer climb out. He doesn't seem to be in a hurry, and has not drawn his weapon.† The officer starts walking toward the front of the car, not keeping his eyes on Oswald but looking down at the ground,‡ his right hand, like a western sheriff, on his gun butt as the young man on the passenger side puts his hands in his pockets and takes two steps back. Suddenly, the young man pulls a gun out from under his jacket.

BANG! BANG! BANG! BANG! Bullets fly across the hood of the car.[426]

Scoggins looks up from his sandwich and sees the policeman grab his stomach, then

---

*The conventional wisdom and that of the Warren Commission is that Tippit pulled his squad car over to talk to Oswald because Tippit must have heard the description of the suspected killer of the president, which was sent out over Dallas police radio at 12:45, 12:48, and 12:55 p.m., that he was a "white male, approximately thirty, slender build, height five foot ten inches, weight 165 pounds," and Oswald's description was similar to the suspect (WR, p.165). The argument of conspiracy theorists, seeking to link Oswald to Tippit before Tippit's murder, that Oswald wasn't similar enough for Tippit to have stopped him, is a very weak one. If there ever was a time when a police officer would stop someone if he even remotely resembled a suspect, surely this was it.

†We will never know what words Oswald and Tippit exchanged that caused Tippit to leave his patrol car and start to approach Oswald. But we can safely assume that there was something about Oswald's words, appearance, or demeanor that made Tippit want to check Oswald out further, but that was not suspicious enough at that point for him to have drawn his gun on Oswald.

‡Tippit had a bad habit, which his fellow officers unsuccessfully tried to break him of, of never looking anyone straight in the eye, looking down or sometimes sideways when he approached a person on duty. This may have accounted for how Oswald got the jump on him. (See endnote discussion.)

fall.[427] Benavides is almost abreast of the squad car when the shooting erupts. He jerks the wheel hard right, bumps his '58 Chevy pickup into the curb, and throws himself down on the front seat.[428]

Tatum is passing through the intersection of Tenth and Patton when he hears the crack of several pistol shots behind him. He jams on the brakes and turns to look back. The police officer is lying on the ground beside the left front tire of the squad car. Tatum sees a man in a light tan-gray jacket start off in Tatum's direction, hesitate at the rear of the police car, then step back into the street and fire one more shot, right into the head of the officer on the ground.[429]*

Mrs. Markham is screaming. The man walks calmly away, back toward Patton Street, fooling with his gun.[430]

Tatum, realizing the gunman is coming his way, drives off, with an eye on his rearview mirror.[431]

The gunman spots Mrs. Markham across the street and looks straight at her. She thinks he's fixing to kill her too. She falls to her knees and covers her face with her hands, but when she pulls them down enough to see, she realizes that he is veering off, cutting across the yard of the corner house.[432]

Barbara and Virginia Davis are babysitting when they hear the shots. The young women (nineteen and sixteen, respectively) have been sisters-in-law for a couple of months, ever since they married brothers. Their husbands are in the home-repair business, and the two couples each live in an apartment in the corner house at Tenth and Patton. Barbara slips on her shoes and rushes to the screen door, Virginia on her heels. She sees Mrs. Markham across the street on the corner, screaming and pointing toward the man coming across her yard, "He killed him! He killed him!" Barbara glances to her right and sees a Dallas police car parked in front of the house next door. The gunman is now less than twenty-five feet away as he cuts across her front walk. He looks at her coolly as he shakes spent cartridges from an open revolver into his hand. She dashes to the phone and calls the police.[433]

Scoggins has been driving a cab for less than two years, but if there's one thing he's learned, it's to get as far away from the cab as possible when trouble starts. He doesn't fancy being commandeered by some nut with a gun. Scoggins is already getting out when he sees the gunman cutting across the yard of the house on the corner, and realizes he'd better get out of sight, fast. He starts to cross the street, but there's no time to run and hide. He quickly crouches down behind the cab, then steals a look as the man runs through the bushes of the corner house. Scoggins can see the side of the man's face as the killer looks back over his shoulder and mutters, "Poor damn cop," twice. Or maybe it was "poor dumb cop." Scoggins isn't sure.[434]

1:13 p.m.

Ted Callaway is in his office, a small clapboard building at the back of Dootch Motors, the used-car lot on the northeast corner of Jefferson and Patton, when he hears five shots. The office boys with him laugh about the "firecrackers," but the forty-seven-year-old Callaway, knowing instantly what it is, says, "Firecrackers, hell! That's pistol shots!"[435]

The used-car manager is a Marine Corps veteran who fought on the Marshall

---

*I asked Tatum at the London trial if he got "a good look" at the man who shot Tippit and whom he identified at the trial. "Very good look," Tatum responded. I asked if there was "any question in your mind" that the man was Oswald. "None whatsoever," he answered. (Transcript of *On Trial*, July 23, 1986, p.200)

Islands during World War II, and later trained recruits during the Korean War. He's on his feet in a flash, running out to Patton Street. He looks to his right, up toward Tenth and the sound of the shots. He can see the cabdriver Scoggins crouched down next to his taxi as a man leaps through the bushes and cuts across Patton, running toward him. The fleeing man has both of his hands on a pistol he holds straight up, elbow high— what the Marines call a "raised pistol position." As the gunman gets kitty-corner across the street—less than sixty feet away—Callaway hollers to him, "Hey, man, what the hell is going on?"

The killer slows, almost stops, says something unintelligible, shrugs his shoulders, and walks briskly on toward Jefferson Boulevard, then turns right and proceeds in a westerly direction down Jefferson.[436]

Callaway turns to B. D. Searcy, a car-lot porter, and tells him, "Keep an eye on that guy, follow him. I'm going to go down there and see what's going on!"

He takes off on the double, a good hard run.

"Follow him, hell," Searcy calls after him. "That man will kill you. He has a gun." Searcy proceeds to find refuge behind the office building.[437]

Warren Reynolds is standing on the balcony of the two-story office building at his brother's used-car lot—Reynolds Motor Company—across Jefferson Boulevard from Dootch Motors. Three men are on the lot below him—Harold Russell, L. J. Lewis, and B. M. "Pat" Patterson. They all heard the shots and now see a man running down Patton toward them. As he nears the corner, they can see he is reloading a pistol, which he promptly tucks into his belt. As he heads west on Jefferson, Reynolds descends the stairs and tells the others that he's going to trail the guy. Patterson goes with him, Lewis runs back to the office to phone police, and Russell trots down toward the scene of the shooting.[438]

On Tenth Street, when the killer is about half a block away, Mrs. Markham runs over to the policeman's body to see if she can help. The gurgling sounds coming from Tippit's body lead Markham to think he may be trying to say something. But it's only death gasps. Markham screams in despair, "Somebody help me!" but she is all by herself, and no one responds to her pleas for what seems to her like several "minutes."[439]

Frank Cimino, who lives at 405 East Tenth Street, directly across the street from the shooting, had been listening to his radio at the time he heard "four loud noises that sounded like shots," after which he heard a woman scream. He puts on his shoes, runs outside, and sees a woman dressed like a waitress (Markham) shouting, "Call the police." She tells him the man who shot the police officer had run west on Tenth Street and pointed in the direction of an alley between Tenth and Jefferson off Patton, but he sees no one when he looks in that direction. Cimino approaches the officer, who is lying on his side with his head in front of the left front headlight of the police car. Cimino can see that Tippit has been shot in the head. Tippit's gun is out of his holster, lying by his side. Tippit moves slightly and groans but never says anything that Cimino can understand. Soon people start coming from all directions toward the police car.[444]

1:15 p.m.

Benavides has been sitting in his truck for two or three minutes, very afraid that the gunman lives in the corner house and might come back shooting. He finally gets out, walks across the street, and cautiously approaches the fallen officer. A big clot of blood bulges at the officer's right temple, his eyes sunken into his skull. It makes Benavides feel sick, and "really" scared.[441]

1:16 p.m.

The mechanic gets into the squad car, grabs the microphone, and tries to call the police dispatcher. Unfortunately, Benavides has no idea how the radio works. He fumbles with the controls and keeps clicking the button on the mike, but from the chatter on the police radio he can tell they can't hear him.[442]

A small crowd has gathered at the squad car by the time Ted Callaway gets there, closely followed by Sam Guinyard, a porter at Dootch Motors, who had been waxing and polishing a station wagon at the back of the lot when he saw the gunman run by. More people from the neighborhood are arriving every minute.[443] Callaway kneels down next to the body. He doesn't have to look very hard to see the officer has been hit at least three times, once in the right temple. Callaway had seen a lot of dead men during the Korean War. This officer looks just like them.[444]

In New York, CBS News anchor Walter Cronkite tells the nation for the first time that the president has reportedly died. Calling it "only a rumor," he leads to Eddie Barker, the news director of CBS's Dallas affiliate KRLD, who is on the scene at Parkland Hospital. Barker says, "The word we have is that President Kennedy is dead. This we do not know for a fact . . . The word we have is from a doctor on the staff of Parkland Hospital who says that it is true. He was in tears when he told me just a moment ago. This is still not officially confirmed, but . . . the source would normally be a good one."[445]

1:17 p.m.

T. F. Bowley, who just picked up his twelve-year-old daughter at the R.L. Thornton school in Singing Hills and was on his way to pick up his wife from work at the telephone company at Ninth and Zangs, drives up on the scene at Tenth and Patton. Bowley tells his young daughter to wait in the car as he walks over to see what's happened. He takes one look at the officer and knows there is nothing anyone can do for him. He walks over to the open driver's door of the squad car. Benavides looks up and says, "I don't know how it works."[446] Benavides gets out of the car and hands the mike over to Bowley, who calls in the shooting, "Hello, police operator?"

"Go ahead," dispatcher Murray Jackson answers. "Go ahead, citizen using the police—"

"We've had a shooting out here," Bowley blurts out.

"Where's it at?" Jackson asks.

Bowley hesitates. He isn't sure.

"The citizen using police radio—" Jackson continues.

"On Tenth Street," Bowley cuts in.

"What location on Tenth Street?"

"Between Marsalis and Beckley," Bowley answers. "It's a police officer. Somebody shot him—what—what's this?" Someone at the scene tells Bowley the address and he repeats it to the dispatcher, "404 Tenth Street."[*]

---

[*]Actually, Tippit pulled over and stopped his squad car on the street in front of the driveway between 404 and 410 East Tenth Street (CE 523, 17 H 229; photo of car parked on East Tenth: Barnes Exhibit D, 19 H 114).

Jackson knows his friend, Officer J. D. Tippit, is in that general area and immediately calls over the police radio, "[Unit] 78?"

Bowley says, "You got that? It's in a police car." Someone at the scene tells him the number of the police car. Bowley repeats it: "Number ten."

Now Jackson knows. That's Tippit's squad car number. In fact, he and J. D. had once partnered in that same car. He can't believe what appears to have happened. He doesn't want to believe it. Both he and the other dispatcher working channel 1, C. E. Hulse, shout into their mikes, "Seventy-eight."

Seconds tick by. No response. It can't be true, Jackson thinks. But it is.

"You got this?" Bowley asks the stunned dispatcher.

Hulse takes command, "Attention all units—"

"Hello, police operator? Did you get that?" Bowley asks, talking over the dispatcher.

"—Signal 19 [police call number for a shooting] involving a police officer, 510 East Jefferson."*

"The citizen using the police radio, remain off the air now," Jackson orders, as he recovers from the shocking news.

"[Unit] 91?" Hulse calls, trying to contact Patrolman W. D. Mentzell, who checked out a few minutes earlier at a traffic accident near the Tippit shooting scene. No response.

"[Unit] 69's going out there," Patrolman A. R. Brock calls in to Jackson.

"Ten-Four, 69," Jackson replies, relieved to know that help is on the way.[447]

It isn't long before law officers throughout the city learn that one of their own has been shot. First, it was the president. Now, for the Dallas police, it's personal.

On the street in front of the Texas School Book Depository Building, Sergeant Gerald Hill had run into Lieutenant J. C. "Carl" Day of the crime lab, just as he arrived at the scene. Hill told him about finding spent cartridges up on the sixth floor, and Day had gone on up. Now, Hill is giving Inspector Sawyer the same information, as *Dallas Morning News* reporters James Ewell and Hugh Aynesworth stand nearby, listening intently to the conversation. Hill, a former newsman, knows how tough it is to gather facts without good police sources. He speaks clearly so the newsmen get it right.

Sergeant C. B. "Bud" Owens and Assistant District Attorney Bill Alexander join the group. In a moment, Sheriff Bill Decker walks up. He's grimfaced. Decker was in the lead car of the motorcade and had seen the carnage at Parkland Hospital. But all he says is, "It looks bad."[448]

They are all standing there but a moment when they hear T. F. Bowley's voice break in on a nearby police radio with the news that a Dallas police officer has been shot.

Sergeant Owens, acting lieutenant in charge of the Oak Cliff area, listens with growing horror to the dispatcher calling in vain for Unit 78. He knows immediately that it's one of his men, J. D. Tippit—a longtime friend.[449] Owens jumps into his car as Hill and Alexander pile in behind him. Owens puts the pedal to the floor and the car squeals away

---

*Hulse has gotten the 510 East Jefferson address (the site of Reynolds Motor Company) from the call sheet passed through the conveyor belt to the dispatch room from the adjacent room manned by civilian employees of the police department taking calls from other civilians—the result of the phone call made by L. J. Lewis from that location. The confusion resulting from the two addresses given for the shooting delayed the arrival of many police officers in getting to the shooting scene.

toward Oak Cliff.[450] Hill grabs the radio in the front seat: "Give me the correct address on the shooting."

"501 East Tenth," dispatcher Jackson replies, giving an address from another call sheet just handed to him from an officer who had received this address from a telephone operator who in turn had been given the address by a resident calling in from East Tenth Street. The police are being flooded with call sheets—notations that record telephone calls from citizens.

Patrolmen Joe Poe and Leonard Jez, also racing to the scene, are equally confused by the multiple addresses.

"Was 519 East Jefferson correct?" Poe asks.

"We have two locations, 501 East Jefferson and 501 East Tenth," Jackson says, not mentioning the correct address of 404 East Tenth Street (Tenth and Patton) that he had also been given. "[Unit] Nineteen [Owens], are you en route?"

"Ten-four," an unknown officer says, "nineteen is en route."[451]

At 1:18 p.m., the channel 2 dispatcher, Gerald D. Henslee, informs "all squads" of the correct address of the shooting.[452]

Back in front of the Depository, reporters Ewell and Aynesworth confer briefly. The shooting in Oak Cliff *has* to be connected to the president's death, they think. They decide to split up—one will stay at the Depository and the other will go out to Oak Cliff. Aynesworth draws the Oak Cliff assignment. After he runs off, Ewell has second thoughts about staying behind. He spots Captain W. R. Westbrook, in charge of the Dallas Police Department's Personnel Bureau, running for his car. He's headed for Oak Cliff too. Ewell asks permission and joins him.[453]

At Tenth and Patton streets, ambulance attendants J. C. Butler and William "Eddie" Kinsley swing their 1962 Ford ambulance around in front of the squad car and jump out. (Though they had received the incorrect address of 501 East Tenth Street from the police, they had no trouble spotting the squad car, and people around it, less than a block to the east.) They've been dispatched from the Dudley Hughes Funeral Home, less than three blocks away, but there's nothing they can do for Tippit. Ambulance attendants at that time are basically just drivers whose job is to get victims to a nearby hospital as quickly as possible. Their ambulance is equipped with little more than a stretcher.

Butler kneels next to Tippit's body and rolls him on his back as Kinsley pulls the stretcher cot from the back of the station wagon. Tippit's pistol is out of its holster, lying on the pavement near his right palm. Ted Callaway moves the gun to the hood of the squad car, then, with Scoggins and Guinyard, helps the attendants lift the body onto the stretcher. As they do so, the first Dallas police officer to arrive at the murder scene, reserve sergeant Kenneth Croy, pulls up. Butler and Kinsley push the cot into the back, slam the door, and are off in a flash to Methodist Hospital about a mile away.[454]

1:20 p.m.

Out at Parkland, the hospital's senior engineer, Darrell Tomlinson, has been manually operating the elevator, shuttling it between the emergency room on the ground floor and the operating rooms on the second floor. Coming down from the second floor, Tomlinson notices that on the ground floor a gurney, which was left in the hallway, has been pushed out into the narrow corridor by someone who may have used the men's room. There is barely enough room in front of the elevator doors as it is, so Tomlinson pushes the gurney back. As it bumps the wall, Tomlinson hears a "clink" of metal on metal. He walks over and sees a bullet lying between the pad and the rim of the gurney.[455]

O. P. Wright, personnel officer of Parkland Hospital, has just entered the emergency unit when he hears Tomlinson call to him. Wright walks over and Tomlinson points out the bullet lying on the edge of the stretcher.[456] Wright, a former deputy chief of police for the city of Dallas, immediately looks for a federal officer to take charge of the evidence. At first, Wright contacts an FBI agent, who refuses to take a look at the bullet, saying it wasn't the FBI's responsibility to make the investigation, in apparent deference to the Dallas Police Department. Next, Wright locates a Secret Service agent, but he too doesn't seem interested in coming to look at the bullet on the stretcher. Frustrated, Wright returns to the stretcher, reluctantly picks up the bullet, and puts it into his pocket. There it remains for the next half hour or so, until Wright runs into Secret Service agent Richard E. Johnsen, who agrees to take possession of the bullet, which will later become a key piece of evidence in the assassination.[457]

In Oak Cliff, Ted Callaway can hear the confusion and desperation of the police over Tippit's car radio as they struggle to locate the scene of the officer's shooting. He lowers his big frame into the patrol car and grabs the mike, "Hello, hello, hello!"

"From out here on Tenth Street," he continues, "five-hundred block. This police officer's just shot, I think he's dead."

"Ten-four, we [already] have the information," dispatcher Jackson replies, exasperated. "The citizen using the radio will remain *off* the radio now." The last thing he needs is some gung-ho citizen tying up the airwaves.[458]

Ted Callaway climbs out of the squad car and spots his mechanic, Domingo Benavides.

"Did you see what happened?"

"Yes," Benavides says.

Callaway picks up Tippit's service revolver.

"Let's chase him," he says.

Benavides wants no part of it. Callaway snaps the revolver open—and Benavides can see that no rounds have been fired. Callaway tucks the gun in his belt and turns to the cabdriver, Scoggins.

"You saw the guy, didn't you?" the former marine asks.

Scoggins admits he had.

"If he's going up Jefferson, he can't be too far. Let's go get the son of a bitch who's responsible for this."

In his blue suit and white shirt, Callaway looks like some kind of policeman, or Secret Service agent. Scoggins doesn't find out until later that he's simply a used-car manager. They go back to Scoggins's cab and set off to cruise along Jefferson, the last place Callaway saw the gunman.[459]

Two blocks away, Warren Reynolds and Pat Patterson wonder whether the gunman went into the rear of one of the buildings near Crawford and Jefferson. They've been tailing him since he headed west, walking briskly along Jefferson Boulevard. They saw the killer turn north and scoot between a secondhand furniture store and the Texaco service station on the corner.

Eventually, they approach Robert and Mary Brock, the husband and wife employees of the service station, and ask if they've seen a man come by. Both say, "Yes." They last saw him in the parking lot behind the station. Reynolds and Patterson run back and check the parking lot, then the alley behind it. Nothing. He's escaped. Reynolds tells them to call the police, then heads toward Tenth and Patton to tell the others.[460]

1:21 p.m. (2:21 p.m. EST)

In Washington, FBI Director J. Edgar Hoover calls James J. Rowley, chief of the Secret Service, to offer any assistance. He tells Rowley it has been reported that a Secret Service agent has been killed, but he had not been able to get his name. Rowley states he did not know one of his agents had been killed. Hoover says the information he has is that the shots came from the "fourth floor of a building" and that "apparently a Winchester rifle was used." The two speculate about who was behind the shooting, Rowley mentioning subversive elements in Mexico and Cuba, Hoover mentioning the Ku Klux Klan.[461]

At the Dallas FBI office, Special Agent-in-Charge Gordon Shanklin, a chain-smoker who buys cartons of cigarettes by the grocery bag, is on the telephone with the third in command at FBI headquarters in Washington, Alan Belmont. With his thin hair, glasses, and comfortable attire, Shanklin looks like a rumpled professor, but all the agents understand his nervousness. It isn't easy to work for J. Edgar Hoover, with his whims and moods. Shanklin tells Belmont that from the information available, it appears the president has died of his wounds and that Governor Connally is in fair condition. He adds that, contrary to prior reports, a Secret Service agent has not been killed in Dallas.

"The director's specific instructions on this," Belmont says, "are that we should offer all possible assistance to the Secret Service and local police, and that means exactly that— give *all* possible assistance."

"Do we have jurisdiction?" Shanklin questions.

"The question of jurisdiction is not pertinent at the moment," Belmont replies. "The Secret Service will no doubt regard this as primarily their matter, but the essential thing is that we offer and give all possible assistance. In fact, see if the Secret Service wants us to send some laboratory men down to assist in identifying the spent shells found in the Depository."

"I've already made the offer," Shanklin tells him. "I've got our men with the Secret Service, the Dallas police, and the sheriff's office. I've even got a man at the hospital where Mrs. Kennedy is."

Shanklin fills Belmont in on the latest developments—shots appear to have been fired from the fifth floor of a five-story building at the corner of Elm and Commerce, where a Winchester rifle was reportedly used.* Shanklin tells him that the building has been roped off and the Secret Service and police are going through it.

"Has anyone been identified?" Belmont asks.

---

*This, and Hoover's statement about a Secret Service agent being killed, are two examples of the kind of erroneous information that was being passed along immediately after the assassination during the initial phases of the investigation. Shanklin's source was apparently the Dallas police radio where similar information had just been broadcast.

"No, not yet," Shanklin answers.

"We'll send out a Teletype to all offices to check and account for the whereabouts of all hate-group members in their areas," Belmont tells him. "If you need more manpower down there, let us know and we'll send it."

"Okay," Shanklin says, and hangs up.

Belmont promptly starts working on a Teletype to alert all FBI offices to immediately contact all informants and sources regarding the assassination and to immediately establish the whereabouts of bombing suspects, Klan and hate-group members, racial extremists, and any other individuals who on the basis of information in bureau files might have been involved.[462]

1:22 p.m.

The cavernous sixth floor of the Texas School Book Depository is crawling with officers looking for evidence. Since the discovery of the sniper's nest, the search has been concentrated there.[463] They have all heard about the shooting out in Oak Cliff and are tense, jumpy. *Dallas Morning News* reporter Kent Biffle, caught up with the officers involved in the search, wonders whether he risks getting shot by a nervous officer.[464]

A flashbulb pops in the southeast corner window as crime-lab investigators Lieutenant Carl Day and Detective Robert Studebaker photograph the three spent cartridges lying on the floor of the sniper's nest. Nearby, Captain Will Fritz of homicide converses with Detectives L. D. Montgomery and Marvin Johnson, who've just arrived.[465] Across the floor, in the northwest corner, near the top of the back stairwell, two sheriff deputies comb through a stack of boxes for the umpteenth time. Deputy Eugene Boone shines his high-powered flashlight into every gloomy crack, crevice, and cranny, looking in, under, and around the dusty boxes and pallets. Alongside him is Deputy Constable Seymour Weitzman, who has been over this area of the sixth floor twice already, though without the aid of a flashlight. Now the bright beam of light picks up something on the floor stuffed down between two rows of boxes, another box slid on an angle over the top of it. Weitzman crawls down on the floor, as Boone shines the light down into the crevice from the top. They spot a rifle at the same moment.

"There it is!" Weitzman shouts.

"We got it!" Boone hollers to other officers across the sixth floor. It was pretty well concealed from view—eight or nine searchers must have stumbled over it before they found it. Boone checks his watch—1:22 p.m.[466]

Captain Fritz tells Detectives Montgomery and Johnson to stay with the hulls, while he and Detectives Sims and Boyd walk over to where the rifle has been found. They can see it down among the boxes. Detective Sims goes back to the area of the sniper's nest and tells Lieutenant Day that they need him, the camera, and the fingerprint dust kit over where the rifle has been found. Detective Studebaker takes another picture of the position of the three empty cartridges lying below the half-open window as Day tells him they've got the pictures they need.

Detective Sims reaches down and picks up the empty hulls and drops them into an evidence envelope that Lieutenant Day is holding open. With the empty hulls secured, Day packs up the camera and dust kit and immediately goes to the officers gathering around the rifle near the stairwell in the northwest corner of the sixth floor. As Day leaves, Detectives Montgomery and Johnson start to collect other evidence in the area of the sniper's nest, including the long, brown paper bag. The bag has been folded twice and is lying to the left of the sniper's nest window. As Montgomery unfolds it, he and Johnson speculate that it may have been used to bring the rifle into the building.[467]

Within minutes, Lieutenant Day and Detective Studebaker are photographing the rifle from several points of view. When they're satisfied they have enough, Fritz carefully lifts the weapon out by its homemade sling. A local TV cameraman records the scene for posterity.[468]

None of the officers crowding around, many of them gun enthusiasts, are able to identify the rifle positively, although it's clearly an infantry weapon with a Mauser action. It is stamped "Made Italy," with a date of 1940 and serial number C2766. Along with some other more arcane markings, it bears the legend "Caliber 6.5" across the top of the rear iron sight. It has the distinctive magazine—designed by Ferdinand Ritter von Mannlicher, who worked on the Mauser bolt action—built on the leading edge of the trigger guard, and capable of holding up to five rounds, or six of a smaller caliber. Day notices that the detachable cartridge clip in the magazine is empty. The rifle has been fitted with a cheap Japanese telescopic sight and an improvised, homemade sling. Whatever the sling came from, it didn't start out as a rifle sling.

Before the rifle is touched or moved, Captain Fritz has Day photograph the rifle and surrounding boxes. Fritz then gingerly opens the bolt and finds one live cartridge in the chamber, which he ejects.[469] The cartridge is printed with the caliber, 6.5 millimeter, and the make, "WW"—symbol of the Western Cartridge Company of Alton, Illinois.[470]

Sergeant Bud Owens races his car south on Beckley with passengers Gerald Hill and and Bill Alexander. In Dallas law enforcement at the time of the assassination, two names stood out: Captain Will Fritz, who headed up the Homicide and Robbery Bureau of the Dallas Police Department, and Bill Alexander, the chief felony prosecutor for the Dallas district attorney's office. Alexander had been with the office for eleven years, had had ten murderers he convicted or helped convict executed at the state prison in Huntsville, and had a 93 percent conviction rate in felony jury trials, above average in his office of twenty-five assistant district attorneys. Both men, though not social friends, liked and respected each other and worked closely on the major homicide cases in Dallas. Both liked their respective bosses, Police Chief Jesse Curry and District Attorney Henry Wade, but viewed them charitably as administrators (though both, particularly Wade, had distinguished careers in their respective departments before leading them) who really didn't know what the hell was going down in the cases handled by their offices.

Alexander, an infantry captain during the Second World War who saw combat in Italy, to this day wears a "John B. Stetson" hat—"with embroidered lining," he hastens to add—and carries a .380 automatic underneath his belt on his left side. Perhaps no other incident illustrates the lore of Bill Alexander more than one involving a Dallas con-artist named "Smokey Joe" Smith. It seems that Smith had the practice of reading obituaries and then preying on and swindling the decedents' vulnerable widows. Alexander did not take kindly to this and started to investigate Smith. One day, word got back to Alexander that Smith was in the Courthouse Café (a popular hangout for court regulars across the street from the courthouse) flashing his .45 and saying he was going to put a few holes in Alexander. There's always been an element of Texas justice that pronounces the word *justice* as "just us," and Alexander walked into the busy coffee shop, jerked Smith's "overfed" body off the counter stool, and with Smith on his knees, put his automatic to Smith's head and said, "Beg me for your life you no good son of a bitch or I'll kill you right here." After first pleading with Alexander, "Don't kill me. Please put the gun away," Smith, becoming more brazen when no projectile was on its way, told Alexander, "I'm going to tell the sheriff." "Well, go ahead and tell that one-eyed, old son of a bitch [Dallas sheriff Bill Decker]. That won't help you if you're gut-shot." Alexander left Smith with this cheerful admonition: "If you ever walk up behind me, I'll kill you dry." Smith, in fact, did call Decker, who called Alexander with this friendly advice: "You really shouldn't talk like that, Bill. Don't kill him."

But anyone led into thinking that because of Alexander's tough talk he was just a raw-boned hick who happened to have a law degree would be wrong. One can't spend more than a few minutes with Alexander without sensing that he is very intelligent and has a dry and pungent wit that he enjoys just as much as the person he's sharing it with.

On the day of the assassination, Alexander was returning to his office from a lunch-hour trip to a hardware store in the Oak Cliff section of Dallas to get supplies for the deer-hunting season coming up, when he heard sirens and saw traffic gridlock near his office in the old Records Building off Dealey Plaza. Learning the president had been shot, he went to his office on the sixth floor. It was virtually empty, since Wade, in view of the president's visit and motorcade, had told his office to take the afternoon off. Knowing there would be a flood of calls coming in, Alexander asked the switchboard operator to stay on the job, and immediately went to the sheriff's office in the Jail Building, which was joined to the Records Building, to "see what was going on." Within minutes he walked to the assassination scene, where his friend, Dallas deputy chief Herbert Sawyer, was coordinating things from a makeshift command post he had set up on Elm in front of the Book Depository Building. When a call came in that a Dallas officer had been shot in the Oak Cliff area, as indicated, he got in the squad car with Bud Owens and Gerald Hill and went to the scene. Alexander knew what all good prosecutors know. If at all possible, you join in the police investigation. It's much easier to present a case in court that you helped put together than to rely solely on the police. If you do the latter and they do a good job, fine. But if they don't, it's legal suicide. Alexander was at ground zero and starting to put his case together against the killer of Officer Tippit.[471]

As Owens, Hill, and Alexander proceed to the Tippit murder scene, they see an ambulance, sirens wailing, cross in front of them, a police car close behind. The officers know it's heading for the emergency unit at Methodist Hospital.[472] The ambulance bearing Tippit's body had picked up a patrol car, driven by Officer Robert Davenport and partner W. R. Bardin, a block earlier. In a moment the two are wheeling into the emergency entrance. When Butler and Kinsley open the back of the ambulance, Officer Davenport is shocked to see J. D. Tippit, whom he knew well and had worked with for three years. Davenport and Bardin help get Tippit into the emergency room. Though he appears to be dead, the officers observe "the doctors and nurses trying to bring [Tippit] back to life."

Up in the call-room of the hospital, Dr. Paul C. Moellenhoff, a twenty-nine-year-old surgery resident, is watching TV coverage of the presidential shooting. Someone from the emergency room calls and asks for the doctor on duty. He's out, so Dr. Moellenhoff runs down to cover for him.[473]

At Tenth and Patton, Officer Roy W. Walker pulls to the curb and recognizes an old school friend, Warren Reynolds, who gives him a description of the suspect.[474] Officer Walker grabs his radio mike as more police cars approach.

"We have a description on this suspect," Walker broadcasts, "last seen about 300 block of East Jefferson. He's a white male, about thirty, five-eight, black hair, slender, wearing a white jacket, white shirt, and dark slacks."

"Armed with what?" dispatcher Jackson asks.

"Unknown," Walker replies.[475]

Patrol partners Joe Poe and Leonard Jez pull up just as Walker finishes the broadcast. Owens, Hill, and Alexander are right behind them. Police cars are now arriving at Tenth and Patton en masse.[476] Sergeant Owens takes command of the area, instructing Officers Poe and Jez to talk to as many witnesses as possible and guard the crime scene. Someone at the scene informs them that the gunman had cut through a parking lot on Jefferson and dumped his jacket. Sergeant Owens and Assistant District Attorney Alexander and a posse of officers leave in search of the gunman.[477]

Sergeant Hill tells eyewitness Harold Russell to come with him. Hill takes Poe's squad car and drives off with Russell in the hopes of spotting the gunman in flight.

Eyewitness Jack Tatum walks up to Officers Poe and Jez with Mrs. Markham in tow. Hysterical, incoherent, and on the verge of fainting, Mrs. Markham recounts the brutal murder for police. It's tough to understand Markham's story through her tears. She keeps telling them that she'll be late for work, and they reassure her that everything will be okay.[478]

Ted Callaway and cabdriver William Scoggins return to the scene after failing to find the gunman. Callaway swears he would have shot him if he had found him. Police are just glad to get Tippit's service revolver back from this gung-ho Dallas citizen.[479]

1:23 p.m.

At Methodist Hospital, Dr. Moellenhoff is joined in the emergency room by Dr. Richard A. Liquori. The physicians make no further effort to resuscitate J. D. Tippit. Dr. Liquori thinks the bullet wound in the temple could have caused instant death. He turns to Officer Davenport and tells him he's declaring Tippit dead on arrival. Davenport shakes his head in despair and leaves the room to notify police headquarters. Tippit's body will be transported to Parkland Hospital for an autopsy. Before it is, Captain Cecil Talbert asks Dr. Moellenhoff to remove a bullet from Tippit's body, one that had not penetrated deeply, so the police can determine what caliber weapon was used in the shooting. "One 38 [caliber] slug and a button from Tippit's shirt" are removed from the wound.[480]

1:25 p.m.

FBI agent James P. Hosty Jr. hurries into the FBI squad room on the eleventh floor of the Santa Fe Building in downtown Dallas. He scans the room for Kenneth C. Howe, his immediate supervisor. Hosty was eating a cheese sandwich in a café when he heard that Kennedy had been shot. He's already been out to the Trade Mart, Parkland Hospital, and now, under orders from Howe, back at the bureau offices.

Hosty sees that Howe, in his fifties, is visibly close to the edge.

Because of Kennedy's progressive civil rights stance, Howe, like so many, suspects that the right wing may be behind the assassination, and Hosty is the only Dallas agent that monitors the right-wing groups. He knows he's in the hot seat now. Just then, Agent Vince Drain calls from Parkland Hospital to report that the president is dead of a gunshot wound to the head. Silence falls over the FBI office. A few secretaries start to sob quietly.

Hosty jumps on the telephone and calls Sergeant H. M. Hart, his counterpart in the Dallas police intelligence unit. In a matter of minutes, they agree to coordinate their investigation of right-wing extremists. As he hangs up the telephone, Hosty, like most of the law enforcement officers involved, can't help but think that the shootings of Officer Tippit and President Kennedy are somehow connected. But how?[481]

In the 400 block of east Jefferson, Sergeant Owens climbs from the squad car and directs a flock of arriving officers into the parking lot behind the Texaco service station. Another group of lawmen, including Assistant District Attorney Alexander, storm into two large vacant houses on Jefferson used for the storage of secondhand furniture. Warren Reynolds had told the police he saw the gunman running toward the houses. *Dallas Morning News* reporter Hugh Aynesworth is with the police searchers. A handful of cops run up a flight of rickety stairs, while another posse paws through the clutter of furniture, weapons cocked.

"Come out of there you son of a bitch, we've got you now!" one of them hollers.

Suddenly an officer falls through a weak section of the second-story flooring with a thunderous sound, his descent stopping at his waist. Before witnessing the humorous sight of the officer being half in and half out of the ceiling, all of them had instantly drawn their guns. Aynesworth, realizing he's the only one in there without a gun, runs for the exit, leaving police to do their duty. It doesn't take long for police to determine that there's nothing but junk in either building.[482]

Captain Westbrook and several officers proceed to the adjacent parking lot behind the Texaco service station, where the suspect lost his civilian pursuers, to conduct a further search. Quickly, an officer points out to Captain Westbrook a light-colored jacket tossed under the rear bumper of an old Pontiac parked in the middle of the parking lot. Westbrook walks over and inspects the clothing. Looks like their suspect has decided to change his appearance.[483] Motorcycle officer J. T. Griffin reaches for his police radio to notify the dispatcher, and fellow officers, of the discovery.[484]

"We believe we've got [the suspect's] white jacket. Believe he dumped it on this parking lot behind this service station at 400 block east Jefferson."[485] A moment later, dispatch supervisor Sergeant Gerald Henslee contacts Captain Westbrook on police radio channel 2.

"Go ahead," Westbrook says as he reaches a nearby radio.

"D.O.A. [dead on arrival], Methodist [Hospital]."

"Name?" Westbrook asks.

"J. D. Tippit."[486]

1:26 p.m.

At the makeshift headquarters in Parkland Hospital's emergency section, Secret Service agent Lem Johns reports to Agent Youngblood that he has lined up two unmarked police cars, along with Dallas Police Chief Curry and Inspector Putnam, who'll act as drivers, to get Johnson back to Love Field.

"Let's go," Johnson says.

They rush out in a football formation, Johnson the quarterback surrounded by a wedge of agents, those at the rear walking backward, hands on their guns. A second formation comprising Mrs. Johnson and two congressmen, Jack Brooks and Homer Thornberry, are close behind. The bewildered crowd at the emergency entrance scarcely has time to react before Johnson dives into the rear seat of Chief Curry's car. Youngblood crowds in behind him, as Thornberry slides in front. Mrs. Johnson and Congressman Brooks and a bevy of agents jump into the second car. As the cars begin to pull away, Congressman Albert Thomas runs up, calling out, "Wait for me!" Youngblood, not eager to present a sitting target right in front of the hospital, tells Curry to drive on, but Johnson overrules him. "Stop and let him get in."

The cars are stopped momentarily by a delivery truck on the access road to the hospital, but the police motorcycle escort gets them through, and they are off again, sirens wailing. Both Youngblood and Johnson ask Curry to turn off the sirens. They don't want to attract any more attention than absolutely necessary. Youngblood radios ahead to have Air Force One ready to receive them. They will be coming on board immediately.[487]

Malcolm Kilduff stands outside Parkland Hospital watching as the new president heads for Love Field. He turns and heads back into the hospital, where he knows he'll have to make the hardest announcement of his life. A crowd of journalists crazy for something official, anything at all, flock around him. All of them know, from Father Huber's indiscretion, that President Kennedy is dead. Someone has already lowered the flag out in front of the hospital to half-mast. Kilduff refuses to oblige them, repeating mechanically that he will make no further statement until the press conference begins.[488]

1:29 p.m.

For the first time, Dallas police headquarters learns that there may be a connection between the Kennedy and Tippit shootings. When Deputy Chief of Police N. T. Fisher calls into channel 2 police radio dispatcher Gerald Henslee and asks if there is "any indication" of a connection between the two shootings, Henslee radios back, "Well, the descriptions on the suspect are similar and it is possible."[489]

1:30 p.m.

Vernon B. O'Neal, proprietor of O'Neal's Funeral Home, and his bookkeeper, Ray Gleason, arrive at Parkland's emergency entrance and open the back of the Cadillac ambulance. Secret Service agents and White House correspondents spring forward to help lug the four-hundred-pound casket requested by the Secret Service out onto the undertaker's lightweight, portable cart assembled there.* Ken O'Donnell gets the signal that the casket has arrived. He returns to the corridor outside Trauma Room One and finds Jackie Kennedy still sitting on the folding chair surrounded by Clint Hill and members of President Kennedy's staff.

"I want to speak to you," he says to Mrs. Kennedy, motioning for her to follow him. They move a short distance down the passageway, away from the casket being wheeled in. The First Lady guesses that he doesn't want her to see it. Dr. Kemp Clark appears beside O'Donnell, and Jackie pleads with him, "Please—can I go in? Please let me go back."

"No, no," he said softly.

Finally, she leans toward him.

---

*Seventeen of O'Neal's eighteen employees are out to lunch when he got a call from Secret Service agent Clint Hill, shortly after 1:00 p.m., who wanted him to bring the best casket he had to Parkland Hospital. His most expensive model, at $3,995, was the Elgin Casket Company's Handley Britannia, a four-hundred-pound, double-walled, hermetically sealed, solid-bronze coffin manufactured by the Texas Coffin Company. O'Neal had to wait until three more of his men came back from lunch before he could wrestle the behemoth into his 1964 Cadillac hearse. (ARRB MD 131, Texas Coffin Company reorder card; Bishop, *Day Kennedy Was Shot*, p.267; Manchester, *Death of a President*, pp.291–292)

"Do you think seeing the coffin can upset me, Doctor? I've seen my husband die, shot in my arms. His blood is all over me. How can I see anything worse than what I've seen?"

There is nothing left for Clark to do but accede to her wishes.

Mrs. Kennedy is right behind Vernon O'Neal as they push the casket into Trauma Room One. She wants to see her husband one more time before they close the coffin, to touch him and give him something. She moves to the president's side, takes off her wedding ring, which he had bought her in Newport, Rhode Island, just before their grand wedding there, lifts her husband's hand, and slips it on his finger. She wants desperately to be alone with him, but she knows it cannot be. She steps into the passageway outside.

"Did I do the right thing?" she asks Ken O'Donnell. "I wanted to give him something."

"You leave it right where it is," he says.

"Now I have nothing left," she says.[*][490]

After seeing the condition of the president's body, Vernon O'Neal knows that it's going to take some time to make sure that the casket's expensive pale satin lining isn't irretrievably stained. Nurses Margaret Henchliffe and Diana Bowron, along with orderly David Sanders, line the coffin with a sheet of plastic, then wrap the body in a white sheet before placing it in the casket. Additional sheets are wrapped around the head to keep it from oozing more blood. The whole process takes twenty minutes.[491]

Meanwhile, Dr. Earl Rose, the Dallas County medical examiner, with an office at Parkland Hospital, rushes into the emergency area and grabs a phone off the wall of the nurses station.

"This is Earl Rose," he says into the mouthpiece, presumably to a Parkland Hospital official. "There has been a homicide here. They won't be able to leave until there has been an autopsy."

He hangs up and turns to leave when Roy Kellerman, who overheard Rose's directive, blocks the door.

"My friend, I'm the special agent in charge of the White House detail of the Secret Service," he says. "This is the body of the president of the United States and we are going to take it back to Washington."

"No, that's not the way things are," Rose snaps, waving his finger.

"The president is going with us," Kellerman argues.

"You're not taking *the body* anywhere," Rose lashes back. "There's a law here. We're going to enforce it!"

"This part of the law can be waived," Kellerman insists, every muscle tightening.

Rose shakes his head, no.

"You'll have to show me a lot more authority than you have now," Kellerman says.

"I will!" Rose shoots back, reaching for the phone.

The law, of course, is on the medical examiner's side. The president was murdered on a Dallas street, and unbelievably, killing a president was not a federal crime at the time unless it was committed on federal property, which wasn't the case here.[†] Also, since Texas

---

[*]At 1:00 a.m. the next morning at Bethesda Hospital, O'Donnell slipped into the room where Kennedy's body lay, removed the ring, and brought it back to Jackie (O'Donnell and Powers with McCarthy, *Johnny, We Hardly Knew Ye*, p.35; *New York Times*, December 5, 1963, p.32).

[†]One of the most prominent misconceptions that has been parroted by virtually everyone, including the Warren Commission, is that in 1963 it wasn't a federal crime to murder the president. "Murder of the president has never been covered by federal law," said the Warren Commission in 1964 (WR, p.454). "At that time

law required an inquest by a justice of the peace for all homicides, and then, if ordered—as it automatically would have been done in this case—an autopsy,[492] Rose has a legal obligation to Dallas County to make sure an autopsy is conducted. Telephone calls to the sheriff's office and police department assure him that he is right, that an inquest and autopsy are mandatory.

Ken O'Donnell and others in the presidential party, imagining the ordeal for the widow if she has to remain in Dallas for another day or two, take turns arguing with the medical examiner. This is not an ordinary homicide, but an assassinated president. He has been examined by doctors and will certainly undergo a federal-level autopsy on his return to Washington, D.C. Further delay will serve no purpose and could cause undue misery for his widow. And so on.

Dr. Rose concedes that he could legally release the body to a Texas justice of the peace functioning as a coroner, but without that, there's no way he will permit them to remove the body from his jurisdiction. The president's men start making phone calls to find an authority who can overrule him.[493]

At the Texas School Book Depository, police officers are conducting a roll call outside of Supervisor Bill Shelley's office, and collecting the names and addresses of the build-

---

it was not a federal crime to assassinate a president," said Chief Justice Earl Warren in his memoirs (Warren, *Memoirs*, p.355). Indeed, even FBI Director J. Edgar Hoover said that "it is not a federal crime to kill the president" (5 H 98, WCT, Hon. J. Edgar Hoover). For *almost* all practical intents and purposes, this is true, but the statement, technically, is not. Under Section 1111 of Title 18 of the U.S. Code, murder was, of course, a federal crime in 1963. And just as obviously there was no language in Title 18 that said, "However, if the victim of the murder is the president of the United States, then it's not a federal crime." Where the limitation came in is in subdivision (b) of Section 1111, which provided (and still does) that for there to be federal prosecutorial jurisdiction over any murder, it has to take place "within the special maritime and territorial jurisdiction of the United States," which the courts have held to be places owned, possessed, or controlled by the U.S. government (most importantly, the president's residence, the White House, but also, for example, federal buildings like the Pentagon, military installations, U.S. highways, national parks, islands like Palmyra in the Pacific that are U.S. possessions, etc.). Since a Dallas street is not a U.S. highway and would not qualify, there could not be a federal prosecution of Oswald for having killed Kennedy. It is highly anomalous that even in 1963, if it could have been shown that Oswald had entered into a conspiracy to murder the president, or even threatened harm to him, since Sections 372 and 871, respectively, of Title 18 contain no such territorial limitation, federal jurisdiction to prosecute Oswald for those separate offenses would have existed. But not for the actual act of murdering the president.

As a direct result of Kennedy's assassination, and pursuant to one of the recommendations of the Warren Commission (WR, pp.26, 455), this loophole in the federal law was plugged on August 28, 1965, when Congress enacted Section 1751 of Title 18 specifically making the assassination of a president (or president elect or vice president) murder under Section 1111, and conveying federal jurisdiction irrespective of where the killing occurred, even if on foreign soil. Section 1751(k) provides that "there is *extra*territorial jurisdiction over the conduct prohibited by this section." Also, anomalously, although the jurisdictional limitation wasn't removed for the president until 1965, in 1963 it already was a federal crime to murder (anywhere) federal judges, U.S. attorneys and marshals, and other "officers and employees of the United States." (18 USC §1114; WR, p.454)

Congressional efforts to make, without limitation, the assassination of a president a prosecutable federal crime (a House bill in 1901 and Senate bill in 1902 following the assassination of President McKinley in 1901, and a House bill in 1933 following the attempted assassination of President Roosevelt on February 15, 1933) failed to be enacted into law (WR, pp.454–455; H.R. 10386, 57th Cong., 1st sess., 1901; S. 3653, 57th Cong., 1st sess., 1902; H.R. 3896, 73rd Cong., 1st sess., 1933).

Attempted assassination is also covered under Section 1751, and the indictment of Charles Manson follower Lynette "Squeaky" Fromme for her attempted assassination of President Gerald Ford on September 5, 1975, in Sacramento, California, was the first under the new law. Fromme was subsequently convicted and is now serving a life sentence.

ing's employees. Superintendent Roy Truly notices that Oswald isn't among the dozen or so stockroom boys talking to the police. In fact, Truly hasn't seen Oswald since he and Officer Baker ran into him in the second-floor lunchroom right after the shots. That encounter may be the only reason Truly is thinking of him now.

"Have you seen Lee Oswald around lately?" Truly asks Shelley.

"No," Shelley replies.[494]

Truly approaches O. V. Campbell, the Book Depository vice president.

"I have a boy over here missing," Truly says. "I don't know whether to report it or not."

Truly thinks that another one or two boys are also missing,* but the only one who sticks in his mind is Oswald, if for no other reason than that he had seen Oswald on the second floor of the building (when almost all of his other employees were out on the street) just an hour or so earlier.

Truly calls down to the warehouse personnel office to get Oswald's telephone number, home address, and description from his employment application. He jots it all down, and hangs up. Deputy Chief Lumpkin is a few feet away.

"I've got a boy missing over here," Truly tells him, instinctively focusing in, again, only on Oswald. "I don't know whether it amounts to anything or not."

"Let's go up and tell Captain Fritz," Lumpkin says as the two head upstairs.[495] They find Captain Fritz on the sixth floor at the top of the stairs, standing with a group of officers and reporters. Lumpkin pulls Fritz aside to listen to Truly, who repeats his story and gives him Oswald's address and general description: age twenty-three (he was now twenty-four), five foot nine, about a hundred fifty pounds, light brown hair.[496]

1:33 p.m.

The large double classroom in the medical school, room 101–102, is jammed with noisy, excited reporters who have difficulty calming down when Malcolm Kilduff takes his place at the teacher's lectern. He starts to speak, then stops. "Excuse me, let me catch my breath." Kennedy has been dead for half an hour and everyone in the room knows it, but Kilduff still can't think of what to say or how to say it. He wonders whether he will be able to control his quivering voice. Finally, he begins, "President John F. Kennedy . . ."

"Hold it," someone calls, as cameras click. Kilduff starts over.

"President John F. Kennedy died at approximately one o'clock Central Standard Time today here in Dallas."

"Oh God!" a reporter blurts out.

Kilduff welcomes a moment of respite as the wire reporters rush out to find a telephone.

"He died of a gunshot wound in the brain," Kilduff continues. "I have no other details regarding the assassination of the president. Mrs. Kennedy was not hit. Governor Connally was not hit. The vice president was not hit."

---

*Actually, only one other of the boys was missing: Charles Douglas Givens (CE 705, 17 H 419; CE 1974, 23 H 873), who went to the corner of Main and Record (two blocks from the Depository) to watch the motorcade. When he returned to the Depository sometime after 12:40 p.m., police wouldn't let him back inside (7 H 382, 385–386, WCT Roy Sansom Truly; 6 H 355, WCT Charles Douglas Givens). Givens, who had a prior police record for narcotics violations, was spotted in the crowd an hour later by Dallas police lieutenant Jack Revill, who recognized Givens from his past dealings with him. Givens was subsequently taken to police headquarters, where he was questioned and gave a statement (5 H 35–36, WCT Jack Revill; 6 H 355, WCT Charles Douglas Givens; CE 2003, 24 H 210).

Reporters will discover Kilduff's error about the governor soon enough.

Tom Wicker, the *New York Times* White House reporter, starts to ask whether Johnson has been sworn in as president, but breaks down. Kilduff's voice also breaks as he tries to answer. Another correspondent asks, "Has the vice president taken the oath of office?"

"No," Kilduff says. "He has left."

The reporters demand a briefing by the attending doctors, and Kilduff, who hadn't thought of it, promises to see what he can do.[497]

1:34 p.m.

In the parking lot in back of the Texaco station, Captain Westbrook turns around and starts toward the Abundant Life Temple, a four-story brick church at the corner of Tenth and Crawford, located right behind the Texaco parking lot. But he sees it's already covered. Officer M. N. "Nick" McDonald was standing at the rear of the Temple and McDonald calls in to the radio dispatcher, "Send me a squad over here at Tenth and Crawford. Check out this church basement."[498]

1:35 p.m.

Dallas police officer Charles T. Walker drops a couple of newsmen off at the Tippit killing scene and drives off to comb the neighborhood. Turning onto southbound Denver, he spots a man, fitting the description of the suspect, running into the library a block ahead, at Jefferson and Marsalis. Walker punches the gas and grabs his radio mike, "He's in the library, Jefferson—East 500 block!"

The radio suddenly comes alive with excited chatter.

"What's the location, 223?" the dispatcher asks.

"Marsalis and Jefferson, in the library, I'm going around the back, get somebody around the front . . . Get 'em here fast!" Walker shouts as he wheels to the curb, tires screeching.

Police and sheriff deputies, including the officers about to search the church, scramble for their cars. Within a minute, the library is ground zero, surrounded by nearly every squad car in the area. Police feel certain they have the cop killer cornered.[499]

1:36 p.m.

Six blocks west of the library on Jefferson Boulevard, twenty-two-year-old Johnny C. Brewer, manager of Hardy's Shoe Store, listened to the president's arrival at Love Field and the motorcade on a little transistor radio, and has been riveted since the first vague reports of the shooting of the president were heard. From what he can gather, a policeman has also been shot, less than three-quarters of a mile away.[500] He's been hearing the periodic wail of sirens for nearly twenty minutes.

Now, Brewer can hear police sirens coming west on Jefferson, their wail growing so strong it sounds like it might land on his doorstep at any moment. Suddenly, a young man walking west on Jefferson steps into the lobby—a large recess, fifteen feet deep, between the sidewalk and the door of the shop, with display windows on either side. The fellow, wearing a brown sports shirt over a white T-shirt, his shirttail out, is behaving very strangely. Brewer is only about ten feet away, just beyond the display window, and is looking directly at his face. Brewer finds it quite unusual that with all the commotion going on outside, the man keeps his back to the street. His hair is messed up, he's breathing

heavily and looks like he's been running, and he also looks scared. Brewer thinks he recognizes him as a particular persnickety customer who once took an agonizingly long time
to make up his mind to purchase a cheap pair of black crepe-soled shoes.[501] (Police did
recover a pair of "black low quarter shoes, John Hardy Brand," from Oswald's Beckley
room on November 23, 1963.)[502]*

Just as the man stepped into the foyer, Brewer can see the approaching police cars make
a U-turn at Jefferson and Zangs, a few stores away, and head back east on Jefferson toward
the library, sirens screaming. The man in the foyer turns and looks over his right shoulder toward the receding police cars, then, seemingly after making sure they have gone by,
steps out of the foyer and continues west on Jefferson. The more Brewer thinks about it,
the more suspicious he becomes. About a half minute later, curiosity gets the better of
him, and Brewer steps out onto the sidewalk to see where this character is going. The
suspect is already fifty yards away, walking at a good clip, nearing the marquee of the Texas
Theater, which is showing a double-feature, *Cry of Battle* and *War Is Hell*.[503]

Julia E. Postal, the forty-seven-year-old ticket-taker, has been listening to the radio too.
Just before the Texas Theater opened for business at 12:45 p.m., her daughter called to
tell her that someone had shot the president, and she has been listening right there in the
box office ever since. Though most of the police cars had turned around, one continued
on, its siren blasting as it shot past the theater box office. John Callahan, the theater manager, who is standing next to Mrs. Postal, says, "Something's about to pop."

They both scramble out onto the sidewalk. The squad car looks like it's stopping up
the street. Callahan gets into his car at the curb to go see what's happening.[504]

Shoe store manager Johnny Brewer, on the sidewalk east of the theater, sees the suspicious man, "walking a little faster than usual," slip into the Texas Theater behind Postal's
back.[505] For Brewer, it's all adding up.

Postal watches her boss drive off, then turns to go back to the box office. Brewer is
standing there, having walked up from the shoe store. He asks her if the man that just
ducked into the theater had bought a ticket. "No, by golly, he didn't," she says looking
around, half expecting to see him. She saw the man out of the corner of her eye when she
walked out with Mr. Callahan.[506]

Brewer tells her the man's been acting suspiciously. He goes inside and checks with
concessionaire Warren "Butch" Burroughs, but he was busy stocking candy and didn't
see anyone come in. Brewer returns to the box office.[507]

"He *has* to be in there," Postal says. She tells him to go get Butch and have him help
check the exits, but don't tell him why because he's "kind of excitable." Brewer goes back
in and asks Burroughs to show him where the exits are. The concessionaire wants to know
why? Against Postal's advice, Brewer tells him he thought "the guy looked suspicious."[508]

The Texas Theater, an architecturally decorative structure built in 1932, was the very
first in a chain of theaters built by inventor Howard Hughes. Upon entering the theater
lobby from Jefferson Boulevard, patrons find themselves to the rear of the theater, where

---

*The Tippit murder occurred at approximately 1:12 p.m. and the murder scene at Tenth and Patton is not
even quite seven blocks from the shoe store and Texas Theater. Also, we know Oswald was running at least
part of the time after he shot Tippit, yet Oswald doesn't reach the shoe store until close to twenty to twenty-
five minutes later. Even given the somewhat circuitous path he must have taken to reach the shoe store area,
the likelihood is that although the area was swarming with police officers searching for him, Oswald succeeded,
along the way, in secreting himself from human view, where he most likely stayed hidden for several minutes
at a time.

a concession stand is set up. A staircase near the stand leads up to a spacious balcony above the main seating area. Another staircase at the far end of the lobby leads to the theater office. Being an L-shaped theater, from the concession stand a theater-goer can only enter the main seating area by walking farther into the lobby and turning right down one of four aisles. The main seating area in the middle of the theater has an aisle on each side of it, and smaller seating areas to the left and right have an aisle adjacent to the left and right walls. The seats descend downward in typical theater style toward a large movie screen rising above a narrow area ("stage") not large enough for live performances, though the theater was built during the vaudeville era. There are five (today, six) fire exits, one to the left of the stage, one at the far end of the lobby, two on the balcony level, and a fifth on the small floor above the balcony, where the projection room is. Four of the fire exits lead directly into an alley running parallel with Jefferson Boulevard.[509]

The flickering images of *War Is Hell* dance across the screen as Brewer and Burroughs check the lock bars on the two ground-floor exits. They are still down, meaning whoever ducked into the theater is still there.[510] There are twenty-four patrons in the theater who have purchased their ninety-cent tickets for the double-feature.[511]

1:38 p.m. (2:38 p.m. EST)

On CBS television, Walter Cronkite again repeats details of the shooting as he awaits official word on the president's death. Viewers can see two newsmen ripping fresh wire-copy from the Teletype machine in the background, then race over to the anchorman, and hand him the sheet. Cronkite slips on his heavy, dark-frame glasses and glances at the copy. Now, for the first time, without equivocation, Cronkite tells a waiting nation, "From Dallas, the flash apparently official, President Kennedy died at one o'clock Central Standard Time—two o'clock Eastern Standard Time—some thirty-eight minutes ago."

The words catch in his throat, and for a moment, the most respected news anchor in the business is about to lose his composure. Choking back tears, Cronkite clears his throat and continues, "Vice President Lyndon Johnson has left the hospital. We don't know to where he has proceeded. Presumably, he will be taking the oath of office and become the thirty-sixth president of the United States."[512] During a later break, Cronkite answered a network telephone and heard a snobbish-sounding woman caller say, "I just want to say that this is the worst possible taste to have that Walter Cronkite on the air with his crocodile tears when everybody knows that he spent all his time trying to get the president." The newsman shot back, "Madam, *this* is Walter Cronkite and you're a goddamned idiot!" and slammed the phone down so hard he thought for a moment he had damaged it.[513]

With the news of the president's death, men and women across the country "sobbed in the streets of the cities and did not have to explain why," historian Theodore White wrote. "Not until he was dead and all men knew he would never again point his forefinger down from the platform in speaking to them, never pause before lancing with his wit the balloon of an untidy question, did Americans know how much light the young president had given their own lives—and how he had touched them."[514] Comedian Bob Hope wasn't trying to be funny when he said, "The lights had blown out in Camelot and the whole nation was stumbling around in the dark."[515] The *New York Times'* Tom Wicker wrote, "People were unbelieving, afraid . . . desperately unsure of what would happen next. The world, it seemed, was a dark and malignant place; the chill of the unknown shivered across the nation."[516]

Many in America, a nation of 190 million people, "simply stood, stupefied, no longer listening to the staccato voices that sounded unceasingly on the radios. Church bells tolled and the churches began to fill . . . Strangers spoke to each other, seeking surcease," wrote Relman Morin, a Pulitzer Prize–winning correspondent who covered the assassination for Associated Press and was a personal friend of the president's. In Boston, he continued, "the Boston Symphony broke off a Handel concert to play a funeral march by Beethoven. The gong sounded in the New York Stock Exchange, suspending trading. Hundreds of football games to have been played Saturday were postponed. Race tracks closed . . . Sessions in the United Nations came to a halt . . . Television and radio networks announced that they were withdrawing all entertainment programs and commercials from their schedules to devote full time to . . . the assassination; normal programming would not be resumed until after the funeral."[517]

What happened in New York City is a microcosm of the country as a whole. The *New York Times* reported,

> The cry rang across the city, echoing again and again: "Is it true?" Another cry quickly took its place as the news of the death of President Kennedy swept with sudden impact: "My God!" . . . In all parts of the five boroughs, motorists pulled up their cars and sat hunched over their dashboard radios . . . Hundreds of thousands reached for so many telephones that the system blacked out and operators had to refuse calls . . . Uptown, midtown, downtown, work in offices came to an abrupt halt . . . The biggest city in the nation turned into something of a ghost town. All Broadway theaters and all musical events . . . were cancelled . . . One common scene was the tight grasp of one's hand on another's arm as they discussed the assassination . . . Those who had no one familiar at hand walked up to strangers . . . The grief and the acts of mourning knew no special group, no particular section of the city . . . The sorrow and shock were unfolded in the human vignette, the collection of individuals who stared as though in a trance from their subway seats, their stools at luncheon counters, their chairs near television sets . . . A postman . . . encountered many housewives who wept as they told him the news. They talked about it just as if they had lost their son or daughter. . . . A dentist, weeping, said: "I can't work. I've sent two patients home and I've closed my office." . . . A bartender said: "Everybody feels dead, real dead." . . . A department store saleswoman declared: "I would do anything to bring him back." . . . As dusk came, automatic devices turned on the huge, gaudy signs that normally blot out the night in Times Square. Then, one by one, the lights blinked out, turning the great carnival strip into what was almost a mourning band on the city's sleeve.[518]*

It was not too different in most foreign countries, people weeping in the streets of the world's great capitals—Berlin, London, Paris, Rome. Even peoples who did not under-

---

*The almost reflexive belief was that a southern segregationist had shot the president. "A lawyer in Riverdale commented: 'We have allowed certain factions to work up such furor throughout the South with fanatic criticism [of Kennedy] that a demented person can feel confident that such atrocious action is justifiable' " (*New York Times*, November 23, 1963, p.5).

The terrible irony is that the man who killed the president was not the product of that segment of the South that despised the president for championing civil rights for the black population, but someone who admired the president for it.

stand a word of English that Kennedy spoke had sensed that he was special, and he some-how touched the heart of these millions. "To them, Kennedy symbolized youth, new ideas, a fresh approach, the New Generation. Indeed, he had sounded that chord himself in his Inaugural Address. 'Let the word go forth from this time and place, to friend and foe alike, that the torch has been passed to a new generation of Americans, born in this century, tem-pered by war, disciplined by a hard and bitter peace.'" Kennedy had come to power after the greatest and most destructive war ever, "only to be followed by the specter of an even greater war in which new weapons could decimate the human race." Because of his lead-ership, soaring oratory, and innate charisma, millions throughout the planet felt that a peaceful resolution to the world's problems was more likely with him leading the way. Peo-ple somehow believed in the possibilities of his vision of "a new world . . . where the strong are just, and the weak secure and the peace preserved . . . Let us begin."

"That young man," Kennedy's cold-war counterpart, Soviet premier Nikita S. Khrushchev, reminisced in sorrow, without the need to say another word. West Berlin mayor Willy Brandt said, "A flame went out for all those who had hoped for a just peace and a better life."[*] Eighty-nine-year-old Winston Churchill, hearing the news in Lon-don while peering at his TV set with his Clementine, said, "The loss to the United States and to the world is incalculable." Around the world, "groups divided by deep ideologi-cal chasms found common cause in mourning John F. Kennedy . . . For an hour, at least, he drew men together in universal mourning."[519] In Latin America, grief was pervasive. Brazilian president João Goulart declared three days of official mourning and canceled all of his official engagements. Chilean president Jorge Alessandri Rodriguez declared national mourning, and radio stations replaced all programs with funeral music. Rómulo Betancourt, president of Venezuela, attempting to read to newsmen the message of con-dolences he had sent to Washington, broke into tears and was unable to go on.[520]

But if one were to think that grief over Kennedy's death was universal, they would be wrong. "An Oklahoma City physician," author William Manchester writes, "beamed at a grief-stricken visitor and said, 'God, I hope they got Jackie [too].' In a small Con-necticut city a doctor called ecstatically across Main Street—to an internist who wor-shiped Kennedy—'The joy ride's over. This is one deal Papa Joe can't fix.' A woman visiting Amarillo, the second most radical city in Texas [after Dallas], was lunching in the restaurant adjacent to her motel when a score of rejoicing students burst in from a high school directly across the street. 'Hey, great, JFK's croaked!' one shouted with fla-grant delight, and the woman, leaving as rapidly as she could, noticed that several din-ers were smiling back at the boy. In Dallas itself a man whooped and tossed his expensive Stetson in the air, and it was in a wealthy Dallas suburb that the pupils of a fourth-grade class, told that the President of the United States had been murdered in their city, burst into spontaneous applause."[521] Similarly, in the fifth grade of a private school in New Orleans, the teacher was called out of the room by another fifth-grade

---

[*]On the evening of Monday, November 25, 1963, a quarter of a million West Berliners crowded into newly dedicated John F. Kennedy Square, where just five months earlier Kennedy gave his famous "Ich bin ein Berliner" (I am a Berliner) speech, to mourn Kennedy's death, thousands openly crying. The Associated Press reported that "never in memory has this tortured city grieved more than in the last four days since the death of the President." (*Dallas Morning News*, November 26, 1963, p.16)

Earlier on Monday the *Telegraph*, a conservative London paper, said that "few of the 35 American Presi-dents have touched the minds and hearts of British people as have Abraham Lincoln, Franklin Roosevelt and John Kennedy." The paper opened a fund drive to build a statue of Kennedy in London with a contribution of one thousand pounds. (*Dallas Morning News*, November 26, 1963, p.15)

teacher to listen to a transistor radio bearing the news. When he returned to his class to announce that Kennedy had been shot and killed, spontaneously the pupils cheered and applauded—one girl, the exception, cried.[522]

Because of JFK's open support for civil rights for the nation's blacks, as indicated, many in the South had detested him. And when news of the shooting and later the death of the president became known, although most in the South—including those like the former Birmingham police commissioner T. Eugene "Bull" Connor, and John Birch Society founder Robert W. Welch Jr., who opposed Kennedy's civil rights policies—expressed their profound grief over the assassination, some southern newspapers received anonymous, jeering telephone calls: "So they shot the nigger lover. Good for whoever did it." "He asked for it and I'm damned glad he got it . . . trying to ram the damn niggers down our throats."[523] Radio also heard from the racial bigots. Before the announcer cut him off, a man who had called a station in Atlanta got in his belief that "any white man who did what [Kennedy] did for niggers should be shot."[524] And it wasn't just in the South. A young man wearing a swastika on his left arm walked around the state capitol in Madison, Wisconsin, proclaiming that Kennedy's death was "a miracle for the white race" and telling bystanders he was "celebrating."[525]*

Ralph Emerson McGill, publisher of the Atlanta, Georgia, *Constitution*, wrote of the antipathy for Kennedy before his death that spilled over, among some, to his demise: "There were businessmen who, in a time when profits were at an all-time high and the domestic economy booming, nonetheless could speak only in hatred of 'the Kennedys.' There were evangelists who declared the President to be an anti-Christ, an enemy of God and religion. This hatred could focus on almost anything the President proposed. When he asked for legislation for medical aid for the aged, for example, there were doctors who succumbed to the fever of national unreason and began abusing the President. In locker rooms and at cocktail parties, luncheons and dinners, it became a sort of game to tell vulgar and shabby jokes about the President, his wife and his family. Most of these were repeats of stories in vogue at the time Franklin D. and Eleanor Roosevelt were in the White House."[526]†

In Irving, Texas, Marina Oswald and Ruth Paine are sitting side by side on the sofa watching the television coverage when they hear the news.

"What a terrible thing for Mrs. Kennedy," Marina sighs, "and for the children to be left without a father." Ruth walks about the room crying, while Marina is too stunned to cry, although she feels as though her blood has "stopped running."[527]

---

*The venom was flying both ways. Republican Senator John Tower of Texas, regarded as a right-wing conservative, had always been highly critical of Kennedy. When he was informed at a Republican conference in St. Louis that his office in Washington had received about a dozen anonymous and threatening phone calls and a number of similar telegrams, he arranged to have his wife and three daughters stay at the home of friends in Maryland until he returned to the capital. Republican Representative Bruce Alger of Dallas was also reported to have received a number of threatening phone calls and telegrams. (*New York Times*, November 23, 1963, p.7)

†One such story about Roosevelt became a favorite of Roosevelt's, and he delighted in telling it to friendly Democratic audiences. It seems there was a wealthy businessman commuting from heavily Republican Westchester County in New York who would hand the newsboy at the train station a dime every morning for the *New York Times*, glance at the front page, then hand the paper back as he rushed out the door to catch his train. Finally, one day, the newsboy, unable to control his curiosity any longer, asked the man why he always only looked at the front page.

"I'm interested in an obituary," the man said.

"But the obituaries are on the back pages of the paper, and you never look at them," the newsboy retorted.

"Son," the man said, "the son of a bitch I'm interested in will be on page one."

In Oak Cliff, police order everyone out of the library at Marsalis and Jefferson, hands high. Officer Walker points out the man he saw run in—Adrian Hamby, a nineteen-year-old Arlington State University student who had dashed into the library, where he worked part-time as a page, to tell friends that the president had been shot. Hamby is terrified as the cops realize the truth. A disappointed Sergeant Owens informs the dispatcher, "It was the wrong man."[528]

1:39 p.m. (2:39 p.m. EST)

The FBI dispatches its first Teletype, from Director Hoover, to all fifty-five of its field offices. Stamped "Urgent" it reads:

> All offices immediately contact all informants, security, racial and criminal, as well as other sources, for information bearing on assassination of President Kennedy. All offices immediately establish whereabouts of bombing suspects, all known Klan and hate group members, known racial extremists, and any other individuals who on the basis of information available in your files may possibly have been involved.[529]

Meanwhile, at Love Field, because he had been alerted to prepare Air Force One for immediate takeoff if necessary, the pilot, Colonel James Swindal, had had the ground air-conditioner disconnected, and the interior of Air Force One is hot and stuffy.[530] Since the plane's own air-conditioning works only when the engines are running, the interior temperature continues to rise slowly but steadily. The shades have been drawn (Agent Youngblood fears a sniper on the roof of the terminal building), the doors locked, and a Secret Service sentinel posted at each one. More agents ring the aircraft on the ground. The Dallas police are patrolling both inside and outside the terminal. Some of them are checking the departure gates for every youngish man who comes close to meeting the broadcast descriptions of the assassin.[531]

Johnson could have left Dallas three-quarters of an hour ago, but feeling, he said, a "sharp, painful, and bitter concern and solicitude for Mrs. Kennedy," he resolves not to leave without the president's widow, knowing that she would not leave without her husband's body.[532]

He is also anxious to take the oath of office as soon as possible. Johnson's aides and the congressmen present aren't quite sure of the procedure. Two of the congressmen, Jack Brooks and Albert Thomas, are in favor of doing it immediately. The third, Thornberry, advises waiting until they get to Washington. No one is clear on the law as mandated by the Constitution, and no one can think where the actual text of the oath might be found. The steadily rising heat in the stateroom* makes clear thought increasingly difficult. The men loosen their ties, open their shirt collars, and fan themselves with papers. The question of how to dramatize the presidential succession is more than symbolic—there is already news of a panic on Wall Street that has wiped out eleven billion dollars of stock values in the little more than an hour since the shooting.

Johnson goes into the bedroom of the presidential cabin to make private phone calls. He calls Robert Kennedy at his home in Virginia. Relations between the two men have

---

*The presidential cabin located toward the rear of the plane consisted of three rooms: the stateroom—the president's "office" on the plane—and an adjacent bedroom and bathroom.

always been frosty. Johnson offers Kennedy words of condolence, and they briefly discuss what is known and what remains unknown about the assassination. The murder, he says, "might be part of a worldwide plot." Kennedy is unresponsive. He doesn't understand what Johnson is talking about.

"A lot of people down here think I should be sworn in right away," Johnson says, moving closer to the point of the call. "Do you have any objection to that?"

Kennedy is stunned by the question. It has only been an hour since his brother was shot and he doesn't see what the rush is. Johnson forges ahead.

"Who could swear me in?" he asks.

Bobby is in a daze. The events are swirling too fast. He'd like his brother's body to be returned to Washington before Johnson becomes the new president, but he decides that his feelings are all personal.

"I'll be glad to find out," he tells Johnson. "I'll call you back."[533]

Johnson then calls a number of political friends in Dallas, finding few of them in their offices. He is particularly anxious to reach federal district judge Sarah Hughes, an old friend and political protégée, on the assumption that she might be able to administer the oath. Judge Hughes is contacted by phone and she agrees to do so.[534]

Youngblood, national security uppermost in his mind, hates the idea of remaining parked on the apron at Love Field any longer than necessary. He thinks there are several people on board the plane who can administer the oath—anyone who himself has taken an oath of office, even a Secret Service agent, for example—but he has to wait while Johnson makes a few more calls to Washington, one to his chief aide, Walter Jenkins, another to McGeorge Bundy.[535] Neither of them can think where to find the exact text of the oath. Meanwhile, Robert Kennedy has consulted Assistant Attorney General Nicholas Katzenbach, who finds it easily—in the Constitution itself, Article II, Section 1 [8]. Katzenbach also resolves the question of who is legally empowered to administer the oath—anyone who can take a sworn statement under state or federal laws. Even a justice of the peace will do. Kennedy calls Johnson back with the information, and tells Johnson that the oath should be administered immediately, before taking off for Washington.[536]

At Tenth and Patton, police question Barbara and Virginia Davis. Domingo Benavides and Sam Guinyard are nearby as the two young women describe how the gunman ran across their front walk, shaking shells from his revolver into his hand. It doesn't take long for Benavides to find one of them, near the bushes at the corner of the house. He picks it up in his hand before he thinks that police might check for fingerprints. He drops it, picks it up again with a twig, and puts it into an empty Winston cigarette package. A minute later, he finds a second cartridge shell in a bush. He turns them over to Officer Joe Poe, standing nearby.[537]

1:41 p.m.
Sergeant Gerald Hill takes Patrolman Poe's squad car back to the scene and hands him the keys. Poe shows the sergeant a Winston cigarette package containing the two spent cartridge casings found by Benavides.[538] Hill tells the patrolman to turn them over to the crime lab and radioes the police dispatcher.

"The shells at the scene indicate that the suspect is armed with an automatic thirty-eight, rather than a pistol," Hill informs him, unaware that eyewitnesses saw the gunman manually removing the spent shells.[539] Police are reconverging on the Tippit murder scene after the false alarm at the Jefferson Branch Library when a civilian witness at the scene gives Hill information that he immediately radios in to the channel 2 dispatcher: "A witness reports that he [the gunman] last was seen in the Abundant Life Temple . . . We are fixing to go in and shake it down."[540] (If Hill had called into channel 1, the dispatcher would have told him the church had been checked out just seven minutes earlier by Officer M. N. McDonald.) Two women emerge from inside the church and tell Hill they are employees. He asks them if they had seen anybody enter the church. They say no, nobody entered the church but invite him and his people to go inside and check for themselves,[541] which the police do,[542] finding no one hiding inside.

At the Tippit murder scene, Captain Westbrook and Sergeant Owens question Mrs. Markham to learn exactly what happened before the shooting. She describes how the gunman seemed to lean on the passenger side of the squad car when he spoke to the officer inside. Crime-lab sergeant W. E. "Pete" Barnes arrives and Westbrook orders him to dust the right passenger side of the car for fingerprints.[543] Just below the top part of the right passenger door and also on the right front fender, Barnes finds some smudged prints.[544]*

Nearby, Sergeant Richard D. Stringer contacts the channel 2 dispatcher.

"Could you pass this to someone. The jacket the suspect was wearing over here on Jefferson in this shooting bears the laundry tag with the letter B 9738. See if there is a way you can check this laundry tag."[545]

1:44 p.m.

Johnny Brewer and Butch Burroughs come out to the box office. They tell Julia Postal that it was too dark to see anything, but they think the man is still inside.[546]

"I'm going to call the police," Postal tells Brewer. "You and Butch get on each of the exit doors and stay there.[547]

1:46 p.m.

Patrolman Bill Anglin, a close friend and neighbor of the slain officer, leans against his own squad car at Tenth and Patton. He still can't believe it's true. Yesterday afternoon he and Tippit had installed a new wheel bearing on J. D.'s 1953 Ford. Just a couple of hours ago the two of them knocked off for coffee at the Rebel Drive-In, as they often did. Now, J. D. was dead. For Anglin, it's nothing short of a nightmare.[548]

---

*Barnes told the Warren Commission that after he took the prints he had "lifted" from the right side of Tippit's car back to the crime lab, "no legible prints were found" (7 H 274). Contrary to popular belief, this is typical. In working with the Los Angeles Police Department when I was with the Los Angeles district attorney's office, I learned that approximately only 30 percent of the times that fingerprint experts are dispatched to the scene of a crime are they able to secure clear, readable, latent prints belonging to anyone. In most cases the prints found are just too fragmentary, smudged (the Tippit car), or superimposed with other prints to be used for comparison with a fingerprint exemplar of someone (here, Oswald) taken at a police station. (To compound the problem in the Tippit case, Barnes testified that the exterior surface of Tippit's car was "dirty," making it much more difficult to lift a readable print.) Indeed, even in those cases where readable prints are secured, only 10 percent of the time do those prints match up to those of a suspect. The rest belong either to the victim or to some third party. A simple equation: 10 percent of 30 percent equals 3 percent. Hence, in only 3 percent of the times that fingerprint experts go to a crime scene are they able to secure the latent prints of the accused. Ninety-seven percent of the time they are unsuccessful. As a prosecutor I would present this "negative fingerprint testimony" from my expert, and I found it to be a powerful statistical rebuttal to the common defense argument that since the defendant's prints were not found at the scene, he was never there.

The police dispatcher is trying to contact Sergeant Owens, who Anglin can see is engrossed in conversation with homicide detective James R. Leavelle. Officer Anglin reaches through the car window and picks up the radio mike. "I'm here at [Unit] 19's [Owens] location. Message for him?"

"Ten-four. Have information that a suspect just went in the Texas Theater on West Jefferson," the dispatcher says. "Suppose to be hiding in the balcony."[549]

Anglin hangs up the transmitter and hollers across the street, "It's just come over the radio that they've got a suspicious person in the Texas Theater!"[550]

Everyone sprints for their vehicles, adrenaline pumping.

The Texas Theater, on Jefferson Boulevard, is about six-tenths of a mile from where Tippit was shot. In less than two minutes, every police car in the area descends on the theater's two-dozen or so unsuspecting patrons.

1:48 p.m.

Julia Postal punches the intercom in the box office and tells the projectionist that she has called the police. He wonders whether he should cut the film off, and she says, "No, let's wait until they get here."[551]

It seems the minute she hangs up the intercom, the place is swarming with squad cars, police officers, plainclothesmen, and deputy sheriffs—armed to the teeth.

"Watch him! He's armed!" one of them shouts.

"I'll get that son of a bitch if he's in there," another replies.[552]

Some of the officers remain outside trying to control the excited crowd materializing from nowhere, a real mob scene.[553] Inside the theater, officers order the theater staff to turn up the house lights.[554]

Behind the stage Johnny Brewer is standing near the curtains that separate the audience and the exit door on the left side of the screen. When the house lights come up, he steps to the curtain and scans the astonished audience. There he is—the man he saw slip into the theater. He's sitting in the center section, six or seven rows from the back of the theater. No sooner do the lights come up than the man stands up, and scoots to the aisle to his right. Police are pouring into the lobby. The suspect turns around and sits back down,[555] this time in the third row from the back. Suddenly, Brewer hears someone rattling the exit door from the outside. The shoe store manager pushes the door open and is immediately grabbed by two officers as he is exiting. The alley is crawling with cops, some up on the theater's fire escape.[556]

Officer Thomas A. Hutson puts a gun into Brewer's stomach. "Put your hands up and don't make a move." Brewer is shaking.

"I'm not the one," he stammers. "I just came back to open the door for you. I work up the street. There's a guy inside that I was suspicious of."

The officer can see that Brewer's clothing—sport coat and tie—is different from the description of the suspect.

"Is he still there?" Hutson asks.

"Yes. I just seen him," Brewer tells him, and leads the lawmen into the theater.[557]

1:50 p.m.

Patrolmen M. N. "Nick" McDonald, C. T. Walker, Ray Hawkins, and Thomas Hutson gather around Brewer as he points out the man in the brown shirt sitting in the main section of the theater on the ground floor, three rows from the back, fifth seat over. From the orientation of the stage looking out toward the audience, McDonald and Walker step out from behind the curtain and walk up the left center aisle and approach two men seated near the front—a diversionary tactic—and order them to their feet. They search them for weapons, all the while keeping an eye on the man in the brown sport shirt. McDonald then walks out of the row to the right center aisle and advances up the aisle. Officers Walker, Hawkins, and Hutson are shadowing McDonald from the left center aisle—the suspect between them. McDonald feigns interest in a man and woman seated across the aisle from the man in the brown shirt, but just as he gets even with him, McDonald spins and faces the suspect.[558]*

"Get on your feet," McDonald orders.

The man obeys and starts to raise his hands. Officers Walker, Hawkins, and Hutson are moving toward him from the opposite side. McDonald reaches for the suspect's waist to check for a weapon.

"Well, it's all over now," the suspect says in a tone of resignation. In a flash, the man cocks his left fist and slugs McDonald between the eyes, knocking his cap off and forcing him backward into the seats. McDonald quickly recovers and swings back as they topple into the seats, McDonald shouting out, "I've got him," though they end up with the man on top of McDonald.[559]

Officers Hutson, Walker, and Hawkins rush in from the other side. Nick McDonald is trying to push the suspect off, but he's holding Nick down with his left hand and reaching for something in his waistband with the other hand. Hutson, in the row behind, reaches over the seats, wraps his right arm around the suspect's neck and yanks him back until he's stretched over the top of the seat. Officer Walker grabs the suspect's left arm and struggles to hold on to it. McDonald jumps forward and grabs the man's right hand, which is trying to pull a revolver out of his beltline. For a second or two, McDonald keeps the suspect from getting the gun out, but then it springs free.

"Look out! He's got a gun!" someone yells.

McDonald, on the receiving end of the barrel, quickly grabs the cylinder of the revolver with his left hand to keep it from turning and firing a bullet. The suspect thrashes as the gun waves in McDonald's direction.[560]

The officers are in a frenzy, a half-dozen hands desperately trying to get the damn gun out of the man's hand.

*The Warren Commission never pinned down what row or seat Oswald was in, and the arresting officers were all in disagreement. McDonald said Oswald was in the "second seat" over from the "right center aisle" and mentions no row (3 H 299); Hawkins said "three or four" seats over from the right center aisle as you face the screen, and "three or four rows from the back" (7 H 93); Walker: "fourth or fifth" row from the back, "third seat" in from where McDonald was (7 H 38–39); Captain W. R. Westbrook: "third or fourth row from the back," seated "in the middle" (7 H 112; see also Sneed, *No More Silence*, p.314). Hutson not only seemed to be the most precise, but on a trip I took to Dallas on September 22, 2004, Ken Holmes, a Dallas student of the assassination with an emphasis on historical detail, said he was very confident, from his studies, where Oswald was seated in the theater, and he pointed out the seat to me. In Hutson's December 3, 1963, report to Chief Curry, Hutson said that Oswald was "sitting in the third row from the back" in the "fifth seat" of "the center section," which he later told the Warren Commission. In his Commission testimony, however, he didn't say fifth seat from what side, but in his report to Curry he did. It was "the fifth seat north of the south aisle [from the stage looking toward the audience, the north aisle is on one's right, the south aisle to one's left] of the center section." (Report from Officer T. A. Hutson to J. E. Curry, Chief of Police, December 3, 1963, p.1; 7 H 31, WCT Thomas Alexander Hutson) That's the same seat Holmes pointed out to me. Holmes, a member of the Dallas Historical Society, has run a popular tour of JFK assassination sites for several years under the name Southwestern Historical Inc.

"Let go of the gun!" a cop commands.

"I can't," the suspect says.[561]

Punches fly as an officer slams the butt of a shotgun against the back of the suspect's head. McDonald gets his right hand on the butt of the pistol and starts to rip it out of the man's hand. Just before he jerks it free, McDonald hears what he believes to be the snap of the hammer and feels a sting to the fleshy web of skin between his thumb and forefinger. The gun continues across his left cheek, leaving behind a four-inch scratch, from which blood trickles.[562]

Captain Westbrook can't quite see what's happening. "Has somebody got the gun?" he yells out. McDonald holds the gun out toward the aisle, where Detective Bob Carroll grabs it, saying, "I've got it!"[563]

Officer Walker pulls the suspect's left arm around and Officer Hawkins snaps handcuffs on him.

"Don't hit me anymore. I am not resisting arrest!" the suspect shouts, loud enough for nearby patrons to hear him. "I want to complain of police brutality!"

Captain Westbrook, who's just heard Mrs. Markham tell him how Tippit's killer shot him down like a dog, at point-blank range, can't believe the gall of the man. Westbrook pushes his way into the aisle in front of the suspect and looks him right in the face—less than ten inches away.

"What's your name?" Westbrook asks.

The suspect is silent.

"Get him out of here!" Westbrook shouts above the commotion.[564]

The officers on the suspect's right start to pull him toward the center aisle, but the officers on the left are pulling in the opposite direction—inadvertently stretching the gunman between them.

"They're violating my civil rights!" the suspect screams.

FBI agent Robert M. Barrett, standing nearby, can only shake his head. They're not violating anything, he thinks to himself. Barrett has been observing the police actions since his arrival at the Book Depository nearly an hour ago. As the FBI agent who handles civil rights violations, Barrett knows that he'll have to write a report on what he's just witnessed.[565]

A WFAA-TV cameraman is in the lobby filming the suspect as police hustle him toward the front entrance. The suspect uses the opportunity to berate the police as he passes: "I want my lawyer. I know my rights. Typical police brutality. Why are you doing this to me?"[566]

Julia Postal, though safe in her box office, is shaking. She's never seen a mob like the one on the sidewalk in front of the theater. Since police stormed into the theater, word has spread among the crowd that they've cornered the president's killer. Few know that a police officer was shot nearby—not even Mrs. Postal.[567]

The doors to the theater are slammed open as a wedge of officers bursts into the sunlight. The suspect shuts up quickly when he sees the size of the crowd on the sidewalk in front of the theater—maybe a hundred people. A half-dozen uniformed officers and several deputy sheriffs are doing their best to prevent a lynching by holding the crowd back and clearing a passage to an unmarked police car at curbside, but the crowd is ugly.

"That's him!" they shout as he comes into view. "Murderer! Kill the son of a bitch! Hang him! Give him to us, we'll kill him!"

The flying wedge just keeps moving, pushing the suspect toward the waiting squad car, its back door open. The suspect complains that the handcuffs are too tight. Detective Paul Bentley, on the suspect's left, cigar stub firmly clenched between his teeth, isn't too sympathetic, thinking to himself that Oswald was in much better shape than Tippit was. He reaches back and tightens the cuffs even more. They're actually a little loose, he later recalls, and he doesn't want to take any chances.[568]

An officer squeezes into the box office to use the phone. Mrs. Postal hears him say, "I think we have got our man on both accounts."

"What two accounts?" Postal asks as he hangs up.

The shootings of both the president and Officer Tippit, the officer tells her. Mrs. Postal is shocked. She knew J. D. Tippit. He had worked part-time at the theater on Friday and Saturday nights a number of years ago.[569]

1:52 p.m.

Police push the suspect into the backseat of the four-door sedan, where he's sandwiched between Officer C. T. Walker on the right and Detective Paul Bentley on the left. Three officers pile into the front seat, Detective Kenneth E. Lyons on the right, Sergeant Gerald Hill in the middle, and the driver, Detective Bob Carroll. As Carroll slides behind the steering wheel, he hands a .38 caliber snub-nosed revolver to Hill.

"Is this yours?" Hill asks.

"No, it's the suspect's," Carroll replies.

Hill snaps the cylinder open and sees that it's fully loaded. He grabs the radio transmitter as the car pulls away from the curb.[570] "Suspect on the shooting of the police officer is apprehended. En route to the station," he announces.

"Ten-four. At the Texas Theater?" the dispatcher asks.

"Caught him on the lower floor of the Texas Theater after a fight," Hill confirms.[571]

The suspect is asked his name, but the guy is dead silent.

"Where do you live?" someone asks. Again, nothing.

"Why don't you see if he has any identification?" Hill asks Bentley.

The detective reaches down and feels the suspect's left hip pocket. There's a wallet in it. As Bentley pulls it out, the suspect breaks his silence.

"What is this all about? I know my rights. I don't know why you are treating me like this. Why am I being arrested? The only thing I've done is carry a pistol in a movie," he says.[572]

One of the cops turns to the suspect. "Sir, you've done a lot more. You have killed a policeman."

"Police officer been killed?" the suspect asks innocently.

The cops remain silent, as the squad car rolls along.

"I hear they burn for murder," the suspect adds.

"You might find out," Officer Walker replies.

"Well, they say it just takes a second to die," the suspect answers coolly.[573]

Detective Bentley flips through the billfold and finds a library card.

"Lee Oswald," Bentley calls out from the backseat. In a moment, Bentley thumbs across another name in the wallet—A. J. Hidell. He asks the prisoner which of the two names is his real name, but Oswald is silent.

"I guess we're going to have to wait until we get to the station to find out who he really is," someone remarks.

One thing they all notice is that Lee Harvey Oswald is showing absolutely no emotion.[574]

1:55 p.m.
FBI special agent Gordon Shanklin telephones Alan Belmont in Washington again.

"Dallas police have captured the man who is believed to have shot the policeman," he tells Belmont, "and police think he may be the man who killed the president. They're en route to police headquarters right now. I'll report as soon as I have the facts."

Belmont prepares a Teletype and takes it in to FBI Director Hoover.[575]

1:58 p.m.
As the unmarked squad car carrying Lee Oswald pulls into the basement garage of City Hall, a gray stone structure in downtown Dallas where police headquarters are located, Sergeant Hill tells Oswald that there will be reporters, photographers, and cameramen waiting there, but he doesn't have to speak to them. They will hold him in such a way that he can turn his head down and away from the cameras.

"Why should I hide my face?" Oswald responds. "I haven't done anything to be ashamed of."[576]

The arresting officers form their wedge around the suspect and rush him into the building. Sure enough, photographers and cameramen are there to film the event. The officers take Oswald to a waiting elevator for the ride up to the Homicide and Robbery Bureau on the third floor.[577]

2:00 p.m.
At the sheriff's office, *Dallas Morning News* reporter Harry McCormick, sidetracked in his quest to locate Secret Service agent Forrest Sorrels, telephones his office to report that he's heard a man was captured at the Texas Theater. The paper already has the news. He hangs up the telephone and spots his initial quarry, Agent Sorrels, standing in a nearby office.[578]

"Forrest, I have something over here you ought to know about," McCormick tells him.

"What have you got?" Sorrels says.

"I have a man who got pictures of this whole thing," McCormick answers.

"Let's go see him," Sorrels replies.

The two men make there way over to the Dal-Tex Building, directly across the street from the Book Depository, and up to the office of dress manufacturer Abraham Zapruder. There are already a few magazine and newspaper representatives there, McCormick's worst fear. Zapruder is a basket case. His business partner, Erwin Schwartz, stands nearby, unable to help.

"I don't know how in the world I managed to take those pictures," Zapruder whimpers. "I was down there taking the thing and—my God, I saw the man's brains come out of his head."[579]

"Mr. Zapruder, I wonder if it would be possible for us to get a copy of those films," Sorrels asks politely. "Please understand that it would be strictly for the official use of the Secret Service."

Zapruder was already expecting to sell the film for as high a price as he could get, and agreed to Sorrels's request with the understanding that it not be shown or given to any newspapers or magazines. McCormick, ever mindful of a scoop for his paper, suggested that the *Dallas Morning News*, just three blocks away, might be able to develop the film for them. The men agree and Zapruder removes the camera from a small office safe, where he put it upon his return to the office. Sorrels, McCormick, Zapruder, and Schwartz hurry down to the street below, where the Secret Service agent commandeers a Dallas police car.

"Take us to the *Dallas Morning News* building immediately," Sorrels says.[580]

Back at the Book Depository, crime-lab technicians are focused on completing the evidence-gathering process. It will be several more hours before they finish dusting the stacks of boxes in the sniper's nest for fingerprints, and combing the sixth floor for possible additional evidence. Word passes quickly that the suspect in the murder of Officer J. D. Tippit has been arrested in Oak Cliff, but no name is given. Captain Fritz, still concentrating on the murder of Kennedy, instructs Detectives Sims and Boyd to come with him, he wants to go out to Irving and check on this missing employee named Oswald. The three men head downstairs and are out in front of the Depository when an officer tells Captain Fritz that Sheriff Decker would like to see him at his office, and he proceeds to Decker's office a block away at the corner of Main and Houston for a conference.[581]

2:02 p.m.
Homicide detective C. W. Brown is taking an affidavit from Book Depository foreman Bill Shelley in a small interrogation room inside the Homicide and Robbery office when the arresting officers bring Oswald in. Mr. Shelley looks up at the man in custody and remarks to Detective Brown, "He works for us. I'm his supervisor."[582]

Detectives Richard S. Stovall and Guy F. Rose begin to question Oswald in the interrogation room as Brown takes Shelley to another room to complete Shelley's affidavit. When they ask him his name, Oswald replies, "Hidell." Finding two identifications in his billfold, one card saying Hidell and the other Lee Oswald, Rose asks him which of the two is his correct name and Oswald replies, "You find out," but later gives the officers his real name.[583]

In the outer office, Sergeant Hill is showing Oswald's pistol to newsmen. In a corner, Detective Brown finishes taking the statement from Bill Shelley. The telephone rings. It's Captain Fritz calling from the sheriff's office. Brown tells him that the officers just brought in a suspect for the shooting of the police officer and how Mr. Shelley identified him as an employee of the Book Depository. Fritz says, "I'll be right up in a few minutes."[584]

The third-floor hallway at police headquarters is beginning to fill with a flood of reporters from newspapers, television, radio, and the wire services. UPI cub reporter Wilborn Hampton had been out at Parkland, where he felt the situation was chaotic. As he ran across the front lawn of Parkland Hospital to nearby Harry Hines Boulevard, hoping his car, which he had abandoned alongside the road because of the clogged traffic, hadn't been towed away, he paused and leaned on a live oak tree, crying, "He's dead, he's really dead." He then continued on to his car, which was still there. When he arrived at City Hall, he took his press card out of his wallet, ready to show it to anyone who challenges him, but security was so lax no one does. He quickly sees on the third floor that it's not merely chaotic, like Parkland, it's pandemonium, and so crowded he is virtually unable to move. It's as if, he thinks, someone had ordered a fire drill and told everyone in the building to show up at this one place.[585]

Less than a half hour after the shooting of the president—twenty-six minutes after the first news moved on the wires of United Press International—68 percent of all adults in the United States, about seventy-five *million* people, had heard about it. That percentage rises steadily through the afternoon, particularly after the president's death, until it reaches an astounding 99.8 percent. This is the story of the century and it's being followed around the world. Reporters and correspondents are already catching planes that will eventually bring them, in the next few hours, to as close as they can get to the tiny hallway outside room 317—Homicide and Robbery Bureau, Dallas Police Department, Dallas, Texas.[586]

2:04 p.m.

By the time the president's body is ready to be moved from Parkland Hospital, the row over the state of Texas's jurisdiction over the body has turned into a major imbroglio. Medical examiner Dr. Earl F. Rose refuses to listen to the pleading of Dr. Kemp Clark, the head of neurosurgery, who sides with the presidential party, or to the advice of Dallas district attorney Henry Wade, who advised him by phone to give it up. Tempers are at the melting point. Kennedy's men have had about all of Dallas law they can stand. Rose sees the casket bearing the president's body being pushed out of Trauma Room One, Mrs. Kennedy at its side. The medical examiner blocks the way with his own body, his hand flying up like a traffic cop. "We are removing it," Admiral Burkley says, enraged. "This is the president of the United States and there should be some consideration in an event like this."

"We can't release anything!" Rose screams. "A violent death requires a postmortem! There's a law here. We're going to enforce it."

A crush of forty sweating men are clustered around the wide doorway as curses fly back and forth. One of them looks like he might belt the medical examiner at any moment.

Admiral Burkley, in an attempt to calm everyone down, informs the conclave that a justice of the peace has arrived and has the power to overrule the medical examiner. Theron Ward, a young justice of the peace for the Third Precinct of Dallas County, makes his way down the corridor. Too timid to buck the medical examiner, the young justice tells them there is nothing he can do.

"In a homicide case, it's my duty to order an autopsy," Ward says in a tone much too weak for Dr. Rose's pleasure. "It shouldn't take more than three hours."

Special Agent Kellerman tells Ward there must be something inside of him that tells him it wouldn't be right to put Mrs. Kennedy and all of the president's people through any further agony in Texas, but Ward can only say, "I can't help you out."

Ken O'Donnell pleads with him, "Can't you make an exception for President Kennedy?"

Incredibly, Ward tells him, "It's just another homicide case as far as I'm concerned."

O'Donnell's response is instantaneous. "Go fuck yourself," he yells. "We're leaving!"

A policeman next to Rose points to the medical examiner and the justice of the peace and says to the president's men, "These two guys say you can't go."

"Move aside," shouts Larry O'Brien, moving toward the officer.

"Get the hell out of the way," O'Donnell hollers. "We're not staying here three hours or three minutes. We're leaving *now*! Wheel it out!" he orders.

The Secret Service men shoulder their way into the patrolman, who wisely capitulates. Rose, overpowered by circumstance, steps out of the way as the casket is wheeled toward the emergency exit, Mrs. Kennedy hurrying alongside, her fingertips touching the bronze finish.

As they move out toward the waiting hearse, Justice Theron Ward dashes to the nurses station and telephones District Attorney Wade and is stunned to hear him say the same thing he told Earl Rose earlier—he has no objection whatsoever to the removal of the president's body.[587]

2:14 p.m.

By the time Jackie Kennedy and the president's men arrive at Love Field with his body in the casket, Secret Service agent Lem Johns, assistant special agent in charge of LBJ's security detail, and the air crew have removed the last two rows of seats from the rear port-side section of the plane,[*] the small area located directly behind the presidential cabin and to the front of the rear galley (kitchen). There is now room on the port side for the casket to rest on the floor, but no one thought to arrange for a hydraulic lift. Kennedy's men—O'Donnell, Powers, and O'Brien—and the Secret Service agents, all unwilling, for Jackie's sake, to delay the departure, even by as little as the few minutes it would take to fetch a forklift, proceed to carry the heavy bulk by hand up the steep steps of the plane. Since none of them know that such a casket comes with a device that automatically pins it to the floor of the hearse, and a catch that releases the lock, they manage to rip a piece of trim from a hinge and the top of a handle housing as they remove it from the hearse. They struggle with the appallingly heavy bronze casket, which, they learn, is actually wider than the steps of the ramp to the rear entrance. As they shuffle the casket the last few feet, Ken O'Donnell keeps checking over his shoulder for police cars, half expecting the Dallas County medical examiner to roar up waving an injunction.[588]

2:15 p.m.

At the FBI's Dallas office, Agent James Hosty is immersed in putting together a list of right-wing extremists when his supervisor, Ken Howe, grabs his elbow. "They've just arrested a guy named Lee Oswald and they're booking him for the killing of the police-man over in Oak Cliff," Howe tells him. "The officer's name was Tippit."

It takes only a second for Hosty to shift from the pile of right-wingers to Lee Oswald. Hosty is in charge of the active file on both Oswalds—Lee and Marina—whom the FBI has considered to be possible espionage risks since their arrival in the United States in 1962. Hosty had learned on November 1 that Lee worked at one of the Texas School Book Depository buildings in Dallas, but he did not know which one.

"That's him! Ken, that must be him. Oswald has to be the one who shot Kennedy!" Hosty exclaims, having no basis to believe this other than his instinct that the Kennedy and Tippit murders are probably related. Three weeks ago he received a lengthy report from New Orleans special agent Milton Kaack describing Oswald's arrest after an alter-cation that broke out while he was passing out leaflets for the Fair Play for Cuba Com-mittee. The incident was banal enough. People who pass out flyers on the street, even for kooky organizations, are not necessarily potential assassins.

"Do you have the Oswald file?" Howe asks.

"It should be in the active file cabinet," Hosty replies as they rush over to it. The file is gone, which means the mail clerk probably has it to update it with incoming mail. They hurry to the mail clerk's office and frantically dig for it as another supervisor comes over to help.

In a few minutes, the FBI men find the file. Paper-clipped to the top is a one-page

---

[*]"We were sort of in a bind," Air Force One pilot Colonel Swindal would later recall, "because there was no place on Air Force One for a casket, and we sure didn't want to put it in the cargo hold" (*Los Angeles Times*, May 2, 2006, p.B11).

communiqué from the Washington, D.C., field office—and it's a shocker. According to the communiqué, Oswald had written to the Soviet embassy in Washington, D.C., about a trip he had made to Mexico City at the end of September, during which he had a conversation with "Comrade Kostine" at the Soviet embassy there. Hosty had read something about the Mexico City trip in October but was forbidden to question Oswald about it for fear of tipping off Oswald, and presumably the Soviets, to FBI surveillance methods in Mexico.[589]

This was a bombshell—*if* Lee Harvey Oswald was in contact with the Soviet government, he may have been some type of agent for them, which would mean a potentially explosive international situation. Had they been negligent and allowed a Soviet agent to assassinate the president? The press would come down very hard on the bureau, and J. Edgar Hoover would come down even harder on everyone in the bureau who had any responsibility with respect to Oswald.

Hosty takes the file to the special agent-in-charge, Gordon Shanklin. Hosty sits down while Shanklin calls Alan Belmont in Washington and advises him that a suspect named Lee Harvey Oswald is under arrest for the murder of Officer Tippit, and that police are questioning Oswald and have his handgun. Hosty hands him the Oswald file. Shanklin glances over the communiqué regarding Oswald's contacts with the Soviet embassy, then, with no visible reaction, says, "Alan, I've got Jim Hosty here. He's the agent who was working our file on Oswald. He's got the file here with him now."

Over the next few minutes, Hosty assists Shanklin by leafing through the Oswald file, locating pertinent information, and handing it to Shanklin as he talks with Belmont at headquarters.

"Oswald is the subject of an Internal Security-R-Cuba case," Shanklin tells Belmont. "The file shows that Oswald works at the Texas School Book Depository where the rifle and shells were found. The file also shows that three years ago Oswald left the U.S. and went to Russia, where he tried to renounce his American citizenship. He returned to the U.S. on June 13, 1962, and brought with him a Russian bride whom he married in Russia.

"Our agents have interviewed him twice since his return," Shanklin continues, "in an attempt to determine why he went to Russia and whether he was given an assignment by the Russians. He was completely uncooperative. He said he came back because he wanted to; denied being given an assignment; and said that why he went to Russia was his own business.

"He has since lived in Fort Worth, Dallas, New Orleans, and is currently back in Dallas. He was arrested in New Orleans in August 1963 on charges of creating a disturbance by passing out leaflets on the street which were published by the Fair Play for Cuba Committee. He drinks, has a violent temper, and has beaten his wife, who has recently had a baby."

"Do the files show whether Oswald has ever made a threat against the president or any public official?" Belmont asks.

"No," Shanklin says. "The agents who have interviewed him have the impression he is a mental case. He withdraws within himself when being questioned."

"Have you given this file information to the Secret Service?" Belmont asks.

"No, not yet," Shanklin replies.

"Well, get this information to the Secret Service," Belmont commands, "and arrange to have the agents who have questioned Oswald to sit in on the interrogations. They might be helpful to the police."

Shanklin puts his hand over the phone, and tells Hosty, "Belmont wants you to get down to the police department and take part in the interrogation of Oswald. Cooperate fully with the police and give them any information we have on Oswald. Get going. Now." Hosty's heart starts beating wildly as he heads out the door for City Hall.[590]

2:17 p.m.

The third-floor hallway at police headquarters resembles Grand Central Station when Captain Fritz and Detectives Richard Sims and Elmer Boyd return to the homicide office. The first order of business is to have some officers get a search warrant and go out to Ruth Paine's residence at 2515 West Fifth Street in Irving, the address on Oswald's employment card at the Book Depository. Lee Oswald, the employee who Fritz was told wasn't present at a roll call of employees, supposedly lived there. But before Fritz starts to round up the officers, Lieutenant T. L. Baker tells him that the man who shot Tippit is in the small interrogation room. The homicide captain enters the room and learns from Detectives Stovall and Rose that the man's name is Lee Oswald, the prime suspect in Kennedy's murder. He immediately dispatches Rose, Stovall, and a third detective, J. P. Adamcik, to go to the Paine residence and rendezvous there with three Dallas deputy sheriffs to conduct a search of the residence. (The presence of the Dallas County deputy sheriffs was needed because although the city of Irving was in Dallas County, it was outside the jurisdiction of the Dallas city police.) He then has Oswald brought into his room to be interrogated.[591]

It's pretty clear to the officers in Homicide and Robbery that the man arrested for the murder of Officer J. D. Tippit is most likely responsible for the assassination of the president of the United States.

2:18 p.m.

With the casket safely aboard Air Force One, Ken O'Donnell hurries forward to ask General McHugh, the ranking air force officer on board, to tell the pilot to take off immediately. But McHugh advises O'Donnell shortly thereafter that President Johnson had ordered the pilot to delay taking off until he was sworn in.[592]

Meanwhile, Jackie Kennedy wants to be by herself for a moment. She doesn't want to leave the coffin but knows that the private presidential cabin that she and Jack had last shared was adjacent to the tail compartment, where the coffin lay. With feelings of nostalgia sweeping over her, she thought it proper that she go there to compose herself. Moving quietly down the dim, narrow corridor, she enters the cabin and proceeds to the bedroom. When she turns the latch and opens the door, she sees Lyndon Johnson, reclining across the bed, dictating to his secretary, Marie Fehmer, who sat in a desk chair. Mrs. Kennedy stops dead. The new president scurries to his feet and hurries past her out the bedroom door, his secretary close behind. Jackie stares after them.[593]*

---

*It has to be noted that this is Mrs. Kennedy's version of what happened. Although President Johnson never addressed himself directly to the matter, his brief statement to the Warren Commission suggests a different version from what Mrs. Kennedy told author William Manchester. He says that when Mrs. Kennedy and President Kennedy's body arrived, "Mrs. Johnson and I spoke to her. We tried to comfort her, but our words seemed inadequate. She went into the private quarters of the plane" (5 H 564). Mrs. Johnson's version is more directly at odds with that of Mrs. Kennedy. She told the Warren Commission that "we had at first been ushered into the main presidential cabin on the plane, but Lyndon quickly said, 'No, no,' and immediately led us out of there; we felt that is where Mrs. Kennedy should be" (5 H 566).

Everyone settles back in the stale air of Air Force One to await the arrival of Judge Hughes. O'Donnell keeps looking out the window, still fearing the sudden arrival of a squadron of howling police cars and an apoplectic medical examiner.[594]

Lady Bird Johnson reenters the presidential cabin by herself to try to offer whatever comfort she can to Jackie, but Jackie is beyond comfort. Seeing that the always exquisitely dressed Jackie had blood on her dress and her right glove was soaked in blood, she asks Jackie if she can get someone in there to help her change. "Oh, no," Jackie says. "Perhaps later . . . but not right now," then tells Mrs. Johnson, "What if I had not been there? . . . I'm so glad I was there."[595]

2:20 p.m.
Detectives Elmer Boyd and Richard Sims move Oswald across the hall, from the small interview room to room 317, the Homicide and Robbery office, and then into Captain Fritz's office, a cozy, nine-and-a-half-by-fourteen-foot room, surrounded by waist-high windows looking out onto the outer office. Venetian blinds offered Captain Fritz privacy when needed. As Oswald settles into a chair beside the captain's desk, Boyd asks him how he bruised his eye.

"Well, I struck an officer and the officer struck me back, which he should have done," Oswald replies.[596]

2:25 p.m.
Captain Fritz enters his office and strolls around behind his desk.[*] Oswald, handcuffed behind his back, tries to look comfortable in the straight-back wooden chair adjacent to the homicide captain's desk. Detectives Sims and Boyd stand guard nearby. They know that Oswald is about to face a grueling interrogation. One, the other, or both, would be present at every subsequent interrogation of Oswald.[597†]

John William Fritz has been a Dallas cop since 1921 and chief of the Homicide and Robbery Bureau since its inception in 1934. He regards it as his own private and independent fiefdom. Fritz's Homicide and Robbery Bureau, consisting of two lieutenants and twenty detectives below him, is the top unit of the department and even has its own sartorial signature, the "Will Fritz" cowboy hat, always a Stetson. The hat designated one as a member of the elite homicide unit, since the only people in the Dallas Police Department who were allowed to wear those types of hats were members of homicide. If you purchased a hat like that but were not in homicide, you were told to get rid of it. And if an on-duty detective in Fritz's unit happened to be caught without his Stetson on, even on a very hot Texas summer day, it meant three days' suspension without pay. Three detectives in Fritz's unit worked on each investigation. Each team of detectives had a senior

---

[*]Dallas district attorney Henry Wade, a law enforcement power in his own right, would later tell the Warren Commission, "Fritz runs a kind of one-man operation there where nobody else knows what he is doing. Even me, for instance, he is reluctant to tell me, either, *but I don't mean that disparagingly*. [But, of course, it *is* disparaging.] I will say Captain Fritz is about as good a man at solving a crime as I ever saw, to find out who did it, but he is the poorest in the getting [of] evidence that I know, and I am more interested in getting evidence" (5 H 218). Without further explanation, unless Wade was speaking loosely, it is difficult to know how one "solves" a crime without a successful gathering of evidence, unless Wade meant that Fritz's intuition was usually accurate.

[†]There would eventually be three more interrogations of Oswald. All four, totaling approximately twelve hours, took place intermittently between 2:30 p.m. on November 22 and 11:10 a.m. on November 24, 1963. (WR, pp. 180, 633)

officer and a rookie, even though the rookie may have been on the force for many years. Each homicide detective carried two guns.[598]

Because of Fritz's sober, and many feel intimidating demeanor, and because he has headed the most important and powerful bureau on the force for over three decades, most officers respect and fear him more than Chief Curry. Fritz was born in Texas, grew up near Roswell, New Mexico, and was a cowhand and mule trader before he started walking a beat in the downtown area of Dallas known as "Little Mexico." He was involved in the hunt for the famed desperados of the early 1930s, Bonnie and Clyde, and won a shootout in an attic with Dagger Bill Pruitt, a robber responsible for several ugly murders, when Pruitt surrendered. Divorced, Fritz has lived alone for years in a hotel room (the White Plaza) located across the street from police headquarters. He has a daughter and some grandchildren, but no one knows much else about his private life, if he has any. His only topic of conversation is whatever case is at hand, and he sometimes works two or three days around the clock to sew up a case. You'd never know his nickname was "Will" because everyone called him Captain Fritz.[599]

Fritz is what one subordinate calls "a straight-laced perfect gentleman" who never uses improper language, is always 100 percent truthful and straightforward, and isn't the least bit political. He has above-average intelligence, understands people very well, seems to be able to know when people are not being truthful with him, and is able to analyze personalities quickly.[600] In particular, Fritz has a phenomenal memory for the details of cases he's worked on over the years, and he's quick to pick up on the contradictions in a suspect's story. If a suspect can't tell his story the same way a second or third time, or a tenth time, Fritz will catch him because he knows exactly what the suspect said the first time.[601]

His style of interrogation is quiet and soothing, a disarming approach for even the most cunning of criminals. His reputation in law enforcement is impeccable and his record of confessions is the best in the Southwest. His men often relate how Fritz even got a confession over the telephone once. An Ohio sheriff had picked up a Texas fugitive wanted for murder. When Fritz was informed, he called the sheriff and asked if the man had confessed. The sheriff told him, "No," then asked Fritz if he wanted to talk to him. Fritz said, "Sure." When the fugitive got on the line, Fritz made small talk, found out they knew someone in common, then told him, "Kind of a bad thing you done here."

"I didn't kill him," the prisoner snapped back.

"You don't strike me as the type that does this every day," Fritz said softly. "Is this the first time you ever killed anybody?"

"Yes, sir, first time" the man answered, without thinking.[602]

Captain Fritz is considered to be the finest interrogator on the Dallas Police Force. This time he faces his ultimate challenge. After asking Oswald his "full" name and Oswald replies, "Lee Harvey Oswald," Fritz begins, as he always does, with casual questions, asking Oswald about where he was from, his background and education, service in the Marines, and so on.*

---

*Although the Sixth Amendment to the U.S. Constitution has provided since 1791 that an accused has the right to counsel to assist him in his defense, in Texas in 1963 the police did not have to *advise* a suspect or person arrested of this right. In this case, Oswald asked Fritz if he had the right to counsel and Fritz told him he did (4 H 215, WCT John Will Fritz; WR, p.602). However, Texas statutory law at the time *did* require that someone under arrest be advised that he did not have to make a statement, and if he did, it could be used against him. Although there is nothing in the report of Captain Fritz on his interrogation of Oswald (WR, pp.599–611) that he advised Oswald of this right against self-incrimination, Dallas assistant district attorney

His grandfather-like manner almost compels people to talk with him, and in that regard, this young suspect is no different.

"Where do you work?" Fritz asks, getting into the present.

"Texas School Book Depository," Oswald says without hesitation.

"How'd you get the job?" Fritz asks.

"A lady that I know recommended me for the job," Oswald replies. "I got the job through her." Fritz asks about the "Hidell" name found in his wallet, and Oswald says that it was a name he "picked up in New Orleans."[603]

Fritz asks Oswald if he lives in Irving.

"No," Oswald replies. "I've got a room in Oak Cliff."

"I thought you lived in Irving?" Fritz asks, a little confused. Oswald says, no, he lives at 1026 Beckley. Although he doesn't know whether the address is North or South Beckley, Fritz and his detectives can tell from Oswald's description of the area that it's North Beckley.

"Who lives in Irving?" Fritz asks.

"My wife is staying out there with friends," Oswald says.[604] Fritz steps out into the outer office and instructs Lieutenant Cunningham of the Forgery Bureau, along with Detectives Billy Senkel and Walter Potts, to go out to 1026 North Beckley and search Oswald's rented room.[605] The homicide commander then gathers Lieutenants James A. Bohart and Ted P. Wells and Detective T. L. Baker around him.

"We've got a lot of work to do," Fritz tells them. "Who's working Officer Tippit's killing?"

"Leavelle and Graves," Baker answers.

"Fine, let them stay on that," Fritz says. "Everybody else will work on the president's killing."[606] Fritz returns to his office and Oswald.

2:30 p.m.

As federal district judge Sarah Hughes, a kindly faced woman of sixty-seven, climbs aboard Air Force One, someone hands her a three-by-five-inch card on which Johnson's secretary has typed out the text of the oath of office. Only a few minutes after Barefoot Sanders, the U.S. attorney in Dallas, whose office was just a floor below hers, had left a message for her, she had returned to her office. Her old friend Lyndon Johnson wanted her immediately at Love Field. She knew what that meant. Judge Hughes goes on into

---

Bill Alexander, who sat in on many interrogations of arrestees by Fritz through the years, said that Fritz always would comply with Texas law and he assumes the reason this was not in Fritz's notes is that it "went without saying" that he gave Oswald this admonition (Telephone interview of William Alexander by author on February 17, 2002). In any event, once FBI agents James Bookhout and James Hosty joined in Oswald's interrogation, the agents advised Oswald of both rights (WR, p.619; 7 H 310, WCT James W. Bookhout; see also 7 H 353, WCT, Forrest V. Sorrels).

In the landmark cases of *Escobedo v. Illinois* (378 U.S. 478), a year *after* the assassination, and *Miranda v. Arizona* in 1966 (384 U.S. 436), it became a federal constitutional right that a suspect (and certainly an arrestee) has to be advised at the commencement of questioning of his right to have counsel during his interrogation, and if he doesn't have funds for a lawyer, one will be appointed. He also has to be told he has a right to remain silent, and anything he says can be used against him, and if this is not done, any statement made by him thereafter that was elicited by the police during the interrogation cannot be introduced against him at his trial.

It should be noted that even before *Escobedo* and *Miranda*, the widespread practice, particularly by *federal* law enforcement agencies like the FBI and Secret Service, was to tell a suspect or arrestee of these rights and help him get a lawyer by allowing him to make a phone call for this purpose, as Captain Fritz allowed Oswald to do in this case. It's just that there was *no legal requirement* to advise arrestees and suspects of these rights before they were questioned.

the stateroom of the presidential cabin and embraces the president, Mrs. Johnson, and several fellow Texans.

"We'll get as many people in here as possible," Johnson says, sending Jack Valenti, Rufus Youngblood, Emory Roberts, and Lem Johns to round up witnesses. "If anybody wants to join in the swearing-in ceremony, I would be happy and proud to have you."

When O'Donnell comes up from the aft compartment where the casket is stowed, he finds the group around the president sweltering in the increasingly unpleasant air of the small stateroom, a room that can accommodate eight to ten people seated. UPI reporter Merriman Smith, one of two pool reporters on the plane, the other being *Newsweek*'s Charles Roberts, wedges himself inside the door, and for some reason begins counting. There are twenty-seven people in the room. It turns out that Johnson is waiting for Mrs. Kennedy. "She said she wanted to be here when I take the oath," he says. "Why don't you see what's keeping her?"

O'Donnell locates her nearby in the dressing room of the presidential cabin, combing her hair. He tactfully explains that she doesn't need to take part in the ceremony if she doesn't feel up to it.

"I think I ought to," she says. "In the light of history, it would be better if I were there."

She wonders whether she should take the time to change out of her bloodstained suit. O'Donnell urges her not to go to the trouble.[607]

2:38 p.m.

Captain Cecil Stoughton, the official White House photographer, records the crowded scene on Air Force One as Judge Hughes reads the oath, from Article II, Section 1 [8] of the U.S. Constitution, with Johnson resting his left hand on top of a Catholic prayer book,[*] his wife on his right, John Kennedy's widow, her Chanel suit stained with her husband's blood and her white gloves caked with it, on his left. Mac Kilduff holds a microphone out to catch the words of the swearing-in ceremony on a scratchy Dictaphone.

After the sixty-seven-year-old jurist tells Johnson, "Hold up your right hand and repeat after me," he says, "I do solemnly swear that I will faithfully execute the Office of President of the United States, and will to the best of my ability, preserve, protect and defend the Constitution of the United States."

Judge Hughes impulsively adds the formulaic "So help me God"—not part of the prescribed oath—and the president, in a deep voice, repeats it. In twenty-eight seconds, it's over.[†]

---

[*]Author William Manchester wrote that JFK's Bible, "his most cherished personal possession," was found on the plane, and LBJ had rested his hand on it (Manchester, *Death of a President*, pp.324, 328). But Lady Bird took the "Bible" off the plane with her as a memento, and later inquiry revealed it was not a Bible but a Catholic prayer book or missal, which, to all appearances, had never been opened (Holland, *Kennedy Assassination Tapes*, p.310).

[†]Johnson's elevation to president from vice president marked the fourth time in American history when an assassin's bullet has elevated a sitting vice president. Andrew Johnson was the first so elevated when John Wilkes Booth, a fierce proponent of the Confederate cause, shot Abraham Lincoln at the Ford Theater in Washington, D.C., on April 14, 1865. Lincoln died the next day. Booth was shot to death during his capture on April 26, 1865. Next was the elevation to the presidency of Chester Alan Arthur, when Charles Julius Guiteau, a self-styled "lawyer, theologian, and politician" who claimed he had worked for President James A. Garfield's election and was entitled to a prominent foreign service post in payment for it, which he never got, shot Garfield as he was walking to a train in the Baltimore and Potomac Station in Washington, D.C., on July 2, 1881. Garfield did not die from his wound until September 19, 1881, and Guiteau was later hanged, on June 30, 1882. The next vice president to be elevated was Theodore Roosevelt when President William McKin-

The new president then turns to his wife, hugs her around the shoulders, and kisses her cheek. Then he turns to John Kennedy's widow, puts his left arm about her, and kisses her cheek. As others among the group move toward President Johnson, he seems to back away from any act of congratulation. Instead, he says firmly, "Now, let's get airborne."[608] In an oath-taking ceremony approaching, in the uniqueness of its setting, the one that Calvin Coolidge took by lamplight in a Vermont farmhouse in 1923, Lyndon Baines Johnson was now the thirty-sixth president of the United States, an office he had dreamed of attaining—he had even run for the office three years earlier, losing the Democratic nomination in Los Angeles to JFK—but not this way.[*]

The pilot starts Air Force One's engines as Judge Hughes, Chief Curry, and Cecil Stoughton, who will not be making the flight to Washington, deplane. Johnson and Lady Bird remain in the stateroom, and Jackie excuses herself, returning to her husband's casket in the small aft cabin, where Ken O'Donnell, Dave Powers, Larry O'Brien, Brigadier General Godfrey McHugh, and for awhile, Admiral Burkley, will keep her company.[609]

Jackie sits in the aisle seat, directly opposite the casket, O'Donnell beside her in the only other seat available. When their eyes meet, she begins to cry hard. When she finally regains her composure, she cries, "Oh, Kenny, what's going to happen?"

O'Donnell knows that she is wondering what is going to happen to all of them now that Jack is dead.

---

ley was shot by Leon F. Czolgosz, an anarchist who said McKinley was "the enemy of the working people," on September 6, 1901, at the Pan American Exposition in Buffalo, New York. McKinley didn't expire until September 14. Czolgosz was electrocuted on October 29. (McConnell, *History of Assassination*, pp.310–312, 314–317; WR, pp.504–510)

That the job of the president of the United States is the most dangerous elected job in the world cannot be too vigorously contested. In addition to the two attempted assassinations of President Gerald Ford in 1975 (by Lynnette "Squeaky" Fromme in Sacramento on September 5, 1975, and Sarah Jane Moore in San Francisco on September 22, 1975), the attempted assassination of President Richard Nixon by Samuel Joseph Byck on February 22, 1974, and the attempted assassination of President Ronald Reagan by William Hinckley in Washington, D.C., on March 30, 1981, two other presidents were attacked before Kennedy, but the attempts failed. Additionally, attempts were made on one president-elect and even one former president. On January 30, 1835, an English-born house painter, Richard Lawrence, fired two pistols, both of which misfired, at President Andrew Jackson. Like William Hinckley, Lawrence was found by a jury to be not guilty by reason of insanity and died in a mental hospital sixteen years later. On November 1, 1950, two Puerto Rican nationalists, Oscar Collazo and Griselio Torresola, attempted to shoot their way into Blair House, where President Harry Truman and his wife were temporarily residing while the White House was being repaired. Torresola was shot to death by White House guards in a hail of gunfire (one of the guards was also killed). Collazo was seriously wounded and sentenced to death, but Truman commuted his sentence to life imprisonment. President-elect Franklin D. Roosevelt was shot at in his car five times at a political rally in Miami's Bayfront Park on February 15, 1933 by Giuseppe Zangara, a thirty-two-year-old bricklayer and stonemason. All five of Zangara's shots missed Roosevelt. However, one of them hit Chicago mayor Anton Cermak, who was riding with Roosevelt. Cermak died of his wound on March 6, and Zangara was electrocuted on March 20, only thirty-three days after his attempt on Roosevelt. The former president who escaped was Theodore Roosevelt, who was running for president again as the candidate of the Progressive or "Bull Moose" Party. On October 14, 1912, a German-born New York bartender, John Schrank, fired one shot at Roosevelt as he entered his car outside a hotel in Milwaukee. The bullet hit Roosevelt in the chest, but a folded manuscript of the speech he was about to make and the metal case for his eyeglasses absorbed part of the bullet's thrust, and he survived. Schrank was found to be insane and died in a mental hospital in 1943. (WR, pp.505, 509–513)

So starting with Lincoln in 1865, approximately one out of every three American presidents either has been assassinated or had an attempt on his life.

[*]Speaking of his early days in office to his biographer, Doris Kearns, LBJ said, "I took the oath. I became president. But for millions of Americans I was still illegitimate, a naked man with no presidential covering, a pretender to the throne, an illegal usurper. And then there was Texas, my home, the home of both the murder and the murder of the murderer. And then there were the bigots and the dividers and the Eastern intellectuals, who were waiting to knock me down before I could even begin to stand up. The whole thing was almost unbearable" (Kearns, *Lyndon Johnson and the American Dream*, p.170).

"You want to know something, Jackie?" Ken says. "I don't give a damn."

When Admiral Burkley tries to persuade the young widow to change out of her blood-stained clothes, she says quietly, "*No*. Let them see what they've done."[610]

2:40 p.m.

Over in Fort Worth, Marguerite Oswald, Lee's mother, dressed in her nurse's uniform, is driving to work at the Hargroves Convalescent Center, listening to the news on the radio of her old, run-down Buick. She had been sitting on the sofa at home watching the television coverage, but had to leave at two-thirty if she wanted to get to work by three. Now, just seven blocks from home, she hears that police have picked up a suspect—Lee Harvey Oswald. Stunned, she immediately turns around and goes back home. She must call Robert Oswald, the younger of Lee's two older brothers. Robert works for Acme Brick, a Fort Worth company. He travels a lot, but they'll know how to get in touch with him.[611] She's also going to call the *Fort Worth Star-Telegram*. She figures there's a way to turn this into cash. And maybe someone there can give her a lift to Dallas.

Twenty-six-year-old *Fort Worth Star-Telegram* police reporter Bob Schieffer is lamenting the fact that he wasn't a political reporter covering the biggest story in the world when he picks up the ringing phone on the city desk. A woman wants to know if there is anyone there who can give her a ride into Dallas. "Lady, this is not a taxi company, and besides, the president has been shot." "I know," the woman says. "They think my son is the one who shot him." Schieffer and a colleague, Bill Foster, drive out to Fort Worth's west side and find Marguerite, waiting for them on the front lawn of her small, white stucco bungalow. The short, pudgy woman in large, dark, horn-rimmed glasses gets in the backseat with Schieffer for the close-to-an-hour trip into town.[612] En route, Schieffer is taken aback by Marguerite's attitude. She not only seemed somewhat mentally deranged but for most of the trip he sensed that she was less concerned about Kennedy's death and her son's predicament than she was with herself. She kept railing about the fact that her son's wife would get all the sympathy but no one would "remember the mother" and that she would probably starve.* However, she did cry quietly and her talk was punctuated with sobs. "I want to hear him tell me he did it," she said at one point. Schieffer never did get around to asking her why she had called the paper for a ride but learned later that she had at one time worked briefly as a governess in the home of Ammon Carter Jr., the owner of the paper, but had been discharged because the children complained that "she was mean." Schieffer ends up depositing Marguerite in what looked like some kind of interrogation room at Dallas police headquarters.[613]

Robert Oswald has not seen his brother Lee for a year and hasn't even heard from him for about eight months. He had heard the news of the assassination just as he was leaving Jay's Grill, a steak and seafood restaurant not far from Acme Brick's new plant in Denton, Texas, where he worked as a sales coordinator linking the marketing and plant departments, scheduling production to meet orders, and following through on customer

*Marguerite told her biographer, Jean Stafford, in 1965, "I'm a mother in history. I'm all over the world . . . and *my* son's the one accused. You know, here is Mrs. Kennedy, a very wealthy woman, Mrs. Tippit, a very wealthy woman, Marina, very wealthy [referring to the donations from the public Marina and particularly Mrs. Tippit received], but *I* am wondering where my next meal is coming from. It's almost unbelievable" (Stafford, *Mother in History*, p.54).

service.[614] Now, Robert is back at the office going over some invoices and wondering whether Lee had taken a few minutes off to watch the motorcade. He goes down to the timekeeper's office to get some of the invoices checked. The receptionist at the front desk has her radio on, and, as he passes by, they both hear a news announcer say the name "Oswald."

Robert stops. He thought someone had called his name until he realizes that the voice came from the radio.

The announcer repeats the name, this time in full—"Lee Harvey Oswald."

Robert is paralyzed. "That's my kid brother," he says, stunned.

He calls his wife Vada and tells her he will be home shortly, but before he can leave he gets a call from the credit manager at the company's Fort Worth office.

"Bob, brace yourself," he says. "Your brother has been arrested."

"I know. I just heard."

The credit manager tells him his mother is trying to reach him. Robert calls her and arranges to meet her in Dallas at the Hotel Adolphus later in the evening.[615]

At the Terminal Annex Building overlooking Dealey Plaza, a box clerk bursts into the office of U.S. postal inspector Harry D. Holmes to tell him it's just come over the radio that police have arrested someone named Lee Harvey Oswald for the murder of Officer Tippit.

"I think you ought to know, Mr. Holmes," the clerk says, "that we rented a box downstairs to a Lee Oswald recently. Box number 6225." The clerk, who has already retrieved the original box application, dated November 1, 1963, hands it to Holmes and tells the inspector that he can't recall what the applicant looked like, but he does remember one thing. The man definitely filled out the application himself.[616]

The form lists "Fair Play for Cuba Committee" and "American Civil Liberties Union" in the space for firm or corporation. Under "kind of business" is the word "nonprofit." No business address is given, but in the space for home address, the applicant has written, "3610 N. Beckley." This is a variation of Oswald's actual address, 1026 North Beckley. At the bottom of the form is the applicant's signature, "Lee H. Oswald."[617]

Inspector Holmes telephones the Secret Service, who order a twenty-four-hour, round-the-clock surveillance of the box to see if anyone attempts to retrieve mail from it.[618]

2:45 p.m.
Secret Service agent Forrest Sorrels is beginning to realize that getting Zapruder's film developed is not going to be easy. The amateur movie camera takes 8-millimeter color film, something that neither the *Dallas Morning News* nor their companion television station, WFAA, can handle. Both are set up for 16-millimeter black-and-white newsfilm.

While the WFAA television news department telephones Eastman Kodak Company, *Dallas Morning News* reporter Harry McCormick manages to arrange a live television interview with Zapruder, who provides a graphic description of the shooting to a stunned Dallas audience.

Sorrels is told that the people at Eastman Kodak Company, located near Love Field, have the capability of developing Zapruder's footage and are standing by right now to assist. Within minutes, the Secret Service agent, with Zapruder, Schwartz, and McCormick in tow, is speeding toward Eastman Kodak in a Dallas police car.[619]

2:47 p.m.

The wheels of Air Force One[*] clear the runway at Love Field as the pilot takes it to an unusually high cruising altitude of forty-one thousand feet, where at 625 mph the great plane races toward Andrews Air Force Base, just outside Washington, D.C., in Maryland. John Fitzgerald Kennedy, in office for 1,037 days, is going home.[620]

2:50 p.m.

The basement garage of City Hall is an incredible hive of activity. Police cars swing in and out of the cavernous space, shouts and hollers echo over parked cars, and officers rush frantically about. FBI agent Jim Hosty jumps from his bureau-issued '62 Dodge and heads for the elevator. Car doors slam to his right as Dallas police lieutenant Jack Revill and several detectives emerge from their autos and head briskly toward him.

Although Hosty and Revill, a thirty-four-year-old veteran of the Dallas police narcotics unit who was recently promoted to head the intelligence unit, have disagreed and clashed a number of times over politics and police work, they have remained friends.[621] Revill tells Hosty he's got a "hot lead" on the Kennedy killing, an unaccounted-for employee at the Texas School Book Depository named Lee. Why Revill only knew Oswald's first name when the full name of the unaccounted-for employee (Oswald) was known from the very beginning is not known. But in the frenetic exchange of information in these first minutes of the investigation, incomplete (and, indeed, incorrect) information was the norm.

"Jack, the Lee you're talking about is Lee Harvey Oswald," Hosty blurts out. "He was arrested an hour ago for shooting Officer Tippit. He defected to Russia and returned to the U.S. a year ago. Oswald is the prime suspect in the Kennedy assassination."[622]

A look of doubt crosses Revill's face. Revill, a conservative who saw Kennedy as being soft on Communism, can't believe what he's hearing, particularly that a Communist, of all people, had killed the president. Revill explodes as they get on the elevator that will take them to the third floor. "Jim, if you *knew* all this [about Oswald's background], why the hell didn't you tell us?"

"I couldn't," Hosty replies, referring to the bureau's long-standing need-to-know policy regarding espionage cases, in which local police were not considered by the FBI to be in the need-to-know group.[623]

The third-floor hallway is in an uproar. Cameramen and reporters are crammed everywhere. The giant television cameras of the era are trained on newsmen as they broadcast live reports. Flashbulbs are going off continuously and people are moving quickly in opposite directions, bumping into each other. It's a three-ring circus without out a ringmaster.

The elevator doors open and Agent Hosty and Lieutenant Revill wade into the chaos and make their way toward room 317—Homicide and Robbery Bureau. As they push their way inside, they find that Captain Fritz is in his private office, behind closed doors. Revill leads Hosty into Lieutenant T. P. Wells's office across the hall from Fritz's private

---

[*]Two other planes leave Love Field following Air Force One: Air Force Two, the vice presidential plane, tail number SAM86970, now occupied mostly by Kennedy staffers forced to leave Air Force One to make room for President Johnson and his entourage; and SAM86373, the C-130 cargo jet carrying the blood-spattered presidential limousine and other trappings of the presidency, such as the president's seal and a special American flag (Holland, *Kennedy Assassination Tapes*, pp.48–49; see also TerHorst and Albertazzie, *Flying White House*, pp.210, 212).

door, introduces Hosty to Wells, and leaves. FBI agent James Bookhout is already in Wells's office when Hosty arrives.[624]

2:58 p.m.
In Oak Cliff, Detectives Senkel and Potts and Lieutenant Cunningham bang on the door at 1026 North Beckley. The housekeeper, Mrs. Earlene Roberts, answers the door and invites the officers inside, where they meet the landlady and her husband, Mr. and Mrs. Arthur C. Johnson. The officers ask if they have a boarder registered under the name of Lee Harvey Oswald or A. J. Hidell.

"No," none of them had heard of either name.

The officers ask to see the register. Earlene Roberts gets out the book and opens it on the table as Mrs. Johnson tells them that she has seventeen rooms and sixteen boarders at the moment. The officers quickly run down the list of names in the register. Neither name is listed. They run through the listings again, this time more carefully. Nothing. There is no record of either Oswald or Hidell.

"Can I use your telephone?" Detective Senkel asks.

"Sure," Mrs. Johnson replies. The housekeeper leads him to a hall phone.

"What's he look like?" Mrs. Johnson asks one of the other officers. He describes the man they have in custody.

"I do have two new tenants that fit that description," Mrs. Johnson says. "Their rooms are around back, in the basement. Let me get the key."[625]

3:00 p.m.
A telephone rings inside the homicide office. Lieutenant T. L. Baker answers. It's Detective Senkel out on North Beckley.

"There's no one registered out here as either Oswald or Hidell," Senkel tells him.

"Maybe it's under a different name," Baker says.

"She's got sixteen boarders here," Senkel replies.

"Sit tight, I'll get someone out there with a search warrant," Baker orders.[626]

At the rooming house, Mrs. Johnson returns with a key to the basement rooms and offers to let the police look if they want. Mrs. Roberts and Mrs. Johnson lead the officers out the back door toward a separate entrance to the basement. Meanwhile, in the living room, Mr. Johnson is watching television coverage of the assassination when the screen flashes the image of Lee Harvey Oswald.

"Hey!" he hollers at his wife as she heads out the door. Mrs. Johnson hands the keys to the housekeeper, "Go ahead, I'll see what he wants." Returning to the living room, her husband tells her, "Why, it's this fellow that lives in here," gesturing to the little room a few feet away. "Go tell them."[627]

Mrs. Roberts has unlocked the doors in the basement, and the officers have just stepped in, when Mrs. Johnson comes running up. "Oh, Mrs. Roberts, come quick. It's this fellow Lee in this little room next to yours."[628]

They run back upstairs to the living room, where images relating to the assassination continue to flicker across the television screen. For a moment, they all stand transfixed on the screen. Suddenly, there he is again—Lee Harvey Oswald.

"Yes, that's him," Mrs. Roberts confirms. "That's O. H. Lee. He lives right here in this room."[629]

Mrs. Roberts points to the two french doors off the main living room. There is no number on the door, just the designation "O." The light, aqua-colored room, just five feet wide and thirteen and one-half feet long, is hardly more than a large closet.*

The police return to the table and look back through the register. They quickly find the listing for "O. H. Lee," now known to be Lee Harvey Oswald. He had rented the room under the fictitious name on October 14, 1963, and is paying eight dollars a week.[630]

3:01 p.m. (4:01 p.m. EST)

In Washington, D.C., FBI Director Hoover calls Attorney General Robert F. Kennedy at his home to inform him he thinks they have the man who killed his brother in Dallas, that the man's name is Lee Harvey Oswald, that he was working in the building from which the shots were fired, that he left the building and "a block or two away ran into two police officers and, thinking they were going to arrest him, shot at them and killed one of them with a sidearm."[631]

Hoover may have been the head of the nation's most famous law enforcement agency, but that doesn't mean he knows what's going on, in real time, in Dallas.

3:08 p.m.

Inside the inner sanctum of Captain Fritz's private office, where the serious questioning of Oswald was just beginning, the telephone rings. It's the Dallas FBI's Gordon Shanklin and he wants to speak to Agent Bookhout. Fritz steps across the hall to Lieutenant Wells's office and tells Bookhout he can take the call in Wells's office, then quietly picks up an extension in his office to listen in.

"Is Hosty in that investigation?" Fritz hears Shanklin say.

"No," Bookhout replies.

"I want him in that investigation right now!" Shanklin says angrily. "He knows those people [the Oswalds]. He's been investigating them." Shanklin finishes by telling Bookhout what he can do if he doesn't do it right quick, using language that Fritz would later tell the Warren Commission, "I don't want to repeat." Fritz slips the receiver back into its cradle.[632] (Fritz was already aware that the FBI would be sitting in on the interrogations prior to the call from Shanklin. A few minutes earlier, Chief Curry had received a call from Shanklin requesting that they have a representative in on the interrogations. Curry had called Fritz and asked him to permit the FBI to sit in.)[633]

Bookhout hangs up. "We'd better get in there," he tells Hosty.

Before they can make a move, Captain Fritz appears and invites the two agents to sit in on the interrogation.[634] Fritz leads the FBI agents back into his office. Bookhout and Hosty pull out their identification badges and lay them on the desk next to Oswald.

"I'm Special Agent James Hosty of the Federal Bureau of Investigation," the agent begins, "and this is Special Agent James Bookhout."

As soon as Oswald hears Hosty's name, he reacts.

"Oh, so *you're* Hosty," Oswald snarls, clearly agitated. "I've heard about you."

"You have the right to remain silent," Hosty says as Oswald eyes him. "Anything you

*But there are five small windows in the room, all with venetian blinds and curtains connected to one five-and-ten-cent-store-type curtain rod. There is a single iron-rail bed, a large wooden movable wardrobe dresser drawer, a small plastic-top table, and a nightstand with a table lamp next to the head of the bed. Two small throw rugs are on the linoleum-tiled floor. (CD 705, pp.1–2, March 28, 1964; CE 2046, 24 H 460–461; 10 H 297, WCT Mrs. Arthur Carl Johnson)

say may be used against you in a court of law." Hosty can barely finish the words, when Oswald explodes. "You're the one who's been harassing my wife!"

Fritz and his detectives glance at one another. Oswald curses both agents with a string of profanities. Hosty tries to calm Oswald down, but only manages to whip him into a frenzy.

"My wife is a Russian citizen who is here legally and is protected under diplomatic laws from harassment by you or anyone else from the FBI," Oswald argues, his face flush, his voice quivering. "You're no better than the Gestapo of Nazi Germany! If you want to talk to me, you should come to me directly, not my wife."[635]

Fritz jumps in and tries to soothe Oswald with a calm voice. Hosty has struck a nerve, and Fritz doesn't want to lose the trust he's been working hard to establish with Oswald. The fact is, Fritz doesn't like it one bit that the federal agents are horning in on his investigation. Anyone in law enforcement knows that when you conduct an interrogation with large groups of people present, you decrease the likelihood of satisfactory results. But, under the circumstances, Fritz knows he'll have to put up with the unwelcome company.

"What do you mean, he accosted your wife?" Fritz asks, thinking he meant some kind of physical abuse.

"Well, he threatened her," Oswald snaps. "He practically told her she'd have to go back to Russia. He accosted her on two different occasions."[636]

Agent Hosty had indeed spoken briefly to Marina, and at somewhat greater length to Ruth Paine, early in November when, in the course of trying to determine where Lee and Marina were living, he located the two women living together out in Irving. But he's never laid eyes on Oswald before, and knows him only from the FBI file, which has been building up ever since he attempted to defect to Russia in 1959.[637]

What strikes Hosty at the moment is the realization that it might have been Oswald who had left an angry note for him at the FBI office about ten days earlier. The note was unsigned, but Hosty recalled that it stated in no uncertain terms that Hosty should not "bother my wife," and threatened to "take action against the FBI" if he didn't stop.[638]*

---

*The date that Oswald came to the FBI office is not known, although it is inferable from Ruth Paine's testimony that Oswald indicated to her it was sometime during the week preceding the weekend of November 9–10, 1963 (3 H 18). Hosty, in his 1996 book, *Assignment: Oswald* (p.29), says it was "ten days before" the assassination. And in a July 15, 1975, affidavit given to the FBI, Nannie Lee Fenner, the FBI receptionist to whom Oswald gave the note, said it was around ten days before the assassination. But there seems to be little basis for this certitude. Indeed, when Hosty testified under oath about it in 1975, he said Oswald dropped the note off "probably November the sixth, seventh, or eighth," which would have been sixteen to eighteen days earlier. And Fenner testified in 1975 that "I do not know the exact date . . . It would have been in November. It could have been before that. I have racked my brain up one side and down the other and I cannot come up with the date." Fenner said Oswald, not identifying himself, came to the FBI office during the noon hour and said to her, "S.A. Hosty, please." He had a "wild look in his eye" and was "awfully fidgety." While she was checking to see if Hosty was in, she said the "bottom portion" of the note Oswald was holding was visible to her and she recalls "the last two lines" of the note, which said, "I will either blow up the Dallas Police Department or the FBI office." When Fenner learned, and told Oswald, that Hosty was not in, he gave her the note to give to Hosty. After Oswald left, she decided to see "what was above" those two lines and said it "was something about [Hosty] speaking to his wife and what he was going to do if they didn't stop." Fenner said the note was signed "Lee Harvey Oswald," and when Hosty came back to the office, she gave the note to him. Hosty, who disposed of the note following the assassination (see later discussion), did not recall the note being signed, and said the note did not contain the language Fenner recalls. When asked at a House Judiciary subcommittee hearing in 1975, "It [the note] didn't say anything about the blowing up of the office?" he replied, "No, sir, I would have remembered that." Hosty characterized Fenner as unreliable and someone with "a distinct reputation for gross exaggeration," saying he was "almost certain that Fenner had never even read the note. It is more likely that she heard about it and embellished her knowledge." A coworker of Fenner's, Joe Pearce, gave an affidavit on July 22, 1975, that Fen-

At the time, Hosty, who was juggling thirty-five to forty cases simultaneously, had no idea who had written the note and simply put it in his file drawer. Now, it seems Oswald may have been the author.

Oswald asks Fritz to take off his handcuffs.

"That sounds reasonable," Hosty quickly interjects, hoping to buddy up. Oswald can only glare at him.

Detectives Sims and Boyd look at Fritz. They know who's in charge here. Fritz tells them he wants Oswald to remain in handcuffs, but tells the detectives Oswald's hands don't need to be cuffed behind his back. As they make the adjustment, Oswald starts to settle down.

"Thank you, thank you," he says to Captain Fritz. He turns to Agent Hosty, and offers an apology, "I'm sorry for blowing up at you. And I'm sorry for writing that letter to you."

Hosty now knows that Oswald was the author of the note. Captain Fritz and the detectives in the tan Stetson hats are wondering just what kind of relationship exists between Oswald and FBI agent Hosty.[639] As Oswald begins to relax, Captain Fritz turns back to the matter at hand. "Do you own a rifle, Lee?"

"No," Oswald says dryly. "But I saw Mr. Truly, my supervisor at work, he had one at the Depository on Wednesday, I think it was, showing it to some people in his office on the first floor."

"Have you *ever* owned a rifle?" Fritz asks.

"Oh, I had one a good many years ago," Oswald says. "It was a small rifle, a twenty-two or something, but I haven't owned one for a long time."[640]

Hosty is eager to find out about Oswald's contacts with the Soviet embassy in Mexico City, which were discussed in the communiqué received by his office that morning. Now that Oswald is somewhat relaxed, Hosty decides to broach the subject.

"Ever been in Mexico City?" Hosty asks, interrupting Captain Fritz's line of questioning.

Oswald hesitates for just a moment, one of the few times he doesn't have an immediate answer.[641]

"Sure," he says. "Sure, I've been to Mexico. When I was stationed in San Diego with the Marines, a couple of my buddies and I would occasionally drive down to Tijuana over the weekend."[642]

Hosty knows he dodged the question, but lets it go, for the moment.

"You said you have a wife who is a Russian?" Fritz asks.

"That's right," Oswald says.

"Have you been to Russia?" Fritz asks.

"Yes," Oswald replies, slightly annoyed. "My wife has relatives over there, and she and I still have many friends."

---

ner had "a tendency to exaggerate." Actually, Fenner's testimony before the House Judiciary subcommittee that when she saw Oswald on TV after the assassination and recognized him as the man who had given her the note, yet told no one at the office about this fact when she came in to work because "there was no one for me to talk to" and "what I didn't know was none of my business," throws her entire story about the contents of the note into question. And of course her recalling that the note said Oswald threatened to blow up the Dallas Police Department for a grievance he had against the FBI has no ring of truth to it. (*FBI Oversight*, December 11 and 12, 1975, pp.37–38, 40–41, 47, 53 [Fenner's testimony on December 11]; pp.129–130, 145–146 [Hosty's testimony on December 12]; Hosty with Hosty, *Assignment: Oswald*, pp.185, 195–199; Telephone interview of James Hosty by author on April 9, 2004; Joe Pearce affidavit: DOJCD Record 186-10006-10077, July 29, 1975; see also Church Committee Report, pp.96–97)

"How long were you in Russia?" Fritz asks.

"About three years," Oswald says, growing increasingly edgy every time Agent Hosty asks a question.

"Ever own a rifle in Russia?" Fritz asks.

"You know you can't own a rifle in Russia," Oswald smirks, figuring that Fritz probably knows nothing about life in the Soviet Union. "I had a shotgun over there. You can't own a rifle in Russia."[643]

"Do you have any political beliefs, Lee?" Fritz asks.

"No," Oswald replies, "but I'm a supporter of the Castro revolution."[644]

Captain Fritz picks up a piece of paper from his desk that was found in Oswald's wallet.

"What is the Fair Play for Cuba Committee?" he asks.

"I was the secretary of that organization in New Orleans a few months ago," Oswald says.

"What is the organization about?" Fritz probes.

"Why don't you ask Agent Hosty?" Oswald replies.[645]

Hosty is itching to grill Oswald about his Soviet contacts in Mexico City and can't understand why Fritz is fooling around with this line of questioning. He jumps in.

"Mr. Oswald, have you been in contact with the Soviet embassy?"

The question instantly unnerves Oswald.

"Yes, I contacted the Soviet embassy regarding my wife," Oswald snaps back. "And the reason was because you've accosted her twice already!"[646]

Oswald is growing steadily out of control, and Captain Fritz knows it. Hosty's questions continually undo the calm and talkative demeanor Fritz is working hard to establish. Hosty presses Oswald further—this time, too far.

"Mr. Oswald, have you ever been to Mexico City? Not Tijuana; Mexico City?"

Oswald jumps up like a live wire and slams his manacled fists down on the desktop.

"No! I've never been there!" he shouts. "What makes you think I've been to Mexico City? I deny it!"[647]

Oswald is shaking and starting to sweat. Hosty has hit a raw nerve. Fritz works quickly to soothe Oswald.

"All right, all right, let's calm down," Fritz says. Oswald sits back down, smoldering, and Hosty wisely retreats to a corner of the office to scribble notes. Fritz steps out to take a phone call. That'll give Oswald a chance to cool off, he thinks.

A detective approaches the homicide captain and tells him that an eyewitness to the Tippit shooting, Helen Markham, may have to be taken to the hospital to be treated for shock. Markham has been across the hall, in the burglary and theft office, for over an hour. The prospect of having to face Tippit's murderer in a lineup has her teetering between vomiting and fainting.

Captain Fritz can't have his key eyewitness leaving the premises, not yet anyway. He needs an identification as soon as possible. Fritz carries some ammonia, which he keeps in the office, across the hall to help get Markham back on her feet. He instructs officers to take her down to the first-aid room in the basement, to get her away from the noise and excitement, and call him when she's ready.[648]

Detective Leavelle follows her downstairs and tries to calm her down. Markham's biggest fear is that Oswald will be able to see her during the lineup.

"Aw, he ain't going to see you," Leavelle tells her. "All you have to do is just stand there and you've got to say just one word—repeat the number over the man's head that you saw shoot the officer. That's all you've got to do. Say one word."[649]

3:14 p.m.

In the morgue at Parkland Hospital, Dr. Earl Rose commences the autopsy on Officer Tippit. Measuring Tippit's height at five feet eleven inches and estimating his weight at 175 to 180 pounds, he finds four separate bullet entrance wounds in Tippit's body, two in the right side of his chest, one in his right temple, and a fourth superficial wound to his left rib. (The bullet had hit Tippit's uniform button and the button had prevented it from penetrating deeply.) There was extensive damage to the brain and penetration of the lung and liver with massive hemorrhaging. The three bullets entering Tippit's chest and temple had not exited the body and were removed by Rose, who listed the cause of death as "gunshot wounds of the head and chest." Rose found "no powder tattooing at the [wound] margins," tattooing or "powder burns" being the term used to describe an embedding into the skin surrounding the entrance wound of splayed grains of burned gun powder exploding from the muzzle. The absence of powder burns in this case indicates that although Oswald shot Tippit at close range, the revolver's muzzle was probably never closer than three feet.[650]

3:15 p.m.

From Air Force One in flight, twenty-eight minutes after the plane left Dallas, President Johnson makes his first telephone call as president, to the mother of his murdered predecessor. The conversation, taped by the U.S. Signal Corps, is to Rose Kennedy in Hyannis Port, Massachusetts, but put through the White House line. Above the static and the sound of the jet engines, the president, his wife, and Mrs. Kennedy shout out their words:

Voice: "AF-1 [Air Force One] from Crown [a code name for the White House]. Mrs. Kennedy on. Go ahead, please."

Sergeant Joseph Ayres [chief steward on Air Force One]: "Hello, Mrs. Kennedy. Hello, Mrs. Kennedy. We're talking from the airplane. Can you hear us all right, over?"

Rose Kennedy: "Thank you. Hello?"

Ayres: "Yes, Mrs. Kennedy, I have . . . uh . . . Mr. Johnson for you here."*

Rose Kennedy: "Yes, thank you."

LBJ: "Mrs. Kennedy?"

Rose Kennedy: "Yes, yes, yes, Mr. President."

LBJ: "I wish to God there was something that I could do and I wanted to tell you that we are grieving with you."

Rose Kennedy: "Yes, well, thank you very much. That's very nice. I know. I know you loved Jack and he loved you."

Lady Bird Johnson: "Mrs. Kennedy, we feel lucky—"

Rose Kennedy: "Yes, all right."

Lady Bird: "We're glad that the nation had your son as long as it did."

Rose Kennedy: "Well, thank you for that, Lady Bird. Thank you very much. Good-bye."

Lady Bird: "—thought and prayers—"

Rose Kennedy: [weeping] "Thank you very much. Good-bye, good-bye, good-bye." [She hangs up.][651]

---

*Ayres would later tell author William Manchester that he started to say "President" Johnson, but checked himself, apparently not wanting to further hurt Mrs. Kennedy with the declared reality that her son was no longer the president (Manchester, *Death of a President*, p.371).

At Parkland Hospital, two of Parkland's surgeons, Drs. Malcolm Perry and Kemp Clark, hold an impromptu press conference. Dr. Perry bears the brunt of the questioning, manfully trying to impart what he knows in response to a hysterical crossfire of badly put questions. Before he can finish one answer, he is interrupted by another question and another. Answers about complicated medical procedures are shouted down by questions the doctors aren't able to answer. They don't really know how many times the president was struck nor from which direction. Perry can't really answer those questions but thinks the wound in the throat they enlarged for the tracheotomy was an entrance wound.[652] As to the bullet wound to the right side of the president's head, Perry doesn't know if that wound and the wound to the throat "are directly related" (i.e., caused by one bullet) or if the two wounds were caused by "two bullets." Though Perry's conclusions were not categorical, in the headlong rush to print it would be reported by some in the media that at least one of the shots definitely came from the front, not where Oswald was believed to be, to the president's right rear.[653]

At the Eastman Kodak Company near Love Field, Secret Service agent Forrest Sorrels and Abraham Zapruder meet with Phillip Chamberlain, acting laboratory manager, and Richard Blair, customer service representative. Within minutes, the laboratory begins the developing process, which will take about an hour.

Sorrels calls his office for the first time since leaving Love Field that morning in the lead car of the motorcade. He learns that Captain Fritz has been trying to get a hold of him, that he has a suspect in custody. Sorrels hangs up and tells Zapruder that he must leave, but will contact him later about getting a copy of his film. The agent hurries out to the Dallas police car and has the waiting patrolmen take him to Dallas police headquarters.[654]

3:30 p.m.
Across town, six plainclothesmen move quickly toward the small ranch-style, brick home at 2515 West Fifth in Irving. The Dallas police detectives had been waiting up the street for nearly forty minutes until the three Dallas County sheriff deputies arrived.[655]

Detective John Adamcik and Deputy Sheriffs Harry H. Weatherford and J. L. Oxford circle around toward the back door; Deputy Sheriff Buddy Walthers and Detectives Rose and Stovall bound up to the front entrance. The front door is standing open, screen door shut, and the officers can see Ruth Paine and Marina Oswald, a baby in her arms, watching television. Rose knocks on the door and fishes for his credentials.[656]

Ruth Paine answers the door and the officers identify themselves.

"It's about the president being shot, isn't it?" Mrs. Paine asks.

"Yes," Rose responds. "We have Lee Harvey Oswald in custody. He is charged with shooting an officer."

They explain that they want to search the house. Mrs. Paine asks if they have a warrant and they tell her they do not, but can get the sheriff out there right away with one if she insisted.

"That won't be necessary," Mrs. Paine says, as she pushes the screen door open. "Come on in. We've been expecting you. Just as soon as we heard where it happened, we figured someone would be out."[657]

Guy Rose, as the senior detective, does most of the talking. Ruth introduces him to Marina, who is holding June in her arms, and explains that she is Lee's wife, a citizen of Russia.

Detective Stovall goes to the back door and lets the other officers in.[658] They spread out and begin searching the premises.

Detective Rose asks to use the phone and calls Captain Fritz, asking him whether there are any special instructions.

"Ask her if her husband has a rifle," Fritz says.

Rose keeps the line open while he asks her, but she doesn't understand. Mrs. Paine explains that Marina speaks very little English and offers to translate for him. Ruth asks Marina the question in Russian, then turns back to Rose and says, "No." But then Marina says something to Ruth, who suddenly tells Rose, "Yes, he does have."

Rose relays the information to Captain Fritz, who tells him to gather everything they can and bring it downtown. Rose hangs up the phone and asks Marina if she would show him where the rifle is. Mrs. Paine translates the request and Marina indicates the garage.[659] They go to the garage, attached to the house just off the kitchen, and Marina points to a blanket rolled up and lying on the floor near the wall. A piece of white twine is tied around one end of the blanket, the other end is loose. To the detective, it looks like something might still be there, the blanket retaining the outline of a rifle.[660]

"Well, now they will find it," Marina thinks to herself.[661]

Detective Rose reaches down and picks up the blanket. It falls loosely over his arm—obviously empty. Marina lets out an audible gasp.[662] About a week after arriving at the Paine residence from New Orleans, she was in the garage looking for a metallic part to put June's crib together. When she came across the blanket with something wrapped in it, she opened it up and saw the rifle.[663] She knows, now, it was Lee who shot the president. Until that moment, she had thought the rifle was in the garage, and therefore Lee couldn't have done it. She had convinced herself that the police had come out simply because her husband was always under suspicion—something the FBI visits in November had reinforced. Now she knows better.[664]

Ruth Paine looks at Marina and sees that she is pale white. Ruth senses what that means. For a moment, Detective Rose thinks Marina might be about to faint.

"I'm going to have to ask both of you to come downtown with us," Detective Rose tells them.[665]

As they return to the house, Ruth Paine's estranged husband Michael arrives. Seeing only Ruth, he says to her, "I came to help you. Just as soon as I heard where it happened, I knew you would need some help."[666]

When Michael Paine heard the news, his first thought was that Oswald could have been the one who had done it.[667]

3:40 p.m.

Captain Fritz returns to his office and resumes his methodical questioning of Oswald. "Lee, I'm a little confused about why your wife is living in Irving and you're living in Oak Cliff. Can you tell me about that?"

"My wife is staying with Mrs. Paine who's trying to learn Russian," Oswald says, gradually regaining his composure. "My wife teaches her and Mrs. Paine helps her out with our small baby. It makes a good arrangement for both of them."

"How often do you go out there?" Fritz asks.

"Weekends," Oswald says.

"Why don't you stay out there?"

"I don't want to stay there. Mrs. Paine and her husband are separated. They don't get along too well," Oswald answers unresponsively.

Fritz asks Oswald if he has a car and Oswald says, "No," adding that the Paines had two cars but he didn't use either one of them.[668] Asked about his education, Oswald tells Captain Fritz that he went to school in New York for a while, then Fort Worth, then he dropped out of high school to go into the Marines, but eventually finished high school while in the service.

"Did you win any medals for rifle shooting in the Marines?" Fritz asks in an innocent way.

"Just the usual medals," Oswald says, heading off the inquiry.

"Like what?" Fritz asks.

"I got an award for marksmanship," Oswald says matter-of-factly.[669]

Fritz suddenly changes subjects.

"Lee, why were you registered at the boarding house as O. H. Lee?"

"Oh, she didn't understand my name correctly," he shoots back. "I just left it that way."[670]

Fritz leans back in the chair, "Did you work at the Depository today?"

"Yes," Oswald replies.

"How long have you worked there?" Fritz asks.

"Since October fifteenth."[671]

"What part of the building were you in at the time the president was shot?" Fritz quizzes.

"I was having lunch about that time on the first floor," Oswald says dryly. "We broke for lunch about noon and I came down and ate."[672]

"Where were you when the officer stopped you?" Fritz asks, referring to the story that Roy Truly, the building manager, had told him earlier.

"I was on the second floor drinking a Coke when an officer came in," Oswald replies. "There's a soda machine in the lunchroom there. I went up to get a Coke."

"Then what did you do?" Fritz prompts.

"I left," Oswald says, like it's nothing.

"Where did you go when you left work?" the homicide captain asks.

"I went over to my room on Beckley," Oswald says, "changed my trousers, got my pistol, and went to the movies."

"Why did you take your pistol?" Fritz asks.

"I felt like it," Oswald says snidely.

"You felt like it?"

"You know how boys are when they have a gun," Oswald smirks, "they just carry it."

"Did you shoot Officer Tippit?"

"No, I didn't," Oswald says. "The only law I violated was when I hit the officer in the show; and he hit me in the eye and I guess I deserved it. That is the only law I violated. That is the only thing I have done wrong."[673]

The answers seem to be coming easy now for Oswald. Like an experienced cross-examiner, Fritz changes the subject abruptly.

"What did you do during the three years you lived in the Soviet Union?"

"I worked in a factory," Oswald says casually.

"What kind?" Fritz asks as he peers at Oswald through his owlish spectacles.

"A radio electronics factory," Oswald answers.[674]

"Why did you leave the Depository after the shooting?" Fritz asks, returning suddenly to the present. The questions are coming from all angles now, but Oswald handles the changeups with ease.

"I went out front and was standing with Bill Shelley," Oswald tells him, "and after hearing what happened, with all the confusion, I figured there wouldn't be any more work done the rest of the day, so I went home. The company's not that particular about our hours. We don't even punch a clock."

"What kind of work do you do at the Depository?" Fritz asks.

"I fill orders," Oswald says.

"Which floors do you have access to?"

"Well, as a laborer," Oswald replies, "I have access to the entire building."

Oswald explains that the company offices are on the first and second floors and that they store books on the third, fourth, fifth, and sixth floors.[675]

"Did you shoot the president?" Fritz asks.

"No, I emphatically deny that," Oswald snaps. "I haven't shot anybody."[676]

A detective opens the door to Fritz's office and pokes his head in. "Captain Fritz, they're ready downstairs."

"Okay," Fritz says, rising from his chair, "let's take a break."[677] Not the best session Fritz has ever had with a suspect, but certainly not the worst, either. Oswald thinks he is being cagey, answering only the questions he thinks he can answer without being caught, but he's talking too much anyway. Fritz didn't know a damn thing about him except his name, where he worked, and one of his addresses, but now he already knows quite a bit more, a lot of little details his men can check out—and who knows what they'll find?

4:05 p.m.

Secret Service agent Forrest Sorrels and a small group of fellow agents are waiting in the outer office of Homicide and Robbery when Fritz comes out of his office. Sorrels greets Fritz, whom he's known for some time.

"Have you gotten anything out of him?" Sorrels asks the homicide captain.

"No," Fritz replies, "he hasn't made any admissions yet, but I'll be talking to him again very soon."[678]

Sorrels sees two detectives preparing to escort Oswald out of Captain Fritz's office.

"Captain, I'd like to talk to this man when I have the opportunity," Sorrels says.

"You can talk to him right now," Fritz answers, deciding to keep the lineup waiting a few minutes. Fritz makes arrangements to have Sorrels question Oswald in a small squad room tucked behind his private office.[679] When Oswald is led in, the cool demeanor is gone, replaced with an arrogant and belligerent attitude.[680]

"I don't know who you fellows are, a bunch of cops?" Oswald asks.

"Well, I will tell you who I am," the agent begins. "My name is Sorrels, and I am with the United States Secret Service. Here is my commission book [the Secret Service term for the small leather folder that contains the agent's ID on top and badge on the bottom]."

Sorrels holds it out in front of the prisoner.

"I don't want to look at that," Oswald says, holding his head up, refusing to look. "What am I going to be charged with? Why am I being held? Isn't someone suppose to tell me what my rights are?"

"Yes, I will tell you what your rights are," Sorrels replies calmly. "Your rights are the same as that of any American citizen. You do not have to make a statement unless you want to. You have the right to get an attorney."

"Aren't you suppose to get me an attorney?" Oswald asks.

"No," Sorrels says.

"You're not?" Oswald says with surprise.

"No," Sorrels answers, "because if I got you an attorney, they would say I was probably getting a rakeoff on the fee." A slight smile creeps across Sorrels's face. He hopes his bit of humor will help loosen the suspect up. But Oswald will have none of it, not finding Sorrels's attempt at humor amusing.

"You can have the telephone book and you can call anybody you want to," Sorrels continues. "I just want to ask you some questions."

Sorrels asks if Oswald has ever been in a foreign country. Oswald says that he had traveled in Europe and spent a good deal of that time in the Soviet Union. Then suddenly, Oswald says, "I don't care to answer any more questions."[681]

With that, the just-started interview is terminated. Fritz instructs his men to take Oswald down to the basement show-up room, then turns to two plainclothes vice squad officers, William E. Perry and Richard L. Clark, waiting to take part in the lineup. Normally, available prisoners are pulled from jail and used in the lineups. But Captain Fritz is afraid that prisoners might try to hurt Oswald, due to the high feeling in Dallas over the assassination of the president. His own office doesn't have any men the right size to show with Oswald, so he had called down to vice to borrow a couple of their men. Fritz tells Officers Perry and Clark to take off their sport coats, loosen their ties, and generally change their appearance before heading down to the show-up room.[682]

4:10 p.m.

Detectives Sims, Boyd, and M. G. Hall escort Oswald toward the exit that leads out of the Homicide and Robbery office. The door opens and they wade into the crowd of reporters jammed in the corridor outside. Flashbulbs pop incessantly as questions are fired at the prisoner. Oswald raises his manacled fists for the photographers.[683] The crowd is shoulder to shoulder, pressing in as the detectives shuffle Oswald twenty-three feet to the jail elevator at a snail's pace. Reporters, frantic for information, shout questions over each other. The huge TV cameras blocking the corridor manage to catch a few seconds of the young man upon whom the attention of the whole world is now focused. Oswald catches one question from the deafening storm directed at him, "Did you kill the president?"

"No, sir." He answers calmly. "Nobody charged me with that."

When they arrive downstairs in the basement holdover room, Sims and Boyd search Oswald—remarkably, no one has yet. Boyd finds five live rounds of .38 caliber ammunition in the left front pocket of Oswald's trousers.

"What are these doing in there?" the detective asks.

"I just had them in my pocket," Oswald says nonchalantly.[684]

Detective Sims finds a bus transfer issued by the Dallas Transit Company in his shirt pocket.[685] Oswald takes off his silver Marine Corps ring and hands it to Sims.[686] Also recovered from Oswald's pockets are a small white boxtop with the name "Cox's, Fort Worth" printed on the top; a paycheck stub from American Bakeries dated August 22, 1960; a brass key marked "P.O. Dept., Do Not Dup." with the number 1126; eighty-seven cents in change; and thirteen dollars in paper money—a five-dollar bill, and eight singles.[687]

The telephone rings in Shanklin's Dallas FBI office. It's Belmont in Washington. He wants an update.

"Well, Alan, our agents are interviewing the suspect Oswald," Shanklin tells him. "Hosty and Jim Bookhout, a good criminal agent, are in with the police right now."

"If there's any question that a polygraph might be productive," Belmont says, "go right ahead and use it. Have you talked with the Secret Service?"

"They don't appear to be doing much," Shanklin replies. "Most of them have gone back to Washington with the vice president."

"You should make sure that all possible investigative steps are being taken," Belmont orders him. "For example, make sure that the gun is checked for fingerprints; determine Oswald's whereabouts throughout the day; and make sure that the locations where the gun and shells were found is examined carefully."

"Well, I think the police have that covered," Shanklin says.

"Don't assume the police are going to handle this properly," Belmont says. "We must conduct a vigorous and thorough investigation if we expect to get answers."

"Right," Shanklin responds.

"Now, if you need additional personnel to accomplish that," Belmont adds, "you should let us know."

"Well, if it turns out Oswald is not the person who shot the president," Shanklin says, "we're going to need more manpower down here. We should know something very soon."[688]

Returning to his office, Chief Curry finds television trucks all around City Hall, the building itself overrun with newsmen and television cameras, their heavy cables snaking through hallways and offices. The Dallas police have always permitted free movement of the press around City Hall, but they have never been faced with anything like this before, with the national and international press descending on them.

Chief Curry knows that his men have a suspect in the Tippit killing, possibly in the assassination, and from the reports coming in it seems that everything that can be done is being done. Curry calls the personnel office and requests the file on the officer killed in Oak Cliff.

Checking the record of the eleven-year veteran patrolman, Curry finds that J. D. Tippit had two previous brushes with death while on the force. Back in April 1956, he and his partner, Daniel Smith, had intervened in a domestic dispute involving a suicidal husband with an icepick. When the two officers moved in to arrest the man, he managed to stab Smith once in the left shoulder and Tippit twice, in the stomach and again in the right knee. Surgeons later found a half inch of the icepick's tip embedded in his right kneecap. It left him with an occasional slight limp and a much more cautious attitude. Four months later, on September 2, 1956, Tippit and partner Dale Hankins shot Leonard Garland to death at Club 80 in Dallas, after Garland pulled out a semiautomatic pistol, shoved it into Tippit's face, and pulled the trigger. Garland had failed to remove the safety, and luckily for Tippit, the gun didn't fire. Tippit and Hankins returned fire, killing the gunman, who turned out to be wanted by the FBI. Tippit (as did Hankins) received a

Dallas Police Department Certificate of Merit for his "outstanding judgment and quick thinking." Bud Owens, Tippit's immediate supervisor for nearly ten years, vouched for him as a well-liked officer who used good common sense.[689]

4:15 p.m.
Lieutenant Jack Revill, the man in charge of the Dallas Police Department's Criminal Intelligence Section, dictates a memo to one of the clerks in the Special Services Bureau office. After leaving FBI agent Hosty in the homicide office, Revill had returned to his office and immediately reported the conversation with Hosty to his boss, Captain W. Pat Gannaway, telling Gannaway that Hosty had said the FBI knew all about Oswald before the assassination and knew he was capable of it. If true, this was explosive information. Why hadn't the FBI told the Dallas Police Department about Oswald before the president came to town? Indeed, why hadn't they and the Secret Service been watching Oswald?

"Put it in writing," Gannaway told him.

Revill said that he hated to do that. After all, Hosty might have been simply stating his personal opinion.

"Put it on paper," Gannaway replied adamantly, "and give it to me and I will take it to Chief Curry."

With the help of an office clerk, Revill follows Gannaway's order:

> On November 22, 1963, at approximately 2:50PM, the undersigned officer met Special Agent James Hosty of the Federal Bureau of Investigation in the basement of City Hall. At that time Special Agent Hosty related to this officer that the Subject was a member of the Communist Party, and that he was residing in Dallas. The Subject was arrested for the murder of Officer J. D. Tippit and is a prime suspect in the assassination of President Kennedy. The information regarding the Subject's affiliation with the Communist Party is the first information this officer has received from the Federal Bureau of Investigation regarding same. Agent Hosty further stated that the Federal Bureau of Investigation was aware of the Subject and that *they had information that this Subject was capable of committing the assassination of President Kennedy.*[690]

When the clerk hands Revill the typed copy, he reads it over carefully before signing it.

"Are you sure this is the way you spell *assassination*?" he asks.

"Yes, sir," the clerk replies. "I looked it up in the dictionary."[691]

4:20 p.m.
Bill Alexander had been in a police squad car parked behind the Texas Theater along with many officers who were watching the backdoor of the theater for a possible escape. When word was received that the Tippit murder suspect was apprehended inside, and was being taken to police headquarters at City Hall, Alexander returned to his office. His old friend, Captain Fritz, was on the phone shortly thereafter, asking Alexander to prepare a search warrant pronto for Oswald's Beckley apartment. Alexander prepared the warrant and called Justice of the Peace David Johnston, whom he needed to sign the warrant, to meet him at the sheriff's office for the trip to Beckley. Alexander meets with Johnston and Dal-

las police detectives F. M. Turner and H. M. Moore at the sheriff's office, and the four immediately leave for Beckley; Johnston, because of the rush, signed the warrant in the squad car en route to Beckley.[692]

4:35 p.m.

The darkened detail room in the basement, where the officers get their assignments at the beginning of each shift, is full of men, some in uniform, others not. At one end of the room is a narrow stage, about two and a half feet high, screened off from the rest of the room by a one-way black nylon scrim. The stage is hotly illuminated by floodlights overhead and at the floor level, making it easy for the witnesses standing in the darkness to see the suspects through the scrim, but impossible for the suspects to see them in the darkness beyond.[693] Detectives Sims, Boyd, and Hall have Oswald in a holdover room next to the stage. They are joined by Officers Perry and Clark, and a jail clerk (a civilian employee), Don Ables, who will appear in the lineup with Oswald. Each of them is handcuffed to the other.[694]

Helen Markham, who had been close to fainting before being given ammonia, is brought out of the first-aid room and into the darkened area of the detail room by Detectives Leavelle and Graves. Captain Fritz, Chief Curry, and Detective C. W. Brown join them momentarily.[695] Mrs. Markham, who still hasn't recovered from the shock of seeing the murder, is terribly jittery, and the darkened roomful of policemen isn't all that reassuring.

The word is given and Detectives Sims, Boyd, and Hall troop the four men out onto the stage.[696] As soon as Oswald comes out, Mrs. Markham feels cold chills run over her and begins to cry.[697] The four men come to a stop, each positioned underneath a large number. Left to right, from Markham's position, the four men are W. E. Perry (under number 1), Lee Harvey Oswald (2), R. L. Clark (3), and Don Ables (4).[698]

Though Markham is confident Oswald is the man she saw shoot Officer Tippit, she wants to be sure and whispers to one of the policemen that she wants them to turn Oswald sideways, which was standard procedure anyway. Detective Leavelle tells the men to turn to their right, left, to the rear, then back to the front. Each man is then asked a question or two so that Markham can hear them speak. Leavelle doesn't ask Oswald his name because Markham might have heard it since the shooting.

Mrs. Markham can't forget the way the killer looked at her on Tenth Street—the glassy, wild look in his eyes.

"The second one," Markham says.

The police aren't sure what she means—second from the left, or the right?

"Which one?" they ask.

"Number 2," she says.

There's an immediate stirring of voices in the room, and Mrs. Markham, faint again, falls over.[699]

Detectives Sims, Boyd, and Hall march the men off the stage and Oswald is taken back up to Captain Fritz's office on the third floor.[700]

4:45 p.m.

The unmarked squad car pulls up in front of the rooming house on North Beckley in Oak Cliff and four men, armed with a search warrant, climb out.

After showing the search warrant to the landlord, Mr. Johnson, Alexander and the detectives enter Oswald's room. They notice the sagging single bed framed in a metal headboard, and the movable wardrobe, an old blonde oak dresser with missing handles. When they open two dresser drawers, some clothing spills onto the floor. Alexander finds an empty leather holster hanging from a doorknob. A shelf on a wall has some food atop it. The room, Alexander sees, is "messy but not dirty."[701]

The detectives begin piling everything on the bed for the trip downtown: clothing, shoes, a shaving kit; a city map of Dallas with some suspicious pencil markings on it, including some at the Texas School Book Depository and Elm Street; an address book, some paperbacks—*A Study of the USSR and Communism* and a couple of James Bond books—a Gregg shorthand dictionary, a copy of *Roberts Rules of Order*; a pair of binoculars; several pamphlets and handbills; a certificate of Undesirable Discharge from the U.S. Marine Corps, and a lot of other documents.

The detectives are particularly struck and alarmed by the stuff in Russian and the left-wing literature. It's not the kind of thing they find too often in Dallas. There's a letter about photography from Gus Hall, leader of the American Communist Party, one in Russian from the Soviet embassy in Washington, and another from someone called Louis Weinstock of the Communist Party's paper, the *Worker*. There are two letters from the Fair Play for Cuba Committee, sent to Oswald at an address in New Orleans, a letter from the Socialist Workers Party—a Trotskyite organization—regarding membership, and a Russian passport with Oswald's photo in it. Alexander thinks to himself that there's a lot of difference between a homegrown killer and someone who appeared, from what he could see, to be a card-carrying Communist with overseas connections. The possibility of a Communist conspiracy enters his mind. Even the thought of Russian military transport planes, landing in Dallas, flashes across his mind.

Over the next hour and a quarter, they nearly strip the room, using the pillow cases and one of Oswald's own duffle bags to carry everything to the waiting patrol cars. Only a banana peel and some uneaten fruit are left behind when they leave just after 6:00 p.m.[702]

Aboard Air Force One, the flight back to Washington has been abuzz with a continuous and overlapping series of communications with the outside world, some to pick up the threads of the American government so brutally ripped asunder just hours ago, some to let profoundly worried officials and congressmen have a reassuring word with the new president, but most of the conversations are about the fallen president.[703] As Air Force One zoomed through the sky to its Washington, D.C., destination at more than 600 mph, there are conflicting reports about the extent, if any, of the tension existing between the old and the new presidential administrations. At a minimum, the ride to Washington, as Mrs. Johnson says, was "strained."[704] And it's clear that the aides to Kennedy and Johnson were separated on the plane, Kennedy's aides in the rear of the plane with Mrs. Kennedy and the casket. A top Kennedy aide is said to have told a news reporter, "Make sure that you report that we rode in back with our president, and not up front with him [LBJ]."[705] Was a lot more involved? Kennedy assistant press secretary Malcolm Kilduff was quoted as telling one source, "That was the sickest airplane I ever was on." And he told the *Los Angeles Times* that there was friction between Kennedy and Johnson factions on the flight. "I think that there are things that happened that could be embarrassing to both the Kennedys and the Johnsons," he said, though he would not describe the events referred to. Another passenger, wishing to remain anonymous, said, "They refought the battles of 1960," during which Johnson and Kennedy had bitterly contested for the Democratic nomination. But, under the circumstances, much of this seems unlikely, and Jack Valenti, an LBJ aide, remembered no such discussion and acrimony, adding that the extreme grief of Kennedy's top aides, Kenneth O'Donnell and Larry O'Brien, was "simply beyond anything as casual as hostility." Charles Roberts of *Newsweek*, who was aboard, wrote, "As an unbiased witness to it [the transition of power], now that questions have been raised, . . . it was careful, correct, considerate and compassionate."

As far as President Johnson's conduct on the plane, rumors abounded that he had been "rude," "overbearing," and "boorish," one anonymous source even saying he had been impatient with Jackie when she did not "immediately come forward to witness the oath-taking." However, the evidence from named sources contradicts this. William Manchester himself, who, in writing *The Death of a President*, probably interviewed more people, including all the Kennedy entourage on the plane, than anyone else, said, "I think Johnson acted in incredibly difficult circumstances. I think he behaved well," particularly, Manchester said, in being solicitous and caring to Jackie throughout, a view which sounds much more believable to me. And Roberts of *Newsweek* said that although Johnson was very "capable of crudities," the new president's conduct during the four hours of flight was completely proper and "four of Johnson's finest." Indeed, even Kilduff, who spoke of hostility on the plane between the two camps, said in a radio-television interview on November 21, 1966, on the Westinghouse Broadcasting network, "I can't help but feel that he [President Johnson] showed the utmost . . . personal concern for Mrs. Kennedy, all members of the Kennedy family, and the whole Kennedy party that was with us."[706]

About certain things, everyone agrees. As author Relman Morin writes, as the plane thundered toward Washington it was "heavily freighted with grief and horror and memories and the aching sense of loss." Also, that Johnson, with the levers of power now in his hands, started working immediately at his new job. He was on the phone to Washington calling for a cabinet meeting the next morning, requesting that Robert S. McNamara, the secretary of defense, and McGeorge Bundy, the special assistant to the president for national security affairs, be at Andrews Air Force Base when Air Force One landed so they could instantly bring him up to date on the very latest developments flowing from the assassination throughout the world, and so on. The transition of power was also filled with the unavoidable poignancies that strike at the heart. During the flight, in the Oval Office "a sad task was going forward. They were removing some of [JFK's] most prized mementos: the coconut shell in which he had sent the message for help after the Japanese destroyer *Amagiri* rammed and sank PT-109, the framed photographs of his wife and of Caroline and John-John at different ages, the silver calendar that marked the dates of the beginning and end of the Cuban missile crisis, his famous rocking chair."[707]

During the flight, Rufus Youngblood and Roy Kellerman conferred frequently by phone with the head of the White House Secret Service detail in Washington, D.C., Gerry Behn, to arrange security and procedures at Andrews Air Force Base. Behn wanted President Johnson to come immediately to the White House, where both security and communications were best, but Youngblood told him that the president was adamantly against it. "That would be presumptuous on my part," Johnson said. "I won't do it." Instead, Johnson instructs Youngblood to have the Secret Service secure the Johnsons' Washington, D.C., residence instead.[708]

A dispute over how and where to take the body broke out. Admiral Burkley advised Captain Taz Shepard, the president's naval aide, to make arrangements with Bethesda

Naval Hospital, while Ted Clifton informed Dr. Leonard Heaton, the army's surgeon general, that the autopsy would be performed at the Walter Reed Army Medical Center, the great hospital in the nation's capital that since 1909 had treated grunts and generals, even presidents and Winston Churchill.[709] General McHugh ordered an ambulance, but was informed that it was illegal in the District of Columbia to move a dead body by ambulance without a coroner's permit. McHugh didn't give a damn.

"Just *do* it," he snapped. "And don't worry about the law. *I'll* pay the fine."[710]

Eventually, the choice of hospital was left to Mrs. Kennedy. Dr. Burkley made his way back to the tiny rear cabin area where she held vigil next to her husband's coffin. He knelt in the aisle beside her, and explained to her that the president's body would first have to be taken to a hospital. "Why?" she asked. To have the bullet removed for evidence, Burkley improvised, not knowing if there was a bullet inside the president's body. He was careful not to use the word *autopsy*, which would conjure up the image of a dissection. Burkley told her that he would be willing to arrange to have it done at any place that she felt it should be done, although for reasons of security it should be done at a military hospital. The president was, after all, the commander in chief. That effectively narrowed the choice down to two hospitals in the Washington, D.C., area: the army's Walter Reed or the U.S. Naval Medical Center in Bethesda, Maryland.

"The president was in the navy," Burkley said softly.

"Of course," Jackie said, "Bethesda."[711]

Then she thought of Secret Service agent Bill Greer, the driver of the limousine in Dallas. Greer had been remorseful all afternoon, feeling that somehow he might have been able to save the president if only he had swerved the car, or sped away before the fatal shot. Mrs. Kennedy felt sorry for him and requested that Greer drive the casket to the naval hospital.[712]

There had been a steady stream of visitors to the cramped cabin in the rear of the plane throughout the flight, but, with the casket at their feet and so many seats removed, there was not enough room for them to stay long. President Johnson, otherwise closeted with his advisers Cliff Carter and Bill Moyers, came back for a visit, telling Kennedy's men that he hoped they would stay on at the White House: "I need you now more than President Kennedy needed you." Later Moyers came back and asked Ken O'Donnell, Dave Powers, and Larry O'Brien to join the president for a conference about arranging a meeting of the congressional leadership, but they didn't want to leave Jackie.

"We understand perfectly," Moyers agreed.

By then, a small Irish wake, full of melancholy reminiscences, had been unrolling in the rear compartment. Jackie recalled how much Jack enjoyed the singing of tenor Luigi Vena at their wedding, and decided to ask Vena to sing "Ave Maria" and Bizet's "Agnus Dei" at the president's funeral mass. Dave Powers and Ken O'Donnell told her about Jack's meeting with Cardinal Cushing at the North American College in Rome a few months ago. Many U.S. cardinals attended the coronation of Pope Paul VI, but only Cushing was there when the president arrived. "They've all gone home, Jack," the cardinal laughed. "I'm the only one who's for ya! The rest of them are all Republicans." It was decided that Cushing, who married Jack and Jackie, would say the low requiem mass, because Jack liked that better than the solemn high ritual.

Powers told Jackie about the president's last visit to the Kennedy family compound at Hyannis Port on October 30, when he spent the whole day with his crippled and speechless father. The next day, when the president's helicopter arrived, Jack kissed his father on the forehead, started off, and then went back to kiss him again—almost, Dave thought, as though he sensed he would never see his father again. They told how they had accompanied Jack to his son Patrick's grave in Brookline that same afternoon and how they heard him remark, "He seems so alone here."

"I'll bring them together now," Jackie said quietly. At first, Dave and Ken thought she was thinking of burying the president in Boston, but she had already decided on Arlington and planned to have Patrick's body moved from Massachusetts for reburial beside his father.[713]

They told her about their trip to Ireland in June, which Jack had described to her as the most enjoyable experience of his whole life. He was impressed by the drill of the Irish military cadets at Arbour Hill when he placed a wreath on the graves of the leaders of the Easter Rising of 1916. Jackie decides to have them attend the funeral too, if they can, along with the pipers of the Royal Highland Black Watch Regiment, who performed for the president and his family only last week on the grounds of the White House.

Now, as the plane begins its descent into Andrews Air Force Base, O'Donnell, Powers, and O'Brien learn that a detachment of military pallbearers is waiting to carry the coffin from the plane. Overcome with Irish sentiment, Ken O'Donnell speaks up.

"We'll carry him off ourselves."[714]

In a quiet Maryland suburb of the nation's capital, Naval Commander James J. Humes strolls purposefully toward the entrance of Bethesda Naval Hospital. There is a cordon of marines and military police around the hospital, with additional guards stationed at all three entrance gates to the grounds with instructions to admit only employees, patients in serious condition, their relatives, and cars with White House clearance. The thirty-nine-year-old Humes senses that the president's body must be en route.

Earlier, around noon, he had left Bethesda, where he is director of laboratories of the Naval Medical School, and had gone home to help his wife, Ann, get ready for a dinner party they were having that evening for twenty-four people, almost all of them military colleagues. In addition to the dinner party, they were busy taking care of last-minute details related to their son's First Communion, scheduled to take place the following morning at their parish church. Both Jim and Ann were far too busy to listen to the radio, and neither had any idea of the tragedy gripping the country until a couple of their older children—they have five in school and two at home—came home on the school bus and told their mother, "The president's been shot."

"That's a terrible thing to say," she scolded, only to switch on the television and find that it was true. Jim and Ann both knew the dinner party was off, which meant they had a lot of telephoning to do. But the Washington telephone system had given out, overloaded by thousands of people wanting to talk about and share their grief over news of the tragedy, and Ann was finding it impossible to reach any of their guests.* In the interim, Jim decided to take his son out for a haircut. They had just returned when his wife was finally able to get an open line, only to have an operator interrupt her for an

---

*Most of the nearly one and a half million telephones in service in the Washington metropolitan area on November 22 were used during the first half hour. A staggering quarter-million long-distance calls alone were made on Friday, resulting in overloaded exchanges, delayed dial tones, and intermittent service. Normal telephone operations were not completely restored until 4:15 p.m. EST. (Manchester, *Death of a President*, pp. 205–206, 253–254)

emergency call from Admiral Edward Kenney, surgeon general of the navy. "Jim," Kenney told him, "you better hurry over to the hospital."

Humes could hardly have imagined at this time that he would someday be accused by many conspiracy theorists as being an accessory after the fact to Kennedy's murder, and indeed, by necessary extension from their arguments, a part of a plot to murder the president.

Now Humes bounds toward Admiral Kenney's office, where the surgeon general gives the commander his orders: "Be prepared to do an autopsy on the late president." As the words sink in, Humes is told that Commander J. Thornton Boswell, the forty-one-year-old chief of pathology at the Naval Medical School, will be assisting him. He can add anyone else to the team he deems necessary in helping him to determine the cause of death, but he's instructed to limit the personnel as much as possible.[715] Retiring to the solitude of his office, Commander Humes gets a phone call from his friend Dr. Bruce Smith, acting deputy director of the Armed Forces Institute of Pathology (AFIP), who offers whatever help he might need. Humes is grateful and tells him he may call him later.

A short time later, Humes gets in touch with Dr. Boswell and together they decide that Dr. Humes should be the senior autopsy surgeon, considering that he was Boswell's superior at the hospital.[716] Both men have performed autopsies, although neither has been trained or certified as a forensic pathologist, a fact that will ultimately be used to great advantage by conspiracy theorists.[717]*

4:58 p.m. (5:58 p.m. EST)

At two minutes before the hour in the East Coast darkness, Air Force One, the superb blue and white plane of the nation's chief executive, touches down at Andrews Air Force Base in Maryland, about fifteen miles southeast of the nation's capital.[718] The plane taxis into the glare of the reception area, now thronged with hundreds of government officials and other VIPs.

The first person to board Air Force One is President Kennedy's brother, Attorney General Robert Kennedy, who bounds up the ramp and races from the front of the plane to the rear, ignoring President Johnson's outstretched hand as he passes. Johnson is miffed, but O'Donnell, realizing that Bobby's only thought is to get to Jackie as quickly as possible, doubts whether he even saw the president's gesture.[719]

In the tail compartment, Bobby Kennedy rushes to Jackie's side.

"Hi, Jackie," he says quietly, putting an arm around her. "I'm here."

"Oh, Bobby," Jackie sighs. It is so like him, she thinks. He is always there when you need him.[720]

Most of the civilized world is riveted to the live television coverage of the arrival. A huge "catering bus"—an outsized forklift, roofed and painted a garish yellow, used to load meals aboard military transports—is brought to the left rear of the plane and attached to the exit twelve feet above. A military casket team moves forward to secure the

---

*When Boswell was informed that the autopsy would take place at Bethesda, he said, "That's stupid. The autopsy should be done at the Armed Forces Institute of Pathology [AFIP]," located just five miles up the road from Bethesda at the Walter Reed Army Medical Center. The AFIP was "the apex of military pathology and, perhaps, world pathology," according to Boswell. However, his suggestion was rejected. "That's the way it is," he was told. "Admiral Burkley wants Bethesda." (Breo, "JFK's Death—The Plain Truth from the MDs Who Did the Autopsy," p.2796; ARRB MD 26, Memorandum, Andy Purdy to Jim Kelly and Kenneth Klein, August 17, 1977, Notes of interview with Dr. J. Thornton Boswell, pp.1–2)

casket but is pushed out of the way by the dead president's friends and aides, who, along with the assistance of Secret Service agents, start to move the casket onto the compartment of the catering bus.[721]

The compartment containing both the casket and the Kennedy entourage slowly begins to descend, then comes to a stop five feet above the ground. Not being designed for such uses, it's the lowest the forklift can go. It is almost impossible to unload the casket from this height, even with two teams of pallbearers, one on the ground, the other on the lift. Television cameras relentlessly record the awkward scene in black and white. The men struggle to move the cumbersome burden into the rear of a gray U.S. Navy ambulance, its rotating beacon throwing flashes of light over their faces, and finally succeed after several minutes. Meanwhile, the men in the Kennedy entourage begin jumping off the catering bus to the ground below. Robert Kennedy, one of the first on the ground, turns back to help Mrs. Kennedy down to the tarmac.[722]*

Jackie Kennedy walks toward the navy ambulance. Clint Hill assumes she'll ride in the front seat, but she makes her way to the rear door. She tries to open it but can't. Fastened from the inside, the driver quickly reaches back to release the lock. She and Robert Kennedy climb into the back with General McHugh. Secret Service agent Bill Greer takes the wheel, while Kellerman, Paul Landis, and Dr. Burkley crowd into the front seat beside him.[723]

Still aboard the plane, President Johnson glances at a brief statement on the three-by-five card in his hand. The words were drafted in longhand by Liz Carpenter, the press attaché of Lady Bird Johnson, honed by LBJ aide Bill Moyers, and finally typed up for the president. Studying it on the plane, Johnson reversed the order of the last two sentences.

"Bird?" Johnson inquires of his wife. She is ready. Bareheaded in the freezing November cold, Lyndon Johnson, Lady Bird at his side, moves down the ramp into the glare of the airport and television lights, steps up to a podium encrusted with microphones, and speaks to the world for the first time as president of the United States, amid the deafening thwacking of helicopter rotors, which await the task of transporting the new president to his next destination.

"This is a sad time for all people," Johnson intones solemnly. "We have suffered a loss that cannot be weighed. For me it is a deep personal tragedy. I know the world shares the sorrow that Mrs. Kennedy and her family bear. I will do my best. That is all I can do. I ask for your help—and God's."[724]

Because of this event, television has taken on an important new dimension. In addition to meting out bits of new information about the day's events as the drama unfolds, it has now become a vehicle through which the nation's grief is both shared and amplified. NBC's cameras, filming people's reactions to the news on a New York street, caught a middle-aged woman in dark glasses and a fashionable hat at the moment the news of the president's death came over a nearby car radio. The woman jerked as though hit with a

---

*In spite of all the planning for the landing, the ambulance is waiting there not by design but by order of Captain Robert Canada Jr., USN, commanding officer of Bethesda Naval Hospital. Canada, unaware of the role his hospital would play, had sent the navy ambulance to Andrews Air Force Base in case Lyndon Johnson, a navy veteran, whom Canada had treated after his massive heart attack in July 1955, had suffered another one. (Manchester, *Death of a President*, p.381)

physical object, and cried out loudly in disbelief. Similar responses were caught on camera throughout America.[*]

ABC begins rerunning the footage shot by its Dallas affiliate at Love Field earlier that morning in the sparkling sunshine after the rain cleared, showing Jack Kennedy, trailed by Jackie, working his way along the fence to shake some of the hundreds of hands reaching out to him, his enjoyment so obviously unfeigned, his whole being seeming to exemplify a vibrant hope for the future.

"This," Jim Hagerty, former President Eisenhower's press secretary, says, commenting on the ABC footage, "is the president's way of saying thank you to the people. How can you stop it? I don't think you want to stop it . . . It's rather difficult, while guarding the president, to argue that you can't shake hands with the American people or ride in an open car where the people can see you."

In the world of television, where recording and rebroadcasting somehow erase the distinction between past and present, the event can be shown over and over again, but it remains tragically unstoppable.

Harry S. Truman, contacted in retirement in Missouri, is reported to be so upset he is unable to make a statement. Dwight D. Eisenhower feels not only shock and dismay but indignation. He angrily mentions this "occasional psychopathic thing" in the American people, but expresses his belief that it is nonetheless a nation "of great common sense" that will not be "stampeded or bewildered."

General Douglas McArthur says, "The president's death kills something in me."

Adlai Stevenson, speaking from the UN and for millions, says, "All men everywhere who love peace and justice and freedom will bow their heads," adding later, "It's too bad that, in my old age, they couldn't have spent their violence on me and spared this young man for our nation's work."

There's footage too of President Johnson being sworn in aboard Air Force One by Judge Hughes, with the stunned but dutiful widow of his predecessor at his side. The nation, as one, sees an orderly transition of government.

The network anchors—Ed Silverman and Ron Cochran of ABC, Bill Ryan, Chet Huntley, and Frank McGee of NBC, Charles Collingwood and Walter Cronkite of CBS—are addressing the largest television audience in history, unconsciously weaving—out of fact, history, and emotion—a shared experience that will hold the nation in its grip into an unforeseeable future.[725]

5:10 p.m.
In Irving, Texas, at the Paine residence, police are just about finished loading everything they have seized into the police cars.

It isn't quite clear to Ruth Paine whether she and Marina are under arrest or not, although it feels as though they are. Earlier, when the officers asked them, as well as Ruth's husband, Michael, to come down to the police station, Ruth, wanting to cooperate, had gone to see whether she could get a babysitter.

---

[*]In a large-sample national poll in March of 1964 by the National Opinion Research Center, an affiliate of the University of Chicago, an astonishing 53 percent of those interviewed said they had wept when they heard the news of Kennedy's death (*New York Times*, March 7, 1964, p.11). This percentage is remarkable by itself, and becomes even more so when you factor in the number of people who, though grieving as much, cannot bring tears to their eyes.

As Ruth left to walk next door to her neighbor's house, one of the police officers moved to accompany her.

"Oh," she said, "you don't have to go with me."

He said he would be glad to, and she told him to come along, but with a sinking feeling as she realized he was probably assigned to escort her. She called on Mrs. Roberts next door, but Mrs. Roberts was just on her way out and couldn't help. It was after school by that time, though, so Ruth went to another neighbor's house and managed to get one of her teenage daughters to come stay with the kids. As she came back to her own house, still under police escort, she saw the other officers carrying boxes of things from the house to their cars. In a backseat she spotted three cartons of phonograph records, her old 78s.

"You don't need those," she protested, "and I want to use them on Thanksgiving weekend. I promised to lead a folk dance conference that weekend. I'll need those records, which are all folk dance records, and I doubt that you'll get them back to me by then."

They paid no attention to her. The records went. She complained about her 16-millimeter projector too, but her escort took her by the arm and told her they were wasting "too much time."

The brusque treatment continued inside the house, and Ruth began to resent it more and more. Now, she changes from her slacks to a suit, but the officers prevent Marina from doing the same.

"She has a right to," Ruth explains to them icily, a note of proper Quaker decency in her voice. "She's a woman, she has a right to dress as she wishes before going." She tells Marina in Russian to go to the bathroom to change, but while Ruth is talking to the babysitter, one of the cops opens the bathroom door and tells Marina she has no time to change. Ruth's protests were useless. Marina, her emotions whipsawing, is suddenly angry. "I'm not a criminal," she says to herself. "I didn't do anything."

"We'd better get this straight in a hurry, Mrs. Paine," one of the officers says, "or we'll just take the children down and leave them with Juvenile while we talk to you."

Ruth doesn't take this lying down. She makes a point of saying to her daughter, who, unlike her son Christopher, was up and about, "Lynn, you may come too."

For the trip downtown Michael was put in another car, but Marina and Ruth, Lynn, Marina's little girl, and her baby were all jammed in together with three police officers.

Marina, who had been shaking all over with fright before they got into the car, calms down as they drive toward Dallas, and the two women speak quietly in Russian. One of the officers, Adamcik, tries a little Czech on them, but they don't understand him. Marina can tell how shaken Ruth is. Ruth had never ridden in a police car before, had never even envisioned doing so, and the experience is unnerving.

One of the officers in the front turns back to ask Ruth, "Are you a Communist?"

"No, I am not," she replies firmly, "and I don't even feel the need for the Fifth Amendment."[726]

On the trip downtown, Ruth Paine starts to be tormented by "if only" thoughts. If only she had known that Lee had hidden a rifle in her garage. If only she had appraised him as someone capable of such terrible violence. If only the job she helped him find had not put him in a building overlooking the president's parade route. If only she had done a dozen things differently, the country might have been spared this tragedy, and Marina, whom she has come to love as a sister, would not have been made into an assassin's wife, bullied by overbearing policemen in a language she doesn't comprehend.

Ruth wonders whether her determination to look for the good in everyone prevented her from seeing Lee clearly. Just three days ago she learned that Lee was using a false name in his Dallas rooming house. How much truth was there in anything he ever told her? What sort of a man was he beyond the confines of Ruth's house, where he was simply Marina's husband and Junie's and Rachel's father?

Is it possible that he is a Soviet agent? She finds that impossible to believe. He's neither bright nor organized enough for such an assignment. Even if he had volunteered his services to the Russians, they wouldn't have accepted him, or they are bigger fools than she ever dreamed.[727]

5:26 p.m. (6:26 p.m. EST)

Just twenty-eight minutes after Air Force One landed at Andrews Air Force Base, a helicopter delivers President Johnson to the south lawn of the White House. The president, his wife, Secretary of Defense McNamara, and McGeorge Bundy, special adviser to the president, walk in the chilly night through the rose garden on the White House grounds on their way to the Oval Office. When they come to the french doors of the president's office, all stop except Johnson, who pauses, then walks in, alone, and stays for but a minute.

After Johnson closed the door behind him and exited the Oval Office, he and his party went across the street (West Executive Avenue, a blocked-off street across from the West Wing of the White House) to his vice presidential office on the second floor of the Executive Office Building, where congressional leaders from both parties stopped by to pledge their bipartisan support for the good of the grief-stricken nation.[728]

Before he meets with anyone though, the president takes the time to pen two notes to a little boy and a little girl, the first two letters of his presidency:

> Dear John—It will be many years before you understand fully what a great man your father was. His loss is a deep personal tragedy for all of us, but I wanted you particularly to know that I share your grief—You can always be proud of him.

He signs it "affectionately," as he does the next letter.

> Dearest Caroline—Your father's death has been a great tragedy for the Nation, as well as for you at this time.
> He was a wise and devoted man. You can always be proud of what he did for his country.

It is 7:30 p.m. as Lyndon Johnson hands the letters to his secretary, gets up, and goes out to the anteroom to meet the men upon whom the continuity of the government of the United States now depends.[729]

5:55 p.m. (6:55 p.m. EST)

It is near dusk as the presidential motorcade, having left Andrews at 6:10 p.m. EST, takes the Suitland Parkway to Bethesda. FBI agent James Sibert, in a car right behind the navy ambulance carrying the president's body, will never forget the sight of people lining the many bridges over the parkway, holding white handkerchiefs to their eyes. At 6:55 p.m., the navy ambulance with its escort of cars and motorcycle police arrives at Bethesda.[730]

By the time the navy ambulance with its escort of cars and motorcycle police arrives at the Bethesda hospital,[731] crowds, alerted by the television coverage of the arrival of the president's body at Andrews, are waiting silently. More than three thousand people have worked their way inside the grounds because of the hopelessly inadequate cordon improvised by Captain Robert Canada Jr., commanding officer of the hospital. Canada had only twenty-four Marine guards at his disposal, so he mobilized all of his off-duty corpsmen, but still hasn't got nearly enough men to keep the ever-growing crowd from surging toward the ambulance.[732] It's one solid mass of humanity, people standing shoulder to shoulder, between the semicircle drive in front of the hospital (which comes off Wisconsin Avenue and returns) and Wisconsin Avenue a few acres away.[733]

The ambulance, now joined by a sedan with a chaplain and nurses, sweeps up to the main entrance. Robert and Jacqueline Kennedy disembark and are met by Captain Canada, Rear Admiral Calvin Galloway, and a chaplain. After a brief exchange, Secret Service agents Clint Hill and Paul Landis accompany RFK and Mrs. Kennedy to one of the two VIP suites on the seventeenth floor of the hospital's high, stone tower.[734] Jackie had been expected to join her children, John-John and Caroline, before their bedtime and tell them of their father's death, but she decides instead to spend the night at the hospital so as not to leave her slain husband. Although the children were shielded from the news throughout the afternoon, Caroline will be told that evening and John Jr. sometime later (see later text).[735]

The hospital suite consists of three rooms—a bedroom and a kitchen facing each other across a small hallway, at the end of which was a long narrow drawing room. While it is comfortable enough, with air-conditioning, wall-to-wall carpeting, and a bedroom television, the walls, furniture, carpet, and drapes were depressing because of their lifeless and uniformly beige color. The entourage is met at the suite by the president's sister, Jean Kennedy Smith; Jacqueline's mother and stepfather, Janet and Hugh Auchincloss; and Ben Bradlee, Washington bureau chief of *Newsweek* and a longtime friend of the president and his family, along with his wife, Toni. Secret Service agents Hill and Landis move quickly to secure the entire floor, taking control of communications and making sure that no one will be allowed to enter without authorization. Since Mrs. Kennedy is determined to wait until the autopsy is over, they know it's going to be a long night.[736]

An overnight bag and makeup case with Jackie's initials, J.B.K. (B is for Bouvier, Jackie's maiden name), on it are brought to Jackie, but both remain unopened in the long hours ahead. Among the friends who will come to the seventeenth floor to try to console her are political columnist Charles Bartlett and his wife, Martha. It was they who had contrived to introduce Jackie to JFK at a dinner party in their Georgetown home in May of 1951. At the time, Jackie was a Georgetown socialite with blue-blood roots (like JFK, her schooling had been at the best private schools—Miss Porter's, Vassar, the Sorbonne in Paris)who was excited to be working as an "inquiring photographer" and celebrity reporter about town for the *Washington Times-Herald*, and he was a young, dashing war hero who was a member of the House of Representatives from Massachusetts.[737] It wouldn't be until September of 1953, when JFK had become a U.S. senator, that the two would wed in Newport, Rhode Island, *the most* correct social address at the time. A church ceremony attended by over three thousand guests was followed by a grand, *beau monde* reception at Hammersmith Farm, an estate overlooking Narragansett Bay. JFK may have been twelve years her senior (ages thirty-four and twenty-two at the time they met two years earlier), but Jackie would later say, "I took the choicest bachelor in the Senate." Few would disagree that by the time JFK was elected president, "Jack and Jackie were America's royal couple."[738]

Below the seventeenth floor, at the main entrance, Larry O'Brien, Kenny O'Donnell,

General McHugh, and other members of the Kennedy party are standing in front of the hospital talking. The navy ambulance carrying the president's body is nearby, with Secret Service agent Bill Greer still in the driver's seat. Secret Service agent Roy Kellerman has gotten out and gone in to find out where the entrance to the morgue is located.[739] After several minutes, Baltimore FBI agents James W. Sibert and Francis X. O'Neill Jr., who had been ordered to accompany the procession from Andrews Air Force Base, witness the autopsy, take custody of any bullets retrieved from the president's body, and deliver them to the FBI laboratory,[740] approach the group of men and ask what the delay is all about. Larry O'Brien says they don't know where the autopsy room is. The FBI men tell them to follow them around to the rear of the hospital.

When the caravan reaches the morgue entrance, Secret Service agent Roy Kellerman comes out onto the rear loading dock. FBI agents Sibert and O'Neill approach him and identify themselves and their mission.

"Yes, I've already been informed," he tells them and moves down the stairs toward the rear of the ambulance, where Secret Service agent Bill Greer waits. First Lieutenant Samuel R. Bird's honor guards quickly assemble and help Secret Service and FBI agents pull the casket out of the back of the ambulance and onto a conveyance cart, and shuffle it toward the steps leading to the small landing at the rear door.[741] At the base of the stairs, the cart is abandoned and the casket is hand-carried up to the loading-dock entrance.[742] Along the way, General McHugh insists on helping to carry the commander in chief into the hospital and relieves one of the casket team members. One end of the casket dips precariously as General McHugh struggles to carry his share of the weight.[743] Just inside the loading-dock entrance, the team returns the casket to the cart and wheels it a short distance down the corridor toward a naval attendant holding open a double-door marked "Restricted—Authorized Personnel Only."

The Bethesda Naval Hospital morgue is stark and spotless. It was newly renovated just four months earlier. They enter an anteroom equipped with eight refrigerated lockers labeled "Remains." To their right is a swinging-type double-door, with glass panels, that leads to the main room where the autopsies are performed. The tiled autopsy room is lined with equipment specialized for postmortem work: scales, a sterilizer, a washing machine, and a power saw. Situated near the center of the room are two eight-foot-long, stainless-steel autopsy tables, their tops perforated with hundreds of drain holes that feed into pipes set in the floor. Against one wall, on a two-step riser, is a small gallery section that contains a short tier of bleacher-style benches, enough for thirty to forty medical students and young doctors to observe autopsies being performed. This night, the students and young doctors are absent.[744]

The casket team rolls the casket through the doors into the autopsy room and veers to the left, where they come face-to-face with Drs. Humes and Boswell and several other Bethesda personnel dressed in surgical garb, who direct the team to move the casket next to autopsy table number one.[745] Major General Wehle orders his aide, Richard Lipsey, "not to leave the body for any reason,"[746] as Lieutenant Sam Bird's casket team takes up guard duty outside the two entrances to the autopsy room, with the assistance of a detachment of marines.[747]

5:57 p.m.
Detectives Stovall, Rose, and Adamcik march Michael and Ruth Paine and Marina Oswald and her two small children up to the third floor to Homicide and Robbery's outer

office. They are unaware that Lee Oswald sits a few feet away, behind the closed venetian blinds of Captain Fritz's private office. It is near bedlam in the homicide office, full of the noise of incoming telephone calls and constant traffic. Within a few minutes, the detectives move them to the Forgery Bureau office next door, to get away from the congestion of homicide.

After getting the Paines and Marina Oswald settled and calling for an interpreter, Detectives Stovall and Rose turn their attention to locating Wesley Frazier. If for no other reason than that he had driven Oswald to work that day and his present whereabouts are unknown, Frazier has become a suspect. Although they'd been told that Frazier was at Parkland Hospital visiting his ailing father, it takes the detectives nearly forty-five minutes to determine that he is actually at the Irving Professional Center, a medical facility. The detectives telephone the Irving Police Department and make arrangements for Frazier to be arrested.[748]

6:16 p.m.

In the fourth-floor crime lab, Lieutenant Carl Day examines the rifle carefully, looking for fingerprints that the gunman might have left behind. Captain Fritz walks in and tells Day that Marina Oswald has arrived[*] and is downstairs in the Forgery Bureau office.

"I want her to look at the gun and see if she can identify it," Fritz says. "But there's an awful mob down there. I don't want to bring her through that crowd. Can you bring the rifle down there?"

"I'm still working with the prints," Day replies, "but I think I can carry it down there without disturbing them."

In a minute, Day is ready and the two of them make their way downstairs. When they get to the third floor, Day hoists the rifle high over his head and wades into the throng of reporters, who shout questions, "Is that the rifle? What kind is it? Who made it?"

Day says nothing as Fritz clears the way to the Forgery office. They step inside and close the door, shutting out the maddening noise. Marina Oswald is there, holding an infant daughter. Ruth and Michael Paine sit nearby with Detectives Senkel and Adamcik and Russian interpreter Ilya A. Mamantov.[749]

Lieutenant Day shows Marina the rifle as Fritz asks through the interpreter whether this is the rifle her husband owns. Marina says it looks like it, they both have dark wood, but she can't be sure. She only saw the stock and can't remember if it had a telescopic sight. To her, all guns look the same.[750]

As the two detectives prepare to take affidavits from Marina Oswald and the Paines, Captain Fritz and Lieutenant Day push back into the sea of reporters in the outer hall. Fritz heads back to his office, while Day, rifle again lofted over his head, slowly makes his way toward the elevators that will take him and the weapon back to the crime lab.

At the corner of Commerce and Harwood, two detectives wait patiently for Piedmont bus number 50. Just a few minutes earlier, the bus transfer found in Oswald's pocket was traced to the driver of that bus, Cecil McWatters. The detectives have orders to intercept

---

[*]Despite Marina's suspicion that her husband had murdered the president, as she walked past the media at police headquarters upon her arrival, she said loyally, "Lee good man—he no shoot anyone" (*JFK/Deep Politics Quarterly*, April 2006, p.8).

the bus and bring the driver to City Hall. When it arrives as scheduled, McWatters is shocked to find that two potential passengers are, in fact, police. They tell him they want to ask him a few questions and escort the befuddled bus driver into police headquarters. Once inside, they show him the bus transfer found in Oswald's pocket.

"Do you know anything about this?" they ask.

McWatters surely does. He's absolutely positive that he issued the transfer, number 004459, on the Lakewood run about one o'clock that afternoon, give or take fifteen minutes. Each driver has a distinctive punch mark, registered with the company, and McWatters recognizes the crescent shape mark as one made by his hand punch. He even takes his hand punch out of his pocket and punches a sheet of paper to prove it. McWatters also remembers that he only gave out two transfers on that run, both at the same stop, the first to a lady and the second to a young man who got off right after her.[751]

6:20 p.m.

Captain Fritz enters the homicide office where Detective Jim Leavelle informs him that downstairs he's got two eyewitnesses from a car lot near the Tippit shooting who are ready to view Oswald in a lineup.

"Good," Fritz tells him. "Have the bus driver take a look at him too."

Detectives Sims, Boyd, and Hall lead Oswald out of the office and wade into the madhouse of reporters in the outer corridor. As the door closes behind them, Fritz walks over to Jim Allen, a former assistant DA now in private practice, and Secret Service agent Forrest Sorrels. The agent tells Fritz that he has a witness he has talked to and that he would very much like for him to get a chance to see Oswald in a lineup.

"That'll be fine," Fritz says.

Sorrels turns to Secret Service agent William Patterson and asks him to track down Howard Brennan and bring him to City Hall.[752]

6:30 p.m.

The lights are dim in the back half of the basement detail room at Dallas police headquarters in anticipation of the second lineup police are about to conduct. Ted Callaway, the manager of Dootch Motors in Oak Cliff, one of his porters, Sam Guinyard, and bus driver Cecil McWatters wait nervously as police make the last-minute preparations. Detective Leavelle leans over toward Callaway and speaks in hushed tones.

"When I show you these guys, be sure, take your time, see if you can make a positive identification," Leavelle says. "We want to try to wrap him up real tight on killing this officer. We think he is the same one that shot the president. But if we can wrap him up tight on killing this officer, we have got him."[753] Callaway steps to the back of the detail room so he can view the lineup from a distance similar to the distance from which he had seen the gunman on Patton Street. When everything is ready, Detectives Sims, Boyd, and Hall march the shackled men onto the brightly lit stage—the same men, in the same order as the first lineup.[754] As soon as Oswald comes out, Callaway recognizes him. No doubt about it. Detective Sims puts the men through the routine—turn left, face forward, then answer a few brief questions so the witnesses can hear them speak.[755] Detective Leavelle walks over to Callaway, "Which one do you think it was?"

"He's the number 2 man," Callaway says firmly.

Sam Guinyard agrees. Number 2 is the man he saw run past him while he was waxing and polishing a station wagon.[756]

Bus driver Cecil McWatters is less certain. There's one man in the lineup, number 2 (Oswald), who is about the same height, weight, and complexion as the person who got on his bus, but he tells the police he cannot make a positive identification.[757]

As the four men are led off stage, Detective Leavelle takes Ted Callaway and Sam Guinyard up to the crime lab on the fourth floor, where they both identify the light gray Eisenhower-style jacket found in the parking lot behind the Texaco station as the one the man they saw was wearing.[758]

6:35 p.m. (7:35 p.m. EST)

At the Bethesda Naval Hospital morgue, autopsy pathologists Drs. Humes and Boswell open the bronze casket and find the naked body of John F. Kennedy wrapped in a bloody sheet labeled "Parkland Hospital," lying on a heavy-gauge clear plastic sheet, placed there to prevent the corpse from soiling the satin interior of the coffin. An additional wrapping, soaked in blood, envelops the president's shattered head.[759] Paul K. O'Connor and James Curtis Jenkins, student lab technicians in charge of the admission and discharge of morgue bodies, lift the body out of the casket and place it on the autopsy table, where the bloody wrappings are removed.[760]* In spite of his training, Dr. Humes is still shocked by the sight of the president's body. His eyes are open, one lid hanging lower than the other. His mouth is also open, in sort of a grimace, his hands are knotted in fists, and there is a ghastly head wound. Still, the well-known facial features are intact and Dr. Humes can't help but think that apart from the horrible head wound, John Kennedy, who is only a few years older than he is, looks perfectly normal. In fact, at a little over six feet and 170 pounds, Kennedy was "a remarkable human specimen," he would later put it, who "looked as if he could have lived forever."[761] Humes shrugs off the moment of hypnotic shock and fascination, reminding himself there is a lot of work to do.

Several of the nearly two-dozen people in attendance,† particularly the military offi-

---

*Dr. Boswell said Humes was "afraid the sheets would end up in somebody's barn on Highway 66 as exhibits" and immediately threw them into the morgue washing machine to be laundered (ARRB MD 26, Memorandum, Andy Purdy to Jim Kelly and Kenneth Klein, August 17, 1977, Notes of interview with Dr. J. Thornton Boswell, pp.2–3; ARRB Transcript of Proceedings, Deposition of Dr. J. Thornton Boswell, February 26, 1996, p.14).

†FBI agents O'Neill and Sibert noted the following were in attendance at the beginning of the autopsy: Admiral Calvin B. Galloway, USN, commanding officer of the U.S. Naval Medical Center, Bethesda; Captain John H. Stover, commanding officer, U.S. Naval Medical School; Admiral George G. Burkley, USN, the president's personal physician; Commander James J. Humes, chief pathologist; Commander J. Thornton Boswell, chief of pathology at Bethesda; Jan G. Rudnicki, laboratory assistant to Dr. Boswell; John T. Stringer Jr., medical photographer; John H. Ebersole, assistant chief radiologist at Bethesda; Floyd A. Riebe, medical photographer; Paul K. O'Connor, laboratory technologist; James Curtis Jenkins, laboratory technologist; Jerrol F. Custer, X-ray technician; Edward F. Reed, X-ray technician; James E. Metzler, hospital corpsman, third-class; and Secret Service agents Roy Kellerman, William Greer, and John J. O'Leary (who stayed only briefly) (ARRB MD 44, FBI Report of O'Neill and Sibert, November 26, 1963, p.2). Admiral George Burkley reported that Admiral Edward Kenney, the surgeon general of the navy; Captain Robert O. Canada, commanding officer of Bethesda Naval Hospital; and Brigadier General Godfrey McHugh, air force aide to the president, were also present when the president's body was moved to the autopsy table (NARA Record 189-10001-10048, Report of George Burkley, November 27, 1963, 8:45 a.m., p.7, ARRB MD 48). During the course of the autopsy Pierre A. Finck, chief of the wound ballistics pathology branch at Walter Reed medical center, arrived to assist Humes and Boswell. In addition, Lieutenant Commander Gregory H. Cross, resident in surgery, and Captain David Osborne, chief of surgery, entered the autopsy room. (ARRB MD 44, FBI Report of O'Neill and Sibert, November 26, 1963, p.2) At one point, Major General Philip C. Wehle, commanding officer of the U.S. Military District of Washington, D.C., entered the autopsy room to make arrangements with the Secret Service regarding the transportation of the president's body back to the White House. Near the end of the autopsy, Chester H. Boyers, chief petty officer in charge of the pathology division, entered the room to type

cers in command of the naval hospital, retreat to the benches in the gallery as Drs. Humes and Boswell begin an initial examination of the body.[762] In addition to the cutdowns (i.e., small incisions for the insertion of tubes) on the arms, ankles, and chest, Dr. Humes notes a tracheotomy incision in the throat. The body is then rolled briefly onto its side and Humes notes a bullet wound in the president's right upper back. As they complete the initial examination, Admiral Burkley reminds the pathologists that the president's brother and wife are waiting upstairs and that they should expedite the autopsy procedure.

"They've captured the guy who did this, all we need is the bullet," Burkley tells them.

Drs. Humes and Boswell disagree. They feel a complete and thorough autopsy is needed. A discussion ensues, one that Burkley ultimately wins—for the moment.[763]

Dr. Humes requests that all nonmedical personnel leave the autopsy room and retire to the adjacent anteroom so that X-rays and photographs of the body can be made.[764] At Humes's instruction, medical photographer John T. Stringer Jr. begins taking photographs of the body from a variety of angles in both color and black-and-white, being careful to bracket the exposures* of the large (four-by-five-inch) images.

As soon as the photographs are complete, John H. Ebersole, assistant chief radiologist at Bethesda Naval Hospital, begins taking X-rays of the president's skull, with help from X-ray technicians Jerrol F. Custer and Edward F. Reed. Unlike the autopsy photographs, which will not be developed until after the autopsy is completed, the X-rays, which see what the eye cannot, are developed in the hospital's fourth-floor lab and returned to the morgue a quarter of an hour later for viewing.[765]

6:40 p.m.
Assistant Dallas DA Bill Alexander pushes through the crowd in the third-floor hallway of Dallas police headquarters.

After completing the search of Oswald's Beckley room, Alexander had returned to his office and, believing there was more than enough evidence to conclude that Oswald had murdered Officer Tippit, filled in the blanks on State of Texas Form No. 141, a form denominated an "AFFIDAVIT" but referred to by all in Texas as a criminal complaint. In clear hand printing, he charged that Oswald "did . . . voluntarily and with malice aforethought kill J. D. Tippitt [*sic*] by shooting him with a gun." Gathering up some additional blank affidavits, Alexander beats a path over to police headquarters.

Now, Alexander raps lightly on Captain Fritz's private office door and steps in. Fritz is grilling Oswald as a few Dallas police officers stand against the wall, their eyes fixed on the homicide captain's prey. "What struck me about Oswald," Alexander, who did not take part in the questioning, says, "is that even under the circumstances he found himself in, he was in control of himself and acted like he was in control of the situation. It was almost as if everything he said had been pre-rehearsed by him. He was quite skillful in deflecting questions, often answering questions with other questions. He was very arro-

---

up receipts for items given to the FBI and Secret Service. At the end of the autopsy, John VanHoesen, Edwin Stroble, Thomas E. Robinson, and Joe Hagan (personnel from Gawler's Funeral Home) prepared the president's body for burial. Also in attendance at that time were Brigadier General Godfrey McHugh and Dr. George Bakeman, USN. (ARRB MD 44, FBI Report of O'Neill and Sibert, November 26, 1963, pp.2–3) The HSCA also noted that Richard A. Lipsey, personal aide to General Wehle, and Samuel A. Bird were also present at various times (7 HSCA 9).

*This is a standard practice in professional photography wherein each angle is photographed three times at three different exposures—one slightly underexposed, one slightly overexposed, and one at the presumed proper exposure setting—ensuring that at least one of the three images will be perfectly exposed.

gant and defiant with Fritz. I would say his whole behavior was completely inappropriate to the situation. You ought not to be ugly to the man [Fritz] who has the option to
prosecute you." Alexander said that Fritz was very courteous with Oswald, as he always
was with all defendants. "I was very pissed off at Oswald because of his having killed
Kennedy and Tippit, but even if he was only in there for spitting on the sidewalk, I was
so infuriated with him for his insolence to Fritz [someone, Alexander says, he had feelings about almost like those he had for his father], I felt like beating the s—— out of him.
Oswald didn't know this. I kept my composure. But I didn't like that little son of a bitch."[766]

Not too far into this latest round of questioning, Oswald suddenly says he doesn't want
to talk any further without first talking to a lawyer. "You can have an attorney anytime
you like," Fritz tells him.

"I'd like Mr. [John] Abt, in New York, to represent me," Oswald says. "He represented
people who were charged with violating the Smith Act.* I don't know him personally, but
that is the lawyer I want. However, I don't have any money to call him."

"That won't be a problem," Fritz replies. "Just call collect. We allow all prisoners to
use the phone."

Fritz tells the two detectives present to be sure that Oswald has a chance to use the
telephone.[767]†

Alexander nods to Fritz that he wants to talk to him privately. The homicide captain
instructs the Dallas detectives to take Oswald out to the little holding room off Fritz's
office, while Fritz and Alexander remain behind.

"I've got the complaint for Oswald on shooting Officer Tippit," Alexander says, knowing that the Dallas police have more than enough to file charges. Although he doesn't
need Fritz's approval to file the complaint, he seeks his support. "I'm ready to go when
you are."‡

Fritz nods in agreement. Indeed, the evidence is already substantial in the Tippit case.
They tick it off to each other. They know Oswald took a bus to his room in Oak Cliff—
they found the transfer he was issued. His landlady can testify that he came in about one
o'clock, changed clothes, and left a couple of minutes later in a big hurry. He admits he
picked up his pistol at the room. They have an eyewitness to the Tippit shooting, Mrs.
Helen Markham, who identified Oswald in a lineup. Two other eyewitnesses—Ted Callaway and Sam Guinyard—who saw Oswald running from the scene also picked him out
of a lineup. He resisted arrest at the Texas Theater, attempting to shoot the arresting officer. And the revolver he had in his possession at the time of his arrest is the same caliber
as the one used to kill Officer Tippit.

---

*Oswald was referring to an antisedition law enacted in 1940 to combat the threat of global Communism
that prohibited advocating the overthrow of the U.S. government "by force or violence." Abt, himself a member of the Communist Party, won his biggest victory in 1965 when the U.S. Supreme Court held that the
nation's 1950 Internal Security Act (commonly called the McCarran Act), which required that all Communists and Communist organizations register with the federal government, was unconstitutional because it violated the Fifth Amendment's right against self-incrimination. (*Albertson v. Subversive Activities Control Board*,
382 U.S. 70 [1965]; *Los Angeles Times*, August 14, 1991, p.A14)

†Despite Captain Fritz's instructions, there is no record that Oswald made any attempts to contact Attorney Abt in New York on November 22.

‡When I asked Alexander if at that time he also believed Oswald had killed Kennedy, he responded, "Yeah.
We felt it was clear that the same person who killed Tippit killed Kennedy. That's why he killed Tippit, because
he was stopped while in flight from Kennedy's murder. It was pretty obvious to all of us—I don't remember
anyone that was thinking otherwise—that Oswald had committed both murders" (Interview of William Alexander by author on December 11, 2000).

"All in all, that's a lot of good evidence," Fritz says.[768] A call is put in immediately to have Justice of the Peace David Johnston come to police headquarters for the arraignment of Oswald on the Tippit murder charge.

6:50 p.m.

Across the hall from Captain Fritz's office, Lieutenant T. P. Wells answers the telephone. The caller is Barbara Davis, an eyewitness to the Tippit murder case, who says her sister-in-law, Virginia Davis, found a .38 caliber shell in their yard after police left this afternoon. "Okay, we'll be right out," the lieutenant tells her. He hangs up and instructs Detectives C. N. Dhority and C. W. Brown to drive out to Oak Cliff and retrieve the shell.[769]

Secret Service agent Forrest Sorrels informs Captain Fritz that eyewitness Howard Brennan has been located and is at police headquarters now and ready to view Oswald in a lineup. "I wish he would have been here a little sooner," Fritz tells Sorrels. "We just got through with a lineup. But we will get another one fixed up."[770] Fritz stops Detectives Brown and Dhority as they head out the door and instructs them to bring the Davis women back with them, get a statement, and arrange for them to also view Oswald in a lineup.[771]

7:00 p.m. (8:00 p.m. EST)

At Bethesda Naval Hospital, Humes and Boswell, followed by a flock of FBI, Secret Service, and navy personnel, retreat to a small alcove within the autopsy room and snap the newly developed X-rays of the president's head up on a light box. Thirty or forty white specks can be seen scattered throughout the right hemisphere of the brain, like stars in a galaxy. These dustlike metallic particles mark the path of the missile as it passed through the right side of the skull. The largest fragment of metal, still much too small to represent any significant part of a whole bullet, lies behind the right frontal sinus. The next-largest fragment is embedded in the rear of the skull.[772] Humes figures that he can probably retrieve the two larger fragments but is beginning to wonder if it might be a good idea to have an expert in wound ballistics present during the autopsy. He and Boswell confer briefly away from the group. Humes mentions the offer of assistance made by the Armed Forces Institute of Pathology (AFIP) and suggests they take it. Boswell agrees and suggests they contact Lieutenant Colonel Pierre A. Finck, chief of the Wound Ballistics Pathology Branch of the AFIP, whom Boswell had worked with before.[773] Boswell remembers him as sharp, hard-working, and a top-notch forensic pathologist.[774] Humes is convinced and places a telephone call to Finck's home, asking the pathologist to come to the Bethesda morgue at once.[775]

7:04 p.m.

Police Chief Curry enters Captain Fritz's office and finds Fritz, Assistant DA Alexander, and Justice of the Peace Johnston. "How's the case coming?" he asks.

"We're getting ready to file on him for the shooting of the officer," Fritz replies.

"What about the assassination?" Curry asks.

"I strongly suspect that he was the assassin of the president," Fritz says. As Curry leaves, Fritz reads over and signs complaint number F-153 charging Lee Harvey Oswald with the murder of Officer J. D. Tippit. Bill Alexander also affixes his signature to the complaint and a minute later files it—not with the clerk of the court, but by merely handing it to Judge Johnston.[776]

7:10 p.m.

Detectives Sims, Boyd, and Hall march Oswald back into Captain Fritz's private office. The door closes behind them, stifling the noise of the outer office. Oswald faces Captain Fritz, Bill Alexander, David Johnston, and at least one FBI agent.[777]

"Mr. Oswald, we're here to arraign you on the charge of murder in the death of Officer J. D. Tippit," Judge Johnston says.

"Arraignment!" Oswald snarls. "This isn't a court. You can't arraign me in a police station. I can only be arraigned in a courtroom. How do I know this is a judge?"

Alexander thinks the suspect "is the most arrogant person" he has ever met and tells him, in no uncertain terms, to "shut up and listen." Oswald complies, but not before snapping back, "The way you're treating me, I'd might as well be in Russia."[778]

Johnston opens the complaint form and tells Oswald that he is charged in the complaint with having "unlawfully, voluntarily, and with malice aforethought killed J. D. Tippit by shooting him with a gun" earlier that day.[779]

Oswald mumbles a stream of sarcastic, impudent little things.[780]

Johnston advises Oswald of his constitutional right to remain silent and warns him that any statement he makes may be used in evidence against him for the charges stated. "You'll be given the opportunity to contact an attorney," Johnston says as he completes the formalities. "Bond [bail] is denied on this capital offense. I hereby remand you to the custody of the sheriff of Dallas County, Texas."[781] In most states, the defendant pleads guilty or not guilty to the complaint at the time of the arraignment. In the few situations where he declines, the court enters a plea of not guilty for him. But in Texas, even to this day, a defendant is not even asked to plead to the complaint, and Oswald did not plead not guilty to the charge of murder against him.[782]

7:15 p.m.

Robert Oswald walks into Dallas City Hall at the Harwood Street entrance (106 South Harwood), where one enters the headquarters of the Dallas Police Department. Robert, intending to go to the third-floor Homicide and Robbery Bureau, mistakenly takes an elevator to a different floor and approaches a police officer who is eating supper out of a paper bag at his desk.

"Could you tell me where I could find the officer in charge of the homicide division?" he asks. "I'm Robert Oswald, Lee Oswald's brother."

The officer's expression changes immediately. He jumps up, dropping his sandwich on the desk, mumbles a few words, then regains control and says, "Let me call Captain Fritz."

After leaving his office in Denton, Texas, earlier in the afternoon, Robert had driven home and told his wife Vada that he planned to drive to Dallas and that she should take their children to her parents' farm outside Fort Worth, where they would be safe. He was worried about someone retaliating against anyone who knew Lee.

Robert then called the Acme company office in Fort Worth and told them of his plans to go to Dallas, and they told him that the FBI had been out there looking for him and wanted him to contact them. He arrived at a quarter after five at the Federal Building and spent the next two hours being interviewed by Dallas FBI agents interested in finding out what he knew about his brother's recent activities. Robert couldn't help them much, he hadn't seen Lee since the previous November. When he asked to see Lee, an agent said, "We don't have any jurisdiction over your brother," and tells Robert he'll have to go to City Hall and speak to Captain Will Fritz in the Homicide and Robbery Bureau of the Dallas Police Department. Now, Robert waits to see the man in charge.

The officer finally puts the phone down. He can't get through, so he offers to take Robert up to the third floor. As they wait for an elevator, Robert reaches into his hip pocket for a handkerchief. The officer flinches. Robert senses what the officer is thinking and freezes—then slowly withdraws his hand clutching the handkerchief. Robert suddenly realizes just how tense the situation is in Dallas.[783]

District Attorney Henry Wade marvels at the amount of reporters—it seems like three hundred—who have managed to shoehorn themselves into the small, narrow third-floor corridor outside the Homicide and Robbery office. Wade was on his way to dinner with his wife and some friends when he decided to stop by police headquarters to see how the investigation was progressing. He fights his way through the press and into the homicide office, where he learns from his assistant, Bill Alexander, that they had filed on Oswald for the Tippit murder.[784] Shouldering back through the crowd, he makes his way to the administrative offices, where Chief Curry sits behind his desk.

Wade is not surprised that Curry knows so little about how the case is coming. Relations between Fritz and Curry are better than they were with Curry's predecessor, but Fritz, as usual, is determined to run his own one-man show.

Wade himself has no power at all over the police. Under the city charter, the police are responsible to the city manager, not the district attorney. All of Wade's assistant prosecutors—Bill Alexander in particular—work closely with the police, but his office has no authority over them. For the moment, Wade and Curry are equally helpless.

Chief Curry slides Jack Revill's memo (the one saying the FBI had advance knowledge that Oswald was "capable of committing the assassination") across the desk to the district attorney.

"What do you think about that?" Curry asks.

Jack Revill is, to Wade's mind, one of the brightest of the young Dallas police officers, but his memo is highly disturbing.

"What are you going to do with it?" Wade asks.

"I don't know," Curry replies.[785]

Even in the midst of the catastrophe it's a bombshell. Curry knows that the security of the president depends not just on the Secret Service, which has the primary responsibility, but on the closest possible cooperation between the Secret Service and the FBI as well as local police authorities. Revill's memo suggests that someone wasn't playing ball, and both men know that a firestorm of public recrimination between the FBI and the Dallas Police Department is not the kind of press the city fathers are going to want to see. Wade is an astute politician. He knows that the press and public will be looking around for someone to blame. Historically, relations between the FBI and local police have never been easy, and this won't make them any easier.

Although the chief of police doesn't have to stand for reelection as Wade does, his position is scarcely less political. The son of a Dallas policeman who became a Baptist preacher, Jesse E. Curry attended police school without pay to get on the force during the Depression, then worked his way up through the ranks, finally becoming chief in January 1960, less than four years ago. He played a key role in the integration of the Dallas public schools in the fall of 1961, demonstrating his talent for careful advance planning.

He works long and hard and is proud of his department, constantly fretting about the lack of manpower—1,123 men covering a vast area and a population of over half a million—and adequate equipment. Most of his men, finding it tough to live on their $370-a-month base pay, are moonlighting. Even Curry's annual salary is only $17,500—after twenty-seven years with the department.[786]

Curry is reluctant to make waves, careful of his relationship with city officials. He's even more sensitive, as is Wade, to the desires of the real powers in the city, the Dallas Citizens Council—the elite group of business and social leaders who largely control the city's destiny, and who always have the city's image in mind. Perhaps that is why Curry hasn't moved forcefully to control the melee of pressmen and their din, wanting to demonstrate to the worldwide press that the Dallas Police Department is willing to cooperate to the fullest extent, even under conditions of dire emergency. There's little question that the assassination has put Curry under a tremendous amount of pressure, from all sides.

At the moment there is little Wade can do to console the police chief.

"I'll see you later," Wade tells him and heads out for dinner.

Robert Oswald follows the police officer as he leads him through the dense crowd of reporters on the third floor. No one is paying attention to either one of them, even though the officer occasionally bellows, "Where's Captain Fritz?" Finally, someone points toward the end of the corridor. The two men squeeze through the crowd until they come face-to-face with Captain Fritz. The homicide captain looks coldly at Robert after the officer whispers an introduction.

"I'm tied up right now," Fritz says, "but I do want to talk with you later. I think your mother is still here." Fritz tells the officer to take Robert down to where Mrs. Oswald is waiting.[787] (This is the only meeting Robert Oswald has with Fritz, who never gets around to questioning him.)

The two men make their way back through the crowded hallway and enter the Burglary and Theft Bureau, where Robert finds his mother along with two *Fort Worth Star-Telegram* reporters and two FBI agents. "I see you found me," Marguerite Oswald says, rising from her chair.

The FBI men have barely finished introducing themselves when Mrs. Oswald interrupts and asks to speak to her son alone. The agents show them to an empty office. As soon as they enter the room, Marguerite leans toward him and whispers, "This room is bugged. Be careful what you say." The comment annoys Robert, but doesn't surprise him. All his life Robert has heard his mother talking about conspiracies, hidden motives, and the maliciousness of others, and has long since discounted most of what she says.

"Listen," Robert says to his mother, not bothering to lower his voice, "I don't care whether the room is bugged or not. I'd be perfectly willing to say anything I've got to say right there in the doorway. If you know anything about what happened, I want to know it right now. I don't want to hear any whys, ifs, or wherefores."

His words don't seem to register. As Robert learned by the time he was four years old, Marguerite has the ability to block out whatever she doesn't want to hear. Apparently forgetting her own words of warning about the room being bugged, she sets out her belief that Lee, whatever he had done, was carrying out official orders. Ever since his defection to Russia, Marguerite has been convinced that Lee is some sort of secret agent, recruited by the U.S. government while in the Marine Corps, and thereafter sent on mysterious and dangerous missions.[788]

But there is something else about his mother now that gives Robert a sickening feeling. It is evident to him that his mother is not really crushed at all by the terrible charges against Lee. If anything, he senses she seems actually gratified at the attention she's receiving. She has always had an inflated sense of her own ability and importance, a trait reflected in her son Lee. But her quarrelsome nature and limited work skills have created instead a life of obscurity. Now, she seems to instantly recognize that she will never again be treated as an ordinary, unimportant woman.[789]

7:28 p.m.

FBI agent Manning C. Clements steps into the homicide office and spots fellow agent James Bookhout. Clements has been at police headquarters since one o'clock when, under instructions from his supervisor, he had offered the assistance of the FBI in the investigation of the president's assassination. For the last several hours he has been acting as a liaison, relaying instructions to the other agents on the premises.[790]

Clements approaches Bookhout and asks if anyone from the bureau has gotten a detailed physical description of Oswald, and more importantly, questioned him in depth about his background. Bookhout tells him no (though Captain Fritz *has* obtained some background information on Oswald), and suggests that Clements do it. Clements seeks out Captain Fritz and asks if there is any objection to his interviewing Oswald to get this information.

"I've got no objection," Fritz says.

Clements enters Captain Fritz's office and finds Oswald seated and two detectives—Hall and Boyd—standing guard nearby.[791]

The FBI agent introduces himself, shows Oswald his credentials, advises him of his right to an attorney, and explains his purpose for being there. Oswald is slightly haughty, but cooperative. Clements proceeds to elicit biographical information from Oswald—date and place of birth, height, weight, and other personal data. He then turns to the obviously fictitious Selective Service card found in Oswald's wallet.

Clements can tell the card is a fake because of the photograph mounted on it, something not contained on an authentic Selective Service card, and the number of obvious erasures made in typing the information on it. Besides, the card is in the name of "Alek James Hidell," but bears Oswald's photograph.[792]

Asked about the purpose of the card, Oswald refuses to answer.

Ten minutes into the interview, the door to the office opens and Detective Sims tells the agent that Oswald is needed downstairs.[793] They lead Oswald once again out into the crush of reporters. Flashbulbs pop and questions are hurled in waves at the prisoner as reporters press in. As the detectives struggle to move Oswald toward the jail elevators, Oswald seizes the moment to exploit his situation.

"These people here have given me a hearing without legal representation," Oswald, referring to his arraignment, says into a microphone shoved in his direction.

"Did you shoot the president?" a reporter asks.

"I didn't shoot anybody," Oswald replies. "No, sir."[794]

7:30 p.m. (8:30 p.m. EST)

At the Bethesda Naval Hospital, a hot white light illuminates the hands of the two pathologists huddled over the body of the late president. In the interests of time, Dr. Humes decided not to wait for Lieutenant Colonel Finck to arrive at Bethesda. Instead, he and Dr. Boswell set about the task of recovering the two largest bullet fragments seen in the X-rays of the president's skull. The hole in the right side of the head was immense (over five inches in its greatest diameter), making access to the brain relatively easy. Portions of the skull, literally shattered by the force of the bullet, fall apart in the hands of the two pathologists as they try to reach the minute fragments behind the right eye and near the back of the skull.[795] Both are recovered, placed into a glass jar with a black metal top, and turned over later in the evening to FBI agents for transport to the FBI laboratory.[796]* To remove the brain, Humes and Boswell use a scalpel to extend the lacerations of the scalp downward toward the ears. Normally, a saw would be used to cut the skullcap and remove the brain. Here, the damage is so devastating that the doctors can lift the brain out of the head without recourse to a saw.[797] The left hemisphere of the brain is intact, while the damage to the right one is massive.[798]

Just as the brain is fixed in formalin for further study, Lieutenant Colonel Finck walks into the autopsy room wearing military pants and a green scrub suit.[799] The three autopsy surgeons begin an examination of the president's head wound. What is immediately obvious to all three is a small oval-shaped hole in the back of the president's scalp. Peeling the skin away from the skull, the doctors find a corresponding but larger hole in the bone beneath the scalp. From inside the skull, the area surrounding the hole is cratered. From the outside, the skull bone around the hole is smooth. The surgeons recognize the wound to the backside of the head as having all the characteristics of an entrance wound.[800]

After taking photographs of the outer layer ("table") of the skull at the entrance wound, the photographer, John Stringer, positions himself at the head of the table. It is difficult to properly illuminate the inside layer or table of the back of the skull, in order to record the cratering effect the doctors have observed, so the doctors hold the head up slightly while Stringer snaps several exposures looking down into the cranial cavity.[801]

As to the massive hole on the right side of the president's head, it is presumably the result of the bullet exiting the head, although no specific exit point in the margins of the defect is discovered.[802]

7:45 p.m.
FBI agent James Hosty pulls out of the police garage and heads back toward the Dallas FBI field office. Oswald's words still resonate in his head, "Oh, so *you're* Hosty. I've heard about you. You're the one who's been harassing my wife!" Hosty couldn't help but think of the two visits he had paid Marina Oswald, the two visits that Oswald was clearly referring to. Hosty hadn't given the visits, or Lee Oswald for that matter, a lot of thought. Oswald was, after all, only one of the forty or fifty cases that made up his normal caseload.

Hosty had remembered reading a front-page article in the Dallas newspapers in 1959 about a former marine, Lee Oswald, who had defected to the Soviet Union. The article also grabbed the attention of Fort Worth FBI agent John Fain, who opened the case file in an effort to determine if Oswald posed any national security risks. In early June 1962, the Dallas newspapers ran another article, this time reporting that Oswald was returning to the United States with a Russian bride. Fain interviewed Oswald twice, in June and August of 1962, and the following month, after concluding that Oswald was not a security risk, closed the file on Oswald. Hosty inherited all of Fain's case files.

*No bullet, or significant portion thereof, was found in either Kennedy's or Connally's body.

Because Hosty had reviewed Marina's records at the Immigration and Naturalization Service office in Dallas for Fain, he had an uneasy feeling that she could possibly be a Soviet intelligence agent, and decided to try to locate the Oswalds, particularly after learning that Lee Oswald had subscribed to a U.S. Communist paper after Fain closed the file. But they had left no forwarding address when they moved from the last address he had on them, Neely Street in Dallas. He later learned they had moved to New Orleans, and shortly after being informed months later by the New Orleans FBI office that the Oswalds had disappeared from New Orleans, Hosty's Dallas office received a communiqué that Oswald, while in Mexico City in early October 1963, had visited the Soviet embassy there and spoken to one Valeriy Kostikov, a vice counsel at the embassy.

Eventually, the FBI's New Orleans office sent Hosty what was believed to be the Oswalds' new address at Ruth Paine's home in Irving, Texas, and asked that he verify their presence before it transfers the case file back to his jurisdiction.

On Friday, November 1, 1963, Hosty stopped at the Paine residence. Ruth Paine told him that Mrs. Oswald and her two children were living with her, and that Mrs. Oswald was temporarily separated from Lee, who visited his wife and children on weekends. Paine knew Oswald was working at the Texas School Book Depository and living somewhere in the Oak Cliff section of Dallas, but she wasn't quite sure where.

While they were talking, Marina came into the room. She looked as though she had been napping. Through her body language, Hosty could see she was frightened and he didn't try to interview her that day. He did intend to later, but he needed some of the materials from the Oswald file, which he had not yet gotten from New Orleans, to do it properly. He told Marina through Ruth that he would come back to see her at a later time. Ruth Paine told Hosty that she would find out where Lee was living and let him know.

On November 5, Hosty and a fellow agent dropped by Ruth Paine's again. The two agents chatted with Mrs. Paine briefly while standing at the front door. Ruth still didn't have Lee's address, and the only new information she volunteered was that Lee had described himself to her as a Trotskyist Marxist. They had been there less than five minutes and didn't see Marina until they were about to leave. Neither of the agents said anything to her.

Having confirmed that both Marina and Lee were living in the Dallas area, Hosty was waiting for the FBI's New Orleans office to send him copies of their entire file at the time of the assassination.[803]

As he pulls into the FBI's parking area, Hosty shakes his head and wonders how it could have come to this. What could he have possibly done differently that might have prevented the assassination? His actions concerning the Oswald file might be explainable, but Hosty knows it won't do his career any good.

Hosty heads up to his office, where a secretary tells him that he is wanted in Gordon Shanklin's office, pronto. Hosty finds his supervisor, Ken Howe, waiting there with Shanklin. They tell him to shut the door.

"What the hell is this?" Shanklin asks, clutching what appears to be a letter.

Hosty takes it and immediately recognizes it as the anonymous note delivered ten days or so earlier, the note he now realized had been delivered by Oswald.

"It's no big deal," Hosty says, trying to shrug it off. "Just your typical guff."

"What do you mean, 'typical guff'? This note was written by Oswald," Shanklin screams, "the probable assassin of the president, and Oswald brought this note into *this* office just ten days ago! What the hell do you think Hoover's going to do if he finds out about this note?" Shanklin is more upset than Hosty can remember, pacing behind his desk, puffing a cigarette.

Hosty again tries to convince Shanklin that the note is not a big deal, that Oswald hadn't threatened the president. But Shanklin knows much more will be made of the note.

"If people learn that Oswald gave you guff a week before the assassination, they'll say you should have known he'd kill the president," Shanklin cries. "If Hoover finds out about this, he's going to lose it."

Howe looks on gravely, arms folded. Hosty pleads that once they explain everything, the note, the background of the case, everyone will understand that there was no way in hell anyone could have guessed that Oswald was going to kill anyone, much less the president. Shanklin rubs his neck, unconvinced. Finally, he orders Hosty to write a memo surrounding the circumstances of the note.

Hosty returns a short while later with a two-page memo and hands it to Shanklin, with the note. The agent-in-charge shoves it into his "Do Not File" desk drawer, that special place in Hoover's FBI where every special agent in charge of an FBI field office kept personal notes on all his agents. The material in the drawer never enters the official record, and gives Hoover "plausible deniability" if anything objectionable ever reaches the public eye.[804]

7:50 p.m.

The assembly room in the basement of City Hall is once again abuzz with activity, as officers prepare for the third lineup. In the holdover area, adjacent to the stage, Detectives Sims, Boyd, Hall, and H. M. Moore arrange and handcuff the men who will appear with Oswald in the lineup. This time a pair of city prisoners have been included—Richard Walter Borchgardt, held for carrying a prohibited weapon and investigation of burglary and theft, and Ellis Carl Brazel, in custody for failing to pay some long-overdue traffic tickets. Borchgardt takes the number 1 position, Oswald is 2, Brazel is 3, and Don Ables, the jail clerk who participated in the first two lineups, takes the fourth spot.[805]

Detectives C. W. Brown and C. N. Dhority accompany sisters-in-law Barbara and Virginia Davis into the darkened end of the assembly room and have them sit down. The women, who haven't seen pictures of Oswald in the evening paper or on television, are nervous.[806] In a moment or two, Secret Service agents Forrest Sorrels and Winston Lawson, who had tracked Brennan down at his home, escort Howard Brennan into the room. The construction worker is petrified that he is the only witness who saw the gunman firing from the sixth-floor window and could give a fair description of him,[*] and over the last few hours has convinced himself that he may be putting his family in danger by stepping forward and identifying him. "Howard, I'm afraid, we don't know who might be out there looking for you," his wife, Louise, had said when he returned home earlier in the day, around three o'clock, and told her, "Louise, I was there. I saw him do it. I saw the man shoot President Kennedy. It was the most terrible thing I've ever seen in my life." Brennan thinks of moving his wife, daughter, and grandson, who was living with them at the time, out of town, but Louise seems to think there is no way to really get away.[807] Brennan is looking for a way out of his predicament.

---

[*]The young lad Amos Euins also saw a gunman firing from the window, but his description of the gunman, as we have seen, was of little value, Euins first describing the gunman as being a colored man, and later, a white man.

"I don't know if I can do you any good or not because I have seen the man that they have under arrest on television," Brennan told Sorrels when he first arrived at the police station. He adds, "I just don't know if I can identify him positively or not."[808]

As they walk into the assembly room, Brennan tells Sorrels that he would like to get back a ways and view the man from a distance, closer to what it was at the time of the shooting. "We will get you clear on to the back," Sorrels says, "and then we can move up forward."[809]

The signal is given and the detectives begin marching the prisoners under the bright lights of the stage. As soon as Oswald appears, and before each man has even settled under a number, the Davis women react.[810]

"That's him," Barbara says. "The second one from the left." When the officers have the men turn sideways, and Barbara sees Oswald from the same angle she saw him crossing her front yard, she is positive.[811]

Her sister-in-law, Virginia Davis, agrees. The man they saw running from the Tippit murder scene is the number 2 man in the lineup—Oswald.[812]

Howard Brennan looks over the men carefully. He will later confide that he recognized the number 2 man, Oswald, immediately, but was afraid to say so.[813] Brennan figures that the authorities don't really need his positive identification anyway. It's not as if they'll let Oswald go if he doesn't identify him. After all, the police are already holding the man for the murder of Officer Tippit. Brennan calculates that he can always tell police what he really thinks at a later date, when it really matters, and not risk endangering his family.[814]

Sorrels has Brennan move a little closer.

"I cannot positively say," Brennan finally says.

"Is there anyone there that looks like him?" Sorrels asks.

"The second man from the left," Brennan answers cautiously, referring to Oswald. "He looks like him. But the man I saw wasn't disheveled like this fella."[815] (Of course, Oswald hadn't yet been roughed up by the police during his arrest at that point.)

Brennan can tell that Sorrels is disappointed.

"I'm sorry," Brennan says, "but I can't do it. I was afraid seeing the television might have messed me up. I just can't be positive. I am sorry."[816]

The agent turns and makes arrangements for Brennan to be taken home.

In New Orleans, a telephone rings at the home of Abraham Plough, foreman of the mails for the U.S. Post Office at Lafayette Square Station. The caller is Postal Inspector Joseph Zarza, who wants Plough to come to Lafayette Square Station immediately to open up the premises. When Plough arrives, Inspector Zarza tells him that postal investigators in Dallas want him to retrieve the application form for post office box 30061. Plough flips on a light, walks over to the file cabinet containing the application forms, and within a few minutes locates the one in question.[817] The form shows that box 30061 was rented to "L. H. Oswald" on June 3, 1963, and Oswald showed his home address as "657 French" Street. The box had been closed on September 26, 1963, with mail forwarded to 2515 West Fifth Street, Irving, Texas. Under the entry, "Names of Persons Entitled to Receive Mail Through Box," Oswald had written the names, "A. J. Hidell" and "Marina Oswald."[818]*

---

*Inspector Zarza checks the box and finds two copies of the *Militant* that had not yet been forwarded (7 H 296, WCT Harry D. Holmes).

Inspector Zarza calls Dallas inspector Harry Holmes and notifies him of the discovery.[819]

7:55 p.m.
In the third-floor hallway at Dallas police headquarters, detectives lead Oswald off the jail elevator and back through the crowd of reporters toward Captain Fritz's office. Oswald tells newsmen that the only reason he is in custody is because of his stay in the Soviet Union, defiantly adding, "I'm just a patsy!"[820]

8:05 p.m.
With Oswald again seated in Fritz's office,[821] FBI agent Clements continues his interview of the suspect, asking Oswald to provide the names, addresses, and occupations of relatives, as well as a sequential list of his own occupations and residences.[822] Oswald answers the agent's questions readily enough, even courteously, although he doesn't volunteer any information. Finally, on a perfectly innocuous question about his present occupation, Oswald balks.

"What started out to be a short interrogation turned out to be rather lengthy," he complains. "I refused to be interviewed by other law enforcement officers before and I've got no intention of being interviewed by you. I know the tactics of the FBI. You're using the soft touch. There's a similar agency in the Soviet Union. Their approach would be different, but the tactics would be the same. I believe I've answered all the questions I'm going to answer, and I don't care to say anything else."[823]*

Nevertheless, when Clements ignores his complaint and asks the same question again—what his present occupation is—Oswald answers. At that, Clements terminates the interview.[824]

8:18 p.m. (9:18 p.m. EST)
Alan Belmont, at FBI headquarters in Washington, is on the phone with Dallas special agent-in-charge Gordon Shanklin. The head of the Dallas office tells Belmont that he has made arrangements with Carswell Air Force Base in Fort Worth to fly one of his agents back to Washington with the rifle, cartridge cases, and metal fragments removed from Governor Connally just as soon as police release the evidence to the FBI.

"See if the police want us to make a ballistics test on the pistol that was used to kill Officer Tippit," Belmont asks. "If so, have it forwarded for examination along with the bullets removed from Tippit's body. If they don't want to release the pistol to us, find out all you can about the make, caliber, how many bullets were fired."

"Okay," Shanklin agrees. "I also realize that it's extremely important to locate and interview Oswald's coworkers to determine his whereabouts and actions at the time of the shooting. This is being done as we speak."

"Good," Belmont says. "President Johnson has been in touch with Mr. Hoover and

---

*Under the 1966 U.S. Supreme Court case of *Miranda v. Arizona*, even if a suspect or arrestee has waived his right to have a lawyer present during his interrogation, and also waived his right against self-incrimination, once he indicates, at any time during the interrogation, that he does not want to answer any further questions, "the interrogation must cease," and any statement he makes thereafter, even if apparently free and voluntary, cannot be used against him because said statement is deemed to be, as a matter of law, "the product of compulsion, subtle or otherwise" (*Miranda v. Arizona*, 86 S. Ct. 1627, 1628). Here, as we shall see, Oswald continued to be interrogated and continued to answer questions for two more days. But *Miranda* wasn't yet in existence back in 1963.

wants to be sure that the FBI is on top of this case and is looking to us to solve it. You understand what that means, don't you?"

"Yes," Shanklin answers.

"It is imperative that we do everything possible in this case," Belmont says firmly.

"Understood," Shanklin reaffirms.

To handle the number of leads pouring into the Dallas office and expedite the interviewing of Depository employees, Belmont tells Shanklin that he's ordering an additional twenty agents, four stenographers, and ten cars to go to Dallas immediately.[825]

8:30 p.m. (9:30 p.m. EST)

At Bethesda Naval Hospital, the three pathologists have rolled the president onto his left side and are examining the oval-shaped bullet wound located to the right of his spine and just above the right shoulder blade. Dr. Finck can see that the edges of the wound are pushed inward and recognizes the reddish brown skin around the margins as an abrasion collar, characteristics typical of entrance wounds.[826] After taking photographs of the bullet hole,[827] Dr. Humes probes the wound with his little finger, but finds that the bullet path seems to stop less than an inch into the hole.[828] Dr. Finck attempts to explore the wound using a flexible metal probe, but after repeated attempts he can't seem to find the path of the bullet. Afraid of making a false passage, Finck removes the probe and examines the front of the body. There are no corresponding exit wounds, only a tracheotomy incision in the front of the throat. Finck, Boswell, and Humes examine the margins of the incision, but cannot find any evidence of a bullet exit.

The doctors are perplexed. Where did the bullet go? Dr. Finck asks to examine the president's clothing, hoping that it might give a clue as to what happened to the bullet, but finds that the clothing is not available.[829] Dr. Finck then suggests that a whole-body radiographic survey be conducted before proceeding any further with the autopsy. All three of the pathologists know from experience that bullets can do crazy things when they enter the human body and might end up anywhere. The only way to be sure they haven't missed it is to x-ray the entire body.[830] Finck's decision doesn't set well with Admiral Burkley, who can see his idea of a quick recovery of evidence giving way to hour after hour of difficulties and delays.* Burkley says that Mrs. Kennedy had only granted permission for a limited autopsy, and questions the feasibility of finding the bullet that entered the president's back without conducting a complete autopsy.

"Well, it's my opinion that the bullet is still in the president's body," Dr. Humes tells him. "And the only way to extract it is to do a complete autopsy, which I propose to do."

As tempers flare, Secret Service agent Roy Kellerman confers quickly with FBI agents Sibert and O'Neill. They agree that from an investigative and prosecutorial standpoint, the bullet must be recovered, no matter how long it takes. They advise Admiral Burkley of their position, but he remains resistant to furthering the probe. Admiral Calvin B. Galloway, commanding officer of the U.S. Naval Medical Center, steps up to break the deadlock and orders Dr. Humes to perform a complete autopsy.[831] Now, to Admiral Burkley's annoyance, they will have to wait more than a hour for the entire body to be x-rayed.[832]

---

*Some of the military men present talked of bringing in metal detectors to expedite the search for any bullets in the president's body (ARRB MD 19, Memorandum to File, Andy Purdy, August 17, 1977, p.10).

At Dallas police headquarters, Captain Fritz ambles back to his office to face Oswald once again. The prisoner doesn't seem to be tiring as the night drags on, although the detectives around him are beginning to feel the wear of the day.

Detective Elmer Boyd never saw a man answer questions like Oswald. He never hesitates about his answers. He shoots back an answer just as soon as the questions are asked, sometimes even before the questions are finished. Though most of the time he is calm, rather frequently his attitude suddenly changes and he gets mad, especially if he is asked something he doesn't like.[833]

"Did you keep a rifle in Mrs. Paine's garage in Irving?" Captain Fritz continues with his questioning.

"No," Oswald replies, having apparently decided to answer more questions despite his earlier refusal.

"Didn't you bring one with you when you came back to Dallas from New Orleans?" Fritz asks.

"No, I didn't," Oswald says.

"Well, the people out at the Paine residence say you did have a rifle," Fritz states firmly, "and that you kept it out there wrapped in a blanket."

"That isn't true," Oswald shoots back.[834]

Fritz lets the response hang there in the silence. He circles the desk.

"You *know* you've killed the president," Fritz says bluntly. "This is a very serious charge."

"No, I haven't killed the president," Oswald responds dryly.

"He *is* dead," the captain says.

"Yeah, well, people will forget that in a few days and there will be another president," Oswald replies, as if the day's events mean nothing.[835]

8:40 p.m.

In Chief Curry's third-floor office, Dallas FBI head Gordon Shanklin informs FBI agent Vince Drain that the FBI in Washington wants their Dallas agents to acquire the rifle found on the sixth floor, the revolver used to shoot Officer Tippit, and other various items, and bring them all to Washington immediately for examination. Drain discusses it with Chief Curry, telling him that he will personally stay with the evidence the entire trip to and from Washington to keep the chain of evidence intact.[836] Personally, Curry doesn't give a hoot what the FBI wants. This is a Dallas case under Dallas jurisdiction and the responsibility is his. Wanting to appear cooperative, though, Curry promises Drain that he'll consider the FBI's request.[837]

8:52 p.m. (9:52 p.m. EST)

The FBI sends a second Teletype to its fifty-five field offices:

> The Bureau is conducting an investigation to determine who is responsible for the assassination. You are therefore instructed to follow and resolve all allegations pertaining to the assassination. This matter is of the utmost urgency and should be handled accordingly, keeping the Bureau and Dallas, the office of origin, apprised fully of all developments.[838]

8:55 p.m.

Crime-lab sergeant W. E. "Pete" Barnes makes his way through the throng gathered on the third floor outside Homicide and Robbery. The size of the mob there is unbelievable, and frankly, Barnes finds it disgusting. He can't imagine how anyone can carry on an investigation properly with this kind of commotion going on.[839] Barnes has been ordered by his boss, Lieutenant Day, to make paraffin casts of Oswald's hands to see if there is any evidence that he has fired a weapon recently. Crime-lab detectives J. B. "Johnny" Hicks and R. L. Studebaker have come along to assist him.[840]

Also called a GSR, the gun residue test involves heating paraffin, a wax substance, to about 130 degrees. It's then brushed onto the suspect's hands and reinforced with alternating layers of bandage gauze. As the wax cools, it extracts from the skin particles of nitrates (acid elements in gunpowder residue that are deposited on the skin by the gases from a fired bullet), and these nitrates become embedded in the wax casts. The casts are then cut from the hands and sent to the crime lab for testing. There, technicians apply one of two chemicals to the casts to determine the presence of nitrates. A positive result will show up as a pattern of blue or violet dots.[841]

Barnes has been known to get exceptionally good paraffin casts, much better than some of the other detectives in his division. He once quipped, "The other detectives don't get the paraffin hot enough. They are afraid they'll burn the suspect, but I don't mind if I burn the bad guys a little in order to get a good cast."[842]

Contrary to myth, the paraffin test is not conclusive for the simple reason that the two chemicals used by laboratories to test for nitrates—diphenylamine and diphenylbenzidine—will react to most oxidizing agents, including urine, tobacco, cosmetics, pharmaceuticals, soil, fertilizer, and many others. The list is so large that a positive nitrate result doesn't preclude the possibility that the cause might be due to something other than gunpowder residue.[843] Moreover, the mere handling of a weapon may leave nitrates on the skin, even without firing it.[844] Because of their unreliability, paraffin tests have fallen into increased disfavor by law enforcement agencies in the United States.

As Barnes steps inside Captain Fritz's office, Fritz tells him that in addition to Oswald's hands, he wants Barnes to make a cast of Oswald's right cheek. Barnes knows immediately how unusual a request it is. Since 1956, when he started doing paraffin tests, this is the only time anyone had ever requested a paraffin test of a suspect's cheek. In fact, common sense tells a man of Barnes's experience that anyone firing a rifle has got very little chance of getting powder residue on his cheek. The reason is that the cartridge is sealed into the chamber by the bolt of the rifle being closed behind it. Upon firing, the cartridge case expands even farther inside the chamber, completely filling it up and preventing the nitrate gases from escaping onto the face. Barnes doesn't question Fritz's judgment though. He has an order, and that's good enough for him.[845]

The crime-lab sergeant begins unpacking his equipment as Oswald sits nearby, watching.[846]

"I know why you're doing this," Oswald says boastfully.

"Why?" Barnes replies, in his right-to-the-point style.

"You want to find out if I fired a gun," Oswald replies.

"I'm not trying to prove anything," the sergeant replies, as the wax begins to heat up. "We have the test to make and the people at the lab will determine the rest."

"Yeah, well you're wasting your time," Oswald says in a self-assured manner. "I don't know anything about these shootings."[847]

As soon as he's done, Barnes places the paraffin casts from Oswald's right cheek and two hands into three separate manila envelopes. A couple of patrolmen assist Barnes in wending his way through the news media to get to the elevators that'll take him to the fourth-floor Identification Bureau. A storm of questions are thrown at him as he snakes through the press: "What have you got in that sack? You owe it to the news media to tell us! What have you got there?" Barnes refuses to reply to the boisterous horde.[848] Arriving at the Identification Bureau, Sergeant Barnes initials the casts, seals them, and locks them in the evidence room. They'll be delivered to the county crime lab at Parkland Hospital in the morning for testing.[849]*

Barnes immediately returns to Captain Fritz's office, and with the assistance of Detective Hicks, takes Oswald's finger and palm prints.[850] Oswald says nothing. When they finish, Barnes asks Oswald to sign the fingerprint card on the line that says "prisoner's signature."

"I'm not signing anything until I talk to an attorney," Oswald replies.

"That's all right with me," Barnes says, and gathers up the identification kit.[851]

In New York City, the city that never sleeps, the streets are deserted, Broadway theaters are closed, Radio City is closed, and the only nightclub that is not deserted is the famed Stork Club, "but the people there," ABC's Barbara Walters observed, "are like the people there on Christmas Eve, people with no home, no place to go."[852]†

9:00 p.m.

Detectives Stovall and Rose lead Wesley Frazier, his sister, Linnie Mae Randle, and their pastor, Reverend Campble of the Irving Baptist Church, into the back room of Homicide and Robbery. Since being arrested an hour and a half ago, Frazier has been very cooperative with police, allowing officers to search his car and his home, where they confiscated a .303 caliber rifle, a full clip, and a partial box of ammunition.[853]

Captain Fritz comes back and questions both Wesley Frazier and his sister. Wesley tells him about Oswald's placing a large bag in the backseat of Frazier's car on the morning of the assassination and telling Frazier the bag contained curtain rods.[854]

---

*Predictably, the paraffin cast for Oswald's right cheek showed no reaction, that is, no nitrates indicating he had fired a weapon (4 H 276, WCT J. C. Day), but the paraffin cast on his hands, also predictably, showed a positive reaction, indicating, though not conclusively, he had recently fired a weapon. Though, as indicated, there is no gap between the chamber and the barrel of a *rifle* through which gases can escape (resulting in no nitrate residue being found on Oswald's right cheek from firing his Mannlicher-Carcano), there is a gap between the barrel and the cylinder on a *revolver* through which gases do escape; hence, nitrate residue was found on Oswald's hands, most likely from his shooting Officer Tippit with his .38 caliber Smith & Wesson revolver (4 H 276, WCT J. C. Day). Indeed, the gun residue test was devised only for the firing of small arms, not rifles.

To confirm that firing a rifle will not leave nitrate residue on the firer's cheeks, the FBI had one of their agents, Charles L. Killion, fire three rounds in Oswald's Carcano rifle. The result of the paraffin test conducted thereafter was negative for his cheeks and hands (3 H 494, WCT Cortlandt Cunningham; WR, pp.561–562).

†Virtually all high school, college, and professional sporting events were canceled or postponed throughout the nation that coming weekend. By far the most prominent exception (for which it has received criticism by many down through the years) was the National Football League. Although the American Football League postponed all of its Sunday games, NFL Commissioner Pete Rozelle said that "it has been traditional in sports for athletes to perform in times of great personal tragedy," and announced that the NFL's schedule of seven games would be played on Sunday. CBS announced it would not televise the games. (*Dallas Morning News*, November 23, 1963, sect.2, p.1; Rozelle quote: *Sunday Press* [Binghamton, NY], November 24, 1963, sect.D, p.1)

Rose and Stovall begin taking affidavits from Frazier and his sister as Captain Fritz makes his way down the hall to the Forgery Bureau, where he asks Marina Oswald if she saw Oswald carrying anything when he left that morning, but she says she didn't see him leave.[855] He probes both Marina and Ruth Paine further. Had Oswald mentioned putting curtain rods in his room? Neither of them know anything about it.[856]

Captain Fritz ponders this latest piece of the assassination puzzle as he makes his way back to his office. Oswald's curtain rod story is terribly suspicious to the homicide captain. If the rifle was in the package, and Fritz strongly suspects it was, then it must have been dismantled slightly to fit the bag Frazier described as twenty-six to twenty-seven inches long. At the moment, Fritz is hesitant to question Oswald about it until he finds out more.[857] Were any curtain rods found at the Depository, or in Oswald's room? Did his apartment need curtain rods? Fritz likes to play his cards close to the vest, then pounce once he is certain of the facts.

Marguerite and Robert Oswald are brought across the hall to the Forgery office, where Marina is being held. Marguerite breaks into tears and hugs her daughter-in-law. She hasn't seen her or Lee in a year. Marina hands her baby, Rachel, to Mrs. Oswald. Neither Marguerite nor Robert had been told of the child's birth. Before Robert has a chance to greet Marina, Ruth Paine bolts toward him.

"I'm Ruth Paine," she says. "I'm a friend of Marina and Lee. I'm here because I speak Russian. I'm interpreting for Marina." (But Mr. Ilya A. Mamantov, a local research geologist who is a native of Russia, has been employed by the Dallas Police Department to interpret for Marina during questioning by police, and has been doing so.)[858]

To Robert, Mrs. Paine comes across as a dominating, controlling woman. She seemed eager to tell anyone who would listen, almost boastfully, that both Lee and Marina had been to her house. Robert's impression of her estranged husband, Michael, was equally unfavorable.[859] Robert later recalled Mr. Paine's eyes as having a cold distant look, as if he wasn't really looking at you, and described his handshake as that of a "live fish." He can't quite put his finger on it, but Robert feels that the Paines are somehow involved in this affair.[860]

Ruth turns to Marguerite and says, "Oh, Mrs. Oswald, I am so glad to meet you." Marina, she tells her, wanted to get in touch with her, especially when Rachel was born, but Lee didn't want her to. The words are not very soothing to Marguerite, who takes an instant dislike to the woman.

"Mrs. Paine," Marguerite snaps angrily, "you speak English. Why didn't *you* contact me?"

Ruth tries to explain that Marina didn't know how to contact Marguerite. Also, because the couple were separated—Lee living in Dallas, Marina in Irving—Ruth didn't want to interfere.[861]

Within five minutes of the introductions, preparations are made to leave the police station. Robert Oswald says that he is going to remain there, where he hopes to talk with Captain Fritz, and will see them tomorrow. Mrs. Paine says she will take Marina and the babies back to her house for the night.[862] Marguerite expresses her desire to stay in Dallas so that she can be close to Lee and help as much as possible.[863] When Mrs. Paine offers to put Marguerite up for the night, Robert says something about not wanting to inconvenience her and Mr. Paine. Ruth immediately shoots back, "Mr. Paine and I aren't living together," adding, "It's a long story." Michael Paine shrinks behind his domineering wife, as they head out the office door.[864]

Dallas police officers attempt to clear the way as reporters descend upon the group in the corridor. Flashbulbs snap and cameras whirl as they face a barrage of questions, none of which are answered, while Marguerite pleads to the cameras about Lee, "He's really a good boy."[865]

Remaining behind, Robert Oswald takes a seat and soon strikes up a relaxed conversation with Lieutenant E. I. Cunningham, who was present at Lee's arrest. Cunningham explains the circumstances surrounding Oswald's apprehension in a calm, sympathetic tone. Robert realizes that there are police officers in Dallas with some genuine compassion. He also realizes, for the first time, just how strong a circumstantial case the police have against his brother for the shooting of Officer Tippit. Equally disturbing to Robert is the thought that it is difficult to explain Tippit's death unless it was an attempt to escape arrest for the assassination of the president.[866]

In the Homicide and Robbery office down the hall, Captain Fritz walks over to Assistant DA Bill Alexander, Jim Allen, the former assistant DA now in private practice, and Secret Service agent Forrest Sorrels. "We need to talk about the case we've developed so far," Fritz says to Alexander, who suggests they find a quieter place.

The four men push their way through the mob of reporters, walk out of City Hall, and stroll north on Harwood to the Majestic Steak House, an eatery in Dallas's theater district favored by Dallas law enforcement officials. Ordering steaks and coffee, the men marvel over the day's events, then get down to business.[867]

"Have you got enough to file on him, Captain?" Alexander asks.

Fritz reviews what they have so far. They can place Oswald on the sixth floor of the Depository a few minutes before the shooting—the same floor where they found the hulls, the rifle, and the paper bag in which the rifle was apparently carried into the building. His wife says he owned a rifle, and it is missing from the storage area where he kept it. She says the rifle they found looks like his, but she can't be sure. The crime lab has lifted good latent prints from the boxes and the bag and hope to get some from the rifle. If they turn out to be Oswald's, they'll have him. Fritz notes that Oswald is the only employee who left the Book Depository after the shooting and didn't return. More important, all of the evidence points to Oswald as being the killer of Officer Tippit.

"All in all, that's a lot of good evidence," Fritz says. "But, I'd like to wait until we develop the firearm and fingerprint evidence before proceeding with any charges in the assassination."

They decide to hold off for an hour or so before filing against Oswald in the Kennedy case.[868]

9:40 p.m.
Ruth Paine's home in Irving is a relief after the circus at City Hall. After police drop them off, Ruth sends Michael out to get hamburgers at a drive-in so she won't have to cook. Marina feeds her two small children, then sits down to eat in front of the television, which is rerunning all of the day's events. Marina even catches a glimpse of Lee being led through the third-floor corridor at police headquarters.[869]

Marguerite begins to complain to everyone present that if they were prominent people, three of the best lawyers would be at the city jail right now defending her son. But, because they are "small" people, they won't get the same kind of attention. Ruth Paine tries to tell her that this is not a small case and will get the most careful attention possible, but she is unable to penetrate the years of self-pity that Marguerite has wrapped herself in.[870]

"Don't worry," Ruth finally says. "I'm a member of the Civil Liberties Union and Lee will have an attorney, I can assure you." Marguerite can't help but wonder why Mrs. Paine hasn't already called for an attorney.[871]

The doorbell rings and two men from *Life* magazine appear unannounced, reporter Tommy Thompson and photographer Allen Grant, two of nine *Life* correspondents and photographers who had flown into Dallas that day from around the country. (Considering the day's events, Ruth is surprised that not more newsmen have been able to locate them by now.)* She lets them in and flips on an extra light in the dimly lit room. Thompson, of course, realizing the difficulty of speaking to Marina through Mrs. Paine, immediately begins questioning Mrs. Paine, while his partner pulls out a camera and begins snapping photographs.[872]

"Mrs. Paine, tell me, are Marina and Lee separated, since Lee lives in Dallas?"

"No, they are a happy family," Ruth says, explaining that Lee works in Dallas and has no transportation to get back and forth from Irving every day. Marguerite is fuming, partly because she doesn't think her son needs this kind of publicity but more importantly because she's beginning to realize that *Life* magazine is going to do a "life story" segment and she wants to be paid. In her paranoid mind, Marguerite is beginning to suspect that Ruth Paine invited *Life* magazine to come over and that she and Marina, while speaking in Russian, have conspired to sell Lee's life story without her.[873]

After a few more questions about Oswald's family life, Thompson asks how Lee got the money to return to the United States.

"He saved the money," Ruth replies. Marguerite finally hits the roof.

"Now, Mrs. Paine, I'm sorry," Mrs. Oswald interrupts, "I appreciate that I am a guest in your home but I will not be having you make statements that I know are wrong. To begin with, I do not approve of this publicity. But if we're going to have a story in *Life* magazine I would like to get paid. After all, we're going to have to pay for lawyers to defend my son."[874]

Suddenly there are angry words between Marguerite and Ruth, who defends Marina's right to have her story told to the reporters.

"I'm his mother," Marguerite shrieks. "I'm the one who's going to speak!" Ruth translates for Marina as Marguerite tries to explain to Marina that neither of them should speak to the reporters without getting paid. Marina, confused by the whole scene, nonetheless understands one thing quite clearly. It's all about money.[875]

Thompson says he will telephone his office and see what he can do about her request, then withdraws to another room to make the call. Meanwhile, the photographer follows Marina into the bedroom, snapping photographs of her as she undresses her daughter June and puts her to bed. Marguerite hovers nearby until Thompson comes back and tells her that *Life* will not pay them for the story, but will pay their food and hotel accom-

---

*The way Grant explained it, when he and Thompson were at Dallas police headquarters earlier in the day, there were "so many reporters and photographers pushing and shoving" in the crammed corridor on the third floor, some "standing on chairs, some on their camera cases, all trying to get in position" for a "photograph of suspect Lee Harvey Oswald" whenever he happened to appear "being led from one room to another," that he suggested to Thompson they "get out" of the madhouse and "look for a more exclusive angle to the story." With Thompson, born in Texas, "using his Texas accent and disarming demeanor" to extract information out of a deputy sheriff, they got the address of Oswald's rooming house, and Earlene Roberts, the housekeeper, then told them of the phone calls that Oswald used to make to Irving. They headed out there and after inquiring around town, finally found the Paine residence. (Allen Grant, "Life Catches Up to Marina Oswald," *Los Angeles Times*, November 22, 1988, part V, pp. 1, 8)

modations while they stay in Dallas. The picture taking continues until Marguerite becomes indignant.

"I have had it," she complains loudly. "You're taking my picture without my consent! Now go find out what accommodations you can make for my daughter-in-law and I so that we can be in Dallas to help my son, and let me know in the morning!"[876]

Thompson and Grant leave the house, but not the area. They sit in their rented car on the dark street in front of the house. Twirling the keys to the car on his index finger as he watches the house, Thompson says, "This, my friend, is probably going to be the scoop of my career. I will kill the first newsman that approaches that house." Grant, with slightly different priorities, says, "Let's go. I want to get this film off to New York." "We're not leaving here," Thompson says, "until those lights go out."[877]

9:50 p.m.

After talking with Lieutenant Cunningham for nearly an hour, Robert Oswald gives up any hope of speaking with Captain Fritz. He leaves the ruckus of City Hall and walks back to his car seven blocks away. The reporters don't have any idea who he is, so his stroll through the cool night air is free of pesky newsmen. Getting in his car, Robert starts driving. He has no particular destination in mind. He only wants to still the turmoil in his mind. If anyone were to ask him what he feels, he would say "unspeakable horror."

Some people are already speculating that the killing of the president was not the isolated act of one man, but the result of a great conspiracy. Robert wonders if it could be true. Is it possible that Marina could have played a role in some plot? What about the Paines? Whom could Lee have possibly become involved with? As the miles click by, he tries to assemble his thoughts and fears into some coherent order, but to no avail. Robert soon finds himself out on Highway 80, approaching the western outskirts of Fort Worth, and suddenly realizes how far he has already driven. He stops for gas, turns around, and heads back to Dallas.[878]

10:00 p.m.

No sooner than Fritz and Alexander get back to City Hall from dinner than the telephone rings in the Homicide and Robbery office of Dallas police headquarters and Alexander takes the call. It's Joe Goulden, a former reporter for the *Dallas Morning News* who is now on the city desk of the *Philadelphia Inquirer*.

"What's going on down there? We're not getting anything straight. It's all garbled. Is Oswald going to be charged with killing the president?" the reporter asks.

"Yeah, we're getting ready to file on the Communist son of a bitch," Alexander tells him. When Goulden asks Alexander why he called Oswald a Communist, Alexander tells him about all the Communist literature and correspondence they found at Oswald's Beckley address. "We have the killer," Alexander says, "but we're not sure what his connections are."

Goulden wants to know exactly when the charges will be filed against Oswald. "As soon as I can draw up the complaint," Alexander replies.

Goulden says his editor won't print the part about Oswald being a Communist for fear of a libel suit. The only way he'd print that is if he could say it was part of the formal charge.

Alexander, who would later allow that "I let my mouth overload my ass," says sarcastically, "Well, how about if I charge him with being part of an international Communist conspiracy? Could you run with that?"

He knew he couldn't draw up a complaint like that, but Alexander was itching to show Oswald for what he was, a damn Communist. Goulden was more than eager to oblige.

"You got it!" the reporter says.[879]

Ever since his meeting with Vince Drain an hour and a half ago, Chief Curry has been getting calls from Washington, insisting that the police send all of the evidence up to the FBI laboratory in Washington, although nobody will tell him exactly who it is that is making the demands, always insinuating it's someone in high authority. Curry manages to get a moment with Captain Fritz and asks him if they are in a position to release some of the evidence to the FBI for testing.

"I need the evidence here," Fritz argues. "I'd like to have some of the local gun shops take a look at this rifle and pistol and see if they can identify them. How can I do that if they're in Washington?"

Curry knows he's right. This case is not under the jurisdiction of the FBI or the Secret Service. Although Curry wants to go all out and do whatever he can to allow these agencies to observe what is taking place, in the final analysis this crime happened in Dallas and would have to be tried in Dallas and therefore it was their responsibility to gather and present the evidence. If they fail, the blame will fall on him. For the moment, the Dallas police chief is unwilling to give in to the demands from Washington.[880]

In New York City, FBI agents watch employees as they rummage through the files of Crescent Firearms Company. Louis Feldsott, president of the company, has been very cooperative, keeping employees after hours to help investigators track the assassination weapon.[881] Earlier in the afternoon, Dallas FBI agents had canvassed Dallas gun dealers to determine if any of them had ever sold surplus World War II vintage Mannlicher-Carcanos. They found only one who did—H. L. Green Company on Main Street. Albert C. Yeargan Jr., manager of the sporting goods department at H. L. Green, spent the late afternoon with agents reviewing sales receipts for the past few years to determine if his company had ever handled a Mannlicher-Carcano with serial number C2766. The search proved fruitless; however, their records did identify the importer of these Italian 6.5-millimeter rifles as Crescent Firearms Company of New York.[882]

The investigation quickly switched to New York, where for the last several hours Crescent Firearm's employees have been looking for a record of serial number C2766. Suddenly, they have a break. Their records show that C2766 had been wholesaled to Klein's Sporting Goods in Chicago.[883]

Within the hour, Chicago FBI agents are pounding on the front door of the home of William J. Waldman, vice president of Klein's. Waldman agrees to accompany agents to the office to start a search, but first he'll need some help. He calls Mitchell Scibor, general operating manager of Klein's, and asks him to meet him at the office. As Waldman gets ready, he tells waiting agents that this is not a simple matter.

"Klein's purchases a lot of sporting goods," he warns them, "of which guns are but one. It could take hours to go through our purchase records."[884]

In a small alcove of the autopsy room at Bethesda Naval Hospital, the acting chief of radiology, Dr. John Ebersole, clips the last of the X-rays onto a light box. Nothing. No bullet. The president's entire body has been x-rayed and still the doctors have been unable to determine what happened to the bullet that struck his back.[885]

"Where did it go?" someone asks.

The doctors have no idea.[886] A discussion ensues about what might have happened to it. Someone suggests the possibility that a soft-nosed bullet struck the president and disintegrated. Others contemplate that the bullet could have been "plastic," and therefore not easily seen by X-rays, or that it was an "Ice" bullet, which had dissolved after contact.[887] None of the suggestions made much sense, but then neither did the absence of a bullet. FBI agent Jim Sibert decided to call the FBI laboratory and find out if anyone there knew of a bullet that would almost completely fragmentize. He managed to reach Special Agent Charles L. Killion of the Firearms Section of the lab, who said he'd never heard of such a thing. After Sibert explained the problem, Killion asked if he was aware that a bullet had been found on a stretcher at Parkland Hospital. Sibert hadn't and is nearly certain that no one else at the morgue has either. Sibert hangs up the phone, returns to the autopsy room, and informs the three pathologists that a bullet had been recovered at Parkland Hospital.[888]

"That could account for it," Humes said of the missing bullet. He suggested that in some rather inexplicable fashion the bullet might have been stopped in its path and thereafter worked its way out of the body and onto the stretcher, perhaps during cardiac massage.[889]

10:15 p.m.

Jack Ruby, by all accounts, was having one of the worst days of his life. "He cried harder when President Kennedy was killed than when Ma and Pa died," his sister Eva would later tell me.[890] But his day had started out with anger, not mourning. He had awakened to find a large advertisement in the *Dallas Morning News* in the form of a letter captioned "Welcome Mr. Kennedy" taken out by one Bernard Weissman in which Kennedy is criticized for aiding and abetting international Communism.[891] Jack is very patriotic, has been all his life. He loves America and can't tolerate anyone saying anything negative about our government.* He was even known to insist that someone he was attending a sporting event with put out his cigarette during the playing of the "Star Spangled Banner."[892] And Jack was a great admirer of President Kennedy and his wife and family, bringing them up in social conversations and praising them.[893] In fact, when someone at the Carousel Club made a disrespectful remark not too long ago about Kennedy, Jack threw him out of the club.[894]† And Jack had forbidden his comics at the club from saying anything or using any

---

*Although Ruby was highly patriotic, he was completely apolitical, though a lifelong Democrat, "being devoid of political ideas to the point of naivete" (CE 2980, 26 H 469–470; CE 1747, 23 H 355). Carousel comic Bill Demar, who knew Ruby well, said he "never recalled ever having heard him discuss politics" (15 H 102, WCT William D. Crowe Jr. [Bill Demar]). His rabbi, Hillel Silverman, told the FBI that Ruby was a very shallow person intellectually, and he considered Ruby to be someone "who would not know the difference between a communistic philosophy and a totalitarian philosophy, in that he was not well-read and spent little time concerning himself with this type of information." The rabbi, however, appears to have missed the mark when he said that although Ruby thought the president of the United States was the greatest individual in the world, it wasn't because of the president himself, but because of Ruby's respect for the position involved and of his high respect for the American government. (CE 1485, 22 H 906–907, FBI interview of Hillel Silverman on November 27, 1963) Though that was probably a large part of Ruby's feeling for Kennedy, the consensus of others, including those who were much closer to Ruby than Silverman, is that Ruby had an extraordinary feeling for Kennedy personally.

†The fact that Barry Goldwater, who was already gearing up to run against Kennedy for president in 1964, was brought up in the discussion by the emcee at the Carousel around the same time as the remark about Kennedy, indicates the incident probably happened within months of the assassination.

material that reflected adversely against "Negroes, Jews, or the Kennedys."[895] How could this fellow Weissman attack "our beloved President," Ruby thought.[896] Indeed, he thought that John F. Kennedy was possibly the greatest man who ever lived,[897] and after the assassination started carrying a small picture of the president on his person, kissing it "like a baby" in front of his sister Eva. "My brother had such a great admiration for this man, it's unbelievable," Eva would recall.[898]

After seeing the Weissman ad, Jack called Eva, he was so upset about it. He told her he had called the *News* and bawled them out. "Where the hell do you get off taking an ad like that? Are you money hungry?" It was a rotten thing for any person to question the way the president was running the country. "If this Weissman is a Jew," he told her, "they ought to whack the hell out of him." He figured Weissman might actually be a Commie himself trying to discredit the Jews, and Ruby later clips the Weissman ad from his sister Eva's copy of the *News*, even though he still has his.[899] Jack seems to almost be more upset about the audacity of Weissman dishonoring the president by addressing his letter to "Mr. Kennedy," rather than "Honorable President" or "Mr. President," than the letter itself.[900]

When Ruby heard at the *News* that Kennedy had been shot, he turned an ashen color, very pale, and sat completely dazed, a fixed stare on his face that was remarkable enough for people in the office to notice. He said nothing, very uncommon for Ruby.[901] He eventually came out of it enough to verbally grieve with those around him on the horror and tragedy of what had happened. Ruby used John Newnam's phone to call his sister Eva, and she was crying hysterically.[902] Ruby asked Newnam to listen to his sister and held the phone up to his ear. Newnam could hear that Eva sounded very upset.[903] Ruby told Newnam, "John, I will have to leave Dallas. John, I am not opening tonight."[904] He left the building and got in his car, sobbing.[905] After returning to the Carousel, he ordered that the club be closed for the night, and his employee Andrew Armstrong made the first phone call, to a stripper, Karen "Little Lynn" Carlin, at 1:45 p.m., to tell her not to come in, but he was unable to reach her.[906] Ruby's coworkers saw that he was taking the president's death harder than even they, and he called what happened an "outrageous crime that would ruin the city of Dallas."[907]

Ruby started making a flurry of phone calls from the club,[908] the first at 1:51 p.m. to his friend Ralph Paul at Paul's Bullpen Drive-In in Arlington, Texas, telling Paul "I can't believe it," and urging him to close his drive-in restaurant "in honor of the president," which Paul told him he couldn't afford to do.[909] He called his sister Eileen, in Chicago, and was crying. "Did you hear the awful news," he asked. "Yes," she said. "Oh, my God, oh, my God," Jack said. "Maybe I will fly up to be with you tonight," he suggested, but she reminded him that Eva, who had just returned home from the hospital from abdominal surgery, needed him now more than she did. "You better stay there," she told her brother.[910]

Later in the afternoon he called Billy Joe Willis, the drummer at his club. "How could any man do such a thing?" he asked Willis, crying. He also said to Willis—not trying to connect the two acts—"Remember that man making fun of President Kennedy in the club last night?," referring to a man in the audience who called Kennedy a bum when Ruby, on stage with his twistboard, said, "Even President Kennedy tells us to get more exercise." Completely broken up over the president's death, Ruby said, "This is the most horrible thing that has ever happened," and hung up. Willis was taking the president's death hard too, but he told his girlfriend later that he couldn't understand the extent that Ruby was torn up over it.[911]

Before the day was out he also called his brother, Hyman Rubenstein, in Chicago, to lament the president's death—"Can you imagine, can you imagine?" he asked Hyman.[912]

Ruby also called Al Gruber, a friend of his from Chicago now living in Los Angeles whom he has known for many years and who had stopped by the Carousel to see Jack just two weeks earlier when he was passing through town. "Did you hear what happened?" he asked Gruber. "You mean the shooting of the president?" "Yes, ain't that a terrible thing. I'm all upset and my sister is hysterical." Gruber heard Ruby crying at this point, and Ruby said, "I'm crying and can't talk to you anymore," whereupon he hung up the phone.[913]

When Ruby heard of Officer Tippit's murder, his grief was intensified, believing it's the Officer Tippit he knows, though he will later learn it's a different Tippit. Ruby knew Dallas police detective Gayle M. Tippit, who worked in the Special Services Bureau, and who on numerous occasions had stopped by the Vegas and Carousel clubs on official business.[914] After leaving the Carousel Club in midafternoon, Ruby goes to his sister Eva's apartment to lament and cry over the president's death, and talks about sending flowers to the place right off Elm Street near the spot where the president was shot. It was the first of three visits to her apartment that day, and he called her eight times on the phone.[915]

Though his financial condition was such that he could ill afford to do it, he made the decision at Eva's place to close his two clubs for not just one but three days, the first time the Carousel had ever been dark.* Ruby had first told Don Safran, the entertainment columnist for the city's evening paper, the *Dallas Times Herald*, that his club would be closed that evening as well as the entire weekend. He then tried to cancel his ads at the *Dallas Morning News* for the weekend, and when he was told that his space had already been reserved for him, he told the paper to just say in the ads that his Vegas and Carousel clubs would be closed for the weekend.[916] Eva had asked Jack to bring some food over when he came, but he brought enough "to feed twelve people," Eva explaining that Jack was so out of it "he didn't know what he was doing then." She said her brother was so upset over what happened that he only took one "spoonful or forkful," then started making more phone calls. At one point, he was sick in the stomach enough to go into the bathroom, but he did not vomit. "Someone tore my heart out," he told Eva, who herself was experiencing great grief, literally screaming over the telephone to a friend earlier that "the president is dead." Jack told Eva, "I didn't even feel so bad when Pops died because Papa was an old man. He was close to ninety." Eva looked at her brother sitting in front of her and got the sense that he felt life wasn't worth it anymore, "like he thought they were out to get the world, and this was part of it." "This man," Jack said to Eva about Kennedy and his efforts with his brother Bobby toward integration in the South, was "greater than Lincoln." When Jack left her apartment in the early evening "he looked pretty bad, a broken man."[917]

At the Shearith Israel Synagogue, where he went to pray for the fallen president, arriving near the end of a two-hour service that had started at 8:00 p.m., the day's events preyed on his mind. When a friend, Leona Lane, remarked to him after the services "how terrible" the assassination of President Kennedy had been, Ruby said, "It is worse than that."[918]

---

*At some time during the afternoon, Ruby stopped in to see a friend of his, Joe Cavagnaro, the sales manager at the Statler Hilton Hotel. He told Cavagnaro about his plans to close the Carousel for three days. Cavagnaro said, "He asked me what *we* were going to do. I told him, 'Jack, you can't just close a hotel. People have to have a place to eat and sleep.' But he expected the whole city to close down." (Wills and Demaris, *Jack Ruby*, pp.38, 40)

The rabbi, Hillel Silverman, noticed that Ruby appeared to be "in shock" and in a daze, though Ruby didn't mention the assassination to him, merely thanking him for visiting Eva at the hospital a few days earlier.[919] When he left the synagogue for the parking lot, he got his pistol, a .38 caliber Colt Cobra, out of the trunk and slipped it into his right front trouser pocket. It's a lightweight revolver with a two-inch barrel, and a shroud over the hammer makes it easy to carry in his pocket without snagging the cloth.[920] He wouldn't take it into the synagogue, but he usually carries the pistol when he has a lot of cash on him from the Carousel, which he does tonight.[921]

Now, around 10:15 in the evening, he's worried about the other Dallas clubs and whether they are properly respecting the death of the president, so he makes a point of driving by the Bali-Hai Restaurant, and notes grimly that it is open. He drives past the Gay Nineties too. It is closed.

As he goes on down Preston Road, he listens to the car radio, hungry for any new information about the assassination. He hears that the police are working overtime, and is overcome by a feeling of respect and admiration for them. He has always felt close to the police department—he doesn't even know why—and believes Dallas has the greatest police force in the world. He has many friends on the force and often visits the police at the station, encouraging them to come to his clubs when they are off duty. Jack gives them the cut rate on drinks he normally reserves for newsmen, hotel receptionists, bellboys, and others who might help to generate business.[922] And if all an officer wanted was a snack, "Jack kept coffee and sandwiches in the back for the police."[923]

On an impulse he stops at Phil's Delicatessen on Oak Lawn Avenue and tells the counterman, John Frickstad, to cut him ten corned beef sandwiches with mustard. And ten soft drinks—eight black cherries and two celery tonics. He chats a bit with the owner, Phil Miller.

He goes to the phone, calls police headquarters, and gets Detective Sims, a fifteen-year acquaintance.

"I hear you guys are still working," he says. "I want to bring you some sandwiches."

"Jack, we wound up our work already. We finished what we were doing. I'll tell the boys about your thoughtfulness. Thank you."[924]

Those sandwiches are already being made, and it's a shame to let them go to waste. Ruby remembers Gordon McLendon, and how good McLendon has always been to him, giving him a lot of free plugs for his clubs on his Dallas radio station. McLendon owns many radio stations, including KLIF in Dallas, the one Ruby had been listening to in the car. One of the disk jockeys, Joe Long, is down at the police station, phoning information to the station as it comes in, and others are working late too—the guy on the air and the engineers at the station. He tries calling KLIF, but because it's after six no one answers. He knows there is a hotline right into the control room, but he doesn't know the number.

He calls out to Frickstad, "These sandwiches are going to KLIF, and I want you to make them real good."

There's another disk jockey he knows at KLIF, Russ Knight, big with the kids in the late-afternoon hot spot, but he can't get his home number from information. He tries Gordon McLendon, who lives out near the synagogue and whose number he does know. A little girl answers. Maybe her name is Christine, Jack thinks.

"Anyone home?"

"No."

"Is your daddy or mommy home? I would like to get the number of the station, so I can get in the building at this time." The little girl leaves the phone and comes back with a number in the Riverside exchange.

Jack dials the Riverside number but it has been disconnected. He calls Eva, tells her he's at Phil's getting sandwiches and is going to the station, and if she needs him, she can reach him there, though he still doesn't have the station's number. The sandwich bill only comes to $9.50 plus tax—Frickstad made only eight sandwiches instead of the ten Jack ordered. Frickstad helps Jack with the sandwiches out to his car and receives Jack's customary tip, a free pass to the Carousel or Vegas, for his pains.[925]

It's four or five miles from Phil's to downtown, and Ruby still doesn't know how he's going to get into KLIF to bring the sandwiches to the gang on duty. He drives up McKinney Avenue to check on some more clubs, and finds more open. Jack simply can't understand how they would remain open at such a tragic time. Jack proceeds to the KLIF station, near City Hall. He knew the front door would be locked, of course, but he hopes his knocking is loud enough for them to hear him, but because of the long distance between the bottom of the flight of stairs and the studio, no one does, so he proceeds to City Hall to look for KLIF reporter Joe Long to get the control-room phone number.[926]

It's about eleven in the evening when he parks at Commerce and Harwood, leaving the sandwiches and his dog Sheba in the car, and goes to the police department, taking the elevator to the second floor. Ruby's an experienced gatecrasher, he can get in anywhere by putting on a busy, peremptory manner, "taking," as he puts it in his weirdly mangled way of talking, "a domineering part about me."

"Where is Joe Long?" he speaks assertively to the officer at the desk. "Can I go look for him?" The officer lets him in.

Emerging from the elevator on the third floor into a throng of reporters, Ruby asks everyone, cops and reporters, if they know where he can find Joe Long, determined to find Long so he can deliver his load of sandwiches out at KLIF. He even has an officer page Long, but with no luck. He knows a lot of the officers, and stops to chat with Lieutenant Leonard and Detective Cal Jones. Roy Standifer, the desk officer in the Burglary and Theft Bureau, calls out, "Hi, Jack," and Jack calls out, "Hi, Sandy"—he calls Roy that, short for Standifer. No one else, Standifer notes wryly, ever does. Standifer, who has known Jack for thirteen years, recognizes Ruby's use of a first name as one of his tricks. On Jack's frequent visits to police headquarters, Standifer has seen him ask someone for the first name of an officer he doesn't know and then greet the man by his first name like an old friend.[927]

Ruby sticks his head in the Burglary and Theft door and is delighted to spot Detective A. M. Eberhardt. The detective's work on the vice squad used to bring him to the Carousel regularly a few years back, and he even brought his wife there once on a night off. Ruby gave "Michael"—for some reason he uses Eberhardt's middle name—a couple of tips too. He reported one of his own girls when he discovered she was forging checks and using drugs, and Eberhardt busted her right there in the club. Another time Ruby heard from some parking-lot boys that a guy under indictment for white slavery was in town and staying at the Baker, half a block down the street from the Carousel, and Eberhardt went in with a squad and made the collar. Later, when Eberhardt was transferred to burglary, he managed to run down a couple of burglars Ruby surprised in the Carousel. Eberhardt always lent a sympathetic ear to Ruby's complaints about his competition, those damned Weinsteins. He knows Jack usually carries a large sum of money in his pocket and worries about Jack leaving the club at two or three in the morning with the night's take in a bag. They are old friends.

Ruby shakes hands, asks, as he always does, about Eberhardt's wife and kids, and tells him he's there as a "translator for the newspapers," brandishing a little notebook. "I'm a reporter," Jack says, tapping something in his lapel (had he purloined a press badge?) with the notebook. The only foreign language Eberhardt knows that Jack speaks is Yiddish, but the corridor outside is crammed with foreigners, shouting in languages he never heard before. Ruby tells him about the sandwiches he made up for the radio reporters, corned beef. "Nothing," Jack boasts, "but kosher stuff is all I bring."

Jack starts talking about how terrible it is for the assassination to have happened in the city. "It's hard to realize that a complete nothing, a zero like that,* could kill a man like President Kennedy was."

Eberhardt is busy. Even though he is only on standby, he's using the opportunity to catch up on his paperwork. So, after a few minutes, Ruby plunges back into the hubbub in the hall, and situates himself where the height of the activity is, right outside Captain Fritz's office door. Oswald, of course, is being interrogated inside. Ruby proceeds to put his hand on the door knob, turn it, and starts to step into the room when two officers stop him. "You can't go in there, Jack," one says. No problem. Ruby is content to be close to the action, right outside the door.

You have to shout to be heard in that corridor, but Ruby enjoys being able to provide information to the reporters, many of them bewildered out-of-towners, about everyone who was coming in or out of the door. "No, that's not Sheriff Decker, that's Chief Curry, C-u-r-r-y," or "That's Captain Fritz, Will Fritz. He's the homicide captain." He really likes to be helpful, particularly to important people like reporters. A detective who recognizes him bellows at the top of his voice over the heads of the reporters, "Hey Jack, what are you doing here?"

Ruby manages to get one arm free to wave to his friend. "I'm helping all these fellows," he shouts back, pointing to the foreigners.

Jack's activity is taking his mind off the tragedy and he is feeling a little better than he has all day. In a way, he feels he is being temporarily deputized as a reporter. He is, he realizes, "being carried away by the excitement of history."[928]

10:30 p.m.
Robert Oswald crosses the lobby of the Statler Hilton Hotel across the street from Dallas police headquarters. For a moment, he considers registering under a false name, to keep reporters at bay, but then decides he isn't going to start hiding. No matter, the desk

---

*Throughout the rest of his life, Ruby rarely permitted the name "Oswald" to come from his lips, either purposefully or instinctively refraining from uttering the word. "I don't know why," he told the Warren Commission. "I don't know how to explain it." One explanation is that he unconsciously sensed that to do so would invest it with a human dignity it did not have. Authors Gary Wills and Ovid Demaris wrote that "Ruby could not bring himself to call *the thing* by name. It is the instinct that kept [Carl] Sandburg from using [John Wilkes] Booth's name in his long description of Lincoln's death. When he must refer to the assassin, he calls him 'the Outsider.'" The authors note that William Manchester, who does use Oswald's name many times in his book, is nonetheless "sickened by the need to do so." Manchester writes, "Noticing him [Oswald], and even printing his name in history books . . . seems obscene. It is an outrage. He is an outrage." (5 H 187, WCT Jack L. Ruby; Wills and Demaris, *Jack Ruby*, p.264; Manchester, *Death of a President*, pp.276–277)

In their book *Johnny, We Hardly Knew Ye*, JFK's two closest aides, Kenneth P. O'Donnell and David F. Powers, never used Oswald's name once, though they wrote about the horrors of JFK's death.

clerk doesn't seem to pay any attention to the name on the registration card. When he arrives on the sixteenth floor, Robert finds a small, rather drab room with two chairs, a small table, and a sofa bed. Unable to face the depressing room, he returns to the hotel coffee shop and nibbles on a ham sandwich.[929]

Henry Wade is returning home after dining with his wife and some friends when he hears a report on the radio that Oswald is going to be charged with being part of an international Communist conspiracy to murder the president.[930] Wade, the Dallas DA since 1951, can barely believe his ears. There is no such law on the Texas books, and anyone familiar with Texas law knows that if you allege anything in an indictment, you have the burden of proving it.[931]

Wade barely gets in the door when the telephone rings. The caller is Waggoner Carr, attorney general for the state of Texas. He had just received a long-distance call from someone in the White House who had heard a similar report. Carr wants to know if Wade has any knowledge of it. Wade said he didn't.[932]

"You know," Carr says, "this is going to create a hell of a bad situation if you allege that he's part of a Communist conspiracy. It's going to affect international relations and a lot of things with this country."

"I don't know where the rumor got started," Wade says, "but even if we could prove he was part of an international conspiracy, I wouldn't allege it because there's no such charge in Texas."[933]

Within a few minutes, Henry Wade gets phone calls from his first assistant, Jim Bowie, and U.S. Attorney Barefoot Sanders—both of whom have gotten very concerned calls from Washington. Wade assures both of them that he will check into the rumor.[934]

Wade immediately decides to take "charge" of the matter and goes down to the police department to make sure that no such language appears in any complaint against Oswald. His man down there, Bill Alexander,* denies to Wade that he had anything to do with the rumor, not telling Wade that his own loose lips had given birth to it.[935]

In Richardson, Texas, Gregory Olds, editor of the local newspaper and president of the Dallas chapter of the American Civil Liberties Union (ACLU), reaches for the telephone ringing on his nightstand. The caller is one of the ACLU board members, who tells him he just got a call from the president of the Austin affiliate. Lee Oswald has been seen on television complaining that he's been denied legal representation and they think that someone should check into Oswald's complaint. Olds agrees and tells him that he will do it.

In a moment, Olds has the Dallas Police Department on the line and asks to speak to the chief of police. He's told that Chief Curry is busy. Olds then asks to speak to one of the deputy chiefs, but no one seems to know where they are. When Olds is asked if he would be willing to speak to a detective, he informs the officer on the phone that he is the president of the Dallas Civil Liberties Union and that he will speak with the man in charge

---

*When I asked Alexander if Wade had immediately assigned him to the Oswald case, the tall, angular-faced Texan who speaks slowly, and sometimes sprinkles those words with salty, ranch-hand profanity, responded, "There was no *need* for any conversation between Henry and me. It was understood" (Telephone interview of William Alexander by author on December 11, 2000).

of the investigation and no one else. An officer eventually comes to the phone and tells him, "Captain Fritz isn't available, but you can tell me."

"I'll wait," Olds tells them through clenched teeth. He has learned to be persistent when dealing with the police.[936]

When Captain Fritz finally comes on the line, Olds explains to him that the ACLU was deeply concerned over Oswald's apparent lack of legal counsel and stands ready to provide him with immediate assistance. Fritz blithely tells him that the suspect had been informed several times of his right to representation and offered opportunities to contact a lawyer, but he declined them. Olds thanks the captain and hangs up.[937]

The situation is nothing new for the ACLU chapter president. He knew that every city had prisoners who refuse the services of an attorney on the assumption they don't need one, deciding to represent themselves in court. Most of them pay for their mistake in prison. It would be easy for Olds to accept the word of the police department that Oswald's legal rights have been safeguarded. Instead, he rubs the sleepiness from his eyes and telephones a few ranking members of the ACLU, telling them to meet him at once in the lobby of the Plaza Hotel, across the street northwest from City Hall.[938]

10:40 p.m.
After having just left police headquarters about ten to fifteen minutes ago, Detectives Guy Rose and Richard Stovall park their car in the basement garage of City Hall and walk back into the basement entrance with Wesley Frazier, his sister, and the Reverend Campble in tow. After taking an affidavit from Frazier, they were driving the three of them back to Irving and were halfway there when they received a call over the radio to return to City Hall with Frazier and contact Captain Fritz. When Detective Rose telephones upstairs, Captain Fritz tells him to take Frazier to the fourth-floor Identification Bureau and give Frazier a polygraph test. Fritz wants to know if he's telling the truth about the curtain rod story. Did Oswald really tell him he was bringing curtain rods to work? Or is this some kind of cover story Frazier has cooked up?

"Okay, Cap'," Rose replies.[939]

Horace Busby, LBJ's longtime aide, speechwriter, and confidant, is waiting for President Johnson to arrive at Johnson's home, the Elms, a large brick home in the Spring Valley section of Washington, D.C., Johnson had purchased from well-known society figure and political hostess Perle Mesta. In the past sixteen years Busby had been through the highs and the lows and everything in between with LBJ, and knew him, he said, better than he wanted to know any man. Yet he knows he is not now waiting for any man he had ever known. He was waiting for the president of the United States. The Elms is being overrun with Secret Service agents and telephone people installing new lines. After LBJ arrives and has a meeting with his close aides, friends, and Mrs. Johnson, he retreats to the sunroom with Busby. A large portrait of LBJ's mentor, former House Speaker Sam Rayburn, looks down on the room. LBJ raises his hand to the portrait, saying quietly, "How I wish you were here." Settling in a chair, he asks Busby to turn on the television set, saying, "I guess I am the only person in the United States who doesn't know what happened today." When he hears talk out of Dallas about a possible Communist conspiracy being behind the assassination, he says, "No, we must not have that. We must not start making accusations without evidence."[940]

11:00 p.m.

At the Paine house in Irving, the rumblings of a long day are coming to an end. Ruth and Marina talk quietly as they prepare for bed. Marina tells her that just the night before Lee had said to her that he hoped they could get an apartment together again soon. She is hurt and confused, wondering how he could say such a thing when he must have been planning something that would inevitably cause their permanent separation. For an instant, Mrs. Paine's politeness was overcome by her curiosity.

"Do you think he killed the president?" she asks.

"I don't know," Marina answers.

There is an awkward moment, and then Marina says that she doesn't think she'll be able to sleep anytime soon and asks to borrow Ruth's hair dryer. She wants to take a shower, which she has often said renews her spirits. Mrs. Paine hands her the dryer and bids her goodnight.[941]

Alone, later, in her own bedroom, Marina runs across June's baby book, which the police had failed to confiscate. She suddenly remembers the pictures Lee had given her from the set he had her take of him in the backyard when they lived on Neely Street. She peels the book open. There they are, pasted into the album, two small snapshots of Oswald wearing a pistol and holster strapped to his waist, a rifle in one hand, two left-wing newspapers in the other. On the back of one he had written, "For Junie, from Papa." When he had given them to her, Marina was appalled and asked, "Why would Junie want a picture with guns?"

"To remember Papa by sometime," Oswald had said.[942]

She realizes now that they will only hurt Lee. She carefully removes them from the baby book and calls Marguerite into the bedroom. She shows them to Mrs. Oswald and tries to explain to her that Lee shot at General Edwin Walker in early 1963[*] and that he might have been shooting at the president too. But her thoughts only come out as a series of gestures and very broken English.

"Mama," she says, pointing at the photographs. "Walker . . . "

Marguerite doesn't seem to understand what she means by "Walker" but understands the significance of the guns in the photos. "You take, Mama," Marina says.

"No," Marguerite resists.

"Yes, Mama, you take," Marina says, shoving the photos at her.

"No, Marina," Marguerite whispers. "Put back in the book."

Marguerite then places a finger across her lips, points toward Ruth's room, and shakes her head, warning Marina, "Ruth, no." Marina understands that she is not to show the photos to Mrs. Paine, or anyone.[943]

After Marguerite leaves the room, Marina makes another discovery that takes her breath away. The police, in their hasty search, also overlooked a pale, translucent, blue-green china cup with violets and a golden rim that her grandmother had given her. Inside it she finds Lee's wedding ring. Lee had taken the ring off at work before, but this was the first time in their marriage that he had ever taken it off and left it at home. Marina immediately realizes that the shooting was not a spontaneous act, but that Lee had intended to do it when he left that morning. Apparently, he didn't expect to return.[944]

---

[*]On the evening of April 10, 1963, retired Major General Edwin A. Walker, a prominent right-wing figure in Dallas, was shot at through the window of his suburban Dallas home. The bullet intended for him was deflected by the window frame and missed Walker's head. (See later text.)

Marina didn't sleep that night. She knew little about American law. She thought it would all be over in three days and Lee would be strapped in the electric chair and executed. Would she be found a criminal too for her knowledge of Lee's involvement in the Walker shooting? Would she find herself in prison? She lay awake wondering what would become of her children.[945]

Henry Wade plows his way through the field of reporters lined up in the corridor outside the Homicide and Robbery Bureau.* Inside, Assistant DA Bill Alexander, FBI agent Jim Bookhout, and Captain Fritz await him. At Wade's request, Fritz begins to outline the considerable amount of evidence the Dallas Police Department has impressively gathered so far—the gun, the witnesses, the arrest, and the fingerprints and probably false statements by Oswald during his interrogation. It all looks pretty good to Wade.[946]

For nearly the past five hours, thirty-five-year-old Richard B. Stolley, the Pacific Coast regional editor for *Life* magazine, has been ringing the home telephone of Abraham Zapruder every fifteen minutes or so without success. Stolley flew into Dallas from Los Angeles earlier in the afternoon with *Life* reporter Tommy Thompson and photographer Allen Grant. The team had set up headquarters at the Hotel Adolphus in downtown Dallas, and within hours Stolley learned from a local correspondent that Zapruder had reportedly taken amateur movies of the shooting.

Stolley dials the number again, and this time a sleepy voice answers, "Hello?"

Zapruder had been driving around the last few hours trying to shake the gruesome images from his mind. Stolley explains that he represents *Life* magazine and might be interested in Zapruder's film. Zapruder says Stolley is the first journalist to contact him and confirms that he does have a film that shows the shooting. Not wishing to lose an exclusive, and knowing others will soon be hot on the trail, Stolley tries to talk Zapruder into letting him come out to his home now to view the film and talk. Zapruder replies that he is too tired and distraught to discuss it tonight. He tells Stolley to come by his office at nine o'clock tomorrow morning, and hangs up.

Stolley decides to show up an hour early, just in case.[947]

It's just after midnight on the East Coast as the three pathologists near the end of their autopsy of the president's body at Bethesda Naval Hospital, when three skull fragments recovered from the floor of the presidential limousine during a Secret Service examination at the White House garage are brought into the morgue.[948] Interest in the three skull fragments grows when the three pathologists note a distinct crater on the outer surface

---

*Wade would later tell the Warren Commission, "You just had to fight your way down through the hall through the press . . . To get into homicide it was a strain to get the door open enough to get into the office" (5 H 218). One problem is that the third-floor hallway was only about 113 feet long and just 7 feet wide (CE 2175; 24 H 848; WR, p.197), and this space was further reduced by all the radio and TV equipment, such as cables and tripods, in the corridor. To compound the problem of all the members of the media and Dallas Police Department mingling or moving about in the narrow hallway, throughout the three days of Oswald's detention the Dallas police were obligated to continue normal business in all five of its bureaus located along the same hallway. Therefore, many persons, such as witnesses and relatives of defendants, had occasion to visit the third floor on matters unrelated to the assassination. (WR, p.204)

of the largest fragment, characteristic of an exit wound.[949] Their suspicions are soon confirmed when X-rays of that fragment reveal minute metallic particles embedded in the margins of the crater.[950] There is no doubt about it. The fragment contains a portion of the exit wound.[951]

FBI agents Sibert and O'Neill, eager to submit a report on the autopsy findings, ask Dr. Humes what his findings will be?

"Well, the pattern is clear," Humes tells them. "Two bullets struck the president from behind. One bullet entered the president's back and probably worked its way out of the body during the external cardiac massage at Parkland Hospital. A second bullet struck the rear of the president's skull and fragmented before exiting."

"Is that then the cause of death, Doctor?"

Humes nods, affirmatively. "Gunshot wound of the head."[952]

As the autopsy team removes its equipment from around the examination table, a group of morticians from Gawler's Funeral Home move their portable embalming equipment into position to prepare the president's body for burial.[953] Secret Service agent Roy Kellerman signs for the photographs[954] and X-rays[955] taken during the autopsy, which will be delivered to Secret Service special agent-in-charge Robert I. Bouck at the White House in the early morning hours of November 23.[956]

Though most in attendance at the autopsy quietly leave the room, for the weary doctors the night is not over; they stay to assist the morticians. No one seems to know whether the coffin will be open or closed while the president lies in state. Although Mrs. Kennedy has expressed her wish that the casket be closed, the issue has been left unresolved. Neither Brigadier General Godfrey McHugh, the president's air force aide, nor Admiral George Burkley, the president's personal physician, can assure the morticians that the body will not be viewed. McHugh decides that it would be better to be on the safe side and have the body fully prepared and dressed.[957]

For the next three hours, the men from Gawler's are absorbed in the tedious task of putting as good a face as possible on death. The president's cranium is packed with a combination of cotton and plaster of Paris to provide the support necessary to reconstruct the head. After the hardening agent dries, the scalp is pulled together and sutured.[958] The organs from the thoracic and abdominal cavity, preserved in formaldehyde, are placed in a plastic bag and returned to the body cavity, which is then stitched closed.[959] The tracheotomy wound is sutured up and a small amount of dermal wax is used to seal the wound. Restorative cosmetics are used to hide some bruising and discoloration on the face.[960]

At the conclusion of the embalming process, the body is wrapped in plastic, then dressed in a blue-gray pinstripe suit, a white shirt, a blue tie with a pattern of light dots, and black shoes, which have been picked out and brought to the morgue by the president's friend and aide, Dave Powers. The president's hands are folded across his chest and a rosary laced through the fingers.[961] When they are finished, the body is lifted into a new casket—made of hand-rubbed, five-hundred-year-old African mahogany—lined in white rayon* that has been brought in to replace the Britannia casket damaged in Dal-

---

*The total bill for the 255-pound Marsellus 710 coffin from Gawler's and its accompanying 3,000-pound Wilbert Triune/copper-lined vault is $3,160 (ARRB MD 130, Embalmers Personal Remarks; ARRB MD 134, Funeral Arrangements for John Fitzgerald Kennedy, November 22, 1963, p.1).

las.[962] Those who might look upon the president's face now will never know the brutal condition of his head just a few hours earlier.

11:15 p.m.
Robert Oswald finishes his light supper—a ham sandwich and a glass of milk. Perhaps Captain Fritz will finally be free to talk with him, he thinks. Leaving the hotel coffee shop, Robert heads back across the street to City Hall and is taken to Fritz's office, but again the captain is too busy to see him.[963]

In the lobby of the Plaza Hotel, Gregory Olds, president of the Dallas chapter of the American Civil Liberties Union, meets with three prominent members of his local organization. Olds rapidly outlines the situation to them as they try to work out a plan. A call to Mayor Cabell seems in order, but Olds comes back to them after a few moments to report that the mayor is busy. They wonder whether he is really busy or just too busy to deal with the ACLU. Olds has learned to deal with disappointment, and he will not be deterred.

"The best thing for us to do," he tells his fellow representatives, "is to go across the street and talk to the police directly."[964]

11:20 p.m.
Chief Curry enters the Homicide and Robbery office and joins District Attorney Wade, Assistant DA Alexander, Judge Johnston, and Captain Fritz in discussions about the evidence against Oswald. "Have we got enough to charge Oswald with the president's murder?" Curry asks. All are in agreement that there is sufficient evidence to file charges.[965]

Assistant DA Alexander drafts the language of complaint number F-154, charging Oswald with the assassination. The words are nearly identical to those used in the Tippit murder charge, only the name of the victim is different. When it is completed, Captain Fritz pulls out a pen and affixes his signature to the complaint, then hands the single-sheet document to District Attorney Wade, who adds his own signature. Judge Johnston takes the form, looks at his watch, then accepts the charge by scribbling his own name and title, along with the words "Filed, 11:26 pm, November 22, 1963."[966]*

There is a certain amount of satisfaction felt by all in attendance. The Dallas police have done an incredible, some would even say a near-impossible job over just the last eleven and a half hours. In that short span since the president's murder, they have apprehended the man they believe is responsible, and amassed evidence against him that is destined to withstand years of intense scrutiny. Despite the thousands of government man-hours yet to come, the basis of the case against Oswald is collected and assembled by the Dallas police in these first crucial hours. It is a feat the world would soon forget.

11:30 p.m.
Captain Fritz instructs Detectives Sims and Boyd to make out an arrest report on Oswald for the president's murder.[967] As they get to work, the discussion in the homicide office

---

*"We wanted to file on him [Oswald] before midnight," Alexander would later recall. "It just would look better that we got the SOB on the same day he killed Kennedy" (Telephone interview of William Alexander by author on December 12, 2000).

turns to evidence in the case. Once again, Chief Curry asks Fritz if they are in a position to release some of the evidence to the FBI for testing. Fritz tells him that he's got a local gun dealer coming down to look at the rifle to see if he can identify it.[*]

"How about after that?" Curry asks. Fritz looks at him, clearly agitated.

"How do we know, Chief, that we can get this evidence back from them when we need it?" Fritz asks. "I don't think we should let them have it."

"You know, this is a Dallas case," Alexander chimes in. "It happened here and it's going to have to be tried here. It's our responsibility to gather the evidence and present it."

Chief Curry is keenly aware that the FBI and Secret Service have no jurisdiction over the case. It's Dallas's baby, and it'll be up to them to see it through to the end. He also knows that it'll be their fault if something gets screwed up. Still, this isn't your average, garden-variety murder case. This is an investigation involving the assassination of an American president. Curry feels that his department has to make every effort to cooperate with the federal agencies and let them see what Dallas is doing. Besides, the FBI laboratory in Washington is the best of its kind in the nation and its support could certainly help expedite the investigative process.[968]

"Chief, I think you ought to let them take it up to Washington and bring it back tomorrow night," Wade suggests, trying to break the deadlock. "Let them have it twenty-four hours."[969]

The group argues some more over whether that is a wise course of action. Finally, an agreement is reached. The Dallas police want two things to ensure an unbroken chain of possession—photographs of everything sent to Washington, and an accountable FBI agent, Vince Drain, to sign for and accompany all of the evidence to and from the nation's capital.[970] Chief Curry calls upstairs to the Identification Bureau and tells Captain Doughty to have Lieutenant Day stop all processing of the rifle and to prepare the rifle, and other key pieces of evidence, for release to the FBI.[971]

Agent Drain telephones the Dallas FBI office, telling Special Agent-in-Charge Shanklin that Curry has agreed to lend the FBI the evidence. Shanklin notifies FBI headquarters and within ten minutes a C-135 jet tanker and crew are waiting on the runway at Carswell Air Force Base in Fort Worth to fly the evidence to Washington.[972]

11:45 p.m.

FBI agents Vince Drain and Charles T. Brown sign for and receive the items to be transported to Washington, which include the Mannlicher-Carcano rifle, serial number C2766, found on the sixth floor;[973] two of the three spent hulls found under the sniper's nest window[974] (the third spent hull[975] was retained by Captain Fritz and kept in a desk drawer in his private office[976]); one live 6.5 caliber cartridge found in the rifle chamber;[977] and the paper sack found near the sniper's nest window.[978]

Lieutenant Day scribbles some instructions on a corner of the paper sack found on the sixth floor: "FBI: Has been dusted [for prints] with metallic powder on outside only. Inside has not been processed. Lieut. J. C. Day."[979] The paper sack already had the words "Found next to the sixth floor window gun fired from. May have been used to carry gun. Lieu-

---

tenant J. C. Day."[980] When Day hands the rifle, the weapon believed by Dallas police to have murdered Kennedy, to FBI agent Drain, he says, "There's a trace of a print here," pointing to the trigger housing. The agent says nothing as he takes possession of the rifle.[981] The rest of the items are loaded into a box and FBI agents Drain and Brown hustle them down the elevator to the basement and out to their waiting car for the short trip to Carswell.[982]

11:50 p.m.
Chief Curry, District Attorney Wade, and Captain Fritz step out of the Homicide and Robbery office into the crush of reporters gathered in the third-floor corridor and announce that charges have been filed against Oswald in the assassination of the president.

"We want to say this," Curry tells them, "that this investigation has been carried on jointly by the FBI, the Secret Service, the [Texas] Rangers, and the Dallas Police Department. Captain Fritz has been in charge."

The newsmen want to know if Oswald has confessed.

"He has not confessed," Curry says.

"Any particular thing that he said," a reporter asks, "that caused you to file the charges regarding the president's death against him?"

"No, sir," Curry answers. "Physical evidence is the main thing that we are relying on."

Asked to name the physical evidence, Curry declines.

"When will he appear before the grand jury?"

Curry doesn't know, although that would be the next step. "We will continue with the investigation. There are still many things that we need to work on."

"Mr. Wade, could you elaborate on the physical evidence?"

"Well," the district attorney tells them, "the gun is one of them."

"Can you tell us if he has engaged a lawyer?"

"We don't know that," Captain Fritz says. "His people have been here but we don't—"

The homicide captain's hoarse voice is drowned out by a flood of other questions: Are there any fingerprints on the gun? Can we get a picture of him? Can we get a press conference where he could stand against a wall and we could talk to him? Do you expect a confession from this man?

"No," Wade says, picking the last question to answer.

"Do you have a strong case?"

"I think it's sufficient," Wade replies.

"What is the evidence that links him to the gun?"

"I don't care to go into the evidence now," Wade says firmly.[983]

The three officials huddle to discuss the possibility of showing Oswald to the press. A nearby microphone picks up fragments of the conversation.

"We could take him to the show-up room," Fritz is heard saying, "and put him on the stage and let him stand up. They couldn't, of course, interview him from up there, you know, but if you want them to look at him or take his picture—I'm not sure whether we should or shouldn't."

"We've got the assembly room," Curry says. "We could go down there."[984]

"Speak up!" the reporters shout.

"We're going to get in a larger room," Wade tells them, "that's what we're talking about here."

"What about the assembly room?" a reporter shouts.

"Is that all right?" Wade says. "Let's go down there."[985]

Most of the reporters make their way downstairs to the City Hall basement, awaiting Oswald. A few continue to grill Wade as Fritz and Curry slip back into the homicide office.

"Will there be a way to take any pictures?"

"I don't see any reason to take any picture of him," Wade replies.

"Of Lee?" a reporter asks, incredulously.

"Yes," Wade replies.

"Well, the whole world's only waiting to see what he looks like [now]," the reporter says.

"Oh, is that all," Wade answers matter-of-factly, "the whole world."

"That's all," the reporter says. "Just the world."[986]

NBC national television is shutting down its live coverage on the East Coast, where it's approaching 1:00 a.m. David Brinkley sums up the feelings of a nation to his dwindling audience: "We are about to wind up, as about all that could happen has happened. It is one of the ugliest days in American history. There is seldom any time to think anymore, and today there was none. In about four hours we had gone from President Kennedy in Dallas, alive, to back in Washington, dead, and a new president in his place. There is really no more to say except that what happened has been just too much, too ugly, and too fast." The network signs off at 1:02:17 a.m.[987]

Saturday, November 23

12:05 a.m.

Gregory Olds and three ACLU representatives, wanting to know if Oswald is being denied legal assistance, are not satisfied by the statement to them of Captain Glen King, the administrative assistant to the chief of police, that as far as he knew Oswald had not requested such assistance. Two members of Olds's group locate and speak directly to Justice of the Peace David Johnston. Johnston assures them that Oswald's legal rights have already been explained to him and that he had "declined counsel." They report this back to Olds. Satisfied that Oswald, despite his earlier protests in the third-floor corridor, had probably not been deprived of his legal rights, the men from the ACLU decide to go home for the night.[988]

It's been dark for hours, and most of Dallas law enforcement would normally be in bed and sleeping by now. But not tonight. In the Homicide and Robbery Bureau, Captain Fritz and Chief Curry confer in hushed tones just outside Fritz's private office, where Oswald awaits them. Their discussion centers around how to make Oswald available to the press. If Captain Fritz had his way, he'd have cleared the third floor of all reporters a long time ago. To his way of thinking, they're nothing but a nuisance to the investigation. Dealing with them has been a thorn in his side all day, because there's only been one way to get Oswald to and from Fritz's office, and that's through the crowd of reporters in the third-floor corridor. Every time they move him, Oswald faces a verbal assault from the press. Some of the things they holler at him are provocative, some seem to please him, others aggravate him, but none of them help the interrogation process. In fact, Fritz thinks, he would have been "more apt to get a confession . . . from [Oswald] if I could have . . . quietly talked with him." The constant barrage by the press has a tendency to keep Oswald upset.[989]

What bothers Chief Curry the most is the beating the city of Dallas, and the police department in particular, is taking in the press. It especially disturbed him to hear a reporter telling a television audience, as he held up a picture of Oswald, "This is what the man who is charged with shooting President Kennedy looks like, or at least this is what he did look like. We don't know what he looks like now after being in the custody of the police."[990] Of course, Curry knew Oswald wasn't being mistreated. He himself had checked with Captain Fritz to make sure that Oswald had been given something to eat and wasn't being subjected to long, drawn-out interrogation sessions. But the comments, no matter how inaccurate, sting just the same. Curry had always maintained very good relations with the local press, and they respected him for it.[991] But this is different. The halls are overrun with reporters from all over the world, each one putting Dallas under a magnifying glass. Under the pervasive glare of the world media, Curry feels that he has to defend the city and his beloved department. In no uncertain terms, he wants the press to know that Oswald isn't being mistreated, which, in his mind, means marching him out to within an arm's length of the mob of reporters waiting downstairs.

"I'm a little afraid something might happen to him," Fritz says. "Let me put him on the stage so nobody can get to him."

"No," Curry says. "I want him out in front of the stage."[992]

Acceding to his boss's request, Fritz steps into his office, where Oswald sits under the watchful eye of two detectives. "Take him on down to the assembly room," Fritz tells them, then orders the rest of his men to go down as part of a security detail. Oswald says nothing, sensing that this isn't going to be just another lineup.[993]

A few minutes later they bring Oswald out of homicide into the narrow, crowded corridor, and Jack Ruby, standing in the hallway right outside of Fritz's office, and with a loaded revolver in his right trouser pocket, finds himself within two to three feet of the man he now hates for killing the president, but the thought of shooting Oswald never enters his mind. Strangely, though he despises Oswald, he thinks Oswald is good-looking and resembles actor Paul Newman.[994] Learning they are taking Oswald down to the assembly room in the basement (next to the show-up room), Ruby follows. He feels perfectly free in what he is doing, with no one asking him any questions. As crowded as the assembly room is, he manages to get in and stand on top of a table to the rear, his back to the wall.[995]

An FBI agent returns to the office where Robert Oswald is being questioned by another agent.

"Robert," he says, "you might as well know now. They are charging your brother with the president's death."[996]

Robert sags in his chair and shakes his head. He realizes that there is not much more he can do tonight and starts for his hotel. For eleven hours he's managed to keep his emotions reasonably in check, but now, as he walks along the quiet streets of downtown Dallas, his body suddenly begins to tremble until he is sobbing. Not yet thirty years old, Robert feels like an aged and decrepit man. He stifles his emotions by the time he reaches the hotel lobby and returns to his room. In the dark, he lies awake unable to sleep.[997]

In the offices of Klein's Sporting Goods in Chicago, general operating manager Mitchell Scibor paws through invoices with company vice president William Waldman. The FBI agents nearby wait patiently as Scibor and Waldman search for a record of having received a Mannlicher-Carcano rifle, serial number C2766, from Crescent Firearms Company of New York. After a little more than an hour of searching, they uncover an invoice dated February 7, 1963,[998] for a shipment of one hundred, six-shot, model 91TS 6.5-millimeter Mannlicher-Carcano rifles from Crescent Firearms, packed in ten cartons, ten rifles to a carton, at a unit cost of $8.50. Attached to the invoice are ten memo pages indicating the serial numbers of the rifles in each case.

Waldman quickly looks over the list of serial numbers. There it is—carton number 3376 had a rifle with serial number C2766.[999]

"There's no question about it," Waldman tells the FBI agents. "We handled this rifle."

Klein's records show the rifle in question arrived on its loading dock on February 21, 1963,[1000] was unpacked the following day,[1001] and assigned control number VC-836,[1002] a number used by Klein's to track the history of the gun while it's in their possession.

"Is there any way to tell who it was sold to?" an FBI agent asks.

"Yes," Waldman says, "the next move will be to hunt through microfilm records of our mail-order customers until we find this serial number. It's going to take some time because there is no specific order of filing."[1003]

Waldman and Scibor move over to two microfilm reading machines and begin the tedious task of looking through hundreds of microfilmed mail-order receipts for the customer who ordered the Mannlicher-Carcano rifle with serial number C2766 found on the sixth floor of the Texas School Book Depository.[1004]

12:10 a.m.

The assembly room at Dallas police headquarters is so crowded with newsmen and cameras that by the time Captain Fritz gets downstairs, Fritz, Oswald's chief interrogator, can't even get in the room as the crowd had jammed clear back out into the hall. Inside, rival reporters jostle for what they hope will be the best position to get a picture or a statement from the prisoner. For any newsman worth his salt, this is the center of the universe. Those at the back of the room can barely hear Chief Curry trying to explain the ground rules over the clamor. "If anything goes wrong with his being down here, if there's a rush up here, he's immediately going out and that's it. Now, do we understand each other?"[1005]

A chorus of voices answers, "Yes! Right! Yes!" until it disintegrates into a wall of incomprehensible sound. Curry shuffles his way back into the hallway as the newsmen crane their necks in the direction of the doorway. The homicide detectives in the Stetson hats appear first and then, suddenly, there is Oswald, sandwiched between them as they inch their way toward the front of the stage.[1006]

A huge, bulky, pool television camera from Dallas CBS affiliate KRLD-TV is mounted on a tripod near the doorway, its four-inch barrel lens trained on Oswald's face. A late-night national audience (only NBC has stopped coverage) holds its collective breath as it gets its first really good look at the man accused of murdering the president of the United States. A flock of flashbulbs pop from dozens of still cameras as police come to a stop near the center of the front of the stage.

"Down in front! Down in front!" the unfortunate newsmen in the back of the room shout in frustration. A crush of reporters are only inches from Oswald, a semicircle of handheld microphones thrust forward toward the suspect's face in eager anticipation of his first words. The noise level dips as Oswald responds to a question he has picked out of the din.

"I was questioned by a judge without legal representation," he says in his peculiarly dry, Texas-tinged boy's voice, before being drowned out by a torrent of frustrated voices.

"Louder! Down in front, down, down!" reporters holler.

Oswald stops for a moment and purses his lips, a habit that gives him a prissy, dogmatic air. When the noise subsides a little, he starts again.

"Well, I was questioned by a judge; however, I protested at that time that I was not allowed legal representation . . ."

"Hey! Down! Down!" a chorus of back-of-the-room voices again shouts at the men blocking their view. Several finally give up complaining and begin dragging metal chairs into position on which to stand for a better vantage point. The sound of clanking metal only helps to drown out Oswald's weak voice.

". . . during that . . . ah . . . that . . . ah . . . very short and sweet hearing. Ah, I really don't know what this situation is about. Nobody has told me anything except that I am accused of . . . ah . . . of . . . ah . . . murdering a policeman. [Oswald has not yet been arraigned for the murder of Kennedy and is unaware that he has been charged with Kennedy's murder.] I know nothing more than that and I do request . . . ah . . . someone to come forward . . . ah . . . to give me legal assistance."

"Did you kill the president?"

"No, I have not been charged with that. In fact, nobody has said that to me yet. The first thing I heard about it was when the newspaper reporters in the hall . . . ," Oswald's voice cracks nervously, ". . . asked me that question."

"You *have* been charged," a reporter in the front tells him.

"Sir?" Oswald says, somewhat confused, looking at the reporter kneeling in front of him.

"You have been charged," the reporter repeats.

Oswald purses his lips, then a look of astonishment crosses his face, but he says nothing.

"Nobody said *what*? We can't hear you back here," someone complains from the back of the room.

The jostling continues unabated and Curry decides he's seen enough.

"Okay, men," Curry says to the two detectives flanking Oswald. "Okay."

The men in the Stetson hats turn and begin pushing Oswald slowly toward the exit as reporters kneeling in the front continue their verbal assault.

"What did you do in Russia?"

Oswald ignores the first question.

"How did you hurt your eye?" another reporter asks.

Oswald moves along in silence. The reporter asks again.

"Oswald, how did you hurt your eye?"

Oswald leans toward the microphone.

"A policeman hit me," he whines.

After just six minutes, it is over. Newsmen in the back of the room plead for someone up front to fill them in on what Oswald had said during his brief moments in front of the cameras.[1007]

Exiting the assembly room, Detectives Sims and Boyd lead Oswald into the basement jail office, where they encounter Deputy Chief George L. Lumpkin and Sergeant Wilson F. Warren. Entering the jail elevator, the four men take Oswald up to the fourth-floor jail office, where he is searched once again and also booked, nearly eleven hours after his arrest.[1008] He is then taken to his fifth-floor jail cell.

The jail cell that Deputy Chief Lumpkin, who is in charge of jail security, has assigned Oswald isolates him from other prisoners. It's a maximum-security cell, number F-2, on the fifth floor. The maximum-security area is a group of three cells away from the rest of the units, with lockable doors that open into a narrow corridor, which itself has another lockable door that is controlled from a master control panel. Lumpkin orders Oswald to be placed in the middle cell, the two cells on either side kept empty. It is virtually impossible for any other prisoners to see or talk with him.

Oswald is ordered to strip to his underwear, and his belt and other potentially harmful personal effects are taken from him. His clothes and effects are shoved into a paper bag for retrieval the next time he's removed from the cell. The jail guard leads Oswald through the first heavily barred door. It bolts behind them. Four bare lightbulbs, screened in wire, hang in the small hallway. The jailer opens the middle cell, Oswald steps inside, and the door shuts behind him with a loud metal clang.

Oswald's twelve-by-twelve-foot cell has four bunk beds inside, the upper two made of metal, the lower two of wood, a stainless-steel sink, a toilet, and a water fountain. Bars that cross overhead give the cell a sense of a cage.[1009] Oswald flops onto a bunk while two guards take up residence right outside the cell as part of an around-the-clock vigil, a suicide watch. Chief Lumpkin is taking no chances with the prime suspect.[1010]

12:19 a.m.

After Oswald was taken from the assembly room, some of the press boys had run out to make deadlines. Others stuck around to interview District Attorney Henry Wade, hoping to pick up something juicy for their morning papers.

Wade's concern is to make sure he doesn't prejudice the rights of the accused to a fair trial. His real problem this night is his lack of knowledge about the investigation. He'd been briefed only once, little more than an hour ago. And then, only on the basics of the case.

Wade tells the reporters that Oswald has been "formally charged . . . with both killing Officer Tippit and John F. Kennedy. He's been taken before the judge and advised of his rights." (Oswald, in fact, had not yet at this point been taken before any judge on the Kennedy charge, arraigned, and advised of his rights.)

"Can you tell [us] any of the evidence against him so far, sir?"

"No," Wade replies. "We are still working on the evidence . . ."

"Do you have a good case?"

"I figure we have sufficient evidence to convict him," Wade answers.

"Are there any indications that this was an organized plot," a reporter inquires, "or was it just one man?"

"There's no one else but him," Wade says, adding, "so far."

Someone, again, asks a question about the evidence gathered so far.

"Well, there is a lot of physical evidence that was gathered," Wade says, "including the gun, that is on its way by air force jet to the FBI crime lab in Washington. It will be back here tomorrow. There are some other things that's going to delay this [until] probably the middle of next week before it's presented to the grand jury."

"Do you have witnesses to use against him in the killing of President Kennedy?"

"We have approximately fifteen witnesses," Wade answers.

"Who identified him as the killer of the president?"

"I didn't say that," Wade corrects.

A reporter asks to clarify whether he's talking about fifteen witnesses in the murder of the police officer or the president.

"Both," Wade replies.

The question of motive is raised.

"Well, he was a member of the movement—," Wade grapples for the word, "—the Free Cuba movement—"

"What's the make of the rifle, sir?"

"It's a Mauser, I believe," Wade answers erroneously.

"Does the suspect deny the shootings?"

"Yes," Wade says, "he denies them both."

"Are you through questioning him?" someone asks.

"No, we have further questioning to do. We will probably let him sleep and talk to him in the morning." It's very late, and Wade is wondering when the questions will end.[1011]

12:35 a.m.
Oswald has been in his cell less than ten minutes when Sergeant Warren opens the door and tells him to put on his clothes. Lieutenant Karl P. Knight of the Identification Bureau is there to see that Oswald is taken to the fourth floor to be photographed and finger-printed.

"I *have* been fingerprinted," Oswald protests.

Knight knew that Oswald was referring to prints taken of him around 9:00 p.m. to compare with the latent prints discovered on the rifle and cardboard boxes found on the sixth floor. Now that felony charges had been filed against him, Knight needs some-thing a little more permanent for the Dallas police files. As part of standard procedure, copies of these new prints will be sent to the FBI to find out if the prisoner is wanted elsewhere.* Sergeant Wilson F. Warren and jail assistant Tommy V. Todd take Oswald downstairs to the Identification Bureau to be processed. Knight and Captain Doughty see that another set of fingerprints is made and mug shots—front and profile—are taken. Oswald is arrogant and irritable. He drags his fingers across the inkpad, until a cop takes each digit one by one and rolls and prints them properly. When they ask him to sign his name at the bottom of the fingerprint card, Oswald refuses. His thumb print is added to indicate that his fingerprints had been taken and placed in police files. They finish the formalities in about thirty-five minutes, and the sullen Oswald is taken back to his fifth-floor jail cell.[1012]

1:00 a.m.
While Bill Alexander and some police detectives were going over the names and back-grounds of Oswald's coworkers at the Book Depository Building before midnight, the name Joe Molina, the credit manager at the Depository, came up. It immediately "rang a bell" with Alexander. "He was a known, card-carrying Communist—at that time there were damn few Communists in Dallas, and they actually carried cards on them— that I knew from a big publicity murder case I had prosecuted a year or so earlier," Alexander would later recall. "Because of the publicity, the defense made a motion for

---

*Why Oswald wasn't fingerprinted when he was booked into the jail just after midnight is not known.

a change of venue and Molina testified for the defense that the defendant couldn't get a fair trial in Dallas. We had no evidence of any connections between Molina and Oswald except the Book Depository Building and their Communist Party affiliation."

Alexander proceeds to prepare a search warrant for Molina's house, gets Judge Johnston to sign it, and "since Fritz's boys were busy" goes to serve the warrant with Captain Pat Gannaway, the head of the Special Services Bureau, and a few of his men, including Lieutenant Jack Revill, who is in charge of the criminal intelligence section that, among other things, investigates subversive activities. Molina, a short, stocky, and prematurely graying man of forty, lives in a small home close to downtown Dallas with his wife and four kids, one of whom is adopted. Alexander and his people arrive around one in the morning, and the loud knocking on the door at this hour scares Soledad, Molina's wife, half to death. The whole family, asleep in the two-bedroom home, was awakened. Joe comes to the door in his pajamas and is served with the warrant. Alexander doesn't say what this is all about but Molina assumes it has some connection with the assassination because of his employment at the Depository.

"Joe," Alexander says, "go back to bed. We won't ransack the house." "Go ahead and look around," Molina said, indicating he had nothing to hide. But before Joe can get back in bed, Gannaway and Revill have other plans and, during the search, question Molina about his acquaintanceship with Oswald (he has seen him at work, but is not acquainted with him and has never spoken to him) and the political affiliation of members of the GI Forum, a local veterans group Molina, a navy vet, belonged to that had several other known Communist members. Molina says he doesn't know the political affiliation of the members of the group, but declines to write a statement to that effect. The search of Molina's house will continue for two hours.[1013]

1:10 a.m.
In the basement assembly room, remarkably, Henry Wade is still held captive by an inquisitive collection of reporters. Judge David Johnston has joined him.

"Does he have a lawyer?"

"I don't know whether he has or not," Wade says.

"Does he appear sane to you?"

"Yes, he does," Wade replies firmly.

"Is he a member of any Communist-front organization?"

"That I couldn't tell you at the present time," Wade says.

"Any organizations that he belongs to that you know of?" a reporter hollers.

"Well," the district attorney answers, "the only one I mentioned was the Free Cuba movement or whatever that—"

Ruby, recalling what he heard on the radio earlier, shouts out a correction from the back of the room, "Fair Play for Cuba Committee." Wade, surprised at getting a correction from his audience, recognizes the man in the horn-rimmed glasses and slicked black hair as someone he's seen around, but thinks he must be a journalist of some sort.

"Fair Play for Cuba, I believe it was," Wade continues, acknowledging the correction.

"Why do you think he wanted to kill the president?"

"The only thing I do," Wade tells the throng, "is take the evidence, present it to a jury, and I don't pass on why he did it or anything else. We . . . we're just interested in proving that he did it, which I think we have."[1014]

"Are you planning to charge anyone else in this at all at this moment?"

"As of this moment," Wade says, "we are not."

"Are you looking for any other suspects at all now that you've got—"

"Well, we're always looking for other suspects," Wade shoots back, "but we have none at present."

"Henry, do you think this is part of [a] Communist conspiracy?"

The question cuts at the district attorney's nerves.

"I can't say that," he answers diplomatically.

"Well, do you have any reason to believe that it might be?" the reporter pursues.

"No," Wade answers, "I don't have any reason to believe either way on it."

"Has he said under questioning that he is either a Communist or a Communist sympathizer?"

"I don't know whether he has or not," Wade replies.

"Can you say whether you have a witness who says he saw the man pull the trigger?"

"No, I cannot," Wade answers carefully.

"What was the result of the paraffin test?" someone asks.

"I am not going into the evidence here," Wade says.

There is some continuing confusion over whether Oswald has been advised of the charge in the assassination. Judge David Johnston, standing behind Wade, steps forward to try to clear up any misunderstanding.

"He has not been advised," Johnston says.

"He has been charged?"

"He has not been arraigned on the second charge," Johnston says.

"No, but has he been charged?" the reporter presses.

"Yes," the judge replies, "he is formally charged."

The reporters question when the arraignment for the assassination will take place, but both Wade and Johnston seem uncertain. They imagine sometime that night, then suggest that it might be morning before Oswald is arraigned.[1015] Wade continues to answer questions for a few more minutes, but has little to add to what he has already said.

"Mr. Wade, was he under any kind of federal surveillance because of his background prior to today, today's events?"

Wade, no doubt thinking of Jack Revill's memo, prefers not to open that can of worms. "None that I know of. We didn't have any knowledge—We didn't have any information on him. When I say we, being the Dallas police or the Dallas sheriff's office."[1016]

Several questions return to the issue of whether this was an organized plot or just one man out to get the president.

"We don't know that answer," Wade replies. "He's the only one we have."

"Are you willing to say whether you think this man was inspired as a Communist or whether he is simply a nut or a middleman?"

"I'll put it this way," Wade says. "I don't think he's a nut."[1017]

1:20 a.m.

After Wade's press conference, he continues to be interviewed by individual reporters outside the basement assembly room, and Jack Ruby persists in his pursuit of Joe Long, who mysteriously remains elusive to Ruby. But Jack finally manages to get the control room number of the station from two reporters, Jerry Cunkle and Sam Pease, who worked for rival KBOX. Calling the control room, he's shuttled to Glenn Duncan in the newsroom, whom he tells, "I have sandwiches for you. I want to get over there," and then adds,

"By the way, I see Henry Wade talking on the phone to someone. Do you want me to get him over here?"

"Yes, do that."

"Just a second, he's talking to someone from New York. I'll get him."

He goes over, collars the district attorney, and brings him back to the phone, not even telling him what station it is.

The newsman at KLIF is elated over scoring the brief interview, and tells Ruby he can "only leave the door open for five minutes."

On the way out, Ruby spots Russ Knight of KLIF with a tape recorder. Glenn Duncan rushed him over from the station a few blocks away to get another interview with the district attorney—they didn't get the first one on the phone on tape, and Duncan wants something for the morning news. Ruby, only too happy to oblige, takes Knight to Wade.

"Ask him if Oswald is insane," Ruby suggests to Knight.

"Okay," Knight says. "That's a point well taken."

Ruby introduces them.

"Oh," Wade says, recognizing Knight's name, "you're the Weird Beard!"

Knight cringes a little—his on-the-air persona is great for the kids who have made him the top-rated DJ in Dallas, but it sounds just a mite foolish here.

Wade obliges Knight with an interview and tells Knight that Oswald is not insane. His brutal act was entirely premeditated. While Knight is interviewing Wade, Ruby leaves for the station three blocks away. But arranging the interview with Henry Wade for Russ Knight delayed Ruby beyond the five-minute window he'd been offered, and he finds the door to the KLIF studios locked when he gets there, so he waits, with Sheba, for Knight to get back.[1018]

1:30 a.m.

Wade and Judge Johnston finally escape the persistent journalists and make their way back to the third-floor homicide office. On the way, the district attorney tells Johnston that they should arraign Oswald on the Kennedy killing immediately. When the pair get to Captain Fritz's office, they confer with Chief Curry, Captain Fritz, and Assistant DA Maurice Harrell.[1019] It may be approaching the middle of the night but with all the activity one would never know it. Curry agrees that Oswald should be arraigned on the murder charge regarding the president's death soon. The U.S. Supreme Court recently ruled that a prisoner must be arraigned and informed of the charges against him as soon as possible. Curry doesn't want anyone saying that they haven't followed the law.

Curry picks up the phone and calls the jail supervisor, Sergeant Warren.

"Bring Oswald back down to the fourth-floor ID bureau," he says. "We'll meet you there."[1020]

Oswald has been asleep,* though not for very long, when Sergeant Warren awakens him.

"What's going on?" Oswald says angrily, half asleep.

"I've got my orders from the chief," the jail supervisor says. "He says to bring you down to ID again."

---

*The only source for Oswald ostensibly being asleep is author Jim Bishop. However, Bishop does not say who his source was, but the implication is that it was Sergeant Warren. (Bishop, *Day Kennedy Was Shot*, p.651) Even if it were Warren, Warren may simply have assumed that a physically still Oswald was asleep and called out to awaken him.

The man who would arguably become the most famous murderer in history, as well as the most consequential one, doesn't bother to protest. He swings his legs to the floor and holds his wrists out in front of him as the cuffs are snapped in place. Sergeant Warren and jailer Tommy Todd escort him toward the stairway.[1021]

1:35 a.m.

Oswald and his escorts emerge from the stairwell into the fourth-floor jail office. A half-dozen police officials are standing behind the counter when Oswald arrives. He purses his lips and surveys the familiar faces.

Judge David Johnston stands squarely behind the counter, with complaint number F-154, the Kennedy murder charge, in his hand. The men grouped around him are some of the top brass of Dallas law enforcement: Captain Fritz, Chief Curry, Assistant Deputy Chief M. W. Stevenson, District Attorney Henry Wade, and Assistant District Attorney Maurice Harrell. A few Identification Bureau officers who happen to be on duty, including crime-lab lieutenant Carl Day, hover nearby.[1022]

"Well, I guess this is the trial," Oswald sneers sarcastically.

"No sir," Judge Johnston replies, "I have to arraign you on another offense."

For the second time this night, Johnston advises Oswald of his constitutional right to remain silent and warns him that any statement he makes may be used in evidence against him. Then, Johnston reads the complaint to Oswald, that "Lee Harvey Oswald, hereinafter styled Defendant, heretofore on or about the twenty-second day of November, 1963, in the County of Dallas and State of Texas, did then and there unlawfully, voluntarily, and with malice aforethought kill John F. Kennedy by shooting him with a gun against the peace and dignity of the State."[1023]

"Oh, that's the deal, is it," Oswald says. "I don't know what you're talking about."[1024]

Johnston ignores the comment and advises Oswald of his right to an attorney.

"I want Mr. John Abt of New York," Oswald demands, spelling the name out. "A–B–T."

"You'll be given the opportunity to contact any attorney you wish," Judge Johnston answers calmly. "Bond is denied on this capital offense. I hereby remand you to the custody of the sheriff of Dallas County, Texas."[1025]

In ten minutes it is over. Lee Harvey Oswald has been formally arraigned on the charge of assassinating the president of the United States. Chief Curry, who has seen little of Oswald in the course of the evening, is not impressed by his truculence and arrogance. Curry nods to the jailers, who spin and take the prisoner back upstairs to his fifth-floor cell.[1026]

1:50 a.m.

Most of Dallas is asleep when Ruby finally enters the KLIF building after Russ Knight gets back from City Hall and opens the door. Several of the guys on duty are glad to see Jack's big paper sack full of corned beef sandwiches and soft drinks. "I figured you guys would be hungry," Jack tells them, "and I brought these up for you." Knight and DJ Danny McCurdy were intrigued by Doctor Black's celery tonic in its peculiarly shaped bottle and expensive-looking gold foil, which neither of them had ever seen before. Whoever heard of a soft drink with celery in it? Jack explains that it's something you normally get only in New York and is especially pleased when McCurdy thinks it's the best soft drink he's ever had.

Five minutes later Jack has worked his way into the control room, where he chats with McCurdy between announcements while Duncan and Knight get the two o'clock news ready.

Jack appreciates the way the station has switched from Top Forty to album music—easy listening, McCurdy calls it. Ruby is pale and keeps looking at the floor. McCurdy is feeling awfully low himself and thinks little of it.

"I'm closing my club down this weekend," Jack tells him morosely. "I'd rather lose twelve or fifteen hundred this weekend than not be able to live with myself later on." He gives McCurdy a card for the Carousel Club. McCurdy already has one Ruby gave him some time back, one with a picture of one of the strippers on it.

Ike Pappas comes in with a lot of tapes he wants to relay back to WNEW in New York, and the KLIF guys are happy to let him use their facilities. Pappas also gets one of the corned beef sandwiches, but is so busy with his work he never sees Ruby.

Though Duncan is getting ready to go with his two o'clock news bulletin, he chats a little with Ruby, who seems somewhat excited and happy that the case against Oswald is going well. He seems to get a real charge out of being close to the police and the news developments. Duncan is intrigued by Ruby's description of Oswald—that he looks a little like the movie star Paul Newman.

Ruby stays right there in the newsroom for the bulletin, and after Duncan leads to Knight, the latter says, "I have just returned from a trip to the Dallas County Courthouse [actually City Hall] and, on a tip from Jack Ruby, local night club owner . . ."

Jack is tickled pink at the mention of his name on the air. After Ruby chats with the guys for a quarter of an hour or so, Knight walks Ruby down to his car, parked right in front of the door, the little dachshund, Sheba, patiently awaiting his return. Ruby wants him to urge Gordon McClendon to devote one of his on-the-air editorials to the assassination and the turgid, right-wing political atmosphere in Dallas that he feels led to it. He's a great admirer of McClendon, a Kennedy supporter who ran unsuccessfully as a Democrat for the senate and the only radio broadcaster in Dallas to do editorials, and outspoken ones at that. Ruby fishes a one-page flyer from the mess in his car and hands it to the disk jockey. "You look like a square guy, why don't you look this over and read it?"

Ruby's story about the flyer is complicated to Knight, but it has something to do with right-wing radicalism in Dallas, though Ruby doesn't use those exact words.

Ruby had gotten the flyer when he was selling a contrivance called a twistboard out at the Texas Products Show at the Exhibit Hall off the Stemmons Freeway a couple of weeks ago. Ruby's friend Ed Pullman, a furniture designer, had a booth there, and Ruby took some of his girls out there every night during the week the show was on to demonstrate and sell the device. One of them got her picture into the *Dallas Times Herald*. Ruby had stopped by the booth of H. L. Hunt, the right-wing Dallas oil tycoon, which was giving away free bags of groceries, and in his Ruby found the flyer, a script called "Heroism" for Hunt's radio show, *Life Line*. He was outraged by the script and steamed back to Pullman's booth on the mezzanine, George Senator in tow.

"I'm going to send this stuff to Kennedy," Jack raged breathlessly. "I want to send this stuff to Kennedy. Nobody has the right to talk like this about our government."

Pullman was philosophical. "Well, you just learned about it now, but *Life Line* has been out for some time, and that's what he does and that's how he gets his materials around."

"I'm going to do something about this, I'm going to see that this is taken up in Washington," Ruby insists. He even mentions the FBI. Pullman recalls to Ruby that Hunt had not been allowed to have a display at some New York fair because of that type of literature. "I'm sure that Kennedy knows all about this, and Washington knows about this."

"Maybe they don't. I'm going to send it in."

"Well, you do what you want," Pullman said.

It's all a bit of a mystery to Knight, but he takes the broadsheet from Ruby and goes home.

It's hard to figure out why Ruby had gotten so exercised about the flyer out at the fair. The flyer was all pretty harmless stuff, although it did contain this language:

> Personal heroism is a vital part of the American character and the American dream . . . Nearly all nations, *when they do fail,* have forgotten what heroism is.

And,

> A nation and a people which truly value their heroes *have no use for a paternal government which always claims to know best.* Such a nation cannot be coaxed or conned out of their fundamental liberties.

It's bylined "Gene Scudder from Washington." At the bottom of the back of the sheet is a list of two-dozen stations in the Dallas–Fort Worth area which carry the program, and a short list of "some of the other three hundred *Life Line* stations," almost all in the South.[1027]

Robert Donovan, Washington bureau chief for the *Los Angeles Times,* finally gets back to his Dallas hotel after an incredibly hectic day that went by without his eating since breakfast the previous morning in Fort Worth. He and some of his colleagues, equally famished and exhausted, were able to send out for food. They give the old black waiter, dressed in a young bellboy's outfit, some extra money to also get them "a jug" of liquor, telling him they had worked for hours, were frazzled, and needed it. But you couldn't buy liquor over the counter in Dallas, it being a "closed" city, and the waiter wasn't about to find some other way, illicit, to get the hooch. "No," he says evenly, "you couldn't do that because that would be breaking the law." He then adds in a voice that Donovan knows he will remember to his dying day, "There've been enough laws broken in Dallas today."[1028]

2:00 a.m.
Eventually, in the early hours of Saturday morning, Dallas police headquarters begins to quiet down for the night. Captain Fritz sends his troops home, with instructions to be back by ten, but remains in his office conferring with Wade, Judge Johnston, and some of the other officers on the case until around 3:45 a.m., when they all go home. Deputy Chief Stevenson remains in his office on the third floor, where, with a couple of detectives, he continues to work, available for anything that might need to be investigated during the night. He doesn't get home until around 12:30 Saturday afternoon.[1029]

2:30 a.m. (3:30 a.m. EST)
At Bethesda Naval Hospital, the morticians are winding up the embalming and casketing of the president's body.[1030]

2:45 a.m.
After leaving KLIF, Jack Ruby decides to drive over to the *Times Herald* building. He rarely goes there to place his weekend ad, because once he gets the ad into the *Morning*

News, which comes out first, he just calls the afternoon newspaper to have the ad "transpired," as he puts it, into the *Times Herald*, but he promised one of the boys over there on the night shift one of his twistboards. He had put off going there for some time, but since he hadn't called in his ad today, he feels this might be a good time to take out an ad in the *Herald* that his clubs will be closed Saturday and Sunday nights.

As he drives past a parking garage at the corner of Jackson and Field, he hears a horn honk and sees a police officer he knows, Harry Olsen, sitting in a car. He's sitting there with one of Jack's girls, Kathy Kay. The thing with Kathy is supposed to be a secret, but Jack knows all about it. Kathy's real name—most of the strippers use stage names—is Kay Coleman.

Harry's divorce came through last month, and Kay has been divorced for a time, but it would be difficult for a police officer to marry a woman who is working as a stripper. Kay is from England and, young as she is—just twenty-seven—has two little girls, ages seven and nine. Jack likes Kay a lot, and he has stopped over at her place with a few other people for a late-night breakfast a couple of times—it's only four or five blocks from his apartment out in Oak Cliff, on the same street, Ewing.

Jack climbs into the car with Harry and Kay. They had driven over to Dealey Plaza earlier, just to see where the president was shot, stopped in at the Sip and Nip on Commerce Street for a couple of drinks, and then went to see their friend Johnny Johnson, who works at the garage. They are drinking beer, ruminating on the day's sad events, and glad to see Jack. They think he's a great guy for closing his clubs. They are all upset about the assassination and find it hard to talk about much else. Harry's leg is in a cast so he has been on light duty for a while. He was off that day and spent most of it moonlighting, guarding the estate of an elderly lady out in Oak Cliff near Kay's place.

Earlier Kay had called Andy Armstrong at the Carousel from her house to find out whether the club would be open that night.

"What's Jack doing?" she asked.

"Oh, he is all upset and he is crying," Andy told her, adding, "We are closed tonight."

Harry and Kay have known Jack for a couple of years and can see that he's really upset. Harry used to work the downtown area and made routine checks of the Carousel. He's seen Jack so mad that he would shake, usually at his employees, but sometimes at customers too. Jack can fly off the handle about almost anything. Harry would take him aside and get him to calm down, and Jack, with his respect for police officers, listened to Harry.

Jack tells them he saw Oswald down at the police station, calls him an "SOB," and says, "It's too bad that a peon could do something like that," referring to the killing of Kennedy and Tippit. Kay thinks Jack is wild-eyed, with a sort of starey look. He is awfully tired, sits back, and stares off into space. He doesn't cry or anything, but he just keeps saying over and over how terrible it is. He also keeps mentioning Jackie Kennedy and her children, whose plight especially touches him. Harry thinks they should cut Oswald into ribbons inch by inch, and Jack recalls all the citizens who went out that morning with banners and posters stirring up hate against the president. "I just wonder how they feel about that now." The three commiserate about the death of Kennedy for over an hour.[1031]

2:56 a.m. (3:56 a.m. EST)
At Bethesda Naval Hospital, Secret Service agent Roy Kellerman telephones the seventeenth-floor suite where the Kennedy family and friends have been waiting for almost nine hours.

"We're ready," he tells them.

Secret Service agents escort the Kennedy entourage—Mrs. Kennedy, Robert and Ted Kennedy and Robert's wife, Ethel, the president's sisters, Dave Powers, Kenneth O'Donnell, Larry O'Brien, Robert McNamara, and others—down to a small room near the rear loading dock.[1032]

In the morgue, the casket team, under the leadership of First Lieutenant Samuel R. Bird, conducts a small ceremony placing the American flag on the casket.[1033] Finally, as a last sign of respect for the commander in chief, the Secret Service agents who have been present all night carry the casket out to the loading dock and toward the navy ambulance.[1034] The marines who have been guarding the Bethesda morgue this night snap to attention and salute as the casket passes.[1035] After the president's body is secured in the ambulance, the Kennedy entourage emerges from the rear of the hospital. Mrs. Kennedy and the president's brother Robert are helped into the rear of the ambulance. Jackie sits on a jump seat next to the coffin; Bobby crouches on the floor beside it. The others enter a bevy of limousines assembled near the loading dock.[1036]

Before leaving, Admiral Burkley turns to autopsy pathologist Jim Humes.

"I would like to have the [autopsy] report, if we could, by 6:00 p.m. Sunday [November 24] night," he says.[1037] Humes nods, in agreement.

Before the three pathologists leave the morgue, they confer on how to handle the task. It's obvious to them that a committee cannot write it. One person will have to take charge and the others can critique and refine the final language. Commander Humes volunteers to write the initial draft. They plan to meet again in Admiral Galloway's office on Sunday morning (November 24) to finalize the autopsy report.[1038]

In a few minutes, under very heavy security, the procession of cars makes its way at thirty miles an hour over the 9.5 miles toward the northwest gate of the White House.[1039] An impromptu escort of hundreds of cars, driven by ordinary citizens, trails the procession as it slips silently through the streets of Washington in the early-morning darkness. Those in the official cars look out the windows and see ordinary men of every color on their way to work standing at attention as they pass, caps held over their hearts.[1040]

At the White House, the six members of the casket team reassemble at the rear of the navy ambulance, which has pulled up close to the portico steps. They seem to be straining as they carry the casket into the White House foyer. Their commander, Lieutenant Bird, steps up quickly and slides his hands under the back of the heavy casket. A soldier in front of him whispers, "Good God, don't let go." They shuffle across the marble floor, past Marine honor guards, and into the East Room, where the casket is placed on a replica of the catafalque on which Abraham Lincoln's coffin rested.* As soon as the pallbearers step back, a Roman Catholic priest moves toward the casket and instructs an altar boy to light the candles that surround the catafalque. The priest sprinkles the coffin with holy water, kneels, and quietly reads from Psalm 130: "Out of the depths I cry to you, O Lord; Lord, hear my voice!" At the end of the brief ceremony, the honor guards are inspected and posted at parade rest, near the casket.

Air Force Brigadier General Godfrey McHugh and Secret Service agent Clint Hill

---

*"Someone had neglected to pass the word that the original Lincoln catafalque had been located in the basement of the Capitol building," and based on a book on the Lincoln funeral that included steel-point engravings, White House carpenters had quickly constructed the replica (Bishop, *Day Kennedy Was Shot*, pp.486, 548; Manchester, *Death of a President*, p.437).

stand momentarily alongside the casket in the hushed and cavernous East Room. It is so quiet they can hear each other breathe. An usher comes up to Agent Hill and informs him that Mrs. Kennedy, who had gone to her room, will come down shortly and would like the casket opened for a few minutes. The flag is removed from the coffin in anticipation of her arrival and the casket lid unsealed, though kept closed. In a moment, the First Lady appears, escorted by Bobby Kennedy. Several members of Kennedy's inner circle are also present, bunched together at one end of the room. Jackie looks exhausted, still wearing her "strawberry dress" caked with the president's dried blood. General McHugh orders the honor guards to leave the room. The men do a quick about-face and start to leave, when Mrs. Kennedy pleads, "No, they can stay." The guards freeze in place, their backs to the coffin. As the First Lady steps to the side of the casket, the lid is opened. She stands gazing for a moment upon her husband's face, then turns to Secret Service agent Clint Hill, the one who had sprung to her aid seconds after the shots, and asks for a pair of scissors. He gets them for her. She reaches in and snips a lock of the president's hair. She then turns away, saying "It isn't Jack."

When Jackie silently leaves the room, "the rest of us followed," presidential aide Arthur Schlesinger would later recall. As Jackie, exhausted, mounts the stairway and makes her way for the night to her second-floor room,[*] the group of Kennedy intimates stand awkwardly outside the East Room, waiting for Bobby Kennedy to direct their next move. Bobby, his cheeks damp with tears, turns to them and asks them to come back in and take a look at the body. He wants to settle the issue of an open casket before he retires, as he had promised the First Lady he would do when they were standing together beside the catafalque. "Jackie wants it covered," he tells them.

RFK had not been able to bear looking at his brother at that time, but now, for the first time, he does. Of the seven who view the remains, including Secretary of State Robert McNamara, Schlesinger, and Nancy Tuckerman (Jackie's social secretary), only two believe the president is presentable. The rest are appalled at the waxen figure.

"Don't do it," Bill Walton, a family friend, pleads.

"You're right," Bobby says. "Close it."[1041]

Bobby turns away and goes upstairs to the Lincoln bedroom with Charles Spalding, a close friend of both Kennedy brothers.

"There's a sleeping pill around somewhere," Spalding says.

"God, it's so awful," Bobby says, sinking onto the bed. "Everything was really beginning to run so well." He is exhausted, but composed. Spalding finds a sleeping pill, hands it to him, and steps out of the room. As he closes the door, he hears Bobby break down.

"Why, God?" he sobs.[1042]

---

[*]Earlier in the day, Jackie's mother, Mrs. Janet Auchincloss, had told Maud Shaw, Caroline and John Jr.'s nanny, that she and Jackie felt that Miss Shaw "should be the one to break the news to the children, at least to Caroline," who was five years old and would be six in a little less than a week. "Oh, no," Shaw said, "please don't ask me to do that." "Please, Miss Shaw," Mrs. Auchincloss said. "It is for the best. They trust you, and you know how to deal with them. I am asking you as a friend, please. It has to be you." In writing about the matter later, Shaw does not pinpoint the time she did this, merely indicating it was after she had tucked the children into bed for the night. She says she went into Caroline's room and started reading to her from one of her books. When Caroline asked her why she was crying, she told her she had "very sad news." She says, "Then I told her what had happened. It was a dreadful time for us both." Caroline eventually fell asleep, with Ms. Shaw still petting her. She said John Jr. still did not know and "was really too young [two, though he'd be three in a few days] to understand." Later, she said, it was decided that Mrs. Robert Kennedy would tell him the best she could. (Shaw, *White House Nannie*, pp. 14, 20–21)

3:00 a.m.

Alexander and his people have just concluded their search of Joe Molina's home, and Molina had been cooperative throughout. "We really searched his home, up and down, not finishing until around three in the morning," Alexander would later recall. "We found nothing to connect him to Oswald or the assassination." But after a conference in Molina's kitchen, the searchers agree that they should interrogate Molina further, and ask him whether he'd prefer to come with them down to police headquarters at that time, or come on his own in the morning. Molina opts to go back to bed and says he'll see them in the morning.[1043]

4:00 a.m.

Mitchell Scibor, general operating manager of Klein's Sporting Goods in Chicago, looks up from one of the company's two microfilm machines at waiting FBI agents. It has taken nearly four hours, but he has found it at last—the order form for the rifle with serial number C2766.[1044]

This particular Mannlicher-Carcano was among those advertised in a number of magazines under catalog number C20-T750, which indicates that it was sold with a four-power telescopic sight,[1045] the sight purchased separately by Klein's from Martin B. Retting Company in Culver City, California, and mounted on the rifle at Klein's by gunsmith William Sharp.[1046] The rifle-scope assembly was then placed in a sixty-inch corrugated cardboard box,[1047] and readied for shipment. The retail price was $19.95, plus $1.50 for shipping and handling.[1048]

Although the original order form or coupon for the C2766 rifle was routinely destroyed, Klein's microfilmed records include a picture of the original order form or coupon clipped from the February 1963 issue of *American Rifleman* magazine and its accompanying envelope, postmarked March 12, 1963.[1049] Enclosed with the order was a U.S. Postal Money Order, number 2, 202, 130, 462, for the total amount, $21.45.[1050] The order had been processed by Klein's on March 13, 1963, and shipped via parcel post on March 20, 1963.[1051] The customer had filled out the coupon and envelope in his own hand. The name is "A. Hidell" and the address is "P.O. Box 2915" in "Dallas, Texas."[1052]

The FBI agents look at each other knowingly. They know from bureau reports that Lee Harvey Oswald was carrying identification in that name at the time of his arrest.

Jack Ruby leaves Harry and Kay and proceeds to the *Dallas Times Herald*, where he delivers the twistboard to Arnold Clyde Gadash, a thirty-four-year-old printer whom Jack has known for years. The twistboard regularly sold for $3.98, and Jack had promised it to Gadash for $2.00, but since he kept him waiting so long for it, he gives it to Gadash. Gadash can see that Ruby, who takes out a black-bordered ad that his club will be closed that evening and Sunday evening, is very upset and emotional about the assassination, and Ruby brings up the Weissman ad with him, saying, as Gadash notices Jack's eyes watering, "The son of a bitch [Weissman] is trying to put the blame [for the assassination] on the Jews . . . Poor Mrs. Kennedy—Jackie and the kids," Ruby says emotionally. Other employees, some of whom know Ruby, are nearby and he temporarily starts to feel better by regaling them with stories of how close Oswald had come to him at City Hall and how he had corrected the district attorney, Henry Wade, at a press conference, intimating he was in good with the DA. He tells them he had seen Oswald being interviewed, that he looked like "a little weasel" and had "a smirk on his face." Gadash asks Jack to show him how the twistboard exerciser works, and though Jack really doesn't want to get into the hilarity of frolicking when he's so upset about the president's death, he gets on top of the board and gives a demonstration for Gadash and the other employees.[1053] God knows they can all use a good laugh.

At four-thirty Jack goes home and rouses George Senator from a sound sleep.

Senator has been staying at Jack's place for the past couple of months. A fifty-year-old World War II veteran, Senator has worked at more jobs than he can remember, mostly as a salesman, mostly without a lot of success. Ten years ago he was working out of Atlanta, selling women's apparel, when his boss said, "George, we are releasing a couple of men in Dallas and we want you to go to Dallas." George didn't want to, but the boss said, "George, you are going." He went. His wife didn't want to go either, and she didn't. A couple of years later they divorced. She kept the kid.

For a long time he lived mostly in motels, and for a period he shared rent with a couple of other guys who weren't doing well enough to afford places of their own. There were some long stretches when he wasn't employed at all, but the guys let him stay on because he was cooking and doing odd jobs for them. Soon after George first came to Dallas, in 1955 or 1956, a friend took him to the Vegas Club, where he met Jack Ruby, and after that they bumped into each other from time to time. In February or March of 1962 Jack sensed that George wasn't doing too well and invited him to move in with him for a while, over on Marsalis Avenue. George tried to hold up his end, cooking sometimes when Jack was home, but after five or six months he got a chance to go into the postcard business with the Texas Postcard & Novelty Company and he moved in with a fellow named Stan Corbat on Maple Avenue. He had been getting along fine with Jack, but he knew that Jack really liked to live alone. And Jack's place is too messy for George. Jack's clean in his person, but if he finishes reading a newspaper or something like that, it goes right on the floor.

At Corbat's, George had to sleep on the couch until he really started to get into selling postcards, and he and Stan were able to take a two-bedroom apartment on South Ewing. George told Jack about how great the building was, and within a week Jack moved into apartment 207, right next door to Corbat and George's 206. Then in August, Corbat got married and moved out, leaving George with all of the rent to pay on the apartment. George tried to stick it out for two months, but coming up with that much rent, at $125 a month, was too much of a struggle. Eventually, in late October, he moved in with Jack again into Jack's extra bedroom, which Jack had always kept available for anyone who needed a place to stay for a night or two, including homeless strippers at his club. They call George a "sales manager" at Texas Postcard, but his draw is only $61.45 a week, so the move was a terrific break for George because Jack didn't even ask him to share the rent. George occasionally helps Jack out at the club, running the lights or taking in the cash at the door, mostly on Fridays and Saturdays, but sometimes he will pop up during the week too.

George would be glad to cook regularly for Jack, but Jack is a funny guy about his food and George just can't cook it right for him. If George doesn't broil something just right, Jack complains. If he makes him eggs, he has to worry about the butter because Jack's always on some diet, and George finally got tired of it and said, "Make your own eggs." George doesn't even eat breakfast, just grabs a cup of coffee downtown once he's up and about. He can't get over Jack's habit of putting two grapefruits, skin and all, through the wringer in this machine he has, and then drinking the juice, his number one thing when he wakes up—sometimes in the middle of the afternoon.[1054]

Now it's the middle of the night and Jack is hollering and shaking him to wake up. He's all upset about that Weissman ad and some sign he saw saying "Impeach Earl Warren." He insists that George get up and get dressed. "You will have to get up, George. I want you to go with me."

It's a bit much at four-thirty in the morning, but George is truly grateful for Jack's many kindnesses to him, and he is always ready to do anything he can for Jack. As he is getting his clothes on, Jack calls Larry Crafard, the drifter kid Jack has been letting sleep in a backroom in front of his office at the club in return for answering the phone, helping to clean up, serving as a part-time bartender, and doing other odds and ends. There is no set salary, but any time Crafard needs a couple of bucks, he puts a draw slip in the till and takes some cash. It isn't a regular job, but Larry Crafard isn't choosy. Since getting out of the army four years ago he has often been unemployed, and the dozens of jobs he's had, from fruit picker to poultry butcher, to carney roustabout and barker (in fact, he met Jack while working at the Texas State Fair the previous month), lasted days or weeks rather than months. He doesn't believe this job is going to last much longer either. "Larry, get up, get dressed, and get the Polaroid with the flashbulbs and meet me downstairs. I'll be right down," Ruby commands. The camera is for taking pictures of the customers when they dance with the girls, and Larry has worked it a couple of times.

Larry had just dressed and got the film and bulbs and was starting to get the camera when he gets a call from the parking garage next door telling him that Jack is already there and to hurry up.

They drive over to the corner of Hall and the North Central Expressway, and sure enough, there it is, a poster about three feet by four, pasted right up on the side of a building, with a photograph of Warren with the legend "Impeach Earl Warren."

They all get out of the car and Jack has Larry take three pictures of the sign with the Polaroid. It's all a mystery to Larry, since he's never heard of Earl Warren, and the conversation between Jack and George isn't all that enlightening. It strikes Larry as funny that Jack suddenly seems more excited about this billboard than he is about the assassination. Jack says, "I can't understand why they want to impeach Earl Warren. This must be the work of the John Birch Society or the Communist Party," two polar opposites politically.

After Larry takes the photos Jack wants, they stop for coffee at Webb's Waffle Shop on the ground floor of the Southland Hotel, located just a few blocks from the Carousel. Jack knows all the all-night places. At this predawn hour, the coffee shop is almost empty. He picks up a paper abandoned on the counter and reads the Weissman ad again. Jack is very suspicious about the coincidental appearance of the ad and the Warren billboard just when the president was coming to Dallas. He thinks there's a connection. Even the post office box numbers are close—1792 for the Weissman ad and 1757 for the billboard, though the latter is in some town in Massachusetts. Larry finds the conversation hard to follow, what with Jack rereading aloud the Weissman ad in the *News* from a newspaper someone left behind, and breaking off to show the Polaroids to the guy at the counter. Jack wants to go to the post office to see what he can find out about the Weissman ad. To Larry's relief, they drop him back at the club first.[1055]

At the Dallas post office Jack and George find a box with the number for the Weissman ad, 1792, and there's a lot of mail in there. Jack presses the buzzer and asks the night clerk, "Who bought this box?"

"I can't give you any information," the clerk tells them. "Any information you want, there is only one man who can give it to you and that is the postmaster of Dallas."

George realizes that Jack is very, very disturbed. He has seen Jack hollering in those sudden outbursts of anger that he seems to forget about within seconds—George is well used to them—but this is completely different. "He had sort of a stare look in his eyes," George would later say. "I don't know how to describe it. I don't know how to put it in words," and it was nothing George had ever seen before in Ruby. When Jack talks about the president's family, he has tears in his eyes. George has known Jack for around eight years and it's the first time he has seen tears in his eyes. "Gee, his poor children and Mrs. Kennedy," he says over and over again. "What a terrible thing to happen." George sees that Jack is "deeply hurt" about the president's death, and although everyone George knows is grieving Kennedy's death, with Jack "it was worse."

The day is beginning to lighten by the time they get home from the post office, around 6:30 in the morning. Jack, back in the apartment, starts to cry "out loud." When he wasn't crying, Senator says "he looked like he was out in space." Jack calms down to watch a review of Friday's events on television for a while with George, but after a quarter of an hour they call it a day and turn in.[1056]

7:00 a.m.
Robert Oswald is already moving about after a sleepless night in the Statler Hilton Hotel's uncomfortable rollaway bed. After taking a shower, he waits in the lobby for the hotel drugstore to open. He hadn't brought a comb or toothbrush when he came from Denton, so he picks the personal items up and returns to his room to comb his hair. Rather than buy a razor and shaving cream, he decides to wait until the hotel barbershop opens and go there.

There are two barbers, both obviously unaware of Robert's identity. As one of them begins lathering up Robert's scruffy face, the barbers engage in a lively discussion of the assassination. One of the barbers has already made up his mind, Lee Oswald killed the president and should be executed immediately.

"Wait a minute," the barber shaving Robert says. "He may be guilty, or he may not. The only way to find out is to give him a fair trial."

Robert says nothing, but is so pleased with his barber's call for a fair trial that he tips him fifty cents. Robert skips breakfast and walks across the street to police headquarters in hopes that he might get in to see the chief of police, or even perhaps the man questioning his brother, Captain Fritz.[1057]

At the Dallas FBI office, Agent-in-Charge Gordon Shanklin calls his men together for their regular daily briefing. The agents have been arriving in virtual silence for the last half hour, whispering in hushed tones about yesterday's events. The office has the air of a funeral parlor.

Shanklin, rumpled, sleepless, and exhausted, reviews the events of the night.

"While you've been sleeping," he begins, "there have been some important developments. Last night at about 1:30 a.m., the county prosecutor filed first-degree murder charges against Oswald for the killing of the president. In addition, our agents in Chicago were able to trace the ownership of the rifle found on the sixth floor of the depository to Oswald."

Shanklin proceeds to outline the assignments for the day.

As the meeting ends, Bardwell Odum, a senior agent on the criminal squad, shows Hosty a surveillance photograph that had been flown up to Dallas in a two-seat navy jet fighter from Mexico City during the night. It was thought to be a photograph of Lee Oswald as he walked out of the Soviet embassy. Hosty takes one look and knows immediately that it isn't Oswald. Odum asks if it might be an associate of Oswald's.

"Not so far as I know," Hosty tells him.

"Well, I've been ordered to show this to Oswald's wife," Odum says.

"Bard," Hosty replies, pointing to the background of the photograph, "you can't show that photo to people outside the bureau. Look, you can see the doorway to the Soviet embassy." Using a pair of scissors they crop out the doorway so no one will know where the photo was taken. They don't want the Soviets to learn that the Soviet embassy in Mexico City is under photographic surveillance, something, however, that the Soviets had to assume.[1058]

8:00 a.m. (9:00 a.m. EST)
Lee Oswald is roused at eight o'clock for breakfast. It was a short sleep, since it was nearly two when they finally locked him up in his solitary cell. The breakfast is no great treat either, just standard city jail fare, stewed apricots, oatmeal, plain bread, and black coffee. They won't let him handle a razor, but a jailer shaves him, making him roughly presentable for the long day ahead.[1059]

Meanwhile, in Washington at the White House, high drama is being played out. President Johnson arrives there, presumably to move into the Oval Office. Indeed, he appears at the door of the office of JFK's longtime secretary, Evelyn Lincoln, and asks her if she would come into the Oval Office with him. "Yes, Mr. President," she says. He proceeds to tell her that "because of overseas" (a presumed reference to nations abroad concerned about whether the country that led the free world in the cold war was as strong as ever), he needed "a transition," adding, "I have an appointment at 9:30 [EST]. Can I have my girls in your office by 9:30?" Remarkably, he was giving her a half hour to clear out of the office she had been in for three years. "Yes, Mr. President," she says quietly.

Lincoln had known that she would have to clear the West Wing of the corporeal evidence of her and her boss's presence, but she never imagined it was going to be so quick. Returning to her office, she saw RFK, and sobbed to him, "Do you know he asked me to be out by 9:30?" RFK was appalled at Johnson's insensitivity. "Oh, no," he said. When he encountered LBJ in the hall shortly thereafter, he told him that crating all of his brother's belongings out of the Oval Office (some had already been) was going to take time. "Can you wait" to move in? he asked LBJ. It wasn't he, Johnson replied, that wanted such a quick transition, but his advisers. RFK's body language let Johnson know he wasn't too impressed with that answer. Johnson, the most powerful man on earth, had been put in his place by one of perhaps only two people (the other being Jackie) capable of doing so at this moment in time, and he returned, with his people, to the Executive Office Building to conduct the affairs of state. It wouldn't be until after JFK was buried two days later that LBJ moved into the Oval Office.[1060] However, at LBJ's invitation, Jackie and the two Kennedy children continued to live in the upstairs presidential quarters until December 7, at which time they moved temporarily into the large and elegant Georgetown home of the aristocratic diplomat

Averell Harriman, and LBJ and Lady Bird moved out of their twelve-room mansion into the White House.[1061]

9:00 a.m.

In Irving, the Paines are having breakfast with Marguerite and Marina Oswald when the two representatives from *Life* magazine, Tommy Thompson and Allen Grant, arrive unannounced with a female Russian interpreter.[1062]

As indicated, Marguerite had decided to take *Life*'s offer to put her and Marina up in a hotel room in Dallas so they could be near Lee. Marguerite was convinced that she would be besieged by reporters anxious to hear the life story of the accused assassin's mother. Why not rest in comfort in a posh hotel at their expense, she reasoned.[1063] It doesn't take long for Marina to get her children dressed and ready to go, packing enough diapers and baby bottles for the day. After all, she expects to return.[1064]* Marguerite is annoyed at the *Life* photographer, who is snapping pictures, and particularly with Mrs. Paine, who seems to be enjoying the media attention. The clear light of morning hasn't diminished the bitterness set off by the previous night's feud between Marguerite and Ruth. Each sees the other as an opportunist, eager to cash in on this unpleasant situation.[1065] Eventually Marguerite and Marina and her two children set off for town, where the *Life* people book them into Hotel Adolphus, right across the street from Jack Ruby's Carousel Club. Ruth Paine only wishes Marina had taken time to finish her breakfast. She knows it's going to be a trying day.[1066]

*L*ife magazine representative Richard Stolley has been waiting outside Zapruder's office in his dress factory, Jennifer of Dallas, for about an hour when the short, balding man in glasses arrives carrying a projector. Stolley is glad that the men waiting with him are Secret Service agents and not his competitors.

Zapruder invites them in, sets up the projector, threads the film, darkens the room, and almost apologetically shows it to the small gathering. The tension in the room is incredible and there is no sound except the cranking of the old projector as it clicks away. There is the president's limousine rounding the corner and everyone knows something awful is about to happen. Suddenly there is a spray of red, a halo of pink mist as part of the president's head is shot off. A horrific silence envelopes the Secret Service men, whose job had been to protect the man in the film.

Additional journalists from the Associated Press, United Press International, and several other magazines begin arriving. Zapruder shows the film a few more times, each replay revealing more details. When he finishes, the Dallas dressmaker looks ill, then uneasy. The number of bidders has grown in the last few minutes.

Stolley knows that *Life* magazine *has* to have this film, and asks to speak privately to Zapruder. Since Stolley had been the first one to contact him, Zapruder agrees to see him first, ushering Stolley quickly into a cluttered inner office. The press outside shouts that Zapruder shouldn't make up his mind until he's heard their offers too. Zapruder wastes no time telling Stolley how he feels. First, he wishes he had never taken the film. Second, now that the film exists, he realizes that it could help financially secure his family's future; however, he is determined not to let it fall into the hands of unscrupulous exploiters. He

---

*In fact, Marina Oswald doesn't return as expected. Ruth Paine won't see her again until March 9, 1964, the beginning of an estrangement that exists to this day.

describes his worst fear to Stolley—the film being shown in sleazy movie theaters in Times Square, while men on the streets hawk it like some pornographic film. The look on Zapruder's face reveals his genuine disgust over the thought.

Stolley knows he has to find out if Zapruder understands just what his film is worth.

"Our magazine is just as anxious as you are to give your pictures a respectable display," Stolley says. "We may even be able to go as high as $15,000."

Zapruder smiles. He understands.

Stolley mentions a new figure, adding that he doesn't think the magazine can go higher. Zapruder hesitates, and Stolley goes higher. The negotiations follow this pattern for a few minutes, while the fearful cry of Stolley's competitors grows louder in the corridor outside.

Finally, *Life*'s reputation, the fact it was the most popular weekly magazine in America, with a circulation in excess of seven million, and Stolley's assurances that the pictures will not be sensationalized win Zapruder over. Stolley types up a crude contract at Zapruder's desk and the two men sign it. It calls for a payment of $50,000 for print rights only.[*]

Stolley picks up the original film and the one remaining copy.

"Is there a back door?" he asks Zapruder.

Having orchestrated one of the journalistic coups of the century, Stolley slips out and leaves Zapruder to face the press, who are still clamoring just outside his office door for a chance to bid.[1067]

Across Dealey Plaza from Zapruder's office, Postal Inspector Harry Holmes arrives for work at the Terminal Annex Building. As Holmes walks into the lobby, the postal inspector on duty tells him that an FBI agent had phoned to inquire as to how the bureau could obtain an original postal money order, and had been told they would have to get it in Washington, D.C.[1068]

Although the FBI already has a microfilmed copy of the money order used to purchase the Carcano rifle, in preparing for trial prosecutors always want the original document. After depositing the money order into its bank account, Klein's, of course, no longer had the original money order.

9:30 a.m. (10:30 a.m. EST)

In Washington, Commander Humes returns to his office at Bethesda Naval Hospital, having gotten hardly any sleep since leaving the morgue six hours earlier. His early morning was consumed attending his son's First Communion at the family parish. However, the puzzling problems the three pathologists encountered during the autopsy, particularly the disposition of the bullet that struck the president's back, has been eating away at him.

Humes telephones Parkland Hospital and speaks to Dr. Malcolm Perry, the surgeon who performed the tracheotomy on the president. Humes explains the problems the pathologists had run into in trying to determine what happened to the bullet that struck the president in the back.

---

[*]After viewing the copy in New York, *Life* publisher C. D. Jackson instructed Stolley to purchase all rights to the film, including television and movie rights, for $150,000 paid in six annual installments of $25,000. The agreement was consummated November 25 in the office of Zapruder's lawyer, Sam Passman. Zapruder asked Stolley not to reveal the fact of the sale because it might intensify the already existing anti-Jewish sentiment in Dallas. Stolley felt that Passman earned his legal fee by suggesting that Zapruder donate the first $25,000 he received for the film to the widow and family of Officer Tippit. Zapruder readily agreed and his donation of $25,000 two days later earned public applause. Zapruder died of cancer in 1970, two years after he received his last payment. (Trask, *National Nightmare*, pp. 146–150; Stolley, "What Happened Next . . .," p. 262; Wrone, *Zapruder Film*, p. 36)

"We surmised that it worked its way out of the wound during cardiac massage," Humes says.

"Well, that seems unlikely, in my opinion," Perry replies. "Are you aware that there was a wound in the throat?"

The light flashes on for Humes when Dr. Perry tells him that he performed his surgery on an existing wound there, a small, round perforation with ragged edges.

"Of course," Humes realizes, "that explains it."[1069]

Suddenly, everything the pathologists had encountered when they explored the chest cavity made sense—the bruise over the lung, the bruised muscles surrounding the trachea. It was obvious. The bullet had exited the throat. Dr. Humes felt a great weight lift from his shoulders. He thanked Dr. Perry and hung up.

Humes figures that the bullet must have struck the president's back, slipped between the muscles without striking any major blood vessels, passed over the top of the right lung, bruising it, and exited the throat just below the Adam's apple.[1070]

His major dilemma solved, Commander Humes has only to write up the final report. He plans to get started later today, but first he needs some sleep.

10:00 a.m.

Bill Alexander didn't get home from the search of Joe Molina's house, and to bed, until around 4:15 in the morning, but by 8:00 a.m. he was down at the DA's office for a full day of work interviewing witnesses and preparing to take the case against Oswald for Kennedy's and Tippit's murders to the grand jury on Monday. At that time he would seek an indictment against Oswald on the murders that would supersede the two existing criminal complaints, and announce that his office would be seeking the death penalty against Oswald. To Alexander's absolute astonishment he receives a phone call from the Dallas police that Jimmy "Rughead" Martin, a local attorney, was at the police station saying he represented Oswald and presenting a writ of habeas corpus signed by Judge Joe B. Brown with bond set at $100,000. If Oswald could pay the 10 percent premium of $10,000 on the bond, he was entitled to be released on bail! Alexander knew that Judge Brown, being a District Court judge, had the authority to overrule Judge David Johnston, who was only a justice of the peace. "Pissed," Alexander immediately calls Judge Brown.

"Judge, what in the hell is going on here? We've already filed on Oswald for the Tippit and Kennedy murders and Judge Johnston has denied bond and we're not going to honor your writ."

Brown immediately backs down, acting as if he didn't know what had already transpired. He promises to immediately recall his writ, and that was the end of it.[1071]

Robert Oswald has been hanging around police headquarters for thirty or forty minutes, and still there doesn't seem to be any hope of talking with police officials. He figures that since his brother has been charged with the president's assassination, perhaps the district attorney will be amenable to talking to him. He goes down to the first floor of City Hall and telephones the DA's office from a pay phone. Assistant DA Jim Bowie answers and tells him that District Attorney Henry Wade isn't in yet, but is expected any moment.

"Come on down," Bowie advises him.

By the time Robert walks the many blocks down to the DA's office, located in the same building as the sheriff's office, Wade has arrived and asks Robert to come right in. They talk for an hour, mostly in generalities, but also about the likely date of Lee's trial. Henry Wade assures Robert that Lee will be tried in a state court, for a reason Robert finds really odd—something about there being no federal law prohibiting the killing of a president.

Wade wonders when Robert had last seen his brother. Robert says that it was about a year ago, at his home in Fort Worth.

"What can you tell me about him?" Wade asks.

Robert tells him a bit about his brother's defection to Russia and other general information. The district attorney decides to play cop for a moment.

"Now, let's see, you last saw Lee . . ." Wade repeats, casually, much of what Robert has just told him, but purposely gets some of the details wrong. The ruse is pretty transparent to Robert, who finds Wade's attempt at trickery to be fairly amusing. He just smiles at Wade, who grins broadly at having been caught. The DA leans back in his leather chair and chats amicably about subjects other than the assassination. Robert begins to realize that Wade is just a plain politician who, after a blundered effort to trick him, now only wants to make sure he leaves with a favorable impression.[1072]

"I was wondering, Mr. Wade," Roberts finally asks, "if you could arrange for Marina, my mother, and myself to see Lee today?"

"I don't see why not," Wade tells him, and telephones Captain Fritz, who tells him that arrangements have already been made for all of them to see Oswald at noon. Wade relays the information to Robert.[1073]

"You appear to be a good citizen," Wade tells him, "and I think you will render your country a great service if you will go up and tell Lee to tell us all about this thing. The evidence is very strong against your brother in the assassination," Wade adds cautiously. "What do you think about it?"

"Well, he is my brother," Robert says, "and I hate to think he would do this. I want to talk to him and ask him about it."

Robert is curious about the shooting of the police officer. Wade tells him that there are several eyewitnesses to the crime, and their accounts have convinced the DA of Lee's guilt on that murder too.[1074]

The two men rise and shake hands. Wade warns him that reporters are waiting outside.

"I won't have anything to say," Robert says and walks out.

Wade steps to the window and looks out front to see Robert Oswald push through the throng of pesky newsmen and walk off, without a word. The district attorney is impressed by the young man from Denton.[1075]

At the compound of the Kennedy family in Hyannis Port, Massachusetts, the family decides that as frail as the patriarch of the family, Joe Kennedy Sr., is from his massive stroke on a Palm Beach golf course in 1961, which left him partially paralyzed on the right side and no longer able to speak, they could no longer keep the truth from him. His wife, Rose, had learned the previous day over television of the shooting in Dallas even before her son Bobby had telephoned her. Tragedy was no stranger to Rose, having already lost a son and daughter in air crashes, but she quietly sank into a chair, trembling. She then went down to the lawn by the sea, where she strode back and forth for the rest of the afternoon. Now, the late president's youngest brother, Ted, tells his father that "there's been a bad accident. The president has been hurt very badly." Though the stroke had also caused aphasia in the old man—an impairment in the ability to understand the spoken or written word—his head snaps back and he stares directly into his son's eyes. "As a matter of fact," Ted says to his father, "he died." The elder Kennedy, as tough an Irishman as they come, immediately starts to sob. Ted and his sister Eunice try to comfort him, but it is unavailing. Even a sedative administered to him doesn't seem to alleviate the emotional response.

The next day, Rose, her daughter Eunice Shriver, and her son Teddy will board a plane, *The Caroline*, at the Hyannis Port airport for the trip to Washington, D.C., for Monday's funeral. Joseph Kennedy will remain behind in the care of his niece, Ann Gargan, and a trained nurse, Rita Dallas. Both have been with him since his stroke.[1076]

10:10 a.m.

Shortly before Oswald was brought down from the fifth-floor jail for interrogation, Chief Curry was stopped by reporters as he made his way down the third-floor corridor toward his office.

"What evidence has been uncovered so far, Chief?"

"I wouldn't want to elaborate on all the evidence that has been uncovered," Curry says hesitantly.

"How would you describe his mood during the questioning?"

"Very arrogant," Curry snaps back. "Has been all along."

"What does he still say, Chief?"

"He just denies everything," Curry says.

"Does he say anything else?" a reporter asks, hoping for more details.

"Not too much," Curry answers, looking for words, then admits, "I don't know. I haven't personally been interrogating him."[1077]

"Is there any doubt in your mind, Chief, that Oswald is the man who killed the president?"

"I think this is the man who killed the president, yes," Curry says firmly.

"Chief, could you tell us what you might have found in his rooming house in the way of literature or any papers connecting him—?"

"We found a great, great amount of Communist literature, Communist books," Curry replies. "I couldn't tell you just what all of it was, but it was a large box."

"Chief, we understand you've had the results of the paraffin tests which were made to determine whether Oswald had fired a weapon. Can you tell us what those tests showed?"

"I understand that it was positive," Curry tells them.

"But, what does that mean?"

"It only means that he fired a gun," Curry says.[1078]

"Chief, is there any plan for a reenactment of the crime? To take him to the scene or to do anything in that respect?"

"No."

"Is there any evidence that anyone else may have been linked with Oswald to this shooting?"

"At this time, we don't believe so," Curry answers. "We are talking to a man [Joe Molina] that works in the same building that we have in our subversive files and we are talking to him but he denies any knowledge of it."

One reporter wants to know how Oswald covered the distance between the Depository and the Tippit shooting scene in Oak Cliff. "I don't know," Curry says. "We have heard that he was picked up by a Negro in a car."[*]

"That is not confirmed?"

"No, it is not confirmed, as far as I know," Curry replies.

"Have you been able to trace the rifle? Do you know where it was purchased?"

"No," Curry says, "we are attempting to do that at this time."

"With this man's apparent subversive background, *was there any surveillance*? Were police aware of his presence in *Dallas*?"

"We in the police department here did not know he was in Dallas. I understand that the FBI did know he was in Dallas," Curry replies, the thought of Lieutenant Jack Revill's memo fresh in his mind.

"Is it normally the practice of the FBI to inform the police?"

"Yes," Curry says curtly.

"But you were not informed?"

"We had not been informed of this man," Curry reiterates.[1079]

It doesn't take long for FBI Director J. Edgar Hoover to get wind of Curry's statements to the press and become livid. Hoover calls Dallas FBI special agent-in-charge Gordon Shanklin and orders him to call Chief Curry and tell him to retract his statement about the FBI having prior knowledge of Oswald being in Dallas.

"The FBI is extremely desirous that you retract your statement to the press," Shanklin tells Curry over the phone, assuring him that what he said could suggest that the FBI had interviewed Oswald in Dallas and had him under surveillance, neither of which was true, he assured Curry.[1080]

Curry agrees to make a retraction and orders Lieutenant Jack Revill to remain silent about the matter as well.[1081]

Lieutenant T. L. Baker answers the telephone jangling at his desk in Homicide and Robbery. The caller is one of the supervisors at City Transportation Company, a taxi service. He's calling to report that one of his drivers, William W. Whaley, came in this morning and said that he had recognized Oswald's picture in the morning newspaper and believed he was the same man he drove out to North Beckley in Oak Cliff yesterday afternoon. Baker informs Captain Fritz, who instructs him to bring Whaley and the cabdriver who was a witness to the Tippit shooting, William Scoggins, to police headquarters to view Oswald in a lineup.[1082]

In the meantime, Fritz asks his detectives to bring Oswald down to his office for further questioning.

10:20 a.m. (11:20 a.m. EST)
The FBI sends another Teletype to all of its field offices:

---

[*]This is apparently a reference to the claim of Deputy Sheriff Roger Craig, who told police Friday evening that he saw a man who resembled Oswald get into a station wagon driven by a Negro. Evidence, including a bus transfer and Oswald's own admissions, proved Craig's claim to be false. The fact that Curry is still unaware that Oswald took a bus and a cab to Oak Cliff after the shooting, something homicide investigators learned Friday night, demonstrates how little Curry knew about the details of the assassination investigation.

Lee Harvey Oswald has been developed as the principal suspect in the assassination of President Kennedy. He has been formally charged with the President's murder along with the murder of Dallas Texas patrolman J.D. Tippet [*sic*] by Texas state authorities . . . All offices should [continue] normal contacts with informants and other sources with respect to bombing suspects, hate group members and known racial extremists. Daily teletype summaries may be discontinued. All investigation bearing directly on the President's assassination should be afforded most expeditious handling and Bureau and Dallas advised.[1083]

In Washington, D.C., even the weather appears to have taken respectful cognizance of the tragedy that has befallen the nation's capital more than any other American city. Rain falls slowly from a bleak, overcast sky through most of the day. A shaken capital tries to piece together a new mosaic of national rule "to replace the one shattered by an assassin's bullet 24 hours before." President Johnson, the eighth vice president to be elevated because of the death of a president, has taken over the machinery of government amid pledges of support from leaders of both parties as well as from leaders throughout the civilized world. He holds his first cabinet meeting, with Attorney General Robert Kennedy present[*] and asks all members to continue to serve under him.[†] Later in the day, he receives former presidents Harry S. Truman and Dwight D. Eisenhower in the Oval Office. Though the Kennedy family has requested of the public that no flowers be sent, encouraging people to contribute instead to their favorite charity, bouquets of flowers arrive throughout the day and are accepted by the White House guard.

At midmorning in the East Room of the White House, where the fallen President and First Lady had once presided over their famous, glittering White House affairs and danced gaily with their friends, seventy-five intimates and relatives of the Kennedy family attend a private mass with Mrs. Kennedy and her two children said by the Reverend John J. Cavanaugh, the former president of the University of Notre Dame and a longtime friend of the family. It is believed to be the first Roman Catholic mass ever said in the White House. (Almost concurrently, in New York City, where the day is also bleak and overcast, twenty-five hundred mourners crowd into the twenty-three-hundred-seat Saint Patrick's Cathedral on Fifth Avenue for a pontifical requiem mass in which 250 clergymen take

---

[*]Quite apart from his unfathomable grief, RFK did not want to attend, finding it difficult to accept that anyone, particularly LBJ, whom he disliked, would be taking his brother's place, and he showed up five minutes late. As alluded to earlier, Johnson had a deep sense of illegitimacy following the assassination and "desperately needed affirmation." Though the American public and Congress gave it to him, it was clear to him RFK had not, and in Bobby's attitude, Johnson felt the rejection of his legitimacy he had feared from others. (Shesol, *Mutual Contempt*, p.119) "During all of that period," LBJ would later say, "I think [Bobby] seriously considered whether he would let me be president, whether he should really take the position [that] the vice president didn't automatically move in. I thought that was on his mind every time I saw him in the first few days. I think he was seriously considering what steps to take" (Tape-recorded interview of LBJ by William J. Jorden, LBJ Library, Austin, Texas; Shesol, *Mutual Contempt*, p.119).

[†]Bobby Kennedy agreed to stay on as LBJ's attorney general, if for no other reason than he didn't have anywhere else to go, at least in government. His friend Dean Markham warned RFK that to resign could "boomerang," benefiting Johnson. "Public sentiment will be on his side," Markham told RFK, "and the feeling will be that he tried to cooperate and work with you, but you didn't want to." (Shesol, *Mutual Contempt*, p.124) After serving as attorney general until September 2, 1964, when he resigned to run for and win the U.S. Senate seat from New York, on March 16, 1968, Kennedy announced his decision to run against Johnson for the Democratic nomination that year, but fifteen days later, on March 31, 1968, Johnson told a stunned nation on national television that he would not seek reelection.

part.) After the mass, a procession of government leaders begins to file into and out of the East Room, where the president's body lies in a flag-draped coffin.

"The medium of television," the *New York Times* observed, "which played such a major part in the career of President Kennedy, is the instrument that is making the tragedy of his death such a deeply personal experience in millions of homes over this long weekend. In hushed living rooms everywhere, the uninterrupted coverage provided by the three national networks and their affiliated stations is holding families indoors to share in history's grim unfolding, the home screen for the first time fulfilling the heart-rending function of giving a new dimension to grief."[*]

In countries throughout the world there is mourning.[†] "From Madrid to Manila churches filled and American embassies were thronged with people who wanted to sign memorial books." American viewers see downcast crowds gathering outside the American embassy in London, where the twelve bells of St. Paul's Cathedral announce the national memorial service there. More than ten thousand Poles line up eight abreast to sign the book of condolences at the U.S. embassy in Warsaw. In Berlin, Mayor Willy Brandt asks his people to light candles in their darkened windows. Within minutes, candles are flickering throughout the city. "We all feel somewhat left alone," Brandt said. Radio Moscow broadcasts a concert of memorial dirges. In Tokyo Bay, Japanese fishing boats, flags at half-mast, drift alongside U.S. warships. Buddhist monks offer prayers in front of black crepe–draped images of President Kennedy. In Paris, French men and women gather solemnly around outdoor radios, their tears hidden by the pouring rain. In Kenya, weeping Kipsigis warriors in ceremonial feathers and body paint listen as their leader extols the virtues of the murdered president. America learns just how many people around the world considered John F. Kennedy *their* president too.

World leaders also weigh in. England's prime minister, Sir Alec Douglas-Home, notes that John Kennedy left "an indelible mark on the entire world. There are times in life when the mind and heart stand still, and one such is now." Premier Khrushchev appears at the American embassy in Moscow to pay his respects, lamenting the blow the president's death has dealt Soviet-American relations. Unable to travel to Washington because of illness, Italian president Antonio Segni, attending a mass in Rome, openly sobs. The words of a "profoundly saddened" Pope Paul VI to a crowd of thirty thousand gathered in St. Peter's Square in Rome are relayed around the world by satellite. The pope expresses his hope that "the death of this great statesman may not damage the cause of the American people, but rather reinforce it." Nineteen chiefs of state and three reigning monarchs let it be known that they will attend the president's funeral on Monday, among them France's General Charles de Gaulle.

Jack Kennedy's political opponents are no less sincere in their grief. The man he defeated to win the presidency, Richard Nixon, speaking from his home in New York, tells the viewers, "President Kennedy yesterday wrote the finest and greatest chapter in

---

[*]Not all Americans were accepting of the uninterrupted coverage. All three networks received calls, in the low hundreds, from viewers complaining about the cancellation of their favorite shows and asking when regular programming would be resumed.

[†]While the rest of the world, including the Soviet Union, eulogized the slain president, Communist China, in sharp contrast, stood virtually alone, Peking not only not offering condolences and eulogies, but defiling, even ridiculing him. The Official New China News Agency did not let up in its attacks on Kennedy and his successor. The *Worker's Daily* went so far as to publish a cartoon of Kennedy sprawled face down in blood on the ground, his necktie bearing a dollar sign, with the caption "Kennedy Bites the Dust." (United Press International, November 25, 1963, p.24)

his *Profiles in Courage*. The greatest tribute we can pay is to reduce the hatred which drives men to do such deeds." Senator Goldwater, at a news conference in Muncie, Indiana, also speaks warmly of the president. Even the two implacably segregationist, Democratic governors of Alabama and Mississippi, George Wallace and Ross Barnett, whose fierce political opposition may have damaged Kennedy more than that of the Republican Party, publicly honor his memory.

An avalanche of mail pours into the networks, as though the viewers feel the necessity to enter into a dialogue with them. Many write poems. At CBS, Walter Cronkite realizes that people are "desperate to express themselves about this thing. And poetry seems a natural form. They seem intent either on finding a way to accept the guilt we are all feeling or laying it on someone or something else, or simply eulogizing the man."

NBC's Chet Huntley and ABC's Edward P. Morgan are also swept away by the outpouring of grief. "It is probable that when all this is over," Morgan muses prophetically, "we will find it created a more personal response than any other event in history."[1084]

10:25 a.m.

As the newsmen in the third-floor corridor grow anxious for Oswald's anticipated reappearance en route to Homicide and Robbery for further questioning, Deputy Chief Stevenson steps into the hubbub and in a commanding voice instructs them that there will have to be some order when Oswald is brought through the hallway.

"Gentlemen!" Stevenson shouts above the din. "Whenever this door [pointing to the jail elevator door] is open and they come through here, we don't want any of you questioning this boy. We don't want any of you pushing him. We want to cooperate with you. We want to help you every way in the world that we can but we're going to have to have room to work."

"Do you mind if we shout a question at him?" a reporter ignorantly asks.

"I don't want you shouting a question at him in no way!" Stevenson barks. "The more you upset him the more difficult it is for us to talk to him."

"We want to do whatever you want us to, so if you say no questions—" a reporter says cooperatively.

"Back up as far as you can against that wall," Stevenson orders as the reporters try to melt into the wall, but there is no place to move.

"Let's make it clear we have all agreed with the chief that we will not ask Oswald any questions," a reporter yells to fellow journalists.[1085]

A moment later, the jail elevator door opens and Oswald is led through the subdued crowd by Detectives Hall, Sims, and Boyd. The reporters follow orders and refrain from bombarding Oswald with questions. He soon disappears behind the closed doors of Captain Fritz's office.

10:35 a.m.

This morning, Oswald faces a formidable array of faces, including FBI agent Jim Bookhout, Dallas Secret Service agent-in-charge Forrest Sorrels, Secret Service inspector Thomas J. Kelley (in from Washington, D.C.), Secret Service agent David B. Grant, and Dallas U.S. marshall Robert I. Nash. Homicide detectives Boyd and Hall remain in the office as security.[1086] As usual, it is the soft-spoken, gravely voiced Captain Fritz who takes the lead.

"Lee, tell me what you did when you left work yesterday?" Fritz begins.

"I took a bus to my residence," Oswald says, self-assuredly, "and when I got off I got a transfer and used it to take another bus over to the theater where I was arrested. A policeman took the transfer out of my pocket at that time."[1087]

Fritz nods agreeably, although he knows that officers actually took the transfer out of Oswald's pocket several hours after his arrest, *not* at the theater. The fact that Oswald said he took a bus to his residence, not the cab Fritz knows he took, hasn't escaped the homicide captain.

"Lee, did you bring curtain rods to work with you yesterday morning?" Fritz asks.

"No," Oswald replies.

"You didn't bring any curtain rods with you?" Fritz asks again.

"No, I didn't," Oswald shoots back.

"Well, the fella that drove you to work yesterday morning tells us that you had a package in the backseat," Fritz tells him. "He says that package was about twenty-eight inches long, and you told him it was curtain rods."

"I didn't have any kind of package," Oswald says. "I don't know what he's talking about. I had my lunch and that's all I had."

"You didn't have a conversation with Wesley Frazier about curtain rods?" Fritz probes.

"No."

"When you left his car, did you go toward the building carrying a long package?" Fritz inquires.

"No, I didn't carry anything but my lunch," Oswald repeats.[1088]

"Didn't you tell Wesley you were in the process of fixing up your apartment . . ."

Oswald doesn't wait for the rest of the question, "No!"

". . . and that the purpose of your visit to Irving on the night of November 21st was to obtain some curtain rods from Mrs. Paine?"

"No, I never said that," Oswald replies.[1089]

Oswald's denials are meaningless to the thirty-year homicide investigator. He has learned long ago that if someone has the immorality to commit a serious crime, he certainly possesses the far lesser immorality to deny having done it. Fritz is sure, in his own mind, that Oswald carried the rifle wrapped in a long package into work Friday morning. Fritz just wants him to admit it.[1090] The homicide captain saunters over behind his desk, taking his time with his line of inquiry.

"Did you ride in a taxicab yesterday?" Fritz finally asks.

"Well," Oswald says hesitantly, "yes, I—"

"I thought you said you rode a bus home?" Fritz snaps back.

"Well, that's not exactly true," Oswald says with a smirk, like a child caught with his hand in the cookie jar. "Actually, I did board a bus at the Book Depository but after a block or two it got stalled in traffic, so I got off and took a cab back to my room. I remember a lady looking in the cab and asking the driver to call her one as I got in."

Oswald is good at volunteering details that don't amount to much.

"Did you talk to the driver during the ride home?" Fritz asks.

"Oh, I might have said something just to pass the time," Oswald answers.

"Did he say anything to you?"

"He told me the president had been shot," Oswald says.

"How much was the fare?" Fritz asks.

"It was about eighty-five cents," Oswald replies.

"This the first time you ever rode in a cab?" Fritz asks innocently.

"Yeah, but that's only because a bus is always available," Oswald answers.

"What'd you do when you got home?" Fritz asks. The question has been put to Oswald before, but Fritz is keenly aware that repetition will frequently trip up liars. They just can't keep their story straight because they don't have the truth as their framework of reference. That's why there's an expression that liars have to have very good memories—they only have their verbal lie to remember, not the full experience of the truth.

"I changed my shirt and trousers and went to the movies," Oswald says.

Fritz makes a mental note that Oswald has again changed his story. Yesterday, Oswald said he only changed his trousers.

"What did you do with your dirty clothes?" the homicide captain asks.

"I put them in the lower drawer of my dresser," Oswald says matter-of-factly.

"Lee, would you describe this clothing?"

"The shirt was a reddish color with a button-down collar and the trousers were gray."[1091]

11:00 a.m.

Robert Oswald arrives at the Hotel Adolphus and finds that room 906 is a suite. A stranger answers his knock.

"I'm Robert Oswald. Is my mother here?"

"In the next room," the man says. "Just come on through."

The suite has been transformed into the local headquarters for *Life* magazine. A Teletype machine clatters away as Robert makes his way past several reporters and photographers. In the next room he finds his mother, Marina and her children, an interpreter, and FBI agent Bardwell Odum. Not surprising to Robert, Odum is in the middle of an argument with Marguerite. The FBI agent wanted to ask Marina some questions, but the controlling Mrs. Oswald had intervened.

"I'm not going to let Marina say anything to anybody, and that's final," Marguerite says, her voice rising to a shout. Odum tries to get around Mrs. Oswald by addressing Marina's interpreter, only to be repeatedly interrupted by the shrill woman. Odum decides he might have better luck with Robert.

"Come on out here for a minute," Odum says, as he pulls Robert into the next room. "You seem to be a sensible guy. All we want is a yes or no from Marina herself, not from your mother. Could you help us?" Robert agrees to try, although he doesn't think his sister-in-law should answer any more questions without the assistance of counsel. On the other hand, he doesn't want to speak for her.

"I'll find out just what she wants to do," Robert says. The two men walk back into the room and Robert holds out his hand to stifle his mother before she can get started again.

"Now, wait a minute," he says, "let me handle this." He explains quietly to Marina through the interpreter what Odum wants. Marina's answer is short and simple, "*Nyet.*"

Odum is disappointed, but Robert assures him that Marina will very probably cooperate fully once things settle down a little. Odum gives him a card with his telephone number and asks Robert to call him when Marina feels like answering some questions.[1092]

Back at the Homicide and Robbery Bureau, Captain Fritz focuses his questions to Oswald once again on the time of the assassination.

"Did you eat lunch with anyone yesterday?" he asks.

"I ate with two colored boys I worked with," Oswald says.

"What are their names?" Fritz asks.

"One of them is called Junior," Oswald says, "and the other one is a short fellow. I don't remember his name, but I would recognize him on sight."*

"What did you have for lunch?" Fritz asks.

"I had a cheese sandwich and an apple," Oswald answers, "which I got at Mrs. Paine's house before I left."[1093]

Captain Fritz changes the subject and begins probing Oswald's relationship with the Paines. He asks Oswald to explain again the living arrangements he has for his wife, Marina.

"Mrs. Paine doesn't receive any pay for keeping my wife and children there. What she gets in return is that she's interested in the Russian language and having Marina around helps her with it."

"What do you know about Mr. Paine?" Fritz asks.

"I don't know Mr. Paine very well," Oswald says. "He usually comes by the house on Wednesday or Friday. He has his own car. Mrs. Paine has two."

"Do you keep any of your belongings at the Paine residence?" Fritz asks.

"I've got some things in her garage that I brought back with me from New Orleans in September," Oswald says.

"Like what?" Fritz inquires.

"Well, let's see," Oswald says, "two sea bags, a couple of suitcases, and a few boxes of kitchen articles—dishes and such."

"That it?"

"I've got some clothes there too," Oswald adds.

"What about a rifle?" Fritz asks.

"I didn't store a rifle there," Oswald says, very perturbed. "I've already told you, I don't own a rifle."[1094]

Fritz switches gears.

"Lee, do you have any other friends or relatives living nearby?"

"My brother Robert lives in Fort Worth," Oswald replies.

"Anyone else? Any other friends?" Fritz asks.

"The Paines are close friends of mine," Oswald answers.[1095]

"Anyone ever visit you at your apartment on North Beckley?" Fritz asks.

"No," Oswald says.[1096]

"Have you ever ordered guns through the mail?" Fritz asks.

"I've never ordered guns," Oswald sighs, tiring of the game, "and I don't have any receipts for any guns."

"What about a rifle?"

"I don't own a rifle," Oswald snaps, "nor have I ever possessed a rifle. How many times do I have to tell you that?"[1097]

Captain Fritz doesn't answer him.

---

*Depository employees James Jarman Jr., called "Junior" by friends (3 H 198, WCT James Jarman Jr.), and Harold Norman are believed to be the men referred to by Oswald. Both men ate lunch while on the first floor, but both said they did not have lunch with Oswald (3 H 188–189, WCT Harold Norman; Transcript of *On Trial*, July 28, 1968, p.72 [never saw Oswald after around ten in the morning]; 3 H 201, WCT James Jarman Jr.).

"Are you a member of the Communist Party?" Fritz asks instead.

"No," Oswald says. "I never joined and have never had a card."

"What about the American Civil Liberties Union?" Fritz asks.

Oswald smiles at the thought that Fritz would ask about the Communist Party and the ACLU in the same breath.

"Yes," he says, "I'm a member of the ACLU. I pay five dollars a year in dues. Does that make me a Communist?"[1098]

Oswald snickers under his breath.

"Lee, if you never ordered a gun or purchased a gun like you say," Fritz says calmly, "then where did you get the pistol you had in your possession at the time of your arrest?"

"Oh, I bought that about seven months ago," Oswald says, avoiding the obvious contradiction.

"Where?" Fritz asks.

"I'm not going to answer any more questions about the pistol or any guns until I've talked to a lawyer," Oswald fires back.[1099]

"Lee, have you ever been questioned before?" Fritz continues to ask questions of the young suspect, but for the moment, less probing questions.

"Yeah, I've been questioned a number of times by the FBI in Fort Worth after returning from the Soviet Union," Oswald says, glaring at the FBI men present in the room. "They used all the usual interrogation techniques—the hard and soft approach, the buddy system—all their standard operating procedures. Oh, I'm very familiar with all types of questioning. And I've got no intention of answering any questions concerning any shooting. I know I don't have to answer your questions, and I'm not going to answer any questions until I've been given counsel. Frankly, the FBI has overstepped their bounds!"

"What do you mean by that?" Captain Fritz asks.

"When the FBI talked to my wife, they were abusive and impolite," Oswald says angrily. "They frightened her with their intimidation. I consider their activities to be obnoxious."[1100] Oswald tells Captain Fritz that he's trying to reach the New York attorney named "Abt," but so far has been unsuccessful. "If I can't get him, then I may get the American Civil Liberties Union to get me an attorney." Captain Fritz advises Oswald that arrangements will be made so he can call Mr. Abt again.[1101]

"Where did you live in New Orleans?" Fritz asks.

"I lived at 4907 Magazine Street," Oswald says.

"Where did you work?"

"The William Riley Company," Oswald answers.

"Were you ever in trouble in New Orleans?" Fritz asks.

"Yes," Oswald replies. "I was arrested for disturbing the peace and paid a ten-dollar fine."

"How'd that happen?" Fritz asks.

"I was demonstrating on behalf of the Fair Play for Cuba Committee," Oswald explains, "and I got into a fight with some anti-Castro Cuban refugees who didn't particularly agree with me. Even though they started the fight, *they* were released and *I* was fined."[1102] Oswald shakes his head in disbelief. Like his mother, he plays the martyr well.

"What do you think of President Kennedy?" Fritz asks.

"I have no views on the president," Oswald replies. "My wife and I like the president's family. They're interesting people. Of course, I have my own views on the president's national policy. And I have a right to express my views but because of the charges, I don't think I should comment further."

"Anything about him bother you?" Fritz presses.

Oswald knows where Fritz is going with the question.

"I am not a malcontent," Oswald snaps, almost annoyed that the cops must think he's that stupid. "Nothing irritated me about the president."[1103]

"Lee," Captain Fritz asks in his grandfatherly tone, "will you submit to a polygraph examination?"

"Not without the advice of counsel," Oswald replies. "I refused to take one for the FBI in 1962, and I certainly don't intend to take one for the Dallas police."[1104]

Captain Fritz reaches into his desk and pulls out one of the two Selective Service cards Oswald had in his wallet at the time of his arrest.[1105] The card is made out in the name of Alek James Hidell, and includes a signature in that name, but bears a photograph of Lee Harvey Oswald. Even a cursory examination reveals the card to be a crude forgery.* Fritz shows the card to Oswald.

"Did you sign this card, 'Alex J. Hidell'?" Fritz asks.

"I don't have to answer that," Oswald says.

"This is your card, right?" Fritz asks.

"I carried it, yes," Oswald replies.

"Why did you carry it?" FBI agent James Bookhout asks.

Oswald is silent.

"What was the purpose of this card?" Fritz asks. "What did you use it for?"

"I don't have any comment to make on that," Oswald says stoically.[1106]

Captain Fritz pulls another item out of his desk drawer—an address book filled with Russian names and addresses—and asks who the people are whose names are in the book.

"Those are just the names of Russian immigrants living here in Dallas who I've visited since my return from the Soviet Union," Oswald says, half-amused.[1107]

The homicide chief looks up at the surrounding faces of law enforcement and lets them know that they can question the subject if they'd like. Secret Service inspector Thomas Kelley rises to the challenge.

"Mr. Oswald, did you view the parade yesterday?" he asks.

"No, I didn't," Oswald says.

"Did you shoot the president?"

"No, I did not," Oswald claims.

"Did you shoot the governor?" Kelley asks.

"No, I didn't know that the governor had been shot," Oswald says.[1108]

"Okay," Captain Fritz says, "that's it for now. Take him back to his cell."

As Detectives Sims, Boyd, and Hall escort Oswald from the room, Dallas Secret Service agent-in-charge Forrest Sorrels can't help but think that Oswald's defiant manner and obvious lying during this session is perhaps an attempt on his part to provoke Fritz into doing or saying something he shouldn't.[1109] Whatever Oswald had up his sleeve, it didn't work. None of Oswald's sass or lying bothered Fritz. As Dallas postal inspector Harry Holmes would later observe about a subsequent interview by Fritz of Oswald, "It

---

*The fact that the card contains a photograph at all is evidence of forgery since a genuine Selective Service card, including the one Oswald had in his wallet at the time of his arrest in his own name, does not include a photograph of the card bearer (CE 801, 17 H 686).

was like water off a duck's back. He was too old a hand to be taken in by something like that."[1110]

11:27 a.m.

As detectives whisk him past newsmen in the crowded third-floor corridor, Oswald leans toward a microphone pointed in his direction. "I would like to contact Mr. Abt, A-B-T," Oswald says, spelling the name. "Mr. Abt in New York to defend me."

Detectives push Oswald through the doorway leading to the jail elevators.* The mob of reporters begins to pass the word, "Oswald wants a New York attorney named Abt to defend him." It's the first indication they've heard about whom Oswald wants to handle his case.[1111]

11:45 a.m.

Shortly after Oswald is taken back to his fifth-floor jail cell, the assistant police chief, Captain Glen D. King, is stopped by reporters as he makes his way through the third floor.

"Captain, could you detail the information you gave us a little while ago about the search for additional suspects?"

King tells a television audience about the search earlier that morning conducted by representatives of his office and the DA's office of the man (Joe Molina) who worked with Oswald at the Book Depository Building, and that the man was presently being interrogated by his office.

"Do you regard this man as a suspect in this case at this moment?" a reporter asks.

"All we regard him as right now is a person to interrogate," King says. "Certainly there's not an adequate amount of information on him to indicate he is a suspect . . ."

"Does this indicate that Oswald has said something that would lead you to believe other people were associated with him in this alleged—?"

"Not necessarily, no," King answers.

"What's the name of the man involved?" someone asks.

"I don't want to identify him, no," King says, "because there's not an adequate amount of evidence of any involvement on his part to warrant identification of him."†

"Could we ask you, sir," a reporter says, "what do you know about the report that the FBI knew that Oswald was [a] priority one?"

---

*"Those people [press] were in our way every time we moved that man from my office to the jail and back," Captain Fritz would later tell the Warren Commission. "We had to push him and pull him through the crowd" (15 H 150).

†But later in the day, Chief Curry does, indeed, identify Molina by name over TV. Indeed, Molina is mentioned over national television on Saturday afternoon as someone who has been a previous subject of U.S. Department of Justice scrutiny as a possible subversive, with the vague implication that, who knows, maybe he could have been involved in the assassination in some way. FBI Director Hoover would later say that there had never been a file on Molina, and he wasn't even known to the FBI prior to November 22, 1963. Molina's wife, Soledad, had dropped him off at police headquarters at City Hall at 9:45 Saturday morning, and between then and 5:00 p.m., when the police drove him home after they were satisfied he had no connection to Oswald or the assassination, he was grilled off and on throughout the day by Dallas police detectives as well as the FBI. Though never told he was under arrest, when he once, between interviews, got up to leave, a Dallas police officer blocked his exit and told him to go sit down. Upon returning home, he learned from a horrified Soledad that he had been all over the news, and cast in a suspicious light. When his Book Depository Building employer thereafter started getting crank calls and warnings from some customers that if the company didn't let the "subversive" working for it go, they would stop doing business with the company, the employer finally let Molina go on December 30, after sixteen years of employment, telling him that automation had required his firing, but he knew better. (6 H 369–371, WCT Joe R. Molina; CE 1937, 23 H 732; CE 2036, 24 H 448–449)

"I know nothing about that," King says dryly.

"Did you give special consideration to the persons on your subversive list before the president came to town, know where they were, what they were doing?"

"Yes," King says.

"Then if the FBI had known about him ahead of time and had informed your office, you would have checked up on Oswald as well?"

"I'd rather not speculate on what might have happened if something else had happened," King tells him.

"We've been given information earlier today that the FBI did know he was here and had interviewed him during the last couple or three weeks," a reporter says.

"On this I have no answer," King replies.[1112]

12:00 noon

Marina, Marguerite, and Robert Oswald arrive at police headquarters for their scheduled meeting with Lee. After being escorted to the third-floor Forgery Bureau office, they are informed there will be a slight delay because they have picked up another suspect (Molina).

"Oh, Marina," Marguerite says to her daughter-in-law, "they think another man might have shot Kennedy."[1113] Whether Marina could understand these words is not clear, but in any event, she had somehow convinced herself that maybe it was a mistake after all— that Lee may be under suspicion because he has been to Russia and that this horrible nightmare will all be over and they can go back to their ordinary lives.[1114]

A female officer from the Juvenile Bureau comes in and takes the two women to another room so that Marina can nurse the infant Rachel in privacy.[1115] Meanwhile, Secret Service agent Mike Howard approaches Robert.

"We're interested in everything we can possibly find out about your brother," Howard says. "Would you mind answering a few questions?"

"I'll do my best to answer anything I can," Robert replies.

Agent Howard wanted to know whether Robert thought that Lee had shot at Governor Connally because of the dishonorable discharge* the Marine Corps had handed Lee following his defection to the Soviet Union.

"I don't think that was the motive," Robert says, explaining that he never heard Lee express any kind of resentment toward Connally and knew for a fact that Lee had received a letter notifying him that Fred Korth had succeeded Connally as secretary of the navy and would be the one to rule on Oswald's efforts to have his discharge changed to honorable.

As the conversation drifts toward the quirky relationship between Marguerite and Lee, Agent Howard tells Robert that the kind of personal details about the Oswald family that he's providing will be of interest to Mrs. Kennedy. Robert takes the agent's comments to mean that Mrs. Kennedy herself had requested the information and Agent Howard will be delivering Robert's responses to her in person. Robert felt that he should express his family's sympathy to her.

"I would like to take this opportunity to express to Mrs. Kennedy, through you," Robert begins, and then his voice suddenly cracks. He stops and hangs his head.

---

*Actually, Oswald received an honorable discharge from the Marines following active duty, but later received an "undesirable" discharge from the Marine Corps Reserves because of his defection to the Soviet Union (WR, pp.386–387).

"That's all right," the agent says, "I know what you are trying to say."[1116]

Under earlier instructions from Captain Fritz, Detectives Sims, Boyd, Hall, and Dhority pull up at Oswald's rooming house on North Beckley to make absolutely sure that nothing was missed in yesterday's search, but Oswald's room has little to tell them. The detectives find a paperclip and a rubber band, which they confiscate, but nothing else. In fact, as Earlene Roberts points out, not only did the police clear all of Oswald's things out the day before, but they made off with a pillow case, two towels, and some washcloths belonging to the landlord. In less than thirty minutes, they're headed back to City Hall.[1117]

12:10 p.m.
When Chief Curry learns that reporters have been bombarding his assistant Glen King with questions about the FBI's possible prior knowledge of Oswald, he knows he'd better get out there and make a statement to the press—the retraction he had earlier promised Dallas FBI agent-in-charge Gordon Shanklin that he would make.

"There has been information that has gone out," Curry tells reporters at a press conference, with a live television audience looking in, "and I want to correct anything that might have been misinterpreted or misunderstood. And that is regarding information that the FBI might have had about this man."

Curry looks hesitant, his eyes shifting quickly from the microphones in front of him to the floor at his feet. He chooses his words very carefully as he picks his way through the political minefield he knows is enveloping his department.

"Last night someone told me, I don't even know who it was,* that the FBI did know this man was in the city and interviewed him. I wish to say this. Of my knowledge, I do not know this to be a fact, and I don't want anybody to get the wrong impression that I am accusing the FBI of not cooperating or of withholding information because they are under no obligation to us, but have always cooperated with us 100 percent."

The conference quickly moves on to other topics. Asked whether Oswald was asked to take a lie detector test, Curry says that it was offered to him but he refused to take it.

"Chief Curry, what are your plans now in dealing with Oswald himself?" a reporter asks. "Will he be interrogated here further or will he be transferred to the county jail to await presentment to the grand jury?"

"He will go to the county jail," Curry replies. "I don't know just when. But I am thinking probably sometime today . . . It is more convenient here to have him near us where we can talk to him when we need to, but we will probably transfer him soon."[1118]

After returning to his office, Curry calls Captain Fritz and asks if he will be ready to transfer Oswald by 4:00 p.m. Fritz says he doesn't think he will be finished questioning Oswald by then.[1119]

Under normal circumstances, an arrested person becomes the responsibility of Sheriff Bill Decker and goes to the county jail as soon as he has been booked. Details of the

---

*Contrary to his statement, Curry certainly knew where he had learned that the FBI purportedly had prior contact with Oswald—Lieutenant Jack Revill. It was Revill's memo regarding FBI agent James P. Hosty Jr.'s alleged remarks in the basement of City Hall that had put Curry on alert. And Curry also may have known from Captain Fritz about Hosty's contact with Oswald's wife, which came out the previous day in Fritz's interrogation of Oswald.

transfer are usually left to Decker, who has deputies from his office pick the prisoner up at the police department and transport him to the county jail. But this one may be too hot for the relatively small sheriff's department to handle. The Dallas Police Department has far more men and resources. The transfer will be from City Hall straight down Main Street to the Criminal Courts Building at Main and Houston, less than a mile away, ironically following the path of yesterday's motorcade. The problem of how and when to move Lee Oswald to the county jail will occupy much of the chief's time and attention over the next twenty-four hours.[1120]

12:35 p.m.
Captain Fritz orders Detectives Senkel and Turner to bring Oswald down from the jail for another interview. This time the questioning is perfunctory, aimed at getting a list of addresses where Oswald lived in Dallas, and in particular, where the bulk of his personal property might be stored. The questioning lasts about a half hour, during which Oswald says that most of his belongings are stored in the garage at Mrs. Paine's house in Irving.[1121]

Captain Fritz steps outside his office and dispatches Detectives Guy Rose and Richard Stovall to Irving with instructions to pick up anything and everything in storage there. This will be the second search of the Paine residence, but the first thorough search of the Paine garage. Only the blanket that had been used to store the rifle had been recovered from the garage on Friday.[1122]

As they head out the door, Fritz orders two visitor passes for Oswald's wife and mother to see Oswald in the fourth-floor jail office.[1123]

1:07 p.m.
Robert Oswald is rather put out that three passes haven't been arranged so that he too can see his brother. Secret Service agent Mike Howard tells him that he'll see what he can do about arranging another pass for him. Robert reluctantly agrees to remain behind and let his mother and Marina use the two passes to go up and see Lee.[1124]

The policewoman from the Juvenile Bureau takes care of the babies, and the two women are led through the pack of reporters in the hallway toward the fourth-floor elevators. They are forced to wait momentarily for the next elevator car, giving the reporters a chance to descend on them like hungry vultures. The two women ignore the bushel of questions tossed at them until Marguerite finally caves in and tells them they are going up to see Lee now. The elevator doors finally open and they escape the onslaught of questions, gliding up the elevator shaft to the floor above.[1125] A gaggle of reporters turn their attention to District Attorney Henry Wade, who is leaning against a corridor wall nearby. "Mr. Wade, do you expect to call Mrs. Kennedy or Governor Connally, if he's able, in this trial as witnesses?"

"We will not, unless it's absolutely necessary," Wade tells them, "and at this point I don't think it'll be necessary."

"How soon can we expect a trial?"

"I'd say around the middle of January," Wade answers.

"Has Mr. Oswald expressed any hatred, ill will, toward President Kennedy or, for that matter, any regret over his death?" a reporter asks.

"He has expressed no regret that I know of," Wade replies.

"This man, it seems, wasn't close to anybody," a reporter interjects. "Have you discovered any close friends in Dallas?"

"No, sir," Wade replies, agreeing with the reporter that this suggests an introverted personality.

"It's rumored that perhaps this case would be tried by a military court because, of course, President Kennedy is our commander in chief," a reporter suggests.

"I don't know anything about that," Wade corrects. "We have him charged in the state court and he's a state prisoner at present."

"And you will conduct the trial?"

"Yes, sir," Wade says. "I plan to."

"And you will ask the capital verdict?"

"We'll ask the death penalty," Wade says firmly.

"In how many cases of this type have you been involved, that is, when the death penalty is involved?"

"Since I've been district attorney we've asked—I've asked the death penalty in twenty-four cases," Wade replies.

"How many times have you obtained it?"

The district attorney looks the reporter in the eye.

"Twenty-three," he says. Elected district attorney five consecutive times over the last twenty years, Wade is confident that the Oswald case will bring him a twenty-fourth death penalty verdict. Texas juries—Texans, period—are strong believers in capital punishment.[1126] In a recent Dallas murder case of Wade's, after a long and impassioned plea by the defense attorney asking the jurors to spare the life of his client, Wade rose and gave one of the shortest summations ever delivered. "Ladies and gentlemen of the jury," the DA said, "this boy belongs in the electric chair." The jury returned a verdict of death after three hours of deliberation.[1127]

1:15 p.m.

Marina and Marguerite Oswald wait nervously in the fourth-floor visiting room to meet Lee for the first time since the murders. The long, narrow room is divided in two by a heavy glass window, one side for visitors, the other for prisoners. Rounded-off plywood wings divide the partition into several cubicles. There are no chairs in the booths, just a wood shelf and a telephone—the only communication across the grimy, dusty glass barrier. It is a stale, claustrophobic room haunted by the thousands of visitors who have crossed its threshold over the years.[1128]

Although Marina has managed to convince herself of Lee's innocence, the minute she sees him caged in glass, troubled, pitiful, and alone, her confidence deserts her. They pick up the telephones on each side of the barrier.

"Why did you bring that fool with you?" Lee says in Russian, glancing over her shoulder at his mother. "I don't want to talk to her."

"She's your mother," Marina says. "Of course she came."

Marina stares at the cuts and bruises on her husband's face.

"Have they been beating you?" she asks.

"Oh no," he answers. "They treat me fine. Did you bring Junie and Rachel?"

"They're downstairs," Marina says, anxious to talk to Lee about something weighing on her mind. "Alik [Marina's Russian nickname for Lee], can we talk about anything we like?"

That morning, Marina had tucked two photographs of Lee and his rifle inside one of the shoes she was now wearing. They were there now. She desperately wants to ask him what she should do with them.

"Oh, of course," he said sarcastically. "We can speak about *absolutely* anything."

Marina could tell from his tone that he was warning her to say nothing.

"They asked me about the gun," she says,

"Oh, that's nothing," he answers, his voice rising, the words coming quickly.[1129]

Marina can't bring herself to ask him if he did it. After all, he is her husband.

"I don't believe that you did that," she finally manages to say. "Everything will turn out well."[1130]

"Oh sure," he says, "there is a lawyer in New York who will help me. You shouldn't worry. Everything will be fine."

On the surface, it is the same old Lee, full of bravado. But this time there is something different. This time, the pitch of his voice is higher. There is also fear in his eyes, betraying his guilt. He is telling her everything will turn out all right, but Marina feels that even he does not believe it. Tears start to roll down her cheek.

"Don't cry," he says tenderly. "There's nothing to cry about. Try not to think about it. And if they ask you anything, you have a right not to answer. You have the right to refuse. Do you understand?"

"Yes," Marina says, wiping the tears away. She looks him in the eye. There are tears in his eyes too, but he's working hard to hold them back.[1131]

Marguerite doesn't understand a word they're saying, since the entire conversation is in Russian. Finally, Marina hands the phone to her.

"Honey, you are so bruised up, your face," Marguerite says. "What are they doing?"

"Mother, don't worry," Lee says. "I got that in a scuffle."

Marguerite thinks that Lee is simply shielding his mother from the truth about the awful beatings behind the jail walls.

"Is there anything I can do to help you?"

"No, Mother, everything is fine," Lee replies. "I know my rights. I have already requested to get in touch with an attorney, Mr. Abt. Don't worry about a thing."[1132]

Marguerite isn't about to insult him by asking him whether he shot President Kennedy. She heard him on television saying he didn't do it and that is enough for her. Eventually she yields the phone back to Marina. Lee again tells Marina not to worry.

"You have friends," he says. "They'll help you. If it comes to that, you can ask the Red Cross for help. You mustn't worry about me. Kiss Junie and Rachel for me."

"I will," Marina promises, tears welling up in her eyes.

Two guards enter the room behind him.

"Alka," Marina says, using a variant of Alik she often used, "remember that I love you." It was her way of letting him know that he could count on her not to betray him.

"I love you very much," he says. "Make sure you buy shoes for June."[1133]

Oswald backs out of the room so that he can look at her until the very last second.

Marina now knows Lee is guilty. She knows that if he were truly innocent, he would be raising the roof about his persecution, the denial of his rights, and the evils of the system, just as he had always done over the slightest perceived transgressions by others. His very docility in his predicament tells her more than he could ever say in words. There is also a certain tranquility about his personality. She remembers how tense he was after the failed attempt to shoot General Walker. Now he is altogether different. There seems to almost be a certain glow of satisfaction. As she watches him leave, it seems he is saying good-bye with his eyes.

The door shuts behind him and Marina starts crying.

Downstairs, the women are forced once again to run the gauntlet of reporters, some of them shouting questions in Russian.

"What did he say? What did your husband say?"

"Leave me alone, it is hard for me now," Marina wants to cry out. Instead, she maintains a stoical silence.[1134]

1:40 p.m.

Lee Oswald has just been returned to his cell when word comes from the Homicide and Robbery office to let him make any telephone calls he wishes. Assistant jailer Arthur E. Eaves and the patrolman assigned to the suicide watch, Buel T. Beddingfield, take Lee from his cell and lead him over to the telephone, which is in a booth.

"Who do you want to call?" the assistant jailer asks.

"New York City, collect," Oswald replies.

The jailer gets the City Hall operator on the line and tells her that the prisoner would like to call New York City collect. The jailer hands Oswald the phone and overhears Oswald call New York City, then place a local call, after which he is returned to his cell.[1135]

In Irving, Ruth Paine is out in the front yard with her children. She's thinking about doing some grocery shopping so that she'll be prepared to stay home and deal with the press and the police, who'll no doubt want to ask her questions. She's about to go inside when Dallas police detectives Rose, Stovall, Adamcik, and Moore arrive with Detective McCabe of the Irving Police Department. The men have a warrant signed by Judge Joe Brown Jr. and want to search the premises again.[1136]

She has no objection to the search but doesn't want to wait for them. They assure her that this time they are looking for something specific—the items Oswald keeps stored in the garage. Mrs. Paine takes them to the garage and shows them where the Oswalds kept their things.[1137]

"I want to go to the grocery store," she says. "I'll just go and you go ahead and do your searching."

As Mrs. Paine leaves, the detectives begin pawing through the Oswalds' effects that they missed in their first search the day before—two seabags, three suitcases, and two cardboard boxes of odds and ends. It doesn't take long before Detective Rose finds some things Marina would have surely destroyed or hidden had she known they existed.

"Look at this!" he says to the others, waving two negatives and a snapshot showing Oswald, dressed in black, holding a rifle that looks very much like the weapon found on the sixth floor of the Texas School Book Depository, the same photo Marina had been hiding from the authorities and trying to give to Marguerite. On Oswald's hip, a holstered pistol—probably, they assume, the gun he used to shoot Officer Tippit. A moment later, Detective McCabe finds the second snapshot that matches the other negative.[1138]

In the same cardboard carton Stovall finds a page torn from a magazine advertising weapons available from Klein's Sporting Goods in Chicago. One of the offerings is circled. It is for a Mannlicher-Carcano rifle.[1139]

That's not all the detectives find. They turn up some more interesting negatives, shots of a Selective Service card with something on the back of the negative to block out the space where the name would be typed in. Several prints made from the negatives were bundled with them. The resulting prints were, in effect, blank Selective Service cards.

The detectives immediately recognized them as identical to the false Selective Service card that Oswald had in his wallet in the name of "Alek James Hidell."[1140]

The detectives take their time combing through the rest of the inventory, careful not to overlook anything. It takes two and a half hours to complete the task. When they're finished, they cart everything off to their car. Mrs. Paine hasn't returned from her shopping trip, so they flip the latch, lock the front door, and head back toward Dallas City Hall.[1141]

2:05 p.m.

Captain Fritz emerges from the Homicide and Robbery office and wades into the newsmen, Chief Curry at his side. "Captain, can you give us a resume of what you now know concerning the assassination of the president and Mr. Oswald's role in it?" a television reporter asks.

"There is only one thing that I can tell you," Fritz replies in his gravely voice, "without going into the evidence before first talking to the district attorney. I can tell you that this case is cinched—that this man killed the president. There's no question in my mind about it."

"Well, what is the basis for that statement?" the reporter asks.

"I don't want to go into the basis," Fritz says. "In fact, I don't want to get into the evidence. I just want to tell you that we are convinced beyond any doubt that he did the killing."

"Was it spur-of-the-moment or a well-planned, long-thought-out plot?"

"I'd rather not discuss that," Fritz answers, "if you don't mind, please, thank you."

The homicide captain brushes the reporters aside and begins making his way toward the stairwell, near the elevators. A trail of reporters follow.

"Will you be moving him today, Captain? Is he going to remain here?"

"He'll be here today," Fritz finally answers, "yes, sir."[1142]

2:14 p.m.

Detective Jim Leavelle leads cabdrivers William Whaley and William Scoggins into the show-up room to view Oswald in a lineup. Whaley drove Oswald to his Oak Cliff apartment after the assassination, and Scoggins witnessed the shooting of Officer J. D. Tippit. In a moment they are joined by Detective C. N. Dhority and Assistant District Attorney Bill Alexander.[1143]

In the hallway just outside, Detectives Hall, Senkel, Potts, and Brown meet the fifth-floor jailers, who have brought Oswald and three other prisoners down in handcuffs. This time, Oswald is in the number 3 position.[1144] Oswald is complaining bitterly about not being allowed to put on a shirt over his T-shirt. A nearby NBC cameraman captures a snippet of Oswald badgering the jailers.

"I've been photographed in a T-shirt," Oswald is heard to say, "now they're taking me to a lineup among these men. Naturally, I will be picked out. Right?"[1145]

The detectives tug Oswald toward the stage entrance.

Inside the show-up room, the lights are dimmed as Detective Leavelle instructs Whaley and Scoggins to look over each man carefully. "If you recognize any of these men as the one you saw yesterday," Leavelle tells them, "just hold up the number of fingers that match the number over the man in the lineup."[1146] Oswald is belligerent, complaining in a loud voice as the prisoners are led out under the bright lights of the stage.

"It's not right to put me in line with these teenagers,"* Oswald cries. "I know what you're doing. You're trying to railroad me! I want my lawyer!"[1147]

Oswald shows no respect for the detectives around him, and tells them what he thinks of them. It matters little to Whaley, though. As soon as he sees Oswald, he knows he is the man he drove to Oak Cliff yesterday. When you drive a cab as long as Whaley has—thirty-seven years—you learn to judge people by looking them over very carefully. It's the way he's learned to determine whether he can trust them or not.

When Whaley saw Oswald's picture in the newspaper this morning, he recognized him immediately. Now, in the flesh, there is no doubt that Oswald is the man who got in his cab.[1148]

Leavelle asks each of the prisoners a question so that the witnesses can hear them speak, although Oswald is spared the procedure.[1149]

"Anybody up there look like the man you saw?" Leavelle asks Whaley.

"Yes, number 3, the man in the T-shirt," Whaley says. "That's him all right."[1150]

Detective Leavelle turns to Scoggins, who is holding up three fingers at his waist.[1151]

"Are you sure?" Leavelle asks.

"Well, he can bitch and holler all he wants," Scoggins says to Detective Leavelle, "but that's the man I saw running from the scene. Number 3."[1152]

The prisoners are taken away as Detectives Dhority and Assistant DA Alexander lead Whaley and Scoggins up to the third-floor Auto Theft office to take affidavits.[1153] Shortly after Oswald is returned to his cell, Bobby Brown of the Crime Scene Search Section of the Identification Bureau and Officer Jack Donahue come up to the fifth-floor jail. With Oswald's consent they obtain scrapings from under the fingernails of both of his hands and specimens of hair from his head, right armpit, chest, right forearm, pubic area, and right leg. The specimens are turned over to FBI special agent C. Ray Hall for comparison tests to be conducted at the FBI's Washington, D.C., crime lab.[1154]

2:25 p.m.

After their visit with Lee,[1155] Marguerite and Marina and her children climb into a squad car, which circles the city for twenty minutes to shake any members of the press who might be following them on their way back to the Hotel Adolphus. At the eleventh floor in the hotel, the police ask Tommy Thompson of *Life* for his credentials—something Marguerite realizes she hasn't thought to check herself. Satisfied of Thompson's bona fides, the police officers leave the Oswalds in his care. Thompson opens the door and lets Marguerite, Marina, and her children into the suite.

"Mrs. Oswald, what do you plan to do now?" Thompson says, turning to Marguerite.

Marguerite fears he is about to renege on his promise.

"Well," she reminds him, "the arrangement was that we are going to stay here in the hotel for a few days, and you are going to pay expenses."

"But you haven't given us any facts," Thompson shoots back.

Marguerite finds it strange that Thompson doesn't ask about her visit with Lee, even though he knew they left that morning to talk to him.

"Mrs. Oswald," Thompson continues, "reporters will be coming here in flocks. They know where you are . . . Just a minute."

---

*The three other young men in the lineup with Oswald, age twenty-four, were John Thurman Horne, seventeen; David Edmond Knapp, eighteen; and Daniel Gutierrez Lujan, twenty-six (7 H 200, WCT Walter Eugene Potts).

Thompson gets on the telephone and calls the ninth-floor room where the rest of *Life*'s representatives are staying.

"Come up here," he says into the phone.

In a few minutes, Allen Grant and another *Life* rep show up. Marguerite helps Marina change the baby's diaper while the men converse with Thompson in hushed tones. Thompson then tells Marguerite that they intend to move her and Marina to the outskirts of town, so reporters won't know where they are. "Here is some money," he tells her, "for your expenses in case you need anything." He gives her a fifty-dollar bill for expenses. She stuffs it into the pocket of her nurse's uniform without even looking at it. A few minutes later, Grant drives Marguerite, Marina, and the kids out to the Executive Inn, a hotel not far from Love Field.

"Mrs. Oswald," he says, "I've arranged for you to stay here for two or three days. I have to be back in San Francisco. Anything you want, you have the cash that Mr. Thompson gave you. He'll be in touch with you."

Grant and a porter escort the women and children up to the rooms—two very nice adjoining suites. Marguerite is pleased with the arrangements. It is only after Grant leaves that she begins to have misgivings about her predicament, stranded with a Russian daughter-in-law she barely understands and two small children. Marguerite orders room service and shoos Marina out of sight when the food comes, to avoid being recognized—they had, after all, been paraded in front of those television cameras up at City Hall.

Marguerite sees Marina hunched over an ashtray on the dressing table. Marina has torn up the photographs of Lee and his rifle that she's kept hidden in her shoe and thrown them into the ashtray. She strikes a match and sets the pieces on fire. But the heavy photographic paper doesn't burn very well. Marguerite decides to help and empties the remains into the toilet, flushing them away.[1156]

3:00 p.m.
With the help of Secret Service agent Mike Howard and his partner, Charley Kunkel, Robert Oswald has been trying to wrangle a visitor's pass to see his brother for the better part of two and a half hours, with little success. Agent Kunkel heads down the hall again to see what he can do.

Secret Service inspector Thomas J. Kelley comes into the Forgery Bureau a moment later and introduces himself. Howard explains to Kelley that Robert is being cooperative and answering any questions he can. The three men speculate as to whether Lee Oswald will admit anything to his brother when he sees him.

"I'm just as anxious as anyone to learn the reason behind the assassination," Robert tells them, "and to discover whether anyone else is involved."

Kelley sends Mike Howard down the hall to help Kunkel arrange the pass, then fights his way through the mob of reporters to retrieve some peanut-butter cookies and a soft drink for Robert from the machine at the end of the hall. It's thirty minutes before Kelley returns. He picks up the telephone and checks on the pass several times. Finally, he turns to Robert, "Okay, we've got it."[1157]

3:37 p.m.
Inspector Kelley, holding the pass signed by Captain Fritz, and a Dallas police officer take Robert Oswald upstairs in the elevator to the visiting room.[1158]

Inspector Kelley and the officer wait outside. For a moment Robert is alone in the stifling atmosphere of the room, the only sound that of the portable camera in the hands of a cameraman who plants himself in the doorway and, without saying a word to Robert, grinds away, collecting footage to sell to television.

Robert doesn't even hear the clank of the steel door, and Lee is almost at the smudged glass before Robert realizes he has come in. Lee points to the telephone on Robert's side of the transparent partition, as he picks up the one on his side. His voice is calm as he says, "This is taped."*

Robert realizes that Lee is warning him to be careful of what he says.

"Well, it may or may not be," Robert answers.

"How are you?" Lee asks evenly.

"I'm fine," Robert replies. "How are you?"

Robert is surprised at his brother's physical appearance. He knew about the scuffle in the theater but didn't know that Lee had sustained cuts and bruises. The liberally applied Mercurochrome makes it look worse than it is.

"What have they been doing to you?" Robert asks. "Were they roughing you up?"

"I got this at the theater," Lee says. "They haven't bothered me since. They're treating me all right."

Robert is astonished at how completely relaxed Lee is, as though the world's frenzied consternation over yesterday's events had nothing to do with him. Lee talks as if they're discussing a minor incident at the Depository. Robert doesn't know how long he's got to talk with Lee, but resists the temptation to ask the one question he wanted to ask most. Instead, they talk casually for a few minutes.

"Mother and Marina were up earlier," Lee says.

"Yes, I know," Robert replies.

"What did you think of the baby?" Lee asks with a grin.

"Yeah," Robert says, "thanks a lot for telling me. I didn't even know you had another one."

"Well, it was a girl," Lee says, "and I wanted a boy, but you know how that goes."

Finally, Robert can't resist anymore.

"Lee, what the Sam Hill is going on?" he asks bluntly.

"I don't know," Lee answers.

"You don't know?" Robert says, disbelieving. "Look, they've got your pistol, they've got your rifle, they've got you charged with shooting the president and a police officer. And you tell me you don't know? Now, I want to know just what's going on."

Lee stiffens, his facial expression suddenly becoming tight.

"Don't believe all this so-called evidence," he says firmly.

Robert studies his face, then his eyes, looking for some expression of the truth. Lee realizes what his brother wants.

"Brother, you won't find anything there," he says.

After an awkward silence, Lee, now more relaxed, mentions Marina again.

"Well, what about Marina?" Robert interrupts. "What do you think she's going to do now, with those two kids?"

"My friends will take care of them," he answers.

"You mean the Paines?"

"Yes," Lee replies, obviously surprised that his brother knew of them.

---

*Oswald's warning was unnecessary. Truth is, the visitors' telephones were not tape-recorded by the police (4 H 154, WCT Jesse E. Curry).

"I don't think they're any friends of yours," Robert tells him, revealing his distrust and suspicion.

"Yes, they are," Lee snaps back.

Another awkward silence.

"Junie needs a new pair of shoes," Lee finally says.

Robert had noticed yesterday that one of the little girl's shoes was practically worn through.

"Don't worry about that," Robert says sympathetically. "I'll take care of that."

Robert asks about the attorney, Mr. Abt, that Lee has been asking for.

"He's just an attorney I want to handle my case," Lee says.

"I'll get you an attorney down here," Robert answers.

"No, you stay out of it," Lee commands.

"Stay out of it?" Robert says, incredulously. "It looks like I've been dragged into it."

"Well, I'm not going to have anyone from down here," Lee says firmly. "I want this one."

"All right," Robert concedes.

A police officer suddenly enters the room behind Lee, taps him on the shoulder, then steps back and waits for them to finish. Robert is surprised and disappointed at the interruption. He feels that they were just beginning to talk easily with each other.

Robert hadn't expected his brother to flat-out admit his guilt. But he felt it was conceivable that Lee had made up his mind that the assassination was necessary for some reason that was sufficient to him, and that he would have wanted to make that motive clear to someone, and Robert felt that he was closer to Lee than anyone else in a lot of ways. He had hoped he would tell him. But he hasn't.

"I'll see you in a day or two," Robert says.

"You've got your job and everything," Lee replies. "Don't be running back and forth all the time and getting yourself in trouble with your boss."

"Don't worry about that," Robert tells him. "I'll be back."

"All right," Lee says. "I'll see you."

They are the last words Robert ever hears him say.[1159] Secret Service inspector Kelley is still waiting for Robert outside the visiting room.

"What did he say?" the inspector asks.

"Let's wait until we're downstairs," Robert replies, miffed that the persistent cameraman is still grinding away. It makes him feel like a zoo specimen. Back in the Forgery Bureau, and away from the prying ears of the news media, Robert tells Mike Howard and Inspector Kelley, "He didn't say anything because he said the line was tapped."

"If that were true," Kelley replies, "I wouldn't be asking you, would I?"

Robert can only shrug. Inspector Kelley asks Robert to reconstruct their conversation as carefully as he can, and Robert does exactly that. He is deeply unsatisfied by his brother's demeanor, which he found disturbingly machine-like, with an uncanny lack of emotion for a man in Lee's predicament, innocent or guilty. Robert was not talking to the brother he knew. The man in jail was a stranger to him.[1160]

3:51 p.m. (4:51 p.m. EST)

President Johnson, from the White House, issues a "Proclamation" which is "to the People of the United States," in which he calls John F. Kennedy "a man of wisdom, strength and peace" who "molded and moved the power of our nation in the service of a world of growing liberty and order. All who love freedom will mourn his death." Johnson proceeds to "appoint Monday next, November 25, the day of the funeral service of President

Kennedy, to be a day of national mourning throughout the United States," urging Americans to "assemble on that day in their respective places of divine worship."[1161] Other than an exhortation to go to one's place of worship, the proclamation, of course, is unnecessary, as the shock, grief, and tears of millions of Americans had not even begun to subside.

4:00 p.m.

Dallas police lieutenant Thurber Lord is the jail lieutenant in charge on the 2:30 p.m. to 10:30 p.m. shift on November 23. Around 4:00 p.m. he gets a call from Detective M. G. Hall of the Homicide and Robbery Bureau telling him that Oswald had requested permission to use the telephone again and that it would be okay for him to do so. Lord telephones Officer J. L. Popplewell on the fifth floor, where he had been assigned to guard the area in front of Oswald's cell.

Popplewell takes Oswald to the phone and Oswald tells the operator he wants to call Mr. John Abt, an attorney in New York. Oswald apparently didn't keep the number he had used earlier to call Abt because the operator looks up the number and gives it to him. Oswald hangs up, but can't remember the number he was just given. He asks Popplewell for a pencil and a piece of paper to write on. The officer tears a corner from a telephone contact slip and gives it to Oswald, along with a pencil. Oswald calls the operator again and this time writes down the number she gives him. He then tries to place the call collect, but there is no answer.[1162]

4:22 p.m.

After Oswald unsuccessfully attempts to reach attorney John Abt in New York City from the phone booth on the fifth floor of the jail, he places a local call. In Irving, the telephone rings at the home of Ruth Paine. She answers it.

"This is Lee," a voice says. She knows who it is—Lee Oswald.

"Well, hi!" she says, unable to hide the surprise in her voice that he would telephone her at all.

"I would like you to call Mr. John Abt in New York for me after six o'clock this evening," Oswald says. "I've got two numbers for you." Mrs. Paine grabs a nearby pencil and notepad. He gives her two telephone numbers—an office and a home number. Mrs. Paine quickly scribbles the numbers down.

"He's an attorney I would like to have represent me," Oswald tells her. "I would be grateful if you would call him for me."

She is very irritated by the fact that he sounds as if nothing out of the ordinary has happened. It seems to him, she feels, that this is a call like any other call, a favor like any other favor. He doesn't mention the assassination, the fact that he is in jail, or the reason he needs a lawyer. He seems so apart from the situation. Still, she agrees to make the call.

"Okay," Mrs. Paine manages to say.

Oswald thanks her and hangs up. The receiver is barely back in the cradle when the telephone rings again. Ruth answers it.

"Hi, this is Lee."

It's Oswald, calling back again. Mrs. Paine is stunned to hear Oswald repeat his request, nearly word for word. It all seems so strange to her.[1163]*

---

*Mrs. Paine attempted to reach attorney John Abt after six o'clock, as Oswald requested, but was unable to get an answer at either number. She testified that she could not recall if she conveyed the results of her efforts to Oswald during a subsequent conversation at 8:00 p.m. Saturday evening. Mrs. Paine made another attempt to reach Mr. Abt at home on Sunday morning, again without success. (3 H 88–89, WCT Ruth Hyde Paine)

5:45 p.m.

H. Louis Nichols, president of the Dallas Bar Association, trots up the concrete steps leading to City Hall. Nichols, a member of the American Bar Association since 1949, has been on and off the telephone since two o'clock this afternoon. He had gotten a call from the dean of an eastern law school who said that the media back there were reporting that Lee Oswald couldn't get a lawyer to represent him in Dallas and he wanted to know if Nichols was doing anything about the situation. Nichols acknowledged that he hadn't, but promised he would look into it. Under Texas law at the time, an attorney had to be appointed for an accused (if he didn't already have one) only after he had been indicted by a grand jury, which Oswald hadn't been yet. But if any defendant needed a lawyer immediately to make sure his rights were being protected, it was Oswald.

Nichols had worked in the city attorney's office, still represented the city's credit union, and has a brother on the police force, so he knows many of the top men there. He telephones the assistant police chief, Captain Glen King, who tells him that so far as he knows, Oswald hasn't asked for a lawyer.

"Well, Glen," Nichols says, "if you know at any time that he asks for a lawyer, or wants a lawyer, or needs a lawyer, will you tell him that you have talked to me? And that as president of the Bar Association, I have offered to get him a lawyer if he wants one?"

"Why don't you come down here and talk to him," King says.

"I don't know whether I want to do that at this point or not," Nichols replies.

Within an hour, Nichols got a call from another law school dean, questioning whether the Dallas Bar was doing anything about Oswald's right to an attorney. That was enough for Nichols, who decides he might as well go down and talk to Oswald directly.

The Dallas Bar Association president takes an elevator to the third floor, where he knows he'll find the Dallas police administrative offices. When the doors open, Nichols is flabbergasted to find an ocean of reporters and photographers stepping over and around a tangle of television cameras, cables, and electrical cords stretched out across the corridor. He pushes his way through the jam to the eastern end of the building and into Chief Curry's outer office. Nichols can see Chief Curry in his office talking with three or four men.

"Is Captain King in?" Nichols asks an officer standing nearby.

"I don't think so," the officer replies.

Just then, Chief Curry looks up, recognizes Nichols, and motions for him to come in. Nichols tells Curry why he is there.

"Well, I'm glad to see you," Curry says. "I'll take you up to see Oswald myself." They walk out into the hallway and take an elevator to the fifth floor.

The jailer opens the outer door of the maximum-security area of the fifth-floor jail and Nichols and Chief Curry step inside the narrow corridor. Oswald, in trousers and a T-shirt, is lying on his bunk. Oswald gets up as Curry asks the officer seated in the corridor to open Oswald's cell.

"Mr. Oswald," Curry says, "this is Louis Nichols, president of the Dallas Bar Association. He's come here to see whether or not you need or want a lawyer."

With that short introduction, Chief Curry steps back into the outer hallway, so that they can talk freely, without interference. Curry is far enough away that neither Nichols nor Oswald can see him from inside the cell.

Oswald sits back down on the edge of the bunk. Nichols takes a seat on the bunk across from him, three or four feet away.

"Do you have a lawyer?" Nichols begins.

"Well, I really don't know what this is all about," Oswald says. "I've been incarcerated and held incommunicado."

"It's my understanding that you're under arrest for the shooting of President Kennedy," Nichols tells him. "I'm here to see if you need or want a lawyer."

"Do you know a lawyer in New York named John Abt?" Oswald asks.

"No, I don't," Nichols says.

"Well, I would like to have him represent me," Oswald says in a calm and clear voice. "Do you know any lawyers who are members of the American Civil Liberties Union?"

"I'm sorry," Nichols says, "I don't know anybody who is a member of that organization."

"Well, I'm a member of that organization," Oswald says, "and if I can't get Mr. Abt, I would like to have somebody from that organization represent me."

Nichols can see that Oswald is in full control of his faculties. He is neither belligerent nor does he appear to be frightened or subdued.

"If I can't get either one of those to represent me," Oswald adds, "and if I can find a lawyer here who believes in my innocence . . ."

Oswald hesitates for a moment, then continues.

". . . as much as he can, I might let him represent me."

"What I am interested in knowing, Mr. Oswald," Nichols responds, "is do you want me or the Dallas Bar Association to try to get you a lawyer right now?"

"No, not now," Oswald replies. "I talked with members of my family this afternoon and they're trying to get in touch with Mr. Abt." Oswald adds, "You might come back next week and if I don't get some of these other people, I might ask you to get somebody to represent me."

Satisfied that Oswald knows what he is doing and is aware of his right to counsel, Nichols leaves the cell. As he and Curry climb back into the elevator for the ride back to the third floor, Curry asks if he wants to make a statement to the press.

"I don't know," Nichols says. "I don't know whether it's the thing to do or not."

"Well, they are going to be right outside the door here," Chief Curry warns him, "and if you want to say anything this would be an opportunity to do it." Curry adds, "Incidentally, I am very glad you came up here. We don't want any question coming up about us refusing to let him have a lawyer. That takes the burden off us."[1164]

6:15 p.m.
The elevator doors open and they step into a swarm of photographers and cameramen. When the media see who it is, they pack in closer. Chief Curry raises his voice above the ruckus.

"This is Mr. Nichols, president of the Dallas Bar Association," Curry announces. "He has been talking to Mr. Oswald and he will make a statement for you if he desires."

Flashbulbs pop and microphones are pushed toward Nichols's face as he suddenly finds himself on live television, wholly unprepared.

Nichols explains what has just transpired.

"Did he seem to be in possession of all his faculties? Did he deny the shooting to you?"

More questions follow until little can be understood. Nichols picks one out of the noise and answers.

"He appeared to be perfectly rational and I could observe no abnormalities about him at all in the short time that I visited with him," Nichols says.

"Do you know anything about John Abt?" someone asks.

"I don't know anything about him," Nichols says.

"How long did you talk with him?"

"About three minutes," Nichols replies.

"Do you think he can get a fair trial in Dallas?" a reporter asks skeptically.

"I think he can get a fair trial in Dallas," Nichols says with assurance.

"Would you be willing to represent him?" someone asks.

Nichols's answer is quick and direct.

"I do not practice criminal law," he says, "and I've never tried a criminal case so I don't know the answer to that."[1165]

Lieutenant Robert E. McKinney of the Forgery Bureau appears at the office of Justice of the Peace David Johnston in Richardson, Texas, with a criminal complaint ("Affidavit" number F-155) he's prepared and signed as an affiant charging Oswald with assault with intent to murder Governor John Connally. Johnston affixes his signature to the complaint and it is officially filed at 6:15 p.m.[1166] Oswald will never be arraigned on this charge.[1167]

Back in Homicide and Robbery, Captain Fritz picks up the telephone and calls the Identification Bureau on the fourth floor. "Have them bring those pictures down to my office," he orders.

They know what pictures he's talking about—the photographs of Oswald holding a rifle.

6:24 p.m.

Under orders from Captain Fritz, Detectives Sims, Hall, and Graves escort Oswald down from his jail cell to the Homicide and Robbery office for another interrogation session. Once again, Oswald is marched through the third-floor corridor. He's getting good at playing to the crowd of reporters, using their microphones to take jabs at the police department and build sympathy. This time he complains about being denied "the basic fundamental hygienic rights like a shower."[1168]

The smirk quickly evaporates from Oswald's face as he's brought into the homicide captain's office. Three homicide detectives in white Stetson hats stand guard, silently.[1169] Fritz walks in, followed by Secret Service inspector Thomas Kelley, FBI agent James Bookhout, and homicide detective Guy Rose, who is carrying an envelope.

Oswald immediately complains about not being allowed in the last lineup to put on clothing similar to that worn by some of the other individuals in previous lineups.[1170] No one says anything. The hostile prisoner braces himself for another onslaught of questions, but Fritz begins slowly with a methodical list of mundane questions designed to relax and settle Oswald down. Oswald is eager to talk about anything that doesn't pertain to the assassination investigation and eventually softens with the gentle banter. Soon, Oswald is rambling on about how life is better for the colored people in Russia than it is in the United States.[1171] Finally, Fritz turns to the business at hand.

"Now, you told me yesterday that you'd never owned a gun," Fritz says innocently.

"That's right," Oswald replies. "I never owned a gun."

"Okay," Fritz says, reaching for the envelope Detective Rose has laid on his desk. "I want to show you something."

Oswald purses his lips and eyes the envelope the captain is reaching into. Like Houdini pulling a rabbit out of a hat, Fritz suddenly produces an eight-by-ten-inch black-and-white photograph and holds it out in front of Oswald.

"How do you explain this?" he says.

The photograph is an enlargement of one found earlier in the afternoon among Oswald's possessions stored in Mrs. Paine's garage. After returning to City Hall, and showing it to Captain Fritz, Detective Rose has been working with officers in the Identification Bureau to produce this slightly cropped blowup.[1172] Everyone present can see that Oswald is flustered.

"I'm not going to make any comment about that without the advice of an attorney," Oswald replies smugly.[1173]

"Well, is that your face in the picture?" Fritz asks, pointing at the image.

"I won't even admit that," he sneers.[1174]

"That's not your face?" Fritz asks, scarcely believing that Oswald would deny what is so obvious.

"No," Oswald says. "*That's not even my face*. That's a fake. I've been photographed a number of times since I got here—first by the police, and now every time I get dragged through that hallway. Someone has taken *my picture* and put *my face* on a different body."

"So that *is* your face?" Fritz asks.

Oswald answers quickly to cover his own contradiction.

"Yes, that's my face," he says, "but that's not my body. I know all about photography, I've worked with photography a long time. Someone has photographed me and then superimposed a rifle in my hand and a gun in my pocket. That's a picture that someone has made. I've never seen that picture before in my life."[1175]

Fritz lays the photograph on his desk.

"We found this photo in Mrs. Paine's garage, among your effects," Fritz tells him.

Oswald rolls his eyes toward the ceiling.

"*That* picture has never been in my possession," he snaps.

"Wait a minute," Fritz shoots back, "I'll show you one you probably have seen."

The captain reaches back into the envelope and pulls out a small snapshot, the original photograph used to produce the enlargement. He shows it to Oswald, who squirms.

"I never have seen that picture either," he says, defiantly. "That picture's been reduced from the big one."[1176]

Fritz asks him how that's so, and Oswald gets into a long argument with Fritz about his knowledge of photography, asking Fritz a number of times whether the smaller photograph was made from the larger or whether the larger was made from the smaller.

"We made this enlargement from the snapshot we found in the search," Fritz finally acknowledges.

"Well, I understand photography real well," Oswald says arrogantly, "and at the proper time I will show that they're fakes. Right now, I have nothing more to say about them."[1177]

7:00 p.m.

In the third-floor corridor outside, reporters scramble toward Chief Curry, who is about to make a statement. He waits for everyone to settle down.

"The FBI has just informed us," Chief Curry begins, "that they have the order letter for the rifle that we have sent to the laboratory. They . . . received it from a mail-order house in Chicago. This order letter has been to the laboratory in Washington, D.C., and compared with known handwriting of our suspect, Oswald, and the handwriting is the

same on the order letter as Oswald's handwriting. The return address on this order letter was to the post office box in Dallas, Texas, of our suspect, Oswald, and it was returned
under another name. But it has definitely been established by the FBI that the handwriting is the handwriting of Oswald."

The reporters shout questions at once. One can be heard clearly above the others.

"Was it a recent purchase?"

"This purchase was made on March the twentieth of this year," Curry tells them.

"What about the ballistics test, Chief?"

"The ballistic test—we haven't had a final report, but it is—I understand [it] will be
favorable," Curry replies.

"Is this the development you referred to today as making this case ironclad in your
opinion?"

"This was not what I had reference to earlier," Curry says.

"Will you give us an indication of what that is?" a reporter shouts. "Were you referring to the photograph earlier?"

The media are already aware of the photographs of Oswald holding a rifle found by
police in Mrs. Paine's garage. Curry doesn't have time to answer the question before
another is shouted out.

"Where did these photographs come from, Chief?" a newsman asks.

"The photographs were found in his—out at Irving, where he had been staying and
where his wife had been staying," Curry says.

"Does [the rifle in the photograph] look like the one that you have, that you think is
the murder weapon, sir?"

"It does," Curry responds.

"How is he taking this information as it builds up?" someone asks.

"I don't know," Curry says.

"Chief, just a moment ago he came out . . . bitterly complaining about being deprived
of his citizenship rights because he can't take a shower. Do you have any comment on
that?"

"I didn't know he had asked to take a shower," Curry says. "We have a shower up there
where he could take a shower if he wants one."

"What was the name under which he ordered the rifle?" a reporter asks.

"The name—the return—the name on the return address was A. Hidell," Curry tells
them.

"Do you consider the case shut tight now, Chief?"

"We will continue to work on it," Curry replies, "and try to get every shred of evidence that's possible."[1178]

The chief's statements set off alarm bells at FBI headquarters. FBI Director J. Edgar
Hoover can't believe that Curry is willing to give the press details about the evidence
against Oswald. Curry's comments are being broadcast nationally, and Hoover doesn't
think that cases should be tried in the newspapers. The bureau has a policy of "no comment" until it has a warrant and makes an arrest. Then a release is prepared, briefly stating the facts of the case and the charges. The details of the evidence are kept secret until
the case goes to trial. The kind of information Curry is blabbing about would never,
under any circumstances, be given out to the press by the FBI. Hoover is particularly

incensed that Curry is talking about evidence that is being developed in the FBI's Washington, D.C., crime lab. Hoover gets Gordon Shanklin, agent-in-charge in Dallas, on the phone.

"Talk to Chief Curry," Hoover tells Shanklin, "and tell him that I insist that he not go on the air any more and discuss the progress of the investigation."

Hoover has little direct authority over the Dallas police chief. The FBI crime lab furnishes free service to all law enforcement agencies throughout the country. What they do with the FBI's lab reports, once they've received them, is their business. But because of the fact that President Lyndon Johnson has asked Hoover to take charge of the case, Hoover feels justified in asking Curry to abide by his wishes.

"You tell him," Hoover adds, "that I insist that he and all members of his department refrain from public statements!"[1179]

The IBM computers at the U.S. Postal Records Center in Alexandria, Virginia, have been humming for nearly seven hours now (though state-of-the-art at the time, these computers are a far cry from today's technology) searching for the original money order used to purchase the assassination weapon. There's no telling how many man-hours it might take to do a manual search.

Suddenly, a match is found, and the money order is located.

The center rushes the original money order by special courier to the chief of the Secret Service in Washington. A handwriting analysis by a questioned-documents expert for the Department of the Treasury shows that the handwriting on the money order is that of Lee Harvey Oswald.[1180]

If there is one thing that is now unquestionably certain, it is that Lee Harvey Oswald ordered and paid for the Mannlicher-Carcano rifle that was found on the sixth floor of the Texas School Book Depository Building shortly after the assassination.

7:10 p.m.
Secret Service inspector Thomas Kelley is very impressed by Captain Fritz, who has shown great patience and tenacity in his efforts to uncover the truth from Oswald about the rifle photographs. But Oswald remains arrogant and uncooperative. Fritz asks Oswald about some of the places where he's lived, trying to get him to admit where the pictures were taken. Oswald tells him about one of the places he lived in Dallas, but is very evasive when Fritz questions him about living on Neely Street.[1181]

"You never lived there?" Fritz asks.

"No!" Oswald says, defiantly.

"You didn't take any photographs there?" Fritz persists.

"No!" Oswald snaps back.

"I've got statements from people* who say they visited you when you lived there," Fritz tells him.

"They must be mistaken," Oswald answers.[1182]

Fritz can only shake his head in frustration. It is apparent to everyone that Oswald, though shaken by the photographic evidence, has no intention of furnishing any more

---

*Michael Paine had told Fritz that he and Ruth had visited the Oswalds when they lived on Neely Street. Fritz later determined that the photographs were taken in the backyard at Neely. (CE 2003, 24 H 268)

information about the rifle pictures. After forty-five minutes of trying to pull impacted teeth to get answers, Captain Fritz orders Oswald returned to his cell.[1183]

7:15 p.m.
Detectives Hall, Sims, Graves, and Boyd lead a very hostile Oswald into the bright news lights basking the third-floor hallway.[1184] A reporter yells, "Here he comes!" to his colleagues as a live television camera swings around and zooms in on the T-shirt–clad Oswald. Newsmen rush toward him, arms outstretched, microphones searching for a brief statement.

"Did you fire that rifle?" a reporter shouts.

Oswald is smoldering, his voice finally exploding in anger.

"I don't know what dispatches you people have been given," he roars, "but I emphatically deny these charges!"

The officers pull him sharply through a doorway into the vestibule of the jail elevator, and out of sight of the live television audience.

"What about Connally?" a newsman hollers, shoving his microphone into the doorway.

Like Dr. Jekyll and Mr. Hyde, another persona seems to slip under Oswald's skin as his anger suddenly gives way to a gentler side.

"I have nothing against anybody," he says, his voice returning to its usual calm state. "I have not committed any acts of violence."[1185]

7:20 p.m.
Marguerite Oswald is in her robe and slippers when there is a knock on the door of the suite at the Executive Inn, where she and Marina are staying.

"Who is it?" Marguerite says, moving toward the door.

"This is Mr. Odum," a voice responds.

She opens the door a crack to see two FBI agents. They are wet from the pouring rain.

"Mrs. Oswald," Agent Bardwell Odum says, "I would like to see Marina."

She peers at him through her heavy, black-framed glasses, the door barely open.

"Mr. Odum, we're awfully tired," she says.

"I just want to show her a photograph," Odum replies.

"She's completely exhausted," Marguerite pleads. "I am not calling my daughter-in-law to the door. As a matter of fact, she's taking a bath."

Marina isn't really in the bathtub. Marguerite will say anything right now to get rid of the FBI men.

"Mrs. Oswald," Odum says, "let me ask you a question then."

"Yes, sir."

Odum holds up his hand to the crack in the door. Cupped in his palm is a glossy black-and-white photograph, its corners carefully trimmed with a pair of shears. It's the image of an unknown individual, originally thought to be Oswald, leaving the Soviet embassy in Mexico City in early October 1963. Only the head and shoulders of the man are visible in the photo. The FBI knows that it's not Oswald, but they wonder if it could be an accomplice.

"Do you recognize this individual?" he asks.

Marguerite looks at the photo briefly through the crack in the door.

"No, sir, believe me," she says.

The rain pelts the ground around the two men. Odum lowers his hand.

"Thank you," he says, as she closes the door.[1186]

7:46 p.m. (8:46 p.m. EST)

ABC commentator Chet Huntley announces that "all the personal effects of the late president have now been removed from the White House."[1187]

8:00 p.m.

In Irving, Ruth Paine answers the phone and hears Lee Oswald say in Russian, "Marina, please." That's the opening phrase he normally uses when he wants to speak to his wife, and he's used it on many occasions.

"She's not here," Mrs. Paine replies, in English.

Oswald is clearly irritated that his wife is not available to speak with him.

"Where is she?" he asks, an edge to his voice.

"I've got an idea where she might be, but I'm not at all certain," Ruth answers. "I'll try to find out." She doesn't tell Lee, but earlier today, while FBI agent Bardwell Odum was at her home, she overheard Odum talking on the telephone to the *Life* magazine people staying at the Hotel Adolphus. He was trying to find out where Marina was staying and she heard him say, "Executive Inn," and saw him jot it down. She thinks that Marina may be there.

"Tell her she should be at your house," Oswald says tersely.

"I'll try to reach her and give her your message," Mrs. Paine answers.

Oswald hangs up. Mrs. Paine had been waiting to hear from Marina since she left that morning. She had no intention of attempting to reach her. She felt that if Marina wanted to talk to her, she would call. Of course, she was hurt that Marina hadn't called or made any attempt to contact her. But now that Lee is trying to reach Marina, Ruth Paine decides to make the first move. She telephones the Executive Inn and asks the hotel operator to speak to Tommy Thompson, the *Life* representative. There is a short pause, then a female voice answers, "Hello?" It's Marguerite Oswald.

"Hello, this is Ruth Paine. I'd like to talk to Marina."

There is no love lost between Mrs. Paine and Oswald's mother, who is suspicious of Ruth and her husband.

"Marina's in the bathroom," Marguerite tells her.

"Lee called me," Mrs. Paine tells her, "and he wanted me to deliver a message to Marina."

"Yes?"

"He wants me to contact an attorney for him," Ruth says, "and he was very upset that Marina was not at my house."

"Well, he is in prison," Marguerite replies callously. "He don't know the things we are up against, the things that we have to face. What he wants doesn't really matter."

Ruth is shocked that Marguerite doesn't have any respect for Lee's wishes.

"Please let me speak to Marina," Ruth asks.

Marguerite finally relinquishes control of the telephone to her daughter-in-law. Mrs. Paine repeats Lee's message to her, in Russian. Marina only says that she is very tired and wants to get to bed. Ruth agrees that it's best that she stay at the hotel tonight. Ruth is disappointed that Marina doesn't tell her what she plans to do tomorrow.

"Did you see Lee today?" Ruth asks.

"Yes, around noon," Marina says.

It's obvious she doesn't want to talk, so Mrs. Paine says good-bye and hangs up.[1188]

Marguerite asks Marina what Mrs. Paine said, but Marina doesn't answer her. Marguerite's suspicions escalate and she begins to imagine that everyone is working against her. She begins to wonder how Mrs. Paine knew where they were staying? What did she say to Marina that caused Marina to withdraw and not want to tell her what Mrs. Paine said? In her conspiratorial mindset, FBI agent Odum's earlier visit and insistence on seeing Marina, and Mrs. Paine's call are somehow tied together. And whatever these people are up to, it's no good.[1189]

On the third floor of City Hall, reporters approach Assistant Police Chief Charles Batchelor outside the administrative offices. They are hungry and want to go out to dinner, but they don't want to miss anything if the Dallas police decide to move the prisoner to the county jail. Just then, Chief Curry walks up.

"How about it, Chief?" they ask. "Are you going to move Oswald tonight?"

"No," he tells them. "It probably will be in the morning."

"When?" they want to know.

"I think if you fellows are back here by ten o'clock in the morning you won't miss anything," Curry says.

With that, the newsmen head out for dinner. Curry decides he'd better double-check with Captain Fritz to see when he plans to transfer Oswald. He walks down the hall to Fritz's office.[1190]

Fritz doesn't think it's a good idea to transfer Oswald at night. An attacker could use the cover of darkness to his benefit and hinder the police from preventing trouble. Fritz suggests they wait until daylight. Besides, Fritz would like to question Oswald again in the morning.

"Okay," Curry says. "What time do you think you will be ready tomorrow then?"

"I don't know exactly when, Chief," Fritz answers.

"Do you think about ten o'clock?" Curry suggests. "I need to tell these people something definite."

Fritz nods his head.

"I believe so," he replies.[1191]

Curry returns to his office and tells Assistant Chief Batchelor of the plans. Then Curry decides that he might as well make an announcement to the press in the corridor. Otherwise, they'll be there all night.[1192] Once again, Chief Curry steps into the crowd of reporters gathered in the third-floor hallway and tells them that Oswald will be transferred to the sheriff's office tomorrow. "If you men would be here by no later than ten o'clock in the morning . . . that will be early enough."

"Are you through with him for the night, sir?" someone asks.

"Captain Fritz says he is finished with him unless possibly some witness might show up that we needed to bring him out for a show-up," Curry says. "But, I think—I don't believe there will be any more questioning tonight."

Someone wants to know what progress has been made toward a confession in the assassination.

"I don't think we've made any progress toward a confession," Curry replies.

"You don't think so?"

"No," Curry answers firmly.

"Why are you so pessimistic about a confession?"

"Well," Curry says with a smile, "you know we've been in the business a good while—"

Laughter ripples through the crowd of reporters.

"—and sometimes," Curry continues, "you can sort of draw your own conclusions after talking to a man over a period of time. Of course he might have a change of heart but I'd be rather surprised if he did."

Someone asks why Oswald's mother and wife were at police headquarters today. The chief says they visited Oswald and are attempting to get in contact with his attorney, John Abt, out of New York.

"Has anyone heard anything from Abt?" a reporter asks.

"Well, it's hearsay with me," Curry responds, "and I don't know who said this but somewhere back in the office someone said that they understood John Abt did not want to handle the case."*

"Chief, will you transfer him under heavy guard?"

"I'll leave that up to Sheriff Decker," Curry says. "That's his responsibility."

"The sheriff takes custody of him here?" someone asks.

"Yes," Curry answers.† "That's all I have, gentlemen, thank you."

A chorus of thank-yous follows the chief as he retreats down the hall for the night.[1193]

Sunday, November 24

12:00 midnight

The press having been told they could go home for the night without missing anything, the pressroom at Dallas City Hall has been nearly deserted for two hours.[1194] Only two reporters—*Dallas Times Herald* reporter Darwin Payne and the longtime police beat reporter for the *Dallas Morning News*, Johnny Rutledge—remain to cover the late shift, their normal assignment.

The telephone rings. It's the *Times Herald* news editor Charles F. Dameron asking for Payne, who takes the phone. Dameron has heard that Dan Rather was on WCBS radio saying that the Dallas Police Department had an eyewitness in protective custody who could identify Oswald as the one who pulled the trigger in the Book Depository. Dameron wants to know if there's any truth to the vague report.

"I'm not sure," Payne says in a whisper, afraid his competition might overhear him.

"Find out," Dameron commands.

Payne hangs up and eyes Rutledge sitting quietly across the room. Payne can't help but think that the *Dallas Morning News* already has the story wrapped up and is going to run it as a big banner in the morning paper. How would that make the *Times* look? Darwin Payne has only been at the newspaper three months, but he knows one thing. He *has* to get that story.

Payne slips out of the pressroom and runs down the night-watch commander. He says it might be true, but he doesn't know anything about it. Payne scrounges around a bit more, but comes up empty-handed.[1195]

---

*Abt testified that he told reporters who called him at his cabin in the Connecticut woods, where he had gone to spend the weekend, that "if I were requested to represent him, it would probably be difficult, if not impossible, for me to do so because of my commitments to other clients." Abt said he was never contacted directly by Oswald or any member of his family. (10 H 116)

†Normally, except in rare instances, men from Sheriff Decker's office handle the transfer of prisoners between the city and county jails. Decker testified that the city police handle "maybe one-tenth of maybe 1 percent" of the transfers (12 H 45).

1:00 a.m.

With the deadline for the final edition rapidly approaching, Darwin Payne, desperate, calls his office. He has no details to report to Dameron. They confer briefly and decide that Payne should call Chief Curry at home. Payne hates the thought of waking the chief, who surely is in bed at this hour. Dameron gives Payne the police chief's home telephone number anyway.

"Call him," Dameron says.

When the telephone rings, Curry's wife answers, obviously awakened from a sound sleep.

"Yes," she mumbles, "I'll give you the chief."

In a second or two, Curry comes on the line, half-asleep. Payne tries to explain to him the information he has and asks if the story is true or not? Curry is nearly incoherent, mumbling softly as if he's in a dream. The reporter frantically scribbles down notes, hoping to make sense of them later. Finally, he gives up trying to make Curry understand and hangs up. Payne's notes are useless. The frustrated reporter is forced to telephone his boss and report that he is unable to confirm the story.[1196]*

The chief of police rolls over and drifts back into a deep sleep. His wife knows just how exhausted he feels. There's been a constant barrage of phone calls since he came home. She reaches over and takes the telephone off the hook so that she and her husband can get a much-needed night of uninterrupted sleep.[1197]

2:30 a.m.

FBI security patrol clerk Vernon R. Glossup receives a telephone call while working the night desk at the Dallas FBI office.

"I would like to talk to the man in charge," a male voice says calmly.

"The special agent-in-charge is not in at the present time," Glossup answers. "Is there someone else that could help you?"

"Just a minute," the anonymous caller says. There is a brief pause, and Glossup is under the impression, though he can't be sure, that the caller hands the telephone to someone else. A second, more mature-sounding voice speaks next.

"I represent a committee that is neither right nor left wing," the man says, "and tonight, tomorrow morning, or tomorrow night we are going to kill the man that killed the president. There will be no excitement and we will kill him. We wanted to be sure to tell the FBI, police department, and sheriff's office. We will be there and we will kill him."

The caller hangs up.

Glossup immediately notifies FBI special agent Milton L. Newsom and quickly prepares a memorandum on the call.[1198]

3:00 a.m.

FBI agent Newsom telephones the Dallas County sheriff's office to advise them of the call, only to learn from Deputy Sheriff C. C. McCoy that he too got such a call. The message was nearly identical except that the anonymous caller said that he represented a group

---

*There actually was no person in protective custody as described in the story. Darwin Payne later stated that the report may have been a distorted reference to Howard Brennan, who had been assured by police that he and his home would be under surveillance by law enforcement. (Hlavach and Payne, *Reporting the Kennedy Assassination*, p.94)

of around one hundred people "who have voted to kill the man who killed the president." The caller said they were advising the sheriff's office because they didn't want any of the deputies to get hurt, but that they were going to kill Oswald anyway. The two lawmen shift into action. Newsom tells McCoy that he'll contact the Dallas police and let them know what's going on. Meanwhile, McCoy calls Sheriff Decker at his home and informs him of the threats they've received.

"Call in a pair of our supervisory personnel," Decker orders, "and have them stand by at the office in case the Dallas police decide to transfer Oswald tonight."[1199]

3:20 a.m.

Captain William B. Frazier, the senior man on duty at the Dallas Police Department, takes the call from FBI agent Newsom.[1200] Informed of the threats, Frazier tells Newsom that the Dallas police haven't received any threatening calls at the department. He will, however, notify his superiors and the FBI will be advised of any change in the transfer plans.[1201]

5:15 a.m.

Nearly two hours later, Frazier calls the apartment of homicide captain Will Fritz, a notorious early riser. Frazier relates the threatening calls, but Fritz reminds him that Chief Curry is handling the particulars of the transfer and that he should be contacted directly.[1202]

A few minutes later, Deputy Sheriff McCoy telephones the Dallas Police Department and tells Captain Frazier that Sheriff Decker would like Chief Curry to call him as soon as possible about the transfer plans, adding that Decker thinks the police should transfer Oswald immediately to the county jail.[1203]

6:00 a.m.

Frazier telephones Chief Curry's residence but is unable to get through. He continues to ring the line for the next fifteen minutes, with no success. Finally, Frazier calls the telephone operator and asks her to check the phone to see if a conversation is in progress or if the line is out of order. The operator calls back in a few minutes and tells him that the telephone is out of order.[1204]

6:15 a.m.

By now, the second shift is beginning to arrive at City Hall, including Platoon Captain C. E. Talbert, who is scheduled to relieve Captain Frazier. Before going off duty, Frazier tells Talbert of the overnight threats and his repeated attempts to contact Chief Curry. Talbert immediately calls the assistant chief of police, Charles Batchelor, and informs him of the threat and the fact that they can't raise Curry on the telephone. Batchelor instructs Talbert to send a squad car over to Curry's house and wake him. Not long thereafter, officers are pounding on the chief's front door to tell him of the death threats against Oswald.[1205]

6:30 a.m.

Captain Fritz's homicide team, the big, taciturn Texans in sober, off-the-rack suits and obligatory Stetsons who are the top drawer on the force and operate on their own time schedule, are also on the job early. Detective E. R. Beck arrives at 6:30, getting there even before the indefatigable and early-rising Captain Fritz. C. W. Brown gets in at seven. Most of the crew is in well before nine.[1206]

7:28 a.m.

Captain Talbert telephones the Dallas FBI office and informs Special Agent Newsom that the police chief has been advised of the threat against Oswald and that Curry expects to be in the office sometime between eight and nine o'clock this morning.

"What about the transfer plans?" the FBI agent asks.

"Well, I don't know," Talbert tells him. "But personally I don't think there'll be any effort to sneak Oswald out of the city jail. We want to maintain good relations with the press and right now extensive coverage has been set up to cover the transfer. I don't think that Chief Curry will want to cross the media."[1207]

8:00 a.m.

Marguerite Oswald is up early at the Executive Inn near Love Field. She has been worried all night. She and Marina haven't heard from the *Life* representatives since they arranged their suite at the inn. Marguerite feels stranded, alone in a strange motel with a Russian daughter-in-law and two babies. She wonders whom she can call for help. She doesn't want to call Mrs. Paine, a woman she has no use for. Nor does she want to telephone Robert, who is clear out in Boyd, Texas, at his farm.[1208] Instead, she remembers Peter Gregory, a Fort Worth petroleum engineer who taught Russian language classes at the library. Gregory was a Russian émigré who came to the United States in 1923 to attend the University of California.[1209]

About three weeks ago Marguerite read an advertisement in the Fort Worth newspaper announcing that free Russian classes were being offered at the public library beginning November 12. Although she had not heard from either Lee or Marina for nearly a year, she hoped in her heart that they would contact her some day, and she thought the instruction might help her communicate with her daughter-in-law. As it turned out, her car broke down just one block from the library before the second class started—just three days ago—and had to be towed. She walked to the class, and Gregory, when he found out that she lived only about ten blocks from his house, kindly drove her home.[1210]

Marguerite approaches Marina, who is up with the babies.

"Marina," Marguerite says, "we need help, honey. I am going to call Mr. Gregory."

She tells Marina about taking Russian language lessons.

"Oh, Mama," Marina exclaims, "I know Mr. Gregory. Lee know Mr. Gregory."[1211]

Marguerite had no idea that Lee and Marina had already met Peter Gregory, Lee having gone to Gregory's office in June of 1962 seeking his help in getting a job as a Russian translater or interpreter. She thinks it's a terribly odd coincidence that they already know him, but feels that somehow her guardian angel is guiding her actions.[1212] She picks up the telephone, gives a fictitious name to the hotel operator, and has her dial Mr. Gregory's residence.

"Mr. Gregory, I can't say who I am," she tells him when he answers, "but you know my son and you know my daughter-in-law, and I am in trouble, sir."

"I'm sorry," Mr. Gregory says, "but I won't talk to anybody I don't know."

"I would rather not tell you who I am," she replies, "but I shall identify myself by saying I am one of the students in the Russian class in the library."[1213]

Mr. Gregory recognizes the voice of Mrs. Oswald.

"You know my son real well," she adds.

Gregory realizes for the first time who the woman caller is.

"Oh, you are Mrs. Oswald," he says, sitting up in bed.

"Mr. Gregory, I need your help," she confesses. "The reporters, the news media are badgering me."

This is a lie, of course. But Marguerite has learned to twist the truth to suit her own ends.

"My daughter-in-law Marina and I are at the Executive Inn in Dallas, stranded," she continues. "I wonder if some of your friends, or you, could provide a place for me to hide from them."

To Peter Gregory, it sounds as if Marguerite is crying on the telephone, although he finds it hard to believe that Mrs. Oswald cries easily. Still, he's not entirely unsympathetic.

"I'll tell you what I will do, Mrs. Oswald," Gregory says. "You stay where you are and I promise you that I will come to see you sometime today."[1214]

In fact, Peter Gregory already knows where Marina and Marguerite Oswald are. Secret Service agent Mike Howard had called him on Saturday and asked him to come out to the Executive Inn and translate an interview with Marina. He hadn't done it because it turned out that his services weren't necessary—the interview didn't take place.

As soon as Gregory hangs up the telephone, he calls Agent Howard, who lives just north of Fort Worth, and reports his conversation with Mrs. Oswald.

"Well, that's fine," Howard tells Gregory, "we'll find a hiding place for Marguerite and Marina Oswald and the babies." He offers to come by Gregory's house in forty-five minutes to an hour or so and they can go over to the Executive Inn together.[1215]

8:05 a.m.

Chief Curry pulls his car into the basement garage at City Hall, parks, and heads for the elevators that'll take him upstairs to his office, where he meets Assistant Police Chief Charles Batchelor and the assistant police chief in charge of investigations, M. W. Stevenson, to discuss the Oswald death threats, the word of which had spread quickly through the police department. The men discuss security precautions that might thwart such an attempt. They even discuss the possibility that a detective or some police officer might be so emotionally charged that he tries to make some move against Oswald. They agree that the men assigned to the basement security detail should be men they know to be emotionally stable.[1216]

8:17 a.m. (9:17 a.m. EST)

Cardinal Cushing, presiding over a pontifical mass in Boston, says, "The world stands helpless at the [president's] death." He speaks of the "unprecedented sorrow" and that "millions lament in a silence which will never be broken."[1217]

9:00 a.m.

Detective Jim Leavelle, along with Detectives Dhority and Brown, has already run over to the Statler Hilton Hotel after receiving a tip from the hotel security officer that a man who said he represented a California munitions company had checked in. The detectives determine very quickly that there is nothing to be concerned with. Such is the tension and concern in Dallas this Sunday morning.[1218]

The Dallas police may believe Oswald is the ultimate scum, but they have to make sure he is protected so he can stand trial for murdering the nation's president.

Across town, Postal Inspector Harry Holmes pulls up in front of a church with his wife and daughter. All the way there, Holmes has been thinking about the whirlwind of events that have driven him to near exhaustion. On the seat next to him is a folder with the postal documents he's been busy gathering on Oswald all weekend. He figures on running them over to Captain Fritz later that day. As his wife and daughter climb from the car, Holmes suddenly has a change of heart.

"You know, I think I'll run down and see if I can help Captain Fritz with anything," he tells his wife. She knows that look in his eye, and she knows there's no use talking to him about why he should spend Sunday with his family at church services. She agrees to find a ride home with friends. Holmes spins the family car around and heads downtown.[1219]

9:10 a.m.
At Dallas police headquarters, Chief Curry calls Captain Fritz's office and asks when he'll be ready to have Oswald transferred.

"We'll be talking to him shortly," Fritz says. "I suppose we'll be ready around ten o'clock."[1220]

"Fine," Curry says. He hangs up and dials Sheriff Decker. The two decide that since the Dallas Police Department is investigating the case and also has a lot more manpower, it would be better to depart from protocol and have the police, rather than Decker's boys, transport Oswald to the county jail.[1221]

Curry hangs up the telephone, tells Deputy Chief Stevenson and Assistant Chief Batchelor that their office will be moving Oswald, and asks, "What do you think about getting an armored truck?"

"I think I know where I can get one," Batchelor replies, telling Curry that he knows the vice president of Armored Motor Car Service, an outfit that serves the Fort Worth–Dallas area. Curry nods his approval. The three discuss a possible route and settle on leaving the jail office in the basement* via the Commerce Street exit ramp, taking Commerce to the Central Expressway, north on Central to Elm, west on Elm to Houston, and south on Houston to the entrance to the county jail. It's decided that Chief Curry's car will lead the caravan, followed by a car of detectives, the armored car, another car of detectives, and Batchelor and Stevenson in the rear car.[1222]

Batchelor returns to his third-floor office and looks up the home number of the armored car company's vice president, Harold Fleming, in the city directory. When the phone rings, Fleming is shaving, getting ready for church. Batchelor makes a pitch for the use of an armored truck.[1223] Fleming replies that he has two that he can send down— one large, one small—and the police can take their pick once they see them.

"I'll need them here about ten o'clock," Batchelor says.

"I'll call you as soon as I can arrange a couple of drivers," Fleming responds.[1224]

Downstairs, in the police garage, Captain Cecil Talbert notices a crowd beginning to build just outside the Commerce Street exit, apparently in anticipation of the transfer. To avoid the chaos of a last-minute security check, Talbert, who is a captain of a patrol division and not assigned to any security detail for Oswald's transfer, takes the initiative to begin securing the basement area of City Hall against anyone or anything that could pose a threat to Oswald. He orders Lieutenant Rio S. Pierce to pull three squads from each of the three outlying police substations and four from the central station; then, using

---

*There are two jail offices in the police building, one in the basement next to the parking area, the other on the fourth floor.

two-man squads, they are to search the basement area, clear it, and keep it cleared of everyone but authorized personnel. He also moves three tear gas grenade kits into the basement, just in case a large threatening crowd storms the jail entrance for a good old-fashion lynching.[1225]

Lieutenant Pierce assigns Sergeant Patrick T. Dean to be in charge of the security detail in the basement garage, to be assisted by Sergeant James A. Putnam. Pierce, apparently, didn't tell Dean who was supposed to conduct the search, but Dean commandeers thirteen reserve officers (including their captain, Charles Arnett) who were congregated in the police assembly room, and together with himself, Putnam, Officers L. E. Jez and Alvin R. Brock, they proceed to empty everyone out of the basement garage, including other officers and members of the media who had already started to wait there.[1226] Dean's group searches the entire garage basement, including the air-conditioning and heating ducts, even the trunks of the cars that are in the basement.[1227] Other than four hunting rifles in the squad cars of officers who were going deer hunting, nothing is found.[1228] Two doors that would give ingress into the basement garage, one just east of the Commerce Street exit ramp, the other in the interior parking area of the garage just north of the adjacent elevators (a service elevator is nearby), are also checked and seen to be locked. In addition to Dean's assigning officers to cover every door or other possible entryway into the basement garage, Dean assigns Officer R. E. Vaughn to the Main Street entrance ramp leading down to the basement garage and Officer B. G. Patterson to the Commerce Street exit ramp.[1229] Sergeant Putnam assigns Officer A. R. Brock to cover the elevator area.[1230] Dean then lets the press and any other authorized personnel back into the garage.[1231]

On the third floor, Captain Fritz turns to Detectives Leavelle, Graves, and Dhority and orders them to bring Oswald down for further questioning.[1232]

9:30 a.m.

George Senator doesn't even know what time it is when he hears Jack Ruby get up and go to the bathroom, always his first stop when he awakens for the day, but it's probably around 9:30. George himself has been up since eight or so. He notices that Jack looks a little worse than the day before and was "even mumbling, which I didn't understand." Jack turns on the TV, which is carrying the preparation for the elaborate state funeral of the president. Over Jack's breakfast of scrambled eggs and coffee (George only had a cup of coffee) George notices that Jack had "this look about him that didn't look good." It was almost as if he was "in shock."[1233]

The previous day, Saturday, was almost a carbon-copy extension of the day before for Ruby, who continues in his grief over the assassination and in his impulsive, frenetic activity with respect to it. The morning got off to a bad start when around 8:30 a.m. Crafard awakens Ruby with a phone call from the club to say he needs dog food for Ruby's dogs he's taking care of for Ruby at the club. Jack chews Crafard out royally for wakening him after only two hours' sleep, but he doesn't go back to bed again. (Crafard, not appreciating Jack's vitriol, gathers his meager belongings, takes from the till the five dollars Ruby owes him, and begins hitchhiking to Michigan to visit his sister.)[1234]

Ruby turns on the TV to hear a rabbi eulogizing about Kennedy that here was a man who fought in the war, went to every country, and had to come back to his own country to be shot in the back.[1235] When a stripper calls Ruby around noon to find out if the club will be open that night, he tells her no. She notices his voice is shaking, as he talks about the "terrible" events of yesterday.[1236] With Ruby leaving his apartment shortly after 1:00

p.m., there is irreconcilable confusion as to the chronology of his movements that Saturday afternoon, irreconcilable to the point where no one, at this late date, will ever know for sure what the chronology was. But the conflict is only as to the sequence. With one exception (see endnote), everyone agrees that Ruby went to all the places mentioned. Each separate view has its advocates, but the confusion is so great that each view is itself internally inconsistent. The following is one view.

After leaving home, Ruby drives downtown to his club, the Carousel. Stopping by the Nichols garage next door to the club, where he and Carousel customers park their cars, he uses the garage phone to call someone and advises that person, in the presence of the garage attendant, Tom Brown, where he could find Chief of Police Jesse Curry. He then tells Brown that two men would probably be coming to the club to see him and to inform them that the club would not be open that night.[1237] Garnett "Claud" Hallmark, the parking-lot manager, overhears Ruby in a separate call talking to a newsman about having heard that Oswald was going to be transferred to the county jail that afternoon and telling the newsman that he'd be there. Ruby tells Hallmark, "I am acting like a reporter."[1238]

On the other end of the line is Dallas radio station (KLIF) announcer Ken Dowe. Dowe hardly knows Ruby, but Ruby says, "I understand they are moving Oswald over to the county jail. Would you like me to cover it, because I am a pretty good friend of Henry Wade's and I believe I can get some good news stories." Dowe, who needs all the help he can get, says "Okay."[1239] The word, incorrect, had gone out to some that Oswald was going to be transferred at 4:00 p.m.[1240]

Ruby then proceeds to Sol's Turf Bar and Delicatessen a few blocks away at 1515 Commerce Street. It is around 2:00 p.m. when Frank Bellocchio, a self-employed jeweler who had known Ruby casually for seven or eight years, sees Ruby near the back of Sol's. Bellocchio had been seated at the bar with a friend, Tom Apple, discussing the assassination. It is Bellocchio's position that the city of Dallas is responsible for the assassination, but his friend, Apple, disagrees. Bellocchio leaves his seat at the bar and approaches Ruby and they get into it on the cause of the assassination, Bellocchio taking from his pocket a folded copy of the full-page ad taken out in the *Dallas Morning News* the previous day by Bernard Weissman. Bellocchio was confused by Ruby's response. On one hand, Bellocchio said, Ruby, who was very upset about the ad, said he had learned that there was no person named Bernard Weissman, and that the ad was probably taken out by a group trying to stir up racial problems. Bellocchio "assumed" that Ruby meant arousing feelings against the Jews, and it was this group, not Dallas, that was responsible for the assassination. But then Ruby takes two of his "Impeach Earl Warren" photos out of his pocket to show Bellocchio, from which Bellocchio felt that Ruby was taking the contrary position that Dallas was responsible. "He seemed to be vacillating between the two sides . . . He seemed to be very incoherent," Bellocchio said. Bellocchio asks Ruby for one of the two copies of the Earl Warren impeachment photo but Ruby refuses to give him one, Bellocchio saying he "believed" Ruby said something about the photos being "some sort of a scoop" for him and he wanted to see that the right persons got the photos.[1241]

After leaving Sol's Turf Bar around three o'clock, Ruby drives over to Dealey Plaza, where he looks at all the wreaths there for the president and talks to a police officer he knows, James Chaney, about the "tragedy" of what had happened. Ruby walks off because he starts to choke up and doesn't want Chaney to see him crying. When Ruby sees Wes Wise, a newsman at KRLD in town whom he also knows, parked in his car near the Book Depository Building (Wise was calling back to his station that he couldn't gain entrance into the building), he knocks on the window of Wise's car, and when Wise rolls it down, they talk for around ten minutes about the tragedy. When Wise tells Ruby that he had been at the Trade Mart waiting for the president's arrival the previous day and had seen in the president's waiting room two large presents meant for Caroline and John Jr.— western saddles—that were going to be given to the president to give to his children, Wise notices tears in Ruby's eyes, and Ruby walks away. But he returns to Wise's car shortly thereafter to give him a tip, that Captain Fritz and Chief Curry were "over there looking at the flowers" for the president and hints that Wise should go and take their picture. Wise is grateful to Jack and he does just that.

Ruby then walks the short distance over to the entrance to the county jail on Houston between Elm and Main, where a large crowd has gathered in anticipation of Oswald's arrival at four o'clock, but the transfer doesn't take place and Ruby drives off for his home, leaving shortly thereafter for his sister Eva's apartment.[1242]

Ruby stays at his sister Eva Grant's apartment "for a good four hours." Eva, who herself feels like "the world was coming to an end" with the president's murder, feels for her brother, "sitting like a broken man crying." Jack starts up again on the Weissman ad, and Eva senses that Jack feels that "Bernard Weissman" may very well be a gentile using a Jewish name trying to get Jews in trouble. He's also still upset about the Earl Warren sign, and he calls Russ Knight over at KLIF and asks him, "Who is Earl Warren?"[1243] reflecting that Ruby had only known that the billboard words were an attack on a high official of the U.S. government, a government Ruby honored and was protective of. In the late afternoon at his sister's apartment Ruby calls Stanley Kaufman, a lawyer friend of his, brings up the Weissman ad with which he has become obsessed, and suggests to Kaufman that the black border of the ad was a tipoff that Weissman knew the president was going to be assassinated. He asks Kaufman if Kaufman knows how he, Ruby, could locate Weissman, but Kaufman has no idea. He tells Kaufman that he "doesn't know why" he wants to "connect" the ad and the Warren sign "with Oswald, but I do." He leaves no doubt in Kaufman's mind that he sees a connection between the ad and the assassination. Though Kaufman has known Ruby for almost ten years, and knows how very quick-tempered he is, Kaufman has never seen Jack so upset.[1244]

Jack asks Eva if she feels up to going to Officer Tippit's funeral with him. It doesn't surprise her. Other than the wife of an officer, she feels that no one in Dallas loves the police more than her brother Jack. He goes to the funerals of all Dallas police officers who die in the line of duty, and if he knows an officer personally, even to the funerals of their loved ones. In fact, when one officer, Johnny Sides, was killed in the line of duty a while back, Ruby held a benefit at his club and turned the proceeds over to Sides's family. But Eva is still weak and sick from her recent surgery and tells him she won't be up to it.[1245]

Ruby leaves Eva's apartment and returns home to his apartment five miles away around 8:30 p.m. Around 9:30 he receives a call from one of his strippers, Karen Bennett "Little Lynn" Carlin. Little Lynn and her husband, not getting the message that the Carousel was closed, find it locked when they arrive. She calls Jack from the Colony Club next door to find out if he's going to open the club, and Jack erupts. "Don't you have any respect for the president?" he barks at her. "Don't you know he's dead?" He adds, "I don't know when I will open. I don't know if I will ever open." Little Lynn feels Jack is "very hateful" to her, but since she and her out-of-work husband only have forty to fifty cents on their person together, she still asks him if he could pay her an advance on her salary so they can get back home to Fort Worth. He tells her he'll be down to the club in an hour to help her, but he doesn't show up, so her husband calls back from the garage next to the Carousel. Jack gets the garage attendant on the phone and gets him to give Little Lynn five dollars, which he'll reimburse him for, and when Lynn gets back on the phone and tells him she'll need rent money tomorrow, he tells her to call him.[1246]

Ruby places a few calls from his apartment that night, including to a friend from Chicago, Lawrence Meyers, who is in town. Ruby talks of the "terrible, terrible thing" that has happened and is very critical of his main competitors, Abe and Barney Weinstein, whom he refers to as "money-hungry Jews," for keeping their clubs (the Theatre Lounge and the Colony Club) open, and tells Meyers he's "going to do something" about it. Meyers, also Jewish, feels there are just as many "money-hungry Christians," but now was not the time to argue with his old friend, who kept repeating, to the point of almost being incoherent, "these poor people, these poor people, I feel so sorry for them," referring to Jackie and her two children. Meyers has never seen his old friend anywhere near like this before, and feels like Jack has "flipped his lid." When Ruby invites Meyers to join him for a cup of coffee, Meyers declines, saying he didn't want to get up and get dressed, but tells Jack that if he wants to talk, to come over to his motel for a cup of coffee, but Jack also declines, and they agree to meet the following evening for dinner.[1247]

Shortly after 11:00 p.m., after repaying the five dollars the garage attendant had given Little Lynn,[1248] he goes to his office at the Carousel and makes some more calls, among them to his friend Ralph Paul in Forth Worth, and Breck Wall, an entertainer friend of Jack's who had gone to Galveston to visit a friend when his show in Dallas suspended its performance out of respect for the president. Wall had just been elected president of the Dallas branch of the American Guild of Variety Artists (AGVA), and Ruby wants to know if AGVA, which includes among its members striptease dancers, had met to discuss his beef with the union—their failure to enforce AGVA's ban on "striptease contests" and performances by "amateurs," both of which the Weinsteins were guilty of—but AGVA hadn't met yet on the issue. Ruby, Wall can tell, is "very upset" about the assassination and curses the Weinsteins for not having the decency to close their two clubs out of respect for the dead president.[1249]

Ruby caps his evening around midnight at the Pago Club, about ten minutes from the Carousel, where he orders a Coke (Ruby rarely drinks alcohol) and asks the waitress in a very disapproving tone, "Why are you open?" "Ask my employer," she says, and leaves Ruby's table. The manager of the club, Robert Norton, knows Jack, and when he sees him sitting alone he joins him to chat. He tells Jack he doesn't know whether he should keep his club open and Ruby tells him he has closed his. During their short visit Norton brought up the assassination, saying "it was terrible" and "an insult to our country," adding that "we couldn't do enough to the person that had done this sort of thing." For once, Ruby, apparently already all talked out for the day about the assassination, shows no emotion and says nothing except he was "tired" and was "going home."[1250] Ruby then heads home and goes to bed around 1:30 a.m.[1251]

Jack's ugly mood when he awakens worsens when he sees in the Sunday morning's *Times Herald* a heartbreaking letter to "My Dear Caroline" dated two days earlier from a Dallas resident who tells her that "even as I write, you probably have not yet received" the news of her father's death. "This news is now being transmitted to all parts of the world . . . In all of this, my thoughts turn to you." Saying that though she was "old enough to feel the awful pain" but not yet "mature enough to understand this sorrow," he tells her he is a man of forty with two young daughters whom he had taken out of school "in order that they might get to see your mother and daddy" when they visited Dallas. From a position on the street not too far from Love Field, he said Caroline's mother and father looked "so very nice and appeared so happy." He said when the limousine passed by, "your daddy . . . did something that made me love him very much. It seemed like such a little thing, but it made me appreciate him the more for it. He looked at the grownups for just a second, and then he looked squarely at my youngest and then my eldest daughter. He smiled broadly and waved just to them in his warm way. Caroline, it was then I first thought of you. I thought your daddy must love little boys and little girls very much. Only one who loves and understands little children would realize just how much it would mean to them to be noticed in the presence of so many adults. I thought then how much he must love you."

He goes on to conclude, "No one can erase this day . . . You will cry. (My children did, my wife did, and I did). You will miss him. (We will). You will be lonely for him . . . You will want to know why anyone would do a thing like this to your father." Telling her he wished there was something he could do to help her, he says that she would be given strength and help and love by her mother and friends. "Most of all, God will help you. You see, God loves little girls, too," and closes by praying that Caroline would "be cradled in God's love."[1252]*

The letter has a devastating effect on Ruby. He also reads in another article in the *Times Herald*, captioned "State's Biggest Trial Expected," that when asked about "the possibility of Jacqueline Kennedy" being used as a witness at the trial of Oswald, DA Henry Wade said, "We will try to avoid [issuing a] subpoena" for Mrs. Kennedy, that she wouldn't "necessarily" have to come to Dallas to testify.[1253] Ruby seethes. If something happened to the president's killer, his jumbled mind thinks, then Mrs. Kennedy won't have to come back for the trial. He decides that he just *has* to kill Oswald. He suddenly gets this tremendously emotional feeling that someone owes a debt to the slain president to spare his wife the ordeal of coming back to Dallas. He doesn't know what the connection is, but he also has this feeling about wanting to show his love for his Jewish faith and demonstrate to the world that a Jew has guts. In the welter of emotions is his hatred for the SOB who had killed his president. If he had confessed, then Jack could know he'd get what was coming to him. But he hasn't and there apparently is going to be a trial. Jack recalls that hotel guy who killed a Dallas police officer a while back and he beat the rap and got away with the killing. It's possible Oswald could get turned loose too.[1254]†

He knows there are people going about their regular activities, out dancing at the clubs and having a good time, not suffering the way he is. The civic leaders of Dallas are probably sincere in their sorrow, but they're helpless to overcome the everlasting stain on the reputation of Dallas, a city he loves and is proud of. The officers of the Dallas Police Department are helpless to do anything to Oswald for killing the president and one of

---

*See photo section for photo of November 24, 1963, *Dallas Times Herald* found on the floor at the foot of Ruby's bed after he shot Oswald. The paper is opened to page A3, the facing page, A2, being the "My Dear Caroline" letter. (CE 2426, 25 H 525; WR, p.355)

†A Dallas police detective, Leonard Mullenax, was shot to death the previous year in a hotel room while working undercover on a drug case. Though Ruby didn't know Mullenax well, he was sufficiently depressed over it to contribute two hundred dollars to his widow, close his club, and take his strippers with him to the funeral. Because of lack of sufficient evidence, Mullenax's alleged killer was never prosecuted. (Kaplan and Waltz, *Trial of Jack Ruby*, pp.66–67; Hall [C. Ray] Exhibit No. 2, 20 H 43)

their own. He saw Bobby Kennedy on television, saw how much he loved his brother, and thought how much Bobby would like to do something to Oswald, but of course he can't do anything either. Somebody ought to do something, something that no one else can apparently do. Though Jack is not insane, most people know he's not all there either, and his limited intellect gets carried away emotionally by the power of his thought to kill Oswald, though he has no idea exactly when or where he will attempt to do this.[1255]

Jack is in another world when Elnora Pitts, the aging, colored maid, calls to see whether Jack wants her to come clean the apartment, as she has for the past eight months or so. He paid her $7.50 the first time she came, because it was pretty dirty. The next time it was $4.00 and bus fare, and then one day he said, "Well, it's getting pretty dirty, I'm going to give you a little raise today," and from then on he paid her $5.50 for a half day's work. She came Tuesdays first, then on Saturday, but eventually they settled on Sunday, because Jack liked to have it clean in case he had guests that day.

Jack sounds very strange to Elnora on the phone. "What do you want?" he asks.

"This is Elnora."

"Yes, well, what? You need some money?"

"No," Elnora says, puzzled. "I was coming to clean today."

"Well, what do you want?" Jack kind of hollers.

"I was coming to clean today." She doesn't think she should have to tell him that, much less repeat it.

"You coming now?"

"No."

"When?"

She says she'll try to be there before two.

"Why so late?"

"I have to go to the store, and I have got some things to do. You seem so funny to me," Elnora says. "Do you want me to come today?"

"Well, yes, you can come," Jack says, "but you call me."

"That's what I'm doing now, calling you so I won't have to call you again."

"Are you coming to clean today?"

"Who am I talking to? Is this Mr. Jack Ruby?"

"Yes. Why?"

"Oh, nothing," she says. Jack is sounding terribly strange to Elnora, doesn't sound like himself, so she says, "Well, I'll call you."

"Yes, so I can tell you where the key will be and the money," he says.

"Okay," Elnora says, completely bewildered, and she hangs up.

Elnora thinks there is something wrong with Jack, wrong enough to scare her, wrong enough for her to call her daughter, who asks, "Well, are you going over there now?"

"No, he don't sound right to me over the phone," Elnora tells her daughter. "I am going to wait."[1256]

P ostal Inspector Holmes hurries up the steps at City Hall and takes the elevator to the third floor. Holmes spots Captain Fritz standing in the corridor just outside the Homicide and Robbery Bureau. Fritz motions to him.

"We're getting ready to talk with Oswald one more time before we transfer him to the county jail," Fritz says. "Would you like to join us?"

"I sure would," Holmes replies.

"Well, come on in," Fritz says, pushing the door open. "I'm waiting here now for them to bring him downstairs from the holdover."[1257] Fritz leads Holmes into his office and closes the door. Secret Service agent Forrest Sorrels and Dallas police detective L. D. Montgomery are already there. So is Chief Curry, who has stopped by briefly to talk with Captain Fritz.[1258]

In a moment, Detectives Leavelle, Graves, and Dhority bring Oswald into the office, his hands cuffed in front of him. Oswald slouches into the wooden chair next to Fritz's desk. Oswald appears in a particularly arrogant mood.

"Are there any FBI men in here?" Oswald asks, looking at the faces around him.

"No," Fritz says, "no FBI men."

"Well, who is that man?" Oswald snaps back, motioning toward Holmes.

"He's a postal inspector and he has a few questions for you," Fritz says calmly.

Oswald seems to relax at the answer.

"Okay," he says.[1259]

Captain Fritz hands Oswald a telegram from an East Coast attorney who is volunteering to represent Oswald. Oswald reads it.

"Maybe you should call him," Fritz says.

"I'll call him later, if I can't reach Mr. Abt," Oswald replies, predictably.[1260]

There is a light knock at the door. It opens a crack and Secret Service inspector Thomas Kelley comes in, slightly out of breath, and takes a seat next to Agent Sorrels. Captain Fritz circles his desk, reaches into a drawer, pulls out the photograph of Oswald holding the rifle, and lays it on the desk next to the prisoner. Oswald purses his lips.

"Lee, why don't you tell us where this picture was taken?" Fritz asks.

Oswald is silent.

"You know, you'll save us a lot of time if you'll just tell us," Fritz continues, slow and methodical. "We'll find the location sooner or later."

"I don't have anything to say about it," Oswald answers defiantly.[1261]

"Did you shoot the president?" Fritz suddenly asks.

"No," Oswald says.

"Do you have any knowledge of the shooting?"

"No," Oswald replies.

"What about the shooting of Officer Tippit?" Fritz asks.

"Look, I don't know why you're asking me these questions," Oswald says, shaking his head negatively. "The only reason I'm here is because I popped a policeman in the nose at the theater on Jefferson Avenue. Okay, I admit it. But the reason I hit him was because I was protecting myself. As far as the rest of it, I emphatically deny having anything to do with shooting an officer or killing the president."[1262]

Chief Curry has had enough of Oswald's arrogance. Besides, he has transfer arrangements to see to. The police chief silently pulls open the office door and slips out.[1263]

9:45 a.m.

Curry hooks up with Batchelor and Stevenson and the three descend in the elevator to the basement garage to survey the security requirements for the forthcoming transfer.[1264]

The press has been arriving in force since nine and have nearly taken over the basement jail office. Cameramen, reporters, and all of their equipment are everywhere, including on top of the booking desk. The media have been insisting all morning that Chief Curry gave them permission to be there. When Curry comes down, they learn otherwise.[1265]

"Let's clear this area out," Curry tells jail lieutenant Woodrow Wiggins. "Move the patrol car and paddy wagon from those first two parking spaces and have the television cameras set up there. If the media want to be down here, put them over behind the rail." Curry is pointing to an area across the ramp from the jail office.[1266]

The top brass are pleased to learn that Captain Talbert has already begun, on his own, making security arrangements for the transfer.[1267]

Back up in Homicide and Robbery, Captain Fritz motions to Inspector Holmes to go ahead and question Oswald. Holmes introduces himself and opens the folder he brought.

"Did you have a post office box here in Dallas?" Holmes asks.

"Yeah."

"What number?"

"Box 2915," Oswald answers. "I rented it at the main post office for a few months before moving to New Orleans."

"Did you rent it in your own name?" Holmes asks.

"Yes."

"How many keys did you have?"

"Two," Oswald says. "When they closed the box I had them forward my mail to my new address in New Orleans."[1268]

Holmes glances at the forms in his folder as Oswald answers. Everything he offers is correct, although Holmes is surprised that Oswald is willing to volunteer so much information about the post office box that the assassination rifle was shipped to. Of course, Oswald isn't telling him anything that he doesn't already know. Holmes quickly learns that this is Oswald's game.

"Did anyone else receive mail in that box, other than yourself?" Holmes asks.

"No."

"Did anyone have access to the box, other than yourself?" Holmes asks.

"No," Oswald says again.

"Did you permit anyone else to use the box?"

"Well, it's possible that I may have given my wife one of the keys to go get my mail," Oswald replies, "but that was rare. Certainly, no one else used it."

"Did you ever receive a package in that box?" Holmes asks.

"What kind of package?" Oswald asks innocently.

"Did you ever have a rifle shipped there?"

"No," Oswald says, testily. "I did not order any rifle!"

"Ever order a rifle under another name?" Holmes asks.

Oswald emphatically denies that he ever ordered a rifle under his name or any other name, nor permitted anyone else to order a rifle to be received in his post office box.[1269]

"In fact," Oswald says, "I've never owned a rifle. I haven't practiced or shot a rifle since I was in the Marine Corps."

"You've never shot a rifle since your discharge?" Fritz asks, disbelievingly.

"No," Oswald says, then backs up. "Well, maybe a small-bore .22 or something."

"You don't own a rifle?" Fritz questions.

"Absolutely not!" Oswald insists. "How can I afford a rifle on my salary? I make $1.25 an hour. I can hardly feed myself on what I make."

"What about this?" Fritz asks, pointing to the photograph of Oswald and the rifle.

"I don't know what you're talking about," Oswald sneers.[1270]

"You mentioned that when you moved to New Orleans you had your mail forwarded to your new street address," Holmes says. "Did you rent a post office box while you were in New Orleans?"

"Yes," Oswald says. "Box 30061."

"Why did you have a post office box if you were getting mail at your residence?" the postal inspector asks.

Oswald explains that he subscribed to several publications, at least two of which are published in Russia, one being the hometown paper published in Minsk where he met his wife at a dance.[1271] "I took the two newspapers for her benefit, because it was local news to her," Oswald says. "She enjoyed reading about the hometown folks."[1272] He explains that he moved around so much that it was more practical to simply rent post office boxes and have his mail forwarded from one box to the next rather than going through the process of furnishing changes of address to the Russian publishers.[1273]

"Did you permit anyone other than yourself to get mail in the post office box in New Orleans?" Holmes asks.

"No," Oswald answers.

Holmes looks at the original application for Oswald's New Orleans post office box, which Oswald filled out in his own hand. Under the entry, "Persons entitled to receive mail through box," Oswald has written "Marina Oswald" and "A. J. Hidell."*

"Your application here lists Marina Oswald as a person entitled to receive mail in the box," Holmes reminds Oswald.

"Well, so what?" Oswald says mockingly. "She was my wife. I don't see anything wrong with that. It could very well be I did put her name on the application."

"Your application also shows the name A. J. Hidell as another person entitled to receive mail in the box."[1274]

Oswald simply shrugs his shoulders.

"I don't recall anything about that," he says.[1275]

Secret Service inspector Thomas Kelley jumps into the fray.

"Well, isn't it a fact that when you were arrested you had an identification card with the name Hidell on it in your possession?"

"Yes, that's right," Oswald grunts.

"How do you explain that?" Kelley asks.

"I don't explain it," Oswald says flatly.[1276]

Holmes refocuses on the Dallas post office box.

"Did you receive mail through box 2915 under any name other than Lee Oswald?"

"Absolutely not," Oswald says.

"What about a package to an A. J. Hidell?"

"No!" Oswald snaps.

"Did you order a gun in that name to come there?" Holmes asks.

"No, absolutely not."

"If one had come under that name, could this fellow Hidell have gotten it?" Holmes presses.

---

*In accordance with postal regulations, the portion of Oswald's application for his post office box in Dallas that listed names of persons other than the applicant who were entitled to receive mail was thrown away after Oswald closed his box on May 14, 1963 (7 H 527, WCT Harry D. Holmes; Cadigan Exhibit No. 13, 19 H 286). But the New Orleans post office did not comply with this regulation, and that portion of Oswald's application for his New Orleans post office box still existed (7 H 527, WCT Harry D. Holmes).

"Nobody got mail out of that box but me," Oswald retorts.[1277]

Holmes has the impression that Oswald has disciplined his mind and reflexes to the point that the inspector personally doubts he will ever confess.[1278]

10:15 a.m.

Lieutenant Rio S. Pierce walks through the City Hall basement garage and checks security arrangements. Pierce can see that Sergeant Dean and his men have done a fine job. He deems the basement secure and returns to the third-floor homicide office to await further instructions.[1279]

In Washington, Commander Humes arrives at Bethesda Naval Hospital for a conference in Admiral Calvin B. Galloway's office with his colleagues from the autopsy, Drs. Boswell and Finck. Dr. Humes has been up half the night* working on a longhand draft of the autopsy report, incorporating notes made during the autopsy with the information he had obtained from Dr. Perry on Saturday morning. The result is the fifteen-page draft he now has in his hands. Humes, Boswell, and Finck carefully review the language of the handwritten draft, making minor corrections and clarifications.[1280] Although the details are extensive, the conclusion is short and to the point:

> It is our opinion that the deceased died as a result of *two* perforating gunshot wounds inflicted by high-velocity projectiles fired by a person or persons unknown. The projectiles were fired from a point *behind* and somewhat *above* the level of the deceased. The observations and available information do not permit a satisfactory estimate as to the sequence of the two wounds.
>
> The fatal missile entered the skull above and to the right of the external occipital protuberance. A portion of the projectile traversed the cranial cavity in a posterior-anterior direction (see later skull roentgenograms), depositing minute particles along its path. A portion of the projectile made its exit through the parietal bone on the right, carrying with it portions of cerebrum, skull, and scalp. The two wounds of the skull combined with the force of the missile produced extensive fragmentation of the skull, laceration of the superior sagittal sinus, and of the right cerebral hemisphere.
>
> The other missile entered the right superior posterior thorax above the scapula and traversed the soft tissues of the supra-scapular and supra-clavicular portions of the base of the right side of the neck. This missile produced contusions of the right apical parietal pleura and of the apical portion of the right upper lobe of the lung. The missile contused the strap muscles of the right side of the neck, damaged the trachea, and made its exit through the anterior surface of the neck. As far as can be ascertained, this missile struck no bony structures in its path through the body.
>
> In addition, it is our opinion that the wound of the skull produced such extensive damage to the brain as to preclude the possibility of the deceased surviving this injury.

---

*Humes completed the autopsy report between 3:00 and 4:00 a.m. EST (1 HSCA 330; ARRB Transcript of Proceedings, Deposition of Dr. James Joseph Humes, February 13, 1996, p.135).

A supplementary report will be submitted following more detailed examinations of the brain and of microscopic sections. However, it is not anticipated that these examinations will materially alter the findings.[1281]

It will take some time to type up the final draft, but Commander Humes is confident that he can deliver it to Admiral George Burkley at the White House by Sunday evening as promised.

10:19 a.m.

Jack Ruby and his roommate George Senator are still in their underwear when the phone rings, and George can tell from Jack's end of the conversation that it's Little Lynn.

She says she is calling "to try to get some money, because the rent is due and I need some money for groceries, and you told me to call."

"How much will you need?"

She confers with her husband Bruce and asks for twenty-five dollars.

"I have to go downtown anyway," Jack says, "so I'll send it to you by Western Union."

She asks him to use her real name, Karen Bennett, and wonders what time she should expect it to arrive at the Western Union office in downtown Fort Worth, but he can't say. He's not dressed yet and he has to do something about the dog, but he promises to take care of it this morning.

"I sure would appreciate it," she says.

He still seems sort of hateful and short with her, but not as much as last night, and she's grateful that he doesn't give her any problem about the money.

Jack finally gets it together enough to shower, shave, and get dressed—an elaborate process that never takes him less than half an hour—but his mood doesn't change. Even after he's fully dressed and ready to go out, he paces nervously from bedroom to living room and back for another ten minutes or so, mumbling to himself, too low for George to catch any of it, and George is too wrapped up in his newspaper to pay much attention in any case.[1282]

10:20 a.m.

In the anteroom of Chief Curry's office, a dozen or so members of the news media have come up from the basement and lay in ambush for the chief, hoping to get some advance word on Oswald's transfer. Comfortable with the security arrangements, Curry steps out of his office and holds an impromptu news conference while he waits for Captain Fritz to finish this morning's interrogation.

"Chief, you say you're going to take him to the county jail in an armored car," a reporter asks. "Have you ever had to do this with another prisoner?"

"Not to my knowledge," Curry says.

"Is it a commercial-type truck, the kind that banks use?"

"Yes, sir."

"Did [the] threats on the prisoner's life . . . did they come in right through the police switchboard?"

"Yes," Curry replies.

"Do you have any details at all on them?" someone asks.

"No."

"Is there any way we can get some [details] on [the calls], sir?"

"I don't know who took the calls or what was said," Curry says, feigning ignorance. Someone asks again about the possibility that Oswald might have had accomplices.

"This is the man, we are sure, that murdered the patrolman and murdered . . . assassinated the president," Curry says confidently. "But to say that there was no other person that had knowledge of what this man might do, I wouldn't make that statement because there is a possibility that there are people who might have known this man's thoughts and what he could do, or what he might do."

"Does he show any signs of breaking—to make a clean breast of this, [and] tell the truth about what happened?"

"No, sir," Curry answers, "there is no indication that he is close to telling us anything . . ."

The press questions Curry about Oswald's relationship with his wife, whether Oswald has any friends, about the backyard photographs showing Oswald holding a rifle, and other topics, but Curry isn't really telling them anything they don't already know.[1283]

Jerry O'Leary of the *Washington Star* is less interested in what Curry has to say and more interested in coming up with a plan to cover Oswald's descent to the basement. O'Leary wants to be on the third floor when Oswald is led to the elevator, in case Oswald makes a statement, and also wants to be in the basement when Oswald is put in the armored truck. He figures the only way he'll be able to cover both events is to race down the stairwell once Oswald is safely on his way down in the jail elevator. O'Leary and New York radio reporter Icarus "Ike" Pappas set up a test race to see if it can be done, with O'Leary and Pappas starting to run down the stairway at the same time the public elevator starts down. When O'Leary and Pappas reach the bottom, they can dash out of the stairwell just ahead of the elevator. The reporters can only hope the jail elevator will be as slow as the public elevator when the time comes. Neither thinks about it until later, but curiously no one questions or asks them for their credentials while running up and down the stairwell.[1284]

In Captain Fritz's third-floor office, Holmes grills Oswald about his current post office box rentals. Oswald says that after he came back to Dallas from New Orleans and shortly after he went to work at the Book Depository, he rented a new post office box in Dallas, number 6225.

"Rented it in your own name?" Holmes asks.

"Yes," Oswald says. "I checked out one key."

All of this was true. The police confiscated the key, which they found in Oswald's pocket after his arrest. Holmes has already compared it to the master key for box 6225 and found them identical.[1285]

"Did you show [in your application for the box] that anyone else was entitled to get mail in the box?" Holmes asks.

"No."

"What did you show as your business?"

"I didn't show anything," Oswald replies.

"Well, your box rental application here says Fair Play for Cuba Committee and the American Civil Liberties Union," Holmes tells him.

"Maybe that's right," Oswald admits.

Holmes wants to know if he rented the box for these groups, but Oswald denies it. "I paid for it out of my own personal money," he says.

Asked why he put them on the application, Oswald only says, "I don't know why."[1286]

"How did you get involved with the Fair Play for Cuba Committee?" Captain Fritz interrupts.

"Well, I first became interested when I went to New Orleans," Oswald says. "It started out as simply a group of individuals who thought and had political opinions like my own. We decided to organize, and did after a while."

"Who is the head of the organization?" Fritz asks.

"We don't have any elected officers," Oswald replies.

The homicide captain presses Oswald, trying to get him to admit that he is the head man of the New Orleans chapter, but Oswald is very evasive.

"Well, I could probably be considered the secretary," Oswald finally admits, "since I wrote some letters on their behalf and tried to collect dues."

"How much were the dues?" Fritz asks.

"A dollar a month," Oswald shoots back.

"Isn't there a Fair Play for Cuba Committee in New York?" Fritz asks.

Oswald smiles. "Yes, but they're much better organized than we are."[1287]

"Did you contact them?" Fritz asks.

"Yes, I wrote to them," Oswald replies, "and they sent me some Communist literature and a letter signed by Alex Hidell."*[1288]

Oswald's statement about Hidell, someone he previously claimed he knew nothing about, doesn't escape the lawmen, but for the moment they let him go on.

"I distributed the literature in New Orleans," Oswald tells them, "and it was at that time that I got into an altercation with a group of Cuban exiles and was arrested. I appeared on Bill Stuckey's television program in New Orleans on a number of occasions and was interviewed by the local press often.† So you see my opinions on the Fair Play for Cuba Committee are well known."

"Did you know Hidell in New Orleans?" Secret Service inspector Kelley asks.

"I never knew him or ever saw him in New Orleans," Oswald replies.

"Do you believe in what the Fair Play for Cuba Committee stands for?" Kelley asks.

"Yes," Oswald says. "Cuba should have full diplomatic relations with the United States. There should be free trade with Cuba and freedom for tourists from both countries to travel within each other's borders."

"Is that why you came to Dallas," Postal Inspector Holmes asks, "to organize a cell of the Fair Play for Cuba Committee in Dallas?"

"No, not at all," Oswald says.

"Did you work on it or intend to organize here in Dallas?"

"No, I didn't," Oswald chuckles. "I was too busy trying to get a job."[1289]

"Do you think that the attitude of the U.S. government toward Cuba will change since the president has been assassinated?" Kelley asks.

Oswald turns to Fritz. "I'm filed on for the president's murder, right?"

"Yes," Fritz says.

"Under the circumstances," Oswald says to Kelley, "I don't believe I will answer the question because whatever I say might be misconstrued."

---

*There is no evidence that the Fair Play for Cuba Committee in New York ever sent Oswald a letter signed by Alex Hidell.

†In fact, Oswald appeared on Stuckey's television program once, a related radio program once, and was interviewed once by the press in relation to his court appearance.

Despite his declaration, Oswald answers the question anyway. "When the head of any government dies," he says, "there is always a second in command who takes over and in this particular case it will be Johnson. So far as I know, Johnson's views and President Kennedy's views are the same, so I don't think the attitude of the U.S. government will change toward Cuba."[1290]

"Are you a Communist?" Captain Fritz asks.

It's the kind of question Oswald likes. "No, I am not a Communist," Oswald says. "I am a Marxist, but not a Marxist-Leninist."

"What's the difference?" Fritz asks.

"It would take too long to explain," Oswald replies, enjoying the fact that he knows more about the subject than the homicide captain.

"Try me," Fritz shoots back.

"Well, a Communist is a Leninist-Marxist," Oswald explains, "while I am a true Karl Marxist. I've read just about everything by or about Karl Marx."[1291]

"Do you read a lot of Communist publications?" Fritz asks.

"I'm an avid reader of Russian literature," Oswald says, "whether it's Communist or not."

"Do you subscribe to any Russian magazines or newspapers?" Agent Kelley inquires.

"Yes, I subscribe to the *Militant*," Oswald replies. "That's the weekly of the Socialist Party in the United States."

Oswald is suddenly intrigued by Agent Kelley.

"Are you an FBI agent?" he asks.

"No, I'm not," Kelley tells him. "I'm a member of the Secret Service."

"Oh, I see," Oswald says, nodding his head. "When I was standing in front of the Depository, about to leave, a young crew-cut man rushed up and said he was from the Secret Service, showed me a book of identification, and asked where the phone was."

"Did you show him?" Kelley asks.

"Well, I pointed toward the pay phone in the building," Oswald says, "and he started toward it, and then I left."[1292]*

10:45 a.m.

The vice president of the Armored Motor Car Service, Harold Fleming, calls Assistant Chief Batchelor and tells him he has two armored trucks, a smaller and a larger one, with drivers ready and waiting for instructions.

"Send them down to the Commerce Street ramp," Batchelor tells him, adding that after picking the one they want, "we're going to back the truck into the ramp so they'll be leaving the ramp in the right direction when they pull out." They already know that the low ceiling in the basement garage will prevent the driver from backing the truck all the way down into the basement. They're simply hopeful that they can get the truck backed down far enough so that they can get Oswald into it without exposing him to the street traffic.[1293]

---

*Later investigation revealed that Oswald's encounter was probably with a young, crew-cut WFAA radio newsman named Pierce Allman, who ran into the Depository to telephone the radio station about the shooting. Allman reported encountering a young man on the front steps who pointed toward the telephone inside, although Allman told the Secret Service he couldn't say for sure whether the man was Oswald or not (CD 354, p.2, Secret Service interview of Pierce Allman on January 29, 1964).

Deputy Chief Stevenson approaches Captain Orville A. Jones of the Forgery Bureau and directs him to take any remaining detectives who are available on the third floor down to the basement to assist the officers already stationed there. Stevenson and Assistant Chief Batchelor then head down to the basement to meet the armored trucks and check the security arrangements again.

Captain Jones makes his way down the hall and tells the duty officers in the Juvenile, Forgery, and Burglary and Theft Bureaus to have all available officers report to the basement jail office for security detail. Two or three detectives accompany him at that time to the basement, where he stations them at the jail office.

Jones then walks to the head of the Commerce Street ramp. He instructs the two officers there to clear the way and assist the armored truck that will be arriving at any moment.[1294] Nearby, Batchelor and Stevenson are going over the proposed route of the caravan with Captain Talbert.

"Are you planning to use sirens to stop traffic at each intersection?" Talbert asks.

"I don't want to attract any more attention to the transfer than we already have," Stevenson says. "Do you have enough men available to cover each of the intersections along Elm Street?"

"I'm sure we can get them," Talbert replies, calling Sergeants Patrick T. Dean and Don F. Steele over and instructing them to get some officers and station them along the Elm Street route to cut cross traffic at all the intersections as the convoy comes through. When Sergeant Steele says he doesn't have enough men available, Talbert orders him to get any additional forces he needs from Captain Perdue Lawrence of the Traffic Division.

"Instruct the men stationed along Elm," Talbert tells Steele, "to fall in line behind the convoy as they come past and be prepared to handle any trouble that develops down at the county jail," where a crowd of around six hundred people has gathered.[1295]

Batchelor and Stevenson can see officers stationed at the top of the Main and Commerce Street ramps. The two men walk up the Commerce Street ramp and survey the crowd that is gathered across the street. A police supervisor advises the deputy chiefs that no one but police officers are allowed on the side of the street next to City Hall. Batchelor can see a few officers stationed across the street, helping to control the crowd. Everything seems to be in order.[1296]

In the third-floor homicide office, Secret Service inspector Kelley can sense, like many others before him, that Oswald likes to talk about himself and express his opinions. Perhaps this is the key to cutting through his denials.

"What do you think about religion?" Kelley asks Oswald.

"Karl Marx is my religion," Oswald replies.

"What I mean is, what faith are you?" Kelley inquires.

"I have no faith," the prisoner answers, then a moment later, "I suppose you mean the Bible?"

"Yes, that's right," Kelley says.

"Well, I've read the Bible," Oswald begins. "Some people might find it interesting reading, but not me. As a matter of fact, I'm a student of philosophy and I don't consider the Bible to be even a reasonable or an intelligent philosophy."

"You don't think much of it?" Kelley sums up.

"You could say that."[1297]

"As a Marxist, do you believe that religion is an opiate of the people?" Agent Kelley asks.

Oswald is in his element, and lights up at the chance to talk about ideology.

"Most definitely so," Oswald says. "All religions tend to become monopolistic and are the causes of a great deal of class warfare."

"Do you consider the Catholic Church to be an enemy of the Communist philosophy?" Kelley probes.

"Well, there is no Catholicism in Russia," Oswald answers. "The closest thing to it are the Orthodox Churches. But, I'm not going to discuss my opinions about religion any further since this is an attempt to get me to say something which could be construed as antireligious or anti-Catholic."[1298]

"Do you believe in a deity?" Fritz interjects, trying to pick up the ball. But Oswald will have none of it.

"I don't care to discuss that with you," Oswald replies sharply.[1299]

The homicide captain turns back to the issues of evidence.

"I understand you were dishonorably discharged from the Marine Corps—"

Oswald bristles noticeably and cuts him off.

"I was discharged *honorably*," Oswald snaps. "They later changed it because I attempted to renounce my American citizenship while living in Russia. Since my change in citizenship did not come to pass, I wrote a letter to Mr. Connally, who was then secretary of the navy, to have this discharge reversed, and after a considerable delay, I received a very respectful reply in which Mr. Connally stated that he had resigned to run for governor of Texas, and that my letter was being referred to the new secretary. I'm still waiting."

Some reporters had been speculating that Oswald's intended target was Governor Connally, rather than the president. But Captain Fritz doesn't detect any animosity toward the governor in Oswald's voice.[1300]

"Lee, we found a map in your room with some marks on it," Fritz says, shifting subjects. "What can you tell me about those marks? Did you put them on there?"

"Oh, God!" Oswald says, rolling his eyes. "Don't tell me there's a mark where this thing happened?"

No one says anything.

"What about the other marks?" Oswald says. "I put a lot of marks on that map. I was looking for a job and marked the places where they were interviewing."

Oswald explains that he has no transportation and either walks or rides a bus and that he was constantly looking for work. He says that as he got leads he would chart them on the map to save time in traveling.

"Why was there an X at the location of the Book Depository?" Fritz asks.

"Well, I interviewed there for a job," Oswald replies. "In fact, I got the job. That's all that map amounts to."[1301]

11:00 a.m.

In the basement jail office, Captain Frank Martin and a posse of detectives walk up to assist in the security measures, having just come down from the third-floor Juvenile Bureau.[1302] They're there only a moment when someone hollers, "The armored trucks are here!"

Assistant Chief Batchelor heads up the Commerce Street exit ramp and after a quick inspection of the vehicles, he decides that the larger truck, with room for two guards, is better suited for the mission. There wasn't sufficient clearance for the truck to be taken to the bottom of the ramp, and the driver believed that because of the truck's weight, if he parked the truck on the incline, when he started to pull out he might stall the truck on the ramp. It was decided to leave the truck at the top of the ramp, the front wheels on the sidewalk on Commerce Street, and the rear wheels on the incline of the ramp.

"That's fine," Batchelor tells the driver, and points out the car that he will be following when they get ready to leave. There is very little room for anyone to squeeze by the truck—a foot to two feet on either side is all. It's effectively plugging the ramp.[1303] Batchelor then opens the back of the truck to make sure it's clean. An empty Nehi soft-drink bottle rolls out and pops as it shatters on the concrete. The sound causes a commotion among the reporters at the bottom of the ramp. What was that? A shot? A group of them break toward the armored truck to see what happened.[1304]

On the third floor, time is growing short, and Captain Fritz makes one more attempt to shake Oswald's story.

"Lee, why did you go to Irving to visit your wife on Thursday night instead of Friday, like you normally did?" the homicide chief asks.

"I learned that my wife and Mrs. Paine were giving a party for the kids," Oswald tells him, "and that they were going to have a house full of neighborhood kids there. I just didn't want to be around then. So, I went out Thursday night."

"Did you bring a sack with you the next morning?"

"I did," Oswald says.

"What was in the sack?" Fritz asks.

"My lunch."

"How big of a sack was it?" Fritz asks. "What was its shape?"

"Oh, I don't recall," Oswald replies, tiring of the cat-and-mouse game. "It may have been a small sack or a large sack, I don't know. You don't always find one that fits your sandwiches just right."

"Where did you put the sack when you got in Wesley's car?" Fritz questions.

"In my lap," Oswald says, "or possibly on the front seat next to me. That's where I always put it because I don't want it to get crushed."

"You didn't put it in the backseat?" Fritz asks.

"I didn't put any package in the backseat," Oswald says vehemently.

"Wesley Frazier says that you brought a long parcel over to his house and put it in the backseat of his car," Fritz tells him. "Do you deny that?"

"Oh, he must be mistaken," Oswald claims, "or else thinking about some other time when he picked me up."

"Didn't you tell him you had curtain rods?" Fritz asks.

"Absolutely not!" Oswald snaps. "I *never* said such a thing."[1305]

Captain Fritz asks Oswald again where he was at the time of the shooting.

"When lunchtime came," Oswald says, "one of the Negro employees invited me to eat lunch with him, and I said, 'You go on down and *send the elevator back up* and I will join you in a few minutes.'" He said that before he could finish what he was doing, all the commotion surrounding the assassination took place, so he said, "I just went on downstairs" to "see what it was all about." On the way, he says, he stopped to get a Coke, and before he could proceed on his way out of the building, "a police officer stopped me" to ask some questions, but "my superintendent stepped up and told the officer that I am one of the employees of the building. So, he told me to step aside for a little bit and we will get to you later. Then I just went out the front door and into the crowd to see what it was all about."[1306]

Postal Inspector Holmes notices that Oswald didn't say what floor he was on at the time of the shooting, or whether he had taken the elevator or stairs down.* He also wonders why Oswald left the scene and how he got away, but figures that Fritz had covered these areas in a previous session.[1307] What Holmes doesn't realize is that Oswald, like thousands of guilty people before him who incriminate themselves by telling inconsistent stories, has changed his story significantly.

Shortly after his arrest, Oswald told Fritz that at the time of the shooting he was eating lunch on the first floor. Also, that he *had gone up* to the second-floor lunchroom to get a Coke when he was stopped by Officer Baker and the building superintendent, Roy Truly. Now, Oswald was *admitting that he was on an upper floor of the Depository when the shooting occurred* and was on his way down to the front door when he was stopped.

Through the venetian blinds, Captain Fritz can see Chief Curry milling about impatiently in the outer office. Finally, the chief raps lightly on the door and opens it a crack.

"We'll be through in a few minutes," Fritz tells him.[1308]

Curry closes the door and the questioning continues, with Dallas Secret Service agent-in-charge Forrest Sorrels and Fritz returning one final time to Oswald's use of the name A. Hidell at his post office box in New Orleans and elsewhere.

"Now, you say that you have not used the name A. Hidell," Sorrels says, "but you show the name on this change-of-address card† as a person entitled to receive mail at this address. If you don't know anyone by the name Hidell, why would you have that name on this card?"

"I never used the name of Hidell," Oswald says, dodging the issue.[1309]

The door to Fritz's office opens again, and this time Chief Curry steps inside.[1310] Although no words are spoken, it's clear that he wants the interrogation to come to an end. But Captain Fitz, following up on Sorrels's question, once again asks Oswald, "Lee, do you know anyone by the name of A. J. Hidell?"

"No," Oswald says.

"Have you ever used that name as an alias?" Fritz presses.

"No!" Oswald insists. "I never used the name and I don't know anyone by that name."

"What about the draft registration [Selective Service] card we got out of your wallet showing the name A. J. Hidell?" Fritz fires back.

Oswald boils over.

"I've told you all I'm going to about that card!" Oswald flares. "You took notes! Just read them for yourself, if you want to refresh your memory. You know as much about it as I do."[1311]

That's it. There'll be no more from Oswald, at least until after the transfer. Both Fritz and Sorrels plan to question Oswald further in the days ahead. Captain Fritz and Chief

---

*But Holmes testified that Oswald made it clear that "he was still up in the building" when the shooting started and had "rushed downstairs to go out to see what was going on" (7 H 302, 306).

†Sorrels probably misspoke here since the Warren Commission investigation never came up with a change-of-address card, if there ever was one, for Oswald in New Orleans. Sorrels probably was referring to the portion of the application for Oswald's post office box in New Orleans that listed "A. J. Hidell" as someone entitled to receive mail through the box.

Curry huddle briefly, whispering in hushed tones, then step out into the outer office to confer in private.[1312]

Secret Service inspector Kelley tells Oswald that the Secret Service is responsible for the safety of the president, and that as soon as he has secured counsel, the Secret Service is very anxious to talk with him to make sure that the correct facts are being developed regarding the assassination.

"I would be glad to discuss your proposition with my attorney," Oswald says, "and after I have talked with one, you can discuss it with me or my attorney, if my attorney thinks that it is a wise thing to do. But, at the present time, I have nothing more to say."[1313]

It's around eleven by the time Jack Ruby starts to leave his apartment to send Little Lynn her money. He tells George he's also going to take Sheba down to the club, and he puts his revolver in his right coat pocket. He normally carries it in his right trouser pocket because he doesn't want to get his coat out of shape.[1314] In the fifteen-minute-or-so drive downtown on the Thornton Expressway, Ruby listens to his car radio but doesn't hear anything that informs him Oswald hasn't yet been moved. He decides to go by Dealey Plaza once again to see the wreaths there, and takes the Industrial Street turnoff to Main, where he takes a right and proceeds past the Criminal Courts Building. He is surprised to see a crowd gathered outside the county jail on the other side of rope barricades since he had heard Oswald was going to be moved to the county jail at ten, and it's now well past eleven. But as he passes City Hall, he notices quite a crowd there too, so he figures maybe they haven't moved Oswald yet and he makes an illegal left turn into a parking lot across the street from the Western Union office on Main, just one block away (at the end of the same block and on the same side of the street) from police headquarters. Leaving Sheba in the car, he takes his keys and locks the trunk—there's over eight hundred bucks in cash in a grocery bag in there, half of it in five-dollar bills. He then puts the trunk key and, oddly, his billfold, with all of his identification in it, in the glove compartment of his car, a 1960s Oldsmobile. Leaving the car itself unlocked, he walks across the street to Western Union. In addition to the gun, he's carrying more than two thousand dollars in cash, wads of it, bundled in rubber bands, stashed in every pocket. He often carries the cash from the Carousel around with him for a couple of days, sometimes as long as a week, and there's almost always money in the trunk of the car, particularly by Sunday night, when he has to make the payroll.[1315]

11:05 a.m.
With the armored truck in place, Captain Jones walks back down the ramp to the basement jail office, where he meets the men who have come down from the Juvenile and Forgery Bureaus, as well as the Burglary and Theft Bureaus. He instructs them to form a line on each side of the passageway leading from the jail office to the ramp and parking area so that Oswald and his escorts will have a protective lane to pass through on their way to the armored car once they emerge from the jail office. Altogether, there are around seventy members of the Dallas Police Department in the basement to make sure there are no problems.

"Don't allow anyone into this area," Captain Jones barks over the noise of the basement garage. "Do not allow the press to approach or even attempt to converse with the prisoner. And don't allow anyone to follow the caravan until after it's left the basement. Is that clear?"

"Yes, sir," a chorus of officers answers. Jones than commands the media horde, "Do not speak to the prisoner as he is led from the building."[1316]*

Of course, few newsmen plan to heed the captain's order.

"I'll go let them know we're ready," Chief Stevenson says to Batchelor as he heads for the elevators.[1317]

On the third floor, Captain Fritz and Chief Curry are discussing the transfer plans in the outer office of the Homicide and Robbery Bureau. A small group of investigators surrounds them—Postal Inspector Harry Holmes, Secret Service agent-in-charge Forrest Sorrels, Lieutenants Rio S. Pierce and Richard E. Swain, and Detective Jim Leavelle.[1318]

"Are you ready for the transfer?" Curry asks.

"When the security downstairs is ready, we're ready," Fritz replies.[1319]

Curry tells Captain Fritz that everything is ready, that an armored truck is in position at the Commerce Street ramp and will transport the prisoner to the county jail. But Fritz suddenly shakes his head.

"Chief, I don't think it's a good thing to try to move him in that money wagon," he tells Curry. "I don't think it's a good idea at all. For one thing, we don't know the driver or anything about that wagon, and if someone tries to take our prisoner, we should be in a position to be able to cut out of the caravan, or to take off, or do whatever is necessary to protect him. That heavy money wagon will be too awkward in that kind of a situation. I would prefer to transfer him in an unmarked car."[1320]

Curry can see the merit to his plan and isn't about to argue with Fritz.

"Well, okay," Curry says, "but we'll still use the armored car as a decoy and let it go right on down Elm just as we planned and if anyone tries to take the prisoner away from us, they'll find themselves attacking an empty armored car."[1321]

"I'll transport him in one car, with myself and two detectives," Fritz says, "and we'll have another carload of detectives as backup. We can cut out of the caravan at Main Street and head straight west on Main Street to Houston, then make a right turn to the county jail. The rest of the convoy can go on to Elm Street to Houston, turn left, but not enter the jail. We'll be in the county jail before they even get there."[1322]

Curry nods his approval, "Okay."

The door to the homicide office opens and Deputy Chief Stevenson comes in and tells Chief Curry that the armored truck is in place. Chief Curry tells him there has been a change in plans and that they're going to move Oswald in an unmarked police car.

"You know, Chief," Fritz says, "we ought to get rid of the television lights and cameramen so they don't interfere with our getting to the car."[1323]

Curry knows that Fritz is suggesting he get rid of the press entirely.

---

*As can be seen in the sketch of the layout of the basement in the photo section of this book, looking out from the jail office to the garage basement ahead, there is a traffic lane that starts at the top of the Main Street entrance ramp on the left. The lane descends into the garage basement and continues past the jail office until it exits the basement by way of the Commerce Street ramp on the right. Most of the media are on the far side of the lane behind a railing that runs alongside the lane, their backs to the parking lot behind them, their eyes facing the jail office. To enable those reporters craning their necks behind others to have a better view, Assistant Chief Batchelor has given permission for them to stand in a semicircle extending from the end of the railing across the bottom of the Main Street ramp. However, on their own, many have also spilled over beyond the railing on the Commerce Street side and are on the jail side of the railing close to the armored truck. (15 H 119–120, 12, H 17–18, WCT Charles Batchelor; 12 H 101–102, WCT M. W. Stevenson; Batchelor Exhibit No. 5001, 19 H 116; 12 H 119, WCT Cecil E. Talbert; CE 2179, 24 H 851; Talbert Exhibit No. 5070, 21 H 668; 15 H 150, WCT John Will Fritz)

"The lights have already been moved back," Curry replies, "and the media have been moved back in the basement, back of the rail, and the spectators have been moved across the street. You won't have any trouble."[1324]

Detective Leavelle takes Fritz aside. "Why don't we take him out on the first floor and put him in a car on Main Street," Leavelle says to Fritz. "We could be in the county jail before they even know we've left the jail."[1325]

"Well, we wouldn't have much protection getting off on another floor," Fritz replies. "You can only get so many men on the elevator." Fritz adds that he didn't think Curry would go for it because the chief had given his word to the press that they would be able to witness Oswald's transfer.[1326]

11:10 a.m.

There is a flurry of activity now as the police brass make last-minute changes to the transfer plan. Captain Fritz instructs Detectives C. N. Dhority, C. W. Brown, and E. R. Beck to go to the basement and get two cars set up for the transfer. Dhority will drive the car transporting Oswald. Fritz tells him to park it near the entrance to the jail office, the door Oswald will emerge from in the basement. (The car will be between Oswald and the media behind the railing on the other side of the ramp.) Beck will drive a posse of detectives in the lead car,* parked directly ahead of Oswald's car. When both cars pull out of the Commerce Street exit behind the armored car, they will turn left two blocks to Central, turn left one block to Main, turn left and go west on Main to Houston, then right a half block to the county jail. Beck will drive past the entrance, and Dhority and Fritz, behind them, will pull right in to the jail entrance.[1327] Someone is already on the telephone to Sheriff Decker, making arrangements to have the steel gate at the county jail entrance open when they arrive.[1328]

"Get going," Fritz tells the detectives, who head downstairs.

Curry turns to Lieutenant Rio S. Pierce and instructs him to get a third car, to be used as a decoy, park it in front of the armored truck, and when the signal is given, lead the caravan left two blocks to Central, turn left up to Elm (while the Oswald vehicle breaks away from the caravan by turning left a block earlier on Main), turn left on Elm to Houston, then left past the jail.[1329]

Captain Fritz is so intent on preventing anyone from harming Oswald or allowing him the opportunity to escape that he pulls Leavelle aside and orders him to handcuff himself to the prisoner.[1330]

"Lee, I want you to follow Detective Leavelle when we get downstairs," Fritz says, "and stay close to him."

Fritz realizes that Oswald is clad only in a T-shirt.

"Do you want something to put over your T-shirt?" he asks.

"Yes," Oswald says.

Fritz orders a detective to go and get some of the clothing police confiscated from Oswald's room. No more than a minute later, they bring in some clothes on hangers and hand Oswald one of the better-looking items, a light-colored shirt.

"If it's all the same to you," Oswald says, "I'd rather wear that black sweater. That might be a little warmer."

---

*For whatever reason, Brown, not Beck, will end up being behind the wheel of this car (CE 2003, 24 H 295; 12 H 19, WCT Charles Batchelor).

Oswald points at a black, Ivy League–type, slip-over sweater that has some ragged holes near the right shoulder. Someone makes a remark that the other shirt looks better, but Oswald insists on the black sweater. They hand it to him as Detective Leavelle releases one of the handcuffs from Oswald's wrists. Detective Graves helps him pull it over his head.[1331] In his black trousers and black sweater, Oswald looks very much the way he did in the backyard photographs, the snapshots where he posed proudly with a rifle and pistol. Captain Fritz asks whether Oswald would like to wear a hat to camouflage his appearance during the transfer, but Oswald doesn't want to do that.[1332]

11:15 a.m.
In the City Hall basement, Deputy Chief Stevenson corrals Chief Batchelor and Captain Jones.

"There's been a change in plans," he advises them. "We are going to put two cars on the driveway and transfer him in one of them." Stevenson quickly outlines how the armored truck will now be used as a decoy.

"Why?" Batchelor wants to know.

"Curry and the others in homicide have decided using the decoy would be a wise move in case anyone attacks the caravan," Stevenson says.[1333]

By the time Ruby fills out the money order in the Western Union office, there's only one client ahead of him in line. Doyle Lane, the thirty-five-year-old senior delivery clerk on duty, recognizes Ruby as a fairly frequent customer. Ruby has already filled out the order in large printing, "$25.00, to KAREN BENNETT, WILL CALL, FTH WORTH," but Lane crosses out "FTH WORTH" and, according to the company regulation, which requires the full destination on the body of a money order, writes "Fort Worth, Texas" in the space provided. He asks Ruby for his own name and address and fills in Ruby's reply: "Jack Ruby, 1312½ Commerce." Doyle writes "Mod FTW," for "Money Order Department Fort Worth" and "rates" the order, adding a charge of $.55, a toll charge of $1.20, and the tax of $.12, for a total of $26.87. He makes change from $30.00 in bills Ruby gives him, stamps the money order and the receipt with the time clock, which rotates on the counter on a minute-to-minute basis, and hands a copy of the receipt and the change back to Ruby. The time, signifying the end of the transaction and synchronized to the U.S. Naval Observatory time in Washington, D.C., as are all Western Union clocks at eleven every morning, reads 11:17.

As Doyle puts the money order into the pneumatic tube that blows it upstairs for transmission, he sees Ruby turn from the counter, walk out the door and turn left, toward City Hall at the other end of the block, walking at an ordinary gait.[1334]

It will be more than an hour before the money order is wired to Fort Worth. Normally it takes no more than about twenty minutes for a transmission to Fort Worth, but the office has had a lot of reporters running in with their scribbled notes, and the extra traffic has slowed the wire way down.[1335]

11:18 a.m.
In the third-floor Homicide and Robbery Bureau, Captain Fritz steps out into the outer office, where Chief Curry waits.

"Is everything ready?" Fritz asks.

"Yes, as far as I know," Curry replies. "Everything is ready to go. I'll go on down to the basement. Chief Stevenson and I will meet you at the county jail."[1336]

As Curry leaves, Secret Service agent Sorrels approaches Fritz.

"If I were you, I would not move Oswald to the county jail at an announced time like this," Sorrels says. "I would take him out at three or four in the morning when there's no one around."

Personally, Fritz couldn't agree more. But this is not his show.

"Chief Curry wants to go along with the press and not try to put anything over on them," Fritz tells him.[1337]

Curry has just exited the Homicide and Robbery Bureau when an officer walks up to him.

"Mayor Cabell is on the phone for you, Chief."

Curry heads to his office down the hall, where he takes the call. Cabell wants to know how everything is progressing, and when Curry plans to transfer Oswald to the county jail.

"We're getting set to transfer him now," Curry says, and quickly brings the mayor up to speed on the transfer.[1338]

Four floors below, the public elevator opens onto the basement corridor just outside the jail office, and a crowd of detectives piles out followed by two WBAP cameramen, struggling to push a rolling tripod with a large TV camera perched atop it. When it nearly topples over, a third crewman from the WBAP basement team rushes over and helps them roll it out to the ramp. The word from the two crewmen who have just come from the third floor is that Oswald could be brought down at any moment.[1339]

11:19 a.m.

In Captain Fritz's office, Oswald stands quietly, his hands manacled in front. Detective Leavelle snaps one end of a second pair of handcuffs on Oswald's right wrist, the other end on his own left wrist.

"Lee, if anybody shoots at you, I hope they're as good a shot as you are," Leavelle says half-jokingly, not only meaning that he hopes Oswald gets hit and not him, but that he knows Oswald killed Kennedy.

"Aw, there ain't going to be anybody shooting at me," Oswald replies with a laugh, one of the few jovial moments he's had since his arrest, "you're just being melodramatic."

"Well, if there's any trouble, you know what to do?" Leavelle says. "Hit the floor."

"Captain Fritz told me to follow you," Oswald answers. "I'll do whatever you do."

"In that case," Leavelle tells him, "you'll be on the floor."[1340]

With the Commerce Street exit blocked by the armored truck, Lieutenant Rio S. Pierce, who has been assigned to drive a car with two detectives in front of the armored truck, decides to exit the basement with his squad car via the Main Street ramp (which is actually the entrance into the basement), circle the block, and back up in front of the armored truck. It will mean he'll have to travel the wrong way on what is normally a one-way ramp, but he has little choice. With Sergeant James Putnam in the passenger seat and Sergeant Billy Joe Maxey in the left backseat, Pierce flips on the flashing red lights, cranks the steering wheel to the right, and inches toward the newsmen lined up across the bottom of the ramp. Captain Talbert splits the group apart so Pierce can get through. As soon as the squad car moves through the line of reporters, the line closes up like water behind a boat.[1341] Two more cars, driven by Detectives C. N. Dhority and C. W. Brown, one of which will transport Oswald, begin to move into position at the base of the Commerce Street ramp behind the armored truck.[1342]

8

In the third-floor hallway outside Homicide and Robbery, uniformed officers and plain-clothes detectives have begun moving the dozen or so reporters still on the third floor against the far wall of the corridor. They're told not to move toward Oswald when he comes out, or ask any questions or shout at him. In the basement, two lines of Dallas detectives form to protect Oswald from the jail office door to where the vehicle to be used for the transfer of Oswald will soon appear. They have instructions to close in behind the prisoner as he walks past them.

Inside the homicide office, Captain Fritz turns to Lieutenant T. L. Baker.

"Call down and tell them we're on our way," he orders.

The door opens into the third-floor hallway and Lieutenant Swain leads the way out, followed by Captain Fritz. As reporters jostle for position, Detective Leavelle steps out the door with Oswald's right wrist cuffed to Leavelle's left wrist. Detective L. C. Graves is close behind, holding Oswald's left arm. Detective L. D. Montgomery follows, cover-ing the rear.[1343] As soon as Oswald emerges, several reporters ignore police orders and begin shouting questions at him. A microphone picks up part of Oswald's response to one question.

"I'd like to contact a member . . . representative of the American Civil Liberties Union . . ."

Oswald's words are broken off as he is pulled into the anteroom of the jail elevator. As soon as he disappears, reporters Jerry O'Leary of the *Washington Evening Star* and Ike Pap-pas, from New York's WNEW radio, accompanied by Maurice "Mickey" Carroll of the *New York Herald Tribune*, bolt for the stairway in their planned bid to get to the basement before Oswald does.[1344]

11:20 a.m.
The telephone in the jail office rings and Lieutenant Woodrow Wiggins, standing at the booking desk, answers it.

"They're on their way down," Lieutenant Baker says. "Is everything ready?"

"All clear," Wiggins replies. He hangs up the phone and sees the jail elevator lights cascading downward as the elevator makes its descent.[1345]

Patrolman Roy E. Vaughn, assigned to guard the entrance to the Main Street ramp, is surprised to see the squad car driven by Lieutenant Pierce exiting from the entranceway. As the squad car approaches the top of the ramp, Vaughn, who was not standing at the top of the ramp but inside a few feet (apparently to see as much of what was going on below as he could), is forced to step to his right to get out of the way of the car, all the while backing up to the top of the ramp that faces the sidewalk. There are small groups of people on each side of the ramp exit on the sidewalk. He clears them, steps out into the sidewalk, checks for traffic on Main, and waves the car through. Pierce turns left onto Main Street and heads for the top of the Commerce Street exit ramp to position himself in front of the armored truck.[1346]

As Ruby, who has walked the long block on Main from the Western Union office to City Hall, approaches the top of the Main Street ramp, he sees, with a quick glance, the offi-cer at the entrance (Vaughn) backing up and stepping to his right, his back toward Ruby. By the time Ruby reaches the entrance to the ramp, Pierce's car has temporarily stopped at the sidewalk outside the ramp, and Ruby recognizes Pierce. Jack is one of many who call the detective by his middle name, Sam, rather than his first, Rio. Ruby sees Vaughn stoop down to acknowledge the officers in the car. Without breaking his stride, Ruby turns left toward the ramp, slips past the car, and hurries down the ramp, not sure whether Vaughn has seen him or not. He knows from a lifetime of gatecrashing that the best way to get in is to look as though you belong there. Halfway down the ramp he hears someone shout something like, "Hey, you," but he pays no attention, just keeps walking down the ramp into the basement.[1347]

At the bottom of the ramp, there is considerable excitement as the reporters know it's just a matter of moments before Oswald appears. Adjacent to them, in the level area between the Main Street entrance ramp and the Commerce Street exit ramp, the two unmarked police cars driven by Detectives Dhority and Brown are having a difficult time maneuvering in the tight quarters behind the armored truck.

Detective Brown swings a pea-green Ford up behind the armored truck, his partner, Detective Dhority, right behind him in an unmarked white sedan. But Brown doesn't pull far enough forward for Dhority to get his vehicle in line behind it.

Captain Talbert can see the predicament and hollers to Brown, "Pull forward!"

When he does, Dhority drives the white sedan onto the Commerce Street ramp, then puts the car into reverse and begins backing up toward the jail entrance to wait for Oswald, but a mass of reporters, who have defied instructions and come out from behind the railing, is blocking his path.

Chief Stevenson and Captain Jones shout out to them, "Get out of the way."

Captain Talbert, along the sedan's left side, pushes at the newsmen, who do not respond instantly because their attention is fixated on the door where Oswald is expected to emerge.

"Get back, get back," he repeats, tugging on their shoulders.

Detective Dhority finally resorts to blowing the horn at the reporters as he rolls the car back toward the door of the jail office.

Suddenly, someone shouts, "Here they come!"

Television floodlights flip on, bathing the garage in a blinding white light as newsmen start rushing as close as they can get to the jail office entrance, craning their necks over the cordon of detectives who are in place to shield Oswald, trying to get a glimpse of him. Stevenson, Jones, Talbert, and other officers hopelessly shout at the wave of humanity, their commands falling on deaf ears, "Get back! Get back!"[1348]

Reporters Jerry O'Leary, Ike Pappas, and Mickey Carroll burst out of the basement stairwell as planned, arriving just before the jail elevator. As they rush through the public corridor and out into the garage, a police officer asks O'Leary and Carroll to show identification. They flash their press credentials and Ike Pappas manages to squeeze in close to the doorway where Oswald will emerge from the jail office.[1349]

The jail elevator doors open and Lieutenant Swain and Detective Montgomery step off into the jail office, then move aside as Captain Fritz emerges. Fritz turns back and grabs Swain by the arm.

"I want you to lead the way," Fritz tells him and motions for him to take the point position.

As Swain begins making his way around the booking desk toward the exit door, Detectives Leavelle and Graves cautiously step out of the elevator with Oswald between them.

Multiple voices ripple through the crowd of reporters: "Here he is. Here he comes."[1350]

Two of the three national television networks are on hand to broadcast Oswald's departure from the City Hall basement. (ABC television opted to cover Oswald's arrival at the county jail and consequently had no live camera coverage in the basement.)[1351] The NBC television network is just concluding a two-minute report from the Kennedy family compound at Hyannis Port when Frank McGee, the anchor in New York, hears through his earphone correspondent Tom Pettit in Dallas shouting, "Give me air! Give me air!" A switch is flipped in New York and the live camera feed from the basement of City Hall comes up on the screens of millions of viewers.[1352]

CBS correspondent Nelson Benton is also shouting into his microphone, "Take it, take it, take it! They're at the door!" CBS cameras are picking up the scene, but the program controllers in New York refuse to cut away from the preparations in Washington, D.C., to move the president's body from the White House to the Capitol rotunda. Dan Rather, in the local CBS affiliate control room in Dallas, leans on the guys in New York, "You've *got* to come to us now!"

"Hold on a just a minute," New York says. "We have to get through this Roger Mudd piece, then Harry Reasoner has a one-minute essay." Rather can't believe it. It is clear to him that by the time New York switches over, the transfer will be over.* Only NBC is broadcasting live to the nation.†

Detectives Leavelle and Graves fall in behind Swain and Captain Fritz as they escort Oswald through the jail office and toward the doorway leading out into the basement garage. Detective Montgomery is right behind them. Fritz looks toward the booking desk, where Lieutenant Wiggins stands.

"Are they ready?" Fritz asks.

Wiggins indicates that everything is in place, walks out from behind the desk, and steps through the doorway to the garage just ahead of Swain.[1353]

WNEW radio reporter Ike Pappas, just six feet from the doorway, speaks into his microphone, "Now the prisoner, wearing a black sweater, is being moved out toward an armored car. Being led out by Captain Fritz."

Lieutenant Swain steps through the doorway of the jail office and into the bright television floodlights. Captain Fritz is a few feet behind him. Swain walks toward the sedan that will carry Oswald as it continues to roll back into position. The driver, Detective Dhority, hits the car horn again to clear the media away.

---

*Roger Mudd was still ten seconds from the end of his piece when the shot was fired. Since CBS television was taping Mudd, it missed the live broadcast from the Dallas basement. Dan Rather partially redeemed CBS's blunder by coming up with the idea of a televised slow-motion playback of the shooting with freeze frames and analysis. This was a national television first, but Dallas's KRLD-TV had been using the technique occasionally for local sporting events. Unbeknownst to Rather and the technicians working with him at KRLD-TV, in New York, Don Hewitt, one of two executive editors of CBS News, was on the telephone trying to reach Rather to suggest the same idea. An hour and a half after the shooting, Rather was on the air with a slow-motion version of the shooting, using a pointer to draw the audience's attention to the critical frames and movements. (However, it was not the first slow-motion showing of the shooting of Oswald [without freeze-frame analysis] on national television. At 12:42 EST, NBC television commentator Frank McGee at NBC headquarters in New York tells his national audience, "We will replay the tape of this bizarre shooting in slow motion.") (Rather with Herskowitz, *Camera Never Blinks*, pp.120, 139–140; NBC News, *Seventy Hours and Thirty Minutes*, p.93) In *Air Time: The Inside Story of CBS News*, author Gary Paul Gates writes, "November 22, 1963, was, in career terms, the most important day in Dan Rather's life. His swift and accurate reporting on the Kennedy assassination and its aftermath that weekend transformed him from a regional journalist into a national correspondent. A few days after the assassination, he received a call from [CBS headquarters in New York] informing him that he was being transferred to Washington to cover the White House" (Gates, *Air Time*, p.293).

†However, less than a minute later, CBS headquarters in New York, upon seeing the tape of the shooting from its local affiliate's live coverage in Dallas, which was received over closed circuit in New York, puts the tape on over the network to a national audience (*New York Times*, November 25, 1963, p.1).

Leavelle and Graves hesitate momentarily at the doorway, holding Oswald just inside the jail office. "Is it okay?" Leavelle asks. Detective Wilbur J. Cutchshaw, standing just outside the doorway, answers Leavelle, "Okay, come on out, Jim."[1354]

Detectives Leavelle and Graves march out, Oswald firmly between them, but manacled only to Leavelle. For a moment Leavelle and Graves are blinded by their first exposure to the lights, making it impossible for them to observe any movements originating from their left front. But they soon regain their vision and are surprised that nothing is ready. The white sedan that is supposed to be parked about thirteen to fourteen feet just outside the door is still rolling back, struggling to get into position against the tide of reporters who have come around or over the railing they had been ordered to remain behind and are now surging toward Oswald.[1355] The driver blasts the horn again as Captain Fritz reaches for the backdoor handle.[1356] Oswald and his police escorts nearly come to a halt as the protective lane around Oswald begins to collapse. Detective Graves finds himself rubbing elbows with reporter Ike Pappas on his left.[1357]

Pappas thrusts his microphone forward and shouts a question as Oswald turns slightly toward him.

"Do you have anything to say in your defense?" Pappas asks Oswald.

Suddenly, a man with a hat lunges from the crowd to Oswald's left front, his arm outstretched with a gun in his right hand. Detective Don Ray Archer, to the man's left, thinks it's someone who has jumped out of the crowd to "take a sock" at Oswald.[1358] The man's face is familiar to Leavelle, and in a split second he realizes the man is Jack Ruby.[1359]

Detective Billy H. Combest, who is part of the line of officers forming a protective lane on each side of Oswald and his escorts, also recognizes Ruby and shouts, "Jack, you son of a bitch, don't!"[1360]

11:21 a.m.
BANG! The shot reverberates through the basement garage.* Several police officers jump at the sound. There is a cold moment of silence, a split second, then Oswald lets out a loud cry, "Ohhh!" and grabs his stomach, his face contorting in pain. No one can believe it. The unthinkable has happened.† Tom Pettit, the NBC News correspondent broadcasting television's first live murder, instantly utters into his NBC microphone what would become the most famous and replayed live words in the entire Kennedy assassination

---

*An FBI examination of Pappas's tape at the FBI laboratory "revealed that no identifiable utterances were made by Ruby at the time he shot Oswald . . . Two groans are heard on the tape immediately following the shot. However, it cannot be said whether any utterance by Ruby would have been picked up by the microphone at this time" (FBI Record 124–10072–10368, July 17, 1964, Letter from J. Edgar Hoover to J. Lee Rankin; see also CD 1314, July 29, 1964). The Ike Pappas tape recording (CD 1314a) is available at the National Archives and reveals that the shot was fired one minute and fifty-eight seconds after Oswald left the third-floor Homicide and Robbery office (see also 15 H 368–369, WCT Icarus M. Pappas).

The famous photo of Ruby shooting Oswald (see photo section) was snapped by *Dallas Times Herald* photographer Robert Jackson. It won Jackson a Pulitzer Prize. Another photo, taken six-tenths of a second before by rival *Dallas Morning News* photographer Jack Beers, did not. Beers's daughter said that this six-tenths of a second bothered her late father to the day he died, her father feeling he had been cheated by fate. He had a "depression that went untreated" and it was "all due to that picture." Bitter and despondent, Beers died of a heart attack in 1975 at the age of fifty-one. (Michael Granberry, "Six Tenths of a Second, Two Lives Forever Changed," *Dallas Morning News*, June 30, 2002, pp.1A, 33A)

†The Dallas Police Department had failed to protect the accused presidential assassin, and hence he would never be brought to trial for a jury to decide whether he was guilty, a fact that will reverberate, to the benefit of those who question the official position of the Warren Commission, down through the centuries. "If we had had jurisdiction," J. Edgar Hoover would later say, "we would have taken custody of him and I do not believe he would have been killed by Rubenstein [Ruby]" (5 H 115).

saga: "He's been *shot*," Pettit exclaims. "He's been *shot*. Lee Oswald's been *shot*," he repeats in a tone more declaratory than incredulous. "There's been a shot," Ike Pappas shouts out almost simultaneously, his astonishment captured on his personal audiotape. "Lee Oswald has been shot." The police spring into action as Oswald's knees crumple and he falls to the garage floor.

Leavelle pushes back on the gunman's shoulder as Graves grabs the pistol. He can feel the man trying to squeeze the trigger again.

"Turn it loose! Turn it loose!" Graves yells, wrenching the revolver from the gunman's hand with a twisting motion.[1361] A platoon of detectives pile on the gunman, knocking him to the concrete, his hat tumbling under their feet. "I hope I killed the son of a bitch," Ruby manages to say while being held down on the floor of the basement.[1362]

Chaos breaks out as the crowd of reporters push madly toward the scuffle. NBC's live national audience hears correspondent Tom Pettit shouting above the din, "There's absolute panic, absolute panic here in the basement of the Dallas Police Headquarters . . . pandemonium has broken loose here!" The appalled anchormen at NBC headquarters in New York cannot contain their shock and outrage. While none of them are sure of what just happened, they know they have witnessed a disaster.[1363]

Captain Talbert vaults over the trunk of an unmarked squad car, throwing himself between the reporters and the melee on the floor.

"Get back! Get back!" and "nobody out," he shouts, shoving the newsmen back hard against the railing.[1364] Several officers draw their pistols and Dick Swain, a burly detective, jumps in with his arms outstretched, fists tight. "I'll knock you on your ass!" he yells at reporters.[1365]

Bob Huffaker, reporting live for CBS through its local channel, KRLD, reports excitedly into his microphone that "police have ringed the inside." He gets only four words into a sentence, "And no one is . . . ," when he falters, buckling under the weight of reporters who are moving and pressing in on him. He holds on tight to his mike cord as they step on it, pulling him farther down. Still not uttering another word into his mike, he manages to regain his footing, but only at a low crouch as he thrusts upward as hard as he can, shoving men off his shoulders on the way up through the brawl.[1366]

Someone shouts, "Get a doctor!" as Detective Combest helps Jim Leavelle drag Oswald back into the jail office. Oswald is moaning as they take the handcuffs off him, his sweater ripped open by the gun blast.[1367]

Police detectives bring the gunman to his feet and rush him back into the jail office. Captain Jones spots some people running up the ramp out to the street. A number of reporters are trying to escape with the news.[1368]

"Block the exits! Don't let anybody out!" Jones yells.[1369]

Fellow officers join in.

"Nobody out! Nobody out!"[1370]

An officer at the top of the ramp pulls his gun, "Get back down!" The reporters quickly retreat, a few managing to escape through the corridor near the jail office to the floors above, where they telephone their newspapers.[1371]

One of them is *Washington Star* reporter Jerry O'Leary, who rockets up the public elevator to the third floor in search of a phone. He notices Chief Curry in his office, apparently unaware of what has happened. He pokes his head in.

"Oswald's been shot," O'Leary says.[1372]

Curry's face turns ashen as the phone in the next office begins ringing.

A police officer comes in and confirms the news.[1373]

Secret Service agents Sorrels and Kelley are standing just outside Deputy Chief Batchelor's office when they hear of the shooting. They both run for the basement.[1374]

Captain Talbert pushes his way into the basement jail office and over to the group of detectives who have the gunman on the floor. One of them has his knees on the man as they slap a pair of handcuffs on him. Everyone is talking all at once.

"Who is this son of a bitch?" Talbert asks.

"Oh, hell! You guys all know me, I'm Jack Ruby!" the gunman says.

Indeed, many of them do.

"He operates the Carousel Club," an officer chimes in. Talbert, his mind swirling, manages to remember being introduced to Ruby by Lieutenant Pierce a while ago at a restaurant in Dallas.[1375]

A few feet away, Detective Combest bends down over Oswald as Leavelle unleashes the two pairs of handcuffs. Combest pulls Oswald's sweater up and sees a bullet hole in the lower left part of his chest, the flesh around it bruised and purple. There doesn't seem to be a lot of blood. Combest thinks that maybe the point of entry has been seared by the gun blast, or that perhaps the wound is not too serious. He reaches around Oswald's right side and feels a lump. The bullet is just below the skin. It has almost passed completely through him. Oswald continues to moan and seems conscious.

"Is there anything you want to tell me?" Combest asks him. "Is there anything you want to say right now before it's too late?"

Oswald's eyes are open. He seems to recognize that Combest is speaking to him.

"Do you have anything you want to tell us now?" Combest asks again.

Oswald only shakes his head slightly, as if to say, "No."*

Combest goes on appealing to him, but Oswald is fading before his eyes. Finally, the detective is no longer sure that Oswald even hears him.[1376]

At the booking desk a few feet away, Patrolman Willie Slack, who was telephoning the dispatcher's office at the time of the shooting to tell them that Oswald was on his way to the county jail, instead tells the dispatch operator, "This is Slack at the jail office. Somebody just shot Oswald. We need a doctor."[1377]

The operator picks up the hotline to O'Neal's Funeral Home, a direct connection to its ambulance service, and tells the man on the other end that Oswald has been shot, they need an ambulance at City Hall as fast as possible. He tells her that an ambulance is on its way. The operator then immediately informs police dispatcher Clifford E. Hulse.[1378]

Dispatcher Hulse recalls that Michael Hardin and Harold Wolfe, another ambulance

---

*There's a rather interesting addendum to this. Although Combest never mentioned this in his testimony before the Warren Commission, he told author Anthony Summers in August of 1978 that Oswald accompanied his shaking of his head with "a definite clenched-fist salute" (Summers, *Not in Your Lifetime*, p.407 note 85). Anti-conspiracy author Joan Davison wrote in 1983, "When Combest testified [before the Warren Commission] in 1964 he probably didn't know what a clenched-fist salute was. Although the gesture had been a socialist salute in Spain in the 1930's, it didn't become a widely recognized symbol of political militancy in this country until the late 1960's. It was probably then that Combest reinterpreted Oswald's gesture as a political statement. Second, a news photograph taken of Oswald after his arrest [see photo section of this book] shows him raising his right manacled arm in what very clearly appears to be a clenched-fist salute. In any event, a raised fist was Oswald's last comment" (Davison, *Oswald's Game*, p.254).

Davison limits the salute to Spanish socialists in the 1930s, but no one was watching the Communists more in 1963 than the John Birch Society, and in a February 1964 article in its publication, *American Opinion*, a contributor wrote that what Oswald gave was "the Communists' clenched-fist salute" (Oliver, "Marksmanship in Dallas," p.14; Oliver Exhibit No. 2, 20 H 721).

team from O'Neal's, have just become available a short distance from downtown. The dispatcher contacts them via radio and orders them to report to the City Hall basement, Code 3. The ambulance driver switches on his red lights and siren and races toward Main Street.[1379]

11:22 a.m.
Frederick A. Bieberdorf, a twenty-five-year-old medical student at Southwestern Medical School and the on–duty first-aid attendant for inmates at the city jail, frantically bangs on the door leading into the basement jail office, but the man standing guard, Detective Wilbur J. Cutchshaw, won't let him in.

"I'm a doctor! Someone called me!" Bieberdorf cries.

Cutchshaw finally opens the door and quickly runs his hands down the young man's coat. He discovers a stethoscope in his right coat pocket and lets him through.[1380]

Bieberdorf dashes around the booking counter, and drops to his knees. Oswald's pupils are slightly dilated. The young medical student is unable to detect a pulse, heartbeat, or any signs of breathing, although there is so much noise and confusion he's not sure whether he'd be able to hear one anyway. Bieberdorf reaches around and feels the bullet bulging between the ribs on Oswald's right side. He starts to massage Oswald's sternum in an effort to get a heartbeat.[1381]

Assistant Chief Batchelor makes his way over to where officers have Jack Ruby on the floor. Captain Talbert asks Batchelor for permission to put all the media in the assembly room for an immediate search when someone says, "Graves has the gun."[1382]

"Let's get him onto the elevator and take him to the fifth-floor jail," Captain Glen King roars. The detectives assist Ruby to his feet and march him past Oswald's body toward the jail elevator.

"I hope I killed the son of a bitch," Ruby hollers out again. "It'll save everybody a lot of trouble."[1383]

As they crowd him into the elevator for the ride to the fifth floor, Ruby adds, "Do you think I'm going to let the man who shot our president get away with it?"[1384]

Captain Talbert grabs a batch of memo pads from the jail office and begins passing them out telling officers to get the names, identification, and location of each person in the basement at the time of the shooting.[1385]

Chief Batchelor checks with Lieutenant Wiggins to make sure an ambulance has been called,[1386] then orders Captain Talbert to go to Parkland Hospital immediately and secure it for Oswald's arrival.[1387]

Secret Service agent Forrest Sorrels enters the jail office and sees Oswald on the floor, being attended to. Sorrels uses the Signal Corps security telephone mounted on the wall to call Secret Service deputy chief Paul Paterni in Washington and tell him of the shooting. Sorrels believes the assailant's name is "Jack Rubin."[1388] Paterni instructs him to get as much background information on the man as possible and report back immediately. Sorrels hangs up and takes the elevator back to the third floor, believing that "Rubin" has been taken to Captain Fritz's office.[1389]

Outside the basement jail office, the newsmen, desperate for any information at all, begin interviewing each other. Almost none of them actually saw what happened—all eyes were focused only on Oswald. They cluster around Francois Pelou, a French journalist, who excitedly tells them he saw the blue muzzle flash against the background of Oswald's black sweater. Ike Pappas recalls seeing the flash too.[1390]

Immediately after the shot, someone came running from the left of KRLD film cameraman-reporter George Phenix and nearly knocked him down. His eye came away from the eyepiece as his unipod slipped to a lower level, but he just kept shooting, not knowing whether he captured anything on film or not. He later learned he got it all—the shooting and the struggle for Ruby's gun.[1391]

John McCullough of the *Philadelphia Bulletin* was on the other side of the ramp from the action, but high enough to see Ruby's sudden lunge toward Oswald. At first he thought it was just a photographer disobeying the instructions not to move toward Oswald when he came out. When Ruby's right hand came up, he wondered for a fraction of a second whether he was going to shake hands with him. Only at the last instant did he see the gleam of metal in Ruby's hand and the muzzle flash against Oswald's sweater.[1392]

The millions of viewers who were watching the event on television hardly fared better. Although the tape of the incident is already being rebroadcast over and over, the shooting lasts just a fraction of a second and all anyone can really see is Oswald's grimace as the shot rings out.[1393]

11:23 a.m.

Up on the fifth floor of the jail, Detectives Archer, McMillon, and Clardy push Ruby against the wall and tell him to "spread-eagle." With help from the jail officer, they frisk him, tossing the items they find into Ruby's hat, including a sizable roll of money. They remove the handcuffs and have Ruby strip down to his shorts, searching his clothes completely for weapons. In his underwear, Ruby no longer seems all that threatening.[1394]

"Jack, I think you killed him," Archer says, recalling the look on Oswald's face as he lay on the jail office floor.[1395]

"Somebody had to do it," Ruby says. "You all couldn't."[1396]

"Did you think you could kill the man with one shot?" someone says.

"Well, I intended to shoot him three times," Ruby replies. "I didn't think that I could be stopped before I got off three shots."[1397]

"How'd you get into the basement?" Detective Barnard Clardy asks.

"Rio Pierce drove out in the car," Ruby says, referring to the Main Street ramp, "and the officer stepped out from the ramp momentarily to talk to Pierce, or said something to him, and I came in behind him right on down the ramp. When I got approximately halfway down the ramp I heard somebody holler, 'Hey, you,' but I don't know whether he was hollering at me or not, but I just ducked my head and kept coming . . . It was one chance in a million . . . If I had planned this, I couldn't have had my timing any better."[1398]

Down in the basement, reporters wander about like sleepwalkers among the noise and chaos, trying to get some information, any information, that might make sense out of the past few minutes.

"How would it have been possible for him to slip in?" NBC's Tom Pettit asks Sergeant Dean above the din. Dean, whose job it was to make sure that no one like Ruby could slip in, is wondering the same thing, but he isn't about to discuss it on television. "Sir, I can't answer that question." Although Dean knows Ruby, he refuses to name him.[1399]

Pettit manages to corner Captain Fritz next. "Do you have the man who fired the shot?"

"We have a man, yes," Fritz replies tersely.[1400]

Although the Dallas Police Department has just sustained the greatest blemish on its record ever in not protecting a presidential assassin for his historic trial, and the officers are visibly upset and humiliated, others aren't upset at all. Outside the entrance to the Dallas county jail on Houston Street, several hundred people had congregated in a roped-off area across the street awaiting Oswald's expected arrival. When Dallas sheriff Bill Decker walks out into the middle of the street and announces, "Ladies and gentlemen, Lee Harvey Oswald has been shot and is on his way to Parkland Hospital," very loud cheers and applause immediately erupt from the crowd of smiling faces.[1401]

11:25 a.m.
It doesn't take long for the ambulance to get to City Hall, arriving just four minutes after the shooting.[1402] Newsmen jump out of the way as the ambulance comes down the Main Street ramp into the basement garage, its flashing red lights sweeping over the concrete walls. Police scramble to move the two unmarked sedans still parked at the foot of the ramp.

Twenty-three-year-old ambulance driver Michael Hardin leaps from the station wagon and scurries toward the back of the wagon. A police officer shoves him back into the crowd of reporters, before realizing that he's the driver. Hardin and assistant Harold Wolfe flop open the back hatch and roll the stretcher into the jail office. They find Oswald on the floor surrounded by officers. There is little they can do at the scene. It is long before the days of trained paramedics, and attendants Hardin and Wolfe are simply there to get the victim to a hospital as fast as possible, their ambulance being equipped with little more than an oxygen tank and a resuscitator cup. They pick up Oswald's limp body and put him on the stretcher and within seconds are wheeling him out toward the ambulance, his left arm dragging along the floor.

Ike Pappas breathlessly describes the scene, his tape recorder capturing the chaos of the moment for posterity.

"Here is young Oswald now," Pappas says in a rush of words. "He is being hustled in, he is lying flat, to me he appears dead. There is a gunshot wound in his lower abdomen. He is white."

The attendants lift the stretcher and slide it into the back of the station wagon.

"Pull the truck out! Pull the truck out!" several anxious policemen yell, suddenly realizing that the armored truck is still blocking the Commerce Street exit.

"Let the driver by," someone pleads to newsmen crowding around the ambulance. Detectives Graves and Leavelle, along with first-aid attendant Fred Bieberdorf, pack into the back of the wagon alongside the stretcher. The tail gate is slammed shut as an officer hollers again, "Get the truck out of the way!"

"Oswald—white, lying in the ambulance," Pappas says into his microphone, now nearly shouting over the noise. "His head is back. He is out—unconscious! Dangling—his hand is dangling over the edge of the stretcher."[1403]

The armored truck crawls out onto Commerce Street as the ambulance slips up the ramp, turns left, passes the armored truck, and screams off to Parkland Hospital, sirens wailing.[1404] Captain Fritz, along with Detectives Beck, Montgomery, and Brown, follow in Beck's car.[1405] The detectives are all talking about Jack Ruby.

"Who is Jack Ruby?" Fritz asks.

"He's a man that runs the Vegas Club out in Oak Lawn," Montgomery tells him.

"Do you know him?" Fritz wants to know.

"Yes," Montgomery says, "I used to have a district for about four years out there."[1406]

11:27 a.m.

At the foot of the ramp, newsmen plead with police officials to allow them to leave the basement so they can file their stories.

"Who is he?" Pappas asks, as he slips his microphone into the group.

"Jack Ruby is the name," a police official replies. "He runs the Carousel Club."

"He runs the Carousel Club," Pappas repeats into his mike.

The name rings a bell with several of the newsmen gathered there.

"He handed me a card the other day," a reporter says.[1407] Suddenly, Pappas remembers a curious little man he met Friday night in the third-floor hallway of police headquarters.

Pappas was standing at a telephone, waiting for District Attorney Henry Wade to join him for an interview he had arranged with WNEW in New York. The line was open and Pappas was frustrated because Wade was tied up on another telephone interview a short distance down the hall. Just then a nattily dressed man in a gray fedora hat, who Pappas first thought was a detective, walked up and asked, "Where are you from?" Pappas told him he was a reporter from New York and was in town to cover the story. The man reached into his pocket and handed him a business card with the words, "Carousel Club, Jack Ruby your host" on it. Pappas asked if he was Jack Ruby and Ruby said, "Yes, come on over to the club if you get a chance and have some drinks. There are girls there." Pappas slipped the card into his pocket and Ruby disappeared into the crowd. A short time later, Ruby passed him again, Pappas still waiting for Wade. The reporter must have looked cross because Ruby asked, "What's the matter?" Pappas explained that he was trying to get Wade over to the phone. Ruby asked, "Do you want me to get him?" Pappas said, "Sure," grateful for any kind of help. He watched as Ruby pushed through the crowd, said something to Wade, who was on another phone, pointed over at Pappas, and disappeared again into the crowd. Whatever he said worked, because a short time later, Wade finished his call and came over to be interviewed by Pappas.[1408]

Now, Pappas reaches into his pocket and thumbs through a stack of business cards he's been collecting all weekend.

"I know him," Pappas announces. "Here it is."

"I got a card from him the other day," another reporter says. Apparently Pappas isn't the only one Ruby gave a card to.

"Here he is," Pappas says, fishing the Carousel Club card out and showing it to police officials. "Jack Ruby. Is this him? Carousel Club?"

"That's him!" a reporter says.

"Yeah, yeah," police officials agree.

"Jack Ruby," another reporter says, "I seen him around several times."

"Who's going to give a complete briefing on this?" someone calls out.

"Chief Curry, at his office on the third floor as soon as we can get one set up," a police official says with a thick Texas drawl.

Excited reporters repeat the name, Jack Ruby.

"Jack Ruby," Pappas sputters into his microphone, "who we noticed the other day, he was hanging around police headquarters. Apparently he's very well known here. And he was in the offices and mingling around and now, so we understand, he has shot Oswald."

Pappas turns and starts sprinting up the basement ramp.

"Holy mackerel!" he says into his mike between breaths. "One of the most sensational developments in this already fantastic case."[1409]

11:28 a.m.

At the Executive Inn near Love Field in Dallas, Robert Oswald and Mr. Paul Gregory, the Russian language instructor, are trying hard to get Marguerite and Marina Oswald packed and into the car outside, where Secret Service agents Mike Howard and Charley Kunkel wait.

Marguerite is having kittens over the state of her and Marina's clothes, the lack of clean diapers, and last night's visit by FBI agent Bardwell Odum, who had shown Marguerite a photograph of an unknown individual. Robert doesn't want to hear it.

"Mother," he says, "will you stop talking and hurry up. We have to get you out of here."[1410]

Robert simply wants to get them out to his in-laws' farm in Boyd, Texas, about forty-five miles from Dallas, with as little fuss as possible.[1411] None of them has any idea what has happened. But his mother won't listen.

"What's your hurry?" she asks. "All we have been doing is running from one place to the other. The diapers are wet. And I want you to know how we got here. Mrs. Paine called last night and said that Lee called, and then I was shown a picture of this man—"

"Mother," Robert says again, his patience wearing thin, "*stop talking*. We have got to get you out of here."

Robert tells her he is going down to the desk to take care of the bill while they finish packing. Marguerite hands him the fifty-dollar bill given to her by the *Life* representatives. It is just enough to cover the charges.[1412]

Robert walks back out to the car, where the two agents have been listening to a Dallas police radio channel. Agent Mike Howard comes over to him.

"Now, don't get excited, Robert," he says, "but we've just gotten word that Lee's been shot. It isn't serious, and they've captured the man who shot him."

The weight of the news pushes Robert up against the side of the car. The only thing that seems reassuring about the news of his brother's shooting is the calmness in Mike Howard's voice.

"Where are they taking him?" Robert finally manages to ask.

"Parkland Hospital."

Robert stares into space a moment, lost in thought.

"What do you want to do now?" Agent Kunkel asks.

"I believe I'll go to Parkland," Robert replies. "But I wish you'd take Mother and Marina and the children on to the farm."

Kunkel suggests that Marina go with him to Parkland, but Robert doesn't think that will be best. "I'll find out how serious it is and let you know then," he says firmly. Robert asks the two agents not to tell his mother or Marina what has happened.

"If they knew," he says, "I'm sure they'd insist on going to the hospital with me."[1413]

Marguerite and Marina and the children come down to the cars and climb into one with Mr. Gregory and the two agents. Robert gets into his car and heads off for Parkland Hospital. Marguerite demands to know where they are going. "We're taking you to Robert's in-laws' house," Mr. Gregory tells her.

"No!" Marguerite complains. "You are not taking me out in the sticks. I want to be in Dallas where I can help Lee."

The Secret Service agents explain that it's for security reasons, but Marguerite won't hear of it.

"You can give me security in a hotel room in town," she whines.

Mr. Gregory has finally had enough of this self-centered woman.

"Mrs. Oswald," he snaps, "you called me at my home and asked me to come and help you, to provide a place for you to stay, and here I am. Now, if you don't like it, then I am through with you!"[1414]

Marguerite is momentarily stunned by Mr. Gregory's forthrightness. The agents start the car and pull away from the Executive Inn. It isn't long before Marguerite insists that they need clothes and diapers for the babies. She suggests that they stop in Irving at Mrs. Paine's house and pick up some of the necessities. The agents radio the FBI dispatcher and learn that a cluster of reporters is staked out in front of the Paine residence. The dispatcher suggests they avoid the media and go to the nearby home of the chief of police of Irving. From there they can telephone Mrs. Paine and have some things brought over. The agents agree and for the moment don't tell the women why they are making the detour.[1415]

11:30 a.m.

The ambulance carrying Oswald speeds down Harry Hines Boulevard toward Parkland Hospital.[1416] First-aid attendant Fred Bieberdorf has placed an oxygen resuscitator cup over Oswald's mouth and continues to massage his sternum in the cramped rear bed of the station wagon. Oswald has been unconscious the entire trip and quite still. Beiberdorf thinks he may already be dead. Five blocks from the hospital, Oswald suddenly starts thrashing about, resisting Beiberdorf's efforts to massage his chest and pulling at the resuscitator cup over his mouth.[1417]

The ambulance swings around to the hospital's emergency entrance, the same one President Kennedy was brought to less than two days earlier. A police contingent is already in place and assists the ambulance driver as he backs up to the entrance. A crowd of citizens, reporters, and cameramen are also on hand as Oswald is quickly unloaded and wheeled into the hospital.[1418]

To Parkland's assistant administrator, Peter N. Geilich, it looks as though a wave of humanity is coming through the door with the stretcher. Flashbulbs seem to be popping everywhere. He gets a good look at Oswald, dressed in black, his face ashen. The police, besieged by reporters and photographers, set about clearing the emergency area and closing off the hallway.[1419]

At the suggestion of a Parkland doctor who felt that it would be tantamount to a sacrilege to treat Oswald in Trauma Room One, Oswald is rushed into Trauma Room Two, across the hall from where President Kennedy had been treated.[1420] Orders are given to clear Trauma Room Two of all unnecessary personnel. An enterprising reporter, Bill Burrus of the *Dallas Times Herald*, evades the sweep for a time by hiding behind a curtain in Trauma Room One across the hall but is eventually discovered and ejected.[1421]

Drs. Malcolm Perry and Ronald Jones, who had both worked to save the president's life on Friday, rush down from the surgical suite and meet the stretcher as it's wheeled into Trauma Room Two. A battery of doctors and nurses, many of the same faces from Friday's ordeal, are already there. Dr. Perry makes a rapid assessment of Lee Oswald's condition. Unconscious and very blue, due to a lack of oxygen, Oswald has no blood pressure. An infrequent, barely audible heartbeat is accompanied by agonal attempts at respiration. Dr. Marion T. Jenkins, an anesthesiologist, immediately inserts an endotracheal tube down Oswald's throat to facilitate breathing, while Dr. Perry quickly examines his chest. Noting the bullet wound in the lower left part of the chest, Dr. Perry reaches around and feels for an exit wound. He encounters a lump on the right side. The bullet is just under the skin at the margin of the rib. Perry knew at a glance that the bullet had likely traversed every major organ in the abdomen. Detective Leavelle, who is in the room, wants the bullet as evidence and he says that someone, maybe Perry, "pinched the skin and the bullet just popped out in a tray, like a grape seed." Leavelle realizes that if the bullet hadn't been stopped by a rib on the right side, it would have automatically gone on to exit Oswald's body and hit him.[1422]

The emergency team swings into action, starting resuscitation routines designed to stabilize the patient. Three small venous incisions are performed on each of Oswald's legs, as well as his left forearm, to introduce fluids. A chest tube is inserted to prevent the left lung from collapsing, and the front of the gurney is lowered to help get blood to Oswald's heart and brain. The irony is not lost on some that every effort is now being made to save the life of someone who virtually everyone believes extinguished the life of President Kennedy just two days earlier.

Dr. Tom Shires, the chief of surgery at Parkland, and Dr. Robert McClelland enter the room just as Dr. Perry orders Oswald taken to the second floor and prepped for surgery. Perry quickly fills in the chief surgeon.[1423]

Dr. Shires knows that it will be virtually impossible to save Oswald's life. Had the shooting happened right outside the operating room, they might have some chance, but Oswald has lost too much blood during the twenty minutes that have elapsed since the shooting. There are no doubt multiple internal bleeding points that will take considerable time to get under control. The tremendous blood loss will result in anoxia, the state of being deprived too long of blood-supplied oxygen, a fatal condition.[1424]

Hospital administrator Steve Landregan manages to get a word with Dr. Shires as he and the other surgeons come out of Trauma Room Two, and he immediately passes it on to the press—Oswald has a gunshot wound in his left side with no exit. He is in extremely critical condition and is being taken immediately to surgery. For the moment, that's all anyone is willing to say.[1425]

11:34 a.m. (12:34 p.m. EST)

Jackie Kennedy, her two children, and RFK enter the East Room of the White House, where the president's body lies in state for a private viewing. Jackie had earlier written a letter to her lost husband, and minutes earlier upstairs in the family quarters, she had Caroline, soon to be six years old, write a letter to her father in which she said, "Dear Daddy. We're all going to miss you. Daddy I love you very much. Caroline." Then Caroline, holding John-John's hand, had him scribble up and down something illegible on a separate sheet of paper. Now at the casket, it is opened. "It isn't Jack, it isn't Jack," Jackie thinks, repeating her observation of several hours earlier as she looks at the grotesquely familiar figure before her, happy that the casket had been closed for the rest of the world. She places the three letters, from herself, Caroline, and John-John, along with a scrimshaw (a decorative article carved from whale ivory) and a pair of cufflinks she had given JFK, in the coffin. Bobby, kneeling beside Jackie at the coffin, places a silver rosary his wife, Ethel, had given him at their wedding, and the PT-109 tie clip his brother had given him, next to his brother's body in the coffin. The coffin is closed, and Jackie and Bobby quietly and slowly leave the room, their minds and souls racked with inconsolable pain.[1426]

11:38 a.m.

At Dallas police headquarters, the public elevator opens onto the third floor and Sergeant Patrick Dean steps off. He's hoping to find someone in Captain Fritz's office who can tell him if it's all right to release to the press the name of the man who shot Oswald. Dean is unaware that the name "Ruby" is already spreading like wildfire through the press corps in the basement below. As soon as Dean steps off the elevator, he encounters Chief Curry and a Secret Service agent.[1427]

"This is Mr. Forrest V. Sorrels, head of the Secret Service in Dallas," Curry says. "Here's my keys. Take him to the fifth floor to interview Ruby."[1428]

Curry hands Dean a packed key ring, including the one Dean will need to operate the third-floor jail elevator.[1429] As the two men ascend to the fifth floor, Agent Sorrels wrestles with a dilemma. He knows that before questioning Ruby he should advise him of his constitutional right to remain silent under the Fifth Amendment.[*] However, Sorrels also knows that it is paramount that he find out if Ruby is involved with Oswald in the assassination, or if Ruby has accomplices. Sorrels figures that if he warns Ruby of his right to remain silent, Ruby might not tell him what he wants to know. By the time Dean and Sorrels reach the fifth floor, Sorrels decides not to warn Ruby, believing that at the moment it's far more important to the Secret Service to determine whether or not Ruby has accomplices, and of critical interest to determine whether or not Oswald and Ruby know each other.[1430]

The elevator doors open onto the fifth floor of the jail and Sergeant Dean and Secret Service agent Sorrels step off. Sorrels surrenders his sidearm to the officer just outside, and they walk over to where three detectives are standing with Jack Ruby, stripped to his shorts.

"This is Mr. Forrest V. Sorrels," Dean says, introducing the two men.

Ruby stops him.

"I know who he is," Ruby says. "He's with the FBI."

"No, I am not with the FBI," Sorrels replies. "I'm with the Secret Service."

"Well, I knew that you were working for the government," Ruby answers.

"I want to ask you some questions," the Secret Service man says.

"Is this for the magazines or press?" Ruby asks.

"No, it's for myself," Sorrels tells him.[1431]

Ruby seems to be mulling over whether he's going to answer any of Sorrels's questions. The agent tries to think of a way to make Ruby feel comfortable talking to him. He remembers looking out Assistant Chief Batchelor's window just before the shooting and seeing Honest Joe Goldstein, a pawnbroker and one of the town's more colorful characters, across the street. It's not easy to overlook Goldstein, who's often seen in his garishly painted Edsel with its plugged .50 caliber machine gun mounted on the top. Honest Joe is well off and generous, always willing to cut prices for a police officer, and a publicity hound to boot. He likes to lend money on oddities, like artificial limbs, just to get his name in the paper—"Honest Joe Goldstein, the Loan Ranger."

"I just saw Honest Joe on the street," Sorrels says. "I know a number of Jewish merchants here that you know." It seems to break the ice.

"That's good enough for me," Ruby says. "What is it you want to know?"[1432]

"Are you Jack Rubin?" Sorrels asks.

"No, it's Jack Ruby," the fifty-two-year-old nightclub owner says. "I was born Jack Rubenstein, but had my name changed legally when I came to Dallas."

---

[*]Prior to the *Escobedo* case in 1964, federal law enforcement agencies had a *policy* of doing this, but as indicated earlier, there was no *legal requirement* that they advise suspects of this constitutional right, and if they didn't, any statement made by the defendant thereafter would be inadmissible at the defendant's trial.

In answer to a series of questions, Ruby says he is in the entertainment business, operating the Carousel Club on Commerce Street and the Vegas Club on Oak Lawn. He has an apartment on South Ewing Street in Dallas.

"Jack—why?" Sorrels finally asks.

Ruby is longing to talk, and it all comes tumbling out.

"When this thing happened," Ruby says, "I was in a newspaper office placing an ad for my business. When I heard about the assassination, I canceled my ad and closed my business and have not done any business for the last three days. I have been grieving about this thing. On Friday night, I went to the synagogue and heard a eulogy on the president. I thought very highly of him."

Tears come to Ruby's eyes.[1433]

"My sister," he continues, "who has recently had an operation, has been hysterical. When I saw that Mrs. Kennedy was going to have to appear for a trial, I thought to myself, why should she have to go through this ordeal for this no good son of a bitch. I had read about a letter to little Caroline. I had been to the Western Union office to send a telegram. I guess I had worked myself into a state of insanity to where I had to do it. I was afraid he might not get his just punishment. Sometimes they don't, you know?"

Jack looks up at Sorrels.

"I guess I just had to show the world that a Jew has guts," he says.[1434]

Sorrels asks him if he was ever politically active and Ruby tells him that he was a labor organizer years ago. Asked if he ever was convicted of a felony, Ruby says he was not.

"I was arrested and taken before a justice of the peace in 1954," Ruby says, "but I was released."

"What for?" Sorrels asks.

"Investigation of violation of state liquor laws," Ruby replies.

"Why were you carrying a gun today?" Sorrels asks.

"I often have a large amount of money on me from my business," Ruby tells him.

Now, Sorrels gets to what he really wants to know. "Was anyone involved with you in the shooting of Oswald?"

"No."

"Did you know Oswald before?"

"No," Ruby says again, "there is no acquaintance or connection between Oswald and myself."[1435]

Before it's all over, Ruby says that he has the highest regard for the Dallas police and that they all know him. After getting the answers to a few more questions about Ruby's background and family, Sorrels excuses himself and leaves.[1436]

The interview has lasted less than seven minutes, but Sorrels has all the information he needs to get an investigation rolling and needs to find a telephone to call Washington immediately. He retrieves his sidearm, steps into the jail elevator, and is whisked back to the third floor.[1437]

Now, Sergeant Dean turns to face the prisoner.

"Jack, I want to ask you a couple of questions myself," he says.

Dean has known Ruby since about 1960 when he commanded a downtown patrol and routinely checked out the Carousel Club. He had even gone there three or four times with friends when he was off duty. Occasionally he would run into Ruby on the street, and Jack was always very friendly, inviting him up to the club to see the latest show. However, Dean didn't want to get cozy with Jack, and kept his contacts on an impersonal basis.[1438]

"How did you get in the basement?" the sergeant asks.

"I walked in the Main Street ramp," Ruby says calmly, repeating what he's already told Detective Clardy. "I had just been to the Western Union to mail a money order to Fort Worth. I walked from the Western Union to the ramp and saw [Rio] Sam Pierce drive out of the basement. At the time the car drove out is when I walked in."[1439]

"How long had you been in the basement before Oswald came out?" Dean asks.

"I just walked in," Ruby replies. "I just walked to the bottom of the ramp when he came out."[1440]

11:40 a.m.

In the Dallas FBI office, Agent Jim Hosty heads down the stairs to the eleventh floor, having just finished an interview with Katya Ford, a Russian-born refugee who had befriended Marina Oswald and knew Lee as an abusive husband. Just as Hosty reaches the bottom step, his supervisor, Ken Howe, scrambles toward him, dodging desks and chairs.

"Goddamn it, Jim, they've just killed Oswald!" he shouts.

Hosty is stunned. His mouth opens but nothing comes out. Howe pushes him aside and dashes up the stairs. Hosty can't believe it. The police had been warned of the threats against Oswald. Why had they not taken them seriously?

Hosty's desk phone rings and he answers. It's W. P. "Pat" Gannaway, captain of the Dallas police intelligence unit. "What do you guys have on a Jack Rubenstein, alias Jack Ruby?" Gannaway asks. "We've arrested him for shooting Oswald."

"Let me check," Hosty says. "I'll get back to you, okay?"

"Sure. As soon as you can," Gannaway says, and hangs up.

Hosty quickly locates the FBI file on Jack Ruby, which shows that Ruby was classified as a PCI—potential criminal informant. There are four pages in it. The first is a memo from Agent Charles Flynn saying he is opening the file. The second is a "contact" page, showing that Flynn had several contacts with Ruby but no information had been developed. The third page was a memo saying the Ruby file was closed because Agent Flynn had been routinely transferred to another city. The final page was a misfiled item that had nothing to do with Ruby.

Hosty knew Flynn as a young, new agent in the Dallas office who, like most new agents, aggressively sought out new potential informants. It was department policy and an easy way to keep bureau authorities off a new agent's back. Hosty ran the file over to Ken Howe's desk.

"Gannaway just called and said they've arrested a guy named Jack Ruby for shooting Oswald," Hosty tells him. "He wants to know what we have on Ruby. Here it is."

Hosty hands Howe the file. "Ruby was one of our PCIs."

Howe grabs the folder and scans the contents a moment.

"Don't call Gannaway back," Howe orders. "I'll take care of it."

Obviously, Howe was worried about how Ruby's PCI status would be viewed if it were ever made public that the gunman in the Oswald shooting was also one of the FBI's potential criminal informants. He knew the press would eat it up. The FBI ultimately decides to handle it the easy way. They bury it—for thirteen years.[1441]

11:42 a.m.

On a second-floor operating table at Parkland Hospital, Dr. Malcolm Perry, under the supervision of chief surgeon Tom Shires, quickly lays open Oswald's abdomen in an operation called a laparotomy. The damage is, much as they suspected, massive. Both of the major vessels leading to and from the heart, the aorta and the inferior vena cava, have been ripped open, with catastrophic loss of blood and circulation. The abdomen is swamped with an excess of three quarts of blood, both liquid and in clots. The whole team—Shires, Perry, McClelland, and Jones—assisted by three anesthesiologists and five nurses, work quickly to remove the blood by suction, lap packs, and their own latex glove–covered hands. Sixteen 500-milliliter bottles of whole blood, along with huge quantities of lactated Ringer's solution, are given to Oswald as the doctors feverishly work to stop the bleeding points one by one. The bullet has shattered the top of the spleen, damaged the area around the pancreas, and torn off the top of the right kidney and the right lobe of the liver before lodging in the right lateral body wall. Along the way the bullet has also injured the stomach. The doctors first concentrate on the right side, using packing to control the bleeding around the kidney, then turn to focus on the left where the bleeding is massive. A multitude of organs and tissues are dissected free, then clamped, only to reveal more damage. Dr. Perry finds the source of most of the bleeding, a ruptured aorta, and uses his fingers to clamp it while Dr. Shires tries to stop the bleeding from another main artery that has been sheared away. Working at a breakneck pace for the next hour, the surgical team manages to stop all the major bleeding and restore Oswald's blood pressure to 100 over 85. They begin to think that they may be able to save Oswald after all.[1442]

In New York, CBS anchor Walter Cronkite calls a cousin of his in Dallas whom he grew up with and was like a brother to him. The cousin was the vice president of the local branch of the National Distillers. As such, he knew all the bars in Dallas. "Do you know anything about Jack Ruby?" Cronkite asks. "Oh, Jack Ruby, he's a nut. Why are you calling me [about him]?" It hadn't been on the air yet but Cronkite said it is believed he's the person who shot Oswald. "No kidding," the cousin says. "Tell me more about him," Cronkite says. "Well, he's kind of a nut. He's been around town a long time. He's owned several bars. He has always been a strange sort of character. I can't imagine why he'd be shooting Oswald. He didn't strike me as the kind of patriot who would want to get rid of this assassin."[1443]

11:45 a.m. (12:45 p.m. EST)
On all three networks, most of America is watching the televised proceedings in Washington, where the weather is crisp and sunny.

Jackie Kennedy, in black, her eyes swollen from hours of crying, holds the hands of her two children as she watches the president's coffin being carried by military pallbearers from the North Portico of the White House and placed in an artillery caisson, a gun carriage without its gun. Six magnificent white horses (which equestrians always call, no matter how white they may be, "grays") will pull it up Pennsylvania Avenue to the Capitol. Immediately behind the caisson is Sardar, a riderless bay gelding given to Mrs. Kennedy by the president of Pakistan, and a ten-car procession—with Mrs. Kennedy and her two children, Robert Kennedy, and Lady Bird Johnson in the first car. An estimated three hundred thousand people line the procession route on Pennsylvania Avenue. Seldom have so many people made so little noise. The crowd's silence is uncanny—loud to the senses. The sound of muffled drums—sticks beating slowly on slackened drumheads—from the corps of military drummers following the caisson increases the emotion of the moment for the hushed throngs. Many have never heard the oppressive and ominous sound before, but few will ever forget its monotonous expression of unremitting and unrelievable grief.

Upon the arrival of the caisson, the same one that bore Franklin D. Roosevelt, at the Capitol steps, and with the Kennedy entourage now standing nearby, a military officer shouts, "Pre-sent! Arms!" the words echoing across the square. In nearby Union Station Park an artillery battalion commences firing a twenty-one-gun salute, after which the navy band breaks into a dramatically melancholy version of "Hail to the Chief." As the notes ring out, Jackie Kennedy's heretofore incredible public poise crumbles, her head bows and beneath the mantilla of black lace, she sobs openly. It is a scene that brings a nation to its knees.

When the last measure has been played, the nine-man casket team from the United States Army, Navy, Marines, Air Force, and Coast Guard unbuckles the coffin and carries it slowly up the thirty-seven steps of the Capitol, the widow and her two children following behind. Inside the rotunda, they ease the coffin onto the catafalque, the honor guards take their positions, and the circle of mourners closes in around them.

They endure a few brief eulogies, starting at 2:02 p.m. (EST), by Senate Majority Leader Mike Mansfield, Speaker of the House John McCormack, and Chief Justice Earl Warren. The rotunda, with its vast spaces and hard reflective surfaces, is a very poor sound studio, and Mansfield's voice is faint, often buried under the barrage of nervous coughing from the onlookers.

"He gave us of a good heart," Mansfield says, "from which the laughter came . . . Of a profound wit, from which a great leadership emerged. He gave us of a kindness and a strength fused into a human courage to seek peace without fear."

Chief Justice Warren speaks of a man who was a "believer in the dignity and equality of all human beings, a fighter for justice and apostle of peace," and that he had "been snatched from our midst by the bullet of an assassin . . . The whole world is poorer because of his loss."

It is not the words, though, but the images that are seared into the collective consciousness—Jackie Kennedy once again poised and collected, little Caroline by her side,[*] unable to understand fully what the chief justice is saying.

The president's brother looks drained, deaf to the words of Speaker McCormack, who says, "Thank God that we were privileged, however briefly, to have had this great man for our president. For he has now taken his place among the great figures of world history."

President Johnson follows a soldier bearing a wreath of red and white carnations to the catafalque. Johnson pauses in momentary prayer, then retreats to his place. The rotunda falls silent. The ceremony has ended, but no one seems to want to leave. Mrs. Kennedy suddenly realizes that everyone is waiting for her. She turns to Robert Kennedy and whispers, "Can I say good-bye?" He nods once.

"We're going to say good-bye to daddy," the First Lady says quietly, turning to her daughter, "and we're going to kiss him good-bye, and tell daddy how much we love him and how much we'll always miss him."

They step forward solemnly toward the casket, Caroline keeping her eyes on her mother to see what to do. Mrs. Kennedy kneels at the coffin, then Caroline, as the whole world watches.

---

[*]During the ceremony, John-John, age three, was kept busy in a room off the rotunda.

"You know, you just kiss," whispers Jacqueline.

She leans forward to brush her lips against the flag, and Caroline does the same, her small white-gloved hand slipping beneath to touch the closed casket. The microphones are too distant to capture the whispers, but the image strikes a deep chord in the hearts of the world. A cutaway to the faces of the Joint Chiefs of Staff shows them standing at attention with tears streaming down their faces. It is one of the most moving moments of the entire four days of television broadcasting.

As the family emerges from the rotunda, squinting in the stabbing sunlight, they see the immensity of the crowd that has gathered and is still growing—people as far as the eye can see waiting to walk past the president's coffin in the rotunda. The streets leading from the Capitol are filled, an ocean of people everywhere, between the congressional office buildings, around the Supreme Court, the Library of Congress, and the Folger Library, from the Botanic Gardens to the Taft tower. The fact that the rotunda would remain open was announced on television, and people are already flowing toward it in a tide that cannot be stemmed. Cars on New York Avenue are bumper to bumper and by dusk will stretch all the way back to Baltimore, thirty miles away.[1444]

12:35 p.m.

FBI agent C. Ray Hall is in Chief Curry's office when a call comes in from the man in charge of the Dallas FBI office, Gordon Shanklin. Hall walks out and picks up a phone just outside Curry's office.

"Get in and interview Ruby," Shanklin orders.

Hall slips the phone back into the cradle, returns to the police chief's office, and requests permission to interview Jack Ruby.

"Of course," Curry replies, and asks a uniformed officer to take Agent Hall up to Ruby's fifth-floor jail cell, immediately. When he arrives, Hall finds Ruby in the same block of maximum-security cells where Oswald had been imprisoned. The jailer, K. H. Haake, opens the outer door that leads into a small corridor in front of the three cells. There is a table and some chairs there. Detective T. D. McMillon is seated on one of them. A few minutes later, Detective Barnard Clardy joins him. Agent Hall enters the maximum-security block and sees Ruby sitting alone in the center cell, clad only in shorts. Like Oswald, the cells on either side are empty.

Ruby is led out of the cell and told to sit down at the table. Agent Hall sits across from him and introduces himself.

"Be advised, Mr. Ruby," Hall tells him, "that you do not have to make any statement. You have the right to talk with an attorney before making any statement. Any statement you do make could be used against you in a court of law."[1445]

Ruby tells him he understands. With that, Agent Hall begins to question the prisoner in his search for answers as to why Ruby shot Oswald.

"When were you born?" Hall asks.

"March 25, 1911," Ruby says. "In Chicago."

Under a string of questions during a long interview, Ruby tells the FBI man of his childhood in Chicago, how he grew up on the west side, how he was hustling refreshments at rodeos and sporting events and scalping tickets as soon as he was old enough. He says he drifted to California in the mid-1930s and sold tip sheets at the race track and subscriptions to the Hearst newspapers to get by. A year later he returned to Chicago and, with the help of attorney Leon Cooke, became secretary/treasurer of the

Scrap Iron and Junk Handlers Union. Two years later, his life came crashing down when Cooke was shot and killed during an argument at a union meeting. Ruby says he often uses "Leon" as his middle name, as a tribute to the man he admired so much.

In early 1940, he quit the union and drifted east, where he hawked punch boards at area factories until he was drafted in 1943. He served state side in the Army Air Corps as a mechanic and was honorably discharged three years later at the rank of private first class. He returned to Chicago and helped his brother Earl with a mail-order business and then moved to Dallas in 1947 to help his sister open the Singapore Club, a nightclub. After a brief return to Chicago, Ruby says he eventually settled in Dallas and struggled to stay in the nightclub business. By the late 1950s, Ruby had owned or had an interest in several nightclubs, all failures except one, the struggling Vegas Club, which his sister Eva still operates. In 1960, with financial help from his brother Earl, and Bull Pen restaurant owner Ralph Paul, Ruby bought the Carousel Club on Commerce Street in Dallas.

Ruby says that through the years he has become personally acquainted with many Dallas police officers.[1446]

12:50 p.m.

Robert Oswald's head is a dull, numbed mass of confusion. He has learned little about his brother's condition since arriving at Parkland twenty minutes ago. It took ten minutes just to get past two Secret Service agents, who, for whatever reason, wouldn't let him inside. Eventually, they escorted him to the hospital's volunteer office, but only after frisking him for a concealed weapon. How ironic, Robert later thought. If only they had done this to the man who had slipped into the City Hall basement.

The hospital is swarming with police officers and Robert waits to be told where to go to get a report on Lee's condition. A Secret Service agent comes into the room and says, "Robert, he's going to be all right. Don't worry about it." It's not much, but it's the first clear report he's heard since the shooting and it sounds reassuring. Robert finally begins to relax and starts chatting with Secret Service agent John Howlett, who seems willing to help him pass the time.[1447]

Upstairs, Dr. Shires's operating team has managed to stop the massive bleeding in Oswald's abdomen. The doctors take a moment to determine how to best go about repairing the damage done by Jack Ruby's bullet. They realize that clamping the aorta has stopped the bleeding, but it's also preventing blood from flowing to the kidneys, a hazardous situation if prolonged. They decide that this major artery must be repaired immediately in order to restore blood to the kidneys and the lower portion of Oswald's body.

Suddenly, Dr. Jenkins reports that Oswald's heart is weakening. The pulse rate abruptly drops from 85 to 40, then seconds later, to zero. Dr. Perry reaches in and feels the aorta. No pulse. The tremendous blood loss has set the stage for irreversible shock and cardiac arrest. Dr. Perry grabs a knife, opens the left side of the chest, and reaches in to massage the heart. It is flabby, dilated, and apparently contains little blood. Perry vigorously massages the organ and manages to obtain a palpable pulse in the blood vessels feeding the neck and head, but he's unable to get the heart to pump on its own. Calcium chloride and then epinephrine-Xylocaine are injected directly into the left ventricle of the heart, causing fibrillation, an uncontrolled twitching of the heart muscles, but no heartbeat. They hit Oswald with 240, 360, 500, and finally 700 volts of electricity, but still no heartbeat. A thoracic surgery resident hands Dr. Perry a cardiac pacemaker, which he quickly sews into the right ventricle of the heart, hoping to artifi-

cially induce the heart to pump. The pacemaker creates a small, feeble, localized muscle reaction but no effective heartbeat. After a frenzied, almost instinctual struggle, Dr.
Jenkins calls a halt. Oswald's pupils are fixed and dilated, there is no retinal blood flow,
no respiratory effort, and no effective pulse. They have done everything they know
how to do and it isn't enough. Oswald is dead. It is seven minutes after one o'clock,
almost exactly two days after Kennedy expired.[1448]

1:00 p.m.
Dallas detectives Guy Rose, H. M. Moore, and J. P. Adamcik arrive at the Marsala
Place Apartments, where Ruby lives, to search his unit, but the search warrant has an
apartment number on it other than number 207, Ruby's apartment, and the manager
won't open the door to 207 until after Rose calls Joe B. Brown Jr., the Oak Cliff judge
who had the original warrant, and Brown comes out to correct the error. The detectives examine everything in the apartment, find nothing of evidentiary value, and leave
Ruby's apartment around 2:00 p.m. without taking anything with them.[1449]

1:16 p.m.
Parkland's assistant administrator, Peter Geilich, dashes up the stairs to the second-
floor operating room to get more news for the press he has corralled into the hospital's makeshift pressroom. As he gets there, Dr. Shires and the other members of the
surgery team are coming out the door and tell him the news. Geilich sees Dr. Malcolm Perry among the group and can't help thinking that Perry has certainly been in
the thick of things over the last few days. Geilich grabs Dr. Shires by the arm.
    "The press wants to talk to you," he says. "We have promised them that you would
make a statement as soon as you came out of surgery."
    Dr. Shires looks down and sees that he is covered in blood. He slips into the doctors'
locker room and puts on a clean lab coat. Then, he and Mr. Geilich make their way down
to the classroom-turned-pressroom to face the live television cameras.[1450]
    "Is he alive, Doctor?" a voice asks from the battery of reporters and cameramen crowd-
ing around.
    Dr. Shires shakes his head, "No, he has died."
    "Let Dr. Shires make his statement, please," hospital administrator Steve Landregan
pleads.
    "When did he die, Doctor?"
    "He died at 1:07 p.m.," Dr. Shires replies, "of his gunshot wounds he had received."
    Shires fields dozens of questions regarding Oswald's final moments, his condition
when he arrived at the hospital, the damage caused by the bullet, and the names of the
other doctors in attendance during surgery.
    "Did you first inform his relatives of the death before you came here?" one reporter
asks.
    "No, I came right here from the operating room," Shires tells him.[1451]
    In the volunteer office down the hall, Secret Service agent John Howlett picks up the
telephone and listens intently as Robert Oswald looks on. After thirty seconds or so,
Howlett says, "Would you repeat that?"
    His tone of voice fills Robert with dread.
    Howlett hangs up and starts around the desk toward him.
    "Robert," he says, "I'm sorry, but he's dead."

Robert slumps in his chair, crushed by the intolerable weight of the news. His hand rises to his face, but it can't cover the sobs that follow.[1452]

Agent Howlett is trying to locate the other Oswalds by telephone through the Dallas police radio system when Geilich comes in and asks Robert whether he wants to talk to the press.

"No, no, not at this time," Robert sobs. "Can I see my brother?"

Geilich calls Jack Price, the county hospital administrator, to see if he can arrange for Robert to see his brother's body.

"Most certainly," Price tells Geilich, "let them have whatever we give any other patient's family."

Geilich checks with the operating room supervisor, Audrey Bell, who says it's not a good idea to bring Robert up to the operating room, which is a mess. The body, she says, will be taken to the morgue within ten or fifteen minutes. Geilich hangs up the phone.

"It'll be a few minutes, Mr. Oswald," Geilich tells him. "The hospital chaplain is in the next room. Would you like to see him?"

Robert nods. Geilich leaves for a moment and returns with one Chaplain Pepper. He and Robert speak quietly for a moment, then pray together.[1453]

The office door opens and Secret Service inspector Thomas Kelley barges in with several other agents. Kelley looks at Robert's tear-stained face.

"Well, what do you expect?" Kelley says. "Violence breeds violence."

The coldness of his remark cuts to the bone.

"Inspector," Robert replies, "does that justify anything?"

Kelley leaves the room without answering.[1454]

1:20 p.m.

En route with the Secret Service to the farm of Robert Oswald's in-laws, Marguerite mentions that Marina's two little babies are all wet, that there are no clean diapers for them, that she and Marina have no change of clothing for themselves, and so forth. Marguerite insists that they turn the car around and go by Ruth Paine's house to pick up what they need. Since the Secret Service learned there were many reporters and people at the Paine residence, they stop at the home of the Irving chief of police. Outside the chief's home now, Marguerite waits in the car with Marina's children and Secret Service agent Mike Howard. Marina is inside with Agent Kunkel and Peter Gregory, making arrangements on the phone with Ruth Paine to have some clothes and diapers picked up and brought over from Ruth's house nearby.[1455] (Irving police are already at Mrs. Paine's home to ferry the items from her house to the police chief's house at the time Marina called.)[1456]

The Secret Service men hid the fact that Lee had been shot until they arrived at the police chief's house several minutes ago. They realized then that the chief's wife was sure to have the television on and that the Oswalds would find out soon enough. When the car rolled to a stop in front of the house, Agent Howard turned around and bluntly told Marguerite, "Your son has been shot."

"How badly?" Marguerite asked, stunned.

"In the shoulder," the agent told her.

Now, the radio on the front dash crackles to life. Agent Howard picks up the microphone. "Go ahead," he says. Marguerite can't quite make out what is being said.

The agent mashes the radio microphone button. "Do not repeat. Do not repeat."

Marguerite can tell that something has happened.

"My son is gone, isn't he?" she asks.

Howard doesn't answer.

"Answer me!" Marguerite demands. "I want to know. If my son is gone, I want to meditate."

"Yes, Mrs. Oswald," Agent Howard tells her, "your son has just expired."

Howard can't keep Marguerite from getting out and going into the chief's house.

"Marina," she cries out, "our boy is gone."

Marina already knows. Peter Gregory had told her moments before.[1457]

The two women weep as the agents watch replays of the shooting on the television, which has been turned around so the women can't see it. The chief's wife brings the women coffee as they sit on the sofa.

"I want to see Lee," Marguerite insists.

Marina joins in, "Me, too, me want to see Lee."

The chief and Peter Gregory both tell her, "It would be better to wait until he is at the funeral home and ready to view."

"No," Marguerite persists, "I want to see Lee now."

Marina is equally stubborn, but the agents have real concerns for their safety. To pacify them, Agents Howard and Kunkel take them back to the car and start for the hospital, all the while trying to convince them to turn back.

"Mrs. Oswald," Mike Howard says as he drives, "for security reasons it would be much better if you would wait until later on to see Lee, because this is a big thing."

"For security reasons," Marguerite retorts, "I want you to know that I am an American citizen, and even though I am poor I have as much right as any other human being. Mrs. Kennedy was escorted to the hospital to see her husband. And I insist on being escorted and given enough security so that I may see my son too."

Agent Howard doesn't bother to argue with her anymore.

"All right, we'll take you to the hospital," he says. "But I want you to know that when we get there we will not be able to protect you. Our security measures end right there. The police will be in charge of your protection. We cannot protect you."

"That's fine," Marguerite replies. "If I'm to die, I will die that way. But I am going to see my son."

Gregory turns and glares at Marguerite sitting in the backseat.

"Mrs. Oswald, you are being so selfish," he snaps. "You are endangering this girl's life, and the life of these two children."

Marguerite is appalled that he would speak to her, a mother who has just lost a son, in that tone. It also ruffles her feathers that he is thinking of Marina's well-being, and not hers. She sees Mr. Gregory as another "Russian" sticking up for her Russian daughter-in-law, and it bothers her. "These Russian people are always considering this Russian girl," she thinks. "What about me?"

"Mr. Gregory, I am not talking for my daughter-in-law," she finally says. "She can do what she wants. I am saying, I want to see my son."

"I, too, want to see Lee," Marina says, somewhat diffusing the tension in the car.[1458]

Inside the rotunda, cameras rove over the statue of Abraham Lincoln as television commentator Edward P. Morgan puts into words what millions of Americans are feeling as they watch Jack Kennedy's family pay their last respects: "It is not the great solemn grandeur but the little human things that are almost too hard to bear . . ."

Suddenly, the network abruptly cuts into the flow of images with a bulletin: FLASH . . . LEE HARVEY OSWALD IS DEAD.

Morgan comments to his colleague, Howard K. Smith, "You keep thinking, Howard, that this is a dream from which you will awake—but you won't."[1459]

1:29 p.m.

The third-floor hallway at Dallas police headquarters has been packed with reporters for nearly two hours, awaiting a statement from Chief Curry. Unlike the previous two days, the corridor leading to the administrative offices is blocked by three uniformed police officers standing shoulder to shoulder.

When Chief Curry finally emerges from his office, he passes through the crowd without a word. The look on his face says everything. The press follows him down to the assembly room, where Curry takes a position at the front of the room. There is a scramble and a slight delay as cameramen and television crews get their equipment set up. Curry stands waiting, the very picture of dejection.

When the press is ready, Curry steps to the battery of microphones assembled before him. "My statement will be very brief," he says. "Oswald expired at 1:07 p.m."

"He died?" one addled reporter in the back of the room asks.

"He died," Curry repeats, "at 1:07 p.m. We have arrested the man. The man will be charged with murder."

Curry then identifies the man as Jack Rubenstein and tells the media he goes by the name of Jack Ruby.

When the press start asking questions about Ruby, Curry responds firmly, "I have no other statements to make at this time," and promptly leaves the room.[1460]

Seth Kantor, a Scripps-Howard reporter in the assembly room, later writes, from his tape-recorded impression of what has transpired, "The boner of the Dallas Police Department [in failing to protect Oswald] would rank now with the building of the Maginot Line by the French to keep the Germans from marching into their country during World War II, when the Germans merely went around the thing. Remember the picture of the Frenchmen crying in the streets of Paris then? Only the tears were missing from the tragedy on Curry's face."[1461]

"Up until Oswald was shot," Dallas police sergeant Gerald L. Hill said, "we were smelling like a rose. Within a short period of time, street cops, sergeants, detectives, patrolmen, and motorcycle officers had caught the man who had killed the President of the United States, had lost an officer in the process, and had managed to do so without the FBI, Secret Service, or any of the other glory boys. Nobody could have faulted us for anything at that point."[1462]

1:58 p.m.

The metal door clangs open as a uniformed jail guard steps into the narrow corridor of the fifth-floor maximum-security block where FBI agent C. Ray Hall is interviewing Jack Ruby. "There's an attorney downstairs who wants to talk with Mr. Ruby whenever he's available," the jailer says.

"He's available right now," Hall says, then turns back to face Ruby. "Jack, why don't you go down and talk with him and we'll continue this when you get back."

The police give Ruby his clothes back and he gets dressed.

With Agent Hall and Detectives McMillon and Clardy in tow, Ruby is led down to the fourth-floor jail office and into a room where he confers privately with attorney Tom Howard, an old acquaintance who had represented him in the past. Their meeting lasts four minutes.[1463]

When Ruby comes out, Detective McMillon asks Dr. Fred Bieberdorf, who had returned from Parkland Hospital, to take a look at Ruby to see if he had any complaints or injuries as a result of the scuffle in the basement garage.

"I'm okay," Ruby says, taking off his suit coat. He shows Dr. Bieberdorf a few bruises on his right arm and wrist and assures him that they aren't bothering him.

"I have a great deal of admiration for the Dallas police," Ruby says. "They only did what they had to do. They didn't hurt me more than was necessary, no more than what I would expect. They were just doing their job and doing it very well."

In a few minutes, the doctor finishes the examination and Ruby is returned to his fifth-floor cell, where he is again stripped to his shorts, and FBI agent Hall resumes his questioning.[1464]

2:11 p.m. (3:11 p.m. EST)

Less than an hour after the eulogies ended in the rotunda of the Capitol on Sunday afternoon, the District of Columbia police reported that a serious problem was developing as people surged toward the Capitol building. The original plan called for closing the rotunda to the public at nine Sunday evening, but no one dreamed there would be such an incredible multitude of people who would show up for the opportunity to pay their final respects to the president, each allowed a maximum of thirty seconds of meditation at the president's casket. The decision is ultimately made to keep the rotunda open all night to accommodate the crowds.[1465]*

For the millions watching television at home, both in America and around the world via satellite, there is little relief from the images of people streaming into the rotunda. As has been the situation with all three networks since the assassination, there are no breaks for commercials or indeed for any of television's routine news, weather, or sports reports. To relieve the monotony there is little but endless replays of earlier events, although by now many viewers have seen the clips several times. With the constant regressions and recyclings of black-and-white footage, time seems to loop back on itself, becoming both fluid and petrified. Saturday afternoon exists in the same frame with Friday morning and Sunday evening. When time does advance, it does so in tiny, almost imperceptible increments. Early this morning the cameras caught a glimpse of the president's mother, Rose Kennedy, emerging from a church in Hyannis Port. At half past three in the afternoon she was briefly seen again, this time with her daughter Eunice Shriver and son Ted as they left Hyannis Port for Washington and tomorrow's funeral. An hour later the cameras' view shifted to Dulles International Airport to cover the arrival of France's head of state, General Charles de Gaulle, where he was met by Secretary of State Dean Rusk and a crew of State Department officers who will be on hand all evening to receive an unprecedented inflow of dignitaries—King Baudouin of Belgium, Chancellor Erhard of West

---

*At midnight, police begin warning those at the rear of the line that extends for miles from the Capitol, that they might as well go home—the rotunda would be closed at nine in the morning in preparation for the burial later that day. Most paid no heed. (*New York Times*, November 26, 1963, p.10)

Germany, Emperor Haile Selassie of Ethiopia, President Eamon De Valera of Ireland, and an English delegation including Prince Philip, Sir Alec and Lady Douglas-Home, the Duke and Duchess of Devonshire, and Harold Wilson and Jo Grimond, heads of the British Labour and Liberal parties.[1466]

Nearly a hundred nations have sent representatives—usually several—to form the largest assembly of ruling statesmen ever gathered in the United States, probably anywhere, for any event. Even the Soviet Union, which plans to broadcast the funeral in its entirety on state-run television, sends its first deputy premier, Anastas I. Mikoyan. The UN contingent includes Secretary-General U Thant, Dr. Ralph Bunche, and seven others. The European Coal and Steel Community sends two, the European Economic Community and Euratom one each, while the Vatican is represented by the Most Reverend Egidio Vagnozzi, archbishop of Myra and an apostolic delegate. Thirty state governors, twenty Harvard professors, and three Roman Catholic prelates arrive and scatter to their various destinations without any notice from television at all.[1467]

Among the televised arrivals there are a sprinkling of special programs. A memorial concert by the New York Philharmonic Orchestra, quickly organized and conducted by Leonard Bernstein, is broadcast, as well as "Largo" and "Requiem" performed by the Los Angeles Philharmonic Orchestra.[1468]

No one really knows how much the television coverage is costing the networks and local radio and television stations. The three networks normally earn a total of about fourteen million dollars each night alone from the sale of advertising during prime time, but when the revenues lost to hundreds of local stations is added in, the cost to the industry altogether could run to one hundred million dollars.[1469]

Although the waning day had been almost cloudless, it was cold and windy, the temperature dipping to thirty-nine degrees at midnight, but neither the cold nor the prospect of the long ordeal ahead daunt very many. As late as eleven o'clock, the line of people, several abreast, is still nine miles long.[1470] Everyone is there, toddlers as well as the elderly and infirm. Men and women on crutches and in wheelchairs wait as long as fourteen hours in the bitter cold. People accustomed to being driven to the Capitol entrance in limousines rub shoulders with those who have come by city bus, but they seem united in a single outpouring of grief. However controversial the young president had been to some just two days before, everyone is equally grieved at his passing and draws sustenance from being so tangibly a part of the vast multitude sharing their feelings. Here and there guitarists keep spirits up with folk songs, including the president's favorite, "Won't You Come Home, Bill Bailey?" There are spirituals like "Swing Low, Sweet Chariot" and songs from the burgeoning civil rights movement like "We Shall Not Be Moved." Some weep, some pray, almost all ask themselves and others, "Why?" The sheer senselessness of it all remains incomprehensible, indigestible, unbearable.[1471] In a way, not really believable.

As the evening wears on, the ropes around the coffin are moved inward to allow more people to circle it at the same time. The flow of humanity widens into a river, seemingly endless. Edward P. Morgan describes the atmosphere as a "mood of mutinous, somber sadness."[1472]

2:25 p.m.
Secret Service agent Mike Howard delivers the two Oswald women to a rear entrance at Parkland Hospital. All his attempts to dissuade them from going there have been stubbornly rejected by the voluble Marguerite. The agents escort the Oswald women and chil-

dren into the freight entrance, where they are met by Nurse Doris Nelson and taken to the Minor Medicine and Surgery room near the emergency entrance.

"I'll have the doctor come in and talk to you," she tells them, and leaves to inform the medical examiner, Dr. Earl F. Rose, that they are there.

The hospital staff has already cleared and prepped the X-ray Department down the hall so that the family can view the body there. Under Dr. Rose's supervision, Oswald's body is placed on a hospital gurney and wheeled down from the second-floor operating room to the X-ray Department under heavy police guard. Nurse Nelson and several police officers help drape the body with sheets for viewing, while Dr. Rose heads down the hall to talk with the family.[1473]

Two nurse's aides attend to the babies while Marina and Marguerite, and their Secret Service escorts, follow Dr. Rose into the room near emergency.[1474] For some reason, no one thinks to go to the volunteer office and get Robert Oswald, or even inform him that his mother and sister-in-law are in the hospital.

"Now, you know," Dr. Rose warns them, "that Texas law says that we have to have an autopsy on the body."

"Yes, I understand," Marguerite says. She is sure that Marina, who was a pharmacist in the Soviet Union, understands as well.

"I understand that you wish to see the body," Rose continues. "Now, I will do whatever you ladies wish. However, I will say this. It will not be pleasant. All the blood has drained from him, and it would be much better if you would see him after he is fixed up."

"I am a nurse," Marguerite says. "I have seen death before. I want to see my son now."

"I want to see Lee too," Marina cries.

With that, Dr. Rose leads them down the hall into the X-ray Department and closes the door. Lee Oswald's body is lying under a sheet, his face visible. Several Dallas police officers are standing nearby.

Marina approaches the body and, to Marguerite's astonishment, pulls open his eyelids.

"He cry," Marina whimpers in broken English. "He eye wet."

"Yes," Dr. Rose replies softly.[1475]

Marina wants to see the wound that had killed him. She *has* to see it. She reaches out to lift the sheet away and someone grabs her arm and stops her. She leans down and kisses her husband. His flesh is cold. "In Russia," she thinks to herself, "it wouldn't have happened. They would have taken better care of him."[1476]

Marguerite doesn't touch the body, but sees enough to know beyond a shadow of a doubt that it is her son. She leaves the room with a parting shot for the police officers.

"I think some day you'll hang your heads in shame," she says. "I happen to know, and know some facts, that maybe my son is the unsung hero of this episode. And I, as his mother, intend to prove this if I can."[1477]

Down the hall, Robert Oswald waits in the purchasing agents' office, where the Secret Service has moved him in anticipation of seeing Lee's body.[1478] Soon, Marguerite, who is quite upset, and Marina, who has a look of shock about her, are brought down to join Robert.[1479] Marguerite, who believes Lee was an agent of the U.S. government, suggests to Robert that he should be buried at Arlington National Cemetery in Washington.

"Oh, Mother, forget it," he tells her.[1480]

The Oswald children are brought in and reunited with Marina. Chaplain Pepper asks that the hospital staff bring something for Marina to drink as she has had nothing all day and is trying to nurse the baby. The staff complies and brings in a tray of coffee.

Secret Service agents announce that they are leaving the case and that the Dallas police will be in charge of protecting the Oswald family. However, a few minutes later, after receiving orders to stay with the Oswalds until further notice, the agents tell them that they will continue to provide protection services.[1481]

Marguerite asks to speak to Chaplain Pepper in private. They adjourn to a side room and she tells him that she believes her son was an agent of the U.S. government and wants to have him buried in Arlington Cemetery.

"I would like you to talk to my son Robert," she says. "He does not listen to me, never has, ever since he joined the Marines. I don't know how the public will take the news that the FBI helped a Marxist, but I think my son should be buried in Arlington. Will you talk to Robert about it?" Marguerite rambles on in some detail about it, although she never really explains why she thinks Lee is an agent. She tells Pepper that financially she is in very poor straits and that she wants him to speak to Robert about having Lee buried in the national cemetery.[1482]

2:45 p.m.
Meanwhile, Mr. Geilich, Parkland's assistant administrator, is at the morgue entrance trying to get permission for Robert to view his brother's body. Rebuffed by the police, Geilich tells the Secret Service agents, who insist that Geilich return to the morgue and ask the medical examiner directly. "Under no circumstances can anyone else view the body," Dr. Rose tells him, after being called to the morgue entrance. "The legal requirements of family identification have been met and I'm not going to let anyone else in to view the body."

In fact, Dr. Rose has already begun taking a series of postmortem photographs of the corpse. Mr. Geilich returns and tells the Secret Service agents, who ask him to break the news to Robert since they would have to be with the family for the next several days and don't want to increase tensions. Geilich is relieved to find Chaplain Pepper in an adjoining room already telling Robert the medical examiner's decision. In a few minutes, Robert emerges and seems composed for the first time since hearing of his brother's death.[1483]

The Secret Service agents have two cars brought around to the freight entrance, but two-dozen photographers and reporters guessed right and are waiting for them.

"Do you have any comments?" they shout at the family as the agents hustle them into the cars. "Do you have anything to say?"

One of the photographers is nearly run over as the cars pull out at top speed.[1484] Several reporters jump into two waiting taxicabs and try to catch up. They nearly do, even though the two Secret Service cars are traveling at high speed. The agents with Robert Oswald radio the Dallas police and ask for assistance. Within minutes, four Dallas police cars appear, roar up behind the taxicabs, and force them to the side of the road. The two Secret Service cars bearing the Oswalds quickly disappear out of sight.[1485]

2:50 p.m.
On the fifth floor of Dallas police headquarters, following a meeting with attorney Tom Howard, FBI agent C. Ray Hall and Jack Ruby once again face each other across a table set up in the maximum-security cell block.

"Tell me about this morning, Jack," Hall says. "What did you do?"

"I left my apartment at about ten o'clock," Ruby replies, "and drove to the Western Union office at the corner of Main Street and the North Central Expressway. Before I left home, I put my revolver, a .38 caliber Colt, in my right coat pocket. After parking my car, I went into the Western Union office and sent a twenty-five-dollar money order to one of my employees, Karen Bennett. She had requested it. Sometime after sending the telegram, I entered the basement of City Hall."

"From which side?" Hall asks.

"From the Main Street side," Ruby replies.

"Did you use a press badge?" Hall asks.

"No," Ruby says.

"Did you help bring in a camera or press equipment?"

"No," Ruby says again. "I really don't want to say exactly how I got in, what time, or anything like that, but I will say that no one helped me in any way to get into the building."[1486]

"Then what happened?" Hall asks.

"When Oswald was brought out through the door," Ruby says, "I pulled my revolver and shot him. Believe me, I didn't plan to shoot him when I went into the basement."[1487]

"Then why did you bring your revolver with you?" Hall asks.

Ruby refuses to say.[1488]

"Did you talk to anyone about shooting Oswald?"

"No, I didn't," Ruby answers.

"Did you make any telephone calls to anyone about it?" Hall persists.

"No."

"Did you tell anyone directly or indirectly that you intended to shoot Oswald?" Hall asks.

"No," Ruby says again, "I made no plans to shoot Oswald. If he had confessed to shooting the president, I probably would never have even shot him."

"Why is that?" Hall asks.

"Because I think he would have been convicted in court," Ruby says, "but since he hadn't confessed, I was afraid he might be turned loose."

After a moment, Ruby says, "You know, hundreds of people probably had thought about doing what I did, but I knew that no one would do anything about it. Although, I must say, after I shot him, I wondered if I'd been a sucker."

"You acted alone then?" Hall asks.

"I was not involved in any conspiracy with anyone," Ruby replies. "No one asked me or suggested to me that I shoot Oswald."

"It was simply a compulsive act?" Hall asks.

"That's right," Ruby says.[1489]

3:15 p.m.

Amid a crush of reporters, Jack Ruby is escorted by detectives through the third-floor corridor to the Homicide and Robbery Bureau in a scene eerily reminiscent of those played out by Oswald over the past two days.[1490]

Captain Fritz, Secret Service agent-in-charge Forrest Sorrels, and Judge Pierce McBride await Ruby in Fritz's office. McBride reads a complaint signed by Captain Fritz to Ruby advising him that he is charged with shooting and killing Lee Harvey Oswald with "malice aforethought." A capital offense, no bond is set. Ruby is to remain a prisoner.[1491]

As Judge McBride leaves the room, Captain Fritz tells Ruby he would like to ask him some questions.

"I don't want to talk to you," Ruby answers. "I want to talk to my lawyers."

"Do you have an attorney?" Fritz asks.

Ruby says that he might get Tom Howard, Fred Bruner, Stanley Kaufman, Jim Arnton, or C. A. Droby to represent him[1492] and that he's already been advised by Mr. Howard.[1493] Captain Fritz asks a couple of questions about Ruby's legal name change and the prisoner begins to relax.

"If you'll level with me," Ruby tells him, "and you won't make me look like a fool in front of my lawyers, I'll talk to you."[1494]

In answers to Fritz's questions, Ruby says he bought his Colt revolver at Ray's Hardware and Sporting Goods store in Dallas, and that his roommate was George Senator. When the subject gets to Oswald, Ruby calls him a "Red."

"Do you think the Communists were behind the assassination?" Fritz asks.

"No, I think Oswald was alone in what he did," Ruby replies.

"How did you know who to shoot?" Fritz asks.

"I saw Oswald in the show-up room Friday night," Ruby tells him. "I knew who I was going for." Then Fritz asks Ruby point-blank, "Why did you shoot him?"

"I was all tore up over the president's killing," he says. "I built up a grief, and I just felt terribly sorry for Mrs. Kennedy and I didn't want to see her have to come back to Dallas for a trial."[1495]

The answers are coming quicker now. Secret Service agent Sorrels notices that Ruby is considerably more composed than he was when Sorrels questioned him shortly after the shooting.

"How did you get down in the basement?" Fritz asks.

"I came down the Main Street ramp, from outside," Ruby answers.

"No, you couldn't have come down that ramp," Fritz argues, "because there was an officer at the top and an officer at the bottom,* so you couldn't have come down that ramp."

Ruby senses a trap of some kind.

"I am not going to talk to you any more," he says. "I'm not going to get into trouble."[1496]†

Ruby doesn't say any more about how he got into the basement, but he does continue to talk to Captain Fritz, covering much of the same ground he did in previous interviews with the Secret Service and FBI agents. Ruby reiterates that the shooting of Oswald was due to a buildup of grief; that Saturday night he had driven around and that people were in nightclubs laughing and no one seemed to be in mourning; that he saw eulogies for the president on television and saw his brother Bobby Kennedy; that he had read about a letter that someone had written to "Little Caroline"; and that all of this had created a moment of insanity.

Ruby tells Fritz that he has a fondness for the police department, that he knows the Dallas Police Department is wonderful and that his heart is with them and that he had hopes that if ever there was an opportunity for participation in a police battle that he could be part of it with them. At one point he looks at Captain Fritz and says, "I don't want you to hate me."[1497]

---

*Fritz may have misspoken here, as there is no evidence that any Dallas officer was stationed at the bottom of the ramp.

†In a December 6, 1963, meeting between Captain Fritz and Tom Howard, attorney for Jack Ruby, Fritz asked Howard if Ruby knew the officer at the top of the ramp, to which Howard replied no. Fritz asked why, then, did Ruby refuse to discuss this point with him during questioning, and Howard stated that "the reason was because Ruby did not want to get the officer in trouble." (CE 2025, 24 H 438–439)

For the most part, Ruby is cooperative. Some of Fritz's questions, however, are either met by a quick "I will not answer that," or ignored all together. When Fritz asks him when he first decided to kill Oswald, Ruby simply talks about something else.[1498]

It doesn't take long for the interrogators to figure out that Jack Ruby is a colorful character. Agent Sorrels later wrote that at one time during the interrogation, Ruby asked Fritz, "I would make a good actor, wouldn't I?"[1499]

4:00 p.m.

Homicide detectives escort Jack Ruby past reporters and back to the jail elevator, where he is returned to his fifth-floor jail cell to face additional questioning from FBI agent C. Ray Hall.[1500] A few minutes later, Captain Fritz steps through the homicide office door and faces the press.

"Captain, is there any doubt in your mind that Oswald was the man who killed President Kennedy?" a reporter asks.

"No, sir," Fritz says, "there is no doubt in my mind about Oswald being the man. Of course, we'll continue to investigate and gather more and more evidence, but there is no question about it."

"Is the case closed or not, then, Captain?"

"The case is cleared," Fritz says, "but we'll be anxious to find out more about it—all we can find out."

"Captain, was anyone else connected with Oswald in the matter?"

"Well, now, not that I know of," Fritz replies.

"Did Jack Ruby say why [he shot Oswald], Captain?"

"Some of those things I can't answer for you," Fritz says. "And he, of course, has talked to his attorney, and there are certain things he didn't want to tell me. He did tell me that he had built up a grief. Those are his words, 'built up a grief.'"

"Captain, what excuse [is there for] letting him get that close?" someone finally asks.

"What excuse did *he* use?" Fritz asks back.

"No, what excuse do *you* all have, you know, that he got that close?"

Fritz can't believe the nerve of some people.

"I don't have an excuse," he snaps.[1501]

4:30 p.m.

FBI agent C. Ray Hall resumes his questioning of Ruby in Ruby's fifth-floor jail cell. Agent Hall asks Ruby to relate the events leading up to his shooting of Oswald.

"After I heard that the president had been assassinated," Ruby says, "I put signs in both my clubs, saying that they'd be closed until after the funeral on Monday. I didn't think anyone would be dancing until then." But as it turned out, they did, Ruby notes, clearly at a loss to understand how.

"That night," Ruby continues, "I went to the synagogue and heard Rabbi Silverman tell the assembly there that the assassination should make them better people. After services, I went to a delicatessen and had some sandwiches made up to take over to the Dallas Police Department. I called homicide detective Richard Sims and told him I knew how hard the police were working and that I wanted to bring some sandwiches down, but Sims said they had already eaten. So, I called radio station KLIF to see if they wanted them but I couldn't raise anyone on the phone."

Ruby explains that he went to the police station to see if he could get the control booth phone number from one of the KLIF reporters there. Ruby says he was in the hall when Oswald was taken to the assembly room late that night. He remembers that Oswald mumbled something as he went past him. After the midnight press conference, Ruby says he returned home, where he watched coverage of the assassination on television and read the newspapers.

Ruby tells Hall that on Saturday morning, November 23, he went down to Dealey Plaza and talked with Dallas police officer Jim Chaney, who was on duty there. Chaney had been one of the motorcycle escorts riding alongside the presidential limousine when the shots were fired.

"Then, what did you do?" Hall asks.

"I went home, watched television, and cried a great deal," Ruby tells him.

"Why?" Agent Hall asks.

"Because President Kennedy was my idol," Ruby says, his voice straining, "and it grieved me that this nut Oswald had done such a thing that brought so much grief to the people of Dallas and people all over the world."

Ruby says that on Saturday night he called Tom O'Grady, a friend and former member of the Dallas Police Department, and talked with him about the president's death.

"Did you talk about shooting Oswald?" Hall asks.

"No," Ruby says, "such a thought hadn't occurred to me at that time."[1502]

Agent Hall asks Ruby for a more detailed account of his activities, and the names of any other persons he has been in contact with during the past few days, but Ruby declines to do so.[1503]

Ruby does say that many grievances built up inside him until he reached the point of insanity. He says he was upset over the advertisement placed by Bernard Weissman that appeared in the *Dallas Morning News* the day of the assassination.

"I am proud that I'm a Jew," Ruby says, "and ashamed that anyone named Weissman would criticize the president."[1504]

Ruby says that he also read in the newspapers about Oswald's forthcoming trial and he thought that Jackie Kennedy would have to return to Dallas for the trial and he did not think she should have to undergo that ordeal.

"I saw Bobby Kennedy on television," Ruby says, "and I thought about how much he must have loved his brother. I read articles about the president's children and thought of the sorrow that had been brought upon them. I thought about how Bobby Kennedy would like to do something to Oswald but couldn't. I knew the Dallas police were also helpless to do anything to Oswald."[1505]

Ruby tells the FBI agent that he entered the basement from the Main Street side, but says he did not wish to say how he got into the basement (which he had already told Detective Clardy and Sergeant Dean).

Ruby says he's proud of the city of Dallas, thinks it is the greatest city in the world, particularly the way it's handled racial problems.

"I wanted to be something," Ruby says, "something better than anyone else."[1506]

5:00 p.m.
With the murder of Oswald, the Secret Service knew that it needed a more secure place for the Oswald family (Marguerite, Marina, Lee and Marina's two children, and Robert) to stay, and the Service chooses the Inn of the Six Flags, a large modern motel in Arlington, Texas. It becomes like an armed camp. Secret Service men, carrying M-1 carbines,

and Arlington police officers patrol the perimeter around two adjoining rooms, 423 and 424, in the most isolated part of the inn. A few months out of the year the inn is overrun with people eager to see the "Six Flags over Texas" exhibition, but at this time of the year the place is nearly deserted. It becomes the perfect spot to keep the Oswalds under Secret Service protection. More Secret Service men turn up at the motel every few minutes, flying in from Washington, D.C., California, and other parts of the United States. It seems that the motel is serving as some sort of regional headquarters.

"All we need is to have one more of you killed," an agent tells Robert Oswald.

Although at least some of the agents have been thinking they would be turning the operation over to the FBI at any moment, it doesn't turn out that way. After a telephone call from Secret Service inspector Kelley, Agent Howard tells Robert Oswald, "It looks like we are going to take care of Marina and your mother." But Howard adds that "it seems to me that they're overlooking you." Mike Howard checks back with Inspector Kelley, who apparently consults with a higher authority in Washington. Later, Howard tells Robert, "They've talked to the president and he has expressed concern for you and the entire family. So has the attorney general."

Robert is struck by the reference to Robert Kennedy. Is the attorney general concerned simply because he is the nation's top law enforcement official, or can Kennedy, out of the depths of his own grief, have fashioned some genuine personal concern for the mother, wife, brother, and children of the man accused of assassinating his brother?[1507]

6:00 p.m.
The eleventh-floor offices at the Dallas headquarters of the FBI in the Santa Fe Building at 1114 Commerce Street (just two blocks west of Jack Ruby's Carousel Club) are quiet. Most of the stenographers and clerks, having worked late on Friday and Saturday, are off duty. Jim Hosty is filled with foreboding when Ken Howe, his supervisor, stops at his desk to tell him that both of them have been summoned by the special agent-in-charge, Gordon Shanklin. They make their way to the twelfth floor together.

Shanklin, it seems to Hosty, is not bearing up well under the strain. Working on as little sleep as his men and under far more pressure, Shanklin is additionally fielding repeated calls from Hoover and other top bureau officials in Washington. Hosty knows that every aspect of the bureau's conduct concerning the Oswald file is under intense scrutiny and that both he and Agent John Fain, who handled parts of the case earlier, are in the hot seat.

Now, to make things worse, the bureau has turned up some newspaper articles from a couple of years ago, interviews with Marguerite Oswald when she visited Washington, D.C., to buttonhole lawmakers about her son, then living in Russia. Even then, she was telling anyone who would listen that Lee was an FBI agent. There isn't a scrap of evidence in the files that points to any FBI involvement with the defector, but that will hardly mollify J. Edgar Hoover, whose jealous guardianship of the bureau's reputation is a watchword in the FBI.

The interview is short, tense, and unpleasant. Shanklin, standing behind his desk, does not invite Hosty to be seated. Looking over his shoulder, Hosty sees that Howe is standing in the doorway, watching. Shanklin reaches down into a desk drawer and comes up with Oswald's scrawled threat and the memorandum Hosty filed on it.

"Jim, now that Oswald is dead, there clearly isn't going to be a trial," Shanklin says, handing the note and memorandum to Hosty. "Here, take these. I don't ever want to see them again."

Hosty looks perplexed and Shanklin can read it in an instant.

"Look, I know this note proves nothing," Shanklin says, cigarette smoke billowing from his nostrils, "but you know how people will second-guess us."

Hosty knows that those "people" are Hoover and his assistants, whose Monday-morning quarterbacking is legendary within the bureau. Hosty begins tearing up the Oswald note on the spot.

"No! Not here!" Shanklin practically screams. "I told you, I don't want to see them again. Now get them out of here."

Hosty walks back to his desk. There's a shredder in the office, but Hosty realizes he can't do it there—he has to be alone. He walks out to the stairwell, down a half flight of stairs, and into an empty men's room. He continues tearing up the note, and his accompanying memorandum, into tiny bits and tosses them into the toilet.

Two short paragraphs, poorly written by a half-wit no one could have taken seriously, have become dynamite. To some, they might prove that the FBI knew, or should have known, two weeks before the president's visit, that Lee Harvey Oswald was potentially dangerous, and should have notified the Secret Service so Oswald could have been put on the Secret Service's "risk list," or security index, of the loonies who are detained or watched when the nation's chief executive comes to town. Worse yet, someone might even conclude that it was Oswald's rage at the FBI that tipped him over the edge and sent him off to murder the president.

Hosty flushes the toilet and watches the swirling water suck the fragments of paper into the oblivion of the Dallas sewer system. He fears his career with the Federal Bureau of Investigation is going down with them.[1508]

7:30 p.m.
Robert Oswald gets a call from Parkland Hospital from somebody who wants to know what is to be done with his brother's body. In the rush of the afternoon, Robert hasn't even thought about funeral arrangements. He turns to Secret Service agent Mike Howard for help. Howard puts in a call to a friend, Paul J. Groody, the director of the Miller Funeral Home. In a moment, Groody is on the line and asks Robert, "What kind of casket do you want?"

Robert isn't interested in an elaborate casket, but he does want an outer vault that will be safe from vandals. The funeral director promises to take care of everything as soon as the hospital releases the body to him.[1509]

Official Washington is increasingly concerned about the wave of paranoia building up in the country as the inevitable result of the fragmentary and halting flow of information from Dallas about the assassination. The media in the United States have been remarkably reluctant to speculate about the possibility of involvement of others in an assassination plot, but the Europeans have not been so circumspect. Speculation in the foreign press is running wild, partly because unlike the United States, European leaders are rarely assassinated by lone gunmen, conspiracies being the norm.

Communist Party newspapers in France, unable to cope with the idea that the killing of Oswald by Ruby is without broader political significance, are convinced that Oswald was eliminated in the execution of a plot. Even the staid *Le Monde*, France's journal of record, hit the streets in the early afternoon with an entire page devoted to "serious doubts" about the Dallas police and to what the two killings appear to reveal about American society. That question is of peculiar interest to Europeans, who, although they rarely question America's assumed right to lead the world, are often uneasy about it.

"What's happening, what's going on?" a bewildered diplomat asks as he leaves the requiem mass for the president in the cathedral of Notre Dame in Paris. "This isn't the America we look to for leadership. How do we answer our anti-American radicals now?"

The state of Texas and the Dallas police have already emerged as the villains. *Le Monde* notes that Texas, "rich and conservative," is a state that largely financed the late Senator Joe McCarthy. Reporting on the pamphlets distributed in Dallas accusing the president of treason, the paper says this indicates "the enormous publicity Americans give to the most fantastic accusations." The French want to know how Jack Ruby ever got close enough to kill Lee Oswald, and they frankly do not believe the story given by the Dallas police.

The English are putting the same questions to the American press: Is there a plot in which the Dallas police are involved, and is lawlessness taking over in the United States? Americans in London—or anywhere else, for that matter—have no easy answers, but there is a general feeling that the evidence against Oswald must be brought out fully and very quickly.

The Justice Department is moving swiftly to do just that, insofar as it is able. Although there is "strong evidence" for Oswald's guilt, a department spokesman assures the press that "the case will not be closed until all the facts are in and every lead followed up."[1510]

Premier Fidel Castro, one head of state who was conspicuously not invited to the funeral, airs his views on the assassination in a two-hour televised address to the Cuban people. He calls Kennedy's murder "grave and bad news from the political point of view." He notes that it could change U.S. foreign policy regarding Cuba from bad to worse.

"As Marxist-Leninists," he says, "we recognize that the role of a man is small and relative in society. The disappearance of a system would always cause us joy. But the death of a man, although this man is an enemy, does not have to cause us joy. We always bow with respect in front of death. The death of President Kennedy can have very negative repercussions for the interests of our country, but in this case it is not the question of our interest, but of the interest of the whole world." Noting that President Johnson has assumed office without the moral authority of having been elected, Castro fears the ascendancy of reactionary forces.[1511]

9:25 p.m.

Around five o'clock, Dallas district attorney Henry Wade awakened from a brief nap and heard a national television commentator accuse the Dallas police of letting Oswald be killed, and giving Wade hell for saying the "case was closed," even though Wade knows he never made any public statement to this effect. Three hours later, Wade makes his way to police headquarters on the third floor and meets with the police brass; everyone except Chief Curry, who is not available.

"People are saying that you had the wrong man and you led Oswald out there to have him killed, intentionally," Wade tells them. "Somebody ought to go out on television and lay out the evidence that you have on Oswald and tell them everything." Wade is told that Curry would have to approve. Meanwhile, determined to see that it is done, the district attorney walks down the hall to Captain Fritz's office, grabs a notepad and pencil, and begins listing from memory the crucial pieces of evidence against Oswald. It isn't long before the police brass get a hold of Curry and he tells them no statement will be made like this by the Dallas police, that he had given his word to the FBI that he would no longer speak out on the evidence.

"Look, you're the ones that know about this," Wade pleads. "If you've got the right man, the American people ought to know. You can't use the evidence anyway, he's dead. You can't try him. Tell the public what you have on Oswald. I think you've got a good case."

Wade's pleas have no effect on Curry's decision; the police will not make a statement and that's final. When Wade asks police to give him details about the evidence so he can present it to the press, they refuse to cooperate. Stubbornly, and foolishly, Wade decides to face the press anyway.[1512]

"The purpose of this news conference," Wade tells an assembly room full of reporters and cameramen, "is to detail some of the evidence against Oswald for the assassination of the president."

Pulling from his memory and a page of hastily jotted notes, the district attorney offers a hodge-podge of fact and misinformation that ultimately causes more harm than any good he intended.

"As all of you know," he says, "we have a number of witnesses that saw the person with the gun on the sixth floor of the Book Store Building." (Many took Wade to mean that Oswald was seen by a number of witnesses; however, the only eyewitness who claimed to have seen Oswald, specifically, was Howard Brennan.) Among many accurate statements in his recitation of the evidence against Oswald, Wade went on to make about nine or ten misstatements, including, for example, telling the press that right after the shooting in Dealey Plaza, Oswald's name and description had gone out over the police radio (only his description had); that Oswald told the bus driver the president had been shot (he didn't); that the Tippit killing took place a block or two from Oswald's rooming house (the distance was nine-tenths of a mile); and that three witnesses saw Oswald shoot Tippit three times (the evidence thus far is that Tippit was shot four times, and only one witness, at that time, was known to have actually seen Oswald kill Tippit).

After running through the list of evidence, Wade fields questions from the reporters.

"Do you know whether Oswald's been recognized as a patron of Ruby's nightclub here?" a reporter asks.

"I don't know that," Wade replies.

"Do you know of any connection between Mr. Ruby and——?"

"I know of none," Wade shoots back.

"Are you investigating reports that [Oswald] might have been slain because Ruby might have feared he would implicate him in something?"

"The police are making an investigation of that murder," Wade says. "I don't know anything about that. Although charges have been filed, it will be presented to the grand jury on Ruby immediately within the next week and it'll probably be tried around the middle of January."

"Has the district attorney's office closed its investigation of the assassination of the president?"

"No, sir," Wade replies. "The investigation will continue on . . . with reference to any possible accomplice or—that assisted him in it."

"Do you have any suspicions now that there were?" someone asks.

"I have no concrete evidence nor suspicions at present," Wade says.

"Would you be willing to say in view of all this evidence that it is now beyond a reasonable doubt at all that Oswald was the killer of President Kennedy?"

"I would say that without any doubt he's the killer," Wade answers firmly.

"That case is closed in your mind?" a reporter asks.

"As far as Oswald is concerned, yes," Wade tells them, asserting the very thing that angered Wade when a national television commentator accused Wade of saying it.

"What do you think Oswald's motive was?" someone asks.

"Don't—can't answer that," Wade says.

"How would you evaluate the work of the Dallas police in investigating the death of the president?" a reporter asks.

"I think the Dallas police did an excellent job on this," Wade replies, "and before midnight on [the day Kennedy] was killed had the man in custody and had sufficient evidence to convict him."

"Is there any doubt in your mind that if Oswald was tried that you would have him convicted by a jury? With the evidence you have?"

"I don't think there's any doubt in my mind that we would have convicted him," Wade replies. "But, of course, you never know what—we've had lots of people we thought—but somebody might hang the jury or something, but there's no question in my—"

"As far as you are concerned," a reporter interrupts, "the evidence you gave us, you could have convicted him?"

"I've sent people to the electric chair on less," Wade replies.

Speaking of the electric chair, a reporter wants to know if Wade will also seek the death penalty against Ruby. Wade says, "Yes."[1513]

By the time the district attorney gets back to the third-floor police administrative offices, there is a phone call from an FBI inspector, asking him, "Please don't say anything more about the case."[1514]

9:45 p.m.

Robert Oswald finds that getting his brother's body released from the morgue for burial turns out to be more difficult than it sounds. Parkland Hospital refuses to release the body merely on the basis of a phone call, even from a Secret Service agent. Eventually a procedure is worked out. Parkland will give a message to the Dallas police with a secret password. The police will pass it on to the Secret Service at the Six Flags motel. They will tell Robert, and Robert will call the hospital, saying only the password to the person who answers. When the time comes, Robert places the call to Parkland. Administrator Bob Struwe answers the phone.

"Malcolm," Robert says.

"All right," Struwe replies and hangs up.

The password was the first name of one of the emergency room surgeons, Malcolm Perry, who tried so hard to save the lives of both Jack Kennedy and Lee Oswald.[1515]

All through the night, the three national TV networks silently cover the endless procession of mourners past the president's bier, only making periodic observations, such as that the music in the background in the rotunda is Beethoven's Seventh Symphony, second movement—a dirge; of the changing of the guard every half hour; of Washington police announcing that mourners were still lined up for three miles, five abreast; the temperature dipping to thirty-two degrees, freezing, at 3:15 a.m. EST; Jersey Joe Wolcott, former heavyweight champion of the world, filing past the coffin; and so on.[1516] The president's body would lie in state for eighteen hours. By the time the viewing in the rotunda is over at nine Monday morning, a quarter of a million mourners have filed silently past the body of the fallen president, and five thousand have been turned away. At the tail end of the line allowed in before the rotunda was closed were a group of nuns, who had been waiting since 1:00 a.m.[1517]

Monday, November 25

8:30 a.m.

Robert Oswald has been up for two hours in his two-room suite at the Inn of the Six Flags. He telephones Paul J. Groody, funeral director at the Miller Funeral Home, and learns that Laurel Land Cemetery on Old Crowley Road in Fort Worth will hold the burial service. Groody admits, though, that he is having a hard time locating a minister to give the service. Robert can only shake his head in disgust and says he'll start telephoning ministers in the Dallas–Fort Worth area to find one to conduct the burial services. They both agree to set the funeral for four o'clock that afternoon.

Marguerite Oswald pounces on the photograph of Jack Ruby in the morning newspaper, her first glimpse of the man who killed her son. She brings it to Robert. "This," she whispers to him dramatically, "is the same man the FBI showed me a picture of Saturday night" (referring to the man outside the Russian embassy in Mexico City).

"All right, Mother," he barks. "If that's so, don't tell me. Tell the Secret Service man right over there."

Robert is offended, impatient. He has had a lifetime of his mother's cunning conspiracies, all of them somehow designed to prevent Marguerite from being recognized as the pivotal figure she has always imagined herself to be. If the FBI had really showed Marguerite a photo of Jack Ruby before Ruby shot Lee, Robert is certain that the Secret Service agents will report the episode to the proper authorities. Right now, he doesn't want to hear any more about it.

Robert begins telephoning ministers in the Dallas–Fort Worth area. He is absolutely astonished at the reactions of the ministers he speaks to. One after another flatly refuses to even consider his request to have someone officiate at his brother's funeral. One minister, a prominent member of the Greater Dallas Council of Churches, says sharply, "No, we just can't do that."

"Why not?" Robert asks.

"We just can't go along with what you have in mind."

Robert has only the simplest possible funeral service in mind and can't understand what the minister means. Then he hears the minister say, "Your brother was a sinner."

Robert hangs up and breaks down.

Robert Oswald is still making phone call after phone call into the late morning to find a clergyman when Marina tells him she wants to watch the funeral service for President Kennedy. Robert switches the television on. As they wait for the sound to come on, one of the Secret Service agents says, "Robert, I don't think you all should watch this." He leans down to switch it off.

"No," Marina says firmly. "I watch."

As they watch the funeral services in Washington, a call comes in for Robert. It is Chaplain Pepper, from Parkland Hospital, asking whether all the funeral arrangements have been taken care of. Robert tells him about the reactions he's been getting from the ministers in the area.

"It seems to me that there are a lot of hypocrites around," Robert tells him. "After all, can the assassination be the act of a sane man?"

"Maybe I can convince some of the ministers by raising that question," the chaplain says. "They surely would agree that you can't hold an insane person responsible for his acts."[1518]

9:23 a.m. (10:23 a.m. EST)

In Washington, D.C., the weather, milder than yesterday, is still raw and wintry with whipping winds. But the day is crystal clear, with deep and hard-edged shadows. Six limousines wait in the White House driveway to convey the Kennedy family to the Capitol rotunda. Jackie Kennedy appears first, quickly followed by Pat Lawford, Bobby, Teddy, Eunice Shriver, and other Kennedy in-laws and children. The late president's children, Caroline and John-John, are notably absent—their mother is sending them on ahead to St. Matthew's Cathedral, where she will meet them for the Low Pontifical Mass. She has planned to spare the children the trip to the cemetery as well.

It takes thirteen minutes for the motorcade procession to reach the Capitol plaza, where Jackie and the president's brothers once again climb the broad, imposing flight of steps to the rotunda. They kneel briefly at the coffin, back away, and leave, reentering their limousine for the trip back to the White House.

It takes another seven minutes for the military pallbearers to remove the flag-draped casket from the rotunda and place it on the caisson that will bear it down Constitution Avenue and then Pennsylvania Avenue to the White House and then to St. Matthew's on Rhode Island Avenue, N.W. The huge crowds lining the streets are so quiet that the clop of hooves, the grating of the caisson's iron tires on the pavement, and the mournful tolling of the bell at nearby St. John's Episcopal Church are easily heard on the radio and television broadcasts being listened to and seen by a global audience.

It is now a full military funeral procession, including the Marine Band—called "the President's Own"—and crack drill units from all four academies, army, naval, air force, and coast guard, and it takes about three-quarters of an hour for the slow-moving cortege to reach the front of the White House.[1519] The funeral procession stops in front of the White House around 11:35 a.m. EST, where the Kennedy family leaves its limousines and joins the ranks of foreign heads of state, reigning monarchs, and dignitaries who had gathered in front of the White House. After several minutes, the procession sets out on foot, with Mrs. Kennedy, the first First Lady ever to walk in her husband's funeral procession, and the slain president's two brothers on each side of her, leading the way on the long eight-block march to St. Matthew's Cathedral.

It's a bodyguard's nightmare. Walking bareheaded, in plain view of any potential sniper, are twenty-two presidents, ten prime ministers, and much of the world's remaining royalty—kings, queens, princes, and emperors. There are more than two hundred officials from a hundred countries, the United Nations, other international organizations, and the Roman Catholic Church. An estimated one million people line the funeral procession route.[1520] The Secret Service, seeing the obvious danger, urges the president to ride to the funeral in a bulletproof car, and Johnson considers it for a moment, but refuses. He and Lady Bird walk along right behind the Kennedys, trailed by the color guard with the presidential flag.[1521]

The great phalanx of luminaries marches straight into the lens of the television camera, the front line dominated by the towering figure of General Charles de Gaulle.* Queen Frederika of Greece is remarkable as the only woman dignitary visible.[1522] They set out to the skirl of pipes played by the band of the Royal Highland Black Watch Regiment, which interrupted an American concert tour to appear at the funeral, at Jackie's behest. Just twelve days earlier the renowned pipers had played on the White House south lawn for the Kennedy children and seventeen hundred other children, and the president put aside his own duties to view their performance. It would be the last public appearance of the presidential family together.[1523]

Shoulders erect and her eyes straight ahead, Jackie Kennedy, as one observer noted, bearing her grief "like a brave flag," walked with a poise and grace as regal as any king or queen who followed her. Indeed, the *London Evening Standard* was moved to say extravagantly, "Jacqueline Kennedy has given the American people from this day on the one thing they have always lacked—majesty." UPI's Helen Thomas said, more soberly, that Mrs. Kennedy had "hidden tears and kept a decorum that few women could under such circumstances."[1524]

Arriving at the cathedral just before noon (EST) the family is greeted by Richard Cardinal Cushing, an old and beloved friend, who comes out to meet them. Cushing, the archbishop of Boston, had married John and Jacqueline, christened their two children, and only last August buried their infant son, Patrick Bouvier Kennedy, who died thirty-nine hours after his birth. He bends to the two children, kissing Caroline and patting John-John on the head, then puts a comforting arm around Mrs. Kennedy's shoulder.[1525]

As the military pallbearers, who seem to be carrying the weight of the world, struggle up the steps of St. Matthew's, the familiar voices of the television commentators are drenched in emotion.[1526] By far the largest television audience in history, perhaps even to this day, had been watching the historic events unfold. In America alone, an estimated 93 percent of all sets, and 175 million people, were transfixed by the images on the screen, and Relay, a U.S. communications satellite orbiting the globe, brought segments of the events into the homes of twenty-three other countries; for the citizens of Russia, it was the first time they had ever been permitted to watch live television from abroad. The apex of the viewing audience seemed to be the funeral. *National Geographic* magazine, with representation worldwide, captioned a portion of their 1964 article, "World Stops at Moment of Funeral." The magazine reported that "for the next few minutes [referring to the casket being brought from the limousine to the cathedral portico], whatever the hour in other lands, countless millions of the earth's people paused to honor the dead President . . . Across our nation trains stopped. Jets halted on airport runways. The Panama Canal suspended operations. Motorists paused in New York's Times Square. Evening traffic halted in Athens, Greece. Around the world flags stood at half-mast."[1527]

11:00 a.m.
At police headquarters, Jim Leavelle, the lead detective in the Tippit murder case, is sipping coffee in the squad room with a couple other detectives, waiting for Captain Fritz when Fritz calls.

---

*Murray Kempton and James Ridgeway would write in the *New Republic*, "It had been less than three years since Mr. Kennedy had announced that a new generation was taking up the torch. Now, old General de Gaulle and old Mr. Mikoyan were coming to see him buried" (Kempton and Ridgeway, "Romans," p.10).

"Are you in a position to talk?" Fritz asks.

"No, not really," Leavelle says.

"Well, go into my office and pick up the phone in there," Fritz tells him.

Leavelle quietly saunters to the privacy of Fritz's office.

"What's up?" he asks.

"I'm down here at the Greyhound bus station with Graves and Montgomery," Fritz says. "We've cased the county jail and it looks clear. I'm going to make a suggestion to you, and if you don't think it will work, I want you to tell me."

"Okay," Leavelle replies, wondering just what Fritz has up his sleeve.

"Go get Ruby out of jail any way you want to, and bring him down in the elevator to the basement," Fritz says. "We'll pull through the basement at a prearranged time, load him up, and whisk him right on down to the county jail with another squad car following us. Do you think it will work?"

"Yes," Leavelle agrees. "I think it will the way you've got it set up."

"I haven't called [Sheriff Bill] Decker or asked the chief about it," Fritz admits.

"Well, all you can do is get bawled out," Leavelle says, "but a bawling out is better than losing a prisoner."

The two homicide men set about conspiring to move Ruby in secret.

"How many men you got there to help you with him?" Fritz asks.

"Three or four," Leavelle answers.

"Okay. Don't tell anybody where you're going," Fritz orders. "Just get them like you're going after coffee and get downstairs or somewhere and tell them what you're going to do. I'll meet you in the basement at exactly eleven-fifteen."

The two men synchronize their watches.

"Okay, Captain," Leavelle says, and hangs up. He walks out into the squad room and without a word motions to Detectives Brown, Dhority, and Beck to follow him. The men follow, their curiosity piqued.

A reporter squares off with Leavelle the minute the detectives step into the third-floor hallway.

"When are you going to transfer Ruby?" the newsman asks.

"Oh, I don't know," Leavelle says coyly, and keeps walking.

When they get downstairs, Leavelle outlines the plan. He tells Brown and Beck to get another car out of the garage and get it in position to go out the ramp. He and Dhority go up to the fifth floor and check Ruby out of jail. They bring him down to the basement in the jail elevator, the same elevator Oswald rode on his fateful journey. Leavelle, who has known Ruby and been friendly with him (though not friends) since 1951, says to Ruby on the way down, "Jack, in all the years I've known you, you've never deliberately caused any police officer any trouble that I know of [but] you didn't do us any favor when you shot Oswald. You've really put the pressure on us." Ruby replied, "That's the last thing in the world I wanted to do. I just wanted to be a damned hero and all I've done is foul things up."

"Wait here," Leavelle tells Dhority, who has a tight grip on Ruby's arm, as they reach the basement.

Leavelle slips out of the elevator, letting the door close behind him. He looks at his watch. They're only two minutes early.

"Don't let anybody ring for this elevator," he tells the unaware lieutenant standing behind the booking desk. "We're going to have it tied up."

Detective Brown talks casually with one of the jail officers just outside the jail office door, his eyes glancing at the top of the Main Street ramp every now and then. A few feet away, Detective Beck sits behind the wheel of an unmarked squad car, its motor running.

Brown spots Captain Fritz's car, with Detective L. D. Montgomery driving and Fritz in the passenger's seat, pulling into the Main Street ramp. Brown turns and nods toward Leavelle, who opens the elevator door so Dhority and Ruby can step out.

"I don't want to have to push or shove you," Leavelle tells Ruby, whom he hasn't bothered to shackle himself to. "But I want you to move."

Ruby is shaking, afraid another vigilante is lying in wait for *him*. Captain Fritz's car glides to the bottom of the ramp and stops. Detective Graves, in the rear seat on the far side, leans over to open the rear door and when he does, Ruby dashes away from Leavelle and Dhority, as astonished jail officers look on, running to the open door where he crawls on his hands and knees onto the floorboard in the backseat and lies on his stomach.* Leavelle follows Ruby into the backseat and places his feet on Ruby's back. "Jack was frightened and that's where he wanted to stay," Leavelle said, referring to Ruby's prone position on the car floorboard, which he would stay in all the way to the county jail. The car leaves the basement garage with Dhority, Brown, and Beck in the backup car. The two-car caravan catches every green light en route to the county jail. When they arrive, the detectives in the lead car get out and cover the jail entrance. In a matter of seconds, Jack Ruby is safely inside the county jail.[1528]

11:18 a.m. (12:18 p.m. EST)

At St. Matthew's Cathedral in Washington, the cameras inside pick up the last of the mourners as they crowd into the church. Admission is by invitation only, but in spite of the planners' best efforts, the green-domed edifice is overflowing with a thousand people, many uninvited. The casket rests at the foot of the altar as Cardinal Cushing, in the Pontifical Low Requiem Mass, prays "for John Fitzgerald Kennedy and also for the redemption of all men . . . May the angels, dear Jack, lead you into paradise." First Mrs. Kennedy, then Robert and Ted Kennedy and hundreds in attendance receive Holy Communion from the cardinal, and Bishop Philip Hannan gives an eleven-minute sermon in which he quotes liberally from the late president's speeches.[1529]

New York Times reporter R. W. Apple describes his city as being "like a vast church," where schools and businesses are closed and four thousand people stand silently in Grand Central Station to watch the funeral rites on a huge television screen, some of them genuflecting or making the sign of the cross. At anchor at Bayonne, New Jersey, the aircraft carrier *Franklin D. Roosevelt* fires its deck guns twenty-one times, once a minute from 12:00 noon to 12:21.[1530]

"For those who are faithful to You, Oh Lord, life is not taken away; it is transformed," Cardinal Cushing says solemnly. He blesses the casket with holy water.[1531]

Outside the cathedral, after the one-hour funeral service, John-John stands hard by his mother as the casket is brought out, still clasping a pamphlet he was given as a distraction while sitting out the main body of the mass with a Secret Service agent in a cathedral anteroom. As the coffin is returned to the caisson, Jackie bends to her young

---

*"How come you weren't handcuffed to Ruby?" I asked Leavelle. "No need to," Leavelle said. "Jack wasn't going anywhere I didn't want him to. If he did, I'd know where to find him," he added in the special dry wit of Texans. (Telephone interview of James Leavelle by author on November 19, 2004)

son, takes the pamphlet from his tiny hand, and whispers something. In a heartbreaking gesture, the president's son, who turned three today, cocks his elbow and salutes his father's casket. Spectators standing across the street almost buckle at the sight. Of all the images burned into the consciousness of America, nothing comes close to the power of that tiny salute.[1532]

As the caisson starts to roll, the heads of state and other dignitaries stand about waiting for their cars—the distance to Arlington National Cemetery is much too far to walk. Two former presidents, Dwight Eisenhower and Harry Truman, passionate political enemies only a few years earlier, walk to their car together. The muffled drums begin again, a constant rumble that nonetheless fails to drown out the spirited clack of the hooves of Black Jack, the magnificent sixteen-year-old riderless horse with a sword strapped to the empty saddle and stirrups holding empty boots pointed backward, a part of an ancient tradition in the funeral procession of a fallen leader, symbolizing that he will never ride again. The family cars roll slowly in behind the honor guards, followed by President Johnson's automobile and the ever-present Secret Service. One by one the other vehicles fall into position in the one-hour, three-mile-long procession, which snakes along Connecticut Avenue to Seventeenth, and then Constitution to the Lincoln Memorial, where it crosses the Potomac River on the Memorial Bridge to Arlington National Cemetery, where only one other president is buried, William Howard Taft. David Brinkley muses that the first cars are quite likely to arrive at Arlington before the last cars depart St. Matthew's Cathedral. The cameras mark time by showing faces from the crowd of ordinary Americans: a young priest, a soldier in dark glasses, a college boy holding a radio to his ear, an older woman clutching a large purse, and a family eating their lunch on the curb.[1533]

As the cortege starts across the bridge, the cameras catch stunning shots from the heights on the Virginia side, the Lincoln Memorial perched majestically in the background. Waiting at attention at the bridgehead, facing the memorial in the far distance, are members of the army's ceremonial Old Guard Fife and Drum Corps in their blazing red tunics and tricorn hats, a colorful reminder of the country's revolutionary origins.[1534]

The matched gray horses begin to labor as they pull the caisson up the winding roadway that leads to the 420-acre, one-hundred-year-old cemetery situated on land once owned by Confederate general Robert E. Lee. Last spring President Kennedy stopped here to relax and enjoy the view of the sparkling city across the river. "I could stay up here forever," he remarked.[1535] Just fourteen days ago, November 11, the president, himself a decorated navy veteran of World War II, had driven here with his son John Jr. to lay a Veterans' Day wreath on the Tomb of the Unknown Soldier, which is close to his grave site.[1536]

As the procession nears the site of the open grave on a sloping hillside, the Irish Guard, a crack drill unit President Kennedy admired on his recent trip to Ireland, stands at parade rest. The casket advances slowly to the wail of bagpipes. As it reaches the grave site, a flight of fifty jet fighters, one for each state, thunders overhead at a speed so fast they precede their own sound. One position, in the otherwise perfect V-formation, is left empty, in accordance with air force tradition. The last plane to fly over, at a terrifying altitude of just five hundred feet, is the president's personal jet, Air Force One, dramatically dipping its wings in tribute.[1537]

The roar of the jet engines soon gives way to the silence of a hillside of somber faces. Cardinal Cushing intones the final prayer: "Oh God, through Whose mercy [the] souls of the faithful find rest, be pleased to bless this grave and . . . the body we bury herein, that of our beloved Jack Kennedy, the thirty-fifth President of the United States, that his soul may rejoice in Thee with all the saints, through Christ our Lord. Amen."[1538]

The network pool camera sweeps over the line of military graves to the Custis-Lee Mansion on the hill above the ceremony, then cuts to Mrs. Kennedy. As each fusillade of the twenty-one-gun salute from three 76-millimeter canons is fired over the grave by the riflemen of the Old Guard, she shudders.

Cardinal Cushing asks the Holy Father to grant John Fitzgerald Kennedy eternal rest, and bugler Sergeant Keith Clark steps forward to play taps. His lips are chilled blue—he has been waiting in the cold wind on the exposed hillside for three hours—and one note cracks, adding an unexpected poignancy to the mournful air.[1539]

The flag folding begins. The camera moves in for close-ups of the white-gloved hands rapidly creating the traditional triangular bundle of the great flag, which has until now draped the casket. The flag is rapidly passed through the honor guards from hand to hand until it reaches John C. Metzler, superintendent of the cemetery, who turns and places it in the hands of the young widow, whose lips, for the first time in public, visibly tremble. The Cardinal sprinkles holy water on the coffin, and Mrs. Kennedy, touching a torch to a jet of gas, lights the eternal flame.* Their hands locked in embrace, Bobby Kennedy then leads Jackie from the grave.[1540]

Although the rites are concluded at 3:15 p.m. EST,[1541]† television lingers at the scene, giving the commentators a chance to recall special moments from the four-day ordeal. Somehow television itself, improvising blindly to cover a unique event in the history of the medium, has become a major component of the larger historical event, and those who constructed that effort are already beginning to realize that some of them are inextricably woven into the texture of the experience—the sad eyes of Walter Cronkite, the poetic irony of Edward P. Morgan, the righteous anger of Chet Huntley. The television images have also conveyed the feelings of a nation, something that was impossible to adequately express in words.

Jacqueline Kennedy has one further official duty to attend to, and despite her mental state, it is of her own choosing. She will receive the foreign dignitaries who had come to the funeral from more than one hundred countries at the White House. "It would be most ungracious of me not to have all those people in our house," she says, and manages a smile and thank you for each of them. JFK had once said of Jacqueline, "My wife is a shy, quiet girl, but when things get rough, she can handle herself pretty well."[1542]

Approaching midnight, Bobby Kennedy, alone with Jacqueline on the second floor of the White House, says quietly, "Should we go visit our friend?" After gathering up lilies of the valley she had kept in a gold cup on a table in the hall, they arrive at the cemetery

---

*The idea of the eternal flame at Kennedy's grave site, one that would glow forever, was Jackie's. She had seen one under the Arc de Triomphe in Paris (one of only two in the world, the other at Gettysburg), and insisted on one for her husband, saying she didn't want the country to ever forget him. Her request threw those around her, as well as those in charge of the funeral, into a tizzy, no one knowing how to produce such a device—at one point prompting Richard Goodwin, a JFK assistant and writer, to bark into the phone at an officer at nearby Fort Myers, "If you can design an atomic bomb, you can put a little flame [one that wouldn't die] on the side of that hill." The military ended up passing, resorting instead to the yellow pages of the telephone directory under "Gas Companies," and securing a modified road torch supplied by the Washington Gas & Light Company. (Manchester, *Death of a President*, pp.550–552)

†A quarter hour after the Kennedy family had left the cemetery, the president's coffin was lowered into the grave under the vigilant eyes of the network television cameras. It's 3:32 p.m. Three minutes later, under orders from John C. Metzler, Arlington Cemetery's superintendent, the power to the network cameras was cut to allow the final stages of the burial to be carried out in private. Shortly thereafter, the burial vault was sealed, the grave filled with dirt, a picket fence erected around the plot, and the surrounding ground dressed with evergreen boughs and flowers. (Manchester, *Death of a President*, p.604; 3:32 p.m.: ARRB MD 134, Funeral Arrangements for John Fitzgerald Kennedy, November 25, 1963, p.3, "at precisely 3:32 p.m., the casket was slowly lowered into the ground"; see also *New York Times*, November 26, 1963, pp.2, 4)

at 11:53 p.m. in their black Mercury, followed by a car with two Secret Service agents. In the presence of only Secret Service agent Clint Hill, two military policemen, and the cemetery superintendent standing at a distance, and the only light being that from the flickering eternal flame, blue in the night, the attorney general and former First Lady drop to their knees and pray silently. Rising, Jackie places the spray of lilies on the grave. Together, they turn and walk down into darkness and into lives that would never be the same.[1543]

1:30 p.m.

Earlier in the day Robert Oswald had gotten a call from Miller Funeral Home director Paul Groody and learned, to his horror, that Laurel Land Cemetery was refusing to accept his brother's remains for burial. Groody had also called other area cemeteries, but everyone had refused, staying away from Oswald's body the way the devil stays away from holy water.

"What do they say?" Robert asked.

"The one in Fort Worth is associated with Laurel Land Memorial in Dallas," Groody explained, "which is where Officer Tippit will be buried."

That, Robert can understand.

"The rest offer vague reasons," Groody continued.

Robert and the funeral director agreed that the rest of the cemeteries are acting out of nothing short of prejudice. Christian charity, it seems, doesn't extend to the presumed assassin of President Kennedy. Groody promised to make arrangements elsewhere as soon as possible.[1544]

Groody now finally calls back and tells Robert, to his great relief, that arrangements for Lee's burial have been secured with Rose Hill Cemetery in Fort Worth, and he is continuing in his search for a minister. The burial will take place at four o'clock and Robert knows he has just three and half hours to find a minister. He thanks Groody for his help and hangs up.

Shortly thereafter, two Lutheran ministers show up at the Inn of the Six Flags. While one waits in the lobby, the other, Reverend French, is escorted to meet with Robert and his family. The minister takes a seat on the sofa, with Robert and Marguerite on each side of him. It is obvious from the start that Reverend French is not eager to officiate at any services for Lee Oswald, and refuses, despite Robert's request, to hold any kind of service in a church. Robert begins crying, trying to get the minister to agree to his wishes, but the reverend only quotes scriptures, referring to Lee as a "lost sheep."

"If Lee is a lost sheep," Marguerite snaps, "then he is the one who should go to church! The good people do not need to go to church. If he is a murderer, then it is he we should be concerned with."

A Secret Service agent steps over to them.

"Mrs. Oswald, please be quiet. You are making matters worse," he says, rankling Marguerite.

Reverend French reluctantly gives in, agreeing to officiate at the services as long as they are held in a cemetery chapel, not a church. Two Secret Service men who are in the room confirm with the minister the time for the service—4:00 p.m.—and make sure he knows how to get to Rose Hill.[1545]

1:50 p.m.

At the Dallas county jail, Jack Ruby is interrogated once again, this time by FBI agents C. Ray Hall and Manning C. Clements. In the presence of his lawyers, Melvin Belli, Joe

Tonahill, Sam Brody, and William Choulous, he talks about seeing Oswald coming out of the jail office just as he got to the bottom of the Main Street ramp. "To me," he says, "he had this smirky, smug, vindictive attitude. I can't explain what impression he gave me, but that is all I can . . . well, I just lost my senses. The next I know I was on the ground and five or six people were on top of me." He said that when Oswald killed Kennedy, "something in my insides tore out."[1546]

2:00 p.m.

In Dallas seven hundred uniformed policemen from throughout the state of Texas congregate at the Beckley Hills Baptist Church to honor the other victim of Friday, Officer J. D. Tippit, gunned down by Lee Oswald on a quiet back street of Oak Cliff. Largely overlooked by the millions absorbed in the grand spectacle in Washington, the funeral of Tippit nonetheless attracts around fifteen hundred citizens of Dallas, over a thousand of whom, unable to find room inside the 450-seat red-brick church, mill around outside, while many others watch the ceremony on local and closed-circuit television. An organist, nearly hidden by a bank of flowers five feet high, plays "The Old Rugged Cross," and the choir, perhaps overly conscious of the cameras trained on them, sing with unusual stiffness.

In the front row, Tippit's widow, Marie, is flanked by her brother Dwight and J. D.'s neighbor and fellow officer, Bill Anglin, while Marie's other brother, Norvell, looks after two of the thirty-nine-year-old fallen officer's three children, Brenda, ten, and Curtis, four. His oldest son, Allen, thirteen, sits next to them. The pews behind them are filled with J. D.'s mother and father, brothers, sisters, nieces, nephews, cousins, and close friends; their faces stained with tears as they bid farewell to the man that they, and many others, considered "a lovable guy."[1547]

Others, some from far beyond the southern suburbs of Dallas where J. D. was a familiar and reassuring figure, have not forgotten the fallen hero. Contributions to the bereft family's welfare have been flowing into the police department ever since the nation learned that the policeman's $7,500 life insurance policy wouldn't take his family very far. Donations have been arriving from all over the country—Boy Scout troops, police departments, church groups, mothers, fathers, and even children have been reaching out from every state. In a child's handwriting, one letter contained the simple words, "This money is yours because your daddy was brave." Enclosed was a dollar bill. Each member of the Detroit Lions football team contributed $50 for a total of $2,000, two brokers colleccted $5,000 on the floor of the New York Stock Exchange, and Walter H. Annenberg, the publisher of the *Philadelphia Inquirer*, paid off the $12,217 mortgage on the Tippit home. Newspapers even report that two prisoners serving life terms raised $200 for the Tippit fund from the inmates of a Texas prison.[1548]

Within months, forty thousand pieces of mail containing close to $650,000 in donations are given to the Tippit family, the largeness of the amount perhaps being partially attributable to ABC commentators Chet Huntley and David Brinkley, each telling a national television audience that calls were coming in to the network urging that in lieu of flowers for the late president, money should be sent to J. D. Tippit's family, care of the Dallas Police Department.* Marie Tippit is grateful for the nation's kindness, and treas-

---

*In a court distribution on October 21, 1964, Mrs. Tippit received $312,916 in cash, and a trust fund for $330,946 was set up for the Tippit children. Also, $3,716 went to policemen's and firemen's funds. ("$650,000 for Family of Man Killed by Oswald," p.9)

ures forever a gold-framed photograph of the president's family inscribed by his widow: "There is another bond we share. We must remind our children all the time what brave men their fathers were." And the president's brother, Attorney General Robert F. Kennedy, and President Johnson personally call the thirty-nine-year-old widow to express their sympathies.[1549] President Johnson wanted her to know, Marie Tippit said, that her husband "gave his life for a good cause"—that Oswald may not have been caught "had he not given his life."[1550]

"Today we are mourning the passing of a devoted public servant," the Reverend C. D. Tipps Jr. says. "He was doing his duty when he was taken by the lethal bullet of a poor, confused, misguided, ungodly assassin—as was our President."[1551]

After the eulogy, Mrs. Tippit is helped forward. She weeps softly as she takes a long, last look at her husband in the open casket. Then, she turns away, dabbing her eyes with a handkerchief, and is helped from the church. Six police pallbearers carry Tippit's gray casket to the waiting hearse.[1552]

A fifteen-man motorcycle escort then leads the cortege to the rolling hills of Laurel Land Memorial Park where J. D. Tippit will be laid to rest in a special plot set aside for Dallas's honored dead.

At the grave site, three-dozen red roses are laid across the casket as family and friends gather under the green awning that brings a bit of relief from the hot Texas sun. Tippit's slender, blue-eyed widow is unconsolable as the minister says a final prayer. Tears can be seen on many of the faces of the stiff-backed policemen standing at attention nearby.[1553]

Marie Tippit and her three children turn away at last.

"Oh God, oh God," she sobs.[1554]

4:00 p.m.

Just outside Fort Worth, two unmarked cars hurry along a back road toward Rose Hill Cemetery. Secret Service agents Mike Howard and Charley Kunkel are riding with Marguerite, Marina, and the children in one of them; Secret Service agent Roger Warner, Arlington police officer Bob Parsons, and a Tarrant County sheriff's deputy accompany Robert in another. Robert Oswald finds the long ride unusually depressing, largely because of the attitudes of the people he has encountered while making the arrangements for his brother's funeral. As they near the cemetery, the driver breaks the gloomy silence.

"What about that car behind us?"

Bob Parsons, cradling an M-1 carbine in the backseat next to Robert, turns around.

"It's just two old ladies," Parsons says, "but one of them has a burp gun."

Everyone laughs, even Robert, who hasn't laughed in three days. He knows that Parsons is trying to shake him from his depression, and he's grateful.

The Secret Service and the Fort Worth police have set up a heavy guard at Rose Hill, with uniformed officers posted every few yards along the fence surrounding the cemetery.

At least financially, Mrs. Tippit would now have no worries. In an AP interview during the weekend after her husband's death, Marie Tippit said, "We always kept thinking we'd put money [aside], but with three kids it just never worked out. It was one payday to the next." Tippit's police salary when he died was $490 per month. She said that to get by, her husband "worked at Austin Barbecue Friday and Saturday nights and at the Stevens Park Theater Sundays." Her eyes swollen with tears as she sat in her neat, three-bedroom, pink-brick home, she spoke lovingly of her husband. "He was very quiet, likeable—almost a lovable guy . . . He was a good father. He always told the kids, 'If you're going to do a job, do it right or not at all.' There was no hollering around here. He wanted me to stay at home and take care of the children." (*Pittsburgh Post-Gazette*, November 25, 1963, p.2)

All cars are stopped and thoroughly searched at the main gate.

They drive to the chapel perched on a low hill. A number of people are standing quietly at the fence line, staring at the grave at the bottom of the hill. They enter the chapel and find it completely empty. There is no sign of any preparation for a funeral service.

"I don't understand," Robert says to Mike Howard and Charley Kunkel. The two agents are equally puzzled. Two or three minutes later one of them comes back with the story.

"We were a few minutes late," he says. "There's been some misunderstanding and they've already carried the casket down to the grave site. We'll have a graveside service down there."

It is the final emotional straw. Robert hits the wall with his fist. "Damn it!" he says loudly.

The agent decides that it's probably better not to tell Robert the rest of the story just now. In the absence of pallbearers—the accused assassin has no close friends—Lee's coffin, an inexpensive, cloth-covered wooden box, had to be carried down to the grave from the chapel by six of the reporters assigned to the story, three from the *Fort Worth Star-Telegram.*

On the way out of the chapel, as Robert hurries back to the car, a photographer walks backward in front of him, snapping off pictures. Robert wants to punch him, but manages to control himself, and climb into the car. Bob Parsons, ordered to stay in the car with the carbine, is waiting for him.

"You're doing all right now," Bob says soothingly. "Just hold on."

They drive down a curving road to the grave site. One of the Secret Service men turns to Parsons and says, "All right now, you stay in the car with the carbine. If anything happens, come out shooting."

"Nothing would give me greater pleasure than to mow down fifteen or twenty reporters," Parsons quips.

The funeral director, Paul Groody, introduces the caretaker of Rose Hill to Robert, explaining that the man agreed without hesitation, though at some risk to his own job, to sell the plot to the family. Groody tactfully suggests that the man's risk might be lessened if Robert, in speaking of the plot, were to create the impression that the plot has been in the family for some time—as though the cemetery itself had no choice in the matter. Robert, moved by the caretaker's warmth and compassion, readily agrees.

The Lutheran minister who had promised to officiate over the services is not there. The Secret Service learn that he won't be coming out at all. Fortunately, Reverend Louis Saunders, executive secretary of the Fort Worth Council of Churches, is willing to step in. Hastily summoned by Fort Worth police chief Cato Hightower, Saunders drove out to Rose Hill to do what he can. He hasn't presided at a burial in over eight years, but felt that "someone had to help this family."

The Oswalds take their seats on several of the five battered aluminum chairs placed at the grave site under a faded green canopy. Marina, dressed in a simple black dress and beige coat, holds June while Marguerite cradles the baby, Rachel, in her arms. Inexplicably, there are two floral arrangements, a white blanket of carnations and a spray of red carnations, from someone named Virginia Leach.

Marguerite is annoyed at the crowd of police, Secret Service men, reporters, and Rose Hill employees gathered there. "Privacy at the grave," she pleads, "privacy at the grave."[1555]

When a French reporter whispers something to Marina in Russian, Robert tries to shoo him away. When the reporter persists, Robert stands up and starts to move on him, but Marina quickly turns to her brother-in-law and says in broken English, "He says sorrow."

Robert turns to Secret Service agent Mike Howard and tells him he plans to have the coffin opened and would like to have all reporters and spectators moved back. The agent nods and in the late-autumn afternoon a dozen plainclothes officers move the seventy-five or so newsmen back from the grave, forming a protective, semicircular barrier. Beyond the cemetery fence there is a scattering of onlookers, who have guessed what is going on at the grave.[1556]

The undertaker opens the coffin to give the family one final look at Lee Oswald. Marina kisses her husband, dressed for burial in a dark brown suit, white shirt, brown tie, and brown socks. She slips two rings on his finger. Her stoic, almost distant composure dissolves into bitter sobs. The two infants, hearing Marina, cry loudly as Robert and Marguerite take a long, last look at Lee's face. As they return to their chairs, the gaunt Reverend Saunders steps up to conclude the stark service.

"God of the open sky and of the infinite universe, we pray and petition for this family who are heartbroken. Those who suffer and who have tears in their hearts will pray for them . . . Their need is great."

For Lee Harvey Oswald he reserves the final words: "May God have mercy on his soul."

It's over in twenty minutes. After the service, Marguerite, Marina, and the children are escorted back to the car to return to the Inn of the Six Flags. Robert lingers for a moment to watch his brother's coffin lowered into the steel-reinforced concrete vault. He finally returns to his waiting family and the two-car caravan drives off.

The grave diggers work hard to get the grave filled before dark, watched by a sprinkling of reporters and a few spectators. Finally, a light bulldozer moves in to help. The two floral arrangements are tossed onto the mound of raw earth. Two policemen are ordered to start an around-the-clock watch on the grave.

"We like to think Fort Worth folks are even-tempered," Chief Hightower explains, "but we can't take any chances. We don't want this grave bothered."

As the crowd melts away, a few more of the onlookers beyond the fence slip over and come down to collect a few souvenir clods of dirt from the assassin's grave.[1557]

Four of the darkest days in American history are finally over.

In an address to a joint session of Congress two days later, President Johnson says:

> All I have I would have given gladly not to be standing here today.
>
> The greatest leader of our time has been struck down by the foulest deed of our time. Today John Fitzgerald Kennedy lives on in the immortal words and works that he left behind. He lives on in the mind and memories of mankind. He lives on in the hearts of his countrymen.
>
> No words are sad enough to express our sense of loss. No words are strong enough to express our determination to continue the forward thrust of America that he began.
>
> The dream of conquering the vastness of space, the dream of partnership across the Atlantic—and across the Pacific as well—the dream of a Peace Corps in less-developed nations, the dream of education for all of our children, the dream of jobs for all who seek them and need them, the dream of care for our elderly, the dream of an all-out attack on mental illness, and above all, the dream of equal

rights for all Americans, whatever their race or color—these and other American dreams have been vitalized by his drive and by his dedication. And now, the ideas and ideals which he so nobly represented must and will be translated into effective action . . . No memorial or oration or eulogy could more eloquently honor President Kennedy's memory than the earliest possible passage of the civil rights bill for which he fought for so long. We have talked long enough about equal rights in this country. It is time now to write the next chapter and write it in the books of law.

The landmark Civil Rights Act of 1964 quickly followed.

The Investigations

The Warren Commission

From the moment the shots rang out in Dallas, the need for some trustworthy and reasonably definitive official account of the events became immediately apparent. The swelling tide of speculation, rumor, and paranoia threatened the credibility of American institutions, not just with the American public but with foreign nations too, which somehow had to be persuaded that the new government to which leadership of the world had been passed had not come to power by some sort of silent coup. Already the rumor mills were filled with speculation about Oswald's visit to Russia, his marriage to Marina, his trip to Mexico City, and his being pro-Castro. People everywhere wondered whether there was a connection between Ruby and Oswald and how the Dallas police could have "allowed" Oswald to be killed.

Because of the unprecedented importance of the case, and though no official announcement had yet been made, on the evening of the assassination President Johnson asked FBI Director J. Edgar Hoover to investigate the president's murder.[1] And as we have seen, at 9:52 EST, the FBI sent a Teletype to its fifty-five field offices saying, "The Bureau is conducting an investigation to determine who is responsible for the assassination." (However, it should be noted that as early as forty-five minutes after Oswald's arrest, two FBI agents were already present during the first interrogation of Oswald.)[2] An editorial on November 23, 1963, in the *New York Times* stated that President Johnson "must convince the country that this bitter tragedy will not divert us from our proclaimed purposes or check our forward movement."[3] Later that day, Director Hoover sent Johnson the results of the bureau's preliminary investigation. The report detailed the evidence known to that point, and it indicated Lee Harvey Oswald's guilt.[4] The next day, the *New York Times* reported that *Pravda* was charging right-wingers in the United States with trying to use the assassination of President Kennedy to stir up anti-Soviet and anti-Cuban hysteria, adding, "Moscow radio said Oswald was charged with Mr. Kennedy's slaying after 10 hours of interrogation, but there was no evidence which could prove this accusation."[5]

Ruby's murder of Oswald at approximately 11:20 a.m. on Sunday, November 24, immediately changed the complexion of the entire saga. There would be no trial of Oswald during which, it could be presumed, or at least hoped, all the relevant facts of Kennedy's assassination would be revealed. Only an investigation by a blue-ribbon commission appointed by the president of the United States could possibly get to the bottom of the matter and allay the doubts and anxieties of the American public.

It is not known for sure who first proposed such a commission, or even whether it was prompted by Oswald's death, but assassination researcher Donald Gibson has come up with the best evidence thus far that it was Eugene Rostow, dean of Yale Law School. Rostow called LBJ aide Bill Moyers on the afternoon of November 24[*] and suggested that "a presidential commission be appointed of very distinguished citizens in the very near future." In the tape-recorded conversation, Rostow says he had already spoken about his suggestion to Acting Attorney General Nicholas Katzenbach "about three times" that day but decided to call Moyers directly to make sure LBJ got the message because he said Katzenbach "sounded so groggy that I thought I'd pass this thought along to you."[6]

Later that Sunday afternoon, Hoover telephoned another Johnson aide, Walter Jenkins, and said, "The thing I am most concerned about, and so is Mr. Katzenbach, is having something issued so we can convince the public that Oswald is the real assassin."[7] Conspiracy theorists have maintained for years that this statement by Hoover means Hoover was trying to set Oswald up. It wouldn't enter their minds that another interpretation of these words was that Hoover (like virtually everyone else in law enforcement at the time) was convinced that Oswald was guilty and Hoover wanted to help make sure a vulnerable and severely traumatized American public, susceptible to rumors and speculation, also became convinced of this reality.

In 1978, Katzenbach, who prior to the assassination had been the deputy attorney general under Robert F. Kennedy, recalled his reasons for wanting some kind of statement issued: "I think . . . speculation that there was a conspiracy of various kinds was fairly rampant at that time, particularly in the foreign press. I was reacting to that and . . . to repeated calls from people in the State Department who wanted something of that kind . . . to quash the beliefs of some people abroad that our silence in the face of those rumors was not to be taken as substantiating it in some way. That is, in the face of a lot of rumors about conspiracy, a total silence on the subject from the government neither confirming nor denying tended to feed those rumors."[8]

On November 25, 1963, Katzenbach wrote a memorandum to Moyers stating, in part, that "the public must be satisfied that Oswald was the assassin; that he did not have confederates who are still at large; that the evidence was such that he would have been convicted at trial."[9] Conspiracy theorists have had a field day with Katzenbach's choice of words, using the memorandum to support their claims that the Warren Commission was created to cover up the truth in the Kennedy assassination. As you'll see later in this section, nothing could be further from the truth.

---

[*]The exact time of the conversation is not known, but we know it was after Oswald's death at 2:07 p.m. EST because Rostow refers to Oswald's death in the conversation.

On the evening of November 25, the same day Katzenbach drafted his memo, the White House announced a statement from President Johnson instructing the Department of Justice and the FBI to conduct a "prompt and thorough investigation of all the circumstances surrounding the brutal assassination of President Kennedy and the murder of his alleged assassin."[10]*

In telephone conversations that Monday morning, Johnson had said he was persuaded by his lawyer's advice that "the president must not inject himself into local killings." Instead of a presidentially appointed commission, he hoped that a two-pronged attack (an FBI report submitted to the attorney general, and a Texas Court of Inquiry headed by Texas attorney general Waggoner Carr, who had met with Johnson for an hour and a half the previous evening and proposed such an inquiry) would satisfy the nation's desire for the truth.[11]

Meanwhile, the foreign rumor mill persisted in pounding at the notion of conspiracy in the Kennedy murder. A TASS dispatch published in the *New York Times* on November 26, concluded, "All the circumstances of President Kennedy's tragic death allow one to assume that this murder was planned and carried out by the ultra-right-wing, fascist, and racist circles, by those who cannot stomach any step aimed at the easing of international tensions, and the improvement of Soviet-American relations."[12] An editorial in the *Washington Post* that day stated, "President Johnson has widely recognized that energetic steps must be taken to prevent a repetition of the dreadful era of rumor and gossip that followed the assassination of President Abraham Lincoln. A century has hardly sufficed to quiet the doubts that arose in the wake of that tragedy."[13]

On November 27, 1963, Senator Everett M. Dirksen proposed in Congress that the Senate Judiciary Committee conduct a complete investigation of the assassination, and Congressman Charles E. Goodell suggested that a joint committee of seven senators and seven representatives conduct an inquiry.[14]

By November 28, President Johnson was beginning to come around to the idea of a presidential commission, believing that a "bunch of Congressional inquiries" might not be the advisable way to get to the bottom of what happened, and could spiral out of control.[15]

Katzenbach later told investigators, "I doubted that anybody in the government, Mr. Hoover, or the FBI or myself or the president or anyone else, could satisfy a lot of foreign opinion that all the facts were being revealed and that the investigation would be complete and conclusive and without any loose ends. So, from the beginning, I felt that . . . it would be desirable . . . for the president to appoint some commission of people who had international and domestic public stature and reputation for integrity that would

---

*Since, as indicated earlier in the text, in 1963 there was no federal jurisdiction over the murder of President Kennedy on a Dallas street (as opposed to on federal property), how did the FBI, a federal agency, even have jurisdiction to investigate the murder? Under Title 18 of Section 372 in the U.S. Code, it *was* a federal crime (no matter where committed) to *conspire* to murder any federal official on account of, or while he was engaged in, the lawful discharge of his duties, language that would have covered the murder of the president. And at the time of the assassination, in the eyes of many, including President Johnson, the possibility of a conspiracy was very real. However, the Warren Commission acknowledged that "once it became reasonably clear [they never identified this point in time] that the killing was the act of a single person, the State of Texas had exclusive jurisdiction . . . [and the FBI handled the investigation thereafter] only upon the sufferance of the local authorities." (WR, pp.454, 456; 5 H 25, WCT Alan H. Belmont; Cushman, "Why the Warren Commission?" pp.478–479) The above in no way militates against the inherent power of President Johnson to have established, by executive order (11130), the Warren Commission, or that of Congress (by Senate Joint Resolution 137) to have empowered the Commission to issue subpoenas and grant immunity in carrying out its mandate. It only deals with the issue of whether Texas law enforcement or the FBI had investigative jurisdiction over the case.

review all of the investigations and direct any further investigation."[16] Katzenbach talked over his idea with Attorney General Robert Kennedy and on November 29, 1963, a memo to President Johnson from presidential aide Walter Jenkins set forth Katzenbach and Kennedy's recommendation that "a seven-man commission—two senators, two congressmen, Chief Justice Earl Warren, Allen Dulles,* and a retired military man (general or admiral)."[17] Johnson liked the idea of Warren being on the commission and dispatched Katzenbach and Solicitor General Archibald Cox that same day to the Supreme Court to ask Warren if he would chair the Commission, but Warren politely said no. He was opposed in principle to Supreme Court justices engaging in extrajudicial activities while a member of the court and felt, for instance, that Supreme Court justice Robert Jackson should not have served as the chief prosecutor of the Nuremberg trials in 1945–1946,[18] and that the appointment of associate Supreme Court justice Owen J. Roberts in 1946 to investigate Pearl Harbor "served no good purpose."[19]† Warren suggested a few people who might serve well in his stead, and when Katzenbach and Cox departed, Warren thought that was the end of it.[20]

That same day, President Johnson spoke with Hoover over the telephone and asked him if he was "familiar with this proposed group that they're trying to put together on this study of your report?"

"I haven't heard of that," Hoover replied, and predictably registered his opposition, adding that it would be "very, very bad to have a rash of investigations on this thing."‡

LBJ: "Well, the only way we can stop them is probably to appoint a high-level one to evaluate your report and put somebody that's pretty good on it that I can select . . . and tell the House and Senate not to go ahead [with their proposed separate investigations] because they'll get a lot of television going and I think it would be bad."

Hoover: "It would be a three-ring circus."§

At this point, the conversation quickly progressed to a discussion of people LBJ was thinking of appointing and Hoover's opinion of them.[21]**

---

*When Johnson telephoned Dulles, who was now in retirement, on November 29 and said, "You've got to go on" the Commission "for me," the always reserved Dulles said, "You think I can really serve you?" "I know you can . . . There's not any doubt about it," Johnson replied, probably thinking of Dulles's vast experience in the CIA as being helpful in clarifying and evaluating Oswald's defection to Russia and his trip to Mexico City. "If I can be of any help," the longtime civil servant said. But perhaps anticipating criticism of his selection, he added, "and you've considered the effect of my previous work and my previous job?" "I sure have," LBJ said. "We want you to do it . . . that's that. You always do what's best [for your country]. I found that out about you a long time ago." (Telephone conversation between LBJ and Dulles at 5:41 p.m., November 29, 1963, in Holland, *Kennedy Assassination Tapes*, p.167)

†As with Warren eighteen years later, Roberts was appointed by the president (Franklin Delano Roosevelt), and the presidential commission he headed and the report it submitted were named after him (Roberts Commission, Roberts Report).

‡Courtney Evans, one of Hoover's assistant directors, would later acknowledge what most everyone already knew. "He wanted to get credit for solving [this] thing," Evans said, "and he wanted to get it fast" (Thomas, "Real Cover-Up," p.71).

§Although Hoover never expressly stated to LBJ his opposition to what LBJ was proposing in lieu of congressional investigations, he did state his opposition to LBJ's proposal of a "high-level" commission in an internal memo to his assistants that day (Church Committee Report, p.46; Memorandum from Hoover to Messrs. Tolson, Belmont, Mohr, DeLoach, Rosen, and Sullivan, November 29, 1963).

**Johnson and Hoover also got into a discussion of the case. Johnson asked Hoover, "How many shots were fired?" "Three," Hoover replied. "Any of them fired at me?" Johnson inquired. "No. All three at the president." Hoover went on to illustrate how much confusion there was about the facts of the case, even by the FBI director himself, when he told Johnson that the shot that hit Kennedy in the head "wasn't shattered" (it was). It was a "complete bullet . . . that rolled out of the president's head" at the hospital "and fell onto the stretcher." (Holland, *Kennedy Assassination Tapes*, p.141; LBJ Record 177-10001-10237, Transcript of telephone conversation between LBJ and Hoover at 1:40 p.m. on November 29, 1963, LBJ Library)

Later that afternoon, Johnson, not about to accept Earl Warren's no for an answer, summoned the chief justice to the Oval Office and applied his famous combination of charm, flattery, and muscle in trying to convince Warren to head the commission. Still, Warren was reluctant to take the job.[22] Warren later recalled in his memoirs that he told Johnson there were several reasons why such an appointment was not in the best interests of the court. "First, it is not in the spirit of constitutional separation of powers to have a member of the Supreme Court serve on a presidential commission; second, it would distract a Justice from the work of the Court, which had a heavy docket; and third, it was impossible to foresee what litigation such a commission might spawn, with resulting disqualification of the Justice from sitting in such cases."

But Johnson would hear none of it. "You were a soldier in World War I, but there was nothing you could do in that uniform comparable to what you can do for your country in this hour of trouble," Johnson told him, invoking the words of Kennedy's inaugural address. "He then told me," Warren recalls, "how serious were the rumors floating around the world. The gravity of the situation was such that it might lead us into war, he said, and, if so, it might be a nuclear war. He went on to tell me that he had just talked to the Defense Secretary Robert McNamara, who had advised him that the first nuclear strike against us might cause the loss of 40 million people. I then said, 'Mr. President, if the situation is that serious, my personal views do not count. I will do it.'"[23] According to Johnson, Warren had "started crying" when he refused to let him off the hook during the face-to-face meeting.[24]

That evening (November 29), in order "to avoid parallel investigations and to concentrate fact-finding in a body having the broadest national mandate,"[25] President Johnson signed Executive Order 11130 creating the President's Commission on the Assassination of President Kennedy, thereafter called the Warren Commission.[26] Seven people were appointed to the Commission: Hale Boggs, Democratic representative from Louisiana who was the majority whip; John Sherman Cooper, Republican senator from Kentucky and former ambassador to India; Allen W. Dulles, former director of the CIA; Gerald R. Ford, Republican representative from Michigan; John J. McCloy, former U.S. high commissioner of Germany after World War II and former president of the World Bank; Richard B. Russell, Democratic senator from Georgia; and Earl Warren, chief justice of the United States Supreme Court.[27] All seven were lawyers. Unlike their staff of prominent attorneys who worked full-time, all of the members of the Commission, except Dulles (who was retired), had full-time jobs, and hence could not devote all their waking hours to the Commission's work.[*]

Like Warren, the other commissioners cited national interest as their motivation for participating. Allen Dulles was highly conscious of the fact that the atmosphere of suspicion interfered with the functioning of government and its foreign relations. John J. McCloy felt it necessary to "show the world that America is not a banana republic where a government can be changed by conspiracy." Senator John Sherman Cooper wanted to lift "the cloud of doubts that had been cast over American institutions."[28] Gerald Ford

---

[*]One hears various figures for the length of time the Warren Commission was in existence. And I suppose that's because of when one starts counting. The Commission was created on November 29, 1963, but no work was done until December 5, 1963, when the Commission had its first executive session (WR, p.x). It called its first witness on February 3, 1964 (1 H 1), and submitted its final report to the president on September 24, 1964 (Letter from Commission to President Johnson dated September 24, 1964, WR, p.vii). I would think the reasonable computation of time would be from December 5, 1963, to September 24, 1964, a period of a little over nine and a half months.

said that he and the other Commission members "were asked by the president to undertake this responsibility as a public duty and service, and despite the reluctance of all of us to add to our then burden or operations we accepted."[29]

Senator Richard B. Russell, the conservative leader of the Southern Democrats who had been LBJ's mentor in the Senate and the one most responsible for his rise to power, nominating him to be majority leader in 1953, had objected vigorously to the idea of serving with Warren, whom he loathed for the unanimous 1954 Supreme Court decision declaring public school segregation unconstitutional.* Johnson bluntly refused to bow to the senator's homegrown scruples, calling him on the evening of November 29, 1963, to advise him that he had appointed him to the Commission.

"But I just can't serve," Russell protested. "I don't like that man [Warren]. I don't have any confidence in him."

"Dick, it's already been announced, and you can serve with anybody for the good of America," LBJ tells his friend. "You're not gonna be in *Old Dog Tray* company [a reference to the 1853 Stephen C. Foster song by that name where Tray is a servile friend], but you never turned down your country . . . I can't *arrest* you and I'm not going to put the FBI on you, but you're *goddamned* sure going to *serve*—I'll tell you *that*!" Johnson roared at Russell.

"Mr. President, you ought to have told me you were going to name [Warren]," Russell said.

When LBJ puts a mutual friend, a local Texas judge who hunts with LBJ and Russell, on the phone to help him with Russell, Russell tells the judge, "I don't know when I've been as unhappy about a thing as I am this. This is awful." With LBJ back on the phone, Russell says, "I think you're sorta takin' advantage of me, Mr. President."

"I'm not," LBJ says, "'cause you *made* me and I know it, and I don't ever forget . . . But you gonna serve your country."

Russell reiterates that "I just don't like Warren."

"Well, of course you don't like Warren, but you'll like him 'fore it's over with."

"I haven't got any confidence in him."

"Well . . . you can *give* him some confidence. *Goddammit*! *Associate* with him!"

Russell, beaten into submission, tells LBJ, "If it is for the good of the country, you know damned well I'll do it, and I'll do it for you . . . I'm at your command . . . I'll do anything you want me to."[30]

Warren, not wanting to forsake his enormous responsibilities as the chief justice of the Supreme Court, would later recall in an interview that he "got them to rent the building right across the street here from the Court and I would just come here to the Court for every conference, come here for every session of the Court, and then as soon as that was over I would run over there to that building [Warren Commission headquarters] and work on that [Commission business] until maybe midnight . . . I think it took a good bit out of me . . . to be doing that, [but] I didn't want to give up my work on the Court . . . and I did carry on my work throughout the year."

Warren was grateful to Johnson for all the support and latitude he and his Commission were given, saying in a later interview that there was no interference by the White House in anything.

---

*The May 17, 1954, landmark decision in *Brown v. Board of Education* (347 U.S. 483) held that segregation in public schools was prohibited by the equal protection clause of the Fourteenth Amendment.

"The White House never gave us an instruction, never, never even looked at our work until I took it up to the President."

Question: "The President never made any suggestions?"

"Never once in any way, shape or form."

Question: "Was there anyone that you felt you should have seen that you couldn't get at?"

"I've never been able to think of one person that we should have called that we did not call . . . The president gave us the broadest powers . . . to get anything in the government . . . We could get any documents or anything else that we wanted."

Question: "You had no budget limitations?"

"Oh no. There was just no problem of that kind at all, nothing. No limitations of any kind [were] put on us. We were just free agents, and did everything we wanted."

Warren's interviewer asked him whether his Commission's investigation was influenced in any way by the fact that it was during an election year for President Johnson, whereupon Warren replied, "This wasn't in the election that we did this, was it? This was in 1963." The interviewer informed him the year was 1964 and observed, "It must not have been much of a factor."

Warren: "No, no, really it was no factor. It was no factor at all."[31]

Gerald Ford confirmed this position. "President Johnson," Ford later wrote, "did not push us, and most importantly, we were encouraged to thoroughly pursue all possibilities—even those that sounded like something out of a James Bond or an X-Files script. We were not given any parameters or restricted by any assumptions or agencies. Everyone and everything were open for scrutiny. We didn't accept anyone's word at face value. There were no . . . sacred cows . . . We didn't assume any answer but investigated all possibilities and let the facts reveal the truth."[32]

The purposes of the Warren Commission, as stated in the executive order, were "to examine the evidence developed by the Federal Bureau of Investigation and any additional evidence that may hereafter come to light or be uncovered by Federal or State authorities; to make such further investigation as the Commission finds desirable; to evaluate all the facts and circumstances surrounding such assassination, including the subsequent violent death of the man charged with the assassination, and to report to me its findings and conclusions."[33] Although accurate, there are indications that a secondary task was expected. It was apparent, at least to Chief Justice Warren and President Johnson, that rumors and speculation had to be quelled.[34] Staff counsel Norman Redlich believed that allaying public fears was "a byproduct of the principal objective which was to discover all the facts." There was an additional, humanly selfish motive for getting at the truth too. Staff counsel Burt Griffin recalled, "I think it is fair to say, and it certainly reflects my feeling, and it was certainly the feeling that I had of all of my colleagues, that we were determined, if we could, to prove the FBI was wrong, to find a conspiracy if we possibly could. I think we thought we would be national heroes in a sense if we could find something sinister beyond what appeared to have gone on."[35]

Although the executive order authorized the Warren Commission itself to conduct further investigations if the commissioners found it desirable, Chief Justice Warren originally did not believe that additional investigations, beyond what the investigative agencies—FBI, Secret Service, and CIA—provided, would be necessary.

On December 5, 1963, just thirteen days after the assassination, the Warren Commission met for the first time in a long, two-hour-and-forty-minute executive session in a hearing room at the National Archives. During the session, Chief Justice Warren told the members of his commission, "Now, I think our job here is essentially one for the *evaluation* of evidence as distinguished from being one of *gathering* evidence [that would soon change], and I believe at the outset, at least, we can start with the premise that we can rely upon the reports of the various agencies that have been engaged in investigating the matter— the FBI, the Secret Service, and others that I may not know about at the present time." Warren continued by saying that he didn't think it would be "necessary for us to bring witnesses before us" (that would also soon change) and didn't believe that the Commission needed independent investigators or the power of subpoena. Most of the other Commission members, however, disagreed with him on the power of subpoena, and in a voice vote, all members, including Warren, agreed to seek it from Congress.[*]

The Commission members began the process of deciding on a general counsel. Chief Justice Earl Warren suggested one of his own protégés, Warren Olney. Senator Russell brought out that since Olney had been the chief of the Criminal Division at the Department of Justice for five years, working closely with the FBI, and the FBI would be "the principal source of our information," that choice might "cause some criticism."[†] And the opinion of John McCloy and other members was that although they did not want to exclude Olney, they wanted to consider several other leading lights in the legal profession before settling on a general counsel.

On another matter, some members expressed concern about apparent leaks to the press attributed to FBI sources while the Commission was still awaiting the first FBI report. Senator Russell questioned, "How much of their findings does the FBI propose to release to the press before we present the findings of this Commission?"[36] The senator's rhetorical remarks were not entirely misplaced.

Acting Attorney General Nicholas Katzenbach, who represented the Department of Justice at the opening session to answer questions, informed the Commission that he had asked Hoover and the FBI's man in charge of the JFK assassination investigation, Assistant FBI Director Alan Belmont, about the leaks. "They are utterly furious at the information that got into the press. They say they are confident it could not have come from the FBI," Katzenbach reported, "and I say with candor to this committee, I can't think of anybody else it could have come from, because I don't know of anybody else that knew that information." But Katzenbach then allowed that "some agent" or "a clever reporter" who "put together a, b, and c" may have been responsible for the information leaks.

Warren had some good news to announce to the Commission members. That morning he had been advised that the proposed Texas Court of Inquiry on the assassination (which could have resulted in a duplication of effort with the Commission and sensational headlines that could have interfered with the larger and more deliberate Commission investigation) was going to be postponed until after the Commission finished its investigation.[‡]

---

[*]On December 13, 1963, Congress passed a joint resolution granting the Commission the power to issue subpoenas, compel testimony, administer oaths, examine witnesses, receive evidence, grant immunity from prosecution, and seek a federal court to hold someone in contempt if he or she refused to give requested testimony (Public Law 88-202, S. J. Res. 137, 88th Congr., 1st sess., December 13, 1963, in WR, pp.473–474).

[†]Although it did not appear in any Commission document, according to J. Edgar Hoover, Olney had a "hostility" toward the FBI, and Commission members Russell, Dulles, and Ford "all threatened to resign if Olney were appointed" (FBI Record 124-10103-10087, Memo from Hoover to Tolson, Belmont, Rosen, and DeLoach, June 22, 1964, p.2).

[‡]No Texas Court of Inquiry proceedings were ever conducted on the assassination. The Texas attorney general's office worked closely with the FBI and Warren Commission throughout the life of the Warren Com-

In a prescient precursor of what experienced hands knew lay ahead for a case of unprecedented importance, Katzenbach told the Commission that the FBI had already set up a "crackpot file" for all the solutions to the case the FBI knew would be offered up by amateur sleuths around the country. "My staff is not that generous," Senator Russell said. "They call it the 'nut file.'"[37]

At the next meeting, on December 6, the Commission agreed that it should have not only the power of subpoena and to administer oaths to witnesses to tell the truth, but also the power to grant immunity. And Warren, seeing the opposition, no longer urged the appointment of Olney, and several other respected and well-known lawyers were mentioned for the job of general counsel. The name J. Lee Rankin, a fifty-four-year-old prominent Republican and former solicitor general of the United States under President Eisenhower who had argued cases before Warren's Supreme Court, was among those mentioned. Warren knew Rankin, was impressed with him, and believed he could work with him. No one had any objection to Rankin and it was unanimously agreed to offer him the job.[38]

On December 8, Warren telephoned Rankin, who was now New York City's corporation counsel, and asked him to be general counsel for the Commission. "The chief called me out of the blue and asked me to serve," Rankin would later say. "I told him I had put in my time with the government and was just starting to build a practice. I told him some members of the commission wouldn't want me. I told him lots of things. I had the job by the end of the conversation. Earl Warren was a very persuasive man."[39] Rankin left for Washington the next day, where he spent the next ten months attending to the Commission's work as its general counsel. If the commissioners set broad general policy, it was Rankin, a formal and intellectually rigorous man, who actually implemented the policy, overseeing both the investigation and the writing of the eventual report, examining many of the important witnesses who testified in the hearings, organizing the Commission staff, and functioning as liaison to other government agencies.[40]

The evidence clearly shows that from the beginning, although FBI Director J. Edgar Hoover did nothing to directly impede the investigation, and complied with all Warren Commission requests, he viewed the Warren Commission more as a competitor than a partner in a search for facts about the assassination. Former assistant FBI director William Sullivan told investigators in 1975 that Hoover was afraid the Commission would criticize the FBI's investigation. "Hoover did not want the Warren Commission to conduct an exhaustive investigation for fear that it would discover important and relevant facts that we in the FBI had not discovered in our investigation, [since] it would be greatly embarrassing to him and damaging to his career and the FBI as a whole."[41] Though Sullivan had had a bitter break with Hoover, his observation was supported by the Church Committee, which noted that Hoover "repeatedly told others in the Bureau that the War-

---

mission, helping in the investigation whenever asked, including serving as a liaison between the Commission and the city and county officials of Dallas, and had a representative attend many of the Commission hearings. On October 5, 1964, Texas attorney general Waggoner Carr sent a very thin report (perhaps seven or eight pages stretched out to twenty) to Governor John Connally in which he said he did "not have the slightest hesitancy in concurring in the conclusion of the Warren Commission" that Oswald killed Kennedy and acted alone. (*Texas Supplemental Report*, pp.8, 10)

ren Commission was 'looking for gaps in the FBI's investigation' and was 'seeking to criticize the FBI.'"[42]

According to Sullivan, the FBI director received frequent updates on the Commission's investigation, as well as its criticisms of the bureau, from one of the Commission's own members—Gerald R. Ford. "[Ford] was one of our [FBI] members of the congressional stable when he was in Congress," Sullivan explained. "[When] he became a member of the Warren Commission . . . he was 'our man' on the Warren Commission and it was to him that we looked to protect our interests and keep us fully advised of any development that we would not like, that mitigated against us, and he did."[43] On December 12, 1963, Ford asked to see FBI Deputy Director DeLoach in Ford's office. Though the Commission had only been in existence one week, DeLoach wrote in a memorandum that Ford said he wasn't pleased that Warren had attempted to establish a "one-man commission" by having his protégé, Warren Olney, appointed chief counsel. Ford reported the activities-to-date of the Commission (including information he had learned about the CIA's investigation in Mexico City) and "indicated he would keep [the FBI] thoroughly advised as to the activities of the Commission. He stated this would have to be on a confidential basis; however, he thought it should be done."[44] However, Ford, who said he had been meeting with DeLoach for years on congressional matters, disputes that he was the FBI's eyes and ears on the Commission. He testified under penalty of perjury that he only met with DeLoach on two occasions, December 12 and 17, 1963, both of which times, he noted, were "during the organizational period of the Commission and before any investigations or hearings were undertaken by the Commission."[45] And no one has been able to show any contact between Ford and the FBI subsequent to December 17, 1963.

As indicated, Hoover's fears led him, at the beginning, to oppose the formation of the Warren Commission,[46] and according to Sullivan, who went from Hoover's most obsequious flatterer to his most severe critic during the later Nixon presidency and was eventually forced out of the bureau by Hoover, when Hoover failed to do that, he attempted to limit the scope of the Warren Commission's investigation. Hoover's principal method, Sullivan said, was to leak to the press the FBI investigation, "believing that this would tend to satisfy everybody and perhaps the authorities would conclude that an investigation of great depth and scope by any entity other than the FBI would not be necessary."[47]*

On December 9, the FBI submitted a 384-page, five-volume report (one volume dealing with the assassination, one with Ruby's killing of Oswald, and three volumes of

---

*James Malley, the FBI inspector from the bureau's General Investigative Division who was assigned by Hoover to serve as liaison to the Warren Commission, and who led the FBI's field investigation of the assassination, disputes Sullivan's allegations, stating that he was not aware of any negative feelings Hoover had toward the Commission. Malley added that "he would not necessarily trust any statements that [Sullivan] made about the assassination investigation and Director Hoover's role in it." (11 HSCA 54–55; Malley led field investigation: DeLoach, *Hoover's FBI*, pp.127–128) However, we do know that on December 1, 1963, before the FBI turned over its report on the investigation to the Warren Commission, the *Washington Post* reported (obviously through a leak) that "all the police agencies with a hand in the investigation . . . insist that [the case against Oswald] is an unshakable one" (*Washington Post*, December 1, 1963). And on December 10, the day after the FBI's supposedly secret report on the assassination was delivered to the Commission, the *New York Times* ran the page-one headline, "Oswald Assassin beyond a Doubt, FBI Concludes," along with an accompanying story announcing the delivery of the report to the Commission and details about the final conclusions reached by the FBI (*New York Times*, December 10, 1963, p.1). More leaks followed shortly (e.g., "Assassination: History's Jury," pp.25–27).

exhibits) to the Warren Commission summarizing the bureau's entire investigation to date, and concluding that Oswald killed Kennedy and acted alone.[48]*

At its next meeting, on December 16, after Supreme Court justice Stanley F. Reed administered an oath to all its members, the Commission set about to determine the scope of the investigation. The first order of business was to consider the FBI's summary report.

"Well, gentlemen," the chief justice said to his fellow Commission members, "I have read that report two or three times and I have not seen anything in there yet that has not been in the press."

"I couldn't agree with that more," Senator Richard Russell said. "Practically everything in there has come out in the press at one time or another, a bit here and a bit there."

But that wasn't the biggest problem. It was the obvious deficiency of the report, mostly attributable, John McCloy said, to the fact that "they [FBI] put this thing together very fast."

Representative Hale Boggs pointed out that, remarkably, "There's nothing in [the report] about Governor Connally."

Senator John Cooper: "And whether or not they found any bullets in him."

After reading the report, McCloy said that "this bullet business leaves me confused."

"It's totally inconclusive," opined Chief Justice Warren.

Representative Gerald Ford: "[The report] was interesting to read but it did not have the depth that it ought to have."

There were so many unanswered questions. For instance, Representative Boggs observed, "There is still little on this fellow Ruby, including his movements, what he was doing, how he got in there [City Hall basement garage]."

Warren: "His relations with the police department."

Boggs: "Exactly."

Talking about the issue of precisely what took place among the occupants of the presidential limousine at the time of the shooting, Warren said, "I wonder if the report we get from the Secret Service wouldn't pretty much clear that up . . . They were there, right at the car, and know exactly what happened."

Representative Boggs: "Well, this FBI report doesn't clear it up."

Warren: "It doesn't do anything."

Boggs: "It raises a lot of new questions in my mind."

General Counsel Rankin summed up the feelings of practically all of the Commission members when he noted that "the report has so many holes in it. Anybody can look at it and see that it just doesn't seem like they're looking for things that this Commission has to look for in order to get the answers that it wants and it's entitled to."[49]

Very momentously, it was during this December 16 session that the Commission decided it could not rely solely on the FBI report or reports from any of the other federal agencies either. "After studying this [FBI] report," Chief Justice Warren said,

---

*A sixty-seven-page supplemental report was sent by the FBI to the Warren Commission on January 13, 1964, with additional exhibits. Most of this supplementary report dealt with Oswald's biography, associates, and affiliations (CD 107). A separate thirty-nine-page FBI report dealing exclusively with Ruby, with emphasis on his background, was also submitted to the Warren Commission on January 13. That same day, the FBI issued a twenty-six-page supplementary report on Ruby, with more emphasis on Ruby's killing of Oswald. Both reports concluded that up to that point the FBI's investigation had not established that Ruby and Oswald had any connection or that Ruby had conspired with anyone to kill Oswald. (Both Ruby reports are listed under FBI Record 124-10062-10290.)

"unless we have the raw materials [i.e., interviews, affidavits, recordings, photographs, etc.] that went into the making of the report and have an opportunity to examine those raw materials and make our *own* appraisal, any appraisal of this report would be [worth] little or nothing." Warren went on to move "that the Commission request at once from all investigative agencies and departments of the Government the raw materials on which their reports to the Commission are based," and his motion was seconded and adopted.

The FBI, which would end up doing a monumental amount of very detailed investigation into the assassination, had failed its first test, badly.

In addition to the commissioners wanting to see and appraise the "raw materials" so they could determine the legitimacy of the conclusions in the reports from the federal agencies, they decided that among the commission staff there had to be a lawyer of high caliber who, as Senator Russell said, "would take this FBI report and this CIA report and go through it and analyze every contradiction and every soft spot in it . . . as if [in the case of an FBI report] he were going to use them to prosecute J. Edgar Hoover." "I agree with you one hundred percent," Warren said.

General Counsel Rankin raised the possibility with the Commission that he and his staff "might have to come back to you and ask for some investigative help . . . [in] situations where we can't get answers" from a federal agency like the FBI, but Senator Russell interjected that if such a situation arose where there was a need for "an independent inquiry," it could be presented to the Commission for resolution, but it would be unnecessary to set up an investigative staff "at this time." The commissioners, however, left no doubt that they themselves were in a very investigative mood.

Senator Cooper: "I think that we ought to have a list of the people we want to interrogate."

Allen Dulles: "I think one who you should see fairly soon . . . would be [U.S. Secret Service chief U. E.] Baughman."

Mr. McCloy: "I think we should get that film [Zapruder] in our possession [before] it deteriorates."[50]*

And so on.

Ultimately, the Commission decided to rely on its own legal staff to direct the efforts of the FBI and other federal investigative agencies, being convinced that since the president had promised it the full cooperation of these agencies, the Commission's counsel would be able to play a significant role in directing the FBI's field work, which the evidence clearly shows the Warren Commission largely did (see later text). Accordingly, Rankin was authorized to employ and organize a staff of lawyers (assistant counsels) whose job would be to review, analyze, and evaluate the thousands of pages of investigative reports that were expected. Assistant Counsel Howard Willens, Robert Kennedy's deputy at the Department of Justice, was in charge of recruiting the staff and forwarding their resumés to Rankin. Eventually, twenty-eight different agencies would send the

---

*Rankin would later tell the HSCA that he gave some thought to an independent investigative staff "and I finally concluded that I would lose more than I would gain, that the whole intelligence community in the government would feel that the Commission was indicating a lack of confidence in them and that from then on I would not have any cooperation from them. They would universally be against the Commission and try to trip us up." He said the Commission, pursuant to his recommendation, made the decision not to employ a separate unit of investigators. (JFK Document 014027, Transcript of deposition of J. Lee Rankin before HSCA on August 17, 1978, pp.43, 97–98) But as we will see (see later text), the Warren Commission did from time to time, on an ad hoc basis, employ independent experts and investigators to verify the conclusions of federal law enforcement agencies.

Commission more than three hundred cubic feet of paper, most of it catastrophically unor-
ganized and unevaluated. It would largely be up to the staff to identify the issues that
required verification and further investigation.[51]

Virtually all conspiracy theorists believe that the Warren Commission did not conduct
an independent investigation of the assassination, and instead relied almost exclusively
on the FBI's investigation to reach its conclusions. For example, in *Crime of the Century*,
Michael Kurtz writes, "Rather than conduct its own independent investigation, the commission relied *entirely* on the FBI report."[52] "The Warren Commission" was "*totally
reliant*" on the investigative reports and functions of J. Edgar Hoover's FBI," wrote
Bernard Fensterwald Jr. in his book *Assassination of JFK by Coincidence or Conspiracy?*[53]
    Indeed, this myth created by the conspiracy theorists has been trumpeted so much
that even most Warren Commission supporters have bought into it. "The [Warren Com-
mission]," says anti-conspiracy author Gerald Posner, "*was almost entirely dependent* on
agencies such as the FBI to conduct the actual investigation."[54]
    Let's briefly jump ahead to discuss this issue, and then we'll return to the chronology.
Because of the Commission's supposed subjugation to the FBI, and the assumption by
the conspiracy theorists that the FBI (under Director J. Edgar Hoover) could not be
trusted to conduct a truthful investigation, critics believe the Warren Commission's conclusions—that Oswald was the lone assassin and that there was no conspiracy— were
compromised. But this is simply an enormous myth that has taken hold and could hardly
be more incorrect. First of all, as you've just seen, on December 16 the Warren Commission came to the conclusion that it could not rely exclusively on the reports of the FBI
and other federal agencies to reach its conclusions. In fact, even before this, on December 13 the Commission obtained the necessary powers to conduct its own independent
investigation with the enactment of Senate Joint Resolution 137,[55] which empowered the
Commission to issue subpoenas requiring the testimony of witnesses and the production
of documentary evidence. The resolution also gave the Commission the power to grant
immunity and thereby force the testimony of witnesses who invoked their Fifth Amendment right against self-incrimination.[56] The Commission never had occasion to grant
immunity.
    Pursuant to these powers, the Warren Commission, *by itself and independent of the FBI*,
took the sworn testimony of 489 witnesses, many in great depth. (This hardly constitutes
relying exclusively on the FBI.) Of these 489 witnesses, 94 testified before one or more
members of the Commission itself, and 395 were questioned in depositions by members
of the Commission's staff, with the Commission members not being present. In addition, 61 witnesses gave sworn affidavits and 2 gave statements, for a total of 552 witnesses.
More than 3,100 exhibits were received into evidence.[57]* Although Commission member
John McCloy complained early on, and *before* the taking of any testimony, that the Com-

---

*Two misconceptions about the Warren Commission hearings need to be clarified. First, Commission hear-
ings were closed to the public unless the witness appearing before the Commission requested an open hearing.
No witness except one (Mark Lane) requested an open hearing, and the testimony of that witness was taken in
a public hearing. (WR, p.xiii; 2 H 33, WCT Mark R. Lane) Second, although the hearings (except one) were
conducted in private, they were not secret. In a secret hearing, the witness is instructed not to disclose his testimony to any third party, and the hearing testimony is not published for public consumption. The witnesses
who appeared before the Commission were free to repeat what they said to anyone they pleased, and *all* of their
testimony was subsequently published in the first fifteen volumes put out by the Warren Commission.

mission was "so dependent on them [FBI] for the facts,"[58] *if examining 489 witnesses under oath is not conducting an independent investigation, then what is?*

If I were the lead prosecutor on a major murder case and I personally interviewed all of the key—and many of the supplementary—witnesses (roughly analogous to the Warren Commission and its staff taking testimony and depositions of the witnesses), and someone denigrated my involvement in the case by saying I relied almost exclusively on the police department (analogous to the FBI) in the case, my response would be to say, "Either you are joking or you are just completely unaware of what took place in this case."

The argument that even if the Warren Commission did independently and thoroughly investigate the assassination by taking testimony and depositions of key and secondary witnesses, the FBI still controlled the investigation by informing the Commission members whom they should examine under oath, is, for the most part, invalid. Indeed, before the FBI even started interviewing witnesses, the Dallas Police Department and the Dallas County Sheriff's Department were interviewing key witnesses in the case. And the media, with their unprecedented scrutiny of the case, were locating and reporting on witnesses to the event in Dealey Plaza and related circumstances. And, of course, witnesses themselves were coming out of the woodwork reporting their stories to the authorities. To suggest that without the FBI the Warren Commission wouldn't have known whom to talk to is ludicrous. Even without the aforementioned sources, let's take a representative witness like George Senator, Jack Ruby's roommate whom the Warren Commission examined under oath in considerable depth. I don't know how Senator came to the attention of the Warren Commission. The FBI may have informed the Commission of Senator's existence. But let's assume for the sake of argument that the FBI did not inform the Commission of Senator's existence. All seven Commission members, General Counsel J. Lee Rankin, and his fourteen assistant counsels were distinguished lawyers. Though most didn't have substantial trial experience, any lawyer, civil or criminal (in fact, any rational person, lawyer or not), would know that if they are investigating any event, it is imperative that they interview all witnesses who might have knowledge about an issue relevant to the case. Does anyone really believe that if the FBI had not informed the Warren Commission of Senator's existence, the Commission (with members like Earl Warren, a former district attorney and attorney general of the state of California) and the assistant counsels (like Joseph Ball, one of the most experienced trial lawyers in the land; Arlen Specter, a former assistant DA in Philadelphia; Albert Jenner, a former special assistant attorney general of Illinois; Burt Griffin, a former assistant U.S. attorney in Ohio; and Frances Adams, a former chief assistant U.S. attorney in New York and police commissioner of New York City, etc.) would not have sought to find out, on their own, what people were closest to Ruby and knew him well (which would include Senator as well as Ruby's key employees at his club, and his sisters and brothers) and then taken their testimony or had them interviewed? Please. Let's not get foolish.

And whom did the Commission rely on the most in writing its famous Warren Report? The FBI's interviews of witnesses or its own examination of these and other witnesses? The official record is clear that for the most part the Commission based its report on its examination of the witnesses, not FBI reports.[59] As the Commission stated, "In addition to the information resulting from these [federal] investigations, the Commission has relied *primarily* on the facts disclosed by the sworn testimony of the principal witnesses to the assassination."[60]

And the Commission didn't limit itself to taking testimony, which would alone immunize it from the total-reliance-on-the-FBI argument. Its staff went beyond this, going out into the field, mostly in Dallas. Assistant Warren Commission counsel Joseph Ball said, "As lawyers we investigated the case thoroughly. We got some leads as to who to talk to from the FBI. *But we went into the field*, we talked to every witness that we reported on. We took depositions. We took people before the Commission. We handled this like we would handle . . . any lawsuit."[61] As Assistant Counsel David Belin wrote, "In the middle of March [1964], Joe Ball and I flew to Dallas to conduct our initial field investigation . . . The first evening there, I telephoned Rabbi Silverman (Ruby's rabbi) and arranged to see him the following Friday night."[62] As just part of his investigation, Arlen Specter said he "sent ahead a list of witnesses whom I wanted to see at" Parkland Hospital, then went "to Parkland Hospital . . . and I interviewed . . . some 20-odd witnesses" there.[63] Does this sound as if the Warren Commission relied exclusively on the FBI? In fact, by the end of March, most of the assistant counsels had arrived in Dallas to conduct their field investigation with respect to witnesses they would eventually take sworn testimony from.[64] "At Chief Justice Earl Warren's insistence," Assistant Counsel Joseph Ball said, "every witness [called before the commission] was privately questioned . . . by commission counsel . . . before being called to testify."[65]

In July 1964, Specter said he traveled "to the West Coast to track down some matters relating to Ruby on some individuals we hadn't been able to locate earlier."[66] Some members of the staff even traveled outside the United States. On April 8, 1964, Assistant Counsels William Coleman Jr., W. David Slawson, and Howard P. Willens flew to Mexico City, where for seven days they investigated Oswald's stay in Mexico City, being briefed by and asking questions of not just the Mexico City station of the CIA, but the FBI office in Mexico City and the Mexican federal authorities who conducted their own investigation of the case. When the Mexico City daily *La Prensa* reported on April 9 that "three investigators of Kennedy case" had come to Mexico City, they weren't referring to the FBI, but to Warren Commission assistant counsels.[67]

Although the assistant counsels did most of the field and grunt work, Commission member John McCloy would later say that the Commission members themselves dug in. "We went [over to] Dealey Plaza," McCloy said, and walked it "foot by foot. We . . . visited . . . the boarding house that Oswald had lived in; retraced, step by step, [Oswald's] movements from the School Book Depository to the point at which he was apprehended in the theater. We chased ourselves up and down the [Book Depository] stairs, and timed ourselves. I sat in the window and held the very rifle . . . and sighted down across it [and] snapped the trigger many times . . . We had a car moving at the alleged rate. Well, I can go on. But I'm trying to give you the . . . fact that we did, assiduously, follow [the] evidence, and work out as best we could our own judgments in relation to it."[68] Indeed, the chief justice himself went up to the sniper's nest, and with a stopwatch, per Arlen Specter, who was present, "made the long walk . . . from the window . . . down one corridor and up another and over to the dimly lighted steps where he descended four flights to the second floor to see if he could get to the Coke machine within the time" Oswald had available to meet Officer Marrion Baker, "and he made it."[69]

And at one point, all seven commissioners traveled to Dallas and, among other things, stood on the fifth floor of the Book Depository Building where the three young black men were at the time of the assassination, and conducted a test wherein a cartridge shell was dropped to the floor directly above them and "*all* the commissioners heard a sound which they . . . concluded . . . was the sound of a shell which had fallen to the floor."[70]

In addition to taking testimony and personally interviewing witnesses, the Warren Commission double-checked the FBI's scientific work, as assistant Warren Commission counsel Wesley J. Liebeler pointed out in his testimony before the HSCA: "The work the FBI did on the physical evidence, the ballistics work, the fingerprint work, the hair and fibers work, that sort of thing, in many, if not in all cases, was checked by independent criminal laboratories."[71] Just two examples: Warren Commission assistant counsel Melvin A. Eisenberg sent a latent right index fingerprint and latent left and right palm prints found on book cartons in the sixth-floor sniper's nest to New York City Police Department detective Arthur Mandella, a fingerprint expert in the department's Bureau of Criminal Identification, and Mandella, after comparing the latent prints with finger and palm print exemplars of Oswald, concluded that the latent prints belonged to Oswald, the same conclusion reached by the FBI's fingerprint expert, Sebastian Latona.[72] And in addition to FBI firearms expert Robert Frazier, the Warren Commission employed Joseph D. Nicol, a firearms expert who was the superintendent of the Bureau of Criminal Identification and Investigation for the state of Illinois, to examine the bullet fragments found at the assassination scene and the whole bullet found at Parkland Hospital to see if they matched up with bullets test-fired from Oswald's Carcano rifle. Nicol's conclusion, the same as Frazier's, was that they did.[73]

In fact, in some very important areas, the FBI did no work at all. For example, the Commission's wound ballistics experiments, conducted to determine critical issues like whether the bullet that struck Kennedy in his upper right back could have physically been the same one that caused all of Governor Connally's injuries, were handled by the Wound Ballistics Branch of the U.S. Army Chemical Research and Development Laboratories at the Edgewood Arsenal in Maryland.[74] And who conducted the all-important tests to determine if Oswald's Mannlicher-Carcano rifle was a sufficiently accurate weapon to have accomplished what the Warren Commission believed Oswald accomplished on the day of the assassination? Not the FBI, but the Infantry Weapons Evaluation Branch of the Department of the Army.[75]

Indeed, Warren Commission assistant counsel David Belin even employed private investigators at various points to cross-check information and give an independent evaluation.[76]

As early as January 21, 1964, we see Chief Justice Earl Warren saying in a Warren Commission executive session, "One of the important things in *our investigation* is to be able to trace every dollar that we can in the possession of Oswald . . . because we don't know where his money came from. There is no evidence of any affluence or anything of that kind . . . but we ought to know as far as we can every dollar that came into his possession and every dollar he spent, and we have taken that up with the [Department of the] Treasury and they have assigned two of their top-flight investigators to run that matter down."[77]

Perhaps nothing is reflective of the Warren Commission's independent state of mind more than General Counsel Rankin's oral request to Director Hoover on February 24, 1964 (unquestionably, on a sensitive matter such as this, with the knowledge and consent of Earl Warren and the other Commission members), which was memorialized in an internal FBI memorandum to Hoover on February 24, 1964, asking that the FBI "set up coverage of Marina Oswald's activities."[78] "Coverage," of course, includes wiretaps. Per FBI agent James P. Hosty, "against the FBI's advice" the bureau acceded to the Warren Commission's request and sought and secured a wiretap warrant, Marina's phone being tapped and her living quarters bugged by the FBI from February 29, 1964, to March 12, 1964. (FBI special agent Robert Gemberling, a supervisor in the Dallas FBI office at the time, testified before the HSCA that "no information gleaned from either of these [two] sources" contained anything pertinent to the assassination.)[79] According to Arthur Schlesinger Jr., RFK's biographer, as attorney general, RFK "authorized . . . an undisclosed number [of wiretaps] in 1964 at the request of the Warren Commission."[80]

In addition, and pursuant to the Warren Commission's request, the bureau set up round-the-clock physical surveillance of Marina, and its reports back to the Warren Commission were captioned "re: FISUR [code name for physical surveillance] of Marina Oswald."[81]

Very importantly (and as previously indicated) a healthy part of the FBI's investigation was being *directed* by the Warren Commission. The FBI was constantly being besieged by the Commission with requests that the agency do all manner of things. For instance, the FBI, in a tone suggesting that the Warren Commission was being too demanding, said that just in the period between February 21 and March 5, 1964, "the General Investigative Division has a total of nine pending requests from the President's Commission." A few examples: "A three page request for technical and other related information concerning the rifle used in the assassination. This request is very extensive and requires the obtaining of *original* documents of numerous items, such as shipping documents, invoices, bills of lading, etc. This request also requires technical examination by our Laboratory as well as extensive work by our Dallas Office"; "[a request] that we obtain copies of Immigration and Naturalization Service records of Jack L. Ruby's parents, Joseph and Fannie Rubenstein. Also, that we obtain all available records of toll calls made by Ruby, his three brothers and four sisters and twelve persons known to have been in contact with Ruby between September 26, 1963 and November 22, 1963"; "[a request] that this Bureau initiate a full scale background and intelligence investigation of Michael Paine and his wife, Ruth Paine . . . and of George and Jeanne De Mohrenschildt"; and so on.[82]

Examples of the Warren Commission directing the FBI in the investigation are too numerous to cite. Here are two more to illustrate just how detailed that direction was. The reenactment of the assassination was conducted by the FBI in Dallas on May 24, 1964, with the assistance of the Secret Service. But the Warren Commission staff not only requested the reenactment, but in Warren Commission general counsel J. Lee Rankin's May 7, 1964, letter to FBI Director Hoover making the request, he instructed the FBI, in detail, as to everything that had to be done, telling Hoover where the limousine should be placed on Elm for each shot. For instance, in part II of his letter, he writes, "the third shot was fixed at a particular frame in the Zapruder film (frame 313), as well as a particular frame in the other two films (frame 24 of the Nix film and frame 42 of the Muchmore film). A car should be placed at the point which we believe to be the approximate location corresponding to these frames and then photographed from the point where the three cameramen were standing to establish the accuracy of this location. Distances should be measured from this point to the various points described in part I, and angles and distances established between this point and the assassination window to establish the view which the assassin had when he fired the third shot." Directions like this— even the direction that all of the many points referred to in parts I and II of his letter should be "mapped on a survey" and "trigonometric readings should be taken" to determine distances and angles—run throughout the letter.

Another example: After the Commission established through its questioning of Dallas Secret Service chief Forrest Sorrels that it wouldn't have been feasible to get to Stemmons Freeway from Main Street,[83] Rankin wrote to Hoover on August 10, 1964, saying the Commission needed photographs to demonstrate that "traffic proceeding westbound on Main Street is directed to turn right on Houston Street and left onto Elm Street if it wishes to proceed north on the Stemmons Freeway. We would like to demonstrate, in short, that the motorcade was not able to proceed on Main Street and gain access to the Stemmons Freeway proceeding northbound without departing from normal traffic patterns." Rankin asked for six photographs depicting six separate points, including one that showed "instructions which are posted on Main Street instructing westbound traffic as to how it should proceed to gain access to Stemmons Freeway," and a photograph showing that "the barricade separating Main Street traffic from Elm Street traffic extends beyond the point where Elm Street traffic can gain access to Stemmons Freeway."[84]*

Moreover, the Commission relied on many other federal agencies besides the FBI for information about the assassination. For instance, the Secret Service launched an extensive investigation, conducting 1,552 interviews and submitting eight hundred reports totaling some forty-six hundred pages. When HSCA member Christopher J. Dodd, in his questioning of former Warren Commission assistant counsel Burt Griffin, stated that the Commission and its staff seemed to be limited to merely "evaluating the evidence that they [FBI] are handing you," Griffin responded this was not so. "We did have other agencies," he said. "We had a countercheck on them [the FBI]. We were getting to a certain extent parallel investigations from the Secret Service. We were also getting information back from the Dallas Police Department. A lot of people who were being interrogated by the FBI were being interrogated by other agencies, even the Post Office Department." He went on to say that "in terms of the scientific information," in addition to the FBI the Warren Commission "deliberately went to find people independent of the federal government."[85] Indeed, Warren Commission assistant counsel W. David Slawson said, "We had special people . . . who were investigators . . . assigned from the CIA, FBI, and Secret Service who were with us more or less full-time, especially the Secret Service."[86] Other agencies that participated in the investigation in a meaningful way were the Department of State, IRS, the military intelligence agencies, and the Dallas Police and Sheriff's Departments. The Commission "directed requests to the 10 major departments of the Federal Government, 14 of its independent agencies or commissions, and 4 congressional committees for all information relating to the assassination or the background and activities of Lee Harvey Oswald and Jack Ruby."[87] And the Commission staff critically reviewed in detail the actions and investigative efforts of all these agencies, even calling the heads of the main agencies (i.e., J. Edgar Hoover, director of the FBI; John A. McCone, director of the CIA; and James J. Rowley, chief of the Secret Service) to testify under oath about the conduct of their respective agencies in the investigation.[88]

But above all, it was the testimony and depositions taken by the Warren Commission and its staff that give the lie to the myth that the Commission was totally dependent on the FBI. Considering that in a state or federal criminal prosecution, as opposed to a civil case, depositions by the prosecution (as well as the defense) are not allowed, the Warren Commission conducted an investigation of Kennedy's murder far, far more independent

---

*For yet another example very representative of the Warren Commission's being on top of the details of the assassination and literally directing the FBI's investigation, as opposed to, as commonly believed, being completely reliant on whatever information the bureau chose to give it, see endnote for a verbatim letter from the Warren Commission General Counsel Rankin to FBI Director Hoover dated March 26, 1964.

of the FBI or local and state law enforcement than any other previous or subsequent case in American legal history.

My foregoing reference to the Warren Commission's independent investigative efforts is not meant to depreciate the FBI's contribution to the assassination investigation. In fact, there's no question that the FBI was the main investigative arm of the Warren Commission *out in the field* and obviously conducted the bulk of that field investigation. A total of 169 FBI agents worked on the assassination, resulting in approximately twenty-five thousand interviews, and over twenty-three hundred reports approximately 25,400 pages.[89]

But even if the Warren Commission had not conducted an independent investigation of the assassination, and had relied on the FBI as the only investigative agency (as some critics claim), and even if the Warren Commission had not sought corroboration for information given to it by the FBI, and had relied solely on the FBI, how bad would that be? Since the FBI was the largest and arguably the best investigative agency in the world, whom would the Warren Commission be expected to rely on? The Cincinnati Police Department? Some foreign law enforcement agency, like Scotland Yard? Since when is it a negative in a federal investigation to rely exclusively on the FBI, which *all* U.S. attorneys in the country routinely do in federal prosecutions? Since when does an FBI investigation of a crime have to have some *other* agency corroborating or investigating the FBI's investigation? And if so, who is supposed to investigate this other agency's investigation? As Plato observed, "That a guardian should require another guardian to take care of him is ridiculous."

Ah, but the Warren Commission critics say, the reason the Warren Commission shouldn't have relied on the FBI in *this* case is that FBI Director J. Edgar Hoover was certainly not someone to be trusted, and they proceed to cite references that suggest that Hoover did not want the Warren Commission to conduct an exhaustive investigation for fear it might uncover malfeasance on the bureau's part. But although the HSCA faulted the FBI's investigation here and there—such as its purported failure to make use of the Cuban section of its Domestic Intelligence Division, and its investigation of organized crime[*]—the committee nonetheless was forced to admit that the FBI "generally exhausted its resources in confirming the case against Lee Harvey Oswald as the *lone* assassin . . . Indeed, [the FBI investigation] was an effort of unparalleled magnitude in keeping with the gravity of the crime, and resulting in the assignment of more Bureau resources than for any criminal case in its history. In terms of hours worked, interviews conducted, and tests performed, the FBI's [investigation] was, in fact, unexcelled."[90] In a September 19, 1964, memo to the file by Hoover, five days before the Warren Report was issued, he wrote, "We left no stone unturned." By that he obviously meant the bureau's exhaustive pursuit of every tip and lead, no matter from whom, including a mentally unstable woman in Cuba, a drunken Aztec Indian, and a Bavarian cabdriver.[91]

---

[*]The HSCA said that "the FBI's investigation into a conspiracy was deficient in the areas that the committee decided were most worthy of suspicion—organized crime, pro- and anti-Castro Cubans, and the possible associations of individuals from these areas with Lee Harvey Oswald and Jack Ruby. In those areas in particular, the committee found that the FBI's investigation was in all likelihood insufficient to have uncovered a conspiracy" (HSCA Report, p.242).

Even assuming the FBI could have done a better job in these areas, the HSCA's observation would have far more virility if, as a result of the committee doing what it said the Warren Commission and FBI should have done (i.e., conduct a more expansive investigation), it had uncovered evidence of a conspiracy. But it did not. So in essence the HSCA is telling the FBI and Warren Commission, "You should have conducted a more in-depth investigation into these three areas so you could have come up with the same conclusion that we did, namely, that there was nothing." I write this not in defense of the FBI and Warren Commission, but to put the HSCA's observation into a proper perspective and thereby reduce it to its true dimensions.

Earlier, the Church Committee reached the same conclusion on the extent of the FBI effort, saying, "The FBI investigation of the assassination was a massive effort. Literally thousands of leads were followed in the field by hundreds of agents, many of whom worked around the clock during the days immediately following the assassination.[92] Even inveterate conspiracy theorist Harrison Edward Livingstone acknowledges that "the FBI . . . performed a massive job of trying to track down many leads."[93]*

According to the HSCA, the bureau made this tremendous effort despite the fact that Hoover "seemed determined to make [the case against Oswald as the lone assassin] within 24 hours of the assassination."[94] The HSCA was referring to a five-page letter Hoover sent to President Johnson on November 23, 1963, in which he apprised Johnson of what his agency had learned about the assassination up to that point. But although Hoover naturally set forth the evidence tying Oswald to the assassination (I mean, what else could he do—the murder weapon, for instance, was sent to Oswald's post office box, not Bob Hope's), there is no way that one can infer from the letter that Hoover "seemed determined" to nail Oswald. Nowhere does he offer an opinion on Oswald's guilt, and there isn't even any vague allusion to the absence of a conspiracy.[95]

However, on November 25, two days later, Hoover did issue a statement to the media that the available evidence indicated Oswald killed Kennedy and "not one shred of evidence" connecting anyone else to the assassination had yet been found by his agents.[96] Though Hoover unprofessionally acted with too much haste in suggesting that Oswald was the lone assassin, he obviously was basing this on information he was receiving from his investigative staff. Moreover, he was simply reporting a fact—*that up to that point in time*, Oswald appeared to be the assassin and there was no evidence he acted in concert with others.

The proof that the FBI had not closed its mind to any subsequent evidence that might have pointed toward a conspiracy is an internal November 27, 1963, memorandum from Assistant FBI Director Alan Belmont, the number-three man at the bureau who headed up its investigation of the assassination, to Associate FBI Director Clyde Tolson, the number-two man, in which Belmont said that although a preliminary FBI report on the assassination would be available on November 29, "The investigation . . . will, however, continue, because we are receiving literally hundreds of allegations regarding the activities of Oswald and Ruby, and these, of course, are being run out as received . . . We must check out and continue to investigate . . . any allegation or possibility that he [Oswald] was associated with others in this assassination. Likewise, we have to continue to [try to] prove the possibility that Jack Ruby was associated with someone else in connection with his killing Oswald."

---

*For people to say that the Warren Commission and the FBI conducted a superficial investigation is the equivalent of their saying that they haven't gotten within a hundred miles of the Warren Commission's twenty-seven volumes. Though many don't agree with his conclusions, virtually everyone agrees that the late Warren Commission critic Harold Weisberg studied the Kennedy assassination longer and more thoroughly than any other known person. And he certainly has written the most about it in his eight books. And Weisberg says the Warren Commission "checked into almost every breath Oswald drew." As an example, he says the FBI "traced and chased all over the world those who traveled on the bus to Mexico City with Oswald . . . to collect every particle of information, no matter how minute, how seemingly inconsequential." (Weisberg, *Oswald in New Orleans*, p.214) Weisberg's criticism of the Warren Commission dealt mostly with his belief that the Commission itself suppressed much information and that its own documents reveal Oswald's innocence and the existence of a conspiracy. Another severe Warren Commission critic, Sylvia Meagher, acknowledged the Commission's and FBI's "microscopic research into Oswald's life" (Meagher, *Accessories after the Fact*, p.243).

But let's assume, for the sake of argument, that Hoover could not be trusted in the Kennedy assassination case and investigation, and tried to emasculate the Warren Commission by convincing everyone early on that Oswald, despite his innocence, killed Kennedy and acted alone, and hence there was no need for a thorough investigation by the Warren Commission. That argument, like virtually all conspiracy arguments, "doesn't go anywhere" since we know Hoover did not succeed. As indicated, the HSCA concluded that the Warren Commission and FBI did, in fact, conduct a massive investigation. Warren Commission assistant counsel Norman Redlich, a self-proclaimed civil libertarian who was a professor of constitutional law at the time of his appointment to the Warren Commission staff, says that he "did not come to Washington with the view that the Federal Bureau of Investigation was a model that I should choose to follow." But he said that "notwithstanding my predisposition" against them, "I left Washington . . . with a feeling of respect for the FBI," finding it to be "a very cooperative agency . . . There is nothing that we asked them to do that they didn't do and do promptly." Perhaps most importantly, he found "they were fair, cautious, and did not try to overstate their case. They were not trying to convict Lee Harvey Oswald . . . They were a very professional organization."[97]

Finally, some conspiracy theorists have made the argument that Hoover couldn't be trusted and was out to sabotage the investigation because he was behind the assassination and was out to cover up his complicity. But no serious and responsible conspiracy theorist believes this. Only those on the far-out fringes do. So where does the argument that Hoover cannot be trusted go? Nowhere. With conspiracy theorists, however, none of their arguments have to "go anywhere." The argument (based on a contradiction, anomaly, rumor, etc.) is the end in itself.

The bottom line is that even if the Warren Commission did rely exclusively on the FBI for its investigation (which clearly wasn't the case), it would only compromise the Commission's conclusions if the FBI itself was involved in Kennedy's murder or in trying to cover up for those who did. In other words, when the critics say the Warren Commission was crippled by the reliance on the FBI as its chief investigative arm, they are for the most part presupposing that the FBI was involved in Kennedy's murder or cover up. But as you'll see later in this book, there is not a scintilla of evidence to support that proposition.

Resuming the chronology, on December 20, four days after the Warren Commission established an investigative direction, the individual reports filed by FBI agents in the field, upon which the bureau had based its summary report to the Commission, began arriving at the Commission's headquarters. That same day, Howard P. Willens, a thirty-two-year-old graduate of Yale Law School and high-ranking Justice Department lawyer in the Criminal Division, joined the staff at the request of Deputy Attorney General Nicholas Katzenbach, who wanted Willens to serve as liaison between the Commission and the Justice Department. Willens got the impression that it was going to be a part-time job, but when confronted with the amount of work piling up, he went back to his Justice Department office, packed up his belongings, and moved into the Commission offices, which occupied two floors of the new Veterans of Foreign Wars Building at 200 Maryland Avenue, N.E., located diagonally across the street from the Supreme Court and only a short distance from the Capitol. He was to become a key player as Rankin's executive officer, organizing and scheduling the staff's work and getting assistance from other agencies. Young, energetic, and occasionally abrasive, he was often thought to be too aggressive, although some finally deemed him to be the "hero of the investigation."[98]

The troika at the top was filled out by Norman Redlich, a thirty-eight-year-old professor at New York University School of Law who had been the executive editor of the *Yale Law Journal*, whom Rankin selected as his special assistant. A perfectionist who sometimes stepped on toes, Redlich was also gifted with prodigious energy. It was said that he could work from eight in the morning until three the next morning, seven days a week. The three men—Rankin, Willens, and Redlich—were indispensable to the Commission's work, each influencing, in his own way, the outcome of the investigation.[99]

In late December, Rankin announced the names of his "senior assistant counsels," men from all parts of the country who were held in high esteem by their regional bar associations and whose reputations would add weight to the final report. These men of stature consisted of the aforementioned Francis W. H. Adams, the former New York City police commissioner who was a partner in a Manhattan law firm and recommended by New York City mayor Robert Wagner; Joseph A. Ball, a close friend of Warren's (who recruited him) from California and the most experienced trial lawyer on the staff, who was a member of the U.S. Judiciary Conference Advisory Committee and past president of the California State Bar; Albert E. Jenner Jr., the former assistant attorney general for Illinois and vice chairman of the National Joint Committee for the Effective Administration of Justice; William T. Coleman Jr., a former special counsel for the city of Philadelphia and a consultant with the U.S. Arms Control and Disarmament Agency, and the only black attorney on the Commission staff; and Leon D. Hubert Jr., a former U.S. attorney and Tulane University professor from New Orleans who was recommended to the staff by U.S. Representative Hale Boggs, a member of the Commission.[100]

While lawyers of such prominence lent credibility to the Commission's eventual report, none of them were able to give up months of their lucrative practices in order to participate in the hard, day-to-day labor of the investigation, and it was understood that although they would supervise their particular area of the investigation, they would only be spending about one full day a week on the job, more at their discretion. Of the five senior assistant counsels, Adams was the least involved, Ball the most. The real work, not surprisingly, was done by the "junior assistant counsels," young lawyers who had been at or near the top of their law school class but who were not "government men." Within days of the formation of the Commission, resumés began flooding the Commission headquarters on Maryland Avenue. But, as it turned out, nearly all the lawyers who were picked for the Commission staff were not those who applied. "They were chosen because they were bright, credentialed, and were in the right place at the right time. And they were known by the right people."[101]

The staff lawyers were told that their work should last three months but that it could go on, depending on developments, for six months. Some junior counsels later testified that there was some grumbling about the amount of work being done and who was shouldering the vast majority of it as the investigation wore on. W. David Slawson stated, "I felt overworked and I think many of the staff members felt the same way. I think one of the main problems was the great underestimation of the size of the task at the time . . . It is my recollection they said it would only be three to six months on the outside and of course we ended up taking about eight."[102] Most of the junior counsels were recruited by Howard Willens, who wanted men who could work sixteen hours a day. They were paid only seventy-five dollars a day, but for many of them it was as much or more than they were making in private practice so early in their careers.[103]

Twenty-nine-year-old Melvin A. Eisenberg, a New York corporation lawyer who had topped his class at Harvard and edited the *Harvard Law Review*, became Redlich's assistant. Also added to the team were Arlen Specter, the former assistant district attorney of Philadelphia with whom Willens had coedited the *Yale Law Journal*; Samuel A. Stern, a developmental editor of *Harvard Law Review* and former law clerk to Chief Justice Warren; Burt W. Griffin, a note and comment editor of the *Yale Law Journal* and the former assistant U.S. attorney for the Northern District of Ohio; David W. Belin, an associate editor of the *Michigan Law Review* and an Iowa trial lawyer; W. David Slawson, a note editor of the *Harvard Law Review* and Denver attorney; and Wesley J. Liebeler, a former Wall Street lawyer and managing editor of the *University of Chicago Law Review* who was recommended to Willens by the dean of the University of Chicago Law School.[104]

Arlen Specter, responding in part to the allegation that the Warren Commission concealed evidence, said that the entire staff of assistant counsels was chosen with the aim of getting not just men of high intellectual stature and probity, but men who were independent of the Washington bureaucracy. The Commission, he said, "did not select people who had ties or allegiances to Government who might have been beholden to some department or another for their jobs, but instead, chose men of outstanding reputation, like Joe Ball from California, a leader of the California bar for many years . . . Similar selections were made . . . from New York and Chicago and Des Moines and New Orleans and Philadelphia and Washington, so that every conceivable pain was taken to select people who were totally independent, *which is hardly the way you set out to organize a truth-concealing commission*."[105]

Slawson said that junior assistant counsels worked very hard "for eight months, six days a week, and usually until ten o'clock in the evening."[106] Specter would later write that the distinction between junior and senior lawyers was eventually dropped, and all the lawyers were classified as "assistant counsel."[107] With all the junior lawyers, and senior lawyers like Willens, Redlich, and General Counsel Rankin, the unrelenting pressure, tension, and concomitant exhilaration in investigating the biggest murder case in this nation's history left an ineradicable mark. "How often in your life do you have a chance to devote a 100 percent effort to one honorable thing—in this case, a national tragedy?" Redlich asked. "Next to high school in Russell, Kansas, it was the best experience I've ever had," Specter said. "I didn't have any gray hairs until the Warren Commission," Willens observed.[108]

An additional eleven "staff members," six of whom were lawyers and recent graduates of major law schools who again were near or at the top of their class (including Warren's law clerk, John Hart Ely), were appointed to do research and "gofer" work for the assistant counsels and Commission members. Five nonlawyers (an editor from the Department of State, a historian from the Department of Defense, and three accountants from the IRS who worked exclusively on Oswald's and Ruby's finances) completed this section.[109]

Per Arlen Specter, though the assistant counsels did most of the day-to-day work, "the Commissioners themselves paid close attention to the work" of the staff. "The Chief Justice was a dominant figure moving throughout the entire investigation, and so were the other commissioners in terms of knowing and understanding and participating in the scope and depth of the Commission work."[110]

On December 28, 1963, Howard Willens drafted a memorandum that laid out the Commission's plan of attack. A senior and a junior lawyer would be assigned to each of six major areas* of concentration: Area I was "Basic Facts of the Assassination," assigned to Francis Adams and Arlen Specter, and focused primarily on determining the location from where the shots were fired; Area II was "Identity of the Assassin," given to Joseph Ball and David Belin; Area III was "Lee Harvey Oswald's Background," handled by Albert Jenner and Wesley Liebeler, and included seeking to determine if there was a domestic conspiracy apart from the questions involving Jack Ruby; Area IV was "Possible Conspiratorial Relationships," assigned to William Coleman and W. David Slawson, and was concerned with the possibility of a foreign conspiracy; Area V was "Lee Harvey Oswald's Death," with Leon Hubert and Burt Griffin, and concentrated on Jack Ruby and his possible involvement in a conspiracy, including whether Oswald and Ruby had a previous association with each other; and Area VI was "Presidential Protection," assigned to Samuel Stern, with General Counsel Rankin assisting, which included an evaluation of the quality of protection afforded the president under existing standards. The organizational plan did not call for a separate investigation into the murder of Dallas police officer J. D. Tippit, which was considered a part of Area II, "Identity of the Assassin."[111] Norman Redlich worked on special projects including the drafting of procedural rules for the Commission, and worked with Ball, Belin, and Specter on the investigation itself. Redlich also attended as many Commission meetings as possible and reviewed and edited drafts of the report. Willens assisted Rankin in organizing the work, reviewing materials received from the various investigative agencies, and requesting further information when necessary.[112]

Several former staff members testified in 1978 that they generally believed the organization of the Commission was effective in producing a professional and thorough investigation aimed at finding the truth.[113] Of those who testified, only Burt Griffin expressed some dissatisfaction, stating that the Commission looked upon Jack Ruby's activities (Griffin and Hubert's area of investigation) as "largely peripheral to the questions that they [the Commission] were most concerned with."[114]

Toward the end of December, Willens and Rankin arranged for the appointment of liaisons to the Commission with the four principal government agencies in the investigation: Inspector James J. Malley from the FBI, Inspector Thomas Kelley from the Secret Service, Raymond G. Rocca from the CIA, and Abram Chayes from the State Department.[115]

During the first three weeks of January 1964, the lawyers reported for work and were each assigned a secretary and an office in the Commission's headquarters. Willens brought in two more lawyers, Charles N. Shaffer Jr. and Stuart Pollak, to assist on clerical and administrative procedures, and the FBI installed a scale model of the assassination site, film projectors, and other equipment in the basement.

The massive task of investigating the assassination events began by dividing more than twenty thousand pages of reports from the FBI, Secret Service, and other agencies into the preassigned areas and handing them over to the responsible teams. Joe Ball, who arrived in Washington from Los Angeles on January 2, 1964, and had the biggest investigative area of all, "Identity of the Assassin," recalled that on the first day "about 10,000 pieces of paper were rolled into my office, the written reports of the various investigative agencies . . . During the first month of the investigation, we classified the information

---

*Initially, Willens suggested five areas. A sixth, "Presidential Protection," was added at the Commission's request. (Epstein, *Inquest*, p.12)

found in the reports by means of a card index system. This permitted the immediate retrieval of this information when needed."[116] Wesley Liebeler, realizing that a lawyer in one area, like Ball, might not perceive the importance of information to another area, proposed that at least one attorney should read all of the reports. Rankin thought it more important for each team to get to work on its own material right away. Later, "if time permitted," a staff member could read all of the material.[117]

On January 20, 1964, Chief Justice Warren met with the Warren Commission staff at their first formal staff meeting. In discussing the role of the Commission with the staff, Warren "placed emphasis on the importance of quenching rumors, and precluding further speculation such as that which has surrounded the death of Lincoln. *He emphasized that the Commission had to determine the truth, whatever that might be.*"[118] Wary of questions of national security which might turn up, he asked the staff not to discuss their work outside the Commission.[119] Rankin warned them against forming conclusions too quickly, before they had a chance to evaluate all of the material, and told them not to accept the FBI's summary report as final. Rankin told his team, "Gentlemen, your only client is the truth."[120] "No one knew," Assistant Counsel Arlen Specter said, "where the Warren Commission investigation would lead, and that was just as it should have been."[121]

The next day, the Commission met to discuss procedural questions, including whether its hearings, scheduled to begin in February, would be open or closed. The Commission decided to keep them closed (unless, as indicated, the witness appearing before the Commission requested an open hearing). The commissioners were concerned that open hearings might interfere with Ruby's right to a fair and impartial trial. They also realized that some of the testimony presented would be inadmissible in a real trial, which this was not, and might prejudice innocent parties in subsequent lawsuits if it were to be made public out of context. Finally, since sworn depositions, affidavits, and statements would not be taken in a logical sequence, the premature release or partial publication of such testimony might start more rumors than it allayed. Other housekeeping matters were also resolved, like who would attend the hearings involving testimony (they wanted a minimum of two commissioners always present, and hoped General Counsel Rankin would be present at all of them), who would do the questioning (in the main, it should be by the assistant counsel who prepared and worked with the witness), and how to deal with the prying media (they did not want a press agent, but agreed they had to be careful, accurate, and limited in what was said; also, the media had to be told certain things or "they will speculate," which would be bad).

The Commission set a flexible "target date" for its report of June 1, 1964. The Commission also rejected a request by Mark Lane, representing Marguerite Oswald, to represent the interests of her son before the Commission. Five of the seven Commission members were already on the federal payroll and hence precluded from receiving additional compensation for their work on the Commission. And the two who weren't, Dulles and McCloy, agreed to serve without compensation, all seven agreeing to only receive reimbursement for their expenses, mostly anticipated to be for travel.[122]

The following morning, January 22, a bombshell exploded on the Commission. Texas attorney general Waggoner Carr telephoned the Commission's general counsel, J. Lee Rankin, to inform him that an allegation was floating around Dallas that Oswald had been an "undercover agent" (the "undercover agent" designation quickly evolved into that of "paid informant") for the FBI, receiving two hundred dollars a month "for an account designated as number 179." Rankin immediately informed Chief Justice Warren, who called an emergency meeting of the Commission that evening.[123] In a hushed, tense, executive session, Rankin explained the allegation to the Commission. They speculated about what the FBI might have been using Oswald for, then turned their attention to the implications of the allegation. Rankin found it unusual that the FBI was insisting that Oswald was the lone assassin, yet the bureau hadn't yet run down "all kinds of leads in Mexico or in Russia." This, he said, "raises questions."

Rankin told the Commission members that he and Chief Justice Warren had reflected on this and "we said if [the allegation] was true and it ever came out and could be established," then simply because of it, some people would think "that there was a conspiracy to accomplish this assassination" and "nothing the Commission did" could change this impression.

Representative Boggs: "You are so right."

"Oh, terrible," Allen Dulles moaned.

"[The] implications of this are fantastic, don't you think so?" Hale Boggs observed.

"Terrific [possibly a typographical error for *terrible*]," Chief Justice Warren answered.

When Dulles asked the question of why, if Oswald were an FBI informant, "it would be in their [FBI's] interest . . . to say [Oswald] is . . . the only guilty one?" Warren answered, "They would like to have us fold up and quit."

"This closes the case, you see," Boggs interjected. "Don't you see?"

"Yes, I see that," Dulles acknowledged.

"They found the man," Rankin continued. "There is nothing more to do. The Commission supports their conclusions, and we can go home and that is the end of it."

"But that puts the men [typo for *burden?*] right on them," Dulles argued. "If he was not the killer, and they employed him, they are already it, you see. [This sentence would seem to make sense only if Dulles had not used the word "not." He could have misspoken or the stenographer could have made a mistake.] So your argument is correct if they are sure that this is going to close the case, but if it [doesn't] close the case, they are worse off than ever by doing this."

"Yes, I would think so," Boggs replied ". . . I don't even like to see this being taken down."

"Yes," Dulles agreed. "I think this record ought to be destroyed. Do you think we need a record of this?"

Rankin: "I don't, except that we said we would have records of meetings."[124]

On January 23, 1964, Texas attorney general Waggoner Carr, along with two of his special counsels, Dean Storey and Leon Jaworski, and Dallas County district attorney Henry Wade and his assistant, Dallas DA William Alexander, flew to Washington, D.C. The following day they met with Chief Justice Warren and General Counsel Rankin to discuss the explosive allegation. At the meeting, the Texas contingent said the rumor was "constant" in Texas, and that "the source of their information was a man by the name of Hudkins [newspaper reporter Alonzo Hudkins]."

Although the source of the allegation has become almost permanently mired in dispute and obfuscation, one thing is very clear. It was a fabricated story with no substance (see in-depth discussion in FBI conspiracy section), but at the time, the Warren Commission did not know this and took the allegation very seriously. The first suggestion on how to handle the rumor was to have the U.S. attorney general look into it, but Rankin said he had already spoken to high officials in the Department of Justice who told him that since the FBI is a part of the Justice Department and the attorney general's office works so closely with the FBI, "such a request [to the attorney general] might be embarrassing, and at least would be difficult for the attorney general." To put, what Rankin called, this "dirty rumor" to rest, he suggested that he talk with Hoover directly and ask him to demonstrate by the bureau's records that the rumor was untrue. In a nod to the power of the FBI, Rankin said he would seek Hoover's permission to do an independent investigation of the Oswald-FBI rumor should it prove necessary. Although Chief Justice Warren said he disliked the idea of going to Hoover without investigating the rumor on their own first, other members were worried that eliciting a statement from the FBI, then conducting a subsequent investigation, would appear to undermine the FBI's authority and cause "grave embarrassment to everybody." The Commission then discussed the problem of proving or disproving the allegation.

"If Oswald never had assassinated the president," Senator Richard Russell said, "[but] . . . had been in the employ of the FBI, and somebody had gone to the FBI they would have denied he was an agent."

"Oh, yes," Dulles, the former CIA director, answered.

"They would be the first to deny it," Russell continued. "Your agents would have done exactly the same thing."

"Exactly," Dulles confirmed.[125]

The commissioners, following a suggestion by Warren, decided to approach the problem from two sides: ask Hoover to investigate, and conduct their own inquiry into the matter. They decided on this course despite their fear that in the process they might anger Hoover. The reason for their fear was simple. *At this very early point*, the Commission was almost totally dependent on the FBI for its investigation. But it became clear to Commission members that they could either, in Senator Russell's words, "just accept the FBI's report" on the Oswald-FBI informant issue, "or else we can go and try to run down some of these collateral rumors."

Representative Boggs: "I think we must do the latter."

Senator Russell: "So do I."

Warren: "I think there is no question about it."

Acknowledging the "awkward" nature of this two-pronged approach, Commission member John McCloy said, "But as you [referring to Rankin] said the other day, truth is our only client . . . I don't think that we [can] recognize that any door is closed to us . . . in the search for the truth."

Representative Boggs: "[We] have got to do everything on earth to establish the facts one way or the other. And without doing that . . . everyone of us is doing a very grave disservice."[126]

Highly illustrative of the Warren Commission's state of mind vis-à-vis not accepting and being limited by the FBI's investigation is this exchange at the January 27, 1964, executive session:

Rankin: "Part of our difficulty . . . is that . . . they [FBI] have decided that no one else was involved [in the assassination]."

Russell: "They have tried the case and reached a verdict on every aspect."

Boggs: "You have put your finger on it."

Rankin: "Yes . . . They decided the case, [but] we are going to have maybe a thousand further inquiries that we say the Commission has to know . . . before it can pass on this."

McCloy: "Yes . . . it isn't only who killed cock robin . . . We have to go beyond that."[127]

During the long discussion of the Oswald informant issue by Commission members, this amusing dialogue arose:

Dulles observed that one reason he didn't believe Oswald was working for the FBI in any type of paid capacity was that "this fellow [Oswald] was so incompetent that he was not the kind of fellow that Hoover would hire . . . He was so stupid. Hoover didn't hire this kind of stupid fellow."

McCloy responded: "I wouldn't put much confidence in the intelligence of all the agents I have run into. I have run into some awfully stupid agents."

Dulles: "Not this irresponsible."

McCloy: "Well, I can't say that I have run into a fellow comparable to Oswald but I have run into some very limited mentalities both in the CIA and FBI. [Laughter]"[128]

Coincidentally, on the very same day (January 27) that the Commission was in session, its office received a letter from Hoover stating that "Lee Harvey Oswald was never paid any money for furnishing information [to the FBI] and he most certainly never was an informant of the Federal Bureau of Investigation."[129] This did not satisfy the Commission, however, and the next day Rankin met personally with Hoover and asked him to conduct a further inquiry into the rumor.[130] On February 6, 1964, Hoover wrote a letter accompanied by his affidavit under penalty of perjury stating that search of FBI records showed that Oswald had never been an informant.[131] However, a letter from Hoover to Rankin on February 27, 1964, acknowledged for the first time that Jack Ruby "was contacted by an Agent of the Dallas Office [of the FBI] on March 11, 1959, in view of his position as a night club operator who might have knowledge of the criminal element of Dallas . . . He expressed a willingness to furnish information along those lines. He was subsequently contacted on eight occasions between March 11, 1959, and October 2, 1959, but he furnished no information whatever and further contacts with him were discontinued." Hoover said that, as was the case with Oswald, "Ruby was never paid any money, and he was never at any time an informant of this Bureau."[132]

For its part, the Warren Commission, which had decided to conduct its own investigation, ended up doing very little. The HSCA said the Commission "quizzed" Hudkins. But it didn't. The citation the HSCA gives for its assertion that the Warren Commission quizzed Hudkins is an interview of Hudkins by the Secret Service on December 17, 1963, almost a month and a half *before* the Warren Commission's executive session on January 27 in which the Commission concluded it had to conduct its own investigation into the matter. Hudkins told Secret Service agent Lane Bertram that Allen Sweatt of the Dallas sheriff's office had told him that it was his opinion Oswald was an FBI informant.[133] (See the FBI conspiracy section for a fuller discussion.) Also, on the evening of January 24, Secret Service inspector Thomas Kelley told Warren Commission general counsel F. Lee Rankin that Hudkins was "not very reliable" based on previous unfounded reports that he had furnished to the Secret Service.[134] However, the only affirmative things that the Warren Commission is known to have done on its own to get to the bottom of the Oswald informant issue was to conduct an independent review of FBI files, which uncovered no evidence that Oswald was an informant,[135] and to have the Internal Revenue Service do an audit on Oswald's income on the assumption that if the FBI had been paying Oswald money the IRS might discover unaccounted-for income.[136] No unaccountable income was found.[137]

In late January, the Warren Commission staff met with FBI and Secret Service experts and viewed for the first time what was to become the single most critical piece of physical evidence in the whole investigation: the twenty-five seconds of 8-millimeter color film shot by a Dealey Plaza spectator to the motorcade, Abraham Zapruder. There was no audio on the film, so it was impossible to time the shots exactly, but it seemed, after a cursory examination, that two of the shots may have come too close together to have been fired by Oswald's bolt-action rifle, the one found in the Texas School Book Depository Building. These initial doubts were based largely on the apparent reactions of President Kennedy and Governor Connally as seen in the film. (See Zapruder film section later in the text.)

The hearings formally opened on February 3, 1964, at 10:35 a.m. with the testimony, through two interpreters, of Marina Oswald. Rankin himself handled the interrogation and began by asking Lee Oswald's widow if she wanted to correct anything she had told FBI agents in the many interviews they had had with her to date. She did.

"Yes, I would like to correct some things because not everything was true," she told the Commission. "It is not just that it wasn't true, but not quite exact."

She couldn't at that point recall any specific instances, "but perhaps in the course of your questioning if it comes up I will say so."[138]

The veracity of Marina Oswald was viewed as imperative by the Commission since she was in a unique position to shed light, directly or indirectly, on her husband's motivations and guilt, she being the only witness to most of Oswald's life from the time she met him in Minsk to the night before the assassination. As such, the Commission was heavily dependent on her testimony.

According to author Edward Jay Epstein, the Warren Commission staff counsel did not believe Marina was a credible witness. He said senior assistant counsel William Coleman wanted her subjected to a more rigorous examination and had prepared a "trappy deposition" for her, and threatened to resign when Rankin said that the Commission members had decided they believed her and saw no need to question her further.[139] But when I spoke to Coleman, he said, "You know, this was many years ago, but I can tell you without any hesitation that I never at any time threatened to resign from the Commission. That's just not true. As to the first matter, I don't recall at all that I was dissatisfied with Marina Oswald's testimony and had prepared a trappy deposition for her. The reason it makes no sense is that my assigned area was the possibility of a foreign conspiracy, and Marina's testimony didn't really go to that issue. Furthermore, I had tremendous respect for those who questioned Marina, like Rankin and Warren, and I can't even imagine thrusting myself into the matter with a so-called 'trappy deposition' for her. Where did Epstein get this? Certainly not from me."[*] When I asked Cole-

---

[*]Because Epstein's book started as his master's thesis in government at Cornell University and he was a doctoral student at Harvard by the time it was published, most readers assumed its accuracy without question since it came clothed in the robes of academe. But the reality is that although Epstein is far more sensible than most Warren Commission critics, and his book is valuable in that it was, for years, the only in-depth analysis of the inner workings of the Warren Commission and its internal fighting, disputes, and dynamics, it unquestionably suffers from a serious lack of credibility in one of its very most important areas: where he purports to quote Warren Commission staff. The Coleman example cited in the text is just one of many.

In a 1967 article in the *Law Quarterly Review*, Professor Arthur L. Goodhart, who went directly for confirmation to some of the persons on the Commission staff whom Epstein quoted, published his findings (Goodhart, "Mysteries of the Kennedy Assassination and the English Press," pp.23–63). They were startling. Joe Ball said that all the quotations attributed to him by Epstein were "wrong or false." Wesley Liebeler denied telling Epstein that the Warren Commission members (as opposed to the staff) had done "nothing," and was very angry overall about Epstein's distortions and misstatements in his book. Norman Redlich said, "I am appalled by the inaccuracies of the book and the statements which he has attributed to me which I never made." (Sparrow, *After the Assassination*, pp.36–37; Roberts, *Truth about the Assassination*, pp.122–123) And General

man whether the majority of the Commission members and staff thought Marina was lying, he replied, "No, not at all. The strong consensus, and I was a part of that consensus, was that she was telling the truth. But after her first four days of testimony, there were several assistant counsels who wanted to ask further questions of Marina, not because they felt she was lying but because there were areas that hadn't been gone into or needed further clarification or amplification."[140]

The overwhelming consensus in the conspiracy community is that Marina Oswald was not a truthful witness. This perception started mostly because of a very ill-advised statement by one of the Commission's most distinguished assistant counsels, Norman Redlich, who said in a February 28, 1964, memorandum to General Counsel Rankin, "We cannot ignore, however, that Marina Oswald has repeatedly lied to the [Secret] Service, the FBI, and this Commission on matters which are of vital concern to the people of this country and the world."[141] These loose and incorrect words have been seized upon by Warren Commission critics to rebut Marina's devastating testimony against Oswald. The Warren Commission staff, as indicated, consisted of very bright lawyers who graduated from the nation's finest law schools. Most of them, however, did not have trial lawyer backgrounds[*] and, hence, were unaware how extremely common it is for even truthful witnesses to give inconsistent, contradictory, and incorrect testimony. And witnesses, of course, flat-out lie all the time on the witness stand. The late Francis L. Wellman, a distinguished member of the New York Bar, once observed, "Scarcely a trial is conducted in which perjury does not appear in more or less flagrant form." In fact, perjury is so common that instead of being surprised by it, seasoned prosecutors expect it.

Redlich was a very bright and highly respected professor at New York University School of Law at the time he was appointed to the Warren Commission staff, but he had never been inside a courtroom, at least as a trial lawyer,[†] and therefore didn't have any framework of reference for the inconsistencies in some of Marina's testimony; hence, he erroneously concluded she had "repeatedly lied." Yet it should be noted that Redlich made his observation about Marina near the start of the Commission's investigation in February of 1964, and even Redlich would later conclude that "based upon everything that I knew," by "the time we were finished with our investigation, I would find her a credible witness."[142]

I am very familiar with Marina's testimony, and I can say that based on the known record, she was every bit as consistent and truthful in her testimony as ninety-eight or ninety-nine out of a hundred witnesses during a trial. In fact, in view of her circumstances, she was surprisingly consistent and truthful. Here's someone who, in 1964, testified for more than *six days* before the Warren Commission, her testimony in the Commission vol-

---

Counsel J. Lee Rankin told *Look* magazine about *Inquest*, "This book is full of distortions" (Knebel, "New Wave of Doubt," p.72).

*This is evident when in reading the testimony of Warren Commission witnesses, one becomes, in many instances, exasperated over a Commission counsel beating around the bush without ever asking the obvious question, sometimes to the point where the witness will volunteer the relevant information without the question having yet been asked. And the lack of trial experience by most of the Warren Commission members and their assistant counsels was particularly betrayed in their frequent failure, at the beginning of their examination of a witness, to get the time and place (i.e., date, time of day, and location) of the event about which the witness would be testifying (something routinely done by experienced trial lawyers), the information coming out in bits and pieces later in the examination. Assistant Counsel Arlen Specter would later speak of the "limited courtroom experience" of the Warren Commission staff as a whole (Specter with Robbins, *Passion for Truth*, p.47).

†"I had appeared in court before appellate judges, but had never tried a case or appeared in court at the trial level," Redlich said (Telephone interview of Norman Redlich by author on September 6, 2005).

umes consuming 215 pages. The pages are small print, so this translates to at least 500 pages of typical courtroom transcript. In addition, she was interviewed in depth, over and over again (an unbelievable *forty-six* times *before* her Warren Commission testimony) by the FBI and Secret Service. In 1978, she gave an additional 201 pages of testimony to the HSCA, and was interviewed in great depth by HSCA investigators. When you couple this prodigious, virtually unprecedented amount of interviews and testimony with the fact that at the time of her Warren Commission testimony she was but twenty-two years old, had a natural and instinctive desire to protect her husband as much as she reasonably could, was highly insecure living as an expatriate in a foreign country whose popular president had been murdered by her late husband,* and was operating under the substantial handicap of not speaking or understanding English and had to communicate through an interpreter (Chief Justice Warren describing her testimony as "laborious because of the interpreter"), it's absolutely remarkable she did as well as she did.[143] With typical witnesses at a trial giving just one-tenth of the vast amount of testimony Marina gave, I can guarantee you I normally would find many, many more examples of inconsistencies and discrepancies in their testimony than were present in Marina's.

When I first read Redlich's remark, I asked myself what was he referring to specifically? Such a question apparently also entered the mind of HSCA counsel Kenneth Klein, and when he asked Redlich, the latter answered, "Now, I have tried to recollect any specific matter that I may have had in my mind, and I have to say that I do not recall anything specific. It may have been, and one would have to go back into the investigatory report, it may have been that at first she may not have told the truth in connection with the attempted killing of General Walker. I am really just surmising she may have been asked if Oswald ever engaged in violence, and she may have at first said, 'No,' and then [she] brought out the fact about the General Walker shooting."[144] Although Redlich is unclear in his memory, what *is* very clear is that the first time Marina was asked, *under oath*, about the attempted murder of General Walker, she readily acknowledged her husband's attempt to kill Walker.[145]†

The following represent the type of inconsistencies in Marina Oswald's statements and testimony, as set forth by the HSCA: "Marina Oswald was subsequently questioned by the FBI about the [backyard] photos. She said they were taken at the Oswald home on Neely Street in Dallas, in the backyard. But Marina gave two different versions of when the pictures were taken. She first told the FBI it was in late February or in early March 1963 . . . Nevertheless, in an FBI interview made after her initial appearance before the

*In testimony before the HSCA, when Marina was asked about the "inconsistencies" of some of her prior statements, which were not given under oath, she said, "At the beginning, if it is possible to understand for people, I am just a human being and I did try to protect Lee . . . Some things I did not want to talk about because I tried to protect Lee. So they can hold this against me, there is nothing I can do about it. I had to protect myself too. I didn't have any home to turn back to. I was not eligible or qualified to live right here . . . But it was not because I was afraid that I might betray some secrets that [I could] be punished for . . . I swear that I never worked for any government of any country [and] I was not aware of the crime he [Oswald] was planning" (12 HSCA 433). Marina had told the Warren Commission on her first day of testimony in 1964, "You must understand this was my husband. I didn't want to say too much." Shortly thereafter, Marina's Russian interpreter, Leon I. Gopadze, volunteered to the Commission, "She says she was not sworn in before. But now inasmuch as she is sworn in, she is going to tell the truth." (1 H 14, WCT Marina N. Oswald)

†Marina explained to her biographer, Priscilla McMillan, that she didn't tell the authorities about the Walker matter because the attempt by her husband on Walker's life was unsuccessful and Walker was alive. She decided that she would be a witness against him only in a situation where she felt it really mattered. (McMillan, *Marina and Lee*, p.560; but see also 1 H 18, WCT Marina N. Oswald)

Warren Commission she said that the first time she ever saw the rifle was toward the end of March. She recalled taking the photos seven to ten days thereafter, in *late March* or early April. [Boy, that's serious stuff. But I don't remember what tie I wore yesterday, and am sometimes off by more than an entire year in trying to recollect the date of an event.] Other evidence available to the Warren Commission supported her later version." And: "Marina Oswald, in addition to giving two different versions of when the backyard pictures were taken, gave different versions of the number of pictures taken. At first she testified that she took one picture. She later testified that she took two pictures."[146] (Wow. Again, this is serious stuff.)

The late Sylvia Meagher, who usually had absolutely no trouble with the hundreds upon hundreds of deliberate, flat-out lies told by her colleagues in the conspiracy theory community in their books, had no tolerance or understanding at all for someone like Marina, who, as indicated, answered literally thousands of questions by the authorities on and off the witness stand and didn't even speak English. Meagher, nitpicking over minutia, did her best to gather up all the examples she could muster of the contradictions in Marina's testimony, but failed miserably, only citing a small handful—all, I believe, while Marina was not under oath.[147]

The very few times Marina was caught in a lie were when she understandably was trying to *protect* her husband shortly after the assassination. An example is her lie (not under oath) to the FBI, which she subsequently admitted to the Warren Commission, that she had no knowledge that Oswald had taken a trip to Mexico,[148] probably thinking this would somehow be incriminating to him in view of his having instructed her not to tell anyone.[149] (She told the Warren Commission that she did "not like [the FBI] too much. I didn't want to be too sincere with them.")[150] But when someone does the opposite and incriminates a loved one (as Marina's testimony before the Warren Commission did concerning the night before, and the morning of, the assassination), there's hardly any reason to disbelieve what that person says. In fact, it could be said that if someone's lies are almost always in favor of another individual, this only increases the former's credibility when he or she says something damaging about that person.

Rather belatedly, on February 25, 1964, the Commission, wanting to ensure the fairness of its inquiry to the alleged assassin and his family, requested Walter E. Craig, president of the American Bar Association, to participate in the hearings and investigation and advise the Commission whether the proceedings "conformed to the basic principles of American justice." In effect, he was to look after Oswald's interests and was even authorized to question witnesses if he desired. Marina Oswald agreed with the arrangement. Craig accepted the appointment but he (and two associates of his who attended the hearings whenever he was absent) was virtually a nonexistent presence at the hearings, asking very few questions (and those innocuous and non-adversarial) of very few witnesses. In no way could they be considered conventional cross-examination. He could have performed the function of a responsible devil's advocate, asking key Warren Commission witnesses questions that a competent defense attorney would have, but he failed abysmally in this effort and, through no fault of the Warren Commission, turned out to be mere window dressing for the expressed goal of helping to guarantee that a deceased accused be treated fairly and objectively.[151]

In mid-March, after Jack Ruby had been convicted of the murder of Lee Harvey

Oswald and sentenced to the electric chair, Joseph Ball and David Belin flew to Dallas to begin, as the FBI had been doing for a few months, their own "field investigation," held off until now so that Commission staffers would have sufficient time to prepare for their fieldwork and to avoid potential future charges that the Commission had interfered with Ruby's right to a fair trial.[152] They set up in the offices of U.S. Attorney Barefoot Sanders in the Dallas Post Office Building, Sanders serving as their liaison to local authorities. They interviewed police officials and witnesses about various aspects of the assassination and the two killings that followed it, and arranged for some of them to testify to the Commission in Washington the following week. On March 20, Ball and Belin staged a reconstruction of Oswald's believed movements at the time of the assassination, in which many of the eyewitnesses participated. By March 23, most of the assistant counsels were in Dallas starting their field investigations. While the staff immersed itself in the field investigation, the most important eyewitnesses to the assassination testified before the Commission in Washington during fourteen days of hearings conducted that month.[153]

Inevitable staff changes were made during the month of March, the kind any large organization goes through as schedules change. Francis W. H. Adams, the senior counsel for Area I, investigation of the actual assassination, was unable to participate very much because of unavoidable responsibilities at his prestigious law firm, so even more of the work of this crucial investigation fell on the shoulders of Arlen Specter. Belin later described Adams's noninvolvement as one of the best-kept secrets inside the Commission. "He should have been asked to resign," Belin wrote, "when it first became apparent that he was not going to undertake his responsibilities, but because of some mistaken fear that this might in some way embarrass the Commission, Mr. Adams was kept on in name only and the entire burden in Area I fell upon Arlen Specter. Fortunately for the Commission, Arlen Specter was able to carry the entire weight of Area I on his own shoulders. Nevertheless, it is indicative of the nature of investigations by governmental commissions that the need for a second lawyer in Area I was outweighed by a political decision. The ramifications of the fact that this decision was made by the Chief Justice of the United States are indeed chilling."[154]

Another senior counsel, William Coleman, was unable to devote as much time as he would have liked to the Commission, and so a young lawyer from the Justice Department, Stuart Pollak, was assigned to work with the junior counsel, David Slawson, in Area IV. With Ball and Belin otherwise occupied in Dallas, Melvin Eisenberg was given the job of examining expert witnesses (e.g., on firearms, fingerprints, etc.) at the Washington hearings. John Hart Ely, Warren's law clerk, was appointed to help Albert Jenner and Wesley Liebeler develop Oswald's history.[155]

To many of the junior counsels in the trenches, the seven commissioners often seemed out of touch with the investigation. Senior counsel Joseph Ball thought the Commission "had no idea what was happening. We did all the investigating, lined up the witnesses, solved the problems, and wrote the report." Eisenberg saw the Commission as a corporation's board of directors, with Rankin as president and the staff as its officers. Howard Willens commented that "the commissioners were not in touch with the investigation at all times." But J. Lee Rankin countered that some of the younger lawyers "simply didn't understand how a government inquiry worked" and that the collective experience and wisdom of the commissioners provided the inquiry with its direction.[156] Norman Redlich, Rankin's assistant, agreed. "I have never known a staff that thought that the group that it worked for was as well informed as the staff was, and the Warren Commission was no exception," he told the HSCA in 1978. Contrary to other staff opinions, Redlich thought that several of the commissioners were "tremendously well informed," citing in particular the chief justice, Gerald Ford, and Allen Dulles. He described the chief justice's almost daily appearances at the Commission, in particular, as "heroic."[157]

The investigation in Dallas continued into the first two weeks in April. Nearly one-half of all the depositions taken by the Commission staff were taken in Dallas during this period. Ball, with the help of Belin, Samuel Stern, Ely, and Alfred Goldberg (a member of the staff who was a U.S. Air Force historian), established Oswald's movements from the time of the assassination until his arrest; Leon Hubert and Burt Griffin investigated Oswald's death, and Liebeler and Jenner interviewed Oswald's relatives and acquaintances in the hope of shedding light on his motive.[158] Back in Washington, Redlich, Specter, Willens, Eisenberg, and others wrestled with problems emanating from the Zapruder film. Rifle tests had determined that the murder weapon could not fire two bullets in the time period that the film *seemed* to show both Kennedy and Connally being hit. The assistant counsels began to develop the hypothesis that came to be known as the "single-bullet theory," the concept that the president and the governor were hit by the same bullet.[159]

The April 30, 1964, executive session of the Warren Commission dealt with a potpourri of matters, such as additional areas of inquiry that should be explored (e.g., taking Ruby's deposition); reaching a decision that two or more Commission members should go to Dallas to examine the entire assassination scene; the problem with the Kennedy family not wanting the autopsy photos to become a part of the record because they didn't want the president "to be remembered in connection with those pictures" (the tentative position was to honor the family's request but to have at least "a doctor and some member of the Commission . . . examine them sufficiently so that they could report to the Commission," if such be the case, that there was "nothing inconsistent with the other findings in connection with the matter in those pictures"); the realization of the "very serious problem now in the record" that Governor Connally had testified earlier in the month that he was sure he wasn't struck by the same bullet that struck Kennedy; taking time, near the end of the session, to look at the front windshield of the presidential limousine, which was brought into the conference room; and even such matters as agreeing to buy and read the first ever pro-conspiracy book, *Who Killed Kennedy?*, published in London that month by an American Communist expatriate named Thomas Buchanan. (Dulles: "I think I can get it through London [by asking] my former associates [at the CIA] to arrange through the British [intelligence] services there to get us a copy of this book immediately.")[160]

At an early May staff meeting, Rankin told the attorneys to wrap up their investigations and submit their first draft chapters of the report by June 1, with June 30 set as the deadline for publication. To the hardworking staff lawyers, these dates seemed rather more exhortative than mandatory. Some teams had yet to resolve thorny problems in their areas, others had turned up new evidence requiring still further investigation. Junior counsel Arlen Specter, working virtually alone in his area, felt the time pressure as keenly as anyone, but never believed it jeopardized the integrity of the results. "No one ever said sacrifice thoroughness for speed," he told the HSCA years later.[161] Arlen Specter and Joseph Ball were the only ones who made the June 1 deadline, the others still trying to wrap up their fact-finding.[162]

The Warren Commission members met in executive session on May 19, 1964, to resolve the most politically sensitive issue they had yet to be confronted with. Several

months earlier, General Counsel Rankin had asked the FBI to conduct full field investigations on each member of the Commission staff for security clearances, since they would
be reading classified documents in their work. The FBI took much longer than Rankin
had anticipated, but all the reports were now in and there were problems with two assistant counsels. A few years earlier, Joe Ball had joined in with other members of the California Bar Association to denounce the House Un-American Activities Committee
(UAAC) for the way it conducted itself during a trip to the West Coast. The Commission members had no problem dismissing the issue with regards to Ball, all agreeing, without even a vote, that his employment should continue.

But the FBI field investigation also found that Norman Redlich had been a member
of the Emergency Civil Liberties Council, which not only was against the UAAC, as many
Americans were, but was considered to be a Communist-front organization by the UAAC
as well as the Internal Security Committee of the Senate, though it was not on the attorney general's list. The FBI check on Redlich was so thorough that it included interviews
with elevator operators at Redlich's New York City apartment building, neighbors of his
at his vacation home in Vermont, even, remarkably, with the obstetrician who had delivered him. Someone obviously had leaked the FBI report and Redlich had become subjected to attacks in the conservative media as well as from speeches on the floors of the
House and Senate, questioning his loyalty to America and whether the Commission could
possibly issue an objective report with such an important leftist staff member like
Redlich on it.

Rankin, who knew Redlich from Yale Law School and had been the one who hired him
to work on the Commission, opened the discussion by saying that Redlich was a brilliant
man who had been working "long hours, longer than anybody else," someone who was
"more familiar with our work than anyone else, and has been of great assistance to me
and other members of the staff," all of whom were "very much disturbed about the attack
on him. They have worked intimately with him and are fully satisfied of his complete loyalty." Rankin added that with a deadline for the report set for June 30, he absolutely needed
Redlich to help him, particularly since the staff was soon to be depleted by several members who had to go back to their law firms in early June, such as Eisenberg, Jenner, and
Hubert. Rankin felt there was "no question of Mr. Redlich's loyalty as an American citizen" and asked the Commission members to formally determine that he had a "right to
a security clearance." Rankin noted the irony that Redlich had already been working with
"classified materials" for months.

The Commission members then started a spirited debate on the issue, which consumed
almost fifty pages of transcript. The member who led the argument to terminate Redlich's
employment was Gerald Ford, who acknowledged that the FBI report did not contain "a
scintilla of evidence that he is a member of the Communist Party. As I read the report,
he's given in this connection a clean bill of health." And Ford didn't question Redlich's
loyalty. The problem, Ford pointed out, was that the report of the Commission "will be
a part of American history as long as the country exists. And it is vitally important, because
of the nature of the assignment, that we be as free of any criticism as possible. The image
of the Commission, in my opinion, is something that just cannot be tarnished in any way."
Ford's most telling point, which he reiterated several times, and with which all of the
members other than Warren seemed to agree, was that a person with Redlich's affiliations (he was a member of several other left-wing "cause" groups), if they had been known
at the beginning, would not have been hired. "Since I would not have approved an indi-

vidual with these affiliations then," Ford said, "I have a terrible time trying to convince myself that we ought to continue the employment" now, though Ford felt it was "very regrettable," since he liked Redlich, admired his work, had "no doubt whatsoever about his loyalty," and didn't want to "hurt him in the slightest." Boggs, Cooper, Russell, and Dulles agreed with Ford that Redlich should be let go, Dulles saying he should be terminated even though his departure would "cripple us a great deal."

Warren made it clear that in his mind, Redlich would have to be retained since the only issue was whether he was a loyal American, and since no Commission members thought he was not, there was no basis to terminate him. Warren added that if, indeed, the Commission were to decide that there was "any question of his loyalty, the least we could do" would be to give Redlich an opportunity to defend himself, saying the courts had held that in government employment, "before you discharge a man for security reasons . . . he has a right to an administrative hearing." If the other members were concerned about the "image" issue with Americans, "we would at least want to have an image of fair play . . . to those who have worked for us, and who have been loyal to us . . . if we expect people to think we have been fair to Oswald." Warren said that to fire Redlich now without cause would be "un-American," tantamount to "dropping him as a disloyal individual. And that is a hurt that can never be remedied as long as a man lives." Warren added that "there will be very little morale left in the staff of this Commission" if Redlich was let go, the staff already "deeply offended" by the assault on Redlich.

McCloy joined in strongly with Warren, noting that "if we dropped [Redlich] at this point, we would be in the middle of as great a controversy as if we did not," receiving "as much criticism" as they would "if we retain him." He also made the point that at the heart of the attacks on Redlich was that he could influence the report, which McCloy felt was ill-founded, since the Commission, not the staff, was "going to be responsible for this report." Cooper agreed that "the Commission is going to make the report," not the staff. Rankin had said that the staff, of course, would only prepare drafts for the Commission's revisions and ultimate approval.

Since no one on the Commission personally questioned Redlich's loyalty as an American, and all had a high opinion of him and his work, the Commission finally decided to issue a press release not even mentioning Redlich, simply saying that "all" Commission staff had been cleared for security purposes.[163]

Meanwhile, arrangements were made to test the single-bullet hypothesis in Dallas on May 24 with an elaborate reenactment of the assassination in Dealey Plaza. The tests confirmed the theory of Specter, Redlich, and other assistant counsels that the alignment of Kennedy's and Connally's bodies to each other in the presidential limousine was such that the bullet that struck Kennedy in his upper right back and exited his throat would have had to go on to hit Connally.[164] Two weeks later Specter, Rankin, and Warren went to Dallas. Specter's assignment was to take Warren to the sniper's nest window and explain the single-bullet theory to him. After Specter did so, Warren walked away from the window, silent, apparently absorbing and understanding the theory for the first time.[165] "It was the only time he was quiet and listened for a few minutes," Specter would later recall. "He didn't say anything, but I think I convinced him."[166]

In late May, Chief Justice Warren announced that other than the Commission's report, the supporting volumes of testimony and evidence would not be published owing to the prohibitive cost.[167] General Counsel Rankin and a number of assistant counsels felt it was virtually obligatory that these volumes be published. Rankin asked the Government Print-

ing Office for an estimated cost. The figure he received was "something around one million dollars, or thereabouts." Warren was shocked.

"My, we can't spend money like that," he told Rankin.

"Well," Rankin replied, "I think the report without it is not going to have the validity that it will have if it is supported and people can check out what we did."

Warren advised Rankin to speak to the congressional members of the Commission.
Rankin approached Senator Russell first and told him what he recommended and why.
Russell agreed immediately. "Go right ahead," he told Rankin, "don't worry about it. We
will get the money for you." Russell himself enlisted the support of the three other congressional members of the Commission—Boggs, Ford, and Cooper—and the funding
was arranged.[168] The cost of printing the report and the first fifteen hundred copies of its
twenty-six volumes eventually came to $608,000.[169]

When Redlich and Willens told Warren that the June 30 deadline could not be met,
he became so agitated and flush that Willens, for a moment, feared that Warren might
have a heart attack. Calming down, Warren said with a tone of resignation, "Well, gentlemen, we are here for the duration."[170] The deadline for the report was extended to July
15.[171] Although Rankin constantly urged his staff to keep moving, the general feeling
among them was that there was more emphasis on getting it done right rather than quickly.
Specter noted that "as we moved along . . . there were comments on attitudes that we
should be moving along, we should get the investigation concluded," but he was clear
that they "did not seek to sacrifice completeness for promptness."[172]

The Warren Commission met in executive session again on June 4, 1964, to address a
single issue, a spate of articles in major newspapers and national magazines that the Commission had already reached a decision that Oswald killed Kennedy and there was no
conspiracy—he had acted alone. There had been speculation about this before, but now
the stories were adding the imprimatur of the Commission itself by saying the source of
their story was "a Commission source" or a "source close to the Commission" or even
"a spokesman for the Commission." Warren was confident that no Commission member
was the source of this information, but he wondered who was leaking it. Without accusing anyone, he said, "Now, the staff of the Commission, individually or collectively, may
have come to certain conclusions such as this. However, the staff, individually or collectively, have no right to make such implications to the press."

There were two problems with the story. Number one, the media was essentially, as
Representative Ford said, "preempting what we may or may not say." Obviously, if the
story the media was presently peddling, and could be expected to peddle right up to the
time the Commission's report was issued, turned out to be accurate, the report would be
completely anticlimactic and bereft of all weight. The other problem was that the story
just happened to not be true. Not only hadn't the Commission made a final judgment yet
on the issue of Oswald's guilt and conspiracy, but not once in all its executive sessions
had the Commission even, Warren said, "discussed these matters as a Commission to my
knowledge. I don't like being quoted when I have not made any final judgment."

Ford: "When we see this practically every day now, and in responsible and highly
regarded newspapers, I think it has gotten to a point where something ought to be done."

McCloy agreed that something should be done and recommended that the Commission put out a statement that no final judgment had been reached on either of the two
issues. Indeed, as Warren said, the Commission was still taking testimony. The Commission agreed to issue an immediate statement to the press.

Warren: "We will see if this won't stop it. I hope so."[173]

On June 7, Warren and Congressman Ford held a special hearing for Jack Ruby in the interrogation room of the Dallas county jail. The room, overlooking Dealey Plaza, was crowded with a menagerie of attorneys and law enforcement personnel. At his trial, Ruby had wanted to testify in his own defense but had been talked out of it by his counsel, the flamboyant San Francisco attorney Melvin Belli, who had tried to convince a Texas jury that Ruby was a victim of something called psychomotor epilepsy, a novel medical theory which implied that at the very moment of the shooting, Ruby had been temporarily "insane" and was not really responsible for his actions. Now, touchingly eager to tell his story to the chief justice, Jack regaled Warren and the other Commission members with a confused, harrowing account of his agonized thoughts and actions over the weekend of the assassination. Ruby seemed unable to understand why the city he loved and for which he had committed his act of heroism had turned on him and brought him so low.[174]

The Commission announced the completion of its hearings on June 17,[175] and ten days later General Counsel Rankin told the press that the report would not be released until after the Republican National Convention, due to begin on July 13.[176] All five senior counsels—Adams, Coleman, Ball, Hubert, and Jenner—returned to their private practices, leaving only junior assistant counsels to continue working for the Commission full-time. The arduous task of writing the final report fell on the shoulders of twenty or more different staffers, including Norman Redlich and Alfred Goldberg, the Department of Defense historian. The basic approach was for the assistant counsels to submit draft chapters on the area they worked on to the Commission members for their review.[177] Howard Willens reported in 1978 that "each chapter of the Warren Commission report went through six or more substantial redrafts, with different persons assuming editorial responsibility at different times."[178] Willens would later tell the HSCA that author Edward Jay Epstein's summary of who wrote the final report was "seriously flawed and should not be relied upon," adding that "it is a matter of record that [Epstein] interviewed only a few members of the Warren Commission staff . . . Accordingly, his summary substantially overstates the contributions of some members of the staff, understates the contributions of others, and does a disservice to the twenty or more members of the staff that participated significantly in preparation of the final report."[179]

Redlich, working up to eighteen hours a day, seven days a week, thought the work "would go on forever." Goldberg finally told Warren that it was "impossible" to finish by July 15, and the deadline was extended to August 1, then August 10. Because of staff disagreement on the use of psychological terminology to describe Oswald's behavior, Rankin arranged for three psychiatrists to meet with staff and Commission members for an all-day colloquium, which ultimately concluded that there was not enough evidence for reaching any firm conclusions about Oswald's motives and psychology. When a draft chapter on the subject was submitted on July 20, Redlich and Rankin thought it too psychological and sent it back for a rewrite.[180]

The August deadline came and went as Commission staffers struggled to reach a consensus on the particular language. The deadline for the completed report was soon extended to mid-September. Meanwhile, the pressure to publish the report kept increasing. Most of the commissioners and staff wanted to publish the report as soon as possible to keep it from becoming a political issue in the fall elections. Finally, on

September 4, galley proofs of the final draft were distributed to commissioners and staff for correction.*

That very same day, however, Assistant Counsel Wesley Liebeler wrote a memorandum to General Counsel J. Lee Rankin in which he recommended that further investigation be conducted to resolve the implications in the testimony of Sylvia Odio.[181] (See discussion of the Odio matter in conspiracy section.) It elicited a response from Rankin that has become a famous part of the imperishable lore of the assassination that Warren Commission critics love to cite for the proposition that the Warren Commission was never really interested in getting to the truth. Rankin told Liebeler, "At this stage, we are supposed to be closing doors, not opening them." The conspiracy theorists,[182] up to their old tricks, never bother to tell their readers the precise context in which Rankin made this remark—the very day that the final draft of the Warren Report was being distributed to the commissioners and staff. When I spoke to Liebeler about Rankin's remark, he said that because of the circumstances, Rankin's words "were not inappropriate at the time. From the beginning we were all after the truth, and there were no limitations on that. We could do anything we wanted to do. But this was at the very end, when the report was about to go to press, so he [Rankin] said something to the effect that *at that* point we should be closing doors not opening them."[183] In other words, Rankin, it seems, was simply showing his irritability over the fact that after all this time, the Commission *should* be in a position of closing all doors. There shouldn't be any doors still to be opened.

On September 6, two days after receiving the galley proofs of the chapter on the identity of the assassin, Liebeler, the Warren Commission's in-house devil's advocate, submitted a twenty-six-page critique of the chapter, forcing publication of the report to be held up again while the chapter was revised.[184]

In later years, Arlen Specter would note, "It is hard to specify the people or Commissioners who were pushing for a prompt conclusion, but it was an unmistakable aspect of the atmosphere of the commission's work."[185] On the other hand, Specter said that in the last analysis "the Commission used ample time in finishing its investigation and coming to its conclusion. The Commission was flexible in its timetable. It started out with the thought that the investigation could be in the three-to-six-month range. When the investigation required more time, more time was taken."[186] Howard Willens thought the time to complete the report was "sufficient," although he could not deny "that the work could have gone on for another month or two or six."[187]

However anxious the country was to know what had happened and whether any conspiracy was involved, Rankin did not think there was any undue pressure. "There was no indication at any time," he told the HSCA in the late 1970s, "that we should try to get it out for any such [political] purpose and not adequately make a report or investigate whatever sources we were able to find." Commissioner John McCloy summed up the final month's work when he told HSCA investigators, "We had no rush to judgment. We came to a judgment," adding that by the time of the report, "We had already arrived at [our] conclusions."[188]

Although there is no evidence of a rush to judgment, the media at the time was full of speculation (speculation that has persisted through the years) that LBJ had exerted pres-

---

*Although Commission members had their biggest disagreement among themselves over the single-bullet theory (see Zapruder film section), the biggest dispute they had with the staff was in the area of conspiracy. Gerald Ford would recall that "the staff draft said there was no conspiracy. Categorically, saying there was no conspiracy. And the Commission—and I don't recall who raised the issue—said that goes too far. And so we inserted the language, 'The Commission found no evidence of a conspiracy' . . . And there was a unanimous vote to have that language." (Specter with Robbins, *Passion for Truth*, pp.119–120)

sure on the Warren Commission to come out with its findings before the presidential election in November of 1964. LBJ, worked up about this charge, telephoned his press secretary, George Reedy, to complain to him about Reedy's profession when it went beyond speculation into fabricated conversations. He tells Reedy what Reedy already knows, that "reliable newspapers" are "quoting me" as pushing for an early report, that these false reports were "not very complimentary to your profession . . . Allen and Scott [two reporters] say Johnson is 'strongly urging' the report of the Warren Commission be made before the Democratic [convention]." LBJ lectures Reedy, "[I] haven't seen either one of 'em. Haven't talked to any of their stringers. And [it] never entered my *mind*. And [Earl] Warren's gonna get it out whenever he *wants* to. That's *pure* makeup."[189]

The Warren Commission's final report was submitted to President Johnson on September 24, 1964, and four days later the Warren Report, as it came to be called, was presented to the press and public. After an exhaustive ten-month effort, the Commission concluded that Lee Harvey Oswald, acting alone, fired the shots that killed President Kennedy and wounded Governor Connally from the sixth-floor window of the Texas School Book Depository Building; that Oswald also killed Dallas police patrolman J. D. Tippit and attempted to shoot another Dallas police officer while resisting arrest at the Texas Theater; that Jack Ruby acted alone in killing Oswald; that Ruby and Oswald did not know each other; and that "no evidence" could be found that either Oswald or Ruby "was part of any conspiracy, domestic or foreign, to assassinate President Kennedy."[190]*

The Commission could not make any definitive determination of Oswald's motive but cited his deep-rooted resentment of all authority, his inability to enter into meaningful relationships with people, his urge to find a place in history and his despair at times over his failures, his capacity for violence as evidenced by his attempt to kill General Edwin Walker, and his avowed commitment to Marxism and Communism as factors that contributed to his character and might have influenced his decision to assassinate the president.[191]

The Warren Report was greeted by many, particularly the establishment press, with praise and a great sigh of relief. *Time* magazine said the report was "amazing in its detail" and "utterly convincing in its major conclusions."[192] The *New York Times* said it was a "comprehensive and convincing account of the circumstances of President Kennedy's assassination" and that "readers of the full report will find no basis for questioning the commission's conclusion that President Kennedy was killed by Lee Harvey Oswald, acting alone."[193] The *Times* went on to publish nearly the entire Warren Report in a forty-eight-page supplement to its September 28, 1964, edition. But the report was greeted by others with profound suspicion and hostility. The truly paranoid immediately decided that Chief Justice Earl Warren, the commissioners, and the staff had to be in on a "conspiracy" to withhold the "truth" of the assassination from the American people.

---

*In addition to the basic conclusions noted, the Commission found that except for the force required to effect his arrest, Oswald was not subjected to any physical coercion by any law enforcement officials; that he was advised of his rights; and that he was given the opportunity to obtain legal counsel and was even offered legal assistance from the Dallas Bar Association, which he rejected. The Commission also reproached the Dallas Police Department for allowing the press to have uninhibited access to the area through which Oswald had to pass, thereby subjecting Oswald to harassment and creating chaotic conditions not conducive to orderly interrogation; and for making numerous, and sometimes erroneous, statements to the press that would have presented serious obstacles to the obtaining of a fair trial for Oswald. See WR, pp.18–25, for a complete listing of the Commission's twelve conclusions.

There was hardly a junior counsel on the staff who did not harbor—and vent—his own criticisms of some of the Commission's decisions and procedures, some of them quite pungent. David Belin complained that the work of the Commission staff was hampered here and there by political considerations and errors of judgment by the commissioners, including the chief justice. He cited mistakes ranging from overzealous marking of evidence as "top secret" to the lack of direct access to parts of the record he and other assistant counsels considered vital, particularly the autopsy photographs and X-rays of President Kennedy's body. He complained of inaccurate reports from all of the investigating agencies, including the FBI, the Secret Service, and the police forces in Dallas. Belin and his fellow investigators were bedeviled by the myriad contradictions, anomalies, and false leads that peppered the record, even though, as practicing lawyers, they were all too conscious of the fact that real evidence—as opposed to a concocted case—is rarely free of contradictions, and the very depth and range of their investigation multiplied them geometrically. Nevertheless, Belin, who in the days following the assassination felt it probable that there was a conspiracy,[194] came to believe, in the course of his work, that Oswald alone killed both the president and Officer Tippit, and that there was no conspiracy.

Easily one of the very most irrational viewpoints about the Warren Commission that has ever been taken in the assassination debate—particularly inasmuch as it emanates from otherwise completely rational people who don't even necessarily buy into the conspiracy nonsense, just that the Warren Commission wasn't of a mind to even try to find out if there was a conspiracy—is exemplified in the following two observations, the essence of which I have heard from a considerable number of otherwise perfectly intelligent people through the years.

Respected author and presidential historian Michael Beschloss wrote on the thirtieth anniversary of the assassination that "U.S. leaders . . . men like Lyndon Johnson, J. Edgar Hoover, Robert Kennedy, Nicholas Katzenbach and others *feared that an unfettered investigation of the crime would lead in dangerous directions. Nervous at the prospect of pursuing the investigation wherever it led, they instead sought to ensure that the American people's suspicions were put to rest as soon as possible.* Their motives were both self-protective and honorable. Johnson, for instance, was justifiably worried that if Americans promptly learned the depth of Oswald's apparent connections to Moscow and Havana, they might demand that he retaliate with force that could lead to a third World War. The effect was to purchase short-term political calm at the price of thirty years of doubt."[195]

And equally respected author and book editor Evan Thomas wrote, "*America's leaders feared that a hysterical public would demand revenge for the death of their President.* At the very least, they worried, the small steps that Kennedy had taken toward detente would be dashed. With remarkable speed and unanimity, officials at the top levels of the U.S. government decided they must convince the country that the President's death was the work of a lone madman, not of some vast Communist plot . . . *The U.S. government did not try very hard to unearth the truth about the assassination of JFK.*"[196]*

---

*When even people of the stature of Beschloss and Thomas, and writing with the implied endorsement of an important magazine like *Newsweek*, say that the Warren Commission engaged in a cover-up, no wonder the vast majority of everyday Americans believe they haven't been told the whole truth about the assassination.

Neither Beschloss nor Thomas give any citation or source for their contention, for the simple reason that no such citation or source exists. Both Beschloss and Thomas, like so many before and after, were merely repeating what they had heard sometime, somewhere, in their past. The long-forgotten (in their minds) source? Conspiracy theorists, of course. A few examples among a great many. Author Walt Brown, in his book *Treachery in Dallas*, writes what the conspiracy community had been saying for years: "The Warren Commission, hardly eager for full disclosure based on [President] Johnson's concern that a nuclear holocaust would follow, acquiesced and enlarged on the FBI cover-up."[197] Conspiracy authors DeLloyd J. Guth and David R. Wrone write, "To allay fears and restore public confidence in law and elected officials, the executive branch [i.e., LBJ] directed that the murdered Oswald be identified as the sole killer."[198] Chief Justice Warren, per conspiracy author Carl Oglesby, was faced with a "choice between covering up a murder and sending a whole world to the brink of war." For the Warren Commission, Oglesby said, the word *conspiracy* actually meant "international Communist conspiracy (i.e., Russia), such that the alternative to the lone assassin concept was axiomatically the next thing to war."[199]

The part of Beschloss's and Thomas's statements about America's leaders fearing that if the American people believed Russia or Cuba had Kennedy killed they might demand retaliation is undoubtedly true. You don't need to cite any source for this since it's just common sense and had to have entered the minds of some, if not all, of America's leaders. As Max Frankel, reporting from the nation's capital, wrote in the *New York Times* on November 24, just two days after the assassination, "Their [America's leaders] greatest fear was that the assassination and the left-wing background of the prime suspect, Lee H. Oswald, would generate anti-Communist passions and cries for vengeance" against, obviously, the leading Communist nation in the world, Russia. But Frankel goes on to write, "No responsible official here believed that any foreign power or movement had any connection with the assassination."[200]

This, however, was not true in the *immediate* wake of the assassination, when, without time for contemplation, the possibility of a Soviet takeover instantaneously entered the minds of many in our government, including Kennedy's successor. LBJ would later say that immediately after the shooting, and before even being sworn in on Air Force One, "I was fearful that the Communists were trying to take us over . . . What raced through my mind was that if they had shot our President . . . who would they shoot next? And what was going on in Washington? And when would the missiles be coming?"[201] CIA Director Richard Helms recalled that immediately after the assassination "we all went to battle stations over the possibility that this might be a plot—and who was pulling the strings. We were very busy sending messages all over the world to pick up anything that might indicate a conspiracy had been formed to kill the President of the United States—and what was to come next." Pursuant to this, "CIA men were staggered to learn that they could not locate Nikita Khrushchev . . . Could there be a plot, perhaps by the Chinese, to murder the leaders of both superpowers? [Or] was the Soviet leader staying away from Moscow in anticipation of an American nuclear strike in revenge for a Soviet plot against the President?"[202]

Indeed, the possibility of a foreign conspiracy was such that at 2:15 p.m. (1:15 p.m. Dallas time) on the afternoon of the assassination, the Joint Chiefs of Staff declared "Defense Readiness Conditions" for all U.S. forces around the world.[203] And "the super-secret National Security Agency and allied eavesdropping agencies went into overdrive to decipher intercepted conversations, cable traffic, and radio and telephone communications at the highest levels of the Soviet and Cuban governments . . . In about forty-eight hours the intercepts showed beyond a reasonable doubt that both the Soviet and Cuban governments had been as shocked as anyone by the news from Dallas." Indeed, late Saturday, November 23, not even forty-eight hours after the shooting in Dealey Plaza, the State Department "issued a public statement declaring that there was no evidence of a conspiracy involving a foreign country."[204]

So although the fear of a Communist plot entered the minds of our nation's leaders in the immediate aftermath of the assassination, this fear was quickly dispelled.

Moreover, the suggestion by Beschloss and Thomas that U.S. leaders actually feared being forced, by this nation's citizens, into a retaliatory war with Russia seems wholly devoid of merit. As Frankel wrote, after reflection no "responsible" official believed that Russia or any other foreign power had any connection with the assassination. So irrespective of what the nation's citizens believed or came to believe, obviously under no circumstances would our leaders go to war with a nation they believed was innocent. That is a verity which cannot be seriously challenged.

Most importantly, where Beschloss and Thomas (neither of whom go on to say they believe Kennedy died as a result of a conspiracy) err is in their contention that America's leaders, fearing this demand for retaliation and possible war, decided not to vigorously pursue the truth in the assassination. I doubt that either gave too much thought to their allegation, because if they did, they would have to realize that by definition, they were accusing members of the Warren Commission and other high American public officials (whom people like Beschloss and Thomas, I would wager, respect) of being criminal accessories after the fact to murder for whatever nation they felt may have been responsible for the president's death. They were also accusing America's leaders, again by definition, of telling any adversary nation at the time or in the future, "We will not, of course, tolerate your murdering any American citizen—with one exception, the president of the United States. Because we don't want to risk war with you, the president is a freebie for you." The Warren Commission defined its role as a "fact-finding agency committed to the ascertainment of the truth."[205] But Beschloss, Thomas, and others are accusing the Warren Commission and its members of going through a ten-month charade of purporting to be interested in the truth, but really having no real interest in it, in effect engaging in a deliberate conspiracy—that all seven members of the Commission, including the chief justice of the U.S. Supreme Court, agreed to—to suppress the truth from the American people.

This is essentially the position of Edward Jay Epstein, who changes the focus away from Russia to the politics of LBJ, who formed the Commission. "I think the members of the Warren Commission were all *honest* men," Epstein generously allows. "It was their mission that was corrupt. And the mission was corrupt from the day they received it. And that was to have a report out by election time that restored stability to the country."[206] But the intelligent Mr. Epstein neglected to ask himself, why in the world would Johnson be stupid enough to appoint *honest* men to carry out his *dishonest* mission? Further, why would men who had been honest all their lives (one of whom was retired, and most in the latter part of their career) decide, at this late point in their lives, to suddenly become corrupt and carry out a corrupt mission? I wonder if Epstein (and others like him) had asked himself these two intelligent questions, how his intelligent mind would have answered them in an intelligent way.

There is an additional reason why the Beschloss-Thomas position has no merit. It would apply only, if at all, if the Warren Commission believed or suspected that Russia was behind the assassination—that is, the whole notion *necessarily presupposes Russia's guilt*, or at least a belief in it.[*] But of all the alleged conspirators behind Oswald's act, Russia was the very least suspected by the Warren Commission and all other sensible people. And this opinion of Russia not being involved was, as Max Frankel wrote, formed *almost immediately after the assassination*. So even if we assume, just for the sake of argument, that the Warren Commission, at the beginning, wanted to suppress the truth about the assassination to prevent a war with Russia (I mean, no one was pointing the finger at Sweden, Portugal, or Chile, were they?), once it became obvious *very early on* that Russia would never have committed such a reckless act as to kill our president, and there was absolutely no evidence of this, what conceivable reason would the Warren Commission have for *thereafter continuing to suppress the truth for the ten months of its existence?*—which is exactly what Beschloss, Thomas, and others are alleging. Was the Commission also trying to suppress the truth that far more suspected bogeymen like the CIA, organized crime, anti-Castro Cuban exiles, and so on, were involved? But if so, *what type of war would such suppression help prevent?* A civil war in this country? You know, half the country thinking it was okay for the CIA, for instance, to murder Kennedy, the other half opposed to it? The silliness is numbing.

Not only are the representative allegations of Beschloss and Thomas that the Warren Commission wasn't interested in investigating the possibility of conspiracy irrational on its face, but as indicated, they have absolutely no evidence to support it. The evidence supports, 100 percent, these two statements made by the Warren Commission: "The Commission has investigated each rumor and allegation linking Oswald to a conspiracy which has come to its attention, regardless of source."[207] And, "Based upon the investigation . . . the Commission concluded that there is no credible evidence that Lee Harvey Oswald was part of a conspiracy to assassinate President Kennedy. Examination of the facts of the assassination itself revealed no indication that Oswald was aided in the planning or execution of his scheme. Review of Oswald's life and activities since 1959, although productive and illuminating the character of Lee Harvey Oswald, did not produce any meaningful evidence of a conspiracy. The Commission discovered no evidence that the Soviet Union or Cuba was involved in the assassination of President Kennedy."[208]

In his sworn testimony before the HSCA on November 8, 1977, Warren Commission assistant counsel Norman Redlich was asked, "What were the real objectives of the Warren Commission?"

He responded, "Perhaps I can best answer that by repeating what [Warren Commission general counsel] Mr. [J. Lee] Rankin said when he convened the staff of the Warren Commission for the very first meeting [January 30, 1964] . . . He said, 'Gentlemen, your only client is the truth.' Those were his opening words of that talk."

Question: "Was it an objective of the Warren Commission to allay public fears?"

Redlich: "I never considered that as an objective. That was not put to me other than in the context of the fact that there were a great many doubts about what had happened, there

---

[*]Syndicated columnist Jack Anderson came up with a slight variation of this. Anderson felt that because of Johnson's suspicion that Castro was behind the assassination, "President Johnson felt, rightly or wrongly, that the American people could not be told this. They would demand retaliation against Cuba which could have . . . involved the Soviet Union . . . and meant World War III. So Johnson and his advisors felt that it was better that Americans not know the truth" (Jack Anderson, "Who Murdered JFK?" *An American Exposé/The Jack Anderson Specials,* television documentary, Saban Productions, November 1988).

was great concern about what had happened, and of course to the extent that we could find all of the truth about the assassination, we would be allaying public fears. I always felt that that was a by-product of the principal objective which was to discover all the facts."

Redlich went on to say that Chief Justice Earl Warren also spoke to the staff at this first meeting and his remarks were the same in their tenor as Rankin's, among other things telling the staff they were to "leave no stone unturned" in pursuing their investigation.[209]

It is nothing short of mind-boggling that even though the proponents of the belief that the Warren Commission wasn't interested in uncovering the truth about a foreign conspiracy in the assassination can't cite one stitch of evidence, not one statement from any member of the Commission or its staff, and surely not one fragment of common sense to support their theory, nevertheless this nonsensical notion, untethered to anything but itself, continues to exist, hearty and hale, to this very day, even among the intellectual elite. This is why, just four years ago, Warren Commission assistant counsel Burt Griffin felt constrained to say on national television, "The accusation that we had a predetermined idea to find that there was no conspiracy . . . is completely false. Let me say to you—the one thing I wanted to do *was* find a conspiracy. I was a thirty-two-year-old lawyer. I had political ambitions. If I could have found [a conspiracy and] that Oswald didn't do it, I'd have been the senator from Ohio, not John Glenn."[210] And this wasn't true only of himself, he felt. As he told the HSCA, "It was certainly the feeling that I had of all of my colleagues that we were determined, if we could . . . to find a conspiracy. I think we thought we would be national heroes . . . if we could find something that showed that there had been something sinister beyond what appeared to have [happened]."[211] Warren Commission assistant counsel David Slawson told me that he and his fellow assistant counsels were always "alert to the possibility of a conspiracy and *looked for one*, but at no time can I remember when anyone on the staff was saying they found any evidence of a conspiracy."[212]

How did all this unbelievable nonsense about the Warren Commission not wanting to investigate and uncover a conspiracy get started? From a clumsily written memorandum (referred to earlier) from Acting Attorney General Nicholas Katzenbach to President Johnson's press secretary, Bill Moyers, on November 25, 1963, just three days after the assassination, and *before* the Warren Commission was even formed. (Katzenbach remained the acting attorney general until December 4, when RFK, who had gone to Florida with his wife shortly after the assassination to mourn his brother's death, resumed his duties at the Department of Justice.) The conspiracy theorists, predictably, have cited the memorandum out of context. Let's take the original dean of distortion, conspiracy theorist Mark Lane. (See discussion of Lane later in text.) In his book *Plausible Denial*, he quotes Katzenbach saying in the memo that the "public must be satisfied that Oswald was the assassin; that he did not have confederates who are still at large"; that "speculation about Oswald's motivation" be "cut off"; and "we need something to head off speculation or congressional hearings of the wrong sort."[213] The implication is clear. Katzenbach didn't want all of the facts of the assassination to be known. They should be suppressed. But Lane, naturally, doesn't tell his readers that the very first words of Katzenbach's memorandum read, "It is important that *all of the facts* surrounding President Kennedy's assassination be made public."* Katzenbach, a World War II bomber

---

*And if Lane can mislead his readers about the Katzenbach memo, why can't another conspiracy theorist mislead his students? Michael Kurtz has taught a class on the Kennedy assassination for years at Southeastern Louisiana University. In his conspiracy book, *Crime of the Century*, he actually writes (and hence, undoubt-

pilot and Rhodes scholar, later goes on to say in the memo that "facts have been mixed with rumor and speculation. We can scarcely let the world see us totally in the image of the Dallas Police when our President is murdered. I think this objective may be satisfied by making public as soon as possible a *complete and thorough* FBI report on Oswald and the assassination." You can't suppress evidence of a conspiracy if you release "all of the facts" to the American people. It was obvious that Katzenbach believed (and he, of course, was correct) that there was no evidence at that time, nor has any surfaced since, supporting the rumor of a Communist conspiracy, and the best way to dispel that rumor with the American public was by releasing all of the true facts then known.[214]

In his testimony before the HSCA on September 21, 1978, and in an earlier deposition on August 4, 1978, Katzenbach conceded that his memo was not "artistically [i.e., artfully] phrased," going on to say to Congressman Christopher Dodd, who was questioning him, "Perhaps you have never written anything that you would like to write better afterwards, Congressman, but I have." Mr. Dodd: "You won't get me to say that." Katzenbach, in his testimony, rejected the notion that conspiracy theorists have drawn from his memo that the Warren Commission was a self-fulfilling prophesy, and he put more emphasis where he acknowledged it should have been put in the memo. He said his state of mind was that

> *if* you are going to conclude, *as the Bureau* [FBI] *was concluding*, that this was not part of a conspiracy, that there were no confederates, *then* you had to make that case, with all of the facts . . . Now, if there was a conspiracy . . . you put *those* facts out. But if you were persuaded Oswald was a lone killer, you had better put all of the facts out . . . I think my basic motivation was the amount of speculation both here and abroad as to what was going on, whether there was a conspiracy of the right or a conspiracy of the left or a lone assassin or even in its wildest stages, a conspiracy by the then vice president to achieve the presidency, the sort of thing you have speculation about in some countries abroad where that kind of condition is normal. It seemed to me that the quicker some information could be made available that went beyond what the press was able to uncover and what the press was able to speculate about was desirable in that state of affairs . . . That was the advice I was giving Moyers and . . . the president.

Katzenbach said, "I thought that everything had to be done that would give public opinion all over the world confidence that the true facts had been revealed, that everything was out on the table, whether they were difficult facts or whether they were not, that they be made public and not subject to later discovery."[215]

In a little-known internal FBI memorandum from Assistant FBI Director Alan Belmont to William Sullivan, the director of the FBI's Domestic Intelligence Division, writ-

---

edly teaches) that "the purpose of such a commission [Warren Commission] was *not to* investigate the facts of the case. Rather, 'the public must be satisfied that Oswald was the assassin.'" (Kurtz, *Crime of the Century*, p.144)

Another college professor, Gerald D. McKnight, goes further than Kurtz, telling his readers that not just Katzenbach but also Johnson and Hoover "had settled on . . . the 'facts' of Dallas that they deemed safe for the ordinary understanding of the American people." The remarkable professor, then, feels that the president of the United States, the head of the FBI, and the nation's acting attorney general all agreed, early on, to cover up the assassination. (McKnight, *Breach of Trust*, p.22) And McKnight is actually a professor emeritus of history at Hood College in Frederick, Maryland.

ten on the very same day (November 25) as the now infamous Katzenbach memo, Belmont says, "The Director [Hoover] advised that he talked to Katzenbach who had been talking to the White House relative to the report that we are to render in the Oswald case. It is Katzenbach's feeling that this report should *include everything* which may raise a question in the minds of the public or the press regarding this matter."[216] In my opinion, Katzenbach comes out as clean as a hound's tooth on this matter, and it is ironic that someone who the record shows championed the cause of complete openness in the investigation would be the one the conspiracy theorists have accused of promoting secrecy and suppression.

But even if, just for the sake of argument, the most sinister inference is drawn from Katzenbach's memo, and the conspiracy theorists are correct that he was urging a suppression of the true facts in the assassination, it is ridiculous in the extreme to presume that Katzenbach, the deputy attorney general who, as indicated, was running the attorney general's office during the period that RFK was immobilized by grief, would be in a position to actually determine and dictate the conduct of the FBI *and* the independent Warren Commission in the future. This sinister inference bears no relationship to common sense or reality.

And yet, none other than Gary Cornwell, the intelligent and savvy deputy chief counsel to the HSCA (Chief Counsel G. Robert Blakey's number-one man) wants us to believe just that. He says, "Katzenbach and those acting with him decided that it was more important to get on with the business of running the government and to quash the rumors than it was to find the truth or to tell the American public what the truth was." Cornwell goes on to say that because of this, "the tragic legacy of the Warren Commission is that we will in all probability always have to live with doubt about the questions that we want real answers to."[217]

It should be noted that since the FBI is under the jurisdiction of the attorney general's office (Department of Justice), and Katzenbach was Attorney General Robert Kennedy's chief deputy, if Katzenbach wanted the facts of the assassination to be suppressed (i.e., although he's working right under the brother of the slain president, he wants to help ensure that the president's alleged murderers are not brought to justice), wouldn't this objective of his more likely be achieved if the FBI kept jurisdiction over the assassination? Instead, it is well documented that Katzenbach, very early on, urged President Johnson to appoint an independent, blue-ribbon commission to investigate the assassination. As the HSCA said, "Officials at [the Department of] Justice, notably Deputy Attorney General Nicholas Katzenbach, were instrumental in creating the Warren Commission, in effect *transferring* the focus of the investigation from the FBI to a panel of distinguished Americans."[218]

The notion that the Warren Commission wouldn't seek the truth about the president's murder because of national security reasons is so far out that in Katzenbach's long testimony and deposition, of the hundreds of questions asked him, only one indirectly touched on this issue. When he was asked, "How big a role in the thinking of yourself and those who were making decisions at those levels of government during 1963 was the consideration that any investigation should be possibly forgone if it had the possibility of creating additional rumors?" he responded, "It never entered my mind or anybody elses that I ever talked to. This was the president of the United States who had been assassinated. Not only would the government want to know everything they could about it, but so would the public and so would the world."

Moreover, as far as the allegation that our nation's leaders decided to suppress the truth about a foreign conspiracy in the assassination, Katzenbach testified, "Everybody appeared to believe that Lee Harvey Oswald had acted alone fairly early."[219] (The facts that the murder weapon was a twelve-dollar mail-order rifle, that Oswald had to fend completely for himself in escaping from the scene of the crime, that he was a completely unstable malcontent, among many other things, pointed clearly in that direction *immediately*.) Therefore, there wouldn't have been any reason for the thought of suppressing the truth to enter the minds of our nation's "leaders," no motivation for them to contemplate such an outrageous course.

Except for the moments right after the assassination when no one knew who the killer or killers were or whether a massive domestic or international conspiracy was involved, the closest reference to national security being an issue is a February 17, 1964, memo to the file (far, far less known than the Katzenbach memo) by Warren Commission assistant counsel Melvin Eisenberg about the first meeting, on January 20, 1964, that Chief Justice Warren had with his staff. Eisenberg quotes Warren as telling his staff that when President Johnson first asked him to head up the investigation (November 29), Warren said that the president spoke "of rumors of the most exaggerated kind . . . circulating in this country and overseas. Some rumors went as far as attributing the assassination to a faction within the Government wishing to see the presidency assumed by President Johnson. Others, if not quenched, could conceivably lead the country into a war which would cost forty million lives. No one could refuse to do something which might help to prevent such a possibility." Of course, there is nothing in Warren's address to his staff about suppressing the truth to avoid a war. Indeed, as indicated earlier, Eisenberg goes on to say that Warren "emphasized that the Commission had to determine the truth, *whatever that might be*." Naturally, as with his surgery on the Katzenbach memo, Mark Lane, in *Plausible Denial*, told his readers only about the "war" part of the Eisenberg memo, deleting all reference to Warren telling his staff they had to find the truth whatever it might be.[220]

And Lane makes no reference in his book to a January 21, 1964, "Memorandum for the Record" by another Warren Commission assistant counsel, Howard Willens, about the same subject meeting Warren had with his staff, in which he writes that Warren "stated that the President had instructed him to find out the whole truth and nothing but the truth and that is what he [Warren] intended to do."* It bears repeating what Liebeler told me— that "from the beginning we were all after the truth, and there were no limitations on that. We could do whatever we wanted to do."[221]

What is elliptical in Katzenbach's and Warren's reference to "rumors" is they obviously were referring to rumors "which had no evidence to support them." The conspiracy theorists have converted Katzenbach's and Warren's desire to squelch *rumors* that had no basis in fact into Katzenbach's and Warren's desire to suppress the *facts* of the assassination. But how could Katzenbach and Warren have known way back then that they had to spell out that *only* false rumors, rumors without a stitch of evidence to support them, had to be squelched for the benefit of the American public? How could they have known back then that there would actually be people like Mark Lane who would

---

*In his testimony before the HSCA on July 28, 1978, Willens was asked, "Were you ever instructed by anyone while you served on the Warren Commission staff not to pursue any area of inquiry because the area might endanger the national security?" Answer: "No." Question: "Did anyone ever suggest to you that certain matters should not be explored for whatever reason?" Answer: "No." (11 HSCA 442)

accuse men like Warren, Congressman Gerald Ford, Senator John Cooper, and so on, men of unimpeachable stature, honor, and probity, of getting in a room and all deciding to deliberately suppress, or not even look for, evidence of a conspiracy to murder the president (thereby jeopardizing their reputation and legacy and making them criminal accessories after the fact), or that there would be intelligent, rational, and sensible people of the considerable stature of Michael Beschloss and Evan Thomas who would decide to give their good minds a rest and actually buy into this nonsense?

Another assertion that has been made over and over again by conspiracy theorists is that Jack Ruby's killing of Oswald prevented this nation from ever finding out the truth about the assassination,[*] and concomitantly, Oswald's unavailability was an inherent weakness of the Warren Commission. Indeed, even the Warren Commission has given a partial nod to this view. "After Lee Harvey Oswald was shot by Jack Ruby," the Commission wrote, "it was no longer possible to arrive at the complete story of the assassination *through normal judicial procedures* during a trial of the alleged assassin."[222]

But the assertion that Oswald's death precluded us from finding out the truth presupposes that Oswald had something to tell us other than precisely *why* he killed Kennedy. (I mean, we could scarcely have more evidence of the fact that he *did* kill Kennedy.) It also necessarily presupposes that he acted with others. If he did not—and there is no evidence that he did—then his death does not diminish at all the total relevant knowledge we already have about the assassination.

Actually, and ironically, because of the laws concerning the admissibility of evidence, chances are we learned more about the assassination *because* Oswald was killed. For instance, all trial lawyers know that just because a statement is hearsay does not, perforce, make it unreliable. Hearsay is simply any oral or written statement (or conduct, when intended as a substitute for words) made outside of court (i.e., not from the witness stand at the present proceeding) that is offered into evidence to prove not merely that the statement was made, but that it was true. Although there are twenty-two recognized exceptions to the hearsay rule, if Oswald had not been killed and had been prosecuted, a great amount of inadmissible hearsay that was published by the Warren Commission, much of it true and very relevant, would not have been received into evidence at his trial.

Also, although Marina Oswald offered a great amount of very incriminating evidence against her husband in her testimony before the Warren Commission, because of the marital privilege (which Oswald would have had a right to invoke), Marina would not have been able to testify at Oswald's trial,[†] for example, about Oswald's attempt to murder

---

[*]Nothing done by the Warren Commission has convinced Americans more of a conspiracy in the assassination than the Commission's allegedly "sealing the records" of the Commission for seventy-five years, thereby preventing Americans from learning "the real truth" about the assassination. The thinking goes that if the Warren Commission didn't have anything to hide, why seal the records? This is a major misconception of the American people, and the entire matter is discussed in depth in an endnote on the Assassination Records Review Board. To summarize, the Warren Commission expressed, in writing, its desire that the American people have access to all the records. The sealing of the records (they are no longer sealed) was the result of a National Archives regulation that had nothing to do with the Warren Commission.

[†]Under Texas law, "The husband and wife may, in all criminal actions, be witnesses for each other; but they shall in no case testify against each other except in a criminal prosecution for an offense committed by one against the other" (Vernon's Ann. C.C.P. art. 714).

General Walker, or to his use of the alias A. Hidell, or about his leaving $170 and his wedding ring behind for her on the morning of the assassination. She wouldn't have been able to identify the backyard photos or the light-gray jacket of his found in the parking lot near the Tippit murder scene, or furnish so much other testimony and evidence at his trial. And there is much other evidence that was presented to the Warren Commission and published that would not have been admissible at any trial of Oswald. As pointed out in the May 1965 *New York University Law Review*, "The Commission was not inhibited by an elaborate system of evidentiary rules, or procedural restraints, [and] its area of inquiry was not circumscribed."[223]

Show me a conspiracy theorist who doesn't believe that Jack Ruby silenced Oswald for the mob. In fact, the majority of American people believe this. Well, Ruby wasn't killed and he was brought to trial for murdering Oswald, wasn't he? Yet virtually nothing we didn't already know came out at Ruby's trial. In fact, Ruby never even testified at his trial, and Oswald, like so many other criminal defendants, may not have testified at his trial either. And let's not forget that even assuming, just for the sake of argument, there was a conspiracy, in over three years before Ruby's death, he never said a word implicating anyone else in the alleged conspiracy.[224] And Ruby was a notorious blabbermouth. Oswald always played things pretty close to the vest, and those who had personal contact with him believe that he never would have confessed. U.S. postal inspector Harry D. Holmes, who interrogated Oswald, said, "I don't think Oswald would have ever confessed. He was that adamant."[225] Dallas detective L. C. Graves, whose right arm was locked inside Oswald's left arm at the moment Ruby shot Oswald, said, "If Ruby hadn't shot Oswald, I doubt seriously if much more would have been clarified. I don't think Oswald would have ever confessed to anything.[226]

These realities throw into question the conventional belief that the murder of Oswald prevented us from finding out the whole truth about the assassination.

The Other Investigations

Succumbing to the never-ending and lurid cries of the Warren Commission critics and conspiracy theorists that there was a conspiracy and cover-up in the Kennedy case, over the years there have been three investigations on very limited areas of the assassination and one complete reinvestigation. In February 1968, a panel of four medical experts appointed by Attorney General Ramsey Clark reexamined the photographs and X-rays from the Kennedy autopsy and confirmed the Warren Commission's finding that President Kennedy was struck by two bullets, both fired from behind.[227]

In 1975, President Ford set up a commission under the leadership of Nelson Rockefeller to determine whether any domestic activities of the CIA exceeded the agency's statutory authority and to make appropriate recommendations. Although it was not specifically part of its charge, the Rockefeller Commission did look into allegations that the CIA participated in the assassination of President Kennedy, concluding, after investigating several allegations, that "there was no credible evidence of any CIA involvement." The Rockefeller Commission also reviewed the medical evidence, and again substantiated the earlier findings that President Kennedy had been struck by only two bullets, both fired from the rear.[228]

In 1976, a select committee of the Senate under the leadership of Senator Frank Church was directed to study governmental operations with respect to intelligence activities. Book V of its final report is dedicated to issues generated by the assassination and the Warren Commission's investigation. The Church Committee* was critical of the response of both the FBI and the CIA to the original investigation, concluding that "the investigation of the assassination was deficient, and that facts which might have substantially affected the course of the investigation [particularly the CIA efforts to assassinate Castro] were not provided the Warren Commission." However, the committee said it wanted to emphasize that it had "not uncovered any evidence sufficient to justify a conclusion that there was a conspiracy to assassinate President Kennedy."[229]

Finally, in late 1976, a major effort to address and resolve remaining problems in the assassination of President John F. Kennedy raised by conspiracy theorists and Warren Commission critics was mounted by the House of Representatives Select Committee on Assassinations (HSCA). (The committee also reinvestigated the murder of Reverend Martin Luther King Jr.) The scope of the select committee's investigation in 1977–1979 was essentially unlimited, except by the inevitable budgetary considerations. It was free to reinvestigate any aspect of the assassination it chose. The HSCA's major contribution was to subject the existing physical evidence to searching scientific analysis, often with techniques unavailable to the Warren Commission fifteen years earlier. All of this added many more volumes to the extensive record, filled in some of the gaps, answered many questions, and refined interpretations of the existing evidence.

The swift acquittal of Clay Shaw in New Orleans in 1969† had dealt the conspiracy movement a severe blow (see conspiracy section). How then did it happen that just eight years later Congress decided to reinvestigate the Kennedy assassination with primary emphasis on the issue of whether there was, indeed, a conspiracy? In addition to the Watergate scandal in 1972–1974, which introduced America as never before to criminal malefaction in the highest corridors of our government, there were two events, it would appear. One was the sensational revelation of the Church Committee in 1975–1976 that the CIA had actually conspired with organized crime to kill Castro. If the CIA not only plotted to murder Castro, but worse, had gotten in bed with organized crime to do so, the thinking among many was that maybe all these allegations about a conspiracy to kill Kennedy by the CIA and organized crime had some merit. But the publicity about the Church Committee findings had a short shelf life for the average American, who may have read an article or two about it in the newspaper or heard about it on the evening news. And, after all, it is quite a leap from conspiring to kill a foreign dictator to conspiring to kill

---

*The mandate of the Church Committee was very broad: to investigate all improper and unlawful activities, domestic and foreign, engaged in by the FBI and CIA as well as American military intelligence agencies. It was not contemplated, however, that it would investigate the allegation that federal intelligence agencies like the CIA and FBI were involved in the murder of President Kennedy. But when a committee member, Senator Richard Schweiker of Pennsylvania, proposed that the committee expand its mandate into an investigation of the assassination, Senator Church appointed Senator Schweiker and fellow committee member Senator Gary Hart of Colorado to be a two-member subcommittee of the Church Committee looking into the assassination. Though it was just a subcommittee of the Church Committee, many assassination researchers refer to the Church Committee as the Schweiker Committee (or Subcommittee). Since the ultimate report on the assassination came from the Church Committee, not the subcommittee, this book will only refer to the Church Committee.

†In 1969, New Orleans district attorney Jim Garrison charged Clay Shaw, a local businessman, with having conspired "with David W. Ferrie, Lee Harvey Oswald [both of whom were now deceased] and others" to murder President Kennedy. The investigation and trial of Shaw are covered in the conspiracy section of this book.

the president. If there had only been the Church Committee finding of CIA–organized crime complicity to kill Castro, and the withholding of this plot from the Warren Commission, it is not at all certain that the HSCA would have come into existence.

What almost assuredly put the reinvestigation movement over the top was the first showing of the Zapruder film (which was not authorized by *Life* magazine or the Zapruder family) to the American people on ABC on the evening of March 6, 1975.* Since the Geraldo Rivera–hosted show *Goodnight America* was on network television, a vast audience of everyday Americans saw, for the first time, the president's violent head snap to the rear, ostensibly indicating a shot from the front, not the rear where Oswald was supposed to be. As conspiracy theorist Jim DiEugenio puts it, "The effect of this public showing of the Zapruder film was, in a word, electrifying. The day after, the Kennedy assassination was topic number one in bars and barber shops across America. The case was back on the front burner,"[230] the *New York Times* noting the "widespread response" the show had "generated."[231]

It was conspiracy theorist Robert Groden's pirated copy of the Zapruder film that had been shown on the ABC network, and Groden around that time was showing the film on a lecture tour with comedian Dick Gregory on college campuses, the most familiar cradle for dissent in contemporary America. He hit pay dirt at the University of Virginia. Andy Purdy, who would go on to become an assistant counsel for the HSCA, was a senior law student at the university who co-chaired the committee that invited Groden to speak at the Charlottesville campus. Purdy said that the large student audience (including himself) was captivated and swayed by Groden's presentation. In the audience that night was the son of Congressman Thomas Downing (D-Va.). Purdy, Downing's son (Dickerson), and a few other law students arranged for Groden to show the congressman the Zapruder film at his office in Washington, D.C., on April 15, 1975. Purdy said Downing, who had never seen the film before, was deeply troubled by it ("The Zapruder film really shook me," Downing would later recall) and arranged for Groden to show the film to over fifty of his congressional colleagues, most of whom, per Purdy, were equally troubled.[232] Downing decided to lead the charge in the House of Representatives (eventually joining forces with Congressman Henry Gonzalez [D-Texas], who already had a bill, which was foundering and going nowhere) to reinvestigate all three assassinations in the 1960s, those of JFK, RFK, and Martin Luther King Jr.

With the climate of the times already heated by the CIA–organized crime–Castro revelations and particularly the showing of the Zapruder film on network television, the Downing-Gonzalez bill (House Resolution 1540) creating the HSCA passed in the House by a vote of 280 to 65 on September 17, 1976. Downing became the chairman of the HSCA, with Gonzalez heading up the subcommittee on the assassination of Kennedy. (There was a separate subcommittee on Martin Luther King's assassination. No reinvestigation of RFK's assassination was authorized.)

In early October 1976, Downing appointed Richard A. Sprague as chief counsel to the HSCA (the person literally in charge of the investigation). Although Sprague was origi-

---

*The first time the Zapruder film was ever shown to everyday Americans, albeit a very small number, was when Jim Garrison subpoenaed the film from *Life* magazine on February 13, 1969, and showed a multigenerational copy of it to the jury and a packed courtroom of spectators in the trial of Clay Shaw. And starting with its November 29, 1963, issue, *Life* magazine showed selected frames of the Zapruder film to its millions of readers at various times, such as in its undated memorial edition in December 1963 and its October 2, 1964, cover story on the Warren Commission's findings.

nally recommended to the HSCA by, of all people, Mark Lane, Downing selected him from a list of six candidates. Sprague was a very prominent and well-respected former prosecutor from Philadelphia who had worked there as the first assistant district attorney under former Warren Commission assistant counsel Arlen Specter when Specter became district attorney of Philadelphia. Sprague had no preconceived biases about the assassination and appointed, as his chief deputy (on the JFK side of the HSCA), Robert Tanenbaum, the leading prosecutor for the Manhattan district attorney's office at the time. Together, Sprague and Tanenbaum were prepared to launch a no-holds-barred, in-depth criminal investigation of the assassination, for which their backgrounds made them both eminently qualified.

But things started to unravel when Downing retired from the House a few months later (January 1977) and was replaced by Gonzalez as chairman of the HSCA on February 2. No one seems to know for sure why Gonzalez and Sprague didn't get along, but their relationship quickly degenerated into ad hominem attacks, almost all of them by Gonzalez, who apparently resented the fact that although he was chairman, the other eleven members of the House select committee listened to and respected Sprague more on matters of HSCA policy, resulting in a charge by Gonzalez that Sprague was deliberately usurping his, Gonzalez's, authority. Indeed, when Gonzalez fired Sprague on February 10, the other eleven committee members defied Gonzalez and signed a letter directing Sprague to disregard Gonzalez's order and remain in his post, which he did. The letter said that Gonzalez "did not have the power unilaterally to discharge Mr. Sprague. It is only the committee which has this power." And the committee wanted Sprague to stay.[233]

Gonzalez and Sprague also locked horns over Sprague's proposed $6.5 million funding request, which Gonzalez felt was bloated, and was determined to trim substantially. The feuding became so bitter that Gonzalez eventually resigned his chairmanship on March 2, 1977, calling Sprague "an unconscionable scoundrel who was insubordinate and insulting, not to mention disloyal." Gonzalez had his supporters, such as Representative Thomas O'Neill Jr., the Speaker of the House, and Representative Jim Wright of Texas, the latter saying that "unless Henry can be prevailed upon to continue as chairman, the House probably will not vote to continue the investigation."[234] But a new chairman, Louis Stokes (D-Ohio), was named to take Gonzalez's place on March 9.[235]

There were other problems. One was that while all this was going on, since the HSCA had, like all congressional committees, officially expired with the end of the congressional term in which it was created (in this case, just over two months later on January 3, 1977, when the 94th Congress ended), a new resolution had to be passed to reconstitute the committee. In view of the fact that the predecessor resolution (HR 1540) had passed rather easily, the new resolution on January 4 should have likewise passed easily, but this time there seemed to be more resistance from Congress. Many in Congress, in addition to Gonzalez, had already been upset with Sprague's proposed December 9, 1976, $6.5 million budget* (for the way Congress spends more money on far less serious matters, seem-

---

*Sprague said the budget for the second year would be for the same amount—a total of $13 million, more than the $10 million the Warren Commission spent. However, he pointed out that in addition to the HSCA also investigating the assassination of Martin Luther King, the HSCA would be employing and paying for its own investigators, whereas the Warren Commission's eighty-three-member staff was supplemented by 222 investigators borrowed from the FBI, CIA, and Secret Service, whose services the Warren Commission never had to pay for. (*New York Times*, December 10, 1976, p.19)

ingly, a reasonable request), believing it was excessive. Also, the internal warfare that they had witnessed had soured some.

And finally, Sprague himself unwittingly contributed partially to his ultimate departure. His budget included funding for polygraphs (a very valuable investigative tool used by virtually every major law enforcement agency in the country), voice stress evaluators (an investigative tool almost universally rejected by U.S. law enforcement as a worthless gimmick), and, what most frightened several members of Congress, miniature phone recording devices. Sprague wanted to secretly wire HSCA investigators with these mini-recorders while interviewing witnesses and then subject their responses to the psychological stress evaluator. Representative Don Edwards (D-Calif.), the chairman of the House Judiciary Subcommittee on Civil and Constitutional Rights, said that this "would constitute intentional invasions of the most fundamental rights of Americans. I believe the use of these techniques by a committee of Congress to be wrong, immoral, and very likely illegal."[236] Congressman Frank Thompson (R-N.J.), the chairman of the House Administrative Committee, said that Sprague had "run amok."[237]

Sprague's state of mind was that *if* there had been a conspiracy to murder the president, there was no need to treat the alleged perpetrators gently. But the sense in Congress among civil libertarians was that while they wanted to get to the bottom of the assassination, they didn't want to do so by a bare-knuckle fight, and in the face of criticism, Sprague announced that his committee would not use the mini-recorders or stress evaluators. But the assault on Sprague continued when the media started resurrecting controversies surrounding Mr. Sprague's handling of a few cases during his many first-rate years with the Philadelphia district attorney's office, which he characterized as a campaign "to smear" him without foundation.[238]

In a four-hour meeting on the evening of March 29, 1977, the day before Congress was scheduled to vote on whether the HSCA should be reconstituted,[*] Sprague and Tanenbaum met with Stokes and Congressmen Richardson Preyer, Walter E. Fauntroy, and Christopher Dodd, all members of the JFK subcommittee, in Stokes's office. Tanenbaum recalls that the congressmen specifically asked Sprague not to resign, to stay on. "These were good people," Tanenbaum says, "and they were willing to fight for Sprague," but it was equally obvious to everyone in the room, Tanenbaum added, that they felt the resolution the next day might not pass if Sprague stayed.[†] "Dick [Sprague] took the high road and resigned," Tanenbaum says, and it was clear the congressmen felt "unburdened."[239][‡]

The *New York Times* quoted another (unnamed) participant at the meeting in Stokes's office as saying the group had concluded that with Sprague remaining as chief counsel,

---

[*]On February 2, by a vote of 237 to 164, the House of Representatives (House Resolution 222) had given the HSCA the authority to continue temporarily.

[†]The lobbying of congressional members to get the HSCA reconstituted, mostly delegated by Sprague to Tanenbaum and his staff, was heavy, time-consuming, and not always pleasant. At a dinner meeting with several congressmen at a restaurant called the Chicken Place in Maryland, after Tanenbaum made his pitch, John Ashbrook, a conservative Republican from Ohio, said, "Well, we really don't mind funding the Kennedy assassination, although I didn't think much of the man, but we'll be damned if we're going to fund that nigger King's." (Telephone interview of Robert Tanenbaum by author on March 10, 2004. See also Fonzi, *Last Investigation*, pp.204–205. Gaeton Fonzi says Ashbrook called Tanenbaum aside to tell him this, but Tanenbaum told me it was right at the dinner table in front of everyone.)

[‡]At an April 11, 1977, press conference after he left the HSCA, Sprague described Gonzalez's conduct as "McCarthyism," but added that he had also begun to have friction with Gonzalez's successor, Stokes, before he left, though he did not elaborate (*New York Times*, April 12, 1977, p.18).

they were about twenty-five votes short of the majority needed to reconstitute the committee and prevent it from going out of business the next day. Speaker of the House Thomas P. O'Neill Jr., who was not present, said that "with Sprague resigning, they [the committee] claim it means 40 more votes." Walter E. Fauntroy (D-D.C.) said that the allegations that had weakened Mr. Sprague had "absolutely no basis in fact" and added that Sprague's resignation to allow the investigation to continue "in my judgment merits the Congressional Medal of Honor."[240]

The next day, March 30, 1977, House Resolution 433 passed after a sharp debate on a vote of 230 to 181, officially reconstituting the HSCA for a term to expire on January 3, 1979. Among other things, opponents of the close-to-two-year extension claimed the committee had come up thus far with nothing but hearsay. Supporters argued that terminating the committee at this point would convince the American public that a cover-up was going on.[241] When Stokes asked Tanenbaum to become the new chief counsel, Tanenbaum, if possible, took an even higher road than Sprague by declining this prestigious position out of loyalty to Sprague, who had brought him aboard and who had even urged him to accept. Further, with Tanenbaum's background and investigative style being almost a carbon copy of Sprague's, he anticipated having the same problems Sprague had with Congress. But he agreed to stay on until a new chief counsel was named.[242] A week and a half later, on April 10, Stokes appointed Alvin B. Hayes, a lawyer on the sixty-four-member staff of the HSCA, to serve as interim chief counsel while the committee sought a permanent replacement for Sprague.[243]*

The committee's real work did not get underway until June 20, 1977, when G. Robert Blakey, a forty-one-year-old Cornell law professor who was a former prosecutor from 1960 to 1964 in the Organized Crime and Racketeering Section of the Department of Justice under Robert Kennedy, was appointed chief counsel and staff director.[244] Blakey was well known in federal law enforcement circles for being the chief author, in 1970, of the Racketeer Influenced and Corrupt Organization Act (widely referred to as RICO), which gave the FBI and Department of Justice new tools to effectively combat organized crime.[245] (Blakey was later described by William G. Hundley, chief of the Organized Crime and Racketeering Section, as having "perhaps the finest analytical mind of the some sixty competent lawyers" in his section.)[246] The committee accompanied its appointment of Blakey by placing a gag order on its investigation. Blakey, quoting the words of Thomas Dewey when he was appointed as a special prosecutor to investigate organized crime in New York City, told the media at a news conference that "in general, it is my belief that a talking prosecutor is not a working prosecutor." The *Washington Post* reported that former Watergate special prosecutor Archibald Cox and former Supreme Court justice Arthur Goldberg "had turned down earlier overtures" to become chief counsel, although Representative Christopher Dodd (D-Conn.) said that "Blakey was our principal choice."[247]

---

*The mandate of the final HSCA had been set forth in the earlier, September 1976 House resolution, as well as House Resolution 222 on February 2, 1977, which authorized the HSCA to "conduct a full and complete investigation" of the assassination of President John F. Kennedy and Martin Luther King, each crime the province of a separate subcommittee. The eventual, permanent Kennedy subcommittee was chaired by Representative Richardson Preyer of North Carolina, the King subcommittee by Walter Fauntroy. Each subcommittee had its own task force, each headed by a deputy chief counsel: Gary T. Cornwell for the Kennedy investigation, Gene R. Johnson for the King investigation. Each task force comprised a dozen or so senior and junior staff counsels, investigators, researchers, and administrative personnel. (HSCA Report, pp.9–10, 514) On April 28, the funding of the committee for 1977 was cut drastically to $2.5 million (Blakey and Billings, *Plot to Kill the President*, p.67).

Thirteen candidates for the position were interviewed and HSCA chairman Louis Stokes said that he picked Blakey.[248]

The committee recognized from the outset that it had to operate under finite constraints of time and resources. The Warren Commission, as indicated, spent over $10 million in its ten-month existence. The HSCA, by contrast, spent about $5.8 million, although it operated, at varying levels of intensity, for about thirty months, from mid-September 1976 to the end of March 1979, the last seven months of which were mostly used "to write the final report, edit the drafts, check the galleys, print up the hearings, clear everything through agencies, and get [all the volumes] printed."[249] The Warren Commission employed some four hundred people; the select committee about two hundred and fifty,[250] and that was for an investigation of two assassinations separated by five years, with no common links.

In order to fulfill its mandate, the committee identified four main issues to be addressed with respect to the Kennedy assassination. First, who was or were the assassins? Second, did they have any aid or assistance either before or after the assassinations? Third, did the agencies and departments of the U.S. government adequately perform their duties and functions in collecting and sharing information before the assassination and in investigating the president's murder? Fourth, and finally, given the evidence the committee uncovered, was the amendment of existing legislation or the enactment of new legislation appropriate?[251]* Of paramount concern was the prevailing view of the public. The select committee knew from a Gallup Poll that 80 percent of the American people believed that Lee Harvey Oswald had not acted alone. Since it was clear that many Americans believed that agencies of the federal government itself were implicated in the assassination, the committee felt a keen responsibility to determine the facts and present detailed evidence on that score. Committee members knew that the credibility of the American government was at stake.[252]

Although their objectives were the same, the select committee's work was substantially different from that of the Warren Commission. For the most part it had to deal with evidence that was already fifteen years old. (Despite the already vast and steadily growing literature on the assassination, very little new evidence had turned up since the first investigation in 1963 and 1964.) That evidence fell naturally into three categories: forensic evidence still amenable to scientific investigation, the recollections of the events by witnesses who were still alive and available in 1978–1979, and documentation in the files of governmental agencies. In the committee's judgment, the most reliable of these was the forensic evidence—autopsy, firearm and ballistic, handwriting, fingerprint, photographic, acoustical, and so on. The HSCA proceeded to hire highly credentialed national experts in each of the subject forensic fields, who subjected all of the scientific evidence[253] to a thorough review and testing that often produced fresh insights and interpretations. "A major focus of our investigation was science," Blakey would later recall. "We figured that the witnesses were now only repeating stories . . . While witness testimony was in stone, we figured the science had progressed in the years since the Warren Commission. We hoped to take advantage of that progress. That is where we put our main emphasis. It paid off."[254]

---

*Although Blakey and his staff brought in many highly qualified experts in various fields to answer these questions (which applied equally to the King assassination), no one on the HSCA legal staff could compare with Sprague and Tanenbaum in the area of experience in handling major criminal murder investigations and prosecutions.

Blakey knew, of course, that his committee was not set up to bring the murderers of Kennedy and King to trial and convict them; that was not the function of a congressional committee. He also realized that the trail was not just cold now. "It had been trampled into a state of confusion by amateur sleuths," he wrote later, "witnesses had died, and the memories of those who were still around had been altered by secondhand perceptions (witnesses, too, read the conspiracy books) and dimmed by the passage of time; and evidence had been misplaced or destroyed." He decided, given his limited resources, to concentrate "primarily on the hard data of science and technology."[255]

In March 1978 the committee was refunded for the year. Blakey had asked for $3 million and was again accorded only $2.5 million, facing him with "unattractive alternatives." The money was enough to keep the full staff on through December but only if travel were disallowed. To keep both staff and travel through December, the staff would have to be halved, which, he felt, "would effectively shut down both the Kennedy and the King investigations." Blakey, with his Washington insider's feel for the art of the possible, realized that if they got a break in either case before July, they could get more funding. If they didn't, no one would care whether they shut down or not. He decided to risk it, cutting only thirty members of the staff and keeping both investigations going with those who were left.

By July 1978 the HSCA was running low on money. On July 13 Blakey met with the committee to review the funding needs. Blakey informed the committee that they had a break on the King case—they had developed evidence of a conspiracy. Spurred by the news, the committee agreed to seek a supplemental appropriation of $790,000.

Later that afternoon, Dr. James Barger, chief scientist at the acoustical firm of Bolt, Beranek and Newman Inc. (BBN) of Cambridge, Massachusetts, called with electrifying news. Barger had been looking at the graphs made from a recording of the Dallas police radio transmissions of November 22, 1963, and, although the sound patterns he saw would have to be verified by comparison gunshots recorded in Dealey Plaza, there appeared to be more than three gunshots, possibly as many as five, which virtually assured a second shooter and, therefore, a conspiracy. The effect on the committee and its staff was galvanic. Barger came to Washington to brief the HSCA with a graph twenty-three feet long. Until now the staff's painstaking reexamination of the assassination had only confirmed the conclusions of the Warren Commission. Even in those areas where the committee felt the Commission's investigation had been careless, inept, or scant, the HSCA's more detailed and scientific examination of the evidence had only strengthened the Commission's conclusions. Now, a twenty-three-foot graph was about to turn the HSCA's investigation on its head. "We were pulling on a thread from an intricate tapestry that was the Kennedy assassination, as it had been understood since 1964," Blakey wrote. "If we pulled hard enough, it might all unravel."[256] They did pull hard enough and it did unravel but not in the sense Blakey meant and not before the HSCA seriously injured its own credibility.

Following an acoustical reconstruction in Dallas, a revised analysis of the Dallas police radio recordings, and seventeen days of carefully orchestrated and televised public hearings, the HSCA closed shop in January of 1979 and began the task of writing a final report.

On March 29, 1979, a substantially divided HSCA, with three out of the twelve members filing written dissents (later followed by a fourth member's dissent)* released its final report concluding, with nearly a total reliance on the acoustical evidence, that President

---

*Compare that to the report of the Warren Commission, which was unanimously agreed upon by all seven members.

Kennedy was "probably assassinated as a result of a conspiracy." (The HSCA's acoustical evidence has been totally discredited. See later text.) Although the committee confirmed that Lee Harvey Oswald fired three shots from the Book Depository, striking Kennedy twice and Governor Connally once, it also claimed to have "established a high probability" that a second gunman fired from the infamous grassy knoll, but that this second shooter apparently missed the limousine and its occupants. The report added, "The committee was unable to identify the other gunman or the extent of the conspiracy."[257] Indeed, the HSCA expressly exonerated every group (organized crime, CIA, FBI, KGB, anti-Castro Cuban exile groups, etc.) suspected by conspiracy theorists throughout the years of complicity in the assassination.

Although the final report concluded that it was unable to identify the "extent of the conspiracy" it had found, or name the alleged second gunman, it did hint at two possibilities. The committee carefully pointed out that "as groups," neither anti-Castro Cuban exiles nor organized crime were involved, but added that "the available evidence *does not preclude* the possibility [how could it?] that individual members [of these two groups] may have been involved."[258]*

At a press conference, Blakey took things a step further than the committee report stated or even implied. "I am now firmly of the opinion that the Mob did it," he told reporters. "It is a historical truth." Then, he quickly added, "This Committee report does not say the Mob did it. *I* said it. I think the Mob did it."[259]† But Blakey's assertion, and the committee's allegation, that there was a conspiracy behind the president's murder, like most of the myths surrounding the assassination, will unravel before you on the pages of the conspiracy section of this book.

HSCA staff investigator Gaeton Fonzi, a well-known antagonist of Blakey, charged in his book on the HSCA's investigation that Blakey not only was predisposed to the mob theory from the beginning, but pushed it on his staff throughout the investigation. He quotes Jim McDonald, an attorney in charge of the Organized Crime Unit on Blakey's staff, as telling him that most of the members of the organized-crime team never bought Blakey's mob theory, which he said Blakey had formulated many months before the HSCA issued its final report. "The team never made the link. But at our meetings it was obvious that Blakey wanted that. He wanted to make the link more than anything else."[260]

---

*Although Blakey, as chief counsel for the HSCA, had much influence on the direction of the investigation toward organized crime more than any other alleged conspiratorial group, he turned out to have little, if any, influence on the committee's ultimate conclusion. The HSCA said the same thing about individual members of anti-Castro Cuban groups as it did about organized crime, and no one was pushing the HSCA toward its conclusion about the anti-Castro Cubans.

†Blakey's conclusion of the mob being behind the assassination is quite surprising given his background, inasmuch as the murder of Kennedy bore none of the indications of a mob hit. And with the mob's history of never going after public figures, starting out with the most powerful man on earth is more than improbable. It's completely far-fetched. (See organized-crime section for full discussion of issue.) And here we had Blakey—who had worked in the organized-crime section of the Justice Department under RFK, was considered one of the country's top experts in the field of organized crime, and was a fixture at organized-crime seminars, having personal contacts with detectives in the organized-crime section of every major police department in the country—reaching that precise conclusion.

It must be noted that other than the acoustical fourth-shot conclusion of the HSCA, which, as indicated, has been completely discredited, the HSCA in large part did an excellent job of reinvestigating the assassination of President Kennedy, and much of the credit for this has to go to Blakey, who shepherded the investigation. This is why it is further surprising to me that someone of Blakey's stature could say "the mob did it," and then proceed to write a book (Blakey and Billings, *Plot to Kill the President*) that doesn't offer one piece of credible evidence to support his conclusion.

Some pieces of circumstantial evidence support Fonzi's and McDonald's position. Blakey chose as his number-one assistant (deputy chief counsel) an organized crime–fighting colleague of his, Gary Cornwell, who as a Justice Department prosecutor had served as the chief of the Organized Crime Strike Force in Kansas City, and for his editorial director a former editor at *Life* magazine who had written a series of articles for *Life* on organized crime, Richard Billings. Indeed, although the HSCA thoroughly investigated nearly every major alleged conspiratorial group, among the twelve volumes published by the HSCA, their 1,160-page volume on organized crime[261] dwarfs all others.

But Andy Purdy, the University of Virginia law student who was on the ground floor of the HSCA's existence, and served as a deputy counsel throughout, does not agree with the charges by Fonzi or with the inference drawn from the size of the massive HSCA Report on organized crime. "Blakey did not push organized crime on the staff. Yes, much more was written on organized crime, but not necessarily more of an investigation was conducted. Pre-acoustics, the investigative effort into each alleged conspiratorial group was proportionate to the complexity and promising nature of the issue presented, with no discernible tilt towards organized crime. Post-acoustics, yes, there was an increased emphasis on organized crime by Blakey to come up with evidence supportive of the acoustics finding of a fourth bullet and therefore a conspiracy. But the main reason for this emphasis was that the work on the other groups had already been completed whereas the work on organized crime had not."[262]

Blakey himself says that Fonzi's charges are "unequivocally not true. In fact, when I first started out as chief counsel, I believed that organized crime was not involved. That the mob just didn't kill public figures. But as the evidence started to develop, I came to the conclusion that Carlos Marcello and Santo Trafficante were behind the assassination. But I at no time pushed my staff in that direction." When I told Blakey I *still* did not believe the mob went after public figures and asked him what caused him to change his position and conclude the mob decided to break with its long-standing tradition and kill a public official, "the biggest one of all," his only answer was that "the evidence" had convinced him the mob killed Kennedy. Among that evidence, he would later write me, was "Jack Ruby's organized crime–related background in Chicago and Dallas" (discussed in depth in the conspiracy section of this book), his belief that Ruby had "stalked Oswald" following the assassination, and FBI surveillance tapes showing the mob's hatred for the president and his brother, including the desire of some individual members of the mob to kill Kennedy.[263]

Because of the disparity between the HSCA conclusion on organized crime and that of Blakey, which he later repeated in his book, I asked Blakey who, specifically, wrote the HSCA Report.

"I wrote the report with the help of Dick Billings, who was with us almost from the beginning. Billings not only had a background as a reporter for *Life* magazine on true-crime stories and organized crime, but he was a professional writer. A lawyer's prose [referring to himself] leaves something to be desired with its legalese, and Billings made my writing, and the report, readable."

"Did the HSCA have to approve of everything you wrote?"

"Yes, the committee [HSCA] had to approve every word in the report. And the report was written by Billings and me with full knowledge of who was on the committee and what their conclusions were. The report was written to express, in our words, *their* conclusions. So the *real* author of the report was the committee."[264]

There was actually one further reinvestigation of the assassination, one that received virtually no attention in the media since it was conducted, without fanfare, behind the scenes. When the HSCA submitted its final report to the clerk of the House of Representatives on March 29, 1979, it made several recommendations, one of which was that the Department of Justice "review the committee's findings" on the assassination of President Kennedy and "report its analysis to the Judiciary Committee."[265] By the end of 1983, the department said it had completed "virtually all" of its investigation, but did not issue its formal report at the time because it wanted to review "all public comment responsive" to the National Academy of Science's review of the acoustical evidence. On March 28, 1988, the Justice Department submitted its formal report to Senator Peter W. Rodino Jr., chairman of the Committee on the Judiciary. The department's report was a rebuke to the HSCA's conclusion of conspiracy. The department said that its "attorney and investigative personnel reviewed the entire Select Committee report as well as all relevant Federal Bureau of Investigation reports." Before it reached its conclusion, the department said it had also asked the FBI "to further investigate any aspect of the assassination which Departmental attorneys felt had even an arguable potential of leading to additional productive information." The Justice Department concluded that "no persuasive evidence can be identified to support the theory of a conspiracy" in the Kennedy assassination, and that "no further investigation appears to be warranted . . . unless new information which is sufficient to support additional investigation activity becomes available."[266]*

The Warren Commission, coming first, couldn't comment on the HSCA, but the HSCA had good words to say about its predecessor. Although faulting the Warren Commission for failing "to investigate adequately the possibility of a conspiracy to assassinate the President," the HSCA said the Commission "conducted a thorough and professional investigation into the responsibility of Lee Harvey Oswald for the assassination." It went on to take note "of the high level of professionalism, dedication, and integrity it found to have characterized the members and staff of the Commission. The committee noted that criticisms leveled at the Commission had often been biased, unfair, and inaccurate. Indeed, the committee believed that the prevailing opinion of the Commission's performance was undeserved. The competence of the Commission was all the more impressive, in the opinion of the committee, in view of the substantial pressure to elicit findings in only nine months."[267]

---

*There was one other "investigation" of the assassination. Though under the auspices of the federal government, it was an unauthorized one. On October 26, 1992, Congress enacted "The President John F. Kennedy Assassination Records Collection Act of 1992," popularly referred to as the "JFK Act," to release to the American public all previously classified documents relating to the assassination. Pursuant to the JFK Act, the Assassination Records Review Board (ARRB) was created to implement the objective of the act, and the board was in operation from October 1, 1994, to September 30, 1998, a period of exactly four years. Among the documents released, not one remotely resembling a smoking gun was found that would call into question the findings and conclusion of the Warren Commission. As the reader will see, particularly in the section on the president's autopsy, certain overzealous members of the ARRB staff took it upon themselves to go beyond the ARRB's limited mandate to release assassination-related documents, and decided to investigate what they perceived to be certain acts of conspiracy in the assassination. For those readers who want to know all about the ARRB and what it achieved, see endnote to this section.

In general, the official investigations of the assassination of the president were well done. No investigation is ever perfect and it is rare for any major and complex case to come to trial without some problems—discrepancies, slipups, unanswered questions, incompetence, evidence that has been lost, leads not properly followed up, breaks in the chain of custody of evidence, flawed interrogations, and so on. A thousand things can go wrong, and at least some of them inevitably do.

The Dallas police certainly made their mistakes, including their critical lapse of failing to adequately protect Oswald from any possible assassin, resulting in his death. Still, by and large, Dallas homicide captain J. Will Fritz, in his dogged, taciturn way, had, within two days of the assassination, managed to build a very powerful case against Lee Harvey Oswald, a case that has stood the test of time. The principal investigation of the assassination, by the Warren Commission, is, of course, unparalleled in history, not just in the sheer, staggering volume of information collected by the FBI and other federal agencies, but in its monumental thoroughness and attention to detail. Likewise, the House Select Committee's modern scientific analysis of the hard, physical evidence in the case produced a corroborative foundation of fact that previous investigations couldn't have hoped to obtain, and thereby contributed appreciably to our knowledge of the case. When taken as a whole, as you'll soon see, the body of evidence collected by these official investigations leaves *absolutely no doubt* that Lee Harvey Oswald murdered the president, and *no reasonable doubt* that he acted alone.

The only doubt that was raised by any of the investigations that Oswald acted alone was the aforementioned bizarre conclusion of the HSCA that Kennedy was "probably assassinated as a result of a conspiracy."[268] I say *bizarre* not because of the conclusion of conspiracy but because of what the conclusion was based on. The committee proceeded through almost all of its inquiry with the conviction that Oswald had acted alone, and in December 13, 1978 (near the very end of its investigation), even wrote a draft of its final report concluding that there was no conspiracy in the assassination.[269] But although Dr. Barger had ultimately been unpersuasive, at the eleventh hour two acoustics experts from Queens College in New York, Mark Weiss and Ernest Aschkenasy, sold the majority of the committee an incredible bill of goods based on their mathematical computations and a static-filled Dallas police Dictabelt recording (from an open microphone on a police motorcycle presumed to be in Dealey Plaza) on which no one could hear the actual sound of gunshots. They claimed they were able to discern, from "impulse sounds" and "echo pattern predictions," that there was a "95 percent or better" probability that a fourth shot was fired from the grassy knoll, and hence, a conspiracy.[270] It *had* to be an incorrect conclusion since all the physical evidence showed that all shots were fired from the sniper's nest on the sixth floor of the Book Depository Building, and there was no credible evidence of any gunman firing from the grassy knoll. (See grassy knoll section of book.) But the Warren Commission's critics and conspiracy theorists were so excited about the HSCA's conclusion that they were practically levitating.

What brought them crashing down to earth was when the smoke-and-mirrors conclusion of the HSCA was exposed as such in 1982 by a panel of twelve physicists and scientists under the aegis of the National Research Council. Hailing from places like MIT, the Lawrence Berkeley Laboratory at the University of California, and the Bell Telephone Laboratory in New Jersey, and headed by Harvard professor Norman Ramsey, the panel of experts analyzed the subject Dictabelt and heard the same impulse sounds that the two Queens professors did. The only problem was that the "sounds" the Queens professors heard occurred "one minute after the assassination," when the presidential limousine was long gone down the Stemmons Freeway on its way to Parkland Hospital.[271] The HSCA conclusion was blatantly incorrect and unprofessional, an unfortunate, serious blemish on its otherwise excellent effort. (For those who want to read more about this entire acoustics issue, see the very long endnote to this section.)

As with all criminal homicides, the first area of inquiry is the autopsy of the victim, the coroner usually being one of the first witnesses the prosecutor calls to the stand in a criminal trial.

President Kennedy's Autopsy
and the Gunshot Wounds to Kennedy
and Governor Connally

In nearly every criminal investigation, something goes wrong—sometimes *terribly* wrong. The one phase of the Kennedy investigation that most experts agree was decidedly botched was the autopsy, a conclusion I do not completely agree with, particularly in view of the circumstances surrounding the autopsy. In any event, the main conclusion of the autopsy—that two shots hit the president from the rear—remains unassailable to this day. It is here that our exploration of the physical evidence in the murder of President Kennedy begins.

The forensic pathology panel of the HSCA (one of several panels of the HSCA that reinvestigated the assassination) noted that John F. Kennedy was the fourth American president to be assassinated. In each of the four cases, pathologists performed an autopsy to determine the cause of death and the nature of the injuries. "It is quite remarkable," the panel reported in classic understatement, "that despite major advances in medical technology, the autopsy of President Kennedy created more controversy than that of any of the others."[1] Dr. Michael Baden, chairman of the panel, put it more bluntly in his 1989 book, *Unnatural Death: Confessions of a Medical Examiner*: "Where bungled autopsies are concerned," he wrote, "President Kennedy's is the exemplar."[2]

In its 1978 critique of the president's autopsy, the forensic pathology panel (often referred to as the medical panel) concluded that the three pathologists who performed the postmortem examination committed a number of procedural errors resulting in an incomplete autopsy. The failings, it said, were extensive. In a considerably overstated indictment, the panel stated that the autopsy pathologists didn't confer with the Parkland Hospital doctors prior to their examination of the president's body; failed to examine the president's clothing, which could have provided clues about the direction of the shots (the autopsy surgeons *did* attempt to examine the clothing, but the clothing was not available [see later text]); failed to determine the precise exit point of the bullet causing the head wound (something the HSCA itself, after the benefit of hundreds of hours of study, was unable to do with 100 percent certainty); didn't dissect the back and neck, and didn't determine the angles of the bullet tracks through the body relative to the body axis, which would have aided in determining the source of the gunfire (there was pressure from the president's family to keep dissection and hence mutilation of the president's body to a minimum, but the surgeons did determine that both bullets were fired on a downward angle); didn't have proper photographs taken (this is a gross exaggeration and probably untrue); and failed to properly examine and section the brain, which would have irrefutably established the path of the bullet (this was not done out of deference to the president's family, which wanted to bury the brain with the body; however, some very limited sectioning was done).

The HSCA panel further said that the autopsy report itself (known technically as the autopsy protocol) was equally incomplete and inaccurate in a number of areas: The location of the entrance wound to the head was incorrectly described; the location of the entrance wound in the upper back and exit wound in the throat were not referenced to fixed body landmarks to permit a precise trajectory reconstruction;[*] the neck areas, which were not dissected, were not described; the report didn't mention that the pathologists, during the autopsy itself, failed to detect the presence of an exit wound in the throat (a strange objection in that the main failure was to detect the exit wound—perfectly understandable because it was obstructed by the tracheotomy—not the failure to mention in their report that they didn't discern this until after the autopsy); and there wasn't any description of the adrenal glands or other organs (hardly critical, and the abdominal organs *were* described).[3]

The question that presents itself is how this critique of the autopsy, which misled its readers into believing that the autopsy was conducted by rank amateurs, made it through all the HSCA's pathologists and lawyers who worked on or looked at it and was permitted to see the light of day.

Few, if any, of these procedures neglected by the autopsy surgeons would have been overlooked in a standard medicolegal autopsy,[†] but as we've seen, the circumstances surrounding *this* autopsy were anything but typical.

The admittedly less-than-perfect autopsy performed at Bethesda that night, which Warren Commission critic Harold Weisberg cried was "unworthy of a Bowery bum,"[4]

---

[*]Though the autopsy surgeons should have used the more conventional technique of setting forth distances from the top of the head (or soles of the feet for lower wounds) and the midline of the body, the HSCA's language here is loose and very misleading. The autopsy report did say that the entrance wound in the back was "situated on the upper right posterior thorax just above the upper border of the scapula . . . This wound is measured to be 14 cm. from the tip of the right acromium process and 14 cm. below the tip of the right mastoid process." The autopsy report said that the exit wound in the throat was "situated in the low anterior neck at approximately the level of the third and fourth tracheal rings." And with respect to the head wound, the autopsy report said it was "situated in the posterior scalp approximately 2.5 cm. laterally to the right and slightly above the external occipital protuberance." (CE 387, 16 H 980–981) What person reading the HSCA's harsh criticism would imagine that the above words appeared in the autopsy report?

[†]Normally, a medicolegal autopsy is part of a criminal investigation by a *forensic* pathologist—a pathologist who has a thorough understanding of death by so-called unnatural causes (homicide, suicide, and accidents)—who evaluates the circumstances of the death, including anticipating and answering questions that might arise later in legal proceedings. Forensic pathology, per Dr. Baden, is an "untaught speciality, a stepchild of the medical profession." The only way to learn the specialization is to serve, after graduation from medical school, in a medical examiner's office. (Baden with Hennessee, *Unnatural Death*, pp.ix–x) The medicolegal autopsy is often a multidisciplinary effort that requires the cooperation of and continuing communication with other scientific disciplines like toxicology, anthropology, and odontology. And in a criminal case, the pathologist works closely with the prosecutor and chief detective on the case as well as representatives from the crime laboratory of the law enforcement agency having jurisdiction.

has fueled skepticism about the president's death for over four decades. The 1978 HSCA forensic panel fixed most of the blame on the three pathologists who, in its view, weren't qualified to perform a forensic autopsy.

Dr. James J. Humes, the senior pathologist and director of laboratories at the Naval Medical School at Bethesda, was the chief autopsy surgeon. Although Humes was board–certified in clinical and anatomic pathology, the panel noted that his training in forensic pathology was limited to a course "at the Armed Forces Institute of Pathology," and although Humes had conducted upward of a thousand autopsies, they overwhelmingly involved deaths from natural causes, not deaths from violence, accidents, or suicides.[5] Dr. Milton Helpern, one of New York City's leading forensic pathologists, though having a point to make, made himself look far sillier than Humes looked incompetent by saying that selecting Humes (who, as we've already seen, was board-certified in anatomic pathology and was the senior pathologist at Bethesda) to perform a medicolegal autopsy was "like sending a seven-year-old boy who has taken three lessons on the violin over to the New York Philharmonic and expecting him to perform a Tchaikovsky symphony. He knows how to hold the violin and bow, but he has a long way to go before he can make music."[6]

Actually, neither the HSCA forensic panel nor Dr. Helpern were being completely accurate regarding Dr. Humes's experience with gunshot wounds. A 1992 article in the *Journal of the American Medical Association (JAMA)*, based on an interview with Dr. Humes, mentions that by 1963 he "had performed several autopsies on military personnel killed by gunshot wounds."[7] Asked about the article during his February 13, 1996, deposition before the Assassination Records Review Board (hereinafter "ARRB") and whether the statement was true, Humes testified, "Yes."

Question: "When did you conduct the autopsies for gunshot wounds?"

Humes: "Well, ones that stand out in my mind, two were in Tripler Army Hospital in Hawaii. The truth of it, I can't recall . . . where else. In San Diego, we did 800 autopsies a year. It's really kind of hard for me to specifically recall the details of many of those. I never held myself forth as an expert in gunshot wounds. That's why I called Pierre Finck, who *was* an expert."

Question: "Had you had experience with gunshot wounds prior to 1963?"
Humes: "Yes."
Question: "And those were, as best you recall now, at Tripler Hospital in Hawaii?"
Humes: "Yes."
Question: "And in San Diego?"
Humes: "Possibly San Diego."[8]

J. Thornton Boswell, the chief of pathology at the Naval Medical School who assisted Humes, was board-certified in clinical and pathological anatomy but was not trained in forensic pathology either.[9] The autopsy team fortunately included Dr. Pierre A. Finck, who *had* been a board-certified forensic pathologist since 1961, although the HSCA panel concluded that Humes would have been better served by a forensic pathologist who was "engaged in the full-time practice of forensic pathology, not merely in a consulting or review capacity," which was the current situation with Dr. Finck.[10] At the time of the autopsy, Finck was chief of the Wound Ballistics Pathology Branch of the Armed Forces Institute of Pathology, where he had been since he received his board certification as a forensic pathologist in 1961. During that time he had reviewed over four hundred armed forces and civilian autopsy cases, many of them involving bullet wounds. Between 1955 and 1958, several years before the president's autopsy, Finck had personally performed approximately two hundred autopsies, many of them pertaining to trauma, including bullet wounds, as pathologist at the U.S. Army Hospital in Frankfort, Germany.[11]

While conspiracy theorists roundly agree with Dr. Helpern and the HSCA's assessment of the autopsy pathologists' relative inadequacies to conduct a forensic examination, the critics most hotly contended argument is that the autopsy was incomplete, largely owing to orders from the military, the Kennedy family, or both. The allegation that the military controlled the autopsy stems from a comment made by Dr. Finck during cross-examination at the 1969 trial in New Orleans of businessman Clay Shaw for Kennedy's murder. When asked if Humes was "running the show," Finck replied, "Well, I heard Dr. Humes stating that—he said, 'Who is in charge here?' and I heard an army general, I don't remember his name, stating, 'I am.'"[12] Oliver Stone's largely fictional (see conspiracy section) film *JFK*, which alleged that the military-industrial complex was behind Kennedy's murder, included this scene in the movie, and conspiracy theorists have taken this to mean, and have reported in countless books and articles, that an unidentified army general was directing the autopsy. However (and naturally, the conspiracy theorists don't put this in their books), when Finck was asked to give "the name of the general that was in charge of the autopsy," he quickly responded, "*There was no general in charge of the autopsy.*" Finck went on to say that the general's statement "may have been pertaining to operations other than the autopsy. It does *not* mean the army general was in charge of the autopsy . . . And by 'operations,' I mean the over-all supervision." That Finck (and unquestionably the general who made the remark) was making this distinction was corroborated by the fact that elsewhere in his testimony Finck said, "*There were several people in charge. There were several admirals, and, as I recall, the adjutant general of the navy.*"[13]

Consistent with the practice of conspiracy theorists knowingly omitting and citing material out of context, the conspiracy authors of the book *Trauma Room One* do not tell their readers about Finck's clarifying the implications of the remark made by an army general, instead referring to "Finck's astounding claim that a non-physician was calling the shots" at the autopsy, thereby totally misleading their readers on this point. Likewise, the authors quote Finck as testifying at the Shaw trial, "There were admirals, and when you are a lieutenant colonel in the Army [referring to himself] you just follow orders," to further support their thesis that the military was in charge of the autopsy, and Finck "was out of his league and out of his element."[14] But they don't tell their readers that *immediately* after the words "you just follow orders," Finck said, "And at the end of the autopsy we were specifically told . . . by Admiral Kenney, the Surgeon General of the Navy, . . . not to discuss the case," a reference that had nothing to do with the conduct of the autopsy.[15]

Just who were the generals and admirals at the autopsy? According to conspiracists, there were a considerable number, many of whom were unknown, and among whom were members of the conspiracy to murder Kennedy who were now attending the autopsy to begin the cover-up. But let's look at them, since we know exactly who they are. During the autopsy, FBI special agents Francis X. O'Neill Jr. and James W. Sibert recorded the names of all those present, including the admirals and generals, of whom there were only four. In addition to their report, which identifies them,[16] listen to what O'Neill said in an October 12, 2001 interview: "There was the commanding officer of the hospital [Admiral Calvin B. Galloway]. There was a rear admiral [Admiral George C. Burkley, the president's personal physician]. There was a General Godfrey McHugh, who was on the airplane with Kennedy and was his military attaché; he was a one-star general. And there was a Major General Philip Wehle [commanding officer of the U.S. Military District, Washington, D.C.] who tried to enter and I kicked him out and he came back and told me he was there to get another casket because the other one was broken. There was no one else."[17] If someone can find a likely conspirator in this group who was covering up the assassination, please let me know.

Bethesda medical corpsman Paul Kelley O'Connor told an interviewer that he remembers the "I am" coming "from the area of Admiral Burkley."

Question: "So you think Admiral Burkley is the one who said, 'I'm in charge'?" "Yes."[18]

Dr. Humes told *JAMA* in 1992, "I was in charge from start to finish and there was no [military] interference—zero . . . Nobody made any decision in the morgue except me. Nobody . . . influenced me in any way, shape, or form."[19] Dr. Finck agreed. "I will repeat this. There was no military interference with the autopsy. There were many people in the morgue—all very upset—and this made it difficult for us. But there was no military interference."[20]*

Although the military did not interfere with the autopsy, it is clear that the Kennedy family did. FBI agent Francis O'Neill wrote that as he understood it, "Mrs. Jackie Kennedy gave permission for a partial autopsy and Dr. George Burkley, the president's personal physician, reiterated her remarks," and that "there was no question that Burkley was conveying the wishes of the Kennedy family."[21] The family's request for a "partial autopsy" was not, however, an attempt to circumvent the investigation, as some have claimed. Dr. Humes explained to the HSCA that "initially, Admiral Burkley said that they had caught Oswald and that they needed the bullet to complete the case, and we were told initially that's what we should do, . . . find the bullet."[22] Dr. Boswell reported much the same thing, that Dr. Burkley said the police had "captured the guy who did this, all we need is the bullet." Boswell added that they argued with Burkley, saying the autopsy must be "complete and thorough."[23] Autopsy photographer John T. Stringer Jr. reported that Dr. Burkley urged that they "shouldn't do a complete one if [they] didn't have to."[24] The issue was expediency, not the suppression of facts. This is underscored by the testimony of Dr. Humes, who said in 1996 that Burkley's "main concern was let's get this over with as fast as we could . . . [But] we had big problems, and we couldn't get it over with as fast as he would have liked it to have been completed."[25]

The deadlock over whether there would be a complete or a partial autopsy was broken by the commander of the National Naval Medical Center, Rear Admiral C. B. Galloway, who ordered a "*complete autopsy*" after checking with the FBI and Secret Service agents in attendance.[26] No doubt, the FBI and Secret Service were, at that point, more interested in the criminal aspects of the case than the feelings of the Kennedy family. So ironically, rather than the military suppressing and controlling the autopsy, as conspiracy theorists have claimed and filmmaker Oliver Stone's movie *JFK* shows, *it was the military who was responsible for ordering a complete autopsy* against the personal wishes of the Kennedy family, who had hoped to expedite the process.

---

*When Dr. Michael Baden of the HSCA's forensic panel asked Dr. John Ebersole, the assistant chief of radiology at Bethesda who was present at the autopsy, if he had any impression "that somebody in the room was in any way giving orders" to Humes "as to how the autopsy should be done," Ebersole responded, "Absolutely not" (Transcript of hearings before HSCA medical panel, March 11, 1978, p.15).

Although Admiral Galloway had ordered a complete autopsy, U.S. Air Force Brigadier General Godfrey T. McHugh, an aide to President Kennedy who was present throughout the autopsy and embalming procedure, told the HSCA that Attorney General Robert Kennedy and presidential friend and aide Kenny O'Donnell frequently telephoned him from the seventeenth floor of the naval hospital, where Jackie and other members of the Kennedy family were waiting, asking about the autopsy results and why it was taking so long. They also kept emphasizing the need for "speed and efficiency." McHugh said that he related this information to the pathologists, never implying that they should limit the autopsy.[27] Autopsy photographer John Stringer confirmed that while McHugh was emotional, he did not issue any orders.[28] While he may not have meant to, McHugh's remarks certainly caused undo anxiety for the pathologists. Humes told the HSCA, "There was no question but we were being urged to expedite this examination as quickly as possible, that members of the president's family were in the building, that they had refused to leave the premises until the president's body was ready to be moved, and similar remarks of that vein, which we made every effort to put aside [so we could] approach this investigation in as scientific a manner as we could. But did it harass us and cause difficulty. Of course it did, how could it not?"

Boswell added, however, "I don't think it interfered with the manner in which we did the autopsy."

Humes: "I don't either."[29]

The proof that the autopsy was not conducted quickly and therefore superficially is that it lasted at least three hours. I say "at least" because although Dr. Humes testified it started at 8:00 p.m. and ended at 11:00 p.m., later in his testimony he said that three pieces of bone were brought to the autopsy room by the FBI "later on that evening or very early the next morning while we were all still engaged" in conducting the autopsy.[30] So the autopsy could have lasted over four hours. Dr. Michael Baden told me that a typical forensic autopsy, in which the clothing would also be examined (here, as indicated, it was not available for examination), and involving two gunshot wounds "would take four to five hours." But Baden hastened to add that an autopsy of the president "could be expected to take all day, eight hours."[31]

One of the problems slowing up the autopsy was gaining access to the president's adrenal glands, which could not be reached through an opening in the chest cavity, necessitating going in through the abdomen. The president's adrenal glands have long been a focal point of the conspiracy theorists' interest. One of the well-kept secrets about President Kennedy's medical history during his lifetime was that he was being treated for Addison's disease, an insufficiency of hormonal secretions by the adrenal glands, which, if left untreated, can be fatal. The treatment in the early 1960s was to supplement the lack of adrenal secretions with the drug cortisone, which allowed many of those afflicted to lead relatively normal lives.[32] Although word of the president's condition had circulated during the 1960 presidential campaign (the charge was that having Addison's disease made him physically unfit for the presidency), it was never publicly confirmed or documented until 1967, when Dr. John Nichols of Kansas deduced circumstantially that case number 3, referred to in a 1955 *American Medical Association Archives of Surgery* article involving a thirty-seven-year-old man with a seven-year history of well-documented and therapeutically controlled Addison's disease who had undergone major back surgery on October 21, 1954, at the Hospital for Special Surgery in New York, was in fact John F. Kennedy. Dr. Nichols offered as evidence reports in the *New York Times* of October 11 and 21, 1954, and February 26, 1955, but he stopped short of claiming confirmation, calling his deduction "strongly presumed."[33]

In a 1965 memorandum to Brigadier General J. M. Blumberg, Dr. Finck wrote that Kennedy "suffered from adrenal insufficiency," though this apparent confirmation was not a public record.[34] In August 1992, *JAMA* confirmed with hospital officials that Dr. Nichols's earlier deduction was correct, the patient was Kennedy.[35] But at the time of the assassination, these facts were not known to the public.

It seems clear that the Kennedy family didn't want the president's adrenal condition publicly known. Dr. Boswell told the HSCA in 1977 that Dr. Burkley told Dr. Humes that he didn't want a report on the adrenal glands, preferring instead for the information to be reported to him informally (i.e., orally).[36] Dr. Robert F. Karnei Jr., a twenty-nine-year-old, second-year resident who was "on duty" on the evening of the assassination, which meant that any autopsy that had to conducted after hours would normally have been his to perform, was merely assigned to "miscellaneous duties," such as obtaining food for the military security guards and FBI and Secret Service agents and, most importantly, trying to control who was and who was not admitted into the morgue during the autopsy. Although Karnei even left the morgue occasionally to perform other duties, he nonetheless did observe, firsthand, several aspects of the autopsy. He told *JAMA* in 1992 that "no adrenal tissue could be found grossly on routine dissection," a fact confirmed by Dr. Boswell, who said that "serial sections of the perirenal fat pads demonstrated no gross evidence of adrenal cortex or medulla." Dr. Boswell's findings are confirmation that the president did, indeed, suffer from severe Addison's disease.[37]

As indicated, according to the HSCA forensic panel, the Kennedy autopsy pathologists failed miserably.[38] However, despite these deficiencies, and the claims by conspiracy theorists that the autopsy pathologists were in essence amateurs, the HSCA forensic panel proceeded on the very next page to contradict itself to the extent of saying that the autopsy report did contain "sufficient documentation" for the panel to arrive at "correct and valid conclusions" regarding the precise nature of the wounds that caused the president's death.[39]

Much more importantly, the HSCA's forensic pathology panel came to the same, identical conclusion that the autopsy surgeons came to: that "President Kennedy was struck by two, and only two, bullets, each of which entered from the rear."[40]

One important footnote, I believe, to the above discussion: If one were to set forth the top-five allegations of the Warren Commission critics and conspiracy theorists in the Kennedy assassination, one of the five would most likely be that Kennedy's body was unlawfully spirited away from the Dallas authorities at Parkland Hospital (mainly, from Dr. Earl Rose, the Dallas medical examiner who physically resisted the appropriation of Kennedy's body by the Secret Service) to be taken to Bethesda for the autopsy. And if the autopsy *had* been conducted in Dallas, no cover-up would have taken place by the incompetent and/or complicit (in the conspiracy to cover up) autopsy surgeons, and therefore the autopsy findings would have been different.

The only serious problem with this is that ironically, and very unfortunately for the conspiracy theorists, they don't even have support for their argument from the very person whom they wanted to conduct the autopsy—Dr. Earl Rose. In 1968, Rose left his job as Dallas medical examiner to become a professor of pathology at the University of Iowa in Iowa City. And in 1978, he was appointed by the HSCA to be one of the nine forensic pathologists to review the autopsy findings. Now retired in Iowa City, Dr. Rose told me no one ever calls him regarding his one year on the HSCA forensic panel and he was "enjoying" his "anonymity." My key question to Dr. Rose was this: "Were you satisfied from your review of the autopsy photos and X-rays that the autopsy surgeons reached the same conclusion you would have reached if you had conducted the autopsy back in 1963 in Dallas?"

Rose immediately and unequivocally answered, "Yes, there's no question their conclusions were correct. Two shots entered the president from behind, the entrance wound to the back exiting in the throat at the site of the tracheotomy and the entrance wound to the back of the head exiting in the right frontal temporal area." The only place he said he disagreed with the autopsy surgeons is that they reported the entrance wound to the back of the head "too low. It was in the cowlick area."

Rose said that although "more experienced" forensic pathologists should have been chosen to conduct the autopsy, the three autopsy surgeons were not, as so often said, inept and did a "competent job considering they were operating under the most trying, tremendously difficult circumstances," with the Kennedy family "limiting" the extent of the autopsy. He said, "You can't blame the autopsy surgeons for the fact that the autopsy should have been more complete."[41] And Rose is not the only member of the HSCA's forensic pathology panel who feels this way. Dr. Charles Petty, the chief medical examiner for Dallas County, and my medical expert at the London trial, told me in preparation for the trial that he felt the autopsy surgeons had done "an adequate job." In 2003, he said the autopsy, overall and considering all the circumstances, was "well done and well reported."[42]

With respect to the autopsy surgeons' lack of experience (with the exception of Finck) in conducting gunshot wound autopsies, Rose said that "Humes was an extremely competent pathologist. Here's someone who became president of the American Society of Clinical Pathologists."[*] With respect to the issue of whether the autopsy surgeons took enough time to conduct the autopsy, when I asked Dr. Rose how long a typical autopsy would take, where, like the president, there were two bullet wounds and the decedent's clothing was not examined, Rose, who at the time of his service on the HSCA panel had conducted around four thousand autopsies, said, "Oh, I think you should be able to do a very competent autopsy in around two hours," which by all accounts is *less* time than the autopsy surgeons in the Kennedy case took.

Concerning his confrontation with the Secret Service at Parkland, although he said he was in the right, "I think they were doing what they thought was right under the circumstances and I believe that their motivations were completely aboveboard."[43]

For over forty years, conspiracy theorists have claimed that the autopsy findings offer clear evidence of a conspiracy. But where? In the following pages we'll take a detailed look at the facts and allegations surrounding the bullet wounds of both President Kennedy

---

[*]Perhaps one of the best indicators that Humes was not out of his depth during the autopsy is a reading of his testimony before the Warren Commission in 1964, or better yet, before the HSCA forensic pathology panel on September 16, 1977, when he was, in effect, grilled by some of the top medical examiners in the land (e.g., Drs. Baden, Petty, John Coe, Joseph Davis, etc.) not only on the president's autopsy but also on the extremely complex interpretation of the autopsy photos and X-rays taken under Humes's direction at the time of the autopsy (2 H 347–376, WCT Dr. James J. Humes; 7 HSCA 243–265, Transcript of Dr. Humes's testimony before the HSCA). I didn't get the slightest impression from the give-and-take that major leaguers (the forensic panel) were talking to a minor leaguer, or, if we're to believe Dr. Helpern, a sandlotter. It couldn't be more obvious that Humes spoke knowledgeably and confidently about all aspects of the autopsy.

and Governor Connally and reveal how conspiracy theorists have bamboozled the general public into believing that even if a shot or two was fired from the sniper's nest to the president's right rear, where Oswald was believed to be, the fatal bullet to the president's head was fired from the grassy knoll to the president's right front. Also, the wound to the front of the president's throat was an entrance, not an exit wound, and it too was fired from the grassy knoll to the president's front.

Early in its investigation, the HSCA realized the importance of establishing the authenticity of the autopsy photographs and X-rays housed at the National Archives—that is, to determine whether they were taken of President Kennedy at the time of his autopsy and whether anyone had altered them, both of which questions have been raised by the conspiracy community. (The 1964 Warren Commission never had to deal with this issue because the autopsy photographs and X-rays were never part of its published record.) This important step of the committee's investigation was essential since the conclusions of its forensic medical panel of experts would rely chiefly on this photographic and radiological (X-ray) record.[44]

To facilitate the scientific analysis of the photographs and X-rays, the HSCA brought in experts in anthropology, forensic dentistry, photographic interpretation, forensic pathology, and radiology. Anthropologists studied the autopsy photographs to verify that they all depicted one individual, John F. Kennedy, and in particular that the photographs of the rear of the head were consistent with other views in which President Kennedy's facial features are recognizable. They also did a comparison study of the autopsy X-rays and premortem (i.e., prior to death) X-rays known to have been taken of President Kennedy over several years. The anthropologists focused on a number of anatomic characteristics (including cranial sutures, vascular grooves, and air cells of the mastoid bone) that would enable them to tell if the premortem and autopsy X-rays depicted one or two separate individuals. They concluded that there could be no reasonable doubt that the person depicted in both the autopsy photographs and X-rays was in fact John F. Kennedy and no other person.[45] In addition, the committee's forensic odontologist, Dr. Lowell J. Levine, who was experienced in identifying the victims of unnatural death through dental records, examined premortem X-rays of President Kennedy's teeth and compared them with those visible in the autopsy X-rays. Dr. Levine concluded, based on the unique positions of the teeth (relative to each other), the shapes and sizes of fillings of the teeth, and a myriad of other anatomic characteristics, that the three autopsy skull X-rays were "unquestionably of the skull of President John F. Kennedy."[46] Dr. Levine's final report also concluded that the "unique and individual dental and hard tissue characteristics which may be interpreted from [the skull X-rays] could not be simulated [i.e., faked]."[47]

In addition to the above-mentioned experts, the HSCA turned to members of its own photographic panel to determine if any of the photographs or X-rays had been altered, and concluded there was no evidence of tampering.[48]

One comment before we continue our examination. As with the HSCA, the actual photographs of the president's wounds are not being published as a part of this book, not just because their release was never authorized (only bootlegged copies have since become available and have appeared in various publications), but also because the exit wound to the president's head is almost indescribably gruesome. I am, however, including a number of sketches produced for the HSCA by Ida Dox, a professional medical illustrator who was recommended to the HSCA by the Georgetown University School of Medicine. It was her task to illustrate the dimensions and location of the two entrance and two exit wounds in the president. She testified that she went to the National Archives and selected *original* autopsy photographs "that best showed the injuries." Four photographs were used, per Dox. One, she said, showed "the back of the [president's] head, another one . . . the upper back, then the side of the head and the front of the neck." She said the subject photographs were copied by her "by placing a piece of tracing paper directly on the photograph, then all the details were carefully traced. Later on, while working on the final drawing, I had to have a photograph in front of me at all times. In this way I could be constantly comparing and looking back and forth at the drawing and the photograph so that no detail could be overlooked or omitted or altered in any way." She said she had access to the original autopsy photographs "a great number of times" and also reviewed the autopsy X-rays.[49]

President Kennedy's Wounds

Early in the autopsy, the three pathologists—Humes, Boswell, and Finck—turned their attention to the most obvious cause of death, the hole in the upper right back of the president's head (which exited, they found, in the right frontal portion of his skull [see later discussion]). It was located, they wrote in their autopsy report, "approximately 2.5 cm. [approximately 1 inch] laterally to the right and slightly above the external occipital protuberance," and the bullet causing the hole was fired, they concluded, "from a point *behind* and somewhat *above* the level of the [president]."[50] This is entirely consistent, of course, with the known location of Oswald on the sixth floor of the Book Depository Building, to the president's right rear.

The wound to the head bore all the characteristics of an entrance wound. For one, it was small, being 6 × 15 millimeters (approximately ¼ × ⅗ inch), slightly less, on the smaller dimension, than the diameter of the bullet, which was 6.5 millimeters. This is so, Humes testified before the Warren Commission, because of the "elastic recoil of the tissues of the skin. It is not infrequent . . . that the measured wound is slightly smaller than the caliber of the bullet that traversed it."[51] The HSCA estimated that the bullet was descending "at an angle of 16 degrees below horizontal as it approached" the president and "from a point 29 degrees to the right of true north from the president," which, of course, would be consistent with its having been fired from the vicinity of the southeasternmost window on the sixth floor of the Depository Building where Oswald was.[52]

As to the long length of the wound, the bullet "struck at a tangent or an angle causing a fifteen-millimeter cut. The cut reflected a larger dimension of entry than the bullet's diameter of 6.5 millimeters (about a quarter of an inch), since the missile, in effect, sliced along the skull for a fractional distance until it entered."[53] This is also consistent with the location of Oswald not being directly behind the president, but to his *right* rear. Humes testified that when he "reflected the scalp [i.e., peeled the scalp skin away to see the skull bone beneath], there was a through and through defect [in the skull] corresponding with the wound in the scalp."[54]

Additional evidence that it was an entrance wound was the "beveling of the margins of the bone when viewed from the inner aspect of the skull."[55] This is the "inward beveling" that one always finds in an entrance wound. When a bullet passes through a skull bone, it creates a beveling (or, as it is sometimes called, a coning or cratering) on the side of the skull opposite the side which was struck first by the bullet—in the same way a BB shot creates a crater on the opposite side when striking a plate of glass. In other words, in an entrance wound, the diameter of the wound is larger on the inside of the skull than on the outside where the bullet first hits. This physical reality has been known for centuries and has been the main basis for determining whether a wound is an entrance or exit wound. For instance, Assistant U.S. Surgeon General Dr. J. J. Woodward, who conducted the autopsy on President Lincoln on April 15, 1865, wrote in his autopsy report that "the ball [bullet] *entered* through the occipital bone about one inch to the left of the median line and just above the left lateral sinus . . . The wound in the occipital bone was . . . circular in shape, with beveled edges, the opening through the internal table being larger than that through the external table."[56] A bevel, then, on the inner surface of the skull is character- istic of an entrance wound, while a bevel on the outer surface of the skull indicates an exit wound. Dr. Finck, one of the autopsy surgeons, told the HSCA that "the hole in the skull in the back of the head showed no crater when examined from the outside of the skull, but when I examined the inside of the skull at the level of that hole in the bone I saw a crater, and to me that was a positive, unquestionable finding identifying a wound of entry in the back of the head."[57] Nine years earlier, Finck told a New Orleans jury in the Clay Shaw trial the same thing, adding, "The bullet definitely struck in the back of the [president's] head . . . The wound was definitely inflicted by a shot from the rear."[58]

In a 1967 CBS interview, Dan Rather asked Dr. Humes, "Can you be absolutely cer- tain that the wound you described as the entry wound was, in fact, that?"

Humes: "Yes, indeed, we can, very precisely and incontrovertibly." Humes said that as the bullet "passed through the skull, it produced a characteristic coning, or beveling effect on the inner aspect of the skull, which is scientific evidence that the wound was made from behind and passed forward through the president's skull."

Rather: "Is [this] conclusive, scientific evidence?"

Humes: "Yes, sir, it is."

Rather: "Is there any doubt that the wound at the back of the president's head was the entry wound?"

Humes: "There is absolutely no doubt, sir."[59]

And there was yet another strong indication that the wound to the back of the presi- dent's head was an entrance wound. The HSCA said that the "margin of this wound [to the president's head], from 3 to 10 o'clock, is surrounded by a crescent-shaped reddish- black area of denudation . . . presenting the appearance of an *abrasion collar* resulting from the rubbing of the skin by the bullet *at the time of penetration*."[60] Dr. Baden testified that "an abrasion collar is characteristic of an entrance wound."[61] Entrance wounds usually have abrasion collars or rings only because the bullet usually enters the skin at least at some angle, resulting, as Dr. Charles Petty, my pathologist at the London trial testified, in "little tiny tears" of skin[62]—thus, the word *abrasion* for abraded skin. Per Dr. Cyril Wecht, a member of the HSCA medical panel who is a conspiracy theorist, the reason why the term *abrasion collar* or *ring* is so popular in law enforcement circles is because "it can be seen by the naked eye." But he added that "if a bullet enters a body straight on without any angularity at all, there might not be an abrasion collar. In the Kennedy head wound there was a collar because the bullet came in at an angle."[63]

Obviously, no other scientific or medical evidence is necessary to convince any rational person that the wound to the back of the president's head was an entrance wound and the bullet that caused the wound was fired from the president's rear.

But though unnecessary, there is additional medical evidence—indeed, conclusive proof—that the wound to the back of the president's head was an entrance wound. The autopsy surgeons found "coagulation necrosis of the tissues" at the inner margins of the head wound.[64] Dr. Wecht acknowledged in 1967 that coagulation necrosis is a "sure sign" of an entrance wound.[65] Although I haven't looked at more than fifty autopsy reports in my career, I don't believe I've ever seen the term *coagulation necrosis* in any of them. When I asked Dr. Wecht to define the term for me, he wrote that "in gunshot wounds of entrance, the dermis [outer layer of skin] . . . shows microscopic changes in the collagen, the protein material that comprises the dermis to a great extent. These changes in the collagen fibers are caused by the thermal [heat] effects of the bullet in distant wounds. In close range wounds, the changes are produced by the hot gases emerging from the muzzle of the weapon. These collagen alterations are referred to as coagulation necrosis. They cannot be seen by the naked eye."[66]

In a follow-up phone conversation, Wecht said that although, as he indicated earlier, not all entrance wounds have abrasion collars, "*all* have coagulation necrosis." He acknowledged that findings of coagulation necrosis normally do not appear in his autopsy reports or those of other prominent forensic pathologists, repeating that changes to the dermis can only be seen by use of a microscope.

"Doctor," I said, "you would agree that a finding of coagulation necrosis in an autopsy report is a very sophisticated one, would you not?"

"Yes, I would."

"How do you reconcile that, then, with the almost universal view that the autopsy surgeons in the Kennedy case conducted a very inferior and amateurish post-mortem?"

All Dr. Wecht could say was, "I'll tell you where the coagulation necrosis finding came from—Dr. Finck. He specializes in this type of thing. I can guarantee you it didn't come from Humes or Boswell."[67] It didn't come from too poor a source. As indicated, Dr. Finck at the time was the chief of the Wound Ballistics Pathology Branch of the Armed Forces Institute of Pathology, and as Finck said, he "was asked" by Humes to participate in the autopsy "specifically to interpret the wounds . . . It was my mission in that autopsy room. My main mission was to study the wounds."[68]*

So we see that despite the insistent and strident claims by conspiracy theorists that the fatal wound to the president's head was fired from his right front, *all* of the medical and scientific evidence proves not just beyond a reasonable doubt but beyond all doubt that it was fired from his rear, and the wound to the backside of the president's head was an entrance wound. Based on the evidence, the Warren Commission naturally concluded that "the . . . hole in the rear of the President's skull was the point of entry" of the fatal bullet.[69]

Warren Commission critics and conspiracy theorists never stop pointing out that the Warren Commission never viewed the autopsy X-rays and photographs. Hence, they say, the Commission's conclusions were invalid. But nearly all of them fail to add that three other later groups *did* examine the autopsy X-rays and photographs and unanimously reached the same conclusion as the Warren Commission.

In 1978–1979, the House Select Committee, based on the findings of nine forensic

---

*That may have been his main mission, but Finck acknowledged that "although to start with I was there as a consultant" to study the wounds, he very definitely became "a part of the autopsy team," signing, with Boswell and Humes, the autopsy report as one of the three autopsy surgeons (HSCA Record 180-10102-10409, p. 71; CE 387, 16 H 983). Indeed, FBI agent Francis X. O'Neill, who was present throughout the autopsy, told the HSCA that Finck seemed to "take over the autopsy when he arrived" (JFK Document 006185, HSCA staff interview of O'Neill on January 10, 1978, p.6).

pathologists on its panel who examined close-up photographs and X-rays of the president's head wound, concurred with the Warren Commission's conclusion, saying, "The President was struck by [a] bullet . . . that entered in the right rear of the head near the cowlick area." The committee added that "there is no medical evidence" that the president was struck from the front.[70]

The Clark Panel in 1968 and the Rockefeller Commission in 1975, which also examined the photographs and X-rays, came to the same conclusion, that the president was struck once in the back of the head by a bullet fired from his rear.* The four-member Clark Panel concluded that "the decedent's head was struck from *behind* by a *single* projectile. It entered the occipital region 25 mm. to the right of the midline and 100 mm. above the external occipital protuberance . . . Photographs and X-rays indicate that it came from a site above and slightly to his right."[71]

The five-member Rockefeller Commission, citing the specific location of the head entrance wound found by the Clark Panel, concluded that this "head shot" was "fired from the rear" and that there was "no evidence to support the claim that President Kennedy was struck by a bullet fired from either the grassy knoll or any other position to his front, right front or right side . . . No witness who urged the view [before the Rockefeller Commission] that the Zapruder film and other motion picture films proved that President Kennedy was struck by a bullet fired from his right front was shown to possess any professional or other special qualifications on the subject." The Rockefeller Commission noted that even Dr. Cyril Wecht had testified before the commission that the evidence establishes there was only one head shot, and it was fired from the rear.[72]

What this means is that the three pathologists who conducted the autopsy, the nine pathologists for the HSCA, the three pathologists (and one radiologist) from the Clark Panel, and the three pathologists, one of whom, Dr. Werner V. Spitz, was also on the HSCA medical panel from the Rockefeller Commission—that is, *seventeen pathologists*,

---

*In addition to the three pathologists who conducted the autopsy, just who were all of these other pathologists who agreed 100 percent with the conclusion of the autopsy surgeons? Were they qualified experts? You be the judge. Dr. Wecht estimates that the following pathologists had collectively conducted "around 100,000 autopsies" by the time of their work on the Kennedy case. As of 1978, when he was on the HSCA forensic pathology panel, he alone had conducted "around 6,000" autopsies. (Telephone interview of Dr. Cyril Wecht by author on October 22, 2002) *HSCA*: Dr. Michael M. Baden, chief medical examiner (coroner) of New York City; Dr. John I. Coe, chief medical examiner of Hennepin County, Minneapolis, Minnesota; Dr. Joseph Davis, chief medical examiner of Dade County, Miami, Florida; Dr. George S. Loquvam, director of the Institute of Forensic Science, Oakland, California; Dr. Charles S. Petty, chief medical examiner, Dallas County, Dallas, Texas; Dr. Earl Rose, professor of pathology, University of Iowa, Iowa City, Iowa; Dr. Werner V. Spitz, chief medical examiner, Wayne County, Detroit, Michigan; Dr. James T. Weston, chief medical investigator, University of New Mexico School of Medicine, Albuquerque, New Mexico; and Dr. Cyril H. Wecht, coroner of Allegheny County, Pittsburgh, Pennsylvania. *Clark Panel*: Dr. William H. Carnes, professor of pathology, University of Utah, Salt Lake City, Utah; Dr. Russell S. Fisher, professor of forensic pathology, University of Maryland, Baltimore, Maryland; and Dr. Alan R. Moritz, professor of pathology, Case Western Reserve University, Cleveland, Ohio, and former professor of forensic medicine, Harvard University, Cambridge, Massachusetts. Dr. Wecht said that between them, Fisher and Moritz, two of the most experienced forensic pathologists in the field, would have conducted "upwards of 30,000 autopsies" at the time. (The panel also included Dr. Russell H. Morgan, professor of radiology, Johns Hopkins University, Baltimore, Maryland.) *Rockefeller Commission*: Lieutenant Colonel Robert R. McMeekin, chief, division of aerospace pathology, Armed Forces Institute of Pathology, Washington, D.C.; Dr. Werner V. Spitz (see HSCA above); and Dr. Richard Lindenberg, director of neuropathology and legal medicine, state of Maryland, Baltimore, Maryland. (The commission also included Dr. Fred J. Hodges, professor of radiology, Johns Hopkins School of Medicine, Baltimore, Maryland, and Alfred G. Olivier, chief of the Wound Ballistics Branch at the U.S. Army's Edgewood Arsenal in Maryland.)

even Dr. Wecht—*all* agreed that the wound to the back of the president's head was an entrance wound.

The precise location of this entrance wound as stated by the autopsy surgeons in the autopsy report ("slightly above the external occipital protuberance"), however, has been established as being incorrect by every pathologist who has subsequently studied the autopsy photographs and X-rays. Although the pathologists for the Clark Panel said the entry wound was "approximately 100 millimeters" (10 centimeters, close to 4 inches) above the external occipital protuberance (a little, bony bulge we can feel at the base of the skull), the HSCA forensic pathology panel measured it precisely as being 9 centimeters above the protuberance in the so-called cowlick area of the scalp.[73] Since 9 centimeters is approximately 3½ inches and the autopsy surgeons said the wound was "slightly above" the protuberance (without specifying how far), we can roughly say the surgeons were 3 inches off in their calculation. Is it possible we are talking about two separate wounds to the back of the head? No. All seventeen pathologists said there was only one gunshot wound to the back of the president's head. So, by definition, we have to be talking about the same wound. Moreover, the fourteen pathologists who followed the three autopsy surgeons were able to demonstrate that the wound they found was the same wound (same dimensions) the autopsy surgeons described in their report.

Not only do the autopsy photos and X-rays definitively show that the entrance wound is in the upper part of the president's skull, but they show a bullet track (deposit of small metal fragments as the bullet proceeded forward) "only in the upper portion of the skull." Additionally, if the bullet had entered the president's skull at the lower point the autopsy surgeons said it did, there would have been damage to the cerebellum, the lower part of the brain, which there was not. Dr. Baden testified that his forensic pathology panel "did not see any photographic or X-ray evidence . . . indicating any injury of the brain other than the extensive damage to the right upper part of the brain, consistent with the upper track which the panel agrees to." In concluding that the autopsy surgeons were wrong about the precise location of the entrance wound (as described in the autopsy report), the HSCA also noted that photographs show the lower area of the president's brain to be "virtually intact"—an *impossibility* had the bullet entered the skull as low as the three autopsy pathologists contend.[74]

How have the three autopsy pathologists reacted to this apparent gaffe in their report? Not very well, I'm afraid. By and large, most people don't want to admit they made a mistake. The three autopsy surgeons were no exception.* When asked about the discrepancy in 1977, both Drs. Humes and Boswell repeated their 1964 testimony, insisting that the entrance wound was low in the skull (this time both said the wound was slightly *below* the external occipital protuberance)[75] and that the photographs were misleading—a consistent theme in numerous subsequent interviews.[76] An HSCA memo says that Dr. Humes, obviously reluctant to second-guess what he had written fourteen years earlier, stated categorically "that his physical measurements are correct and emphasized that he had access to the body itself and made the measurements of the actual head region." In addition, he said that "photographs and X-rays have inherent limitations which are not present when

---

*Much has been made in the assassination literature of the fact that the autopsy surgeons were wrong on the location of the entrance wound. But is there any real significance to the head entrance wound being 3

one is examining the subject."[77] Also, in 1978, Dr. Finck testified to the HSCA that the entrance wound was low in the back of the head, identifying a small piece of white brain tissue, seen in autopsy photographs near the hairline, as the point of entry.[78] Finck, too, pointed out to the committee that interpreting photographs of the body after the fact is never as good as examining the actual body, and chalked up the discrepancy as "the difference between the interpretation of photographs and the [actual] autopsy wounds."[79]

The HSCA pathology panel reported that the lead autopsy surgeon, Dr. Humes, had changed his mind during the committee's public hearings and "supported the panel's conclusion as to the location of the wound."[80] But actually, Humes wasn't quite that clear. In fact, when he was asked specifically by HSCA counsel to explain the discrepancy between the language in the autopsy report, which placed the entrance wound "slightly above" the occipital protuberance, and the forensic panel's conclusion, which placed the entrance wound 4 inches above the occipital protuberance, Humes replied, "Well, I have a little trouble with that; 10 centimeters is . . . significant—4 inches."[81]*

But in the final moments of his appearance before the HSCA, as the committee sought to come to some understanding how a nearly 4-inch error might have been made, Dr. Humes offered something that helps to answer the question and furnish the reason for Humes's error. After explaining that he didn't get much sleep between the conclusion of the autopsy and the writing of the report, Humes was asked if he had any notes from which to work in the preparation of his autopsy report. Humes said that he had "draft notes" that were written in the autopsy room.

Question: "Was the distance between the wound and the external occipital protuberance noted on those notes?"

Humes: "*It was not noted in any greater detail than appears in the final report.*" (Remember, the autopsy report says only that the wound was "slightly above" the occipital protuberance.)

Question: "So, the *exact* distance, then, above the external occipital protuberance was not noted—?"

Humes: "*It was not noted, with the feeling, of course, that the photographs and X-rays that we had made would, of themselves, suffice to accurately locate this wound.*"

Indeed, the autopsy photographs and X-rays *do* locate the wound precisely, though, to Dr. Humes's chagrin, not where the autopsy report says. Humes added to his concession by saying that he and his colleagues were "hampered by our inability, number one, to never have seen, after about midnight of that night, the X-rays, and to never have seen at any time until a year or two after the Warren Commission the photographs which we made. I think had we had those opportunities, some of the confusion and difficulties which seem to have arisen might not have arisen."[82]

---

inches higher than the autopsy surgeons said it was other than as a reflection on the *alleged* incompetence of the surgeons? "No, not really," Dr. Werner Spitz, the German-born member of the HSCA's forensic pathology panel and the Rockefeller Commission, said. "It's just a red herring. We know from the autopsy photos and X-rays that there was only one entrance wound to the back of the president's head. The only significance this matter has is academic. If the bullet had entered where the autopsy surgeons said it did—and we know from the photos and X-rays they were wrong—it would have been an unusual deflection for the bullet to have exited where it did. This was a military-type bullet and it is unlikely that it would be deflected so sharply upwards" (Telephone interview of Dr. Werner Spitz by author on March 26, 2005).

*Ten centimeters, which is close to 4 inches, was bandied loosely about, including by the HSCA (7 HSCA 107), ever since the Clark Panel said the wound was "100 millimeters" (10 centimeters) above the external occipital protuberance. But as indicated, the more precise measurement was 9 centimeters.

 $\mathbf{W}$ hat happened to the bullet once it entered the rear of the president's head? Once again, the opinion of all the pathologists who either conducted the autopsy or examined close-up photographs and X-rays of the president's head and wounds was unanimous. As the HSCA medical panel concluded, the bullet "proceeded in an essentially straight and forward path" and exploded out of the right front of the president's head.[83] (See drawing in photo section for path of bullet.)

The autopsy report describes the damage caused by the exiting bullet as "a large irregular defect of the scalp and skull on the right involving chiefly the parietal bone [above the ear] but extending somewhat into the temporal [front] and occipital [rear] regions." The report also notes that there is an "actual absence of scalp and bone" producing a very large hole "that measures approximately 13 cm [5 ¹⁄₁₀ inches] in greatest diameter."[84]* The HSCA forensic pathology panel concurred. It found that the lacerated area caused by the exit wound was "in the right parietal region, anteriorly to the right frontal region . . . and posteriorly toward the occipital region."[85] Likewise, the Clark panel of pathologists concluded that the bullet wound to the back of the head "explosively fractured the right frontal and parietal bones as it emerged from the head."[86]†

Clearly visible and exuding from this defect, the autopsy report said, was "lacerated [torn] brain tissue which on close inspection proves to represent the major portion of the right cerebral hemisphere."[87] X-rays support these observations, revealing multiple fracture lines (the longest measuring approximately 7½ inches) radiating from both the large defect on the right and the small entrance wound on the back of the skull.[88] More importantly, with respect to the path of the bullet, Dr. Humes testified to the Warren Commission that the X-rays also showed "multiple minute fragments of radio opaque material [missile fragments] traversing a line *from the wound in the occiput [rear head bone] to just above the right eye*, with a rather sizable fragment visible by X-ray just above the right eye. These tiny fragments that were seen dispersed through the substance of the brain in between were . . . extremely minute, less than 1 mm. in size for the most part."[89]‡ In other words, the X-rays conclusively showed that all of the minute missile

---

*The outwardly exploding bullet in the parietal area lifted "a large plate of [parietal] bone upward," causing it to "protrude from the wound" (Sullivan, Faccio, Levy, and Grossman, "Assassination of President John F. Kennedy: A Neuroforensic Analysis—Part 1," p.1023).

†Dr. Alfred G. Olivier, chief of the Wound Ballistics Branch at the U.S. Army's Edgewood Arsenal in Maryland, supervised experiments in 1964 in which Western Cartridge 6.5-millimeter bullets were fired from Oswald's Mannlicher-Carcano rifle (at the appropriate distance, simulating that from the sixth-floor window to the point on Elm Street where Kennedy was struck in the head) at reconstructed and inert human skulls filled with a 20 percent gelatin substance to see whether the president's exit head wound could have been caused by the subject rifle and bullets. In one skull that was struck at a point closely approximating the wound of entry to the backside of Kennedy's head, the bullet "blew out the right side of the reconstructed skull in a manner very similar to the head wound of the president." (WR, p.87; CE 861–862, 17 H 854; 5 H 75–77, 87, 89, WCT Dr. Alfred G. Olivier)

‡As can be seen, the autopsy surgeons saw the X-rays they took of the president's body. "We had to see those right then as part of our examination," Dr. Humes said, and "the X-rays were developed in our X-ray department right on the spot." However, the photos taken of the president during the autopsy were not seen by them that night or before the autopsy report was prepared. "They were turned over to the Secret Service in their cassettes unexposed [that night], and I have not seen any of them since," Dr. Humes told the Warren Commission. (2 H 372, WCT Dr. James J. Humes; ARRB Transcript of Proceedings, Deposition of Dr. James Joseph Humes, February 13, 1996, pp.96–98) The first time Humes saw the autopsy photos was at the National Archives, and Boswell at the National Archives, on November 1, 1966 (ARRB Transcript of Proceedings, Deposition of Dr. James Joseph Humes, February 13, 1996, p.96; HSCA Record 180-10093-10429, HSCA interview of James Humes on August 17, 1977, p.7); HSCA Record 180-10097-10151, p.1, January 26, 1967). Dr. Pierre Finck didn't see the photographs at the archives until January 20, 1967 (HSCA Record 180-10097-10151).

fragments lay in a *back-to-front* pattern on the right side of the president's head. None were seen on the left side of his head, as there would have been if the shot to the head had come from the grassy knoll or any other location on the right side of the presidential limousine (as conspiracy theorists maintain), since the bullet would be expected to proceed forward into the left side of the president's brain.

The HSCA concurred with the Warren Commission in this essential finding. "The [forensic pathology] panel examined X-ray films of the . . . skull with the naked eye and with 10× magnification . . . Within the *right side* of the head are randomly distributed, irregularly shaped, radiopaque shadows which are missile fragments. These shadows, measuring from 0.2 to 0.6 centimeters in diameter, extend from the *back to the front*."[90] The Clark Panel found that the bullet that entered the back of the president's head left "a trail of fine metallic debris as it passed forward and laterally" through the head.[91]

In an interview with *JAMA* editor George D. Lundberg in October of 1991, Humes said,

> In 1963, we proved at the autopsy table that President Kennedy was struck from above and behind by the fatal shot. The pattern of the entrance and exit wounds in the skull proves it, and if we stayed here until hell freezes over, nothing will change this proof. It happens 100 times out of 100, and I will defend it until I die. This is the essence of our autopsy, and it is supreme ignorance to argue any other scenario. This is a law of physics [referring to the fact that with a through-and-through wound of the cranium it is "always the pattern," he said, that "the beveling or crater effect appears on the inside of the skull at the entrance wound and on the outside of the skull at the exit wound"] and it is foolproof—absolutely, unequivocally, and without question. The conspiracy buffs have totally ignored this central scientific fact, and everything else is hogwash.[92]

After examining the head wound, the three autopsy pathologists focused on a wound in the upper right part of the president's back. According to the autopsy report, and the testimony of Drs. Humes, Boswell, and Finck, this wound was a "7 × 4 millimeter" (approximately ¼ × ⅙ inch) oval *entrance* wound "just above the upper border of the scapula [shoulder blade]" located "14 centimeters [5½ inches] from the tip of the right acromion process" (the acromion is the extreme, outermost edge of the shoulder blade) and an equal distance "below the tip of the right mastoid process" (the bony protuberance just behind the ear).[93] This terminology makes the location of the wound difficult to visualize for a layperson. The HSCA presented a sketch of the wound's location (see photo section) and said that the right edge of the ruler that is on top of the president's spinal column is "approximately 2.5 centimeters" (around 1 inch) away from the wound.[94]

The Warren Commission concluded that the wound just above the president's right shoulder blade was a wound of entrance.[95] Likewise, the nine-member HSCA forensic pathology panel, eight of whom, as we have seen, were chief medical examiners (coroners) in major cities throughout the United States, "unanimously concluded that a bullet *entered* the upper right back of the president"—that is, the president was shot from behind.[96]

Dr. Finck testified at the Clay Shaw murder trial in New Orleans that the edges of the wound to the president's back were *pushed inward* and contained an abrasion collar: "I looked at it very closely and I had the opinion based on the characteristics I mentioned—

regular edges, with abrasion, and turned inward—that this was a wound of entry."[97] The HSCA forensic panel later concurred with Dr. Finck's assessment, concluding that autopsy photographs of the back wound showed it to be oval and surrounded by a sharply defined "abrasion collar resulting from the bullet scraping the margins of the skin at the moment of penetration," characteristic of "wounds of entrance and not typical of exit wounds."[98] The forensic panel noted that the abrasion collar, though surrounding the entrance wound, was "most prominent between the 1 and 7 o'clock positions,"[99] leading the panel to conclude that the bullet was moving "from right to left,"[100] consistent with a shot from the Book Depository Building.

From this and also trajectory studies (see later text), the HSCA estimated that as opposed to the shot to the head, which was descending at a 16-degree angle below horizontal and from a point 29 degrees to the right of true north from the president, this earlier shot to the president's back was descending at an angle of 21 degrees below horizontal as it approached him and from a point 26 degrees to the right of true north,[101] that is, "moving from right to left,"[102] again consistent with Oswald's perch above and to the right rear of the presidential limousine.

Further, a microscopic examination of the tissues surrounding the back wound (as noted in the supplementary autopsy report) found "coagulation necrosis of the tissue at the wound margins,"[103] conclusively establishing, as with the wound to the back of the president's head, that the wound was an entrance wound. It should be noted that no beveling or cratering was found on the inner surface of the back wound, since this is a phenomenon that only exists in gunshot wounds to the skull. "In all my years," Dr. Cyril Wecht says, "I've never seen a beveling effect on soft-tissue gunshot wounds."[104]

Finally, an FBI examination of the president's clothing at its laboratory in Washington, D.C., also confirmed that the bullet wound in the back was an entrance wound. Robert Frazier, the FBI agent who conducted the examination, told the Warren Commission that it revealed a small hole in the back of the president's suit coat approximately 5⅜ inches below the top of the collar and 1¾ inches to the right of the middle seam.[105] The hole was circular in shape and "the cloth fibers around the margins of the hole were pushed inward."[106] A spectrographic examination of the fabric surrounding the hole in the back of the coat revealed minute traces of copper[107] consistent with the copper-clad ammunition fired from Oswald's rifle.

Frazier testified that his examination of the back of the president's shirt revealed a hole with similar characteristics located 5¾ inches below the top of the shirt collar and 1⅛ inches to the right of the midline of the shirt. In other words, the hole in the shirt matches up fairly well with the hole in the president's suit coat, and both the Warren Commission and HSCA so found. The torn threads surrounding this hole in the shirt, which was slightly oval in shape (½ inch vertical by ⅓ inch horizontal), also, he said, "had been pressed inward." Both holes were considered typical of bullet entrance holes.[108]

In addition to the Warren Commission and the HSCA, the four-member Clark Panel likewise concluded that the wound to the backside of the president was an entrance wound.[109]

So we see that there is unanimity of opinion as to the back wound (as we saw earlier with the head wound) being an entrance wound. This unanimity extends to Dr. Cyril Wecht, "the darling of the conspiracy buffs," as I referred to him at the London trial over Gerry Spence's objection. I asked Wecht at the trial, "Doctor, even though from a professional perspective you don't think too much of the autopsy surgeons' report, you do agree 100 percent with their findings; to wit, that the bullet wound to the president's upper back and the bullet wound to the back of the president's head were both entry wounds and not exit wounds, and hence, the bullets were fired from the president's rear. Is that correct?"

Wecht: "Yes."[110]

After taking photographs of the wound to the president's back, Drs. Humes and Finck made attempts to probe the wound and determine its track through the body. Humes, using his little finger, was only able to penetrate the wound a short distance (less than an inch),[111] whereas Finck, using a flexible metal probe, was able to penetrate a distance described by observers as 2 to 4 inches.[112] In both cases, observers testified that the probing conducted by Drs. Humes and Finck indicated a downward trajectory. Humes testified that "attempts to probe in the vicinity of this wound were unsuccessful without fear of making a false passage . . . We were unable . . . to take probes and have them satisfactorily fall through any definite path."[113] Dr. Boswell told investigators in 1996, "We probed this hole which was in his neck with all sorts of probes and everything, and it was such a small hole, basically, and the muscles were so big and strong [they] had closed the hole and you couldn't get a finger or a probe through it."[114]

Next, Dr. Finck took a look at the tracheotomy incision performed by Dallas physician Malcolm Perry in the front of the throat, and examined the trachea in an attempt to locate an exit for the back entrance wound, but could not find "any evidence of a bullet wound."[115] (Of course, we know that the tracheotomy incision had almost completely obscured the exit wound in the throat.) In an effort to resolve where the bullet went, Dr. Finck asked to examine the president's clothing to correlate it with the wounds and found it "most unfortunate" that the clothing was not available.[116] It had been taken into custody at Parkland Hospital by the Secret Service.[117] Asked in 1996 if it would be standard practice to have the clothing available for inspection, Dr. Boswell stated, "Well, under normal circumstances, but these were not normal circumstances."[118]

Not seen by the three pathologists until they testified to the Warren Commission in 1964, the president's clothing* would have confirmed that the bullet had exited at the throat. In a 1965 memorandum describing his examination of the clothing, Finck wrote that "immediately below the upper button of the front [of the president's shirt] is a bullet hole perforating both flaps of the shirt, right and left. There is dry blood on the margins of both holes. *The innermost hole reveals fibers directed outward, which indicates an exit perforation.* The outermost hole also shows this outward orientation of the bloody shirt

---

*Though Ernest Hemingway once opined that the only difference between the rich and the poor is that the rich have more money, it has been said that *old* wealth comes through, regardless of the raiments worn by their possessors; that there is a well-scrubbed aspect to those born to the manor; and that the wealth is even heard in their voices. But President Kennedy, a Brahmin by birth and rearing, though dressing in an understated fashion—as is the usual custom of the privileged class—was clothed in the finest of garments and accessories on November 22, 1963. Though the FBI didn't note the make of Kennedy's gray suit, it was well known that he bought his suits at Brooks Brothers, the oldest haberdashers in America dating back to 1818, and in 1963 a more exclusive store than it is today. His black leather belt, size 34, was made by Farnsworth-Reed. The blue-and-white striped shirt he wore was custom made by Charles Dillon shirtmakers at 444 Park Avenue, New York. His white shorts were made for Brooks Brothers by D. & G. Anderson, Scotland. His size 10½ shoes were black mocassin, no make given. He had a white linen handkerchief, and a tortoiseshell comb by Kent of London. (HSCA Record 180-10087-10096, Report of FBI agent Robert L. Bouck, November 23, 1963) He was wearing a gold Cartier wristwatch with a black leather band (HSCA Record 180-10087-10095, December 2, 1963). His blue silk tie was labeled "Monsieur" Christian Dior.

fibers, but to a lesser extent."[119] In the FBI's laboratory examination of the hole in the shirt shortly after the assassination, investigators too found that the "fibers of the cloth" were "protruding outward," characteristic of an exit hole for a projectile, but did not find any bullet metal in the fabric surrounding the hole.[120]*

Unfortunately, the autopsy pathologists wouldn't learn of all the facts about the clothing until after the autopsy had been completed. For the time being, they were perplexed. *What happened to the bullet that entered the president's upper right back?* Knowing that bullets can unexplainably end up in strange places, and thus far only X-ray films of the head having been taken, Dr. Finck requested a radiographic survey (X-rays) of the entire body before going further with the autopsy. After they waited more than an hour for the results, they proved to be negative.[121] There was no bullet in the president's body except for the metallic fragments seen earlier in the skull X-rays.[122]

The autopsy pathologists then subsequently learned that a bullet had been recovered from a stretcher at Parkland Hospital,[123] which caused Dr. Humes to theorize that the bullet that struck the president in the back, "in some rather inexplicable fashion, had been stopped in its path" and had fallen back out of his body onto the stretcher, perhaps during cardiac massage at Parkland Hospital.[124] FBI agent Francis O'Neill reported that Dr. Humes appeared "greatly relieved" and grew more and more confident that this is what happened. By the end of the autopsy, O'Neill reported, the three pathologists were convinced that the bullet that entered the president's back had worked its way out through the back wound and dropped on the Dallas stretcher.[125]

As previously indicated, the following morning Dr. Humes placed a telephone call to Parkland Hospital surgeon Malcolm O. Perry in which he expressed his inability to determine what happened to the bullet that caused the back wound. He and his fellow autopsy surgeons couldn't figure out where it went, Humes told Perry, surmising that perhaps it had fallen out during cardiac massage. "It seemed like a very unlikely event to me, to say the least," Perry recalled in 1978. "But at any rate, when I told him that there was a wound in the anterior [front] neck, lower third, he [Humes] said, 'That explains it.'"[126]† With the knowledge that the tracheotomy had obscured the bullet wound in the throat, Dr. Humes realized that the bullet had entered the back, slipped between the muscles of the

---

*Dr. Finck reported that the *tie* worn by Kennedy showed "a tear of the cloth to the left side of the knot and *corresponding to the two anterior holes in the shirt*. The tie knot was not perforated but glanced by the bullet, which is indicated by the fact that the white padding of the tie is visible and . . . the blue cloth on the internal aspect of the knot is intact, which indicates a tangential path of the left side in relation to the knot." (AFIP Record 205-10001-10002, Memorandum, Finck to Blumberg, p.7; also ARRB MD 28) The tear to the tie was described by the FBI laboratory as a "small elongated nick" on the "left side of the knot of the tie" (CD 205, p.154; 5 H 62, WCT Robert A. Frazier; 7 HSCA 89). An FBI examination found no metallic residue on this nick in the tie, and unlike the shirt, the FBI could not find any characteristic disturbance in the fabric around the tie hole that "would permit any conclusion" as to the direction of the missile (5 H 62, WCT Robert A. Frazier; 7 HSCA 89–90; FBI Record 124-10024-10173; Gallagher Exhibit No. 1, 20 H 2).

†Warren Commission critics have pointed out that Dr. Perry told Dr. Humes that the wound in the throat was 3 to 5 millimeters in size (CE 397, 17 H 29), and a 6.5-millimeter bullet that did not fragment (as we know Commission Exhibit No. 399, as opposed to the later bullet that struck the president in the head, did not) could not exit through a hole "between 3 and 5 millimeters in diameter" (Thompson, *Six Seconds in Dallas*, p.51). But clearly, Perry had to be wrong in his estimate of the size of the wound, since there is no evidence the bullet that entered the president's back exited anywhere else, and no bullet was found inside the president's body. Moreover, Perry, who later told the Warren Commission that the wound was "perhaps 5 millimeters in diameter," admitted that he "did not examine [the wound] minutely," giving it and the head exit wound a "cursory examination" (6 H 15, 3 H 368, 375). The critics never mention, naturally, that Dr. James Carrico, the first Parkland doctor to see the president, estimated the throat wound to be "5 to 8 millimeters in size" (3 H 361), which would be consistent with the exit wound of a 6.5-millimeter bullet.

upper back and neck (without striking any major blood vessels), continued over the top of the right lung, and exited at the throat just below the Adam's apple.[127]

After talking to Dr. Perry, something else that Humes had observed the night of the autopsy suddenly made sense too. Late in the autopsy, Humes had made a standard Y incision in the chest and pulled back the skin and tissues in order to examine the interior of the chest and neck. Humes recalled that while examining the area of the tracheotomy incision, he noted that there was "some bruising of the muscles of the neck in the depths of this wound as well as [a] laceration or defect in the trachea," perhaps caused, he thought at the time of the autopsy, by Dr. Perry's knife.[128] (He had also found bruising on the apex [top] of the right pleural cavity containing the right lung.) Yet, the incisions in the president's chest, left arm, and ankle at Parkland (for the purpose of administering bodily fluids) showed "no evidence of bruising or contusion," leading the autopsy doctors to conclude that these incisions were made during the death throes of the late president, when blood circulation had virtually ceased.[129] Thirty minutes after his first conversation, Humes telephoned Dr. Perry again and asked him about the chest tube incisions.[130] Perry doesn't recall the conversation but he would have informed Humes that the tracheotomy and chest incisions were performed at about the same time.[131]

The bruises in the neck region, then, *couldn't* have been caused by the tracheotomy because the circulation of blood in the body was nearly nonexistent at that point. Without blood, there could be no bruise—that is, there could only be damage to tissue, not discoloration of the tissue. The bruising of the neck muscles and right lung *had* to have been caused while the president's heart and lungs were still operating sufficiently to permit a bruise to occur.[132] In short, these bruises, which lay along a path between the president's back and his throat wound, *could only have occurred prior to the incisions that were made at Parkland Hospital* (i.e., they had to have been made at the time of the shooting), and hence, the damage found there had to have been the result of a bullet *entering the president's back and exiting the throat.*

Based on the testimony of Dr. Humes, which was agreed upon by fellow pathologists Boswell and Finck in the autopsy report, the Warren Commission concluded that the bullet that entered the president's back "proceeded in a straight line" on a "downward angle" through the "soft tissue of the neck," moving in a "slight right to left lateral direction," hitting "no bony structure" before emerging in the front area of the president's neck "that had been cut away by the tracheotomy."[133] This conclusion of the Warren Commission on the track of the bullet was "unanimously" confirmed by all nine of the HSCA's panel of forensic pathologists, who noted that the straight path of the bullet was "adjacent to the spine," though not touching it.[134] Although the Warren Commission merely said the bullet passed on a "downward angle" through the president's body, the HSCA's sketch of the angle of decline shows 23 degrees from the horizontal.[135]

The 1968 Clark Panel also agreed with the autopsy surgeons on the path of the bullet, adding that "the possibility that this bullet might have followed a pathway other than one passing through the site of the tracheotomy wound was considered. No evidence for this was found. In addition, any path other than one between the two cutaneous [skin] wounds [upper back wound and wound in front of throat] would almost surely have been intercepted by bone, and the X-ray films show no bony damage in the thorax or neck."[136]

At the London trial, before getting into the details supporting the conclusion, I asked Dr. Charles S. Petty, a member of the nine-man forensic pathology panel of the HSCA, what conclusion his panel had come to with respect to the number of bullets that struck the president, and their points of entrance and exit on his body.

Petty: "The conclusion of the panel was that the president was struck by two bullets, one entering the right upper back and exiting in the front of the neck, the other entering the right back of his head and exiting in what we call the right frontal area, that is, the front and side of the head."

Question: "You found no evidence of any other entrance or exit wounds anywhere else on President Kennedy's body?"

Petty: "That is absolutely correct."[137]

Thomas Noguchi, the famed Los Angeles "Coroner to the Stars" (including Marilyn Monroe, Robert F. Kennedy, Janis Joplin, Natalie Wood, Sharon Tate, and John Belushi), is fond of saying that an autopsy is a homicide victim's opportunity to testify. "The victim is talking to you," he says. President Kennedy's autopsy, whose findings were confirmed by the HSCA, leaves no doubt that two bullets struck the president from the rear, one exiting the front of his body, the other the right front.

How do conspiracy theorists challenge this incontrovertible evidence? By trotting out the observations of the Parkland Hospital doctors, a group of mostly young interns and residents who were not pathologists and who had only twenty-two frenzied minutes in Kennedy's presence, and then *only* to try to resuscitate him. Their observations, as unfocused and unconcentrated as they must have been regarding anything not directly related to saving the president's life, supersede, in the conspiracy theorists' minds, autopsy photographs and X-rays, and the positive conclusions of seventeen forensic pathologists, along with other experts (radiologists and anthropologists), who, with almost unlimited time, could coolly and dispassionately evaluate all the medical and scientific evidence. Don't misunderstand me, here. I'm not saying that we should disregard out of hand everything that was not the primary focus of these physicians who were trying to save the president's life, particularly in the absence of an explanation for their supposedly erroneous observations. This brings us to the central question in this matter. Starting with the head wound, what did the Parkland doctors "see"?

Most saw the large defect as being not to the right front but the *right rear* of the president's head, lending support to the conspiracy theorists' position that the fatal shot to the head was fired from the front.[*] For instance, Dr. Malcolm Perry, along with Dr.

---

*For years, one of the very biggest allegations among conspiracy theorists is that every one or virtually all of the Parkland doctors said the exit wound was to the rear or right rear of the president's head, which would be in direct contradiction of the autopsy findings. An example: "*All* the doctors and nurses at Parkland Hospital who saw the body described a large exit wound in the *back* of the President's head" (Groden and Livingstone, *High Treason*, p.26). But this is simply not true. A significant minority of Parkland doctors saw the exit wound essentially, or close to, where the autopsy and X-rays clearly showed it to be. Dr. Charles Baxter testified that the head exit wound was in the "temporal and parietal" area (6 H 44), as all the later scientific and medical evidence proved. Dr. Robert Grossman, the neurosurgeon who accompanied Dr. William Kemp Clark, the chief neurosurgeon at Parkland Hospital, into Trauma Room One, said that the large defect he saw was "in the parietal area above the right ear" (Ben Bradlee, "Dispute on JFK Assassination Evidence Persists," *Boston Globe*, June 21, 1981, p.A23), although Grossman's credibility on this matter may be questioned (see endnote). Dr. Adolph Giesecke Jr. testified the exit wound extended "from the brow line [ridge above eye] to the occiput on the left [*sic*] hand side of the head" (6 H 74). Dr. Marion T. Jenkins, the Parkland anesthesiologist, said he saw "a great laceration on the right side of the head (temporal and occipital)" (CE 392, 17 H 15). Dr. Kenneth Salyer told the Warren Commission that the exit wound was in the "right temporal region" (6 H 81). And Dr. Donald Seldin, chairman of the Department of Medicine at Parkland, said that "the entire frontal, parietal and temporal bones were shattered . . . I believe that the official story is accurate in all details" (Letter from Dr. Donald Seldin to Vince Palamara dated August 27, 1998).

Charles Carrico, one of the two primary doctors administering emergency care to the president, said the large defect was to "the right posterior parietal area."[138] Dr. Carrico thought it to be in the "right occipital parietal area."[139] Dr. William Kemp Clark and Gene Akin also said the large wound was in the "right occipital parietal region."[140] Dr. William Zedelitz, a second-year general-surgery resident at Parkland whose presence in the president's recovery room was mentioned in the Warren Commission volumes,[141] but who never testified before the Commission, was tracked down by assassination researcher Vincent Palamara, and in a November 4, 1998, letter to Palamara also said that the president "had a massive head injury to the right occipital parietal area of the cranium." Dr. Ronald C. Jones testified he saw a "large defect in the back side of the head."[142] But Mark Redhead, the London Weekend Television producer of the 1988 Oswald docu-trial, wrote that in a June 13, 1986, telephone conversation with Jones, "He cooled off a little on his testimony about the head wound. He said that, though his initial impression was that the bullet had hit JFK in the throat and exited from the back of the head, he had not gone around to the head and examined the wound."[143]

Dr. Robert McClelland, who would later become the main Parkland doctor the conspiracy theorists would cite for the proposition that the large exit wound was not just to the occipital parietal area but completely to the rear of the president's head, originally told the Warren Commission that the *"right posterior* portion of the skull had been extremely blasted . . . The parietal bone was protruded up through the scalp and seemed to be fractured almost along its *right* posterior half," with "some of the occipital bone being fractured in its lateral half."[144] Two months before McClelland's Warren Commission testimony on March 21, 1964, the *Texas State Journal of Medicine* contacted the Parkland doctors who had actually treated the president (which the journal concluded numbered only seven) and asked them to record their separate impressions for the journal's readers. McClelland wrote that "the cause of death was the massive head and brain injury from a gunshot wound of the right side of the head."[145] McClelland's view would soon change radically.

McClelland eventually drew a sketch for conspiracy theorists, which appears in their books,[146] showing the massive gaping wound to the president as being *solely* in the occipital (rear bone) area of the president's head. To fortify his position about seeing a large hole in back of Kennedy's head, he has also said he saw a piece of cerebellum (a portion of the brain located to the rear of the cerebrum, the front part of the brain) fall out of the back of the president's head onto his stretcher.[147] But although the autopsy report notes that "the major portion" of the right cerebrum was "exuding" from the large defect on the right side of the president's head, there isn't one word in the report indicating that any part of the cerebellum was missing or even lacerated.[148] And Dr. Michael Baden of the HSCA told me that "X-rays and autopsy photos show that although there was damage to the cerebrum, the cerebellum was intact. Any doctors at Parkland, none of whom were pathologists, who said they saw damage to the cerebellum were wrong. They saw some brain tissue on Kennedy's hair and they incorrectly assumed it was cerebellum tissue."[149] Indeed, with the entry wound to the president's head being as high up as it was, it would have been virtually impossible for the cerebellum, in the lower part of the brain, to have been damaged, at least by the bullet.[150]

The relevance of this issue, of course, is that since the cerebellum is located near the back of the head, finding pieces of cerebellum on the stretcher would be consistent with there being a large exit wound to the rear or right rear of the president's head, where conspiracy theorists claim the head exit wound was. Cerebellum certainly wouldn't likely have been expelled from any defect in the right front of the president's head, where the Warren Commission and the autopsy surgeons concluded the exit wound was. Yet several Parkland doctors claim they saw damaged and exposed cerebellum tissue (e.g., Dr. Charles Carrico,[151] Dr. William Kemp Clark,[152] Dr. Charles Baxter,[153] Dr. Malcolm Perry,[154] and Dr. Marion Jenkins).[155] In his hospital report dated November 22, 1963, Dr. Jenkins wrote that "the cerebellum had protruded from the [head] wound,"[156] and later testified to the Warren Commission in 1964 that the "cerebellum . . . was herniated from the wound."[157] However, Jenkins changed his mind after seeing autopsy photographs in 1988, telling author Gerald Posner that "the photos showed the President's brain was crenelated from the trauma, and it *resembled* cerebellum, but it was *not* cerebellar tissue. I think it has thrown off a lot of people that saw it."[158] And after interviewing Jenkins in 1992, Dennis Breo reported in *JAMA* that when Jenkins wrote in his 1963 report that the "cerebellum had been blown out, he meant cerebrum."[159]

When I spoke to Dr. Carrico, one of the doctors who testified he had seen damaged cerebellar tissue, I asked him if there was any possibility that the Parkland doctors were confused about the cerebellum being damaged.

"Oh, absolutely," he immediately replied.

"Why?" I asked.

"Looking at the shredded pieces of brain on the gurney, it looked like some of it had the characteristics of cerebellum, which kind of has a wavy surface. But because these brain pieces were shredded, this could easily have led to confusion as to whether it was all cerebrum—which has broader bands across the surface—or some cerebellum."[160]

And in a telephone conversation in 1994, Dr. Boswell, in response to Parkland doctor Kemp Clark's claiming to have seen "exposed . . . cerebellar tissue," told Dr. Gary Aguilar, "He was wrong. The right side of the cerebrum was so fragmented. I think what he saw and misinterpreted as cerebellum was that."[161] Parkland doctor Robert Grossman, who said he was present in Trauma Room One during the effort to resuscitate the president,[162] would later write that "the autopsy demonstrated that the cerebellum was intact and that the physicians, including myself, who had thought that they had observed cerebellar tissue must have mistaken macerated brain for cerebellar folia."[163] It bears repeating that the autopsy report only mentioned damage to the cerebrum, not the cerebellum.

When I spoke over the telephone to Dr. McClelland in late September and early October of 2002, McClelland, a respected Dallas surgeon whom no one accuses of trying to deliberately mislead anyone, only of being completely wrong in what he thought he saw (the most honest people in the world can think they saw the darndest things), said he was positive the president had a "massive hole to the back of his head." He said at the time of his observation he was holding a metal retractor that was pulling the skin away from the president's trachea so Drs. Perry and Carrico could perform their tracheotomy. "I had nothing else to do or to distract me so I fixated on this large, gaping hole to the back of the president's head for ten to twelve minutes." When I wondered how he could see the large hole when the president was always lying on his back, he said the wound was so large that he nevertheless could see "most of it." If what he said was true, I asked, how is it possible that on the Zapruder film itself, the explosion is clearly to the right frontal portion of the president's head with a large amount of brain matter spraying out, and the back of his head appears to be completely intact? Dr. McClelland gave an answer that deserves some type of an award for inventiveness: "What the explanation for this is, I just don't know, but what I believe happened is that the spray of brain matter and blood was kind of like a bloodscreen, similar to a smokescreen, that precluded a clear view of the occipital area."

If, I pursued the matter, the exit wound was to the back of the president's head, where was the entrance wound for this bullet? McClelland, who believes the shot to the head came from the grassy knoll, said he believed the president was struck "around the hairline near the middle of his forehead." If that was so, I asked, how was it that seventeen pathologists, including Dr. Wecht, all agreed that the president was only struck twice, both times from the rear, and none of them—from photographs, X-rays, and personal observation (by the three autopsy surgeons)—saw any entrance wound to the president's forehead? Again, McClelland, who acknowledged, "I'm not a pathologist and I've never conducted an autopsy," said, "I don't know the answer to your question." But he remained sincerely inventive in his imagination. "What I believe happened is that none of the pathologists saw the entrance wound because it became a part of the destruction to the whole right side and top of the president's head. In other words, it was no longer a separate hole that could be identified." (Of course, none of the autopsy photographs show any such massive injury to the president's forehead extending to the right side of his head, and none is referred to in the autopsy report, nor in the reports of the Clark Panel and Rockefeller Commission. As the HSCA said, "There is no evidence that the president was struck by a bullet entering the front of his head.")[164]

"So you do acknowledge," I said, "the explosion to the *right front part* of the president's head?"

"Oh, yes," the doctor said, "but that's not where the bullet exited. It exited in the occipital region of his head, leaving a hole so big I could put my fist in it."

When I pointed out to the doctor again that not only didn't the Zapruder film show any large hole to the back of the president's head but autopsy photographs never showed any large hole there either, he said that although it was pure "supposition" on his part, at the time the photographs were taken, someone "could have pulled a flap of the president's skin, attached to the base of his neck, forward," thereby covering the large defect. When I asked him if he saw any such loose flap of skin at Parkland, he acknowledged, "I did not."

It was getting late in the evening, Dallas time, but before I ended the interview I reminded Dr. McClelland of the fact that in his Parkland Hospital admission note at 4:45 p.m. on the day of the assassination, he had written that the president died "from a gunshot wound of the *left* temple."[165] "Yes," he said, "that was a mistake. I never saw any wound to the president's left temple. Dr. Jenkins had told me there was a wound there, though he later denied telling me this."[*] Since there was no bullet wound to the left side of the president's body, and since the conspiracy theorists allege that Kennedy was shot from the grassy knoll to his *right* front, conspiracy author Robert Groden solves the prob-

---

[*]It clearly appears that Dr. McClelland is telling the truth on his accusation. In author Gerald Posner's book, *Case Closed*, he writes that Dr. Jenkins told him what happened. "When Bob McClelland came into the room, he asked me, 'Where are his wounds?' And at that time I was operating a breathing bag with my right hand, and was trying to take the President's temporal pulse, and I had my finger on his left temple. Bob thought I pointed to the left temple as the wound" (Posner, *Cased Closed*, p.313 footnote). It's rather amazing that Jenkins would say this when close to thirty years earlier, when he testified on the record before the Warren Commission, he said, "I don't know whether this is right or not, but I thought there was a wound on the *left* temporal area" (6 H 48).

lem and avoids having his star witness, Dr. McClelland, look very confused and non-credible simply by changing McClelland's words "left temple" to "right temple" in his book, *The Killing of a President*.[166]

When I called Dr. McClelland the following evening to discuss further one of the points he had made, he quickly told me he was glad I had called because "since we hung up last night, I've had some second thoughts about the exact location of the exit wound." Unlike the many conspiracy theorists who have exploited Dr. McClelland's obvious errors to their benefit, he told me, "I don't question the integrity of all the pathologists who disagree with me" (he wasn't so kind to his colleague, Dr. Charles Crenshaw: "Chuck had a lot of problems and fabricated a lot of things"), saying, for instance, that he and the three autopsy surgeons were "obviously looking at the same head and the same wound," but that the area on the head where they placed the wound differed because of "the different positions from which we viewed it and also because of the different interpretations of what we saw, which is normal." But he made a major concession in an effort to reconcile his position with theirs. "I have to say that the sketch I first drew for Josiah Thompson's book a few years after the assassination was misleading. Since last night, I've been thinking that I placed the large hole in the president's head farther back than it really was, maybe. It may have been a bit more forward." When I asked him where he now put it, he said, "Partially in the occipital region and partly in the right back part of the parietal bone" (which I told him was actually consistent with the original position he took in his Warren Commission testimony), but he still insisted that this large exit wound was not to the right frontal area of the president's skull as concluded by all the pathologists.

Dr. McClelland told me he believes there were two gunmen, Oswald and someone else, and further believes that "the CIA and FBI, mostly the CIA, were behind the conspiracy to kill Kennedy, and they brought in the Mafia, who carried out the killing." He said he didn't know but suspects that "the Warren Commission covered up the conspiracy." On that note, I thanked the good doctor for his time and bid him a good night.[167]

Even apart from Dr. McClelland's wandering completely off the reservation in the sketch he drew for Josiah Thompson, what is the explanation for several of the other Parkland doctors erroneously thinking that the large exit wound was to the right rear of the president's head as opposed to the right frontal region, where all the medical and scientific evidence proved it to be? Dr. Michael Baden, the chief forensic pathologist for the HSCA, has what I believe to be the answer, one whose logic is solid.[*] "The head exit wound was not in the parietal-occipital area, as the Parkland doctors said. They were wrong," he told me. "That's why we have autopsies, photographs, and X-rays to determine things like this. *Since the*

---

[*]I sought the advice of Dr. Baden on many of the medical issues in this case because of his background and qualifications. A board-certified forensic pathologist who is presently the codirector of the New York State Police Medicolegal Investigative Unit, he has an impressive curriculum vitae. Among many other things, he has been the chief medical examiner for New York City; been the president of the Society of Medical Jurisprudence; held professional appointments at several institutions of higher learning, including New York Law School and the Albert Einstein Medical School; and served as an expert in forensic pathology on numerous prominent cases, among them the examination of the remains of Czar Nicholas of Russia and his family, the reexamination of the Lindbergh kidnapping and murder, autopsies of the victims of TWA Flight 800, and the O. J. Simpson and Claus von Bulow murder trials. He has written a number of articles in medicolegal professional publications and coauthored the book *Unnatural Death: Confessions of a Medical Examiner*. Most importantly, of course, I sought him out because he was the chairman of the nine-member forensic pathology panel of the HSCA's investigation into the deaths of President Kennedy and Dr. Martin Luther King Jr., a chairmanship that shows the very high esteem he has in his profession.

thick growth of hair on Kennedy's head hadn't been shaved at Parkland, there's no way for the doctors to have seen the margins of the wound in the skin of the scalp. All they saw was blood and brain tissue adhering to the hair. And that may have been mostly in the occipital area because he was lying on his back and gravity would push his hair, blood, and brain tissue backward,* so many of them probably assumed the exit wound was in the back of the head. But clearly, from the autopsy X-rays and photographs and the observations of the autopsy surgeons, the exit wound and defect was not in the occipital area. There was no defect or wound to the rear of Kennedy's head other than the entrance wound in the upper right part of his head."[168]

Indeed, in a letter to conspiracy theorist Vince Palamara on October 13, 1998, Dr. Ronald Jones wrote that "President Kennedy had very thick dark hair that *covered the injured area*." Where was that injured area? Jones said it was only his "opinion" (i.e., without being able to see it) that the large defect "was in the occipital area in the back of the head."

A few other explanatory observations relative to Dr. Baden's comments: Dr. Marion Jenkins, the Parkland anesthesiologist, says, "I was standing at the head of the [cart] in the position the anesthesiologist most often assumes closest to the patient's head . . . The President's great shock of hair and the location of the head wound was such that it was not visible to those standing [on] each side of the gurney where they were carrying out their resuscitative maneuvers."[169] And Dr. Carrico, the first Parkland doctor to treat the president, told me, "The president was lying on his back, so we couldn't see the rear portion of his head. Consequently, what we did see appeared to be further back than it was since we were not viewing it in relation to his whole head. But really, none of us were looking closely at where the defect was and making mental notes. We were just trying to save his life."[170] And Dr. Charles Baxter told author Gerald Posner that Kennedy "had such a bushy head of hair, and blood and all in it, you couldn't tell what was wound versus dried blood or dangling tissue."[171]

Not only does Baden's observation make immense sense, but the photographs of the dead president bear him out. Two terribly gruesome autopsy photos of the president's face and head (which, as previously indicated, I chose not to put in this book) that appear in Robert Groden's *Killing of a President*[172] clearly show that the president's thick hair, drenched in blood, is all going in the direction of the rear—matted tufts of bloody hair literally extending way beyond the rear of his head.

Author Jim Moore has added another possible explanation for the error made by many of the Parkland doctors. He points out that since the president was lying on his back and they could not see the rear of his head, most described the large exit wound as being to the right *rear* of the president's head "because the *side* of the president's head was the most rearward portion of the skull they observed."[173]

I n addition to the testimony of the Parkland doctors, conspiracy theorists cite the recollections and testimony of several eyewitnesses in attendance at the autopsy as further "proof" that the exit wound was to the right rear or back of the president's head.† Once

---

*Baden said that Kennedy's head wasn't even shaved of its hair at the time of the autopsy, and hence, any observations by onlookers of the autopsy (as opposed, he said, to the autopsy surgeons themselves, who were working directly with the president's head) would also likely have been skewed.

†In an assertion by the HSCA forensic pathology panel that is so incorrect it can only be categorized as strange, someone (no one, thus far, has admitted authorship) wrote, "In disagreement with the observations of the Parkland doctors are the 26 people present at the autopsy. *All* of those interviewed who attended the

again, these eyewitness accounts (some of them, recollections over three decades old) are supposed to supersede the autopsy photographs and X-rays that show the large defect was primarily to the right front. Remarkably, the list by conspiracy theorists of eyewitnesses to this supposed back-of-the-head exit wound is so expansive it frequently even includes two of the autopsy pathologists, Drs. Humes and Boswell, who we know concluded that the bullet exited in the *right front of the skull*. Apparently the fact that they mentioned in their autopsy summary that the large exit defect "extended somewhat into the temporal and *occipital regions*" got them a ticket into the club of *rear*-exit believers. Indeed, even Captain John H. Stover, commanding officer of the Naval Medical School, who reported in 1978 that he saw "a wound on the *top of the head*,"[174] qualified for the back-of-the-head list.

The list includes three Secret Service agents (William Greer, Roy Kellerman, and Clint Hill) and two FBI agents (James Sibert and Francis O'Neill) whose testimony points to a right-rear or back-of-the-head exit wound.[175]*

The above is not to suggest that all of the lay witnesses at the autopsy thought the exit wound was to the right rear or back of the president's head. For instance, James Curtis Jenkins, a lab technician during the autopsy, told HSCA investigators that the large head wound was to the "middle temporal region back to the occipital."[176] Chester Boyers, the chief petty officer in charge of the lab at Bethesda who was present at the autopsy, said the exit wound was to the "right side of the head above the right eyebrow and [extending?] towards the rear."[177] Richard A. Lipsey, a personal aide to General Wehle, told the HSCA it was obvious that a bullet "entered the back of his head and exited on the right side of his head."[178]

Also, at the London trial, Paul O'Connor, the naval hospital corpsman who assisted in the president's autopsy, testified he "assumed" that the bullet to the president's head "had hit him from the rear and had come out the front only because of what other physical evidence was present." When I said to O'Connor, "You told me over the phone that this large massive defect to the right frontal area of the president's head gave all appearances of being an exit wound, is that correct?"

O'Connor: "Yes, on the front."[179]

None of the aforementioned people or witnesses had a close-up view of the president's

---

autopsy corroborated the general location of the wounds as depicted in the [autopsy] photographs; none had differing accounts" (7 HSCA 37). However, though they clearly were wrong, several autopsy witnesses thought the exit wound was to the right rear or rear of the president's head.

*Sibert's 1977 drawings for the HSCA place the head wound square in the back of the head. Shown the drawings in his appearance before the ARRB in 1997, Sibert, who didn't recall making them, said, "I would have moved [the wound on the back of the head] over a little bit to the right on the back of his head here, rather than dead center" (ARRB Transcript of Proceedings, Deposition of James W. Sibert, September 11, 1997, p.70). O'Neill's 1997 drawing for the AARB shows the exit wound encompassing the right-rear quadrant of the head (ARRB MD 86, Interview Report of Francis X. O'Neill, January 10, 1978, pp.10–11). In an October 24, 1978, affidavit to the HSCA, Sibert said there was "a large head wound in the upper back of the head." But in a November 8, 1978, affidavit to the HSCA, he said "the massive head wound pointed towards the right side of the head." It is instructive to note that there was an increased likelihood for Agents Sibert and O'Neill to make an error in the placement of the wound because as Sibert testified before the ARRB—and he told me in a telephone interview—he and O'Neill were standing next to each other at the head of the autopsy table, looking at the top of the president's head (as he lay on the autopsy table) rather than the side of his head. (Telephone interview of James Sibert by author on July 21, 2000; ARRB Transcript of Proceedings, Deposition of James W. Sibert, September 11, 1997, p.123) Dr. Boswell said in 1994 that the "FBI people . . . were never out of the morgue. They stayed there the entire time and . . . stayed on the telephone [in a May 7, 1992, *JAMA* interview, Boswell said the agents were "talking on their radios to people outside the room"] all the time . . . They were causing an awful lot of distraction" (Transcript of taped telephone interview of Dr. J. Thornton Boswell by Dr. Gary Aguilar on March 8, 1994, p.7). And while causing a distraction they were obviously distracted themselves—hardly reliable, percipient witnesses to the precise location of the president's wounds.

head. Only four people in the autopsy room did, the three autopsy surgeons and John Stringer, the chief medical photographer for the navy at the autopsy who took the only photographs of the president's head. When I spoke to Stringer, he said there was "no question" in his mind that the "large exit wound in the president's head was to the right side of his head, above the right ear." And in an ARRB interview on April 8, 1996, Stringer said, "There was a fist-sized hole in the right side of his head above his ear."[180] Though, as we shall see later, Stringer's recollection of matters is questionable, he said he remembers this very clearly. When I asked him if there was any large defect to the rear of the president's head, he said, "No. All there was was a small entrance wound to the back of the president's head. During the autopsy, Dr. Humes pointed out this entrance wound to everyone."[181]

So we see that all four people who were much closer to the president's head than anyone else, and whose business it was, as opposed to the many other people in the room, to know where the wounds were, have no question in their mind that the exit wound was to the right front side of the president's head, not the rear.

In the final analysis, it's difficult to accept the testimony of any of these lay witnesses as irrefutable truths given the fact that their accounts run directly contrary to the conclusions of the three autopsy surgeons and fourteen other pathologists whose position is supported by the autopsy photographs and X-rays. In other words, lay observations, notoriously problematic, have to yield to hard, scientific evidence.

One footnote to all of this, and a possible explanation for the claim by some of the autopsy eyewitnesses that the exit wound was farther back on the head than the photographs and X-rays show, is the fact that the condition of the head wound *changed as the autopsy progressed*. As Dr. Humes testified in 1964, the skull came apart "very easily" in the pathologists' hands as they conducted their examination. Some bone fragments fell into the head wound, others onto the autopsy table,[182] thereby necessarily causing an *enlargement* of the large exit defect, *including to the rear*. When we couple this with the fact that the president was lying on his back during the autopsy, and therefore, the blood and brain tissue would naturally fall toward the rear of the head, we would *expect* the head wound to appear differently to the autopsy witnesses, depending on their viewpoint and the time of their observation. Add to the mix a generous sprinkling of erroneous observations and a few outright fabrications (not uncommon in a case of this magnitude) and you have a recipe for the kind of contradictions that fertilize the growing number of unfounded allegations made year after year after year by conspiracy theorists.

Lest anyone still has any doubt as to the location of the large exit wound in the head, as indicated, the Zapruder film itself couldn't possibly provide better demonstrative evidence. The film proves conclusively, and beyond all doubt, where the exit wound was. Zapruder frame 313 (when the president's head exploded) and frame 328 (almost a second later) (see photo section) clearly show that the large, gaping exit wound was to the *right front* of the president's head.* *The back of his head shows no such large wound and clearly is completely intact.* And yet, silly conspiracy theorists cite witness after witness,

---

*Abraham Zapruder himself, who was looking through the zoom lens of his camera at the moment the president was struck in the head, testified that he saw the right side of Kennedy's head open up and brain matter spray out (7 H 571–572). In his office, within an hour of the shooting, Zapruder was interviewed by *Dallas Times Herald* writer Darwin Payne. Payne's shorthand notes reflect Zapruder telling him that blood was coming out the "side" of Kennedy's head, that it "looked like blobs out of his *temple . . .* forehead" (Trask, *National Nightmare*, p.97). And at about 2:10 on the afternoon of the assassination, during a live interview with Dallas's WFAA-TV program director, Jay Watson, Zapruder put his hand to the right front side of his head to demonstrate where he saw the president's head "practically open up" (Trask, *Pictures of the Pain*, pp.77–78).

and write article after article—even in prestigious academic journals—alleging that the large exit wound was to the back of the president's head. There is simply nothing that will take the air out of their tires of advocacy for the conspiracy position.

The president's throat wound has received an equal amount of attention from critics seeking to knock down the conclusion that the president was struck by a bullet fired from behind. And again, as in the case with the president's head wound, conspiracy theorists have seized on the testimony of some of the Parkland doctors, as well as statements a few of them made to the press around the time of the president's death, for the proposition that the wound to the president's throat was an entrance wound rather than an exit wound, as the evidence clearly shows it was. "It is clear that the Parkland Hospital doctors [formed] an opinion of the anterior neck wound—they thought it was an entrance wound," says Sylvia Meagher in her book *Accessories after the Fact*.[183] "The [Parkland] doctors were unanimous [not true, as we shall see] about the nature of the throat wound: it was an entrance wound," Mark Lane asserts in his book *Rush to Judgment*.[184] Another conspiracy theorist, Harrison Edward Livingstone, writes that "all the doctors in Dallas" who saw the wound thought "it was a wound of entry."[185] The conspiracy theorists, convinced the shot came from the front, and citing the Warren Commission's position that Oswald was to the president's right rear in the Book Depository Building at the time of the shooting, conclude that Oswald could not have fired the bullet that caused the throat wound. And therefore, they argue, he is completely innocent, or at a minimum, there were two gunmen and hence a conspiracy.

What has complicated the correct characterization of the wound and kept this from being a nonissue is the fact that as previously indicated, Dr. Malcolm Perry, a Parkland Hospital doctor, used the wound in the president's throat as the point to make his tracheotomy incision (cutting into the president's trachea, or windpipe, to enable the insertion of a tube to maintain breathing), and in the process enlarged the wound, destroying most of its original configuration.[186] Indeed, when the Warren Commission asked Dr. Humes, "In spite of the incision made by the tracheotomy, was there *any* evidence left of the exit aperture?" he answered (erroneously), "Unfortunately not that we could ascertain, sir."[187] But although the tracheotomy had destroyed much of the exit wound's original configuration, it had not completely obscured the wound. Looking at black-and-white photographs of the wound to the throat (which were sharper and clearer than similar color photographs), the nine-member panel of forensic pathologists for the HSCA noticed "a semicircular *missile* defect near the center of the lower margin of the tracheotomy incision." The committee said it was an "*exit* defect."[188] Dr. Baden, who headed up the HSCA panel, said, "The semicircular defect was caused by the exiting bullet. I saw it right away in the photographs, even though they weren't of the best quality."[189] The four-member 1968 Clark Panel of physicians and pathologists also saw a portion of the exit wound that was not obliterated by the tracheotomy.[190]

Before we look at and evaluate the observations of the Parkland doctors, it should be noted that by their own admission, they did not even attempt to make a determination of whether the wound to the president's throat was an entrance or exit wound. They were only trying to save his life.[191] Among the later pathologists who *did* attempt to determine whether it was an entrance or exit wound, all fifteen of them not only concluded that it was an exit wound, but that it was the exit wound of the bullet that entered the president's upper right back.[*] And as I pointed out in my cross-examination of Dr. Cyril Wecht at the docu-trial in London, even Wecht, a member of the nine-doctor HSCA panel and the leading medical voice for years for the conspiracy theorists, agreed in his testimony before the HSCA that the throat wound was a wound of exit when he conceded, by necessary implication, that no bullet that struck the president entered from the front. "The president was struck definitely twice," Wecht said, "one bullet entering in the *back*, and one bullet entering in the *back* of [his] head."[192]

Dr. Perry testified before the Warren Commission that he did not know whether the throat wound was an entrance or exit wound.[193] However, at a press conference at Parkland Hospital commencing at 3:16 p.m. on the day of the assassination, he told the assembled media that "the wound appeared to be an entrance wound in the front of the throat."[194] Confronted with this apparent contradiction when he was interviewed by the HSCA, he tried to explain his press conference remarks by saying that "I thought it looked like an entrance wound because it was small, but I didn't look for any others, and so that was just a guess."[195][†] In a subsequent interview with author Gerald Posner on April 2, 1992, Dr. Perry said that the press "took my statement at the press conference out of context. I did say it looked like an entrance wound since it was small, but *I qualified it by saying that I did not know where the bullets came from*. I wish now that I had not speculated. Everyone ignored my qualification."[196]

The reason the press ignored Dr. Perry's qualification is that he did not, in fact, make one. To the contrary, the transcript of the press conference, which Posner had and cites as a source, reflects just the opposite of what Perry told Posner and what Posner led his readers to believe. In response to the question "Which way was the bullet coming on the neck wound?" from a member of the press, Perry answered, "It appeared to be coming *at him*." (In Dr. Perry's mind, he may have *felt* unsure about what type of wound the wound to the throat was. His telling Dr. Robert McClelland, another attending physician, that the wound had "somewhat irregular margins," which is indicative of an exit wound, supports this. But he never qualified at the press conference, at any point, his conclusion it was an entrance wound.)[197][‡]

Dr. Charles Carrico was the first Parkland doctor to see the president and to start the resuscitation effort. He testified before the Warren Commission that he made no determination whether the throat wound was an entrance or exit wound. "It could have been either," he said.[198] However, in his 4:20 p.m. Parkland Memorial Hospital "Admission

---

[*]The fifteen were the three pathologists who conducted the autopsy of the president on the night of the assassination (CE 387, 16 H 983), the nine doctors in 1978 on the forensic pathology panel of the HSCA, and the three pathologists in 1968 on the Clark Panel (ARRB MD 59, Clark Panel Report, 1968, p.15). The 1975 Rockefeller Commission did not address itself to the back and throat wounds, only focusing in on the allegation by conspiracy theorists that Kennedy was struck in the head by a shot fired from the grassy knoll.

[†]Of course, when a bullet entering the body passes through soft tissue before it exits, the exit wound is going to be as small or almost as small (and as circular or almost as circular) as the entrance wound. Striking bone damages the bullet, normally causing it to leave a ragged, irregular, and larger exit hole. The bullet that entered the president's body in the upper right part of his back only passed through soft tissue before exiting from his throat (CE 387, 16 H 983).

[‡]The Warren Commission, in a transparent effort to reconcile Perry's remarks with its ultimate conclusion, selectively cited the November 23 *New York Herald Tribune*'s account of the press conference, which quoted Perry as only saying it was "possible" the wound in the throat was an entrance wound (WR, pp.90–91). But Tom Wicker of the *New York Times*, who attended the conference, got the distinct impression from Perry that the wound "had the appearance of a bullet's entry" (*New York Times*, November 23, 1963, p.2; Gary L. Aguilar and Kathy Cunningham, "How Five Investigations into JFK's Medical/Autopsy Evidence Got It Wrong," May 2003, p.2, available at http://www.history-matters.com/essays/jfkmed/How5Investigations/).

Note" on November 22, 1963, he described the wound as a "penetrating" wound.[199] Conspiracy theorists have alleged that by the word *penetrating*, Carrico meant an entrance wound (e.g., "Dr. Carrico . . . described the throat wound as one of entrance, using the phrase: [a] small *penetrating* wound").[200] When I asked Dr. Carrico what he meant by the word *penetrating*, he responded, "I was not using the word *penetrating* to be synonymous with entry, because I didn't know at the time whether it was an entry or exit wound. Although Mr. Webster might not agree, we physicians differentiate the mechanism causing injury into two broad groups. One is *blunt* trauma, which is, for instance, broken bones from car wrecks, bruises and lacerations from aggravated assault, or other wounds caused by machine or blunt force or instrument. The other is *penetrating* trauma, which is a wound caused usually by a knife or gunshot, or by impalement from other sharp objects."[201] Although Carrico was unable to determine whether the throat wound was an entrance or exit wound, he did observe that the wound was "ragged,"[202] virtually a sure sign of an exit wound as opposed to an entrance wound, which is usually round and devoid of ragged edges.

Several points should be kept in mind about the observations of Drs. Perry and Carrico. Neither was a pathologist. In fact, of the many doctors in the resuscitation room at Parkland Hospital, none were pathologists,[203] much less forensic pathologists, whose specialty is determining, for legal purposes, the cause of death and, among other things, the nature (e.g., entrance as opposed to exit) of wounds. To do this, forensic pathologists examine the track of the bullet through the victim's body, examine the victim's clothing, take measurements and photographs, and so on. The Parkland doctors did none of these things. In fact, as recently as 1992, all four of the principal doctors on the medical team that treated the president at Parkland (Drs. Marion "Pepper" Jenkins and Charles Baxter as well as Perry and Carrico) emphasized, in an interview with *JAMA*, that their experiences in the trauma room at Parkland Hospital did not qualify them to reach conclusions about the direction from which the fatal missiles were fired—that is, whether the wounds were entry or exit wounds.[204] Indeed, Dr. Perry, thirty-four years old at the time, had just completed his residency the previous year, and Dr. Carrico, only twenty-eight, was still a resident at Parkland, which means he hadn't even yet completed all of his training to become certified in his specialty of surgery.[205] Why, one may ask, were such young and relatively inexperienced doctors given the responsibility of saving the president's life? (The conspiracy theorists have overlooked a natural argument for them: Parkland Hospital may have been in on the conspiracy to make sure the president died.) The reason is that nearly all the senior doctors at Parkland were attending a medical conference in Galveston, and only relatively junior doctors were available at Parkland to treat the president.[206]

Most importantly by far, the Parkland doctors, as previously alluded to, weren't there to determine the nature of the president's wounds. Dr. Perry said that whether the wounds were entrance or exit wounds "really made very little difference [to us]. Some things must take precedence and priority, and in this instance the airway and the bleeding [had to] be controlled."[207] "We were trying to save a life, not worrying about entry and exit wounds," Dr. Carrico told *JAMA* in the 1992 interview, echoing his 1964 testimony before the Warren Commission that "this was an acutely ill patient and all we had time to do was to determine what things were life-threatening right then and attempt to resuscitate him . . . after which a more complete examination would be carried out [by others]."[208]

Question by Warren Commission counsel: "Why did you not make an effort to determine the track of the bullets?"

Carrico: "The time to do this was not available. The examination conducted was to try to establish what life-threatening situations were present and to correct these."[209] *New York Times* White House correspondent Tom Wicker, who was at the press conference at Parkland when the media was informed of Kennedy's death, wrote that the doctors "gave us copious details, particularly as to the efforts they had made to resuscitate the president. They were less explicit about the wounds, explaining that the body had been in their hands only a short time and they had little time to examine [them] closely."[210]

Illustrating the rushed circumstances, Dr. Perry told *JAMA* in the 1992 interview, "Jim [Carrico] was having trouble inserting the endotracheal tube because of the wound to the trachea and I didn't even wipe off the blood before doing a 'trach.' I grabbed a knife and made a quick and large incision."[211]

Briefly, the following Parkland doctors, in addition to Perry and Carrico, gave an opinion on the nature of the president's throat wound, or passed on hearsay information about the wound:

> Dr. Charles Baxter: "We . . . did not determine at that time whether this represented an entry or an exit wound. Judging from the caliber of the rifle that [was] later found . . . this would more resemble a wound of entry. However . . . depending upon what a bullet of such caliber would pass through, the tissues it would pass through on the way to the [throat], I think that the wound could well represent either an exit or entry wound."[212]
>
> Dr. Marion Jenkins: "I thought this was a wound of exit because it was not a clean wound, and by 'clean,' [I mean] clearly demarcated, round."[213]
>
> Dr. Robert McClelland: "The neck wound, when I first arrived, was [already] converted into a tracheotomy incision . . . The description that [Dr. Perry] gave me was . . . a very small injury, with clear-cut, although somewhat irregular margins."[214]
>
> Dr. Ronald Jones: "[The] small hole in anterior midline of neck [was] thought to be a bullet entrance wound."[215]
>
> Dr. Gene Akin: "[The wound] was slightly ragged around the edges . . . The thought flashed through my mind that this might have been an entrance wound. I immediately thought it could also have been an exit wound."[216]

Undoubtedly, one of the main reasons, if not *the* main reason, why the Parkland doctors were clearly confused as to whether the throat wound was a wound of entry or exit, with several actually believing it was an entry wound, is the simple fact that none of them were aware at the time of the corresponding wound (the real entrance wound) in the president's back. "We were not aware," Dr. Carrico testified before the Warren Commission, "of the missile wound to the back . . . *We knew of no other entrance wound*."[217] Common sense tells us that seeing only the wound to the front of the president's neck, the Parkland doctors would instinctively have been more inclined to think of it as an entrance wound. Almost anyone would be so predisposed. But if the Parkland doctors had been aware of the corresponding wound to the president's back, and particularly that it was small and oval with clean and not ragged edges,[218] the very strong likelihood is that they all would have concluded that the throat wound was the exit wound every pathologist later found it to be.

Why weren't the Parkland doctors aware of the wound to the president's back? Because they did not turn the president's body over. Why didn't they? Again, they weren't there to examine bullet wounds and their trajectory, but were engaged in a frantic effort to save the president's life. And turning the president's body over to examine his back for bullet wounds when you're right in the middle of an attempt to save his life would be clearly counterproductive. As Dr. Perry testified when asked by Commission counsel Arlen Specter why he didn't turn the president's body over, "At that point it was necessary to attend to the emergent procedure, and a satisfactory effective airway is uppermost in such a condition."

Specter: "Did you *ever* turn him over?"

Dr. Perry: "I did not."[219]

When Specter asked Dr. Carrico, "Why did you not take the time to turn him over?" Carrico replied, "[A] thorough inspection would have involved . . . considerable time which at this juncture was not available. [It] would have involved washing and cleaning the back, and this is not practical in treating an acutely injured patient. You have to determine which things . . . are immediately life-threatening and cope with them."

Specter: "Was any effort made to inspect the president's back *after* he had expired?"

Carrico: "No, sir."

Specter: "And why was no effort made at that time to inspect his back?"

Carrico: "I suppose nobody really had the heart to do it."[220]

Carrico told me, "Once the president died, we discontinued all examination of the president's body. That was for the medical examiner. It would have been needless meddling on our part."[221] Dr. Jenkins spoke similarly. Explaining why the president's body was never turned over, he said, "I think as we pronounced the president dead, those . . . who were there just sort of melted away; well, I guess 'melted' is the wrong word, but we felt like we were intruders and left. I'm sure that this [would have been] beyond our prerogative and . . . [it] would have been meddlesome on anybody's part after death to have done any further search."[222]

The very nature of an emergency trauma room at a hospital is such that forensically precise and accurate descriptions of the character of a gunshot wound cannot be expected. In fact, a 1993 article in *JAMA* reported that "the odds that a trauma specialist will correctly interpret certain fatal gunshot wounds are no better than the flip of a coin." A study conducted by investigators at Bowman Gray School of Medicine at Wake Forest University in Winston-Salem, North Carolina, from 1987 to 1992, compared the postmortem findings of a board-certified forensic pathologist with the medical records of emergency medicine physicians, trauma surgeons, and neurosurgeons. It was discovered that out of forty-six cases, trauma specialists made errors in 52 percent, either in differentiating the exit and entrance wound or in determining the number of bullets. In 15 percent of the cases, the trauma specialist made both types of error. As expected, multiple gunshot wounds (the situation with the president) were more often misinterpreted, accounting for 74 percent of the errors. Even single gunshot wounds were misclassified in 37 percent of the cases.[223]

Even under the most optimum of circumstances, people's perceptions of what they think they saw are more often than not seriously conflicting. For instance, there's the famous law school experiment where the professor has someone run into the classroom and do several things (such as speak some words, pick up a book, turn over a small trash can, etc.), then immediately run out. The students, sitting calmly in their seats with nothing to do except observe what is taking place in front of them, give wildly divergent descriptions of the person, his clothing, and his conduct. Yet here we have the Parkland doctors, in the middle of their desperate attempt to save the life of the most powerful man on earth, and with absolutely no need or desire on their part to determine the correct physical characteristics of his wounds, and the conspiracy theorists expect them, in the chaotic frenzy of the moment, to make observations that should be treated like immutable mosaic truths, trumping photographs and X-rays and subsequent contrary conclusions by the autopsy surgeons and all other pathologists who have studied and examined the available evidence.

Though conspiracy theorists are almost unanimous in believing that the president was shot from the front and his throat wound was an entrance wound, they are strangely silent as to what happened to this bullet after it entered the president's throat. Unlike the fatal head wound, which most conspiracists also say came from a shot from the front and exited to the rear of the president's head, they don't say what happened to the bullet that entered the president's throat from the front. Since no bullet was found inside the president's body at the time of the autopsy, by definition, it would have had to exit the president's body. But where? Virtually the only argument the conspiracists have ever made about this bullet is the contention, by some of them, that it was the "missile" given to the FBI agents by Dr. Humes at the time of the autopsy. But they don't even contend this anymore since the agents said it was not a bullet, only two fragments, and the naval corpsman who typed up the word *missile* has conceded that it was not a missile, only fragments, and he had made a mistake.[224] Moreover, it would be virtually impossible for a bullet entering the soft tissue of the neck at a speed of two thousand feet per second to stop inside the neck and not exit the body.

And since the conspiracy theorists have never claimed[225] that the wound to the upper right back of the president was not an entrance wound but actually the wound of exit for the bullet that entered his throat, their conspicuous and glaring lack of a theory or even an argument at all as to what became of this bullet should alone convince them that their contention of a bullet striking the president in the throat from the front is entirely without merit. Talk about a magic bullet—this one didn't change flight in midair as they claim the bullet in the Warren Commission's single-bullet theory did. Instead, it simply vanished.

One of the most outlandish allegations made regarding the president's wounds came from Parkland doctor Charles A. Crenshaw, who had become an icon to the conspiracy theorists before his death in 2001. A hardcover publisher sent Crenshaw's unpublished manuscript about the Kennedy assassination to me in 1991 for my view of whether there was any merit to Crenshaw's charges. I responded that I didn't believe there was, and they passed on publishing it. But he got it published in paperback with a different publisher the next year and it became a *New York Times* best seller.

Although the four main Parkland doctors who attended to the dying president (Perry, Carrico, Jenkins, and Baxter) now all agree that, in Carrico's words, "nothing we observed contradicts the autopsy finding that the bullets were fired from above and behind by a high-velocity bullet,"[226] in Crenshaw's book, *JFK: Conspiracy of Silence*, he says that before the president died, he observed "two frontal-entry bullet wounds," charging that there was a later alteration of the wounds by someone to make it look like the shots came from the rear. "There was something rotten in America in 1963," he writes. Crenshaw charges that Dr. Perry's tracheotomy was later "enlarged and mangled, as if someone had conducted another procedure. It looked to be the work of a butcher. No doubt, someone had gone through a great deal of trouble to show a different story than we had seen at Parkland."[227]

Even though the grief and mourning in the air of Trauma Room One must have been thick enough to cut, and even though the wound to Kennedy's throat had been virtually obliterated by the tracheotomy, and even though the direction of fire wasn't yet an issue to anyone, much less the people in Trauma Room One, Crenshaw, just a junior resident at Parkland, said that before "we placed him [Kennedy] in a coffin . . . I looked at the [neck] wound again. I wanted to know and remember this for the rest of my life. And the rest of my life I will always know he was shot from the front."[228]

Crenshaw was even more unbelievable in his remarks when the FBI interviewed him in 1992. He claimed he supervised the placing of the president's body into the coffin, but that prior to this, even though the president had already died, he moved the president's head and placed his fist next to the large exit wound (which he first said was in the center of the back of the president's head, then said it was in the right read of his head) in order to compare the wound's relative size, and he found the wound to be about the size of his fist.[229] The probability that Crenshaw, at that time, would have any reason or desire to do what he did, or that his superiors would permit a junior resident like him to disturb the president's corpse to measure the exit wound with his fist, is virtually nonexistent.

Perhaps Crenshaw's main charge is that all of his colleagues at Parkland knew the truth and deliberately engaged in a conspiracy of silence. "I believe," he wrote, "there was a common denominator in our silence—a fearful perception that to come forward with what we believed to be the medical truth would be asking for trouble . . . I reasoned that anyone who would go so far as to eliminate the President of the United States would surely not hesitate to kill a doctor."[230] But he gave no reason why he decided, after almost *twenty-nine years*, to finally enlighten the world with his knowledge of what happened.

Some in the anti-conspiracy community have questioned whether Crenshaw was even in Trauma Room One, and cite as support Dr. Perry's statement to *JAMA* in the 1992 issue that "in 1963, Chuck Crenshaw was a junior resident and he absolutely did not participate in a meaningful way in the attempt to resuscitate the President . . . I do not remember even seeing him in the room."[231] However, as conspiracy theorists have pointed out, Dr. Crenshaw *was* present, a fact confirmed by several Parkland doctors and nurses in their testimony before the Warren Commission. Yet, rather than being supportive, their testimony undermines Crenshaw's claims. For instance, two provided details that are quite damaging. Dr. Robert McClelland told the Commission that he was "showing a film on surgical techniques to a group of students and residents on the second floor of Parkland Hospital in the surgical suite [when] I was notified [by Dr. Charles Crenshaw] of the fact that President Kennedy was being brought to the Parkland emergency room after being shot."[232] McClelland then accompanied Crenshaw to Trauma Room One, where Kennedy had been taken. Contrary to Crenshaw's later claims, McClelland testified that by the time they arrived, Dr. Perry *had already made the tracheotomy incision through the throat wound*,[233] which would have precluded Crenshaw from seeing the wound and identifying it as a wound of entrance. When confronted with McClelland's testimony in 1994, Crenshaw claimed that McClelland must have "looked away" just as Dr. Perry made the incision, but that he (Crenshaw) saw the bullet hole for a "fraction of a second." This admitted split-second assessment of the bullet hole was made despite the fact that Crenshaw had no training or background as a pathologist, forensic or otherwise.[234]

And as to Crenshaw's actual role in the resuscitation efforts, Dr. Kenneth E. Salyer told the Warren Commission, "Dr. Crenshaw participated to about the extent that I did. We were occupied in making sure an I.V. was going, and hanging up a bottle of blood . . . That's the reason I remember him specifically because we were sort of working there together on that."[235] Yet, to listen to Crenshaw one would think he was one of the lead doctors. In his book, he says things like, "I removed the President's shoes and right sock, and began cutting off his suit trousers . . . I made a small incision to expose the saphenous vein . . . I inserted a catheter toward the heart, then tied the space between the vessel and the catheter to prevent leakage," and so on.[236] Crenshaw ultimately blamed his coauthors, Jens Hansen and J. Gary Shaw, two longtime conspiracy theorists, for taking "poetic license" and inflating his role in the attempt to save Kennedy's life.[237]

The four main Parkland doctors, in a May 27, 1992, interview in *JAMA*, were unanimous in their rejection of Crenshaw's allegations about a cover-up by the Parkland doctors. Perry said, "When I first heard about Crenshaw's claims, I was considering a lawsuit, but after I saw Charles on TV one day, all my anger melted. It was so pathetic to see him on TV saying this bogus stuff to reach out for his day in the sun that I ended up feeling sorry for him." He added, "Crenshaw says that the rest of us are part of a conspiracy of silence and that he withheld his information for twenty-nine years because of a fear his career would be ruined. Well, if he really felt he had valuable information and kept it secret for all those years, I find *that* despicable."[238] Dr. Baxter said that when Crenshaw's sensationalistic book came out, he and the other main Parkland doctors received calls from other members of the Parkland medical team who were on the scene on November 22, 1963, and "there has not been one call supporting [Crenshaw's] position." He added, "Charles and I grew up in Paris, Texas, and I've known him since he was three years old. His claims are ridiculous." Dr. Jenkins said, "Crenshaw's conclusions are dead-wrong."[239]

But what would motivate Crenshaw to make the outrageous charges he made? Dr. Carrico pointed out that Crenshaw himself inadvertently has given us the answer. On page 15 of *JFK: Conspiracy of Silence*, Crenshaw writes, "Many of us have dreamed that history's grand scheme will involve us in some far-reaching role or experience thrusting us into notoriety and dramatically changing our lives." Carrico said, "There's your answer, in Charles' own words. I don't have those kind of dreams."[240]

Crenshaw also claims in his book that two days after the assassination, while he was helping to save the life of Lee Harvey Oswald at Parkland Hospital, a nurse asked him to "take a telephone call in the supervisor's office." Crenshaw claims that none other than the president of the United States was on the line. He quotes President Johnson as telling him, "Dr. Crenshaw, I want a deathbed confession from the accused assassin. There's a man in the operating room who will take the statement. I will expect full cooperation in this matter." The man in the operating room, per Crenshaw, was a mysterious stranger, an Oliver Hardy look–alike "with a pistol hanging from his pocket." Oswald died, Crenshaw said, before any attempt to extract a confession from him could be made.[241] "Did that happen? Heavens no," Dr. Baxter says. "Imagine that, the President of the United States personally calls for Chuck Crenshaw."[242]

To be fair, Dr. Baxter's characterization that LBJ personally called for Crenshaw is inaccurate—as indicated, Crenshaw simply said that a nurse had asked him to take the call. Also, Dr. Phillip E. Williams, an intern administering fluids to Oswald's right leg, supported the basics of the story in 1992 (though he didn't say whether Crenshaw was the one who took the call), telling the *New York Times*, "I vividly remember someone said, and I can't say who it was, *the White House* is calling and President Johnson wants to know what the status of Oswald is." Williams added, however, that he didn't hear that LBJ wanted a confession and didn't know whether it was Johnson himself or a presidential aide who was on the phone.[243]*

However, the administrator at the hospital, Charles Jack Price, who supervised, among others, all the switchboard operators at Parkland, said he did not believe that any call had ever come through from President Johnson,[244] as Crenshaw alleged, and a switchboard operator who claimed, almost thirty years later, that Johnson called, failed to mention, in her detailed report to Price of the period November 22–24, 1963, receiving a call from the president of the United States, though she found the space in her report to mention the substance of calls from many everyday citizens. There's not even a reference to receiving a call from anyone at the White House. (For further discussion, see endnote.)

The capper on all of this is that in 1992, assassination researcher David Perry received from the LBJ Foundation at the LBJ Library in Austin, Texas, the "White House Detail" for November 24, 1963. The fifteen-page detail lists all telephone calls from the White House as well as all presidential appointments and activities on any given day. It does not show any phone call made from the White House, which would include calls from a mobile phone patched through the White House switchboard, to Parkland Hospital at any time on November 24, 1963.[245]†

As far out as Crenshaw's LBJ phone call story is, apparently his first story about the alleged call was ten times worse. Author Gus Russo writes in an e-mail to John McAdams on August 25, 2003, "When Oliver Stone was in Dallas prepping for [his movie] *JFK*, a number of us were around as 'technical advisors,' which was a bit of a joke, since Stone only listened to people with crazy conspiracy info. One night at the Stoneleigh [Hotel] . . . Stone ushered Gary Shaw [a coauthor of Crenshaw's later book, *JFK: Conspiracy of Silence*], Robert Groden and Crenshaw into his room. I was not invited, but I [later] pressed Shaw for info in the lobby. He was the first to tell me that LBJ ordered Oswald killed. Later, Crenshaw came down, and we happened to be in the Stoneleigh men's room at the same time . . . It was there that he told me that Johnson

---

*There is also testimony that may corroborate the presence of Crenshaw's "mysterious stranger," but once again the facts are less sensational. Homicide detective L. C. Graves, one of the two Dallas detectives who were escorting Oswald at the time he was shot by Ruby, testified that he rode in the ambulance to Parkland Hospital, changed into "one of those scrub uniforms and crepe-soled shoes," and stationed himself outside the second-floor operating-room door, where he was joined later by an FBI agent. Crenshaw may have been referring to Graves, who said he remained at the door until Oswald was declared dead, then made arrangements for an autopsy and security in the morgue. (13 H 9–10, WCT L. C. Graves)

†The first entry in the White House Detail for November 24, 1963, records an 8:30 a.m. breakfast in bed by the president and his wife at their home, "The Elms," and the entries end with a telephone call by the president from his home to a "Judge Moursand" at 11:15 p.m.

The relevant times for any alleged call by LBJ to the operating room at Parkland are from 11:32 a.m. (12:32 p.m. EST), when Oswald was brought into the emergency room at Parkland, to 11:42 a.m. (12:42 p.m. EST), when he was brought into the operating room, to 1:07 p.m. (2:07 p.m. EST), when Oswald was pronounced dead. (Times of Oswald at Parkland: "Three Patients at Parkland," p.71) The White House Detail entries between 12:26 p.m. and 2:19 p.m. EST, which would encompass the 12:32 p.m. to 2:07 p.m. time frame, are these: "12:26 p.m. After having coffee with members of the [St. Mark's Church] congregation, the President, accompanied by Mrs. Johnson, departed church; 12:35 p.m. Arrived at North Portico of the White House; 12:45 President Johnson called Secy. [of State Dean] Rusk, probably to have him join Pres. after ceremonies at the Capitol since Secy. Rusk did join Pres. at EOB [Executive Office Building] at 2:40 p.m.; 1:08 p.m. The President, accompanied by Mrs. Kennedy, Mrs. Johnson, The Attorney General, Caroline & John Jr. Kennedy and Colonel Jackson departed the White House in the Funeral Procession; 1:46 p.m. Arrived at Steps of the Capitol; 2:19 p.m. The President, accompanied by Colonel Jackson, departed the Capitol." (White House Detail, November 24, 1963)

had ordered the Parkland staff to 'kill the son-of-a-bitch.' It was decided to 'drown Oswald in his own blood,' i.e., transfuse him until his lungs collapsed."[246] Crenshaw told author Harrison Livingstone that his publisher had his two coauthors, Shaw and Jens Hansen, tone down in the book what Johnson actually told him.[247]

On November 22, 1992, Crenshaw and one of the two coauthors of his book, Gary Shaw, sued the American Medical Association, *JAMA*'s editor, George Lundberg, and the *JAMA* staff writer of the article who interviewed the Parkland doctors, Dennis Breo (there were other defendants, including the *Dallas Morning News*), for libel, asking for $35 million in damages. At the core of the lawsuit was Lundberg's statement to the media at a New York City press conference on May 19, 1992, that "the recent Crenshaw book is a sad *fabrication* based upon unsubstantiated allegations." In October of 1994, the defendants agreed to settle the case with Crenshaw and Shaw for monetary damages of $213,000 plus an agreement to publish a rebuttal article in *JAMA* by Crenshaw and Shaw, which they did in the May 24/31, 1995, edition. However, *JAMA* did not admit liability, made no apology, and published no retraction. Although conspiracy theorists see this settlement as a victory (i.e., that *JAMA* admitted Crenshaw was right), for anyone familiar with litigation, the above three facts could just as well indicate settlement of a "nuisance" lawsuit, a very common occurrence where the defendant settles the lawsuit with the plaintiff not because the defendant believes the suit has any merit, but because, in addition to the enormous aggravation and consumption of time of a protracted lawsuit, the legal fees for defending the case would end up costing more than the amount of the settlement. One of the defendants confirmed that this was in fact the case.[248] What *did* come out of the depositions of Lundberg and Breo prior to the settlement is that Breo did not interview Crenshaw prior to his article, which he clearly should have done, and did not read the testimony of the Parkland doctors before the Warren Commission, some of whom, as we have seen, established Crenshaw's presence at the autopsy.[249]

Before moving on to a key issue in the Kennedy case, let's once again observe that all of the disagreements among the many Parkland and Bethesda witnesses we've seen are normal and to be expected. But conspiracy theorists, consistently divorcing themselves from life and human experience, invariably conclude that disagreements add up to conspiracy and cover-up, when all they really add up to is life. When today's conspiracy theorists get tired playing with the sinister (in their mind) discrepancies in Kennedy's autopsy, I can give them a good start with Lincoln's autopsy, conducted by Assistant U.S. Surgeon General Dr. J. J. Woodward on April 15, 1865. In the first place, the autopsy report is only four paragraphs long, which, to me, is highly suspicious. Why so superficial? Whom was Woodward covering up for? By the way, Woodward said that the "ball" (slug) came to rest "in the white matter of the cerebrum just above the anterior portion of the left corpus striatum" (i.e., above the *left* eye). Baloney, said Dr. Charles Taft, acting assistant surgeon in the U.S. Army. He was present at the autopsy and said the bullet ended up above Lincoln's *right* eye. But then Taft later contradicted himself and said it was the left eye.[250] What does all this mean? One of two things. If Taft's first version is correct, John Wilkes Booth may not have been in the location the authorities said the assassin was in at the time Lincoln's killer pulled the trigger, meaning that Booth may not have killed Lincoln after all. (By the way, why did Taft later change his story? Did conspirators threaten him?) Or, since we know the bullet couldn't have ended up in both places, maybe it didn't end up in either, meaning that either Lincoln wasn't shot in the head, or there was a giant cover-up. I, for one, demand a reinvestigation.

One of the few legitimate questions that critics have raised about the president's wounds (legitimate in the sense that the solution, though simple, is not so obvious), and the very first and most troubling problem I had to deal with concerning the medical evidence in the docu-trial in London, was this: with respect to the president's back wound, how could a bullet coming from Oswald's rifle on the sixth floor of the Book Depository Building, and fired on a downward trajectory[*] enter the president's back, pass through soft tissue (and hence would not likely have been deflected upward or in any other direction), and yet emerge from an area of the throat that is slightly higher than the point of entry? I could see Gerry Spence arguing that it couldn't; ergo, the shot did not come from up above on the sixth floor, where I was alleging Oswald was, but from his front, where Oswald was not; that is, if the throat wound was not an exit wound, it would have had to be an entrance wound. As author Edward Jay Epstein put it in his 1966 book, *Inquest*, "The decisive question here is: Was the *entrance wound* in the back *above or below* the '*exit*' *wound* in the *throat*? [If the shot was fired from above], the entrance wound . . . *had* to be *above* the exit wound."[251]

Dr. Cyril Wecht, a member of the HSCA's forensic pathology panel, testified, "The bullet wound of entrance on the president's back—[when] lined up with the bullet wound of exit on the front of the president's neck, drawing a straight line—showed that vertically the bullet had moved slightly upward. *That is extremely important* . . . How in the world can a bullet be fired from a sixth-floor window, strike the president in the back, and yet have a slightly upward direction?"[252] The HSCA forensic panel did say that "when seen in the autopsy position, the outshoot wound was described as being at about the same height, (or slightly higher) relative to the inshoot wound."[253]

When I asked my pathologist for the London trial, the chief medical examiner for Dallas County, Dr. Charles Petty, about this problem, he explained to me during preparation for the trial that from an analysis of the Zapruder film, the HSCA determined that at the time the president was struck in the back, his upper body (though not his head) was inclined forward at "an approximate angle of 11 to 18 degrees" relative to the horizontal plane,[254] and *because of this*, Petty said, even though the bullet was at all times traveling downward (from the horizontal, i.e., relative to Elm Street) through the president's body, from an *anatomic* standpoint (i.e., if the president had been seated ramrod straight— referred to medically as the "anatomic" or autopsy position) it was proceeding on a slightly *upward* path through his body.[255] Therefore, diagrammatically, the bullet that struck the president *appears* to be going upward—in that it is exiting at a point on the president's body higher than where it entered—"but it is only doing so anatomically," he said, adding that "the president was *not* in an anatomic or autopsy position at the time he was shot. If he had been, the bullet, even anatomically speaking, would have exited at a lower point on his body then it entered, because it would have entered higher up." As the HSCA photographic panel of experts concluded, "The bullet was moving . . . downward by 4.0° relative to Kennedy *if he was sitting erect* (not inclined forward or aft)."[256]

I literally struggled for an hour or so that afternoon to comprehend the points Dr. Petty had told me, eventually using my left hand and my right index finger to grasp this

---

[*]The downward angle of a bullet striking President Kennedy between Zapruder frames 190 and 225, the period during which most agree he was hit, was found to range between 16 and 21 degrees, with the angle decreasing as the limousine moved farther away from the muzzle (6 HSCA 34; WR, pp.105–107; 5 H 162, WCT Lyndal L. Shaneyfelt; HSCA Report, p.82).

simple, yet deceptive reality. To follow what I did, extend the palm and fingers of your left hand (representing a human body) straight up and perpendicular to the ground. Now incline your hand backward, that is, to your left, illustrating the president leaning forward. Now take your right index finger, and keeping it straight, point it slightly downward, putting the tip against the palm of your open hand, the tip representing the descending bullet about to enter the body. Without moving your right finger but keeping the tip touching the palm, now straighten out your left hand. As you do so, though the tip of your right finger hasn't moved, it (bullet) is now touching the palm (entering the body) at a point higher up and would thereby exit at a lower point.[257] Likewise, if you start inclining your hand back again to the left, the same bullet (tip of finger) that would have entered high up on the hand (president's body) if the hand had been straight, now enters at a lower point on the hand (body), and hence would exit at a higher point. Indeed, the more the hand (body) is leaning to the left (forward), the lower the point of entry of the bullet and the higher the exit point.

See Exhibit A on this page for an illustration of the point that the *same* bullet enters and exits Kennedy's body at different points (causing three separate bullet tracks) dependent on the orientation of Kennedy's body at the moment of impact. As illustrated, if President Kennedy had been sitting absolutely straight up in the anatomic position at the time the bullet struck his body, it would have struck a point several inches higher than it actually did and exited a corresponding number of inches lower, in which case the whole issue of the exit point being higher than the entrance point would never have arisen.

Exhibit A

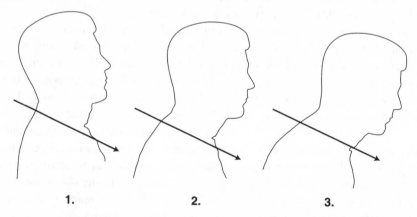

1.   **2.**   **3.**

1. Where the point of impact (on Kennedy's neck) would have been if the president had been sitting in the "anatomic position" at the time he was shot.

2. Where the point of impact would have been if the president had been leaning forward slightly at the time he was shot. Note that the exit wound would now be located higher up on the president's body.

3. This representation of the president's body, a reproduction of an HSCA sketch (HSCA volume 7, page 100), depicts the approximate orientation of the body at the time he was hit by the first bullet, although his head is tilted forward slightly more than it actually was as shown in the Zapruder film. The point of impact is now the lowest on the president's upper right back, and the exit wound is the highest.

But the above only tells you why the orientation of the president's body caused him to be struck precisely where he was, and why the bullet, passing through soft tissue, exited where it did (Exhibit A-3) as opposed to the two other bullet tracks (A-1 and A-2). Now let's take this *single* bullet track (A-3) and see how it looks as the orientation of the president's body changes. Exhibit B-1 (which is identical to A-3) is the actual track of the bullet through Kennedy's body, and it is downward. But as we elevate the president's head (B-2 and B-3), we see that the *same* bullet track, which is going downward through the president's body, is traveling upward anatomically.

With the exception of Dr. Wecht, the HSCA understood this issue, and as opposed to the Warren Commission (see later discussion), dealt with it properly.[258] But in the committee's attempt to explain this elusive and illusive concept visually (see Exhibit C),[259] it presented a sketch that, although correct, might be confusing to some. Although the three arrows (and lines) in Exhibit C are intended to represent the same single bullet track, without elucidation they could easily be erroneously viewed as depicting three separate bullet tracks, each one based on a different orientation of the president's body at the time of impact. Exhibit B eliminates this confusion, and was the one I intended to present to the jury in London if Spence raised the issue, which he did not.

Exhibit B

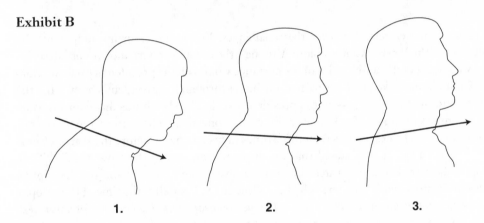

1.   2.   3.

Exhibit C

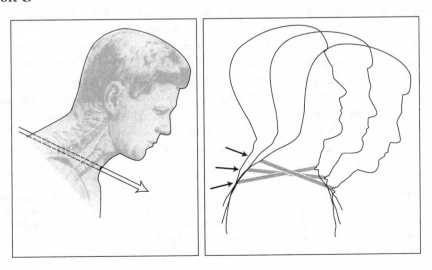

As indicated elsewhere in this book, the Kennedy family has not authorized any autopsy photographs to be released to the public. However, pirated autopsy photos have appeared in some conspiracy books on the assassination. Perhaps the clearest visual evidence of the fact that the entrance wound in the back was definitely above the exit wound in the throat appears in one of these photos taken of the left side of the president's head as he is lying on his back, his head on a metal headrest. Only the wound to the throat is visible, not the wound to his upper right back. However, it couldn't be clearer from this photo that the wound to the back was definitely *above* the exit wound in the throat.[260] And Dr. Humes, in his testimony before the Warren Commission, made it very clear that "the wound in the anterior [front] portion of the lower neck is physically lower than the point of entrance posteriorly [to the rear], sir."[261] Undoubtedly, one factor that has contributed to the mistaken illusion that the bullet entered at a point lower on the president's body than it exited is that one's back is *below* one's neck, and the bullet entered the president's back and exited in his throat (neck). But this ignores the reality (shown in the photo) that the *front* of one's neck extends farther downward (i.e., lower) into one's body than the back of one's neck does.

There is another related matter that challenges, like no other in my judgment, the integrity of the Warren Commission. Although the autopsy report and autopsy descriptive worksheet both put the point of the entrance wound on the president's *back*, the Warren Commission's sketch of the path of the bullet through the president's body[262] has the bullet entering the lower part of the president's *neck*. The sketch was made for the Warren Commission under Dr. Humes's direction from his recollection of the autopsy.[263] Moreover, Dr. Humes, no less than three times in his testimony before the Warren Commission, even specifically stated that the entry wound was in the "low *neck*."[264] This, despite the fact that, as indicated, his own autopsy report states,[265] and the descriptive sheet of the president's body made by his colleague Dr. Boswell at the time of the autopsy shows,[266] that the entrance wound was *not in the president's neck, but lower, in his upper right back*. In fact, the autopsy photographs of the wound clearly show that the wound was almost 2 inches lower than what is shown in the Warren Commission's sketch[267]—in other words, just about where the autopsy report says it is. And the HSCA concluded that the bullet entered "the upper right *back* of President Kennedy."[268]

In any event, I am compelled to conclude that the Warren Commission staff, in not challenging Dr. Humes's testimony and sketch on this point, either was medically naive in not knowing (or negligently overlooked the fact) that the autopsy report's description of the entry wound being in the "upper right posterior thorax just above . . . the scapula" (the shoulder blade) would put the wound in the upper right part of the back, not the low neck,* and hence did not realize that Dr. Humes's testimony and his sketch varied materially from his own autopsy report and the autopsy descriptive sheet; or, erroneously

---

*There is no question that the Warren Commission staff was aware of how Dr. Humes described the location of the wound in his autopsy report. For example, Commission counsel asked Dr. Malcolm Perry, "And have you noted in the autopsy report the reference to the presence of a wound on the upper right posterior thorax just above the upper border of the scapula?" (6 H 14, WCT Dr. Malcolm O. Perry; see also 2 H 351, WCT Dr. James J. Humes)

believing they had no plausible explanation for the exit wound being *ostensibly* higher than (or even approximately the same height as) the entrance wound, changed the location of the entrance wound for the purpose of solving the higher-exit-wound problem.

USA Today reported on July 3, 1997, that Warren Commission member Gerald R. Ford had changed the Commission staff's draft of its report from the language that the bullet had entered Kennedy's "*back* at a point slightly above the shoulder,"[269] to its entering "the back of his *neck*" in its final report.[270] To immediate charges by conspiracy theorists that Ford did this to cover up a conspiracy in the assassination, Ford is quoted in *USA Today* as responding, "My changes had nothing to do with a conspiracy theory. My changes were only an attempt to be more precise." Though Ford may have been responsible for changing the draft to reflect the entry wound as being in the neck, he would have had no influence over the sketch of the wound[271] showing the *same* erroneous point of entry. As stated earlier, the sketch was made under Dr. Humes's direction in preparation for his testimony before the Warren Commission.

In response to a June 15, 1999, letter from me in which I asked him to elaborate on *why* he made the subject change in the draft, former president Ford, in his June 28, 1999, reply to me, merely said, "I will not comment on any 'media' report of the deliberations of the [Warren] Commission" except that "I reaffirm my comment in the July 3, 1997, edition of *USA Today* that 'my changes had nothing to do with a conspiracy theory. My changes were only an attempt to be more precise.'" He added that "as the sole, surviving member of the Warren Commission, I reiterate my support for the Commission's fundamental conclusions. I re-emphasize my endorsement that Lee Harvey Oswald was the assassin and he acted alone. I also reaffirm that the Commission found no evidence of a conspiracy, foreign or domestic."

With respect to the central issue of whether the Warren Commission made a mistake on the back-neck location of the wound, or deliberately changed the facts to solve the high-exit-wound problem, based on the fair manner in which I found the Warren Commission to have evaluated and handled the mountains of evidence in this case, of these two interpretations I am inclined to accept the first one (i.e., they were medically naive in not knowing, or negligently overlooked the fact), particularly when Dr. Humes himself told the Commission that the entrance wound was in the "low neck," and then went on in the very same paragraph to use the precise language he used in his autopsy report, which stated that the wound was situated "just above the upper border of the scapula" (which is the upper back).[272]

It also has to be noted that the Warren Commission staff did not have access to the autopsy photographs and X-rays, as the HSCA later did,[273] because the commissioners had made a commitment to make public all the evidence they examined, and they felt that if they examined the photographs and X-rays, they might be published, and the subsequent viewing of them (particularly the gruesome photographs) by the American public would constitute an invasion of privacy of the Kennedy family.[274] Commission assistant counsel Arlen Specter, in an April 30, 1964, memorandum to the general counsel, J. Lee Rankin, urged that the Warren Commission obtain the photographs and X-rays, saying it was "indispensable" that the staff examine them to, among other things, "corroborate the autopsy surgeons' testimony that the holes on the President's back [recall that the draft of the Warren Report said "back"] and head had the characteristics of points of entry" and "determine with certainty that there are no major variations between the [X-ray] films and the artist's drawings."[275] However, Specter's request was not met.

Perhaps one reason why the Commission turned Specter down is that when he asked Dr. Humes, during the latter's testimony, "In what way the availability of the X-rays would assist in further specifying the nature of the [president's] wounds?" Humes answered, "I do not believe, sir, that the availability of the X-rays would assist in further specifying the nature of the wounds." As to the photographs, though Humes said they "would show more accurately and in more detail the character of the wounds," in answer to a question from Chief Justice Warren, he said that if he had the photographs in front of him while testifying, "it would not" change any of the testimony he had given.[276]*

Inasmuch as the Commission felt that the photos and X-rays were "only corroborative," it decided that they "should be excluded for other reasons of taste."[277] It's my sense that if the Commission had felt the photographs and X-rays were necessary to make the determinations it had to make, that fact would definitely have overridden the fear of the Kennedy family that they may someday be seen by the American public.

In 1967, former Warren Commission member John J. McCloy told Walter Cronkite on a CBS News Special, "I think that if there's one thing that I would do [differently], I would insist on those photographs and the X-rays having been produced before us. In the one respect, and only one respect there, I think we were perhaps a little oversensitive to what we understood was the sensitivities of the Kennedy family against the production of colored photographs of the body, and so forth."[278]

Although the House Select Committee said that "there was no evidence that any members of the Warren Commission or its staff ever viewed any of the autopsy photographs or X-rays of President Kennedy,"[279] apparently Chief Justice Warren was an exception, at least as to the photographs.† In his book *The Memoirs of Chief Justice Earl Warren*, Warren wrote,

> It has been contended that the reason these pictures were not filed [in the National Archives] was because they would show that the shots which struck the President did not come from behind and above him. While I have never before entered into that discussion, I feel that it is appropriate to do so here because I am solely responsible for the action taken, and still am certain it was the proper thing to do.
>
> The President was hardly buried before people with ghoulish minds began putting together artifacts of the assassination for the purpose of establishing a museum on the subject. They offered as much as ten thousand dollars for the rifle alone. They also wanted to buy . . . various things at the Depository, and they were even making inquiries about the availability of the clothes of Presi-

---

*The fact that Humes, when he gave this categorical answer, had no way of knowing if the photographs and X-rays, when they emerged at some point in the future, would confirm or refute his testimony, is fairly strong circumstantial evidence that he was very confident in the correctness of his conclusions, indicating not only that the conclusion he reached was very obvious to him, but also that he was no insecure amateur doing a professional's work, as Warren Commission critics want everyone to believe.

†In an informative behind-the-scenes look in 1992 at the operation of the Warren Commission, in which the twelve surviving assistant counsels on the Warren Commission staff as well as the lone surviving Commission member, Gerald Ford, were interviewed, *U.S. News & World Report* disclosed that Robert Kennedy gave his family's approval for Chief Justice Warren and Commission counsel Lee Rankin to look at the photos, but only Warren elected to see them (Gest, Shapiro, Bowermaster, and Geier, "JFK: The Untold Story of the Warren Commission," p.40). See also endnote for fact that Warren Commission assistant counsel Arlen Specter was privately shown one autopsy photo by a Secret Service official while on a trip to Dallas.

dent Kennedy. They also, of course, wanted the pictures of his head. I could see in my mind's eye such a 'museum' preying on the morbid sentiments of people and perhaps planting seeds of assassination in the minds of some deranged persons who might see opportunity for personal notoriety or expression in assaulting yet another President. *I saw the pictures when they came from Bethesda Naval Hospital, and they were so horrible that I could not sleep well for nights.* Accordingly, in order to prevent them from getting into the hands of these sensation mongers,* I suggested† that they not be used by the Commission, but that we rule on the convincing testimony of the Naval doctors who performed the autopsy to establish the cause of death [and the] entry, exit, and course of the bullets . . .

Sometime in the latter part of President Johnson's administration, when the aforementioned charge was made, he set up a Board [Clark Panel] of outstanding pathologists from various parts of the country and submitted the pictures to them for comparison with the findings of the [autopsy] doctors . . . on which the Commission had relied. That Board confirmed the findings of the Commission.[280]

Warren Commission general counsel J. Lee Rankin pointed out to the HSCA that if the Commission had seen the photographs and X-rays, they would necessarily "become a part of the official record of the Commission," so they would have to be published.[281]

Returning to the key issue, even if we assume, for the sake of argument, that my innocent interpretation of what happened here is incorrect, and the Warren Commission and its staff knowingly raised the entrance wound from the back to the neck so the entrance wound would not be lower than the exit wound, I feel it would be a non sequitur to conclude that the misconduct of the Warren Commission in this matter contaminates the immense and irrefutable evidentiary logic and power of its ultimate findings. Moreover, even if the Commission did do this, it in no way changed the actual location of the wound in the upper right part of the back as shown in the autopsy photographs and X-rays, a location agreed upon by all of the pathologists who reviewed them, nor the reality of the bullet, as indicated, always proceeding in a downward trajectory.

There can be no escape from the simple fact that the wounds in the president's body were the result of two bullets that had been fired from above and behind. *All* pathologists who examined the evidence in this case for four national commissions (seventeen pathologists for the head wound, fifteen for the back wound) reached the same conclusion: that

---

*Chief Justice Warren's fears were not unfounded. In 1991, Robert J. Groden, a leading conspiracy theorist and consultant to the HSCA's photographic panel, sold pirated copies of the gruesome color photographs taken at the autopsy, along with an accompanying story, for $50,000 to the tabloid *Globe*, which published them on the front cover (and across five internal pages) under banner headlines like "Shocking Autopsy Photos Blow Lid Off J.F.K. Cover-Up!" "Jackie Crawled Out of Limo to Grab Her Dying Hubby's Brains—and She Had Them in Her Hand!" and "JFK Autopsy Photos Were Faked & Here's How & Why Feds Did It" (Ken Harrell, "Shocking Autopsy Photos Blow Lid Off J.F.K. Cover-Up!" *Globe*, December 31, 1991; Reporters Daily Transcript, *Superior Court of the State of California for the County of Los Angeles, Sharon Rufo, et al., Plaintiffs, vs. Orenthal James Simpson, et al.,* Defendants, Case No. SC031947, December 20, 1996, vol.36, pp.60–63).

†This suggests that the Kennedy family did not care, but they did and they let their reservations be known to the Commission. Warren goes on in his book to indicate this (Warren, *Memoirs*, p.372).

the two wounds to the back side of the president's body (i.e., the upper back and back of the head) were *entrance*, not exit wounds, and that both exited toward the front of the body. And this group of pathologists includes, as I indicated earlier, the leading forensic pathologist for the conspiracy community, Dr. Cyril H. Wecht.

And yet, allegations (many of them offered by respected professionals who should know better) that the president was shot from his right front continue to appear in books, magazines, and newspaper articles, accomplishing little other than to titillate the public's fascination for such exotic imaginings and, more importantly, to throw into question the clear and incontrovertible tower of facts that prove that no such thing ever happened.

One allegation that conspiracy theorists are particularly fond of (and one they *had* to invent to counter the irrefutable conclusions of the autopsy) is that the autopsy photographs and X-rays have been doctored, phonied up, or otherwise faked to hide the conspiracy to kill the president. We know this charge is false because, as discussed earlier, the photographs and X-rays were authenticated by the HSCA in 1978. But conspiracy theorists have never let facts stand in the way of a good, sensational story. In this case, critics point to a comment made by one of the two FBI agents at the autopsy in his deposition before the ARRB that reportedly suggests the autopsy photographs in evidence are forgeries.

In 1997, Jeremy Gunn, the ARRB general counsel, showed former FBI agent Francis O'Neill autopsy photograph number 42 (depicting the back of the president's head) and asked whether the photograph resembled what O'Neill saw at the time of the autopsy *thirty-four years earlier*. O'Neill answered, "This [photograph] looks like it's been doctored in some way. *Let me rephrase that.* When I say 'doctored,' [I mean] like the stuff [brain matter] has been pushed back in, and it looks like [the photograph was taken] more towards the end [of the autopsy] than at the beginning. All you have to do was put the flap [of scalp] back over here, and the rest of the stuff is all covered on up."[282]

The conspiracy theorists have had a good old time with O'Neill's "doctored" photograph remark and naturally have posted their distortions on Web sites all over the Internet, where they can quickly and eagerly trade misinformation with each other. (I know this not because I have a computer—I'm still in the nineteenth century, working with a yellow legal pad and pencil, although recently I graduated from a number-three to a number-four pencil, so I'm inching my way into modernity—but because people sometimes send printouts from the sites to me.) Naturally and predictably, and in the best tradition of the conspiracy theorists' discipline, a conspiracy newsgroup posting of January 5, 2000, quoted O'Neill as testifying about the subject photograph: "This looks like it's been doctored in some way." The author of the message, of course, fails to include what O'Neill said immediately thereafter to explain what he meant. Likewise, Warren Commission critic and conspiracy theorist Dr. Gary Aguilar writes that "the theory of some kind of photographic 'doctoring' is not mere lunacy. It has significant support in the record." But after quoting O'Neill's testimony that "this looks like it's been doctored in some way," Aguilar proceeds to insert " . . . " instead of including O'Neill's words immediately thereafter, where he makes it clear he was not referring to a doctoring of the photograph.[283] Aguilar is a polished writer, a reputable doctor, and an excellent researcher. It is beneath him to play this dot-dot-dot game. The three dots (" . . . "), he knows, are only supposed to be used when the words they replace don't alter or modify the words quoted. But at least Dr. Aguilar gave researchers a heads-up with his dots, which thereby announced he had deleted *something*. Most conspiracy theorists don't even do that.

One of the very biggest mysteries concerning missing evidence in the Kennedy assassination, one that continues to fascinate, and one that may never be solved—but, fortunately, one that doesn't need to be, since it has only academic value—is *what happened to President Kennedy's brain*? At the London trial, Gerry Spence zeroed in on the issue with my pathologist, Dr. Charles Petty.

Spence: "Did you ever see the brain?"

Petty: "No."

"Do you think it's important for a doctor, before he gives his opinion, to see the brain to determine what the course of the bullet was?"

"It would be nice if the brain were available."

"Now, please, Doctor, let's not be silly. You're a professional. You're under oath. Tell the ladies and gentlemen of the jury if it isn't essential for you to see the brain?"

"No, it's not essential to see the brain."

"You didn't see the brain in this case?"

"No, I did not."

"Do you know where it is?"

"No, I do not."

"Did you look for it?"

"Well, not really."

"As a matter of fact—well, now, please, Doctor, you smiled. But as a matter of fact, didn't your committee ask some twenty different people where the brain of the president was?"

"We asked, but we did not look for it."

"You couldn't find it, could you?"

"No."[284]*

Conspiracy theorists have always been certain that the conspirators who killed Kennedy somehow were able to expropriate his brain as a part of the cover-up.

Here's what we do know. As the HSCA summarized it, "shortly after" the supplemental examination of the president's brain (the date of which has never been confirmed—see later discussion), Kennedy's personal physician, Admiral George Burkley, directed the Bethesda Naval Hospital to transfer all the physical autopsy material in its possession to Robert I. Bouck, the special agent in charge of the Protective Research Section of the Secret Service, at the White House. Captain John H. Stover, the commanding officer of the Naval Medical School at Bethesda, gave Burkley "the [president's] brain in a . . . stainless steel bucket," and Burkley "personally transferred it to the White House where it was placed in a locked Secret Service file cabinet" along with the other autopsy-related material, such as photographs, X-rays, and tissue sections.[285] Bouck took the containers of autopsy-related material and stored them inside a four-drawer file cabinet safe with a dial combination lock in a basement location in the White House adjacent to the control room occupied by White House police.[286]

---

*In his final summation, Spence argued, "I'll tell you this much, if one of us was charged with murder, and the most important piece of evidence in the whole trial was gone, and it was evidence that we needed to prove our innocence, we needed it to prove our innocence, and it was gone . . . what would we say? We would say, 'What has happened to this country?' We would say, 'What kind of procedure is this?' We would say, 'What kind of judicial system is this?' We would say, 'What's going on with the FBI?' . . . I can hear Lee Oswald saying, 'I'm a patsy' " (Transcript of *On Trial*, July 25, 1986, p.1015).

On April 22, 1965, Senator Robert Kennedy sent a letter to Admiral Burkley, directing Burkley to transfer, in person, all of the aforementioned autopsy material being kept at the White House to the president's personal secretary, Mrs. Evelyn Lincoln, at the National Archives for safekeeping.[287] Mrs. Lincoln did not work at the archives, but the archives gave her an office there to assist in the transfer of the president's official papers to the archives. Pursuant to this request, on April 26, 1965, Burkley, accompanied by Bouck, said he personally took the brain and tissue sections, with all the other materials, which were now inside a locked footlocker, to Mrs. Lincoln.[288] Accompanying the transfer was a cover letter of the same date on White House stationery from Burkley to Lincoln memorializing the transfer to Lincoln. An attached list set forth an inventory of nine items of autopsy-related materials that were transferred. Item number 9 (the other eight items being predominantly autopsy photos, negatives, and X-rays, although item number 1 was "one broken casket handle"), the last item on the inventory, contained paraffin blocks of tissue sections of the president's brain, four boxes of slides, one of which was of "blood smears," and "1 stainless steel container," 7×8 inches in diameter, "containing gross material"—that is, what was left of the president's brain.[289] Admiral Burkley told the HSCA that item number 9 represented "the container of the brain."[290]

As of this point in time, the materials had only been transferred, per the April 26, 1965, letter to Lincoln, to "your [Mrs. Lincoln's] custody," not the custody of the archives. It's from this point on that the situation gets very murky. Mrs. Lincoln gave an affidavit to the HSCA in which she said that approximately one month after she received the footlocker, Robert Kennedy telephoned to inform her that he was sending Angela Novello, his personal secretary, over to her office to move the footlocker. Lincoln, who said she had never opened the footlocker while it was in her custody,[*] assumed it was going to be moved to another part of the archives where Robert Kennedy stored other materials. Novello, accompanied by Herman Kahn, assistant archivist for presidential libraries, came and took physical possession of the footlocker. Lincoln gave Novello both keys to the footlocker and never saw it again.[291]

No one knows what Novello did with the footlocker. It was either kept in a personal storage area set aside for Robert Kennedy within the archives or, more likely, removed from the archives building altogether, since it turned up one and a half years later in the possession of Burke Marshall, a Kennedy family friend.[292]

At the request of the U.S. Department of Justice, on October 29, 1966, Marshall, on behalf of "the executors of the estate of the late President John F. Kennedy," transferred ownership of the autopsy materials and other items (such as the "personal clothing" and "personal effects" of the president that were "gathered as evidence" by the Warren Commission) to the U.S. government. The seven-page letter transferring title to the government, from Marshall to Lawson B. Knott, the administrator of the General Services Administration (GSA), constituted a "deed of gift" from the Kennedy family, and per the letter, the items transferred thereunder "should be deposited, safeguarded and preserved" in the National Archives. The letter said that the Kennedy family "desires to prevent the undignified or sensational use of these materials . . . or any other use which would

---

[*]Mrs. Lincoln mentioned in a 1978 interview that although "she had no intention of looking inside the various containers [within the trunk] because she was very upset about the assassination of the president and was upset at the prospect of having to handle the autopsy materials," she was very careful with them "and noted that they fit neatly into the trunk," indicating that at some point she did look inside the footlocker (HSCA Record 180-10077-10138, Interview of Mrs. Evelyn Lincoln, July 5, 1978, pp.5–6; also ARRB MD 128).

tend in any way to dishonor the memory of the late President or cause unnecessary grief or suffering to the members of his family and those closely associated with him. We know the Government respects these desires."[293]

The "gift" had restrictions. Although access to the president's clothing and personal effects would be immediately available to any federal government investigative agency and any "serious scholar or investigator" whom the administrator approved of, access to the autopsy photographs and X-rays would not be authorized "until five years after the date of this agreement [October 29, 1966] except with the consent of the Kennedy family representative," designated in the document as Burke Marshall. Also, per the deed of gift, no public display of the items would be permitted and the limitations on the gift would remain in effect throughout the lifetime of Mrs. Kennedy, the president's parents, his brothers and sisters, and his two children.[294]

Two days later, on October 31, 1966, Marshall delivered the footlocker back to the archives, and in the presence of many people, including Novello (who furnished the key to open it) and several officials from the GSA, archives, and attorney general's office, the footlocker was opened and all the materials contained within were removed so they could be inspected and reinventoried. Per a document signed on November 4, 1966, by Robert Bahmer, the archivist of the United States, James B. Rhoads, the deputy archivist, and three other officials, "Inspection of the footlocker disclosed that it contained items 1 through 8, inclusive, referred to in the attachment to Admiral Burkley's letter of April 26, 1965. It did not contain *any* of the material [i.e., not just the stainless steel container holding the brain, but the slides and tissue sections] referred to in item 9 of the attachment."[295]

So sometime between April 26, 1965, when Burkley transferred the footlocker to Evelyn Lincoln and confirmed that the steel container holding the president's brain was inside, and October 31, 1966, when it was discovered the container was no longer there, someone removed the container from the footlocker.

The question of who it was has mystified students of the assassination for years, and the HSCA conducted a very thorough and comprehensive investigation to answer the question, interviewing or deposing over thirty people who were believed to have possible knowledge about the disappearance,[296] all of whom claiming to the HSCA that they had no knowledge. One person they naturally sought out was Novello, who gave them an affidavit saying she had no recollection of handling the footlocker, of possessing a key or keys to such a footlocker, or handling any of the autopsy materials. The HSCA did not believe Novello, particularly in view of the fact that when the footlocker was opened for inspection on October 31, 1966, it was she, in the presence of many witnesses, who produced the key to open the locker.[297]

Burke Marshall told the HSCA it was his opinion that Robert Kennedy obtained and disposed of the brain and slides himself. "Marshall said Robert Kennedy was concerned that these materials would be placed on public display in future years in an institution such as the Smithsonian, and wished to dispose of them to eliminate such a possibility.[*]

---

[*]In a similar vein, and fortifying the natural inference that RFK (or, for that matter, any member of the Kennedy family) would have had every motive to have expropriated his brother's brain, on April 5, 1988, RFK's brother-in-law, Stephen Smith, telephoned Los Angeles County deputy district attorney Steven Sowders, and asked him, on behalf of RFK's widow, Ethel, to return RFK's bloodstained suit jacket and shirt to her from his assassination in Los Angeles in June of 1968, and if that couldn't be done, to make sure that these items were kept at the DA's office and never given to any third party. Sowders said RFK's clothing was not returned to the

Marshall emphasized that he does not believe anyone other than Robert Kennedy would have known what happened to the materials and is certain that obtaining or locating these materials is no longer possible."[298] Marshall's strong suggestion that Robert Kennedy disposed of the items is strengthened by the testimony of Evelyn Lincoln, who told HSCA investigators in 1978 that Robert Kennedy came to the National Archives four or five times during the key period of 1965–1966, when the autopsy materials are known to have disappeared. After Robert Kennedy was assassinated in 1968, Mrs. Lincoln reportedly became concerned about the autopsy materials stored at the archives. She called Ken O'Donnell, who contacted Ted Kennedy. O'Donnell called back and said, "Everything is under control."[299]

The HSCA noted that "the *only* materials" removed from the footlocker were "physical specimens from the body of [RFK's] brother: tissue sections, blood smeared slides, and the container of gross material [i.e., the president's brain]. He [RFK] may have understandably felt more strongly about preventing the misuse of these physical materials than the photographs and X-rays. Second, the Justice Department . . . pushed hard to acquire the photographs and X-rays but did not request the physical materials."[300]

After its extensive inquiry, the HSCA concluded "that Angela Novello *did* remove the footlocker . . . from the office of Mrs. Lincoln at the direction of Robert Kennedy" and that "circumstantial evidence tends to show that Robert Kennedy either destroyed these materials or otherwise rendered them inaccessible."[301]

As indicated, the conspiracy theorists maintain the president's brain was stolen as part of the cover-up and that only with an examination of the brain itself could we "determine whether all the shots were fired from the rear or if shots came from the right front. The path of the bullet through the brain could be discerned, and the location of the gunman determined."[302] But we've already seen that the three autopsy surgeons, as well as every one of the many other forensic pathologists who looked at the X-rays and photographs of the president's brain, already reached firm and irrefutable conclusions as to the location of the entrance and exit wounds and the path the two bullets took through the president's body. If both of the wounds to the rear of the president's body (upper right area of the back and right rear of his head) were determined to be entrance wounds, as they were, it would be physically impossible for an examination of the president's brain to reflect that the bullets, in fact, entered from the front or the side.

The conspiracy theorists also seem to forget that this "missing brain" that they go on and on about was not always "missing." The three autopsy surgeons *saw* the brain, held it in their hands, examined it, even weighed it. And they said the left hemisphere of the brain was "intact." If they saw any damage to the left hemisphere of the president's brain or any bullet track through the left hemisphere, they obviously would have mentioned it in their autopsy report. And the only bullet track the autopsy surgeons noted through the right hemisphere was one that "traversed the cranial cavity in a posterior-anterior [i.e., back to front] direction . . . depositing minute particles along its path."[303] And Dr. Michael Baden, the chief forensic pathologist for the HSCA, testified before the HSCA that an examination of the photographs and X-rays of the brain and a description of the

---

Kennedy family, and is still in the office's "evidence locker," not available for public scrutiny. (Telephone interviews of Steven Sowders by author on July 20, 1999, and June 25, 2002; see also *Washington Post*, April 20, 1988, p.C3) Greg Stone, a dedicated student of the RFK assassination who got to know the Kennedy family, told me years ago that the family didn't want RFK's clothing on display anywhere for the public.

brain by autopsy surgeons did not indicate "any injury of the brain *other than* the extensive damage to the right upper part of the brain consistent with the upper track" of the bullet that entered the rear of the president's head.[304] In other words, there was absolutely no evidence of any second bullet entering the president's head. So finding the "missing brain" would not have any evidentiary value.

The majority of the HSCA forensic pathology panel (eight of the nine members, the exception being Dr. Cyril Wecht) concluded that "the documentation that is available—photographs and X-rays of the brain and the autopsy report—are sufficient to permit accurate evaluation of the gunshot injury to the head and brain, and . . . examination of the brain itself *would only further confirm* the panel's conclusion that one, and only one, bullet struck the president's head from behind."[305]

On February 13, 2002, I called Dr. Wecht, who in assassination literature is the leading proponent of the position that the president's brain, if it could be found, could unlock all kinds of mysteries in the Kennedy assassination. Dr. Wecht told the *Washington Post's* Michael Isikoff that "there's something very sinister" about the brain's disappearance, adding that "it's the most important piece of physical evidence in the case."[306] Wecht agreed with me, as he had to, that all forensic pathologists, including himself, who either physically examined the president's head or looked at X-rays and photographs of it, agreed that the only entrance wound discernible from the physical examination and the X-rays and photographs was a wound to the upper right rear of the president's head, meaning the shot came from the rear. I then asked Dr. Wecht, "Doctor, since the wound to the back of the president's head was an entrance wound, meaning the bullet would have had to travel from the back of the president's head to the front, how would it be physically possible for the brain itself to reflect that the bullet actually came from a different direction?"

Wecht responded, "Well, of course, it could not. I agree that the brain could only show that that bullet passed from the back of the president's head to the front."

"So then you agree, do you not," I said, "that finding the president's brain would not have any evidentiary value?"

"No," Dr. Wecht said, proceeding to reprise a position he had taken with me in an earlier conversation. "The brain," he said, "could show a second track through the president's brain from a second missile entering the right side of the president's head in the area of the large exit wound."

But since there's absolutely no evidence that this ever took place, and even Dr. Wecht agrees that such a bullet (if it were a normal bullet) would have had to penetrate into the left hemisphere of the president's brain, and Wecht agrees the left side of the president's brain "was intact," the bottom line is that even if the president's brain were to be found, it would not have any evidentiary value.

Dr. Wecht did point out a theoretical value the brain could have. It could help determine where, based on the path of the bullet through the president's brain, the shooter was located *to* Kennedy's rear. But all the evidence, including, but not limited to, the trajectory studies (see later text), shows that the bullet came from the vicinity of the sniper's nest window. And we know from the physical evidence (e.g., Oswald's Mannlicher-Carcano, his finger and palm prints, etc.) that Oswald fired the rifle. There's no evidence the bullet was fired, for instance, from a lower floor in the Book Depository Building or from the Dal-Tex Building to the president's rear.

As a side note, if Senator Robert Kennedy came into possession of his brother's brain, as appears likely, what did he do with it to make it inaccessible to others? For years, there have been rumors that when President Kennedy's body was moved from its temporary site and reinterred at a new and permanent granite and marble site at Arlington National Cemetery* under floodlights on the evening of March 14, 1967,[307] the brain was placed in the president's grave. In a photo at the grave site (see photo section), Robert and Edward Kennedy stand between the Eternal Flame on their left and a curious box to their right. No one knows what this box's purpose at the grave site was, or what it contained, if anything, but the speculation is that it contained the president's brain. The subject photograph surfaced after the HSCA concluded its investigation in 1979, but the HSCA did interview the few people (it was a very private ceremony that the press was not privy to) who were present at the grave site, and they could not recall any additional package or material being placed in the grave. John Metzler, the superintendent of the cemetery, now deceased, told the HSCA that the coffin was in a sealed vault. He was present throughout the entire process—from the opening of the old grave site through the transfer by crane of the vault to the reinterment at the new site—and said there was no way anyone could have placed anything in the coffin or vault without his seeing it, and no one placed anything in the new grave site.[308]

Robert Tanenbaum, the chief assistant to Richard Sprague, the first chief counsel for the HSCA, told me that in a personal conversation he had years ago with Frank Mankiewicz, Robert F. Kennedy's press secretary and close confidant, Mankiewicz told him that he was present at the grave site when JFK's body was reburied, and that Bobby Kennedy had "put Jack's brain in the coffin."[309] When I asked Mankiewicz about this, he denied expressly telling Tanenbaum this, though he conceded talking to Tanenbaum about the president's brain and further acknowledged that he may have speculated to Tanenbaum that this could have happened. But since Mankiewicz was at the grave site, his "speculation" position doesn't have nearly the believability it would have if he hadn't been present, and it is unlikely that someone of Tanenbaum's stature would have misunderstood what Mankiewicz told him about such an important matter.

Mankiewicz told me, "I do believe that the president's brain was reburied with the president when his body was moved from its temporary grave to its permanent one," adding, however, that he had no firsthand knowledge of this. Mankiewicz told the HSCA's G. Robert Blakey in 1978 that after the reinterment, Edward Kennedy "seemed" to confirm that the brain was buried in the grave site, but when I asked Mankiewicz to elaborate on this, he said, "I honestly just don't recall either Ted confirming this in any way, or telling Blakey this."[310]

If, indeed, Robert Kennedy somehow placed the president's brain in the president's coffin when the president was reburied, we have a situation where the dead president was not "taking a secret to his grave," but someone else's secret.

Easily one of the most obscenely irresponsible documents ever promulgated in the assassination debate, and yet one whose contention is being hailed and widely accepted today in the conspiracy community, is the one written by Douglas P. Horne, the ARRB's chief

---

*The Kennedy's infant son Patrick, who died in August of 1963 after only thirty-nine hours of life, and their unnamed stillborn infant daughter who died in 1956, were both reburied beside their father's grave.

Lee Harvey Oswald with the rifle he later used to kill President Kennedy and the pistol he used to kill Officer Tippit. This backyard photograph eventually came to national attention on the cover of the February 21, 1964, issue of *Life* magazine. (*National Archives*)

Top left: Marina and Lee Harvey Oswald on the balcony of their apartment building in Minsk, in what was then the U.S.S.R. (*National Archives*)

Top right: Lee Harvey Oswald as a fifteen–year–old in New Orleans. He had an older brother and half brother, but always seemed to be the favorite of his mother, Marguerite. He gave little indication of reciprocating that love. (*National Archives*)

Bottom: Oswald, a fervent supporter of Fidel Castro's Cuban Revolution, passing out "Hands off Cuba" flyers on the streets of New Orleans in the summer of 1963. (*Johann Rush*)

Top: Oswald's Mannlicher-Carcano rifle, the murder weapon. (*National Archives*)

Bottom: The same gun shown disassembled alongside the brown wrapping-paper bag found on the floor near the sniper's nest window at the Texas School Book Depository Building. The blanket was found in Ruth Paine's garage, where Oswald had stored his rifle. (*National Archives*)

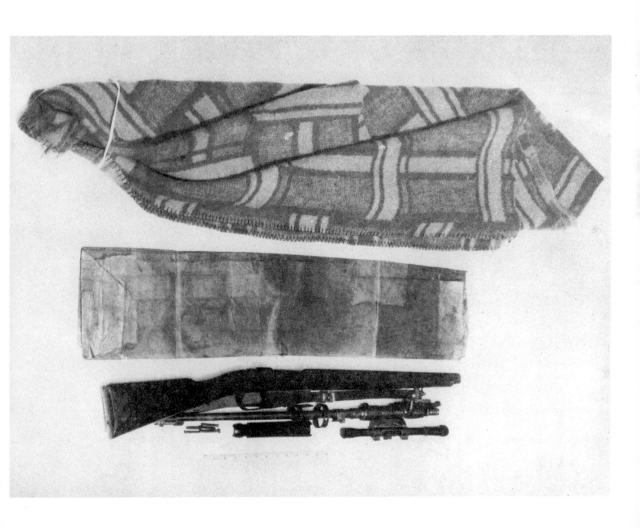

Left: Three cartridge shells, as they were found on the floor of the sniper's nest on the sixth floor of the Texas School Book Depository Building. The sniper's nest window is to the left of the boxes in the left rear of the frame. (*Dallas Municipal Archives*)

Below: The sniper's nest, with Oswald's fingerprint and palm print locations as marked by the Warren Commission. Southwest is the same direction in which the presidential limousine was proceeding down Elm Street. (*National Archives*)

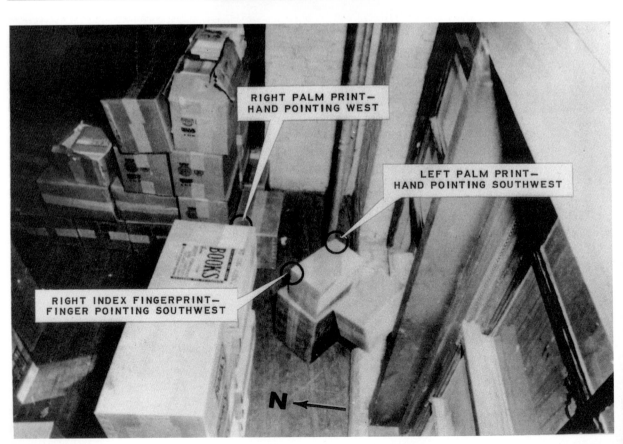

RIGHT PALM PRINT—
HAND POINTING WEST

LEFT PALM PRINT—
HAND POINTING SOUTHWEST

RIGHT INDEX FINGERPRINT—
FINGER POINTING SOUTHWEST

N

Left: While the crowds gathering near the end of the motorcade in Dealey Plaza are comparatively sparse, here in the heart of downtown Dallas the president is met by record numbers of enthusiastic well-wishers. (*Courtesy the Sixth Floor Museum at Dealey Plaza, Photographer William Beal*, Dallas Times Herald *collection*)

Below: Within seconds after the shooting in Dealey Plaza, *Dallas Morning News* photographer Tom Dillard takes this photograph of the southeasternmost windows on the fifth and sixth floors of the Texas School Book Depository Building. The top open window is the sniper's nest window. The small visible portion of a box toward the right side of the window was one of the three boxes Oswald used to construct a gun rest for his rifle. Depository employees Bonnie Ray Williams (left) and Harold Norman (right) are in the windows below. Both heard the shots being fired just above them. Norman, directly below Oswald, even heard the operation of the bolt and the three cartridge shells hitting the floor. (*Courtesy the Sixth Floor Museum at Dealey Plaza, Tom Dillard Collection*, Dallas Morning News)

Left: With thousands of supporters waiting to greet them, President and Mrs. Kennedy emerge from Air Force One on the gloriously bright morning of November 22, 1963. "They looked like Mr. and Mrs. America," one reporter would say. (*Cecil Stoughton, White House / John F. Kennedy Library*)

Below: Conspiracy theorists would later point out that the entry hole in the back of the president's suit was lower than, and did not match up with, the entry wound to his upper back, and hence, the Warren Commission's single bullet theory was destroyed. This photograph, taken around two and a half seconds before the first shot that hit Kennedy, clearly shows Kennedy's suit bunched up on his back, so that fabric meant to hang below his shoulders is covering them when the bullet hits. (*Robert Croft*)

Top: Zapruder frame 133. This is the first frame of the Zapruder film that shows the presidential limousine, which has just turned onto Elm from Houston. Each frame of the film represents one-eighteenth of a second. (*Courtesy the Sixth Floor Museum at Dealey Plaza, Zapruder Collection, © 1967 [renewed 1995] the Sixth Floor Museum at Dealey Plaza, All Rights Reserved*)

Bottom: Frame 161. The consensus of most assassination researchers is that the first shot was fired around the time of this frame. Some people in Dealey Plaza thought it sounded like a firecracker or the backfire of a car. This shot missed the limousine completely. (*Courtesy the Sixth Floor Museum at Dealey Plaza, Zapruder Collection, © 1967 [renewed 1995] the Sixth Floor Museum at Dealey Plaza, All Rights Reserved*)

Top: Zapruder frame 193. As the limousine proceeds down Elm Street, the president waves to the crowd, showing no signs of physical distress. (*Courtesy the Sixth Floor Museum at Dealey Plaza, Zapruder Collection, © 1967 [renewed 1995] the Sixth Floor Museum at Dealey Plaza, All Rights Reserved*)

Bottom: Frame 204. While almost all of the limousine has disappeared from Zapruder's view behind the Stemmons Freeway sign, Kennedy, now past most of the spectators on his right, begins to lower his right arm. (*Courtesy the Sixth Floor Museum at Dealey Plaza, Zapruder Collection, © 1967 [renewed 1995] the Sixth Floor Museum at Dealey Plaza, All Rights Reserved*)

Opposing page: Frames 222 to 224. Connally emerges from behind the Stemmons Freeway sign. The House Select Committee on Assassinations panel of photographic experts said that he seems to be "reacting to some sort of external stimulus. He appears to be frowning, and there is a distinct stiffening of his shoulders and upper trunk." (*Courtesy the Sixth Floor Museum at Dealey Plaza, Zapruder Collection, © 1967 [renewed 1995] the Sixth Floor Museum at Dealey Plaza, All Rights Reserved*)

Above: Zapruder frames 225 and 226. As Connally shows increased distress, Kennedy comes into Zapruder's view. The president can clearly be seen reacting to a severe external stimulus, as he begins to move his elbows upward and his forearms inward. This strongly indicates, *through the film alone*, that Kennedy and Connally were struck by the same bullet.

Top: Zapruder frame 237. This frame shows Kennedy's full reaction to being shot in the upper back. The awkward angle of his arms and elbows has mistakenly been thought by some to be the so-called Thorburn position, which was described in an 1887 article and sketch in a British medical journal by Dr. William Thorburn about a patient with a lesion to the cervical region of the spinal cord whose body took a similar but different posture. In a Thorburn position the elbows are elevated as Kennedy's were, but the forearms are thrust upward, not inward toward each other. Most importantly, the elbows of Thorburn's Manchester, England, patient were locked into their position for twelve days. (*Courtesy the Sixth Floor Museum at Dealey Plaza, Zapruder Collection, © 1967 [renewed 1995] the Sixth Floor Museum at Dealey Plaza, All Rights Reserved*)

Bottom: Frame 264. Kennedy's elbows are shown returning from his Thorburn position a second and a half later, which would not have happened had he been in a true Thorburn position. (*Courtesy the Sixth Floor Museum at Dealey Plaza, Zapruder Collection, © 1967 [renewed 1995] the Sixth Floor Museum at Dealey Plaza, All Rights Reserved*)

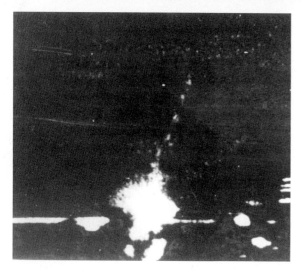

Above: Zapruder frames 312 and 313. Right: Frames 314 to 316. This series shows Kennedy's reaction to the fatal shot. The bullet comes either at frame 312, as some believe, or within the next one-eighteenth of a second, before the explosion of the head seen at frame 313. Note that in frame 313, the impact of the bullet pushes the president's head slightly *forward* (2.3 inches), indicating a shot from the rear, where Oswald is, not from the grassy knoll, which is to the president's right front. At frame 314, his head begins to reverse direction, now moving to the rear in what is believed to be a neuromuscular reaction. (*Courtesy the Sixth Floor Museum at Dealey Plaza, Zapruder Collection, © 1967 [renewed 1995] the Sixth Floor Museum at Dealey Plaza, All Rights Reserved*)

Left: A high-contrast photo of frame 313 by the Itek Corporation. Note that the spray of blood and tissue is to the front, again indicating a shot from the rear. (*Courtesy the Sixth Floor Museum at Dealey Plaza, Zapruder Collection, © 1967 [renewed 1995] the Sixth Floor Museum at Dealey Plaza, All Rights Reserved / Itek Optical Systems*)

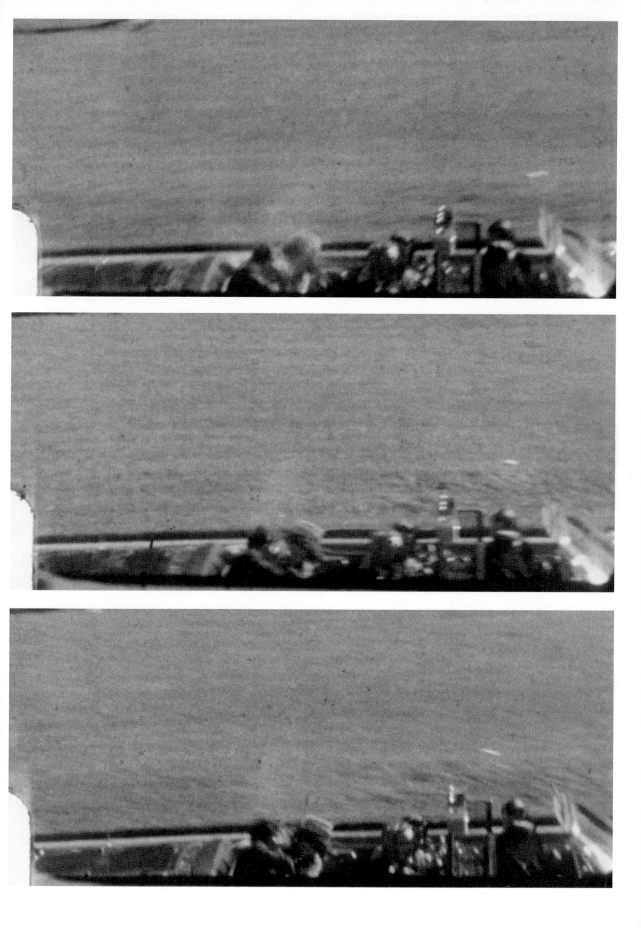

Top: Zapruder frame 321. By this point, the backward motion of Kennedy's head, which is often referred to as the "head snap to the rear," is virtually completed. (*Courtesy the Sixth Floor Museum at Dealey Plaza, Zapruder Collection, © 1967 [renewed 1995] the Sixth Floor Museum at Dealey Plaza, All Rights Reserved*)

Bottom: Frame 328. Many conspiracy theorists, arguing that Kennedy was shot from his right front, maintain that the bullet exited explosively out of the back of his head, leaving a very large wound there. But as this Zapruder frame and all others subsequent to the head shot at frame 313 show, there is no visible damage to the back of the president's head. The entrance wound there was very small and obscured by his thick hair. (*Courtesy the Sixth Floor Museum at Dealey Plaza, Zapruder Collection, © 1967 [renewed 1995] the Sixth Floor Museum at Dealey Plaza, All Rights Reserved*)

Top: Perhaps the most famous Dealey Plaza photograph. Taken by Associated Press photographer James Altgens, this is the only photograph that shows people in the motorcade indicating, by their movement, where any of the shots came from. Here, Secret Service agents look to their right rear, where Oswald was. The photo is also famous for showing a man on the front stairs of the Depository Building who resembles Oswald (Oswald's coworker Billy Lovelady, who is just inside the columns framing the entrance). Many conspiracy theorists insist it is Oswald, proving he was not in the sniper's nest. (*AP/Wide World Photos*)

Center: Mary Moorman's Polaroid is the only known still photograph of the president at the time of the fatal head shot (about one-ninth of a second after it) and the only known photograph of the famous grassy knoll at that moment. Conspiracy theorists are convinced that the president's assassin was hidden somewhere behind the fence to the left. In various places in the foliage, some even believe they can make out figures of assassins. (*Mary Ann Moorman Krahmer*)

Bottom: Wilma Bond's photograph, taken approximately twenty seconds after the shooting, shows the full area around the grassy knoll. (*Wilma Irene Bond/Lorene Bond Prewitt*)

Above: Lyndon B. Johnson, with his wife, Lady Bird Johnson, to his right and a stricken Jacqueline Kennedy to his left, is sworn in as the nation's thirty-sixth president aboard Air Force One, two hours and eight minutes after the shooting in Dealey Plaza. The plane would transport two presidents, both LBJ and the slain Kennedy, back to the nation's capital. (*LBJ Library Photo by Cecil Stoughton*)

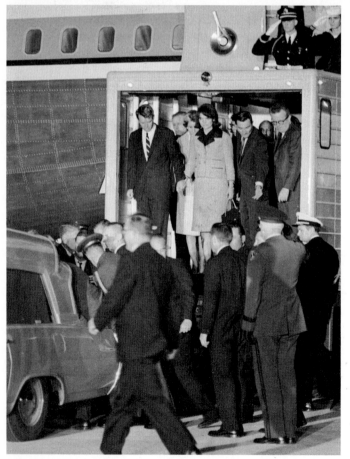

Left: Attorney General Robert Kennedy, who had hurried aboard the plane when it landed at Andrews Air Force Base outside Washington, D.C., stands alongside Mrs. Kennedy as the president's coffin is moved into a waiting car. (*© Wally McNamee/Corbis*)

analyst for military records. The ARRB, established in 1994, was not authorized by Congress to be an investigative agency. Its sole function was to determine what previously unreleased documents pertaining to the assassination should be released to the American public. (See discussion in endnote to "The Investigations" section.) But the authorization to determine what records could be released enabled the board members to stretch their narrow mandate here and there by taking depositions under oath to "clarify points that weren't clear from the original records." Nowhere did they do this more, and cause more harm and confusion, than in the area of Kennedy's autopsy.

The juggling of dates by Horne unfortunately will make this section confusing to many readers, despite my effort to present Horne's theory in an understandable way. Before we get into Horne's theory, the reader should know that even before the ARRB hired Horne for his jurisdictionally narrow job, one that required objectivity, Horne was already a strong supporter and believer in perhaps the craziest theory ever to come out of the conspiracy community, David Lifton's theory that Kennedy's body was stolen and his wounds altered before his autopsy.[311]

Horne wrote a "Memorandum for File" on June 2, 1998 (released by the National Archives on November 9, 1998), that has achieved iconic status in the conspiracy community. Its main conclusion belongs on the cover of the weekly tabloid *Sun*, which features stories like "Hitler Is Still Alive" and "Actual Photos of Heaven." Unbelievably, Horne said that the depositions taken by the ARRB caused him to conclude that there were two (not one) supplemental brain examinations following the autopsy, and the second one—are you ready?—wasn't on the president's brain, but on another brain from some anonymous third party. Horne, accusing Drs. Humes and Boswell of criminal conduct to cover up the true facts of the assassination, said that what happened was a "carefully controlled, compartmented operation in regard to orchestrating who was present, and what procedures were performed, at the two separate brain examinations."[312] Horne's star witness in reaching his conclusion was John T. Stringer Jr., the autopsy photographer.

The three autopsy surgeons negligently did not say, on the autopsy report they each signed, the date of its preparation. However, the chief autopsy surgeon, Dr. James Humes, testified that he prepared and delivered the final report on Sunday, November 24, 1963.[313] One of the other autopsy surgeons, Dr. Pierre A. Finck, also has written, and testified, that it was the twenty-fourth.[314] And a January 26, 1967, affidavit signed by all three autopsy surgeons reads, "The autopsy report, written by Dr. Humes with the assistance of Dr. Boswell and Dr. Finck, was . . . delivered by Dr. Humes to Admiral Burkley, the President's physician, on November 24 at about 6:30 P.M."[315]

The last page of the subject autopsy report reads, "A supplementary report will be submitted following more detailed examination of the brain and of microscopic sections."[316] But the surgeons continued their negligence in not saying, on their supplementary report, the date of their supplementary examination of the brain, or the date of the supplementary report, and as opposed to the date of the autopsy and autopsy report, the date of the supplemental examination of the brain, and the report thereof, has never been determined to anyone's complete satisfaction. The handwritten date "12/6/63" in the upper right corner of the supplemental report was only determined to be the date Humes hand-delivered the report to the president's personal physician, Admiral George Burkley.[317]

The supplementary autopsy report said, among other things, that "in the interest of preserving the specimen, coronal sections are *not* made. The following sections *are* taken for microscopic examination [seven sections are listed, e.g., "from the margin of the laceration in the right parietal lobe"]."[318] So serial, coronal sectioning, sometimes called cross-sectioning, where the brain is sliced through and through—in small parallel intervals from one side of the brain to the other for interior analysis—was *not* done.[*] Only small sections of the brain were taken for analysis.

But in his appearance before the ARRB on July 16, 1996, when asked if the sections the autopsy surgeons took of the brain were "small pieces, or cross-sections," John Stringer responded, "*If I remember*, it was cross-sections."[319] Apart from the fact that Stringer wasn't absolutely sure and the supplementary report signed by all three autopsy surgeons clearly refuted his testimony, Humes had already testified in his ARRB deposition on February 13, 1996, that "we didn't divide the brain like we often do . . . a so-called bread loaf-type incision."[320] The reason? Humes told *JAMA* that Admiral Burkley told him, "The family wanted to inter the brain with the President's body."[321] Dr. Thornton Boswell, the second autopsy surgeon, in his February 26, 1996, ARRB deposition, also testified that the president's brain was not serially cross-sectioned, only small sections being taken.[322] And the other autopsy surgeon, Pierre Finck, in a February 1, 1965, report (based on his notes taken around the time of the brain examination) to his superior, Brigadier General J. M. Blumberg, wrote, "Commander [Humes] takes sections from [the brain] but does *not* make coronal sections in order to preserve the specimen."[323]

That should have been the end of it, right? But not for Mr. Horne. With Stringer speaking of cross-sectioning, and the three autopsy surgeons speaking only of small sections of the president's brain being taken, he was off and running, concluding that there must have been two supplementary brain exams (all three autopsy surgeons have only referred to one), one of which was on the morning of November 25, 1963, and attended by Humes and Boswell, Stringer, and others. Drs. Humes and Boswell, Horne concludes, did not invite Dr. Finck to this exam. (The only supplementary report of a brain exam in the Warren Commission volumes is signed by Dr. Humes,[324] and Humes testified that "Dr. Boswell, *Dr. Finck* and I convened to examine the brain.")[325] This was an examination that even Horne agrees was of the *president's* brain. But Horne alleges there was a *second* brain exam, this one of someone else's brain being represented as the president's, on November 29, 1963, at which time Humes, Boswell, and this time Finck were present, but not Stringer.

It was critical to Horne's mad theory that the "first" exam be *no later* than the morning of November 25 because he concludes the brain was buried with the president's body, and the funeral was that afternoon.[326] Hence, per Horne, the president's brain wasn't even available to be examined on November 29, when Horne says the "second" supplementary exam took place.[†] But to arrive at the twenty-fifth as the date of the "first" supplementary brain exam, Horne had to engage in what appears to be deliberate distortion. The only other option is serious incompetence. His main source for his conclusion of the twenty-fifth was an interview of autopsy surgeons Dr. James Humes and Dr. Thornton Boswell by *JAMA* editor Dr. George D. Lundberg and *JAMA* reporter Dennis Breo in

---

[*]Most brain sectioning for examination purposes is coronal—from ear to ear, that is, side to side—but some are sagittal, that is, the slices are from front to back.

[†]Also, Horne knew that if the first supplementary examination of the brain was not on November 25, the argument could be made that the second exam, which Horne said took place on November 29, was really the first and only exam.

the May 1992 edition of *JAMA*, in which Breo writes, "On December 6, 1963, Humes alone submitted to Burkley his supplementary report . . . *Shortly afterward* [i.e., *after* December 6, 1963], Humes [and Captain John Stover, the commanding officer of the Naval Medical School at Bethesda] turned over everything from the autopsy to Admiral Burkley—bullet fragments, microscopic slides, paraffin blocks of tissue, undeveloped film, X-rays—*and the preserved unsectioned President's brain.*" Breo then quotes Humes as saying, "Admiral Burkley gave me a receipt for the autopsy materials, including the brain. It was my understanding that all the autopsy materials, except the brain, would be placed in the National Archives." Although, Humes said, he didn't know whether the brain was ultimately buried with the body, he did recall Burkley telling him that "the family wanted to inter the brain with the President's body."[327]*

Horne conveniently omits from his report the reference to the brain being turned over to Burkley *after* December 6, 1963. If he had, this would have proved that his theory that the president's brain was buried with his body on November 25, 1963, was wrong. Instead, he focuses only on the desire of the Kennedy family to inter the brain with the body, and since the president's funeral was on the afternoon of November 25, 1963, he concludes that "the supplementary brain examination [took place] prior to the November 25, 1963 state funeral of President Kennedy."[328]

Could the highly unlikely argument be made that Horne was unaware of the *JAMA* interview with Humes? This argument, even if accepted, doesn't save Horne. In fact, the situation gets much, much worse for him. Four years after the *JAMA* interview, Dr. Humes himself testified before the ARRB. *And Horne was present at the deposition.* Humes

---

*Since Burkley told Humes that the president's family wanted the brain to be buried with the body, and the president's funeral was on November 25, this certainly sounds as if the conversation between Burkley and Humes (which took place around the time Humes turned the president's brain over to Burkley) occurred before November 25. But since we know (see later text) that the examination of the president's brain took place *after* November 25 (i.e., after the funeral), two possibilities come to mind to explain this apparent contradiction. One is that the wishes of the Kennedy family could have been expressed after the funeral, and it would not have been a pointless desire, since the brain could be put in the coffin even after the original burial. For instance, we know that on the evening of March 14, 1967, the president's body was reburied. Indeed, when ARRB counsel asked Humes in 1996 whether he had asked Burkley how the Kennedy family "would be able to inter the brain if the president had already been buried?" he responded, "I didn't worry about it one way or the other. I would presume that they could devise a method of doing that without too much difficulty, however" (ARRB Transcript of Proceedings, Deposition of Dr. James Joseph Humes, February 13, 1996, pp.148–149). What is also possible, and more likely, is that the Kennedy family expressed its wish about the brain being buried with the body *before* the funeral, and Humes, looking back almost thirty years later in his *JAMA* interview, confused when Burkley told him about the Kennedy family's wish, thinking it was when he transferred the brain to Burkley after December 6, when it may have been at some time before the funeral on November 25.

But all this is irrelevant since we know the brain was not buried with the body at the time of the president's funeral on November 25. Among other reasons why we know this, Admiral Burkley told the HSCA that when he received the brain from Humes he decided to keep it because he thought they could do serial sections of both the damaged and undamaged portions of the brain (HSCA Record 180-10093-10429, Memorandum to File, Andy Purdy, August 17, 1977, p.5). In a handwritten cover note to his subsequent November 28, 1978, affidavit to the HSCA, Burkley wrote that he "retained the brain" because, for instance, "the possibility of two bullets having wounded President John F. Kennedy's brain would have been eliminated" by such a sectioning, and "had the Warren Commission called me" to testify, he said he would have told them why he kept the brain (HSCA Record 180-10104-10271, HSCA affidavit of George G. Burkley, November 28, 1978, handwritten cover note to affidavit). Indeed, as late as April 26, 1965, the president's brain was inside a container in a footlocker at the National Archives (HSCA Record 109-10364, Memorandum, SAIC Bouck to Chief, Transfer of Material—Assassination of President Kennedy, April 26, 1965; ARRB MD 70).

testified that Admiral Burkley told him that Robert Kennedy, as the "spokesperson" for the Kennedy family, told Burkley that the family wished "to inter the president's brain with the body."

ARRB counsel then asked him, "Did you give Dr. Burkley the [president's] brain prior to the time President Kennedy was interred?"

Humes: "No, no, no, no, no, no. It was *afterwards*."

Question: "Approximately when?"

Humes: "I can't remember. I would say it was within ten days, probably."[329]

Horne, with full knowledge of this, didn't tell the readers of his memorandum report what Humes had testified to because, again, it would destroy his whole theory. And whether Horne believed Humes or not is completely irrelevant. You don't write a single-spaced, fifteen-page report with footnotes and eighteen pages of supporting documents accusing Humes of this terrible crime without finding space to include what Humes had to say, under oath, about the matter. Nor, of course, did Horne tell his readers that Admiral Burkley had given an affidavit (which was also under oath) that *after* the supplementary autopsy examination of the president's brain he had delivered the president's brain, in a steel container, to the White House, and that on April 26, 1965, when the container was transferred to the National Archives, the brain was *still* in the container.[330]

Inasmuch as Drs. Humes and Burkley have given statements under penalty of perjury that the president's brain was not buried with his body, I wonder if Doug Horne would be willing to testify under penalty of perjury that he didn't know about Burkley's affidavit, or about Breo's article, and that he had also forgotten what he personally heard Humes testify to. Or that yes, he was aware of all three of these things, but he never included them in his memorandum because he didn't think they were relevant?

By the way, at least as to Dr. Humes, could one make the argument that Humes lied under oath to protect himself from Horne's accusation? No. Humes testified on February 13, 1996, and Horne didn't even write the first draft of his unbelievable theory until more than six months later, on August 28, 1996.

Trying to construct his nonexistent case, Horne goes on to say in his memorandum that since Dr. Finck, in his letter to Dr. Blumberg, specifically says the supplementary brain examination was on November 29, this must have been a *second* supplementary exam, the only one of the two, Horne says, that Finck attended. Horne says that "although John Stringer did photograph the supplemental brain examination [the one that Horne says occurred on November 25, not the later one on November 29 that Horne claims took place], the photos of a brain in the National Archives today are *not* the photographs that he took at that event . . . Those photographs . . . are photographs of a different brain, and *are not images of President Kennedy's brain*."[331] Horne doesn't know who took these photos at the alleged second brain exam on November 29, but it wasn't Stringer, he says. So according to Horne, the photographs held today at the National Archives that researchers are told are of the president's brain, really are photographs of the brain of some anonymous third party, and all of the photographs of President Kennedy's brain are missing. I see.

Horne's modus operandi in reaching his incredibly far-out conclusion is standard conspiracy fare. All normal people know that people's recollections of an event vary widely, sometimes just moments or a day after it happened, and it doesn't mean anything at all. It's to be expected. For instance, Dr. Finck himself, whose recollections Horne relies on for his sinister scenario, stated at the end of his deposition before the ARRB, "that there are things I remember, others I don't . . . And to me, it is a real burden to have to repeatedly answer questions, being asked, 'Do you remember this, do you remember that,' and quite often I have to answer, 'Well, I don't remember,' or 'I cannot answer that question with precision.'"[332]

But exactly like his congenitally suspicious predecessors, who apparently have different experiences in life than normal humans, whenever Horne spots a discrepancy in the recollection of two or more people trying to remember a long-ago event that supports his theory of what happened, he immediately smells the sweet (to him) aroma of a conspiracy. For example, Dr. Finck, in his report to General Blumberg, writes that "color and black and white photographs are taken by the U.S. Navy photographer: superior and *inferior* aspects of the brain."[333] Horne writes in his report, "Navy photographer Stringer, who was present at the earlier brain exam [the first one, he says, of the president's brain] . . . *is on record* [ooh!] in his ARRB deposition transcript that he did not shoot basilar [meaning *base, below*], or *inferior* views of the brain* . . . This Finck recollection of witnessing a photographer shoot *inferior* views of the brain, therefore, corroborates that he was at a different examination than was John Stringer."[334] I get it. If five witnesses to an automobile accident each give different versions of what they saw, there must have been five separate automobile accidents. Someone with this mentality was being paid with *our* tax dollars.

But when a discrepancy can't be used to support Horne's theory, he suddenly becomes normal and doesn't think anything of it. For instance, FBI agents O'Neill and Sibert watched the entire autopsy proceeding together. Yet Horne has no difficulty at all with O'Neill testifying before the ARRB that he saw the president's brain being removed from his cranium and measured, weighed, and put in a jar, and Agent Sibert not being able to recall seeing the president's brain ever being removed from his cranium or seeing the brain at any time outside the body.[335]

Now why would Humes and Boswell, who testified that there was only one supplementary brain exam, have conducted a second one of a different brain? Of course, Horne has an answer, in effect accusing Humes and Boswell of being a part of a vast conspiracy to cover up the true facts of the assassination, which pointed away from the guilt of Oswald. He writes that there *was* coronal sectioning of the president's brain on November 25, but photographs of the damage to these sections couldn't be allowed to see the light of day. Why? Because they would have documented the damage to the president's brain "in great and irrefutable detail" and hence, "was considered knowledge which had to be suppressed." Therefore, "an examination of a second (different) brain (exhibiting a more acceptable pattern of damage), with photographs to record [that] different pattern of damage (such as those now in the Archives)," was deemed "necessary."[336]

In other words, the shots really didn't come from behind, where Oswald was, but from the president's right front, that is, the grassy knoll. As a contributing writer in the book *Murder in Dealey Plaza*, Horne wrote,

> The real brain, examined on or about Monday, 25 November 1963, constituted unassailable evidence of a shot from the front, and was incompatible with the

---

*Horne doesn't bother, of course, to tell his readers that although Stringer did first tell the ARRB that he did not shoot the basilar view of the president's brain shown to him, when asked again, "You did not take a basilar view of the brain, is that correct?" he backpedaled considerably, answering, "I *think* so, yeah. Whether I took that [photo of basilar view shown him], *I don't know*" (ARRB Transcript of Proceedings, Deposition of John T. Stringer, July 16, 1996, pp.216–218, 221).

"cover story" of a lone shooter from behind . . . The condition of the real brain was consistent with the reports of the Dallas doctors, who said President Kennedy had an exit wound in the right rear of his head . . . Allowing it to remain in evidence would have confirmed that the President was shot from the front, and would have made it impossible to sell the "cover story" to the American people. Removing the real brain from evidence and substituting photographs of another brain . . . with a pattern of damage roughly consistent with a shooter from above and behind, would support the "cover story" that a lone man in a building shot a man in a car from above and behind.[337]

Horne also goes on to say he believes "that President Kennedy's *body* was altered—tampered with—prior to the commencement of the . . . autopsy, presumably to remove evidence (i.e., bullets or bullet fragments) inconsistent with the lone-assassin-from-behind cover story."[338] (See discussion of this body-alteration allegation in conspiracy section.) Since Horne and his fellow conspiracy theorists passionately believe that the conspirators shot Kennedy from the grassy knoll to the president's right front, then tried to frame Oswald by making it look like the shots came from the president's rear, where Oswald was, did the thought ever enter their mind that rather than get surgeons beforehand to alter the wounds on Kennedy's body and remove bullets or fragments, and then have the autopsy surgeons engage in a monumental charade of having two separate brain exams, why wouldn't the conspirators avoid the necessity for all of this by simply shooting Kennedy from the rear instead of the front? That way they wouldn't have to pull off an operation of staggering difficulty and complexity and wouldn't have to bring into the conspiracy all these surgeons and doctors, each one of whom could expose it and put all the conspirators on death row.

Since Dr. Finck's letter to General Blumberg was based on "personal notes" of his that he presumably made around the time of the events to which they relate, his date of November 29, 1963, for the one and only supplementary brain exam is probably correct.[*] But if, as Horne suggests, the first supplementary brain exam was on November 25, and the conspirators, Humes and Boswell, made sure they didn't invite their colleague Finck

---

[*]The November 29 date for the one and only supplementary brain exam is partially corroborated by Chief Petty Officer Chester Boyers, who was in charge of the Pathology Department at Bethesda Naval Hospital in November of 1963. Boyers told an HSCA investigator his records reflected that he prepared tissue slides of sections of the president's brain for analysis on December 2, 1963, very close to the November 29 date. (ARRB MD 62, Interview of Chester H. Boyers, April 28, 1978, p.4) One of the strongest reasons to believe that the supplementary brain exam did not take place on November 25 (the date, to repeat, that Horne believes the first of two supplementary brain exams took place), and was no earlier than November 29, is that, as Dr. Baden told me, when a brain is put in formalin, it's "never put in for just a few days. In fact, it's usually for two weeks. The reason is that it takes time for the brain to harden and fix to the point where it's easier to make thinner slices. Even November twenty-ninth is early, but November twenty-fifth wouldn't make any sense for a brain examination" (Telephone interview of Dr. Michael Baden by author on July 14, 2000).

When Humes testified before the Warren Commission on March 16, 1964 (less than four months after the autopsy, when we can assume his memory would have been more fresh), that the supplementary brain exam was "some days after" the autopsy, it is doubtful that he would have been referring to November 25, because he left the embalming room in the early morning hours of November 23, just fifty or so hours earlier. "This delay" he referred to for the brain exam (2 H 355) was probably six days later, on the twenty-ninth. In his testimony before the ARRB in 1996, Humes says the brain exam was "a couple of days after" he delivered the autopsy report to the White House on Sunday evening, November 24, not a couple of days after the autopsy (ARRB Transcript of Proceedings, Deposition of Dr. James Joseph Humes, February 13, 1996, p.148).

to attend, we can be sure that when they conducted their second exam—this one of a different brain, the one that Humes and Boswell purloined from the morgue, and apparently fired a bullet (or drilled a hole) through from the rear—they would be double and triple sure not to invite him to this one also, since the likelihood of his recognizing the brain as different from the one he saw at the president's autopsy on November 22 could expose their participation in the conspiracy.

I mean, since Horne claims this second exam took place on November 29, only seven days after the November 22 autopsy, and Finck saw and was present when the president's brain was removed from the cranium at the time of the autopsy, he could be expected to remember how the president's brain looked, particularly since the right hemisphere was so badly damaged. Yet Finck never, in his personal notes and in his various testimonies since then, suggested the brain examined on November 29 was not the brain he saw removed from the president's skull on the evening of November 22. The only difference he noted was that the convolutions (ridges) of the brain were flatter, and the sulci (furrows or grooves) were narrower than at the time of the autopsy, two normal changes brought about by formalin fixation, a fact he recognized in his personal notes.[339*]

Horne, however, desperate to prove his theory, in effect rejects what Dr. Finck says and totally accepts the testimony of former FBI agent Francis O'Neill before the ARRB in 1997. O'Neill, many years after he probably looked over someone's shoulder in the crowded autopsy room to get a quick glimpse of the president's brain, said that the photos he was shown by ARRB counsel, supposedly of the president's brain, didn't look like the brain he saw at the time of the autopsy. "It [the brain seen in the photo from the National Archives he was shown] appears to be too much." On the night of November 22, 1963, he said, "More than half the brain was missing."[340] But if Dr. Finck noticed a change in the brain as minute as the width of the many grooves, surely he would have noticed if the size of the brain was markedly and demonstrably different, as O'Neill said. Yet Mr. Horne takes the word of a former FBI agent in the autopsy room, *thirty-four years after the fact*, over the word of one of the autopsy surgeons writing notes of his observations shortly after the autopsy. By the way, if Humes and Boswell were going to go through all the trouble of getting another brain, mangling and tearing part of it away to resemble Kennedy's, and drilling or shooting a hole through it from behind, wouldn't you think— if O'Neill's observation that the president's brain was much smaller than the photo of the brain he was shown was correct—they'd also do the much easier and obvious thing of making sure this other brain was the approximate size of Kennedy's?

Horne does his best to protect his credibility on his memorandum by burying in a footnote near the very end of it some information that severely damages the credibility of his star witness, autopsy photographer John Stringer. (But it's too late. There is nothing that can possibly restore the credibility of Doug Horne for the main conclusions he sets forth in the body of his memorandum.) Stringer, it turns out, told the ARRB that he had no recollection whatsoever of ever having spoken to, or having any contact with, anyone from the HSCA. Yet he was interviewed over the phone by an HSCA investigator on August 12, 1977, and accompanied HSCA personnel to the National Archives on August 15, 1977.

---

*Dr. Michael Baden, the chief forensic pathologist for the HSCA, confirmed for me the normalcy of these changes resulting from formalin fixation. On a broader note, Baden only had one word for Horne's whole theory: "ridiculous." (Telephone interviews of Dr. Michael Baden by author on July 14, 2000, and March 25, 2002)

And on September 11, 1977, he wrote a letter to Andy Purdy of the HSCA staff. Additionally, although he told Purdy of the HSCA on August 12, 1977, that he believed the doctors had "sectioned" the brain, on August 15 he told Purdy the doctors "didn't section the brain serially." They "cut some pieces from the brain . . . while normally they would cut it right in half."[341] "Within a few days," Purdy told me, "Stringer completely changed his story."[342]

With this type of witness who, though well intentioned, has no memory of three contacts with the HSCA staff, and through confusion or faulty memory has flatly contradicted himself on the principal point of whether the brain was sectioned—the point that launched Horne on his harebrained theory—Horne decides to build a case around him. Horne thereby rejected the language in the autopsy and supplementary autopsy reports, and sworn testimony of Drs. Humes and Boswell, that the brain was not cross-sectioned or coronally sectioned (only small sections were taken), taking Stringer's word in his 1996 testimony before the AARB over all of theirs that the brain was cross-sectioned. By doing so, he in effect accuses these honorable men of being in on a conspiracy to suppress the truth from the American public.

It obviously would be bad enough to take the word of someone whose credibility on this issue was as diminished as Stringer's was over that of Drs. Humes and Boswell,[*] but since Horne writes it was estimated that fifteen people were present at the supplementary exam of the president's brain, he must have been referring to more than just Humes and Boswell when he writes that Stringer's "recollection of the sectioning of the brain" was "at variance with every other witness to that event who can be located today."[343] No matter. Stringer's weak, lone, and self-contradictory recollection of the cross-sectioning of Kennedy's brain makes for a conclusion of two brains, a cover-up of the truth, and a sensational story. Everyone else's version, plus that of common sense, produces no story at all. When a reporter asked Dr. Boswell about Stringer's recollection of photographing cross-sections of Kennedy's brain, Boswell sneered, "He's full of [expletive]."[344]

Knowing that Stringer's memory and credibility are suspect, when I interviewed him over the telephone on September 21, 2000, I nonetheless sensed that the entire Stringer issue of whether or not Kennedy's brain was "sectioned" may have all been the result of a simple misunderstanding of terms. Now living in retirement in Vero Beach, Florida, Stringer told me he is certain the autopsy surgeons cut sections of the president's brain out, and that he photographed them. When I asked him if he meant by this that the surgeons made coronal, through-and-through sectioning, he said, "I don't recall if they cut it [the brain] through and through." Nor could he recall at this late date the size of the sections that were cut out. What was very illuminating, however, is that when I asked him how many photographs he took of the sections during the brain examination, he said, "I took around six or eight photos." Of each cut-out section? I asked. "No, no. You would only take one, or two at the most, of each section. I took six or eight total." The relevance of this, of course, is that as set forth earlier, and this bears repeating, in the supplementary report of the autopsy surgeons on the brain examination, it reads, "In the interest of preserving the specimen, coronal sections are not made. The following sections *are* taken for microscopic examination," whereupon *seven* sections are set forth (e.g., "from the right cerebellar cortex").[345] The seven sections cut out of the president's brain match up almost

---

[*]Not Finck, since, as indicated, Horne concludes that Finck was only present at the alleged second supplementary exam, and unaware of the fraud being perpetrated by his colleagues.

perfectly with the "six or eight" photographs (assuming he didn't take more than one photo of each section) Springer said he took. One additional point on this issue. Although Stringer testified in his ARRB deposition, "If I remember, it was cross-sections," launching Horne into a world whose dwellings are booby hatches, he had said earlier that the autopsy surgeons "*took* some sections" of the brain,[346] language one would be more apt to use if, as the supplementary autopsy said, "sections are *taken*" of the brain, than one would use if through-and-through, bread-loaf incisions were made.

Before Doug Horne, the main beef that most conspiracy theorists had with the autopsy surgeons was their alleged incompetence. But thirty-five years after the assassination, Horne showed all these naive, whippersnapper conspiracy theorists a thing or two. Humes and Boswell weren't incompetent. They were criminals and co-conspirators.

One would think that Horne would be ashamed of himself for writing the memorandum he did. But to the contrary, he is very proud. In an introduction to his memo that he wrote for *Probe*, a small, informative conspiracy publication that has since folded, he said his view of his memo as being "extremely significant, even seminal" was confirmed by the reaction of others of its importance, and that while he was writing it he "felt electrified" because of his "unique and revelatory interpretation" of the evidence "that was critical to proving that there was a massive government cover-up of the medical evidence in the JFK murder." Horne goes on to say in his introduction that he was "still surprised" that no one else previously saw what he did and published the hypothesis before he did.[347] But he has no reason to be surprised. Most people don't have thoughts this irrational. And if, perchance, such a vagrant thought enters their mind, they recognize it as such. When you have such a virtually insane thought and you don't realize it, that's when, you know, there's a problem.

There is one delightful gem that I must add to this section to lighten it up. Dr. David Mantik, a Loma Linda, California, cancer specialist, is, like Dr. Gary Aguilar, a part of the new wave of conspiracy theorists. Taking Horne's theory to vertiginous heights, listen to what he has to say about Horne's substitute brain. "If there was a surrogate brain, it *also* has disappeared . . . It is not likely that RFK would have wanted even a surrogate brain placed on public display as if it were his brother's. *Most likely*, RFK placed the authentic brain into the coffin for initial burial on Monday, November 25, and was therefore fully aware that a surrogate brain had later surreptitiously appeared . . . If RFK understood the role that the surrogate brain had played, as he probably did, he could have used any convenient waste disposal site [to dispose of it]."[348] My God. RFK somehow finds out that Humes and Boswell, as part of an apparent conspiracy to cover up the assassination of his brother, used a brain other than his brother's to conduct their examination. So he goes out and finds, seizes, and then gets rid of his brother's substitute brain. Is there any end to the silliness?

Dr. Mantik, as is obvious from his scholarly research in the Kennedy case as well as his background, is a person of considerable intelligence. Not only is he an oncologist, but also a radiologist with a doctorate in physics. How, then, can Mantik and thousands like him in the conspiracy community—many of lesser intellect—end up uttering absurdities like this, as well as countless others throughout the years? The answer is that within the world of insanity there is an internal logic. By that I mean one can frequently have a perfectly intelligent conversation with an insane person if one is willing to enter that person's world of insane suppositions. Mantik is clearly a very rational person and not insane, but for whatever reason he is starting out with an insane premise (in this case, Horne's theory). The internal logic that flows from this premise makes perfect sense. But only from the outside peeping into this mad world can one see how utterly crazy his "logical" conclusions are.

A great number of nuts have kept pumping out conspiracy theories for years. But these are private nuts, on the outside as it were. But when someone like Horne, working for an official review board of the federal government, someone we expect to be responsible, can author a document that couldn't possibly be any sillier or transparently irresponsible, then unfortunately we know that the notion of a conspiracy in the Kennedy assassination will be alive and well until the crack of doom. I suppose it is a given that there will be other Doug Hornes who will breast-feed the conspiracy loonies for generations to come with their special lactations of bilge, blather, and bunk.

One wants to take earnest, well-intentioned, and intelligent people like Drs. David Mantik and Gary Aguilar seriously, even though neither of them are pathologists. But when they take someone like Doug Horne seriously, and accept his outrageous and patently false theory as completely valid,[349] it becomes much more difficult to take them seriously.

It would be reassuring to know that Doug Horne was just an ARRB aberration, an unaccounted-for loose cannon. But very unfortunately, the evidence seems to indicate that Horne had soul mates, important ones at that, at the ARRB. Jeremy Gunn, the one-time executive director, no less, for the review board, told George Lardner Jr. of the *Washington Post* that he thought it was "highly plausible" that there were two different brain examinations.[350] In other words, in Gunn's view, it is "highly plausible" that Drs. Humes and Boswell joined in the conspiracy by getting another brain, altering it to reflect a shot from where Oswald was, when they knew the fatal shot came from the front, then lied under oath to everyone about their findings. And I repeat. This was an executive director of the ARRB!

In case the reader is wondering, I did not call Doug Horne to have him comment on his highly defamatory (to Drs. Humes and Boswell) and scurrilous memorandum. I would not be interested in anything further he had to say. But on August 21, 2000, I did call and speak to Horne's superior, Jeremy Gunn. Gunn immediately tried to distance himself from Horne. When I said to him, "You of course have read Douglas Horne's memorandum," he said, "I try to avoid reading anything written by Douglas Horne." When I told him that in Horne's introduction to the *Probe* republication of his memo Horne said he had shown him (Gunn) the first draft of his memorandum on August 28, 1996, and that Gunn had told him he liked what Horne had written about the two-brain discovery "very much" and that it was "very persuasive," but that it was "a little bit too one-sided, and a little bit too biased in tone" and that he could be more effective in making his argument if he included "devil's advocate" arguments on the other side,[*] Gunn said, "Anything that Horne said about any conversation I had with him I would not consider reliable."

Gunn refused to give me his opinion on the merits of Horne's theory, saying, "I don't want to get into any of this. It's no longer a part of my life. I want to stay away from all of this as far as I can." When I reminded him that he had told the *Washington Post*'s George Lardner Jr. on November 10, 1998, that he found Horne's position "highly plausible," he responded that so often in interviews, remarks are taken "out of context," adding he would "neither confirm nor deny" he told Lardner this.

---

[*]We can probably thank Gunn for small favors—the aforementioned negative footnote on Stringer, which Horne buried near the end of his memorandum.

The bottom line is that finally, in 1996, Doug Horne, after thirty-five long years, proved what the conspiracy theorists had only been alleging—Oswald was innocent, and the killer or killers were firing from the grassy knoll. Most of the conspiracy community has welcomed Horne with open arms. He is routinely praised in conspiracy publications and articles and has been the guest of honor at gatherings of conspiracy buffs. "This man is a hero," gushed conspiracy writer Joseph Backes in a 1999 article.[351]

Before I get into Governor Connally's wounds, let me point out that Horne, without expressly saying it, at a minimum accused Drs. Humes and Boswell not only of perjury, but also, as indicated, of being criminal accessories after the fact to Kennedy's murder by joining a conspiracy to suppress the truth. He writes that "Drs. Humes and Boswell were present at *two different* brain examinations, and that they have intentionally tried to obscure this fact from all official parties to whom they have spoken *or testified* about this matter over the past thirty-three years."[352] In other words, Horne wants us to believe one of two possibilities. The first is that someone (one of the conspirators who was behind Kennedy's murder) "got to," or "reached" Drs. Humes and Boswell—you know, tapped them on the shoulder and whispered into their ears, or some variation thereof—*after* Kennedy was killed, but before the autopsy, and got them to join the conspiracy. And I imagine it was easy for the doctors to decide to help frame Oswald for Kennedy's murder. After all, everyone else in the world was in on the conspiracy. Why shouldn't they be? Why should they rain on the parade?

But that's really the most unlikely of the two scenarios by far. If Humes and Boswell were going to be called upon by the conspirators to do what they did, the people behind this incredibly complex conspiracy obviously would never wait until after Kennedy was killed to start feverishly rounding up pathologists (in the few hours before the autopsy) to carry out that end of the plan. Those pathologists would necessarily have to be already on board. Meaning what? That Humes and Boswell weren't just accessories *after* the fact to Kennedy's murder, but *part of the conspiracy to murder him*. This is what Horne, and all of the many in the conspiracy community who have embraced his theory, have, in effect, accused Humes and Boswell of. In other words, they knew, *before* Kennedy's murder, that he was going to be murdered, and agreed to be part of this conspiracy to murder him—their role being to help cover it up. And since, under the law of conspiracy (the so-called vicarious liability rule), each member of a conspiracy is criminally responsible for all crimes committed by his co-conspirators to further the object of the conspiracy, under federal law and the law in every state, if Horne's allegations were true, Humes and Boswell would be guilty not only of the crime of conspiracy to commit murder, but also of Kennedy's murder itself. Again, as I've said so many times in this book, it's just too insane for words.

And by the way, the conspirators would have had to have a team of pathologists ready at two hospitals to perpetrate the cover-up that Horne is sure took place. What I'm saying is that even if we exclude Parkland Hospital (which one can't really do, since the conspirators couldn't know, for sure, that the autopsy would not be conducted there), since it looked like the autopsy was going to be conducted at Walter Reed Army Medical Center in Washington, D.C., until Jacqueline Kennedy, midair between Dallas and Washington, D.C., decided on Bethesda, the conspirators would have also had to line up some pathologists at Walter Reed—in other words, if the autopsy was at Walter Reed, almost for sure the pathologists would not have been Humes and Boswell, who were naval doctors, but instead army pathologists. So the conspirators, cold-blooded murderers from the Mafia or CIA or KGB, and so on, would have necessarily had to approach not only

Humes and Boswell, but also their counterparts at Walter Reed. And since other pathologists would be available at both places and the conspirators wouldn't know until *after* Kennedy died who among them would be assigned to the case, the superiors of Humes and Boswell and the superiors at Walter Reed would also have had to have been approached* and told that they intended to murder the president and asked if they would be willing to join in the conspiracy. And of course, after they heard the conspirators' proposal, none of the pathologists told them, "Are you crazy? The moment you leave I'm going to call the police." Instead, every single pathologist the conspirators approached apparently agreed to participate in the conspiracy to murder Kennedy.

At the time of the president's autopsy, Dr. Humes was a commander in the Medical Corps of the U.S. Navy and senior pathologist and director of laboratories of the Naval Medical School at the Naval Medical Center in Bethesda. Humes received his undergraduate training at Villanova University in Philadelphia and his medical degree from Jefferson Medical College in Philadelphia. His internship and postgraduate training in his special field of pathology took place at various naval hospitals and at the Armed Forces Institute of Pathology at Walter Reed Hospital in Washington, D.C.

Dr. Boswell was also a commander in the Medical Corps of the U.S. Navy and the chief of pathology at the Naval Medical School at Bethesda. Receiving his medical degree from Ohio State University College of Medicine, he interned at naval hospitals and took his pathology training at St. Albans Naval Hospital in New York.

But of course, according to Mr. Horne, all of this background of Drs. Humes and Boswell was simply preparation for their date with infamy—becoming big-time felons by joining shadowy conspirators who clandestinely approached them and enlisted their participation as conspirators in the murder of John F. Kennedy. Why would they want to jeopardize their lives and careers and legacy to do something so incredibly reprehensible as this? You'd have to ask the eminent Mr. Horne that question. So far he hasn't said.

Just as the discredited acoustic evidence has left an indelible stain on the legacy of the HSCA with its unwarranted conclusion of conspiracy, Doug Horne (and those who allowed him to do his thing) to a lesser degree has left a stain on the legacy of the ARRB, which overall did an excellent job under the chairmanship of John R. Tunheim. In a form letter sent to people around the country seeking assassination-related documents they might have, the then executive director of the ARRB, David Marwell, pointed out that the ARRB was a federal agency "whose members were appointed by the President and confirmed by the Senate" and "charged with the responsibility of collecting records related to the assassination of President Kennedy." The letter went on to say that the ARRB "*is not seeking to reach any conclusions*" regarding the assassination, but is primarily concerned with "identifying, clarifying, locating and making available assassination records." From that very clear and limited mandate, the atmosphere at the ARRB apparently was such that someone like Doug Horne was allowed to pursue his fantasies to such an extent that not only was a prohibited and crazy conclusion reached and published, but it was one that accused innocent and honorable men of murder.

Not that Humes's and Boswell's characters have to be vouched for, but when I asked

---

*Dr. Humes testified before the Warren Commission that when it first became known on the afternoon of November 22 that the autopsy would be at Bethesda, "I was called to the [Bethesda Medical] Center by my superiors and informed that the president's body would be brought to our laboratories for an examination, and I was charged with the responsibility of conducting and supervising this examination" (2 H 348).

John Stringer what he thought of Douglas Horne's two-brain theory, he chuckled and said, "What these people won't come up with next?" About the possibility that Humes and Boswell (both of whom, he said, he knew very well and worked with for many years) would ever do what Horne accused them of, Stringer, who is now in his late seventies, said, "Oh, no. Not even a chance. They were both honest and sincere men, real gentlemen. I would trust anything they said."[353]

What is Humes's take on all of the conspiracy theories, some of which, like Horne's, involve him? He called them "general idiocy" and "a tragedy" themselves. "It almost defies belief," he said. "But I guess it is the price we pay for living in a free country. I can only question the motives of those who propound these ridiculous theories for a price and who have turned the president's death into a profit-making industry."[354]

Governor Connally's Wounds

Of course, President Kennedy wasn't the only one shot during the motorcade. Texas Governor John B. Connally was also wounded, although the nature of his wounds is far less controversial than that of the president's. According to both the Warren Commission and the HSCA, the governor suffered five wounds caused by a single bullet that struck the upper right area of his back, exited the right side of the chest (just below the right nipple), reentered the back of his right wrist, exited the opposite side, and finally came to rest after causing a superficial entrance wound in the left thigh.[355] Three surgeons attended the governor: Dr. Robert R. Shaw (chest), Dr. Charles F. Gregory (wrist), and Dr. Tom Shires (thigh).

Dr. Shaw's postoperative report describes the "wound of entrance" in the governor's upper right back as being "just lateral to the right scapula [shoulder blade] close [to] the axilla [armpit]."[356] The HSCA medical panel described the location of the entrance wound more precisely as 20 centimeters (7 9/10 inches) right of the midline and 18 centimeters (7 1/10 inches) below the top of the first thoracic vertebra.[357] In other words, just below and to the left of the right armpit. Shaw wrote that the entrance wound was "approximately 3 centimeters [1 1/5 inches] in its longest diameter."[358] This was later corrected by Dr. Shaw to 1.5 centimeters (3/5 inch) in its longest diameter during testimony before the Warren Commission and again during an interview for the HSCA.[359] (Shaw explained to the HSCA that when the edges of the wound were later surgically cut away, this effectively enlarged the entrance wound to about 3 centimeters.)

During the HSCA interview, Dr. Shaw prepared a drawing of the entrance wound in which the longest dimension is in the *vertical* plane.[360] However, on September 6, 1978, Dr. Michael Baden conducted a physical examination of Governor Connally's wounds in the governor's room at the Mayflower Hotel in Washington, D.C., and found that the scar from the entrance wound was actually longest in the *horizontal* plane.[361] This fact coincides with the hole in the back of Connally's suit coat, which also was found to be longest in the horizontal plane.[362] The egg shape, as opposed to a circular shape, of the wound indicates it had hit an intervening object (almost assuredly President Kennedy's body) before it hit Connally, causing it to "tumble." (See discussion in endnote and in text of the Zapruder film section.)

Because of the back wound's small size and relatively clean-cut edges, Dr. Shaw, who had a considerable amount of experience evaluating gunshot wounds (having attended to over nine hundred gunshot cases as head of the Thoracic Center in Paris, France, during World War II), concluded that it was an entry wound.[363]

After entering the governor's back, the bullet passed downward through the chest, where it tangentially struck the midpoint of the fifth rib, shattering approximately 10 centimeters (4 inches) of the rib before exiting. The exiting bullet (and accompanying rib fragments) blew a 5-centimeter (2-inch) ragged hole in the governor's chest at a point 7.5 centimeters (3 inches) to the right of the midline and 2.5 centimeters (1 inch) below the right nipple.[364] Dr. Shaw described it as a sucking wound, meaning that air was allowed to pass freely between the chest cavity and the outside of the body.[365]

During Governor Connally's appearance before the Warren Commission, Dr. Robert Shaw measured the angle of declination between the entrance and exit wounds in the governor's chest and concluded that the bullet that struck the governor proceeded on a downward angle of 25 degrees.[366] In a 1964 analysis based on an examination of the bullet holes in the governor's suit coat, the FBI reported that the bullet "passed through Governor Connally at an angle of approximately 35 degrees downward from the horizontal and approximately 20 degrees from right to left if he were sitting erect and facing forward [neither of which he was doing] at the time he was shot."[367] The right-to-left trajectory is consistent, as we saw earlier, with the right-to-left path the bullet took through Kennedy's body.

Considering the nature and location of the entrance and exit wounds, the bullet that struck the governor's chest, then, was fired from above and behind and was moving slightly right to left, consistent with Oswald's firing position on the sixth floor of the Book Depository Building, located to the right rear of the presidential limousine.

The second entrance wound the governor suffered was caused by the bullet exiting just below the governor's right nipple and going on to enter his right wrist. Dr. Charles Gregory, who attended to the governor's wrist wound, wrote in his postoperative report that the wound was located "on the dorsal aspect [i.e., the back] of the right wrist over the junction of the right distal fourth of the radius and shaft," and testified that the wound was "approximately 5 centimeters [2 inches] above the wrist joint."[368] The wound was approximately 0.5 centimeter wide ($\frac{1}{5}$ inch) and 2 centimeters ($\frac{4}{5}$ inch) in length, rather oblique (i.e., the bullet had entered at an angle), with a loss of tissue and considerable bruising at the margins.[369] X-rays showed that as the bullet passed through the right wrist it caused a comminuted (i.e., shattering) fracture of the radius (one of two bones connecting the hand to the arm) into seven or eight pieces. Near this radial fracture were found a number of bits of metal.[370] Several were removed during surgery; however, no effort was made to recover all of the tiny fragments seen in the X-rays. The few fragments recovered from the governor's wrist were found by chance as the wound was cleaned.[371]

All of the evidence surrounding the governor's wrist wound indicates that a bullet, tumbling and distorted from having struck a previous object, impacted the back of the right wrist, shattered the right radius (depositing small fragments of metal), and exited on the palm side of the wrist close to an inch above the wrist joint.[372]

The governor's third entrance wound occurred when the bullet that exited the right wrist went on to hit his left thigh, causing a superficial injury. Dr. Tom Shires, who examined the wound, testified that there was a puncture or entrance wound 1 centimeter ($\frac{2}{5}$ inch) in diameter over the junction of the middle and lower third of the left thigh. X-rays of the wound revealed only a small fleck of metal lying about $\frac{1}{2}$ inch beneath the surface of the skin.[373] The doctors thought the bullet might have ended up somewhere else in the left leg and so additional X-rays were taken, but no bullet was seen. The doctors knew that a fragment so small could not have produced the nearly ½-inch–diameter puncture wound in the thigh, and were perplexed that they could not find a bullet of sufficient size to account for the three wounds in the governor's body.[374] Of course, we know that a bullet (Commission Exhibit No. 399) *was* found that afternoon by a hospital maintenance worker on a stretcher at Parkland Hospital believed to have been occupied by Governor Connally.

Dr. Gregory opined that the stretcher bullet could very well have struck the thigh in reverse fashion (i.e., base end first), shed a small fragment immediately beneath the skin, then, because it hadn't penetrated the thigh deep enough, worked its way out of the wound.[375] The reduced velocity of the bullet after having passed through Kennedy's and Connally's bodies would be the main factor causing it to penetrate the governor's left thigh only slightly. Although the muzzle velocity of the Mannlicher-Carcano rifle is 2,296 feet per second,[376] the FBI estimated that the speed of the bullet at the time it struck Kennedy in the back was around 1,900 feet per second.[377] It is believed to have lost speed of about 100 feet per second in passing through the soft tissue of Kennedy's body and over 400 feet per second after having struck Connally's rib and radius.[378] The HSCA estimated that the speed of the bullet when it exited Connally's wrist and struck his left thigh would probably have been reduced down to around 1,100 to 1,300 feet per second.[379]

Dr. Shires told the Warren Commission that during the operation on Governor Connally, all three attending surgeons, as well as their assistants (Drs. McClelland, Baxter, Patman, Osborne, Parker, Boland, and Duke), thought that *one* bullet had caused all of the governor's wounds.[380] The majority of the nine-member HSCA medical panel (Dr. Cyril Wecht was the only dissent) agreed.[381]

Although the medical findings *alone* do not provide enough evidence to state with absolute certainty that the bullet that passed through the president's body went on to hit the governor, the majority of the HSCA forensic panel members (with the exception of Dr. Cyril Wecht) felt that the medical evidence was "consistent with this hypothesis" (i.e., the single-bullet theory) and "much less consistent with other hypotheses."[382] In fact, as you'll see later in this book, when other nonmedical evidence is considered, there can be *no reasonable doubt* that both men were struck with the same, single bullet.

The Most Famous Home Movie Ever,
the "Magic Bullet,"
and the Single-Bullet Theory

No other issue in the Kennedy assassination has given birth to more literature and argument among Warren Commission critics, supporters, and students of the assassination than the timing and number of bullets that were fired in Dealey Plaza, the resolution of which involves no less than whether or not there was a conspiracy in the death of the president. The principal source and starting place for their inquiry is always the Zapruder film, the twenty-six-and-a-half-second, 8-millimeter color film of 486 frames shot by Dallas dressmaker Abraham Zapruder, for certain the most famous and examined film footage in history.

It is also, in the estimation of the *New York Times*, "the most valuable piece of film in the world,"[1] the U.S. government paying Zapruder's heirs $16 million in 1999 for the original footage. After Time-Life purchased the film from Zapruder for $150,000 in 1963 for its magazine, *Life*, payable in six installments of $25,000 per year (the first $25,000 of which Zapruder contributed to the family of slain police officer J. D. Tippit),[2] Time-Life returned the film and copyright back to the Zapruder family for one dollar in 1975. On April 24, 1997, the Assassination Records Review Board, on a 5-to-0 vote, declared that the Zapruder film was "an assassination record," and hence, the historic film became the property of the federal government, the board's ruling being effective as of August 1, 1998.[3] However, the U.S. Constitution (the Fifth Amendment in 1791) requires the government to pay the owners of private property "taken for public use" a "just compensation," and the question became what was the original film worth. The government originally offered $750,000 but hinted it might go as high as $3 million. The Zapruder family, led by Zapruder's son, Henry, a Washington, D.C., tax attorney, countered that it believed the half minute of history captured on the film would auction for as high as $30 million, but asked for $18 million. A three-member arbitration panel, in a 2-to-1 vote, agreed to the sum of $16 million, plus $800,000 in interest.[4] Today, the film and two original copies sit in a refrigerated, fireproof safe at the National Archives in College Park,

Maryland, too fragile ever to be run through a projector again. A third original copy was donated by Zapruder's heirs to the Sixth Floor Museum located inside the old Book Depository Building in Dallas.[5]*

Although entire books and millions of words have been written to analyze and interpret the Zapruder film, my personal view, for whatever it's worth, is that while the film is very important to the assassination inquiry, it has been given more attention than it deserves, its examination to determine the timing and number of shots being more of an intellectual, academic exercise than providing conclusive evidentiary value. There are several reasons why I say this, among which is the fact that the Zapruder film is a silent one (if there were sound on the film, we'd *know* the number of shots and their timing), making interpretation of it subjective and speculative for the most part. Moreover, we don't need the Zapruder film at all to tell us what happened. Indeed, less than .01 percent of all murders, if that, are captured on film, yet law enforcement has done quite well, thank you, without such films in proving beyond a reasonable doubt exactly what happened. And here, even without the Zapruder film, there were well over a hundred witnesses to the murder in Dealey Plaza—here again, a fact that sets the assassination apart from nearly all other murders. The overwhelming majority of premeditated murders don't even have *one* eye or ear witness, yet law enforcement normally is successful in proving the defendant's guilt beyond a reasonable doubt.

It is because virtually all authors of books on the assassination have had no background in law enforcement that a remark like the following, from anti-conspiracy author Gerald Posner, could be made: "To think that if the Zapruder film did not exist we would *never* be able to prove with *any* certainty what happened in Dealey Plaza."[6]

So traditionally—and the Kennedy case is no exception—guilt (and the existence or nonexistence of a conspiracy) in a murder case is proved not by a film or eyewitnesses, but rather by other evidence. And in this case, the physical evidence isn't just persuasive or even overwhelming, it's *absolutely conclusive* that only three shots were fired, and that one of the two shots that hit Kennedy also went on to hit Connally. Hence, Connally was not hit by a separate bullet, which would have established a second gunman and a conspiracy.

Yet the Zapruder film remains the focal point for most conspiracy theorists who are drawn to this unique and grisly spectacle. Over the past forty years, the film, for many, has become the Holy Grail of the case for conspiracy. At first, the *apparent* backward snap of the president's head at the moment of the head shot, and the *alleged* delayed reaction between Kennedy and Connally around the time the Warren Commission claimed they

---

*The Zapruder film, art historian David Lubin wrote in his book *Shooting Kennedy: JFK and the Culture of Images*, may be "the saddest movie ever made." Saying that the "internal architecture" of the film even conforms "to the three-act structure" of modern motion pictures, "whether comedy, drama, or melodrama" (Act I being the smiling and radiant first couple; Act II, the tragedy; and III, the ending of the "terrible tale" as the limousine disappears into a dark tunnel), he writes that if major works of cinematic art "combine beauty . . . happiness, tragedy and horror," then the twenty-six-second film "may qualify as such a work." He sees JFK and Jackie as movie stars, "two of the biggest ever to pass before the eyes of a motion picture camera." (Lubin, *Shooting Kennedy*, pp.1, 4, 15) Playing off these and other observations by Lubin, *New York Times* reporter Richard B. Woodward writes that the very brief movie, "beginning in anticipation" as the limousine turns the corner into Dealey Plaza, ends "in national despair" less than half a minute later, the film suddenly over. Unlike the film of Ruby killing Oswald two days later, which provided sound for its viewers and showed the killer, not only is the Zapruder film eerily silent, but the killer is "off-screen, his presence announced only by the hero and heroine [JFK and Jackie] reacting to the gunshots." (Woodward, "The 40th Anniversary of a 26-Second Reel," *New York Times*, November 16, 2003, p.40; Lubin, *Shooting Kennedy*, pp.4, 17, 35)

were hit by a single bullet, were touted as absolute proof of two assassins. Today, even though the overwhelming majority of evidence has shown that neither allegation is true, most conspiracy theorists, embracing the philosophy of "Don't confuse me with the facts, I've already made up my mind," still cling tenaciously to these arguments. However, some theorists, knowing that the evidence has obliterated their position, are now actually arguing that the film itself has been altered as part of a massive cover-up to hide the truth about the "conspiracy." In this chapter, we'll examine the facts and the myths surrounding the timing and number of shots, the single-bullet theory, the president's head snap to the rear, the source of the gunfire, and allegations that the most famous home movie of all time has been altered to conceal the truth. We'll also learn that the "magic" bullet was not magic and the "pristine" bullet (same bullet) was not pristine.

Several hundred Dealey Plaza photographs relating directly to the assassination were taken by approximately thirty-one photographers on November 22, 1963, making the assassination of President Kennedy, arguably, the most photographed murder in history.

Contrary to popular belief, Zapruder was not the only one to capture the assassination on film.[*] Three other amateur films (by Marie Muchmore, Orville Nix, and Charles Bronson) did, but they are not nearly as valuable as the Zapruder film. All three were taken on the opposite side of the street from where Zapruder saw the right side of the president's head open up, and whereas Zapruder was only 75 or so feet away from the president at the time of the fatal head shot, Bronson was around 240 feet away, Nix around 215 feet, and Muchmore around 140 feet.[7] Moreover, the frame of the Bronson film that corresponds to the shot to the head is so unclear that nothing taking place can be identified, and the Muchmore frames corresponding to the head shot are partially obstructed by Dealey Plaza spectators. Only the Nix frames capture the fatal shot and snap of the head to the rear, though not with the clarity of the Zapruder film. Also, Nix did not shoot any film around the time of the first two shots.

Abraham Zapruder's home movie is unique in that it shows the presidential limousine throughout the entire period of the shooting. It was, and remains, the only complete film of the assassination, Zapruder first picking up the limousine with his camera as it made the turn onto Elm Street from Houston Street and, except for a few frames when the limousine was behind the Stemmons Freeway sign, continuing to take a motion picture of the limousine until it disappeared from sight to his right.

Born in czarist Russia in 1905, Zapruder emigrated to the United States in 1920 and landed a job at a New York City dress factory. He and his wife moved to Dallas, Texas, in 1941, where they raised two children. In 1954, Zapruder and a partner went into business as "Jennifer Juniors, Inc., of Dallas," which manufactured a line of young women's and children's clothing. By 1963, the company occupied the fourth and fifth floors of the Dal-Tex (Dallas Textiles) Building, located on the northeast corner of Elm and Houston

---

[*]The assassination of President William McKinley at the 1901 Pan-American Exhibition in Buffalo, New York, was also captured on film. Unlike the Zapruder film, investigators who studied Kinematographs (produced by the original Edison Laboratory) of President McKinley's speech easily identified the assassin, Leon F. Czolgosz, as he made his way through the large crowd toward the president. Attempts to detect Czolgosz exchanging glances with possible confederates failed, despite the use of enlargements. Another motion picture camera was a few feet from McKinley just as Czolgosz came through the receiving line and fired the fatal shots. (Olson and Turner, "Photographic Evidence," p.400)

across the street from the Texas School Book Depository.[8] On the morning of November 22, Zapruder left his Model 414PD Bell & Howell Zoomatic Director Series 8-millimeter movie camera at home, figuring that the drizzly overcast morning wouldn't allow him to get good movies of the president's scheduled motorcade trip past his office building. By late morning, however, sunshine began breaking through the thick cloud cover that shrouded Dallas. At the urging of his assistant, Lillian Rogers, Zapruder drove home and retrieved his amateur camera. He first thought of filming the motorcade from his office window, but decided to go down to the street for a better view. He found a good spot—a two-and-a-half-by-four-and-a-half-foot rectangular concrete pedestal about four feet high—on the north side of Elm Street in front of the decorative pergola. The perch would afford Zapruder, a tremendous fan of the president, a commanding view of the motorcade as it passed from his left to his right down Elm. Only the Stemmons Freeway sign, which stood between the concrete pedestal and Elm Street, would interrupt Zapruder's view for a moment.

Wearing his customary fedora hat and bow tie, the fifty-eight-year-old Zapruder climbed atop the pedestal, then urged his office receptionist, Marilyn Sitzman, to stand behind him on the pedestal in case "he got dizzy."[9] His camera loaded with a twenty-five-foot roll of 16-millimeter film (which in effect afforded him fifty feet of 8-millimeter silent film for his 8-millimeter camera), half of which had already been exposed, Zapruder checked to make sure it was fully wound, pushed the zoom lens to the maximum telephoto position, and set the camera to its "normal" run mode (approximately 18 frames per second).[10]

The first scene Zapruder shot of the motorcade was a seven-second sequence of the three lead Dallas police motorcycles (traveling a half block ahead of the motorcade's lead car) turning the corner from Houston onto Elm Street. Zapruder, unaware of the makeup of the motorcade, stopped filming as soon as he realized that the president wasn't coming into view. A moment later, the presidential limousine, its flags fluttering in the breeze, appeared among the cheering crowd gathered at the southwest corner of Elm and Houston. Just after the limousine had turned onto Elm and straightened out, Zapruder started filming again at frame 133, the first frame of the Zapruder film that shows the presidential limousine. The next ten seconds captured the presidential party waving to the crowd and then, in a moment of horror, coming under gunfire. Zapruder told the Warren Commission eight months later, "I heard the first shot[*] and I saw the president lean over and grab himself like this (holding his left chest) . . . For a moment I thought it was, you know, like you say, 'Oh, he got me,' . . . you've heard these expressions, and then I [said to myself]—I don't believe the president is going to make jokes like this, but before I had a chance to organize my mind, I heard a second shot and then I saw his head open up and the blood and everything came out and I started—I can hardly talk about it." Zapruder started crying. After taking a moment to compose himself, he continued, "Then I started yelling, 'They killed him, they killed him,' . . . and I

---

[*]The shot Zapruder describes as the first one was actually, from all the evidence, the second in the sequence. Zapruder was confused, testifying that "I thought I heard two, it could be three [shots], because to my estimation I thought he was hit on the second—I really don't know . . . I never even heard a third shot" (7 H 571). However, according to a *Dallas Times Herald* reporter's shorthand interview notes (jotted down on November 22), Zapruder said he "heard 3 shots . . . after the first one Pres slumped over grabed stomac . . . hit in stomac . . . two more shots . . . looked like head opened up and everything came out" (Trask, *Pictures of the Pain*, p.149 note 13).

was still shooting the pictures until he got under the underpass—I don't even know how I did it."[11]

In the hours after the shooting, Zapruder took the film to the Eastman Kodak Company in Dallas, where it was processed (developed), and later to the Jamieson Film Company, where three color copies were made. Zapruder turned two of the first-generation copies over to the Secret Service that night and sold the third copy and the original film to *Life* magazine the following morning (November 23).[12] One of the Secret Service copies was subsequently loaned to the FBI, which made a second-generation copy and sent it to the FBI laboratory for analysis. There, FBI special agent Lyndal Shaneyfelt, the FBI's photographic expert, assigned numbers to each of the frames, beginning with the first frame that showed the Dallas police motorcycles turning the corner from Houston onto Elm.[13] It has become customary to refer to each frame of the Zapruder film by Shaneyfelt's number, preceded by the letter *Z* for *Zapruder*, for example, Z186.

The Warren Commission's study of the film began in earnest on January 27, 1964. During seven, day-long examination sessions (not consecutive), Commission representatives (always in the company of Secret Service representatives) viewed a second-generation copy of the film at regular, slow-motion, and freeze-frame modes in an attempt to sort out exactly what happened. By day two, Special Agent Shaneyfelt suggested that the Commission try to get access to the original film, which no doubt would be clearer. On February 25, the assistant chief of *Life*'s photographic lab, Herbert Orth, brought the original film to Washington and projected it a number of times for the Commission (as well as representatives from the FBI and Secret Service). Shaneyfelt was right. The original film contained far more detail and clarity than the Commission's second-generation working copy.[14] Reluctant to loan out the original film because of the possibility of damage, *Life*, which jealously guarded the original film, publishing only selected frames in its November 29 and December 6, 1963, editions, agreed to make available to the Commission a set of 35-millimeter color slides, taken directly from the original film, of all pertinent frames of the assassination, determined by Shaneyfelt to be Z171–334.[15]

It wasn't long before the Commission's examination of the Zapruder film turned up a serious problem. FBI tests had determined that Oswald's Mannlicher-Carcano could not be fired twice in less than 2.3 seconds[16] (a figure that would later be revised). The FBI had also determined that Zapruder's Bell & Howell camera had been operating at an average speed of 18.3 frames per second on the day of the assassination.[17] The Commission noted that the Zapruder film showed the president waving to the crowd until he disappears from Zapruder's view behind the Stemmons Freeway sign at Z205. When he emerges a little over a second later, at Z225–226, he seems to be reacting to a shot. Yet an undiscerning view of the Zapruder film shows Governor Connally apparently reacting to a shot between Z235 and Z240.[18] As Raymond Marcus puts it in his 1966 book, *The Bastard Bullet*, "Even assuming that the shot to which JFK is reacting in 226 had struck him as early as 210 (the first frame in which he would have been clearly visible from the sixth floor window after emerging from behind the oak tree), there still would not be time for a second shot from the Mannlicher-Carcano rifle [to hit Connally] until at least 42 frames (2.3 seconds) later, or 252."[19] So at a minimum, 42 frames would have had to elapse between any first and second shot with Oswald's Carcano. In other words, at this very early stage in the analysis of the Zapruder film, it appeared that unless there was a delayed reaction by Connally, Connally was hit too late to have been hit by the same shot that hit Kennedy, and clearly too soon for Oswald to have gotten off another shot with his bolt-action Mannlicher-Carcano rifle. Ergo, four shots were fired in Dealey Plaza, not three, and hence, there was a conspiracy. Indeed, upon seeing the Zapruder film for the first time, several assistant counsels thought there must have been two assassins. One, David Belin, even called his wife to say there was a second gunman.[20]

It is a maxim in the conspiracy theorist community that to get around the apparent slight discrepancy in the reaction times of Kennedy and Connally, the Warren Commission "came up with" (as out of whole cloth) or "made up" the "single-bullet theory," the notion that irrespective of what the Zapruder film shows, the same bullet that hit Kennedy must have gone on to hit Connally. But the Commission didn't have to make the theory up. In view of all the evidence that there was only one gunman in Dealey Plaza (e.g., only one rifle and one gunman were seen, the bullets that killed Kennedy were connected to only one rifle, etc.), the Commission's conclusion became inevitable. However, what solidified the theory was the FBI and Secret Service reenactment of the shooting in Dealey Plaza on May 24, 1964 (see later text). When three points—the sniper's nest, the bullet wound to Kennedy's back, and the bullet wound to Connally's back—were found to exist along a straight line, the Commission's single-bullet theory was "substantiated."[21]

The Commission staff's hypothesis didn't exactly receive a warm welcome from all of the Warren Commission members. At the Commission's last meeting on September 18, 1964, and with its report scheduled to reach President Johnson's desk in just six days, the majority of Chief Justice Earl Warren, Representative Gerald Ford, Allen Dulles, and John McCloy sided with the staff's single-bullet theory, but Representative Hale Boggs and Senators Richard Russell and John Cooper thought it improbable. Boggs told author Edward Jay Epstein that he had "strong doubts" about the theory and felt the question was never resolved. Cooper claimed that "there was no evidence to show both men were hit by the same bullet." Russell was the most adamant and wanted his opposition to the single-bullet theory to be acknowledged in a footnote at the bottom of the page in the Commission's report.[*]

But Warren felt it was vital that the Commission release a unanimous report. After haggling over the language of the report, Russell relented (as did Cooper and Boggs) if his dissent was acknowledged by reducing the word the majority wanted ("compelling") down to "persuasive," and the Commission finally held that: "Although it is not necessary to any essential findings of the Commission to determine just which shot hit Gov-

---

[*]It is perhaps worth noting that out of the seven Commission members, the three who had problems with the single-bullet theory were among the least faithful in attending Commission hearings during which testimony was given, two of them the worst. Cooper missed 44 out of the 94 hearings, the fourth worst attendance record; Boggs missed 74 hearings, the second worst. Living up to Benjamin Franklin's adage that an empty drum sounds the loudest, Russell, who should have been the quietest, was the loudest dissenter. Shockingly irresponsible, Russell only attended 6 out of the 94 hearings, having more important things to do at the time, namely, being the leader in the Senate of the South's opposition to the passage of the 1964 Civil Rights Act. In fairness to Russell, he did write a letter to Johnson on February 24, 1964, saying that because of his "legislative duties," he did not have enough time to serve on the Commission, but Warren ignored the letter, and Russell continued to serve. (Fite, *Richard B. Russell*, pp.406, 416, 421) Chief Justice Warren, who was busier and had more responsibilities outside the Commission than anyone else on the Commission, had the best attendance record, commendably attending all or a portion of all 94 hearings. Representative Gerald Ford had the next best attendance record, showing up at 70 of the 94 hearings. Dulles attended 60, and McCloy 35. (Meagher, *Accessories after the Fact*, p.xxx)

ernor Connally, there is very persuasive evidence from the experts to indicate that the same bullet which pierced the President's throat also caused Governor Connally's wounds."[22]

As tape-recorded on the evening of September 18, President Johnson called Senator Russell at his home in Winder, Georgia. Russell complained to LBJ, "That danged Warren Commission business, it whupped me down so, I'm just worn out fighting over that damned Report." Russell proceeds to talk about his opposition to the single-bullet theory, saying, "The commission believes that the same bullet that hit Kennedy hit Connally. Well, I don't believe it."

LBJ responded, "I don't either," as if he had studied the issue and was very knowledgeable about it, both of which we can reasonably assume are not true.

Russell goes on to say, "I couldn't sign it [the Report]. And I said that Governor Connally testified directly to the contrary and I'm not going to approve of that. So I finally made 'em say there was a difference in the commission, in that part of [us] believed that that wasn't so." Russell, who, as indicated, attended far fewer hearings of the Warren Commission than any other member, apparently was so out of it and ill-informed he never understood that the Commission agreed to no such thing. The members did make a concession to Russell, but only in the language used about the single-bullet theory conclusion. Nowhere does the Commission report refer to the division of beliefs among the Commission members about the theory. One typed transcription of the telephone conversation has Russell telling LBJ, "I tried my best to get in a dissent, but they'd come 'round and *trade me* out of it by giving me a little old *threat*."[23] But when assassination researcher Max Holland listened to the tape, he concluded that Russell had actually said, "Little old *thread* of it."[24] Russell most likely was referring to the "thread" or tidbit the Commission had given him in reducing the language from "compelling" down to "persuasive."

Russell tells LBJ that "I don't think you'll be displeased with the Report. [But] it's too long."[25]

A point that never, ever is mentioned by the conspiracy theorists who speak about the division among the Warren Commission over the single-bullet theory is that although a minority of members found the theory hard to accept, the report that all seven Commission members signed off on said, "There was no question in the mind of any member of the Commission that all the shots which caused the President's and Governor Connally's wounds were fired from the sixth floor window of the Texas School Book Depository."[26]

Despite the Warren Commission's assertion that the single-bullet theory was not essential to its conclusion that there was no evidence of a conspiracy, as critics would correctly point out, the single-bullet theory *was* essential to its findings. Commission assistant counsel Norman Redlich put it more bluntly: "To say that [Kennedy and Connally] were hit by separate bullets is synonymous with saying that there were two assassins."[27]

It may be advisable to step back for a moment and reflect on what the dispute among the Warren Commission members over the single-bullet theory really says about the Commission. With the single-bullet theory being so important to the Commission's finding that there was no evidence of a conspiracy in Kennedy's murder, if—as virtually all conspiracy theorists allege—the Warren Commission deliberately set out to suppress the truth about a conspiracy from the American people, how would it be possible that three out of the seven members of the Commission voiced, for the public record, their skepticism about the theory's validity? Are the conspiracy theorists at least willing to alter their decades-old argument that "the Warren Commission" conspired to suppress the truth from the American people, by changing it to "four members of the Warren Commission" conspired to do so? Because if the other three members (Boggs, Russell, and Cooper) were trying to suppress the truth about a conspiracy, why in the world would they be advocating a position (i.e., the invalidity of the single-bullet theory) that could only serve to reveal the conspiracy's existence? And if the Warren Commission critics are willing to make this concession, as it would seem they almost have to, do they then really want us to believe that whoever (Warren?) decided to keep the truth from the American people only approached Ford, Dulles, and McCloy with his conspiratorial idea, not Boggs, Russell, and Cooper? Or that he also approached those three and they refused to join in the conspiracy, but agreed not to tell anyone about it?

Indeed, the very fact that the Warren Commission, by its noncategorical language ("very persuasive evidence"), did not unequivocally rule out the possibility that Kennedy and Connally were struck by separate bullets (in effect, not ruling out the possibility of a conspiracy) is itself extremely powerful evidence that not only didn't the Commission, or any portion thereof, set out to suppress the truth from the American people, but that its conclusion of no evidence of a conspiracy was not, as conspiracy theorists believe, a predetermined conclusion.

Although the HSCA, with more sophisticated technology at its disposal fifteen years later, and employing more experts to reach its determination, had little difficulty concluding that Kennedy and Connally were, indeed, struck by the same bullet,[28] the almost universal position of the conspiracy community is that the Warren Commission's single-bullet theory has "no basis in fact"[29] and was invented by the Warren Commission out of thin air. Actually, the single-bullet theory was only arrived at by the Warren Commission after a very comprehensive examination of all the evidence, including the Zapruder film. But at the start of the investigation, the FBI at first thought that three separate bullets caused the wounds to Kennedy and Connally. "Three shots rang out. Two bullets struck President Kennedy, and one wounded Governor Connally," the FBI wrote in its first preliminary report on the assassination on December 9, 1963.[30] FBI Director J. Edgar Hoover would later say that this error was based on oral comments made by the autopsy surgeons on the night of the autopsy (and picked up by the two FBI agents in attendance) that the bullet which struck Kennedy in the back had not passed through his body, a conclusion they reached because they couldn't find the exit wound. Although we've seen that the chief autopsy surgeon, Dr. James Humes, found out the following morning where the probable wound of exit was and incorporated this into the final autopsy report, the FBI and the Warren Commission did not get a copy of the autopsy report from the Secret Service until December 23, 1963, two weeks *after* the first FBI report on the assassination.[31]

A s I said at the beginning of this chapter, an examination of the Zapruder film to determine the timing and number of shots, and in particular, whether or not the bullet that hit Kennedy also went on to strike Connally, is mostly academic. We can have all the confidence in the world, by an examination of the physical evidence and the utilization of common sense, that it did do so. When you can establish the single-bullet theory by reference to evidence other than the film, you necessarily know that the film itself cannot, by definition, show something else. Therefore, anything in the film that is perceived to contravene the single-bullet theory is either a misinterpretation by the viewer or explainable in some other way. One could say, Wait a minute. Are you saying that even if it's very clear from the film that Kennedy and Connally were hit by separate bullets, we should ignore this fact? That the film can never count? No, I am not saying that at all. If, indeed, the film showed Kennedy and Connally being hit by separate bullets, then the film evidence would be powerful and persuasive. But since we *know* Kennedy and Connally were not hit by separate bullets, we know, before we even look at the film, that it *cannot* show otherwise. That the best that conspiracy theorists can possibly hope for in the film is confusion and ambiguity, not clear, visual evidence that Kennedy and Connally were hit by separate shots.

Let me give a different example of the point I'm making here. If, indeed, you can prove beyond all doubt that Oswald killed Kennedy, then you thereby know, by definition, that even if someone else confesses to the murder, he is either lying or crazy. An extension of this logic answers the contention made by conspiracy theorists that with every single point they make, the anti-conspiracy theorists claim they have a good answer. How can that be, they ask? The reason it can be is that all of the evidence proves Oswald's guilt and there is no credible evidence of a conspiracy. If, for the sake of argument, we accept these two propositions as realities, then naturally there *necessarily* and *automatically* are answers that satisfactorily explain away all contrary inferences and allegations, *irrespective of how many allegations there are*. Likewise, again by definition, if we were to accept the opposite proposition, that Oswald is innocent and there is credible evidence of a conspiracy, there could not be satisfactory answers to all adverse allegations.

So, what evidence is there, *unrelated* to the Zapruder film, that only three shots, not four (or more), were fired on the day of the assassination, and hence, the single-bullet theory is more than a theory, it's a reality? I can think of five reasons, based on evidence and logic, that are conclusive and overwhelming:

1. Perhaps the biggest argument the anti–single-bullet-theory advocates make is that the alignment of Kennedy's and Connally's bodies to each other was such that any bullet passing through Kennedy would have had to make a right turn in midair to go on and hit John Connally—thus, the "magic bullet" of conspiracy lore. As conspiracy author Robert Anson puts it, "After CE 399 emerged from the President's throat, evidently it stopped in midair, made a ninety degree [right] hand turn, traveled on a few inches, stopped again, made a ninety degree [left] hand turn, and then plunged into Governor Connally's body."[32] But actually, the alignment of Kennedy's and Connally's bodies to each other is, all by itself, virtually conclusive evidence in support of the single-bullet theory.

In a gross and brazen misrepresentation of the facts, sketches in conspiracy books and literature have consistently and falsely placed Connally seated directly in front of Kennedy in the presidential limousine. In fact, Connally's jump seat not only was situated a half foot inside and to the left of the right door, but also was three inches lower than the backseat[33]—placing him to the left and below Kennedy's position on the extreme right side of the limousine's backseat. (See photo section.)[34] The HSCA said, "A photogrammatic analysis of several pairs of pictures taken from the Zapruder movie" and viewed through a "stereoscopic viewer . . . clearly showed that Kennedy was seated close to the right-hand, inside surface of the car, with his arm resting atop the side of the car and his elbow extending . . . beyond the body of the car. Connally, on the other hand, was seated well within the car on the jump seat."[35] Moreover, at the moment Kennedy was hit with the bullet to his back, Connally's body was turned to his right, causing their bodies to be aligned in such a way that a bullet traveling on a downward trajectory, entering the upper right part of the president's back, passing through soft tissue in a straight line, and exiting his throat (which the Warren Commission and HSCA found), *had* to go on and hit the governor in the upper right part of his back. As Warren Commission assistant counsel Norman Redlich testified before the HSCA, the bullet that entered the president's back and emerged through the front of his throat "had nowhere else to go other than to hit Governor Connally."[36] But conspiracy theorists have avoided all this by simply placing Connally directly in front of the president, as the chief proponent of this false alignment, Robert Groden, does in a sketch that appears in a book he wrote with Harrison Livingstone, *High Treason*. (Note that in addition to Connally being seated directly in front of Kennedy as opposed to Kennedy's left front, Groden also doesn't show Connally's body turned to the right, as it was at the moment he was struck.)[37]

I encountered this misrepresentation on the alignment of Kennedy's and Connally's bodies to each other at the trial in London. On direct examination, Gerry Spence had Dr. Cyril Wecht testify about a schematic illustration introduced as a defense exhibit and supposedly based on the Zapruder film. It was the Groden sketch.* Wecht testified, "The Zapruder film, which I have seen countless times, shows that the two men were seated in essentially a straight line, the governor *directly in front of the president*." (On cross-examination, I introduced an illustration based on a photograph taken by Dealey Plaza spectator Hugh Betzner[38] showing Connally not directly in front of Kennedy, as Wecht asserted, but to the president's left, and his body, as opposed to the president's, being turned fairly sharply to the right.) Using the Groden sketch, Spence asked Wecht to tell the jury what the bullet that struck Kennedy in the back would have had to do to hit Connally. Answer: "When it [the bullet] exited from the front of the president's throat, it would have continued in a straight line. There's simply no way possible for that bullet to have entered Governor Connally's posterior right axillary area, which is a fancy way for saying behind the right armpit. If it hit him behind the right armpit, it would have had to come out of the president's neck and in some way veered back to the right and then stopped and turned around and started once again in a path towards the left. Bullets do not react that way, not even in comic books."[39]

On cross-examination I explored what happened to the bullet *after* it exited Kennedy's throat.

"Now, Doctor, if the bullet was coming on a downward path as it entered the presidential limousine, as you say it was, is that correct?"

Answer: "Yes."

Question: "And it missed Governor Connally, is that correct?"

Answer: "Yes."

Question: "Why didn't it hit the driver of the car or do any damage to the car?"

Answer: "Mr. Bugliosi, you are conveniently ignoring the fact that Elm Street is on a downward path which progresses in a more downward fashion as it goes away from the Texas [Book Depository] Building; and therefore, as the car is going downward and the

---

*The genesis of the Groden sketch was a copyrighted sketch drawn by conspiracy theorist R. B. Cutler in 1969 (Letter from R. B. Cutler to author dated December 14, 1986). Groden alludes to this in his testimony before the HSCA when he says the sketch he was using "was drawn by a Warren Commission critic" (1 HSCA 65). Although Cutler erroneously had Connally seated directly in front of Kennedy, he at least correctly had Connally turning to his right at the time he was hit.

bullet is going downward, then the declination, the angle downward of the car more than compensates for the slight downward angle of the bullet."

Question: "Oh, but Doctor, please, the degree of declination of Elm Street is 3 degrees,* and certainly the bullet [coming] from the second floor [where Wecht had speculated the assassin was] would have been 3 degrees higher on a horizontal plane than the presidential limousine."

Answer: "Not considerably higher."

When I asked Wecht once again why that bullet, after entering Kennedy's body, did not go on to hit anyone inside the presidential limousine or cause any damage to the interior of the limousine, he responded, "What happened? . . . Where is it? You're asking me to be responsible for the bullets in this case."

Question: "I'm asking you what happened to the . . . bullet."†

Answer: "I can't tell you where all the bullets are. I didn't conduct the investigation."

After I firmed up that he agreed the bullet passed through soft tissue on a "straight line through the President's body," yet he believed it did not hit Governor Connally, I derisively accepted the defense's notion of the prosecution's magic bullet by saying, "Doctor, the prosecution has its own magic bullet, and frankly, we're jealous of it . . . Now you've got *your* magic bullet, a bullet that is coming on a downward path into the presidential limousine, 2,000 feet a second, passes through President Kennedy's body . . . and it misses the driver and it misses the car. It must have zigzagged to the left?"

Answer: "No. It need not have zigzagged to the left."

Question: "Did it broadjump over the car?"

Answer: "No . . . It need not have performed any remarkable feats."

Question: "But you don't know what happened to it?"

Answer: "No, I do not. There is a lot of things I don't know about what happened to it in this case."[40]

If we're to believe Dr. Wecht and his fellow conspirators on this matter, after the bullet passed through Kennedy's body, it apparently vanished without a trace.

To further illustrate how untenable Dr. Wecht's position was, I proceeded to underline in the jury's mind how vulnerable he was in being the only one of nine pathologists on the HSCA medical panel to reject the single-bullet theory. I drew his attention to his testimony before the committee that his conclusion, as opposed to that of the other eight, was so obviously correct that it "is not in the realm of interpretative or speculative or conjectural opinion, but is related to things which I truly believe do not even require the expertise of a forensic pathologist to see and interpret."[41]

Question: "Well, Doctor," I then asked, "it seems to me that you're saying that if the other eight pathologists disagreed with you, and they did, is that correct?"

Answer: "Yes."

Question: "It seems to me, Doctor, that by necessary implication they are either hopelessly and utterly incompetent—if you say it's so obvious anyone can see it, [you] don't even have to be a doctor—or they deliberately suppressed the truth from the American people."

Answer: "That is up to other people to determine."

---

*For years, books and assassination researchers have loosely said 3 degrees, and I was guilty of this myself. But actually, the degree of declination was found to be 3.9 degrees (WR, p.106), which is almost 4 degrees.

†Another way of looking at this point is this: If Kennedy was hit by two bullets and Connally, as the conspiracy theorists maintain, by a third and separate bullet, what physical evidence is there (the bullet itself or even one single fragment of it) of this third bullet's existence?

Question: "No, I'm asking, is there any other alternative to these two?"

Answer: "Yes, there is a third alternative, which would be a hybrid to some extent to the deliberate suppression, sir. To some extent, a subconscious desire not to injure or aggrieve the government [to] whom they look for various research grants and appointments and lectureships at the Armed Forces Institute of Pathology, and a variety of reasons."

When I asked Wecht whether it wasn't true that these other doctors were "of good reputation and standing?" he responded, "You bring them here, sir, and present them to the jury. I can only present my testimony, show the pictures for his Honor and the jury. You bring the other eight in and let them present their views." (I did have one in London, Dr. Petty.)

Raising my voice considerably in irritation and disbelief, I said, "So of the nine pathologists, Dr. Wecht, you're the only one who had the honor and the integrity and the professional responsibility to tell the truth to the American people. Is that correct, Doctor?"

Dr. Wecht shouted back, "I'd prefer to put it this way. [I'm the only one] who had the courage to say that the king was nude and had no clothes on. Yes. That's correct."[42] Wecht had given me the answer that I was hoping to elicit from him in my line of questioning, and I was confident that his final words weren't helpful to him in the eyes of the jury.

If, as the conspiracy theorists allege, the bullet that exited the president's throat did not go on to hit Connally, it would have inevitably gone on to hit the driver or caused some significant penetrating damage to the interior of the car. Yet no such damage was found when the limousine was examined by Secret Service and FBI agents at the White House garage on the evening of the assassination. So to accept the proposition that the bullet that hit Connally didn't first hit Kennedy, you'd necessarily have to accept the further proposition that once the Kennedy bullet passed through his body, it literally, as I've said, vanished into thin air. When Robert Frazier of the Firearms Identification Unit of the FBI was asked by Warren Commission counsel what effect a whole bullet exiting Kennedy's throat and not hitting Connally "would have had on any . . . portion of the automobile which it might have struck in the continuation of its flight," Frazier answered, "In my opinion it would have penetrated any . . . metal surface and, of course, any upholstery surface."

Question: "Was there any evidence in any portion of the car that the automobile was struck by a bullet which exited from the president's neck under the circumstances which I have just asked you to assume?"

Answer: "No, sir, there was not."

Question: "And had there been any such evidence would your examination of the automobile have uncovered such an indication or such evidence?"

Answer: "Yes, sir, I feel that it would have."[43]

Since the bullet, after exiting Kennedy's throat on a downward trajectory, never struck the interior of the car, *it must have struck someone in the car.* And other than Kennedy, only Connally was hit by a bullet. This simple logic cannot be controverted. And the Warren Commission's most vocal proponent of the "single-bullet theory,"* Arlen Specter, told *Life* magazine in a 1966 interview, "Where, if it [the bullet that hit Kennedy in the back and exited his throat] didn't hit Connally, did that bullet go? This is the single most com-

---

*Although it is almost universally believed that Arlen Specter was the sole architect of the "single-bullet theory," a belief that he himself has promoted, there is evidence that he was not. (See endnote discussion.)

pelling reason why I concluded that one bullet hit both men."[44] In other words, since we know that the bullet exiting Kennedy's throat did not go on and hit the interior of the car, or Mrs. Kennedy, or Mrs. Connally, or either of the two Secret Service agents in the front seat, the only remaining place it could have possibly gone was into Connally's body.

To this very day, Arlen Specter (now a U.S. senator from Pennsylvania) has been the recipient of endless vitriol and condemnation by conspiracy theorists. The story of one of them is instructive. Andrew Purdy, the law student at the University of Virginia who brought conspiracy theorist Robert Groden to speak at his school in 1976, told me, "Groden told us the single-bullet theory was a complete fraud perpetrated by Arlen Specter, and most of us bought what Groden said hook, line, and sinker. I was convinced Specter was a liar and could never pass a polygraph test. In fact, I became the head of a group of around a hundred law students who lobbied Congress, by letters and actually knocking on their doors, to reopen the investigation [of the assassination]." When Congress, by its House Select Committee on Assassinations, did so in 1977, Purdy got a plum assignment as one of the leading assistant counsels to the committee, ready to expose the fraud and get the truth out. "But amazingly and astonishingly," he said, "when I closely looked at and examined all the evidence, I came around full circle. I am now certain the single-bullet theory is correct. And if I ever see Arlen Specter, I will apologize to him."[45]

An extension of the above argument comes at the question from a different direction and focuses on the allegation that the bullet that hit Connally *only* hit him: to my knowledge, everyone, even the extremists on the conspiracy fringes, agrees that Governor Connally was shot in his upper right back, not from the side or right front, as most conspiracy theorists believe Kennedy was. Some representative examples: "[the] bullet struck Governor Connally in the back";[46] "the missile that hit the Governor in the back";[47] "the [bullet] entered Connally's body at the rear of his right armpit";[48] and "this shot . . . struck the Governor in the back."[49] And they likewise all agree that the bullet was proceeding from back to front, not right to left or left to right. For example: "[The bullet] exited by the right nipple,"[50] and "the missile traversed Connally's chest, blasting out approximately four inches of the [right] fifth rib and collapsing the right lung. It exited below the right nipple."[51] Indeed, when Governor Connally testified before the Warren Commission on April 21, 1964, he took his shirt off in front of six out of the seven Commission members, General Counsel Lee Rankin, five assistant counsels, and four other observers, including Waggoner Carr, the attorney general of Texas, and Dr. Robert Shaw, the doctor who operated on him, and all looked at his wounds. As Arlen Specter, one of those present, put it, "It was perfectly plain as to the fact that the bullet had struck the governor in the back and had exited below the right nipple at a lower angle on the front of his body."[52]

A question I have for the anti–single-bullet conspiracy theorists is that if Connally did not receive the wound to the upper right part of his back in the way that the Warren Commission and HSCA concluded he received it, then just how in the world did Connally receive a wound to his back from a bullet fired from his rear without the bullet having struck Kennedy (whose upper body completely covered, looking from the rear, the right upper part of Connally's back, where he was hit) first? Who was it, if not Oswald, who fired this bullet that they say only hit Connally, and from what conceivable position in Dealey Plaza did he fire it?

2. A second powerful reason to believe in the validity of the single-bullet theory without any reference to the Zapruder film is the lack of any physical evidence supporting a second gunman. As has already been established, *three* shell casings ejected from Oswald's

Mannlicher-Carcano rifle were found on the sixth floor of the Book Depository Building beneath the southeasternmost window. If, indeed, a fourth shot had been fired that day (and hence, there was a second assassin), how is it possible that not one person, out of an estimated crowd of four to five hundred spectators in Dealey Plaza, saw a second gunman? Furthermore, how is it possible that a blanket search of the plaza by law enforcement agents right after the shooting failed to turn up any physical evidence of a second gunman (e.g., a shell casing, a fourth bullet, a second rifle, etc.)? Are we to believe, then, that the second gunman simply vanished into thin air? Not only he himself, but all *evidence* of his existence? Is that life in the real world? Or is that nonsense? Again, the lack of any physical evidence of a second gunman, all by itself, is extremely powerful evidence supporting the single-bullet theory.

3. Another fact that, all by itself, is virtually conclusive evidence proving the single-bullet theory is that the entrance wound in Governor Connally's back was not circular, but oval. Drs. Charles Gregory and Robert Shaw, who attended Connally at Parkland Hospital, described the wound as "linear" and "elliptical" in shape,[53] indicating that the bullet was out of alignment with its trajectory just before striking Connally's body. The HSCA said that a factor which "significantly" influenced its conclusion that the bullet that struck Connally had first struck and passed through Kennedy "was the ovoid shape of the wound in the Governor's back, indicating that the bullet had begun to tumble or yaw before entering. An ovoid wound is characteristic of one caused by a bullet that has passed through or glanced off an intervening object . . . The forensic pathology panel's conclusions were consistent with the so-called single bullet theory advanced by the Warren Commission," to wit, that one bullet had passed "through both President Kennedy and Governor Connally."[54]

My firearms expert at the London trial, Monty Lutz, told me that "no bullet traveling at 2,000 feet per second is going to start to tumble or yaw on its own until around 200 yards. When Connally was struck he was around 60 yards from the window, so the bullet had to have hit something before it hit him, and other than Kennedy's body, there was nothing between the sixth-floor window and him. Not the oak tree, or its leaves. Nothing."[55] It has to be emphasized that at the time Connally was struck by a bullet (somewhere between Z frames 210 and 222),* the oak tree to the north of Elm close to the Depository Building was no longer in the line of fire from the sniper's nest to Connally's body.[56] So Kennedy's body was the only intervening object that the Connally bullet could have first hit. HSCA physical scientist Larry M. Sturdivan told the committee that the Carcano bullet was a "very stable bullet, perhaps one of the most stable bullets that we have ever done experimentation with." He said that it would only start yawing—and then very little, "perhaps less than a degree"—at "about 100 meters" (about 110 yards) and "if it had struck [Connally] without having previously encountered another object, it [Connally's back wound] would never have been elongated. This bullet is too stable. It would have had to be a nice round hole."[57]

4. Another reason why we know Connally was hit by the same bullet that had struck Kennedy is that the argument that there wasn't enough time to fire a second shot from the bolt-action Mannlicher-Carcano rifle, and hence Connally must have been hit by a sec-

---

*Connally can first be seen reacting to being hit by a bullet at frame 222 of the Zapruder film, when his upper body can be seen for the first time emerging from behind the Stemmons Freeway sign (see photo section of book; HSCA Report, p.82).

ond assassin, *doesn't go anywhere*. It would only go somewhere if Commission Exhibit No. 399, *the bullet that struck Connally* (and which the Warren Commission and HSCA concluded had first struck Kennedy), hadn't been fired from Oswald's Mannlicher-Carcano. But firearm tests showed that it *was* fired from Oswald's rifle to the exclusion of all other weapons.[58] Therefore, even if we assume that Commission Exhibit No. 399 did not first pass through Kennedy's body, *we still know that it was fired from Oswald's rifle, not a different rifle,* and we don't have any evidence of a second assassin, only Oswald. Or did Oswald, after shooting Kennedy in the back, hand his rifle to a second gunman standing beside him and say, "I just shot Kennedy, now you shoot Connally?"

5. Finally, there's another reason, almost too embarrassingly simple to mention, why, independent of all the conclusive reasons set forth above, we can almost be certain that the shot that hit Kennedy also hit Connally: *no separate bullet was available to hit Connally!* Let me explain. No one alleges anymore that the first shot around Z frames 160 to 165 hit Kennedy or Connally. (See later text.) And everyone agrees that the last shot, at frame 313, only struck Kennedy. (See later text.) So if only three shots were fired, that only leaves one more bullet, folks, to have hit both Kennedy and Connally. At least last time I heard, three minus two leaves one. *Were* only three shots fired? Well, only three empty cartridge cases were found on the floor of the sniper's nest, and no other empty cartridge case was found anywhere else in Dealey Plaza. Also, of the two major studies of the number of bullets fired in Dealey Plaza, by author Josiah Thompson in his "Master List of Assassination Witnesses" in 1967, and the HSCA in 1978, 79 percent (Thompson) and close to 75 percent (HSCA) of the witnesses only heard three shots. *Only 3.5 percent of the witnesses in each study heard four shots.* (Small percentages of witnesses heard other numbers of shots, one claiming to have heard eight shots.) So the very, very high probability is simply that no other shot was fired that day that could have hit Connally without also having hit Kennedy. To be cruel to the buffs, *they simply ran out of bullets for their second-gun theory*. There was no other bullet flying through the air that could have *only* hit Connally.[*] To accept the position of the conspiracy theorists, one would have to reject the physical evidence (only three cartridge cases), but accept the hearing acuity of 3.5 percent of the people in Dealey Plaza over that of around 75 percent of the witnesses. Actually, the percentage of people the theorists would have to thumb their noses at would be 85 percent, since 10 percent of the witnesses in the HSCA study only heard two shots.[59]

Each of the above five reasons, alone and by themselves, proves the single-bullet theory *independent* of the Zapruder film. (I would defy any conspiracy theorist to come up with even one—much less five—logical arguments that are independent of the Zapruder film and support the proposition that Kennedy and Connally were hit by separate bullets.) All five of these reasons, when taken together, prove the proposition that Connally was hit by the same bullet that hit Kennedy not just beyond all *reasonable* doubt, but beyond *all*

---

[*]But conspiracy theorists shouldn't despair. If they need an extra bullet or two, I would refer them to Warren Commission critic Nord Davis Jr. Nord is a serious student of the assassination who has studied all twenty-six volumes of the Commission, and he is confident that *twenty-one bullets* were fired in Dealey Plaza. Now, I can't vouch for Nord's credibility. After all, he is the same fellow who says that the Parkland doctors confused Officer Tippit's body for that of President Kennedy. (Nord Davis Jr., "Dallas Conspiracy, Pardon Me, but . . . ," vol.44, self-published, 1968, pp.12, 16) But hey, with the desperate position the conspiracy theorists are in having run out of bullets, they can't be picky about who is trying to help them.

possible doubt. Therefore, the film itself cannot, by definition, show something else. As I said earlier, any interpretation of the film that contravenes the single-bullet theory either must be a misinterpretation by the person analyzing the film, or is explainable in some other way.

Although the Zapruder film, by itself, can never conclusively prove that Kennedy and Connally were struck by the same bullet, it will soon be obvious to the reader that a close examination of the film tends to corroborate, not refute, the single-bullet theory. Before we examine the sequence of shots fired during the assassination, I must point out the many built-in limitations in trying to analyze the Zapruder film.

First of all, the difficulties of extracting information from a film whose images are small are formidable. Film as small as that used in Zapruder's camera is limited in its ability to capture photographic detail, owing partly to the relatively large size of the film's grain (i.e., the chemical dots that compose the image). Those who have never seen 8-millimeter film might find it hard to imagine just how tiny each frame is. The film strip itself is 8 millimeters wide, less than a third of an inch. Since a part of this width is taken up by the borders of the frames and the sprocket holes running down one side of the film, the actual image area is much smaller—just nineteen-hundredths by fifteen-hundredths of an inch (about one-fifth the size of a postage stamp). The area that Kennedy and Connally occupy within that image is even smaller. When the film first begins, the images of both Kennedy and Connally fit into an area that is only one-sixty-fourth of an inch square, less than the head of a pin. Even at the point where they appear the largest in the frame (their image size grows as the limousine draws closer to Zapruder's camera), their combined images cover an area that is just one-thirteenth of a square inch. At Z225, around the time we can see they have been hit with a single bullet, Kennedy and Connally fit into an area one-twenty-sixth of a square inch. These images are so minuscule that the grain of the film obscures details, leaving us with a soft, slightly blurred image, a condition that is not improved by the enlargement of the individual frames.

Second, although one constantly hears how the film has been digitally enhanced with the very latest computer technology (mostly, film stabilization techniques designed to remove the "jitter" inherent in hand-held home movies, and amplifying the contrast between bright and dark portions of the film), to this very day most frames of the film available to researchers (second and later generations of the film) remain grainy and blurry, making interpretation virtually as difficult as it has always been. As Richard Trask, the leading authority on photographic evidence in the Kennedy assassination, points out, "In a 4 or 5 frame cycle [of the film], a pattern was found of a good frame preceded and followed by several less sharp [actually, frustratingly fuzzy] frames. This was very common in these cameras at the time and was attributable to the mechanized system of the camera itself."[60]

And let's not forget that, like all film, literally half of the movements of Kennedy and Connally were never captured by the film and have been lost forever. Why? Contrary to popular belief, a film does not provide a continuous image to the viewer. Instead, a sequence of still images is recorded in rapid succession by the motion picture camera, and when the sequence is played back at the proper speed, it creates the illusion of motion (through a natural human phenomenon known as "persistence of vision"). It takes a little more than twice as long to advance and stabilize each frame behind the closed shutter of the camera as it does to expose it, which means that for roughly half the overall time no image is being recorded at all. This lost time, seen as a screen "flicker" during projection, is more pronounced in home movies like the Zapruder film, which run at 18 frames per second, than in typical motion picture film shot for movie theaters, which runs at 24 frames per second. More frames (or images) per second results in less screen flicker during projection.

Another limitation is the subjective nature of film interpretation. Just as beauty lies in the eyes of the beholder, life's events are seen differently by different people, and nothing will ever change this phenomenon. Since interpretations of the movements of Kennedy and Connally in the Zapruder film are subjective (only the explosion to the president's head at frame 313 requires no interpretation), their value is inherently limited by the fact that the interpretations and the conclusions based thereon can never be proved or disproved scientifically. Moreover, it is a mission impossible to try to divine whether Kennedy and Connally, even if they were hit at the same time, showed this by their physical reactions. Since we know people can react to being struck by a bullet literally hundreds of seconds after the fact, then certainly either Kennedy or Connally could have reacted a second or so after being shot.

I elicited this well-known phenomenon of a "delayed reaction" from one of my Dealey Plaza witnesses at the London trial, Charles Brehm. Over many objections by defense counsel Gerry Spence, the judge allowed me to pursue the matter. To counter Spence's argument that Connally reacted too long after Kennedy did for them to have been hit by the same bullet, but too soon after Kennedy did for Oswald to have been able to fire two rounds, I wanted to offer to the jury a plausible reason for this in the event the jury accepted Spence's position.

Question: "Do you have any personal knowledge of a person being hit by a bullet and having any delayed reaction to having been shot?"

Brehm: "Yes, sir." Brehm said it was in 1944, during the Battle of Brest in France during the Second World War. He noticed a soldier on his left who got wounded in his right arm.

Question: "How do you know that?"

Answer: "Because he bloodied up in that area."

Question: "You saw a reddening of his jacket?"

Answer: "That's correct."

Question: "And you presumed it was blood?"

Answer: "Yes."

Question: "At the time you saw the blood, what was he doing?"

Answer: "We were all on a dead run across the field."

Question: "He was continuing on?"

Answer: "Yes."

Question: "He didn't stop?"

Answer: "No."

Question: "He didn't put his left hand over his right arm?"

Answer: "No."

Question: "Nothing at all?"

Answer: "No."

Question: "He showed no visible signs of his reaction to being hit?"

Answer: "None at all."

Brehm testified that "in the months that I spent with him in the hospital, he said that he could not remember being hit in the arm. It was only after he was [also] hit in the side that he was aware he was wounded."[61] In this case, Connally himself testified before the HSCA that although he was aware of being struck in the back, he did not realize until much later that he had also been struck in the rib and wrist by the bullet.[62] And Dr. Michael Baden, the chief forensic pathologist for the HSCA, told the committee, "There's no way to compare how people react to . . . gunshot injury. There often is delay time between an injury and a person manifesting the effects of such injury."[63]

The essence of what I'm saying is that determining the timing[*] and number of shots (or the validity or invalidity of the single-bullet theory) by only analyzing the Zapruder film is really like an existential discussion about how many angels can dance on the head of a pin (i.e., it's more of an intellectual exercise than anything else). Fortunately, since we have other more reliable evidence, we are not hostage to, nor bound by, whatever results this exercise produces.

Two final thoughts before we examine the Zapruder film in detail: In dealing with the frames of the film, one is wise not to think of the numbers of frames in the same context as other numbers. By that I mean that the difference between, for instance, the numbers 200 and 209 is 9, a substantial, meaningful number in our minds. But in the context of the Zapruder film, 9 frames only represents one-half of one second. So one shouldn't place too much importance in, let's say, a hypothetical reaction time difference between Kennedy and Connally of 5 frames, which is *less than one-third of one second*!

Second, one should be aware that in the study of the timing of the shots in the Zapruder film, one is always dealing with at least two moments in time, and usually three, for each shot being analyzed. One moment is the first frame that we notice Kennedy or Connally showing some physical reaction to a severe external stimulus. Even where there's no delayed reaction, this moment is usually at least a frame or two *after* Kennedy or Connally has been hit—a "frame or two after" meaning that Kennedy or Connally was actually struck one-eighteenth to two-eighteenths of a second earlier. And since the time it takes the bullet to travel eats up frames before it reaches its target, the actual firing of the bullet (at the distance the bullets were fired in Dealey Plaza) is around two frames earlier. For instance, as to the head shot, we see the president's head exploding at frame 313, but the HSCA deduced that it actually struck Kennedy at frame 312. It went on to say, "The distance from that window [sixth-floor sniper's nest] to the limousine at frame 312 is approximately 265 feet. Since a Mannlicher-Carcano bullet travels at approximately 2,000 feet per second, the bullet flight time would have been 0.13 second, or the passage of approximately 2.4 frames in Zapruder's camera. Subtracting these two frames from frame 312, it is apparent that the fatal head shot was fired at approximately frame 310."[64]

The First Shot

Although the HSCA concluded that the first shot was fired around Zapruder frame 160,[65] and there is overwhelming evidence to support this, the Warren Commission did not conclude that a shot was fired around frame 160, though it did not rule it out either.[66] As everyone who has studied the assassination knows, from the sniper's perch at the south-

---

[*]In a letter to FBI Director J. Edgar Hoover in May of 1964, Warren Commission assistant counsel Norman Redlich wrote that "the Commission is aware that it is impossible to determine the exact point at which the first two shots were fired" (Letter from Norman Redlich to J. Edgar Hoover, May 7, 1964).

easternmost window on the sixth floor of the Book Depository Building, there is an oak tree that obscured the sniper's view of the presidential limousine on Elm Street starting at frame 166 and continuing on to frame 210. The exception is an eighteenth-of-a-second interval at Z186.[67] The Warren Commission acknowledged that the first shot may have been fired before the oak tree when it said, "If the first shot missed, the assassin perhaps missed in an effort to fire a hurried shot before the president passed under the oak tree."[68] But the Commission also cited the fact that some eyewitnesses believed that the first shot the assassin fired hit the president, and it may have been around Z210. Indeed, the Commission seemed confident that Kennedy didn't manifest any reaction to being shot until around Zapruder frame 225. So if a shot were fired around Z160, it must have missed, and the Commission showed its slight preference for the position that no shot was fired around Z160 when it said, "The greatest cause for doubt" that a shot was fired before the oak tree (i.e., before Z166) "is the improbability that the same marksman who twice hit a moving target would be so inaccurate on the first and closest of his shots as to miss completely, not only the target but the large automobile."[69]

However, there can hardly be any serious doubt, despite the Commission's reservation, that the first shot *was* fired around Z160 and missed the limousine. First of all, many witnesses said the first shot was fired just after the limousine had completed its turn from Houston onto Elm, which would be *before* the oak tree at frame 166. A sampling: Governor John Connally testified before the Warren Commission, "We had *just made the turn* . . . when I heard . . . this noise which I immediately took to be a rifle shot. I instinctively turned to my right because the sound appeared to come from over my right shoulder . . . at an elevation. The only thought that crossed my mind was that this is an assassination attempt."[70] Vice President Lyndon Johnson's wife said, "We were rounding a curve . . . and suddenly there was a shot . . . from the right, above my shoulder, from a building."[71] Secret Service agent Paul E. Landis, on the right running board of the car immediately following the president's car: "The president's car and the follow-up car *had just completed their turns* and were both straightening out. At this moment I heard what sounded like the report of a high-powered rifle from behind, over my right shoulder."[72] Barbara Rowland, standing with her husband on the west side of Houston Street midway between Elm and Main Streets, testified that "*as they turned the corner* we heard a shot."[73] Presidential aide Kenneth O'Donnell, in the Secret Service car right behind the presidential limousine, testified that the president's car was "just about [through] turning [and had started] to step up the speed a little bit" when the first shot rang out "from the right rear." He said that "the agents [in his car] all turned to the rear."[74] Geneva Hine, watching from a window on the second floor of the Book Depository Building, testified the presidential limousine had just "turned the corner" when she heard the shot.[75] Many other witnesses gave essentially the same testimony.

Second, although the indication is that the Warren Commission never focused too much on the earliest frames (Z133–170) of the president's limousine on Elm Street, taken as the car was straightening out after its turn,* the HSCA, with a larger staff of scientific

---

*As previously indicated, although the Warren Commission had a copy of the entire Zapruder film, *Life*, in response to a request by FBI photographic expert Lyndal Shaneyfelt, only provided the Warren Commission with enlarged color slides of Zapruder frames 171–334, which were thought by Shaneyfelt, at the time, to include "all of the pertinent frames of the assassination" (5 H 139, 142; CE 885, 18 H 1–80). The fact that the Warren Commission, when it published its volumes, only published *sequenced* frames 171 forward is evidence, author Gerald Posner points out, that they were "under the assumption that nothing of interest

experts, did closely examine this section of the Zapruder film. The committee concluded that "the first shot . . . occurred at approximately frame 160," noting, among other things, that this was "consistent with the testimony of Governor Connally, who stated that he heard the first shot and began to turn in response to it. His reactions, as shown in Z162–167, reflect the start of a rapid head movement from left to right."[76]*

As we just saw, the Warren Commission testimony of many witnesses strongly supports the conclusion that the first shot was fired as the president's limousine was completing its turn onto Elm Street. One other witness, Bonnie Ray Williams, pinpointed the moment further. Viewing the motorcade from a fifth-floor window immediately below the sniper's nest window, Williams testified, "After the president's car had passed my window, *the last thing I remember seeing him do . . .* was he pushed his hand up like this. I assumed he was brushing his hair back. And *then* the thing that happened then was a loud shot."[77] We can see Kennedy brushing his hair back (just as Williams describes) between Z133 and Z143. One second later (Z162), Governor Connally begins to react.[†] Clearly, then, the first shot is fired between Z143 and Z160, just *before* the limousine passes under the branches of the oak tree shading Elm Street.

Many have questioned how Oswald could possibly have missed the president on the first shot, when Kennedy was closest to him, especially since his next two shots were hits. As the Warren Commission put it, "The greatest cause for doubt that the first shot missed is the improbability that the same marksman who twice hit a moving target would be so inaccurate on the first and closest of his shots as to miss completely, not only the target, but the large automobile."[78] The reason typically given for Oswald missing Kennedy and the car on his first shot is that it was the first shot he was firing at the president of the United States that day, and like any actor first walking on stage (only multiplied a hundredfold) his nervousness affected his shooting. While this may be true, it is pure conjecture and thus entitled to little, if any, weight. What is not conjecture is that he fired

---

happened earlier" (Posner, *Case Closed*, p.323 footnote). However, in fairness to the Warren Commission and FBI, they did analyze and draw inferences from frames 161 and 166 (5 H 147–149, 161, WCT Lyndal L. Shaneyfelt; WR, p.98; CE 888–889, 18 H 86–87).

*If Governor Connally were reacting to the sound of a shot between Z162 and Z167, when might that shot (with its contemporaneous sound) have been fired? Human reaction times in response to the sound of gunshots were measured and published in the 1939 experimental work of C. Landis and W. Hunt (Landis and Hunt, *Startle Reaction*). For "head movement," "movement of neck muscles," and "initiation of arm movement," Landis and Hunt found that the reaction time was 0.06 to 0.20 second—that is, the equivalent of 1.1 to 3.7 Zapruder frames (6 HSCA 28). Since Connally's reaction begins at Z162, the sound of the shot would have been heard by Connally at about Z158–161. The caveat to the Landis and Hunt study is that it presupposes that one always reacts to hearing the sound of a gunshot instantaneously. This is, on its face, a clearly unwarranted assumption. One may hear a shot and react only in the mind, not moving at all. (Even if, in this case, Connally reacted instantaneously by the "movement of [his] neck muscles," that obviously would not be discernible on the Zapruder film.) This is why I asked Cecil Kirk, my photographic expert at the London trial, "When you say that your [HSCA] panel concluded that the first shot was fired around frame 160, that's on the assumption that Connally turned immediately?" "Yes." "If he took just one second to react, that would put the first shot back around 140, is that correct?" "That is correct." (Testimony of Cecil Kirk, Transcript of *On Trial*, July 23, 1986, pp.280–281) What I'm saying is that the HSCA, as well as virtually the entire anti-conspiracy community, has been gratuitously generous (a trait the conspiracy community seems to be incapable of in the assassination debate) to the conspiracy theorists in placing the first shot around frame 160, meaning Oswald may have had more time than believed to get off his later, second shot.

†Because the president also turns sharply to his right during this period (Z157–160), some have suggested that he too is reacting to the sound of the first shot. It should be noted, however, that unlike Connally, he continues to smile and wave to crowds along the north side of Elm Street. Although we can never be sure, it is difficult to believe that the president would have responded this way had he interpreted the sound as a shot the way Connally and some others did.

around frame 160, and since the oak tree started to obscure his vision of Kennedy at the time of frame 166, only one-third of a second away, he *necessarily* would have felt very hurried and hence rushed the shot.[79]

But there is perhaps an even better reason why Oswald missed this first shot. Contrary to the conventional wisdom, it was actually the most difficult shot he fired that day. I've been up to the southeasternmost window on the sixth floor of the Book Depository Building, holding an imaginary rifle in my hand, and *at shots two and three* the movement of the president would be on almost a straight line from the barrel of the rifle. Monty Lutz, the head of the Firearms Unit of the Wisconsin State Crime Laboratory and a member of the HSCA's firearms panel, testified for me at the London trial. Here is an excerpt of my direct examination of Lutz:

Question: "I take it you have been to the Book Depository Building in Dallas?"

Answer: "Right."

Question: "And from the southeasternmost window on the sixth floor you observed . . . cars going down Elm Street, is that correct?"

Answer: "Yes."

Question: [Directing his attention to a diagram of Elm] "Looking at the alignment on Elm Street vis-à-vis a sniper's position at the sixth-floor window, would the presidential limousine proceeding in a southwesterly direction down Elm Street be proceeding on *almost a straight line from the barrel of the rifle?*"

Answer: "*Yes, it would.*"

Question: "This would obviously make it easier for the firer?"

Answer: "Yes, it would."

Question: "You're aware that there is an approximate 3-degree slope on Elm Street going down [from the Depository Building]?"

Answer: "Yes."

Question: "Would this fact in any way make it easier for a sniper in that sixth-floor window to hit a moving target proceeding away from him?"

Answer: "Yes, it would."

Question: "Why is that?"

Answer: "It would require less movement, or less elevation of the rifle barrel to compensate for the target as it's moving away from him."

Question: "Assuming a sniper at the sixth-floor window with the presidential limousine proceeding at a very slow speed, about eleven and a half miles per hour, and with the limousine being almost on a straight line with the barrel of the rifle, coupled with the 3-degree downward slope on Elm—I don't want to put words in your mouth, you answer the question—would the president be almost a stationary target?"

Answer: "Yes, he would."[80]

However, between Z143 and Z160 (the time during which the first shot was fired), the president was not a stationary target proceeding on a straight line away from the barrel that Lutz had described. He wasn't far enough away from Oswald to be such a target, and he was moving from Oswald's left to his right—that is, he was a *moving* target.

In my preparation for the trial, Lutz pointed out to me an additional reason why the first shot was the most difficult one for Oswald. The windowsill, and the three boxes stacked next to it, could only be used to stabilize the rifle when the limousine was farther down Elm Street and the barrel could rest on top of them. The steeper angle at the time of the first shot prevented Oswald's rifle from having the stability it needed. What would that angle be? Though it could not look to the Zapruder film for help, the Warren Commission was able to determine the first point on Elm Street in which a person in the sniper's nest window could have gotten a shot at the back of the president after the car rounded the corner from Houston onto Elm, and the angle from the window to the car at that point was 40.10 degrees.[81] Compare this steep and insecure angle with the 17.43-degree downward angle for the shot that entered the president's upper back, and the 15.21-degree angle for the subsequent shot to the head.[82]* But apparently, Oswald couldn't resist a target so temptingly close.

As we know, the bullet fired by Oswald around Z160, which missed both Kennedy and the presidential limousine, has never been found. What happened to it? We know that if it was fired between Z143 and Z160, it would not have hit any significant twig or branch of the oak tree (from the sniper's nest only a few leaves and branchlets are visible, at the edges of the tree, around frame 160),[83] as some have theorized, since the bullet would have been fired *before* the limousine disappeared under the branches. And since there's no evidence the bullet hit the car, the only other possibility is that the bullet hit the pavement or earth and ricocheted elsewhere. Mrs. Donald Baker, a bookkeeper at the Book Depository, was standing in front of the building watching the motorcade. She testified before the Warren Commission that after the limousine drove by (she told the FBI on November 24, 1963, it was "immediately" after the car drove past her)[84] and neared "the first sign,"† she "heard a noise and I thought it was firecrackers, because I saw a shot or something hit the pavement . . . It looked just like you could see the sparks from it." She told the Commission that the bullet struck the pavement in the middle of the lane that was to the left of the limousine, though she wasn't sure.

Question: "Where was the thing that you saw hit the street in relation to the president's car?"

Answer: "I thought it was, well, *behind* it."

Question: "You saw this thing hit the street *before* you heard the second shot, is that correct?"

Answer: "Yes, sir, yes."

Question: "Are you absolutely sure of that?"

Answer: "I hope I am. I know I am."[85]

The probability is that a fragment of the bullet that hit the pavement went on to strike the south curb on Main Street at the base of the Triple Underpass, propelling a bit of the concrete (or a bullet fragment) into the right cheek of James Tague, a motorcade spectator who was standing on the narrow concrete strip or island between Commerce and Main at the east edge of the Triple Underpass. Tague was twelve to fifteen feet west of where the bullet hit the curb and over five hundred feet from the Book Depository Building.[86]

Assassination researcher Dan Curtis points out that the Tague curb shot does not perfectly line up with any of the three shots from the Texas School Book Depository Building; that is, a line drawn from the sniper's nest to the point on Elm where the limousine was believed to be at the time of the first shot (Z160), if extended, would not hit the concrete curb near where Tague was. Likewise with the second and third shots, though they

---

*Ironically, when the president was closest to Oswald—when the limousine was directly below Oswald's window—he was the most difficult shot for Oswald, which Oswald would know. Directly below, the president would be traveling from Oswald's left to right the most, and Oswald's rifle would have virtually no stability.

†There were three signs along the north side of Elm Street between Houston and the Triple Underpass—the R.L. Thornton Freeway, Stemmons Freeway, and Fort Worth Turnpike signs (CE 2114, 24 H 544). From Mrs. Baker's position in front of the Depository, the "first sign" would have been the R.L. Thornton Freeway sign, which was nearly in line with the west end of the Depository.

are closer to an alignment.[87] So Curtis concludes that one of the three shots (he assumes the first, being satisfied that the second and third shots came from the Book Depository Building) must have been fired from a different source, namely, a second-floor window of the Dal-Tex Building where a shot could be hypothesized to line up with the curb shot.[88] Of course, Curtis's analysis presupposes that the first shot was not deflected in any way after striking one or more objects, a presupposition that cannot be made.

The Second Shot

To this day, the most controversial segment of the Zapruder film by far is the period corresponding to the second shot (which various assassination researchers put anywhere between Z190 and Z240), which was the first shot that hit the president and, according to the Warren Commission's single-bullet theory, Governor Connally. Part of the reason why questions still linger about this second shot is the fact that *during* this crucial segment Zapruder's view of Kennedy and Connally is momentarily blocked[*] by a traffic sign—the Stemmons Freeway sign—located on the north side of Elm Street. Although the interruption lasts only approximately one second, the sign, along with the subjective nature of film interpretation (as discussed earlier), has led many down a road mired in frustration as they try to pinpoint the exact moment that both men were hit. Consequently, every attempt to explain what the Zapruder film shows (including the efforts of two separate government investigations) usually results in slightly different conclusions. Because an analysis of this area of the Zapruder film is very complex, I'll be taking some time to examine the key issues. In my defense, readers should know that the thicket I will try to navigate them through is not avoidable.

The first official investigative body to take a crack at determining the precise moment of the second shot based on the Zapruder film was, of course, the Warren Commission. In 1964, Lyndal Shaneyfelt, the FBI's photographic expert, testified to the Commission that right up to around Z205, when Zapruder's view of the president is blocked by the freeway sign, "it is obvious he [Kennedy] is smiling, you can actually see a happy expression on his face . . . and his hand is in a wave."[89] Shaneyfelt said that as the president fully emerges from behind the Stemmons Freeway sign at Z225, "his right hand that was waving [just a little over a second earlier, in the frames before Z205] . . . has been brought down as though it were reaching for his lapel or throat . . . His left hand is . . . rather high, as though it were coming up, and he is beginning to go into a hunched position."[90] Shaneyfelt testified that frame 225 is the first frame on the Zapruder film that reveals the president responding to a severe external stimulus, though the reaction, he said, is "barely discernible" at frame 225, but "clearly apparent in 226."[91]

Because of photographs taken by the FBI during its on-site reenactment on May 24, 1964, the Warren Commission concluded that it was "probable that the president was not shot before Z210," since with the exception of the fleeting instant at Z186 when the president appeared in an opening among the leaves of the oak tree,[†] Z210 was the first time

---

[*]The Stemmons Freeway sign begins to block Zapruder's view of Kennedy and Connally as early as Z201, although the top of Kennedy's head is visible as late as Z207. While Connally begins to emerge from the sign at Z221, Kennedy doesn't fully reappear until Z225.

[†]Actually, the likelihood is that on the day of the assassination, November 22, 1963, there was no opening even at frame 186. When I asked Gary Mack, the curator of the Sixth Floor Museum, "How would the foliage on the live oak tree differ from November 22, 1963, to May 24, 1964, when the FBI took its reenactment

(from the moment the limousine disappeared under the oak tree at Z166) that an assassin at the sixth-floor window would have had a clear shot at the president.[*] "It is unlikely," the Commission said, "that the assassin would deliberately have shot at [Kennedy] with a view obstructed by the oak tree when he was about to have a clear opportunity." Consequently, the Commission concluded that "the President was not hit until at least frame 210 and that he was probably hit by frame 225."[92] This conclusion, of course, was only the first of many opinions as to when the president was first hit by the bullets fired in Dealey Plaza.

Unlike the Warren Commission, which saw no reaction in Kennedy until after he emerged from the Stemmons Freeway sign, the 1978 House Select Committee on Assassinations, in this necessarily imprecise and subjective endeavor, concluded that Kennedy was first struck by a bullet at Z190 and exhibited signs of being hit before he disappeared behind the Stemmons sign. The HSCA's photographic panel concluded that "at approximately frame 200 [ten frames, or just over a half second after being hit] Kennedy's movements suddenly freeze; his right hand abruptly stops[†] in the midst of a waving motion and his head moves rapidly from [his] right to his left in the direction of his wife. Based on these movements, it appears that by the time the President goes behind the sign at Z207 he is evidencing some kind of reaction to severe, external stimulus. By the time he re-emerges from behind the sign at Z225, the President makes a clutching motion with his hands toward his neck, indicating clearly that he's been shot."[93]

The very awkward and unusual position of Kennedy's arms during the sequence Z226–236 (see photo section) is perhaps the most persuasive evidence that Kennedy has been hit by Z225. Both elbows eventually become flexed and raised to a point above the shoulders, his right and left forearms are pulled inward, and his hands become clenched—the right in front of his mouth, the left just below his chin. Oddly, though both the Warren Commission and the HSCA concluded that Kennedy's movements at Z225–226 indicate he had been shot, each failed to comment on the very unusual position of his hands and arms, describing them as if they were in a completely pedestrian

---

photo?" Mack, who has two live oak trees on the front lawn of his home in Dallas, said, "Live oak trees start to drop their leaves in March. So on May 24, there would most likely be less foliage than on November 22, but in no case more." (Telephone interview of Gary Mack by author on January 24, 2006) With the foliage, then, almost assuredly being thicker and more abundant on November 22, the likelihood is that there would have been no opening for the assassin even at frame 186. "Live oaks are green all year," longtime Dallas resident Ken Holmes said, "but they shed a little starting in March" (Interview of Ken Holmes in Dallas by author on January 26, 2006). On the other hand, the Secret Service took some photographs of the scene of the assassination way back on December 5, 1963, just two weeks after the assassination, and U.S. Secret Service inspector Thomas J. Kelley testified that from the photographs the foliage on the live oak tree on May 24 was "very similar, practically the same" as it was on December 5 (5 H 134).

[*]Although around Z210 is the first time that a sniper in the sixth-floor window would have had a completely clear view of the president emerging from under the oak tree, the president's body, in reenactment photographs, can be seen clear enough from the sixth-floor window as early as Z207 (CE 892, 18 H 88).

[†]Itek Corporation, after its multimonth analysis of the film for CBS in 1976, disagreed. Stating that it "has been suggested that from around frame 189 to 195 [Kennedy's] hand appears to move very little and could be construed to be frozen in position," Itek's report said its specialists found that "his hand continues the relatively even sweep across his face aand down until no longer measurable at frame 206" (HSCA Record 180-10001-10396, "John Kennedy Assassination Film Analysis," Itek Corporation, May 2, 1976, p.35). Itek's conclusion was that "no evidence could be found that would indicate that President Kennedy was struck before the Stemmons Freeway sign blocked Zapruder's view. President Kennedy was first wounded most probably after frame 212 and before frame 223" (HSCA Record 180-10001-10398, May 2, 1976, p.11).

position. The Warren Commission said that at Z226 the president had raised "his hands to his throat,"[94] while the HSCA said the president "leans forward and clutches his throat."[95] In fact, the president's hands are not "clutching" or even touching his throat.

Could the bullet's passage close to the president's spine[96] have caused enough trauma to the nerves in that area to result in Kennedy's odd raised-elbow posture? The answer seems to be yes, and, if true, it likely would have caused an instantaneous reaction. The HSCA's forensic pathology panel noted that as a bullet passes through tissue, considerable radial motion is imparted to the surrounding area, creating a large temporary cavity. The panel agreed that this kind of tissue disruption "might have produced fractures of the transverse processes of one or several of the lower cervical and/or upper thoracic vertebrae in President Kennedy's neck, as indicated by the post-mortem X-rays." The muscles attached to this vertebra would have received a "tremendous shock, even if several inches distant from such a missile."[97] In addition to the muscle masses present, the neck region contains nerve bundles that control both arm muscles. These nerves would also be affected by any tissue disruption. The resulting effect would be immediate—like flipping a light switch. Dr. Baden testified, "If a nerve is injured, this would produce a quicker response than if a nerve weren't injured. That is why, if the bullet injured the president's spinal nerves in the neck area, which is rich with nerves, a reflex, rapid reaction might ensue."[98]

If the nerves in Kennedy's neck had been sufficiently stimulated by the passage of the bullet, as Dr. Baden suggests, how soon after being struck could we expect to see the president react? In other words, how quick is a reflex, or involuntary reaction, as opposed to the slower voluntary reaction? Larry M. Sturdivan, a research physical scientist involved in wound ballistic studies for the U.S. Army, showed the HSCA high-speed films of a goat being shot in the head. The films show that neuromuscular, involuntary reactions in the goat begin one-twenty-fifth of a second after the bullet impact.[99] If the same time frame were applied to humans, and the president's reaction in Z225–226 was involuntary, it could be the result of a bullet impact less than one frame earlier, at Z224, although the president's reaction, of course, could also have started several frames earlier, only becoming visible for the first time as he emerged from behind the Stemmons Freeway sign at Z225.

Despite the suggestion that Kennedy's reaction to being hit might have been immediate, the HSCA panel of forensic pathologists was unable to determine, based on the medical evidence alone, "whether President Kennedy's reaction was voluntary or involuntary."[100] The majority of the panel (including Baden) believed the president's physical reaction around Z225 was a voluntary reaction (i.e., Kennedy consciously brought his arms up in reaction to the shot through his back and neck), though they recognized that his movements "could have been involuntary had the bullet caused sufficient shock to his spine and spinal cord. The majority [of the panel] cannot say definitely, based on the available evidence, whether this more serious injury occurred and precisely when the president was struck."[101] The reason for the uncertainty is that, as indicated, specific human reactions to gunshots are difficult, if not impossible, to predict or prove given all of the variables involved. This might partly explain why there was a discrepancy between the conclusions of the two government investigations that attempted to pinpoint when the president was first hit—the Warren Commission concluding that Kennedy was struck somewhere between Zapruder frames 210 and 225 and first showed a reaction at frame 225, and the HSCA concluding that Kennedy was first struck around Z190 and first showed a reaction at frame 200. In either case, I think we can all agree that the position the president was in, at Z225–226, is a very unusual position and that the president is undoubtedly reacting in these frames to having been struck by a bullet.

W hat about Governor Connally's reaction as seen in the Zapruder film around the time of the second shot? Though Warren Commission counsel elicited much testimony from experts analyzing the president's reactions in the Zapruder film, they, perhaps inadvertently, did very little of this during their hearings with respect to Connally. There was *testimony* as to when he could have been hit, and when he was hit (Connally himself, after watching the Zapruder film, testified he felt he was hit somewhere between frames "231 and 234"),[102] but not an analysis of his specific facial or bodily movements from which an inference could be drawn as to what Zapruder frame he was struck at. Representative Ford did ask Shaneyfelt, "Isn't it apparent in those pictures [never spelled out precisely which ones, but frames 222, 231, 248, and 249 are discussed in no discernible pattern in the preceding paragraphs] that after a slight hesitation Governor Connally's body turns more violently [to the right] than the president's body?"

Shaneyfelt: "Yes."

When asked by Senator Cooper when Connally commenced this turn, Shaneyfelt responded, "Approximately at frames 233 to 234."[103]

Commission members John McCloy and Allen Dulles expressed puzzlement over the fact that Connally did not seem to exhibit a reaction until Z233–234, whereas Kennedy was reacting by Z225–226—a difference of seven to eight frames, the equivalent of less than a half second.[104] Absent an explanation, this pointed in the direction of Connally being hit by a separate bullet and hence, necessarily a conspiracy. The Warren Commission noted that "there was, conceivably, a *delayed reaction* between the time the bullet struck [Governor Connally] and the time he realized he was hit . . . The Governor didn't even know he had been struck in the wrist or in the thigh until he regained consciousness in the hospital the next day."[105] The Commission's receptiveness to the delayed-reaction theory was not quixotic on its part.

It is well known, of course, that men can sometimes experience a delayed reaction when struck by bullets. Recall the testimony I elicited from Dealey Plaza witness Charles Brehm at the London trial. Another example among many—Secret Service agents reported that President Ronald Reagan was not aware, until being told, that he had been shot by John W. Hinckley in 1981. And Dr. James Humes, the chief autopsy surgeon, testified before the Warren Commission that "people have been drilled through with a missile and didn't know it."[106] Likewise, Dr. Arthur J. Dziemian, a physiologist at the U.S. Army Chemical Research and Development Laboratories and the chief of the Biophysics Division, told the Commission, "All I can say is that some people are struck by bullets and do not even know they are hit. This happens in wartime. But I don't know about [Connally's reaction]."[107]

The Commission said that by merely looking at the film, it appeared Connally "could have" received his injuries as late as Z235–240.[108] This conclusion strangely ignores the important testimony of FBI firearms expert Robert A. Frazier, who participated in the FBI's 1964 reenactment of the assassination utilizing frames from the film. Frazier testified that with respect to the trajectory from the sixth-floor window and the location of the governor's wounds, Connally "could have been struck anywhere . . . from [frames]

207 to 225." Asked if the same were true for frames after 225, Frazier replied that from frames 226 to 239 Connally's body was facing "too much towards the front" for the bullet to enter Connally's back where it did, and from 240 on he was turned "too far to the right" to be hit where he was—that is, the governor's wounds would have been misaligned with the trajectory of the bullet.[109] In its final report, the Commission noted Frazier's testimony and Connally's belief, after viewing the film, that he was hit between Z231 and Z234.[110] But then the report erroneously states, "At some point between frames 235 and 240 . . . is the last occasion when Governor Connally could have received his injuries [in fact, Frazier's testimony—which, as indicated, the report cites—reflects the opposite], since in the frames following 240 he remained turned too far to his right."[111] It was FBI photographic expert Lyndal L. Shaneyfelt, not Frazier, who testified that Connally might have been in the requisite alignment position to be shot as late as Z240. However, Shaneyfelt deferred his opinion to that of FBI expert Frazier who, he pointed out, was "in the window with the rifle scope and made a more thorough study of the possible path of the bullet [than I]."[112]

Although the Warren Commission's analysis of Connally's reactions to determine just when he was struck by the bullet in the back was superficial, Commission members did opt for common sense in reaching their ultimate conclusion that the bullet that hit Connally had previously exited from the president's throat, inferentially concluding, therefore, that Connally, like Kennedy, was struck by a bullet somewhere between Zapruder frames 210 and 225.[113] They were aided in this commonsense conclusion by the testimony of experts. Robert Frazier testified before the Commission that because Kennedy and Connally were in direct alignment with each other during those frames from the vantage point of the rifle in the sniper's nest, "the [bullet] through the president *had* to cause Connally's wound, otherwise it would have struck somewhere else in the car and it did not strike somewhere else. Therefore, it *had* to go through Governor Connally."[114] Among other Warren Commission witnesses, Dr. Frederick W. Light Jr., a wound ballistics expert, testified, "Perhaps the best, the most likely thing is *what everyone else has said so far*, that the bullet did go through the president's neck and then through the [governor's] chest and then through the wrist and then into [his] thigh."

Question: "You think that is the most likely possibility?"

Answer: "I think that is probably the most likely, but I base that not entirely on the anatomical findings but as much on the circumstances."

Question: "What are the circumstances which lead you to that conclusion?"

Answer: "The relative positions in the automobile of the president and the governor."[115]

As opposed to the Warren Commission, the HSCA photographic panel spent a considerable amount of time studying Connally's movements in the Zapruder film. As we discussed earlier, the governor's initial reaction was to turn to the right at the sound of the first shot, believing the sound to have originated from his right rear. Calvin McCamy, a member of the photographic panel who studied the Zapruder film for the HSCA, testified that Connally's entire torso remained twisted to the right as he disappeared behind the Stemmons Freeway sign.[116] When he emerged from behind the sign, about a second later, at Z222–224, the panel perceived that Connally was reacting to a severe external stimulus: "He appears to be frowning, and there is a distinct stiffening of his shoulders and upper trunk. Then there is a radical change in his facial expression and rapid changes begin to occur in the orientation of his head."[117] Hence, the HSCA, and without the use of the delayed-reaction argument, has Connally first showing a reaction to being hit by a bullet at the same time Kennedy clearly showed a reaction—as the two of them were emerging from behind the Stemmons Freeway sign.* As with Kennedy, Connally, of course, could have been struck several frames earlier when his body was hidden from Zapruder's camera by the sign.

However, the HSCA ultimately concluded that "the second shot hit the limousine's occupants (both Kennedy and Connally) at about Zapruder frames 188–191,"[118] and the committee says that Kennedy "does not appear to react to anything unusual prior to 190," although it does not say what change in Kennedy it noticed at frame 190.[119] The HSCA goes on to say that "at approximately Zapruder frame 200, Kennedy's . . . head moves rapidly from right to his left in the direction of his wife."[120]

There are many reasons why the HSCA was wrong in its Z188–191 conclusion, one of which is obvious to even a lay reader. Z frame 193 (see photo section), three frames after Kennedy was supposedly reacting at frame 190 to being hit, clearly shows Kennedy still waving to the crowd. But more importantly, it is difficult to see how the HSCA photographic panel can say that at Z frame 200 Kennedy's head moves rapidly from right to left in the direction of Mrs. Kennedy. Z frames 200 to 203 in the Warren Commission volumes[121] show that Kennedy is still very definitely looking to his right. In fact, as late as Z frame 204 (see photo section) he is still looking to his right. And Willis photo number 5, taken from the motorcade's rear at around frame 202, shows Kennedy looking to his right.[122]†

One support the HSCA has cited for its Z188–191 conclusion is that a jiggle or blur analysis of the Zapruder film showed a jiggle around that time. But there was also a jiggle around frames 220–228.[123] Since even the HSCA agrees that shots were not fired both at 181–191 *and* at 220–228, this only confirms the unreliability of jiggle analysis, the reason being that blurs can be caused by things other than the sound of a gunshot. Inasmuch as the HSCA can't have it both ways (i.e., it accepts the jiggle analysis supporting a shot hitting the limousine occupants around frames 188–191, but does not accept the jiggle analysis showing a second shot being fired around frames 220–228), the jiggle analysis is negated and is no support for the HSCA's conclusion that the bullet that hit Kennedy and Connally struck them both around frames 188–191.

Second, though the Warren Commission's conclusion on this issue cannot be automatically accepted, it cannot be cavalierly ignored either, and as we've seen, the Warren Commission's conclusion is that the Kennedy-Connally bullet struck them between frames 210 and 225.

Indeed, the HSCA's own forensic pathology panel didn't agree with its conclusion, saying that "the *first* visual evidence that the president was struck was the movement of his hands to a position in front of his neck."[124] Of course, that was around frames 225–226, two full seconds after the HSCA said Kennedy was hit.

---

*But to remind the reader, the HSCA, unlike the Warren Commission, concluded that Kennedy first showed a reaction to being hit at frame 200, when the HSCA saw, as few others have, Kennedy's right hand freeze in the midst of a waving motion.

†Only at frame 205 can Kennedy's head be seen to start moving to his left to face the front (CE 885, 18 H 18). But this could very well have been because he had just passed the last large group of people on his right—who appear to be women office workers—waving to him, as shown in photo number 3 by Dealey Plaza spectator Hugh Betzner, which corresponds to around Z frame 186 (Betzner photo and correlation to Z186: 6 HSCA 51; Telephone interview of Richard Trask by author on October 23, 2006).

Finally, and most importantly, logic and human experience would seem to dictate that the HSCA was wrong on this score. We know that from the sixth-floor sniper's nest, with the exception of one-eighteenth of a second at Z186,[125] the oak tree obstructed a view of the president from around the time of Z166 up to Z210.[126] A bullet striking Kennedy around Z188–191 would mean that the sniper who fired this bullet (who the HSCA itself concluded was Oswald in the sniper's nest of the Book Depository Building)[127] fired the shot a fraction of a second earlier—around Z186—which seems to fit the one-eighteenth-of-a-second moment when an opening in the leaves would have afforded him a clear view. But even making the illogical assumption that one-eighteenth of a second (Z186) is long enough for a gunman to have realized that he had a clear shot and to fire the rifle, which seems extremely unlikely, why would a sniper fire almost blindly through the leaves of the oak tree, when he would know that *in just one second* or so he would have a completely clear and unobstructed view of the president for the rest of the road ahead?

But since HSCA members nevertheless embraced their seemingly illogical position that Kennedy and Connally were hit by the same bullet back at Z188–191, they had a problem. Though they saw Kennedy first reacting at Z200[128] to the shot at Z188–191, the first reaction they saw in Connally was when he emerged from the Stemmons Freeway sign at Z222–224.[129]

Because of the differences in apparent reaction times between Kennedy and Connally, the HSCA forensic pathology panel was compelled to deal head-on with the *allegation* that the "observable interval" between the reactions of Kennedy and Connally in the Zapruder film was inconsistent with the single-bullet theory, which the HSCA had accepted. The committee's report noted that, contrary to the allegation, a majority of the panel "believes that the interval is consistent with the single-bullet theory. At issue is the time delay between bullet impact and the observable reactions of each man to his injury, which in turn is determined by many factors, including whether or not their reactions were voluntary or involuntary. If involuntary, they would have occurred almost simultaneously with the injuries. If voluntary, there is often a slight delay in reacting."[130] As mentioned earlier, the majority of the panel thought the movement of Kennedy's arms around Z225 was voluntary, although they recognized that it could have been involuntary had the bullet caused sufficient shock to the president's spinal cord. Turning to Connally, the medical panel said that they were unable to say precisely when the governor was hit, but the majority of the panel felt that the "nature of his injuries could have resulted in a voluntary motion, which would mean a delayed reaction. Thus, the majority believes that there could have been *sufficient delay* in Governor Connally's reaction to account for the interval seen in the film and to permit the conclusion that a single bullet injured both men."[131] In other words, both men were hit by the same bullet around Z190, with Kennedy first showing a visible reaction at around Z200 and Connally at around Z225.

Why, one may ask, was the HSCA forensic pathology panel more inclined to think that Connally was more likely than Kennedy to have had a voluntary response? Dr. Charles Petty, a member of the HSCA pathology panel, testified at the London trial that the bullet that entered Kennedy's back went closer to his spinal cord, where there is a concentration of nerves. (Petty felt Kennedy "had an involuntary response.") "Governor Connally," Petty went on, "had no such wounds. He was wounded in the chest, the wrist, and the thigh. These were not close to any major nerve system."[132]

Despite the numerous medical opinions and documented empirical evidence relating to delayed reactions in the wake of bullet strikes to human flesh, critics have, predictably, opted for the notion that a separate shot struck Governor Connally, necessitating a second gunman, and hence, a conspiracy. One of the first such critiques appeared in Josiah Thompson's 1967 book, *Six Seconds in Dallas*, in which he writes,

> In Z236–237 [Connally's] mouth opens in what appears to be an exclamation. Then, suddenly, in Z238 his cheeks puff [out] and, in succeeding frames, his mouth opens wide—he gives the appearance of someone who has just had the wind knocked out of him. Dr. [Charles F.] Gregory told me in Dallas that a necessary consequence of the shot through Connally's chest would be a compression of the chest wall and an involuntary opening of the epiglottis, followed by escaping air forcing open his mouth. Dr. Gregory estimated the interval between impact and mouth opening to be on the order of ¼ to ½ second. Thus the surge of air to the cheeks in Z238 and the subsequent mouth opening indicate the impact of a bullet only the barest fraction of a second earlier. Had both victims been hit by the same bullet, we would expect Connally to be manifesting the signs of impact at least *sixteen* frames earlier.[133]*

Not only is Thompson incorrect about the time that Connally first reacts (subsequent investigations agree that Connally is shown reacting immediately after emerging from behind the Stemmons sign, at Z222), but the medical premise Thompson bases his observations on is apparently flawed. When I read the above passage to Dr. Baden, he asked, "Was Thompson quoting Dr. Gregory?"

"No," I said, "it's a paraphrase. There are no quotation remarks."

"I thought so," Dr. Baden replied. "It's easy for a layperson to misinterpret what a doctor says. For one thing, unless we're eating or drinking, the epiglottis [the thin cartilaginous valve that covers the opening at the upper part of the larynx during swallowing to permit the entrance of food and liquid into the larynx] is *always* open. Also, a bullet cannot cause the chest wall to collapse. Thompson probably meant lung as opposed to chest wall, but he would have misunderstood Dr. Gregory even on this point. When the lung is punctured, as Connally's was,[†] the air in the lung goes out into the chest cavity, *not out* of the mouth, so Connally's cheeks puffing would not have been caused by air trying to escape." Baden attributed the puffing of the cheeks to just one of the many unpredictable ways one reacts to a physical trauma. He added that Connally's right lung only partially collapsed and his left lung remained intact. Could Connally's attempt to breathe have caused the puffing of

---

*There's an old adage—be careful what you ask for: you might get it. The conspiracy theorists have made a desperate effort to refute the single-bullet theory on the rationale that if they do, Oswald wouldn't have had time after hitting Kennedy to fire the shot that hit Connally; hence, there must have been a conspiracy. But they may be creating a scenario which, if accepted, could seriously damage or destroy their cherished conspiracy hypothesis. Let's look at the theoretical possibilities, which I personally reject. We saw that the HSCA concluded that Kennedy was first struck by a bullet at around frame 190 (HSCA Report, p.47). If Connally, per Thompson, was first struck around Z235 (the "barest of a fraction" before Z238) that leaves 45 frames, or, at 18.9 frames of the Zapruder film per second, about 2.4 seconds between both hits. Since, using the scope on the Carcano, Oswald could get off two shots in 2.3 seconds, the theory of the conspiracy theorists comes tumbling down. And if, as believed, Oswald used the iron sights, in which case he could fire two rounds in 1.6 seconds (see later text), Oswald would have had time to spare in getting off two rounds. Therefore, since all the evidence points to only Oswald having fired a weapon in Dealey Plaza on November 22, 1963, Oswald is the sole assassin, with or without the single-bullet theory.

†Baden said the panel was divided on whether the puncture was caused by the bullet entering the lung or the injury to Connally's fifth rib. Connally's Parkland Hospital operative record only said "the middle lobe [of the right lung] had a linear rent" (CE 392, 17 H 17).

the mouth, I asked. "I don't see how," he said. He added that we breathe about fifteen times a minute, meaning once every four seconds, which translates to more than seventy-three Zapruder frames. And here, we're talking about a matter of just a few frames.[134]

Governor Connally's observation that he was not hit by the same bullet that hit Kennedy has given aid and comfort to, and been embraced by, the conspiracy theorists for years. In the November 25, 1966, edition of *Life* magazine, he said, "They talk about the one-bullet or two-bullet theory, but as far as I am concerned, there is no theory. There is my absolute knowledge . . . that one bullet caused the President's first wound, and that an entirely separate shot struck me. It's a certainty. I'll never change my mind."[135] Governor Connally said in many interviews through the years that he did not believe there were two assassins, that only one gunman fired all the shots at the presidential limousine. But of course, were one to accept his assertion that he and Kennedy were struck by separate bullets, his conclusion of one assassin would have to be wrong.

It was Connally's belief that the president's first wound was caused by the first bulled fired. He believes the second bullet hit him, and the third hit the president.[136] But perhaps one of the least likely persons in the world who would know things such as this would be the person being shot. At the moment he was hit, Connally shouted out, "My God, they're going to kill us all," meaning he was in the ultimate state of fear and panic, which can only cloud, not sharpen, perception. Moreover, a bullet piercing a human body is an enormous, physiologically neutralizing assault on all the senses of the victim, including, of course, cognition. I mean, even when we are sitting in a comfortable chair watching a slow-motion film of the assassination, we cannot be absolutely positive exactly when Connally was hit and whether it was by the same bullet that first hit Kennedy. We must make recourse to other evidence to prove this point. So how in the world would Connally know these things? The governor himself, in his Warren Commission testimony, acknowledges as much when he said he was "in either a state of shock or the impact [of the bullet] was such that the sound didn't even register on me . . . I was never conscious of hearing the second shot [the one, we should add, he nonetheless testified he was sure hit him] at all."[137]

Quite apart from the fact that the governor, having been shot, would be one of the least likely people to know what happened, the governor's own testimony refutes his conclusion that the president was hit by the first shot. Connally testified that after the first shot, which he said he heard as "we had just made the turn" onto Elm, "I turned to look back over my right shoulder . . . *but I did not catch the president in the corner of my eye.*"[138] He said he was in the process of "turning to look over my left shoulder into the backseat to see if I could see him [the president]. I never looked. I never made the full turn."[139] Even if Governor Connally had seen the president, there would be no way for him to know for sure if the same bullet that struck him had struck the president, but since he admits not seeing the president when the president was hit or at any time during the shooting, it would be impossible on its face for him to know, or even have a sensible opinion, of whether or not he was hit by a separate bullet. If he *had* seen the president, he would have seen that the president was in no physical discomfort at all after the first shot. Rather, he was smiling and waving to the crowd for at least two full seconds after Z160.

Governor Connally's conclusion that the president was hit by the first shot is based solely, it seems, on the recollection of his wife, Nellie. "Nellie was there, and she saw it," he said in 1967 on CBS television. "She believes the first bullet hit him [the president] because she saw him after he was hit."[140] But the governor's wife was understandably equally confused. In her Warren Commission testimony, she testified that immediately after hearing the first shot, she "looked back and saw the president as he had both hands at his neck." We know from the Zapruder film, of course, that Kennedy showed no visible reaction to the first shot around Z160, so we know Mrs. Connally was wrong. She also said that after the *first* shot, she recalls her husband exclaiming, "Oh, no, no, no." But he testified, "When I was hit" (which he said was by the *second* shot) is when "I said 'Oh, no, no, no.'"[141] All of this is perfectly understandable confusion.

In the governor's September 6, 1978, testimony before the HSCA, he retreated from his categorical position: "Now, there's a great deal of speculation that the president and I were hit with the same bullet. *That might well be*, but it surely wasn't the first bullet, and Nellie doesn't think it's the second bullet. I don't know. I didn't hear the second bullet. I felt the second bullet."[142] In one of his last pronouncements on whether he thought he was hit by the same bullet that hit Kennedy, Governor Connally, who died at age seventy-six on June 15, 1993, departed from his ambivalence before the HSCA and went back to his earlier position. In a January 29, 1992, letter to Dr. Michael West, a proponent of the single-bullet theory, Connally wrote that "I disagree with the thesis that President Kennedy and I were both hit by the single bullet." *Case Closed* author Gerald Posner says that just a few months later "during a telephone conversation in May of 1992" with the governor, Connally again suggested that the Warren Commission was right, saying, "The second bullet could have hit both of us."[143]

The only thing that rings true to me about the governor's reflections on what was happening around the time he was hit is not when he tries to be precise, but when he said things like this in his 1978 testimony before the HSCA: "*When* I was hit, or *shortly before* I was hit—no, I guess it was *after* I was hit . . ."[144] All of his hesitation and confusion is more in keeping with what I would expect from a witness who had sustained the kind of injuries Connally did. Before Warren Commission assistant counsel Arlen Specter took the testimony of Connally and his wife in front of the Commission, he had them witness the Zapruder film. Even looking at the film, Specter said, "Connally and his wife argued over whether the Governor had fallen into his wife's lap or she had pulled him into her lap. Connally insisted he had fallen. Mrs. Connally insisted she had pulled him. 'No, Nellie,' 'No, John,' they shot back and forth several times." Eventually, Nellie prevailed.[145]

As previously indicated, the Warren Commission concluded that the first time they could see a reaction by Kennedy to a severe external stimulus was when he emerged from behind the Stemmons Freeway sign at frame 225. But they didn't see a reaction from Connally until around frame 235. The HSCA, on the other hand, saw a reaction by Connally at around frames 222 to 226;[146] the following frame, 225, being the time the Warren Commission saw Kennedy reacting.

My sense of when the second bullet was fired is this. Kennedy's arm completely disappears behind the Stemmons Freeway sign at frame 207 of the Zapruder film.[147] The president, per FBI photographic expert Lyndal Shaneyfelt, was still seen waving to the crowd at frame 205, and he testified that he saw "nothing in the frames" around this point to "arouse my suspicion about his movements" that he had been shot.[148] We also know that frame 210 was the first frame at which the assassin in the sniper's nest window had a completely clear shot at Kennedy,[149] although as early as frame 207, the assassin would have had a clear enough shot.[150] Since all the evidence confirms the single-bullet theory, and since Connally, when seen emerging from behind the Stemmons Freeway sign at frame 222, and Kennedy at frame 225, are already showing signs of reacting to a severe external stumulus,[151] we can reasonably assume that the second shot was fired somewhere between frames 207 and 222 of the Zapruder film.

As we have seen, good minds have differed and will continue to differ on when Kennedy and Connally were hit by a bullet, what precise frame of the Zapruder film Kennedy and Connally *first* reacted to being hit by a bullet, what the nature of their reactions was, what position Kennedy and Connally were in relation to each other at the time each was first hit, what movements they made that resulted from their being hit, and what overall interpretation should be put on the totality of the observations. A year before he died, Governor Connally wrote, in a letter to Dr. Michael West, that "this dispute [about the single-bullet theory] will go far beyond our time on earth to engage in it." I would only add this elliptical clause to the governor's words: that is, as long as we try to resolve the dispute by referring primarily to the Zapruder film. For fertile minds and susceptible eyes, the Zapruder film can be, as Winston Churchill once said about the Soviet Union, "a riddle wrapped in a mystery inside an enigma." But the overwhelming evidence is that whenever Kennedy and Connally were hit, or first reacted to being hit, they were both struck by the same bullet.

The Third Shot

Of the three shots fired that day in Dallas, there is no doubt as to when the third (and according to nearly all of the witnesses, the last) shot was fired. The Zapruder film graphically shows the results of the impact of that shot on the president's head at frame 313,[*] when the president was exactly 265.3 feet from the sniper's nest window.[152] Here, the controversy is centered on what happens next—in just four-tenths of a second (Z314–321) the president's head snaps violently to the rear. Perhaps the majority of Americans have

---

[*]Though we can *know* from the evidence the approximate time Oswald's aforementioned three shots were fired, and hence, the spacing of the shots, earwitnesses, for the most part, didn't agree. The space between Z160 and Z207–222 is shorter than that between Z207–222 and Z313, yet most Dealey Plaza witnesses thought there was more time between the first and second shots than between the second and third (WR, p.115). (Examples of each: "Following the first shot, there was a slight pause, and then two more shots were discharged, the second and third shots sounding closer together" [Lillian Mooneyham: CE 2098, 24 H 531]; "It seemed to me that there was less time between the first and the second [shots] than between the second and third" [4 H 149, WCT Mrs. John B. Connally Jr.].) What explanation can there be for the considerable majority hearing the opposite of what the evidence shows? Apart from the fallibility of eye and ear testimony, though the earwitnesses heard the first shot, it could have been such a shock to their senses that only the sound (which many erroneously thought was that of a firecracker or car backfire) registered, not the sound in relation to the very next sound they heard. By the time of the second shot they may have regained their mental and auditory acuity, now knowing shots were being fired, but they were in no position to compare the space between the second and third shots with that of the first and second. At the London trial, when I asked Dallas deputy sheriff Eugene Boone, who as a member of law enforcement was very accustomed to the sound of shots from a weapon, what was the spacing of the shots he heard that day in Dealey Plaza, he said, "The first two shots and then the third shot was a little longer." Question: "So the first and second shots were closer together, then there was an interval, and then the third shot?" "Yes, sir." I then proceeded to have Boone demonstrate to the jury by the use of the word *bang* the three shots. There was a meaningful interval between the first and second, and second and third shots, but the latter interval was greater. (Testimony of Eugene Boone, Transcript of *On Trial*, July 23, 1986, pp.125–126)

Quite a few witnesses thought the shots were evenly spaced. "I distinctly remember three shots . . . and the three shots were evenly spaced" (7 H 475, WC affidavit Clifton C. Carter).

seen this portion of the Zapruder film at least once on television. The conspiracy theorists have argued, and millions of Americans have agreed, that this head snap conclusively proves that the president was shot in the head from the front. Indeed, it would be safe to say that the single thing that has convinced people more than anything else that the fatal head shot to the president came from the front, not the rear where Oswald was, is the head snap to the rear. "No layman can watch these frames," author Henry Hurt wrote, "and avoid the clear impression that the shot came from the right front of the President, the grassy knoll area."[153] Mark Lane declared, "So long as the Commission maintained the bullet came almost directly from the rear, it implied that the law of physics vacated in this instance, for the President did not fall forward."[154] New Orleans district attorney Jim Garrison said, "You don't have to be a genius. It takes no arguments, no words. When you look at the Zapruder film you see that the president of the United States was shot from the front, and there's no question about it. He's so clearly hit from the front the force almost catapults him out of the back of the car. Any American seeing the film would know at a glance that the entire Warren Commission conclusion was a complete hoax, was absolutely false, and every man on the Warren Commission had to know it was a lie."[155]

This impression was not just limited to those who would end up being hard-core conspiracy theorists, but was widespread. When Robert Healey, the executive editor of the *Boston Globe*, saw the Zapruder film in his office during a presentation to him and his staff on April 23, 1975, by members of the Assassination Information Bureau, a conspiracy-oriented group, he wrote the following editorial just two days later: "Oswald could not have fired all the shots that killed President Kennedy . . . The visual presentation is far more convincing than all the books and all the magazine articles that have ever been advanced . . . No words can make the case better than the Zapruder film. It is as simple as that."[156]

In the London trial, there was little doubt in my mind that if I didn't satisfactorily explain away the problem of the head snap to the rear for the jury, their verdict would most likely be not guilty. And I knew I couldn't use the sudden acceleration of the presidential limousine to explain the backward lurch since the Zapruder film shows that the acceleration was several frames after the president's head had lurched backward.[157]

Perhaps the biggest shock I had in my investigation of the facts and evidence in preparation for the London trial was how this most overshadowing point was completely disregarded by the Warren Commission. In the Commission's report and accompanying twenty-six volumes, I could not find one single word of reference to the president's head snap to the rear. Warren Commission assistant counsel Wesley J. Liebeler, on the *Louis Lomax* television program in Los Angeles in 1966, acknowledged that the Commission did not focus in on the president's head movements. "It is only since the critics have raised this point that anybody has ever looked at it closely," Liebeler said.[158]

Upon reflection, I realized that the Warren Commission probably believed it never had to concern itself with the head snap because it had conclusive medical evidence that the president was struck by two and only two bullets, both of which entered the president's body from the *rear*.[159] Therefore, whatever caused the head snap to the rear was irrelevant to its inquiry since it could not have been a bullet from the front. While the Warren Commission was correct in this regard, its conclusion did not suffice for my purposes at the London trial. It was one thing for my medical expert to testify that an examination of the autopsy photographs and X-rays of the wound to the right rear of the president's head revealed that it was an entrance, not an exit wound, and hence, the bullet that caused the wound had to have been fired from the president's rear. But Kennedy's head dramatically being thrust to the rear would, I feared, be more powerful evidence of a shot from the front in the eyes of twelve lay jurors, probably enough, indeed, to raise a reasonable doubt of Oswald's guilt, which would result in a not-guilty verdict. The old saw that a picture (here, a motion picture, no less) is worth a thousand words was never more applicable.

Fortunately, the HSCA did address itself to the issue, though extremely briefly, concluding that the sharp rearward movement of the president's head was probably caused by a neuromuscular reaction—that is, nerve damage caused by the bullet to the president's brain caused his back muscles to tighten, which in turn caused his head to be thrust backward.[160] Among other things, Larry Sturdivan, a research wound ballistics scientist at the Biophysics Laboratory at the federal Aberdeen Proving Ground in Maryland, showed the HSCA a film of an experiment in 1948 conducted at Aberdeen where live goats were shot in the brain by a bullet, causing the subject neuromuscular reaction, resulting in the goat's back arching backward.[161]

Although no evidence was presented that a goat's back and abdominal muscles are the same as a human's, when Sturdivan was asked whether he was "troubled" by the president's head being thrust backward, he said, "No, sir . . . The neuromuscular reaction in which the heavy back muscles [of a human] predominate over the lighter abdominal muscles would have thrown him backward no matter where the bullet came from, whether it entered the front, the side, or the back of the head."[162]*

But this was a *technical* explanation, and although I certainly intended to present it to the jury in London, I felt it might not carry the day for me on this critical issue. The first and most fundamental question I asked myself was why the bullet coming from the rear, irrespective of the neuromuscular reaction, didn't propel the president's head forward at least at the moment of impact, that is, *before* the reaction came into play? Rather ironically, I first learned that my assumption that the president's head had not been pushed forward was an erroneous one while reading the pro-conspiracy, but serious and scholarly book *Six Seconds in Dallas* by Josiah Thompson, in which Thompson treated the whole head snap issue in considerable depth, though ultimately incorrectly.[163] Thompson's book pointed out that Kennedy's head *was* propelled slightly forward between Z312 and Z313 (the frame in which blood and tissue are seen spraying forward from the president's head).

Thompson's observation was confirmed when in 1975 CBS asked Itek Corporation, a Massachusetts photo optics company, to study the *original* Zapruder film using the most advanced photo analysis techniques and instrumentation then available. (CBS had purchased, from Zapruder's heirs, the right to use the original for analysis purposes.) Over several months, Itek, with a staff of a dozen specialists, studied the film. Among the many findings in its ninety-four-page report to CBS in 1976, Itek proved that *before* the president's head snap to the rear commenced at Z314 and continued until Z321, "at [Zapruder frames] 312–313 [the president's] head goes forward approximately 2.3 inches, his shoul-

---

*While it was clear that the House Select Committee preferred the neuromuscular-reaction explanation for the president's head snap to the rear, it allowed, in its official conclusion, for another cause. It said that the head snap to the rear could also have been caused "by a propulsive effect resulting from the [brain] matter that exited through the large defect [on the right side of the president's head] under great pressure, or a combination of both." (7 HSCA 178) The president's head can be seen on the Zapruder film as going not only backward but slightly *leftward*. This movement to the left can be explained by the explosive exiting of the brain matter on the right side of the president's head creating a corresponding propulsive momentum (commonly called a "jet effect") in the opposite direction, as a rocket recoils in a direction opposite to that in which its jet fuel is ejected. (See endnote for further discussion.)

der about 1.1 inches."[164] Although at one point Itek's report says that "frame 313 is the frame in which the President is fatally struck in the head," it is clear from the report that Itek's experts believed the shot struck at frame 312, at another point saying, "Prior to impact at frame 312," and referring "to the impact at frames 312–313." Itek found that "by [frame] 314 Kennedy's head has reversed direction" and continues in a backward direction until "it reverses direction at about frame 321 as his body contacts the back of the seat."[165]

In the CBS television broadcast "Inquiry: The American Assassins," part 1, presented on November 25, 1975, host Dan Rather told the TV audience, "According to John Wolf, president of Itek's optical systems division, when the fatal [head] bullet struck, the president's head went forward with extreme speed, almost twice as rapidly as it subsequently traveled backwards."

Wolf: "In the three frames following 313 he reversed his direction and came back where he was before. It took him three frames to do it, so he's moving considerably slower moving back than he moved forward."

Rather: "That's not the impression one gets just sitting in a room and looking at the film."

Wolf: "That, of course, is the whole point of doing this kind of [analysis]. It's to get away from the subjective impressions that are developed by looking at a blurred motion picture."[166]

Remarkably, the twenty-six volumes of the Warren Commission contain only one reference to the absolutely critical and paramount fact of the president's head being propelled forward, and it's not by any member of the Commission or its staff. Associated Press photographer James W. Altgens, in testifying about the shot to Kennedy's head, said, "What made me almost certain that the shot came from behind was because at the time I was looking at the president, just as he was struck, it caused him to move a bit forward."[167] And there is only one sentence and four additional words on the subject in the entire twelve volumes of the HSCA.[168] The official investigations treated the matter so dismissively that neither of their final reports mentioned the forward movement of the president's head at all.

Watching the Zapruder film in my study, I could not discern the slight forward movement at Z313, one-eighteenth of a second before the head snap to the rear. But looking at the individual frames, I could see that from Z312 to Z313 the forward movement, though slight, was distinct and unmistakable.[169] (See Z312 and Z313 for the forward movement and Z314–321 for the head snap to rear in the photo section.) I now had, for the first time, clear, *photographic* evidence to present to the London jury that Kennedy was struck by a bullet from the rear—powerful evidence I very much needed as a counterpoint to the defense's evidence indicating a shot from the front.

One other point, often overlooked, worked in my favor. The president's head was pushed not only forward at impact but also downward. Only a shot from a high elevation (the sixth-floor sniper's nest) could be expected to push the head downward to the degree it was. A shot from the much lower grassy knoll could be expected to push the president's head to his left, not downward.

On May 24, 1986, I flew to Phoenix, Arizona, to spend the day working with my photographic expert, Cecil Kirk, on a multiplicity of photographic issues. Kirk, who helped me understand the intricacies of the Zapruder film, had been the sergeant who headed the Mobile Crime Lab and Photographic Services Unit for the Metropolitan Police Department of the District of Columbia. This unit was responsible for the preparation of the photographic exhibits for the HSCA hearings and final report. Retired from the force in 1980, Kirk, considered one of the nation's leading experts in forensic photography and forensic crime-scene technology, and a former lecturer on forensic crime photography at the FBI Academy, was now director of the Support Services Bureau for the Scottsdale Police Department. On the dining room table of his suburban home, I witnessed an enormous mound of photographs from the HSCA's investigation of the Kennedy assassination. The photographs were all mixed up, with no discernible pattern. Five or so minutes into my necessarily indiscriminate perusal of the photographs, one photograph suddenly stood out, startlingly so.

"What in the hell is this?" I asked in amazement.

He answered, "A high-contrast photo of frame 313."* I asked, "This is an absolutely incredible photo. I've never seen it before. Why wasn't it published in the volumes?"

He said, "I don't know," that he had nothing to do with the determination of what photographs appeared in the volumes.

I asked why wouldn't a similar photo have been in the Warren Commission volumes.

"They didn't have the necessary photographic image enhancement technology to do this back then," Kirk answered.

It had to be pure oversight on the part of someone at the HSCA to not publish this enhanced reproduction of Z313 (see Itek's high-contrast enhancement of Zapruder frame 313 in the photo section), for this reproduction is almost, if not equally, as dramatic as that of the head snap to the rear, only it shows vivid, graphic evidence that the fatal shot to the head at Z312–313 was fired *from* the rear. As can be clearly seen, the terrible spray of blood, shell fragments, and brain matter a millisecond after the president was shot appears to be to the *front*.†

I now had more than enough evidence, of every species I would possibly need, to demonstrate to the jury that at the all-important moment of impact, Kennedy's head was pushed forward, not backward, proving the head shot came from the rear. As I indicated earlier, if I hadn't been prepared to prove this fact to the jury, the verdict most likely would

---

*The enhanced photograph was published as part of Itek Corporation's report in 1976 on their analysis of the Zapruder film (HSCA Record 180-10001-10396, "John Kennedy Assassination Film Analysis," Itek Corporation, May 2, 1976, p.57).

†And indeed, from Governor Connally's wife, we know that the shot to the president's head caused "brain tissue" to land on "both of us" (she and her husband), each of whom was seated in *front* of the president (4 H 147). In fact, Secret Service agent Roy Kellerman, seated in the front passenger seat of the presidential limousine (even farther forward of the president than the Connallys), testified that the blood spray from the president's head shot landed "all over my coat" (2 H 78).

Not only were the blood, brain tissue, and skull fragments all blown to the *front* of the president's body, but the five bullet fragments found in the presidential limousine were all to his front. The fragment of the base of a bullet (CE 569) was found on the floor beside the right side of the driver's seat, and the fragment of the nose of a bullet (CE 567) was found on the driver's seat right beside the driver (5 H 67, WCT Robert A. Frazier). And then there were the three small fragments found beneath the left jump seat (CE 840, 17 H 840; 5 H 66). Also, the three skull fragments found inside the limousine were all to the president's front, one in the footwell in front of the backseat, another on the floor in the middle of the car, the other on the floor near the jump seat (HSCA Record 180-10075-10174, January 6, 1964; ARRB MD 259, Interview of Floyd Boring by ARRB investigators Joan Zimmerman and Doug Horne, September 19, 1996; HSCA Call Report of phone call to Douglas Horne by Floyd Boring on September 19, 1996).

The main argument from conspiracy theorists that the "law of physics" requires that an object hit by a projectile has to be pushed in the direction the projectile is traveling, and therefore, the head snap to the rear compels the conclusion of a shot from the front, can easily be used against them. In addition to the fact that the president's head moved *forward* at the moment of impact, how do the conspiracists explain what would be the ridiculous anomaly of blood, brain tissue, three skull fragments, and five bullet fragments all flying to the front of the president's body at the same precise time they claim Kennedy's head was being propelled backward by a shot from the front? They don't. And can't.

have been different. That my opposition, Gerry Spence, knew it was a pivotal issue at the trial was demonstrated when Spence, being the devil of a great advocate that he is, had the head snap portion of the film shown to the jury (without objection from me) *five* times at the very beginning of his cross-examination of one of my first witnesses, Charles Brehm, even though Brehm was merely a Dealey Plaza witness and not my photographic expert. Spence made the commentary (proper only in summation) during his cross-examination, which I elected not to object to, that the head snap to the rear "looked as if somebody walked right up to the president with a baseball bat and took a full swing as hard as they could, like Babe Ruth, and hit him right square in the middle of the forehead and knocked his head back."[170] But the Sultan of Swat actually struck out in this case.

This new evidence I now possessed, that the head shot to the president was fired from the rear, still did not negate, by itself, the far-fetched conspiracy argument that the president was struck by a second head shot perhaps a millisecond after the shot from the rear, and it was *that* head shot that caused the violent head snap to the rear. To furnish scientific support for the head snap to the rear being caused by a projectile (i.e., a bullet), the grassy knoll advocates invariably cite Newton's second law of motion, to wit, that the rate of change of momentum is proportional to the impressed force, and is in the direction in which the force acts. Thompson asserts,

> Basically, the law says that an object hit by a projectile will be given a motion that has the same direction as that of the projectile. At a shooting gallery, for instance, the ducks fall away from the marksman, not toward him . . . Applying Newton's Second Law to the case in question and supposing that a bullet fired from the rear struck the President's head, we would expect to see his head and body driven forward . . . We [do] see the beginning of such a movement at Z312–313 . . . If we account for the sudden forward movement as a consequence of the bullet's impact, *only a similar hypothesis could account for the equally sudden backward movement.* What we see on the Zapruder film are the effects of a double transfer of momentum—one forward, the other backward. At Z313 we witness the effect of a virtually simultaneous double impact on the President's head. One shot was fired from the rear, and the other from the right front.[171]

The italicized language, referring to the movement of the president's head to the rear, which we know was considerable, is what immediately caught my eye and attention. It was only at this point that I asked myself, how *does* a human body react to being hit by a bullet? Though I had tried quite a few murder and ADW (assault with a deadly weapon) cases in my career, I was embarrassed to learn I had no idea. I had never witnessed an actual shooting of a human being, and the issue had simply never arisen in any case in my career. The only issue was whether the defendant shot and killed the victim, not how did the victim's body react at the precise moment it was struck by the bullet. Now, suddenly, it appeared to be perhaps *the* critical issue at the trial in London.

In early May of 1986, I drove down to the University of California at Irvine and spent the entire day with Dr. Vincent Guinn, a professor of chemistry at the university. Guinn was the nation's leading authority on neutron activation analysis (NAA) and was to be one of my key expert witnesses in London. At dinner that evening, after we left the complex subject of NAA, I casually mentioned to the doctor and his young assistant the problem I was having with the head snap to the rear issue:

"Doctor," I asked, "this is probably outside your expertise, but if a bullet hits the head of a human being, do you have any idea how much the head would be moved in the direction the bullet was traveling?"

"Rudimentary physics will tell you that the head would move very slightly," Dr. Guinn said.

I asked, "Why is that?"

Dr. Guinn replied, "The weight of the bullet as compared to the weight of the human head."

I said, "Let's take the Kennedy case."

He said, "Okay. As you know, the Western Cartridge Company bullet that struck the president weighed approximately 161 grains, about a third of an ounce. If Kennedy's head was a normal head, it weighed between ten and fourteen pounds. Also, heads don't just lie on top of our torso unattached. There is muscular resistance to the head being propelled in the same direction in which the bullet is traveling. One-third of an ounce striking a resistant ten to fourteen pounds, particularly where there is penetration, as there was here, with a resulting loss of momentum, is going to move those ten to fourteen pounds very slightly." (In other words, the transference of momentum onto the head from the bullet has got to be small because of the very small weight or mass—only one-third of an ounce—of the bullet.)

When I told Dr. Guinn about the slight forward movement of Kennedy's head at Z313, which he had been unaware of, he said this was precisely how much he would have expected the president's head to move.

"So, the head snap to the rear could not possibly have been caused by the force of a bullet from the front?" I asked.

He replied, "That's correct. Kennedy's head simply would not be pushed anywhere near that far back by one-third of an ounce, even traveling in excess of two thousand feet per second."

I told the doctor that although I had avoided taking physics in high school, millions upon millions of Americans who have taken physics have seen the dramatic head snap to the rear in the Zapruder film, and been convinced it was caused by a shot from the front. "Why is this?" I asked.

He said, "I haven't the faintest idea."

Dr. Guinn had given me exceedingly valuable information which, if correct, was the precise type of commonsense fact I could give the jury to support my medical evidence that a shot from the front could not have caused the president's head snap to the rear, and that the sole shot that struck the president's head entered from the rear.[*]

---

[*]In 1990, four years after the London trial, I asked Dr. Art Hoffman, a physicist out at UCLA, to give me his views on this matter. In a written report to me, Hoffman hypothesized the situation of a man lying on his back. "How far," he asked, "will his head rise if struck by a bullet fired directly upward from below? Using the known mass (161 grains) and muzzle velocity (2,165 feet per second) of the Mannlicher-Carcano bullet and 15 pounds for the weight of the head, and assuming that the bullet is completely stopped within the head for maximum momentum transfer [here, the bullet wasn't completely stopped by bone in the head, most of it exiting the head in fragments, which would even decrease the transference of momentum] and assuming that no other forces than gravity retard the motion of the head, we [Hoffman worked with a colleague, Dr. Robert Ditraglia] find that it *would rise only two inches* . . . The height that a head would be lifted against gravity is a reasonable estimate of how far it might [be propelled] when struck horizontally. The resisting forces of the neck muscles and connecting tissue are comparable to gravity since these muscles normally function to stabilize the head against gravity. Indeed, they are capable of exerting forces several times that of gravity . . . These considerations lead us to conclude that the Mannlicher-Carcano bullet would not impart a particularly large [movement]

During a telephone conversation the next day, Dr. Charles Petty in Dallas confirmed what Guinn had told me, saying that the reaction of a head of a human struck by a bullet would be "roughly similar to that of firing a bullet through a half-open door. The door, on hinges, is penetrated, but would move very slightly to the rear." I asked Dr. Petty if he knew of any shooting of a human recorded on film that I could show the jury in London to support what Guinn and he had told me. Petty said that during Mao's Cultural Revolution, Mao had a number of major drug dealers lined up and executed by a firing squad. They were all shot in the head, and the film of this was shown on worldwide television. Dr. Petty said he had seen the footage and distinctly recalled that the heads of the victims hardly moved upon the bullet's impact. I immediately called Mark Redhead in London and told him it was very important that his staff get this film for me. He said the London Weekend Television (LWT) film library was immense, but that if the library did not contain the footage, they could get it elsewhere. (As it turned out, LWT never did come up with the film footage.) However, during the trial, after establishing for the jury through Dr. Petty the fact that a bullet weighing one-third of an ounce was simply incapable of having propelled the president's head backward the way the jury saw it on the Zapruder film, that it would only move his head very slightly, I asked him, "So the killings that people see on television and in the movies, which is the only type of killings most people ever see, where the person struck by the bullet very frequently is visibly and dramatically propelled backward by the force of a bullet [sometimes to the point of toppling over] is not what happens in life when a bullet hits a human being?"

"No, of course not."[172]

Author Josiah Thompson clearly was unaware of this reality. He wrote in his book, "Supposing that a bullet fired from the rear struck the President's head. We would *expect* to see his head and body driven forward, *the force of the impact perhaps forcing him out of the rear seat onto the floor*."[173] But this is not what happens in real life. Further demonstrative evidence that a human body is not substantially propelled by the force of a bullet in the direction in which the projectile is traveling is the Zapruder film itself, which does not show either Kennedy or Governor Connally, when struck in their backs by the other bullet from their rear, being pushed noticeably forward in their seats in the presidential limousine. Though one's back admittedly would provide more resistance to such a thrust than one's head, it obviously wouldn't be to the point of completely negating Thompson's proposition.

So in the final analysis, even if one were forced to rely only on the Zapruder film, we have seen that from the film alone, there is strong evidence of three, and *only* three shots, fired during the assassination. This is completely consistent with all the physical evidence in the case, and flies in the face of over four decades of allegations made by conspiracy theorists that the film contains conclusive "proof" of two or more assassins.

With respect to the second shot fired in Dealey Plaza, the "single-bullet *theory*" is an obvious misnomer. Though in its incipient stages it was but a theory, the indisputable evi-

---

to the head." From measurements based on his analysis of the Zapruder film, Hoffman found a "2 inch forward movement" of Kennedy's head "owing to the entrance of the Mannlicher-Carcano bullet" from behind. He concluded that Kennedy's head snap to the rear was "8½ inches," obviously far too much for the impact of any bullet to have caused. (Letter from Dr. Art Hoffman to author dated March 20, 1990, pp. 1–3)

dence is that it is now a proven *fact*, a wholly supported conclusion. As one of the authors of the single-bullet theory, Arlen Specter, says, "It began as a theory, but when a theory is established by the facts, it deserves to be called a conclusion."[174] And no sensible mind that is also informed can plausibly make the case that the bullet that struck President Kennedy in the upper right part of his back did not go on to hit Governor Connally.

Left with evidence of only three shots, the next obvious question is whether Oswald, using the Mannlicher-Carcano rifle found on the sixth floor of the Depository Building, could have gotten off two out of three shots with accuracy in the time period shown in the Zapruder film. Critics of the Warren Report have argued from day one that it couldn't be done, not by Oswald or any other lone gunman. The main reason they normally cite is that a bolt-action rifle takes too much time to operate between each shot. Though it does sound as if the hand movements of the firer, on paper, are time-consuming—after a shot, he has to push the bolt handle up, pull the bolt to the rear (which ejects the shell), push the bolt forward (which positions the next cartridge in the chamber), and then turn down the bolt handle to lock the bolt in place—these are not really four separate steps in the true sense of the word. As a Los Angeles Police Department firearms expert told me, "They [the steps] are all done in one continuous action; for instance, like turning a door knob, pushing it forward, and walking in. The operation of the bolt by an experienced rifleman is very fast."[175]

Early press reports "guesstimated," without the benefit of the Zapruder film, that the assassination occurred in a span of only 5 seconds, which helped make the general public predisposed to accept the critics' argument. In attempting to resolve this issue, the Warren Commission cited the FBI's conclusion (based on test-firing the Mannlicher-Carcano) that with telescopic sight, "the minimum time" for a person to fire two "successive, well-aimed" shots with the weapon was "approximately two and a quarter [2.25] seconds,"[176] which is usually rounded out to 2.3 seconds. What this means is that the "minimum firing time *between* shots was 2.3 seconds"[177]—that is, *after* a shot, it takes a minimum of 2.3 seconds to operate the bolt, reaim, and fire the second shot.* This firing time was based on the premise, which I believe to be false (see following), that Oswald *must* have used the telescopic sight.

The HSCA later found that Oswald's rifle, using the iron sights rather than the scope, could be fired twice in a shorter time than 2.3 seconds. "The Committee test-fired a Mannlicher-Carcano rifle using the open iron sights. It found that it was possible for two shots to be fired within 1.66 seconds."[178] Monty Lutz of the HSCA firearms panel, and my firearms expert at the London trial, told me that "at distances below a hundred yards [Kennedy was about sixty yards from the sixth-floor window at the time the first shot hit him and almost precisely eighty-eight yards for the head shot], a shooter can not only fire faster with the open iron sights, which he can do at any distance, but, if rapid firing, more

---

*The Warren Commission has no firm opinion as to when the first shot was fired in Dealy Plaza (saying it could have been as late as Z210), or whether it hit either Kennedy or Connally. But it did note that at 18.3 frames per second on the Zapruder film, the time between Z210–225 (when the Commission believes both Kennedy and Connally were struck by the same bullet) and Z313 (the head shot to the president) was "4.8 to 5.6 seconds." With the 2.3 seconds required between two shots, and only 4.8 to 5.6 seconds to fire them in, the Commission said, "The gunman would have been shooting at very near the minimum allowable time" to fire them, adding, "Although it was entirely possible for him to have done so." (WR, pp.111–112, 115)

accurately. My assumption is that Oswald would know this and that he used the iron sights."[179]*

The one small piece of circumstantial evidence, which could easily be a coincidence, that Oswald used the telescopic sight is that the FBI found the scope to be defective, causing shots to land "high and slightly to the right."[180] The two shots that struck the president from behind hit slightly to the right of the center of the president's body. However, assistant Warren Commission counsel Arlen Specter believes that the scope (irrespective of the issue of whether Oswald used it when he shot Kennedy) may very well have become misaligned when Oswald dropped it in haste onto the sixth floor of the Depository Building during his quick getaway. "A very reasonable inference," Specter says, is that Oswald "most assuredly didn't place it [his Carcano] on the ground with great care to preserve it for its next use; he gave it a pretty good toss, . . . [and] that could have damaged the sight."[181] FBI agent James Hosty made the same assumption as Specter.[182]

Supportive of Specter's and Hosty's assumption is the testimony of FBI firearms expert Robert Frazier that when he got the Carcano back at the FBI lab in Washington, D.C., the scope tube had a "rather severe scrape" on it, and the "scope tube could have been bent or damaged." Ironically, though, if the scope had become defective *before* the assassination, the defect would have actually assisted the assassin in his aiming at a target moving away from him. Frazier testified that the weapon firing high "would actually compensate for any lead which had to be taken. So that if you aimed with this weapon as it actually was received at the laboratory, it would be necessary to take no lead whatsoever in order to hit the intended object. The scope would accomplish the lead for you."[183]

Quite apart from the fact that the Mannlicher-Carcano, then, could be fired twice within 1.66 seconds, since the HSCA determined that the first shot was fired around Z160, not between Z210 and Z225, the committee had ample evidence to conclude that contrary to the popularly accepted 5 seconds, the assassin had over 8 seconds (18.3 frames per second divided into 153 frames between Z160 and Z313 gives 8.4 seconds), a point I made very clearly to the London jury through my photographic expert, Cecil Kirk.[184] But, to be even more precise, Oswald really had 8.4 seconds to operate the bolt, aim, and fire *two*, not three shots. Most people forget that for the first shot, the cartridge was already in the chamber and Oswald had all the time in the world to prepare for that shot, so the clock doesn't really start to run until the time of the first shot. Deducting the millisecond it took him to pull the trigger for the first shot, Oswald had at least 8 seconds from that point forward to fire two more rounds, hardly the impossible timing problem that conspiracy theorists have alleged throughout the years.

---

*To help explain why he felt Oswald could have fired more accurately in rapid rather than slow fire at a short range (as opposed to great distances, where the advantage of the telescopic sight for accuracy trumps other considerations), Lutz testified at the London trial that "the ability to fire the rifle with the telescopic sight requires that you readjust your head, raise it from the stock. With the open sight . . . the face can be placed on the stock of the rifle and be fired a lot more quickly as result of being able to recover to the same spot." (Testimony of Monty Lutz, Transcript of *On Trial*, July 24, 1985, p.453)

A firearms expert for the Los Angeles Police Department elaborated on this point for me: "With the old type optical sight that they had on rifles in those days," he said, "there was a narrow field of view. Just for example, at 100 yards it could have a view of only twenty feet across or wide. Upon discharging the weapon, you normally did lose sight of the target and had to reacquire the sight on the target. With the open iron sight, however, you're only limited by what your eye can see, and if you're really experienced with a firearm, you won't lose your target at all after firing the weapon, but even if you do, it won't take you as long to reacquire your sight on the target as it would with a telescopic sight" (Telephone interview of LAPD firearms expert by author on March 17, 2006).

Even when we analyze the amount of time Oswald had available to him between individual shots, we find that the feat was not impossible. Virtually everyone agrees that President Kennedy and Governor Connally were showing a reaction to being hit at frame 225 of the Zapruder film, 65 frames or 3.5 seconds after the first shot at around Z160. *Even if we use the 2.3-second (telescopic sight) figure as the minimum amount of time to fire two shots*, at 3.5 seconds Oswald would have had 1.2 seconds *more* than the minimum time needed to fire a second shot at the time of Z225. If we assume Kennedy and Connally were hit at Z210 (the earliest time, according to the Warren Commission, they were probably shot), this would be 50 frames or 2.7 seconds after frame 160, which is 0.4 second *more* than the minimum time needed to fire two shots.

Using the more likely open-iron-sights figure of 1.66 seconds, if the shot that hit the president was fired at frame Z210 (50 frames or 2.7 seconds after Z160), Oswald would have had 1.04 seconds *more* than he needed for the second shot. It is only when we consider the HSCA's conclusion that Kennedy and Connally were hit at about Z190[185] (a highly dubious conclusion which every other major study of the Zapruder film has disagreed with, and which is sorely lacking in common sense—see earlier text) that we find Oswald would have been left with only 1.6 seconds (30 frames) to get off his second shot, a very tight window of opportunity to be sure but a period still possible, according to HSCA estimates, if he used the rifle's open iron sights to aim.

With respect to the third shot, the head shot at Z313, if the second shot was at Z225 (the latest time, according to the Warren Commission, that Kennedy and Connally were hit), as the Warren Commission concluded, this would have given Oswald 4.8 seconds (88 frames) to fire the third shot. Assuming Kennedy and Connally were first hit at Z210, Oswald would have had 5.6 seconds (103 frames) to fire his third shot. If we accept the HSCA's questionable conclusion that the second shot was fired at Z190, Oswald would have had 6.7 seconds (123 frames) to fire the third shot, *four times* the minimum time required. What follows is a summary of the relevant times:

First Shot	*Second Shot*	*Third Shot*
Frame 160	Frame 190 (1.6 sec after first shot)	Frame 313 (6.7 sec after second shot)
	Frame 210 (2.7 sec after first shot)	(5.6 sec after second shot)
	Frame 225 (3.5 sec after first shot)	(4.8 sec after second shot)

As these figures show, as opposed to what the conspiracy theorists have been alleging for years, whether Oswald used the telescopic sight or iron sights, he would have had, in nearly every case, *more than enough time* to fire the three shots. At the London trial, I felt it was relevant to ask those who actually heard the three shots in Dealey Plaza that day, and who had fired a bolt-action rifle, for their on-the-spot sense and impression of whether one person could have fired all three of the shots. For example, I asked Charles Brehm, the combat veteran who was a part of the D-day invasion of Normandy, who was on the south side of Elm Street with his five-year-old son as the motorcade came by, and who was "very familiar" with bolt-action rifles, "Did it appear from the timing of the shots that you heard that you, yourself, could have operated, aimed, and fired a bolt-action rifle as quickly as those shots came?"

Answer: "Very easily."

Question: "So you definitely believe that the three shots you heard that day could easily have been fired by one person?"

Answer: "Absolutely."

Question: "From your experience with rifles and the report of rifle shots, did you hear any difference at all in the report of the three shots that indicated more than one rifle or firing location was involved?"

Answer: "No. All three shots were from the same origin."[186]

I also asked Dallas police officer Marrion Baker, who was riding a police motorcycle in the motorcade, "Have you personally had occasion to fire a bolt-action rifle and fire shots in rapid succession?"

Answer: "Yes, sir. I have."

Question: "Did it appear from the timing of the shots you heard that you could have operated, aimed, and fired a bolt-action rifle as quickly as those shots came?"

Answer: "Yes."

Question: "So you believe the three shots you heard that day could have been fired by one person?"

Answer: "Yes."[187]

The conspiracy crowd has three arguments for the proposition that although the Carcano could be fired twice within 1.66 seconds, the accuracy simply wouldn't be there, none of which have merit. One argument is that, as conspiracy theorist Walt Brown puts it, Oswald's Mannlicher-Carcano was a "piece of junk" that "certainly lacked accuracy."[188] Even if Oswald's Carcano was the worst piece of junk in the world, this is an irrelevant argument since we have seen that firearms experts for the Warren Commission (FBI) and HSCA proved that it was, in fact, the weapon that fired three bullets in Dealey Plaza, two of which struck the president. But in point of fact, the Carcano was not a piece of junk that lacked accuracy. Ronald Simmons, the chief of the Infantry Weapons Evaluation Branch of the Department of the Army, had his people test-fire Oswald's Carcano rifle (not *a* Carcano rifle, but Oswald's, the one found on the sixth floor, Warren Commission Exhibit No. 139) forty-seven times, and testified the rifle was "quite accurate"— in fact, just as accurate as the American military rifle being used at the time, the M-14.[189] Indeed, the exact type of rifle Oswald used to kill Kennedy was still being used at the time by the Italian NATO rifle team in competition.[190]*

Another argument made by the conspiracy theorists is that Oswald's Carcano had a "hair trigger" that would affect its ability to be fired with accuracy. The problem with this argument is that although the trigger pull of the Carcano, at approximately three pounds, is below average for most military rifles, a hair trigger only requires an extremely

*Oswald's particular Carcano, serial number C2766 (stamped on the left side of the barrel), was manufactured at the Italian government's arsenal at Terni, Italy (fifty miles north of Rome), sometime during the year 1940, a version of an older design. Its first name came from the designer of the weapon's predecessor in 1880, the Austrian, Ferdinand Ritter von Mannlicher; the second name, from one of two men who modified the original into its 1940 form, M. Carcano. Soon after the assassination, many Italian people referred to the rifle as *il fucile maledetto*—that "cursed gun." How the weapon was used from the time of its origin in 1940 to the time it made its way into history is not known, but because the Mannlicher-Carcano rifle was the rifle of the Italian army, it is believed it was used during the Second World War before Italy's surrender in September 1943, after which it returned to the military warehouse at Terni. FBI firearms expert Robert Frazier described Oswald's Carcano thusly: "The stock is worn, scratched. The bolt is relatively smooth, as if it had been operated several times. I cannot actually say how much use the weapon has had. The barrel is not . . . in excellent condition. It was, I would say, in fair condition. In other words, it showed the effects of wear and corrosion . . . It is a surplus type of weapon." (3 H 394, WCT Robert A. Frazier; Wheeler, "Cursed Gun," pp.62–65)

light pull, normally measured at one pound or less. So the Carcano's trigger pull was three times that of a hair-trigger rifle.[191]

Perhaps the biggest argument of the conspiracy theorists is that even apart from the rifle, no one could possibly have hit Kennedy twice in the time Oswald had available to him, particularly Oswald. But of course, the very best evidence that Oswald had the ability to fire his Carcano rifle within the subject time and with the requisite accuracy is that we *know*, from all the evidence, that he did. Conspiracy thorists, naturally, don't accept this. "Oswald was known as a poor shot, . . . missing the target [in the military] altogether as often as he hit it," says conspiracy theorist Harrison E. Livingstone.[192] Kirk Wilson says that "to those who knew him in the Marines, Oswald's marksmanship was a joke."[193]

Robert Groden, the self-proclaimed photography expert and Zapruder film guru, told readers of *Rolling Stone* magazine, "Unfortunately for the Commission, not one man in this entire country could duplicate the incredible feat attributed to Lee Harvey Oswald, who was, according to his Marine Corps records, 'a rather poor shot.' The Commission hired some of the nation's best marksmen, gave them every advantage, and they still couldn't duplicate the shots."[194]

In the first place, Oswald's Marine Corps records do not show he was a "rather poor shot" and a "joke" as a marksman. To the contrary, as set forth earlier in this book, on December 21, 1956, during Oswald's most important shooting for the record, he fired a 212 out of a possible 250, which qualified him as a sharpshooter.[195] Even when he was about to leave the corps, and his good or poor marksmanship could no longer help or hurt him in his Marine Corps career, on May 6, 1959, he fired a 191, which still qualified him as a marksman.[196]* And we know from Marina that during Oswald's time in New Orleans in the summer of 1963, she frequently saw him dry-firing his Carcano.[197] And in Dallas that year he told her he practiced firing the rifle at Love Field and at a shooting range.[198] Indeed, Oswald's friend George de Mohrenschildt told the Warren Commission that Marina, in referring to Oswald, said, "That crazy idiot is target shooting all the time," and that Oswald himself had told him, "I go out and do target shooting. I like target shooting."[199]

Second, even a cursory review of the record on this issue shows the charges of Groden and others in the conspiracy community to be false. As alluded to in the introduction, way back in 1964 the Warren Commission had three expert riflemen fire Oswald's Mannlicher-Carcano rifle at stationary targets (head and shoulder silhouettes) located at distances of 175, 240, and 265 feet, the distances of 175 and 265 feet corresponding to the distances from the sniper's nest window to the presidential limousine at Z frames 210 and 313, respectively. The fact that the targets were stationary does not quite warrant the criticism the Commission has gotten from critics like Groden, since the critical point in trying to simulate what Oswald did was to compel the riflemen to move the muzzle

---

*At the London trial, I elicited from Oswald's Marine squad mate in Santa Ana, Nelson Delgado, that the score on the range one gets during basic training (when Oswald fired as a sharpshooter) is extremely important because "that score is going to follow you throughout your military career. Your promotion is going to be based, in part, upon that." But when you're about to leave the military (as Oswald was when he only qualified as a marksman), there is no incentive to do well. I asked Delgado if he "got the impression that Oswald wasn't even trying" when he shot for the record just before leaving the corps. Answer: "Yes." Delgado said that during that period Oswald wasn't even taking care of his rifle. I asked Delgado if he felt Oswald could have done better if he had tried during this last firing for the record and Delgado said he felt Oswald could have. (Testimony of Nelson Delgado, Transcript of *On Trial*, July 24, 1968, pp.596–599; see also 11 H 304, WCT Maj. Eugene D. Anderson)

The Marine rifle ratings are marksman, 190–209; sharpshooter, 210–219; and expert, 220–250.

between shots. And since the targets were *separated* from each other, the riflemen would have to move their muzzles in the same way they would have if the target were moving as Oswald's target was. Even given this, however, it would seem to be easier to fire at stationary rather than at moving targets, although as we have seen, the 3.9-degree declination of Elm Street made it less difficult. On the other hand, it is noteworthy that none of the riflemen had any practice with Oswald's rifle except to operate the bolt for about "two or three minutes," and did not have any practice with the trigger at all because of concern "about breaking the firing pin."

In any event, the best rifleman, one "Specialist Miller," got off three shots (using the telescopic sight) within 4.6 seconds on the first of two series of three shots, and within 5.15 seconds on his second series. Using the iron sights, he got off three rounds in 4.45 seconds. (The second and third riflemen, using only the telescopic sight, took 6.75 and 6.45, and 8.25 and 7.00 seconds, respectively, for the two series.) As for the accuracy, the Warren Commission's witness, Ronald Simmons, who interpreted the scoring for the Commission, was unprepared for his testimony, and therefore his answers could have been much clearer, part of the lack of clarity being his jumping from the telescopic to the iron sights without clear demarcation.

Question by Warren Commission counsel: "What was the accuracy of Specialist Miller?"
Simmons: "I do not have his accuracy separated from the group."
Question: "Is it possible to separate the accuracy out?"
Answer: "Yes, it is, by an additional calculation . . . Mr. Miller succeeded in hitting the third target on both attempts with the telescope. He missed the second target on both attempts with the telescope [he makes no reference to the first target], but he hit the second target with the iron sight. And he emplaced all three rounds on the . . . first target."

In the last sentence, he's presumably (though his language is too sloppy to be sure) talking about Miller's use of the iron sights. But when Simmons was asked the follow-up question, "How did he [Miller] do with the iron sight on the third target?" he responded, "On the third target he missed the boards completely."[200] (The other two marksmen hit the first target, missed the second, and both of them, it can be inferred from loose testimony, hit the third.) It appears, though it is by no means crystal clear from Simmons's imprecise language, that using the iron sights, Miller hit two out of the three targets, the same as Oswald. What *can* be clearly inferred from the information is that Oswald's rifle was certainly capable of being fired three times within as short a period as 4.45 seconds with the iron sights and 4.6 seconds with the telescopic sight, both of which are more than three full seconds less than we know Oswald had.

It should be added that in an example of investigative sloppiness, the three experts who test-fired for the Warren Commission did so from atop a thirty-foot tower, less than half the height of the sixth-floor window from Elm Street below. I have been told by firearms experts that this difference in elevation was inconsequential to the validity of the tests, but why not construct a tower as high as the sixth-floor window from which to fire?

Three years later, as part of a four-part television special hosted by Walter Cronkite and Dan Rather from June 25 to 28, 1967, CBS improved on the Warren Commission's simulation. Although CBS investigators did not use Oswald's Mannlicher-Carcano (they used an identical model), they used a tower and target track constructed to match exactly the heights, distances, and angles in Dealey Plaza. Also, the target, a standard FBI silhouette, moved by electric motors at eleven miles an hour, approximately the speed of the presidential limousine. "Eleven volunteer marksmen" were given time to practice with the Mannlicher-Carcano at a nearby practice range and then each took turns firing clips of three bullets at the moving target. All using a telescopic sight, which we know is slower than the iron sights, the average time of the eleven riflemen to fire three shots was 5.6 seconds, much faster than the 8.4 seconds we know Oswald had. And one rifleman hit two out of three targets (Oswald's accuracy) in "slightly less than five seconds." A weapons engineer had the best score, making three out of three hits in 5.2 seconds, meaning he was operating the bolt and firing accurately every 1.7 seconds, clearly besting Oswald's marksmanship on November 22, 1963.[201]*

This should have forever put to rest the argument by conspiracy theorists that no one has ever duplicated what Oswald did, yet hundreds of books have come out since the 1967 CBS demonstration alleging that very thing, conditioning millions of Americans to believe the allegation.

To repeat, because it is so important, what everyone seems to forget is that Oswald qualified as a sharpshooter in the Marines, firing a score of 212. Much more importantly to the issues in this case, for some curious reason Oswald was an even better shot when rapid firing. In an analysis of Oswald's targets and score cards when he fired his M-1 rifle during several days in December of 1956,[202] my London trial firearms expert, Monty Lutz, found that Oswald fired better in rapid than in slow fire.† For instance, at two hundred yards (six hundred feet, well over twice as far away as Kennedy was on November 22, 1963, when Oswald fired the last shot, the head shot), his proficiency rate, Lutz said, averaged "76 percent slow fire, *but 91 percent rapid fire.*" Lutz said that "some shooters are better at firing rapid or timed courses once they get into a rhythm or conditioned reflex situation." He added that "on the day of the assassination, Oswald hit two out of three shots, a 67% proficiency rating. So he was shooting *below* his average for rapid fire on that day."[203]

And so, despite the erroneous claims of the conspiracy theorists, the evidence is very clear that Oswald, with his background with a rifle, had plenty of time to accurately fire two out of three shots in the 8.4 seconds available to him and at the intervals suggested by the various studies of the Zapruder film.

And let's not forget that at the time Oswald hit Kennedy with his two shots, Kennedy was relatively close, around fifty-nine yards for the shot that hit him in the back and around eighty-eight yards for the shot in the head.[204]‡ Qualifying with a rifle in the Marines starts at two hundred yards (in the infantry at one hundred), and proceeds to three hundred, then five hundred. And, as I demonstrated for the London jury by my questioning of Monty Lutz, Kennedy was "almost a stationary target."

Major Eugene D. Anderson, assistant head of the Marksmanship Branch of the Marine Corps, testified before the Warren Commission that based on Oswald's record in the Marines, the shot to the president's head was "not a particularly difficult shot" and

---

*Indeed, one rifleman got off three shots at the target in 4.1 seconds, less than 1.4 seconds per round, though he only had one hit. And on March 21, 1979, an HSCA marksman, firing at distances of 143, 165, and 266 feet, hit three of the three targets (though he missed the head portion of the target at 266 feet) in "less than 5 seconds for all three shots" (8 HSCA 184).

†Relevant to this issue, I asked Lutz at the London trial, "How does the recoil of the Carcano compare with the recoil of other military rifles?" Answer: "It is considerably less." "Would that tend to improve the shooter's marksmanship under rapid-fire conditions?" "Yes, it would." (Testimony of Monty Lutz, Transcript of *On Trial*, July 24, 1986, p.454)

‡As indicated earlier, the reasonable assumption is that Oswald used the iron sights on his Carcano. But if he had, indeed, used his four-power scope, the first shot at approximately sixty yards would have appeared to him to be only fifteen yards away, and the second shot at eighty-eight yards, only twenty-two yards away.

"Oswald had full capabilities to make such a shot."[205] Sergeant James A. Zahm, the non-commissioned officer in charge of the Marksmanship Training Unit at the Marine Corps school in Quantico, Virginia, told the Warren Commission that compared to the average civilian in America, Oswald was "an excellent shot." Even in the Marine Corps, Oswald would be considered to be "a good shot, slightly above average." Zahm went on to say that he considered the shot from the sniper's nest that hit Kennedy in the back to be a "very easy shot" and the later one that struck him in the head "an easy shot" for a man with the equipment Oswald had and with his ability."[206]

Finally, when you stop to think about it, the standard argument made by conspiracy theorists that what Oswald accomplished demonstrated incredible marksmanship on his part (a marksmanship, they say, he did not possess) is further refuted by the fact that he really hit his "target" not two out of three times, *but only one out of three times*. What *was* Oswald's target? It could only be Kennedy's head. I mean, we have to assume that Oswald was aiming at Kennedy's head when he fired all three shots since that would be the most vulnerable (and, if hit, fatal) part of Kennedy's body. It makes no sense that Oswald would be aiming to hit Kennedy in his back. In addition to the back being far less vulnerable than the head, very little of Kennedy's back was visible to Oswald, being hidden by the backseat of the limousine. So with Kennedy's head being the target, Oswald's first shot not only missed the target, but also completely missed the limousine; his second shot also missed the target (Kennedy's head) when it struck Kennedy in the back; only his third shot hit the target, Kennedy's head. I ask the conspiracy theorists, How can hitting your target only one out of three times, particularly when your target is relatively close and essentially stationary, be considered incredibly great marksmanship, as you've been successfully peddling to the American public for over forty years?

The Zapruder film has also proved useful to official investigators in determining the location from which the gunfire came in Dealey Plaza and the trajectory of the bullets. By combining information about the location and track of the wounds (as determined by the autopsy of the president and the postoperative reports on the governor) with the relative positions of Kennedy and Connally as seen in the Zapruder film, both the Warren Commission and the HSCA sought to establish the location of the assassin, though the Warren Commission's tests were more about proving Oswald's involvement and validating the single-bullet theory than determining the source of the gunfire.

Since the Warren Commission had already found that the "cumulative evidence of eyewitnesses, firearms and ballistic experts and medical authorities demonstrated that the shots were fired from above and behind President Kennedy and Governor Connally, more particularly, from the sixth floor of the Texas School Book Depository," the Commission's trajectory analysis was only designed to ensure that all data was "consistent" with this premise.[207] At the Commission's request, the FBI and the Secret Service conducted an elaborate reenactment of the assassination in Dealey Plaza on May 24, 1964, using the 1958 Secret Service Cadillac follow-up car (which is similar in design to the actual 1961 Lincoln presidential limousine, which was being remodeled),[*] stand-ins for the president

---

[*]Owing to the differences in the automobiles, the reenactors were sitting ten inches higher than the president and governor were on the day of the assassination. This variance was accounted for by investigators in their calculations. (5 H 148, WCT Lyndal L. Shaneyfelt)

and governor (played by FBI agents with approximately the same physical characteristics), and Oswald's Mannlicher-Carcano rifle. The rifle was outfitted with a camera (to photograph the view the assassin had through the telescopic sight) and mounted on a tripod in the sixth-floor window of the Book Depository Building. The locations of the president's and governor's back wounds (as determined by the medical evidence) were circled in chalk on the back suit coats of the stand-ins. The agents ascertained that the foliage of the oak tree between a gunman in the sniper's nest and his target was "practically the same" on May 24, 1964, as it was when photographs were taken on December 5, just two weeks after the assassination.

Using frames from the Zapruder film (as well as the Nix and Muchmore films), investigators attempted to match, as closely as possible, the positions of their mock car and stand-ins with the positions of the president's limousine and occupants as seen at various points in the films. As these alignments were completed, a straight line from the telescopic sight at the window through the chalk-marked wounds of Kennedy and Connally became very evident when the car was at the location recorded in Zapruder frames 210–225. A surveyor's sighting equipment then measured the angle of declination from the rifle in the window to the entrance point on the back of the president's stand-in to be 21.34 degrees at Zapruder frame 210 and 20.11 degrees at Z225, giving an average angle of 20.52 degrees. Allowing for the 3.9-degree downward slope of Elm Street, the Commission concluded that the probable downward angle of the bullet at impact was 17.43 degrees. (The angle of declination for the fatal shot to the president's head was determined to be approximately 15.25 degrees.) The tests led the Warren Commission to conclude that the trajectory of the bullet that passed through the president and struck Governor Connally, and that of the bullet that hit the president in the head, were consistent with Oswald's believed position in the southeasternmost window of the sixth floor of the Book Depository.[208]

Critics were quick to point out that the Commission's approach assumed that the shots came only from the sixth floor of the Depository. Mark Lane wrote in *Rush to Judgment* that the Commission "employed the unproved assertion that the bullet which struck the President came from the rear as the basic premise to prove that it 'probably' hit Governor Connally as well."[209] Sylvia Meagher charged, in *Accessories after the Fact*, that the Commission did not give "adequate consideration to the possibility of assassins at locations other than the window or the overpass."[210] Josiah Thompson's analysis in *Six Seconds in Dallas* concluded that four shots were fired from three different locations.[211] "It would seem that the critics have at least one point in their favor in attacking the Commission's analysis," G. Robert Blakey, HSCA chief counsel, told the HSCA in 1978. "The analysis assumes the firing position of the assassin as a known, then proceeds to compute the angle to the target."[212] True, but if the trajectories failed to match up with the subject sixth-floor window, the assertion that the sixth-floor window was the source of the shots would automatically fall.

In any event, the HSCA took a different approach, one that made no assumptions as to the origin of the shots. It was an interdisciplinary effort, principally based on the expertise of the forensic pathologists, photographic analysts, and an engineer from the National Aeronautics and Space Administration (NASA), Thomas Canning, who plotted the trajectories by starting with the location of the wounds and working backward to the source.[213] "To the best of my ability," Canning told the HSCA, "I put myself in the position of assuming that no gun was found and simply say, Where would I look?"[214] Like the Warren Commission, Canning's trajectory analysis relied heavily, of course, on the

Zapruder film and Zapruder's line of sight (his location was determined from photographs taken of him by photographers on the south side of Elm Street) to pinpoint the location of the car and the positions and relative alignment of the president and the governor within it. However, unlike the Commission, Canning's analysis did not require an on-site reenactment. The location of the president's limousine was instead determined through analytical photogrammetry conducted by the U.S. Geological Survey in Reston, Virginia. Using enlargements of six frames from the Zapruder film, the U.S. Geological Survey group plotted the position of the limousine, at various intervals throughout the assassination, on a survey map of Dealey Plaza.[215] Armed with the position of the limousine, the position of its occupants (as deduced from the Zapruder film by the photographic panel), and the precise location of the wounds in President Kennedy's and Governor Connally's bodies (as provided by the HSCA's forensic pathology panel), Canning proceeded to calculate three separate trajectories to ascertain the source of the bullets—one for the bullet that caused the president's upper back and neck wounds, one to test the hypothesis that the bullet that exited the president's neck also went on to cause the wounds to Governor Connally, and a third trajectory for the bullet that caused the president's head wound.[216]

Canning concluded that the bullet that struck Kennedy in the upper back was descending at an angle of 21 degrees below horizontal as it approached him (recall the Warren Commission concluded 17.43 degrees) and was 26 degrees to the right of true north from the president. (The Warren Commission made no such computation, though its trajectory analysis showed that the source of the bullet was to the president's *right* rear at the sniper's nest.) He concluded the bullet that struck Kennedy in the head was descending at an angle of 16 degrees below horizontal (recall the Warren Commission concluded 15.25 degrees) and came from a point 29 degrees to the right of true north from the president.[217] (Again, the Warren Commission made no such computation.)

With respect to the first trajectory, Canning used the locations of the entrance and exit wounds to the president's upper back and neck, and the position of the limousine at Zapruder frame 190. (Canning was instructed by the HSCA to calculate a trajectory based on Z190 because of the committee's conclusion of a shot at Z188–191.) Canning connected the entrance and exit wounds with a straight line and projected that line backward to determine the source of the shot. He found that the line representing the trajectory of the shot through Kennedy's upper back and neck originated from a point just west of the first window at the southeast corner of the sixth floor of the Texas School Book Depository Building, where all the physical evidence shows Oswald was at the time of the shooting in Dealey Plaza. Canning then went through each stage of his analysis and made a point-by-point estimate of how accurate each step was and by how much an error might shift the calculated source of the gunfire. Adding the possible errors together generated a circle around the subject window with a radius of thirteen feet, which simply meant that the shot that hit the president, even when all errors in calculation are taken into account, was fired from somewhere within that area or cone. Oswald's sixth-floor sniper's perch was within the region described by Canning's analysis.[218]

To determine the validity of the theory that the bullet that pierced the president's upper back and neck (already shown by Canning to have originated from the sixth-floor sniper's nest) went on to strike Governor Connally, Canning next used the exit wound on the front of the president's neck and the entrance wound in the governor's back to calculate a second trajectory. (The governor's other wounds were not used because of the photographic panel's belief that the missile had been "significantly deflected" during its course through his body when it struck "at least two bones at oblique angles.")[219] Canning concluded that the bullet that struck Connally's back was proceeding on a downward trajectory of 25 degrees below horizontal.[220]

Projecting this trajectory backward* from the position of the two wounds and the limousine's location at Z190, Canning found that it again terminated on the front face of the Depository, this time at a point approximately two feet west of the southeast corner of the building and about nine feet above the sill of the sixth-floor corner window. A similar set of calculations for the cumulative margin of error produced a circle with a seven-foot radius.[221] This not only clearly identifies the sixth-floor sniper's nest as the source of the second shot, but is strong evidence in support of the validity of the single-bullet theory. In fact, Canning told the HSCA, "The bullet would have had to have been substantially deflected by passing through the president in order to miss the governor. It seems almost inevitable that the governor would be hit with the alignments we have found."[222]

Finally, Canning and his team felt that the trajectory of the shot to the president's head would be the easiest to calculate, partly because they knew the time and location of the injury so precisely, and partly because the head is a rigid object and less subject to the vagaries of posture and bodily movement. The key evidence for the third shot was, of course, Zapruder frame 312 (one-eighteenth of a second before the explosion to the president's head at Z313), supported by corresponding frames from the films by Orville Nix and Marie Muchmore. To project this third trajectory path, Canning relied on two sketches (frontal and right lateral view) of the entrance and exit wounds crafted by the HSCA's forensic pathology panel from measurements they made of the autopsy photographs and X-rays.† The orientation of the president's head in relation to Zapruder's camera was determined by comparing Zapruder frame 312 with a series of calibration photographs (photographs of a likeness or replica) of Kennedy's head prepared by the Physical Anthropology Section of the Federal Aviation Administration. The calibration photograph that best matched the features seen in Z312 (such as the back of the head, the position of the right ear, the projection of the nose beyond the rest of the facial profile, and the shape of the brow) was used to obtain the relative positions of the head wounds to Zapruder's camera.[223] A straight line was then drawn between the exit and entrance wounds and extended rearward from Kennedy's position in the limousine at Z312. Canning found that line tracked back to a point approximately eleven feet west of the southeast corner of the Texas School Book Depository Building and fifteen feet above the sixth-floor windowsill.[224] An estimate of the margin of error in the calculations, like before, produced a circle with a twenty-three-foot radius, a cone area much larger than what previous error calculations showed, owing to the fact that the limousine was now more than a hundred feet farther down Elm Street. This larger error circle included the top four floors and the roof of the southeastern end of the building, extending slightly beyond the southeastern corner. But the only open, unaccounted-for window (the three open win-

---

*For those who feel that any projection backward shows a presumption toward Oswald's guilt, note that the trajectory could not be projected *forward*. Since we know from the entrance wounds to the backs of Kennedy and Connally that the bullet was traveling on a straight line downward, any such projection forward to a possible source would have the assassin lying on the pavement of Elm Street flat on his back in front of the limousine. Even were that the alleged case, the body of the presidential limousine would be in the way of any of his bullets.

†The pathology panel concluded from the X-ray evidence that although the bullet struck bone, it was undeflected and "proceeded in an essentially straight and forward path" to its point of exit (7 HSCA 176, 125–126).

dows on the fifth floor were occupied by the three black Depository employees) within the margin of error was the sixth-floor sniper's nest window.[225]

The HSCA concluded that "all three trajectories intercepted the southeast face of the Texas School Book Depository Building. While the trajectories could not be plotted with sufficient precision to determine the exact point from which the shots were fired . . . the margins of error were indicated as circles within which the shots originated. [And] the southeast corner window of the [sixth floor] of the Depository [where police found the three spent cartridges and where eyewitnesses saw a rifle being fired] was inside each of the circles."[226] (See the three trajectories back to the southeasternmost area of the Book Depository Building, with ovals representing margins of error, in the photo section. This photo of the front of the Book Depository Building was taken by *Dallas Morning News* photographer Tom Dillard just moments after the third shot was fired.)[227]

Although Canning's trajectory analysis may not have been perfect, he had successfully determined the source of gunfire: the vicinity of the sniper's nest in the Book Depository Building.

Fifteen years later, in what can only be characterized as a terrible, terrible slap in the face to the personnel of the HSCA and Warren Commission, whose painstaking efforts had established scientific proof that the alignment of Kennedy and Connally in the presidential limousine assures us of the validity of the single-bullet theory, and that all of the gunfire originated from the Texas School Book Depository, *Case Closed* author Gerald Posner claimed that the single-bullet theory was still an open question—one that *he* apparently was instrumental in finally solving. In his 1993 book, Posner wrote that "Failure Analysis Associates applied the latest computer and film enhancement technology *to answer the question* of whether one bullet could have caused the wounds [to Kennedy and Connally]."[228] He quotes Dr. Robert Piziali, described as overseeing the Failure Analysis tests, as stating that in Failure Analysis's reenactment of the assassination, "the most important factor was to have the President and the Governor in the exact locations [alignment] they were at [at] the time they were shot." You mean we had to wait almost thirty years to find this out? Unbelievably, the *Case Closed* author could only find space in his book to say, and then in *just one single sentence* of his book, that "the Warren Commission and the House Select Committee did the best they could with photo and computer technology as it existed in 1964 and 1978" to solve the problem. He goes on to say, "However, scientific advances within the past five years allow significant enhancements of the Zapruder film, as well as scale re-creations using computer animation, which were unavailable to the government panels. *As a result, it is now possible to settle the question of the timing of Oswald's shots and to pinpoint the moment when both Kennedy and Connally were struck.*"[229]*

There's only one way, not two, to read what Posner wrote: that the Warren Commis-

---

*Remarkably, as late as 2004, Posner wrote that "it would take nearly 30 years [by Failure Analysis, as reported by Posner in his book in 1993] for science to establish the [single-bullet] theory as fact" (*Los Angeles Times*, August 29, 2004, p.R5). But the Warren Commission clearly established the single-bullet theory by the testimony of scientists back in 1964, and the HSCA did likewise with scientists in 1978. Actually, science was never required, as Posner suggests. Only common sense. A bullet passing through soft issue in Kennedy's body and then exiting the body had nowhere else to go *but* to Governor Connally's body, which was in perfect alignment with Kennedy's body to be hit by the exiting bullet. No more than ten seconds of reflection is necessary to *know* this.

sion and HSCA were both *unsuccessful* in solving these critical issues. ("They did the best they could" with the technology that was available to them in 1964 and 1978, the author allows generously.) Nowhere in his book does Posner tell his readers that the Warren Commission and HSCA reached the *same* result that Failure Analysis did many years later. Indeed, nowhere in his discussion of the alignment of Kennedy's body to Connally's and the issue of the single-bullet theory does the *Case Closed* author describe the elaborate 1964 on-site reconstruction of the assassination conducted by the Warren Commission to confirm the single-bullet theory.* And remarkably, NASA's Thomas Canning and the comprehensive, sophisticated tests he conducted for the HSCA, which were far more sophisticated and in-depth than anything even attempted by Failure Analysis, involving frequent coordination with experts as diverse as the HSCA's forensic pathology panel and the Federal Aviation Administration's Civil Aeromedical Institute, are not even mentioned in Posner's book. Not one word. Instead, as indicated, the *Case Closed* author presents the results of Failure Analysis's work on the alignment and single-bullet theory issue as if it was a new revelation.[230]

As we've already shown, the Warren Report, way back in 1964, concluded that "the bullet that hit President Kennedy in the back and exited through his throat most likely could *not* have missed both the automobile and its occupants. Since it did not hit the automobile . . . it probably struck Governor Connally."[231] The Warren Commission, of course, was being far too circumspect in its conclusion. As FBI firearms expert Robert Frazier and wound ballistics expert Dr. Frederick W. Light Jr. testified, the bullet that passed through the president's neck *had* to cause Connally's wound, a fact demonstrated by Arlen Specter, a chief expositor of the single-bullet theory, in a 1964 photograph.[232] And, as we have seen, the HSCA in 1978 went over the entire single-bullet theory in even more depth than the Warren Commission and reached the same conclusion. When HSCA counsel asked Thomas Canning whether a bullet fired from the southeasternmost window of the sixth floor of the Book Depository Building and passing through Kennedy would "of necessity" have gone on to hit Connally, he answered, "The bullet would have had to have been substantially deflected by passing through the president [and everyone agrees, even the conspiracy theorists, that it was not, passing through soft tissue on a straight line] in order to miss the governor. It seems almost inevitable that the governor would be hit with the alignments that we have found."

Question: "So that if we assume, as apparently is the fact, that this jacketed bullet did not hit anything solid in the way of bone in the president but only traversed the soft tissue of the neck, and presuming the approximate location of the limousine at the time, and the posture as nearly as can be determined of the president at that time, that in your view then, absent a deflection of that bullet, it could not have missed Governor Connally."

Answer: "That is my view, yes."[233]

And all of this was decades before the apparent "revelation" the *Case Closed* author tells us about.

Just as remarkably, *Case Closed* goes on to tell its readers, "*The second question resolved by the Failure Analysis re-creation* is where the sniper would have to be located for the single bullet to have the correct trajectory."[234] But, of course, this is not a second, separate

---

*The author devotes only one clause in one sentence to the reconstruction. And this clause actually suggests the opposite of a single-bullet conclusion. Also, buried as part of a caption for three photos in the photographic section, the author makes reference to the fact that there was a 1964 reconstruction (Posner, *Case Closed*, p.327, photo section between pp.320 and 321).

question. In answering the first question posed by the *Case Closed* author—whether one bullet could have caused Kennedy's *and* Connally's wounds—one necessarily has to analyze and determine the trajectory of fire. And when you do that, you also necessarily determine the location of the sniper. The suggestion by the *Case Closed* author that the validity of the single-bullet theory and the question of the location of the sniper were "resolved by the Failure Analysis re-creation [of the shooting]" at the American Bar Association's 1992 five-hour mock trial must have made those FBI agents who were a part of the FBI's May 24, 1964, reenactment of the shooting to determine the location of the sniper's rifle, and who have since passed on, spin in their graves. The precise location of the presidential limousine on Elm Street at the time of the second shot and the position of Kennedy's and Connally's bodies as they were in the limousine at the time of the shot, the trajectory of the bullet, and the determination of the location of the sniper at the sixth-floor window were all analyzed in depth at that time, leading the Warren Commission to conclude that the single bullet that struck Kennedy and Connally traced back to the sixth-floor sniper's nest window.[235] And as we saw on the preceding pages, in 1978 the HSCA likewise, in determining whether Kennedy and Connally were struck by the same bullet, had to determine the trajectory of the shot. It, too, with three separate trajectories, concluded that the shot was fired from the vicinity of the sixth-floor window behind which Oswald's fingerprints and Mannlicher-Carcano weapon were found.[236] All of this occurred many, many years before the *Case Closed* author told his readers these questions were finally "resolved."

The further implication in *Case Closed* that the author commissioned or was somehow a part of the Failure Analysis study was equally deceptive. As I indicated in the introduction, this was the inference drawn by several leading newspapers who reviewed *Case Closed*, even though Posner had nothing to do with the Failure Analysis study. In his book *Final Judgment*, Michael Collins Piper writes that the *Case Closed* author "essentially leaves his readers to believe that the computer analysis was somehow prepared exclusively for his use, when, in fact, it was prepared for a mock trial of Lee Harvey Oswald conducted by the American Bar Association."[237]

Perhaps Posner's biggest deception is simply the title of his book, *Case Closed*, suggesting that the author, after nearly thirty years of unsuccessful effort by others, had finally closed the case. Warren Commission critic Harold Weisberg sarcastically wrote, "All hail Gerald Posner. He has done the impossible—what had not been done in thirty years. He solved the JFK assassination case, what the Warren Commission, the FBI, and CIA, and all those other government agencies . . . were not able to do. Thus . . . his title: *Case Closed*."[238]

Indeed, in the very preface to his book, Posner goes way beyond the single-bullet theory, making it clear to the reader that he has accomplished what no one before him, including the Warren Commission and HSCA, had. He writes, "Many people, *understandably*, believe that the truth in the Kennedy assassination will *never* be discovered. [In other words, no one, prior to his book, has yet proved the truth in the Kennedy case.] But the troubling issues and questions about the assassination *can* be settled, the issue of who killed JFK resolved . . . *Presenting those answers is the goal of this book*."[*] But the reality is that we already knew the full truth about the assassination—at least as to *all* of its essen-

---

[*]The inside flap to Posner's book declares that "after thirty years, *Case Closed* finally succeeds where hundreds of other books and investigations [i.e., the Warren Commission and House Select Committee on Assassinations] have failed—it *resolves* the greatest murder mystery of our time, the assassination of JFK."

tial matters—and we've known it since way back on September 24, 1964, the date the Warren Report was published. Admittedly, since that time, hundreds of additional issues have been raised by Warren Commission critics and conspiracy theorists, but they go nowhere and are almost embarrassingly devoid of substance.

Before we leave the subject of the Zapruder film, I want to address one of the craziest allegations that conspiracy buffs have ever latched onto in their efforts to pull the conspiratorial wool over the eyes of gullible people everywhere. The Zapruder film, of course, was originally touted by the vast majority of conspiracy theorists as incontrovertible proof of the conspiracy that killed the president (Connally reacting later than Kennedy, head snap to rear, etc.). As prosecutor Jim Garrison argued in his final summation in the Clay Shaw murder trial in 1969, the head snap to the rear on the film proves the fatal head shot "came from the front." Though the Warren Commission's investigation of Kennedy's death, he said, was "the greatest fraud in the history of our country," how wonderful, he told the jurors, that they had seen the "one eyewitness which was indifferent to power— the Zapruder film. The lens of the camera tells what happened . . . and that is one of the reasons two hundred million Americans have not seen the Zapruder film."[239]*

Even the zany Garrison would have never believed that the latest big rage in the conspiracy community today is its charge that the film, through alteration, is a forgery, created by photographic experts (hired by the "conspirators") in an effort to conceal the truth about the shooting in Dallas and frame Oswald. Can you imagine that, folks? The deliriously wacky conspiracy buffs are now claiming that the Zapruder film itself, the film of the assassination, is a hoax, a fraud, a forgery. What's next? Kennedy is still alive in a suite on the top floor of Parkland Hospital? G. Gordon Liddy was the grassy knoll assassin? Oswald was, as rumored, Ruby's illegitimate son? Just stay tuned to the buffs' wacko network.

The absurd arguments made on behalf of the Zapruder film "alteration theory," as it has come to be called, stem from conspiracy theorists who refuse to accept the explanations, discovered through scientific inquiry, that have successfully answered all of the earlier conspiracy allegations about the Zapruder film. But to concede to these scientifically based explanations, for many conspiracy theorists, is tantamount to high treason. And so, in recent years, a movement, nurtured by the Internet, has been growing around the allegation that the Zapruder film (as we know it) is a sophisticated forgery, altered by the conspirators in the days, weeks, and months following the assassination. Prominent conspiracy theorist Harrison Edward Livingstone, speaking for many in the conspiracy community, writes that "the famous Zapruder film is the biggest hoax of the twentieth century."[240] The evidence of alteration, according to proponents, is plentiful and has been lying right under our noses for over four decades. In other words, the *Life* editor who wrote (presumably echoing the view of all of us) in an early issue of the magazine that "of all the witnesses to the tragedy, the only unimpeachable one is the eight-millimeter movie camera of Abraham Zapruder"[241] was either blind or terribly naive.

Actually, though completely unlike the current rage, the idea that the Zapruder film might have been tampered with goes back to the beginning. The first allegation (and one that is still making the rounds among the uninformed) is that several frames of the Zapruder film had been cut out and are mysteriously "missing." This claim arose when

*The Zapruder film was not shown to the American public until 1976 (see later discussion).

early students of the assassination discovered that frames 208 through 211 were missing from the sequence (Z171–334) reproduced in volume 18 of the Warren Commission's exhibits.[242] The two frames adjacent to the "missing" images (Z207 and Z212) show a splice line, indicating that the four missing frames had been edited from the film. Conspiracy theorists immediately alleged that these missing frames, which are among the frames when the presidential limousine was hidden, from Zapruder's viewpoint, behind the Stemmons Freeway sign, must have shown something the Warren Commission didn't want the world to see. Since these frames (less than one-fourth of a second) could only show, like those just before and after them, the back of the freeway sign, the buffs had a difficult time explaining what the Warren Commission could possibly have seen that it did not want to reveal.

On January 30, 1967, George Hunt, managing editor of *Life* magazine, the owner and custodian of the film, cleared up the missing frames mystery when he released copies of frames Z208–211 to the American media, along with a statement: "[In] handling the film . . . we accidentally damaged not four but six frames of the original—frames 207 through 212. *Before* that happened, however, and before we came into possession of the original print, [Abraham] Zapruder had ordered three color copies made by a Dallas Laboratory— two for federal agents and one for *Life*. These are and always have been intact . . . Thus, there never have been any missing frames."[243]

Another early allegation that the Zapruder film was tampered with revolves around the reproduction of Z314 and Z315, which were inadvertently printed in reverse order in volume 18 of the Warren Commission's exhibits.[244] The conspiracy theorists naturally smell a rat here but fail to articulate how it would have benefited the Commission to have switched the frames. As switched, Kennedy's head seems to go forward at Z313, backward at Z314, forward again at Z315, and finally backward at Z316. This wouldn't be compatible with any theory postulated by the Warren Commission. In fact, it would be in direct opposition, since it not only could give rise to the inference of four shots to the head (and hence, automatically a conspiracy, since no one gunman could fire even two shots, much less four, in four-eighteenths of a second), but inasmuch as the Warren Commission concluded that the *sole* shot to Kennedy's head was at Z313,[245] two separate backward movements at frames 314 and 316 would indicate (despite the neuromuscular reaction) that at least one shot came from the front, which is what the conspiracy theorists have always claimed.

In a December 14, 1965, letter responding to Judith R. Schmidt, an assistant to well-known conspiracy theorist Mark Lane,[246] FBI Director J. Edgar Hoover wrote, "You are correct in the observation that frames labeled 314 and 315 of Commission Exhibit 885 are transposed in Volume 18 as noted in your letter. This is a printing error and does not exist in the actual Commission Exhibit. For your information, the slides from which Commission Exhibit 885 was prepared are correctly numbered and are being shown in their correct sequence. The National Archives is aware of this printing error."[247] This whole matter is really a nonissue, since there are a great number of copies of the Zapruder film in existence, and frames developed from any of them show Z314 and Z315 in their proper sequence.

With respect to the alterationists, there is no rhyme or reason to their allegations. Indeed, they aren't even unified in their beliefs as to *what* has been altered. Suffice it to say, the claims of editing, digital airbrushing, compositing, and general image manipulation run deep and wide.

For instance, some alterationists claim that a large block of Zapruder frames show-ing the limousine nearly hitting the north curb of Elm Street as it made its turn were cut—the critics never bother to say *why*—from the very beginning of the shooting sequence.[248] The allegation is based on the testimony of Book Depository superintend-ent Roy Truly, the only witness who claimed driver William Greer swung the limousine too wide, nearly clipping the north curb.[249] However, amateur films taken by Elsie Dor-man and in particular Tina Towner show the limousine making a smooth, tight turn from Houston to Elm, never veering far from the center lane.

One of the critics' biggest allegations, which, they say, proves the Zapruder film has been altered, is that the presidential limousine came to a complete stop just prior to the time of the head shot (part of the conspiracy, they say, to make the president an easier target for the assassin), but the Zapruder film does not show this. It clearly shows that the limousine did not stop. However, the charge has been made so often that even anti-conspiracy author Gerald Posner almost accepts it, saying that the driver of the vehicle, William Greer, "slowed the vehicle to almost a standstill."[250] The charge that the presi-dential limousine did is based on a number of eyewitnesses (forty-eight at last count) who testified that the limousine either "slowed," "almost came to a halt," or "stopped com-pletely" as the shots rang out. One of the proponents of this theory, James H. Fetzer, asserts that "the driver [of the presidential limousine], William Greer, actually brought the vehicle to a stop in Dealey Plaza after bullets had begun to be fired. This was such an obvious indication of Secret Service complicity in the assassination," he says, "that it had to be edited out."[251] In this case, critics have accepted eyewitness testimony—which can be very reliable, but so very often, as we know, is not—over what the film of the event actually shows—that the limousine did not stop. Since the witnesses are judged to be cor-rect by the theorists, the film, they deduce, must be fake.

One would think the "alterationists" (the name applied to those in the conspiracy com-munity who believe the Zapruder film was altered) would have a difficult time with the fact that the Zapruder film shows that the back of the president's head always looks intact (negating the conspiracy position that there was a large exit wound to the rear of the pres-ident's head) and also shows a large exit wound to the right front of the president's head (validating the Warren Commission's and HSCA's position that the head wound shot came from the president's rear, not the grassy knoll). But where there's a will there's a way. Alterationist David Lifton, while conceding "it wasn't easy" for the conspirator-forgers of the film to do it, claims that they "blacked out" the back of the president's head to con-ceal the large exit wound, and "painted on" what looked like a large exit wound to the right front of the president's head. But Lifton offers no evidence to support his absolutely incredible allegation, nor is he troubled in the least, apparently, by the fact that Zapruder testified that while viewing the motorcade through his telephoto lens he saw the right side of the president's head open up and "blood and everything" come out.[252]

Some critics even contend that two separate and distinct head shots (one at Z313 from the rear, and one at Z358 from the front) were combined into a single head shot and "sim-ply imported to where it now appears as a composite image."[253] But again, the propounders of this allegation offer not a speck of evidence to support it.

The conspiracy alterationists are so incredibly zany that they have now gone beyond their allegation that key frames of the Zapruder film were altered by the conspirators to support their false story of what took place, to claiming that the conspirators altered all manner of people and objects in Dealey Plaza that couldn't possibly have any bearing on the president's murder. The book *The Great Zapruder Film Hoax* gives many such examples. Just one: conspiracy buff Jack White points out that in frame 360, Jack Franzen, his wife, and son Jeff are seen watching the presidential limousine from the south side of Elm Street as it speeds away toward the underpass, but at frame 367, while the three are still there, Mrs. Franzen's head appears a few inches closer in height to her taller husband than it did in frame 360. What he doesn't tell his readers is that between frames 360 and 367, Mrs. Franzen clearly seems to have stepped very slightly backward, and from Zapruder's elevated camera position across Elm Street, this would automatically put her higher on the frame in relation to her husband, who hasn't moved his feet; that is, if she had moved backward even farther than she had, such as three steps, though her height would of course be the same, her head would be much higher on the frame than that of her husband's. But the looney White has other ideas. He says that "Mrs. Franzen has *grown* half a head taller while Jack and Jeff remain the same height. There is no explanation which would cause this—except alteration." White doesn't say what the conspirators could possibly gain by altering the Zapruder film between frames 360 and 367 (close to three seconds *after* the last shot) to cause Mrs. Franzen to get taller.[254]

The alterationists have even claimed that "at some point after the assassination, all the curbside lampposts in Dealey Plaza were moved to different locations and/or replaced with poles of different height. Researchers think this was part of a cover-up plan to confound and confuse attempts to replicate photos in the plaza."[255] I know that conspiracy theorists have a sweet tooth for silliness, but is there absolutely nothing that is too silly for their palate?

Perhaps the goofiest assertions that have emerged from all of this alteration hocus-pocus are the ideas that—are you ready?—"the Zapruder film itself may have not been taken by Abraham Zapruder,"[256] but that if it was, Zapruder himself was in on the plot. Conspiracy author Harrison E. Livingstone writes, "Is it possible that Zapruder was a plant? I think the masterminds that planned this wanted to document the assassination on film so they could alter it, if need be, to support their story. It just seems too convenient, otherwise. If they could control the autopsy photos and X-rays, getting someone to film the assassination would be a piece of cake."[257]

The list of alleged discrepancies, contradictions, and anomalies seems to grow in direct proportion to the number of amateur Internet-based film experts who take up the challenge of finding the "proof of conspiracy" that they believe is imbedded *somewhere* in the frames of Zapruder's film, just waiting to be extracted, like DNA from a crime scene. Most of this thoughtless nonsense is sold on the strength of what is theoretically possible today using modern computer technology. However, twenty-first-century technology is hardly a measuring stick for events that allegedly occurred more than four decades ago. In fact, there is *nothing* simple about the kinds of wholesale changes that are alleged to have been made during the course of altering the Zapruder film, even with today's technology. The myriad of technological problems associated with such an effort (i.e., manipulating photographic images in such a way that they can escape detection by stereoscopic viewing techniques, such as those used to authenticate the Kennedy autopsy photographs) are never explained by the alterationists. In the "Alice in Wonderland" world of conspiracy buffs, incredibly tedious film editing at a micro level, and miracle composites that would stagger the imagination of even today's special effects professionals (who are armed with sophisticated computer tools only dreamed of when the Zapruder film was supposedly altered), are all possible with a single addled thought and a wave of the hand.

Indeed, some conspiracy theorists, unable to control themselves, have left the alterationists, with their apparent naivete, in the dust. Conspiracy theorist James H. Fetzer flat-out declares, "There is no other conclusion other than that the film was not just altered, but is a complete fabrication."[258] Fetzer is not alone. John Costello, an Aussie with a PhD in theoretical physics and hell-bent on showing his American counterparts that an Aussie can be just as crazy as they, chimes in that he has studied the Zapruder film in depth and concluded "that the extant Zapruder film is a complete fabrication, rather than simply an alteration of an original film."[259] In other words, folks, and pardon the pun, the Zapruder reel is not real.[*]

Although it could hardly be more far-out, the notion that the Zapruder film has been altered has continued to gain such support in the conspiracy community that I am constrained to set forth seven solid reasons why we *know* the Zapruder film hasn't been altered, as conspiracy theorists claim. (For how the alterationists claim the conspirators came into possession of the Zapruder film so they could alter it, see long endnote discussion.)

1. There is an immutable reality that would preclude anyone from even making an effort to alter the Zapruder film. We know of at least eight other spectators in Dealey Plaza who, *standing in plain view and visible to others*, were filming the presidential motorcade—Robert Hughes (standing on the curb at the southwest corner of Houston and Main); Mark Bell (on a pedestal at the north peristyle on the south side of Elm Street); Orville Nix and Charles Bronson (both near the southwest corner of Houston and Main); Marie Muchmore (on the west side of Houston close to the north peristyle); thirteen-year-old Tina Towner (standing with her parents on the southwest corner of Elm and Houston); and John Martin Jr. (at first on the west side of Houston Street, a few feet north of Main, and then running with the limousine up Houston to a position at the northern end of the reflecting pool across the street from the Texas School Book Depository Building on Elm). And then there is the unknown woman in a blue dress running on the grass north of the reflecting pool on the south side of Elm holding what appears to be a camera with a long lens, indicating a motion picture camera.[260] How would the conspirators know they only had to secure Zapruder's film and didn't have to seize the films of these other people?[†]

---

[*]For those conspiracy theorists who say that the Zapruder film is a hoax and probably feel that they are the bold avant-garde in the conspiracy community, I am here to tell them that they really are just pikers in this regard. Author Bernard M. Bane writes that the assassination *itself* never even took place! "President Kennedy's assassination was a hoax," he writes, "masterminded by social engineers in furtherance of promoting social reform." He doesn't spell out how these people did it, but in his book *Is President John F. Kennedy Alive—and Well?* he answers his question with a confident yes. "So what has kept JFK from surfacing all these years, given that he is not being held against his will as in the case of a house arrest? . . . In order to implement a revisionist face-saving surfacing, he needs the cooperation of the powers that be, his erstwhile adversaries, which, not surprisingly, he is not getting." (Bane, *Is President John F. Kennedy Alive—and Well?* pp.viii, 120–121) So there.

[†]Although the conspirators would be able to see that Zapruder was in a better position to film the assassination they knew was about to take place, Zapruder's film, if they tried to alter it, would still have to be 100 percent consistent with films taken from less favorable vantage points, like the Nix and Bronson films. Moreover, how could the conspirators have known, in advance, that only Zapruder would be in the position he was in—that there wouldn't be other spectators with motion picture cameras on the north side of Elm Street?

Indeed, since we know that in addition to the many motion picture cameras in plain view, there were many Dealey Plaza spectators taking still photographs, unless the conspirators had a helicopter hovering over Dealey Plaza with several telescopic sights trained tightly on everyone in the plaza, how could they possibly know which of the cameras took stills and which were the more dangerous (to them) motion picture cameras they had to seize?

Or, for that matter, the films of NBC cameraman Dave Wiegman and Dallas WFAA–TV cameraman Malcolm Couch (both of whom took film of the motorcade in Dealey Plaza from their respective "camera cars" to the rear of the presidential limousine); Jim Underwood from Dallas radio and TV station KRLD; and television newsman Jimmy Darnell of Dallas station WBAP-TV, all four of whom jumped out of their cars after the shooting and were seen by everyone shooting film up and down Elm Street? How would the conspirators know they wouldn't have to seize these films? Or the film of Ernest Charles Mentesana, who arrived at the assassination scene right after the shooting, and from his position on the west side of the Dal-Tex Building, filmed the turmoil in and around the Book Depository Building? Though he, unlike the others, showed up *after* the shooting, how would the conspirators know this? Not knowing this, wouldn't they have to seize his motion picture camera too? Or the motion picture camera of Tom Alyea, who was in a car at a stoplight at Commerce and Houston at the time of the shooting. Alyea grabbed a fully loaded motion picture camera, jumped out of his car, and ran across the plaza, filming the emerging scene and chaos on Elm and Houston as he ran. How would the conspirators know not to try to seize his camera too?[261]

Since the alleged conspirators couldn't have known at the time that it was Zapruder's film, not any of the many others, that they had to seize because it was the only one that captured the entire assassination sequence, their only going after his film makes absolutely no sense. If we're to govern our reasoning on this issue by common sense, the above reality, all by itself, would tell any reasonable person that the Zapruder film was not altered.

2. Another reason why it's obvious the Zapruder film was not altered is that, as we know, at the very heart of nearly all conspiracy arguments is the contention that the fatal shot to the president's head came from the grassy knoll to the president's right front, not from the right rear where Oswald was. We also know that the head snap to the rear has convinced Americans more than any other thing that, indeed, the head shot came from the president's front, and this, without an explanation, *exonerates* Oswald at least as to the fatal shot. Since the whole alleged purpose of the forgery of the Zapruder film, per the conspiracy theorists, was to *frame* Oswald* as the *lone* gunman[262] and conceal the truth from the American public (the truth, per the buffs, being that the shot to the head came from the grassy knoll), if there were *one* thing, and one thing only that the forgers would have altered, they would have altered the Zapruder film to make it look like Kennedy's head had been violently thrust forward (indicating a shot from the rear, where Oswald was), not backward, as the film shows. Instead, if we're to believe the conspiracy-theorists, the conspirator-forgers decided to alter everything else in the film, including the height of a spectator, but not the most important thing of all, the head snap to the rear. Leading alterationist Dr. David Mantik claims that the conspirator-forgers excised frames that he said would have shown "tissue debris" from Kennedy's head going backward. "Backward going debris would have been overwhelming evidence of a frontal shot (or shots) and would have posed too serious a threat to the official story of only posterior [from the rear] shots."[263] But if the forgers would delete the backward movement of the spray, they all the more so would want to delete the much more visible head snap to the rear.

---

*If it weren't to frame Oswald, and the conspirator-forgers didn't want something in the film to be known, they obviously (assuming, as the theorists contend, the conspirators had possession of the original film) would have simply destroyed the film rather than engage in the incredibly complex effort to alter it.

3. Itek Corporation and the HSCA[264] demonstrated that many of the adjacent frames on the Zapruder film can be viewed as a stereoscopic pair, analogous to the stereoscopic effect achieved when photographing a stationary object with two cameras, representing the left and right eye. That the film's frames can be viewed stereoscopically means the alteration ball game is over. It is virtually impossible (even with modern computer technology) to create images (i.e., forgeries) containing digitally painted effects* and composite imagery that can escape detection during stereoscopic viewing. The reason is that when digitally painted or altered portions of any two images are viewed stereoscopically, the painted or altered area appears to "float" above the original image, betraying the forgery. The fact that the Zapruder film can be viewed in stereo, without any evidence of "floating" imagery, assures us of its authenticity.

4. The original Zapruder film was proved to have been shot using Zapruder's camera, which effectively eliminates the alterationist argument that the film is actually a forgery of selected frames created by using an optical printer. In 1998, at the request of the ARRB, Roland J. Zavada, the retired standards director for imaging technologies at Kodak, and Kodak's preeminent 8-millimeter film expert, analyzed the "out-of-camera" original film (i.e., the actual film that Zapruder had loaded into his camera on November 22, 1963), several first-generation copies, and a number of prints of the Zapruder film, as well as the actual Bell & Howell camera used by Zapruder to create the film. Edge print codes embedded in the original film show that the film was manufactured in 1961 at Kodak in Rochester, New York, and processed (i.e., developed) in November 1963, both of which are very strong indications that the film being examined was, indeed, the original film. The processing number 0183, perforated vertically along the width of the film (a common practice used to match up processed films with customer orders), was traced to the Kodak developing laboratory in Dallas where Zapruder took his film to be processed. The link between the processing number (0183) and Zapruder's film was confirmed by the technicians involved in the developing process, and proves that the Zapruder film, as we know it, was developed in Dallas on the afternoon of November 22, 1963, and not at some other time and place after alterations had been made. Further, Zavada concluded that whatever "anomalies" there were in the Zapruder film "can be explained by the design and image capture characteristics of [Zapruder's] Bell & Howell 414 PD Camera."[265]

5. We all know that human movements are harmonious with each other and are therefore essentially predictable from any chosen interrupted point. Common sense tells us, then, that if the forgers altered any frames, juxtaposition of the altered frames with the unaltered frames would necessarily result in extremely jerky movements, making the Zapruder film look almost cartoonish in the altered areas. No such Charlie Chaplin–like movements have been evident on the Zapruder film to the hundreds of experts who have studied it and the millions of people who have seen it.

6. Even hypothetically assuming that a forgery were possible, the forgers would have had to alter the original Zapruder film before any copies were made, since an altered copy could immediately be exposed as a fraud when it was compared with the original.† But

---

*These are additions or alterations to an image using computer technology to manipulate the pixels (i.e., colored dots) that make up the image.

†Alterationist David Lifton is satisfied that the original Zapruder film was processed and developed at the Kodak plant in Dallas, but believes a copy was altered at a supersecret Kodak facility in Rochester, New York, and thereafter passed off as the original (David S. Lifton, "Pig on a Leash, a Question of Authenticity," in Fetzer, *Great Zapruder Film Hoax*, pp.387–388, 413). Apart from the fact there is no evidence this was done,

we know from the record that Abraham Zapruder kept the original film in his possession until it was sold to *Life* magazine on Saturday, November 23, 1963, which means, of course, that no one could have altered the film before then. Yet by *that* time, multiple copies of the film were already in the hands of the Secret Service and the FBI, both of whom were, in turn, making second- and third-generation copies for their files. Or do the alterationists want us to believe that the "conspirators" altered the original film *after* these second- and third-generation copies had been made? But in that case, any one of the copies could expose the fact that the original had been altered.

The fact that each of the many copies of the Zapruder film matches all others as well as the original film proves *beyond any doubt* that no alterations were made.

7. Finally, even if by some miracle of miracles the conspirator-forgers were able to get possession of and alter the original and all copies of the Zapruder film, and had the time and technology to do what had to be done, they would, of necessity, have to also commit themselves to finding and altering all *other* films and still photographs of the motorcade on Elm Street so that they all agreed with the altered Zapruder film. Because if they didn't, any one of those photos and films could immediately expose the Zapruder film as being a fraud and forgery, something the conspirator-forgers would never want to be known. Yet, we know that none of these other films and photographs have ever been shown to be in conflict with the Zapruder film, but instead are completely consistent with it. As Josiah Thompson says, to believe that all of these other films are consistent with the Zapruder film because they too were altered to match the altered Zapruder film is to "end up claiming that the whole photographic record of the assassination has been falsified. When we reach that point, don't we have to turn away in disgust mumbling to ourselves, 'This is just crazy!?'"[266]

Even assuming, for the sake of argument and without any evidence to support it, that the conspirator-forgers seized and altered the Hughes, Bell, Nix, Muchmore, Towner, Martin, and Bronson films, how in the world would they even presume to have knowledge of the identity of every other person in Dealey Plaza who took a photo or film of the motorcade (people like Elsie Dorman, who filmed part of the motorcade from a fourth-floor window of the Texas School Book Depository Building, or Patsy Paschall, who filmed part of the motorcade from an upper-story window of the old Dallas Court House on Main Street),[267] locate them, and seize their photos and films?[*] And even if they could somehow manage to do this impossible task, they could never be certain that a photo or particularly a film wouldn't surface in the future (and the fact remains that such a film could still, even decades later, emerge from someone's attic or closet) and expose the alteration as being a giant hoax.

Gary Mack, the curator at the Sixth Floor Museum at Dealey Plaza, said that "for years our staff used to joke about someone one day showing up here with an old shoe box containing assassination or motorcade photos or film. And in early 2003, Jay Skaggs, an

---

surely Lifton has to realize that this altered copy could be immediately exposed as a forgery when it was ultimately compared with the out-of-camera original.

[*]How, indeed, would they know that presidential assistant David Powers, in the car right behind the president's limousine, who had a movie camera and *did* stand up in his car to take home movies at various places along the parade route starting at Love Field, would not have taken any pictures on Elm Street during the assassination (Trask, *Pictures of the Pain*, pp.37, 63, 369; Letter from Dave Powers to Richard Trask dated March 28, 1989)? If he had, why would they think they'd be successful in stealing his film so they could alter it to make it consistent with their altered Zapruder film?

eighty-two-year-old Dallas citizen, who was watching the motorcade at the northeast corner of Main and Houston, showed up here with a small box containing twenty 35-mil-
limeter color slides and photos of the motorcade, seventeen of which showed the
motorcade or aftermath. Because none captured the assassination, Skaggs didn't feel they
were important enough to turn over to anyone, but his wife finally encouraged him to do
so, and the guy was apologetic for having waited so long."[268] All of this only illustrates the
suicidal venture of any conspirators who might set out to forge the Zapruder film.

In conclusion, it is instructive to note that although the Warren Commission has been
severely maligned in its interpretation of the Zapruder film, and although it was demonstrably off in its ambivalence as to when the first shot was fired, its conclusion way back
in 1964 on the much more important issue that the bullet that entered Kennedy's back
also went on to hit Connally was reaffirmed by the in-depth Itek Corporation study in
1976[269] and by the HSCA in 1978. It is also completely consistent with all the other available evidence as well as simple common sense.

  Before getting into the case against Lee Harvey Oswald, just who was this killer and
historical figure?

Lee Harvey Oswald

Oswald is not, I put it in simple words, an easy man to
explain.
—G. Robert Blakey, former chief counsel of the
House Select Committee on Assassinations[1]

Robert Oswald, the brother of the president's killer, says that to understand how and why
his "kid brother" ended up in the sniper's nest window, "people need to look at what transpired before that, everything, from childhood on up, especially that last year of his life."[2]
That proposition cannot be quarreled with. English psychologist and writer Havelock
Ellis notes that "a man's destiny stands not in the future, but in the past. That, rightly
considered, is the most vital of vital facts."

The long road to the sniper's nest for a man who would change history started just over
twenty-four years earlier, when Lee Harvey Oswald was born at the Old French Hospital on Orleans Avenue in New Orleans, Louisiana, on October 18, 1939, to thirty-two-
year-old Marguerite Frances Claverie Oswald.[3] The delivering physician was Dr. Bruno
F. Mancuso.[4] Two months earlier, Lee's father, named Robert Edward Lee Oswald for the
famous Confederate general, Robert E. Lee, had died of a stroke while mowing his lawn
on a hot and muggy August morning. He was only forty-three years old. Marguerite, seven
months' pregnant, buried him that afternoon, an act his family considered shockingly
cold, causing them to never speak to her again.[5] Marguerite was Robert's second wife.
He had divorced his first wife in 1933 and married Marguerite six months later.[6]

   Marguerite's ancestors were part of the working class in the great port at the mouth
of the Mississippi, many working in trades associated with shipping, although Marguerite's father, John, was a motorman on the city's tramlines for forty years. Her grand-
parents on her father's side, the Claveries, were immigrants, Catholics from France. Her
mother Dora's parents, named Stucke, were Lutherans from Germany. Marguerite, her
three sisters, and two brothers were brought up as Lutherans, even though their mother
died in 1911 when all were still children. Marguerite, who was born in 1907, was four at
the time and was raised by her widowed father, housekeepers, and her older siblings.[7] It
was not easy to raise six children on a motorman's salary of ninety dollars a month, even
if the rent was only "twelve or fourteen dollars a month," but Marguerite's older sister
Lillian remembered it as a happy time. "We were singing all the time," she would later

recall, "and I often say that we were much happier than the children are today, even though we were poor. My father was a very good man. He didn't drink, and he was all for his family. He didn't make much money, but we got along all right."[8]

Marguerite also remembered having "a very happy childhood," and the pleasures of life centered on the home on Phillips Street in a poor, racially mixed part of New Orleans, the Claverie children playing with the Negro family next door.[9] Lillian recalled skating parties around Jackson Square in the French Quarter and parties at an aunt's who had a piano and who didn't mind when the teenagers took up the rug to dance. Eventually, Mr. Claverie bought a piano for five dollars and Marguerite learned to play a little by ear. Marguerite was "very entertaining," according to Lillian. "She could sing very well, not, you know, to be a professional singer, but she had a very good voice." The girls were given a dollar a day to feed the family, and they were allowed to keep whatever was left over after shopping for the beans and rice and spinach and vegetables and bananas.[10]

Lillian and Marguerite's brothers died young, Charles, a gunner on transport ships during the First World War, at age twenty-three, John at the age of eighteen, both of tuberculosis.[11]* Marguerite dropped out of McDonogh High School in New Orleans her first year, lied on a job application that she had completed high school, and went to work as a receptionist for a firm of lawyers.[12] On August 1, 1929, with the Great Depression about to explode on America, Marguerite, pretty, vivacious, but quick-tempered, married Edward John Pic Jr., a stevedoring company clerk in Harrison County, Mississippi. Both were twenty-two years old.[13] Pic, who had lost the sight of one eye as a youth when a loose lace on a basketball struck him in the eye, and Marguerite rented a house off Canal Street in New Orleans, but the marriage was in difficulty from the outset and they separated after about a year. Marguerite was three months' pregnant. Money was one of the big issues—as it would be with Marguerite throughout her life. She told her sister Lillian that Pic had lied to her about his salary, but Lillian, who found Pic oddly silent, never heard his side of the story. Marguerite also claimed that Pic left her because he didn't want children, although Pic claimed that he had no objection to them, that the legal separation would have happened with or without the pregnancy. "Marguerite was a nice girl," he told the Warren Commission in 1964. "We just couldn't get along, you know, so we finally decided to quit trying and call the whole thing off . . . Our dispositions would not gel." He said that she was aware of his earning capacity when they married and that it did not worsen during the year they lived together. Marguerite did not work during that time, he claimed, but lived as a housewife.[14]

Their son, John Edward Pic, was born on January 17, 1932. The father went on sending Marguerite forty dollars a month and claiming their son as a dependent until 1950, when the boy was eighteen and started filing an income tax return on his own behalf, claiming Marguerite as a dependent. Otherwise, the separation was nearly total—Pic never saw his son after the boy was a year old, or even a photo of him, until Marguerite sent him one of eighteen-year-old John Edward Pic in his Coast Guard uniform.[15]

Marguerite met Robert Edward Lee Oswald shortly after her separation from Pic. A friend of Lillian's, Robert saw Marguerite and her baby coming home from a park, picked them up in his car, and started dating her.[16] Robert Oswald collected insurance premiums

---

*Little is known of Marguerite's two younger sisters, except Pearl married and had already died at the time of the assassination, and Aminthe was married and living in Knoxville, Tennessee (8 H 96, WCT Lillian Murret; Armstrong, *Harvey and Lee*, p.13).

door-to-door for the Metropolitan Life Insurance Company. Lillian was already married to Charles "Dutz" Murret when the energetic and affable Robert began to collect the Murrets' premiums. He too was separated from an earlier marriage, and eventually both he and Marguerite arranged divorces in order to marry on July 20, 1933. Oswald, a divorced Catholic, could not remarry in the church, so he had to marry Marguerite in her Lutheran church on Canal Street. He wanted to adopt young John Edward Pic, but Marguerite, aware that the boy's support payments from his father would cease, was against it.[17]

A son was born on April 7, 1934, nine months after the marriage, and named after his father, Robert E. Lee Oswald. The couple settled down to what Lillian perceived as a happy marriage, a family that flourished as the Depression raged, eventually buying a house on Alvar Street. The Oswalds even had a car.[18] That period with her husband, their son, and her son by her previous marriage, Marguerite would recall later, "was the only happy part of my life."[19]

Two months after her husband died on August 19, 1939, Marguerite gave birth to their second son, Lee Harvey Oswald. (*Harvey* was Oswald's paternal grandmother's family name.) Although the young couple had been hoping for a girl, the baby's two older brothers, then five and seven, were not. "If it's a girl," John told Robert, "we'll throw it out the hospital window."[20]

At times the boy would pretend that the death of his father before he was born was of no consequence, as a psychiatric social worker who examined him at the age of thirteen noted. "He has no curiosity about his father," Evelyn Strickland wrote, telling Strickland he never missed having one and never thought to ask about him.[21] Nevertheless, one chilling phrase from a draft of a book he was writing about his experiences in Russia has lodged itself in the consciousness of many: "Lee Harvey Oswald was born in Oct 1939 in New Orleans, La." he wrote, "the son of a Insuraen Salesmen whose early death left a far mean streak of indepence brought on by negleck."[22]*

The early death of Oswald's father plunged the family into economic difficulties. The Depression was all but over by October 1939 as the country geared up for the Second World War, which had just started in Europe, but for Marguerite and her boys, life would soon become harsh. For over a year after her husband died on August 19, 1939, Marguerite remained at the Alvar Street home with her three children without working, probably living on the life insurance proceeds from her husband's death.[23] Her oldest two children went to the William Frantz Elementary School, which was across the street from the Alvar Street home. In January of 1940, Marguerite removed her two sons from the Frantz school and placed the boys in the Infant Jesus College, a Catholic boarding school in Algiers, just across the Mississippi River from New Orleans proper.[24] John Pic believed Marguerite had done this to save money,[25] though it is not known how much it cost to board the two boys, and why that would have been cheaper than to keep them at home. Evidence that Marguerite was feeling a financial pinch is that at some time in late September of 1940, she applied for Aid to Dependent Children assistance.[26]

*Oswald was a voracious reader of serious literature who had intellectual proclivities, and most who came in contact with him felt he was bright and spoke very well, but he was dyslexic. Throughout this biography, the reader can expect to see a great number of misspelled words and defective grammar by Oswald, which I've decided to quote as is, for historical accuracy.

The boys did not like it at the Catholic school. "The nuns were terribly strict," Robert would recall, "and we were afraid of them. We saw boys who broke the rules beaten with a broomstick. The whole place was gloomy and cold and we felt like outsiders because we were Lutheran."[27] With the advent of the new school year in September of 1940, Marguerite reenrolled her two sons at the Frantz school.[28] Also, sometime in late September of 1940, Marguerite rented the house on Alvar Street to Dr. Bruno F. Mancuso, the doctor who had delivered Lee,[*] and at the end of September moved to a smaller home at 1242 Congress Street.[29] She soon transferred her two sons to the nearby George Washington School.[30]

In early March of 1941, Marguerite purchased and moved into a small-frame house on Bartholomew Street for $1,300.[31] Her nine-year-old, John, recognized the move as a step down in life but recalled the house as pleasant enough. It was in an older, "upper-lower-class" neighborhood, but it had two bedrooms and a large backyard, and they had a dog called "Sunshine."[32]

Marguerite opened a shop in the front room, "Oswald's Notion Shop," where she sold needles, thread, ribbon, and other sewing materials, as well as candy—which the boys occasionally swiped. She hoped to be able to make enough money to stay at home and keep her children with her, but she couldn't.[33] In December 1941, as war broke out, Marguerite turned to the Lutheran church, which ran the Bethlehem Children's Home (Evangelical Lutheran Bethlehem Orphan Asylum), a place that took in orphans or children with just one parent for a fee tailored to the circumstances. Marguerite paid ten dollars a month for each of her sons, John and Robert, plus provided shoes and clothing, and hoped to place Lee there too, but the home did not take children under the age of three.[34]

Robert thought Lee must have already begun to realize that Marguerite considered all of her boys a tribulation to her. "I don't know at what age mother verbalized to Lee to the effect that she felt he was a burden to her. Certainly by age three he had the sense that, you know, we were a burden."[35]

The older boys got on well at Bethlehem. Robert remembered it as a cheerful place, far less rigid than the Catholic boarding school at Algiers. Marguerite, flitting like a butterfly from job to job, would fetch John and Robert on weekends and return them on Sunday morning so they could go to church with the other children.[36][†] John recalled pleasant interludes at Aunt Lillian's too—"Whenever we had a chance we were more than glad to go there."[37]

In January of 1942, Marguerite sold the Bartholomew Street house back to the seller from whom she had purchased it for a profit of $800,[38] and moved again, to an apartment on Pauline Street. She tried as best she could to look after Lee, with the help of babysitters,[39] while she worked as a switchboard operator.[40] But it wasn't working and her sister Lillian, already with five children of her own, the youngest about the age of Robert, volunteered to take Lee in as well. He was "a very beautiful child," she said. She took him to town in his sailor suit, where the friendly tyke would call out "hi" to everybody and

---

[*]Dr. Mancuso continued to rent the house until 1944, when Marguerite obtained a judgment of possession against him. She then sold the home for $6,500 to a bank, which resold it to Dr. Mancuso. (WR, p.670; CE 2197, 25 H 76)

[†]Though Marguerite is quite specific about this, her sons, though less specific, disagree. John said that "maybe once every two weeks," Marguerite "would drop around" (11 H 20). And Robert said that later, when Lee was also at Bethlehem, "on weekends she came to the home to visit us" (Oswald with Land and Land, *Lee*, p.35).

people would say, "What an adorable child he is." He got along well with Lillian's children too, but he could be troublesome, particularly in the morning when Lillian had her hands full getting all five of her own kids off to grammar school. Lee, still in his nightclothes, would slip out of the house, go down the street, and sit down in someone's kitchen. "You could have everything locked in the house," Lillian said, "but Lee would still get out."[41]

Although Lee's Aunt Lillian got on well enough with Lee, her relations with her quick-tempered sister Marguerite were often prickly. The women usually settled their differences, as they had ever since they were children—"Marguerite was easy enough to get along with," Lillian would say, "as long as she gets her own way," adding, "You see, she was always right." Also, "She would fly off too quick," and no matter how much anyone did for her, such as Lillian taking in Lee, "she never thought that anyone was actually helping her."[42]

Lillian is unsure of the length of time she kept Lee, though she believes it was two years. Robert recalls a much shorter time and says that Marguerite, evidently feeling Lee would be better off in his own home, took him back from Lillian. Marguerite advertised in the newspaper and found a couple willing to accept free room and board and fifteen dollars a month in return for caring for Lee while she was at work. The arrangement lasted only two months. Marguerite came home one day to find the child crying, red welts on his legs. She fired the couple, who claimed that Lee was "a bad, unmanageable child," on the spot. Marguerite did not believe that a child that young could be that bad. She moved back nearer to her sister, to a house on Sherwood Forest Drive, and made a new arrangement: Lillian would look after Lee during the day while Marguerite went out to work.[43]

As Lee's third birthday approached in October of 1942, Marguerite again inquired about his admission into the Bethlehem Children's Home, offering to contribute ten dollars a month toward his upkeep as well as provide his shoes and clothing, and he was accepted. When John and Robert went back to the children's home after the Christmas holidays in December of 1942, three-year-old Lee went with them.[44] Marguerite took a job as a telephone operator for, it is believed, the Pittsburgh Plate Glass Company.[45]

Eight-year-old Robert in particular enjoyed having Lee with them at what they called the orphanage. Used to the protection of his older brother, John, Robert now became the protector of Lee, and the two of them began to feel a brotherly closeness for the first time, a feeling that persisted throughout their lives. Robert thought he and Lee were always closer than Lee and John, or, for that matter, Lee and their mother. It was to Robert that Lee turned when he had something important to discuss.[46]

Robert remembers Lee "as a happy baby and a happy little boy" at that time, "not too quiet nor too rambunctious," and filled with curiosity about how things worked. He didn't seem to miss his mama all that much, but Robert didn't find that surprising—he had spent more time with babysitters, housekeepers, and aunts than with his mother anyway, and it wasn't as if the boys didn't get to see Marguerite. Once a week they would take a streetcar over to Canal Street to visit their mother at her latest job as manager of the newly opened Princess Hosiery Shop. They would have lunch there and then go to a movie. And on weekends she would go to the Children's Home to visit them.[47]

Lee remained in the Bethlehem Home until late January of 1944, about thirteen months, but according to John, he left on several occasions to spend short periods of time with his mother or the Murrets.[48] Marguerite also seemed to like her new job; she was given a free hand and was able to hire four girls in six days to help her.[49] Her employer, Edward Aizer, remembered her as a neat, attractive, and hardworking woman, a "very aggressive individual" who would make a good manager, but she was not good with figures—she apparently could not even add or subtract—and after a few months he had to discharge her.[50]

By this time, however, Marguerite—looking much younger than her thirty-seven years and a "remarkably pretty and vivacious woman," according to her son Robert, with dark hair worn long and vivid blue eyes—had begun dating Edwin Ekdahl, an electrical engineer from Boston who was then working for the Texas Electrical Service in New Orleans. Ekdahl, a tall, white-haired, well-educated man with a Yankee accent, was much older than Marguerite. The boys liked him because he seemed to like them. He was good-natured and friendly, and he seemed to know how to talk with them. He also had a car, a 1938 Buick, which was important.[51] By the time Marguerite brought Ekdahl out to the orphanage to meet her three children, she had already been seeing him for several months and he had asked her to marry him.[52] He had one powerful advantage in the eyes of the hard-strapped widow. He was a "ten-thousand-dollar-a-year man with an expense account,"[53] excellent remuneration in those war years, when a worker might be glad to pull down forty or fifty dollars a week. However, Ekdahl was not only a good bit older, he had been married to a woman to whom he was only separated, his job required him to travel a lot, he had a bad heart, and Marguerite was not overly eager to marry him. She took her time to decide, even after Ekdahl's sister came to New Orleans to urge his suit, telling Marguerite he was lonely.[54]

Marguerite dithered, the affair continued, and finally, in January of 1944, she decided to marry Ekdahl. She made an arrangement with Bethlehem to leave the two older boys there until they completed the school year, and took Lee with her to Dallas, where Ekdahl had been transferred. There, however, she changed her mind about marriage, and using money from the sale of her Alvar Street property in New Orleans,[55] and possibly help from Ekdahl, for a very small downpayment she bought her own place, a white, two-story duplex on Victor Street in Dallas with rooms lined up like railroad cars—living room, bedroom, bathroom, bedroom, kitchen. She settled down in one of the apartments, while renting the other.[56] When the two older boys finished the school year at Bethlehem in June of 1944, they moved to Dallas to reunite with Lee and their mother. They were enrolled in a summer school and then, in the fall, in a public school three blocks away, Davy Crockett Elementary. Marguerite dropped Lee off at a nursery school on her way to work in the morning and picked him up when she came home in the evening. Robert was now ten, John twelve, and Lee not quite five.[57]

Ekdahl visited Marguerite on weekends and stayed at Victor Street with her and the boys.[58] Early in the following year, 1945, Marguerite decided she would marry Ekdahl after all, and she tried, in February, to return the older boys to the Bethlehem Children's Home. Although she knew the home did not accept children with two parents, Marguerite explained that her prospective husband's work would require her to travel a great deal.[59] When the home refused them, she made other plans, enrolling both of them, for the fall semester of 1945, in Chamberlain-Hunt Academy, a military school in Port Gibson, Mississippi. She paid the tuition herself from what remained of the proceeds from the sale of the Alvar Street house in New Orleans the previous year.[60] With that taken care of, she and Ekdahl married on May 7, 1945.[61] After a honeymoon that may have lasted only a day or two, Ekdahl moved into the Victor Street house.[62]

Ekdahl got along well with the boys, and they thought it a treat to have a stepfather who had a genuine interest in them, talked to them, took them out for ice cream, and made every little excursion a special event. He asked them to call him Ed, and it made them feel very grown-up to do so. Robert would later say that both he and John could remember having "a father to play with us when we were little and picking us up when we fell, but Lee had never known a normal family life" and he was thrilled to have a father at last. Robert also thought that their mother was easier to please when Ekdahl was around.[63]

In early September 1945, Ekdahl, with Marguerite and Lee, drove Robert and John to Port Gibson, Mississippi, dropping them off for their first year at Chamberlain-Hunt on their way to visit Ekdahl's son by a previous marriage, who lived in Boston.[64] Chamberlain-Hunt would be John and Robert's home over the next three years. It was a small school, with about 110 boys, each of whom got a good deal of individual attention. The commandant, former Marine captain Herbert D. Farrell, taught them math as well as military science and became something of a substitute father and role model. Listening to his stories of life in the corps, the boys formed an early predilection for military life that would resonate with Lee in later years.[65]

In the meantime, Lee traveled the country with his mother and new stepfather on his stepfather's business trips. The boys at school got letters from Boston and snapshots from Arizona.[66] Traveling with a small child did put something of a strain on the marriage, though. Marguerite's friend from New Orleans, Myrtle Evans, who visited the Ekdahls in Dallas around this time, thought that Marguerite would have had a better life if she could have put Lee into a boarding school with the other two boys. As opposed to Lee's brother Robert, who always said that Marguerite acted as if all three children were a burden to her, Evans felt that Marguerite "loved [Lee] to death and spoiled him to death . . . She was too close to Lee all the time and I don't think Ekdahl liked that too much" and she feels it "contributed" to their eventual divorce.[67]

Sometime that fall of 1945, the Ekdahls moved to Benbrook, a suburb just northwest of Fort Worth that at the time was not much more than a "wide spot in the road," according to Robert. They leased a comfortable stone house on a rural mail route. It was on a large plot of land and there was a creek four or five hundred yards from the house. Lee entered first grade at the Benbrook Common School on October 31, 1945, a few days after his sixth birthday—although his application gives July 9, 1939, as his birth date instead of October 18, presumably to satisfy the age requirement that he be six by September 1. He did well there—all As and Bs, including an A in citizenship.[68]

It was not until Christmas of 1945 that John and Robert, on vacation from military school, saw their new home. They were impressed. John recalled that one of President Roosevelt's sons was supposed to have a house nearby.[69]* Over the holidays, Lee's cadet brothers taught him close order drill with wooden practice rifles and marched him around, and he tagged along with them whenever they would let him. He also liked to play cowboys and Indians, and his brothers obliged him, even though they felt too old for such games. Lee's older brothers were almost unaware of the rapid erosion of their mother's

---

*Robert told the Warren Commission that he and John did not come home this Christmas of 1945 because Marguerite, Lee, and Ekdahl had been living in Boston and their stay there had included the Christmas holidays (1 H 278). Not only does this clearly conflict with John's testimony (11 H 25), but we know from school records that Lee, Marguerite, and Ekdahl were back in Dallas at least as early as October of 1945 since Lee entered in the first grade on October 31, 1945 (CE 1874, 23 H 679).

marriage, the arguments, disagreements, and separations. Ekdahl began to spend more and more time away from home. Lee, who was around the house far more than his brothers, was more upset by these conflicts. Robert thinks he was more sensitive than they realized at the time, being worried over "the danger of losing the only father he had ever known," but the six-year-old was already learning to keep his feelings to himself.[70]

Marguerite began to suspect Ekdahl of infidelity and was also distressed by Ekdahl's closeness with money. Even though they stayed in good hotels when they traveled and lived lavishly because of his expense account, he gave her only a hundred dollars a month for household expenses and demanded a strict accounting of it. She continued to use her own dwindling supply of money for the boys' expenses at the military school.[71]

In early February of 1946, Lee was admitted to Harris Hospital in Fort Worth with "acute mastoiditis" on the left side, which was successfully treated by a mastoidectomy (the removal of part of the mastoid bone, behind the ear, to drain the infection). He left the hospital in four days.[72]

After the spring semester in 1946, arrangements had been made for Robert and John to remain at Chamberlain-Hunt to attend the summer session. They didn't much mind, as they liked the school, and they were enjoying the two- or three-week hiatus before the summer session was to start when Marguerite showed up with Lee and told them she and Ekdahl had separated. Instead of having them attend school, she took them to Covington, Louisiana, for the rest of the summer. John thinks she may even have consulted Commandant Farrell, who was an attorney, about divorce proceedings. The four of them spent the rest of the summer in Covington, a pleasant resort town on the shore of Lake Pontchartrain (near New Orleans). Marguerite took a house on Vermont Street, where they seemed to be a "very happy family," at least according to one observer, Marguerite's friend Myrtle Evans. They went swimming, ate watermelon, and owned a couple of dogs, though she noticed that little Lee always preferred his own company. Myrtle admired the way Marguerite, never well-off, provided for her children, and she thought the boys were aware of how hard she worked to put them through school and give them what they needed.[73]

In the fall, John and Robert returned to the military academy, but Marguerite and Lee stayed on. She enrolled him in Covington Elementary School, again in the first grade since, in spite of his good record at Benbrook of all As and Bs, he hadn't completed his first year.[74] Mother and son attended the only Lutheran church in Covington, and six-year-old Lee distinguished himself by singing a solo "Silent Night" in church during the Christmas season.[75] Lee did well during the four-month period he attended Covington Elementary School, receiving Bs, including one in "conduct."[76] But his mother and Ekdahl reconciled, and on January 23, 1947, Lee was withdrawn from Covington Elementary School[77] and Marguerite and Lee moved back to Fort Worth to an upstairs apartment at 1505 Eighth Avenue that Ekdahl had been renting.[78]

Four days later, Lee was enrolled in Clayton Elementary School in Fort Worth. This was already his third school and he was still in the first grade, which he finally completed that May, although he seems to have done well enough, with Bs in every subject except physical education and health, in which he earned As.[79]

Whatever Marguerite hoped for from the new start, the reconciliation did not last long. She was convinced that Ekdahl was leading a double life. A day or two after she and Lee had moved into the upstairs flat on Eighth Avenue, she went downstairs to hang clothes out in the yard. There she met a neighbor to whom she introduced herself as Mrs. Ekdahl. The woman's expression betrayed her astonishment and aroused Marguerite's suspicion.

Later the woman told her that until recently there had been another woman living in the apartment with Ekdahl, a woman whom she had thought was the engineer's wife.[80]

By the time the boys returned from the military academy at the beginning of summer, the ill feelings between Ekdahl and Marguerite could no longer be hidden—they fought every other day and frequently separated. There's no doubt the turmoil in the household had its effect on Lee. Fifteen-year-old John came home from his summer job as assistant manager of the Tex-Gold Ice Cream Parlor shortly after ten one night and found his step-father and mother in Ekdahl's car, on their way to spend the night at a downtown hotel—yet another reconciliation period. When John passed the word on to his seven-year-old brother, Lee was clearly delighted. Robert thought that Lee wanted more than anything else for his parents to make up their differences and get back together.[81]

The reprieve was temporary at best. One day toward the end of that summer of 1947 Marguerite got a telegram from Ekdahl saying he would not be home from his business trip for several more days. So she rang his secretary at the company office in Fort Worth to pass the news along, but before she could do so, the secretary told her that Ekdahl was not in, that he was out to lunch. That afternoon she drove to his office, watched him leave the building, and followed him to another apartment house, that of a married woman named Mrs. Clary. Marguerite went home and consulted a neighbor who was an attorney, John McClain. He suggested she call Mrs. Clary and let her know she knew her husband was there, but Marguerite realized her husband could say he was just there on business. She wanted to trap her husband.

By this time John had come home from his job and was there with several friends—Sammy, two years older than himself, and Sammy's friends, a young married couple named Marvin and Goldie. All four of them and Marguerite piled into Marvin's car and drove over to Mrs. Clary's, where Sammy went to the door pretending to deliver a telegram. Mrs. Clary told him to push it under the door, but Sammy told her she had to sign for it. As Mrs. Clary, in a negligee, answered the door, Marguerite pushed inside and surprised her husband, who was seated, in his shirt sleeves—in his "athletic shirt," according to Marguerite's sister Lillian—in the living room. "Marguerite, Marguerite," he protested, "you have everything wrong, you have everything wrong. Listen to me."

"I don't want to hear one thing," she snapped. "I have seen everything I want to see. This is it."[82]

According to her sister Lillian, who recalled only what Marguerite had told her, Marguerite consulted her pastor about getting a divorce, but he warned against it because of Ekdahl's heart problem. Ekdahl was in the hospital shortly thereafter, and when Marguerite went to visit him, Lillian thought "they had a roar-up right there at the hospital."[83] The marriage nonetheless dragged on several more months. The older boys returned to Chamberlain-Hunt in the fall, and Lee went back to Clayton Elementary, where he started second grade.[84] Philip Vinson, a classmate at Clayton, recalled Lee at that time as a "quiet type of kid" who "didn't make a lot of noise" but was nonetheless a leader of one of the small gangs among the fifteen or so boys in the second grade. Lee was a year older than most of the boys and was sturdily built and husky, which made other boys look up to him. Though he was "a tough guy type," he was not a bully. Vinson had the impression that Lee rarely played with his friends or brought them home after school.[85]

When Lee's older brothers came home for the Christmas holidays, Ekdahl was nowhere in evidence, and on January 10, 1948, Marguerite ordered Ekdahl out of their home for good.[86]

Evidently somewhat to Marguerite's surprise, Ekdahl was the one who started divorce proceedings against her on March 23, 1948.[87] "I thought I was sitting pretty," she would later say. "He didn't have anything on me. I had him for adultery with witnesses and every-thing and I didn't have any idea that he could sue me for a divorce, but Mr. Ekdahl did."[88] He also made plenty of charges in his complaint, alleging that shortly after February 1, 1947—less than two years after the marriage—Marguerite "commenced a course of harsh and cruel treatment . . . which has continued with very slight interruptions until the date of the filing of this petition." She nagged him about money, accused him of infidelity, threw a bottle at him, scratched him on the arm, had outbursts of uncontrollable temper, and on one occasion threw a glass at him accurately enough that he moved to avoid it but it still hit him, causing partial paralysis of his right arm. This "ill treatment" took place "with the full knowledge of plaintiff's condition"—severe heart disease. The petition added "that a continuation . . . of the marital relationship would result in a serious impairment of plaintiff's health."[89]

Marguerite, not surprisingly, denied all of these allegations and asked for attorney's fees.[90] While the divorce was pending, Marguerite moved yet again, from Eighth Avenue to a house at 3300 Willing Street in Fort Worth, "right slap" next to the railroad tracks, which is where John and Robert came home in May for the summer. From the house they could hear the sound of trains throughout the day and night. What had happened to the family was clear, at least to John, who noted that they "were back down in the lower class again." He had a feeling that Robert and he would not be going back to Chamberlain-Hunt.[91] Lee had withdrawn from the Clayton school in mid-March of 1948 and started in the George C. Clark Elementary School shortly afterward. Although he spent only two and a half months at Clark, he did complete the second grade with a record of mostly Bs and As.[92]

In early June, both John and Lee went downtown to testify in the divorce proceeding, which Marguerite contested in the hope of getting financial support from Ekdahl, but eight-year-old Lee told the court he wouldn't know the truth from a falsehood and he was excused from testifying.[93] In any case, Marguerite lost and Ekdahl was granted a divorce. The jury found her "guilty of excesses, cruel treatment, or outrages toward the plaintiff" that had not been provoked by Ekdahl. Since there was no appeal, there was no transcript, but we can assume Marguerite presented evidence of Ekdahl's infidelity. By the jury's finding that Marguerite's cruel treatment of Ekdahl was unprovoked, one can only assume the jury concluded that, as the expression "you're driving me to drink" goes, Ekdahl had been driven into his infidelity. The court ratified a property agreement which gave Marguerite $1,500 in "full and final" settlement and whatever community property had been acquired during the marriage, mostly furnishings and clothing. The defendant also recovered her name, Marguerite C. Oswald, and was awarded $250 as rea-sonable attorney's fees.[94] The divorce became final on June 24,1948.[*]

Lee had lost not only the first father he had ever known, but also the last. To a degree, he also lost a full-time mother, since Marguerite, without Ekdahl's support, had to return to work.[95]

Shortly after the divorce became final, the Oswalds moved yet again, to a small L-

---

[*]Ekdahl died shortly after the divorce proceedings, and there seems to be no record in the literature as to how Lee reacted to his death (Thomson, Boissevain, and Aukofer, "Lee Harvey Oswald—Another Look," p.122).

shaped house in Benbrook, though not so far out in the country as the large Benbrook house Ekdahl had leased. Marguerite had bought the house a year earlier with a small downpayment and had leased it out for $50 a month.[96] The house was the only one built on a street that didn't even have a name, although it was later christened San Saba Street.* There was only one bedroom, where Lee slept in the same bed with his mother, and a screen porch, where John and Robert slept on studio couches.[97] Marguerite got a job at Leonard Brothers Department Store in Fort Worth.[98] A neighbor, Mrs. W. H. Bell, recalled the family's brief sojourn in Benbrook. The talkative Marguerite constantly complained that she was very poor and that "society was against her," that it was very hard for a widow to provide for her family. Lee, Bell observed, was a boy who liked to be alone and did not like discipline. Mrs. Bell thought his older brothers got along better with other children in the neighborhood than Lee did.[99]

Another neighbor, Otis R. Carlton, had good reason to remember Marguerite and Lee. She asked him to come over one night in 1948 and estimate what she might get for her house if she sold it. He told her he was a schoolteacher, not a real estate agent, but when she insisted, he guessed she might get $2,750 for the house and lot.[100] Carlton himself wound up buying the house from Marguerite for that amount, although the sale wasn't completed until November 6, 1951, three years later.[101] He later told the FBI that the night he went over, while talking with Marguerite in her living room, he saw Lee chase John through the kitchen door brandishing a long butcher knife. He threw the knife at John but missed, hitting the wall. Marguerite passed it off by saying, "They have these little scuffles all the time . . . Don't worry about it."[102]†

Presumably renting out the San Saba house in Benbrook again before it was sold a few years later, Marguerite moved in the fall of 1948 into Fort Worth, buying a two-bedroom frame house at 7408 Ewing. It was a small step up in the world. The house was still small, but it did have two bedrooms, asbestos siding, a small porch on the front, and a garage, all on an average-sized lot, and it was within the city limits, not "out in the sticks," as John put it.[103] Lee could walk to his third-grade class at Arlington Heights Elementary School.[104] John was not to be so lucky. Although Marguerite finally told John and Robert that they would not be returning to Chamberlain-Hunt in the fall, which they had wanted to do, sixteen-year-old John was at least looking forward to starting eleventh grade in Fort Worth. To his dismay, Marguerite ordered him out to work (though Robert, fourteen, returned to school, as did Lee, nine). His income, she said, would be needed to support the family. He got a twenty-five-dollar-a week job as a shoe stock boy at a downtown department store. His take-home pay came to about $22.50, out of which he handed over $15.00 to Marguerite. After bus fare, there wasn't anything left for himself. For the first time he began to feel real hostility toward his mother, and he began to ignore her as much

---

*Two snapshots given the Warren Commission by John Pic suggest the barrenness of the neighborhood. The only building visible, at some distance, is a small, low, single-story building that Pic said contained both the local grocery store and the laundromat. The photos show Lee, a dog named Blackie they had acquired, and a ten-year-old car belonging to Marguerite. (Pic Exhibit Nos. 54 and 55, 21 H 122; 11 H 30, WCT John Edward Pic) The kids all wanted Marguerite to get a new car because this one didn't work. Marguerite would have the boys out on the street every morning waving down people to push the car to get it started so she could get to work. (11 H 77, WCT John Edward Pic)

†Somehow, at least to me, the story just doesn't have the ring of truth to it, not only because there's no corroboration, and no evidence that Lee had ever engaged in conduct designed to kill either of his brothers, but also because Marguerite's ho-hum attitude about this most serious and dangerous of conduct is not too believable.

as he could. Though John had never been affectionate with Marguerite, from then on he felt no "motherly love feeling" at all toward her.[105]

These early years had proved to be the best years of young Lee's life, not only because he had gained a "father," but because of the one brother he had and the other one (John) he had acquired. The age gap between them—five years with Robert and seven with John—naturally limited the relationship, but the older boys clearly cared for and looked after Lee, and he idolized them. But now it would become a much more lonely life for a child increasingly thrown upon his own resources.[106]

For one thing, Marguerite and John would return home late from work, well after Lee got home from school.[107] And although Robert, like Lee, was going to school, he had taken on a part-time job after school at a nearby grocery store to pitch in with family support, so he wasn't home when Lee returned from school either.[108] Marguerite worked at a variety of jobs during this period, but she always worked. At one time she apparently sold insurance, at others she worked in department stores—she became an assistant store manager for Lerner Shops. She seldom kept any employment longer than half a year.[109]

Although Lee came home to an empty house every day, Marguerite instructed him to stay there. She thought it safer for him to be in the house doing minor chores like taking out the garbage or playing with his dog Blackie than to be out playing with other children—she felt he could not get in much trouble alone in the house.[110] There were few children his age in the neighborhood anyway—most were closer in age to John and Robert.[111] But Lee did not seem to mind the solitude at home.[112] And despite his nomadic existence, his schoolwork did not suffer. He completed third grade with As in social studies, arithmetic, music, and physical education; Bs in citizenship, handwriting, English, and art; and a D in spelling[113]—no doubt an indication of his struggle with dyslexia, a learning disability that had not yet been identified in America, much less treated at the time. In September of 1949 he transferred to the newly built Ridgelea West Elementary School, where he continued to perform satisfactorily over the next three years with mostly Bs in the fourth and fifth grades, Bs and Cs in the sixth. Dyslexia may again account for the Ds he got in fifth- and sixth-grade spelling and arithmetic. On achievement tests in each of the three years at Ridgelea (the longest he had ever been at one school), he twice did his best in reading, twice his worst in spelling. He got Cs in Spanish in the fourth and sixth grades, which may account in part for his rudimentary acquaintance with that language as an adult.[114] He scored 103 on a fourth-grade IQ test.[115]

Mrs. Clyde Livingston, a sympathetic teacher who had Lee in her homeroom in the fourth grade, recalled that the boy, quiet and shy, took a long time to make friends with other students. She took extra pains to coach him in spelling and worried about the fact that he was left at home so much. "Lee left an empty home in the morning, went home to an empty home for lunch, and returned to an empty home [after school]," she told *Life* magazine. When she asked him if his mother would leave a lunch for him, he told her, "No, but I can open a can of soup as well as anyone." He responded to her warmth and solicitude by presenting her with a puppy at Christmas of 1949. She sensed that his visiting the puppy became a pretext for further visits with her.[116]

One Ewing Street neighbor, a tool inspector at General Dynamics named Hiram Conway, who had a daughter about the age of John and Robert, took a liking to John and taught him to play chess. His friendship with John lasted for many years—John never came through Fort Worth without stopping to call on him. He nonetheless formed a highly negative impression of Lee, saying that Lee was "a bad kid" and "just ornery . . . vicious almost . . . is the best word I can describe it," and "quick to anger." He said Lee would walk up and down the street looking for other kids to throw stones at. He recalled Lee trying to fight with John and Robert too, trying to kick their shins while they fended him off. He also thought Lee was bright, but overall "very strange." His chess students told him that Lee had picked up the game from them and had occasionally beaten them, but also that he got angry when he lost.[117]

Lee filled a lot of his lonely hours with reading, an odd pastime for a child troubled by dyslexia. He liked comic books, but he read books as well, some of them, his mother thought, beyond his depth. Before they got television, he listened to the radio a great deal, particularly the news, which he would break off reading for. "He was always reading," John would later recall. Lee particularly liked animals, about which he read a good deal, and maps, which held a particular fascination for him.[118] Years later his Aunt Lillian noted that "he always carried a map with him to find directions. If he wanted to go to a certain place, he would never ask you how to get there. He would always take this map and mark the route out himself."[119] Taking a cue from John and Robert, he started his own stamp collection, and played chess and Monopoly with his brothers when they had the time. And he'd love to climb up on the roof of their house so he could get closer to the stars, the heavens fascinating him, and Marguerite would have to fetch the older boys to get him down. John thought Lee was a "normal, healthy, robust boy who would get in fights and still have his serious moments."[120]

John and Robert were already planning to leave home at the first opportunity. Both were fed up with Marguerite. Money, John said, was "her God," and she was constantly trying to get as much as she could out of him and Robert. More importantly, even as a ninth grader, Robert had become keenly aware that their mother felt the world owed her a living. Although she worked, and worked hard, to support them, she made it clear that she resented the responsibility, felt the children should be grateful to her for her taking care of them, and now that they were teenagers, wanted them to take on some of her burden, though the latter would not seem to be unreasonable. Their education was of little importance to her—college was never even mentioned. Marguerite had gotten by with a ninth-grade education and assumed that her boys could do as well or better with or without high school diplomas.[121]

Food was no great priority for Marguerite either. Though John felt that with their contributions Marguerite had enough money to provide better food, he remembered that "we didn't eat that good." John, who had to figure out how to feed himself from leftovers from the others' dinner when he came home from work, had weighed around 130 or 140 pounds in military school. But now at home his weight fell precipitously to 118, and it was only after he left home for good that it shot back up to 145.[122] Marguerite has a slightly different take on the food issue. "I never neglected my children," she would later recall. "Oh, yes, we didn't have steak, but we never even thought about steak—I didn't anyway, I was always grateful to eat. And the children never really and truly complained. I know of one or two occasions when the boys said, 'Mother, why don't you have a platter of chops? I was at such and such a house yesterday and they served seconds,' and I said, 'Well, now, honey, this is all Mother can do.' If, say, three days before payday, I had a dollar and a half to my name, I would cook up a big pot of beans and cornbread or a big pot of spaghetti and meatballs and make it last, but I happen to know some women in that position who would take that dollar and a half and go to the corner restaurant and come home with hamburgers and Coke, and there's the difference. I have always done what I thought was right, and I always did it in a true Christian way. And even though we were poor and I was a widow and I had to support myself and three children, I always seemed to manage."[123]

Even though John was working full-time, Marguerite pressed him to join the Marine Corps Reserve to bring in a little income to supplement the fifteen dollars a week he was giving her, probably not more than another two or three dollars for each monthly meeting. John resisted—he had his eye on the Coast Guard and he was too young anyway. And he still deeply resented not being able to finish high school. Marguerite won the argument: she took John to a notary and signed an affidavit saying he was born in 1931 rather than 1932, and in October 1948 he entered the Marine Corps Reserve, where he served with Fort Worth's 155th Howitzer Battalion.[124]

In January 1949, John enrolled in Arlington Heights High School as a junior without asking his mother for permission. He could not continue in his full-time job, but he found another part-time job at Burt's Shoe Store, working afternoons and Saturdays.[125]

Robert was equally disenchanted with his mother's idea of discipline. Both boys had lived apart from Marguerite for a good many years and both had submitted easily to the discipline at the Bethlehem Children's Home and Chamberlain-Hunt Academy. Marguerite, though, threw tantrums about everything, trivial or serious, and either ranted at them or gave them "the silent treatment." When Robert was about sixteen, a friend gave him two or three Danish cigarettes to try. When he came home from school, he laid them on the table with his books, seeing no reason to keep them secret, since his mother already knew he smoked from time to time. Marguerite was incensed. "Now you're on dope!" she screeched. "I'm going to take those cigarettes to the police and have them analyzed. I'll find out what's in them! You can't get away with this in my house!" Robert, accustomed to Marguerite's constant threats to call the police for one thing or another, told her to go ahead. She took the cigarettes and he heard no more about it.[126] While the older boys could shrug off Marguerite's tirades, it wasn't so easy for Lee. Robert recalls that Lee would get very upset. He would sulk and pout, but he never talked back to Marguerite. He would often go off on his own to brood for hours, although he usually recovered his spirits by the next morning. At the same time, though, Marguerite would hear no criticism of her youngest son. Any dispute among the three boys was always the fault of John and Robert, never Lee.[127]

In January 1950, just three days short of graduating from high school, John, now eighteen, quit school and joined the Coast Guard and left for Cape May, New Jersey.[128]

After John left, Lee moved out of his mother's bed and into John's bed, sharing a room with Robert, and the two brothers grew even closer. Lee followed Robert around more than ever, trying to identify more and more with him, even trying to read Robert's books, some of which were heavy-going for a ten-year-old. They often worked together on John's stamp collection, which Robert eventually passed on to Lee. Robert noticed his brother's love of fantasy. Lee watched the clock to be sure not to miss *Let's Pretend*, a Saturday-morning radio show dramatizing fairy tales, and he seemed to stay enmeshed in the story long after the program was over. "All of us had our dreams and fantasies," Robert recalls, "but Lee's always lingered a little bit longer." When Marguerite bought a television set, Lee was fascinated with it. One of his favorite programs was *I Led 3 Lives*, the dramatized adventures of Herbert A. Philbrick. The opening narrative is, "This is the fantastically true story of Herbert A. Philbrick, who for nine frightening years led three lives: average citizen, high-level member of the Communist Party, and counter-spy for the FBI."* Lee watched *I Led 3 Lives* every week without fail. Robert wondered whether he had taken on a suspicious cast of mind from their mother, who saw "a spy behind every door and tree."[129]

Meanwhile, Marguerite's constant complaints about money had their effect on Robert. Although she was selling insurance at that point, and doing well enough to put food on the table, he knew she was under great strain to provide for them. In June of 1950, after he completed the tenth grade, he left Arlington Heights High School and got a full-time job at an A&P Supermarket, starting at forty dollars a week. By the fall he had been granted one raise and was expecting another, since he was soon to be made a checker, at which he would earn sixty-five or seventy dollars a week. He contributed almost all of his earnings to the family.[130]

Around this time Marguerite was having a harder time of it financially than usual, and she reached out to her sister Lillian for help. Lillian offered to assist by taking Lee off Marguerite's hands once again until Marguerite "got on her feet," and Uncle Dutz—Lillian's husband Charles—wired Marguerite seventy-five dollars. She sent Lee to New Orleans by train and he stayed with the Murrets for a few weeks.[131] Lillian found it a trying experience. They wanted to take Lee out to ball games and to entertain him, but he never wanted to leave the house. He would take a little radio of his into a back room and listen to it for hours while reading comic books. Lillian didn't think this was healthy and did her best to encourage him to go out and play with other kids in the neighborhood, and he would make a stab at it, but after a day or two he would hole up in the back room again. Lillian saw the letter he wrote to Marguerite telling her that nobody there liked him, which astonished Lillian since, to her mind, they were "knocking themselves out for him."[132]

Robert, after a year of working full-time, came to understand John's feelings about being forced to drop out of school, and like his older brother, he went back to Arlington Heights High School as a junior in the fall of 1951. He continued, though, to work afternoons and Saturdays at the A&P. He completed his junior year, but by the following July he too had had enough, and three months after his eighteenth birthday he joined the Marine Corps. Lee, who was twelve, was fascinated and full of questions for his older brother about the Marines. Soon after Robert left home to fulfill his military obligation, Lee bought a copy of the Marine Corps handbook. He wanted to learn everything Robert was learning in boot camp.[133] Eventually, he too would take the same escape route as his brothers.

The following month, August of 1952, Marguerite sold the Ewing Street house and moved with Lee to New York City. She did not want Lee to be alone while she was working, which he would be with no brothers at home anymore. Her eldest son, John Pic, by now a staff sergeant in the Coast Guard, was living in New York with his wife of one year, Margaret, or Marge, and a three-month-old baby. "The main thing was," she said, "to be where I had family. And I moved to New York for that reason."[134]

New York turned out to be a disaster from the outset. For one thing, John and Marge had understood that Marguerite and Lee were just coming for a visit, which was fine with them—Marge's mother, in whose apartment they were living, was visiting Marge's sis-

---

*Conspiracy theorists, as much dreamers as the young Oswald, have always believed that in later years Oswald became a rendition of the main character in the show he was fascinated by, a double (some even say triple) agent. The fact that they have no evidence to support this belief, and that millions of others were fascinated by the popular TV show, is not troubling to them.

ter in Norfolk, Virginia, so they even had a room free for a time. They were, however, disconcerted when Marguerite and Lee turned up in Marguerite's 1948 Dodge not only with a lot of luggage but also with their own TV set.[135]

John's job at the U.S. Coast Guard Port Security Unit at Ellis Island kept him away from home for one night and one weekend out of four, but he took ten days of his accumulated leave to spend more time with Lee. As he walked home from his subway stop to their apartment at 325 East 92nd Street, he was delighted to spot Lee in the street coming to meet him, and in the following days he took pains to introduce his little brother to some of the landmarks of the city: the Staten Island Ferry, the Museum of Natural History, and Polk's Hobby Shop on Fifth Avenue—John had taken to building model ships.[136] But the "visit" had gotten off to an unpleasant start. Twelve-year-old Lee was beginning to rebel against Marguerite, as his two older brothers had. On the first day, Marguerite came out of her room crying, saying that Lee had slapped her when she asked him to look out the window to make sure their car was all right. The house guests were particularly difficult for eighteen-year-old Marge, who was already struggling with caring for an infant son and maintaining the apartment. When Marguerite, shortly after arriving, took Marge aside and informed her that it was her desire that she and Lee live permanently with Marge and her husband, Marge immediately let Marguerite know that that would be wholly unsatisfactory with the Pics. Marguerite was taken aback by Marge's rejection, and Marge firmly believed that from that point on Marguerite did everything to turn her husband against her.[137]

John was looking forward to the end of his enlistment in January 1953 and thinking of leaving the service to enter a university, so Marguerite drove him around to several colleges—Fordham and a few others. She took the opportunity to explain to him that Marge was not as good as he was.[138] Marguerite thought that Marge had grown up in a very poor section of New York, "cursed like a trooper," and was "not of a character of a high caliber."[139] John was distinctly not interested in Marguerite's views—he put his wife before his mother any day.[140]

There were other irritations for John and Marge. Marguerite made no contributions to the grocery bill, and John, who was making only about $150 a month, did not find it easy to feed two extra mouths. And every night when he came home, his wife recounted a litany of the day's arguments with Marguerite and her growing feeling that Marguerite was encouraging Lee to be antagonistic toward her. Marge liked Lee, though, and she and John discussed how they would be willing to keep Lee with them if Marguerite weren't there, although they knew that such an arrangement would be impossible. They never even bothered to mention it to Marguerite.[141]

In the meantime, Lee was enrolled briefly in the seventh grade at the Trinity Evangelical Lutheran School on Watson Avenue.[142] On September 30, after several weeks of irregular attendance, he transferred to Public School (P.S.) 117, a junior high school in the Bronx,[143] and the boys there made fun of his Texas drawl and the way he dressed.[144]

At about the same time, the problems at the apartment came to a head. When Marge had some kind of an argument with Lee over the television one Sunday afternoon, Lee pulled out a small pocketknife with the blade opened and moved toward her in Marguerite's presence. Very frightened, Marge backed away, and Lee did not advance further.[145] This is Marge's version. Marguerite denies all of this. Without saying why, other than Marge's alleged hostility toward Lee, she says Marge struck Lee, and Lee only had his pocketknife out because he was whittling a wooden ship with it at the time. "He did not use the knife," she said, though he had "the opportunity" when he and Marge "struggled."[146] Robert Oswald, based on hearsay in the family, had a slightly different version, saying that when Lee advanced toward Marge with the knife, Marguerite intervened and Lee struck his mother.[147] When John came home and heard what happened, he tried to talk it over with Lee but found him suddenly impenetrably hostile toward him. Lee ignored him, and John was never able to get to the boy after that day. John had already noticed that his youngest brother was no longer the sunny, well-behaved kid he'd left behind when he joined the Coast Guard nearly three years before. Lee, now on the verge of thirteen and adolescence, had no respect for his mother and she had no authority over him. If anything, he dominated her, to the point of hitting her. John knew that he and Robert had rebelled against their mother too, but they would never have thought to strike her—they just walked away when her nagging became intolerable. In any case, the knife incident brought about the end of any emotional intimacy between John and his brother, and the Oswalds moved out a few days later.[148]

Marguerite found a one-room basement apartment at 1455 Sheridan Avenue, just off the Bronx's Grand Concourse. The single room was quite large, and Lee had his own bed while Marguerite slept on a studio couch.[149] Within days she also found a job at one of the Lerner Shops, the same chain of dress shops for which she had worked briefly in Fort Worth.[150]

John dutifully kept trying to maintain relations with his mother. He dropped in on her from time to time at the Lerner Shops store on East 42nd Street where she was working—at least once with Marge, although Marge did not really care to see his mother—and he inquired about Lee to little avail. "He is okay," Marguerite would say, "but he doesn't have an older brother to talk to or no one to do anything with." She did not tell him until much later that Lee had virtually quit going to school. By January of 1953, Lee would be absent for an astonishing forty-seven out of sixty-two days of school. He was, naturally, failing in all his classes.[151] What was he doing during all his absences from school? Sometimes just watching television in his apartment. Sometimes spending the whole day exploring the subways to see how far he could travel on one dime. Other days he spent at the Bronx Zoo.[152]

That January Marguerite moved once again, to an apartment in a four-story brick building in the Bronx at 825 East 179th Street, and Lee was transferred to a school in his new district, P.S. 44, but continued his truancy. Although years later Marguerite would tell an author that "boys do play hooky. I don't say it's the right thing to do, but I certainly don't think it's abnormal,"[153] at the time she wasn't nearly as blasé. She used to talk to a neighbor, Mrs. Gussie Keller, all the time and cry about Lee's conduct, including his insisting on playing by himself. "If he had a father," she would tell Mrs. Keller, "maybe he wouldn't act that way."[154] On January 16, 1953, before Lee's transfer to P.S. 44, Marguerite, after consulting the Federation of Protestant Welfare agencies, had applied to New York's Community Service Society for help. She had earlier been summoned to a hearing by P.S. 117's Attendance Board and warned that she would have to do something about getting Lee to school,* although the board stopped short of threatening suspen-

---

*One wonders just how much pressure Marguerite was putting on Lee to go to school. Though she undoubtedly urged him to do so, we also know that Marguerite, who had since started selling insurance, would occasionally allow Lee to go with her during the day, but he found it too boring waiting for her in the car as she made her frequent stops (Siegel Exhibit No. 1, 21 H 485).

sion. Although Marguerite told the Service Society that since the Attendance Board hearing she hadn't been able to get Lee back to school and he was "nearly driving me crazy," the society, unfortunately, had a substantial backlog and could not grant her an appointment before the end of January. In the meantime, however, a caseworker for the society called P.S. 117 and talked with an assistant principal, a Miss Kahn, who was not able to provide much information since she had only seen Lee at school once or twice. Kahn volunteered, though, that she thought the boy was rather withdrawn.

The caseworker went on to talk with a Mr. Keating of the Attendance Bureau of the city's Board of Education. Keating had spoken with Marguerite, and told the caseworker that she had complained to him that she simply could not handle Lee, that he refused to go to school and wanted to return to Texas, where he was more at home. She also admitted that she nagged Lee a great deal and said she would try to ease up on that to see if it would help.

Responding to Lee's truancy at his new school, P.S. 44, a "visiting teacher" was dispatched to see Lee at home. Lee told the teacher that he would think about going to school but hadn't made up his mind yet. On January 30, 1953, the Community Service Society file on the case was closed with the unexplained notation that on that date "Appointment failed," perhaps signifying that Marguerite had failed to show up for the appointment she had sought with the society.[155]

Meanwhile, Marguerite and Lee had failed to appear at two hearings, on January 13 and 20, before the Board of Education's Bureau of Attendance, and on January 27 Lee was finally placed on probation until June 20 and warned that failure to attend school in the interim would result in truancy charges being brought against him.[156] But Lee's truancy continued to the extent that between January 15, 1953, and March 11, 1953, he never attended one class.[157]

In February, John, with his wife and infant son, visited Marguerite and Lee at their Bronx apartment for Sunday dinner, but as they arrived, Lee walked out, probably, according to Marguerite, on his way to the Bronx Zoo. Marguerite finally broached the subject of Lee's truancy to John and told him that the school officials had advised her to seek psychiatric help for him.* Marguerite wondered how she could get him to a psychiatrist. John told her just to take him. But Marguerite told him that she couldn't control Lee and he simply would not see a "head shrinker or nut doctor," and it was evident to John that Lee had become the boss. Shortly thereafter, John's ship went to sea, and he heard nothing further about Lee's problems during that time.[158]

Finally, on March 12, the attendance officer in charge of Lee's case filed a petition in New York City's Domestic Relations Court, Family Division (referred to as "Children's Court"), which declared that the boy had been "excessively absent from school" and was "beyond the control of his mother." Marguerite appeared alone before a Justice Delaney that day, and reported that Lee refused to attend the court proceeding.[159] Indeed, one spring day an attendance officer for the school district, Victor Connell, found Lee at the Bronx Zoo. He noted that Lee was clean and well dressed but surly—he called Connell a "damned Yankee." Connell returned Lee to school.[160] On April 16, with Lee present (having been picked up pursuant to a warrant), Justice Delaney declared Lee a truant and remanded him to Youth House for three weeks of "psychiatric study."[161] This time it was serious. Two bailiffs

*"I was never told my son needed psychiatric treatment, believe me," Marguerite would later tell author Jean Stafford (Stafford, *Mother in History*, p.22).

took Lee from Marguerite right there in the courtroom. She saw him briefly a few minutes later, when the officers gave her a Marine Corps ring that Robert had sent to Lee, along with Lee's other personal effects. They also gave her a slip of paper to inform her of the location of Youth House and when she might visit him there.[162] A few days later, Lee's probation officer, John Carro, interviewed Lee and found him to be "friendly and likable" and "fairly bright," but indifferent to the situation. Lee told him he didn't like his teachers or his classmates and just wanted to be left alone. Carro had a lower opinion of Marguerite, whom he interviewed on April 21, finding her "self-involved," someone who blamed everyone else for Lee's problems, and was reluctant to get involved in Lee's treatment, seeing herself "as removed, as this having nothing to do with her."[163]*

Youth House, New York City's detention home for delinquent boys who were remanded by the courts for a brief period of diagnostic study, was a dingy, jail-like building on Manhattan's Lower East Side, between First and Second Avenues, with barred windows looking out on tenements of the teeming city.[164] Youth House ran its own school, P.S. 613, and maintained workshops for the children, a recreation department, facilities for group therapy, even its own hospital.[165] Marguerite disliked Youth House intensely from her visit there with Lee. She complained that she had to wait in line with Puerto Ricans and Negroes and that her pocketbook was emptied by a guard because "the children in this home were such criminals and dope fiends and had [committed] criminal offenses." They even removed the wrappers from the sticks of chewing gum she had brought for Lee. Lee didn't like it either, according to Marguerite. He cried when he saw her. "Mother, I want to get out of here," he said. "There are children in here that have killed people, and smoke. I want to get out."[166]

A psychologist, Irving Sokolow, subjected Lee to several tests, the Wechsler Intelligence Scale for Children, the Monroe Silent Reading Test, and Human Figure Drawings. Lee scored 118 on his IQ test, some fifteen points higher than on the earlier test administered in Fort Worth, and indicating, per Sokolow, "present intellectual functioning in the upper range of bright normal intelligence." All of Lee's scores, Sokolow's report of May 7, 1953, said, were above average for his age group, "appreciably so in verbalization of abstract concepts and in the assembly of commonly recognizable objects." Sokolow thought "his method of approach was generally an easy, facile and highly perceptive one." (As indicated earlier, the dyslexia from which Lee suffered was not yet recognized as a common disability, and it is impossible to tell how much higher he might have scored on an IQ test if he had not had this problem.)[†] By contrast, the report said that "the Human Figure Drawings are empty, poor characterizations of persons approximately the same age as [Lee]. They reflect a considerable amount of impoverishment in the social and emotional areas." Sokolow went on to note that Lee exhibited "some difficulty in relationship to the maternal figure suggesting more anxiety in this area than any other."[167]

Robert Oswald, who first read Sokolow's report long after the assassination, was not

*Marguerite had since left the employ of Lerner Shops and was now working at Martin's Department Store in Brooklyn. The next month she went to work for Lady Oris Hosiery on Park Avenue South in Manhattan, a chain of hosiery shops she had worked for in New Orleans in 1943. (Carro Exhibit No. 1, 19 H 309; CE 2213, 25 H 110)

†The consensus of many observers is that Oswald was not bright and was intellectually shallow. I'm not a psychiatrist, but I have always been puzzled by this assessment. In my opinion, his words and thinking process in his late teens and early twenties have always struck me as being those of someone not only above average in intelligence, but much more intellectual than I would expect most people of his young age to be.

surprised by it. He thought Lee had good cause to feel anxiety about "the maternal figure." Neither he nor John had been able to cope with Marguerite either, but they at least had each other for support, and after they escaped, both tried to have as little to do with her as possible. Lee had been left to cope with her all alone, and Robert didn't think he had the strength to do that.[168]

A week after Lee's psychological test, Mr. Rainey, on the Youth House staff, recommended that Lee see a caseworker: "Lee has constituted a problem here of late. He is a non-participant in any activity on the floor. He has made no attempt at developing a relationship with any member of the group, and at the same time not given anyone an opportunity to become acquainted with him. He appears content just to sit and read whatever is available."[169]

The case was assigned to Evelyn Strickman, a young New Yorker and Hunter College graduate who had earned her master's degree from Columbia's School of Social Work the year before.[170] She wrote the most extensive and perceptive report on Lee at this period of his life. The draft runs to seven closely typed pages, the rewritten version to five and a half, and includes a detailed account of an interview with Marguerite.[171] Strickman found Lee to be a "seriously detached, withdrawn" boy who was "laconic and taciturn." She also found "a rather pleasant, appealing quality about this emotionally starved, affectionless youngster which grows as one speaks to him, and it seems fairly clear that he has detached himself from the world around him because no one in it ever met any of his needs for love." Strickman asked him what his mother's reaction to his truancy was, and Lee told her that Marguerite had told him to go to school, "but she never did anything about it." Strickman asked him if he wished that she might do something about it, and Lee finally said that his mother "never gave a damn about him."[172]* This would not have surprised Robert either. At least since he was at Chamberlain-Hunt Academy he had been aware that the relationship between the other cadets and their parents "was not at all like the relationship we had with our mother. Maybe because she had to worry about supporting us she never had time to enjoy us. Other parents, it seemed to me, enjoyed their children. I just know that we learned, very early, that we were a burden to her."[173]

Strickman's report said that "questioning elicited the information that he feels almost as if there is a veil between him and other people through which they cannot reach him, but he prefers this veil to remain intact." She also persuaded him, with some difficulty, to talk about his fantasies, and he "acknowledged that some were about being powerful, and sometimes hurting and killing people, but refused to elaborate on this."[174]

Strickman also interviewed Marguerite, whom she described as "a smartly dressed,

---

*As with the common perception about Lee's intelligence, I also tend to disagree, although not as confidently, in the general impression of Marguerite. Obviously, Lee and his brothers knew Marguerite and I didn't. But from the cold written record, and taking cognizance of the fact that everything in life is relative, I don't find Marguerite to have been that bad a mother. She may have been deficient in several respects, but she was always working hard and providing for them. And the record seems to reflect, as her friend Myrtle Evans would agree, that at least with regard to Lee, alongside of whom she is now buried for eternity, she did love him dearly. One wonders if it wasn't her offending personality, rather than her conduct and attitude, that turned people off so, and that the two somewhat separate realities seemed to slop over onto each other and get blurred, influencing people's perception of her. As an example of her disobliging personality, journalist Hugh Aynesworth, who got to know the members of the Oswald family better than any of his peers, wrote, "Few people have ever so deeply annoyed me as Marguerite Oswald. And of all the things I disliked about her, none irritated me more than her voice. It was strange—unique in my experience—a jarring combination of birdlike sing-song, childish whine, and predatory threat that invaded your head like a dental drill. She would not stop talking" (Aynesworth with Michaud, *JFK: Breaking the News*, pp.123–124).

gray haired woman, very self-possessed and alert and superficially affable. Essentially, however, she was revealed as a defensive, rigid, self-involved person."[175] Remarkably, Marguerite began the interview by demanding to know why Lee had been remanded, and refusing to wait for an explanation, wanted to know if he had been given a complete physical examination, and was particularly concerned about his genitalia. When she was told the examination had revealed "nothing unusual, she looked at once relieved and disappointed." She had noticed that Lee had of late gotten big "down there," and her worries about the genital area stemmed from the fact that Robert, on induction to the Marine Corps, had been found to have a hydrocele, a sort of watery blister in the penis of little significance.[176]

In the draft of her report, which she dictated, Strickman said about Marguerite, "I honestly don't think that she sees [her son] as a person at all but simply as an extension of herself. Interestingly enough, by the way, although Lee was a planned-for-baby, because her husband [and] herself wanted a girl, I take it she was rather disappointed at having a third boy."[177]

Strickman concluded that she believed "the root of Lee's difficulties, which produced warning signals before he ever came here [New York], seems to lie in his relationship with his mother. Lee feels that while she always cared for his material needs she was really never involved with him and didn't care very much what happened to him." She thought Marguerite had "little understanding of this boy's behavior nor of the protective shell he has drawn around himself in his effort to avoid contact with people, which may result in hurt for him. It is possible that her own negative attitude about casework help and probation officers may communicate itself to Lee, interfering with his chances for help." She nonetheless recommended against placing Lee in an institution without first seeing whether he could be reached by therapy. "Despite his withdrawal," she wrote, "he gives the impression that he is not so difficult to reach as he appears, and patient, prolonged effort and a sustained relationship with one therapist might bring results. There are indications that he has suffered serious personality damage, but, if he can receive help quickly, this might be repaired to some extent."[178]

Years later, Evelyn Strickman, testifying before the Warren Commission under her then-married name of Siegel, had a very vague recollection of Oswald, but from what she wrote in her report she told the Commission he was "a youngster who was teetering on the edge of serious emotional illness. Now, whether that included violence I am not prepared to say."[179]

The chief psychiatrist at Youth House, Dr. Renatus Hartogs, exhibited no such professional caution in his testimony before the Warren Commission, giving the flip side of the opinions offered in defense of Oswald by the Warren Commission critics. In the process, he embarrassed himself. Hartogs was a German emigré who had been educated in Frankfort on the Main and received his medical training in Belgium. He came to America in 1940 and took two further medical degrees, from the University of Montreal and New York University. Dr. Hartogs said he was used to dealing with children with serious mental problems, some of whom committed very serious crimes. He was intrigued by the "discrepancy" between the rather trivial reason for Lee's remand to Youth House—inveterate truancy—and the seriousness of what he perceived to be the boy's underlying personality disturbance.

Hartogs interviewed Oswald and then selected him as the subject of one of the Youth House's informal Monday-afternoon "seminars," at which all of those who had dealt

with the subject child would discuss the case in great detail. Typically, the house director opened the seminar; the social worker talked about the boy's development, background, and early history; staff from the recreation department and household gave
their views; the psychologist reported his findings; and the psychiatrist—in this case
Hartogs himself—discussed the recommendations he was prepared to make to the
Children's Court.[180]

The report to the court he dictated on May 1, 1953, is the only known report from a
psychiatrist who interviewed Oswald. It reads,

> This 13 year old, well built, well nourished boy was remanded to Youth House
> for the first time on a charge of truancy from school and being beyond the con-
> trol of his mother as far as school attendance is concerned. This is his first con-
> tact with the law. He is a tense, withdrawn and evasive boy who dislikes intensely
> talking about himself and his feelings. He likes [to] give the impression that he
> doesn't care about others and rather likes to keep to himself so that he is not
> bothered and does not have to make the effort of communicating. It was difficult
> to penetrate the emotional wall behind which this boy hides [but] he provided us
> with sufficient clues, permitting us to see intense anxiety, shyness, feelings of
> awkwardness and insecurity as the main reasons for his withdrawal tendencies
> and solitary habits. Lee told us: "I don't want a friend and I don't like to talk to
> people." He describes himself as stubborn, and according to his own saying he
> likes to say "No." Strongly resistive and negativistic features were thus noticed
> but psychotic mental content was denied [psychiatric term meaning not present
> or found] and no indication of psychotic mental changes was arrived at.
>
> Lee is a youngster with superior mental endowment, functioning presently on
> the bright normal range of mental efficiency. His abstract thinking capacity and
> his vocabulary are well developed. No retardation in school subjects could be
> found in spite of his truancy from school. Lee limits his interests to reading mag-
> azines and looking at the television all day long. He dislikes to play with others or
> to face the learning situation in school. On the other hand he claims to be "very
> poor" in all school subjects and would need remedial help. The discrepancy
> between these claims and his actual attainment level show the low degree of self-
> evaluation and self-esteem at which this boy has arrived presently, mainly due to
> feelings of general inadequacy and emotional discouragement.
>
> Lee is the product of a broken home as his father died before he was born. Two
> older brothers are presently in the United States Army while the mother supports
> herself and Lee as an insurance broker. This occupation makes it impossible for her
> to provide adequate supervision of Lee and to make him attend school regularly.
> Lee is intensely dissatisfied with his present way of living, but feels that the only
> way in which he can avoid feeling too unhappy is to deny to himself competition
> with other children or expressing his needs or wants. Lee claims that he can get
> very angry at his mother and occasionally hits her, particularly when she returns
> home without having bought food for supper. On such occasions she leaves it to
> Lee to prepare some food with what he can find in the kitchen. He feels that his
> mother rejects him and really has never cared very much for him. He expressed the
> similar feeling with regard to his brothers who lived pretty much on their own
> without showing any brotherly interest in him. Lee has a vivid fantasy life, turning
> around the topics of omnipotence and power, through which he tries to compen-

sate for his present shortcomings and frustrations. He did not enjoy being together with other children and when we asked him whether he prefers the company of boys to the one of girls, he answered, "I dislike everybody." His occupational goal is to join the army. His mother was interviewed by the Youth House social worker and was described by her as a "defensive, rigid, self-involved and intellectually alert" woman who finds it exceedingly difficult to understand Lee's personality and withdrawing behavior. She does not understand that Lee's withdrawal is a form of violent but silent protest against his neglect by her—and represents his reaction to a complete absence of any real family life. She seemed to be interested enough in the welfare of this boy to be willing to seek guidance and help as regards her own difficulties and management of Lee.

Neurological examination remained essentially negative with the exception of slightly impaired hearing in the left ear, resulting in a mastoidectomy in 1946. History of convulsions and accidental injuries to the skull was denied. Family history is negative for mental disease.

Dr. Hartogs then appended a summary for the probation officer, which included his recommendations to the court:

This 13 year old well built boy has superior mental resources and functions only slightly below his capacity level in spite of chronic truancy from school which brought him into Youth House. No finding of neurological impairment or psychotic mental changes could be made. Lee has to be diagnosed as "personality pattern disturbance with schizoid features and passive aggressive tendencies." Lee has to be seen as an emotionally, quite disturbed youngster who suffers the impact of really existing emotional isolation and deprivation, lack of affection, absence of family life and rejection by his self-involved and conflicted mother. Although Lee denies that he is in need of any other form of help other than a remedial one, we gained the definite impression that Lee can be reached through contact with an understanding and very patient psychotherapist if he could be drawn at the same time into group psychotherapy. We arrive therefore at the recommendation that he should be placed on probation under the condition that he seek help and guidance through contact with a child guidance clinic, where he should be treated preferably by a male psychiatrist who could substitute, to a certain degree at least, for the lack of a father figure. At the same time, his mother should be urged to seek psychotherapeutic guidance through contact with a family agency. If this plan does not work out favorably and Lee cannot cooperate in this treatment plan on an out-patient basis, removal from the home and placement could be resorted to at a later date, but it is our definite impression that treatment on probation should be tried out before the stricter and possibly more harmful placement approach is applied to the case of this boy. The Big Brother Movement could undoubtedly be a tremendous value in this case and Lee should be urged to join the organized group activities of his community such as provided by the PAL or YMCA of his neighborhood.[181]*

---

*On the day after the assassination, Dr. Hartogs was interviewed on television about why anyone might want to murder a president. At the time he did not recall having Lee in observation and his remarks were entirely generalities. Such an assassin, Hartogs thought, would be mentally disturbed, with a personal grudge

On May 7, 1953, Lee was released from Youth House and he and Marguerite appeared in court once again, this time before a Justice McClancy, who reviewed Lee's record and psychiatric report at some length. He warned Lee that he would have to return to school and stay there. There was no change in who Lee's probation officer would be, John Carro.[182] Marguerite was beside herself. She had taken an immediate dislike to Carro and, as she said, she was not one to "mince my words." When Carro told Lee that he would have to report once a week, Marguerite said, "Mr. Carro, my son is not reporting to you once a week. This is not a criminal offense. He was picked up for truancy. He has assured the judge, promised the judge, that he would be back to school. He has promised you he would be back to school. Let's give this boy a chance, and let's see if he will go to school. And then, Mr. Carro, if he doesn't go to school, then you can have him report to you." Mr. Carro did not, according to Marguerite, "take that graciously."[183]

Carro was, however, touched by the boy's plight. For one thing, Lee seemed like a little lost boy, particularly compared to some of the mentally defective, even psychotic kids—often hardened criminals, burglars, and murderers—with whom Carro had been dealing. Carro also understood something of the culture shock Lee underwent when he came to New York, still wearing the jeans that were common in Texas but unknown in the city, and speaking with a soft southern accent amid the harsh accents of the Bronx. Carro himself had come to New York from Orocovis in his native Puerto Rico at the age of nine, speaking not a word of English, and lived in a tiny Puerto Rican enclave surrounded by black East Harlem. Carro understood what it was like for Lee to be taunted for his accent and dress by New York kids who "wore pegged pants and talked in their own ditty-bop fashion," but he also understood that not all boys reacted as overtly as he had as a Spanish-speaking nine-year-old injected into East Harlem. Carro told the Warren Commission that looking back, he saw no propensity for violent behavior in Oswald at the time, nothing he could equate with the Puerto Rican and Negro youth with whom he was familiar,

---

against authority figures, and likely a person seeking to overcome his own insignificance and helplessness with an act that frightens others, even one that would shatter the world, discharging his own insecurity by making others insecure. (8 H 219–220)

Oddly, Hartogs found fit to tell the Warren Commission (perhaps to impress others that he had foreseen Oswald as doing what he did, and without there being any indication he knew of the two knife incidents) that he had found Oswald "to have definite traits of dangerousness. In other words, this child had a potential for explosive, aggressive, assaultive acting out" (8 H 217). But if Hartogs actually believed this back in 1953, he knew he obviously should have recommended that Oswald not be returned to the community and that he be institutionalized immediately. In his Warren Commission testimony, he said, "I recommended that this youngster should be committed to an institution." Question: "Immediately?" Hartogs: "Yes, that is right." But Hartogs did not make this recommendation, only recommending institutionalization as a last resort. In his testimony before the Commission, when confronted with his earlier report by Warren Commission counsel, Hartogs was forced to concede that his earlier report in 1953 "contradicts" the recollection of Oswald's character and disposition he gave the Commission. Trying to cover himself on another point, he said that he "implied" Oswald's potential for explosive violence by his "diagnosis of passive-aggressive," but the latter is hardly a synonym for the former. Hartogs told the Commission that although he did not use the words "potentially dangerous" in his report, he believed that violence was always a possibility with a passive-aggressive personality, whose aggressivity can be triggered by a situation of high stress, particularly if he "nourishes his hate and hostility for [a] considerable length of time." (8 H 218, 221–222, WCT Dr. Renatus Hartogs)

Author Gerald Posner, apparently trying to explain away Hartogs's contradictory testimony, says Hartogs did not mention in his 1953 report his belief that Oswald was capable of explosive violence "since that would have mandated institutionalization," and Hartogs only wanted "probation" with "guidance" (Posner, *Case Closed*, p.13). But Posner gives no source for this, and Hartogs himself never said this in his testimony. Further, if one were to embrace Posner's logic, it's understandable and acceptable for a psychiatrist to recommend only probation and guidance, not institutionalization, for someone he believes is dangerous and capable of explosive violence.

kids that cried out to say "that they exist and that they are human beings" and who committed violent acts "just to get their one day in the sun, the day when all the papers will focus on them and say 'I am me. I am alive.'"[184] For the moment, Carro, to Marguerite's chagrin, made it very clear that Lee would indeed have to report to him once a week, like it or not, and then set out to find an appropriate place for treatment for Lee, which, because of waiting lists, et cetera, he was unable to do.[185]

In the few remaining weeks of the spring semester, Lee returned to school at P.S. 44 and, even with his long absences from class, managed to finish with generally low but passing marks. Surprisingly, a teacher gave him an "O" or "Outstanding" for "Social-Participation." This makes no sense since it contradicts all we know about Oswald at the time, and in fact, the very same report refers to him as "Quick-Tempered, Constantly Losing Control, Getting into Battles with others."[186] Indeed, the lack of social participation was a large part of Lee's problem, in Carro's view. Lee told him he didn't like the teachers, the school, or the children. "I like myself," he said. And his mother? "Well, I've got to live with her," Lee said. "I guess I love her."[187]

Marguerite was another problem. Carro felt the boy would respond to therapy, that he needed to be brought out of his shell, but for the therapy to work, Marguerite had to be involved, and Carro realized that Marguerite herself felt threatened, and was convinced that she had nothing to do with Lee's problems. Even if Lee did go into the therapy he needed, if his mother communicated her own resentment, resistance, and negativity about it to the boy, the time and effort would be wasted. Carro saw that Marguerite was so involved with herself that she would blame anything and anybody but herself for Lee's problems. These, she insisted, would take care of themselves if the authorities stopped pestering him and her.[188]

In July, Robert came to New York while on leave from the Marine Corps, and was on his way to the Marine base at Opa-locka, Florida. It had been a year since he had left his mother and brother in Fort Worth to enlist, and he had a lot of catching up to do. They were very glad to see him, but, oddly, he heard nothing of the troubles Lee had been having, or the family's knotty involvement with the Children's Court. Eventually, Marguerite did mention to Robert that Lee had had to appear before "a Negro judge" because he had been absent from school too much, but Marguerite brushed it off as something that never would have happened in Texas, and Robert did not get the impression it was a serious matter.[189]

Lee couldn't wait to take Robert to the nearby Bronx Zoo and, proud of knowing his way around, give him a detailed explanation of the New York subway system. Lee, all of thirteen, took Robert to the top of the Empire State Building, pointed out places of interest, and planned his brother's itinerary for the next week, from Wall Street to the Museum of Natural History.[190] One Sunday Robert went up to Marguerite and Lee's apartment in the Bronx for a Sunday dinner with a date that John's wife, Marge, had arranged for him. When John, Marge, and their child arrived shortly thereafter, Lee left the room. Rather than join everyone for dinner, he came to the table, took what he wanted, and went into the next room to watch television. John tried to talk to him, but Lee, uninterested in anything John had to say, shrugged him off.[191]

When Robert's leave was up, Lee accompanied him to the bus terminal to see him off to Florida. To Robert, Lee still seemed to be just a normal, healthy, happy thirteen-year-old boy who was enjoying himself.[192]

Carro continued through the summer to try to find some help for the boy. Early in September, he was turned down by the Salvation Army, which thought Lee, according to his psychiatric report, too severely disturbed for them to be able to help.[193]

On the day Lee's probation was up and he was due in court, September 24, 1953, Marguerite rang Carro to explain that she was unable to appear and there was no need for it anyway, as Lee had made a "marvelous adjustment" and was now regularly attending his school classes. Apparently Marguerite told Carro—brazenly gilding the lily—that Lee had even been elected president of his class at P.S. 44. Indeed, Warren Commission assistant counsel Wesley Liebeler, misreading Carro's summary report to the Children's Court in 1953, said Carro's report reflected that Oswald had been elected president of his class. But a closer reading of his report shows that Carro had only been told this by Marguerite, and Carro told the Warren Commission that Lee "had not become president of the class that I recall."[194]

Marguerite's fabrications and protestations didn't work. Carro explained that Lee would still have to continue under supervision for a time, and suggested group therapy at the court's own treatment clinic, an outpatient facility on 22nd Street, since intake had finally opened up there. Marguerite would have none of it. Later that day, a Justice Fogarty continued Lee's probation another five weeks, to October 29.[195] In mid-October, just before Lee's fourteenth birthday, Carro was informed by Lee's homeroom teacher at P.S. 44 that Lee's attendance record had indeed improved—he had been absent only one day and three half days—but that his conduct was atrocious, and Marguerite was refusing to cooperate with the school authorities. "During the past two weeks," Mr. Rosen reported to Carro, "practically every teacher has complained to me about the boy's behavior. He has consistently refused to salute the flag during early morning exercises. In many rooms, he has done no work whatsoever. He spends most of his time sailing paper planes around the room. When we spoke to him about his behavior, his attitude was belligerent. I offered to help him," Rosen said, but Oswald said, "I don't need anybody's help." As indicated, notations on his report card said he was "quick-tempered," "constantly losing control," and "getting into battles with others." On October 29, when Lee was again due in court, Marguerite rang Carro to explain she couldn't be present owing to her work. The judge, his patience exhausted, told Carro to try to refer Lee to the Berkshire Industrial Farm or, if they were unable to take the boy, to Children's Village.[196]

By the next court day, November 19, the situation seemed to be improving. Lee's teacher told Carro that Marguerite had finally appeared at the school and that Lee was now getting along very well in school. He had even resumed saluting the flag. Marguerite asked a Justice Sicher to discharge Lee from the court supervision, as he was no longer a problem and she was capable of coping with him. Sicher didn't buy it. He explained to Marguerite that Lee was in need of treatment and that it was in Marguerite's interest to cooperate with whatever plan the court offered. He told Carro, who apparently was still unable to place Lee, to refer Lee to the court's own psychiatric clinic, which Carro himself had earlier suggested to Marguerite, and at the same time try a referral to the Protestant Big Brothers organization.[197]

Marguerite, again, did not want Lee to get the recommended psychiatric treatment nor did she want him to get involved in the Big Brothers program. She told Carro, "Why are you bothering me? You're harassing me. He's back in school. Why do you want him to go to the clinic for? Why do we have to see the Protestant Big Brothers for? He has brothers. What does he need [more] brothers for? Leave me alone. I don't like New York."[198]

On the evening of January 4, 1954, when a Mr. Groetz, a member of the Big Brothers program, called on Marguerite and Lee at their apartment, Marguerite was as adamantly opposed to outside help for Lee as ever, and told the representative she had quit her job and was planning to leave New York for New Orleans. He advised that Lee was still on probation and could not be removed from the court's jurisdiction without the court's permission.[199]

When Marguerite testified to the Warren Commission ten years later, her story was different. According to her, Groetz had told her that absconding to New Orleans was a good idea. "So, I said, 'Is it alright? They won't arrest us and bring us back?' He said, 'No, there's no extraditing'—that was his words."[200] When Carro heard about Marguerite's plans, he wrote to ask her to come in to see him. The letter was returned with the notation "Moved, address unknown."[201]

Marguerite was right about one thing: there was no "extraditing." The Children's Court had no extra-state jurisdiction, and, after ascertaining that the Oswalds were no longer in New York—although it had not been able to determine whether they were then in New Orleans, or, according to one story, in California—the court finally closed Lee's case on March 11, 1954.[202]

Carro, who had been sympathetic to Oswald's plight at the time, remained sensitive to Oswald in his testimony to the Warren Commission in 1964. For instance, he was not inclined to make too much of the fact that the thirteen-year-old had been refusing to salute the flag, putting it down to little more than being "a little disruptive in class," and he had even deliberately refrained from mentioning it to the press after the assassination for fear they would say, "See, fifteen years ago he refused to salute the American flag. This is proof." Carro said he did not want to see that type of newspaper headline. He also told the Warren Commission he did not see Oswald exhibit any Marxist leanings.[203]

But something that Carro knew nothing about had happened to Lee. Many years later Lee told Aline Mosby, a reporter interviewing him in Moscow about his defection to the Soviet Union, "I became interested [in Marxism] about the age of fifteen. From an ideological viewpoint. An old lady handed me a pamphlet about saving the Rosenbergs . . . I looked at that paper and I still remember it for some reason. I don't know why."[204]

Actually, Lee left New York City with Marguerite when he was fourteen, and he was probably thirteen at the time of the incident, which most likely took place on Mother's Day, May 10, 1953, just three days after he was released from Youth House. Julius and Ethel Rosenberg, convicted in March of 1951 of conspiracy to commit espionage in providing atomic secrets to the Soviet Union, were then on death row at Sing Sing in New York, awaiting execution on June 19. (Both were executed.) Oswald biographer Jean Davison determined from the files of the *New York Times* and the Communist Party's *Worker* newspaper that women recruited by an ad in the *Worker* had passed out leaflets for the New York Committee for Clemency for the Rosenbergs on May 10. While the content of the leaflet is unknown, Davison wrote that the committee harped on two themes. First, the Rosenbergs were innocent victims of an unjust court—much as Lee, in his mind, probably thought he was a victim of Children's Court. The other theme was linked to the use of women for the leaflet team and the choice of Mother's Day for the demonstration—the fact that Ethel Rosenberg would leave behind two small boys orphaned if she were executed.[205]

While it's too much to assume that a single pamphlet turned a thirteen-year-old into a committed Marxist, Lee had probably found a metaphor for the outward expression of his disaffection with life, for the rage of a child who believed he had been abused and neglected, not only by his mother but also by the schools, the courts, the entire system. Here were others decrying persecution and exploitation, people who were potential friends and allies in what appeared to be a friendless world.

Lee's Communism had always been an attitude rather than an activity. He never even found out how to join the Communist Party, either in the United States or in the Soviet Union—where, after all, it wasn't much more difficult or dangerous to do than joining the Elks or Odd Fellows here in the states. He claimed to many that he had read *Das Kapital* by Karl Marx and *The Communist Manifesto* by Marx and Engels, but beyond its most fundamental principles and cosmetic generalities, such as rectifying inequality, which he undoubtedly sincerely believed in, there's not too much more trace of Marx and Engels in his rhetoric, and no indication that he ever read, much less studied, other important Marxist authors like Trotsky, Gramsci, Marcuse, and Adorno. Much of his Marxism was in the vein of *Let's Pretend*. However, it gave him the concept and theme he needed so badly to express himself. He was never comfortable talking about himself or his feelings, and it was only when he resorted to the political that he became fully animated and expressive.

Lee's fantasy had once been nourished by the television series called *I Led 3 Lives*, about a man who had been a Communist for the FBI. Now he was about to become a Communist for Lee Harvey Oswald.

Marguerite and Lee fled New York in early January 1954 and turned up in New Orleans, where, for the time being, they stayed with Marguerite's sister Lillian and her family on French Street. Both of the Oswalds seemed happy to be back, after what Marguerite described in a May letter to her son John as "the ordeal in New York." She wrote to him that "it was almost a tragedy, but a little love and patience did the trick."[206] Lee enrolled in the eighth grade at Beauregard Junior High School on January 13.[207] Beauregard was at the far end of Canal Street—the city's main thoroughfare—three stops from the end of the streetcar line, down by the famous cemeteries with the elevated graves owing to New Orleans's high water level. The school drew its students from a pleasant, largely working-class, residential area called Lakeview.[208]

The Oswalds stayed with the Murrets for only a few weeks before Marguerite found an apartment on St. Mary Street, which she rented from her old friend, Myrtle Evans, who gave her a bit of a break on the rent for old times' sake.[209] The move put Lee in a different school district, but Marguerite continued to use the Murrets' address to avoid moving Lee to yet another school when only four months of the term remained.[210]

Life in the "Big Easy," the sweltering seaport on the Mississippi River, was not all that easy for the Oswalds, although Lee did seem to get along a little better at school there than he had in New York. But if he had been taunted for his southern accent in New York, here, in the city of his birth, his speech was thought to be offensively Yankee,[211] some of his fellow students at Beauregard even calling him "Yankee" as a nickname.[212]* His grades of 73 in English, 70 in mathematics and social studies, 78 in industrial arts, 72 in physi-

---

*There were differences of culture between New York City and New Orleans that resulted in Oswald getting beaten up one day. Lee got on a crowded school bus headed for Beauregard and sat where a seat was available. It happened to be in the section of the bus to the rear for colored people. Coming from New York City, Lee didn't have the faintest idea that he had done anything wrong. He found out differently at the end of the line in front of the school. White boys on the bus jumped and pummeled Lee when they got off the bus, loosening his front teeth. (8 H 124, WCT Lillian Murret; 8 H 159, WCT Marilyn Dorothea Murret)

cal education, and 74 in science were above the passing grade of 70 at Beauregard, though below the average grade of 79–80,[213] but his attendance improved—he was absent only a few days in what remained of the school year.[214]

Lillian saw Lee off and on during this sojourn in New Orleans. He liked seafood and knew she followed the Catholic practice of meatless Fridays, so he showed up on several Friday evenings for dinner. He sometimes came on Saturday mornings too, and Lillian would give him money to rent a bike in City Park. She and her daughter bought Lee new clothes.

"Why are you all doing this for me?" he asked.

"Well, Lee, for one thing," Lillian said, "we love you, and another thing we want you to look nice when you go to school, like the other children."

Lee was not gracious about it. "I don't need anything from anybody," he told her on one occasion.

She took issue with him. "Now listen, Lee, don't you get so independent that you don't think you need anyone, because we all need somebody at one time or another."[215]

Lee made an attempt at team sports at Beauregard. He told Aunt Lillian that he wanted to get on the baseball team at school but had neither glove nor shoes, and Lillian not only gave him a glove one of her sons had used but also arranged to get a pair of cleated baseball shoes, which her son-in-law sent over from Beaumont, Texas. Lee got off the team as quickly as he got on, but he never discussed it with Lillian and she never found out what happened.[216] Relations between Marguerite and her friend Myrtle Evans became strained, partly, it seems, because Marguerite had difficulty meeting even the reduced rent, and partly because of Lee, whose conduct Evans didn't approve of. He was no longer the small boy she had once known, but a "difficult teenager," and Evans was shocked at the way he would, on his return from school, demand to be fed. If Marguerite was downstairs visiting with her, Lee would come to the head of the stairs and shout, "Maw, how about fixing me something to eat?" Marguerite would "jump up right away and go running upstairs to fix something for him." Lee, she said, was very spoiled because Marguerite "poured out all her love on him, it seemed like."[217]

Myrtle's husband Julian thought that Lee was "arrogant, and no one liked him." He too noticed Lee's impudence with his mother, but saw other unpleasant behavior as well. He once took Lee on a weekend trip to his sister-in-law's place across Lake Pontchartrain, where there was a private pond for fishing. Lee went fishing with some other boys, but Julian noticed that he wouldn't talk to them and fished by himself. Lee caught some fish, but then just threw them down on the bank of the pond, and when he had enough he just walked away and left them lying there. Julian, who felt you ought to eat the fish you catch or throw them back in the water, found that very hard to understand. He thought Lee was "a psycho."[218] Julian sympathized with Marguerite, whom he thought to be a "fine woman, intelligent, very soft-spoken, a beautiful woman with black hair streaked with a little gray" (hardly the short and stocky, very assertive woman the world would come to know years later when her son shot the president), but she was spoiling Lee, who was "real demanding" with her and "had absolutely no patience with her." Marguerite, he said, "would do just about anything he wanted."* Lee had a nice speaking voice, but

---

*To elaborate on the earlier footnote on Marguerite, the knock on her by virtually everyone who knew her that she was almost impossible to coexist with and not a good mother has a few dissenters, at least as to the issue of whether she was a loving and caring mother. The Evans are two of the few dissenters. And Lee's jun-

he didn't use it in his relationship with his mother. Julian said he was always "very loud and insolent," and the Evans always knew when the Oswalds were at home upstairs. Lee made no effort to control his "foghorn" voice and it disturbed other tenants—there were twenty-seven units in the building.[219]

After about six months, when Marguerite, despite the reduced rent, continued to complain it was too high, and was already a month in arrears, even her good friend Myrtle had had enough. "It seemed," Myrtle said, "that the situation was getting worse all the time, so I thought maybe it would be better if I didn't have them around. So . . . she upped and moved, and that's when she moved to Exchange Alley." It was around April of 1955, and Myrtle never saw her friend Marguerite again.[220]

Number 126 Exchange Place—earlier known as Exchange Alley—is in the Vieux Carré, the heart of inner New Orleans, and the apartment was located just above a pool hall. The apartment was nice, according to Lillian, who noted that the downtown district, in spite of its rough character, was attractive to many people, so rents tended to be high there, although she thought Marguerite's was modest enough, particularly in view of the bedroom, bath, large living room, and breakfast room she had. Lee got the bedroom, and Marguerite, who was working at a department store on Canal Street, slept on a studio couch in the living room. She also fixed the apartment up "real nice," according to her sister.[221]

There's little evidence that Lee partook of the seaminess of the neighborhood, beyond the occasional game of pool or darts in the poolroom below.[222] He continued to behave much as he had in New York, returning home from school alone long before Marguerite came in from work and spending his time in solitary pursuits, including reading books he brought home from the library.[223] Aunt Lillian continued to give him money to rent a bicycle in the park, which he seemed to enjoy a lot, and he sometimes visited museums or walked in the park by himself.[224]

The picture people had of Lee in the eighth and ninth grades at Beauregard Junior High School in 1954–1955 when Lee was fourteen and fifteen years old is not so much muddled as it is dim. He made very little impression on his schoolmates. After the assassination, when a local television station tried to find people who had known Lee Oswald at that time, they were mostly reduced to canvassing neighbors who had merely seen him around. Three girls who did remember him from junior and senior high school—Bennierita Smith, Anna Alexander Langlois, and Peggy Zimmerman—had to put their heads together to remember much of anything at all about him, and that mostly was about the way he dressed (distinctively unfashionably, in jeans and sweater vests), his erect carriage, his aloofness—he never belonged to any of the cliques that young people are prone to form in these years—and "he was always getting in fights."[225]

---

ior high school friend in New Orleans, Ed Voebel, was another, telling the Warren Commission that "I think she [Marguerite] tried to take care of him," adding that "if he wanted something, no matter what it was . . . she would try to get it for him" (8 H 11). These testimonials cannot be disregarded, though it has to be noted that neither the Evans nor Voebel lived in Marguerite's household, and Voebel only personally met Marguerite one time and did sense that "something was lacking" in Lee's relationship with his mother. But more importantly, even if we ignore the negative observations about Marguerite by the professionals like the psychiatrists, psychologists, and social workers in New York, even, indeed, those of her own sister Lillian—sisters, of course, can be catty—the relationship a son has with his mother is so special that virtually nothing can tear it asunder. Yet not just one, but all three of Marguerite's sons seemingly had no respect for her and felt she left much to be desired as a mother. That assessment, coming from such a source, is even more difficult to disregard, although the available record of that assessment from the three sons is mostly conclusionary about their feelings concerning Marguerite, as opposed to supporting their conclusions with chapter and verse.

One fight at school brought him the only real friend he made in those years. At Beauregard, Lee ran afoul of the Neumeyer brothers—John Neumeyer claimed that Lee had been picking on his little brother Michael. One day after school, Lee and John fought in the street in a long, rambling battle that crossed sidewalks and lawns, was broken by adults who tried to intervene, and then started up again. Edward Voebel witnessed the fight, largely because it followed the route he took home from school. Eventually little Mike Neumeyer came to the aid of his older brother, Lee hit Mike in the mouth hard enough to start blood, and the crowd turned against Lee, apparently because Mike was so much smaller than he, but Voebel thought Lee had every right to defend himself. It was, after all, two against one.[226]

Voebel went home, but a couple of days later he found himself right behind Lee when they left the school building. An older boy, Robin Riley—Voebel thought he must have been a high school kid—punched Lee in the mouth without warning, possibly in retaliation for the Neumeyer fracas. In the schoolyard slang of the day, this was called "passing the post" on Lee, but it was a serious blow that cut Lee's lip and loosened his teeth, possibly even causing him to lose one; Voebel and a couple of other boys took Lee to the boy's restroom and tried to clean him up. Aunt Lillian paid the dentist bill.[227] Voebel, blond and corpulent, came from a family of florists—mother, uncle, and grandmother—and eventually went to work in the family business. He played both the piano and the clarinet in junior high school and, like Lee, had no interest in belonging to any clique. On several occasions he went with Lee to Exchange Place, where they played darts and pool.[228]

They never became really close friends, but Voebel appears to be the only school friend Oswald had ever had, and he visited Oswald at home and met Marguerite, but Lee never visited Voebel at his home. Voebel, who went out of his way to avoid trouble with the gangs in and around the school, admired Oswald's willingness to stand up for himself. "He didn't take anything from anybody," Voebel said. Another difference between them was that Voebel had a lot of friends and acquaintances, while Lee simply did not make friends. "People . . . just didn't interest him generally," Voebel said. "He was just living in his own world."[229]

One day, when the two of them went over to the local high school, Easton, for an orientation for students about to graduate from Beauregard, Lee shocked Voebel by presenting him with a plan to steal a pistol from a shop on Rampart Street. Voebel didn't pay too much attention to Lee, but several days later at Lee's home Lee broached the plan again, bringing out a glass cutter and a plastic pistol, presumably to use in the heist. Voebel had recently heard of thefts from Canal Street jewelry stores by thieves who cut through the show windows. He was flabbergasted but agreed to accompany Lee to the store to see the pistol. "Well, what do you think?" Lee asked. Voebel didn't know what to say, until he noticed the metal tape of the burglar alarm running through the glass. He pointed out that any attempt to cut the glass—unlikely as it was that anyone could get through plate glass with a cheap glass cutter—would set off the alarm. Voebel heard no more about the scheme, and he suspected that Lee had really wanted to be talked out of it.[230]

While the boys were still in junior high school, they were recruited into the Civil Air Patrol, largely by a schoolmate and athlete named Frederick O'Sullivan. O'Sullivan concentrated on three of his classmates, Joseph Thompson, Edward Voebel, and Lee. Lee had impressed him by his military bearing, "head straight, shoulders back," and O'Sullivan thought he would not only be an asset to the squadron's drill team but might make a pretty good leader. He talked all of them into coming out to New Orleans Airport (Lakefront Airport) to attend a couple of meetings. Thompson stayed with the squadron, but after a few meetings, Voebel and Oswald left and joined the Civil Air Patrol group at New Orleans's Moisant International Airport.[231]

Voebel recalled talking Lee into joining and that Lee may even have taken a paper route to earn enough money to buy a uniform, but he dropped out after attending two or three meetings. Voebel sensed Lee liked the uniform more than the classes they had to attend.[232]

During this period, Marguerite worked for a time at Burt's Shoe Store on Canal Street in New Orleans and then for the Dolly Shoe Company.[233] Her employer at Dolly Shoe, Maury Goodman, recalled her as a pleasant person and a good worker, and he agreed when she asked him to employ Lee to help keep the boy off the streets and out of trouble. He found Lee to be a "nice, pleasant little boy, but not with much sense." Lee worked for about ten weeks in 1955, mostly on Saturdays and an occasional weekday, as a stock boy. They tried to train him to be a salesman, but with no success.[234]

At the end of the ninth grade at Beauregard, in June of 1955, he filled out a "personal history" form. On it, he indicated that the subjects he liked the best were "Civics, Science, Math"; those the least as "English, Art." His vocational preferences were listed as biology and mechanical drawing. His plans after high school were checked off as "military service" and "undecided." Reading and outdoor sports were given as his recreational activities, with football being his favorite sport. He said he had no close friends in school. Lee was five feet five inches tall at the time and weighed 135 pounds.[235]

Lee's ninth grade at Beauregard was marked by a rising scholastic average, getting a 70 in English, 70 in mathematics, 81 in art, 83 in civics, 76 in science, and 78 in physical education, for an average grade of 76. And again, his attendance wasn't bad, for him. He missed math class the most, nine times, the other classes no more than five.[236] However, on an aptitude and achievement test, his scores were 49 in reading, 48 on vocabulary, and 43 on mathematics.[237] The averages in New Orleans schools on these tests were 62, 63, and 63. The national averages were 60, 60, and 68.[238]

In July of 1955, Robert was discharged from his three-year enlistment in the Marine Corps. On his return from Korea he went to Fort Worth, where he intended to live and work, but after a couple of days seeing old friends he bought a 1951 Chevy and drove to New Orleans to visit his mother and brother, arriving there on July 14 and staying with Marguerite and Lee at Exchange Place. It was midsummer and Lee had no job, so the two boys spent a good bit of time together wandering the city—Audubon Park and City Park, the French Quarter, and along the waterfront. Lee pumped Robert mercilessly about the Marine Corps. He intended to enlist as soon as he was old enough, less than a year and a half away.[239]

In the fall of 1955, Lee entered tenth grade at Warren Easton High School. On October 7, he presented the school with a handwritten letter that he had signed with his mother's name:

> To whom it may concern,
>   Becaus we are moving to San Diego in the middle of this month Lee must quit school now. Also, please send by him any papers such as his birth certificate that you may have. Thank you.
>
>   Sincirely
>   Mrs. M. Oswald[240]

Marguerite was astonished when the principal of the school called her a few days later at Kreeger's Specialty Shop on Canal Street, where she was then working, to verify the note. Marguerite went along with it and covered for Lee, who later that afternoon showed up at the shop with the news that he was quitting school and, although he was still a few days short of his sixteenth birthday, wanted to join the Marines. He begged her to falsify his birth certificate. Although an old childhood friend who was now an attorney advised her not to do it, eventually she signed an affidavit to the effect that she lost Lee's birth certificate and that he was born in 1938 rather than 1939. A few days after his birthday he tried to enlist in the Marine Corps. He even went off to the recruiting station with a packed duffel bag, but he was sent home again—though it is not known why the recruiters did not accept the affidavit.[241]

According to Marguerite, Lee continued to live for the day when he could join the Marines, and he read and reread the Marine Corps manual, even got her to hold the book and quiz him on it—"He knew it by heart," she said. She also recalled a "small book" from the library that was "about Communism." (Oswald later told newswoman Priscilla Johnson McMillan, when she interviewed him in 1959 in Moscow, that he began at this time to get books out of the New Orleans library by "Marx, Engels, and American Communist writers," although he couldn't think of any other authors' names.)[242]

On October 10, three days after he wrote the forged note, Lee dropped out of Warren Easton High School, where he had been getting Cs and Ds,[243] and the next month he got his first full-time job. On November 10, he started work as a messenger boy for a Canal Street shipping company, Gerard F. Tujague Inc., where he earned $130 a month.[*] For a little over two months, Lee delivered shipping papers to the U.S. Customshouse export office, steamship lines, and foreign consulates. He kept to himself, apart from the other employees, and usually went home for lunch, as Exchange Place was nearby. Mr. Tujague recalled Oswald complaining that the work was too strenuous, but he didn't remember why Lee left his employ on January 14, 1956, and the company's employment records only noted tersely that Oswald had resigned.[244]

Robert recalled that Lee had started well at Tujague's, that he was "eager, animated, and genuinely enthusiastic" about his job. He liked having money to spend and used some of it to buy presents for his mother. "The very first pay that Lee got from this job at Tujague," Marguerite told the Warren Commission, "he came home with a birdcage on a stand that had a planter. It had ivy in the planter, it had the parakeet, and it had a complete set of food for the parakeet." It was the first money that Lee had ever earned. "And then he paid his room and board."

He also bought Marguerite a thirty-five-dollar coat and opened a savings account with the hope of going on some sort of tour with a group of young people. With his regular earnings, he also bought an electric football machine, a bow-and-arrow set, and a real gun.[245]

Robert remembered the gun well. It was a Marlin bolt-action .22 caliber clip-fed rifle—that didn't work. The firing pin was broken. Robert recalled that Lee had paid sixteen or eighteen dollars for it, about what he spent a few years later for the Carcano rifle, and that he eventually bought it from Lee for ten dollars and had it fixed.[246]

Three days after leaving Tujague's, Lee went to work as an office boy and runner at another Canal Street firm, J. B. Michaels Inc. Two weeks later he was gone, and by the

---

[*]Some confusion has been caused by the fact that there were two businesses under the name Tujague in New Orleans, one of them a restaurant reputed to be an underworld hangout involved in gambling. The HSCA checked to see where Oswald had actually worked, and it turned out to be the shipping company. Frank DiBenedetto, who took over the business when Gerald Tujague died, told the committee that Tujague had once told him that he was in no way related to the owners of the restaurant. (9 HSCA 101–102)

time of the assassination no one at the company remembered him at all. Even Marguerite forgot he had worked there.[247] Shortly thereafter he went to work as a messenger for the Pfisterer Dental Laboratory.[248] There, he finally succeeded in striking up something of a friendship with a fellow messenger, Palmer McBride, a boy nearly two years older who was struggling hard to get an education. McBride, learning of Oswald's interest in classical music, invited him to his home to listen to records. When the talk turned to the world situation, McBride offered the opinion that President Eisenhower was actually doing quite well, although McBride felt there should be more emphasis on the space program. He was taken completely aback when Lee denounced Eisenhower as one of the exploiters of the working class and that he would like to kill him. McBride didn't take the remark seriously enough to notify the authorities because he didn't believe Oswald's statement was made in the nature of an actual threat on the president's life, but he didn't think Oswald had made the remark in jest either. He realized that Lee was quite serious about the virtues of Communism. Lee praised Khrushchev for improving the lot of the workers in the Soviet Union and predicted that the workers of the world would soon rise up and throw off their chains[249]—heavy sentiments for a teenage boy in the depths of the cold war, at a time when Joe McCarthy had passed from the scene, but McCarthyism in America had not yet been laid to rest.

On another occasion, McBride went to Lee's home, where Lee showed him copies of *Das Kapital* and *The Communist Manifesto*. Although they were just library books, McBride thought Oswald was "quite proud to have them."[250] Years later, when he defected to Moscow, Lee told journalist Aline Mosby, "Then we moved to New Orleans and I discovered one book in the library, *Das Kapital*. It was what I'd been looking for. It was like a very religious man opening the Bible for the first time . . . I read the *Manifesto*. It got me interested. I found some dusty back shelves in the New Orleans library, you know, I had to remove some front books to get at the books. I started to study Marxist economic theories. I thought the workers' life could be better. I continued to indoctrinate myself for five years."[251]

McBride also took Lee to a meeting of a citywide astronomy club and introduced him to the club's president, William Wulf, a LaSalle High School student the same age as Lee. At their first meeting, Wulf was unimpressed by Oswald's knowledge of astronomy, to the point of trying to discourage him from joining the club, since few of the members would be interested in teaching him the fundamentals.[252]

Lee spoke with Wulf again, this time at Wulf's house, where McBride took him sometime in early 1956. Wulf, who had a lively interest in history, got into a heated argument with Oswald about Communism. Lee had brought the subject up, telling Wulf he was "highly interested in Communism" and that "Communism was the only way of life for the worker," becoming, Wulf said, "loud-mouthed, boisterous." Wulf said Lee bemoaned the fact he could not find a Communist cell to join in New Orleans. Eventually, Wulf's father, a merchant mariner and native of Hamburg, Germany, who had seen all he cared to see of Communism in Germany after World War I ended in 1918, took Oswald by the arm and politely ejected him from the house.[253] Wulf found Lee's ideas alarming enough to warn his friend McBride, who hoped for a career in rocketry, that a friendship with Oswald might later be construed as a security risk. Wulf was surprised, since Oswald was only sixteen, at Oswald's ideological vehemence over Communism, describing his attitude as "militant" and impressing him as someone "who could get violent over Communism." Wulf told the Warren Commission that Oswald seemed to be a young man who had "very little self-identification," someone who was "looking for something to belong to . . . and he just happened, I guess, to latch on to this particular area to become identified with."[254]

Both Wulf and McBride soon lost track of Lee when the Oswalds moved in early July 1956 back to Fort Worth.[255] Oswald was still only sixteen, but this was the seventeenth time he had moved in his gypsy-like existence.[256] Marguerite had several reasons for the latest move. She told the Warren Commission that she knew Lee was intending to join the Marine Corps on his seventeenth birthday, coming up in October, and she thought that if they lived with Robert, he might be able to dissuade Lee from enlisting. She may equally have hoped that Robert would take over some of the burden of supporting his brother and herself. "I have always been broke, and I mean broke," she told the Commission about her move back to Fort Worth. "About a month before rent time, we had it pretty hard in order to have that rent." In any case, Marguerite rented an apartment at 4926 Collinswood Avenue for all three of them. Robert was less than thrilled. He had his own plans—he was going to marry Vada Marie Mercer in November and intended to find their own apartment. Nevertheless, he had agreed to move in with Marguerite and Lee and to help out with the bills until then.[257]

Robert did indeed try to talk Lee out of joining the Marine Corps before finishing high school during their brief period together at Collinswood Avenue, but Lee, after giving his older brother's advice some serious thought, was determined to join up when he turned seventeen. Marguerite quickly found a job in a Fort Worth shoe store, and the family, minus John, was temporarily back together again, Robert working and contributing to the household expenses.[258]

In September, Lee enrolled in the tenth grade—again—at Arlington Heights High School, which his brothers had attended some years before, but his stay there was short-lived.[259] One student recalled later that Lee had tried to interest him in Communism, but the temper of the times only caused the student to "shy away from him."[260] Lee also went out for the football team. When it came time to run the sprint at the end of practice, Oswald announced to the coach that "this is a free country, and I don't have to do it." The coach told him to hang up his cleats.[261] This incident recalled Lee's behavior at Youth House in New York City, where a social worker said he had been a "non-participant in any activity." Robert had noted Lee's difficulty in taking orders from other kids—if he couldn't be the boss, he didn't want to play at all—a characteristic Robert thought Lee had in common with their mother. "I've known her to lose a good job," he wrote, "because she was too bossy and wanted to be the manager or a partner instead of just another employee. She always felt she was somebody special and people should recognize that fact."[262]

Before the month of September was out, and after receiving four Ds and a C on tests, Lee dropped out of Arlington altogether.[263] A few days later, on October 3, 1956, he wrote to the Socialist Party of America in New York City:

> Dear Sirs:
>   I am sixteen years of age and would like more information about your youth League, I would like to know if there is a branch in my area, how to join, ect., I am a Marxist, and have been studying socialist principles for well over fifteen months I am very interested in your Y.P.S.L. [Young People's Socialist League]
>
> Sincerely
Lee Oswald

He enclosed an advertisement coupon that had three boxes for checking off items—one for a three-dollar subscription to the *Socialist Call*, another to get information about the Socialist Party, and another to join the party—but Lee checked only the box requesting information.[264] Mostly, he was waiting to turn seventeen and realize the dream he had nurtured since he was twelve, to join the Marine Corps. Clearly, the young Lee never found—or perhaps never gave a thought to—the incompatibility between his nascent Communism, whose goal was to end capitalism, and the U.S. Marines, the corps whose gallantry on the battlefield was intended to preserve America's way of life—capitalism.

Lee's brother Robert told the Warren Commission, "I believe that the reason Lee joined the United States Marine Corps was to follow in my footsteps in that same service," adding he felt his younger brother was always closer to him than his mother or half-brother, and he "looked up to me" and wanted to emulate Robert not only in the Marine Corps but in other respects.[265] Indeed, Oswald told reporter Aline Mosby in Moscow in 1959, "I joined the Marine Corps because I had a brother in the Marines."[266] In Robert's book, however, he writes that "after John left for the Coast Guard and I decided to join the Marines, he [Lee] talked of nothing else. He had seen us escape from mother that way. To him, military service meant freedom [from Marguerite]."[267] Lee's other brother, John, agreed. While not addressing himself to the Marines as an issue, he simply said that Lee joined the service "for the same reasons that I did it and Robert did it, I assume, to get from out and under" the "yoke of oppression from my mother."[268]

Perhaps the even greater incongruity was someone like Oswald, who was fiercely independent and resisted any type of authority, joining an organization whose trademark and way of life was authority and regimentation. But what was probably more important to Lee, at least for the moment, was that consistent with his adventuresome nature, as manifested by his exploration, as a child, of the streets of New York, he was going to be exploring another world, and it couldn't be worse than the very unhappy one he was leaving behind. Also, the young man who even his youthful peers noticed was in search of an identity had now found a brand-spanking new and impressive one, a marine, as discordant as it was with his Marxist ideology. But all that could be sorted out later.

On the eighteenth of that month, October, Lee reached his seventeenth birthday, and on October 24 he enlisted for a six-year military obligation (three active duty, the remaining three in the reserve) and was now a marine. That same day he boarded a bus to Dallas, where he was given a physical examination and sworn in, then flown to San Diego for recruit training. For the first time in his life, he was on his own.[269]

He arrived at the San Diego Recruit Depot on October 26, 1956, and was assigned to the Second Recruit Training Battalion. He had now grown to five feet eight inches tall, but still weighed 135 pounds, and had no physical defects. He scored above the Marine Corps average on tests for reading and vocabulary, below average on arithmetic and pattern analysis. His composite general classification score (GCT) for the battery of six tests was 105, two points below the corps average. He scored near the bottom of the lowest group on a radio code test and failed to qualify as a swimmer. He gave as his preference for duty "aircraft maintenance and repair"—his brother Robert's specialty—and he was recommended for such training. He also managed to get a satisfactory—but not distinguished—score on a test of general educational development.[270] His starting basic pay as a private was a grand spanking $78 per month, not a princely wage. On the other hand, he got free room and board.[271] (By the time Oswald was discharged from the military in September of 1959, he was a private first class and his basic pay was $108 per month.)[272]

Boot camp, ten grueling weeks starting at five every morning under a barking drill sergeant, is a living hell for all recruits—it is specifically designed to be—but Oswald somehow managed to survive it. The recruits were trained on the standard American military rifle of the period, the Garand M-1, a .30 caliber weapon with iron sights. Lee, per a fellow recruit, Sherman Cooley, had difficulty firing the M-1 accurately during training.[273] However, on December 21, when his company fired for the record, Lee not only qualified, but managed a score of 212, two points above the threshold for a "sharpshooter," the middle of three Marine Corps qualification classifications, twelve points better than "marksman," and eight points below the level of "expert."[*]

His overall marks as a recruit were 4.4 for both conduct and proficiency—5.0 was the highest mark possible, and 4.0 was required for an honorable discharge.[274]

After ten weeks of basic training, in January of 1957 Oswald was transferred to an Infantry Training Regiment at Camp Pendleton outside of San Diego, sort of an advanced boot camp that concentrated on the basic skills of combat and the amphibious techniques and methods all marines must know.[275] One of the men in Oswald's squad, Allen R. Felde, mostly remembered Oswald's mouth. Lee railed against the American intervention in Korea and blamed "one million" useless deaths on President Eisenhower—in spite of the fact that Truman was president for all but the last six months of that war. Felde said that such political talk did not endear Oswald to his fellow marines, who had little interest in politics at all, much less in Lee's view of politics. Felde said he also wasn't popular because he was very "argumentative," seemingly taking an opposite side of an argument "just for the sake of a debate." And although he would share a cab to Tijuana with his squad mates when they went on liberty, Lee would part from them when they arrived and rejoin them only back at Pendleton. The same thing happened when they went several times to Los Angeles—Oswald rode with them on the bus but went off on his own as soon as they got there. Felde, who considered Oswald a "good talker" with an "excellent vocabulary," said that Oswald, whom he described as "left-winged," expressed a dislike for people with wealth, championed the cause of the "workingman," and spent much of his time reading in quarters or in the base library.[276]

Lee completed the course at Pendleton with a 4.2 in conduct and 4.0 in proficiency, and on February 27 he went on leave for two weeks, visiting his mother and brother in Fort Worth.[277]

The two brothers had a lot to talk about. Robert was married and anxious for Lee to get to know Vada, and he had a job at Condar, where he was testing and working on fuel component systems for the B-58 bomber. Lee was full of enthusiasm for the Marines and eagerly looking forward to his next training assignment. One weekend they went out to the dairy farm operated by Vada's parents, where Lee got a very rough ride from a palomino mare that belonged to Vada's brother and had a mind of its own. He managed to hang on and seemed proud of that fact, but he didn't try any more rides. He had more success when the brothers went hunting. They found no squirrels at all, but Lee shot a

---

[*]Apparently, Oswald wasn't bad with a pistol either. At the naval air base in Japan where he was later stationed, his pistol instructor, Marine sergeant Arnie Vitarbo, said, "Everyone was required to train with a pistol and rifle, and he showed a special interest. He was better than average . . . but everyone seemed to think he was different. A loner" (*Los Angeles Daily News*, April 21, 1992; see also 11 H 305, WCT Maj. Eugene D. Anderson).

strange animal they couldn't identify, one with a sharp snout, a long, thin body, and a bushy tail like a coon. Vada's father told them it was a ring-tailed cat—the first he had seen in fifteen or twenty years. Lee was delighted with his rare bag.[278]

Although Lee was staying with his mother, he spent most of his time with Robert and Vada. Robert saw little of Marguerite. They had had a falling out over the fact that the young couple refused to live in a house with a garage apartment for Marguerite, but Robert knew that they would never have a life of their own with Marguerite nearby, and he was pleased to keep a safe distance from her.[279]

On March 18, 1957, Lee reported to the Naval Air Technical Training Center at the Naval Air Station in Jacksonville, Florida.[280] His training detachment there was schooled in the work of the air wing of the Marine Corps, including courses in the security of classified matter, missions and systems, navy plotting symbols, basic theory of radar, air traffic control procedures, map reading, and weather and aircraft recognition.[281] At the conclusion of the training on May 3, he was given clearance to deal with "confidential" materials—the lowest grade of security clearance but a necessary one for the next step of his training, one requiring a "careful records check."[282] He did fairly well at Jacksonville. Although he ranked forty-sixth in a class of fifty-four, his scores of 4.7 for conduct and 4.5 for proficiency were the highest he would ever attain.[283] He was also promoted to private first class, effective back to May 1.[284]

The same day the course ended, May 3, 1957, he was sent by train, along with five other marines, to Keesler Air Force Base in Biloxi, Mississippi, to learn to be a ground radar operator responsible for locating and guiding aircraft aloft.[285] One of the six marines who traveled to Keesler with Oswald and served with him there, Daniel Powers, thought that Lee might have been striving for a relationship with the others, but that his personality alienated the group, some of whom called him "Ozzie Rabbit," undoubtedly because of the Walt Disney cartoon "Oswald, the Lucky Rabbit." Powers even suspected Oswald of having homosexual tendencies, although he had little evidence for this other than saying "a lot of his mannerisms were closely related to other homosexuals that I had seen in my life up to that period of time." Oswald kept to himself and didn't play cards, work out in the gym, or go on liberty with the others.[286] They had most of their weekends free, and Oswald usually spent them alone in nearby New Orleans, which he always considered his home more than Fort Worth, and where he still had the Murrets to visit.[287]

Lee did well in his six-week school, finishing seventh in a class of thirty—and those thirty had already been selected for their aptitude.[288] He also earned a 4.2 for conduct and a 4.5 for proficiency.[289] On June 20 he went on ten days' leave, again visiting his mother and Robert in Fort Worth.[290] Robert remembered very little about that visit, except that it was "too hot to do anything we didn't have to do." One incident did stand out. Robert ran a red light to avoid getting rear-ended by a driver tailgating him and was promptly stopped by a police officer. Robert explained that he would have been hit had he stopped, and the policeman said, "But the other guy would have been at fault"—as he handed Robert the ticket. As they drove off, Lee looked back over his shoulder and said, "That dumb cop!" Robert forgot about it until November 1963, when witnesses reported that the man who gunned down Officer J. D. Tippit had muttered, "Dumb cop" or "Damn cop."[291]

On July 9, he reported to the Marine Air Corps Station at El Toro, California (close to Santa Ana), a base located between San Diego and Los Angeles, where he was classified as a "replacement trainee" and attached to the Fourth Replacement Battalion—in effect, he and his mates were simply waiting for their first real assignment in the fleet, although it was not until August 22 that they embarked on the USS *Bexar* for transport to Yokosuka, Japan, and eventual duty at nearby Atsugi Naval Air Station. On the ship Oswald taught Powers how to play chess, and they sometimes wiled away up to four hours a day. Powers got good enough to beat Oswald occasionally, and he noticed how much that irritated his mentor. Oswald was always very happy to win, "like," Powers remembered, "he was accomplishing something in life."[292]

Powers was three years older than Oswald, had completed a year at the University of Minnesota, and was determined to finish his education when he mustered out of the Marines—he eventually became a teacher in Wisconsin. He was also married and had been promoted to corporal while they were still at Keesler. He felt "somewhat above" the boys like Lee, who he thought had enlisted largely because "there wasn't anything better for him to do at [the] time . . . He was somewhat of a rolling stone." Powers was nonetheless impressed by the quality of Oswald's reading. There isn't a lot to do on a troopship, and many of the men read a lot, but Oswald showed some taste. Powers thought Oswald might have read *The Age of Reason* and *The Age of Enlightenment* (from Will and Ariel Durant's popular history of philosophy, then published in several paperback volumes), as well as some books about American presidents and democracy. The one book Powers was sure that Oswald read was Walt Whitman's *Leaves of Grass*.[293]

The *Bexar* docked at Yokosuka, a seaport on Tokyo Bay, on September 12, 1957, and Oswald, Powers, and their fellow marines were sent on to Marine Air Control Squadron No. 1 (MACS-1), then attached to Marine Air Group 11 of the First Marine Air Craft Wing based at Atsugi Naval Air Base, about thirty-five miles southwest of Tokyo.[294] Atsugi had been the main training base for Japanese kamikaze pilots (pilots on a suicide mission who flew planes laden with explosives into American ships) during World War II, and the hills were riddled with caves where the Japanese air force had stowed fighter planes to keep them safe from American strafing raids. Beyond the barbed wire lay rice fields. Hangars on the west side of the long main runway housed Marine fighter squadrons, while on the east were the facilities for the navy patrol and antisubmarine squadrons. One huge hangar in the northwest housed the U-2 spy planes, and there was a complex of about twenty buildings housing a "joint technical advisory group"—one of the CIA's main bases in Asia. Everyone who worked at or visited the base had to have at least a minimum security clearance. It was even rumored that nuclear weapons were stored there, in violation of U.S. treaties with Japan.[295]

The still-mysterious U-2 plane was operated under conditions of the utmost secrecy—even its name, U-2, was a common navy designation for a "utility" aircraft, a sort of catchall for general-purpose planes with no distinct military role. The single seater had been conceived in 1954, built by Lockheed, and first flown in prototype in 1955. The U-2A production version was powered by a Pratt and Whitney J57-P-37A Turbojet engine with 11,200 pounds of static thrust. It had a range of 2,600 miles and an astounding initial climb rate of 7,500 feet—well over a mile—per minute. Called by the Soviets "the black lady of espionage," it was capable of soaring to an altitude of about 75,000 feet, an altitude never before reached by a human, and remaining there for over nine hours at a time. The U-2 entered service with the U.S. Air Force and the National Aeronautics and Space Administration in 1956, and it must have appeared in Atsugi not long after. It represented a dramatic advance in the capabilities of aerial reconnaissance. More a powered glider than a conventional jet plane, the U-2's wingspan, at 80 feet, was more than twice

the length of its slender body. It was fitted with an array of cameras and sensitive electronic equipment designed to record and monitor radio and radar transmissions, and
before being shot down in 1960, "for four years [it] provided the United States with invaluable intelligence data on Russia's nuclear testing, missile and space launches, and other
war-making potentials."[296]

While the enlisted marines at Atsugi knew nothing about the U-2's capabilities or mission, and were in fact ordered not to discuss it, it was impossible to ignore. The long silver or—after 1957—matte blue-black craft was hauled out to the strip by a tractor, its
fragile, drooping wings supported by tiny wheels on the wingtips—pogos, the pilots called
them.[297] The pilot, in a rubber uniform, arrived by ambulance and climbed into the cockpit of the plane, whose ground crew had removed all identifying markings from the plane.
The high whine of the Pratt and Whitney Turbojet engine was so distinctive that the
marines often rushed outside to watch it take off. They were dazzled by its short take-off
run and incredibly steep rate of climb. Landings were equally spectacular. The plane could
not be flown into a landing. It had to be stalled just off the ground, and it landed not on
the conventional tricycle landing gear, but on a nose and a tail wheel, more like a bicycle.
It could be kept upright as long as it was moving, but as it slowed, it tipped over on one
wingtip, the wingtip with its small wheels beneath often giving off a shower of sparks as it
scraped the tarmac. Two jeeps covered with canvas held the wings up as the tractor towed
the U-2 back to its hangar, which was guarded by men armed with submachine guns.[298]

The radar operators at Atsugi were also intrigued. The planes simply vanished from
their radar screens when they exceeded 45,000 feet, the altitude limit on their MPS-11
antennae, and the U-2 pilots would sometimes request information on winds at 90,000
feet, well above the known world altitude record of 65,889 feet.[299] While anyone might
easily have surmised that the plane was flying aerial reconnaissance missions over China
and the Soviet Union—other patrol planes had been doing that for a long time—it's
doubtful whether anyone could have guessed just how deep their penetration of enemy
airspace might be.

Although conspiracy theorists have made much of Oswald's brief proximity to the U-
2, suggesting he traded his knowledge of the U-2 to the KGB in exchange for special
treatment when he later defected to Russia, there is no evidence that his particular unit
actually dealt with the spy plane's operations, nor is there any evidence that Oswald displayed more than a normal curiosity about the plane.

Oswald's unit at Atsugi, MACS-1, code-named "Coffee Mill," had just under a hundred men[300] whose duty was to man a semicircular radar room called "the Bubble," usually in groups of three officers and about seven men. The room was kept dark to improve
the visibility of the hooded UPA-25 radar scopes, and the noise and temperature levels
were very high owing to the many pieces of heavy electrical equipment. The grease pen-
cils the men used to plot positions and courses would sometimes melt on the translucent
plotting board. The men worked in their skivvy shirts and mopped the perspiration from
their faces as they shouted over the din of the machinery.[301]

The crew members worked four-hour shifts staggered in such a way that over the
course of time they worked at all hours of the day or night—not that it made much difference in the Bubble, where it was always so dark that they couldn't recognize their
coworkers more than a few feet away. They monitored a quadrant of airspace stretching
from due west to due north, tracking all aircraft movements and radio communications
with the pilots. They directed friendly planes to their destinations and detected incom-

ing foreign aircraft, notifying their presence to the Tactical Air Control Center at Iwakuni as well as plotting fighter intercepts of the intruder. They also served as communication liaisons with Japanese air defense forces.[302]

The new men arriving for duty at Atsugi were appropriately hazed by the veterans, and most of them laughed it off or responded with good-natured insults. One marine in Oswald's barracks, Jerry E. Pitts, thought Oswald took it too personally. Once the men discovered that Lee reacted badly to being called "Harve" or "Harvey," they called him that relentlessly, infuriating him. It was, of course, his middle name, but it was also the name of the famous invisible rabbit in a popular Broadway play. "We all had to go through the same thing," Pitts recalled, "but Oswald never understood that . . . He just never knew how to read the system. If he could have just taken the initial insults, he would have become one of the boys."[303]

Daniel Powers thought Lee became more aggressive and outgoing at Atsugi. "He took on a new personality, and now he was Oswald the man, rather than Oswald the rabbit.[304] Other marines reported, though, that Oswald would mimic Bugs Bunny by wiggling his ears, squinting, and pushing his teeth out over his lower lip, which earned him another nickname—"Bugs."[305] And other marines who served with Oswald at Atsugi remembered him in diverse ways. Zack Stout was quite impressed with Oswald, finding him to be "honest and blunt . . . and that's what usually got him into trouble . . . He was absolutely truthful, the kind of guy I'd trust completely." Stout said that Oswald "would read deep stuff like *Mein Kampf* or the *Decline and Fall of the Roman Empire*" and was one of the few men in his unit whom he could hold an intelligent conversation with. Another friend at Atsugi was George Wilkins, who thought Oswald's resentment of young officers fresh out of college entirely natural. "Hell," Wilkins told author Edward Epstein, who did some valuable investigative work on Oswald's entire military period, "we all thought we were smarter and better than any of the officers, and Ozzie was just like the rest of us. We all resented authority." Wilkins taught Oswald how to use a 35-millimeter camera, and Oswald bought a camera for himself—the famous Imperial Reflex that Marina eventually used to take the backyard shots of him holding his rifle, pistol, and left-wing publications.[306]

Another marine, David Christie Murray, said that Oswald had a "chip on his shoulder" and "did not often associate with his fellow marines." And Murray said he had his own reasons for staying away from Oswald. "I had heard a rumor to the effect that he was homosexual. I personally observed nothing to support this rumor, and am not sure that I heard it from more than one person."[307]

Yet another marine, John Rene Heindel, told the Warren Commission that Oswald was frequently in trouble for failing to adhere to rules and regulations and for his express and open dislike of authority exercised by his superiors in the Marines. Heindel also said he, Heindel, was often called, as a nickname, "Hidell"—pronounced "to rhyme with 'Rydell' rather than 'Fidel'"—by other marines, although he could not specifically recall Oswald doing so.[308]*

---

*There's no way to know for sure if Oswald used the alias Hidell because of his exposure to Heindel or not. The likelihood is that he did not, it just being a coincidence, the further coincidence being that Heindel was also from New Orleans, though there's no evidence the two knew each other before Atsugi. Because Marina, who had firsthand knowledge, said Oswald came up with Hidell as an "altered Fidel" due to his reverence for Fidel Castro (1 H 64), and Heindel saying the "i" in his nickname was hard, not soft, as in *Fidel*, it's safe to assume that Oswald's alias had nothing to do with Heindel.

After a few weeks at Atsugi, Lee seemed to be coming out of his shell, and he occasionally went with other marines to carouse in local bars that doubled as cheap brothels for the troops. As author Epstein noted, "Oswald had found a camaraderie with a group of men that he had never experienced before," and in one of the bars he found a Japanese bar girl he lost his virginity with. He started to drink for the first time that anyone knows of, sometimes drinking to excess. He watched the other guys' late-night poker games—watch standers kept very odd hours—but never played himself. Occasionally, when the weekly rotation of watchers brought him two days' liberty, he took off for Tokyo. He apparently scored with a striking Japanese woman he seemed to be crazy about and who he told a friend was a hostess at the expensive Queen Bee nightclub in Tokyo. His mates, seeing Oswald with the woman when he brought her on base, wondered how the rabbity Oswald rated such a classy and expensive woman. They never got an answer.[309]*

On October 27, just five weeks after Lee reported for duty at Atsugi, Oswald's resurgence came to an end. Another marine, Paul Murphy, heard a pistol shot and rushed into Oswald's cubicle in the barracks. He found Oswald sitting on a footlocker looking at a wound in his arm. "I believe I shot myself," Oswald told him calmly. He had been keeping a loaded .22 caliber Derringer pistol in his locker. As he was removing some gear, the gun fell to the floor and discharged, the bullet hitting him in the left elbow.[310] The injury was serious enough to keep him in the U.S. Naval Hospital at Yokosuka, where the slug was excised from his arm, until November 15.[311]

The shooting put Oswald in trouble with the office of the Judge Advocate General, the military's legal branch for enforcing the Uniform Code of Military Justice (UCMJ). The officers who reviewed his case were, however, lenient, concluding that Oswald had "displayed a certain degree of carelessness or negligence," but that the injury was incurred "in the line of duty" and not as a result "of his own misconduct."[312] He was, however, charged with a violation of Article 92 of the UCMJ for "having in his possession a privately-owned weapon that was not registered,"[313] and punishment would have to be meted out. Zack Stout told author Epstein that the unit was scheduled to leave Japan on maneuvers to the Philippines, and Oswald wasn't happy about it, possibly because of trouble he was having with the hostess. Some of the marines thought Oswald may have shot himself deliberately in the hope of remaining at Atsugi while the rest were shipped out.[314]

The trial for Oswald's minor court-martial offense would have to wait, because on November 20, 1957, just five days after he was released from the hospital, his unit was sent aboard a landing ship called USS *Terrell County* to the Philippines.[315]

The unit expected to return to Atsugi in fairly short order, and in fact after less than a week of amphibious landing maneuvers, the men were already embarked on the *Terrell County* for the return trip, but a crisis growing out of a civil war in Indonesia caused a long delay in their return—they spent the next thirty days or so, including Christmas, sailing about the South China Sea without ever seeing land. By the time that crisis was resolved, further maneuvers in the Philippines planned for February or March 1958 were

---

*There was another puzzling question. On Oswald's take-home pay of eighty-five dollars a month, how was he even able to afford going to the Queen Bee, one of the three most expensive nightclubs in Tokyo whose "strikingly beautiful hostesses . . . catered to an elite clientele, . . . not impoverished marine privates"? A night at the club "could cost anywhere from sixty to one hundred dollars." (Epstein, *Legend*, p.71) But one should remember that Oswald was notoriously close with his money all of his life and did not gamble like his fellow marines, so he could have easily saved enough to go to the Queen Bee. After all, we know that no one thought any bigger than Oswald. And of course he could have met the hostess at some place other than where she worked.

looming, and it made little sense to send them back to Atsugi only to return them almost immediately to the Philippines.

Right after Christmas, MACS-1 arrived at Cubi Point in the Philippines, where they set up a temporary base. Cubi Point was adjacent to Subic Bay on Bataan, the famous peninsula where U.S. and Filipino troops surrendered to the Japanese on April 9, 1942. Though there was a landing strip at Cubi, the marines did not set up a radar station there. The temporary assignment in the Philippines ended up lasting for months, until March 18, 1958.[316]

While at Cubi Point, Oswald passed an examination that made him eligible for the rating of corporal, although he was never promoted.[317] He also learned, according to his November 1959 interview with Priscilla Johnson McMillan, to "sympathize with local Communists and conceived a hatred for U.S. 'militarist imperialism' for exploiting the Filipino natives."[318]

Cubi Point was also the scene of an incident that to this day continues to intrigue conspiracy theorists who believe Oswald may have had a hand in it. Around seven o'clock on the night of January 5, 1958, Private First Class Martin Elmo Schrand, one of Oswald's classmates at Jacksonville and Biloxi, was found lying on his back in a pool of blood, having been shot to death near a hangar where he was on guard duty. A January 1958 investigation by the Marine Corps at Cubi Point concluded that the shooting was caused when Schrand's weapon, a Winchester Model 12 riot-type shotgun, was "accidentally discharged." An investigative report ruled out "suicide" and said the "investigation disclosed beyond doubt that no other person or persons were involved in the incident." It also revealed that the weapon was discharged within eight inches of Schrand's left armpit.[319]

Pursuant to a request from Warren Commission general counsel J. Lee Rankin in 1964, the Department of the Navy's Office of Naval Intelligence conducted a reinvestigation into Schrand's death, including a determination of the position of the body at the time he received the wound, and concluded that "Schrand's death was accidental and the result of a malfunction in the receiver section of his weapon caused by an impact on the butt of the piece incurred in the course of [Schrand] conducting Manual of Arms evolutions." Interviews with three of Schrand's close associates at Cubi Point revealed "that Schrand was a 'bug' for drill and spent considerable time practicing the Manual of Arms."[320]

A few days after Schrand's death, Coffee Mill was sent to the island of Corregidor forty miles away, where the unit set up another temporary camp, this time including a radar "bubble" in a tent. The unit remained at Corregidor, another island where U.S. troops were defeated by the Japanese (May of 1942), until the end of its Philippine maneuvers. Oswald had been doing mess duty throughout this entire three-month Philippine period—probably as a sort of informal punishment, since he was still awaiting court-martial on the weapons charge. One of the marines to whom author Epstein talked recalled that "Ozzie could really put on a show with those eggs. He could have three gallons of eggs on the griddle and take a mess tray and slide it under the puddle of eggs and flip them all at once. It was quite a sight."[321] However much he pretended to enjoy mess cooking, though, his military career was definitely slipping. At the end of January he received his lowest marks yet on his semi-annual evaluation—4.0 for conduct and 3.9 for proficiency.[322]

Shortly after setting up camp at Corregidor, actor John Wayne, on location filming *The Barbarian and the Geisha*, landed in a helicopter. Wayne, a grizzled veteran of many heroic Marine battles on the back lots of RKO and Republic Pictures in Hollywood, was besieged by the marines, and in a photo of Wayne dining with the troops in their mess hall, Oswald can be seen standing in the doorway to the Duke's left rear.[323]

On March 7, 1958, MACS-1 was loaded aboard another landing ship, the USS *Wexford County*, and sent back to Atsugi, where the men arrived eleven days later.[324] For Oswald, homecoming also meant facing the music: on April 11, 1958, he was finally court-martialed on the weapons charge, and on April 29 sentenced to twenty days' confinement at hard labor, docked twenty-five dollars a month for two months, and busted to private. The confinement at hard labor was "suspended for six months, at which time, unless the suspension is sooner vacated, the sentence to confinement at hard labor for twenty days will be remitted without further action."[325] Oswald began to go haywire. In addition to the formal punishments, he was not returned to the radar crew, as he requested, but was formally reassigned to serve as a mess cook. According to the marines Epstein talked to, Oswald's carping about the corps became extremely bitter and may well have led to a second incident less than two months later. Technical Sergeant Miguel Rodriguez, the man who reassigned Oswald to mess duty, said that Oswald approached him at a party in the Enlisted Men's Club at Atsugi, looked at him with "those small, dreamy eyes," and said, "You've got guts to come in here." Rodriguez laughed it off, assuming that it was an instance of prejudice against Mexican-Americans. A few days later, though, on June 20, Oswald again accosted Rodriguez in the Blue Bird Café, a squadron hangout just off the base, in Yamoto. Oswald spilled a drink on Rodriguez—who rose and shoved him away—and then cursed the sergeant, calling him yellow and inviting him outside. Rodriguez, who was more sturdily built than Oswald, nevertheless turned down the invitation to duke it out and filed a complaint against Oswald.

Oswald had a right to be represented at the ensuing court-martial trial on June 27, but elected to represent himself. There were two charges under two different articles of the UCMJ, one of "wrongfully using provoking words to a Staff Non-Commission Officer," the other of "assault [on] a Staff Non-Commission Officer by pouring a drink on him."[326] Oswald cross-examined Rodriguez and tried to get him to admit that the spilling of the drink had been accidental, and to some extent he prevailed—the court decided the question could not be proved one way or another and found Oswald not guilty on that charge. Oswald also testified on his own behalf that Rodriguez had been picking on him, that he had requested to be transferred away from the sergeant's supervision, and that he had merely approached him in the Blue Bird Café to discuss the situation. He admitted to inviting Rodriguez outside, but denied calling him yellow. He also claimed to be slightly drunk at the time. Oswald was convicted on the charge of wrongfully using provoking words and sentenced to twenty-eight days' confinement at hard labor and forfeiture of fifty-five dollars out of one month's pay.[327]

The conviction and sentence were approved by the First Marine Aircraft Wing on July 14, 1958, by which time Oswald had already been incarcerated for over two weeks. Because of his second conviction, he would now also have to serve the twenty-day sentence originally suspended at his first court-martial in addition to the twenty-eight days meted out in the second.[328] There were other blows to whatever hopes Oswald may have had for a successful career in the Marine Corps. When he was busted to private on the first conviction, it dashed any immediate hopes for promotion to corporal, in spite of the fact that he had passed the examination. His military obligation period would also be extended by the time served in incarceration.[329] Further, a request he had made in mid-April to extend his tour of overseas duty to May 1959, routinely approved the same day, was revoked in

June.[330] However much Oswald may have wished to stay in Japan, he would be returned to stateside duty in mid–September, and most of his time in that interval would be spent in a place worse than boot camp—a Marine brig.

Little is known about Oswald's stint in the brig, except that it amounted to nearly the full forty-eight days he had to serve on the two sentences—he was confined on June 29 and released on August 13, a total of forty-five days, and he made it tougher than it had to already be by getting into a fight with a brig guard.[331] It is well known that a Marine brig can humiliate the strongest of men. A 1963 play at New York City's avant-garde Living Theater, *The Brig*, by Kenneth H. Brown, was a depiction of an hour in a typical Navy–Marine Corps prison, filled with shouting, brutal guards and their utterly silent, utterly cowed prisoners, who are kept hard at work at menial, demeaning tasks or braced at rigid attention every moment of the day. It no doubt depicts the living hell—much worse than any civilian prison other than the Alabama chain gang—Oswald lived through for a month and a half in 1958.

The experience left Oswald a changed man, more embittered than ever before. He told a fellow marine, "I've seen enough of a democratic society here in MACS-1. When I get out I'm going to try something else."[332] He also backed away from his nights out with the boys, tending once again to keep to himself and disappearing into Tokyo on his longer liberties. One of the marines who spoke with Epstein told him that he had been surprised to meet Oswald in a private house in Yamoto with a woman who worked there as a house-keeper for a naval officer. Also present was a young Japanese man for whom Oswald had bought a T-shirt from the base PX. The marine was impressed that Oswald had a girl-friend who was not a bar girl and who was cooking sukiyaki on a hibachi grill for him.[333] In her testimony before the HSCA, Marina said Oswald had mentioned "his Japanese girlfriend" to her. He said that "she was very nice and . . . a very good cook and . . . she prepared special dishes for him, that he was pampered."[334]

"Fortunately, I moved around, began visiting places where youngsters meet, and established contacts with some more progressive and thinking Japanese," Lee told Dallas friend George de Mohrenschildt many years later, "and this is what led me to Russia eventually." De Mohrenschildt remembered the conversation in a manuscript he was writing at the time of his death in March 1977, quoting Oswald as saying, "I also learned there of other, Japanese ways of exploitation of the poor by the rich. Semi-feudal, industrial giants which act paternalistically yet exploiting the workers—proletarians. The wages in Japan were ridiculously low." Lee spoke glowingly of Latin American revolutionary Che Guevara, saying he, like Lee, had awakened to the fate of the poor in Central America.[335]

On September 14, 1958, just a month after his release from prison, Lee was with his unit aboard an attack cargo ship, the USS *Skagit*, which steamed out of Yokosuka for the South China Sea.[336] The occasion was the shelling of the disputed offshore islands Quemoy and Matsu by the Chinese army, who regarded them as Chinese territory although they were occupied by the Nationalist Chinese forces settled on Taiwan (or Formosa, the Japanese name it was often called then). A week later, Coffee Mill set up its radar bubble at P'ing-tung, North Taiwan, as part of an effort to forestall a major war between the two Chinese forces. Very little happened, although an air control officer at the site, Lieutenant Charles R. Rhodes, told author Epstein that MACS-1 soon discovered that their IFF (Identification Friend or Foe) codes had been seriously compromised. When Chinese pilots were challenged to identify themselves, they obligingly sent back codes that identified them as friendly, allowing them to sail right through the airspace MACS-1 was trying to control. "We really caught hell about that," Rhodes told Epstein.[337]

One night Rhodes, on duty as officer-of-the-guard, heard several shots from one of the guard posts. He ran to it, drawing his .45 caliber pistol, and found Oswald slumped against a tree with his rifle on his lap. "When I got to him he was shaking and crying," Rhodes told Epstein. "He said he had seen men in the woods and that he challenged them and then started shooting." Rhodes put his arm around Oswald and walked him slowly back to his tent. "He kept saying he just couldn't bear guard duty." A few days later, on October 6, Oswald was sent back to Japan by plane for "medical treatment." Rhodes suspected that Oswald had staged the shooting incident with the hope of being sent back to Japan, which he liked. "There was nothing dumb about Oswald," Rhodes said.[338]

Oswald was also, however, trying to cope with a dose of the clap. On September 16, just after embarking from Atsugi for Taiwan on September 14, he had reported to sick bay with a discharge and slight burning sensation in the urethra. The doctor took a smear, and the official diagnosis was that organisms were detected "resembling neisseria gonococci" (almost certainly gonorrhea, a disease that was nearly a rite of passage for millions of young men in those years), and that Oswald had "urethritis, acute, due to gonococcus" with a "slight discharge and a stinging sensation on urination." The origin was listed, strangely, as "in line of duty [in line of duty?], not due to own misconduct." But the Marine captain who interpreted Oswald's medical record on this matter for the Warren Commission was unable, either because of his lack of knowledge or the ambiguity of the records, to explicitly tell the Commission whether or not Oswald had actually contracted gonorrhea, though he said, "We *assume* he had gonorrhea," and Oswald was given antibiotics for gonorrhea.[339] The infection was tenacious, resisting treatment by several different antibiotics,[340] and it is probable the doctor thought that Oswald would get better care in a hospital in Japan than could be provided in what was a very hastily assembled temporary camp in Taiwan.

The day after Oswald's arrival back at Atsugi from Taiwan on October 5, he was assigned to "Sub-Unit 1" of MAG-11, apparently a rear guard unit that had not gone with the rest of the squadron to Taiwan, and the following day Oswald entered the Atsugi Station Hospital, where he remained from October 7 to October 13 to receive treatment for his gonorrhea.[341]

Two weeks later he departed Yokosuka, on November 2, aboard the USS *Barrett*, and arrived in San Francisco on November 15. His tour of foreign duty was over.[342] He had about a year left to serve on his enlistment, but he had already hatched a new plan, one in accordance with his brother Robert's perception of him: try a job, fail, do something dramatic. He was planning to defect to the Soviet Union.

In November of 1959, when he had been in Moscow for several weeks, Oswald told journalist Priscilla Johnson McMillan, "For two years I have been waiting to do this one thing"—that is, to defect.[343] Two years before that date he was still with his unit in the Philippines, and even if the plan began in fantasy, he had plenty of time to brood over it, particularly during his weeks in the brig. McMillan says that he also told Marina that he had been exposed to Soviet propaganda in Japan, both in the form of people who were pro-Soviet and in Soviet magazines. "Soviet propaganda," he would tell Marina, "works well."[344]

Though he may have begun laying his plans to defect while still in Japan, he kept the fact well to himself. Four days after he arrived in San Francisco for processing at the receiving station, he went on leave, taking a bus to Fort Worth. Again he stayed with Marguerite but spent a lot of time at Robert and Vada's place on Davenport Street. He had just missed seeing his half brother John Pic and his family, who about a month earlier had passed through Fort Worth on their way to John's new duty station in Japan.[345] It had been six years since he had last seen John in New York, and it would be another three before the three brothers would be together again.

The vacation was uneventful, and Lee apparently revealed nothing of his new cast of mind to his brother. He visited the farm at least twice and hunted squirrels and rabbits with a .22 rifle. Three days before Christmas, 1958, Lee arrived at his new duty station in El Toro, California. Lee's new unit, Marine Air Control Squadron No. 9 (MACS-9), was attached to the Third Marine Aircraft Wing at Marine Corps Air Station at El Toro.[346] He had once been stationed briefly at El Toro while awaiting transfer to Japan, but this time he went back to work in his specialty, aircraft surveillance, as an aviation electronics operator ("scope dope"), to use the jargon of the era.[347] His actual duty station was an old blimp base, LTA (Lighter Than Air), under the administration of El Toro but about ten miles away in Santa Ana. Fixed-wing aircraft flew out of El Toro, while the old LTA base was now being used principally by helicopters, which were housed in two of the largest wooden hangars ever constructed.[348] Oswald's work there was the same as his work in Japan, with the significant difference being that no one expected enemy planes to penetrate the airspace of sprawling, wealthy, conservative Orange County, which bridged the tract home suburbs of San Diego to the south and Los Angeles to the north. With the exception of a few days when his squadron was sent to Yuma on the Arizona-California border for air defense exercises, Oswald would serve out the remainder of his enlistment at Santa Ana.[349]

It was deadly boring duty. "All we did was look at radar screens," a fellow marine named Mack Osborne commented. "It was the sort of work a left-handed monkey could do . . . The only thing to do at that base was to play around."[350]

It was clear to all of his mates that Oswald was now concentrating on learning Russian—he would sit in his room for hours on end poring over Russian newspapers bought in Los Angeles and a Russian-English dictionary,[351] but when he took the Marine Corps proficiency test in Russian on February 25, 1959, less than two months after his arrival, he scored a minus 5 on understanding, which meant he got five more answers wrong than he got right; 4 on reading, four more answers right than wrong; and 3 on writing. His composite score for the entire test was 2. His marks were rated as "poor" in all categories.[352] However, since the test was designed to assess the proficiency of native speakers and students at the military's rigorous language schools, and Oswald had apparently acquired the language entirely on his own, his grades were not that bad. He apparently had the rudiments of the language and a base on which to build. It was also apparent that he must have been studying for some time before he arrived in Santa Ana, mainly in Japan. "I remember that Oswald could speak a little Russian," says Paul Murphy, who served with Oswald at Atsugi.[353] Most of the marines who knew him at Santa Ana were aware of—and amused or even awed by—his studies and predilection. They often kidded him, calling him "Oswaldovich," and he enjoyed it, answering their questions with "*da*" and "*nyet*" and addressing them as "comrade,"[354] while at the same time referring, seriously, to "American capitalist warmongers."[355] Oswald took it in good humor when some of the guys accused him of being a Russian spy.[356] When he and Richard Call played chess, Oswald always took the red chessmen because he said he preferred the "red army."[357] On the other hand, one of Oswald's superior officers said he never heard Oswald "confess" to being a Communist or say he "thought about being a Communist."[358]* Many of the men who served with Oswald at LTA Santa Ana recalled a Russian-language paper Oswald read, and one was certain that Oswald read the American Communist Party paper, the *Daily Worker*.[359]

According to Epstein, Oswald subscribed to a Russian-language newspaper as well as the *People's World*—a publication of the Trotskyist Socialist Workers Party—and the arrival of the papers caused consternation in the mailroom. When mail clerks brought it to the attention of Captain Robert E. Block, the operations officer, Block asked Oswald about it. Oswald blithely explained that he was merely carrying out Marine Corps policy of getting to know the enemy. Block knew he was being conned but didn't make an issue of it.[360] The only conclusion one can come to is that Oswald's Marine superiors, in never curtailing or giving Oswald any trouble over his Soviet affinity, must have concluded that the lowly, eccentric private, on his way out of the military anyway, could not possibly be a security risk. Besides, Oswald wasn't being secretive. He was advertising his pro-Soviet sentiments.

On March 9, Oswald was promoted back to private first class, the appointment retroactive to the first of that month,[361] but it seems not to have encouraged him to make a fresh start in the corps. Although he would attract no further disciplinary action, the unofficial record is strewn with instances of his wiseguy attitude, almost always accompanied by pursed lips and a petulant expression on his face that people up until his death often referred to as a smirk. He frequently baited his superiors (noncommissioned officers and officers) by asking them questions on foreign affairs about which he already knew they were uninformed, all to demonstrate he knew more than they did; was deliberately sloppy, including not shining his shoes; would sleep late; wear his hat as low over his head as possible to avoid having to look at anyone; and engage in other acts of recalcitrance and rebellion against an existence in the Marines he analogized to being like George Orwell's *1984* with its mythical leader Big Brother.[362] Oswald's marks for conduct and proficiency continued to hover during this period barely at the threshold of acceptability.[363]

That spring a young officer, Lieutenant John E. Donovan, joined Oswald's radar squadron. Donovan was a 1956 graduate of Georgetown University's School of Foreign Service, a background that attracted Oswald's interest. Donovan often chatted with Oswald, especially on long night-watches, when they had to stay on duty until the last plane came in, often with little to do but talk. Donovan thought Oswald competent in all the jobs he was called on to do—surveilling unidentified aircraft or planes in distress, plotting on the board, relaying information to air force and navy radar sites, et cetera—and he did not hesitate to let Oswald serve as crew chief when neither of the two sergeants normally entrusted with that responsibility were available. He also found Oswald fairly bright and surprisingly well versed in foreign affairs, and Oswald would take great pride

*Most of the former squad mates whom the Warren Commission took testimony or affidavits from were only with Oswald in Santa Ana, not Japan. Of three squad mates who were stationed with Oswald at Atsugi, one never mentioned one way or the other whether he had heard of Oswald's pro-Russian and anti-American bent (8 H 318, WC affidavit of John Rene Heindel), and another said, "I never heard Oswald make any anti-American or pro-Communist statements" (8 H 317, WC affidavit of Peter Francis Connor). However, as indicated, fellow marine Paul Murphy did say that Oswald spoke "a little Russian" in Japan (8 H 320, WCT affidavit of Paul Edward Murphy).

in his ability to mention not only the leader of a country but five or six subordinates in that country who held positions of importance. Donovan was less impressed by Oswald's knowledge of philosophy, although he knew many philosophers' names. "It was obvious," Donovan said, "that he often knew the names and that was it." Donovan was also aware of Oswald's high opinion of himself and his sense of grievance that the Marine Corps did not recognize his talent, even without the magic college degree, and place him in a position of prominence in the corps. "There is something wrong," he told Donovan, "when I have more intelligence and more knowledge" than the men "that are leading us." Donovan suggested that if Lee felt he had the necessary qualities—and Donovan seemed to think he had—that he put in for noncommissioned officer leadership school, or even leave the corps, get a commission as an officer, and reenter the service.[364]

Donovan said that Oswald played end on the squadron football team and would quite often argue with the quarterback in a huddle as to what play should be called. Some of the players reported to Donovan that if a play was called that was not to Oswald's liking, he would slack off on that play. Because he was not getting along with the other players, Donovan had to drop Oswald from the team.[365]

Another marine, Nelson Delgado, also saw Oswald in heated discussions with officers. "He didn't like the immediate people over him . . . All of them weren't as intelligent as he was in his estimation," Delgado recalled. "They'd be talking about . . . politics, which came up quite frequently during the break . . . and I would say . . . Oswald had them stumped about four out of five times. They just ran out of words, they couldn't come back, you know . . . He thought himself quite proficient with current events and politics . . . He used to cut up anyone who was high-ranking, and make himself come out top dog."

Delgado, who said Oswald always had a "very sarcastic sneer" on his face, also noticed that Oswald was a poor loser. "Whenever he got in a conversation that wasn't going his way he would just get mad, he'd just walk off, you know, and leave." When Warren Commission counsel asked Delgado if he spotted "any homosexual tendencies" in Oswald, Delgado responded, "No, never once . . . In fact we had two fellows in our outfit that were caught at it, and he [Oswald] thought it was kind of disgusting that they were in the same outfit with us."[366]

Delgado told the Warren Commission that "anything, anything that [Oswald's superiors] told him to do, he found a way to argue it to a point where both him and the man giving him the order both got disgusted and mad at each other . . . For him there was always another way of doing things."

Question: "He didn't take too well to orders that were given to him?"

"No, he didn't."[367]

In addition to reading *Mein Kampf* and *Das Kapital*, Oswald told Delgado about this other unnamed book he was reading, one that provided one of the few lighthearted moments at the hearings of the Warren Commission. Delgado told an amused Wesley Liebeler, who was questioning him, that the book was "about a farm, and about how all the animals take over and make the farmer work for them. It's really a weird book, the way he was explaining it to me, and that struck me as kind of funny. But he told me the farmer represented the imperialistic world, and the animals were the workers, symbolizing that they are the socialist people, you know, and that eventually it will come about that the socialists will have the imperialists working for them."

Liebeler informed Delgado of the name of the book.

"The *Animal Farm*," Delgado mused. "Is that a socialist book?"

"No," Liebeler said.

"That is just the way *you* interpret it, right?" Delgado said.

"Yes, I think so," the Commission counsel replied. "It is actually supposed to be quite an anticommunist book . . . Didn't Oswald tell you," Liebeler asked, that after "the pigs took over the farm . . . they got to be just like the capitalists before?"

"No," Delgado said. "Just that the pigs and animals had revolted and made the farmer work for them."[368]

If Oswald read the whole book, he almost undoubtedly would think about it when he eventually saw firsthand what happened to Lenin's revolution of 1917—that the only solution was not revolution, but a surgical operation on human nature.

The book may have also contributed to one of the few jokes ever ascribed to Oswald. Master Sergeant Spar, Oswald's section chief, in calling a bunch of marines to him, had said, "All right everybody, gather around." Oswald muttered in a thick Russian accent, "Ah, ha, collective farm lecture."[369]

Of the many events under the rubric of foreign affairs that were current in 1958—the Algerian War, the coming to power of Archbishop Makarios against British rule in Cyprus, the bold new economic goals for overtaking the West by the Soviet Union's premier and party secretary, Nikita Khrushchev—the one that absorbed Oswald most by far was Fidel Castro's successful revolution in Cuba. Donovan found nothing untoward in Oswald's sympathetic support of Castro (who at that time was not known as a Communist) and his burgeoning revolution—many Americans, including *Time* magazine and Harvard University, agreed with him in those first months that it was a godsend that somebody had overthrown the Cuban dictator, Fulgencio Batista.[370]

Because of Oswald's passion for the Cuban Revolution, he was interested in Delgado, the Brooklyn-born Puerto Rican who was a fellow radar operator, because Delgado was proficient in Spanish—he not only spoke it at home but also had studied it in high school. The first time they met, just before Christmas 1958, they talked about the news from Cuba, where the revolution coming down from the Sierra Maestra mountains was just coming to a head. On New Year's Day 1959, Batista fled Havana, and Castro's victorious forces rolled into the Cuban capital. The two young men, both nineteen, continued to discuss the Cuban Revolution and imagined going there to take part. They were particularly fascinated by an American adventurer, William Morgan, who had been dishonorably discharged from the American army but went on to become a hero of Castro's revolutionary army, earning the battlefield rank of major.[371]

Delgado, Oswald's squad leader, got to know Oswald well and described him (when he wasn't fighting or arguing) as a "very quiet, intellectual young man. A loner, who liked to listen to classical music and play chess." Someone who believed "our present form of government didn't have anything to offer to the common people, and he resented our way of life, you know."[372]

That spring of 1959, on May 5, the men in the company who weren't noncommissioned officers went out to the firing range to qualify again with the M-1 rifle. Oswald's score dropped from a 212 (sharpshooter) two and a half years before to a 191, just barely qualifying him as a marksman. Throughout the years, most conspiracy theorists have ignored Oswald's score of 212, only mentioning his 191 (which, after all, still meant he qualified with the M-1 rifle) for the proposition that Oswald was a poor shot and, hence, could not have achieved what the authorities said he did in Dealey Plaza. I wanted to put this in its proper perspective for the jury in London, particularly since I knew defense counsel Gerry Spence would call Delgado, if I didn't, to repeat his Warren Commission testimony that Oswald's performance "was a pretty big joke." Delgado said that Oswald got a lot of "Maggie's drawers" (when one misses the target completely, and at the pits behind the target they wave a red flag from left to right).[373] So I called Delgado as my own witness. Delgado conceded that although he viewed himself as a good shot, he had only fired a 192. More importantly, and as previously indicated, he acknowledged what is well known, that in the U.S. Army and the Marine Corps, one's score on the rifle range when "shooting for the record" is very important, that promotion during one's military career "is going to be based, in part, upon that." It's so important, in fact, that if you don't qualify, "you have to start basic training all over again." When Oswald fired for the record at the beginning of his military career, when his score would be very important to him, we know he fired a 212. But at Santa Ana, Oswald was about to be released from the Marines and therefore his performance on the range no longer meant anything to him. When I asked, "So you got the impression that he wasn't even trying on the range, is that right?" Delgado answered, "Yes." He said Oswald demonstrated his lack of interest by not taking care of his rifle like his fellow marines did, and he, as Oswald's squad leader, would get in trouble because the gigs (demerits for minor infractions) Oswald got were a reflection on him. When I asked Delgado if he felt Oswald "could have done better [on the range] if he tried," he responded, "Right," and said that he did not attribute his relatively poor showing on the range in Santa Ana to his being a poor shot.[374]

Another marine who became friends with Oswald around this time at Santa Ana was Kerry Thornley, an acting corporal who was in a different squadron (Thornley in MACS-4, Oswald in MACS-9) but barracked next to Oswald, and they'd talk off-duty. Thornley was someone on whom Oswald made a vivid impression. When, months later, news of Oswald's defection to the USSR reached Thornley, he realized that he had the subject for a novel—the story of a marine disillusioned by experiences in Japan who defects to the Soviet Union. The novel, *The Idle Warriors*, was completed but still unpublished by the time of the assassination—and in fact it would not be published in full until 1991.

"My first memory of him," Thornley told the Warren Commission, "is that one afternoon he was sitting on a bucket out in front of a hut, an inverted bucket, with some other marines. They were discussing religion . . . It was known already in the outfit that I was an atheist. Immediately somebody pointed out to me that Oswald was also an atheist." Oswald took no offense at the remark. Instead, he asked Thornley with a little grin, "What do you think of Communism?" Being an atheist obviously didn't necessarily mean one was a Communist (though the converse would almost necessarily be so), and Thornley told Oswald he "didn't think too much of Communism." Oswald replied, "Well, I think the best religion is Communism." Thornley said he "got the impression that he said this in order to shock. He was playing to the galleries I felt."[375]

They were an odd couple, united by amorphous leftist views—by 1964 Thornley had no compunction about describing himself to the Warren Commission as an "extreme rightist" or libertarian, but at the time of his brief acquaintance with Oswald he was still thinking of himself as a radical leftist, an example of the observation that people on the opposite fringes of the political spectrum are closer to each other than to those in the middle. Thornley was under no illusions as to Oswald's views. "Definitely he thought that Communism was the best—that the Marxist morality was the most rational morality to follow that he knew of. And that Communism was the best system in the world."[376]

For all of Oswald's talk, Thornley thought that Oswald's Communism was largely theoretical, even "idle." Oswald, he judged, "'was not militant,' the type who would be 'storming the Bastille, so to speak.'" In other words, he didn't think Oswald would get personally involved in trying to overthrow this country by force or violence. "I don't think he felt he had to do that. I think he felt that would inevitably happen some day and he was just getting into the swing of things by doing this his way. I don't think he felt that he could do much to promote the Communist cause or hinder it."[377]

From a personal standpoint, Thornley thought Oswald to be "extremely unpredictable," with a "definite tendency toward irrationality at times, an emotional instability." He said Oswald "got along with very few people" in the unit and "seemed to guard against developing real close relationships."[378]

Throughout early 1959, Nelson Delgado shared Oswald's enthusiasm for the Cuban Revolution and Castro, whom he wholeheartedly supported, and he played along with Oswald's fantasies—they were going to leave the corps and go to Cuba, where, unlike their hero William Morgan, they would even have the benefit of honorable discharges. They believed Delgado's speaking Spanish would be useful, and Oswald had ideas of how a government should be run much in tune with Castro's, so they would become officers and lead expeditions to the other islands in the Caribbean still under the yoke of tyranny, get rid of Trujillo in the Dominican Republic, and so on.[379]

When Oswald asked Delgado how one could get close to the Cubans, and Delgado told him, "The best way to be trusted is to know their language, know their customs," and offered to teach him Spanish, Oswald took him up on it, bought a paperback Spanish-English dictionary, and really worked at it. Before long, he was speaking and understanding at least rudimentary Spanish. "He could speak a common Spanish like 'How are you? I am doing fine. Where are you going? Which way is this?'"[380] When Oswald kept asking Delgado further questions on how to get in touch with the Cubans, Delgado, at a loss, suggested the Cuban embassy. Eventually, Oswald told him that he had, indeed, gotten in touch with the Cubans, but Delgado thought Oswald was fibbing—that is, until one day when he went into Oswald's room to borrow a tie and noticed a letter from Los Angeles addressed to Oswald in his open footlocker. It had an official Cuban government seal and "he was telling me there was a Cuban Consul [there]" and he "was in contact with them."[381]

One Friday night shortly thereafter, Delgado was waiting for his train to Los Angeles in the Santa Ana station when Oswald walked in. Delgado spent every other weekend in Los Angeles, but to his knowledge Oswald never left the base—"He always had money, you know, he never spent it. He was pretty tight." Delgado recalled that when they went to movies on the base, "nine times out of ten I ended up paying for it."[382] The two chatted amiably on the trip up to Los Angeles but never discussed where Oswald was going or why, and they parted company on arrival. Later Delgado learned that Oswald did not stay for the weekend but returned on Saturday night. Delgado was curious about where Oswald had gone because he normally dressed casually in sport shirts, but on that occasion he wore a dark suit, white shirt, and tie.[383]

Around the same time that Oswald began to receive much more mail than he had before, he had an odd visitor at the main gate. The man must have been a civilian, otherwise the guards at the gate would have let him in, and it must have been after nine at night, because civilians could not come on the base after that hour. Delgado and Oswald were both on guard duty that night, so Delgado had to persuade a marine to relieve Oswald for a few minutes. Oswald spent a very long time in conversation with the visitor at the gate, a lot more than an hour, while the marine who relieved Oswald bitched constantly at Delgado to get Oswald back on the job. Delgado connected this visit in his mind to Oswald's letters from the Cuban consulate, although he had no real evidence for that.[384]

It wasn't too long before Delgado started to have questions about Castro. Like many Americans, Delgado was increasingly disturbed by the direction the Cuban Revolution was taking, and the show trials and executions reported in the American press rapidly cooled his ardor for Castro. "I couldn't see that," Delgado said, "when they started executing these people on just word of mouth."* Oswald, though, dismissed the news reports as biased, distortions of the facts, retaliations for the fact that the Cubans had stemmed the outflow of profits to the United States. Delgado didn't buy that.[385] It was clear to Delgado that Oswald revered Castro, was obsessed with him, and thought he was a great man.[386]

Some of the things Oswald wanted to talk about were becoming distinctly odd. He wondered where someone who committed a crime in the United States might be safe from extradition—although why he thought nineteen-year-old Delgado could provide sound advice on that score is a question. Delgado guessed that, apart from Cuba and the Soviet Union, a criminal might be safe in Argentina. Oswald then showed him a safe route for defecting to the Soviet Union—he believed you could evade official interference by going through Mexico and Cuba, something that he had apparently learned from stories about two other defectors. He even sketched a map of the route on a piece of scrap paper.[387]

It finally dawned on Delgado that all this was something more than the usual barrack's bull. Oswald was really making plans, and "that's when I started getting scared." Delgado even put in for a transfer to another barrack in order to put some distance between himself and Oswald, although Oswald was gone before any such change came through.[388]

There was one other incident that stuck in Delgado's mind, a trip to Tijuana, the big border town in Mexico just south of San Diego that was a favorite haunt for randy servicemen. In late May or early June, a couple of marines offered to pay for the gas if Delgado would drive them down there. To his surprise, Oswald agreed to go along—he had never taken up any of Delgado's invitations to accompany him to Los Angeles or anywhere else. After wandering around and drinking in a few of the night spots in downtown Tijuana, Oswald said, "Let's go to the Flamingo." The club was about two miles out in the country, but Oswald was able to tell Delgado how to get there and where to turn, as though he had been there before. No one recognized Oswald there, but he did seem to know his way around, which was odd because it was Delgado's impression that his buddy, who was so assiduously trying to save money, never left the base.[389]

Other than the Tijuana visit, the trip on the train to LA, two dates in Santa Ana that had been arranged by a squad mate who thought Oswald would like to meet his attractive aunt, an airline stewardess who was studying Russian preparing for a U.S. Department of State foreign-language test,[390] and one time to apply for a passport, there doesn't seem to be any other evidence of Oswald leaving his El Toro base in eight months.

One of Oswald's fellow marines, Mack Osborne, once asked Oswald why he never went off base, and Oswald told him he was saving his money "because one day he would do something which would make him famous."[391]†

---

*At the trial in London, Delgado said that Castro ended up executing an American, Major Morgan, who had assisted him in the revolution, and whom Oswald and he had spoken of emulating, and that execution in particular disillusioned Delgado about Castro (Transcript of *On Trial*, July 24, 1986, p.593–594).

†A much more famous remark of this nature has been attributed to Oswald, but he may not have made it. Kerry Thornley told the Warren Commission that Oswald "looked upon history as God. He looked upon the eyes of future people as some kind of tribunal, and he wanted to be on the winning side so that ten thousand

At some point after Oswald's probable contacts with the Cuban embassy or consulate in Los Angeles, he abruptly mentioned other plans to Delgado—to attend a college in Switzerland.[392] As early as March 19, he had applied to Albert Schweitzer College in Churwalden, Switzerland, a small institution in the central canton of Graubünden that specialized in religion, ethics, science, and literature. He wrote to the school that he hoped to attend it for the third term, running from April 12 to June 27, 1960. Still only nineteen, he gave his age as twenty (possibly because he would be that age by the starting date), described his occupation as "student," and claimed fluency in Russian equal to a year's schooling. He boldly lied that he had completed high school by correspondence with an 85 percent average, equal to a B+. His special interests, he wrote, were "Philosophy, Psychology, Ideology" and "Football, baseball, tennis, Stamp collecting." His private reading consisted of "Jack London, Darwin, Norman V. Peal, Sciencetific books, Philosophy, ect." He had taken part in a "Student body movement in school for controll of Juvenile Delinquency" and claimed membership in "Y.M.C.A. and A.Y.A. associations." His vocational interest was "To be a short story writer on contemporary American life."[393]

He wished to attend Albert Schweitzer "in order to aquire a fuller understanding of that subject which interest me most, Philosophy. To meet with Europeans who can broaden my scope of understanding. To recive formal Education by Instructers of high standing and character. To broaden my knowledge of German and to live in a healthy climate and Good Moral atmosphere." He also claimed, "I do speak a very little German" and gave the names of two fellow marines as his references.[394] He was accepted, and on June 19 he sent the college a letter enclosing his registration fee of twenty-five dollars.[395] In the meantime, on March 23, he took steps to cover his lack of a high school diploma by taking a General Educational Development (GED) test from the Armed Forces Institute, often accepted by colleges in lieu of the diploma. The standard scores on five tests were correlated to a percentile of the population: in English literature, on which he scored best, he placed in the 34th percentile; in English composition, in the 76th; in social sciences, in the 69th; in physical science, in the 79th; and in mathematics, in the 58th percentile. The results were then reduced to three grades, unsatisfactory, satisfactory, and with distinction—Lee passed, being rated satisfactory.[396]

Since Oswald's passion for Castro and the Cuban Revolution was white-hot at the time, his intention to attend the staid Albert Schweitzer College is jarring to say the least, and cannot be taken at face value. On the other hand, it is equally hard to see, if it were all a ruse, what the purpose of that ruse would be.

On June 6, Lee wrote to his brother Robert, "Well, pretty soon I'll be getting out of the corp and I know what I want to be and how Im going to do it, which I guess is the most important thing in life." He offered, however, no further details.[397]

At that time, Lee did not expect to leave the Marine Corps until December 8, 1959, six long months later, since the forty-five days of his confinement in the brig had to be added to the term of his enlistment, which otherwise would have been up on October 24.[398] But something that offered a quicker out occurred to him. The previous December, while Lee was home on leave, Marguerite had injured herself while working at the candy counter at the Fair Ridgelea store in Fort Worth. She had dropped a large glass jar

years from now people would look in the history books and say 'Well, this man was ahead of his time.'" Oswald, he said, "was concerned with his image in history." (11 H 97–98) From the context it is not clear whether Thornley came up with the ten-thousand-year observation himself, or Oswald mentioned it to him first.

of candy while trying to get it from a shelf above her head, and it hit her on the nose.[399] Marguerite had presented a workman's compensation claim[400] that she was getting nowhere with, and wrote Lee to tell him of her woes. In her letter he saw his opportunity to get an early discharge. He wrote back,

> Dear Mother
> Recived yur letter and was very unhappy to hear of your troubles, I contacted the Red Cross on the base here, and told them about it. They will send someone out to the house to see you, when they do please tell them everything they want to know, as I am trying to secure an Early (hardship) discharge *in order to help you* such a discharge is only rarely given, but If they know you are unable to support yourself than they will release me from the U.S.M.C. *and I will be able to come home and help you.*

He went on to stress the importance of making the "right impresstion" on the visitor from the Red Cross and suggested that she make it clear that "I have been your only source of income."[401]

That was pure scam, since he had not been a source of any income to her, much less the only one, but he immediately moved to give that claim some credibility by opening, on July 22, two allotments to her from his service pay, a Q Class and a D Class allotment. The latter was a fixed amount deducted from the serviceman's pay and sent directly by the government to whomever the serviceman designated. The Q allotment could be made only to dependents, and the government, after verifying the dependency, contributed part of the amount. Marguerite would receive her first—and last—monthly checks for August, $91.30 on the Q allotment and $40.00 on the D.[402]

Though it had all started from the injury to Marguerite's nose that her son Robert noticed, "a little swelling" in the upper part,[403] Marguerite rose to the occasion, supplying Lee with compelling documentation to use with his application for an early discharge. When he filed for a dependency (popularly known as a hardship) discharge on August 17, he attached a letter from Marguerite's attorney and two affidavits from friends, one of whom stated that Marguerite's doctors had told her that "there is no cure for her." The other friend noted that Marguerite "was very nervous and has a great deal of trouble breathing." Both stated that her health did not permit her to hold down a job. Her doctor, a doctor of osteopathy, described her condition as "traumatic arthritis of tempero-mandibular and cervical joints and also right maxillary sinusitis and 5th cranial nerve neuritis." Marguerite's affidavit stated that as a result of her injury she had for awhile received disability payments of twenty-one dollars a week, but they had been discontinued because the insurance company doctors thought there was nothing wrong with her. With no income she had to sell all her furnishings for two hundred dollars and work for two weeks as a housekeeper at twenty-one dollars a week plus room and board, but had to quit because her employer was a drunk. She was incapable of holding an eight-hour-a-day job because she could not breathe or sleep at night, and "also, I must constantly blow my nose." Neither of her two older sons, Robert or John, were able to help her because they had families of their own. "I have no money to use for living expenses and I must have my son at home now to provide for me."[404]

It worked. The application passed up the chain of command swiftly, and on August 28, 1959, the Dependency Discharge Board recommended that Oswald "be released from active duty . . . for reasons of dependency."[405] When the men in Oswald's squadron learned about his mother's financial hardship, they offered to pitch in, but Oswald turned down their offer.[406]

On September 4, he was transferred out of MACS-9 to the H & HS MCAS Squadron, which would process the discharge.[407] That same day he left the base to apply at the Superior Court in Santa Ana for a passport. He gave as his purpose for travel "to attend the college of A. Schweitzer, Chur, Switzerland, and the Uni of Turku, Turku, Finland. To vist [visit] all other country as a tourist." His proposed destinations were Cuba, the Dominican Republic, England, France, Switzerland, Germany, Finland, and Russia; his length of stay four months. He expected to depart from New Orleans by ship on the Grace Lines on September 21.[408]

The passport, requested on September 4, was granted on September 10, 1959.[409] The next day, September 11, Lee Oswald was released from active duty* on a "Dependency Discharge" and was on his way home to Fort Worth.[410]

Lee arrived at Marguerite's apartment in Fort Worth at two in the morning on September 14. Marguerite wanted to stay up and talk about their future, but Lee said they could talk in the morning. She set up half of a studio couch in her tiny apartment for him, and in the morning, Marguerite, who was not working because of her "injury" at work, excitedly told Lee of her plan to find a better place with more room for them. "We will be able to manage," she said. "I can babysit or pick up a few dollars," and Lee could "get a job." But Lee had no intention of staying in Fort Worth or, for that matter, helping to support her. He told her he was going to get a job on a cargo ship. She was let down and didn't like the idea, even when he proposed a crafty inducement—he would make much more money on a ship than he could hope to make in Fort Worth and would consequently be able to send money home to her.[411]

Lee spent a day with Robert and Vada at their house, where they did little but sit and talk, but he told them a different story from what he had told Marguerite. He was going to New Orleans to work for an export firm—no mention of shipping out himself. Late that afternoon they went out to the yard to take pictures. Cathy, Robert and Vada's two-year-old, wanted to show her uncle her birthday present, the swings Robert had erected in the backyard. The photo Robert took of Lee and little Cathy shows a decent-looking, smiling young man with a trim haircut, well dressed in shined shoes, slacks with a razor-sharp crease, and a plaid sport shirt, holding a blissful toddler in his arms amid the lengthening shadows. He looks like a young man with a real future.[412]

Oswald moved quickly. The same day he had arrived in Fort Worth he registered his dependency discharge and transfer to the Marine Corps Reserve with the Selective Service Board in Fort Worth. Two days later, on September 16, he emerged from Marguerite's kitchen with his suitcase and told her he was leaving for New Orleans. He showed Marguerite his passport, gave her a hundred dollars, and ignored her entreaties.

"Lee, why don't you stay?" she said, "we can get along" financially.

"Mother, I am off," he said, and left.[413]

The following day he presented himself at a New Orleans travel agency, Travel Consultants Inc., where he answered questions for a "Passenger Immigration Questionnaire,"

---

*He was transferred to the Marine Corps Reserve, in which he was expected to serve until December 8, 1962, his unit headquartered at the Naval Air Station in Glenview, Illinois (WR, pp.688–689; Folsom Exhibit No. 1, 19 H 679).

giving his occupation as "shipping export agent" and saying he would be abroad for two months on a pleasure trip. He booked passage on SS *Marion Lykes*, due to leave for Le Havre, France, the next day, and paid his one-way fare, apparently in cash, of $220.75.[414] The travel agent, Lewis Hopkins, thought him ill-informed about travel in Europe and, had he known where Oswald really intended to go, could and would have recommended a ship that would have docked at a port more convenient to Russia than Le Havre.[415] That night Lee registered at the Liberty Hotel on South Liberty Street in New Orleans.[416]

The next afternoon, still carrying his simple suitcase, he boarded the *Lykes* docked at "Army Base Berth 2" in New Orleans. The departure was delayed until early the next morning, 6:24 a.m. on September 20.[417] Before departing, Lee posted a letter to Marguerite:

> Dear Mother:
> Well, I have booked passage on a ship to Europe, I would of had to sooner or later and I think It's best I go now. Just remember above all else that my values are very different from Robert's or your's. It is difficult to tell you how I feel, Just remember this is what I must do. I did not tell you about my plans because you could harly be expected to understand.
> I did not see aunt Lilian while I was here. I will write again as soon as I land.
>
> Lee[418]

The *Lykes* was a freighter that, as many such ships did, also provided a half-dozen cabins for passengers, and there were three others on this crossing: a retired army officer and his wife, and a boy who had just graduated from high school in Midland, Texas, and was on his way to France to continue his education in Tours and Paris.[419]

Eighteen-year-old Billy Joe Lord and nineteen-year-old Lee Oswald were assigned to the same cabin, introduced to each other by a ship's officer, and left to their devices. Billy Joe found Lee "standoffish" and even unfriendly. Although they didn't "hit it off," they were thrown together for the next two weeks, and Billy Joe heard that Lee was recently separated from the Marine Corps where he worked with radar, was planning to travel in Europe, possibly to attend school in Sweden or Switzerland, and would probably return to the United States to get a job. He mentioned with some bitterness that his mother had to work in a drugstore in Fort Worth and was having a hard time, but oddly, they did not discuss politics. Lee got off on another hobbyhorse, though, possibly because he noticed Billy Joe's Bible. Lee informed his young cabin mate that there was no supreme being and that it should be apparent to anyone with intelligence that nothing existed but physical matter.[420]

The Churches, a couple in their forties, saw less of Oswald, since they met him only at dinner in the officers' mess, where they dined at the same table, and Lee missed a number of meals, possibly owing to seasickness. George B. Church Jr. had retired from the army as a lieutenant colonel and was teaching junior high school in Tampa. He thought Lee "rather withdrawn," and said Lee did not participate in any of the social activities onboard. But he did hear Lee talk of his plan to attend a college in Switzerland. He also heard that Lee was just out of the Marines and had not liked the service. Oswald apparently displayed his bitterness about the hard time his mother had suffered during the Depression of the 1930s, but Church himself had survived the Depression, along with millions of other Americans, an observation that apparently "made no impression" on his fellow passenger. Church indicated he wasn't too interested in getting to know Oswald.[421]

Mrs. Church made more of an effort but also found that Lee "did not enter into friendly conversations." She thought him "peculiar." Lee evaded naming the Swiss college he meant to attend and had no very clear educational goal in mind—Mrs. Church noted the contrast to Billy Joe, who worked on his French and was exuberant about his course of study and purpose in life. When Billy Joe dropped off at La Rochelle-Pallice, three days before the ship reached its final destination of La Havre, Mrs. Church got Billy Joe's address so she could send him Christmas cards, but only with some reluctance did Lee give her Marguerite's address in Fort Worth.[422]

Lee's sympathy for the workingman did not appear to extend to stewards—he rebuked Frank Mijares for not mopping the floor of his cabin to his satisfaction and failed to tip him when he left the ship after it berthed at the Cotton Dock in Le Havre on October 8, 1959.[423]

Oswald left Le Havre that day, and after an overnight trip, he entered England at Southampton on the ninth.[424] He told British custom officials there that he had seven hundred dollars and that he planned to remain in the UK only one week before going on to school in Switzerland,[425] but the next day, October 10, he flew on to Helsinki,* where he registered at the Torni Hotel, located in the center of the city, the same day. The following day he registered at another Helsinki hotel, the nearby Klaus Kurki,[426] where he stayed for five days and four nights.

What flight Oswald took out of London to Helsinki and what happened while he was in Helsinki are among the enduring puzzles of the assassin's history and fertile ground for conspiracy theorists who are convinced Oswald was a U.S. intelligence agent, and holes in a story can only be explained and filled in by conspiratorial mush. The first problem here was that the only direct flight from London to Helsinki that day, October 10, arrived too late in the evening, at 11:33 p.m., for Oswald to have cleared customs and checked into the Torni by midnight, which we know he did. But unhappily for the conspiracy theorists, this fact was brought to the Warren Commission's attention by Richard Helms, then deputy director of the CIA, someone whose agency most conspiracy theorists believe was involved in Kennedy's murder.[427] Moreover, the CIA failed to note that there were two indirect flights he could have taken out of London,[428] one through Copenhagen, which would have landed him in Helsinki at 5:05 in the afternoon, and the other through Stockholm, which arrived only a half hour later.[429] But Oswald's change of hotels is also curious, since there seems to have been no particular advantage to do so. The fact that the Torni and Klaus Kurki are each quality hotels seemingly beyond the finances of Oswald has also raised suspicions in some.[430]

More of a problem is that Oswald was issued a visa to the Soviet Union in just two days, which ostensibly seemed unlikely in that era. Oswald's passport is stamped with an exit visa showing he left London Airport on October 10,[431] which is highly unlikely to be wrong, so he probably did arrive in Helsinki that day, a Saturday, but not in time to deplane and get to the Soviet embassy at noon, when it closed for the weekend.[432] Thus, his first chance to apply for a visa at the Soviet consulate in Helsinki would have been Monday, October 12, 1959.[433] The questionnaire he filled out, probably at a Finnish travel agency,

*Where Oswald spent the night of October 9 is not known, but it's likely he spent it in an airport waiting room. The Warren Report (p.690) says, "On the same day [he arrived at Southampton] he flew to Helsinki," but the visas in his passport (CE 946, 18 H 162–163) showed that he arrived at Southampton on October 9 and left London Airport (now Heathrow) for Helsinki on October 10.

and that was handed in at the Soviet consulate in Helsinki and preserved by the KGB in Belarus, is dated in Oswald's hand, October 13.[434] And his six-day tourist visa was issued by the Consular Section of the Soviet embassy in Helsinki on October 14, just two days after he applied for it.[435] Passport stamps show his exit from Finland and entry into the Soviet Union on October 15.[436]

The problem of how Lee Oswald might have gained an entry visa for the Soviet Union in two days troubled the Warren Commission. J. Lee Rankin asked both the State Department and the CIA for information, and both told the Commission that it normally took five days to a week at the Helsinki embassy or elsewhere to obtain permission for any stay in Russia longer than twenty-four hours.[437] Eventually, the HSCA took up the question by reviewing classified information about Gregory Golub, the Soviet consul in Helsinki who issued Oswald's visa. Golub was suspected of being a KGB official—which was hardly surprising. But quite apart from the fact that if the KGB were facilitating Oswald's travel to Russia, why would it have taken Oswald even two days—why not only one—to get his visa, the HSCA came up with two communications from the American embassy in Helsinki to the State Department concerning Golub's handling of visas. The first disclosed that Golub had once told his counterparts at the American embassy during a luncheon conversation that "Moscow had given him the authority to give Americans visas without prior approval from Moscow." Golub stated that this would make his job much easier, and as long as he was convinced the American was "all right" he could give them a visa in a matter of minutes.[438] Here, Oswald being only nineteen, and listing his present job as "student," Golub probably had no trouble issuing the visa.[439]

A second dispatch, dated October 9, the day before Oswald's arrival in Helsinki, mentioned a case involving two American businessmen that occurred about a month earlier. The U.S. consul "advised them to go directly to Golub and make their request, which they did. Golub phoned [the U.S. consul] to state that he would give them their visas as soon as they made advance Intourist reservations. When they did this, Golub immediately gave them their visas."[440]

In addition to Golub's practices, Oswald, per a KGB official, also seems to have benefited from the fact that the Helsinki consulate was partial to granting visas to the Soviet Union owing to the "geographical proximity of Finland to the Soviet Union as well as the good relations between Intourist, the Soviet national travel bureau, and the local Finnish travel agencies."[441]

In any case, Oswald left Helsinki by train the following day, October 15, crossed the Finnish-Russian border at Vainikkala, and arrived in Moscow on October 16, 1959. He was met at the Leningradsky station by an Intourist representative who took him by car to the Hotel Berlin, where he registered as a student on a "five-day luxury" tour.[442] Very soon after his arrival he was introduced to the Intourist guide assigned to him for that period, a young Russian woman named Rimma Shirokova, who would take him sightseeing.[443]

Lee Oswald's dream of defecting to the Soviet Union, the plan he seems to have first contemplated two years before,[*] was within his grasp, and Rimma was going to play a part in it. He was on the eve of his twentieth birthday.

---

[*]Oswald told UPI reporter Aline Mosby in November in Moscow, "For two years I've had it in my mind, don't form any attachments, because I knew I was going away. I was planning to divest myself of everything to do with the United States. I've not just been thinking about it, but waiting to do it. For two years, saving my money" (CE 1385, 22 H 705).

Rimma Shirokova, slender, blond-haired, and good-looking, was only about two years older than Oswald. A student at Moscow's Foreign Language Institute, she spoke English, which was just as well, since Lee seemed to speak hardly passable Russian. She was surprised that a client on the "deluxe tour" (which meant that she would guide only him over the next few days—no group activities) looked so unprepossessing. Those who took the deluxe tour were usually rich and looked it. She started by listing all of the things they might do in the next five days and explained that she could get tickets for the theater or the ballet, but he seemed withdrawn and uninterested in anything she had to offer. Nevertheless, they went for a chauffeured drive around Moscow and they saw what Rimma regarded as the most important sights the city had to offer, like the Tretyakov Gallery, the cathedrals, and Red Square, saving the Kremlin, the highlight of the tour, for the afternoon.[444]

At midday, she dropped him back at the Hotel Berlin, where he lunched by himself, and she came back for him later, but he did not really want to see the Kremlin. They sat outdoors on a bench, where he began to talk a little about himself,[445] one of the few times in the detailed record where he seems to have wanted to do so. By contrast, the reports of conversations in which he railed about capitalist exploitation of the workingman are so numerous as to be almost unworthy of mention. On the other hand, this was the first time in his life where he realized that pontificating to someone about the evils of capitalism and virtues of Marxism would be about as pointless as watering one's lawn in the rain.

Rimma recalls his telling her that he was from Texas, had served in the Marine Corps, hated the loss of American life in war, and spoke about the unjust wars caused by U.S. imperialism. He gave her the distinct impression that he had been in combat, and he told her as well that his mother had remarried and was no longer interested in him. In fact, he said, no one was interested in him in America. Whatever he told her, it worked. She was moved by him and eager to help when he told her that he wanted to remain in the Soviet Union. That seemed natural enough to her—after all, she felt the Soviet Union was the best country on earth—but she was nonetheless surprised. She asked him for his motives and "he said that it was his political views. He said that he was a Communist. He [didn't] approve of the American way of life."[446]

Oswald set out his own recollection of the conversation in what he called his "Historic Diary" under the date of October 16, 1959, the day of his arrival: "I explain to her [Rimma] I wish to appli. for Rus. citizenship. She is flabbergassed but aggrees to help. She checks with her boss, main office Intour; then helps me add. a letter to Sup. Sovit asking for citizenship, mean while boss telephons passport & visa office and notifies them about me."[447]

The Historic Diary, Oswald's handwritten account of his life in Russia, was completed before he left that country. The earlier entries were probably written, according to Marina, some time after the particular event occurred and may have been reconstructed from notes Oswald made at the time. However, in Minsk, it is believed he kept a more contemporaneous record of his experiences.[448] The Warren Commission took the diary to be Oswald's own record of his feelings and impressions, but with future readers in mind, and hence, the Commission relied whenever possible on independent evidence.[449] The HSCA found Oswald's diary to be "generally credible."[450]

The "passport & visa office" Oswald mentions in his diary was the Visa and Registration Department (OVIR, hereinafter "Passport Office") of the Ministry of Internal Affairs (MVD).[451] The MVD was roughly equivalent to the American Justice Department. It was responsible for the enforcement of civil law (though not criminal, like the U.S. Department of Justice) and the administration of prisons and forced-labor camps.[452]

Rimma's boss at Intourist was not happy about her commitment to Oswald. "What have you done?" he barked. "He came as a tourist. Let him be a tourist."[453] Unfortunately for Lee, and ultimately for history, the Soviet Union was not particularly interested in defectors from the West who were not top-level scientists or intelligence agents. Their experience with so-called blow-ins had never been too encouraging, as the HSCA would discover from a "Defector Study" carried out by its staff. Of 380 Americans in the USSR between 1958 and 1964 whom the CIA knew of, the HSCA selected 23 whose situations most closely resembled Oswald's for detailed study. Most of them were disgruntled people, some seriously disturbed, and some had simply chosen a spectacularly inappropriate way to solve personal problems. Many applied for Soviet citizenship, but few were granted it. In most cases the defectors experienced a change of heart and tried to return. The case histories strongly suggest that the Soviet Union gained nothing but trouble from its hospitality.[454]

Rimma's boss told her that Oswald would have to request citizenship from the Supreme Soviet, and Oswald mailed such a letter, written with Rimma's help,* that same day, October 16:

> To the USSR Supreme Soviet, 16th October 1959:
> I, Lee Harvey Oswald, am asking to be granted citizenship of The Soviet Union. My visa is valid from 15th of October and expires on 21st of October. My citizenship should be granted before this date. In the mean time I am waiting for your decision about my citizenship. Currently I am a citizen of the United States of America. I want citizenship because I am a Communist and working class person. I have lived in a decadent capitalist society, where the workers are slaves. I am 20, I served in US marines for three years, I served in the occupation forces in Japan. I have seen American militarism in all its forms. I do not want to return to any other country outside of the Soviet Union's borders. I wish to reject my American citizenship and accept the responsibility of a Soviet citizen . . . I do not have enough money to live here indefinitely or to return to any other country . . . I am asking you to consider my request as soon as possible.
>
> Sincerely yours,
Lee Harvey Oswald[455]

Although Oswald had no idea of what was happening, the Soviet authorities reacted quickly. The Fifteenth Department of the First Chief Directorate of the KGB memorial-

---

*The reader will note in reading the many writings of Oswald in this section that his dyslexia caused various degrees of errors in spelling, punctuation, and grammar, ranging from really bad to almost passable. The only explanation that makes sense for why his dyslexia was not as obvious in some of his letters is that, like the above referred-to letter to the Supreme Soviet, he had third-party help, or he deemed a particular letter important enough to rewrite it several times to make it better. For instance, Marina told the Warren Commission that with respect to the envelope alone on his November 9, 1963, letter to the Soviet embassy in Washington, D.C., "Lee retyped it some ten times or so" (1 H 45), although she later told her biographer Priscilla McMillan it was more like four times (McMillan, *Marina and Lee*, p.624 note 17). The Warren Commission noted the varying quality of his letters and dismissed a third possibility, at least as to the letters coming from Oswald in the United States. "There is no evidence," the Commission's report said, "that anyone in the United States helped Oswald with his better written letters or that anyone else wrote his letters for him" (WR, p.666).

ized Oswald's status in a "Report on the Stay in Moscow of American Citizen Lee Harvey Oswald," which clearly drew on what Rimma was reporting to her superiors at Intourist, since it includes a paragraph reading, "Oswald showed absolutely no interest in sightseeing, but was completely consumed by the thought of staying in the Soviet Union."[456]

Oswald, along with everyone he was bringing into his orbit, was obviously on the fast track. On October 17, just one day after he arrived in Moscow, Oswald's letter, accompanied by a cover letter marked "urgent," was forwarded from the Chancellory of the Presidium of the Supreme Soviet to the KGB deputy chairman, Aleksandr Perepelitsyn. An attachment suggested a review of Oswald's request by the First and Second Directorates of the KGB—the organs responsible, respectively, for intelligence and counterintelligence in the Soviet Union. That same day the Registry and Archives Department of the KGB opened a *spetsproverka*, a "control file," on Oswald and he was given the code name Nalim, meaning "turbot" or "river fish."[457]

In Oswald's diary he records that Rimma's attitude changed the next day when they again went sightseeing. He noted that she was politely sympathetic but uneasy. He thought Rimma felt sorry for him and had tried to be a friend because he was "someth. new." On his twentieth birthday, October 18, two days after he arrived in Russia, she gave him a copy of Dostoevsky's novel *The Idiot*,[458] in which she had written, "Dear Lee, Great congratulations! Let all your dreams come true! 18 X 1959 Moscow Yours Rimma." The book, FBI item number 291, was found among his effects after the assassination.[459]

As they waited for word about Lee's request for residence and citizenship, they continued their sightseeing, attending an exhibition and visiting Lenin's tomb. There were moments when she sensed that Lee wanted to kiss her, but although they were getting closer, she had a boyfriend she saw once a week, a young engineer who recently graduated from the Moscow Power Institute. Besides, if she let Lee kiss her and it somehow got back to her superiors, she knew she could lose her job. When these moments occurred, Rimma would dispel them by patting Lee on his hand.[460] Meanwhile, Oswald counted the rapidly dwindling days left on his visa.[461]

On October 19, Oswald was interviewed in his hotel room by a man named Lev Setyaev, who told Lee he was a reporter for Radio Moscow seeking statements from American tourists about their impressions of Moscow,[462] but who was probably also acting for the KGB.[463] According to author John Newman, Setyaev was also known to the CIA and the FBI, but Newman was unable to ascertain in what context.[464] In 1991, Setyaev was located and interviewed by journalist Peter Wronski. Setyaev said he tape-recorded his interview of Oswald but erased it immediately because Oswald's remarks were too political for the light tourist chatter that he needed for his show.[465] Two years later, Oswald told officials at the American embassy that the interview had lasted no more than three minutes and he had said nothing of political significance. It may well have been, however, an attempt by the KGB to evaluate Oswald's sincerity or to provoke compromising statements from him. If the interview was ever broadcast, the American embassy and the Associated Press, which monitored Radio Moscow, remained unaware of it.[466] Setyaev may also have taken a photograph of Oswald in his hotel room,[467] which is a rather odd thing for a radio interviewer to do—less odd for a KGB agent.

Most everyone Oswald met in the Soviet Union was at least a KGB informant if not an outright agent. The Committee for State Security, or KGB, was a lineal descendant of the Cheka, the security force established by Lenin in 1917 to protect his Bolshevik Revolution against counterrevolutionary elements.[468] In addition to its foreign intelligence and counterintelligence operations, in which it resembled the American CIA, the KGB was responsible for the internal security of the Soviet state and the safety of its leaders.[469] A section in the Seventh Department of the Second Chief Directorate of the KGB was responsible for the surveillance of all American tourists, and it expected, and got, full cooperation of all Intourist guides, hotel concierges and porters, and anyone else who might come in contact with a tourist like Lee Oswald.[470]

On October 20, Oswald wrote in his diary that Rimma was able to tell him that the "pass. and visa dept." wanted to see him. "I am excited greatly by this news," he wrote.[471] The next morning, October 21, he was interviewed by an official concerning his application for citizenship. The official, Oswald wrote in his diary, "Balding stout, black suit fairly good English, askes what do I want?, I say Sovite citizenship, he ask why I give vauge answers about 'Great Soviet Union' He tells me 'USSR only great in Literature wants me to go back home.'" Lee is "stunned" and reiterates his desire but gets no encouragement. The official tells him only that he will check to see if the visa can be extended. Oswald returned downcast to the Hotel Berlin.[472]

His interlocutor, Abram Shaknazarov, was in fact a KGB official who had worked in the organs of State Security since the late 1920s. He spoke several languages, including English, and the interview, although Oswald seems not to have realized it, was essentially a KGB debriefing. Shaknazarov was not impressed with Oswald. Even if Oswald had offered classified information in a bid for special favors, it's doubtful that the KGB would have been ready to rely on information from such a clearly disturbed youth. Oswald was distinctly unappetizing small fry, and even to use him as a propaganda device would be ill-advised during this period of warming U.S.-Soviet relations.[473]

That same day, the heads of both the First and Second Chief Directorates wrote to the KGB's Registry and Archives Department, which was maintaining Oswald's control file and stated that they had no interest in "American Citizen Oswald," and that "it was not advisable to grant him Soviet citizenship."[474] The quickness of the reply can only be interpreted to mean one thing: they were so certain they would never have any interest in Oswald that there wasn't even any need to sleep on it, not even for one night.[*]

Later in the morning of October 21, the Passport Office ordered his ticket for the train back to Helsinki and sent him a message at his hotel to report to the Passport Office at three o'clock. He must leave Moscow by eight that evening.[475]

"I am shocked!! My dreams!" Oswald exclaimed in his diary entry of October 21. "I retire to my room. I have $100. left. I have waited for 2 year to be accepted. My fondes dreams are shattered because of a petty offial; because of bad planning I planned to much!" In a passage clearly meant to be affecting, Oswald describes his next moves: "7:00 P.M. I decide to end it. Soak rist in cold water to numb the pain. Than slash my left wrist. Than plaug wrist into bathtub of hot water. I think 'when Rimma comes at 8. to find me dead it will be a great shock. somewhere, a violin plays, as I wacth my life whirl away. I think to myself. 'how easy to die' and 'a sweet death, (to violins) about 8:00 Rimma finds [me] unconscious (bathtub water a rich red color) she screams (I remember that) and runs for help."[476]

As stated earlier in the text, not all of Oswald's diary entries appear to have been made on the day of the event to which they related, and this invited errors. Almost assuredly,

---

[*]In a memorandum dated October 22, 1959, the KGB also decided that "it was not advisable to give [Oswald] refugee status in the Soviet Union" (Nechiporenko, *Passport to Assassination*, p.34).

his October 21, 1959, entry that at 6:00 p.m. he received word that he had to leave the country that night at 8:00 p.m.[477] is an error. On its face, most likely the Passport Office would not be open at 6:00 p.m. And even if it were, it's highly unlikely they'd call him at 6:00 p.m. and tell him he had to leave the country two hours later. There'd be no reason for them not to give him a few more hours' notice. More conclusively, the Moscow hospital records show that Oswald was admitted, unconscious, at 4:00 p.m. on October 21, 1959,[478] which would have been two hours *before*, according to Oswald, he received notice he had to leave the country. And Rimma told author Norman Mailer that when Oswald did not appear outside the Hotel Berlin by 2:30 p.m., she went to his room with her associate from Intourist to knock on his door. He was discovered inside his room in his bathtub shortly thereafter.[479] Just as Oswald's diary entry of 6:00 p.m. was in error, his entry for the same day, October 21, that he tried to commit suicide at "7:00 p.m." and was discovered in his room "about 8" has to correspondingly be in error.

According to KGB files,

> On October 21, a phone call was placed from OVIR [Passport Office] to the Hotel Berlin with a message for Oswald and his translator [Rimma] to appear at OVIR at around three o'clock in the afternoon. OVIR wanted to know if tickets for Oswald's departure had been purchased and, learning that they had not, suggested that they be ordered immediately, since the time of his stay in the country had expired. To the question of whether it made sense to extend his tour for one to two days, the reply was negative. At twelve o'clock noon the hotel informed Oswald, in the presence of his translator, that he must be at OVIR at three o'clock and that train tickets to Helsinki had been ordered for him. Oswald said that he would come down at 2:45 and went back to his room. When he did not appear at the appointed time, the translator became worried and went to his room. The door was locked from the inside, and no one responded to the sound of knocking. When the door was opened with an emergency passkey, Oswald was discovered lying in his bathtub unconscious and with a cut vein on his left arm. Before opening his vein, he had written a note of the following content: "I have made such a long journey to find death, but I love life."[480]*

Rimma rode with Oswald to the Botkin Hospital in Moscow—one with a special section for diplomats and foreigners—and saw him taken into a locked mental ward.[481]

The evidence as to whether this was a serious suicide attempt on Oswald's part is not clear. The doctor who treated Oswald's wound when he first arrived at Botkin (she did not want her name to be given) told author Norman Mailer thirty years later that the wound was hardly more than a scratch, it never reached his vein, and he wouldn't have been kept in the hospital had he been an ordinary Russian patient.[482] Author Jean Davison makes the point well for the proposition that it was not a suicide attempt. She writes, "There's reason to believe that this incident was another one of Oswald's dramatic

---

*Thirty years later, Rimma told *Frontline* that "I saw Lee in the bath. It was water there and it was reddish, so it was blood. Lee cut his wrist" (Transcript of "Who Was Lee Harvey Oswald?" *Frontline*, PBS, November 16, 1993, p.8). But two years later she told author Norman Mailer that she stayed out in the hallway and did not see Lee in the tub, and was told he had "cut his wrists." When they brought him out on a stretcher she said he was unconscious, his cheeks were hollow, his face was bluish, and he looked like a person about to die. (Mailer, *Oswald's Tale*, p.50)

manipulations. He knew Rimma was scheduled to arrive at his hotel room within the hour and would find him. The hospital records, provided by the Soviets after the assassination, state that his injury was 'light' and that Oswald told his doctor he had cut his wrist to 'postpone his departure' from the Soviet Union. In fact, this 'apparent suicide attempt' was similar to the minor gunshot wound Oswald had inflicted on himself in Japan. Each incident seemed to have had the same purpose—to avoid being sent where he did not want to go. The emotion expressed was probably not suicidal despair but extraordinary willfulness—a determination to act decisively and even violently to manipulate events."[483] Davison's strongest point is Oswald's apparently saying himself that he inflicted the wound to delay his departure. But one can't be certain that Oswald said this. Although there is a paragraph of the medical report at the Moscow hospital that quotes Oswald as having said these words, the words had no quotation marks around them and the paragraph prefaces this supposed remark by saying, "According to his statement in the Admission Ward, *with the aid of an interpreter* . . ."[484]

The evidence that Oswald had, indeed, attempted suicide is substantial. After the alleged remark made at the time of admission, Oswald's injury is later referred to in the hospital records more than once by the medical staff as a "suicide attempt."[485] Elsewhere, the records said Oswald "tried to cut the blood vessels of his left arm" and "tried to commit suicide in order not to leave for America."[486] One of the psychiatrists who examined Oswald, Dr. Maria Ivanovna Mikhailina, told *Frontline* in 1993 that "this was a sure suicide attempt."[487] And although one notation in Oswald's hospital records does refer to the wound as "light without functional disturbance," the wound ("incised wound of the lower third of the left forearm" by use of a "safety razor blade") is described in one place as "3 cm. long," elsewhere as "5 cm. in length" (in other words between 1¼ and 2 inches long), it required "four stitches," and there was "injury to the blood vessels." Moreover, Oswald "lost consciousness."

As indicated, Oswald was admitted to Botkin Hospital at 4:00 p.m. on October 21, 1959. He was discharged seven days later on October 28. The first three of those days were in the "Psychosomatic Department," where one psychiatrist (Dr. I. G. Gelershtein) concluded that Oswald's "mind is clear . . . No psychotic symptoms were noted. The patient is not dangerous for other people . . . He has a firm desire to remain in the Soviet Union." But another psychiatrist who examined Oswald (the aforementioned Dr. Mikhailina) wrote that "he claims he regrets his action. After recovery he plans to return to his homeland."[488]

The Warren Commission, after reference to Oswald's diary and the medical records, concluded that Oswald's inflicted wrist slashing was "an apparent suicide attempt."[489] If Oswald had attempted suicide in Russia, as appears to be the case, and if, as so many conspiracy theorists allege, Oswald went to Russia as a CIA agent, then, as anti-conspiracy theorist Mel Ayton asks, "why did he attempt suicide in Moscow?"[490]

Oswald's diary entries during this period are interesting. During his first day, October 21, at Botkin, he writes, "Poor Rimmea stays by my side as interrpator (my Russian is still very bad) far into the night, I tell her 'go home' (my mood is bad) but she stays, she is 'my friend' She has a strong will." He adds that "only at this moment I notice she is preety." His entry for October 22 reads, "Hospital I am in a small room with about 12 others (sick persons.) 2 ordalies and a nurse the room is very drab as well as the breakfast. Only after prolonged (2 hours) observation of the other pat. do I relize I am in the Insanity ward. This relization disquits [disgusts? disquiets?] me."[491]

As seen, Rimma did not abandon him. She visited him faithfully over the next days, partly to scold him for his foolishness, partly to help get him transferred to an ordinary ward, partly to interview him for the KGB. She also began to develop a sisterly affection for him, and started calling him "Alik"—the Russian nickname for Alexei that he started using for himself throughout his stay in the Soviet Union—since the name Lee didn't sound Russian at all.[492]

After his three-day stint in the psychiatric ward, Oswald found the hospital more pleasant. The new ward, which he shared with eleven other patients, was, he wrote, "Airy, good food." He noted in his diary, "Afternoon. I am visited by Roza Agafonova of the hotel, tourist office who askes about my health, very beautiful, excelant Eng., very merry and kind, she makes me very glad to be alive."[493]

When he was released from Botkin on October 28, Oswald was driven back to the Hotel Berlin in what appeared to be an Intourist car. His doctor thinks not. Dr. Mikhailina told PBS's *Frontline* in 1993 that he was taken away by the KGB. She says that she received a call from the KGB just before he was to be discharged, asking her to keep him there until they arrived. "Sometime later," she said, "about forty minutes, a large black car arrived and three young men came in. They confiscated his medical history, his discharge paper, and all his documents, and then they told me they were taking him away."[494]

Frontline asked Vladimir Semichastny, the then chairman of the KGB, about this, and although the KGB had never previously acknowledged any direct contact with Oswald, he admitted that "there were conversations, but this [what Oswald told them] was such outdated information, the kind we say the sparrows have already chirped to the entire world, and now Oswald tells us about it. Not the kind of information that would interest such a high-level organization like ours." The KGB did, however, consider recruiting Oswald as a spy. "Counterintelligence and intelligence—they both looked him over to see what he was capable of, but unfortunately, neither could find any ability at all," Semichastny said.[495]

If Semichastny was telling the truth and if his memory of what happened thirty years earlier was accurate, what we don't know is whether Oswald was aware, in these "conversations," that he was speaking to the KGB. His Historic Diary has no mention of any such conversations, nor even a reference to any discussion with those who removed him from the hospital.

Nearly out of money and technically in the country illegally since he had outstayed his visa by several days, Oswald moved to the Hotel Metropole, a large hotel under the same administration as the Hotel Berlin, probably by order of the government. He was impressed that the authorities returned his watch, ring, and money "to the last kopeck," and with the farewell he received from Lyudmila Dmitrieva, head of the Intourist Office at the Berlin, and Roza Agafonova, her assistant who, per his diary, invited him to "come and sit and take [talk] with them anytime." At the Metropole, by contrast to the Berlin, where he had started to make friends, he felt lonely, but he must have been cheered by the fact that Rimma told him on the day he was released from the hospital that the "pass & registration office whshes to see me about my future."[496]

Oswald later thought that the interview with the Passport Office, which, per KGB records, took place on October 29 (Oswald's diary records it as October 28), the day after his release from the hospital, did not go well. According to his diary, "We entered the officies to find four ofials waiting for me (all unknown to me) they ask How my arm is, I say O.K., They ask 'Do you want to go to your homeland. I say no I want Sovite citizen I say I want to reside in the Soviet Union. They say they will see about that. Than they ask me about the lone offial with whom I spoke in the first place (appar. he did not pass along my request at all but thought to simply get rid of me by not extending my Soviet visa . . . [They asked me] what papers do you have to show who and what you are?"

It seems likely that they wanted some proof of Lee's vaunted Marxism—membership in the Communist Party in the United States, or something like that, but all he had to offer them was his discharge papers from active duty in the Marine Corps. By his own account they were not impressed. "They say wait for our ans. I ask how long? Not soon."[497]

The KGB report of the interview notes that "Comrade Ryazantsev [head of the Passport Office] said that the matter was still unresolved and that he [Oswald] could remain for the time being in Moscow and wait for a definitive answer from the Supreme Soviet . . . At the present time Oswald resides at the Hotel Metropole, does not go out, and spends whole days in his room. He has to pay thirty rubles a day for his room [and] has eight hundred rubles in his possession. The translator Shirakova R. S. continues to work with Oswald." The author of the report also thought that "Oswald left OVIR [the Passport Office] in a good mood. He said he hoped his request would be granted."[498]

That's not the way Oswald remembered it. He said the interview left him in a rotten mood. Rimma dropped by the Metropole that evening to check on him, and he wrote that "I feel insulted and insult her."[499]

Over the next couple of days he remained worried and edgy. He wrote in his diary, "Oct. 29. [probably October 30] Hotel Room 214 Metropole Hotel. I wait. I worry I eat once, stay next to phone worry I keep fully dressed." The entry for the next day reads, "I have been in hotel three days, [it] seems like three years I must have some sort of showdown!"[500]

When he met Rimma around noon on October 31, she must have sensed that he was loaded for bear. Although he told her nothing of his plans, she warned him to stay in his room "and eat well."[501] A few minutes after she left, though, he took a taxi to the American embassy, where one of two Russian guards asked to see his passport, then waved him in. Inside, he found a receptionist on duty typing. When he asked to see the consul, she asked him to sign the "tourist register," and went back to her typing. "Yes, but before I'll do that, I'd like to see the consular." He laid his passport on her desk and, as she looked up, puzzled, he added, "I'm here to dissolve my American citizenship."[502]

It was a half hour past noon that Saturday and the embassy was already closed for business for the weekend, but the receptionist, Jean Hallett, alerted Richard E. Snyder, the senior consulate official, who had her show Oswald into his office.[503]

Oswald selected an armchair to the left front of Snyder's desk. Snyder's assistant, John McVickar, was also in the room. Oswald's diary reads, "I wait, crossing my legs and laying my gloves in my lap. He finishes typing, removes the letter from his typewriter and adjusting his glasses looks at me. 'What can I do for you he asks' leafing through my passport. 'I'm here to dissolve my U.S. citizenship and would like to sing the legle papers to that effect.' have you applied for Russian citizenship? yes."[504]

Snyder, an experienced Foreign Service officer having served in Frankfurt, Munich, and Tokyo, examined Oswald's passport and noticed that Oswald had inked out the space for his address in the United States. Snyder asked him where he lived, but Oswald refused to answer. Oswald, very presentable in Snyder's eyes, is at once proper and extremely curt, although not insulting. Snyder could see from the passport that Oswald was only just twenty, still a minor hardly out of his teens.[505]

Snyder noticed that Oswald seemed to "know what his mission was. He took charge, in a sense, of the conversation right from the beginning . . . In general, his attitude was quite arrogant."[506] He presented Snyder with a note he had written out by hand on the printed stationery of the Hotel Metropole:

> I Lee Harvey Oswald do hereby request that my present citizenship in the United States of america, be revoked. I have entered the Soviet Union for the express purpose of applying for citizenship in the Soviet Union, through the means of naturalization. My request for citizenship is now pending before the Supreme Soviet of the U.S.S.R. I take these steps for political reasons. My request for the revoking of my American citizenship is made only after the longest and most serious considerations. I affirm that my allegiance is to the Union of Soviet Socialist Republics.
>
> Lee H. Oswald"[507]

Snyder groaned inwardly. He had recently had some headaches with a few American defection cases, and just three days earlier had written a thoughtful letter to the State Department in which he recommended a certain elasticity in dealing with them.[508] Warily, he began to question Oswald, but he ran into a solid wall of refusal. "Don't bother wasting my time asking me questions or trying to talk me out of my position," Oswald told Snyder. He was cocksure. "I am well aware . . . of exactly the kind of thing you will ask me and I am not interested, so let's get down to business."[509]

Oswald told him his principal reason for his wanting to defect: "I am a Marxist." In that case, Snyder said to Oswald, he was going to be very lonesome in the Soviet Union— a witticism that was lost on Oswald. The boy appeared to be "intense" and "completely humorless."[510]

By way of a test, Snyder asked Oswald his opinion of Marx's theory of labor value— a basic Marxist theory presented in the very early chapters of *Das Kapital*—and noted that Oswald did not know what Snyder was talking about. Snyder then spoke a little to Oswald in Russian, and concluded from Oswald's responses that Oswald knew very little Russian. He guessed that Oswald's Marxism was about as good as his Russian—in other words, he had no knowledgeable background at all.[511]

But Oswald suddenly became more talkative and offered that he had recently been separated from the Marine Corps and that his service in the Far East had given him "a chance to observe American imperialism." Oswald went on to mention the hardships his mother had endured as a "worker" in America, and announced that he did not intend that to happen to him. It seemed to Snyder that Oswald felt little real affection for his mother—or much of any sense of obligation toward her—in spite of his complaints about her plight.[512]

Oswald, becoming exasperated by the chitchat, went over to the attack and told Snyder that he had been a radar operator in the Marine Corps and that he had already— voluntarily—told the Soviets that if they made him a Soviet citizen he would make known to them whatever knowledge he had.* He intimated to Snyder that he knew of something that would be of special interest to the USSR, though he did not claim to possess knowledge or information of a highly classified nature.[513] For someone who many conspiracy

---

*It is not known if Oswald ever made this offer, or if he was just bluffing Snyder. As indicated earlier, Oswald made no reference to offering the Soviets anything in return for citizenship, although Semichastny claims Oswald, in one or more conversations with the KGB, offered the Soviets information he called "outdated."

theorists are convinced was a double agent for the CIA and KGB, this was not a very bright thing for him to do. Snyder could certainly be expected to send that information back to the State Department, giving the military authorities a chance to nullify the value of any information that Oswald might actually possess. And the Soviets, even if they took the kid seriously, would hardly appreciate his telling American officials that he was passing information on to them.[*]

Snyder suggested that Oswald come back at a later time to discuss the matter, giving the reason that the embassy was closed and preparation of the documents required some time. Actually, Snyder was reluctant to allow Oswald to cash in his citizenship, an irrevocable step, and he felt Oswald fell into the category of "quixotic types of uncertain mentality and doubtful emotional stability" or those who do things on an "irrational impulse or other transient influence." Snyder told the Warren Commission, "Particularly in the case of a minor [Oswald], I could not imagine myself writing out the renunciation form, and having him sign it, on the spot, without making him leave my office and come back at some other time, even if it is only a few hours intervening."[514][†]

When Oswald left, he gave no indication to Snyder when, if at all, he would return.[515] Years later, Snyder gave his impression of Oswald to author Gus Russo. Referring to him as a "flaky kid," he said Oswald "had all the earmarks of a sophomore Marxist, someone who'd just discovered a religion" and didn't have "the faintest idea of what this country [the Soviet Union] is about."[516]

As soon as Oswald left the embassy, Snyder fired off a telegram to the State Department, outlining the interview and specifically mentioning Oswald's threat to reveal information derived from his service as a radar operator for the Marine Corps.[517]

A copy of Snyder's telegram was sent to the FBI,[518] and the CIA received an expanded version of the telegram on November 2.[519] Immediately after sending off his telegram, Snyder called Robert J. "Bud" Korengold, Moscow bureau chief for United Press International, "to try and get another line on Oswald." He gave Korengold Oswald's room number at the Metropole, and Korengold wasted no time—he knocked on Oswald's door at two that afternoon. Oswald was astonished. "How did you find out?" he asked. Korengold told him he had been alerted by the embassy, but Oswald refused to say anything except that he knew what he was doing and did not want to talk to anyone.[520]

Korengold, stymied, went back to his bureau and talked with another UPI correspondent, Aline Mosby. Within minutes, she was on her way to the Metropole. "I went up in the creaky elevator to the second floor and down the hall," Mosby wrote in her

---

[*]Of course, the situation was rife with other considerations and possibilities. Though Oswald couldn't be expected to know the complex law of subversive activity by U.S. citizens, even treason, surely he had to know that what he was threatening to do was flirting with a violation of some federal law, although in his unschooled mind he probably felt safe since he knew he hadn't actually passed any information to the Soviets yet. And then there is the possibility that Oswald may very well have assumed that the Soviets had bugged the U.S. embassy and Snyder's office and he was speaking to them and attempting to establish his bona fides.

[†]McVickar, possibly being influenced by the occurrence of later events, in responding to a request after the assassination from Thomas Ehrlich, a special assistant to the legal adviser to the Department of State, to set forth his impressions of Oswald in Moscow, wrote, "I recall thinking at the time that Oswald was behaving with a great deal of determination and purpose for such a young and relatively uneducated person. He was certainly very independent and fearless in a rather blind way and it seemed to me that he could have acquired all these ideas himself . . . On the other hand, there also seemed to me to be the possibility that he was following a pattern of behavior in which he had been tutored by person or persons unknown . . . It seemed to me that there was a possibility that he had been in contact with others before or during his Marine Corps tour who had guided him and encouraged him in his actions" (CE 941, 18 H 155; 5 H 384, WCT Frances G. Knight).

notes, "past the life-sized nude in white marble, the gigantic painting of Lenin and Stalin and the usual watchful floor clerk in her prim navy blue dress with brown braids wrapped around her head. An attractive fellow answered my knock on the door of Room 233."[521]

She didn't get much from Oswald on her first visit, but it was enough for UPI to file the story that went out over the wires on October 31, 1959, that Oswald had applied to renounce his citizenship and intended to become a Soviet citizen for "purely political reasons." He also told UPI he would never return to the United States.[522] The story of Oswald's defection appeared the next day in many papers throughout the United States. The young American who always wanted to make a splash was not starting out poorly. That Sunday he made page 3 of the *New York Times*, the paper of record of the nation he was leaving behind, with a six-paragraph article captioned "Ex-Marine Requests Soviet Citizenship."[523]

Oswald's October 31 entry in his diary reads, "From this day forward I consider myself no citizen of the U.S.A. . . . I leave Embassy, elated at this showdown, returning to my hotel I feel now my enorgies are not spent in vain. I'm sure Russians will except me after this sign of my faith in them. 2:00 a knock, a reporter by the name of Goldstene* wants an interview I'm flabbergassed 'how did you find out? The Embassy called us.' He said. I send him away I sit and relize this is one way to bring pressure on me. By notifing my relations in U.S. through the newspapers . . . A half hour later another reporter Miss Mosby comes. I ansewer a few quick questions after refusing an interviwe. I am surprised at the interest. I get phone calls from 'Time' [magazine] at night a phone call from the States I refuse all calles without finding out who's it from. I feel non-deplused because of the attention 10:00 I retire."[524]

Lee's brother, Robert, was halfway through his milk delivery route for Boswell's Dairy in Fort Worth on Halloween and was writing up a customer's order in his ledger when a man got out of a taxi and walked up to his truck. "Are you Robert Oswald?" the man asked. He said he was a reporter for the *Fort Worth Star-Telegram*. "I have a report here that your brother is in Russia . . . I have a copy of the teletype and thought you might want to read it and comment." Robert read it and felt his stomach tighten as he said, "Oh no." He was floored, taken completely by surprise. The reporter asked him if he believed the story. "There doesn't seem to be any doubt," Robert said. "Lee is awfully young. He's looking for excitement. I don't believe he knows what he is doing." Robert wasn't entirely sure of that, though. The more he thought about it, the more he realized how carefully Lee had planned his defection.[525]

Robert finished his milk route and rushed home, where he found that Marguerite had already heard the news on the radio. Among the reporters besieging him and Marguerite was one who suggested he send two telegrams, one to Secretary of State Christian Herter and the other to Lee at the Metropole.[526] Robert agreed, and the next morning sent the telegrams, the one to Herter asking to have his office get Lee to call Robert,[527] and the one to Lee, which was personal and beseeching. Thinking Lee would remember his many admonitions, when Lee was little, to keep his nose clean, Robert wired, "LEE, THROUGH

---

*Oswald may have conflated (a poor conflation at that) the names Korengold and A. I. Goldberg, a reporter for the Associated Press, to come up with "Goldstene." Goldberg did try to interview Oswald at the Metropole, he says before Mosby, and Oswald, speaking to him through the slightly opened door of his room, refused to talk, confining himself to "I've got my reasons" in response to Goldberg's "Why?" Goldberg never saw him again. (CE 2719, 26 H 99–100)

ANY MEANS POSSIBLE CONTACT ME. MISTAKE. KEEP YOUR NOSE CLEAN." Both he and Marguerite tried to call Lee in Moscow, but they failed to get through.[528]

A couple of reporters from the *Fort Worth Press*, Kent Biffle and Seth Kantor, went to extraordinary lengths to arrange a three-way conference call among Marguerite at her home, the two reporters in their city room, and Lee at the Metropole. It took hours to set up on the primitive international phone network—it was 1959—but eventually Biffle heard Lee come on the line, he recalls, with "two husky hello's." The moment Lee heard that reporters set the call up so he could talk to his mother, he clanked down the receiver as Marguerite was pleading, "Hello! Hello! Lee?" A shattered fifty-two-year-old Marguerite wept softly.[529] "All those hours," Kantor would later write, "down the drain."[530] Robert Oswald also attempted to reach Lee on the phone, but Lee refused to talk to him.[531]

The aborted calls gave Lee a lift, though. He wrote in his diary on November 1, "More reporters, 3 phone calls from brother & mother, now I feel slightly axzillarated, not so lonly."[532]*

Oswald's "axzillaration" was short-lived. He covered the next two weeks of his sojourn in the Metropole in a single diary entry for November 2 through 15: "Days of utter loneliness I refuse all reports phone calls I remaine in my room. I am racked with dsyentary."[533] Nor did he return to the American embassy, contenting himself with a handwritten letter to the embassy:

> I, Lee Harvey Oswald, do hereby request that my present United States citizenship be revoked.
>
> I appered [appeared] in person, at the consulate office of the United States Embassy, Moscow, on Oct 31st, for the purpose of signing the formal papers to this effect. This legal right I was refused at that time.
>
> I wish to protest against this action, and against the conduct of the official of the United States consuler service who acted on behalf of the United States government.
>
> My application, requesting that I be considered for citizenship in the Soviet Union is now pending before the Surprem Soviet of the U.S.S.R. In the event of acceptance, I will request my government to lodge a formal protest regarding this incident.
>
> Lee Harvey Oswald[534]

The fact that Oswald said the U.S. embassy had "refused" to let him renounce his U.S. citizenship when it hadn't done this at all is revealing. Snyder merely told Oswald to return on another date, and when Snyder responded to Oswald's November 3, 1959, letter on November 6, he informed Oswald that he did, in fact, have the "inherent right" to renounce his citizenship and all he had to do was return to the embassy during the hours the embassy was open (set forth in the letter) and follow the prescribed procedures, including the taking of an oath.[535] Yet Oswald elected not to return to the embassy, which per-

---

*Though he was lonely, he apparently was not alone. A June 4, 1964, internal memorandum of the CIA on KGB operations against foreign tourists noted that "Rm 233, Hotel Metropole, Moscow" [Oswald's room] was "equipped with infra-red camera for observation of occupants" (Newman, *Oswald and the CIA*, pp.9, 531 note 46).

Meanwhile, on November 2, the U.S. State Department (even before receiving a November 2 Moscow embassy dispatch to them from Snyder proposing "to delay action on Oswald's request") sent a telegram to its Moscow embassy that read in part, "If Oswald insists on renouncing U.S. citizenship, Section 1999 Revised Statutes precludes Embassy withholding right to do so" (CE 908, 18 H 97–99; CE 916, 18 H 114).

haps speaks loudly for one point. Renouncing his citizenship was only ancillary to the main thing he wanted, becoming a Soviet citizen.

But since his interview at the Soviet Passport Office on October 29, Oswald had heard nothing from the Soviet authorities. Finally, on November 4, Oswald was visited by one "Andrei Nikolayevich," ostensibly an employee at Intourist, who chatted with Oswald about his reasons for requesting Soviet citizenship and promised to help him get settled in the USSR after the November holidays—in five days. This was, of course, just another camouflaged interview by the KGB. When Oswald heard nothing further from Niko- layevich, he got Rimma to try to arrange a meeting with him, but they discovered that there was no such person at Intourist. That organization, alerted to the monkey business by Oswald's attempt to locate "Nikolayevich," asked the KGB for an explanation and was told that its spy had spoken to Oswald "on the subject of possible use abroad."[536]

But as indicated, since the KGB had no *use* for Oswald, the Nikolayevich meeting was most likely just another KGB contact with Oswald to check up on him, not to use him, and the fact that Oswald apparently never heard from Nikolayevich again supports this inference.

Oswald would have no further contacts with the Soviets for weeks to come. He did hear from the U.S. embassy, however. It had received Robert's November 1, 1959, telegram to Christian Herter at the State Department, urging that State have Lee get in touch with his brother. Snyder had his secretary, Marie Cheatham, call the Metropole on November 2 to ask Oswald to come and pick up Robert's telegram. He was not inter- ested. Snyder told her to call back and ask Lee if she could read the telegram over the phone. "Not at the present time," he said, and hung up.[537] Robert's telegram was finally sent to Oswald from the embassy by registered mail.[538]

Lee undoubtedly would have been gratified to learn of the commotion he was caus- ing, although, holed up in his room at the Metropole, he had no way of knowing about the cables flying back and forth between Moscow and Washington, or of the consider- able traffic between agencies of the U.S. government on the one hand and those of the Soviet government on the other.

Although there is no indication in the Warren Commission volumes that the Depart- ment of Defense, which oversees the nation's military defense, received a copy of Snyder's October 31, 1959, telegram to the Department of State about Oswald offering to furnish the Soviets with his radar knowledge, only that the FBI and CIA got copies,[539] on Novem- ber 3, 1959, the naval attaché at the American embassy in Moscow sent a confidential "mes- sage" to the chief of naval operations (CNO) at the Department of Defense at the Pentagon in Washington that Oswald had stated he "has offered to furnish Soviets info he possesses on US radar."[540] The following day, the CNO messaged back to the attaché that the depart- ment had found "no record of [security] clearance at HQ [Headquarters], Marine Corps, but possibility exists he may have had access to Confidential info . . . Request significant developments in view of continuing interest of HQ, Marine Corps, and U.S. intelligence agencies."[541] In view of what potentially was at stake, this seemed to be a rather tepid response to Oswald's threat. A layperson would naturally expect his threat to be a bomb- shell to the military, in that at that time no one knew for sure just what confidential infor- mation Oswald might have stumbled on that might be of any use to the Soviets (that is, unless just a few quick calls from the Pentagon that we don't know about to Oswald's supe- riors at Atsugi revealed that he was, to be cruel, a military cipher). However, apparently the military did do something as a result of Oswald's threat, but the only evidence I could find in the Commission volumes comes not from the Department of Defense or any military command, but from Lieutenant John Donovan, the officer in command of Oswald's radar crew in Santa Ana, who recalled what happened when "we received word that he had shown up in Moscow. This necessitated a lot of change of aircraft call signs, radio frequencies, radar frequencies."[542] "We had to spend several thousand man-hours changing everything and verifying the destruction of the codes."[543]

Inasmuch as Donovan's credibility has been severely thrown into question on another matter related to Oswald (see endnote), we cannot automatically accept his words here at face value.

Donovan went on to say that Oswald's low grade of clearance, confidential, gave him potential access to, in Donovan's words, "the location of all bases in the West Coast area, all radio frequencies for all squadrons, all tactical call signs, and the relative strength of all squadrons, number and type of aircraft in a squadron, who was the commanding officer, the authentication code of entering and exiting the ADIZ, which stands for the Air Defense Identification Zone. He knew the range of our radar. He knew the range of our radio. And he knew the range of the surrounding unit's radio and radar."[544]

Much of this information was look-up stuff, not something anyone would be likely to remember several weeks after working with it, but if Oswald had written it down he might make it available to the Soviets. The authentication and identification codes were changed routinely anyway, and anything Oswald might reveal about them would be short-lived, but there was other information, Donovan said, that could not be changed. Oswald had worked with the new MPS16 height-finder radar, which vastly improved the service's ability to determine the altitude of aircraft, which could not, like the codes could, be changed. He had also been schooled in a piece of gear called TPX-1, which transferred radio and radar signals over great distances, allowing the radar operators to be far away from the radar antennae, which would be electronically targeted by incoming aircraft and missiles. That fact could not be changed either.[545]

If Donovan's words are to be believed, Oswald's defection had gone far beyond a mere teenage prank.

After the flurry of activity in the first week of November 1959, things turned dismal for Lee Oswald. The penetrating, cold bleakness of a Moscow November had little on him. He heard nothing from his Soviet hosts. Out of money, and poorly clothed against Moscow's weather, he rarely if ever left his room in the Hotel Metropole. Finally, on November 8, he wrote to his brother. The spelling and punctuation are so clearly better than his atrocious diary entries that we can assume he had some help, or simply spent a lot of time in its preparation, using a dictionary for spelling.

> Dear Robert
>
> Well, What shall we Talk about, the weatter perhaps? Certainly you do not wish me to speak of my decision to remain in the Soviet Union and apply for citizenship here, since I'm afraid you would not be able to comprehend my reasons. You really dont know anything about me. Do you know for instance that I have waited to do this for well over a year, do you know that I [a few words in Russian to illustrate knowledge of language] speak a fair amount of Russian which I have been studing for many months.

I have been told that I will not have to leave the Soviet Union if I do not care to. This than is my decision. I will not leave this country, the Soviet Union, under any conditions, I will never return to the United States *which is a country I hate*.

Someday, perhaps soon, and then again perhaps in a few years, I will become a citizen of the Soviet Union, but it is a very legal process, *in any event*, I will not have to leave the Soviet Union and I will never [do so].

I recived your telegram and was glad [to hear] from you, only one word bothered me, the [word] "mistake." I assume you mean that I have [made a] "mistake" it is not for you to tell me [that. You] cannot understand my reasons for this very [full word not shown] action.

I will not speak to anyone from the United States over the Telephone since it may be taped by the americans.

If you wish to corespond with me you can write to the below address, but I really don't see what we could Take about, if you want to send me money, that I [could] use, but I do not expect to be able to send it back.

                                                                        Lee

Lee Harvey Oswald
Metropol Hotel RM 233
Moscow U.S.S.R.[546]

Oswald's claim that he had been told that he could remain in Russia does not appear to be true—according to his own diary, he was not told until a week later that he could remain even temporarily in the Soviet Union.[547]

Several days later, the U.S. embassy in Moscow received a cable from the U.S. embassy in Tokyo, forwarding a message for Lee from his half brother, John Pic, who had by now left the Coast Guard to join the U.S. Air Force and was stationed at Tachikawa Air Base in Japan. Pic had learned of his brother's defection from an Armed Forces Network broadcast, which was confirmed the next morning by the Pacific edition of *Stars and Stripes*. John found it all but unbelievable, although in the back of his mind was the grim thought that "ever since he was born and I was old enough to remember, I always had a bad feeling that some great tragedy was going to strike Lee in some way or another, and when this happened, I figured this was it."[548]

Eventually, John contacted the U.S. embassy in Tokyo, which forwarded to Moscow a few words for Lee: "PLEASE RECONSIDER YOUR INTENTIONS. CONTACT ME IF POSSIBLE." On November 9, Snyder's assistant John McVickar took a typed copy of the message over to the Metropole to deliver it by hand, at least partly in the hope of putting the lost sheep back in touch with his family and possibly dissuading him from his reckless course. Lee wasn't in so McVickar sent it to Oswald by registered mail.[549]

The following Saturday, November 14, Aline Mosby, who had broken the first story on Oswald for United Press International, finally managed to wangle a real interview with him.[*] She had given him her card at their first meeting but was surprised when he called and

---

[*]Although Oswald's diary entry of November 15, 1959, says he was interviewed by Mosby that day (CE 24, 16 H 97), and in his handwritten account of the interview, which was found among his personal effects, he also says it was on November 15 (CE 2717, 26 H 91), this has to be incorrect, since Mosby's published story on the interview in the *Fort Worth Star-Telegram* ("Fort Worth Defector Confirms Red Beliefs"), published on Sunday, November 15, 1959, was datelined "Moscow, November 14 (UPI)," and in the article Mosby said she interviewed Oswald the previous day, "Saturday" (CE 2716, 26 H 90).

offered to talk. She drove straight over to the Metropole. When she met him in his hotel room and thanked him for the opportunity, he told her that indeed "other reporters have been trying to get up here," but he thought she might "understand and be friendly because you're a woman."

Mosby was also young, outgoing, and good-looking. A native of Montana, she had brought her white MG-A roadster to Moscow, which guaranteed her a great deal of interested attention. Her colleague, A. I. Goldberg from the rival Associated Press, speculated that Oswald had granted her the interview instead of him because Oswald fancied himself a "ladies' man," but Lee did not make a particularly favorable impression on Mosby. Scarcely out of cultural shock herself—she had arrived in Moscow only in February—there were times when the sheer frustration of life in Russia had reduced her to tears,[550] but even so it was difficult to empathize with Lee Oswald. Mosby wrote,

> As he talked he held his mouth stiffly and nearly closed. His jaw was rigid. Behind his brown eyes I felt a certain coldness . . . Sometimes he looked directly at me, other times at the plush furniture. Now and then he gazed out the tall window, hung with lace curtains and gold draperies,[*] to Sverdlovsk Square and the Lenin Museum and the gold onion-shaped domes of the ancient Kremlin churches beyond. He talked almost non-stop like the type of semi-educated person of little experience who clutches what he regards as some sort of unique truth. Such a person often does not expect anyone else to believe him and is contemptuous of other people who cannot see his "truth." A zealot, he is not remotely touched by what anyone else says. In fact, at times in my two hours with Lee Harvey Oswald I felt we were not carrying [on] a conversation, but that two monologues were being delivered simultaneously.

Oswald seemed full of confidence, often showing a "small smile, more like a smirk." He admitted his Russian was bad but was convinced it would improve rapidly. He told her a bit about his childhood in New Orleans, Fort Worth, and New York, and mentioned his discovery of Karl Marx's *Das Kapital* with fervor, eyes shining.

Having grudgingly surrendered as much about his personal life as he cared to, Oswald, who she said was "inexpensively but well and neatly dressed in a suit, white shirt and tie," launched into his standard disquisition on Marxism, which Mosby found as entertaining as recitations from *Pravda*. Since she took down his words in shorthand, her account, though written a few years later from the notes of her interview of Oswald, preserves much of the tone of the twenty-year-old's mind:

"I would not care to live in the United States where being a worker means you are exploited by the capitalists . . . I could not be happy." Oswald said that in New York City, he "saw the luxuries of Park Avenue and the workers' lives on the East Side" and could see

> "the impoverishment of the masses before my own eyes in my own mother . . . I could not live under a capitalist system. I would have a choice of becoming a worker

---

[*]Though this sounds like an elegant suite, something Oswald could not be expected to be able to afford, Mosby says the room was the standard "thirty dollar a day room with meals that all tourists must buy" (CE 1385, 22 H 702).

under the system I hate, or becoming unemployed. Or I could have become a capitalist and derived my profit and my [living] under the exploitation of workers. I
will live now under a system where no individual capitalist will be able to exploit
the workers . . .

"Capitalism has passed its peak. Unemployment is growing. An era of depression is on the way . . . The forces of communism are growing. I believe capitalism
will disappear as feudalism disappeared . . . The hysteria in America has gotten
worse. If practice makes perfect, the U.S. is getting better," he said sarcastically.
"You know, fashions, mode, clothes, food—and hating communists [and] niggers.
You go along with the crowd. I am against conformism in such matters, such as
fashionably hating minority groups. Being a southern boy, I've seen poor niggers.
That was a lesson, too. People hate because they're told to hate . . . People in the
United States are like that in everything."

When Mosby "got a word in edgewise" and asked Oswald if he was a member of the
Communist Party, Oswald seemed surprised. "Communist?" he said. "I've never met a
communist. I might have seen a communist once in New York, the old lady who gave me
the pamphlet, 'Save the Rosenbergs.'" Oswald acknowledged he had been "influenced
by what I read" about Marxism, and had made "careful plans to go to Russia . . . to observe
that which I had read." He said intensely, "When I was working in the middle of the night
on guard duty [in the Marines] I would think how long it would be and how much money
I would have to have. It would be like being out of prison. I saved about $1,500."

After two hours, Mosby had enough. When she started on "the ebb and flow of communism" again, she took her leave. At the door, though, she finally had a twinge of sympathy for him, someone she perceived as still "a boy," and a stranger in a strange land,
without a family or friends, trying to digest the Hotel Metropole's food every night. She
thought it might do him some good to meet some other westerners in Moscow. She invited
him to dinner at her place—she lived in an apartment with a TASS Teletype, as it was
also her office—in a building where many of the other foreign press also lived and worked,
a kind of ghetto for foreign journalists. She thought he might enjoy it.

He thanked her but declined. It was obvious to her that he had no intention of ever
seeing her again.[551]

For the date of November 16, Oswald wrote in his diary, "A Russian official comes to my
room askes how I am. Notifies me I can remain in USSR till some solution [is] found with
what to do with me, it is comforting news to me."[552]

During the month he waited to hear from the Soviets, Rimma came to see him faithfully—she had been assigned the task as her job and she wrote reports to her chief whenever it seemed useful. She always tried to give a good impression of Lee. She and Roza
Agafonova worried about his clothing, which was not weighty enough for the steadily
worsening weather. Together they broached the problem to Alexander Simchenko, head
of the Passport Office, and he authorized them to purchase a good hat from the GUM
(State Universal Store) Department Store. Lee was delighted with it, became emotional,
and kissed them both.[553]

The day before Lee finally heard that he would be allowed to stay in the Soviet Union,
Priscilla Johnson returned to Moscow from a visit to the United States, where she had

been covering Premier Khrushchev's dramatic and colorful tour of America, his second visit there. Johnson was then a thirty-one-year-old expert in the Russian language. At college she had been a World Federalist, out of hope that the Soviet Union could be persuaded to join a world government, and toward that goal she had majored in Russian at Bryn Mawr and received an MA in Soviet area studies from Radcliffe College in 1953. Because of her background in Russian studies, she applied for employment at the CIA in the summer of 1952 as an intelligence analyst. It was one of a number of places she applied for work at the time. She was eventually turned down by the CIA after a long check on her background, her association with the liberal United World Federalists almost assuredly proving fatal to any hopes of a career in the CIA. But by the time of her rejection in March of 1953, she had already started to work elsewhere— as a researcher for a dashing newly elected senator from Massachusetts named John F. Kennedy.[554]

By 1959 she was the Moscow correspondent for the North American Newspaper Alliance. Having just returned from the states, she stopped in at the American embassy late on Monday afternoon, November 16, to pick up mail that might have landed there in her absence.[555] When she walked past John McVickar's office, he came out to welcome her back to Moscow. "Oh, by the way," he said, "there's a young American in your hotel trying to defect. He won't talk to any of us, but maybe he'll talk to you because you're a woman."[556] McVickar pointed out to her that there was a narrow line between her duty as a correspondent and her duty as an American, the message being McVickar and Snyder needed help with Oswald.[557] She went straight back to the Metropole and when she knocked on the door to Oswald's room, which was one floor below her own, he did not invite her in but agreed to come upstairs to her room to be interviewed later that evening.

He appeared around "eight or nine," she would later write, neatly dressed in a dark gray suit, white shirt, and dark tie, with a tan cashmere sweater vest, looking not unlike college boys she had known on the East Coast in the 1950s. Johnson, living on a shoe-string in Moscow—about fifty dollars a week—often cooked in her room to save money. She made him a cup of tea on a little burner she kept on the floor, and they settled down for what was to become the longest interview anyone ever had with Lee Harvey Oswald, Oswald staying until "two o'clock in the morning."[558]

She was startled, almost above all else, by his youth—he seemed no more than about seventeen to her—and like Mosby, referred to him as "a boy."[559] Also like Mosby, she found his ideological spiel heavy going, but she liked him and wanted to establish communication with him, and she realized his incantations about the exploitation of the American worker by the capitalist system were practically the only means he had for speaking about himself. Ever mindful that her room might be bugged, she nonetheless tried to suggest to him that life in the Soviet Union was not going to be a rose garden. There is, she told him, poverty and injustice everywhere. She hoped that if she could at least meet him partway on his own ground, she might encourage him to hesitate, to think his decision over, but it didn't work.[560] Seeing he was interested in economics, she tried to engage him in a discussion on economic principles but quickly came to the conclusion that he really didn't have the capacity for "a logical sustained argument about an abstract point on economics or on non-economic political matters, or any matter philosophical,"[561] observing he had "a very primitive understanding of economics,"[562] which, ironically, was virtually the entire reason for his defection. She wondered what socialist literature he might have read, and he came up with his standard response, Marx and Engels, but was then unable to name any work by Engels. He claimed to have read the work of American Marxists, but couldn't name any of them either.[563]

To Priscilla Johnson several things stood out about Oswald, the callow American who "seemed lonely . . . very, very young. He seemed lost in a situation that was beyond him,"[564] among them being that "he was the first and, as it turned out, the only ideological defector I met in Moscow." There weren't many, and none claimed to be motivated by a belief in Communism. "All appeared to be fleeing some obvious personal difficulty, such as an unhappy marriage back home." But Oswald, whom Johnson saw "as a little lost boy," insisted that "my decision is not an emotional one." He was acting, he maintained, solely out of an intellectual conviction that Marxism was the only just way of life. "For this alone he was memorable," she would later write. Also, in the contemporaneous notes she took as they talked, there was the repeated marginal reminder to herself that "he's bitter." Finally, she sensed in him "the desire to stand out from other men," that he saw himself as "extraordinary." For instance, she said this "came out unexpectedly when I asked him why he had been willing to grant me an interview. I expected a simple response. That he was homesick, maybe, and wanted somebody to talk to. Instead, he surprised me. 'I would like,' he replied, 'to give the people of the United States something to think about.'"[565] *That* he would eventually do, in spades, but it would have nothing to do with his beliefs or defection to Soviet Russia. When he left at two that morning to return to his own room, she felt a twinge of pity for him: "I felt that I had failed," she wrote later. "I had reached out, and my fingers had not touched anyone."[566]

Four Americans—Snyder, McVickar, Mosby, and Johnson—had tried, in their way, to help Lee Oswald. But help doesn't visit those who do not welcome it.

Near the end of the week, Priscilla Johnson paused on the second floor on her way back to her own room on the third floor of the Metropole. She stopped to ask the *dezhur-naya*, a diminutive concierge in white who sat on the landing, "How about Number 233? Is he in?" The woman checked her drawer of room keys and her arms flew up. "Out," she said. Lee had forgotten his promise to say good-bye and she never saw him again.[567]

Johnson told McVickar that Oswald was no longer at the Metropole, and on December 1, the U.S. ambassador to Russia, Llewellyn Thompson, informed the State Department that "Lee Harvey Oswald believed departed from Metropole Hotel within last few days . . . apparently quickly and with no forwarding address."[568]

Oswald had ostensibly vanished into Russia, a country twice the size of the United States, practically a continent in its own right, and no one on the American side had any idea of what happened to him.

In fact, Lee Oswald, his funds all but depleted, had gone no farther than another, smaller room in the Metropole—a chambermaids' cubbyhole room on the top floor arranged for by Rimma's superiors. For the next six weeks he did little but wait for the Soviet authorities to decide what they were finally going to do with him.

Moscow in December is brutally cold, and Oswald did not have clothes warm enough to permit explorations in the city, so he mostly sat in the little room for which he was no longer able to pay rent and waited, even taking his meals there, though they were of poorer quality than the regular hotel fare. The reliable Rimma continued to visit him.[569] He later covered the whole period from November 17 through December 30 in a paragraph entry in his Historic Diary. He wrote that "I have bought myself two self-teaching Russian Lan. Books I force myself to study [them] 8 hours a day. I sit in my room and read and memorize words . . . I have $28. left," he said, from the fifteen hundred dollars he had managed to save over the previous two years for his Russian adventure. "It is very cold on the streets," he wrote, "so I rarley go outside at all . . . I see no one speak to no-one accept every-now-and-than Rimmea."[570]

On November 26, he undertook a very long, handwritten reply to a letter from his brother Robert. It is a shockingly cold, fanatical document. In one of the softer, early paragraphs he writes,

> I will ask you a question Robert. what do you surpport the american government for? What is the Ideal you put forward? . . . Ask me and I will tell you I fight ["fight" is encircled] for communism. This word brings to your mind slaves or injustice. This is because of american propaganda. Look this word up in the dictionary or better still, read the book which I first read when I was fifteen, "CAPITAL," which contains economic theorys and most important the "communist manifesto."
>
> I will not say your grandchildren will live under communism, look for yourself at history, look at a world map! america is a dieing country, I do not wish to be a part of it, nor do I ever again wish to be used as a tool in its military aggressions.

He tells Robert that "happiness" for him "is taking part in the struggle" for Communism.

He later gets into the heart of his letter: "I want you to understand what I say now, I do not say lightly, or unknowingly, since I have been in the military as you know, and I know what war is like: 1. In the event of war I would kill any american who put a uniform on in defense of the american government—any american. 2. That in my own mind I have no attachment's of any kind in the U.S. 3. That I want to, and I shall, live a normal happy and peaceful life here in the Soviet Union for the rest of my life." In case Robert missed the import of "no attachment's," Lee's fourth paragraph spelled it out: "4. That my mother and you are (in spite of what the newspaper said) not objects of affection, but only examples of workers in the U.S."

After this diatribe, he writes, "You should not try to remember me in any way I used to be, since I am only now showing you how I am. I am not all bitterness or hate, I come here only to find freedom, In truth, I feel I am at last with my own people."[571]

Unless Oswald was lying to himself in his own diary entry covering the period of November 17 to December 30, in which he said he had twenty-eight dollars to his name, he tells Robert in the letter the lie that "I have no money problems *at all*. My situation was not nearly as sable [stable?] then, as it is now, I have no troubles at all now along that line." He also made it clear in the letter that he was disappointed that his grand gesture had put him in the spotlight for only two days before he was plunged once again into obscurity. "I wish you would do me a favor since that other bad newspaper story went [out], I have been thinking I would like to give people, who are interested [in] the real reasons," he wrote. "If you would, give the contents of this letter . . . to some reporter, it will clarify my situation, use your own judgement, however."[572]*

Oswald seemed to realize that his fifteen minutes of fame had come and gone, and he knew his life was presently even gloomier than it had been before. He might have been

---

*Oswald ended his letter lightheartedly: "It is snowing here in Moscow now, which makes everything look very nice from my hotel window. I can see the Kremlin and Red Square and I have just finished a dinner of meat and potatoes. So you see the Russians are not so different from you and I" (CE 295, 16 H 822).

cheered had he known anything of the progress of his case through the Soviet bureaucracy, but he did not. On November 27, Andrei Gromyko, minister of foreign affairs, and Aleksandr Shelepin, chairman of the KGB, addressed a joint memo to the Central Committee of the Communist Party of the Soviet Union that concluded with a recommendation: "Considering that other foreigners who were formerly given Soviet citizenship (Sitrinell, Afshar) left our country after having lived here for awhile and also keeping in mind that Oswald has not been sufficiently studied, it is advisable to give him the right to temporary residence in the USSR for one year, with a guarantee of employment and housing. In this event, the question of Oswald's permanent residency in the USSR and granting of Soviet citizenship can be decided during the course of this term."[573]*

Sometime in December, the Central Committee, not having yet ruled on the recommendation, once again called Oswald to the Soviet Passport Office, where he met three new officials who put to him the same questions the others had asked a month before, as though his case were only then being taken up for the first time. "They appear not to know me at all," he wrote, disconcerted, in his diary.[574]

Rimma, during her visits, didn't even try to help him with his Russian, as she felt he was too distraught to learn very much, and she noticed no particular improvement in his skills from all the hours of study he put in alone. He kept asking her for news about his case, but when she passed his query on to her chief at Intourist, he said to her, "What can he do for a living?" She had no answer to that.[575]

Robert received a third letter on December 17 in which Oswald said that he would be moving from the hotel and would not be writing again. He asked Robert not to write to him. The letter concluded, "I'm sure you understand that I would not like to recive correspondence from people in the country which I fled. I am starting a new life and I do not wish to have anything to do with the old life. I hope you and your family will always be in good health."[576]

Within a week or two, his mood had softened, if all but imperceptibly. Marguerite had mailed him a personal check for twenty dollars dated December 18. He returned it to her on January 5 with a note terse to the point of insult, scribbled on the torn-off flap of her envelope: "I can't use this check, of course. Put the $20 bill in an envelope and send it to me I'm also short of cash and need the rest. Love Lee."[577] The "rest" may have been in reference to the hundred dollars he supposedly had given, not lent, her in September. In any case, she did send him a twenty-dollar bill, and almost immediately thereafter a money order for about twenty-five dollars, both of which failed to get through and were eventually returned to her.[578]

---

*How did the decision on Oswald come about? Former KGB colonel Oleg Nechiporenko, with access to KGB files, writes in his book *Passport to Assassination* that "the news of Oswald's visit to the [U.S.] Embassy, in conjunction with his attempt at suicide, upset the people who ran Intourist . . . Now the Western mass media were clued into events, which could lead to reports that in the Soviet Union tourists are 'driven to commit suicide.' This could damage the image and the commercial interest of Intourist by scaring away potential tourists to the USSR. Therefore, the Intourist brass again began to sound all the alarms. This time it sent another strictly confidential message on November 12 straight to Anastas Mikoyan, Deputy Chairman of the USSR Council of Ministers. As First Deputy Chairman, Mikoyan was in charge of all Soviet foreign trade organizations, including Intourist. In this capacity he could issue orders to the Ministry of Foreign Affairs and the Chairman of the KGB. Mikoyan forwarded the letter to the head of the Seventh Department of the Second Chief Directorate, the division of counterintelligence that handled tourists" (Nechiporenko, *Passport to Assassination*, p.39). The implication is that the mere forwarding of the letter carried the imprimatur of Mikoyan that he was not opposed to Oswald being permitted to stay in the Soviet Union.

Christmas came and went. On New Year's Eve 1959, Roza Agafonova was on duty in the hotel, and Oswald sat up with her to see the new year in. He had only just learned that she was married and the mother of a child born crippled, which was why, he wrote in his diary, "she is so strangly tender and compeling." She gave him a small "Boratin" clown as a New Year's present.[579]

Still unknown to him, on November 27, 1959, his fate had already been decided by the highest entity in the Soviet Union, the Central Committee of the Communist Party, which passed a resolution on his behalf:

> In regard to the petition by the American citizen Lee Harvey Oswald for Soviet citizenship, let it hereby be resolved: 1. To agree with the proposal of the Ministry of Foreign Affairs and the KGB to grant U.S. citizen Lee Harvey Oswald temporary residence status for one year and to resolve the questions of his permanent residency in the USSR and Soviet citizenship during this period. 2. To oblige the Belorussian National Economic Council to place Oswald in a job in electronics and the Minsk City Council of Worker's Deputies to assign him his own small apartment. 3. To instruct the executive committee of the Societies of the Red Cross and the Red Crescent to assign five thousand rubles for equipping the apartment for Oswald and to issue him an allowance of seven hundred rubles a month over the course of one year.[580]

KGB defector Yuriy Nosenko told author Gerald Posner, "After years of cold relations between the superpowers, they were just starting to warm up. We didn't want to do anything to hurt this new atmosphere or to give a pretext to those who wanted to ruin better relations. By telling Oswald he had to leave, he was so unstable he might try and succeed in killing himself. Then we would be criticized for a KGB murder of an American tourist. If we forced him onto a plane for deportation, there was still an image of a student being manhandled by the Soviet security forces. Considering the options, we decided to let him stay. He seemed harmless enough. We could decide where he worked and lived, and maintain surveillance over him to insure he did not cause any trouble or was not an American sleeper agent."[581]

Finally, on January 4, 1960, Oswald was summoned to the Soviet Passport Office and given Identity Document for Stateless Persons Number 311479, although he was technically not stateless—he had never returned to the American embassy either to renounce his citizenship or to recover his passport.[582] He was told he was being sent to Minsk in the Soviet republic of Belorussia (also spelled Byelorussia—Belorussia became known as Belarus following the demise of the Soviet Union in 1991). He asked the official, "Is that in Siberia?" The official laughed.[583] Minsk is in the opposite direction, an industrial city located about 450 miles southwest of Moscow with a population of about 510,000 in 1959.[584] Further, he was told that a factory job had been arranged for him there. His disappointment that he had not been granted Soviet citizenship and was not going to remain in Moscow, where he wanted to be, was balanced by relief that the uncertainty was ended; he told Rimma Shirokova that he was happy.[585]

The next day he went, by direction of the Passport Office, to an agency the Russians called the Red Cross, although it was not a private charity like the International Red Cross or the Muslims' Red Crescent, but an organ of the Soviet government. They gave him five thousand rubles, or about five hundred dollars at the official exchange rate, a not inconsiderable sum. Oswald thought it "a huge sum!" He used 2,200 rubles to pay his hotel bill and 150 rubles to purchase his railroad ticket to Minsk.[586]

Always faithful Rimma saw him off at the station. He was depressed and wanted her to accompany him on the overnight train trip, but by now he understood that such things were not as simple in the Soviet Union as they might have been in the states. It was snowing as they said their good-byes. Both of them were crying.[587] But through the tears there was a sense of defiance and renewal. After writing in letters to his mother and brother that "I do not wish to every contact you again," he wrote in his diary, "I am beginning anew life and I don't want *any part* of the old."[588] Oswald was met at the station in Minsk by two Soviet Red Cross workers who took him to the Hotel Minsk, an impressive five-hundred-room establishment built less than three years before at the direct order of Khrushchev[589]—Rimma had been there and thought it especially nice.[590] Two women from Intourist, both of whom spoke English, were waiting there for him. One, Roza Kuznetsova, would become a close friend and attend his twenty-first birthday party later that year. "Excellant English," Oswald wrote as his first impression of her, "we attract each other at once."[591]

Two days before his arrival in Minsk, KGB officers in that city were informed of Oswald's pending arrival. They were given minimal details about how he had arrived in Moscow, his alleged suicide attempt, and how he had insisted on remaining in the Soviet Union. Their mission was to determine if Oswald was an American intelligence plant. Surveillance began the moment he got off the train in Minsk.[592]* The following day Oswald met the mayor, Comrade Sharapov, who welcomed him to Minsk, promised him a nearly rent-free apartment, and warned him against "uncultured" persons who sometimes insulted foreigners.[593]

The new life for which Lee Oswald had yearned and planned so long was finally to begin—in the city of Minsk, a town about the size of Tucson, Arizona. It had been destroyed twice during World War II, once when the Germans swept through on their advance on Moscow and again when the German army pushed back toward Poland and their homeland by the Red Army. Ninety percent of the town, originally a warren of small, ramshackle wooden buildings, had been destroyed, so the city that presented itself to Oswald in the frosty January of 1960 was, by Russian standards anyway, quite modern.[594] After he returned to America he eventually wrote a description of it for a book he hoped to write.[595]

The tallest building was still only nine stories, and the more distant landscape of factory chimneys and construction cranes testified to its largely industrial character. The main street, the Prospekt Stalinskaya, contained most of the city's attractions—the five-hundred-room hotel Lee was staying at, the stuffy four-hundred-seat cinema, and the big GUM Department Store, where you could sign on to a three-month waiting list for a refrigerator or vacuum cleaner or even a car, a Moskvich (one year's wait) or a Victory

---

*Author Norman Mailer, in research for his book *Oswald's Tale: An American Mystery*, spent six months in Russia in 1993. While there he tracked down and interviewed the KGB agents who were assigned to monitor Oswald's every move. Undoubtedly aided by his international stature as an author, he was also given access to the Belarus KGB files on Oswald, including transcripts of conversations overheard by the KGB (through electronic surveillance) in the apartment in Minsk that Oswald shared with his wife, Marina. I have availed myself, in this book, of some of Mailer's seminal research on Oswald in Russia along with that of KGB colonel Oleg Maximovich Nechiporenko, who also had access to KGB files on Oswald, which he used for his book *Passport to Assassination*.

or a Volga (six or seven months' wait). In a society where there was no commercial competition, Minsk had mostly just one of everything, except restaurants—there were five of those, including two almost identical stand-up cafeterias across the street from each other where Stalinskaya ended in Stalin Square. Stalinskaya was the longest, straightest street in the state of Belorussia, while its cross-streets were narrow, cobbled, and picturesque, ending at the end of the outskirts in pleasant public parks.[596]

Among the prominent public buildings were the Ministry of Internal Affairs, run by a tough MVD colonel, and right around the corner, the headquarters of the Belorussian KGB. A building Lee would come to know well was the Trade Union Building, which was used more for education and entertainment than business—real union affairs were handled in the factories. A large Greek revival building, it housed offices and work spaces for the performance groups that entertained there, an auditorium, and a small dance hall that Lee would come to frequent. Its architrave bore, in place of Greek heroes and gods, a surveyor with his transit, a bricklayer, a sportswoman in a track suit, and a man in a double-breasted suit carrying a briefcase, "either a bureaucrat or an intellectual, apparently," Oswald wrote.[597]

On January 10, his third day in the city, Oswald's diary is confined to a single, terse, run-on sentence: "The day to myself I walk through city, very nice."[598]

Here is the KGB's more detailed account of his day:

> At 11 o'clock, Lee Harvey left Hotel Minsk and went to GUM. There he came up to the electrical department, asked a salesperson some question, then took money out of his pocket and went to a cashier of this department. He did not pay for anything but just put money back into his pocket and started pacing first floor of department store up and down looking at different goods. Then he went back to electrical department, paid 2 rubles 25 copecks for electrical plug, put it into his pocket and went up to second floor. There he spent some time in department of ready-made clothes, looked through available suits, then left GUM store walking fast. He was back at his hotel by 11:25. At 12:45 he came out of his hotel room and went to restaurant. He took seat at vacant table and began to eat. (No observations were made during this meal because no other people were in there.) 13:35 [1:35 p.m.] Lee Harvey left restaurant and went back to his room. 18:10 [6:10 p.m.] he left his room and went to restaurant. He took vacant table, had his meal, left restaurant at 18:45, and took elevator to fourth floor where he went to his room. He did not leave his room up to 24:00 [midnight] after which time no observation was made until morning.[599]

Although Lee was probably never more than fleetingly aware of it, one feature of his new life was that he would never walk alone. A few weeks earlier, on December 21, 1959, the KGB opened an espionage file on him. As alluded to earlier, the Central Committee had given the KGB one year to "resolve the questions of his permanent residency in the USSR and Soviet citizenship," and the spy agency was frankly puzzled as to why he had come to their country at all. Opening a file on him under the rubric of espionage, a very serious matter, guaranteed that whatever manpower, equipment, and resources were needed to keep him under surveillance would be available.[600]

Curiously, or perhaps not so, they never chose to confront Oswald openly. According to Vladimir Semichastny, then chairman of the KGB, "those who met with him were under the cover of different organizations: Belorussian Ministry of Foreign Affairs, USSR Ministry of Internal Affairs, OVIR [passport office]," but there were no direct contacts.[601]

Indirectly or directly, however, the KGB had determined that Oswald's knowledge of radar was "very primitive and did not extend beyond the textbooks." The head of the First Chief Directorate of the KGB, Aleksandr Sakharovsky, saw no particular use for him, but the intriguing possibility remained that he might have been planted on them by the CIA. He would, therefore, according to Semichastny, be handled "with the usual control measures. Routine surveillance, involving agents, observation, and standard operative techniques." Even then, however, "we didn't . . . involve our most skilled surveillance agents, because we didn't want to risk compromising them for future, more important use."[602]

Colonel Oleg Nechiporenko, who studied the KGB files on Oswald and interviewed the KGB operatives and their superiors charged with his control and surveillance, thought that the intelligence agency might have taken a different attitude toward him if they had known that the U-2 spy plane had been housed at Atsugi when Oswald was stationed there.[603] Though Oswald apparently never mentioned that to anyone in Moscow (in spite of his silly threat at the American embassy), it appears likely that the KGB, as effective as well as incompetent as virtually all official bodies are, never knew that Oswald was even stationed at Atsugi. Oswald made no reference to this in the questionnaire he completed for Russia's Passport Office in Moscow on January 4, 1960,[604] or the earlier questionnaire he filled out when he applied for a Soviet visa at the consulate in Helsinki on October 12, 1959.[605] Indeed, KGB defector Yuriy Nosenko told author Gerald Posner, "as for Atsugi, we didn't know he had been based there."[606] And Nosenko told the HSCA back in 1978 that the KGB "didn't know" Oswald had any connection with the U-2,[607] which he, in fact, did not.

But surely Soviet intelligence was well aware of the fact that U-2 missions had been flown from Atsugi, whether or not they knew it was, along with Adana in Turkey, one of the aircraft's two main bases. It didn't take any military intelligence capacity to know about the U-2 at Atsugi. As indicated earlier, not only was the unique plane clearly visible to anyone in the vicinity at Atsugi, which, unlike Adana, is in a populated area, but in September 1959, just before Oswald's arrival in the Soviet Union, the pilot of U-2 plane number 360, outfitted with the new and more powerful engine that increased its range and altitude, decided to test the machine by setting a new altitude record. He did, but at the cost of too much fuel. The plane ran out of gas and landed ten miles short of Atsugi at the airstrip of the Japanese Glider Club, where it bogged down in mud. The pilot, wearing the uncomfortable rubber bodysuit and unable to get out of his jammed cockpit unaided, radioed to Atsugi for help. Military police quickly arrived to cordon off the area and drive onlookers away at gunpoint, but not before hoards of Japanese with omnipresent cameras had crowded around the plane and snapped innumerable photos, some of which appeared the next day in Japanese newspapers and magazines. Editorial writers wondered in print why, if the U-2 was engaged only in high-altitude weather research, it bore no distinguishing identification marks and occasioned such elaborate security.[608]

After CIA U-2 pilot Francis Gary Powers was shot down over Sverdlovsk on May Day (May 1) 1960, his interrogators at Moscow's Lubyanka Prison showed him articles about plane 360's crash near Atsugi and asked him whether he knew about it. He did, but he didn't bother to tell them that it was the same plane they had just shot down, the remains of which they had put on display in nearby Gorky Park.[609]

In any case, there is no suggestion in the Soviet intelligence documents that have become available since the collapse of the USSR that Oswald ever gave the Soviets intelligence information or that they were interested in him as a source. One of the great, eternal problems of intelligence gathering is and always has been the reliability of the information acquired—false or faulty information is often more harmful than no information at all—and the Soviets simply did not believe that a disturbed youth had anything to tell them that they could trust.

While the KGB obsessively followed Lee around on his first, tentative forays into the cityscape of his new home, American security services were also showing an interest in him. Although they didn't actually know where he went after they lost track of him in Moscow, they were beginning to open files on him. Eventually, CIA, FBI, Department of Defense, U.S. Navy, U.S. Army, and State Department files would be opened, closed, reopened, neglected, and stuffed with odd bits of information of very little use to anyone, but they would testify to a continuing interest in their subject.

In the meantime, the subject of all this scrutiny was getting acquainted with Minsk and meeting the people who would become his new circle of friends. On January 11, 1960, he visited the Belorussian Radio and Television factory, referred to by everyone as the "radio factory" or "Horizon," where he would be working,[610] a massive facility on a twenty-five-acre site two miles north of the center of town. This haphazard collection of buildings, workshops, and sheds reminded author Norman Mailer of a rundown movie studio.[611] About five thousand employees produced radio and television sets there for Russian consumers. Lee noticed that there were no "pocket radios"—the tiny "transistors" that had recently become the rage in America. These were not available anywhere in the Soviet Union.[612]

On Oswald's first visit to the factory he met Alexander Ziger, a Polish Jew who had emigrated to Argentina in 1938, where he worked for an American company until he returned to Poland in 1955. His Polish homeland had been annexed by the USSR and was now a part of Belorussia. Ziger, an engineer in his forties who headed a department in the factory, spoke English well, and both he and his family, including two daughters born in Argentina, would become good friends to Oswald.[613]

Two days later, Oswald began work at the factory as some sort of machinist. In his diary he described the job as a "checker," in quotation marks. One of his work documents describes him as an "adjuster," another as a "locksmith or metal worker."[614]

He was assigned to an "experimental shop," a drab two-story red-brick building in the center of the factory complex. While in other parts of the plant, workers, three out of five of them women, toiled at long assembly lines, the experimental shop employed only fifty-eight hands, five of whom were foremen, and a commissar from the Communist Party. Work began at eight sharp with the ringing of a bell. Ten operators worked on lathes on the lower floor, the rest upstairs. Apparently the work involved the construction of prototypes. Oswald later wrote that they often worked directly from blueprints.[615] Oswald's base pay was seven hundred rubles per month (about seventy dollars on the official exchange rate), normal pay for his type of work. However, he also received seven hundred rubles monthly from the Soviet Red Cross, and he thought his total of fourteen hundred rubles per month was about as much as the director of the factory made.[616] Since he was paid based on his production, he could make up to nine hundred rubles per month.[617]

Oswald found his coworkers "friendly and kind," almost too friendly at times—some offered to call a mass meeting so he could tell everyone about himself. Oswald declined the honor. The first small hint of a collision between his uncommonly independent nature and the antithetical climate for this in Soviet life surfaced in his diary entry for January 13 to 16, where he writes, "I don't like" the fact that there was a picture of Lenin which "watchs" the workers from up above, and the fact that there was "complusery" physical training "at 11-11.10 each morning." But he seemed otherwise content. He was taking Roza, one of the two Intourist representatives who had met him at his hotel when he first arrived in Minsk, to the movies, theater, or opera almost every night. "I'm living big . . . and very satisfied," he wrote in his diary.[618] He came to rely on the other official who had met him at the railroad station, Stellina (named for Stalin), a twenty-eight-year-old married woman with a year-old daughter. She was the head of the Service Bureau at the hotel and lived only two blocks away. Since her job required her to be on call at all hours, she didn't mind Lee dropping in for help with a problem, and she even dubbed him "Aloysha," a name she believed to be rather distinguished. She thought him oddly secretive, but she was well disposed toward Americans. She remembered, when she was living in an orphanage after the Great Patriotic War (the Russian name for the Second World War), the good things the Americans had sent the children: beds, clothes, sugar, chocolate, and nuts. She was also touched by Lee's helplessness and began to mother him a bit. She tried to teach him Russian, sometimes on walks with him out to the Dynamo Sports Stadium with her child in a stroller.[619]

Comrade Libezin, the party secretary at the plant, was solicitous of Oswald's inability to speak passable Russian and assigned two coworkers of Oswald's to help improve his Russian, one working with Oswald on the job, the other after work.[620] Neither of the two men "hung out" with Oswald, but the relationship changed for one of them, Pavel Golovachev, one night when he was accosted by a KGB agent who showed his ID and asked for a talk. The agent was Stepan Vasilyevich Gregorieff (to borrow the pseudonym used by Norman Mailer). He was the main agent in the Minsk headquarters of the KGB who had been assigned the task of watching Oswald. His job was to keep his distance and to try to determine whether Oswald was an agent or some kind of CIA plant. He had several questions he wanted answers to. One had to do with the nature of Oswald's service in the Marine Corps and his experience with radar and electronics. Another was the nature of his commitment to Marxism, since Oswald seemed to know so little of Marxist-Leninist theory. Yet another was his proficiency in Russian—was he really as inept and unskilled as he seemed, or only pretending to be?

Gregorieff wanted eighteen-year-old Pavel Golovachev's cooperation in providing regular reports on the activities and attitudes of the American defector, and Pavel was not in a position to refuse, although he wasn't happy about having to do it. Pavel was the son of a famous Soviet fighter pilot who had been twice decorated as a hero of the Soviet Union, which could have bought Pavel a certain level of privilege, but he had not done well on his own. Following his father around from base to base, he had attended eleven schools in ten years, and his last school report was a disgrace. He'd also been kicked out of Komsomol, the party's youth organization. He was working at the plant only as a stepping stone to a career as an engineer—he was at the same time attending the Minsk Polytechnic Institute four nights a week. The KGB suspected him of small transactions in the black market as well. He didn't want to tell his father that the KGB had spoken to him, and he thought it best to go along quietly with Gregorieff's plan. Pavel, whose "first reaction to Oswald was that he looked like an extraterrestrial who had all of a sudden ended up in their factory," felt that Oswald did not seem to be up to much that would interest the KGB in any case.[621]

"It was like this," Pavel said. "He [the KGB man] said, 'Your country asks you—your country demands. There is a foreigner here. It's in the country's interests for security, and so on.'"[622]

In the end, Pavel became Lee's best and closest friend in the Soviet Union—although Pavel learned more English from Lee than Lee learned Russian from Pavel. "I told him [Oswald] about it [the KGB's contact with Pavel] a year later," Pavel says. "I had three or four meetings with the KGB people. They gave me little assignments to provoke him, saying try this out on him and see what he says."[623] By the time Marina entered Lee's life the following year, the two men almost always spoke English with each other.[624] Pavel wrote to Lee and Marina after they went off to America, the last time less than two months before the assassination.[625]*

On March 16, Oswald was given a fourth-floor apartment in a riverside building reserved for employees of his factory that was surprisingly ornate for Minsk. Apartment number 24 was very tiny but attractive, and to get any apartment there at all was remarkable, since many of his coworkers spent months or even years on a waiting list for such an accommodation, sometimes delaying marriage for however long a time it took. Oswald knew he was getting special treatment, describing the one-room apartment with a kitchen, bathroom, and a balcony overlooking the Svisloch River, as "a Russian dream."[626] Pavel and some other friends from the factory helped Lee move in, with some furnishings provided by the factory: a bed, a table, some chairs, a gas cooker. The kitchen was very small and the room was only about ten by seventeen feet, but the building itself was very grand and located in the best part of town, and the view of the river four stories below and just across Kalinina Street was outstanding.[627] Oswald described the place as "almost rent-free," and with some justice—it cost him only sixty rubles, or about six dollars, a month. The preference shown him was not all that remarkable. Foreigners residing in the Soviet Union were often given financial subsidies and other aid, and foreign students were paid a stipend double that of Soviet citizens.[628] Oswald's Russian friends were in no way surprised that he was receiving certain advantages "below the waist," as Pavel put it, since, as indicated, they knew it was normal in Russia for foreigners to be treated better than Russian citizens.[629] It also went without saying that the place was bugged—the electric meter kept running even when all the appliances and lights were off, and surveillance was a common assumption. After Marina married Lee and moved in, she and Lee took it for granted that their mail was opened and read, and it was.[630]

As spring turned into summer, Lee enjoyed his new life, which involved a lot of new

---

*Meanwhile, since Marguerite hadn't heard from Lee for several months, she became worried, and wrote her congressman in Fort Worth, Jim Wright, on March 6, 1960, asking him for help in locating Lee (CE 1138, 22 H 118). Wright forwarded her inquiry to the Department of State, which in turn sent it to the American embassy in Moscow. The embassy responded to the Department of State on March 28 that embassy officials had had no contact with Oswald since November 9, 1959, and had "no clue as to his present whereabouts." The embassy suggested that Mrs. Oswald write a personal letter to Lee, send it to the embassy, and they'd forward it to the Soviet Foreign Office. (CE 923, 18 H 122; CE 927, 18 H 126) There's no evidence that Marguerite did that, but the day after she wrote to Wright she wrote a letter to U.S. Secretary of State Christian Herter, also asking him for assistance in locating Lee. "Lee is probably stranded," she wrote Herter, "and even if he now realizes that he has made a mistake he would have no way of financing his way home. He probably needs help." (CE 206, 16 H 594–595; see also CE 928–930, 18 H 128–130)

friends—it is the only period of his life where he was involved in social activities with others, many of whom were his own age. May Day 1960 was his first holiday in Russia, marked by the customary, spectacular parade of the region's armed forces and workers, drawn from the ranks, passing the reviewing stand waving flags and large banners with Khrushchev's portrait on them. That evening he went to the Zigers for a party with forty guests, many of them Argentinians, and there was a great deal of dancing and singing.[631] His friend Pavel, who was also there, was impressed by the relaxed, joyful atmosphere and the Latin decor, music, and manners of the Zigers, who served coffee and wine on a tray—very unlike Russians. The Zigers' daughters scandalized the neighborhood by sun-bathing on their balcony, a barbarity put down to the fact that they were not only foreign but Jewish.[632]

Lee took notice of both of the daughters. Eleonora, twenty-six, divorced, was a talented singer. He thought he "hit it off" with the younger Anita, who was twenty and "not so attractive" but a gifted pianist who was studying music and played everything from Beethoven's "Moonlight Sonata" to Argentine tangos on the Zigers' piano.[633] He was also attracted to a friend of Anita's, a girl who worked in the central post office, Albina, at whom he made an unsuccessful pass. She in turn introduced him to Ernst Titovets, also called Erich, a handsome, blond charmer who was drawn to Lee at least in part because of the opportunity it gave him to improve his English. Erich was a bit of a nerd. He spoke a cultured English, played chess, and was going to medical school. He would become another of Lee's pals.[634]

Needless to say, none of this escaped the notice of the KGB, whose dogged appetite for banality was insatiable. Their account of Lee's first holiday in the USSR runs as follows:

> At 10:00 Lee Harvey came out of house N4 on Kalinina Street [Lee's apartment], came to Pobedy Square where he spent 25 minutes looking at passing parade. After this he went to Kalinina Street and began walking up and down embankment of Svisloch River. Returned home by 11:00. From 11:00 to 13:00 [1:00 p.m.] he came out onto balcony of his apartment more than once. At 13:35 Lee Harvey left his house, got on trolley bus N2 at Pobedy Square, went to Central Square, was last to get off bus, went down Engelsa, Marksa and Lenina Streets to bakery store on Prospekt Stalina. There he bought 200 grams of vanilla cookies, then went to café Vesna, had a cup of coffee with patty at self-service section and hurried toward movie theater Central. Having looked through billboards he bought newspaper *Banner of Youth*, visited bakery for second time, left it immediately, and took trolley bus N1 to Pobedy Square and was home by 14:20 [2:20 p.m.]. At 16:50 Lee Harvey left his house and came to house N14 on Krasnaya Street (Residence of immigrant from Argentina—Ziger). At 1:40 Lee Harvey together with other men and women, among whom there were daughters of Ziger, came home. Observation was stopped at this point till morning."[635]

Apparently, the KGB missed something by not going to the party. "Zeber [Ziger] advises me to go back to U.S.A.," Lee wrote in his diary, "its the first voice of opposstion I have heard. I respect Zeger, he has seen the world. He says many things, and relats many things I do not know about the U.S.S.R. I begin to feel uneasy inside, its true!"[636]

Something else happened on that May Day in 1960—the aforementioned shooting down of Francis Gary Powers's U-2 spy plane over Sverdlovsk by Soviet rockets, an event that stunned the world, although it would be almost a week before ordinary citizens in either the Soviet Union or the United States would hear about it. The worldwide press was full of the international incident for months. Lee, with his still awkward Russian and little if any access to English news sources, could not have failed to notice the way the story galvanized his friends—it was the Soviet Union's greatest propaganda triumph since the beginning of the cold war. However, when Lee got around to making entries in his diary for the months of May, June, and July, although he apparently was disturbed about the U-2 incident, fearing it might hurt him since he was an American (see later text), he didn't mention one word about it, writing instead of the May Day parade, the party at the Zigers, picnics and drives in the countryside with Anita and the Zigers' "mos.vick" car, summer months of "green beauty," and pine forests that were "very deep." Unfortunately, Anita Ziger's Hungarian boyfriend Alfred always came along.[637]

By this time, though, Lee's eye had already been caught by a new worker at the factory, Ella German, a slim, pretty Jewish girl who had worked at the factory before. She had always wanted to attend Minsk University but had trouble getting accepted, possibly because she was Jewish, possibly because she didn't bribe the right people. However, when a law was passed that factory workers were to be given priority, she finally got into the university on a scholarship. Two years later she got a low grade on an important exam, lost her scholarship, and had to switch from full-time study to night classes—and she had to return to the assembly line at the factory.[638] "A silky black haired Jewish beauty with fine dark eyes skin white as snow a beauifel smile and good but unpredictable nature," Lee would write of her. "Her only fault was that at 24 she was still a virgin, due entirely to her own desire. I met her when she came too work at my factory. I noticed her, and perhaps fell in love with her, the first minute I saw her."[639]

Ella recalled she was twenty-three when they met. She was introduced to Lee the first morning she came back to work, and one day she asked him to help her with some pages of English she had to translate. They began to walk to the park and go to the movies about twice a week. She thought he was a kindhearted person with a good sense of humor. Ella sensed that Lee was very lonely in Minsk and consequently pitied him enough that she didn't want to reject him. But she didn't like him enough to consider marrying him either.[640]

Soon after they met, information about the U.S. spy plane being shot down was in the news. "What do you think, Ella?" Lee asked her. "Can it damage me because I'm an American?" She reassured him that "no one can say you are responsible."[641]

On June 18, 1960, Lee obtained a hunting license and soon after purchased a 16-gauge single-barrel shotgun.[642] Lee joined a local chapter of the Belorussian Society of Hunters and Fishermen, a hunting club sponsored by his factory. But according to KGB records, it was not until September 10 that he actually went out with seven others to hunt for small game in the farm regions around Minsk.[643]*

Coupled with his lukewarm (if that) Marxist activism, Oswald's yen for hunting set

---

*Author Norman Mailer was told by the KGB agent in charge of Oswald's detail that by now the agency had given Oswald a new code name. Mailer writes, "It was Likhoi. That sounded like Lee Harvey, but the word meant valiant, or dashing. It was KGB humor. Likhoi never seemed to do anything but go to work, walk around, and shop." (Mailer, *Oswald's Tale*, p.114)

off alarm bells at the KGB. Vacheslav Nikonov, an aide to the first KGB chief after the fall of Communism, reviewed the entire Oswald file and told PBS's *Frontline*, "Oswald looked very suspicious to the KGB and to the factory authorities because he was not interested in Marxism. He didn't attend any Marxist classes. He didn't read any Marxist literature and he didn't attend even the labor union meetings. So the question was, what was he doing there?"[644]

One of Oswald's hunting companions, Leonid Sepanovich Tzagiko, a lathe operator at Oswald's plant, said "We set off to hunt. There were five of us . . . Suddenly, a shot rang out. I asked Oswald, 'Why are you shooting?' He said, 'Look! Look! A hare!' The others fired, too, but missed. And then we all stopped and discussed why he had shot too soon. He explained that the hare had jumped from under his feet and he was startled and so he shot. I said, 'You could have killed me. Your gun was pointing right at me.'"[645]

Being startled and firing wildly doesn't mean you're a bad shot, and missing a rabbit once when you shoot at it also obviously doesn't mean you're a bad shot, but somehow, from this meager evidence, conspiracy theorists have concluded Oswald was a poor shot as a hunter and, hence, an unlikely assassin of Kennedy. But his brother Robert doesn't buy into Lee's being a poor shot at shooting rabbits, maintaining that Lee had plenty of experience at varmint hunting and knew how to handle himself. "We have shot cottontail rabbits with .22's on the run, okay? We've shot squirrels in the trees with .22's," he told ABC in 1993. "My experience with him in the field with a shotgun or a .22 was he usually got his game."[646]

According to Tzagiko, "We didn't take him [Oswald] again because the head of our group had been warned [presumably by the KGB] not to."[647]* Although the military installations in the district were off limits to hunters, his KGB minders feared that Oswald might have some sort of sensing equipment that would allow him to spy on the facilities from a distance.[648]

But Pavel Golovachev told author Gus Russo in 1993, "I would say that he wasn't a spy because when he bought a camera, he couldn't even put film in it. And it was a very basic camera, a Smena-2, which even a Soviet schoolchild could use, and he couldn't." Pavel also said that Oswald couldn't repair the simplest defect in a radio while working at the Belorussian Radio and Television factory in Minsk.[649]

Regarding a report in the KGB files that a coworker of Oswald's at the radio factory, code-named Zorin, said that Lee was possibly working on a secret radio transmitter at the plant, Pavel says this is nonsense. "He bought one of the cheapest radio sets, and it only had short and long-wave frequencies. He complained that he couldn't receive certain broadcasts. So, with a kitchen knife, I adjusted the capacitor and it worked fine. I have no doubt he was not a CIA agent. His knowledge was too primitive." Pavel also reported that Lee managed to rip two wires out while trying to insert batteries into another portable radio.[650]

If Lee Harvey Oswald were really a spy for the CIA, as so many conspiracy theorists believe, he seemed to be a singularly inept one.

Lee settled into Soviet life easily. He found a nearby café where the food wasn't very

---

*It is not clear how many times Oswald went hunting with the club. Although Tzagiko suggested only once, Lee suggested it was several times, later telling a group of college students in Alabama that the group of hunters he went with sometimes spent the night in outlying villages, which were so poor that they "often" left their bag with the villagers, who did not seem to have enough to eat (CE 2678, 26 H 34–35; CE 2679, 26 H 35–36; WR, p.699).

good and depressingly unvaried, although it was cheap and he really didn't care about quality "after three years in the U.S.M.C."[651] In August he applied for membership in the union at his plant and became a dues-paying member in September.[652] With the help of friends Golovachev and Titovets, his ability to speak Russian improved. Both likewise improved their English skills and wound up speaking more English with him than Russian. Titovets and Oswald improvised a grisly, taped "interview" with a fictional murderer:

Titovets: "Will you tell us about your last killing?"

Oswald: "Well, it was a young girl under a bridge. She came in carrying a loaf of bread and I just cut her throat from ear to ear."

Titovets: "What for?"

Oswald: "Well, I wanted the loaf of bread, of course."

Titovets: "Okay. And what do you think—what do you take to be the most—your most famous killing in your life?"

Oswald: "Well, the time I killed eight men on the Bowery sidewalk. They were just standing there, loafing around. I didn't like their faces, so I just shot them all with a machine gun. It was very, very famous. All the newspapers carried the story."

According to Titovets, "We were just having a great time and, actually, we were laughing our heads off."[653]

Around the same time, Oswald's diary reflects that he began to view his new homeland with a more critical eye. "As my Russian improves I become increasingly concious of just what sort of sociaty I live in. Mass gymnastics, compulsary after work meeting, usually political information meeting. Complusary attendance at lectures and the sending of the entire shop collective (except me) to pick potatoes on a Sunday, at a State colletive farm. A 'patriotic duty' to bring in the harvest. The opions [opinions] of the workers (unvoiced) are that its a great pain in the neck. They don't seem to be esspicialy enthusiastic about any of the 'collective' duties a natural feeling. I am increasingly aware of the presence, in all thing, of Lebizen [Libezin], shop party secretary, fat, fortyish, and jovial on the outside. He is a no-nonsense party regular."[654]

In October, he invited Ella to a party at his apartment. When Lee's pal Pavel showed up with a young woman named Inna Tachina and made it rather obvious that he had brought her for Lee, Ella, who wasn't really all that serious about Lee, was nonetheless miffed, and she quarreled with him about Inna. He left his own party to walk Ella to her nightshift at the plant about eight minutes away and apparently smoothed things over, for the relationship continued, but he also started an affair with Inna.[655]

Oswald wrote of Inna on a page in his diary he kept separate from the others, one dedicated to his amorous affairs in the Soviet Union: "Enna . . . from Rega, [Riga] Esonia [Estonia—Riga is actually in Latvia, not Estonia]. Studing at Conservatorie I met her in 1960 at The Zegers. her family (who sent her to Minsk) apparently well off. Enna loves fancy cloths well made shoes and underthings in October 1960 we began to get very close and clemingating [culminating?] in intercourse on October 21 she was a virgen and very interesting we met in such a fashion on 4 or 5 occiations ending Nov. 4 1960 later upon completion of her last year at the Music Con. she left Minsk for Rega."[656]

By December 1, he was having a light affair with one Nellya Korbinka.[657] She also made it to the same, separate, long page of his diary dedicated to intimate relations: "Nell . . . large, five ft. 11. inch, 150 lbs, built proportionly, large . . . breast hips wide and lovely but very pleasly proportioned, from a village near the polish border of strictly Russian peasents stock. gentle kind womenly and understanding, passionate in heart . . . she combined all the best womenly features with the kind, simple, Russian hearth I met her through one of her room-mates, Tonka, Nell and Tonka together with three other girls lived in a room at the for. lan. Insit. [Foreign Language Institute] dorm. in Minsk near the victory circle. I began to notice Nell serously only after I had parted ways with ENNA. Nell at first [does] not seem to warrant attention since she is rather plain looking and frieihtingly large. but I felt at once that she was kind and her passions were proportional too her size . . . after a light affair lasting into Jan and even Feb, we [continued] to remain on friendly but conventional terms."[658]

Lee did not understand that a few of the young women who showed an interest in him were, so to speak, professionals—informants to the KGB. One, Anna Byeloruskaya, wrote the following report to them: "The general mental development of Oswald is low. His views are limited, and he has a very poor appreciation of music, art, and literature." The KGB, however, thought she might be able to trap him as a spy. They asked her to tell Oswald that a relative of hers was a physicist at the Academy of Sciences, but she got no response from him, Oswald showing as much interest as being told about a new fly in the forest.[659]

The woman he remained serious about was Ella German. They continued to see each other and mostly enjoyed each other's company. After a New Year's Eve party at her parent's home, he wrote in his diary, "I think I'm in love with her. She has refused my more dishonourable advanis, we drink and eat in the presenec of her family in a very hospitable atmosfere. Later I go home drunk and happy. Passing the river homeward, I decide to propose to Ella."[660] The next day, January 2, 1961, Lee made his move. He wrote, "After a pleasent handin-hand walk to the local cinima we come home, standing on the doorstep I propose's She hesitates than refuses, my love is real but she has none for me. Her reason besides lack of love; I am american and someday might be arrested simply because of that example Polish Inlervention in the 20's. led to arrest of all people in the Soviet Union of polish oregen 'you understand the world situation there is too much against you and you don't even know it' I am stunned she snickers at my awkarness in turning to go (I am too stunned too think!) I realize she was never serious with me but only exploited my being an american, in order to get the envy of the other girls who consider me different from the Russian Boys. I am misarable!"[661]

It was difficult for Ella too, "because I knew he was in love with me, and he was all alone here. But I had no deep feelings for him."[662] "I am misarable about Ella" Oswald wrote the day after they parted. "I love her but what can I do? It is the state of fear which was alway in the Soviet Union."[663]

The very next day brought a fateful meeting at the Passport Office in Minsk, which called Oswald in to find out whether he still wanted Soviet citizenship. "I say no simply extend my residental passport . . . and my document is extended untill Jan 4. 1962."[664]

He covered the remainder of the month in his diary with a single entry: "I am stating [starting] to reconsider my disire about staying The work is drab the money I get has nowhere to be spent. No nightclubs or bowling allys no places of recreation acept the trade union dances I have had enough."[665]

Although he was well off by Soviet standards, he had learned about the peculiar quality of Soviet money, which was more like a sort of military scrip than the money in capitalist countries. You could not invest Soviet money in anything at all except a low-interest savings account, and you didn't need to save it for medical expenses or your children's education, since these were covered by the state. It's only real use was to exchange it for consumer goods and services, and those were severely limited in variety, quantity, quality, availability, and style. It's not that the parsimonious Oswald didn't have enough money, just that there was nowhere to spend it.

It probably wasn't the bleak Soviet lifestyle, however, that caused Oswald to give up on Russia. It was something much more fundamental. He defected to Russia, of course, because he thought it embodied Karl Marx's core tenet of a classless society, where the proletariat (working class) was not exploited as he perceived it to be under the capitalism he loathed. But to his considerable dismay, what he found in Russia was not Marxism but Russian Communism, a bastardization and pale imitation of what Marx had envisioned in *Das Kapital*. Russia's "classless society" was only a heady theory, not a reality. The commissars drove around in their fancy Ziln cars and spent their idle time at their comfortable dachas, while 99.9 percent of the Soviet population remained poor, were depressed, and led a marginal existence. This jolting realization rekindled—but with much more intensity this time—Oswald's interest in Cuba, leading him to the view that Castro and Cuba were the last bastion of true Marxism on the face of the globe. It also caused him thereafter to never fail to proclaim that he was a Marxist, not a Communist, which he at one time had assumed was simply a synonym for Marxism.[666]

When he later returned to the states, he told a New Orleans police detective that Russia had "fat stinking politicians over there just like we have over here," and that "they do not follow the great concepts of Karl Marx—the leaders have everything and the people are still poor and depressed."[667] The Warren Commission found that Oswald's "most frequent criticisms" of Russia concerned the contrast between the lives of the ordinary workers and the Communist Party elite.[668] He told an acquaintance in Dallas that the people in the Soviet Union "were poor. They worked and made just enough to buy their clothes and their food . . . The only ones who had enough money to buy anything else . . . the luxuries of life, were those who were Communist Party officials . . . high ranking members in the party."[669] Another Dallas acquaintance said that Oswald "seemed to classify all members of the Communist Party as opportunists who were in it just to get something for themselves out of it . . . and [he] thought they were ruining the principles which the country should be based on. In other words, they were not true Communists. They were ruining the heaven on earth which it should be."[670] A Dallas friend said that Oswald was "quite bitter" about the disparity between the elite and working class, including the fact the former could take vacations down to the Black Sea. When he reminded Oswald, "You were saying everyone got a month's vacation," Oswald responded, "That's true, but you had to pay your transportation," and it would take, for instance, a year's salary to go from Minsk to the Black Sea.[671] He told another Dallas friend that for the average worker or citizen in Russia, "travel was nonexistent; that a person who grew up in Minsk would probably spend his whole life without venturing far from the city."[672] "I didn't find what I was looking for," he summed up his feelings about Russia to yet another Dallas friend.[673]

Many have ridiculed Oswald for the superficiality of his understanding of Marxism, and it clearly did not appear to be deep, but his writing reflects that he was also very aware of an important adjunct to Marx's classless society, the "withering away of the state," a situation that would exist for a short, unspecified period following the revolution during which time a police state would be necessary to avoid anarchy. But the Bolshevik Revolution was way back in 1917, and Oswald said, "This is not the case, and is better observed [as he did] than contemplated." If anything, he concluded, the state had actually increased, not decreased the regimentation of every ordinary Soviet citizen.[674]

A friend of Oswald's in Dallas said that in a discussion between the two of them, Oswald indicated that average Russian citizens "didn't have any freedoms, as we think of freedom, in other words, to get in our car and go where we want to, do what we want to, or say what we want to."[675]*

Oswald's February 1, 1961, entry in his diary reads, "Make my first request to American Embassy, Moscow for reconsidering my position, I stated 'I would like to go back to U.S.'"[676] Although this February 1, 1961, diary entry says that Oswald made his "first request" to return to the United States on that date, he had done so two months earlier. On February 13, 1961, the American embassy in Moscow received a letter from Oswald postmarked Minsk, February 5:

> Dear Sirs,
>   Since I have not received a reply to my letter of December 1960, I am writing again asking that you consider my request for the return of my American passport.
>   I desire to return to the United States, That is if we could come to some agreement concernig the dropping of any legal proceeding's against me, If so, than I would be free to ask the Russian authorities to allow me to leave. If I could show them my American passport, I am of the opinion they would give me an exit visa.
>   They have at no time insisted that I take Russian citizenship. I am living here with non-permanent type papers for a foreigner.
>   I cannot leave Minsk without permission, therefore I am writing rather than calling in person.
>   I hope that in recalling the responsibility I have to america that you remember your's in doing everything you can to help me since I am an american citizen.
>
>   Sincerly
>   Lee Harvey Oswald[677]

The letter is noteworthy in two respects. For one thing, Oswald's dyslexia is largely absent, which suggests that it was very carefully crafted and recopied, possibly with the help of one of his friends or acquaintances. It's tone of mixed humility and bluster suggests that Oswald had not forgotten his foolish threat to betray military secrets to the Soviets, although he was at the same time prepared to demand his rights as an American citizen. Then there's that mention of a previous request, from December, which he said went unanswered. Richard Snyder, still in his post at the embassy, was puzzled by that. They had heard nothing of Oswald since November 1959.[678] The Warren Commission

---

*In a typed narrative to a book he was contemplating writing on Russia and his experiences there, Oswald described life in Russia, and at the factory, as centered around the "Kollective." He wrote that the head of the Kollective in his factory, Comrade Lebizen, saw to it that everyone maintained shop discipline, attended party meetings, and received all the new propaganda as it came out. Meetings of the Kollective were "so numerous as to be staggering." In a single month were scheduled one meeting of the professional union, four political information meetings, two young Communist meetings, one meeting of the production committee to discuss ways of improving work, two Communist Party meetings, four meetings of the "School of Communist Labor," and one sports meeting. All but one of the fifteen meetings were compulsory for Communist Party members and all but three were compulsory for everyone. They were scheduled so as to not to interfere with work (meaning at lunch or after work), and were anywhere from ten minutes to two hours in duration. "Absenteeism," he said, "is by no means allowed." Oswald said that no one liked the meetings. (CE 92, 16 H 285, 290–292)

concluded, partly because of Oswald's statement in his Historic Diary that he made his "first" request in early February, that the claim of an earlier request was probably not true.[679] That little mystery was finally cleared up in November 1991, however, when ABC broadcast a special *Nightline* investigation into Oswald's KGB files, which its investigator had inspected in the Soviet Union. One of the questions Forrest Sawyer put to the KGB officer showing him the files had to do with the missing letter. The first letter, written in December but intercepted by the KGB and for some reason never forwarded to the embassy, was still there in Oswald's file.[680]

That all mail sent to every embassy in Moscow was intercepted, read, and possibly photographed was no secret—Richard Snyder told the Warren Commission in 1964 that "every embassy there knows the system and operates within it. All mail from or to a foreign embassy in Moscow goes to a separate section of the Moscow Post Office called the international section, and this is the screening office for all mail to and from any embassy."[681]

It is interesting that Oswald had already requested help in returning to the United States even before he proposed to Ella German, although he never intimated that to her. It is also interesting that the KGB already knew that he wanted to return to the United States when it called him to the Passport Office and asked him whether he still wanted Soviet citizenship, although it is possible that the KGB branch responsible for intercepting the embassies' mail in Moscow had not yet told the KGB office in Minsk about the letter.

Oswald's second letter, the one from February, not only got through to the American embassy, it got results, though delayed. Snyder, who, as indicated, had not heard from Oswald since November of 1959 and had no idea of his whereabouts since then, wrote back to Oswald about two weeks after receiving his letter ("Mr. Oswald had no claim to any unusual attention of mine," he would later say) to say that Oswald would have to appear at the embassy personally to discuss a return to the United States. "Inasmuch as the question of your present American citizenship status can be finally determined only on the basis of a personal interview," Snyder wrote, "we suggest that you plan to appear at the Embassy at your convenience."[682]

That same day, Snyder wrote to the State Department to report on Oswald and included Oswald's address in Minsk as taken from the envelope containing his letter. He also suggested that State might want to forward Oswald's address in Minsk to Marguerite, who was increasingly frantic about her son's disappearance, even enlisting the services of her Fort Worth congressman, Jim Wright, and, as previously noted, U.S. Secretary of State Christian Herter, but up until now they had been unable to help her locate Lee. In the bitterest of ironies, on January 26, 1961, Marguerite had even gone to Washington, D.C., in the hope of moving the newly elected administration of John F. Kennedy to locate her son in the Soviet Union, undoubtedly so she could try to induce him to come back to the United States. After asking to see President Kennedy and told he was in a conference, she asked to see the new secretary of state, Dean Rusk, who, she was told, was also tied up in a conference. She kept persisting, however, and finally found someone, in fact three people, willing to listen to her at the State Department: representatives of the Passport Office, Office of Special Consular Services, and the Office of Soviet Union Affairs. Typically, she had developed a conspiracy theory regarding her son's disappearance. She thought Lee had gone to the Soviet Union as a "secret agent" and that the State Department was not doing enough to help him. Perhaps even more typically, she thought she might be able to make some money out of this. She told the three State Department officials that she was destitute and should receive some compensation from the appropriate authorities. The officials hastened to assure her that they had no reason to believe that Lee had gone to the USSR as an "agent," but they did offer to do what they could to locate him. A few days later, on February 1, they sent a new instruction to the American embassy in Moscow to seek the help of the Soviet Foreign Ministry to locate Oswald.[683] The riddle was finally solved when Oswald's letter from Minsk arrived on the thirteenth of that month.

Oswald sent another letter postmarked March 5, which reached the embassy only on March 20. He once again noted that, as a resident alien, he was unable to leave Minsk without permission, and therefore asked that "preliminary inquiries . . . be put in the form of a questionaire" and sent to him. He did not want to be in a position of "abusing" his "position" in Minsk.[684] He wrote a diary entry covering the first two weeks in March and noted, "I now live in a state of expectation about going back to the U.S.," but he also "confided with Zeger he supports my judgment but warnes me not to tell any Russians about my desire to reture [return]. I understade now why."[685]

The last remark, otherwise unexplained, may have to do with the fact that his monthly payments from the Soviet "Red Cross" were cut off, effectively halving his income. Although he had not approached any Soviet authorities about returning to the United States, he did not think it was a coincidence that the Red Cross subsidy ceased as soon as he started to correspond with the U.S. embassy in Moscow to come home.[686]

The embassy responded to Oswald's letter on March 24, insisting that he would indeed have to come to Moscow. Richard Snyder suggested he show the embassy's letter to the Russian authorities and ask for permission to travel to Moscow, which he felt would be granted since it was not the Soviet government's policy to raise obstacles to foreign citizens visiting their embassies.[687]

Meanwhile, on March 17 Oswald went to a dance organized by his trade union at the Palace of Culture for Professional Workers with his pal Erich Titovets. His diary entry for March 17 describes what turned out to be a red-letter day: "Boring but at the last hour I am introduced to a girl with a French hair-do and red-dress with white slipper I dance with her. than ask to show her home I do, along with 5 other admirares [admirers] Her name is Marina. We like each other right away she gives me her phone number and departs home with an not-so-new freiend in a taxi, I walk home."[688]

Marina Prusakova was born in Molotovsk (now Severodvinsk), a village about thirty miles from Archangel, a seaport in the northwestern part of the Soviet Union, on July 17, 1941, less than two months after the German invasion of Russia.[689] For reasons she does not know, her mother, Klavdia Prusakova, was unable to marry her father, and she would use her mother's last name until she married. Marina was born two months prematurely and weighed only a little over two pounds. It was a while before it became certain that she would survive at all, but when she did, Klavdia, a twenty-three-year-old laboratory worker, took her into Archangel and turned her over to Klavdia's mother, Tatyana Yakovleuna Prusakova, who would rear Marina until she was almost six. Like Lee, but for different reasons, Marina would later say, "I had no father. I never knew him."[690]

Although the war brought disaster to much of eastern Russia, there was no combat around Archangel itself, and Marina's memories of the medium-sized, woodsy city with some cobblestone streets on the White Sea were mainly pleasant. Her grandmother doted on her, and her mother's sister Lyuba lived with them in a clean and relatively spacious three-room apartment. Tatyana's husband, Vasily Prusakov, was the captain of a Soviet commercial vessel working overtime on the resupply of the Soviet Union. Unlike Murmansk, the only other usable port in northwestern Russia, Archangel's river and harbor froze for about six months of the year, but it was kept open by ice breakers, and, with the major port of Leningrad under siege and most land routes cut, the town was vital to the war effort. Vasily was seldom home during those years. Marina recalled, though, tasting Spam from America and special treats—peppermint sticks or gingerbread—sent to her by another aunt, Taisya, who worked as an accountant on a commercial ship that traveled between Russia and the United States.[691]

In 1942, Marina's mother married a wounded soldier named Alexander Medvedev, but Marina never saw him until 1945, after the war, and then she was under the impression that he was her real father. Medvedev and Marina's mother went off to live in Murmansk, while Marina continued to live with her grandmother until her grandfather finally came home to die of throat cancer. Marina then joined her parents in Murmansk, where her half brother Pyotr was born in 1945.[692] In 1947, the family moved to Zguritza, a small rural village in Moldavia, a largely agricultural province of the Soviet Union wedged between Rumania and the Ukraine. There, her mother had another daughter, Tanya.[693]

In 1952, the family moved to Leningrad, where Marina's stepfather, an electrical worker, obtained a job in a power plant.[694] In 1955, when Marina completed the seventh grade, she convinced her mother, who was very frail and ill at the time, and who knew that when she passed on Marina would have to stand alone without her, to let her enter a pharmacy school (Pharmacy Technikum). She told her mother the white coats pharmacists wore and the extremely clean shops in which they worked greatly appealed to her. In November 1957, when she was in her second year, Marina received a terrible shock. From a school friend whose aunt was friendly with Klavdia, Marina learned that she was illegitimate. As indicated, she had begun by believing that Medvedev was her father. She later thought that her real father had been killed in the war, and now, finally, she learned that an unknown father had never married her mother. Klavdia refused to provide details, only telling Marina, from her sickbed, "Not now. I'll tell you when you've grown up a bit." All Marina ever found out about her real father came from her school friend, who knew only that he had been an engineer denounced as an enemy of the people when he was blamed (possibly framed) for drawing up a faulty blueprint for a bridge or some other public project. As happened all too frequently in the Soviet Union during those years, he had simply vanished forever. Marina would never even learn his last name. Although about one in five of the children born in the late 1930s and early 1940s in Russia were illegitimate, Marina took the news very hard. It seemed to italicize her feelings of worthlessness. She desperately wanted to believe—but was never able to find out—that her mother's relationship with her father had been a serious one, that she had not resulted from an unloving and brief sexual tryst.[695]

Marina's mother died of cancer in April of 1957 after a long, agonizing struggle. Marina was fifteen, and she continued to live with her stepfather, his mother, and her half brother and half sister. But she didn't get along with her stepfather, who had never adopted her, Marina being too willful and difficult to discipline for him.[696] There was another problem.

Marina's stepfather was of the firm opinion that she was leading a very loose life morally in Leningrad. The day after her mother's funeral, he said to her, "And when will you be taking yourself out of here?" Later, he would put it even more bluntly: "You're not my daughter. I'm under no obligation to feed you." She stayed, but the situation at home became worse and eventually Alexander and his mother told Marina she could no longer take her meals with the family.[697] Marina undertook to feed herself at home. Since her birth certificate listed no father and her mother was dead, she qualified for a small orphan's pension worth about sixteen dollars a month. In addition, she had her student's stipend of about eighteen dollars a month. Over the year-end holidays, she took a job delivering telegrams, and somehow she managed to squeak by. But she was much on her own and began to live what was, by the puritanical standards of Leningrad in the late 1950s, something of a wild life, going to many parties and frequently coming home very late. She continued in school but became, not surprisingly, apathetic. The long day was too much for her—six hours of school and four hours of practical work in the pharmacy. She began to cut classes. Her grades plummeted, so much so that by the middle of the year her student's stipend was withdrawn and she had to get by on her pension and whatever her grandmother Tatyana could send her from Minsk, where Tatyana had since moved to live with her son Ilya and his wife. Just two weeks before Marina's examinations she was expelled for "academic faults and systematic non-attendance at class."

Emaciated and often ill, Marina found a somewhat informal job at a "commission shop" where a friend was a deputy director. This was not unlike a pawnshop, a place where goods from abroad or before the revolution were sold on commission. The shop was frequented by the young Estonians and Latvians who worked in the Soviet commercial fleet and who brought in foreign shoes, cigarettes, and clothes for resale. Many were eager to ask her out, and by accepting she found a solution to the problem of feeding herself. She later recalled one two-week period during which she had eaten dinner every night in one or the other of the best hotel restaurants in Leningrad.[698]

In this rendition of her life in Leningrad that Marina gave author Priscilla McMillan, who studied Marina more than anyone ever has and wrote the definitive book on her relationship with Oswald, she speaks of many dates and relationships, but never of losing her virginity, though she said she was willing with one young man, and another attempted to rape her.[699] But when an interviewer for author Norman Mailer said to her he had been told she felt very bad about her life in Leningrad, "and that you had to resort to things to survive, to eat," she responded, "I never once in my life was paid money," which certainly implies a rather loose sexual life, and a rather loose one for a girl still in her teens, particularly in morally strict Russia. But then Marina added, "I was looking for love in some wrong places and sometimes I had to pay for that. I actually was raped by a foreigner [presumably the same incident in which she told McMillan there had only been an attempt] . . . He threw me against him. He said, 'Well, if I knew you were a virgin, I would not have touched you,'" a statement that tends to confirm, if this was near the end of her Leningrad years, that she in fact had not been sexually promiscuous.[700]*

Whether warranted or not, what has hurt Marina's reputation through the years perhaps more than anything else is her own acknowledgment to author Priscilla McMillan that one time during the heated apex of her life in her stepfather's home after the demise of her mother, he said to her, "Don't come to me bringing a baby in your skirts . . . I don't want any prostitutes around me."[701] That pejorative word has stuck, and most likely unfairly. Indeed, even if Marina had been sexually promiscuous in Leningrad (and, the evidence does not appear clear one way or the other), as author Gus Russo points out,

---

*In the same interview Marina acknowledged that when she wed Oswald, she was not a virgin, that she was terrified he might ask but he did not.

"In many cultures, a beautiful woman who likes to have carnal fun is often [erroneously] branded a prostitute."[702]

Marina was eventually readmitted to the pharmacy school and graduated with a diploma in June of 1959. She was now eighteen and only too happy to leave her stepfather (but not Leningrad, one of the world's most beautiful cities, which she loved) shortly thereafter and move to Minsk, where she arrived with the equivalent of sixty cents in her pocket at two in the morning in early August to live with her aunt and uncle, Valya Prusakova and Ilya Prusakov.* Marina's grandmother (Valya's mother), who had been living with them, had died the previous year.[703] Although the Prusakovs had no children and there was ample space in their home for Marina, the advance notice from relatives in Leningrad that Marina may have become a prostitute made Ilya at first reluctant to let her stay with him and his wife.[704]

Ilya Prusakov had been very successful by Soviet standards, rising to the rank of lieutenant colonel in the MVD, the Ministry of Internal Affairs. His job, as head of the Belorussian Republic's Timber Administration, appears to have involved supervision of the convict labor that produced much of the country's lumber. He had necessarily become a high-ranking member of the Communist Party and would be held to very high standards of propriety, not only in his own conduct but in that of his relatives. His high responsibilities brought equally high privileges. Prusakov and his wife lived in a part of the town reserved for high government officials. The house was across the street from the Suvorov Military Academy and a wooden house with a stockade that once belonged to Marshall Timoshenko, a towering hero of the Second World War. It was now occupied by the head of the republic's Communist Party, Kirill Mazurov. It was not a part of town where a young woman suspected, say, of prostitution could go in and out of at all hours without attracting a great deal of extremely unfavorable notice.[705]

Work for Marina was a problem. A work permit was not easy to come by, and at first, Ilya, a man of vigorous probity, refused to pull strings for her. Eventually, against his principles and better judgment, he finagled a work permit, which carried residence permission as well, from the MVD. An actual job was almost as difficult, but after several more weeks, Marina found employment as one of four assistants in the pharmacy at the Third Clinical Hospital, where she was paid the equivalent of about forty-five dollars a month. It was poor pay, particularly in view of her responsibilities, but she loved her work and it was the standard rate everywhere in the Soviet Union. Besides, she did not have to pay rent. Uncle Ilya preferred that she spend her money on herself.[706]

At about the same time, Marina joined the local Komsomol, the Communist youth organization.[707] She soon fell in with a group of young people who passed, in the Soviet Union of 1960, for Bohemian, and with her good looks, taste in clothes, and upper-class address, she attracted a number of male admirers. Her friends were mostly students who, like Marina, had irreverent proclivities and whose social life consisted of reading and discussing serious literature as well as current news they heard on Voice of America broadcasts, going to the opera, the theater, and restaurants, and dancing to the music of Elvis, Eartha Kitt, and Louis Armstrong. But their tastes were more eclectic than that, includ-

---

*In Russia, an *a* is added to a last name for a wife. When a husband and wife are spoken of as one, the husband's name is used—hence, "the Prusakovs."

ing an appreciation for Latin classics like "La Paloma." Slang words borrowed from English were very popular in her set, with a hint of the forbidden. They called Minsk's main street "Broadway" and an apartment was a "pad." An evening's get-together was a "do" or a "carouse."[708]

Marina seemed to be enjoying this life at the time she met Lee at the Palace of Culture dance in March of 1961.[709] Lee asked to see her again and begged her to name a time and place. She was noncommittal, saying only that she might see him at the Palace of Culture dance the following week.[710]

She did go to the dance, with a girlfriend, the next week, and Lee was there. They danced together most of the evening, and she allowed him to walk her home. Aunt Valya was prevailed upon to meet him and was suitably impressed. She liked his modesty and politeness and the fact that he was neatly dressed, although neither Valya nor Marina really thought of Lee Oswald as a potential husband. Marina, however, did agree to a date the following weekend.[711]

But on March 30, 1961, before they could see each other again, Oswald was admitted to a hospital because of a discharge and loss of hearing in his right ear, which had periodically become inflamed during his youth, though his childhood mastoidectomy had been to his left ear.[712] Marina visited Lee the next day, bringing a jar of apricots, which seemed to delight Lee, particularly since it was his favorite dessert, and she continued to visit him until, after the removal of his adenoids, he was discharged from the hospital on April 11.[713] While he was in the hospital, he wanted to become engaged to her and didn't want her to see anyone else. She indicated acquiescence but did not take his proposal seriously. At that point, she did not love him and was mostly visiting him because he seemed to be all alone and she felt sorry for him. Besides, she cared much more for another suitor, a twenty-six-year-old medical student named Anatoly Shpanko, with unruly blond hair and a fetching smile, whose kisses made Marina's head spin but whose proposal of marriage she had declined.[714] Nonetheless, on the suggestion of her Aunt Valya, Marina invited Lee over for supper, and her aunt and uncle were favorably impressed with him. At one point, Uncle Ilya put his arm around Lee's shoulder and said, "Take care of this girl. She has plenty of breezes in her brain."[715]

The next night Marina visited Lee at his apartment in the company of several friends, and her girlfriend Lyalya thought Marina was insanely lucky to have acquired an American boyfriend who was so handsome. Was he a better catch than Anatoly? Marina asked. "Of course," was the reply. After several days of long walks on the cold streets and along the frozen river of Minsk, punctuated by tender kisses, Lee, just one week after having left the hospital, asked Marina to marry him, and told her he wanted to stay in Russia forever. She did not say no, but thought it wise to wait for a while. He would not hear of it. He wanted to marry immediately. She agreed to let him speak to her Uncle Ilya the next day.

He arrived at the Prusakovs' flat in a black suit, white shirt, and tie, topped off by a dark blue hat. Thoroughly intimidated, he nonetheless conferred with Ilya while Marina and her aunt waited breathlessly in the kitchen. Ilya put Lee through a battery of grueling questions and tried to make sure that Lee fully realized what a flighty creature Marina, in his view, was. He even examined Lee's documents and asked Lee if he intended to stay in the Soviet Union. Lee solemnly stated that he intended to stay. It wasn't true, of course. As we have seen, he had started proceedings to return in December and had been pursuing them for four months already—but he hadn't told Marina about them either. He had told her several other lies too, that his mother was dead ("I don't want to talk about it—it's too painful"), that he was almost twenty-four (he was twenty-one), and that he had renounced his American citizenship and could thus never return to the United States. Prusakov gave them his blessing, somewhat reluctantly perhaps. He thought it was too soon, but he didn't want Marina to blame him for her unhappiness later on.

"If you fight or if anything goes wrong," he told them, "settle it yourselves. Don't come to me with your troubles."

"Does that mean you are saying yes, Uncle Ilya?" Marina asked like a young girl.

"I am," he said. "Let's drink to it," he added, and they retired to the kitchen table where they drank cognac.[716]

The next day, April 20, Marina agreed to marry Lee and they met during their lunch hour for a trip to the registry office to sign documents starting the ten-day waiting period. Marina noticed that Lee was born in 1939.

"You are only twenty-one," she said, a slight irritation in her voice. "Why did you tell me you were twenty-four?"

"I was afraid you wouldn't take me seriously," he responded evenly.

They were married on April 30, 1961, in a civil ceremony at Marina's home, with two of Marina's girlfriends as bridesmaids, followed by a festive dinner reception for about twenty people.[717] "It was one of the happiest days in my life," Marina would later write.[718]

M any have asked the question of whether Marina loved Lee, and there is no simple answer since Marina herself has given conflicting stories. But although Marina had dreamed of one day coming to America, that apparently was not one of the reasons for marrying him, because at the time she thought he had renounced his citizenship and could not return.[719] Marina told the FBI shortly after the assassination that she married Oswald because she loved him,[720] and in a summary of her life with Lee for the Warren Commission, said that even before he asked her to marry him she "had already fallen in love with him." But years later she told author Priscilla McMillan, "Maybe I was not in love with Alik as I ought to have been. But I thought I loved him."[*] If she did, it clearly did not appear to be a deep love. If it were, it wouldn't have been possible for the following words, taken down by McMillan, to come out of her mouth: "I married him because I liked him. He was neat and clean and better looking than Anatoly. I was more in love with him than anyone else at the time."[†] And: "I married Alik because he was American." McMillan writes, "It was almost as if, being the only American in Minsk, he had the right to pick anyone he pleased. It would have been an act of *lèse-majesté* to refuse." Marina also conceded to McMillan that Oswald's apartment played a role in her decision and that she might not have married him without it. McMillan writes, "All her life she had always felt unwanted and 'in the way' . . . Because of her illegitimate birth she had felt like an outsider all of her life . . . All of her life she had dreamed of having a room of her own

---

*In September 1992, Marina told a Moscow correspondent for the *Toronto Star*, Jennifer Gould, "I was never in love with Lee." Marina, fifty-one at the time and living as man and wife with Kenneth Porter, a rancher in Rockwell, Texas, was in Moscow for the filming of *Marina's Story*, a $3.7 million NBC made-for-television movie about her life—ironically billed as a "love story." (Jennifer Gould, "Oswald's Soviet Friends Come to His Defense," *Toronto Star*, January 31, 1993; "Marina's Turn," p.71)

†Tamara, an older coworker of Marina's at the pharmacy, was convinced that of the two men Marina had been seeing, it was Anatoly whom she loved (McMillan, *Marina and Lee*, p.101).

. . . And for her, as for many girls she knew, the great lottery of Soviet life was to find a man you loved—who had an apartment."[721]

If Marina's love for Lee was not the kind novelists write love stories about, you couldn't tell it by Lee, who wrote in a diary entry for May of 1961, "She is maddly in love with me from the very start."[722]

What about Lee's reasons for marrying Marina? Were they as impure as hers? In his May 1 diary entry, he writes, "Inspite of fact I married Marina to hurt Ella I found myself in love with Marina." In a following May entry he writes, "The trasistion of changing full love from Ella to Marina was very painfull esp. as I saw Ella almost every day at the factory but as the days and weeks went by I adjusted more and more [to] my wife mentaly." He added, "I still hadn't told my wife of my desire to return to US."[723]

To make their union even more confusing, there was one thing that bothered Marina. Lee, curiously, had never yet actually *told* her that he loved her. When she expressly asked him once, he only replied, "You ought to know how I feel from the way I act."[724]

By midnight, the wedding reception was over and Oswald had escorted Marina to her new home, carrying her up the four flights of stairs (he didn't tell her it was an American tradition) to his apartment. On their wedding night sex did not come easily to the two, who were, after all, only nineteen and twenty-one years old. Marina, to disguise the fact that she was not a virgin, resorted to some preparation from the pharmacy where she worked to create the impression that she was. It worked well enough as far as Lee was concerned, who told her, "Thank you for saving yourself for me. Frankly, I didn't think you had."[725]*

Marina thought of the whole month of May as her honeymoon, as they met every evening at 5:30 outside the pharmacy when she got off work, went for a stroll, window shopped, and dined at the dingy Café-Avtomat, where the food was at least not worse than Marina's cooking. Afterward, Lee would water the flowers on their tiny balcony and scan the view across the river with his binoculars.[726]

They both loved classical music—Tchaikovsky was Lee's favorite composer—and they'd play a game of listening to classical music on the radio and see who could name the composer. He was better at it than she, being able to recognize whether a composition was by Bach, Chopin, or Wagner.[727]

Lee's diary entry for the month of June reads, "We draw closer and closer, and I think very little now of Ella. in the last days of this month I revele [reveal] my longing to return to America. My wife is slightly startled. But than encourages me to do what I wish to do."[728]

Oswald must have known of his wife's desire to go to America (even though she had resigned herself to not being able to do so) because even before he told her in late June, per his diary, that he longed to return to America, he wrote an undated letter (postmarked

---

*While Marina, as previously indicated, was not a virgin, the extent of her sexual freedom is somewhat unclear. Her chief accuser in Minsk, Yuri Merezhinsky, was a member of the small group of hip men and women Marina hung out with, and according to him, "everybody" in the group was having sex with Marina except for Sasha Piskalev, the one in the group who was "in love up to his ears" with Marina and "was ready to marry her." Fine. But then it turns out that Yuri himself never had sex with Marina either. (Mailer, *Oswald's Tale*, pp.154–157)

Minsk, May 16, 1961) to the U.S. embassy sometime in May of 1961 (received by embassy on May 25) asking it to include his new wife in his plans:

> Dear Sirs
> In regards to your letter of March 24. I understand the reasons for the necessity of a personal interview at the Embassy, however, I wish to make it clear that I am asking not only for the right to return to the United States, but also for full guarantee's that I shall not, under any circumstance's, be persecuted [prosecuted] for any act pertaining to this case. I made that clear from my first letter, although nothing has been said, even vaguely, concerding this in my correspondence with the Embassy. Unless you honestly think that this condition can be met, I see no reason for a continuance of our correspondence, Instead, I shall endeavour to use my relative's in the United States, to see about getting something done in Washington.
> As for coming to Moscow, this would have to be on my own initiative and I do not care to take the risk of getting into a awkwark situation unless I think it worthwhile. Also, Since my last letter I have gotten married.
> My wife is Russian, born in Leningrad, she has no parents living, and is quite willing to leave the Soviet Union with me and live in the United States.
> I would not leave here without my wife so arrangements would have to be made for her to leave at the same time as I do.
> The marrige stamp was placed on my present passport., after some trouble with the [local] authorities, so my status as far as the U.S.S.R. is concerded, is the same as before, that is, "Without cititzenship."
> So with this extra complication I suggest you do some checking up before advising me futher.
> I believe I have spoken frankly in this letter, I hope you do the same in your next letter.
>
> Sincerly Yours
Lee Harvey Oswald[729]

Even if the United States granted his request to return with his wife, there was still another considerable obstacle. Would the Soviets permit Marina to leave? At some time within a month or two thereafter—exactly when is not clear—Marina began to seek the permission of the Soviet authorities to leave for the United States. She wrote to a government department in Minsk, which forwarded her request for exit documents to the Foreign Office in Moscow. Marina also wrote a letter to the American embassy in Moscow for documents to request permission for herself to emigrate to the United States.[730]

Around this time, Lee started to correspond, after a two-year lapse, with his brother Robert, without apology and as if the 1959 letters had never been written. In a May 5, 1961, letter, he advised Robert he was now married.[731] In a May 31, 1961, letter he hinted, without giving a tad of reason for his 180-degree turnaround, that he might want to return to the United States. He wrote, "I can't say wether I will ever get back to the States or not, if I can get the government to drop charges against me, and get the Russians to let me out with my wife, than maybe I'll be seeing you again. *But*, you know it is not simple for *either* of those two things. So I just can't say for now."[732]

Meanwhile, in Moscow, Richard Snyder wrote to the State Department on May 26 (the day after receiving Oswald's letter) noting Oswald's threat to create problems for the department in the United States, and asking for guidance. "In view of the possibility that the Department may receive further inquiries from Oswald's mother or from other persons in his behalf concerning his case, the Embassy would be glad to have the Department's comments before replying to Oswald." Snyder did include his proposal to State that "should [Oswald] be found not to have lost American citizenship, he would be entitled to return to the United States under the laws and regulations applicable to all American citizens."[733]

State wrote back to approve, with circumspection, Snyder's proposal. "The Embassy's careful attention to the involved case of Mr. Oswald is appreciated," they said. "It is *assumed** that there is no doubt that the person who has been in communication with the embassy is the person who was issued a passport in the name of Lee Harvey Oswald . . . In the absence of evidence showing that Mr. Oswald has definitely lost United States citizenship he *apparently* maintains that technical status."[734]

On July 8, 1961, Oswald, impatient at the lack of a response from the U.S. embassy to his last letter, appeared without warning at the embassy in Moscow. It was a calculated risk for him, since, as a resident alien, he was not supposed to travel without authorization.[735] Marina was anxious and tearful about the trip, but Lee, who as a southern boy (Louisiana and Texas) didn't like Russia's harsh climate, told her, "One more winter in Russia and I'm going to die."[736] And there was now a new factor in the equation: Marina was pregnant. In a narrative of her life with Oswald for the Warren Commission, she wrote, "Lee was very anxious to have a child and was very grieved when the honeymoon was over and there was no sign of a baby. Sometime in the middle of June we were out on a lake near Minsk with one of his friends who spoke English very well, lying in the sun and swimming. That was a wonderful day, and that evening Lee told me that he was sure that after the required time, starting from that day, we would have a baby. I did not believe it, but a week later we were eating in a café and I fainted. I think this was the first sign of the baby."[737]

This news was much on their minds as he boarded an Aeroflot airliner for the two-and-a-half-hour flight to Moscow. He was, according to Marina, quite fearful when he said good-bye to her, and neither of them were able to eat their breakfast at the airport. He told Marina that officials at the embassy were "entitled" to arrest him because he had tried to renounce his citizenship—they weren't, of course, but Oswald seemed to believe they might. He was equally fearful of the Soviet authorities and begged Marina to say nothing to her Uncle Ilya about his risky trip. He sought to minimize that risk by taking a two-week vacation and traveling during it so as not to be missed at work.[738]

But he miscalculated slightly. When he finally arrived at the embassy in the city center at three o'clock on Saturday afternoon, July 8, he found the offices closed. Fortunately he was able to reach Snyder by phone. Snyder, like other embassy employees, lived in the building, and he came downstairs to meet him, advising him to return on Monday.[739]

The pregnancy had made Marina topsy-turvy with emotions she did not understand and could not control. She bristled at his attempts to dominate her. During Lee's whirlwind courtship of her, she had been very much in control, but with their marriage the

---

*The odd language "it is assumed" stems from a June 3, 1960, memorandum from FBI Director J. Edgar Hoover to the Department of State in which he said that the bureau had learned from Oswald's mother that her son had taken his birth certificate with him to Russia and that three letters she had written to him had been returned undelivered, raising the possibility of something having happened to him and someone using his birth certificate. See discussion on the Second Oswald allegation in conspiracy section.

rules began to change and he asserted himself more and more and Marina hadn't been altogether sure that she liked that. And his jealousy and suspicions were oppressive. "Where have you been?" he would ask her when she was only a few minutes late in coming home from her work. "I called the pharmacy and they said you had already left." And their sex life wasn't quite what she expected. She thought there would be more romance to it, but it was mostly, for Lee, just sex, and she started to feel used by him physically, and started, every now and then, to resist his advances. She also began to become a little distrustful of him when she found out (when he received a letter from Marguerite) that his mother was still alive. Here she had thought that "God sent me an orphan like myself." When she asked him why he had lied to her about his mother being dead, his explanation, which he had no time to formulate, was entirely inadequate—something about if people knew he had a mother it might cause his mother some unpleasantness. He then proceeded to tell Marina he didn't love his mother and added another lie to the tableau, that the reason was the way his mother treated his brother Robert's wife. If he did not tell Marina about Marguerite, Lee *did* tell her—and it made her jealous—about the first woman he ever physically knew, a Japanese girl whom Lee spoke glowingly of in terms of beauty and how she had catered to his every need.[740]

As if the foregoing were not enough, Marina, because of her pregnancy, became inordinately sensitive to odors. Even the walls of their tiny apartment seemed to smell to her, and when she tried to escape to the balcony, she smelled everything on the stoves of the neighboring apartments, and she had trouble eating. She even noticed Lee's body odor, which was persistent. She began to wonder if she had erred in marrying him so quickly.[741]

The Saturday afternoon that Lee arrived in Moscow, Marina got a phone call at the pharmacy from a former boyfriend, Leonid Gelfant, a young architect she had seen before she met Lee. She told him she was now married, but he offered her dinner and champagne at a friend's apartment where he was staying for a few days while the friend was away. Marina somewhat foolishly agreed, thinking that the evening might reveal to her whether she had made a mistake in marrying Lee. They first saw a movie together and afterward repaired to his borrowed flat, eventually winding up in bed, although, according to the story Marina told Priscilla McMillan years later, Leonid, making love to a woman for the first time, proved inadequate. Nevertheless, Marina felt dirty afterward. She ran home, where she nearly threw up. She knew she had seriously betrayed Lee.[742] In the evening Marina went to the central post office in Minsk to receive a call from Lee, who asked her to join him in Moscow. She went, arriving on Monday morning.[743] She took the bus into Sverdlov Square and went to the Hotel Berlin, where Lee was staying and where they made love. When Lee returned to the embassy that Monday afternoon, Marina waited outside in the waiting room[744] while her husband was searchingly interviewed by Snyder, who asked to see Oswald's Soviet papers and questioned him closely about his life in Russia and any possible expatriating acts that would preclude his returning to America. Oswald stated he was not a citizen of the Soviet Union, had never applied for citizenship (dubious, since we know he did request it, though not by formal application),[745] had never taken an oath of allegiance to the Soviet Union, and had never become a member of a Soviet trade union, the latter being untrue.[746] He also said that he had never given Soviet authorities any confidential information gleaned from his service in the military, had never been asked to give such information, and doubted that he would have done so had he been asked.[747]

Snyder felt that Oswald had matured while he was in Russia and did not show the bravado and arrogance that characterized his first contact with the embassy. Oswald told him that he had "learned a hard lesson the hard way" and had acquired a new appreciation of the United States and the meaning of freedom.[748]

Lee clearly feared prosecution and lengthy imprisonment if he returned to the United States, but Snyder, speaking unofficially, told him he saw no reason for such fear if everything he had told Snyder was true. He added, however, that there was no way the embassy had the power to grant him any sort of blanket immunity from prosecution.* Oswald appeared to understand but explained that he did not want to apply for an exit visa back to the United States from the Soviet authorities until he "had this end of the thing straightened out."[749]

Snyder had Oswald complete and sign an "Application for Renewal of Passport," and then fill out a questionnaire, under penalty of perjury, on which he wrote what he essentially had told Snyder, including that he had only a residence permit in the Soviet Union and was still an American national. Snyder reviewed his application and questionnaire and, finding everything in order, returned (*not* renewed) Lee's passport, amended for travel only back to the United States, knowing that Lee could make little headway with the Soviets for his exit visa without it.[750] Oswald's passport was scheduled to expire on September 10, 1961, and when Warren Commission counsel asked Snyder, "And you felt he would not be able to get out of the Soviet Union prior to September 1961?" Snyder answered that in his estimation "there was no prospect of his leaving the Soviet Union at that time, and probably not for quite some time to come."[751] Though Snyder didn't explain why, we can only assume that he knew from experience that it would take the Soviets far beyond September to issue Oswald the exit visa he needed to leave the Soviet Union. And ultimately, the State Department would have to conclude whether Oswald had expatriated himself, and if not, renew his passport and allow him to return to America.

The next day, Lee, elated by the return of his passport and the fact that his darkest fears of arrest, at least in Moscow, had not come to pass, went back to the embassy with Marina, where John McVickar took them through the procedures for admitting her to the United States as an immigrant, although there was little McVickar could do but take official notice of her intent until she obtained her exit visa from the Soviet Union. With an exit visa, Marina, being the wife of an American citizen, would have the right to enter the United States under a non-quota status.[752] Pushed by Lee, Marina had not mentioned to McVickar her pregnancy, which might have caused a delay, and she had lied when he had asked her if she was a member of Komsomol. She was, although she took no interest or active role in the communist youth organization.[753] McVickar typed out an immigrant visa application for Marina, which Lee signed.[754]

After Lee and Marina returned to Minsk, he wrote to his brother Robert on July 14, 1961:

> Dear Robert,
>   On the 8th of July [it had been the 10th] I and my wife went into The american Embassy, I cannot write you what went on there, because the Russians, read

---

*There was, of course, one governmental agency that could give Oswald the promise of immunity he wanted so badly. Indeed, if Oswald was the CIA agent or operative on a mission to Russia that conspiracy theorists are so convinced he was, the issue of immunity, and Oswald's fears and anxieties with respect to prosecution, would never have arisen in the first place.

all letters going in and out. But anyway I have the American Passport, and we are doing everything we can to get out . . .

The Russians can be crule and very crude at times. They gave a cross eximanation to my wife on the first day we came back from Moscow, They knew everything because they spy, and read there mails. but we shall continue to try and get out. We shall not retreat. As for your package we never recived it, I suppose they swiped that to, the bastards.

I hope someday, I'll see you and Vada but if and when I come, I'll come with my wife. You can't imagine How wonderful she stood up.

Write offten

> Your Brother
> Lee[755]

The secret was indeed out. The Soviet authorities, who usually check the papers of anyone entering the American embassy in Moscow,[756] were perfectly aware that Lee and Marina had gone there, and the battle, particularly over Marina, was now openly joined. Lee, however, would not waver until he had accomplished his goal, to return to America with his wife and, as it turned out, his child.

If Oswald's diary is correct about the date—always a questionable supposition—Marina was ambushed at work on the very day after their return. She was, he wrote in his diary entry for July 15, "shocked to find out ther everyone knows she entered the U.S. embassy . . . The boses hold a meeting and give her a strong browbeating. The first of many indocrinations."[757]

In a letter to the American embassy dated the same day, July 15, he mentioned Marina's difficulties at what he called "the usual, 'enemy of the people' meeting." She was "condemed, and her friends at work warned against speaking with her." But he also boasted that such "tactics" were "quite useless" since Marina had "stood up well, without getting into trouble."[758]

Lee and Marina's attempt to leave Russia for the United States was not going to be easy. For starters, the Soviets required the completion of four documents, which were submitted by Lee and Marina in July and August of 1961: Lee's application for an exit visa, backed by Marina's application for permission for Lee to leave, Marina's own application for an exit visa, and a statement by Lee guaranteeing Marina's financial support.[759] But Lee's diary entry for the period from July 15 through August 20 suggested that so much more was involved, there being "about 20 papers" in all, including birth certificates and photos. Because of his dyslexia, filling out all the forms he had to was a real strain, and Marina recalls that he would pick up five or six blank forms for every one he was eventually able to complete reasonably well.[760]

But the psychological obstacles for Marina and Lee were much more difficult. He wrote in his diary, "On Aug 20th we give the papers out they say it will be 3½ months before we know wheather they'll let us go or not. in the meantime Marina has had to stade [stand?] 4 different meeting[s] at the place of work held by her Boss's at the direction of 'someone' by phone. The young comm. leauge headquthers also called about her and she had to go and see them for 1½ hours. The purpose (expressed) is to disaude her from going to the U.S.A. Net effect: Make her more stubborn about wanting to go Marina is pregnet, we only hope that the visas come through soon."[761]

For the period from August 21 through September 1, 1961, Oswald's diary reads, "I make expected trips to the passport & visa office also to ministry of for. affairs in Minsk, also Min. of Internal affairs, all of which have a say in the granting of a visa. I extracked promises of quick attention to US."[762] For the period from September through October 18, he wrote, "No word from Min. (They'll call us.)"[763]

If Marina thought her reception by her bosses at work was bad, what she received at the Komsomol was worse. She was harangued not only by the city's Komsomol leader, but also by representatives of every department in the hospital, and even two of the girls from the hospital pharmacy where she worked. She was bitterly offended by the questioning and even more so by the fact that the Komsomol chairman told her they knew everything about her and her husband. "We knew each time you had a date. We knew when you applied for your marriage license," he told her. When they suggested that Lee was a spy, she did not handle it diplomatically. "Actually, what he does every night," she said, "is tap out messages in Morse Code about how the Komsomol is trying to brainwash me." After the meeting she was warned that there would be another meeting to determine whether she should be expelled from the organization. It took place a week later, she refused to attend, and she was indeed expelled and told she had "anti-Soviet views," which Marina did not feel she had. But it didn't matter. "Fine," the defiant Marina told her coworkers at the pharmacy. "Now I'll have money for the movies."[764]

Even more painful was the reaction of her Aunt Valya and Uncle Ilya. Lee had tried to visit them, and Ilya had turned him away at the door, telling him he was no longer welcome there. Marina had not told them of their plans, but Ilya, of course, had already been fully informed by the KGB. It took Marina a week to get up the courage to call him. She was invited over—without Lee—and subjected to a grilling by her appalled uncle. "A fine niece you are," he said. "You're here all the time, then you fly off to Moscow without a word and leave me to hear it from others." Valya interceded and eventually invited both Marina and Lee over, at which time Ilya subjected Lee to an even more heated and thorough third degree. Colonel Prusakov wanted to know everything about Lee's contacts with the American embassy, their trip to Moscow, everything. Lee was infuriated. Marina, who considered her sneaking off to Moscow without telling her aunt and uncle the same as a lie, was angry that she had been forced into a position of lying to her own family. "I can't live like that," she told Lee. "I can't open my mouth without giving you away as a liar. You lied about your mother and your age. You lied when you said you couldn't return to America. Now you're making me lie. When will there be an end to it?"[765]

Years later, in the United States, she would tell Paul Gregory, to whom she gave Russian language lessons, that this period of her life in Minsk was "a very horrible time."[766]

Not long after, Marina discovered yet another deception—Lee had been hoarding five thousand rubles, about five hundred dollars, apparently saved from the days when he was still enjoying the regular stipend from the Soviet Red Cross. He had also started writing something shortly after their return from Moscow, which, he told her only after she insisted, were his "impressions of Russia," but he refused to show her the pages, even though, given her lack of English, there wasn't much she could have made of them. She began to wonder whether he was not in fact a spy. It was already clear to her that her husband was secretive by nature, secretive even when there seemed to be no purpose served. He lied not because he needed to but because he liked to—it was his character.[767]

Lee's suspicions, expressed in a letter to his brother Robert on July 14, that he and Marina were being spied on were, as we already know, far more justified than he knew. Norman Mailer was never able to find out from KGB contacts when the visual surveillance of Oswald extended to an electronic surveillance (bugging) of their apartment (the Oswalds had no telephone to tap), but the earliest transcripts date from mid-July of 1961. Mailer speculated that the microphones were installed during the Oswalds' four-day trip to Moscow. In any case, listeners in a space above the apartment started recording everything that happened in the tiny flat, day and night. Later they moved the operation into a room next door. Mailer believes the KGB may have also inserted a sophisticated fiber-optic viewing device, one that required inserting a special lens into a tiny hole in the wall.[768]

Whatever the Soviet authorities might have been hoping to learn, the transcripts tell us mostly that the young marriage was in trouble from the outset. There was endless bickering, as in this example from a KGB transcript of July 19, 1961:

Wife: All you know how to do is torture . . .
(LHO goes out, yells something from the kitchen)
Wife: Go find yourself a girl who knows how to cook . . . I work, I don't have time to prepare cutlets for you. You don't want soup, you don't want kasha, just tasty tidbits, please!
LHO: I can go eat at a restaurant.
Wife: Go to hell! When are you ever going to leave me alone? I'll probably never live to see the day when you leave me alone.
LHO: But you don't know how to do anything.
Wife: Leave me alone![769]

And from August 3:

Wife: (yells) I'm tired of everything! And what about you? Can't you wash? I suppose you want me to wash floors everyday?
LHO: Yes, wash these floors every day!
Wife: You don't do anything and I'm supposed to spend all day cleaning up. A decent man would help. Remember you used to say: I'll help! You did wash once, and now you talk about it endlessly, and I wash our clothes every time and it doesn't count for anything . . .
LHO: You have to make something to eat.
Wife: (yells) I can't. I'm not going to cook.
LHO: You could make cutlets, put on water for tea . . .
Wife: I won't.
LHO: You haven't done anything.
Wife: Well, what have you done for me?
LHO: Silence!
Wife: I'm not going to live with you.
LHO: Thank God! . . .
LHO: This house has to be cleaned every day. There's dirt in our kitchen, dirt everywhere. What good is that? You sleep until ten in the morning and you don't do anything. You could be cleaning up during that time.
Wife: I need my sleep. *If you don't like it, you can go to your America.*
LHO: (calmly) Please, thank you.
Wife: You're always finding fault; nothing's enough, everything's bad.
LHO: You're ridiculous. Lazy and crude . . .

Wife: Get out! I'm not your housekeeper . . .

LHO: Don't cry. I'm just saying that you don't want to do anything.

Wife: So? I never washed our floors?

LHO: You're not a good housewife, no, not a good housewife.

Wife: You should have married a good one . . .

(they're silent)

Wife: . . . If you don't like it, you can go to your America.

LHO: I've told you for a long time that you don't do anything.

Wife: I wash floors every day.

LHO: It's dirty.

Wife: What's dirty to you is clean to me. I washed floors yesterday and you walk around in shoes . . .

LHO: Calm your nerves.

Wife: Just say: "Marina, it has to be done." Don't yell; it's hurtful . . . Alka,[*] do you hate me when you yell at me?

LHO: Yes.

Wife: Yes?

LHO: Yes.

Wife: . . . Why are you afraid of people? What scared you?

LHO: (yells angrily) Shut up, shut up . . . You stand there and blab.

Wife: *You're afraid of everybody!* . . .

LHO: Shut up!

Wife: Are you afraid that they'll steal everything from you, a pot of gold that you have? (laughing) At times like this you could kill me. You have to have some kind of strong will . . .[770]

Although the quarreling continued and was very heated, Marina told the Warren Commission he had never struck her in Russia.[771] But author Norman Mailer suggests (presumably from interviews of Marina) that "he hit her . . . three or four times."[772] As if their arguments were not enough, their sex life was not fulfilling to Marina, who did not achieve orgasm, and she blamed it on him for always ejaculating before she was ready, making her furious.[773]

The American consul at the U.S. embassy in Russia, Richard Snyder, had already indicated that he believed Oswald had not lost his U.S. citizenship,[774] and a July 11, 1961, Foreign Service dispatch from the Moscow embassy to the Department of State suggested as much.[775] On August 18, 1961, the State Department, after a review of all pertinent documents as well as Oswald's history by the Passport Office of the State Department, stated in an "Operations Memorandum" to the Moscow embassy that "we concur in the conclusion of the Embassy that there is no information and/or evidence to show that Mr. Oswald has expatriated himself under the pertinent laws of the United States," and ruled that his application for the renewal of his passport to return to the U.S. "is authorized."[776][†]

---

[*]According to Marina's biographer, Priscilla McMillan, Marina called Lee either "Lee" or "Alka." She called him "Lee" when she was angry at him. "Alka" was a nickname Marina had given Lee (McMillan doesn't say how she came up with it or its derivation) that was reserved for warm and sentimental moments, as when she was thinking of the happy days in Russia when they first met (McMillan, *Marina and Lee*, p.221).

[†]Although Oswald had verbally told the American embassy in Moscow in October 1959, and even confirmed in a note he wrote on hotel stationery that he had given to them, that he wanted to dissolve his Amer-

It was okay with America for Oswald to come home. Now it was up to the Soviets to decide when they would let him and Marina leave Russia.

On September 25, 1961, Lee made a special effort to listen to the live broadcast of a complete speech to the General Assembly of the United Nations in New York City by America's new young president, Jack Kennedy, then in office less than nine months. According to Marina, Lee was rigid with attention as he listened to the often faint and fading signal, and he indignantly hushed her if she dared to make the slightest noise. After Kennedy's speech, Marina asked Lee what it was about.

"War and peace," he said, and quoted a few of Kennedy's remarks.

"That's funny," Marina observed. "Everybody wants peace here. They want peace there, too. So why do they talk about war?"

"Politics," Lee smiled.

Several days later, Lee hotly defended the president's speech in a discussion with Marina's Uncle Ilya, denouncing the Soviet press for attacking the speech without printing a full and fair account of it. The colonel defended his own government with equal fervor, but on one thing both of them agreed—the Bay of Pigs invasion of Cuba, which had failed so ignominiously right after Kennedy took office. Lee was still an ardent defender of Fidel Castro and the Cuban Revolution.[777]

Two and a half months having elapsed without the Soviet government doing anything on his and his wife's application to leave the country, Oswald wrote to the U.S. embassy in Moscow on October 4 to ask that his government intervene with the Soviet government to facilitate getting exit visas for Marina and himself. He began to revert to that odd mixture of whining and bullying which he had adopted in his initial dealings with the embassy on his arrival in the country and which was to become increasingly his tone whenever he dealt with authorities:

> Dear Sirs, . . .
>
> I believe there is justification for an official inquiry, directed to the department of "Internal Affairs, Prospect Stalin 15, Minsk," and the offices of the "address and passport office," Ulitsa Moskova, Colonel Petrakov director.
>
> Also, I believe it is doubley important for an official inquiry, since there have been systematic and concerted attempts to intimidate my wife into withdrawing her application for [a] visa. I have notified the Embassy in regard to these incidents by the local authorities in regard to my wife, these incidents had resulted in my wife being hospitalized for a five day period, on September 22, for nervous exhaustion . . .

---

ican citizenship and wanted to become a Soviet citizen, this was not enough to constitute expatriation. What would have been? Among other things (none of which Oswald had done) being "naturalized as a citizen of a foreign state"; having "taken an oath or made an affirmation or *other formal* declaration of allegiance to a foreign state"; "entered or served in the armed forces of a foreign state"; having "made a *formal* renunciation of nationality . . . before a diplomatic or consular office of the United States in a foreign state" (recall that Oswald had not returned to the U.S. embassy in October 1959 to fill out the necessary *formal* documents for renunciation); et cetera. (CE 938, 18 H 144; for Oswald erroneously indicating on the Application for Renewal of Passport form that he had renounced his citizenship, or affirmed his allegiance to the Soviet Union, or it being a typographical error, see CE 938, 18 H 144; CE 947, 18 H 176–177; WR, pp.755–756; and 5 H 282–283, 286, WCT Richard Edward Snyder)

I think [it] is within the lawful right, and in the interest of, the United States government, and the American Embassy, Moscow, to look into this case on my behalf.

Yours very truly

Lee H. Oswald[778]

Marina later testified before the Warren Commission that she was not hospitalized over this matter,[779] and since Lee failed to mention it either in his diary or in letters to his family, the Commission concluded Oswald probably lied in his letter.[780] However, near mid-August Marina had, indeed, at least undergone a special medical examination because of "unpleasant sensations in the heart region," probably because of the pregnancy and the heavy strain she was under.[781] Then, in late September, as Marina later told Priscilla McMillan, she was overcome by gas fumes from the bus taking her to work, and after stepping off the bus, she fainted in the street. She was taken to the Third Clinical Hospital, which was right above the pharmacy where she worked, and remained there for about five days. (Oswald obviously got the "five day" reference in his letter to the U.S. embassy from this hospital stay by Marina.) Marina's doctors found that she was rundown, deficient in iron and vitamins, and, worse, had RH–negative blood. Fearing for her pregnancy, they tested Lee's blood and found, to everyone's relief, that he too was RH–negative.[782]

The American consul at the U.S. embassy in Moscow replied about a week later to Lee's letter of October 4 and counseled patience, as the embassy had no way to pressure the Soviet government, which seldom acted rapidly on visa matters. The embassy clearly had no interest in Lee's attempt to set up a fight between the Soviets and American officials. They would have to live with the Soviet government long after Lee Harvey Oswald was gone.[783]

In early October, Marina used her annual three weeks' vacation to visit her Aunt Polina in Kharkov—alone (Lee had already taken his to go to the U.S. embassy in Moscow), even though it would mean missing Lee's birthday on the eighteenth. She sent him a few presents, including a gold and silver cup inscribed "To My Dear Husband On His Birthday," which he appreciated, but he also told Robert that he and Marina had agreed that the "change of scenery was good for her." It was their first separation, after four months of marriage, but hardly the last—there would be many more in the remaining two years of Oswald's life. Mindful of her pregnancy—she could already feel the baby's movements—Marina did little in Kharkov but sleep and eat. Polina and her husband, Yuri Mikhailov, an engineer in the building trades, weren't even there for the first week, so they hired distant relatives to cook and look after Marina, and she must have enjoyed having the relatively luxurious three-room apartment to herself for awhile. But her aunt's remonstrations when she and her husband returned against Marina's going to America with Lee upset Marina, particularly in the pregnant condition she was in, and she left for home a day earlier than planned.[784]

Lee wrote a letter to Marina on October 14, 1961, that sounded as antiseptic as a weather report,[785] but by the eighteenth he responded to the birthday presents she sent him somewhat more warmly: "Well, are you returning soon? I will be glad to see you again—I will love you so!!"[786] That evening, his twenty-second birthday, he went alone to see his favorite opera, *The Queen of Spades*.[787]

By the time Marina returned in the latter part of October, "with several jars of preserves for me from her aunt in Khkov," he wrote in his diary that she was "radient."[788] Later, when he looked back on this period after her return, he wrote in a November–

December entry that "we are becoming anoid about the delay Marina is beginning to waiver about going to the US. Probably from the strain and her being pregrate, still we quarrel and so things are not to bright esp. with the approach of the hard Russian winter."[789]

Given her Uncle Ilya's fears that the Oswalds' attempt to leave the country might jeopardize his own position, Marina knew that the colonel would never intervene on her behalf with the Passport Office at the MVD in Minsk, but she had a more direct line of information, if not influence. Her best friend's (Lyalya Petrusevich's) boyfriend, Tolka, lived as a family friend in the apartment of Colonel Nicolai Axyonov, head of the Passport Office in Minsk. It seems that Axyonov's wife had been entertaining certain male visitors at home during her husband's absences, and Tolka found it easy to worm information from the wife in return for his silence about her dalliances. It was Tolka who was finally able to tell Marina and Lee that their exit visas had been granted sometime between December 12 and 15. However, Marina told author Priscilla McMillan that Lee wasn't content with the good news. He wanted to know exactly when he and Marina would be receiving the official word. And of course, when nothing happened between December 12 and 15 or in the immediate days thereafter, he probably had every reason to believe Tolka's information was not good. Lee, wild with impatience, sought an interview with Colonel Axyonov but was denied access to him by lower-ranking personnel in the office.

He then insisted that Marina try and see the colonel herself. She was fearful of any unnecessary contact with the authorities but eventually gave in. She was surprised when she was shown into his office immediately, though perhaps less surprised when Axyonov kept her waiting for another half hour before he appeared.[790] As is so frequently the case in life, Axyonov was not as fearsome as she imagined. He turned out to be a small, mousy man in civilian clothes. "Why do you want to leave Russia?" he asked Marina, who deflected a direct answer to the question by trying to convince Axyonov that she wished to leave not at all out of disloyalty to the Soviet Union but only out of loyalty to her husband, and Axyonov took no exception to that. She also hoped to leave before her pregnancy came to term, but he suggested that she wait until after the child was born so it would be born in Russia. He was kindly, even soothing. "Tell your husband not to worry," he said, "I believe your request will be granted." He also told her that the decision was not really up to him—which was undoubtedly true. In fact, such decisions were normally made in Moscow, probably by the KGB rather than the MVD, and Axyonov's receiving her in his private office was most likely a courtesy extended to her as the niece of a colleague in the ministry, nothing more. He made it clear to Marina that there were many others seeking visas and told Marina that she and her husband would "have to wait your turn."[791]

On the other hand, they no doubt benefited from the liberalization in Soviet society and the thaw in U.S.-Soviet relations, which was back on track after the temporary derailment occasioned by the U-2 overflight of Francis Gary Powers. While Marina was away in Kharkov, Premier Khrushchev, who had once been one of Stalin's henchmen, had boldly and courageously denounced Stalin and the crimes of the Soviet state during the Stalin era at the Twenty-second Congress of the Soviet Communist Party in Moscow. The fresh wind of "de-Stalinization" raised there (which included removing the dictator's tomb from Red Square—Lenin's would remain) had visible effects even in Minsk, where a monumental statue of Stalin had been demolished—if only with great difficulty—by chains, tanks, and explosives.[792]

In the meantime, Lee, who had rebuilt his bridges back home with his many letters not only to Robert but to Marguerite as well, was rewarded with several shipments of chewing gum and books in English, neither easy to come by in Minsk.[793]

Finally, on Christmas Day 1961, Marina was called to the Soviet Passport Office and told that she and her husband had been granted permission to leave.* Lee noted in his diary, "Its great (I think!)." Marina was surprised—she had never quite believed that she would ever be allowed to leave.[794]

For the Soviet authorities, allowing Oswald to leave the Soviet Union was a desirable solution. By the end of 1961 they had been studying him for over two years—and he had been trying to depart for nearly half that time—and they had come to the conclusion that he was not a spy. His carefully watched trips to the countryside on hunting parties produced no evidence of any interest in military installations. He hadn't even bothered to take his camera to photograph anything he might have come across by accident. Several approaches to him, offering the bait of secret information or access, had also been ignored. And they were confident he had no military secrets to give them that would be of any value. Also, he clearly had shown himself to be someone who could only cause them trouble, someone so tenacious in his determination that he was literally "willing to do anything, including the use of violence against his own person, in order to get what he wanted."[795]

Vladimir Semichastny, the KGB chairman during the period of Oswald's stay in Russia, said, "We [the KGB] concluded that he was not working for American intelligence. His intellectual training, experience, and capabilities were such that it would not show the FBI and CIA in a good light if they used people like him . . . As for Marina, about whether she had been planted by the KGB as his wife, I was often asked this question and I can say with authority that nothing of the sort happened."[796] Semichastny told Soviet author Nechiporenko that "Oswald knew little about Soviet reality. Almost everything he saw was completely unexpected by him. While living in the Soviet Union, he made no effort to augment and deepen his theoretical knowledge of Marxism. He was incapable of adapting himself to our reality. Incidentally, based on this, we concluded that he was not employed by any special intelligence service. Oswald's actions in Minsk were not those of a foreign agent. His primary interest was in attending dances."[797]

Oswald also didn't seem to be much of a worker. His radio plant had forwarded a report on his performance at work to the Minsk City Militia Department, which found nothing favorable to say about him: "During his employment as regulator his performance was unsatisfactory. He does not display the initiative for increasing skill as a regulator.

---

*Conspiracy theorists, ever suspicious, believe that Marina was granted an exit visa more quickly than normal, and they thus infer that she (and hence, her husband) was a KGB agent. Although Marina formally applied for her Soviet exit visa on August 21, 1961, she initiated her request in a letter to the Soviet authorities more than a month earlier, though the exact date is not known. However, we know that as early as July 17, 1961, her husband gave the Soviets a statement guaranteeing the support of his wife if they allowed her to leave for America. (CE 985, 18 H 405) So we know that at least five months transpired between when the Soviets received a document of some sort requesting an exit visa and when they granted her permission to leave on December 25, 1961. Of eleven cases examined by the CIA, Soviet wives of American citizens had to wait from five months to a year to obtain an exit visa. Of six cases examined by the U.S. Department of State after 1953, the liberalized post-Stalin era, the approximate waiting periods for Soviet wives of American citizens were, in decreasing order, approximately thirteen months, seven months, three months, one month, and ten days. (WR, pp.279–280; CE 2756, 26 H 141–142)

Citizen Lee Harvey Oswald reacts in an over-sensitive manner to remarks from the foremen and is careless in his work. Citizen L. H. Oswald takes no part in the social life of the shop and keeps very much to himself."[798]

Sending Oswald back to the United States was, all in all, good riddance. Only one very major hurdle remained. The U.S. government had to grant an entrance visa to Marina. But since she was his wife and he was going to be permitted to return to America, Lee was confident it would be just a matter of time before the approval came. Pursuant to this belief, on January 2, 1962, Oswald wrote his mother and asked her to "get in touch with the Red Cross" and ask it to contact an organization called the International Rescue Committee or some other group that helps persons from abroad get settled in the United States. He said he needed eight hundred dollars for two tickets from Moscow to New York and New York to Texas, that she should try to get a gift, not a loan, and not to send any of her own money.[799] Despite instructions, Marguerite asked the Red Cross for a loan, but was told the organization was not in a position to give her a loan.[800]

On January 13, 1962, Oswald himself wrote to the International Rescue Committee in New York to ask for eight hundred dollars to purchase two tickets from Moscow to Texas. "We are in need of help, he wrote, "and would appreciate any help that you can give us. We are expecting a baby the latter part of February."[801] Two weeks later he wrote again, this time upping the request to one thousand dollars.[802]

Curiously, now that the problems with the ponderous Soviet bureaucracy seemed to be solved, Lee's own government took over the endless reel of red tape. The U.S. embassy wrote Oswald on January 5 with the suggestion that he skirt the difficulties of obtaining an American visa for Marina by returning alone to the United States and sending for her later. Among the difficulties mentioned were the fact that she still lacked an affidavit of support or offer of employment in the United States.[803] He replied on January 16 that he would not consider leaving Russia without her. In the same letter he enclosed his own affidavit of support for Marina,[804] but the letters were going back and forth so quickly that the embassy had not received the affidavit by the time Embassy personnel wrote to him that there was no evidence that she would not become a public charge in the United States. They suggested that Oswald's mother or some other close relative file the affidavit of support.[805] The wrangling with letters and affidavits continued, to Lee's growing exasperation, for several months and extended beyond the U.S. embassy in Moscow and the U.S. State Department to the Immigration and Naturalization Service (INS), which had its own set of obstacles and procedures to follow. Meanwhile, in late January, Marguerite wrote to Lee to inform him that he had been given a dishonorable discharge from the Marine Corps.[806] This was incorrect in two respects. The discharge had actually been "undesirable," a less serious category than "dishonorable," and it was an undesirable discharge from the Marine Corps Reserve, not the Marine Corps, where his earlier dependency discharge remained intact.[807] The Marine Corps Reserve, apparently acting in response to the press accounts of Oswald's defection to Moscow, had moved against him almost immediately, and his case had been referred to a board of officers at the Glenview, Illinois, training station of the Marine Air Reserve by July 1960. On August 8, the board recommended that Oswald be "separated from the Marine Corps Reserve as undesirable," and his undesirable discharge was dated September 13 of that year, a time when neither the Marines nor anyone else in America knew where he was.[808]

Oswald, seeking to set aside the dishonorable discharge he thought he had been given, immediately sought the help of John B. Connally Jr., under the mistaken assumption that

Connally was still secretary of the navy. Connally had in fact resigned to become governor of Texas. Lee wrote on January 30, 1962,

> Dear Sir,
>   I wish to call your attention to a case about which you may have personal knowlege since you are a resident of Ft. Worth as I am. In November 1959 an event was well publicated in the Ft. Worth newspapers concerning a person who had gone to the Soviet Union to reside for a short time, (much in the same way E. Hemingway resided in Paris.)
>   This person in answers to questions put to him by reporteds in Moscow criticized certain facets of american life. The story was blown up into another "turncoat" sensation, with the result that the navy department gave this person a belated dishonourable discharge, although he had received an honourable discharge [he had received a hardship/dependency discharge] after three years service on Sept. 11, 1959 at El Toro, Marine corps base in California
>   These are the basic facts of *my* case . . .
>   I ask you to look into this case and take the necessary steps to repair the damage done to me and my family. For information I would direct you to consult the american Embassy, Chikovski St. 19/21, Moscow, USSR.
>
> Thank you
Lee H. Oswald[809]

Connally, to whom Oswald's letter had been forwarded, merely passed the letter on to his successor at the Department of the Navy, Fred Korth, and wrote to Oswald on February 23, 1962, that he had done so.[810] In an undated letter, the department wrote to Oswald in Minsk affirming the propriety of the undesirable discharge and sending him a copy of it, which he had never seen.[811] On March 22, Oswald wrote to the Department of the Navy seeking a further review of his undesirable discharge, but the department referred him to the Navy Discharge Review Board. He filled out the enclosed application for review while still in Minsk but did not send it until shortly after he returned to the United States.[812]

Marina had taken a pregnancy leave from her job early in January 1962, and in the middle of the night on February 15, her water broke. Lee and Marina hastily consulted their copy of *Dr. Spock's Baby and Child Care*, which had been obtained with some difficulty from England by Ernst Titovets, who had asked a pen pal to send it. Somehow they got the idea from the book that they still had fourteen hours before the birth, even though all the signs indicated it was going to happen a lot sooner. Lee wanted to go to the hospital, Marina felt they had time. They finally left at nine in the morning. There was snow on the ground, it was cold and slippery, they were unable to summon a taxi, and they finally had to take a bus to the hospital. Lee then went on to work, since fathers were not allowed in the maternity section of the hospital, but the news got there before he did—his coworkers congratulated him on the birth of his first child, a baby girl, who had been born at ten o'clock.

The following day his colleagues presented Lee with a big box containing a baby blanket, a sweater, overalls, shirts, a yellow blanket, even some of the cloth in which Soviet newborns were customarily swaddled.[813]

Lee wanted to name the child June Marina Oswald, but under Russian custom a child's second name had to be some form of the father's first name, or at least patronymic,* so the little girl was named June (for the month she was conceived) Lee. Both Lee and Marina had wanted a boy, but the fact that June Lee was not a male did nothing to dampen Lee's enthusiasm—he even thought a girl might be better for the mother, and he was willing to wait for a son until the next child. He was so excited when Marina and June first came home he couldn't even talk. He was also terrified that June might get cold, and Marina said that he "even forbade anyone to come into the room where the baby was kept [presumably the bathroom or kitchen since they only had a one-room apartment] until they got warm after coming from the street," to avoid carrying a chill in to the child. Both Marina and Lee laughingly tried to stay awake at night for fear the baby might die without making a sound. June Lee was very quiet and very little trouble, and after two weeks or so the new parents lost their jitters and became, in Marina's words, "normal parents." Marina felt at that time that Lee was "a very good husband and a very good father," and he helped Marina with the chores, even washing and ironing June's diapers.[814]

With the birth of the child, Oswald's nervousness and sense of urgency about getting out of the Soviet Union relaxed.[815] For one thing, he wanted little June to gain weight and strength before they undertook the trip.[816]

Meanwhile, Oswald had received no response to his petition to the International Rescue Committee for a loan of one thousand dollars, and on March 3, the embassy received an undated letter from him applying for a repatriation loan of eight hundred dollars† and advising it of the birth of his daughter, who, of course, would have to come to America with them. The embassy replied that it was authorized to lend him no more than five hundred dollars.[817]

On March 15, 1962, he finally received notification from the INS office in San Antonio, Texas, that Marina's application for a visa had been approved,[818] and on March 20, Marina, still on maternity leave, quit her job.[819]

Things were falling into place for Lee and Marina's new life in America, but Marina's aunt and uncle were still urging her not to leave Russia. Valya feared that Marina's leaving would harm her husband's career. "He has so little time left until his pension. He's done so much for you. What a blow if he loses it because of you," she told Marina.[820] The fear was not just paranoia—Ilya had been interviewed by the KGB as recently as February 23, the day baby June came home from the hospital with Marina, and he had assured

---

*A name derived from that of the father, especially by the addition to his first name of a prefix or suffix.

†Section 423.2-1 of the U.S. State Department regulations in force at the time provided that repatriation loans could be made to destitute U.S. nationals: "(a) Who are in complete and unquestioned possession of their citizenship rights; (b) Who are entitled to receive United States passports; (c) Whose loyalty to the United States is beyond question, or to whom the provisions of Section 423.1-2(b) apply" (7 FAM [Foreign Affairs Manual] § 423.2–1; 5 USC § 1701; WR, p.771).

Oswald clearly satisfied the qualifications of items (a) and (b), although not (c). Surely, his statements at the embassy at the time of his "defection" rendered his loyalty to the country of his birth highly suspect, but the State Department felt that an escape clause, appended to Section 423.1-2 (b), was applicable here. It permitted such loans when "the United States national is in or the cause of a situation which is damaging to the prestige of the United States Government or which constitutes a compelling reason for extending assistance to effect his return." (7 FAM § 423.1–2; CE 950, 18 H 310) The State Department did indeed feel that Oswald's "continued presence in Russia was damaging to the prestige of the United States because of his unstable character and prior criticisms of the United States." Government officials knew about his botched suicide attempt when he first tried to gain residence in the USSR, and no one could be sure that he would not pull some other crazy stunt that would create an international incident embarrassing to the United States. (CE 950, 18 H 309–311; WR, p.771)

the concerned agent that he had spoken to Marina about the necessity of her never doing anything in America that could be used as anti–Soviet propaganda.[821]

Uncle Ilya and Aunt Valya were not Marina's only relatives who found her plan to leave Russia with her husband repellant. One day Valya read to Marina a passage from a letter she had recently received from Marina's Aunt Polina in Kharkov: "I've never been inside a church in my life. But the day Marina goes to America I'll go to church. I'll light a great big candle and pray that her soul may rest in peace. I'll say a prayer for the dead. Then she'll be dead to me. I'll forget that I ever had a niece. As for her, she can forget that I was ever her aunt."

Marina was devastated. According to Priscilla McMillan, to whom she later told the story, Polina's letter was a curse, and Marina was superstitious enough to believe it might have the power to kill. She went home, brooded, and finally told Lee that she would not accompany him to the United States. She could not jeopardize the positions of her relatives that way.

"Okay, if that's how you feel," Lee said, "if you care more for them than for me, you can stay."

Hurt by the coldness of his response, Marina took the baby and fled to the Prusakovs, where she arrived in tears. Valya was sympathetic, Ilya forbidding—she might spend that night with them, he said, but she was not to come running to them every time she had a fight with her husband. She lay awake all that night, miserable at the thought that the two men, Lee and Ilya, cared so little for her, and that her two aunts, Polina and Valya, were sure to be deeply hurt by her defection. In the morning, things looked rosier though, and she set off for home. When she met Lee on the street, they returned to Valya's, where they found her other aunt from Minsk, Musya. Musya scolded Lee bitterly for being so self-ish as to take Marina off to America. When Lee decided to leave for his and Marina's apartment, he wanted to take the baby with him. Aunt Musya grabbed little June and told him he had no right to take a child from its mother.

Lee went into the other room and stood by the window, quietly crying, while Valya shuttled back and forth as the peace emissary. "Look what you've done," she told Marina. "He's as pale as a ghost by the window. The tears are streaming down his face. I even heard him say, 'What have I to live for? What am I to do now?'"

In the end, Lee's distress proved to be far more eloquent than anything he might have said. Marina wanted proof that he cared for her, and she agreed to leave with Lee for America when she realized that she had no more right to separate him from their child than he had to take June from her. Back at their own apartment, Lee took off June's swad-dling and kissed her tiny hands and feet. "Bad mama," he said. "She wanted papa to never see his good girl again."[822]

On May 10, the U.S. embassy in Moscow wrote Oswald that it was "pleased to inform" him that it was "now in a position to take final action on your wife's visa application." Telling him to have Marina gather up a few more documents (such as one more copy of her marriage certificate and a certification of smallpox inoculation), the letter suggested that Oswald come to the embassy with his wife to sign the final papers.[823]

The days were winding down before they would leave for Moscow, then America, but Lee hadn't quit his job yet. One day he approached Ella German at work. She had recently married a fellow worker, Max Prokhochik. Lee had not spoken to her in the fifteen months since they broke up and even pretended not to know her, but he turned up at her work-bench just as she was preparing to go to lunch with her husband. "Can we meet today?"

he asked. "There's something I want to talk to you about." Ella, fearful that Max would be jealous, shook her head and explained, "I just got married." Lee asked if it was anyone he knew. "Yes," she said. Lee walked away without another word.[824] Marina, too, had an encounter with an old attachment, Anatoly Shpanko, whom she ran into in a shop by the Oswalds' apartment. He had heard that she was leaving. "Take me with you," he joked. "Write. Let me know where I can find you. One day I'll get to America, too. You'll have money over there. You'll come back for a visit. Someday we will see one another again."

Marina, uneasy, told him she had to go home to feed her baby. *That*, he had not heard about. He was surprised, since the last time he had seen her, about three months ago, she had not appeared to be pregnant. "You didn't see right," Marina said, although she recalled that at the time she had carefully arranged her coat to conceal her pregnancy.[825]

On May 22, Lee picked up his exit visa at the MVD office in Minsk,[826] and wrote to Robert with the news that they would be leaving for Moscow by train the following day and that he expected to depart for England, also by train, ten to fourteen days later. They would then travel by ship, probably to New Orleans, so it might be nearly a month before they arrived home. He now took up a theme that was to preoccupy him over the next few weeks—how to deal with the press:

> Dear Robert, . . .
>
> In case you hear about our coming, or the newspapers hear about it (I hope they won't), I want to warn you not to make any comment whatsoever about us. None at all!! I know what was said about me when I left the U.S. as Mother sent me some clipping's from the newspaper, however I relize that it was just the shock of the news which made you say all those things. however I'll just remind you again not to make any statements or comments if you are approuched by the newspapers, between now and the time we actally arrive in the U.S. Hope to see you soon.
>
> Your Brother
> Lee[827]

When the Oswalds finally did leave by train for Moscow on May 23, 1962, after spending their last night in friend Pavel's apartment, it appeared that none of Marina's family turned up to say good-bye, only a number of friends. Some of them brought flowers, reminding Marina of a funeral.[828] The ubiquitous KGB spy, without which no Soviet social gathering would be complete, may have turned up as well. At least Eleonora Ziger thought so. She focused on a fellow half hidden behind a pillar and told him, "Listen in if you like. We have no secrets here." Eventually, Marina noticed that her Uncle Ilya and Aunt Valya had indeed come. They stood a long way off, by themselves, in a corner, forlorn and furtive. Marina and Lee went over to them. "We didn't want to be in the way," Valya said. The Prusakovs kissed Marina, the baby, and even Lee, whom they begged to take good care of Marina, and then scuttled away.[829]

The Oswalds came to the Moscow embassy on May 24, where Marina picked up her American visa.[830] And Lee's passport was finally renewed, for thirty days, and amended to include little June Lee.[831] They spent much of the next ten days waiting around in embassy lobbies of several countries for the transit visas that would allow them to travel by train across Poland, East and West Germany, and the Netherlands.[832]

The American embassy made arrangements for them to sail from Rotterdam to New York on a Dutch passenger ship, the *Maasdam*, on June 4, and approved of a repatriation loan to Lee of $435.71, which, with their savings, was just enough to cover the cost of their hotel room in Moscow, the train trip, one night in unpretentious but clean lodgings in Rotterdam before boarding the ship, and the ocean passage to New York, where they would arrive all but penniless.[833]

The Oswalds spent their last evening in Moscow visiting Marina's friends from Minsk, Yuri and Galina Belyankin, at their apartment. The following morning, June 1, 1962, Lee went back to the U.S. embassy, signed a promissory note, and received Russian money equivalent to $435.71, the amount of his State Department loan, to cover the purchase of two railroad tickets from Moscow to Rotterdam (Baby June traveled free), for which Lee contributed ninety rubles, and three steamship tickets (June's ticket only cost $20.00) from Rotterdam to New York.[834]* Late that afternoon when they boarded their train at Moscow's Belorussian Station, Galina was the only one to see them off.[835] And with that, Lee Harvey Oswald's Soviet odyssey came to a close.

We know, of course, that Oswald was not a KGB agent—my God, the KGB was spying *on him* in Russia—but those who believe Oswald had been infiltrated into the Soviet Union as an agent of some American intelligence agency—and there are many who do—would do well to ask themselves just what his mission could possibly have been. There's no evidence that he had any social or professional contact with ranking officials or diplomatic or military people, nor access to restricted locations. He had no special expertise or experience, and only a marginal, though improving, competence in the Russian language, and what he did learn about the Soviet Union probably could have been gathered by an alert journalist in a few days. It is just about as plausible to imagine that the KGB would have taken pains to gather sensitive information about America by infiltrating an uneducated teenager who spoke virtually no English into the United States to work in a bicycle factory in Bakersfield, California. It could be done, of course, but what could possibly be the point?

It should be noted that well over half of the time that Oswald was in the Soviet Union, he was trying very hard to get out of it. The Warren Report devotes thirty-two pages to "transactions between Lee Harvey Oswald and Marina Oswald, and the U.S. Department of State and the Immigration and Naturalization Service of the U.S. Department of Justice,"[836] an analysis based on the hundreds of documents, letters, cables, and reports generated by the government in dealing with Oswald, and there is no hint in any of them that Oswald was in any way encouraged to defect or given special help to reverse his defection by any of the agencies involved—indeed, it doesn't appear that any of them even knew where he was for the first year of his two-and-a-half-year stay in the country. Apart from a few clerical errors and bobbles in administrative procedures, there are no noteworthy anomalies in the paper trail, no indication that Oswald's case was handled differently from that of other defectors who wished to return, or indeed, from that of other American citizens who found themselves stranded abroad in other countries and needed State Department assistance to return. Given the temper of the times, there were no doubt some in the government who would have happily left Oswald to stew in his own juices by

---

*Although transportation to Texas was not provided for, it still appears that the eight hundred dollars, then one thousand dollars, that Oswald had earlier requested from the International Rescue Committee for transportation was more than he actually needed.

denying him a renewal of his passport, but two 1958 decisions of the U.S. Supreme Court, *Kent v. Dulles* and *Dayton v. Dulles*, made it impermissible to deny passports to American Communists or any other American suspected of going abroad "to engage in activities which will advance the Communist movement." The opinion in the *Kent* case made it clear that the right to travel was one of those liberties of which no American citizen may be deprived without due process of law. The majority held that "freedom of movement across frontiers in either direction, and inside frontiers as well, was a part of our heritage. Travel abroad, like travel within the country . . . may be as close to the heart of the individual as the choice of what he eats, or wears, or reads. Freedom of movement is basic in our scheme of values."[837]

For the Oswalds, leaving the Soviet Union was a momentous, life-changing event. Marina was leaving a country which, however repressive, was well known to her and with which she was comfortable. Her relations with her family had always been trying, at best, but she nonetheless maintained them assiduously, and she relied heavily on her relatives, particularly her aunts. As far as she knew, she was leaving these people forever to go to a country whose language she could not speak at all and where she would be surrounded by strangers. If she were to find any work at all, it would almost for sure not be as a pharmacist, and she would never again enjoy the easy camaraderie of coworkers who were young women very much like herself, with similar backgrounds and experience. In addition, Lee had already demonstrated a desire to control her, to make her live up to his image of what a wife should be. Even though he had already bullied Marina, according to the KGB transcripts of the goings-on in their apartment, Marina was not a shrinking violet (I would find this out firsthand years later) and she had always fought back stoutly or fled to her Aunt Valya, never capitulating. Her new life in America, with its isolation, would greatly exacerbate her problems.

It was also an enormous change for Lee. He had arrived in the USSR as a nineteen-year-old and became a man in the two and a half years he lived there. He had lost his baby fat and prematurely some of his hair, and he had lived independently, out from under the yoke of his mother and the U.S. Marines, for the first time in his life. He had had a job—the longest one he would ever hold and the only one he would neither quit nor be fired from—that did not pay badly by Soviet standards, but his incompetence and insufferable attitude had been tolerated in a way they would never be in a highly competitive and rough-and-tumble capitalist society. He had been exposed to communism in the raw and saw it was not the same as he had read about in the yellowing pages of Marxist literature from the New Orleans public library.

Since the train's route led back through Minsk, where they would stop briefly in the early morning of June 2, Marina wired ahead in the hopes that Valya would come for one last meeting. Marina and Lee walked up and down the platform looking for Valya, but she was not there. Lee grasped Marina, who was crushed and crying. "Don't worry, don't cry," he said. "Everything will be alright."[838]

Later in the day, as the train passed the border at Brest crossing into Poland, one of the guards asked Lee and Marina whether they had any gold or other valuables to declare, and just grinned when Marina pointed to Baby June.[839]

All that day the train plied its way across the broad expanse of Poland. They had a brief respite in Warsaw, where they bought beer and Lee took photographs. They crossed into

East Germany at Frankfort on the Oder, and later that night Marina woke long enough to notice the stark contrast between East and West Berlin—the former dark, the latter brightly lit in the western manner. They were in the West at last. The next day the contrast was even greater, as the train crawled across the storybook landscape of Holland to Rotterdam, where they were scheduled to stay overnight. Although the shops in Rotterdam were closed for Sunday, Marina could see they were overflowing with what were to her unimaginable luxuries. Lee bought her the first Coca-Cola she ever tasted. That night, in the modest pension booked for them by the embassy, the sheets were so clean Marina didn't want to lie down in the bed.[840]

The next day, June 4, 1962, they boarded the SS *Maasdam*, bound for New York and the New World.[841] During their voyage across the Atlantic, Marina spent most of her time in their cabin with the baby while Lee would disappear to the ship's library, where he spent many hours writing.[842] What Lee was writing on the voyage appears to have been a preparation for the interviews or interrogations he at once half hoped and half feared to be subjected to on his arrival in the United States. Although he may have started work on this before he boarded the *Maasdam*, he at least rewrote or recopied the pages while on the ship, because they are written on the back of the ship's stationery. There are two separate drafts of answers to an identical set of eight questions—one, for the most part, seemingly designed to alarm and infuriate his questioners, the second much more velvety in tone with an exonerating spin on them. Although the two sets of questions and answers were written separately, they are presented here with both answers to each question:

Q: Why did you go to the USSR?
  1. I went as a mark of discuss [disgust] and protest against American political policies in forenign countrys, my personal sign of discontent and horror at the misguided mind of reasoning of the U.S. Government.
  2. I went as a citizen of the U.S. (as a tourist) residing in a foreing country which I have a perfect right to do. I went there to see the land, the people and how there system works

Q: What about those letters?
  1. I made serval letters in which I expressed my above feeling to the American Embassy when in Oct 1959 I went there to legally liquate my american citizenship and was refused this legalle right.
  2. I made no letters deriding the U.S.!! In correspondence with the U.S. Embassy I made no anti-american statements, any critizem I might have had was of policies not our government

Q: Did you make statements against the U.S. there?
  1. yes
  2. no

Q: What about that type [tape] recording [a very brief recording undoubtedly made as a favor to Rimma for her employer when he first arrived in Moscow]?
  1. I made a recording for Radio Moscow which was broadcast the following sunday in which [I] spoke about the beauiful capital of the Socialist work [world?] and all its progress.
  2. I made a recording for the Moscow Tourist Radio travel log, in which I spoke about sight-seeing and what I had seen in Moscow tourist circles. I expressed delight in all

the interesting places, I mentioned in this respect the University, mesuem of art, Red Square, the Kremlin I rember I closed this 2 minute recording by saying I hoped our peoples would live in peace and fr.

Q: Did you break laws by residing [or] taking work in the USSR?

1. I did in that I took an othe of allignce to the USSR.

2. Under U.S. law a person may lose the protection of the U.S., by voting or serving in the armed forces of a foringn state or taking an othe of alligence to that state. I did none of these

Q: Isn't all work in the USSR considered State work?

1. Yes of course and in that respect I allso broke US law in accepting work under a forign state.

2. No. Technically only plants working directly for the State, usually defense, all other plants are owned by the workers who work in them.

Q: What about statements you made to UPI agent Miss Mosby?

1. I was approched by Miss Mosby and other reporters just after I had formally requested the American Embassy to legally liquate my U.S. citizenship, for a story, they were notified by the U.S. Embassy, not by me. I answered questions and made statements to Miss Mosby in regard to my reasons for coming to the USSR, her story was warped by her later, but in barest esscens it is possible to say she had the thruth printed.

2. I was approcaed just after I had formally notified the U.S. Embassy in Moscow of my future residence in he USSR by the newspaper agenties in Moscow including U.P.I. API and time inc. who were notified by the Embassy. I did not call them. I answered questions and gave statements to Miss Mosby of U.P.I. I requested her to let me OK. her story before she released it, which is the polite and ususal thing. She sent her version of what I said just after she sent it. I immially called her to complant about this, at which time she apolizied but said her editor and not her had added serval things. She said London was very excited about the story (there is how I deduced that she had allready sent it) so there wasn't much else I could do about it. and I didn't relize that the story was even more blown out of shape once it got to the U.S.A. I'm afriad the printed story was faricated sensenlionilizism.

Q: Why did you remain in the USSR for so long if you only wanted a look

1. I resided in the USSR from Oct 16 1959 to sprig of 1961 a period of 2½ years I did so because I was living quite comfortably. I had plenty of money, an apartment rent-free lots of girls, ect.. why should I leave all that?

2. I resided in the USSR until February 1961 when I wrote the Embassy stating that I would like to go back. (My passport was at the Embassy for safekeeping) they invited me to Moscow for this purpose however it took me almost ½ year to get a permit to leave the city of Minsk for Moscow. In this connection I had to use a letter from the head consular, to the Russian authrities in Minsk (the Russians are very beaurocratic and slow about letting foreingrs travel about the country hence the visa) when I did get to Moscow the Embassy immiately gave me back my passport and advised me as to how to get a exit visa from the Russians for myself and my Russian wife, this long and ardous process took months from July 1962 untill _____ 1962, therefore you see almost 1 year was spent in trying to leave the country. thats why I was there so long not out of desire!

Q: Are you a communits?

1. Yes basically, allthough I hate the USSR and socialist system I still thank marxism can work under different circumstances.
2. No of course not.

Q: have you ever know a communist?

1. not in the U.S.A.
2. I have never even know a communist, outside of the ones in the USSR but you can't help that.

Q: What are the othestanding [outstanding] differants between the USSR and USA?

1. None, except in the US the living standard is a little higher, freedoms are about the same, medical aid and the educational system in the USSR is better than in the USA.
2. freedom of speech travel outspoken opposition to unpopular policies freedom to believe in god.[843]

It is difficult to know what Oswald had in mind with this schizophrenic performance, but he added a significant clue at least with respect to his second set of answers when, at the end of that set, he assigned these words to his anticipated questioner, whom he assumed to be reporters for "newspapers." They say to him, "Thank you sir, you are a *real* patriot!!"[844]

Also on the trip back to America he wrote notes on what he called "speech before," suggesting he was contemplating the possibility of giving a speech, somewhere, upon his return. In the speech notes, he scores segregation in America, writing,

> It, is, I think the action of the active segregationist minority and the great body of indiffent [indifferent] people in the South who do the United States more harm in the eyes of the worlds people, than the whole world communist movement . . . Make no mistake, segregationist tendencies can be unleared. I was born in New Orleans, and I know.

He refers to the "major short comings and advantages" of both the American and Russian systems of government, but notes that

> only in ours is the voice of dissent allowed opportunity of expression . . . I have done a lot of critizing of our system I hope you will take it in the spirit it was given. in going to Russia I followed the old priciple "Thou shall seek the truth and the truth shall make you free" In returning to the U.S. I have done nothing more or less than select the lesser of two evils.[845]

Other dissertations he worked on aboard the SS *Maasdam*, written on the front of the ship's logoed paper, could be construed to reveal the considerable thought he gave to the damage his second defection—from the Soviet Union—did to his claim to be a Communist. He put time and effort into a new statement of his political beliefs:

> I have often wondered why it is that the communist, capitalist and even the fasist and anarchist elements in America, allways profess patrotistism toward the land and the people, if not the government; although their movements must surly lead to the bitter destruction of all and everything . . .
> I wonder what would happen if somebody was to stand up and say he was utterly

opposed not only to the governments, but to the people, too the entire land and complete foundations of his socially.[846]

It's a rhetorical question, and one senses that one day he would like to be that "somebody." But first he gropes for some third position between capitalism and communism:

> too a person knowing both systems and their factional accesories, their can be no mediation between the systems as they exist to–day and that person.
>
> He must be opposed to their basic foundations and representatives and yet it is imature to take the sort of attitude which says "a curse on both your houses!"
>
> their are two great represenative[s] of power in the world, simply expressed, the left and right, and their factions . . .
>
> any practical attempt at one alternative must have as its nuclus the triditionall ideological best of both systems, and yet be utterly opposed to both systems.[847]

After some confused exegesis of the Industrial Revolution, which he seemed to believe began at "the turn of the [twentieth] century," he decides that the two systems are incompatible because of their competition for markets. The communist system is as much at fault as the capitalistic system.

> In the communist experamint serveal factions and unavoidable developments have emerged which Marx and Engels could not possibly have foreseen . . . Marx envisualized that the aboliaton of class'es would lead to the gruaual [gradual] reduction of state apparous [apparatus]. however this is not the case and is better observed than contemplated. the state rather becomes more extensitve.[848] . . . In the late 1800's Engels wrote Vanti Dühring which rightly critized Eugen Duhring's, a german idealist who was supposably not consistent enough in his materialism for the dialectical materilist Marx. [But in] his critical anylis of Dühring Engles said with much heavy sarcism that Dühring only changed a word in his putting forward of his social revolutionary ideas that [the] changed word "was the word community from the word state" whereas Dühring wanted Social Democracy at a local or community level, Marx and Engels advocated a centrilized state which would later "wither away!" But . . . as history has shown time again the state remains and grows whereas true democracy can be practiced only at the local level, while [as long as] the centralized state, administrative, political or supervisual remains their can be no real democracy.[849]

Oswald goes on to write that he intends to "put forward" an "allturnative" to the two systems of capitalism and communism, and "supporters" of his alternative "must prepare now in the event the situation [he writes the word "melatarist," by itself, below "situation"] presents itself for the practical application of this allturnative."[850] But then he loses his focus, does not present an alternative (other than to resort to the meaningless platitude that "what is needed is a constructive and practical group of persons desiring peace but steadfastly opposed to the revival of forces who have led millions of people to death and destruction"), and proceeds to make his emotional rejection of both the communist USSR and the capitalist USA very clear:

We have lived into a dark generation of tenstion and fear. But how many of you have tried to find out the truth behind the cold war clic'es [cliches]! I have lived under both systems, I have *sought* the answers and although it would be very easy to dupe myself into believing one system is better than the other, I know they are not.

I despise the representatives of both systems weather they be socialist or cristan democrats, [whether] they be labor or conserative they are all products of the two systems.[851]

He finishes his paper, mostly devoted to abstractions he can't quite get a handle on, with two peculiar codas. The first is a confession that he had in fact taken Russian gold:

Whene I first went to Russia in the winter of 1959 my funds were very limited, so after a certain time, after the Russians had assured themselfs that I was really the naive american who beliyved in communism, they arranged for me to recive a certain amount of money every month. OK it came technically through the Red-Cross as finical help to a . . . polical immigrate but it was arranged by the M.V.D. I told myself it was simply because I was broke and everybody knew it. I accepted the money because I was hungry and there was several inches of snow on the ground in Moscow at that time but what it really was was *payment* for my denuci-ation of the U.S. in Moscow in November 1956 [1959] and a clear promise that for as long as I lived in the USSR life would be very good I didn't relize all this, of course for almost two years.

As soon as I became completely disgusted with the Sovit Union and started negotitions with the American Embassy in Moscow for my return to the U.S. my "Red Cross" allotment was cut off. this was not diffical to understand since all cor-respondece in and out of the Embassy is censored as is common knowledge in the Embassy itself. I have never mentioned the fact of these monthly payments to any-one. I do so in order to state that I shall never sell myself intentionly or uninten-tionly to anyone again.

The second coda is another peek into Lee's fantasy life, not unlike the imagined admi-ration by the newspapers who would be interviewing him. It assumes that what he has written will be published and that he would be offered an appropriate fee for it:

as for the fee of $_____ I was supposed to recive for this _____ I refuse it. I made pretense to except it only because otherwise I would have been considered a crack pot and not allowed to appear to express my views. after all who would refuse money?!?[852]

The SS *Maasdam* put into Hoboken, New Jersey, and the Oswalds cleared immigration on June 13, 1962.[853] The hordes of reporters eager to hear Lee's story were notably absent. But INS inspector Frederick Wiedersheim was there to briefly question Lee about his Soviet interlude. Oswald told Wiedersheim that he had been employed as a mechanic in Russia, had threatened to renounce his U.S. citizenship but had never carried out the threat, had never voted in Russia, and had not held any position in the Soviet government.[854] Also there to meet Oswald was a representative of the Traveler's Aid Society, Spas T. Raikin, who had been alerted by the State Department. Lee did need Raikin's help, as he had only sixty-three dollars to his name, nowhere to spend the night, and was without funds to go on to Texas as he wanted to do. Raikin helped Lee and Marina get through Customs and then sent them on to the New York City Department of Welfare.[855]

The Welfare Department put the Oswalds up for the night in the Times Square Hotel[856] and called his brother Robert's home in Fort Worth. A case worker spoke to Robert's wife Vada, who offered to help. She called Robert at work, and he immediately wired two hundred dollars.[857] The next morning Oswald tried to refuse Robert's money on the grounds that his brother, raising a family on a milkman's wages, could hardly afford it. Lee wanted the Welfare Department, not Robert, to lend him the money, which he'd repay when he could. When that didn't work, he suggested that he and his family could take the train as far as his sixty-three dollars would take them, and then apply to the welfare services wherever that was for transportation the rest of the way. He was advised that this plan was highly unrealistic and dangerous, and he finally accepted, grudgingly, Robert's money. A case worker for the department then escorted him to a Western Union office and a bank to help him cash Robert's money order, to the West Side Airlines Terminal to buy the tickets for the flight reserved for them, Delta Airlines flight number 821, and back to the hotel to pay their room rent and pick up their luggage. The worker then took them to Idlewild airport and remained with them until they boarded their flight for takeoff at 4:15 p.m.[858]

When Lee, Marina, and June Lee descended from the plane at Dallas's Love Field in the early evening of June 14, 1962, Robert and his family were there to greet them. Lee's first words to his brother were, "No reporters?"

"I managed to keep it quiet," Robert said, "as you asked in your letter." Robert thought Lee was a little disappointed, but Lee said nothing more about it.[859]

Lee had stated his intention, in his affidavit of support for Marina, to reside with his mother in Vernon, Texas,[860] but he was probably relieved when Robert had offered in a letter to let Lee and his family stay with them instead, and after Lee arrived, he asked how everyone was doing without even mentioning Marguerite.[861]

Robert found his younger brother only a little changed after his two and a half years in the Soviet Union. He was thinner, beginning to bald, his curly hair somewhat kinkier— Lee blamed his hair loss on the Russian weather, while Robert wondered if Lee had received shock treatments in Russia that caused the loss—but he also seemed rather tense and anxious the first couple of days. He might have picked up a hint of an accent as well. Nonetheless, Robert said that "to me, [Lee] acted the same as he did in 1959 prior to going to Russia . . . He appeared to be the same boy I had known before."[862]

The brothers got on well together, although Lee avoided talking politics with Robert, who, as Lee knew, considered himself a born conservative.[863] Robert, for his part, was delighted to have Lee, Marina, and June with him on Davenport Street, out on the western edge of Fort Worth. The house had two bedrooms. Their infant son, Robert Lee, had his baby bed in Robert and Vada's room, and their daughter, Cathy, slept in the other bedroom. So all they had to do was shift little Cathy onto a couch in the living room to give Lee, Marina, and June a room to themselves. The two young wives communicated happily by sign language as they washed, ironed, and looked after their infants, and Marina pitched in to help Vada with the other housework.[864] Marina was ecstatic about everything in her new surroundings, from the kitchen equipment to the shrubs in the yard, and she asked Lee wonderingly, "Will we be able to live like this?" After the first few days she even prevailed upon Vada, a licensed hairdresser, to give her a short, fluffy haircut like Vada's own. Both she and Lee were delighted with the result.[865]

Robert and Vada were just "tickled to death" to be able to show Marina things in America she had never seen before, and Vada gave her some lightweight summer clothes to replace her heavy Russian woolens, which were a misery in the Texas heat. But Marina hesitated to accept a pair of walking shorts because she feared they were immodest, even though they came nearly to her knees. In Russia, shorts were only worn at the beach, and the thought that she could wear them elsewhere was revolutionary.[866]

Robert was perplexed by the fact that although Marina seemed happy, she seldom smiled, until Lee explained that, embarrassed by a crooked tooth, she had pulled it herself before they left Minsk. She wasn't smiling because she didn't want to reveal the gap. Her first trip to an American supermarket, though, finally evoked plenty of smiles. It was a fairyland for her and she couldn't wait to push the shopping cart.[867]

The first weekend home Lee showed Robert the sheaf of notes he had been keeping for a book he was writing about the living and working conditions in Minsk, and Robert read the first fifteen or twenty pages of them.[868]

On Monday morning, June 18, Oswald went to the offices of Mrs. Pauline Virginia Bates, a public stenographer whose name he got out of the telephone directory, and asked her to type a manuscript he had started working on in Russia that was supplemented by the sheets of paper on which he had recorded his impressions of the Soviet Union. After Oswald told her that he had just returned from Russia and smuggled his notes out of the country, she was immediately intrigued, enough for her to agree to type the notes for one dollar per page or two dollars an hour, fifty cents less than her usual hourly rate. Over the next three days, Bates spent eight hours typing for Oswald while he helped her translate portions of the notes written in Russian. At the end of each session, Oswald took home with him all of his notes and as much of the manuscript that she had completed. After paying ten dollars for ten single-spaced pages, he told her he had no more money to give her. Fascinated with what she was typing, she offered to continue to type for nothing, but he declined, telling her, "No, I don't work that way."[869]

He continued to work on the book at Robert's house, sometimes spending hours at a stretch reworking his notes. What remains from this projected book are reprinted in fifty-one pages of a Warren Commission exhibit, the typed (by the Commission) narrative of Oswald's handwritten manuscript,[870] along with ninety-seven other pages of Warren Commission exhibits (forty-one of which consist of Oswald's original handwritten manuscript) of other handwritten and typed thoughts of Oswald's that he may or may not have intended to be a part of the book.[871] That he intended to write a book is beyond doubt: the manuscript even includes, in Oswald's handwriting, a "furword" (foreword), an "About the Author" profile (the latter containing, as alluded to earlier, one of the most famous phrases ever attached to Oswald: "Lee Harvey Oswald was born in Oct 1939 in New Orleans La, the son of a Insuraen Salesman whose early death left a far mean streak of indepence brought on by neckleck"), and a table of contents with forty-five sections or chapters.[872]

Nowhere in the historical record is there any indication that Oswald even got around to making any attempt to get his writings published, either as a book or as a long article. However, someone else was planning a book on Lee's defection—Marguerite. She had received notification from the State Department that Lee was returning to the United States, and although he hadn't bothered to tell her he was home and staying at Robert's, she figured that out. About a week after his arrival, she took a few days off from her practical nursing job in Crowell, Texas, where she looked after an elderly invalid woman, to travel to Fort Worth to meet her new grandchild and daughter-in-law. Renting a motel room paid for by her client's daughter, she visited her sons and their families every day. She was happy to see Lee again, loved to hold June in her lap, and was thrilled to death with Marina, raving over her looks.

"Marina doesn't look Russian," she told her son. "She is beautiful."

"Of course not," he said. "That's why I married her, because she looks like an American girl."

"You know, Lee," she said, "I am getting ready, I *was* getting ready to write a book on your so-called defection."

Lee was alarmed, only hearing the "am" not the "was." "Mother, you are not going to write a book!" he asserted.

She told him that she didn't like his telling her what to do, since it was her life, and his defection had an impact on it, but went on to say, "I cannot write the book now because honey, you are alive and back." She told the Warren Commission that she was contemplating a book at the time because she had no way of knowing "whether my son was living or dead."[873]

Marguerite proceeded to make an offer to Lee that clearly didn't please him. She said she planned to give up her job and move back to Fort Worth to take a place where Lee, Marina, and June could live with her. Lee told her that they would find their own place as soon as he landed a job, but Marguerite was insistent.[874]

However, that was some time off, and Lee's main concern now was to get a job. Indeed, he had already visited the Fort Worth office of the Texas Employment Commission to check job possibilities on the same day he started work on his manuscript with Pauline Bates. He also asked if there was anyone in town who spoke Russian. He was given two names, one of them Peter Paul Gregory, a Siberian-born consulting petroleum engineer who taught classes in Russian at the public library. He called Gregory in his office the following morning and asked whether he would be willing to give him a letter certifying his ability to translate Russian into English. Gregory suggested he drop by the office.[875]

Oswald turned up the next morning, ludicrously attired for the summer heat in a heavy gray flannel suit and atrociously clunky Russian shoes. Gregory gave him a passage from a high school text in Russian to read aloud and then asked him to translate it into English. Oswald did very well on both tests, and Gregory had no hesitation in writing out a "To Whom It May Concern" letter attesting to his qualifications, that he was "capable of being an interpreter and perhaps a translator." Gregory warned Lee that there were no jobs for translators in Fort Worth, but asked for his address and a way to reach him.[876] A week later, Gregory and his son, Paul, a college student, visited the Oswalds at Robert's home and arranged for Marina to give Paul lessons in Russian during the summer, Gregory feeling that his own conversational Russian had probably deteriorated after living in this country for forty years.[877]

That night, Lee jubilantly told Marina, "Mama, Mama, I've found you some Russians in Fort Worth. Now you won't be lonely anymore." Curiously, though, he lied to Marina about how he located the engineer—claiming to have gotten his name and address from the public library rather than the Texas Employment Commission. What he thought to gain from the lie is a mystery, but Lee seldom resorted to the truth when he thought a lie would do. Although here, perhaps, he wanted to convince Marina he had gone out of his way to get her the information.

He was less successful with the other name he had been given by the Employment Commission, Gali Clark, the Russian-born wife of Fort Worth attorney Max Clark. Clark was not as forthcoming as Gregory—unlike him, she had an inkling of who Lee was from a news story in a Fort Worth paper describing him as a defector. She didn't like the sound of him, and she fobbed him off, saying she had to speak to her husband. However, following the suggestion of her husband, she called back the following Sunday and invited Lee to bring Marina to her house, but apparently miffed by her earlier chilly reception, he told her they could not come.[878]

That night at Robert and Vada's dinner table Lee told Marina—in Russian—about his telephone conversation with Gali Clark. Marina thought he had been rude to Mrs. Clark, and scolded him for it, the conversation developing into a fight. Lee, humiliated by the fact that Robert and Vada could certainly understand the tone of their interchange, if not the words, ordered Marina to smile. When she refused, he called her a dirty word in Russian and she left the table. Lee followed her into the bedroom, and with a coldness she had never seen before, and as quietly as he possibly could, so Robert and Vada would not hear, hit her several times across the face, then told her he would kill her if she told Robert.

Marina spent the next couple of hours wandering alone around the neighborhood, stunned by the realization of the degree to which she was now at his mercy—there was no Aunt Valya in Fort Worth, Texas, to run to. She was also amazed at his capacity to mask his cruelty to her behind the affable exterior he presented to his brother and sister-in-law. Eventually, she returned—where else was she going to go? He was lying awake in bed when she came in, but he said not a word to her.[879]

However interested Lee may have been in making a splash in the American press on his return from the Soviet Union, he thought better of it once he settled down at Robert's home in Fort Worth. He fended off inquiries from several reporters. But there was one interview he could not so easily fend off. On May 18, 1962, Fort Worth FBI agent John Fain had interviewed Vada Oswald, Robert's wife, who informed him that Lee and his wife were going to return to the states. She promised to advise him when they did, but when he learned on June 22, from the New York office of the FBI and independently from an assistant manager of Holland-America Line, that Oswald and his wife and child had arrived in the United States on June 13 and their destination was 7313 Davenport, Fort Worth (Vada and Robert Oswald's address), he contacted Vada by phone on the morning of June 26. Vada confirmed that Lee and his family had arrived in Fort Worth on June 14 and had been living at her and her husband's residence since then.

"Why didn't you let me know about it?" Fain inquired.

"Well, actually the whole family had been so harassed and . . . he just didn't feel like letting his face be shown outside of the house."

Fain had Vada put Oswald on the phone, and Lee agreed to come downtown to talk with Fain and a colleague that afternoon. Fain had set up a file on Oswald when Oswald defected in 1959, and had interviewed Marguerite and Robert while Lee was in Russia, Marguerite for the first time in January of 1960 when she purchased a "foreign money transfer" of twenty-five dollars to send to Lee in Russia.[880]

Though he already had a moderately comprehensive file on Oswald, the afternoon of June 26, 1962, was the first time Fain met Oswald face to face. Another agent, Tom Carter, sat in on the interview. They found Oswald "tense, kind of drawn up, and rigid. A wiry little fellow, kind of waspy." Lee declined to discuss his reasons for going to the Soviet Union as he was unwilling to "relive the past." He told the agents that he did not try to renounce his citizenship and had not tried to acquire Soviet citizenship. He also said the Soviets had neither asked nor had he offered them information about his experience in the U.S. Marines. He promised to notify them if he were ever contacted by Soviet agents.* He also reminded the FBI that Marina was required by Soviet law to keep her embassy in Washington informed of her whereabouts, so they would have to have at least that much contact with Soviet authorities.[881]

As little as Fain liked Oswald, he was inclined to be charitable. "He had just come to town and he was out there at his brother's place," Fain explained to the Warren Commission. "He had a wife and a little four-month-old baby that he had brought from Russia, and he didn't have any established place to live, and I can see how the newspapers may have harassed him." Reflecting on Oswald's arrogance and insolence later, Fain suspected that Oswald might well have been "just scared."

Fain was not, however, entirely satisfied with Oswald's answers. The FBI agent's information was that Oswald had in fact attempted to renounce his American citizenship and had applied for Soviet citizenship, and Fain felt that under the circumstances "he ought to be talked to again, he ought to be interviewed in detail about these same things."[882]

Lee never mentioned the interview to Marina, but he did tell Robert about it that evening, saying that he had been treated "just fine." He told Robert that at the end of the interview, "they asked me was I a secret agent" for the U.S. government. He laughed at recalling his retort to the agents: "Well, don't *you* know?"[883]—a rather illuminating observation for those conspiracy theorists who believe he was.

In early July, Marguerite Oswald followed through on her promise to move from Crowell back to Fort Worth. She took an apartment at 1501 West Seventh Street. Lee, perhaps feeling that he had imposed on Robert's hospitality long enough—almost a month— agreed to move in with her. She would later say that the month Marina and Lee lived with her was a "very happy month," but Robert claims it was only two weeks and Lee told him that he quarreled constantly with his mother. Marina agreed. Although she got on well enough with Lee's mother at first, Marina remembered times when Lee would not talk to Marguerite, and it became apparent to Marina that Lee "did not love his mother, she was not quite a normal woman." She was amused to note, though, that he, always a finicky eater, lustily demolished everything Marguerite cooked for him. Lee didn't even bother to file a change of address with the post office, so it is likely that he never meant to stay with his mother a moment longer than necessary.[884]

Marguerite eventually began to complain about her son's wife. Marguerite, who slept on a couch in the living room so the young couple could have the bedroom, said that Marina let her do the lion's share of the housework. She also complained that Lee made no effort to include her in their conversations. Marguerite even began to suspect that Marina was a spy because she heard her singing "Santa Lucia" and didn't realize that it was a song known abroad as well as in the United States. Lee paid no attention to her

---

*Though not included in the Warren Commission volumes, the cover letter of Agent Fain's July 10, 1962, report to FBI headquarters of his June 26 interview of Oswald says that Fain asked Oswald if he'd be willing to take a polygraph test on whether he had furnished any information to the Soviets, or had been recruited by Soviet intelligence agents, or had made any deals with the Soviets in order to obtain permission to return to the United States. Oswald declined to take the test without giving any reason. (FBI Record 124-10010-10033, July 10, 1962, Cover page C)

complaints, so Marguerite took to scolding Marina directly. During one particularly unpleasant scene, Marina was able to make out Marguerite's English: "You took my son away from me!"[885]

Shortly after Lee and Marina moved to West Seventh Street, in the third week of July Lee found, through the Texas Employment Commission, a job as a sheet metal worker at the Louv-R-Pak Division of Leslie Welding Company, and started work there on July 17, 1962. He didn't like the work, but it paid $1.25 an hour and made an early escape from Marguerite possible.[886]

Lee didn't even tell Marguerite he was looking for a place, but in late July he was finally able to rent a furnished one-bedroom apartment at 2703 Mercedes Street. He paid $59.50 in advance for the first month's rent. That same night, he called Robert and asked him if he could help them move the next day. When Robert drove up the next morning, he heard Marguerite screaming even before he got to the door. Marguerite was hysterical, Lee stony, and Marina somewhat bewildered, but Robert and Lee carried the suitcases and boxes to the car and left Marguerite to her own devices.[887]

The new apartment was half of a shabby bungalow across an unpaved street from a Montgomery Ward store. It was a neighborhood with a lot of duplexes and small bungalows, and Marina was especially pleased with it—it was the first chance that she and Lee had had to live alone together since they left Minsk three months before. Later American friends of theirs, used to a higher standard of living, thought it atrocious, "a shack," "a slum," but the apartment was reasonably clean and had a bedroom, living room, dining area, kitchen, and bath, even a little yard with some grass. Marina told author Priscilla McMillan that in Russia she and Lee could have worked a lifetime and not had so much space.[888] In early August, Oswald resumed his nexus with Marxism by mailing in his $2.00 three-month subscription to the *Worker* (formerly the *Daily Worker*), and the *Midweek Worker*, newspapers of America's Communist Party.[889]

On August 16, Special Agent Fain came to interview Lee again. He told the Warren Commission that he and Special Agent Arnold Brown waited in their car down the street out of sight of the Oswalds' home and approached Lee as he walked home from work, but Marina told Priscilla McMillan it was a hot summer night, the front door was open, and one of the agents came to the screen door just as she was about to serve dinner. Lee, sitting on the sofa, was reading the *Worker*, which he hastily stuffed down between the cushions. He invited the agents into the house, but they asked him to come out to their car. She had to keep warming up the dinner while Lee spoke to them.[890]

Lee got into the backseat with Brown and talked with Fain in the front seat. Fain explained that they didn't want to embarrass him by contacting him at his work, and they preferred to keep the conversation informal. Fain found Lee less tense than before, perhaps because Lee now had a job and a place to live, and he talked more freely with them. He told them that he had notified the Soviet embassy in Washington of Marina's whereabouts, and he answered all of their questions readily except when they again asked why he had gone to the USSR. That, Lee told them, was no one's business except his own. "I went and I came back," he said. "It was just something I did."

Fain was particularly interested in whether the Soviets had made a deal with him for permission to leave with Marina, whether they had asked any favors of him? "No," Lee answered, adding "I was not that important," and Fain was inclined to agree with him. But Oswald again said he would contact the FBI if the Soviets did try to contact him.[891]

Although Fain was dissatisfied with Lee's refusal to talk during the interview about why he went to the USSR, he did not really think that Lee constituted any serious security risk, and, after dictating a report of the interview, he closed his file.[892]

Ironically, just as the FBI was closing its file on Oswald, Lee thought the two interviews with the FBI were going to be the beginning of his "persecution" by the bureau. "Now it's begun," he told Marina gloomily. "Because I've been over there they'll never let me live in peace. They think anyone who has been there is a Russian spy." The next few days he remained in a bad mood.[893]

Shortly after Marina and Lee settled into their new abode, Marguerite somehow located them, and when Lee was at work one day, she showed up at their front door laden with gifts. Marguerite had recently gotten a job as a private nurse in Fort Worth, the first time she had ever received a regular nurse's salary. She was earning sixty-three dollars a week, very good money for her, and she wanted to bring clothes for Marina and Baby June, kitchenware for Marina and Lee, and a high chair for June. The latter puzzled Marina, who had never seen one before. In Russia, babies are held on the mother's lap when they are fed.

Lee was furious when he came home and discovered that his mother had been there. He told Marina never to let her in again. When she protested that Marguerite was, after all, his mother, he snapped, "You know nothing about her. You're not to let her in again." The next day Marguerite came again, this time bringing the green and yellow parakeet Lee had given her nearly seven years earlier in New Orleans, the one he bought with the wages of his first job. She was taking snapshots of the baby when Lee came home from work, and he told her to leave, but she stood her ground, insisting on her right to see her grandchild. He also told her he did not want her to buy any gifts for his family, that he would take care of whatever they needed. Besides, he said, if Marguerite got sick, he'd have to take care of her because she was spending all her money on them.

The moment Marguerite left, Lee scolded his wife and told her again never to let his mother in the house. Marina, who felt sorry for Marguerite, protested that Lee had no right to turn his back on his mother, but he warned her that Marguerite would try to move in—"You'll be sorry then." He ordered her to obey. When she refused, he slapped her four or five times across the face. About a month later, Lee took the bird outside and let it fly away.[894]

While Lee was immersed in his new job and life in America with his new wife, he did not jettison his old interests. On August 12, 1962, he wrote to the Socialist Workers Party (SWP) in New York City, a party aligned with the ideology of Leon Trotsky, the Russian political leader and colleague of Lenin who espoused a Communism based on the power of the proletariat (working class) of all nations rather than the domination of the Soviet Union. Stalin forced Trotsky into exile in the late 1920s and had him assassinated in Mexico City in 1940. In his letter, Oswald asked the SWP to "send me some information as to the nature of your party, its policies, etc., as I am very interested in finding out all about your program." On August 23, he received back a pamphlet titled *The Socialist Workers Party—What It Is, What It Stands For* by Joseph Hansen, who reportedly had been a secretary to Trotsky.[895]

On August 28, Oswald ordered a copy of *The Teachings of Leon Trotsky* from Pioneer Publishing in New York, a subsidiary of SWP at the same address, enclosing twenty-five cents. The company wrote back saying the "book" (actually a thirty-five-page booklet by Jack Warwick written in 1944) was out of print but telling him he had a twenty-five-cent credit due on any other purchase.[896] (The booklet, as of 2004, was in only two libraries in

America.) Author Albert Newman writes, perhaps correctly in view of Oswald's subsequent attempt to get to Cuba in search of a purer form of Marxism, that "turning thus towards Trotskyism in disillusionment with the Soviet Union, Oswald was following a path well-worn by more than a few American Communists in 1939. Horrified at the Nazi-Soviet friendship pact of late August that year which triggered World War II and left Poland a helpless victim of dismemberment by both signatories, these ideological refugees sought asylum and comfort in the 'purer,' more revolutionary form of Marxism embodied in the *Manifesto of the Fourth International* of the Trotskyites."[897]

Lee also, though always strapped for money, continued his subscription to at least three Russian journals. He received literature from the Soviet embassy in Washington too, having asked the embassy to send him "any periodicals or literature which you may put out for the benefit of your citizens living, for a time, in the U.S.A.," suggesting an ambivalence on his part as to the wisdom of his return to America.[898]

Marina remembered the early days on Mercedes Street as idyllic. "Alka, do anything," she began saying to Lee, "but don't ever, ever make me go back." Often, she would take June and walk down the road to meet Lee coming home from Leslie Welding in the evening. Seeing them a long way off, he'd wave, and when they'd meet, he'd pick up June in one arm, and with his other arm around Marina, they'd happily walk back to their home together. Sometimes Lee took her to a delicatessen, where they found some of the kinds of food she had known in the Soviet Union, even caviar. Though he loved caviar himself, he could not really afford it, so he bought it only for Marina and lovingly watched her eat it. She often went to Montgomery Ward across the street to marvel at the profusion of products on display, even if she had no money to buy them—Lee rarely let her have as much as two dollars at a time. After the first couple of weeks, he stopped giving her any money at all.[899]

The beatings also resumed, sometimes to the point of leaving obvious bruises. When Marguerite, on a visit one day, saw that Marina, who was nursing Junie, kept her head down, she came around to Marina's front and noticed she had "a black eye." Marguerite called her son on it: "Lee, what do you mean by striking Marina?" He told her to mind her own business, and she did. As she told the Warren Commission, there were occasions when her son would come home from work and there would be no supper waiting for him, and "there may be times that a woman needs to have a black eye."[900]

Marina hoped that Robert might intervene, and Robert did see her at least once when she had an obvious black eye, but he said nothing. The beatings became routine—as frequent as once or twice a week after Marguerite's first visit. What followed was the by-now-familiar, dreary pattern of wife battering. Each time Lee physically abused Marina, he would offer an abject apology and assure her of his love, and Marina would eagerly seize on the assurance of his love, forgiving and no doubt to some extent accepting the blame for the incident herself. With the progressive loss of her self-esteem, she lost more and more of the will to resist. She began to collaborate in fabricating the excuses offered to others for increasingly serious injuries. Underlying it all was Lee's need to control Marina, with alternating abuse and tantalizing offers of affection.[901]

His control of her world, however, would soon be threatened by a new group of friends, who not only noticed and deplored the beatings but also were able to speak to Marina in her native tongue. Near the end of August, Peter Gregory arranged a small dinner party at his residence to introduce Lee and Marina to a couple of friends from the tiny Russian-speaking community in the Dallas–Fort Worth area. In those days, before the advent of large-scale immigration from the Eastern Bloc countries, there weren't many Russian-born people in the United States, and those who were tended to know and socialize with each other. They naturally were interested in new arrivals who could give them firsthand accounts of present-day conditions in their countries of origin.

Gregory had mentioned to his friend George Bouhe, a Dallas accountant, that Marina had lived and studied in Leningrad, where Bouhe had been born and raised when the city was still called St. Petersburg. Bouhe wanted to meet her, and so Gregory arranged a dinner. Bouhe brought along a friend from Belgorod, a Russian town on the Ukrainian border, Anna Meller, whose husband was unable to attend.[902]

Bouhe had become proficient enough in English early on, thanks to an English governess, to work as an office boy for Herbert Hoover's American Relief Commission in Leningrad after the revolution. Denied permission to leave the Soviet Union, in September 1923 he waded across a river into Finland in the middle of the night and made his way to the United States. In his first years in Dallas he knew only three Russian people, but the early 1950s saw a small wave of immigration that brought in as many as fifty more. There were Estonians, Lithuanians, and Poles as well as Russians, but all spoke the Russian language. Bouhe took a very active interest in them, helping them to find jobs and directing them to English language classes in night school. He organized a congregation of the Greek Orthodox Church for anyone who wished to worship in the Russian or Slovenian languages. Now he was prepared to be very helpful to Marina and her husband.

He came to the Gregorys' dinner with an album called *Plans for St. Petersburg*, which held maps of the city at every phase of its development from its creation in 1710 by Peter the Great to the present, and for a while he sat on the floor with Marina, asking her about the old places and buildings he had known as a boy. He found her engaging, well mannered, and well spoken, a testament to the education and culture of her grandmother. Lee he found less engaging, someone with a "diseased" mind. Nevertheless, he continued to play an important role in the Oswalds' lives, as did Anna Meller.[903]

When the German forces retreated from Russia back to Germany in 1943, they forcibly took many Russians with them to work in the war effort. Anna Meller was among those taken by train, at the age of twenty-six, against her will, though she never cared for the repressive Russian regime anyway. She met her husband in Germany and emigrated with him to America in 1952, becoming a citizen in 1959. Meller had trained as a dentist in Russia, but the war started before she got her "main diploma," so at the time she met Marina she had been working as a "draftsman" for ten years with the Dallas Power and Light Company. Like Bouhe, she liked Marina but not Lee. "The first impression of Lee Harvey is a man absolutely sick. I mean mentally sick . . . He's against Soviet Union. He's against United States. He made impression he did not know what he likes, really." Like Bouhe, she felt that Lee spoke Russian well, "better," Meller said, "than I would expect." Meller would see the Oswalds several times in the next year. When she noticed the Marxist and Communist literature of Lee's in their home, it made her "real upset," and she also disapproved of Lee's not wanting Marina "to speak English, not a single word," claiming he wanted to learn better Russian and "she doesn't need English."[904]

The circle of Russian-speaking acquaintances of the Oswalds rapidly expanded. Before the end of August, Lee and Marina were invited to lunch at Anna Meller's. Other guests were invited for cocktails afterward, and the young couple met Declan Ford, a consulting geologist in the Dallas area, and his Russian-born wife, Katya, who, like Anna Meller, was taken to Germany by the German army.[905] Later, the Oswalds were introduced to Elena Hall, born in Teheran to Russian parents. She worked as a technician in a dental factory. In order to obtain dental aid for Marina, George Bouhe had brought the Oswalds to Miss Hall's home in Fort Worth, offering to pay fifty, even seventy-five dollars if she could find a dentist for Marina. But this was not nearly enough money for what Marina needed.[906] In early September, the Oswalds met Alexander Kleinlerer, a Polish survivor of Buchenwald who was fluent in several languages, including Russian. He was then courting Miss Hall, who was between marriages to the same husband.[907] Gali Clark—the woman Oswald had telephoned based on information from the Texas Employment Commission that she spoke Russian, but did not meet—was eventually introduced to Marina by George Bouhe and Anna Meller, and Gali's husband, Max, met the Oswalds later.[908]

The Oswalds also came to know George de Mohrenschildt, a petroleum engineer born of nobility in czarist Russia who was such a fascinating character that Warren Commission assistant counsel Albert Jenner, incredibly, ate up fifty-eight pages in a Warren Commission volume just talking to de Mohrenschildt about his background and life before even getting into a discussion about Lee Harvey Oswald. "You are an interesting person," Jenner at one point told de Mohrenschildt. De Mohrenschildt had first heard of Lee and Marina from Bouhe, who told him of this "interesting couple," the woman a pretty young girl from Russia, living in "dire poverty somewhere in the slums of Fort Worth." In Fort Worth on business one day, he and an associate stopped by the Oswalds' residence in the late afternoon and met Lee and Marina. The description de Mohrenschildt had been given had not been an exaggeration, recalling that the two were living in "horrible surroundings" in a "very poorly furnished, decrepit . . . little shack" on a dusty, unpaved road.[909] De Mohrenschildt would come to play a major role in the lives of the Oswalds, and an even more consequential one in the fancies and fantasies of conspiracy theorists. He introduced the Oswalds to his fourth wife, Jeanne, who was born in northern China to Russian parents.[910]

By and large, to the small Dallas–Fort Worth Russian emigré community, Marina was the sensation, the genuine article, "a relic of their old and much loved homeland that had suddenly been dug out of the Russian earth." Her physical and emotional fragility evoked the desire in them to help and nurture her. Lee was someone they could have very easily done without. Though he had recently come from Russia, he had little to say that they were interested in hearing—Marxism was a dated and worthless philosophy to them. Besides, they were older, more cultured, and more worldly than young Lee, and their social life was set aside for rich and interesting discourse, not confrontation, Lee's raison d'etre.[911]

Oswald's Russian-speaking acquaintances had any number of reasons to dislike him, neatly summed up by Alexander Kleinlerer as "his political philosophy, his criticism of the United States, his apparent lack of interest in anyone but himself and because of his treatment of Marina."[912]* Katya Ford believed that all of them thought he was "mentally

---

*But some in the Russian emigré community felt that Marina was as much to blame for their difficulties as was Lee. One was Katya Ford. Though she liked Marina and agreed that Oswald was "mentally unstable," she felt Marina was "a rather immature girl" who deliberately provoked Oswald by saying things to him that she knew would anger him, such as that he was "badly brought up or something like that." (2 H 300, WCT Katherine N. Ford) Jeanne de Mohrenschildt said that Marina "ribbed him even in front of us. She ribbed him so, that if I would ever speak to my husband that way we would not last long." When

unstable."[913] But because they felt sorry for Marina and the child, they were willing to put up with Oswald's boorish behavior to continue to help his wife.[914] For his part, Lee felt the emigrés, with the exception of de Mohrenschildt, whom he liked, were a superficial lot who measured everything by money. But Marina wondered if he was just envious of what they had, a notion he angrily rejected when she suggested it.[915]

In the half-dozen weeks Oswald worked at Leslie Welding, he was intent on trying to pay off his two debts, one to his brother and the other the loan from the State Department, and the couple hadn't a dime to spare. On a visit to the Oswalds' home, one of the emigrés was "shocked to find that [June] had no baby crib or bed but was kept on the floor in the bedroom either in a suitcase or between two suitcases."[916] Many in the emigré group were generous with gifts of small amounts of money, groceries, clothing, and furniture. George Bouhe, Anna Meller, and Elena Hall were the primary contributors, but others also helped with transportation and groceries when they'd see the icebox was empty. Bouhe, in particular, adopted a fatherly attitude toward Marina and even prepared some simple English lessons that she could do at home and mail to him for correction. Several of these new friends visited Marina in Fort Worth all through September, and the Oswalds in turn visited some of them in Dallas.[917]

It soon became apparent, however, that Oswald did not really appreciate the help of these new friends, even resented and got angry about it, saying he didn't need any help to take care of his family.[918] He went out of his way to offend them. Jeanne de Mohrenschildt described him as "very, very disagreeable," and said he was "sort of withdrawn within himself . . . His greatest objection was that people helped him too much, they were showering things on Marina. Marina had a hundred dresses given to her . . . He objected to that lavish help because Marina was throwing it into his face . . . He could never give her what the people were showering on her. So that was very difficult for him."[919] In Lee's view, the Russian community was helping Marina in order to humiliate him. "It's not that I don't want to buy you things," he bristled, "but I can't. I haven't any money to spare. Besides, they're spoiling you." When Marina questioned why they shouldn't spoil her since he couldn't, he slapped her hard across the face. "Don't ever say that again. I'll be the one to spoil you—when I can. I don't want you depending on other people anymore."[920]

On several occasions Lee embarrassed and shocked their guests by verbally abusing Marina in their presence,[921] and some of the visitors noticed the telltale bruises of his physical abuse, although it would be a while before any of them attempted to intervene.

On September 30, 1962, a mob of segregationists, believed by the authorities to have been instigated by former major general Edwin A. Walker, rioted against federal troops and marshals protecting James Meredith, a twenty-nine-year-old black student who tried to enroll in the all-white University of Mississippi at Oxford, and Walker was arrested for insurrection. (Walker had resigned from the army in West Germany in 1961 after charges that he had indoctrinated his troops with the ultra-right-wing philosophy of the

---

asked by Warren Commission counsel for an example of the ribbing, Mrs. de Mohrenschildt said Marina would say, "Oh, big hero" or "Look at that big shot, something like that." (9 H 312–313) But George de Mohrenschildt seems to be the only one that went beyond this, claiming that Marina was always nagging Oswald over the fact that they weren't as well off as others, and said that he and his wife finally told her to stop annoying him, that "he is doing his best" (9 H 233).

John Birch Society.) Since his resignation in 1961 and the University of Mississippi incident, Walker, a national icon of the conservative right, was in the news speaking out against Communism and urging a U.S. invasion of Castro's Cuba. When Walker, who was based in Dallas, was released on bond on the Ole Miss riot charges and arrived back in Dallas at Love Field on October 7, he was greeted by two hundred cheering supporters.[922]

That same day, a Sunday afternoon, Oswald announced to the group of visitors in his home that he had lost his job at Leslie Welding in Fort Worth, the rent was overdue, he was moving to Dallas, and he needed another job fast.* Marguerite was there, as well as a good many from the Russian community—George Bouhe, Anna Meller, Elena Hall and her former husband John, the de Mohrenschildts, their daughter Alexandra, and Alexandra's husband Gary Taylor.[923] Lee's story was not true—he "hated" his job at Leslie Welding and was planning to walk away from his employment there in a day or so without even giving notice—but none of his friends knew that, and they immediately addressed the problem. The group agreed that Dallas was a better place for Lee to seek employment since it was a much larger city than Fort Worth, and Elena Hall saw a way to make that possible. She invited Marina and the baby to live with her on Trail Lake Drive in Fort Worth until Lee found work in Dallas.[924] John Hall interjected that he would call his father, who was with the Murray Gin Company in Dallas, where Lee might find work in the machine shop.[925] It was agreed that Marina could stay in Dallas for the first couple of days with the Taylors, since she was scheduled to have six teeth, rotted to the roots, extracted at the Baylor University Dental Clinic in Dallas on Monday and Wednesday. (George Bouhe paid the fee of sixteen dollars or so for Baylor University senior-class students, who practiced on people who could not afford a regular dentist, to perform the dental work on Marina.)[926]† In the meantime, the Oswalds' skimpy belongings would be stored in Elena Hall's garage in Fort Worth.[927] Marina and Lee accepted the invitation, and she and the baby left with the Taylors for Dallas that night.[928]

The next night, Monday evening, Robert Oswald helped his brother remove Lee and Marina's belongings from Mercedes Street, and the Halls drove the belongings over to Elena's home in a pick-up truck that belonged to the dental laboratory where Elena worked. That night, October 8, Lee took a bus to Dallas.[929]

For Oswald the move would be a new beginning. He would not see his mother again until after the assassination, which was more than a year in the future. He would shun his brother Robert too. He would never say or write anything about his real reasons for closing out one phase of his life and starting yet another, but the news about General Walker, who lived in Dallas, may have had something to do with it.

Oswald's last day of work at the Leslie Welding Company was October 8, 1962. The following day he simply failed to appear on the job. The company had no idea what happened to him until it received his letter stating that he had moved permanently to Dal-

---

*Lee told Marina he had been fired at Leslie Welding but didn't say why (1 H 5, WCT Marina N. Oswald). Shortly thereafter, he filled out an application card at the Texas Employment Commission in Dallas and said he was "laid off" by the Fort Worth employer, again without explanation (10 H 135, WCT Helen P. Cunningham). However, he implied to the group at his home that the reason he lost his job was that it was "seasonal" (McMillan, *Marina and Lee*, p.252; 8 H 366, WCT George Alexandrovich Bouhe).

†Mrs. Taylor got the job of babysitting June while Marina was at the dentist. It wasn't easy. "The minute Marina left, the child would start to cry. She whimpered all the time. I couldn't feed her. Every time I got near her she'd scream. She never slept. She's a very difficult child to get along with. She was not affectionate at all to anybody else but to her own parents" (11 H 127–128, WCT Mrs. Donald Gibson [Mrs. Gary Taylor, formerly Alexandra de Mohrenschildt]).

las.[930] As indicated, the story he had told Marina and their friends from the Russian community about losing his job was not true. His foreman at Leslie Welding, Tommy Bargas, regarded him as a good employee, one who might have turned out to be a pretty good sheet metal man, and Bargas never had any intention of terminating him.[931]

Why did Lee lie about being laid off? He may have felt that Marina's Russian friends would be more likely to relieve him of the need to support her while he engineered the move. He didn't really need to lie, as the emigré circle would no doubt have helped her anyway, whatever their distaste for her husband, but he probably wanted to ensure their help in taking care of Marina and June until he could get on his feet in Dallas. In other words, while continuing to sneer at their materialism, he may have now been consciously reaching out to them in making a move to Dallas he could not have pulled off without them.[932]

The first day in Dallas, October 9, Oswald rented a box at the main post office on Ervay Street, number 2915, giving his address as 3519 Fairmont Street in Dallas, the address of Alexandra (George de Mohrenschildt's daughter) and Gary Taylor, though he never lived there.[933] He had asked Gary Taylor for permission to do this, and Gary had said all right.[934] Two days later he submitted a change-of-address form asking that mail addressed to Mercedes Street in Fort Worth be forwarded to the box in Dallas.[935]

At some time between October 9 and 11, Lee was interviewed for a job by Samuel Ballen in Dallas. Ballen, a close friend of George de Mohrenschildt's, was a financial consultant, a senior officer in several corporations, and the head of an electric log reproduction service company. De Mohrenschildt had called Ballen and asked him if he could help Lee with a job. Ballen spent two hours with Lee, and told the Warren Commission that although "I started out being attracted somewhat toward him . . . and I also started out feeling very sorry for the chap . . . and wanting to help him . . . I just gradually came to the feeling that he was too much of a rugged individualist for me, and that he was too much of a hardheaded individual, and that I probably would ultimately regret" employing him at Electrical Log Services, one of his firms, feeling that he "probably would not fit in" with his coworkers.[936]

On October 9 and 10, Lee also appeared at the Dallas office of the Texas Employment Commission, where he was interviewed by an employment counselor in the clerical and sales division, Helen Cunningham. She was expecting him because Anna Meller's husband, Teofil, had called her, explaining the Oswalds' predicament, and told her that he and other friends had been trying to help the young family. Lee scored well on a battery of aptitude and other tests. A note on his application form states that he had "outstanding verbal-clerical potential," and further, that he was "well-groomed and spoken, business suit, alert replies—expresses self extremely well."[937]

Lee told the counselor at the commission that he hoped to qualify in the future for a work program at Dallas College or Arlington State and get a BBA, but because of financial problems and family responsibilities, these plans would have to be delayed.[938]

The next day he was referred to a graphic arts firm, Jaggers-Chiles-Stovall, which was looking for a photo print trainee. There he made a good impression on John Graef, head of the photographic department, and was hired. The next day he started training to make prints of advertising material at $1.35 an hour, decent wages at the time. He had been out of work less than a week.[939]

He did not, however, send for Marina in Fort Worth because he really did not have the money, in spite of his penny pinching. According to the Warren Commission's meticulous reconstruction of his income and expenses, he had at most $22.34 to his name at the end of September, less if he had bought anything not covered by the Commission's estimates.[940] In the four months he had been in Fort Worth he had earned or otherwise had taken in about $476, but he had also repaid about $140 of the $200 Robert had lent him, plus $60 of the State Department loan.[941] He did not have enough money for the first month's rent on even a very modest apartment.

On October 15, three days after starting at Jaggers-Chiles-Stovall, he moved into the YMCA,* where he stayed through October 19 at $2.25 a night. In a goofy, spur-of-the-moment flash of inspiration, he gave "Toro, California" as his place of residence.[942] He could hardly have expected that the YMCA would bother to check on his residence, so he was muddying a trail that no one was following. Moreover, his *Let's Pretend* spy tradecraft left something to be desired: the childish deception, as with many more he would devise in the coming months, still left an arrow pointing back to him in his one-time duty station at El Toro in a way that giving any one of thousands of other American towns and cities would not have.

Although Lee left the Y after the night of October 19, it would be nearly two more weeks before he and Marina moved in together again. Nobody, including Marina, who merely recalls that Lee "rented a room in Dallas," knows where he stayed between October 19 and November 3 when he wasn't with her,† although he worked through that period at Jaggers-Chiles-Stovall. The separation from Marina was not a result of the quarrels between them, however much some of the Russians hoped it might be.[943] Lee kept in touch with Marina during the three days she was at the Taylors in Dallas, visiting her there,[944] and during the month and a half she returned to Fort Worth to live with Elena Hall, visiting and telephoning her as well as sending her letters there.[945]‡

Thinking about this period later, Marina wrote, "No matter how much we quarreled, I knew he loved me and the family, and I trusted him. We quarreled only because he had a difficult character and because that was the only way he could love. But he did not think that these quarrels could break up the family, so I forgave him everything."[946]

As for the Russian community, once Lee secured a job, he apparently felt free to be as directly insulting to them as he liked, despite the fact they were continuing to help Marina. For instance, on the first evening after he started work at Jaggers-Chiles-Stovall, Lee rang Bouhe, the one who had helped Lee and Marina the most, from a pay telephone, and informed him that he was "doing fine," with no word of thanks, no small talk, nothing, though he did, only in response to Bouhe's question, say he was doing some type of pho-

---

*It is not known where Oswald spent the nights of October 8 through October 14, 1962, in Dallas, which raises all types of sinister alarm bells for conspiracy theorists. But other than the fact that Oswald had been a defector—not a terribly important event—he was of no interest to anyone. Before the assassination, no one had any reason to have Oswald under surveillance, watching his every move. The conspiracy theorists, however, do not accept this obvious fact, and expect every day and minute of his time to be accounted for. Whenever a day is unaccounted for, it must be because Oswald eluded those who were watching him (but no one was), and snuck off to meet with those he was conspiring with to kill Kennedy.

†During part of this period Oswald stayed with Marina at Elena Hall's residence in Fort Worth. Hall had an automobile accident on October 18 that resulted in her being hospitalized until October 26, and four days after returning from the hospital, she left for New York to visit friends, not returning until after Marina and Lee had moved into an apartment on November 3. So Marina was all alone at Hall's residence and Oswald stayed overnight with her on several days. (11 H 137, WCT Mrs. Donald Gibson; 1 H 8, WCT Marina N. Oswald; 11 H 120, WC affidavit of Alexander Kleinlerer; WR, pp.719–720)

‡And with the contacts came the beatings, even though Lee wasn't living with Marina at the time. Elena Hall told the Warren Commission that the first time Marina came to live with her after Marina's stay at the Taylors, Marina "had black and blue over half of her face . . . He would beat her all the time" (8 H 395).

tographic work before he quickly hung up. To underline his contempt for Bouhe, he repeated the childish stunt of calling Bouhe, saying, "I am doing fine. Bye," and promptly hanging up several times over the next few days. Bouhe had had enough. He resolved to do nothing more for Oswald, a conclusion reached by the other emigrés as well. They would continue to do what they could for Marina, but Lee—probably to his perverse satisfaction—they wrote off. He was incorrigible.[947]

Around this time, Lee started receiving copies of the *Worker* through his new post office box. The front page of the October 2 and 7 issues focused on "the fascist character of Gen. Edwin A. Walker" and warned "the Kennedy administration and the American people of the need for action against him and his allies." Two weeks later the *Worker* asserted that Walker's financial backers were "extreme right-wing groups."[948]

Lee was settling down to work at Jaggers-Chiles-Stovall. For the first couple of days, he did little but follow John Graef—the man who hired him—around to learn the ropes. The company's business involved producing special photographic effects, principally for advertising. The work was meticulous, demanding not only in terms of correct measurements and angles but also in the use of many different development processes as well as grades and contrasts of printing paper. The company expected the on-the-job training to take two or three months.[949]

Since Graef could not work with Oswald full-time, some of the burden of training Oswald fell on another employee, Dennis Ofstein, who was Oswald's age and also a military veteran. Ofstein had started at Jaggers about seven months earlier and had already begun to work with the complicated cameras on simpler jobs, and he showed Lee, he said, "how to operate the cameras, and how to opaque negatives and make clean prints, and just the general work around there."

Ofstein found his new colleague difficult. Oswald barely got along with the people who worked alongside him, speaking to them only enough to learn what he had to do, and his relations with them worsened as time went on. Space in the darkroom was tight, and a worker might have to squeeze by a colleague working with tongs over a developing tray, but Oswald would just burst through head-on. He would take over the Bruning machine, which produced proofs of their work, with no regard for whoever might still be using it or the jobs they were trying to finish. He never asked anyone to go to lunch with him, nor did anyone ever eat lunch with him, although Ofstein, at least, asked him. Both Ofstein and Graef offered him rides home or to catch a bus after work, but Oswald never accepted.[950]

Ofstein had studied Russian for a year at the army's foreign language school at Monterey. He did not do well there but understood a little of the language. Like Oswald, he too had resided abroad. He had been stationed in Germany. It would be many months, though, not until February 1963, before he learned anything about his coworker's sojourn to the Soviet Union or even, for that matter, that Lee's wife was Russian.[951]

On November 3, Lee, now having a steady job and income, rented a sixty-eight-dollar-a-month apartment for himself, Marina, and June at 604 Elsbeth Street in the Oak Cliff district of Dallas.[952] On Sunday, November 4, the Taylors helped Lee and Marina move their belongings from Elena Hall's home in Fort Worth to the apartment using a rented trailer.[953]

The reunion of the Oswald family in a new place for a new start did not turn out to be a happy one. Marina was disheartened by the crummy apartment Lee had chosen for them. Alexandra Taylor agreed. It was a hole. "It was terrible," she said, "very dirty, very badly kept, really quite a slum." The floor slanted and had big bumps in it, and the exterior was as depressing as the interior, "a small apartment building . . . two stories, over-run with weeds and garbage and people."[954]

That night, Marina described the place as "filthy dirty—a pigsty," and didn't even want to move in, but she was a trooper and stayed up until five in the morning trying to scrub it clean, without much help from Lee. After he cleaned the icebox, he told her he still had a night left at the YMCA that he had paid for so he might as well use it. It was another lie. He hadn't been at the Y for days, and he probably went back to wherever he had been staying the previous two weeks that no one seemed to know about.[955]

The new beginning was really just a resumption of their old fights, but with a new savagery, and the small Russian community of friends was still hanging on to Marina, off stage.[*]

Mr. and Mrs. Mahlon Tobias, the managers of the apartment who lived in one of the units, were aware of the frequent fights, and other tenants complained about the noise from the fights and the baby crying so much that she kept them awake at night. One reported that a window in a backdoor to the flat was broken, apparently in connection with a fight.[956]

Marina was making no secret of her sexual problems—she told the de Mohrenschildts, right in front of Lee, "He sleeps with me just once a month, and I never get any satisfaction out of it." George was somewhat taken aback by her crude and straightforward confession to "relative strangers," as he still regarded themselves to be at the time.[957] Relative strangers they may have been, but the fact is that by the time of the move to 604 Elsbeth Street, the de Mohrenschildts were just about the only friends Lee had left.

Baron George de Mohrenschildt is God's gift to the conspiracy theorists. Foreign born, intelligent, urbane, multilingual, well connected, well traveled, eccentric, unconventional, with contacts in the CIA, he seems too extravagantly endowed with qualities *not* to have played some hidden role in the assassination.

De Mohrenschildt was born in 1911 in a small town near the frequently shifting Polish-Russian border, bearing the blood of many nationalities in his veins, which was not uncommon among the European aristocracy with their international family ties. The name, originally Mohrensköldt, was Swedish, and the family descended from Baltic nobility at the time of Sweden's Queen Christina.[958] All of the men in the family, including George, were entitled to call themselves "Baron," although none of them did. George's Uncle Ferdinand had been first secretary of the Russian embassy in Washington in the time of the Romanovs and married the daughter of Woodrow Wilson's son-in-law, Secretary of the Treasury William Gibbs McAdoo. George's older brother, Dimitry, a prestigious scholar at Dartmouth, also shunned the title.[959] George and Dimitry's father, Sergei von

---

[*]Indeed, a harbinger that nothing had changed occurred at Elena Hall's home in Fort Worth the day before the Oswalds moved into the Elsbeth apartment. Elena was away in New York and pursuant to Lee's asking him, Alexander Kleinlerer came to Elena's to discuss and help in the moving arrangements. While there, Oswald noticed that the zipper on Marina's skirt was not completely closed. "He called to her in a very angry and commanding tone of voice, just like an officer commanding a soldier. His exact words were 'Come here!' in Russian and he uttered them in the way you would call a misbehaving dog in order to inflict punishment. He was standing in the doorway. When she reached the doorway he rudely reprimanded her in a flat imperious voice about being careless in her dress and slapped her in the face twice. Marina had the baby in her arms. Her face was red and tears came to her eyes. I was very much embarrassed and also angry but I had long been afraid of Oswald and I did not say anything" (11 H 120, WC affidavit of Alexander Kleinlerer).

Mohrenschildt, had been marshall of nobility in the province of Minsk and a representative elected by the landowners in the local government. At the same time, he was opposed to both czarist repression and the prevailing anti-Semitism of the period. He eventually resigned his post in order to direct the affairs of the wealthy Swedish family Nobel in Russia, a post that took the family to the oil fields of Baku, then to Moscow, and eventually to St. Petersburg, where they were when the revolution broke out in 1917. George was then six years old. The family fled back to Minsk, but when the Bolsheviks drove out the German occupying forces, they also jailed Sergei von Mohrenschildt, who, though a classic liberal, openly opposed the Bolsheviks. He was released through the good auspices of some influential Jew whom he had protected from persecution years before.

He was thereafter appointed by the Bolsheviks to the Belorussian Commissariat of Agriculture in Minsk, but it wasn't long before he was in trouble again, arrested, convicted, and sentenced to live out his life in exile in Siberia with his wife and younger son. Sergei had opposed on principle, even though he was not very religious himself, the atheistic Bolsheviks forcing their irreligion and godlessness on others. And when they asked him at a court hearing, "What kind of government do you suggest for Soviet Russia?" and he answered, "A constitutional monarchy," that sealed his fate. While their mother searched everywhere for influential friends who could help the family, young George "remained on the street making my own living somehow." He was ten years old.

Jewish doctors in Sergei von Mohrenschildt's prison came to his aid. They told him to eat little and feign illness, while they advised the government to allow him to return home until he grew well enough to survive the journey to Siberia and the harsh life there. The ruse worked. Sergei was released and promptly fled with his wife and young George in a hay wagon to a family estate just across the border in Poland, near Wilno. Meanwhile, George's brother, Dimitry, who had been under a sentence of death by the Bolsheviks for being, as George said, "a ferocious anti-Communist" who was a member of the Russian czarist navy at the time of the revolution, was later released in an exchange of prisoners with Poland. For Dimitry's mother, the relief was short-lived. She died in 1922, when George was eleven. The de Mohrenschildts lost the estate to expropriation by the Communist regime, somehow managed to get it back, then sold it off piecemeal to the tenants. Dimitry left for America and an academic career, while George remained with his father in Poland until he was eighteen, when he briefly attended the Polish Cavalry Academy. At twenty he went to Antwerp, Belgium, to take a master's degree at the Institute of Higher Commercial Studies. Five years later he went on to the University at Liège, where he earned his doctorate in international commerce in two years. He also owned, with a girlfriend, a successful boutique for ski clothing, but in 1938, as Austria fell to the Anschluss and Czechoslovakia was occupied by the Wehrmacht as a result of Chamberlain's concessions to Hitler at Munich, he broke with his partner and departed for the United States.[960]

That summer he stayed with his brother and his American sister-in-law at Bellport, near East Hampton on Long Island, where he quickly made friends with the smart set, including a young woman, Janet Lee Bouvier, who was estranged from her husband, John "Blackjack" Bouvier. Blackjack had more or less dropped out of the picture, but George spent a lot of time with the rest of the Bouvier clan, including Janet's nine-year-old daughter Jacqueline, who would one day be the nation's First Lady. George even dated Janet to the point of wanting to marry her, but according to Jacqueline's brother Jack, his mother "wanted a very rich man," and George didn't qualify.[961]

Despite his easy entree into high society, assured by his aristocratic background, his superior education, his mastery of Russian, Polish, French, German, and Spanish, and even more by his good looks and fabled charm,[*] life was rough in those last years of the Great Depression, and George had to scramble to make a living as a salesman for a series of New York perfume, wine, and fabric companies. His degrees counted for little, but his contacts eventually paid off. Through letters of introduction from Margaret Clark Williams, whose family owned vast oil holdings in Louisiana, he landed a very well-paid job with Humble Oil, even if the work was physical. He enjoyed the hard labor until he was badly injured in an accident on a rig, and then contracted amoebic dysentery. He failed to get a job as a polo instructor at an Arizona boy's school, tried selling insurance in New York—he was spectacularly unsuccessful, failing to sell even a single policy—and was then called up for service in the Polish army, which he narrowly avoided because the last ship for Poland, the *Battory*, had already sailed. He then made a documentary film, with a distant cousin named Baron Maydell, about the Polish resistance to Soviet aggression. The film was very popular with supporters of the resistance but made no money.[962]

It is during this period, at the outset of the war in 1939, that de Mohrenschildt began to develop contacts with intelligence agencies. He is reported to have done odd jobs for Polish intelligence, and in 1941 did work with a friend and business associate, Pierre Fraiss, for French intelligence. The two men traveled the country purchasing American oil for France, as much to keep it out of German hands as anything else. This activity came to a natural end when Germany declared war on the United States in December of 1941 and there was no further possibility of Germany buying oil in the United States.[963]

Around that time he pursued a romance with a woman he thought of as "the love of my life," Lilia Larin, a Mexican to whom de Mohrenschildt was introduced in the United States by Dr. Declo de Paulo Machado, a fabulously wealthy Brazilian. Larin had been divorced once, but was now married to a Frenchman named Guasco, with whom de Mohrenschildt had a fistfight. George having just been declared 4-F by the draft and thus ineligible for military service, Larin invited him to go to Mexico City with her, which he did, devoting himself to her and to the painting of watercolors for about nine months, an idyll that was brutally interrupted when a Mexican general fell in love with Larin and eliminated the competition by having de Mohrenschildt expelled from the country. George proceeded to New York, where he exhibited his watercolors. Though they were well received by critics, they failed to sell.

George's Mexican adventure also produced his first run-in with American authorities. On the drive down to Mexico, he and Lilia stopped at a lonely spot on the Gulf Coast between Corpus Christi and the Mexican border for a swim and some sketching. On the way back from the beach their car was stopped by federal agents—he believes they were the FBI—who searched the car, were very insulting, he said, to Larin, and worst of all accused George of being a German spy. It seems his sketches were made too

---

[*]He would come to be described as "six feet one or two inches tall, handsome, dark, broad-shouldered, a man of arresting physique who frequently wore bathing trunks on the street the better to display it, loud, hearty, humorous, a man who was forever dancing, joking, and telling off-color stories, and who would drink all night and never show it, lover of innumerable women, a European aristocrat so secure of his lineage that there was no one whose friendship could demean him" (McMillan, *Marina and Lee*, p.264). Albert Jenner, de Mohrenschildt's questioner at the Warren Commission who clearly was taken with George, and whose enjoyment at questioning George leaps from the transcript pages, gratuitously added, for the record, that the witness was "athletically inclined . . . quite tanned, [and] an outdoors man" (9 H 180).

close to a Coast Guard station near Aransas Pass, although they apparently did not include the station itself. George protested that he wasn't spying for anyone at the time, not even the French, and although George and Larin were let go, the incident left him with a lifelong grudge against the FBI. Larin complained to the Mexican ambassador about the incident.[964]

Back in New York City with a wounded ego, in 1942 de Mohrenschildt sold an investment he had made in sugar in Mexico at a tidy profit and started to work on a book of his early life, which he called "A Son of the Early Revolution." He took a trip to Palm Beach, where he met and married a teenage girl, Dorothy Pierson, daughter of a woman who was, by a second marriage to a Florentine, the Countess Cantagalli. On Christmas Day of 1943, Pierson bore him a daughter, Alexandra, or Alexis, as she came to be known. Pierson also left him a month later, seeking a divorce on grounds of physical cruelty and infidelity. Alexis was transferred to the care of her aunt, Nancy Tilton, whom she came to think of as her mother and lived with for fourteen years while growing up in Arizona and Florida in the winter, and Vermont in the summer.[965]

After the divorce in early 1944, de Mohrenschildt decided that his efforts at writing and painting were getting him nowhere but he was still interested in the oil business. He enrolled at the University of Texas to study petroleum geology with a minor in petroleum engineering. He supplemented his income by teaching French at the university and received another master's degree, this one in petroleum geology, in 1945.[966]

De Mohrenschildt had a job waiting for him in Venezuela as a field engineer, but it didn't last long. He got in "some personal trouble" with the company's vice president, which led to his resignation. He wanted to come back to the United States anyway to renew his application for American citizenship, as he was still traveling on his prewar Polish passport. So in 1946 he passed through New York and soon went on to Houston, where he found a job that took him to Rangely, Colorado, then the largest oil field in America. He spent three years there, working for the Rangely Field Engineering Committee, a joint operation of all the oil companies charged with compiling statistics and engineering data for the whole field. There, in 1947, he married his second wife, Phyllis Washington, the daughter of a diplomat with the State Department. Both job and marriage failed to survive. He terminated his employment in January 1949 and divorced Phyllis around that time too. He worked for a time as a consultant out of the Denver office of a friend in the business, Jimmy Donahue, and then realized that everyone was making money in the oil business except him, that he was little more than a flunky for the big operators. He got in touch with Eddie Hooker, a nephew by marriage who worked for Merrill Lynch, Fenner, & Beane in New York, and, in 1950, they went into business together, with de Mohrenschildt in Denver buying oil leases and Hooker raising New York money for exploratory wells. The partnership lasted two years before it foundered, and George developed reputations for square dealing in business but hanky-panky with other men's wives. "We made money, we lost money," he would later say of the partnership, "but it was a pleasant relationship. We are still very good friends."[967]

During this period, in 1951, at the age of forty, de Mohrenschildt took a third wife, Wynne "Didi" Sharples, a physician from a wealthy Philadelphia Quaker family involved in the oil business. They met through Hooker in New York, where she was just graduating from Columbia University's College of Physicians and Surgeons. They settled in Dallas, plunged into a giddy social whirl, and had children, a son and a daughter, both of whom suffered from cystic fibrosis. George and Didi set up the National Foundation for

Cystic Fibrosis, of which Jacqueline Kennedy—then the senator's wife—eventually became the honorary chairman. In 1956, George and Didi divorced.[968]

De Mohrenschildt, becoming skittish for the first time in his life, decided he had had enough of the oil promotion business and started to take a series of consulting jobs that took him mainly to Mexico, but to Cuba and several African and Latin American countries as well. One eight- or nine-month job in Yugoslavia, under the auspices of a governmental agency called the International Cooperation Administration, resulted in extensive debriefing by the CIA on his return, although there is no record of his ever having been employed by the CIA or any other American intelligence agency.[969]

Before he left for Yugoslavia, he met Jeanne LeGon, a Russian woman who had been born in Harbin, Manchuria, as Eugenia Fomenko, daughter of the Russian director of the Chinese Far East Railway. The director was killed by Communists during the war, although Jeanne never knew whether they were Russian, Japanese, or Chinese. She married her first husband, Robert LeGon, in Harbin in 1932. Neither were qualified architects, but they had done well in the business of designing and building houses there until the encroachment of the Japanese forced them to flee southward. They got by for a time in Tientsin and Shanghai as a dance team under the name of LeGon, until in 1938 they fled again, this time to the United States. They were about to open in New York's Rainbow Room when Jeanne became pregnant and was no longer able to dance. She became a model and then a successful fashion designer, living in both New York and California, and her profession took her often to Europe. As she flourished, LeGon waned, becoming increasingly depressed about the loss of his family's fortune in China and eventually wound up in serious mental trouble.[970]

The LeGons were living apart, he in California with their daughter, she in Dallas, when she met George de Mohrenschildt. She spent several weeks with George in Yugoslavia when he was on a mission for the International Cooperation Administration and, after their return, LeGon came to Dallas to break up their affair, hiring a private detective and threatening George with a pistol. Eventually, however, he agreed to divorce his wife provided George would marry her. George called LeGon "a charming fellow" and married Jeanne.[971]

A year or so later, George's son by Didi Sharples died, and George, in his fifties, made another astounding change in his life: in 1960 and 1961, he and Jeanne left the states and took an incredible walking trip from Mexico through Guatemala, El Salvador, Nicaragua, Honduras, Costa Rica, and Panama. Though Jeanne would say it was an "exciting, wonderful time . . . a trip I would never forget," it was also exhausting physically and financially, and the de Mohrenschildts were still trying to recover from it when they met the Oswalds in the summer of 1962. George hoped to publish a book about the adventure and had even written to President Kennedy—perhaps relying on his long friendship with the president's wife Jacqueline—in the hopes that Kennedy would write a preface for it. Jeanne, meanwhile, was supporting them with a job in the millinery department of Dallas's Sanger-Harris store.[972]

De Mohrenschildt's experience with money paralleled his relationship with his friends. Ever profligate, he needed great quantities of both, but he also tended to squander both. Few of those who knew him well were able to resist his charm entirely, but everyone tended to reach a point where they had had rather more of it than they could take. It seemed that he was compelled to test people's affection for him by assaulting their sensibilities however he could. He would show up at people's homes without invitation. Though he was a "fighting atheist," he would turn up at one of the two Russian Orthodox churches in Dallas, clad in shorts, because he wanted to sing along with the church choir, then say, "The Communists don't believe in God and neither do I. We will all be fertilizer after we die." He would show up at a formal party in bare feet, or a social get-together bare-chested. To call him a free spirit would be to dishonor the term.[973]

Though he was liberal, and felt most people were bigots, just to provoke shock he hurt close Jewish friends at a meeting of the Bohemian Club, a small group of Dallasites who got together "to argue," by opining in a speech that Heinrich Himmler, head of the infamous SS, had not been so bad. He greeted his Russian immigrant friends, the Voshinins, who particularly loathed Hitler, with "*Heil Hitler!*" He jumped enthusiastically into discussions of political and social matters but would always "take the opposite side of whatever anybody would say."[974]

Natalie Voshinin, a geologist and one-time employee and friend of George's, thought him neurotic, noting that he would flare into a rage for no reason and complained several times to her that he couldn't concentrate very well, one time speaking about seeing a psychiatrist.[975]

It would be nice to say that George's wife Jeanne tried to be a moderating influence on him. But alas, she was not. Author Priscilla McMillan, who interviewed members of the Dallas–Fort Worth Russian community, writes of Jeanne,

> Middle-aged and spreading a bit, she had platinum blond hair and went around in tight pants and a very tight top—"like a teenager," one of the Russians sniffed. Jeanne insisted on playing tennis clad only in the briefest of bikinis, years before the bikini was "in." In Jeanne, in fact, George had at last found a helpmate so wildly unconventional as to make him seem staid by comparison. Her conduct was often more outrageous and antagonistic than his. Like her husband, she thought religion a "fraud" and lost no opportunity of saying so. But the worst thing was her passion for her dogs. Jeanne had two little Manchester terriers with whom it was not too much to say that she had fallen in love. She would go nowhere without them, and friends who asked the de Mohrenschildts to dine found that they had asked the dogs too. She dressed them in diapers and fondled them ostentatiously the entire time.[976]

Mrs. Voshinin, who knew the de Mohrenschildts well, said that both of them were "like children."[977] But because the de Mohrenschildts were the only members of the small Russian community in Dallas and Fort Worth who weren't ultimately driven away from the Oswalds by Lee's offensive behavior, and continued to see and try to help them (Jeanne told Katya Ford it was their duty since everybody else had dropped them and they still needed help),[978] and because the Warren Commission painfully and minutely examined every single aspect of Oswald's life that could possibly lead to the complicity of others, the life and background of one of these "children," George de Mohrenschildt, came under the intense scrutiny of the Commission.[979]

For all his byzantine cosmopolitanism, George de Mohrenschildt is in one respect an odd choice to be one of the primary villains for the conspiracy theorists, because he was a conspiracy theorist himself, convinced from first to last that his friend Lee had been set up to be the patsy.[980] Never tired of talking, even writing about it, at the time of his death he was still working on a book-length exoneration of Oswald entitled "I am a Patsy! I am a Patsy!"[981] Nevertheless, the screaming incongruities between the vigorously outgoing, well-educated, well-connected man-of-the-world de Mohrenschildt and the hopelessly awkward, reclusive, and inadequate Oswald are striking, fueling speculation that something else just had to be behind their relationship. Moreover, as de Mohrenschildt would say, "Marxism," Oswald's guiding star, "is very boring to me. Just the sound of that word is boring to me . . . When it comes to dialectical materialism, I do not want to hear that word again."[982] Intellectually, the contrast is also conspicuous, de Mohrenschildt with several graduate degrees, Oswald the "semi-educated hillbilly," as de Mohrenschildt himself once called him, with his unremarkable elementary school education.

Lee had no real friends, according to Marina, but he did have, per Marina, "a great deal of respect for de Mohrenschildt," because he considered George to be "smart, to be full of the joy of living, a very energetic and very sympathetic person." Marina liked him too. "He would bring some pleasure and better atmosphere when he came to visit."[983]

The fact that de Mohrenschildt took Oswald seriously was no doubt a major part of his attraction for Lee. Why de Mohrenschildt took him seriously is more perplexing, but there are clues in his manuscript. Here is de Mohrenschildt's description of their first meeting, at the Oswalds' place in Fort Worth: "He wore overalls and [had] clean workingman's shoes on. Only someone who had never met Lee could have called him insignificant. 'There is something outstanding about this man,' I told myself. One could detect immediately a very sincere and forward man. Although he was average-looking, with no outstanding features and of medium size, he showed in his conversation all the elements of concentration, thought, and toughness. This man had the courage of his convictions and did not hesitate to discuss them. I was glad to meet such a person."[984]

In Lee's very cantankerousness and rebellious ways, so offensive to others, George seems to have seen some reflection of his own youth. He was "carried away back to the days of my youth in Europe, where as students we discussed world affairs and our own ideas over many beers and without caring about time." He was also impressed by Lee's social consciousness, the fact that he was a "seeker of justice" with "highly developed social instincts," the lack of which George had come to deplore in his own children.[985] Lee was also of an age to be George's son—he mentioned that in his testimony to the Warren Commission.[986] As indicated, George's only boy had died, and at his age (fifty-one) it was unlikely that he would ever have another.*

A few days after that first meeting in Fort Worth, Lee called George and offered to visit the de Mohrenschildts in Dallas—an offer almost unique in Lee's history. He rarely offered to visit anyone, never with his family in tow. George was willing to drive over to Fort Worth to fetch them, but Lee politely declined. He, Marina, and June would go over to George and Jeanne's home on the bus.

The two men sat on a couch and talked the whole evening. George was naturally curious to hear anything of recent vintage about Minsk, which he thought of as a hometown,

---

*Though de Mohrenschildt was impressed with certain character traits of Oswald's, he did, on the other hand, discount the possibility that Oswald was a Soviet spy, saying, "I never would believe that any government would be stupid enough to trust Lee with anything important . . . an unstable individual, mixed-up individual, uneducated individual, without background. What government would give him any confidential work? No government would. Even the government of Ghana would not give him a job of any type" (9 H 237).

but he also encouraged Lee to talk about his childhood, his military service, how he had come to his radical ideas, what drove him to try the Soviet Union. They even traded some of those wonderfully cynical jokes people in Communist countries tell about their predicament. ("Comrade Secretary, I want to ask you four questions: What happened to our petroleum, wine, and meat, and also what happened to the comrade who asked the first three questions some time ago?") Above all, George paid attention to Lee, an experience for the younger man that had heretofore been almost unknown. That visit was to be only the first of several to the de Mohrenschildts.[987] The friendship was extraordinary for one so brief. Priscilla McMillan estimates that they saw each other only fifteen or twenty times in all over a period of less than a year.[988] They met in the late summer of 1962 and the de Mohrenschildts moved to Haiti in May of 1963 on an oil- and gas-drilling venture.[989]

When relations between Lee and Marina turned really ugly in early November of 1962 after the move to Elsbeth Street, George de Mohrenschildt and his wife Jeanne were the only ones in the emigré community with the will and courage to confront Lee directly. Lee had accused Marina of "whoring" after her Russian friends—using a particularly abominable Russian word for "whore," *blyad*—because they gave her money and possessions she could not get from him. He invited her to leave: "If you like them so much, go live with them." Marina was so offended she ran out the door, with Lee shouting after her, "Go. I don't care, I don't need you!"[990]

She ran to a nearby filling station, where an attendant listened to the name she kept repeating, finally understood she wanted to speak to Teofil and Anna Meller, found the number, and dialed it for her. Marina asked if she and her baby could come to her home.[*] Anna, after a brief argument with Teofil, who was dead set against her coming, told Marina to take a cab, which the Mellers would pay for when she arrived.

Marina went back to the apartment just long enough to get the baby and a couple of diapers and ducked out again, while Lee was stretched out on the bed. She didn't tell him what she was doing or where she was going. She somehow managed to convey to a waitress at a donut shop not far from the apartment that she needed a cab, and around eleven she turned up at the Mellers, upset and shaking but dry-eyed. She was wearing only a skirt and light blouse—on a chilly November night. Meller recalls that Marina was holding her "baby . . . a couple of diapers and that was all. No coat, no money, nothing." Marina and Junie stayed with Anna and her husband for several days, at which time Anna took Marina to the doctor because she was "as skinny as she could be" and the doctor said she was "very undernourished."[991]

The day after Marina came to the Mellers, some of the Russians met with Marina to confer about the problem, and George Bouhe encouraged her to leave Lee. "I don't think you could have a good life with him." Everyone was still willing to help her, he said, but if she went back to Lee, no one would want to help her again. Marina told herself, "I will never go back to that hell."[992]

After four or five days at the Mellers though, Lee and Marina agreed that they'd meet at the de Mohrenschildts' apartment to see if they could iron out their differences. On the morning of November 11, a Sunday, Bouhe drove over to the Mellers, picked Marina up,

---

[*]Anna thinks that Marina said Lee had beaten her, but Marina said Lee hadn't, and she didn't tell Anna he had, but "perhaps [Anna] understood that he had beaten me, because it had happened [before]." Meller did say she saw no bruises on Marina when she arrived at her home. (1 H 34, WCT Marina N. Oswald; 8 H 386–387, WCT Anna N. Meller)

and drove her to the de Mohrenschildts, where she met Lee. Bouhe did not want to be present at the meeting. He was literally afraid of Lee, telling Marina, "I don't want to listen to his threats. If he sticks his fists in my ears it will suit neither my age nor my health." The Mellers shared his view that Lee was a "megalomaniac," "unbalanced," a "psychopath."[993]

The meeting did not go well. Lee was nervous and embarrassed over being lectured by the booming George de Mohrenschildt ("Do you think it's heroic to beat a woman who is weaker than you?") and patronized by Jeanne, who told the two of them, "If you cannot live with each other peacefully, without all this awful behavior, you should separate, and see. Maybe you don't really love each other." When Marina said she couldn't take Lee's brutality anymore, Lee interjected, "I'm not always in the wrong, Marina has such a long tongue, sometimes I can't hold myself back."[994]

Eventually, the de Mohrenschildts left the two of them alone for awhile to sort it out. Lee, realizing that things had gone too far, shifted to contrition. He told Marina he didn't want to go on living without her. She was adamant, wanting to hurt him as he had hurt her. He grandly informed her that he was unable to change, that she had to accept him as he was. She told him she wanted a divorce. When it broke up, the de Mohrenschildts drove Marina as well as Lee back to Elsbeth Street so she could pick up her things for transfer to the Mellers' apartment. Lee grew very angry, threatened to get even with them all, including George, and boasted, "By God, you are not going to do it. I will tear all her dresses and I will break all the baby things." George, enraged, threatened to call the police while Jeanne tried to calm things down. (One hearsay account has George picking Oswald up by the front of his shirt and shaking him like a dog, telling Oswald he would really work him over if he laid another hand on Marina—a story that may be far-fetched but seemed plausible to some of their friends.) "Do you love your wife?" Jeanne asked Lee. "If you want your wife back sometime, you better behave."

His bluff called, Lee seethed silently for a while, and then caved in and started helping to carry Marina's things out to the car. Before she left, he took Marina into the kitchen and begged her one last time to stay. She refused. "Go this minute," he bellowed. "I don't want to see you another second."[995]

Later that afternoon, George Bouhe picked up Marina, the baby, and all their belongings at the Mellers and transferred them to the home of Declan and Katya Ford, who had a small baby and a four-bedroom house. Declan Ford was attending a convention of the American Association of Petroleum Geologists in Houston for a week, so there was more room for Marina there than in the Mellers' cramped two-room apartment, where she and the baby had to sleep on improvised beds in the living room.[996]

Lee called Marina twice every evening until she eventually consented to speak to him. He told her that Robert had written to him to tell him that their brother, John Pic, and his family would be coming for Thanksgiving, and he needed her for the planned family reunion in Fort Worth. (Robert had written to his post office box, as Lee never divulged any of his addresses in Dallas to him.) She knew he was worried about being humiliated in front of his family, for whom he would have to concoct some explanation for his runaway wife, and she was beginning to weaken. Her position was tenuous anyway—how long could she count on the generosity of friends?

Katya Ford was also aware of the fragility of Marina's situation, and her advice was practical. Katya was revolted by Lee, whom she regarded as an animal, but she recognized that Marina was not entirely faultless, that her personality played some role in provoking Lee's brutality. Further, Marina's lack of English narrowed her choices. All the women with whom Marina stayed knew that she was a terrible housekeeper, and it was unlikely that she could find employment even as a domestic, with or without English. Until she learned the language, she had no hope of building a life for herself in the United States. For the time being, it seemed that she would have to return to Lee, although Katya counseled her to start learning the language as fast as she could so that by the time June was old enough for day care, she might hope to find useful employment.[997]

What Katya didn't know is that Marina was starting to miss Lee. Her life with Lee was combative, and the icebox was always half-empty, but she thought it was "home all the same." However, she would hold out a little while longer, hoping to teach Lee a lesson and value her more.[998]

George Bouhe, who believed Marina's break with Lee was permanent, continued to help. He took her to lunch with Anna Ray, a Russian married to an American, and Ray immediately offered Marina a refuge in her own home. Even though the Rays had two small children of their own, they had enough room for Marina and June, and Anna had an uncommon generosity. She was ready to teach Marina English and put her in night school. Marina's plight touched Anna and she made it clear that Marina would be welcome to stay with her and her husband Frank virtually indefinitely, at least until she became able to make it on her own. Bouhe was delighted when Marina accepted.[999]

The same day that Marina moved in with the Rays, Lee called Mrs. Ray and asked for permission to visit Marina and the baby, which she gave, telling him how to get there on the bus. When Lee arrived, he and Marina went into a room by themselves, and Lee begged for forgiveness. "Why do you torture me so?" he complained. "I come home and there's nobody there. No you, no Junie."

"I didn't chase you out," Marina said, "you wanted it. You gave me no choice."

Lee got on his knees and begged her to come back, eyes filled with tears. He knew he had a "terrible character," but now he promised to try to change and if she did not return to him he did not want to continue living. Marina, embarrassed and fearful that someone could come in and find him weeping on his knees, was moved. He refused to get up until she forgave him. She did, and they both cried. Lee covered baby June with kisses and crooned, "We're all three going to live together again. Mama's not going to take Junie away from Papa anymore."

After supper, Frank Ray drove them all back to Elsbeth Street. Marina's rebellion was over and the bridges burned. There was little chance that anyone in the emigré community would ever again offer her the help she would need to escape. For better or worse, she was now committed to life with Lee.[1000] And for a few days thereafter, Lee and Marina were happy, playing childlike games with each other and going for walks every night, stopping for coffee and donuts. He even offered to teach her how to bowl, but the balls turned out to be too heavy for her to hold.[1001]

The same night she had come home from the Rays, November 17, Lee wrote a letter to Robert, accepting his invitation for Thanksgiving and asking Robert to pick them up at the bus station in Fort Worth.[1002] Lee had gotten Marina back just under the wire. Thanksgiving was just five days away.

Lee and Robert's half brother, John Pic, had returned from Japan with his family and was now living in San Antonio, so Thanksgiving was a chance for a rare family reunion. Although Robert had kept in touch with both brothers, Lee and John had not seen each other or even exchanged letters in ten years, not since Lee was a young teenager in New York. Robert made a point of not inviting Marguerite—he wanted the reunion to be "a happy meeting for everybody, with no bitterness or unhappy reminders."[1003]

On the morning of November 22—just one year before the assassination—John and Robert drove down to the bus station to pick up Lee, Marina, and June. They were all happy and cheerful, Robert having no idea of the recent storm in Lee and Marina's life. While waiting for John and Robert, Lee and Marina and the baby crowded into a photo machine to pose for pictures of themselves, and they were still laughing about the "silly pictures" they had taken when Lee's brothers arrived. John was a little worried as to whether Lee would be as hostile to him as he had been ten years before, but there was no sign of that until they arrived at Robert's house, when Lee greeted John's wife Margie, whom he had threatened with a knife so many years before, and then never again addressed her for the rest of the day.[1004]

While the women occupied themselves with the Thanksgiving dinner in the kitchen, the brothers sat in the living room and talked. Lee and John, in particular, had a lot to talk about, ten years to catch up on, experiences in Japan to swap. Two subjects were avoided, Lee's trip to the USSR and Marguerite. Nobody wanted to spoil the holiday mood. They played with the children, and Robert shot some film of them, all in color. They had dinner in the late afternoon and sat around the table for around two hours.[1005]

Marina would later write that the day was "very gay," that she liked "this good American holiday" and found it "very agreeable to celebrate it."[1006] Apart from Lee not talking to Margie, there was only one other disagreeable moment, one that would be remembered for a lifetime. Paul Gregory, Marina's one-time Russian-language student, was home from college for the holiday and Marina called him to come over for a brief visit. John Pic was shocked when Lee introduced him to Paul as his "half brother," a designation Marguerite's three sons had avoided using all of their lives.[1007] Lee had a long memory. But everything is relative, and for the three children of Marguerite and their wives it had been a good day, the last one they would ever spend together.

Indeed, it would be the last time Lee would see any member of his family until November 23, 1963.[1008]

When Marina refused to grasp the lifeline held out to her by the Rays, the Russian community for the most part, with the exception of the de Mohrenschildts, gave up on her. George Bouhe, who had helped the most, never tried again—he even asked her to return the Russian-English dictionaries he had lent her.[1009]

Actually, one other compassionate soul did make one more attempt to help the Oswalds. Lydia Dymitruk had been captured by the German army in the Soviet Union as a teenager and brought, with her sister, to Düsseldorf. Freed by the advancing American army at the end of the war, Dymitruk became a Belgian citizen, eventually married an American, and settled in Dallas, where she became friends with Anna Meller. Shortly after Marina went back to Lee, Anna told Lydia that she received a phone call from Marina, who was distraught because the baby was ill and Lee would not take them to the hospital because he didn't have money to pay the bill. The next day, while Lee was at work, Lydia advised Marina to dress both herself and the baby warmly, and she would drive them to a hospital. It was a very cold December day, and June was running a temperature of 103 degrees.

They went to the emergency room at Parkland Hospital in Dallas but were told there was no pediatrician on duty until five in the afternoon. They gave June some medication to reduce the fever and suggested they return after five or try a children's hospital. Lydia and Marina went to a children's clinic, but there were dozens of children ahead of them and a three- to four-hour wait. Lydia couldn't spare that kind of time, so she drove Marina and June to their home, took care of her business, and came back around six. Marina then wanted to wait until Lee got home from work—but when he came home shortly thereafter, he was still opposed to taking June to a hospital. Lydia heard them arguing heatedly in the kitchen about it, but when they finally emerged, Lee had agreed to take June to the hospital with Lydia and Marina.

At Parkland, a doctor gave the baby a blood test, a chest X-ray, and examined her carefully. When he was finished, he gave Lee some forms to take to a service desk. Lydia and Marina waited in line with him there and heard him tell the nurse who looked over his forms that he had no money, was unemployed, drew no unemployment benefit, and was living on money borrowed from friends. Lydia, who was standing in front of Marina in the line, could hear Marina, who apparently was able to make out what Lee was saying in English, hiss, "What a liar." The nurse gave Lee a slip of paper, requiring a small payment because of his financial condition, and told him to take it to the cashier. But Lee jammed the paper in his pocket and ducked out without paying anything at all.

During the car ride back home Lee complained that medical care in America ought to be free, as it had been in the Soviet Union, and Marina was on Lee's case, in a harsh tone, all the way home. By the time Lydia had dropped them off at Elsbeth Street, she was heartedly disgusted with both of them, but more with Marina. "No wonder he's so mean to you," she told Marina. "I'm sorry for Lee, I don't see how he takes it. You have a dreadful disposition. I couldn't live with you a single second. You simply ate him alive." At least someone was on Lee's side in the small Russian community. Marina didn't object to Lydia's criticism, knowing she did, indeed, have a poor disposition, but thought to herself, "Just you try living with Lee, and then see how you behave."[1010] Eventually a bill arrived in the mail from Parkland and Lee paid it without complaint. It was for two dollars.[1011]

There were few enough other visits to the Oswald household in the late months of 1962. Gary Taylor, the de Mohrenschildts' son-in-law, dropped by one day shortly after Thanksgiving to return the manuscript about Lee's life in the Soviet Union, which Lee had given him.[1012] Christmas Day, Elena Hall, who had remarried her husband John in November, dropped by with him to bring a toy for June. They noticed that the Oswald home had no Christmas tree or decoration of any kind, which they thought strange since in those days you could get a small tree for as little as thirty-nine cents. Oswald protested he did not want a tree, and told John that Christmas was nothing but a commercialized holiday.[1013] Later, Marina brought home a stray evergreen branch that she found. She also found nineteen cents that Lee had untypically left lying around and used it to buy colored paper (which she shredded into tinsel) and miniature decorations for the branch at a five-and-dime store. Parsimonious Lee was pleased for once. "I never thought you could make a Christmas tree for nineteen cents," he said to Marina.[1014]

In mid-December 1962, Oswald had subscribed to the *Militant*,[1015] the Troskyite publication of the Socialist Workers Party (SWP) in America which was so often critical of Moscow. The *Militant*, more supportive of Castro's brand of Marxism than the Kremlin's, was known to publish "more complete texts of the speeches of Fidel Castro and other documents of the Cuban Revolution in the English language than any other news source in the world."[1016] It was also highly critical of General Edwin Walker and of Kennedy's policies on Cuba.[1017] In late October, Oswald had sought to join the SWP,[1018] but the party wrote him back saying, "It is not our practice to take in individual members when no branch [of our party] yet exists. Unfortunately, we don't have any branches at all in Texas."[1019] (Not a surprise.) As we've seen, way back in August, Oswald had also subscribed to the *Worker* and the *Midweek Worker*, publications of the Stalinist "Communist Party, United States of America" (CPUSA).[1020] It is not known whether he was aware that the two parties (CPUSA and SWP) were, at a minimum, rivals of each other (though both glorified Castro), and that Stalin had had Trotsky murdered.

Around this time at his job, Oswald asked his coworker Dennis Ofstein whether the company equipment could be used to make copies of prints and enlargement of photographs that had been taken in small-format cameras. Ofstein told him that while Jaggers didn't sanction the use of company equipment for private projects, people did it now and then. He showed Oswald how to do it and watched as Oswald made photographic enlargements of snapshots taken in Minsk and while Oswald was in the service in Japan.[1021] Lee would later also do some other work that Ofstein never knew about, making calling cards for George de Mohrenschildt as well as Marina and himself. He also experimented with making photographic copies of some of his own documents—his birth certificate and his military and draft registration ID cards—which he would soon use in attempts to create crude forgeries.[1022] It was also during this period that Oswald started sending samples of his photographic work, apparently carried out in stolen moments at Jaggers, to leftist organizations back East. It isn't known what he sent to the SWP to aid the party in connection with its posters and advertising, but his offer was diplomatically declined in a letter to him dated December 9, 1962.[1023] And when Gus Hall and Ben Davis, two leaders of the American Communist Party, were on trial in Washington, D.C., for violating the McCarran Act (which required the registration of agents of the Soviet Union to fight subversive activities in America), Oswald sent a poster to the Hall-Davis Defense Committee reading,

> The Gus Hall–Benjamin J. Davis
> Defense Committee
> END McCARRANISM

The executive director of the defense committee wrote back on December 13, 1962, thanking him, but politely declining his offer of help.[1024]* And in response to another poster Lee had submitted, this time to the *Worker* ("Read *The Worker* If you want to know about Peace, Democracy, Unemployment, Economic Trends"), on December 19, 1962, Louis Weinstock, general manager of the *Worker* in New York, wrote Lee and, in as delicate a way as he could find, told him the paper wasn't interested in using the poster-like blowup Lee had submitted. "Your kind offer," Weinstock said, "is most welcomed and from time to time we shall call on you." In other words, thanks but no thanks.[1025]†

---

*Hall and Davis were convicted by a federal jury shortly thereafter. Their lawyer, John Abt (whom Oswald would later want to represent him after his arrest for Kennedy's murder), had argued that the act of registration violated the Fifth Amendment's prohibition against self-incrimination, and the conviction was later reversed in 1965 when the U.S. Supreme Court ruled the McCarran Act was unconstitutional (*Albertson v. Subversive Activities Control Board*, 382 U.S. 70, 86 [1965]).

†Oswald's appetite for the revolutionary cause carried over to the New Year, Lee celebrating the first day of 1963, when most other men his age were watching football games on TV, by sending thirty-five cents to

On December 28, George de Mohrenschildt picked up Lee and Marina in his big convertible to take them to a holiday party at Declan and Katya Ford's house. En route they stopped by the Sanger-Harris department store, where Jeanne worked as a designer, to pick her up. The de Mohrenschildts pitied the young couple for their isolation and wanted to do something to relieve the gloom of the holidays. Jeanne had called Katya and asked permission to bring them, and she even arranged for one of her neighbors to babysit June. Katya had hoped she had seen the last of the Oswalds—a sentiment no doubt shared by many of her guests, some of whom thought the de Mohrenschildts were again being deliberately provocative—but she could hardly say no.

Marina was delighted to see George Bouhe again and kissed him on the cheek, to Lee's palpable scorn. "Why are you sucking up to him?" he asked her when he got the chance. He then put on another display of caddishness by devoting virtually all of his time and attention, to Marina's increasing concern, to Yaeko Okui, a young Japanese woman who had come with Lev Aronson, a Latvian who played first cello in the Dallas symphony. Lee and Yaeko sat on the steps at one end of the room and talked about Japanese and American customs as well as ikebana, the art of flower arrangement, which Yaeko was certified to teach, while Marina ate her fill and gathered at the piano with others to sing Russian songs.

Lee was also attracted to the Fords' daughter Linda, who found him staring solemnly at her while the rest of the party laughed at comedian Vaughn Meader's takeoff on President Kennedy on the best-selling album *The First Family*. Linda was so troubled by that stare that she remembered nothing else about the party.[1026]

Whatever joy Marina got from getting out of the house for the Fords' holiday party was dashed just three days later, on New Year's Eve, traditionally a much more important celebration in the Soviet Union than Christmas, which the atheistic Communist government shunned. To her great disappointment, Lee turned in early, about ten, and left her to celebrate by herself. When the momentous year of 1963 began at midnight, she was in the bathtub, imagining it was full of champagne and thinking of her friends in Minsk and the good times they were having. Later, so troubled she could not sleep, she sat at the kitchen table and wrote a letter to Anatoly Shpanko, the medical student who had asked her to marry him. Might she not have been happier with him?

Much later she reconstructed the letter for Priscilla McMillan. In the letter, which she starts with "Anatoly Dear," she tells Anatoly she is writing him, as he requested, about her life in America. She tells him she feels "very much alone," that her relationship with Lee had changed from what it was in Minsk, and that he no longer loved her. She says she is "sad" that an ocean separates her from Anatoly and she has "no way back" to him. "How I wish you and I could be together again," she writes.

Marina then alludes to a time in Minsk when Anatoly had held himself back (presumably a reference to sexual intimacy), saying, "You did it for me, I know," but adds that if he hadn't, "everything might have turned out differently. But maybe, after the way I've hurt you, you would not take me back." She closes with "I kiss you as we kissed before" and a postscript: "I remember the snow, the frost, the opera building—and your kisses. Isn't it funny how we never even felt the cold?"

Pioneer Publishers, the literary arm of the SWP, for three pamphlets by J. B. Cannon: *The Coming American Revolution*, *The End of the Cominterm*, and *The 1948 Manifesto of the 4th International Period*. And he said he'd appreciate it if they would send him the English words to the song "International." (Dobbs Exhibit No. 7, 19 H 573)

Marina was in tears as she finished the letter. She kept it for several days before mailing it.

On Monday, January 7, 1963, Lee came home from work with the letter in hand. Marina had mailed the letter showing Lee's post office box as a return address. The postage rates had gone up one cent and the letter was returned for insufficient postage. Lee asked Marina what the letter was about and asked her to read it to him. When she refused, he read it to her, although he broke off before he finished.

"Is it true what you wrote?" he demanded.

"Yes," she said. Marina recalls, "And of course he hit me, but he did not believe this letter was sincere."

"Not a word of it is true," he insisted. "You did it on purpose. You knew they changed the postage and the letter would come to me. You were trying to make me jealous. I know your woman's tricks. I won't give you any more stamps. And I'm going to read all your letters. I'll send them myself from now on. I'll never, ever trust you again."

Marina would recall that "it was a very ill-considered thing" she had done, and Lee's hitting her had been "the right thing to do. There [were] grounds for it."

He made her tear up the letter in front of him. And he was true to his word. From then on he made Marina hand him all of her letters in an unsealed envelope so he could search them for secret messages to Shpanko or anyone else who presented a threat, however distant, to his domination of her.[1027]

Apart from his pathological need to keep Marina a prisoner at home, and continuing to be physical with her on occasion, Lee, perhaps chastened by Marina's letter to a former suitor, was now a more considerate and affectionate husband, according to Marina. He did the vacuuming, carried out the garbage, washed the dishes, turned down the bed at night, and generally made himself useful. On weekends, when Lee was off from work, he followed Marina around wherever she'd go, even coming with her to the landlady's to borrow the vacuum cleaner shared by all the tenants. He "wore me out with his kisses," Marina told Priscilla McMillan. Lee granted Marina two indulgences—deciding if and when they would have children, and staying in bed when he awoke in the morning. He got up by himself, made his own breakfast, and left coffee on the stove for her. His increased affection for Marina was not at little Junie's expense. He did not trust Marina to bathe June without endangering her, and would happily climb into the bath to play with his baby, ordering Marina to bring them the baby's bath toys and clean up the water they splashed on the floor.[1028]

That first month of the year brought very disquieting news to Oswald—there could be another invasion of his beloved Cuba. One of the first issues of the *Militant* that Oswald received early in January commented on the speech Kennedy gave at the Miami Orange Bowl on December 29, 1962, in which he declared to the anti-Castro Cubans who had been repulsed by Castro's forces at the Bay of Pigs, "I can assure you that this [battle] flag will be returned to this [Cuban] brigade in a free Havana." The *Militant* called Kennedy's remarks "the most barefaced and disgusting display of immorality, ignorance, and bad taste ever put on by a U.S. President."[1029] In the January 21 edition, which Oswald would have gotten, the *Militant* quoted Castro as saying Kennedy was acting "like a pirate," Castro declaring, "Mr. Kennedy, too much blood has flowed between you and us."[1030]

On January 14, Oswald enrolled in a night-school typing course at Crozier Technical High School in Dallas, paying a tuition fee of $9.00.[1031] How serious Oswald's interest in typing was is open to question. Evidence suggests that he was already planning a change of career, as an assassin, and he may well have undertaken the typing classes as a cover for more sinister activities.

If there is one thing Lee Harvey Oswald had, it was pride. That undoubtedly was the main reason he normally resisted help from third parties for him and his family. Concomitantly, the thought of owing his brother Robert and the U.S. State Department weighed on him. As his friend George de Mohrenschildt observed, "I ask you where do you find another man in Lee's position, on the verge of starvation [obvious hyperbole], who would be in such a hurry to repay a government loan, which would be very difficult to collect from a poor man like Lee? But somehow Lee felt this obligation very sincerely."[1032] Although Oswald usually didn't have two nickels to rub together, by October 7, 1962, he had finally managed, through scrimping, to pay off his loan to Robert, even though Robert had insisted he wait until he was making more money, and, after paying $10.00 month on his $435.71 State Department loan, he sent in two money orders totaling $106.00 on January 25 to pay that off.[1033]

Just two days free of debt for the first time since he returned to America, on January 27, 1963, Oswald ordered a .38 caliber Smith & Wesson revolver from a Los Angeles company named Seaport Traders Inc., enclosing $10.00 in cash as a downpayment on the full price of $29.95, the balance to be paid COD. He signed the order form, "A. J. Hidell," age "28." (He was twenty-three.) He gave his Dallas post office box, 2195, as his address. The form had to be countersigned by a witness who could attest that the person ordering the gun was an American citizen who had never been convicted of a felony. Oswald obliged by signing as his own witness, using the name "D. F. Drittal."[1034]

The gun was in fact a very poor one in terms of accuracy. First, Seaport had arranged for the gunsmith, L. M. Johnson, to shorten the barrel from five inches to two and a quarter inches, considerably reducing its accuracy—the company had a demand for the shorter weapons, presumably from those who wanted to conceal them on their persons. The muzzle had been recrowned, the front sight reset, and the cylinder rechambered to take the more popular .38 Special cartridges (as opposed to .38 Smith & Wesson cartridges), although the barrel had not been changed. Since the .38 Special cartridge was of slightly smaller diameter, the bullet wobbled slightly in the barrel, which further reduced the weapon's accuracy. The pistol might be okay at very close range, but no target shooter would want to use it.[1035]

January also brought new troubles for Oswald, both at work and in his marriage. By mid-January he must have realized that his days at Jaggers were numbered. He had been employed there over three months and was expected to start pulling his own weight, but his work, which required a great deal of precision, was sloppy, and, as indicated, his manner annoyed his fellow workers in the cramped darkroom quarters. John Graef was being remarkably patient with Oswald, even though the finished jobs Lee turned in had to be redone far too frequently, much more often than the work of other employees. Oswald had to know that Graef's patience would not be without limit.[1036]

Also in January, the Oswalds' marriage took a sharp turn for the worse. They continued to bicker, and Lee slapped Marina from time to time, but there were sweeter moments too. Then one night, while laying in bed together in the dark, Lee told Marina something about his old girlfriends. Marina jumped from the past to the future, asking him to tell her if he ever intended to be unfaithful.

"If I were planning it, I wouldn't tell *you*," he said. He was suddenly struck by a new thought. "Have you been with any other man since we were married?"

Marina, always brutally candid, answered yes. She told him about her assignation with Leonid Gelfant in Minsk when Lee had gone to Moscow. She told him everything, including the fact that Leonid had proved impotent.

"Why?" Lee asked.

"Because he was a virgin. And I wasn't about to be his teacher. I never wanted to see him again."

"And you didn't?"

"I ran into him once or twice on the street."

"And nothing happened?" Lee pressed.

Marina laughed. "You were home. Where on earth could we go?"

Lee could not or would not believe her. "You're making the whole thing up," he insisted.

"No, I'm not," Marina said, insisting on telling him the painful truth, with nothing to lose if she told him the lie she knew he wanted to hear except a splinter of her own honesty. But perhaps sensing she had gone too far, she tried to explain that the experience had taught her a lesson, and it had taken away any desire she would ever have for anyone but Lee.

Lee still wasn't convinced that Marina had been unfaithful. They had agreed that if either of them used the phrase "word of honor," the other had to tell the truth—he made her give him her "word of honor" that everything she told him was true. She did, and he still did not believe her.

The next morning he returned to the subject. "I don't believe it," he said. "You women are all alike. You want to make a man jealous." Then Lee, the arch-nonconformist, took the modern male conformist view, adding, "If I ever see you with another man, I'll kill *him* right off," as if the male stranger, more than his wife, would have been the one who breached a moral responsibility to him.

Marina, amused, and perhaps wondering about his logic, asked, "And what will you do to me?"

"We'll see about *that*."[1037]

It is impossible to tell what the real impact of Marina's confession had on Lee or how much it contributed to the darkness that was beginning to fall on him. Overtly, though, he claimed not to believe her. He made it clear to Marina that he thought she had written her letter to Anatoly Shpanko knowing it would fall into his hands and make him jealous, and he now decided that her tale of the encounter with Leonid Gelfant was another ruse for the same purpose. Since he was an inveterate liar himself, it was an explanation that came easily to mind, and it may be that it was what he really needed to believe. There were, after all, only two elements of his life over which he had any control, his baby daughter and his wife, and his control of Marina was slipping, as her brief escape from him had shown. Keeping her ignorant of English would work only for awhile, and the act of beating her was only an admission that he could not keep her in line except by physical force.

For the moment, Lee and Marina were locked in the deadly symbiotic embrace of emotional neediness, each of them utterly reliant on the other to fulfill this need. The descending spiral of the battered woman syndrome, neediness leading to ever-dwindling self-esteem and lack of confidence, is well known. Priscilla McMillan had come to believe from exhaustive conversations with Marina that Lee was in fact much the weaker of the two. The proposition is easy to entertain. One has only to imagine which of the two would have thrived if he or she had come to the United States separately: Marina, with her new-found friends who were so willing to help, or Lee, whose abrasive personality and towering ego, unsupported by even normal capabilities, made him so offensive to everyone. Lee seemed doomed to fail at everything, including his marriage, which he was keeping together by intimidation and brute force. And he seemed to be keeping himself together, as he had as a child, by his turn to fantasy. His wife's confessed infidelities were just attempts to trick him. And if the world would not present him with the grand position he imagined as his due, he would invent one all of his own.

On January 28, the day after he ordered the pistol, he started the typing course at Crozier Tech. The classes met only three evenings a week, Mondays, Tuesdays, and Thursdays, from a quarter after six to a quarter after seven. Not only did Lee miss a lot of classes (he was dropped from the class after a little over two months because of his absences),[1038] but Marina noticed he rarely got home from work before seven on any evening of the week, whether there was a class or not. He would then spend a lot of time in the kitchen, ostensibly to practice typing on a printed keyboard there, but he was also studying bus schedules and a map of Dallas. When Marina asked why, he told her he was trying to figure the quickest way home from Crozier Tech, but that couldn't have required much planning. The night school was a few blocks from Jaggers, and he had been returning home from there for months.[1039]

Apparently what he was really doing was plotting the assassination of Major General Edwin Walker.

Lee Oswald was still in the Soviet Union when Major General Edwin A. Walker received worldwide attention stemming from an April 13, 1961, story in the tabloid *Overseas Weekly* that Walker, a decorated war hero in the Second World War, had been indoctrinating the troops of his command in West Germany, the Twenty-fourth Infantry Division, with literature published by the ultra-right-wing John Birch Society, and had given a speech to a group of mainly military dependents in which he said that Harry Truman, Eleanor Roosevelt, and former secretary of state Dean Acheson were "definitely pink."[1040]

Walker denied the allegations, denouncing the *Overseas Weekly* as "immoral, unscrupulous, corrupt, and destructive." The controversy snowballed all through the spring of that year. President Kennedy eventually ordered an investigation by the Defense Department and Walker was relieved of his command and transferred to army headquarters in Heidelberg, Germany. On June 12, the army gave him an administrative "admonition" (not considered punishment by the army) for his speech and for refusing to heed superior officers' advice against participating in "controversial" activities beyond the scope of his military duties. But he was cleared of the main charge against him. The army concluded that the "pro-blue" program initiated by Walker in his division was "not attributable" to any program of the John Birch Society.[1041] Although originally destined to command the Eighth Corps in Texas, he was derailed to Hawaii as assistant chief of staff for training and operations, a much less glamorous position.[1042] It looked as though a third star might never be pinned to his collar.

The American Right took up the general as a cause celebre. Several senators put together a subcommittee of a Senate Arms Services subcommittee to investigate the Kennedy administration's "muzzling" of military officers. But on September 6 and 7, Secretary of Defense Robert McNamara testified that Walker's activities had violated a federal criminal statute[1043] in attempting to influence senatorial and congressional elections by indoctrinating his troops, as well as violating noncriminal provisions of the Hatch Act, which prohibit political activities by federal employees. However, McNamara also gave the subcommittee a copy of the army's report on Walker, which called him eccentric but "a sincere, deeply religious, patriotic soldier" and a passionate anti-Communist. The report also confirmed that he was a member of the John Birch Society and that his indoctrination programs were "remarkably identical" to the tenets promulgated by that ultra-right-wing group.[1044] On November 2, 1961, when Oswald was still struggling to leave the Soviet Union, Walker resigned from the army, a celebrated martyr among the nation's right wing. He announced that he would "find other ways to serve my country in this time of her great need."[1045]

How much of this story Oswald knew before his return to the United States cannot be determined, but he certainly knew something. Among the notes he wrote aboard the *Maasdam* as it carried him and his family toward New York is this: "The case of Gen. Walker shows that the army, at least, is not fertail enough ground for a far right regime to go a very long way."[1046] He probably got the story in Russia from two articles that appeared in the *Worker* on November 12 and December 10, 1961: "Gen. Walker Bids for Fuhrer Role" and "Walker Defends American Nazis," the former denouncing the general with the label "Fascist," the latter citing Walker's defense of George Lincoln Rockwell, head of the American Nazi Party.[1047] Marina told the Warren Commission that Lee read the English-language edition of the *Worker* while in Russia.[1048]

General Walker continued to command headlines after his retirement to Dallas, where he rented a gray mansion high up from the street in the upscale Turtle Creek area, and promptly raised the American flag and the flag of the state of Texas on the front lawn. In the spring of 1962, the six-foot four-inch Walker ran against Governor John Connally in the Democratic primary for governor of Texas and finished last in a field of six, but he received 138,387 votes, which was a respectable 10.46 percent of the total. Connally, who won the primary, received 431,498 votes.[1049] On September 14, 1962, by which time Lee and Marina were living on Mercedes Street in Fort Worth, the city's *Star-Telegram* published a story about a speech Walker gave to Lampasas County ranchers protesting the army's intention to hold maneuvers on their land. He told them, "If Fort Hood needs any maneuvering or training grounds, it should be training in Cuba now." On September 28 he hit the headlines again: the previous day he had called for ten thousand civilian volunteers to go to Oxford, Mississippi, to oppose any federal troops trying to enforce the court-ordered admission of the black student James Meredith to the state university there.[1050]*

On September 29, President Kennedy started massing hundreds of army troops and five hundred U.S. marshals at a large naval air station near Memphis, some twenty miles away, to be dispatched to Oxford to force Meredith's admission, which was bitterly opposed by the state's governor, Ross Barnett, a rabid segregationist. The next day, September 30, Kennedy called Mississippi's National Guard into service and in the evening made an unprecedented plea on national television and radio for peace, but it was unavailing. Shortly thereafter, Walker, who heard the president's speech on radio in an Oxford café and called it "nauseating," was on the scene as rioting broke out that night when

---

*Ironically, in 1957, Walker, stationed with his army unit in Arkansas, subjugated his segregationist impulses and carried out his duty, commanding the "federalized" National Guard troops that forced integration on Little Rock's Central High School (Cartwright, "Old Soldier," p.59).

Meredith was admitted to the campus for enrollment the following day. Two people, one a French newsman, were killed and another severely wounded in a bloody riot in which over three thousand U.S. soldiers, federalized Mississippi guardsmen, and federal marshals fired rifles, threw tear gas grenades, and used clubs to overcome the bottle- and brick-hurling rioters. Soldiers, Negroes, and newsmen were beaten and homes and automobiles were damaged. The fifteen-hour rioting persisted through the night, and Governor Barnett eventually gave up the fight, saying he was "physically overpowered." Two hundred rioters were arrested on various charges.

The next morning, October 1, Meredith enrolled and started attending classes without further violence, although white students shouted racial epithets and threats at him as he was guarded by seventy-five U.S. marshals. Walker was arrested on several charges, including inciting insurrection, and conspiracy to commit sedition, and flown to the U.S. Medical Center for federal prisoners in Springfield, Missouri, for psychiatric observation. On October 6 he was released on a $50,000 bond and his agreement to submit to further psychiatric examinations in Dallas.[1051]

A subplot had begun on the night of the Oxford rioting, though many miles away in Dallas, when police stopped a car driven by Ashland F. Burchell and found a .357 Magnum and three .22 caliber pistols, a rifle, three thousand rounds of ammunition, blankets, a change of clothes, two or three hundred card files, and a switchblade knife. Texans toting small arsenals were neither uncommon nor outside the law—only the switchblade knife was actually illegal—but Burchell, a twenty-two-year-old graduate of Walker's "special warfare" unit in West Germany, was known to be one of the general's disciples. He had come to Dallas that spring to work on Walker's failed run for governor in the Democratic primary. He denied he was on his way to Oxford, said the guns were his hobby and the index cards belonged to a friend. In the end the story did not amount to much. Burchell quickly made bail and was later slapped on the wrist for possession of the switchblade, but that did not keep the October 21 issue of the *Worker*, to which Oswald was subscribing, from reading the utmost sinister significance into it all— "Oxford Campus Plot for Bloodbath Bared." The paper asserted that "hundreds" of other cars "carrying arms and ammunition were stopped on the way to Oxford on Sunday night and Monday morning," something that escaped the attention of other news-reporting agencies. Only the Burchell incident appeared in the October 2 edition of the *Dallas Morning News.*[1052]

None of this, of course, could have escaped the attention of Oswald, who always followed the news. It is worth being reminded that on the same day, October 7, that General Walker returned to Dallas to a welcoming crowd of two hundred supporters waving signs, including those urging Walker to run for president in 1964,[1053] Oswald announced to the small group of Russian emigrés at his Fort Worth apartment that he had decided, without giving them any explanation, to move to Dallas.

Over the next three weeks, stories about Walker appeared almost daily, many on the front page, in the Dallas papers, as his attorneys denounced the government's persecution of their client. There weren't too many literate Americans that October who did not know anything about General Walker, but the Dallas newspapers, of course, gave the story much more play than it got nationally—Walker was, after all, a resident of the town. The friendship between George de Mohrenschildt and Lee was just beginning to flower during what George called Walker's "big show-off" period, and the general was a hot topic of their conversations. George knew that Lee hated the man. Quite apart from the fact that Lee revered Castro and Walker reviled him, Lee was, per George, "ferociously" in favor of integration, and Walker was just as fanatically a segregationist.[1054]

On January 21, 1963, an all-white federal grand jury in Oxford, Mississippi, declined to return an indictment against Walker on insurrection and other charges (including seditious conspiracy and assaulting, resisting, and impeding federal officers), and the federal U.S. attorney there had the federal District Court judge dismiss all charges against Walker. "I am glad to be vindicated," Walker told the press. "Today my hopes returned to the [anti-Castro] Cubans . . . who long to return to their homes." The dismissed charges against Walker made the front page in the January 22 edition of the *Dallas Morning News*.[1055]

When Oswald ordered his revolver five days later, on January 27, he started talking about sending Marina and June back to Russia. "I told him that . . . if he wanted me to go," Marina would later tell the Warren Commission, "then that meant he didn't love me." But Lee "said he loved me but that it would be better for me if I went to Russia, and what he had in mind I don't know."[1056] What Lee had in mind very likely was his plan to murder General Walker.

Marina would tell Priscilla McMillan that the month of February in 1963 was the worst month of her married life. The beatings grew more frequent and more savage. Before that February he would slap her once or twice with the flat of his hand; now, Marina told McMillan, he began to hit her with his fist five or six times. "When he started to strike her, his face became red and his voice grew angry and loud. He wore a look of concentration, as if Marina were being paid back for every slight he had ever suffered by her, and he was bent on wiping her out, obliterating her completely. To Marina, it seemed that it was not even a human being he saw in front of him. Most horrifying of all was the gleam of pleasure in his eyes," as he would say things like, "I'm not hitting you just for *this*, but because I'll never forgive you for running off to your Russians. Oh, what humiliation you made me suffer. Always you go against me! You never, ever do what I want!"[1057]

Marina, naturally, sought some affection from Lee during this period, and whenever she did he would say, "I know what you want," referring to sex. But he himself made violent sexual attacks on her, insisting on having her when and where he wanted, pinning her down and forcing himself on her, even if she was crying. "You're my property," he told her, "and I'll do with you as I please."[1058]

Perhaps even worse than the beatings, which Marina had almost accepted as a part of her life, was his talk about her returning to the Soviet Union. She had no way of guessing that this might be part of his plot to murder General Walker. If Lee survived the killing of Walker and got away, he might make his escape, perhaps to Cuba, and then find some way to send for Marina and June. This, of course, is speculation, but by this time he had already ordered the pistol, and he was staying out late in the evening, probably scouting Walker's home on Turtle Creek Boulevard across town. He was also busy forging a couple of ID cards for the fictitious "A. Hidell" at Jaggers by photographing his own Marine Corps and Selective Service cards and other documents, blanking out the data, rephotographing the documents, and then typing the new false data directly on the resulting prints. The separate prints for the front and back of the cards were then glued together.[1059] He would soon need such identification when he had to pick up "Hidell's" pistol at the post office.

On February 14, 1963, the *Dallas Morning News* ran a front-page story on General Walker's cross-country speaking tour with the fire-and-brimstone right-wing evangelist Billy James Hargis* to warn against the dangers of Communism. Three days later, the *Morning News* carried another story on General Walker's speaking tour, emphasizing the anti-Castro side of his "crusade."[1060]

Later that same day, February 17, Lee forced Marina to handwrite a letter to the Soviet embassy asking to return to the USSR:

> Dear Comrade Reznichenko!
>
> I beg your assistance to help me return to the Homeland in the USSR where I will again feel myself a full-fledged citizen. Please let me know what I should do for this, i.e., perhaps it will be necessary to fill out a special application form. Since I am not working at present (because of my lack of knowledge of the English language and a small child), I am requesting you to extend to me a possible material aid for the trip. My husband remains here, since he is an American by nationality. I beg you once more not to refuse my request.
>
> Respectfully
> Marina Oswald[1061]

Marina told the Warren Commission that on her own she had never once considered returning to the Soviet Union, but that Lee insisted on it. "He handed me the paper, a pencil, and said, 'Write' . . . What could I do if my husband didn't want to live with me? At least that is what I thought."[1062]

Marina told Priscilla McMillan that the week after she wrote the letter to the Soviet embassy was the most violent of all. They had celebrated June's first birthday on February 15, and the next day she confirmed she was pregnant again. "Very good," Lee said. "Junie is one year old and Marina is cooking up a present. A baby brother. What better present could there be?" But after a day or two of exulting over the prospect of another child, Lee soon resumed showing no compassion for its mother. On one occasion he hit Marina so hard that she started bleeding from the nose. He seemed contrite and made Marina lie down, but his anger persisted. He stormed out and didn't return for hours.

---

*The Tulsa-based Hargis, whose oratorical style of preaching was what Oklahomans call "bawl and jump" (shouting to the point of hoarseness while flailing one's arms), weighed in at 270 pounds and was known more for his anti-Communism than for his preaching the Gospel of Christ, though one of his favorite lines was *"for Christ and *against* communism."* In the 1960s and early 1970s his fame and influence was on its way to rivaling Reverend Billy Graham's. The Christian Crusade, which Hargis founded, had an enormous budget by 1972 and his message was being delivered in over 500 radio and 250 television stations around the country, mostly in the South. On the air and in his many books (e.g., *Communist America—Must It Be?*, *The Real Extremists—The Far Left*, *Why I Fight for a Christian America*"), Hargis routinely accused the likes of President Kennedy, his brother Robert, and network news anchors like Walter Cronkite, Chet Huntley, and David Brinkley of being soft on Communism. He himself had a soft side, shown by his establishment, in 1966, of a missionary foundation that ran medical clinics and orphanages in Asia and Africa. His power and reach substantially and irrevocably waned in 1974, when he resigned as president of the Christian college he had founded in Tulsa amid allegations he had had sex with a few male and female students. *Newsweek* noted in 1987 that Hargis was "the first televangelist brought down by allegations of sexual misconduct." (Myrna Oliver, "Rev. Billy James Hargis, 79, Pastor Targeted Communism," *Los Angeles Times*, November 30, 2004, obituary, p.B10; *New York Times*, November 29, 2004, p.A23) Likewise, it was charges of sexual misconduct against General Walker (arrested and convicted of public lewdness after making sexual advances to an undercover Dallas police officer in the men's room of a public park) that brought his downfall as a significant force two years later in 1976 (Cartwright, "Old Soldier," p.59).

Marina had locked both front and back doors, but Lee just broke the window in the back door, came in, and went to bed without even speaking to Marina. Even as he feigned regret for his violence, he contrived to lay the blame on her: "You see I'm in a bad mood, try not to make me mad. You know I can't hold myself in very long now."[1063]

In mid-February the de Mohrenschildts invited Lee and Marina to dinner and a screening of the film on their walking trip through Mexico and Central America. Among the guests were the Dallas chemist Everett Glover and his roommate, Volkmar Schmidt—Glover was between marriages at the time. Lee had already seen the film and preferred to spend the time in earnest conversation with Schmidt, a young German geologist who had recently come to the United States to work at Magnolia Laboratory in Dallas, owned by Standard Oil of New York. Schmidt, who spoke English but little Russian, was interested in Lee's story.[1064] "Lee Harvey Oswald brought up in the conversation with me," Schmidt told *Frontline* in 1993, "the fact that he really felt very angry about the support which the Kennedy administration gave to the Bay of Pigs invasion. It turned out that Lee Harvey Oswald really idealized [the] socialism of Cuba, while he was critical of the socialism in the Soviet Union. And he was just obsessed with his anger towards Kennedy."[1065]

The credibility of this statement has to be questioned. Although there is evidence of Oswald's opposition to Kennedy's support of the Bay of Pigs invasion, in all the literature on the Kennedy assassination this is the only reference to Oswald being obsessed with anger against Kennedy prior to the assassination. Much more importantly, when the FBI interviewed Schmidt thirty years earlier on November 29, 1963, the agents' report said that Schmidt told them that "Oswald did not speak of President Kennedy or his politics. On one occasion, Schmidt praised Kennedy by stating that President Kennedy would improve the welfare of the working man in the United States. Oswald made no objection to this statement."[1066]

George drove the Oswalds home afterward and spoke Russian when he discussed the evening. Getting around to Schmidt—George called him "Messer Schmidt"—George said to Marina and Lee, "Just imagine, such a young man. Yet a fascist from his brains to his bones."

It was the first time Marina had heard George or Lee use that word—readily comprehensible even when they spoke English, since it is virtually the same word in Russian. It was news to her that there were fascists in America. George told her about the John Birch Society and said Schmidt's ideas were like theirs, enough to "make your hair stand on end."[1067]

A few days later, on February 22, Glover invited some friends interested in the Russian language to his own apartment to meet the Oswalds. It was a chance for the Oswalds to shine, in spite of their shabby clothing, as they were the only ones there who had fresh knowledge of the Soviet Union. The de Mohrenschildts put in an appearance but left early. Among the guests was a tall, thin, freckle-faced young woman, an acquaintance of Glover's who would come to play a very large and critical role in the Oswalds' lives, Ruth Hyde Paine.[1068]

Ruth Paine, thirty years old and a housewife at the time, would become, over the next nine months of Marina and Lee's life, the single person closest to both of them, and for that reason she has attracted a great deal of attention from assassination conspiracy theorists. (Paine would become one of my star witnesses at the London trial.) At the Second

National Conference of the Coalition on Political Assassinations (COPA) in 1995, three researchers, Barbara LaMonica, Carol Hewett, and Steve Jones, who had been working together compiling information on Paine and her estranged husband Michael, each presented research papers based on "all the Paine files they could find, including FBI and Secret Service background reports, Warren Commission testimony, and CIA documents—over two thousand pages in all," as well as "Ruth's grand jury testimony in New Orleans [in the Clay Shaw case], Dallas police files, and reports of a Quaker activist who was with Ruth Paine in 1991." They found mighty slim pickings, mostly things like the fact that Ruth's father, William Avery Hyde, had been in the Office of Strategic Services, the Second World War forerunner of the CIA, became an insurance executive, and in 1965—well after the assassination—took leave from his company to work for a time for the Agency for International Development, "a mysterious agency about which not much is known," in the words of assassination researcher Steve Jones. An FBI document also revealed that the CIA had approached Hyde about running an educational cooperative alliance in Vietnam in 1957, although the plan was dropped. He also "traveled abroad frequently."[1069] Ruth's mother was a Unitarian minister who was still studying for her bachelor of divinity degree at Oberlin College in Ohio. An FBI report said that a confidential informant for "another U.S. Government Agency" advised back in 1952 that Mrs. Hyde had admitted to many neighbors in the past years that she was a "Communist."

The father of Ruth's husband, Michael, was a "notorious Trotskyite" (coincidentally the same wing of the Communist Party that most attracted Oswald), although Michael had little contact with him. Michael's stepfather, Michael Young, was the inventor of the first commercially licensed helicopter, the Bell 47.[1070]

Ruth Paine herself was a member of the American Civil Liberties Union and League of Women Voters in Dallas. She considered herself a pacifist and had been connected with the Central Committee for Conscientious Objectors.[1071] Ruth was a graduate of Antioch College in Ohio, as was her brother, a doctor. She also had a sister living in Ohio. In early 1951 Ruth joined the Society of Friends, commonly known as Quakers, "tremendously excited," she said, "by the idea of the 'inner light'—the possibility of direct communication between God and man—and also by the Quaker concern for other people." She met Michael at a folk dance in Germantown, Pennsylvania, in 1955. Michael had flunked out of Harvard and transferred to Swarthmore College, spending a year there majoring in physics before dropping out of college in 1951. They married at a Friends meeting in Media, Pennsylvania, in December of 1957 and moved to Irving, a suburb of Dallas, where they bought a house in 1959. They had two small children, Sylvia Lynn, three, and Christopher, two.[1072] Although Michael and Ruth, each of serious personality and strong social conscience, were soul mates on political issues, both being very liberal, their marriage had already gone stale by the time Ruth met the Oswalds.[1073]

In September 1962, Michael and Ruth separated, although Michael continued to support the family, came to dinner twice a week, entertained and enjoyed his children, and generally made himself handy when he was there, often working in his workshop in the garage. Although the Paines were planning to divorce, Ruth thought they went out to the movies more often than some of their married friends.[1074] Ruth would later volunteer her view of the marriage to the Warren Commission: "Our marriage is marked both by mutual honesty that is exceptional and by a lack of overt or interior strife, except that it hasn't quite come together as a mutual partnership. My mother recently said to me that 'If you would just look only at what Michael does there's nothing wrong with your marriage at all. It is just what he says,' and I concur with her opinion on that, that he is so scrupulously honest with his own feelings." While they lived together, Michael had been, Ruth thought, "insufficiently attentive" but "always kind and thoughtful."[1075]*

Ruth knew no one at Glover's gathering but Glover himself, whom she had met in a madrigal (old English songs) singing group to which she and Michael belonged.[1076] She was eager for an opportunity to talk with native Russian speakers, as she had been studying the language with a Russian tutor in Dallas, took summer courses in Russian in Pennsylvania and Vermont in 1957 and 1959, and enrolled in a Berlitz course in Russian in 1959. She hoped one day to become a teacher in Russian, and later that summer began tutoring one student.[1077] At Glover's home Ruth had little opportunity to speak with Marina, who spent the first half of the evening trying to get baby June to stop crying and go to sleep. The de Mohrenschildts had a few words of Russian with Marina in the kitchen, but they did not amount to much, and Ruth was too embarrassed by her own poor Russian to do much more than listen.[1078] Ruth also heard Oswald holding forth on his experiences in the Soviet Union in the living room, enough to know he considered himself a Marxist and had thought—before going there—that the Soviet Union's economic system was superior to that of the United States. He complained about censorship, mentioning a letter his brother Robert sent to him in the USSR with a clipping about his "defection" that he never received, probably, he believed, because the Soviet authorities intercepted it. Ruth was puzzled. "His discussion of the censorship made me feel that he wanted his listeners to know he was not blind to the defects of the Soviet system," she told the Warren Commission. "I was left wondering which country he thought conducted itself better," though he did indicate he did not like the capitalist system.

The gathering broke up late, but not before Ruth, who had no idea of the turbulence in the Oswalds' marriage at the time, asked Marina for her address. She wanted to visit Marina to speak Russian with her—the only speaker of contemporary Russian that Ruth had met—in the hope of improving her own language skills. She hoped that Marina was speaking an "educated" Russian, but she was not well enough versed in the language to know whether she was or not.[1079]

The day after the affair at Everett Glover's, Lee ordered Marina to cook red beans and rice for dinner and then went out for the whole day. It was a Saturday, and although he

---

*The considerable and ongoing, to this day, interest by members of the conspiracy community in Ruth Paine is because they have actually entertained the notion that she and her husband were part of a conspiracy to murder Kennedy (e.g., Garrison, *Heritage of Stone*, pp.80, 114–115). Indeed, at the London trial, Gerry Spence, on cross-examination, actually pushed the issue, suggesting that a series of incidents involving Ruth only appeared to be coincidences. "It just is a coincidence that you befriended the wife of the man who was later charged with the murder of our president?" Spence asked Ruth, disbelief in his voice. "And is it a coincidence that it was you, Mrs. Paine, who directed Lee to the job that put him in the Texas School Book Depository?" "And it's just a coincidence that the gun that supposedly killed the president was located in your house?" (Transcript of *On Trial*, July 24, 1986, pp.647–648) To me, and to all or most of the jury I'm sure, the thought of the extremely proper and straight-laced Quaker lady with the rimless glasses conspiring to kill an ant or flower, much less a president, was laughable, and my amusement was apparently picked up by the camera. Paine's biographer, Thomas Mallon, writes, "Spence walks around with a giant photo of Oswald and throws everything he can at Ruth, even the suggestion she might be a KGB agent." (As seen, he suggested much more than this.) Mallon goes on to write that the camera shows "Bugliosi, by contrast . . . beaming with delight [an exaggeration—only a measured smile] as Ruth gently forbears Spence's assault. The prosecutor takes no advantage of several obvious opportunities to object, clearly preferring to let his opponent's aggression backfire." (Mallon, *Mrs. Paine's Garage*, p.147) While Mallon's assessment of my strategy was correct, even if the majority of jurors felt the way I did, if Spence could muddy the waters to the extent of creating a reasonable doubt in the mind of just one of the jurors, he would have succeeded in creating a hung jury.

sometimes worked on Saturdays at Jaggers (taking another day off during the week) to get time-and-a-half pay, he did not work this Saturday. When he returned, he found that she had cooked the rice and beans in the same pot, which infuriated him—he wanted the beans cooked separately and poured over the rice. Tempers flared, Marina threw the dinner out, and again Lee struck her. After she threw a wooden box of jewelry at him, which hit him on the shoulder, he threw her on the bed and grabbed her throat. "I won't let you out of this alive," he said. Just then, Junie started crying, and Lee went to comfort her. Marina went into the bathroom, found a rope she used for hanging the baby's diapers up to dry, tied it around her neck, and climbed onto the toilet seat. Lee caught her in time and hit her in the face, shouting, "Don't ever do that again. Only the most terrible fools try that."

"I can't go on this way, Alka," she wailed. "I don't want to go on living."

The crisis was followed by the ritual contrition—and a memorable night of sex—and the equally inescapable laying of the blame on Marina.

"I'll try and change if you'll only help me," he said.

"But why, Alka, why do you do it?"

"Because I love you. I can't stand it when you make me mad."[1080]

The fighting in the Oswald apartment finally became intolerable for the other tenants in the building, and the owner, Mr. William Martin Jurek, told Lee he and his wife had to stop fighting or leave. Lee decided to leave.[1081] He said nothing to Marina about Jurek but went out to look for another place. He spotted a "For Rent" sign on an upstairs apartment of a ramshackle, wooden, two-unit building, about a block and a half away, around a corner, at 214 West Neely Street. The rent was sixty dollars a month, eight dollars less than what he had been paying at Elsbeth Street. He presented the idea of the move to Marina as an improvement in their lives, and on March 3, 1963, the Oswalds piled their belongings on June's stroller and walked them over in several trips to their new place. Marina liked it—it had a porch and seemed more suitable for the baby. As poor as it was, at least visitor Gary Taylor thought it an improvement over Elsbeth Street.[1082]

About two weeks after their first meeting at Everett Glover's, Ruth wrote to Marina and offered to visit. Marina wrote back to say that they had just moved to Neely Street and needed time to tidy up the new apartment, so Ruth should come in about a week. Ruth did, arriving in the midmorning after a thirty-five- to forty-minute drive from Irving. The two young mothers took their children to a nearby park. It was a warm Dallas day and Marina was grateful for the opportunity for one-year-old June to play with other small children (Christopher was two, and Sylvia Lynn three), which was rare, and for the chance to talk with another woman—Ruth felt her desperate need for friendship. Marina did most of the talking, in Russian, taking care to speak slowly and use small simple words, which Ruth understood easily.

Ruth visited Marina again on March 20. At either their first meeting or the second one, Marina told Ruth of her pregnancy and asked Ruth not to mention it to the Russian community. Ruth really didn't know anyone in that community but assured Marina that she wouldn't say anything until Marina chose to make the news public. Marina asked Ruth about birth control too—the pregnancy had been a surprise and not entirely welcome. She would not consider an abortion, but she was interested in preventing further surprises. They also talked about Lee's refusal to help Marina learn English, which Ruth found inconsiderate, even cruel. Ruth hadn't warmed to Lee when they met at Everett Glover's, and nothing Marina told her made her feel better about him.[1083]

Throughout this period, Lee was quite obviously proceeding with his plans to murder General Walker, aided by a curious feature of the new apartment: Off the living room was a sort of small storeroom, hardly larger than a double closet, which he immediately appropriated as his "study." There he could compose the notebook with the information and photographs he would use in plotting the assassination of Walker. Oddly, the tiny room had two entrances, one through a door from the outside at the top of the stairs, another through a door in the living room. Both doors could be locked. He gave Marina strict instructions that he was not to be disturbed when he was in there "working," and the door from the exterior enabled him to come and go without her knowing.[1084]*

Meanwhile, General Walker was back in the news in Dallas. In a speech on his tour on March 5 in Savannah, Georgia, reported in the *Dallas Times Herald,* Walker said to a standing ovation, "I challenge the commander in chief of the United States of America to take one U.S. Army division, the 82nd Airborne Division at Ft. Bragg, North Carolina, properly supported and joined by Cubans who want to be free, and liquidate the scourge that has descended upon the island of Cuba."[1085]

On March 12, Oswald ordered a Mannlicher-Carcano carbine from Klein's Sporting Goods, a mail-order house in Chicago, using the name "A. Hidell" in accord with the fake ID cards he had fabricated at Jaggers-Chiles-Stovall. He paid $21.45 for it, less than he had paid for the pistol for which he was still waiting.[1086]

Two days before, on Sunday, March 10, Oswald had gone to General Walker's home at 4011 Turtle Creek Boulevard and taken a series of photographs. Four of them survive, having been found in a cardboard box in Ruth Paine's garage in Irving, Texas, by the Dallas Police Department on November 23, 1963.[1087] One shows the alley behind Walker's house,[1088] two the back of the house itself,[1089] and one more is of railroad tracks in a wooded area about half a mile away.[1090] It may not have been his first such visit, but one of the photographs shows some construction work on a building located at 21 Turtle Creek Square in the background.[1091] The FBI consulted the supervisor of the work and he determined that the building was in that state of completion on the weekend of March 9 and 10.[1092] The time card at Jaggers showed that Lee worked too late at the photo lab on Saturday, March 9, to have taken the snapshots that day,[1093] so almost for sure they were taken on March 10. When Marina saw the photographs in Lee's office, she asked him, "What kind of photographs are these?" but she said that "he didn't say anything to me."[1094]

Oswald would have had little fear of getting caught snooping around the general's house on March 10 since, as indicated, Walker was off on his well-publicized sleeper-bus tour of twenty-six cities in seventeen states with evangelist Billy Hargis, one of the then-popular crusades against Communism. "Operation Midnight Ride," as they dubbed it, started in Miami on February 27 and was scheduled to finish on April 3 in Los Angeles. It was well reported in the newspapers, so Oswald knew the general would not be in Dallas on March 10.[1095]

What was Oswald's plan? How did he think he was going to kill General Walker with

---

*When I saw the "room" on a trip to Dallas on September 22, 2004, I wondered how anyone could possibly use this small room as any type of functional study. The current tenant, John Thompson, who has lived there for four years, was kind enough to measure the room for me. It's three feet nine inches by four feet five inches, a room he uses as a closet to put his "junk." Incidentally, the door leading out of this small room to the outside, which enabled Oswald to come and go without Marina knowing, is no longer there.

his pistol—perhaps ring the doorbell, hope that Walker himself would answer, and shoot the man at point blank? What if someone else opened the door? No one can know what was in Oswald's mind, but his photographic reconnaissance of the Walker home may have led him to a more practical idea. In any case, it was only two days later, March 12, that Oswald, as indicated, ordered the Mannlicher-Carcano carbine from Klein's Sporting Goods store in Chicago.

By coincidence, both weapons, pistol and carbine, were shipped to him on the same day a little over a week later, March 20.[1096] Marina noticed the rifle several days later in Lee's "office." He later draped a coat over it for concealment.[1097]

At the same time Oswald was laboring over his notebook and carrying out surveillance of General Walker, he had come to the attention of the FBI again. John Fain, the special agent in the Fort Worth bureau, had closed the case on Lee Oswald in September of 1962 and retired a couple of weeks later, right in the middle of the Cuban missile crisis. His caseload fell to Special Agent James P. Hosty Jr. in the Dallas office. In July 1962, Fain had asked Hosty to run over to the Immigration and Naturalization Service in Dallas to review Marina's file and forward information to him in Fort Worth about it, which Hosty did. Hosty had just taken an in-service training course in Washington, D.C., on security and counterespionage cases, and it occurred to him that Marina, a recently arrived twenty-three-year-old Russian immigrant, fit the profile of a "sleeper" agent, one who might lie dormant for years and be activated only if the cold war boiled over and diplomatic communications were severed. Hosty even went to his superior and asked for permission to open a file on Marina as a potential espionage agent. That permission was denied on the grounds that new immigrants were always allowed a six-month period of grace before the FBI interviewed them, but he did allow Hosty to open a "pending inactive" file on Marina.

In late February of 1963 that six-month period was well over, and Hosty had not forgotten about Marina. He activated her file and drove over to Fort Worth and talked with the Oswalds' landlady at the Mercedes Street address, who told him that the Oswalds had moved and left no forwarding address. A couple of weeks later he checked with the INS and found that Marina had registered, as she was required to do, her new address at Elsbeth Street in Dallas. On March 11, the day after Lee's photographic surveillance of Walker's house, Hosty called on Mrs. Tobias, only to learn that the Oswalds had been thrown out of there because of their constant, noisy fighting. Mrs. Tobias gave Hosty the Oswald's new address at 214 West Neely Street. In Hosty's book and in his testimony before the Warren Commission, he said Mrs. Tobias only told him the Oswalds had moved nearby, but didn't know where, and he got their address from the postal authorities. But in his first statement on the matter, his FBI report of September 10, 1963, he said he got the Oswalds' address from Mrs. Tobias. Hosty checked the mailbox at the Neely address and found the name Oswald on it, but he decided to hold off awhile on interviewing Marina, given what he thought he knew about their recent marital difficulties—it was FBI practice to try to conduct interviews under tranquil circumstances.

Hosty had to write a report on his efforts to locate Marina, and so he also reviewed Lee's closed file. He discovered that the New York office of the FBI had noted the fact that Lee had taken out a subscription to the U.S. Communist Party newspaper, the *Worker*, in December. Hosty by now was definitely intrigued, and on March 31 he requested permission from Washington to reopen the file on Oswald.[1098]

Meanwhile, the target of Hosty's interest was sitting in his office closet writing out a document,[1099] a political statement in the tradition of Hitler's *Mein Kampf* in which he switches gears, for the first time, to a leadership role. He starts by denouncing the Communist Party of the United States. Calling Communism "that most sublime ideal," he says, "There can be no sympathy for those who have turned the idea of communism into a vill [vile] curse to western man." He turns on the Soviets, who have "committed crimes unsurpassed even by their early day capitalist counterparts, the imprisonment of their own peoples, with the mass extermination so typical of Stalin, and the individual surpresstion [suppression] and regimentation under Krushchev." He then proposes the formation of a new party—and seems to be addressing a host of prospective followers: "In order to free the hesitating and justifiably uncertain, future activist for the work ahead we must remove that obstacle which has so efficiently retarded him, namely the devotion of Communist Party U.S.A., to the Soviet Union, Soviet Government, and Soviet Communist International Movement." Then he gets to his apocalyptic vision: "It is readily foreseeable that a coming economic, political or military crisis, internal or external, will bring about the final destruction of the capitalist system, assuming this, we can see how preparation in a special party could safeguard an independent course of action after the debacle, an American course steadfastly opposed to intervention by outside, relatively stable foreign powers, no matter from where they come, but in particular, and if necessary, violently opposed to Soviet intervention." He writes that "whereas our political enemies talk loudly now, they have no concept of what total crisis means."

Entertained by his apocalyptic dream, Oswald can afford a certain bemused tolerance of the United States: "We have no interest in violently opposeing the U. S. Government, why should we manifest opposition when there are far greater forces at work, to bringabout the fall of the United States Government, than we could ever Possibly muster."

"We," he says rather grandly, invoking a nonexistent cadre of dedicated followers, "do not have any interest in directly assuming the head of Government in the event of such an all–finising crisis." He recognizes that patience will be required: "These prefered tactics now, may prove to be too limited in the near future, they should not be confused with slowness, indesision or fear, only the intellectualy fearless could even be remotly attracted too our doctrine, and yet this doctrine requirers the utmost restraint, a state of being in itself majustic in power. This is stoicism." To those for whom too much stoicism is cold comfort, he offers hope: "Armed Defenses of our ideals must be an accepted doctrine after the crisis, just as refrainting from any demonstrations of force must be our decision in the mean time."

Oswald concludes with the most eloquent prose of his that I am aware of: "No man, having known, having lived, under the Russian Communist and American capitalist system, could possibly make a choice between them, there is no choice, one offers oppresstion the other poverty. Both offer imperilistic injustice, tinted with two brands of slavery. But no rational man can take the attitude of 'a curse on both your house's.' There *are* two world systems, one twisted beyond recognition by its misuse, the other decadent and dying in its final evolution. A truly democratic system would combine the better qualities of the two upon an American foundation, opposed to both world systems as they are now. This than is our ideal."[1100]

It is difficult to divorce these political writings of Oswald's from his contemplated assassination of General Walker. We know that Oswald was very busy during this period. He didn't miss a day of work at Jaggers for the months of February and March of 1962,[1101] and we know he was also busy working on his plans to murder Walker during this time because he later told Marina this.[1102] So he obviously had no free time to spare—that is, he had to have *made* time by staying up until midnight or later many nights during March working on his political statement.[1103] Why the urgency? We can never know for sure, but we do know that Oswald did not view himself a mere foot soldier in the Marxist struggle but a potential leader. We also know he knew there was a chance he would be apprehended in his attempt to murder Walker, and if such an event happened, it's reasonable to assume he wanted these writings to be accepted as a moral (though not a legal) justification for what he had done, and hoped he would be rightfully perceived by those of similar mind as not the equivalent of a hit man or a member of a firing squad carrying out a sentence of death, but as an important historical figure who not only pulled the trigger but conceptualized its rationale, and hence should be greatly respected for his visionary and leadership qualities. If there were not some umbilical cord between his political manifesto and his plans to murder Walker, it's hard to imagine why, during this turbulent period, he would have set aside time to write it.

Marina had not been happy when she discovered the carbine standing in a corner of Lee's closet study. "What do you need a rifle for? What do we need that for?" she asked, and he only responded that it might come in handy some day for hunting.[1104] Though she said no more about it, still it bothered her that he would buy a "toy" like this when they were scrimping, even on their food. But Marina was from the old school and felt that Lee worked for his money, and ought to spend it as he pleased.[1105]

Lee's rages in February subsided in March and he seemed more relaxed. She believed this was due to his "little closet," since he could lock himself away where Marina could not get on his nerves, and he seemed to be preoccupied anyway during this period since, she said, "I know that Lee was planning for something," though she didn't know what.[1106]

On March 8, V. Gerasimov of the Soviet embassy replied to Marina's letter seeking readmission to the Soviet Union, explaining that it was not going to be easy. Among other things, she had to fill out an application in three copies and furnish three copies of a detailed biography of herself. In addition, she needed to indicate the profession she would pursue back in the Soviet Union and the place she wanted to reside. She also had to supply three passport-sized photos of herself and three of her child, as well as one or two letters from her relatives in the USSR who would be inviting her to live with them.[1107]

Since Marina didn't want to go back anyway, she was pleased the embassy was making it so difficult. She was particularly heartened by the fact that Gerasimov said the "time of processing" her application "requires five to six months." Wise in the ways of the Soviet bureaucracy, she was sure that five or six months really meant much longer, by which time the whole thing with Lee hopefully will have blown over. When Lee made her sit down and fill out the application on March 17, she did so with a much lighter heart than when she wrote the first letter.[1108] It looked as though things might still turn out all right.

But on March 29 or April 1, John Graef took Oswald aside in the laboratory. Graef had no office at Jaggers, just a desk out in the open among some others, so he sought out a quiet corner of the darkroom where he could talk to Lee without being overheard. He didn't want to embarrass the boy. Business had slackened off somewhat and Graef figured it was a good time to let Lee go. "Lee," he said, "I think this is as good a time as any to cut it short. Business is pretty slow at this time, but the point is that you haven't been turning the work out like you should [and] there has been friction with other peo-ple." Graef was also thinking about a recent incident when he had looked up from his desk and saw Lee reading a Russian paper—*Krokodil*, he thought it might have been. Graef advised him to put it away. In the political climate of America in the early 1960s—hotly anti-Communist and anti-Soviet—it didn't seem wise to flaunt such a thing. That wasn't why Graef was firing him, of course, but it didn't help Lee's case.

"I think you tried to do the work," Graef told him, "but I just don't think that you have the qualities for doing the work that we need."

Lee just looked at the floor the whole time Graef was talking. Graef gave Lee until April 6 and suggested he get in touch with the Texas Employment Commission again, adding that he would be happy to give him a reference for any prospective employer—with a reservation he kept to himself. Graef felt he would have to warn future employers about the fact that Oswald found it so difficult to get along with his coworkers. When Graef was finished talking, Lee, who had said nothing at all, finally said, "Well, thank you," turned, and walked away.[1109] When Lee came home that night, he did not tell Marina that he had lost his job.[1110]

On Sunday, March 31, Oswald wrote to the Fair Play for Cuba Committee (FPCC) in New York City telling them, "I do not like to ask for something for nothing but I am unemployed. Since I am unemployed, I stood yesterday for the first time in my life, with a placare around my neck, passing out fair play for Cuba pamplets [almost undoubtedly Corlis Lamont's basic pamphlet, *The Crime against Cuba*, about America's offenses against Cuba] ect.[*] I only had 15 or so. In 40 minutes they were all gone. I was cursed as well as praised by some." Oswald asked for "40 or 50 more of the fine basic pamplets."[1111]

This was not Oswald's first communication with the FPCC, but it appears to be the earliest dated one that survived the chaotic conditions of that office.[1112] The reason we know it was not the first communication is that among the piles of evidence accumulated by the Warren Commission is an empty envelope found in Lee's rooming house. The printed return address is "Rm.329, 779 Bway NY," the address of the FPCC. Although the only part of the postmark that is legible is "1962," the envelope is addressed to 2703 Mercedes Street in Fort Worth,[1113] where Oswald had not lived for nearly six months by the time he wrote the letter of March 31. In any case, the letter that Lee wrote to the FPCC at the end of March 1963 was to be followed by an exchange of several more let-ters extending over the next few months, to at least August 12. On May 26, Oswald requested "formal membership" in the organization, the leading pro-Castro group in the United States.[1114†]

---

[*]Sometime in the "late spring or early summer of 1963," a Dallas police officer, W. R. Finigan, who was posted on the corner of Main and Ervay not far from Jaggers-Chiles-Stovall, spotted a man across the street passing out literature. He had a sign on his back (probably the placard Oswald wore around his neck) read-ing, "Viva Castro." When Finigan's superior, Sergeant D. V. Harkness, stopped to talk to Finigan for a moment, the man removed the "Viva Castro" sign, ran into a department store, and disappeared. Harkness told Fini-gan to forget about it. A passerby who had seen the leaflet peddler close up reported to the police that the guy had muttered, "Oh hell, here come the cops" as he fled. (CE 1409, 22 H 796, Letter from Finigan to J. R. Curry, May 15, 1964)

[†]*New Yorker* writer Albert H. Newman, in his fine book *The Assassination of John F. Kennedy: The Rea-sons Why*, argues that all of this activity by Oswald, as early as March of 1963, revolved around a desire to get to Cuba and be recognized as a hero of the Cuban Revolution (Newman, *Assassination of John F. Kennedy*, p.329), a plan he had first broached years before with Nelson Delgado, his buddy in the Marine Corps at El Toro. And Marina testified to Oswald's interest in Cuba and Castro's revolution while they were still in the Soviet Union (1 H 24; CE 944, 18 H 631–632).

Also on Sunday, March 31, the day after he passed out pamphlets on behalf of Castro in downtown Dallas, Lee surprised Marina, who was hanging out diapers in the backyard at Neely Street, by coming down the outside backstairs dressed all in black as if he represented the return of Zorro. He was carrying some essential props: his rifle and some recent issues of the *Worker* and the *Militant*. His pistol was tucked into his waistband. He wanted her to take his picture.

Marina laughed. "Why are you rigged out like that?" she demanded, thinking that Lee had gone "crazy." She wasn't interested in taking photographs either. She had never used a camera, didn't care to learn how, and had diapers to dry. Nevertheless, she allowed herself to be persuaded. He showed her how to point his cheap Imperial Reflex camera and which button to push. She snapped the shutter at least three times as Lee smugly brandished the carbine and newspapers.[1115]

When Marina asked Lee what he planned to do with the photographs, he told her he was going to send them to the *Militant* to show he was "ready for anything."[1116] Oswald apparently did what he promised. Sylvia Weinstein, who handled the *Militant*'s subscriptions, told author Gus Russo that she opened the envelope containing the pictures that Oswald had sent, and the man in black appeared "kooky." She was struck by the fact that Oswald was holding both the *Worker* and the *Militant* in his hand, two newspapers that were ideologically at war with each other over Soviet dominance of socialist movements as well as interpretations of Stalin's role in history. She figured that Oswald would have to be "really dumb and totally naive."[1117]

Oswald probably intended the backyard photographs to be of great historical significance, telling Marina the photos were "for posterity."[1118] He may have intended to leave them for inclusion in the dossier he was compiling on his assassination of General Walker. Or they could have been another exhibit he could flash at Cuban leaders who were going to welcome him with open arms when they realized that he was the one who killed one of Castro's greatest American enemies.

If anything went wrong with his plan, the photo could still serve as a memento. Several days later, after developing and printing at least three of the negatives at Jaggers, he gave Marina a print, on the back of which he had written, "For Junie, from Papa." Marina was appalled.

"Why would Junie want a picture with guns?" she asked Lee.

Newman noticed the likelihood that Oswald was listening to nightly broadcasts of shortwave radio from Cuba, something the Warren Commission overlooked. The Commission sent the small Russian radio found in Oswald's rooming house after the assassination to the National Security Agency at Fort Meade, which reported that the radio "appears to be a normal receiver and there's no evidence of its use for any other purpose" (CE 2768, 26 H 155). Newman, a shortwave listener himself, easily determined that Oswald's "tourist" brand radio was capable of receiving Radio Havana's twice-nightly English-language broadcasts on both the normal broadcast and the shortwave band. Oswald was certainly familiar with the shortwave band and Soviet attempts to jam it. He wrote in his notes on the Soviet Union, "But the jamming frequences are only half those of the 'Radio Moscow' propaganda programs, which may be heard on any short wave radio in the United States and without jamming" (CE 95, 16 H 406). He also referred to a Voice of America broadcast he had heard in Minsk in a letter to his brother Robert (CE 316, 16 H 875). Mr. Johnson, the landlord of Oswald's final residence in the Oak Cliff rooming house, said that Oswald retired early and listened to his small radio (Hugh Aynesworth, "Oswald Rented Room under Alias," *Dallas Morning News*, November 23, 1963, p.6).

In the summer of 1966, Newman used the cheapest portable, transistor shortwave radio he could find—it cost less than twelve dollars—to check Radio Havana's signal in Dallas and found it to be consistently the strongest on the forty-nine-meter band (at 6.135 megacycles), three times stronger than it was in New York. Newman, in referring to Cuban radio, writes, "If soap and cigarettes can be sold over radio, so can hatred of the United States, its policies and its leaders." (Newman, *Assassination of John F. Kennedy*, pp.23–27)

"To remember Papa by sometime," he said.[1119]

Sadly, the photographs did in fact turn out to be of historical significance, not because of Lee's bungled attempt to kill General Walker but because of his all too successful attempt to murder John F. Kennedy. One of the three received the accolade of becoming a front cover of *Life* magazine, and it has been reprinted countless times in newspapers, magazines, books, and television documentaries. The photograph Marina took that Sunday afternoon has become the enduring universal image of, for some, the assassin of President Kennedy, for others, the helpless patsy caught in the vortex of a dark conspiracy. Whichever it is, one thing is reasonably certain. It is the image by which, more than any other, Lee Harvey Oswald wanted to be remembered, not just by his baby daughter but by the entire world. And that wish came true.

On March 26, Ruth Paine had written Marina to invite the Oswalds to dinner on April 2.[1120] Marina had already been out to Irving with the children, but neither Lee nor Ruth's estranged husband had been at any of the three meetings between the young women.

On the appointed night, Michael Paine drove into Dallas to pick the Oswalds up at Neely Street. Michael, who had a lively interest in things political—though the only arguably political organization he ever belonged to was the American Civil Liberties Union—was intrigued by what Ruth had told him of the Oswalds. Marina was not prepared to go when he got there, and spent a half hour or so packing up the baby's things and getting ready, while Lee sat in the living room with Michael talking politics, occasionally interrupting himself to bark orders in Russian at Marina, though he did nothing to help her. Michael was astonished that he would speak so harshly to his wife, particularly in front of a guest. "Here is a little fellow," Michael thought to himself, "who certainly insists on wearing the pants," and who, by keeping Marina from learning the English language, was intent on "keeping her vassal to him."

Michael noticed that Lee spoke as derisively of the USSR as he did of the United States, and he found that odd for someone who had taken the trouble to go and live there. What really struck Michael about Lee was his deep resentment of the exploitation of workers by their bosses, which occasioned a discourse by Lee on the Marxist theory of surplus value—the notion that profit is generated when employers pay employees less than their labor is really worth in order to profit from the difference—calling this "an unforgivable moral sin." Michael thought that Lee's obvious resentment of employers could scarcely be hidden from his current employer and must cause him problems at his job; he had no idea that Lee had already been given his notice and had only four more days of work.

Michael told the Warren Commission that Oswald felt that "all the working class was exploited, and he also thought they were brainwashed, and . . . thought that churches were all alike . . . they were all apparatus of the power structure to maintain itself in power." When Michael pointed out to Lee that his church was supported by dollars donated by the members themselves, Oswald simply shrugged his shoulders. As far as he was concerned, his views were still valid. According to Michael, Oswald dismissed others' arguments because he saw them as a product of their environment and they didn't know any better. He was in a state of "enlightenment" and knew the truth and therefore those who disagreed with him were just "spouting the line that was fed to [them] by the power structure."[1121]

During dinner in Irving, the conversation moved more slowly, since Michael and Ruth tried to involve Marina, and everything had to be translated. They both noticed that her opinions often differed from his and that he didn't much like that. (Later, Ruth told Michael that Lee had disparaged Marina in Russian, calling her a fool and telling her she didn't know what she was talking about.) In an effort to find more common ground, Michael asked Lee what he thought of Major General Walker, who was still appearing in the newspapers several times a week as his Operation Midnight Ride encountered angry demonstrations across the country. Oswald was oddly noncommittal, although they seemed to share a low opinion of Walker. But only one of them was going to try to murder him in a week or so.[1122]

J ust five days later, Ruth Paine sat down to write Marina a letter, which she had been mulling over ever since the night of the dinner party. She knew that Marina was expecting another child and that Lee was insisting that she return to the Soviet Union. Even worse, Lee would not divorce her, leaving her abandoned in the Soviet Union but not free. Ruth also knew that Marina was very much opposed to leaving the United States, and she was angry that Lee would so cavalierly shrug off his responsibilities to his wife and children. She had talked the matter over with Michael and decided she had to intervene somehow, but she was afraid her Russian was not up to such a serious discussion. She wanted to offer Marina the chance to come live with her in Irving, and she wrote the letter as a way to gather her thoughts and hoped she was expressing them in passable, although halting Russian.[1123]

Dear Marina,
    I want to invite you to move here and live with me both now and later when the baby is born. I don't know how things are for you at home with your husband. I don't know what would be better for you, June and Lee—to live together or apart. It is, of course, your affair, and you have to decide what is better and what you wish to do. But I want to say that you have a choice. When you wish, for days, weeks, months, you could move here. I have already thought about this invitation a lot, it is not a quick thought.
    It seems to me that it would be pleasant and useful for us both to live together. We can easily help one another. When you converse it helps me. If you sometimes correct my mistakes in conversation and letters, I would be very happy. It is so helpful for me that I would consider it proper to buy all which we need from the grocery store: food, soap, etc. Lee would have to give you enough money to pay for clothes and medical expenses. You can get rest here such as you need during pregnancy. During the day it is rather quiet here, but not so quiet as at your place. You and June would be by yourselves in the room which fronts on the street. There you would find privacy. Here, I think, it would not be difficult to learn English. From me and from my children you would learn words. In the course of two weeks you could learn all I know about cooking. I'm bad at housecleaning. Perhaps you could help me with this a bit. I don't want to hurt Lee. Of course I don't know what he wants. Perhaps he feels like Michael, who at one time wants and doesn't want to live with me. You know, you could live here [on Lee's] workdays and return home on weekends. You would only need to carry back and forth clothes, diapers,

etc. The other things necessary for June and you are here all the time: beds, sheets, towels, a high chair for June, etc.

Please think about this invitation and tell me (now or later) what you think. If you are interested in coming here earlier than September or October (about which we have already spoken), I want to write an official letter to you and Lee, and I want him to know all that I have said to you. Where you and June live—that is of course a matter which touches him deeply. Therefore, I want to speak directly with him about it.

She signed the letter "Your Ruth" and then added a postscript: "Do you have the book by Petrov: Self-Teacher in English Language? My neighbor has promised us a bassinette after the birth of the baby."[1124]

It had not been an easy letter to write. It was not an easy letter to send either. In fact, Ruth never mailed it. For the time being she kept it in her purse, thinking she might give it to Marina personally, but she never did. Eventually, she turned it over to the Warren Commission, with the notation "Not sent" on it.[1125]

According to Marina, Lee cleaned his rifle on four or five occasions during the short period between the time he received the rifle in the mail and the attempt on General Walker's life on April 10.[1126] It is not known precisely where or when Oswald practiced shooting the new gun, only that he did it. Marina said she thought Lee had practiced with his rifle "once or twice" before the Walker shooting.[1127] And she told the FBI that Lee, before the shooting, had told her he had been practicing, the implication being that it was more than once.[1128] The Warren Commission never even hazarded a guess as to when and where he might have done so.[1129] So we are left with only one occasion we can rely on since Marina vividly recalls it. And again, we don't know the date except Marina says it was "shortly before" the attempt on Walker's life, which would put it sometime in early April.[1130] Marina recalls that Lee had arrived home from work just as she was taking the baby out for a ride in her stroller. He told her to go ahead and he would catch up to her so they could all walk together. When he caught up though, he was carrying the carbine underneath his green Marine Corps raincoat. He told her he was going to practice with the rifle, which upset her because he had led her to believe that he would accompany them on their walk.

"Instead of coming with us," she complained, "you just go someplace to shoot."

"It's none of your business," he snapped. "I'm going anyway." The bus was coming, and he ran to catch it.

"Don't bother to come home at all," she shouted. "I won't be waiting for you. I hope the police catch you there."[1131]

No one knows exactly where Oswald went, but Trinity River is the most likely place. The river cuts through Dallas from the northwest to the southeast and is bounded by high levees on both sides. Certain stretches of the levees were popular with gun owners for shooting practice, using them as safe backstops for their bullets. The bus that Marina saw Lee get on had a Love Field sign on its front, and at one point she told the Warren Commission that Lee told her when he returned that evening that he had practiced at Love Field,[1132] but at another point in her testimony she was less sure about Love Field.[1133] The FBI checked the whole area out and found that part of the route of the Love Field bus lay along the Trinity River, and Oswald could have gotten off the bus at West Commerce and Beckley and easily gotten down into the sandy riverbed—if there was any water there it would have been restricted to a narrow channel down the middle of the bed. But the FBI could find no area at Love Field itself or immediately adjacent thereto that would have been suitable for rifle practice.[1134]

Lee checked out of work between 5:00 and 5:30 p.m. during the first week of April, his last week of work, and sundown was around 6:45 p.m., so he didn't have too much time to take the bus home, get his rifle, and take the bus to his practice site.[1135] But he didn't have to do much. To "sight in" a rifle all one has to do is fire several rounds to determine how far off the target the bullets are hitting and then adjust the iron or telescopic sight to accommodate for "windage"—horizontal error—and "elevation"—vertical error. Marines were expected to sight in their rifles with just three shots. Oswald also needed some time and a few shots to get a feel for the carbine's bolt action and trigger pull and to get used to the telescopic sight, since there's no evidence he had any experience with that. One of the Marine Corps' top marksmen, Master Sergeant James A. Zahm, told the Warren Commission that an ex-marine like Oswald could easily have done all he needed to do with just ten shots.[1136]

During the last days of March and that first week of April, Marina knew something troubling was on Lee's mind because he talked in his sleep a lot during that time. She had no idea what he said, since he spoke in English, but he seemed so distressed that she felt she had to wake him, sometimes as often as twice a night.[1137]

On Saturday, April 6, Lee's last day on the job at Jaggers, he worked until 5:30, a full day. The only one there who was sorry to see him go was Dennis Ofstein, who had made a special effort to befriend Lee. He didn't know Oswald had been fired until that last day. Oswald was calm enough about it, though rueful. He had liked the work. Ofstein tried to be helpful, named some of the other firms around Dallas that did similar work and suggested that Oswald try to find jobs there. Lee laughed and said if he couldn't find work in Dallas, he could always go back to Russia. Ofstein hoped they might continue to see each other, perhaps socially with their wives, and he got the number of Oswald's post office box. About a week later he wrote to propose that they all get together, on a Saturday evening, but he never got a reply and never saw Oswald again.[1138]

The next day, Sunday, April 7, Oswald left his Neely apartment with his rifle.[1139] No one knows what he did on that day, but what he eventually told Marina is probably true: he told her he went out to Turtle Creek and secreted the rifle in the isolated, wooded area by the railroad tracks he had photographed a month earlier, a spot about a half mile from General Walker's house.[1140] It is equally probable that he spent the rest of the time watching Walker's house and exploring the neighborhood for useful escape routes.

On Monday morning, Lee's first day out of work, he dressed as if for work, left at the usual time, and stayed away all day. He visited the Texas Employment Commission, which had referred him to Jaggers, but this time there were no leads for him.[1141] He came home for supper around six and went out again afterwards—Marina assumed he went to the typing class, not knowing he been dropped from the class because of his poor performance. He came home too early if that was where he really was, but she didn't bother to ask him about it. Nothing else is known about his activities that day, and again it is likely he visited the scene of the crime. If so, he might have seen the hitherto empty Walker residence come back to life, since General Walker returned from Operation Midnight Ride that night, April 8.[1142]

On Tuesday, Lee didn't even pretend to go to work. He told Marina it was a holiday and that he was just going to collect his paycheck, but once again he was gone for the whole day. After supper he walked down the street to buy a newspaper and a Dr. Pepper, then sat out on his porch to drink it. He asked Marina to come out and sit with him, chatted amiably with her about news from their friends in the Soviet Union, and insisted she finish his Dr. Pepper. Marina was struck by his friendly demeanor, not that it was anything special in and of itself, but it was so different from his constant, grinding irritability of the past two months.

The morning of Wednesday, April 10, 1963, Lee seemed pensive and sad. He finally told Marina he had been let go at his job. "I don't know why," he told her tearfully. "I tried. I liked that work so much. But probably the FBI came and asked about me, and the boss just didn't want to keep someone the FBI was interested in. When will they leave me alone?"

When he went out later,* he dressed in his gray suit and Marina assumed he would be looking for work.[1143]

Lee did not come home for supper. At seven Marina cooked something for herself, and then spent an hour or so putting June to bed. By nine o'clock, she began to worry, even though in the past two months she had become used to his unexplained absences. She was aware that Lee was not a social butterfly nor, because he seldom drank, likely to be spending his evenings in a bar somewhere. Then, too, he had been so tense in the past weeks, plagued by bad dreams, restlessness, and a shorter temper than usual. And he was preoccupied. She knew that the loss of his job had been a blow, one that could set a match to the powder keg. Worried, unable to relax, she prowled the apartment.

It was around ten o'clock when she opened the door to Lee's tiny study. Lying on his desk was a letter handwritten by Lee to her in Russian, with a key on top of it. It read (translated into English without Oswald's dyslexia):

1. Here is the key to the post office box which is located in the main post office downtown on Ervay Street, the street where there is a drugstore where you always used to stand. The post office is four blocks from the drugstore on the same street. There you will find our mailbox. I paid for the mailbox last month so you needn't worry about it.
2. Send information about what has happened to me to the Embassy [the Soviet Embassy in Washington] and also send newspaper clippings (if there's anything about me in the papers). I think the Embassy will come quickly to your aid once they know everything.
3. I paid our rent on the second so don't worry about it.
4. I have also paid for the water and gas.
5. There may be some money from work. They will send it to our post office box. Go to the bank and they will cash it.
6. You can either throw out my clothing or give it away. *Do not keep it*. As for my personal papers (both military papers and papers from the factory), I prefer that you keep them.

---

*The April 8, 1963, edition of the *Militant* to which Oswald subscribed carried a story datelined Denver, March 27, and headlined "United Picket Line in Denver Greets 'Night Riding' Walker" and mentioned that Walker had challenged President Kennedy to drop the Eighty-second Airborne Division on Cuba and get rid of Fidel Castro (Newman, *Assassination of John F. Kennedy*, p.342). It cannot be known whether Oswald got his copy of the edition on April 9, or before he left to shoot Walker on April 10, or sometime thereafter.

7. Certain of my papers are in the small blue suitcase.
8. My address book is on the table in my study if you need it.
9. We have *friends* here and the *Red Cross* will also help you.
10. I left you as much money as I could, $60 on the second of the month, and you and Junie can live on $10 a week.
11. If I am alive and taken prisoner, the city jail is at the end of the bridge we always used to cross when we went to town. (the very beginning of town, after the bridge.)[1144]

It was eleven-thirty when Lee finally returned home. Marina immediately showed him the note and asked, "What is the meaning of this?"

He was in something of a panic, sweating, out of breath. "I shot Walker," he gasped.

"Did you kill him?" Marina asked.

"I don't know."

"My God. The police will be here any minute," Marina exclaimed. "What did you do with the rifle?"

"Buried it."

Marina was appalled, very frightened, and started to tremble, sure that the police would turn up to lay hands on her husband at any moment. Lee turned on the radio to see if the killing was reported in the late news. It wasn't. He finally undressed and threw himself down on the bed, where he fell asleep immediately. He slept the whole night through.

Marina could not. She lay awake, in panic, wondering what on earth she could do. Under Soviet law she had a duty to inform the police immediately—in fact, if witnesses didn't, that made them accomplices to the crime. She had no way of knowing that the criminal justice system in America was different, so different, in fact, that Lee could prevent her from even testifying against him because he was her husband. She was terrified. She did not know what to do. She did nothing.[1145]

At nine o'clock on the night of April 10, 1963, General Walker was seated at his desk in the rear of his residence bending over his 1962 income tax return, due in just five days. Most of the lights in the house were on, although he was alone, as he was most nights—unlike the daytime, when the rented house was often full of political aides and colleagues. The shades were up, windows closed—that afternoon the temperature had broken all records for April 10, ninety-nine degrees, and Walker had the air-conditioning on. Suddenly, he was startled by a blast and sharp crack right over his head to the left of where he was sitting. At first he thought one of the neighborhood kids had tossed a firecracker through the window. They often played in the alley out there and in the parking lot of the Mormon Church next door, but he immediately saw that the window screens were intact. Puzzled, he got up, walked around his desk, and looked back at where he had been sitting. There was a bullet hole in the wall not more than three or four inches from where his head had been. He dashed upstairs to get his pistol.

As he ran back down the stairs at the front of the house, he caught a glimpse through a rear window of a car leaving the driveway of the church and turning left onto Turtle Creek Boulevard. All he really saw were the taillights. It was dark and his view was blocked by the branches of a tree. It could have been a getaway car—the timing was about right, as the alley that ran behind his house turned into the parking lot behind the church and continued between his house and the church until it reached the boulevard.

Pistol in hand, he went out the back door to see what was going on. Halfway to the alley he turned back and eventually saw that one of the windows of his study was shattered. Somebody had fired at him in the dark from a position to the rear of the house toward the alley. He realized that his right forearm was bleeding from a few slivers of the bullet's jacket. Later, others would notice plaster debris from the wall in his hair.[1146]

Walker called the police, who turned up shortly in force, a couple of patrolmen followed by a couple of detectives. Two of the officers checked the room on the other side of the wall the bullet had gone through, which was stacked high with pamphlets and literature that Walker used in his political campaigns. Rummaging through the papers, they quickly found a "mushroomed bullet" lying on top of one of the stacks of literature near the hole in the wall.[1147]

The double-window through which the bullet had been fired had a wooden frame running horizontally in the middle of it. The police saw that the bullet had struck the "upper portion" of the "window frame near the center locking device" as it smashed through both the screen and the window, thus deflecting the bullet just enough to save the general's life. The projectile's contact with the window frame had stripped away part of its metal jacket, accounting for the splinters of metal in Walker's arm. When the Dallas detectives went outside to line up the bullet hole in the wall with the damage to the window, the line led to the back fence on the alley. It was latticed, with large, square holes. They even found a "fresh chip" in the wood on the top part of the fence. In lining up the path of the bullet, they concluded that the bullet was fired "from just below the chipped portion of the fence," the rifleman resting his weapon in the latticework opening below the top of the fence. It was amazing that he had missed his target, not more than forty yards away. Walker, motionless, thoroughly engrossed in his tax return, had been a sitting duck. The sniper, Walker thought, must have been a lousy shot, and one of the policemen said, in awe, "He couldn't have missed you!" That sounded all right to Walker then, but, as he mulled it over later, he realized that the glare of light from the room would have blurred the horizontal frame of the window, making it all but invisible to the shooter (particularly if he was using a telescopic sight, which would have been focused well beyond the window itself). The shooter might well have been a very good shot indeed, Walker thought, just very unlucky because of the confluence of circumstances.[1148]

The next morning, when Marina woke up, Lee was listening to the radio. "I missed," he told her angrily. He was sure he had taken very good aim, and kept repeating, "It was such an easy shot," but they were saying that Walker was uninjured. Marina was hugely relieved. He went out and came back a few minutes later with the morning paper, which carried front-page accounts of the incident. He had a good laugh over the fact that the police had misidentified the smashed bullet. "They say I had a .30 caliber bullet when I didn't at all," he told Marina. "They got the bullet and the rifle all wrong . . . What fools." The papers also reported that a fourteen-year-old neighbor of Walker's, Walter Kirk Coleman, rushed outside at the sound of the shot and saw two cars, one with one man in it, the other with several, speed away from the church parking lot nearby.* "Americans are

_____
*Coleman lived in the house on the other side of the church parking lot and apparently was the only witness to have heard the sound of the rifle shot, though he originally thought it was a car backfire. Coleman told

so spoiled," Oswald sneered, "they always think you have a car. It never occurs to them that you might use your own two legs."[1149] Lee was unusually forthcoming with Marina about what he had done and how he had done it. He told her he hadn't waited to see whether his shot struck home but had taken off running. He said that "several kilometers away" he got on a bus, and indicated that he later got off the bus to hide the weapon, either in the bushes or in the ground, she does not recall which.[1150] He also told her he had gone to Walker's residence at some earlier time to shoot him but had returned. "I don't know why," she told the Warren Commission, but suggested Lee had told her that on the evening he did shoot at Walker, there were church services nearby and "there were many people there, and it was easier to merge in the crowd and not be noticed," the inference being that on the earlier occasion he had noticed a sign saying that the church had services on Wednesday evening.[1151]

Marina finally got around to asking Lee the question that had troubled her as soon as she heard Walker's name. Just who was Walker and why would Lee want to kill him? "He's a very bad man," Lee said, "the leader of a fascist organization." Marina told him he still had no right to try to kill him, but when he responded that "many lives" could have been saved if someone had killed Hitler earlier, she didn't have a response. Lee told her he had been planning to kill Walker "for two months."[1152]

Marina was outraged at what Lee had done and threatened him by telling him she intended to keep the letter he had left behind for her on the night he went to kill Walker, which was obviously a very incriminating farewell letter, and if he ever did something "crazy" like this again, she would go to the police and "have the proof in the form" of his letter. She told him that "it was fated that Walker not be killed," and therefore, he should never "try such a thing again." He promised her he would not do something like this again.[1153]

On April 13, three days after the bungled shooting,* Marina saw Oswald thumbing through the blue looseleaf notebook she had seen before. This time she asked him what it was. "My plan," he told her, handing it to her. It contained all the details—maps, photographs, sketches, bus schedules, pages of notes, some typed, some handwritten, all in English and unintelligible to Marina—of his effort to kill Walker. The snapshots were of Walker's house. Marina asked him what he meant to do with this book. "Save it as a keepsake," he told her. "I'll hide it somewhere."

"Some keepsake! It's evidence! For God's sake Alka, destroy it."[1154]

---

the FBI that he ran out to his backyard, stepped up on a bicycle, and looked into the floodlit church parking lot, where he saw about eight cars parked and a man hurrying to one of them, a white or beige 1950 Ford, with its headlights on and its motor running. The man was a white male, nineteen to twenty years old, about five feet ten inches tall and weighing around 130 pounds, "real skinny," and had dark bushy hair, a thin face, and a large nose. A second man was walking to a 1958 black-over-white Chevrolet sedan. This man, also a white male, was around six feet one inch tall and weighed about 200 pounds. The first man got into the Ford and drove out of the lot, he said, at a "normal rate of speed" to Turtle Creek Boulevard—this is probably the car Walker saw as he came down the stairs with his pistol. The second man went to the Chevy, pushed the driver's seat forward, and leaned into the backseat. At that point Coleman went back into the house and saw no more. (CE 2958, 26 H 437–438, FBI interview of Walter Coleman on June 3, 1964; position of cars in lot: CE 953-B, C, D, 23 H 773–775)

*Marina told her biographer, Priscilla McMillan, that the incident took place on Thursday morning, April 11, the day after the attempt on Walker's life (McMillan, *Marina and Lee*, pp.356–358). However, earlier, on July 24, 1964, just eight months after the event, Marina clearly told the Warren Commission that this incident took place "three days after this [attempt on Walker] happened." Question: "Three days after he shot at General Walker you saw him destroy the [notebook], is that correct?" "Yes." (11 H 292)

He seemed reluctant to do so, but some moments later she found him setting fire to the pages he had written and dropping them one by one into the toilet.[1155] He destroyed most of the evidence that tied him to the Walker shooting—notes, sketches, and bus schedules—but he saved the pages containing his political philosophy. And, as we know, several photographs he had taken of Walker's home also survived the burning, as did a piece of evidence that more than anything else tied him to the crime—the handwritten note in Russian he left for Marina in case he did not come home that night.

So deeply shocked was Marina by her husband's crime and what she imagined to be her shared complicity—according to her understanding of Soviet law—that she told no one about it, not even after the murders of President Kennedy and Officer Tippit and Lee's own death at the hands of Jack Ruby. She had kept the letter Lee had left for her on the night he went out to shoot Walker as a means of forcing him to behave, but it was not found in the searches of the Oswalds' possessions at Ruth Paine's house. Several of Lee's surveillance photographs of Walker's place and its environs, which he had made prints of at Jaggers, were found, but the searchers who found them had no idea of their significance. And they overlooked the two Russian books Marina had left in Ruth Paine's kitchen, a cookbook and a book on child care. Ruth noticed them about a week after the police had carted everything away and turned them over to the Irving Police Department to be delivered to Marina. But the police instead turned the books over to the Secret Service on December 2, 1963, and Lee's letter of instructions to Marina was found in one of the books, a cookbook titled *Book of Helpful Instructions*.[1156]

Since we know that Oswald attempted to murder General Walker because he confessed to his own wife that he did, nothing further is required to make the point. But in addition to his letter of instructions to Marina, which has survived, and has been confirmed to be in Oswald's handwriting,[1157] as well as the photos Oswald took of Walker's residence, there is some other independent evidence, though not conclusive by itself, connecting Oswald to the attempted murder of Walker.

The Dallas police took the slug found at the Walker residence to the Dallas City-County Investigation Laboratory at Parkland Hospital on April 25, 1963, to see if lab technicians could determine the type of gun from which it was fired. Within a few days the lab reported back that it could not do so "because of the battered condition of the bullet."[1158] On November 30, 1963, the FBI, thinking there possibly could be a connection between the Kennedy assassination and the Walker shooting, requested the bullet from the Dallas Police Department for examination,[1159] and the local office of the FBI sent the slug by registered mail to the FBI lab in Washington, D.C., on December 2, 1963.[1160]

Robert Frazier, the FBI firearms expert, testified before the Warren Commission that because of the mutilated condition of the Walker bullet, he was "unable to reach a conclusion" as to whether or not the bullet was fired from Oswald's Carcano rifle, the one he determined was the weapon that killed President Kennedy. However, he said that "the general rifling characteristics of the rifle 139 [Commission Exhibit No. 139, Oswald's Carcano] are of the same type as those found on the bullet, [Commission] Exhibit [No.] 573 [Walker slug]," and therefore, at least on this basis, "the bullet could have been fired from the rifle." The general rifling characteristics on the Walker bullet and the barrel of the Carcano were "four lands and grooves" with a "right" twist. Frazier said the Walker bullet was fired from a Mannlicher-Carcano rifle or one with similar barrel characteristics. Frazier also said the "remaining physical characteristics of this bullet, 573, are the same as Western [Cartridge Company] 6.5mm Mannlicher-Carcano bullets . . . made for this rifle, 139."*

Although the bullet was too damaged to find the essential "microscopic characteristics" (markings) to match up with the barrel of Oswald's Carcano that would enable Frazier to connect the Walker bullet to the Carcano to the exclusion of all other weapons, importantly, Frazier said he found *no* microscopic characteristics on the bullet that would indicate it was *not* fired from the Carcano.[1161]

Joseph D. Nicol, the superintendent of the Illinois Bureau of Criminal Identification and Investigation, conducted an independent examination of the Walker bullet for the Warren Commission, and went a small step further than the FBI, concluding that he found sufficient markings on the Walker bullet as compared to those test-fired from Oswald's Carcano to say "that there is a fair probability" that the Walker bullet was fired from Oswald's Carcano. However, he did not find enough to make "a positive finding."[1162]

Even before the attempt on Walker's life, we knew that Oswald was a severely disturbed and dysfunctional human being. With the attempt, we now also know that he was capable of murdering a fellow human being—indeed, didn't mind doing so, was even excited by it.

On Friday, April 12, 1963, the *Dallas Morning News* reported that Walker's home was under close police surveillance and corrected what it had printed the previous day that "a slight movement by Walker apparently saved his life." It now reported correctly that the bullet had been deflected by the window frame. "If it hadn't hit that," Dallas chief of police Jesse E. Curry said, "it would have hit him right in the head." Oswald undoubtedly read the paper and also learned, to his relief, that the police had no clues to the identity of the shooter.[1163] Even so, he did not dare go out to recover the carbine from its hiding place.

That afternoon Oswald again dressed in his best suit and went downtown to the Texas Employment Commission. They still had nothing for him.[1164] He also filed a claim for unemployment compensation, giving his occupation as "photographer" and describing his departure from Jaggers as a layoff due to lack of work.[1165]

Sometime the following day, Saturday, April 13, which was the day before Easter, Lee went out and retrieved his rifle from its hiding place and brought it back to his apartment. That evening brought a surprise visit: George de Mohrenschildt, just back from a trip to New York, came bouncing in with Jeanne. They had come to visit Lee and Marina with a "big pink rabbit for the baby" for Easter. Lee and Marina went downstairs to greet and open the door for the de Mohrenschildts. George was in high spirits.

"Hey, Lee!" he bawled as soon as he walked in the door. "How is it possible that you missed?"

Lee and Marina, following their guests up the stairs, looked at each other, stunned. How on earth did the de Mohrenschildts know that Lee had taken the shot at Walker? Lee, of course, thought that Marina must have told them; Marina thought it must have

---

*When Dr. Vincent Guinn made his neutron activation analysis of the bullet for the HSCA, he determined that it was "extremely likely" that the Walker bullet was a Mannlicher-Carcano bullet manufactured by the Western Cartridge Company, the same as the ammunition used in the Kennedy assassination (1 HSCA 502, HSCA testimony of Dr. Guinn on September 8, 1978). The Dallas Police Department's "General Offense Report" on April 10, 1963, its first report on the Walker shooting, described the bullet as a "steel-jacketed bullet" (CE 2001, 24 H 39), whereas the 6.5-millimeter Mannlicher-Carcano bullets were copper-jacketed. Frazier told the Warren Commission that "some individuals commonly refer to rifle bullets as steel-jacketed bullets, when they actually in fact just have a copper alloy jacket" (3 H 439).

been Lee. They were speechless. Actually, George was just being George, not truly serious, but since what he said was so true, Lee and Marina were convinced he knew. Lee managed to change the subject.[1166] "Shhh," Lee said to everyone, "Junie's sleeping."

Jeanne spoke to her husband. "You always forget the baby. Let's go out on the balcony." The Oswalds readily agreed to that—it was dark out there and no one could see their faces. Lee scurried about getting them all chairs, making coffee, and trying to avoid getting into a conversation with George about the Walker shooting. When George started talking about it, Lee never said a word, finally dismissing the subject with an offhand, "Oh, yes, wouldn't it be fascinating to know who did it and why and how?"[1167] George, in any case, had a more interesting topic of conversation—himself. While Marina and Jeanne left so Marina could show Jeanne the apartment, George proceeded to tell Lee how really excited he was about the business deal he had finally clinched during his trip to New York. The complicated venture would take him to Haiti within a few weeks and possibly make him the fortune that had been as elusive as mercury to him all of his life. He had been working on the deal ever since the Oswalds first met him and even before. In some ways his interest in Haiti started in 1947 when he first visited the country as a tourist, and was reanimated in 1956 when he worked there on an oil exploration project that eventually fell through. He had devoted the past two years to the organization of his present project, which involved a $300,000 two-year contract between his company and the government of Haiti to carry out a magnetic survey of oil and other mineral deposits on the island.[1168]

When Marina opened the door to a room of the apartment (Lee's office) that looked more like a "closet" to Jeanne, Jeanne immediately saw Lee's rifle in full view standing against the wall. Surprised, she asked Marina "what on earth" Lee was doing with a rifle, and Marina, at a loss for words, came up with a story about Lee going to the park and shooting at the leaves.[1169]

Jeanne called out to George, "Look, George, they have a gun here." George didn't enter the small room (with Marina and Jeanne already in the closet-sized room, from my recollection it would have been difficult for him to do so even if he had tried), but heard Marina say, "That crazy idiot is target shooting all the time." When George asked Lee why he did that, Lee merely parroted Marina, "I go out and do target shooting. I like target shooting."[1170]

Enough had happened for both couples to be uncomfortable and the de Mohrenschildts left very soon thereafter.[1171]

As soon as they were gone, Lee rounded on Marina, "Did you telephone them and tell them it was me?"

"Of course not," Marina said, "I thought you did."

"You're out of your mind," he said. "But isn't it amazing how he guessed? It's a lucky thing he couldn't see my face. I was hardly able to speak. Maybe he was only kidding, but he sure hit the nail on the head."[1172]

That night Lee again had some sort of anxiety attack in his sleep. This time he broke out in violent trembling from head to toe fours times at half-hour intervals, although he never woke up. He was still frightened the following day, and that night he again slept the sleep of the damned, shaking all over.[1173]

Although no one could know it at the time, it would be the last the two couples would ever see each other. A few days later the de Mohrenschildts left on a trip to New York, Washington, and Philadelphia. They did not return until six weeks later, at the end of May, by which time the Oswalds had already moved to New Orleans. The de Mohrenschildts were preoccupied by the necessity of shipping some of their belongings to Haiti and putting the rest in storage in Dallas. Jeanne recalled getting a card from New Orleans with the Oswalds' new address, but she misplaced it. A larger package that Lee sent escaped their notice altogether. It just got dumped into storage with everything else.[1174]

Four years later, after the de Mohrenschildts returned from Haiti to Dallas and recovered the things they had put into storage, they found the package, which contained some English language records they had lent to Marina and a photograph neither recalled having seen before. It was one of the famous backyard snapshots taken by Marina showing Lee with pistol and carbine, brandishing copies of the *Militant* and the *Worker*. On the back were the words, written in Russian and in apparently two different handwritings, "Hunter of Fascists, ha, ha, ha" and "To my friend George from Lee Oswald." It was dated "5/IV/63" a typical Russian way of designating April 5, 1963.[1175] Only the words "To my friend George from Lee Oswald" were proved to be written by Oswald.[1176]

In the week following Easter, Marina and Lee had begun to talk about moving to New Orleans, where Lee still had family, the Murrets. Marina, fearing that Lee, despite his word to her, would try to shoot Walker again, had pleaded with him to get rid of the rifle, but he had not done so.[1177] So now she encouraged Lee to move to New Orleans. If she couldn't get the rifle away from Lee, she might at least be able to get Lee away from the target. There seemed to be no jobs in Dallas anyway, and his luck might be better in the city of his birth. She told him she wanted to see his hometown.[1178] Sometime in that week Lee received a letter from the Texas Employment Commission denying his claim for unemployment benefits on the grounds that he had insufficient employment credits. That was a mistake—the Commission had credited him only for his work at Leslie Welding because Jaggers-Chiles-Stovall had been reporting his income under an incorrect Social Security number—but the time it would take to set that right made Lee's predicament worse.[1179]

Another letter brought more bad news—for Lee if not for Marina. The Russian embassy replied to her letter of March 17 by telling her that "it would be desirable" if she could visit the consulate section in person. "If it is difficult for you to come to Washington at the present time," wrote Comrade Reznichenko, "we request you to give us [the] reasons which made you start proceedings for permission to enter the Soviet Union for permanent residence."[1180] Marina's government was not going to allow her to return as easily as Lee had hoped.

On Friday, April 19, the Fair Play for Cuba Committee in New York sent fifty more copies of Corliss Lamont's pamphlet *The Crime against Cuba* to Lee's Dallas post office box.[1181]

On Saturday, Ruth Paine brought her kids into Dallas for a picnic with the Oswalds in the small park near Neely Street, where Lee spent the whole time fishing in its tiny lake. Ruth was struck by his absolute refusal to be sociable—the best he could manage was to come to eat when it was time—but Ruth knew it was not a happy period for the Oswalds.[1182]

The next day, Sunday, April 21, 1963, Lee set out, at least ostensibly, to murder former vice president Richard M. Nixon.

That Sunday morning, Lee's copy of the *Dallas Morning News* carried a front-page banner headline: "Nixon Calls for a Decision to Force Reds out of Cuba." The subheadline read, "Open U.S. Support of Rebels Urged." The story reported Nixon's speech in Washington, D.C., on Saturday to the American Society of Newspaper Editors in which he had flayed Kennedy for curbing the Cuban exile raids against Cuba and also declared, to thundering applause, "The United States cannot tolerate the continued existence of a Soviet military and subversive base 90 miles from our shores."[1183]

Shortly after reading the Sunday paper, Lee dressed in a suit and started to go out. His pistol was at his waist. Marina asked him where he was going.

"Nixon is coming," he said. "I want to go and have a look."

Marina did not know who Nixon was but that was irrelevant to her. "I know how you look," she said sarcastically, adding that he had promised her never to go out and repeat what he had done with General Walker, but Lee merely said, "I'm going to go out and find out if there will be an appropriate opportunity and if there is I will use the pistol."[1184] Furious, Marina was determined to stop him. Thinking quickly, she went into the bathroom and told Lee to come in there with her, which he did. Once both were inside, she immediately jumped outside the door, closing it as she left. The door could only be locked from the inside, but Marina used all the frantic power she could muster to keep him inside, bracing her feet against the nearby opposite wall, as he pushed from the inside to get out.

"Let me out," Lee yelled. "Open the door."

But Marina kept pushing against the door, crying out that he had gone back on his word to her and all of this could cause her to lose their baby, and he would have thus killed his own child.[1185]

Marina told the Warren Commission, "I remember that I held him. We actually struggled for several minutes and then he quieted down. I remember that I told him that if he goes out it would be better for him to kill me than go out." Warren Commission counsel wondered how the five-foot two-inch, hundred-pound Marina would be strong enough to keep her husband inside the bathroom. She had an answer. Number one, she said, Lee "is not strong." (George de Mohrenschildt told the Commission, "He was small, you know, and he was a rather puny individual." Oswald was five feet nine inches tall, and weighed around 140 to 150 pounds.) Secondly, she said—I'm sure to the obvious delight of her questioner, Allen Dulles—"When I want to and when I collect all my forces and want to do something very badly I am stronger than he is." Dulles asked her if she meant "mentally or physically," and Marina eventually had to acknowledge that "I don't think it was physically, physical prevention because if he—I couldn't keep him from going out if he really wanted to* . . . Possibly he didn't want to go out at all but was just doing this all as a sort of joke, not really as a joke but rather to wound me, to make me feel bad . . . My husband had a sadistic streak in him and he got pleasure out of harming people."[1186]

In any event, when Lee gave up the struggle, Marina, trembling all over, demanded Lee's gun, which he gave her, and then instructed him to take off all his clothes, which he also did, down to his T-shirt and shorts. "If you're going to keep me here all day," he

---

*Not only could the bathroom door be locked only from the inside, but also critics point out that most bathroom doors open inward. If this one did (as of September 22, 2004, when I visited the apartment, the door did, but it is unknown whether this was the same door that was on the hinges forty-one years earlier), and Marina was pushing forward, as she said she was, unless Oswald got so caught up in the moment that he forgot to turn the knob (in which case there wouldn't have even been a struggle), she would only be pushing the door open, not keeping it closed. Hence, the critics question Marina's story about the entire incident (e.g., Summers, *Not in Your Lifetime*, p.124).

said, "at least give me something to read." She fetched one of his books for him and he sat on the toilet seat for two or three hours before he came out, neither exchanging a word with each other until supper.[1187]

The purpose of this Oswaldian Theater of the Absurd cannot be known for sure, but Marina may have been correct in deducing that it possibly was staged entirely for her benefit. The FBI checked all editions of the *Dallas Morning News* and *Dallas Times Herald* between March 16 and May 15, 1963, and neither paper mentioned any visit or proposed visit by Nixon between these times.[1188]

Also, Nixon himself said the only time he came to Dallas in 1963 was in November,[1189] and Lee told Marina the next day that Nixon had not come to Dallas.[1190] So Nixon was not in Dallas on Sunday, April 21, 1963.

Another vice president did visit the city, though, two days later, on Tuesday, April 23—Lyndon Baines Johnson. That visit had been well publicized all through April.[1191] The FBI suggested that Marina had confused Nixon with Johnson, but she was sure that "in this incident it was a question of Mr. Nixon." She told the Warren Commission, "I remember distinctly the name Nixon."[1192]

Marina's interpretation of the incident—that he was only trying to hurt her—is supported by the fact that even if, because of his dyslexia, it was he, not she, who confused Nixon with Johnson (not overly difficult to imagine since Johnson was the "vice president" and Nixon was the former "vice president"), as indicated, Johnson's scheduled visit was listed for April 23, not April 21. So why was Oswald going out the door on April 21? And Marina also noted that it "was rather unusual" for Lee to have given up so quickly with her.[1193]

On Wednesday, April 24, Ruth Paine dropped in for a prearranged visit with Marina and was surprised to find Lee preparing to leave for New Orleans. In fact, he was fully packed and evidently waiting for Ruth—he asked her if she would take all of his suitcases to the bus station. Marina rode with them to the station, where Lee bought a ticket not only for himself but for Marina too, which she was to use as soon as she heard from him that he found a job. Ruth had a better idea: if Marina and June came to stay with her, instead of waiting at Neely Street, Lee could reach Marina more quickly by phone (the Oswalds had no phone at Neely), and then Ruth would drive Marina and June down to New Orleans in her car. Ruth knew that a twelve- or thirteen-hour bus trip with a baby in the gathering heat and humidity of May, and having to transport all the baby's gear and more, would not be a pleasant experience for a four-month-pregnant woman.

For once Oswald did not disdain the proffered help. He cashed in the extra bus ticket and gave Marina some of the money. Since his bus did not leave until that evening, they all went, after he had checked in his baggage, back to Neely Street. He had taken virtually all of their things, leaving behind only what Marina and the baby would need for a brief period, such as the crib, playpen, stroller, some dishes, and some clothing, and he loaded all that into Ruth's car. About four that afternoon, Ruth drove Marina and June back to Ruth's home in Irving, leaving Oswald alone at the apartment.[1194]

Around three weeks later, FBI agent Jim Hosty decided he had given the Oswalds enough time to cool off, so Hosty drove over to Neely Street to interview them. This time they had disappeared without a trace. Neither the INS nor the post office had an address for them. Hosty wrote up a report but he wasn't too concerned—he was sure they would turn up somewhere before long. He had other more pressing matters on his mind anyway. He was investigating former major general Edwin Walker. Even though the case against Walker for his involvement in the riot at the University of Mississippi had been dismissed by the court back in January, the bureau saw that Walker's group was clearly a militant right-wing organization that had to be investigated, and it had put Hosty under intense pressure about it. In fact, he had made it his top priority. As far as he was concerned, the problem of locating the Oswalds could be put on the back burner for awhile.[1195]

Lee rang his Aunt Lillian Murret, his mother's sister, from the bus station in New Orleans on Thursday, April 25. He didn't know how he would be received, since the conservative Catholic Murrets had never replied to the one letter he had written them from the Soviet Union. He needn't have worried. Lillian was glad to hear from him again. He told her that he was married and had a baby daughter, which she didn't know. She was taken aback at the prospect of putting up his whole family, but he was alone for the time being, and Lillian, as kind as ever, welcomed him to their house at 757 French Street, where he could stay until he found work. He came out right away on the streetcar and arrived with just one small bag. That evening, Lillian had her husband Dutz drive Lee back to the bus station to pick up the rest of his things, which Lee stored in their garage.[1196]

Lee wrote a postcard to Marina at the Paine residence: "All is well. I am living with Aunt Lillian. She has very kindly taken us in. I am now looking for work. When I find it I will write you."[1197]

On Friday, the day after his arrival, he registered at the Louisiana Division of Employment Security, seeking work as a commercial photographer, shipping clerk, or darkroom man.[1198] After the weekend he went back to file a request for reconsideration of the ruling by the Texas Employment Commission denying his claim for unemployment benefits.[1199] On May 3, he wrote another postcard, this one to the "Girls" (Marina and June), saying he had not yet found work, but "Uncle [Dutz]" had offered him "a loan of two hundred dollars if needed. Great, eh?"[1200]

On May 8, his request was ruled valid and he was granted maximum benefits of $369, payable at the rate of $33 per week.[1201]

Life with the Murrets was peaceful and pleasant. The Louisiana Division of Employment gave Oswald some referrals, but primarily he sought jobs on his own. Every morning he checked the small employment ads in the New Orleans *Times-Picayune* and then went out, newspaper in hand, and applied for jobs until the end of the workday.[1202] After supper, he would watch television with the Murrets for a while and then retire early.[1203] Only two of his five cousins were living at home—John, the youngest, and Marilyn. John, or "Bogie," was four years older than Lee. The Murret's other daughter, Joyce, was married and living in Beaumont, Texas; another son, Eugene, was studying for the priesthood in Mobile, Alabama; and a third son, Charles, was a dentist in the New Orleans suburb of Chalmette.

John had trained to be a high school teacher and played professional basketball but was now working as a salesman for E. R. Squibb and Company. Lee's cousin Marilyn was thirty-five, a graduate of Tulane and a teacher, and somewhat of a kindred spirit to Lee insofar as travel and adventure were concerned—she had spent three and a half years traveling on tramp steamers and teaching in Australia, New Zealand, and Japan.[1204] One evening Marilyn tried to engage Lee on the subject of religion—Marilyn was a practicing Catholic—but Lee announced he was an atheist and otherwise avoided the discussion.[1205] The Murrets were all distressed by Lee's lack of suitable clothes, but Lee refused his aunt's offer to buy him new things.[1206] He wore his heavy woolen Russian suit on his first visit to the unemployment office,[1207] which was clearly impractical in sultry New Orleans. Eventually, John almost bullied him into accepting a short-sleeve white shirt, which John claimed was too small for himself, and a tie, insisting Lee take them to help him get a job.[1208]

On the first Sunday Lee spent with the Murrets, he suddenly showed an interest in his family, asking Lillian if she knew anything about the Oswalds. She didn't. She had known only his father and had met one of his uncles one time. "Well, you know," he said to her, "you are the only relative I know." That Sunday he took the Lakeview streetcar, which ran past the Murrets' home, to the end of the line, where there's a cemetery. A cemetery worker helped Lee locate his father's grave. He also called all of the Oswalds in the New Orleans phone book and managed to locate an elderly aunt, Hazel Oswald, the widow of his father's brother, William Stout Oswald. Lee paid her a visit out in Metairie. She had never met Lee and she had last seen Marguerite in New Orleans when Lee was about fourteen. She had had no idea what had become of Marguerite and her three boys, although she had seen something in the papers about Lee's defection to Russia. Lee said he wanted to visit and obtain some information about his father's relatives. They talked about the family, including Lee's grandfather, Harvey Oswald, and Hazel gave Lee a large picture of his father. She told Lee she had a son and grandson in New Orleans. Lee thought Hazel was "very nice," though he winced when he showed her a photograph of Marina and she asked, "Is she Russian?" Hazel said she hoped Lee would drop by again, but she never heard from him.[1209]* The photo of Lee's father eventually disappeared—it was not found among his possessions after his death.

On May 9, two weeks after his arrival in New Orleans, his job seeking paid off: he was taken on at William B. Reily and Company Inc. (a coffee company) at 640 Magazine Street as a sort of general laborer, cleaning and oiling the heavy equipment used in the grinding, canning, bagging, and sale of coffee, and started to work the next day, May 10. On his application he had listed as references, in addition to John Murret, "Sgt. Robert Hidell" (a composite of his brother Robert and his own alias, Hidell) and "Lieut. J. Evans," the surname and initial of the husband of Myrtle Evans, Marguerite's old friend.[1210] His pay was to be sixty dollars a week, about what he had made at Leslie Welding and Jaggers-Chiles-Stovall.

"I got it, I got it," he exclaimed happily as he got back to the Murrets' residence.

"Well, Lee, how much does it pay?" Lillian asked.

"It don't pay very much," he told Lillian, as he hugged and kissed her, "but I will get along on it."[1211]

On May 9, the day before he started work, Lee went to the apartment of his mother's old friend Myrtle Evans, who had known him as both a child and a willful teenager. Lee rang the doorbell and Myrtle's husband answered the door. Lee said he wanted to rent an apartment. Myrtle told him she didn't have any apartments in the building but she was fixing up another building and she might be able to find something suitable for him.

---

*In addition to the Murrets, who were Lee's relatives on his mother's side, Lee had many other aunts and cousins in the New Orleans area, all on his father's side. But other than Aunt Hazel, all of them told the FBI they had never met him and could furnish no information concerning him. (CD 107, pp.14–16, January 13, 1964)

He told her he had a wife and child in Texas and that he was going to bring them over as soon as he could find an apartment.

"I want something right away," he told her.

It wasn't until they were walking down her steps that she took a hard look at him and asked, "I know you, don't I?"

"Sure," he said. "I'm Lee Oswald. I was just waiting to see when you were going to recognize me."

She was surprised. She thought he was still in Russia. She wanted to be helpful, and she called a friend who had a place to rent, but it was too small and had no laundry facilities. Myrtle suggested they drive around the area and look for signs. They drove up and down Baronne and Napoleon, Louisiana Avenue, Carondelet, and finally down Magazine Street. Since the Reily coffee company was on Magazine, Myrtle said, "You might as well get as close to your work as possible."

They spotted a sign at 4907, pulled up around the corner, and went to have a look. There were two apartments available. Lee liked the one that had a large living room, a screened-in front porch, and a long yard. He also liked the "Page fence," a metal lattice-work fence characteristic of New Orleans that would easily keep little Junie in the yard. Myrtle thought it was all right and very good for the money.

The caretakers, a cabdriver named Jesse Garner and his wife, Lena, lived in the rear on the other side of the house, at 4911 Magazine. Lee paid Mrs. Garner the monthly rent of sixty-five dollars and a five-dollar deposit so the electricity and lights could be turned on right away. This made Lee a little short on money, and he would borrow a few dollars from Dutz around this time, which he repaid when he got his first check from his job.

Lee and Myrtle drove back to her place, where she fixed a lunch of ham sandwiches and Cokes and they spent a while chatting. Lee was happy. "I have wanted to move back to New Orleans," he told her. "New Orleans is my home . . . I felt like I just wanted to come back. You know, I like the old high ceilings and the trees and the French Quarter, and everything in New Orleans."[1212]

Later that day, Lee telephoned Marina at Ruth Paine's and asked her to come to New Orleans. Marina was ecstatic, crooning over and over to baby June, "*Papa nas lubet*"— "Daddy loves us." Characteristically, he lied about his new job, saying it was photographic work similar to the work he had done at Jaggers.[1213]

The two young mothers had gotten along well at Ruth's home in Irving, although their differences were considerable. Ruth, older, better educated, and in many ways more experienced, was nevertheless at one distinct disadvantage with Marina because of her limited ability to speak Russian, and the situation could not have been easy for Marina, who was wholly dependent on Ruth's generosity, hardly having a penny of her own. Marina had no way of knowing whether her predicament was permanent or only temporary. Lee, after all, had been trying to force her to return to the USSR. Marina, ashamed of her dependence on Ruth, did what she could to help with the housework, and tried to help Ruth with her Russian, but she felt she was an imposition on Ruth and had no idea how long that might be necessary. "She was never comfortable accepting bed and board from me," Ruth would later recall. "I don't think I was ever able to convince her how valuable it was to me to have a resident nonpaid tutor [in Russian]." In the meantime, Marina enjoyed Ruth's friendship and liked her, soon calling her "Aunt" Ruth, a common appellative in Russia for close female friends of one's family.

As dissimilar in background as they were, the two young women had two things in common, small children and very unsatisfactory marriages. But Ruth, for all her mature acceptance of Michael's lack of feeling for her, was still hoping for a reconciliation, and she looked forward to his regular visits two nights a week, Tuesday and Friday, when she served dinner by candlelight. Marina was equally encouraged by the postcards Lee sent from New Orleans and his demeanor when they spoke on the phone. Both women hoped things could be patched up with their husbands, and both of them drew comfort from each other.[1214]

There was much that Marina could not or would not tell Ruth. She could not reveal anything about Lee's attempt on General Walker's life, nor would she tell Ruth anything about the physical abuse to which Lee had subjected her. They did talk about Lee's plan to send Marina back to Russia, though, and Ruth again offered her the haven of her home if Marina chose to stay in the United States. In any case, Ruth suggested that Marina come back to her house from New Orleans to have her baby. She knew Lee had not bothered to send Marina to a doctor for prenatal care, and she was equally aware from her own experience of how hard it is for a woman with a child barely out of infancy to have another baby. Although little Junie did not take readily to strangers, she seemed to be comfortable with Ruth, and Ruth felt it would be ideal for her to take care of Junie while Marina was in the hospital.

Nothing Ruth knew about Lee Oswald encouraged her to like or trust him very much, and she was sure that Marina, with her help, could make it on her own in America. Despite Lee making it almost impossible for Marina to learn English by never speaking it to her, Ruth knew that Marina did have an interest in the language and she ordered a book in Russian for her, *The Self Teacher in the English Language*.[1215]

On May 10, the day after he was hired, Lee started work at Reily, and Marina, June, and Ruth, with her two kids, set out for New Orleans, five hundred miles away, in Ruth's station wagon, spending the night in Shreveport and arriving at the Murrets on May 11. After a happy hour of reunion (highlighted by Lee's delight over seeing Junie walking for the first time) and introductions to the Murrets, Dutz Murret drove Lee to the apartment on Magazine Street, Ruth following in her station wagon with Marina and all the kids.

Lee tried hard to sell Marina on the apartment, which he had already cleaned up the night before, but she was not pleased. "This is lovely. How pleased I am," she said tartly. In the confusion, she had thought the home Ruth had first driven her to, the Murrets' cozy house, was where she was going to be living, and the apartment, for all of its attractions, could not match that. Now he led her about, hopefully pointing out the attractions. It was larger than their last apartment in Dallas, the living room was quite spacious, there was a fenced-in yard where little June could safely play and where fresh strawberries could be picked and eaten. Also, it was on the ground floor and there was a screened porch, both of which would be wonderful for baby June. The furnishings were not terrible—Mrs. Garner had described them as "early New Orleans style." But Marina was not impressed and she let Lee know it. It was dark, none too clean, and shabby. And there was little ventilation but many evident cockroaches, which Lee was doing his best to get rid of as he expectantly showed Marina the apartment. To Marina, it was nothing at all like the Murrets' house, or Ruth's house in Irving, which she had enjoyed so much the past two weeks.

Ruth, who found some sympathy for Lee in his effort to please Marina, and her children stayed with them on Magazine Street for three days, but the atmosphere did not improve. On the trip from Texas Ruth had bought a lot of blackberries from a roadside stand, and Lee set out to make wine from those that were left over, a move Marina considered stupid. She bawled him out for wasting good blackberries: "What do you think you are doing? Ruining all this." He defended himself and stubbornly continued, but the next day he threw all the wine out.

Ruth walked through the French Quarter with them and the children one day, but she was too aware of the tension between the Oswalds and it made her uncomfortable. The presence of three outsiders wasn't helping matters. She drove back to Texas a day earlier than planned, on May 14, leaving the Oswalds to sort out their problems.[1216]

During the early New Orleans days, the Oswalds' marriage, though always peppered with verbal bickering, was more harmonious than it had been for some time. Marina would later write that although "the mosquitoes are terribly vicious" and she could "hardly stand the humid and hot weather . . . our family life in New Orleans was more peaceful. Lee took great satisfaction in showing me the city where he was born. We often went to the beach, the zoo, and the park. Lee liked to go and hunt crabs." She added, however, that "it is true he [Lee] was not very pleased with his job . . . We did not have very much money, and the birth of a new child involved new expenses . . . As before, Lee spent a great deal of time reading."[1217]

Marina told Priscilla McMillan that she and Lee were happy to be together again— "'I've missed you so,' Lee said again and again." Though the Oswalds' sexual intimacy bloomed during this early New Orleans period, much to Marina's satisfaction, even that had its trials. Lee liked to watch them making love in a mirror at the foot of their bed, but that made Marina, thinking that the mirror excited him more than she did, uneasy. At the beginning of their marriage, Lee had wanted sex more than she, but the reverse was now true—she, threatened with being sent back to Russia, needed constant reassurance from him, and sex seemed to fill that bill. At the same time, their marriage was no more peaceful than before. Volatility had become the essence (could it have been the sine qua non?) of their relationship, and Marina said that the marriage was a succession of "tears and caresses, arguments and reconciliations." The arguments often turned ugly, enough to annoy the neighbors, as they had in Dallas, although Lee, perhaps out of respect for Marina's advancing pregnancy, no longer physically abused her. Marina simply did not know where she stood.[1218]

The relatively good New Orleans days ended no later than May 25, just two weeks after they had arrived in the Big Easy, when Marina wrote to Ruth in Russian: "Here it is already a week since I received your letter.* I can't produce any excuses [for not respond-ing earlier] as there are no valid reasons. I'm ashamed to confess that I am a person of moods and my mood currently is such that I don't feel much like anything. As soon as you left all love stopped and I am very hurt that Lee's attitude toward me is such that I feel each minute that I bind him. He insists that I leave America which I don't want to do at all. I like America very much and I think that even without Lee I would not be lost here. What do you think? . . . Lee has said to me that he doesn't love me . . . It is hard for you and me to live without a return of our love—interesting, how will it all end?"[1219]†

---

*The letter was not reproduced in the Warren Commission volumes.

†On a lighter note, Marina wrote that she and Lee had recently been to the French Quarter in the evening. "It's a shame you didn't manage to get there in the evening. For me it was especially interesting as it was the first time in my life I had seen such. There were many nightclubs there. Through the open doors were visi-ble barely covered dancing girls (so as not to say entirely unclothed). Most of them had really very pretty, rare figures and if one doesn't think about too many things, then one can like them very much" (CE 408, 17 H 89).

From his first day at the Reily coffee company, Lee regarded the new job as an annoying distraction from what appeared to be his true mission: striking a spectacular blow for Marxism or Castro, or both, that would propel him to celebrity and, probably in his mind, an honored position as a Fidelista in the new Cuba. The experienced maintenance man who was charged with teaching Lee the job at the coffee company noticed the indifference his pupil couldn't be bothered to mask. Charles Le Blanc testified, "Well, when they first hired him, they brought him to me, because I was to break him in on his job." Le Blanc said he started to show Oswald how to grease the machines. But "the first day, I mean when I was showing him, it looked like if he caught on to it, all right, if he didn't, it was still all right. It looked like he was just one of these guys that just didn't care whether he learned it or he didn't learn it."

Not that there was much to learn. Le Blanc expected anyone "with any mechanical knowledge" to get it within a week. You found the grease and oil fittings on every machine and you then greased and oiled them. There were five floors of machinery on one side of the building, four on the other, and you started on the fifth floor and worked your way down. For those who couldn't remember the fittings, there was a check list to follow and initial. But as soon as Le Blanc left Oswald to do the job on his own, which was after about a week, Lee would just disappear. "I would take and put him up there," Le Blanc said, "and about a half hour or forty-five minutes or so, I would go back up and check how he is doing . . . and I wouldn't find him . . . So I would start hunting all over the building . . . I would cover from the roof on down and I wouldn't locate him, and I asked him, I said, 'Well, where have you been?' and all he would give me was that he was around. I asked him, 'Around where?' He says, 'Just around,' and he would turn around and walk off."

Oswald was preoccupied with weightier matters. "On one occasion when I was in the shop and I was working on some sort of piece of machinery . . . ," Le Blanc recalled, Oswald came in the shop "and he was standing there by me and watching me and I asked him, I says, 'Are you finished [with] all your greasing?' He said yes. So he stood there a few minutes, and all of a sudden he says, 'You like it here?' I said, 'What do you mean?' He says, 'Do you like it here?' I says, 'Well, sure I like it here. I have been here a long time, about eight and a half years or so.' He says, 'Oh, hell, I don't mean this place.' I said, 'Well, what do you mean?' He says, 'This damn country.' I said, 'Why, certainly, I love it. After all, this is my country.' He turned around and walked off." Le Blanc quickly came to the conclusion that Oswald was a "crackpot." Apart from his inattention to his work, there was one thing that Oswald did that unnerved Charles Le Blanc more than anything else: he had a habit of walking past Le Blanc and, "like a kid playing cowboys," lift his "finger like a gun" and go "pow." Le Blanc said, "When he would do it he wouldn't even crack a smile. That is what used to get to me."[1220]

Le Blanc told the FBI that on several occasions Oswald overstayed his scheduled fifteen-minute break by "20 to 30 minutes," and was a "loner," even during the lunch period.[1221]

On May 12, the first Sunday after he had started work, Oswald sent a change of address to the Dallas postmaster and asked for his mail to be forwarded to his Magazine Street address.[1222]*

---

*The publications he would continue to receive which he had been subscribing to included the *Worker*, the *Militant*, and *Soviet Belorussia*, an organ of the Soviet government. It's noteworthy that in an April 19, 1963, speech by President Kennedy reported in the *Militant*, he said that "in five years time" it was likely that Castro would be deposed, and the April 29, 1963, edition of the *Militant* quoted a statement by Robert F. Kennedy on April 22, that "we can't just snap our fingers and make Castro go away. But we can fight for this.

Lee did not immediately rent a post office box in New Orleans as he had done so quickly after he moved from Fort Worth to Dallas. However, while he had tried in a number of childish ways to conceal his presence in Dallas, most likely from the FBI (but as we have seen, the FBI did learn about Oswald's presence in Dallas, at two different addresses, although they were at sea on his current whereabouts), he now tried to establish an overt presence in New Orleans. On his application for work at the Reily coffee company he had given his Aunt Lillian's address as his own, and, to the question how long he resided there, he crowded the words "23 yrs. CONTINU" into the tiny space provided—essentially claiming that he had lived his whole life in New Orleans, except perhaps for his last employment, which he gave as "Active duty USMC."[1223] Neither the Soviet Union nor his recent sojourn in Dallas figured in this new scenario. Part of what lay in his mind may have been a desire to erase all traces of Dallas—where he had attempted to commit a murder—from his life story.

Two days later, he mailed a change-of-address card to the Fair Play for Cuba Committee in New York, again giving his Magazine Street address.[1224] On that same day, Oswald visited the New Orleans Public Library, applied for a card, and took out his first book, *Portrait of a Revolutionary: Mao Tse-tung*, by Robert Payne. Marina told Priscilla McMillan that Lee identified with the great men he read about and genuinely believed he was one of them, but his interest in Chairman Mao may have been inspired by an article in the April 29, 1963, edition of the *Militant*, which was about the possibility that Castro, disappointed with the support he was getting from the Soviets, might turn to—and even visit—China. The article's author denied, however, that Castro had become a Maoist.[1225] On May 26, two weeks after starting work, Lee wrote what he must have felt was a very important letter to Vincent Lee at the FPCC. He wanted to formally lead a group in the fight against the foes of Castro.

> Dear Sirs . . .
> I am requesting formal membership in your Organization.
> In the past I have recived from you pamplets ect., both bought by me and given to me by you.
> Now that I live in New Orleans I have been thinking about renting a small office at my own expense for the purpose of forming a F.P.C.C. branch here in New Orleans. Could you give me a charter?
> Also I would like information on buying pamplets ect. in large lots, as well as blank FPCC applications ect.
> Also, a picture of Fidel, suitable for framing would be a welcome touch. Offices down here rent for $30. a month and if I had a steady flow of litarature I would be glad to take the expense. Of course I work and could not supervise the office at all times but I'm sure I could get some volunteers to do it.
> Could you add some advice or recommendations? I am not saying this project would be a roaring success, but I am willing to try . . . so here's hoping to hear from you.
>
> Yours respectfully
> Lee H. Oswald[1226]

We can dedicate all our energy and best possible brains to that effort." (McMillan, *Marina and Lee*, pp. 399–400, 611–612 note 2)

It was clear to Oswald that the Kennedy administration wanted to overthrow his hero, Fidel Castro.

Lee's move to New Orleans not only had brought him closer geographically to Havana but also seemed to clearly signal an increased interest on his part in Castro and Marxist Cuba.

Three days later Vincent Lee sent him a membership card and the FPCC's constitution and bylaws, and welcomed him to the organization. However, he made it clear that *only* if the national committee deemed it was "reasonable" to expect that there was enough interest in New Orleans in their activities would they "issue a charter" to Oswald "for a New Orleans chapter of FPCC." So far they were not convinced. Nonetheless, Lee went on to advise Oswald: "You must realize that you will come under tremendous pressures with any attempt to do FPCC work in that area and that you will not be able to operate in the manner which is conventional here in the northeast. Even most of our big city chapters have been forced to abandon the idea of operating an office in public . . . Most chapters have found that it is easier to operate semi-privately out of a home and maintain a P.O. Box for all mailings and public notices . . . We do have a serious and often violent opposition and this procedure helps prevent many unnecessary incidents which frighten away prospective supporters. I definitely would not recommend an office, at least not one that would be easily identifiable to the lunatic fringe in your community. Certainly, I would not recommend that you engage in one at the very beginning but wait and see how you can operate in the community through several public experiences."

Vincent Lee added a few elementary precautions, which Oswald, with his taste for spycraft, surely found congenial to his instincts. (For example, "Note: When you contact people by mail we recommend that only first class be used and that no full name go on the return address on the outside of the envelope.")[1227]

The same day, May 29, that Lee wrote to Oswald, and hence, before Oswald received Lee's letter, Oswald took matters into his own hands by going to the Jones Printing Company on Girod Street, where, under the fictitious name of Lee Osborne, he ordered a thousand copies of a handbill reading,

HANDS
OFF
CUBA!
Join the Fair Play for
Cuba Committee
NEW ORLEANS CHARTER
MEMBER BRANCH
Free Literature, Lectures
LOCATION:

EVERYONE WELCOME!

Two days later he returned to put down a four-dollar deposit, and on June 4, "Osborne" appeared to collect the handbills, for which he paid $9.89 in all.[1228]

On June 3, Oswald also opened a post office box in New Orleans (number 30061) under the name L. H. Oswald. He listed his address as 657 French Street in New Orleans. (The Murrets lived at 757 French Street.)[1229]

Also on June 3, Oswald visited the Mailers Service Company to order five hundred copies of an application for membership in the projected New Orleans chapter of the FPCC. Again, it was "Lee Osborne" who picked up the order and paid $9.34 in cash for it. According to the layout furnished by "Osborne," an interested party could join the chapter for a one-dollar initiation fee and maintain membership by paying dues of a further dollar a month, or he could subscribe to "mailings" for five dollars a year, or he could make a donation in an amount to be determined by the donor. Several days later "Osborne" returned to order three hundred membership cards with spaces for the name and signature plus a third space to be signed by the "Chapter President."[1230]*

On June 10, Oswald wrote to the *Worker* to apprise them of his activities:

> Dear Sirs,
> As a long time subscriber to the worker I know I can ask a favor of you with full confindence of its fulfillment. I have formed a "Fair Play for Cuba Committe" here in New Orleans, I think it is the best way to attract the broad mass of people to a popular struggle.
> I ask that you give me as much literature as you judge possible since I think it would be very nice to have your literature among the "Fair Play" leaflets (like the one enclosed) and phamplets in my office.
> Also please be so kind as to convey the enclosed "hounery [honorary] membership" cards to those fighters for peace Mr. Gus Hall and Mr. B. Davis.
>
> Yours Faternally
Lee H. Oswald[1231]

Gus Hall and Ben Davis were the Communist Party officials for whose defense committee Oswald had offered to create a poster in December (see earlier text). Even if his letter did not bring the hoped harvest of CPUSA literature, he may have thought it might well provoke a reply from the party that he could add to his bonafides for his eventual arrival in Havana.

Although Oswald's commitment to the FPCC cannot be seriously challenged—he had passed out its literature even in Dallas—surely, being a leaflet peddler on the streets of New Orleans could never satisfy someone of such grandiose dreams. It appears that Oswald was starting to move fast, that he had other plans, but before they came to fruition he intended to pursue his small-bore FPCC endeavor. One can reasonably infer that his real goal at the time was to forge a new life for himself in Cuba. I say that because on June 1, only three days after he placed his printing orders for the FPCC materials, he had himself photographed.[1232] We can fairly presume this was for a passport because a week later, on June 8, he prepared an "International Certificate of Vaccination or Revaccination Against Smallpox," a World Health Organization doc-

---

*On his own membership card, Lee signed his name, then instructed Marina to sign the name "A. J. Hidell" above the typed words "Chapter President." When Marina, perplexed, said, "You have selected this name because it sounds like Fidel," Lee blushed, then said, "Shut-up, it is none of your business." Marina was convinced Hidell was nothing but an "altered Fidel," and she laughed in his face at such foolishness. If it wasn't Fidel, she pressed him, then who was Hidell? He was stuck and muttered the contradiction that Hidell "was his own name and that there is no Hidell in existence." Oh, Marina said, taunting him, so you have "two names?" "Yes," he said, with nowhere else to go. He finally recovered his mental equilibrium and said it was necessary to use this fictitious name so "people will think I have a big organization." Marina played her husband's silly game and wrote the name A. J. Hidell on the card, as Lee insisted she do. (5 H 401, 1 H 64, WCT Marina N. Oswald)

ument for international travelers that he had probably picked up at a government pass-port office.[1233]*

Priscilla McMillan, who, along with Ruth Paine, knew Marina as well as anyone, and through Marina, knew Lee, has this analysis of what Lee was up to during this period: "Four years earlier [in the Marines at El Toro] he had thought about gaining Castro's trust and joining his revolution. Now, in the summer of 1963, he was thinking about the same thing. His effort to establish a chapter of the Fair Play for Cuba Committee in New Orleans appears to have been two-pronged, both an attempt to change American policy toward Cuba by peaceful political action at the grass-roots level, and an attempt to win the trust of the Castro government."[1234] And we do know what Marina told the Warren Commission: "I only know that his basic desire was to get to Cuba by any means, and that all the rest of it was window dressing for that purpose."[1235]

On June 11, Oswald returned to the post office where he had his mailbox list A. J. Hidell and Marina Oswald as people authorized to receive mail there.[1236]

On June 16, Lee made his debut as New Orleans's leading Fidelista. He took some of the leaflets he had printed and some of the pamphlets he had received from the New York headquarters of the Fair Play for Cuba Committee—one-page flyers protesting the recent decision by the government to prevent Americans from traveling to Cuba—and went down to the Dumaine Street Wharf, where an aircraft carrier, the USS *Wasp*, was docked, to pass them out to naval personnel and civilians who were leaving the carrier. The ship, which normally operated out of Boston, had arrived with six other ships several days before and was allowing visits by the public, so Lee expected a good crowd. He attracted the attention of the ship's officer of the deck, who sent an enlisted man to find an officer of the Harbor Police. Patrolman Girod Ray, thus alerted, located Oswald, took two copies of the leaflets he was handing out, and asked him if he had permission to distribute literature on the wharf. Oswald told him he did not, but he was an American citizen and had a right to distribute literature anywhere he wanted. Ray told him that he was mistaken about that. The wharves and buildings along the Mississippi River, encompassing the port of New Orleans, were under the jurisdiction of the Harbor Commissioners, and Oswald could not distribute leaflets on their property without their permission. Oswald objected, insisting he saw no reason why he could not distribute whatever literature he chose wherever he liked, and Ray warned he would be arrested if he did. Oswald finally conceded the point and left the Dumaine Street Wharf.[1237]

During the same period that Lee was busy organizing his political group and hopefully setting in motion his political career, he did not completely neglect implementing his other decision—to send Marina and his beloved Junie back to Russia. He had already sent a change-of-address card to the Soviet embassy in Washington, D.C., giving Magazine Street as his new address.[1238]

---

*On the Certificate of Vaccination document, Oswald used his rubber-stamp kit to imprint the name of "Dr. A. J. Hideel," whose office he listed as P.O. Box 30016, New Orleans. He failed to notice his misspelling of his favorite alias, "Hidell." More seriously, he misprinted Dr. Hideel's post office box address, reversing the last two numbers, an error he repeated, more consequentially, when he stamped some of his handbills— if any potential recruit did try to get in touch with the New Orleans chapter of the Fair Play for Cuba Committee, Oswald might never have known about it. The rubber-stamped location on his handbills exists in two versions, one giving A. J. Hidell's name and the incorrect post office box number "30016, New Orleans, LA" under "Location" and the other stamped "L. H. Oswald" and giving his correct 4907 Magazine Street address. (Cadigan Exhibit No. 23, 19 H 296–297; CE 2966-A and B, 26 H 448)

Although Marina knew nothing of this communication, she knew he had not given up on the plan. He told her she was "in his way." He was planning to go to Cuba, then China, he told her, and she would have to wait for him in Russia. "I love to travel," he said, "and with you I can't."[1239]

On Saturday morning, June 1, Marina, pushing June in her stroller, walked with Lee to the nearby Napoleon branch of the New Orleans Public Library with the hope of finding some books in Russian that she could read. There were none, but Lee checked out Deane and David Heller's *The Berlin Wall* and Hermann Bacher Deutsch's *The Huey Long Murder Case* for himself. Walking home, Marina started to feel faint. "Don't go so fast," she told him, "I don't feel well." She stopped and leaned against a storefront. Thinking Marina was joking, he kept walking. She passed out and found herself lying on the sidewalk when she came to. He carried her into a store, where strangers revived her with ammonia. She was eventually able to walk the rest of the way home but she took to her bed, and Lee, finally alarmed, was particularly caring for the rest of the day.[1240]

Before the week was out Marina received a letter from Comrade Reznichenko on behalf of the consular's section of the Russian embassy in Washington. The letter essentially reiterated what he had written on April 18, asking Marina to give him her reasons for wanting repatriation to the USSR.[1241] She noticed that the letter had not been forwarded from Dallas; it was sent directly to Magazine Street, and only Lee could or would have informed the consulate of their new address. To her it was additional proof that his insistence on her returning to Russia had continued and was deadly serious. The threat was constantly on her mind.[1242]

The Murrets and the Oswalds exchanged visits from time to time during this period, providing temporary, marginal relief to Marina for her anxieties. Marina thought Lee's relatives were very kind. Lee, she said, liked them very much, but he disliked their religiosity and said they were "bourgeois," a term to describe the tastes and values of the middle class and their emphasis on materialism, social respectability, and a secure, conformist existence.

A week after Marina fainted in the street, Lee took her to the New Orleans Charity Hospital for a medical examination. It was nearby and largely free, but as a state institution it was permitted to treat only patients who were legal residents of Louisiana. The Oswalds had not been in the state long enough to qualify. Oswald argued heatedly with the staff for an hour but failed to move them. He was furious and complained that it was just one more proof that nothing but money counted in America. He made no further attempt to get appropriate medical attention for his wife, though he was now working and not completely indigent. Marina would be back in Dallas in her ninth month of pregnancy before she finally saw a doctor for the first time.[1243] Ruth Paine, in Dallas, worried when she heard nothing from Marina for a time and tried to get the names of the secretaries of the Quaker and Unitarian churches in New Orleans to enlist their help. She wrote to ask them to find people who spoke Russian who might call on Marina, but her efforts came to very little—just one visit from Ruth Kloepfer, clerk of the Quaker Meeting in New Orleans who spoke no Russian and had to rely on Lee's interpreting to chat with Marina. One of Kloepfer's daughters was studying Russian but was presently out of the country, and Mrs. Kloepfer never made a serious attempt to locate real Russian contacts for Marina.[1244]

Right from the beginning, Marina had felt more isolated than at any time in her life, and for one reason only. She was trapped behind her language barrier. Other than Lee, she had virtually no other human being to talk to. Dallas had been bad enough, but at least there she had the occasional contact with one or more members of the Russian emigré community who spoke her native language. But in New Orleans, if she wasn't talking to Lee or her baby June, she simply wasn't talking. Several times she told Lee she would appreciate it if he would try to become acquainted with some Russian-speaking people in New Orleans so she could have friends and someone with whom to converse, but he had not done this, and he continued to speak to her, and their daughter June, only in Russian.[1245]

Lee kept up unrelenting pressure on Marina to write the letter required by the Soviet consulate. Every evening when he came home from work he asked her whether she had written it yet. She cried every day and stalled as best she could. Finally she told him she would go back to the USSR if he would give her a divorce. Lee, angry, told her, "There will be no divorce, I may want to come to you some time . . . You're my wife and you'll stay my wife. The children are mine. You'll wait for me just as long as I want." He told her "the conversation is over," but in fact it wasn't. Marina learned that insisting on divorce was a way to get him to ease up, at least for the time being, his insistence on her writing the letter. For Marina, a day's postponement was a day's hope that their relationship might change just enough to forestall a terrible event in her life.

Another weapon at her disposal was, curiously, Anatoly Shpanko. Lee had never gotten over his chagrin at learning of Marina's alleged infidelity while he was in Moscow, and the letter she had written to Anatoly he had intercepted. Any mention of the putative lover's name, whether by Marina or Lee, was enough to change the subject of any argument. But one way or another, the name came up in virtually every fight, and if Marina ever spoke about some incident in Minsk, Lee would assume that Anatoly had been a part of it. "Stop it," he would tell her in her reminiscence of the event. "I can't stand it." And if she herself brought up Anatoly's name, he would tell her, "Shut up. I don't want to hear about your boyfriends." But Marina, on at least one occasion, told Lee, perhaps in sweet revenge for all of his beatings and mistreatment of her, that if Lee spent his whole life trying, he would never learn to kiss as well as Anatoly. Marina often daydreamed about Anatoly. He had been kind to her and she imagined he always would be. If Lee did force her to go back to the USSR, Anatoly was the man she would want to marry. Oddly, Marina thought Anatoly resembled both President Kennedy and actor José Ferrer, and Lee may have somehow inferred this association in her mind between her phantom lover and President Kennedy, who, she told Lee once, was "very attractive as a man." Lee appeared jealous of Kennedy and said, "You mustn't like any other man but me."[1246]

Marina taunting Lee, Lee beating up Marina, Marina running away, Lee begging her to return, blissful moments making up and reuniting, each desperately needing each other, then Lee trying to send Marina back to Russia, more beatings, inducement of jealousy, and so on. Though their marriage, as Marina said, was a succession of arguments and reconciliations, so are many marriages. But Lee and Marina's fell into the much smaller category where both parties always seem to be just beyond the other's reach, both unable, for whatever perversion in their makeup, to give the other what they know the other needs. It seemed that Lee and Marina were each taking turns playing Carmen to the other's Don José, the problem being, as we shall see, that this game they were playing out with their small, ordinary hands would change history for years and years to come.

On June 24, Lee went to the passport office and applied for a new passport. He gave his occupation as "photographer" and his proposed itinerary as "England, France, Poland, USSR, France, Finland, Poland." He said he had intended to travel during the period from October to January.[1247] Absent from the itinerary was Cuba. Recent laws[1248] prohibited travel to the small island nation, and indeed, the passport that was issued the next day was stamped with a warning that a person traveling to Cuba was liable to be prosecuted.[1249]

The speed with which the passport was processed by the State Department—and even the fact that it was issued at all—became an essential suspicion of conspiracy theorists, but in fact the State Department had no legal grounds for denying any American a passport since the Supreme Court had ruled in 1958 that travel abroad was a right of all citizens.[1250] The FBI had not placed Oswald on the watch list for those seeking passports because, the agency would later say, its "investigation of Oswald had disclosed no evidence that Oswald was acting under the instruction or on behalf of any foreign government or instrumentality thereof."[1251] Oswald also benefited from the recent installation in the New Orleans passport office of a Teletype system to Washington that markedly sped up the issuance of passports, their being granted in "24 hours in most cases."[1252] Both the legal adviser to the U.S. Department of State, Abram Chayes, and the assistant chief of the Legal Division of the Passport Office of the Department of State, Carroll Hamilton Seeley Jr., told the Warren Commission that based on Oswald's background he had a right to a passport and he could not legally be denied one.[1253] Seeley added that another former defector, Paul David Wilson, had applied for a passport and received it as a "routine issuance."[1254]

On June 26, a confidential informant for the FBI in New York reported the arrival of Oswald's June 11 letter at the *Worker*. That same day the FBI's New York office sent the post office box information on Oswald to its New Orleans office, but it wasn't until August 5, 1963, after some legwork, that the New Orleans office verified that Oswald was living in New Orleans and at 4907 Magazine Street. The information was forwarded to Special Agent Hosty in Dallas,* but as of that point New Orleans became the "Office of Origin" for Oswald's case file, and Hosty wouldn't have anything to do with the Oswald case until October of 1963.[1255]

On July 1, Marina finally wrote her letter to Comrade Reznichenko at the Soviet consulate in Washington, D.C., giving "family problems" as her reason for the long delay of her reply. They were also, Marina added, one of her reasons for wanting to return to her homeland, although the main one was simple "homesickness." She wished, she said, to return to Leningrad, where she grew up and went to school. She said her husband also "expresses a sincere wish to return together with me to the USSR. I earnestly beg you to help him in this. There is not much that is encouraging to us here and nothing to hold us." She said that since she was pregnant, she "would not be able to work for the time being . . . And my husband is often unemployed."[1256]

Marina's change of heart about writing the letter had been brought about by an astonishing coup de théâtre. The evening before she wrote the letter, Marina was watching Lee read and she sensed he was very sad. He put his book down and went into the kitchen alone. A moment later, Marina put the baby down and followed him. He was sitting in the dark in a chair in reverse, his arms and legs wrapped around the back of the chair, his

---

*Hosty had been doing the usual things to pick up Oswald's trace, and learned in May that Lee and Marina had apparently left the Dallas area (4 H 443, WCT James P. Hosty Jr.).

head resting on top. He was staring at the floor. Marina put her arms around him, stroked his head, and could feel him shaking with sobs. Finally, she said, "Everything is going to be alright. I understand." She held him for fifteen minutes and he told her between sobs that he was lost. He didn't know what he ought to do. Finally, he stood up and returned to the living room, and then suddenly asked, "Would you like me to come to Russia, too?" Marina thought he was kidding. Oswald explained that he wasn't. "There's nothing to hold me here," he said. "I'd rather have less but not have to worry about the future . . . We'll be together, you and me and Junie and the baby. How would I manage without my girls?" Marina was beside herself with joy, dancing around the room and sitting in Lee's lap. It couldn't be clearer that although Marina loved America, she cared for Lee more. A while later, Lee held her by the shoulders in the kitchen and told her to write the Soviet embassy that he would be coming too.[1257]

Marina would have been surprised to read what he wrote on his note accompanying her application for a visa:

> Dear Sirs
>   Please *rush* the entrance visa for the return of Soviet citizen, Marina N. Oswald. She is going to have a baby in *October*, therefore you must grant the entrance visa and make the transportation arrangements before then. As for my return entrance visa please consider *separtably*.
> Thank you
Lee H. Oswald
(Husband of Marina Nicholeyev [Nikolaevna])[1258]

Lee had no plan to go back to the USSR at all, either with Marina and June or without them. As will be very clear in the Mexico City section of this book, he only wanted a visa for the USSR to enable him to get an in-transit visa to Cuba, which allowed travelers on their way to the Soviet Union to enter Cuba temporarily. His crying ruse had persuaded Marina at long last to write the letter to the Soviet embassy. She had no idea he had asked for the separate visa until long after the assassination of the president, which makes the last paragraph of her letter to Reznichenko especially poignant: "These are the basic reasons why I and my husband wish to return to the USSR. Please do not deny our request. Make us happy again, help us to return [to] that which we lost because of our foolishness. I would like to have my second child, too, to be born in the USSR."[1259]

Lee had not told Marina his job involved greasing machines in a coffee factory. He pretended it was a photographic job, but he couldn't explain why he smelled of coffee, and he finally fessed up. Working with grease and oil had an effect, for a brief period, on his own personal hygiene. He grew sloppy in his appearance, wearing sandals, old work pants, and a dirty T-shirt he rarely changed.[1260] He told Marina, "My work isn't worth getting dressed for." Marina told him to do it for himself, or, at least for her. "I simply don't care," he answered.[1261]* Lee's sloppy appearance was in sharp contrast to the cleanliness

---

*The shortness of this period of personal neglect is evidenced by the fact that Adrian Alba, the operator of the garage next door to the coffee company where Lee spent so many of his work breaks, apparently doesn't recall it at all. His only recollection of Oswald in this regard is that he couldn't figure out how someone whose

he had always demonstrated throughout his adult life. For instance, in Russia, Marina noted that no matter how late at night, he would bathe, shave, and brush his teeth before they would be intimate.[1262]

Oswald's work performance at the Reily coffee company was very poor, and the man in the personnel department who hired him, Alfred Claude Jr., considered firing him several times in the first four weeks of his employment, but he didn't only because the maintenance department was short of employees at the time.[1263] His immediate supervisor during those first four weeks, John Branyon, said he would not have given him a recommendation to another employer.[1264]

Typically, Lee made no friends at Reily and was often downright rude. He ate lunch alone at the nearby Martin's Restaurant, and when the men took a break in the alley, Lee would sit on a bench by himself, staring into space and making no reply if any of them sought to include him in their bull sessions.[1265]

He did make one friend (or acquaintance at least), though, Adrian Alba, a part-owner of the auto storage garage next door to Reily's. Alba kept a coffee urn and Coca-Cola machine in his office for his clients, and Lee took to dropping in frequently during his breaks. Lee found Alba interesting in that Alba was a knowledgeable gun enthusiast who often worked at "sporterizing" military rifles and carbines. Surplus military rifles were usually inexpensive, but also heavy and awkward to handle, and Alba eliminated some of the weight, shortened and refinished the stock, and reseated the barrel, sometimes shortening it as well. Alba did most of the work himself right there in his office, although he turned the more delicate and critical problems over to a gunsmith.

Oswald may have wanted to purchase a better rifle than his Mannlicher-Carcano. Alba said Lee expressed an interest in "one 30.06 Springfield rifle" that Alba was "in the process of sporterizing," until Alba told him it would cost him more than a hundred dollars. Lee didn't mention it again.[1266]*

When Lee stopped in at Alba's, he'd put a nickel in the Coke machine and start thumbing through Alba's considerable collection of hunting and gun magazines. Alba thought Lee was very quiet, not ready to talk until he felt like talking. He learned nothing of Lee's personal life, only that he had some guns himself. When they did talk, it was only about guns.

Lee spent so much time with the magazines that on several occasions someone from Reily's had to come warn him that someone was looking for him and he risked getting fired if he didn't get back to work right quick. Sometimes Lee borrowed one or two of the magazines, but was always scrupulous about returning them after a week or so.[1267]

---

job was an oiler "was always extremely neat and clean. At anytime during the day his pants had a neat crease in them and his shirt was always clean—no oil on them at all" (HSCA Record 180-10072-10047, HSCA staff interview of Adrian Alba on January 24, 1978, p.2).

*No wonder. A hundred dollars was about all Lee and Marina had to their names. They never had a bank account or safe-deposit box during their marriage and Marina said that in New Orleans Lee put the family savings in a wallet he kept at their home. She estimated that there "might be $100" or two hundred dollars at the most in the wallet. Since he had no source of income other than the modest compensation he received while working, Oswald could never adequately provide for his family, and he felt shamed by this. Marina said that she was aware of the shame he felt and therefore very seldom spoke to him about finances or money or finding a job. Speaking of the New Orleans period, Lillian Murret, Oswald's aunt, said, "Lee was very poor. They were practically starving." (CE 1781, 23 H 387, FBI interview of Marina Oswald on November 28, 1963; HSCA Record 180-10075-10352, HSCA deposition of Lillian Murret on November 6, 1978, p.15) The situation did not improve much in Dallas. When I asked Ruth Paine at the London trial, "How would you characterize the financial condition of the Oswalds?" she responded, "They were very poor" (Transcript of *On Trial*, July 24, 1986, p.627).

Back on June 5, Marina had written to Ruth telling her that Lee "insists that I go away to the Soviet Union—which I certainly don't want to do." Referring to Ruth's problems with Michael, she said, "I can only console you with this: that you are not the only rejected one in this world. In many ways you and I are friends in misfortune. But surely a person can carry on through all the most heavy losses, trials and misfortunes. I think we will not perish, but that something will smile brightly on us too . . . Soon you will set out on your vacation, and I wish you and the children a good trip. With us everything is as it used to be. A gloomy spirit rules the house. The only joy for me and for Lee (I think) is June . . . Lee either yells at me or is silent, but never talks."[1268] It wasn't until July 11 that Ruth wrote back to Marina with a shortened version of the letter she had written to her in April but had not sent, in which she invited Marina to stay with her. (The reason for the delay was that Michael, who even consulted a friend, had to first consider the possibility that Lee may become violent and "stab Ruth or Marina." He finally concluded that if Lee were handled in a gentle and considerate manner, he would not be a danger.)[1269] "If Lee doesn't wish to live with you anymore, and prefers that you go to the Soviet Union," Ruth wrote to Marina in Russian, "think about the possibility of living with me. It would be necessary, of course, to live dependent upon me for a year or two, while the babies are small, but please do not be embarrassed . . . You know, I have long received from my parents. I lived 'dependent' a long time." Ruth told Marina not to concern herself with the thought of her being a financial burden to her and Michael.

> We have sufficient money. Michael would be glad. This I know. He just gave me $500.00 extra for the vacation or something necessary. With this money it is possible to pay [your] doctor and [the] hospital in October when the baby is born. Believe God. All will be well for you and the children. I confess that I think that the opportunity for me to know you came from God. Perhaps it is not so, but I believe so . . . Marina, come to my home the last part of September without fail. Either for two months or two years. And don't be worried about money.
>
> I don't want to hurt Lee with this invitation to you. Only I think that it would be better that you and he do not live together if you do not receive happiness. I understand how Michael feels—he doesn't love me, and wants the chance to look for another life and another wife . . . I don't know how Lee feels . . . Surely things are hard for him now, too. I hope that he would be glad to see you with me where he can know that you and the children will receive everything that is necessary, and he would not need to worry about it. Thus, he could start life again. Write, please.[1270]

In an undated response to Ruth's letter, Marina wrote:

Dear, dear Ruth!
    There are no words to thank you and Michael for the thoughtfulness you show me . . . Now regarding your invitation to come and live with you for rather a long time. For me, of course, it is very tempting . . . Lee and I have not talked about it. I am afraid to talk to him, as I know he will be very hurt. While I was at your house, I wrote him about Philadelphia—that I could go there with you. Many times he has recalled this matter to me and said that I am just waiting for an opportunity

to hurt him. It has been the cause of many of our arguments . . . I am very happy now, that for a considerable period he has been good to me. He talks a lot about the coming baby and is impatient to have a son . . . We went to the doctor. My condition is normal [Marina would later tell her biographer she had not gone to any doctor, it being a false assurance to Ruth.] . . . I will try to take advantage of [your invitation] if . . . Lee becomes coarse with me again, and treats me badly. Sweet Ruth, I am so thankful to you for your good and sympathetic heart. And wherever I am I will always say that plain Americans are good, peaceful . . . and sensitive people . . . I kiss and embrace you, dear Ruth, and also Lynn and . . . little Chris, I wish you all the very best.

Sincerely,
Marina[1271]

For now, at least, Marina had turned down Ruth's generous invitation.

July 17, 1963, was Marina's twenty-second birthday. Lee forgot the date, and Marina glumly reminded him over supper that night. He moved quickly to repair the damage. "Come on," he said, "let's go out." "The stores are closed now," she said, thinking of the new dress or shoes that Lee had promised for her birthday. He took her to the drugstore and bought her a Coke and some face powder anyway.[1272] Two days later, July 19, he was discharged from his job at Reily because his work there had gotten no better and he showed no interest in improving it.[1273] Marina took the news well, blaming widespread unemployment rather than Lee, and assured him that he would soon find another job.[1274]

On Monday, July 22, Lee again reported to the Louisiana Division of Employment to file a claim for unemployment compensation and to look for another job. He apparently made some effort to find employment but soon gave up, content to live on the thirty-three dollars a week he received for unemployment compensation. Every week he dutifully listed four or five prospective employers he contacted in his search for work, but most of them he never contacted.[1275]

Somewhere around July 25 he received word that the review of his undesirable discharge from the Marine Corps Reserve that he had requested had resulted only in a confirmation of the original decision. The review board found that no "change, correction or modification is warranted."[1276]

Oswald continued to check many books out of the New Orleans Public Library during this period, all serious literature. One he checked out two weeks before he was fired was William Manchester's friendly biography of John F. Kennedy, *Portrait of a President*, and he finished it close to the time he lost his job.[1277]

Both Lee and Marina were already fascinated by the young president and his wife, whom they often discussed—not understanding English it would have been hard for Marina to know much about the president if Lee had not spoken of him often. And Lee also harbored a keen interest in the president's wife. They had been aware of Jacqueline Kennedy's pregnancy since Easter and that it had started around the same time as Marina's. Lee told her that the First Lady already had two failed pregnancies, a miscarriage and a stillbirth, tragedies about which Marina felt deeply sorry. The Oswalds subscribed to *Time* magazine, and the two of them leafed through it and every other magazine they could find for photos and articles to follow the progress of Mrs. Kennedy's pregnancy, which had been announced that spring just after Easter,[1278] and which paralleled Marina's own. Lee would translate everything for the eager Marina.

Marina's fascination extended to the president himself. She also searched every magazine that came to hand for photographs of him. (Marina would later use these words to her biographer, Priscilla McMillan, to describe her feelings about JFK: "I was in love with him.") Marina was insatiably avid for news of the glamorous First Family, and Lee was curiously willing to indulge her in this. He seemed to admire the young president and even believed that Kennedy might have been willing—if he had been free to do so—to moderate the country's loathing of Lee's hero, Fidel Castro, a photograph of whom, clipped from the Soviet magazine *Ogonyok*, adorned their mantel alongside another of John F. Kennedy, that Marina had bought.[1279]

Manchester's biography of Kennedy fed into Lee's fantasy life in an odd way. He began to imagine that the child Marina was carrying—undoubtedly a boy this time, he believed—would one day be president of the United States. Lee, apparently adopting the role of Kennedy's father, Joseph, would see to that. He believed that Joe Kennedy had more or less bought the presidency for his son, but that would not be beyond Lee, since, in twenty years' time, he himself would be "president or prime minister," not troubled, evidently, by the fact that the United States did not have a prime minister. Lee didn't seem to be speaking lightly—he returned to the idea several times and was offended by Marina's refusal to take it seriously. She laughed at his pretensions—perhaps with a note of desperation—hoping to pull him back to a more realistic appraisal of their future.

"Okay," she said, "Papa will be prime minister. Son will be president. And what will I be—chief janitor in the White House? Will I be allowed to clean your room, or will you tell me I'm not to touch your papers even then?"

"We'll have to see what kind of girl you turn out to be," he said, seemingly in all seriousness.

She continued to poke fun at him, saying that when he became the nation's leader he could buy something fancy for her, but for now she'd settle for "something for thirty-nine cents."

"Shut-up," he said.[1280]

Up to the middle of August, Lee was content to live off his unemployment compensation until it ran out, and he read one book after another from the Napoleon branch of the New Orleans Public Library, more on Kennedy than any other political leader, including Kennedy's own *Profiles in Courage*, which he checked out with another book on July 15 and returned on July 29.[1281] But Lee, in his own mind, was a man on the move, one who appeared to look upon himself in a historical light. And this brief interlude of relative calm would soon give way to something he began to mull over in his mind, a darker plan that he was not yet ready to broach to Marina.

But before then, Lee enjoyed a small triumph of sorts. Aunt Lillian's son Eugene, who was studying at a seminary, the Jesuit House of Study in Mobile, Alabama, was interested in Lee's experience in the Soviet Union, and he wrote to invite Lee to come and discuss it with some of his fellow seminarians and the faculty. Lee couldn't have managed the trip on his own, but Lillian and Dutz offered to drive him, Marina, and June there and back. The Murrets' daughter, Joyce, and her two children went along for the ride. Though they would only be gone a day, Marina was excited by the trip, referring to it as a "small vacation." And their route lay along Mississippi's Gulf Coast, which she had been eager to see. They set out for Mobile, Alabama, on Saturday morning, July 27, for Lee's talk that night. En route, Lillian suggested that Lee make some notes, map out his thoughts, so he wouldn't be too nervous, but he airily dismissed the suggestion. "Don't worry about me," he said, "I give talks all the time."

At the event, he spoke well without notes. Women were not allowed in the seminary, so Marina and the Murrets stayed outside and visited the chapel. One of the seminarians who was studying Russian and spoke it rather well came out and chatted for an hour with Marina, while Lee spoke with the small gathering inside. He outlined his experiences in the USSR for about half an hour and then fielded questions. He liked the Soviet social programs, particularly their universal health system, he told his audience, adding, however, that although he wasn't completely happy in the United States, living in the United States was better than living in Russia. But overall, he said, "capitalism doesn't work. Communism doesn't work." He said he was a Marxist and was disillusioned with the Soviet brand of communism, noting that the people were "dominated by roughnecks." But he spoke highly of the Russian people themselves, saying they were "naturally very moral, honest, faithful in marriage."

In spite of the fact that he made it fairly clear that he was not religious, Oswald, neatly dressed in a sport shirt and slacks, made a rather good impression. The two priests in attendance assumed that he had a college degree, and one later told Lee's cousin Joyce that Lee's criticism of stock speculation (which a professor at the school had likened to a form of gambling, a sin in the Catholic Church) and exploitation of the working class under capitalism were not that far off base, since Catholic popes had often addressed the same issues. After Lee's appearance at the seminary, they spent the night at the Palms Motel in Mobile, at Dutz Murret's expense, and drove back to New Orleans the next day.[1282]

A couple of days later, Lee received more encouragement: a letter from someone he considered extremely important—Arnold Johnson, director of the Information and Lecture Bureau of the American Communist Party, in response to the letter Lee had written to the *Worker* in early June. Johnson noted that "it is good to know that movements in support of Fair Play for Cuba [have] developed in New Orleans as well as in other cities. We do not have any organizational ties with the [Fair Play for Cuba] Committee, and yet there's much material we issue from time to time that is important for anybody who is concerned about developments in Cuba." He added that he was sending some literature under separate cover.[1283]

The letter could hardly have been more brief or almost form letter–like, but to Oswald it was proof of his own importance. He told Marina, when she made fun of his pretensions, that Arnold Johnson was a "great man," the "Lenin of our country" whose letter was proof that others valued Lee's activities on behalf of Castro and the Cuban Revolution.[1284]

Encouraged by the response, however belated, by Johnson, Lee wrote once again in the first days of August (the letter is dated August 1 but postmarked August 4) to Vincent Lee at the Fair Play for Cuba Committee in New York. He had written to Lee earlier, around the same time he had written to the *Worker*, but received no reply from Vincent Lee authorizing him to open a branch in New Orleans. Now he wrote,

Dear Mr. Lee
    In regards to my efforts to start a branch [office of] FPCC in New Orleans. I rented an office as I planned and was promply closed three days later for some

obsure [obscure] reason by the renters, they said something about remodeling, ect., I'm sure you understand. After that I worked out of a post office box and by use-ing street demonstrations and some circular work have substained a great deal of interest but no new members. Through the efforts of some Cuban-evial [exile] "gusanos" a street demonstration was attacked and we were officialy cautioned by police.

This incident robbed me of what support I had leaving me alone. Neverthe-less thousands of circulars were distrubed and many, many pamplets which your office supplied. We also manged [managed] to picket the fleet when it came in and I was surprised at the number of officers who were interested in our literature. I continued to recive through my post office box inquires and questions which I shall endeavor to keep answering to the best of my ability.

Thank you
Lee H. Oswald[1285]*

The remarkable thing about this letter is not that virtually none of it was true—Oswald had not rented an office nor had he been attacked by *gusanos* ("worms," Cuban slang for counterrevolutionaries)—but that on August 5, the day after he mailed it, he took steps to make it become true. He walked into Casa Roca, a clothing store run by Carlos Bringuier, a real *gusano*. Bringuier, a slender, light-skinned Cuban lawyer who had emi-grated after the revolution, first to Argentina and then to the United States, was the New Orleans delegate of the Miami-based counterrevolutionary organization called the Cuban Student Directorate (CSD).[1286] His brother, Juan Felipe, had been a member of Brigade 2506, the anti-Castro rebel force that landed on the beach in the CIA-sponsored Bay of Pigs invasion of Cuba in April of 1961.[1287]

Oswald may have been inspired by front-page headline stories on the discovery of bomb material in New Orleans that appeared in the New Orleans *Times-Picayune* on August 1 and 2. On July 31, the FBI had seized more than a ton of dynamite and twenty 100-pound bomb casings three feet long at a cottage on Lake Pontchartrain in St. Tammany's Parish, and the cottage had been linked to the anti-Castro movement. That there were Cuban exiles in New Orleans was no secret—the city boasted the second largest concentration of them after Miami, a fact that could not have escaped Oswald's attention—but there had been little indication that raids against the island were being prepared in New Orleans. The news stories may have induced Lee's venture into freelance undercover work. In any case, he was not merely shopping for clothes. He had called a New Orleans newspaper to get information as to the whereabouts of exile organizations and had been given the address of Bringuier's store at 107 Decatur Street and three others he noted in his address book. He already knew when he walked in that Bringuier was associated with the CSD.[1288]

Bringuier was in the store with his brother-in-law, Rolando Pelaez, and was engaged in conversation with a couple of American ninth graders named Philip Geraci and Vance

---

*Vincent T. Lee later told the Warren Commission that he decided to quit corresponding with Oswald. "He had gone ahead and acted on his own without any authorization [to set up a New Orleans chapter] . . . and then, when somebody goes off like this, violating all the rules that you send him, it comes as quite a dis-appointment because you have had hopes. Obviously, this man was not operating in an official capacity for the organization" (10 H 90).

The hapless Lee was the only member of the "New Orleans branch" of the FPCC, a branch that had never been chartered by the national committee.

Blalock. Geraci had known Bringuier for some time and had even raised about ten dollars for the CSD, but Bringuier told him he was much too young to join the fight against Castro. Bringuier would provide him with anti-Castro literature if he wanted to distribute it, but the best way he could help the struggle against Castro, he told the youth, was to listen to his parents and study hard. Oswald, having looked over several items on sale in the store, joined in the conversation and gave the impression that he too was enthusiastic about the underground war against Castro. Bringuier gave him some of the CSD literature printed in English.

"Is this the Cuban exile headquarters?" Oswald asked Bringuier. Bringuier said it wasn't, but that he was a part of the anti-Castro movement. Oswald told Bringuier that he had been a marine and had training in guerilla warfare. He would not only be willing to train Cubans to fight against Castro, he was ready to go along on a raid. He even offered to make a cash donation to the CSD, but Bringuier would not take his money, giving him instead the address of the national association in Miami.

Bringuier's brother-in-law was impressed by Lee; Bringuier was not. He was suspicious. Oswald could be a pro-Castro agent or an FBI agent. Ever since the CSD had shelled Havana without CIA authorization about a year before, Bringuier feared an attempt by the authorities to infiltrate the organization. Someone, after all, must have tipped off the bureau about those bomb materials in St. Tammany's Parish, a cache that Bringuier himself did not know about until the *Times-Picayune* article. He told Oswald that he had nothing to do with any military activities against Castro, that he was only involved in propaganda and information. Oswald insisted that he wanted to make himself useful and said he would bring Bringuier the Marine Corps manual for enlisted men the next day.[1289]

Young Geraci and Blalock were also impressed with Oswald, who told them how to blow up the Huey P. Long Bridge, derail a train, and construct a zip gun—pretty heavy stuff for high school kids.[1290]

As Oswald was making his crude foray into undercover work, the FBI, his bête noir, was on his trail again, although Lee had no inkling of that fact. That same day, August 5, 1963, the FBI's New Orleans office, by means of an interview of Oswald's landlady, confirmed the fact that he was now residing in the city at 4907 Magazine Street.[1291]* Also on that day, the consulate section of the Soviet embassy in Washington wrote to Marina to inform her that her "request to enter the Soviet Union for permanent residence" had been "forwarded to Moscow for processing."[1292]

---

*After the FBI confirmed Oswald's residence at 4907 Magazine Street, Mrs. Lena Garner, Oswald's landlady, recalled that the agent, Milton Kaack (one of two New Orleans FBI agents—the other, Warren de Brueys—assigned to monitor Oswald's activities), asked her "different little things about if I had seen him go out and did he have company and all this and that." Concerned, she asked Kaack, "I hope I don't have the wrong type of person in my house," and he told her, "Oh, no." He gave her his phone number and told her to call him if any unusual activities pertaining to Oswald took place. (CE 826, 17 H 755, xxii, FBI report of SA Milton Kaack on October 31, 1963; HSCA Record 180-10104-10364, Testimony of Lena Garner before HSCA on May 5, 1978, pp.8–10; HSCA staff interview of Mrs. Jesse Garner on February 20, 1978) Though Agent Hosty had lost Oswald's trail in Dallas, the New York City FBI office learned from an informant that on June 26, Oswald, with a post office box numbered 30061 in New Orleans, had corresponded with the *Worker* in New York, and this information was passed on to the New Orleans office of the FBI. Another informant (almost undoubtedly a New Orleans post office employee) advised the New Orleans FBI office on July 23 that Oswald's post office box had been rented on June 3, and Oswald had given his address as 657 French Street (as indicated, the Murrets lived at 757 French Street) in New Orleans. It is not clear from the record how the FBI got Oswald's address on Magazine Street since the Murrets never indicated the FBI came to their door until after Labor Day. (CE 833, 17 H 794; CE 826, 17 H 754–755; 8 H 146–147, WCT Lillian Murret)

The next day, August 6, Oswald returned to Casa Roca. Bringuier wasn't there, but Oswald left his copy of the *Guidebook for Marines* with Pelaez. The name "L. H. Oswald" was written on the first page.[1293]

On August 7, Lee brought Marina good news: Jackie Kennedy had given birth to a boy, Patrick. He broke the rest of the news gently since it was bound to be disturbing to Marina: there were problems with the Kennedys' baby—he had to be rushed to a special hospital. Lee was sure, though, that the doctors would be able to save the newborn's life. The next day, Lee listened to the news bulletins on the radio, and Marina, who recognized the name "Kennedy" when she heard it, anxiously asked him for the latest news. It was not good, but it was not until later that he told Marina that the doctors held little hope for Patrick.[1294]

Marina probably had something else on her mind. As indicated, even at this late stage of her pregnancy, she had not seen a doctor. Ruth Paine had written the previous month that she had found a hospital in the Dallas–Fort Worth area that could handle a childbirth for only $225.00—certainly a reasonable cost, except that it was $22.25 more than Lee's entire net worth at the moment. When looked at from that perspective, the cost was prohibitive. Lee had $202.75 in cash on hand at the end of July, and rent and other expenses would have to come out of that.[1295] Ruth had gone on to emphasize, in a section of the letter in English and addressed to Lee, the importance of prenatal care and of the medical records Marina should bring with her when she came to Dallas. "Major difficulty," Ruth had written, "can be avoided if the early warning signs available in the urine analysis and blood count are watched for." She went on to mention the dire results of toxemia and eclampsia.[1296] Marina was very worried, and told Lee, but Lee said, "No, no, you're not to worry. You'll be taken care of. Once you're in the hospital, the doctors don't care whose baby it is. They do the same for everyone. I'll borrow money. I promise you, you'll never be thrown out of the hospital."[1297]

Early the next morning, Friday, August 9, came the news that baby Patrick Kennedy had died during the night. Marina wept. Lee tried to reassure her by noting that Jacqueline Kennedy was frail and had lost other babies, while Marina was strong and was already the mother of a healthy, thriving child.[1298]

Later that same day, three days after Lee had delivered the Marine manual to the Casa Roca, around two in the afternoon he started passing out leaflets in the seven hundred block of Canal Street, not far from Bringuier's store. He attracted the attention of Celso Hernandez, a recently arrived refuge from Cuba. Hernandez spoke no English, but he understood very well two of the words on the sign Oswald was carrying: *Viva Fidel.* Hernandez tried to speak to Oswald, but the language barrier between them was impenetrable. Hernandez hurried off to Decatur Street to find Bringuier.

He found him at his store with another recently arrived, teenage Cuban, Miguel Cruz. The three of them decided on a counterdemonstration. Taking a sign Bringuier had in the store, they went back to Canal Street in search of the man passing out pro-Castro leaflets. The sign depicted the Statue of Liberty, with a hand, labeled "Soviet Union," plunging a knife in her back. The caption read, "Danger. Only 90 Miles From The United States Cuba Lies In Chains."

The man was nowhere to be found, so Bringuier, after taking a streetcar the length of Canal Street to scout for him, went back to his store. A few minutes later Cruz came in and said the man was again on Canal Street. Bringuier and Cruz hurried back to the scene. The excitable Bringuier was not just surprised to find that the man he was looking for was Oswald, he was outraged. Oswald smiled and offered Bringuier his hand, which only made Bringuier angrier. A crowd gathered, and Bringuier tried to explain to them that this man with his sign reading "Hands Off Cuba" had been presenting himself only four days earlier as a dedicated anti-Castroist. He warned the crowd that Oswald was a pro-Communist who wanted to kill them and send their children to the execution wall. The three excited Cubans found some allies in the crowd, people shouting at Oswald, "Traitor! Communist! Go back to Cuba! Kill him!" Someone gave Oswald a shove.

A policeman appeared and asked Bringuier and his friends to move on and allow Oswald to pass out his leaflets in peace. He was breaking no law. Bringuier tried to explain Oswald's treachery, but the policeman wasn't interested and went off to phone for help. In the officer's absence, Hernandez grabbed a stack of Oswald's yellow leaflets and threw them into the air, where they blew all over the place. Bringuier was ready to punch Oswald but stopped when Oswald crossed his arms in front of himself and said, "Okay, Carlos, if you want to hit me, hit me." Carlos held his punch. He wasn't going to make a martyr of Oswald.[1299]

A few minutes later two squad cars full of police arrived and arrested all four of them, Oswald as well as the three Cubans, for "disturbing the peace by creating a scene." They were taken to the station house of the First District, New Orleans Police Department, on North Rampart Street.[1300][*]

Each of them was questioned by police officers in the same room and Bringuier was impressed by Oswald's cool self-possession. He was not nervous, not out of control, confident of himself, even when he was asked if he was a Communist. He obliged the police by showing them his literature and explaining that the Fair Play for Cuba Committee was not some weird fringe group but a national organization with offices in New York. About the extent and membership of the organization in New Orleans, Lee was understandably more cagey. He did not want to discuss that in the presence of Bringuier and the other Cubans. The police took Oswald out of the room and Bringuier did not see him again that day. The Cubans put up twenty-five dollars each for bail and were released until a court appearance on Monday morning. Oswald, who did not have the money for bail, spent the night in jail.[1301]

About ten the next morning, New Orleans police lieutenant Francis L. Martello interviewed Oswald. Martello was currently a platoon commander at the First District station. As such, he routinely checked the preceding day's arrest records, and today he was struck by Oswald's police report. The police like to know what fringe groups are in the city and what their politics are, but the Fair Play for Cuba Committee was a new one to Martello. Martello had Oswald brought into an interview room, where he sorted through the contents of Oswald's wallet, making note of his Social Security number, Selective Service draft card, and two membership cards of the FPCC—one from New York and another from New Orleans signed A. J. Hidell.[1302]

Martello was friendly. His purpose was to establish a rapport with Oswald, and he found Lee easy to talk to, nonchalant, and obviously well read if not well educated, with a sort of "academic approach" to the Cuban problem. Oswald told him he had been born

---

[*]Film, which few Americans have ever seen, was shot of this incident. Sixteen-year-old Jim Doyle, walking with his parents on Canal Street, tried out his birthday present, an 8-millimeter camera. The film is somewhat murky, but the participants are clearly identifiable. The footage of Oswald passing out literature that is usually shown to illustrate this incident in television documentaries was actually shot a week later in a different location and without the involvement of any anti-Castro Cubans.

and raised in New Orleans, served in the U.S. Marines, lived for several years in Fort Worth, and moved from there to New Orleans only about four months ago. Martello had no reason to notice that Russia and Dallas had been entirely edited out of Oswald's biography, and his general impression was that Oswald was telling the truth, even though Oswald became evasive when the conversation turned to the New Orleans chapter of the FPCC. Oswald claimed about thirty-five members, whose names he declined to give, and said that about five of them might attend each regular meeting, whose location he likewise declined to give. Martello found this information surprising, since it seemed unlikely that a group with thirty-five members would have escaped the notice of the police department, but he did not make an issue of it. Curiously, Lee also asked to see an agent of the FBI,[*] and Martello obliged him by calling the local office of the bureau.[1303]

Lee turned to the Murrets for help to get out of jail. Unfortunately, only his cousin Joyce, home from Beaumont, Texas, for a visit, was at the house when Lee called from a jail phone. His Aunt Lillian was in the hospital, having undergone a minor ear operation, and his Uncle Dutz was away on a weekend Catholic religious retreat in Manresa, Louisiana, a place where people only go to pray and whose strict rules require that you can't talk to anyone for twenty-four hours. Joyce not only was encumbered by her two small children, but also had to go to the hospital to bring Lillian home and could ill afford the time to come down to Rampart Street to bail him out. But she promised to do so if she could manage.[1304]

For the time being, Oswald had better luck with his request to see a representative of the FBI. It was Saturday and the local office of the FBI was manned only by a skeleton crew. John Lester Quigley was the agent assigned the task. Neither the name nor the person of Lee Harvey Oswald rang any bells when Lee was shown into the police commander's office, where Quigley was looking over the FPCC materials Lieutenant Martello had given him. Quigley knew of the committee as a national organization but had not yet encountered any signs of it in New Orleans. He did know that the bureau had an open file on Oswald and somehow had completely forgotten that about a year and a half before he had gone over to the naval station at Algiers, a suburb across the river from the city, to check Oswald's naval intelligence records in response to a request from the bureau's office in Dallas.[1305]

Quigley took down some basic information about Oswald's background, which he seemed to be fairly forthcoming about. Again, Lee was less forthcoming when the conversation turned to details of the local chapter of the FPCC, although he was willing enough to lecture the agent on patriotism. He had been distributing these throwaways for the FPCC as "a patriotic duty, as a patriotic American citizen." The United States should not, Oswald said, attack Cuba or interfere with Cuban political affairs. The philosophy of the FPCC was that the American people should better understand internal conditions in Cuba and be given opportunities to go there to make up their own minds about it. As to the identity of A. J. Hidell,[†] whose signature appeared on the FPCC membership card,

---

[*]Why Lee would want to talk to the FBI, whom he had tried to elude in Fort Worth and Dallas, and for whom he had a dislike, is not known. The FBI agent who interviewed him, when asked that question, could only say that "frequently, persons who are in custody of local authorities . . . like to talk to the FBI" (4 H 435, WCT John Lester Quigley).

[†]We have seen that, per Marina, Oswald's alias Hidell was derived from Castro's first name, Fidel. The "A." on the membership card was the initial for Alek, which appeared on the forged Selective Service card Oswald had in his wallet at the time of his arrest ("Alex James Hidell"), and probably came from his Russian nickname Alik.

Oswald said he had never met Hidell personally but had spoken with him on the telephone on several occasions. He could not recall Hidell's telephone number but remembered it was now disconnected anyway. He said he had received a note in the mail from Hidell on August 7 asking him to distribute some FPCC literature in the downtown area of New Orleans. FPCC meetings were held, he said, in various members' residences, but he had attended only two of them and everyone there had been introduced by their first name only. He couldn't recall any of the first names. One meeting had been held at his own home, but he declined to say how he had managed to get in touch with these other FPCC members whose names and addresses he did not know. In short, it was obvious that Oswald was not going to provide Quigley with information of any real interest to him or the bureau.[1306]

Late that Saturday, Joyce Murret finally showed up at the police station, ready to put up the twenty-five-dollar bail for Oswald's release. When she saw the "Viva Fidel" sign Oswald had been carrying and the leaflet with its bold heading "HANDS OFF CUBA!" she flinched. "Oh, my God," she said, realizing she did not want to be a part of his being released from jail. Martello told her that Lee's offense wasn't particularly grave, and if she didn't want to put up the twenty-five-dollar bail, she could contact one of the city or state officials who had the "power of parole," and on his instruction Oswald would be released until his case was heard. Not sure what to do, she left and went to bring her mother home from the hospital, but not before she filled in some of the gaps Lee had left in his interview with Martello, telling the lieutenant about Lee's trip to Russia and his poor Russian wife whom Lee did not even allow to speak English.[1307]

Martello, intrigued, had Lee brought out of his cell to talk with him again. He asked Lee whether he was a Communist and Lee said he was not, relying on his increasingly familiar mantra that he was a Marxist but not a Soviet-style Marxist-Leninist. Lee, given the opportunity to talk about his favorite subject, political philosophy, grew expansive. He said he was in full accord with Karl Marx's book *Das Kapital*, but true Communism did not exist in Russia. Marx, he said, was never a true Communist anyway; he was a socialist, as, Lee said, he himself was. Soviet Communism "stunk." Russia had, he said, "fat, stinking politicians over there just like we have over here," and that while the leaders have everything, the people are still poor and depressed. When Martello asked why he did not allow members of his family to learn English, Lee said that he hated America and didn't want them to become "Americanized" and that he planned to return to Russia. As for his views of Khrushchev and Kennedy, he said he thought they got along very well together. There was no other mention of the president, but they did talk about Castro again. Martello asked whether he knew that Castro had recently admitted he was a Marxist-Leninist. Lee did, but he was not going to discuss the merits and demerits of the Cuban premier; he was mainly concerned with the people of Cuba and said the situation in Cuba would be a lot better "if this country would have better relations with the poor people of Cuba and quit worrying about Castro."[1308]

After, Martello had Lee returned to his cell, he stuck his notes and several copies of the evidence—Oswald's leaflets—in a file folder, put them away, and forgot about them. He did not consider Lee Oswald anyone who would be likely to resort to violence. In fact, he found him rather the opposite, rather passive. He hadn't even tried to defend himself when Bringuier had threatened him. When Martello thought about the events of the day before, it seemed to him that Oswald may have set the Cubans up.[1309]

Lee languished in jail—no sign of cousin Joyce and the bail money. Irritated, and not knowing that Joyce had already been to the jail, he called again and found that Joyce had just returned from the hospital with his Aunt Lillian. He was quite rude to Joyce on the phone, wanting to know why she hadn't come to bail him out. When she told him she didn't have any money, he told her to go to Magazine Street and get it from Marina, who should have about seventy dollars in cash. But Joyce absolutely did not want to make yet another trip to Rampart Street or get involved in any way. She told Lillian what Martello had told her about getting an official to "parole" Lee, and Lillian came up with the solution. She had Joyce get in touch with someone the Murrets knew, a local liquor store owner and state boxing commissioner, Emile Bruneau, who called her back later to say he had contacted a local official (A. Heckman, a New Orleans jury commissioner) and that Oswald had been released.[1310]

When Lee finally got home on Saturday evening, he was tired and dirty but quietly jubilant as he informed Marina where and why he had been detained. She had lain awake until three that morning worrying about him and had even gone to check to be sure he did not have the Mannlicher-Carcano rifle with him. He told her that he enjoyed a philosophical conversation with a sympathetic police officer who had been like "a kindly uncle"—no doubt Martello. "He listened to my ideas," Lee told her, "and let me out."[1311]

When Dutz came home from his retreat on Sunday evening and Lillian told him what had happened, he was horrified by the whole story. He drove over to the Oswalds' place on Magazine Street, where he took note of the photograph of Fidel Castro on the mantle. He gave Lee a good talking to, suggesting that he get a job and start taking his family responsibilities seriously.

"You be sure you show up at that courthouse for the trial," he warned Lee.

Lee said, "Don't worry, I'll show up."[1312]

Come Monday morning, August 12, Bringuier, Hernandez, and Cruz arrived early, joining some other Cubans who had taken seats in the half of the small Rampart Street courthouse reserved for white folks. Moments later Oswald arrived and ostentatiously took a seat on the other side, the one reserved for colored people. Bringuier seethed. The Cuban immediately understood what Oswald was up to. He meant to win the blacks over when he made a stirring defense of the villainous Fidel Castro. This would be "a tremendous work of propaganda for his side," Bringuier realized, one of the things that caused him to think "that he was really a smart guy and not a nut."[1313]

But Oswald pled guilty to a charge of disturbing the peace and was sentenced to pay a fine of ten dollars or serve ten days in jail. Oswald paid the fine.[1314] Bringuier, himself an attorney when he was in Cuba, pled not guilty and undertook a defense of himself and his two companions. He showed the judge the *Guidebook for Marines* and pointed to Oswald's name on the first page, clear proof that Oswald was an agent provocateur trying to infiltrate the Cuban Student Directorate. The judge, no doubt eager to see the last of all four of them, dismissed the case against the Cubans.[1315]

Johann Rush, a young cameraman for New Orleans television station WDSU, started filming Oswald walking down the stairs from the second-floor courtroom after the court session. Oswald seemed startled by the TV cameras.

"So you're interested in this, huh?"

"Yes, we are," Rush said.

When Oswald learned he would be seen on WDSU-TV that evening, his interest was piqued. Rush spotted the gleam in his eye, handed him his business card, and suggested that Oswald give him a ring at the station whenever he planned further demonstrations.

Rush was eager to film a good, old-fashioned street brawl. Oswald was noncommital but clearly interested, and Rush was pretty sure he would go for it. The Cubans watched the conversation from a distance, and raged. As soon as Oswald left, they assailed Rush. He ought not be talking at all with a Communist like that, much less giving him publicity. Rush shot footage of them too, and they were temporarily appeased.[1316]

Lee, who had been waiting two months for a reply from Vincent Lee of the national Fair Play for Cuba Committee, felt that the recent events would finally evoke a response from the New York headquarters, and later in the day he wrote to Vincent Lee:

> Dear Mr. Lee
>   Continuing my efforts on behalf of F.P.C.C. in New Orleans I find that I have incured the displeasure of the Cuban exile "worms" here. I was attacked by three of them as the copy of the enclosed summons indicates I was fined ten dollars and the three Cubans were not fined because of "lack of evidence," as the judge said. I am very glad I am stirring things up and shall continue to do so. The incident was given considerable coverage in the press and local T.V. news broadcast. I'm sure it will all be to the good of the Fair Play for Cuba committee.
>   Sincerley yours
>   Lee H. Oswald[1317]

Vincent Lee, already disturbed by Oswald's undisciplined efforts on the committee's behalf, was not inspired to reply.[1318]

That day, August 12, or the next, Rush's friend Bill Stuckey, who had a weekly program on the radio side of WDSU, phoned Bringuier and asked him if he had Oswald's address. Stuckey had hitchhiked around Latin America for awhile after he mustered out of the Marine Corps, and he spoke Spanish pretty well. His program on WDSU dealt with Latin American affairs, and he knew many of the anti-Castro leaders in the city. Within the week Bringuier got the address for Stuckey from the court papers and asked Stuckey why he wanted it. Stuckey, who had heard about the national Fair Play for Cuba Committee but nothing about any local chapter, wanted to interview Oswald. Bringuier protested vehemently—Stuckey shouldn't give a Communist like Oswald airtime when there were plenty of people in town who really knew what was going on in Cuba. Stuckey offered to do a radio interview of Bringuier too, but Bringuier didn't like that idea either. Bringuier suggested a debate.[1319]

When Stuckey didn't take him up on the idea, Bringuier acted on his own. Rush found himself dispatched to Casa Roca to film Bringuier's hastily organized press conference. Bringuier presented two Cuban exiles who had just returned from a raid on their homeland, and he served as their interpreter since neither of them spoke English. The two freedom fighters agreed that conditions in Cuba were now worse than ever. They were angry that the U.S. government, since the missile crisis, no longer supported Cuban exile raids on the island.[1320]

Meanwhile, the August 13 edition of the *Times-Picayune* published an account of the street incident under the caption "Pamphlet Case Sentence Given." It read, in its entirely, "Lee Oswald, 4907 Magazine, Monday was sentenced to pay a fine of ten dollars or serve ten days in jail on the charge of disturbing the peace by creating a scene. Oswald was arrested by First District police at 4:15 p.m. Friday in the 700 block of Canal while he was reportedly distributing pamphlets asking for a 'Fair Play for Cuba.' Police were called to the scene when three Cubans reportedly sought to stop Oswald. Municipal Court charges against the Cubans for disturbing the peace were dropped by the court."[1321]

It wasn't much, but New Orleans's main newspaper had taken notice and Oswald, delighted, made the most of it. He wrote to Arnold Johnson, information director of the U.S. Communist Party, that same day, August 13:

> Dear Mr. Johnson:
>
> I wish to thank you for the literature which you sent me for our local branch of the "Fair Play For Cuba Committee," of which I am the secretary-President. As you can see from the enclosed [newspaper] clipping I am doing my best to help the cause of [a] new Cuba . . . Please accept an honourary New Orleans branch membership card as a token of esteem.
>
> Thank You
>
> Lee H. Oswald[1322]

Johann Rush did not have long to wait on his invitation to Oswald. Oswald left a message for Rush at the TV station to alert him that the Fair Play for Cuba Committee would again distribute literature, this time in front of the International Trade Mart at noon on Friday, August 16. Other newspaper and television stations were also informed, although the papers ignored the event, and only one other cameraman, WWL's Mike O'Connor, showed up.* It was Oswald's best-organized effort. He provided some substance for his phantom FPCC chapter by getting two other young men to help distribute the literature. One of them, a short, young Cuban, only passed out a few of the handful of leaflets Rush saw Oswald give him on the street after talking to him and his taller companion. The short man, who has never been identified, seemed embarrassed by the entire affair, grinning a lot, and soon left with his companion, who seemed to purposefully keep his back to Rush's camera throughout the entire incident. The other leaflet distributor was a kid named Charles Hall Steele Jr., whom Oswald had recruited at the unemployment office, where Steele was waiting for a friend who was taking a test. Oswald offered two dollars for fifteen or twenty minutes of work. It sounded good to Steele, who asked no questions. He didn't even bother to read the literature he passed out. Carlos Bringuier was tipped off, but he got the news too late and failed to get to the scene on time. This time there were no Cuban exiles and no fracas, but the footage of Oswald passing out leaflets in front of the New Orleans Trade Mart shot by Rush and O'Connor was broadcast on television that evening anyway.[1323]

Someone brought one of the leaflets Oswald was passing out to Bringuier's store, and Bringuier noticed that although it was the same leaflet, on yellow paper, from the week before, this time it bore a different address. The original leaflet from August 9 was stamped with the name A. J. Hidell and a post office box number; today's was stamped with Oswald's name and the Magazine Street address. A friend, Carlos Quiroga, came up with an idea to run a counterspy operation on Oswald. That evening, posing as a Castro sympathizer, Quiroga called on Oswald and spent an hour on Oswald's screen porch dis-

---

*Oswald's choice of the Trade Mart, located on Camp Street in a busy part of downtown New Orleans, was a logical one, since his whole plea involved Cuba, and the Trade Mart housed many import and export companies that did business with Latin America. Before the trade embargo on Cuba by the American government, many of such companies did business with Cuba. (Letter from Johann Rush to author dated January 5, 2000)

cussing Cuban affairs with him. Oswald suspected that the Cuban was an agent of Bringuier's or possibly even the FBI and told him nothing in particular,[1324] but while Quiroga was there, little June came out on the porch and—to Quiroga's astonishment—Lee spoke Russian to her. He tried to cover the blunder by telling Quiroga that he was studying Russian at Tulane University and was teaching it to his daughter, but the cat was out of the bag. Quiroga went straight back to Bringuier with the news that Lee Oswald might well have some connection to Soviet Russia.[1325]

Early the next morning, Saturday, August 17, Bill Stuckey finally made use of the address he had gotten from Bringuier. He went to Magazine Street at eight o'clock to catch Oswald before he left for the day. Oswald appeared on his front porch wearing nothing but a pair of U.S. Marine fatigue pants but looking trim and very "neat and clean."[*] Stuckey had expected something more bohemian, a beard and sandals perhaps, more like a folk singer. Stuckey invited Oswald to appear on his radio program, *Latin Listening Post*, that night. If Oswald would come down to the WDSU studios at five, they could record an interview out of which four and a half minutes would be edited for broadcast the same evening at 7:30.

Oswald was more than ready to oblige. The two men talked long enough on the screen porch for Stuckey to form the opinion that Oswald was intelligent, articulate, and serious-minded, the type who could attract some followers to his ideas. Oswald could not invite Stuckey in for a cup of coffee, because, he said, his wife and child were still asleep. Lee probably wanted to avoid the debacle of the evening before when Quiroga heard him speak Russian to his child. He showed Stuckey his membership cards in the FPCC, including the one that designated him secretary of the local chapter. He pointed out that he was only the secretary; A. Hidell was the president of the chapter—a chapter, we know, that was entirely fictitious, not being authorized by the national office of the FPCC. Lee also gave Stuckey some of the literature he had collected, including two speeches by Castro, "The Revolution Must be a School of Unfettered Thought" and "Bureaucracy and Sectarianism." There was a pamphlet by the French existentialist Jean-Paul Sartre, *Ideology and Revolution*, and Corliss Lamont's *Crime against Cuba*. Oswald agreed to meet Stuckey at WDSU at five.[1326]

Stuckey was intrigued enough by Oswald to want to record an interview much longer than the four and a half minutes he could cram into his program. If it went well—from his estimation of Oswald, he thought it would—he would approach station management about running it complete, a half hour or so. He drew up a long list of questions.

Oswald came in about five, dressed as he had dressed for his two street demonstrations—neatly, in a short-sleeved white dress shirt, tie, and slacks. Under his arm he carried a blank looseleaf notebook. He handed Stuckey a reprint of an article about the treatment of the Cuban Revolution in the American press from the 1961 summer edition of *Liberation* magazine.[1327] Stuckey and Oswald sat down before microphones in a studio and began the taped (not live) interview, while the recording engineer, Al Campin, listened to every word. Campin was as intrigued as Stuckey had been. He hadn't encountered anyone with Oswald's views, and he too was curious as to how Oswald thought and why. Oswald obviously already had fully prepared "answers" to Stuckey's questions, which made Stuckey's

---

[*]The frames of Oswald in front of the Trade Mart also show him shaven and clean-cut with a white shirt and tie and dark trousers (see photo section), clearly the old Oswald once again after the brief spell at the greasing job at the coffee company.

questions almost irrelevant. Stuckey realized "how adept [Oswald] was at taking a question, any question, and distorting it for his own purposes, saying what he wanted to say while making you think that he was answering your question. He was an expert in dialectics." Stuckey let the conversation run to thirty-seven minutes.[1328] Of course, he had never heard most of Oswald's take on things before, which lent them a freshness they didn't have; Oswald's views had not developed much from the time he had been interviewed in Moscow by Priscilla Johnson and Aline Mosby.

Lee told one of his characteristically pathetic little lies when asked about his background—he claimed that he had worked his way up through the ranks of the Marine Corps to the grade of "buck sergeant." Notably absent from his account of himself were his recent stay in Dallas, and, naturally, his pilgrimage to the Soviet Union. He didn't even refer to the latter when asked if he knew of any black market in Soviet Russia.[1329]

Most of the rest of the interview was unremarkable, true as far as it went, though lacking any sort of insight into or special knowledge of conditions in Cuba, where Oswald had never been, or the nature of the severely strained Cuban-American relations. On a few occasions Oswald stumbled but displayed some agility in recovering.

He suggested that the suspensions of civil liberties in Cuba were similar to those imposed in the United States in 1950 with the outbreak of the Korean police action: "We adopted an emergency law which restricted newspapers, broadcasters, radio and TV from giving any opinions, any comments which [were] not already checked out by certain administrative bureaus of the United States Government." Such restrictions and administrative bureaus were, of course, figments of Oswald's imagination, and Stuckey, who had earlier been a columnist for the *New Orleans States-Item*, called him on it: "Mr. Oswald, this is very interesting to me to find out about the restrictions of newspapers in 1950 because I was in the newspaper business at that time and I do not recall seeing any such government bureau established . . . to tell us what to print. Exactly what do you have reference to?"

Oswald backpedaled—lamely: "Well, I have reference to the obvious fact that during wartime, haphazard guesses and information are not given by anyone. In regards to military strategical comments, such as comments or leaks about new fronts or movements and so forth, news was controlled at that time to that extent, as it is always controlled during a war or national emergency, always."[1330]

He then claimed that the Fair Play for Cuba Committee had "often approached" the local *Times-Picayune* and *States-Item* newspaper syndicate with information or comments that the paper had "consistently refused" to print because of its anti-Castro position. Stuckey recognized this as claptrap and asked Oswald for the names of people at the paper he might have approached—people Stuckey knew well.

"I do not know the name of the reporter," Oswald explained. "I did speak to the City Editor, I spoke to him one week ago and I spoke to him yesterday, Friday, which was immediately after our demonstration."[1331]

Oswald's resort to Far Left cant about the nature of the exodus from Cuba following the revolution also went astray. "Needless to say, there are classes of criminals; there are classes of people who are wanted in Cuba for crimes against humanity [a reference to members of Batista's regime] and most of those people are the same people who are in New Orleans and have set themselves up in stores with blood money and who engage in day to day trade with New Orleanians." To these he added, "Peasants who do not like the collectivization of Cuban agriculture [and] others who have one reason or the other . . .

for fleeing Cuba. Most of these people flee by legal means. They are allowed to leave after requesting the Cuban government for exit visas. Some of these people for some reason or another do not like to apply for these visas."

Stuckey countered that what Oswald said was "very interesting" because he had been covering the refugees for three years and the last Batista supporter he knew of had left the island at least two and a half years before, "and the rest of them I've talked to have been taxicab drivers, laborers, cane cutters, and that sort of thing," the very people "the revolution was supposed to benefit."

Oswald now admitted that the "Batista criminals" were in the minority and that the majority in the last year were undoubtedly "rather peasant class," but went on to say that revolutions demand certain sacrifices and adaptations that not all are willing to make.[1332]

Oswald slipped again while advocating friendlier relations between Cuba and the "government of the United States and its government agencies, particularly certain covert, undercover agencies like the now *defunct* CIA."

Stuckey was all but speechless. "Now defunct?" he asked.

"Well, its leadership is now defunct. Allen Dulles is now defunct."[1333]

Allen Dulles, who survived to become a member of the Warren Commission, might well have been surprised to hear this description of his current mortal condition, but it was never broadcast. It fell by the wayside when Stuckey, immediately after the recording session, cut the tape down to the four and a half minutes, which was broadcast that night. Stuckey chose what he thought were the best parts, in particular Oswald's definition of democracy, which Stuckey found good. Oswald said that the definition of democracy was now "controversial . . . You know, it used to be very clear, but now it's not. You know, when our forefathers drew up the constitution, they considered that democracy was creating an atmosphere of freedom of discussion, of argument, of finding the truth. The rights, well, the classic right of having life, liberty and the pursuit of happiness. In Latin America they have none of those rights, none of them at all. And that is my definition of democracy, the right to be in a minority and not to be suppressed. The right to see for yourself, without government restrictions, such countries as Cuba, and we are restricted from going to Cuba."

Stuckey told Oswald about his plan to play the original, uncut tape for station management to see if they would be interested in broadcasting it later, and he asked Oswald to call him on Monday, by which time he would have management's decision. It was obvious to Stuckey that Oswald was delighted with his performance and felt he had "scored quite a coup."[1334]

Indeed, so confident was Oswald that he would do well that it appears that before he even went to the station that night for the interview, he tried once again to induce some response from Vincent Lee at the national FPCC office by referring to his interview as if it had already taken place:

> Dear Mr. Lee,
>   Since I last wrote you . . . about my arrest and fine in New Orleans for [distributing] literature for F.P.C.C., things have been moving pretty fast. On August 16th I organized a F.P.C.C. demonstration of three people. This demonstration was given considerable coverage by WDSU-TV Channel 6, and also by our Channel 4 T.V. station. Due to that I was invited by Bill Stucke to appear on his T.V. show called "Latin American Focus" at 7:30 P.M. Saturday's on WDSU-Channel 6.

After the 15 minute interview which was filed on magnetic tape at 4:00 P.M. for rebroadcast at 7:30 I was flooded with callers and invitations to debate's ect, as well as people interested in joining the F.P.C.C. New Orleans branch. That than is what has happened up to this day and hour. You can I think be happy with the developing situation here in New Orleans. I would however, ask you to rush some more literature particularly the white sheet "Truth about Cuba" regarding government restrictions on Travel, as I am quickly runing out.

Yours truly
Lee H. Oswald

On the outside of the envelope Oswald wrote, "RUSH PLEASE."[1335]*

On Monday, Oswald called Stuckey, who told him that the program director had not wanted to broadcast the whole interview but was interested in a debate between Oswald and some local anti-Communists. It would run—live—for twenty-five minutes in one of the station's regular, daily time slots, *Conversation Carte Blanche*, on Wednesday at 6:05 in the evening. "How many of you am I going to have to fight?" Oswald asked. Stuckey told him he had already arranged for two other guests, one whom Oswald knew—Carlos Bringuier. The other was Edward S. Butler, executive director of the Information Council of the Americas (INCA), a rising young star in the anti-Communism field. Butler, along with Dr. Alton Oschner, the famous New Orleans surgeon, founded INCA. Butler's council was a producer of anti-Communist literature and recordings, principally tape-recorded interviews with Cuban and East European refugees from satellite countries of the USSR denouncing the evils of Communism. One of his featured speakers was Fidel Castro's fervently anti-Communist sister, Juanita. The tapes were distributed to over a hundred radio stations in Latin America.[1336] Stuckey and one of the station's radio announcers, Bill Slatter, would be the co-moderators. Oswald cheerfully accepted the challenge.

That same day, August 19, Stuckey called a contact at the local FBI office, who read salient points of Oswald's FBI file to him—Oswald's defection to the USSR, his marriage to a Russian woman, his eventual repatriation, all of which Oswald had not mentioned in the first interview. Stuckey found this new information "so interesting," and offered to let the FBI make a copy of the tape of the full thirty-seven-minute interview he had recorded on Saturday, and the agency did.[1337]

Stuckey had no qualms about ambushing Oswald with Oswald's defection to Russia.

---

*Although it doesn't make too much sense, I am forced by the evidence to conclude that Oswald probably wrote this letter *before* he even went on Stuckey's show. Stuckey is positive that the taped interview with Oswald took place around 5:00 p.m. on Saturday, August 17, 1963, a few hours before his regular Saturday night show at 7:30 p.m. (11 H 160, 162, 165, WCT William Kirk Stuckey). Yet Oswald's August 17 letter to Lee is postmarked, "New Orleans, L.A. 6:06 p.m. 17 AUG 1963" (Lee [Vincent T.] Exhibit No. 7, 20 H 531). There is no way Oswald could have had the long, thirty-seven-minute interview with Stuckey at 5:00 p.m., a discussion with him thereafter, gotten home (presumably by bus), written the letter, and had it postmarked 6:06 p.m. Either he wrote the letter before the interview (his saying the interview lasted only fifteen minutes when it lasted thirty-seven minutes is further evidence it was written before the interview), or Oswald was right about the interview being at 4:00 p.m., not 5:00 p.m. as Stuckey said, and Oswald, who would still, even with this additional hour, be very pressed for time, managed to get home on time to write the letter and get it off at a substation of the post office in his area for the postmarked time of 6:06 p.m. But this is still unlikely since it appears that the various post office substations in New Orleans closed at 5:45 p.m. (CE 2132, 24 H 716), the postmark being made at the post office after the mail was picked up. Oswald most likely put his letter in a mailbox or delivered it to a substation at some earlier time in the day.

He thought that Oswald was so glib that his appearances on WDSU radio might well attract new followers, but in the strongly anti-Communist, anti-Soviet atmosphere of New Orleans, that would be much less likely if his audience knew that Oswald had defected to the USSR. Butler, who had separately gotten hold of newspaper clippings on Oswald's defection to Russia from the files of the House Un-American Activities Committee in Washington, D.C., agreed that Stuckey would spring the trap on Oswald at the very outset when he introduced the participants in the debate.[1338]

Oswald appeared promptly at 5:30 p.m., neatly if incongruously dressed in his heavy, badly cut woolen suit from Minsk—which must have been a misery in the sweltering heat of mid-August in New Orleans—a blue shirt, and a dark tie. He looked hot and uncomfortable. He carried the same black looseleaf notebook.[1339]

Butler came in a little later, and then Bringuier. Both of them carried what looked to Stuckey like "pounds and pounds" of literature. They were well prepared. Oswald approached Bringuier to shake his hand, and Bringuier returned the friendly gesture by explaining to Oswald that he had nothing personal against him, just ideological objections. Bringuier believed that the best thing he could do would be to get a Communist like Oswald out of the party and put him to work against Communism, because a former member of the party would know what Communism truly meant. He told Oswald he found it painful to see any American espouse Communism, because Communism was trying to destroy the United States. He was sure that if Oswald considered it—perhaps when he was in bed and thinking things over—he would see that he could still do something good for his country, for his family, and for himself. If Oswald wanted to do that, he could come to Bringuier, who would receive him with open arms.

It seemed a touchy moment to Stuckey, but Oswald just smiled at Bringuier and observed that he, Oswald, was on the correct side and Bringuier on the wrong side, and they left it at that. Oswald saw that Carlos was carrying Oswald's Marine Corps manual and said, "Well, listen, Carlos, don't try to do an invasion with that *Guidebook for Marines*, because that's an old one and it will be a failure." Bringuier took it as a joke.[1340]

After they took their places in the studio, the red "On the Air" sign went on and Bill Slatter, the radio announcer, introduced the program and then passed it over to Stuckey. Stuckey immediately sprang the trap on Oswald. Speaking of last Saturday's appearance by Oswald on *Latin Listening Post*, Stuckey said, "Mr. Oswald said . . . that he was a native of New Orleans . . . had entered the U.S. Marine Corps in 1956 and was honorably discharged in 1959. He said . . . that he had lived in Fort Worth, Texas, before coming here to establish a Fair Play for Cuba chapter several weeks ago. However, there are a few items apparently that I suspect that Mr. Oswald left out in his original interview, which was principally where he lived . . . between 1959 and 1962 . . . Mr. Butler brought some newspaper clippings to my attention . . . Washington newspaper clippings to the effect that Mr. Oswald had attempted to renounce his American citizenship in 1959 and become a Soviet citizen. There was another clipping dated 1962 saying that Mr. Oswald had returned from the Soviet Union with his wife and child after having lived there three years. Mr. Oswald, are these correct?"

"That is correct," Oswald said. "Correct, yeah."

"You did live in Russia for three years?"

"That is correct, and I think that those, the fact that I did live for a time in the Soviet Union gives me excellent qualifications to repudiate charges that Cuba and the Fair Play for Cuba Committee is Communist-controlled."

Lee kept his composure and tried to change the subject, but his attackers would not let him off the hook. Lee had prepared to put up a spirited defense of the Cuban Revolution but was now forced to defend himself. They bored in relentlessly: Lee was probably a Communist, and the Fair Play for Cuba Committee was thus a Communist front, its strings pulled from Moscow. The so-called revolution in Cuba was a mask for the Soviet colonization of the island, and so on.

Slatter passed the microphone to Bringuier, who wanted to know "exactly the name of the organization you represent here in the city, because I have some confusion. Is [it] Fair Play for Cuba Committee or Fair Play for Russia Committee?"

"Well, that is a very provocative request," Oswald said, "and I don't think [it] requires an answer."

Bringuier dropped his question and launched into a diatribe loaded with statistics about the decline in living standards since the success of Castro's revolution, but Oswald countered that he didn't think that was "the subject to be discussed tonight. The Fair Play for Cuba Committee, and as the name implies, is concerned primarily with Cuban-American relations."

"How many people," Slatter asked bluntly, "do you have in your committee here in New Orleans?"

"I cannot reveal that as secretary of the Fair Play for Cuba Committee."

"Is it a secret society?" Butler asked.

"No, Mr. Butler, it is not. However, it is standard operating procedure for a political organization consisting of a political minority to safeguard the names and the number of its members."

"Well, the Republicans are in the minority," Butler said. "I don't see them hiding their membership."

"The Republicans are not a . . . well . . . the Republicans are an established political party representing a great number of people. They represent no radical point of view. They do not have a very violent and sometimes emotional opposition as we do."

"Oh, I see," Butler said. "Well, would you say then that the Fair Play for Cuba Committee is not a Communist-front organization?"

"The Senate subcommittees who have occupied themselves with investigating the Fair Play for Cuba Committee have found there is nothing to connect the two . . . We have been investigated from several points of view. That is, points of view of taxes, allegiance, subversion, and so forth. The findings have been, as I say, absolutely zero."

Butler asked Oswald if he knew who the honorary chairman of his national committee was. Oswald didn't, and Butler proceeded to tell him it was Waldo Frank, an avowed Communist, citing the title of an article written by Frank in the publication *New Masses* back in 1932 titled "How I Came to Communism—A Symposium." Butler went on to ask Oswald who the national secretary for the FPCC was. After answering, "Well we have a National Director who is Mr. V. [Vincent] T. Lee," Oswald went on to acknowledge that Lee was under indictment for illegally traveling to Cuba, a fact that Oswald did his best to minimize without much success.

"The Fair Play for Cuba Committee," he concluded defensively, "is not now on the Attorney General's subversive list. Any other material you may have is superfluous."

Slatter broke in to put the focus firmly back on Oswald himself, returning to a matter Oswald had already admitted. "I believe it was mentioned that you at one time asked to renounce your American citizenship and become a Soviet citizen, is that correct?"

"Well, I don't think that has particular import to this discussion. We are discussing Cuban-American relations." It was another try to make it back to firmer ground, but they weren't interested in discussing Cuban-American relations. They wanted to discuss whether Lee Harvey Oswald was a Communist, disloyal to his country, and a member of a Communist-front organization, and none of them were satisfied with what they perceived to be Oswald's hairsplitting when he said, "I am a Marxist."

A commercial break brought a momentary respite, but after it Bill Slatter immediately continued the attack, pointing out that even though he agreed that the discussion was supposed to be about Latin American relations, Oswald's secrecy about his organization meant that "anybody who might be interested in this organization ought to know more about you. For this reason I'm curious to know just how you supported yourself during the three years that you lived in the Soviet Union. Did you have a government subsidy?"

Stunned, Oswald stammered, "Well, as I, er, well . . . I will answer that question directly then as you will not rest until you get your answer. I worked in Russia . . . I was not under the protection of the American government, but as I was at all times considered an American citizen I did not lose my American citizenship."

"Did you say that you wanted to at one time, though?" Slatter asked. "What happened?"

Oswald tried to claim that he never renounced his citizenship, which was technically true, and was never out of contact with the American embassy, which was not, so Butler read from two clippings in the *Washington Evening Star*, which said that Oswald had turned in his American passport and applied for Soviet citizenship. Oswald effectively replied that his return to the United States was proof that he had not renounced his citizenship.

Bill Slatter finally gave Oswald a break by asking him—at last—about the Fair Play for Cuba Committee. "I would say that Castro is about as unpopular as anybody in the world in this country," Slatter began. "As a practical matter, what do you hope to gain for your work? How do you hope to bring about what you call 'Fair Play for Cuba' knowing this sentiment?"

"The principles of thought of the Fair Play for Cuba [Committee] consist of restoration of diplomatic, trade, and tourist relations with Cuba," Oswald replied. "That is one of our main points. We are for that. I disagree that this situation regarding American-Cuban relations is very unpopular. We are in the minority surely. We are not particularly interested in what Cuban exiles or . . . rightist members of rightist organizations have to say. We are primarily interested in the attitude of the U.S. government toward Cuba. And in that way we are striving to get the United States to adopt measures which would be more friendly toward the Cuban people and the new Cuban regime in that country. We are not at all communist controlled, regardless of the fact that I had the experience of living in Russia, regardless of the fact that we have been investigated, regardless of any of these facts. The Fair Play for Cuba Committee is an independent organization not affiliated with any other organization. Our aims and our ideas are very clear and in the best keeping with American traditions of democracy."

"Do you agree with Fidel Castro," Bringuier asked, "when in his last speech of July 26 of this year he [described] President John F. Kennedy of the United States as a ruffian and a thief? Do you agree with Mr. Castro?"

"I would not agree with that particular wording," Lee said. "I and the Fair Play for Cuba Committee do think that the United States government, through certain agencies, mainly the State Department and the CIA, has made monumental mistakes in their relations with Cuba. Mistakes which are pushing Cuba into the sphere of activity of, let's say, a very dogmatic Communist country such as China."

The program dragged on for another minute or two, and Oswald managed to make a couple of points, that the American government might have indeed eventually withdrawn its support of Batista but really never supported Castro, and, in answer to Butler's charge that the Cuban people were "starving," responded that the "diversification of agriculture"—from sugar and tobacco to products such as sweet potatoes, lima beans, and cotton—was bound to create temporary shortages. Time ran out and Slatter brought the program to a close.[1341]

Afterward, Bill Slatter asked Oswald to help him make a brief clip that could be used on the television news. They went into a television studio and shot about five minutes of Oswald repeating some of the statements he had made on the radio broadcast. A brief excerpt was used later in the evening.[1342]

Stuckey would later say, "We finished [Oswald] on that program. I think that after that program the Fair Play for Cuba Committee, if there ever was one in New Orleans, had no future there, because we had publicly linked the Fair Play for Cuba Committee with a fellow who lived in Russia for three years and who was an admitted Marxist."[1343]

Oswald was dejected when he came out of the studio, and Stuckey suggested they go for a beer, which Oswald accepted. Oswald let his hair down and spoke with Stuckey as he had with no one since before George de Mohrenschildt left Dallas for Haiti. Before the two young men adjourned to a bar called Comeaux's, about a half a block from the station, Oswald had been guarded with Stuckey, speaking stiltedly, like a lawyer speaking for the record. Now he seemed relaxed, perhaps relieved that the ordeal of the panel discussion was over.

Oswald talked about Sukarno and Communism in Indonesia, about which he had been reading everything he could lay his hands on, and Stuckey was again struck by Oswald's intelligence and was of the "impression he had done a great deal of reading." Oswald's position was that Sukarno was not a Communist but was using the Indonesian Communists for his own purposes.

The conversation became more personal. Stuckey made a remark about Oswald's "gawky suit," and Oswald admitted that it was of Russian manufacture and the Russians didn't know much about making clothes over there. He went on to talk about his impressions of life in Russia, which he described as very bland as well as repressive. A protest organization like the Fair Play for Cuba Committee would never have been allowed there, he said.

When Stuckey mentioned the fact that Oswald was not making much headway with his beer, Oswald told him, "Well, you see, I am not used to drinking beer. I am a vodka drinker."

Stuckey, who had never met a Marxist before, asked Oswald how he became one. From books on the subject at public libraries, Oswald said. When Stuckey asked Oswald if his family had been an influence on him in any way, Oswald said, "No," a little amused. "They are pretty much typical New Orleans types."

He had begun to read Marx and Engels at the age of fifteen, he said, but it was his military service in Japan that made him decide for Marxism. Living conditions there convinced him not only that something was wrong with the system, but that Marxism might be the solution. It was in Japan that he began to think about going to Russia to see for himself how a revolutionary Marxist society works.

He admitted that it hadn't entirely pleased him. Factory life there was pretty much what you would find in an American plant—bad attitudes and a lot of goldbricking. Nepotism. Extra privileges for the bosses. Dishonest, padded production figures. Oswald scornfully observed that there was a sameness to the people—he thought it might be because the Soviets had eliminated too many of the dissenting elements in Russian society and were left, as a result, with a fairly homogeneous population.

Stuckey got the impression that Oswald regarded himself as an intellectual living in a world of clods. He didn't come across as being offensively arrogant, having more the attitude of someone who is aware of his own intelligence and who rarely found anyone to talk to he regarded as an equal. There was something sad about it too. Stuckey realized that Oswald was gratified that the journalist was paying attention to him, which suggested to Stuckey that not many others did.

They talked for about an hour. Stuckey never saw him again.[1344]*

Oswald knew by the time he got home that evening his career as an agitator was over. "Damn it," he fumed to Marina. "I didn't realize they knew I'd been to Russia. You ought to have heard what they asked me! I wasn't prepared and I didn't know what to say."[1345]

His career in politics had lasted less than four and a half months. He had started it by passing out some leaflets in Dallas in April. He had distributed some handbills in the vicinity of the USS *Wasp* in New Orleans in June and twice more on downtown streets in New Orleans in August. He had been arrested, got three inches of coverage in a newspaper, appeared briefly on television twice, and twice, more extensively, on the radio. Although the essence of politics is joining with others of like mind to achieve common goals through weight of numbers, and although New Orleans is a large city and it is certain that some of its residents, in spite of the prevailing atmosphere of anti-Communism, looked rather more favorably on Fidel Castro and his revolution than the press and general public, he had failed to attract one single soul to his fake organization.

The other side of his "political" activity involved his frequent attempts to attract the notice of the Fair Play for Cuba Committee and the Communist Party of the United States of America. And even after the debacle of the panel discussion on WDSU, he made a further attempt to engage the interest of the CPUSA. In a letter dated August 28, a week after the disastrous *Conversation Carte Blanche* show, he wrote to the party again—this

---

*In 1985 and 1986, researchers for London Weekend Television interviewed Stuckey several times by phone at his hotel in Seattle. Stuckey had long since given up on his Latin America specialty and had become something of a gypsy, wandering from university to university in the land picking up stories to write in science journals. They asked him to be a witness in the trial, but he wanted to be paid a substantial fee, and the production company wasn't paying witnesses. Indeed, he wanted $5,000 just to loan out his copy of the tape of the WDSU radio debate. Stuckey said if he were to testify he should be placed into the category of a "character witness for Oswald." He was impressed by Oswald, believing him to be intelligent, sincere, and articulate, and called Oswald's performance on the show "the best run-down of a national liberation philosophy I've heard in a long time." Speaking of how conservative and anti-Communist New Orleans was at the time, and the fact that it was populated by many anti-Castro Cubans, he couldn't get over how Oswald could "go handing out left-wing pamphlets downtown. He was begging for a bullet." Stuckey himself felt isolated from the typical New Orleans scene. He and his French wife had wanted to see Oswald socially after the debate, and were going to invite him to the beach with them, but decided not to, as it would be inviting trouble. (Telephone interviews of Bill Stuckey by London Weekend Television researchers on September 4, 1985, and June 9 and 25, 1986)

time, not to Arnold Johnson, but directly to the Central Committee, whom he addressed as "Comrades."

> Please advise me upon a problem of personal tactics. I have lived in the Soviet Union from Oct. 1955 [*sic*] to July 1962. I had, in 1959, in Moscow, tried to legally dissolve my United States citizenship in favor of Soviet Citizenship, however, I did not complete the legal formalities for this.
>
> Having come back to the U.S. in 1962 and thrown myself into the struggle for progress and freedom in the United States, I would like to know weather, in your opions, I can continue to fight, handicapped as it were, by my past record, can I still, under these circumstances, compete with anti-progressive forces, above-ground or weather in your opion I should always remain in the background, i.e., underground.
>
> Our opponents could use my background of residence in the U.S.S.R. against any cause which I join, by association, they could say the organization of which I am a member, is Russian controled, ect., I am sure you see my point.
>
> I could of course openly proclaim, (if pressed on the subject) that I wanted to dissolve my american citizenship as a personal protest against the policy of the U.S. goverment in supporting dictatorships, ect., But what do you think I should do? which is the best tactic in general? Should I dissociate myself from all progressive activities?
>
> Here in New Orleans, I am secretary of the local brach of the "Fair Play for Cuba Committee," a position which, frankly, I have used to foster communist ideals. On a local radio show, I was attacked by Cuban exile organization representatives for my residence ect., in the Soviet Union. I feel I may have compromised the F.P.C.C., so you see that I need the advice of trusted, long time fighters for progress. Please advise.
>
> With Ferternal Greeting
Sincerely
Lee H. Oswald[1346]

The Communist Party could, perhaps, have regarded this as an attempt by an agent provocateur to lure them into committing some damaging statement to writing, but whether they did or not, Elizabeth Gurley Flynn, one of the party's leaders, passed the letter on to Arnold Johnson, asked him to answer, and left it up to him as to what to say.[1347]

Three days later, August 31, Oswald wrote to a Mr. Bert, managing editor of the *Worker* in New York.

Dear Mr. Bert

> As a commercial photographer I have, in the past, made blow-ups, reverse's and other types of photo work for the "Worker." Mr. Weinstock, in December 1962, expressed thanks for my modest work in a letter. Mr. Tormey, of the Gus Hall–Ben Davis defense committee also has commended some photos I did for his committee. I am familiar with most forms of Photo and art work, and other fazes of Typogrohie.
>
> I am sure you realize that . . . the greatest desire imaginable is to work directly for the "Worker." However, I understand that there might be many loyal comrades who want the same thing, i.e. to work for the "Worker." So if you say there is no opening's I shall continue to hope for the chance of employment directly under the "Worker."

My family and I shall, in a few weeks, be relocating into your area. In any event I'm sure you shall give my application full consideration. Thank you.

> Sincerely
> Lee H. Oswald[1348]

Of course, Oswald had done no work for the *Worker* or the Gus Hall–Ben Davis defense committee that had been accepted or used. And what was this about moving to New York? The following day, September 1, a Sunday, Oswald wrote to the Socialist Workers Party in New York:

> Dear Sirs,
>   Please advise me as to how I can get into direct contact with S.W.P. representatives in the Washington D.C.-Baltimore area. I and my family are moving to that area in October. As you know, there is no S.W.P. branch in the New Orleans area where I have been living. I am a long time subsriber to the *Militant* and other party literature of which, I am sure, you have a record.
>
> > Thank you
> > Lee H. Oswald[1349]

On the same day, Oswald wrote again to the CPUSA:

> Dear Sirs,
>   Please advise me as to how I can contact the Party in the Baltimore-Washington area, to which I shall relocate in October.
>
> > Fraternally
> > Lee H. Oswald[1350]

It can never be known whether Oswald meant every word he wrote in the above flurry of letters or whether he was trying to provoke responses that he could add to a scrapbook he intended to show the Cuban authorities on his arrival. Curiously, for all his assiduous correspondence with the Communist Party, the Socialist Workers Party, the *Militant*, and the *Worker*, he never offered to become an actual member of either party or even, for that matter, ask for information about how he might set about joining. He had only joined the FPCC. And as far as anyone knows, he never had any intention whatsoever of moving his family to New York, Baltimore, or Washington, D.C. He may have thought, however, that letters from the SWP or CPUSA suggesting he contact party officials in Washington or Baltimore or thanking him for his application for a job at the *Worker* would lend weight and credibility to his resumé.

In the meantime, Oswald's determination to get to Cuba grew hotter than ever. So hot in fact that he now planned to hijack a plane. Around the third week in August, possibly just after his appearance on *Conversation Carte Blanche*, he told Marina of his plan and informed her that he would need her help. She rejected the proposal out of hand. "For God's sake, don't do such a thing," she remonstrated. It was so ridiculous it was almost funny.

But Oswald was very serious. He started doing exercises to strengthen himself for the caper—deep knee bends, arm exercises, leaping about the apartment in his underwear—much to the merriment of June, who thought he was playing with her. Afterward, he would rub himself down with some strong-smelling liniment, take a cold shower, and emerge red as a lobster. Marina laughed along with the baby. "Junie," she said, "our papa is out of his mind." But Lee insisted in trying to drag her into the plot.

They would buy tickets separately under different names, he said. Lee would sit in the front of the cabin with a gun, Marina in the rear with a gun. Once Lee had subdued the pilot, Marina would stand up, address the passengers, and urge them to be calm and cooperative. Marina reminded him that she did not speak English. "That script won't do," he admitted, but it barely slowed him down. "I'll have to think of something new," telling her to sit on the bed as he left the room. Shortly thereafter, he bounded into the bedroom shouting to her, "Hands up and don't make any noise!" Marina didn't think she could handle even that much English, but he told her she could speak in Russian and if she stuck her gun out everybody would know what she meant. He begged her and promised to buy her a small handgun, one suitable for a woman. He had already been shopping around for one.

"Do you really think anybody will be fooled?" Marina asked. "A pregnant woman, her stomach sticking way out, a tiny girl in one hand and a pistol in another? I've never held a pistol in my life, much less shot anyone."

Lee offered to teach her, and explained again how easy it would be. Nothing could go wrong. Marina thought plenty of things could go wrong and probably would, things he couldn't even imagine. There was no way she was going to take part in the hijacking of an airliner. "Only a crazy man would think up something like this," she said.

Lee was undeterred. He spent a great deal of time studying a large world map that he hung inside the porch of their house and was always measuring distances between places with a ruler, and talking about the need to hijack a plane that had enough fuel to get to Cuba. He collected flight schedules, some from nearby airports smaller than the one in New Orleans, with smaller planes, which would give him fewer passengers to intimidate and subdue. To solve the fuel problem, he talked of flying from New Orleans to some place nearer to Cuba—Key West, perhaps—and then taking a smaller plane headed inland and forcing it to turn back to Cuba. He told Marina he was looking for someone else who also wanted to go to Cuba and would be willing to help him with the hijacking. He soon gave that up, though, because, he told Marina, "Your accomplice is your enemy for life." This madness lasted only about two weeks, Marina helping to convince him that he should try to find some legal and sane way to get to Cuba.[1351]

Lee now began to work on another plan to get to Cuba. There was no legal way to get to Cuba directly from the United States, but there were regular flights between Mexico City and Havana, and there was a Cuban embassy in Mexico City where he might be able to get a visa into Cuba. "I'll go there," he told Marina excitedly. "I'll show them my clippings, show them how much I've done for Cuba, and explain how hard it is to help in America. And how above all I want to help Cuba." He just knew the child in Marina's womb had to be a boy, a boy he'd call Fidel, he told Marina, to help ensure his welcome in Cuba. She replied there was going to be no little Fidel in her stomach. He told Marina that once he got established in Cuba he would send for her. But she paused. She was sure his vision of Cuba would turn out to be as illusory as his vision of the Soviet Union had. Whatever it was that was eating at him would not be vanquished by a change of scenery. He would only be happy, Marina thought, on the moon.[1352]

He drew a rosy picture of what their life in Havana might become. She could study there—education was free—and get a job. The Cubans would be grateful for the propaganda coup of attracting an American defector, and he would be granted special privileges as he had been in the Soviet Union, including "a nice little house" for the two of them. Marina hated the fact that her country conferred privileges on foreigners and was sure that Castro's Cuba, about which she had heard nothing but good, would not do that. She thought Lee would last a few months there at most. Thus, she felt compelled to abet his scheme, mostly because she knew he would never settle down until he had been to Cuba and seen for himself that it was not really better than anywhere else. Marina would later tell Priscilla McMillan, "I loved him because I felt he was in search of himself. I was in search of myself too. I couldn't show him the way, but I wanted to help him and give him support while he was searching."[1353]

But meanwhile there was a more pressing problem—Marina's pregnancy and the lack of funds to adequately provide for her hospitalization and the child's birth. This was a specter hanging over Lee's head and he had already set in motion a plan to solve it. Back on August 11 (and not knowing that Ruth was only too happy to take care of everything concerning the birth of his and Marina's child), he had gotten Marina to write Ruth to tell her he had lost his job, and therefore, in so many words, they were out of money. She was not to mention to Ruth his plan to send her and June to Russia (which, unbeknownst to him, Marina already had) or his own plan to abscond to Cuba. The letter Marina ended up writing was full of news about their trip to Mobile and the visit by Ruth Kloepfer, the clerk of the local Quaker Meeting whom Ruth had both called and written to in the hope of finding someone in New Orleans with whom Marina might speak Russian. "I liked her very much," Marina wrote. "Don't you think she is a fine woman? And such a pleasant and winsome face." Marina said that she would be happy to see Ruth again when, as Ruth had promised in an earlier letter, she arrives in New Orleans for a visit around September 20.

Eventually, she slipped in the information Lee wanted Ruth to know: "[A] little about our life. June runs about, grows, and is a great joy for me. Lee doesn't have work right now, already for three weeks. But we hope that everything will clear up, right? For the time being it is difficult to find work, but possibly at the end of summer there will be more openings, when some go to study. But we are not downcast and are hoping for better times."[1354]

Marina sent the letter to Ruth in Paoli, Pennsylvania, where Ruth had gone at the end of July for a holiday that would last just under two months. From Paoli, Ruth replied in a letter postmarked August 25 about how "very sorry" she was that Lee was not working, saying she knew it was therefore "hard for him and for you in the meanwhile." Because of their predicament, she added that it was "too bad" that she and Lee were not still living in Dallas. "I found out that you may go to Parkland Hospital and receive everything necessary, and pay only according to your earnings. Those unable to pay do not have to. But, in order to get this aid, you have to live in Texas for one year and in Dallas County for six months." She also told Marina to look for her to arrive in New Orleans on Friday, September 20, "in daytime if I can make it; otherwise, in the evening."[1355]

Lee was confident that Ruth had gotten the message intended, and felt that from that point on Ruth would be thinking about what she could do to ameliorate the fix Marina was in. Ruth did not have to renew her offer to Marina to come to her home in Dallas for the birth of the new baby in early October. She had already done that in the last letter she sent Marina before she left for her vacation.[1356] What Ruth did not know was how much Lee was counting on her to do just that. Ruth had not disappointed. Her letter to Marina of August 25, saying she was coming to New Orleans on September 20 and speaking about the cost at Parkland Hospital to deliver the baby, gave Lee, by implication, the assurance he needed that Ruth would take care of Marina.[1357]

At some point Oswald set out to prepare a resumé of points to use to persuade Cuban authorities of his desirability. He wrote on pages of a looseleaf notebook, each headed by a different title. One was "Military and Far East," which summed up his service in the Marine Corps. He also cited his training in electronics and claimed to have received a high school diploma "at the same time as my [Marine Corps] schooling in Biloxi, Mississippi." At the end, he lists the papers he will produce to document everything he said, including his original discharge certificate, his diplomas from the service schools he attended in Jacksonville, Florida, and Biloxi, Mississippi, and a certificate of "high school completion," which, though he never did complete high school, was proof of his satisfactory results on the high school–level General Educational Development test he took in the Marine Corps. He followed the same format on other pages titled "Resident of USSR," "Marxist," "Russian," "organizer" and "Street Agitation," the latter two dealing with his FPCC activities in New Orleans. He even had sections for "Radio Specker [Speaker] and Lecturer" and "Photograpes" (his work at Jaggers in Dallas).[1358]

What he wrote under all these categories was intended to be, in effect, the official "record" of his adult life up to somewhere around the end of August or the beginning of September 1963. It seems pitiful enough, even if you grant him some of the claims that really don't bear close scrutiny. It was not pitiful to Lee, though. He intended to dazzle the Cuban authorities with it, so he must have thought it reasonably impressive. It is impossible to know with any certainty what Lee was thinking, as his fantasy life was spinning out of control, but the resumé offers an insight into his view of himself at that time. Some writers have assumed that Oswald was in despair over the many failures of his life, but his resumé suggests that at least at this point in time, he had not thrown in the towel and did not think of himself as a failure. He was a man of many accomplishments—which the Cuban authorities were bound to recognize.[1359]

On the morning of Septemaber 2, Labor Day, Lee rang up his Aunt Lillian and asked whether he, Marina, and the baby could come over for the day. Lillian, who was tired and often felt the strain of the language barrier between herself and Marina, suggested they come later, in midafternoon. They took the bus, and Dutz Murret, who just happened to be driving by, picked them up and saved them some of the walk from the bus stop. They arrived at about three or four in the afternoon.

Lillian asked them if they had had "dinner"—which means lunch in New Orleans—and they said they had, but Lillian somehow doubted that. She went to the store and bought some rolls, came back, and made coffee, and the fact that they ate all of the rolls made Lillian think she had guessed right that they probably hadn't eaten. Later that evening she made hamburgers and Marina and Lee each ate two.

It was a pleasant family day, enlivened by the presence of two of Lee's cousins, John and Marilyn. Dutz took the occasion to lecture Lee on his refusal to teach Marina English, which disappointed the Murrets.

"Lee, we love Marina very much," Murret said, "but we feel very bad that we can't converse with Marina because you speak to her all the time in Russian, and we don't know what is going on, and she doesn't know what is going on with us. Don't you think you should teach her the English language?"

Lee said "No." It wasn't the first time Dutz had started this argument. "I'll tell you right now," Lee said, "I will never teach it to her." He said he didn't object to her learning the language on her own somehow, but "I am not going to teach her, because I do not want to lose my Russian."

Why not? Lillian wondered. "Why do you want to keep up your Russian, Lee? Do you intend to go back to Russia?" Something happened right then—Lillian forgets what—but she never did get an answer to her question.

Though the Murrets faulted Lee for keeping Marina from learning English, they felt he was otherwise very attentive to her, noticing that he would always open the car door for her, pull the chair out when she wanted to sit down, and things like that. Lillian's daughter, Marilyn, sensed that Lee was very devoted to Marina, loved his child very much, and was not just well mannered with his wife but with every woman in his presence. After the hamburgers John took them home in his car.[1360]

John was in no rush that Labor Day evening, so he drove the Oswalds around to see the church where he was going to be married on October 5. They also drove by the imposing home of his well-to-do fiancée on Palmer Avenue, where the reception would be held. Lee said nothing, but Marina knew that his fists were clenched in anger, not because he disliked or envied rich people[*] so much but because of his hatred for an economic and political system that made it possible for some people to be so wealthy. She could almost feel his hatred of American capitalism sitting next to him in the car.[1361]

John finally dropped them at home, and that was the last that any of the Murrets ever saw—or even heard from—Lee and Marina.[1362]

Although Lee and Marina were facing a separation the consequences of which could hardly be foreseen—if Lee did manage to get to Cuba and Marina did not, it might be the end of their life together—their daily life on Magazine Street did not change very much. Lee continued to spend most of his days sprawled on the couch reading. Sometimes he also read all night long, in the bathroom so as not to disturb Marina. After he lost his job in July, his interest in serious books on social and economic policy and history and biography tailed off in favor of fiction, particularly science fiction and a sprinkling of spy novels. The only work of history or sociology he checked out of the New Orleans Public Library after he lost his job was *Everyday Life in Ancient Rome* by Frank Richard Cowell. The twenty other books he checked out in the two months before he left New Orleans included two books by Aldous Huxley, *Brave New World* and *Ape and Essence*, Lew Wallace's *Ben-Hur*, and many science-fiction novels and collections by Isaac Asimov, Frederik Pohl, and others. In late July he checked out *Five Spy Novels* selected by Howard Haycraft, and he also took out three of Ian Fleming's James Bond spy novels, *Thunderball* in June and *Moonraker* and *Goldfinger* on September 19, although he had little time to read much of them before he left New Orleans a few days later.[1363] (All three Bond novels turned up in his Dallas rooming house after the assassination.)

The only air-conditioning in the apartment was an old fan, and Lee would sit or lay

---

[*]Priscilla McMillan, in talking over many years with Marina and others who knew Oswald, wrote, "Stingy as he was, and forever saving up in little ways, Lee did not want a lot of money for himself. That was not where his ambition lay. As with virtually everyone who knew him, Marina, too, believes that her husband could not have been 'bought'" (McMillan, *Marina and Lee*, p.457).

bare naked in the suffocating summer heat, reading his books. Marina thought it was bad for Junie to see him naked, but he dismissed her concerns—the child was much too young. He often took baths with the baby that were really just long and loud sessions of play.[1364]

There was one sinister novelty in their lives. One evening at the end of August Marina returned from a twilight stroll with June and found Lee on their screened-in side porch, kneeling on one knee, aiming his rifle into the street and working the bolt—dry firing. It was the first time she had seen him playing with his carbine since they moved to New Orleans. She was horrified.

"What are you doing?" she demanded.

"Get the heck out of here," he said. "Don't talk to me. Get on about your own affairs."

From then on she often heard him dry firing the rifle on the porch in the dark. He had fixed a lamp out there so that he could read in the evening, but he left it off when he was drilling with the rifle so the neighbors could not see him. Marina chided and even ridiculed him about it, but he was deadly serious: "If Fidel Castro needs defenders," he told her, "I'm going to join an army of volunteers. I'm going to be a revolutionary."

Marina did not make an issue of it. As far as she was concerned, he could do what he liked with his plaything as long as he did it at home—or in Cuba, for that matter. She made him promise that he would not take the rifle off to use against anyone in the United States.

"*Ya ne budu* [I won't]," he would say in Russian. Marina let it drop.[1365]

His neighbors would later say they noticed him always reading, either on the side porch or, through the front window, in the living room. Oswald stonily refused to talk with the neighbors. Even when they would pass each other on the sidewalk and the neighbors would bid him a good day, he'd look straight ahead without saying a word. It went beyond that. A. P. Eames, the neighbor who lived next door with his wife, said Oswald actually "projected a real hostile kind of feeling" as he passed by. About the only time the neighbors would see Marina was when she would go to a small neighborhood grocery. She, too, never said a word to any of them, only because she couldn't speak English. But at least she was always friendly, always smiling to let them know she was acknowledging their presence. It was a tight little neighborhood where many people tried to beat the heat at night by sitting on their screened-in porches (which are very common in New Orleans to keep the mosquitoes at bay), and because Lee and Marina, speaking a foreign language, were different, some of the neighbors seemed almost to be keeping watch on them, noting their comings and goings and wondering about the loud arguments they couldn't understand. "I used to hear him and her arguing at night," Mrs. Garner, the landlady, would later recall, "and he would have her crying and the baby crying, and he would be speaking his foreign language. I couldn't understand what he was saying."[1366]

The Oswalds had "very, very few visitors," Mrs. Garner said.[1367] One was a "Latin type" who came to her door one evening and inquired for directions to the Oswalds' apartment. He spoke with a Spanish accent and had some pro-Castro leaflets—undoubtedly Carlos Quiroga (see conspiracy section).[1368] The Garners had had an argument with Oswald about those leaflets. He had posted two pro-Castro signs on his screened porch, and Jesse Garner had to order him to remove them. Oswald wanted to know who objected to the signs, and Garner told him that he, Jesse Garner, did. Lee was to either take them down or vacate the apartment. It would hardly have been a loss to Garner. Lee was always late with the rent, though he paid in cash. Lee took the signs down.[1369]

Although Oswald sought no social intercourse with his neighbors, he didn't mind having a relationship with their garbage cans. The Oswalds didn't have their own cans, and Mrs. Garner often saw Lee, late at night, come out of his apartment clad only in yellow trunks, shirtless, thongs on his feet, and watched as he worked his way up the street, stuffing his garbage in other people's cans.[1370]

Lee's miserly ways now had a point: he would need every penny for the expenses to get to Cuba. He began the month of September, the Warren Commission would later conclude, with $182.21 cash in hand.[1371] His monthly rent of $65.00 was due on September 9, but he would end up not paying that or even for the two weeks he would remain in the apartment after the ninth. He would skip out on the utility bills too.[1372] With his unemployment compensation still flowing in, he would have more than enough money to finance his trip to Cuba. Nevertheless, he and Marina continued to fight over money. One night Lee "lent" her money to play poker with him, and she was absolutely exultant when she won, but Lee refused to pay up because he had lent her the money. He insisted they play another game, and, if she won that one, she could keep the money. If she lost, then she'd owe him again.

Marina exploded. "I'm sorry, Alka," she said, "I see this game in real life every day, you're always greedy for money. You know I don't have a cent. Supposing I do owe you money, where will I get it? Steal it from you? You know I can't steal."

"Then you didn't have to play by those principles."

"I'm tired of your principles," she said. "Even in games I see your petty spirit. I see it in the grocery store. We go in and you give me thirty cents. Afterwards, you want to know what I spent it on . . . You save on everything. What for? To buy a dress for your wife? Food or a toy for your child? No. You have money for a gun. You have money for your Mexico. But for your own baby, no! What joy is your Cuba, your Mexico, your Castro, to me? You never even think about our new baby. I have to ask Ruth to help because papa has got something more important on his mind. I'm tired of your 'important' things. When will you start to think the way normal people do? You imagine that you're a great man. Nobody thought that up but you." Marina's grievances about his penny-pinching came pouring out of her in a way that stunned him into silence. Then she started packing her clothes in a suitcase. She would go stay with the Murrets until Ruth arrived on the twentieth.

He took her clothes out of the suitcase and returned them to the closets and drawers, and she took them out again and repacked them. Eventually she quieted down and went to bed. Lee retreated to the bathroom to read. When he did come to bed, she told him to go sleep on the floor, although she eventually relented on that too.[1373]

The cause of the fight seems trivial enough, but it was probably sparked by the underlying and largely unspoken tensions between them. Marina, after all, was days away from the rupture, perhaps a final one, of her marriage. She knew that Lee was planning to dump her on Ruth Paine, whom he was counting on to cope with the trouble and expense of the birth of their second child. And he still threatened to send her and their children back to the USSR. The only chance that they would ever be reunited was that he might send for them if he succeeded in establishing himself in Cuba. With a resignation or wisdom uncommon in such a young woman—she was still only twenty-two—she realized that Lee would never be able to settle down until he got his Cuban fantasy out of his system. But apart from this, Lee, she was convinced, wanted only to be rid of her. Ruth was her only real hope of staying in America. Yet she clung to a hope that Lee might one day want his wife and children back again.[1374]

Many have asked if Lee and Marina loved each other, and if so, what kind of love it was. I wouldn't presume to know the answer except to observe that the opposite of love in any relationship is indifference, not hate, where at least some passion remains. And one thing that no one could ever say about Marina and Lee—they were not indifferent to each other.

On September 9, 1963, the New Orleans *Times-Picayune* reported on a September 7 interview Castro gave to an AP reporter in Havana. The headline on the article was "Castro Blasts Raids on Cuba; Says U.S. Leaders Imperiled by Aid to Rebels. Havana (AP)." The article read, "Prime Minister Fidel Castro said Saturday night 'United States leaders' would be in danger if they helped in any attempt to do away with leaders of Cuba. Bitterly denouncing what he called U.S.-prompted raids on Cuban territory, Castro said, 'We are prepared to fight them and answer in kind. United States leaders should think that if they are aiding terrorists' plans to eliminate Cuban leaders, they themselves will not be safe.'" The article said that Castro accused the United States of "double-crossing" policies and called President Kennedy a "cheap and crooked politician."[1375] If, in Oswald's mind, there ever was a time that Castro and his tender revolution needed him, it was now.

On September 17 Oswald visited the Mexican consulate in the Whitney Building in New Orleans and filled out an application for a tourist card. He described himself as a twenty-three-year-old, married, American-born "photographer" residing at 4907 Magazine Street. Giving in once again to his congenital lying, he put down 640 Rampart Street as his "business address" and said he was "Catholic." Under the heading "Destination in Mexico" he wrote, "Transit tourist." He would travel by bus, "$300.00" was listed as the approximate amount of money he was taking for the trip, and "10 days" was listed as the duration of the trip.[1376] Lee paid fifty cents for tourist card number 24085, valid for a single journey to Mexico for a period of fifteen days.[1377]

A few days later, Thursday, September 19, Arnold Johnson, information director of the U.S. Communist Party, finally got around to answering Lee's August 28 letter to the Central Committee[1378] and Oswald's September 1 letter a few days later to Communist Party headquarters.[1379] Johnson's letter to Lee was as meaningless as could be. As to the advice Lee sought, Johnson suggested he "remain in the background" in his FPCC activities, whatever that meant, and "not [go] underground." And as to Lee moving to Baltimore, Johnson told Lee to "get in touch with us" once he arrived.[1380] At one point, any contact from the national office of the Communist Party would have been important to Lee, but now that he was headed for the big time in Cuba, Johnson's letter was just another document he would put in his folder to establish his bonafides with the Cuban embassy in Mexico City.

On Friday afternoon, Marina went out to buy some groceries, and Ruth was waiting for her when she got back—September 20, exactly as promised. Lee was entertaining Ruth and her children on the porch in a way Ruth had never seen before. He was in high spirits. It was in marked contrast to her last visit, when she had driven Marina from Dallas to New Orleans. Then he had found fault with Marina constantly, as though he wanted only to rid himself of her.[1381] That first time she found the atmosphere so unpleasant she left, as previously noted, a day early. This time, however, she lingered through the weekend.[1382]

It was a pleasant time, enlivened by the visit of Ruth Kloepfer. Kloepfer brought along her two college-age daughters. The one who had been studying Russian had recently visited Russia, and Lee played the gracious host, looking at her slides of Moscow, a few of which he recognized from his own trip there.[1383]

Marina wanted to take Ruth Paine for another tour of the French Quarter, this time in the evening. Lee could not be prevailed upon to accompany them, so the two young women, with their three very small children, strolled along Bourbon Street, soaking up the special atmosphere of that storied street.

Back at Magazine Street, they found Lee to be in an unusually good mood. He had straightened up the apartment, washed the dishes, and started packing their things into and atop Ruth's station wagon. Looking back, Ruth realized he had been "distinctly" eager to do the packing.[1384] He was probably trying to avoid having her handle, any more than she had to, the Mannlicher-Carcano rifle, which he had disassembled, wrapped in a brown paper package, and tied up in a blanket.*

Other than packing for the trip to Texas, it was a restful weekend, and the two women had plenty of opportunity to talk. But Ruth was never told about Lee's plans to go to Cuba by way of Mexico. He had insisted to Marina that she not tell Ruth about this. Ruth had not even known, before she arrived, that Marina had decided to accept her invitation and that Marina and June would be returning to Dallas with her for Marina's childbirth the next month. She could see that Lee was greatly relieved when she offered to take care of Marina and help ensure that Marina got good care at Parkland. Lee told Ruth that he was going to seek work in Houston or Philadelphia, and that he would leave as soon as Ruth and Marina were gone. He said when he got established there, he would send for Marina once she had given birth. Thus, Ruth thought Marina would be with her for only a brief period.[1385] Lee did tell Ruth about the fracas and his arrest when he was passing out pro-Cuba leaflets on the streets of New Orleans, and it was one of the few conversations she ever had with him in which he deigned to speak English.[1386]

Mr. Garner, noticing Lee packing Ruth's station wagon with his family's personal belongings, approached Lee and asked him if he was moving, since Garner was concerned that Lee already owed about fifteen days' rent. But Oswald reassured Garner that he was not leaving, saying that his wife was only going to Texas to have their baby, after which she was going to return to New Orleans.[1387]

On Monday morning, September 23, Ruth and Marina were finally ready to leave.[1388] The car was severely overloaded with all of the Oswalds' possessions added to Ruth's, which included a boat on the roof rack, to which they attached a playpen, stroller, and other things. Lee kissed Marina tenderly, each struggling not to break down; Marina, knowing Lee was going to Cuba, tried to conceal from Ruth that she might be losing him forever. Lee watched as the car drove away, long enough to see that they made it no farther than a few blocks to a gas station—a tire was about to give out. He went down to the station and Marina took Lee a few steps away, and they kissed tenderly again. She told him to please be careful and take care of himself. "Stop," he told her. "I can't stand it. Do you want me to cry in front of Ruth?" Ruth bought a new tire and had it mounted. "This is sure going to cost a lot, isn't it?" Lee said to Ruth. "Yes," Ruth said, "but car

---

*But of course someone had to unpack the package when Ruth arrived in Texas a few days later, and it was her husband Michael, whom she had called to help her. He was perplexed by the weight and feel of the contents of the package, thoughts like "camping equipment" and "an iron pipe" entering his mind. These guesses didn't seem quite accurate to him, but being the "polite" Quaker he was, and aware of Oswald's "rights to privacy," he never snooped. He would later say he was satisfied it was Oswald's rifle. (2 H 414–415, 417, 419, 9 H 436–441, WCT Michael R. Paine)

owners have to expect that." He did not offer to contribute anything to the trip finan-cially. In fact, Ruth sensed that he didn't even give Marina any spending money to take with her. But Ruth didn't let it bother her. She knew that he had been unemployed for a long time and probably needed every cent he had to find a new job and rent a new apart-ment for them.[1389] Ruth's attitude toward him had softened. When she had seen him kiss Marina good-bye very fondly, she felt that he really did care for his wife, and she recalled that he had told her not to tell anyone at Parkland that he had "abandoned her."[1390] Ruth, Marina, and the kids made it to a motel that night just across the line in Texas, and arrived at Ruth's home in Irving the next day.[1391]

Oswald appears to have spent one more night in the empty apartment on Magazine Street. On Tuesday, September 24, he filed a change-of-address card at the post office to redirect mail from his New Orleans post office box to Ruth's address in Irving, Texas, and Oswald's box was closed on September 26.[1392]

That evening, Tuesday, Lee's next-door neighbor, Eric Rogers, saw him leave the apart-ment in a hurry with two cloth suitcases, one large, the other small, run across the street, and catch a bus at the bus stop headed for downtown.[1393] In a December 11, 1963, inter-view with the FBI, the bus driver recalled picking up a passenger one evening around September 24 near Lee's apartment with two suitcases who asked what was the best bus to take to the Greyhound bus terminal, but he was unable to describe the individual or identify Lee as the passenger. He did recall seeing a station wagon parked in front of the apartment where Oswald lived for one or two days (presumably Ruth Paine's) "several months ago."[1394]

Where Oswald spent Tuesday night is unknown. The Warren Commission concluded that "he probably returned to the apartment to sleep after checking his luggage at [the] bus station, or spent the night at an inexpensive hotel or rooming house."[1395] (But in the possibility that Oswald did not return to his Magazine apartment on the night of Sep-tember 24, 1963, on September 8 and 9, 1964, the FBI checked with the owners, man-agers, or desk clerks of forty-one inexpensive hotels located in the vicinity of the Continental Trailways bus depot, Greyhound bus depot, and main U.S. Post Office in New Orleans, as well as the YMCA and Baptist Rescue Mission, and the name Lee Harvey Oswald did not show up on any of the hotel registers or those of the YMCA and Baptist Mission for the night of September 24, 1963.)[1396] The only reason why Oswald would have to go through the trouble of making a separate trip to check his bags at the bus station would be if he wanted to conceal from his landlord the fact that he was skipping out on his rent, so he left after dark hoping the Garners wouldn't see him, and if they saw him the next day leaving the apartment, he wouldn't be carrying any baggage. But they didn't see him the next day. Moreover, this reasoning falls when his neighbor testified that he saw Oswald leave with his baggage in the early evening. "It was kind of daylight. You could see."[1397] It is therefore likely that if Oswald left New Orleans by bus, he spent the night in the bus station to save money.

Oswald's thirty-three-dollar weekly unemployment check arrived at the main post office in New Orleans sometime between 6:15 and 6:40 on the evening of September 24, well after the post office substation (Lafayette Square) where Oswald had a box had closed to the public, which occurred at 5:45 p.m.[1398] The FBI determined that the earliest possible time Oswald could have obtained this check from his post office box was "subsequent to 5:00 AM on September 25, 1963."[1399] And we know that sometime after 8:00 on Wednes-day morning, September 25, he cashed his thirty-three-dollar check at the Winn-Dixie

Store near his apartment—somewhat oddly, since it was quite a distance back to his old neighborhood and he had cashed checks nearer to the post office before.[1400] He couldn't have been eager to be spotted in the old neighborhood either—that same day his landlord discovered that the apartment was empty and there was no sign of Oswald, who still owed a couple of weeks' rent.[1401]

It has never been conclusively established precisely when Oswald left New Orleans, what route he took from New Orleans to the Mexican border, or even what mode of transportation he took out of New Orleans. All of this will be discussed in considerable depth in the Sylvia Odio part of the conspiracy section of this book. What follows is only one of several reasonable scenarios: that Oswald left New Orleans on Wednesday, September 25, probably on Continental Trailways. One Trailways bus, 5121, departed New Orleans at 12:20 p.m. and arrived in Houston at 10:50 p.m.[1402] Sometime—many believe that evening while Oswald was in Houston—he called Horace Twiford, a Houston member of the Socialist Labor Party who had received Oswald's name from the party's headquarters in New York in July and had sent Oswald the Labor Day issue of the party's publication, the *Weekly People*.

Twiford's wife, Estelle, told Lee that her husband, a merchant seaman, was working aboard the SS *Del Monte* and would not be home for several days. Oswald told her he was a member of the Fair Play for Cuba Committee and would have liked to talk with Horace that evening for a few hours before flying to Mexico. Mrs. Twiford took Lee's name, noted the information about the FPCC, and promised Lee she would tell her husband he had called.[1403]

If Oswald had been in Houston when he called the Twiford residence, he would have had some time to wait there for his connecting bus, Continental Trailways bus number 5133, which left Houston for Laredo, Texas, via Corpus Christi at 2:35 a.m., that is, the next day, September 26. The passengers on that bus, including Oswald, changed to bus number 304 at Corpus Christi at 8:15 in the morning, and that bus arrived in Laredo about 1:20 in the afternoon of the same day.[1404] We do know Oswald was on the bus that started from Houston, because at some time after six in the morning, with the coming of daylight, a couple of British tourists who would be traveling with Oswald and others all the way to Mexico City, Dr. John B. McFarland and his wife Meryl, who were on their way to Yucatan to study Indian culture, noticed him.[1405]

Oswald crossed the border from Laredo to the Mexican city on the other side, Nuevo Laredo, between 1:30 and 2:00 that afternoon, September 26.[1406] This was the end of the line for the Continental Trailways bus, and many of their passengers, including Oswald and the McFarlands, boarded bus number 516 of the Flecha Roja (Red Arrow) Bus Line at Nuevo Laredo for the trip to Mexico City, leaving Nuevo Laredo at around 2:15 p.m. on September 26, 1963. The ticket cost Oswald $5.71 (71.40 pesos).[1407]

That is one story of how Lee Oswald made his way from New Orleans to the Mexican border. But is it the correct one? There is another account that places him not in Houston on Wednesday evening, September 25, 1963, on his way to Mexico, but in Dallas the following evening, Thursday, 244 miles away. Sylvia Odio, a beautiful young Cuban refugee living in the Crestwood Apartments in Dallas, was just getting dressed to go to a friend's house for the evening—her sister Annie had come over to babysit her four young children—when she was reportedly visited at her door by two Latin men and a third man, an American whom Odio later identified as Oswald. Odio thought the visit came no earlier than 9:00 p.m., Thursday, September 26,[1408] but by then Oswald had already been on a bus bound for Mexico for hours, a fact supported by a number of witnesses and documents. Some have suggested that Odio was confusing Thursday night with Wednesday night, or the American was not Oswald. If it was Oswald, it could only have been if he had been driven on Wednesday all the way from New Orleans to Odio's apartment in Dallas (which, at 503 miles, would have been around an eight-hour trip in a car traveling a little over 60 mph). From there, Oswald would have had to be driven south about 244 miles to catch the bus in Houston that left for Laredo in the early morning hours (2:35 a.m.) on Thursday, September 26.[1409] The entire issue, with its considerable implications on the issue of conspiracy, is discussed, as indicated earlier, in depth in the Odio section of the conspiracy part of this book. It is not surprising that this matter has been one of the very most controversial pieces of Lee Harvey Oswald's story. The Warren Commission decided a little too hastily that Oswald was not one of the three men who visited Sylvia Odio.[1410] Years later, the HSCA was more receptive to the notion of conspiracy, and did not discount the possibility that he was.[1411] Neither settled the Odio controversy, which continues to this day.

At the first rest stop after the Flecha Roja bus left the border at Nuevo Laredo on its 750-mile trip to Mexico City, Meryl McFarland, who had been aware of Oswald sitting behind her since early that morning, decided to speak to him. She asked him if he wanted some coffee, and he replied, with typical Oswaldian graciousness, that he preferred to drink his coffee alone. Eventually, however, in spite of his rudeness, they did converse. Meryl had heard him chatting with his seatmate, an elderly gentleman who spoke with a slight northern British accent—Yorkshire, perhaps. She gathered from bits of their conversation that they had not been acquainted since chance threw them together on the crowded, dusty bus.

The McFarlands were surprised when Oswald told them of his plan to travel—illegally—to Cuba, where he hoped to meet Fidel Castro in Havana. The couple, from Liverpool, had been in the United States for a year at that time. John had been working as a research fellow at the University Hospital in Jackson, Mississippi, but they had found time to travel a good deal, and they were well aware that Castro was anathema to most Americans. Meryl was surprised that Oswald would so openly advertise his admiration for the Cuban premier. He also told them that he was the secretary of a chapter of the Fair Play for Cuba Committee in New Orleans, and that he had started his trip to Mexico City from New Orleans. By the end of the conversation the McFarlands decided that it was better not to have too much to do with him. Meryl definitely didn't like his attitude. Though it wasn't the way he dressed—the McFarlands recall Oswald wearing casual slacks, a light pullover, and a zippered jacket—in Meryl's diary she described him as a "weedy, ratty little man."[1412]

Pamela Mumford and Patricia Winston boarded the Flecha Roja bus in Monterrey, Mexico, around 7:30 that evening. They too were bound for Mexico City. Though they had grown up in Australia, both had been born in Fiji. Two years earlier they had set out from Australia on a tour of the world and worked as they traveled. After a year in Great Britain they left for the United States as permanent residents under the Fiji Islands' quota. They had worked for a while in New York to get some money for further travels, Mumford as a legal secretary, Winston as an occupational therapist. After their side trip to Mexico, they were heading to California. Eventually they would return to Australia, but they were taking plenty of time to see as much of the world as possible. Their tickets to Mexico City allowed them to stop at intermediate destinations, and they had just taken a day off to see the city of Monterrey.[1413]

Soon after the bus departed from Monterrey, Oswald came down the aisle to them and started a conversation. He told them he had somehow thought they were Mexican when he first saw them struggling with their heavy luggage to the only open seats in the back of the bus, and, wanting to help them, which he didn't end up doing, had asked his seatmate how to say in Spanish, "How can I help you?" When he heard them speaking English, he wondered where they were from. He was impressed by the story of their travels and told them he too had traveled a great deal. He had been in Japan while he was in the Marines and regretted that he had never traveled to Australia. He had been to Russia though. They hadn't, but a friend of their's had, and they told him about some of her experiences in Moscow. They were curious as to what he had been doing in Russia and whether he had any trouble getting in. He said he had been studying there and lived in an apartment in Moscow. He said he had a hard time getting out of the country. As if he was afraid they might not believe he had been to Russia, he returned to his seat at the front of the bus and came back with his passport to show them the Russian stamps on it—not that the young women were able to read them. But they did see the name Oswald on the passport. He didn't mention the fact that his wife was from Russia. He didn't mention his wife at all, but both young women noticed his gold wedding band on his left hand.

Mumford and Winston were not terribly impressed by Lee. After first talking with him on the bus, they referred to Oswald in conversations between themselves by the nickname "Texas." They noticed that he sat alone at the bus stops, which came at around two-hour intervals, and ate rather too much food—perhaps he could not make himself understood in Spanish and had to order by pointing at the menu.[1414] Apparently the limited Spanish Lee had learned four years earlier from a squad mate in the Marine Corps had not produced much in the way of results.

The sixth English-speaking passenger, out of nearly forty passengers (plus crying babies and small animals) on the completely full bus, was Lee's seatmate, the elderly Albert James Osborne, who turns out to have been even more committed to the romance of falsehoods and flightiness than Lee Oswald. Osborne, a self-described itinerant rug-cleaner, gardener, boys' camp operator, and Baptist preacher, was born in Great Grimsby, Lincolnshire, in England and had migrated to the United States in 1914. Osborne was nearing his seventy-fifth birthday, although he apparently told the McFarlands he was eighty,[1415] a pointless lie that Lee might have appreciated. No one knows what Osborne told Oswald about himself, if anything, on the long ride to Mexico City, but it is likely that very little of it was true. Osborne lived a nomadic existence in Canada, the southern part of the United States, and Mexico for the past fifty years, having mailing addresses like "Will Call," "General Delivery," post office boxes, and hotels, and often staying at the homes of Christian friends who put him up during his many travels. During the summer of 1963 he worked briefly at the Tyler Nursery Company in Tyler, Texas. In the previous twenty-five years, Osborne had spent considerable time doing missionary work in rural Mexico.

Osborne became the eventual subject of a remarkable ninety-five-page FBI report (with its own table of contents and eight-page index) to the Warren Commission investigating his tangled background and true identity. It seems that years earlier Osborne took on a dual identity, known to many people as John Howard Bowen and to others by his real name. This resulted in his being interviewed on several occasions by *different* FBI agents, sometimes as Bowen, other times as Osborne, the bureau believing they were talking to two separate people.* "Bowen" and "Osborne" said they knew each other and "each" sent the FBI on fruitless quests to find the other. When the duplicity was becoming obvious, Osborne finally admitted to the FBI that he had been using the alias John H. Bowen off and on since 1916. It was as Bowen that he had taken the bus from Nuevo Laredo to Mexico City on September 26, 1963. (One strong reason for the use of the Bowen alias on this occasion was that Osborne had been deported from Mexico on April 5, 1958, for selling an automobile without paying the import duties, and if discovered under his true name as having entered Mexico illegally, he would have been detained and deported.) Bowen confirmed sitting next to a young man of Oswald's approximate age and physical appearance on the trip, with one exception. He said that the young man had a dark complexion and was of Mexican or Puerto Rican descent. He did not identify photos of Oswald as the man he sat next to. Moreover, he maintained that there were no other English-speaking fellow passengers on the bus.[1416]

However, the evidence that Oswald was on the subject bus is conclusive, and it therefore follows that Osborne, for whatever personal reason (perhaps simply not wanting his name attached to a presidential assassin in any way), was not telling the truth. Not only does Bowen's name appear along with Oswald's and the McFarlands' on the manifest of Flecha Roja bus number 516 for the September 26 trip from Nuevo Laredo to Mexico City,[1417] but the same immigration inspector who stamped Oswald's tourist card on September 26, 1963, Helio Maydon, also stamped Bowen's.[1418] Osborne also fits the description given by the McFarlands and the two Australian girls as being an elderly male with a British accent who had spent considerable time previously in Mexico.[1419] The McFarlands also identified photos of Osborne as being the man.[1420] The Australian girls were unable to make a positive ID from earlier photos of Bowen (one wearing a sun helmet, the other standing in front of a castle a decade earlier), but as indicated, the McFarlands clearly identified him as being the passenger seated next to Oswald.[1421] Although Osborne claimed there were no other English-speaking people on the bus, both of the McFarlands were aware that Oswald and Bowen were speaking to each other. Indeed, Pamela Mumford got the impression that Oswald and Osborne talked a lot on the trip. And at one of the bus stops, as she and Winston were waiting to reboard the bus she asked Osborne what the weather was going to be like in Mexico City. Osborne just told the two of them

---

*When the FBI first ran Osborne down in February of 1964 near Russellville, Alabama, where he was staying at the residence of one Wylie Uptain, he was going under the name John Howard Bowen, with a bogus Social Security card as well as credit cards under that name, and said he was planning to leave for Laredo by way of New Orleans. He told them he had been born in Chester, Pennsylvania, in 1885 and raised in an orphanage in Philadelphia. That all of his relatives were deceased. That he completed the equivalent of two years of college by correspondence courses and completed a course in theology in 1914. He said he was ordained by the Plymouth Brethren in Trenton, New Jersey, and also by the Northern Baptist Convention in Binghamton, New York. And, he added, he was recognized as an ordained minister by the Missionary Baptist Convention. He said he worked for a time with juvenile delinquents in Knoxville, Tennessee, and had traveled extensively, but had never been to Canada or England. He considered his home to be the Saint Anthony Hotel in Laredo, Texas, where he had resided "intermittently" for twenty years. He told the FBI that Albert Osborne was another Baptist preacher he met in 1958 when they were staying at the same hotel in Oaxaco, Mexico. He said Osborne was about his same size and age.

It took a very long time and dogged footwork for FBI agents to sort out this convoluted fiction. They eventually turned up Albert Osborne's birth certificate at Somerset House in England (where all births, deaths, and marriages in England are recorded) and a clutch of Osborne's equally elderly brothers and sisters, all of whom readily identified him from photographs. However, many of the questions about Osborne-Bowen remain unanswered. (CE 2195, 25 H 25–74; CE 2196, 25 H 75)

that "the young man traveling beside me has traveled to Mexico also. Why don't you talk to him?"[1422]

The Warren Commission concluded, "Osborne's responses to federal investigators on matters unrelated to Oswald have proved inconsistent and unreliable and, therefore, based on the contrary evidence and Osborne's lack of reliability, the Commission has attached no credence to his denial that Oswald was beside him on the bus. Investigation of his background and activities, however, disclosed no basis for suspecting him of any involvement in the assassination."[1423] In any event, Osborne gives new life to the observation that the most seemingly nondescript people we brush up against in life "have a story" to tell. It is ironic that Lee Oswald, who so clumsily fabricated his own fake identity as Alek Hidell, spent a day and a night in the company of a master in the art and undoubtedly never realized it. That it was more than a chance encounter[*] between Oswald and Osborne was briefly in vogue among conspiracy advocates. For instance, conspiracy theorists Robert Groden and Harrison Livingstone went so far as to suggest that Osborne and his true identity provides a "clue to the assassination."[1424] Conspiracy author Anthony Summers reported that Osborne had been a "fanatical supporter of Nazi Germany" during the Second World War but cites no evidence for the claim. Summers also notes that Oswald had used the pseudonym "Osborne" when ordering some of his Fair Play for Cuba leaflets in New Orleans, but fails to recall that Oswald served at the El Toro Marine Air Corps Station with a Mack Osborne, whom he no doubt knew much better than the man sitting beside him on the bus, whose name he may never have even known.[1425] In the end, the wily Osborne-Bowen proved to be as elusive for the conspiracy theorists as he had for the FBI, and he is not usually mentioned in the more popular conspiracy theories today.

Mumford and her friend Winston talked with Lee Oswald once again on the trip, at the last bus and rest stop before Mexico City. He asked if they knew where they were going to stay in Mexico City. They didn't. They were relying on a popular travel book of the period, *Mexico on Five Dollars a Day*, which listed various cheap hotels. He said that on previous trips to Mexico City (there's no evidence or likelihood that he had ever been there before), he had stayed at the Hotel Cuba, and recommended it as being clean and inexpensive.

They did not take his suggestion. The last time they saw him was shortly after the bus, which had traveled throughout the night, arrived in Mexico City around ten o'clock Friday morning, September 27. He was standing alone in the bus terminal. They took a taxi and left without speaking to him again.[1426]

Within an hour of his arrival at the Flecha Roja bus terminal in Mexico City, Lee Oswald registered at the Hotel del Comercio on Calle Bernardino de Sahagun, named for a Spanish colonial missionary who befriended Indians. The modest but clean four-story red-brick establishment catered to traveling salesmen and was good value for the money, which came to $1.28 a night. Although it was well located, about four blocks from the bus station and eight from the commercial heart of the city—which was on famous

---

[*]The other passengers on the bus were of the opinion that Oswald and Osborne did not know each other. For example, Pamela Mumford told the FBI it was her opinion that Oswald "had had no previous contact with any of the English-speaking people on the bus" including Osborne (11 H 220–221). And the McFarlands told me that from what they could gather from pieces of conversation they picked up between Oswald and Osborne, they got the "impression" the two didn't know each other (Telephone interview of the McFarlands by the author on May 12, 1986).

Paseo de la Reforma, Mexico City's main east-west thoroughfare—and the owner was known for a willingness to try out his small English vocabulary, it did not attract a tourist trade, so an American like Lee Oswald was a rarity. Registration was simple: you paid your room rent each day in advance and signed your name in the hotel's register. Lee signed his name as "Lee, Harvey Oswald" and gave his occupation as "photo." His room, with a private bath, suited him fine. He stayed there, in room 18 on the third floor, throughout his visit to the city. All the places he wanted to go were within three miles to the south and west of the hotel—within walking distance if he felt like it, but taxis were plentiful and cheap. He acquired a street map of the city and marked a number of locations on it.[1427]

As soon as he registered, Oswald went straight to work on the problem of getting to Cuba. The Mexican authorities didn't care whether a traveler's passport barred travel to Cuba as long as the citizen had a proper visa from the Cuban embassy, but they would not permit Oswald to board a plane for Cuba without that visa.[1428] Oswald's 1963 passport—stamped invalid for travel to Cuba like all American passports issued that year—had neither a regular Cuban visa nor an "in transit" one, which would permit a short stay in Cuba if he were on his way to another country—Russia, for example. He looked up the telephone number and address, on the nearby Paseo de la Reforma, of Cubana Airlines, which flew from Mexico City to Havana three times a week, and jotted it in his address book.[1429] But first he had to get a Cuban visa.

He went that same morning to the Cuban embassy on the Calle Francisco Marquez, and there he spoke to Señora Silvia Tirado de Duran, a young Mexican woman temporarily employed in the consulate section of the embassy. He was prepared. He showed Duran his Soviet papers, which indicated that he had lived and worked there for three years. His documents attested that he was married to a Russian woman, and several prized documents, including a newspaper clipping, indicated that he was the secretary of the New Orleans chapter of the Fair Play for Cuba Committee. He told Duran that Cuba should accept him as a proven "friend" of the Cuban Revolution.[1430] Duran told the HSCA in 1978 that Oswald told her he was a member of the Communist Party.[1431] Although the day after the assassination she told the Mexican Federal Security Police she did not remember whether or not he did,[1432] the "comments" typed in by her and appended to Oswald's application for a Cuban visa on the day he applied, September 27, state that "the applicant states that he is a member of the American Communist Party," and he displayed a document "in proof of his membership."[1433] It would have had to be a document Oswald had forged. Duran also told the HSCA that Oswald showed her "letters to the Communist Party, the American Communist Party."[1434] Duran thought it odd that, if he was a member of or associated with the CPUSA, he had not asked the party to arrange the visa for him with Cuba. Cuba would have sent it to the Cuban embassy in Mexico City and it would have been waiting for him to pick up. He told her he hadn't had time to arrange it that way. It still seemed strange to her. The Communist Party was illegal in Mexico and had he cleared his travel through the American Communist Party, he would not have had to travel to Mexico with incriminating documents. His passport would have sufficed.[1435]

Oswald said that he was on his way to the Soviet Union but wanted an "in transit" visa allowing him to travel to Cuba immediately and to remain there for two weeks or even longer, if that were possible, before continuing his journey to the Soviet Union.[1436] Duran was sympathetic. At twenty-five, she was only a little older than Lee and was also a Marxist, although not really active politically. Her husband, Horacio Duran Navarro, had written a few articles for *El Dia*, the Communist newspaper in Mexico City, and both of them were sympathizers of the Cuban Revolution. She had worked for a time at the Mexican-Cuban Institute of Cultural Relations, a private organization subsidized to some extent by the Cuban government. Now she was working only temporarily as a secretary to the Cuban consul because the former secretary, a friend of Silvia's, had been killed in an automobile accident in July. Silvia was just filling in until a suitably qualified secretary could be brought over from Cuba.[1437]

As green as she was in the job, she knew it was impossible for Oswald to be granted an immediate visa to Cuba and that there were all types of steps to be followed, including getting authorization from Cuba. When Oswald heard there were going to be problems that would take time to resolve, he said he didn't have any time, that his Mexican tourist visa was going to expire in three days (which wasn't true, he had over a week and a half left), and became angry and agitated, whereupon Duran called Eusebio Azcue out of his office to speak to Oswald.[1438]

Azcue, in his early fifties, had been the Cuban consul in Mexico City for several years. He had been in Mexico since 1944 and had been working as an architect when Fidel Castro's forces swept into Havana in 1959 and ousted Fulgencio Batista and his regime. Azcue had been asked to take charge of the consulate in Mexico City. Now, in September of 1963, he wanted to retire and return to Havana, where he was born. The incoming consul, Alfredo Mirabel Diaz, had arrived on September 2, but Mirabel was still learning the job from Azcue and wouldn't formally take over until November 18. So it was Azcue who emerged to speak with Oswald.[1439]

Azcue explained to Oswald that the visas were issued by the Ministry of Foreign Affairs in Cuba, not in Mexico City, and that would take time, probably fifteen to twenty days. The only exception, he said, would be if Oswald could get a valid visa from the Soviet embassy permitting travel to the Soviet Union, in which case the consulate in Mexico City could issue an in-transit visa to Cuba to Oswald without prior consultation with the authorities in Cuba.[1440]

At this point, Duran also told Oswald that he would have to secure photographs of himself to attach to his application for a visa, and she gave him the addresses of several nearby photo shops and told him that if he wanted to come back that afternoon with the photographs and a visa for travel to the USSR, an application for a Cuban visa could be prepared.[1441]

Oswald had a lot to do, but he apparently decided to go to the Russian embassy first. At about half past noon Lee rang the bell at the gate of the Soviet embassy. It was only a short walk of less than two blocks down Calle Francisco Marquez from the Cuban embassy. Normally, you had to have an appointment to visit the Soviet embassy, but after Lee spoke to the sentry in Russian explaining the purpose of his visit, he was shown into the waiting room of the consul's office, which was located in a small building detached from the main embassy but within the grounds. After a few minutes, a man named Valeriy Vladimirovich Kostikov appeared to interview him.

Lee, taken aback by Kostikov's dark complexion and Zapata mustache—he looked more Mexican or Arabian than Russian—said, "I would like to speak with one of the *Soviet* consular officers." Kostikov, amused, showed Lee diplomatic identification indicating that he was indeed an employee of the consulate. He then led him into the office where he had been receiving visitors since eleven o'clock that morning.

There were three consular officials in the embassy—Oleg Nechiporenko and Pavel

Yatskov, in addition to Kostikov. In public they passed themselves off as the consul (Yatskov) and two vice consuls, but in fact all three were KGB officers of equal rank and responsibilities but in different directorates of the Soviet intelligence service. They were always interested in American visitors. Some could be people with important jobs in sensitive places, people who perhaps wanted to offer information or other kinds of cooperation. Kostikov, a colonel in the KGB's First Chief Directorate, was charged with foreign intelligence, and he was curious as to what Oswald had to say.

Oswald said he wanted a visa for travel to the USSR. He pulled a wad of documents out of his zipper jacket, handed them to Kostikov, and started telling the same story he had just given at the Cuban consulate. Kostikov scanned Oswald's papers, saw that his visitor had indeed lived in the Soviet Union, and quickly decided that this was more of a matter for counterintelligence than his own directorate. He excused himself, went to a telephone in another room, and rang Colonel Nechiporenko in the embassy.

"Listen, some gringo is here," Kostikov said. "He's asking for a visa to the Soviet Union . . . Come over here and get to the bottom of this . . . It seems to be more in your line of work. I'm in a hurry."

As Nechiporenko walked over from the embassy, he saw Oswald standing on the steps of the consulate building. Inside he found Kostikov eager to palm Oswald off on him. "He keeps saying the FBI is after him in that he lived for a while in the Soviet Union. Those are his papers over there. Listen, I got to run, I'll see you later this evening." Kostikov opened the door to the reception area and invited Oswald back into the office, introduced Nechiporenko without mentioning his name, and left. Nechiporenko's impression of Oswald was that he was suffering from some sort of exhaustion, physical or mental. As Oswald talked, he became more and more agitated, and Nechiporenko gave him a chance to calm down by turning his attention to Lee's documents.

Nechiporenko knew that Oswald could possibly be a plant or an agent provocateur sent by the CIA or some other intelligence agency. On the other hand, he could equally be utilized by the Russians as an asset—the problem was to figure out which was which as quickly as possible. When Oswald cooled down a bit, Nechiporenko went straight to the heart of the matter. He asked for specific information on why the FBI might be following him.

Oswald had no convincing explanation. He said that the bureau had started interrogating him and Marina shortly after he returned to the United States from the USSR. His wife was still being questioned in his absence, and the FBI had now started making inquiries among his friends. When Nechiporenko, conversing with Oswald primarily in Russian, asked Lee why he had returned to the United States, Lee flunked the test. (Since he left voluntarily—because he couldn't stand Russia—why did he want to go back?) For all his months of obsessive preparation, he had never invented a persuasive answer to this question by any Communist inquisitor. Nechiporenko would later recall that "Oswald fidgeted, changed the subject, and avoided answering the question." That was all the colonel needed to know. Although it went without saying, Nechiporenko thought that his colleagues in the USSR would have kept Oswald under close surveillance during his stay in the Soviet Union. The only question was whether there had been any deeper contact with the KGB. And actually, from virtually the start of their conversation, Nechiporenko realized that any such operational connection was clearly out of the question—Oswald was in no way suitable agent material.

Nechiporenko had seen Oswald's letter to the Soviet embassy in Washington, D.C., among his documents, but he asked Oswald anyway whether he had appealed to the Washington embassy for help. Oswald had to admit that he had and that it had turned him down, then launched into a cockamamie story about his fear that the FBI would arrest him for having written that letter. That was why, he told Nechiporenko, he had decided to come to Mexico City, because the FBI wouldn't be able to seize him here. He added, as an afterthought, that he also wanted to visit Cuba on his way back to the USSR.

Nechiporenko recalled an earlier drop-in at the consulate, an American who claimed to be in communication with Premier Khrushchev and suddenly said, "Just a minute . . . Khrushchev is speaking to me again." The more the colonel saw of Oswald, the less he wanted to talk to him. He silently cursed his friend Kostikov for having offloaded Oswald on him. He decided to put an end to the interview. He explained to Lee that all matters concerning travel to the USSR had to be handled by the Soviet embassy in the country where the applicant resided. They could make a minor exception in Oswald's case by allowing him to file the necessary application in Mexico City, but Moscow's response would be sent to him at his permanent address in the United States. It would take, at the least, Nechiporenko told him, four months.

Oswald snapped. He leaned forward and practically shouted in Nechiporenko's face, "This won't do for me! This is not my case! For me it's all going to end in tragedy!"

The colonel shrugged and stood up. He noticed that Oswald's hands were shaking as he put his documents back into his jacket. Nechiporenko led him through the reception area out into the grounds and saw him off at the gate. The visit had lasted nearly an hour. Over a beer in a nearby cantina that evening, Kostikov wondered out loud if the young American were "schizoid."

"I don't think so," Nechiporenko said, "but there's no doubt he's neurotic. That's for sure."[1442]

Oswald returned to the Cuban consulate with four photographs after the two o'clock closing time, but somehow managed to get in to see Señora Duran.[*] Duran typed Oswald's visa application for him in four copies, fastened a photograph to each copy, and had Oswald sign each one. He told her again he needed the visa urgently. She again called Azcue, who again explained that he could do nothing without the proper visa from the Soviet Union. Oswald told them he had succeeded in getting a Russian visa, but when Duran asked to see it, Oswald, of course, had nothing to show Duran. Yet, remarkably, Oswald kept insisting that he had a Russian visa, so Duran called the Russian embassy and Nechiporenko told her that Oswald did not, that Oswald was told it would take around four months.[1443]

Azcue proceeded to tell Oswald that he simply would not give him the visa he was demanding, and Oswald, at this point, was at his wit's end. In a rage of frustration, he became abusive. He contemptuously referred to the Cubans as "bureaucrats." Azcue, who had not liked Oswald from the beginning, finding him "never friendly, persistent, not pleasant," was provoked and threw Oswald out, perhaps "somewhat violently or emo-

---

[*]Oswald probably gained admission by using Silvia Duran's name when he spoke to the gatekeeper. It is not known where Oswald went to get his photographs. The FBI checked seven photo studios located within the vicinities of the Cuban and Russian embassies and could find no negative of Oswald. (CE 2449, 25 H 589–590) The negative for the photo stapled to Oswald's application for a visa was found among his effects after the assassination. The Warren Commission speculated that Oswald may have had the photos with him when he came to Mexico. (WR, pp.304, 734)

tionally," as he later admitted to the HSCA. Oswald, mumbling to himself, slammed the door behind as he left.[1444]*

Kostikov and Nechiporenko had naturally assumed that they had seen the last of the strange American. They had no idea of how tenacious he was. The Soviet embassy was closed on the weekends, but all three of the consuls turned up there on Saturday morning, September 28, for a serious volleyball match between two groups working at the embassy, mostly KGB members on one side and GRU (Soviet Military Intelligence) on the other side. The KGB side was called "the diplomats," because of their cover jobs. The embassy teams did well in Mexico City's annual volleyball tournament, and were very competitive with college and university teams of men ten years their junior despite the fact that the latter were more used to the area's heat and altitude—7,415 above sea level. The Soviet sportsmen were dangerous opponents.

Pavel Yatskov was the first to show up. Though considerably older than Kostikov and Nechiporenko, he kept himself extremely fit and played both tennis and volleyball like a professional. While he was getting ready for the game, which would start about ten, the gate sentry came to tell him that someone at the gate—not Mexican by appearance—wanted to speak to the consul. The sentry had refused him entrance, since the embassy was officially closed. Yatskov told the sentry to bring the man to the office.

A young man dressed in a gray suit was brought to him. Yatskov, who had not met Oswald the day before, could see that he was pale and extremely agitated. Without waiting for questions, Oswald launched into his story in English, which was difficult for Yatskov, whose English was limited, to follow. Nevertheless, he understood Lee was American, a Communist, a pro-Cuban, and that he was being persecuted and feared for his life. His hands trembled as he spoke. Yatskov was considerably relieved when Valeriy Kostikov walked in.

Kostikov briefly outlined for Yatskov what he knew of Oswald from the interview of the day before, and Oswald began telling his story all over again to Kostikov. Eventually, Yatskov broke in and suggested that, since Oswald had lived and worked in the Soviet Union, he could probably explain himself in the language. Oswald complied and continued his story in his ragged Russian for the rest of the interview.

In Oswald's trembling state, he proceeded to betray, perhaps unwittingly, what he really was up to, and it had nothing to do with going to Russia,[1445] the whole purpose of why Oswald was supposedly at the Russian consulate. He told them he wanted to help the Cuban people "build a new life."

Oswald, already nervous and agitated, suddenly became hysterical when he started to tell of his persecution by the FBI. He sobbed, "I am afraid . . . they'll kill me." He was,

---

*Duran gave her recollection of the incident to the Mexican Federal Security Police in 1963 and the HSCA in 1978. She said that when Azcue refused to give Oswald his visa, Oswald became "highly agitated and angry," insisting that he "was a friend of the Cuban Revolution, that he had already been in jail for the Cuban Revolution . . . He was red and he was almost crying and, uh, he was insisting and insisting, so Azcue told him to go away because if he didn't go away at that moment he was going to kick him, or something like that. So, Azcue went to the door, he opened the door and told Oswald to go away . . . I was feeling pity for him [Oswald] because he looked desperate." Duran said that at some point during Azcue's argument with Oswald, Azcue had told Oswald that "a person like you, [instead] of aiding the Cuban Revolution, are doing it harm." (3 HSCA 47–49, 51; CE 2121, 24 H 589–590; CE 2445, 25 H 586; see also Interview of Duran, Transcript of "Who Was Lee Harvey Oswald?" *Frontline*, PBS, November 16, 1993, p.28)

Before Oswald left, Duran gave him a piece of paper with her name and the Cuban consulate's phone number so he could inquire at a later time about the decision in Havana regarding his visa application.

he said, even being followed here in Mexico. Suddenly, he stuck his hand into his jacket pocket and pulled out a revolver. "See, this is what I must now carry to protect my life." He put the gun on the desk between himself and Kostikov. Yatskov went pale. Kostikov was dumbfounded.

"Here," Yatskov said to Kostikov, "give me that piece."

Kostikov handed the pistol, a Smith & Wesson revolver, to Yatskov, who broke it open, shook the bullets into his hand, and put them into his desk drawer. He handed the gun back to Kostikov, who put it back on the desk.

Oswald went on sobbing for a while and Yatskov, to calm Oswald down, poured him a glass of water. Oswald took a sip and put it on the table in front of him. At that moment, Nechiporenko, thinking he was late for the volleyball game—it was already after ten— burst into the room with his athletic bag, but stopped in his tracks when he saw who his colleagues' guest was. Oswald barely took notice of him. Nechiporenko saw that his eyes were reddened from crying, and that Oswald was even more disturbed than he had been the day before. Nechiporenko backed out of the room, went to the courtyard, and warned the sentry not to let anyone else in. If any of the other volleyball players asked the sentry where they were, he was to tell them that they were occupied in the consulate and the others should start without them. He then went back into the consulate office next to the one where Oswald was still talking with Yatskov and Kostikov. The door was ajar, and Nechiporenko listened to the conversation.

Yatskov offered Oswald application forms for a visa and explained the rules once again—the application had to be sent to the USSR, and if the visa were granted, it would be at least four months. Nevertheless, they would, if he wished, forward his application to Moscow. Oswald tried another tack. He wanted them to tell the Cubans to give him a visa. That, they explained, was simply not possible. Notwithstanding his ardent desire to "help the Cubans build a new life," Cuba was a sovereign nation that issued its own visas according to its own rules. The Soviet consulate had no influence over the Cubans in that regard.

Yatskov stood up to signal that the interview was over. Oswald, who by now had gone from a state of agitation to one of frustration and disappointment, stood, grabbed the gun, and stuck it somewhere under his jacket. Remarkably, Yatskov retrieved the bullets from his desk drawer and handed them to Oswald, who put them in the pocket of his jacket. Kostikov took him to the door and followed him to the gate. Oswald, as though aware of the possibility that visitors to the Soviet embassy were photographed by nearby CIA cameras, turned up the collar of his jacket to conceal his face and left on foot.[1446]*

Norman Mailer writes, "It is painful to think of Oswald walking down the street, his documents in his ditty bag. All his striving had gone into collecting those documents, yet no one had been stirred by his deeds."[1447]

Nechiporenko later wrote that after Oswald left them that Saturday morning, "The

---

*In his 1995 book, *Oswald's Tale*, Norman Mailer writes that an interviewer employed by him asked Nechiporenko how it was possible that a responsible KGB agent would give back not only a gun but also the bullets to someone as disturbed in appearance as Oswald. "Nechiporenko shrugged. It had happened, he said. He could not speak for why. Yatskov had done it, but it did not seem exceptional at the time. They just had not been afraid that this man Oswald would go out on the street and cause trouble with his gun." Interestingly, when Nechiporenko was further asked if "this same episode had taken place in London, would any of you have returned the bullets?" Nechiporenko responded, "Never," from which Mailer infers "that these three KGB men had served in Mexico long enough to feel it was wrong to deprive a man of his gun. *That*, by the Mexican logic of the cantinas, was equal to emasculation." (Mailer, *Oswald's Tale*, p.640)

three of us remained in the consulate and exchanged our impressions about this strange visitor . . . We decided we could not take Oswald seriously, . . . that his mental state was unstable, or that, at the very least, he suffered from a very serious nervous disorder." But they nonetheless decided to report their two-day experience with Oswald in a coded cable (Special Communication 550) to KGB headquarters in Moscow dated October 3, 1963. Though Oswald had not completed an application for a Russian visa, the cable never-theless mentioned Oswald's request for reentry into Russia. A letter dated October 25 from KGB Deputy Chairman S. Bannikov to Deputy Minister of Foreign Affairs V. V. Kuznetsov said, "It is our opinion it is inadvisable to permit Oswald to return to the Soviet Union."[1448]

Oswald's attempt to enter his paradise of Castro's Cuba had come, finally and irrevo-cably, to an end. In spite of his loutish behavior at the Cuban consulate, Señora Duran did forward his application for a Cuban visa to Havana, but the Cuban Ministry of For-eign Affairs replied on October 15—long after Oswald had left Mexico City—that the visa could be issued only after Oswald had obtained a visa valid for travel to the Soviet Union.[1449]

Oswald knew that his trip had been a complete failure and that it was unlikely he would be able to contrive any other means of getting to Cuba.[1450] Once again he had been thwarted by a government, only this time it was Cuba, the one on which he had fastened his dreams.

Lee, who, from his days as a teenager in New York City, liked to travel and see new places, lingered for several more days in Mexico City, a sprawling metropolis of five mil-lion people in 1963. Since he was alone, what he did there will never be known for sure.[1451]* He did not spend much time at his hotel. The maid, Matilde Garnica, recalled that Oswald was usually gone by the time she arrived at nine in the morning—she only saw him twice— and a night watchman, Pedro Rodriguez Ledesma, said Oswald usually returned at or after midnight. He never appeared to have been drinking, was never accompanied by any-one, and did not use the only telephone at the hotel, which was located at the reception desk.[1452] He ate several times at a small restaurant immediately adjacent to the hotel, usu-ally in the early afternoon. He ordered by pointing to items on the menu, would take the soup of the day, and rice with either meat or eggs, but refused dessert and coffee, possi-bly because he thought they might cost extra. The owner, Dolores Ramirez de Barreiro, guessed that he didn't understand that they were included in the price, but no one spoke enough English to explain that to him. He took no soft drinks either, which was unusual in that class of restaurant, and she estimated he spent five to six pesos (forty to forty-eight cents) for his meals.[1453]

Oswald was never seen with anyone else at the hotel or the restaurant.[1454] And one hotel guest who did sit at Oswald's table once because there were no other places, Gabriel Con-treras Uvina, did not exchange a single word with him. Contreras spoke no English.[1455]

Oswald told Marina that he had attended a bullfight in Mexico City.[1456] One of the

---

*One thing we do know he did (from CIA monitoring of telephone conversations at the Russian embassy) is that at 10:45 Tuesday morning, October 1, Oswald telephoned the embassy. After identifying himself by name, and saying he was at the embassy on Saturday, he said, "They said they'd send a telegram to Washing-ton so I wanted to find out if you have anything new." Oswald was informed that "nothing has been received as yet." (CIA Document CSCI-3778826, November 25, 1963, JFK Document 000169) It is not known to whom in Washington the Soviets had told Oswald they would send the telegram, or for what purpose.

city's two arenas, El Toreo, was closed in September and October of 1963, but on Sunday afternoon (the customary time for bullfights), September 29, 1963, Oswald could have seen a *cartel de novilladas* (literally meaning "baitings of young bulls"), training sessions for young toreadors that do not quite amount to bullfighting, and hence are much less expensive to watch (general admission of two pesos—sixteen cents), at the other arena, Plaza de México, believed to be the world's largest bullfight arena with a seating capacity of fifty thousand.[1457]

Oswald also told her he had visited museums[1458] and done some sightseeing.[1459] In *Esta Semana*, a guide to the week's events in Mexico City, Oswald checked several films, American movies with Spanish subtitles or Mexican films with English subtitles.[1460] From a notation in his guide map of Mexico City, it appears that Oswald at least thought of going to a jai alai game, the ancient sport from Spain.[1461]

Lee bought several postcards depicting bullfights and tourist attractions, which he brought back to Marina,[1462] but, with one small exception, that appeared to exhaust his interest in shopping. Marina had asked him to bring her some Mexican musical records, but he did not.[1463] She had also told him she would like a Mexican silver bracelet, and he did bring her a silver ID bracelet inscribed with her name, but she didn't like it at all. And Marina suspected that the cheap Japanese bracelet did not even come from Mexico. Such jewelry was not sold in Mexico City because of high import duties, but it was common in five-and-dime stores in Dallas, and Marina had seen its like in New Orleans.[1464] Lee did buy Marina one gift from Mexico she hadn't asked for, though after he was gone she would treasure it like nothing else he had ever given her—a miniature straw monkey he had paid only five cents for.[1465]

With the new week, Oswald was making arrangements to return to the United States. On Monday, September 30, at the Agencia de Viajes Transportes Chihuahuenses, he bought two international exchange orders totalling $20.30 to pay for the trip on a Transportes del Norte bus from Mexico City to Laredo and by Greyhound directly from Laredo to Dallas. That same day he reserved a seat on the bus, which was to leave at 8:30 on Wednesday morning, October 2, giving him one more full day in the city. The travel agency reserved seat number 12 for him under the name "H. O. Lee."[1466] This was another of Lee's feeble attempts to be deceptive almost for its own sake, although if he had one-tenth the fear of the FBI that he expressed to the consular agents at the Russian embassy, it may have simply been an attempt to muddy his trail. Oswald would later use the name O. H. Lee, a variation of H. O. Lee, when he rented a room in Dallas in mid-October.[1467]

On Tuesday, October 1, Lee's last full day in the city, he paid his hotel bill in advance for the night.[1468] The next morning, the hotel's night man went out about 6:30 or 7:00 to fetch him a cab.[1469] Transportes del Norte bus number 332 left as scheduled at 8:30 a.m.[1470] Arriving at Monterrey around 9:15 p.m., the passengers were shifted to another bus, number 373, which departed for Laredo at 9:50 p.m. that evening.[1471] A passenger on the bus recalled that Oswald annoyed him by keeping his overhead light on to read after ten at night.[1472] At the Mexican side of the border, Oswald was pulled off the bus by Mexican immigration officials, apparently over some question about his papers, but the questioning only lasted three or four minutes and he was soon back aboard the bus, grumbling about the Mexican authorities.[1473] At about 1:30 on the morning of October 3, Oswald crossed the International Bridge from Nuevo Laredo, Mexico, to Laredo, Texas.[1474] A couple of passengers recall that when the bus reached Laredo and the U.S. Immigration station, Oswald "gulped down" a banana, possibly for fear he could not take fruit into the United States.[1475] Lee, according to Marina, "loved bananas" and ate them often.[1476]

From Laredo, Lee traveled to Dallas via San Antonio on Greyhound bus number 1265, following Interstate 35. The bus left Laredo about 3:00 in the morning and arrived in Dallas about 2:20 p.m. on the same day.[1477] Per the Warren Commission's calculations, Oswald left New Orleans on his Mexican adventure with around $215, and when he arrived back in Dallas he had approximately $130. The entire trip, including transportation, lodging, food, and miscellaneous expenses, had cost him the grand total of $85.[1478]

Lee Oswald's brief stay in Mexico City has become a happy hunting ground for dedicated seekers of a conspiracy to assassinate John F. Kennedy. Less than two months before the murder, Oswald made contact with the embassies of two hostile Communist countries, the Soviet Union and Cuba, and, as would be the case with any ordinary citizen visiting Mexico, there can be no certainty about how he spent all of his time in Mexico City or whom he might have met there. It has been claimed that he met socially with Cubans in Mexico City, that he made open threats against President Kennedy in the presence of Cuban embassy officials, and most improbably of all, that someone else posed as Oswald for the visits to the embassies. All of these matters, and many more, of course, will be discussed in depth in the conspiracy section of this book.

When Oswald arrived at the bus terminal in Dallas on Thursday afternoon, October 3, his financial predicament was tight but not desperate—he had enough, presumably, to rent an apartment, although he needed a job fast. He didn't even take the time to call Marina at Ruth Paine's house in Irving to let her know he was back from Mexico,[1479] instead going straight to the nearest office of the Texas Employment Commission to register for work[1480] and file another claim for unemployment compensation.[1481] That done, he spent the night at the YMCA, where he registered as a serviceman to avoid paying the membership fee.[1482] He also gave his last address as "Toro, Cal"—his last duty station in the Marine Corps had been at El Toro. He had no way of knowing that FBI agents were once again on his trail, but they were. On Tuesday, October 1, Jesse Garner had informed FBI agents in New Orleans that the Oswalds had left their Magazine Street apartment in New Orleans on September 25.[1483] The day that Lee arrived back in Dallas, FBI agent Jim Hosty, notified by the New Orleans office of the bureau that Marina had left New Orleans in a station wagon with Texas plates and driven by a woman who spoke Russian, launched a new search for the Oswalds in Dallas.

There wasn't much to go on, but Hosty went to the immigration office to see if it had any information, and he tried to find out what Russian-speaking American with a station wagon might be a friend of Marina Oswald's. He drove over to Fort Worth to check Lee and Marina's old neighborhood and attempted to locate Robert Oswald, who, he learned, had moved to Malvern, Arkansas. He requested the Little Rock office of the bureau to contact Robert to see if he knew where his brother was. He doggedly searched whole neighborhoods in Dallas and Fort Worth where the Oswalds had been before. It was a lot of work but more or less routine for the FBI. It wasn't particularly urgent and it wasn't very successful. The Oswalds had, at least for the time being, disappeared.[1484]

Hosty might have picked up Lee's whereabouts earlier had he thought to check the records of the Texas Employment Commission in Dallas, since Lee had given the commission Ruth Paine's address and phone number as his address. Oswald also truthfully told the employment commission that his last place of work was the "Wm. B. Reily Co." in New Orleans. He more or less had to do that, since it was already in his record that he had been collecting his Texas unemployment compensation in New Orleans and he needed proof that he hadn't been shirking work. At the same time, he lied and stated on his application for a work form that the type of work he did at the coffee company was "photography," which certainly suggests that he was hoping for another job in that field. He noted his experience with radar in the Marine Corps and claimed four months of employment as a shoe salesman and a year as a general office worker in New Orleans in 1961.

Lee impressed the official who took his application, who noted that Lee was "well-groomed and spoken, business suit, alert replies. Expresses self extremely well."[1485] The next day Lee responded to a newspaper ad for a trainee in typesetting at the Padgett Printing Company. The idea of the severely dyslexic Oswald working as a typesetter is startling, but it suggests that Lee may have been unaware of his own limitations. He claimed on his application that he had been a "cleark" at Louv-R-Pak. Oswald made a good impression on the department foreman at Padgett. However, unfortunately for Lee, the superintendent, Theo Gangl, was a good friend of Bob Stovall's at Jaggers-Chiles-Stovall. He wrote on the bottom of Lee's application, "Bob Stovall does not recommend this man. He was released because of his record as a troublemaker.—*Has communistic tendencies.*"[1486]

That same day Lee enrolled at JOBCO, a private employment agency located in the Adolphus Tower in downtown Dallas. His application there, like the one at Padgett, omitted any mention of his work in New Orleans and listed Jaggers as his last place of employment. He said he had been in the Dallas area for the last fifteen years. He listed George de Mohrenschildt as his closest friend, although George had been in Haiti since June and could no longer be contacted at the Dickens Street address Lee gave for him.[1487]

Later, in the early afternoon, Oswald finally called Marina in Irving to tell her he had arrived back in Dallas from Mexico City the previous day. He asked Marina to have Ruth pick him up in Dallas. Marina, who told Lee she was already upset with him for not calling as soon as he arrived, said that Ruth couldn't come to pick him up. "Ruth has just been to Parkland Hospital this morning to donate blood. She shouldn't be driving now to pick you up."

Ruth left to go grocery shopping, returned in something less than an hour, and was astonished to find Lee already there—he had hitched a ride with an accommodating black man who had gone out of his way to drop him at Ruth's, where he spent the weekend.[1488]

The Oswalds took care to conceal Lee's Mexican excursion from Ruth. He told her that he had been to Houston but had not been able to find work there, so he was now looking for employment in Dallas.[1489] To Marina he told all, about all the places he had been to in Mexico City, and including the fact that he did not like Mexican girls. He told her that the officials at the Soviet embassy refused to have anything to do with him. And he referred to the officials at the Cuban embassy with whom he had dealt as "bureaucrats" and said their system was similar to the Russians—"too much red tape."[1490]

Although Lee, Marina said, had always been "crazy about Cuba," they didn't talk about Cuba any longer after the Mexican trip because, as Marina put it, "I was just sick and tired of this."[1491] They talked about their living arrangements for the next couple of months. Marina, nearing the term of her pregnancy, did not really want to live with Lee for the time being—she preferred to be with "a woman who spoke English and Russian." Lee was not invited to move into the house, which was already sheltering two adult women and their three children, as well as, from time to time, Ruth's husband Michael, a frequent visitor. Lee told Marina he would look for a furnished room in Dallas, as it would be considerably cheaper than renting an apartment until she came back to live with him.[1492]

In the meantime, Ruth was content for him to stay with them that weekend as well as subsequent weekends, even finding Lee to be a welcome visitor. Either that weekend or the next, he planed down some doors that had been sticking and generally ingratiated himself, adding "a needed masculine flavor." Ruth, realizing that Lee had to be depressed about looking for work, came to like him better than she had before and described him in a letter to her mother as a "happy addition to our extended family." He played with her little boy, Chris, watched football on TV,[1493] and read the papers, in one of which, the *Dallas Morning News* of Sunday, October 6, he probably noticed the ad "Furnished Rooms Oak Cliff," reading beneath, "GOOD HOME—Bedroom, living room privileges, café, washateria, cleaner, bus door, $7 up, 1026 N. Beckley."[1494] Oak Cliff was their old neighborhood in Dallas, and the reference to this rooming house attracted him.

On Monday morning, October 7, around noon, Ruth obligingly drove Lee to the intercity bus terminal in Irving, two or three miles he would otherwise have had to walk given the paucity of public transportation in the suburb.[1495] On the way to the bus station, Lee asked Ruth if Marina could stay with her until he found work. Ruth answered that Marina was welcome to stay as long as she liked.[1496]

Inasmuch as his Cuban plans had been dashed, it is unknown at this point what Oswald intended to do with Marina. However, unbeknownst to him, the Ministry of Foreign Affairs in Moscow would narrow, if not eliminate, his options. The same day Ruth drove him to the bus station, October 7, the ministry, acting on the recommendation of the Leningrad KGB (Marina's Leningrad relatives did not want to take her in, her stepfather telling the KGB she was a person of loose morals), refused her request to reenter her homeland.[1497]*

Back in the city, Lee's first order of business was to get out of the YMCA, which he thought too expensive.[1498] He turned up at the rooming house on 1026 North Beckley, but there were no vacancies. Mrs. A. C. Johnson, who owned the place, had just rented her last room, but Lee apparently liked the location, so Mrs. Johnson told him to keep an eye out for the "For Rent" sign she posted whenever she had a vacancy.[1499]

Later that afternoon Lee found another place at 621 North Marsalis in the Oak Cliff area of Dallas. It was about a mile southeast of the Beckley address that had caught his fancy and farther from the city center, but it too was on a bus route. He found Mrs. Mary Bledsoe in the backyard, told her he was just out of the Marine Corps, showed her snapshots of Marina and June, and gave her seven dollars for a week's rent in advance.[1500] About forty minutes later he reappeared with the larger of his two bags and moved in, bringing with him his shortwave radio (which Ruth Paine had recognized as of Russian manufacture), which he apparently retrieved from Irving that first weekend. Mrs. Bledsoe recalled that Oswald came with "a clock wrapped up,"[1501] but there is no record of a clock among his possessions, and the radio was found at Beckley Street after the assassination. With his shortwave radio, Lee was capable of listening to the nightly propaganda broadcast in English emanating from Havana.

Before settling in, Lee walked to a nearby grocery store and returned with some milk, peanut butter, sardines, and bananas. Mrs. Bledsoe discouraged him from using her refrigerator by pointing out it was small, but he put his milk in it anyway, which she didn't like,

---

*There is no record of any letter from the Soviets to Marina informing her of their decision.

then ate the rest of the food in his room, which she also didn't like. But she said nothing because she "wanted to get along" with her new tenant.[1502]

Tuesday, Wednesday, and Thursday, Lee went job hunting, but to no avail. On Tuesday, even Mary Bledsoe tried to help him get a job by making calls for him, because she felt he was a nice-looking young man and really wanted a job. "He was not lazy," Marina would say.[1503]

Worried about Marina's health and little Junie during this period, Lee telephoned Marina twice a day.[1504] Friday, Mary Bledsoe noticed, Lee spent the whole day in his room.[1505] Even though Lee had just moved in, his habits started to wear on her. One day she heard him talking on the phone in a foreign language, and she didn't like that at all. Also, his return from job hunting in the afternoons disturbed her naps, and she didn't like his "big-shot" attitude, his eating in his room, and getting ice from her refrigerator. So she decided to put an end to the rental. On Saturday he appeared with his little overnight bag and said he was leaving for the weekend. She told him no, he was going to move. She would not rent the room to him for another week. She just didn't like him anymore.[1506]

That weekend at Ruth Paine's house was much like the preceding one. Ruth had taken Marina to the hospital on Friday for a checkup, and everything seemed to be in order—Ruth was impressed by the quality of care Marina was being given. Lee wanted to use Michael Paine's drill press to put a hole in a Mexican peso so Marina could wear it. Ruth didn't want him to use Michael's shop tools, but he persuaded her he knew how to do it. On Sunday, she agreed to give him a driving lesson in her car, and he climbed in and started it. Ruth, knowing he did not yet have a learner's permit, did not want him to drive on the streets, but in the end she allowed him to navigate the three blocks to the parking lot of a closed shopping center, where he practiced starting, stopping, turning, backing, and other simple maneuvers. He was not particularly adept at it, and Ruth insisted on driving when they headed for home.[1507] He told her that weekend that he had received the last of the unemployment checks due him, and that it had been for less money than he usually got. She thought he was "very discouraged" that he hadn't been able to find a job.[1508]

On Saturday evening of that weekend, Lee and Marina shared a banana and she put her head in his lap, dozing off now and then while he watched old movies on television, two films back to back, *Suddenly* and *We Were Strangers*. She watched the latter film, but not the former,[1509] although she knew the first one involved "an attempt to kill a president at a railroad station with a rifle from a house."[1510] Eerily, both movies involved political assassinations.

Suddenly was a nine-year-old B-thriller starring Frank Sinatra and Sterling Hayden. Directed by Lewis Allen from a script by Richard Sale, Sinatra plays a psychotic ex-serviceman who has been hired to assassinate the president of the United States when he gets off the train in the small western town of Suddenly for a vacation in the nearby Sierras. Sinatra and two accomplices masquerading as FBI agents take over the house of an attractive young widow whose family they hold hostage. The house overlooks the train stop, and the upper windows provide a perfect location for a shooter with a high-powered sniper's rifle mounted with a telescopic sight. From the window, one sees a dark limousine about two hundred yards away waiting for the president to arrive. In the end, the president's train passes through Suddenly without stopping, and the would-be assassin eventually meets his death at the hands of the local sheriff, played by Hayden.

The second film, *We Were Strangers*, directed by John Huston and written by Peter

Viertel, was even older, dating from 1949, and based on the overthrow of the Cuban dictator Geraldo "the butcher" Machado in 1933, but it was a better film, with splendid performances by John Garfield, Jennifer Jones, and a cast of psuedo-Cubans such as Pedro Armendáriz, Ramon Novarro, and Gilbert Roland. Garfield plays an American expatriate who takes up the cause of China Valdez (Jennifer Jones), who joined the Cuban underground after her brother was killed by the chief of the secret police. Garfield develops a plan, involving the building of a tunnel, to blow up the dictator and his entire cabinet when they congregate for a state funeral. His plot fails and Garfield dies a hero's death, which sparks a popular uprising, and the film ends with the Cuban people dancing in the streets at the fall of the dictatorship.

The impact of these films on Lee's fantasy life cannot be known. He never discussed them with anyone beyond remarking to Marina that the content of the Cuban film was similar to the actual situation then existing in Cuba and that he did not like the conspirators' plans in *We Were Strangers* because, as he said, "that was the way they did it in the old days."[1511]

However, as to the movie *Suddenly*, with someone possessing the unbalanced and homicidal (remember the attempt on General Walker's life) mind Oswald did, there is no way that his seeing the movie can casually and automatically be dismissed out of hand as having played no part in his forming the intent to kill Kennedy from his sniper's nest window at the Texas School Book Depository the following month. Author John Loken, in his book *Oswald's Trigger Films* (in which he includes *We Were Strangers* and *The Manchurian Candidate*, also starring Frank Sinatra, which the author speculates Oswald may have seen when it was shown in Dallas in late December of 1962), wonders about the effect *Suddenly* and *We Were Strangers* could have had on a psyche as combustible as Oswald's, and said that if these movies "provided only five to ten percent of the stimulus for his act, their influence would still be momentous."[1512] After all, it was a newspaper clipping about the murder, by gunshot, of the king of Italy that helped inspire the murder of President William McKinley in 1901.[1513] It is noteworthy that Marina told author Priscilla McMillan that while watching one or both movies, every now and then Oswald would sit up straight and strain toward the television set, greatly excited.[1514]

One person we know felt there may have been a connection or at least a possible one between *Suddenly* and the assassination—Frank Sinatra. Sinatra had enough clout in the movie industry by 1963 to have *Suddenly* "taken out of distribution after hearing that President John F. Kennedy's assassin, Lee Harvey Oswald, had watched '*Suddenly*' only days before November 22, 1963."[1515]

On Monday, October 14, Ruth had to take her Russian typewriter into Dallas for a repair, so she, with Marina and the kids, dropped Lee off near the unemployment office.[1516] Lee picked up his bag from Mrs. Bledsoe's rooming house[1517] and later that day went back to the rooming house at 1026 North Beckley Avenue and rented a room from Mrs. Johnson for eight dollars a week.* The room was tiny, little more than a large closet—Mrs.

---

*As previously noted, the Beckley address, like the unit he rented on North Marsalis, was in the Oak Cliff area of Dallas, an area Oswald obviously showed a preference for, the two places on Elsbeth and Neely he lived in with Marina also being in Oak Cliff. His taste for Oak Cliff, apart from the rents being affordable to him, was understandable. For the most part Oak Cliff is a moderately hilly, homey, and pridefully old residential area of Dallas. Just across the Trinity River, the tall buildings of downtown Dallas appear to be quite close. Indeed, they are. Oswald's rooming house was only 1.9 miles from where he worked at the Book Depository Building on the edge of downtown Dallas. (Assassination researcher Ken Holmes recorded 1.9 miles on the odometer in his vehicle on the evening of September 22, 2004, during my trip to Dallas.)

Johnson called it her "library" because it once did serve as her library and "that's what it was built for," she said, but it had four windows and was light and airy. He told Mrs. Johnson that he would take it until a larger one became available, but by the time one did, he liked it so well he didn't even bother to look at the other room. It was certainly an improvement over Mrs. Bledsoe's. There was a television set in the main room for all the tenants, and when Lee asked Mrs. Johnson if he could put milk and lunch meat in the refrigerator, she said that would be fine with her. Oswald registered—as "O. H. Lee"— and moved in immediately.[1518]

That same Monday afternoon, Ruth and Marina went to visit Ruth's neighbor across the street, Dorothy Roberts, for coffee, and Lee's problem of finding a job came up in the conversation. Linnie Mae Randle, another neighbor from a little farther down the street, was also there, and she mentioned the fact that her younger brother, Wesley Frazier, had recently found work at the Texas School Book Depository in Dealey Plaza. Wesley had mentioned that there might be another opening there. Marina asked Ruth if she would call the Texas School Book Depository, which she did.[1519] Roy Truly, superintendent of the Depository, was encouraging—he told Ruth he would be happy to talk to Lee if he applied in person,[1520] and when Oswald called that evening to speak to Marina, Ruth told him about the opening.[1521]

The next day Oswald went to the Book Depository, where Truly gave him an application to fill out. Lee claimed to have lived in Dallas "continuously," following a pattern of deleting from his records, where possible, all traces of his recent stay in New Orleans. He listed his last job as his three-year service in the Marine Corps, his reason for leaving being his "honorable discharge." There was no point in giving references to Jaggers-Chiles-Stovall or the Reily coffee company, both of which had fired him. Roy Truly was favorably impressed. He had assumed he was interviewing a recently discharged veteran with a young family, and he didn't bother to check Oswald's application, which also claimed experience in clerical accounting from his military service, and with a kind of typing machine and filing system. He thought Lee quiet and well mannered—he was pleased that Lee addressed him as "Sir," a southern custom that was no longer in evidence in Dallas by the 1960s.

Truly wanted to give him a chance. The job was temporary but Lee told Truly he was happy to have any kind of work. Truly told Lee he could start work the next day, Wednesday, October 16, the beginning of a two-week pay period. Lee would be filling book orders, which involved retrieving the required books from the warehouse stocks on various floors of the building and delivering them to the shipping department on the first floor. His hours were 8:00 a.m. to 4:45 p.m., with forty-five minutes off for lunch, and he would be paid $1.25 an hour. Lee filled out a form for withholding tax but asked for permission to leave the entry for the number of dependents blank for a few days, since he was expecting his second child any day.[1522]

Both Lee and Marina were elated with the new job, however temporary and unskilled it might be. "Hurray, he has got a new job," Marina rejoiced to Ruth.[1523] Lee liked, he said, "working with books," and it was a lot cleaner than working on the greasy machines at the Reily coffee company. He liked Roy Truly too, but he still had his sight set on a better job, perhaps another one involving photography.[1524] For the next few weeks he turned up promptly every morning and did a satisfactory job,[1525] but he kept to himself—perhaps even more so than he had in his previous jobs—and none of his fellow employees got to know him. No one reported a real conversation with him.

"The boy . . . talked little to anybody . . . I never heard him talk to anyone," Truly said.

"I don't believe nobody knew him too well. You might say he wouldn't have too much to say to anybody. He just stayed all to hisself," a coworker, Jack Dougherty, said.

Geneva Hine, who worked at the credit desk on the second floor, would always say "good morning" to Lee when she'd occasionally see him at the beginning of the day, but he'd avert her glance and not respond. She never saw him smile or laugh, and asked his supervisor, William Shelley, "Who is that queer duck you have working down here?"

The janitor, Eddie Piper, saw Oswald all the time, but when asked by Warren Commission counsel, "Did you ever talk [with] him?" he replied, "No, sir."

"Did he ever speak to you, say 'Hello' or anything of that sort?"

"No, sir. If he did, you hardly ever heard him."

"Did you ever speak to him?"

"Yes."

"Did he ever reply to you that you can remember?"

"If he did, I didn't ever hear him. He'd mumble something and he would just keep walking."[1526]

Although Oswald had always been uncommonly reclusive and unsocial, at past places of employment he had struck up remotely passable associations with at least one employee (e.g., Dennis Ofstein at Jaggers). Now, if possible, he had withdrawn even deeper into his psychological funk hole, most probably because his Cuban dream had been shattered and he could see he was going nowhere with his life, with little hope of extricating himself from the nothingness of his existence.

Oswald soon met Linne Mae Randle's brother, Wesley Frazier, at work. Frazier introduced himself to Lee and offered to give him a lift to and from Irving every day, but Lee said he wouldn't be going there during the week. However, he did ask Frazier if he could take him there at the end of each workweek for the weekends. Frazier said he'd be happy to, and that Friday, October 18, after work Frazier drove him out to Ruth's place,[1527] where a pleasant surprise awaited him. Lee turned twenty-four that day, and Marina and Ruth had prepared a small birthday party, with wine, table decorations, and a cake Ruth had baked. Michael Paine was there too—he usually came to dinner on Friday evenings. When they brought in the cake and sang "Happy Birthday," Lee was so nervous, touched, and self-conscious that he cried and couldn't blow out all the candles at once, even though there were fewer than the two dozen called for by the occasion.

Lee told them he wanted a special present—he wanted the baby to be born today, on his birthday. "I don't like late birthday presents," he joked. "I don't accept them."

"You won't keep your baby?" Marina asked. "We'll see."[1528]

That night Lee was extremely solicitous of Marina, who was feeling the strain of the long pregnancy. Veins in her ankles and legs had burst and her ankles ached. Lee massaged and kissed them and promised he would never put her through the ordeal of pregnancy again.

The next morning, October 19, he scoured the classified ads in Ruth's newspapers in search of a secondhand car and a used washing machine, which he wanted in preparation for the day when Marina, June, and the new baby would come to live with him in an apartment in Dallas. Of the two, the washing machine was more important. He knew that the upkeep on old cars was costly and he didn't really mind taking the bus, but he did not want Marina washing the diapers of two infants in the bathtub. Marina was happy that his first thought was of her, and her happiness lasted through the whole day. She nevertheless remarked, when the Oswalds went to bed that night, "You know what, Alka? I never think of Anatoly, but last night I dreamt about him."

"And what did you dream?"

"We kissed as we always did. Anatoly kissed so well it made me dizzy. No one ever kissed me like that."

"I wish I did," Lee said.

"It would take you your whole life to learn," Marina said, as subtle as a blunt ax.

According to Priscilla McMillan, whose only source was Marina herself, Lee did not show any trace of the jealousy he usually felt when Marina needled him with remarks about her boyfriends, particularly the glamorous Anatoly, who so much resembled, in her mind, President Kennedy. He just put his hand over her mouth and said with surprising restraint, "Please don't tell me about the others. I don't want to hear." In spite of Marina's staggering tactlessness or her desire to needle him in partial retaliation for all his past abuse of her, he kissed her, they made love, and Marina was exceedingly happy. It was the last time they would ever be intimate.[1529]

On Sunday evening, October 20, Ruth cooked Chinese food for dinner, but Marina felt sick at the sight of it. Even though she felt no labor pains yet, while the others ate she got her things ready for the trip to the hospital, and the pains appeared later in the evening. Lee wanted to go to the hospital with her, but someone had to stay with the children and there was nothing he could do at the hospital anyway—husbands were rarely allowed to attend the birth of their children at the time in Texas—so Ruth drove Marina to Parkland and waited with her until she was taken into the labor room.

Lee had put himself as well as the children to bed by the time Ruth got back from the forty-minute drive, and although Ruth thought he was still awake, she didn't disturb him. She called the hospital around eleven and learned that Marina had had a baby girl after only about two hours of labor. She gave Lee the news on Monday morning before he returned to Dallas with Wesley Frazier.[1530] Frazier brought him back to Irving after work that same Monday evening, but Lee seemed reluctant to go with Ruth to visit Marina at Parkland. Ruth guessed that he was worried the hospital would find out he was employed and charge him for the expenses of the delivery, but she told him that they knew that already. When they were admitting Marina, the staff had asked Ruth whether Lee was employed, and Ruth had told them the truth. It made no difference—the medical care was still going to be free.

Lee then decided to go, and he appeared to be delighted with the new child, even though it was not the boy he had been hoping for. Forgetting his promise the previous night, he told Marina that the next child would be a son, but she informed him that she had had enough—she did not intend to go through ten babies just to get a boy. "You're right," he agreed cheerfully. "Whatever you say. Besides, a girl doesn't cost so much. She gets married. You have to educate a boy."

He didn't like the name Marina had given for the birth certificate: Audrey (for actress Audrey Hepburn) Rachel. He thought Rachel sounded "too Jewish." He preferred "Marina." She went along—the next day the certificate was altered to read: Audrey Marina Rachel Oswald. In fact, though, the new child was always and still is called Rachel.[1531]

Lee asked Marina whether she had had stitches and an anesthetic, and was pleased when she told him she required neither. And she was also pleased that he treated her like some kind of heroine. She later wrote, "Monday evening Lee visited me in the hospital. He was very happy at the birth of another daughter and he even wept a little. He said that two daughters were better for each other—two sisters. He stayed with me about two hours."[1532]

According to his landlady, Oswald spent "95%" of his time in the rooming house sitting in his room, although Mrs. Johnson, who owned and operated a restaurant as well as the rooming house, was not around all the time, and she admitted that the house was large—with twenty-two rooms, seventeen of them let to roomers—and she spent a lot of time at the back, where she might not have been aware of the comings and goings of the tenants. Other than to a nearby washateria, she never saw Oswald go out at night. Earlene Roberts, the housekeeper, was on the premises more often, and said Lee "was always home at night. He never went out." She said she was aware that he was visiting friends "out of town" on the weekends. Both women were also aware that he never spoke to the other roomers, even when he joined them for a few minutes to watch television in the evening. "That man never talked," Mrs. Johnson would recall. "That was the only peculiarity about him. He would never speak." When Warren Commission counsel asked Earlene Roberts, "Did you ever talk to him about anything?" she replied, "No, because he wouldn't talk."

"Did he say, 'Hello'?"

"No."

"Or 'Goodby'?"

"No."

"Or anything?"

"He wouldn't say nothing."

"Did you ever speak to him?"

"Well, yes—I would say, 'Good afternoon,' and he would just maybe look at me—give me a dirty look and keep walking and go on to his room."

Mrs. Johnson recalled that he arrived home about half-past five every afternoon and made a phone call in a foreign language, switching to English if anyone came near enough to the pay phone on the wall to overhear him. Mrs. Johnson thought the effort foolish, and Marina, on the other end of the line, would get perturbed at his suddenly changing to English and also thought it foolish on his part.[1533]

Marina said he normally called her twice a day—once during the day and once from the rooming house after work. He would always ask about June and sometimes tell Marina he loved her.[1534] He occasionally ate breakfast at a small restaurant across the street and down a ways from the rooming house, kept mostly bread, jelly, and lunch meat in the kitchen refrigerator, and drank a half a gallon of milk every day. He would sometimes eat in the kitchen if no one else was there, but more frequently in his room, which was all right with Mrs. Johnson since he kept his room in spotless condition.[1535]

He was very probably listening to his Russian-made shortwave radio too. Although the Warren Commission displayed no interest in Lee's shortwave radio, which was the size "of a small mantelpiece clock," it was recovered from his room at Beckley and is now in the National Archives in Washington, D.C., though it was never assigned a Warren Commission exhibit number.[1536] On the afternoon of the assassination, Mr. Johnson told a reporter from the *Dallas Morning News* that Lee was "always in bed by 9:30 or 10:00 p.m." and that he "would retire early and listen to his small radio."[1537] Radio Havana's first English broadcast began at nine in the evening, Dallas time, the second at eleven, and, as noted earlier, was easily heard in Dallas.[1538] If Oswald had listened to Radio Havana in his room on the first night he moved in, October 14, which is more likely than not, he would have heard, among other things, the announcer speaking about the "hypocrisy" of America offering Red Cross aid to the island, which had just been devastated by Hurricane Flora (the hurricane had missed Florida just ninety miles away), while at the same time "trying to smash the Cuban Revolution in every way it can, . . . trying to deprive the Cuban people of food by its [economic] blockade . . . Just a few days before the hurricane the U.S. government was boasting of the pain and misery it was causing Cuba. That was U.S. policy—to cause Cuba as much pain and misery as possible. That was going to lead to the overthrow of the Cuban government—remember? We cannot be expected to say 'thank you very much' to an offer from the U.S. government that is now, in the middle of our suffering, maintaining a trade blockade with Cuba."[1539]*

Radio Havana kept up a steady drumbeat of propaganda against the United States through October and November, and it is more likely than not that Lee Oswald was hearing Havana's every complaint. Even if he did not, the *Dallas Morning News* he would pick up in the lunchroom at the Texas School Book Depository was full of accounts of ongoing high tension between Cuba and the United States. And he continued to maintain subscriptions to various periodicals, including *Time*, the *Worker*, the *Militant*, and some Russian periodicals.[1540]

In any case, on Wednesday evening, October 23, just three days after the birth of his daughter, Lee reentered the political arena. He attended a meeting (believed to be the first political meeting he had ever attended) sponsored by the Dallas United States Day Committee, an ultra-right-wing group that was proposing "United States Day" as a counterpoint to "United Nations Day," which was to be held the following day in Dallas and featured Adlai Stevenson, the American ambassador to the United Nations, as a speaker.

Lee was more of an observer than a participant in a crowd of a thousand, who heard the main speaker say that they stood on "a battleground identified on this stage as U.S. Day—the symbol of our sovereignty. Tomorrow night there will stand here a symbol of the communist conspiracy and the United Nations." Lee would hardly have thought of Ambassador Stevenson as a fellow Communist, but he was no doubt more interested in the speaker than the message. He had seen him before, including once for a few seconds through the sights of his Mannlicher-Carcano rifle. It was the man he had tried to murder, Major General Edwin A. Walker.[1541]

Over the next two days the news was absorbing, if disquieting, for an ardent supporter of Fidel Castro like Lee Harvey Oswald. Thursday morning's *Dallas Morning News* carried a United Press International account that revealed the presence of "special forces troops of the U.S. Army . . . in Guatemala on a secret mission, apparently either to train Cuban exiles for another strike against Fidel Castro or to instruct Guatemalan troops in anti-communist tactics." Another story told of the State Department's rejection of Castro's request for an end to the economic blockade of the island to help it recover from a

---

*That Lee's small Russian radio had a shortwave capacity was virtually confirmed in his letter to his brother Robert written when Lee was in Minsk, in which he said he had "heard a Voice of America" broadcast about "the Russians releasing [Gary] Powers" (CE 316, 16 H 875).

recent, disastrous hurricane. "Our policies toward the Castro regime," the department said, "have been determined by its communist character, its hostility toward the United States, and its efforts to overthrow other governments in the hemisphere by violence, terror, and subversion."

Radio Havana finished its broadcast Thursday evening, October 24, with a reading from Cuba's official state newspaper *Revolución* that accused President Kennedy personally of the murder and mayhem resulting from recent raids on the island by militant Cuban exile groups: "The CIA acts under the direct orders of the President, in this case Mr. Kennedy, and is responsible solely to him for their activities and adventures. When they launch a pirate attack against the Cuban coastline, and murder a militiaman or a teacher, when they commit acts of sabotage against a Cuban vessel or industry, they are acting under direct orders of the U.S. President."[1542]

It is hard to know what Lee Oswald, if he was listening (as it is reasonable to believe he was), made of such statements. He once told Michael Paine, in referring to the Communist Party's *Worker*, that one could tell what "they" wanted you to do by "reading between the lines."[1543] It is just speculative, but if *Revolución* was ready to blame President Kennedy personally for the CIA attacks on Cuba, Lee Oswald probably agreed, and he may also have discerned, "between the lines," what people sympathetic to Cuba's plight were expected to do.

That same evening, Adlai Stevenson was booed, spat on, and struck with a picket sign as he left Dallas Memorial Auditorium after he tried to depart, under police escort, through a rear entrance. The pickets had blocked his escape from the front. None of the pickets identified themselves to a reporter from the *Morning News*, but many said they had attended the Walker rally at the same venue the night before.[1544]

That Friday evening, October 25, Wesley Frazier drove Lee out to Irving for the weekend with his family, and Michael Paine, Ruth's husband, was there to dine with his own family. Lee told Michael about the Wednesday-evening rally where he had heard General Walker speak. That interested Michael, since he had gone to a meeting of the John Birch Society on Thursday evening. He found it sparsely attended and speculated that some of the regulars had gone down to Memorial Auditorium to spit on Adlai Stevenson.[1545] Michael, a staunch liberal, had been to a number of rightist meetings and seminars—he was interested in seeking more communication between the Right and the Left. There wasn't much "Left" in Dallas, but he was curious about the Right's feelings, fears, and language.[1546]

He also wanted to communicate with Lee, whose rigid attitudes piqued his curiosity. He tried to draw him out on his politics, wondering why, for instance, he still considered himself a Marxist even though he had given up on life in Russia with some disappointment, but Michael was unable to get anything out of Lee that answered this question. What Michael did gather was that Lee seemed to be totally uninterested in the small, incremental improvements that might be made in a democratic society, believing only a total change of the system, by drastic means, would do, one where kindness and good feelings should not stand in the way. Yet he never spelled out, verbally, what he necessarily implied—that there had to be a violent revolution.

Lee refused to be drawn in any further on the subject, and Michael did not press it. He sensed that Lee's political notions were more rooted in his emotions than his reason, and that he was paranoid, but not in the classic sense. Lee seemed to think that the evil of others, of "the system," was not directed against him personally but against the oppressed class in which he counted himself. Michael also sensed that except for his daughter June, people were just like "cardboard" to Lee, and he was repelled by that.[1547]

There was a meeting of the local chapter of the American Civil Liberties Union, to which Michael belonged, that evening out at Southern Methodist University. Michael had arranged to meet a fellow research engineer from Bell Helicopter, Frank Krystinik, and his wife there, and invited Lee to come along.[1548] It was a thirty-five-minute drive to the university, and Michael used the opportunity to explain the purpose of the ACLU, which was pretty much limited to the preservation of civil rights. Oswald knew nothing about the organization and seemed mystified by its lack of political ideology.[1549]

The meeting—Lee's second and last encounter with political activists in America— began with a showing of a film about a popular politician from Washington state who had lost his bid for reelection as a result of a smear campaign based on the fact that his wife had once been a member of the Communist Party. Afterward, the group discussed the film and what might be learned from it. Someone said something to the effect that members of the John Birch Society should not be considered anti-Semitic simply because they were Birchers. Lee objected. He rose and, speaking clearly and coherently, said that he had attended a meeting just two nights before where he had heard a number of anti-Semitic and anti-Catholic statements by people on the platform, including General Walker.

Later in the evening, as everyone went to the back of the auditorium for coffee and private discussion, Michael introduced Lee to Frank Krystinik, who had previously heard about him from Michael and was ill disposed at the outset toward anyone who might be a Communist. Frank was prepared to defend free enterprise. A Catholic himself, he was also interested in the anti-Catholic sentiments Lee heard at the Walker meeting. Michael left Lee and Frank, knowing all too well what kind of discussion would evolve.[1550] Another, older man joined the conversation and was apparently better at controlling his temper than Frank. Frank was irritated by Lee's haughty disdain for his arguments in support of capitalism over communism, and got the impression that Lee was talking down to him. Lee, who told Frank, "I am a Marxist" when Frank called him a "Communist," raised Frank's hackles to the point where he and Frank almost got into a fight when Lee started talking about employers profiting from their employees' labors. Frank said he felt he was paid a "fair salary" by his employer and was "real glad to work for him for the salary I get." Frank proceeded to tell Lee he himself had a small business on the side for which he paid two workers three dollars an hour and they were "tickled to get that." But when Lee found out that Frank was getting four dollars an hour for their work and hence making a dollar per hour off each worker, Lee got personal with Frank and accused him of exploiting his two workers. But they didn't come to blows and Lee did admit to Frank that the Soviet state exploited the workers worse than capitalists did in the United States. He also conceded that the United States was superior to the Soviet Union in the area of civil liberties, and when Frank asked him what he thought of all the opposition President Kennedy was getting in the South over his position on civil rights, Oswald said he thought Kennedy was doing a really good job in the area of civil rights.[1551]

In the car on the way back to Irving, Lee showed no sympathy for the ACLU. He could never join such an organization because it simply wasn't "political." Defending freedom of speech and other freedoms was far too circumscribed a goal in Oswald's mind. For any group to be worth its salt, it had to have a political objective.[1552]

In Moscow this same Friday, October 25, 1963, the KGB deputy chairman of the Secretariat, S. Bannikov, sent a letter to V. V. Kuznetsov, deputy minister of the Ministry of Foreign Affairs, regarding Oswald's request to return to the Soviet Union. After setting forth a history of Oswald in Russia from 1959 until his return to the United States, the letter concludes, "In our opinion, it is inadvisable to permit Oswald to return to the Soviet Union." Former KGB chairman Vladimir Semichastny (1961–1967) stated that "not under any circumstances" did the KGB want the Oswalds to return to Russia. "We were against their return not so much for political reasons as for material considerations. We did not want to waste money on him with nothing in return. He was of absolutely no interest to us. Moreover, his scurrying about caused us headaches on more than one occasion."[1553]*

The rest of the weekend Lee passed at Ruth's house in Irving the same as he always did, playing with his daughters, reading, and mostly watching television. When he finished the evening meal he got up and went back to the living room to read or watch television, even though no one else had finished. Ruth realized that he joined the others at the dining table only to be fed, not for a social event. But it was during these weekends that Ruth concluded that Lee really did care for his wife and children, and she saw that he had tried to make himself welcome in her home although he really preferred to keep to himself. It was also on these weekends that he was the most "human" she had ever known him to be and, in some ways, a rather "ordinary" human being at that.[1554]

Lee went back to work with Wesley Frazier on Monday morning and returned to the Beckley Street rooming house that evening. The following day, October 29, 1963, FBI agent Jim Hosty received a communication from the New Orleans office that agents had finally turned up a new address for Lee and Marina Oswald, 2515 West Fifth Street in Irving, Texas. Oswald's mail in New Orleans was being forwarded there. Just four days earlier, Hosty had received word from New Orleans that Lee had been in contact with the Soviet embassy in Mexico City, and Hosty was eager to follow up on the information. As soon as he received the October 29 communication from New Orleans, he drove out to Irving and did what the FBI called a "pretext interview" with Ruth Paine's neighbor, Dorothy Roberts. Roberts told him that Ruth had a young Russian-speaking woman staying with her who had just given birth the week before and that the woman's American husband visited there from time to time. Hosty was quite sure that he had found the Oswalds at last, but he wanted to check out the Paines before he went any further.[1555] Dorothy Roberts told Ruth Paine, and Ruth told Marina, about the man who had been asking questions about her and Lee. Ruth and Marina guessed it was the FBI.[1556]

On Friday, November 1, Lee rented post office box number 6225 at the Terminal Annex Post Office Station at the southwest corner of Houston and Commerce, directly across from Dealey Plaza and just two blocks south from the building where he worked. His application reveals his intention to reenter the political arena—he indicated that the box would also be used to receive mail for the Fair Play for Cuba Committee and—surprisingly—the American Civil Liberties Union, both of which he described as "none Profit." Just to make sure he kept his trail as muddy as possible, he gave the wrong street number for his residence on North Beckley, 3610 instead of 1026.[1557] Since he had also

---

*As with the decision by the Soviet Ministry of Foreign Affairs on October 7 refusing Marina's request to reenter the Soviet Union, the actual Soviet letter of rejection of Oswald's request to reenter the Soviet Union has never surfaced. At least neither had been received by Marina and Lee as late as November 9. On this date, Oswald wrote, as we shall see, to the Soviet embassy in Washington asking the embassy to inform him and his wife of the arrival of their Soviet entrance visas "as soon as they come." (CE 15, 16 H 33)

registered there as O. H. Lee, he could be fairly sure that the FBI would have a difficult job figuring out where he was living.

Was Lee thinking of organizing a chapter of the ACLU that would be as phony as his FPCC chapter, even though there was already an organized ACLU group in Dallas? He had dismissed the ACLU to Michael Paine because it had no political agenda, but he nonetheless decided to join the organization, mailing a membership application and two dollars in cash to the ACLU's New York office, which it received on November 4, 1963.[1558]

He also sent a change-of-address card to Comrade Reznichenko at the Russian embassy in Washington, giving the post office box as his new address,[1559] and an undated letter (postmarked November 1) to Arnold Johnson at the headquarters of the Communist Party:

Dear Mr. Johnson,

In September I had written you saying I expected to move from New Orleans, La., to the Philadelphia-Baltimore [actually, "Baltimore-Washington"] area. You advised me that I could contact you when I had gotten settled there and the party would contact me in that area. Since then my personal plans have changed and I have settled in Dallas, Texas for the time.

Through a friend, I have been introduced into the American Civil Liberties Union Local chapter, which holds monthly meeting[s] on the campus of Southern Methodist University. The first meeting I attened was on October 25th, a film was shown and afterwards a very critical discussion of the ultra-right in Dallas On October 23rd, I had attened a ultra-right meeting headed by General Edwin A. Walker, who lives in Dallas. This meeting preceded by one day the attack on A.E. Stevenson at the United Nations Day meeting at which he spoke

As you can see, political friction between "left" and "right" is very great here. Could you advise me as to the general view we have on the American Civil Liberties Union? And to what degree, if any, I should attempt to highten its progressive tendencies? The Dallas branch of the A.C.L.U. is firmly in the hands of "liberal" professional people, (a minister and two Law professors conducted the Oct. 25th meeting.) however, some of those present showed marked class-awareness and insight.

> respectfully Yours,
> Lee H. Oswald[1560]

The same Friday afternoon, November 1, that Lee set himself up at the post office as a representative of the FPCC and ACLU, Jim Hosty, driving back to Dallas from Fort Worth, made a short detour to Irving, where he knocked on Ruth Paine's door at about 2:30.

Hosty had been doing his homework. He had run a credit check on Michael and Ruth Paine. Michael was an engineer at Bell Helicopter, the Paines had resided in Irving for several years, and both had good reputations. He had checked the criminal records of the Irving Police Department and the Dallas County sheriff's office and found nothing. He contacted a security officer at Bell, who told him that Michael held a security clearance. He talked to the assistant headmaster at St. Mark's School, where Ruth taught Russian part-time. Edward Oviatt told him that Ruth was both stable and loyal to the United States.

She had told Oviatt about the Russian woman living with her who spoke no English and had just given birth to another child. Oviatt knew that Ruth was a Quaker and a very kind person who would go out of her way to help someone in distress. All this reassured Hosty that Ruth was unlikely to be involved with Lee Oswald in anything inimical to the interests of the United States, and she was his best—his only—lead to locating Lee himself.[1561]

Hosty was alone that Friday, but he did not consider Ruth Paine to be either a subject of an investigation or a hostile witness, which would have required him to be accompanied by another agent, and indeed, Ruth invited him in when he identified himself to her. She had never met an FBI agent before, but she seemed pleased about it and was friendly and helpful. She told him that Marina and her two children were there with her, and when he asked her if she knew where Lee was living, she said she didn't, but believed it was somewhere in Oak Cliff. When he asked her where Lee worked, she told him the Texas School Book Depository Building and the two of them looked up the address of the building, 411 Elm Street, in the phone book, although Ruth hoped Hosty would not visit Lee at his job and cause trouble with his employer. Ruth told Hosty Lee had told her that the FBI "had had him fired from every job he ever had." Hosty assured her that he had never done such a thing and was quite sure that no other agents had either. Curiously, Ruth did not think to give him Lee's phone number at the rooming house, which she had in her address book.

Eventually, Hosty recalls, "a pretty young brunette with beautiful green eyes came out of one of the back bedrooms" and joined them in the living room. He knew it was Marina. Hosty thought she must have been taking a nap—in fact she had just been drying her hair. Although he did not understand anything she said to Ruth, he realized from her eyes and her expression that she was alarmed. He had seen that instinctive fear of the authorities in other people who had come to the United States from Communist countries, Russians equating the FBI with the KGB, which intimidated its own citizens. He asked Ruth to reassure Marina that he was not there to harm or to harass her in any way. He told her that the FBI's job was to protect people like her and their rights. Whatever Ruth said to Marina seemed to work. Marina even liked the idea that this genial, burly, dark-haired representative of American authority was protecting her. She relaxed and smiled. Hosty asked whether Lee was doing anything on behalf of Cuba as he had in New Orleans, and Marina felt comfortable enough to say that she didn't think the American press was fair with regard to Cuba and its leader, but she didn't think Lee had revived his FPCC chapter. "Oh, don't worry about him," she told Hosty (through Ruth) cheerily. "He's just young. He doesn't know what he's doing. He won't do anything like that here."

Although Hosty doesn't recall, and Ruth only remembers for sure telling Hosty that Lee came there for the weekends, Marina remembers suggesting to Hosty that he stay until Lee arrived around half past five that day, since it was Friday and he would be coming for the weekend, but it was only about three in the afternoon and Hosty declined.[1562] Hosty has given several reasons for not having done so: He had other stops on cases to make on his way back to the office. Also, he knew that Marina had just given birth to a second child and he didn't want to upset her. Further, he believed that Ruth would, as she had assured him, find out Lee's home address in Dallas and call him, and he wrote out his name and phone number on a piece of paper so she could do so—FBI agents were not allowed to carry calling cards. And then there was the fact that the Oswald file was still in the New Orleans office, which would still have control of the case until Hosty confirmed for them, as he had not done at that moment, that the Oswalds had definitely moved to his area. New Orleans hadn't yet sent him copies of all the reports in its file, which he wanted to read before conducting an in-depth interview of Lee as well as Marina. He didn't know what contacts the New Orleans office might have had with both of them, and there seemed to be no reason to rush things. Had Lee been working in a sensitive position, the FBI would have been keenly interested, but a stock boy's job in a warehouse was far from sensitive.[1563]

Lee did arrive a couple of hours later, and he was clearly disturbed when he heard from Marina that the FBI had picked up his trail. He questioned her closely about the visit, but she was unable to tell him very much as she had not understood the conversation between Hosty and Ruth. Marina could see that the unexpected visit had unnerved her husband. At supper shortly thereafter, Ruth also told Lee about Hosty's visit, and Lee, feigning unconcern, asked, "Oh, and what did he say?" Ruth told Lee and gave him the slip of paper on which Hosty had written his name and phone number. Since Ruth felt confident that Lee had nothing to fear from the FBI, she suggested that he simply call Hosty, make an appointment, and tell him whatever Hosty wanted to know. But Ruth, of course, knew nothing about Lee's recent attempt on the life of General Walker or his trip to Mexico and attempt to defect to Castro's Cuba.

Lee was subdued during supper and never really recovered, barely speaking a word for the rest of the evening. That night, for the first time since his return from Mexico, he did not initiate any sex with Marina, not even the limited sex that might have been possible so soon after Rachel's birth.

The next day he silently washed the diapers for Marina and hung them out to dry, then watched football, and finally his spirit began to lift. He took Marina aside and gave careful instructions. If Hosty returned, she was to get the license number of his car. Even if another agent came, he would probably use the same car. It might be parked across the street or in front of the neighbors, he told her. He didn't have to instruct her not to give Hosty his address in Dallas. Marina didn't know herself where he was living.

On Sunday, Ruth gave Lee another driving lesson. He wanted to take June along, a sign perhaps of his growing confidence, but Marina would not hear of it. "If you want to break bones, break your own," she told him.

He returned from his lesson in a markedly more cheerful mood. He felt he was making good progress at learning to drive.[1564]

Lee went back to work on Monday, November 4, but did not call Jim Hosty at the FBI Dallas office. However, Hosty was closing in on him. On Monday Hosty called the Texas School Book Depository and asked the personnel department whether Lee Oswald was employed there. They confirmed he was and told him that his address was 2515 West Fifth Street in Irving, a blind alley, since Hosty already knew that Lee was not living at Ruth Paine's. But since he knew that Lee was now living somewhere in Dallas, he sent a letter to the bureau's New Orleans office instructing it to "make the Dallas office the office of origin" on the case. Hosty was once again taking control of the case.[1565] On the same date, November 4, Forrest Sorrels, in charge of the Secret Service in Dallas, was informed of the president's forthcoming trip to Dallas. Gerry Behn, the special agent in charge of the White House detail, called Sorrels and told him the visit would probably take place on November 21, less than two and a half weeks away. He asked Sorrels to check out two possible sites for a formal luncheon on that day, the new Trade Mart near downtown off the Stemmons Freeway, and the Women's Building at Fair Park on the other side of town.[1566]

If Lee had picked up a copy of that day's *Dallas Morning News* in the lunchroom at the Texas School Book Depository, he would have read the front-page headline story: Governor John Connally and the chairman of the state's Democratic Party, Eugene Locke, asked "The Blue-Ribbon Citizens Council" to handle a noontime luncheon honoring the president on either November 21 or November 22. There were no details as to the location of the affair.[1567]

The next day, Tuesday, Jim Hosty made another trip to Fort Worth. Since his route took him past Irving and Ruth had told him she would try to get Lee's address in Dallas for him, he decided to stop by to see if she had done so. His partner, Agent Garry S. Wilson, went up to the door with him, and Hosty spoke with Ruth on the doorstep for a few minutes. She had not asked Lee for his address in Dallas, but she had given him Hosty's telephone number and thought he would call. Ruth mentioned the fact that Lee had told her that weekend that he was a Trotskyite Communist. She found what Lee told her more amusing than anything else, and told Hosty Lee was "an illogical person." Hosty wondered to Ruth whether Lee had mental problems. Ruth responded that she did not understand the thinking of anyone who espoused Marxism, but that was far different from a judgment that Lee was unstable or unable to function in a normal society.[1568]

The interview at the front door lasted only a few minutes, and Hosty and Ruth recalled Marina appearing briefly just as the agents were leaving. She had actually been outside while Hosty was talking to Ruth, memorizing the license plate number of Hosty's official FBI car and walking around the car several times to see if she could determine the car's make, which she could not. The two women watched from the front window as the FBI agents drove away from the curb, made a U-turn, and went back the way they had come, heading for the highway to Fort Worth. Then Marina, in accordance with Lee's instructions and still without Ruth's knowledge, wrote the license plate number down on a piece of paper. Either she got one number wrong or Lee copied it wrong into his address book, where it was found, written in his hand, after the assassination.[1569]

The next day, Wednesday, November 6, Oswald visited the branch of the Dallas Public Library in Oak Cliff, where he checked out a book called *The Shark and the Sardines*.[1570] The book was by the former president of Guatemala, Juan José Arévalo, and was directly addressed to the American people. It accused American policy of being predatory toward the people and governments of Latin America, which Arévalo compared to the policy of the shark toward sardines. (Another Guatemalan president, Jacobo Arbenz, had been overthrown by a CIA-inspired coup in 1954.) Translated from the Spanish by June Cobb and Dr. Raul Osegueda, Arévalo writes to the American reader in the introduction, "This book [does not] seek to cast blame on the North American people, people who, like us, are victims of the imperialist policy of promoting business, multiplying markets, and hoarding money." Symphonic music to Oswald's ears, no doubt.*

The theme of the book, most likely the last book Oswald ever read,[1571] was very much in keeping with Oswald's passionate advocacy of the Cuban cause, and it may have col-

---

*An insolvable mystery attaches to this book. *The Shark and the Sardines* is the only book Oswald failed to return to the Dallas library on time—it was due on November 13. It was not found among his possessions either at Ruth Paine's house or at his North Beckley rooming house after the assassination. Three months after the assassination, the book had not been returned. (CE 2642, 25 H 901–902) Years later, author Albert H. Newman checked with the library and found to his astonishment that the book had indeed been returned; he had gone to the Oak Cliff branch of the library and held it in his hand. But the library kept no records of when and by whom. (Newman, *Assassination of John F. Kennedy*, pp.107–108) Either the library made a mistake when it listed the book as delinquent, which would not be an uncommon error, and is probably what happened, or someone returned it after Oswald's death. The latter opens the possibility that Oswald himself passed the book on to an ideologically like-minded acquaintance who perhaps did not want his association with the

ored his view of President Kennedy as well. Although Arévalo first published the book in Spanish during the Eisenhower administration, he added language to it after the election of John F. Kennedy, who, Arévalo said, owed his presidency to big money as surely as Eisenhower had. After saying that Eisenhower had been "negotiated and bought by Wall Street and the Republican Party," Arévalo wrote that one should not ever forget that "his successor John Kennedy is the son of the number one landlord in the United States, or that Calvin Coolidge was president thanks to the ringing and ready money of the House of Morgan, in which Coolidge was a powerful stockbroker."[1572]

While not expressly about the political situation then existing in Cuba, the book was widely popular with the part of the Left that was concerned with Cuba and the Kennedy administration's general policy on Latin America, including the Alliance for Progress, and it was advertised in leftist political papers and magazines. Newman noticed copies of it displayed for sale at the headquarters of the Socialist Workers Party when he visited there doing research for his 1970 book on the assassination.[1573]

On Thursday morning, November 7, the front-page headline of the *Dallas Morning News* announced that the president's wife would be accompanying him on the forthcoming trip to Texas, the first "political" trip for the First Lady since Kennedy became president (she had accompanied him on foreign excursions). He was definitely scheduled to speak in Houston on November 21, exactly two weeks hence, but other engagements, including appearances in Fort Worth, Dallas, and Austin on the following day, were still "tentative."[1574]

On Friday morning, November 8, the *Dallas Morning News* finally reported that the president's trip to Dallas was set for November 22, fourteen days away. According to Governor Connally, President Kennedy would speak at a luncheon sponsored by the Dallas Citizens Council and the Graduate Research Center, but the site was still uncertain because the Secret Service had not yet cleared the matter. "Under consideration," the *News* said, "are the Trade Mart, with a seating capacity of 1,800 but with security difficulties, and the Women's Building at the State Fair which is larger." However, Connally assured his Texan constituents immediately after a conference with the White House that the plans were "as firm as can be at this time."[1575]

Back in Washington, the Secret Service was working on security problems. Agent Winston Lawson, the advance man for Dallas, was briefed on his assignment by Roy Kellerman, the assistant special agent in charge of the White House detail,[1576] and immediately afterward went to the Secret Service's Protective Research Section in the Executive Office Building. He informed them of his assignment as advance man for Dallas and asked them to comb their files for "active subjects"—people who potentially would be a danger to the president in the Dallas area. He waited for them to do the work and was relieved when they failed, astonishingly, to produce a single name in the Dallas area.[1577]

That evening, Lee again drove out with Wesley Frazier to spend the weekend in Irving, a long one, since Monday was Veterans Day.[1578] Ruth had discussed with Marina whether they ought to tell Lee that the FBI had paid a second call earlier in the week— she knew that he had been deeply upset by the first visit, though not why. Although they didn't resolve what to do, Marina settled the issue by telling Lee soon after he arrived Friday evening. Lee had gone out to where Marina was hanging diapers and asked her, "Have they been here again?" Marina told him yes, earlier in the week, but she had forgotten to tell him when he called each day on the phone. "How on earth could you for-

---

assassin to become known but who was sufficiently civic-minded to return the book discreetly to the library long after the assassination. The question is unlikely to ever be answered.

get?" he asked. She said she was afraid to upset him. "It upsets me worse if you keep it from me. Why must you hide things all the time? I never can count on you." Marina insisted that Hosty was a nice man and only wanted to protect her rights. Oswald snapped, "You fool. He doesn't care about your rights. He comes because it's his job." Lee softened slightly when he learned Marina had done one thing he asked her to—she got Hosty's license number.[1579]

When Lee questioned Ruth about what Hosty had said during this last visit, she said that he had inquired whether Lee had mental problems, to which Lee laughed scoffingly. When Lee complained bitterly to Ruth that the FBI was "inhibiting his activities," Ruth did not see how exactly. She assumed he meant his activities such as passing out pro-Cuba pamphlets or expressing support for Fidel Castro as he had done in New Orleans, which she told him he had every right as an American to do.[1580]

Ruth Paine told the Warren Commission that at some point around this time, Oswald told her that he had gone to the downtown office of the FBI in search of Hosty, and finding him out, had left him a note "saying what he thought" about the FBI "bothering him and his family." Although, because of poor questioning by Warren Commission counsel, it is not 100 percent clear when Ruth Paine was saying Oswald told her this, and she herself said she wasn't positive,* the garbled context and her testimony seemed to indicate that she thought he told her this on the weekend of November 9–10, 1963.[1581] If this is accurate, then Oswald probably left the note at some time during the previous week. As the reader knows, the date that Oswald stopped by the FBI office, as well as the contents of the note he left, are mired in conflict and have already been discussed in a long footnote in the "Four Days in November" section.

On Saturday morning, November 9, Lee asked Ruth whether he might use her typewriter, and she agreed. It was a letter he didn't want Ruth to see—when she put June down in her high chair beside him, he covered his work, which only aroused her curiosity.[1582]

There was nothing of any real significance in the letter dated November 9, 1963 (though he continued to work on it off and on through November 11), that Oswald sent to the Soviet embassy in Washington. He wrote about his problems at the Russian embassy in Mexico City (but found no fault on the Russians' part because they hadn't been prepared for his visit) and the "gross breach of regulations" at the Cuban consulate. He just didn't want Ruth to know about his trip to Mexico City and his effort to get into Cuba. He also told a few lies in his letter—that the FBI was "not interested in my activities" but "warned" him that if he engaged in FPCC activities in Texas the bureau would again take an "interest" in him, and that the FBI was trying to get Marina to defect to the United States. He closed by telling the embassy of the birth of his new daughter.[1583]

The lone significance of Oswald's letter is that by his asking the embassy to "please inform us of the arrival of our Soviet entrance visa's as soon as they come," Oswald, at this late date, was apparently still holding out the possibility of getting to Cuba (we know he didn't want to have anything further to do with Russia) by way of an in-transit visa based on a final-destination visa to Russia. As previously indicated, what this necessarily means is that either the Soviet government had not sent a letter to Oswald informing him

---

*Ruth Paine, after discussing the previous weekend of November 2 and 3, testified, "Then he told me, it must have been the following weekend, that same weekend of the 9th." At this point, instead of letting her say what Oswald told her about the note he had left at the FBI office and trying to firm up the date, Warren Commission counsel completely changed the subject by asking her, "Did he say anything when you gave him Agent Hosty's name on the telephone?" (Paine had *handed* Oswald the paper with Hosty's name and phone number on it, not told him over the phone.) "No," Ruth said. Question: "Nothing at all?" "I don't recall anything Lee said." Paine then returned, on her own, to relating what Oswald had told her about the note. (3 H 18)

of its October 25, 1963, decision to deny him his request for a Soviet visa, or if the Russians did send it, with all the moving and changes of address, he had not received it. It is also clear that he had not received notification of the Soviet government's decision on October 7, 1963, denying Marina's request (forced on her by Lee) to return to Russia.

After Lee finished typing the first draft of his letter to the Soviet embassy early Saturday morning, the anger and fright of the previous night seemed to dissipate, and all seven of the Oswalds and Paines piled into Ruth's station wagon so Ruth could drive Lee all the way into Oak Cliff and Dallas to a Texas Driver's License Examining Station to get his learner's permit. Unfortunately, it was a local election day and the office was closed.[1584] As a consolation, they trooped into a nearby dime store and did some shopping. Oswald bought rubber pants for both Junie and Rachel. He was in high spirits, crowing about his purchases, singing, and making puns in Russian that struck Marina, at least, as screamingly funny. His good mood persisted throughout the day. When Ruth left the house in the early afternoon to vote, he persuaded Marina to cook him a favorite Russian dish, potatoes and onions mixed with flour and eggs, and for once was pleased with the result, which he wolfed down while watching football on the television. At halftime he took the kids down the street for a popsicle and came back with Ruth's Chris on his shoulders. After the game, he played "horsey" with the boy, galloping around on all fours with the boy on his back. Marina sensed that in spending so much time with Chris, Lee was pining to have his own son.[1585]

That night in bed, Lee teased Marina, obviously not knowing that each of them had already been denied reentry into Russia, about returning to the Soviet Union, the thought of which he knew depressed her. And he continued his deception with her, telling her he wanted to go back too, and they would both work and see old friends. She didn't want to go back to Minsk. He didn't want to go to Leningrad. She didn't like Moscow.

"Come on, Alka, let's not go to Russia at all."

"Okay," he said.

"Hooray," Marina cried. "Do you swear?"

"I swear."

"Word of honor?"

"How come you need my word of honor?"

"Because sometimes you promise one thing and do another."

"I won't betray you this time," he assured her.

It was not all back-and-forth chitchat. For some reason, Lee proceeded to tell Marina of all the previous women in his life, including eight during the time he was in Japan, the first one almost twice his age who taught him about sex and wanted to marry him, another he went to see more for her cooking than for love. He also told her of a one-year drought of women after he first arrived in Russia but then there had been a whole succession. "But it's all in the past," he said. "I was only tricking them. Then a girl came along with a red dress [Marina]—and she tricked me." He did admit asking one of the girls, Ella German, to marry him, but "her grandmother scared her away," Lee said. "Being American, she thought I must be a spy." Lee told Marina that of all of the women he had ever known, she was the only one he had ever loved.

"Oh, Alka, you don't love me. Look at the way we fight."

"Everyone does that," he replied.

"If you loved me, maybe we wouldn't fight," she rejoined.

"You silly, don't you see that I love you?" he said as he stroked her hair. "Did you grow your hair long especially for me?"

"Who else but you," she purred.[1586]

Ruth was up before the others on Sunday morning. The previous night she had noticed on her desk what appeared to be the letter Lee had been working on. It was still there. At least the original handwritten draft was. The paper was folded over, but some of the text was visible, and she read, "The FBI is not now interested in my activities." Struck by the fact that this obviously was a patent lie, she unfolded the letter and read the rest of it. It was a rough draft of the letter with many cross-outs. She was appalled and alarmed at the implications of it, with its talk of contact with the Soviet embassy in Mexico City, and she wondered just whom she was harboring in her home. It sounded like a report from some sort of spy, even though she realized it was actually like someone trying to give the impression that he was a spy more than someone who really was. She was dismayed by the lies—the suggestion that the "notorious" FBI was trying to get Marina to defect to the United States, that he had met with Agent "Hasty" and had protested vigorously. She was offended that he was using her typewriter to write lies. Why, she asked herself, is Lee Oswald writing this kind of letter? What kind of a man is he after all?

She thought the FBI should see the letter. Someone, probably Lee, was in the shower, and she hurried to make a handwritten copy of the letter, which she put in an envelope and buried in a drawer in her desk before he finished. If Hosty came again as she thought he would, she would hand her copy of the letter over to him.[1587]

Otherwise, Sunday was a typical weekend day. Lee again watched football in the afternoon. Michael came over for a while and had to step over Lee's body sprawled on the floor. He didn't begrudge Lee his leisure, but the thought crossed his mind that the would-be revolutionary did not seem to be working very hard to bring about the revolution. In the afternoon Ruth gave Lee another driving lesson, mostly on parking, and felt he was getting the hang of it.

But Ruth could not get the letter out of her mind. Late that evening she could not sleep, so she came out to the living room to join Lee, who was watching a late movie—a spy story. She wanted to confront him about the letter but finally could not. She didn't want him to feel she was spying on him. In any case, it wasn't just the letter that was troubling her, and Lee, for once, was perceptive and sensed her unease. "I guess you are real upset about going to the lawyer tomorrow," he said.

She was going to discuss the possibility of a divorce from Michael, and she said she was indeed upset about the idea. She let it rest there, quietly watched a little more of the movie with him, and then went to bed.[1588]

Ruth did go to see the lawyer on Monday morning, but since it was Veterans Day and Lee did not have to return to work, she parked her kids with a neighbor to give the Oswalds some welcomed time to themselves. Lee seemed self-absorbed, sitting alone in the backyard for a while before going back in and getting back to work on revising his letter. He eventually admitted to Marina that the letter he was working so assiduously on was to the Soviet embassy, but only to complain about the FBI. He even asked her to sign it along with him, but she would not. Later that afternoon, they talked more about the FBI while they hung the laundry out to dry. Lee told her that when they finally moved to a new apartment, after Christmas, he wanted her to keep their new address a secret from Ruth. Marina objected that she could not repay Ruth's many kindnesses by doing such a thing. He eventually dropped the subject.[1589]

On Tuesday morning, November 12, Oswald rode back to his job with Wesley Frazier. Since Frazier told the Warren Commission that once he and Oswald started to drive from Irving to Dallas that day, he never stopped anywhere,[1590] Oswald probably mailed his letter to the Soviet embassy earlier in a neighborhood mailbox. The letter was postmarked "Irving Nov 12 5-PM 1963 Tex."[1591]

That evening, Agent Winston Lawson flew into Dallas from Washington and the next morning, Wednesday, November 13, conferred with Forrest Sorrels. They discussed the Adlai Stevenson incident, which they did not want to see repeated during the president's brief appearance in Dallas ten days hence. The danger posed by "extremist . . . right wing groups" preoccupied them throughout the time they worked on arrangements for the visit. Both the Trade Mart and the Women's Building at the fairgrounds presented certain security drawbacks, but they were confident they could handle the problems once the decision was made in Washington.[1592] The next day, Thursday, November 14, Kennedy's special assistant, Ken O'Donnell, informed Special Agent Gerry Behn that they had decided on the Trade Mart. Behn immediately called Dallas to inform Lawson.[1593]

Late that afternoon, when Lee made his usual after-work phone call to Marina, she asked him not to come out to Irving that weekend. She was growing uncomfortable about the burden she and the children were placing on Ruth, and Lee had been there three days the preceding weekend. Ruth had said nothing to her, but she knew that Ruth was planning a birthday party for her little girl on Saturday and that Michael was going to attend it, and Marina definitely felt that all four Oswalds would be too much for what would be a family occasion. Lee made no objection and said he would do as she wished. Marina told him not to stay cooped up in his room the entire weekend, to take a walk in the park. Ruth got on the phone to tell Lee that because of the birthday party, she wouldn't be able to take Lee back to the driver's license place in Dallas. Lee was under the impression that he needed a car to get his learner's permit but Ruth assured him that he didn't, that he could go there without a car, which surprised him.[1594]

That Friday, November 15, a week before President Kennedy was expected to visit Dallas, the *Dallas Morning News* reported that it was "unlikely" there would be a motorcade through the city. According to the *Morning News*, the decision as to whether the luncheon would be given at the Trade Mart or the Women's Building had not been made— though it had been—but it was likely that the president would be driven to the luncheon directly from Love Field by the most convenient artery. That afternoon, the *Times Herald* was able to announce that the luncheon would indeed take place at the Trade Mart off Stemmons Freeway.[1595] The next day's *Morning News* now said there *would* be a motorcade but that "the route of the Dallas motorcade has not been firmly established. The President is expected to travel over Lemmon Avenue or Cedar Springs Road to the downtown area, then west on Main Street before turning north after driving through the Triple Underpass. If he stays on schedule he would pass through the downtown area about noon." Nothing was said about turning right off Main at Houston and left again on Elm in front of the Texas School Book Depository Building.[1596]

Lee got over to the Driver's License Examining Station on Saturday morning well before the regular noon closing hour, but he found a big crowd of people before him waiting to be served—the result of the station's having been closed the preceding Saturday for the election and again on Monday for Veterans Day. He told Marina over the phone that afternoon that officials told him there was no use waiting in the long lines because he wouldn't have had time to take the test anyway. He did, however, get an application form, which he took home to fill out. It was found among his belongings at his North Beckley rooming house after the assassination. He had not yet completed it.[1597] Lee told Marina he had taken her advice and visited the same park they had been to in the spring. She told him to be sure to "eat better" over the weekend, knowing he was prone to eat poorly, almost starve himself when they were apart. In another phone call that evening he assured her that he was not starving himself, that he found a restaurant where he could get a steak and fries with salad and dessert for just $1.25.[1598] Marina told Priscilla McMillan that Lee did not call her on Sunday, November 17, which was uncommon for him, but Ruth Paine says she is not sure he did not call. In any event, Marina missed Lee, and when she noticed June playing with the telephone and saying, "Papa, Papa," that evening, she impulsively asked Ruth to call him at the number he had given them—she could have dialed the number herself, but she knew someone other than Lee would probably have answered the pay phone and she would be unable to converse in English with that person. Ruth made the call and asked for Lee Oswald. The man at the other end told her that there was no one in the house by that name. Ruth, astonished, asked, "Is this a rooming house?" and when she was told it was, asked, "Is this WH 3-8993?" "Yes" came the answer. But there was no Lee Oswald rooming there. Baffled, Ruth thanked the man and hung up.[1599]

The next day, Monday, November 18, Oswald turned up at work as usual,[*] and he called Marina, as he usually did, at lunchtime. She told him that Ruth had tried to call him and asked him where he had been. "I was at home watching TV," he told her. "Nobody called me to the phone. What name did she ask for me by?" Marina told him that Ruth had asked for Lee Oswald. There was a long silence from Lee. "Oh, damn," he said finally. "I don't live there under my real name." Lee proceeded to scold Marina for trying to reach him at his rooming house. But Marina was even more angry with him. What was all this foolishness about? He told her he didn't want his landlady to know his real name because she might read in the paper that he had been to Russia and been questioned by the authorities.

"It's none of her business," Marina said.

"You don't understand a thing," he said. "I don't want the FBI to know where I live, either." He ordered her not to tell Ruth about his alias.

Marina remained angry. "Starting all your foolishness again," she said. "All these comedies. First one, then another. And now this fictitious name. When will it all end?"

He told her he had to get back to work and hung up.

Although he had ordered her not to say anything to Ruth, Marina couldn't contain herself and told Ruth. She felt herself between "two fires," loyalty to Lee and the fear that he was once again up to no good. That night he called again. Marina told Ruth she didn't want to speak to him, but Ruth insisted—she couldn't tell him that his wife would not come to the phone. When Marina did, Lee was insulting, addressing her as a *devushka*, a word that means something like "wench," but more cruel in Russian than it would be in English.

"Hey, wench," he said, "you are to take Ruth's address book and cross my name and telephone number out of there."

Marina would not hear of it. "It's not my book and I have no right to touch it."

"Listen here," Lee snarled, "I order you to cross it out. Do you hear?"

Marina responded, "I won't do it."

He started to scold her in a way she had never heard before. She hung up on him.[1600]

On Tuesday afternoon, November 19, 1963, the *Dallas Times Herald* ran a page 1A headline about President Kennedy's major foreign policy speech given the previous night before an audience of one thousand at the Inter-American Press Association convention in Miami Beach, Florida: "Kennedy Virtually Invites Cuban Coup." The first paragraph

---

[*]He didn't miss a day of work from the day he started, October 16, through November 22 (CE 1949, 23 H 749–751).

read, "President Kennedy all but invited the Cuban people today to overthrow Fidel Castro's communist regime and promised prompt U.S. aid if they do . . . The president said it would be a happy day if the Castro government is ousted."[1601]

That morning's *Dallas Morning News* reported, for the first time, the exact motorcade route: "From Love Field to Mockingbird Lane, along Mockingbird Lane to Lemmon, then Lemmon to Turtle Creek, Turtle Creek to Cedar Springs, Cedar Springs to Harwood, Harwood to Main, Main to Houston, Houston to Elm, Elm under the Triple Underpass to Stemmons Expressway and on to the Trade Mart."[1602]

Even if Oswald, who avidly read newspapers (the previous day's *Dallas Morning News* at work each morning in the domino room,[1603] and the evening *Dallas Times Herald*, which he frequently bought out on the street), never read this article, there can be no question that by word of mouth, everyone at the Texas School Book Depository Building had to know that the presidential motorcade would pass by the building that Friday. It was clear to Oswald, then, that in three days President John F. Kennedy, the leader of worldwide capitalism and an avowed enemy of Fidel Castro and the Castro revolution, would be driven past the Book Depository Building, presumably in an open car, right past the building where he worked, right below those windows he had looked out so many times.

No one can possibly know what was going through Oswald's mind during these three days before the assassination. But a few things we do know. He had once written, "I wonder what would happen [if] somebody was to stand up and say he was utterly opposed not only to the governments, but to the people, [to] the entire land and complete foundations of his socially [society]."[1604] He had also once written to his brother Robert from Moscow, "In the event of war I would kill any american who put a uniform on in defence of the american government—any american."[1605]

In a sense, Oswald had been at war with America ever since he could remember. He had been at war with the whole world. He had tried to fashion a new life for himself more than once, only to be thwarted at every turn. His career in the Marine Corps had ended in ignominy. His defection to the Soviet Union had petered out in a dead-end job in a factory. His return to America had been ignored. His job as a "photographer" led to nothing. He shot at General Walker and missed. His career as leader of a pro-Cuban political group had failed to attract a single follower. In Mexico City, representatives of Cuba and the Cuban Revolution seemed utterly uninterested in his devotion. Was there any battle in this war of his he could win? Oswald's motive for killing Kennedy is discussed in depth in the "Motive" section of this book. But was it possible he was thinking that if he killed Fidel Castro's most powerful enemy, he might avert the assassination of Castro, forestall the invasion of Cuba, and bring him at last to the status he craved as a hero of the Cuban Revolution? And that if he died in the attempt, Castro would see what Cuba had lost when its petty bureaucrats frustrated his ardent desire to serve the cause?

Additionally, since we know Oswald wanted to leave his footprints on the sand dunes of history, even naming his diary the Historic Diary, could it be that, like so many people, he felt fate was intervening in his life and sending him a message, nay, a command? I mean, could it really be pure chance, and nothing more, that the most powerful man on earth was going to pass right beneath his window? No one can ever know, but is it possible that, along with other toxic currents, the thought entered his mind that he had a historic duty, for whatever reason or reasons he conjured up, not to deny the hand that fate was now giving him? That he couldn't fail to show up for his rendezvous with history?

That Tuesday, Lee worked all day, but very uncharacteristically did not call Marina even once, much less twice, as he virtually always did.[1606] On Tuesday evening, Radio

Havana's English-speaking broadcast said that "since last March the [U.S.] Central Intelligence Agency has itself been organizing all attacks on Cuba . . . We know the ships they came on, including the famous *Rex* that sails out of West Palm Beach on missions against Cuba."[1607]

He worked a full day on Wednesday, November 20, also, but again did not call Marina.[1608] Marina told Ruth Paine, "He thinks he's punishing me." She was angrier with him than he was with her, and she was perfectly willing to let him sulk.[1609]

Late that Wednesday night, Oswald took a load of his clothes to Reno's Speed Wash, a washateria a half block away across the street at 1101 North Beckley. While his clothes were being washed and dried, the janitor noticed that he spoke to no one, sitting and reading magazines until closing time at midnight. When the merchant patrolman requested him to leave because the speed wash was closing, Oswald ignored him and continued to read for an additional five minutes.[1610]

On the morning of Thursday, November 21, Oswald dressed and left for work, his head roiling with the grandiose scheme that, if he dared to carry it out, would finally ensure his place in history. Based on his conduct later that evening with Marina at Ruth Paine's residence, he probably had not made up his mind yet. But all the circumstantial evidence shows the thought clearly was in his mind, and it had to be intoxicating. Befitting the moment, he expansively offered himself a treat. Instead of making his breakfast in the rooming house, as he usually did, he went over to the Dobbs House restaurant at 1221 North Beckley, just short of two blocks away on the other side of the street. He had been there before, often enough for the waitresses to recognize him. Dolores Harrison cooked a couple of eggs for him, but when the other waitress, Mary Dowling, served him, Oswald complained that he had ordered them "over light," and they were "cooked too hard." He accepted them anyway.[1611]

Later that morning, but before the ten o'clock break, Lee asked Wesley Frazier if he could ride out to Irving with him that evening. That was okay with Frazier, but it dawned on him it was only Thursday, and with the exception of the Monday night in October the day after Marina had given birth to their daughter Rachel, Lee had never driven out to Irving with him on anything but a Friday. "Why are you going home today?" he asked Lee.

"I'm going to get some curtain rods," Lee said. "You know, put in an apartment."

By telling Frazier this, a lie that was demonstrated to be such (see later text), Oswald showed he had already come up with a story to cover up the fact that, absent a reconciliation with Marina, he was going back to Irving a day early to pick up his rifle for the following day.

"Are you going to go out to Irving tomorrow night too?" Frazier asked Oswald.

"No," Oswald answered.[1612]

Probably sometime during the course of that day Lee improvised a bag to contain his rifle from the heavy, brown wrapping paper and three-inch paper tape used in the shipping department.[1613]

Marina was surprised when she saw Wesley's car stop in front of Ruth Paine's house to let Lee out early that evening. Not only had he never come out on a Thursday evening before, but even on the weekends he had always asked Ruth's permission to come.[1614] At the London trial I asked Mrs. Paine, "On Thursday, November 21, 1963, did anything unusual happen with respect to Mr. Oswald?"

Paine: "Well, yes, he came out that night. And it was the first night he had come out on a weeknight, and it was the first time he had ever come without asking permission."

"You were surprised?"

"I was very surprised, yes."

"Was Marina a little embarrassed and surprised at this?"

"She was, yes. She said to me—she apologized for his not asking whether he could come, and she expressed her surprise."[1615]

Marina was still angry about his use of a false name at his rooming house and did not go to greet him. In fact, she was pleased that he had come, but she wasn't about to let him know that. He found her in the bedroom. She asked him why he had come.

"Because I'm tired of living alone and because I got lonesome for my girls," he said. He told her he didn't want her to continue living with Ruth Paine, and if Marina wanted him to, he would "rent an apartment in Dallas tomorrow."

He tried to kiss her, but she turned away and ordered him to clean up and change his clothes. Docilely, he did as he was told. When he had showered and changed, he again demanded a kiss, and this time he blocked her exit from the bedroom until she submitted, unwillingly, still angry.

"He tried to talk to me," Marina would later tell the Warren Commission, "but I would not answer him, and he was very upset . . . He tried to start a conversation with me several times, but I would not answer."

"Enough," he finally said, angered by her rejection. "You get too much spoiling here." He told her he was "going to find an apartment tomorrow and take all three of you with me."

"I won't go," Marina said.

He said she would, or he would take the children.

"That's fine," she said. "Just you try nursing Rachel. You know what that's like."

He told her he had gone to see the FBI and told the agents not to bother her anymore. She didn't care about that. She went out to the backyard to gather the laundry from the line, and Lee went into the garage.[1616]

Since we know from all the evidence that he brought his Mannlicher-Carcano rifle to work with him the next morning, it was probably then that he attended to it. Neither Ruth nor her children were at home; Marina would be occupied at the clothesline for a few minutes. He didn't need much time. We know the carbine, wrapped and tied in its blanket, was lying on the floor. He quickly removed the two parts—the short barrel with its mounted telescopic sight and the stock with a sling improvised from a camera strap—and placed them both in the heavy, brown wrapping paper bag he had fashioned most likely earlier that day. From somewhere he gathered the cartridges. He carefully arranged the blanket to look exactly as it had when the carbine was still in it, left the new package containing the rifle someplace where it would not attract attention,[*] and went out to the backyard to help Marina bring in the clothes.

Again he asked her to come live with him and their children in an apartment in Dallas. When she once again refused, he told her she preferred her friends to him, and that she obviously didn't love or need him anymore. She responded that they had already agreed that she would stay with Ruth through the coming holiday season, and they might as well save their money till then. Besides, she said, she would just be lonely in an apartment in Dallas while he was at work.

"Don't worry about the money," Lee said. "We have a little saved up. I'll take an apartment and we'll buy you a washing machine." In fact, they had $183 and another payday in two weeks, easily enough to rent a cheap apartment and, with a bit of scrimping, to

---

[*]Though we were not present in the garage, when we look at all the evidence, we can know, with every confidence, that each of the above actions took place precisely as stated, for the simple reason they *had* to take place.

buy a secondhand washing machine to boot. Although Marina wanted a washing machine, it always seemed more important to Lee than Marina that she have one, and she told him now to forget about getting her a washing machine. If there was money, she said, "it would be better" if he got himself a car, that she "would manage." Indeed, Michael had just bought an Oldsmobile, which Lee and Marina had looked at out on the street and admired, for $200, and it was only seven years old.[1617]

"I don't need a car," Lee told Marina, saying he would continue to take the bus. But she, he told her, would need a washing machine now that she had two children in diapers. She couldn't go back to washing things in the bathtub.[1618]

Marina was noncommittal. Secretly, she was pleased he was making a strong effort to heal the rift between them. "I was smiling inside, but I had a serious expression on my face," she would later recall, to the very end playing their little game of *Carmen*, not giving the other what they knew the other needed. Although she did want to stay at Ruth's until the new year, she was not adamantly opposed to Lee's plan. If he persisted, she might just give in—sooner or later she would have to anyway—but she still had to teach him a lesson for scaring her over the recent alias thing. Now she was additionally upset because he had come out to Irving on a weeknight, in violation of their understanding with Ruth and without even asking permission.[1619]

When Ruth drove up with her station wagon full of groceries, Lee and Marina went out to help her carry them into the house. Marina lagged behind to make a quiet apology for Lee's unannounced and unexpected visit, but Ruth was not at all put out. She guessed that Lee had come out to Irving unannounced in the hope of smoothing over the rift with Marina.[1620]

As they entered the house, Ruth said to Oswald in Russian, "Our president is coming to town," but he merely replied, "Uh, yeah," as he brushed past her, communicating to her that he didn't want to talk about it.[1621]

Later, as the Oswalds sat together on the couch folding diapers, Marina, ever the fan of the Kennedys, also brought up the president's visit. "Lee," she said, "Kennedy is coming tomorrow. I'd like to see him in person. Do you know where and when I could go?"

"No," he said.

It seemed odd to her that Lee, who had been almost as interested in the Kennedys as she had—or at least indulged her fascination with them—had nothing to say about the forthcoming visit. Lee went out to the front lawn to play with the children—some of the neighbor's children as well as the Paines' and June—and Marina watched them. He carried June piggyback as they galloped about in pursuit of a butterfly, then Lee tried to catch oak wings drifting down from the trees. Later he sat with June on a red kiddie cart, talking with the children in English. He said to Marina, in Russian, "Good, our Junie will speak both Russian and English . . . but I still don't like the name Rachel. Let's call her Marina instead."

He started talking again, for the final time, about getting an apartment in Dallas so they could all be together again. He was much kinder now than he had been in the bedroom, and Marina softened. She was at the point of saying yes, but Marina told Priscilla McMillan, "I was like a stubborn little mule. I was maintaining my inaccessibility, trying to show Lee I wasn't that easy to persuade. If he had come again the next day and asked, of course I would have agreed. I just wanted to hold out one day at least."[1622]*

The rest of the evening was much like any other, with both of the women preoccu-

---

*In a handwritten narrative prepared by Marina at the request of the Warren Commission, Marina, again displaying her brutal honesty, lamented, "Of course, if I had known what was going to happen, I would have

pied with their chores and their children. At dinner, the conversation was so unremarkable that neither Ruth nor Marina remembered it. But Ruth was pleased. Her friends were not bickering, for once, and they looked to her like any married couple making up after a spat.[1623]

After dinner, Marina stacked the dishes while Ruth bathed her children and read to them in their beds for an hour. Lee put June to bed while Marina nursed Rachel, and then he settled down in front of the television with the baby on his lap, getting her to sleep. He watched an old movie from the Second World War while Marina put the toys away and did the dishes.[1624] Around nine, Lee came into the kitchen and told Marina that he was going to bed, earlier than usual for him. He seemed sad. "I probably won't be out this weekend," he told her. "It's too often. I was here today."[1625]

Not long after, Ruth went out to the garage to paint some children's blocks and noticed that the light was already on, which was odd. She thought Lee might have been rummaging around in their things for some warmer clothing—it was approaching the end of November and getting chilly. But she thought it careless of him to leave the light on.[1626]* When she went back in, she sat with Marina for a while folding laundry and chatting about nothing very important. Eventually, Ruth went off to bed too, leaving Marina, as usual, the last one up. Marina took the opportunity to soak herself in a hot tub for another hour.

When she finally crept off to bed, Lee was lying on his stomach with his eyes closed, oddly tense. Though he was not asleep, he did not speak.[1627]

Tomorrow was going to be a big day.

Now let's get into the case against Oswald, and some related as well as miscellaneous topics, before setting forth a summary of Oswald's guilt.

---

agreed without further thought. Perhaps (if Lee was planning anything) he staked everything on a card. That is, if I agreed to his proposal to go with him to Dallas, he would not do what he planned, and, if I did not, then he would" (CE 994, 18 H 638).

One well-recognized exception to the rule of evidence that hearsay (a statement made outside of court that is offered into evidence to prove not merely that the statement was made but that it is true) is not admissible in a legal proceeding because of its untrustworthiness (not under oath, not subject to cross-examination at the time the statement was made) is when the statement made is against the declarant's own interest, the reasoning being that people may lie to hurt others, but not themselves, thereby investing the statement with an inherent trustworthiness. If saying something (as Marina did) that, in effect, places the blame for the murder of a president on your shoulders is not a sufficient reason to believe it, few other things would be. And if we believe Marina's rendition of what took place the evening before the president's murder, as all sensible people must, then two things would necessarily seem to follow: one, that Oswald's decision to kill Kennedy was tentative—that he would not have killed Kennedy if Marina had agreed to come back to him; and two, *by this fact alone*, the likelihood of his being a part of a conspiracy to murder Kennedy, in which others got him to do what he did, is virtually nonexistent.

*At the London trial, Ruth Paine testified that when she entered the garage around 9:00 p.m. and saw the overhead light on, she knew it wasn't she who had left it on because she hadn't been in the garage earlier in the evening. What about the possibility of Marina? I asked. She answered, "It couldn't have been Marina. She was very good at turning out the lights whenever she went in there, and then I could hear her moving about. I knew where she was during the evening. So as I walked into the garage and found the light on, it was my clear impression that Oswald had been there and left it on carelessly." (Transcript of *On Trial*, July 24, 1986, pp.617–618)

Oswald's Ownership and Possession of the Rifle Found on the Sixth Floor

A 6.5-millimeter Mannlicher-Carcano rifle found on the sixth floor of the Book Depository Building was ultimately determined by the authorities to have been the weapon that fired the bullets that killed Kennedy. If it belonged to Oswald, that fact alone would almost conclusively make him the assassin, since the alternative inference that some third party had gotten possession of Oswald's rifle without his knowledge (in his interrogation, Oswald never made any such claim, denying even owning a rifle) and killed Kennedy with it stretches credulity. Thus, the need to examine this issue in depth. The reader will recognize some of the matters being discussed as having been touched on in the "Four Days in November" section of this book.

Approximately a half hour after the shooting in Dealey Plaza, Dallas deputy sheriff Luke Mooney squeezed between stacks of boxes clustered around the southeast corner window of the sixth floor of the Texas School Book Depository and discovered what looked to him like a sniper's nest. He saw three expended cartridges on the floor and a stack of boxes at the window, and noticed a "slight crease" on the top of one box that he thought might have been used for a gun rest.[1] He noted that the crease was "at the same angle that the shots were fired from." No more than twenty-five minutes later, on the same floor, Dallas deputy sheriff Eugene Boone and deputy constable Seymour Weitzman found a bolt-action rifle with a telescopic sight partly hidden between stacks of boxes in the northwest corner near the stairs. Neither of them touched it. Instead, they called it to the attention of senior officers.[2] Initially thought to be a 7.65-millimeter Mauser, investigators later determined that the rifle stuffed behind the boxes was a 6.5-millimeter Mannlicher-Carcano military carbine, model 91/38, manufactured for the Italian military in 1940 and stamped with serial number C2766.[3]* FBI expert Robert Frazier told the Commission that

---

*In America, the caliber of a firearm is the diameter of the interior of its barrel, and with American weapons it is expressed in inches. Thus, a .30 caliber weapon is one whose interior barrel is thirty-hundredths, or three-

the original rifle, designed in 1891 by Ferdinand Ritter von Mannlicher and M. Carcano,[4] was a 6.5-millimeter caliber weapon, but a later model 38, designed shortly before the outbreak of World War II, was 7.35 millimeters. Early in the war, the Italian government discovered that it had far more 6.5-millimeter ammunition than rifles, so a number of model 38s, like Oswald's, were manufactured in the Italian army with the smaller barrel, and were in every respect (other than the barrel) identical to the 7.35-millimeter model 38.[5]

As previously indicated, it didn't take long for police to link the rifle to Oswald. At four o'clock in the morning on November 23, less than sixteen hours after the assassination, agents of the FBI discovered that the Mannlicher-Carcano, serial number C2766 (Klein's control number VC-836, catalog number C20-T750), had been shipped from Klein's Sporting Goods of Chicago on March 20, 1963, to one "A. Hidell, P.O. Box 2915, Dallas, Texas."[6] Indeed, in a search pursuant to a search warrant by Dallas Police Department detectives of Oswald's belongings in Ruth Paine's garage on November 23, 1963, portions of two Klein's magazine ads for the rifle were found inside a box.[7]

The rifle, without the scope, cost $12.78.[8] With the four-power telescopic sight that Oswald ordered, the cost was $19.95, and shipping charges were $1.50, for a total of $21.45.[9] The rifle was designated by the Warren Commission in 1964 as Commission Exhibit No. 139. Expert document examiners from the Treasury Department and the FBI determined that the *hand printing* on the mail-order coupon ("A. Hidell, P.O. Box 2915, Dallas, Texas," etc.) clipped from a February 1963 advertisement by Klein's in *American Rifleman* magazine touting the "fast loading and fast firing" weapon, and the *handwriting* on the envelope (name and address of addressee, Klein's store in Chicago, and name and return address of sender, A. Hidell in Dallas), which was postmarked March 12, 1963, were those of Lee Harvey Oswald.[10]

The rifle and its cheap Japanese telescopic sight had been paid for with a $21.45 postal money order purchased on March 12, 1963. The written words designating the payee as "Klein's Sporting Goods," and the purchaser of the money order and his address as "A. Hidell, P.O. Box 2915, Dallas, Texas," were all determined to be in Oswald's handwriting.[11]* Klein's shipped the rifle by parcel post to A. Hidell's post

---

tenths, of one inch in diameter. The caliber of continental European weapons like Oswald's is measured not in inches but in millimeters. Therefore, his 6.5-millimeter Carcano would be the same as an American .257 caliber weapon, the interior barrel diameter being about one-fourth of an inch.

Oswald's bolt-action, clip-fed military rifle had many markings on it, among which were "MADE IN ITALY"; "TERNI," referring to being manufactured and tested at the Terni Army Plant in Terni, Italy; "CAL. 6.5," to the rifle's caliber; "1940" and "40," to the year of manufacture; and "2766," to the weapon's serial number. The scope was stamped "4 × 18 COATED," "ORDNANCE OPTICS INC," "HOLLYWOOD CALIFORNIA," and "MADE IN JAPAN." The ammunition clip, which did not come with the rifle, bore the letters "SMI" (for "Soc. Metallurgica Italiana") and the number "952" (a part of the full code number "Partita No. 1A/1/1952").

After the Second World War, when the Italian army switched to a different rifle, the Carcano was imported into this country from Italy as surplus military equipment and was fairly common in America at the time. (WR, pp.81, 553–555; 3 H 392–396, 398, WCT Robert A. Frazier; Trask, *Pictures of the Pain*, pp.549–550; clip did not come with rifle: 3 H 398, WCT Robert A. Frazier); Fuhrman, *Simple Act of Murder*, p.46)

*Handwriting identification, though not as conclusive as fingerprint identification, is nonetheless considered to be definitive when done by qualified experts, and is "based upon the principle that every handwriting is distinctive." However, since any *single* distinctive characteristic in handwriting as well as hand printing may not be unique to one person, in order to make an identification the handwriting expert (normally referred to as a "questioned-documents" expert or examiner) must find a sufficient number of corresponding distinctive characteristics (and a general absence of distinctive differences) between the *known* writing of the person and the writing on the document in question. The possibility that one person can imitate the handwriting of another and successfully deceive an expert document examiner is considered to be very remote, though it has been

office box in Dallas on March 20, 1963. The post office box that the rifle had been sent to was rented by Oswald, who was receiving periodicals through it at the time the rifle was shipped.[12] One would think that with this kind of evidence, no reasonable person could ever doubt that Oswald bought the weapon found on the sixth floor of the Book Depository. But then, conspiracy theorists, for the most part, are not reasonable people when it comes to the Kennedy case.

The identification of the rifle as a Mannlicher-Carcano, and not a Mauser, as the earliest news accounts reported, caught the attention of the earliest conspiracy theorists, particularly attorney Mark Lane, who brought up the issue during his testimony before the Warren Commission[13] and later devoted an entire chapter of his 1966 book, *Rush to Judgment*, to it. To hear Lane tell it, the police switched the "real" murder weapon (a Mauser) with one traceable to Oswald (the Mannlicher-Carcano). Most of the smoke and mirrors that Lane, and others, have used to sell this story originate with a remark made to the press by one of the men who discovered the rifle.

The rumor that a Mauser was found in the Depository began when Captain John Will Fritz of the Dallas Police Department, while waiting for Lieutenant J. C. Day of the police crime lab to photograph the rifle as it lay on the floor between stacks of boxes, remarked that he thought it looked like a 7.65-millimeter Mauser. Deputies Boone and Weitzman, who were present, agreed and later repeated it.[14] Neither Weitzman nor Boone ever touched the rifle, and Weitzman said he only had "a glance" at it.[15] Weitzman, formerly in the sporting goods business,[16] included the misinformation in an affidavit filed the following day.[17] Within hours, a Dallas radio station reported the misidentification, attributing the story to "sheriff's deputies."[18] Lieutenant Day recalled in 1987 that as he came out the door of the Depository carrying the rifle, a reporter asked, "Is that a Mauser?" Day didn't answer, but about thirty minutes later radio and television stations were reporting that a Mauser had been found. The story was picked up by the television networks and quickly spread. Late Friday night, during an impromptu press conference, District Attorney Henry Wade seemed to add weight to the reports when he told a reporter asking about the make of the gun, "It's a Mauser, I believe."[19] What the press couldn't have known is that Wade, at the time, didn't have a firm grasp on many of the details about the official investigation and, in fact, didn't know much more about the investigation than what had been reported by the media—including the "fact" that a Mauser had been found.

The suggestion that the early reports of a German-made Mauser being found is evidence of a "police switch" has not worn well. To begin with, it is easy to confuse the Italian-made Mannlicher-Carcano with the German Mauser[*] as well as with several

---

done. Not only does the forger have the problem of simulating every distinctive characteristic, but the forger is drawing, not writing. Forged writing is therefore distinguished by defects such as "tremor, waver, patching, retouching, noncontinuous lines, [and] pen lifts in awkward and unusual places." (4 H 364, 372, WCT Alwyn Cole)

The two experts who compared handwriting and printing exemplars or "standards" of Oswald's (i.e., known writing of Oswald's, such as endorsements on his payroll checks, applications for employment, for a passport, for membership in the American Civil Liberties Union, and letters to the Immigration and Naturalization Service, the Marine Corps, the State Department, and the American embassy in Russia) with the writing on the postal money order were Alwyn Cole, a questioned-documents examiner for the U.S. Treasury Department with twenty-eight years of experience, and James C. Cadigan, an FBI agent and examiner of questioned documents in the FBI laboratory in Washington, D.C., for over twenty-three years. (WR, pp.566, 569)

[*]In one of the leading books on rifles and other small arms, the author writes that the Mannlicher-Carcano is even "known occasionally as the Mauser Paravicino" and is, in fact, "a modified Mauser" (Smith, *Small Arms of the World*, p.474). FBI firearms expert Robert A. Frazier testified that "the Mauser was one of

other European military rifles. Firearms expert Monty C. Lutz prepared an exhibit for the HSCA showing five European-made rifles—the German Mauser among them—of very similar shape and size, all containing the same right-sided bolt handle (common on all bolt-action rifles), an ammunition magazine protruding below the receiver (immediately in front of the trigger guard), and bayonet studs (allowing a bayonet knife to be attached to the barrel of the rifle).[20] Lutz testified that "many of these rifles could very easily have been confused with the [Italian-made] Mannlicher-Carcano to the person who did not make a complete and thorough examination of that particular rifle."[21] Further, Lutz noted that the difference in caliber between the Italian Carcano and the German Mauser, about forty-thousandths of an inch, could hardly be determined by the naked eye.[22]

While Lane argued that a rifle clearly marked "CAL. 6.5" couldn't possibly be misidentified by seasoned police officers,[23] there is no evidence to suggest that the officers peering down at the weapon between two stacks of boxes ever read the rifle's markings. Moreover, the legend "CAL. 6.5" was stamped across the rear iron sight, which was partly obscured by the scope sight mounted above it, and therefore hardly visible to Boone and Weitzman.[24]

In a 1967 interview, Weitzman said he had "no doubt" that the rifle identified by the Dallas Police Department as being a 6.5-millimeter Carcano, and as having been found on the sixth floor of the Book Depository Building, is "the rifle we found. It was strictly a mistaken identity which anybody could make. If you know anything about guns, a Mauser is a Mauser. What make it is, what country it was made in, can easily be misidentified because mostly your Mauser mechanism looks very similar." Weitzman went on to say that the Carcano "was a Mauser-action rifle" and really was "an Italian Mauser."[25] Although the evidence clearly shows, then, that the early reports of a Mauser being found were mistakes, in the world of conspiracy theorists there are no mistakes, only sinister implications.

In addition to the documentary record of his purchase of the Carcano rifle, some of the most damning pieces of evidence against Oswald, demonstrating his actual possession, as opposed to mere ownership, of the weapon used to murder John F. Kennedy, are three photographs, taken well before the assassination, that depict Oswald posing (in two different poses) in his backyard with a rifle, a pistol (believed to be the one he used to murder Officer J. D. Tippit), and two Communist newspapers—the *Militant* and the *Worker*.[26] Together, these pictures have become known as the "backyard photographs."

On November 23, 1963, police discovered at least two prints and one negative (from which one of the prints had been made) during a search of the Oswalds' possessions in Mrs. Paine's garage.[27] Taken to police headquarters, one of the pictures was enlarged and shown to Oswald that evening by Captain Fritz. As previously indicated, Oswald declared it a fake, that he had never seen it before, and that someone had superimposed his head on someone else's body. Fritz then showed him the small, original photograph found in the garage. Oswald claimed it too was a trick photo, adding that he knew a lot about photography and would, in time, prove that they were fakes.[28]

---

the earliest, if not the earliest," of "bolt-action" rifles "from which many others were copied. And since [the Mannlicher-Carcano] uses the same type of bolt system, it may have been [erroneously] referred to as a Mauser for that reason" (3 H 394, WCT Robert A. Frazier).

Marina Oswald later told the Warren Commission in 1964 that she had taken the photos, at Oswald's request,[29] with his Imperial Reflex camera[30] while they were living at a small rented house on Neely Street.

One of the backyard photographs, later designated as Commission Exhibit No. 133-A, appeared on the cover of the February 21, 1964, edition of *Life* magazine,[31] which had purchased the rights to the photo for $5,000 through Marina Oswald's business manager at the time. Other copies also appeared in the *New York Times* and several other publications.[32]

In 1964, FBI photography expert Lyndal L. Shaneyfelt testified that he determined, by comparing the negative of one of the other backyard photographs (Commission Exhibit No. 133-B) with test pictures taken with the Imperial Reflex camera, that the negative had been exposed in Oswald's camera *to the exclusion of all other cameras.*[33] Although he could not test the other known photograph (Commission Exhibit No. 133-A), since the negative was never recovered,[34] he did note that both pictures were nearly identical, containing similar backgrounds and lighting, and based on the shadows, both had been taken at about the same angle.[35] Consequently, the Warren Commission was reasonably certain that both images had been taken with the same camera and at the same time, as Marina Oswald had testified.[36] Shaneyfelt was also reasonably certain that the photographs were not composites, and that Oswald's face had not been pasted on someone else's body, as Oswald had claimed. Shaneyfelt testified that his opinion, based on the expertise and technology available in 1964, contained "very, very minor" reservations, "because I cannot entirely eliminate an extremely expert composite." He did add, however, that a composite can "nearly always be detected under magnification," and that in his magnifications he "found no such characteristics in these pictures."[37]

Finally, Shaneyfelt compared the actual rifle with the rifle depicted in backyard photograph 133-A, as well as with five new prints of 133-A that were produced to provide greater detail, and found them to have "the same general configuration. All appearances were the same," and he found "no differences." However, he "did not find any really specific peculiarities" (other than "one notch" on the stock "that appears very faintly in the photograph") from which he could make a "positive identification" that the rifle seen in the backyard photographs was the rifle found on the sixth floor "to the exclusion of all other rifles of the same general configuration."[38]

Despite the Warren Commission's best efforts to dispel questions about their authenticity, the backyard photographs spawned an entire branch of Kennedy assassinology. As G. Robert Blakey, chief counsel and staff director of the HSCA, pointed out in public hearings in 1978, "If the backyard photographs are valid, they are highly incriminatory of Oswald, and they tend to strongly corroborate the basic story told by Marina Oswald. If they are invalid, how they were produced poses far-reaching questions in the area of conspiracy for they evince a degree of technical sophistication that would almost necessarily raise the possibility that more than private parties conspired not only to kill the president, but to make Oswald a patsy."[39]

It was because of the importance of the backyard photos that the HSCA brought its photographic panel, consisting of twenty-two experts in all aspects of photography, including photogrammetry, photointerpretation, and forensic photography, to bear on the subject. The committee knew that if the rifle held by Oswald in the photos did not match up with the one found on the sixth floor, that alone would be strong circumstantial evidence that the backyard photos may have been fakes.

Although by 1978 the Carcano could theoretically have accumulated scratches and marks it did not have in 1963, fortunately for the photographic panel, besides having, of course, the actual rifle found on the sixth floor, the rifle had been photographed many times shortly after the shooting in Dealey Plaza, beginning with the crime-lab photographs that showed where it was found.[40] A cameraman for Dallas television station WFAA, Thomas Alyea, present on the sixth floor when the rifle was discovered, also captured the weapon on 16-millimeter film. And both *Dallas Morning News* photographer Jack Beers and *Dallas Times Herald* photographer William Allen took multiple shots of the rifle as Lieutenant Day carried it from the Depository.[41] It was photographed again at Dallas police headquarters by many different photographers from all over the world as Lieutenant Day carried it high overhead while en route to the Forgery Bureau to show it to Marina Oswald for identification.[42]

The HSCA photographic panel, with a far larger staff of experts than the Warren Commission, and utilizing photographic technology not available back in 1964, determined that all of the photos and footage of the rifle taken right after the assassination in 1963 proved "that the rifle in the [National] Archives is the same weapon that Oswald is shown holding in the backyard [photos], and the same weapon that was seized by Dallas police and appears in various post-assassination photographs." The rough wooden stock of Oswald's rifle had been heavily used, and there were many identifying scratches, marks, and gouges on it. A comparison of the marks on the rifle in the archives with those visible in the earlier photographs showed all of the photos to be of the same rifle—Oswald's Mannlicher-Carcano.[43] The most prominent mark, a large gouge in the forestock, also appears in the Alyea film of the rifle and in the backyard photo, as well as three other post-assassination photographs,[44] which proves beyond *any* doubt that it was Oswald's Mannlicher-Carcano that police found. Despite over forty years of allegations by Mark Lane and other conspiracy theorists, if there is one thing even a child should walk away from this case knowing for sure, it's that only *one* rifle was found in the Texas School Book Depository and that rifle, a Mannlicher-Carcano, serial number C2766, was bought and paid for by Lee Harvey Oswald.

As indicated, the HSCA took note of the fact that Marina told the committee (and earlier the Warren Commission) that she took the subject backyard photos. So we absolutely know the backyard photos of Oswald are genuine because Marina herself said she took the photos. That alone and all by itself should end all debate. And for those diehard conspiracy theorists who maintain that what Marina told the Warren Commission in 1964 cannot be relied on because the FBI put pressure on her to lie, and that in 1978 she was merely continuing the lie with the HSCA, even today, many years later when no one is putting pressure on her to say anything other than what is the truth, and even though she now wholeheartedly embraces the conspiracy theory of the assassination, she told me and my Fort Worth lawyer friend Jack Duffy on November 30, 2000, in Dallas that she took the photos.

And if even this is not enough (nothing ever is for the buffs) to refute the argument that someone framed Oswald with fake photos, there is the fact that Oswald himself *signed and dated* one of the prints. As alluded to earlier, in February 1967, George and Jeanne de Mohrenschildt, friends of Oswald, ran across a set of instructional English language record albums that Jeanne had loaned to Marina Oswald. The records were found stuffed among their belongings that had been in storage since before the couple's departure to Haiti in May 1963. Leafing through the records to make sure they had not been broken, they discovered an enlargement of one of the backyard photographs (133-A). On the back was an inscription, "To my friend George from Lee Oswald," and the date, "5/IV/63," interpreted by George de Mohrenschildt as April 5, 1963, a common Russian method of date notation. Above the autograph were the words, written in Russian, "Hunter of Fascists, ha, ha, ha," which George thought might have been added by Marina jeering at her husband's antifascist feelings.[45] The de Mohrenschildt print was turned over to the HSCA in April 1977, and its panel of handwriting experts determined that the inscription to George, and the Oswald signature, were both in the handwriting of Lee Harvey Oswald.[46]*

Responding to the allegation of many in the conspiracy community that the backyard photos were "fakes," after subjecting all aspects of the photos (not just the rifle, but the background, lighting and shadows, dimensions, etc.) to excruciatingly detailed and sophisticated analysis, the HSCA concluded that "there was no evidence of fakery in the [backyard] photographs, and the rifle in the photographs was identical to the rifle found on the sixth floor of the depository on November 22, 1963."[47]

Near the conclusion of his appearance during the HSCA's public hearings, photographic panel expert Calvin McCamy remarked, "The allegations [of fakery in the backyard photographs] have been based on observations made by people [the] least qualified to make the observations. This has resulted in false observations, and, therefore, false premises on which to base theories. The lesson I think is very clearly taught, and I might say taught at extreme expense, and it is the age old lesson that a little learning is a dangerous thing."[48]

A perfect example of McCamy's on-the-nose observation is seen in the work of conspiracy author Robert J. Groden, a photographic consultant to the House Select Committee[†] and coauthor of the book *JFK: The Case for Conspiracy*. Despite its exhaustive and conclusive findings, Groden disagreed with the photographic panel's conclusion that the backyard photos were genuine. While he generally agreed that many of the questions concerning the background of the photos "were no longer issues and that some of them never really were," the backyard photographs were, in his opinion, "beyond question fakes." He remained convinced that the head of Lee Harvey Oswald had been added on from the middle of the chin up.[49]

Groden has continued to defend this thesis in his more recent books, *High Treason* (1989) and *The Killing of a President* (1993), as well as in several video cassettes. He even found a curious parallel in the evidence against O. J. Simpson, when he testified at the 1996 wrongful death civil suit against Simpson arising out of the murder of his former wife, Nicole Brown, and an acquaintance of hers, Ronald Goldman. Simpson's defense team, after finding no one else who would call photographs of Simpson (commentating, on the field, for NBC at a Buffalo Bills football game on September 26, 1993) wearing Bruno Magli shoes fakes,[‡] hit upon Groden, who obliged by telling the jurors that the

---

*Although the HSCA did not exclude Oswald, the committee was unable to conclude whether it was he, Marina, or de Mohrenschildt who had written the phrase "Hunter of Fascists, ha, ha, ha" (12 HSCA 52–53).

†The HSCA was careful to point out that Groden was "not a member of the committee's photographic evidence panel," but was a consultant (unpaid at that) providing background information on the issues that had been raised by Warren Commission critics in the area of photographic evidence (6 HSCA 294; unpaid: Trask, *National Nightmare*, p.208).

‡The killer of Nicole Brown and Ron Goldman had left bloody shoe prints as he walked away from the murder scene on the evening of June 12, 1994. The shoe (sole) prints were those of the rare, Italian-made Bruno Magli shoe.

shoes had been superimposed onto Simpson's body (apparently the same way Oswald's head had been superimposed onto someone else's body).

Groden's appearance at the Simpson civil trial resulted in a blistering attack on his qualifications as a photo expert. Because Groden is by far the leading photographic expert for the conspiracy community, and was Oliver Stone's photographic consultant on his movie *JFK*, let's look at what came out on his background. The plaintiffs' counsel brought out the fact that Groden was a high school dropout, and had never taught a course or written anything in the field of questioned photographs. Moreover, he hadn't taken any course, attended any schools, or had any formal training in analyzing photographs, and consequently had no particular qualifications as a questioned-photographs examiner. Indeed, he couldn't even name a professional association to which such experts might belong. His credibility was further seriously impeached when he first denied selling purloined copies of the Kennedy autopsy photos to the supermarket tabloid *Globe*, but then, when confronted with a copy of the contract under which he had received fifty thousand dollars from *Globe*, he claimed that he had been paid that sum for his "story," for which the photos (the *only* thing, obviously, the *Globe* wanted) were only illustrative examples. Only once before had he ever been paid to establish the authenticity of a photo, that of an apparition at a voodoo ceremony.[50]

Unable to qualify as an expert, Groden was nonetheless allowed to testify as someone with "experience" that he found clear signs of photographic manipulation on two color photographs of Simpson taken by one Harry Scull at a football game in Buffalo on September 26, 1993.[51] (The photos surfaced *after* Simpson's criminal trial, but before the civil trial.) To frame Simpson, apparently someone had, according to Groden, carefully doctored the photos *after* the murders to show Simpson wearing the rare, "ugly-ass"[*] shoes the killer wore.[52]

Unfortunately for Groden, by the time he was called to the stand again after the Christmas holidays, the plaintiffs had come into possession of thirty more photographs of Simpson at the same game, *every one of them* clearly revealing the same ugly-ass shoes. All had been taken by another photographer, the son of the owner of the Buffalo Bills, and worse, one of them had been *published* in a Bills promotional publication in November 1993, six months *before* the murders in June 1994.[53] Groden, badly shaken, insisted that the existence of the thirty newly found photographs did not change his opinion that the two Scull photographs had been insidiously manipulated.[54] So if we're to believe Groden, the conspirators out to frame Simpson doctored not only Scull's two photographs but also thirty additional photographs taken by the son of the Buffalo Bills' owner. And one of them (the one published in November of 1993) had been *doctored* by the conspirators six months *before* the murders even took place in June of 1994. Apparently the conspirators were clairvoyant and knew that a half year later Simpson's former wife and male companion would be murdered and Simpson would be charged with their murders.

Why the conspirators out to frame Simpson would want to give the authorities thirty-two fake photographs instead of just one, thereby increasing the likelihood of their fakery being discovered thirty-two-fold, is not known. Even more stupefying is the conclusion that the conspirators, having gone to so much trouble and expense to frame Simpson, then forgot to make their doctored photographs available for the much more important criminal trial, and only remembered them in time for the later civil trial. It

---

[*]Simpson's dismissive characterization of the shoes, saying he'd never wear such shoes.

should be noted that Gerald Richards, a photographic expert for the plaintiffs who the judge said qualified as an expert in his field, testified at the civil trial that all of the subject photographs were genuine and had not been doctored.[55]

Groden's career as a two-thousand-dollar-a-day expert witness in the Simpson case[56] may have been, like Simpson's legs allegedly were in the photographs, cut off at the knees.

While Oswald's ownership and possession of the Mannlicher-Carcano is established beyond doubt, the question of whether Oswald was in continuous possession of it (the only rifle there is any evidence Oswald ever possessed) from the moment he received it in the mail until it reached the sixth floor on the day of the assassination is more difficult to determine, although *all* of the evidence points to that conclusion.

Marina recalled seeing the rifle in their house on Neely Street shortly after Oswald ordered it in early 1963. She also saw him cleaning it on a number of occasions.[57] She noticed it again immediately after they moved to New Orleans. As we have seen, they had a screen porch and Oswald, particularly after his arrest while distributing pro–Castro leaflets in the summer of 1963, during one period spent several nights a week working the bolt of the rifle and aiming the rifle.[58]

Ruth Paine told the Warren Commission that when Oswald loaded the family's household goods, clothing, and possessions—including the rifle—into her station wagon in New Orleans so Ruth could transport them, along with Marina and her baby, back to Ruth's home in Irving, Texas,[59] "he did virtually all the packing and all the loading of the things into the car. I simply thought that gentlemanly of him at the time. I have wondered since whether he wasn't doing it by preference to having me handle it."[60] Although Ruth never saw it, Marina knew that the rifle was among those possessions.[61]

Since Oswald did not accompany the women back to Texas, and left for Mexico instead, many of the family's belongings were stored in Ruth's garage without being unpacked, including, undoubtedly, the rifle wrapped in a green and brown blanket. About a week after arriving in Irving, less than two months before the assassination, Marina saw the bundle on the floor in the garage and lifted a corner of the blanket enough to recognize the rifle's wooden stock.[62] So Marina, though unknowledgeable about rifles, had seen her husband's rifle many times and knew what it looked like. When she was shown the rifle found on the sixth floor by Warren Commission counsel, she not only identified it as being her husband's rifle, but even identified the telescopic sight as being the one he had on the rifle.[63]

Both of the Paines recalled seeing the bundle on the garage floor from time to time, though neither realized that it might contain a rifle. Michael Paine had moved the bundle several times while working in the garage, but never opened the bundle to see what it contained.[64]

As we know, on the afternoon of the assassination, Marina led several police officers into Ruth Paine's garage, where they found the bundled blanket, looking very much as though the disassembled rifle was still in it, but the bundle went limp when they picked it up. It was empty.[65]

While the evidence does not prove conclusively that the rifle was continuously in Oswald's possession or in Ruth Paine's garage from late in March when he received it to November 22, 1963, that is the most reasonable assumption and there is no evidence to suggest that it was anywhere else.

More to the point is how it came to be on the sixth floor of the Texas School Book Depository. As we saw earlier in the text, from the time he returned to Dallas from New Orleans, by way of Mexico City, in early October Oswald lived alone in the Oak Cliff section of Dallas, while his wife continued to stay with Ruth Paine in Irving, fifteen miles away.[66] Summarizing what is set forth in the "Four Days in November" section of this book, beginning in mid-October when he found a job at the Texas School Book Depository, Oswald spent most weekends at Ruth Paine's house, invariably riding out from work on Friday evening and returning to work on Monday morning with coworker Wesley Frazier, Paine's neighbor.[67] But on the week of the assassination, for the very first time he came out to Irving on a Thursday evening, the night before the president's motorcade was scheduled to pass beneath the windows of the Texas School Book Depository.[68]* That morning Oswald asked Frazier for a ride out to Irving after work. Frazier wondered why Oswald was going there on a Thursday evening rather than the more customary Friday, and Oswald told him he was going home to get some curtain rods "to put in an apartment."[69] Frazier's sister, Linnie Mae Randle, with whom Frazier was living, also noticed the oddity of Oswald's midweek trip home, and Frazier mentioned the curtain rods to her as well.[70]

On the morning of the assassination Frazier's sister saw Oswald arrive for the ride back to work carrying a long brown paper package. Frazier saw it on the backseat of his car, asked about it, and was told that it was curtain rods. Later he watched Oswald walk into a back door of the Depository with the package under his arm.[71]

After the shooting, a bag, handmade from brown wrapping paper and three-inch-wide packing tape, was found folded on the floor directly east of three book cartons stacked at the sniper's nest window.[72] Since the bag appeared to have been custom-made to a size that conveniently fit the rifle when disassembled (the longest component of the rifle, when disassembled, is the wooden stock, which measures $34\,4/5$ inches,[73] while the homemade bag found on the sixth floor was 38 inches[74]),† there was a good presumption that it had been used for that purpose.[75]

FBI agent James C. Cadigan, a questioned-documents expert, testified that although he observed "some scratch marks and abrasions" inside the bag that were caused by "a hard object," he found "no marks on this bag that I could say were caused by [the Carcano] rifle or any other rifle or any other given instrument."[76] However, prints from Oswald's left index finger and right palm were found on the bag by the supervisor of the FBI's Latent Fingerprint Section, Sebastian F. Latona.[77] No other finger or palm prints were found on the bag.[78] These findings were reconfirmed fifteen years later by HSCA fingerprint expert Vincent J. Scalice.[79]

On the day of the assassination, samples of the wrapping paper and tape used in the Texas School Book Depository were forwarded to the FBI laboratory for fiber and spectrographic analysis. They were found to be in all respects identical to the materials used to construct the bag.[80] The packing tape even bore the impression of the knurled roller in the shipping room's tape dispenser.[81] The Commission pointed out that "the complete identity of characteristics between the paper and the tape in the bag found on the sixth floor and the paper and tape found in the shipping room of the Depository on November

---

*The only other time Oswald had come out to Irving on a day other than Friday was on Monday, October 21, but that was when he visited Marina in the hospital after the birth of their second child (3 H 40, WCT Ruth Hyde Paine).

†The overall length of the Carcano rifle, when fully assembled, is $40\,1/5$ inches (3 H 395, WCT Robert A. Frazier).

22 enabled the Commission to conclude that the bag was made from these materials."[82] Also, a "single brown, delustered, viscose fiber and several light-green cotton fibers found inside the bag . . . matched in all observable microscopic characteristics" fibers from the blanket in Ruth Paine's garage, where Oswald stored his Carcano. However, because there were so few fibers found inside the paper bag, and the blanket in the garage also consisted of other fibers (e.g., brown and green woolen fibers), the FBI crime lab was unable to make a positive match between the fibers found inside the bag and the blanket.[83]

Oswald's claim that he went out to Irving on Thursday to get some curtain rods turns out to be another of the many lies he told both before and after the assassination. His rented room on North Beckley was already fitted with curtains and rods, and his landlady testified that Oswald never discussed redecorating with her.[84] Nor did Oswald mention curtain rods to either Marina or Ruth Paine.[85] Mrs. Paine did in fact have two curtain rods in the garage among her stored household goods, but they were still there after the assassination.[86] Additionally, no curtain rods were ever discovered in the Texas School Book Depository Building.[87]

Starting with Oswald's journey out to Irving on Thursday night, an odd departure from his routine of going out only on the weekends, all of the evidence points toward his going there to retrieve his rifle from its place of storage in Ruth Paine's garage and carrying it to the Depository the next morning in a bag he constructed himself from materials evidently taken from his place of employment. The Warren Commission also gave weight to the fact that Oswald lied twice to Wesley Frazier, since he neither went to Irving for curtain rods nor returned with curtain rods the next morning.[88]*

Lee Harvey Oswald's ownership and possession of the rifle found on the sixth floor is further demonstrated by the fact that he physically handled it, as evidenced by his right palm print being found on it. Like everything else in the case against Oswald, though, this palm print was to become embroiled in controversy. And there were fingerprint problems too.

Shortly after the rifle was discovered, Lieutenant J. C. Day of the Dallas police crime lab pulled it carefully from its hiding spot, grabbing it by the wooden stock, which he

---

*Further evidence showing that Oswald was in physical possession of the Carcano is that a tuft of several cotton fibers of dark blue, gray-black, and orange-yellow shades were found in the crevice of the butt plate of the rifle, and the FBI laboratory found that the colors and even the twist of the fibers matched perfectly with the shirt Oswald was wearing at the time of his arrest, the same shirt the Warren Commission believed he was wearing when he was on the sixth floor in the sniper's nest.

The FBI expert testified that the fibers "were clean, they had good color to them, there was no grease on them and they were not fragmented," causing him to conclude they "had just been picked up . . . in the recent past," although at another point he couldn't categorically say they had not been there for a long time. However, the Warren Commission noted that "the fact that on the morning of the assassination Oswald was wearing the shirt from which these relatively fresh fibers most probably originated provides some evidence that they transferred to the rifle *that day* since there was limited, if any, opportunity for Oswald to handle the weapon during the two months prior to November 22." (WR, pp.124–125; 4 H 82–87, WCT Paul Morgan Stombaugh; CE 673, 17 H 330; CE 674, 17 H 331) Indeed, when Marina was first asked whether she knew what shirt her husband was wearing on the morning of the assassination, she answered, "I don't remember." But when she was shown Commission Exhibit No. 150, the shirt he was wearing at the time of his arrest, and was asked if she recalled him wearing it on the morning of November 22, she answered, "Yes, it was a dark shirt" (which Commission Exhibit No. 150 is). Question: "You think that was the one?" Answer: "Yes." (1 H 121, WCT Marina N. Oswald) In any event, the tufts of fibers certainly are further substantive evidence that Oswald was at least in possession of the Carcano at some point, as opposed to merely owning it.

had determined was too rough to hold fingerprints. After examining the polished surface
of the bolt knob with a magnifying glass and determining that it contained no prints, Day
allowed homicide captain Will Fritz to grab the bolt knob and pull it, ejecting a live round
from the firing chamber. Day then turned his attention to the trigger housing, dusting
the metal surface with a fine, black fingerprint powder. He quickly noticed traces of three
fingerprints on the left side of the trigger housing, two of which showed ridge patterns.
He turned to Captain Fritz and told him he wanted to take the rifle to the crime lab, where
he had the proper equipment to develop the fingerprint traces.[89]

Lieutenant Day carried the rifle from the building around 2:00 p.m. and took it to the
fourth-floor crime lab in the Identification Bureau at police headquarters, where he locked
it in an evidence box until later that evening. Day returned to the Depository and supervised the taking of fifty photographs of the southeast corner of the sixth floor, the dusting of the boxes in the sniper's nest for fingerprints, and the drawing of a scale map of
the sixth-floor crime scene.[90]

Returning to the crime lab about 7:00 p.m., Day began examining the fingerprint traces
he had seen on the trigger housing earlier that afternoon. Despite the fingerprint powder adhering to them, the traces were still unclear. Day decided to photograph them rather
than try to lift them with an adhesive material similar to Scotch tape, since the latter actually removes some of the oil, dust, and fingerprint powder making up the visible print.[91]
Day later testified that because the prints were only "traces" and "unclear," he "could
not positively identify them." However, Day added he "thought" the fingerprints
"appeared to be the right middle and right ring finger" of Lee Harvey Oswald.[92] (Day,
long since retired, told me that "the general pattern of the two prints were the same as
Oswald's but the ridges just were not clear enough for me to say they were his.")[93]

Day then began dusting the rest of the rifle and noticed a print on the bottom of the
barrel, partially covered by the wooden stock. Taking the stock off, it looked to him like
a palm print, and he could tell by the way the powder was sticking to the print that it had
been there quite a while. Day placed a strip of two-inch cellophane tape over the print,
then peeled the tape off, lifting "a faint palm print" off the barrel. He made a quick comparison between the palm print lifted from the rifle and Oswald's palm prints taken earlier in Captain Fritz's office[94] and tentatively identified the palm print on the rifle as
Oswald's, but he wanted to do some more work before declaring that he had a positive
match. He did, however, tell both Captain Fritz and Chief Curry that night that he had
a tentative match.[95]

After doing the lift, Day was about to photograph what remained of the palm print on
the barrel when he was interrupted by crime-lab captain George M. Doughty, who
instructed him to stop working on the rifle and prepare to release it to the FBI. Arrangements had been made for FBI agent Vince Drain to fly the rifle and other pieces of important evidence to the FBI laboratory in Washington, D.C., that night.[96]*

At 11:45 p.m., the rifle and film negatives of the prints were turned over to the FBI's

---

*It's no secret that the Dallas police were put off by the intrusion of federal law enforcement and the fed-
eral request to turn over all of the physical evidence to the FBI for analysis. The implication, of course, was
that the federal government thought the Dallas police were not equipped to resolve the basic facts of the assassination, or worse, were incompetent. Early in the afternoon of the assassination, Dallas crime-lab detective
W. E. "Pete" Barnes said he was approached by a Secret Service agent who wanted Barnes to turn the rifle
over to him "to make sure we didn't mess up the prints on it." Barnes told him, "Pardner, I'll bet I've dusted

Vince Drain. In a 1984 interview, Day said that he pointed out to the FBI man the area where the palm print was, adding that he "cautioned Drain to be sure the area was not disturbed."[97] Though Drain denied that Day showed him the palm print,[98] crime-lab detective R. W. "Rusty" Livingston, who was standing nearby, recalled that another FBI agent was there pressuring Drain to leave. "Drain was half listening to Lieutenant Day and half to the other FBI man and evidently didn't get the word about the palm print at that time."[99] (The FBI agents were in a hurry to catch a C-135 jet tanker, its crew waiting on the runway at Carswell Air Force Base in Fort Worth to fly the evidence to Washington.)[100] Also, Day told me that technically he didn't "show" Drain where the print was because "you couldn't see it. It was under the stock. But I told him where it was."[101]

The morning after the assassination (November 23), FBI fingerprint expert Sebastian Latona examined the rifle in Washington. His attention was first drawn to the cellophane used to protect the surface of the trigger housing. Removing the cellophane, he could see "faint ridge formations." Latona testified before the Warren Commission that he then took a look at the three film negatives of the trigger housing that Day had enclosed, but he didn't think the photographs were of any help in clarifying the ridge formations. Latona had an experienced photographer rephotograph the trigger housing in hopes of improving the condition of the fingerprint traces, but the effort was unsuccessful. Although Latona could see that the pattern formations were consistent with those on Oswald's hands, they were "insufficient" to make a definitive determination. The lack of detail forced Latona to conclude that the fingerprint "fragments" were of "no value" in determining with certainty who had handled the rifle.[102]

Latona then proceeded to dust the entire rifle for prints, including the clip, the bolt, and the underside of the barrel, where, according to Lieutenant Day, traces of the palm print he had lifted remained. Despite a careful examination, Latona was unable to find any identifiable print.[103] The rifle was returned from Washington, by the FBI's Drain, to the Dallas police on Sunday morning, November 24, around the same time Oswald was being rushed to Parkland Hospital after having being fatally shot by Jack Ruby. Lieutenant Day told me the FBI put the Carcano in a box in his office "and I was instructed not to do anything with it. The FBI had pretty well taken over the case."[104] Five days later, on November 29, the card containing the palm print that Day had lifted on the night of November 22, along with the notation "off underside of gun barrel near end of foregrip C 2766"—the serial number of Oswald's Mannlicher-Carcano— reached the FBI crime lab.[105]

Though he had been unable to see or lift any palm print of Oswald's on his own at the FBI crime lab on November 23, Latona told the Warren Commission that when he received Day's actual lift card on November 29, "the palm print which appears on the lift was identified by me as the right palm print of Lee Harvey Oswald."[106]

Lee Harvey Oswald, if he had lived, was now precluded from making the argument that even if the *ownership* of the Carcano was linked to him, he had never been in *posses-*

---

more fingerprint powder than you've ever seen in your lifetime." (Savage, *JFK First Day Evidence*, pp.80–81) Later in the evening, and before Day received instructions from Captain Doughty, Secret Service agent Forrest Sorrels approached Day and warned him, "The FBI is trying to get that gun." Day told him it was fine with him if they wanted to work on it. Yet the request must have been a blow to the twenty-three-year veteran crime-lab lieutenant who had amassed fifteen years of experience reading fingerprints for the Dallas Police Department's Identification Bureau. (4 H 249–250, WCT J. C. Day)

sion of the weapon. This is so because fingerprint and palm print evidence is conclusive. There has been no reported case of two people having the same finger or palm prints. Desperate attempts by criminals to destroy or alter their fingerprints, for instance, by burning or filing the skin, have proved unsuccessful. The original patterns reappear with the healing of the epidermis (outer layer of skin), the most famous FBI case like this being of fugitive Roscoe Pitts. Only skin grafts have worked.[107]*

Lieutenant Day, in looking back on the event, told me, "I don't fault the FBI for not being able to find the palm print. It was already faint when I lifted it, and it's even more difficult to lift the same print a second time because some of the detail has been removed from the first lifting of the print."[108]

For the great numbers of conspiracy theorists who maintain that the Carcano did not belong to Oswald and was planted on the sixth floor, how do they then explain Oswald's right palm print being found on the weapon? How did it get there if he wasn't in possession of it?

Predictably, many conspiracy authors have drawn sinister implications from these events, strongly suggesting that the Dallas police had framed Oswald by fabricating the palm print and its connection to the Oswald rifle after the FBI's expert fingerprint examiner was unable to find any identifiable prints on the rifle.[109] Apart from the absurd notion that for some reason Lieutenant Day would decide to frame Lee Harvey Oswald for Kennedy's assassination, as he told me in 2002, "I don't even think such a thing [transferring Oswald's prints on the finger and palm print samples, or exemplars, he gave to the Dallas Police Department, onto the Mannlicher-Carcano rifle] could be done. In this day and age they might be able to figure out some way to transfer the ink print on the card to the weapon, but I wouldn't know how to do it myself. Sounds like an impossible task to me."[110]

Conspiracy author Mark Lane also alleged that an investigation by the Warren Com-

---

*Fingerprint analysis in this country dates back to 1903 in New York. The FBI "went into the fingerprint business in 1924." The French (with its famous Bertillon system), British, and Argentinians were into fingerprint analysis as early as the 1880s, and the first article believed to have been published on establishing identity by fingerprints was written by a Scottish doctor in 1880 and titled, "On the Skin-Furrows of the Hand." (Moenssens and Inbau, *Scientific Evidence in Criminal Cases*, pp.350–351; 1903 and 1924 dates: 4 H 14–15, WCT Sebastian F. Latona)

Latent fingerprints (as opposed to a fingerprint *exemplar*, which is the model for comparison taken in ink at the police station) is the technical term for fingerprints left on everyday objects. These prints are transmitted to the surfaces of objects by a residue of oil secreted from the body, and are eventually "lifted" from the objects by fingerprint specialists. Contrary to popular belief, the perspiration from one's fingers and palms contains no such oily substance. The fingers and palms acquire that residue of oil when they come into contact with parts of the body that do have such secretions, such as the hair and face. Fingerprints are more popularly known than palm prints, most likely because people generally touch objects with their fingers rather than their palms.

Most American law enforcement agencies consider ten "points of similarity" (between the latent prints and those on the exemplar) enough for a fingerprint expert to give an unqualified conclusion. In Europe, the minimum requirements are usually higher, going all the way up to sixteen at Scotland Yard. The FBI has never accepted the minimum-requirement doctrine, and the FBI expert in the Kennedy case, Sebastian F. Latona, told the Warren Commission he has given an opinion in court as to identity with as few as seven points of similarity. Arthur Mandella, a fingerprint expert for the New York Police Department who also compared the latent prints in the Kennedy assassination with Oswald's exemplar, also said that no given minimum number of points of similarity is necessary for a conclusion. "A sufficient amount determined by the expert is the important factor," he said, though he added that the usual range for him has been between eight and twelve. (4 H 13–14, WCT Sebastian F. Latona; 4 H 53, WCT Arthur Mandella; WR, p.563)

The FBI found twelve points of similarity between Oswald's right-palm-print exemplar and the latent palm print found "off underside gun barrel near end of foregrip" (CE 640, 17 H 292).

mission of this issue raised more questions than it answered.[111] In the finest traditions of the conspiracy theorists' profession, Lane neglected to tell his readers that the central question of whether the palm print originated from the rifle *was* answered, *conclusively*, by that very inquiry. Warren Commission assistant counsel Wesley Liebeler told the HSCA that in "late August or September" of 1964, he suggested questioning Day further in an attempt to resolve the multitude of questions that remained surrounding the discovery of the palm print. It had occurred to Liebeler and a few other assistant counsels, as it would later to Mark Lane, that perhaps the palm print didn't come from the rifle at all. The Commission, at that time, only had Day's word for it. It wanted something stronger. But when Liebeler approached Chief Counsel J. Lee Rankin about it, he objected. "Mr. Rankin was not terribly enthusiastic about having a couple of Commission lawyers go down to Dallas and start questioning the Dallas Police Department," Liebeler told the HSCA in 1978. "Quite frankly . . . it would have raised all kinds of questions at that time as to what in the hell was going on, what are we doing going down and taking depositions from the Dallas Police Department two months *after* the report was supposed to be out?"[112]

But Liebler said they realized the problem could be resolved "in another way." Several Commission assistant counsels subsequently met with FBI inspector James R. Malley, the bureau's liaison with the Commission, and FBI fingerprint expert Sebastian Latona. Liebeler asked Latona whether there was a way to prove that the lift came from the rifle. Latona reexamined the lift submitted by Lieutenant Day and noticed pits, marks, and rust spots on it that corresponded to *identical areas on the underside of the rifle barrel*—the very spot from which Day said the print had been lifted.[113] J. Edgar Hoover sent a letter by courier to the Commission on September 4 to confirm this finding, along with a photograph showing the corresponding marks on the barrel and the lift.[114] Liebeler was satisfied. Now, there was *no doubt whatsoever*—the palm print Day had lifted had come from Oswald's rifle.[115]

Lost amid all of the controversy and politics swirling around the palm print lift are the fingerprint traces that Day had first discovered on the trigger housing. Dallas police crime-lab detective Rusty Livingston was with Lieutenant Day during the evening of the assassination and managed to squirrel away a set of first-generation photographic prints from five negatives Day had taken of the Carcano's trigger housing. Photographic prints from three of the five negatives were never seen by the Warren Commission or the HSCA. In 1991, Livingston turned the five photographs over to his nephew, Gary Savage, who in turn asked Captain Jerry Powdrill, a fingerprint expert from Savage's hometown of West Monroe, Louisiana, to compare fingerprint traces on the Mannlicher-Carcano's trigger housing, as seen in the photographs, with a known fingerprint exemplar of Oswald's. Powdrill only found three matching "points of identity" (in earlier years, the term was *points of similarity* and my sense is that the earlier term was more accurate) and said he was unable to conclude that the latent prints in the photographs belonged to Oswald, adding, however, that there were "enough similarities to suggest" that they possibly did.[116]

In 1993, Savage turned the photographs over to *Frontline* for its thirtieth-anniversary special on the assassination. *Frontline* asked Vincent J. Scalice, the leading fingerprint expert for the New York City Police Department who had also been the HSCA's fingerprint expert, to compare the latent prints in Livingston's photographs with fingerprint exemplars of Oswald's. Scalice had already examined two of the five Dallas police photos depicting the latent fingerprints on the trigger guard for the HSCA in 1978. At that time, he agreed with the FBI and Warren Commission that the photographs of the latent prints were not clear enough to make an identification.[117] After examining all five photographs for the first time in 1993 for *Frontline*, he said, "I found that by maneuvering the photographs in different positions, I was able to pick up some details [of the fingerprints] on one photograph and some details on another photograph. Using all of the photographs at different contrasts, I was able to find in the neighborhood of about 18 points of identity . . . These are definitely the fingerprints of Lee Harvey Oswald and . . . they are on the rifle. There is no doubt about it."[118]

Scalice told the press that had he seen all of the photographs in 1978 (not just two of them), "I would have been able to make an identification at that point in time." After consulting with Scalice, Captain Jerry Powdrill also agreed with Scalice's judgment—that the fingerprints on the trigger guard were those of Oswald.[119]

So, in addition to Oswald's palm print being found on the underside of the Carcano's barrel, we know that Oswald's fingerprints were found within an inch of the trigger of the rifle found on the sixth floor of the Texas School Book Depository Building. The evidence is clear and unimpeachable—Lee Harvey Oswald bought, owned, and handled the Mannlicher-Carcano rifle found on the sixth floor. And as you're about to see, it was *this* weapon that was used to murder John F. Kennedy.

Identification of the Murder Weapon

In addition to the unfired cartridge found in the chamber of Oswald's Mannlicher-Carcano, you will recall that police also found three 6.5-millimeter cartridge cases[1]—or casings, shells, or "hulls," as the Dallas police frequently called them—scattered on the floor of the sniper's nest in the southeast corner of the sixth floor of the Texas School Book Depository Building. Two of the empty shells were lying directly under the sniper's window, about six inches apart and a foot or so west of the two book cartons that had been used as a gun rest. The other shell was another yard farther west, lying about sixteen inches back from the window.[2] (See photo section.) Two firearms experts, Robert A. Frazier of the FBI's Washington laboratory, and Joseph D. Nicol, superintendent of the Bureau of Criminal Identification and Investigation for the state of Illinois, examined these spent shells for the Warren Commission.[3] By comparing the individual microscopic marks and impressions that the bolt (or breech) face and firing pin of the rifle left on the head (base) of the expended cartridge cases with those on the cases of cartridges test-fired in Oswald's rifle, both experts concluded that all three cartridge cases found on the sixth floor had been fired in Oswald's Mannlicher-Carcano to the exclusion of all other weapons in the world.[4] Fifteen years later, the firearms panel of the HSCA reached an identical conclusion.[5]

In their bid to exonerate Oswald, critics have attacked these rock-solid conclusions by suggesting that the three cartridge cases were neatly planted to frame the hapless ex-marine. The suggestion that there might have been hanky-panky with the three hulls arose during a 1968 interview with former Dallas deputy sheriff Roger Craig,* who told the *Los Angeles Free Press*, "The shells found on the floor in front of the window—I saw 'em—they were laying, all the shells were facing the same direction—there was not one of them more than ¾ of an inch apart, and I've fired many a bolt action rifle and I have never had two shells land in the same place."[6] Craig embellished the tale further in his unpublished 1971 man-

---

*Craig also claimed to have been present during an Oswald interrogation, though he was not. See later text.

uscript, "When They Kill a President": "Luke Mooney and I reached the southeast corner at the same time. We *immediately* found three rifle cartridges [actually, cartridge cases] laying in such a way that they looked as though they had been carefully and deliberately placed there—in plain sight on the floor to the right of the southeast corner window. Mooney and I examined the cartridges very carefully and remarked how close together they were. The three of them were no more than one inch apart[*] and all were facing the same direction, a feat very difficult to achieve with a bolt action rifle—or any rifle for that matter."[7]

Roger Craig's embellishments could have easily been exposed early on had anyone bothered to look at his sworn testimony to the Warren Commission in 1964. When asked whether he saw the cartridge cases at the time they were found, Craig said that he was at the far north end of the building when someone yelled across the room, "Here's the shells!"[8] Craig said that after "a couple of minutes" he went over to the sniper's nest and saw three shells lying about a foot away from the window. Craig said that he didn't get "too close" and went back to where he was because he didn't want to bother the area.[9] Asked if he recalled any of the shells being up against the wall, Craig replied, "No, I don't. I didn't look that close."[10] So much for Craig's immediate discovery and careful examination of the shells. It should be added that when the FBI conducted tests to see where shells ejected from the Carcano at the window would land, the test landings were found to be "consistent" with where the three shells were found after the assassination, all at right angles from the ejection port on the rifle and all ricocheting in a random pattern within a forty-seven-inch circle.[11] And Luke Mooney, the Dallas deputy sheriff who first discovered the shells, said they "appeared as though they had been ejected from the rifle and had possibly bounced off the cartons of the books to the rear."[12]

It should be noted that the three empty shells found in the sniper's nest don't necessarily prove that three shots were fired from that location, even though common sense dictates that this must be the case. Science can only prove that the three cartridge cases were fired in and ejected from Oswald's rifle at some point prior to their discovery. It does, however, support and is consistent with all the other evidence—including earwitnesses—that three shots were indeed fired from the Book Depository.

The principal evidence connecting the bullets that struck Kennedy with Oswald's rifle, and therefore establishing the identity of the assassin, are two bullet fragments that were found in the presidential limousine on the night of the assassination.[†] As anyone who has ever watched an episode of a TV detective show knows, guns fire bullets that can be matched to the weapons that fired them. Gun barrels, even those manufactured in the same factory on the same day and drilled by the same machine—even two successive barrels—have unique markings, called striations, that distinguish one barrel from the other, the individual markings being different. That's because the drilling and cutting tools used in the manufacturing process leave behind a microscopically rough surface that is unique to each barrel and that engraves its imprint on all bullets subsequently fired through the barrel. As time goes by, normal wear and tear, cleaning, and corrosion add

---

[*]By 1975, the space between the shells had grown from one inch to "no more than two inches" (Letter, Roger Craig to Ed Tatro, April 9, 1975, p.2). A year later, conspiracy authors J. Gary Shaw and Larry Ray Harris tacked on an additional inch to the spread—"about three inches apart" (Shaw with Harris, *Cover-Up*, p.28).

[†]A third set of lead fragments (CE 840), found under the left jump seat occupied by Mrs. Connally, were too small to connect to Oswald's rifle. They were, however, linked to the shooting through neutron activation analysis. (See later text.)

even more points of unique detail to the gun barrel, which are also engraved onto the surface of subsequently fired bullets. All of these markings compose the "signature" or fingerprint of the gun and can be used by firearms experts to determine whether bullet or bullet fragments recovered at a crime scene were fired in a particular weapon to the exclusion of all other weapons in the world.[13]

In addition to the striations on the inner surface of the barrel (known in firearms identification parlance as "microscopic [or individual] characteristics"), weapons also have "rifling [or "general" or "class"] characteristics," which, although not unique to each weapon, can, together with the diameter of the bore, aid a firearms identification expert in determining whether a bullet was fired from a particular gun. "Rifling" is the manufacturing process by which spiral grooves are cut into the inner surface of the barrel of a gun from end to end. The raised portions of the surface remaining from the process (the ridges between the grooves) are called lands. The purpose of the grooves is to impart to the bullet passing through the barrel a rotating or spinning motion that, like a tossed football as it passes through space, gives it stability and keeps it true to its intended course. The number of lands and grooves, which are imprinted on the bullet as it passes through the barrel, and the direction (left or right) of the spin or twist, are additional characteristics that help to identify a gun as the murder weapon. The science of firearms identification* is precise, exacting, and conclusive.

One of the two large fragments recovered from the front seating compartment of the president's limousine (on the driver's seat just to the right of the driver) and designated by the Warren Commission as Commission Exhibit No. 567, consisted of a piece of the copper metal jacket of a bullet with part of its lead core still attached to it. It weighed 44.6 grains (a tenth of an ounce), less than a third of the weight of an intact 6.5-millimeter Mannlicher-Carcano bullet. FBI firearms expert Robert A. Frazier, who examined the fragment at the bureau's Washington lab on the morning of November 23, and independent expert Joseph D. Nicol, superintendent of the Bureau of Criminal Identification and Investigation for the state of Illinois, found that the sides of the bullet fragment contained sufficiently distinctive barrel markings for the firearms experts to compare them, under a comparison microscope (two separate microscopes mounted side by side), with the markings on bullets test-fired from Oswald's Carcano. The experts identified the bullet fragment as having been fired in Oswald's rifle to the exclusion of all other weapons.[14] In 1978, a panel of five firearms experts from the HSCA came to the same conclusion.[15]

The second fragment, found on the floor to the right side of the driver's seat in the president's limousine and designated by the Commission as Commission Exhibit No. 569, weighed less than half as much as the first, 21 grains (about an eighth of a whole bullet), and came from the base of a bullet. This was evident because the cannelure, a groove that rings a bullet near its base, was clearly visible. The fragment consisted entirely of the metal jacket, with no part of the lead core remaining. In spite of the heavy mutilation caused by the bullet striking a hard object, about a third of the surface area was sufficiently intact to show, under a comparison microscope, markings identical to those of test bullets fired from

---

*In the common vernacular, and in books, television shows, and movies, a firearms identification test for a suspect weapon is almost always erroneously referred to as a "ballistics test." But in the real world, very few criminal cases involve ballistics, which is a highly specialized branch of firearms identification dealing with the *motion* of a fired bullet through the barrel of a gun (interior ballistics), its movement and trajectory once it leaves the muzzle to its point of impact (exterior ballistics), and its movement after impact (terminal or wound ballistics). In the Kennedy case, of course, the issues of the trajectory of the bullets fired and their movement after impact *do* have enormous significance. But an expert in ballistics may be untrained in (and hence incapable of) identifying, from the striations (markings) on the surface of a bullet, whether it was fired from a particular gun.

the Mannlicher-Carcano—again, to the exclusion of all other weapons.[16] The HSCA firearms panel came to the same conclusion.[17]

So we know that Oswald's Carcano was the weapon that murdered the president.

The experts were unable to determine whether the two fragments (Commission Exhibit Nos. 567 and 569) were parts of one bullet or came from two separate bullets, since they did not fit together, nor was the combined weight of the two fragments more than a whole bullet (which would have indicated two bullets).[18]

There has been very little controversy about the identification of these bullet fragments, but the same can hardly be said for the nearly intact bullet found on a stretcher at Parkland Hospital on the afternoon of the assassination, designated as Warren Commission Exhibit No. 399, the notorious "magic" bullet. After a comparison, by microscope, with markings on test bullets fired from Oswald's rifle, FBI firearms expert Robert Frazier (and later, independent expert Joseph Nicol) concluded that the bullet[*] had been fired from Oswald's rifle to the exclusion of all other weapons in the world.[19] The HSCA firearms panel came to the same conclusion.[20] The Warren Commission would eventually decree the bullet to be the cornerstone of its single-bullet theory, concluding not only that it had been fired from Oswald's rifle, but that it had passed through the president's body and caused all the wounds to Governor Connally—shattering one of his ribs, breaking a right wrist bone, and puncturing his left thigh.[21]

Ever since the release of the Warren Report, critics have had a field day with Commission Exhibit No. 399, dubbed the "pristine bullet" or "magic bullet" in assassination literature largely because it remained substantially intact after passing, as the Warren Commission maintained, through Kennedy's and Connally's bodies.

Though it has become an accepted part of the lore of the assassination that the stretcher bullet was pristine (defined as something in "its original condition"), that is, completely undamaged, remarkably, the only authority for this statement is one single photograph of the bullet published in the Warren Commission Hearings and Exhibits.[22] Yet, it is almost impossible to see how damaged the bullet really is from this single-view photograph that does not show the base of the bullet. That left the critics free to burn the image of a pristine bullet into the consciousness of America without fear of their lie being exposed by accurate photographs. In 1978, the public got its first good look at the so-called pristine bullet during the televised hearings of the HSCA. Later published as part of the committee's exhibits, the HSCA photographs depict the bullet from four views (not just one)—two sides, one frontal, and one base.[23] The base view (see photo section) shows the base of the bullet badly smashed into an ovoid shape.[†] It is also evident that lead is slightly extruding from the base, like toothpaste from a tube.[‡] Indeed, a portion

---

[*]The FBI laboratory "determined that the bullets used in the assassination of President Kennedy on November 22, 1963, were a military type manufactured by the Western Cartridge Company, East Alton, Illinois" (CD 107, p.2, January 13, 1964; 3 H 399, WCT Robert A. Frazier). The cartridges, which include the cases enclosing the bullets, were also manufactured by the same company, and were, as previously indicated, 6.5-millimeter Mannlicher-Carcano cartridges (3 H 399, WCT Robert A. Frazier).

[†]Also, though no photograph of the bullet from the National Archives reflects it, visual inspection reveals it is "somewhat flattened in its lower half" (DOJCD Record 186-10006-10449, June 3, 1996, p.4). And my firearms expert at the London trial, Monty Lutz, who was also a member of the HSCA firearms panel, saw the bullet close up at the National Archives and testified at the London trial that "there was a slight curving to that bullet" (Transcript of *On Trial*, July 24, 1986, p.444).

[‡]The HSCA's wound ballistics expert, Larry Sturdivan, told the committee that extrusion of lead from the base is the first thing that happens when a bullet begins to deform. Under great pressure, the metal jacket begins to peel off and "the softer lead core is extruded through the only opening, that is, the opening in the base." (1 HSCA 411–412)

of the lead is missing, causing the bullet to weigh less, 158.6 grains, than in its original state, 161 grains.[24] So much for the pristine bullet. But the myth has long survived the public hearings (which few watched) right up to the present day.

Dr. Michael Baden, the medical examiner who headed the forensic pathology panel for the HSCA, scoffed at the notion that the bullet was pristine, labeling it an inaccurate media description. "It is like being a little bit pregnant—it is either pristine or it is not pristine," he told the committee. "This is a damaged bullet . . . not a pristine bullet. This is a bullet that is deformed. It would be very hard to take a hammer and flatten it to the degree that this is flattened."[25]

He went on to explain that the bullet, in its course through the president and the governor, "did not strike much that would cause it to be damaged." It passed through soft tissue on its course through the president's body. The first hard structure it hit was the governor's fifth rib, but it was a glancing blow to what Dr. Baden called "a very thin bone." The only impact likely to have caused damage of any significance to the bullet was on the lower part of the forearm. His panel of experts felt that striking the radius there probably caused some flattening of the bullet, but they were not particularly surprised that the bullet was not more deformed. The radius in the wrist, unlike the bones of the skull or spine, is not very hard—it could damage some bullets but not others.[26]

At the trial in London, Dr. Charles Petty, chief medical examiner for Dallas County and a member of the HSCA forensic pathology panel, gave even stronger testimony. With a photo of the stretcher bullet on the screen, I asked, "Could this bullet have ended up in this *relatively* pristine condition if it had entered the president's back, exited his throat, then entered Governor Connally's back . . . and taken the path through Governor Connally's body you have just described?"

Dr. Petty: "Yes, of course."

"Would you explain to the jury how you arrived at this conclusion?"

"This bullet is a full, metal-jacketed military [type] bullet, designed to pass through [i.e., without fragmenting] the soft tissue of an individual, exactly as it did in President Kennedy's instance. It then contacted bone only in two areas. First, the rib in Connally, and second the wrist bone in Connally. In neither instance did it penetrate the rib or the wrist bone." He went on to add that the bullet could "easily" have traveled the course it did "without [sustaining] great deformity. I've seen that many times."

Question: "You have seen a bullet causing the damage that was caused to the president's body and Governor Connally's body and not having any more damage than that bullet on the screen, is that correct?"

"Yes, of course." Petty added that no metal fragments were found in Governor Connally's chest, further evidence that the bullet had only struck a glancing blow to the governor's fifth rib.[27]

The first metal fragments found along the supposed path of the bullet were discovered in the governor's wrist, and, in Petty's opinion, this was the place where the bullet became deformed.[28]

Among the experiments carried out for the Warren Commission was one in which a test bullet was fired into the wrist bone of a human cadaver, the result being that the nose of the bullet was damaged more than the base of the bullet that hit Connally's fifth rib and wrist bone,[29] as Commission critics like Mark Lane[30] and Dr. Cyril Wecht[31] are fond of pointing out. The problem is that shooting a bullet at full muzzle velocity directly into a wrist sheds little light on what might happen to a bullet striking a wrist at a little over half its original velocity. Dr. John Lattimer, who himself conducted tests with the Carcano bullet, told author Gerald Posner that "the Warren Commission did not conduct the proper experiments. They fired a 6.5 mm [bullet] traveling at over 2,000 feet per second *directly* into a wrist bone. Of course you are going to get deformation of the bullet when it strikes a hard object at *full* speed."[32]

The HSCA's physical scientist and wound ballistics expert, Larry Sturdivan, who took part in the Warren Commission tests conducted by the Army's Wound Ballistics Branch at the Edgewood Arsenal laboratories in Maryland in April and May of 1964, pointed out to the committee that the relatively intact state of Commission Exhibit No. 399 was "direct proof that the bullet that struck Governor Connally's wrist was not at high velocity." If it had been, he said, it would have been more deformed than it was.[33*]

Sturdivan explained how the bullet that hit the wrist would have lost velocity and energy as it was successively slowed in its flight. He said the original velocity at the muzzle varied from 2,000 to 2,200 feet per second. In the distance it traveled before striking the president, it would have slowed to about 1,800 feet per second—fast enough to traverse the soft tissue of the body, with very little loss of velocity. By the time the tumbling bullet (the tumbling accounting for almost all the damage being to its base) struck the governor, it would have been traveling, he said, at about "1,700 feet per second or a little less." Sturdivan calculated that the loss of velocity of the bullet on its passage through the governor's chest (where it hit a rib) resulted in its exiting the governor's chest and striking his wrist bone at "somewhere between 1,100 and 1,300 feet per second." That was sufficiently fast to break the bone (any velocity above 700 feet per second would do that), but not fast enough to shatter the bullet. Sturdivan also reckoned that the bullet in this case would have been slowed to about 700 feet per second or less by the time it struck the governor's thigh, too slow to penetrate very deeply.[34†] Sturdivan concluded that a bullet like Commission Exhibit No. 399 was "quite capable" of passing through Kennedy's and Connally's bodies, striking the tissue and bone that it did, and end up in the same condition that Commission Exhibit No. 399 is presently in.[35]

There is a frequently overlooked reason (briefly alluded to earlier) why the stretcher bullet did not have more damage than it did. It was a military-type bullet, the very type

---

[*]Unlike other areas (like firearms and ballistics) where the HSCA conducted its own tests, the committee elected not to undertake further tests to determine if the stretcher bullet could have caused the wounds it did and end up in the condition it did. It did consider doing so, contacting the H. P. White Laboratory in Bel Air, Maryland, but was told that the "number of shots required to produce the chance result of Commission Exhibit 399 could range from one up to infinity." And the first series of tests alone would cost $20,000, a lot for the austere budget of the HSCA. Because the number of shots fired to obtain a match or "statistical sample" could not be "reasonably determined," plus the expense and the further realization that the "results of tests with materials other than human bodies could always be theoretically questioned by those who would quarrel with [the] results," the HSCA decided to rely on the Warren Commission tests and Sturdivan's testimonial interpretation and elucidation of them. (1 HSCA 382–383)

[†]In Sturdivan's 2005 book, *The JFK Myths*, he elaborates on and refines his HSCA testimony, adding, from an evaluation of the damage to the bullet and the wounds to Kennedy and Connally, the orientation of the bullet at the various points along its path. Starting with a muzzle velocity of 2,160 feet per second, at impact on Kennedy's upper back it was traveling 2,015 feet per second, give or take 30 feet, and its orientation was nose first. At impact on Connally's back it had lost 175 feet per second in velocity and was traveling 1,830 feet per second, give or take 50 feet, and its orientation was 60 degrees. Upon striking Connally's right rib the bullet was traveling 1,450 feet per second, give or take 100 feet, and its orientation was sideways. At impact with Connally's right wrist it was traveling 500 feet per second, give or take 100 feet, and its orientation was nearly backward. At impact with Connally's left thigh, its velocity all but spent, it was traveling 135 feet per second, give or take 20 feet, and its orientation was backward. (Sturdivan, *JFK Myths*, p.144)

expected to cause great damage to what it strikes but minimum damage to the bullet itself (unless, of course, it hits the hardest of bone head-on). "There is nothing here that is unusual or spectacular or unexpected," Dr. Petty told the committee. "This is the behavior of a full *metal* jacketed bullet, a bullet covered in all areas except the base by means of the firm, hard, tough, not easy to deform jacket."[36]

The allegedly "mysterious" circumstances surrounding the discovery of Commission Exhibit No. 399 on a stretcher at Parkland Hospital gave rise to one of the main issues the conspiracy theorists have seized on in the Kennedy assassination—that the facts surrounding the bullet's discovery could only add up to one thing: the bullet was planted by the real conspirators who killed Kennedy to frame Oswald. But do they?

The movements and handling of President Kennedy's stretcher negates the possibility that the bullet could have originated from the president's stretcher. We know President Kennedy remained on his stretcher in Trauma Room One until the arrival of the casket at 1:40 p.m.[37] After his body was placed into the casket, the stretcher was stripped and wheeled across the hall into Trauma Room Two, where, by all accounts, it remained until after the presidential party left the hospital at 2:00 p.m.—roughly forty minutes after Darrell Tomlinson discovered the bullet in a completely different part of the emergency room area.[38] After ruling out the president's stretcher as the source of the bullet, the Warren Commission concluded that the bullet had come from the stretcher carrying Governor Connally.[39]

But conspiracy theorists maintain that the finding of the bullet on Connally's stretcher at Parkland Hospital, not in more normal places such as inside the presidential limousine, or somewhere in Dealey Plaza, somehow is too convenient and smacks of a planting of the bullet. And if it was planted, we're talking conspiracy. They point out that even if the stretcher bullet was conclusively proved to have been fired in Oswald's rifle, this does not, perforce, mean that it was fired in Dealey Plaza on the day of the assassination.

To buttress that which is already obvious (except to conspiracy theorists)—that the stretcher bullet was the bullet that struck Kennedy and Connally, and that the bullet fragments that were removed from Connally's right wrist must have come from this bullet— we turn to the HSCA and the passionate, dogged determination of two scientists, Drs. John Nichols and Vincent Guinn, who spent fourteen years in their quest to trace the source of the stretcher bullet.

On the day after the assassination, FBI special agent John F. Gallagher examined some of the bullet fragments recovered during the Kennedy assassination investigation using emission spectrography, a process in which a tiny part of a bullet fragment is burned and the resulting spectrum of light is analyzed to determine its elemental composition. The test was unable to determine more than the fact that the lead portion of all the fragments (which included those recovered from the limousine, the president's brain, and Connally's wrist) were "similar in metallic composition."[40] It could not distinguish how much of any given "trace element" (such as copper, silver, antimony, aluminum, manganese, sodium, and chlorine) was present in any fragment, nor, more importantly, which bullet each fragment had come from.[41]

In May 1964, Gallagher used a scientific technique—neutron activation analysis (NAA)—to more precisely identify the fragments. NAA had been around since the 1930s and by the early 1960s was a fairly common process in a number of industries (though not in firearms and ballistic examinations), but had never been used by the FBI.* Gallagher went down to the Oak Ridge National Laboratory in Tennessee, a major nuclear facility where scientists were working with NAA. Two of the Oak Ridge people showed him how to handle the equipment and calculate the results, and over the course of several days there they worked together, Gallagher making and recording his own measurements. Unfortunately, the men at the nuclear facility, who were highly conversant in NAA, had never performed any forensic work. Likewise, Gallagher, who was a highly qualified forensic expert, had never worked with NAA.[42]

On July 8, 1964, J. Edgar Hoover wrote to Warren Commission chief counsel J. Lee Rankin to inform him of the disappointing results of Gallagher's efforts. "While minor variations in composition were found by this method," Hoover wrote, "these were not considered sufficient to permit positively differentiating among the larger bullet fragments and thus positively determining from which of the larger bullet fragments any given small lead fragment may have come."[43]

There the matter rested. But when early critics learned that spectrographic tests had been performed (they were mentioned in the testimony of FBI firearms expert Robert Frazier), but the specific results were not reported by the Warren Commission, they speculated that the Commission may have suppressed the results because they disproved the single-bullet theory.[44] Unaware that NAA tests had also been performed, critics began screaming that the Commission didn't submit the fragments to the superior NAA tests because the FBI was afraid that the fragments in Connally's arm wouldn't match the stretcher bullet.[45]

Dr. Nichols, a pathologist at the University of Kansas Medical Center with an abiding interest in the assassination, tried for a number of years to convince FBI Director J. Edgar Hoover, and later his successor, Clarence Kelly, to release the bullet fragments for independent NAA tests. He also enlisted the aid of Dr. Vincent Guinn, a professor of chemistry at the University of California's Irvine campus and a twenty-year veteran of NAA, who agreed that such an examination might well produce new information about the assassination. Neither of them, however, were originally successful in convincing the FBI to release the fragments for analysis.

Finally, in September of 1977, the HSCA succeeded with the FBI where Nichols and Guinn had not, and gave Dr. Guinn a chance to develop his own data from the remaining fragments in the FBI's custody to determine if the stretcher bullet matched up in the concentration of its metallic elements with bullet fragments found in the presidential limousine and those removed from Connally's wrist.[46†] By the time Dr. Guinn, who had a PhD in chemistry from Harvard University, performed his NAA tests on the Kennedy assassination evidence at his Triga Mark I nuclear reactor at the University of California

---

*Two years later, in 1966, the FBI established an NAA group within the FBI laboratory (1 HSCA 559).

†There were small differences in the tiny samples (taken from the fragments) examined by Guinn as opposed to the samples examined by the FBI, which were no longer available, owing to the fact that some of the 1964 FBI tests, those carried out by emission spectrography, were partly destructive in nature, and the FBI disposed of the rest of the minuscule samples (HSCA Report, p.599 note 33). As you might have guessed, conspiracy theorists chalk the discrepancies up to more evidence tampering by an ever-expanding list of conspirators. Partially addressing myself to this issue, I elicited from Guinn at the London trial that James Geer, of the National Archives in Washington, flew out to California and personally delivered the fragments to him. Question: "What security measures were taken to guard the evidence while in the state of California?" "Well, all the time that I was working with the samples, every place that I went with samples in my possession, I had two armed guards [U.S. marshals] on either side of me." (Transcript of *On Trial*, July 24, 1986, p.501)

at Irvine, he had served as an expert witness on NAA in approximately fifty trials, had examined 165 different types of bullets, and had published fifty-three articles on forensic NAA. His research on NAA was supported by the U.S. Atomic Energy Commission (AEC) as well as the Law Enforcement Assistance Administration of the U.S. Department of Justice.[47] Throughout his career, he had applied NAA techniques to many other kinds of materials involved in criminal cases—gunshot residues, glass, paint, paper, cloth, oil, greases, and many others.[48] He first analyzed general Mannlicher-Carcano ammunition in 1973 after Dr. Nichols offered him samples for NAA testing,[49] and discovered a peculiarity of this ammunition that turned out to have great significance for the fragments in the Kennedy case.

Dr. Guinn found that when it came to most manufactured rounds of ammunition, NAA could not detect any differences in metallic composition between bullets of the same production lot (a lot consisting of several batches or melts of lead)—they were essentially carbon copies of each other. However, Mannlicher-Carcano ammunition was very "unusual" in that the bullets seemed to have very little uniformity within a production lot. Bullets (which consist of 98 to 99 percent lead, the rest being trace elements) from a single box of twenty cartridges from the same lot varied widely in their composition, particularly with respect to the *most important* (for NAA purposes) of the three major trace elements, antimony, which manufacturers add to harden the bullet. (The other two most common elements are silver and copper.) In fact, the Mannlicher-Carcano ammunition made by Western Cartridge varied so much that individual bullets from a single box of ammunition could be identified and distinguished from each other, and hence are ideal for NAA since the possibility of a mere coincidence when you find a match is substantially reduced.[50]

In performing NAA on bullets, a sample of bullet lead—which can be extremely small—is first cleaned to remove any contamination by dust, moisture, or salt from handling or perspiration, and then put into a small vial, which in turn is placed in a small nuclear reactor,* where it is bombarded with neutrons until it becomes radioactive. The emissions given off by the sample as the radioactivity decays are then recorded, in Guinn's case by a "high-resolution germanium" detector or counter, an instrument that is a great deal more sensitive and sophisticated than the relatively crude Geiger counter featured so prominently in movies made at the dawn of the atomic age.[51] Since various elements form different radioisotopes, the counter not only distinguishes them in the sample material, but also is capable of measuring their relative quantities with extraordinary precision.

Ten different bullet samples were given to Dr. Guinn to analyze, each with an identifying Warren Commission exhibit number or an FBI "Q" number ("Q" for "questioned item").[52] Three of these were not suitable for testing, and the examination of two others added only basic, supportive knowledge to the case.

The five remaining specimens proved to have great value in corroborating what was already known about the assassination of President Kennedy. The first was the bullet found on the stretcher at Parkland Hospital (Commission Exhibit No. 399). The second (Commission Exhibit No. 567) was one of the two large fragments recovered from or near the front seat of the limousine, which had already been matched by firearms tests to

---

*The nuclear reactor I saw at the University of California at Irvine, where Guinn was headquartered, was purchased in 1967 at a cost of around $350,000. It is still there and is submerged in a pool of water twenty-five feet deep and ten-by-fifteen feet in size. The reactor itself is only a four-by-four-foot cylinder, but with auxiliary equipment and pipes heading to it, it takes up a good part of the pool.

Oswald's rifle. (The other large front-seat fragment that was connected to Oswald's rifle to the exclusion of all other weapons by the firearms experts, Commission Exhibit No. 569, was not subject to NAA because only the metal jacket remained, and there was no lead for analysis.) A third specimen (Commission Exhibit No. 843) consisted of two fragments recovered from President Kennedy's brain during the autopsy at Bethesda. The fourth specimen (Commission Exhibit No. 842) consisted of three fragments removed by surgeons from Governor Connally's wrist at Parkland. The fifth specimen (Commission Exhibit No. 840) included the small fragments found on the rug of the limousine under the left jump seat.[53]

When subjected to NAA by Dr. Guinn, all five of the specimens produced a profile highly characteristic of the Western Cartridge Company's Mannlicher-Carcano ammunition. Even more interesting, the results fell into two distinct groups. Of the five samples, two had a concentration of antimony of about 800 parts per million, and three had a concentration of antimony of around 600 parts per million. This could mean only one thing: all five specimens had come from just two bullets. "There is no evidence for three bullets, four bullets, or anything more than two, but there is clear evidence there are two," Guinn told the HSCA.[54]

Guinn concluded that the large fragment found in the limousine, the smaller fragments found on the rug of the limousine, and the fragments recovered from Kennedy's brain were all from one bullet.[55]

His most important conclusion by far, however, scientifically defeating the notion that the bullet found on Connally's stretcher had been planted, was that the elemental composition and concentration of trace elements of the three bullet fragments removed from Governor Connally's wrist matched those of a second bullet, the stretcher bullet. The stretcher bullet, then, had to be the one that struck Connally, which all of the other evidence had already shown.*

Even without NAA, the idea that conspirators planted a bullet on the stretcher to frame Oswald makes no sense at all. You can only frame an innocent person, not a guilty one. And if Oswald were innocent, that would mean he wasn't in the sixth-floor window firing at Kennedy with his Mannlicher-Carcano. Someone else (the hit man for the conspirators) was up there or elsewhere firing with a *different* rifle.

Note that at the time the conspirators supposedly planted the stretcher bullet (which, if we're to follow the logic of the conspiracy theorists, must have been fired from Oswald's rifle at some earlier time in order to frame him with it), they'd have to assume that at least one of the *real* bullets fired at Kennedy would be recovered, either from Kennedy's body or inside the presidential limousine or elsewhere. And since they would know that firearm tests would reveal the bullet (or bullets) was not fired from Oswald's Mannlicher-Carcano, this would automatically exonerate Oswald as the assassin, when the whole purpose of the alleged planting was to frame Oswald.

---

*There is another piece of circumstantial evidence pointing to the stretcher bullet as the bullet that passed through Kennedy's and Connally's bodies. If it weren't, then what happened to that bullet, which, its velocity nearly spent, barely penetrated the governor's left thigh? Since we know that the FBI and Secret Service scoured the limousine for evidence and even found several small bullet fragments, surely they would have found the bullet, *inside* the limousine, that dropped from the governor's left thigh. As author Larry Sturdivan writes, it would be "inevitable that the bullet that worked its way out of the governor's thigh would be found" in the search (Sturdivan, *JFK Myths*, p.132 footnote 62). The fact that no such bullet was found in the presidential limousine is fairly strong circumstantial evidence that that bullet is the same one found on the governor's stretcher.

Moreover, the conspirators would have to know that if the *real* bullet (or bullets) was recovered and determined not to have been fired from Oswald's Carcano, the presence of a planted bullet on Connally's stretcher that *had* been fired from Oswald's rifle would immediately signal to the authorities that a second gun (and hence, a conspiracy) was involved in the assassination. Since we can assume that the conspirators would not want the existence of a conspiracy to be known, why would they do something that could only advertise their existence? For their plan to plant the stretcher bullet to work, the conspirators would have to feel extremely confident, at the time they planted it, that they would be able to retrieve and destroy all of the *real* bullets that were fired, even those that, for all they knew, might still be lodged in Kennedy's body. But how could they possibly believe they could do this?

Or are we perhaps to believe that the conspirators' hit man did not fire from a different rifle, but with the Carcano itself, which was then left behind on the sixth floor, knowing it would be found and Oswald would be implicated in the murder? But if the hit man for the conspirators fired three shots *from* Oswald's rifle and left it on the sixth floor, why would the conspirators have felt the need to plant a fourth bullet on the stretcher at Parkland to frame him? Wouldn't the authorities finding the murder weapon (Oswald's Carcano), as well as three shells from that weapon, on the sixth floor be enough to frame Oswald? What more could they possibly hope to achieve by gilding the lily and taking the additional risk of being caught by planting the fourth bullet at Parkland?

And if we follow the illogic of this scenario, how in the world did the conspirators come into possession of Oswald's Carcano in the first place? Did they break into Ruth Paine's garage sometime before the assassination, steal the Carcano, take it out and fire a bullet into some object from which they could recover it, then fire the Carcano from the sixth-floor window and leave it behind, then plant the earlier, recovered bullet on a stretcher at Parkland? Under that scenario, I guess the conspiracy theorists would want us to believe that *Oswald was really having lunch on the first floor of the Book Depository Building at the time of the assassination while some stranger who had stolen his rifle was firing it on the sixth floor.* Nurse, call the doctor. Our fine-feathered conspiracy friends seem to be hallucinating.

I hate to reduce myself to talking about such silliness, but if Oswald wasn't the one who fired his Carcano that day, then after his arrest when the authorities asked him questions about the Carcano and showed him a picture of himself holding the murder weapon—the main piece of evidence, he knew, that connected him to the assassination—why did he deny holding the rifle, or even owning a rifle, two blatant lies that showed an unmistakable consciousness of guilt? If it wasn't he who fired his Mannlicher-Carcano at the president, wouldn't the automatic and natural thing for him to say be, "Yes, that's of course my rifle, but some SOB stole it from me about a week or so ago. You find the person who stole it from me and you'll find the person who killed the president." Instead, Oswald told one lie after another about his own rifle because he knew, of course, that it was the murder weapon.

There necessarily is another piece of evidence against Oswald that would have had to be planted by the conspirators under this latter scenario—the famous backyard photograph of Oswald holding the Mannlicher-Carcano taken by Marina when she and Oswald were living on Neely Street in Dallas. As previously indicated, this photo was recovered from the inside of a brown cardboard box found in Ruth Paine's garage the day after the assassination by Dallas police pursuant to a search warrant.[56] Oswald, we know, told his police interrogators that his head in the photo had been superimposed on someone else's body.[57] Let's see what the conspirators would have had to do to bring this about. After stealing Oswald's Carcano from Ruth Paine's garage at some time prior to the assassination, they had to take an Oswald stand-in to the backyard of the Neely address and photograph this person holding the Carcano, since irrespective of the alleged superimposition of Oswald's head in the photo, the backdrop of the photo is the Neely backyard.[58] Then the conspirators would have had to get a photograph of Oswald's head and superimpose it on the other person's body. They'd then have to sneak back into Ruth Paine's garage to return the Carcano, and then plant this photo there, hoping the authorities would find it to implicate Oswald further in the assassination. I see. But wait. Even if the conspirators could have pulled this off, how could it possibly be that their fabricated scene with a stand-in for Oswald holding the Mannlicher-Carcano in the backyard just happened to match the actual photo Marina herself said she took of Oswald holding the Carcano in the same backyard, and with the stand-in dressed the same way Marina said Oswald was dressed that day? The alleged fabricated photo even shows Oswald's stand-in with a pistol strapped to his waist and holding two newspapers, the very same situation that Marina clearly recalls when she took her actual photo.[59] I could continue this safari into delirium, but enough.

With respect to the Tippit murder, critics as well as many supporters of the Warren Commission often say that it is the "Rosetta stone" to the solution of the Kennedy assassination, referring to the stone slab found in Rosetta, Egypt, in 1799 that was inscribed with ancient pictorial script (hieroglyphics) that proved to be the key to understanding Egyptian writing. The implication is that if it can be proved that Oswald killed Tippit, *that* would finally prove conclusively he had also killed Kennedy. I reject this thinking out of hand because it presupposes that without the Tippit killing, the evidence against Oswald for Kennedy's murder, standing alone, might not be enough. But that, we know by now, is simply not true. Even if there were no evidence that Oswald murdered Tippit, the other evidence against him already proves *beyond all doubt* that he murdered Kennedy; hence, proof of this guilt does not depend on proving that he killed Tippit. However, the Tippit killing, showing that Oswald was in flight from some awful deed, does *confirm* Oswald's guilt for the murder of Kennedy.[*]

Note that unlike the Carcano rifle, which the Warren Commission had to connect to Oswald, no such burden has to be met with the .38 caliber Smith & Wesson revolver, which was ultimately determined (see later text) to be the Tippit murder weapon, inasmuch as it was found on Oswald's person at the time of his arrest.[60] And in addition to his possession of the revolver, as with the Carcano, he was the owner of the weapon. As noted earlier, sometime after January 27, 1963, Seaport Traders Inc., a mail-order business in Los Angeles, received through the mail a mail-order coupon for a Smith & Wes-

---

[*]Because of space limitations and the *comparatively* lesser importance of the Tippit murder in proving Oswald's guilt for Kennedy's murder, plus the fact that there were actual eyewitnesses to Oswald killing Tippit, this book has not gone into the same depth on the Tippit slaying as it has on the president's murder. Although there are hundreds of books on the Kennedy assassination, remarkably only one, Dale Myers's *With Malice*, has ever been written on the Tippit murder, and it fortunately provides an in-depth, detailed, and excellent analysis of the entire case. Since the Warren Commission and the HSCA did not examine the Tippit case in the depth they should have, Myers performed a singular service for the historical record by his work on this important and integral part of the case.

son .38 caliber revolver costing $29.95. Ten dollars in cash was enclosed, with the balance of $19.95 due on receipt (COD). The order was dated January 27 (no year given) and was signed "A.J. Hidell, age 28," a little departure from Oswald's "A. Hidell" on the purchase order for the Carcano, and the address listed was P.O. Box 2915, Dallas, Texas, Oswald's post office box.[61]

Handwriting experts from the Warren Commission concluded that the handwriting on the mail-order coupon was Oswald's, and that the name "D. F. Drittal," written on the coupon as a witness attesting to Hidell's representation that he was an American citizen and had not been convicted of a felony, was also in Oswald's handwriting. Marina also identified the writing on the coupon for the revolver as being that of her husband* and when shown the revolver, she immediately recognized it as being the one owned by her husband.[62]

Seaport Traders' records show that a ".38 S & W Special two-inch Commando [revolver], Serial No. V510210" was shipped by Railway Express on March 20, 1963 (coincidentally, the same day that Klein's in Chicago sent Oswald his Carcano), to A.J. Hidell, P.O. Box 2915, Dallas, Texas. The Railway Express Agency shipping documents show that the balance owed of $19.95 plus $1.27 in shipping charges was collected from the consignee, Hidell, although the date that "Hidell" paid the balance and shipping charges for the revolver is not reflected.[63]

So Oswald owned and possessed the .38 caliber Smith & Wesson. Was it also the murder weapon?

Quite apart from all the eyewitnesses who actually saw Oswald kill Tippit or saw him at or running from the murder scene, the firearms evidence, as with the Carcano, but not quite as strongly, shows that Oswald's revolver was the Tippit murder weapon. Four lead bullets were retrieved in this case, one by Dr. Paul Moellenhoff at Methodist Hospital in Dallas, where Tippit was first taken by ambulance. This bullet had hit a button, which prevented the bullet from penetrating far beneath the skin, allowing Dr. Moellenhoff to easily remove it.[64] The other three bullets were removed from Tippit's body by Dr. Earl Rose, who performed the autopsy later that afternoon at Parkland Hospital.[65]

When the FBI firearms expert, Cortlandt Cunningham, test-fired Oswald's revolver and then tried to match up the striations (marks or individual characteristics) on the test-fired bullets with those on the four slugs, he had difficulty, for two reasons. All of the slugs were badly mutilated, one being completely useless for comparison purposes. The other three did have microscopic marks, but although the barrel of this particular revolver (which, as indicated earlier in the text, had been shortened by 2¾ inches) had been *rechambered* before being sold to handle a .38 Special cartridge, the kind used to kill Tippit, the revolver had not been correspondingly *rebarreled* to handle a .38 Special bullet from the cartridge. Since a .38 caliber Smith & Wesson Special bullet has a slightly smaller diameter than a regular .38 Smith & Wesson bullet, the bullets were "slightly undersized" for the barrel, causing "an erratic passage down the barrel," thereby causing "inconsistent individual characteristic marks to be impressed or scratched on to the surface of the bullets." Cunningham said it was therefore "not possible" to positively determine whether the bullets removed from Tippit's body were fired from Oswald's revolver, since "each time it [revolver] was fired, the bullet would seem to pass down the barrel in a different

---

*The HSCA neglected to have its handwriting experts, who examined the Carcano purchase documents and many others, examine the revolver purchase documents (8 HSCA 230).

way."[66] However, the other firearms expert employed by the Warren Commission, Joseph D. Nicol, the superintendent of the Illinois Bureau of Criminal Identification and Investigation, was able to find "sufficient individual characteristics" on one of the four bullets to conclude it was fired from Oswald's revolver to the exclusion of all other weapons.[67]

The HSCA firearms panel had the same problem with the bullets that the FBI did. After attempting to match up the individual characteristics on bullets they test-fired from the revolver with those on the four slugs, the HSCA experts were unable to positively conclude that the evidence bullets were fired from Oswald's revolver.[68] In addition to the barrel of Oswald's revolver being too large for the bullets, one of the experts on the HSCA's firearms panel, Monty Lutz, testified at the London trial that the barrel itself "had been enlarged through corrosion and multiple shooting,"[69] exacerbating an already existing problem. However, both the FBI and the HSCA firearms experts were able to determine that the four slugs or bullets had the same rifling characteristics imprinted on them as the barrel of Oswald's revolver—five lands and grooves with a right twist.[70] Additionally, Cunningham testified that the widths of the lands and grooves on the evidence bullets were the same as those on the test bullets. However, rifling (or class or general) characteristics, as opposed to individual characteristics (marks and striations), are never enough for a positive match in that a great number of revolvers would also have five lands and grooves with a right twist, and with the same widths on the lands and grooves. But because of the matching rifling characteristics, Cunningham concluded that the four bullets or slugs "could have been" fired from Oswald's revolver.[71]

The inability to positively connect the four bullets in the Tippit murder case with Oswald's revolver has naturally given hope and comfort to conspiracy theorists through the years.[72] But this completely ignores the fact that there are other ways (as we saw with the Carcano rifle) to prove that a particular firearm was the murder weapon. In this case, in addition to the four bullets recovered from Tippit's body, four cartridge cases were found near the Tippit murder scene near Tenth and Patton, two by Domingo Benavides, who actually saw Oswald throw the shells in the direction of some nearby bushes,[73] and one each by Mrs. Barbara Jeannette Davis and her sister-in-law, Mrs. Virginia Davis, both of whom lived with their husbands in an apartment house located on the southeast corner of Tenth and Patton, and both of whom saw Oswald emptying his gun as he ran across the yard of their apartment house. Benavides and the two Davis girls turned the four shells they found over to the police.[74]

FBI firearms expert Cortlandt Cunningham compared the markings on the four cartridge cases with those that had been test-fired from Oswald's revolver and found identical breech face and firing pin marks on the head of the cases, concluding that the four shells found at the Tippit murder scene had been fired in the revolver in Oswald's possession at the time of his arrest to the exclusion of all other weapons.[75] Two other FBI firearms experts, Robert Frazier and Charles Killion, independently conducted the same test and came to the same conclusion.[76]

In 1978, the five experts on the firearms panel of the HSCA conducted their own comparison tests of the shells with test-fire shells and reached the same conclusion as the FBI in 1963—the four shells found at the Tippit murder scene had been fired in Oswald's revolver.[77]

Oswald at the Sniper's Nest and "Evidence" of His Innocence

In 1964, the Warren Commission evaluated the physical evidence found near the southeasternmost sixth-floor window of the Texas School Book Depository Building and the testimony of eyewitnesses to Oswald's actions both before and after the assassination and concluded that Oswald, who had ready access to the sixth floor and whose rifle, the murder weapon, was found there, was the person present at the window at the time of the assassination, and hence, that it was Oswald, and not some unknown individual, who murdered President Kennedy.[1] Critics have since laboriously argued that the physical evidence establishing Oswald's presence at the window is, at best, "circumstantial," and that the eyewitness testimony the Commission relied on was subject to a second interpretation, one that either raised serious questions about Oswald's involvement or completely exonerated him from complicity. Let's examine the evidence.

As we recall, on the day of the assassination Oswald arrived for work at the Depository a few minutes before 8:00 a.m., having been driven there by one of his coworkers, Wesley Frazier, following an overnight stay at the Irving home of Mrs. Ruth Paine. According to Frazier, Oswald was carrying a long package which he told Frazier contained curtain rods.[2] Curiously, and very suspiciously, Oswald didn't accompany Frazier as they walked the distance between the employee parking area and the Depository Building, which he usually did.[3] Instead, Oswald kept an increasing distance between them. By the time he reached the back door of the loading dock, Oswald was fifty feet or so ahead of Frazier.[4] And by the time Frazier entered the same door a moment later, Oswald had already disappeared into the confines of the warehouse.[5]

No one knows what Oswald initially did with the package once he entered the Depository. Only one person, forty-year-old Depository employee Jack Dougherty, claimed to have seen Oswald come in the back door that morning. Dougherty told authorities, "I recall vaguely having seen Lee Oswald when he came to work at about 8 a.m.," and "didn't see anything in his hands at the time." However, he said, 'I just caught him out of the corner of my eye."[6] The Warren Commission later wrote that Dougherty "*does not remember* that Oswald had anything in his hands as he entered the door."[7] Conspiracy author Sylvia Meagher chastised the Commission for its "subtle and disingenuous transformation of what Dougherty really said," suggesting that the Commission's choice of words was yet another example of how testimony that was helpful to Oswald (suggesting, of course, that Oswald didn't bring a package to work at all that morning) was altered to cast a negative light on Oswald.[8] However, it is quite clear from other documents in the Commission's possession that Dougherty's veracity as a witness is questionable at best and no doubt is why it didn't put much stock in his testimony. During a statement given to the FBI on November 23, 1963, Dougherty's father told agents that "his son received a medical discharge from the U.S. Army" and indicated his son "had considerable difficulty in coordinating his mental facilities with his speech."[9] A few weeks later, Depository superintendent Roy S. Truly told the Secret Service that "although Dougherty is a very good employee and a hard worker, he is mentally retarded and has difficulty in remembering facts, such as dates, times, places, and has been especially confused since the assassination." The Secret Service noted that Dougherty was "not questioned further" about the events of November 22.[10] Obviously, Dougherty is not the kind of witness one can rely on to substantiate whether Oswald carried a package into the building that morning or not.

Very few people had personal contact with Oswald throughout the morning hours, although several saw him. Their recollections are necessarily hazy since, not knowing he would be accused of murdering the president later that day, none of them would have had any reason to pay any more attention to him than normal. But Roy Truly, the man who hired Oswald, is almost certain that when he arrived at work that morning around 8:00 a.m., he saw Oswald on the first floor and greeted him, as was his usual habit.[11] Danny G. Arce, an order filler, also saw Oswald on the first floor, near the book racks, at about that same time,[12] as did Bonnie Ray Williams, a general warehouse worker, who remembered Oswald walking in the area with a clipboard in his hands.[13] A half hour later, Charles D. Givens, another order filler, saw Oswald on the first floor near the order bins when Givens came down to use the restroom.[14] James "Junior" Jarman, an order checker, corralled Oswald on the first floor between 8:00 and 9:00 a.m. and told the Warren Commission he had Oswald correct an order that was improperly filled. Then, sometime between 9:30 and 10:00 a.m., Jarman saw Oswald standing between two rows of order bins on the first floor looking out one of the windows overlooking Elm Street. Jarman walked over and Oswald asked him why all the people were gathering at the corner of Elm and Houston. Jarman replied that the president was supposed to come by sometime that morning, and Oswald asked which way he would be coming. Jarman told him that the parade would probably come down Main Street, turn on Houston, and then go down Elm Street. Oswald said, "Oh, I see," and walked off.[15] Billy N. Lovelady, one of six employees helping to lay new flooring on the sixth floor, saw Oswald at about 10:00 a.m. when Oswald approached him on the sixth floor "and asked where a certain book was stored." Lovelady told him the book was out of stock. This was the last Lovelady saw of him.[16] Harold Norman, an order filler, saw Oswald at about 10:00 to 10:15 a.m. on the first floor near the order bins on the south side of the building.[17] Roy E. Lewis, another order filler at the Depository, saw Oswald at about 10:30 a.m. (exact floor not mentioned) as he went about filling orders.[18]

A half hour later, around 11:00 a.m., Oswald was seen on the sixth floor. Danny Arce, part of the floor-laying crew there, reported that Oswald had a piece of paper in his hand, and although Arce said nothing to him, other members of the floor-laying crew teased Oswald about getting a haircut, which Oswald laughed off.[19] Bonnie Ray Williams, who was also part of the floor-laying crew, thought he remembered seeing Oswald on the sixth floor "messing around" with some of the book cartons stacked near the east elevator on the north side of the floor, although he couldn't be sure it was Oswald or what time he might have been there. According to Williams, Oswald "always just messed around, kicking cartons around."[20] Williams told the FBI that he saw Oswald at "about 11:40 a.m." and at "that time Oswald was on the sixth floor on the east side of the building," but that Williams "didn't pay particular attention to what he was doing."[21] Sometime after 11:30 a.m., Jarman said he saw Oswald taking one of the elevators (he didn't say from what floor) "up," and he assumed he was going after some books.[22]

William H. Shelley, Oswald's immediate supervisor, told the Secret Service that at "about 11:50 a.m." he saw Oswald on the first floor and Oswald appeared to be going about his normal duties.[23] Eddie Piper, a janitor at the Depository, said he saw Oswald around noon on the first floor.[24]

Piper and Shelley may very well have seen Oswald sometime before noon on the first floor, but chances are they (particularly Piper) saw Oswald a little earlier than they thought. I say that because four other Book Depository Building employees recall seeing Oswald on the fifth floor about ten to fifteen minutes before noon. Charles Givens testified that around 11:45 a.m.,* when he and several fellow workers left the sixth floor on two elevators to go down to have lunch, as they were descending they saw Oswald on the fifth floor and Givens hollered out, "Boy, are you going downstairs? It's near lunchtime."

"No sir," Oswald said, adding, "When you get downstairs, close the gate to the elevator," which was necessary for Oswald to have gotten the elevator back to him on the sixth floor.

Givens said, "Okay," but neglected to do so.[25] Danny Arce said that while he was on an elevator descending for the noon lunch (he assumed it was around five minutes before noon because that was the normal time they broke for lunch), he also saw Oswald on the fifth floor, and he recalls someone on the elevator asking Oswald if he wanted to go down with them, and Oswald saying, "You all close the door on the elevator. I will be down."[26] Billy Lovelady said that "a little before 12" he came down with other employees from the sixth floor to have lunch, and "on the way down" they saw Oswald (though Lovelady wasn't asked where, presumably on the fifth floor) and "I heard [Oswald] holler to one of the boys to stop, he wanted the elevator," but "they said, 'No, we're going down to lunch.'"[27] Bonnie Ray Williams said that around five minutes before noon, he was on an elevator descending from the sixth floor to have lunch when he heard Oswald holler out from either the fifth or sixth floor, "Close the gate on the elevator and send the elevator back up."[28] But the elevator was not sent up.[29]†

---

*Givens and his fellow workers almost assuredly came down to lunch at least five or more minutes after when he says they did. Not only would 11:45 a.m. be very early for the lunch break at noon, but their supervisor, William Shelly, didn't come down until around 11:50 a.m. (6 H 328, WCT William H. Shelley), and they would not likely have left for lunch before he did. Also, Givens's coworkers testified they came down for lunch later than 11:45 a.m. (see text).

†Only the west elevator could be called, by push button, to any floor, but only as long as the two gates on it were closed. The east elevator required someone to be onboard to operate it by hand pedal. (3 H 171, WCT Bonnie Ray Williams)

From all of this, it is *inferentially* clear that only Oswald was on the upper floors of the Book Depository Building close to noon, and the weight of the evidence was that he was on the fifth floor, not the sixth floor, where the shooting took place a half hour or so later. The fact that Oswald appeared to be by himself, and had all the time in the world to get to the sixth floor in time to shoot Kennedy, is not enough for the conspiracy theorists. No one, they say, placed him on the sixth floor after he was last seen on the fifth floor. No one, that is, except Charles Givens, whose testimony they reject on this point.

Givens testified before the Warren Commission that after he descended to the ground floor for lunch, "I discovered I left my cigarettes in my jacket pocket upstairs, and I took the elevator back upstairs to get my jacket with my cigarettes in it. When I got back upstairs, he [Oswald] was on the sixth floor in that vicinity coming from that way."

Question: "Coming from what way?"

"Toward the window up front where the shots were fired from." Givens says this was "about 5 minutes to 12."[30] He said Oswald had a clipboard with orders in his hand, and when he, Givens, asked Oswald if he was going to come downstairs, Oswald replied, "No, not now."[31]

The problem, however, is that on the afternoon of the assassination (which is long before his testimony to the Commission on April 8, 1964) Givens *supposedly* told FBI agents Will Griffen and Bardwell Odum that at around 11:50 a.m. he saw Oswald reading a newspaper in the domino room, the lunchroom on the first floor, and there's no mention in the report of Givens claiming to have seen Oswald on the sixth floor.[32] How does one resolve this contradiction? For years, conspiracy theorists have maintained that obviously Givens's first statement to the FBI was the truthful one, and for whatever reason, he fabricated his Warren Commission testimony and never saw Oswald on the sixth floor at any time that morning.[33] But why would Givens make up such a story? What would be in it for him? The conspiracy theorists don't expressly say. The reality is that it would appear to make no sense that Givens would make up his Warren Commission testimony.

Moreover, if Givens were to make up such a story, or someone put him up to it (presumably for the purpose of implicating Oswald in the assassination), why in the world would he tell the Warren Commission he saw Oswald on the sixth floor around 11:55 a.m.? That's *thirty-five minutes before the assassination*, hardly strong evidence that Oswald was still there at 12:30 p.m. If, for whatever reason, Givens was trying to nail Oswald, why wouldn't he say he saw Oswald on the sixth floor much closer to the time of the shooting, like 12:25 p.m.? Or 12:20, 12:15, or even 12:10?

Since Givens's invention of the story makes little sense, what is much more likely is that the FBI report is in error. The report is very brief (only four short paragraphs), and it is not a signed statement or affidavit by Givens. Summary reports of what someone allegedly told a report's author, whether it be an FBI agent or someone else, so very, very frequently contain misinformation. I've given interviews to many reporters in my day, some of them even tape-recorded, yet when the interview sees the light of day, very often dates and incidents are garbled, sometimes beyond recognition. Here, Givens may have mentioned details like 11:50 a.m., first floor, Oswald, newspaper, et cetera, to the FBI, and the agent who prepared the report from his notes* the *following* day, November 23, when the report was dictated, put the separate facts together incorrectly. (Indeed, we can

---

*The FBI policy in 1963 was not to tape-record interviews, only to take notes. That remained the bureau's policy for many years thereafter, although today, FBI agents do tape-record many interviews.

virtually be certain that he did not tell the FBI that he saw Oswald around 11:50 a.m. in the domino room on the first floor, or if he did, he was incorrect. His testimony to the Warren Commission that he saw Oswald on the fifth floor around that very time is supported by three other witnesses—Arce, Lovelady, and Williams.)

Conspiracy theorists could justifiably criticize the above rationalization if I had nothing more to go on here. But I do. If the conspiracy theorists are going to argue that Givens's "first" statement to the FBI was the honest one and his subsequent story, therefore, must have been a fabrication, this rationale can be used against them. Givens's statement to the FBI on the afternoon of the assassination was not, it turns out, his *first* statement on the matter. Lieutenant Jack Revill, who was in charge of the criminal intelligence section of the Dallas Police Department, said that during the search of the Book Depository Building right after the shooting, he "talked to a Negro by the name of Givens, and we handled this person in the past for marijuana violations and I recognized him, and in talking to him I asked him if he had been on the sixth floor, and . . . as I recall, and Detective [V. J.] Brian was present at this same time, he said yes, that he had observed Mr. Lee *over by this window*. I asked him who Mr. Lee was, [and] he said, 'It is a white boy.' . . . So I turned this Givens individual over to one of our Negro detectives and told him to take him to Captain Fritz for interrogation."[34] We can assume that Revill and Givens were talking about the sniper's nest window at the southeasternmost corner of the sixth floor. (Note again that this took place right after the shooting and hence was *before* the FBI's formal interview of Givens later in the afternoon.) And to repeat Givens's testimony on this point, he said that when he went back up to the sixth floor to get his jacket and cigarettes, he saw Oswald "on the sixth floor in that vicinity coming from that way."

Question: "Coming from what way?"

"Toward the window up front where the shots were fired from."[35]

So we see that although Givens's testimony was inconsistent—at least on the face of it—with an earlier statement he made to the FBI, it is in fact entirely consistent with an even earlier statement he made to Dallas Police Department detectives.

All totaled, the foregoing sightings of Oswald account for only a few minutes of the four and a half hours he was in the building that morning, which means that Oswald had ample time to hide the package he brought to work, retrieve it later, remove the rifle from the bag, assemble it,[*] and prepare the sniper's nest—all without being detected. In fact, two employees, Carl E. Jones, an order filler, and Troy West, a wrapper in the shipping department, reported that they usually saw Oswald every day somewhere in the building, but oddly, on the day of the assassination, they didn't see him at all—an indication, though certainly not conclusive, that he might have been making himself a little more scarce than usual.[36]

Although there are no credible reports that anyone saw Oswald on the sixth floor during the thirty-five-minute period between 11:55 a.m. and the time of the shooting at 12:30 p.m., there can be little doubt that he was on the sixth floor preparing for his murderous deed. In addition to Oswald's Mannlicher-Carcano rifle being found on the sixth floor, and the expended rifle shells (fired in and ejected from Oswald's rifle to the exclusion of all

---

[*]FBI firearms expert Cortlandt Cunningham testified that Oswald's rifle could be assembled in a little over two minutes using a screwdriver. It could also be assembled, though more slowly, with virtually "any object that would fit the slots on the five screws that retain the stock to the action," including a dime. Cunningham then proceeded to demonstrate the process for the Warren Commission using a ten-cent piece, assembling the rifle in six minutes. (2 H 252)

other weapons) being found by police in the sniper's nest on the sixth floor, there is other circumstantial evidence that points to Oswald's presence in the sixth-floor sniper's nest.

First, Oswald's finger and palm prints were found on two of the four boxes inside the sniper's nest. When Dallas police, around 1:00 p.m. on November 22, located the place where the shots were fired, they found a large carton of books at the foot of the windowsill; a smaller, lighter carton marked "Rolling Readers" sitting on top of it; and a third, Rolling Readers carton lying in front of the other, resting partially on the windowsill. Behind these three boxes was another carton on the floor on which someone could sit and look in a southwesterly direction down Elm Street over the top of the two Rolling Readers cartons.[37] The large carton on the floor[38] at the foot of the windowsill, and the Rolling Readers carton on the windowsill[39] did not contain any identifiable fingerprints.[40] The other Rolling Readers carton,[41] however, contained prints identified by FBI fingerprint expert Sebastian Latona (after comparison with inked fingerprint and palm print exemplars of Oswald's) as coming from Oswald's left palm and right index finger, Latona finding thirteen points of similarity between the left palm print and Oswald's exemplar, and ten points on the right index fingerprint.[42] *Oswald's left palm print and right index fingerprint were both pointed in a southwesterly direction, the same direction the presidential limousine was proceeding down Elm Street.*[43] Three other fingerprint experts, Arthur Mandella of the New York City Police Department, and Ronald G. Wittmus and Cortlandt Cunningham of the FBI, also conducted independent examinations of the finger and palm prints found on the boxes. All concluded that the two prints were Oswald's.[44]

Another palm print of Oswald's, his right palm print,[45] was found by Dallas police lieutenant J. C. Day on the top northwest corner of the fourth box inside the sniper's nest, the large carton on the floor located behind and to the east of the three cartons stacked near the windowsill.[46]* An FBI fingerprint expert and an expert from the New York Police Department came to the same conclusion.[47] Eleven points of similarity were found.[48]

Vincent J. Scalise, a fingerprint expert for the HSCA from the New York City Police Department, also concluded that Oswald's right index and left palm print were found on one of the cartons in the sniper's nest, and his right palm print on another carton.[49] (See photo section for location of Oswald's prints inside the sniper's nest.)

Of course, conspiracy theorists are quick to emphasize that the fact that Oswald's finger and palm prints were found on some of the boxes in the sniper's nest doesn't prove Oswald was the assassin since the prints can't tell us precisely *when* he might have touched them. Oswald was, after all, an order filler at the Depository, which meant that his duties involved handling many boxes throughout the warehouse, including those stored on the sixth floor, where nearly all of the books that Oswald was most familiar with—and therefore more likely to handle in the course of his work—were located.[50] In addition, Oswald's prints were *not* the only ones found on the four cartons examined by police. The FBI also discovered twenty-five additional finger and palm prints, which they felt were of sufficient clarity that they could be identified, along with "many extremely fragmentary latent impressions" that were impossible to identify.[51] They subsequently compared these additional prints with those obtained from sixteen Depository employees (according to Roy Truly, the building superintendent, the only employees, including himself, besides

---

*Detective Robert Lee Studebaker, who lifted the print with Day at the crime scene, marked it as a "Left Palm" print. But later at the crime lab Lieutenant Day determined from a closer examination that it was a *right* palm print. (CE 649, 17 H 297)

Oswald who could possibly have handled the cartons) as well as with the prints of members of the Dallas police and FBI who handled the boxes in the course of their investigation.[52] All but one print were subsequently identified as belonging to either Dallas police crime-lab detective Robert Lee Studebaker or FBI clerk Forest L. Lucy.[53] The remaining print—a palm print—remains unidentified to this day.[54]*

This fact shouldn't cause anyone to begin imagining the presence of some unknown assassin lurking in the sniper's nest. These cartons were handled by many people throughout the normal course of manufacturing, warehousing, and shipping, and consequently could have contained the fingerprints of many people having nothing to do with the assassination.[55] In addition, any number of unknown individuals handled these boxes after the shooting and before they were turned over to the Dallas police crime laboratory on the morning of November 25, 1963, three days after the assassination.[56] Roy Truly, the building superintendent, told the FBI that a number of newspaper, radio, and television reporters from all over the world had access to the sixth floor after the assassination and might have handled the four cartons.[57] Dallas police lieutenant J. C. Day concurred, telling the FBI that many unknown individuals had been on the sixth floor on Saturday, November 23, taking photographs, as evidenced by the fact "that he noticed many empty film pack cartons near where the boxes were located, and *the boxes had been re-arranged, apparently for the purpose of taking photographs.*"[58] Detective Studebaker confirmed Day's observations and added that dozens of newspaper and television people from England, France, Spain, and Germany were "all over the building, particularly on the sixth floor," on Sunday, November 24, taking photographs and "generally looking for and *examining anything* that might have been related" to the assassination.[59]

In evaluating the significance of finding Oswald's prints on two of the boxes in the sniper's nest, it's important to remember that although a person could handle a carton and not leave identifiable prints, being too fragmentary or smudged for comparison purposes,[60] no Depository employees other than Oswald left identifiable prints on the sniper's nest boxes even though none of them wore work gloves.[61] Roy Truly testified that the two, small, lightweight cartons marked "Rolling Readers" found at the sixth-floor window were ordinarily stored "40 feet away or so."[62] William Shelley, the Depository foreman, testified that the Rolling Readers cartons were normally stored "at least halfway across the building from [the southeasternmost] corner."

Question: "Would it have been unusual for two Rolling Readers to be out of the stack and over there?"

Shelley: "Very unusual, because they are different size cartons . . . from any box on that floor . . . They were little boxes. The rest of them are pretty good sized."[63] The fact that those two smaller cartons, which were obviously put there for the purpose of creating a gun rest, were even there suggests that they were moved by someone who not only was familiar with the different-size cartons available on the sixth floor but also knew where

---

*Author Gus Russo reported that an FBI source told him in 1993 that the unidentified palm print belonged to Dallas police homicide captain Will Fritz, who didn't have his own prints compared with the carton prints back in 1964. Fritz reportedly had his prints taken shortly before his death in 1984, allowing the FBI to do the comparison. (Russo, *Live by the Sword*, p.583, appendix A, note 2) The National Archives, which is now the repository of all FBI documents related to the assassination, says, "We have not been able to locate any documentation to substantiate the claim made by Gus Russo in his book" (Letter from James R. Mathis, archivist, special access and FOIA staff, to author dated September 24, 2004). Since the FBI would have every reason to make it known that the palm print belonged to Fritz, and no reason to keep it a secret, Russo's FBI source was probably not a good one.

to find them—in other words, a Depository employee. The likely candidate, of all the Depository employees, was of course Oswald.

Finally, the handmade paper bag found on the floor of the southeast corner of the sniper's nest alongside the window was determined by fingerprint experts Latona, Wittmus, Cunningham, and Mandella to have Oswald's right palm print and left index fingerprint on it. Oswald's palm print was on the bottom of the paper bag, indicating not only that he had carried the bag but also that he had done so with his right hand, the same hand with which Wesley Frazier saw him carrying a bag into the Book Depository Building.[64] Fifteen points of similarity were found on the right palm print,[65] and nine points of similarity were found on the left index fingerprint.[66]

Perhaps one of the most damning pieces of circumstantial evidence indicating Oswald's presence on the sixth floor at the time of the shooting is the fact that the clipboard he'd been carrying around all morning was later discovered on the sixth floor. Whether Oswald had actually filled *any* orders at all that day (outside of the one James Jarman asked him to correct) is a matter of conjecture. Roy Truly testified that there wasn't any way to determine how many orders, if any, Oswald might have actually filled on November 22.[67] However, Frankie Kaiser, who had given Oswald the clipboard to use when he first came to work at the Depository, found it on December 2, 1963, lying behind a stack of books between the west elevator shaft and the back stairwell, a few feet from where police found Oswald's Mannlicher-Carcano rifle. There were three orders on the clipboard. Oswald had not filled any of them.[68]

Critics have argued for over four decades that *none* of this evidence—the fact that Oswald brought a mysterious package to work the morning of the assassination, and it was found in the sniper's nest with his finger and palm prints on it; the fact that Oswald was seen on the sixth floor around thirty minutes before the shooting in Dealey Plaza; the fact that the clipboard Oswald was carrying all morning was found on the sixth floor; the fact that two of Oswald's palm prints and one of his fingerprints were found on two of the sniper's nest boxes; even the fact that Oswald's rifle, the proven murder weapon, and the three expended rifle shells fired in and ejected from that same weapon, were found on the sixth floor—*proves* Oswald was the one who actually pulled the trigger. Anthony Summers, author of the book *Conspiracy* and one of the more respected critics, writes, "The evidence does certainly cast enormous suspicion [only suspicion?!?] on Oswald. Quite apart from the evidence linking him to the rifle, his own statements—above all the implausible 'curtain rod' tale—leave him looking guilty of *something*. The evidence does not, on the other hand, put him behind a gun in the sixth-floor window. A mass of information, indeed, suggests that others were manning the sniper's perch." But Summers doesn't go on to say, because he can't, what this "mass of information" is or whom else it points to. He merely adds, "Oswald *may* have been, as he claimed so urgently before he died, 'just a patsy.'"[69]

If we were to accept Summers's logic, the *only* thing that could connect Oswald to the assassination would be an eyewitness seeing Oswald shoot Kennedy. And the inescapable extension of that logic is that if a killer can make sure that no one sees him kill the victim, he cannot be convicted of the murder, no matter how much other powerful evidence shows he killed the victim.

The reader should already know by now that even if there were an eyewitness to Oswald killing Kennedy, this would never satisfy the conspiracy theorists. They would simply attempt to savage the credibility of the witness, including making the allegation that the CIA or whoever else was really behind the assassination put the witness up to his testimony. Indeed, even if Oswald were shown on film shooting at Kennedy, the conspiracy theorists would argue either the film was a hoax or the man in the window was simply an Oswald look-a-like.

The essence of conspiracy theorists' argument is that they apparently want us to believe that some mysterious stranger or strangers were up on the sixth floor shooting at the president with Oswald's rifle while Oswald himself was elsewhere. And where do conspiracy theorists say Oswald was if he wasn't on the sixth floor shooting the president? For over forty years, critics have accepted Oswald's own claim to police that he was on the first floor eating lunch at the time of the assassination. To support Oswald's rather weak alibi, conspiracy theorists cite a handful of witnesses who said they saw him on the first and second floors between 12:00 and 12:30. They also offer up what they believe is the linchpin in Oswald's alibi—a chance encounter between Oswald and Dallas police officer Marrion Baker in a second-floor lunchroom less than ninety seconds *after* the last shot was fired—which they believe proves Oswald didn't kill Kennedy. But, as you'll see, these so-called proofs of Oswald's innocence all vanish, like shadows before sunlight, when exposed to scrutiny.

Before I begin, I should point out that in virtually every criminal case that doesn't result in a plea bargain and actually goes to trial, the defendant presents evidence of his innocence to the trier of fact (a judge in a court case, a jury in a jury case). Many times the evidence is fabricated, but sometimes it is legitimate, even when the defendant did, in fact, commit the crime and is ultimately found guilty. The latter is possible because of two reasons. First, the reality in life is that even when a person is guilty, he very often engages in an act or makes a statement that, when looked at in isolation, incongruously points toward his innocence. Second, evidence is not synonymous with proof. Evidence is that which is offered (legitimate or not, whether it is believed or not) to prove a fact in dispute. Proof, on the other hand, occurs when the trier of fact is satisfied that the fact in dispute has been established by the evidence. In other words, if the evidence offered proves the fact for which it is offered, it is proof. If it doesn't prove the fact, it isn't. But *proof of guilt is never dependent on a showing of no evidence of innocence.*

In the Kennedy assassination, those who subscribe to the theory of Oswald's innocence have struggled mightily to find supposed evidence of his innocence. And they have failed miserably. As opposed to so many guilty defendants who offer legitimate (though ultimately not persuasive) evidence of their innocence, one would have to be magnanimous to characterize anything that Oswald said or did as meaningful evidence of his innocence. Surely his denial of guilt does not rise to the dignity of being legitimate evidence of innocence. Whether Oswald was guilty or innocent, we could expect the same, identical denial of guilt from him. I mean, if a man possesses the extraordinary immorality to murder the president of the United States, surely he would possess the infinitely lesser immorality of denying having done so.

And certainly the fact that "no one saw" Oswald shoot Kennedy, as conspiracy theorists love to point out, is not affirmative evidence of his innocence. Indeed, in the vast majority of premeditated murders (as this one obviously was), as opposed to killings where the intent to kill was formed on the spur of the moment, there are no eyewitnesses, yet convictions are obtained every day based on circumstantial evidence. And I've never seen a case with anywhere near as much circumstantial evidence of guilt as there is against Oswald in the Kennedy case. In murder cases I prosecuted where defense counsel would argue that there were no eyewitnesses to his client committing the murder with which he was charged, after pointing out that there rarely are eyewitnesses to a premeditated murder, I'd say, "Certainly, counsel isn't suggesting that if a man commits a murder where there are no eyewitnesses, he is home free. It's not quite that easy, ladies and gentlemen of the jury. And when you come back into this courtroom with your verdict of guilty, you are going to tell this defendant," I'd say with a sudden, staccato loudness, "*it's not quite that easy!*"

What evidence has been offered as proof of Oswald's innocence? You'll recall that Oswald told police shortly after his arrest that at the time of the assassination he was eating his lunch—a cheese sandwich and an apple[70]—in the first-floor lunchroom. At some point, according to Oswald, he went up to the second-floor lunchroom to get a Coke. It was there that he was stopped by Officer Marrion Baker, who had dashed into the Depository believing that shots had been fired from the building.[71]

According to the critics, Oswald had descended from the sixth floor to the first floor— apparently via the staircase, since by all accounts no one bothered to close the west elevator gate on the first floor, as Oswald had requested so he could summon the elevator to eat lunch.[*] Critics cite the testimony of William Shelley and Eddie Piper as being supportive of Oswald's story.[72]

However, as you'll see, neither Piper's nor Shelley's testimony puts Oswald on the first floor *after* he was seen and heard on the fifth and sixth floors shortly before noon. In fact, their testimony only adds additional support to the conclusion that Oswald *remained* on the upper floors of the Depository, obviously preparing to shoot Kennedy.

To elaborate in more depth on what was touched upon earlier, William Shelley testified that he encountered Oswald on the first floor at about 11:50 a.m., after he descended for lunch from the sixth floor, where he had been supervising a six-man crew laying new flooring.[73] Piper claims he saw Oswald on the first floor around noon,[74] though he probably saw Oswald on the first floor around the same time Shelley did. I say that not just because Givens saw Oswald ostensibly dallying on the *sixth* floor shortly before noon, but because Piper's testimony linked the time of his conversation with Oswald to the time just before lunch.[75] And we know that virtually all of the Depository employees *broke early for lunch* on the day of the assassination, beginning with Shelley[76] in anticipation of watching the president's motorcade pass their building. In fact, it may very well have been Shelley's appearance on the first floor that triggered Piper's remark to Oswald, "It's about lunch time. I believe I'll go have lunch."[77] We also know, from a signed affidavit Piper gave the Dallas Sheriff Department the day after the assassination, that Oswald responded to him, "I'm going *up* to eat."[78] Two weeks later, Piper told the Secret Service that Oswald had said, "I'm going up to eat lunch."[79] Much later, in April of 1964, Piper told the Warren Commission that Oswald said he was "going up or going out" (Piper forgets which).[80] In either case, whether he went up to a higher floor in the Depository Building or outside (which there is no evidence of), Oswald apparently didn't intend to eat lunch *on* the first floor, as he later claimed. That Oswald subsequently *did* go up to the upper floors *after* talking with Piper (and consequently didn't remain on the first floor,

---

[*]In fact, James Jarman and Harold Norman found that the west elevator was still on the first floor thirty-five minutes later, when they used it to ascend to the fifth floor to watch the motorcade (3 H 210, WCT James Jarman Jr.).

as critics contend) is supported, as we have seen, by four witnesses—Givens, Williams, Lovelady, and Arce—who saw and heard Oswald calling to them from the fifth floor as they descended past him in two elevators on their way down to lunch,[81] and by Givens, who saw Oswald minutes later on the sixth floor with a clipboard.[82]

The Warren Commission critics don't deny these Oswald sightings. They simply believe that they occurred *before* Piper spoke to Oswald on the first floor and, therefore, are still consistent with the belief that Oswald, *after* he was seen on the fifth and sixth floors, came down to the first floor for lunch. But there is a very good reason to conclude that Oswald was spotted on the fifth and sixth floors *after* the conversation with Piper and not before, and hence, remained on the upper floors.

We know that when Shelley left the sixth floor around 11:50 a.m. or a little earlier to go down to the first floor for lunch, this was before the rest of the work crew did, since he was not part of, nor did he testify about, the elevator descent from the sixth floor that subsequently took place. That means that the sixth-floor work crew was still on the sixth floor, with *one* remaining freight elevator, when Shelley saw Oswald on the first floor. This is an important point because we know that when the sixth-floor work crew broke for lunch a few minutes later, they used *both* elevators. As Danny Arce said, "Me and Bonnie Ray and . . . I believe it was Billy Lovelady were on the same elevator, and Charles Givens and the other guys were on the *other one* and we were racing down."[83] That means that the elevator Shelley likely used to descend to the first floor had been returned (either manually or by remote control) to the sixth floor during the intervening few minutes. It seems pretty obvious that it was Oswald himself who took the freight elevator back up to the sixth floor after talking with Piper, considering the fact that Oswald was seen on, and heard calling from, the fifth floor shortly thereafter by his coworkers descending past him on their way to lunch.

Once again, the cohesiveness of all of the evidence—Oswald's statement to Piper ("I'm going *up* to eat lunch"), his presence on the upper floors of the Depository shortly thereafter (as determined by eyewitness testimony and from the movements of the freight elevators), and all of the physical evidence (Oswald's finger and palm prints in the sniper's nest, his ownership of murder weapon found on the sixth floor, etc.)—easily overwhelms the allegation that Oswald was eating lunch on the first floor of the Depository at the time of the shooting. Even if Oswald had descended to the first floor to have lunch *after* being seen by his coworkers on the fifth floor, this would obviously not preclude his having a quick lunch and then going up to the sixth floor to await the motorcade. If Harold Norman could be eating lunch on the first floor after 12:00 noon and still be on the fifth floor to hear the shots being fired above him on the sixth floor at 12:30, why couldn't Oswald have gotten from the first-floor lunchroom to the sixth floor just as quickly?

In addition to citing Piper and Shelley, critics also point to the testimony of James Jarman Jr. and Harold Norman as supportive of Oswald's claim, in his interrogation by Captain Fritz, that at the time of the assassination he was "having lunch" on the first floor "with some of the colored boys" who worked with him.[84] Pressed to name the employees, Oswald said that one of them was called "Junior" and the other was a short man whose name he did not know.[85]* Oswald was undoubtedly referring to James "Junior" Jarman

---

*Secret Service inspector Thomas Kelley also recalls, like Fritz, that Oswald said he had lunch with the two black employees (Kelley Exhibit A, 20 H 440). However, FBI agent James Bookhout, who was also present during the interrogation of Oswald, recalls Oswald's covering his bases by saying that "possibly" Jarman and another black employee "walked through" the first-floor lunchroom while he was there (WR, p.622).

and most likely Harold Norman (who was short and with whom Jarman spent most of his lunch break that day), two of three men who would later watch the motorcade from the fifth floor. Conspiracy theorists are quick to emphasize that both men did, in fact, eat lunch on the first floor.[86]

Conspiracy author Anthony Summers writes, "If Oswald was not indeed on the first floor at some stage, he demonstrated almost psychic powers by describing two men—out of a staff of seventy five—who were actually there."[87] Of course, Oswald's claim can hardly be considered psychic given the fact that he undoubtedly was, *at some stage*, on the first floor, being seen there not too long before noon by Shelley and Piper. Also, Oswald could easily and safely have said that Jarman and Norman were also on the first floor at some point during the lunch period. The real question is whether Oswald had lunch *with* Jarman and Norman, as he told Captain Fritz he did, in the first-floor lunchroom.[*] The big problem with Oswald's story is that when Warren Commission counsel asked Jarman, "After his [Oswald's] arrest, he stated . . . that he had had lunch with you. Did you have lunch with him?" Jarman answered, "No, sir, I didn't."[88]

What about Norman? Norman testified that while he was having lunch in the domino room, though he never said Oswald was in the room with him, he did say, "I think there was someone else in there."[89] Summers, like critic Sylvia Meagher, suggests that the "someone else" Norman recalled seeing in the lunchroom after 12:00 noon might have been Oswald.[90] But Danny Arce told the Warren Commission that he and Jack Dougherty ate their lunch in the domino room during the period Norman described. In fact, Arce was one of those who joined Norman and Jarman when they walked outside a moment later.[91] Obviously, Arce and Dougherty were the "someone else" Norman had referred to. Indeed, at the London trial, after Norman testified he saw Oswald around "10, or ten after 10" in the morning at the first-floor window looking out at Elm Street, I asked him, "Did you see him at any other time that day?"

Norman: "No, sir."[92]

So much for Oswald's claim that he was having lunch in the first-floor lunchroom with Jarman and Norman at the time the president was shot. But that's not the end of the conspiracy theorists' arguments that Oswald had an alibi for the time of the shooting.

The principle witness whom conspiracy theorists rely on to establish an alibi for Oswald *just prior* to the shootings in Dealey Plaza is Carolyn Arnold. Mrs. Arnold reportedly saw Oswald on one of the lower floors of the Depository at about the same time Dealey Plaza witness Arnold Rowland saw a man with a gun in a sixth-floor window, which of course suggests that someone other than Oswald was waiting to shoot the president.

The twenty-year-old Mrs. Arnold was employed as a secretary at the Book Depository Building. She came into prominence for the first time in 1978, fifteen years after the assassination, when she told the *Dallas Morning News* that around 12:25 p.m. on the day of the assassination, five minutes before the shooting, she left the building to watch the motorcade. On her way out, she claims she saw Oswald in the second-floor lunchroom. "I do not recall that he was doing anything," she said. "I just recall that he was sitting

*Oswald's telling Fritz this was understandable, since, as previously indicated, the domino room is where the stock boys normally had their lunch—that is, with the exception of this day, when, in anticipation of the president's motorcade coming by, most employees apparently took their lunch outside or to a window facing Elm Street, (e.g., 6 H 383, WCT Eddie Piper; 6 H 338, WCT Billy Nolan Lovelady; 3 H 168–169, WCT Bonnie Ray Williams).

there . . . in one of the booth seats on the right hand side of the room as you go in. He was alone as usual and appeared to be having lunch . . . I recognized him clearly."[93] That same month, Arnold told author Anthony Summers that "she went into the lunchroom on the second floor for a moment" (she was pregnant at the time and had a craving for a glass of water) and saw Oswald there, alone and having lunch. Instead of the 12:25 p.m. time she had given the *Dallas Morning News*, she told Summers she saw Oswald "about a quarter of an hour before the assassination . . . about 12:15. It may have been slightly later."[94] Why, fifteen years after an alleged incident, Arnold saw fit to give, within the same month, different times to separate interviewers is not known. But that is the least of the problems with Arnold's story.

Not only is Mrs. Arnold's 1978 story diametrically opposed to what Oswald told police (he claimed he ate lunch on the *first* floor, not the second floor as Arnold said, then went to the second to get a Coke), but when she was interviewed by the FBI just four days after the assassination, she said she saw Oswald a few minutes before 12:15 p.m., and it wasn't in the second-floor lunchroom at all. The FBI report reads, "As she was standing in front of the building, she stated she *thought* she caught a fleeting glimpse of Lee Harvey Oswald standing in the hallway between the front door and the double doors leading to the warehouse, located on the *first* floor. She could not be sure that this was Oswald, but she felt it was."[95] So in 1963 she *thinks* she saw Oswald on the first floor, and in 1978 she *knows* she saw him on the second floor. And in 1963 Oswald was standing, whereas in 1978 he was sitting down having lunch.

Arnold told both the *Dallas Morning News* reporter and Summers that the FBI report was wrong and the agent misquoted her. Being misquoted, of course, is not uncommon, but it is somewhat unlikely the FBI agent would have misquoted her on not just one but three significant parts of her story. It should be noted on her behalf that this was an FBI report of an interview with her, not a statement signed by Mrs. Arnold. But on March 18, 1964, she did give two FBI agents a signed statement that made no reference to seeing Oswald in the second-floor lunchroom, not mentioning the incident at all, or even that she thought she might have seen him on the first floor. The only reference to Oswald is her saying, "I did not see Lee Harvey Oswald at the time President Kennedy was shot."[96] Conspiracy theorists like author Howard Roffman claim that Mrs. Arnold was not asked about seeing Oswald *before* the shooting, but was only responding to the specific question of whether she saw Oswald *at the time of the shooting*, and therefore her reply has no relevance to the issue of whether she saw Oswald in the lunchroom before the assassination. Roffman adds, "There is no reason to expect that the agents who obtained the statements would have sought any further detail, and the final reports reveal that indeed none was sought."[97]

But that's not true. Although the Warren Commission asked the FBI to interview all of the Depository employees and ask them six specific questions,[98] many of the respondents volunteered information that was not requested, including the fact that they had not seen Oswald *at any time* on November 22.[99] In fact, two of the four women who accompanied Mrs. Arnold outside—Virgie Rackley and Judy Johnson—reported that they did not see Oswald *at any time* that day.[100] Obviously, Carolyn Arnold had an opportunity in March of 1964 to report seeing Oswald on the morning of the assassination, and common sense would dictate that she would have, had she actually seen him. It may simply be that by 1964 she had decided that she was wrong about catching a "fleeting glimpse" of Oswald. But fifteen years later, Arnold, who had to know by then (the conspiracy theorists had made it well known to the world) that Oswald claimed he was having lunch at the time of the assassination, comes up, *for the very first time*, with her allegation of see-ing Oswald eating lunch inside the second-floor lunchroom just before the shooting in Dealey Plaza.

Quite apart from all the inconsistencies in Mrs. Arnold's story, it is also not believable because there is a mountain of evidence conclusively proving that Oswald shot Kennedy at 12:30 p.m. (and therefore would not likely be having lunch on the second floor at 12:25 p.m., but would be on the sixth floor getting ready for his murderous mission), *and because Arnold is the only witness who claims to have seen Oswald in the lunchroom on the second floor, or on the first floor* (Arnold's 1963 statement) *shortly before the assassination or at any time between noon and 12:30.* (Piper says he saw him at noon.) The Warren Commission took statements from several Book Depository employees, some of whom had lunch in the second-floor lunchroom on the day of the assassination, where the office personnel nor-mally had their lunch, and some of whom had lunch in the domino room on the first floor, where the regular workers (like Oswald) usually ate their lunch. Although the Commission attorneys could have done a better job in asking specific questions of each of them as to pre-cisely when and where each had lunch that day and whether Oswald was in their presence, it is very inferable (e.g., "Did you see [Oswald] at *all* on November 22nd?" Answer: "I never did see him")[101] from each of their testimonies that none of them saw Oswald during their lunch break starting at noon up to the time of the assassination at 12:30 p.m.[102]

So again, the bottom line is that no Book Depository employee other than Mrs. Arnold claims to have seen Oswald on the first or second floor between 12:00 and 12:30 p.m. And she claimed she did, for the first time, fifteen years after the assassination.

Additionally destructive of Mrs. Arnold's fifteen-year-old claim, Mrs. Pauline Sanders, a fifty-five-year-old clerk-accountant at the Depository, reported *leaving the second-floor lunchroom* at "approximately 12:20 p.m." to await the president's arrival in front of the building. So here we have an employee who was actually in the lunchroom at the precise time that Carolyn Arnold claimed to have seen Oswald there. Yet Mrs. Sanders told the FBI that although she knew Oswald "by sight," she did not see him "*at any time*" on November 22, 1963.[103] Obviously, there's no reason or basis to give any credibility at all to the statement Carolyn Arnold made fifteen years after the assassination.

One final observation about the contention that someone other than Oswald was at the sixth-floor sniper's nest shooting at Kennedy. There is no record of any Book Depository employee seeing a stranger or strangers in the building on the morning of the assassina-tion. In fact, sixty-four Book Depository employees gave signed statements affirmatively declaring that they saw no stranger or strangers in the building that morning. Only one employee, Danny Arce, said that around 11:45 a.m. he saw an "elderly white man" around eighty years old at the entrance of the building. The man asked Arce to direct him to a restroom. Arce did, saying the man was feeble and could "hardly make it up the steps." Five minutes later the man left the building and Arce saw him enter an old Buick with three women in it and drive off.[104] Some sinister stranger.

So if it wasn't Oswald who shot Kennedy from the sixth-floor window, and no stranger was in the building at the time, it must have been some other Book Depository employee, right? But who? Charles Givens? James Jarman? Victoria Adams? (Why not? Women can pull triggers too, you know.) Or maybe there was a stranger in the building who shot Kennedy from the sixth-floor window, and like his counterpart, the grassy knoll gunman, he had the unprecedented ability to become invisible. Or then again, maybe he exists only in the minds of desperate conspiracy theorists.

A few Dealey Plaza witnesses gave statements of observing men on the upper floors of the Book Depository Building, which, if true, would support the conclusion that whoever shot Kennedy from the building may have had someone else with him. Since this would conflict 100 percent with the Warren Commission's conclusion of no conspiracy, it arguably spills over and throws into question the Commission's main conclusion that Oswald killed Kennedy, and I am therefore including this discussion under the "evidence of Oswald's innocence" rubric. Undoubtedly, a fact that has contributed greatly to the confusion about men on the upper floors is that three Book Depository employees— Harold Norman, Bonnie Ray Williams, and James Jarman—were watching the presidential motorcade go by from the fifth floor (Norman and Williams at the double-windows directly below the sniper's nest window Oswald was at, Jarman at the double-window immediately to their west) and no Dealey Plaza witness who happened to see them or Oswald in these windows before the shooting commenced would have had any reason at all to make a mental note of exactly who was at what window, and whether they were on the fourth, fifth, or sixth floor. (See the photo section for a photo of Bonnie Ray Williams on the left and Harold Norman on the right in the half-opened double-windows on the southeasternmost side of the fifth floor. The photo, by *Dallas Morning News* photographer Tom Dillard, was taken within seconds following the third shot.[105] Note that the sniper's nest window, as opposed to the double-windows below, is only one-quarter open—the bottom quarter.[106])

The most famous (and most widely quoted by conspiracy theorists) of all the Dealey Plaza witnesses who claim they saw people and happenings on the upper floors of the Book Depository Building that differ from the weight of the evidence and conclusion of the Warren Commission is Arnold Rowland. Rowland was a clearly intelligent and fairly articulate eighteen-year-old high school student who was watching the motorcade with his wife in front of the sheriff's office on the east side of Houston Street. While waiting for the president's arrival, they discussed the security measures being taken to protect the president, noting the number of police officers in the Plaza.[107]

Rowland spoke to several members of law enforcement in Dealey Plaza right after the shooting. It appears he first spoke to Dallas deputy sheriff Roger Craig. Craig testified that Rowland told him that around 12:15 p.m., he saw *two* men, one holding a rifle with a telescopic sight on it, walking back and forth two windows over from the west side of the sixth floor, not the east side where the sniper's nest was located. He assumed they were Secret Service agents. When he looked back a few minutes later, he only saw the man with the rifle.[108] In Craig's report filed the day after the assassination, he not only does not mention the Rowlands, he makes no reference to anyone claiming to have seen two men (one with a rifle) on the sixth floor of the Depository moments before the shooting.[109] C. L. "Lummie" Lewis, the Dallas deputy sheriff who escorted the Rowlands to the sheriff's office to make a statement, *did* mention the Rowlands in his report of November 23, noting that Arnold Rowland "saw man in bldg about 15 min before shooting with a gun. Wife Barbara was with him," but not one single word about Arnold Rowland seeing a second man.[110] Rowland then told Dallas police detective F. M. Turner that he saw a white man with a rifle that had a telescopic sight standing in the background of an open window on the southwest side of the sixth floor, but made no reference to seeing any second man on the floor.[111] And he told Forrest Sorrels, the special agent in charge of the Dallas office of the Secret Service, that he saw a man (he again made no reference to seeing any second man) standing with a rifle several feet back from an open window that was two windows from the westernmost side of the building. (If Rowland told him what floor, Sorrels didn't say.) The man, whom Rowland said he "could not" identify, was holding the rifle, per Rowland, at the ridiculous formal military position of "port arms."[112]

Rowland was taken inside the sheriff's office that same afternoon, where he gave a notarized affidavit that reiterated what he had told Turner and Sorrels, except that now the man was holding the rifle at the military position of "parade rest," but again made no reference to seeing a second man.[113] In two separate FBI interviews on the day of the assassination and the following day, Rowland told the FBI essentially the same story, again not referring to a second man.[114] On November 24, Rowland gave a signed statement to the FBI. He said he only saw the man "momentarily" on the sixth floor, and this time he was once again back to holding the rifle at "port arms." Again, there was no reference to seeing anyone else in the window, or anywhere else on the sixth floor.[115]

Three and a half months later, in his March 10, 1964, testimony before the Warren Commission, Rowland repeated the essence of his previous statements about the man with the rifle he claims he saw around 12:15 p.m. He definitely was holding the "high-powered" rifle, he said, at "port arms," not parade rest, either one of which would be a laughably inappropriate way to hold a rifle for a man about to kill the president. But the devil was in the details he added and his additional observations.[*] Unbelievably, even though he told the FBI he only saw the man "momentarily" (indeed, he told the Commission that he told his wife about the sighting of the man immediately after he saw him, and when she looked up the man was already "gone from our vision"), he gave the Commission incredible details. The man had "dark hair" that was "well-combed or close cut," was a "light Latin or Caucasian," had on a "very light-colored shirt" that was "open at the collar" and (get this) "unbuttoned about halfway," was wearing "a polo shirt under" the shirt, and was wearing "dark slacks or blue jeans." Rowland didn't mention the state of the man's shoeshine, but only because he couldn't see more than "six inches below his waist." This was not looney bird time. This clearly was fabrication time. "There was nothing dark on the man's face, no mustache," Rowland testified, but he allowed that "there could have been a scar, if it hadn't been a dark scar."

Rowland now added, for the first time that has been recorded in any statement of his, that on the same floor the man with a rifle was on, he saw, around five minutes before the shooting, an elderly "colored man . . . hanging out the window . . . that they said the shots were fired from," the "southeast corner" of the building, and that on the floor directly below the colored man, he saw "two Negro women" (obviously, the two black men, Harold Norman and Bonnie Ray Williams) looking out adjacent windows.[116] But when his wife was asked by Warren Commission counsel if her husband "ever told you that he had seen anyone else on the sixth floor other than this man with the gun," she responded, "No, sir."

"Has he ever told you that he told anyone else that he saw anyone else on the sixth floor?"

"No, sir."[117]

---

[*]Although there was some slight ambiguity in Rowland's previous statements as to precisely which window he allegedly saw the man with the rifle in, the matter was clarified in his testimony before the Commission when he placed an arrow on a photograph of the Book Depository Building at the window where he claimed to have seen the man. In the first pair of windows, it was the second window to the east on the westernmost side of the sixth floor. (2 H 169; CE 356, 16 H 952)

It was obvious that Rowland had no credibility left to squander, but Rowland tried hard to prove this conclusion wrong in the remainder of his testimony. He said he saw "three women" and a "couple of boys" on the freeway overpass (though we know from the testimony of several witnesses that neither were there), and that "*all* the officers . . . 50, maybe more" converged on the railroad yards behind the picket fence right after the shooting[118] (again, we know this is not true).

Since no one else but Arnold Rowland claimed to see a man holding a rifle on the west side of the sixth floor of the Book Depository Building, and since there is no physical evidence that Kennedy was shot from a window on the west side of the building (e.g., no cartridge cases were on the floor), and certainly no evidence at all that Oswald had any accomplice helping him that day, there appear to be several possible explanations of what happened here. Rowland may have seen Oswald himself holding the rifle, around fifteen minutes before the shooting, on the west side of the sixth floor. Another possibility is that Rowland was simply mistaken as to what he thought he saw. This would be consistent with the well-known phenomenon that whenever there are multiple witnesses to an event, almost invariably there is very wide divergence as to what people think they saw. But if I were to guess, I'd say that Rowland made the story up for his wife, and then later ran with it, exaggerating and embroidering his yarn along the way. Rowland said that just prior to his alleged sighting of the man in the window, he and his wife "were discussing . . . the different security precautions. I mean, it was a very important person who was coming and we were aware of the policemen around everywhere, and especially in positions where they would be able to watch crowds . . . *We had seen in the movies before where they had security men up in windows . . . with rifles.*"[119] His wife, Barbara, confirms this conversation.[120] Further support that Rowland may have made his sighting up is that it doesn't ring true—that he immediately told his wife of his sighting, but when she looked up shortly thereafter, the man who had been holding his rifle at port arms, no less, suddenly vanished, her husband telling her "the man had moved back."[121] True, his wife was nearsighted and she wasn't wearing her glasses at the time, but she said she "saw the window plainly, and I saw some people . . . looking out of some other windows."[122]

Was Rowland the type of person to make a story up? Though he was only eighteen, he had already caused people who knew him to conclude he was not truthful. The assistant principal at his Dallas high school told the FBI that he had learned from his contact with Rowland that Rowland "would not hesitate to fabricate a story."[123] And the dean of the technical high school he had earlier attended told the FBI that from her dealings with him she "determined he could not be trusted and would not tell the truth regarding any matter."[124] As to Rowland's exaggerating and embroidering the story as he told it to subsequent people, we've seen that he conducted his own self-immolation on this point, even his wife telling the Warren Commission he was "prone to exaggerate," though she was quick to add that his exaggerations were usually "not concerned with anything other than himself. They are usually to boost his ego . . . that he is really smarter than he is or that he is a better salesman than he is, something like that."[125]

Another Dealey Plaza witness quoted often by conspiracy theorists is Carolyn Walther. She told the FBI on December 5, 1963, that from her vantage point on the east side of Houston near Elm, within a minute before the shooting she saw a man standing in the southeasternmost window of either the fourth or the fifth floor of the Book Depository Building. (She said she was "positive" the window wasn't as high as the sixth floor.) The man was leaning out the window holding a weapon that looked like a machine gun. He had blond or light brown hair. In the same window, to the left of this man, she saw a portion of another man in a brown suit coat. She could not see his head and she gave no description of him.[126] Walther repeated her story to "the investigators" for a 1967 book[127] and in 1978 to the *Dallas Morning News*.[128]

Apart from the fact that we know from photographs and testimony that the fourth-floor window was closed and the fifth-floor window occupied by identified Book Depository employees (James Jarman, Bonnie Ray Williams and Harold Norman, one of whom, Norman, can be seen leaning out the window in the Robert Hughes film, and undoubtedly is the person whom Walther saw), there is another very serious problem with Walther's statement. She was watching the motorcade with her friend, Pearl Springer, who told the FBI that not only didn't she see any armed man standing in the window, but much more importantly, Walther, after the shooting, did not mention to her anything about seeing any man in the window holding a rifle, machine gun, or any other type of weapon.[129] Apparently Walther never considered her observation important enough to waste a breath on. I understand.

The last witness in this category is John Powell. Powell told Earl Golz of the *Dallas Morning News* in 1978, fifteen years after the assassination, that on the day of the assassination he was an inmate in the county jail (at the corner of Houston and Main) and that several minutes before the shooting he and others in his cell on the sixth floor of the jail saw two men in the sniper's nest window who were "fooling with" the scope of a rifle. (In other words, Oswald didn't need a second gunman firing a second rifle from the window, but he did need someone there to hold his hand, tinker with the scope of his rifle, or what have you.) Powell, seventeen at the time and in jail for three days on charges of vagrancy and disturbing the peace, told Golz, "Quite a few of us saw [the two men]." The two men "looked darker" than whites and seemed to be in "work clothes." There's no reference in Golz's article that Powell had ever spoken to the authorities. Indeed, the opposite is suggested when Powell told Golz, "I didn't tell very many people."[130]

The Golz article, coupled with the allegation in Anthony Summer's book, *Conspiracy*, two years later that the jail cells provided "an ideal vantage point for observation of the famous Depository window,"[131] created a new stir in the conspiracy community.

Although it is not known whether law enforcement ever spoke to John Powell, the entire allegation of inmates at the Dallas county jail witnessing the assassination was investigated by the Dallas sheriff's office and the FBI in November and December of 1964. The allegation was made to the FBI on December 11, 1964, by one Fay Leon Blunt, who wasn't even incarcerated in the jail at the time of the assassination but claimed there were seventeen witnesses to the assassination who were in the hospital ward on the fifth floor of the jail, and none had been interviewed. The FBI contacted Sheriff Bill Decker on December 14 about the allegation and Decker told them a "thorough investigation [was] conducted at the County Jail immediately subsequent to the assassination and no witnesses to same [were] located among the inmates." This, of course, would include not only the fifth floor, where the seventeen witnesses allegedly were, but also the sixth floor, where Powell claims he and others were. The search by the sheriff's office for witnesses to the assassination at the jail would seem to have been an automatic one, and therefore appears to be a clear refutation of Powell's story, one that he, Powell, saw fit to keep secret from the media and the authorities for fifteen years. The Powell allegation is not only silly on its face (someone apparently helping Oswald with the telescopic sight), but he is the only Dealey Plaza "witness" to have made it.

As far as Blunt's allegation about the fifth floor is concerned, Ernest Holman, the Dallas County chief jailer, took the FBI on a tour of the jail on December 14, 1964, and pointed out that the hospital section of the jail on the fifth floor had three cells. One cell was for mental inmates, and the windows from this cell allowed a view of the motorcade, but the sniper's nest window, per the FBI report, "is not visible from this cell area." Another cell area in the hospital section was "only used on weekends by persons serving three day sentences for 'Driving While Intoxicated' charges" and there were "no DWI prisoners in this particular cell at the time of the assassination." The third cell in the hospital section did have a view of the sniper's nest window, but the FBI report said the cell window "is very dirty and is backed by an iron mesh type grid guard." The view from this window is "very distorted" and Holman told the FBI he believed it would be "impossible to identify anyone" from this window. The FBI report said that "Holman and Chief Identification Officer James H. Kitching advised that Fay Leon Blunt . . . is well known to them as a person completely unreliable who has been arrested on several occasions in the past on lunacy charges."[132]

More than the eyewitness testimony already discussed, conspiracy theorists rank Oswald's second-floor lunchroom encounter with Dallas police officer Marrion L. Baker near the very top of the list of reasons to believe Oswald didn't kill Kennedy. According to the critics, Oswald couldn't possibly have gotten from the sixth-floor sniper's nest to the second-floor lunchroom in the ninety-second time frame estimated by the Warren Commission. Howard Roffman, who offered a critical analysis of Oswald's and Baker's movements in his book *Presumed Guilty*, wrote, "Thus, Oswald had an alibi. Had he been the sixth floor gunman, he would have arrived at the lunchroom *at least* five seconds *after* Baker did, probably more . . . [Therefore] Oswald *could not* have been the assassin."[133] Once again, however, the critics have exaggerated and misrepresented the circumstances surrounding this encounter in their curious zeal to exonerate Oswald of the crime he so obviously committed.

You'll recall that Officer Baker was one of the motorcycle escorts riding in the motorcade approximately two hundred feet behind the president's car. Baker had just turned onto Houston Street and was heading north toward the Depository when the shooting started. His immediate thought (though later proved incorrect) was that the shots were being fired from the roof of the Book Depository directly ahead of him. Racing his motorcycle to the front entrance, Baker dashed into the building and together with building superintendent Roy Truly ran to the freight elevators at the back of the building. After a brief delay (trying unsuccessfully to bring an elevator down by remote control so they could ascend to the upper floors), they ran up the nearby staircase. As Baker rounded the second-floor landing, he caught a glimpse of someone walking away from him in the vestibule leading to the second-floor lunchroom. Baker approached the lunchroom door, pistol drawn, and spotted Oswald, now inside the lunchroom, continuing to walk away from him. "He was in the center of the room walking away from me," Baker testified at the London trial.[134]

When Warren Commission counsel asked Baker if, when he saw Oswald, Oswald was "carrying anything in his hands," Baker answered, "He had nothing at that time." Oswald's statement to Captain Fritz that he "was on the second floor drinking a Coca-Cola when the officer came in"[135] became so famous and written about that Officer Baker himself would later have to catch himself for buying into it. In a September 23, 1964, handwritten statement he gave to the FBI, he wrote, "I saw a man standing in the lunchroom drinking a coke." He immediately crossed out the words "drinking a coke" and placed his initials above the words crossed out.[136] Conspiracy theorists were quick to pounce on this as evidence that Oswald was in fact drinking a Coke when Baker confronted him, and Baker, like everyone else in the world, was trying to cover up the truth in the assassination and falsely implicate Oswald. But Baker's credibility in this matter couldn't be any better. After all, if he were trying to implicate Oswald he obviously would never have told the Warren Commission that Oswald was calm and collected when he, Baker, first confronted Oswald.

It should be noted that Roy Truly's testimony is corroborative of Baker's testimony before the Warren Commission. When Warren Commission counsel asked if Oswald "had anything in either hand," Truly responded, "I noticed nothing in either hand."[137] Author Gerald Posner is probably correct when he concludes that after Baker and Truly left him, Oswald "was now left in the empty lunchroom, and almost instantly he must have thought of the alibi he later used after his arrest—that he was eating lunch during the shooting. He went to the soda machine and purchased a Coke as he decided how to leave the Depository."[138] The Warren Commission concluded that the "full bottle of Coca-Cola" Oswald was holding in his hand when Depository employee Mrs. R. A. Reid saw him was "presumably purchased *after* the encounter with Baker and Truly."[139]

On March 20, 1964, the Warren Commission had Baker and Truly repeat their movements as the first step in determining whether Oswald could have descended to the second-floor lunchroom from the sixth floor by the time Baker and Truly arrived.[140] Two trial runs were made, beginning with Baker's position on Houston Street at the time of the first shot and ending at the moment Baker saw Oswald. (It is not clear whether the Commission's timing ended when Baker first saw Oswald in the vestibule or a moment later in the lunchroom.) Using a stopwatch, the Commission timed Baker's reconstructed movements at *ninety seconds* during the first test, and *seventy-five seconds* during the second.[141]

That same day, Oswald's presumed descent from the sixth floor was also reconstructed and timed. Secret Service agent John Howlett, playing the role of Oswald, carried a rifle from the southeast corner of the sixth floor north along the east aisle to the northeast corner of the floor, then west to the top of the northwest corner staircase, near where Oswald's rifle was found.* He placed the rifle on the floor there, descended the stairs to the second floor, and entered the lunchroom. Again, two test runs were conducted. The first, covering the route from the sixth floor to the lunchroom at a "normal walking" pace, was clocked at seventy-eight seconds. The second test run, at a "fast walk," took seventy-four seconds.[142] In a test the HSCA conducted, running from the sixth floor to the lunchroom, the same or close to what we could have expected Oswald to do, took just forty-six seconds.[143]

The Warren Report noted that even the minimum (fastest) time it took Baker to reach the second-floor lunchroom (seventy-five seconds) would have put him in the lunchroom just three seconds *before* Oswald reached it by merely walking at a normal pace (seventy-eight seconds), though the time taken by Baker (and Truly) on November 22 was "prob-

---

Case Closed author Gerald Posner concluded that after Oswald left the sniper's nest, he "hurried *diagonally* across the sixth floor, toward the rear staircase" (Posner, *Case Closed*, p.264). An illustration in the back of Posner's book (pp.480–481) also depicts this conclusion. But Oswald *could not* have cut diagonally across the sixth floor because of the numerous boxes stacked throughout the floor, a fact demonstrated by virtually every photograph and film taken on the sixth floor that weekend (e.g., CE 719, 17 H 502; CE 723, 17 H 504).

ably longer than in the test runs," in which case Oswald would have had *more* time to get to the second-floor lunchroom before Baker arrived. For example, the Commission wrote, "No allowance was made for the special conditions which existed on the day of the assassination," including Baker's possible delayed reaction to the sound of the shots, his taking time (after parking his motorcycle) to survey the area along Elm Street before entering the building (as he testified he did),[*] and jostling with the crowd of people on the steps leading to the entrance of the Depository.[144] Even Baker acknowledged that his reconstructed times of ninety and seventy-five seconds "would be the minimum, because I am sure that I, you know, it took me a little longer [on the day of the assassination]."[145] Just as obviously, we can assume that Oswald would have moved faster than merely a "normal walking pace" or even a "fast walk" from the sniper's nest to the second floor. Indeed, we would expect him to have run, although when Warren Commission counsel asked Baker if, when he confronted Oswald, Oswald was "out of breath, did he appear to have been running?" Baker answered, "It didn't appear that to me. He appeared normal, you know."[146] However, running downstairs and running upstairs are two very different things. When I asked Baker at the London trial if he was out of breath himself from his "fast walk" simulation, he said he was not.[147] Truly would later say, "He [Oswald] didn't have to hurry. He just walked down the stairway from the sixth to the second floor."[148]

On the basis of the time tests, the Warren Commission concluded "that Oswald could have fired the shots and still have been present in the second-floor lunchroom when seen by Baker and Truly."[149]

Of course, the critics vehemently disagree with the Commission's conclusion. But, like many other aspects of the assassination, their arguments ultimately crumble in the face of abundant physical and testimonial evidence that shows Oswald killed Kennedy. Because of the strength of this evidence, we know that Oswald, of necessity, was able to beat Baker to the second-floor lunchroom. There can be no other reasonable answer that is compatible with the overwhelming evidence of Oswald's guilt.

There are three further points often cited by conspiracy theorists as affirmative, circumstantial evidence of Oswald's innocence. Rejecting Lord Byron's dictum that calmness is not always the attribute of innocence, they point out, most notably, that when Warren Commission counsel asked Baker whether Oswald was "calm and collected" when he confronted Oswald in the second-floor lunchroom, Baker responded, "Yes, sir."[150][†] As previously noted, Roy Truly, superintendent at the Book Depository Building, was present with Baker and Oswald and also said Oswald "didn't seem to be excited or overly afraid or anything."[151] Surely not the conduct of someone who just shot the president, conspiracy theorists say. But this is very naive thinking. Did they expect Oswald to act guilty? Obviously,

---

[*]At the London trial, I asked Baker if, before he ran into the building, he paused "at all to survey the situation on Elm." Baker: "Yes, sir." Question: "How long would you estimate you paused?" "Oh, two to three minutes. Just a short time." Question: "Two to three minutes or two to three seconds?" "Two to three seconds." He then said that as he "was going into the building, there were a lot of people going in with me that couldn't get in." Question: "So that slowed you down a little bit?" "Yes, it did." Because of these things, he said the simulated reconstruction was not precise. (Transcript of *On Trial*, July 23, 1986, pp.170–171, 176)

[†]Though Gerry Spence's question at the London trial called for an inadmissible conclusion, the judge permitted Spence, on cross-examination of Baker, to ask Baker if Oswald acted like a man "who had just, seconds before, killed the president of the United States." Baker answered, "No, sir." (Transcript of *On Trial*, July 23, 1986, p.190)

if he had just shot the president, he would have acted as calmly as he possibly could when confronted by the authorities. That's just common sense.

But there is another important point to be made here. Though clearly in the minority, it is known that there are those who curiously become very calm in moments of crisis. Oswald gave every indication of being one of these people.* Indeed, we have absolute proof that even when we are 100 percent sure that Oswald had every reason to act nervously, he acted in the same, calm way.

For instance, Howard Brennan, who saw Oswald in the sixth-floor window, said that Oswald "didn't appear to be rushed. There was no particular emotion visible on his face."[152] Helen Markham testified that when she saw Oswald shoot Officer Tippit, "it didn't seem like it bothered him . . . He was very, very *calm*." And after she saw Oswald shoot Tippit, "He just walked *calmly* [away], fooling with his gun."[153] And after Oswald was arrested in the Texas Theater, following a struggle over his gun, for the murder of Officer Tippit, and he was surrounded by the media and an angry crowd, other than his hollering out that he was going to protest the police brutality on him, he was very calm. Dallas police officer M. N. McDonald, the first officer to confront Oswald in the Texas Theater, and who was struck by Oswald in the face, described Oswald thereafter as being "quite *calm* and cool."[154] Dallas police officer Bob Carroll, who wrested Oswald's gun from him and admits hitting Oswald on the side of the head thereafter, said, "The way he acted you'd think he'd barely been arrested for a traffic ticket because he never had the usual symptoms of nervousness, or breaking out in a sweat, or shaking, or anything like that. He was just a real cool individual."[155] Dallas police officer C. T. Walker, who had snapped the handcuffs on Oswald at the theater, said that Oswald "was real *calm*. He was extra *calm*. He wasn't a bit excited or nervous or anything."[156] Dallas Police Department detective Richard Sims was present during much of Captain Will Fritz's interrogation of Oswald, and said Oswald "was calm" during the questioning.[157]

When Oswald called Ruth Paine to ask her to contact attorney John Abt for him, she said Oswald, who had just been charged with murdering the president of the United States, "sounded to me almost as if nothing out of the ordinary had happened."[158]

"He seemed *calm*?" Gerry Spence asked Mrs. Paine at the London trial.

"Yes," she answered.[159]†

So throughout the assassination event, those who saw and spoke to Oswald were unanimously struck by his calmness, most using that very word. And therefore, in addition to the fact that if he killed Kennedy (which all the other evidence shows he did) he would have every reason to feign calmness when confronted by Officer Baker, it apparently was natural for him to be that way anyway.

---

*Is there any inconsistency between Oswald being calm in front of Baker, yet, as we saw earlier, somewhat frantic at the Russian and Cuban consulates in Mexico City when he couldn't get his visa to Moscow and an in-transit visa to Cuba? No. Being stopped by a police officer moments after killing the president of the United States is a real crisis, and one that can't be compared with having your request for a visa turned down, which is not a crisis situation at all, only one that induces anger and disappointment. Moreover, this ability to be calm in a crisis frequently exists in the very people you wouldn't expect to be that way—excitable and high-strung people.

†Even in the Marines back in 1959, Lieutenant John Donovan, Oswald's superior in the Air Control Squadron in Santa Ana, California, noticed that in his job in front of the radar screen as a "radar plotter," Oswald appeared to be "very cool and deliberate *under periods of tension*." He said that emergency conditions (referred to as "May Day") discovered by radar plotters would arise, and that "on at least one occasion [which was] identified as an emergency," Oswald responded in a "*matter-of-fact*" voice, did not get excited, and did the right thing at the right time." (CD 87, pp.2–3, Secret Service interview of John Donovan on December 4, 1963)

Against the massive amount of evidence pointing toward Oswald's guilt, the conspiracy theorists point to another small incident that, if it were accurate, would point in the direction of innocence. But it almost assuredly is not accurate. William Whaley, the taxi driver who drove Oswald in his cab after the shooting in Dealey Plaza, testified before the Warren Commission on March 12, 1964 (almost four months after the assassination), that right after Oswald got in his cab at the Greyhound bus station, "an old lady" stuck her head in the window of his cab and said, "Driver, will you call me a cab down here," whereupon Oswald said, "I'll let you have this one," and she said, 'No, the driver can call me one." Whaley said he didn't call her a cab because he knew one would be there shortly.[160] If true, it doesn't sound like Oswald was in too much of a rush to escape. And conspiracy theorists have so argued.[161] But Whaley's memory must have failed him, because on the very day after the assassination, he gave a signed affidavit under penalty of perjury in which he recalled the incident completely differently. He said that after Oswald got in his cab, "a lady came up to the cab and asked if she could get [my] cab. As I recall, I said there will be one behind me very soon. I am not sure whether the man passenger [whom he identified in a lineup as Oswald] repeated this to her or not, but I think he may have. I then drove away."[162] So what we have here is that on the day after the incident, Whaley remembers it one way, not even being absolutely sure of all of the details, yet nearly four months later he recalls the incident differently and remembers all the details, even the exact words uttered. Human experience would cause one to conclude that Whaley's first rendition of the incident is the one that is accurate. This is particularly true here since the version of the incident that Oswald himself gave Captain Fritz is more consistent with Whaley's original account than his later one. He told Fritz that when he got in the cab a lady also wanting a cab came up, and the driver told Oswald to tell the lady to "take another cab." Without saying anything more on the matter to Fritz, Oswald was therefore implying that this is what he did.[163]

Finally, we have the most famous and enduring words ever uttered by Lee Harvey Oswald, "I'm just a patsy," which surprisingly were only recorded in one place in assassination literature. Scripps-Howard newspaper reporter Seth Kantor jotted the words down when Oswald spoke them to reporters, Kantor's notes say, at 7:55 p.m. on the evening of the assassination.[164] Oswald's declaration, which is audible in TV footage, has been repeated for years by conspiracy theorists far and wide as evidence of his innocence. "Maybe, just maybe," New Orleans DA Jim Garrison tells his staff in Oliver Stone's movie *JFK*, "Lee Oswald was exactly what he said he was—a patsy."

The only problem is that Oswald's declaration has been taken out of context by the conspiracy theorists, who want people to believe that when Oswald said he was just a patsy he was referring to being a patsy for the conspirators behind the assassination. But it appears from the context that he was not. From TV footage we hear this exchange:

First reporter: "Were you in the [Book Depository Building] at the time [of the shooting]?"

Oswald: "Naturally, if I work in that building, yes, sir."

Second reporter: "Back up, man!"

Third reporter: "Come on, man!"

Fourth reporter: "Did you shoot the president?"

Oswald: "No. *They've taken me in because of the fact that I lived in the Soviet Union.* I'm just a patsy."[165]

It is clear from the context that Oswald is saying that the Dallas authorities (who he obviously is *not* suggesting are responsible for and behind Kennedy's murder) are blaming him for the assassination simply because of the fact that he had defected to the Soviet Union and he was a convenient person for them to accuse.

But let's assume, just for the sake of argument, that Oswald was not referring to the authorities. The gist of the conspiracy theorists' position is that Oswald didn't just simply deny guilt. He got specific and said he was a "patsy," which suggests, they say, that Oswald was a part of some group that, most likely with his unwitting cooperation,[*] conspired to kill Kennedy. They allege he was the "designated fall-guy who takes the rap while the real culprits escape unscathed,"[166] "the designated patsy."[167] So they place special significance in Oswald's use of the word *patsy*.[†]

But should they? Perhaps most conspiracy theorists are unaware that the principal defense, by far, that defendants in criminal cases use is the so-called alibi defense. When prosecutors don't have evidence, such as eyewitnesses or fingerprints, to put the defendant in the area of the crime, and frequently even when they do, the defendant says he has an alibi; that is, he has witnesses, usually members of his family, close friends, or relatives, who say he was somewhere else with them at the time of the crime. However, when it is incontestable that the defendant *was* in the area of the crime—here, Oswald worked at the Book Depository Building and several people saw him in the building around the general time of the crime—he obviously couldn't say he had an alibi. He couldn't say, for instance, that he was somewhere across town at the time of the shooting in Dealey Plaza. Therefore, he could use only one other defense to the president's murder—that he was "set up" or "framed," or was a "patsy" or "fall guy," and so on. I mean, short of confessing, what else could he say?

Just saying he didn't kill Kennedy (which he also said) would obviously not be enough for him. He'd want to say something else to help convince the authorities of his innocence. And since he was precluded from saying he was somewhere else (i.e., the alibi defense), he was forced to use one of the very few words that mean he was set up or framed. Why he chose the word *patsy* over words of similar meaning to express himself, I don't know—and it is immaterial. However, I would ask conspiracy theorists to ask themselves this question. If Oswald, instead of using the word *patsy*, had said he was "set up" or "framed" or was a "fall guy," wouldn't you have the same, identical feeling you have from his use of the word *patsy*? Once you concede the word *patsy* is not special, and since Oswald couldn't say he had an alibi, what other word in the English language *could* he have used to defend himself that would not have caused you to draw the inference of conspiracy that you have? Since there is no such other word, the argument that his use of the specific words "I'm just a patsy" points toward his innocence has to fall.

If, as so many conspiracy theorists believe as an article of faith (even though they have absolutely no evidence, of any kind, to warrant such a belief), Oswald was just a patsy for a group of conspirators responsible for Kennedy's assassination, and he never fired one

---

[*]Although the evidence is overwhelming that Oswald was a very independent person who disliked being led by others, at the heart of the conspiracy lore is the belief that he was the opposite and was used by the true conspirators in the assassination. New Orleans district attorney Jim Garrison, saying what most conspiracy theorists say, told an interviewer that Oswald "was influenced and manipulated rather easily by his older and more sophisticated superiors in the conspiracy" ("Playboy Interview: Jim Garrison," p.163).

[†]That Oswald was a "patsy" is one of the most widely accepted and popular of all conspiracy dogma. But at least one conspiracy theorist elevated the patsy argument to a new level, believing that the CIA used drugs, hypnosis, and mind control to program Oswald to kill Kennedy, Oswald being completely unaware he was a Manchurian candidate (Leonard, *Perfect Assassin*, pp.1–2, 17, 21).

shot at Kennedy, the only purpose the conspirators would have in making Oswald such a patsy, of course, would be to divert law enforcement away from them, the investigation ending with the arrest, conviction, and execution of the patsy, Oswald.

But such a notion in this case makes no sense. Why in the world would anyone agree to be arrested, convicted, and put to death for a murder he didn't commit? Certainly we know Oswald wouldn't, since we know he tried to escape and resisted arrest. So we know he wasn't a knowing patsy, chosen, with his consent, to take the fall. That only leaves us with the one remaining possibility, that he was an unwitting patsy, as many conspiracy theorists boldly speculate without any evidence at all to support their speculation. Under this scenario, Oswald may not have even known that Kennedy was to be murdered,[*] and was simply instructed by his "handlers" to go to a certain place at a certain time in the Book Depository Building and await further instructions.

The immense problem with this speculative theory is that it would necessarily mean that the conspirators (CIA, mob, etc.) made a decision to place the entire fate and success of their killing the president of the United States and getting away with it *completely* on the shoulders of the *completely* unreliable Lee Harvey Oswald—that they trusted him implicitly to do exactly what they told him to do, without the slightest deviation. Because if Oswald (who we know disliked taking orders from anyone) did not follow their orders exactly, *at the precise moment in time of the shooting in Dealey Plaza* by the real killer, some employee of the Book Depository Building might have seen Oswald at a place such as the lunchroom on the second floor, or walking on the stairs between the second and third floors, and so on. If so, this witness's sighting of Oswald at the moment of the shooting, and without a rifle in his hands, would automatically eliminate Oswald as Kennedy's killer. And with his exoneration, the whole patsy operation would be dead and the police would be in hot pursuit of the conspirators, not Oswald.

Indeed, even if Oswald did do exactly what he was instructed to do by his "handlers," the conspirators would still have no assurance that one or more people would not see him at the exact moment of the shooting, again exonerating him of Kennedy's murder and thereby killing the whole patsy plan.

Likewise, how could the conspirators possibly know that some employee or employees of the Book Depository Building wouldn't see the *actual* killer of Kennedy at the sixth-floor window? I mean, we know that three Book Depository Building employees watched the motorcade pass by from the fifth-floor windows. What if they had watched it from the sixth floor? They would have seen the true killer, and again, Oswald wouldn't be a patsy and the conspirators would be on the run from the authorities.

So in addition to there not being one speck of evidence to support the patsy theory, it doesn't even make sense. Further, as discussed earlier, it appears from the context of Oswald's declaration that he wasn't even suggesting he was a fall guy for the true conspirators behind the assassination.

It should be noted that if Oswald weren't a knowing or even unwitting member of an alleged group that conspired to murder Kennedy, but simply, as some conspiracy theorists claim, someone they chose to frame for the murder, then the frame-up or patsy argu-

---

[*]I guess one could make the argument that if Oswald truly was completely unaware that Kennedy was to be murdered, and was a completely unwitting patsy, the conspirators wouldn't have had any reason thereafter to have Ruby "silence" Oswald, as conspiracists believe. But the conspiracy community also believes that Oswald had been associated with those who set him up, like David Ferrie and Clay Shaw, so that his connection with Kennedy's killers would alone be enough to silence him.

ment becomes even more far-fetched, if that's possible. How would the framers possibly know where Oswald was going to be at the time of the shooting? And therefore, and again, how would the framers know that Oswald wouldn't be somewhere at the time of the assassination where witnesses could vouch for his innocence? For instance, he may have called in sick that day, and not even be at the Book Depository Building, or he may have been out on Elm Street watching the motorcade. When you frame someone, it's always done in a manner where the framers know, in advance, that the party being framed will be unable to prove his innocence or have a very difficult time doing so. Here, the framers would have every reason to believe that Oswald, even if he were at work, *would* be out on the street with other Book Depository employees, who would be witnesses to his innocence. Nearly all Book Depository employees *were* outside the building watching the motorcade, and the framers, who would have to play the percentages, would have to anticipate that Oswald would be too. So this scenario of framing Oswald makes no sense either.

The bottom line is that evidence of Oswald's innocence in the Kennedy assassination is about as rare as hundred-dollar bills on the floor of a flophouse.

The Grassy Knoll

No term has been associated with the assassination of President Kennedy as much as *grassy knoll*, which refers to a patch of sloped lawn on the north side of Elm Street leading up to a wooden picket fence[*] on top of the knoll, with a concrete retaining wall and pergola to the fence's northeast.

The origin of the term *grassy knoll* as applied in the Kennedy assassination to this patch of land has not been conclusively determined. Among assassinologists, it is not even certain what area of the sloping lawn constitutes the knoll. Gary Mack, the curator of the Sixth Floor Museum, says that the grassy knoll is "considered to be from Zapruder's pedestal [on the concrete wall] west," thereby excluding most of the pergola area, an area that many researchers believe is a part of the grassy knoll. Mack's position is fortified by the fact that the gradual slope of the lawn starts to become more of a hill or knoll from the Zapruder platform west.

As the reader can see from the map in the photo section of this book, the grassy knoll was located to the president's right front at the time he was hit by the two bullets. The knoll's fame is understandable. Since the majority of Americans believe there was a con-

---

[*]Though usually referred to as a picket fence, technically the structure is not a picket fence. As Gary Mack, curator of the Sixth Floor Museum since 1994, points out, "In a picket fence, the wooden slats are not touching each other across the width of the fence. Here, they are. The fence is more properly referred to as a stockade fence" (Telephone interview of Gary Mack by author on August 18, 2005). However, in this book, since the term *picket fence* is the one that nearly all Americans know the fence by, I will use the terms *picket* and *stockade fence* interchangeably.

The picket (stockade) fence is five feet high (5 HSCA 603). Starting near the northeast tip of the Triple Underpass, the fence, which has been called "the most famous fence in the world," runs in an easterly direction parallel to Elm Street for around 125 feet and then turns in a northerly direction for around 40 feet. When I spoke to Mack in 1999, he said that "the original fence—as far as the metal posts, brackets, and hardware, such as clamps and cross-bars—is still there, but the pickets, the wood, have been replaced many, many times" (Telephone interview of Gary Mack by author on December 17, 1999). The next year the fence was torn down (because of considerable deterioration) and replaced by the present replica fence.

spiracy in the assassination, and the conspiracy theorists have controlled and dominated the dialogue in the debate for well over four decades, the theorists' belief that the deadly shots emanated from the grassy knoll has been burned into the consciousness of nearly all Americans. The term has become so much a part of the American lexicon and culture that it is routinely used metaphorically (e.g., "He has a grassy knoll mentality," referring to a highly suspicious person who believes there's a conspiracy behind every major tragedy) and as an element of humor (e.g., "Everyone and their grandmother was on the grassy knoll that day" and "I saw Nixon that day. He was on the grassy knoll talking to G. Gordon Liddy"). For years, a Manchester, Vermont, conspiracy theorist even published the *Grassy Knoll Gazette*. There's no question that the grassy knoll, which the evidence shows was not the source of any of the shots, is far better known than the Texas School Book Depository Building, which was.

Just as the validity of Christianity rises or falls on the Resurrection (i.e., if Christ did not rise up from his grave, then he was not divine and the son of God, and Christianity no longer has the very foundation for its existence), the validity of conspiracy theories rises and falls on the grassy knoll. Since virtually all conspiracy theorists believe that either all the shots came from the grassy knoll or, even if Oswald did shoot at the president from the Texas School Book Depository Building, at least one or more shots were also fired from the knoll, if it can be demonstrated that no shots came from that area, the very heart of conspiracy allegations and lore ceases to beat.

Before presenting the various reasons why it couldn't be clearer that no shots were fired from the grassy knoll, I want to discuss four points, all of which deal with the origin of fire in Dealey Plaza. The first one is the contention of many conspiracy theorists that shots were fired from *both* the front (grassy knoll) and the rear (Book Depository Building and/or Dal-Tex Building) in a so-called triangulation of fire. I believe it to be a verity that the various groups the conspiracy theorists have alleged were behind the assassination would never in a thousand years have risked murdering the president of the United States. Obviously, the conspiracy theorists do not agree with me on this point. But there is another verity even all of these theorists would have to agree with me on—namely, that if one of these groups did attempt to murder the president, they certainly would not want to advertise the existence of a conspiracy, thereby increasing the risk immeasurably that law enforcement would eventually find them and they would know they'd be facing almost certain death by legal execution.

And because the alleged conspirators obviously didn't want anyone to know there was a conspiracy behind Kennedy's murder, they would never have gunmen of theirs firing from different directions, since they would have to know that witnesses and evidence would establish two separate gunmen and, hence, a conspiracy. Having more than one gunman would itself be a highly risky venture since the more gunmen (many conspiracy theorists believe there were multiple assassins firing at the president), the greater the likelihood that one would be apprehended and eventually point the finger at whoever was behind his act. But if the alleged conspirators did decide to employ more than one gunman, they'd obviously have them firing from the same direction (e.g., if from the rear, from the Book Depository Building and/or the Dal-Tex Building), not from nearly opposite directions, which would conclusively betray and disclose the existence of a conspiracy. Indeed, to conceal the existence of a conspiracy, conspirators would have their multiple gunmen firing not only from the same direction, but also from the very same kind of weapon using the same type of bullets. Yet conspiracy theorists throughout the years have had their imagined gunmen firing at the president from all manner of weapons (e.g., New Orleans DA Jim Garrison: the Carcano and a .45 caliber revolver used by an assassin emerging from a manhole on Elm Street) and bullets (e.g., Dr. Cyril Wecht: the Carcano's Western Cartridge bullets, as well as frangible bullets).

The second point is the confusion among Dealey Plaza witnesses as to the origin of the shots on the day of the assassination as demonstrated by their testimony, statements, and affidavits.* In a 1967 study of the witnesses, Warren Commission critic Josiah Thompson found that out of 64 who gave an opinion to the authorities around the time of the assassination, 33 said the shots came from the grassy knoll, 25 from the Texas School Book Depository Building, 2 from the east side of Houston Street, and 4 from two directions.[1] In a 1978 study by the HSCA, of 178 witness statements, 46 witnesses said the shots came from the Texas School Book Depository Building, 21 from the grassy knoll, 29 from "other" directions, and 78 were unable to tell.[2] The London Weekend Television staff, in 1986, examined the testimony and statements of 88 witnesses who expressed an opinion as to the origin of fire. Forty thought the shots came from the area of the grassy knoll, 41 from the Texas School Book Depository, and 7 from other directions. Anti-conspiracy author Jim Moore found that "eyewitnesses standing nearer the Book Depository *generally* thought that the shots came from within or close to the building, while those standing nearer the knoll or the underpass were convinced that the shots had been fired near their position."[3]

There are several reasons for the disagreement between witnesses as to the origin of fire, among which are the hysteria and mass confusion that reigned in the plaza among virtually everyone at the time of the shots. Even under ideal conditions, witnesses can be expected to give conflicting accounts of a sudden event taking place before them. But in the circumstances existing in Dealey Plaza, it's remarkable that there was any coherence at all as to what they thought they saw and heard. "There was a lot of confusion and everyone was running around," presidential motorcade spectator Mary Elizabeth Woodward said.[4]

Moreover, Dealey Plaza resounds with echoes, the multistory buildings on the north, south, and east sides making it a virtual echo chamber. Dr. David Green, then chairman of the National Research Council Committee on Hearing, Bioacoustics and Biomechanics, was present in Dealey Plaza in August of 1978 when the HSCA conducted its acoustic tests by firing shots in the plaza, and reported that "there are strong reverberations and echoes present in the plaza."[5] Many witnesses, in their testimony before the Warren Commission, spoke about the echoes. A few examples: When Deputy Sheriff Roger Craig was asked, "Where did the noises or shots sound to you like they came from?" he answered, "It was hard to tell because—uh—they had an echo, you know . . . There was the—uh—the shot and then the echo from it. So, it was hard to tell."[6] Lee Bowers, who worked in the railroad yards next to Dealey Plaza, testified it was difficult to tell where the source

---

*Surprisingly, although we have the testimony of many Dealey Plaza witnesses that it was their opinion, based on their auditory senses, that the shots came from the Book Depository Building, grassy knoll, or some other direction, we have virtually no photographic evidence capturing their bodies responding to their minds' message as to the origin of the shots. One exception is arguably the most famous Dealey Plaza photograph taken, by AP photographer James Altgens around the time of the second shot. As can be seen in the photo section, Secret Service agents on the right running board of the follow-up car to the presidential limousine, as well as several of the spectators on the north side of Elm Street, are seen looking backward, indicating a shot from the rear.

of any loud sound was coming from "because there is a reverberation that takes place" in the plaza.[7] Dallas police officer Joe E. Murphy, who was on the Stemmons Freeway overpass, said that as he heard the shots, "there were so many echoes."[8]

Remarkably, the HSCA, when visiting Dealey Plaza, found twenty-two structures "that would have produced echoes,"[9] and gave an example of the confusion they caused. "One hears," the committee wrote, "a very strong reflection [echo] from the Post Office Annex that arrives about 1 sec[ond] after the shot, regardless of whether the rifle is fired from the TSBD [Texas School Book Depository] or the [grassy] knoll. Because of the long delay, a listener located on the knoll would recognize this as an echo but might place the source somewhere in back of him, anywhere from the TSBD to the railway overpass. From near the TSBD, a listener would hear a strong echo from the general vicinity of the railway overpass."[10]

Abraham Zapruder testified before the Warren Commission that he "assumed" the shots had come "from back of me" because he saw police running to the area after the shots. But when he was specifically asked, "Did you form any opinion about the direction from which the shots came by the sound?" he responded, "No, there was too much reverberation. There was an echo which gave me a sound all over. In other words that square is kind of—it had a sound all over."[11]

Gary Mack, who leans toward the conspiracy theory, told me that when the HSCA acoustics people came to Dealey Plaza in August of 1978 and fired, he recalls, around fifty to sixty shots from the sixth-floor window at the Book Depository Building and from the grassy knoll, he first went to the top of the Dal-Tex Building. "From up there, there weren't as many echoes, and I had a better sense of where the shots were coming from. But when I moved down to the street level, even though I knew where the shots were coming from, I, on my own, was confused. You could hear the shots bouncing around off the buildings and monument structures in the plaza, and I can understand from the echoes why people were confused or uncertain about where the shots were coming from. And when you add all the additional sounds that were present on November 22, 1963—all the people in Dealey Plaza, all the cars and motorcycles, and the immediate chaos following the shooting—it's understandable why no one knew for sure where the shots were fired from."[12]

Even in the absence of echoes, as firearms experts Major General Julian Hatcher (former director of the technical staff of the National Rifle Association) and Lieutenant Colonel Frank Jury (former chief of the Firearms Identification Laboratory of the New Jersey State Police) point out in their authoritative textbook *Firearms Investigation, Identification, and Evidence*, "It is extremely difficult to tell the direction [from which a shot was fired] by the sound of discharge of a firearm."[*] The authors go on to say that "little credence . . . should be put in what anyone says about a shot or even the number of shots. These things coming upon him suddenly are generally extremely inaccurately recorded in his memory."[13]

The third point I want to discuss deals with the number of shots fired in Dealey Plaza. There is concrete, physical evidence (the three empty cartridge cases on the floor of the sniper's nest) that three shots were fired from the Book Depository Building. Was a fourth

---

[*]I'm not a hunter, but more than one whom I have asked has told me that if there are several people out in the forest and there's a sudden gunshot, it's very common for them to have diverging opinions as to the direction the shot came from.

shot (believed by conspiracy theorists to have been fired from the grassy knoll) fired in Dealey Plaza? In the summary of witness observations by author Josiah Thompson referred to earlier, Thompson looked at the statements of 172 witnesses and found that 136 (79 percent) thought they heard three shots and only 6 (3.5 percent) heard four shots.[14]* According to the HSCA study of 178 eyewitness statements, 132 witnesses (74.2 percent) heard three shots and, again, only 6 (3.3 percent) heard four shots.[15]† London Weekend Television examined the statements of 189 witnesses and, in a report to defense attorney Gerry Spence and me, said that 144 (76 percent) heard three shots and only 8 (4.2 percent) heard four shots.[16]

If, indeed, a fourth shot was fired that day, why did only 6 witnesses hear four shots according to two studies and only 8 witnesses according to another, whereas the vast majority of witnesses (136 in one study, 132 in another, and 144 in a third) heard only three shots? With ratios like 136, 132, and 144 to 6, 6, and 8, respectively, if you had to wager your home on who is right, whose opinion would you endorse? Can there really be any question?

One complementary addendum to the above is that although echoes in Dealey Plaza may have confused many as to the origin of fire, if a second gunman was firing at the presidential limousine that day from the grassy knoll, why is it that only 4 of Thompson's 172 witnesses, 4 of the HSCA's 178, and 5 of London Weekend Television's 189 thought they heard bullets being fired from *two* directions?[17] Even given all the confusion and reported echoes in Dealey Plaza at the time of the assassination, it would seem that a second shot fired from a completely different location would be distinctive enough to cause more than four or five witnesses to report hearing more than one origin of fire.[18] I mean, if Oswald was firing from the Book Depository Building and the conspiracy theorists' assassin was firing from the grassy knoll, how can it be that 168 of Thompson's witnesses, 174 of the HSCA's, and 184 of London Weekend Television's heard bullets coming only from *one* direction? Again, if you had to wager your home, whom would you believe, the 168, 174, and 184, or the strikingly low 4, 4, and 5? The above direct evidence by way of the witnesses' sense of hearing (as difficult as it was with the echoes) is very powerful support for the proposition that only three shots were fired in Dealey Plaza, all from one location, the Book Depository Building.

The final point I want to discuss concerns the many Dealey Plaza spectators and members of Dallas law enforcement who ran to the grassy knoll area after the shooting. It is accepted wisdom in the conspiracy community that they did so because they all thought the fatal shot had "come from the top of the grassy knoll."[19] But while this may have been the reason why some ran there, it certainly wasn't the reason why others, perhaps most, did. I say this because those who maintain people ran to the knoll because they thought the shot or shots came from there almost always add that the people did so to "pursue the assassin."[20] But if one stops to think about it, where else but the parking lot area behind the top of the knoll *could* people possibly run if they wanted to "pursue the assassin"? No one has ever claimed that any of the shots came from the south side of Elm Street, most likely because everyone knows that the south side of Elm is literally

---

*Thompson noted that 10 witnesses heard "two or three" shots and 5 heard "three or four shots." When Thompson included these 15 witness reports under "three shots," he calculated a total of 88 percent; excluding all of these reports yielded a figure of 79 percent. Thompson split the difference and reported a figure of 83.4 percent hearing three shots. (Thompson, *Six Seconds in Dallas*, p.23 footnote)

†In the HSCA study, "7 other witnesses reported [hearing] 1, 4–5, 5, 6 or 8 shots" (2 HSCA 122).

out in the open and wouldn't provide the assassin any cover from detection. For the very same reason, no assassin would run *to* the south side of Elm, where there would be nothing to shield him from view. So that only leaves the north side of Elm (no one ran down Elm or up Elm in pursuit of any possible assassin). And on the north side of Elm, though many people ran toward the Book Depository Building, it wasn't to "pursue the assassin," but simply because they thought the shots came from the building. How would the spectators pursue the assassin inside the building? Moreover, any assassin in the building would have to leave it in order to escape. That only leaves one other possible area where a Dealey Plaza spectator might think, at least on the spur of the moment, an assassin would conceivably fire from—the grassy knoll and pergola area, with its walls and heavy foliage. And if a spectator made that assumption, he would know that the parking lot area behind the knoll and pergola would be the only area the escaping assassin could run through. Hence, the natural and intuitive place for many of the police and spectators to run toward to pursue or see a fleeing assassin would be the railroad yard area behind the knoll and pergola.

Is there any evidence, apart from logic, to support the above? Yes. Among others, Dallas deputy sheriff Luke Mooney said, "We . . . ran over into Dealey Plaza, crossed Elm, jumped over the wall of the embankment on what's now called the grassy knoll and headed toward the railroad yards. At that time, it seemed to have been the most logical place to begin looking unless you had actually known from where the shots originated, which I didn't."[21] Dallas police officer David V. Harkness said, "I . . . started searching behind the railroad yards, *not because I thought shots had come from there*, but because we were looking for . . . somebody running, trying to get away."[22] And Dallas U.S. postal inspector Harry D. Holmes, who was watching the motorcade with his binoculars from one of the windows in his office in the Terminal Annex Building at the southwest corner of Main and Houston streets, said that after the shooting, he kept using his binoculars "to see if anybody left the area, especially the parking area and the railroad tracks where a guy would likely try to escape."[23]

One Dealey Plaza witness, Charles Brehm, goes a step further, believing there was no valid reason for people to run up the knoll. "They were running up to the top of that hill, it seemed to me, in almost *sheep-like fashion following somebody running up those steps*. There was a policeman who ran up those steps also. Apparently people thought that he was chasing something, which he certainly wasn't. There were no shots from that area, but *some of the people followed him* anyway."[24] Another Dealey Plaza witness, Bill Newman, essentially supports Brehm's conclusion. He says, "I don't know why they were running up that way. Maybe the Secret Service men, or whoever, *initiated* it, but I just think it was more or less a *crowd reaction*. I doubt if the people saw or heard anything up there."[25]

The above is not to suggest that there were very few witnesses who believed one or more shots came from the grassy knoll. Quite a few did. For instance, it couldn't have taken Dallas police motorcyclist Clyde A. Haygood too much time after he heard the shots to get from where he was at Main and Houston to halfway down Elm Street, where the president was shot, yet when he got there, some people were already "pointing back up to the railroad yard," which is where he searched.[26] But if Mooney, Harkness, Holmes, Brehm, and Newman are correct, and knowing how our subconscious minds influence our conscious words and deeds, one wonders how many Dealey Plaza witnesses who testified or gave statements that they thought the shots came from the grassy knoll said this not because they thought so *at the time of the shots*, but because they clearly remember running up to that area after the shooting, and that reality, over time, convinced them they heard shots coming from there.

W̲ith respect to shots allegedly coming from the grassy knoll, where, specifically, on the knoll do the conspiracy theorists claim the triggerman was? The consensus among theorists, including the HSCA, is that he was standing behind the stockade fence at a point about eight feet to the west of the southeastern corner of the fence (see photo section).[27] The HSCA determined the location through the mathematical computations of its acoustic experts. A celebrated Polaroid photo taken by Dealey Plaza spectator Mary Moorman at the time of the shot to the president's head includes this spot as well as other locations in the knoll area that conspiracy theorists have claimed was the location of the second gunman. Many conspiracy theorists are convinced they see the human figures of assassins in several places amidst the heavy foliage on the knoll shown in the Moorman photo.[28]

The photographic evidence panel of the HSCA examined the Moorman photo and said, "It was not possible to determine the nature of the images [in the photo] with the naked eye . . . Enhancement attempts in the region of the retaining wall produced no significant increase in detail and no evidence of any human form. Because the stockade fence region of the photograph was of even poorer quality than the retaining wall area, no enhancement attempts were recommended."[29] The HSCA went on to say, somewhat sheepishly, that if the photo "did not contain images that might be construed to be a figure behind the fence, it would be a troubling lack of corroboration for the acoustical analysis" (subsequently discredited), which alleged a fourth bullet was fired from this general area of the grassy knoll.[30]

Suffice it to say that anyone who can actually see human figures at the aforementioned encircled points in the Moorman photograph, or anywhere else in the background of the photo, should be thoughtful enough to bequeath his or her eyes to the scientific and medical communities for study and analysis.

It is important to note that the HSCA photographic panel examined several other photos that conspiracy theorists have maintained, throughout the years, show the outline and existence of a gunman on the grassy knoll or in the retaining wall area on the north side of Elm Street. Its conclusion was that "we find *no* [photographic] *evidence* [emphasis by panel] to support the contention that there were [other] gunmen in the Dealey Plaza area . . . We believe that the best available science and technology in photography and computer manipulation of images was utilized in preparing the evidence that led to the above conclusion."[31]

L̲et's briefly set forth the points that not only conclusively prove that the shots did not come from the grassy knoll, but also show that if conspirators had indeed set out to murder the president, selecting the grassy knoll as the place where they would position their triggerman would make absolutely no sense at all. I want to emphasize that *most* of these points, all by themselves and independently of the others, *alone* demonstrate the obvious invalidity and absurdity of the conspiracy theorists' grassy knoll argument.

During the discussion of these points the reader should remember that the three cartridge cases, which we know were ejected from Oswald's rifle, were found on the floor beneath the southeasternmost window on the sixth floor of the Book Depository Building shortly after the shooting. Indeed, without even knowing who Lee Harvey Oswald was, without even having heard his name or knowing he existed and worked at the Book Depository Building, within minutes of the shooting in Dealey Plaza law enforcement primarily focused not on the grassy knoll, but on the Book Depository Building, specifically the sixth floor.

1. Although the conspiracy theorists have written countless words about the grassy knoll and presented all manner of theories, at the end of the day, as the expression goes, the cold hard fact remains that *no witness saw any human, with or without a rifle, standing behind the picket fence on the grassy knoll at the time the president's limousine proceeded down Elm Street, and although many people, ran to the knoll after the shooting to investigate, they didn't see anyone, with or without a rifle, running or even walking away from behind the picket fence after the shots rang out.* Certainly, no reasonable person would say that people like Virgil Hoffman and Jean Hill, who said for the first time, fifteen to twenty years after the assassination, they saw someone with a rifle behind the fence (and even then in complete contradiction with their earlier statements that they saw nothing), should be considered as refuting this assertion.

Lee Bowers, the Union Terminal Railroad switchman who was up inside the north tower 120 yards or so behind the picket fence at the time of the shooting, was looking "directly towards" the picket fence area as he watched the motorcade go by. He had a view of the entire rail yard area behind the fence,[*] *the only route of escape for an assassin behind the fence,* and he saw no one running or even walking away from behind the fence after the shooting, much less someone holding a rifle or any other type of weapon.[32] Right after the shooting, Dallas County deputy sheriff Eugene Boone ran behind the picket fence into the parking lot in the railroad yards, and he told the Warren Commission that he "searched the freight yards" behind the fence and was "unable to find anything." He also said he asked a man "up in the tower [obviously, Bowers] . . . if he had seen anybody running out there in the freight yards" and the man said he "hadn't seen anybody racing around out there in the yard."[33] At the London trial, after Boone repeated all of this, I asked him to elaborate on the search behind the picket fence. He said there were flower beds behind the fence and the soil had recently been turned over. He said he checked the entire area for footprints because someone firing from behind the picket fence "would have had to stand in the flower bed," but he found "no footprints" at all.[†] Neither did he find "any powder burns or anything like that on any of the foliage" near there.[34]

Additionally, although the many people standing on the railroad overpass above Elm, Main, and Commerce streets would not have been able to see directly behind the picket fence on the grassy knoll (since the overpass is at approximately the same height as the fence), they would have had a clear view of anyone running away from behind the fence into the parking lot and railroad yards to the rear, and there's no evidence they saw anyone. Austin Miller, one of the people on the railroad overpass, said that after the shots "I stepped back [since, as indicated, he was at the same level as the fence] and looked on the

---

[*]Although a railroad spur of the Union Terminal Railroad Company ran in a southwesterly, diagonal position across the "railroad yards" behind the fence, this area was used as a lot for cars, which parked on both sides of the spur.

[†]Warren Commission witness S. M. Holland told the Warren Commission he saw "about a hundred foot tracks" just behind the picket fence (6 H 246), and told author Josiah Thompson he saw "four to five hundred footprints" there (Thompson, *Six Seconds in Dallas*, p.122). Between Holland's observation (which is ludicrous on its face, and he is the only witness who ever said he saw *any* footprints right behind the picket fence) and Boone's observation, the latter should have far more credibility.

tracks to see if anybody [was running] across the railroad tracks, and there was nobody running across the railroad tracks."[35] S. M. Holland, who was also standing on top of the railroad overpass and thought a shot may have come from the grassy knoll, told the Warren Commission that "immediately" after the shots were fired, he ran to his left off the overpass "to see if I could see anyone up there behind the [picket] fence," but he saw no one.[35] Holland said that he and several policemen and plainclothesmen "looked for empty shells around there for quite awhile," but found none.[36]

As already indicated, the gunman would have had to flee through the railroad parking lot and over the tracks and would have easily been observed and noticed by many people. Yet no one saw such a figure. Indeed, Dallas deputy sheriff W. W. "Bo" Mabra said that right after the shots he went to the rail yards and parking area "behind the knoll behind a wooden fence" and "helped search this area." He said that while in the area behind the picket fence, "I talked to a [uniformed Dallas police] officer who said 'I was stationed in the rail yards and had this entire area in view. Nobody came this way.'" In an interview later, Mabra said the officer added, "There hasn't been a thing move back here in a hour or more because I've been here all that time."[37] True, there were some cars in the parking lot, but Dallas police officer Joe Smith said, "I checked all the cars. I looked into all the cars."[38]

In fact, behind the picket fence on the grassy knoll would have been such a bad location for any assassin to have placed himself that when Warren Commission counsel asked Dallas deputy sheriff Buddy Walthers (who was standing in front of the sheriff's office on Main Street at the time of the shooting) if he thought of it as the source of the shots, Walthers said, "No, it never even entered my mind . . . Knowing how this thing is arranged, and I have chased a couple of escapees across the thing before, and knowing what was over there, the thought that anyone was shooting from [there]—I've heard some people say he was behind the fence, and I'm telling you, it just can't be, because it's a wide open . . . area as far as you can go . . . The thought that anyone would be shooting off of there would almost be an impossible thing. There's no place for him to go. There's nothing."[39]

Also, no rifle was found behind the picket fence or nearby. For that matter, other than Oswald's Carcano rifle found inside the Book Depository Building, no other rifle or weapon was found anywhere in Dealey Plaza following the assassination.[*] In addition, as indicated, no expended cartridge cases ejected from any rifle were found on the ground anywhere near the area. As Walter Cronkite, in the 1967 CBS special on the assassination, put it so cogently, to accept the grassy knoll theory we'd have to believe that an assassin "materialized out of thin air [behind the fence], fired a shot, and then vanished again into thin air, leaving behind no trace of himself, his rifle, his bullet, or any other sign of

---

[*]In the December 1994 issue of *Vanity Fair*, conspiracy theorists Anthony and Robbyn Summers wrote, "We now have an FBI report revealing that at 7:30 on the morning after the assassination, 'a snub nose thirty eight caliber Smith and Wesson, Serial Number 893265, with the word "England" on the cylinder was found . . . in a brown paper sack in the general area of where the assassination took place.' It is a scandal that the public had to wait 30 years to learn that a second gun was found *at the scene of the crime*" (Summers and Summers, "Ghosts of November," p.100). But the FBI report on the recovered revolver contains information the Summers didn't tell their readers: "On 11-23-63, Patrolman J. Raz brought into the Homicide and Robbery Bureau, Dallas PD, a brown paper sack which contained a snub-nosed .38 caliber Smith & Wesson, SN 893265. This gun had the word 'England' on the cylinder and had been found at approximately 7:30 A.M. in a brown paper sack, together with an apple and an orange, near the curb at the corner of Ross and Lamar Streets and was turned in by one Willie Flat, white male, 9221 Metz Drive, employed at 4770 Memphis, to the Dallas PD" (FBI Record 124-10005-10210, November 25, 1963). The corner of Ross and Lamar streets is about five blocks northeast of the Book Depository Building and Dealey Plaza, hardly "the scene of the crime."

[his] existence[*] . . . If the demands for certainty that are made upon the [Warren] Commission were applied to its critics, the theory of a second assassin [on the grassy knoll] would vanish before it was spoken."[40]

We know that among other evidence, a gunman was seen in the sixth-floor window, Oswald's finger and palm prints were found on boxes and a large bag in the sniper's nest, and his rifle, as well as expended cartridge casings from the rifle, were found on the sixth floor. So we have the incredible irony that the grassy knoll assassin is so completely incompetent that he can't even hit the presidential limousine (see later text), yet he impeccably vaporizes into thin air without leaving any evidence whatsoever that he was there, whereas Oswald, in the sixth-floor window, is competent enough to hit Kennedy twice but litters his shooting site with all kinds of evidence of his presence.

Or as former Dallas sheriff Jim Bowles persuasively observed, "Isn't it strange that an assassin firing from a concealed position up on the sixth floor and inside a building was observed by several people, but the supposed second assassin, comparatively out in the open and in front of the action in the line of sight of many bystanders and photographers, was not seen before, during or after by a single living soul?"[41] In other words, there is *no* eyewitness evidence and no physical evidence of any kind whatsoever that any gunman fired at the president from the grassy knoll, and because of this reality, there's really not too much more to say.

But for the record, there are a host of other reasons why the grassy knoll theory is completely barren of evidence as well as common sense.

2. As discussed in depth earlier, every one of the pathologists who examined the president's wounds and/or photographs and X-rays of the wounds, even Dr. Cyril Wecht, concluded that there was no entrance wound to the front or right front of the president's body, thereby eliminating not only the grassy knoll as the source of the bullets but also any other position to the president's front. I mean, if the president were shot from the right front, as the conspiracy theorists allege, why weren't there any entrance wounds to the front or right front of his body? As Dr. Pierre Finck, one of the autopsy surgeons, put it in less-than-impressive prose, "Although there had been rumors that shots came from the front, I did not see any evidence on the dead body of President Kennedy of wounds of entry in the front portions of the cadaver."[42]

3. We know from all the medical evidence that the throat wound to the president was an exit wound, although the conspiracy theorists allege that it was an entrance wound caused by a bullet fired from the right front. Suppose, for the sake of argument, that it was an entrance wound. Then where was the exit wound for that bullet? As can be seen from the sketch in the photo section of this book, if the throat wound was caused by a bullet fired from the grassy knoll, since the knoll was to the president's right front, the bullet would be traveling from his right to his left. Hence, the exit wound would have to have been to the *left* upper back of the president. But there was no bullet hole, entrance or exit, to the left upper back or to any other place on the left side of his body.

What I am saying, of course, presupposes that the bullet passed through soft tissue in the president's body and was not deflected, which all the medical evidence, discussed earlier, shows to be the case.[43] Even the conspiracy theorists have never disputed that the bullet causing the throat wound passed through soft tissue on a straight line through the

---

[*]Author Larry M. Sturdivan explained the absence of this evidence in his pithy observation that "non-events leave no evidence" (Sturdivan, *JFK Myths*, p.249).

president's body.* They only disagree on the direction the bullet was traveling. The only wound to the president's back, as we know, was an *entrance* wound to his upper *right* back, and the conspiracy theorists cannot use this wound as an exit wound since a bullet fired from the grassy knoll to the president's right front and passing through soft tissue could never end up on the right side of the president's body, only his left side. For the bullet to exit where we know the entrance wound is, the president's upper right back, the gunman would have to have been located across the street from the knoll to the president's *left* front, standing in full view of everyone without even a picket fence to hide behind.

4. If the fatal shot to the president's head was fired, as the conspiracy theorists allege, from the grassy knoll—that is, from the president's right *front*—it would be traveling toward the president's left *rear*. Yet the two large bullet fragments found inside the presidential limousine were found on or near the front seat of the limousine—that is, in *front* of the president, not behind him as one would expect if the bullet were fired from the front of the president. Indeed, even the three small lead fragments found in the limousine were found on the rug beneath the left jump seat, which again would be in *front* of the president, not behind him. As author John Canal writes, "I've heard of 'frangible' and 'explosive' bullets, but not 'bouncing' bullets."[44] In other words, did the bullet hit the president from the front, as the grassy knoll devotees maintain, and bounce backward after impact instead of continuing to proceed forward toward the president's rear? Not too likely. Additionally, even if it was slightly deflected by bone in the president's skull, a bullet traveling at 2,000 feet per second and entering the right front of the president's head would have inevitably passed through to the left side of the president's brain, yet we know from the autopsy report and X-rays that the left hemisphere of the president's brain was "intact."[45]

5. The triggerman, who the conspiracy theorists want us to believe fired from the grassy knoll, would have to have had a proven record as an expert shot, or the mob, CIA, KGB, et cetera, obviously would never have employed him to get the job done. But if this were so, how come this high-powered triggerman, this top professional assassin, turned out to be so bad a shot that not only couldn't he hit any part of the president's body at a close range ("the shot from the grassy knoll missed President Kennedy," the HSCA reported),[46] *he couldn't even hit the very large presidential limousine*? No bullet struck any part of the car. To emphasize the absurdity of it all, I should point out that Kennedy would have been only fifty-seven and thirty-five yards from the grassy knoll gunman at the time of the head shot, and less than sixty (around fifty-eight) yards at the time of the first shot that struck him (see scaled map in photo section of book),[47] both relatively close shots. And if either shot had been fired at the president from the grassy knoll and missed both him and the car, what happened to the bullet? Not only do we know it did not go on to hit anyone[†] in the crowd on the south side of Elm, but also after

---

*As Dr. Cyril Wecht, the most prominent medical doctor for the conspiracy theorists, told me, "Whichever direction the bullet was traveling in, it passed through soft tissue. There was no bony or cartilaginous damage in the neck and throat area of the president" (Telephone interview of Dr. Cyril Wecht by author on December 14, 1999). At the trial in London, Wecht testified that the bullet "did not strike any dense bone. There was nothing to deflect it whatsoever. Nothing to alter its path. When it exited from the front of the president's throat, it would have continued on a straight line" (Transcript of *On Trial*, July 25, 1986, p.728; see also Wecht's testimony before the HSCA, 1 HSCA 344).

†Not only didn't any bullet hit anyone on the south side of Elm Street, but no one reported hearing the sound of any bullet passing by. If the speed of the alleged bullet from the grassy knoll area were faster than the speed of sound (around 1,100 feet per second)—for instance, the Carcano bullet traveled in excess of 2,000

many years have gone by, no one has ever found a bullet anywhere on the south side of Elm Street.

6. Each of the aforementioned reasons provides solid, concrete evidence that proves to the satisfaction of any unbiased observer that no shots were fired at the president from the grassy knoll. But even if we were to throw all this evidence out the window, there are several points of simple common sense that tell us that someone shooting at the president would do so *when* we know the assassin did, and *from* the Book Depository Building as opposed to the grassy knoll. Yet conspiracy theorists as well as independent impartial observers have stated a great many times that one point militating against the conclusion that Oswald shot the president is that if he were at the southeasternmost window on the sixth floor of the Book Depository Building (as the evidence shows he was), "the perfect shot [for him] would have been when the limousine was on Houston Street, heading north toward the Book Depository."[48] But nothing could be further from the truth. In the first place, if Oswald had taken such a shot as the limousine was proceeding northbound, most of the president's body would have been shielded by Governor Connally's body even though Connally was not seated *directly* in front of the president, and so the gunman would not have had a clear, unobstructed view of the president. But there's a more important reason why such a shot would have made no sense at all. Whoever killed the president—forget about Oswald for the moment—was a sniper. How do we know he was a sniper? That's simple. He didn't want to get caught.[*] In fact, the headline in the *New York Times* the day following the president's murder read, "Kennedy Is Killed by Sniper as He Rides in Car in Dallas." The *Los Angeles Times* headline said, "Sniper's Bullet Kills President in Dallas." Now, if you're a sniper who doesn't want to get caught, why in the world would you fire any shots at the president from a position directly in front of him and with all eyes looking in your direction? Obviously, you wouldn't.[†] What you would do is exactly what we know Oswald did—wait until the presidential limousine had turned onto Elm Street and then, with most eyes to the front, shoot the president from behind with an unobstructed view.

7. For the very same reason that a sniper at the sixth-floor window wouldn't shoot the president while he was proceeding northbound on Houston, no sniper in possession of his faculties would decide to position himself on the grassy knoll to the president's right front, since he would know he would easily be within the range of vision of all eyes (and potential cameras) looking to the front. So the notion of some group like organized crime, the CIA, or the military-industrial complex positioning their gunman on the grassy knoll is irrational beyond belief.

8. As is well known, Oswald was up on the sixth floor of the Book Depository Build-

---

feet per second—this supersonic speed would have caused a "high-pitched sonic cracking sound" (*not* the *report* of the weapon being fired) as it passed by people on the north and south sides of Elm Street, which would not be loud but "clearly audible." Even a subsonic speeding bullet causes a lesser sound called a "ballistic wind" due to the movement of air being displaced by the traveling bullet, which would also have been audible to someone whom the bullet passed by. (Telephone interview of LAPD firearms expert by author on August 26, 2002)

[*]He wasn't, for example, like John Hinckley, who tried to assassinate President Ronald Reagan in 1981. Hinckley shot at Reagan in plain view of many witnesses and made no attempt to escape.

[†]Since your location would immediately expose you as the assassin, the great likelihood is that you wouldn't be able to escape from the building. The considerable number of law enforcement personnel in Dealey Plaza would immediately surround the building and it would be sealed off before you could get from the sixth floor down to the ground level to escape from the building.

ing. The relevance of this is that the overwhelming majority of people down in Dealey Plaza were only looking—as would be expected—at people and objects at the ground level. They would not be looking up to the top floors of buildings. And because of this, one could expect a sniper to be where Oswald was, high above, not where he would be more likely to be observed, at ground level.

If you were a conspirator and you were planning the assassination of the president of the United States, since you obviously would not want the existence of your conspiracy to become known, would you place a second gunman (or a sole gunman, for that matter) on the ground level (the grassy knoll) where there is a good chance that either he or his rifle would be captured on film or photographs by at least one and maybe more of the many people you know are going to be filming and photographing the event in Dealey Plaza? Since people with a camera, like a regular eyewitness, could be expected to be photographing and filming things almost exclusively at ground level, the obvious answer is no. You'd place him high above, where the likelihood of a photograph or film capturing him would be dramatically reduced.

9. Can anyone criticize my logic for saying that the CIA or organized crime, et cetera, would not want to place a hit man in a place where local law enforcement parked their cars, and hence, could be expected to be coming in and out of the area at any time? Speaking of the parking lot owned by the Union Terminal Railroad behind the picket fence, Warren Commission counsel asked S. M. Holland, signal supervisor for the railroad, "This is an area in which cars are regularly parked?" Holland: "Yes." Counsel: "A parking area for the School Book Depository?" Holland: "No. It is a parking area for the sheriff's department and people over [at] the courthouse [Dallas County Criminal Courts Building on Houston Street]." Counsel: "I see." Holland: "Sheriff's department parks in there. District attorneys' cars park in there."[49]

To make the parking lot area behind the picket fence even more improbable than it already is as the site for a presidential assassin, Lee Bowers, who operated the switches regulating the movement of trains from his Union Terminal tower overlooking the parking lot, said that this area between his tower and the fence "had been covered by police for some 2 hours" before the motorcade came through on Elm. "Since approximately 10 o'clock in the morning traffic had been cut off into the area so that anyone moving around could actually be observed."[50]

10. Moreover, are we really to believe that conspirators planning the biggest murder in American history would place their hit man on the grassy knoll knowing full well that people watching the motorcade might be sitting or standing very close to, or perhaps even at, the place where the hit man was to fire his deadly shots? And if that were to occur, what would their instructions to him be? "Quickly find some other place to shoot Kennedy—maybe from on top of the railroad overpass"?

11. There is another reason (not that any additional ones are necessary) why a conspiratorial group would not want to place a hit man on the grassy knoll: shooting at the president from the knoll would be a more difficult shot than from the Book Depository Building. I've been up to the sixth-floor window and I can tell you that if you imagine holding a rifle in your hand at the window as you look down Elm Street, the barrel of the gun is on a straight line with the presidential limousine proceeding down Elm. Moreover, the limousine was only traveling around eleven miles per hour, and Elm Street at this point has a declination of about 4 degrees, virtually eliminating the necessity of elevating the muzzle of the rifle as the limousine proceeded farther away from the sixth-

floor window. What I am saying is that the president, as my firearms specialist testified at the London trial, was for all intents and purposes a "stationary target" from the vantage point of the sniper's nest. But as can be seen from the sketch in the photo section of this book, from the grassy knoll not only would Governor Connally's body be more than partially shielding the president's body at the time of the first shot, but the gunman would be firing at a moving target (one moving, in constant motion, from left to right in front of his rifle), the presidential limousine traveling at an angle from the gunman's barrel. For the second shot, the head shot, as you can see from the sketch, the limousine is traveling at an increased angle from the gunman's barrel, making it an even more difficult shot than one from the sniper's nest window. Of course, if you are an expert rifleman hired by the mob or CIA, a shot from the grassy knoll was still very doable, but for a job of this enormous importance, why not select *the* optimum location?

Even though there's no credible evidence that any shot was fired from the grassy knoll, one could still have shouting rights if one could at least argue that logic and common sense dictate that one or more of the three shots emanated from there. But when you have no evidence and no common sense on your side, isn't it time to put the "Closed" sign on your door and go home?

A Conversation with
Dr. Cyril Wecht

Dr. Cyril H. Wecht has been, throughout the years, by far the most prominent and vocal medical critic of the Warren Commission. One of nine doctors selected to be on the panel of forensic pathologists convened by the House Select Committee on Assassinations to address and evaluate the medical issues relating to the president's death, he frequently was the lone dissenter (primarily in that he does not accept the single-bullet theory, as the rest of the panel did, believing that Governor Connally was hit by a separate bullet, and hence there was a second gunman and a conspiracy).[*] However, as indicated earlier in this book, on a critical point he was in agreement with the other eight. "I believe that the president was struck definitely twice, one bullet entering in the back, and one enter-

---

[*]Dr. Wecht's consistent disagreements with the other forensic pathology panel members was such that in its final report, the HSCA was constrained to say that "in all references to conclusions of the [forensic pathology] panel, unless it is specifically stated that it was unanimous, it should be assumed that Dr. Wecht dissented" (HSCA Report, p.43 note). In a parting shot to his colleagues on the panel, Wecht wrote to G. Robert Blakey, the HSCA's chief counsel, that "I do not intend to sign the final report of the Forensic Pathology Panel." After setting forth a litany of disagreements with his colleagues on the panel, he closed by saying, "Serving as a member of the HSCA's Forensic Pathology Panel has not been a pleasant or satisfying experience for me, and I continue to be disgusted and appalled at the manner in which this entire matter has been handled. I believe that the record will clearly show the partisan bias of the members of the House Committee, staff (with individual exceptions), and the Forensic Pathology Panel. I plan to continue my criticisms of the original Warren Commission Report and all the subsequent sycophantic reports that have followed under the imprimatur of the Federal Government." (HSCA Record 180-10109-10256, Letter from Dr. Cyril Wecht to G. Robert Blakey, December 15, 1978, pp.1–4)

One of the panel members, Dade County (Miami, Florida) medical examiner Dr. Joseph H. Davis, wrote Wecht a personal letter expressing his umbrage at Wecht's suggestion that he had not been impartial in his findings. "Most assuredly," Davis wrote, "if I felt there to be a preponderance of scientific evidence to support your conclusions, I would have so stated. The X-rays, photographs and other relevant evidence furnished to the panel cannot be interpreted by me as supportive of your conclusion." Davis went on to say that Wecht's suggestion that he had not been impartial, an absolute requisite of all scientific professions, was "a libelous attack most unworthy of our profession." (Letter from Dr. Joseph H. Davis to Dr. Cyril Wecht, October 30, 1978, pp.1–2)

ing in the back of the head," he testified before the HSCA.[1] Wecht is agnostic on the source of these two bullets, not conceding or rejecting that Oswald fired them.

And throughout the years, Wecht, at different times, has spoken of the possibility of two other shots hitting the president, one hitting Kennedy in the throat and the other the right side of his head. In a 1967 written critique of the president's autopsy, he suggested that the "size of the throat wound" was more indicative of a bullet entrance than an exit wound. He also noted that "an FBI examination of a slit in the president's shirt near the collar button, and a nick in [his] tie failed to disclose the presence of any metallic traces," concluding that "all of this indicates that the autopsy conclusion of a back to front transit" of the bullet that entered the president's back "has become progressively more unacceptable"—that is, the wound in the president's throat may possibly have been an entrance wound from a separate shot.[2] Wecht has also postulated the "possibility" of a second gunman firing a shot that entered the right side of Kennedy's head which was "synchronized with the head shot that struck the president in the back of the head."[3]

Dr. Wecht has not always been consistent about these two additional shots, however. Ten years after the assassination, though highly critical of the president's autopsy, he wrote, "So far as the available evidence shows, *all* shots were fired from the rear. No support can be found for theories which postulate gunmen to the front or right front of the presidential car."[4] In a May 7, 1975, staff interview of him by Rockefeller Commission senior counsel Robert Olsen, when Olsen asked Wecht, "In 1972, you [made] an examination of all the autopsy photographs, X-rays, and the materials at the National Archives . . . and on the basis of your studies . . . you concluded that there was no medical evidence which would support a theory that a shot fired at the president, or that had struck the president, [came] from the front, or the right front?" Wecht responded, "Yes, that is correct." However, troubled by the head snap to the rear, Wecht proceeded to qualify his answer by saying there were other possibilities that he acknowledged were "remote" and "not very likely."[5] And in a June 12, 1975, press release, Dr. Wecht said, "I see no evidence for gunmen in front of the President."[6]

Dr. Wecht has a very impressive curriculum vitae, being not only a doctor but also a lawyer associated with a Pittsburgh law firm. Up to early 2006, he had been the coroner of Allegheny County for twenty-one years, president of the American Academy of Forensic Sciences (1971–1972), and author, coauthor, or editor of thirty-six medical and forensic books as well as three mainstream ones (*Cause of Death, Grave Secrets,* and *Who Killed JonBenet Ramsey?*)—clearly, not someone whose views can be ignored. Dr. Michael Baden, the chief forensic pathologist for the HSCA, though disagreeing with many of Dr. Wecht's conclusions, told me he had "the greatest respect for Dr. Wecht."

Dr. Wecht is an expansive individual, and now and then he is given to wild and outrageous statements that I doubt he truly believes beyond the moment, such as the following remark in the 1988 British production *The Men Who Killed Kennedy*: "There's no question in my mind that the twenty-six-volume set [Warren Commission volumes] should be taken from the shelves of all the libraries where they now rest in the United States for nonfiction and placed in the fiction shelves along with *Tom Sawyer, Huckleberry Finn,* and *Gulliver's Travels.* That's where they belong."[7] But despite this, as well as the rather heated exchanges he and I had during my cross-examination of him at the London trial in 1986, and my disagreement with his pro-conspiracy views, I recognize that he is a rationalist in principle, and as contrasted to the overwhelming majority of his colleagues in the conspiracy community, he will readily acknowledge points that cannot be reasonably disputed. Indeed, for years Dr. Wecht has been, and continues to be, a thorn in the side of the small, anti-conspiracy community because unlike most other conspiracy theorists, who can easily be written off as kooks or lacking in qualifications, he has excellent credentials. Because Dr. Wecht has been a student of the Kennedy assassination for over a quarter of a century, and for most of those years he was virtually the only credible expert in the area of forensic pathology to speak for the conspiracy theorists, I had two telephone conversations with him at his home and office on December 14, 1999, and January 5, 2000, about his hypothesis of two other "possible" shots.

With respect to the throat wound, I asked Dr. Wecht, "If the bullet entering the president's upper right back did not exit in the front of his throat at the site of the tracheotomy, where *did* it exit?" He responded, "I have no exit wound to give you for the entrance wound to the president's back. I can't tell you what happened to *that* bullet."

I reminded Dr. Wecht that at the London trial I had asked him to be more specific as to the location of his possible second gunman, and he ended up positioning the triggerman not on the grassy knoll but "around the second floor of the Texas School Book Depository Building, and more down towards the other end [far west side] of the building."[8] When I pointed out to him in our phone conversation that from that position—not as far behind the president as Oswald was believed to be, but still to the president's right rear at the time of the first shot that hit him—it would have been physically impossible for a bullet shot from there to enter the front of the president's throat, he replied, "Yes, of course. And that's why I want to drop that position of mine and put the possible second gunman more to the west [right front] in the area of the grassy knoll. I know I testified to the other position in London and also wrote that in one of my articles in the past[9] but I no longer believe that to be true."

Wecht conceded in our December 14 conversation that if the wound to the president's throat was an entrance wound from a bullet fired from the grassy knoll to the president's *right* front, since the bullet passed through soft tissue there would have to have been an exit wound somewhere on the *left* side of Kennedy's body, and none was found there. I therefore asked Dr. Wecht why not concede that the throat wound wasn't caused by a bullet from the president's right front, but was the exit wound of the bullet that entered the upper right back, an entrance wound he acknowledges? Because, Wecht said, if a bullet were fired in a "slightly upward" trajectory from the president's right front on the grassy knoll, it could have entered where the throat wound was and "exited at the president's lower left occipital protuberance, which was covered with his thick hair, and the autopsy surgeons may not have seen the exit wound, and may not have seen the actual pathway of the bullet." Wecht says this is "only a possibility" and he has "no evidence" of any such exit wound to the left side of the president's head. Of course, engaging in such speculation where there is no evidence to support your position is more appropriate to fiction than historical nonfiction.

My follow-up question of the doctor was that assuming this "possible" shot from the right front was fired at the president, where, specifically, did he propose the gunman was located *on* the grassy knoll? After the doctor said, "From behind the picket fence on the grassy knoll," and I pointed out to him that that would be *above* the president and that he had earlier postulated that his possible shot had traveled on a slightly *upward* trajectory, he countered, although not robustly, that "we don't know if there was an aperture somewhere lower on the fence." I responded that even if the imaginary gunman fired through an aperture at the bottom of the fence, it would still be at the top of the knoll, and the top of the knoll was around twenty-five feet *above* Elm Street. Since, in fact, *everything* to the president's right was above him (and the doctor said, "I don't buy any gunman firing from a manhole on the street"), where in the world, I asked, could his second gunman have been located? The doctor said, "That's a fair question. I cannot answer that. I'll have to take a further look at the topography of Elm Street and Dealey Plaza and get back to you on this point."

When Dr. Wecht called back on January 5, 2000, I knew what his research about Elm Street and Dealey Plaza *had* to tell him, and I wasn't indelicate enough to even raise the issue. I didn't have to. Dr. Wecht told me to "forget about" his previous statement to me about the "possibility" of a shot being fired from the grassy knoll entering the wound in Kennedy's throat and then exiting in the left occipital area of his head. "That's no longer a possibility," he said, adding that he had reconsidered his position and now accepts that the bullet that entered the right upper back of the president "must have" exited the front of the throat where the Warren Commission and HSCA said it did.[*]

However, he still maintained there was a possibility of a second gunman located somewhere to the president's right side who fired a shot at the president's head. But the shot to President Kennedy's head also creates insurmountable directional problems for Dr. Wecht. We see from frame 312 of the Zapruder film (see photo section) that Kennedy's head was tilted to the *left* at the moment he was hit. Thus, a bullet fired from his right rear, where Oswald was, and hitting him on the *right* rear of his head could logically be expected to exit (as both the Warren Commission and HSCA concluded) on the *right* side of his head, which we know it did. But if the bullet had come from Kennedy's right side, wouldn't it be expected to exit on the left side of his head, or at least penetrate far enough to cause *some* damage to the left side of his brain? Or at least leave some metal fragments there? Yet the autopsy showed that "the left cerebral hemisphere is intact," and the HSCA said that X-ray film of the skull reveals "the absence of any metal fragment within the left cerebral hemisphere."[10] Dr. Wecht has always felt he had a possible answer for this. He theorized in his testimony before the HSCA that the bullet may have entered the right side of the president's head in the very same spot that the bullet that struck the president's head from the rear had exited. Such a bullet, he said, "would have been fired in synchronized fashion[†] simultaneously with the shot that did strike [Kennedy] in the rear of the head," and the reason it didn't exit or even penetrate any part of the left side of his head was that it was a "frangible" (dumdum) bullet, a bullet that immediately disintegrates into a great many pieces. But Wecht testified before the HSCA that if such a shot were fired, it did not come from the right front (grassy knoll) but from the president's

---

[*]But Wecht added that based on the trajectory of that bullet through the president's body, it could not have been fired from as high up as the sniper's nest on the sixth floor of the Depository Building. It had to be from a lower floor, and possibly from the Dal-Tex Building. This latter observation was not a new one for Dr. Wecht; he has maintained this for years. See earlier text.

[†]On cross-examination of Dr. Wecht at the trial in London, I made the point about the utter improbability of synchronized shots. If there were synchronized shots, the two shooters would have had to know, in advance, that the presidential limousine would be passing within their cross-hairs at the agreed-upon time, which they could never know (i.e., at the agreed upon time, the limo could have been on Main or Houston, or past Elm onto the Stemmons Freeway). Even if they were to have this unachievable foreknowledge, there would virtually be no way for the two shooters, in different locations, to fire at the same, precise time. Since a gunman can't look at his watch and fire simultaneously, a watch would literally have to somehow be attached to the cross-hairs. To add to the extreme improbability of such an occurrence, the shot from the grassy knoll would have to have hit Kennedy's head at the precise point where the bullet from behind was exiting. (Transcript of *On Trial*, July 25, 1986, pp.778–780)

"right side or the lower right rear." And he conceded that his synchronized frangible-bullet theory was "extremely remote" and "the evidence is not there" to support it.[11]

Dr. Charles Petty of the HSCA forensic pathology panel responded to Dr. Wecht's frangible-bullet theory in his testimony before the committee. "I happen to be the coauthor of the only paper that has ever been written about the wounding capabilities of frangible bullets . . . [They are] used in shooting galleries . . . [and] are specifically designed to break up on the backdrop of the . . . gallery so as not to ricochet and cause injury to either the shooters or the people who work in the gallery . . . Such bullets and the breakup products of [these] bullets are easy to detect in X-rays. There are no such fragments in the X-ray of the late president's head. There was no frangible bullet fired. I might also add that frangible bullets are produced in .22 caliber loads and they are not produced [for] larger weapons."[12] In fact, all eight of Dr. Wecht's colleagues on the HSCA forensic pathology panel rejected his frangible-bullet hypothesis as well as any hypothesis concerning a bullet striking the president's head in the area of the exit wound. "We believe strongly that another missile did not enter the right front of the head within the area of the large defect. We find no evidence supporting this speculation in the photographs of the head or brain, or in any of the X-rays of either adjacent bone fragments or the left side of the head where, in such an event, one might expect such a bullet to lodge. No other missile was found, and the majority [of the forensic panel excluding Dr. Wecht] knows of no bullet that would completely disintegrate on hitting the soft tissue of the brain, as Dr. Wecht suggests."[13] Additionally, the HSCA's wound ballistics expert, Larry Sturdivan, concluded that the bullet was not a frangible one.[14] Dr. James Humes also dismissed the frangible-bullet theory for the head wound. "Had this wound . . . been inflicted by a dumdum [frangible] bullet, I would anticipate that the [wound] would not have anything near the regular contour and outline which it had."[15]

In my January 5, 2000, telephone conversation with Dr. Wecht, I asked him, "If the synchronized bullet you postulate, but acknowledge have no evidence to support, was *not*, in fact, a frangible bullet, do you concede that it would have exited the left side of the president's head, or at least penetrated far enough to cause *some* damage to the left hemisphere of his brain or have left metallic fragments there?" "Yes," he responded. "It would have had to go over to the left side of the president's brain." When I asked, "So do you concede that if the bullet was *not* a frangible bullet, your theory about the possible synchronized shot coming from the president's right side is no longer viable?" he answered, "Correct." When I also reminded Dr. Wecht that the autopsy X-rays of the president's head did not show any metallic fragments from a bullet proceeding from the right side of Kennedy's head to the left, only from the back to the front, he conceded this was another problem with the theory postulating a shot from the president's right side. He added, "I have no basis to set forth a theory that a bullet fired from the president's right side was comprised of nonradiopaque [that is, transparent, and hence, not seen on X-rays] material such as plastic or glass."

Larry Paul, a firearms expert with thirty years of experience with the Philadelphia and Los Angeles police departments, told me he had never heard of a glass bullet. And plastic bullets, he said, weren't manufactured until "the late sixties or early seventies and are only used as training ammunition. This is because they are fired without gunpowder—only a primer in the shell is used—and there is minimum velocity and minimum amount of impact and destructive capability. No assassin would ever use such a bullet." Paul added that all the plastic bullets he had ever seen were painted black, so they "*would* be visible in X-rays." But even if they weren't, he noted that the "wad" (the plastic component of a shotgun shell) frequently appears in X-rays, "even when they are white, and not painted a different color."[16]

Wecht's theory about frangible bullets only pertains to the shot to the president's head. He has never suggested that such a bullet may have entered the president's throat, and he confirmed this position in our telephone conversations. "If it had been a frangible bullet, there would have been much more soft-tissue damage in the area of the president's throat and neck," he said. I therefore said to him, "Doctor, you've always said you believed there was only one gunman firing from the president's right. You've never suggested two gunmen there, is that correct?"

"That's correct."

"But if the shot that you originally thought may have struck the president in the throat was *not* a frangible bullet, yet the synchronized bullet that you say may have struck the president on the right side of his head may have been, you'd have to have two gunmen on the president's right side, one firing frangible bullets, the other regular ones."

"Yes."

"You agree this is pretty far-fetched, don't you?"

"I agree that would not be likely at all," Dr. Wecht acknowledged, still not backing down, however, from his rejection of the single-bullet theory, only being forced into the conclusion that both gunmen were firing from the president's rear.

What all of the above shows, of course, is that in addition to the points made in the previous section—that there is no credible evidence whatsoever that any shots were fired from the president's right side or right front (grassy knoll), and the selection of the general area around the knoll as the site from which to shoot the president makes absolutely no sense at all—the conspiracy theorists' leading medical forensic expert cannot even *hypothesize* a shooting from the right side or right front that is intellectually sustainable. Even with as fine a forensic mind as Dr. Wecht's, by definition no one can defend a position that is indefensible.

Secret Service Agents
on the Grassy Knoll

Although the notion of a grassy knoll assassin has no basis in the evidence or common sense, before we move on we must discuss one of the very most enduring of all grassy knoll allegations. Three members of Dallas law enforcement testified before the Warren Commission that after the shooting they encountered Secret Service agents behind the picket fence on the grassy knoll as well as behind the Book Depository Building. The immediate problem that presents itself is that, as the Warren Commission found, "none [of the sixteen Secret Service agents protecting the president] stayed at the scene of the shooting . . . Secret Service procedure requires that each agent stay with the person being protected and not be diverted unless it is necessary to accomplish the protective assignment. Forrest V. Sorrels, special agent in charge of the Dallas office, was the first Secret Service agent to return to the scene of the assassination, approximately 20 or 25 minutes *after* the shots were fired."[1]

The HSCA likewise stated, "Except for Dallas [Secret Service] Agent-in-Charge [Forrest] Sorrels, who helped police search the Texas School Book Depository, no agent was in the vicinity of the stockade fence or inside the book depository on the day of the assassination."[2]

The conspiracy theorists have naturally alleged that these Secret Service impersonators were involved in the assassination, and hence, there was a conspiracy. What, specifically, did the Dallas law enforcement witnesses say? An examination of their testimony and interviews reveals that they are not quite as unambiguous as conspiracy theorists have led people to believe. Dallas County deputy constable Seymour Weitzman testified that after the shooting he ran into the parking lot in the railroad yards behind the grassy knoll, where he saw "other officers, Secret Service as well," and he later turned over what looked to him "like human bone" found on Elm Street to "one of the Secret Service men."[3] But in a report on his 1978 interview of Weitzman, HSCA investigator Leodis C. Matthews writes that Weitzman said "he did not know if the man was a law enforcement agent or not. I reminded him of his testimony before the Warren Commission identifying the person as a Secret Service agent. He recalled that he just didn't know who it was."[4]

Dallas police officer D. V. Harkness testified that around 12:36 p.m., six minutes after the shooting, he was in the back of the Book Depository Building and saw "some Secret Service agents there. I didn't get them identified. They told me they were Secret Service."[5] But again, in a report on his 1978 interview with Harkness, HSCA investigator Harold Rose writes that "Harkness told me that there was quite a bit of confusion and he would have to say that he may have assumed that the men were Secret Service. They could have been from some other agency."[6]

Dallas police officer Joe M. Smith testified that after the shooting he was one of the first officers who ran into the railroad yards* behind the fence to look around. He said, "Of course, I wasn't alone. There was some deputy sheriff with me, and *I believe* one Secret Service man when I got there." Smith said that because a woman had told him just before he went behind the fence that "they are shooting the President from the bushes," he pulled his pistol from his holster and approached the man he believed to be a Secret Service agent. But "I thought, this is silly, I don't know who I am looking for, and I put it back. Just as I did, he showed me [presumably with his badge] that he was a Secret Service agent."

Warren Commission counsel: "Did you accost this man?"

Smith: "Well, he saw me coming with my pistol and right away he showed me who he was."

Warren Commission counsel: "Do you remember who it was?"

Smith: "No, sir, I don't, because then *we* [presumably Smith, the deputy sheriff, and the "Secret Service" agent] started checking the cars."[7]

Note that Smith said he *believed* (not that he was sure) the man was a Secret Service agent. Also, he doesn't say how the person showed him who he was. It almost undoubtedly was by displaying a badge, but unless Smith examined the badge closely and saw the words *Secret Service* on it (which he had no reason to do, particularly in the frenzy of the moments following the shooting), Smith may have assumed the man was a Secret Service agent and therefore further assumed that the badge was a Secret Service badge when it could very well have been the badge of some other law enforcement agency.

Several people could have been the person Officer Smith encountered behind the picket fence. FBI special agent James P. Hosty told the committee that Frank Ellsworth, a plainclothes Dallas agent for the Alcohol and Tobacco Tax Unit of the Treasury Department (the predecessor to today's Bureau of Alcohol, Tobacco and Firearms), told him that he had been in the grassy knoll area right after the shooting and for some reason had identified himself to someone as a Secret Service agent.[8] But when the HSCA took Ellsworth's deposition, he denied telling Hosty this, adding, however, that "when ATF agents were detailed [to] Secret Service on the presidential protection, we were commonly mistaken for Secret Service agents."[9] Between Hosty and Ellsworth, whom should one believe? Experience with human nature would tell us that Hosty wouldn't have any reason to lie about what he said Ellsworth told him, whereas we know how very common it is for people to deny something that would be embarrassing to them. (The reason Hosty had contact with Ellsworth is that Ellsworth was the Treasury Department agent in Dal-

---

*The terms *parking lot* and *railroad yards* behind the stockade fence are used constantly in assassination literature. Are they one and the same? For the most part, yes. "The parking lot was *on* railroad property, and at least one railroad track passed through the parking lot." (Telephone interview of Gary Mack by author on August 18, 2005) Of course, there is a considerable area behind the stockade fence that is part of the railroad yards but is not a parking lot.

las whose investigative responsibilities included illegal trafficking in firearms and explosives in the Dallas region, and Hosty was his FBI contact. In fact, both Hosty and Ellsworth told the HSCA that they had met the very morning of the assassination to discuss the possible theft of rifles at nearby Fort Hood involving right-wing elements.)

What has to be taken into consideration is that, as the HSCA said, "because the Dallas Police Department had numerous plainclothes detectives on duty in the Dealey Plaza area, the Committee considered it possible that they were mistaken for Secret Service agents."[10] Several of these Dallas Police Department detectives, we can reasonably assume, went to investigate behind the grassy knoll. And many plainclothes detectives from other local and federal agencies, all with badges, were also in Dealey Plaza at the time of the shooting and went to investigate in various areas of the plaza. For example, Dallas deputy sheriff Roger Craig, a plainclothes officer, testified that he "ran up to the railroad yard and—uh—started to look around."[11] Dallas deputy sheriff Luke Mooney testified that immediately after the shooting, he and fellow deputy Ralph Walters "jumped over the [picket] fence and went into the railroad yards . . . and began to look around there." He said that "of course, there were other officers . . . there." Two of the officers, he said, were "Webster and . . . Vickery . . . *They were plainclothes officers like myself.*" He added, "We were trying to clear the area out and get all the civilians out that [weren't] officers."[12]

I couldn't find any record of Mooney having ever spoken to the media or assassination researchers through the years, and when I tried to reach him through the Dallas County Sheriff's Department, he was not amenable to talking to me. Finally, through the intercession of a friend of his, former Dallas assistant district attorney Bill Alexander, who had promised me he would "deliver" Mooney to me, I got Mooney on the phone for a few minutes on the afternoon of March 15, 2000. He is a very plainspoken man of few words who clearly wants to put his limited role in the assassination inquiry behind him. I really only had one important question to ask him. Were there any Secret Service agents in the railroad yards behind the picket fence after the shooting? "If there were, I didn't see them," Mooney said. I told him about the allegation by conspiracy theorists that Secret Service agents were there. "That's all bull," he responded, then added, "but now, I only looked around the area for two or three minutes before I left for the Book Depository Building. So I can't say who was there after I left." But while he was there, the only plainclothes officers in the yards besides himself whom he remembers by name were "Sam Webster, Ralph Walters [both now deceased], and Bill Vickery [I was unable to locate Vickery]." When I reminded him of his Warren Commission testimony that besides these three officers there were "other officers" in the yards, but "who they were, I don't recall at this time," and asked him if these other officers were plainclothes officers, he told me they were. "Could they have been from the Secret Service?" I questioned. "No," he said, "they definitely were all from my department, but I wasn't with them, and I don't recall who they were. But they were our boys."[13]

Mooney was in the yards for a very brief period. Undoubtedly, other plainclothes detectives from *other* agencies came there after Mooney left.

And according to a January 14, 1964, memorandum from Carl R. Booth Jr., the supervisor in charge of the Dallas office of the Alcohol and Tobacco Tax Unit of the Treasury Department, to Forrest Sorrels, special agent in charge of the Dallas office of the Secret Service, right after the shooting, nine of his investigators (all plainclothes) "ran from our offices . . . to the Texas School Book Depository Building . . . [and] participated in [the] search." One of the nine officers listed in the memo is the aforementioned Frank Ellsworth.[14] That one or more of these officers also went to the railroad yards behind the grassy knoll is not unlikely.

More significantly, the HSCA also learned from the testimony of Robert E. Jones, a retired army lieutenant colonel who was the operations officer for the 112th Military Intelligence Group headquartered at Fort Sam Houston, Texas, in 1963, that on the day of the assassination, his group "provided a small force . . . between eight and twelve" men to "augment" the Secret Service protection of the president. Jones said this was not unusual. That "at any time the president, or vice president" or anyone else under Secret Service protection would come to the area, the Secret Service would contact his group to assist in the protection of the subject official. He said on November 22, 1963, all of his men, who "were under the control and supervision of the Secret Service," were in *plain-clothes* and carried credentials, which included a photograph of themselves. If asked to identify themselves, they would "identify themselves as special agent John Doe and present their credentials," an identification that clearly could have made one assume that they were Secret Service agents. He said if the identification went further, they would say "they were working in conjunction with the Secret Service," but would not be authorized to say they were Secret Service agents, adding, however, he could not vouch that they did not do so. Jones testified he did not know where his detail of men were around the time of the shooting. "Some of them may have accompanied the motorcade and some of them may have stayed there [in Dealey Plaza]. Some of them may have been with the Secret Service. Some of our agents may have been with the FBI."[15]

The HSCA said it "sought to identify these agents so that they could be questioned. The Department of Defense, however, reported its files showed 'no records . . . indicating any Department of Defense Protective Services in Dallas [on the day of the assassination].' The Committee was unable to resolve the contradiction."[16]

The person Dallas police officer Joe Smith took to be a Secret Service agent in the parking lot behind the picket fence could easily have been one of Colonel Jones's men from the 112th Military Intelligence Group who was assigned to assist the Secret Service that day. But perhaps the most likely candidate for the person Smith confronted—a person whose identity has bewildered students of the assassination for over four decades—was James W. Powell, at the time of the assassination a Specialist E4 for the same 112th Military Intelligence Group who was stationed in Dallas but not assigned to protect the president that day. Powell told HSCA investigators in 1978 that he had taken the day off to see the president and was in his civilian clothes standing on the southeast corner of Elm and Houston when the president was shot. When someone in the crowd pointed to the Texas School Book Depository exclaiming the shots came from that direction, he took a picture of the building. Powell then "ran across the street and followed a group running towards the railroad tracks" because someone said the shots came from that direction.[17] In an interview with an investigator from the ARRB in 1996, Powell elaborated on this. He said the specific area he ran to was "the parking area" (i.e., behind the picket fence) and he ran there with some police officers and sheriff's deputies. Most importantly, when he was asked whether he showed anyone his identification at that time, he replied, "*I recall that I, I basically recall that I did*, because the officers were curious as to why I was joining them and *I just flashed my credentials to show them*." He said his ID was "a fold-out type," and when the ARRB investigator asked, "Something like this?" (described for the record as a "wallet-type credential showing the owner's picture and employing federal agency"), Powell said, "Like that exactly." Powell said he assumes he said what he normally did when showing his credentials: "I'm a special agent" or "I'm a special agent with Military Intelligence." Powell said that after he and the others checked the parking lot area and "didn't see anything obvious," he went back to the Book Depository Building, where he called his office.[18]

And, indeed, when the FBI interviewed Powell way back on January 3, 1964, he identified himself as a "special agent" for Army Intelligence.[19] The probability is substantial that the person Dallas police officer Joe Smith encountered behind the picket fence whom he took to be a Secret Service agent was none other than James W. Powell.

With respect to the issue of whether a Secret Service agent was behind the picket fence on the grassy knoll, the story of Special Agent Thomas "Lem" Johns has to be told. Johns was riding in the vice presidential security car (right behind the vice president's car), the fourth car in the motorcade. When the Warren Commission said that "none [of the Secret Service agents protecting the president] stayed at the scene of the shooting," it forgot about Johns, who stayed there for awhile, though unwillingly. As Johns explained it in a November 29, 1963, memorandum to Secret Service chief James Rowley, when the second shot rang out, he leaped out of his car to run to the vice president's car, saying, "I felt that if there was danger due to the slow speed of the motorcade, I would be of more assistance and in a more proper location with the Vice President's car." But he said that "before I reached the Vice President's car, a third shot had sounded and the entire motorcade then picked up speed and I was left on the street at this point." Johns doesn't say how long he remained at the assassination scene or what he did while he was there, only adding in his report, "I obtained a ride with White House movie men and joined the Vice President and ASAIC [Assistant Special Agent-in-Charge Rufus] Youngblood at the Parkland Hospital."[20]

However, in 1989, NBC cameraman David Wiegman, who had been in one of the press cars in the motorcade, told author Richard Trask that after the shooting he jumped out of his car and when he saw the police officer getting off his motorcycle and running up the slope toward the pergola on Elm, "I figured he knows something's up there, so I ran up there. I found myself there with Lem [Secret Service Agent Johns] close by, a few feet away . . . Lem was sort of looking around. Couldn't see anything. I knew now I'd better get . . . some footage. I saw these people lying on the ground, and I took them. I saw a lady being pulled down to the ground . . . You could sense she just wanted to get away from there, and somebody pulled her down." Note that there's no indication that Wiegman (and Johns, who allegedly was just a few feet away) ran to the parking lot and railroad yard area *behind* the picket fence, where Dallas police officer Joe Smith supposedly saw the "Secret Service" agent, only that he ran to the top of the slope. And the people Wiegman refers to as seeing lying on the ground were on the street side of the fence and pergola, not in the parking lot area on the other side.

Wiegman then told Trask something possibly contradictory when he said that "when I [not he and Johns] came back down the hill Lem Johns didn't have a ride and I said 'Come on, get in our car,'" which he said Johns did.[21]

Since Johns doesn't say in his report that he went up the grassy slope, and Wiegman said he did, I contacted Johns by phone. Now living in retirement in Alabama, Johns chuckled when he heard Wiegman's story. "I never got out of the street," he said. When

I asked him if he could have at least stepped a little off the street to the grassy area at the bottom of the slope, he said, "No, I never did. I never left the street." He chuckled again over Wiegman's story that implied he was checking around the assassination scene. "Our job is not to investigate. Our only job is to remove the vice president from danger." He reiterated, "I never left the street," adding, "I don't know where that fellow came up with his story." Johns said that he was on the street for "two to three minutes" before he hitched a ride to Parkland with the people "in the photographers' convertible."[22]

We don't know the definitive answer to the question concerning the *alleged* presence of Secret Service agents on the grassy knoll shortly after the shooting, but whatever it is, we know there is an innocent explanation for it. Why? Because the scientific and medical evidence could not be any more conclusive than it is: no shot was fired from the grassy knoll, the grassy knoll as the site where one would place an assassin makes no sense, no one saw anyone with a rifle behind the stockade fence or running away from it, and no rifle or expended cartridge casings from a rifle were found there. Since we know these things to be a fact, even if we assume for the sake of argument that there were twenty people on the grassy knoll claiming to be Secret Service agents, that wouldn't change this fact. And by definition and necessarily, this reality would dictate that they would have to be up there for some reason other than complicity in the assassination. What I'm saying is that the Secret-Service-agents-on-the-grassy-knoll argument "doesn't go anywhere."

Moreover, in the same "doesn't go anywhere" mode, even if there had been a gunman firing at the president from behind the picket fence, what purpose could Secret Service agents have served? The two Dallas officers who thought they encountered Secret Service agents behind the fence never said the agents were doing anything that could possibly help any assassin who had shot the president from behind the fence. Both Weitzman and Harkness merely said they saw these "agents" there, not that they were trying to keep people away from behind the fence so someone could escape, or prevent legitimate law enforcement from searching behind the fence for evidence. So whoever gave the impression of being a Secret Service agent clearly wasn't acting in any way indicative of complicity in the assassination.

And how can anyone draw any conspiratorial inference from the *supposed* Secret Service agents standing around behind the Book Depository Building six minutes after the shooting? I personally don't see where the Secret-Service-agent-impersonation story goes.

As indicated, the Secret-Service-agent-behind-the-picket-fence story has been heavily cited by authors of pro-conspiracy books as strong evidence of a conspiracy. As one example among many, author Sylvia Meagher, in referring to the alleged Secret Service agent Dallas police officer Smith encountered, writes, "I suggest that he was one of the assassins, armed with false credentials."[23] And the conspiracy authors never fail to mention the main witnesses who thought they saw Secret Service agents that day on the grassy knoll, like Sergeant Harkness and Officer Joe Smith.[24]

But with one commendable exception,[25] they predictably do not mention the most prominent person of all who fell victim that day to the phenomenon that afflicts most humans—as Henry Thoreau put it, "We see what we expect to see." It's a rich irony that this person is the very person whose memory the conspiracy theorists fight so endlessly to defend, using the Secret-Service-impersonation story as one of the quills in their conspiratorial quiver. The reader has to know by now that I'm talking about Lee Harvey Oswald. In an interview of Oswald in Captain Fritz's office on the morning of November 24, 1963, just an hour or so before Jack Ruby shot him, Oswald asked one of his inter-viewers, Secret Service inspector Thomas Kelley, if he was an FBI agent. When Kelley said he was not, that he was a member of the Secret Service, Oswald said that "when he was standing in front of the Textbook Building and about to leave it, a young crew-cut man rushed up to him and said he was from the Secret Service, showed [his] identifica-tion, and asked him where the phone was. Oswald said he pointed toward the pay phone in the building and that he saw the man actually go to the phone before he left."[26]*

Others that day made the same erroneous assumption as Oswald. Dealey Plaza motor-cade witness Ronald Fischer testified before the Warren Commission that after the shoot-ing, he "ran up to the top of the hill [grassy knoll] where all the Secret Service men had run."[27] But he told an HSCA investigator he did not know the men were Secret Service men, except that they wore suits and ties and appeared to have been law enforcement peo-ple.[28] And Mrs. Arnold Rowland testified that when her husband saw a man in the win-dow of the Book Depository Building minutes prior to the shooting, "we assumed that it was a Secret Service man."[29]

From all the evidence it clearly appears that the Secret Service sightings on the grassy knoll and behind the Book Depository Building after the shooting are entitled to about the same weight as Oswald's statement in Captain Fritz's office about being confronted by a Secret Service agent in front of the Book Depository Building.

---

*It has been widely assumed throughout the years that that person was NBC reporter Robert MacNeil. Indeed, in his book *The Right Place at the Right Time*, MacNeil says that as he ran up the steps of the Book Depository Building right after the shooting, he asked a young man in shirt sleeves who was coming out of the building where there was a phone, and the man pointed to another man inside who was talking on a phone and said, "Better ask him." He adds that although it is "possible" that Oswald was the man he encountered, he had "no way of confirming" that he had spoken to Oswald, and when he saw Oswald on television later that day, "there was no leap of recognition" on his part. "My hair was very short then and I was wearing a White House press badge [Oswald] may have mistaken for Secret Service ID." (MacNeil, *Right Place at the Right Time*, pp.208, 213)

Although it is not important just whom Oswald spoke to that day, there is a possibility it was someone other than MacNeil. On January 29, 1964, the Secret Service interviewed Pierce Allman, who was a reporter for Dallas TV station WFAA at the time of the assassination. Allman was described in the report as a "white male" with a "crew cut." The Secret Service report reads that Allman also ran into the Book Depository Build-ing right after the shooting, "where he met a white male whom he could not further identify. He asked this white male for the location of a telephone . . . The person pointed out a phone to him which was located in an open area on the first floor of the building." The interview report's "Synopsis" is that Allman is "believed to be [the] one mentioned by Lee Harvey Oswald as identifying himself as a Secret Service agent." (CD 354, p.2, Secret Service File 00-2-34,030) Gary Mack, curator at the Sixth Floor Museum in Dallas, agrees: "Pho-tos of MacNeil on November 22 [1963] show he had short hair, but it definitely was not a crew cut. Allman's the guy Oswald spoke to" (Telephone interview of Gary Mack by author on April 20, 2000).

The Zanies (and Others)
Have Their Say

Comedy feeds on tragedy. And whenever there's a major catastrophe or tragedy, as sure as death and taxes a chorus of cuckoo birds will voice their bizarre observations. It's automatic, as automatic as the bird whistles in the stands when there's a controversial call in an athletic event. But unfortunately for the conspiracy theorists in this case, although an enormous number of crackpots have surfaced to tell their silly stories about every single aspect of the Kennedy assassination, not nearly as many cuckoo birds as the conspiracy theorists would have liked, nor as many as one would have expected given the bedlam and chaotic circumstances following the shooting in Dealey Plaza,[*] have surfaced to say they *saw things* at or around the time of the assassination from which an inference of conspiracy could be drawn. Those who did ranged in credibility from nonexistent to—well—nonexistent. But no matter how far-fetched, fantastic (as in fantasy), and lacking in credibility their stories were, the conspiracy theorists have seized on these stories as holy writ and totally worthy of belief.[†]

---

[*]As Dealey Plaza spectator James L. Simmons told the Warren Commission, "Immediately after the shots were fired, people were running in every direction through the whole area, and there was a scene of mass confusion" (CE 1416, 22 H 833).

[†]Regarding this cuckoo bird phenomenon, let's look at what just a few among many have said about the death of Elvis Presley on August 17, 1977, in Memphis, Tennessee, at the age of forty-two. The following are from letters written to Ann Landers that were published in her syndicated column of October 23, 1988. From Stamford, Connecticut: "The King lives! I attended his funeral and lingered at the casket for quite awhile before the guards made me move on. Elvis was not in that casket. It was a wax dummy. I stood very close and had the opportunity to look at him for a long time. I would bet my life on it." From Henderson, Kentucky: "My uncle works in a place that manufactures coffins. The elaborate coffin that Elvis was buried in can be obtained only by special order because it takes a long time to construct. Elvis' coffin was ordered several weeks in advance, which proves that his 'death' was planned long before the public was told that he died." From Bismarck, North Dakota: "My sister's niece works in the courthouse where Elvis' death certificate was processed. The original certificate stated that the body weighed 170 pounds. The paramedics who picked him up said he weighed at least 250 pounds. Looks like there were two corpses, doesn't it? To add to the mystery, the first death certificate disappeared and was never found."

One of the Dealey Plaza witnesses whom conspiracy theorists have dearly embraced (to the extent of paying for his autograph at their conventions) as an important rebuttal to the conclusion of the Warren Commission that no shots came from the grassy knoll is Virgil "Ed" Hoffman, a deaf-mute. Conspiracy theorist Jim Marrs, in his book *Crossfire*, says, "It is [a] strange irony that the one person who apparently witnessed men with guns behind the wooden picket fence on the grassy knoll at the time of the Kennedy assassination was unable to tell anyone what he saw. Virgil Hoffman of Dallas has been deaf since birth and, as is common with that disability, he cannot speak."[1] Hoffman could make sounds, but nothing that was comprehensible to a third party.[2]

Virgil Hoffman first came to the attention of the authorities almost four years after the assassination when Jim Dowdy, his supervisor at Texas Instruments in Dallas, called the FBI on June 26, 1967, and told them that an employee, Hoffman, desired to tell the FBI what he saw at the time of the assassination. The FBI told Dowdy that Hoffman, being a deaf-mute, should put in writing everything he saw on that day.

Two days later, Hoffman appeared at the Dallas FBI headquarters. Because he did not read lips and was only semiliterate in reading and writing, he had a difficult time communicating with the agents, but he managed to convey to them, per an FBI report of that day, that when the motorcade was passing through Dealey Plaza, he was standing off the Stemmons Freeway (often referred to as the Stemmons Expressway) near the Texas and Pacific Railroad bridge that crosses over the freeway (not the railroad overpass above Elm, Main, and Commerce, but the one about a hundred yards to the northwest). He said that right after the shooting he saw two white males, clutching something dark to their chests with both hands, running from the rear of the Texas School Book Depository Building. The men ran north, then east, and Hoffman lost sight of them. The report doesn't say whether the interviewing agent (Special Agent Will Hayden Griffin) told Hoffman that from Hoffman's vantage point he wouldn't have been able to see the rear of the Texas School Book Depository Building because of a six-foot fence west of the building running for about 150 feet north of the building. In any event, the report goes on to say, "Approximately two hours after the above interview with Hoffman, he returned . . . and advised he had just returned from the spot on the Stemmons Freeway . . . and had decided he could not have seen the men running because of a fence west of the Texas School Book Depository Building. He said it was possible he saw these two men on the fence or something else."[3]

Since Hoffman admitted that he couldn't have seen what he said he saw, that should have been the end of him as a purported witness. But Hoffman was not about to go away.

In the meantime, the FBI interviewed Roy Truly, the superintendent of the Book Depository Building, on July 6, 1967, and he said that the subject fence was constructed approximately two years *before* the assassination. The previous day, July 5, the FBI interviewed Hoffman's father, E. Hoffman, and brother, Fred. The FBI report of the interview said, "Both advised that Virgil Hoffman has been a deaf mute his entire life and has in the past distorted facts of events observed by him. Both the father and brother stated that Virgil Hoffman loved President Kennedy and had mentioned to them just after the assassination that . . . he saw numerous men running after the President was shot. The father . . . stated that he did not believe his son had seen anything of value and doubted he had observed any men running from the Texas School Book Depository, and for this reason did not mention it to the FBI."[4] Hoffman would later claim that his father and uncle had told him it would be "dangerous" for him to say what he saw because of the "C.I.A. or other persons."[5]

It should be noted that way back in 1964, two men, James E. Romack and George W. Rackley, told the FBI they were standing about thirty-five yards to the rear of the Depository Building at the time of the shooting, facing the rear doors of the building, and they saw no one come out of the rear of the building right after the shooting.[6]

At this point, everyone (including apparently Virgil Hoffman's own family) intended to put the matter behind them. Everyone, that is, except Virgil Hoffman. Almost another ten years went by before Hoffman, this time with bells and bangles, emerged once again. Thoughts about the assassination obviously had not died within him, but instead had been gestating. By 1977, when he reemerged, allegations about Kennedy's assassin being behind the picket fence on the grassy knoll and about a "puff of smoke" being seen in the vicinity at the time of the shooting (much more on this later) had become the currency of discourse in the conspiracy theory community, and Hoffman had a much better tale for the authorities. He appeared at the Dallas FBI office on March 21, 1977, and this time told agents that the two men he had seen were not, as he had first told them, behind the Texas School Book Depository Building, but instead were—yes, you guessed it—behind the picket fence on the grassy knoll, and one had a rifle and the other a handgun. (The conspiracy theorists, in their books, have always put one assassin behind the picket fence. Hoffman put two there. Both were obviously real, professional hit men for the mob or CIA, etc. If the rifle doesn't get Kennedy, a good old revolver will for sure.) The FBI report says, "Hoffman made hand motions indicating that one of the men disassembled the rifle and placed it in a suitcase" and that he had also seen a puff of smoke prior to that.[7]

Four days later, on March 25, one Richard Freeman, a coworker of Hoffman's at Texas Instruments, called the FBI to advise that he knew sign language and Hoffman was concerned that the FBI perhaps did not fully understand what he was trying to communicate. But it turned out the FBI had gotten the story pretty straight. Freeman told the FBI that Hoffman had communicated the following to him: From his position atop the Stemmons Freeway overpass, "Hoffman saw two men, one with a rifle and one with a handgun, behind a wooden fence . . . this fence is located on the same side of Elm Street as the Texas School Book Depository Building but closer to the Stemmons Freeway. Since he is deaf, he naturally could not hear any shots but thought he saw a puff of smoke in the vicinity of where the two men were standing. As soon as he saw the motorcade speed away and saw the puff of smoke in the vicinity of the two men, the man with the rifle looked like he was breaking the rifle down by removing the barrel from the stock and placing it in some dark type of suitcase that the other man was holding. The two men then ran north on the railroad tracks" out of Hoffman's sight. Hoffman told Freeman, "Both men were white males, both [were] dressed in some type of white suits, and both wore ties."[*]

On March 28, 1977, FBI special agent Udo H. Specht had Hoffman take him to where he said he was at the time of his alleged observations. Specht estimated the distance from the vantage point to the area behind the wooden fence "at approximately 200 yards." Hoffman communicated to Specht that after he saw what he claims he did, he tried to get the attention of a Dallas policeman nearby but he could not communicate with the officer.[8]

---

[*]In 1986, Hoffman changed the clothing of the men considerably. He told conspiracy theorist Jim Marrs that the man with the rifle was "wearing a dark suit, tie and overcoat" and the second man "was wearing light coveralls and a railroad worker's hat" (*Coverups*, March 1986, no. 25, p.1).

On the 1988 British television production *The Men Who Killed Kennedy*, Hoffman said the FBI didn't want him to tell anyone what he saw and "offered me money to keep me quiet." The conspiracy theorists are so impoverished in their desperate search for evidence to support their cause that they are compelled to descend to such whimsical, ever-changing, and obviously untrue accounts as that of Virgil Hoffman.[*]

One of the very biggest favorites of the conspiracy community is the late Jean Hill, the famed "Lady in Red" who parlayed her Dealey Plaza experience into a commercial enterprise, speaking for a fee at buff conventions (always signing autographs in red ink in memory of the red raincoat she was wearing that day), making many appearances on radio and TV, and even writing a book, *JFK: The Last Dissenting Witness*. London Weekend Television contacted her about testifying for the defense in the London trial and she agreed, but after Gerry Spence and his staff either interviewed her or looked at her record, they elected not to call her to the stand as a witness. It's not hard to figure out why. It has something to do with credibility.

At the time of the assassination, Mrs. Hill, with her friend Mary Moorman, was watching the motorcade pass by from the south side (to the president's left) of Elm Street. At approximately 1:20 p.m., NBC national news cut to its Fort Worth affiliate, WBAP, for a live interview of Mrs. Hill by reporter Tom Whalen. Hill told Whalen that just before the president's car came right in front of her and Mary Moorman, "the shots came directly across the street from us. And just as the president's car became directly even with us," the president and his wife "were looking at a dog that was in the middle of the seat,[†] and about that time two shots rang out." Hill said she heard "more shots" right after these two. She elaborated that "the shots came from the hill—it was just east of the underpass" (i.e., the grassy knoll) and said she thought she saw "this man running . . . up there."[9] Shortly thereafter, Mrs. Hill gave a sworn statement to the Dallas County Sheriff's

[*]Hoffman sent a letter on October 3, 1975, to JFK's brother, Senator Edward Kennedy, telling him of his observations on the day of the assassination, and adding in broken syntax, "I talked F.B.I.'s office in Dallas last 1968 or can't remember date and year ago. If you will find to see F.B.I.'s report about I talked them. I guess, maybe F.B.I. did not know understand what I talked a thing, because I am deafness and hard to talk F.B.I. . . . If you will help me and tell some things. Thank you much. Respectfully, Virgil Edward Hoffman."
Kennedy replied on November 19, 1975: "My family has been aware of various theories concerning the death of President Kennedy . . . I am sure that it is understood that the continual speculation [about the case] is painful for members of my family. We have always accepted the findings of the Warren Commission Report . . . Our feeling is that, if there is sufficient evidence to re-examine the circumstances concerning the death of President Kennedy . . . this judgment would have to be made by the legal authorities responsible for such further examination." (FBI Record 124-10163-10464, pp.5–6)
[†]When the interviewer pressed Hill as to what kind of dog it was, she said she didn't know but it was "white and fuzzy" (6 H 214, WCT Jean Lollis Hill). Since there was no dog in the president's car, Hill took a lot of ribbing for this, and in later years conspiracy theorists tried to restore her credibility on this point by claiming that photographs taken at Love Field show that Mrs. Kennedy had been given a white, stuffed toy representing the famous Sheri Lewis TV puppet Lamb Chop. The claim, however, was based on poor-quality images posted on the Internet. High-quality images show that what critics thought was a Lamb Chop toy was, in fact, a bouquet of white flowers (asters) that someone in the greeting party at Love Field (it is not known who) had given the First Lady in addition to a larger bouquet of red roses given to her by the mayor's wife. (Trask, *That Day in Dallas*, pp.27, 29) In Richard Trask's 1994 invaluable book, *Pictures of the Pain*, he said film footage showed that Mrs. Kennedy "was apparently presented with a small stuffed animal . . . She may have kept the stuffed toy among the roses with which she was also presented" (Trask, *Pictures of the Pain*, p.260 footnote 17). However, no photo of the interior of the car ever showed the toy, and such a toy never surfaced. Four years later, in his 1998 book, *That Day in Dallas*, Trask corrected himself and noted that the "stuffed toy" among the red roses was really a "gift bouquet of white asters" (Trask, *That Day in Dallas*, p.29).

Department in which she repeated the dog story, did not indicate where the shots came from, but added, "I thought I saw some men in plain clothes shooting back" (none were), acknowledging that "everything was such a blur." After the shooting, she said she "looked across the street and up the hill [grassy knoll] and saw a man running toward the monument [pergola]" and she "started running" across the street in his direction but was eventually turned back by police officers.[10]

At this point, Mrs. Hill was just one of many Dealey Plaza witnesses who thought the shots came from the grassy knoll. As to the running man, with chaos reigning after the shooting and people running in every direction, a man running toward the pergola, in and of itself, is meaningless. So there was nothing of any special significance to the assassination inquiry in Hill's two statements on November 22, 1963. But not to worry. Like wine, Mrs. Hill's self-described "blur" became clearer and better with time and she came to embrace virtually everything about the grassy knoll any conspiracy buff could ever hope for.

In her testimony before the Warren Commission on March 24, 1964, in addition to repeating that she thought the shots came "from the [grassy] knoll," she elaborated on the running man. He was wearing a brown overcoat and hat and when she first saw him, "he was at the top of [the] hill . . . right up there by the School Depository," she said, "more to the west-end" of the building, and he was "running, or getting away, or walking away or something—I would say he was running." He was going "toward the railroad tracks to the west." When Warren Commission counsel asked if the man had a weapon in his hand, she answered, "No, I never saw a weapon during the whole time, in anyone's hand." She said she ran after the man to "catch" him, and while she was running after him she "looked down and saw some red stuff and I thought 'Oh, they got him, he's bleeding,' . . . but it turned out to be Koolade or some sort of red drink." By the time she looked up from the grass, she had lost sight of the man and "couldn't find him again . . . By that time everyone was screaming and moving around."

Whom did this man look like?

"The person that I saw looked a lot like . . . Jack Ruby."

Question: "Do you think he was, in fact, Jack Ruby?"

"That, I don't know," she said.[11]

By 1986, she was convinced it was Ruby, telling an interviewer, "Of course, I didn't know who Jack Ruby was at the time. But when I saw Ruby on television, when he shot Oswald, I called to my daughter to look, and said 'This is the man I saw run that day.'"[12]

Mrs. Hill testified that "quite a lot of people" had made "an awful lot of fun" of her over her observations that day, including her husband, and she was "real tired of it." But she concluded her testimony by saying, "You are not proud to say it, but I think it was part of history and I was glad I was there . . . because I got publicity . . . I think my children will be interested to know . . . someday that I was in it someway."[13]

In her Warren Commission testimony in 1964, when Hill was asked why she thought the shots came from the grassy knoll area, she said, "That was just my idea where they were coming from." She made no reference at all to seeing any man firing a weapon from behind the picket fence.[14] As indicated, she testified expressly that she "never saw a weapon during the whole time, in anyone's hand." In fact, at 3:16 p.m. on the day of the assassination, Hill was interviewed by a WBAP newsman (believed to be either Jimmy Darnell or Floyd Bright). When asked, "Did you see the person who fired the—?" Hill answered, "No, I didn't see any person fire the weapon."[15] But twenty-six years later, in 1989, Hill told conspiracy theorist Jim Marrs that "I saw a man fire from behind the wooden fence [on the grassy knoll]. I saw a puff of smoke and some sort of movement on the grassy knoll where he was."[16] In a February 20, 1989, television interview, she further embroidered her story by saying she saw a "flash of light" in the area behind the stockade fence where some conspiracy theorists claim the "Badge Man" (see later text) was firing.[17] By 1992, writing in the third person in her book, she says, "It was a sight that was destined to haunt her for the rest of her life: a muzzle flash, a puff of smoke, and the shadowy figure of a man holding a rifle, barely visible above the wooden fence at the top of the knoll, still in the very act of murdering the president of the United States."[18]

In her book, Hill said she was puzzled as to why she wasn't called as a witness in the London trial, and wondered ominously, and conspiratorially, "Had pressure been applied from some covert source to stifle [my] story? Had that pressure somehow reached all the way across the Atlantic ocean?" Hill writes in her book that since the docu-trial's producers had already promised, in writing, to pay for all of her (and a guest of her's) expenses to London, she threatened, through an attorney son-in-law, to sue if they didn't live up to their agreement, and she and her mother had an all-expense-paid trip to London for two weeks. However, she was "ordered" by the producers "to stay completely away" from the courtroom.[19]

Although it would not be too easy to have any less credibility than Mrs. Hill, conspiracy buffs, in their desperation, have elevated her to an iconic stature, Hill being one of the very brightest stars in the conspiracy theory constellation. Oliver Stone, in his movie *JFK*, treated the Hill character with utmost seriousness, and her Dealey Plaza observations are cited and accepted without criticism in virtually all the major conspiracy books on the assassination. To hell with the official record, even, as indicated, Mrs. Hill's own husband. We know a credible witness when we see one, the buffs in effect are saying.

Another favorite of the conspiracy theorists who would fall in a general way under the category of "grassy knoll" witness is a former Dallas police officer named Tom Tilson. Gerry Spence called him as a witness at the London trial, and after my having interviewed Tilson no fewer than four times over the phone in May and June of 1986, and cross-examining him at the trial, my feeling about Tilson, at least in 1986, was that he was somewhat pathetic and a good-old boy who was more confused than anything else. However, I'm probably being too charitable in my assessment of him,[*] because his story is so obviously silly and false on its face that one has to wonder whether it was an intentional fabrication on his part, back in 1978, the first time I'm aware he told it.

On August 20, 1978, fifteen years after the assassination, Tilson told *Dallas Morning News* reporter Earl Golz that on November 22, 1963, he had taken the day off from his job as a Dallas police officer, and as he was driving downtown with his daughter, Judy, to pick up another daughter who was watching the presidential motorcade, he heard on his police radio that Kennedy had been shot. While he was driving east on Commerce approaching the Triple Underpass, he told Golz, "I saw all these people running to the

---

[*]Spence was even more so, telling the jury in his summation that "Mr. Bugliosi can laugh him out of the courtroom," but actually "old Tom Tilson" was a believable witness, a really genuine, salt-of-the-earth type of person who "would be one of my best friends . . . if I lived in Dallas . . . We'd go out . . . He's the kind of people I would congregate with" (Transcript of *On Trial*, July 25, 1986, pp. 1016–1017).

scene of the shooting . . . but here's one guy coming from the railroad tracks. He came down that grassy slope on the westside of the triple underpass [not the "grassy knoll," which is to the east of the Triple Underpass, but an embankment to the west of it], on the Elm Street side. He had a car parked there, a black car. And he threw something in the backseat and went around the front hurriedly and got in the car and took off . . . I said 'That doesn't make sense. Everybody running to the scene and one person running from it.'" Tilson told Golz he pursued the car on to the Dallas–Fort Worth Turnpike but the car eventually eluded him. He described the man as being about five feet nine inches tall and weighing 185 to 190 pounds, and told Golz he telephoned the Dallas Police Homicide and Robbery Bureau that day and gave the bureau the license plate number (which he had his daughter write down) and a description of the driver and car, "but they never contacted me or did anything about it." Golz writes, "City police radio logs for that day do not reflect any alert for the vehicle that Tilson says he pursued." Tilson said he didn't keep the paper on which his daughter had written the license plate number.[20]

Although several books quote Tilson as telling Golz in the August 1978 interview that if the man he pursued "wasn't Jack Ruby, it was someone who was his twin brother,"[21] the name Ruby isn't even mentioned in that interview. However, Tilson was just getting warmed up. Six days later, he told essentially the same story to investigators for the HSCA, adding the man was "slipping and sliding down" the embankment, and because of the speed of his movement, the man rammed against the side of the "dark" car he got into. Also, if the man he pursued wasn't Ruby, he looked enough like Ruby to be his "twin."[22]

At the trial in London, Tilson elaborated on his story and became even more certain it was Ruby. On direct examination by Spence, he said that Ruby "had a Silver Spur Dance Hall on my beat" and therefore he knew Ruby very well because he saw him "just about every day." He said he got a good look at the driver because he "pulled up beside [his] car." But since his daughter was with him and he feared she might get shot, he said to himself, "It's not worth it," whereupon he took the first exit off the turnpike and called homicide with his information. He said the man looked "exactly like [Ruby] . . . If it wasn't Ruby, it was a twin brother."

Leaving aside the fact that we know where Jack Ruby was at the time of the assassination (see "Four Days in November" section); that a photo of the specific area where Tilson claimed the black car was parked (west of the Triple Underpass on the north side of Elm), and taken at the very time Tilson said he saw the car, reveals no car of any kind or color parked there; and that Dallas police radio logs (examined in detail throughout the years by a great number of people) do not contain any record on November 22, 1963, of Tilson's call, there are a host of other problems with Tilson's story. He told Golz that the reason the Dallas Homicide and Robbery Bureau didn't pay any attention to the information he phoned in was that "homicide was that way. If you didn't have a big white hat on, they didn't even want you in the office . . . They didn't want to have to look for anybody else and they didn't even want to know about it really." In other words, according to Tilson, on the day of the assassination, Dallas homicide detectives weren't interested in finding out who murdered the president, and under no circumstances did they want to even consider information about the president's murder if it came from someone who didn't wear a "big white hat," referring to a Stetson, which, as indicated earlier, only Dallas homicide detectives on the force were allowed to wear.

On cross-examination in London, these were just a few of the points I made:

Question: "When you pursued this man in your car, you told me [in pretrial interviews] that he did not drive fast at all. Is that correct?"

Answer: "That's right. He didn't drive fast . . . No hurry."

Question: "In fact, he drove at the minimum speed without getting a ticket on the turnpike, forty-five miles an hour, is that right?"

Answer: "That's right."

(I then brought out before the jury that although Tilson was now testifying that the driver of the car was driving relatively slowly, and he, Tilson, gave up the chase, in a December 31, 1978, interview with Golz, he said he "chased the speeding car" and told Golz in the August 20, 1978, interview that the driver of the car had eluded him. At the trial he denied telling Golz the latter.)

On direct examination Spence had sought to bolster Tilson's credibility by establishing that he had been a Dallas police officer since 1946 and had received four awards for outstanding police work. On cross-examination I said to Tilson that the president of the United States had just been assassinated, and he, a well-decorated police officer, called homicide and reported seeing a man running from the scene of the murder, get in a car, and drive off, and he gave homicide the license plate number of the car, "and you're telling this jury, Tom, that they weren't interested?"

Answer: "They probably thought just like I did. Who would use their own car and their own license number to kill a president of the United States?"

Question: "You never once called Dallas homicide to find out, did you, Tom, whether they had followed up on what you had given them?"

Answer: "No. I didn't dare go into the office. I didn't have a wide [Stetson] hat."

Then I started having a little fun with Tilson:

Question: "So the fellow you saw running away, whom you believe to be Jack Ruby, you feel that he is the one who killed the president?"

Answer: "He's the killer."

Question: "Well, by putting two and two together, then, you feel, that not only did Ruby kill President Kennedy, but when Oswald was getting credit for it, Ruby killed Oswald, too."

Answer: "Looks like it, doesn't it."

The Court: "Alright, alright."

I asked Tilson why, if he believed the man he pursued was Ruby, didn't he give Dallas homicide Ruby's name when he called them with his information? Unbelievably, Tilson answered, "Well, I couldn't. Somebody might go get Jack Ruby and he might not have been guilty." (Translation: Never pursue any suspect to a crime because there's always a chance the suspect might not be guilty.)

Question: "Well, now, Jack used to give you free drinks at his club, is that right?"

Answer: "When I was off."

Question: "You weren't trying to protect him, were you?"

Answer: "Oh, no."

Question: "Later on TV you saw that Oswald was arrested for the murder of the president, right?"

Answer: "Correct."

Question: "Didn't you say to yourself, hey, they've got the wrong guy. They should pick up Jack?"

Answer: "No. Not until Jack shot him. When Jack shot Oswald, [I said,] 'I'll be. I'll be durned. That's old Ruby, alright.'"[23]

In the introduction to this book, I spoke, among many other things, of the meaningful contribution the trial in London had made to the study of the assassination in that both pro– and anti–Warren Commission witnesses were cross-examined. I also spoke of how a reader would have no way of knowing if the author of a book on the assassination were conveying something worthy of belief unless the reader had access to the official record, which few have. With this in mind (and this is just one typical example among hundreds of others), and knowing what you now know about the Tilson story, picture an innocent reader dealing with Jim Garrison's take on Tilson in his number-one *New York Times* best-selling book on the assassination, *On the Trail of the Assassins*: "Tom Tilson, an off-duty police officer, had heard about the shooting over his radio . . . As he drove near the overpass, he saw a man 'slipping and sliding' down the slope west of the overpass . . . This was the only man Officer Tilson could see running away from the shooting, so he watched him. The man came down against the side of a car parked there, threw something in the backseat, then jumped in the front seat and took off at high speed. Tilson followed the car in a wild chase. When he got close enough, he called out the license number and the make and model of the car to his daughter riding with him. She wrote the information down, and after the car got away, he called it in to the Dallas Homicide Squad. But there was no response from homicide. Officer Tilson never heard another word about the suspect he had chased." Period. Nothing more. The reader would think Tilson was a completely credible witness.[24]

The distortions, omissions, lies, and nonsense have continued for well over forty years.

The Tilson experience is simply illustrative of something at the heart of the conspiracy culture, something that provides its oxygen: the uncritical acceptance, at face value, of any statement made by anyone that in any way supports the conspiracy position. Examples of erroneous statements about the case that turn out to be untrue once they are challenged are countless and ongoing. Just one quick one before we move on: Early on, New Orleans DA Jim Garrison alleged that Kennedy was killed as a result of a homosexual conspiracy involving David Ferrie (who was homosexual), Oswald (who Garrison said was a "switch-hitter"), and Jack Ruby. And indeed, one Leona Kirilenko told the FBI a month after the assassination that she worked at Ruby's Carousel Club for about two weeks in 1957, and that it was "common knowledge" at the club that Ruby was a "queen" whose male "girlfriend" was named Carmen. But when the FBI reinterviewed her and told her that Ruby didn't even start operating the Carousel Club until early in 1960, she conceded she had been in error and had confused Ruby with someone at another club she had worked at who was very similar in appearance to Ruby.[25] Absent the FBI's going back to reinterview Kirilenko, her false declaration about Ruby (whether Ruby was, in fact, a homosexual or not, is irrelevant) would have been, as the *New York University Law Review* put it, "an acceptable part of the historical record, there to lurk and mislead tomorrow's historians."[26] Multiply Kirilenko's original statement by a thousand to get an idea of the enormous amount of misinformation peddled as fact in books, articles, and radio and TV shows, and movies for conspiracy theorists to use with their particular brand of mischief.

Then there's the story of Richard Randolph Carr, which ultimately becomes funny. But first, the serious part. In 1964, Carr told the FBI that at the time of the shooting in Dealey Plaza he was seeking employment at the construction of a new courthouse at the corner of Houston and Commerce streets in Dallas. When told that the foreman was on the ninth floor, he started walking up the stairway. "As I reached a point at approximately the sixth floor of the building framework, I looked toward the Texas School Book Depository Building . . . and at that time I observed [almost two hundred yards away] a man looking out of a window on the top floor" of the building. Carr said he was "a heavyset individual, who was wearing a hat, a tan sport coat, and horn-rimmed glasses" and was located "in the second window over from Houston Street." Carr told the FBI that from his vantage point he could not see the lower floors and entrance of the Book Depository Building, that he could "only see the top floor and roof" of the building. (The top floor is the seventh floor, a floor above where we know Oswald was.)

After he heard the shots, he immediately proceeded down the stairway of the building, and when he got out on the street near Houston and Commerce, he said, "I saw a man whom I believe was identical with the man I had earlier seen looking out of the window." Carr went on to say that the man walked very fast *south* on Houston Street to Commerce, then walked east on Commerce to Record Street, where he got into a car driven by a "young Negro." The car drove north out of sight.[27] James Worrell Jr., a Dealey Plaza witness, testified before the Warren Commission that after he heard the shots, he got frightened and started running north on Houston. When he stopped to get his breath, he turned around. "I was there approximately three minutes," Worrell testified, "before I saw this man come out the back door" of the Book Depository Building, though, he said, "I am not positive," just "pretty sure" that's where he first saw the man.[*] The man proceeded to run south on Houston toward Elm. Conspiracy theorists have long maintained this was the same man Raymond Carr saw walking very fast south on Houston. But apart from the fact that Worrell's man was running and Carr's man was walking (albeit, very fast), the description by Worrell and Carr of the man each saw varies quite a bit. Worrell's man weighed between 155 and 165, Carr's was "heavyset." Worrell's man never had a hat on, Carr's was wearing a hat. Worrell's man was wearing a sports jacket "dark in color," Carr's a "tan sport coat."[28]

It should be noted that several days prior to his testimony before the Warren Commission, which was on March 10, 1964, Worrell told the *Dallas Times Herald* the same thing. When James Romack (mentioned earlier in relation to Virgil Hoffman) read this in the March 6, 1964, edition of the *Times Herald*, he called the Dallas office of the FBI that very evening to report that Worrell's story simply could not be true. Romack, an employee of the Coordinated Transportation Company located a few blocks northeast of the Depository Building, told the FBI that he and a coworker, George Rackley, were standing approximately 110 feet north of the northeast corner of the Depository Building at the time of the shooting. Romack and Rackley had gone there hoping to see the presidential motorcade as it passed the intersection of Houston and Elm. Romack said they had a clear view of the three doors to the rear of the Texas School Book Depository Building, the back door and the two loading dock entrances, and he was "positive that no one came out of this door or the loading dock doors" after the shooting. Indeed, Romack paid particular attention to the rear of the building since he recognized the sounds he heard as gunshots, and when he saw a uniformed police officer running alongside the building, he realized that "someone might come out of the back of the building." He said he remained in back of the building for some time and did "not believe it is possible that

*Indeed, Dealey Plaza witness Amos Lee Euins, though not seeing anyone emerge from the back of the building, said that shortly after the shooting he heard someone tell a police officer "he seen a man run out the back" (2 H 205–206).

anyone came out of the back door of the building" without his seeing the person. George Rackley, on March 9, 1964, confirmed to FBI agents what Romack had told them and said he "saw no one leave the Texas School Book Depository Building by way of the rear exit."[29] Romack and Rackley not only told the FBI this, but testified under oath before the Warren Commission to this fact. Their observations of the rear of the building, including the back door, continued, they said, for sometime thereafter, Rackley saying "probably ten [minutes]," Romack, "four or five minutes."[30]

Even assuming the two witnesses, Worrell and Carr, saw what they said they saw, and even if we make the further assumption they saw the same man, the fact remains that running out of the Book Depository Building or running up or down any of the streets in Dealey Plaza right after the assassination, when absolute chaos reigned, would not seem to be abnormal behavior. And if anyone involved in the assassination were to have run out the back door of the Book Depository Building (the north side of the building), one would think the normal direction he would have taken for his escape would be to go *north* on Houston, where virtually no one was, not south toward Elm Street, where all of law enforcement had congregated.

Since that time, Carr has changed his story as well as added substantially to it. In New Orleans district attorney Jim Garrison's unsuccessful prosecution of Clay Shaw in 1969 for conspiring to murder Kennedy (see conspiracy section), Garrison called Carr to the stand. But he had a problem. Garrison couldn't have Carr testify he saw the man on the top floor (the seventh floor), since no one saw anyone on that floor, and he couldn't say the sixth floor, because Oswald was there. So the very accommodating Carr now said the man he saw in the window was really on "the fifth floor of the School Book Depository" Building, totally contradicting what he told the FBI in 1964, which was that he couldn't see, from his vantage point, any of the floors beneath the seventh floor. And now the man was "at the third window" from Houston, having apparently moved not only two stories down from where Carr saw him on November 22, 1963, but also one window over. Carr further embroidered his statement to the FBI by testifying in New Orleans that while the man was walking fast, "every once in a while he would look over his shoulder as if he was being followed."

Then Carr added something completely new: "*Immediately* after the shooting," he told Garrison and the Shaw jury, he saw "three men that emerged from behind the School Book Depository." (How he saw them when he told the FBI in 1964 that he could not see anything beneath the seventh floor is not known.) One of the three men, Carr testified, was "real dark-complected" and the three got into a Rambler station wagon driven by the dark-complected man and sped north on Houston. This new version of the story by Carr corroborated, for Garrison, the story of Roger Craig (see later text), who testified for Garrison that he saw Oswald running out of the Book Depository Building and getting into a "Rambler station wagon" driven by a "dark-complected" man. The problem with fabricated stories is that inconsistencies frequently occur. As opposed to the truth, which is compatible with its environment, falsehoods, as Daniel Webster said, not only disagree with truths, but usually quarrel among themselves. As we shall see, Craig's Rambler was going west on Elm; Carr's, north on Houston. Craig's Rambler drove off from Dealey Plaza fifteen minutes after the assassination; Carr's, immediately after. Moreover, there were only two people (Oswald and driver) in Craig's Rambler, three in Carr's Rambler. But we'll get to Craig later. As for Carr, we know he made up the story about "three men speeding away in the Rambler" because in his first interview with the FBI on January 4,

1964, and in the three-and-a-half-page comprehensive signed statement he gave the bureau on February 1, 1964, he mentioned no such thing.

Carr came up with yet another story at the Shaw trial. He told the FBI in 1964 that he heard three shots and they seemed to be coming from the Triple Underpass area. But in New Orleans, he testified he heard four shots and "the last three" came from—you guessed right—*behind the picket fence at the top of the grassy knoll*. How could he tell? Listen to this. From his position almost two hundred yards away (close to two football fields) he saw that one of the three bullets "knocked a bunch of grass up . . . and you could tell from the way it knocked it up that the bullet came from this direction (pointing to a photomap of the picket fence on the grassy knoll)."[31]

Now for the somewhat funny part. Though Carr has no credibility and no one in authority is in the least bit interested in what he has to say, apparently the conspirators who murdered Kennedy are still terrified that the authorities might listen to him one day, and according to him, they have been trying to intimidate and even murder him for years, all to no avail. Carr told conspiracy theorist Gary Shaw in 1975 that when FBI agents interviewed him and he told them the man he saw in the Book Depository Building window wasn't Oswald (the FBI report of the interview, as indicated earlier, only says that Carr described the man as a "white male" and described the way he was dressed, not that Carr said the man was not Oswald), one of the agents said to him, "If you didn't see Lee Harvey Oswald in the School Book Depository with a rifle, you didn't witness it." When Carr persisted that the man wasn't Oswald, the agent said to him, "You better keep your mouth shut." Not long after, he told Shaw, his home was raided by more than a dozen Dallas policemen and detectives armed with a search warrant looking for "stolen articles." They ransacked his home, he said, while holding him and his wife at gunpoint. The day after the police raid, Carr said he received an anonymous phone call advising him to "get out of Texas." Carr heeded the warning and left for Montana, but the Kennedy assassination conspirators apparently pursued him there. One day, he found dynamite in his car. Another time, before he was scheduled to testify in the Clay Shaw trial, someone fired a shot at him, trying to murder him. He added that after the Shaw trial he was in Atlanta when he was attacked by two men who stabbed him in the back and left arm, and he says he fatally shot one of his assailants.[32]

Obviously, the conspirators found it easy to eliminate President Kennedy, but they never could find a way to eliminate the person they feared the most, the dreaded Richard Randolph Carr.

Another enduring conspiracy favorite, Julia Ann Mercer, really had a handle on what "went down" (law enforcement jargon) on the day of the assassination, trying to put Jean Hill, Tom Tilson, and others to shame. On the afternoon of the assassination the twenty-three-year-old gave a notarized statement to the Dallas County Sheriff's Department that as her car approached the Stemmons Freeway overpass on Elm Street (in a subsequent statement she said the time was around 11:00 a.m.) on November 22, 1963, her passage was blocked by a green Ford pickup truck parked with "one or two wheels up on the curb" on the right side of Elm. The hood of the truck, which had the words "Air Conditioning" printed on the driver's side, was open. She said, "A man was sitting under the wheel of the car and slouched over the wheel." (I defy any student of the English language to explain, from these words, the position the man was in.) Another man, at the back of the truck, "reached over the tailgate and took out . . . what appeared to be a gun case." She said the man then "walked across the grass and up the grassy hill." Apparently, Miss Mercer's grassy knoll assassin needed an hour and a half (11:00 a.m. to 12:30 p.m.) to set himself up behind the picket fence. All of this evidently took place in broad daylight in the virtual presence, she said, of "three policemen standing talking near a motorcycle on the bridge just west of me."[33] And since the approach to the Stemmons Freeway overpass is close to a hundred yards from the top of the grassy knoll, Mercer's gunman had quite a long walk carrying a gun case in front of potential witnesses, something I would think he would want to avoid.

Mark Lane, in his book *Rush to Judgment*, writes that "the truck was parked illegally and blocked traffic while a man carried what appeared to be a rifle case up a grassy slope in the presence of Dallas Police Officers." ("At that very spot later that same day," Lane assures his readers, "the President was shot and killed.")[34] But why presidential assassins, hired by the CIA or mob or anyone else, would deliberately draw attention to themselves by parking illegally and blocking traffic on a busy street in the presence of three Dallas police officers as well as lay witnesses like Miss Mercer is not known. Of course, conspiracy theorists never let common sense get in the way of their hallucinatory theories.

On December 9, 1963, Dallas police officer Joe E. Murphy, whose assignment for the motorcade was on the Stemmons Freeway overpass above Elm Street just west of the Triple Underpass, told the FBI that around "10:30 to 10:40 a.m." on the day of the assassination, a green pickup truck stalled on Elm Street. He ascertained that it belonged to a construction company working on the First National Bank Building at Elm and Akard in Dallas. The FBI report reads, "There were three construction men in this truck, and [Murphy] took one to the bank building to obtain another truck in order to assist in moving the stalled one." Murphy said the other two men remained with the pickup truck in the company of "two other officers" Murphy was working with. "Shortly prior to the arrival of the motorcade, the man [Murphy] had taken to the bank building returned with a second truck, and all three of the men left with the two trucks, one pushing the other . . . Murphy further stated that it was probable that one of these men had taken something from the rear of this truck in an effort to start it. He stated these persons were under observation all during the period they were stalled on Elm Street because the officers wanted the truck moved prior to the arrival of the motorcade, and it would have been impossible for any of them to have had anything to do with the assassination of President Kennedy."[35] Forrest V. Sorrels, special agent in charge of the Secret Service's Dallas office, told the Warren Commission that he learned a truck "had stalled down there on Elm Street and I . . . found out that [it] had gone dead." Sorrels said the truck "apparently belonged to some construction company, and that a police officer had come down there and they had gone to the construction company and gotten somebody to come down and get the [truck] out of the way."[36]

If we went no further, to believe Mercer's story would stretch credulity beyond all tolerable boundaries, but the very creative Miss Mercer was determined not to let well enough alone. Adopting the motto "Anything she [Jean Hill] can do, I can do better," in a 1983 interview with conspiracy-leaning author Henry Hurt she said she told the FBI that the two men she had seen were—yes, you guessed right—Jack Ruby and Lee Harvey Oswald. "Ruby, she said, was the driver, and Oswald the man with the rifle."[37]*

---

*However, on November 27, 1963, when the FBI showed Miss Mercer photos of Ruby and Oswald, she could not identify either as the two men she saw, saying only that the driver had a round face like Ruby, and the one with the alleged gun case was the same general build, size, and age as Oswald (12 HSCA 17).

One of the most bizarre stories that has emerged in assassination literature comes from a respected conspiracy theorist (there is such a species, though rare), the aforementioned Gary Mack. The former program director of radio station KFJZ in Fort Worth, Mack, since 1994, has been the curator at the Sixth Floor Museum at Dealey Plaza.[38] Although Mack, who has been an assassination researcher since 1975, tends to believe in a conspiracy, he is respected by both sides in the debate, and as opposed to 95 percent of his colleagues, you can engage in a spirited give-and-take exchange with him with neither side becoming incoherent.

As indicated earlier, the photo of the presidential limousine taken by Dealey Plaza spectator Mary Moorman at almost the precise moment of the shot to the president's head, the second of two photographs she took with her Polaroid camera that day,[39] corresponds approximately to frame 315 of the Zapruder film. We know the president was shot in the head at frame 313—when we see the explosion in the head—or somewhere between 312 and 313, and each frame of the Zapruder film represents about one-eighteenth of a second; therefore, she took her photo about one-ninth of a second *after* the president was hit—virtually contemporaneous with the head shot. "My picture, when I took it," Moorman told ABC's Bill Lord on the afternoon of the assassination, "was at the same instant that the President was hit, and that does show in my picture . . . It shows the President, he, uh, slumped. Jackie Kennedy was leaning towards him to see, I guess."[40]

The background of the subject photo picks up the area of the grassy knoll around the eastern part of the stockade fence and the retaining wall to the east of the fence. But the image of the retaining wall area is so blurred that enlarging the photo and seeking to enhance it at the Rochester Institute of Technology "produced no significant increase in detail and no evidence of any human form." And since the "fence region of the photograph was of even poorer quality than the retaining wall area, no enhancement" was even attempted.[41] Mack says the HSCA was dealing with the original Moorman photo, but it had deteriorated. But around 1983, he came into possession of an eight-by-ten-inch UPI print of Moorman's photo taken after the shooting on the day of the assassination, and it was in good condition. Mack says that in an area of the photo different from where most conspiracy theorists place the grassy knoll assassin (which is behind the picket fence, eight to ten feet *west* of the southeast corner of the fence)—behind the fence but about sixteen feet north from the southeast corner[*]—can be seen a man who "appears to be dressed in a manner that's certainly consistent with a police uniform."[42]

In the 1988 British Television Production *The Men Who Killed Kennedy*, Mack spoke about the origin of the "Badge Man" theory. He said that in studying the Moorman photo he saw an image behind the stockade fence that looked like "eyes and ears and forehead and hair. And little by little the pieces of the image started to make sense to me. And that's when I first called Jack [White, someone, Mack says, who is "knowledgeable about pho-

---

[*]If you've been there, as I have, Mack's man would only be about twenty feet to the left rear of the main alleged grassy knoll assassin, both men behind the fence and each necessarily aware of the other's presence, since nothing but the ground would be between them. Hence, if there was a grassy knoll assassin where most conspiracy theorists and the HSCA say he was, and Mack's man was where Mack says he was, the grassy knoll assassin and Mack's man (who Mack believes may be the grassy knoll assassin) had to be co-conspirators. (I say "may be" because although the conspiracy community seems to have the impression that Mack believes the man *was* the grassy knoll assassin, in a 2006 letter to me Mack expressly wrote, "I've never said that Badge Man was the knoll assassin, but I have said he's a possibility, that's all" (Letter from Gary Mack to author dated August 10, 2006, p.1).

tography and dark room technique"]. And with his photographic work doing the blowups we could see more and more detail. And at one point we realized this fellow was probably wearing a police uniform, or close enough to what the Dallas police were wearing to pass as a police officer." Mack and White would later identify a "shining object" in the Moorman photo image as being the badge on the figure's police uniform—hence, the birth of the "Badge Man" in conspiracy theorist mythology as being the grassy knoll assassin.

But there's so much more to the story. In the British television production, Jack White also claims that the Moorman photo shows "another image standing directly behind the Badge Man. This appears to be a person in a hard hat and a white T-shirt." It's obviously just a matter of time before White will be able to tell us the color of the two men's eyes, the condition of their teeth, and perhaps, someday, the number of hairs on their heads. White and Mack call this second man the "Back Up Man," and say the Back Up Man was not in a uniform of any kind.[43]

Remember that the Moorman photo was taken at almost the precise moment of the shot to the president's head. So for the Badge Man to have fired the fatal shot, not only would the badge he was supposedly wearing have to have been high up on his body (perhaps attached to his neck) so that it was visible behind the five-foot fence, but also the Badge Man would have to have been standing up tall, his head far above the top of the fence, at the time he shot Kennedy, for the badge to have been seen in the photo. And if that's the case, then he wasn't stooped down so his head was on a line with the rifle barrel and sight, which most likely would have been resting on the top of the fence for stability and accuracy. This makes a lot of sense, doesn't it? With respect to the rifle the Badge Man would have had to have had if he fired at the president, Mack said he has "never been able to see any rifle" in the Badge Man's hands,[44] but added that was "because the smoke and/or flash in front of it obscured it from my view. I've also noted that specific area seems to also be in shadow."

"The so-called Badge Man image, if legitimate, would have to be of a man who is standing a considerable distance behind the stockade fence," says Dale Myers, a computer graphics expert. "I used a computer model of Dealey Plaza to duplicate Mary Moorman's position at the time she took the photograph that allegedly shows the Badge Man image. Using that position and placing a computer model of an average size man at the fence line where Badge Man is alleged to have stood reveals that the Badge Man image is too small to be a man standing at the fence line. In order to get the computer model to match the size of the Badge Man image, the model, to be as small as the Badge Man image, would have to be placed 32 feet behind the fence line and 4.5 feet off the ground. Other photographs taken at the time of the assassination show a Coke bottle sitting on the wall of the pergola between Moorman and the so-called Badge Man position. The Badge Man image is more than likely a distortion of this Coke bottle."[45]

As if the Badge Man firing at Kennedy from behind the stockade fence is not fantastic enough, Mack, White, and a few other conspiracy theorists have tried to bolster and connect the Badge Man with an even more bizarre story. In 1978, *fifteen years* after the assassination (not too long, after all, just a little longer than the Second World War, Vietnam War, and the Korean War all put together), one Gordon Arnold came from behind the curtains and appeared for the first time on the conspiracy stage. Arnold says that at the time of the assassination he was a twenty-two-year-old soldier home on leave. He told reporter Earl Golz of the *Dallas Morning News* that minutes before the motorcade came by, he was moving toward the railroad overpass to film the motorcade when "this guy walked towards me and said I shouldn't be up there." When he challenged the man's authority, he said the man "showed me a badge and said he was with the Secret Service." As we've seen, several people said that *after* the shooting they confronted men who indicated or said they were Secret Service agents. Now, for the first and only time on record we have someone (someone, to repeat, who materialized fifteen long years after the assassination) who says he met someone *before* the shooting who said he was a Secret Service agent.

Arnold said he then took a position in front of the picket fence high up on the grassy knoll. He told Golz that when he heard the first of two shots that came from behind him, over his left shoulder, he immediately "hit the dirt." He added that after all the shots were fired, and while he was still on the ground, "the next thing I knew someone was kicking my butt and telling me to get up. It was a policeman. [Arnold would later say the policeman asked him if he was taking pictures and he told him he was.] And I told him to go jump in the river. And then this other guy, a policeman, comes up with a shotgun and . . . that thing was waving back and forth. I said you can have everything I've got. Just point it [the gun] someplace else." He told Golz he gave the officer with the gun the film from the canister and two days later he was on a plane reporting for duty in Alaska. He didn't come forward with his story throughout the years because, he said, he heard that "a lot of people making claims about pictures and stuff . . . were dying sort of peculiarly."[46] But this is a bogus argument on its face. The completely unmeritorious argument that many witnesses associated with the assassination were dying mysteriously (see conspiracy section later in book) didn't start until 1966, when conspiracist Penn Jones started peddling it. What excuse did Arnold have for not coming forward in the more than two years before then?

Ten years later, in the 1988 British television production *The Men Who Killed Kennedy*, Arnold changed his story in two significant ways. The plainclothes agent who told him not to go up on the railroad overpass was no longer a Secret Service agent. Arnold said the man said to him, "I'm from the CIA." Much more importantly, only one police officer, he now said, accosted him after the shooting, not two. The one who kicked him on the ground was the same one who had the gun. Arnold said that before he hit the ground, he was standing with his back almost to the picket fence, and the officer (officers) who accosted him came from behind him, from the opposite side of the fence.

There are several photos, including film, of the precise area where Arnold said he was on the grassy knoll, and none of them, taken at the very time Arnold said the incident happened, show Arnold. This is conclusive photographic proof that Arnold's story was fabricated. And many people who ran up the grassy knoll after the shooting, several of whom were on the south side of Elm and were facing where Arnold supposedly was, testified before the Warren Commission and have been interviewed untold times, and not one has ever said they saw the extraordinary sight of a police officer, right after the shooting, standing over a prone man on the knoll, kicking him. The reason why no one saw, and no camera or film shows, Arnold on the grassy knoll is that—and this is being very charitable to Arnold—this incident only took place in Arnold's mind. In fact, in the British television production, he used a rather curious (for someone who was really there, but not for someone who was lying about the matter) way of expressing his presence on the knoll. He said, "There's no doubt *in my mind* I was there."[*]

---

[*]Curiously, over four months after Golz published his article, U.S. Senator Ralph Yarborough called Golz and told him, "Immediately *on the firing of the first shot* I saw the man you interviewed throw himself on the ground. He was down within a second of the time the shot was fired and I thought to myself, there's a combat veteran who knows how to act when weapons start firing" (Earl Golz, "Panel Leaves Question of Imposters," *Dallas Morning News*, December 31, 1978, p.2A). Conspiracy theorists say this confirms Arnold's

Arnold's story inspires only one thing, disbelief. But as indicated, he has many believers in the conspiracy community, and two particularly avid supporters—Gary Mack and Jack White, the main Badge Man advocates.

So we're obviously being asked to believe that the Badge Man, the assassin who was in a police uniform *behind* the stockade fence (Arnold, Mack says, was in front of the fence), is the same person in a police uniform who ended up kicking Arnold and taking his film.[*] Apparently, Kennedy's assassin, instead of trying to hide in the trunk of a car in the railroad yard parking lot or trying to escape from behind the picket fence after shooting Kennedy, had much more important things to do—mainly, climb over the fence (at which point he'd be in plain view of everyone on Elm Street) so he could beat up on that louse Gordon Arnold and take his film.

Mack and White also have a big problem with the "light blob" being Arnold. The light blob is in a tall vertical position in front of the alleged Badge Man. But again, Moorman's photo was taken around the exact time as the head shot, which was the *third* and last of the three shots. By that time, according to Arnold, he was already lying down, having immediately dropped to the earth after, he says, the *first* shot was fired. So he could not have been the "light blob."

Neither the Badge Man nor Gordon Arnold benefit from scrutiny, disappearing back into nothingness in the grassy knoll landscape.

The next three witnesses fall under the "and others" part of this section. They are not, in other words, downright silly people whose stories are almost laughable. But their observations are nearly as lacking in credibility as their loony bird cousins.

Roger Craig was a twenty-seven-year-old Dallas County Sheriff's Department deputy. In a composite summary of what he says he saw on the day of the assassination, he told the Dallas sheriff's office on November 23, 1963,[47] the FBI on November 23[48] and November 25,[49] and the Warren Commission, in testimony before it, on April 1, 1964,[50] the fairly consistent story (there were minor discrepancies, which is normal) that at the time the presidential motorcade approached Dealey Plaza, he was waiting for it in front of the sheriff's office on the north side of Main Street (corner of Main and Houston). A short time after the president's car had passed, he heard three shots. He said he ran across Houston Street and then Elm up to the railroad yards behind the grassy knoll and Texas School Book Depository Building and "began moving people back out of the railroad yard." He then went to the front of the Book Depository Building and began talking to people "to see if they'd seen anything." After speaking to a husband and wife (Arnold and Barbara

---

presence on the knoll. But it almost certainly does not. At the time of the first shot, the presidential limousine, we know, had just turned from Houston on to Elm. Yarborough's car, two cars behind Kennedy's, would have been right at the intersection of Houston and Elm, and from that position the pergola wall would have completely blocked Yarborough's view of the place where Arnold claims he was. So Yarborough did not see Arnold for two reasons. One, photographs and film show that Arnold was not there, and two, even if he were, Yarborough couldn't have seen him. It is difficult to know whom Yarborough saw, since several people dropped to the ground immediately. He may have been referring to Bill Newman, who testified for me in London. Newman was at the bottom of the knoll on the north side (picket fence side) of Elm and would have been visible to Yarborough at the time of the first shot. However, Newman didn't drop to the ground until after the third shot. Also, if Yarborough were referring to Newman, it's hard to believe he wouldn't have mentioned Newman's wife and their two young children, all of whom dropped to the ground together.

[*]If not, since the Back Up man, per Mack, was not in a police uniform, then who was the person kicking Arnold? Another co-conspirator of the Badge Man who was dressed in a police uniform? This is all terribly silly.

Rowland) for a few minutes, he and Deputy Sheriff Clinton "Lemmy" Lewis crossed Elm and walked down to where they were told one of the bullets had ricocheted off the curb. As they were searching, which he testified was about "fourteen or fifteen minutes" after the shooting, he heard a "shrill whistle," looked up, and saw a man "start to run down the hill on the north side of Elm Street" (across the street from Craig) coming from the direction of the "southwest corner of the [School Depository] Building." At that point, Craig saw a white Nash Rambler station wagon with a luggage rack on the top driving slowly westbound on Elm. In Craig's first interview he described the driver as a "Negro," then later a "dark-complected white male," then finally said he "couldn't say." The running man, who he said was around five feet eight or nine inches tall, 140 to 150 pounds, with medium-brown sandy hair, got in the station wagon, which continued southbound on Elm out of sight. Craig had wanted to talk to the running man and the driver, but the "traffic was so heavy" he couldn't get across the street before the station wagon drove off without his even getting the license plate number.

When he heard later in the day that the authorities were trying to see if there was a connection between the murder of Officer Tippit and the assassination, he called Captain Fritz's office, told one of his officers what he had seen, and was asked to come up and look at the suspect (Oswald) in Fritz's office. According to Craig's testimony before the Warren Commission (all of what follows is heavily disputed), he entered Fritz's small office and identified Oswald as the running man he had seen get in the car. He says when Fritz asked Oswald, "What about the station wagon?" Oswald responded, "That station wagon belongs to Mrs. Paine . . . Don't try to tie her into this. She had nothing to do with it."* When Fritz said to Oswald, "All we're trying to do is find out what happened, and this man saw you leave the scene," Oswald, according to Craig, said, "I told you people I did," then added, "Everyone will know who I am now." Craig said he then left.

There are three basic parts to Craig's story: a running man getting into the Nash Rambler, the identification of the man as Oswald, and the alleged conversation in Fritz's office. It's my sense that Craig was more likely than not telling the truth about the first part, lying or simply wrong about the second part, and almost assuredly lying about the third part. For those who find it hard to believe that Craig would make up any part of the story, police are human beings like everyone else, and a few have been known, in their effort to be looked upon as heroes, not only to magnify what they did or saw, but actually to make false claims, for example, that they were shot at by mobsters or drug traffickers, and so on.

With respect to the running man, there are two strong inferences, going in opposite directions, on the issue of whether or not Craig should be believed. With over two hundred people, including many police officers, milling about on Elm Street after the shooting, one would assume that a significant number of them—I would think at an absolute minimum, ten—would have seen what Craig claims he saw. Yet, of all the police officers who should have seen this, including his fellow deputy, Lemmy Lewis,† only Craig

---

*In Craig's Warren Commission testimony he said the station wagon he saw was a "Nash Rambler" and "it looked white to me" (6 H 267). But actually, Ruth Paine owned a green Chevrolet station wagon (2 H 506, WCT Ruth Hyde Paine; CE 2125, 24 H 697). This, apparently, created a problem for Craig. Seven years later, in his 1971 unpublished book manuscript, "When They Kill a President," he wrote that the Rambler station wagon was "light green" in color (p.12).

†Deputy Sheriff Lewis, now deceased, submitted a report to his office on the afternoon of the assassination concerning his activities and observations that day and made no mention of seeing what Craig allegedly saw (Decker Exhibit No. 5323, 19 H 513).

reported seeing what Craig claims to have seen. On the other hand, two people, not afoot in Dealey Plaza but passing through in cars, *did*, indeed, support Craig's story. And if what Craig said he saw didn't happen, how is it possible that *anyone at all* (assuming they are not connected in some way with Craig, of which there's no evidence) would say they saw essentially the same thing Craig says he saw? It would seem there's a greater improbability of the second thing happening than the first, and this is why I give the benefit of the doubt to Craig here.

Marvin C. Robinson told the FBI on November 23, the day after the assassination, that at sometime "between 12:30 and 1:00 p.m." the previous day he was driving westbound on Elm Street. After crossing the intersection of Elm and Houston, "a light-colored Nash station wagon" suddenly appeared before him. The vehicle stopped and a "white male came down the grass-covered incline between the [School Book Depository] building and the street and entered the station wagon." The station wagon then proceeded westbound on Elm. Robinson said he did not "pay any particular attention" to the person who entered the station wagon and told the FBI he would be unable to identify him.[51] Roy Cooper told the FBI the day after the assassination that he was driving behind Marvin Robinson, his boss, in his car, when he saw a "white male somewhere between 20 and 30 years of age wave at a Nash Rambler station wagon, light colored, as it pulled out . . . real fast in front of the Cadillac driven" by his boss. Cooper could not see who was driving the station wagon and could not give any further description of the man who got into it.[52] Although Robinson and Cooper did not say the man running was Oswald, they did corroborate the essence of Craig's story.

As far as Craig's observation that about fourteen or fifteen minutes after the shooting in Dealey Plaza he saw Oswald get in the Rambler, either this was a sincere mistake on his part or he deliberately lied to magnify his importance in this historic event. In any case, we can be certain he was wrong because we already know where Oswald was at the time: Just two minutes after the last shot was fired, a Book Depository employee, Mrs. Robert Reid, saw Oswald on the second floor of the building walking toward the front stairway leading out of the building. Then, within minutes after the shooting, Oswald boarded a bus seven blocks from the Book Depository Building, and two blocks later the driver issued a bus transfer to him, which was found on his person after his arrest. A former landlady of Oswald's was on the bus at the time and positively identified him. Getting off the bus, he picked up a cab another two blocks away and was driven to within a few blocks of his home. The cabdriver also positively identified Oswald. Not that Oswald's word, by itself, should be given any credibility at all, but during his interrogation, even he confirmed the bus and cab rides (right down to some of the details told by the bus and cab drivers) as the transportation he used to get home from the Book Depository Building on the day of the assassination. Fourteen to fifteen minutes after the assassination, then, Oswald was far away from the Book Depository Building.

With respect to Craig's alleged encounter with Fritz and Oswald in Fritz's office, the high probability is that Craig lied about it. T. L. Baker, one of the three Dallas Police Department lieutenants who were assistants to Captain Fritz, confirmed to me that it was he whom Craig called in the late afternoon of November 22 with his information about the running man. Baker said that when Craig, who Baker said was in plainclothes, thereafter came to the Homicide and Robbery Bureau, "I met him at the door and took him into my office, where he sat down. I knocked on Captain Fritz's door, the captain stepped out, and I told him what Craig had told me, and he told me, 'We already know how he

[Oswald] left. Thank him [Craig] for coming down.' I told Craig this and walked back to the door with him."

Baker said that he did not know Craig and didn't see him again. When I asked Baker if he had any opinion on whether Craig had made up his story about the running man, he said, "I don't know about this because I wasn't there, but I know he made up the story about being in Captain Fritz's office. He didn't enter the room. I'm absolutely positive about that."[53]

Captain Fritz, in an affidavit to the Warren Commission, confirmed the essence of Baker's version of events. He said, "I do remember a man coming into my outer office and I remember one of my officers calling me outside the door of my private office. I talked to this man for a minute or two, and he started telling me a story about seeing Oswald leaving the building. I don't remember all the things that this man said, but I turned him over to Lieutenant Baker who talked to him."[54]

Baker told me, "Everything was hectic at that time and the captain was incorrect here about talking to Craig. He simply forgot. He was confusing my telling him what Craig said with Craig having told it to him. He never spoke to Craig."[55]

And in his Warren Commission testimony, counsel asked Fritz, "Now this man . . . has stated that he came to your office and Oswald was in your office, and you asked him to look at Oswald and tell you whether or not this was the man he saw, and he says that in your presence he identified Oswald as the man that he had seen run across this lawn and get into the white Rambler sedan. Do you remember that?"

Fritz: "If he saw him [Oswald] he looked through that glass and saw him from the outside because I am sure of one thing, that I didn't bring him into the office with Oswald."

Counsel: "You are sure you didn't?"

Fritz: "I am sure of that. I feel positive of that. I would remember that. I am sure."

Counsel: "He also says that in that office . . . after he had said 'that is the man,' that Oswald got up from his chair and slammed his hand on the table and said, 'Now everybody will know who I am.' Did that ever occur in your presence?"

Fritz: "If it did, I never saw anything like that. No, sir. No, sir."

Counsel: "That didn't occur?"

Fritz: "No, sir. It didn't. That man is not telling a true story if that is what he said."[56]

A further indication that Craig made up the encounter inside Fritz's office was that Oswald's alleged remark, "Don't try to tie her [Ruth Paine] into this. She had nothing to do with it," and particularly his alleged assertion, "Everybody will know who I am now," together almost constitute an implied confession to Kennedy's murder by Oswald, which is totally inconsistent with Oswald's repeated remarks after his arrest, some captured on television film, that he was innocent and didn't know anything about what happened. It should be noted further that if, indeed, Oswald said what Craig claimed he did, why would Fritz deny it if it actually happened? The alleged remarks could only serve to bolster Fritz's case against Oswald, not weaken it.

Dallas police detective Elmer Boyd knew Craig, and told me when I asked him about Craig's reputation for truthfulness, "Well, I could tell you a few stories, but I won't. Let's just say he had a tendency to exaggerate."[57]

But assuming the running-man incident Craig reported did take place, which, in view of existing, albeit limited corroborative evidence, is a reasonably fair assumption, we have to ask ourselves, What significance does it have? My view is very little. I say that for several reasons. One is the very time the event occurred, assuming, again, that it did. Though not impossible, it is highly improbable that anyone running from the direction of the Book Depository Building a *quarter of an hour* after the shooting (recall that Craig said it was "fourteen or fifteen minutes" after) would have been the shooter of the president, or a second gunman. If he had successfully avoided detection (despite the fact that swarms of law enforcement personnel almost immediately converged on the Book Depository Building and surrounding area) for that very considerable period of time, why would he suddenly choose to draw attention to himself by running away and letting out a shrill whistle to his accomplice in the getaway car rather than casually walking into, and getting lost among, the crowd? It doesn't make too much sense.

Second, it's hard to pull off the biggest murder ever without leaving not one speck of evidence of your existence. As we have seen, there is much evidence putting Oswald and the murder weapon at the sniper's nest window. Yet no one saw this second gunman or accomplice before or during the shooting, and there's no evidence that any other rifle or cartridge case from said rifle was found anywhere in Dealey Plaza, much less the Book Depository Building, after the shooting. So unless the man Craig said he saw running had taken his rifle and any cartridge case or cases with him (and Craig never reported that the man was carrying a rifle or anything else), this man would seem to have been a benign figure. Finally, as we have seen, the vast majority of witnesses that day only heard three shots. And as we know, three cartridge casings, all ejected from Oswald's rifle alone, were found beneath the window on the sixth floor of the Book Depository Building, where we know Oswald was. So even if Craig's mysterious running man had intended to shoot Kennedy that day, he in fact didn't fire any weapon at Kennedy, and would have been running, if at all, for some other reason, not because of having physically participated in the crime of the century.

One thing arguing against everything Craig said is his overall lack of credibility. In his 1971 unpublished book manuscript, "When They Kill a President," he unwittingly lays out his own brief for being a highly paranoid, unbalanced person. He strongly suggests that Sheriff Bill Decker, with the full knowledge of the FBI, was a part of the conspiracy to kill Kennedy. The motive? Decker and most of his deputies hated Kennedy, in large part because he "was a Catholic." Craig alleges that Warren Commission assistant counsel David Belin changed his (Craig's) testimony before the Commission "fourteen times" in the published volumes. He also wants the reader to believe that after he was fired by the sheriff's office in July of 1967 ("because of a disturbance growing out of personal matters, according to the Dallas Sheriff's personnel officer"),[58] he started being followed everywhere. When he arrived in New Orleans in late 1967 after volunteering to help New Orleans DA Jim Garrison* in Garrison's prosecution of Clay Shaw, "four men followed" him around town. He writes, "Upon returning to Dallas . . . I was picked up by another 'tail.' I was followed constantly. My wife could not even go to the grocery store without being followed. Sometimes they would go so far as to pull up next to her and make sure she saw them talking on their two-way radios. [He doesn't say why the people were following his wife, or him, everywhere.] They would also park across from my house and sit for hours."

He claimed that on November 1, 1967, in Dallas, someone shot at him, and "the hair

---

*Craig not only volunteered to testify for Garrison but also privately started investigating the case for him. An example of his work: knowing that one of Garrison's zany theories was that a vast homosexual ring conspired to kill Kennedy, Craig wrote a December 7, 1967, memo to Garrison stating that Marina Oswald's personal physician in Dallas was associated at a hospital there with four doctors (whom Craig identifies by name), all of whom, Craig says, "are reported homosexuals."

just above my left ear parted." Unable to hold down a job and in failing health, he was eventually befriended by Penn Jones, the architect of the "mysterious deaths" theory, who provided a home for Craig and his family on his property near Dallas. But strangers continued to follow him. "One day," he writes, "after being followed by this truck for several days . . . the driver stuck a revolver out the window and was about to fire, when another car pulled up behind me and he withdrew the pistol." He also said he got threatening calls in the middle of the night reminding him, "You have a family." He claims that on October 27, 1970, when he turned his car's ignition on, his car exploded, causing severe injuries.[59]

Craig's unpublished manuscript was dated 1971. But he told others that the attempts on his life continued: being run off the road in West Texas in 1972, causing him to break his back, and being shot in his left shoulder in January of 1975. All in all, according to Craig, there were five unsuccessful attempts on his life.[60]

The conspiracy theorists who have accepted Craig's entire story without qualification hint darkly that Craig did not commit suicide as reported, but was murdered on May 15, 1975, in Dallas because of what he says he saw on the day of the assassination. One example among many: "At the age of 39, Roger Craig, suffering from the stress of the constant back pains he endured and the financial pressures he encountered because of finding it difficult to get work, succumbed, *they said*, and committed suicide. *They said*."[61] Even the more scholarly conspiracy theorists like David E. Scheim have implicitly bought into the possibility of the Craig murder scenario. Scheim quotes a source for the proposition that it was the mob who was out to kill Craig.[62]

The Dallas Police Department and coroner's office both concluded that Craig, who in 1960 was named the Dallas County Sheriff's Department's officer of the year by the Dallas Traffic Commission, shot himself to death with his own rifle inside the home he shared with his father. He left a suicide note that said in part, "I am tired of all this pain." His father, who found Craig's body in a back bedroom when he came in from mowing the lawn, told police that his son had been taking painkillers because of injuries received in an auto accident two years earlier, and just that week had received notice from the Social Security Administration that he had been turned down for benefits. Dallas police detective Robert Garcia said that the gunshot wound to Craig's upper chest was "self-inflicted," and Craig's .22 caliber rifle was by his side.[63]

But if we're to believe the clear implications of the conspiracy theorists like Matthew Smith, the conspirators (CIA, mob, etc.) were apparently trying to kill Craig, eventually doing so. Apart from the absurdity that these high-powered conspirators, who could kill the president on their first attempt and get away with it, found it almost impossible to kill the completely unprotected but apparently Rasputin-like Craig, finally succeeding only after an eight-year effort, why would they want to kill him anyway? To silence him? He had *already* told his story to the authorities, many times over. So what could possibly be achieved?

If Craig was murdered by the alleged conspirators in the Kennedy assassination, here is the essence of what their decision would have had to have been: "I know this guy Craig has already told his story to the local police and feds, and they didn't buy a word he said. And I know twelve years have already gone by. But who knows? What if he tells it again to them, and this time they believe him because, I don't know, maybe his voice or body language will be more convincing this time. Best thing to do is kill him. Oh, by the way, and this goes without saying, we'll have to reach the Dallas police and coroner's office to let them know that even though he was murdered, they both have to report it as a suicide. If they refuse to go along with it, then we could be in real trouble for approaching them, so we'll have to kill the detectives and coroner who worked on the case, too." You see, if you play out the countless conspiracy theories, something the theorists never bother to do, the absurdity of their original position only degenerates into greater absurdity.

One of the most sacred and iconic beliefs by conspiracy theorists resulted from the testimony of S. M. (Sterling Mayfield) Holland, a signal supervisor for the Union Terminal Railroad. Holland testified to the Warren Commission that at the time of the motorcade, he was "on top of the Triple Underpass"[*] watching it with two uniformed Dallas police officers (J. W. Foster and J. C. White) and about eight or nine other coworkers of his, who had to identify themselves to the police for security reasons.[64] Holland testified that at the time of the shots he saw "a puff of smoke," presumably from a shot, coming from the trees on the grassy knoll.[†] Warren Commission counsel asked Holland to draw a circle on a photo indicating the area to his left front where he saw the puff of smoke, which he did. But when this photo was reproduced for the Warren Commission volumes, the entire grassy knoll area came out so dark that no circle is visible.[65][‡]

It should be mentioned that Holland says he heard four shots and, per his affidavit to the Dallas County Sheriff's Department on the afternoon of the assassination, only saw the puff of smoke after the *first* shot.[66] But in his Warren Commission testimony, and partly because of imprecise questions by Warren Commission counsel, although at one point he again indicated he saw the puff of smoke after the first shot,[67] at another point in his testimony he implied it was after the third or fourth shot.[68] When Warren Commission counsel asked, "What was your impression about the source of these noises?" he answered, "Well, the impression was that . . . the first two or three shots came from the *upper part of the street* . . . from where I was."

Counsel: "East on Elm?"

Holland: "Yes, up in here somewhere [indicating] . . . That is what it sounded like to me from where I was."

Counsel: "You are indicating on this [Holland] Exhibit C. Why don't you put a square around the area that you just pointed to. You had no idea, I take it, that the shots were coming from your area?"

---

[*]Per Ken Holmes, president of Southwestern Historical Inc., which runs tours of all the Kennedy assassination sites, the official words on the plaque next to the underpass are "Union Terminal Underpass," but he said most people in Dallas refer to it as the "Triple Underpass" (Telephone interview of Ken Holmes by author on March 11, 2004). However, assassination literature is filled with references to the site as the "triple overpass," including, for instance, by the two Dallas officers who were assigned to positions above the underpass on November 22, 1963 (6 H 249, WCT J. W. Foster; 6 H 254, WCT J. C. White). For purposes of this book I use the term "Triple Underpass" to refer to the convergence of the three roads of Commerce, Main, and Elm, and "railroad overpass" to the railroad tracks (and walkway) on top of the three converging roads.

[†]Clemon Earl Johnson, a machinist for the Union Terminal Company who was on the overpass with Holland, also said he saw "white smoke," but it was "near the pavillion" (which some people, including Sixth Floor Museum curator Gary Mack, feel is not part of the "grassy knoll"). Further, Johnson felt the smoke came not from a shot but "from a motorcycle abandoned near the spot by a Dallas policeman." (CE 1422, 22 H 836) Another Union Terminal Company employee (described as a "hostler helper") atop the railroad overpass on Elm who saw smoke was Nolan H. Potter, but Potter told the FBI that the smoke he saw was "in front of the Texas School Book Depository Building rising from the trees" (FBI Record 124-10026-10153, FBI interview of Nolan H. Potter on March 17, 1964).

[‡]However, in a clearer copy sent to me by Steven Tilley of the National Archives, who reproduced the negative for me with special equipment, Holland's markings on the photograph can be made out, although just barely, and not clear enough for reproduction in this book.

Holland: "No."[69]

The square Holland drew is at the southeast corner of the Book Depository Building. As Warren Commission assistant counsel David Belin says in his book, *November 22, 1963: You Are the Jury*, "[The November 22, 1963] affidavit by Sam Holland is the fountainhead for speculation that there might have been another source of rifle shots."[70] In his affidavit to the Dallas County Sheriff's Department that afternoon, Holland said that at the time of the first shot he "saw a puff of smoke come from the trees," but he said the trees were in the "arcade" area (i.e., pergola or pavillion area).[71] However, in his testimony before the Warren Commission, when Holland said he saw "a puff of smoke [come] out about six or eight feet above the ground right out from under those trees," although he continued to refer to "the arcade area," he drew a circle on a photograph on the grassy knoll (not the arcade area) for the Warren Commission counsel.[72]*

If we give the benefit of the doubt to the conspiracy theorists that what Holland claims he saw did not come from the exhaust of a motorcycle (as a coworker of Holland's on the railroad overpass believes), a question that presents itself is whether any smoke would emanate from the muzzle (and be visible upon the firing) of a modern rifle using so-called smokeless powder. In a September 23, 1964, letter from FBI Director J. Edgar Hoover to J. Lee Rankin, general counsel for the Warren Commission, Hoover said that in test-firing a Mannlicher-Carcano rifle, "a small amount of white smoke was visible."[73] My firearms expert at the trial in London, Monty Lutz, later told me the same thing, saying that "a very small amount of light gray smoke" would be visible. Lutz told me that the smoke would "dissipate almost immediately," and on "a windy day, such as this was, it would be gone almost immediately and it would be virtually impossible to see it." He continued, "You'd almost have to be alerted to where the muzzle was and concentrating and looking for the smoke to see it." He added that an additional factor made it even more difficult to see the smoke. "By all accounts," he said, "this was a very bright and clear day." When I asked him why that would make a difference, he said, "Imagine if the background were dark. The light gray smoke would show up better because of the contrast. All in all, even if there had been a grassy knoll shooter, I doubt very, very much that anyone would have seen any smoke coming out of the muzzle of his rifle."[74] In fact, in Oliver Stone's movie *JFK*, he didn't even use a rifle to create his puff of smoke, machine-generating the smoke instead.[75]

It would seem, then, almost impossible for Holland, about sixty-five to seventy yards away, to see any "puff of smoke," particularly since it was a very windy day, and such a

---

*Holland told the Warren Commission that "immediately after the shots were fired," he ran behind the picket fence to see if he "could see anyone . . . behind the fence," but he saw no one. He said by the time he got there "there were twelve or fifteen policemen and plainclothesmen" there, and "we looked for empty shells around there for quite awhile." Though they found no shells, he did see several cars parked behind the picket fence, including "a station wagon backed up toward the fence" and in "one little spot" around there in an area of three by two feet, it looked to him "like somebody had been standing there for a long time." Remarkably, and as alluded to earlier, he said there were about "a hundred foot tracks in that little spot." (6 H 245–247) I should think this would be impossible enough, but in a taped interview with author Josiah Thompson on November 30, 1966, Holland said there were "four or five hundred footprints" in the area behind the station wagon (Thompson, *Six Seconds in Dallas*, p.122). Apparently, the conspirators who had Kennedy killed didn't bring in just one assassin to shoot Kennedy from behind the picket fence, but imported the Russian army. If Holland's testimony about footprints was strange, the testimony of Seymour Weitzman, the Dallas deputy constable who misidentified the Carcano, was close. He said that "in the railroad yards" used as a parking lot behind the picket fence, "we noticed numerous kinds [of] footprints that did not make sense because they were going in different directions" (7 H 107). Say what? It's a parking lot for cars yet all footprints are supposed to be going in the same direction?

puff would not linger in the air but would immediately dissipate before Holland could even direct his attention away from the motorcade and over to the grassy knoll. Dallas deputy sheriff Luke Mooney, who was in Dealey Plaza at the time of the shooting, testified, "The wind was blowing pretty high."[76] *Dallas Morning News* photographer Tom Dillard, who was also there, testified there was "a very brisk north wind."[77] Associated Press photographer James Altgens testified that at one point, "Mrs. Kennedy was looking at me . . . [and] just as I got ready to snap it the north wind caught her hat and almost blew it off."[78]* Indeed, the velocity of the wind was such that at the trial in London, Gerry Spence, referring to the wind "blowing very hard," said to Dallas police officer Marrion Baker that because of the way "the wind was blowing . . . you were about blown off your bike, isn't that true?" and Baker responded, "That is correct."[79]†

In addition to all of the above, one must view Holland's unequivocal testimony that he saw a puff of smoke on the grassy knoll at the time of the shooting in relationship to all the other evidence. Since we know that no gunman was seen behind the picket fence at the time of the shooting nor was one seen running away from the grassy knoll with his rifle, and no rifle or expended shells from said rifle were found behind the picket fence or anywhere else in Dealey Plaza other than on the sixth floor of the Book Depository Building, we cannot logically and reasonably give any meaningful weight at all to Holland's testimony. If an ephemeral wisp of smoke—even if it existed—can overcome several mountains of solid evidence to the contrary, then the investigation into the truth in the assassination is more of an existential exercise fit for black coffee–sipping Left Bank philosophers who have always been more interested in asking questions than in getting answers to those questions.

It should also be noted that on at least two occasions Holland saw things that no other human did. As previously indicated, the famous photograph by Dealey Plaza witness Mary Moorman of the grassy knoll at the time the president was shot in the head is very blurry and of poor quality. Photographic experts for the HSCA concluded that the images behind the picket fence in the photo may "represent parts of a tree, or they may be photographic artifacts. Due to the poor quality of the photograph . . . it was *not possible* to determine the nature of the images with the naked eye."[80] In other words, no human figure can possibly be made out behind the fence. But when conspiracy theorist Josiah Thompson showed Holland this same photo in 1966 during the writing of his substan-

---

*At least out at Love Field, the Department of Commerce records reflect that the wind was going in an easterly direction. But more than one witness in Dealey Plaza felt it was going in a northerly direction.

†One wonders how to reconcile these undoubtedly accurate on-site testimonials from Dealey Plaza witnesses as to the stiffness of the wind at the time of the assassination, with Weather Bureau records from the U.S. Department of Commerce, which show that the velocity of the wind at 12:30 p.m. on November 22, 1963, at nearby Love Field in Dallas, where the measurements were taken, was 13 knots, translating (a knot equals about 1.15 statute miles per hour) to around 15 miles per hour, a good but not a strong wind (U.S. Department of Commerce, Weather Bureau, Local Climatological Data, Dallas, Texas, Love Field, November 22, 1963, p.3; see also HSCA Record 180-10104-10458, November 1, 1978). When I posed this question to William Brown, a research meteorologist at the Department of Commerce Weather Bureau in Asheville, North Carolina, he said, "I've been to Dealey Plaza, and as you know there are many tall buildings in the area. When wind, like water, is funneled through a smaller channel—here, between buildings—the wind will *always* speed up, sometimes considerably. You're forcing the same volume of air through a smaller area. It's simple physics. In a water example, a wide river may not flow rapidly, but when funneled through a narrow canyon its velocity picks up immediately" (Telephone interview of William Brown by author on January 9, 2003). In other words, prairie winds, which are famous, are not strong because of the prairie, but because they are simply strong. A strong wind in the prairies surrounding Oklahoma City, for instance, will be even stronger in the city, not less strong.

tive and well-researched book, *Six Seconds in Dallas*, Holland said, "Well, now you have something here . . . I didn't see this man before . . . Well, you know, I think you're looking right down the barrel of that gun right now."[81]

And in Holland's sworn affidavit to the Dallas County Sheriff's Department on the afternoon of the assassination, he said that "after the first shot the Secret Service man raised up in his seat with a *machine gun* and then dropped back down in the seat," the context of Holland's observation clearly being that the subject Secret Service man was in the presidential limousine.[82] No Secret Service agent in the entire presidential motorcade had a machine gun that day (Agent George Hickey did stand up in his seat in the vice president's car holding a rifle), and no Dealey Plaza witness, other than Holland, reported seeing one. In 1966 Holland told an interviewer that the agent was "in the President's car," and the agent "pointed this machine gun right towards that grassy knoll behind that picket fence," then, after standing up, "fell backwards, like he was shot."[83] No other witness that day saw Hickey fall backward or down.

Finally, there is another enormous problem for conspiracy theorists who desperately want to avail themselves of Holland's "puff of smoke." *All* of the conspiracy theorists who believe that one or more shots were fired from the grassy knoll area place the alleged assassin *behind* the picket fence on top of the knoll, or at least behind the retaining wall or some other structure in the pergola area. *None* of them place the alleged assassin on the grassy knoll itself, in front of the fence and in plain view of everyone. The problem for the buffs is that even if we accept Holland's observation, he himself didn't say he saw any puff of smoke at the top of the picket fence, which, if a weapon had been fired from there, would have been the only place (right at the muzzle) where a puff of smoke could have been seen. Instead, he told the Warren Commission that he saw the smoke "under those trees." In using the plural, he had to have misspoken, meaning the many branches of the single tree in the photograph on which he placed a circle for the Commission. In his November 30, 1966, interview with author Josiah Thompson, he first said "trees," then said "right under this tree, [this] particular tree."[84] It's the same location he encircled for the Warren Commission. And that location is eleven feet in front of the picket fence. So the puff of smoke that Holland claims he saw would not likely have been from the muzzle of any rifle on top of the picket fence.

If Holland is an example of the well-known phenomenon that witnesses to a sudden, startling, and dramatic event genuinely think they see things that aren't there, I'm not sure what phenomenon Lee Bowers would be an example of. Bowers was in the Union Terminal's north tower operating the switches and signals controlling the movement of trains at the time of the assassination. I've been at the south window on the second floor of the tower, and from that vantage point, about fourteen feet above the ground, one has a clear, unobstructed view of the area behind the picket fence atop the knoll, which is only approximately 125 yards away.[85] This is the location where most conspiracy theorists allege the president's assassin was.[*]

[*]The fact that Bowers had a very busy day controlling trains on thirteen separate tracks that passed in front of the tower causes one assassination researcher to wonder whether Bowers was even at the window as he says he was. Jim Moore, author of *Conspiracy of One*, lives in Dallas and over the years has spent much time examining Dealey Plaza and the surrounding area. He makes this telling observation in his book: "[Bowers's] work position required him to throw signal switches located on a panel in the center of the room. Sitting at

Bowers told the Warren Commission that he saw "one or two" men "in the area" before the shooting, presumably, from the context of the questioning, *somewhere* behind the fence, though inept questioning by Warren Commission counsel failed to establish *just where* these men were. At one point he said, "They were some distance back, just a slight distance back," suggesting they were not at the fence itself. Just who were these men? Bowers said he recognized one because he was "a parking lot attendant that operates a parking lot there." This man and the other man, whom Bowers didn't indicate he knew, "each had uniforms similar to those custodians at the [county] courthouse." Bowers did not indicate that he saw anything suspicious or out of the ordinary with these two men.

Although Bowers saw nothing suspicious about the two men, he told the Warren Commission that "at the moment" he heard the shooting he was "looking directly towards the area" (again, presumably the area behind the fence, though he never expressly says this, and remarkably, Warren Commission counsel never nailed down what specific "area" Bowers was talking about) and "there seemed to be some commotion" atop the grassy knoll. When Warren Commission counsel asked Bowers what he meant by that, he said, "It was something out of the ordinary, a sort of milling around, but something occurred in this particular spot which was out of the ordinary, which attracted my eye for some reason which I could not identify."

Counsel: "You couldn't describe it?"

Bowers: "Nothing that I could pinpoint as having happened."[86]

But there's a strong reason to believe that what Bowers said is not credible. His testimony before the Warren Commission came on April 2, 1964. But on the afternoon of the assassination, over four months earlier, he gave a sworn "State of Texas, County of Dallas" affidavit, which he signed before a notary public[87] and in which he said absolutely nothing at all about the commotion and unusual activity behind the picket fence that attracted his attention. And it's not as if he was just answering someone else's questions, or that no one asked him a question that would have allowed him to furnish this information. This was an affidavit he himself prepared and signed. The very purpose for the taking of all the affidavits in this case was to see if the person giving such an affidavit had any information relevant to the assassination, as the alleged commotion behind the picket fence surely would be. Bowers had to know this.

And it's not because Bowers wasn't trying to recollect suspicious activity. In fact, he wrote in his affidavit about seeing three separate cars in the parking lot behind the fence that attracted his attention, one at 11:55 a.m. with an out-of-state license plate and a "Goldwater For 64" sticker on it, one at 12:15 p.m. whose driver seemed to have a "mike or telephone in the car," and another one a few minutes later that also had a Goldwater sticker on it. In his Warren Commission testimony, he said that the area between his tower and Elm Street "had been covered by police for some two hours. Since approximately ten o'clock in the morning, traffic had been cut off into the area so that anyone moving around

---

the panel, Bowers could not have seen the area at the apex of the wooden fence where [Mark] Lane and [Sylvia] Meagher [conspiracy authors], among others, place their mythical assassin. Bowers, in order to view the area in question from a window somewhat removed from his control panel, would have had to leave his switches and walk over to the window. By all accounts, Bowers was a good employee, not a shirker of duty. It is inconceivable to me that he walked away from his control panel at a particularly busy time to stare at the back of a picket fence. Indeed, Bowers testified that he 'threw red-on-red'—a signal that effectively blocked all trains—just after the fatal shot. He had to be sitting at his control panel to take this action." (Moore, *Conspiracy of One*, p.32)

could actually be observed." The Dallas police and sheriff's office did not report seeing any suspicious cars in the area, but Bowers apparently saw three that attracted his attention. So three cars in the parking lot behind the picket fence, all of which he said left the parking lot *before* the shooting, were suspicious enough to mention in his affidavit, but the suspicious activity *right behind* the picket fence *at the very time* of the shooting was not. Right. Later in the afternoon of the assassination, Bowers was interviewed by the Dallas County Sheriff's Department as well as the FBI and again spoke of the cars, but not one word about the suspicious activity right behind the picket fence.[88] But four months later, for the very first time, Bowers remembers all the "out of the ordinary activity" behind the picket fence. Lee Bowers finds his way into virtually all conspiracy books on the assassination, but one would have as much luck finding a reference in *any* of these books to Bowers's failure to mention (in his affidavit and two interviews on the day of the assassination) his seeing any suspicious activity behind the fence as finding hair on a bald man.

Bowers couldn't describe what he saw for the Warren Commission. But when conspiracy theorist Mark Lane interviewed him on March 31, 1966, over two years after his Warren Commission testimony, Bowers became a poster child for recovered memory. Suddenly, he remembered what he saw that attracted his attention. It was "a flash of light or smoke."[89]* To paraphrase the song "Smoke Gets in Your Eyes," a lot of smoke would have to get in one's eyes to believe Lee Bowers. If Bowers hadn't died when his car struck a bridge abutment near Midlothian, Texas, in August of 1966, it probably would have been just a matter of time before he had Jack Ruby with a machine gun on the grassy knoll.

Setting aside the whole area of the recovery of unconscious memories and perceptions (hypermnesia), we know, as an almost ironclad rule, that accurate memories of an event or statement tend to fade with time.† So how do we deal with the many Warren Commission witnesses like Bowers whose memory supposedly got better with time? Assuming their first statement was intended to be a complete one, and there is no question that the witnesses said what they are reported to have said, we must, almost by definition, reject *sensational* additions to their original story.

Are these "additions" by witnesses in the Kennedy case always flat-out lies on their part? In many cases, yes, just as some of their original statements are often completely fabricated in the hope of getting five minutes of fame or attention. But many times, witnesses are not knowingly telling a falsehood. As time goes by, they naturally forget some of what they saw or heard, and these new voids in their memory are frequently filled in with details derived from the power of suggestion or their own imagination, or from knowledge of later events that make the details more likely or even inevitable, or from the

---

*The HSCA, in an allusion to Bowers as well as Holland, said that "none of the photographs of the grassy knoll that were analyzed by the photographic evidence panel revealed any evidence of a puff of smoke or flash of light" (HSCA Report, p.86).

†I say "almost" because it's not uncommon for a person, when first asked about something, to be unable to recall it or some of the details, but when given help in the form of linkage by the questioner, the person finally does recall it. For example, "Do you recall telling Joe that _____?" "No." "Don't you remember he said to you that _____ and then you started laughing and said to him _____?" "Oh yes, I do remember telling him that now." In the legal context, this is called "refreshing the memory," and is usually achieved by documents the person is shown on the witness stand.

recollections of others that witnesses unconsciously embrace as their own—that is, the witness ends up saying he saw something that he himself never saw. David L. Schacter, professor of psychology at Harvard University, says that in these cases, "with the passage of time, memory shifts from a reproduction of the past to a reconstruction of it."

As author Elizabeth Loftus says about the passage of time causing memories to fade, "In its weakened condition, memory, like a disease-ridden body, becomes especially vulnerable to repeated assaults [of information from others]."[90]

With so many people trying to attach themselves, in some way, to the biggest murder case in American history, the addition of new elements to their stories, particularly important details that would never have been omitted by them in the original telling if they were true, has to be taken, as they say in Latin, *cum grano salis* (with a grain of salt). One has to be highly skeptical of witnesses who, for no convincing reason, tell their story about some aspect of the Kennedy case for the first time years later.

No hard and fast rules can be employed, without exception, to determine the credibility of the various witnesses dealt in this book other than the dictates of logic and common sense.

Other Assassins

As Warren Commission member Allen Dulles put it back in 1966, if the Warren Commission critics find an assassin other than Oswald, "Let them name names and produce their evidence."[1] Since that time, the critics and conspiracy theorists have indeed named names—eighty-two at last count—but haven't produced one single, solitary piece of credible evidence connecting any of these other alleged assassins to Kennedy's murder.

In the conspiracy section of this book, I set forth the list of eighty-two men who one or another conspiracy theorist has alleged assassinated Kennedy. I feature some of the more prominent ones on the following pages. Among them are a few nuts, publicity seekers, and those after easy money who actually volunteered the fact that they themselves killed Kennedy or knew someone who did.

I should candidly acknowledge that I will not include in this section allegations of other assassins that are just too difficult for me to debunk. For instance, conspiracy author Milton William Cooper alleges, as others have, that America and the world are controlled by the American Council on Foreign Relations (Henry Kissinger, Dr. Edward Teller, David Rockefeller, etc.) and the international Trilateral Commission, which, he says, included, at the time of Kennedy's assassination, American members like George H. W. Bush, John McCloy, and Dean Acheson. These groups learned of space aliens invading the United States and apparently had no objection to them, even establishing, with selected Americans and representatives of the Soviet Union, a joint lunar base with the aliens. One of these leaders, George H. W. Bush, who at the time was president and CEO of the offshore division of Zapata Oil, based in Texas, started to traffic in drugs with the CIA, the CIA controlling "most of the world's illegal drug markets." When President Kennedy found out about this as well as the aliens, he issued an ultimatum to Majesty 12, a permanent subcommittee of the National Security Council dealing with alien issues, that if the subcommittee did not clean up the drug problem, which was destroying American youth, he would reveal to Americans the existence of aliens among us and the base we established with them on the moon. Members of Majesty 12 decided they had to kill Kennedy, which they did on November 22 by having the driver of the presidential limousine, William Greer, shoot him. The reason why I can't knock this theory down is that Cooper says he has a special copy of the Zapruder film, which I don't have, that clearly shows Greer shooting Kennedy. How can I refute photographic evidence, particularly when I don't have access to it?[2]

Now for the assassins I am willing to challenge.

Hugh C. McDonald, a former chief of detectives for the Los Angeles County sheriff's office, says in his little pocket book, *Appointment in Dallas*, that he traveled almost fifty thousand miles through ten countries for close to two years to track down Kennedy's assassin. When, he says, he had just about "run out of cash" and was "eating my credit cards," the chase bore handsome fruit. In a room at the Westbury Hotel in London in June of 1992, the assassin, whom he named Saul (McDonald tells his readers that Saul was the man whose picture was taken by the CIA outside of the Russian embassy in Mexico City in October of 1963, and was erroneously believed to be Oswald in an early, internal CIA memorandum), and who McDonald says was a paid killer and soldier of fortune who participated in the Bay of Pigs invasion, bared his soul to McDonald. A man named Troit, representing powerful interests, had paid him (Saul) fifty thousand dollars to kill Kennedy. Saul said he killed the president with frangible bullets, firing from the second floor of the County Records Building on Houston Street. Oswald was set up to be the patsy, firing "cover shots" from the Book Depository Building, and the plan was that the Secret Service would fire back at Oswald and miss, but Saul would then kill Oswald and the Secret Service would have gotten the credit for it. "I don't know why they didn't fire. I seemed to have him [Oswald] in my crosshairs for an eternity," Saul tells McDonald.

Since there is no statute of limitations for murder, why would Saul confess to a murder for which he could get the death penalty? "You just don't kill the President of the United States, walk away from it and then not mention it to anyone forever," McDonald writes. That answer certainly satisfies me, Hugh. McDonald, who goes out of his way to inform his readers about his credentials, background, and many friends and connections in law enforcement, even referring to the congratulatory wire he received from FBI Director J. Edgar Hoover when he retired, did not take his explosive information to the authorities. Why not? "Who would listen?" he asks his readers. No one, Hugh. No one. But at least you got to tell your story in a book.[3]

Three alleged Corsican hit men hired by the mob to kill Kennedy were memorialized in the disgraceful documentary *The Men Who Killed Kennedy*. The initial four-part, two-hour British production (there have been five subsequent episodes under the same title, *The Men Who Killed Kennedy*, but different subtitles) was first shown in England on October 25, 1988, and discredited there shortly thereafter[4] (see following). The documentary wasn't shown in America until October 1991 on the A&E cable network and has been shown many times in the United States since then (since 1996 all segments or episodes have been shown on the History Channel). It has been very popular, having been viewed by an estimated 100 million people worldwide.

The highlight of the "documentary" is *Part 4*, where the producer, Nigel Turner, is nice enough to tell us who killed Kennedy. He does this through a Hollywood scriptwriter, Steve Rivele, who, we are told, devoted almost four years of his life (since

1985) to getting to the bottom of the case. Rivele, the film says, "was given the name [by conspiracy theorist Gary Shaw] of a French drug smuggler in prison in the United States who, it was rumored, had some first-hand knowledge of the President's assassination." His name? Christian David, who, Rivele tells the audience, was "a member of the old French Connection heroin network and then the leader of a Corsican drug trafficking network in South America called the Latin Connection." In exchange for Rivele's promise to help him find an attorney to resist deportation to France after he finished his drug-trafficking sentence at Leavenworth federal penitentiary here in the United States, David agreed to start giving Rivele information about the assassination.

Rivele says David told him that there had been a conspiracy to murder the president, and in May or June 1963, in Marseille, France, he had been offered the contract to kill Kennedy, "but turned it down." Rivele's help was ineffectual and David was deported, but Rivele followed him to a Paris prison (Fresnes prison, and later La Santé prison, where he was awaiting trial for the murder of a police officer—he was subsequently convicted) to continue to interrogate him. Since there was nothing, at that point, that Rivele could offer David for his earth-shaking information, why would David snitch on the murderous conspirators, the type of people, we can assume, who usually have rather harsh ways of dealing with canaries? Rivele comes up with this non sequitur: David talked out of "the fear that he would either be committed to an asylum [in view of the psychotic fairy tale David tells, that part I certainly do understand] or that he would be convicted of an old murder charge." Say again?

Eventually, through David and Michel Nicoli, a former drug trafficker turned DEA informant to whom David referred Rivele for corroboration of what he told Revele, Rivele came up with a whopper of a story. (It should be noted that by the time of their story, all of the hollow and hallowed conspiracy allegations—several professional assassins, not a lone gunman; Kennedy killed in a cross fire; head shot fired from grassy knoll; Badge Man; frangible bullet; Mafia behind the assassination; etc.—were very well known, and David's and Nicoli's story, as told by Rivele, conveniently "corroborated" all of them.)

Here is the story: The assassins of Kennedy "were hired on a contract [by the Chicago mob] which had been placed with the leader of the Corsican Mafia in Marseille," Antoine Guerini, in May or June of 1963. Guerini was asked to supply three professional, "high-quality, experienced killers." Rivele tells the TV audience that in the fall of 1963 the three killers were flown from Marseille to Mexico City where they spent three or four weeks at the house of a contact in Mexico City. They were then driven from Mexico City to the U.S. border at Brownsville, Texas. They crossed the border using Italian passports. They were picked up on the American side of the border by a representative of the Chicago Mafia with whom they conversed in Italian. They were then driven to Dallas where they were put up in a safe house. They spent several days taking photographs in Dealey Plaza, and in the evening they studied the photographs, et cetera, et cetera. Kennedy was killed in a "cross fire," Rivele said. Two of the assassins were in buildings behind the president, and the fatal head shot was fired by Lucien Sarti, who—yeah, you guessed it—was in a uniform (remember the "Badge Man" in an earlier section?) behind the picket fence on the grassy knoll.[*] As soon as Rivele says this, a photo of the Badge Man is put on the

---

[*]Rivele said he was told that the two assassins to the president's rear were firing regular bullets, but Sarti, from the grassy knoll, fired (naturally) a frangible bullet. Four bullets were fired. The first bullet was fired from the rear and struck the president in the back, and the second bullet, also fired from the rear, hit Connally. (As we know, the Warren Commission was originally perplexed by whether or not the shot that hit Kennedy went on to hit Connally, but finally concluded that it did—the single-bullet theory. David and Nicoli,

screen. Lucien Sarti, the film wants you to believe, *was* the Badge Man, who, being the very experienced professional assassin that he was, didn't try to escape after killing Kennedy, but instead jumped over the picket fence to kick Gordon Arnold for taking a photo of Lucien's handiwork, and get the film from Arnold.

Rivele informs the TV audience that after killing Kennedy, all three killers went back to their safe house in Dallas, where they stayed for ten days before being flown by private jet to Montreal, and then back to Marseille. Rivele says the assassins were paid by the Mafia in heroin, which was converted into cash.

A very neat package. A brilliant investigation by a lone Hollywood scriptwriter, Steve Rivele, finally, after all these years, solved, we are told in the film, "one of the greatest murder mysteries of all time." My only question is, Where was Rivele when the Warren Commission and the House Select Committee on Assassinations needed him? By the way, why the conspirators would risk telling David and Nicoli, who were *not* part of the conspiracy to kill Kennedy, all about it, right down to the finest details, is not known.

The Men Who Killed Kennedy names Sarti, Roger Bocognani, and Sauveur Pironti as the three assassins from Marseille who killed Kennedy. The problem is that David, who is supposed to be the main source of all of Rivele's information, publicly exonerated Bocognani and Pironti.[5*]

But we didn't need David to say two of the three were innocent, which alone destroys the credibility of Rivele's entire fable. Within two days of the October 25, 1988, debut of *The Men Who Killed Kennedy* in Britain, French authorities debunked the film's claims as to all three alleged assassins. They ascertained that on the day of the assassination, Pironti was doing his national service onboard a minesweeper based at Toulon, Bocognani was serving time in the Baumettes prison in Marseille, and Sarti, the Marseille crook who is accused in the film of having fired the fatal head shot, was in Fort Ha prison in Bordeaux.[6]

Upon hearing of the three solid alibis, the film's producer, Turner, was undaunted and

---

however, debunked the single-bullet theory out of hand. How they would know this [i.e., how would even the alleged assassin who fired the bullet that entered Kennedy's back know it did not go on to strike Connally?] Rivele does not tell the TV audience.) The third bullet, Rivele said, was the fatal head shot that was fired from the grassy knoll, and the fourth bullet, fired from Kennedy's rear, missed.

*So we know this is a phony story to begin with, but did David even tell it to the Hollywood scriptwriter, Rivele? Someone who should know says he doesn't believe he did. Jim Lesar, the scholarly head of the Assassination Archives and Research Center in Washington, D.C., was the lawyer Rivele got to try to prevent David's extradition back to France. In a last-ditch effort, he almost succeeded. Lesar actually accompanied Rivele on three separate trips to France for Rivele's interviews of David at La Santé prison, and says that although David and Rivele conversed in French, and Lesar's French is very limited, it's his impression that Rivele "inferred" the identity of the three gunmen from what David said, "putting two and two together."

Even though David had previously said that two of the three killers Rivele names in the movie were innocent, David has supposedly written a letter in which he names all three presidential assassins. It is not known who they are (and therefore whether the two he previously exonerated are among the three) since David's Parisian lawyer, Henri Juramy, has the letter, and as recently as the fall of 2003, Rivele told Lesar that he hadn't been able to get Juramy to furnish him with a copy of it. (Telephone interviews of Jim Lesar by author on February 3, 2004, and February 18, 2006; FBI Record 124-10001-10390, March 7, 1988, pp. 1–3) Like Rivele, I can't wait to see who the chosen three are.

Because of David's earlier exoneration of two of the three killers Rivele named, a French publisher whom Rivele had a contract with to publish his story, withdrew, and Rivele has never found an American publisher for his book. I can't imagine why. Years later, Rivele got the book published in Spanish by Ediciones B, a small Madrid publishing house. In great despair over the total disintegration of his case over in Europe, Rivele returned to the United States only to find that his wife was divorcing him, in whole or in part because of his madcap adventure, which had brought him to the brink of bankruptcy, and Rivele contemplated suicide. But he made a comeback, co-writing the script for Oliver Stone's movie *Nixon*, for which he was nominated for an Academy Award. (Telephone interview of Jim Lesar by author on February 3, 2004)

indeed confrontational. "We expected this. People have had 25 years to come up with alibis."[7] But, of course, the three accused assassins didn't "come up" with anything. French
authorities ascertained the bona fide existence of the alibis. On the other side of the water,
Steve Rivele, the writer, backed down quite a bit. "I [still] believe that Sarti was involved,"
he said, "but apparently I was wrong on the other two."[8] Only wrong on two-thirds of
your story? That's all? The charges in the film were so obviously false and lacking in support that several members of the British Parliament called for the revocation of the television franchise of Central Independent Television, the big British production company
that had shown the film on the ITV network.[9]

Central Independent Television, to defend itself against the mounting charges that it
had been sold a bogus bill of goods by producer-director Nigel Turner and hadn't demonstrated professional responsibility in checking the story before showing it on British television, immediately dispatched its own team of investigative reporters to France to verify
if, indeed, the story was all hogwash. The investigators reported back that what the French
authorities had said was correct, finding documentation to support the alibis of all three
of the alleged assassins.[*] The *London Sunday Times* reviewed the file on the matter and
reported that it "revealed evidence from Central reporters that the company had accepted
half-baked theories from an American author who heard a story from a known liar trying
to talk his way out of a jail sentence." An internal memo from one of the reporters on the
investigative team, Peter de Selding, said that the so-called documentary had "sullied the
reputation of a serious broadcasting company." The memo added that "ten days" of investigation "have turned up no evidence supporting the program's accusations against the
three men. On the contrary it has produced evidence that leaves the program's conclusions in a shambles." Another memo from another Central reporter referred to the show
as "total nonsense" dreamt up by an "amateurish" American author from underground
gossip. Another memo said, "We destroyed the allegations concerning the Frenchmen
within a few days." All three of the alleged assassins were found to be petty criminals.[10][†]

When the show was broadcast in England in 1988, Sarti was dead (having been killed
in a shootout with police in Mexico City in 1972), and Bocognani was somewhere in South
America, but Pironti, still in France, told the French newspaper *Le Provencal* on October 26, 1988, "This is the most terrible moment of my life. It is wholly inexplicable. I
agree that when I was younger I did things I should not have done. But I have paid for
that. I was never a killer for the Mafia or anybody."[11] He told the *London Times*, "The
only thing I know about Dallas is the soap opera I have watched on TV."[12]

Talking about Sarti's losing one of his eyes, I'm aware of the expression that in a world
of blind men, a one-eyed man is a king. But unfortunately for Nigel Turner and his Sher-

---

[*]However, as to Sarti they found that on the day of the shooting, "he was undergoing serious medical treatment in France." Whether that was inside or outside of Fort Ha prison in Bordeaux was not stated in the *London Sunday Times* report on the investigation. (*London Sunday Times*, November 24, 1991) The *Manchester
Guardian Weekly* reported that on the day of the assassination, Sarti "was apparently on sick leave from his
job as a dockwasher, following the loss of an eye" (*Manchester Guardian Weekly*, November 6, 1988, *Le Monde*
sect., p.13).

[†]Though Central Television's franchise was ultimately not revoked for presenting untruthful broad-
casts, producer-director Nigel Turner did not fare so well. Turner "was censured by members of the British
Parliament." And the British regulatory agency, the Independent Broadcasting Authority, directed Central
Television to present another broadcast devoted solely to exposing Turner's misleading show and the lack
of ethics he used in producing it. Called a "studio crucifixion" of Turner, the program, which was taped in
Washington, D.C., was aired only in Britain on November 16, 1988, and was the first time that the British
regulatory agency had ever compelled such an action. (*Manchester Guardian*, December 7, 1988;
http://mcadams.posc.mu.edu/holland3.htm)

lock Holmes, Steve Rivele, we are not blind (though even a blind man could see through their farce) and we see very clearly that their film is a prodigious fiction. And across the water, it is treated as that. The fury created by the show was such that it was shelved in England. But when Central Independent Television ran into financial difficulty in the early 1990s, it had no hesitancy about selling the show to America, where American audiences, without objection from American authorities or the television industry, have been eating it up, with gusto, ever since. The *London Sunday Times*, aghast at the American sale, said that "Central Television sold the documentary, which the company must have known was based on false evidence, to American television."[13]

By the way, the absurd conspiracy theorists who have come to believe that the three Corsicans from Marseille, not Oswald, killed Kennedy, and that they did it for "the Mafia," should get together with the conspiracy theorists who believe Oswald killed Kennedy for the Mafia and was later silenced by Ruby for the Mafia, and ask themselves this question: if the mob felt the need to have Ruby silence Oswald, why wouldn't it feel the same need (in fact, three times as urgent, since there is not just one killer but three who could talk) to silence their three hit men from Marseille? Yet all three of them were apparently permitted by their mob employers to go on their merry way after they killed Kennedy for them. Just a thought.

One prominent conspiracy theorist who thinks this completely fictional "documentary" is valid is Gaeton Fonzi, a former Philadelphia writer who worked as an investigator on the Church Committee and for the HSCA. Fonzi actually said that the conspiracy theory in the Kennedy assassination that has impressed him the most "is the French Connection, especially the evidence developed by researcher Steve Rivele."

Interviewer: "He was on *The Men Who Killed Kennedy*?"

Fonzi: "Yes, the French Connection theory always intrigued me as the most likely possibility . . . [It's] the one that makes the most sense to me."[14]

And to think that Fonzi was at one time an investigator on the federal payroll, although I must say that some of his reports for the HSCA seemed professional. Fonzi also said he "always assumed" that Robert Kennedy was murdered because if he became president he intended to reopen the investigation of his brother's murder, and the conspirators who killed his brother couldn't allow that to happen.[15]

At the end of *The Men Who Killed Kennedy*, writer Rivele tells the audience that he turned over all of his investigation to the FBI so the bureau could go after the true killers of Kennedy, but, he laments, "Nothing is being done about it." Again, I can't imagine why. Could it be that, as another writer, Gertrude Stein, once said in a different context about Oakland, California, "There's no there, there"?

Rivele did leave the audience with this bit of insight and wisdom: he is "convinced that Oswald had nothing to do with the assassination and he was carefully chosen and set up to take the blame." For all its silliness, the American public, as indicated, can't get enough of the British film. One would think that those who watch the History Channel would be above average in intelligence and erudition. And they probably are. Yet the channel reports that the most frequently asked question it gets is, "When will *The Men Who Killed Kennedy* repeat?"[16]

Charles Harrelson, the father of Hollywood actor Woody Harrelson, was at one time believed to be the youngest of the "three tramps" arrested in Dealey Plaza.[17] For years, many conspiracy theorists believed the three tramps to be the president's killers (see later text). Harrelson, whose late brother was an FBI agent, is not a nut or a publicity seeker but someone with a long criminal record and reputed mob connections. He was convicted of murdering U.S. district court judge John H. Wood Jr. for a drug kingpin for $250,000 outside the judge's home in San Antonio on May 29, 1979. At the time of his arrest for the murder, Harrelson, high on cocaine, offered the authorities a deal. He was part of a team of assassins who murdered Kennedy, he said, and would be willing to implicate the other members of the conspiracy in return for his freedom. The feds rejected the deal. Harrelson has since admitted making the story up. "On November 22, 1963," Harrelson said, "I was with a friend at twelve thirty in the afternoon having lunch in a restaurant in Houston, Texas. I did not kill JFK . . . I was not in my right mind when I confessed."[18] Harrelson is presently serving a life sentence for Judge Wood's murder at a federal penitentiary in Texarkana, Texas.

Even verifiable nuts who have been committed are too much to resist for conspiracy theorists. Unbelievably, author Henry Hurt devoted *forty-five* pages in his book *Reasonable Doubt* to the claim of one Robert Easterling (who Hurt admits is a "raging alcoholic, diagnosed psychotic and schizophrenic" who has been admitted to mental institutions) that he was involved with David Ferrie (see conspiracy section), Oswald (who was to be the patsy), and anti-Castro Cuban exiles in a New Orleans–hatched plot to kill Kennedy financed by a wealthy Dallas oilman. Kennedy was to be killed because he betrayed the Cubans at the Bay of Pigs. Easterling, who spun his tale to Hurt in September of 1981, claims that his role in the plot was to meet Oswald at a bus station in Dallas at 10:30 on the morning of the assassination and drive Oswald to Mexico City. Oswald's Mannlicher-Carcano was to be planted at the Book Depository Building murder scene as a cover for the real murder weapon, a 7-millimeter Czech automatic, which would fire bullets that would disintegrate into untraceable fragments upon impact. Oswald would eventually be killed in Mexico by the conspirators. Easterling learned later that a Cuban named "Manuel," who originally recruited him into the plot, was the one who shot Kennedy from the sixth-floor window, having entered the building that morning with an Oswald look-alike named Carlo.

Getting cold feet the night before Kennedy's assassination, Easterling, who said he was an FBI informant (the FBI has no record of Easterling being an informant), told Hurt he tried to bail out of the conspiracy by calling FBI headquarters in Washington, D.C., at 9:30 p.m. from a pay phone at a service station in Baton Rouge. He said he told someone who was working late at the headquarters, "They're going to kill the president" the next day, only to be told by the person at headquarters, "We know all about it. We're going to catch them red-handed. You're in too deep. Don't go to Dallas," which Easterling never did. Instead, to provide an alibi for himself in case someone tried to later connect him to the assassination, he burglarized a store in Baton Rouge in the early-morning hours of November 22, 1963, and was later apprehended and sentenced to five years in prison. After the assassination, he told Hurt, several Cubans were sent to kill him by tricking him into taking a drive with them, but he somehow outwitted them and escaped.

Though Hurt tries to protect his own credibility by acknowledging that Easterling is a "terribly sullied witness" whose story, in some respects, is "obviously preposterous," he still says that Easterling's "underlying account is compelling in certain respects," and that "Easterling's confession, with all its ragged edges, provides a persuasive version of events that fills the void of uncertainty" created by the Warren Commission. He adds, "In the final analysis, it is not possible to prove that the Easterling confession is true. [Really? If Henry Hurt hadn't said this, I, for one, was ready to accept it.] What remains is a massive public skepticism over the official account." Right. *A skepticism almost solely created and fueled by conspiracy theorists like Mr. Hurt* who devoted an entire chapter of his book to peddling nonsense like the Easterling yarn.[19] And to illustrate how bad the situation is, Henry Hurt, a former editor at *Reader's Digest*, no less, is one of the most responsible of the conspiracy theorists.

A footnote to the Easterling story. Johann Rush, the assassination researcher who shot the film of Oswald passing out Fair Play for Cuba leaflets in New Orleans in the summer of 1963, is from the same town as Easterling—Hattiesburg, Mississippi—and knows him well. He told me that after Easterling saw his (Rush's) first Kennedy report on local television in 1981, "he began calling me to 'confess' and to ask me to help him sell his story to NBC news. Easterling's tale was a little believable until he started telling me how J. Edgar Hoover used to call him up all during the 1950's and 60's for advice. Easterling told me he was Hoover's chief advisor and that Hoover went to Baton Rouge to meet secretly with him when he had a perplexing problem he couldn't solve by himself. I talked with the local sheriff, Gene Walters, about Easterling, and Walters told me that Easterling had been 'confessing' to various sensational crimes for more than twenty years. Easterling called Walters and the FBI in the early 70's to tell them he knew where Patti Hearst was being hidden, but when they interviewed him, he never would reveal the exact location."[20] Easterling's first known commitment to a mental institution was in 1974, and his second was in 1983.[21]

Marita Lorenz is the soldier of fortune and one-time reputed mistress of Fidel Castro and former Venezuelan dictator Marcos Pérez Jiménez, both of whom she allegedly had a love child with. The thrice-married Lorenz *does* have photos of herself with Castro, whom she met when she accompanied her father, Heinrich, the captain of the MS *Berlin*, a luxury German ocean liner, to Havana in February of 1959, when Lorenz was only nineteen. And there is evidence she lived with him for several months after the revolution in his headquarters in the Habana Hilton. Her sister, Valerie, told *Vanity Fair* that Castro was "the big love of [Marita's] life," having been her first lover. The author of the article on Lorenz in the respected monthly concluded that it was "indisputable" that Lorenz did have a long-term affair with Castro and became pregnant by him, but said that "there is no evidence a child was born . . . So desperate is Lorenz to prove her claim of having had Castro's child that she offers me what looks like an FBI report in order to verify her story. However, misspellings, uncharacteristic language, and the lack of an FBI file number betray the document as a fraud." In her 1993 autobiography, Lorenz says her son by Fidel, Andre, has become a Cuban doctor, and Castro only permitted her to meet him once, on a visit to Cuba in 1981, causing her love for Castro to turn into a love-hate emotion. Pérez Jiménez did pay child support for a while for Lorenz's alleged child by him, Monica (who would one day pose for *Playboy* and become a finalist in the Miss Fitness USA contest), though the latter's Miami lawyer said Pérez Jiménez denied the child was his.[22]

Lorenz has provided the quenchless conspiracy community with another wild and improbable tale of a plot to murder the president. Described by a New York reporter as a "curvy, black-haired American Mata Hari," the German-born Lorenz waited until 1977, fourteen years after the assassination, to inform the world of what really happened. She told *New York Daily News* reporter Paul Meskill in September of 1977 that she had accompanied Oswald and an "assassin squad" to Dallas a few days before the assassination.* Meskill wrote, "[Lorenz] told the *News* that her companions on the car trip from Miami to Dallas were Oswald, CIA contract agent Frank Sturgis, Cuban exile leaders Orlando Bosch and Pedro Diaz Lanz, and two Cuban brothers whose names she did not know. She said they were all members of Operation 40, a secret guerilla group originally formed by the CIA in 1960 in preparation for the Bay of Pigs invasion . . . She claimed the group conspired to kill . . . President Kennedy, whom it blamed for the Bay of Pigs fiasco . . . Ms. Lorenz said she first met Oswald, whom she knew only as 'Ozzie', at an Operation 40 'safe house' in Miami's Little Havana section in the summer or early fall of 1963. She said she asked Sturgis who the stranger was and he replied: 'He's OK. He's one of us.'" Lorenz said that after the group arrived in Dallas she "flew back to Miami the next day. And two days later I was on a plane to New York when the co-pilot announced that President Kennedy had been shot in Dallas."[23]

In sworn testimony before the HSCA in 1978, Lorenz said the group met in September of 1963 at Bosch's home in Miami. She was never told about the purpose of the meeting, but heard the group discussing a trip they were going to take and she assumed "it was an armory hit," a raid to get weapons as she had done before with Sturgis. She noticed one thing that caught her attention, however. The group was studying street maps of Dallas. "About a week or so before November 22nd," she said, the group left for Dallas in two cars. Oswald, whom she said she didn't like, Diaz, Bosch, and Gerry Patrick Hemming,[†] whom Lorenz never mentioned to Meskill, were in one car, and she, Sturgis, and "the Novo's" (Guillermo and Ignacio Novo, the two previously unnamed brothers who were anti-Castro Cuban exiles) were in the other car. After the two-day, 1,300-mile trip, they holed up in a motel on the outskirts of Dallas. The group's two rooms were separated by an open door. Sturgis was in charge. "We were told no newspapers, no phone calls, we don't go out, food will be brought in . . . Once we were inside, the trunk of the car was opened and they brought in . . . three, four automatics." Lorenz sensed this was not going to be a hit on an armory, where she was always used as a decoy,

---

*In an earlier, June 13, 1976, article by Meskill in the *Daily News*, he quotes Lorenz as claiming that in the fall of 1960, Frank Sturgis (real name, Frank Angelo Fiorini), one of the Watergate burglars and an alleged CIA operative, gave her two capsules of poisoned powder that she was supposed to put in Castro's food, but she said that after entering Cuba on her secret mission, the capsules dissolved while concealed in a jar of cold cream in Castro's room at the Havana Hilton, to which she still had a key from the previous year. In her autobiography, she says one of the two capsules slipped out of her hand and fell into the bidet and she flushed the other one down, realizing, since she still loved Fidel, how "utterly preposterous" it was for her to be there to "kill this man." She says when Castro later returned to his suite and found her there, he asked her if she had come for him or to kill him (she acknowledged the latter) before they made love. (Lorenz with Schwarz, *Marita*, pp.77, 80–83; 10 HSCA 156) Gaeton Fonzi, an HSCA investigator who was assigned to investigate Lorenz's claims about the Kennedy assassination, describes her as someone who has always "lived on the edge," and the dominant characteristics of her life were "change and turmoil." Because of her penchant for intrigue and strong anti-Castro sentiments, Fonzi believes he has been an informant at times for the FBI, U.S. Customs, and the DEA. (Fonzi, *Last Investigation*, pp.87–88)

†Hemming is a right-wing, ex-Marine soldier of fortune who keeps popping up in assassination literature. Like Sturgis and others, he went to Cuba to help Castro's rebels overthrow Batista, and ended up trying to overthrow Castro with his own group of fellow adventurers, Interpen (Intercontinental Penetration Forces, which shunned CIA funds and control), when he discovered Castro was pink.

but when she asked Sturgis, "What the hell is going on?"[*] he simply told her, "I will talk to you later." She decided she wanted to return to Miami the very next day, but before she left, a visitor came to the motel room. "It was . . . Jack Ruby."[24] Marita would later tell *Vanity Fair*, "[Ruby] comes into the room. He's like a little Mob punk, a short, balding guy with a cocky hat, heavyset, with a cleft on his chin. He took two steps inside, saw me lounging, and said 'Who's the fucking broad?' And I said, 'Fuck you, punk.'"[25]

The HSCA said it could find "no evidence to support Lorenz' allegation."[26] Edwin Lopez, an HSCA researcher who testified for the defense at the London trial, told *Case Closed* author Gerald Posner, "Oh God, we spent a lot of time with Marita . . . It was hard to ignore her because she gave us so much crap, and we tried to verify it, but let me tell you—she is full of s——— . . . Marita is not credible."[27]

Not that they would be expected to acknowledge it if Lorenz were telling the truth, but Lorenz didn't fare any better with members of the "assassin squad." Bosch told the HSCA that the last time he saw Lorenz was in 1962 when she called him to get involved in anti-Castro activities, and he turned her down, adding he never traveled west of New Orleans in his life. The "Novo" brothers were never located, but Diaz and Hemming both denied ever taking any trip to Dallas with Lorenz. When the HSCA deposed Sturgis on Lorenz's claim that he had participated in a plot to murder Kennedy, he responded, "Sir, that is an absolute lie . . . She is a liar. I took a polygraph examination to that effect that I have never been involved in any conspiracy to kill the president of the United States . . . nor was I with her in any automobile with these people or any other people going to Dallas to plot to kill the president of the United States. She is an absolute liar."[28][†]

In late October of 1977, Lorenz succeeded in having Sturgis arrested in New York City for allegedly making threatening calls to her, which she taped. But when the Manhattan district attorney's office heard the tapes (there were seven) Lorenz provided, they contained "no threats." The prosecutor, Assistant District Attorney Alan Brooms, accordingly made a motion, which was granted, to dismiss the charges against Sturgis because "a lack of any substantiation of her [Mrs. Lorenz's] charges impairs her credibility."[29]

Even the wacky conspiracy theorist A. J. Weberman said he didn't believe Lorenz's story. A measure of Lorenz's lack of credibility is that when her mother (whom, heretofore, not even Marita had alleged was a part of her far-reaching world of espionage and intrigue) died in 1977, Marita exclaimed, "She knew too much. They gave her a shot. Same as they gave Jack Ruby."[30]

Marita should have known that quite apart from the fact that all the evidence shows precisely who killed Kennedy, and there is no evidence that shows her group did, she made it hard on herself by alleging that Lee Harvey Oswald, or "Ozzie," was part of her group. The slightly inconvenient fact for poor Marita is that Oswald could not have been in Miami the week before the assassination and then traveling cross-country with her and the others thereafter, since Oswald was seen every day during this period in Dallas, where

---

[*]By 1993, fifteen years later, Lorenz had apparently forgotten her earlier lie, and told a new one. In her autobiography she wrote that "the weaponry we carried" in the two cars en route to Dallas "would *only* be used for a *murderous* mission. The rifles were excellent assassination tools for fairly long range . . . I knew we were [going to Dallas] to kill somebody" (Lorenz with Schwarz, *Marita*, pp.131, 134).

[†]It is not known what polygraph examination Sturgis was referring to, but three years earlier, when counsel for the Rockefeller Commission asked Sturgis if he were involved in any way in Kennedy's death, he said, "No, sir," and then proceeded to offer to take a polygraph examination on his denial. There is no suggestion in the record that the Commission gave Sturgis such a test. (SSCIA 157-10005-10126, Deposition of Sturgis before Rockefeller Commission, April 4, 1975, pp.10, 14–15)

he was living. Indeed, every day of the week (except on Saturday and Sunday) he was working at the Book Depository Building and accounted for.

But who cares about these minor problems? Marita and her fable would live to see another day in the nurturing arms of someone who could give her a run for her money when it comes to a lack of credibility—the inimitable Mark Lane. In an August 1978 article in *Spotlight*, a small Washington, D.C., weekly published by the ultra-right Liberty Lobby, ex-CIA agent Victor Marchetti wrote that former CIA agent E. Howard Hunt's assertion in a prior lawsuit that he was in Washington, D.C., not Dallas, on the day of the assassination "was not true," and that when the HSCA held its open hearings later that month, his former employer, the CIA, would "admit" that Hunt (one of the Watergate burglars) "was involved in the conspiracy to kill Kennedy." Marchetti's reasoning for why the CIA would do this made a lot of sense—to a child. The CIA, he said, had "decided to sacrifice him [Hunt] to protect its clandestine services." Apart from the non sequitur (in what way would sacrificing Hunt "protect its clandestine services"?), the very strong likelihood is that the CIA would only be in a position to "admit" that Hunt was a part of a conspiracy to kill Kennedy if the agency itself was involved in it. And if it was, the CIA would really be protecting its involvement in the assassination by sacrificing Hunt, wouldn't it? Hunt, being a minnow in the conspiratorial pond, would be a ripe candidate for a plea bargain to implicate the higher-ups at the CIA. But Marchetti assured his readers that Hunt "will not dare to speak out—the CIA will see to that." Right. Sacrifice someone who can implicate you, when he has nothing to lose and everything to gain by doing so, and then see to it (Marchetti doesn't say how the CIA would accomplish this) that he doesn't put the hat on you.

Marchetti, who wrote that there were "many powerful special interests connected with the conspiracy to kill Kennedy," most of whom "are already dead" (Marchetti doesn't say who these special interests and dead conspirators are, nor does he say how he came by this information), also claimed in the article that the CIA "just happened to stumble across" a memo in its old files "dated 1966," which said in essence "someday we will have to explain Hunt's presence in Dallas on November 22, 1963."[31] Marchetti doesn't concern himself with why the CIA would put such a cover-up plot on paper, but he busily goes on in his article to embrace the fairy tale told by Marita Lorenz. One wonders how someone (Marchetti) with this type of fuzzy mind could have been a fourteen-year veteran of the CIA before his resignation in 1969, at one time serving as an assistant to the deputy director. None of Marchetti's silly predictions in the *Spotlight* article* came true, of course. One also wonders why Hunt would pay any attention to

---

*Marchetti also predicted in his article that the CIA, during the HSCA hearings, "may go so far as to 'admit' that there were three gunmen shooting at Kennedy." Where, pray tell, did Marchetti get all this "inside" information? At his deposition in Hunt's lawsuit against him and Liberty Lobby for libel, he was forced to acknowledge that it came from two sources *outside* the CIA (which, I suppose, is the reliable way to get *inside* information, right?), one of whom was the loony conspiracy theorist A. J. Weberman. (Lane, *Plausible Denial*, p.145)

Six days after the *Spotlight* article, Joseph Trento, a reporter for the Wilmington, Delaware, *Sunday News Journal*, perhaps parroting without attribution the *Spotlight* article, wrote in his paper about the existence of the 1966 memo. When Lane took Trento's deposition in the *Spotlight* lawsuit on June 28, 1984, Trento said he got his information about the memo from "sources within the agency [CIA] and outside the agency," but refused to disclose their identity. On cross-examination he claimed he had actually seen the memo and it was initialed by CIA officials James Jesus Angleton and Richard Helms. (Lane, *Plausible Denial*, pp.162–163, 167) Apparently Angleton and Helms, both notorious masters of deceit and secrecy, not only wanted to put the CIA's cover-up of Hunt's participation in Kennedy's murder in writing, but they wanted to make double sure, by their initials, that they got whatever credit they had coming for the cover-up.

this drivel in a low-circulation publication. But he did, suing Marchetti and Liberty Lobby for libel.

Mark Lane, whose politics are as far away from that of Liberty Lobby as night is from day, was the defense attorney for Liberty Lobby and wrote a book about the case, *Plausible Denial*. The book in substantial part deals with matters totally unrelated to the trial, providing Lane with yet another opportunity to regurgitate all of his conspiracy theories and allegations about the Kennedy assassination. *Plausible Denial* is poorly written, very superficial (but then again, maybe it's not, since Lane had nothing to write about), and even lacking in citations (a cardinal sin for any book on the assassination) to give the precise sources of Lane's allegations. Remarkably, Lane doesn't even tell his readers whether or not Marchetti was a defendant in the lawsuit (he *was* in the original complaint, but the case was dismissed against him prior to the trial), waits until page 129 to tell his readers what the *Spotlight* article says, and never finds the space in his 393 pages to inform his readers what Hunt's formal complaint, the basis for the defamation lawsuit, trial, and Lane's book, said. But it is inferable from the book that the main issue at the trial seemed to be the *Spotlight* article allegation that Hunt was in Dallas, not Washington, D.C., on the day of the assassination. Hunt, being the plaintiff, had the legal burden of proving a negative, that he wasn't in Dallas on November 22, 1963, some twenty-two years before the trial, which was held in a U.S. district court in Miami in 1985.* He was unable to prove this to the satisfaction of the jury, something that millions of others might be unable to do also, and on February 6, 1985, the federal jury found "for the defendant, Liberty Lobby, and against the plaintiff, E. Howard Hunt."

Consistent with his MO, Lane led his readers to believe that the reason for the verdict against Hunt was that the Miami jury believed the CIA was responsible for Kennedy's murder. But to support this, he only cites one juror, jury forewoman Leslie Armstrong, who said *she* believed this. But obviously, the issue of whether the CIA was behind the assassination was not for the jury to consider, and they apparently didn't. The tireless and always industrious conspiracy researcher Harrison Edward Livingstone, in his book *Killing the Truth*, says that "UPI wrote that juror No. 11 (Cobb) 'said the jury did not address the allegations brought out by Lane throughout the trial that Hunt was involved in a CIA conspiracy to kill Kennedy.'"[32] And *Newsweek* reported that another juror, Suzanne Reach, told the *Miami Herald* (in support of what Cobb said) that what Armstrong said "wasn't the reason for the verdict."[33]

In classic understatement, Lane announces to his readers in the opening pages of his book that "there is no legal precedent for *Hunt vs. Liberty Lobby*. More than two decades after the murder of John F. Kennedy in Dallas, the case against his killers was finally tried in a civil action suit brought in the federal courthouse in Miami." And, of course, representing the people of this country in seeking justice was . . . Mark Lane.

By Lane's own admission, his "most important" witness at the trial was none other than Ms. Lorenz, who, Lane writes, "traveled with the assassins from Miami to Dallas just before the murder." Lorenz's New York deposition on January 11, 1985, was read to the Miami jury. Since Lorenz's original story was so much of a lulu, one would have thought that there wasn't too much room for improvement. But with Lane holding her

---

*There was an earlier trial in 1981, after which the jury returned a verdict of $100,000 compensatory and $550,000 punitive damages in favor of Hunt, but the judgment was reversed by the U.S. Court of Appeals for the Eleventh Circuit (Case 82-5321).

hand, she managed to do so, big time. After recounting the meeting at Orlando Bosch's home, the car trip to Dallas (the group no longer had just three or four automatic weapons, but "cases of machine guns, rifles, thirty-eights [and] forty-fives"), and the arrival at the Dallas motel, she testified that not only did Jack Ruby come to the door during her very short overnight stay at the Dallas motel, but the plaintiff, E. Howard Hunt, whom she knew as "Eduardo," also came to the room, and she saw Hunt deliver an envelope of cash to her friend Sturgis, obviously, the payoff for the assassination. (She testified she had seen Eduardo make previous payments to Sturgis.) And Sturgis, who Marita had previously indicated wouldn't tell her anything, told her Hunt "had made [all] the arrangements" for their mission and "would provide the operating funds, cover, and plans for exit from the area once the assignment was completed." And though, in her HSCA testimony, she indicated she only *assumed* that the Sturgis-led group had killed Kennedy, she testified in the defamation trial that Sturgis later told her that by leaving Dallas she had missed "the really big one" in Dallas. "We killed the President that day. You could have been a part of it—you know, part of history. You should have stayed. It was safe. Everything was covered in advance. No arrests . . . it was all covered. Very professional." Lane, in his book, adds triumphantly, "It may have been very professional, but after the testimony of Marita Lorenz was read to a jury in a United States courthouse, it was no longer all covered."[34]

In other words, Lane, in 1966, informed the world in his book *Rush to Judgment* that the Warren Commission had covered up the identity of the conspirators in the assassination of President Kennedy, and then, in 1991, finally informed the world in his book *Plausible Denial* just who those conspirators were. The quarter-of-a-century wait was worth it, at least for me. Lane's undoubtedly innocent and unsuspecting publisher for *Plausible Denial*, Thunder's Mouth Press, laments on the book's dust jacket that the Miami trial was "historic, yet curiously unpublicized." I can't imagine why.

One of the most amusing stories on the assassination was told by Chicago mobster Sam Giancana's brother, Chuck, in his 1992 book (written with Sam Giancana's grandson, Sam Giancana), *Double Cross*. I could make a few sardonic asides about the story as it progresses, but I'll respectfully defer to Chuck here. He doesn't need me to make his story funny.

It seems that one day after pasta at Chuck's home three years after the assassination, older brother Sam told Chuck what really went down. Sam started out by saying that he and the CIA "took care of Kennedy . . . together." But as he continued his tale, Sam said a great many other people were also involved. Jack Ruby (who needed help crossing the street on a green light—here I go again—that's the last interruption) was put in charge of overall coordination of the assassination in Dallas because he was Sam's representative in Dallas. (Ruby and Oswald, Sam added, "were queer for each other.") Sam said that "Richard Nixon and Lyndon Johnson knew about the whole damn thing" because he, Sam, told them about it when he met with them in Dallas several times before the assassination. A "half-dozen fanatical right-wing Texans" were also involved in the assassination, per Sam. The nuts-and-bolts planning for the assassination involved some of the top people on the Dallas police force as well as Mayor Earle Cabell.

Chuck writes that his brother solicited from several quarters professional killers who were required to be top-notch marksmen. The killers? Two of New Orleans mafioso Carlos Marcello's men, Charles Harrelson and Jack Lawrence, as well as two of Tampa mafioso Santo Trafficante's Cuban exile friends. Sam told Chuck that he sent three of his killers down too: Richard Cain, Chuckie Nicoletti, and a fellow named Milwaukee Phil (Felix Anthony Alderisio). So seven assassins in all were sent to Dallas to kill Kennedy, but the actual killers, Sam told Chuck, were Cain and Nicoletti, both firing from the Book Depository Building. Chuck writes that "during the operation, Moonie [Sam's nickname] said the CIA upper echelon sequestered themselves in a hotel, surrounded by electronic equipment. With the aid of walkie-talkies, the [killers] were able to secure their firing positions." The CIA, Sam said, had arranged for Dallas police officers J. D. Tippit and Roscoe White to murder Oswald after the assassination, but when Tippit wavered, White was forced to murder Tippit. Oswald's survival, Sam told Chuck, was "probably the only real screw-up in the whole goddamned deal," but it was a big one. Since Ruby was assigned to make sure everything went right and it didn't, he knew that to avoid dying at the hands of "one of Moonie's vengeful enforcers for a screwed-up job," he himself would have to silence Oswald, which he did. Sam told Chuck that after the assassination, "for once, we didn't have to worry about J. Edgar Hoover." Hoover, Sam said, covered up anything and everything his "boy scouts" found because "he hated the Kennedys as much as anybody and he wasn't about to have Bobby find his brother's killers."

Oh, by the way, Chuck, who often speaks fondly of his late brother, Sam, informs the reader in his book that Sam had Marilyn Monroe murdered with a lethal dosage of sedatives, and had also been behind the murder of Robert Kennedy in California in 1968.[35] I'd hate to read what type of book Chuck Giancana would write about his deceased brother if he hadn't been so fond of him.

Not only are brothers fingering their supposedly beloved brothers as being behind the assassination, but sons, still loving their dead fathers, are fingering their fathers. Ricky White, a twenty-nine-year-old unemployed salesman, called a press conference on August 6, 1990, at the JFK Assassination Information Center in Dallas (a haven for conspiracy theorists and literature that is no longer in existence but at the time was run by Larry N. Howard, J. Gary Shaw, and Larry Ray Harris) and said his father, Roscoe White, a Dallas police officer at the time of the assassination,[*] was one of three CIA operatives who fired on the president that day.[†] For good measure, he said his father also killed Dallas police officer J. D. Tippit. Oswald, he said, was also part of the conspiracy but fired no shots. Jack Ruby was a co-conspirator, but his role was not specified.

---

[*]Conspiracy theorists maintain that Roscoe White was a Dallas police officer on November 22, 1963. Indeed, conspiracy icon Beverly Oliver said that she saw White, in his police uniform, walking away from the grassy knoll after the shooting in Dealey Plaza. But on November 22, 1963, White was only a Dallas police officer in a technical sense. Dallas police records show that although White was *hired* as an apprentice policeman on October 7, 1963, he didn't even start his police training at the police academy until December 4, 1963, graduating from Class 79 on February 28, 1964, so he would not have been in any Dallas police uniform on November 22, 1963. White resigned from the force on October 7, 1965, exactly two years after he was hired, going to work for Page Drugs in Dallas.

[†]Roscoe White certainly had the background of someone one would expect to be a top-level CIA operative assigned to murder the president. He entered the U.S. Marine Corps, at the age of twenty-two, on February 19, 1957, and received his honorable discharge as a corporal on December 4, 1962. While in the military, he was trained as an auto mechanic and in artillery ballistic meteorology, and received a Good Conduct medal during his time in the corps. When he was discharged, and before he became a Dallas police officer, he worked in Dallas selling life insurance door to door for the American National Insurance Company and as a part-time agent for Farmers Insurance Company.

Where did Ricky White learn about his father's role in the assassination? His father's diary, he said, which he found in 1982 in a footlocker inside a shed behind his grandfather's home in Paris, Texas. But White was unable to produce the diary, the entire basis for his charge, for the throng of reporters at the press conference, claiming it was stolen by an FBI agent who came to his home in Midland, Texas, to interview him in 1988. Though he didn't have the diary, he recalled for the reporters the diary's entry for November 22, 1963. His father, a covert U.S. intelligence operative code-named "Mandarin" in the diary, fired the two shots that killed Kennedy from behind the picket fence using his 7.65-millimeter Mauser. "Lebanon" was the man in the Book Depository Building that fired two more shots, and "Saul" (the name most likely picked up from Hugh McDonald's 1978 book, *Appointment in Dallas*) fired two shots at the president from the Dallas County Records Building. The reason for the assassination, per his father's diary, was "to eliminate a National Security threat to world-wide peace," and it was a part of Roscoe White's "assignment" to join the Dallas Police Department before the assassination.

White wasn't content to merely tell a ridiculous story. He insisted on bringing a collective smile to his audience by saying that although he wasn't quite three years old at the time of the assassination, he recalled seeing his father and four other men practice for the assassination by firing into an automobile on a remote ranch near Van Horn, Texas. Although his father died in 1971 from third-degree burns on 99 percent of his body sustained in an industrial fire and explosion at a site where he worked as a welder, White claimed his father was probably murdered because he wanted to leave his CIA unit.

None of the allegations Ricky White made at the 1990 press conference had been made in early 1988 when he first indicated to the authorities in Midland, Texas, that he might have some information relating to the assassination. In meetings with representatives of the Midland County DA's office and FBI agents out of the El Paso office in January of 1988, he said nothing about his father being a CIA agent who was one of three people who shot Kennedy, or that his father had killed Officer J. D. Tippit. Nor did he say anything about his father being murdered because he wanted to leave the CIA. He did say he believed that his father and his father's mistress, who worked at the Book Depository Building, arranged for Lee Harvey Oswald to get the job he got at the building, and that it was his opinion that his father, Officer J. D. Tippit, and Lee Harvey Oswald had conspired to kill Kennedy because all three were U.S. marines who were upset with JFK "for leaving Marines on the beach at the Bay of Pigs."

He also had a box of materials he showed the FBI agents. What they found, among the miscellaneous items, was a "hodge-podge of late 1950's vintage letters" from his father to his mother, miscellaneous receipts and insurance policies of his father, a key, a letter, his father's military service papers, an address book, correspondence from the HSCA to his mother, Geneva, and two receipts from the HSCA to his mother for photographs she had sent them of Lee Harvey Oswald, one of which, it turned out, was a companion to the backyard photos of Oswald holding the Carcano rifle taken by Marina.[36]

How did Roscoe White's widow, who told the FBI agents she was a distant relative of JFK's, come into possession of such photos, particularly the backyard one? She told the FBI El Paso agents that her husband was a police photographer for the Dallas Homicide and Robbery Bureau, that he had access to the photographs and simply took some. She said he "put the pictures in a nice album and thought they would be valuable someday." Dallas assistant DA Jim Owens told the Midland DA that many police officers of that era acquired various sets of photographs and other memorabilia concerning the JFK assassination.

What about the diary White claimed, at his later press conference, that he found but was then stolen by an FBI agent who came to his home in Midland in 1988? The FBI never went to White's home in Midland. White went to the Midland office of the FBI, but he told the FBI that in 1976 or 1977 "they" (he did not identify who "they" were, but he presumably meant HSCA investigators who picked up mostly photographs from his mother on December 31, 1976) took the diary and he never got it back, but his mother had a copy. However, neither White nor his mother were ever able to furnish this alleged copy of the alleged diary to the FBI.

The El Paso office of the FBI concluded that because of the photos of Oswald that his father had and because his mother told him his father was a friend of Officer J. D. Tippit's on the Dallas Police Force, Ricky White was "trying to cash in" on the situation with his allegation of a conspiracy involving his father, Tippit, and Oswald. Finding there wasn't "any basis in fact" in anything Ricky White had to say, the El Paso office of the FBI closed its file on the matter on January 26, 1988, unaware that two years later Ricky White would reemerge, full bore, with new and more sensational charges.[37]

Ricky White's story, of course, was pure moonshine, and didn't need any more assaults on its veracity, but assassination researchers Gary Mack and David Perry further exposed Ricky White's claim as a complete hoax. Perry located Dr. Daniel Pearson, who, White claimed, had given electroshock treatments to his mother (since deceased) to force her to erase her memory of the conspiracy. Dr. Pearson told Perry that electroshock treatments can "affect" memory but "don't erase memory," and that although he did administer the treatments to Mrs. White in 1966, they were for her severe depression, not to erase or affect memory. This didn't surprise Perry since he knew Roscoe White had gotten a hardship discharge from the army based on his wife's depression.

And Perry and Mack located a man White had said was a hit man in the conspiracy, but he turned out to be a blueberry farmer.[38]

When Mack told White three weeks after White's press conference that he and Perry "have good news for you. We're convinced your father didn't kill the president," Mack said that White obviously "should have been overjoyed and relieved." Instead, Mack said, White was shocked and speechless. "I waited for him to ask me 'What do you have that convinces you of my father's innocence?' but he never asked. That's when I knew the story was a hoax."[39]

White had previously tried to sell his story as a book and movie. His efforts from the beginning had been financed by a group of seven young oil millionaires from Midland, Texas, incorporated under the name MATSU. Under its 1989 contract with White, the group was to receive an eight-to-one return until they received their eighty-thousand-dollar original investment back, then 20 percent of "any and all income generated from the story."[40] But nothing came of the effort. One member of the group would later say, "Ricky sounded sincere, and if what he said was true, he had the key to the biggest mystery in American history. We were young and naive, and being in Midland, had nothing much better to do. We figured we could spend about as much on this project as it would cost to drill a dry hole."[41]

After some national television appearances by White (e.g., on *Larry King Live*), media interest in his story quickly died, but a conspiracy theorist named Joe West tried to revive interest in the story by calling a press conference claiming that before she died, Roscoe White's widow had found a second diary of his (which Oliver Stone paid $5,300 for) at her home. "Almost everyone who saw the journal believed that it was a fraud," wrote Gary

Cartwright in *Texas Monthly*. The belief, he said, was that "Geneva created the journal." The journal refers to the last assignment for Roscoe by his handlers (the ones who supposedly got him to murder Kennedy) as "Watergate." The only problem, Cartwright writes, "is that the break-in at the Watergate apartment complex [June 17, 1972] didn't occur until [close to nine] months after Roscoe died." Further, though the entries were "supposedly written between 1957 and 1971, it appeared to be written in the same felt pen." Cartwright did confirm that in August of 1957, White and Oswald, coincidentally, sailed aboard the same ship, the USS *Bexar*, from San Diego to Yokosuka, Japan. "White was in the same military division as Lee Harvey Oswald," Cartwright wrote, "the 1st Marine Air Wing. So were about seven thousand other Marines. Geneva swears that her husband and Oswald were friends, but except for her word, there is no proof they even knew each other." It should be noted that White and Oswald were also stationed in late 1957 at Subic Bay in the Philippines and it is certainly possible they could have run into each other at that time.[42]

After White's press conference at the JFK Assassination Information Center back in 1990, the center turned over the key "evidence" in support of White to the Texas attorney general's office so the attorney general could conduct an investigation of the matter. In February 1991, the attorney general's office said that everything it had looked at had "not given any credibility to anything these people have been trying to say."[43]

Though virtually everyone saw that Ricky White's story was fraudulent, one person, predictably, was impressed with his allegation: Oliver Stone's hero, New Orleans DA Jim Garrison. Garrison told the media that White's story "rings true."[44]

Another alleged assassin is James E. Files (true name, James Sutton), the Rodney Dangerfield of Kennedy assassins. For years Files has been begging people to believe that he killed Kennedy, but with a few exceptions, no one, not even those on the fringes of the conspiracy community, respects him or his story. Indeed, Files has fallen on such hard times that few buffs will even talk to him. However, a few promoters and publicity seekers have tried to exploit Files's pathetic story. On August 17, 1992, the late Joe West, who had just failed in trying to promote the Ricky White story, interviewed Files at the Stateville Correctional Center in Joliet, Illinois, where Files is serving a fifty-year sentence for the attempted murders of two Illinois police officers in 1991.[45] West died in 1993, and Bob Vernon, a Houston producer, took over the Files story at the request of West's family. Vernon videotaped an interview with Files at Stateville on March 22, 1994, in while Files confessed to firing the fatal head shot on November 22, 1963, and the tape, called *Confession of an Assassin*, was sold commercially.[46] Also, between 1996 and 2001, conspiracy author Jerry Kroth visited and interviewed Files at the prison on three occasions as well as corresponded with him, and treats Files seriously in his book on the assassination, *Conspiracy in Camelot*. Most recently, in 2005, mobster Sam Giancana's daughter, Antoinette, and two co-authors have featured Files in their book on the assassination, *JFK and Sam*, calling Files "The Real Assassin."*

---

*West and Vernon are the ones who started the whole Files story and got it out there. It is noteworthy that on September 5, 1992, West wrote to Files, "When I get your songs, I'm going to show them to a friend of mine who is a music producer and see if there is anything he can do with them. He was Fats Domino's manager for over ten years." There are no references to songs in West's and Files's letters to each other, so Files wanting help with his songs must have been discussed when West met Files at the Stateville Correctional Cen-

The following is a brief synopsis of Files's story, which I feel is just as good or better than the hugely successful *The Men Who Killed Kennedy*. What I'm saying is that I feel Files is entitled to more respect from the buffs than he is getting, and they should perk up and listen when he talks. I know I do. (I'm being sarcastic.) Files ("Jim" hereafter) says he was a bodyguard and driver for Charles "Chuckie" Nicoletti, a hit man for Chicago mobster Tony Ascardo and, later, Sam Giancana. Six months before the assassination, Chuckie told Jim that Kennedy was going to be killed and Jim was supposed to help out in whatever way he was told. Files said he "never liked Kennedy since he backed out on us" at the Bay of Pigs. A week before the assassination, Jim drove the weapons for the assassination from Chicago (where, Jim says, the assassination was originally scheduled to take place) down to Mesquite, Texas. The next day, Lee Harvey Oswald came by Jim's motel (Files said he was confident Oswald was sent by David Atlee Phillips, who Files said was Oswald's as well as his CIA handler) and took him out to a place near Mesquite where Jim fired the weapons and calibrated the scopes. The next "five days" Oswald and he drove around Dealey Plaza and Dallas (apparently Oswald wasn't at work these days; his supervisors and coworkers only *thought* they saw him) so Jim would know all the streets and not run into any dead-ends "if anything went wrong and we had to flee from the area." He said, "Lee Harvey Oswald and I never discussed the assassination of John F. Kennedy." (That's one statement I'd be willing to bet every penny I have was true.)[*]

On the morning of the assassination, he and mobster Johnny Roselli met Jack Ruby at a pancake house in Fort Worth, where Ruby gave Roselli an envelope that contained Secret Service identification badges and a map of the presidential motorcade route. Per Jim, at the time of the shooting, Nicoletti was firing at Kennedy from the second floor of the Dal-Tex Building (Roselli was present with Nicoletti but did not fire), while he (Jim) was behind the fence at the grassy knoll (Ruby, he said, was at the bottom of the grassy knoll) with instructions from Nicoletti to be a backup shooter *only* if the shots from the Dal-Tex Building didn't kill Kennedy. Since it appeared to him that the Dal-Tex shots had only hurt Kennedy (Jim says Nicoletti hit Kennedy from behind with a 7.62-millimeter rifle), Jim fired the fatal head shot with his "Remington Fire Ball" XP-100 pistol, which he says CIA agent David Atlee Phillips gave to him when he worked for the CIA with anti-Castro Cubans at "No Name Key" in Florida. After Jim killed Kennedy, he said he wanted to leave his personal calling card, so he bit the empty shell that had been the casing for the bullet that killed Kennedy and placed it on top of the picket fence.

Jim said that Oswald's CIA handler, Phillips, had gotten Oswald his job at the Book Depository Building. He said that Kennedy's murder was ordered by the mob and the CIA, with the main figure being Chicago mob boss Tony Accardo. The CIA, at the last moment, tried to call off the assassination but Accardo overruled the agency.

---

ter (Files was not incarcerated in the much more famous Joliet State Prison across the river, which was closed in 2002) for the first time about three weeks earlier, on August 17, 1992. Shortly after Bob Vernon took over the Files case from Joe West on March 10, 1993, he wrote a letter (date of letter not known, but it was on March 10 or a day or so thereafter) to Files. On March 15, 1993, in Files's very first letter to Vernon, he writes, "I received your letter with 'Earlene's' [Joe West's widow] this past Saturday evening. Thank you for writing to me . . . Thank you for wanting to help with my music. It would be really nice to hear some of my songs over the radio." (Dankbaar, *Files on JFK*, pp.360, 392, 394) It could very well be that part of Files's motivation for telling his phony "Kennedy assassin" tale was not just his fifteen minutes of fame, but fifteen or more minutes of turntable time on the radio for his songs.

[*]Files said he had met Oswald earlier in New Orleans, and when Oswald was in Clinton, Louisiana, Files said he "was running semi-automatic 45 caliber submachine guns" down to Oswald for CIA agent David Atlee Phillips, who he said introduced him to Oswald (Dankbaar, *Files on JFK*, pp.51, 173–174).

We learn from Jim that Oswald was set up, that he did not fire a round and wasn't privy to the plan. Oswald also did not kill Tippit. The man who did kill Tippit (Jim wouldn't say who it was) had been assigned to kill Oswald but he "messed up." Jim was later paid thirty thousand dollars for his expert services in killing JFK. He believes that Giancana, Roselli, and Nicoletti were murdered later to silence them from telling the authorities what happened, but doesn't say why "they" haven't silenced him. I assume it's because they think he's a likeable chap. Or maybe they want to hear more of his song. We also learn from Jim that Joe West, the first person who contacted him on this case, was silenced ("they tampered with Joe's medication") in 1993 because he was getting close to being able "to get Kennedy's body exhumed," and that John F. Kennedy is not buried in Arlington National Cemetery.

Personally, a lot of my questions about the assassination were finally and conclusively answered by Jim, and I don't need any proof beyond his word. But Jim told Jerry Kroth that if he is ever set free, he has "solid proof" of everything he says and would retrieve the proof from a box of papers he has outside of prison. Kroth writes that "Files' story . . . is the most believable and persuasive" he has heard or read on JFK's murder. "His account," Kroth says, is "surprisingly credible." Can you imagine that? And Kroth actually found a publisher to publish his book.[47]

Ah yes, and then there is Loy Factor, Mac Wallace, and the book *The Men on the Sixth Floor* by Glen Sample and Mark Collom, which has become a favorite of many on the fringes of the conspiracy community.

The key to the story, Sample and Collom tell us, is Lawrence Lloyd Factor, a Chickasaw Indian from Fillmore, Oklahoma. Factor, a World War II veteran, was declared incompetent by the Veterans Administration in 1948, which required the appointment of a legal guardian for him before he could receive his sixty-dollar-per-month disability payments.[48] In 1969 he was convicted of first-degree manslaughter for strangling his wife, Juanita, the previous year. A diabetic with one wooden leg, he was being treated in 1971 for hepatitis in the hospital ward of the Oklahoma state prison at McAlester. For some undisclosed reason, Factor decided to tell a story—and a whopper it was—to Collom, another hepatitis patient in the ward. According to Factor, in November of 1961 his wife suggested that they and their kids drive to Bonham, Texas (a few hours away), so they could see President Kennedy, who was going to attend U.S. Senator Sam Rayburn's funeral there. While Factor was waiting in the crowd on the street in Bonham, a Spanish-speaking man, whom he later identified as Mac Wallace, approached him and asked about his ability as a marksman. Being a hunter, Factor said it was right good. Wallace gave him twenty dollars and told Factor to take his family to a nice dinner.

A year later, Wallace showed up unannounced at Factor's home. Factor demonstrated his marksmanship for Wallace by shooting bottles with his deer rifle, after which Wallace offered him ten thousand dollars if he would do an unspecified "job" for Wallace and his people, two thousand payable up front, eight thousand when the job was done. A deal was struck. A few days before the assassination, a young Hispanic woman of around twenty named Ruth Ann, accompanied by a man, another young Hispanic, drove to Factor's home in Fillmore to fetch him for the ride to Dallas. Factor suspected they wanted him to kill someone, but he told Collom he was too afraid to back out. Plus, he needed that extra eight thousand dollars. The two Hispanics drove Factor to a small home in Dallas, where Wallace, the group leader, was already present. For a few days, the group discussed (while

Factor sat idly by) their plan to kill Kennedy. Ruth Ann, Factor said, was second in command. Two other people arrived at the house to sit in on some of the planning sessions—Jack Ruby and Lee Harvey Oswald.

Per Factor, just before the assassination Ruth Ann drove him to the Book Depository Building and led him up the stairwell to the sixth floor, where Wallace and Oswald already were. Factor was given a rifle. "Wallace told me that if they [Oswald and Wallace] missed, I would be the backup. They [had] wanted me to shoot, but I told them I wouldn't do it," Factor told Collom in a subsequent interview in which coauthor Glen Sample was also present. Nonetheless, Factor was told to go to the southwesternmost window on the sixth floor. Wallace was two windows to the east, and Oswald was at the sniper's nest window at the southeasternmost corner. Ruth Ann, with a walkie-talkie communicating with other shooters, presumably located on the grassy knoll, gave a countdown to Factor, Wallace, and Oswald, signaling them when to fire. But Factor said that although he "ejected a shell from the rifle," he did not fire it.[*]

Following the shooting, Factor said that he and Ruth Ann fled down the stairs[†] and she dropped him off at the Greyhound bus depot. But before she did, even though he hadn't done what he was paid to do, Ruth Ann was sweet enough to give him his eight thousand dollars. An hour or so later, while he was still waiting for a bus out of town, Ruth Ann came back to the bus depot with Wallace. "They said they had to get me out of town, 'cuz things was too hot there." Ruth Ann and Wallace, or whoever employed them, certainly could have used some of that eight thousand dollars they gratuitously handed to Factor to make sure they had a dependable getaway car, because—well, let's let Factor tell the story: "We was headed up through Mead [Oklahoma] when the car broke down, right outside of Mead. I think the clutch went out," Factor said, so he got out on the highway and hitched his way home, presumably leaving the two masterminds behind the biggest murder in American history sitting in a dead car alongside the road.

Ol' Loy might have been too incompetent to take care of his own personal affairs, but he wasn't too incompetent for people to hire him to kill the president of the United States, and in the process, get them to pay him ten thousand dollars for doing nothing. Factor died in 1994.

No rational person could possibly believe this pathetic story,[‡] even, it seems, the authors themselves. In the acknowledgments section at the beginning of their self-published book, the Garden Grove, California, sign-shop owner (Sample) and Belling-

[*]One of the things that convinced Sample and Collom that Factor was telling the truth and was on the sixth floor that day is his telling them he saw a "table saw" on the sixth floor, and they say that the late Harold Norman told Sample in 1993 that there was a table saw on the sixth floor. How could Factor have known this if he wasn't there? But assassination researcher Dave Perry, who specializes in poking holes in the more-far-out conspiracy allegations, said he and Gary Mack, the curator of the Sixth Floor Museum, looked over film footage and many photographs taken on the sixth floor after the assassination and saw no table saw. (*Los Angeles Times*, Orange County edition, January 16, 1996, p.E5; Telephone interview of Dave Perry by author on December 20, 2004)

[†]Factor said he never saw anyone when he entered the building and proceeded to the sixth floor, or when he descended the stairs and exited the building. Many Book Depository Building employees gave statements to the FBI that they saw no strangers in the building on the day of the assassination. Ruth Ann, Factor, and Wallace, all strangers, must have done a good job hiding not only their physical form inside the building that day, but also the rifles that one or more of them apparently carried into and out of the building that day.

[‡]Although Collom and Sample's book is silly beyond belief, British conspiracy theorist Robin Ramsay couldn't be more impressed with the authors, asserting that they "solved the case" (Ramsay, *Who Shot JFK?* p.67).

ham, Washington, real estate agent (Collom) thanked, among others, their wives, who "not only allowed us our *fantasy*, but encouraged it." In some circles, this is known as a Freudian slip. What Sample and Collom should know is that even if their fantasy was that Lee Harvey Oswald was Kennedy's guardian angel, and it was Jackie Kennedy who was behind her husband's murder, there would be many in the conspiracy community to encourage that fantasy too.

Why did Wallace mastermind Kennedy's death? The authors ask the reader to believe that LBJ ordered Wallace, who allegedly was a part of LBJ's Texas inner circle, to do so. Not too much is known about Wallace, who died in a car accident near Pittsburg, Texas, on January 7, 1971. Wallace, a University of Texas graduate and student body president in 1945 who at one time worked as an economist in Washington, D.C., for the U.S. Department of Agriculture, did, indeed, commit one killing we know about. In 1952, he was convicted in Austin, Texas, of murdering a golf pro, John Douglas Kinser, who had been having an affair with Wallace's estranged wife. He received a five-year suspended prison sentence. The authors see the dark hand of LBJ in the very light sentence, since Wallace's lawyer, John Cofer, was one of LBJ's main lawyers in his successful postelection legal battle for the U.S. Senate against former governor Coke Stevenson in 1948. How Cofer would have the power to bring about Wallace's light sentence, the authors don't say. In a 1986 interview with the *Dallas Times Herald*, D. L. Johnson, one of the jurors in the Kinser case, said that he was the only juror who favored an outright acquittal for Kinser and that he forced the guilty-with-a-suspended-sentence verdict by threatening to cause a hung jury if he didn't get his way.[49]

To fortify their position that Wallace wasn't just a heat-of-passion killer of his wife's lover but a cold-blooded premeditated killer for hire, the authors struggle mightily, without succeeding, to prove that Wallace was responsible for the June 3, 1961, shotgun death of Henry H. Marshall of Bryan, Texas, a regional official for the Department of Agriculture who was in charge of the federal cotton allotment program in central Texas. Marshall, it was claimed, had to be silenced because he could connect Johnson aide Cliff Carter and LBJ with the illegal activities of Billie Sol Estes, an LBJ political ally and fund-raiser Marshall was investigating who had, among other things, been fraudulently obtaining federal cotton allotment payments as well as mortgages on farm equipment that did not exist. As author Alfred Steinberg described Estes, the short, plump young man from Texas "could have written volumes on wheeling and dealing and financial fakery."[50] Estes was eventually convicted in 1963 (after his first conviction in 1962 was reversed because the televising of his trial without his consent was deemed to be a denial of his right to a fair trial) of swindling farmers and banks out of millions of dollars and sentenced to prison. After being paroled in 1971, he was convicted again in 1979 for mail fraud and concealing assets. At Estes' sentencing before the Dallas federal judge, he told the judge, "I have a problem. I live in a dream world." The judge sentenced him to ten years.[51]

In an August 9, 1984, letter to the Department of Justice, Estes' lawyer, Douglas Caddy, said that Estes, who some believe never forgave Johnson for not fixing the case against him back in 1962, was "willing to testify that LBJ ordered . . . the killing of President J. F. Kennedy," and that "Mac Wallace" murdered Kennedy for Johnson. Pretty serious charges, right? The problem is that Estes, who had been released on parole in 1983, said that LBJ had ordered *seven other* murders, and he transmitted his orders through his close aide Cliff Carter to Mac Wallace, who committed the murders. The murders included not just Henry Marshall, but—get this—LBJ's own alcoholic younger sister, Josefa Johnson, who died, per her death certificate, not as a result of a homicide but from a cerebral hemorrhage at the age of forty-nine on December 25, 1961, after coming home from a Christmas party at LBJ's ranch. Also among the seven people whom LBJ, per Estes, had Wallace kill for him was John Kinser, the man who was having an affair with Wallace's wife.[52*] It obviously was loony bird time, but the Department of Justice, to avoid charges of indifference, actually sent three eager investigators down to Texas to interview Estes, but Estes cancelled the interview. A con man to the end.

No remotely believable evidence that Mac Wallace had anything to do with the assassination has ever surfaced, and in fact, around the time of the assassination, Sample and Collom say he was living in Anaheim, California, where he worked for Ling Electronics from 1961 to 1969. (When I called Ling Electronics on February 20, 2002, they said their employment records did not go back to 1963, and hence they were unable to provide documentation for Wallace's employment with them.)[53]

Nevertheless, the myth of Wallace being one of the shooters of Kennedy persists. Conspiracy theorist Walt Brown, the editor of the substantive *JFK/Deep Politics Quarterly*, claimed, in a May 29, 1998, press conference at the Conspiracy Museum in Dallas and in the October 2001 edition of his publication, that a latent print examiner from Texas, Nathan Darby, was furnished with a copy of the only latent print found on the cardboard cartons inside the sniper's nest that was never identified,[54†] as well as the 1951 fingerprint card for Wallace following his arrest for the murder of John Kinser, and that the expert made a positive match, finding fourteen points of identification. (Recall that our boy Loy Factor put Wallace several windows to the *west* of the sniper's nest.) According to Darby's March 9, 1998, affidavit, the match was of "the left little finger."[55]

On November 20, 2001, I spoke over the telephone with Darby. Eighty-seven at the time, he told me he had been the head of the Austin, Texas, police department's Identification and Criminal Records Section for several years. He had retired from the force and was still living in Austin. I told him I had trouble with his finding a "match" between prints found at the sniper's nest on the sixth floor and the fingerprint exemplar card of Malcolm Wallace. "Why?" he asked. "Because," I pointed out, "the unidentified latent print found on the sixth floor was a palm print, not a fingerprint, and unless you've come up with something new, I've never heard of anyone matching a palm print with a fingerprint." Darby, sensing he had been taken, told me that he had been given "two fingerprints, one from a card, the other a latent. It was all blind. I didn't know and wasn't told who they belonged to [it was much later, he said, that he heard Malcolm Wallace's name mentioned], although I recognized the layout of the card [he said all identifying features

---

*In Estes' later memoir, *Billie Sol Estes*, he makes the same incredible charges, suggesting that the reason for all these murders was that all of the victims were "associated with me. Each of these victims could have revealed my connection to Lyndon Johnson" (Estes, *Billie Sol Estes*, pp.90, 98). If this is true, Billie, why didn't LBJ have you killed? Wouldn't you be the most dangerous to LBJ of all people in his eyes?

†In a September 18, 1964, letter to the Warren Commission's general counsel, J. Lee Rankin, FBI Director J. Edgar Hoover wrote that "on our efforts to identify the latent fingerprints and palm prints [on the four cardboard boxes inside the sniper's nest] . . . *only one latent palm print remains to be identified*" (CE 3131, 26 H 799, 809). As we have seen, apart from the prints of Oswald found on the cartons, of the nineteen other fingerprints and six palm prints on the four cartons, all except the one palm print were found to belong to either Dallas detective Robert Lee Studebaker or FBI clerk Forest L. Lucy, both of whom handled the cartons during the investigation (CE 3131, 26 H 809; WR, p.249).

had been blacked out] as that of the Texas Department of Public Safety. I wasn't given any palm print. *They were both fingerprints.* Of course, you can't compare a palm print with a fingerprint."

So much for Malcolm Wallace at the window and another desperate attempt by the conspiracy community to implicate *anyone* other than Lee Harvey Oswald for Kennedy's murder.

Or so one would think. But one Barr McClellan, who at one time was a lawyer in an Austin law firm that represented Lyndon Johnson, came out with a book in 2003 that claims LBJ was behind Kennedy's murder, anchored on the same allegation that Wallace carried it out for LBJ. It seems that it was McClellan and an associate of his, one J. Harrison, who approached Darby with the two prints and engaged his services in March of 1998, McClellan alleging to his readers that the latent fingerprint they gave Darby was found on one of the four book cartons. McClellan says that Wallace put together a three-man hit team (Oswald firing two shots from the sniper's nest window, Wallace firing one shot from the third window over, and one "Junior" firing the head shot from the grassy knoll) to kill Kennedy for LBJ. Indeed, McClellan said he had "confirmed" that LBJ was behind *eleven* murders in Texas, "with nine more possible."

McClellan (the father of Scott McClellan, President George W. Bush's former press secretary, and Mark S. McClellan, the former commissioner of the Food and Drug Administration) was considerate enough to tell us that "the way Wallace and Oswald met is not known, but they did meet and were together on the sixth floor . . . when Kennedy was shot." Though he presents no evidence of Wallace ever meeting or even knowing of Oswald's existence, he writes an entire chapter (without offering one source for anything) about Wallace and Oswald inside the Book Depository Building, with all of the details: when a Depository employee entered the sixth floor, "Wallace had decided to kill the worker but, in that instance, the man left. Wallace grinned and gripped his rifle"; "Oswald walked with Wallace to check out the boxes stacked in the southeast corner to get ready for the shooting"; "Oswald explained to Wallace that the windowsill would be a rest for the rifle"; "Wallace shook his head and moved another carton under the window"; later, "Wallace walked over to Oswald's position"; "Wallace took up his position at the third window to the southwest"; "Wallace cursed" when Oswald's first shot missed; and so on.[56]

McClellan begins his book by telling of his membership in an Austin law firm from 1966 to 1971. The firm was headed by Edward Clark, LBJ's personal lawyer, who, if we're to believe the author, was the most powerful and corrupt lawyer in Texas, one who would do anything at all, including arranging for murders, for LBJ. Remarkably, the author unwittingly seems to acknowledge that he either was complicit in or had full knowledge of all the crimes committed by his law firm. He writes that "the only thing that mattered [in his law firm] was the ruthless exercise of *our* power. If scandals were threatened and murder was necessary, 'so what'? That was the price of power and power was the firm's business. Besides, what *we* did was privileged. *We* only worried about results, about winning."

According to McClellan, in 1973 another member of the law firm, Don Thomas, "told me that our senior partner had engineered the death of John Kennedy. 'Clark handled all of that in Dallas,'" he quotes Thomas as telling him. Conveniently for the author, Clark, Thomas, LBJ, and Wallace are long ago dead, so they can't rebut his accusations. It would have been nice if McClellan hadn't waited thirty years to finally tell the American public what he knew.

Nowhere in McClellan's book does he offer any evidence at all that Clark knew Wallace,* whom McClellan says Clark enlisted to kill Kennedy for LBJ, or that Wallace knew LBJ, other than to say, without citing any authority, that when LBJ was a U.S. senator in Washington, he got Wallace a job as an economist at the Department of Agriculture.† But in one's reveries, such details as showing a real connection between parties to a conspiracy and showing them acting in concert are not essential.

In his book, McClellan repeats all the charges in *The Men on the Sixth Floor* about the murder of Henry Marshall and LBJ being behind it; however, he claims that LBJ and Edward Clark (not LBJ aide Cliff Carter, whom Estes had implicated) decided Marshall would have to be "taken care of for good," and so Clark had Wallace murder Marshall. Since McClellan doesn't suggest or provide evidence that LBJ had anything to do with the *misconduct* of Estes, which was the subject of the Marshall investigation, one therefore wonders if McClellan ever questioned why LBJ would order the murder of Marshall, Estes' investigator. Although it was loosely alleged in *The Men on the Sixth Floor* that Marshall could connect LBJ with Estes' misconduct, no evidence has ever surfaced that Marshall learned of any misconduct by LBJ from his investigation of Estes. Estes *did* acknowledge giving large sums of unreported money from his investments to an LBJ slush fund managed by Cliff Carter.[57] The unreporting of money given to LBJ, if true, was a federal offense. But if LBJ was contemplating murder to prevent harm to his political ambitions, it would have been Estes, not Marshall, whom he would have silenced. Why Marshall? In any event, McClellan goes on to allege that to prevent the attorney general, Bobby Kennedy (whose office was investigating Marshall's murder), from finding out about LBJ's ordering Marshall's murder, LBJ asked Clark to have Kennedy murdered for him so he could become president rather than go to jail. My God. Has this author no shame at all?

McClellan, of course, has no evidence that LBJ asked Clark to have Wallace kill Kennedy, but substitutes a reverie of his in which he lets the listener hear a long conversation he fabricated between Clark and LBJ at LBJ's ranch "soon after" Marshall's murder in which the decision to kill Kennedy was finally made.

One reads McClellan's book with disgust and a certain degree of awe that someone would have the audacity to write a book like this. Just when the reader feels that the author cannot push his despicable fantasy any further, he reaches into his bag and produces one crowning nugget to do the reader in. The author sets forth a long conversation (that Thomas allegedly told the author about) between Thomas and LBJ at LBJ's ranch shortly before LBJ's death on January 22, 1972, in which—are you ready?—Johnson confesses to being behind JFK's murder and—are you really ready?—beseeches Thomas to tell the world about this after he and his wife die because—are you really and truly ready?—his reputation was no good, and if he at least had the honesty to confess to JFK's murder to the American people, "my damned legacy just might improve. Hell. Might just improve my reputation, you know."

---

*The author says that Wallace's first wife was Mary Andre Dubose Barton, and there is a "possible connection with Clark's family line. They share a common name, that of Dubose," and "while the connection [between Wallace and Clark] cannot be made from this, the possibility cannot be excluded."

†Actually, there is a likelihood that LBJ had at least a passing acquaintance with Wallace, though this in no way supports the outrageous and foundationless allegations in McClellan's book. Apparently McClellan was unaware that in 1986, Horace Busby, an LBJ aide, told the *Dallas Times Herald* that around 1949 or 1950, Wallace and Josefa, LBJ's sister, "were having a relationship" in Washington, D.C., and "she may have moved in with him or he moved in with her" (*Dallas Times Herald*, March 31, 1986, p.11A). Also, Busby said that Johnson had met Wallace once, when Cliff Carter had taken Wallace to Johnson's home in Washington, D.C., presumably during this same period of time (*Dallas Morning News*, March 23, 1984, p.5A).

But Thomas disobeyed LBJ, telling McClellan the following year, 1973, instead of wait-ing, and McClellan finally tells the American people in his book *thirty years later*.[58]

Shame on a former member of the American bar* for sinking to such a depth of ignominy. Although McClellan has written a blasphemous and completely false story, his book has sold an incredible seventy-five-thousand copies, and when he repeated his claim on the History Channel in its November 18, 2003, documentary, *The Guilty Men* (*Part 9* of Nigel Turner's *The Men Who Killed Kennedy*), hundreds of thousands of Americans heard the damning allegation, precipitating a flood of angry letters on the LBJ Library in Austin, some of the writers threatening to burn the library down. McClellan's charges were taken seriously enough that a group of LBJ loyalists led by Bill Moyers and Jack Valenti demanded that the History Channel investigate the charges and set the record straight. Indeed, two former presidents, Gerald Ford and Jimmy Carter, formally protested the show by letter to the History Channel, Ford calling McClellan's charges "the most damaging accusations ever made against a former vice-president and president in American history."[59]

Responsibly, the History Channel asked three prominent historians to review McClel-lan's charges and conducted "its own internal review" of the allegations. On April 2, 2004, the History Channel issued a press release saying that the historians reported back that McClellan's allegation of LBJ's complicity in the assassination "is entirely unfounded and does not hold up to scrutiny." The channel also said its own review revealed that its show "fell short of the high standards that the network sets for itself. The History Chan-nel apologizes to its viewers and to Mrs. [Lady Bird] Johnson and her family for airing the show."[60] But former president Gerald Ford, although undoubtedly pleased by the apol-ogy, wasn't completely appeased. Writing later about the incident, he says that it is one thing for an independent writer like McClellan to publish such "despicable . . . trash, but a reputable media organization, which the public trusts to give accurate and unbiased information, [was] swept into this frenzy. Who or what is next? Will I be inducted into the JFK assassination ring when I am no longer around to defend myself? America needs to get a grip on this hysteria."[61]

The search for *any* assassin of President Kennedy other than Lee Harvey Oswald has been so intense and persistent that it has even trespassed beyond the margins of conven-tional irrationality into the allegation—are you ready for this one?—that Kennedy was killed *accidentally* by a Secret Service agent in Vice President Johnson's car. This approaches (but does not rival, since no one can rival) David Lifton's lunacy in theoriz-ing that Kennedy's body was stolen before the autopsy and new bullet wounds were cre-ated to make it look like he was shot from behind (see conspiracy section). Also, if one bought into Lifton's madcap theory, the reputations of many innocent people would be destroyed, whereas in the accidental assassination theory, no one's is.

In *Mortal Error*, author Bonar Menninger chronicles the odyssey of one Howard Don-ahue, a firearms expert who flew thirty-five combat missions over Europe in the Second World War and was one of eleven marksmen employed by CBS in 1967 to see if they could

---

*McClellan was convicted of forging a $35,000 deed of trust in 1982 and the "criminal charges were dis-missed" in 1992 (McClellan, *Blood, Money and Power*, pp.292–294). As of February 19, 2006, he was not listed as a member of the Texas State Bar.

duplicate what Oswald did firing at a moving target. Donahue not only matched Oswald, he beat Oswald, firing three shots with a Mannlicher-Carcano rifle within 5.2 seconds, all of which hit the bull's-eye.[62] This triggered Donahue's interest in the assassination and ultimately led to an obsession in which he said he gave "twenty-five years of my life" to his search for the solution to Kennedy's murder. Donahue clearly is no kook, and when one reads the first fifty or so pages of his book, one is impressed with the fastidiousness of his research and the commonsense inferences he draws therefrom. But then Donahue and Menninger (basically, his friendly biographer) ask the reader to swallow a story unfit for human consumption.

Donahue believes that three shots were fired in Dealey Plaza. However, Oswald only fired two, one that missed and the other that struck Kennedy and Connally. The third, the fatal shot to the head, was accidentally fired by George Hickey, a Secret Service agent seated in the left rear seat of the presidential follow-up car.[63] The weapon, he says, that killed Kennedy was an AR-15, an automatic rifle that is the civilian version of the M-16 rifle, the primary American infantry weapon used in Vietnam.[*]

This is how Donahue (through Menninger) says Kennedy was shot: "Oswald fires again [the second and last shot from Oswald, Donahue believes]. So Hickey reaches down and grabs the AR-15 off the floor, flips off the safety and stands up on the seat, preparing to return fire. But his footing is precarious. The follow-up car [the one Hickey is in] hits the brakes or speeds up. Hickey begins to swing the gun around to draw a bead on Oswald, but he loses his balance. He begins to fall. And the barrel happens to be pointing towards Kennedy's head. And the gun happens to go off," hitting Kennedy in the head and killing him. In other words, per Donahue, "the gun accidentally discharged."[64][†]

Even assuming for the sake of argument that the AR-15 was fired, Donahue's assumption that with the possibility of the shot ending up in thousands of other places in Dealey Plaza (or Hickey's own car or the air above), it just happened to hit Kennedy in the back of his head is more than hard to believe. But to compound the problem, after a quarter of a century of research, Donahue is unable to come up with any evidence at all that the AR-15 was even fired that day. There were nine other people riding in or on the running boards of the presidential follow-up car,[65] each of whom testified before the Warren Commission or gave a statement, and not one of them, including Agent Glen Bennett, who was seated within a foot or two of Hickey, said the AR-15 rifle or any other weapon was fired in the car around the time of the assassination. How is it possible that none of them heard the rifle being fired right next to them if it had indeed been fired? As Kennedy aide

---

[*]The only weapon any Secret Service agent accompanying the president had on his person in Dealey Plaza was his handgun, a four-inch revolver. In the presidential follow-up car there was also a shotgun inside a compartment in front of the jump seats, and the AR-15 automatic rifle lying on the floor of the rear seat between Agents George Hickey and Glen Bennett (2 H 69, WCT Roy H. Kellerman; 2 H 134–135, WCT Clinton J. Hill; CE 1024, 18 H 760).

[†]Though Donahue believes that Secret Service agent George Hickey accidentally shot Kennedy with a fatal shot to the head from behind, two young Canadian sleuths, Ray Dupois and Jason Amelotte, are "positive" that another Secret Service agent, William Greer, the driver of the presidential limousine, intentionally fired a fatal shot into Kennedy's head from the front. Dupois and Amelotte find it "hard to believe that more people" haven't come to this conclusion, since "the evidence is obvious." What is that evidence? They say that if you watch the Zapruder film closely, when the limousine slows down on Elm after Kennedy is shot in the back, Greer can be seen turning around in his seat holding a handgun in his left hand, with which, they say, he fired the fatal shot. So it may have been Greer, not Hickey, who actually killed Kennedy. But Dupois and Amelotte can't take full credit for finally solving the twentieth century's biggest murder mystery. As indicated earlier, author Milton William Cooper, in his book *Behold a Pale Horse*, is the first one to have caught Greer in the act of killing Kennedy. ("Did Chauffeur Murder JFK?" *Windsor (Ontario) Star*, November 22, 1993)

Dave Powers, who was in Hickey's car, put it, "Someone a foot away from me or two feet away from me couldn't fire the gun without me hearing it."[66]

And among the several hundred or so people in Dealey Plaza that day, not one said they saw or heard any weapon being fired inside the subject vehicle, or anywhere close to it. Indeed, Dealey Plaza witness Hugh Betzner Jr., in a November 14, 1967, letter to assassination researcher Richard E. Sprague, specifically said that he saw the rifle in Hickey's hands and "it was not fired."[*]

In Hickey's own November 30, 1963, Secret Service report, he said he heard three shots that day. "At the end of the last report I reached to the bottom of the car and picked up the AR-15 rifle, cocked and loaded it, and turned to the rear. At this point the cars were passing under the overpass and as a result we had left the scene of the shooting. I kept the AR-15 rifle ready as we proceeded at a high rate of speed to the hospital."[67]

To support his contention that the reason Hickey's rifle accidentally went off was that he lost his balance and while falling backward the rifle fired accidentally, Donahue relies exclusively on Dealey Plaza witness S. M. Holland, who told Richard Warren Lewis and Lawrence Schiller in 1967, "I actually thought when they started up, he [Hickey] was shot, too, because he fell backwards . . . It jerked him down when they started off."[68] But neither Hickey nor Bennett nor anyone else said that Hickey lost his balance and fell backward. *Only* Holland said this. And Holland's questionable perceptive abilities have been discussed earlier in this book.

Donahue's other-world conclusion is a textbook example of the fact that if you start out with an erroneous premise, the conclusion based thereon may be logical, but it's wrong. A few, among several, illustrations: Donahue said that since Oswald was located to Kennedy's right rear, a bullet "coming in at a 6% angle from right to left . . . should have exited through the president's face . . . yet the actual exit wound was in the upper right portion of the skull"—in other words, too far to the right. Hence, the only geometric sense for such an exit wound would be if the bullet were fired from where Hickey was, slightly to the president's left rear. But that's because Donahue, a firearms expert but not a photographic one, asserted that at the time of impact, Kennedy's head was tilted 15 degrees to the left. The reality, however, per the HSCA photographic panel of experts, was that Kennedy's head was tilted 25 degrees, not 15 degrees to the left, at the time he was struck in the head.[69] With that orientation of the head, the trajectory that the HSCA (and Warren Commission) concluded the fatal bullet took now makes perfect sense.

Donahue also finds it incomprehensible that both the back bullet and the head bullet were fired from Oswald's Carcano rifle, because if that were the case the two bullets would not "have behaved so differently"—the back bullet having relatively little damage to it but the head bullet fragmenting into many pieces.[70] Of course, as discussed elsewhere in this book, the back bullet passed through soft tissue in Kennedy's body and then, after having slowed down, only struck a glancing blow to Connally's right fifth rib and then struck the small wrist bone, whereas the head bullet, striking Kennedy's skull head-on, could be expected to fragment the way it did.

Donahue also questions how a 6.5-millimeter bullet (Carcano round) could create a

---

[*]The only reference to Hickey having fired the gun was really no reference at all. When Secret Service agent Winston G. Lawson, riding in the lead car (directly in front of the presidential limousine), heard three shots coming from his rear, he turned around and saw Hickey standing up with the AR-15 in his hand. He testified, "The first thing that flashed through my mind . . . was that he had fired because this was the only weapon I had seen up to that time" (4 H 352–353).

6-millimeter hole in the back of Kennedy's head. (The AR-15 round, Donahue points out, is 5.6 millimeters in diameter.)[71] But very frequently the measured wound is slightly smaller than the caliber of the missile that created it because of the subsequent recoil of the tissues of the skin.[72]

We know from the firearms examinations conducted by the Warren Commission and HSCA firearms experts, and the neutron activation test conducted by the HSCA, that *all* the Winchester Western bullets and bullet fragments in this case matched up with each other. No fragment from any other bullet (the AR-15 bullet is manufactured by Remington Arms, not Winchester Western) was ever found. And the stretcher bullet and two large fragments (Commission Exhibit Nos. 567 and 569) found in the presidential limousine were determined to have been fired from Oswald's Carcano rifle to the exclusion of all other weapons.

For Donahue's theory to work, in addition to all of the above problems with it, Oswald would have had to fire (as Donahue contends) only two bullets. But we know that three expended shell casings were found beneath the sixth-floor sniper's nest window where Oswald was. One of the three cartridge shells found on the floor beneath the sixth-floor window, Commission Exhibit No. 543, had a dent on the mouth of it. Donahue says that "the dent in the empty shell found in the depository . . . would have precluded a third shot from that location."[73] Donahue's source? Josiah Thompson, a professor of philosophy, not a firearms expert, who says in his book, *Six Seconds in Dallas*, that because of the dent, the cartridge case "could not have been fired in any rifle—its lip will not receive a projectile." Thompson goes on to speculate that the dent occurred before November 22, and therefore the cartridge was not fired that day.[74] One possibility he failed to consider was what obviously happened. The dent occurred on November 22 when the cartridge shell was being ejected from the Carcano. Not only firearms experts from the Warren Commission, but those from the HSCA concluded that Commission Exhibit No. 543 was fired in and ejected from Oswald's rifle. When asked if the dent could have occurred "during the loading process" of the cartridge into the breach of the Carcano, Donald Champagne, one of the HSCA's five firearms experts, testified, "No sir."

Question: "Could it have occurred during the ejection process?"

Answer: "Yes." Champagne went on to say that Monty Lutz of the firearms panel (my firearms expert in London who was a past president of the Association of Firearm and Tool Mark Examiners) test-fired four cartridges from the Carcano, one of which had a "similar deformation of the mouth of the cartridge case."

Question: "Are you saying then when your panel test-fired CE-139, out of four fired cartridges, one was ejected with a dented mouth?"

Answer: "Yes sir, that occurred during the ejection process in firing the weapon."[75]

Dedicated and sincerely convinced he was correct, Donahue attempted to interview Secret Service agent Hickey himself, but Hickey did not respond. I imagine his position was that Donahue's claim was so absurd it wasn't worth responding to. Donahue also made every effort to testify before the HSCA, even enlisting the support of his congressional representative in the Baltimore area, where he lived. Donahue was interviewed by HSCA investigators but that's as far as it got, the HSCA refusing to allow him to testify and clutter up the official record with such sublime silliness. Though Hickey did not respond to Donahue, some other Secret Service agents did not remain mute. For example, when he called Agent Winston Lawson, Lawson said, "That's about the biggest bunch of bull—— I have ever heard in my life. That's absolutely ridiculous. That's all I've got to say. Thank you for calling. Goodbye." Agent Richard Johnson said, "That's way out. My God, that's way out. That's too far out to even think about."[76]

Donahue was led so far astray by his obsession that Menninger writes, "The more he [Donahue] thought about it, the more he was inclined to believe the government had probably made the right decision in keeping the truth from the American public in 1963 . . . There could have been no way of knowing how the American people would have reacted to news that Kennedy had been killed accidentally."[77] In other words, even before the Warren Commission, the U.S. government knew Hickey had killed Kennedy and suppressed this fact from the American people. My, my.

The back cover of *Mortal Error* reads, "On November 22, 1963, two men shot the President of the United States. They had never met or heard of each other. They did not work for the same people. They knew nothing of each other's existence. One of them meant to kill the President. The other actually did . . . The Warren Commission was wrong. The conspiracy theories about the CIA and the Mafia are wrong. *JFK*, the movie, is wrong. Here is the hard evidence pointing to the bullet, the gun and the man who killed John Kennedy. And the real reason behind the cover-up." Fortunately, *Mortal Error* has not been mortal in its impact. Other than Howard Donahue and his biographer Bonar Menninger, I know of no serious student of the assassination who takes the book or its contents seriously.

P erhaps the most famous (not by their given names) of the "other" assassins are the "three tramps." The fact that there never was any evidence at all of their guilt is irrelevant to the conspiracy theorists. To the buffs, there was one big piece of incriminating evidence against the tramps: *they weren't Lee Harvey Oswald*! And in the balmy and unhinged conspiracy universe, no evidence of guilt is stronger against someone than that he isn't Lee Harvey Oswald. Indeed, if the three tramps, or any of the many other assassins of Kennedy (other than the self-proclaimed ones) whom the conspiracy buffs have pointed their fingers at through the years, were ever put on trial for Kennedy's murder and were to cry out, in desperation, from the witness stand, "Please, tell me what I have done!" the resounding answer from their conspiracy prosecutors would be, "You're not Lee Harvey Oswald, you fool."

Shortly after (no one seems to know the exact time) the president was shot on Elm Street, five Dallas police officers in Dealy Plaza, some of whom had just been ordered to go there on a Code 3 (emergency), were instructed to go to the railroad tower. A civilian had told one of the Dallas police supervisors that a man in the tower "had some information." One of the five, Marvin Wise, told the FBI in 1992 that he went to the tower and spoke to the controller (presumably Lee Bowers, though Wise said he could not remember his name), who told him he had seen three men running down the tracks and climbing into a coal car. The controller directed the officers to the specific car, which Wise said was "several hundred yards from the control tower," and which was south of Dealey Plaza. And then Wise and Officer Roy Vaughn were the two who actually entered the car and rousted the three. One of the three was carrying a bag containing a bar of soap, a shirt, a towel/rag, a can of spam or Vienna sausage, and a jackknife. The three were taken into custody and transported back to the sheriff's office, where Sheriff Bill Decker and some of his deputies talked to the three for a few minutes. Wise was then instructed to take the three to Captain Will Fritz's office, and by himself (he said it was not uncommon in those days to transport several prisoners by yourself), he drove the three to City Hall, two of them handcuffed to each other in the backseat and one, unhandcuffed, riding in the front seat with him.

Wise said that since he was "convinced" the three had nothing to do with the assassination, he felt "guilty and ashamed" to bring the three hoboes to Fritz's office, thinking the elite detectives would "think less" of him. He deposited the three at the Homicide and Robbery office and an hour later was instructed to bring them back to the sheriff's office, which he did. Wise said the three were never booked and were soon released, but he could not remember if they spent the night in a "Hold For Decker" tank.[78]

While they were first being escorted to the Dallas sheriff's office on Houston Street, the transients were photographed several times near the Book Depository Building by photographers from the *Dallas Morning News*, *Dallas Times Herald*, and *Fort Worth Star-Telegram*. Except for these photographs, and the controversy they generated, the transients, who later became known as the "three tramps," dissolved into history for many years because, it was believed, no reports were ever made memorializing their arrest, or if they were, they had been destroyed as a part of the assassination cover-up.[*]

Who were these transients, these tramps? Their anonymity at once frustrated and tantalized conspiracy theorists for years. Because there was no evidence that the authorities ever identified them (which went beautifully in the direction of one of the theorists' favorite arguments, "a cover-up" by the same authorities), and because they did not look quite as disheveled and unkempt as many rail hoboes do (though obviously bedraggled in their appearance, they seemed to be relatively clean shaven, did not have long, uncut hair, and their shoes did not appear to be overly worn),[†] the conspiracy community believed that the three men were somehow involved in the assassination.

The "tramp" photos were first accumulated by conspiracy theorist and computer expert Richard E. Sprague in 1966 and 1967, and he turned them over to New Orleans district attorney Jim Garrison in 1967 when the latter was conducting his investigation of Clay Shaw for the murder of the president. During his January 31, 1968, appearance on *The Tonight Show* starring Johnny Carson, Garrison proceeded to hold up for the camera a photo of the three tramps, suggesting they were involved in the assassination. After a split second, Carson brought Garrison's arm (and hence, photo) down, realizing the potential liability for defamation of accusing someone on national television of murder without any evidence.[79]

An interesting vignette demonstrating the extent to which the three-tramps allegation went involved one of Garrison's first lead investigators in the Shaw case, William C. Wood, a former CIA officer fired from the agency in 1953 because of alcoholism. Garrison gave him the pseudonym Bill Boxley, hoping to conceal his CIA pedigree since Garrison was alleging the CIA had a hand in the assassination. Boxley was known to feed Garrison's fantasies by dredging up bogus evidence to support them. One such fantasy was that a New Orleans construction worker named Robert L. Perrin was actually the gunman on the grassy knoll.

[*]The first reference in print to the three men came in the April 6, 1964, Warren Commission testimony of Lee Bowers, the Union Terminal switchman, who said he had "held off the trains [from continuing on] until they could be examined, and there was some transients taken [off] at least one train" (6 H 288). The first reference to "tramps" came in the April 9, 1964, testimony of D. V. Harkness, one of the five Dallas police officers who arrested the three men at the boxcar, referring to them as "tramps" (6 H 312).

[†]On the other hand, Wise said they were "smelly" and the photos didn't really show how "dirty" they were. Indeed, a female reporter is being seen in a *Dallas Morning News* photo covering her nose as they walked by.

The only inconvenient problem is that Perrin's wife confirmed that Perrin, who had been discharged from the service for hysteria and had a history of mental disturbance, died in New Orleans on August 28, 1962, over a year *before* the assassination, and the coroner ruled the cause of death was suicide from "acute arsenic poisoning." No problem. Boxley told Garrison he found witnesses who saw Perrin alive in Dallas shortly *before* *and after* the assassination, convincing Garrison that Perrin had faked his death. Further, the enterprising Boxley went out and found some neighbors who, although they never had a good look at Perrin in the neighborhood, and couldn't identify him from a coroner's photo, identified, from a photo, one of the three tramps as being someone who lived across the hall from Perrin. The situation got so far out of hand that Garrison was actually planning to indict Perrin (who, as I mentioned, was dead) *and* the three tramps for Kennedy's murder on November 22, 1968, the fifth anniversary of the assassination. When Garrison's staff, fearful he was about to ruin himself and whatever credibility his investigation had, was unable to talk him out of it, they enlisted the help of Warren Commission critics Harold Weisberg and Vincent Salandria. Weisberg made Garrison see how worthless Boxley's work had been and Salandria convinced him Boxley was a CIA "plant," resulting in Garrison firing Boxley. Weisberg said that one of Garrison's assistants, Andrew Sciambra, was so grateful to him for getting Garrison to stop his suicidal plans that "he treated me to a homemade Italian dinner cooked by his wife."[80]

The tramp story remained a heavy topic of conversation and speculation within the conspiracy community for years after Garrison's near indictment of them in 1968. But it wasn't until 1974 that two conspiracy theorists, Alan J. Weberman and Michael Canfield, hit on what they thought was pay dirt. Comparing the photos of the three tramps with every "suspect" imaginable, they concluded that two of the tramps were none other than two of the convicted Watergate burglars: Howard Hunt, the former CIA agent, and Frank Sturgis, the soldier of fortune who ran arms for Castro in the Sierra Maestra mountains of Cuba and who conspiracy theorists have always believed to be a CIA agent or operative. Hunt was thought to be the shortest of the three tramps; Sturgis, the tallest. If true, which Weberman, Canfield, and many in the conspiracy community believed to be the case, this was "proof" of CIA complicity in the assassination. Weberman and Canfield turned the comparison photos (which immediately started appearing in alternative-press newspapers throughout the country) over to comedian-turned-civil-rights-advocate Dick Gregory, and it was Gregory who, because of his celebrity, became the point man on radio and television for the accusation. The next year, 1975, the national print media took notice, with stories about Gregory and his Hunt and Sturgis charges being reported in *Rolling Stone* magazine on April 24, 1975, and *Newsweek* magazine on April 28, 1975.[81]

The story started gaining such momentum that when the Rockefeller Commission conducted its investigation of CIA activities within the United States in 1975, it took testimony from Gregory, Hunt, Sturgis,* and several other witnesses on the issue. Remarkably, of the eighteen pages of its June 1975 report that were devoted to the Kennedy assassination, seven (almost 40 percent) dealt exclusively with the three-tramp

---

*The commission concluded that Sturgis "was not an employee or agent of the CIA either in 1963 or at any other time." Nor was he an "informant or other operative." Sturgis himself testified before the commission that he had never been a CIA agent but that he had engaged in several "adventures" relating to Cuba which he believed to have been organized and financed by the CIA.

issue. The commission concluded that Hunt and Sturgis were not two of the three tramps. It said that the weight of the evidence was that Hunt and Sturgis were in Washington, D.C., and Miami, Florida, respectively, on November 22, 1963. What conclusively proved they weren't the transients in Dealey Plaza was a comparison of the tramp photos with those of Hunt and Sturgis by FBI agent Lyndal Shaneyfelt, a nationally recognized expert in photo identification and analysis. Although two of the tramps bear a resemblance to Hunt and Sturgis, they clearly are not one and the same. Shaneyfelt found, among other things, that the tramp believed to be Hunt was much older than Hunt, was two inches shorter, and had a more pointed chin and more bulbous nose. The Sturgis tramp looked Nordic, whereas Sturgis (real name, Frank Angelo Fiorini) looked Latin. Also, other facial features were different and the tramp was three inches taller than Sturgis.[82] Indeed, even *Rolling Stone* magazine, pro-conspiracy in its early San Francisco years, commissioned the Institute of Forensic Sciences in Oakland, California, to make a comparison of the tramp photos with those of Hunt and Sturgis, and the institute concluded Hunt and Sturgis were not the tramps.[83]

While the Rockefeller Commission was in the midst of its hearings on the CIA,* Weberman and Canfield published their book *Coup d'État in America*, in which they went beyond the mere charge that Hunt and Sturgis were two of the three tramps, alleging that Hunt and Sturgis most likely were two of the actual assassins.

The authors, whose book never rises to the level of elementary-school scholarship, tell their readers that two of the tramps "fit the descriptions of the men seen running" from the assassination scene after the shooting. But they are so inept that they actually say that the older of the three tramps, whom they believe to be Hunt, and whom they described as someone of "very thin build" who wore "no coat," fit the description of the man Jean Hill saw running from the Book Depository Building toward the railroad tracks. But they quote Hill as saying the man she saw was "shorter than Ruby/stocky" and wore a "brown overcoat." How these two descriptions, which the authors themselves give, match up with each other is only known to them. The authors also say the tallest tramp, the one they believe to be Sturgis, and whom they describe as "175–200 lbs./6' tall," fits the description of the man Jesse Rice (see endnote) saw running in the railroad yards, whom they quote Rice as saying was "145 lbs./5'6 or 7"." To suggest that 175 to 200 pounds and six feet tall fits the description of someone who is 145 pounds and five feet six or seven inches tall is not just goofy but *non compos mentis*. The authors said they did not know who the third tramp was, but originally suspected he was an Oswald impersonator. Later, in 1992, they concluded he was Dan Carswell, believed by them to be a CIA operative.[84]

In 1978, the HSCA revisited the issue, and its panel of forensic anthropologists concluded that none of the three tramps were Hunt or Sturgis. The HSCA also compared several other conspiracy "suspects" (including Dan Carswell, whom they also eliminated as a tramp) and concluded that only one, Fred Lee Chrisman, a New Orleans minuteman, had facial measurements "consistent" with any of the tramps. However, the HSCA could

---

*Although the Rockefeller Commission, headed by Vice President Nelson A. Rockefeller, and consisting of many distinguished Americans such as C. Douglas Dillon, Erwin N. Griswold, Lane Kirkland, Lyman L. Lemnitzer, and Ronald Reagan, was a blue-chip body, it clearly made a mistake in appointing former Warren Commission assistant counsel David Belin as its executive director, not because he wasn't more than qualified, but because of the appearance of a potential conflict of interest, Belin being one of the strongest and most vocal defenders of the conclusions of the Warren Commission.

not establish any link between Chrisman and the assassination, and further, it "independently determined that Chrisman was not in Dealey Plaza on the day of the assassination."[85]

Even before the JFK Act, in October of 1992, ordered the release of all records related to the assassination of any "local law enforcement office" that assisted in the investigation of the assassination, the Dallas Police Department released thousands of pages of arrest and investigation reports on January 27, 1992. On February 3, 1992, at the Dallas Municipal Archives and Records Center journalist Mary La Fontaine, after finding nothing of any real value among these recently declassified and released documents, discovered among a different batch of documents voluntarily released by the department back in 1989, the arrest records (which, as indicated, were previously thought to have never existed, or to have been destroyed) of the "three tramps." Their names were Harold Doyle, John F. Gedney, and Gus W. Abrams.[86]

According to their November 22, 1963, arrest reports, filed by Dallas police officer W. E. Chambers, the three tramps, Doyle (age thirty-three, home address Red Jacket, West Virginia), Gedney (thirty-eight, home address "None"), and Abrams (fifty-three, home address "None") were arrested as "investigative prisoners" for vagrancy and robbery. The sparse report says they were "taken off a boxcar in the railroad yards *right after* President Kennedy was shot." The reports said the men "are all passing through [town]. They have no jobs, etc." The three were kept in custody until 9:25 on the morning of November 26 and released.

A front-page article on Mary La Fontaine's discovery written by her and her husband, Ray, in the *Houston Post* on February 9, 1992, prompted an immediate search for the tramps by the FBI and many others. But it was the La Fontaines themselves who tracked down Harold Doyle in 1992 in Klamath Falls, Oregon, and who ended up producing a February 25, 1992, segment on *A Current Affair* on their search for and interview of Doyle which received the highest rating, a 14 share, in *Current Affair* history. In the interview, Doyle said that although he had heard of the tramp controversy throughout the years, he never came forward because to do so might implicate him in the assassination, and "the tramps had nothing to do with it." As for the notoriety of identifying himself, he said, "I am a plain guy, a simple country boy, and that's the way I want to stay. I wouldn't be a celebrity for $10 million."[87] On February 29, 1992, four days later, the Portland office of the FBI interviewed Doyle, who advised the agents that around the time of the assassination, he, Gus Abrams, and John Gedney had been riding the rails in Texas. The three arrived in Dallas during the early morning hours of November 22, 1963, and spent the night at the Irving Street Mission in Dallas, where they "showered, cleaned up," and were fed. After a noon meal, they headed to the railroad yards intending to hop a freight to Fort Worth. While inside a "coal car" they were confronted by several police officers, who told them not to move or they'd be shot. They were arrested, he said, interrogated about the assassination at the Dallas Police Department, and released a few days later.[88]

On February 26, 1992, the Tampa FBI office caught up with John Gedney in Melbourne, Florida, where he was working as a code enforcement officer for the city. Back in 1976, Gedney had obtained a bachelor of science degree from Northeastern University in Boston. His relation of the events was the same as Doyle's, though he describes the railroad car they were arrested in as a "flatbed car with large sheets of steel" inside it. After he, Doyle, and Abrams were released, they rode the rails to Fort Worth, then to

Arizona, where they picked lettuce, then into Mexico and back to the states to Los Angeles, where the three of them split up, never seeing each other after that time.[89]*

The following year, 1993, assassination researcher Kenneth Formet located the sister of the third tramp, Gus Abrams, and she identified him from the Dealey Plaza photos, saying he had died in Ohio in 1987. She recalled that in the years around the assassination, her brother "was always on the go, hopping trains and drinking wine," and speculated he didn't even know who the president of the United States was at the time.[90]

From all appearances, and to the satisfaction of the FBI, the tramps turned out to be exactly what people had called them through the years, the conspiracy theorists coming up empty-handed once again.

There is no question in my mind that the search by conspiracy theorists for an assassin or assassins other than Oswald will continue down through the ages.

---

*In a 2001 book, *The Making of a Bum*, Gedney said that for years up to and including the day of the assassination, he was "a bona fide bum, tramp, hobo, rounder, and all-around drunken scoundrel . . . A scum-bag [who] lived in doorways and cardboard boxes, begged for money to buy a meal but used it for cigarettes or wine . . . My only allegiance was to the bottle" (Gedney, *Making of a Bum*, Preface, p.116).

Motive

One of the biggest unanswered questions that has always bedeviled students of the Kennedy assassination is, Why did Oswald kill Kennedy? What was his motive? Indeed, it was an issue I had to deal with at the London trial. When I say I *had* to deal with it, I do not mean in a legal sense. It should be explained that motive is not the same as intent, two terms that are sometimes erroneously used interchangeably by those unfamiliar with the criminal law. *Motive* is the emotional urge or reason that induces someone to commit a crime. It is different from *intent* in that a person can intend to steal property or kill someone and can be found guilty of that theft or homicide irrespective of what his motive was (e.g., need, avarice, revenge, jealousy, etc.). To say it more succinctly, motive is what prompts a person to act (or fail to act). Intent is the state of mind with which the act is done. Motive, of course, may aid you in determining what one's intent or state of mind was.

While intent is an element of every serious crime and a prosecutor has to prove it beyond a reasonable doubt, motive is *never* an element of the corpus delicti[*] of any crime. Therefore, the prosecution *never* has to prove motive. All it has to prove is that the defendant did, in fact, commit the crime with the requisite intent (e.g., intent to kill, steal, deceive, burn, etc.), not why. I've put people on death row without knowing for sure what their motive was for the murder. All I knew for sure was that they had intentionally put someone in his or her grave and had no legal right (e.g., justifiable homicide) to do it.

However, even though prosecutors have no legal burden to prove motive, it is always better if they can, because juries want to know "why." And just as the presence of motive to commit a crime is circumstantial evidence of guilt, the absence of motive is even stronger circumstantial evidence of innocence. Why? Proving that the defendant had a motive doesn't mean that others didn't also. But a complete lack of motive is very pow-

---

[*]Corpus delicti is not, as many lay people believe, the dead body in a homicide case, but rather the body or elements of the crime.

erful circumstantial evidence of innocence because there is a motive, no matter how irrational or even insane, for every crime.

Since Oswald is dead, we will never know for sure why he killed Kennedy.* Ironically,
the advertisement for the movie Oswald was watching at the time of his arrest, *War Is
Hell*, just over an hour after he murdered Kennedy, contained these words: "There are
some things that only the people that do them understand." Even if Oswald were alive
and wanted to tell us, though he could tell us much, he might not be able to convey all
the psychic and subconscious dynamics swirling about in his fevered mind that led up to
his monstrous act of murder. Even on a conscious level, his demented mind may have
been confused as to the main reason or reasons why he pulled the trigger.† So all we can
do is draw inferences from the available evidence, knowing that trying to divine human
motivation is a rather unprofitable undertaking, and that our quest is circumscribed by
the contradictory reality of trying to find rationality in an inherently irrational act.

The Warren Commission, after saying it had no doubt that Oswald killed Kennedy,
considered "many possible motives" he may have had for doing so. It ended up conceding that it could not "ascribe to him any one motive or group of motives."[1] Former President Gerald Ford, in testimony before the HSCA, said, "We were not able to precisely
pin down a motive for the assassination by Lee Harvey Oswald of President Kennedy.
There was no way of really being definitive as to that motive, and so we could only speculate."[2] "The Commission reached no conclusion on motive," Warren Commission assistant counsel Norman Redlich said.[3] The HSCA in essence agreed with the Commission
that many "factors" were involved in Oswald's decision and that "in the absence of other
more compelling evidence," the ones set forth by the Warren Commission "offered a reasonable explanation of his motive to kill the President."[4]

If the Warren Commission and HSCA conceded that they could not nail down for sure
why Oswald killed Kennedy, I surely am not so presumptuous as to believe that I can.

One thing, however, we should all agree on. Killing a president and thereby negating
a presidential election is the ultimate "political act." And we know that starting with his

---

*Dr. Renatus Hartogs, the psychiatrist who examined Oswald in New York City when Lee was thirteen,
offered a few possibilities of why Oswald killed Kennedy. Remarkably, if we're to believe Hartogs, one is that
Oswald, by his act, may have been shrieking to the world, "I have been deprived of a father, which is every
man's birthright, who would have taken care of me and protected me from my wild impulses, and now I will
deprive everyone else of a father, too," the president being the father of the nation. As far-out as this was, Hartogs wasn't through. He went on to say that Oswald's act may also have been "his unconscious attempt to cas-
trate his father," the "top man in his life as a child [Oswald's father was already dead at the time Oswald was
born], the man who is his rival for his mother. His 'place in history' may have meant what he believed to be
his rightful 'place' in his mother's bed, . . . the secret wish to commit what he unconsciously believed to be
the highest of forbidden pleasures—incest." (Hartogs and Freeman, *Two Assassins*, pp.188–189) So it was all
about the Freudian Oedipus complex. Oswald was just trying to retroactively have sex with his mother, Marguerite. My question is, What can society do to protect itself from such psychiatric silliness?

†One circumstance militating against the conclusion that Oswald knew precisely why he killed Kennedy
is that his decision did not appear to be thought-out, but seemed to culminate more from a potpourri of hemorrhaging emotions. Some have defined emotion as that which is devoid of reason. That may be too simplistic, but surely an extremely emotional act, as killing the president has to be, isn't grounded too much in reason.
Two facts, among others, suggest that Oswald's killing of Kennedy was not too premeditated: First, as known
from earlier in the book, he left a threatening, inflammatory note at FBI headquarters about two weeks before
the assassination. It seems very, very unlikely he would have done that (or would have even concerned himself with a minor matter like being upset with FBI agent James Hosty) if he at that time (two weeks before the
assassination) was right in the midst of his plans to murder the president of the United States. Second, and
also mentioned earlier, he didn't take his revolver with him on the morning of the assassination to aid in his
escape, going back to his rooming house to get it after he shot Kennedy.

reading *Das Kapital* in his early teens, Oswald's life was consumed by politics. "Politics was the dominant force in his life right down to the last days . . .," the HSCA said. "Although no one, specific, ideological goal that Oswald might have hoped to achieve by the assassination of President Kennedy can be shown with confidence, it appeared to the Committee that his dominant motivation, consistent with his known activities and beliefs, must have been a desire to take political action."[5]*

Were Oswald's political imaginings akin to that of a small-town city councilman? We know they were not. Though he may have been a small man in virtually every way, his thoughts were big and grand, thoughts in which he personally played a historically important role. How many people do you know who call their daily diary a "Historic Diary"? That's what Oswald called the mundane journal he kept in Russia.[6]†

Moreover, Oswald viewed himself as a militant soldier of action in the Marxist class struggle to bring about change, not by a slow, evolutionary process but by a violent revolution. The backyard photo of Oswald with a rifle and a pistol and holding two left-wing publications shows this. In a letter from Russia to his brother Robert, he wrote, "I . . . would like to see the present capitalist government of the U.S. overthrown . . . I fight for communism . . . In the event of war I would kill any American who put a uniform on in defense of the American government—any American," he emphasized, implying he'd even be willing to kill members of his own family.[7] Michael Paine, who had several conversations with Oswald about politics, told HSCA investigators in 1978 that it was "Oswald's belief that the only way the injustices in this society could be corrected was through a violent revolution."[8] Paine told *Frontline* in 1993 that Oswald "thought capitalism was rotten, it was a fraud, and it needed to be overthrown. Lee wanted to be an active guerrilla in the effort to bring about a new world order . . . There's no doubt in my mind that he believed violence was the only effective tool. He didn't want to mess around with trying to change the system."[9]

We know that Oswald's life was consumed by politics, especially with regard to Fidel Castro, Cuba, Marxism, and the notion of revolution, and among much other literature found in Oswald's tiny Beckley Street room or stored in Ruth Paine's garage after his

---

*The three prior assassinations of American presidents are compatible with the political motivation factor. Abraham Lincoln's assassin (assassination on April 14, 1865), John Wilkes Booth, was a Confederate sympathizer. So were all of his co-conspirators. James A. Garfield's assassin (July 2, 1881), Charles J. Guiteau, was a would-be officeholder who earlier had unsuccessfully sought to be appointed U.S. ambassador to Austria. Guiteau became enraged when Garfield failed to appoint him as ambassador to Austria. William McKinley's assassin (September 6, 1901), Leon F. Czolgosz, was an avowed anarchist. (HSCA Report, pp.21–23; WR, pp.506–510)

It should be noted that there is no such crime known as assassination, though by definition an assassination necessarily includes murder, which, next to treason, is the ultimate crime. The word *assassination* has come to mean the murder of a public official (e.g., Julius Caesar, Lincoln) or a public figure (e.g., Pancho Villa, Leon Trotsky), and hence, unlike a murder, its occurrence affects the lives of hundreds of thousands, sometimes millions of people, and often the course of public policy and events. Because of this reality, and because of the empirical evidence, we can safely say that most assassinations have, as their primary motive, the changing of history. A personal hatred of the victim by the killer, present in the majority of murders, is frequently absent or of secondary importance in assassinations. Oswald's killing of Kennedy was, of course, a classic assassination. Though we don't know his motive, the evidence is lacking that he "hated" Kennedy.

†Oswald's brother Robert believed that he had gotten this trait from his mother, Marguerite, who he said "had an extraordinary idea of her ability and importance" and felt "the world should recognize her as somebody special and important" (Oswald with Land and Land, *Lee*, pp.23, 48). Marguerite, he said, "had certain characteristics that were so much like Lee. The time and circumstances always seemed to be against her . . . She wanted to be somebody. I think this was passed on to Lee" (Transcript of "Who Was Lee Harvey Oswald?" *Frontline*, PBS, November 16, 1993, p.4).

arrest (including twenty Russian-language books, seven Russian-language newspapers, and the American leftist publications the *Militant* and the *Worker*) were booklets titled *The Coming American Revolution, Cuban Counter Revolutionaries to the U.S., Fidel Castro Denounces Bureaucracy and Sectarianism, Ideology and Revolution, Socialist Workers Party, Speech at the U.N. by Fidel Castro,* and *Continental Congress of Solidarity with Cuba, Brazil*; a book titled *A Study of U.S.S.R. and Communism Historical*; pamphlets titled *The End of the Comintern, The Crime against Cuba, The Revolution Must Be a School of Unfettered Thought, The Road to Socialism,* and *New York School for Marxist Study*; 358 handbills titled "Hands off Cuba, Join the FPCC"; and seven photographs of Fidel Castro.[10]

A person with an obsessive fanaticism for militantly revolutionary politics coupled with personal delusions of historical grandeur automatically removes himself from the general run of men, making a monstrous deed like Oswald's so much more likely. After all, there's always much more reason and motivation to do a bold and dramatic thing if that person is not just going to vicariously share in someone else's reflected glory, but be the principal recipient of the glory himself. And Oswald had such dreams. Recall his telling Marina that someday "he would be prime minister." She felt he had a "sick imagination" and tried to convince him he was just an ordinary man like others around them and "it would be better [for him] to direct his energies to some more practical matters," but she said, "He simply could not understand that . . . His imagination, his fantasy, which was quite unfounded, [was] that he was an outstanding man . . . He was very much interested, exceedingly so, in autobiographical works of outstanding statesmen of the United States" and elsewhere. "I think he compared himself to these people whose autobiographies he read."[11]

No one, of course, knew Oswald better than Marina, and when Warren Commission counsel asked her simply, "Do you have any idea of the motive which induced your husband to kill the president?" she answered, "From everything that I know about my husband, and the events that transpired, I can conclude that he wanted in any way, whether good or bad, to do something that would make him outstanding, that he would be known in history." Later in her testimony she repeated that her husband "wanted . . . by any means, good or bad, to get into history."[12] Earlier she had told the FBI something very similar: Her husband had "an obsession to get his name in history. Everything he did was toward that end."[13] In an even earlier interview with the Secret Service, she had said her husband always tried to improve himself, but mostly concentrated on "reading books about the great men of the world, their achievements and their contribution to the world." She said her husband was "an ego-maniac who wanted to be a 'big man' but that in failing to be so he decided to show the whole world who he was by killing the president so that the whole world would know his name."[14]

"My general impression [of Oswald] was he wanted to become famous or infamous. That seemed to be his whole life ambition . . . He just seemed to have the idea that he was made for something else than what he was doing . . . He seemed to think he was destined to go down in history someway or other," said Max Clark, a Fort Worth lawyer who had become an acquaintance of Oswald's when Oswald sought out Clark's wife, an immigrant from France who was three-quarters Russian and spoke the language fluently.[15] Michael Paine inferred from his political conversations with Oswald that Oswald believed that society was bad and had to change, but "he was of the mind that something small, or evolutionary changes were never going to be of any effect . . . It had to be of a rather drastic nature. Society was all tied together. The church and the power structure and our education was all the same vile system and therefore there would have to be an overthrow of the whole thing. Just how he was going to overthrow it or what he was going to overthrow toward, it was not clear to me."[16] Mack Osborne, who served with Oswald in Marine Air Control Squadron No. 9 in Santa Ana, California, told the Warren Commission, "I once asked Oswald why he did not go out in the evening like the other men. He replied that he was saving his money, making some statement to the effect that one day he would do something which would make him famous."[17] Even those like Volkmar Schmidt, the de Mohrenschildts' friend who did not know Oswald well but had at least one lengthy conversation with him, came away with the clear impression that he "was extremely fixed on making an impression with his life. [He was] enormously ambitious, ambitious to achieve something beyond the normal."[18]

Priscilla Johnson McMillan, the American reporter who interviewed Oswald in her Moscow hotel room in November of 1959 and author of the definitive book on Oswald and his wife, *Marina and Lee*, wrote in 1964, "If there was one thing that stood out in all our conversation [in Moscow], it was his truly compelling need . . . to think of himself as extraordinary . . . the desire to stand out from other men . . . I believe that Oswald yearned to go down in history as the man who shot the President."[19]

Kerry Wendell Thornley was a corporal in Oswald's Marine unit at the El Toro Marine base near Santa Ana, California, in 1959. As indicated earlier, he told the Warren Commission that in conversations with Oswald he sensed that Oswald "looked upon history as God. He looked upon the eyes of future people as some kind of tribunal, and he wanted to be on the winning side so that ten thousand years from now people would look in the history books and say, 'Well, this man was ahead of his time.' "[20]* In other words, Oswald was not someone who wanted to make a ripple or even a wave on this planet. His grandiose dreams were nothing short of changing the tide of history. And as stated earlier in this book, the assassination of John F. Kennedy arguably altered the course of world history.

Conspiracy theorists seek to rebut the argument that Oswald killed Kennedy because he wanted to be known as a revolutionary hero and famous down through the ages, by asking, If this were so, why did Oswald try to escape and, when apprehended, deny that he killed Kennedy? In other words, if Oswald wanted to get credit for the assassination, why did he do everything possible to cover up his perpetration of it? But this is a non sequitur predicated on the belief that his wanting to become famous and his denying guilt right after the assassination are mutually exclusive states of mind. They are only so on the surface. Though Oswald's leaving his wedding ring and most of his money behind on the morning of the assassination shows he thought he probably would not survive his killing of Kennedy, and was willing to sacrifice his own life, if necessary, to accomplish his plan to murder the president, this is not synonymous with saying he *wanted* to die. His conduct after the shooting clearly showed that he wanted to survive, to see another day. More importantly, just because he wanted to be famous for his deed doesn't necessarily mean he wanted this to happen immediately, thus ensuring his apprehension and likely execution. It is much more reasonable to assume that he wanted to disclose his identity on his own terms and at a time and place he, not the authorities, chose, such as in Cuba or Russia. There is no indication that Oswald *only* wanted to be famous *after* he died. In fact, his outsized grandiose dreams

---

*However, as indicated earlier in the book, it is not clear from the context whether Oswald himself used the "ten thousand years" phrase, or Thornley came up with the words to convey the impression Oswald left with him.

always imply his living to reap the rewards (e.g., his telling Marina that someday "he would be prime minister"). Knowing Oswald as he did from the Marines, Kerry Thornley told the Warren Commission that because Oswald had killed Kennedy, "I think he probably expected the Russians to accept him . . . in a much higher capacity than they [had]. I think he expected them to, in his dreams, invite him to take a position in their government . . . that he could go out into the Communist world and distinguish himself and work his way up into the party, perhaps."[21] Of course, you don't get that high position if you've been arrested, prosecuted, and executed in Dallas.

Oswald's obsession with and immersion in politics, as we know, was a constant and integral part of his life. More specific was his passion for Cuba and reverence for its leader, Fidel Castro.[*] We also know that as early as 1959, when Oswald was in the Marines stationed in Santa Ana, he told a member of his squad about his fervent desire to get to Cuba to aid Castro in his revolution.[22] His apparently solitary mission to proselytize for Castro and Cuba to the extent of passing out Fair Play for Cuba literature on the streets of New Orleans during the summer before the assassination, and being arrested for his efforts, clearly demonstrates the extent of his commitment. And his attempt to get to Cuba in late September and early October of 1963, and literally crying at the Cuban consulate in Mexico City when he was denied entry, shows that his devotion and ardor for Cuba knew no boundaries. "His basic desire," Marina testified, "was to get to Cuba by any means, and . . . all the rest of it was window dressing for that purpose." Oswald's "favorite subject," she said, was "Cuba, and he was . . . a little bit cracked about it, crazy about Cuba."[23] In late August 1963, when Marina saw Oswald on the porch of their house in New Orleans aiming his rifle, he told her, "Fidel Castro needs defenders. I'm going to join his army of volunteers. I'm going to be a revolutionary."[24] The Warren Commission reasonably inferred that Oswald's Cuban connection might very well have played a significant role in the assassination, Oswald hoping to thereby "aid the Castro regime, which President Kennedy so outspokenly criticized."[25][†]

Because Robert F. Kennedy, if possible, seemed to take JFK's death even harder than the rest of the Kennedys, being emotionally numb, reclusive, and even incommunicative for hours on end, many have conjectured that the reason was his sense of guilt, that the obsession and personal involvement he had (even greater than that of his brother) in overthrowing Castro may have inadvertently, as writer Max Holland says, "motivated a politicized sociopath."[26]

In this regard, we know Oswald subscribed to the *Militant*,[27] a leftist publication that regularly denounced U.S. foreign policy toward Cuba and reported Castro's extreme dis-

---

[*]Although Oswald may have liked Kennedy (see later discussion on why he would murder someone he may have liked), he revered Castro, and in any clash of interests in his mind, Castro obviously would have prevailed. "Fidel Castro was his hero," Marina Oswald said about her husband (2 HSCA 252). Oswald was so taken by Castro, he even kept a picture of him on the mantel in his apartment in New Orleans (8 H 187, WCT Charles Murret). An anti-Castro Cuban in New Orleans, Celso Macario, recalls seeing a small placard around Oswald's waist on which was written, "Viva Fidel" (HSCA Record 180-10030-10062). Indeed, as indicated earlier, Marina says that the alias "Hidell" was just a variation he used of "Fidel" (1 H 64).

[†]*American Assassins* author James W. Clarke feels Oswald had more than one motive for the assassination, one being that he "hoped to prove his value to the Cubans by killing a president who had effectively intimidated and threatened their small nation." Clarke broke down American assassins and would-be assassins into four classifications, Oswald, he said, falling into type two, assassins "with overwhelming and aggressive egocentric needs for acceptance, recognition and status." Lincoln's assassin, John Wilkes Booth, was put into type one, assassins who "view their acts as a probable sacrifice for a political ideal." (Clarke, *American Assassins*, pp. 126, 14)

pleasure with it. For example, the October 7, 1963, edition reported a September 28 speech by Castro in Havana. "Fidel Castro made it clear," the paper said, "that Cuba would continue its policy of revolutionary opposition to U.S. efforts to crush his government. He said that while Cuba welcomed the current easing of world tensions, *it could not accept a situation* where at the very same time the U.S. was increasing its efforts to 'tighten the noose' around Cuba."[28] A remark Oswald once made to Michael Paine about the *Worker* (like the *Militant*, a Far Left political organ we know Oswald subscribed to) was perhaps forebodingly ominous and revealing. "He told me," Paine testified before the Warren Commission, "if you knew how to read the thing [the *Worker*] and read between the lines a little bit you could see what they wanted you to do."[29] With that type of frazzled mentality, Oswald easily could have interpreted Castro's words about the United States as meaning he (Castro) would be very happy with the demise of Kennedy.

Moreover, we know from Marina and other sources that Oswald read the daily newspaper, and the previous month, on September 9, 1963, while he was still in New Orleans, the New Orleans *Times-Picayune* published (under a three-column headline, "Castro Blasts Raid on Cuba, Says U.S. Leaders Imperiled by Aid to Rebels") an article by AP reporter Daniel Harker quoting Castro as saying, "We are prepared to fight them and answer in kind. United States leaders should think that if they are aiding terrorist plans to eliminate Cuban leaders, they themselves will not be safe."[30] Although there are reasons to believe that Castro didn't quite say what Harker said he did (see conspiracy section on Cuba), Oswald would have had no way to know this. And any reference to Kennedy trying to kill Castro and Castro being agreeable to killing Kennedy could very well have had a combustible effect on a mind as flammable as Oswald's.

The CIA, for one, thought the Harker article could have had a connection to Oswald's act of murder. In response to an April 15, 1975, inquiry from David W. Belin, the former Warren Commission assistant counsel who was then the executive director of the Rockefeller Commission on CIA activities, the agency wrote on May 30, 1975, that since Oswald was "an avid newspaper reader—which we know from the testimony of Marina Oswald and others—" the "assumption" was that Oswald had "read the Castro warning and threat" in the New Orleans *Times-Picayune*. And that if he indeed did, it "must be considered of great significance in light of the pathological evolution of Oswald's passive-aggressive makeup after his attempt to kill [Castro hater] General [Edwin] Walker early in April 1963 and his identification with Fidel Castro and the Cuban revolution, which is directly traceable as far back as his Marine Corps service in El Toro, California."[31]

More immediately, in a major foreign policy speech in Miami Beach, Florida, just five days before the assassination, Kennedy all but invited the Cuban people to overthrow Castro, promising prompt U.S. aid if they did. A front-page headline in the *Dallas Times Herald* (which Oswald most likely saw) the following day, November 19, 1963, said, "Kennedy Virtually Invites Cuban Coup."[32] Coupled with the Bay of Pigs invasion, one can logically assume that Oswald's love for Cuba played at least a part in his ultimate act of violence. In his mind, he could have been striking a blow for Castro and Cuba. Although when Oswald was asked during his interrogation if he thought Cuba would be better off because of Kennedy's death, he replied that he felt that "someone else will take his place, perhaps Vice-President Johnson, and his views will probably be largely the same as those of President Kennedy."[33] However, Oswald would have known that a contrary answer would have pointed in the direction of giving him a motive for the murder.

There are those who say that after the Cuban consulate turned Oswald down, his ardor for Castro and Cuba had cooled, and they cite as evidence Marina's testimony before the Warren Commission: "In New Orleans he used to talk to me endlessly about Cuba, but after we came back [she from New Orleans, he from New Orleans and Mexico City] he didn't talk to me about it any longer." But Marina added that the reason he didn't was "because I was just sick and tired of this."[34] Although Marina said Oswald was obviously disappointed in not being able to go to Cuba, was fed up with the bureaucracy and red tape, and didn't express any "great desire" to try to get there again,[35] this is not the same as saying he had lost one iota of his love for Cuba, Castro, and the Marxist cause. There is no evidence of this. In fact, as late as November 1, 1963, just three weeks before the assassination, Oswald opened up P.O. Box 6225 in Dallas and listed the Fair Play for Cuba Committee as an organization authorized to receive mail at the box.[36] Moreover, Oswald had two Fair Play for Cuba cards in his wallet at the time of his arrest.[37] And a search of Oswald's small room on Beckley Street just hours after the assassination revealed the presence of Fair Play for Cuba circulars.[38] Indeed, during Oswald's interrogation, Captain Will Fritz said that when he asked Oswald if he belonged to the Communist Party, "he said that he had never had a card, but repeated that he belonged to the Fair Play for Cuba organization."[39]

Another important factor the Warren Commission and HSCA cited as probably contributing to Oswald's pulling the trigger was this: he clearly had, as the Warren Commission put it, a "capacity for violence."[40] Perhaps nearly all of us are capable of killing a fellow human being (e.g., in self-defense), but I have never believed that we are all capable of murder. This is why the percentage of murderers among us is an infinitesimal fraction of 1 percent. Oswald fell into this exclusive, as it were, class of humans. His attempt, just seven months earlier, to kill Major General Edwin A. Walker clearly showed his propensity for murder, at least where his target was political.

Oswald biographer Jean Davison says that his attempt to murder Walker, a right-wing extremist whose politics Oswald loathed, "revealed," like his defection to Russia, "Oswald's extreme dedication to his political beliefs. All else was secondary to him—his family, even the question of whether he lived or died."[41] At a minimum, it clearly demonstrated that Oswald not only was willing but appeared to have the desire to commit murder *for a political cause*. As far back as late 1957 or early 1958, he told a friend of his in New Orleans, Palmer McBride, that he would "like to kill" President Eisenhower because he was exploiting the working class. Palmer told the Warren Commission, "This statement was not made in jest, and Oswald was in a serious frame of mind when this statement was made."[42] When we couple his capacity for violence with his deep hostility for people and institutions, there can be little question that Oswald was a ticking time bomb, and it was only a matter of time before something like the Kennedy assassination occurred.*

---

*Remarkably, many major books on the assassination by Warren Commission critics and conspiracy theorists don't even mention Oswald's attempt to murder Walker. Not one word. A few examples: James Fetzer, *Murder in Dealey Plaza*; Jim Garrison, *On the Trail of the Assassins*; David Lifton, *Best Evidence*; David Scheim, *Contract on America*; Jerome Kroth, *Conspiracy in Camelot*; and so on.

Many books mention the Walker shooting but treat it dismissively in a few sentences. For example, in *Mafia Kingfish*, John Davis says that "someone took a shot" at Walker, and Marina Oswald "later claimed" that it was her husband, but this contention "has never been conclusively proved" (Davis, *Mafia Kingfish*, p.135). Period. Michael Kurtz, in his book *Crime of the Century*, says only that the Warren Report stated that Oswald

Along with Oswald's proven homicidal tendencies, both the Warren Commission and the HSCA noted, as contributing factors to his act, the fact that Oswald was a deeply disturbed and frustrated individual. He was "profoundly alienated from the world in which he lived," the Warren Commission said.[43] Marina went so far as to say that he would not have been happy anywhere, "only on the moon, perhaps."[44] Since his dreams were towering and incapable of fulfillment, he was "extremely bitter" and felt "exploited," Michael Paine told the Warren Commission.[45] "He was always speaking of the injustices which had been perpetrated against him," his Marine Corps friend Kerry Thornley said.[46]

Wherever Oswald turned or went, he found rejection and failure: The Soviets wouldn't grant him citizenship, and the Cubans wouldn't even let him in their country. He was ridiculed for his political beliefs and mannerisms in the Marines and received an "undesirable" discharge from the Marine Corps Reserve. He was always short of money and was fired from several jobs. He was estranged from his own mother. At the end, living in a closet-like room and holding down another menial job, he wasn't able to provide for his wife and two daughters, having to rely on the beneficence of another. Indeed, even his own wife confessed to him her infidelity during their marriage, spoke longingly of her past lover, and, the day before he killed Kennedy, rejected his entreaties to come back to him. "He had failed at almost everything he had ever tried to do[*] . . . Even though he had searched—in the Marine Corps, in his ideal of communism, in the Soviet Union and in his attempt to get to Cuba—he had never found anything to which he felt he could really belong," the Warren Commission said.[47]

Despair and frustration are the mother of madness, frequently bursting out into wildly aberrational behavior. It is unreasonable to assume that by this one cataclysmic act of killing Kennedy, Oswald, a loser trying to give meaning to his life, felt he would finally be doing something sublimely important, something that would free him from the dead end of his existence. As author John Clellon Holmes writes, "Oswald's sinister calm before the Dallas police, . . . his perfectly blank-faced denials of any complicity in the assassination, suggest a man whose darker conflicts are at least temporarily at rest, a man at ominous peace" with himself.[48] The terribly gruesome, destructive, but *successful* nature of the act put an end to all the frustration, rejection, and unhappiness forever roiling inside of him—at least for the moment.

There may have also been a sense of self-appeasement for Oswald in firing a destructive, equalizing missile at someone Marina said he may have been jealous of, envied—someone who was everything he was not.

As psychiatrist J. Anderson Thomson and his two associates at the Center for the Study of Mind and Human Interaction, Joy Boissevain and Clare Aukofer, summed it up, "Oswald found himself defeated in all his endeavors . . . He had failed as a Marine, a revolutionary, a husband, a provider, and a lover . . . In his mind, Oswald, in one bold stroke, would undo all his past humiliations and failures."[49]

Perhaps no one got to know Marina after the assassination as well as author Priscilla Johnson McMillan. In her book *Marina and Lee*, based mainly on her conversations with Marina, she writes about Marina's impressions of Oswald when she visited him at the

---

had tried to kill Walker, then adds, "The story of the attempt on General Walker's life is beyond the scope of this book." Why? "Obviously," he writes, "it has little bearing on the question of whether or not Oswald shot President Kennedy over seven months later." (Kurtz, *Crime of the Century*, p.124) Yes, indeed.

[*]Writer Dwight Macdonald says that "the one real success in Oswald's whole life seems to have been the assassination of President Kennedy" (Macdonald, "Critique of the Warren Report," p.137).

Dallas city jail the day after the assassination: "After the Walker affair, when he [Oswald] failed at what he had set out to do, he had remained keyed up and tense . . . Now he was altogether different. He had succeeded. The inner tension was gone. Marina sensed in him a glow of satisfaction that she had not seen there before."[50]

If there's one thing about Oswald that stands out above everything else, it's that he was a very angry human being. I mean, here's someone who, at the early age of thirteen, told his school psychiatrist "I dislike everybody."[51] Priscilla Johnson, remarking about her impression of Oswald during her interview of him in Moscow, noted years later "the repeated marginal reminder to myself [in her notes] 'He's bitter.'"[52] The Warren Commission said essentially the same thing when it reported, after saying it could not ascribe any one motive or group of motives to him, that "it is apparent, however, that Oswald was moved by an overriding hostility to his environment."[53] The inevitable question presents itself—why did Oswald have all this hostility?

Though his relationship with his mother, Marguerite, was strained, it could not be characterized as terrible. Moreover, his brother Robert grew up with the same mother and in the same environment, and nothing in his testimony before the Warren Commission or in his book, *Lee: A Portrait of Lee Harvey Oswald by His Brother*, hints that he was a bitter person mad at the world. So why was Oswald the way he was? No one will ever know the answer to that question, and I don't intend to be a park-bench psychologist, but his severe dyslexia could have contributed to his bitterness toward life and a feeling of frustration. Though there is no known reference to it in his grade-school records, for Oswald to be as dyslexic as he was in his writing as an adult, one can imagine how bad it was in the earlier years. And being severely handicapped by dyslexia, a disability a small percentage of children have, could be expected to give him a feeling of inadequacy among his peers and a sense of anger over the curse that had befallen him, an anger that could likewise be expected to stay with him and perhaps become intensified as the years went by.

The Warren Commission hired Dr. Howard P. Rome, a psychiatrist for the Mayo Clinic in Rochester, Minnesota, to analyze Oswald's writings and give his professional opinion. In a letter to Warren Commission assistant counsel Wesley Liebeler dated September 8, 1964, Rome concluded that Oswald was suffering from "constitutional dyslexia," a "reading-spelling disability" that can exist, he said, "in the absence of intellectual defect or of defects of the sense organs." He went on to say that the phenomenon is a "congenital, neurological deficiency" and that "difficulties in reading[*] are always accompanied by difficulties in writing and spelling." Rome wrote that "the person with this kind of word-blindness does not see and retain the picture of the word as an entity. It is as if he grasps certain features and tries to guess the rest by filling in the blanks, as it were. If he attempts to circumvent this difficulty by an untutored phonetic approach, as the more intelligent do, he encounters a further obstacle in the form of the irregularities, inconsistencies and ambiguities which are characteristic of

---

[*]However, Rome may be overgeneralizing here since, although dyslexia is primarily a reading disability and it is very unusual for a dyslexic to be an avid reader, we know Oswald read voraciously throughout his abbreviated adult life, and there is nothing in the record to suggest he had a difficult time reading the many books he got from the library. The only manifestation of his dyslexia seems to have been in his spelling of words. Indeed, whatever *reading* disability he may have had in his early youth, it was clear that by the age of thirteen, as shown in the Wechsler Intelligence Scale for Children, Oswald had overcome it, showing no retardation in reading speed and comprehension. (WR, p.381)

printed and written English." Rome said it was obvious that Oswald attempted to spell phonetically and more often than not failed in the effort. Dyslexic people like Oswald, Rome said, "are prone to develop a range of alternative ways of coping with their disadvantaged state: apparent indifference, truculent resistance, and other displacement activities by which they hope to cover up their deficiency and appear in a more commendable light."

Rome concluded that "[Oswald's] disability and its consequential effect upon him . . . amplifies the impressions from many sources about the nature of Oswald's estrangement from people." He said that dyslexia frequently gives rise to a "life-experience which [is] marked by repeated thwarting in almost every sphere of endeavor. For a bright person [which I think we can say Oswald was] to be handicapped in the use of language is an especially galling experience. It seems to be that in Oswald's instance this frustration gave an added impetus to his need to prove to the world that he was an unrecognized great man."[54]

The Warren Commission was essentially dismissive of Oswald's dyslexia, devoting only two sentences to it,[55] and then only to explain his misspelling of words. The reason may have been that Rome's letter to Liebeler was mailed on September 8, 1964, and by the time Liebeler wrote a memorandum[56] to fellow Warren Commission assistant counsel Howard P. Willens on September 15 recommending a reference in the report to Rome's belief that Oswald's dyslexia may have been partially responsible for his frustration and need to prove he was a great man, the Warren Report had already gone to press, eventually being published on September 24, 1964.

Although neither the Warren Commission nor the HSCA listed it as a contributing factor to Oswald's decision to kill, there's little question in my mind that to do what Oswald did, one would have to qualify as a first-class "nut." His act could not have been more irrational. We know that Oswald was crazy enough to ask Marina to help him hijack a plane to Cuba.[57] When Marina responded, "Of course I won't help," Oswald proceeded to start increasing his muscle strength by doing knee bends and arm exercises and tearing through their apartment at night in his undershorts to practice leaps, causing Marina to say to their little daughter, June, "Junie, our papa is out of his mind." Oswald went as far as bringing home airline schedules and a large map of the world, telling Marina how he planned to hijack the plane. He would sit in the front row and at some point walk into the pilot's cabin with a gun and order the pilot to turn the plane around.[58]

Oswald was crazy enough to attempt to murder General Walker. Indeed, the evidence that Oswald was a nut is best exemplified by his defection to the Soviet Union. Ever since Gorbachev made the cold war obsolete with his shredding of the Marxist catechism, *Das Kapital*, and gave the Russian people a taste of freedom for the first time, with the exception of a small handful of zanies, who in the hell ever defects to the Soviet Union? It's just not done, Russia, by all accounts, being one of the bleakest countries on earth. And to do this *before* Gorbachev's era, and then to try to commit suicide, as Oswald did, when his request for Soviet citizenship was turned down, further qualifies him for the booby hatch. I mean, how deranged does one's conduct have to be for him to be characterized as a nut? Oswald was so obviously a nut that in an FBI memorandum from J. Edgar Hoover to his staff dictated just five hours after the assassination, when the FBI knew nothing more about Oswald than his defection to the Soviet Union and his apparent murder of Kennedy, he said, "Our agents view him as a nut."[59]

One of the most serious problems I had in preparing for the upcoming trial in London was not that I didn't know for sure why Oswald killed Kennedy. As I indicated, I had dealt with that type of problem before in my career. The problem here—which I knew Spence would bring up—is that at least arguably Oswald had a motive not to kill Kennedy because he supposedly liked him. But I quickly discerned that the remarks made by the chief proponent of that view, Marina, could be broken down into two distinct time periods: the Warren Commission, in 1964, and the HSCA, almost fifteen years later, in 1978. The clear and explicit assertions of Oswald's liking Kennedy were almost all made in 1978, when Marina, having been hounded and courted by the conspiracy theorists every single year after the assassination, was definitely moving away from her Warren Commission testimony that "I have no doubt in my mind that Lee Oswald killed President Kennedy"[60] and closer to the view of the conspiracy theorists that Oswald was innocent and framed. Thus, testimony by her that "he always spoke very complimentary about the president" and whatever he said about President Kennedy, it was "always . . . something good," "I do not recall ever hearing Lee talking badly about John Kennedy," and "my impression was that he liked [Kennedy] very well" and "he was very proud of the new president of his country" when he heard over the radio in Russia that Kennedy had been elected occurred in 1978, a decade and a half after the assassination.[61] When we look at her Warren Commission testimony, however, her remarks are a little more muted and ambiguous. Thus, although she said that in translating articles for her about Kennedy, her husband "always had something good to say" about Kennedy she also said the much less emphatic, "From Lee's behavior I cannot conclude that he was against the president,"[62] and at one point said, "I don't think he ever expressed hatred toward President Kennedy, but perhaps he expressed jealousy, not only jealousy, but envy" over Kennedy's wealth.[63]

This ambiguity in Oswald's feelings toward Kennedy* was also reflected in the observations of other people who testified before the Warren Commission. Raymond Franklin Krystinik, who attended an ACLU meeting in Dallas with Oswald the month before the assassination, said Oswald felt Kennedy was doing "a real good job" in the area of civil rights. "That was the only comment that was made [by Oswald] in reference to President Kennedy," Krystinik testified, clearly not a blanket endorsement of the Kennedy administration.[64] Lieutenant Francis Martello of the New Orleans Police Department, who interviewed Oswald after his arrest resulting from his activities in connection with the Fair Play for Cuba Committee, told the Warren Commission that all of Oswald's thoughts "seemed to go in the direction of the socialist or Russian way of life, but he showed in his manner of speaking that he liked the president . . . or, if he didn't like him, of the two [Khrushchev and Kennedy] he disliked the President the least."[65]

Though the record was somewhat mixed, if anything Oswald had a positive feeling for Kennedy. As late as the summer of 1963 he said something in praise of the president and his wife in a casual conversation at the home of Lillian and Dutz Murret.[66] In any event,

---

*But whatever the ambiguity, there is little question that Oswald liked many things about Kennedy. Paul Gregory, a member of the Russian-speaking community in Dallas, said that Oswald "expressed admiration of Kennedy. Both he and Marina would say, 'Nice young man'" (9 H 148, WCT Dr. Paul Roderick Gregory). George de Mohrenschildt testified that Oswald said Kennedy was "an excellent President, young, full of energy, full of good ideas" (9 H 255, WCT George de Mohrenschildt), and Oswald's aunt, Lillian Murret, told the Warren Commission, "I think he said he liked him [Kennedy]" (8 H 153).

Top: Joined by world and national leaders, Jacqueline Kennedy, her eyes straight ahead, walks between the president's brothers, Attorney General Robert Kennedy (left) and Senator Edward Kennedy, as they follow the late president's caisson from the White House to St. Matthew's Cathedral. An estimated one million people line the funeral procession route—in such silence that the clopping of the horses' hooves can be heard by a global TV and radio audience. (© *Henri Dauman/daumanpictures.com*)

Bottom left: John Kennedy Jr. salutes his father's coffin as the funeral cortege leaves St. Matthew's Cathedral for Arlington National Cemetery. (© *Bettmann/Corbis*)

Bottom right: The procession, with a three-mile line of mourners behind it, nears the president's grave. (*Time & Life Pictures/Getty Images*)

Top left: Crowds gather to mourn all over the world, as in this renamed square in Berlin. (© *Bettmann/Corbis*)

Top right: The president of Italy, Antonio Segni, who had been prevented by his health from traveling to Washington, cries at a memorial service in Rome. (*Time & Life Pictures/Getty Images*)

Bottom left: The Kennedy family—Jacqueline, John Jr., John, and Caroline—dressed for mass in Palm Beach, Florida, Easter 1963. (*Cecil Stoughton, White House/John F. Kennedy Library*)

Bottom right: In sunnier days, Jack and Jackie enjoy a summer afternoon, Hyannis Port, August of 1959. (© *2000, Mark Shaw/MPTV.net*)

Right: Dallas police officer J. D. Tippit, whom Oswald shot and killed when Tippit pulled his squad car over to talk to Oswald just forty-five minutes after the shooting in Dealey Plaza. (*National Archives*)

Below: An aerial photograph of the neighborhood of the Tippit killing, marked by the Warren Commission with the locations of eyewitnesses to the movements of Lee Harvey Oswald. (*National Archives*)

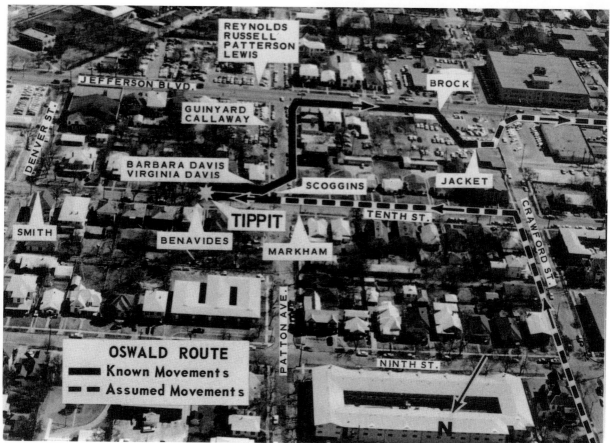

Top left: In custody of the Dallas police, Oswald raises his handcuffs and a rebellious fist. (*Courtesy the Sixth Floor Museum at Dealey Plaza, Bill Winfrey Collection,* Dallas Morning News)

Top right: In the chaotic corridor outside the Dallas Police Department's Homicide and Robbery office the night of the assassination, a Dallas detective thrusts the murder weapon into the air amid the press corps. (© *Bettmann/Corbis*)

Bottom left: Just after midnight on the night of the assassination, during an impromptu press conference, the media question Oswald about his role in the murder of the president. (*AP/Wide World Photos*)

Bottom right: At 11:20 a.m. on November 24, as Oswald is about to be transported from the Dallas Police Department to the county jail, Jack Ruby emerges from the crowd in the police building basement and shoots him fatally. (*Bob Jackson*)

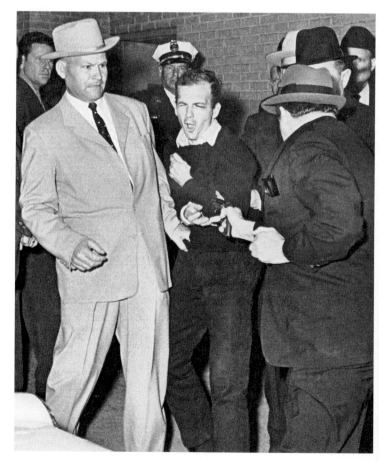

Top left: Jack Ruby outside his strip club, the Carousel, with two of his dancers. The Carousel was always open seven days a week, but in deference to Kennedy, Ruby closed it the entire weekend following the assassination. (*Eddie Rocco*)

Top right: Ruby and dancers in his Carousel office. (*Eddie Rocco*)

Bottom: Allegations by conspiracy theorists that Ruby and Oswald were hired assassins are belied by these photographs of their rooms. The squalid conditions in which they both lived are just the opposite of what one would expect of two hit men paid well for their work. Oswald's almost closet-sized lodgings at 1026 North Beckley in Dallas, as shown by the landlady to a *Life* photographer on the afternoon of the assassination, are on the left. At right, Ruby's bedroom is shown as he left it on the morning he shot Oswald. The newspaper on the floor is open to coverage of the assassination. (*Oswald's room: Allan Grant. Ruby's room: Courtesy the Sixth Floor Museum at Dealey Plaza, Photographer William Allen,* Dallas Times Herald *collection*)

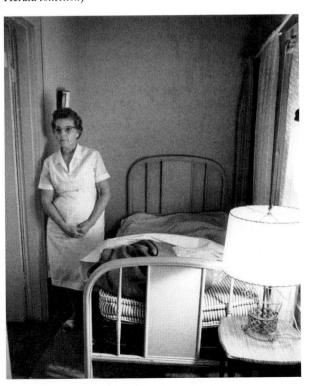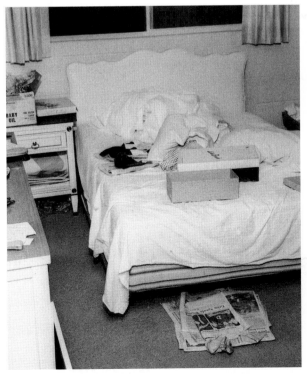

Top: The President's Commission on the Assassination of President Kennedy, led by the chief justice of the United States Supreme Court, Earl Warren, was appointed by President Lyndon B. Johnson to investigate the assassination. Although it would be difficult to come up with a group of more distinguished men, conspiracy theorists are convinced this bipartisan group deliberately conspired to keep the truth from the American people. From left, Gerald Ford, then a member of the House of Representatives; Representative Hale Boggs; Senator Richard Russell; Chief Justice Warren; Senator John Sherman Cooper; former World Bank president John J. McCloy; former CIA director Allen Dulles; and J. Lee Rankin, commission counsel. (*National Archives*)

Bottom left: Lee Harvey Oswald's mother, Marguerite Oswald, is shown here at Dallas Police Headquarters with her daughter-in-law Marina Oswald and her grandchildren Rachel (in arms) and June Lee. Not long after her son's death Marguerite entered the public sphere to speak out on his behalf. She maintained his innocence until the end of her life. (Dallas Morning News/*Jack Beers*)

Bottom right: Many conspiracy theorists have argued that this man was impersonating Oswald in Mexico City less than two months before the assassination. But shouldn't an impersonator at least resemble the man he's standing in for? (*National Archives*)

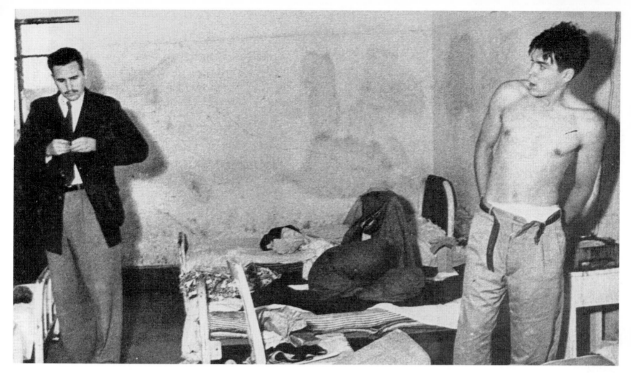

Top: The lawyer (Fidel Castro) and the doctor (Che Guevara) who led the Cuban Revolution are shown together in Mexico City in July of 1955. Castro was in exile from Cuba and Guevara on the run from Guatemala when the two met in Mexico. The Cuban Revolution in 1959 gave rise to the ill-fated, CIA-sponsored Bay of Pigs invasion in 1961, which was fodder for allegations that Castro or anti-Castro Cuban exiles were behind the assassination. (*Cuban Council of State, Office of Historic Affairs*)

Bottom: Robert and Edward Kennedy pause before John Kennedy's grave as his body is reburied, without the knowledge of the media, in March of 1967. Also reburied this night, beside their father's grave, were his son Patrick, who died two days after his birth in August of 1963, and the unnamed Kennedy infant stillborn in 1956. (*Cecil Stoughton, Army Signal Corps/John F. Kennedy Library*)

Left: More than five years after Kennedy died, New Orleans district attorney Jim Garrison charged businessman Clay Shaw (facing page) with conspiracy to murder the president. Garrison said that "the government's handling of the investigation of John Kennedy's murder was a fraud. It was the greatest fraud in the history of our country. It probably was the greatest fraud ever perpetrated in the history of humankind." (*AP/Wide World Photos*)

Below: Perry Russo (left) was Garrison's star witness against Shaw. He said he had heard David Ferrie (right) plotting with Clay Shaw and Lee Harvey Oswald to assassinate Kennedy. The *New York Times* called Garrison's unsuccessful prosecution of Shaw, an obviously innocent man, "one of the most disgraceful chapters in the history of American jurisprudence." (*Russo: Photo by Ralph Uribe © 1968 The Times-Picayune Publishing Co., all rights reserved. Used with permission of the* Times-Picayune. *Ferrie: © Bettmann/Corbis*)

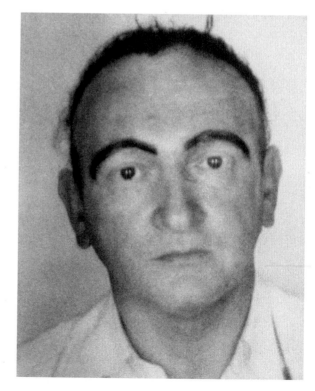

Right: Clay Shaw, who said of his trial, "If a jury could convict me on such shoddy evidence as Garrison presented, I would have gladly gone to jail—it would be the safest place in a world gone mad." (© *Joe Bergeron / Bergeron Studio*)

Below: Hollywood director Oliver Stone (right) and actor Kevin Costner on the set of the movie *JFK*, which convinced millions of young Americans that the CIA and military-industrial complex, opposed to Kennedy's intention to withdraw troops from Vietnam, were behind the assassination. Costner played the role of Jim Garrison. (© *Sygma / Corbis*)

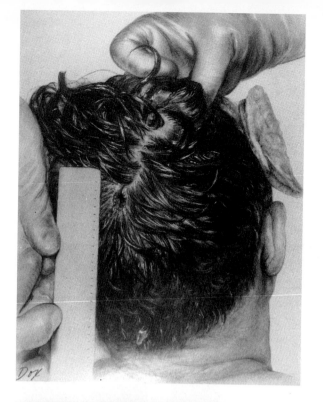

These are not photographs but drawings done for the House Select Committee on Assassinations. They were made from the photographs of the autopsy that was performed at Bethesda Naval Hospital on the night of the assassination. The Kennedy family has never authorized the public display of the actual photographs. The entire autopsy, along with the photos and X-rays taken during it, remains a major source of controversy.

Top: The back of Kennedy's head showing the entrance wound, with a portion of his scalp held in place by the hand at top. (*National Archives*)

Center: The entrance wound on Kennedy's upper back. (*National Archives*)

Bottom: The exit wound from that bullet was obscured by the incision for a tracheotomy performed on the dying president at Parkland Hospital in Dallas. (*National Archives*)

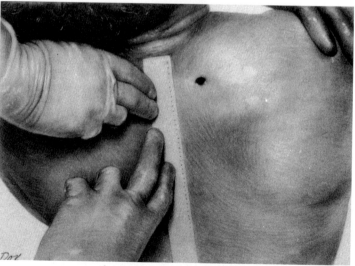

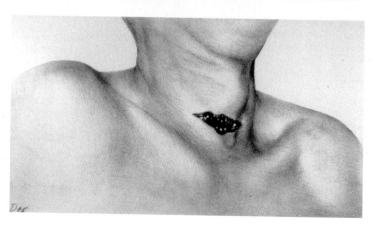

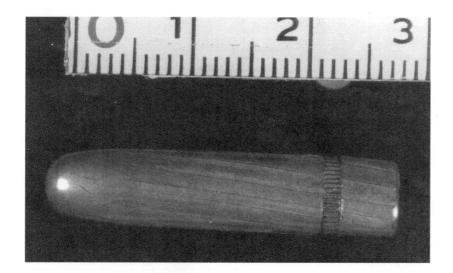

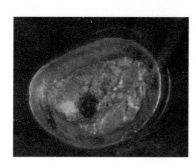

Above: The bullet that struck both Kennedy and Connally, and which conspiracy theorists have called the "magic bullet." (*National Archives*)

Left: One reason the theorists call it the magic bullet is that they maintain it was in "pristine" condition, but this photograph of its base, virtually never shown in a conspiracy book, proves otherwise. (*National Archives*)

Below: Lateral autopsy X-ray of President Kennedy's skull. (*National Archives*)

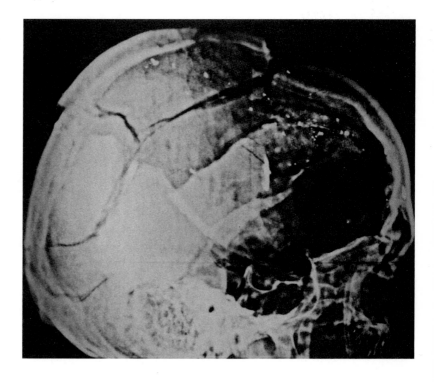

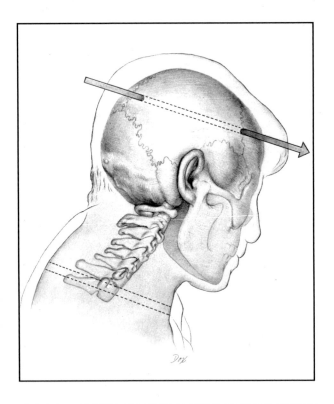

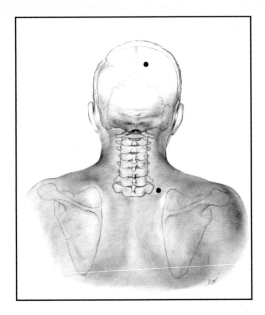

Above: This drawing documenting the two bullet entrance wounds to the president's body was made for the House Select Committee on Assassinations, as were the others on this page. (*National Archives*)

Left: These two drawings by the House Select Committee trace the path of the bullet that struck the president's head from behind (top left) and shattered his skull (bottom left). (*National Archives*)

Below: This Committee drawing shows the resulting severe damage to the upper right hemisphere of the president's brain. (*National Archives*)

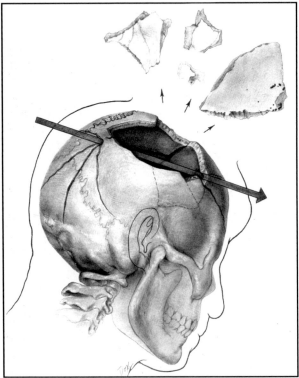

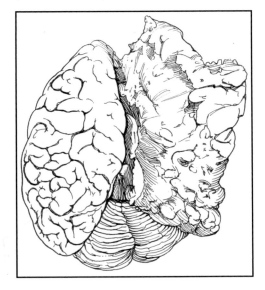

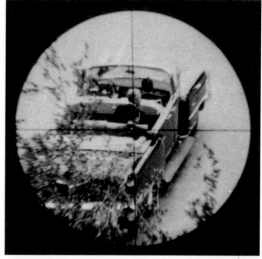

Frame 161

Frame 210

Above and right: On May 24, 1964, the FBI conducted a reenactment of the shooting in Dealey Plaza for the Warren Commission, with FBI agents standing in for Kennedy and Connally. Assuming that Oswald used his telescopic sight, these three photographs depict the approximate view he would have had of Kennedy and Connally from the sniper's nest around the designated frames of the Zapruder film at which the three shots were believed to have been fired: top left, the first shot around frame 161; top right, the second somewhere around frame 210; and at right, the fatal head shot at frame 313. The head of the FBI agent representing Kennedy in the reenactment photo of frame 313 seems to be farther to the left than Kennedy's head actually was. (*National Archives*)

Frame 313

Right: The three ovals drawn onto this photograph of the Texas School Book Depository Building represent the results of a bullet trajectory analysis by the House Select Committee on Assassinations. The smallest oval shows the point of the bullet's origin if a straight line were drawn backward from Connally's back wound to Kennedy's neck exit wound in his throat and through his back entry wound to the oval. The middle oval traces the second bullet backward from the exit wound in Kennedy's throat to the entrance wound in his back, to the point of origin. The largest oval runs from the exit wound in Kennedy's head to the entry wound in his head to the point of origin. Note that whatever the margin of error in the cone calculations, all trajectories lead to and encompass the sniper's nest window on the sixth floor. (*National Archives*)

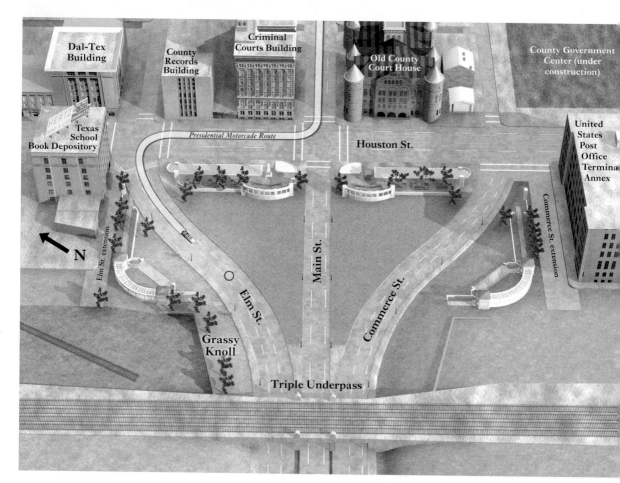

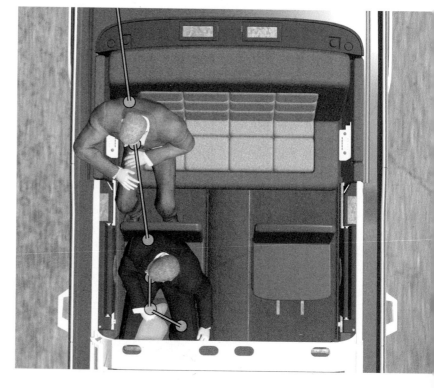

Above: An artist's rendering of Dealey Plaza on November 22, 1963. (*By Patrick Martin; 3D plaza model by Douglas Martin; Artimation of Arizona*)

Right: No one knows the exact Zapruder frame at which the president and Governor Connally were hit by Oswald's second bullet, but it was somewhere within a split second of frame 210. This is a three-dimensional overhead rendering of Kennedy and Connally as they were seated in the limousine at approximately frame 210, with the single bullet's trajectory. (*3D limo by Fred Kuentz, Artimation of Arizona; 3D plaza model by Douglas Martin; assembled by Patrick Martin*)

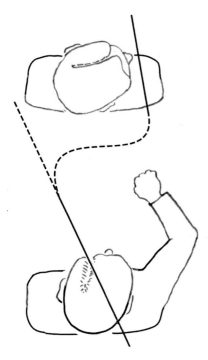

Top left: In a typical drawing seen in conspiracy books, conspiracy theorists improperly place Connally in the limousine directly in front of Kennedy. This enables them to make the argument that for the Warren Commission's single-bullet theory to work, the bullet exiting Kennedy's body would have had to make a right and then a left turn in midair before striking Connally—thus the "magic bullet," a demonstrably fraudulent conspiracy theorist creation. (*Illustration by John McAusland*)

Top right: The limousine leaving Love Field for the motorcade through downtown Dallas. Connally is actually, as can be seen here, seated substantially to the president's left and somewhat lower than the president. (*Courtesy the Sixth Floor Museum of Dealey Plaza, Tom Dillard Collection, Dallas Morning News*)

Bottom: Kennedy and Connally in the presidential limousine at approximately frame 210, from Abraham Zapruder's position (if Zapruder's camera could have seen through the Stemmons Freeway sign), with the bullet trajectory. (*Illustration by Michael McDermott; 3D limo by Fred Kuentz, Artimation of Arizona; 3D plaza model by Douglas Martin; assembled by Patrick Martin*)

Gerry Spence and Vincent Bugliosi were legal adversaries in the twenty-one-hour unscripted docu-trial of Oswald for the Kennedy assassination, held in London. This photograph shows them in 1986 in Dallas at the famous sixth-floor sniper's nest window of the Texas School Book Depository Building, from which Oswald shot President Kennedy. The two were chosen to try the case as a result of a survey of American trial lawyers. The media described them as "bitter rivals" who did not like each other, which was inaccurate. (The *London Observer* noted further that the British producers of the docu-trial "did not realize the extent of each man's desire to win the case. It soon became clear that two great egos were slugging it out.") Although there were some acrimonious exchanges during the pretrial maneuvering, the trial forged a friendship between them. Bugliosi says that Spence is "the finest trial lawyer" he has ever faced, and that he is "this generation's Clarence Darrow." Spence says that "Bugliosi knows more about the prosecution of criminals than Saint Peter himself," and, referring to the London trial, that "no other lawyer in America could have done what Vince did in this case." After a first vote of 10 to 2 for guilty, the Dallas jury returned a verdict of guilty against Lee Harvey Oswald for Kennedy's assassination. *Time* magazine called the trial, which used the original Warren Commission witnesses, "spellbinding, TV's best courtroom drama ever" and "as close to a real trial as the accused killer of John F. Kennedy will probably ever get." (Dallas Morning News/*Ken Gieger photo*)

The dark line on this map of Dallas tracks John F. Kennedy's motorcade from Love Field through Dealey Plaza to Parkland Hospital. The lighter line traces Oswald's route from the Book Depository Building to the point of his arrest. (*By Patrick Martin*)

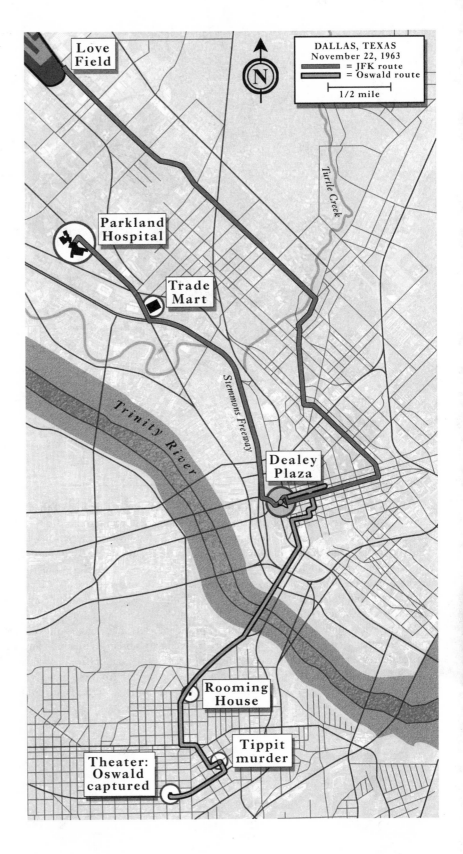

DALLAS, TEXAS
November 22, 1963
= JFK route
= Oswald route
1/2 mile

Love Field

Parkland Hospital

Trade Mart

Turtle Creek

Stemmons Freeway

Trinity River

Dealey Plaza

Rooming House

Tippit murder

Theater: Oswald captured

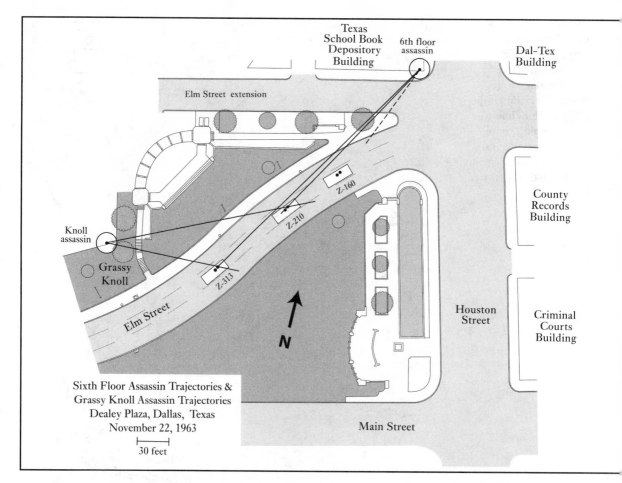

Above: The two lines coming down from the top right show the trajectories of the two bullets that struck President Kennedy, from their common point of origin at the sniper's nest window to the presidential limousine. (The broken line represents the first bullet fired by Oswald that missed the limousine entirely.) The two lines coming from the left show theoretical grassy knoll bullet trajectories from an imaginary assassin located there. It is dogma in the conspiracy community that bullets fired from the grassy knoll (the HSCA and most conspiracy theorists pick the encircled spot behind the picket fence for the location of the assassin) struck Kennedy, one in the throat, the other on the right side of his head. But as we can see from this sketch, if this were so, both bullets would almost automatically have exited the left side of Kennedy's body. At an absolute minimum they would have penetrated into the left side of his body. Yet the autopsy revealed no exit wounds or bullet tracks on the president's left side, nor any injury there. For instance, the autopsy surgeons found that "the left cerebral hemisphere [of Kennedy's brain] is intact." Note further that, from the grassy knoll, the president would have been, because of the angles, a moving target (from left to right in front of the assassin's rifle) and hence, it would have been a more difficult shot than firing at him from the sniper's nest window, where he was on almost a straight line from the rifle's barrel. This fact, among many others, increases the unlikelihood of the grassy knoll being used by any would-be assassin. (*By Patrick Martin; based on plaza survey by Drommer & Associates, Dallas, Texas*)

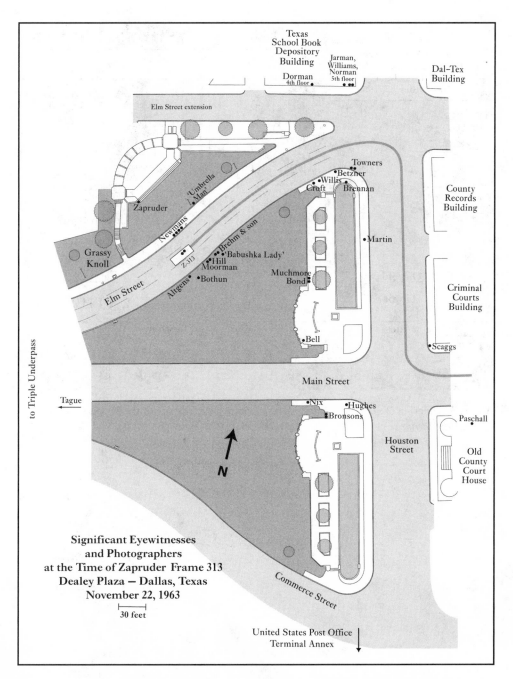

Here, dots mark the positions of significant eyewitnesses and photographers around Dealey Plaza at the time of Zapruder frame 313. (*By Patrick Martin; based on plaza survey by Drommer & Associates, Dallas, Texas*)

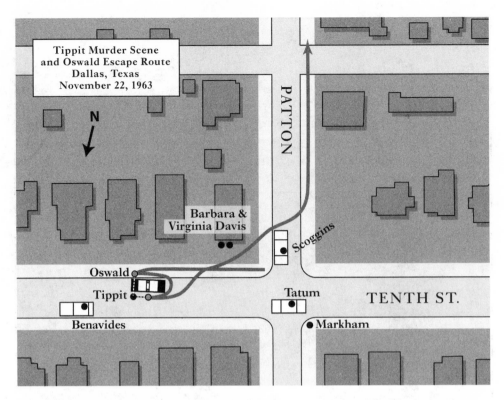

Above: A rendering of Oswald's route toward and away from the site of the Tippit shooting. (*By Patrick Martin*)

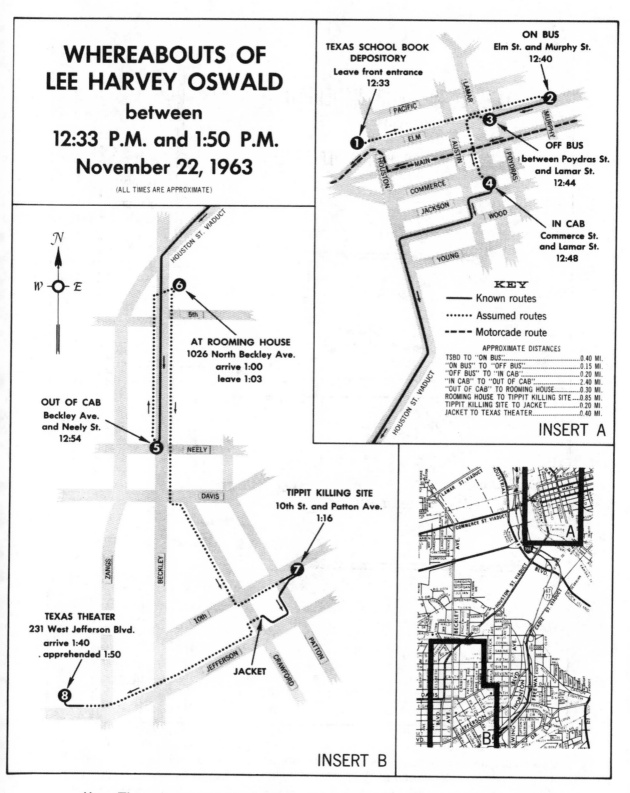

WHEREABOUTS OF LEE HARVEY OSWALD
between
12:33 P.M. and 1:50 P.M.
November 22, 1963

(ALL TIMES ARE APPROXIMATE)

TEXAS SCHOOL BOOK DEPOSITORY
Leave front entrance
12:33

ON BUS
Elm St. and Murphy St.
12:40

OFF BUS
between Poydras St.
and Lamar St.
12:44

IN CAB
Commerce St.
and Lamar St.
12:48

PACIFIC
ELM
MAIN
COMMERCE
JACKSON
WOOD
YOUNG
LAMAR
MURPHY
AUSTIN
POYDRAS
HOUSTON
HOUSTON ST. VIADUCT

KEY
— Known routes
······ Assumed routes
— — Motorcade route

APPROXIMATE DISTANCES
TSBD TO "ON BUS"..............................0.40 MI.
"ON BUS" TO "OFF BUS"......................0.15 MI.
"OFF BUS" TO "IN CAB".......................0.20 MI.
"IN CAB" TO "OUT OF CAB"..................2.40 MI.
"OUT OF CAB" TO ROOMING HOUSE....0.30 MI.
ROOMING HOUSE TO TIPPIT KILLING SITE....0.85 MI.
TIPPIT KILLING SITE TO JACKET..............0.20 MI.
JACKET TO TEXAS THEATER....................0.40 MI.

INSERT A

N
W · E
S

HOUSTON ST. VIADUCT

5th

AT ROOMING HOUSE
1026 North Beckley Ave.
arrive 1:00
leave 1:03

OUT OF CAB
Beckley Ave.
and Neely St.
12:54

NEELY

DAVIS

TIPPIT KILLING SITE
10th St. and Patton Ave.
1:16

ZANGS
BECKLEY
10th
JEFFERSON
CRAWFORD
PATTON

JACKET

TEXAS THEATER
231 West Jefferson Blvd.
arrive 1:40
apprehended 1:50

INSERT B

LAMAR ST. VIADUCT
INDUSTRIAL
PACIFIC
MAIN
COMMERCE ST. VIADUCT
HOUSTON ST. VIADUCT
PEARL ST. VIADUCT
BECKLEY
JEFFERSON

A

B

Above: These maps assembled by the Warren Commission follow Oswald's movements, as indicated, between 12:33 p.m. and 1:50 p.m. The times in this book vary slightly in some places from those calculated by the Commission. (*National Archives*)

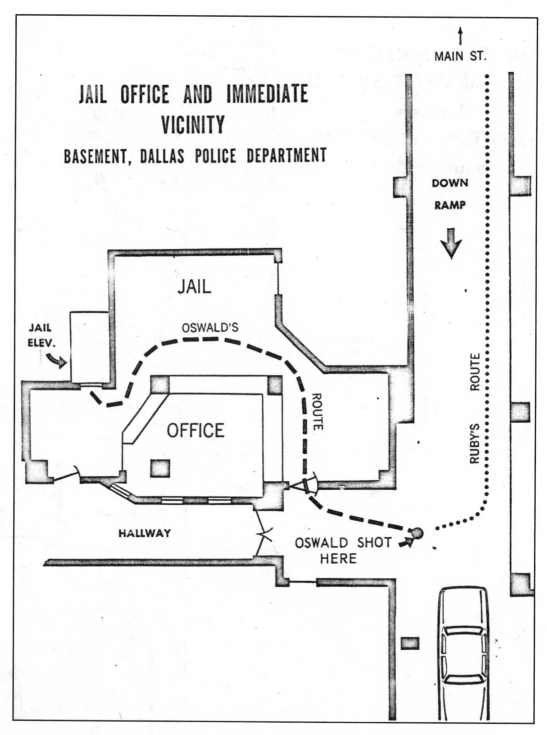

JAIL OFFICE AND IMMEDIATE
VICINITY
BASEMENT, DALLAS POLICE DEPARTMENT

MAIN ST.

DOWN
RAMP

JAIL

JAIL
ELEV.

OSWALD'S

ROUTE

RUBY'S ROUTE

OFFICE

HALLWAY

OSWALD SHOT
HERE

This Warren Commission diagram of the basement of the Dallas Police Department indicates, with a dashed line, the route Oswald was being walked on when he was shot. The dotted line coming down from the top right corner, from Main Street, is Ruby's path toward him. The car at the bottom is the one that Oswald was to ride in, which, because of the surging media, hadn't yet backed up all the way into position. (*National Archives*)

at the London trial I knew I would be asking a jury to believe that someone who did not, apparently, dislike Kennedy had in fact killed him. But quite apart from Oswald's personal feelings, although his trying to kill General Walker made some sense in that it was the Far Left (Oswald) shooting at the Far Right (Walker), why would someone on the political left like Oswald shoot at someone in the middle, or if anything, left of center, like Kennedy?*

I knew I'd have to closely scrutinize the official record to at least find something I could give the jury that went in the direction of Oswald's opposition to Kennedy. I already had one built-in argument. Even if we assume Oswald liked Kennedy, he clearly revered Castro, and Kennedy was Castro's sworn enemy. I also found a nugget, as small as it was, in Captain Fritz's interrogation of Oswald. "I have no views on the president," he told Fritz. "My wife and I like the president's *family*. They are interesting people." And then he added the cryptic, "I have my own views on the president's national policy."[67] Certainly not a ringing declaration of affection by Oswald for Kennedy. But I needed something more.†

I got a little help in the testimony of William Kirk Stuckey, who interviewed Oswald on his New Orleans radio show on the evening of August 17, 1963, following Oswald's altercation with anti-Castro Cuban exiles. Oswald's Marxist rantings on the show are covered elsewhere in this book, but the points of his interview that went to the issue of motive were his telling Stuckey that "Hands off Cuba" was the main slogan of his Fair Play for Cuba Committee. "In other words, keeping your hands off a foreign state," which Oswald said our U.S. Constitution dictated. "Castro," he went on, "is an independent leader of

---

*That Walker was Kennedy's opposite was made clear in many pronouncements by the right-wing zealot. For instance, in a speech before the Annual Leadership Conference of the White Citizens' Council of America on October 25, 1963, in Jackson, Mississippi, Walker declared, "The Kennedys have liquidated the government of the United States. It no longer exists . . . The best definition I can find today for Communism is Kennedy liberalism . . . He is the greatest leader of the anti-Christ movement that we have had as a president of the United States."

†I am assuming here that Kennedy's fierce opposition to Cuba was not enough, by itself, to cause Oswald to kill Kennedy, which it may very well have been. Author Jean Davison, in her fine book, *Oswald's Game*, perceptively points out what nearly all assassination writers have failed to do: although General Walker was on the Far Right and Kennedy was a moderate, even a liberal in the area of civil rights, they both were identical in one very important way to Oswald—their outspokenly strident opposition to his beloved Castro and Cuba. And if we *know* Oswald tried to kill Walker, most likely because of Walker's belligerence toward Cuba, as they say in the law, *a fortiori* (all the more so) he would be willing to try to murder Kennedy, who, unlike Walker, had the capability to physically remove Castro from power. *Did* Oswald try to kill Walker over Cuba? Oswald, of course, hated anti-Communists. But Walker is the only anti-Communist (other than Kennedy) whom Oswald tried to kill. What set Walker apart from other anti-Communists? It may very well have been the emphasis in Walker's heated rhetoric of overthrowing Castro, which Oswald, a diligent reader of the daily newspapers, would have known. The January 22, 1963, issue of the *Dallas Morning News* (the day after a federal judge in Mississippi dismissed charges against Walker for helping to incite the desegregation riots at the University of Mississippi the previous fall) quoted Walker as saying, "I am glad to be vindicated . . . Today my hopes returned to the Cubans . . . who long to return to their homes." The February 17, 1963, issue of the newspaper quotes Walker at length remonstrating against Cuba, calling Cuba "very significant" and the Cuban situation "unacceptable" to America. The caption for a March 6, 1963, article from the same paper (just over one month prior to Oswald's attempt to murder Walker on April 10, 1963) was "One U.S. Division Could Free Cuba, Walker Claims." The article read in part, "Former Major General Edwin A. Walker has called upon President Kennedy to oust Fidel Castro from Cuba. 'I challenge the commander in chief of the United States of America to take one U.S. Army division, the 82nd Airborne Division at Ft. Bragg, N.C., properly supported and joined by Cubans who want to be free, and liquidate the scourge that has descended upon the island of Cuba.'" Those would be frightening words to a devoted and fanatical follower of Castro like Oswald.

Notwithstanding the above, though Oswald would have detested everything about the right-wing extremist Walker, he did not appear to dislike Kennedy, and in fact admired him in some ways. And this is why I felt "I needed something more."

an independent country . . . He is . . . a person who is trying to find the best way for his country . . . We cannot exploit that system and say it is a bad one . . . and then go out and try to destroy it."[68]

Oswald gave Stuckey two speeches by Castro to read, a pamphlet by French existentialist Jean-Paul Sartre and a pamphlet titled *The Crime against Cuba*. Also, and more importantly, he gave him a pamphlet with a sketch on the cover whose message was clear: Kennedy was at the head of the line, leading the military, the intelligentsia, the media, and the people in the unconstitutional and criminal war against Cuba.[69] Whatever else Oswald may have thought of Kennedy's policies—for instance, in the area of civil rights—one thing was very clear: he very strongly opposed Kennedy's belligerent and militaristic (Bay of Pigs) policy toward Cuba.

I certainly would be able to use this to my advantage before the London jury, but I was still looking for a clearer example of hatred by Oswald toward Kennedy. Murder, after all, is an act of passion, and the London trial was a trial for murder, plain and simple. In the Stuckey interview and in the pamphlets Oswald had given Stuckey, the passion against Kennedy, if any, had to be inferred. I wanted (not needed, since motive, as indicated earlier, is not an element of murder that I had to prove) something more direct.

I finally found words of Oswald's which, though not as direct as I had hoped for, I was willing to settle for. In reading Oswald's 1959 Historic Diary, I found two similar entries that literally leaped off the page for me, meaning more to me than perhaps the average person. As the prosecutor of Charles Manson, I knew he didn't know the people he ordered his followers to murder. They were simply representatives of the white establishment he hated, and he was using his minions to vent his spleen on society for him. In other words, the murders were *representative*, symbolic murders. In the first of the two diary entries I came across, Oswald wrote, "To a person knowing both systems [capitalist and communist] . . . there can be no mediation between the systems as they exist today. He must be opposed to their basic foundations *and representatives*."[70]

Although Oswald's being opposed to the representatives of a system he hated is certainly logical and necessarily follows, I nonetheless felt that to go off on a tributary, as Oswald did, and specifically mention the "representatives" of the systems was not what one would normally do in the context in which he was writing—an abstract discussion of the systems themselves. I may be wrong, but to me it showed that Oswald had consciously focused in on the representatives themselves, that it was unlikely the word was just a gratuitous addendum. This inference I drew was fortified in a much stronger later entry by Oswald, in which he wrote, "I have lived under both systems . . . I *despise the representatives* of both systems."[71]

From the moment I saw these two entries—particularly the word *despise*, which certainly connotes passion—I knew that in addition to arguing the motives set forth by the Warren Commission and the HSCA, I would offer for the London jury's consideration an additional possible motive for the murder that, if not necessarily transcendent, was at least working in confluence with the others at the fateful moment Oswald decided to murder Kennedy. To counter Gerry Spence's anticipated argument that his client (Spence referred to him as "Lee" at the trial) would never have killed Kennedy because he liked him, I would use words to the effect that although Oswald may not have hated Kennedy personally, Kennedy, being the president, was the ultimate, quintessential *representative* of a society for which he had a grinding contempt. ("The United States," he wrote to his brother Robert from Russia, "is a country I hate";[72] he told New Orleans police lieutenant

Francis Martello that he "hated America" and that he would not permit his wife to learn the English language because he did not want his family to "become Americanized."[73]) *And therefore, when he fired at Kennedy, in his addled mind he was firing at the United States of America.* And even assuming, just for the sake of argument, that he had positive feelings about Kennedy, those would have been subsumed by his enmity for America. Speaking of Oswald's revolutionary thoughts, Michael Paine said that he "had frequently had the impression" that they were "of a rather drastic nature, where kindness or good feelings should not stand in the way of those actions."[74]

Returning to one of the essential questions—whether Oswald was the type of person to have killed Kennedy—let's briefly reflect on the rudimentary nature of his personality and the life he led. I like Relman Morin's description of Oswald in his book *Assassination*: "Oswald was a loner, a perennial failure, an egotist with small reason for egotism, restless, dissatisfied, highly introverted, quarrelsome, given to fantasies . . . He developed no close relationships and had no close friends . . . He read voraciously, borrowing books from the public libraries. His wife said there were occasions when he read all night, sitting in the bathroom so the light would not disturb her . . . He earned little money . . . [and] lived like an ascetic. He ate little and rented cheap rooms. He spent almost nothing on himself. He was not interested in clothes, automobiles, playing cards, or chasing women."[75]

I've always had the sense that there was something "test-tube," something mechanical, about Oswald, that he simply was not someone who had the normal components of humankind, but rather was someone who was manufactured in a lab with normal cognition yet abnormal "affect," as psychiatrists would say. I mean, as described on the pages of this book, which were gleaned from the official record, how many of you readers have ever met someone like Lee Harvey Oswald? Yes, you *may* have run across a fanatical leftist or rightist. But did they also, as Morin says, chase women? Or have a sense of humor, or like jazz, or have a profane tongue, or dress sloppily, or any of the myriad personal characteristics or eccentricities that are so very human? Oswald seemed to be bereft of these things. What he *did* look like was a presidential assassin.

If anyone ever had the psychological profile of a presidential assassin, it was Oswald. He not only had a propensity for violence, but was emotionally and psychologically unhinged. He was a bitter, frustrated, and beaten-down loser who felt alienated from society and couldn't get along with anyone, including his wife; one who irrationally viewed himself in a historical light, having visions of grandeur and changing the world; one whose political ideology consumed his daily life, causing him to keep time to his own drummer in a lonely obsession with Marxism and Castro's Cuba; and one who hated his country and its representatives to such an extent that he defected to one of the most undesirable places on earth. If someone with not just one but all of these characteristics is not the most likely candidate to be a presidential assassin, then I would ask, Who would be? Oswald cut the mold. If he didn't, what else is missing from the equation that would add up to a likely presidential assassin?

Certainly, and unequivocally, Oswald's background, character, and disposition show that he was the exact type of person who had it within himself, and who had a motive, to kill the president. In other words, his alleged act was completely consistent with his personality. But does all of this mean he did, in fact, do it? No. For the answer to that question we have to turn to the evidence, and, as we have seen, the evidence is more than overwhelming that he shot Kennedy. It is conclusive, leaving no room for any doubt.

For those who, despite all the evidence, still entertain some doubt that Oswald killed Kennedy, or believe there was a massive conspiracy behind his act, writer Jon Margolis says it very well: "*All* conspiracies that have been alleged are unsupported by credible data and *require far more suspension of disbelief than does acceptance of the prosaic likelihood that poor Oswald did it by himself, because he was mad.*"[76]

The fact that Kennedy was a powerful public figure was very relevant to Oswald's motivation for killing him. On the other hand, murders of powerful public figures in America by the groups fancied by conspiracy theorists—the CIA, mob, FBI, and military-industrial complex—are absolutely unheard of. Show me a precedent. I'm sure if Will Rogers were alive, the very suggestion that, for instance, the Joint Chiefs of Staff conspired with the nation's industrial leaders (as depicted in Oliver Stone's movie *JFK*) to murder Kennedy would have prompted his expression, "That's the most unheard of thing I ever heard of." On the other hand, if there was any evidence that one or more of these groups actually had the president killed, that would be different. But there is none (see conspiracy section). None whatsoever.

Summary of Oswald's Guilt

Putting aside for the moment the separate issue of whether or not Oswald was part of a conspiracy to murder Kennedy, there can be no doubt that he shot and killed the president. Yet other than a very small cadre of responsible conspiracy theorists who acknowledge Oswald's guilt but believe he was part of a conspiracy, the vast majority of the conspiracy community believe that Oswald is totally innocent, that he never fired one shot at Kennedy. Nearly all of them also believe that Oswald was framed by others who conspired to kill Kennedy. Here is a small sampling of both states of mind: "A false case against Oswald was constructed."[1] "The idea that Oswald was framed for the crime is supported by several things."[2] "The evidence showed that Oswald had no motive, no means (marksmanship of the highest order) and no opportunity (his presence on the second floor of the Book Depository little more than a minute after the shooting . . . constitutes an alibi)."[3] "Evidence has piled up that Oswald . . . was set up as the patsy, and did not shoot anyone."[4] "The other participants [in the conspiracy] were almost certainly law enforcement officers of one kind or another who were in a position to plant the evidence which would incriminate Oswald."[5] "It is the federal government that maintains the guilt of an innocent Lee Oswald."[6] "President Kennedy was killed by a conspiracy. The man who paid with his life for that crime in the basement of the Dallas City Hall was innocent."[7] "Shots were fired [at Kennedy] by an assassin I consider unidentified."[8] "There is not a shred of tangible or credible evidence to indicate that Oswald was the assassin. It can now be inferred that Oswald was framed."[9] "Oswald was framed for two murders—then was himself murdered."[10] "Oswald was who he said he was, a patsy."[11] "No credible evidence . . . connects [Oswald] to the assassination," and "irrefutable evidence shows conspirators, none of them Oswald, killed JFK."[12] "Lee Harvey Oswald had nothing whatsoever to do with the assassination of John Kennedy. Oswald was a very convenient scapegoat for the murder and was set up for it by the real killers."[13]

It is remarkable that conspiracy theorists can believe that groups like the CIA, military-industrial complex, and FBI would murder the president, but cannot accept the likelihood, even the possibility, that a nut like Oswald would flip out and commit the act, despite the fact that there is a ton of evidence showing that Oswald killed Kennedy, and not an ounce showing that any of these groups had anything to do with the assassination.

It is further remarkable that these conspiracy theorists aren't troubled in the least by their inability to present any evidence that Oswald was set up and framed. For them, the mere belief or speculation that he was is a more-than-adequate substitute for evidence. More importantly, there is a simple fact of life that Warren Commission critics and conspiracy theorists either don't realize or fail to take into consideration, something I learned from my experience as a prosecutor; namely, that in the real world—you know, the world in which when I talk you can hear me, there will be a dawn tomorrow, et cetera—you *cannot* be innocent and yet still have a prodigious amount of highly incriminating evidence against you. That's just not what happens in life. I articulated this fact in my opening argument to the jury in London: "Ladies and gentlemen of the jury, when a man is innocent of a crime, chances are there isn't going to be anything at all pointing towards his guilt. Nothing at all pointing towards his guilt. But now and then, because of the very nature of life, and the unaccountability of certain things, there may be one thing that points towards his guilt, even though he is innocent. In an unusual situation, maybe even two things point to his guilt, even though he is innocent. And in a very rare and strange situation, maybe even three things point to his guilt, even though he is completely innocent. But with Lee Harvey Oswald, everything, everything points towards his guilt. In fact, the evidence against Oswald is so great that you could throw 80 percent of it out the window and there would still be more than enough to prove his guilt beyond all reasonable doubt."[14]

Indeed, the evidence against Oswald proves his guilt not just beyond a reasonable doubt, but beyond *all* doubt, or, as they say in the movies, beyond a shadow of a doubt.[*] In other words, not just one or two or three pieces of evidence point toward Oswald's guilt, but more than fifty pieces point irresistibly to his guilt. And not only does all of the physical, scientific evidence point solely and exclusively to Oswald's guilt, but virtually everything he said and did points unerringly to his guilt.[†] Under these circumstances, it is not humanly possible for him to be innocent, at least, as I said, not in the real world in which we live. Only in a fantasy world could Oswald be innocent and still have all this evidence against him. I think we can put it this way: If Oswald didn't kill Kennedy, then Kennedy wasn't killed on November 22, 1963. You simply cannot have the mountain of evidence that Oswald had against him and still be innocent.

The Warren Commission critics and conspiracy theorists display an astonishing inability to see the vast forest of evidence proving Oswald's guilt because of their penchant for obsessing over the branches, even the leaves of individual trees. And, because virtually all of them have no background in criminal investigation, they look at each leaf

---

[*]Even if we were to reduce, for the sake of argument, the proof of Oswald's guilt from absolute and conclusive (which it actually is) to only probable, as British author John Sparrow points out about Oswald's guilt, "In order not to believe in the probable, there is so much of the improbable that [one] has to believe in" (Sparrow, *After the Assassination*, p.43).

[†]Prosecutors like to argue in their final summation to the jury that "looking at the evidence as a whole" (or "the totality of the evidence," or "all the evidence") makes it clear the defendant is guilty. But in the case against Oswald, one doesn't have to look at *all* or even most of the evidence to reach the conclusion he is guilty. Indeed, there are many individual things he did, like immediately fleeing the Book Depository Building after the shooting, killing Officer Tippit, et cetera, which by themselves point clearly to his guilt.

(piece of evidence) by itself, hardly ever in relation to, and in the context of, all the other evidence.

As I pointed out earlier in this book, within a few hours of the assassination, virtually all of Dallas law enforcement already *knew* Oswald had murdered Kennedy. Indeed, it was obvious to nearly everyone, not just law enforcement. At 4:45 p.m. on the day of the assassination, NBC network news anchorman Bill Ryan reported that "*all* circumstantial evidence points to the guilt of the suspect Lee Oswald."[15] Exactly what happened was *that* obvious within hours of the shooting.

If there was one, and only one, contribution to the assassination debate I would want to make, over and beyond the substance of this book, it's the obvious notion that once you prove the positive or negative of a matter in dispute, all other questions about the correctness of the conclusion become irrelevant. They only have a legitimate life if the matter has not yet been proved. Put another way, the answers to all other questions dealing with the correctness of a conclusion are rendered moot and academic by the answer to the seminal question. Hence, once you truly prove the earth is round, all questions about whether it is flat become irrelevant.

With respect to the Kennedy assassination, once you establish and know that Oswald is guilty, as has been done, then you also *necessarily* know that there is an answer (whether the answer is known or not) compatible with this conclusion for the endless alleged discrepancies, inconsistencies, and questions the conspiracy theorists have raised through the years about Oswald's guilt.[*] This, they simply do not understand. If they did, in all probability their voice would finally, after more than forty years, be silenced. Their inability or unwillingness to grasp this fundamental reality is the precise reason why questions about Oswald's guilt will be broached by conspiracy theorists as long as chickens lay eggs. If they don't have a satisfactory answer to any of their never-ending questions (one among thousands: something as obscure as whether it was Oswald or an imposter who allegedly signed Oswald's name to a guest register at a restaurant in North Dakota in 1963), without thinking they automatically feel the question of Oswald's guilt is still unresolved. In other words, every event, incident, piece of information, inconsistency, and so on, is segregated and becomes the whole story in itself. Nothing is part of the whole. Each incident is its own whole.

What the Warren Commission critics and conspiracy theorists seem incapable of seeing is that the answers to their countless questions are irrelevant since Oswald's guilt has

---

[*]For instance, since we *know* that Oswald shot and killed Kennedy, we *also know* that questions such as, What is the small object resembling a bullet fragment that Dr. David Mantik has become obsessed with, believing it was planted in an autopsy X-ray to frame Oswald by indicating a shot from the rear? Whatever happened to the missing autopsy photos? Was Oswald a good shot or not? Why wasn't Commission Exhibit No. 399 damaged more than it was? Whom did Roger Craig see running out of the Book Depository Building fifteen minutes after the assassination and getting into a Nash Rambler? Did Oswald have time to get to Tenth and Patton from his rooming house in time to kill Officer Tippit? Why, Drs. Gary Aguilar, Cyril Wecht, and Rex Bradford want to know, did a test bullet fired through a test skull cause more damage to the right side of the skull than Commission Exhibit No. 399 caused to the right side of Kennedy's skull? What is the reason for the sharp dent on the lip of one of the three cartridge cases found on the floor of the sniper's nest, which Josiah Thompson believes would have prevented it from being loaded into Oswald's rifle?—and hundreds upon hundreds of other questions and problems the critics have with the case against Oswald—are all irrelevant. Why? Because we *know* that Oswald killed Kennedy. So *by definition*, there *has* to be a satisfactory answer for all of these questions and perceived discrepancies and problems with the case. This is not an opinion I am giving. This is an incontrovertible fact of life and logic. They would have relevance only if the guilt of Oswald hadn't already been established beyond all doubt. But it has.

already been conclusively established by *other* evidence. Now, if it hadn't been, then, indeed, their many unresolved questions would have to be addressed.

I gave an illustration of this reality in my book, *Outrage*, on the O. J. Simpson murder trial. To remind the reader, among much other incriminating evidence, not only was Simpson's fresh blood found at the murder scene, but the victims' blood was found in his car, driveway, and home. With this type of evidence, that's the end of the ball game. There's nothing more to say. To deny guilt under these circumstances, which Simpson did, is the equivalent of a man being caught by his wife in bed with another woman and, quoting comedian Richard Pryor, saying to her, "Who are you going to believe, me or your lying eyes?" Simpson's guilt couldn't have been more obvious. In any event, *Outrage* was an in-depth discussion of all the *major* issues in the Simpson case, and I gave the following example to explain why it was unnecessary for me to discuss every single ancillary issue raised by the defense:

> Say that we know X committed a bank robbery in Detroit, Michigan, on October 25, 1993, at 10:00 a.m. We know this because there are ten eyewitnesses who have positively identified him; his fingerprints are found at the teller's window even though he lives in El Paso, Texas, and there is no evidence he had ever been in Detroit (much less at this bank) to have left the fingerprints on some prior occasion; and at the time of his arrest, all of the bank's marked money is found in his possession.
>
> Now, let's say that a witness comes forward and says X was actually in his presence in El Paso at 10:00 a.m. on October 25, 1993. Since we know X is guilty, we also thereby know that the witness is either honestly mistaken or is lying. Say the bank robbery was a very famous one because of a record amount stolen, and Y steps forward and actually proclaims it was he who committed the robbery (in sensational murder cases, it's not uncommon, for instance, for innocent people called "chronic confessors" to confess to a murder just to be in the limelight). Again, we know Y is either a kook trying to get into the news, or he's clinically psychotic. Why? Because we already know who committed the Detroit robbery.
>
> Likewise, with Simpson in this case. Since we know that in view of the evidence it's not even possible for him to be innocent, we know that whatever evidence the defense offered on his behalf, there's an explanation for it, *even in those cases where we might not know what that explanation is.* Whatever argument the defense makes, we know it is invalid. On the other hand, if we didn't *know* Simpson was guilty, then in the absence of an examination of every single defense argument, we could not feel sanguine about any conclusion of guilt.[*]

Has the evidence in this case proved Oswald's guilt to the point where we know that there must be an innocent explanation, one that in no way disturbs the conclusion of

---

[*]In a related matter, conspiracy theorists are fond of saying that there are just "too many problems and discrepancies" with the Kennedy case for Oswald to be guilty or for there to be no conspiracy. But actually, most of the "problems and discrepancies" in the case are not real but invented by the theorists. In any event, there are, as is normal and can be expected in all complex murder cases, some problems and apparent discrepancies—for example, some Dealey Plaza witnesses thinking the shots came from the grassy knoll. But you know what these same conspiracy theorists would argue if there wasn't one problem or discrepancy in the case? That this was abnormal, that there are problems with all cases, that the case was "too perfect," and for this to happen the case against Oswald must have been contrived by the authorities.

Oswald's guilt, to whatever question a Warren Commission critic or conspiracy theorist has about the case? Yes, unquestionably so. In very abbreviated and summary form, let's look at most of that evidence. (Some of the following is presented without documentation of sources, since this has already been done earlier in the book.)

1. Whenever Oswald had Wesley Frazier drive him out to visit his wife and daughters at the Paine residence in Irving, he'd go on a Friday evening and return to Dallas on Monday morning. The assassination was on Friday, November 22, 1963. For the very first time, Oswald went to Irving with Frazier on Thursday evening, November 21, obviously to pick up his Mannlicher-Carcano rifle for the following day.

2. Oswald told Wesley Frazier he was going to Irving to pick up some curtain rods for his apartment in Dallas. But Oswald's landlady testified that the windows in Oswald's room on North Beckley already had curtain rods and that Oswald never discussed getting curtain rods with her.[16] Indeed, Allen Grant, a photographer for *Life* magazine, took a photo of Oswald's room on the afternoon of the assassination, and it clearly shows the curtain rods that were alreaady in his room.

Additionally, Ruth Paine had two flat, lightweight curtain rods in her garage, and they were still there after Oswald's arrest.[17] Oswald never asked Ruth Paine about curtain rods at any time.[18] When Marina was asked in her Warren Commission testimony, "On the evening of the 21st, was anything said about curtain rods or his taking curtain rods to town the following day?" she answered, "No, I didn't have any." Question: "He didn't say anything like that?" "No."[19] And no curtain rods were found in the Book Depository Building after the assassination.[20]

If Oswald, as he claimed, brought curtain rods to work, whatever happened to them? We know from witnesses (on the bus, the cabdriver, and Earlene Roberts) that he wasn't carrying any long package after he left the Book Depository Building. And, as indicated, no curtain rods were found in the building after the assassination. As with the supposed killer behind the picket fence on the grassy knoll whom no one saw run away, and the bullet that exited Kennedy's throat without going on to hit Connally or anything else in the presidential limousine, did the curtain rods simply vanish into thin air? One would think that things like this would at least give the Oswald defenders and conspiracy theorists pause, but instead, their eyes blazing with certainty, they tell you that you just don't understand.

In addition to the evidence showing that Oswald's curtain rod story was a fabrication, the story, all by itself, is inherently implausible. If Oswald did want to pick up curtain rods at Ruth Paine's home for his apartment, why would that require him to go there on a Thursday evening? Could he only pick them up if he went there on a Thursday evening, not a Friday evening?

3. When Oswald told Wesley Frazier why he was coming to Irving on a Thursday night—to pick up curtain rods—Frazier said to Oswald, "Oh, very well," then added, "Well, will you be going home with me tomorrow also?" and Oswald replied, "No."[21]

4. Oswald and his wife, Marina, shared an abiding interest in President Kennedy and his family and spoke of them often. Yet on Thursday evening, the night before the assassination, when Marina brought up in conversation with Oswald the president's scheduled visit to Dallas the next day, she said, "He just ignored a little bit, you know, to talk about [it] . . . maybe changed subject about talking about . . . newborn baby or something like that . . . It was quite unusual that he did not want to talk about President Kennedy being in Dallas that particular evening. That was quite peculiar."[22]

5. Friday morning, before leaving Ruth Paine's house in Irving, Oswald left behind his

wedding ring and $170, believed to be virtually all of his money, for Marina, demonstrating that he realized he might never see her again—that is, he might not survive the assassination he was contemplating. Moreover, as he left Marina that morning, Oswald told her to use the money to buy shoes for their new baby, Rachel, and "anything" else that she felt was necessary for the children. Marina thought this to be strange since Oswald had always been "most frugal" and hardly allowed her to spend any money at all.[23]

6. Before Oswald got into Frazier's car that Friday morning, the day of the assassination, he placed a long, bulky package on the rear seat, telling Frazier it contained the curtain rods.[24]

7. Wesley Frazier said that on the way to work on the morning of the assassination, he noticed that for the very first time Oswald did not bring his lunch.[25]

8. When Frazier and Oswald arrived in the parking lot for the Book Depository Building on the morning of the assassination, Oswald picked up the long package on the backseat and, for the first time ever, walked quickly ahead of Frazier all the way into the building, Oswald being approximately fifty feet ahead at the time he entered the building. Always previously, they had walked the three hundred or so yards from the car to the building together.[26]

9. Every morning after arriving for work at the Book Depository Building, Oswald would go to the domino room on the first floor of the building and read the previous morning's edition of the *Dallas Morning News*, which another employee had brought in. On the morning of the assassination, for the first time, he did not do this.[27]

10. Despite the fact that the president's visit and route received enormous and inescapable attention in the Dallas papers and on radio and TV, and that Oswald usually read both daily newspapers each day and had to know what was happening, he asked coworker James Jarman somewhere between 9:30 and 10:00 on the morning of the assassination why people were gathering around the corner of Houston and Elm. When Jarman said the president was going to pass by the building, Oswald asked if he knew which way he was coming, whereupon Jarman told Oswald the president's route was from Main to Houston to Elm.[28] Obviously, Oswald was trying to create the false impression that he knew nothing about the president's visit. If not, these were just two nervous, pointless questions by someone who knew he was about to change history.

11. After the first and second shots rang out in Dealey Plaza, a motorcade witness, Howard Brennan, sitting on a short concrete wall directly across the street from the sixth-floor window, looked up and actually saw Oswald in the window holding his rifle. Only 120 feet away from Oswald, he got a very good look as he watched, in horror, Oswald (whom he had seen in the window earlier, before the motorcade had arrived) take deliberate aim and fire the final shot from his rifle.[29] At the police lineup that evening, Brennan picked Oswald out, saying, "He looks like him, but I cannot positively say," giving the police the reason that he had since seen Oswald on television and that could have "messed me up."[30] However, Brennan signed an affidavit at the Dallas sheriff's office within an hour after the shooting and *before* the lineup saying, "I believe that I could identify this man if I ever saw him again."[31] On December 18, 1963, Brennan told the FBI he was "sure" that Oswald was the man he had seen in the window.[32] And he later told the Warren Commission that in reality at the lineup, "with all fairness, I could have positively identified the man" but did not do so out of fear. "If it got to be a known fact that I was an eyewitness, my family or I . . . might not be safe."[33] Although Brennan did not positively identify Oswald at the lineup, he did say, as we've seen, that Oswald looked like the man. And we know Brennan

is legitimate since the description of the man in the window that he gave to the authorities right after the shooting—a slender, white male about thirty years old, five feet ten inches—matches Oswald fairly closely, and had to have been the basis for the description of the man sent out over police radio just fifteen minutes after the shooting.[34]

12. Apart from Brennan, we *know* that Kennedy's assassin was at the subject sixth-floor window. Among other evidence, the rifle that was used to murder Kennedy was found on the sixth floor of the Book Depository Building, witnesses other than Brennan saw a rifle sticking out of the southeasternmost window on the sixth floor, a sniper's nest was found around the subject window, and three cartridge casings from the murder weapon were found on the floor beneath the window.

13. Although in his interrogation on Friday afternoon, November 22, Oswald said he was having lunch on the first floor of the Book Depository Building at the time of the assassination,[35] during Sunday's interrogation Oswald slipped up and placed himself on the sixth floor at the time of the assassination, making him *the only employee of the Book Depository Building who placed himself on the sixth floor, or was placed there by anyone else, at the time we know an assassin shot Kennedy from the sixth floor.* In his Sunday-morning interrogation he said that at lunchtime, one of the "Negro" employees invited him to eat lunch with him and he declined, saying, "You go on down and send the elevator back up and I will join you in a few minutes." He said before he could finish whatever he was doing, the commotion surrounding the assassination took place and when he "*went down-stairs,*" a policeman questioned him as to his identification, and his boss stated that he was one of their employees.[36] The latter confrontation, of course, refers to Officer Marrion Baker, in Roy Truly's presence, talking to Oswald in the second-floor lunchroom within two minutes after the shooting. *Where was Oswald at the time the Negro employee invited him to lunch, and before he descended to the second-floor lunchroom?* The sixth floor. Charles Givens testified that around 11:55 a.m., he went up to the sixth floor to get his jacket with cigarettes in it and saw Oswald on the sixth floor. He said to Oswald, "Boy, are you going downstairs . . . it's near lunchtime." He said Oswald answered, "*No, sir.* When you get downstairs, close the gate to the elevator."[37]

There is another very powerful reason why we can know that Oswald, at the time of his confrontation with Baker in the second-floor lunchroom, had just come down from the sixth floor, not up from the first floor, as he claimed. It is an accepted part of conspiracy dogma to believe what Oswald told Fritz during his interrogation—that he had been eating lunch in the lunchroom on the first floor at the time of the shooting and had walked up to the second floor to get a Coke from the Coke machine just before Baker called out to him.[38] Assassination literature abounds with references to "the Coca-Cola machine in the second floor lunchroom." And indeed there was a Coca-Cola machine in the subject room.[39] But to my knowledge, there is no direct reference in the assassination literature to a *second* soft drink machine in the Book Depository Building, and in a phone call to Gary Mack, the curator at the Sixth Floor Museum in the building, he told me he was "unaware" of any other soft drink machine in the building at the time of the assassination.[40] What prompted my call to him was not the frequent references in the literature to the Dr. Pepper bottle found on the sixth floor after the shooting,[41] since some soft drink machines contain a variety of drinks, but a reference in stock boy Bonnie Ray William's testimony before the Warren Commission to his getting "a small bottle of Dr. Pepper from the *Dr. Pepper machine,*"[42] and stock boy Wesley Frazier's testimony that "I have seen him [Oswald] go to the *Dr. Pepper machine* by the refrigerator and get a Dr. Pepper."[43]

Neither Williams nor Frazier expressly said what floor this machine was on, and I was aware, from a photo,[44] that there was a refrigerator next to the Coca-Cola machine on the second floor. Through a few phone calls I was able to reach Wesley Frazier, whom I hadn't talked to since 1986, when he testified for me at the London trial. Still living in Dallas, he told me that "there was a Dr. Pepper machine on the first floor." Where, specifically, was it? "It was located by the double freight elevator near the back of the building." Was there a refrigerator nearby? I asked. "Oh, yes, right next to it." (And indeed, I subsequently found proof of the existence of the machine, with the words "Dr. Pepper" near the top front of it, in an FBI photo taken for the Warren Commission of the northwest corner of the first floor, and it is located right next to the refrigerator.)[45]

Frazier said that "almost all the guys would get their drinks for lunch from this Dr. Pepper machine. It mostly had Dr. Pepper, but also other drinks like orange and root beer." I asked him, "What about the Coca-Cola machine in the second-floor lunchroom? Did it have other drinks too?" He said it "only had Coca-Cola in it" and "the only time anybody would go to that machine is if they wanted a Coke, which I did from time to time." When I asked him whether or not "it was rare" for the workers to go to the second floor to get a Coke, he said, "Yes. We had our own machine on the first floor, where we ate our lunch. It was more convenient to use the machine on the first floor." Frazier said he could not say whether Oswald ever went to the second floor to get a Coke or ever drank soft drinks other than Dr. Pepper, but "I only recall seeing him with a Dr. Pepper."[46] Author Jim Bishop, in his book *The Day Kennedy Was Shot*, writes (without a citation, however) that Oswald "invariably drank Dr. Pepper."[47] And we know that Marina told her biographer, Priscilla McMillan, that when he was working at Jaggers-Chiles-Stovall in Dallas in 1963, "after supper" he would walk down the street as he often did "to buy a newspaper and a bottle of Dr. Pepper."[48]

So we see that apart from all the conclusive evidence that Oswald shot Kennedy from the sniper's nest, and therefore *had* to have descended from there to the second floor, his story about going *up* to the second floor to get a Coke doesn't even make sense. Why go up to the second floor to get a drink for your lunch when there's a soft drink machine on the first floor, the floor you say you are already on, particularly when the apparent drink of your choice is on this first floor, not the second floor?

14. There is yet another reason why Oswald's statement that he was on the first floor eating lunch at the time of the shooting makes no sense at all. If he had been, once he heard the shots and the screaming and all the commotion outside, if he were innocent, what is the likelihood that he would have proceeded to go, as he claims, up to the second floor to get himself a Coke? How could any sensible person believe a story like that?

15. Though Oswald was probably more politically oriented than all thirteen other warehousemen at the Book Depository Building put together, if we are to believe Oswald's story, he apparently was the only one who had no interest at all in watching the presidential motorcade go by, either from out on the street or from a window, claiming in one version that he was having lunch on the first floor of the Book Depository Building at the time of the shooting, and in another version that he was working on the sixth floor. Indeed, Oswald, the political animal, was so uninterested in the fact that the most powerful politician on earth had just been shot that he had no inclination to stick around for a few minutes and engage in conversation with his coworkers about the sensational and tragic event. Does that make any sense?

16. After the shooting in Dealey Plaza, nearly all of the sixteen warehousemen who

worked in the Depository Building returned to the building and were present at a roll call of employees. Only Lee Harvey Oswald and Charles Givens were not present; Givens was located shortly thereafter.[49] So only Oswald left the building and was unaccounted for. *Dallas Morning News* reporter Kent Biffle, who was inside the Depository Building, wrote in his journal that day, "I listened as the building superintendent [Roy Truly] told detectives about Lee Oswald failing to show up at a roll call. My impression is that there was an earlier roll call that had been inconclusive because several employees were missing. This time, however, all were accounted for but Oswald."[50]*

17. After exiting the front door of the Book Depository Building, if Oswald hadn't just murdered the president but still wanted to go home, he only had to turn left on the sidewalk in front of the building, cross Houston, and wait for the Beckley bus, which stopped at the northeast corner of Houston and Elm.[51] This is the same bus that he took every weekday to and from work, picking it up almost directly in front of his rooming house[52] and getting off at Houston and Elm, and on the way home getting off diagonally across the street from his rooming house on the northwest corner of the intersection of Beckley and Zangs Boulevard.[53]

But instead of waiting at the bus stop at Houston and Elm for his Beckley bus, Oswald walked past the bus stop and continued walking east on Elm, apparently wanting to get as far away as he could and looking for the very first Oak Cliff bus that came along, eventually boarding the Marsalis bus, which was proceeding westbound on Elm about seven blocks from the Book Depository Building.[54] But the closest the Marsalis bus could possibly take him to where he lived was Marsalis and Fifth Street, requiring him, if he had stayed on the bus, to walk five blocks to the west and one block north to get to his home.[55] Why would Oswald take a bus that he knew couldn't take him closer than a half mile from his home (when he knew the next bus, the Beckley bus, would take him to his front door) if he weren't in a frenzied flight from the scene of where he had done something terrible?[56]

18. When the Marsalis bus he had boarded got snarled in traffic, Oswald got off after just a few blocks, again demonstrating he was in flight from the scene of a crime. Flight, in the criminal law, is always considered circumstantial evidence of a consciousness of guilt.

19. When Oswald got in the cab shortly after getting off the bus for the trip to Oak Cliff, and the cab drove off, the cabdriver, seeing all the police cars crisscrossing everywhere with their sirens screaming, said to Oswald, "I wonder what the hell is the uproar?" The cabdriver said Oswald "never said anything." Granted, there are people who are very stingy with their words, and this nonresponse by Oswald, by itself, is not conclusive of

---

*For years, conspiracy theorists have attempted to explain away Oswald's fleeing the Book Depository Building by saying he probably "sensed" that he was being set up as a patsy. But when you ask them what evidence they have to support their speculation, or even what evidence they are aware of that may have caused Oswald to believe this, the silence is deafening. A typical example of this defense of Oswald comes from conspiracy theorist Susan Sloate, who writes that "anyone, realizing the President had been shot *and that he himself might be blamed for* it, would be frightened and insecure," justifying, per Sloate, Oswald "leaving the scene of the crime at the first opportunity [and] going home to get a revolver, his only means of protecting himself" (*Fourth Decade*, January 1995, p.22). But Ms. Sloate doesn't bother to say why she believes Oswald had this realization. She is apparently opposed to even trying to support her fantasy with some evidence.

In the book *High Treason*, the authors nakedly speculate that Oswald "knew he had been set up as the patsy, and so went home," not being nice enough to their readers to say what basis they had for their speculation (Groden and Livingstone, *High Treason*, p.153).

his guilt. But ask yourself this: If a thousand people were put in Oswald's place in the cab, particularly if they, like Oswald, were at the scene of the assassination in Dealey Plaza and knew what had happened, how many do you suppose wouldn't have said one single word in response to the cabby's question?

20. Instead of having the cabdriver, William Whaley, drop him off at his residence, 1026 North Beckley, Oswald had him drive directly past his residence and continue on for about almost blocks before dropping him off close to the intersection of Neely and Beckley.[57] Since we know Oswald was going home, this was obviously a feeble but incriminating effort to prevent the cabdriver from telling the authorities where the passenger he drove that day lived, and/or Oswald, in driving past his residence, was checking to see if the authorities had zeroed in on him yet. So instead of getting out of the cab in front of his residence, Oswald has the cabdriver, William Whaley, drive right past it. And this is the person who conspiracy theorists believe was as innocent as a newborn baby of the assassination that had taken place about a half hour earlier.

21. Oswald entered his rooming house around 1:00 p.m. on the day of the assassination, and per the testimony of the housekeeper, Earlene Roberts, before the Warren Commission, he seemed to be "walking unusually fast . . . he was all but running." When she said to him, "Oh, you are in a hurry," he did not respond.[58] The first person who interviewed Roberts on the afternoon of the assassination was *Dallas Morning News* reporter Hugh Aynesworth. Roberts told Aynesworth, "He came in running like the dickens, and I said to him 'You sure are in a hurry' but he didn't say anything . . . just ran in his room, got a short tan coat and ran back out."[59]

22. Oswald picked up his revolver at the rooming house, not a normal thing to do unless he felt he had a need to protect himself in light of some terrible act he had just committed. That he had no nonincriminating reason for getting his revolver was proved by the fact that when police later asked him why he picked up his revolver, he lamely answered, "You know how boys do when they have a gun, they just carry it."[60]

23. In addition to picking up his revolver at the rooming house, Oswald changed his trousers.[61] So Oswald changed his clothing, in the middle of the day, after the assassination.

24. Forty-five minutes after the shooting in Dealey Plaza, out of the close to three-quarters of a million or so people in Dallas, Lee Harvey Oswald is the one who just happened to murder Dallas police officer J. D. Tippit on Tenth Street near Patton in the Oak Cliff area, only about nine-tenths of a mile from his rooming house. One witness, Helen Markham, identified Oswald in a lineup later in the day as the man she saw shoot Tippit.[62] (Years later, the HSCA found another witness, Jack Tatum, who saw Oswald shoot and kill Tippit).[63] Another witness, William Scoggins, identified Oswald as the man he saw approach Tippit's car after it pulled up alongside Oswald, who was walking on the sidewalk. He lost sight of Oswald behind some shrubbery, but heard the shots that killed Tippit, saw Tippit fall, and then saw Oswald, with a pistol in his left hand, run away south on Patton Street in the direction of Jefferson Boulevard.[64] Another witness, William Smith, heard some shots, looked up, and saw Oswald running west on Tenth Street out of his sight.[65] Two other witnesses, Virginia and Barbara Davis, identified Oswald as the man they saw cutting across the front lawn of their apartment house right after they heard the sound of gunfire from the Tippit murder scene and a woman screaming. Oswald had a revolver in his hand and was unloading the shells from his gun on their lawn. They saw Oswald proceed down Patton toward Jefferson Boulevard.[66] Four other witnesses (Ted Callaway, Sam Guinyard, B. M. Patterson, and Harold Russell), from their position on two used-car lots at the intersection of Patton and Jefferson, identified Oswald as being

the man who, right after the Tippit shooting, ran past them on Patton toward Jefferson Boulevard (where the Texas Theater was located) holding a revolver in his hand.[67] Two men who were on one of the lots, Warren Reynolds (the owner of the lot) and Patterson, followed Oswald until they lost him behind a Texaco gasoline station on Jefferson. Mrs. Mary Brock, the wife of a man who worked at the gas station, identified Oswald as the person she saw walk past her, at a fast pace, into the parking lot behind the station.[68]

One of the canards of the conspiracy theorists that they've sold to millions is that there was only one eyewitness to Oswald killing Officer Tippit, Helen Markham, and she wasn't a strong one. But in addition to Jack Tatum also being an eyewitness to the killing, for all intents and purposes there were eight other eyewitnesses. For instance, with the Davis women, can anyone make the argument that although someone else shot Tippit, it was Oswald who was seen running from the Tippit murder scene with a revolver in his hand unloading shells? And when Scoggins saw Oswald approach Tippit's car and then lost sight of him for a moment, Tippit's true killer appeared out of nowhere, shot and killed Tippit, then vanished into thin air, whereupon Scoggins then saw Oswald again, running away from Tippit's car with a pistol in his hand?

So there were ten witnesses who identified Oswald as the murderer. And we know that the physical evidence was all corroborative of their testimony.

Granted, mistaken identity has resulted in many wrongful convictions. But here, and not counting Mrs. Brock, there were many eyewitnesses who identified Oswald. Show me any other case where *ten* eyewitnesses were wrong.

I argued to the jury in London that "Oswald's responsibility for President Kennedy's assassination explains, explains why he was driven to murder Officer Tippit. The murder bore the signature of a man," I argued, "in desperate flight from some awful deed. What other reason under the moon would he have had to kill Officer Tippit?"[69]* It should be noted that even if we assume just for the sake of argument that Oswald didn't murder Officer Tippit, then who in the world did? The conspiracy community never says. And although we know why Oswald would have had a reason to kill Tippit, what possible reason would the phantom killer have had?

25. Within minutes after the murder of Tippit, the manager of a shoe store on Jefferson Boulevard that was located several doors down from the Texas Theater, hearing police sirens on Jefferson and having heard over the radio of the shooting of the president and Officer Tippit, saw a man enter the recessed area of the store off the sidewalk and stand with his back to the street. After the sirens grew fainter, the man looked over his shoulder, turned around, and walked up the street toward the Texas Theater. The shoe store manager positively identified the man as Oswald. Because Oswald's hair was "messed up and he looked like he had been running, and he looked scared," the manager "thought the guy [Oswald] looked suspicious" and followed Oswald to the theater.[70]

26. The cashier at the theater said that Oswald had "ducked in" to the theater without buying a ticket.[71]

---

*Even without all the independent evidence proving that Oswald killed Kennedy, it was obvious that Oswald's murder of Tippit alone proved it was he who murdered Kennedy. So obvious, indeed, that one of the arresting officers at the Texas Theater who had pursued Oswald to the theater because of Tippit's murder, yelled at Oswald, "Kill the president, will you," and another officer called in to police headquarters from the theater that "I think we have got our man on *both* accounts."

The HSCA "concluded that Oswald shot and killed Officer Tippit. The committee further concluded that this crime, committed while fleeing the scene of the assassination, was consistent with a finding that Oswald assassinated the President" (HSCA Report, p.59).

27. Responding to a call from the cashier, the police approached Oswald in his seat in the theater. When the lead officer told Oswald to stand up, Oswald rose and said, "Well, it is all over now." What else could he have possibly meant by these words other than that he knew the police had been in pursuit of him and were there to arrest him? And how would he have known they were after him if he hadn't killed Kennedy and/or Tippit?[72]

28. After saying, "It is all over now," Oswald immediately struck the officer in the face with his left fist and drew his loaded revolver, but he was subdued by other officers after a struggle and placed under arrest.[73] If Oswald hadn't just murdered Kennedy and Tippit, not only wouldn't he have been likely to have a loaded revolver on him, but there wouldn't have been any reason for him to draw that revolver on the arresting officer and strike him. Is that what an innocent person normally does when a police officer approaches to arrest him—pull a revolver on the officer and physically resist arrest? Or does he say words to the effect, "What's going on? What have I done? Why are you doing this to me?"

29. After Oswald's arrest at the Texas Theater, he refused to give even his name to the Dallas police officers who captured him.[74] As a pretty consistent general rule, when a person is innocent of a crime, he cooperates with law enforcement.

30. While being led by Dallas detectives down the hallway of police headquarters on the day of the assassination, Oswald suddenly lifted his manacled right hand in a clenched-fist salute of some nature (see photo section). One would expect an innocent person to have an expression on his face conveying bewilderment or anger or a plea for help. Instead, it's clear Oswald is making some type of statement by his clenched-fist salute, one closer to that of defiance, satisfaction, even triumph. In no way would he confess to Kennedy's murder, which would ensure his execution, but by the body language of his clenched fist (for which he would suffer no consequences), he seems to be telling posterity that he did it. If not, ask yourself how many people charged with a murder they did not commit would respond the way Oswald did—with a clenched-fist salute? One out of a thousand? One out of a million?

31. When asked to, Oswald refused to take a lie detector test.[75] By contrast, Ruby volunteered to take one. In view of all the other evidence of Oswald's guilt, his refusal to take a lie detector test, though certainly not conclusive, goes in the direction of showing a consciousness of guilt on his part.

32. No one knew Oswald as well as his wife, Marina, and after the assassination, Marina never cooperated with any writer or journalist as much as she did with Priscilla McMillan, who ended up writing the very well-received *Marina and Lee*, a 659-page anatomy of their life together. Marina told McMillan that when she visited her husband in jail on the day after the assassination, she came away knowing he was guilty. She said she saw the guilt in his eyes. Moreover, she said she knew that had he been innocent, he would have been screaming to high heaven for his "rights," claiming he had been mistreated and demanding to see officials at the very highest levels, just as he had always done before over what he perceived to be the slightest maltreatment. For her, the fact that he was so compliant, that he told her he was being treated "all right," was an additional sign that he was guilty.[76] In Marina's appearance before the Warren Commission on February 3, 1964, she testified, as she later told McMillan, that when she visited with her husband on November 23 at the jail, "I could see by his eyes that he was guilty."[77] In her September 6, 1964, testimony before the Warren Commission, she said "I have no doubt in my mind that Lee Oswald killed President Kennedy."[78]

The Physical Evidence

33. A Mannlicher-Carcano rifle, serial number C2766, was found on the sixth floor of the Book Depository Building shortly after the shooting in Dealey Plaza. Handwriting experts determined that the writing on the purchase order and money order for the rifle was Oswald's. And the seller shipped the rifle to Oswald's post office box in Dallas. So Oswald owned the Carcano. Also, photographs taken by Oswald's wife, Marina, in April of 1963 show Oswald holding the Carcano, and Oswald's right palm print was found on the underside of the rifle barrel following the assassination.[*] So we know that Oswald not only owned but possessed the subject rifle.

In the same vein, a tuft of several fresh, dark blue, gray-black, and orange-yellow cotton fibers was found in a crevice between the butt plate of the Carcano and the wooden stock. The FBI laboratory found that the colors, and even the twist of the fibers, perfectly matched those on the shirt Oswald was wearing at the time of his arrest.[79] Though such fibers could theoretically have come from another identical shirt, the prohibitive probability is that they came from Oswald's shirt.

34. Firearms identification experts from the Warren Commission and the HSCA concluded that two large bullet fragments found in the presidential limousine were parts of a bullet fired from Oswald's Carcano rifle to the exclusion of all other weapons. Likewise, the firearms experts found that the whole bullet recovered from a stretcher at Parkland Hospital, believed to be the stretcher Governor Connally was on, was fired from Oswald's rifle to the exclusion of all other weapons.

35. Firearms experts determined that the three expended cartridge shells found on the floor beneath the southeasternmost window on the sixth floor of the Book Depository Building were fired in and ejected from Oswald's Mannlicher-Carcano rifle to the exclusion of all other weapons.[†]

So we know, not just beyond a reasonable doubt, but beyond all doubt, that Oswald's rifle was the murder weapon, the weapon that fired the bullets that struck down the thirty-fifth president of the United States. If there were no other evidence against Oswald, the fact that the murder weapon belonged to him, and that there was no evidence or even likelihood that anyone else had come into possession of the weapon, would be devastating evidence of his guilt.

But likewise, it should be realized that even if, hypothetically, Oswald had succeeded in secreting his weapon and law enforcement never found it, and hence, the murder weapon could never be connected to him, as can be seen from all the preceding pages and those that follow, the evidence against him would still be much more than enough to prove his guilt beyond all doubt. Convictions are secured every day without the prosecution finding the murder weapon.

36. A large brown handmade bag of wrapping paper and tape of the appropriate size

---

[*]This palm print could have been placed on this portion of the rifle only when disassembled, since the wooden foregrip of the rifle covers the barrel at this point (WR, p.124; 4 H 260, WCT J. C. Day; Telephone interview of C. Day by author on August 29, 2002). And, of course, we know that Oswald's Carcano had been disassembled when he took it to work in the paper bag on the morning of the assassination.

[†]Recall that other than Oswald's Carcano and the three expended shells from the Carcano being found on the sixth floor of the Book Depository Building, no other weapon, or even shells from another weapon, were found or seen anywhere else in Dealey Plaza.

to contain Oswald's disassembled Carcano rifle, undoubtedly the bag Wesley Frazier saw Oswald carry into the Book Depository Building on the morning of the assassination, was found inside the sniper's nest on the sixth floor close to the three cartridge cases ejected from Oswald's rifle. Oswald's left index fingerprint and right palm print were found on the bag.[80]

37. Oswald's left palm print and right index fingerprint were found on top of a book carton next to the windowsill of the southeasternmost window on the sixth floor of the Book Depository Building. The carton appeared to have been arranged as a convenient gun rest. Both prints were pointing in a southwesterly direction, the same direction the presidential limousine was proceeding down Elm Street.[81] A print of his right palm was found on top of the northwest corner of another carton just to the rear of the gunrest carton.[82]

38. The revolver in Oswald's possession at the time of his arrest at the Texas Theater was a Smith & Wesson .38 Special caliber revolver, serial number V510210. Handwriting experts found that the mail-order coupon for the revolver contained the handwriting of Lee Harvey Oswald, and the seller of the revolver sent it to Oswald's post office box in Dallas.

39. Four bullets were recovered from the body of Officer Tippit. A firearms identification expert for the Warren Commission concluded that one of the four bullets was fired from Oswald's revolver to the exclusion of all other weapons, and another expert acknowledged that all four bullets "could have been" fired from the revolver, since the bullets recovered from Tippit had the same general characteristic as those test-fired from Oswald's revolver—five lands and grooves (including the same width of the lands and grooves) with a right twist. (Recall that the bullets were .38 Special bullets, not .38 Smith & Wesson bullets, and the barrel of Oswald's revolver was slightly oversized for such a bullet. Therefore, during the passage of these slightly smaller bullets through the barrel, the barrel did not clearly imprint its signature striations or markings on the sides of the bullets to enable a positive identification.)

40. Four expended cartridge cases were found near the site of the Tippit killing. Firearms experts from the Warren Commission and the HSCA concluded that all four were fired in and ejected from Oswald's Smith & Wesson revolver to the exclusion of all other weapons. At the time of his arrest, then, Oswald owned and had in his possession the revolver used to kill Tippit. Also at the time of his arrest, he was carrying in one of his pockets five live .38 Special cartridges.[*]

So we know that not only was Oswald the owner and possessor of the rifle that killed Kennedy, but he was also the owner and possessor of the revolver that killed Tippit. In a city of more than 700,000 people, what is the probability of one of them being the owner and possessor of the weapons that murdered both Kennedy and Tippit, and yet still be innocent of both murders? Aren't we talking about DNA numbers here, like one out of several billion or trillion? Is there a mathematician in the house?

41. Dallas police performed a paraffin test on Oswald's hands at the time of his inter-

---

[*]Just one further observation about the .38 caliber revolver that was used to kill Tippit: As we know, many conspiracy theorists allege, without any evidence to support their allegation, that Oswald's Carcano rifle was planted on the sixth floor of the Book Depository Building by those who, they claim, framed Oswald for Kennedy's murder. But what about the .38 caliber revolver? Oswald himself admitted during his interrogation that after the shooting in Dealey Plaza he went back to his rooming house and got the revolver, the same one he had on his person at the time of his arrest at the Texas Theater. Do conspiracy theorists want us to believe that the framers of Oswald stole Oswald's revolver from him after he left his rooming house with it, murdered Tippit with the revolver, and then between the time of Tippit's murder and Oswald's arrest at the theater somehow got that revolver back into the hands of Oswald, where it was at the time of his arrest? But look, anything is possible.

rogation to determine if he had recently fired a revolver, and the results were positive, indicating the presence of nitrates from gunpowder residue on his hands.[83]

42. When Oswald left the Book Depository Building within minutes after the shooting in Dealey Plaza, he left his blue jacket behind, the jacket being found on December 6, 1963, in a depressed area beneath the windowsill in the domino room on the first floor.[84] Marina Oswald identified the jacket as one of two he owned, the other being a light-colored gray jacket.[85] Several brown head hairs found inside the blue jacket had the same microscopic characteristics as a sample of hair taken from Oswald.[86] Leaving one's jacket behind, particularly where Oswald did, can only go in the direction—though certainly not conclusively—of a consciousness of guilt, not innocence.

43. When Oswald left his rooming house around 1:00 p.m. on the day of the assassination, the housekeeper noticed that he was zipping up his jacket, which he had not been wearing a few minutes earlier when he arrived at the rooming house. When he was arrested around forty-five minutes later, he did not have a jacket. Shortly after Tippit's murder and after Oswald was seen running toward the rear of a Texaco gas station on Jefferson Boulevard, police found a light-colored jacket with a zipper under one of the cars in the parking lot behind the gas station. The last time anyone saw Oswald before he appeared near the Texas Theater was when Mary Brock, the wife of an employee at the gas station, saw him, wearing a light-colored jacket, walk past her into the parking lot at a fast pace.[87] Marina Oswald later identified the jacket as being the second one her husband owned.[88] What is additionally damning to Oswald is that the jacket was found along the path (from Tenth and Patton, south on Patton to Jefferson, then right or west on Jefferson, with a slight detour behind the gas station, then on to the Texas Theater) we know the murderer of Officer Tippit took after the slaying. Finally, dark blue, gray-black, and orange-yellow cotton fibers were found in the inside areas of the sleeves of the jacket, and their microscopic characteristics matched those of the dark blue, gray-black, and orange-yellow cotton fibers composing the brownish shirt that Oswald was wearing at the time of his arrest.[89]

44. Oswald's clipboard was found on the sixth floor after the assassination. Three orders for Scott, Foresman & Company books were on the clipboard, all dated November 22, 1963. Oswald had not filled any of the orders.[90]

Oswald's Own Words during His Interrogation

I told the jury in London that during his interrogation, "Oswald, from his own lips, told us he was guilty. Almost the same as if he had said, 'I murdered President Kennedy.' How did he tell us? Well, the lies he told, one after another, showed an unmistakable consciousness of guilt."[91] Oswald tried very hard to lie his way out of the quickly developing evidence against him. Let's look at some of the more important lies he told, each of which, alone and by itself, is evidence of his guilt because if he were innocent, he wouldn't have had any reason to tell even one of the lies. More often than not in a criminal case, the means a criminal employs to conceal his guilt (here, Oswald's words) are the precise means that reveal his culpability.

45. Oswald lied when he denied purchasing the Carcano rifle from Klein's Sporting Goods Company in Chicago. He even denied owning any rifle at all.[92] Since Oswald knew he had killed Kennedy with that Carcano rifle, he knew he had no choice but to deny that the rifle was his. (It's interesting to note that although Oswald himself knew the obvious,

that ownership of the murder weapon was tantamount to identifying himself as Kennedy's killer, his countless defenders in the conspiracy community apparently do not realize this.)

46. When Oswald was shown a backyard photograph of himself holding the Mannlicher-Carcano rifle, he lied and said it was not he holding the rifle, that someone had superimposed his face on someone else's body.[93]

47. He also lied when he said he had never seen the photograph before, even though handwriting experts concluded it was Oswald's handwriting on the back of a copy of the photograph that was found among the personal effects of a friend of Oswald's who later died.[94]

48. Oswald consciously tried to distance himself from the murder weapon so much that he apparently even went to the following extreme: He and Marina and their daughter June lived at the apartment on Elsbeth Street in Dallas for exactly four months (November 3, 1962, to March 3, 1963),[95] and then moved to the apartment on Neely Street for close to two months (March 3, 1963, to April 24, 1963).[96] However, when he was asked to furnish all of his previous residences since his return from Russia, and the approximate time he lived at each, he gave all of them (including his residences in Fort Worth and New Orleans) with one notable exception. He omitted any reference to the Neely residence, the residence, of course, where he knew his wife had photographed him with the murder weapon in the backyard. He cleverly accounted for the close to two months at Neely by saying he lived *seven* months (not the actual four) at Elsbeth.[97] And when Captain Fritz, during his interrogation of Oswald, asked Oswald about the Neely address, Oswald flat-out denied ever living there.[98] All of this, of course, shows a consciousness of guilt on Oswald's part.

49. Oswald denied telling Wesley Frazier that the reason he came to Irving on Thursday night was to get curtain rods for his Dallas apartment.[99]

50. He also denied putting any kind of long package or bag on the backseat of Frazier's car on the morning of the assassination, saying he only brought a cheese sandwich and some fruit to work with him. But unfortunately for Oswald, not only did Frazier see him put the long package in the car, but Frazier's sister, Linnie Mae Randle, also saw him put such a package in the car.[100] Oswald also denied carrying any long package or bag into the Book Depository Building, which Frazier saw him do.[101] He also denied telling Frazier that curtain rods were inside the large bag.[102]

Warren Commission critics and defenders of Oswald have always steadfastly maintained that the brown paper bag was too short to contain even a disassembled Carcano. But if the Carcano was not in the bag that Frazier and his sister, Linnie Mae Randle, saw Oswald place in the backseat, and something nonincriminating was, instead of lying and saying he never placed a large bag or any other bag on the backseat, why didn't Oswald admit placing the bag there and simply tell Captain Fritz what *was* in the bag? To put it succinctly, if Oswald's rifle wasn't in that bag, he wouldn't have had any reason to lie and say that he did not put the bag on the backseat of Frazier's car and did not carry it into the building that day.

51. Oswald told Fritz that the only thing he brought to work on the morning of the assassination was his lunch, but we know from Frazier that this was the only day he noticed that Oswald did not bring his lunch.[103]

52. Oswald told Fritz that at the time the president was shot, he was having lunch on the first floor with "Junior" (James Jarman Jr.) and another employee he did not identify, but Jarman testified that he did not have lunch with Oswald, that he ate alone.[104]

53. Oswald told Fritz he had bought his .38 caliber Smith & Wesson revolver in Fort Worth,[105] when he actually purchased it from a mail-order house in Los Angeles.[106]

Not that the case against Oswald, which is already absolutely conclusive, needs any more strengthening, but the fact that Oswald never was able to offer any evidence at all to exonerate himself is itself evidence of his guilt. For instance, if, as the conspiracy theorists allege, Oswald was set up, and he knew he had been, then surely he would have known or at least have had some idea who framed him. Yet as we've seen, during his time in custody, instead of trying to clear himself by pointing to the identity of those who allegedly framed him, Oswald dug an even deeper hole for himself by telling one provable lie after another, showing a consciousness of guilt. Is that believable? Obviously, not. Oswald never put the hat on anyone because the hat only fit him. Even if he had no idea at all who framed him (which would be unlikely), if he knew he didn't kill Kennedy with the Carcano rifle, why didn't he, in anger, say something like this to the police questioning him: "Yes, the Carcano is my rifle, but someone stole it from where I had it in Ruth Paine's garage. Find the SOB who stole my rifle and you'll have the person who shot and killed Kennedy."

It should also be noted that after more than four decades of searching by the conspiracy theorists, they haven't been able to come up with one speck of credible evidence that some *other* person killed Kennedy, which is additional circumstantial evidence of Oswald's guilt. As Warren Commission member Allen Dulles told *Look* magazine in 1966, "If the Commission critics have found another assassin, let them name names and produce their evidence." Author Jim Moore asks simply, "If Oswald is innocent, who did shoot President Kennedy and officer Tippit?"[107]

If Oswald didn't kill Kennedy and someone else did, how is it possible that there are, as I've set forth, *fifty-three* pieces of evidence pointing toward his guilt, and after close to forty-four years of an enormously massive investigation, not one single piece of evidence pointing toward the guilt of anyone else? Indeed, even though, as we've seen, everything Oswald did and said reeked of guilt, *who else in Dallas that day was acting and talking guilty?* No one. No one at all except Lee Harvey Oswald. By the way, knowing the conspiracy theorists as I have come to know them, I can assure you that if any one of the fifty-three pieces of evidence against Oswald presented here existed against some third party, that one piece, all by its lonesome, would be more than enough to convince the conspiracy community that he, not Oswald, was the killer of Kennedy.

Coupled with all the evidence set forth, if anyone ever had the psychological profile of a presidential assassin, it was Lee Harvey Oswald. Here is someone who, as I point out in the "Motive" section of this book, not only had a propensity for violence (his attempted murder of Major General Edwin Walker seven months before the assassination, his threat to blow up the FBI building around two weeks before November 22, 1963), but also was emotionally and psychologically unhinged; was a bitter, frustrated, and beaten-down loser who felt alienated from society and couldn't get along with anyone, including his wife; irrationally viewed himself in a historical light, having visions of grandeur and of changing the world; was one whose political ideology consumed his daily life, causing him to keep time to his own drummer in a lonely obsession with Marxism and Castro's Cuba; and hated his country and its representatives to such an extent that he defected to one of the most undesirable places on earth. If someone with not just one but all of these characteristics is not the most likely candidate to be a presidential assassin, then who would be?

As we all know from reading the newspapers and watching the nightly news, with so many killers, including mass murderers, the discovery of their crimes is oftentimes met by incredulity on the part of neighbors, coworkers, and friends. But when Warren Commission counsel asked Fort Worth lawyer Max Clark, who knew Oswald, if, based on his knowledge of Oswald, he thought he was capable of killing Kennedy, Clark replied, "Definitely. I think he would have done this to President Kennedy or anyone else if he felt it would make him infamous."[108] Oswald's disposition, personality, and virulent beliefs were such that when Michael Paine, Ruth Paine's husband, heard of the assassination, he immediately "felt cold sweats." Although he felt he probably was not involved, he thought of Oswald "as soon as I heard the Texas School Book Depository Building mentioned," and "was nervous . . . wondering whether Oswald would do it."[109] Would that thought enter your mind if you learned the president had been shot from a building where a friend or acquaintance of yours worked? John Hall testified before the Warren Commission that when he and his Russian wife, Elena, and Max Clark and his wife, Gali, all friends of Lee and Marina's, learned over television that the authorities believed Oswald had murdered the president, "We said, 'I am not surprised at all. That is the kind of guy that would do something like that.'"[110] And although there were some exceptions, this was generally the feeling among the people who knew him.

Even UPI correspondent Aline Mosby, who met Oswald only once, when she interviewed him in his Moscow hotel room, said, "I was not surprised" when she received a phone call on the night of November 22, 1963, informing her that Oswald was a suspect in the president's slaying.[111] Think of anyone you know or have ever known. Do any of them even remotely come close to Oswald as the type of person who you would not be shocked to learn had killed the president of the United States?

How exceedingly instructive and illuminating it is that those who knew Oswald personally felt that he was the exact type of person who would kill the president, and weren't surprised at all by his arrest. And they felt this way without even being aware of the massive evidence against him that would eventually be gathered. Yet conspiracy theorists and Warren Commission critics around the country, not one of whom knew Oswald, and who are aware of all the evidence against him, are convinced he is innocent.

I told the jury in London, "Ladies and gentlemen of the jury, if Lee Harvey Oswald had nothing to do with President Kennedy's assassination, and was framed, this otherwise independent and defiant would-be revolutionary who disliked taking orders from anyone turned out to be the most willing and cooperative framee in the history of mankind, because the evidence of his guilt is so monumental that he could just as well have gone around with a large sign on his back, declaring in bold letters, 'I just murdered President John F. Kennedy.' Anyone, anyone who would believe that Lee Harvey Oswald was innocent would believe someone who told them that they once heard a cow speaking the Spanish language." I went on to ask the jury, "If Oswald was framed, how could these phantom framers have gotten Oswald, who was supposed to be totally innocent, to act like the guiltiest person imaginable? For instance, how did they get him to tell one lie after another when he was taken into custody, such as that he did not own a rifle, that it wasn't he in the backyard photo, that he never carried a large package into the building that day, et cetera? How, exactly, if Oswald is not guilty, did they get Oswald, within forty-five minutes after the assassination, to murder Officer Tippit? Or was he framed for that murder too?"[112] I mean, why would Oswald, who supposedly, per the conspiracists, was only a patsy for Kennedy's murder, decide, on his own, to murder Tippit?

The case against Oswald consists of both direct evidence and circumstantial evidence. It is so overwhelming and absolute that even his own brother Robert felt constrained to say in 1993 that "a struggle . . . has gone on with me for almost thirty years now. This is mind over heart . . . The facts are there. And I say to people who want to distort the facts, . . . I say, 'What do you do with his rifle? What do you do with his pistol? . . . What do you do with his actions?' To me, you can't reach but one conclusion. There's hard physical evidence there. It's good that people raise questions and say, 'Wait a minute. Let's take a second look at this.' I think that's great, you know? But when you take the second look and the third and the fortieth and the fiftieth—hey, enough's enough. It's there. Put it to rest."[113] But, of course, enough is never enough for the Warren Commission critics and conspiracy theorists. Enough isn't even an hors d'oeuvre. Ten years later, Robert Oswald added, "He was my kid brother . . . If I had the facts that Lee was innocent, I would be out there shouting it loud and clear. It is my belief, my conviction, no one but Lee was involved, period."[114]

British author John Sparrow observes how conspiracy theorists and critics of the Warren Commission, when faced with the overwhelming evidence of Oswald's guilt, are "compelled, in order to supplant the story told by the [Warren] Commission, to treat as [erroneous] or perjured the testimony of witness after witness, and to brand as accomplices in the conspiracy one party after another, each less likely than the last, until the structure becomes top-heavy and collapses under its own weight."[115]

I can tell the readers of this book that if anyone in the future maintains to them that Oswald was just a patsy and did not kill Kennedy, that person is either unaware of the evidence against Oswald or simply a very silly person. Indeed, any denial of Oswald's guilt is not worthy of serious discussion.

Since we can be absolutely sure that Oswald killed Kennedy, he could not have been a "patsy" (i.e., he could not have been "framed") as many conspiracy theorists love to say. By definition, you can't frame someone who is guilty; you frame *innocent* people. To frame, per the dictionary, means "to incriminate an innocent person through the use of false evidence." Since we know Oswald was guilty, we thereby know that no other person or persons killed Kennedy and framed Oswald for the murder they committed.* Therefore, the only remaining issue worthy of discussion is whether Oswald acted alone, that is, whether he was a part of a conspiracy to murder the president.

---

*Since you can't frame a guilty person, what I'm about to say is unnecessary, but one of the very first thoughts I had when I started preparing for the London trial, I ended up articulating for the jury in my final summation. The backdrop is that my opposing counsel, Gerry Spence, was suggesting to the jury that Oswald was framed by sophisticated people; and there were the two facts that although Oswald was a good shot, he was not an expert rifleman, and though the Carcano was a decent rifle, it was not a great rifle. I argued in my final summation to the jury in London, "I ask Mr. Spence, if the conspirators who [supposedly] framed Oswald were so sophisticated and intelligent, wouldn't they make sure that the person they framed was someone whose skill with a rifle was absolutely beyond question, and wouldn't they also make sure that the person they were seeking to frame possessed a modern, expensive rifle that unquestionably had the capacity to get the job done? Wouldn't they have to know, in advance, that failing to do either one of these things would automatically raise a question about whether the person they were seeking to frame was guilty, and therefore be self-defeating? You don't have to have a PhD in logic to know this. Even someone with not too much furniture upstairs would know this. Mr. Spence can't have it both ways. If the people who set Oswald up were so sophisticated as to come up with this incredibly elaborate conspiracy—I mean, to the point where they had people, according to Mr. Spence, who could superimpose Oswald's head on someone else's body, they had imposters down in Mexico City, and so forth—if they were that bright, why weren't they intelligent enough to know the most obvious thing of all? That you don't attempt to frame a man of questionable marksmanship ability who possesses a nineteen-dollar mail-order rifle?" (Transcript of *On Trial*, July 25, 1986, pp. 1056–1057)

BOOK TWO

Delusions of Conspiracy

What Did Not Happen

Introduction to Conspiracy

> One never speaks of this assassination without making
> reckless judgments . . . The absurdity of the accusations,
> the total lack of evidence, nothing stops them . . . One
> must read everything with mistrust.
>
> > —Voltaire, speaking about the incredible stories
> > and conspiracy theories surrounding the
> > assassination of King Henri IV of France[1]

Populus vult decipi—"The public is ready to be deceived."

The following was posted on the Internet on June 22, 2002:

How can Mr. Bugliosi possibly prove the preposterous negative[*] that a conspiracy did not exist in the murder of J.F.K. and that one doesn't continue to exist in the cover up? I don't feel that his work, long in progress, whether it is two volumes or twenty-six volumes, can successfully navigate the mire of evidence and controversial evidence which confronts him. It seems to me that the evidence is conspiracy and the controversial evidence is the Warren Report. Perhaps we will never see this work! I have very much been an admirer of Mr. B's previous work and have purchased and read everything to date that he has published. Perhaps also Mr. Bugliosi's ego cannot tolerate the forthcoming mass of criticism which he must acknowledge will arise. Had he, on the other hand, decided to take the opposite tack in this study, his book would have long since been published and probably given conspiracy an even greater impetus than Oliver Stone's movie.

---

[*]One frequently hears that "it is impossible to prove a negative." But this, of course, is pure myth. In some situations, as in the murder of President Kennedy, it is impossible, but in many situations in life it is very easy. For instance, in a criminal case where a defendant says he did not commit the robbery or burglary, or what have you, because he was somewhere else at the time, the prosecution routinely proves the negative (that he was not somewhere else) by establishing through witnesses, fingerprints, DNA, or sometimes even film, that he did commit the crime and was not where he said he was at the time it happened.

On an even more obvious level, if someone were to say, "I have [or do not have] pancreatic cancer," medical tests can disprove this (i.e., prove the negative), if such be the case.

In the Kennedy case, I believe the absence of a conspiracy can be proved to a virtual certainty.

James Fetzer, PhD, is the editor of the only exclusively scientific books (three) on the assassination. David Mantik, MD, PhD, is among the leading conspiracy researchers and writers in the current conspiracy community. They are both good and sincere men. Dr. Fetzer wrote me on January 23, 2001: "*What Would It Take*, David Mantik has asked me to inquire of you. What would it take to convince you of the existence of a conspiracy and cover-up in the death of JFK? What would it take to persuade you of Oswald's innocence, which is not necessarily the same thing? Are none of our major discoveries—our '16 smoking guns,' for example—convincing? And, if not, why? And, if not, then *what would it take*?"

Only evidence, Drs. Fetzer and Mantik. Only evidence.

Over the past forty-four years, close to one thousand books have been published on the assassination. What follows is the first anti-conspiracy *book*. Lest there be any confusion, several books have taken an anti-conspiracy *position*, but the mere taking of the position with very little supporting text does not make the book an anti-conspiracy *book*. Let me illustrate this (as I must do to support what would seem to be an otherwise incredible assertion—that this is the *first* anti-conspiracy book) with reference to the two best-known books with an anti-conspiracy position. In his book *Conspiracy of One*, Jim Moore devotes one *sentence* (not one page) to rebut the main argument of the conspiracy theorists that the CIA was behind Kennedy's murder; nothing to the FBI, or Castro, or anti-Castro Cuban exiles; two sentences to organized crime; nothing to the military-industrial complex or KGB; and so on. In all deference to Mr. Moore, who wrote a fine book, if you title it *Conspiracy of One*, meaning you believe Oswald acted alone and there was no conspiracy, you have to set forth the various conspiracy theories (e.g., CIA, organized crime, KGB, etc.) and then attempt to refute them. Three sentences (I may have missed a few others) in an entire book just won't do.

Gerald Posner, in *Case Closed*, does much better than Moore, but again, his book cannot be considered an anti-conspiracy *book* (except in the sense of maintaining throughout, as Posner's and Moore's books and several others do, that Oswald killed Kennedy and had no confederates, and seeking to show the fallacy of many contentions made by the conspiracy community). Posner devotes only approximately 50 pages of his 607-page book (again, I may be off by a few pages) to refuting the various conspiracy theories. But at least half of those pages are spent on rebutting New Orleans district attorney Jim Garrison's charges; Posner does not address and try to disprove the theories of right-wing, military-industrial complex, or anti-Castro Cuban exile involvement in the assassination, and though he makes several passing references to the CIA ("CIA domestic spying," "CIA received information," etc.), I could not collectively find more than two or three full pages in his entire book, if that, where it could inferentially be said he was attacking one of the very most important allegations of all, that of CIA complicity in the assassination. Devoting approximately 8 percent of one's book, as Posner does, to presenting evidence and arguments to refute the many conspiracy theories in the murder of John F. Kennedy would not seem to qualify it as an anti-conspiracy *book*.

So the curious and rather remarkable fact remains that with the majority of Americans believing there was a conspiracy in the murder of President Kennedy, and with hundreds upon hundreds of books having been written on the president's murder, no previous author has seen fit to tackle the issue head-on and knock down all the various alleged conspiracies. That clearly is not a boast, just a plain fact that I believe is worth noting about the Kennedy case.

Before going any further, I should define just what a conspiracy is, something that virtually all readers already have a general sense of. The main element of a criminal conspiracy is simply two or more people getting together (they don't have to physically meet or utter any magic words—all that is required is a "meeting of the minds," which can be proved by the circumstantial evidence of their words and/or conduct) and *agreeing to commit a crime.* (To the ever suspicious conspiracy theorists, the definition of a conspiracy is two people talking to each other on a street corner.) For a conspiracy to exist under the law, the prosecutor has to prove one additional element of the crime of conspiracy: that at least one member of the conspiracy committed some "overt act" to carry out the object of the conspiracy (the overt act doesn't have to be unlawful; e.g., in a conspiracy to commit a bank robbery, buying gas for the getaway car would suffice). The purpose of this requirement is to allow the individuals who have agreed to commit the crime an opportunity to terminate the agreement before any decisive action is taken in furtherance of it. Once a conspiracy is formed, under the vicarious liability theory of conspiracy each member of the conspiracy is criminally responsible for all crimes committed by the co-conspirators to further the object of the conspiracy, whether or not they themselves committed the crimes. Hence, if A and B conspire to rob a bank or burglarize a home or murder John Jones, and A commits the robbery or burglary or murder while B is in Madagascar playing volleyball, B is equally criminally responsible for the robbery, burglary, or murder. And if, for instance, A and B conspire to rob a bank, and A kills the bank teller who resists the robbery, B (whether driving the getaway car or playing in Madagascar) is responsible not just for the robbery, the only thing B agreed to, but also the murder, since the murder was committed by A "to further the object of the conspiracy," which was robbery.

The belief in conspiracy (derived from the Latin word *conspirare*, "to breathe together") has appealed to those of liberal as well as conservative mind, to the uneducated as well as the intellectual elite,[*] and has been with humanity—if not in name, then in the sensing of it—since the beginning of time. Witness, for example, the title of a 1798 book by one John Robison, a professor of natural philosophy who was the secretary to the Royal Society of Edinburgh: *Proofs Of A Conspiracy Against All The Religions And Governments Of Europe, Carried On In The Secret Meetings Of Free Masons, Illuminati, And Reading Societies.*

When the term *conspiracy* is applied by one group of people to another (e.g., by Hitler's regime to those in the Third Reich trying to kill him and thereby end the Second World War), the emphasis is always on the hidden, the concealed, not that which is in the open. No one would have said that the Ku Klux Klan was "conspiring" against blacks, or that today's political parties (Democrat and Republican) are "conspiring" against each other.

---

[*]For instance, in the Kennedy case, if a brilliant man like Great Britain's Bertrand Russell, a towering figure in the field of mathematical philosophy and intellectual thought (whose fourth wife, Lady Russell, never forgave a friend who said on television that Russell did not outshine Plato), can say with conviction that "an innocent man [referring to Oswald] was framed and gunned down" (Lewis, "Tragedy of Bertrand Russell," pp.30, 32), you know the idiocy over this case has not discriminated against any mental category of people.

Thus, with the Kennedy case, the main belief is that *hidden* elements in the CIA, military-industrial complex, organized crime, and so forth, got together for the purpose of killing Kennedy. And it has been the objective of thousands of assassination researchers since 1963—in most cases their raison d'etre—to bring these hidden conspirators out into the open so they can face justice.

What causes such a ready suspicion of conspiracy? This has been the subject of several books, which generally conclude that its genesis is in such realities as innate human paranoia and cultural dispositions toward paranoia.* With respect to the latter, many of the conspiracy allegations in the Kennedy case (accepted by millions of Americans far outside the conspiracy community) may be influenced by a distrust of those in power that arguably has deep roots in the thinking that gave birth to this nation. The Declaration of Independence, adopted by the Continental Congress on July 4, 1776, asserts, in its Bill of Indictment, that the "history of the present King of Great Britain [King George III] is a history of repeated injuries . . . abuses and usurpations, all having in direct object the establishment of an absolute tyranny over these states." In the Kennedy case, the belief in conspiracy has certainly been aided and abetted by the confluence of other historical events, such as the cold war intrigue of spies and secret agents, as well as the Watergate and Iran-Contra scandals, the latter two generating an increased distrust of the federal government.[2]

In his book *The Paranoid Style in American Politics and Other Essays*, Richard Hofstadter writes that "the typical procedure of the higher paranoid scholarship is to start with defensible assumptions." He goes on to say, in an observation tailor-made for the conspiracy theorists in the Kennedy case, that "the paranoid mentality is far more coherent than the real world, since it leaves no room for mistakes, failures or ambiguities . . . It believes it is up against an enemy who is as infallibly rational as he is totally evil, and it seeks to match his imputed total competence with its own, leaving nothing unexplained and comprehending all of reality in one overreaching, consistent theory." Hofstadter says the "qualities" of the paranoid style are "heated exaggeration, suspiciousness, and conspiratorial fantasy," and a "heroic striving for 'evidence' to prove that the unbelievable is the only thing that can be believed."[3]

Author Mark Fenster feels that one reason for the success of major conspiracy theories is that they tell a "gripping, dramatic story . . . The conspiracy narrative is compelling in its . . . focus on the actions of the perpetrators of the evil conspiracy and [on] the defender of the moral order."[4]

Warren Commission staff member Richard M. Mosk, in his article "Conspiracy Theories and the JFK Assassination: Cashing in on Political Paranoia," adds that the Kennedy conspiracy theories "allow full scope for the exploitation of political prejudices. No target could be more welcome to the intellectual left than the Texas oil plutocracy, the radical right, the FBI and the CIA. [Likewise], the [political] right could not dream of better suspects than Castro or Russia."[5] Also, it is the view of many liberals and not a few moderates that a moral degeneration of American government started with Kennedy's death (e.g., Vietnam, Cambodia, Watergate, etc.). The continuing angst of these believers requires something large in the body politic against whom they can apply their a priori reasoning.

---

*A far more mundane reason may simply be that the masses, trying to make some sense out of events that are not to their liking, find that a conspiracy theory they can easily understand or adopt, and which fits a bias of theirs, often explains things very well.

An emotionally disturbed misfit and non-entity like Oswald inherently lacks gravitas. But dark, powerful, sinister forces like the CIA and military-industrial complex, out to destroy our individual freedoms and American way of life, fit just fine. Thus, these people were (and are) much more receptive, even eager, to buy the conspiracy theory of the assassination. Indeed, apart from the belief in a conspiracy in the Kennedy case being literally forced on people by the one-sided bombardment of allegations, there is the natural sense among nearly all humans that great events have to have great causes. A lone nut just doesn't work in the calculus of the Kennedy assassination. Or, as Boston University historian Robert Dallek put it, "It's been very difficult to believe that someone as inconsequential as Oswald could have killed someone as consequential as Kennedy."[6]

None of the above is to suggest that there aren't such things as conspiracies. They happen all the time, and in very serious crimes. John Wilkes Booth was the leader of the conspiracy to kill Abraham Lincoln. The CIA conspired with organized crime to kill Cuban dictator Fidel Castro. In the famous Dreyfus affair at the end of the nineteenth century in France (the case that most Kennedy assassination conspiracy theorists so often compare to the Kennedy case), several high-ranking French military officers conspired to frame Alfred Dreyfus, a Jewish army officer, for "high treason" in revealing French military secrets to Germany. (The French Supreme Court ultimately declared Dreyfus innocent in 1906.) I could name a great number of other conspiracies. So actual conspiracies are common. I myself have convicted criminal defendants of the crime of conspiracy to commit murder.

This book thus far has conclusively established one point, that Oswald killed Kennedy, and inferentially established another, that he acted alone. I say *inferentially* because if our thoughts are going to be governed by common sense on this issue, we would agree that no group of top-level conspirators would ever employ someone as unstable and unreliable as Oswald to commit the biggest murder in history, no such group would ever provide its hit man with, or allow him to use, a twelve-dollar rifle to get the job done, and any such group would help its hit man escape or have a car waiting for him to drive him to his death, not allow him to be wandering out in the street, catching cabs and buses to get away, as we know Oswald did.

Because of this reality, no matter what some person or group did or said before or after the assassination that might be deemed suspicious and indicative of a conspiracy, we know there is an innocent explanation for it that is unconnected to any conspiracy. And anyone who thinks it is connected, and that it points to some group as being the conspirators behind the assassination, necessarily has to be willing to also conclude that the subject conspiratorial group *would* get Oswald to murder Kennedy for them, and *would* only provide him with a cheap, mail-order rifle to get the job done, and *would* make no effort to immediately kill him or help him escape so he wouldn't be arrested and interrogated by law enforcement, as Oswald was. For example, anyone who believes that the Secret Service's spiriting Kennedy's body away from Dallas in violation of Texas law (thereby preventing Texas authorities from examining it) is suspicious and points to a conspiracy (as so many conspiracy theorists do) has to be willing to also conclude that the Secret Service, Kennedy's bodyguards, decided to murder Kennedy, hired Oswald to kill Kennedy, provided him with, or allowed him to use, the cheap rifle he had, and did not make any effort to help him escape. And anyone who is *not* willing to draw all of those inferences should immediately put out of his or her mind any suspicious notion about the Secret Service's conduct in removing Kennedy's body from Texas.

What I am saying is that one of the principal frailties in the thinking processes of the theorists is that they rarely ever carry their suspicions, which are based on some discrepancy, anomaly, or contradiction they find, to their logical conclusion. If they did, they'd see the *reductio ad absurdum* of their position. But for them, if something looks suspicious, that's enough. Instead of asking, "Where does this go?"—that is, where does the discrepancy, contradiction, or whatever, lead them?—they immediately give their minds a breather and conclude that what they find is itself proof of a conspiracy (or proof that Oswald is innocent). The discrepancy or contradiction is the *entire* story. And being the entire story, it by itself discredits the entire twenty-six volumes of the Warren Commission. Nothing else has to be shown or even argued.[*]

A few examples: If conspiracy theorists are told that Oswald's Carcano rifle was a poor and inaccurate rifle and could not have been the murder weapon, they immediately conclude Oswald must be innocent, and hence, was framed. What they don't bother to think about is that if they say this, what they are necessarily also saying is that one of the conspirators must have tapped each of the firearm experts for the Warren Commission and HSCA (a total of nine) on the shoulder and said, "Listen, this weapon [the Carcano] is not the murder weapon, but we want you to say it is," and that all of these experts who were approached agreed to go along with this. But since this absurdity would never have happened, the argument that the Carcano was a poor and inaccurate rifle doesn't, as they say in trial practice, "go anywhere."

The rifle found on the sixth floor was originally identified as a 7.65 Mauser. Over and over again, conspiracy theorists who believe Oswald was framed actually cite this fact as part of their proof—that is, it wasn't Oswald's rifle so he's innocent and was framed. But one moment's reflection (one moment more than almost all conspiracy theorists are willing to give) would cause you to ask, If he was framed, why would the framers place a rifle

---

[*]For conspiracy theorists, all discrepancies, contradictions, anomalies, et cetera, are suspicious, and are the heart and soul of the conspiracy movement. In their universe, everything proceeds perfectly and there is no such thing as human error, incompetence, coincidence, or failure of memory. There are no innocent, benign explanations for anything.

With respect to contradictions, a godsend to all conspiracy researchers, eyewitness authority Elizabeth Loftus writes, "If a hundred people were to see the same automobile accident, no two reports [of this] would be identical" on all the details (Loftus, *Eyewitness Testimony*, p.153). This reality of human cognition, that different people see and hear the same event differently, has proved to be the richest of troves for the scavenging Warren Commission critics and conspiracy theorists. Author Quentin Reynolds writes in his book *Courtroom*, "No two persons will give the same account of an incident they both witnessed. They will paint a door black, blue and green, and give more varieties of weather for the same day than the weather bureau does for all the days of the year. They vary the time of the day by minutes or hours. They differ in their measurement of space by inches, feet and miles" (Reynolds, *Courtroom*, p.186). As psychologist and philosopher William James said, "Whilst part of what we perceive comes from the object before us, another part always comes out of our mind."

Warren Commission counsel David Belin points out that because our eyes are not perfect cameras that can recall exactly what took place in a matter of seconds, "if you get two conflicting stories with two witnesses, you can imagine how many arise when there are hundreds of witnesses to a sudden event, as there were in Dealey Plaza on November 22, 1963. Almost anyone who wants to concoct a theory can find one or two witnesses who might support his theory" (Belin, *Final Disclosure*, p.14).

A substantial majority of the conspiracy community is also extremely gullible, believing every story they hear without bothering to check it to see if it is accurate or makes any sense. As long as the story helps their theory, they buy it. They would improve the quality of their research appreciably by simply embracing rule number one of the journalistic profession: "If your mama says she loves you, check it out."

on the sixth floor that was not Oswald's, one that no one could ever connect him to? And if they didn't place or plant it there, how could they possibly think they could successfully frame him if they knew a rifle belonging to someone else was found on the sixth floor? Conspiracy theorists never bother to ask and attempt to answer such obvious questions. Instead, they find it so much easier to make a silly allegation and then simply move on—to their next silly observation.

Another example among countless others: To say, as conspiracy theorists do, that the backyard photo of Oswald, dressed in black with a rifle and revolver, is a composite photo is to also say that Marina Oswald was part of the conspiracy to frame her husband, since Marina says she took the photo. But the notion that Marina was part of any conspiracy to frame her husband for Kennedy's murder is absurd on its face, so the argument that the backyard photo is a composite "doesn't go anywhere"—that is, unless you are willing to say that Marina was, indeed, part of said conspiracy. If people want to use such absurdity and illogic as their guide in analyzing the assassination, I submit that they should not have a ticket into the theater of serious debate on the assassination. The price of admission to the debate, as it were, should be sense, not nonsense.

Not only do the considerable number of conspiracy theories in the Kennedy assassination do violence to the facts and the evidence, but conspiracy theorists, in welcoming as many people and groups as they can get under their tent, are rarely troubled by the fact that many of their theories are incompatible with each other. For instance, if the KGB did it, doesn't that eliminate the theory that the CIA (sworn enemies of the KGB during the cold war) or America's military-industrial complex did it? If organized crime did it, doesn't that eliminate the theory that the Secret Service or LBJ was behind the assassination? I mean, the Secret Service (which is *not* the CIA) is sitting down with the Mafia to kill Kennedy? Please.

Indeed, in addition to conspiracy theories being incompatible with each other, conspiracy theorists are so immediately taken by and enamored of events they can't explain that they blindly find no problem drawing a conclusion of conspiracy that inherently contradicts some other conclusion of theirs. One example among a great many: In his book *"They've Killed the President!"* Robert Anson tries hard to convince the reader that the CIA was not alarmed when Oswald, arriving in Moscow, offered to furnish the Soviets information on U.S. radar, because Oswald was probably working for the CIA (i.e., whatever information he gave the Soviets would be incorrect or valueless). But then, in the very next paragraph, he asks the reader to entertain the possibility that since the Russians had never shot down a U-2 before May 1, 1960, which was seven months after Oswald arrived in Moscow, there may have been a "connection between Oswald, the purveyor of radar secrets, and the Russians' unaccustomed accuracy." In other words, Oswald is now working with the KGB. But then remarkably, Anson goes back to suggesting that Oswald was working for the CIA when he says, "The U-2 incident was all the more reason [for the CIA] to question Oswald [which the CIA did not do] on his return to the United States . . . There would have been no need for the Agency to interview Oswald, of course, if they knew . . . why he had gone to the Soviet Union, and what he had done there—the things they would have known if he had been one of their agents."[7] So does Anson, then, want us to believe that the CIA had Oswald give the KGB radar information that enabled the Russians to shoot down a CIA agent's U-2? Not really. Anson, in his eagerness to go on to his next discrepancy, coincidence, unexplained event, et cetera, wouldn't have taken the time to ask himself that question.

An absolute staple of the conspiracy community—no, a sine qua non, that without which they could not survive—is the interesting but ultimately unproductive and ridiculous notion that if A knows B and B knows C, then A is meaningfully connected to C, which of course is a non sequitur. In fact, the theorists go beyond the above equation. Not only is A connected to C, but whatever nefarious deed C has done (all the more so with B), A must have done also. (Actually, conspiracy theorists frequently go beyond A-B-C into D, E, and F.) So if Jack Ruby is a friend of Dallas mobster Joe Campisi, and Campisi has underworld connections to New Orleans Mafia chieftain Carlos Marcello, then if they posit that Marcello was behind the assassination, it becomes irresistible to the theorists that Ruby must have been involved with Marcello in the assassination or the cover-up.

Here are just two examples representative of literally thousands of A-B-C (and D, E, and F) situations that the conspiracy theorists set forth in their books: Conspiracy author Peter Dale Scott believes that Dallas oilmen, Jack Ruby, and J. Edgar Hoover, along with many others, may have been part of a conspiracy to murder Kennedy. In support of this, he writes, "A businessman told the FBI that Ruby had once introduced him to Dallas businessman E. E. Fogelson and his wife, Greer Garson. Fogelson was a member of the 'Del Charro set.' This was a group of Texas millionaires who frequented [Texas oilman] Clint Murchison's resort, the Hotel Del Charro, near Murchison's racetrack, the Del Mar, in La Jolla, California. Clint Murchison and some of his associates would pay for the annual racing holidays of their good friend J. Edgar Hoover."[8]

Clay Shaw (like thousands of American businessmen who traveled to foreign countries and agreed to submit reports once they returned providing information that might be of interest to the CIA's nonclandestine Domestic Contact Service) wrote in reports dated June 14, 1949, and June 29, 1951, that while in Nicaragua he "heard General Somoza's cattle monopoly bitterly criticized by businessmen in Managua," and while in Buenos Aires he was told that "Juan Peron and Evita are each jealous of the other's power and that they maintain separate and independent political organizations." Conspiracy author William Davy, who believes Clay Shaw was involved in Kennedy's assassination, writes, "*Curiously*, both Somoza and Juan Peron were patients and friends of Shaw's close associate, Dr. Alton Ochsner . . . Ochsner is best known for his association with Ed Butler and the Information Council of the Americas, or INCA . . . INCA was composed of several members of the New Orleans elite. These included . . . Eustis and William B. Reily. The Reily family owned William B. Reily & Co., makers of Luzianne coffee. It was at Reily's where Oswald found work as a machine greaser in the summer of 1963."[9]

Under this infantile reasoning in which guilt by association is elevated to an art form, one should watch whom one has dinner with. If A, a surgeon, is friendly and has frequent dinners with B, the president of a major corporation, then if B ends up embezzling millions from his corporation, A must have been involved too.

Just for example, Dallas police officer Joe Cody, a friend of Jack Ruby's, said, "Yes, Jack knew the Campisis [Joe, whom some believed to be a Dallas organized-crime figure, and his brother Sam], and I'd seen them together on numerous occasions. Jack ate out there at the Egyptian Lounge [owned by the Campisis]. Sometimes Joe Campisi would sit with him. If I came in, I'd sit with Jack Ruby and Joe Campisi. We all knew each other well." So since Cody was friendly with Campisi and it turns out Campisi with Marcello, if Marcello had Kennedy killed, I suppose Officer Cody must have also been involved, right? Better yet, a friend of Ruby's, Pat Morgan, told a Ruby biographer that one night Ruby took him to a big "Italian Night" party "that all the important people of Dallas attended. He took me over and introduced me to [Dallas] Mayor [Earle] Cabell and to Judge Joe B. Brown, who later tried his case. They [Cabell and Brown] were sitting with Joe Campisi."[10]* So now, apparently, since we've connected Cabell and Brown with Campisi, and Campisi with Marcello, they must have also been in on the plot to kill Kennedy.

And if you want an even closer connection to Marcello, Dallas County deputy sheriff Al Maddox says, "One day I was in Joe Campisi's office and he called Carlos [Marcello] on the phone and I talked to Carlos on the phone." I reckon that makes Maddox just dead in the water guilty, along with Marcello, of Kennedy's murder.[11]

How about this: Although there is no credible evidence that Campisi was a mobster (see section on Jack Ruby and organized crime later in text), it is known that Joe Civello (not Joe Campisi) was head of the Dallas Mafia, whatever there was of it. Indeed, Civello, who knew Ruby, was present at the Mafia summit meeting in Apalachin, New York, in November of 1957, which was also attended by Florida Mafia chieftain Santo Trafficante, whom a considerable number of conspiracy theorists believe was behind the assassination. Yet Dallas police sergeant Patrick Dean *volunteered* to HSCA investigators that even though he knew of Civello's background, he was a dinner guest one night of Civello's "at one of them Italian get-togethers when they have, you know, a big dinner."[12] Since Civello was connected to Trafficante, and Dean was a friend of Civello's, maybe Dean was in on the alleged plot to murder JFK, right?

Remarkably, even sensible, intelligent people, such as HSCA chief counsel Robert Blakey, who personally believes Marcello was behind Kennedy's assassination, unthinkingly invoke the buffs' A-B-C reasoning to support their position. On *Frontline*'s 1993 show "Who Was Lee Harvey Oswald?" Blakey said, "When you find David Ferrie, who is an investigator for Carlos Marcello, being a boyhood friend to Lee Harvey Oswald, and with him that summer, and with Carlos Marcello at that very point in time, you have an immediate connection between a man [Marcello] who had the motive, opportunity, and means to kill Kennedy and the man [Oswald] who killed Kennedy."[13] What?!?†

Although common sense alone should tell conspiracy theorists that knowing someone or even being friendly with him is no evidence of a connection to his criminal activity, that you have to show the two were involved with each other in the same enterprise, there is another fascinating phenomenon that the conspiracy theorists must be aware of but seem determined not to acknowledge. I'm referring to the curious but undeniable reality that virtually any two people chosen at random can be connected to each other by the interposition of a very small number of mutual friends or acquaintances. For instance, although most readers of this book don't know and haven't ever met President Bush, they might very well know someone who knows him, or know someone who knows someone who knows him. Hence, most of us are only two, three, or four intermediaries removed from the president of the United States. This reality is the reason why most of us, at one time or another,

*Morgan added, "I don't think he knew these people [Cabell and Brown] except to shake hands with—but he knew them all at least that far. He used to say to me, 'You know, Pat, considering my background, it's really amazing I have come so far'" (Wills and Demaris, *Jack Ruby*, p.43).

†To dilute the connection even further, Ferrie was not an investigator for Carlos Marcello. He was an investigator for lawyer G. Wray Gill, and Gill had Ferrie work on an immigration lawsuit against Marcello in which Gill was representing Marcello. Also, there is no credible evidence that Ferrie was ever a boyhood friend of Oswald's or was with Oswald in the summer of 1963. But even if these assertions were true, so what? They certainly don't add up to a conspiracy to commit murder.

meet someone new in a distant city or country and discover we have mutual friends or acquaintances. And what do we all say at these moments? "It's a small world."[*]

Indeed, a Harvard-sponsored study in 1967 exploring the theory that all of us are connected by no more than a few people (the so-called six-degrees-of-separation theory) asked this question: "Given any two people in the world, person X and person Z, how many intermediate acquaintance links are needed before X and Z are connected?" Although the study never answered that question definitively with reference to the entire world, the implied answer was "not very many," the Harvard study citing another study by a group of workers at the Massachusetts Institute of Technology for its finding that although there is "only about one chance in 200,000 that any two Americans chosen at random will know each other, amazingly, there is better than a 50-50 chance that any two Americans can be linked up with two intermediate acquaintances." The Harvard empirical study found that on the average, only five intermediate friends or acquaintances were needed to link up any two Americans chosen at random.[14]

I have frequently told juries in cases I prosecuted that they should take their human experience with them into the jury room when they deliberate on the issue of the defendant's guilt, that they didn't have to leave these experiences at the door. Likewise, conspiracy theorists should use their human experience and common sense in addressing the issues in the Kennedy case rather than their pet A-B-C theory.

There are several other ways in which the conspiracy community operates in defiance of logic and common sense. A few: Warren Commission critics and conspiracy theorists are constantly scavenging for something, whether in the eighteen thousand pages of the Warren Commission volumes or anywhere else, that supports their theory. If they find it, they embrace it as the absolute truth even if it is inconsistent with the overwhelming weight of the evidence, including physical, scientific evidence—indeed, even if there are twenty other pieces of evidence showing that their point is wrong. And if someone rejects their "truth" as being erroneous or fraudulent, they simply accuse them of being part of the cover-up or groveling apologists for the Warren Commission.

Also, as former Warren Commission assistant counsel W. David Slawson put it, they love to "prove" their version of events occurred by "showing that it *could* have happened that way, without offering any evidence that it actually did."

The dreadful illogic and superficiality of the conspiracy theorists' modus operandi has inevitably resulted in the following situation: Though they have dedicated their existence to trying to poke holes in the Warren Commission's findings, akin to a defense attorney in a criminal trial trying to raise a reasonable doubt of the defendant's guilt in the jury's mind, they have failed abysmally to tell us (if the Warren Commission was wrong) what actually did happen. In other words, other than blithely tossing out names, they have failed to offer any credible *evidence* of who, if not Oswald, killed Kennedy. Nor have they offered any credible *evidence* at all of who the conspirators behind the assassination were. So after more than forty years, if we were to rely on these silly people, we'd have an assassination without an assassin (since, they assure us, Oswald didn't kill Kennedy), and a conspiracy without conspirators. Not a simple achievement.

---

[*]Or we'll say, "What a coincidence," or "What are the odds of this happening?" But in the world of conspiracy theorists, happenstance and coincidences don't exist. What appears to be a random coincidence is really always complicity. Indeed, perhaps the only coincidence they will acknowledge is that the words *coincidence* and *complicity* each start with the letter *C* and each has four syllables.

To elaborate further on this point, the conspiracy theorists claim to have found a million problems with the Warren Commission's conclusions that Oswald killed Kennedy and acted alone, but not one of them has ever offered a coherent and logical alternative theory as to what did happen. All they can do is point out that such and such a group had a motive; claim that Oswald was a poor shot; allege that Oswald left the Book Depository Building after the shooting in Dealey Plaza because he probably sensed he was being framed; and so on. Their charges, which they have repeated in book after book, usually citing each other as the primary source, could be condensed and put into a thousand-page book titled *Discrepancies, Supposed Coincidences, and Unanswered Questions*. However, the totality of what they have written, with any semblance of credibility, as to what precisely did happen would fill only a page or so of a companion book, if that. And if that is all that the conspiracy community can produce after more than forty years, shouldn't they be finally asking themselves if the reason why they have failed to come up with anything is that nothing exists? Not even Houdini could pull a rabbit out of the hat when there was no rabbit in the hat.

But telling the conspiracy theorists they have failed doesn't phase them at all. In fact, it's like waving a red flag in front of a bull. They are so tenacious and desperate to prove a conspiracy that out of their ranks came a book, published in 2002, that actually contained a purported official CIA internal document in which the CIA confesses to the murder and implicates the FBI and Joint Chiefs of Staff as co-conspirators. In that book, *Regicide*, conspiracy theorist Gregory Douglas claims that Robert T. Crowley, a former CIA assistant deputy director of plans, gave him the document in 1996 with the understanding that it not be published in his lifetime (Crowley died in 2000). Crowley said he was part of the conspiracy, but he apparently had no fear that Douglas would turn on him for fame and fortune, in which case he'd be prosecuted, convicted, and most likely executed. Crowley also apparently didn't mind his surviving family and descendants having to live with the infamy that he had helped orchestrate the murder of Kennedy. After all, it was important to this nation's history that all Americans know what happened. That is why Crowley didn't give the explosive document to publications with a small circulation like the *New York Times*, *Time*, or *Newsweek*, but to Douglas, who had the document published in his book by a giant, international media conglomerate, the Monte Sano Media company of Huntsville, Alabama, which, by the way, isn't listed in the phone directory.

Either Douglas (true name, Peter Stahl) is a fraud, or the person who forged the document is. Apart from the obvious insanity that the CIA would confess in writing to the assassination, the document, dated December 22, 1963, and referenced "Operation Zipper," has no "To" or "From" line, no signature or even signature block, and is not even labeled or stamped "Top Secret" or any other level of confidentiality. You see, the CIA, like Crowley, wanted the world to know its agents had killed Kennedy. One wonders why the agency never called a press conference to announce its having murdered him. Laughably, the forger of the document couldn't even get his grammatical tenses to be consistent. In the first paragraph of the document, he writes, "The removal of the President and the Attorney General from their positions because of high treason *has been* determined"—that is, the assassination hasn't taken place yet. (That murder is contemplated is made clear in paragraph 4, which reads, "Removal by impeachment or other legal means is considered unfeasable [the forger had a spelling problem and no dictionary at his side] and too protracted," and paragraph 5, which reads, "Therefore, an alternative solution has been found to effect this removal.") But paragraph 7 of this very same document reads, "This operation, codenamed ZIPPER, *was* under the direction of James Angleton of the Agency, assisted by Robert Crowley and William Harvey, also of the Agency." The forged, internal CIA document[*] is now suddenly in the past tense, speaking about the assassination that has already taken place, and uproariously informing its CIA readers that Angleton, Crowley, and Harvey are members of the CIA.[15] Can you imagine that, folks? The CIA has *confessed* to Kennedy's murder! And in writing!

It couldn't have been more obvious within hours after the assassination that Oswald had murdered Kennedy, and within no more than a day or so thereafter that he had acted alone. And this is precisely the conclusion that virtually all local (Dallas), state (Texas), and federal (FBI and Secret Service) law enforcement agencies came to shortly after the assassination. Nothing has ever changed their conclusion or proved it wrong.

Apart from the fact that no group of conspirators would ever get someone like Oswald to kill for them, no evidence has ever surfaced even linking Oswald to any of the groups the conspiracy theorists believe to be behind the assassination. But remarkably, many in the debate treat this all-important fact as irrelevant and moot. The reason is grounded in a stark misconception. The biggest mistake, by far, that well-intentioned lay people make in concluding there was a conspiracy in the Kennedy assassination, and the biggest argument, by far, that conspiracy theorists use in their books to support their position of a conspiracy, is to maintain that such and such a group "had a motive" to kill Kennedy and, therefore, must have done it. For instance, one hears that organized crime killed Kennedy out of anger because, after they helped finance his 1960 presidential campaign, he betrayed them by allowing his brother, Attorney General Robert Kennedy, to continue his crusade to destroy them; or that they killed the president "to get Bobby Kennedy off their back." Or, Castro had Kennedy killed to get even with him for the Bay of Pigs invasion or before Kennedy had him killed. Or, the military-industrial complex and the CIA killed Kennedy because he intended to withdraw American troops from Vietnam, and they were fiercely opposed to it.[†] You know, if the president of our country is doing some-

---

[*]It has to be noted that along with the allegation of planted evidence, the other main conspiracy argument conspiracy theorists have made over and over again is that much of the evidence against Oswald was forged or tampered with by the authorities. But not once have the theorists ever proved this allegation. Yet, the very group always shouting forgery and tampering has been caught on many occasions forging documents to make its point in the assassination debate. (See endnote discussion.)

[†]Millions of Americans through the years have mouthed these or similar beliefs. Here's just one example, from President Kennedy's own longtime personal secretary, no less: In an October 7, 1994, letter to Richard Duncan, a high school teacher in Roanoke, Virginia, who had inquired of her state of mind vis-à-vis the assassination, Evelyn Lincoln wrote, "It is my belief that there was a conspiracy because there were those that disliked him and felt the only way to get rid of him was to assassinate him. These five conspirators, in my opinion, were Lyndon B. Johnson, J. Edgar Hoover, the mafia, the CIA, and the Cubans in Florida" (Duncan sent me a copy of the letter on January 23, 1997).

This mind-numbing phenomenon is actually more the rule than the exception with everyday people who watch events from afar. At a reception following a speech I gave around the time of Princess Diana's fatal car crash in Paris, a fifty-ish, well-coiffed woman with a doctorate in psychology told me, without batting an eye, that the Royal Family was behind Princess Di's death. How, I inquired, had she come to this rather startling conclusion? "If Di married Dodi and had a son, the son would be half Arab and might someday become king, something they couldn't abide." "Oh, I see," I said, fighting back a smile. I certainly had no difficulty picturing the Queen Mother and her family, aghast at such a possibility, deciding that "Di had to go," and Prince Philip, perhaps, making the arrangements by calling in someone the family normally employs to "take care" of such problems.

thing that a particular group (e.g., Wall Street or unions or environmentalists) doesn't like, the group simply kills him. That's what we routinely do in America, right?

Moreover, for some reason, believers in the conspiracy theory apparently never stop to realize that even assuming, for the sake of argument, that a particular group of people had a motive to kill Kennedy, they also had an even greater motive *not* to do it, namely, that if they did it and got caught, they could be tried, convicted, and sentenced to death. Indeed, they would also know that the probability of their being caught and executed would be increased a hundred times over since their victim was the president of the United States, and his murder would ignite the most massive, dogged, and never-ending pursuit of his killer or killers by local, state, and federal law enforcement that had ever taken place.

But even if this apparently never-considered countervailing motive were treated as if it did not exist, a motive to commit a crime hardly gets one to first base in any criminal prosecution. I mean, if President Bush were assassinated tomorrow, there would be all types of people and groups who one could say would have had a motive to kill him. It is only one of the starting points of the investigation. Irrespective of the presence of motive, prosecutors still have to prove, by solid evidence, that the person or group who had a motive is the same person or group who committed the crime, a little fact that millions of Americans and most conspiracy theorists ignore. Taking the French proverb *Qui en profite du crime en est coupable* ("Whoever profits from the crime is guilty of it") to heart, they are convinced that finding a motive is synonymous with finding the perpetrator. In their mind, finding that a particular group had a motive to kill Kennedy is enough to prove that the group did, in fact, do so—a non sequitur and broad jump of Olympian proportions. For example, Oliver Stone concluded that no fewer than ten separate groups or people had a motive to kill Kennedy, and this is why someone of his intelligence (with his thinking cap turned very tightly to the "off" position) directed a movie (*JFK*) in which, unbelievably, *all ten* were involved in Kennedy's murder, the *reductio ad absurdum* of such an infantile, yet exceedingly prevalent mode of thinking.[*]

Many conspiracy theorists embellish the motive argument to prove that a particular group killed Kennedy, by saying that it had the "motive, means, and opportunity" to do so. They present this almost as a prosecutorial legal brief, but in my years as a prosecutor I never once used the phrase and personally don't know any seasoned prosecutor who has, although I assume some do and I am aware of this legal colloquialism. Much more so than motive, "means and opportunity" are virtually worthless as evidence of guilt (unless, of course, you can show that no other living human, or very few other living humans, had the means or opportunity).

To illustrate how empty the concept of motive, means, and opportunity is, let's take the Kennedy assassination. Any of the thousands of citizens of Dallas who hated Kennedy with a passion would have had a motive to kill him. And any of them who owned a gun or a rifle had the means. And if they were anywhere along Kennedy's motorcade route, they would have the opportunity. Again, "motive, means, and opportunity" hardly gets

---

[*]Fourteen years before Stone's movie came out, another Hollywood director made light of what Stone would take so seriously. In his 1977 picture *Annie Hall*, Woody Allen has his character Alvie ask Allison, "How is it possible for Oswald to have fired from two angles at once? . . . I'll tell you this. He was not marksman enough to hit a moving target at that range. But if there was a second assassin, that's it." Allison responds in exasperation, "Then everybody's in on the conspiracy—the FBI, CIA, J. Edgar Hoover, and the oil companies and the Pentagon and the men's room attendant at the White House?" Alvie: "I would leave out the men's room attendant."

one to first base. As indicated, even if all three are present, a prosecutor still has to show that the person or group who had them committed the crime. Indeed, a prosecutor's focusing heavily on motive, means, and opportunity is almost an implied admission by him that he has very little evidence that the defendant did, in fact, commit the crime. "Yeah, okay," a courthouse wag could say. "He had motive, means, and opportunity. But did he do it?" Motive, means, and opportunity are certainly helpful (and sometimes critical) to a prosecutor in proving his case, but are perhaps more helpful to the police who investigate the case in that the absence of any of them, particularly means and opportunity, enables the police to exclude those who may have otherwise been considered suspects to a crime.

If all the groups and people who Oliver Stone, in his movie, alleges were involved in Kennedy's murder (e.g., FBI, CIA, Secret Service, military-industrial complex, LBJ, etc.) actually *were*, a coup d'état would necessarily have taken place. And, indeed, in Stone's movie New Orleans DA Jim Garrison tells his staff that the assassination of President Kennedy "was a military-style ambush from start to finish, a coup d'état with Lyndon Johnson waiting in the wings." It's a notion that many conspiracy theorists readily subscribe to. In fact, one of their books on the Kennedy assassination, by Alan Weberman and Michael Canfield, is specifically titled *Coup d'État in America*. Kennedy's assassination, writes conspiracy writer James H. Fetzer, could very well have been "the result of a coup d'état involving the CIA, the mob, anti-Castro Cubans, and powerful politicians, such as LBJ, Richard Nixon, and J. Edgar Hoover, fully financed by Texas oil men and elements of the military-industrial complex."[16] "There can be no doubts," conspiracy author L. Fletcher Prouty writes, that the Kennedy assassination "was the result of a coup d'état."[17] Conspiracy icon Vincent Salandria concludes that "the killing of Kennedy represented a *coup d'état*."[18] I suppose that since a coup d'état is defined as a sudden, unconstitutional change of state policy and leadership "by a group of persons in authority," a coup would actually be required in order to pull off the massive conspiracy contemplated by conspiracy theorists; that is, you couldn't even have a coup without the involvement, cooperation, and complicity of groups like the FBI, CIA, and military-industrial complex.

In addition to the fact that the aforementioned groups and people would find it impossible to agree on who should be seated where at a presidential swearing-in ceremony, much less on how, when, and where to murder the president, what the conspiracy theorists fail to realize is that there is absolutely no history of coups d'état in America. They are talking about the United States of America, the most powerful, democratic, and economically stable country in the world, as if it were no different from Nicaragua or Tanzania—in effect, comparing us with banana republics and Third World countries whose weak, vulnerable, undemocratic, and economically unstable conditions lend themselves to, and are fertile soil for, one coup after another. For instance, in the year Kennedy was killed alone, there were attempted but unsuccessful coups in Argentina and Turkey and successful coups in the Dominican Republic, Ecuador, Guatemala, Honduras, Peru, South Vietnam, (Republic), Iraq, Syria, Congo (Brazzaville), and Tanzania.[19]

Even if a coup against Kennedy by powers in America were feasible (and the very thought is repellant to our minds), what Secretary of State Dean Rusk told the Warren Commission in discounting Russian participation in a conspiracy to kill Kennedy, though not directly applicable, is instructive: "Although there are grave differences between the Communist world and the free world, . . . even from their point of view there needs to be some shape and form to international relations, that it is not in their interest to have this world structure dissolve into complete anarchy, that great states . . . have to be in a position to deal with each other . . . and that requires the maintenance of correct relations."[20]

What Rusk was saying is that with respect to stable foreign nations (as opposed to, say, banana republics or Third World countries), it is in the best interests of even adversaries to accept the "legitimacy" of their opposition. And what Rusk observed between these stable foreign nations is equally applicable internally. Even though, as with every president, our elected leader has many factions in the country opposed to his stewardship of government, these factions would have many more reasons to accept the continued legitimacy invested in the president by our constitutional process than to embrace fascistic principles that would only ultimately promote the insecurity and illegitimacy of their own positions. Why would they want to live in an environment where in the future their political opposition would likely do the same thing to them as they did to Kennedy? The notion that major federal agencies of government (or even one such agency) would decide to murder Kennedy because they didn't agree with certain policies of his is sufficiently demented to be excluded at the portals of any respectable mental institution short of an insane asylum.

Because conspiracy theorists believe that once they find a motive, they have found a perpetrator, many books of theirs on the Kennedy assassination devote several hundred pages to a specific group's motive to kill the president, but remarkably never get around to spending any time on whether Oswald, who all the evidence shows to be the triggerman, had any actual and direct connection to the group, or more importantly, even if he did, whether there is any evidence that the group got him to kill Kennedy for them. These conspiracy theorists get so caught up in their fertile delusions that while they spend entire chapters on arcane relationships of groups like the mob and CIA with various people, groups, and events wholly unrelated to the assassination, many don't even bother to devote *one single sentence* in their long books to scrutinizing Oswald's activities during the critical days and weeks leading up to the assassination, an exceedingly important source of information from which to infer the existence or nonexistence of a conspiracy. It's as if these authors believe there's no need to connect Oswald to the CIA or the mob, or show that they got him to kill Kennedy for them. If, as I say, they can prove that one of these groups had a motive to kill Kennedy, then, *if* Oswald was the assassin, he *must* have killed Kennedy *for* them. This crazy, incredibly childlike reasoning is the mentality that has driven and informed virtually all of the pro-conspiracy sentiment in the Kennedy assassination from the very beginning.

Though many people have not stopped to realize it, the issue of conspiracy in the Kennedy assassination is two-pronged, the first of which can be disposed of in one sentence: since we know Oswald killed Kennedy, we also know that no group of conspirators killed Kennedy and framed Oswald for the murder they committed. You can only frame an innocent person, not a guilty one, so this type of conspiracy has been taken off the table by the conclusive establishment of Oswald's guilt.

The second issue, and the subject of this Book Two, involves whether Oswald was a part of a conspiracy—that is, did he kill Kennedy for others?

In the following sections on the various groups who have been accused of being behind the president's murder, the reader will see that none of the conspiracy theories relating to these groups benefit from scrutiny, and that to accept any of them one has to knowingly abandon all conventional notions of logic and common sense. Again, this is not to suggest that there is no such thing as conspiracy to commit murder. It's just that there is no evidence of such a conspiracy in the Kennedy assassination.

I said in the introduction to this book that one of the reasons why everyday Americans believe in a conspiracy in this case is that they find it intellectually incongruous that a peasant can strike down a king, that something more just had to be involved. CBS commentator Eric Sevareid spoke of Americans finding it difficult to believe that "all that power and majesty [could be] wiped out in an instant by one skinny, weak-chinned little character. It was like believing that the Queen Mary had sunk without a trace because of a log floating somewhere in the Atlantic, or that AT&T's stock had fallen to zero because a drunk somewhere tore out his telephone wires."[21]

In explaining that what happened in Dallas was so horrendous, so incredible, so shattering that the American people demanded that the cause or reason for the murder equal the effect, no one, I think, has said it better than William Manchester, the author of the 1967 best seller, *The Death of a President*: "I think I understand why they feel that way. And I think, in a curious way, there is an aesthetic principle involved. If you take the murder of six million Jews in Europe and you put that at one end of the scale, at the other end you can put the Nazis, the greatest gang of criminals ever to seize control of a modern government. So there is a rough balance. Greatest crime, greatest criminals. But if you put the murder of the President of the United States at one end of the scale, and you put that waif Oswald on the other end, it just doesn't balance. And you want to put something on Oswald's side to make it balance. A conspiracy would do that beautifully. Unfortunately, there's no evidence whatever of that."[22]

It might be productive for the reader to keep Manchester's words in mind as he or she reads what follows.

History of the
Conspiracy Movement

Before I discuss the enormous issue of conspiracy in the murder of President Kennedy, a very brief history of the conspiracy movement in America with respect to the assassination is in order.

The very first conspiracy theorists consisted, essentially, of two groups. The first included those who love conspiracies and see one behind every tree and everywhere else in modern society. They are, for the most part, culturally paranoid people. To them there is always much more going on below the radar screen than on it, the powers that be are always up to something, and *that something* is always no good. Not infrequently, their charges happen to be true. This group was screaming conspiracy before the fatal bullet had even come to rest, although the first literary shot fired by this group is believed to be Mark Lane's article, "Defense Brief for Oswald," published in the December 19, 1963, edition of the *National Guardian*, a libertarian newsweekly.

The other group were not conspiracy lovers per se, but the millions among us who instinctively believe that any really important human event that is concomitantly harmful to the interest of many, including them, is never brought about by just one dirty hand.* The automatic and ubiquitous word they employ to express their angst is the anonymous *they*. After employing this pronoun, they usually don't consume their lives with the issue, and go on to other matters of more immediate concern. The easy reliance on *they* to explain away all manner of major occurrences is not confined only to the man on the street. Thus,

---

*Indeed, a national Gallup Poll that started on the day of the assassination and continued through November 27 showed that the first instinct of most Americans was that Kennedy had died as a result of a conspiracy, 52 percent believing "some group or element was responsible," 29 percent believing the "assassin acted on his own," and 19 percent being "uncertain." As indicated in the introduction to this book, this sentiment was reversed the following year with the publication of the Warren Report, a September 1964 Harris Poll showing 55.5 percent of Americans believing Oswald acted alone, 31.6 percent believing he had accomplices, and 13 percent being unsure.

in the moments after the assassination, President Johnson would think, "If *they* shot our president, who would *they* shoot next?" And Jacqueline Kennedy cried, "*They* killed my husband." Suffice it to say that *they*, whoever *they* are, have been responsible for more terrible and cataclysmic events than any group, tribe, or nation in world history.

Although the conspiracy movement throughout the years has had no political agenda, and its adherents run the gamut from members of the Far Left to the Far Right, this was not true at the beginning. Because Oswald was a known Marxist who had defected to Russia and was a pro-Castroite, the belief of many Americans in the wake of the assassination was that Russia, our bitter enemy in the cold war, was behind the president's death. It probably was no coincidence, then, that the first four *conspiracy* books on the assassination[*] were written by old-line Communists or politically active leftists, the first two expressly seeking to deflect suspicion away from the Soviet Union.[1]

The first conspiracy book, *Who Killed Kennedy?*, was published in London in May of 1964 and written by Thomas Buchanan, an expatriate American Communist living in Paris who began writing a series of popular conspiracy articles titled the "Buchanan Report" for the Paris weekly *L'Express* on February 10, 1964. Per the February 29, 1968, *Congressional Record*, "In 1949 [actually, 1948], Buchanan was fired from the staff of a Washington newspaper [*Washington Evening Star*] for being a Communist party member, and is now a frequent contributor to left-wing newspapers and periodicals." Challenging the anticipated findings of the Warren Commission, Buchanan, who argued that two gunmen, firing from different directions, killed Kennedy, pointed out in his book that "it seems clear that from the Chinese point of view, as from the Soviet and Cuban, no political advantage could have been anticipated from the death of Kennedy." He added how ludicrous it was to believe a "plot by leaders of the Kremlin to dispatch a trained assassin to shoot down the only president since Roosevelt they respected."[2]

Joachim Joesten, aka Franz von Nesselrode, Walter Kell, and Paul Delanthuis, a German-born American, wrote the next book, *Oswald: Assassin or Fall Guy?* (published in Germany in mid-June 1964, and soon thereafter in America), attacking the Warren Commission's anticipated findings before its report was published on September 24, 1964. Per the same issue of the *Congressional Record*, Joesten was a "German Communist party member. Joesten's book was published in this country by the recently defunct publishing firm of Marzani and Munsell, . . . one of the most foremost publishers of Communist and extreme left literature in America." Indeed, a copy of some German documents seized by U.S. authorities at the end of World War II contain the statement that Joesten had been a member of the Communist Party of Germany since 1932. A November 8, 1937, memorandum of the Gestapo documents his membership in the party, which was outlawed in Germany at that time.[3]

---

[*]The very first book written on the assassination was the little-known *Red Roses from Texas* by the British author Nerin E. Gun. Published by Frederick Muller in London in February 1964 (and by R. Julliard in France), before the Warren Report came out, it wasn't a conspiracy book at all, over half of its 208 pages not even dealing with the assassination, but with the short period leading up to it. And the assassination part of the book is more a series of claims gathered from rumors, newspapers, tabloids, and newspaper articles on the case (since testimony before the Warren Commission was in private and, as indicated, not yet published). Many were inaccurate, such as that a doctor examining President Kennedy at Parkland Hospital found a bullet on his stretcher; that Dallas deputy sheriff Buddy Walthers found a "fourth bullet" in the grass near the Triple Underpass; that Oswald was not advised of his constitutional rights and not allowed to telephone a lawyer; that the presidential limousine shot down the Stemmons Freeway toward Parkland Hospital at 100 miles per hour. (Gun, *Red Roses from Texas*, pp.111–112, 127, 204–205; see also CE 2580, 25 H 851–852) Because it is the first book on the case, and because it is so rare, I'm told a copy of *Red Roses from Texas* is worth $750.

Joesten, in his book, concludes that Oswald "never was a genuine Communist who looked upon Soviet Russia as the Fatherland of the Oppressed," as he claimed, but was simply "masquerading as a pro-Communist." What Oswald was, per Joesten, was "an FBI agent provocateur with a CIA background and connections" who was a "perfect fall guy, a scapegoat" in the assassination, which was orchestrated by "some officials of the CIA and FBI, as well as some Army figures such as General Walker and reactionary oil millionaires such as H. L. Hunt."[4]

The next two conspiracy books on the assassination, *Whitewash* and *Rush to Judgment*, did not have any kind of political orientation and were not written by Communists, but by, as assassination researcher Johann Rush says, "leftists sympathetic to Marxist ideology."[5] The first of the two authors, Harold Weisberg, self-published *Whitewash* in August of 1965 after, the author says in the book's preface, it had been rejected by sixty-three American publishers over a fourteen-month period and eleven publishers in eight foreign countries.[6] The Dell edition of *Whitewash* was published in 1966. Per the same February 1968 issue of the *Congressional Record*, Weisberg "was earlier, in 1938, discharged from his investigator post on the La Follette Civil Liberties Committee 'for giving confidential matter to the *Daily Worker*, the leading Communist newspaper in the country.' In the summer of 1947, Weisberg was fired from his post with the U.S. Department of State along with nine others for known association with agents of the Soviet Union." *Whitewash* is more about a conspiracy by the authorities to cover up the truth about the assassination than it is about the conspiracy to commit it.

The last of the "original four" books was Mark Lane's *Rush to Judgment*, published in 1966.[*] It accuses the Warren Commission of so many misdeeds and suggests so many things (e.g., one or more shots came from the front, Ruby knew Oswald, Oswald may have been framed) that a gullible reader has no choice but to infer the existence of a conspiracy. The aforementioned *Congressional Record* says about Lane, "He has a long and curious involvement with a host of extreme left-wing causes and is a well-established spokesman for leftist ideology . . . Lane is a former executive secretary and national board member of the National Lawyer's Guild, a cited Communist front . . . This past year he was a member of the Committee of Sponsors for a Veterans of the Abraham Lincoln Brigade dinner. The brigade is also a cited Communist front."

Though Lane's *Rush to Judgment*, to this day the biggest-selling book on the assassination, was the main spark igniting a strong (as opposed to merely visceral) belief in many Americans that there was a conspiracy behind the death of the president, the real genesis of what we think of as the conspiracy movement, and that which has persisted to this day, probably began back on November 23, 1964 (eight weeks after the Warren Report was published), when the Government Printing Office started to sell the twenty-six volumes of the Warren Commission over the counter at its office in Washington, D.C., for seventy-six dollars a set, mostly to the media and private researchers. A total of 1,340 sets were sent free to libraries around the country.[7] As conspiracy theorist David Lifton

---

[*]Another book published after *Whitewash* but before *Rush to Judgment* has been erroneously classified by some as a conspiracy book, but it is not. Sylvan Fox's *Unanswered Questions about President Kennedy's Assassination*, published in October of 1965, is merely a very superficial critique of the Warren Report. After asking boilerplate questions like what was Oswald's motive in killing Kennedy, and how many shots were fired in Dealey Plaza, and from what direction, the author, who posits the possibility of conspiracy, concludes that the only certainty in the case is that "Oswald participated in the assassination of President Kennedy, either alone or in concert with others." (Fox, *Unanswered Questions about President Kennedy's Assassination*, pp. 24, 44, 192)

says, "A small but hardy band of individuals [including Lane and Weisberg], sometimes called the 'first generation researchers,' began going over [the volumes] with a fine tooth comb."[8] And there were many others, some not working with the volumes, all from various walks of life ranging from lawyers (Vincent Salandria), farmers (Weisberg), graduate students (Lifton), and small businessmen (Raymond Marcus), to a Hominy, Oklahoma, housewife (Shirley Martin), a Dallas legal secretary (Mary Ferrell), a researcher at the World Health Organization in New York City (Sylvia Meagher), a Los Angeles bookkeeper (Lillian Castellano, who also later became a major RFK assassination researcher), the wife of a Beverly Hills stockbroker (Marjorie Field), a radio host in Carmel-by-the-Sea (Mae Brussel), and a small-town Texas newspaper publisher (Penn Jones Jr.). Most were idealistic, patriotic men and women who sincerely believed that the official version of the assassination was a lie. Convinced that a vigorous and promising young American president had been cut down by malevolent forces whose interests were dangerously adverse to those of the average citizen, they were willing to consecrate their lives in an attempt to shine a bright, prosecutorial light on these dark forces and reclaim America from them. If it is true, as they say, that one man can make a difference and that passion changes the world, then someone like Martin, the Oklahoma housewife who got in her car and drove down to Dallas with her four children in tow and knocked on the doors of Dealey Plaza witnesses to interview them with her pad and pencil, represents the type of commitment and flame that, in confluence with other currents, can change the status quo.

At the beginning, with the exception of the researchers who did their work at the National Archives, and therefore knew of each other's existence, most researchers around the country, working out of their kitchen, living room, or local library, and not knowing of the others, felt all alone. But here and there, through word of mouth or an occasional article, they learned who their soul mates were, and the "discovery that they were not alone struck most of the buffs as monumental. They finally had someone to *talk* to."[9] It wasn't too long before these amateur "detectives," trying in their mind to educate the vast American public about a crime they perceived to be much greater than a lone nut killing Kennedy,* networked into a community of researchers, meeting at their homes and elsewhere, and excitedly exchanging their findings by phone and letter. They even helped each other with their work, such as furnishing documents and editing each others' writings. What undoubtedly brought them closer together in spirit is that their group was small and they were facing a monolithic establishment that scorned them.† Also, as Josiah Thompson observed, the Kennedy case became an "obsession," and "there's a fan-

---

*The early conspiracy theorists were encouraged and abetted by the Russian press and intellectuals across the water, such as Britain's Hugh Trevor-Roper, Bertrand Russell, and Arnold Toynbee—even London's conservative *Daily Mail* editorialized on November 27, 1963, that "facts can be produced that a right-wing plot against the President had caused his death"—as well as French publications like *Le Figaro, L'Express,* and *Le Monde,* France's leading paper.

†Many of the early researchers considered themselves liberal, which is why they weren't prepared for the disdain or indifference they received from even the liberal establishment and media (such as the estimable *Nation* magazine and leading lights of the Left like Alexander Cockburn and I. F. Stone), who, apart from other reasons to support the findings of such an august body as the Warren Commission, were reticent about attacking a Commission whose chairman, Chief Justice Warren, had become a liberal icon for the civil rights' rulings of his court, and who had been the subject of vitriolic attacks by the nation's right wing. Indeed, a liberal like Vince Salandria was astonished to find his message of questioning the Warren Commission resonating more with Republican groups than with those to the left of center. (Trillin, "Buffs," p.46)

tastic way in which the assassination becomes a religious event. There are relics, and scriptures, and even a holy scene—the killing ground. People make pilgrimages to it."[10]

Apart from the few who would write an entire book about the case (e.g., Josiah Thompson, Mark Lane, Harold Weisberg) or the occasional article in a prestigious publication (e.g., Richard Popkin's 1966 attack on the Warren Commission in the *New York Review of Books*), most needed a non-mainstream home for their articles and essays, since the mainstream press, for the most part, didn't believe in a conspiracy, and still doesn't to this day. They found it in a small, alternative magazine, *Minority of One*, a monthly operating out of Passaic, New Jersey, which started to include articles by conspiracy theorists who became known as "The Philadelphia School" of theorists because most of its members, like lawyer Vincent Salandria and Gaeton Fonzi (editor of the *Greater Philadelphia Magazine*), were from Philadelphia. Though the conspiracy theorists would later branch out and find other homes, such as *Ramparts* magazine (which replaced *Minority of One* in 1967 as the principal journalistic voice of the conspiracy movement) and periodicals of their own (such as the *Decade* series, which ended with the *Fourth Decade*; *Continuing Inquiry*; *Assassination USA*; *Conspiracy Newsletter*; *Investigation*; *Coverups!*; *JFK Honor Guard*; *Echoes of Conspiracy*; *Prologue*; *Grassy Knoll Gazette*; *Kennedy Assassination Chronicles*; *Probe*; and *JFK / Deep Politics Quarterly*) that catered exclusively to those interested in the assassination and its various conspiracies theories, *Minority of One* was the first magazine to routinely publish articles propounding the conspiracy theory. Its most important early one (in the March 1965 issue) was "Fifty-two Witnesses: The Grassy Knoll" by Philadelphia schoolteacher Harold Feldman, who examined the testimony of Warren Commission witnesses and reported (erroneously) that most thought the shots came from the grassy knoll. The article was published as a small book that same year by Idlewild, an alternative-press San Francisco publishing house.

By 1965, the relatively small but unflagging, energetic, and resourceful band of Warren Commission critics and conspiracy theorists were raising such a ruckus that former Warren Commission assistant counsel Joseph Ball became concerned and called Chief Justice Warren. "Chief, these critics of the report are guilty of misrepresentation and dishonest reporting," Ball lamented to Warren. "Be patient," Warren replied. "History will prove that we are right."[11]

The year 1966 was an important one in the history of the conspiracy movement, with the number of conspiracy theorists starting to multiply like bacteria, the original band of lonely doubters now looking more like a small army.[12] In addition to producing a great number of pro-conspiracy and anti–Warren Commission articles in newspapers and magazines, the theorists came out with a spate of conspiracy books, including Edward Epstein's *Inquest* (more an assault on the internal workings of the Warren Commission, with hints in the book of a second gun, and hence, conspiracy), Léo Sauvage's *Oswald Affair* (original French edition in 1965), Richard H. Popkin's *Second Oswald*, Penn Jones's *Forgive My Grief*, and Joesten's second book on the case, *Oswald: The Truth.** Moreover, the passage of the Freedom of Information Act in 1966 guaranteed almost perpetual oxygen to the movement, allowing theorists—after being put through the hoops by federal agencies—to get their hands on many previously sealed Warren Commission documents.

---

*The barrage of books prompted the *New York Times* to comment in an editorial that "debate on the accuracy and adequacy of the Warren Commission's work is now approaching the dimensions of a lively small industry in this country" (*New York Times*, September 1, 1966, p.34; "Playboy Interview: Mark Lane," p.42).

Perhaps more importantly, the critics had made enough noise and charges that for the first time they were making inroads into the nation's establishment in their call for a reinvestigation of the assassination. In July of 1966, JFK speechwriter and adviser Richard N. Goodwin, believing that Epstein's *Inquest*, which essentially alleged that the Warren Report was hastily prepared and inadequate, was "a fairly impressive book," became the first member of JFK's inner circle to publicly call for a small group of prominent citizens who had no connection with public office to review the Warren Report and recommend whether or not there should be a reinvestigation of Kennedy's death.[13] A few months later, in November, Arthur M. Schlesinger Jr., a former assistant to the president whose book on Kennedy's presidency, *A Thousand Days*, had won a Pulitzer Prize, went further than Goodwin, stating there was a "residue of uncertainty" among the American people about the assassination and recommending that Congress should initiate a new inquiry "to reduce, to narrow that zone of uncertainty." That same week, *Life* magazine called for a new investigation (joined by the *Saturday Evening Post* two months later), while its sister publication, *Time*, took the opposite view. But opposition among most members in Congress to a reinvestigation was strong, a typical response coming from Carl Albert, the House Democratic majority leader, that he wasn't troubled by "minor inconsistencies" in the report and felt confident "the Warren Commission answered the basic questions."[14]

But two days later in an editorial, even the nation's leading newspaper, the *New York Times*, joined in the chorus of those who wanted something to be done, not the reinvestigation that most of the other voices wanted, but for the Warren Commission and its staff to address themselves to "the many puzzling questions that have been raised . . . There are enough solid doubts of thoughtful citizens," the paper said, that now "require answers. Further dignified silence, or merely more denials by the commission or its staff, are no longer enough."[15]

The tide against the Warren Commission was gaining so much vigor that on September 25, *New York Times* White House correspondent Tom Wicker wrote, "A public discussion group in New York sought to hold a round-table session about the Warren Report . . . The major difficulty for the group was in finding anyone of stature who was willing to *defend* the Warren Report and its findings."[16]

The next year, 1967, brought two of the best, but inevitably flawed, books the conspiracy community has ever produced. One was Josiah Thompson's classic *Six Seconds in Dallas*, which perceptively focused on the technical part of the case (firearms, bullet trajectories, photographic and medical evidence, etc.) more than any book before it. Thompson, a professor of philosophy who became an ardent student of the assassination, was hired by *Life* magazine to be its special consultant on the assassination. *Life* also allowed him to work with and study one of the first-generation copies of the Zapruder film it had purchased, which put him in an envied position among his fellow critics and theorists. From his examination of the film, he was the first Warren Commission critic to postulate the theory that Kennedy had been hit by two shots in the head almost simultaneously, one from his rear, one from his right front.

The other was Sylvia Meagher's well-researched *Accessories after the Fact*, in which her sense of scholarship is consistently at odds with her strong conspiracy orientation (admitting to her readers she had an "instantaneous skepticism about the official version of what happened in Dallas"), with the former barely managing to prevail, the book being reasonably sober and factual.

The year 1967 also brought the first article about the conspiracy phenomenon: a June article in the *New Yorker* by Calvin Trillin appropriately titled "The Buffs," which was a peek into their world of passion and idiosyncracy. But Trillin didn't coin the term *buffs*, even though he remarked at one point in his article, "They are also known as 'assassination buffs.'" [17]*

Although a plurality of Americans were now accepting the conspiracy argument of the Warren Commission critics, this meant nothing to the theorists if there wasn't going to be a reinvestigation into the assassination to find out just who the actual villains were so they could be brought to a punishing justice. So when New Orleans DA Jim Garrison announced his decision in March of 1967 to prosecute Clay Shaw for the murder of Kennedy, many members of the conspiracy community reached a high-water mark of excitement and hope and flocked to New Orleans to help him in any way they could to get to the bottom of what they perceived to be, so far, an impenetrable mystery. The cafés and bars along the fabled Bourbon Street were now rocking with not only Dixieland jazz but also the tingle of fevered, late-night conversations among the theorists.[†] The conspiracy community was on such a high that nothing could penetrate the armor of their resolve, not even a four-part CBS news documentary hosted by Walter Cronkite and Dan Rather and seen by an estimated 30 million Americans in June of 1967, which concluded that Oswald killed Kennedy and acted alone. Garrison was going to deliver them to Nirvana, and neither the Warren Commission nor the esteemed Cronkite and Rather were going to stand in their way.

Garrison's ultimate, miserable failure in 1969 (see later text), with the world watching, dealt a solar plexus blow to the movement, and many members, angry at the embarrassment Garrison brought to them, denounced him as a fraud and a megalomaniac. As conspiracy theorist Robert Anson put it, because of Garrison, "bills in Congress asking for a new investigation were quietly shelved. The reporters who had spent months digging up leads put away their notebooks."[18] But in the detritus of his ignoble defeat, Garrison had nonetheless inspired a new generation of conspiracy theorists and made a very significant contribution to the movement that has endured to this day. He added a whole new New Orleans subplot to the case "with its own cast of characters. By finding associates of Oswald, naming names, locating addresses of secret rendevous, and logging dates and times of purported plot events, he gave new impetus to conspiracy thinking."[19] Though hurt by Garrison's fiasco, the foot soldiers in the conspiracy movement continued, unabated, in their work and charges. Indeed, the skewering of the Warren Commission's findings by the critics became so intense, and there were so many "new revelations," that by 1969 an article in *Ramparts* was declaring that the critics "were doing the job that the Dallas police, the FBI, and the Warren Commission should have done in the first place."[20]

---

*Why the members of the conspiracy community so loathe the appellation *buff* and consider it as pejorative as they do is not clear, since it's not a new word that applies only to them. For many years before the assassination the word had been used, without a negative connotation, to describe a devotee or well-informed student of some subject, like a Civil War, opera, or trolley-car buff.

†Garrison also had the nation's attention on New Orleans, nearly two out of three Americans telling a nationwide Harris Poll in late May 1967 that they were following the investigation. And Garrison was winning in the court of public opinion. In an earlier Harris Poll conducted in February, 44 percent thought there was a conspiracy, 35 percent thought Oswald acted alone, and 21 percent weren't sure. But the late-May poll, just three months into Garrison's probe, found 66 percent believing there was a conspiracy. Only 19 percent did *not* believe there was a conspiracy, and 15 percent didn't know. ("66% in Poll Accept Kennedy Plot View," *New York Times*, May 30, 1967, p.19)

In a preview of Oliver Stone's 1991 movie, *JFK*, the year 1973 brought *Executive Action*, the first feature film on the assassination, to the big screen. Based on a novel by Mark Lane and Donald Freed, *Executive Action: Assassination of a Head of State*, and starring Burt Lancaster, the screenplay, written by Dalton Trumbo, one of the alleged Communists blacklisted by Hollywood following the McCarthy hearings in the early 1950s, hypothesized the assassination of Kennedy by three professional gunmen (none of whom was Oswald, who, the movie suggests, was just a patsy). The gunmen were commissioned by the right wing and powerful members of the nation's military-industrial complex, who had concluded that Kennedy had to die because they feared he would sign an all-encompassing test-ban treaty, pull out of Vietnam (based on his announced intent to withdraw one thousand troops by the end of 1963), and provoke a black revolution by his proposed civil rights legislation. The 1974 film *Parallax View* also assumes a conspiracy behind the assassination of a Kennedy-like politician with a Warren-like commission that bungles the investigation.

The year 1973 also saw the formation of the Assassination Information Bureau in Cambridge, Massachusetts. The group was led by Carl Oglesby, a sometime instructor at MIT operating out of his home who was the former president of Students for a Democratic Society. He and his four associates (the latter all in their twenties) spoke to increasingly large audiences on hundreds of college campuses, from Maine to Hawaii and parts in between, urging a reopening of the investigation into the assassination, and were very instrumental in helping to get Congress to eventually do so. (The group folded shortly after the HSCA issued its report in 1979.)

In March of 1975, Geraldo Rivera's *Good Night America* show on ABC national television showed millions of Americans, for the very first time, the Zapruder film and the head snap to the rear. As I indicated earlier, this created, overnight, a whole new wave of Warren Commission critics and conspiracy theorists demanding that the federal government—not a clearly irresponsible and inept local DA in New Orleans—order a new investigation. The climate in Washington was heating up: the Rockefeller Commission, also in 1975, revealed that the CIA had trespassed beyond the margins of its jurisdiction (limited to gathering *foreign* intelligence) and had infiltrated and spied on anti–Vietnam War dissidents here in the United States; and the Church Committee in 1976 found that U.S. intelligence agencies (for years one of the main suspected conspirators behind the assassination) had engaged in clandestine foreign operations that most Americans considered far beyond the moral and ethical pale (most prominently the CIA's effort, with organized crime no less, to murder Cuban premier Fidel Castro). With so much accumulated cynicism about national affairs spawned by Watergate and the Vietnam War, the conspiracy movement finally received enough institutional support to get the investigation of the assassination reopened. The result was the HSCA's inquiry from 1977 to 1979, which found that the president "was probably assassinated as a result of a conspiracy."[21]

But the HSCA's conclusion never had the effect on the American public that had been anticipated, a public that already believed in a conspiracy and had no comprehension of the highly sophisticated acoustic basis for the HSCA's conclusion. The committee's nebulous conclusion, in which it named no group or individual as being responsible for the assassination, and then proceeded to seal much of its own documentation, proved to be unsatisfying to the conspiracy theorists, who were hungry for redder meat. Conspiracy theorist Gaeton Fonzi said that the HSCA's investigation was "simply not broad enough, deep enough, ambitious enough, nor honest enough."[22]

Though the HSCA's conclusion never gave the conspiracy movement much of a boost, most television specials, which had started in the 1960s, continued to trumpet the conspiracy theory. And between 1978 and 1990 the cottage industry the assassination had created also continued, without letup, to churn out books and magazine articles, the most notable of which were Anthony Summers's *Conspiracy* and David Lifton's *Best Evidence* in 1980 and Henry Hurt's *Reasonable Doubt* in 1985,* all three of which remain prominent in the conspiracy genre and have devotees to this very day. Summers's *Conspiracy* regurgitated almost every conspiracy theory and allegation that had previously been propounded, but in a more literary and less strident fashion. The book got good reviews from the mainline press and mostly gave the reader a mass of suppositions and innuendos, each pointing toward a conspiracy that even the author seemed to distance himself from for the most part, accepting just enough to leave the reader with a sense that there couldn't possibly be this much smoke without the fire of conspiracy. Lifton's book, which also got good reviews and sold even better than Summers's tome, argued that the conspirators had enlisted the work of surgeons to rearrange the bullet wounds in Kennedy's body to frame Oswald. The book was meticulously researched but so far out in its theory that most responsible conspiracy theorists (perhaps an oxymoron) felt constrained to reject it because of its lack of feasibility. Hurt's *Reasonable Doubt* was a fairly reasonable analysis of the assassination from a conspiratorial perspective, but loses its way when Hurt makes the centerpiece of his book a "confession" to the assassination by a patient in a mental hospital.

Three other best-selling conspiracy books in the 1980s, all in 1989, were Jim Marrs's *Crossfire*, a low-brow version of Summers's *Conspiracy*; *High Treason*, by conspiracy hawker extraordinaire Robert Groden and his more accomplished coauthor, Harrison Livingstone, which argued, among many other things, that the autopsy photos were altered; and *Mafia Kingfish*, by John H. Davis, claiming that Mafia don Carlos Marcello was behind JFK's murder.

But by the second half of the 1980s, interest among the general public in the assassination and the conspiracy aspects of it was definitely on the wane. One reason, writer Pete Hamill pointed out, is that by 1988 "an entire generation had come to maturity with no memory at all of the Kennedy years; for them, Kennedy is the name of an airport or a boulevard or a high school."[23]

That all changed in 1991 with Oliver Stone's successful movie *JFK*, which introduced a whole new generation of young Americans to every hoary conspiracy argument and theory that had been around for years, dressing them up in a well-done fantasy movie with marquee Hollywood actors like Kevin Costner and Joe Pesci to sell the conspiracy psychedelic nostrum as the solution to the question of who was behind Kennedy's murder. Millions of Americans were again talking about the assassination, particularly its alleged conspiratorial ramifications. The national interest the movie ignited actually led to the passage by Congress of the JFK Act in 1992 and the creation of the Assassination Records Review Board (ARRB) to implement the JFK Act's mandate to release to the American public every previously sealed document "related" to the assassination.

---

*The 1980s didn't get off to a good start for the conspiracy theorists. British conspiracy author Michael Eddowes, convinced that an imposter was buried in Oswald's Fort Worth grave, actually succeeded in having the body exhumed on October 4, 1981, and examined by medical experts. The buffs had their fingers crossed but the body turned out to be Lee Harvey Oswald.

The conspiracy theorists and assassination researchers had a field day from 1994 (when the ARRB became operational) to 1998 (when the ARRB closed its doors), poring over the thousands of newly released documents at the National Archives in Washington, D.C., hoping to find that one document which would confirm all their deepest suspicions and finally solve the mystery, in their minds, of the assassination. Coming away completely empty-handed did not deter them in the least. For example, on the fortieth anniversary of the assassination, in November of 2003, no fewer than ten additional books were published by the theorists (e.g., *The Zapruder Film*; *The Great Zapruder Film Hoax*; *Blood, Money and Power: How LBJ Killed JFK*; and the *Triangle of Death*, a book that actually alleges that South Vietnam was behind the assassination).

I see no end in sight. The notion of a plot to murder the president has provided a rich pasture for the minds of conspiracy theorists to frolic in. The beat will continue, with wide-eyed initiates joining the conspiracy community and attending its yearly conventions in Dallas after "discovering" some document or argument on the Internet that convinces them that the official version was all wrong, owing to either gross incompetence or intentional suppression of the truth. Because a little knowledge, as we all know, is dangerous, and because there are always grizzled conspiracy theorists willing to share with these neophytes their madcap theories and all the misinformation they have accumulated through the years[*] and to guide them through the conspiracy thickets, the conspiracy movement will continue, as an old Indian treaty provided, "as long as the water flows and the wind blows and the grass grows."

If I can be so presumptuous as to throw the conspiracy theorists a bone, it would be to say that with the exception of a few charlatans, the overwhelming majority of them definitely have above-average intelligence and are dedicated, patriotic Americans who sincerely believe there was a well-orchestrated conspiracy in the assassination that has been covered up by those walking the marbled corridors of power in our own government. And they fervently want to right this egregious wrong and bring about justice. In their search for justice, they have unearthed much information on the assassination that the authorities missed. But it is also undeniably true that in their uncontrollable zeal to achieve their goal, most of these otherwise honorable people have knowingly and intentionally distorted the official record, under the notion, I suppose, that the end justifies the means.

With the exception of the occasional pro–Warren Commission book, there has been no equivalent of the network of conspiracy theorists to support the findings of the Warren Commission. As author Gerald Posner notes, "When the commission disbanded, the

---

[*]Some of these neophytes have elbowed their mentors out of the way and have themselves become part of a new wave of Warren Commission critics presently comprising the dominant force in the conspiracy movement. They include theorist James Fetzer, who has wisely gathered the best technical minds in the conspiracy community to write scholarly scientific essays in books that he edits. Other members of the new wave include, but are not limited to, Walt Brown, Drs. Gary Aguilar and David Mantik, James DiEugenio, Vincent Palamara, and John Newman. One of the best examples of the old school working with the new is that of Josiah Thompson, one of the most respected Warren Commission critics ever, becoming a friend to and colleague of Aguilar's, who seems to be following Thompson's footsteps in terms of rigorous, high-quality research.

In this book I use the terms *Warren Commission critic* and *conspiracy theorist* somewhat interchangeably, not because they are linguistically so, but because in the context of the assassination they essentially are. One could certainly be a critic of the Warren Commission without being a conspiracy theorist, and some have been, in an article or column. But show me a critic of the Warren Commission down through the years who isn't also attached to one or more conspiracy theories or the general notion of conspiracy in the assassination. For the most part I use one or the other term for a person to describe what I perceive to be his or her primary interest—conspiracy, or being a critic of the Warren Commission's work.

members failed to arrange to defend their work or answer questions."[24] Warren himself, who always was averse to public relations, decided to let the work of his commission and its report stand on its own, like a Supreme Court decision.[25] From the publication of the Warren Report in 1964 forward, Warren Commission assistant counsel David Belin was virtually the lone regular voice on radio, TV, and print to rebut the relentless deluge of conspiracy advocacy, and that continued up to 1993, when Posner published his best-selling book *Case Closed* and very ably joined Belin, as did, even earlier, the very literate Max Holland, preventing the theorists from having the airwaves all to themselves. And former president and Warren Commission member Gerald Ford, on those occasions when he has spoken out, has proved to be an impressive defender of the conclusions reached by the Commission. But for the most part, the Commission members, even when they were still alive, rarely deigned to comment on the charges of the critics, obviously believing, like their chief, that their report spoke for itself, and to respond would only dignify the charges. As indicated, in late 1966, *Life*, one of the most influential magazines in America at the time, joined the critics in its November edition by calling for a new inquiry. Of the seven Commission members whom the *New York Times* went to for a response to the *Life* piece, six were "unavailable for comment." Only Allen Dulles bothered to answer, saying tersely, "I find there is nothing new or startling in this *Life* article—except the conclusions."[26]

So the conspiracy community, a potent and formidable body through the decades, has by sheer force of numbers clearly dominated the debate in front of a national audience, one which apparently hasn't minded hearing, for the most part, only one side of the story.

Before getting into an examination of the various conspiracy theories alleging specific conspirators (e.g., CIA, organized crime, Castro, etc.), I feel a separate, short chapter should be devoted to the aforementioned Mr. Lane, the original granddaddy of all conspiracy theorists, whose misleading and deceptive ways have resonated down through the years, to one degree or another, with nearly all conspiracy theorists who came thereafter.

In addition, I want to clear the table of three separate allegations, which, if true, by their very nature compel the inference of a conspiracy, even though no group of conspirators is specifically named.* The three sections on these allegations are titled "The Second Oswald," "Mysterious and Suspicious Deaths," and "David Lifton and Alteration of the President's Body." But first, Mark Lane.

---

*Book One has already examined some allegations that, if true, spell conspiracy, such as that one or more of the shots came from the grassy knoll, and that the Zapruder film was altered. I made the decision to include them in Book One because they were an intrinsic and inseparable area of inquiry that more properly fit into the subject of discussion—for example, grassy knoll, to the murder of the president in Dealey Plaza; Zapruder alteration, to the Zapruder film.

Mark Lane

Mark Lane, the Pied Piper of conspiracy theorists, was the New York lawyer retained by Lee Harvey Oswald's mother, Marguerite, to represent her son's interests before the Warren Commission, a representation that the Commission did not allow. Through his lectures and best-selling 1966 book, *Rush to Judgment*, Lane has been by far the most persistent and audible single voice in turning the American people against the Warren Commission's conclusions. (Only New Orleans district attorney Jim Garrison, by his prosecution of Clay Shaw for Kennedy's murder, and Hollywood producer Oliver Stone, by his movie *JFK*, have been more famous and had more of a temporary impact, but they were relatively ephemeral stars in the conspiracy constellation.) Over the last forty-plus years, Lane has given at least several thousand speeches on the case, mostly to large and enthusiastic college audiences. To give you just a small representative sample of his college appearances, in a trip to the San Francisco Bay area for a few days in March of 1964, in addition to several other speeches, Lane spoke at San Jose State College on March 16, Oakland City College on March 17, San Francisco State College on March 18, University of California at Berkeley on March 21, and a high school, Garfield High in Berkeley, on March 22.[1] He blanketed the entire nation like this for years. And he was so effective, and his charges so serious, that the Warren Commission asked the FBI to monitor all his public appearances in this country, which the bureau proceeded to do.[2]

Former *Dallas Morning News* reporter Hugh Aynesworth, who in December of 1963 furnished Lane with copies of witness statements he had taken in the case because he thought Lane wanted to be a legitimate devil's advocate for Oswald, now says ruefully that Lane "almost single-handedly invented the lucrative JFK conspiracy industry."[3]

In addition to being the most persistent and audible voice among conspiracy theorists, Lane has clearly been the most influential of all those who have championed the theory of conspiracy—so much so that the *New York Times* said "an examination" by the paper "determined that much of the information on which Congress decided to reopen its investigation" of the assassination of Kennedy came from Lane: "Mark Lane, the author and lecturer, provided the House subcommittee [HSCA] with most of its 'new leads.'" The *Times* said that Lane had confirmed to them "that he was the primary force behind the formation" of the committee, and the paper added that "according to members of the committee staff, Mr. Lane's books, theories and private investigations provided the 'working manuals' for the inquiry."[4]

I was an early witness to Lane's unsettling effectiveness with audiences. Back in December of 1964, I attended a debate at the University of California, Los Angeles, between Lane and Joseph A. Ball, who had been one of the principal lawyers for the Commission. Initially, a majority of the thousand or so people present were plainly skeptical of Lane's claim that Oswald had been framed. But like a human pinwheel, Lane threw off a string of loosely connected challenges to the Commission's findings and created the implication of a cover-up without presenting any theory of his own. Ball found it a hopeless task to refute all of Lane's scattershot allegations, and many members of the audience were obviously left wondering why this or that point had not been adequately refuted. By the end of the evening, sympathy had clearly shifted toward Lane—and away from the Commission's verdict. In fact, hisses could be heard when Ball spoke. Assistant Warren Commission counsel Wesley J. Liebeler says that Lane's antics remind him of "an old legend about frogs jumping from the mouth of a perfidious man every time he speaks. These frogs representing the lies leap out and you have to run in all directions to grab them. It's just incredible to listen to him. If he talks for five minutes, it takes an hour to straighten out the record."[5]

Within a few months after the assassination, Lane, who had been elected to the New York State Assembly in 1960, served one year, then lost in the Democratic primary for Congress in 1962, founded his Citizens' Committee of Inquiry on the assassination, which had headquarters in a little office on Fifth Avenue in New York City and was staffed by student volunteers. Every night for several months he gave a rousing speech on the assassination at a small Manhattan theater he had rented, Theater Four on West Fifth Street.[6] Lane was the slickest and most voluble of the early left-wing group of writers, and the KGB (per copies of documents from KGB files spirited out of Russia by a KGB defector in 1992) even contributed two thousand dollars, through an intermediary whose association with the KGB Lane was probably unaware of, to Lane's efforts. Five hundred dollars of it paid for his trip to Europe in early 1964 to spread his conspiracy gospel,[7] where, unlike the United States, political assassinations resulting from a conspiracy, rather than a lone gunman, are the rule rather than the exception.

It was a heady time for Lane. He was welcomed into Left-leaning European intellectual circles, particularly after he was interviewed by, and received the backing of, the French magazine *Les Temps Modernes*, Jean-Paul Sartre's publication. Noted British philosopher Bertrand Russell headed up the London branch of Lane's inquiry, calling his group "The British 'Who Killed Kennedy?' Committee." Fourteen of the fifteen members of the committee were Oxford or Cambridge University graduates listed in Britain's *Who's Who*, including Oxford University professor Hugh Trevor-Roper, who became very taken with Lane and who, twenty years later, would be deceived by a peddler of Hitler's forged diaries into declaring they were authentic.[8] German Communist Joachim Joesten dedicated his 1964 book, *Oswald: Assassin or Fall Guy?*, to Lane, proclaiming that nothing, including the "police-state tactics of the FBI," could sway Lane "from doggedly pursuing the truth."

Lane's travels were not limited to England and France. On April 5, 1964, he appeared at the convention of the International Association of Democratic Lawyers in Budapest. Alleging that Kennedy's killer was still at large and that U.S. authorities were engaged in a massive cover-up, he "called for an international commission of jurists to investigate the assassination."[9] Two days later he called a press conference in Rome condemning the "silence" of the American press in covering up the problems with the assassination.[10] Lane also made public appearances in Denmark and Czechoslovakia in the course of his seventeen-day swing through the continent.[11]

Lane's appearances even caused concern at the U.S. State Department. An internal memo from Kampala (capital of Uganda) said that Godfrey Binaisa, Uganda's attorney general, had attended the Budapest conference and was telling the press in Uganda it was "likely" Oswald was killed as a result of a conspiracy involving the "U.S. Army, Government, and big business who were opposed to policies that Kennedy stood for."[12] There is no record of Lane speaking in Poland, but based solely on his December 1963 *National Guardian* article, "Defense Brief for Oswald," which appeared before Lane even went to Europe, a cry for help was sent to the U.S. State Department in Washington by a department representative in Warsaw, who complained that the Polish press was giving major attention to Lane's charges of a cover-up, and urged "VOA [Voice of America] review" of the article to "refute Lane's claims which are widely published and accepted here."[13]

At home in the states, Lane did everything possible to stir up a national effort to challenge the Warren Commission's work. He had told a New York City audience on February 18, 1964, that "we're putting together citizens' committees of inquiry in every city in the country," adding that the national office was currently functioning in the city, and he asked all persons in the audience who believed in his message to fill out cards in the hall of the auditorium after his speech.[14]

Lane's *Rush to Judgment*, which was on the *New York Times* best-seller list for six months, leaves the uninitiated reader convinced that the Warren Commission was a national disgrace, having conspired to keep the truth from the American people. Yet, if the reader checks Lane's assertions against the evidence produced by the Commission—which few have bothered to do—he or she will find that Lane's contentions are either distortions or outright fabrications. "I only wish," Warren Commission critic Harold Weisberg told *Mother Jones*, the erudite organ for leftist causes, that Lane "were content to steal from others, but he has this urge to invent his own stuff." Lane, who also thrust himself into the middle of the Jonestown massacre as a lawyer for Jim Jones's "People's Temple" in Guyana, and into the assassination of Martin Luther King as a lawyer for James Earl Ray,* and as the coauthor, with Dick Gregory, of the book *Murder in Memphis*, has become an embarrassment to the Left. For example, in its article on

---

*Ray originally pleaded guilty to the murder of Martin Luther King, but at the time Lane was representing him in 1978 he had recanted his confession, denied his guilt, and declared he was an innocent victim of a large conspiracy. In defense of Ray, Lane alleged that the HSCA's investigators and their agents had suborned perjury, criminally received stolen property, and unlawfully tape-recorded telephone conversations, all to prevent Ray from receiving a fair hearing before the HSCA, which, along with Kennedy's murder, was reinvestigating the assassination of King. Lane added that the HSCA itself had engaged in conduct which was part of a "conspiracy" to prevent a fair investigation. (Anthony Marro, "Mark Lane Charges Panel Conspiracy," *New York Times*, August 8, 1978, p.A10)

Lane, *Mother Jones* referred to him as "the Left's leading hearse chaser," adding that he was a "huckster" who unfortunately couldn't be "written off" because "he is, in some disturbing sense, on our side. His story raises some troubling questions for the Left."[15]

In virtually every criminal case, there is only a handful, if that, of really key witnesses against the accused. The Kennedy case was no exception. Yet Lane devotes page after page of his book to persons who had only the remotest connection to the case—including eleven pages to a woman who worked as a bartender in Jack Ruby's night club over two years *before* the assassination[16]—while completely ignoring key witnesses against Oswald.

For instance, the main issue raised by Warren Commission critics is whether any or all of the bullets fired at the president came from the southeasternmost window on the sixth floor of the School Book Depository Building, where the Commission concluded Oswald was, or from the grassy knoll. Yet there is no mention in any of the 478 pages of *Rush to Judgment* of Robert H. Jackson, the photographer for the *Dallas Times Herald* who was in the presidential motorcade. As set forth earlier, Jackson told the Warren Commission that immediately after he heard the three shots, he looked up at the Depository and saw a pair of black men in a fifth-floor window straining to see directly above them. Following this line of sight, he spotted a rifle being slowly drawn back into the southeasternmost window of the sixth floor.[17]

Even more astounding is Lane's failure to mention Johnny C. Brewer, the person responsible for Oswald's arrest. Recall that Brewer, a shoe store manager, was listening to radio reports on the shooting of the president and the killing of a policeman. As he heard police sirens approaching, he saw a man duck into the entryway to his store with his back to the street. Brewer later told the Warren Commission the man "seemed funny. His hair was sort of messed up and looked like he had been running, and he looked scared." As soon as the wail of the sirens had receded, the man hurried away and Brewer stepped out on the sidewalk and watched him enter a nearby movie house, the Texas Theater, without buying a ticket. Brewer followed him and had the ticket seller call the police. They swarmed into the theater and after the house lights came on, Brewer pointed out the man he had followed into the theater—later identified as Oswald—and he was subsequently arrested.[18] Remarkably, not only doesn't Lane mention Brewer in his book, he doesn't even mention Oswald's arrest.

After Brewer identified Oswald, the first policeman to approach him was Dallas police officer M. N. McDonald. McDonald testified that Oswald said, "Well, it's all over now," and suddenly knocked the policeman down. He drew a revolver and was subdued only after a struggle.[19] Lane fails to mention McDonald in his book. In fact, he makes no reference at all to these very incriminating circumstances surrounding Oswald's apprehension. It is nothing short of incredible that Lane, who finds room in his book for 353 people who he claimed were connected in some way to the Kennedy case, couldn't find room for a single paragraph on people like Jackson, Brewer, and McDonald.

But this is Mark Lane's MO. He repeatedly omits evidence damaging to his side. Just one more example among many: Barbara and Virginia Davis both identified Oswald as the person they saw after the Tippit murder crossing their lawn while emptying his pistol. And Ted Callaway and Sam Guinyard both identified Oswald as the man they saw run south on Patton with a gun in his hand right after the Tippit shooting.[20] But Lane doesn't mention Guinyard in his book at all, and only mentions the two Davis women and Callaway in connection with other issues, like whether the Davis women could identify the empty shells that Tippit's killer had ejected and they picked up (they couldn't) or whether Callaway's description of the jacket the killer was wearing was completely consistent with the description given by other witnesses. He never gets around to finding the space to tell his readers that all of these witnesses identified Oswald as the man they saw.[21]*

Lane also elevated to an art form the technique of quoting part of a witness's testimony to convey a meaning completely opposite to what the whole would convey. A perfect example occurs when he quotes part of Jack Ruby's testimony before the Warren Commission, in which Ruby literally begged Chief Justice Earl Warren to bring him to Washington to give further testimony. "Ruby made it plain that if the Commission took him from the Dallas County Jail and permitted him to testify in Washington, he could tell more there; it was impossible for him to tell the whole truth so long as he was in jail in Dallas," writes Lane. Lane gives the following excerpt from Ruby's testimony before the Warren Commission:

Ruby: "But you [Warren] are the only one that can save me. I think you can."
Warren: "Yes?"
Ruby: "But by delaying, you lose the chance. And all I want to do is tell the truth, and that is all."[22]

The unmistakable implication that Lane seeks to convey is that if Ruby were questioned in Washington, he would divulge the existence of a conspiracy. *Yet the very next words* that Ruby uttered after "that is all" were "There was no conspiracy."[23] These four words, which completely rebutted the entire thrust of Lane's contention, were carefully omitted from *Rush to Judgment*.

Likewise, in his efforts to prove that the shots that killed President Kennedy were fired from his front rather than his rear, where Oswald was, Lane distorted the truth with half-truths. In his book he writes that "none of the [Parkland Hospital] doctors who examined the President in Dallas *observed* in the rear of his head a 'smaller hole' to which the Commission alluded as the entrance point . . . Although eight doctors were unable to locate [such a] hole . . . the Commission apparently felt constrained to insist on the existence of such an entry wound to support its conclusion."[24] In other words, if we're to believe Lane, there was no entrance wound to the rear of Kennedy's head, and therefore, Oswald could not have been the assassin. In addition, the Commission had, somehow, later created a wound in the rear of Kennedy's head to frame Oswald.[†]
But Lane did not tell his readers why the Parkland doctors failed to find an entrance

---

*With respect to the above four witnesses, conspiracy-leaning author Henry Hurt, who overall is not nearly as bad as Lane, doesn't mention their names either in his best-selling book, *Reasonable Doubt*, much less say they identified Oswald as being at or running from the Tippit murder scene with a revolver in his hand.

†Some further examples, among many, of Lane's suggestion that the Warren Commission not only was completely unobjective about the facts of the assassination ("the Commission was biased toward its conclusion before the facts were known . . . The Commission worked from the *a priori* assumption that Oswald was on the sixth floor, was the assassin, and acted alone" [Lane, *Rush to Judgment*, p.71]), but actually attempted to frame Oswald: "[The Commission considered] only such testimony as did not endanger [its] case"; "the symphony of conformity *arranged* by the most active Commission members, Warren, Dulles and Ford, their counsel Rankin, and their eager accomplices among the younger lawyers, David Belin and Arlen Specter"; "In attempting to" prove that no shots came from the grassy knoll, the Warren Commission, in its report, "ignored and reshaped evidence"; "evidence against [Oswald] was magnified, while that in his favor was depreciated, misrepresented or ignored" (Lane, *Rush to Judgment*, pp.193, xxxvi, 45, 378). In a related vein: "Thus, the Commission met its mandate to attempt to quell the many rumors about Jack Ruby, but it did so, apparently, by deliberately suppressing the truth" (Lane, *Rush to Judgment*, p.xiii).

wound in the rear of the president's head. *They testified they never turned Kennedy's body over* because their sole concern was to deal with the immediately visible wounds and save his life.[25] Benjamin Franklin, who once observed that "half the truth is often a great lie," would not have liked Mark Lane.

Lane also showed no reluctance in taking liberties with the statements of witnesses whose testimony got in the way of his theories. In his book he quotes James W. Altgens, an Associated Press photographer, and another eyewitness, Charles Brehm, as supporting his position that the head shot was fired from the grassy knoll.[26] But Altgens told the Warren Commission he believed "the shot came from the opposite side, meaning in the direction of this Depository Building,"[27] and told CBS that the shot came "from behind" Kennedy.[28] And Brehm told CBS, "I never said that any shot came from here [grassy knoll] like I was quoted by Mr. Lane. [He] takes very great liberties with adding to my quotation."[29]

Lane was so bold and blatant in distorting the truth that he even gives citations to the Warren Commission volumes that he knows directly contradict his own arguments. For instance, he states that the Warren Commission's firearms experts were unable to duplicate on the range what Oswald had done. "Not one of them," he says, "struck the enlarged head or neck on the target even once."[30] But an examination of the citations given by Lane himself (Commission Exhibit Nos. 582 to 584, Warren Commission volume 17, pages 261 to 262) shows two hits were scored on the head. Obviously, Lane felt free to do something as outrageous as this because he knew only a handful of readers would bother to look up the citations or have access to the twenty-six volumes of testimony and evidence produced by the Warren Commission.

We've already seen in this book examples of Mark Lane's remarkable ability to get people to change their original story to one favorable to his position; their memories suddenly improve after they speak to Lane. Here's one more for the record: As referred to earlier, Union Terminal Company employee James L. Simmons was one of several people atop the railroad overpass at the time of the shooting in Dealey Plaza. On March 17, 1964, he told the FBI he thought the shots came from the Book Depository Building, and he came down off the overpass and ran to the Depository Building.[31] But over two years later, in the lovin' arms of Lane, Simmons, unbelievably, said he thought the shots came from "the wooden fence" on the grassy knoll and so he immediately ran behind the fence after the shooting.[32]

Nothing, however, exposes Lane's tactics more than his treatment of Helen Louise Markham, who picked Oswald out of a police lineup and identified him as the slayer of Officer Tippit. Lane has always sought to convey the impression that he is a crusader for truth and justice, while the Warren Commission conspired to suppress the truth about the Kennedy assassination. Lane accused the Warren Commission of leading witnesses, putting words in their mouths, and trying to force them to give the testimony it wanted. He states that "the leading questions regularly and persistently asked by counsel for the Commission added up, in my opinion, to an improper effort to develop a favorable record—that is to say, a record consistent with Oswald's guilt."[33] But nowhere does the Warren Commission come anywhere close to what Lane did with Mrs. Markham, a thirty-nine-year-old waitress with an eighth-grade education.

In sworn testimony before the Warren Commission, Lane related that Mrs. Markham had given him a description of the man who shot Tippit that was completely at odds with that of Oswald. "She said he was short, a little on the heavy side, and his hair was somewhat bushy." Oswald, he pointed out, was of "average height, quite slender, with thin and receding hair."[34] The Commission later asked Mrs. Markham if she had ever given such a description to Mark Lane. "No sir," she replied, "I don't even know the man."[35]

As it turned out, she had talked to Lane on the telephone, Lane identifying himself as Captain Fritz of the Dallas Police Department.[36] When the Warren Commission called Lane back to testify, it was only after being pressed by questions from Warren Commission counsel that he made it known that the conversation with Markham had been tape-recorded. When the Commission requested the tape, Lane vigorously, but ultimately unsuccessfully, resisted efforts to make it available.

Rankin: "Do you have any writing from Mrs. Markham in connection with the interview that you referred to in your testimony?"

Lane: "Any document which Mrs. Markham wrote? . . . I have nothing that she signed or that she wrote."

Rankin: "Do you have anything that you made up yourself from any interview with her?"

Lane: "Yes, I do."

Rankin: "Do you have that with you?"

Lane: "No, I do not."

Rankin: "Will you describe that document? Is it a paper or a tape recording, or what form does it have?"

Lane: "It is a tape recording."

Rankin: "Was the tape recording made by you?"

Lane: "I think we are now moving into an area where I would prefer not to answer questions, quite frankly . . . I think that the Commission [is] aware of the fact that I have an attorney-client relationship existing."[37]

The legal theory Lane spun for the Commission was as exotic as some of the allegations of conspiracy he has promoted. As indicated, Lane had originally been retained by Marguerite Oswald to represent the interests of her son before the Warren Commission hearings, but since Oswald was not a defendant in a criminal proceeding, the Warren Commission declined to permit Lane to represent Oswald.[38]* Lane said that the interview of Mrs. Markham was made pursuant to his attorney-client relationship with Marguerite Oswald and that *this* relationship would prohibit him from turning over the tape to the Commission, even though he had already testified to the contents of the tape. Moreover, he argued, the tape was the equivalent of "working papers of an attorney," and the U.S. Supreme Court had spoken of the sanctity of these papers, protecting them from being disclosed.

Rankin: "Mr. Lane, could you tell us whether there was anyone else present at this interview with Helen Markham that you recorded?"

Lane: "I don't believe that I said *I* recorded it."

Rankin: "Was it recorded by someone else?"

Lane: "I decline to answer any questions because the questions you are asking clearly are not for the purpose for which this Commission has been established."

---

*Although he couldn't represent Oswald's interests before the Commission, Lane continued to be retained by Marguerite, and he and she made several joint appearances together, including one at a New York City town hall meeting on February 18, 1964 (FBI memorandum from Mr. Branigan to Mr. Sullivan, March 13, 1964). Marguerite dismissed Lane as her attorney on April 1, 1964 (*New York Times*, April 2, 1964, p.37).

Rankin: "Can you tell us who was present at the time of this tape recording of Helen Markham?"

Lane: "I am not going to discuss any working papers in my possession."

Representative Ford: "Did you know about the tape-recording being made?"

Lane: "I decline to answer that question."

The man who has railed for years about the Warren Commission's refusal to be open and frank with the American public about the facts of the assassination couldn't have been less open and more obstructionist himself when he appeared before the Commission; he was, in fact, far more uncooperative than any of the other 551 witnesses the Commission interviewed or took testimony from.

Ford: "Do you believe Mrs. Markham is an important witness in this overall matter?"

Lane: "I would think so."

Ford: "In order for us to evaluate the testimony she has given us and what you allege she has given you, we must see the information which you have at your disposal."

Lane: "I have told you precisely under oath what Mrs. Markham has said to me."

Rankin: "Are you unwilling to verify [what she has told you] with the tape recording that you claim you have?"

Lane: "I am unable to verify that because of an existing attorney-client relationship."

Rankin: "Can you tell us where the tape recording was made?"

Lane: "I can tell you, but I will not tell you."[39]

The above testimony of Lane took place on July 2, 1964. Chief Justice Warren pointed out to Lane that he had already told the Commission (in his previous testimony on March 4, 1964) what was allegedly said in the tape-recorded conversation. "Now, if you testified concerning it then, why can't you now tell us all the circumstances surrounding that? Why is your privilege any different now than it was then?" Lane responded that since the time he testified to the tape's contents, Mrs. Oswald, over his strong objection, "instructed me not to discuss the entire Markham situation at all."

If Mrs. Markham said on the tape what Lane said she did—that is, give a description of Tippit's killer that did not match Oswald—why would Oswald's mother instruct Lane to suppress this evidence that could only be helpful to her son?

Rankin pointed out to Lane that under the law, if one comes "before any body, the Commission or any court, and purport[s] to disclose part of a matter [here, Lane's testimony as to what Markham allegedly told him], I know of no law that permits you to withhold the rest."[*] But Lane wouldn't budge. The Commission's frustration with him is evident from this remark by the chief justice: "Mr. Lane, you have manifested a great interest in Lee Harvey Oswald and his relationship to this entire affair. According to

---

[*]Lane's "attorney-client" privilege and "working papers" arguments were legally indefensible. This is why, I am quite sure, he came up with a completely new legal argument in his book to shore up his legacy on this point; but his new story didn't hold water either. Lane wrote, "Had the Commission been motivated by an authentic desire to know the truth, surely it would have directed me to give the tape recording up. I was eager to furnish this evidence, but I was reluctant to break the law, for to make and divulge a recording of a telephone conversation may be a violation of the Federal Communications Act," and Lane said he feared being prosecuted (Lane, *Rush to Judgment*, pp.181–182). But number one, at the time the Warren Commission asked Lane for the tape, he had already disclosed its contents, and number two, if Lane knew enough about the law to quote the Federal Communications Act (47 USC § 605), then he almost assuredly also knew that under the act it is not prohibited and not a crime for a party to a telephonic communication to tape the conversation, even without the knowledge of the other party, and to furnish this tape and/or divulge its contents to a third party. Such a taping does not involve an "interception" of the telephone message, which would be prohibited by the act. (*Rathbun v. United States*, 355 U.S. 107, 110 [1957]; see also *U.S. v. McGuire*, 381 F.2d 306, 314 [1967])

you, Mrs. Markham made a statement that would bear upon the probability of his guilt or innocence in connection with the assassination. Mrs. Markham has definitely contradicted what you have said, and do you not believe that it is in your own interest and in the interests of this country for you to give whatever corroboration you have to this Commission so that we may determine whether you or she is telling the truth . . .? You say that you have a recording, but you refuse to give it to this Commission."[40]

Lane finally gave up the tape after being given a promise of immunity from prosecution.[41]* The transcript of the tape, revealing Lane's gross and tawdry effort to put words into the mouth of Mrs. Markham, shows why Lane desperately sought to prevent the Commission from hearing it.

Lane: "I read that you told some of the reporters that he [Oswald] was short, stocky and had bushy hair."

Markham: "No, no, *I did not say this.*"

Lane: "You did not say that?"

Markham: "No sir."

Lane: "Well, would you say that he was stocky?"

Markham: "Uh, he was short [the autopsy report on Oswald gives his height as five feet nine inches]."[42]

Lane: "He was short?"

Markham: "Yes."

Lane: "And was he a *little bit* on the heavy side?"

Markham: "Uh, not too heavy."

Lane: "Not too heavy, but *slightly heavy?*"

Markham: "Uh, well, he was, *no, he wasn't*, didn't look too heavy, *uh-uh.*"

Lane: "He wasn't too heavy. And would you say that he had rather bushy . . . kind of hair?"

Markham: "Uh, yeah, uh just a little bit bushy, uh huh."

Following a discussion of the police lineup in which she picked out Oswald as Tippit's slayer, Lane once again focused on Mrs. Markham's description of the gunman.

Lane: "Did they [the police] ever ask you anything else about Oswald, about whether he was tall or short?"

Markham: "Uh, yes sir. They asked me that."

Lane: "And you said he was short, uh?"

Markham: "Yes sir, he is short. He was short."

Lane: "He was short and they asked if he was thin or heavy, and you said he was a *little on the heavy side?*"

Markham: "He was, uh, well, not too heavy. Uh, say around 100, maybe 150 [the autopsy report on Oswald states he weighed 150 pounds]."

Lane: "Well, did you say he wasn't too heavy, but he was *a little heavy?*"

Markham: "Uh, huh."

Lane: "You did say that?"

Markham: "I did identify him in the lineup."

Lane: "Yeah, and did you tell the officers that the man who shot Tippit had bushy hair?"

---

*Lane claims he voluntarily decided to turn over his tape to the Warren Commission ("Playboy Interview: Mark Lane," p.55).

Markham: "*Uh, no, I did not.*"

Lane: "But, but he did have bushy hair you said, *just a little bushy?*"

Markham: "Well, you wouldn't say it hadn't been combed you know or anything."

Lane: "Yeah."

Markham: "Of course, he probably had been through a lot, and it was kinda tore up a little."[43]

The reason for Lane's reluctance to release the tape of the conversation was now obvious. The tape had revealed his blatant attempt to improperly influence, almost *force* an uneducated and unsophisticated witness to say what he wanted her to say. Under oath, Lane quoted Mrs. Markham as having specifically told him that Officer Tippit's slayer was "short, a little on the heavy side and his hair was somewhat bushy"—while the import of her words was something decidedly less than that.

We have all had the experience of sitting in an audience and feeling embarrassed for someone on the stage either because of his very poor performance or for some other reason. The latter was the situation when I debated Lane before a packed audience at Simmons College in Boston on the evening of December 2, 1986. Though the audience consisted mostly of conspiracy-leaning people, when I started to read to them Lane's shameful questioning of Mrs. Markham, the embarrassment the audience felt for Lane was so pronounced that many began to dip their head, as you would to avert your eyes from someone you don't want to look at. Halfway through my recitation of Lane's performance, I mercifully said to the audience, "Have I read enough?" and the audience, by various sounds, let me know I had.

Lane was so embarrassed by it himself that when I debated him again at Nassau Community College on Long Island on April 15, 1992, and was about to read the Markham matter to the audience, he said something that not only reveals his knowledge of just how bad he was with Markham, but actually was funny. I started out by giving a fifteen-minute summary of the case. He commenced his fifteen minutes by saying that "everything Mr. Bugliosi said was a lie." Later, during the question-and-answer period, I said, "What it comes down to is credibility. Who has credibility, the Warren Commission or Mr. Lane? I'd like to read something to you, Mr. Lane's interview of a woman named Helen Markham, that bears on Mr. Lane's credibility," whereupon Lane interrupted and said, "I'll sue if you get into this. It's defamation," adding that no one had asked me a question about it, and hence, I was just raising the matter myself, which he said I didn't have a right to do. His position, of course, was utterly untenable, but he was so upset that I didn't bother to go into the matter. Such a threatened lawsuit by Lane would stake out new legal ground. Not only is truth a complete defense against defamation, and I was about to read Lane's own words, but defamation is when someone makes a false and harmful statement about you. Here, Lane would be arguing in effect that his own words defamed him, and therefore he didn't want anyone to repeat them. I don't know about you, but I think this is very funny.*

---

*I debated Lane three times, the last time in San Francisco in the late 1980s or early 1990s at a California Trial Lawyers convention. Only the first debate, in Boston, was at night, with no limitation on time. The Long Island debate was during the noon recess at the college, as I recall, and there was a time limitation in San Francisco. At our first debate, when I confronted Lane with Jack Ruby's "there was no conspiracy" omission in his book, he had no answer at all. How could he? Neither did he have any answer for the fact that witnesses whose testimony clearly point to Oswald's guilt, such as Johnny Brewer and Officer McDonald, weren't even mentioned in his book. I was surprised at the poor quality of his presentation. It predictably consisted of one mis-

On a companion matter, Lane had testified before the Warren Commission on March 4, 1964, that an informant told him that Bernard Weissman, a right-winger who had signed an anti-Kennedy advertisement in the *Dallas Morning News* on the morning of the assassination, had met with Jack Ruby and Officer Tippit at Ruby's club, the Carousel, on the evening of November 14, 1963.* Weissman vehemently denied this and called into a radio talk show to ask Lane why he, Lane, had never "taken the trouble to contact" him and ask if it were true. Lane had told the Commission that he would try to get the informant to come forward, identify himself, and testify before the Commission.[44] But when Lane came back to testify on July 2, 1964, he claimed that the informant would not give him permission to disclose his identity. When Rankin informed Lane that this was "no legal justification" for refusing to disclose the man's identity, Lane responded, "I know that is true, there is no legal justification." His position, however, was that "I have given my word to that person that I would not disclose his name."

Chief Justice Warren: "We heard . . . when you were here in March—hopefully you would be able to tell us who this informant of yours was in Dallas concerning the so-called meeting between Jack Ruby and others in his nightclub. And we have been pursuing you ever since with letters and entreaties to give us that information so that we might verify what you said. Here we pay your expenses from Europe, bring you over here, and . . . you won't answer that question. You come before the Commission and refuse to testify. Do you consider that cooperation?"[45]

Lane, in his book, says that his informant first gave this information to Thayer Waldo, a reporter for the *Fort Worth Star-Telegram*. Lane writes, "If the Commission had wanted [the informant's] name, it need only have asked one of its witnesses, Thayer Waldo . . . [Commission] Counsel, however, did not ask Waldo about the meeting." Lane doesn't explain why he told his readers, but not the Commission, that it was Waldo who had this information. He also doesn't explain how the Commission Counsel could possibly have asked Waldo about this alleged meeting when the Commission members had no way of knowing he had any information concerning it.[46] But at the end of the deposition of Waldo on his observations of Oswald and Ruby at the Dallas Police Department on November 23–24, 1963, Commission counsel asked Waldo, "Is there anything you want to add further, sir?" and Waldo, with the opportunity to add at this time the explosive information about the alleged meeting between Ruby and Officer Tippit, answered, "No." Waldo went on to say, "I would simply offer you this, if it's of any interest," whereupon he volunteered that he and a colleague had collaborated on a manuscript about the assassination that they had not yet been able to place with a publisher, and he would let Commission members read it if they liked.[47] But not a word about the Ruby-Tippit meeting. Lane goes on to say, with bottomless audacity, that the information about the Ruby-Tippit-Weissman meeting from Waldo "was valuable as a

---

representation of the facts after another, and I had no difficulty exposing these misrepresentations to the audience. Lane, who is very intelligent, did better at the Long Island and San Francisco debates, where he increased the number of allegations and misrepresentations and I had insufficient time to respond to all of them.

*If Ruby had been involved, as Lane suggests, in a conspiracy with Weissman to murder Kennedy, it is more than highly unlikely that, as we've seen is the case, Ruby would have called so much attention to Weissman and his anti-Kennedy advertisement on Friday and Saturday, November 22 and 23, 1963 (WR, p.369). But Lane has never been deterred by such commonsense observations.

lead, one that merited the serious attention of the Commission. This . . . it failed to receive, for neither the Commission nor its agents appeared willing to investigate it."[48]

In referring to the Markham and Weissman situations, Chief Justice Warren said this to Lane: "It is a matter of great concern to this Commission that you are unwilling to tell us about those things that you considered bear upon the guilt or innocence of Lee Harvey Oswald. And it handicaps us greatly in what we are trying to do, because of the things that you do say when you are away from the Commission, and then when you refuse to testify before us as to those very things that you discuss in public."[49] Speaking of Warren, Commission member Gerald Ford said, "The one time I saw him get irritated, and I mean really irritated, at a witness, was Mark Lane."[50] In a 1964 press conference, Governor Connally said, "It is shocking to me that in the backlash of tragedy, journalistic scavengers such as Mark Lane attempt to impugn the motives of these members of the Warren Commission, cast doubts upon the Commission as a whole, and question the credibility of the government itself."

Lane was up to his old tricks in 1978 when he represented Martin Luther King's assassin, James Earl Ray, before the HSCA. Let's look at what the HSCA had to say about Lane in its final report: "Many of the allegations of conspiracy the committee investigated were first raised by Mark Lane, the attorney who represented James Earl Ray at the committee's public hearings. As has been noted, the facts were often at variance with Lane's assertions . . . In many instances, the committee found that Lane was willing to advocate conspiracy theories publicly without having checked the factual basis for them. In other instances, Lane proclaimed conspiracy based on little more than inference and innuendo. Lane's conduct resulted in public misperception about the assassination of Dr. King and must be condemned."[51]

Lane's bona fides as a skilled and dedicated soldier in the fight for civil liberties, whether as a "Freedom Rider" arrested in June of 1961 in Jackson, Mississippi, or as a lawyer defending beatnik coffeehouses in Greenwich Village in the late 1950s from the harassments of officialdom, are unquestioned, and it's been written he had a sincere belief that the buttoned-down establishment was always a force far more evil than good.[52] However, when we couple his demonstrated infidelity to the truth, and his deliberate distortion of the evidence, with the fact that virtually all intelligent people who are knowledgeable of the facts (both of which Lane is) know that Oswald killed Kennedy and almost assuredly acted alone, one is compelled to conclude that from the very beginning, Lane was a fraud in his preachments about the Kennedy assassination.

As a direct result of the unprincipled work of Lane and so many other conspiracy theorists, the polls show that an entire generation of Americans now "believe" that President Kennedy died as a result of a conspiracy. The students who crowded Lane's lectures in the 1960s and 1970s are the parents and teachers of today. Unless this fraud is finally exposed, the word *believe* will be forgotten by future generations and John F. Kennedy will have unquestionably become the victim of a conspiracy. Belief will have become unchallenged fact, and the faith of the American people in their institutions further eroded. If that is allowed to happen, Lee Harvey Oswald, a man who hated his country and everything for which it stands, will have triumphed even beyond his intent on that fateful day in November.

Mysterious and Suspicious Deaths

One of the very most popular and durable myths about the Kennedy assassination that conspiracy theorists have successfully peddled to millions of Americans is that witnesses who knew things that the conspirators who killed Kennedy didn't want anyone to know met "mysterious" or "suspicious" deaths. The myth has many inherent weaknesses, just one of which is that once someone has already told his story, the cat, as the expression goes, "is already out of the bag." And that's one of the main reasons why the conspiracy theorists' mysterious-deaths argument, first brought to national attention through a promotional campaign for the 1973 movie *Executive Action*, is lame on its face. Many of the witnesses who allegedly died mysteriously had already told their stories.

When I was a prosecutor, there were several occasions where witnesses of mine were afraid to testify because they thought they would be killed if they did. If the witness was fearful of retaliation because his testimony would destroy a friend or relative, and I was unable to provide adequate protection for him, I would never, of course, put pressure on him to testify if he was unwilling to do so. We are all aware of the many examples of people killing others to "get even" with them for "squealing," betraying a trust. But if the witness before me had no relationship at all with the person or group of people against whom he would be testifying, I was always able to convince him of the logic that the very safest thing for him to do *would* be to testify. If the person or group the witness feared knew he had something to say that could destroy them, the only legitimate fear was that they would kill him to *prevent* him from talking, that is, silence him *before* he talked. But once the witness talks and it's part of the public record, not only wouldn't the person or group achieve anything at all by killing the witness, but it could very definitely end up jeopardizing them. They would immediately be drawing attention and suspicion to themselves, since the person who testified *against them* had been murdered.

The genesis of the mysterious-deaths allegation goes back farther than the movie *Executive Action*. Penn Jones Jr., the late editor of a small, four-page weekly newspaper, the

Midlothian Mirror, with a circulation of about five hundred[1] in Midlothian, Texas (a semi-rural, one-yellow-page town of around 1,500 twenty-five miles southwest of Dallas), believed deeply in Oswald's innocence.[*] In 1966 he self-published the first volume of his four-volume *Forgive My Grief* series in which he started alleging that people connected to or associated with the assassination in some way were suffering untimely and mysterious deaths—for instance, Earlene Roberts, the housekeeper of the rooming house where Oswald lived. But as the HSCA said, "There is no indication in the records relating to her death, or in Mr. Jones' book, as to what exactly was mysterious about a 61-year-old woman with large calcium deposits and a case of pneumonia, dying of acute heart failure. The same is the case with other deaths cited in the same book, for example, Dr. Nicholas Chetta, the coroner . . . at David Ferrie's death, and Thomas Howard, Jack Ruby's attorney, both of whom died of heart attacks [Chetta in 1968, Howard in 1965]."[2] Jones tells his readers that his book "gives names and details of the strange deaths of . . . people who knew something, learned something, or saw something that was supposed to have remained secret."[3]

The biggest supporter of Jones's fantastic charges was *Ramparts* magazine, a onetime Catholic quarterly turned New Left monthly out of San Francisco. After interviewing him several times and conducting what the editorial staff suggested was a thorough investigation, they bought his allegations completely, publishing many of his articles on mysterious deaths word for word and concluding "that Penn [Jones] was right when he said the Warren Report was a waste of paper."[4] What gave tremendous aid to Penn Jones's fantasies and mythology was a February 26, 1967, article in the *London Sunday Times* in which an actuary hired by the paper calculated that the odds of fifteen of the people Jones had listed as having died mysterious deaths (a list that included Oswald, Ruby, and Tippit) within a little over a three-year period after November 22, 1963 (up to the date of the article, February 26, 1967), were "100 trillion to one." The article ended by observing that these "statistics are not proof of anything" but said that actuarial "science" pointed to foul play. The HSCA requested, in 1978, a copy of the actuarial study from the London paper and received a response on May 19, 1978, from the legal manager saying the article was "based on a careless journalistic mistake and should not have been published. This was realized by *The Sunday Times* editorial staff after the first edition—the one which goes to the United States and which I believe you have—had gone out, and later editions were amended . . . We asked [the actuary] the wrong question . . . what were the odds against fifteen *named people* out of the population of the United States dying

---

[*]Jones became so obsessed with the assassination that his small, rundown farmhouse in the countryside near Waxahachie, Texas, overflowing with books on the assassination and with the obligatory movie projector to show visitors the Zapruder film, became the headquarters for his crusade to prove Kennedy was killed as a result of a conspiracy. Caught up in this passion, he neglected his newspaper and in the early 1980s began publishing a conspiracy newsletter, the *Continuing Inquiry*, for conspiracy buffs. Not infrequently, he would disappear from his newspaper duties for weeks at a time to chase down witnesses and track rumors. Once, he even crawled through a storm sewer beneath Elm Street to prove that Kennedy's assassin could have fired to Kennedy's front from a gutter opening on Elm. (Brad Bailey, "The Obsessed," *Dallas Morning News*, November 20, 1983, p.55)

"Penn Jones hated me," former Dallas assistant district attorney Bill Alexander told me with a chuckle. "He thought I was a member of the killing team that was doing away with Warren Commission witnesses" (Telephone interview of William Alexander by author on December 11, 2001). The diminutive (5-foot-2½-inch) Jones, who fought as an infantry officer at the battles of Salerno and Anzio in the Second World War, was almost assuredly motivated by patriotism in his assassination research. The only problem was that his beliefs were, to be generous, irrational.

within a short period of time . . . [instead of] the odds against fifteen of those included in the *Warren Commission Index* dying within a given period," which they said would have been "much lower." The editor said this was a "fundamental error . . . for which we apologize."[5]

Apart from the issue of fifteen *named* people out of the U.S. population as opposed to fifteen *un*named people from the Warren Commission Index (there are 2,479 people in the Commission Index),[6] the joker here is "named" people. For instance, if one were to ask what are the odds against one *named* person (out of any number, no matter how big or small) getting multiple sclerosis, they would be about 500 to 1, since about 1 out of 500 people in our population gets multiple sclerosis. However, if the question were what are the odds against one person (one person period, not one named person) out of 500 getting multiple sclerosis, they would be about 1 out of 1—in other words, it's a virtual certainty, since 1 out of 500 people gets multiple sclerosis.

Millions of Americans are unaware of the above, and one hears, to this very day, every-day Americans who have accepted the mysterious-deaths allegation asking, "What is the likelihood that all these people connected with the assassination would end up dying mysterious deaths? One out of a trillion?"

When I asked Robert M. Musen, vice president and senior actuary at Metropolitan Life Insurance Company in New York City, what the likelihood was that 15 out of 2,479 people aged forty (I just hazarded a guess of the median age of the 2,479 people in the Warren Commission Index, and I thought that forty would be a fair age to both sides in this debate) would die within a three-year period, he reported back to me that "based on the United States Life Tables from the Department of Health, Education and Welfare for the closest years, 1959–1961, the likelihood that at least 15 would die would be 98.16 percent; that is, 1 out of 1.2." (Musen said that the "U.S. Life Tables were based on data from the 1960 U.S. Census [180,671,000 people] and deaths occurring in the U.S. from 1959 to 1961." The next census was ten years later.) For those who figure that age forty is too high, the numbers, per Musen, for thirty-five years old would be 57.09 percent and 1 out of 1.75. If forty is too low, the numbers for forty-five years old, he said, are 0.999996 percent; in other words, 100 percent, or 1 out of 1.[7] All of these figures are several light years away from "100 trillion to one," right? So we learn that the number of people somehow associated with the Kennedy case who had died at the time of the *London Sunday Times* survey was completely normal—it was not unusual in any way.

Perhaps the most prominent mysterious death the conspiracy theorists have cited is that of fifty-two-year-old *New York Journal-American* newspaper gossip columnist Dorothy Kilgallen,[*] who died in her New York City townhouse in the early morning hours of November 8, 1965. The reason for her prominence in conspiracy lore is that according to the theorists, she had interviewed Jack Ruby alone in the judge's chambers during his trial and was about to break the case wide open; that is, assuming she had a story to tell, she had *not* yet told it.

Because the whole mysterious-deaths issue is nonsensical, with no merit to the charge ever being found for any of the deaths, and because the Kilgallen death is, as *Newsweek*

---

[*]Kilgallen was best known for her daily newspaper column, "The Voice of Broadway," and for starring on the popular television show *What's My Line?*, which had a seventeen-year run on CBS.

correspondent Charles Roberts said, the *pièce de résistance* of the mysterious-deaths allegation, hers is the only one I shall devote a modest amount of time to. To give similar treatment to the other hundred alleged mysterious deaths would require a book in itself.

It should be pointed out that the *only source* for all the factual allegations surrounding Miss Kilgallen's death (other than her actually dying, of course) is Penn Jones Jr., the original and leading proponent of the mysterious-deaths allegation. Jones writes in his *Forgive My Grief* series that "shortly before her death, Miss Kilgallen told a friend in New York that she was going to New Orleans in five days and break the case wide open." Therefore, Jones says, Miss Kilgallen had to be silenced. But Jones gives no source for his allegation.[8]

It should be noted that even if Kilgallen had interviewed Ruby (more on this later), for him to tell her anything that would break the case wide open presupposes that Ruby had anything to say. But since there's no evidence whatsoever that the mob or anyone else got Ruby to kill Oswald for them (in fact, being who he was, he would be among the very last people to employ for such a mission), other than his psychotic ramblings ("Chief [Justice] Warren, your life is in danger in this city, do you know that"; "The Jewish people are being exterminated at this moment . . . a whole new form of government is going to take over our country"; etc.),[9]* what valid, earth-shaking thing could Ruby possibly have told Kilgallen? And even if he did have something to say, if he didn't want to tell it to the Warren Commission, or to any of his brothers and sisters whom he spoke to while in custody, why would he want to tell it to Miss Kilgallen, a gossip columnist?

Bill Alexander, the Dallas assistant district attorney who was the lead trial prosecutor in the Ruby trial, told me that the story that Kilgallen had a private interview with Ruby during the trial was "pure bull——. The sheriff's office never let any of the reporters talk to Ruby."[10]

When I asked Hugh Aynesworth, veteran investigative reporter for the *Dallas Morning News* and *Newsweek* magazine who was nominated for a Pulitzer Prize in 1964 for his coverage of the Kennedy assassination, Warren Commission, and Ruby trial,[†] what he knew about Kilgallen's supposed interview with Ruby, he said, "I know it didn't happen, and there was never any belief by the press corp in Dallas that it did."

I asked Aynesworth whether Kilgallen herself had ever claimed to anyone or in any of her articles to having had a private interview with Ruby. "No," he said, "never, not in any of her articles on the case, all of which I believe I've read, or to any of us who covered the trial. This allegation surfaced for the first time after Dorothy's death when her New York hairdresser supposedly told Walter Winchell that Dorothy had told her she spoke to Ruby and was going to blow the case wide open." Aynesworth, being a local reporter, knew the judge ("We were drinking buddies"), the DA, and the sheriff, and said if anyone had been

*Sam Ruby, one of Jack Ruby's brothers, told the Warren Commission that while Ruby was in custody, "his mental condition has deteriorated very rapidly. He keeps saying that people are being killed in the streets and he hears screams in the building of people being slaughtered" (14 H 501). Another brother, Earl, told the Commission, "As of now, he [Jack Ruby] don't even think I'm alive. He thinks they killed me and my family, my children" (14 H 428).

†In his distinguished career as an investigative reporter, Aynesworth was nominated six other times for this prize and was a finalist five times. "I'm kind of the Susan Lucci of investigative journalism," he chuckles. He was the only reporter to have been at all four major scenes of the assassination: in Dealey Plaza at the time of the shooting; the Tippit murder scene shortly after Tippit was killed; the Texas Theater when Oswald was arrested; and the police basement when Ruby shot Oswald. (Telephone interview of Hugh Aynesworth by author on January 11, 2000)

allowed to speak with Ruby alone, it would have been he (he was the first member of the media to be granted an exclusive interview with Marina), but he added that no one in the media was allowed to speak with Ruby. "I and everyone else was turned down. The best we could do was shout questions to Ruby when he was being brought to the courtroom from the lockup." When Sheriff Bill Decker (now deceased), whose office had custody of Ruby, heard of Kilgallen's alleged claim to her hairdresser that she had spoken alone to Ruby, Aynesworth said Decker told him, "Hugh, it didn't happen. These New York folks just make up stories." Aynesworth said that the late district attorney Henry Wade also told him it didn't happen. Aynesworth said the only person outside of Ruby's family and close friends who did get into Ruby's cell was a Los Angeles film producer who "somehow snuck in with Earl" (Ruby's brother) and provided the audio equipment for Earl questioning Ruby for a documentary.

Aynesworth said if the authorities had ever granted any reporter an interview with Ruby, "like flies on a horse-dropping, they would have had to let all the rest of us in the media talk to him. It didn't happen," he reiterated.[11]

However, in her biography of Kilgallen, author Lee Israel says that Ruby's co-defense counsel, Joe Tonahill, wrote her on January 12, 1978, that sometime in March of 1964, Kilgallen requested a private interview with Ruby. She told Tonahill she had a message to give to Ruby from "a mutual friend," who Tonahill was led to believe was a singer from San Francisco. Tonahill made arrangements with Judge Joe B. Brown, who Israel writes was "awestruck by Dorothy," for the interview to take place in a small office behind the judge's bench. Kilgallen and Ruby spoke alone for about eight minutes. Israel wrote that "Dorothy would mention the fact of the interview to close friends, but *never* the substance. Not once, in her prolific published writings, did she so much as refer to the private interview."[12]

In any event, Jones's story about Kilgallen having a story about the case from her interview with Ruby that would blow it wide open is wholly uncorroborated and very suspect. To make the tale even more malodorous, there wasn't anything suspicious or mysterious about Miss Kilgallen's death. Dr. James L. Luke, the Manhattan assistant medical examiner who conducted the autopsy, concluded in his report on November 15, 1965, that the cause of death was from "acute ethanol [medical term for alcohol] and barbiturate intoxication." The quantity of alcohol and barbiturates in her bloodstream had not been excessive, but the combination had caused a fatal "depression on the central nervous system, which in turn caused her heart to stop." There was no indication of violence, but it was "undetermined" whether the overdose was accidental or suicide. Dr. Luke told the *New York Times* that "it could have simply been an extra pill. We really don't know. All we know is that depressants such as alcohol and barbiturates, one on top of another, are dangerous."[13] About Kilgallen's legendary drinking, Aynesworth said, "Dorothy was a very heavy drinker. I remember one night at one of Belli's [Mel Belli, Ruby's main defense lawyer] parties, she joked to me, 'Hugh, you may have to write my story tomorrow.'"[14] Bill Alexander told me, "Whatever Dorothy Kilgallen said, she said through the bottom of a bottle of booze."[15]

At the time Miss Kilgallen died on November 8, 1965, her husband, Richard, and twelve-year-old son, Kerry, were asleep in other rooms in the townhouse.[16] When you are alleging murder, as Penn Jones was in his book, this is a rather important detail, one that Jones didn't bother, naturally, to include. Did the conspirators somehow gain entry into Miss Kilgallen's townhouse and bedroom in the middle of the night and force alcohol and barbiturates down her throat without her making any noise that would alert her husband and son? Kilgallen's body was found by the maid, a copy of Robert Ruark's *Honey Badger* by her side.[17] So there was absolutely nothing suspicious and no evidence of foul play. Or are we expected to believe that Miss Kilgallen was murdered by the conspirators who killed the president, but that these conspirators "reached" the Manhattan police and medical examiner and threatened them not to write her death up as a murder?

Finally, assuming that Kilgallen did have a private interview with Ruby, it took place at the Ruby trial in Dallas during *March of 1964*. But wait awhile, folks. Didn't Miss Kilgallen die in November 1965, one year and eight months later? You mean to tell me a *gossip* columnist, or any columnist, would wait *twenty months* to break a sensational story? They wouldn't even wait twenty minutes, would they? Wouldn't they report it immediately so they wouldn't be "scooped" by some other reporter? Yet her biographer confirmed what Hugh Aynesworth said, that Kilgallen never wrote any article about the alleged interview with Ruby.[18]

There is a footnote to all of this: Mrs. Earl E. T. Smith was a New York City society figure who wrote a Sunday column in the Living Section of the *Journal-American* under her maiden name, Florence Pritchett. When she died of a cerebral hemorrhage (Penn Jones tells his readers that the cause of death was "unknown") at her Fifth Avenue home just two days after Miss Kilgallen,[19] it simply was too much of a coincidence for Penn Jones, who ominously linked the two deaths to the Kennedy assassination cover-up. Jones said the two were "close friends" ("Possibly," he speculates, "Mrs. Smith was the trusted friend" to whom Kilgallen allegedly said she was going to break the case wide open; Penn doesn't mention, or didn't know about, the hairdresser story), but again offers not one scrap of evidence to support this assertion of friendship.[20] Other than their working at the same paper (Kilgallen, full-time, Mrs. Smith, probably mailing her column in once a week) and most likely at least being acquaintances, they certainly moved in different worlds. The tart-tongued and aggressive Miss Kilgallen, described by a colleague as a "newspaperman in a $500 dress," worked in the rough-and-tumble field of investigative journalism, almost exclusively male at the time. Mrs. Smith, a member of the Four Hundred in New York, was very active in the arts and in charity work and mingled with the swells from the Social Register. Per her obituary in the *New York Times*, she and her husband (the American ambassador to Cuba just before Castro took power) were close friends to President Kennedy and his wife, were frequent White House guests, and were Palm Beach, Florida, neighbors.[21] In the absence of any evidence presented by Jones that they were "close friends," the assumption (even if they had lived in the same apartment and worked everyday for the same company) has to be they were not. And in Lee Israel's 485-page biography of Kilgallen, there isn't even a single reference to her. Indeed, he writes that Kilgallen had very few female friends, her closest being Jean Bach and Lillian Boscovity.[22] But even if they were friends, so what?

Jones, naturally, doesn't bother to tell his readers that Mrs. Smith, per the *New York Times*, "had been in ill-health since mid-August" (almost three months *before* Miss Kilgallen's death) and "had recently been discharged from Roosevelt Hospital."[23] It should finally be noted that even *Ramparts* magazine, which so effusively endorsed Penn Jones's powerful imagination, could not swallow his claim that Kilgallen was silenced, conceding that "we know of no serious person who really believes that the death of Dorothy Kilgallen was related to the Kennedy assassination."[24]

The vast majority of the witnesses on the various mysterious-death lists of the conspiracy theorists (e.g., conspiracy theorist Jim Marrs's book *Crossfire* lists 104 witnesses) weren't connected with the case in any known way whatsoever, and had absolutely nothing of any known value to say about the case (e.g., Donald Kaylor, FBI chemist in the fingerprint section who wasn't even assigned to the Kennedy assassination investigation and died of a heart failure in 1977; DeLesseps Morrison, New Orleans mayor at the time of the assassination who died in a plane crash in 1964; Francis Gary Powers, U-2 pilot shot down over Russia in 1960 who died in a helicopter crash in 1977; etc.). But of those who did have a connection—such as Roger Craig, Earlene Roberts, Lee Bowers, and Dallas deputy sheriff Eddy Raymond "Buddy" Walthers—all of them, *without exception*, had already told their story, most of them on the public record, so what could possibly be achieved by killing them? For instance, as previously indicated, Craig not only had told his story on radio and TV and to conspiracy writers many times, but also had given an affidavit to the sheriff's office and two affidavits to the FBI and testified before the Warren Commission.

The buffs are so silly that in addition to President Kennedy and Officer J. D. Tippit, they even have people like Abraham Zapruder (heart attack, 1970), J. Edgar Hoover (heart attack, 1972), Lyndon Baines Johnson (heart attack, 1973), and Earl Warren (heart attack, 1974) on their mysterious-death lists.[25]

So silly that when Dorothy Hunt, wife of CIA agent E. Howard Hunt (believed by some buffs to have been in Dallas on November 22, 1963 and a co-conspirator in the assassination), died with sixty other passengers on a United Airlines flight that crashed on landing in Chicago on December 8, 1972, her death was listed as suspicious. Apparently the conspirators were so eager to silence poor Mrs. Hunt that they decided to take sixty other people with her.[26]

So silly that when Edward Benavides, who the buffs say resembled his brother, Warren Commission witness Domingo Benavides, was shot to death in a Dallas bar in February 1964, they allege that it was a case of mistaken identity, Domingo probably being the intended victim, and list Edward's homicide as "particularly suspicious" and, by implication, unsolved.[27] Actually, he was shot by a drinking companion, who confessed to the killing and served twenty months for manslaughter.[28] It should be recalled that Domingo Benavides, who saw Officer Tippit being murdered, never identified Oswald as the killer. He only said Oswald "resembled" the man and refused to make a positive identification.[29]

So silly that when Marilyn "Delilah" Walle, a former Oriental dancer at Jack Ruby's Carousel Club, was shot eight times by her husband in their Omaha apartment in 1966 (he was charged and subsequently convicted of her murder), the zany buffs alleged (without bothering, naturally, to cite any source for this allegation) that Walle was "planning a book on the assassination," so the conspirators murdered her and framed her husband.[30]

So silly that they even list the homicide of Dallas deputy sheriff Buddy Walthers (who searched Dealey Plaza for evidence and helped subdue Oswald in the Texas Theater) as a mysterious death.[31] But there was nothing mysterious about Walthers's death. An escaped convict from Georgia, Walter Cherry, shot Walthers when he and his partner, Al Maddox Jr., entered Cherry's motel room in Dallas on January 10, 1969. Cherry was convicted of Walthers's murder on June 27, 1970.[32] But wait. Maybe, just maybe, the conspirators who killed Kennedy helped Cherry (who was serving a life sentence for a robbery because he had seven prior felony convictions) escape, sent him to Dallas, holed him up in a motel room, and then sent an anonymous tip to Walthers that Cherry was there, thereby setting up Walthers to be killed. But why would they want to kill Walthers? I don't know.

So silly that when Michael D. Groves, the army captain who had directed military honors at President Kennedy's funeral, died of a heart attack while eating dinner at his home in Fort Myer, Virginia, on December 3, 1963, the buffs categorized it as a suspicious death.[33]

Not only did the majority on these mysterious-death lists die completely natural deaths, but if the theorists believe the Kennedy assassination conspirators murdered these people to silence them, why would they wait so long to do it? Marrs's 1989 book includes some who died as late as 1984 (Roy Kellerman, Secret Service agent in the presidential motorcade who died in 1984 of a heart attack), *twenty-one years after the assassination.* Jack Ruby, of course, is on all the buffs' mysterious-death lists, but Ruby died from a pulmonary embolism and cancer of the lungs and brain on January 3, 1967, more than three years after he murdered Oswald, supposedly for the mob. Why would the mob wait 1,137 days to silence Ruby? Weren't they afraid he'd point the finger at them on any of the hundreds upon hundreds of days before then?

In their unharnessed zeal to show that Warren Commission witnesses have been murdered to silence them, the conspiracy theorists haven't stopped to realize that they also have the unnamed conspirators murdering witnesses who could only help, not hurt, their cause. Since these conspirators obviously would not want it to be known that anyone else was involved with Oswald, or that someone other than Oswald killed Kennedy, why would they want to silence people who supported the Warren Commission's position that Oswald killed Kennedy and acted alone? Just a few examples: Why would the conspirators kill J. Edgar Hoover or Earl Warren, both of whom, as indicated, are on the buffs' mysterious-death lists? Or William Whaley (who died in a head-on car collision on December 18, 1965, when an eighty-three-year-old driver, who also died, was traveling north in Whaley's southbound lane without his headlights on in a drizzling rain), the cabdriver who Oswald suspiciously had drive past his rooming house and drop him off a few blocks later? Or James Cadigan (who died from injuries sustained in a fall at his home in August of 1977), the FBI handwriting expert who identified the signature "A. J. Hidell" on the coupon sent to order the Mannlicher-Carcano rifle as being Oswald's handwriting? Why kill Harold Russell (heart attack, 1967), who identified Oswald running away from the Tippit murder scene?[34] I know the buffs believe the conspirators will do anything to silence people who can expose them, but are the conspirators paranoid and crazy enough to kill people who can only help them?

The latest mysterious death some buffs say was a murder to prevent the truth from coming out? None other than JFK's son, John F. Kennedy Jr. The story goes that shortly before his death on the evening of July 16, 1999, he told friends he intended to launch a new investigation into his father's assassination; somehow the word got out to the conspirators and they sabotaged his small Piper Saratoga plane, causing it to crash into the sea off Martha's Vineyard, Massachusetts, with his wife and her sister aboard. The National Transportation Safety Board's conclusion that "spatial disorientation" by JFK Jr. was the cause of the fatal crash? Just a cover-up.[35]

Gerald Posner, in his book *Case Closed*, has a good section on the mysterious-deaths allegation, and perceptively points out that "no *major* writer or investigator on the case—even those trying to expose dangerous conspiracies—has died an unusual death."[36]

Indeed, I'm unaware that *any* of the hundreds upon hundreds of conspiracy theorists and authors have been murdered or died unusual or unnatural deaths. As *New York Times* columnist Tom Wicker points out in his review of Oliver Stone's movie *JFK*, "If a conspiracy as vast and consequential as the one claimed could have been carried out and covered up for three decades, why did the conspirators . . . allow Mr. Stone to make [his] movie? Why not murder him, as they supposedly murdered others? Why, for that matter, didn't they knock off Mr. Garrison himself when—as Mr. Stone tells it with so much assurance—the New Orleans District Attorney began so fearlessly to follow their trail?"[37]

The House Select Committee conducted a thorough investigation of the entire mysterious-deaths allegation. Jacqueline Hess, the House Select Committee's chief of research for the Kennedy assassination investigation who was in charge of the mysterious-deaths project, concluded her testimony before Congress saying,

> We . . . asked the Library of Congress to compile all newspaper articles which had appeared concerning any and all the individuals. We further asked them to give us their evaluation of the critical literature and the press accounts on each individual and to make recommendations with respect to further investigation in each case. Independently, we sent requests to the Bureau of Vital Statistics, the medical examiners' offices and the police departments in the jurisdiction in which each death was believed to have occurred, for the death certificates, medical records, police reports, and any other documents which might exist concerning the death. Because there were many cases in which there was no information indicating the appropriate jurisdiction, we sent letters to the pertinent offices in Dallas and Fort Worth, Texas, in New Orleans, Louisiana, and in Miami, Florida, listing all the names on which we desired information. In the case of some of the individuals, information was requested from federal investigative agencies. In the cases of [Johnny] Roselli and [Sam] Giancana, we requested and received a briefing on the Justice Department investigations of those deaths. In the cases in which further investigation was deemed necessary, it was initiated. Our final conclusion on the issue is that the available evidence does not establish anything about the nature of these deaths which would indicate that the deaths were in some manner, either direct or peripheral, caused by the assassination of President Kennedy or by any aspect of the subsequent investigation.[38]

To accept the mysterious-deaths allegation, one has to believe that in every single one of the more-than-one-hundred mysterious deaths alleged to be murders, the police or coroner's office that investigated each one and concluded the death was by natural causes or resulted from causes unrelated to the assassination must have succumbed to threats by the conspirators and deliberately wrote up a report that they knew was wrong, or, in more than one hundred cases, they were always wrong in their determination as to the cause of death.

There is no evidence whatsoever that conspirators behind the assassination of President Kennedy have been murdering dozens of people throughout the years who they fear will implicate them in Kennedy's death. Not one of these so-called mysterious deaths has ever been connected, in any way, to the assassination. The only thing mysterious is how anyone with an IQ above room temperature could possibly buy into such nonsense.

The Second Oswald

Among the most persistent contentions of the conspiracy theorists is that there was a "Second Oswald," one or more people impersonating Oswald prior to the assassination. For the purposes of this discussion, "Second Oswald" includes not just alleged Oswald impersonations but also Oswald "sightings" before the assassination. The way the conspiracy theorists have it figured out, if the sightings were truly of Lee Harvey Oswald, the things he was doing, or the people he was with, were of such a nature that they went in the direction of a conspiracy. And if the sightings were not of Lee Harvey Oswald, since it could be proved he was somewhere else at the time, then this means there was a Second Oswald, someone impersonating him, which again goes in the direction of a conspiracy. (The issue of an alleged Oswald impersonation in the Sylvia Odio incident is discussed later in this book.)

The leading current proponent of the Second Oswald theory,[*] which has a considerable number of adherents, is John Armstrong, a well-to-do contractor and oilman from Tulsa, Oklahoma, who is convinced that another Lee Harvey Oswald started impersonating the real one when Oswald was only thirteen. He cites as evidence a December 11, 1963, letter to President Lyndon Johnson from a lady named Alma Cole, who claimed that her son befriended Oswald in Stanley, North Dakota, sometime in the 1950s (her son later provided the year as 1953, when we know Oswald was living with his mother in New York City) and told her that Oswald was reading "Communist books" and said he "had a calling to kill the president."[1] Can you imagine that? Oswald is only thirteen and living in New York City, and already, conspirators have set out to frame him for "some" murder they intend to commit, and they start out by sending a teenage Oswald impersonator to Stan-

---

[*]The first conspiracy theorist to raise the issue of impersonation was Léo Sauvage in an article in *Commentary* in the spring of 1964. The Warren Commission treated all of the unlikely or impossible Oswald sightings as either cases of mistaken identity or deliberate falsehoods.

ley, North Dakota, to tell his young friend about his plans to kill a president someday. If that's not crazy enough, how the conspirators could clairvoyantly know, when Oswald was only thirteen, where his life would take him so he could even be in a position to be framed, as opposed, say, to being an ornithologist studying obscure birds in the jungles of Bolivia, or a doctor at a clinic in Grand Rapids, Michigan, Armstrong doesn't say.

As preposterous as this story was, the FBI, as with virtually every kooky story the bureau heard, actually wasted its time and checked it out a month after the assassination by interviewing other people in the small town of Stanley (around eight hundred) who would be expected to know of Oswald's presence in 1953. None of them confirmed the story. For instance, Bud Will, the proprietor of the City Trailer and Motel where Oswald and his mother were believed to have stayed, checked his motel registrations for the period from 1952 through 1955 and there was no record of the Oswalds staying there. Jerry Evanson, a friend of Cole's son throughout the summer of 1953 in Stanley, never recalled anyone by the name of Lee Harvey Oswald being there that summer or any other time. Additionally, Ralph Hamre, the county sheriff, said he was familiar with virtually everyone in the small hamlet and had never heard of a Lee Harvey Oswald living there, and did not consider Cole's son to be a reliable person. Mrs. Harry Merbach, a cousin of Mrs. Cole, said the latter was suffering from a "mental condition" and attempted suicide while living in Stanley by "drinking Lysol."[2]

For his part, Cole's son, William Timmer, told the FBI on December 27, 1963, that he saw Oswald five or six times in the summer of 1953, that Oswald said he was from New York City and was a member of a gang, and that he spoke about Communism and carried a pamphlet with the name "Mark's" (Karl Marx) on it and said, "Someday I am going to kill the president and I'll show them." Timmer told the FBI that after the assassination, his mother sent him some newspaper clippings of Oswald, reminding him that he may have known Oswald, and it was at that point that he recalled he did.[3]

In an interview in early October of 1999, Jack Feehan, one of Timmer's childhood playmates who Timmer believed had met Oswald that summer of 1953, said he could not recall ever meeting Oswald. In a later interview he said that right after the early October interview he called Timmer about the Oswald matter and Timmer denied knowing anything about Oswald being in Stanley.[4]

Conspiracy theorist Armstrong says that confirmation of an Oswald (not the real one, Lee Harvey Oswald, per Armstrong, but Oswald's impersonator) "in North Dakota comes from several sources. Oswald told Aline Mosby, in a November 14, 1959, interview in Moscow, that after living in New York 'we moved to North Dakota.'" Armstrong goes on to say that when Oswald was arrested in New Orleans in August of 1963, he told Lieutenant Francis Martello "that he had moved from New York to North Dakota." However, the Oswald who told Mosby and Martello this story was not, per Armstrong, the real Oswald, but Oswald's impersonator, "Harvey Oswald."[5] (Why the architects of this all-important conspiracy to frame Oswald would not have Oswald's imposter use Oswald's exact name of "Lee Harvey Oswald," Armstrong does not tell us.) In any event, even Oswald's alleged imposter did not make the statements Armstrong says he made. Nowhere in Martello's entire, August 10, 1963, interview did Oswald tell Martello he had ever gone to, or lived in, North Dakota.[6] And nowhere in Martello's testimony before the Warren Commission did Martello say he did.[7] As far as UPI reporter Aline Mosby's November 1959 interview of Oswald in his hotel room in Moscow is concerned, all of her original notes of the interview are set forth in a Warren Commission volume,[8] and Oswald told her, "We moved to New Orleans,"[9] not, as Armstrong says, North Dakota. Oswald never mentioned North

Dakota in the interview.* So much for "Oswald's" brief excursion to the thriving metropolis of Stanley, North Dakota, in the summer of 1953 to announce for posterity that although he was only a youngster, when he grew up he was going to "kill the president."

The Second Oswald theorists, then, have Oswald's imposter—apparently working at the behest of the CIA, FBI, or some other sinister group—impersonating Oswald all the way from Stanley, North Dakota, in 1953 to his grave in a Fort Worth cemetery in 1963, the real Oswald not being killed by Jack Ruby and possibly still being very much alive.

Oswald sightings were a predictable adjunct to the assassination. Shortly after the assassination, the Dallas police, FBI, and other law enforcement agencies were deluged with calls from hundreds of people who thought they had seen Oswald prior to the assassination at places and times when, the evidence showed, Oswald was elsewhere. This phenomenon inevitably arises in every high-visibility criminal or missing-person case. As author Jim Moore points out, "Whenever a sensational event takes place, there are always people who, for one reason or another, proclaim and manage to convince themselves that they have had previous contact with an individual associated with the well-publicized event."[10] Although many of these sightings are by sincere people, just as many are by those who are merely seeking publicity, some of whom will literally do anything to become part of the case. The "anything" can even go to the extreme of confessing to the crime. Indeed, one of the reasons why law enforcement officials routinely withhold (from the media and public) details of a sensational crime that only the perpetrator would know is to eliminate as suspects those who falsely claim to have committed the crime. In the Kennedy case, the sightings of Oswald were as common, and deserving of almost as little credence, as Elvis sightings after his death.

Conspiracy theorists know, as you and I do, that the great bulk of people who claim to be in possession of valuable information on any highly publicized matter are so full of it that it's coming out of their ears. For instance, conspiracy theorist John Davis says that "while writing *Mafia Kingfish*, all sorts of people in Louisiana climbed out of the swamps and bayous to enlighten me on the assassination plotting of Marcello, Ferrie and Banister. They all turned out to be frauds."[11] Yet this same Davis buys the Second Oswald sightings and argument completely, uncritically accepting, at face value, the Second Oswald allegations to be discussed hereafter. In his book, he writes that the evidence is "convincing beyond a reasonable doubt" that conspirators staged "a number of incidents" in and around Dallas in September, October, and November of 1963 that could "some day be used to frame" Oswald. "The conspirators hit upon the idea of deploying two Oswalds, perhaps even three, the real Oswald and one or two imposters, to accomplish this aim."[12]

The Second Oswald allegations and sightings have ranged from the possible (Odio incident) to the preposterous (that an Oswald impersonator was so good he even fooled Oswald's own family). Setting aside the Odio incident (see later text), all of these allegations, with one exception, are either unsupported by any credible evidence or patently unworthy of belief on their face.

Two realities should be kept in mind in any discussion of the Second Oswald theory. First, an attempted impersonation of Oswald would serve no purpose unless the imper-

*On November 23, 1959, Mosby, from Paris, wrote a condensed version of the long interview that was sent out over the wires to hundreds of newspapers throughout the land, and apparently a few (e.g., *New York World Telegram*, November 24, 1959, p.9) erroneously typed up "North Dakota" instead of "New Orleans," furnishing fuel for the Stanley, North Dakota, myth. Oswald's brother Robert informed the FBI his brother Lee had never lived in North Dakota. (FBI Record 124-10010-10361, Letter from J. Edgar Hoover to SACS Phoenix, Dallas, Minneapolis, December 20, 1963)

sonator resembled Oswald to such an extent that third parties thought the impersonator was actually Oswald. The problem that presents itself, however, is the extreme difficulty in finding one human being who looks almost exactly like another. For instance, even when national contests are conducted to find celebrity look-alikes, the likeness is often not that great. Where would these conspiratorial forces find someone who looked just like Oswald (not just facially, but in his approximate height and physique) and get him to go along on some mysterious mission for them, doing things in various cities (even other countries, Mexico and Russia) and giving his name as someone he was not, Lee Harvey Oswald? Second, whomever the framers of Oswald found to impersonate him, once Kennedy was killed and Lee Harvey Oswald was accused as the assassin, the impersonator would immediately know whom he had been impersonating and why.[*] And the threat of his informing the authorities on the people who had employed him would be very real. Even if they killed him, what about his family and friends, people he may have told about his new life? But maybe the CIA, FBI, KGB, or whoever allegedly framed Oswald discovered that one of their very own miraculously looked like Oswald's clone, so they didn't have to go outside their group to get an impersonator. And maybe, just maybe, alligators can do the polka. Of course, in the fantasy world of the conspiracy theorists, there is no room for the aforementioned practical considerations. But to reasonable minds, the high improbability that any group seeking to create an Oswald imposture would be able to overcome these two obstacles is alone good reason to look at the Second Oswald allegation with immense skepticism.

The premise of all these allegations is that the real Oswald was being set up, framed, for the assassination.[13] Without this premise, the impersonation argument makes no sense and is irrelevant. With this premise, if some group were framing Oswald, they would necessarily have their Oswald imposter say and do things which would lead an observer to the conclusion that the real Oswald killed the president. As New Orleans district attorney Jim Garrison, a firm believer in the Second Oswald theory, said, "Someone had been impersonating Oswald. And . . . the reason was obvious. A trail of phony incriminating evidence had been carefully laid down prior to the execution of the president, leading to Oswald as the scapegoat."[14] But the reality is that, as with virtually all of the Second Oswald sightings, the alleged impersonator said and did no such things.

The following, in rough chronological order, is a brief discussion of the more well-known Second Oswald allegations and sightings. As with the mysterious-deaths allegations, to discuss all of them would take an entire book. The reader should know, of course, that because I'm not discussing all Oswald sightings and impersonations, the conspiracy theorists will predictably and automatically say, "Ah, but Mr. Bugliosi failed to mention _____."

Other than the Stanley, North Dakota, impersonation, the first suggestion of an Oswald impersonator, ironically, came from none other than FBI Director J. Edgar Hoover. In a June 3, 1960, memorandum to the State Department's Office of Security concerning Oswald's renunciation of his American citizenship at the U.S. embassy in Moscow on October 31, 1959, Hoover concludes, "Since there's a possibility that an impostor is using Oswald's birth certificate, any current information the Department of

[*]Unless, as some theorists believe, the impersonator was also the actual killer of Kennedy, in which case the conspirators would have had an even more implausible task to meet: find someone who not only looked almost exactly like Oswald but also was willing to kill the president for them.

State may have concerning subject will be appreciated."[15] In his book *Conspiracy*, Anthony Summers (a Second Oswald devotee), true to the hallowed tradition of conspiracy theorists to religiously quote selectively, quotes only this last paragraph of Hoover's five-paragraph memorandum, and then ominously and disingenuously asks his readers, "What led to [Hoover's] feeling that there [was] a possibility of imposture?"[16] Summers wasn't about to answer that question for his readers. Reading Summers, one would naturally think that Hoover's reference to Oswald's birth certificate and the possibility of imposture must have stemmed from some information in the FBI's possession not referred to anywhere else in the memorandum. But the very preceding paragraph, which Summers conveniently makes no mention of, reveals why Hoover made the birth certificate reference and where he most likely got the idea of imposture—from Oswald's mother, Marguerite. Hoover points out in the paragraph that Marguerite had informed the FBI the previous month that Oswald had taken his birth certificate with him when he had defected to the Soviet Union, and that three letters she had written him had been returned to her undelivered. Also, she had recently received a letter addressed to her son from the Albert Schweitzer College in Switzerland indicating that he had been expected to show up at the college on April 20, 1960, but hadn't. The mother, Hoover said, was therefore "apprehensive about his safety." In the infinite research on the assassination, no one has yet been able to dredge up any indication that the FBI had evidence at the time of Hoover's memorandum that someone might be impersonating Oswald. From this fact and from the context in which the subject paragraph was written, it would appear that Hoover used rather loose language in speculating about the possibility of an imposter.

The suggestion that the FBI had deliberately withheld Hoover's memorandum from the Warren Commission[17] is refuted by a May 4, 1964, cover letter from the FBI to the Warren Commission which lists the contents of Oswald's FBI file (up to November 22, 1963) being forwarded to the Warren Commission. Item 14 refers to Hoover's June 3, 1960, memorandum.[18]

Three days after the assassination, one Oscar Deslatte told the FBI that on January 20, 1961, a Latin man and an Anglo man came to the Bolton Ford Dealership in New Orleans, where he was the assistant manager for truck sales, and inquired about the purchase of ten trucks for their organization, Friends of Democratic Cuba, headquartered in New Orleans. No sale was consummated, but during negotiations the Latin identified himself as Joseph Moore and the Anglo said his name was "Oswald," and if the purchase were made, he (Oswald) would be paying for the trucks. Oswald, per Deslatte, did not give his first name. When shown a photograph of Oswald, Deslatte could not identify him as the man who came in with the man named Moore since, he said, the incident happened almost three years earlier.[19] In May of 1967, Deslatte told New Orleans district attorney Jim Garrison that he had no memory of this incident and denied that it ever took place.[20] But four years later, his boss, Fred Sewell, whom Deslatte had not even mentioned to the FBI as being a party to the negotiations, suddenly stepped into the investigative limelight and told the New Orleans DA's office that he also saw the two men, that Oswald gave his first name as "Lee," and from seeing Oswald on TV said he appeared to be the "same man" who came in with the Latin man.[21]

The only problem with Deslatte's original story (subsequently recanted) and Sewell's story is that on January 20, 1961, the real Oswald was in Minsk, Russia.

Assuming this very shaky and questionable story were true, what possible relevance could it have to the assassination? Ask almost any conspiracy buff and he'll tell you it means that someone was impersonating Oswald in New Orleans in January of 1961, ultimately framing Oswald for Kennedy's murder. But let's walk this through. January 20, 1961, happened to be Kennedy's inauguration day. Even before Kennedy angered Castro and anti-Castro Cuban exiles at the Bay of Pigs, and before he failed to call his attorney general brother, Bobby, off the mob's back, and before the CIA and military-industrial complex feared that Kennedy might withdraw from Vietnam, indeed, before Kennedy had done anything at all that might cause anyone to want to kill him, a group of conspirators decided to murder him? And their brilliant plan was to frame a man who at the time was living in Russia—which means they would have no way of knowing if he'd ever return home and even be capable of being framed—and one way they decided to set Oswald up was to have one of two men who were thinking of buying trucks for their organization call himself "Oswald"? Really? Once again, is there no end to the silliness of the conspiracy theorists? Answer: No. And by the way, since those supposedly framing Oswald had to know that he was a Marxist who had defected to the Soviet Union, would it help their cause to have their Oswald impersonator acting like he was anti-Castro, and hence, anti-Communist? Just a thought. Assuming the Bolton Ford incident actually occurred, chances are it was just a coincidence (something conspiracy theorists refuse to acknowledge exists in life) that the man's name was Oswald.[*]

A reported sighting of Oswald took place over two years later, in March or early April of 1963. On November 30, 1963, a Sparta, Wisconsin, barber named John Abbott told the FBI that he had given Oswald a haircut back in March or April. Oswald said he was in town to visit the mother of a drinking buddy of his in Dallas named Philip Hemstock, who was from Sparta. While getting his haircut, Oswald told Abbott that he had been blackmailing, at fifty dollars a crack, some unidentified Texas nightclub operator he used to work for. Oswald stated that when a politician needed a job done, he (Oswald) would do it if the pay was right, and told the barber that he planned to use the blackmail money to buy himself a gun to settle a score he had with the United States.

Hemstock's mother told the FBI that no friend of her son's had ever visited her, and that her son was living in Victorville, California, not Dallas. The Sparta chief of police told the FBI that Abbott, the barber, "uses the truth rather loosely and enjoys telling tall tales." The local sheriff said Abbott was considered "peculiar" by many townsfolk and came from a family with a history of mental instability, though Abbott had no such record.[22]

The next alleged Oswald impersonations occurred in late September of 1963 in Austin, Texas, and Mexico City (Mexico City will be discussed later, out of chronological order). Why those who allegedly were conspiring to kill Kennedy and frame Oswald for the murder decided to take such a long sabbatical from the task at hand is not known. Nor do Second Oswald exponents attempt to explain the hiatus. Mrs. Lee Dannelly, assistant chief of the Administrative Division at the U.S. Selective Service headquarters in Austin, Texas, told the FBI on December 30, 1963, that two days after the assassination

[*]Before he recanted his story, the thoroughly discredited Deslatte had come up with an unnumbered (making its validity impossible to check) price quote sheet dated January 20, 1961, with the name "Oswald" written on it by him in the upper right corner. Each Ford truck, if sold, would sell for $2,088.32. Interestingly, Friends of Democratic Cuba Inc. was an anti-Castro group incorporated in New Orleans on January 6, 1961, whose board of directors included the right-wing Guy Banister (see later text for discussion on Banister) and whose vice president was one Gerard F. Tujague, the owner of a New Orleans shipping company whom Oswald worked for as a messenger boy between November 10, 1955, and January 14, 1956, when he was sixteen. Tujague knew and remembered Oswald (10 HSCA 134, note 64; CE 2227, 25 H 128), so if the group, for whatever reason, wanted its purchaser of the trucks to use a fictitious name, Oswald is a name that was not unfamiliar to at least one member of the group.

she heard over television that as of that time the authorities had no definite record of Oswald's whereabouts between May and the date of the assassination. Dannelly came to the rescue. She said she recognized Oswald as being the person whom a coworker, Jesse Skrivanek, brought to her desk on September 25, 1963. (On September 25, we know that Oswald was either in New Orleans or on his way to Mexico, with a questioned stop en route at the Sylvia Odio residence in Dallas.) Oswald told her he had "just come from the Governor's office" (in Austin) to try to change his dishonorable discharge from the Marines, and that office had referred him to the Selective Service office. Dannelly was unable to personally help Oswald (who told her he was registered with the Selective Service in Florida but living in Fort Worth), but gave Oswald information on how he could go about applying for the change he was seeking.[23]

The FBI was unable to corroborate Dannelly's story with anyone at the Austin office of the Selective Service,* including Skrivanek, who not only couldn't remember seeing anyone resembling Oswald but also could not recall the incident referred to by Dannelly. Further, records at the governor's office for the previous six months did not document any visit from a Lee Harvey Oswald or anyone else with a similar name.[24] The Warren Commission noted that "all of the information which [Dannelly] furnished . . . could have been derived from news media, consciously or unconsciously, by the time she told the FBI her story."

When conspiracy theorist Anthony Summers asked, "Was someone trying to impersonate [Oswald in Austin]?"[25] should he not have gone on to ask what purpose such an impersonation would serve? Again, the whole premise of impersonation would be to frame Oswald by laying a trail of incriminating evidence at his door. If the alleged framers of Oswald were so daffy and inept that they believed they could help frame Oswald for Kennedy's murder by sending an Oswald impersonator to Austin to rectify Oswald's dishonorable discharge, President Kennedy most likely would have survived November 22, 1963.

Since less than two months remained between the time of the alleged impersonation in Austin and the president's fateful scheduled trip to Dallas, one would think that the framers of Oswald would have been stepping up their Second Oswald impersonations. But curiously, they took a holiday for the entire month of October.† Richard H. Popkin, author of the 1966 book *The Second Oswald* and at that time chairman of the Department of Philosophy (not, as we shall soon see, Logic) at the University of California in San Diego, had an explanation for this hiatus. "In October there seems to have been little double-Oswald activity. This may be explained," Popkin writes, "by the fact that Oswald was looking for a job at the time and that his second daughter was born on October 20th."[26] Say what? I know some philosophers, as William Saroyan once said, think they can live "on tap water and Proust," but after awhile such a diet can take its toll on one's mental faculties. As author Jim Moore points out in his perceptive book *Conspiracy of One*, "Why

---

*The Austin Selective Service files listed fifteen Oswalds in the state of Texas.

†The only possible exception doesn't quite rise to the dignity of an Oswald sighting. Mrs. Lovell T. Penn, who lived with her husband on a farm near Dallas, Texas, told the FBI on December 2, 1963, that on October 6, 1963, she saw three men in her cow pasture. One had a rifle and was firing it. When she threatened to call the police, they left. Although she took down the license plate number on their car, she threw it away. She made no reference to Lee Harvey Oswald being one of the three men. Two days later the FBI interviewed her again and this time she said the man with the rifle "might have been Oswald." (CE 2944, 26 H 406; CE 2449, 25 H 588) Penn located one spent shell, a Mannlicher-Carcano cartridge case, that the man with the rifle had fired, but after tests the FBI concluded it could not have been fired from Oswald's Carcano because of "differences in firing pin and breech face marks" (CD 205, p.182).

would the activities of the 'real' Oswald keep the 'second' Oswald from going about his duties as impersonator? Professor Popkin doesn't bother to explain."[27]

Following a month of unexplained rest, an alleged Oswald impersonation took place somewhere between November 1 and 14. The allegation had the aroma of fabrication from its inception. On the afternoon of November 24, two days after the assassination, an anonymous male telephoned Channel 8 news in Dallas and told the news department that Oswald had had his rifle sighted at a gun shop (Irving Sports Shop) located in the 200 block on Irving Boulevard in Irving. That evening, an anonymous male called the Dallas office of the FBI with the same information, claiming to have received it from an unidentified sack boy at an Irving supermarket.[28] The next day, an FBI agent interviewed Dial Ryder, service manager of the Irving Sports Shop, who informed him that while cleaning off his workbench on November 23, he discovered an undated repair tag for a rifle bearing the name "Oswald." The tag reflected the work done to have been "drill and tap $4.50" (mounting a telescopic sight on rifle) and "bore sight $1.50." Ryder said the rifle was of Argentine make. The transaction, Ryder claimed, must have taken place sometime between November 1 and 14 when Charles Greener, the store's owner, was on vacation, because he said that Greener did not recall the transaction.[29]

Even excluding the suspicious anonymous calls (who else, other than Ryder, would have been privy to this alleged transaction?), Ryder's credibility went downhill from that point on. Ryder had told the FBI that although he could not be positive from photos of Oswald shown to him that Oswald had ever been a customer in his store, he was quite sure he had seen or talked to Oswald, probably in the store.[30] But on December 1, 1963, just six days later, Ryder told the Secret Service that Oswald was not the customer and he had never seen him.[31]

Most damning of all is that despite the fact that Ryder worked right alongside his boss, Greener, for several days after the date he allegedly discovered the tag, November 23, and they had discussed the assassination, at no time did Ryder advise Greener that he, Ryder, had located a repair tag bearing Oswald's name. Greener, in fact, told the FBI that he did not learn of the Oswald tag in his store until November 28, when TV reporters called him to comment on the allegation.[32]*

In his later testimony before the Warren Commission on March 25 and April 1, 1964, Ryder, who had told the FBI the rifle was of Argentine make, now claimed he didn't know what kind of rifle he mounted the telescopic sight on (the Carcano mailed to Oswald already had a sight mounted on it), but knew it wasn't a Carcano or any other Italian rifle. He reaffirmed in his testimony that "as far as seeing [Oswald] personally, I don't think I ever have."[33]

For those few who still want to believe Ryder's fable, if it were Oswald in the store, his owning a second rifle would in no way militate against the evidence of his guilt in the Kennedy assassination. However, Marina Oswald said Oswald had only one rifle, and that was the one he kept in Ruth Paine's garage.[34] And the imposture argument here is even

---

*Ryder's credibility was weak enough without author Gerald Posner distorting Ryder's statement and testimony. In *Case Closed*, Posner dismisses Ryder's tale, writing that *"subsequent investigation found* that . . . the gun store tag was in [Ryder's] handwriting, not in Oswald's" (Posner, *Case Closed*, p.214 footnote), implying that Ryder attempted to lead authorities to believe that the handwriting was Oswald's. But Ryder, in his very first interview with the FBI on November 25, acknowledged he had written the name "Oswald" on the tag (CE 1325, 22 H 523, FBI interview of Dial D. Ryder on November 25, 1963). Worse, Posner goes on to say that Ryder "refused to take a polygraph" (Posner, *Case Closed*, p.214 note). The opposite is true. The only polygraph issue that arose was limited to whether Ryder had or had not given the details of his story to a *Dallas Times* reporter, which Ryder denied. The reporter offered to take a polygraph test and Ryder testified that "I'm not one to volunteer for anything, [but] I'll take the thing if you want me to take it" (11 H 238).

more inane than in those cases where the alleged impersonator does nothing that in any way would incriminate Oswald. Here, the imposture would go in the direction of exonerating Oswald. If the framers of Oswald know he owns a Carcano and intend to plant it, the murder weapon, on the sixth floor of the Book Depository Building (as the conspiracy theorists claim the framers in fact did), why would they want to put a different rifle, a nonmurder weapon, that's not even the same make as the Carcano, in Oswald's hands?

Predictably, the conspiracy theorists don't avail themselves of this logic and also have no trouble with Ryder's credibility. Anthony Summers and Mark Lane, in their books, don't tell their readers how Ryder kept changing his story and the fact that he never even mentioned the Oswald repair tag to his boss, concluding, respectively, "somebody who was not Oswald had commissioned alterations for a gun—not Oswald's—in Oswald's name"[35] and "someone laid a trail of evidence leading to Oswald . . . Ryder's testimony regarding the authenticity of the repair tag was unchallenged by the evidence."[36]

An Oswald sighting related to the Ryder incident involved two middle-aged women, Mrs. Edith Whitworth, who operated a used-furniture store in Irving, and her friend Mrs. Gertrude Hunter. Whitworth and Hunter told an American correspondent for a British newspaper that on Wednesday or Thursday afternoon, November 6 or 7 (Hunter said she only visited Mrs. Whitworth on Wednesdays and Thursdays, and she also fixes these dates because of an upcoming high school football game the two were to attend), Oswald had come into the store and asked for a "plunger" (colloquial for a firing pin) for his rifle, presumably because a "Guns" sign was still affixed to the storefront, advertising a gunsmith who had previously leased part of the premises. Whitworth referred "Oswald" to the Irving Sports Shop a block and a half away. Before Oswald left, however, he brought his wife, "two or three week old" baby girl and two-year-old daughter into the store, where for thirty minutes or so he alone looked at a dining room set, remarking, "Most people are buying Early American furniture."[37]

In their later testimony before the Warren Commission, both Whitworth and Hunter identified Oswald and Marina from one or more photos showed to them by Warren Commission counsel, although Hunter's identification of Lee and Marina Oswald was not unequivocal.[38] When Marina appeared at the Warren Commission hearings in front of the women, Hunter said she recognized Marina "by her eyes" and Whitworth said she was sure Marina was the woman in the store but she had changed.[39]

The likelihood of the two women's story being true is practically nil. Texas School Book Depository records show that Oswald worked full days on November 6 and 7, 1963, and there's no evidence he absented himself during working hours on those days.[40]* Further, Mrs. Hunter said that when the "Oswalds" left the store, Oswald drove their car. However, even apart from the fact that Oswald did not have a driver's license and was

---

*Payroll records at the Book Depository Building show that Oswald worked continuously at the Depository from October 16 up to the time of the assassination, working full eight-hour days (8:00 a.m. to 4:45 p.m., with lunch from 12:00 to 12:45 p.m.) Monday through Friday, not missing one day of work. (The payroll records erroneously credited Oswald with a full day's work on November 22, 1963. In view of what happened at the Depository that day, this type of error is more than understandable.) Conspiracy theorists have made much of the fact that since the Depository employees did not punch a time clock, there's no way to know if Oswald was absent from work for a few hours here and there. But this ignores the fact that Book Depository Building supervisors kept fairly close tabs on their employees, making "a notation" if the employee was present at the start of the workday and another notation if he was still at work at the end of the day. Further, the supervisors reported to the payroll department any absence during the day for a period longer than that authorized (such as for lunch), and the time was deducted from the employee's pay. (CE 1334, 22 H 537; CE 2454, 25 H 601–602) No evidence has ever emerged from anyone at the Book Depository Building that Oswald was absent from work at any time during the period between October 16 and November 22, 1963.

learning to drive, there's no evidence he had access to a car. And Marina Oswald testified, "Lee never drove a car with me or the children in it. The only time I saw him behind the wheel was when Ruth Paine . . . was teaching him to drive." After being taken to Mrs. Whitworth's store by Warren Commission counsel, Marina testified she had never been in the store before.[41]

Mrs. Hunter testified that Oswald was driving a 1957 or 1958 two-tone blue Ford, and the reason she is positive of this is that friends of her's in Houston, James and Doris Dominey, "had a car just like this." In fact, she said, she was expecting them to visit her that very day and "had left a note [for them] on my mailbox that I would be at this place [Mrs. Whitworth's store]."[42] However, Mrs. Dominey, whose sister was married to Mrs. Hunter's brother, told the FBI she and her husband did not visit Mrs. Hunter in November of 1963, had no plans to visit her, and never told anyone of any such plans. According to Mrs. Dominey, Mrs. Hunter had a strange obsession for attempting to inject herself into any big event that came to her attention. As examples, she said, Mrs. Hunter was likely to claim some personal knowledge of any major crime that received much publicity. And if a tornado should strike out of a clear sky, Mrs. Dominey said, "Mrs. Hunter will claim that she had known the day before that this event was to occur." Dominey stated that "the entire family is aware of these tall tales Mrs. Hunter tells and they normally pay no attention to her."[43]

As to the connection between this incident and the Ryder one, it should be noted that what "Oswald" was allegedly seeking at the furniture store (a firing pin) bears no relation to the work (mounting a telescopic sight) covered by Ryder's repair tag. Further, in her testimony before the Warren Commission, Mrs. Whitworth said she was uncertain whether she referred the man to the Irving Sports Shop or "down . . . the highway at some pawnshop or something like that."[44]

For many reasons, including the fact that Oswald was at work and couldn't have been in the store, we know that Oswald and Marina were never in the store. And as for the issue of imposture by a second Oswald to frame him, how does buying a firing pin for one's rifle constitute evidence implicating one in the assassination of President Kennedy? Do the conspiracy theorists really want us to believe that for this benign and non-implicating act of buying a firing pin, the conspirators would not only come up with a second Oswald to impersonate the real one, but now, apparently, a second Marina to impersonate Marina? There is no end to the silliness.[*]

The Oswald sighting (or impersonation) that conspiracy theorists have perhaps relied on most strongly, and the only one that is supported by credible evidence, is the one by a car salesman in Dallas named Albert Guy Bogard. In statements to the FBI on November 23, 1963, and September 17, 1964, and in his testimony before the Warren Commission on April 8, 1964, Bogard said that on the afternoon of Saturday, November 9, 1963, a man walked into the showroom of the Downtown Lincoln Mercury dealership he worked for. Bogard said he introduced himself to the man and asked him his name twice before

---

[*]As we have seen, the Irving Sports Shop impersonation and furniture store sighting of Oswald simply "don't go anywhere." Yet conspiracy theorists predictably aren't cognizant of this fact. For instance, conspiracy theorist Michael Kurtz, who believes it *was* the real Oswald at both places, condemns the Warren Commission for not accepting the stories of Ryder and the two middle-aged women, saying this was a "rejection of evidence" (Kurtz, *Crime of the Century*, pp.147–148). But Kurtz doesn't bother to ask the obvious question, "evidence *of what*?" Even if it were Oswald at both places, what would this prove?

the individual gave his name as Lee Oswald. Oswald asked to test-drive a new Mercury Comet. Bogard, who accompanied Oswald on the test-drive, said that Oswald "drove a little reckless" at about 75 to 85 miles per hour on the freeway, taking the curves "kind of fast." When they got back from their drive and Oswald expressed an interest in buying the car, Bogard prepared a "customer's purchase sheet" (which Oswald declined to sign) and told Oswald he would need $300 as a down payment on the $3,000 car. Oswald said he didn't have the money now but he'd have some money coming in "in two or three weeks." Oswald would not give his address but told Bogard he lived in the Oak Cliff area of Dallas, which Oswald, in fact, did. Bogard said he wrote the name "Lee Oswald" on the back of one of his business cards. When Bogard heard over the radio on November 22 that a Lee Harvey Oswald was a suspect in the Kennedy assassination, the name rang a bell with him and "I tore up the card and said 'He won't want to buy a car'" anymore, throwing the card in a wastepaper basket. Bogard said he also recognized Oswald when he later saw him on TV as the man who had come to his dealership on November 9.[45]

On February 24, 1964, the FBI administered a polygraph test to Bogard at its Dallas office and concluded he was not being deceptive in his answers since there was no significant physiological response to the questions.[46]* Little is known about Bogard, but when the FBI reinterviewed him on September 17, 1964, he was being held at the Dallas County jail on charges of "passing worthless checks and theft by conversion."[47] And on February 14, 1966, he committed suicide by carbon monoxide poisoning inside his car in the small racetrack (drag strip) town of Hallsville in East Texas. Nonetheless, his favorable polygraph result cannot be summarily dismissed. Just as obviously, the results cannot be treated as dispositive on the issue. Other evidence has to be examined to see if a reasonable conclusion can be reached.

Since Bogard was about to leave for a visit home to Shreveport, Louisiana, after Oswald left the dealership, he told Oran Brown, a fellow salesman, to handle Oswald if Oswald came back while he was away, giving Brown Oswald's name. And Brown confirms Bogard's story, telling the FBI on December 10, 1964, that Brown wrote the name "Lee Oswald" down "on something." Indeed, even Brown's wife told the FBI that she had seen the name "Oswald" on a piece of one of her husband's papers at the house, but the Browns were unable to find the paper.[48] Brown also confirms that he and Bogard and other salesmen were listening to the radio in the showroom after the assassination, and when Oswald's name was mentioned, Bogard spoke out that this was the same man who had come to the dealership and that Oswald wouldn't be buying a car anymore, and then Brown saw Bogard throw a card from his wallet into the wastebasket.[49]

Another car salesman at the dealership that day, Eugene Wilson, confirmed all of Bogard's story about the customer test-driving the car. Wilson was told by Bogard that the customer drove like a "madman," didn't have enough money for the down payment, and so on, but he could not say, from photos, whether or not the man was Oswald. Anticonspiracy theorists seize on Wilson's statement to the FBI that the man was only about five feet tall. But this observation by Wilson, who told the FBI he had "poor vision," is

---

*It should be noted that contrary to popular belief, a polygraph does not show whether or not one is telling the truth, only whether he believes he is; that is, the test, if it is accurate (which law enforcement feels it normally is when administered by a competent operator), measures the presence or absence of deception from the physiological response (breathing, pulse, perspiration, etc.) to the questions. Sociopaths (those who have no conscience or feeling of guilt or contrition for what they have done) often are able to lie on the test without the lie being betrayed by a physiological response.

outweighed by others who saw the man that day, each of whom describe him as being of average height (e.g., Bogard said, "Medium" height; Frank Pizzo said, "Maybe five feet, eight and a half inches"). Further militating against the accuracy of Wilson's observation is that he didn't give it until September 8, 1964, nearly ten months after the incident in question. There is another point that makes it hard to give Wilson credibility, since Bogard never mentioned it: Wilson claims that when the man was unable to get the car, he said, rather sarcastically, "Maybe I'm going to have to go back to Russia to buy a car."[50]

Jack Lawrence, another salesman, confirmed that he was present at the dealership with other salesmen when Oswald's name was mentioned over the radio, and heard Bogard say Oswald had been to the dealership about ten days or so earlier test-driving a new car. He said Bogard was nervous about calling the authorities, so he, Lawrence, took it upon himself to do so, and he immediately called the FBI. He had already given notice that he was leaving his job at the end of the month, but he feels his discharge was expedited because of his reporting the matter and he was let go that same day by William Faller, the manager of the dealership.[51]

Frank Pizzo, the assistant manager at the dealership, told the Warren Commission that when Bogard was trying to close the deal with Oswald, he asked Pizzo how much money Oswald would need for a down payment and Pizzo said, "Around $200 or $300." When Bogard was unable to close the deal, he brought Oswald to the door of Pizzo's office and told Pizzo, "He doesn't have the down payment, but he will have $200 or $300 in a couple or three weeks," and Pizzo said, "Okay." Pizzo testified that when he saw Oswald on TV, "He looked familiar to me, and at that time I could have sworn it was him." But Pizzo added that he had only seen the man for "a few seconds" at his door and "couldn't say absolutely sure" that Oswald was the man. He also said that the "hairline" on two out of three photos he was shown of Oswald was not quite the same hairline of the man he saw for a few seconds.[52]

In addition to the problem of whether Oswald could have been at the dealership on November 9 (see later text), there are other problems with Bogard's story, perhaps the most important of which is that the day after the assassination, Bogard, Pizzo, and an FBI agent emptied out the large dumpster in back of the dealership where all the refuse had been placed from the wastebaskets and other sources, and a thorough search revealed no card of Bogard's with Oswald's name on it.[53] Nonetheless, Bogard was consistent in telling his story three times and, as indicated, passed a polygraph test, and all of his coworkers who had knowledge of the incident confirmed one or more parts of his story, not one of them negating the essence of it. So although I am not very confident, I feel that one is led to the conclusion that it is just as likely as not that it was Lee Harvey Oswald who came to the car dealership.

One thing is clear. There can be little doubt that the essentials of the incident described by Bogard took place. As indicated, no one disputes this and everyone at the dealership confirms it. The only question is whether the man was Oswald. Despite the aforementioned evidence that it may have been Oswald, anti-conspiracy theorist Gerald Posner, in the finest traditions of his opposition, the conspiracy theorists, not only didn't tell his readers that Bogard passed a polygraph test, but actually wrote this about Bogard in *Case Closed*: "A Dallas car salesman, Albert Bogard, said Lee Oswald visited him on Saturday, November 9, and test-drove a car at high speeds. It could not be the real Oswald since he was occupied with Marina and Ruth in Irving that entire day. Again, the specter of a 'Second Oswald' was raised. Bogard said he had written Oswald's name on a business card, which he had thrown away, and also claimed to have introduced Oswald to his manager [Frank Pizzo], who could not remember such a meeting. [Pizzo, of course, confirmed the meeting.] None of his fellow workers supported Bogard's story [just the opposite is true], although one did remember a five foot tall 'Oswald,' not a very good imposter. Bogard was fired soon after he told his story."[54] (Posner gives no source for this last statement and I am unaware of anything in the Warren Commission volumes or elsewhere indicating that Bogard was fired soon after he told his story. As we've seen, Jack Lawrence, the salesman who called the FBI about Bogard's story, may have been.)

If, indeed, it was Oswald whom Bogard saw, the biggest problem with Bogard's story is that he says the incident occurred on November 9, 1963, which was a Saturday. We know that Oswald arrived at the Paine residence in Irving after work on November 8. The next day, November 9, was the day that Ruth Paine drove Oswald to the Texas drivers' license examining station in Oak Cliff for him to make an application for a learner's permit, but the station was closed because it was an election day in Texas. She drove Oswald back to Irving, where he remained for the rest of the day.[55] However, we don't know, for sure, that the incident took place on November 9. Bogard said, "To be exact . . . I *think* it was . . . the ninth day of November . . . a Saturday."[56] But Pizzo said the incident happened "in the middle of the week, towards the weekend." He said he couldn't swear to it but thought "it was a weekday."[57] And Eugene Wilson said that "it had been raining" on the day of the incident and Bogard had told him the pavement "was slick," making Oswald's driving so fast all the more hazardous.[58] But it was desert dry in Dallas on November 9, 1963, without a trace of precipitation.[59] The next Saturday, November 16, Oswald was not at the Paine residence in Irving; he had stayed in Dallas because Ruth Paine was having a birthday party for her daughter, and Marina asked him to stay in Dallas.[60] We also know that on that day, November 16, Oswald had cars and driving on his mind because he went back to get a driver's permit that morning, but the line was very long and he left.[61] Since we know that Oswald told Wesley Frazier he intended to buy a car, albeit an old one,[62] it's not far-fetched to imagine that he went to the subject car dealership that Saturday, November 16 (when it also didn't rain in Dallas), or at some previous time that month, and on a lark took a spin in a new car. The fact that the subject car dealership was right near the Triple Underpass, and hence within view of the Texas School Book Depository Building where Oswald worked,[63] increases the likelihood that if Oswald did have any interest in buying a car, this dealership, of which he was probably aware, would have been a natural place for him to go.

The argument by anti-conspiracy theorists that the man could not have been Oswald because Oswald couldn't drive has some merit, but not much. Though Oswald was not proficient, Ruth Paine, who was teaching him how to drive, said that by November he had made "considerable" progress and had "learned well."[64] Although the Warren Report cites Marina as saying Oswald was unable to drive, of the three citations it gives to support this, one doesn't deal directly with the issue and one doesn't address the issue at all. Only the third does and it supports the opposite. When Marina was asked in her testimony if he was "able to drive a car," she answered, "Yes, I think that he knew how. Ruth [Paine] taught him how."[65]*

The only relevance of the whole Bogard story, of course, is that if the man was Oswald,

---

*Marina told the FBI that her husband never told her he had seen or spoken to anyone about buying a car (CE 1403, 22 H 780, FBI interview of Marina Oswald on December 16, 1963). But since Oswald was notoriously secretive about everything in his life, not too much weight can be given to this.

his telling Bogard he was going to be coming into some money soon raises the inference that he was getting paid to kill Kennedy and hence, many conspiracy theorists argue, the existence of a conspiracy. But when we look closely at the matter, there's much less to it than meets the eye. What type of money was Oswald (assuming it was he) talking about? It is not clear from Bogard's testimony whether Oswald intended to buy the car outright or just make a down payment.

"Did you tell him you needed a down payment?" Warren Commission counsel asked Bogard.

"He said he would have it . . . in two or three weeks."

"Did you tell him how much?"

"Yes . . . Three hundred dollars."

But later Bogard quotes Oswald as telling him he "would just pay cash for it [the car] at a later date," so there is some ambiguity. But there is no ambiguity in Frank Pizzo's testimony. As indicated, he said Bogard told him, "He [Oswald] doesn't have the down payment, *but he will have $200 or $300 in a couple or three weeks.*" So we may only be talking about $200 or $300. But even assuming Oswald led Bogard to believe he would pay cash for the whole purchase price of the car, nothing can be made of this for two reasons. If a man can tell his wife, as Oswald did, that one day "he would be Prime Minister," certainly he would be very capable of telling a persistent car salesman he'd be coming into some money soon and would pay cash for the car. These words, like those between lovers, are written on the wind. But far more importantly, we know no one paid Oswald to kill Kennedy, not only because there's no evidence of this, but because we know that Oswald virtually hadn't a dime to his name on the day he killed Kennedy. He left $170 behind for Marina on the morning of the assassination, and had $13.87 on his person when he was arrested. In a highly detailed analysis of Oswald's finances from January 13, 1962 (when he arrived back in the United States from Russia), through November 22, 1963, the Warren Commission concluded that Oswald and Marina had $183.87 to their name at the time of the assassination.[66]

The remainder of the conspiracy community believes that the man at the car dealership was not Oswald but an imposter. As conspiracy theorist Walt Brown puts it, "It would seem, on [its] face, that this test-drive event was a bonafide 'Oswald impersonation' which immediately shouts 'conspiracy,' as someone wanted to have it on record that a 'Lee Oswald' would soon be coming into money."[67] But this argument is counterintuitive. Any group of conspirators out to frame Oswald would obviously want the authorities to believe that Oswald acted alone, that no conspiracy was involved. If the Oswald impersonator said or did anything to advertise that he was not acting alone, that there were conspirators behind him, it would immeasurably increase the risk that law enforcement, now knowing there were people behind Oswald, would eventually find them. Apparently Walt Brown's good mind was taking a rest when he wrote those words.* If conspirators had Oswald kill Kennedy for them, the last thing in the world they would do would be to encourage the suspicion that anyone was behind Oswald's act. It should be added parenthetically that a professional imposter, as the conspiracy buffs would want us to believe was impersonating Oswald, would clearly have shown Bogard a fake ID to implant his

---

*Unless—and this is a real possibility that the conspiracy theorists should start writing books about— there was a group of conspirators out to frame the conspirators who were framing Oswald.

name in Bogard's mind. But Bogard said "Oswald" showed him no ID. In fact, Bogard said the man had to be prodded even to give his name.[68] Some imposter.

My sense is that the man in the Bogard incident was either Oswald, in which case no conspiratorial inferences can reasonably be drawn from all the evidence, or someone else whom Bogard sincerely believed was Oswald. But he surely was no imposter.

Several witnesses claim they had seen Oswald firing a rifle at the Sports Drome Rifle Range in Dallas at various times from September through November of 1963. Malcolm H. Price Jr., who helped out at the range, told the Warren Commission he first saw Oswald at the range on September 28 when Oswald asked him to set the scope on his rifle for him, which he said he did, zeroing it in at one hundred yards. Apart from the fact that Oswald, a former marine, would certainly know himself how to set the scope on his rifle, the problem with Price's story is that Oswald is known to have been in Mexico City on that date. Price said he saw Oswald two times thereafter at the range, the last time being the "Sunday before . . . Thanksgiving."

Warren Commission counsel: "Well, the Sunday before Thanksgiving [November 24, the day Ruby killed Oswald] was *after* the assassination."

Price: "It was *after*?"

"Yes, and you saw . . . Oswald at the rifle range *after* the assassination?"

"I believe I did."[69]

Garland Slack, who fired at the range, said that on November 10, when they had a turkey shoot at the range, and November 17, he saw Oswald firing at the range. On the seventeenth he had a run-in with Oswald because Oswald was shooting at Slack's target. Though Oswald was not at the Paine residence on the weekend of November 16 and 17, and hence, it was possible for him to be at the range, it was not possible for Slack to see Oswald at the range on the tenth. Ruth Paine said that "except for the trip to Dallas, Texas, on November 9, 1963 [to get Oswald's driver's permit], Lee Oswald remained in my home from the time of his arrival, the late afternoon of November 8, 1963, until he departed for Dallas, Texas, in the early morning of November 12, 1963." (November 11 was Armistice Day, a holiday, so Oswald returned to Dallas on Tuesday morning.) Slack acknowledged how "you read the papers and you get to where you . . . find yourself imagining you saw somebody." But he said he was positive ("I know") Oswald was the man at the range. What type of hair did "Oswald" have? Slack said he had "hair that grew down his neck, all the way down into his jacket."[70] Certainly sounds like Oswald to me.

Two other shooters at the range, Dr. Homer Wood and his thirteen-year-old son, Sterling, told the Warren Commission they were confident they saw Oswald firing on the range on November 16, 1963.[71]*

Though other witnesses partially corroborated the testimony of the above witnesses, the Warren Commission said, "There was other evidence which prevented the Commission from reaching the conclusion that Lee Harvey Oswald was the person these witnesses saw."[72] In addition to the impossibility of some of the witnesses seeing Oswald on

---

*Two of the aforementioned witnesses said that "Oswald" came to the range with a companion, one saying the companion was around five feet nine inches (10 H 393, WCT Sterling Charles Wood), and the other saying he was a "tall boy" (10 H 381, WCT Garland Glenwill Slack). Several witnesses noted a bearded man at the range and one witness thought the man and Oswald were together, but the bearded man (one Michael Murph) was located by the FBI and found to have no connection to Oswald (CE 2897–2898, 26 H 350–351).

certain days, when we know Oswald was elsewhere, some of the descriptions of him (very long hair, the hair was "blonde," he wore a "Bulldogger Texas style" hat, and had bubble gum or chewing tobacco in his cheek, etc.) simply didn't fit Oswald. Nor did the allegation that Oswald drove up in a 1940 or 1941 Model Ford, since there's no evidence that Oswald had access to a car. Also, neither Oswald's name nor any of his known aliases were found on the sign-in register at the Sports Drome Rifle Range, though customers didn't always sign their names. Moreover, there is no evidence that Oswald owned more than one rifle, and the one the witnesses saw did not match Oswald's Carcano. For instance, Price and Slack said that certain pieces were missing from the top of the weapon, and Dr. Wood and his son recalled that the weapon spouted flames when fired. Price and Slack also said they did not believe the rifle had a sling, but the Carcano did.[73] Also, all casings recovered from areas where witnesses claimed to have seen Oswald firing his weapon were examined at the FBI laboratory, which determined that none had been fired from Oswald's Carcano rifle.[74]

Despite all this, if the man, indeed, was Oswald, his practice firing at the range with his Carcano would be a normal activity and would not implicate him in Kennedy's murder. Some conspiracy theorists believe that the man at the range was not Oswald. "The [Warren] Commission may be correct," Mark Lane says, immediately segueing to the possibility that the man at the range was "impersonating Oswald" for the obvious purpose of a frame-up.[75] But how, may I ask, would impersonating Oswald firing at the range serve to implicate Oswald in the murder of President Kennedy? That's evidence of guilt? And if the man were impersonating Oswald, why would he keep his hair very long (like a "beatnik," Slack told the FBI), wear a type of hat Oswald was never seen wearing, and use a rifle not identical to Oswald's Carcano (which the conspiracy theorists believe the framers of Oswald knew about and indeed planted on the sixth floor)? Why, indeed, didn't he tell some of the people at the range that his name was Lee Harvey Oswald, or even print his name in the sign-in register? The whole rifle range story doesn't add up to a hill of beans.

Leonard E. Hutchison, the owner of a supermarket in Irving, told the Warren Commission that early Friday evening in the first week of November, Oswald tried to cash a personal check payable to him for $189 at his store, but he declined since he never cashed personal checks in excess of $25. Oswald is not known to have received a check for this amount from any source, once again raising in the minds of conspiracy theorists the specter of conspiracy. Hutchison's story broke down when he said he had seen Oswald in his store on weekday mornings four or five times starting in late September. Not only didn't Oswald start coming out to Irving until he got his job at the Book Depository Building in mid-October, but in Hutchison's earlier statement to the FBI on December 3, 1963, he said the $189 check incident in November was the *first* time he had seen Oswald, and Oswald started coming to the store "once or twice a week" thereafter up to the assassination.[76] Hutchison also told the Commission that Oswald would always come into the store between 7:20 and 7:45 in the morning (he said 7:15 to 7:20 to the FBI) to buy cinnamon rolls and milk, presumably for breakfast. But Marina said that Oswald would never eat breakfast. "He just drank coffee and that is all."[77] Moreover, except for rare occasions, Oswald was in Irving only on weekends, and Wesley Frazier testified that he'd pick Oswald up around 7:20 on Monday mornings, and never later than 7:25 to get to work by 8:00.[78] The Paine and Frazier residences were eight-tenths of a mile from Hutchison's store.[79]

Hutchison told the FBI that on Wednesday evening, November 13, Oswald came into the store with a woman he "presumed" was his wife, and this was the only person he had ever seen Oswald with.[80] In his testimony before the Warren Commission, he said the woman was Marina, and the two were accompanied by an "elderly lady."[81] We know that Oswald was not at the Paine residence in Irving on Wednesday evening, November 13, having returned to Dallas on the morning of the twelfth, making his going to the store in Irving with Marina and the "elderly lady" highly unlikely. Marina, as well as Oswald's mother, Marguerite, both told the FBI they had never been to Hutchison's market, and Marina said neither had her husband.[82]

Since it is clear the man Hutchison saw was almost assuredly not Oswald, the question again has to be asked: Is it believable that conspirators trying to frame Oswald with an Oswald imposter would advance their cause by having the imposter try to cash a $189 check at a supermarket? If so, in what way?

For years, students of the Kennedy assassination have wondered where, if anywhere (i.e., he could have been wandering aimlessly trying to figure out what to do next), Oswald was going just before his fateful encounter with Officer Tippit at around 1:15 on the afternoon of the assassination. Was he going to alleged co-conspirator Jack Ruby's apartment (1⅓ miles away and almost on a straight line from the direction Oswald was walking)? Or was he going to the home of retired Major General Walker (about 5 miles away) to kill him for sure this time? Or was he perhaps on his way to rendezvous with Tippit himself, an alleged co-conspirator in Kennedy's assassination? These are just a few of the speculations that have tantalized researchers. Conspiracy author Sylvia Meagher pointed out that Oswald "had no known social or business contacts in [the] immediate area" where Officer Tippit was shot.[83]

Although no one knows where Oswald was headed at the time he met up with Tippit, the probability is that he wasn't thinking about escaping to Mexico or Cuba. With $183.87 to his name on the morning of the assassination, it is highly unlikely he would have only taken $13.87 (the amount on his person at the time of his arrest) of it for himself if Mexico or Cuba were on his mind. The fact that he only took $13.87 with him on the morning of November 22, 1963, suggests he probably thought the likelihood of his escaping was small.

One of the most interesting speculations that the more serious conspiracy theorists have entertained is that Oswald was on his way to Redbird Airport, a small municipal airport in South Dallas, where waiting co-conspirators would fly him away to Mexico or Cuba in his escape from the police dragnet. Dallas assistant district attorney Bill Alexander, whose job it would have been to prosecute Oswald, told me that "this possibility naturally entered my mind, as well as Captain Fritz's."[84] Indeed, though Oswald never went to Redbird Airport on November 22, 1963, assassination lore has it that a small plane, bound for Mexico, did leave Redbird Airport on the afternoon of the assassination.

That Redbird Airport (renamed Dallas Executive Airport on May 1, 2002) even entered anyone's mind is because at the time Tippit pulled his squad car over to talk to Oswald, Oswald was walking eastbound on the south side of Tenth Street near Patton, and if he were to continue eastbound, Interstate 35 (R. L. Thornton Freeway) would have been seven blocks away, with the Redbird Airport being about 5¼ miles southwest down the road from there. The Secret Service said Oswald could have managed to catch a bus near the freeway that would be "routed past the Redbird Airport."[85]

Indeed, some conspiracy theorists depart from the theory that Tippit was part of the plot to kill Kennedy* and depict him, instead, as an unwitting pawn who, as a favor for Roscoe White, an ex-CIA friend, was supposed to pick up Oswald, a stranger, at Tenth and Patton to drive him to Redbird Airport. When Tippit noticed that Oswald fit the vague description of the presidential assassin sent out over the police radio, and threatened to arrest him, White, fearing that Tippit already had learned too much, jumped out of some nearby bushes and killed Tippit.[86] But instead of the aforementioned plan that would thrust Tippit unknowingly into the assassination plot, why White himself wouldn't simply drive Oswald to the Redbird Airport, the conspiracy theorists don't say.[†]

Naturally, the conspiracy theorists would love to have some "evidence" to support this delicious Redbird Airport suspicion of theirs. And they got it when it surfaced publicly for the first time in 1966 in Richard Popkin's book *The Second Oswald*. Conspiracy theorist Jones Harris told Popkin that one Wayne January, "the manager of the Redbird Air Field at the time of the assassination," told him, Harris, that on Wednesday morning, November 20, 1963, three people turned up at the airport. Two of them, a heavy-set young man and a girl, got out of their car and spoke to him, leaving a young man sitting in the car. The couple inquired about the possibility of renting a Cessna 310 on November 22 to fly to Mexico, saying they would return the plane on Sunday, November 24. From their appearance and demeanor, January did not believe they could afford the flight and suspected they might want to hijack the plane and go on to Cuba. He decided not to rent them the plane even if they turned up with the money for the flight, which they did not do, and January never saw them again. However, when January saw Oswald on television he was "convinced" Oswald was the man seated in the car.[87]

One big problem with January's credibility is that Alexander said that because he and Fritz had wondered if Oswald was on his way to Redbird Airport, "either one or two days after the assassination I know that Captain Fritz sent a couple of detectives out to the airport to speak to the people in charge and check all the records of the arrivals and departures for the days leading up to and including the assassination, and everything was negative." (One can assume that either the detectives spoke to January or he at least was aware of their presence at the small airport, and he did not tell them the story about the three people.) Contrary to the allegation in several conspiracy books, Alexander also said that the Dallas police never impounded any plane at Redbird following the assassination, nor, to his knowledge, did anyone else in law enforcement.[88]

January's biggest problem, by far, is that *after* the Dallas detectives had made their inquiries at the airport, he finally did tell his story to authorities. On November 29, 1963, he told FBI agents Kenneth Jackson and John Almon the same story he told Jones Harris in 1966, with these major exceptions: The incident occurred not on the morning of November 20, 1963, but "during the latter part of July, 1963."[‡] Additionally, no mention was made

---

*Per Tippit's wife, Tippit voted for Kennedy in the 1960 election, and those who knew him said he seemed to have no interest in politics (CE 2985, 26 H 486–488).

†The above discussion would be academic if Oswald, as some believe, had been walking west on Tenth Street before the Tippit confrontation, and changed his direction, possibly when he spotted Tippit's police car driving eastbound on Tenth toward him. (See discussion in endnote section.) If, indeed, Oswald's original direction was westbound on Tenth, the Redbird Airport, as well as Ruby's apartment at 223 South Ewing Street, both of which were to the east of Tenth and Patton (Walker's home, at 4011 Turtle Creek Boulevard, was to the northeast), would be eliminated as Oswald's intended destination.

‡As discussed in detail in the Oswald biography, Oswald was living in New Orleans throughout the months of July and August and most of September in 1963.

of the man and woman wanting the plane for November 22, 1963, telling him only that they didn't want to make the flight "for a couple of months." And January said the man waiting in the car only "somewhat resembled Oswald." What a difference a few years make. As indicated, when January spoke to Harris in 1966, "the latter part of July, 1963" had become "November 20, 1963"; "a couple of months" had become "November 22, 1963"; and January no longer only believed the man "somewhat resembled" Oswald, but now was "convinced" it was Oswald. When January told his story once again to conspiracy theorist Anthony Summers in 1978, he had one more important change to make: Oswald was no longer waiting in the car but instead approached January along with the other man and woman.[89] On January 19, 1994, January told author Gus Russo that the three people who approached him at Redbird on November 18 were no longer two men and a woman (what he told the FBI in 1963 and author Popkin in 1966), but "three men," one of the three apparently having metamorphosed from a woman into a man. And oh yes, Oswald was now back in the car, waiting for the two men who were talking to January.[90]*

January was obviously having a difficult time remembering his story. And like so many invented tales, January's story contained within it the evidence of its fabrication. Although the buffs, hanging on desperately to January's story, have floated their stories that a Piper Cub was "revving" its engines at Redbird Airport waiting for Oswald to arrive on the afternoon of the assassination, January himself forgot to include in his obvious fable the assertion that the man and woman with "Oswald" on November 20 were at the airport on the afternoon of November 22 waiting for Oswald to arrive. (Nor did he say anyone else was there waiting for Oswald or anyone else.) And after all, since they weren't, where does January's story "go"?

It should be noted that January, not content with only one fable about Oswald, came up with a second one he didn't tell the FBI agents when they interviewed him. On December 20, 1963, January called the local UPI office in Dallas and told them that "last summer" a man who "looked like Oswald" approached him about chartering a plane in September or October (1963) for five passengers to fly to an island off the Mexican peninsula of Yucatán, but the flight never came about.[91] No one can ever accuse January of not trying to make a name for himself.

In all the alleged Second Oswald impersonations, while the real Oswald is doing what we know he was doing—defecting to the Soviet Union, living on Beckley in Dallas, working at the Book Depository Building, visiting his wife and daughters on weekends in Irving, and so on—an Oswald look-alike was seen elsewhere during these times doing all

---

*In his book *Live by the Sword*, Russo quotes FBI agent Jim Hosty telling him in 1994 that the FBI investigation revealed there was a plane revving up at Redbird (Russo doesn't mention a time for this) that took off around 3:00 p.m. Hosty told Russo, "We ran [the investigation] out but it got nowhere." And the air traffic controller at Redbird, Louis Gaudin, told Russo about three well-dressed people flying out of Redbird in a Comanche-type aircraft somewhere between 2:30 and 3:00 p.m. on the afternoon of the assassination, returning forty minutes later with only two occupants, and being met by a part-time employee at the airport who was moonlighting (in the afternoon?) from the Dallas Police Department. (Russo, *Live by the Sword*, pp. 308–309) Gaudin told the FBI on March 7, 1963, that the plane took off between 2:00 and 2:30 p.m. (Smith, *JFK: The Second Plot*, p.279). But I thought the assassination happened at 12:30 p.m. on November 22, 1963. A plane departing a full two to two and a half hours later wouldn't be that suspicious, would it? I also thought that Redbird Airport was a functioning municipal airport in November of 1963 and actually had planes departing and landing all the time. When they did, under what theory is this suspicious or unusual?

types of other things. But a British solicitor (lawyer) named Michael Eddowes, in his 1977 book, *The Oswald File*, came up with a really wacky variation on the above theme. The Oswald who defected, worked at the Book Depository Building, and eventually murdered Kennedy was not the real Oswald. He was a member of the assassination squad of the KGB who looked like Oswald and was sent to this country to kill Kennedy. The real Oswald, after he defected to the Soviet Union, simply disappeared, never to be heard from again, being disposed of presumably at the hands of the KGB.

Why did the Soviets want to murder Kennedy? Eddowes really doesn't concern himself with this unimportant issue, summarily disposing of it in one sentence by saying that because Kennedy "opposed the aggressive moves of . . . Khrushchev, the latter ordered his assassination" through the Soviet secret police. Eddowes also doesn't concern himself with the problem Khrushchev would have in not knowing whether Kennedy's successor would be just as bad as, perhaps worse than, Kennedy. (The whole notion of the KGB being behind Kennedy's murder is discussed in depth in the KGB conspiracy section.) Eddowes doesn't even try to prove that there was, indeed, a Soviet plot to kill Kennedy, offering naked conjecture and not one iota of evidence.

How was the real Oswald selected for his role in this endeavor? Per Eddowes,

> The plot [was] that a young American serving in the Armed Forces of the United States would be selected (probably by the KGB) and persuaded to visit the Soviet Union at the termination of his military service. The selected American would have to be unmarried, and his immediate family would have to be somewhat disunited. He would have to . . . have exhibited some Marxist or pro-Soviet sympathies which would make it credible that he might visit the Soviet Union. He would have to be of average height, of normal physique, and with a face of regular and no distinguishing features, thus making it comparatively easy for the KGB or the MVD to find a dedicated Soviet look-alike from their hundreds of thousands of members . . . On visiting the Soviet Union, the American serviceman would be seized and his place taken by the look-alike already selected . . . After two or three years and having learned the American's background, habits, gait, speech patterns, and handwriting . . . the look-alike would enter the United States in the identity of the American serviceman and . . . assassinate the President.[92]

Eddowes wants us to believe the absurd—that the imposture was so perfect (right down to getting the face, physique, mannerisms, and even the voice right) that the pretender actually succeeded in fooling Oswald's own mother, brother, and half brother (though they might have noticed some understandable changes in Oswald after his being away for going on three years).[93]

Like all intelligent people with nutty ideas who set out to prove their particular "the earth is flat" theory, Eddowes comes up with evidence that the Oswald who shot and killed Kennedy was not the real Lee Harvey Oswald but a Soviet imposter: for example, at various times during his brief adult life, Oswald's height is listed differently, such as five feet nine inches and five feet eleven inches.* Eddowes isn't troubled by the fact that this is a perfectly common phenomenon. Furthermore, after Eddowes's trained Soviet look-alike for Oswald came to America in 1962, and the real Oswald was still in Russia, only the

---

*Oswald's autopsy report gave his height as five feet nine inches (CE 1981, 24 H 7).

look-alike was being measured or giving his height on employment applications, et cetera, where those different heights turn up, so Eddowes automatically loses his argument that the real Oswald has one height and his imposter another. For example, in his application for employment at William B. Reily and Company in New Orleans on May 9, 1963, "Oswald" gave his height as five feet nine inches,[94] but the next month, on June 25, when applying for a passport he gave his height as five feet eleven inches.[95] Why would an Oswald imposter give two different heights for the person he was impersonating? Some Soviet spy and imposter. Eddowes points out that when the Oswald pretender came (not came back, since he apparently had never been here before) to the United States from Russia in 1962, the real Oswald's mother noted that her son looked "very, very thin," and in the close to three years since she had seen him last, he had lost some hair. Robert Oswald said his brother not only had lost a lot of hair but had a more "ruddy" complexion than the last time he saw him.[96] However, neither gave the slightest indication that the man was not their respective son or brother.

Despite the lunacy of Eddowes's theory, the HSCA addressed itself to the "assertion by some critics that the Lee Harvey Oswald who returned from Russia in 1962 was a different person than the Lee Harvey Oswald who defected to Russia in 1959." When I met with Second Oswald proponent John Armstrong in Tulsa, Oklahoma, on January 21, 1994, he assured me he had photographic evidence of two separate and distinct humans, one the real Oswald, the other an imposter. Armstrong proceeded to send me a collage of sixty photographs, claiming the "two" Oswalds were represented therein. However, the HSCA employed forensic anthropologists to analyze and compare photos of Oswald from the time he was in the Marines (which was before he went to Russia) until the assassination, and they concluded that all the photographs were "consistent with those of a single individual,"[97] and there were "no biological inconsistencies in the Oswald photographs examined that would support the theory that a second person, or double, was involved. The variation observed is that expected in an array of photographs taken by different cameras with varying lens, camera angles, lighting, and other technical differences."[98] The HSCA could have added that the photos the experts examined were taken between 1956 and 1963,[99] a seven-year period, and people's appearances do tend to naturally change over time.

Handwriting experts for the HSCA also examined several known handwriting exemplars of Oswald's (e.g., application for a passport in 1959, purchase order for Carcano in 1963, etc.), and found them all to have been written by the same person.[100] Additionally, the HSCA's fingerprint expert, Vincent Scalice, compared Oswald's fingerprint and palm print exemplar taken when he enlisted in the U.S. Marine Corps on October 24, 1956 (before he left for Russia), with those taken on November 22, 1963, and November 25, 1963, of the Lee Harvey Oswald who was arrested for the assassination of Kennedy, and found that the prints were "identical."[101]*

The HSCA concluded that "accordingly, on the basis of the committee's scientific analysis, there was no evidence to support the allegation that the Lee Harvey Oswald who returned from Russia in 1962 was a different person than the Lee Harvey Oswald who defected to Russia in 1959."[102]

---

*One advantage of being a conspiracy theorist is you don't need any evidence to support your charge. Theories and speculations will do. Eddowes said, "*My theory* [nothing else, folks, just a theory, no evidence] is that . . . the KGB had substituted a forged print card in the FBI fingerprint files [which contained Oswald's Marine Corps prints], the forgery substituting the imposter's prints in place of [Oswald's]" (Eddowes, *Oswald File*, p.139).

Even without the findings of the HSCA, it is interesting that this Soviet pretender, meticulously trained and sent to the United States for the sole and specific purpose of assassinating President Kennedy, decided, apparently on his own, that he'd like to try to murder Major General Edwin Walker too. I guess he felt he needed some target practice for the big day coming up. Also, the Russian agent-imposter, whose real name Eddowes never gives his readers, showed just how professional he was at convincing the world that he, the man who killed Kennedy, was really Lee Harvey Oswald, by ordering the rifle he used to kill Kennedy and the revolver he used to kill Officer Tippit under the alias A. Hidell.[103] And at the time of his arrest on the afternoon of November 22, 1963, he had in his possession a counterfeit Selective Service System Notice of Classification listing his name as Alek James Hidell.[104] You see, although the KGB wanted its agent-imposter to convince people he was Lee Harvey Oswald, and he was willing to murder Kennedy and possibly die in the process to accomplish his goal for his KGB superiors, he apparently felt he could convince people he was really Lee Harvey Oswald by frequently using the alias A. Hidell. It certainly makes sense to me.

Eddowes, in his obsessive belief that a Lee Harvey Oswald imposter killed Kennedy and was then killed by Ruby, was so persistent and created so much fuss on both sides of the Atlantic that he actually succeeded, with the support he had gained from Oswald's widow, Marina (who had come to believe that Oswald's body was no longer in the grave— she was "99% sure" of it), in having Oswald's body removed from its Fort Worth grave on October 4, 1981, to see who, if anyone, really was in it. Oswald's mother, Marguerite, had died on January 17, 1981, but before she died, she refused to cooperate with Eddowes, saying Eddowes's contention was "an asinine theory."[105] And Robert, Oswald's brother, had originally gotten a lower court injunction prohibiting the exhumation. However, a state appeals court overruled the injunction. Eddowes himself paid for all the costs and was present at the grave site. A team of two forensic pathologists and two forensic odontologists under the direction of Dr. Linda Norton examined Oswald's skeletal remains at the Baylor University Medical Center in Dallas. Norton told reporters after the nearly five-hour examination on October 4, "We, both individually, and as a team, have concluded beyond any doubt, and I mean beyond any doubt, that the individual buried under the name Lee Harvey Oswald in Rose Hills Cemetery is Lee Harvey Oswald." Among other things, the pathologists compared and matched the teeth of the remains with Oswald's Marine Corps dental records of October 25, 1956, and March 27, 1958, and also found, in the skull, the scar made by surgeons in 1945 when Oswald, age six at the time, had a mastoid operation.[106]

At the time of the exhumation, Dr. Norton, a former medical examiner of Dallas County, was the associate chief medical examiner in Birmingham, Alabama. The rest of her team consisted of Dr. Irving Sopher, chief medical examiner for the state of West Virginia; Dr. James Cottone, head of the Forensic Odontology Department at the University of Texas at San Antonio; and Dr. Vincent DiMaio, chief medical examiner in San Antonio.* In 1984, the four wrote an article, "The Exhumation and Identification of Lee Harvey Oswald," in which they set forth their medical findings. Though the decomposition of the remains was severe, they "estimated" Oswald's height as "5′8½″." They noted that "a gold wedding band and a red stone ring were removed from the fifth digit

---

*Fifteen people witnessed the examination, including the four team members, four doctors who assisted them, three lawyers and their assistants, and a court reporter (*Dallas Morning News*, October 5, 1981).

of the left hand" and that "Mrs. Porter" (Marina) identified the rings as those which she "placed upon the body at the time of initial burial."[107]

Eddowes estimated to reporters that the multiyear effort on his part to get to what he perceived to be the truth in the assassination had cost him, since 1963, "more than $250,000." Chastened by the medical findings, he told reporters, "Though surprised, I am in no way disappointed in the apparent disproving of my evidence of imposture. Rather, I have accomplished my objective in obtaining the exhumation."[108]

One would think that Eddowes's bizarre theory was laid to rest with the reinterment of Oswald's body, but believe it or not, some conspiracy theorists remain unsatisfied, arguing that the body of the real Lee Harvey Oswald may have been substituted for the body of the impersonator, who was originally buried in the grave.[109] And just four years later, and undaunted by (in fact, totally ignoring) the 1981 findings, conspiracy theorist R. B. Cutler, for years the editor of the *Grassy Knoll Gazette*, and his fellow theorist W. R. Norris self-published their book *Alek James Hidell, Alias Oswald*, in which they allege that the person buried in Oswald's grave is not, as Eddowes claimed, a KGB agent, but a CIA agent whose name was Alek James Hidell. "Oswald was *not* murdered by Ruby," Cutler assertively declared in his letter to me of July 24, 1986. So we learn from Cutler and his coauthor that A. Hidell was not the alias we believed Oswald frequently used, one that his wife, Marina, knew to be "merely an altered Fidel"[110] denoting Oswald's reverence for Cuban premier Fidel Castro, but a real person who impersonated the real Oswald.

Without a tad of evidence to support their crackpot theory, the authors surmised that Hidell was "a Russian student [in the United States] recruited by the CIA to be a spy in the Cold War." They go on to say that "*next to nothing* is known about Hidell's life," which is remarkable since it suggests at least something, however little, is known about someone who never existed. They say it is a "reasonable guess" that Hidell was born in Riga, Russia, in February of 1938. The Russian CIA agent "substituted" himself for Oswald in 1958, the authors tell us, when Oswald was stationed in Japan. Like Eddowes, they say that it is "unknown" what ultimately happened to the real Oswald. According to the authors, the fake Oswald returns to the United States in 1962 under the name Lee Harvey Oswald, and like Eddowes's fake Oswald, fools even the real Oswald's mother and brother as to his true identity. The authors claim that Hidell was a "patsy" who was set up by his "handlers," the CIA and FBI, and that four other men assassinated Kennedy, Hidell finally being murdered by Ruby.

The two authors, who refer to themselves in their book in the third person, leading the reader to believe someone is writing about them, are so hopelessly confused that although they start their book claiming the CIA was behind the assassination, one of them (Norris), after finding a former CIA and FBI "operative" kneeling at Oswald's (actually Hidell's) grave with flowers (he knew "Oswald" from their days as CIA and FBI operatives and felt terrible for what happened to him), is convinced by the man that the John Birch Society, not the CIA and FBI, was behind Kennedy's assassination. But Norris, without any explanation, later in the book returns to the fold in pointing the finger solely at U.S. intelligence.

Cutler and Norris don't seem to be concerned about the fact that at the time they say the CIA substituted their Russian-born agent for the real Oswald in 1958 as part of their master plot to assassinate Kennedy, Kennedy wasn't even president. Eisenhower was, and Kennedy hadn't yet even announced his intention to run for president. But hey, the CIA was clairvoyant. Nor do they seem concerned about the same problem Eddowes had, such as the real Oswald's fingerprints, taken in 1956 (before the "substitution" of Hidell for Oswald in 1958), matching up with the fingerprints taken in 1963 of the man they say was a CIA agent.[111] Now, if they can get around the fact that no two humans have the same fingerprints (more unique than DNA, since identical twins do have the same DNA), maybe they can keep their mad theory alive.

The most significant alleged Oswald impersonation took place during Oswald's trip to Mexico City in late September and early October of 1963. The evidence could hardly be more overwhelming that Oswald (not an impersonator) did, in fact, go to the Cuban consulate and Soviet embassy for the purpose of securing an in-transit visa to Cuba ostensibly to be used by Oswald on his way to the Soviet Union. Yet conspiracy theorists have persisted in claiming, against a tide of irresistible evidence, that it wasn't the real Oswald who did these things. Jim Garrison refers to the alleged imposture in Mexico City as "the most significant of [all the Oswald] impersonations."[112]

As we saw earlier in this book, Oswald crossed the border into Mexico at the city of Nuevo Laredo at around 2:00 p.m. on September 26, 1963.[113] Records of the Flecha Roja bus line show that Oswald arrived in Mexico City around 10:00 a.m., September 27, 1963.[114] He checked into the Hotel del Comercio, per the owner and manager, sometime between 10:00 and 11:00 a.m., and paid for five nights' lodging (at the peso equivalent of $1.28 in U.S. currency per night) at the subject hotel for the evening of September 27 through the evening of October 1, 1963.[115] Oswald left Mexico City for Laredo, Texas, on the Transportes del Norte bus line at 8:30 on the morning of October 2,[116] and crossed the International Bridge from Nuevo Laredo into Texas at about 1:35 a.m. on October 3.[117]

Señora Silvia Tirado de Duran, a twenty-six-year-old native of Mexico who worked in the visa section of the Cuban consulate of the Cuban embassy, processed Oswald's request for his visa on September 27, 1963. In a statement to Mexico's Federal Security Police the day after the assassination, she positively identified Oswald and related the facts of his visit to the consulate.[118] Virtually the sole basis for the allegation of imposture comes from Eusebio Azcue, the former Cuban consul in Mexico City. As we saw earlier in the book, Oswald had told Duran he was a friend of the Cuban Revolution, and felt the documents he presented to her (documents showing he lived and worked in Russia, marriage certificate to a Russian citizen, membership in the Fair Play for Cuba Committee, letters to the American Communist Party, etc.) should entitle him to a visa. When Duran, herself a Marxist and sympathetic with Oswald's objective, told him nonetheless that she could not grant him an immediate Cuban visa, that he would first have to get a Russian one and this would take some time, Oswald became very angry, causing Duran to call for Azcue's assistance.[119] Coming out of his office, Azcue listened to Oswald's request and told Oswald the same thing: it would take time, perhaps ten to twenty days. Azcue testified before the HSCA that the first time he saw Oswald in connection with the assassination was about two months after the incident at the consulate, when he saw the film of Oswald being killed by Ruby. Azcue said he was certain the person in the film was not the same man he saw at the consulate. The man at the consulate, he said, was "over 30 years of age and very thin, very thin-faced. And the individual I saw in the movie was a young man, considerably younger, and [had] a fuller face." Of course, Oswald is only shown for a second or two on the film before his face is contorted almost beyond recognition with shock and pain. And Azcue conceded "that the conditions under which I had seen him in the film at the time he was killed, with distorted features as a result of the pain, it is conceivable that I might be mistaken."

When HSCA counsel showed Azcue the photograph of Oswald attached to the visa application, he said the man in the film more closely resembled the man in the photograph than the man he saw at the consulate. Though he testified that "fifteen years [have] gone by so it is very difficult for me to be in a position to guarantee it in a categorical form," he nonetheless believed that the man in the photograph "is not the person or the individual who went to the consulate."

Azcue did not testify before the Warren Commission, and a full ten years before his HSCA testimony on September 18, 1978, he may have been influenced by New Orleans DA Jim Garrison's pronouncements in 1967–1969 that there was an Oswald impersonator in Mexico City, though Azcue told the HSCA that Garrison merely "reaffirmed [his] view" that the man at the consulate was not Oswald.[120]

If Azcue's opinion were all one had to go on, it would be entitled to great weight. But *all* of the other evidence conclusively establishes that the real Oswald was at the consulate:

1. Silvia Duran spent much more time with Oswald than Azcue did, and upon seeing Oswald's photograph in the Mexico City morning newspaper *El Dia* the day after the assassination, she immediately recognized and identified the person in the photo as being the same person who had come to the consulate.[121] Although later, to the HSCA, she described the American at the consulate as being around five feet six inches and 125 pounds with light blonde hair,[122]* a description that doesn't precisely match that of Oswald, she has never wavered in her belief that it was Oswald.[123]

2. Alfredo Mirabal Diaz, one of only three people—along with Duran and Azcue—to see the man identifying himself as Oswald at the consulate,[124] and who was in training at the time to replace Azcue as Cuban consul, also identified Oswald as the person seeking the visa.[125]

3. As indicated, Oswald arrived in Mexico City from the states around 10:00 on the morning of September 27, 1963. The working hours of the Cuban consulate were 10:00 a.m. to 2:00 p.m., and the American seeking the visa first came to the consulate on the morning of the twenty-seventh.[126] Oswald's visa application also bears the date September 27, 1963.[127] And on the fourth line of the application, the date September 27, 1963, in Spanish, is typed.[128]

4. A photograph of Oswald is stapled to the visa application.[129] And, indeed, Duran testified that she told Oswald he would have to have a photograph of himself to attach to his visa application and she referred him to a few places near the consulate. Oswald left the consulate and returned "in the afternoon" that same day, September 27, with photos of himself, which she checked to make sure they matched up with the man before her.[130]

*We know that people observing the same person or event can almost be expected to give different descriptions. Here, although Duran recalled the American at the consulate to have *light* blond hair, Azcue recalled the very same man to have *dark* blond hair (3 HSCA 136). Oswald himself described his hair color as "medium brown" (WR, p.614). As to Duran's description of Oswald as being around five feet six inches and 125 pounds, Oswald's autopsy report, as previously indicated, reads he was five feet nine inches. His "estimated weight" was 150. (CE 1981, 24 H 7) The estimation of weight seems high. At the time of his interrogation following the assassination Oswald himself gave his weight as 140 pounds (WR, p.614). Virtually every photo of Oswald shows him to be of slight frame. See photo section for a picture of the slender Oswald taken in front of the New Orleans Trade Mart in August 1963, the month before he went to Mexico City. Marina felt he looked like a "skeleton" during this period (McMillan, *Marina and Lee*, p.460). Alfredo Mirabal Diaz, a Mexican consulate employee, recalled Oswald as being "a rather small man, medium height or somewhat less, narrow shoulders" (3 HSCA 177).

5. Handwriting experts from the CIA concluded that the signature "Lee Harvey Oswald" affixed to the visa application is the signature of Lee Harvey Oswald.[131] The HSCA, discovering that the name "Lee H. Oswald" was also signed on a copy of the application, had its own handwriting experts examine each signature. Their conclusion was that both signatures belonged to Oswald.[132]

6. As if the above weren't more than enough, the American seeking the visa acted exactly as Oswald so often did—angry, persistent, and intense. In her statement to the Mexican Federal Security Police, Duran said that when Oswald was informed of the fact that he could not get an immediate visa to Cuba, "he became highly agitated and angry."[133] She told the HSCA, "He was red and he was almost crying, and uh, he was insisting and insisting . . . [Azcue] opened the door and told Oswald to go away . . . I was feeling pity for him because he looked desperate."[134] And Azcue testified before the HSCA that the man "was very anxious we grant him the visa . . . We never had any individual that was so insistent or persistent . . . He was never friendly . . . He accused us of being bureaucrats, and in a very discourteous manner."[135]

Common sense dictates that someone trying to physically pass himself off as Oswald would draw as little attention to himself as possible. By creating such a scene and ruckus at the consulate, he would be immeasurably increasing the likelihood that the personnel at the consulate would get a much better look at his face and overall physical appearance and, hence, be able to recollect that he was not Oswald.

7. The fact that we know Oswald was in Mexico City at the very same time that someone claiming to be Oswald was at the Cuban consulate and Russian embassy is just further evidence that it was indeed he at the consulate and embassy. Handwriting experts for the Warren Commission and HSCA concluded that the signature "Lee Harvey Oswald" on the register of the Hotel del Comercio on September 27, 1963, was Oswald's signature.[136] Oswald stayed in room 18 at the hotel for, as indicated, five nights. Both the owner-manager of the hotel, Guillermo Garcia Luna, and the maid, Matilde Garnica, identified Oswald to the CIA as being at the hotel, Garnica adding that she clearly remembered Oswald because so few Americans stayed there. The desk clerk, Sebastian Perez Hernandez, and the watchman, Pedro Rodriguez Ledesma, who sought out a taxi for Oswald on the morning when Oswald departed the hotel for the states, also clearly identified Oswald. And Dolores Ramirez de Barreiro, the owner, manager, and sometimes cook of the small restaurant immediately adjacent to the hotel, identified Oswald as the young American who had eaten several meals at her restaurant in the late afternoon during Oswald's stay in Mexico City. All five of the above witnesses said that whenever they saw Oswald, he was alone.[137]

8. As conclusive as the above evidence is, none of it is even necessary, since Oswald himself has told us it was he at the Cuban consulate. In his November 9, 1963, letter to the Soviet embassy in Washington, D.C., he recounts the trouble he had at the Cuban consulate in Mexico City and alludes to Azcue by saying that he was "glad the [Cuban consul] has since been replaced."[138] Though Azcue did not, in fact, leave the consulate until November 18, 1963, which was after Oswald wrote his letter, he testified that "since the month of September of 1963 I had started to turn over affairs to the new consul who was to replace me, Mr. Alfredo Mirabal."[139] It appears that Oswald, during his visits to the consulate, had somehow become aware of this fact.

9. Not only do we know that it was Oswald at the Cuban consulate, but we know it was Oswald who, on the afternoon of September 27, 1963, and the morning of September 28, 1963, entered the Russian embassy and met with KGB members of the embassy staff

(Colonel Oleg Maximovich Nechiporenko and Valeriy Kostikov on both days and Pavel Yatskov on September 28) seeking a visa to Russia. When Oswald appeared on television following his arrest in Dallas on November 23, 1963, Nechiporenko, Kostikov, and Yatskov all remembered and identified Oswald as being the person they had spoken to at their embassy.[140]

10. Oswald had told his wife, Marina, earlier about his plans to go to Cuba by way of Mexico City and later about his trip to Mexico City, his trouble at the "two embassies," and that because of all the "red tape" he got nowhere with the "bureaucrats" there in his effort to get to Cuba. Oswald told Marina he was in Mexico City "about a week," which the documentary record confirms.[141]

11. After his arrest, Oswald told his interrogators about his Mexico City trip. Postal Inspector Harry Holmes, one of Oswald's interrogators, testified that "he [Oswald] went to the Mexican consulate or embassy or something and wanted to get permission, or whatever it took to get to Cuba. They refused him and he became angry and he said he burst out of there."[142]

12. And Oswald's own possessions reveal that he was at the Cuban consulate. Silvia Duran said that even though she was unable to give Oswald the immediate visa he wanted, she wanted to be helpful to him so she gave him a piece of paper with her name on it, as well as the telephone number of the consulate, which was 11-28-47.[143] Silvia Duran's name and the consulate's phone number were found on a piece of paper among Oswald's possessions after his arrest.[144] That same piece of paper contained the phone numbers of both the Soviet embassy in Mexico City (15-61-55) and the Soviet Department of Consular Affairs (15-60-55).[145]

13. The linchpin for the allegation that there was an Oswald imposter at the Cuban consulate is that this imposter was the same one who impersonated Oswald at the Russian embassy. This is so because the alleged imposture not only occurred during the same, precise period of time, but the contact by "Oswald" with the Soviet embassy is inextricably connected with his contact with the Cuban consulate. For instance, Consul Azcue told Oswald that the one way he could issue him an immediate in-transit visa to Cuba without the waiting period and protocol of prior consultation with Cuba would be for Oswald to secure a final destination visa to the Soviet Union from the Soviet embassy. Oswald proceeded to the Soviet embassy just two blocks away and attempted to obtain such a visa, but he was unsuccessful. Azcue testified that either the same day he sent Oswald to the embassy (September 27) or the next day, he spoke over the phone to "the consulate of the Soviet Union" at the Soviet embassy and was told that the documents Oswald produced attesting to his residence in the Soviet Union and his marriage to a Soviet citizen (both of which Oswald had previously shown to Duran and Azcue) were apparently valid, but a visa could not be issued without authorization from Moscow, and that would take approximately four months.[146] And Silvia Duran also said she spoke to the "Russian consul" on the same day they sent Oswald there and was told he had been there and that Oswald was informed he'd have to wait for four months.[147]

Since we know that the real Oswald was at the Cuban consulate, we know, then, that the real Oswald was also at the Soviet embassy. To believe otherwise demands answers to the following questions: How would the bogus Oswald know to go to the Soviet embassy around the very time the real Oswald was sent there, and for the identical purpose? Did he have the real Oswald and the Cuban consulate bugged? But even if he did, how would that prevent the real Oswald from going to the Russian embassy too? And if so, why didn't Azcue and Duran say that in their contacts with the Soviet embassy they were told that *two people* claiming to be Lee Harvey Oswald had come to the embassy seeking a final destination visa to the Soviet Union? John Davis, author of *Mafia Kingfish*, has no trouble with such folly. He writes, "As it turned out, Oswald, or his impostor, *or both*, spent six days in Mexico."[148] In *Conspiracy*, Anthony Summers writes, "It should be remembered that the real Oswald almost certainly was in Mexico City at the relevant time, even if it was somebody else who visited the embassies."[149] Such is the infinitely silly world of the conspiracy theorists in the Kennedy assassination.

14. Finally, as with his visit to the Cuban consulate, Oswald himself told us of his visit to the Soviet embassy. In his November 9, 1963, letter to the Soviet embassy in Washington, D.C., he wrote, "This is to inform you of recent events since my meetings with Comrade Kostin [almost assuredly, a reference to the aforementioned Valeriy Kostikov, a KGB officer and member of the consular staff at the Soviet embassy in Mexico City at the time of Oswald's visit] in the Embassy of the Soviet Union, Mexico City, Mexico." Elsewhere in the letter he said, "I had not planned to contact the Soviet Embassy in Mexico so they were unprepared."[150] Further, Oswald told his interrogators after his arrest, per Postal Inspector Harry Holmes, that after he "burst out" of the Cuban consulate, he went "over to the Soviet embassy" seeking authorization from them "to go to Russia by way of Cuba," but "they refused and said 'come back in thirty days' or something like that. And he went out of there angry and disgusted."[151]

Since we absolutely know Oswald went to the Cuban consulate and Soviet embassy during his Mexico City trip, all other matters pertaining to a possible Oswald imposture at the consulate and embassy that have been written about and discussed ad nauseam by the conspiracy theorists become automatically irrelevant and superfluous. But for the historical record, what are some of these matters? Although for the most part they involve simple human as well as bureaucratic errors, they have enjoyed a resonance in the conspiracy community exceeding the half-life of uranium.

One misstatement made *the day after* the assassination—when turmoil, confusion, and extreme pressure understandably led to errors and misstatements—was a paragraph in a five-page preliminary analysis of the assassination (much too soon for *any* kind of analysis to be written), in which J. Edgar Hoover wrote, "The Central Intelligence Agency advised that on October 1, 1963, an extremely sensitive source had reported that an individual identified as Lee Oswald . . . contacted the Soviet Embassy in Mexico City inquiring as to any messages. Special agents in this Bureau [in Dallas], who have conversed with Oswald in Dallas, Texas, have observed photographs of the individual referred to above *and have listened to a recording of his voice*. These special agents are of the opinion that the above-referred-to individual was not Lee Harvey Oswald."[152] This, naturally, was tremendous fodder for conspiracy theorists—someone obviously was impersonating Oswald in Mexico City. In the world of the theorists, there is no room for error, misstatements, incompetence, and so on. Hoover, in the confusion following the assassination, simply misunderstood the information he had received, or someone made an error in giving him this information.*

*Consistent with the confusion and errors Hoover, and many others, made in the immediate wake of the assassination, in a 1:48 p.m. memo to his staff on the afternoon of the assassination, Hoover wrote, "The President and the Governor were shot at the corner of Elm and Commerce Streets" and that he had been told "the shots came from the fourth floor" of the Book Depository Building (FBI Record 124-10012-10169); in a 2:21 p.m. memo to his staff he said that he advised James W. Rowley, chief of the Secret Service, "that one of the Secret Service agents reportedly had been killed, and [Rowley] stated he did not know this" (FBI Record 124-

The HSCA thoroughly investigated the matter and learned that later in the day (7:23 p.m., Central Standard Time, November 23, 1963) Dallas FBI special agent-in-charge Gordon Shanklin advised Hoover of his error, informing him that only a *report* of Oswald's conversation was received by the Dallas field office from the CIA station in Mexico City, not an actual tape recording of the conversation. And on November 25, the Dallas office again apprised Hoover that "there appears to be some confusion in that *no tapes* were taken to Dallas. Only typewritten [reports were] supplied."[153]

The HSCA went on to say, "Shanklin stated in a Committee interview that no recording was ever received by FBI officials in Dallas. Moreover, former FBI Special Agents James Hosty, John W. Fain, Burnett Tom Carter, and Arnold J. Brown, each of whom had conversed with Oswald at one time, informed the Committee that they had never listened to a recording of Oswald's voice . . . The Committee concluded, therefore, that the information in the November 23, 1963, letterhead memorandum [the assassination analysis by Hoover] was mistaken and did not provide a basis for concluding that there had been an Oswald imposter."[154]

As is typical of most conspiracy writers, Jim Marrs, author of *Crossfire*, tells his readers about the November 23, 1963, FBI memo, but then never tells them that the HSCA determined that the memo was in error.[155]

Actually, there were recordings of Oswald's voice secured by the CIA station in Mexico City resulting from its monitoring of all incoming and outgoing telephone calls at the Cuban consulate and Soviet embassy. For instance, the prelude to the typed transcript of the first of two calls made to the Soviet military attaché at the embassy on October 1, 1963, at 10:31 a.m., says the caller spoke "broken Russian." The caller, per the transcript, was told that for the information he was seeking he should call a different number at the embassy, 15-60-55, "and ask for a consul." At 10:45 a.m., the person called the consul, and the prelude to the new transcription again refers to the "broken Russian" of the caller. The transcribed monitored telephone conversation follows:

"Hello, this is Lee Oswald speaking. I was at your place last Saturday and spoke to a Consul, and they said they'd send a telegram to Washington, so I wanted to find out if you have anything new? But I don't remember the name of that Consul."

OP (Other Party): "Kostikov. He is dark/hair or skin?"

Oswald: "Yes. My name is Oswald."

OP: "Just a minute, I'll find out . . . They say that they haven't received anything yet."

Oswald: "Have they done anything?"

OP: "Yes, they say that a request has been sent out, but nothing has been received as yet."

Oswald: "And what . . . ?"

The other party hangs up.

A concluding paragraph to the transcript reads, "Station source, who did transcriptions, says Oswald is identical with person speaking broken Russian who called from Cuban [consulate] 28 September to Soviet Embassy."[156]

A "station source" who heard and transcribed Oswald's voice on some of the tapes was identified years later as Boris Tarasoff, a CIA staff officer in Mexico City whose job in September and October of 1963 was to receive tapes of CIA telephone taps at the Soviet

---

10012-10167); in a 4:01 p.m. memo to his staff he relayed that after Oswald left the Book Depository Building he "ran into two police officers . . . a block or two away . . . and thinking they were going to arrest him, shot at them and killed one of them with a sidearm" (FBI Record 124-10012-10170).

embassy in Mexico City and translate (from Russian into English) and transcribe the tapes. He would receive the tapes from a CIA courier the day after they were made and would return the tapes and their transcriptions to the same courier the following day. Tarasoff only remembers translating and transcribing two Oswald tapes, of telephone conversations on September 28 and October 1, 1963, though he says, "There might have been more. I am not certain."* Oswald only used his name on October 1, not September 28.[157] Anna Tarasoff, Boris's wife, who assisted him with the transcriptions in Mexico City, told the HSCA there was another taped conversation between Oswald and someone at the Soviet embassy for which no transcript has been found, in which Oswald identified himself, said he was broke, and wanted financial aid from either the Russians or the Cubans so he could leave the country. "They definitely turned him down. In fact, if I recall, they finally got disgusted and hung up on him."[158]

What happened to these tapes? In 1963, David Atlee Phillips was the number-three man at the CIA station in Mexico City, and among other responsibilities he was chief of the station's Cuban operations. When I was preparing him for his upcoming testimony at the London docu-trial in 1986,[†] he told me that "95 percent of the recordings our person would listen to would be just junk. With the 5 percent that was relevant, the conversation would be typed up. But the tape of all the conversations would continue to be used. New conversations would simply obliterate the old conversations. There's no question that's what occurred to Oswald's conversations. They don't exist anymore. The tapes were large in those days. If we kept all of the tapes and didn't re-use them, they would have filled a warehouse."

"It would have been nice," I said, "if those tapes still existed."

"Yes, but we didn't know at that time that people like Ed Lopez and Gaeton Fonzi [HSCA conspiracy-minded investigators] would later question whether it was really Oswald on the phone."[159] When London Weekend Television researcher Richard Tomlinson interviewed Phillips three weeks earlier in Washington, D.C., for three hours, Phillips put it even better: "How were we to know that two months later this person, Oswald, would assassinate the president?"

It's interesting to note that even the long report that HSCA investigator Edwin Lopez authored on Oswald's trip to Mexico City concluded that "the CIA telephone surveillance on the Soviet Embassy taped several calls of a man using the name 'Lee Oswald.' [Lopez offers no evidence to support the assertion that Oswald used his name several times.] These tapes were retained for a routine two [the number "one" is handwritten above the typewritten "two"] week period and were *most likely* erased shortly after 16 October 1963."[160] Lopez apparently was unaware that a November 24, 1963, CIA Teletype (No. 7054) from the CIA station in Mexico City to CIA headquarters in Washington, D.C., read, in part, "Hqs has full transcripts [of] all pertinent calls. Regret tapes for this period *already erased*."[161]

---

*Mexico City, at the time, "had the most comprehensive, extensive telephone tap facilities . . . of any [CIA] station in the world," said John Scelso, chief of the WH (Western Hemisphere) 3 branch of clandestine operations at CIA headquarters to whom the CIA station in Mexico City reported. There was only one problem, he said. "They had far more material to deal with than they could possibly handle . . . like ten times." (HSCA Record 180-10131-10330, Testimony of John Scelso before HSCA on May 16, 1978, pp.4, 17, 58)

†Most of the trial preparation I did with my witnesses, who were living around the country (Phillips in Bethesda, Maryland), was by written correspondence and over the telephone from my home in Los Angeles, although once we all got to London, I interviewed each of them again in person before the trial started.

The other major area that has been grist for the conspiracy mill on the issue of an Oswald impersonator in Mexico City is the lack of any photo of Oswald in Mexico City. The CIA had photographic surveillance of people entering and leaving the Cuban consulate and Soviet embassy,[162] but since it was not able to produce photos of Oswald entering or leaving these places, the conspiracy theorists have long since maintained this proves Oswald was never present at either place. The theorists never consider the possibility of incompetence, which is so very common in life, being the answer, or of a failure or breakdown of the equipment from time to time. It turns out that the photographic surveillance of the Cuban and Russian embassies (and their respective consulates) was nowhere as seamless as might be wished. David Phillips told me that although his office in Mexico City had the capacity to photograph the consulate and embassy round-the-clock, seven days a week, the reality was that this was not done. Because the equipment malfunctioned from time to time—the repairs obviously took time—and because personnel were sometimes needed more elsewhere, the surveillance "was not constant and uninterrupted."[163]

Indeed, in 1998 the ARRB conducted a very thorough review of all logs, tapes, and records from the CIA's station in Mexico City with respect to the period of Oswald's visit, and found that a Robot Star camera and a K-100 camera had been installed by the CIA on September 27, 1963, to cover the entrance to the Cuban consulate. (Per the CIA, there was no photographic surveillance of the entrance to the Cuban consulate prior to September 27.) The K-100 camera broke down after one day's operation, and the Robot Star, which was to be tested for eight days, "broke down after four days of operation," meaning it was only operational from September 27 to September 30, and "there is no record of actual photographic takes or test results from the camera." A functioning "pulse camera" was installed on December 17, 1963, weeks after the assassination.

As far as the Soviet embassy was concerned, the ARRB learned that LIMITED, the name for the CIA's photographic surveillance operation located in a first-floor apartment directly across the street from the main Soviet embassy gate, and operating from 9:00 a.m. to 2:00 p.m. each day, was the source of the photographs of the unidentified "mystery" man (see later text) supplied to the Warren Commission, and lived up to its title by not even being operational on September 28–30 and October 5–6. The ARRB found that even on the days of operation, there were many cases where "the log entries documenting observed activities at the site do not correlate with the recorded hours of operation. This suggests that the target site was not being monitored for the entire duration of the surveillance shift."[164]

The documentary history of the photographic surveillance cameras around the time of Oswald's visit to Mexico City, which either were manually operated or had to be triggered by a movement or color in the area of the embassy being "covered," is sorry at best. References to the system like the following appear in an internal CIA document from the chief of the CIA station in Mexico City: the system works "about 80 percent of the time"; the coverage was changed to "only photograph people leaving but not entering the target building"; when a person leaves by this entrance, "the man's shirt or face will trigger the device photographing a front or side view depending on how the subject leaves" the building; "*this system does not work when a person enters the building with light clothing* [unbelievable]"; and the station "requested that a substitute camera be shipped to the Station as soon as possible to replace the Robot Star camera on this project."[165] But if you were to listen to the conspiracy theorists, the surveillance cameras were operating continuously and never missed a thing.

The HSCA dealt with allegations from conspiracy theorists that the CIA did, in fact, obtain a picture of Oswald entering the consulate and embassy, but the CIA denied that any photograph or photographs of Oswald had been thus obtained, and the committee discovered no such pictures of Oswald in its review of the agency's files.[166]

The famous Lopez Report referred to earlier (formally, the HSCA's "Report on Lee Harvey Oswald's Trip to Mexico City"), named after Edwin Lopez, the young HSCA investigator who after much research in Mexico City drafted the report, was finally, after thirty-three years and amid much anticipation in the conspiracy community, declassified from "Top Secret" and released by the ARRB on October 7, 1996.

Though conspiracy theorists thought it would contain some powerful evidence of a conspiracy, the report, despite Lopez's strong, conspiracy orientation, turned out to be, *as it had to be*, a giant dud. Lopez concluded that "the Warren Commission correctly established that Oswald had traveled to Mexico City." What about once he got there? "While the majority of the evidence tends to indicate that [the individual who visited the Cuban consulate and Soviet embassy on the dates in question] was indeed Lee Harvey Oswald, the possibility that someone else used Lee Harvey Oswald's name during this time in contacts with the Soviet and Cuban Consulates cannot be absolutely dismissed."[167]* But nowhere in the 393 pages of his report does Lopez say why an imposter would go to Mexico City at the same time as Oswald and use Oswald's name at the Cuban consulate and Soviet embassy around the very same time that we know, from much evidence, that Oswald was also doing so. What could possibly be achieved by such an endeavor? Moreover, since the Cuban consulate and Soviet embassy in Mexico City are only two blocks apart, wouldn't there be a likelihood that Oswald and his imposter would run into each other? And even if Oswald and his impersonator looked like identical twins, and the impersonator managed to dress exactly like Oswald, and had the identical papers and documents Oswald had, wouldn't the employees at the consulate and embassy be saying to Oswald or his impersonator things like "Weren't you just here?" "Didn't you tell me . . . ?" "I thought I already told you . . ."

One would think that only children in a sandbox could imagine an Oswald impersonator in Mexico City at the same time Oswald was there, right? But among many others, conspiracy theorist John Newman believes all of this. And he's actually an assistant professor on the payroll of the University of Maryland, teaching courses in Soviet, Chinese Communist, East Asian, and Vietnam War history. Why would anyone be impersonating Oswald at the consulate and embassy? "Someone," Newman says, "wanted to make sure that Oswald's Cuban and KGB contacts in Mexico were fully documented." Why? To establish "evidence of an international communist conspiracy" to murder Kennedy. But since Newman, who maintains that Oswald was a CIA operative, admits the real Oswald was also down there at the consulate and embassy around the same time, why the need for the imposter? The good professor doesn't say. And if the imposter had the objective Newman gives him, why wouldn't he want to "do his thing" at some time *other than* when Oswald was also walking back and forth between the consulate and embassy?

---

*At the London trial, although I was able to impeach Lopez's credibility as a witness by other means, I didn't have his own report to the HSCA, since, as indicated, it wasn't released to the public until 1996, ten years *after* the trial. So when Lopez testified on direct examination by Gerry Spence that he had concluded that Oswald "had not" been to the Cuban consulate and Russian embassy in Mexico City and agreed with Spence's assertion "that there must have been an imposter there," I didn't have Lopez's own report to refute his testimony. However, I did have the conclusion of his employer, the HSCA (HSCA Report, pp.251–252), that it was the real Lee Harvey Oswald at the Cuban consulate and Russian embassy in Mexico City, which I introduced to the jury on cross-examination of Lopez. (Transcript of *On Trial*, July 25, 1986, pp.877, 894)

Newman's resumé says he had twenty years of military intelligence training. Apparently, it's in the twenty-first year that the armed forces finally gives you the small commonsense tablet.[168]

Getting back to Lopez, he comes up with an Oswald impersonator possibility in his report that is so far out a hundred fertile minds sitting in a room for an entire week with the express purpose of thinking up impersonator scenarios wouldn't think of it. It's always assumed, of course, that the imposter would impersonate Oswald without his knowledge, that he would be someone Oswald did not know. But Lopez raises the possibility—are you seated? because I don't want to be responsible for anyone falling down and hurting themselves—that maybe the impersonator was "one of his [Oswald's] companions" in Mexico City.[169] To think that our tax money went into the preparation of the Lopez Report.

Elsewhere in his report, Lopez says, "The CIA photo-surveillance operations in Mexico City probably obtained a photograph of Lee Harvey Oswald,"[170] and he hints darkly that the CIA suppressed the photo or photos, though he does not say why the spy agency would want to keep Oswald's entering the Cuban consulate and Soviet embassy a secret. Lopez has always suspected that the CIA, or rogue elements thereof, may have been behind the assassination.[171] Indeed, in my interview of him before the London trial he even said he was "a great fan" of A. J. Weberman, the bearded guru and wacky conspiracy theorist who lived in a loft in Greenwich Village and was, per Lopez, "the leader of the yippies." However, in front of the jury in London he would only acknowledge that he told me he was "impressed" with Weberman's research in the Kennedy case (i.e., when Weberman wasn't rifling through the garbage of Bob Dylan, with whom Weberman was obsessed).[172] On direct examination by Gerry Spence, Lopez said that he felt the CIA was "trying to set Oswald up" for the Kennedy assassination. On cross, I asked him, "[So] you believe that the CIA may have set Lee Harvey Oswald up?"

"Not as an agency, no."

"But some maverick, rogue element?"

"Some type of maverick element, yes."[173]*

But if the CIA, or rogue elements thereof, were responsible for Kennedy's murder and trying to frame Oswald for it by alleging he was a Castro or KGB agent, why wouldn't they want people to see the very evidence (the alleged suppressed photographs of Oswald at the Cuban consulate or Soviet embassy) that could help them do it? Since it would be to their advantage to show Oswald's connection with these people, instead of concealing these photographs, wouldn't they be passing them out on street corners for the world to see?

---

*On cross-examination of Lopez at the London trial, I brought out that he was a young law student without one day of law enforcement investigative experience when he was hired by HSCA chief counsel Robert Blakey, a law professor at Cornell University who met Lopez while the latter was attending law school there. The CIA submitted a formal complaint to the HSCA about Lopez showing up at CIA headquarters in shorts and jeans, and Lopez changed his attire thereafter. Knowing Lopez was a very shaky witness, I deliberately gave him free reign to self-destruct on the witness stand in front of the jury's eyes, and he gladly obliged. Lopez told the jury he had his own opinion of who actually killed Kennedy and it wasn't Oswald. "Just for the record," I asked him, "could we have this chap's name?" Lopez answered, "No, because I [am] under a secrecy oath [at the HSCA] never to disclose that name." Unbelievably, Lopez, an otherwise pleasant and intelligent young man, said he and his colleagues at the HSCA received information from "a reliable source" that there was an actual photograph of this person shooting at Kennedy, but they weren't able to get the photograph, and the FBI and CIA wouldn't let him and his colleagues question Kennedy's killer. I said, "You told me [in a pretrial interview] that this fellow was an agent for Castro, the CIA, and the FBI, but none of

There's a footnote to the weightless allegation that someone was impersonating Oswald at the Soviet embassy in Mexico City. The Mexico City office of the CIA cabled CIA headquarters in Langley, Virginia,[*] on October 9, 1963, that on September 28 and October 1, an "American male who spoke broken Russian" and who identified himself as Lee Oswald had contacted the Soviet embassy, speaking once to Consul Valeriy Kostikov and once with Soviet guard Ivan Obyedkov, asking the latter if any messages had been received for him at the embassy, and being told there hadn't been. The cable goes on to describe the American male, whom Mexico City believed was "Lee Oswald": "Apparent age 35, athletic build, circa six feet, receding hairline, balding top, wore khakis and sport shirt."[174] When the CIA's photographic surveillance of the embassy picked up an American-looking male entering the embassy around the same time, the staff erroneously assumed, David Phillips told me, that it was a photo of Oswald, whom they did not have a photo of in their Mexico City files.[175] The reason they assumed the man was Oswald was that they knew from a tape-recorded phone conversation and the transcript of it that Oswald was a North American, and from their photograph surveillance during the same period of time there was just one person who appeared to be North American. All the rest were Latin.[176] As Phillips describes the gaffe in his book, *The Night Watch*, his office had "put one (Oswald, seeking a visa from the Soviets) and one (an unknown visitor to the Russian Embassy) together and come up with an incorrect two: the assumption that the two men were the same."[177][†]

Upon receiving the October 9 internal cable at Langley, Charlotte Bustos, a twenty-six-year veteran CIA employee working the "Mexico desk" at headquarters, requested a "name trace" on Lee Oswald, and she received Oswald's 201 file, where his name was listed as Lee *Henry* Oswald. Afer reviewing Oswald's file, she sent out a cable (telegraph) on October 10 to three federal agencies (Department of State, FBI, and Department of Navy) passing on the information in the October 9 internal CIA cable, and adding that "Oswald may be identical to Lee Henry [*sic*] Oswald, born on 18 October 1939 in New Orleans, Louisiana, a former U.S. Marine who defected to the Soviet Union in October

them knew this, is that correct?" "They probably know it by now, but they didn't know it back then." "So you're a twenty-one-year-old kid out of Cornell, and the CIA, the FBI and Castro are using this guy and they don't know he is an agent for all three of them, but Edwin Lopez knows?" When Lopez said yes and offered to tell why, I had run out of my allotted time on cross-examination, so I suggested he tell his lawyer, Mr. Spence, on redirect. But Spence, wanting to get Lopez off the stand as quickly as possible before he embarrassed and hurt the defense more than he already had, elected not to ask one single question of Lopez on redirect. (Transcript of *On Trial*, July 25, 1986, pp.892, 897, 903, 916–919)

This is but another example of what happened when conspiracy icons in the Kennedy assassination like Lopez, who had never been cross-examined on the case, were subjected to cross-examination at the London trial. Some of the icons, like Jean Hill (who wanted to testify for the defense very badly at the London trial) and Delphine Roberts, were so pathetically bad that the defense in London decided to not call them to the witness stand, period. By the way, I defy anyone to come up with any witness I called to the stand for the prosecution at the London trial who was made to look ridiculous or noncredible on cross-examination. Since none were either of these, I don't believe you will be able to.

[*]The CIA moved its headquarters from downtown Washington, D.C., to Langley, Virginia, on September 20, 1961, although John McCone, the first CIA director to occupy Langley headquarters, didn't move in until November 29, 1961. However, the CIA, in testimony by its agents and in other ways, has continued to refer to its headquarters as being in "Washington," Langley-assigned agents even saying they are stationed in "Washington." In fact, to this very day, the mailing address for CIA headquarters is "Washington, D.C., 20505."

[†]Phillips told me (as he said in his book) that the CIA case officer at the Mexico City station who was in charge of Soviet operations (he couldn't recall his last name, but said his first name was Craig) was the first person at the station who became aware of Oswald seeking to go to Russia ostensibly by way of Cuba. Craig, Phillips said, should have routinely cabled CIA headquarters in Washington asking for a file check on Oswald.

1959 and later made arrangements through the United States Embassy in Moscow to return to the United States with his Russian born wife, Marina Nikolaevna Pusakova [*sic*], and their child."[178]

The CIA memos between the CIA station in Mexico City and CIA headquarters, where the staff is trying to figure out who Oswald is and what he looked like, by themselves show that Oswald obviously had no connection with the CIA. These weren't memos by the CIA to the outside world, but *internal* memos, that is, *within* the CIA. When Charlotte Bustos, who sent out the aforementioned memo and another on the next day, was asked in her testimony before the HSCA, "Do you have any reason to believe that Oswald had any type of relationship with the Central Intelligence Agency?" she responded, "No, none whatsoever." "When you had access to Oswald's 201 file you saw no indication in there that he had any type of relationship with the Agency as an agent, source, asset, et cetera?" "No, none whatsoever. There certainly would not have gone out all this cable traffic if anybody along the way had known he was an asset. You would not have gone out with [name] traces and things." "If he was an agent would you have notified the Mexico City station?" "Yes." "Would that normally be done as a matter of standard operating procedure?" "Yes. Then somebody would be very upset that [there] was an agent in Mexico without telling the [Mexico City] Chief of Station because the Chief of Station is responsible for all operational activities in his area."[179]

The person described as Oswald in the Mexico City memos (his identity to this day is not known) is shown in a photo in the photo section of this book.[180] As can be seen, he bears no resemblance to Oswald in face or physique.* Yet unbelievably, even though someone attempting to impersonate Oswald would have to bear at least some resemblance to him, several conspiracy theorists aren't willing to accept the matter as a simple case of mistaken identity. Anthony Summers, in his book *Conspiracy*, smells a CIA cover-up: "The CIA did not reveal [to the Warren Commission that the man] had also been at the Soviet Embassy on October 1, the date of an 'Oswald' contact with the Soviets." He goes on ominously: "Who was this mystery man, anyway?"[181] John Davis, in his book *Mafia Kingfish*, and Jim Garrison, in *On the Trail of the Assassins*, also suggest the man in the photo was impersonating Oswald.[182]† Peter Dale Scott, after writing that the man in the

---

When he didn't do it for several days, Craig's wife, who worked part-time at the station, took it upon herself to type up the October 9 cable, the first cable about Oswald from Mexico City. (Telephone interview of David Phillips by author on June 22, 1986)

*Per a CIA memorandum, three photos of the unknown American male were taken by CIA cameras in front of the Soviet embassy around "12:17 hours" (12:17 p.m.) on October 1, 1963; five photos of him, in the same location, around "11:32 hours" on October 4, 1963; and two photos of the same male in front of the Cuban embassy on October 15, 1963. The CIA turned over all ten photographs to the FBI in Mexico City on the afternoon of the assassination. According to the CIA, "CIA did not have a known photograph of Oswald in its files before the assassination of President Kennedy either in Washington or abroad." (CIA Document 1993.6.29.13:15:59:560410, pp.2–4, Undated draft of CIA memorandum re: Garrison Allegations Re CIA Photograph in Warren Commission Report—The Facts, JFK box OSW17, vol.5, folder IV, National Archives)

†Garrison and others believe the CIA was behind the assassination and that Oswald was working for the agency as a member of U.S. intelligence, yet it framed him for the assassination as its patsy. But there's a problem with this. If Oswald was actually working for the CIA, why would it bother to send an Oswald imposter to the Cuban consulate and Russian embassy to make Oswald look like a leftist or Marxist in league with the Cubans and Russians just prior to the assassination? Instead of sending an imposter to Mexico City to set Oswald up for the assassination, why not send Oswald himself to these places? But if, for whatever reason, the CIA wanted to send an Oswald impersonator, obviously it would have to send someone who looks very much like Oswald, right? Since the photos that the CIA took of its Oswald impersonator (the one it supposedly used to help frame Oswald) clearly show that he bears no resemblance to Oswald, wouldn't this only serve to defeat the CIA's whole impersonation, frame-up scheme?

CIA photos is "heavyset, balding, and middle-aged," nonetheless remarkably goes on to agree with most of the critics that the man was not Oswald but an imposter.[183] The conspiracy theorists are so unhinged that they believe Oswald's framers would use an impersonator who looks as much like Oswald as Danny DeVito does.

The allegation that someone was impersonating Oswald in Mexico City is completely devoid of merit. The Warren Report concluded that it was Oswald, not an imposter, in Mexico City.[184] Likewise, the HSCA, though acknowledging that there were "unanswered questions" about Oswald's trip to Mexico City, said that "the weight of the evidence supported the conclusion that Oswald was the individual who visited the Soviet Embassy and Cuban Consulate."[185]

The Second Oswald allegation, like virtually all the allegations by the conspiracy theorists, is ludicrous on its face and goes nowhere. As the Associated Press reported from a review of FBI records in December of 1977, "When Oswald was identified as the suspect and his picture was flashed around the world, people from one end of the country to the other called their local FBI office to report seeing Oswald in their neighborhood in the preceding weeks."[186] This phenomenon would particularly pertain to someone like Oswald, whose features were so common. Even when someone is dead, like Elvis Presley, people continue to swear they've seen him. ("I have seen Elvis in the supermarket. Once he gave me a wink as if to say, 'Don't tell anybody.' Several people in Kalamazoo know where Elvis lives, but they respect his privacy and are protecting him from the media," wrote someone to Ann Landers.)[187]* Take the case of someone who, to put it indelicately, looks like no one else: Michael Jackson. When Jackson, amid allegations of child molestation, called off the remainder of a tour in November of 1993 and went into hiding, "Jackson sightings were reported around the world. A Jackson look-alike stirred paparazzi in London, a hotel operator in the French Alps announced that the singer was staying at his resort, and a local newspaper in Connecticut quoted an 'impeccable source' who said Jackson was recovering at a nearby drug treatment center. All these reports were false."[188]

Conspiracy theorists are well aware of this syndrome; yet, starving for any morsel at all that will feed their obsession, they have seized on almost every one of the Oswald sightings, virtually all of which, even if true, don't intelligently advance any argument, much less a conspiratorial one.

---

*Elvis sightings have been reported in forty out of the fifty states. For instance, he's been seen, since his death, on a parachute ride at a carnival in Denton, Texas; ordering food at a Burger King in Philadelphia; living in a secluded cabin in Orlando, Florida; listening to a rock band in a bar in Riverhead, New York; in a hotel lounge in Atlanta, Georgia; in a 1969 Plymouth with Colorado tags in Tennessee; and at a laundromat in East Lansing, Michigan. Author Gail Brewer-Giorgio compiled all the evidence of Elvis still being alive in her 1988 book *Elvis Alive*, which remarkably got up to number eight on the *New York Times* best-seller list. With all these sightings, many Elvis fans are all shook up, believing the King of Rock and Roll is still among us. Following Brewer-Giorgio's August 6, 1988, appearance on Fox TV's *Late Show*, viewers were asked to call in and vote whether Elvis was alive or dead. Of 30,000 calls, more than 25,000, or 84 percent, believed Elvis was not dead. (Karen Ridgeway, "Fans Say Elvis Is Popping Up All Over," *USA Today*, August 16, 1988)

David Lifton and
Alteration of the President's Body

There have been so many preposterous theories about the Kennedy assassination that it's hard to say which one is the most far-out. One theory that perhaps "takes the cake" is set forth by conspiracy author David Lifton in his book *Best Evidence*. The theory is so unhinged that it really doesn't deserve one word in any serious treatment of the assassination. The only problem is that it comes wrapped in a hefty 747-page book, which was published in 1980 by a prominent publisher (Macmillan), was treated seriously by many people who should know better, got excellent reviews in several major newspapers, was a Book of the Month Club selection, and was on the *New York Times* best-seller list for three months, rising as high as number four. Therefore, I am forced to devote some time to talking about nonsense of the most exquisite nature.

At the time of the assassination, Lifton, age twenty-four, was attending UCLA to get an advanced degree in engineering. To support himself he worked nights as a computer engineer at North American Aviation. What set him off on what would become a lifetime obsession,[*] causing him to eventually quit school and his job and borrow money from his parents so he could pursue shadows of a conspiracy in the Kennedy assassination, was a Mark Lane lecture he attended in Los Angeles in 1964.[1] Before he left UCLA in 1966, he sat in on a course on the Warren Commission taught by former Commission assistant counsel Wesley Liebeler. The law professor and Lifton became friendly adversaries, but when Liebeler learned that Lifton actually intended to write a book on the theory he had come up with, he told Lifton, "I don't think that anybody will ever believe anything you say."[2] Liebeler was wrong. Many have. The good professor failed to take into account that reason only visits those who welcome it.

Lifton is a confirmed grassy knoll devotee. He believes the deadly shots came from

---

[*]"I never got married," Lifton told a reporter in 1993, because "there always came a point when the woman realized I was more interested in the president's body than in her body" (Solomon, "True Disbelievers," p.96).

there as opposed to the Book Depository Building, where Oswald was. But the conspirators, to frame Oswald, somehow got a hold of the president's body, per Lifton, between the time it was at Parkland Hospital in Dallas and the time it arrived at Bethesda Naval Hospital for the autopsy, spirited it away to a place where the bullet wounds to the president were altered to make it look like the shots came from the rear (where Oswald was, not the right front, where the triggerman for the conspirators supposedly was), and then returned the body to the presidential party, all without anyone having any inkling of what had taken place. No self-respecting author of suspense novels would be bold enough to float a theory like this. But then again, Lifton would probably say, this isn't fiction, it's real.[*]

More specifically, knowing that bullet entry wounds are smaller than exit wounds, Lifton says the plotters enlarged the wound in the throat (ignoring the fact that the tracheotomy at Parkland had already done that) and the wound to the right side of the president's head to make them look like exit wounds, when they were really, per Lifton, entry wounds. Believing that the two bullets that he says entered the president's body from the front did not exit his body, and believing further that the president was not shot from the rear, Lifton said the back side of the president originally had no wounds of any kind. So the plotters, he said, "created" two "false . . . entry" wounds to the rear of the president, one in his upper right back and one in his upper right head to make it look as if Kennedy was shot from the rear. Lifton doesn't say if the plotters fired two rounds into the president's corpse or created the two holes some other way.[3] But if they "created" the two wounds in some other way, he doesn't say how the three autopsy surgeons and every other pathologist, including the nine forensic pathologists on the HSCA medical panel, all concluded that the two wounds to the back side of the president were caused by *bullets*.

Lifton believes that only the plotters know what type of rifle and bullets were used to kill Kennedy, because when the conspirators had possession of Kennedy's body, they removed the real bullets that killed him so they would never reach the FBI lab. What about the fragments of one bullet found inside the presidential limousine, and the whole bullet found on the stretcher at Parkland Hospital, each of which was determined to have been fired from Oswald's Carcano rifle? Per Lifton, the plotters planted them there. But how did the plotters come into possession of Oswald's rifle? Lifton doesn't say, but apparently they somehow found out where it was—on the garage floor at Ruth Paine's house—and broke into the garage and stole it. Later, he suggests, they fired it twice at some undisclosed location, retrieved the two bullets, smashed one of them into several fragments, then planted these fragments in the limousine, as well as the whole bullet at Parkland Hospital, and Oswald's rifle itself on the sixth floor of the Book Depository Building.[4]

Since Lifton's theory not only presupposes *but requires* Oswald's total innocence, how does Lifton handle Oswald and the warehouse full of evidence pointing to his guilt? Simply by ignoring both, for the most part, in his book. Out of his 747 pages, he unbelievably devotes no more than 6 or 7 full pages, if that, to Oswald. He dismissively treats Oswald

---

[*]At the beginning of Lifton's immersion in the Kennedy assassination and before he started to write his book focusing on the alteration of the wounds, he had an equally grand theory: that the grassy knoll assassins installed an artificial tree on the knoll prior to the assassination, and camouflaged snipers fired at the president from it. Lifton then magnified, up to twenty times, photos of the trees and shrubbery on the knoll. In the greenery, he saw "several forms which he [interpreted] as assassins firing at the motorcade. One of them looks as if he is wearing a Kaiser Wilhelm helmet. Others wear electronic headsets and man periscopes and machine guns on a platform operated by hydraulic lifts. One of his imagined finds resembles General Douglas MacArthur" (Lewis, *Scavengers and Critics of the Warren Report*, pp.145–146). From this auspicious beginning, Lifton launched into his theory and a book that is paradoxically scholarly yet ridiculous.

almost like an afterthought, not even mentioning, for instance, his attempted murder of Major General Edwin Walker, and devoting only one sentence to Oswald's murder of Dallas police officer J. D. Tippit. I understand. There wasn't room in his book for such trivia.

Getting back to Lifton's theory, is it a legitimate question to ask why didn't the plotters, instead of firing the deadly bullets from the president's right front (grassy knoll) and then, to frame Oswald, engage in the absolutely impossible task of stealing the president's body to remove the bullets and create and alter bullet wounds to make it look as if the shots came from the rear, eliminate the need for this mission impossible by simply using Oswald's rifle (that they had stolen) to fire the deadly shots from the rear—from a different window at the Book Depository Building than where Oswald was, or from the Dallas County Records Building on Houston Street? Lifton, who struggles mightily to convince his readers of the logic of his theory, knows he can't answer that question sensibly, as he comes up with one sentence in his entire book that has no logic behind it, and he hopes the reader will gloss over it and not realize he hasn't answered the question. He says the problem with firing Oswald's rifle from the rear is that "more than one assassin would almost certainly be required to accomplish the assassination with precision because of numerous unpredictable factors: the position of bystanders, the president's posture, etc."[5] Of course, not only is this unresponsive and no answer to the question, but additionally, his assertion itself makes no sense.

Lifton did an enormous amount of thorough and meticulous research over a fifteen-year period (1964–1980) to prove his mad proposition—that conspirators had altered the president's wounds before the autopsy. And miraculously, in his religious zeal and diligence, he actually found, like manna from heaven, evidence to support his theory. That evidence, the centerpiece of his fantasy, was found in a November 26, 1963, FBI document titled "Autopsy of Body of President John Fitzgerald Kennedy" written by FBI special agents Francis O'Neill Jr. and James W. Sibert.[6] On November 22, O'Neill and Sibert had been dispatched to Andrews Air Force Base in Camp Springs, Maryland, to meet Air Force One as it arrived from Dallas with the president's body. At Andrews, they received further instructions to accompany the body at all times, including during the motorcade from Andrews to Bethesda and during the autopsy. In their report, dictated four days later, they said on page 3, "It was ascertained that the President's clothing had been removed and it was also apparent that a tracheotomy had been performed, *as well as surgery of the head area*, namely in the top of the skull."[7] Inasmuch as there was no surgery to the president's head at Parkland Hospital, Lifton had his smoking gun, the proof there was surgical tampering with the president's head by conspirators somewhere between Parkland and Bethesda. Lifton breathlessly tells his readers about his elation upon discovering this language in O'Neill and Sibert's report: "*This* was the missing piece of the puzzle . . . I was exhilarated, terrified . . . Before the coffin arrived in the Bethesda autopsy room, somebody had performed 'surgery' on President Kennedy's corpse . . . The [president's] head was thrust backward by the impact of a bullet from the front, yet the autopsy performed at Bethesda showed an impact from behind. Someone had altered the head. I could hardly believe what I had found." He goes on to say, "The scene conjured up was unbelievable [You're right on that point, Mr. Lifton, unbelievable meaning "not worthy of belief."]—the lid of a coffin raised at some secret location, unknown hands on the body, tools brought to bear, cutting into the corpse of John F. Kennedy."[8]

Before I elaborate on the impossibility of Lifton's theory, let's see what one of the FBI agents has to say about this entry in his report. In an October 24, 1978, affidavit to the HSCA, Agent James Sibert wrote, "When the body was first observed on the autopsy table, it was thought by the doctors that surgery had possibly been performed in the head area and such was reflected in my notes at the time. However, this was determined not to be correct following a detailed inspection."[9]

And in a 1999 telephone conversation from his retirement home in Fort Myers, Florida, Sibert told me that when the casket was opened in the autopsy room, "The president was wrapped in two sheets, one around his body, another sheet around his head." He said the sheet around the head was "soaked in blood," and when it was removed, Dr. Humes "almost immediately upon seeing the president's head—this was before the autopsy—remarked that the president had a tracheotomy and surgery of the head area."[*] When I asked Sibert what Humes was referring to when he used the word *surgery*, he said, "He was referring to the large portion of the president's skull that was missing." When I asked him why he was so sure of this, he replied, "Well, if you were there, it couldn't have been more clear that that's what he was talking about. *He said this as soon as he saw the president's head. He hadn't looked close-up for any evidence of surgery to the head when he said this.* I'm positive that's what he was referring to."[10] (Indeed, in Sibert and O'Neill's five-page report, twelve of the paragraphs pertain to the autopsy, and the "surgery" reference is the first observational entry in the very first paragraph about the autopsy. The tracheotomy and surgery references immediately follow the words "following the removal of the wrapping.") And in a 2001 interview, O'Neill said essentially the same thing as Sibert, that "the doctors'" statement referring to surgery to the head area was made "immediately during a cursory examination . . . It was *not* an exam. First viewing, put it that way . . . I think that was before the washing of the head."[11]

It should be noted that absent a probing with the fingers—which was eventually done during the autopsy—since the scalp was covered with the president's well-known thick growth of hair, any surgery to the scalp would have been impossible to detect visually. So almost necessarily, Humes had to be referring to the open defect. When Dr. Thornton Boswell, the other chief autopsy surgeon, was asked in his appearance before the ARRB in 1996, "Did you see any incisions that appeared to be any form of surgery in the head area prior to the time that you conducted any procedures at Bethesda," he answered, "No."[12]

It should further be noted that the autopsy report on the president (number A63–272), which contains a ten-paragraph, detailed description of the condition of the president's body when it arrived for the autopsy (including such details as "there is edema and ecchymosis of the inner canthus region of the left eyelid measuring approximately 1.5 cm. in greatest diameter"), there is absolutely no reference to observing surgery on the president's head. There *is* a reference, however, to what Sibert referred to: "There is a large irregular defect of the scalp and skull on the right involving chiefly the parietal bone but extending somewhat into the temporal and occipital regions. In this region there is an actual absence of scalp and bone producing a defect which measures 13 cm. in greatest diameter."[13][†]

---

[*]As author Jim Moore very logically surmises, Humes was most likely "unprepared for the massive head wound Kennedy had suffered" (Moore, *Conspiracy of One*, p.97 footnote). Most people would have been. Therefore, a spontaneous, incorrect assessment is understandable.

[†]Dr. Michael Baden told me that "since we know what incisions were made to the president's body at Parkland and by the autopsy surgeons, the photographs and X-rays taken at the time of the autopsy clearly show that no additional incisions were made anywhere on his body after it left Parkland and prior to the autopsy at Bethesda. That's flat and categorical." Baden added that his forensic pathology panel's interviews with the Parkland doctors and autopsy surgeons helped to corroborate this conclusion by his panel. (Telephone interview of Michael Baden by author on January 8, 2000)

So to believe Lifton's theory, not only should one sentence in a report by two FBI agents with no medical background supersede the formal autopsy report written by the three pathologists who conducted the autopsy, but also we'd have to believe that the conspirators had "reached" all three autopsy surgeons who signed the report, and had instructed them (or, if necessary, I assume, threatened them with their lives) not to put in the report that they observed that surgery had been performed to the president's head.

Dr. Michael Baden, chief forensic pathologist for the HSCA, says that "Lifton's theory—and I hate to even call it a theory—is totally bizarre. There is no medical or scientific evidence to support his claims."[14]

Even Dr. Cyril Wecht, who, it should be mentioned again, is the favorite and the most prominent doctor in the conspiracy community, says, "I have never accepted David Lifton's theory. What he concluded can't be done." In the first place, Wecht says, if the president's wounds had been altered before the autopsy, "they would be postmortem wounds and it would immediately be discernible to any pathologist, not just a forensic pathologist, that it had been done." (After death, the heart, of course, stops pumping blood to the rest of the body. Therefore, postmortem "wounds," with their lighter color and created by the alterationists, would be easily distinguishable by the autopsy surgeons from the real wounds Kennedy had sustained while his heart was still pumping blood. Lifton, in his prodigious monument to minutiae, never discusses the difference between postmortem and antemortem wounds.)

Moreover, Wecht adds, "if you try to alter the wounds, how do you know *how* to alter them? Lifton's theory is like this elaborate Shakespearean drama, with the whole plot laid out, and then the plotters have to hope and pray that what later happens fits into their drama." For instance, how could the plotters and doctors altering the wounds have known, Wecht says, "what conclusions the autopsy surgeons would come to later that night, or about the single-bullet theory, which hadn't yet been born, or, for that matter, in deciding before the assassination to alter the wounds, how could they have known there would be a tracheotomy?"[15]

Dr. Wecht, who at one time was called a "traitor" to the cause by Lifton, but who has since had a reconciliation of sorts with him, is being intentionally light-handed about Lifton's thesis. The reality is that Lifton's scenario couldn't possibly be more insane.

Although Dr. Wecht's observations about Lifton's theory are valid, there are much more serious problems with his fantasy. For one, Lifton knew that somewhere in his tale he would have to tell his readers when and how the plotters got possession of the president's body to do what they supposedly did. But instead of Lifton addressing this problem early on (which, if he had, would have caused any sensible reader to put the book down at that point, or to continue to read it but with a continuous smile on his face), the reader has to wait till page 678, right near the end of the book, for Lifton to write, "If my analysis was correct, the President's body was inside the Dallas casket when it was put aboard Air Force One at 2:18 [afternoon of November 22, 1963], but was no longer inside the casket at 2:47, as the plane rolled down the runway." What happened to the body? And how did it get from Dallas, Texas, to Washington, D.C.? Lifton writes, "I considered three possibilities: One, that it was aboard *Air Force Two* [the vice presidential plane]; two, that it was aboard some other plane of which I had no knowledge; three, that it was aboard *Air Force One*, but not in the Dallas casket." Lifton ends up rejecting possibilities one and two as being too unrealistic (in an untethered fantasy world of one's very own making, why would anything be unrealistic?), and settles for number three.[16]

Even though at the Dallas Airport the president's body had to be one of the most secure and protected objects on the face of this earth, with the Secret Service, FBI, presidential friends and staff, and media all either inside the packed plane or nearby on the tarmac, by cobbling together disparate inferences, Lifton postulates that the casket, which was in the aft galley (rear) of the plane—the presidential staff and Secret Service area—was mysteriously left completely "unattended" between 2:18 and 2:32 p.m. And Lifton says that at this point "President Kennedy's body was removed from the casket and hidden somewhere on board *Air Force One* in a body bag . . . Disguised as luggage, it might have been put in the baggage hold, or in the forward galley area."[17] Who removed the body from the casket? Lifton doesn't deign to tell his readers because he admits he doesn't know. Obviously, it had to be either strangers, who, I assume, would immediately be recognized and not allowed on the plane, or Secret Service agents,[*] or presidential assistants on the plane, such as the dead president's "Irish Mafia" friends Ken O'Donnell and David Powers. If, as Lifton speculates, the body was hidden somewhere in the forward galley area, no one on the jam-packed plane apparently noticed when it was carried from the rear of the plane all the way down the aisle, past the press and staff area and crew's quarters, to the front of the plane. Or if they noticed, they probably looked the other way because all of them were in on the plot too.[†]

What about the body being hidden in the rear baggage hold of Air Force One? Conspiracy theorist Craig Roberts, in his book *Kill Zone*, came to Lifton's aid by claiming there was a trapdoor into the baggage hold that the conspirators could have used.[18] But Pittsburgh assassination researchers James Sawa and Glenn Vasbinder conducted extremely extensive research into Air Force One, talking to people very familiar with the plane, including the flight engineer who had flown on it, secured diagrams and floor plans from Boeing, which manufactured the plane, even going to Wright-Patterson Air Force Base near Dayton, Ohio, and personally inspecting and photographing every area of the plane when it was retired in 1998. They learned that "there is no rear trap door into the rear cargo hold into which a body could have been moved."[19]

Lifton then writes, "If the body was hidden aboard Air Force One, how did it get to Bethesda, and where could it have been altered?" He concludes that when Air Force One landed at Andrews Air Force Base, while the nation was watching the Kennedy party and

---

[*]Lifton asserts in his book that "it would hardly be possible to implement" the scenario he describes "without the involvement of some Secret Service personnel." He doesn't even speculate why Secret Service agents, who are trained to literally "take a bullet" to save a president's life, would want to be part of a conspiracy to murder him. Was anyone else involved? Lifton says a "sophisticated appraisal of the evidence must force one to the conclusion that there was a plot involving the executive branch of the government . . . Some government officials must have been recruited into the plot." (Lifton, *Best Evidence*, p.697) Since the president heads up the executive branch, apparently some of Kennedy's own underlings decided to murder him. Lifton doesn't say who these people are or why they'd want to murder their chief.

[†]Gerald Posner, in his book *Case Closed*, writes that the president's casket "had an air-lock mechanism that, when turned, hermetically sealed the lid on the casket. It was sealed at Parkland. Aboard *Air Force One* it had been strapped to the floor. To get the body out, the conspirators would have had to unstrap the coffin and unscrew the lock, allowing the unit to unseal itself. After removing the President's body, something of similar weight would likely have to be placed inside, so people handling the casket would not notice it was too light. Finally, the casket would have to be resealed and strapped back into its original position" (Posner, *Case Closed*, p.298). The reason I have footnoted the above is that Posner gave no citation as a source for this. Though there was a device on the bottom of the casket that "automatically pins a coffin to the floor of a modern hearse," and "there was a catch which released the lock," this device may have been damaged and become inoperable after JFK's aides, who "didn't see it," forcibly removed the casket from the hearse when they lifted it onto Air Force One at Love Field (Manchester, *Death of a President*, p.308).

presidential casket deplaning through the rear door on the left side of the plane, the plotters were removing the body from the front door on the right side of the plane and placing it aboard a waiting helicopter, which quickly flew it to Walter Reed hospital thirteen miles away, arriving at 6:05 p.m.* In Lifton's psychotic (and psychedelic) scenario, this would allow, he says, "about thirty minutes for alterations." Then, Lifton says, the body, in a "plain metal coffin," was transported about five miles to Bethesda Naval Hospital either by helicopter to the rear grounds at Bethesda "for rendezvous" with a black Cadillac hearse, or by the hearse itself, arriving at the hospital "about 6:45" p.m. At this time the body in the casket was carried into the hospital by "a half dozen men in plain clothes," removed from the casket, and placed on the autopsy table. Next, "the body [was] transferred into the Dallas casket" (the expensive bronze one) and taken outside and put into the "correct" ambulance. The casket was then removed from the ambulance by the District of Washington casket team and brought back into the morgue for the commencement of the autopsy at 8 p.m.[20]

Setting aside Lifton's delirious "everybody had their eyes closed and never saw anything" theory for a moment, in addition to praise for his thorough research, Lifton does deserve one other compliment. Unlike the overwhelming majority of conspiracy theorists, he does not deliberately twist, warp, and lie about the official record. Such honesty, together with his being an indefatigable and resourceful investigator, would make him a worthy adversary if he had common sense on his side. Through his compulsive effort, he comes up with a speck of evidence here and a speck there to support his earth-is-flat theory. For instance, he tells us, and I assume he's being truthful, that if one listens to the tape of CBS anchorman Harry Reasoner announcing the arrival of Air Force One at Andrews, "it [is] difficult to hear [Reasoner] because, thundering in the background could be heard the turning rotor of a helicopter,"[21] the one, Lifton assures his reader, that took the president's body to Walter Reed hospital, where his phantom conspiracy surgeons performed the alterations. Assassination researcher Howard Platzman describes this tendency of the conspiracy theorists to stitch together bits and scraps of information to support their grand conclusions "hyperperspicacity. Seeing very clearly what isn't there or what is innocently there. This special kind of seeing is what enabled me, at age 19, to discover 83 pieces of evidence in Beatles' music and paraphernalia pointing inescapably to the conclusion that Paul [McCartney] was dead."[22]

A sine qua non to Lifton's entire premise is that at various points along the way, no one, literally no one, was paying any attention to the president's casket, it being left unattended. Additionally, no one noticed the very busy movements of the plotters removing the body from the casket on the plane, transporting it down the aisle or elsewhere, removing it from the plane for the trip to Walter Reed, and then returning it to the naval ambulance at Bethesda. If you can believe that, then I assume you would believe someone who

---

*When did Air Force One land at Andrews Air Force Base? Although Lifton was very meticulous in trying to nail down every detail to the *n*th degree, he was uncharacteristically imprecise (particularly since time is of the essence in his madcap scenario) when it came to answering this question. Indeed, on page 681 of his book he quotes one Secret Service agent as saying the plane landed with the body at Andrews at 6:05 p.m., but later on the same page, and without quoting a source, he has the plane landing moments before 6:00 p.m. and the body arriving at Walter Reed hospital for alterations, thirteen miles away, at 6:05 p.m. On page 690 he quotes Marie Fehmer, Lyndon Johnson's personal secretary, as noting on a piece of paper that the plane landed at 5:58 p.m. The latter time is the same time that a different Secret Service agent had the plane landing. (CE 1024, 18 H 757) UPI's Merriman Smith, on the flight, records the plane landing at 5:59 p.m. EST (United Press International, *Four Days*, p.33).

told you they had once seen a man jump away from his own shadow. The story, on its face, is unbelievable, and would be so even if no one was watching over the casket—but indeed, people were. Here are just a few: U.S. Air Force Brigadier General Godfrey T. McHugh says,

> From the moment we wheeled the casket out of Parkland Hospital in Dallas and pushed it into the ambulance, I, who was an Air Force aide to the President, never left the coffin except for a few minutes. I did so only to talk to the pilot of *Air Force One*, and this was at Mrs. Kennedy's request. She wanted to expedite our departure. During this time, Mrs. Kennedy, along with Larry O'Brien and Dave Powers, remained at the site of the casket. To suggest that anyone could have taken the body of the President out of the coffin with Mrs. Kennedy and two of his closest and most loyal friends a few feet away is illogical. Aboard *Air Force One* it would have been impossible. Further, the statement [by Lifton] that the ambulance sent to Andrews Air Force Base by the Bethesda Naval Hospital was left unattended at the front entrance of the hospital is false. I remained with the ambulance at all times. After a short while, I entered the ambulance. It was then driven to the emergency entrance, and the casket was immediately wheeled into the operating room.[23]

Secret Service agent Richard Johnsen of the White House detail was specifically assigned to watch over the casket. He said, "On the drive from [Parkland] Hospital to AF [Air Force] #1 I rode the follow-up car. Upon our arrival at AF#1 I assisted in placing the casket upon USAF#26000 [Air Force One]. While awaiting for the departure of AF#1 I was instructed by STSAIC Stout to ride in the rear of the plane with the casket. This had been a request of President Johnson."[24]

Dr. George Burkley, the president's personal physician, said, "Throughout the plane trip, Mrs. Kennedy sat in the vicinity of the coffin talking to Mr. [Kenneth] O'Donnell and various close members of the party."[25] Presidential aide O'Donnell said that "Dave [Powers], Larry O'Brien and I stayed with her [Jackie Kennedy] beside the casket until we landed in Washington."[26]

FBI agents Francis O'Neill and James Sibert were at Andrews Air Force Base before Air Force One arrived from Dallas. At 5:55 p.m. EST they received specific instructions from bureau headquarters to stay with the president's body after it arrived. They were present when the president's coffin was unloaded from Air Force One and placed inside a navy ambulance. They got into the third car in the motorcade, the car right behind the ambulance, and followed the ambulance to Bethesda Naval Hospital, where they assisted in unloading the president's casket from the ambulance and helped carry it into the autopsy room. O'Neill says, "It would have been a physical impossibility for anyone to have tampered with the casket or the body from the time it left Air Force One until the time we took the president out of his coffin." He added that from the moment the president's coffin was placed in the ambulance at Andrews Air Force Base, "the ambulance carrying the president's body was in my line of vision until the time we stopped our vehicle in the rear of the hospital." He goes on to say that he helped remove the casket from the limousine and deliver it "next to [the] autopsy table."[27]

Lifton's theory is so outside the realm of possibility that even inveterate, hard-core conspiracy theorists like Robert Groden and Harrison Livingstone found it too strong for their stomachs. They write in their book *High Treason,*

The evidence indicates that the coffin was never unattended. President Kennedy's entire party, including several of his closest long-time friends and his wife, were crowded into the rear of the plane, since the new President and his party were also on board, filling the plane tightly. Dave Powers, a long-time friend and close aide of President Kennedy, told co-author Harrison Livingstone on June 12, 1987, that "The coffin was never unattended. Lifton's story is the biggest pack of malarkey I ever heard in my life. I never had my hands or eyes off of it during that period he says it was unattended, and when Jackie got up to go to her stateroom where Lyndon Johnson was, Kenny O'Donnell went with her, but we stayed right there with the coffin and never let go of it. In fact, several of us were with it through the whole trip, all the way to Bethesda Naval Hospital. It couldn't have happened the way that fellow said. Not even thirty seconds. I never left it. There was a general watch. We organized it."[28]

Finally, as if this isn't enough, Lifton's fantasy couldn't have happened because the conspirators would have needed *at least* three separate teams of plastic surgeons waiting in hiding, one at each of three hospitals. A team would have had to be waiting at Parkland, since the conspirators wouldn't have known for sure that the autopsy would not be conducted there. (As we've seen in the "Four Days in November" section, almost physical force by the president's inner circle was necessary to prevent the autopsy from being performed at Parkland.) Since the president was taken directly to the emergency trauma room at Parkland in an effort to save his life, if the autopsy was done there after he died, how would the team of conspiracy surgeons have stolen the body away from the emergency room doctors (as well as from the Secret Service, Kennedy's wife and brother, and presidential assistants) to work on it before the autopsy? And where would they have taken the body if they could? To the basement at Parkland?

If the plotters speculated that the autopsy might be back East, Bethesda and Walter Reed would have been the best guesses, but it could only be a guess. And which one? The original plan was to take the body to Walter Reed. As Lifton himself says, "Secret Service Agent Roy Kellerman, in a conversation [from Air Force One] with Secret Service Headquarters, said: 'Arriving Andrews 6:05. The body will go to Walter Reed. Have an ambulance for Walter Reed to take the body there.'"[29] The decision to go to Bethesda Naval Hospital was made *on the plane thereafter* by Jacqueline Kennedy.[30] So if the autopsy was to be at Bethesda, the alterations would have to be at Walter Reed, or some other location, and if at Walter Reed, the alterations would have to be at Bethesda or some other location. Can you imagine that? At a minimum, in addition to all the other impossibilities and absurdities, three separate teams of plastic surgeons were apparently in hiding at hospitals, waiting, with their instruments, to reconstruct the president's wounds and create new ones.

And if that isn't preposterous enough, Lifton, without blinking an eye, compounds the improbability a thousand times when he says that "this was not the way it was supposed to happen. The body was never supposed to be stolen on Air Force One. *It was never supposed to be altered on the East Coast.* Something also was planned and that something went wrong. We're looking at a rather bungled scenario here."[31] We learn, then, from Lifton that the most incredibly sophisticated conspiracy and forgery ever perpetrated managed to be so despite a terribly bungled scenario. Lifton is apparently telling us that after the conspirators somehow goofed in not being able to pull off the alterations in Dallas and they learned the president's body was going to be flown back on Air Force One right away, they had to round up a crew, apparently within minutes, to steal the body aboard the plane, and while the plane was in flight, they had to round up a team of physicians at Bethesda and Walter Reed to perform the required alterations as soon as the body arrived.

Author Jean Davison, in her fine book, *Oswald's Game*, says that "although it is easy to point to anomalies in the mountain of evidence the Warren Commission accumulated, it is something else again to weave those anomalies into a credible scenario that illustrates how a conspiracy might actually have been carried out." Citing Lifton, she says that when a conspiracy author tries to do so (to Lifton's credit, the vast majority never bother, as he did, to even make the attempt) he ends up presenting "stories that are grotesquely improbable."[32]

One could safely say that David Lifton took folly to an unprecedented level. And considering the monumental foolishness of his colleagues in the conspiracy community, that's saying something.

Before moving on, I should mention in fairness to Lifton that although the FBI report by Sibert and O'Neill formed the heart of his theory that the president's wounds had been tampered with, he also relied on his August 25, 1979, interview of one Paul O'Connor, a twenty-one-year-old laboratory technician at the Bethesda morgue whose job was to assist in postmortem examinations. He told Lifton that when the president's body arrived for the autopsy on the evening of the assassination, it "didn't have any brains left." In other words, Lifton asked, "the cranium, for all practical purposes, had been eviscerated?"

"It was gone. Everything was gone. There were bits of brain matter laying around inside the cranium, but . . . that was it."

Lifton asked if the brain being gone also included the left side of the brain, and O'Connor replied it did. "The left side of his brain was gone," he said. "There was no brain on the body, near the body, or in the casket."[33]

If O'Connor's observation that the president's body arrived at Bethesda without a brain was correct, this would indeed be extremely suspicious, since the autopsy report clearly said that the left hemisphere of the president's brain was intact. If that was a lie, then the argument could be made that the entire autopsy report was fraudulent, and all of the autopsy surgeons' conclusions were suspect because they had all agreed to lie. And why would they tell such an egregious lie if they weren't part of some sinister cover-up?

Predictably, Gerry Spence called O'Connor to the stand for the defense at the London trial. On direct examination O'Connor testified that it would have been his job to remove Kennedy's brain, but there was no brain to remove.

Spence: "Are you saying that there was no brain in the president's head?"

O'Connor: "There was no brain. There were pieces of brain matter that were inside the cranium . . . Maybe half a handful . . . at most."

Spence: "And so [the president's brain] was never . . . taken out?"

O'Connor: "We didn't have to . . . The brain was gone."[34]

On cross-examination, one tack I took to diminish O'Connor's credibility was to show the jury the inherent improbability of his story by reviewing the detailed autopsy report, which showed the left side of the president's brain was removed, photographed, and even weighed. It wouldn't be reasonable to assume that three surgeons would make up a fantastic story like this, to the point of getting a photographer to agree to say that he took photos of a nonexistent brain.

Question (Bugliosi): "The official autopsy report in this case, Mr. O'Connor, dated November 22, 1963, states on page 4, 'The brain is removed and preserved for further study following formalin fixation.' Also, 'from the surface of the disrupted right cerebral cortex, two small irregularly shaped fragments of metal are recovered. These measure 7 × 2 millimeters and 3 × 1 millimeter. These are placed in the custody of Agents Francis X. O'Neill and James W. Sibert of the Federal Bureau of Investigation, who executed a receipt therefor.' Now, Mr. O'Connor, three surgeons signed their name to this autopsy report. Are you saying that none of these things happened?"

Answer: "Not to my knowledge, they didn't."

The above was an indirect attack (by reference to the assumed credibility of the autopsy surgeons) on O'Connor's credibility. I then proceeded to attack his credibility directly.

Question: "Now, would you agree, Mr. O'Connor, that the president arriving at Bethesda hospital with his brain already having been removed is one of the most shocking things that you have ever seen in your whole life?"

Answer: "Yes."

Question: "It's the type of thing that if you lived to be one hundred years old—and I hope you do, sir—other than observing a terrible, terrible large defect to the right frontal area of the president's head, certainly [this] is one thing you are never, ever going to forget. Is that correct?"

Answer: "That's correct."

Question: "And it goes without saying that you felt this is something that should have been investigated, right?"

Answer: "Well, I thought it would be."

Question: "In fact, throughout the years you have often wondered what the answer to it was, right?"

Answer: "Oh, I still have questions."

Question: "I believe you told me that you bought a copy of the Warren Report when it came out in 1964, and you looked for it, paying particular attention to the medical aspects of the report. Is that correct?"

Answer: "Yes."

Question: "In fact, you bought and got a hold of virtually every one of the many books on the Kennedy assassination. Is that right?"

Answer: "Just about."

Question: "And you read the medical aspects of it?"

Answer: "Yes, I did."

Question: "At the time you were interviewed by the [House] Select Committee in 1978, you hadn't seen any reference in the Warren Report or in any of these books that you had read about this case mentioning that the brain was missing when it arrived at Bethesda hospital, is that correct?"

Answer: "That's correct."

Question: "And these books, they mention all types of weird things, isn't that correct?"
Answer: "Yes."

Question: "Such as Oswald being Jack Ruby's illegitimate son. You heard that one?"
Answer: "I've heard a lot of stories."

Question: "And that the president is still alive on the top floor of [Parkland] Hospital?"
Answer: "That's a popular story, yes."

Question: "But nothing about that brain being missing?"

Answer: "No."

Question: "With respect to your being interviewed by the House Select Committee, two investigators from that committee, one of whom was Andrew Purdy, interviewed you on June 28, 1978, at your home in Gainesville, Florida, is that correct?"

Answer: "Yes."

Question: "And this was a one-and-a-half-hour interview?"

Answer: "Yes, as I remember."

Question: "Pretty much in depth, right?"

Answer: "Yes."

Question: "They wanted to know about your observations that night?"

Answer: "Yes."

Question: "And that interview is set forth in detail in JFK Document No. 013613. Have you ever heard those numbers before?"

Answer: "No, sir."

Question: "Now, Mr. O'Connor, if the president's brain being missing from his head is one of the most shocking things that you have ever seen in your entire life, a matter that you certainly think should have been investigated, and if they spoke to you for one and a half hours about your observations that night, why wasn't it important enough for you to tell these people about it?"

O'Connor was stumped for an answer, but he managed to come up with a completely inappropriate one: "I was under orders not to talk *until* that time."

That was true, but by his own admission ("*until* that time") he *was* allowed to talk to HSCA investigators. The HSCA had gotten the secretary of defense, Harold Brown, to rescind the November 22, 1963, verbal order of Surgeon General Edward Kenney that personnel present at the autopsy not disclose their observations except under court order.[*] In 1978, letters were sent out to everyone who had been in the autopsy room that night allowing them to speak freely with HSCA investigators, and O'Connor admitted he had received such a letter. Moreover, and more important, he didn't dispute my assertion that he *did*, in fact, talk to the HSCA investigators "for an hour and a half" and "told them all types of things."

Question: "Paul, when I first asked you this question over the phone—it was a Sunday night, about eleven o'clock in Florida, eight o'clock in L.A.—did you tell me, 'the reason I never told them is they never asked me?'"

Answer: "Well, they didn't ask me."

Question: "And *that's* why you didn't tell them?"

Answer: "Yes."[†]

Question: "So, in other words, Mr. O'Connor, even though this was one of the most

---

[*]On November 26, 1963, J. H. Stover Jr., commanding officer at the U.S. Naval Medical School, sent a letter to all interested parties that "you are reminded that you are under verbal orders of the Surgeon General, United States Navy, to discuss with no one events connected with your official duties on the evening of 22 November–23 November 1963. This letter constitutes official notification and reiteration of these verbal orders. You are warned that infraction of these orders makes you liable to Court Martial proceedings under appropriate articles of the Uniform Code of Military Justice." This order of silence was lifted for the HSCA inquiry by Secretary of Defense Harold Brown in 1978.

[†]This is not quite the type of situation where a follow-up question can be, "How would they know to ask you this if you didn't tell them what you knew?" because a considerable number of *other* people were present at the autopsy, and a witness like O'Connor could say, "I assumed they already knew since many other people saw the same thing."

shocking things that you have ever seen, and you're going to remember it until the day you die, and you felt this matter should have been investigated, and you read all these books—the Warren Report and all the others—and no one mentioned it, if those investigators from the House Select Committee didn't ask you the magic question, by golly, you weren't about to tell them. Isn't that correct?"

Answer: "No, sir. I only answered what I was asked, and that was it. I didn't elaborate."

Question: "The problem, Mr. O'Connor, is that on August 25, 1979, over a year after you spoke to the investigators from the House Select Committee on Assassinations, you were contacted by author David Lifton."

Answer: "That's correct."

Question: "And you told me, and I hold you to it now, that he didn't ask you either but you volunteered it to him?"

Answer: "Yes."

Question: "And he wrote a book about this case, right?"

Answer: "Yes."

Question: "And you're a big part of that book, right?"

Answer: "I have a chapter in it, yes."[35]*

It should be noted that of all the doctors, lab assistants, FBI agents, military personnel, and others who were present at one time or another during the autopsy (when we include the four men from the funeral home who prepared the president's body for burial, the total was thirty-two),[36] O'Connor was the only one who said the president's brain was missing. Indeed, seven photographs were taken of the brain at the time of the autopsy.[37]

John Stringer Jr., the photographer for the navy at the autopsy, said he clearly remembered that "Dr. Humes took the brain out of the president's head and put it in a jar of formalin. I personally saw this. I don't know how anyone could say that the president had no brain, except for money."[38]

O'Connor told the HSCA investigators that the president's body arrived inside a pink shipping casket,[39] and told Lifton that the body arrived in a "cheap, pinkish gray casket, just a tin box." But FBI agent James Sibert told me that he, his partner, Francis O'Neill, a few Secret Service agents, and a few others he doesn't recall, carried the casket from the limousine at the back of the hospital to "an anteroom right next to the autopsy room." He recalls that "one of the handles on the casket was damaged." He doesn't remember

---

*I am here to report that years later I came into possession of another HSCA document containing an interview of O'Connor conducted by HSCA investigators at an earlier time, August 25, 1977, in which O'Connor *did* tell them that there was "nothing left in the [president's] cranium but splattered brain matter" (HSCA Record 180-10107-10448, p.2). O'Connor, in London, had apparently forgotten he had told HSCA investigators this earlier and hence did not correct me during my cross-examination of him. Though my misleading cross-examination of him in London was unintentional on my part—only being in possession of his 1978 interview—I owe him an apology, which I am herein giving. But the point also has to be made that he did not reiterate (as he might be expected to do about such an incredible discovery [no brain] that meant so much to him) his observation when he was interviewed in 1978. Even before acquiring the 1977 interview, my overall sense of O'Connor is that his unquestioned error about the president's brain being gone was more the result of confusion than duplicity on his part. His recollection of what took place on the night of the autopsy is very poor, to say the least. Just one more example: in the aforementioned 1978 interview he told the investigators that the autopsy surgeons had not done "a Y incision," but we know they did (CE 387, 16 H 982).

the specific color of the casket but vividly remembers "it was a very expensive one, definitely not a shipping casket" and he recalls it was "very, very heavy."[40] John Stringer also told me that the president's casket was "an expensive, very heavy bronze casket. It definitely wasn't a cheap shipping casket."[41]

Although the body was wrapped in sheets at Parkland, O'Connor told Lifton it arrived at the autopsy room, instead, "in a body bag . . . just a regular, zippered bag." When Lifton asked him, "The kind of body bag they talked about in Vietnam, when they brought soldiers back?" O'Connor said, "It was the same."[42] Lifton also quotes photographic assistant Floyd Riebe as telling him, "I think [the president] was in a body bag," and Dr. John Stover as telling him that "I think I remember seeing a body bag peeled off [the president]."[43]*

But the November 26, 1963, report of FBI agents Sibert and O'Neill reads that when the president's body arrived in the autopsy room, "the complete body was wrapped in a sheet and the head area contained an additional wrapping which was saturated with blood."[44] And in a July 21, 2000, telephone conversation, Sibert told me the body "was not in any body bag when it arrived at Bethesda." John Stringer also told me that when the body arrived at Bethesda, it was "wrapped in two sheets, one around the head, the other around the rest of his body. The body was nude." When I asked him if the body was enclosed within a body bag, he answered, "There was no body bag."[45] In 1992, Dr. Humes said, "I cannot imagine how this talk about the president's body being delivered in a body bag got started, but it is absolutely false." Humes added that Kennedy's body was "wrapped in sheets."[46]

The recollections of Sibert, O'Neill, Stringer, and Humes about the president being wrapped in sheets is consistent with the testimony of the two Parkland nurses who tended to the president's body before it was placed in the coffin at Parkland. Nurse Diana Bowron told the Warren Commission that "after all the work had been done" on the president's body by the doctors, "we wrapped some *extra sheets* around his head so it wouldn't look so bad."[47] Nurse Margaret Henchliffe told the Commission that "after the last rites were said, we . . . wrapped him up in sheets."[48]

But Lifton, although he presents in a footnote the statement of an employee at O'Neal's Funeral Home that the president's body was not in a body bag, elects to go with O'Connor's version that it was. Translation: If we're to believe Lifton (and O'Connor), the conspirators, who performed the most improbable and sophisticated body-snatching caper in history, and along the way performed other magical feats (per Lifton, the successful alterations of the president's wounds) that even Houdini wouldn't have aspired to, somehow neglected to do the simplest, most obvious thing imaginable: put the president's body back into his original wrapping *and* casket. Determined to draw attention to themselves and to what they had done, or because these brilliant plotters suddenly became totally mindless, they apparently went out of their way not only to find a completely different casket to put the president's body back in, but to put it in a body bag instead of keeping the body wrapped in the sheets it was in when they took it away.

*I can see bloody sheets being peeled off the president's body, but how do you peel off a body bag?

Ruby and the Mob

One of the most widely accepted conspiracy theories is that organized crime had Kennedy murdered and then got Ruby to silence their assassin, Oswald. Contrary to what may seem logical, I am starting here with an emphasis on Ruby, not organized crime, because after reading the "Organized Crime" section, which follows, it will be very clear to the reader that the Mafia had nothing to do with Kennedy's murder, and it would be terribly anticlimactic and superfluous for the reader then to go on to a whole chapter on Jack Ruby, his alleged association with the Mafia, and why it's obvious he didn't kill Oswald for them.

But before discussing the allegation that organized crime got Ruby to kill Oswald, I must present the simple facts surrounding Ruby's murder of Oswald, which by them-selves preclude the notion of organized crime, or anyone else, being behind Ruby's act. In fact, the issue of time alone precludes conspiracy. The time it would have taken Oswald, in armed custody, to exit the basement door at the Dallas City Hall garage and walk the ten steps or so to the unmarked police vehicle waiting to transport him to the Dallas sher-iff's office couldn't have been more than fifteen or twenty seconds, if that, since the police car was close to the door Oswald exited.[1] He had only taken a few steps toward the car when he was shot.[2] Several fortuitous things happened, or did *not* happen—*none of which the conspirators would have had any control over*—which enabled Ruby to be in the base-ment at the precise moment he was, and gave him the opportunity to shoot and kill Oswald. If any one of these things had happened otherwise, Ruby would not have been in the base-ment at the right moment, proving that the shooting could not have been a planned event:

1. When Ruby went to the Western Union office, there was only one customer ahead of him.[3] If there had been two customers in front of him, or even if the lone customer had had a transaction that took the clerk just a minute or two longer to complete, or if the clerk, for whatever reason, took longer than he should have, or if he was interrupted

by a telephone call, Ruby would not have been able to shoot Oswald. We know that the twenty-five-dollar money order Ruby sent that morning, and the receipt for it, were both stamped 11:17 a.m. and that Ruby shot Oswald four minutes later at 11:21 a.m., the O'Neal Funeral Home logging the call it received for an ambulance at 11:21 a.m.[4*]

When Doyle Lane, the Western Union clerk, was asked at Ruby's trial, "Did you talk to [Ruby] very much, chat with him?" he answered "Only briefly."

"How did he appear to you?"

"Calm."

"Did he leave then?"

"Yes, sir."

"Which way did he go?"

"Out the door and to the left."

"Was he in a hurry?"

"No, sir."

"Just casually moving along?"

"That's right."

If Ruby had to be at a designated spot two or so minutes later to kill Oswald, how is it possible he would not have been in a hurry?[5]

We also know that the distance from the doorway of the Western Union office to where Ruby shot Oswald was 454½ feet, and that walking at a regular pace—which Ruby was doing, per Lane, at the time he left the Western Union office—it took approximately one minute and thirty-five seconds (one minute and thirteen seconds to walk the surface street, twenty-two seconds to walk down the ramp) to walk the distance.[6]

How long was Ruby in the basement before Oswald appeared and Ruby shot him? Although it is not completely in sync with the above times, we know it was less than a minute, probably in the vicinity of thirty seconds. Local television station KRLD was videotaping everything that was taking place in the basement area and furnished its tape to the Dallas Police Department. Dallas investigating officers Lieutenant C. C. Wallace and Lieutenant P. G. McCaghren, in a report to Chief Jesse Curry, said that they "timed the video tape from the time Lieutenant R. S. Pierce's car left the basement and started out Main Street [the time Ruby entered and started to walk down the Main Street ramp] until the time the shot was fired. The time recorded on the video machine and checked twice was fifty-six (56) seconds."[7] Indeed, an NBC newsman testified before the Warren Commission that he saw Ruby coming down the Main Street ramp into the police basement "not more than fifteen to thirty seconds" before he shot Oswald.[8] Ruby himself says he saw Oswald emerge from the jail office "just as I got to the bottom of the [Main Street] ramp."[9]

If Ruby was a hit man for the mob, how is it, then, that they would cut it that close? Wouldn't this, by definition, have required Captain Will Fritz and one or more of his men to conspire with the mob to kill Oswald? How else could the mob be assured that the Dallas police wouldn't get Oswald into a car a minute or so earlier? But no sensible person could possibly believe that Captain Fritz conspired with the mob to kill Oswald.

If Ruby was a hit man for organized crime, how is it that for at least five minutes or so

---

*Ruby probably had less than four minutes to get to the police basement. The time clock that stamped the money order and receipt rotated on a minute-to-minute basis. (13 H 224, WCT Doyle E. Lane) So the actual time the transaction was completed would have been somewhere between 11:17:00 and 11:17:59.

before he shot Oswald, he wasn't lying in wait for Oswald to appear in the basement garage of City Hall, but instead was approximately *one and a half football fields* away waiting for the person in front of him to complete his transaction so Ruby could wire his money to Karen Bennett Carlin? Only a silly person (i.e., only an avid conspiracy theorist) could possibly believe the hit man theory. No one said it better than author Norman Mailer. If Ruby killed Oswald for the mob, he asks, "Why was Ruby standing [in] line [at the] Western Union waiting his turn to send $25 to a stripper while time kept floating away and Oswald might be moved at any moment? . . . How many confederates—and most of them had to be police—would be necessary to coordinate such a move? No one who is the key figure in a careful schedule that will reach its climax just as the target is being transferred is going to be found dawdling [down] the street at a Western Union office with only a few minutes to go. It would take hours for a stage director to begin to choreograph such a scene for an opera."[10] In simple language, if Ruby had *planned* ahead to kill Oswald in the basement, it is absolutely inconceivable that he would not have been in the basement far in advance of when Oswald was supposed to be brought down. He *never* would have taken a chance on possibly missing Oswald, since he would know it would most likely be the last chance he would ever have to silence him. There are no ifs, ands, or buts about this.

Moreover, the possibility that one or more members of the Dallas Police Department conspired with Ruby and signaled him (how? there were no cell phones in those days) or told him exactly when Oswald was going to be brought down has no merit. Not only is there no evidence to support this rank speculation, but as Dallas police captain Orville A. Jones put it, "If there was some type of conspiracy, [Ruby] . . . would have had to have known what time the man was coming down, which we didn't know, Fritz didn't know, nor did any of the policemen. The only reference to it was made by Curry when he told the press that if they'd get there by 10:00 . . . it would be early enough. He didn't know exactly what time it was going to be. So if there was a signal or something, somebody had to have some rather Divine Knowledge of what was going to happen."[11]

2. Forrest Sorrels, the special agent in charge of the Dallas Secret Service office, testified before the Warren Commission that when the interrogation session of Oswald wound up after 11:00 a.m. on Sunday, November 24, Oswald was told he was going to be moved to the county jail, and "he requested that he be permitted to get a shirt out of . . . the clothes that had been brought in, that belonged to him, because the shirt he was wearing at the time he had been apprehended was taken, apparently for laboratory examination. And so Captain Fritz sent out and got his clothes and, as I recall it, he selected a dark colored kind of sweater type shirt . . . and then he was taken out."[12] Obviously, if Oswald hadn't made the request he did, necessitating a delay of at least one to two minutes, he probably would have left the basement in the police car by the time Ruby arrived. *So unless Oswald was a party to the conspiracy to murder himself,* it would appear from this fact alone that Ruby's killing of Oswald at 11:21 a.m. was not a planned event.

3. Going back even further, how did it happen that Dallas U.S. postal inspector Harry D. Holmes attended the interrogation session of Oswald on Sunday morning, the day Oswald was shot? It was completely fortuitous. In his testimony before the Warren Commission, Holmes said, "I had been in and out of Captain Fritz' office on numerous occasions during this two and a half day period [of interrogation of Oswald]. On this morning I had no appointment. I actually started to church with my wife. I got to church and I said, 'You get out, I am going down and see if I can do something for Captain Fritz. I imagine he is as sleepy as I am.' So I drove directly on down to the police station and

walked in, and as I did, Captain Fritz motioned to me and said, 'We're getting ready to have a last interrogation with Oswald before we transfer him to the county jail. Would you like to join us?' I said, 'I would.'"[13] What's the relevance of Holmes's attending this Sunday-morning session? It's so enormous that by itself it disposes of the hit man theory. As opposed to the previous interrogation sessions, Holmes participated heavily in this one (it is the only one he submitted a memorandum on), thus helping appreciably to lengthen the session beyond the time it had been scheduled to end. Captain Fritz testified that the Sunday-morning interrogation session had been scheduled to end "by ten o'clock," but "we went . . . an hour overtime with the interrogation."[14] Therefore, Oswald's transfer from the Dallas Police Department to the sheriff's office, which had been scheduled for 10:00 a.m., was delayed over an hour.[15]

Following is a four-paragraph excerpt from a "Memorandum of Interview" prepared by Holmes and signed on December 17, 1963, summarizing the portion of the Sunday-morning session he participated in. As can be seen from this excerpt, the interrogation of Oswald by Holmes of Oswald's post office boxes in Dallas and New Orleans was extensive and time-consuming. The memorandum was based on notes Holmes took during the interview as well as his memory.

> P.O. Boxes - - - He [Oswald] was questioned separately about the three boxes he had rented, and in each instance his answers were quick, direct and accurate as reflected on the box rental applications. He stated without prompting that he had rented Box 2915 at the Main Post Office [in Dallas] for several months prior to his going to New Orleans, that this box was rented in his own name, Lee H. Oswald, and that he had taken out two keys to the box, and that when he had closed the box, he directed that his mail be forwarded to him at his street address in New Orleans.
>
> He stated that no one received mail in this box other than himself, nor did he receive any mail under any other name than his own true name; that no one had access to the box other than himself nor did he permit anyone else to use this box. He stated it was possible that on rare occasions he may have handed one of the keys to his wife to go get his mail but certainly nobody else. He denied emphatically that he ever ordered a rifle under his name or any other name, nor permitted anyone else to order a rifle to be received in this box. Further, he denied he had ever ordered any rifle by mail order or bought any money order for the purpose of paying for such a rifle. In fact, he claimed he owned no rifle and had not practiced or shot a rifle, other than possibly a .22 small barrel rifle, since his days with the Marine Corp. He stated that "How could I afford to order a rifle on my salary of $1.25 an hour when I can't hardly feed myself on what I make."
>
> When asked if he had a post office box in New Orleans, he stated that he did, for the reason that he subscribed to several publications, at least two of which were published in Russia, one being the hometown paper published in Minsk where he met and married his wife, and that he moved around so much that it was more practical to simply rent post office boxes and have his mail forwarded from one box to the next rather than going through the process of furnishing changes of address to the publishers. When asked if he permitted anyone other than himself to get mail in Box 30061 at New Orleans, he stated that he did not. It will be recalled that on this box rental application he showed that both Marina Oswald and A. J. Hidell were listed under the caption "Persons entitled to receive mail through box."

After denying that anyone else was permitted to get mail in the box, he was reminded that this application showed the name Marina Oswald as being entitled to receive mail in the box and he replied "well, so what, she was my wife and I see nothing wrong with that, and it could very well be that I did place her name on the application." He was then reminded that the application also showed the name of A. J. Hidell was also entitled to receive mail in the box, at which he simply shrugged his shoulders and stated "I don't recall anything about that."

He stated that when he came to Dallas and after he had gone to work for the Texas School Book Depository, he had rented a box at the nearby Terminal Annex Postal Station, this being Box 6225, and that this box was also rented in his name, Lee H. Oswald. He stated he had only checked out one key for this box, which information was found to be accurate, and this key was found on his person at the time of his arrest. He professed not to recall the fact that he showed on the box rental application under the name of corporation, "Fair Play For Cuba Committee" and "American Civil Liberties Union." When asked why he showed these organizations on the application, he simply shrugged and said that he didn't recall showing them. When asked if he paid the box rental fee or did the organizations pay it, he stated that he paid it. In answer to another question, he also stated that no one had any knowledge that he had this box other than himself.[16]

For those who might say it isn't 100 percent clear from these paragraphs that Holmes himself was conducting the interview,* and therefore his mere presence at the interrogation session did not lengthen it, let's look at some snippets of his testimony on this point: "In questioning him about the boxes, which I had original applications [for] in front of me"; "I brought it up first as to did he ever have a package sent to him from anywhere. I said, 'Did you receive mail through this Box 2915 under the name of any other name than Lee Oswald?'"; "'Well, who is A. J. Hidell?' I asked him"; "I showed him the box rental application for the post office box in New Orleans and I read from it. I said . . ."; "And I said also it says 'A. J. Hidell'"; "When I was discussing with him about [the] rental application for Box No. 6225 at the Terminal Annex, I asked him if he had shown that anyone else was entitled to get mail in that box"; "I said, '. . . What did you show as your business?' and he said, 'I didn't show anything'"; "I asked . . . 'Is that why you came to Dallas, to organize a cell of this organization in Dallas?'"[17]

It is very clear, then, that if Holmes hadn't decided to go downtown to the police station on Sunday morning, November 24, a completely fortuitous event, the interrogation session would have ended quite a bit earlier, and Oswald would have been transferred to the Dallas county jail well before Ruby arrived in the basement—in fact, probably before Ruby even left his apartment to go to the Western Union office.

So unless Postal Inspector Holmes was part of the conspiracy to murder Kennedy or to cover it up—a possibility that would be just fine with conspiracy theorists—Ruby's

---

*A Dallas police detective, C. N. Dhority, testified before the Warren Commission that during the Sunday-morning interrogation session of Oswald, "I don't think Mr. Holmes talked to him too much" (7 H 155). Dhority may be correct only in the sense that the interrogation covered a whole range of issues and matters, and Holmes probably only participated in the portion of it dealing with Oswald's post office boxes. But as to the latter, not only do we have Holmes's testimony that he asked the many questions dealing with the post office boxes, and not only would he be the one to naturally ask those questions, not anyone else, but also Captain Fritz testified, "Mr. Holmes did most of the talking to him [Oswald] about the boxes" (4 H 229).

killing Oswald was exactly as he said it was, a spontaneous decision on his part that was not pursuant to any conspiracy involving others.[*]

Parenthetically, it was stated on radio and television that Oswald was to be transferred to the sheriff's office at 10:00 Sunday morning.[18] In fact, Ruby himself acknowledges knowing this.[19] Since there is no evidence that anyone from the Dallas Police Department was in touch with Ruby to inform him of the new time for transferring Oswald, if Ruby's shooting of Oswald was planned, and part of a conspiracy, why wasn't he down at the police station at 10:00 a.m. to carry out his assignment? We know that Ruby was still at his apartment at 10:00 a.m. Records from Southwestern Bell Telephone Company show that Ruby's employee, stripteaser Karen "Little Lynn" Carlin, called Ruby at his apartment at 10:19 a.m. on Sunday.[20] This was the call asking for money that led to Ruby's going downtown to the Western Union office to wire twenty-five dollars to Carlin. And George Senator, Ruby's roommate, testified that Ruby didn't leave the apartment until around 11:00 a.m., some time after the call, among other things first shaving and getting dressed.[21]

Anthony Summers, in his book *Conspiracy*, sets forth the conspiracy theorists' position that someone did inform Ruby of Oswald's new transfer time and more: "The suspicion is that somebody in the know kept Ruby closely in touch with Oswald's changing timetable."[22] As indicated, cell phones were not in existence in those days, and though the conspiracy theorists have struggled long and hard, they haven't come up with any evidence to support this hypothesis, support for which they would be willing to donate one of their bodily organs. The conspiracy theorists have focused their "suspicion" on four Dallas police officers—Sergeant Patrick Dean, who was in charge of securing the basement garage against unauthorized persons, and three of his men assigned to the security detail, Officer William Harrison, Detective Louis D. Miller, and Lieutenant George Butler—claiming suspicious behavior on the part of all four. But in the process, they rewrite the official record. For instance, shortly after 8:00 that Sunday morning, Harrison and Miller went out for coffee at the Deluxe Diner near the police station. Summers writes that Miller testified that while there, "Officer Harrison received a telephone call from an unknown person."[23] But despite the quotation marks Summers uses, that was not quite Miller's testimony. He testified, "When the person that works there at the diner answered the phone, he said, 'Phone for one of you.' Officer Harrison answered it and came back to the counter and said we were to come back to the office as soon as we finished eating and were to remain there until further notice."

Question: "Did he tell you who made the telephone call?"

Answer: "No, sir, he never did, and I never did ask him."

---

[*]Author Gerald Posner makes the good observation that if there was such a conspiracy, and the morning's events before the shooting were only contrived to "provide Ruby" with the "defense" at his trial that his murder of Oswald wasn't premeditated (which would actually protect the conspirators more than Ruby, since lack of premeditation would only save Ruby from a sentence of death, not a conviction of murder, whereas lack of premeditation would mean Ruby hadn't conspired with anyone, conspiracy necessarily involving premeditation), the conspiracy would include "Karen Carlin, whose plea for money took [Ruby] to the Western Union office . . ., George Senator, for confirming the Carlin story . . ., postal inspector Harry Holmes, for delaying the transfer with his questions, police chief Curry and Captain Fritz, for selecting the basement . . ., Lt. Rio Pierce, for driving his car up the ramp a minute before Oswald was taken from the jail; and Officer Vaughn, for turning his back when Ruby walked down the ramp" (Posner, *Case Closed*, p.397 footnote).

Question: "Do you know whether it was somebody from the police department that made that call?"

Answer: "I presumed it was."[24]

In other words, the caller was not an "unknown person"; the caller was only unknown to Miller. And the call wasn't specifically for Harrison, it was for either Harrison or Miller. Moreover, Harrison himself testified that the call was from the deskman at the police station, Charles Goolsby, telling him and Miller to "come on back to the bureau when we got through eating."[25] In *The Ruby Cover-Up*, conspiracy theorist Seth Kantor writes that Harrison was given a polygraph test "concerning his movements as they could have involved Ruby on that morning" and the results were "not conclusive." Kantor quotes no source for any of this.[26] The only testimony regarding the issue of whether or not Harrison passed the polygraph test came from Dallas police lieutenant Jack Revill. Revill said that Harrison was given a polygraph test on the sole issue of whether Harrison had seen Ruby standing to his left rear before Ruby shot Oswald, and Harrison, who denied seeing Ruby, passed the test.[27]

The Dallas Police Department, naturally very concerned about its failure to protect Oswald, and cognizant of all the whispers that maybe one or more of its officers had helped Ruby sneak into the basement garage, conducted an extensive investigation that revealed no evidence of complicity between Ruby and any Dallas police officer.[28]

It should be noted that at Ruby's trial for murdering Oswald, perhaps more than any other evidence against him, the testimony of Dallas police officers as to what Ruby told them right after he shot Oswald refuted and negated his defense of temporary insanity. (See discussion in Ruby trial section.) Therefore, the charge of Dallas police complicity with Ruby "ignores," as Ruby author and appellate attorney Elmer Gertz points out, "the implications of Ruby's failure to accuse the [Dallas] police *after* the imposition of the death sentence [against] him. Why would Ruby remain silent if the police had aided and then double-crossed him?"[29] Instead, Ruby maintained to the end that the officers in the Dallas Police Department were his friends.[30] After the trial, he even gave Sergeant Patrick Dean, whose testimony of Ruby's statements were the most damaging of all to Ruby's case, a copy of the Warren Report "with a fond inscription in it, and tried to give him his watch and his gun."[31]*

Not that we can persuasively cite Jack Ruby himself to rebut the never-ending suspicions of the conspiracy theorists, but Ruby did testify that when he drove past City Hall (on the way to the Western Union office after 11:00 a.m.) and saw a crowd gathered there, "I took it for granted that he [Oswald] had already been moved."[32] The reason why it is highly probable that Ruby was telling the truth is that he took his beloved dog Sheba with

---

*As indicated earlier in the book, Ruby's affection for the police was not one-sided. Although many of his police friends and acquaintances tried to disassociate themselves from him once he shot Oswald (9 HSCA 1120 note 49), there can be no question about the relatively close relationship Ruby had with Dallas law enforcement. In fact, the gun that Ruby used to kill Oswald, a .38 Colt Cobra, was registered to a friend of his, Dallas police detective Joe Cody! Rather than buying a wall safe at his club, which Cody told him would cost, with wiring, a couple of thousand dollars, Ruby took Cody's suggestion to "just get a pistol" as protection for when he carried the day's receipts home with him. About a year or so before the assassination, Cody and Ruby went to a hardware store in West Dallas that sold guns (Ray Brantley's hardware store), and to save Ruby the eight or nine dollars in sales tax, a tax police didn't have to pay when they bought guns in Texas at the time, Cody paid the $62.50 purchase price himself and Ruby reimbursed him. After Cody heard the announcement that Ruby had shot Oswald, he said, "It all hit me that Jack Ruby was a friend of mine and that I had bought that pistol for him, and the pistol was in my name." (Sneed, *No More Silence*, pp.470–471)

him that morning and, even more tellingly, left her in the car when he entered the basement. As one of his appellate lawyers, William Kunstler, argued to the Texas Court of
Criminal Appeals in Austin, Texas, on June 24, 1966, "Was that the act of a man planning
to shoot another in a crowded basement, knowing he would never get out?"[33] Ruby's
friends have said that his love for Sheba was such that if he had planned in advance to
shoot Oswald in the basement of the police station, he never would have left his beloved
dog in the car, since he would have to know he would be taken into custody and would
not be coming back to the car.[34]

Countless words have been written on the importance of Jack Ruby in the Kennedy
assassination. Every conspiracy book that propounds the "mob killed Kennedy" theory
tries to establish, above all, the connection between Ruby and organized crime. Richard
Billings, a former *Life* magazine editor who wrote extensively on organized crime and
coauthored the book *The Plot to Kill the President*, puts it this way: "If there's a smoking
gun in this case, it's the pistol that was used by Jack Ruby to kill Oswald in the basement
of the police station. *The main piece of evidence of Organized Crime complicity in the conspiracy is Jack Ruby.*" Billings goes on to say that "if you're going to determine the final
answer to this crime, the murder of the president, the character of Ruby is crucial."[35]

To address the character issue, the story of Jack Ruby's life is presented here. It takes
the reader up until the early morning hours of the day of the assassination. "Four Days
in November," as you may recall, took the story from there.

Jack Ruby (born Jacob Rubenstein), arguably history's most notorious avenger and
embodiment of vigilante justice, was born in 1911 in Chicago, Illinois, the fifth of eight
children of Fannie and Joseph Rubenstein, Ruby having one older brother and three older
sisters. Births were not required to be recorded in Chicago prior to 1915, and Jacob's may
not have been. If it was, it's hard to explain why there is so much confusion about his
exact birth date. There is no conflict in the year—it was 1911—but the date has been
listed in various places as March 3, March 15, March 19, April 21, April 25, April 26,
May 15, and June 23.[36] However, Ruby himself most frequently, but not always, gave the
date of March 25, the date that is also on his driver's license as well as in Dallas Police
Department records,[37] though he gave March 19, 1911, as his date of birth at the time
of his arrest for killing Oswald.[38] Later that day he gave the FBI March 25 as the date of
his birth.[39]

Ruby's father, Joseph, was born in 1871 in Sokolov, Poland, a small town near Warsaw.
With Poland under the rule of czarist Russia, Joseph, at age twenty-two, entered the Russian army (artillery).[40] In the army, he was trained as a carpenter. Both his father and brother
were carpenters. He also learned how to drink excessively, being a heavy drinker the rest
of his life.[41] Joseph served in China, Korea, and Siberia, but reportedly hated these places
and army life in general.[42] While in the army, Joseph took a bride through the services of
a professional matchmaker.[43] Her name was Fannie Turek Rutkowski, who is believed to
have been born in 1875 near Warsaw. Fannie came from a well-to-do family and was considered to be very pretty but with little intelligence.[44]

In 1898, tiring of the military, Joseph simply "walked away" from it and about four
years later emigrated to England and then Canada. Eventually, in 1903, he entered the

United States. Fannie followed him in June of 1905 with their two children, Hyman and Hannah (Ann), both born shortly after the turn of the century.[45]

Joseph and Fannie settled in Chicago and had six more children, of whom Jack was the third. Besides Hyman and Ann, his older siblings included two sisters—Marion, born in June 1906, and Eva, born in March 1909. Jack had two younger brothers, Sam, born in December 1912, and Earl (Isadore), born in April 1915, and a younger sister, the last child, Eileen (Ida), born in July 1917.[46] The couple had another child, a girl, who died at the age of five after she tipped over a vat of boiling chicken soup onto herself and suffered fatal burns.[47]

In 1904, a year after his arrival in Chicago, Joseph joined the carpenters' union and remained a member until his death in 1958, although he was mostly unemployed for the last thirty years of his life.[48] He learned to speak a little English, whereas Fannie spoke and wrote virtually no English, though she went to night school around 1920 in a failed effort to learn. In fact, as late as 1940, thirty-five years after she entered this country, she had to write an "X" for her signature in the affidavit for her Alien Registration Form. The language spoken in the Rubenstein household was predominately Yiddish.[49]

Fannie, unlike her husband, felt her children required an education if they were to better themselves. Joseph, having received scant formal schooling himself, argued that his children needed to go only to grammar school.[50]

When Jack was born, the Rubensteins lived near Fourteenth and Newberry streets in Chicago, the first of many Jewish neighborhoods in which they lived.[51] At age ten, Jack and his family were living at 1232 Morgan Street, their fourth different address on Chicago's teeming west side.[52]* All were lower-class Jewish neighborhoods, his brother Earl said, in "the Maxwell Street district." This, he said, "was like the ghetto of Chicago," with people selling their wares out on the street in pushcarts.[53] Sister Eva elevated the description to "below the middle class but yet it wasn't the poorest class."[54] Indeed, the Maxwell Street Market at the time was called "the World's Greatest Outdoor Market."†

They would eventually move farther west (away from downtown) in the city, near "Dago Town," an improvement over the Maxwell Street neighborhood but where fighting in the street between Italians and Jews was the norm,[55] as was the domestic fighting that occurred within the Rubenstein home. Joseph's drinking, coupled with Fannie's uncontrollable temper and constant nagging, led to his frequent arrests for disorderly

---

*The Rubensteins were almost as nomadic as the Oswalds, though, unlike the Oswalds, the changes of address were always to another place in the same city, Chicago. Between 1911, when Jack was born, and 1933, a period of just twenty-two years, the Rubenstein family had moved ten times (CE 1185, 22 H 304).

†All the books on Ruby say he grew up in Chicago's "west side," and those who grew up with him in Chicago told the FBI that Ruby "grew up in the neighborhood of the west side" (CE 1266, 22 H 371). Ruby himself said he was born on the west side of Chicago and grew up there (Hall [C. Ray] Exhibit No. 1, 20 H 37). Yet, his brother Earl told the Warren Commission that the Rubenstein family grew up in "what is known as the east side of Chicago" (14 H 366). Richard Lindberg, a Chicago author and historian who has written eleven books on Chicago's crime and history, says that Ruby's brother, who had long since moved out of Chicago, "spoke loosely and his words should not be interpreted literally. Ruby grew up in Chicago's 'near west side,' the word *near* meaning close to the downtown Chicago area. Back then, and for years, Chicago had no east side. If the term was used at all, it referred, jokingly, to Lake Michigan. The term *east side* was coined in the 1980s by real estate people who created a little development near the Gold Coast, the affluent lakefront area of Chicago." Lindberg did allow that the Maxwell Street area was on the "eastern side of Chicago's near west side," the dividing line between the west side and the commercial development area of Chicago's downtown area being Halsted Street. (Telephone interview of Richard Lindberg by author on February 11, 2005)

conduct and assault and battery charges, some of which Fannie brought against him.[56] Around the neighborhood, Joseph was known as "Poppa Joe," the neighborhood carpenter, and a drunk.[57] Fannie also questioned Joseph's fidelity, accusing him of philandering and spending his money away from home.[58] A July 1922 report from the Jewish Social Services Bureau, dealing with Jack's "truancy from school" and "behavior trouble in school and at home," used these adjectives for Joseph: "alcoholic," "sexually promiscuous," and "quick tempered."[59]

The discord within the Rubenstein household was, as one might expect, taking its toll on the children. Hyman, the oldest, remembered his father and mother arguing constantly, his father drinking to excess, and the arguments erupting into physical fights.[60] Fannie and Joseph eventually separated in 1921.[61] Jack, ten at the time, stayed with his mother.*

"Truancy and incorrigible at home" were the reasons the Social Services Bureau gave in its 1922 report for having eleven-year-old Jack examined by the Institute for Juvenile Research, which was under the Illinois State Department of Mental Health. Based on its psychiatric examination that year, the institute made the recommendation to the Social Services Bureau that he be placed in a new environment, primarily to provide supervision and recreation and thus end his interest in street gangs.[62]

The examination noted the following about his childhood demeanor: he was "quick tempered" and disobedient, he openly disagreed with his mother, he ran away from home, he felt his classmates were picking on him, he felt he could not get along with his friends, and he was destructive. Jack's psychiatric examiner stated, "He [Jack] stated that he does not like to live at home because he does not like his mother. Stated his mother beats him and so he runs away. He could give no adequate reason for running away from school, but said that he went to amusement parks at this time . . . This patient is egocentric, states that he can lick everyone and is as good as anybody at anything he wants to do."[63] The Stanford-Binet intelligence test was administered to Ruby on July 6, 1922, and yielded an IQ of 94.[64] Jack Ruby wasn't quite a moron, but for the rest of his life no one would ever accuse him of being bright either.

Perhaps the best insight into eleven-year-old Jacob Rubenstein's world can be had by reference to the words written about his mother in some of the documents from the Institute of Juvenile Research, which were later provided to the Warren Commission. In a questionnaire regarding young Jacob, a handwritten observation, presumably by a psychiatric examiner in response to the typewritten question "What do you consider the chief trouble in patient's situation?" read, "An extremely excitable and un-understanding mother."[65] A summary sheet dated July 6, 1922, had this notation: "Mrs. Rubenstein has so little self control that during any conversation of the slightest importance, she becomes highly excited, talking most rapidly and often un-intelligently. She admits she loses her temper with the children and beats them, has a very disagreeable and sharp tongue and quarrels with her neighbors—often is ready to come to blows with them. In spite of her temper and severity with the children, she cannot control them and is always getting into

---

*Joseph lived away from home for fifteen years, part of the time with another woman, before returning. Since he worked very sporadically and since Fannie only did crocheting for some shops for a limited period, Jack and his siblings, for the most part, had to support their parents with money they earned from whatever jobs they could get, and Joseph having a separate apartment increased the burden, causing them to ask him to move back home in 1936, which he did. (CE 1281, 22 H 392; CE 1281, 22 H 407) Even when Ruby was in the military, he arranged for a deduction from his pay to be sent to his parents (CE 1706, 23 H 185).

quarrels because of their delinquencies, i.e., principally their destructive tendencies and disregard for other people's property."[66] The institute also noted that "from a superficial examination of his mother who was here with him, it is apparent that she has no insight into [her son Jacob's] problem and that she is thoroughly inadequate in the further training of this boy." The report concluded it was "very advisable" to put young Jack "into a new environment."[67]

No action was taken on the recommendation of a new environment, and in March of 1923, the institute elaborated on its earlier recommendation, stating, "Placement in a home, where intelligent supervision and discipline can be given him will in all probability improve his present behavior and his future conduct."[68]

In a 1964 report to the Warren Commission pursuant to the Commission's request for a summary of the clinical evaluation done at the Institute of Juvenile Research on Jack Ruby in 1922 and 1923, the Illinois State Department of Mental Health stated that Ruby's family relationships were "characterized by a high degree of instability and disorganization . . . All the children apparently were involved in some, more or less minor, delinquent activity."

Regarding Jack's mother, the report said, "It is not possible to reconstruct from the accumulated data the nature of the mother's disturbance. She might have been an emotionally and materially grossly deprived individual suffering from a severe character disorder, but by the same token she could have been of low intellectual endowment or grossly disturbed emotionally to the point of being psychotic."[69]

In another section of its report concerning Ruby, the Department of Mental Health told the Warren Commission, "He was not fond of his parents but still preferred his father to his mother."[70] However, the department, in compiling its summary of records from 1922 and 1923, apparently overlooked a questionnaire in which Ruby, after saying he was not fond of his parents, was reported to have given a "no" reply to the question "Does he like his father better than his mother?" and a "yes" reply to the next question, "Does he like his mother better than his father?"[71] The report included a comment on a finding from the physical examination given Jack in 1922 that "the only medical finding of some interest is the undescended testicles. This may be of a certain physical as well as psychological importance."[72]

A dependency hearing for Jack, his younger brothers, Sam and Earl, and his younger sister, Eileen, was finally held in Chicago's juvenile court on July 10, 1923, where it was alleged the children were not receiving proper parental care.[73] The judge made a finding of dependency, which meant that the Jewish Home Finding Society was appointed guardian of the children, and they were taken from Fannie and placed in foster homes, where they may have remained until November of 1924.[74]

The exact dates and length of time Jack and his younger siblings were away from home is not clear. Court records either are inexact or have been destroyed, and the testimony of the children themselves shows their own uncertainty. Earl testified that "on the farm I was with my brother Sam, and Jack was in another farm some distance away from us. In the foster home Sam and I were together again, I think, just Sam and I. Then in another foster home, I think, Jack was with us. The three of us were in one foster home together."[75]

When Jack and his younger siblings returned to their mother's home, family harmony did not.

Jack exhibited entrepreneurial instincts early on in life, scalping tickets at sporting events, selling peanuts and pennants at football and baseball games, tip sheets at racetracks, chocolates at burlesque shows, cheap costume jewelry, even carnations in dance halls.[76] He was described as "always looking to make a buck,"[77] and two of his sisters said that in his days in Chicago he could be classified as a "peddler or salesman" of novelty items.[78]*

Many of Jack's friends knew him by his nickname, "Sparky," which he did not like. Eva said he acquired the nickname because from age five to eight, being short, fat, and stocky, he wobbled when he walked and thus was likened to a horse in the comics— "Sparky, the slowest darn horse you ever saw." Eva recalled that hearing the name Sparky burned him up, and he would hit the children calling him that name.[79]

Hyman Rubenstein has a different recollection as to how his younger brother acquired the nickname. When questioned before the Warren Commission as to the origin, he said, "Fast, aggressive, quick thinker, always on the ball, you know." Asked if he was sure, he admitted, "No, but how else would a fellow get a name 'Sparky'?"[80] But Hyman admitted that Eva "was at home most of the time and I think she could tell you more about the family than any of us . . . She has a very good memory too, by the way, which is important."[81] However, the consensus of nearly everyone was that Ruby was called Sparky because of the volatility of his personality.[82]

Jack was out on the streets a lot, where he was described as "quite good with his fists."[83]† A childhood friend remembered Jack's proclivity for engaging in arguments, usually about sporting events. If the argument did not go to his liking, he was liable to use his fists or pick up a stick or any other weapon that was readily available. Similar to what many of Jack's other friends through the years would recall, this same friend observed that "when the altercation was over, he immediately returned to his usual likeable self."[84]

The recollections of Jack's friends from his Chicago days were that although he had a quick temper, he was not overly aggressive or apt to pick fights for no reason, but he sure as hell didn't go out of his way to avoid them either.[85] They do remember that he would initiate a fight with anyone showing a pro-Nazi or anti-Semitic attitude, and that whenever he would hear of a meeting of those sympathizers taking place, he would go there and try to break it up.[86] Older brother Hyman said, "Jack went out to the northwest side many times and broke up Bund meetings. That is one thing he wouldn't go for. Other people told me. They said, 'Your brother is terrific. He just goes in there and breaks up the joint.' He just couldn't tolerate those guys. Nobody would dare mention the word 'Jew' in a derogatory form to him because he would be knocked flat in two minutes."[87] Although only five feet eight inches tall, he was solid and muscular. Ruby bragged that he could hit harder than heavyweight champ Joe Louis.[88]

Though volatile and scrappy, Jack was able to avoid any major trouble or legal problems. He hung around with hustlers who could help him make a fast buck‡ and, as Hyman put it, "fellows who loved life and [to] go out and have a good time," but "he

---

*The prophet Mohammed said, "Tell me you can move a mountain, but don't tell me that people change." As we've seen earlier in this book, Jack Ruby, the Chicago street hustler, was selling "twistboards" around the time he murdered Lee Harvey Oswald some forty years later.

†A boyhood friend of Jack's whom he idolized, Barney Ross, was so good with *his* fists that he became the welterweight champion of the world in the late 1930s, by all accounts one of the greatest Jewish fighters in boxing history (15 H 21, WCT Hyman Rubenstein).

‡Ruby hung around with hustlers because that's what he was. When the FBI, days after the assassination, interviewed a series of old friends of Ruby's from his Chicago days, the words that kept coming up to describe him were "hustler" and "ticket scalper," but never "criminal" (FBI Record 124-10070-10295, November 26, 1963, pp.1–2, 4, 6).

never hung around with no hoodlums. We knew hoodlums, sure. If they came into a restaurant where you are, next to them you are sitting, 'Hello, Hy', 'Hello, Joe.' What do you do, ignore them? You have known them all your life, you don't ignore them . . . [They're] kids from the neighborhood."[89]

Hyman did mention the only time he could remember Jack being in trouble: a fight with a policeman, he thought for scalping tickets, where he was clubbed on the back of the head, requiring hospitalization. Hyman didn't recall what year this was, but said he went to court with his brother and the charges were dropped.[90*]

The only other time Jack got into trouble was in his late teens when he served thirty days in 1930 for selling copyrighted sheet music, a fact that he admitted, years later, still embarrassed him.[91]

Jack appears to have been an average student, attending several different public schools in the Chicago area. Records from the Board of Education do not indicate he ever advanced past grade 8B or attended any Chicago high school. However, Jack himself said that he entered the second year of high school but did not complete it, and Eva seemed to remember her brother attending a year and a half of high school.[92] There's no record of Jack having had any schooling outside the public school system,[93] but before his parents separated, when Jack was ten, he and his brothers did receive some Hebrew school training.[94]

At the time of Jack's exam by the Department of Mental Health, he was in the fifth grade, and his best subject was arithmetic and his worst ones were spelling and history.[95] During the two years, 7A and 8B, for which there exists a record of his grades, on the excellent/good/average/poor scale that was used then, Jack had one "excellent," eight "good," seven "average," and three "poor" grades.[96]

There is some difference of opinion among the children as to how Orthodox a Jewish home Joseph and Fannie kept. Earl remembers it as a home where his mother made them all observe dietary rules and the practice of having separate dishes for dairy and meat.[97] However, Hyman remembers the home as "not Orthodox, not strict, nothing strict except for the holidays."[98] And Eileen stated, "We weren't too religious . . . We adhered to certain conservative Jewish principles." Eileen doesn't remember the family having separate dishes, but agreed with Earl and Hyman that their mother's influence made the family abide by strict dietary rules.[99]

The seeming contradiction in the home of Joseph and Fannie Rubenstein in strictly observing the dietary laws of Judaism, but not necessarily the more formal aspects of the religion, was easily understandable to the eldest son, Hyman: "You try to bring up eight kids in Chicago and keep them in shoes and keep them in school, out of jail, out of trouble, that was enough . . . That is more important."[100]

Things weren't made any easier by the fact that Fanny Rubenstein was deficient in so many ways. Her daughter Marion later said that ever since she could remember, her

---

*A boyhood friend of Jack's remembers the incident more clearly. Jack, he said, was probably around fifteen at the time, and was struck hard on the head by a policeman who caught Jack trying to sneak into one of the most famous fights in boxing history, the "long count" heavyweight championship fight in 1927 at Chicago's Soldier Field between Jack Dempsey and Gene Tunney. In the seventh round, Dempsey knocked Tunney down but didn't immediately go to a neutral corner, as required. The referee didn't start counting until four or five seconds later, which, some claim, gave Tunney time to recuperate. (Others say that if the count had started when it should have, Tunney would have simply gotten up earlier.) Tunney went on to win in a unanimous ten-round decision. And Ruby went on, his friend seems to recall, to having a metal plate installed in his head because of the severe injury. (CE 1191, 22 H 311)

mother was "difficult to get along with. She was selfish, jealous, disagreeable, and never cared to do anything in the house but lie around and sleep . . . [She] has never been any kind of a housekeeper, was careless with money, and never took much interest in the children's welfare." The children couldn't invite friends to the house "for fear that she [would] embarrass" the family. Fannie had eventually taken to accusing her children of being "immoral," and they were all "nervous wrecks" living with her under one roof, which they were finding increasingly impossible.[101]

Joseph was still separated from Fannie when Jack, around age twenty-two, left Chicago "sometime in 1933 or 1934."[102] According to Eva, there was no work in Chicago and Jack heard that a lot of jobs were available in San Francisco.[103] First though, Los Angeles beckoned, and Jack and three friends arrived there and found work selling "Collier's Tip Sheet" for handicappers at horse races.[104] Eva recalls that her brother also worked as a singing waiter, but apparently he ruined a lot of good meals and, she says, "nearly starved to death."[105] Moving to San Francisco a few months later, Jack initially continued to sell tip sheets at the Bay Meadows racetrack. Later, he solicited newspaper subscriptions door-to-door. He worked for several of the newspapers that covered San Francisco and the nearby small towns—the *San Francisco Examiner*, the *Call-Bulletin*, the *News*, and the *Chronicle*.[106]

Eva, who had recently divorced, followed Jack to San Francisco approximately six months later with her young son, Ronnie. She also worked with Jack selling newspaper subscriptions door-to-door.[107] They both had good reputations. A former crew manager of Jack's recalled him as an honest and forthright person who associated, not with any hoodlum element, but with the sports crowd and those involved with professional fighting. He was also of the opinion that had Jack possessed a larger physique, he would have liked to have been a police officer since he had a personal liking for law enforcement.[108]

At first Eva and her son shared an apartment with Jack, who helped pay Ronnie's private-school expenses. Then, in 1936, while still in San Francisco, Eva remarried, and for a while, Jack lived with his sister and her new husband and Ronnie in a four-room apartment.[109]

Ronnie recalls that his uncle left the newspaper subscription business and went into the linoleum-laying business while in San Francisco, working for himself.[110] Also, for a short time in 1936, Jack, ever true to his reputation as a hustler who would do anything to make a buck, went into business with Sam Gordon. The two bought small turtles and painted their backs and sold them at a fair in Pomona, California.[111]

On July 14, 1937, Jack's sister Marion had the Cook County sheriff's office take her mother to the Presbyterian Hospital of Cook County. Marion said Fannie "had become unmanageable, and gets into hysterics and screams and shouts day and night."[112] After she was examined by a psychiatrist and found to have "senile deterioration" and to be in a "paranoid state," a Cook County judge committed Fannie, at age sixty-two, to Elgin State mental hospital in Illinois, the committing document referring to "the alleged insanity" of Mrs. Rubenstein.[113] Three months later she was released into daughter Marion's custody only to be readmitted in January of 1938 at the wish of the majority of the family.[114*] The return home had not worked out. A letter from Florence Worthington, chief

---

*That mental illness ran in the Ruby family is clear. Jack himself, we all know, had considerable mental and emotional problems. His brother Earl said that Jack received psychiatric help when he was ten (14 H 414–415, WCT Earl Ruby), though this has never been confirmed. Earl himself was hospitalized in August of 1960 harboring thoughts of self-destruction by sleeping pills, gun, or asphyxiation (FBI Record 124-10062-10290, January 13, 1964, p.1).

social worker, requesting Fannie's readmittance to Elgin State Hospital stated that the family said their mother was "uncooperative and causes constant discord in the family. She is very noisy and uses obscene language."[115] In an earlier letter Worthington stated she had been informed that the "patient eats a great deal. She refuses to do anything—cook, wash dishes, dust, go out, etc. She crochets all the time. If she ever does cook something, she leaves the entire kitchen in such a mess that it takes hours to clean it up . . . The mother and father fight, the mother making up obscene jingles about the relationship between the father and the daughters."[116]

It is interesting to note an observation that was made about the Rubenstein family in a progress report: "The children all seem to be wholesome, nice young people. They manage to leave the impression of living rather comfortably, but in visiting with them longer, one learns that they have little income among them and use great ingenuity to make the house comfortable, meet weekly expenses, etc."[117]

Marion, the only one of the children who had been upset at her mother's readmittance to Elgin in January of 1938, had planned to share an apartment with her.[118] Fannie was released again four months later.[119] A May 1938 letter to Marion from the managing officer at Elgin indicated the rather obvious eagerness of the medical staff to shed themselves of the impossible Fannie and to send her home again, saying, "It has been decided that this parole may be carried out at once. You may call for her at your earliest convenience."[120] Follow-up reports indicated that Fannie, living with Marion in a West End Avenue apartment and away from her husband and children, was doing much better than the first time she was paroled.[121]

Jack, who had returned to Chicago from San Francisco in 1937, was without work until he eventually contacted an attorney friend, Leon Cooke, who had organized the Scrap Iron and Junk Handlers Union.[122] Leon had decided on his own that the low wages at that time made the formation of a union a good idea. According to Earl Ruby, Leon did all the legal work, and Jack became secretary-treasurer of Local 20467 of the union.[123]

The union's application for an affiliation to the AFL-CIO in March of 1937 was accepted, and at that time Leon Cooke was listed as the financial secretary on the application but Ruby's name doesn't appear as a union official.[124] Jack's employment records with the Social Security Administration show that he was employed by the union for approximately two and a half years from the last quarter of 1937 through the first quarter of 1940.[125]

An acquaintance and former executive director of the Waste Trade Industries in Chicago, Theodore Shulman, recalled that Ruby always exhibited a "highly emotional attitude" and seemed to get "overly excited about things that did not go his way." He recalled that Jack would advocate a union strike at the smallest provocation.[126]

On December 8, 1939, John Martin, who had become president of the union, and Leon Cooke, who was no longer an officer of the union, got into an argument at union headquarters and Martin shot Cooke. Cooke went to the hospital under his own power and gave a statement saying that Martin became angry with Cooke's assertion that union members were not receiving adequate salaries, and pulled a gun and shot him. Cooke died a month later. Martin, during his murder trial, maintained that he shot Cooke in self-defense and it was Cooke who had the gun. Martin was acquitted of the murder.[127] Although conspiracy theorists for years have boldly asserted that Ruby was involved in Cooke's murder (e.g., "Ruby was involved in the December 1939 murder of Leon Cooke"),[128] no evidence has ever emerged that he was, and he was never a suspect, although on the morning after the shooting, the *Chicago Daily Tribune* printed a photo of "Jack Rubenstein" alongside a photo of Cooke saying that Rubenstein was the "present secretary" of the union and had been "seized for questioning."[129]

Jack left the union about two months after Paul Dorfman was appointed to run it.[130] Abe Cohn recalls that the union became disorganized after Cooke's death, and although Ruby expressed to a friend that he wanted very badly to take over the union, he later complained to Cohn that "his heart was not in it" and that he was going to quit.[131] Another acquaintance, Ira Colitz, believed that one reason for Ruby leaving the union was that progress was too slow and Jack was more interested in making a "fast buck."[132] In fact, Dorfman recalled that to his knowledge, "Ruby was never a salaried employee of the union but probably drew some expense money from collected dues."[133]

Leon Cooke's death affected Jack, and out of respect and remembrance, or as Jack said, "for sentimental reasons," he adopted *Leon* as his middle name. Although he rarely used it when signing his name, it remained on his driver's license.[134]

The Warren Commission concluded, "There is no evidence that Ruby's union activities were connected with Chicago's criminal element. Several longtime members of the union reported that it had a good reputation when Ruby was affiliated with it, and employers who negotiated with it have given no indication that it had criminal connections."[135] Bill Roemer of the FBI, who led the federal government's drive against organized crime in Chicago, said that "Ruby was nothing in that union. The mob came in and took it over later."[136]

In 1941, Ruby, his brother Earl, and three friends, Harry Epstein, Marty Gimpel, and Marty Shargol, "went on the road." Ruby and Epstein had formed a small company, the Spartan Novelty Company, selling gambling devices known as punchboards, candy, and small cedar chests. They traveled throughout the Northeast, in particular Connecticut, New York, Massachusetts, New Hampshire, and Pennsylvania, with no fixed address, living in hotels.[137] Later that year, Jack returned to Chicago and continued selling punchboards, primarily through mail order, including an advertisement that ran in *Billboard* magazine.[138]

After the Japanese attack on Pearl Harbor, Ruby tried to promote, with two Chicago associates, a plaque in remembrance of the tragedy. He particularly liked this idea because he had always been very patriotic, having busts of Franklin D. Roosevelt and Douglas MacArthur in his room at home while growing up.[139] However, the market became flooded with Pearl Harbor–themed trinkets before their plaque—depicting the Statue of Liberty with a blue background and the words "Remember Pearl Harbor" printed thereon in silver ink—could be developed. One of Ruby's associates described Ruby as a "perfectionist" and said it took anywhere from four to six weeks to develop a proof of the plaque that was acceptable to him.[140]

Another venture of Jack's about this time in which his sister Marion and brother Earl invested $1,500, almost every dime they had, was a bust of President Roosevelt's head with an excerpt from his 1932 inaugural speech.[141] Jack sold quite a few of them for one dollar each. But nothing Jack did ever went really well, only providing him with his next meal, not easy street, even though he was tireless in his efforts and energy.

Jack's younger brothers, Sam and Earl, were already in the military when he registered with the Selective Service in Chicago for duty on October 16, 1940, and was classified 1A, meaning he was eligible for the draft. Later he received a deferment, although the Warren Commission was unable to determine whether he was reclassified as 1A(H), the classification for registrants who have reached their twenty-eighth birthday, or 3A, applying to persons whose entry into military service presents financial hardship to dependents, since the records of the local draft board were destroyed in 1955 in accordance with an act of Congress in 1943. Jack's local board in Chicago, Local Draft Board No. 124, had passed out of existence in 1947.[142] Hyman stated that his brother initially applied for a deferment "because he was the only one home. We were all in. My mother was alone."[143]

However, Jack was later reclassified 1A again and inducted into the U.S. Army Air Force on May 21, 1943.[144] His enlistment records show his occupation at the time as "sells novelties and premiums" and his income as "$3000 annually."[145]

Jack entered active duty at the induction center at Camp Grant, Illinois, on June 4, 1943, and arrived at his first duty station, Keesler Field, Mississippi, about a month later, starting a twenty-two-dollar-per-week pay deduction for his mother and father. From his induction until his discharge some thirty-three months later, Jack would serve in six different states, with later assignments in North Carolina, New York, Georgia, and Florida. His longest assignment would last a little over seventeen months with the 114th Air Force Base Unit (B) at Chatham Field in Georgia.[146]

During that summer of 1943, Hershey Colvin was a corporal in the training unit at Keesler Field and an instructor in "marching, rifle lore, and calisthenics." Hershey had also been a childhood friend of Jack's from the Roosevelt Road area of Chicago. Jack was assigned to Colvin's unit when he arrived, much to Colvin's pleasure, and Colvin later stated that he considered himself to be Jack's closest associate in the unit. Socializing frequently with his old buddy, Colvin later characterized Jack's behavior as nervous, high strung, and "taut as a fiddle," and stated that Ruby left the impression that it was impossible for him to relax, carrying on conversations in an excitable manner. Colvin also reinforced the view of many others with regard to Jack's irritation at anyone making remarks degrading Jews, and his hot temper. Dating back to his Chicago days, Colvin knew of no criminal associates of Jack's and reiterated that although Jack was known as a hustler who made a quick buck on the sale of cheap merchandise, he was definitely not a criminal or "a heist guy."[147]

At Chatham Field in Georgia, Jack's closest friend at the time, fellow airplane mechanic Irving Zakarin, witnessed Jack beating up another crew member with his fists. The man, a buck sergeant from Texas, made the mistake of calling Jack a "Jew bastard." Zakarin described Ruby as someone who would do anything for his friends, including readily loaning money to them, and was "very emotional," crying when President Roosevelt, whom he greatly admired, died in April of 1945.[148]

At Bluethenthal Field in North Carolina, where Ruby had been stationed before being transferred to Chatham, another acquaintance, Sergeant Stephen Belancik, echoed others' feelings about Jack's temper and remembered he liked to gamble in card or dice games near the barracks. And apparently Jack had all the makings of a Sergeant Bilko, the television role made famous years later by the actor Phil Silvers, who played the conniving but likeable army hustler who was continually scheming to make a buck while working as little as possible. Belancik recalled that on one occasion in 1944 Ruby contacted someone in Chicago to send him punchboards and chocolates, which Jack then peddled throughout the base to make extra money. Also, according to Belancik, Ruby had no liking for work, and carefully avoided any situation that would dirty his hands.[149] However, his Chatham Field buddy, Zakarin, differs in his recollection about Ruby's work ethic, remembering that Ruby, who was thirty-four at that time, "always worked harder than the younger men in the group in order to prove he could keep up with them."[150]

Ruby's military records indicate that his military occupational speciality was Airplane and Engine Mechanic 747.[151] He was awarded the World War II Victory Medal, American Theater Ribbon, and Good Conduct Medal. Regular character and efficiency ratings ranged from "Unknown" to "Excellent" and there were no records of any court martials or absences without leave. His proficiency with firearms earned him a "sharpshooter" qualification with the M-1 rifle. Ruby was honorably discharged at Fort Sheridan, Illinois, on February 21, 1946, as a private first class.[152] His discharge physical indicated that with the exception of a sore left thumb, plantar warts, and a case of athlete's foot, he was in good physical condition.[153]

On April 4, 1944, while Jack was still away in the service, his mother was admitted to Michael Reese Hospital with arteriosclerotic heart disease, followed by complications of bronchial pneumonia, which proved fatal. She passed away while in the hospital on the evening of April 11, 1944. Jack came home for the funeral in Chicago and was very upset, having become very fond of and devoted to his mother despite all the family turmoil to which she had contributed.[154]* But years later, he would take the death of his president harder.

After his discharge, Jack returned to Chicago. He and his three brothers, Hyman, Sam, and Earl, teamed up to run Earl Products Company, which Earl, the sole investor, had started after he left the service in 1944 and which involved selling small cedar chests and candy punchboards by mail order. As his brothers were discharged from the military and returned to Chicago, Earl gave each of them equal shares of the business even though they did not invest money in it. Jack recalled that he "prospered" in the business, but dissension soon set in since there wasn't enough money to go around, and Hyman left, leaving Earl, Sam, and Jack to manage the company.[155] However, that too was short-lived as Jack and his brothers had a falling out. Earl and Sam wanted Jack, who was the sales manager, to sell exclusively the products they were manufacturing, but Jack seemed interested in selling products made by others too. Consequently, Jack and Sam had an argument ("a real run out" was how Earl put it, "a little difference as to the politics of the company" were Sam's words), and as Earl said later, "We just couldn't get along so we decided to buy Jack out." And they did for a little over $14,000 in cash,[156] almost assuredly the most money Jack Ruby would ever have to his name.

Two other catalysts to Jack's departure from Earl Products in 1947 were his apparent dislike for traveling outside the Chicago area to secure new accounts, as Earl and Sam would have liked, and sister Eva's moving to Dallas some four or five years previously. She had been writing Jack with tales of how good life was there, and asked him to come and join her. Jack subsequently left for Dallas very shortly after his buyout, but not before he and a partner from Detroit were unsuccessful in a cookware promotion business.[157]

With the help of some money Jack had sent her earlier to obtain a building lease, Eva had purchased a nightclub, known as the Singapore Supper Club, in the 1700 block of

---

*Jack's sister Eileen often felt that Jack was her mother's favorite child (15 H 278 WCT Eileen Kaminsky; see also 14 H 120, WCT Alice Reaves Nichols).

When Jack's father died many years later, while Jack was living in Dallas, Jack, not a devout Orthodox Jew, and accustomed to attending synagogue services only on high holidays, attended the synagogue twice daily for eleven months (CE 1183, 22 H 296, Interview of Rabbi Hillel Silverman by Warren Commission staff member Murray J. Laulicht on July 20, 1964).

South Ervay Street in Dallas. Earl and Hyman had also given money to Eva to help her out. Jack, after his arrival, invested "a lot" of his $14,000 cash windfall and became a 50 percent partner with Eva in the club, which was primarily a dance hall that served beer.[158] But the club was in a bad area, and business was so poor they were lucky they were eating. Jack eventually left Eva by herself to run the Singapore and returned to Chicago for a few months to enter into various "merchandising deals," as he referred to them, but they proved unsuccessful. A pattern was well established. Jack was always selling some cheap item of merchandise, and he was always unsuccessful. When Eva asked Jack to come back to help with the club, he returned to Dallas that same year, 1947.[159]

Jack, who had been using the name Jack Ruby for some time, decided to officially change his name from Jacob Rubenstein, his petition saying he sought the change because the name Rubenstein was too long and because he was "well known" as Jack Ruby. On December 30, 1947, he secured a decree from the 68th Judicial District Court in Dallas effecting the change, which included the addition of a middle initial, L, in memory of his late friend Leon Cooke. Jack's brothers Earl and Sam had already changed their name to Ruby; it's unknown if this prompted Jack to follow suit. Earl stated that he and Jack never discussed the name change. Hyman kept the name Rubenstein.[160]

Now officially "Jack L. Ruby," and having left his failed merchandising deals in Chicago, Jack's main interest in life for the next sixteen years became managing nightclubs and dance halls in Dallas. Though he was an owner of nightclubs, where smoking and drinking were almost automatic, he himself never smoked and rarely drank. Apparently, Jack rarely took a drink because he could not hold his liquor.[161] Eva testified that Jack didn't drink a fifth of liquor a year. When they went out, she said, "We ordered two drinks. I would drink mine and have to drink two-thirds of his." And she added, "I don't remember but once he had a cigar in his mouth . . . and maybe he had three or four cigarettes in his life that I know of." Said Earl, "He didn't smoke at all."[162]

Soon after Jack resumed operating the Singapore Supper Club, he changed its name to the Silver Spur (though it was sometimes referred to as the Silver Slipper), and Eva left for the West Coast, where she operated a restaurant behind a bar on Sunset Boulevard in Los Angeles and later sold fishing tackle and radios on the road. She remained a partner with Jack in the club, gave him power of attorney, and invested money when she could, but she only returned to Dallas sporadically over a ten-year period until her permanent return in 1959.[163]

Jack, meanwhile, in about 1952, purchased another club, the Bob Wills Ranch House, located in an industrial area at Corinth and Industrial streets, with money obtained from a friend, Ralph Paul. Jack had met Paul, as was his style, by simply walking up to him one day in 1948 in the Mercantile National Bank, where they both did business, and introducing himself. Paul, like Jack, had come to Dallas the previous year. He was from New York City and in 1948 was half owner of a nightclub called the Sky Club. Paul invited Jack to see the show at his club, and later Jack reciprocated and invited his new buddy Ralph to see his club. They became fast friends, and a few years later Jack went to Paul and told him he wanted to buy the Bob Wills Ranch House and asked to borrow $2,000 so he could "show" some people he had the money, which he would promptly return the next day. It turned out that wasn't enough. As Paul told the Warren Commission in 1964, "Subsequently he [Ruby] roped me in for $3700." Eventually, Paul ended up with a note, or part ownership, on the Silver Spur.[164]

Norman Weisbrod and his partner, Sam Lasser, operated a photograph and popcorn concession at the Ranch House for a year. Weisbrod, calling Ruby a "Damon Runyon type character,"* said he became convinced that Ruby was "crazy" in the manner he operated his newly purchased club and performed as master of ceremonies. According to Weisbrod, Ruby purchased Western clothing, and at times got up on stage and attempted to entertain the customers with a guitar. Sam Lasser commented on Jack's efforts at being a guitar-playing cowboy by saying that Ruby could not sing or play the guitar.[165] However, Ruby did occasionally have "first-class" entertainment, including Tennessee Ernie Ford, the country western singer Tex Ritter, and big bands including Artie Shaw and other entertainers, many of whom he also, it seems, tried to shortchange. Lasser stated that on one occasion Jack had considerable trouble when he tried to cheat Tex Ritter out of two hundred dollars that Ritter was owed.[166]

With both the Bob Wills Ranch House and the Silver Spur to run, Jack encountered severe financial difficulty in 1952. He apparently had completely dissipated his $14,000 and was doing so badly that he moved out of his apartment and started sleeping and cooking in the back of the Silver Spur. Dallas police officer Gerald Henslee recalls driving with his partner one summer night up the alley behind the nightclub and seeing a man sleeping in his underwear just inside the screen door. When they rousted him, Ruby identified himself as the owner of the place, and they advised him to find safer sleeping accommodations, considering the bad neighborhood. Jack disregarded the advice but told them to return to his club anytime, everything on the house.[167] Jack soon went completely broke and lost both clubs, first the Ranch House and then, about a month later, the Silver Spur, and had a "mental breakdown."[168] Marty Gimple (Jack's friend from Chicago who had sold punchboards with Jack in 1941) and his business associate Willie Epstein assumed some of the debts and took over the Silver Spur.[169] After pulling down the shades and "hibernating" in the flea-bag Cotton Bowl Hotel in Dallas for three or four months, and declining to see his friends, Jack went back to Chicago and was mentally depressed to the point where he told his brother Earl, "Well, it looks like it is the end for me." Jack was penniless and Earl tried to help him out and find a business for him to run. However, he was listless and wouldn't go anywhere. Earl even had to force him to wash and clean himself.[170]

Jack came out of his depression after a month or two and returned to Dallas in 1952, saying he did not like being in Chicago, owed a lot of money to people in Dallas, and wanted to make money so he could pay off his debts.[171]

Starting his "comeback," Jack tried operating the Silver Spur again, taking it back from Gimple and Epstein, who apparently were more than happy to get rid of it. And for a few months in 1952 into 1953 he even operated the Ervay Theater, a motion picture theater next door to the Silver Spur.[172]

In 1953, Jack, with a partner, Joe Bonds, obtained an interest in another Dallas nightclub, the Vegas Club, one he would continue to operate right up to the time he shot Oswald more than ten years later. The Vegas Club (or Club Vegas) was formerly the Studio Lounge, and was located in a semicommercial district on Oaklawn Avenue. The owner, Irving

---

*The Damon Runyon allusion was an apropos one. Runyon, the legendary Broadway reporter and writer, captured in his short stories the era between the 1930s and the 1950s. His stories were populated by small-time crooks, broads, hustlers, and cops on the beat operating in a street world of neon lights, burlesque joints, racetracks, and boxing clubs. Some of these stories were adapted to Broadway and the movies (e.g., *Guys and Dolls*), and one might say that Runyon had been writing the story of Ruby's life right up to the moment Jack fired the shot that forever plucked him out of that world.

Alkana, had purchased the club in the latter part of 1952 or early 1953. However, Alkana, owing the government $6,000, signed a lease purchase agreement with Jack, whom he had met a year earlier while frequenting the Dallas nightclub scene. Jack completely controlled the operation of the club, which sold beer, wine, soft drinks, and some prepared food items, and managed it along with Bonds. Jack bought Bonds out a few months later for $2,500.[173]

It was around this time that Jack discovered—no one remembers how—a ten-year-old black boy from Dallas called "Little Daddy Nelson" (real name, Ben Estes Nelson), who was the greatest little singer, dancer, and piano player Jack and many others had ever seen. Little Daddy started performing regularly at the Vegas Club to highly appreciative audiences. No one recalls how Little Daddy came up with his second name, Sugar Daddy, but it may have been Jack's doing since he felt he had finally struck gold with the young black performer whom he was going to ride to fame and fortune in New York, Vegas, and Hollywood. Jack spent every penny he had on Little Daddy and on March 18, 1952, signed a contract with the boy's legal guardian and father, Columbus Nelson, giving Columbus and his wife, presumably the boy's mother, 25 percent of the action and Little Daddy 50 percent, with Jack getting the remaining 25 percent as his manager. The contract even provided for a tutor for Little Daddy while he was on the road. Jack took Little Daddy to New York and Chicago to line up TV and radio appearances, but just when things were about to happen, a second mother, or a second woman claiming to be Little Daddy's real mother, showed up as the fly in the ointment, and Jack, on the advice of his lawyer, backed off, afraid of all the legal entanglements that would inevitably follow.[174]

In September of 1953, some three months prior to the option date of Jack's lease purchase agreement, Jack informed Alkana that he would not be able to obtain the funds to make the purchase. Alkana took over the management of the club and Jack retained a one-third interest. However, numerous disagreements ensued, including a fist fight in May of 1954. After their brawl, Jack was arrested and charged with carrying a concealed weapon when the police found a .38 caliber snub-nosed revolver in his possession. Alkana said Ruby always had the gun on him because he carried large sums of money. Alkana also told FBI agent Carl Murano Jr. that he could not recall ever seeing Ruby pull his revolver on anyone, nor had he ever heard of Ruby threatening anyone with a gun, including himself when they had their fight and Ruby had the gun on his person. In June of 1954, Alkana sold Jack his two-thirds interest in the Vegas Club.[175]

In 1955 Jack had difficulty paying federal excise taxes for the Vegas Club, so his brother Sam loaned Jack $5,500 to prevent the IRS from padlocking the door of his club. Sam was forced to sue when Jack defaulted on his payments. They went to trial but apparently the matter was settled before a judgment was rendered, Jack agreeing to pay the balance on the loan, $4,500. At the time of Jack's death, Sam was still owed about $1,300.[176] Jack sold his interest in the Silver Spur in 1955 but continued operating the Vegas Club. Right around this time, he opened another club named Hernando's Hideaway on Greenville Avenue in Dallas, but it was not successful and he lost it after less than a year.[177]

Jack continued ownership of the Vegas Club but turned over its operation to his sister Eva in 1959, when she returned from California. She ran the club as a salaried employee with no ownership interest.[178]

Soon, a new club, the one history would forever link him with, was to come his way. An acquaintance, Joe Slatin, got the idea to open a private membership club in Dallas, and with borrowed funds he leased the upstairs second-floor property at 1312½ Commerce Street, located halfway between the county jail and the Dallas Police Department, and began the process of redecorating and finding employees. Slatin, however, had used up all of his initial capital, so he approached Ruby, who had visited the premises during the redecorating, regarding additional financing. Ruby eventually put up $5,000, money he mostly got from his brother Earl and his friend Ralph Paul, and the Sovereign Club was established as part of S&R Inc. S&R (Slatin and Ruby) was a corporation Ruby formed in February of 1960, though Ralph Paul, Slatin, and a third party are listed in the articles of incorporation, not Jack. Earl Ruby is listed on the board of directors with the above three parties, but again, Jack isn't.[179] The club opened in the early part of 1960. Not only was business poor, but Slatin accused Ruby of trying to be "too high class" in the operation of the club, thereby dooming any chance of success. Seeing no hope for success, Slatin voluntarily withdrew. Jack promised to pay Slatin $300, but never did.[180]

With Slatin out and in need of money to pay the rent, Jack turned to his old friend Ralph Paul—the one he had "roped in" for $3,700 in order to buy the Bob Wills Ranch House, and whom he still owed $1,200. Paul advanced Jack another $2,200, enough to pay the Sovereign Club's rent for four months.[181]

As time passed, rent money became due again, and again Jack had difficulty paying. Paul, Jack's personal piggy bank, was there again for Jack with another $1,650, but this time there was a condition. The number of anticipated private memberships had never materialized, so Paul insisted that the club become "an open place"—a burlesque house. Jack, who according to Paul felt the Sovereign Club was dead, agreed. Thus, in late 1960, the Carousel Club, not a private club where members could buy hard liquor, but an open place where customers could buy beer, was born.[182] The Carousel Club, a classic burlesque house* with striptease acts, Jack's first club with strippers,[183] was much more difficult to manage than Ruby's Vegas Club, which had no regular acts and was basically a rock-and-roll dance club in a rougher part of town.[184]

The Carousel Club opened at 8:00 in the evening. The cover charge was paid to an attendant in a tiny cashier's booth at the top of a narrow flight of stairs leading from the street below. The mostly male customers came to the club to see "Ruby's Girls," over twelve in all—waitresses, cigarette girls, cocktail girls, and the main attraction, the four strippers. Though the girls were sexy, Ruby made sure no prostitutes worked at the club.[185] Indeed, if Ruby suspected any of his "girls" of hustling johns out of his club, he would have them followed to see if they were making arrangements to meet the patrons outside. He was even known to have the girls take lie detector tests.[186] Ruby felt so protective, almost paternal, toward his girls, that he had several physical fights with known pimps in the Dallas area who tried to recruit them.[187]

A four- or five-piece orchestra was situated at the back of the stage to play for the performances and between acts. There was no dance floor. The strippers displayed their wares on three short runways into the audience. In addition to beer, the Carousel Club served Coca-Cola, champagne, and pizza, the only food the Carousel served, which was made in the kitchen behind the bar.[188] Customers wanting hard liquor had to bring their own

---

*The Carousel was one of three burlesque houses in downtown Dallas, the other two being the Theatre Lounge and the Colony Club (13 H 319, WCT Andrew Armstrong Jr.; 15 H 212, WCT Thomas Stewart Palmer).

bottle and order a set-up, ice and a glass. Although the club stayed open until 2:00 a.m., seven days a week, drinking of hard stuff had to cease at midnight on Sunday through Friday and at 1:00 a.m. on Saturday night (early Sunday). By Jack's admission, the beer was the cheapest he could buy, and the champagne was "pure rotgut," bought for $1.60 a bottle and peddled to the customers for $17.50 a bottle.[189]

As indicated, the legal ownership of the Carousel Club was S&R Inc., but it's hard to know exactly who all the people were who were putting up the money and owning the shares. Paul was the recipient of half of the shares in the corporation, five hundred.[190] Jack, though, insisted he had no financial interest in the club—he was just the manager.[191] Stanley Kaufman, a lawyer who handled many of Jack's legal matters including the S&R incorporation, agreed.[192] And Social Security Administration files only show Ruby as being "an employee" of the club.[193] No matter. It was Jack's club. He ran the Carousel, paid the bills, and banked the receipts, and it was his favorite of all the clubs he had ever had. "This is a fucking high-class place," he would assure any doubters as he threw them down the dimly lit stairs.[194] *Class.* That meant a lot to Jack. Everyone who knew him knew it. The only problem is that Jack had no class. Tammi True, a stripper who worked for Jack off and on for almost two years and was one of his favorites, thought the world of Jack (though they cursed each other out regularly), but said, "I don't care how much money Jack had. If he had been a millionaire, he wouldn't have been one bit different. He didn't have any class, and he really wanted to . . . He used the word class quite often, so I know it was an important thing with him . . . Everything had to have class, and I think that is what he wanted, but he could never have it, because Jack was just Jack."[195]

The Carousel became Ruby's life, his real home. "You can't write about Jack's life outside the club," Andrew Armstrong, Jack's black bartender, later told a Ruby biographer. "There *wasn't* any. Even when he was outside, he was at the newspaper or the radio stations trying to get more publicity;* he was handing out passes to the club, or thinking of some new scheme to push it."[196]

Sam Ruby said that his other brother Earl told him he had visited Dallas in 1961 in an attempt to get back some money that their sister Marion had loaned Jack for the Carousel and was now regretting. Not only was Earl unsuccessful, but since he was in town, Jack got a further loan from Earl too.[197] Jack's sister Eva told the Warren Commission, "And I understand Jack has taken money from Earl and probably from my sister Mary [Marion] and God knows who else in the family. There was none of his money in there. If he had a thousand dollars of his money, it was a lot of money." She went on to say that after her brother shot Oswald, the beneficent Paul had given her all five hundred shares of S&R stock that he had received from Jack.[198] The stock, perhaps unbeknownst to Paul, had become worthless on July 17, 1961, when the Texas Secretary of State's office in Austin ruled that S&R Inc. had forfeited its right to do business in the state as a corporation (as opposed to a partnership or sole ownership), finding that the corporation had no assets from which a judgment for franchise tax penalties and court costs could be satisfied.[199]

Jack, it seems, never paid back any of Paul's loans to Jack for the club on Commerce,

---

*Everyone agreed that Ruby was, as former Dallas assistant district attorney Bill Alexander said, "a publicity seeker." As an example, Alexander said, "When they had boxing matches at the city auditorium, Jack would come in after the preliminary, just before the main event, and while the house lights were on, he'd walk down the aisles greeting everybody and inviting them to the club that night. He made sure that everybody saw that he was seated ringside." (Sneed, *No More Silence*, pp.549–550)

whether the club was making any profits or not. "He never paid me a dime," said Paul, who didn't seem to be particularly upset about it, possibly because he considered Jack his "best" and "closest" friend and was confident Jack felt the same way about him.[200] When informed by Warren Commission counsel, who added up the loans, that apparently Jack Ruby still owed him $5,050, Paul replied, "Well, what am I going to do?"[201]

What is fairly certain is that Jack collected and deposited all the cash receipts; he seemed to always be behind on his bills; and whether the club seemed to be doing well or not, he always claimed he was going broke. Somehow though, he still had the ability to siphon off funds for new schemes he might be involved in, and to afford the many gratuities he gave to ingratiate himself with members of the Dallas Police Department.[202]

Just what were Ruby's receipts and expenses at his club? Unfortunately, the only tax records in the Warren Commission volumes for Ruby's clubs were for his Vegas Club, not the Carousel Club, and the National Archives has "no tax returns for the Carousel Club." A fairly typical year was 1962, when the gross receipts for the Vegas Club were listed as $48,150, the gross profit as $41,462.77, and the net income as $5,619.65.[203] There is very little reference in the testimony of Warren Commission witnesses as to how much Ruby took in at the Carousel and how much he paid out. One of the few references came from handyman Curtis "Larry" Crafard, hardly a good source, not only because of his low-level job but also because of the short time he was at the club. He told the Commission that on a Friday, Saturday, or Sunday night, Ruby took in "anywhere from $100 to maybe $1,000." When Ruby once took in a total of $1,400 for a Friday and Saturday night, Crafard heard the bartender, Andy Armstrong, say it was the most the Carousel had taken in for a two-day period over the past year or so. Crafard said, "The Carousel made enough to clear the bills," which is why he was puzzled when he heard that Ruby was taking money from his Vegas Club to keep the Carousel going.[204]

Though we have no tax records for the Carousel Club, we do have a two-month snapshot (assuming Ruby wasn't seriously misreporting income and expenses) from which we can extrapolate approximately what Ruby was making at the club in 1961–1963. In his car shortly after his arrest, the Dallas police found two handwritten papers, dated November 13, 1963, one captioned "Aug. Receipts for 30 days," the other "Sept. Receipts for 30 days," prepared for a "Bobby," to whom he writes, "These above records will show everything, and perhaps you will believe me now, that I'm having a rough time. Sincerely, Jack Ruby." For August, he took in $2,945.52 at the "bar" and $4,176.00 at the "door." After deducting an anticipated 10 percent federal tax for the bar income and 20 percent state and federal taxes for the door, he said he had a net of $5,304.68 before expenses. His payroll is interesting. He paid his lead stripper, Jada, $300 per week and the three others $110; his emcee, Wally Weston, $200 weekly; and the house band $330, for a total weekly payroll of $1,160, or $4,640 for the month. (Since Ruby makes no reference to salaries for his waitresses and cocktail girls, apparently he did not pay them any wages and they had to subsist on tips.) After employing a math that didn't compute on the page, he said his average net profit for one week for the month of August was $1,237.74 (for September the net was $1,350.93), but that this was "not counting" what he had to pay for "rent, utilities, advertising, bartender" or "porter," which, for whatever reason, he did not set forth but which must have virtually eliminated the $1,237.74 amount.[205]

Ruby told his strippers once that the most he had netted at the Carousel in a year was $5,000.[206] Though they were inclined to believe he was lowballing it, he may have been telling them the truth. Armstrong, who worked for Ruby for a year and a half, said that the financial condition of the Carousel Club was "not good" and the club was only "making enough [money] to pay the bills and . . . overhead."[207]

Although Jack did buy a safe for his office just two weeks before President Kennedy's assassination,[208] for most of the time that he managed the club he kept his funds in his trouser pockets and the trunk of his car. One acquaintance remarked that Ruby "operated out of his hip pocket."[209] At the time of his shooting of Oswald, Ruby had $2,015.33 in cash on his person, consisting of nine $100 dollar bills, thirty $10 bills, forty $20 bills, two $5 bills, four $1 bills, and $1.33 in change. All the money, Ruby said, was for his club's payroll and money to pay his excise tax.[210] His pockets being his principal bank, at the time of the shooting the Carousel Club's balance at Merchants State Bank on Rose Avenue in Dallas was only $199.78.[211] Murphy Martin, a WFAA (Dallas) radio and TV reporter who knew Ruby, said that Jack was "the type of person that, I think, would have $5,000 in his pocket and not a dime in the bank."[212] And safe-deposit box records showed that Ruby had not used his boxes for more than a year prior to the events in November, and when later opened, they were empty.[213]

As could be expected from someone who was continually late paying his bills, Ruby was also late filing his taxes. His records were in chaos, and one accountant quit because Ruby's habit of having his important papers and tax records and receipts at either one of his clubs, his apartment, or his mobile home (his car)* made doing his returns next to impossible.[214]

When Jack did get his taxes done, he was almost always late, and he frequently requested extensions, citing his inability to get his Carousel and Vegas club records together in time.[215] The Warren Commission, examining Ruby's financial records, found them to be "chaotic" and in "hopeless disarray."[216]

The IRS, of course, breathed down Jack's neck for years with phone calls, letters, and meetings because of tax delinquencies dating back to 1958.[217] In 1960 the government filed two tax liens for the years 1956 to 1959 in the amount of $20,200.21.[218] Jack was put on a monthly payment plan to pay off his income and excise tax obligations, and his frequent offers to pay a lesser amount were always rejected.[219]

---

*The items found in Jack Ruby's white, two-door, 1960 Oldsmobile, with Texas license plate number PD-768, after it was impounded on November 24, 1963, following his shooting of Oswald, were listed in great detail in eighteen pages of an FBI report. Reading through the items found in the glove compartment, trunk, and interior of his car conjures up visions of a homeless person's car overflowing with all of his life's belongings. It is comical, and inevitably sad. To give the reader an idea of what was contained in Ruby's rolling, lowbrow thrift shop, the following incomplete list is offered: numerous business cards, notebooks, unpaid traffic tickets, newspapers and clippings, paint bucket and paddle, bars of soap, pistol holder, adding machine, dog muzzle, phonograph records, door threshold molding, old telegrams, yellow legal pads, income tax book, three American Express traveler's checks, transcript of a radio show, a paper sack containing $837.50, box of razor blades, staples, blanket, bathing cap, umbrella, roll of toilet paper, receipts, golf shoes, several golf balls, jar of Coffee-Mate, jar of dietary food, two spotlight lenses, several "Twist Waist Exercisers," bail bond cards, a suit and pair of slacks, sport coat, empty wallet, several *Dallas Morning News* newspapers, extension cord, four photographs (including one of the "Impeach Earl Warren" signs), partially filled can of varnish stain, chrome fender molding strip, maps, rubber tips for chair legs, microphone, blank bank drafts, book of stamps, bottle of deodorant, one pair of ladies' gloves, car insurance policy, two beer-can openers, twelve cigarette butts, two packets of tooth space cleaners, leather belt, pair of horn-rimmed glasses, two tie clasps, two pairs of aluminum knuckles, various items of advertising, a wristwatch, address book, magazines, box of hardware, box of stationery, box of handkerchiefs, gooney bird in plastic bag, forty-two permanent pass cards to the Carousel to be laminated, another seventeen permanent pass cards, numerous scraps of paper with writing on them, and much more, including a carton of several hundred glossy 8 × 10 photos of exotic dancer Jada. And even with all this, there was still room in his trunk for the spare tire and jack! (CE 1322, 22 H 501–514; see also CE 2417, 25 H 518–520)

The bottom line for Jack Ruby in all of his complicated and convoluted tax dealings with the federal government was that he was liable for close to $40,000 at the time he shot Oswald, mostly in excise taxes. In June of 1963, he had made an Offer in Compromise of $3,000, one-thirteenth of the amount owed, to settle the entire amount, saying he would borrow the money from a friend. On November 24, 1963, the day he killed Oswald, his offer was still pending.[220] Jack's involuntary change of residence on that day to the Dallas city jail rendered moot all of his previous seven years' tax problems, although the IRS, later rejecting Jack's offer, sent a Notice of Levy to Dallas chief of police Jesse Curry on December 9, 1963, advising him that the "taxpayer" in his custody, Jack Ruby (actually, Jack was now in the custody of the sheriff's department), now owed them $44,413.86.[221]

As we have seen, from the time of Jack's arrival in Dallas some sixteen years earlier, he was primarily a nightclub operator, moving into burlesque (or a "girlie club") in his final and most famous venue, the Carousel Club. However, this hardly took all of his time. Those who worked with Jack knew him to show up at the club usually in the early afternoon, when the club was closed, although his comings and goings in the afternoon were "unpredictable," and he'd stay for a few hours before leaving. The first show at the Carousel was at 9:00 p.m., and Jack would usually show up again between 9:00 and 10:00 p.m. and stay until closing time.[222] There was plenty of time for Jack to "make a buck" on other endeavors. And there weren't too many others trying to make a buck who could keep up with Jack, at least as far as motley attempts were concerned.

What follows is only a partial list (some previously mentioned) of the "make a buck" schemes that Ruby tried, at one time or another, in his adult life. They are in no particular order by chronology, longevity, preference, or profitability. The only thing they have in common is that he tried them all and none were successful. He peddled punchboards,[223] cookware,[224] miniature cedar chests,[225] small turtles with painted backs,[226] sporting event tickets,[227] subscriptions to newspapers,[228] racetrack tip sheets,[229] little footballs with school colors,[230] a plaster of paris bust of President Roosevelt,[231] "Remember Pearl Harbor" plaques,[232] chocolates at burlesque houses,[233] peanuts at sporting events,[234] carnations in dance halls,[235] "hot" music sheets,[236] costume jewelry,[237] an arthritis remedy,[238] a liquefied "vitamin" of mineral water with enzymes,[239] gadgets to be used as sewing machine attachments at the Texas State Fair,[240] Wilkinson steel razor blades,[241] pizza crust to Dallas restaurants,[242] and "Twist Waist Exerciser" boards.[243]*

Jack also promoted the sale of prefabricated log cabins at Grapevine Lake between Dallas and Fort Worth[244] and, as we've seen, managed the young, black piano-playing tap-dancer, "Little Daddy Nelson."[245] He promoted records for musicians,[246] entertainment for a Dallas hotel,[247] assisted producers of a "How Hollywood Makes Movies" show at the state fair,[248] and investigated selling jeeps to Cuba,[249] all losing propositions. It wouldn't be fair to say that Jack Ruby never tried to be a success. He just never succeeded. As Tony Zoppi, the nightclub editor for the *Dallas Morning News*, said, "The man was a loser, let's face it. I mean, he was a friend of mine, but he was a loser."[250]

Although Ruby was a loser, that didn't mean he didn't have dreams and ambitions—

*The twistboard was the latest gadget Jack was selling, and he was very serious about it. His roommate, George Senator, said that in the last few weeks before the assassination, Ruby had been getting up many mornings at eight or nine o'clock, earlier than normal, to visit department stores in Dallas in an effort to promote the board (CD 106, p.89, FBI interview of George Senator on December 19, 1963). Just, of course, what you would expect a big mob hit man to be doing in the weeks and days leading up to the biggest day of his mob career, when he would be "silencing" Oswald for them.

they were just limited to the world of nightclubs. Former Dallas police lieutenant Elmo Cunningham, who worked off duty for Ruby for a short time at the Silver Spur, and knew him well, said that "Jack . . . was very ambitious. He told me on more than one occasion that he would rather run a New York nightclub such as the Copa than to be President of the United States."[251]

Much has been mentioned of Ruby's association and friendship with members of the Dallas Police Department. "Jack Ruby knew all the policemen in town," said a close friend.[252] Another friend, boxer Reagan Turman, told the FBI that "Ruby was acquainted with at least 75 per cent, and probably 90 per cent, of the police officers on the Dallas Police Department."[253] While these remarks are undoubtedly hyperbole, it can't be considered exaggeration when a lieutenant for the police department, George C. Arnett, told the FBI that Ruby "was well known among the members of the Dallas Police Department and was rather friendly with them."[254] A higher officer on the force, Captain W. R. Westbrook, said, "I'd say that half the police force knew [Ruby] and called him a friend . . . A lot of policemen went to his clubs. It was an open home for them."[255] Dallas officer Joe Cody, a close friend of Ruby's who would often go skating with him and, as previously indicated, actually had his name on the title to the pistol Ruby used to kill Oswald, said that "everybody that I knew kind of liked Jack, and that included policemen. There'd be ten or twelve of us up [at the Carousel] having a few beers every night."[256] And Dallas police detective Roy Standifer told the FBI that Ruby "frequently" came to downtown headquarters, was "widely known among police officers," and liked to call officers by their first names as though they were close friends of his.[257]

Warren Commission counsel asked Dallas police officer A. M. Eberhardt, "At the time that Oswald was killed, who were the officers on the force outside of yourself that Ruby knew the best, would you say?" Eberhardt replied, "I don't know who he knew the best."

"From your own estimation, who did he?"

"I don't know . . . He knew just about everybody."[258]

A friend and former business associate of Ruby's told the Warren Commission that "because of [Ruby's] character" some people "would take him as a thug," but actually, "he was in thicker with the police in Dallas than anybody else I knew of because they were always in his place."[259]

The evidence is overwhelming that Ruby felt very close to law enforcement, particularly the Dallas Police Department. He knew and was friendly with a considerable number of officers on the force, and was constantly trying to ingratiate himself with them. Ruby's love for the police goes way back. Louis Capparelli, who served as police captain in the area of Chicago where Ruby was born, knew Ruby well back then. He recalls, "I guess you could call him a frustrated policeman because he liked to be seen with a policeman."[260]

Ray Mathis, a former FBI agent who was a Dallas police officer in the early 1960s, told me that Ruby "loved the police" and "always had a pot of coffee for us when we stopped by." He said that Ruby would show up at the scene of murders. He later found out how Ruby knew. He walked into the kitchen of the Carousel one night and there was Ruby listening to police calls.[261]

As author Jim Bishop says, "Ruby had 'copitis.' Many times he had bought the smiles of hardened police officers by bringing them bags of coleslaw, cold cuts, seeded rye bread, rolls and coffee."[262]

According to two of Ruby's Carousel Club employees, "he heroized the police because they represented the good and the decent. He had crashed through life with the bad guys, but he always respected the good guys, and to him the police were the best of the good guys."[263] Each Sunday evening Jack would have "Celebrity Night" at the club and in so doing would entertain as many as eight law enforcement officers with free pizza and drinks. When asked why he went to such expensive lengths when it was not necessary to cozy up to the police (since he was not engaging in any illegal activities), Ruby replied that he wanted to because he liked law enforcement officers and "these men did not make salaries which would enable them to have this kind of entertainment."[264] In the words of one ex-officer, Jack "loved policemen."[265] He thought it was great having police officers at his club, and therefore they always got free coffee and soft drinks, got their liquor at a cut rate, and never had to pay a cover charge.[266]

One of Ruby's dancers reported that from time to time she would see police officers enter the Carousel Club, go to Ruby's office, and then leave with bottles of whiskey under their arm,[267] and a former Dallas police officer, who said "a great many" police officers "attended the club socially," acknowledged that Jack would give numerous policemen whiskey at Christmas time.[268] A Carousel employee recalled how there were always police officers in the club and they would congregate at the end of the bar.[269] Jack gave some of the officers off-duty jobs as a bouncer or "door watcher."[270] One officer remembered that Jack "liked any kind of officer and always wanted to be in a position of helping them." He recalled that on one occasion, three men jumped on two officers in Ruby's club and Jack jumped into the fight and "gave a good account of himself." He believed Ruby could have whipped all three.[271]

One business associate of Ruby's recalls visiting the Carousel Club one evening and seeing approximately six uniformed officers of the Dallas Police Department there. He said he recalled thinking that Ruby must have friends in the police department because drinks were being served after midnight even though policemen were present.[272]*

For his part, Ruby told the Warren Commission, "I felt I have always abided by the law—a few little infractions, but not serious—and I felt we have one of the greatest police forces in the world here, and I have always been close to them, and I visited in the office."[273] It is interesting to note that Ruby's fondness for police officers did not overcome his sense of decorum and his protectiveness—he would never let his girls at the Carousel Club go out with any of them,[274] although one policeman did and ended up marrying the girl, a Carousel Club stripper.[275]

From all of the statements by policemen and others to the FBI regarding Ruby's association with Dallas police officers, it seems very likely that the number of policemen whom Ruby knew was considerably more than what Dallas police chief Jesse Curry estimated to the Warren Commission: "I believe less than 50 [officers] knew him."[276] One musician acquaintance of Ruby's who spent a lot of time at the Carousel over a four- to five-week

---

*One big reason Ruby had for cozying up to the police over and above any fondness for them (one member of law enforcement thought it was *the* reason) was to protect perhaps his most valuable asset, his liquor license, commonly referred to as the "beer license" because beer was by far the main alcoholic beverage sold at the Carousel (which also, as noted earlier, sold champagne) and other clubs in Dallas. The beer license had to be renewed every year, and the Dallas Police Department was one of five agencies (it would seem the most important one) that recommended whether the license should be approved or disapproved. (Sneed, *No More Silence*, pp.540–541)

period, and who sometimes worked with the band, estimated he saw between 150 and 200 police officers at the Carousel at one time or another.[277]

Although Ruby's primary association with law enforcement was unquestionably the Dallas Police Department, he also had friends at the Dallas County Sheriff's Department, legendary Dallas deputy sheriff Eddy Raymond "Buddy" Walthers and his partner, Alvin Maddox, being two of them. In fact, both visited Ruby in jail after he killed Oswald. So did Deputy Sheriff Bill Courson.[278]

With Jack's familiarity with the Dallas Police Department, one might reasonably wonder if he received preferential treatment or got away with breaking the law while his uniformed friends looked the other way. Perhaps the best example of this—though it would have been something the police would have done for others in Jack's situation—is Jack's admission that several Dallas police officers knew he had a gun, and one can presume they also knew he carried it on his person for protection when he had the club's payroll in his pocket, even though he never had a concealed-gun permit. In fact, on a couple of occasions when he was picked up for some violation and released from jail, the police gave him his gun back.[279] Although Jack maintained that he never asked for any special favors from the police in return for what he gave them, one time he did ask a policeman to whom he had given whiskey as a gift on three different occasions if he would fix a three-dollar parking ticket for him. When he was informed that the policeman could but that it would cost the policeman a dollar to do so, Jack said never mind and that he would pay the ticket.[280]

If the Dallas police occasionally looked the other way with Ruby, sometimes they didn't, even when a reasonable person might think they should have. One must remember, of course, the moral climate of Dallas in the conservative 1950s, but one well-documented incident (before Ruby's glory days at the Carousel) went more in the direction of harassment than anything else. On December 5, 1954, Ruby was arrested at his Silver Spur Club for violation of the state liquor law. Under "details which prompted arrest," the "Arresting Officer's Report" stated, "Arresting officers saw bottle party filled with Schlitz beer on the table occupied by Eugenia Mary O'Brien and Mary Jane Schultz." The "Case Report" on the incident stated, "He [Ruby] permitted Eugenia Mary O'Brien and Mary Jane Schultz to consume a part of a bottle of Schlitz beer during forbidden hours on Sunday." Ruby, it seems, was arrested at 1:30 a.m., fifteen minutes into the "forbidden hours."[281] The district attorney's office recommended in a motion to the court that the arrest of Ruby be dismissed because of insufficient evidence since both officers stated that they did not actually observe the customers consuming the beer. The case was dismissed. The two officers who arrested Ruby for this egregious violation of Texas law were later interviewed by the FBI about the 1954 arrest in the wake of Ruby's shooting of Oswald, and both admitted to having been to Ruby's club, neither paid the cover charge, and one paid for his beer, the other didn't.[282]

The Texas Liquor Control Board gave Ruby's clubs numerous suspensions over the years for various infractions, including conducting lewd and obscene shows, consumption of liquor after hours, and passing a dishonored check. He received three-day suspensions in March of 1956 and October of 1961; five-day suspensions in 1949, 1953, and 1954; and a ten-day suspension in 1954.[283]

The Warren Commission's accounting of Ruby's arrest record is contradictory. For instance, although the Commission stated in its report that Ruby was arrested eight times by the Dallas Police Department between 1949 and November 24, 1963, the report in the volume that it cites lists nine arrests.[284] And even this list is incomplete. For instance, it doesn't include a February 1959 disturbance-of-the-peace violation or a February 1954 arrest for presenting a lewd and vulgar show.[285]

The relevant point is that Ruby was arrested a number of times by the Dallas Police Department, and of all the arrests duly documented, he paid two fines—the others resulted in "complaint dismissed," "no charges filed" (including two arrests on charges of carrying a concealed weapon, for which Jack had no permit), and a "not guilty" verdict on a charge of simple assault.[286]

On any given night, even a misstep by one of Jack's dancers or patrons could have been cause for his arrest or suspension as the operator of his clubs. So it might be said that given the nature of his chosen profession—operating a nightclub—and being subject to the strict state liquor laws of Texas, and therefore under the constant surveillance of both undercover and uniformed law enforcement for more than fifteen years, Jack was a relatively law-abiding citizen and, with only a few exceptions, ran a clean club. It was "not a troublesome one" for the Dallas Police Department, in the opinion of the assistant chief of police.[287*]

The same, however, cannot be said of Jack's driving record—it was by no means clean. In fact, he was a terrible driver. His first of many tickets in Texas came in April 1950 as a result of speeding. From then on he accumulated violations at a pretty regular pace, with his most popular violation being to run red lights, totally consistent with his aggressive personality. Jack liked speeding and had a fondness for running stop signs as well. His worst year was 1956. At the end of January he ran a red light. Two weeks later he got caught doing it again. Thirteen days after that he was caught speeding. After the first three of his 1956 violations, his driving privileges were suspended for six months, accounting for the lack of violations on his record for the same period of time. No sooner was his suspension over before Jack was back at it. Between Thanksgiving and Christmas he ran two stop signs. However, not until August of 1959 was a petition filed against him for being a "habitual motor vehicle violator." (At this point, he had had seventeen violations—for which he was caught—in less than nine years.) In December of 1959 he was convicted of this charge and put on twelve months' probation, at the end of which he had to pass a driving test before his license would be reinstated. The records show that Jack apparently didn't have to wait the entire twelve months of his probation before getting his license back. After passing a test in May of 1960, he showed his gratitude by slowing down his frequency of infractions and having only two automobile accidents and running just one red light that we know of in the next three years.[288]

It's interesting to note that on the morning he shot Oswald, Ruby admitted to making an illegal left turn on Main Street after he saw a bunch of people gathered around City Hall.[289] If only an officer had been there to give him a ticket on the spot that day.

---

*Although Ruby never maintained to anyone that he had gotten away with anything because of his association with the Dallas Police Department, an acquaintance of Ruby's did tell the FBI that "he did not personally like Ruby as Ruby always attempted to be the big shot and boasted not only to him but to other people in his presence that he could do anything he wanted in Dallas as he had enough information on the Police Department and judges that he could not be convicted" (CE 1746, 23 H 354, FBI interview of Walter Clewis on November 27, 1963). This is pure braggadocio, of course. Whatever Ruby may have learned about the private peccadillos of some officers or judges could never compromise and immobilize the entire Dallas Police Department and Dallas judiciary.

The one area in Jack Ruby's life that has received by far the most scrutiny is his alleged ties to the underworld, since conspiracy theorists and millions of everyday Americans believe that Ruby "silenced" Oswald for organized crime. Given his continual search to make a quick buck, and particularly in view of the fact that he operated a striptease club, it should not surprise anyone that Jack came into contact with and made the acquaintance of some shady characters and people of questionable reputations. Joe Bonds (Joseph Locurto), for instance, who had been one of his partners in the Vegas Club, was convicted of sodomy in 1954 and sentenced to eight years.[290]

But recalling Hyman Rubenstein's remarks about him and his brother growing up in their Chicago neighborhood, what was Ruby to do when these unsavory characters walked into a Chicago diner he was in, or into his club in Dallas—ignore them? As brother Earl said, Jack "had a plush [hardly] striptease club and the Mafia used to go to his place when they were in town. They were big spenders and I'm sure he wasn't unhappy when they came to his joint to spend their money."[291]

Ruby associated with everyone. One of those people was Joseph Campisi, who with his brother Sam owned the Egyptian Lounge, a restaurant and bar that was one of Jack's favorite haunts.[292] Campisi told the FBI that the only times he had contact with Ruby were at various sporting events in Dallas and when one would visit the other's club.[293] However, there is some evidence that Campisi was closer to Ruby than he indicated. Campisi told the HSCA in 1978 that Ruby also came to his home once but did not stay for long.[294] He also acknowledged visiting Ruby at the county jail on November 29, 1963, for ten minutes after the sheriff's office contacted him to advise that he was one of several people Ruby wanted to have visit him.[295] Indeed, Ruby's roommate, George Senator, told the FBI that Campisi was one of Ruby's three closest friends.[296]

In book after book by conspiracy theorists, Campisi turns up as an alleged "Dallas Mafia figure" with whom Ruby had close ties.[297] But the HSCA thoroughly investigated Campisi and found that although his "technical characterization in federal law enforcement records as an organized crime member has ranged from definite to suspected to negative," the only thing that was clear was that "he was an associate or friend of many Dallas-based organized crime members," including Joe Civello. However, the HSCA went on to say there was "no indication" that Campisi himself "had engaged in any specific organized crime–related activities." Yes, Campisi had mob friends. So did Frank Sinatra and Dean Martin. Although Campisi had been linked with gambling and bookmaking activities, he was never arrested for them, and the sense of the FBI is that he limited his gambling because he feared it would jeopardize the success of his Egyptian Lounge. Like Ruby, Campisi had just as many contacts with members of the Dallas Police Department as he did with those on the seamier side of society, but unlike Ruby, he also had close and friendly contacts with "both state judges and members of the Dallas County District Attorney's office."[298] And former Dallas sheriff Jim Bowles told me, "I had pizza with Joe many times at his restaurant," recalling his days when he was the sheriff.[299]

Another mobster with whom Ruby has been allegedly linked is the aforementioned Joe Civello. Civello, to be sure, was a Mafia figure and the head of the mob, or what there was of it, in Dallas. We know that because he attended the famous Mafia conference of mob leaders from around the country in Apalachin, New York, in 1957.[300] But the Mafia had a very small presence in Dallas, and indeed, the FBI concluded there was "no evidence of illegal activity by Joseph Francis Civello," indicating he was just an associate of leading mob figures who broke bread with them but didn't participate in their crimes. If he did, they never appeared on the FBI radar screen.[301] Civello *was* convicted on a narcotics charge in 1937, and when he later applied for a pardon, guess who was one of his character witnesses? The sheriff of Dallas County, Bill Decker.[302*]

Conspiracy theorists, desperate to connect Ruby to Civello and the Mafia, have been reduced to pointing out that among the many papers found in Ruby's car after his arrest for killing Oswald was a November 18, 1963, *Wall Street Journal* article on the "Mafia and Business," in which Civello, among many other mob figures, was briefly mentioned. Some connection. However, Civello did acknowledge to the FBI in a 1964 interview that he had been a casual acquaintance of Ruby's (as was half of Dallas) "for about ten years," and had seen Ruby "four or five times during that period."[303]

Talking about both Civello and Campisi, former Dallas assistant district attorney Bill Alexander said that around the time of the assassination, "we had no organized crime in Dallas. Our local criminals were too tough for them. I would be the one to have known because I screened all the cases that came through the district attorney's office. Carlos Marcello had no influence here, and as far as two of our locals, Joe Civello and Joe Campisi, they never did anything here. Campisi owned the Egyptian Lounge, an Italian restaurant, which still has the best spaghetti and meatballs. Joe thought it would add a little flavor, a little romance, to his place if he let on like he was Mafia-connected."[304]

Another alleged mob associate of Ruby's was convicted in 1947 of attempting to bribe the Dallas County sheriff, Steve Guthrie, as part of the Chicago mob's attempt to move into Dallas by establishing a nightclub as a front for illegal gambling. Since Ruby, from Chicago, permanently moved to Dallas in 1947, the thought has persisted for years that the Chicago mob had sent him to Dallas to be the front man for its gambling club. The alleged Ruby associate was Paul Roland Jones,[†] whom Jack's sister Eva had met in Dallas in 1947. Later, and while free on bail pending his appeal on the bribery conviction, Jones had a chance meeting with Ruby in the lobby of a hotel in Chicago. He said members of the Chicago Syndicate who were with him recognized Ruby and told him Ruby was "okay." Ruby told Jones he planned to return to Dallas to help his sister in business there. It was only after Jones served the five years for his bribery conviction that he

---

*Though Jack Ruby was no more of a mobster than you or I, he liked to intimate that he had contacts with underworld figures. "Jack would like to put on a facade that he was connected," said former Dallas police sergeant Patrick Dean, who was friendly with Ruby (HSCA Record 180-10073-10050, November 15, 1977, p.19). At least one Ruby acquaintance, Irvin Charles Mazzei, the regional director for the American Guild of Variety Artists, said that on one occasion Ruby actually told him he was connected with the "Syndicate" in Chicago and used to work for it. But Ruby, at the time, was trying hard to get Mazzei to stop Ruby's nightclub competition, Abe and Barney Weinstein, from using amateurs as strippers at their club (see later discussion), and Mazzei felt that Ruby was always trying to impress him, Ruby also showing Mazzei a gun he carried in his belt and an honorary Dallas Police Department membership card, and telling Mazzei he had "ins" with the Dallas Police Department. (CE 1543, 23 H 34–35) He also told a business associate, with whom he had had a fist fight and many disagreements, that he had contacts with various underworld figures, but only mentioned one by name, Los Angeles mobster Mickey Cohen, saying he used to know Cohen (CE 1228, 22 H 336).

Ruby also tried to create the impression he was a "tough guy." Lawyer Luis Kutner, who knew Ruby from his Chicago days, recalled Ruby wearing "sharp" suits back then as well as a pearl gray fedora with the broad brim turned down in front, a style Al Capone had made a hoodlum fad (*New York Times*, November 26, 1963, p.15). But was Ruby, in fact, a tough guy? "He wasn't a tough guy," says Chicago police captain Louis Capparelli, the longtime commander of the Maxwell District of Chicago, where Ruby was born. "But he was a very aggressive salesman when he was selling something." (*New York Times*, November 26, 1963, p.15)

†Jones was just one of about twenty Chicago mobsters who were sent to Dallas in 1946 to open up the city for them. One of them was a reputed friend of Ruby's from Chicago's west side named Paul Labriola, who was slain in 1954. (*New York Times*, November 26, 1963, p.15; Scheim, *Contract on America*, pp.81–83)

returned to Dallas and got to know Ruby fairly well by visiting Ruby's club.[305] Although Sheriff Guthrie stated that Jack Ruby's name came up on numerous occasions in discussions with Jones during a sting operation in November and December of 1946 at Guthrie's house after it was wired, a subsequent review by the FBI of the twenty-two tape recordings showed that "at no time on any of the 22 recordings was the name of 'Jack L. Ruby' or 'Ruby' mentioned."[306] Indeed, Jones, on tape, can be heard telling Guthrie that the front man brought in from Chicago looked like "a preacher" and was "not a Dago, not a Jew."

The chief of police in Dallas at the time the recordings were made was Carl Hansson. When questioned by the FBI in 1964, the former chief did not recall the name of Jack Ruby ever being mentioned. Furthermore, Hansson noted that he did not have a good opinion of Steve Guthrie and would not place any confidence in any statement by Guthrie to the effect that Paul Roland Jones had mentioned the name of Jack Ruby on the tapes. And Jones himself said he did not mention Ruby's name and, in fact, had never even heard of the name Jack Ruby at that point in time. Lieutenant George Butler of the Dallas Police Department, who was part of the sting operation with Guthrie, and tape-recorded the meetings with Guthrie and Jones he participated in, investigated the whole case and said Ruby was not involved in the bribery attempt.[307]

Author Anthony Summers asserts that "Ruby said" his eventual move to Dallas had been "on mob instructions."[308] But Anthony, Ruby could only have said this in one of your dreams, and you would have been better off citing a dream of yours as your source than giving no citation at all.[309]

Of all the evidence the conspiracy theorists cite to connect not just Ruby with the mob, but Ruby and the mob with JFK's assassination, none has been cited or relied on more than Ruby's telephone contact with mob figures in the two months preceding the assassination. And, indeed, Ruby did dramatically increase his contact with mob figures he had known from his Chicago days during this period. Conspiracy author David Scheim writes that "these timely and intensive contacts of Ruby suggest that a mob conspiracy [to murder Kennedy] was in progress."[310] "[Ruby's] calls" to the underworld before the assassination, says conspiracy author John Davis, "suggest some sort of conspiracy."[311] But an analysis of these calls and their purpose by the Warren Commission and HSCA clearly reveals that this most promising of conspiratorial trees bore no fruit for the theorists. *All of the calls* related to Ruby seeking help in getting the American Guild of Variety Artists (AGVA) to enforce its rules against two competitors of his, Abe and Barney Weinstein.*

Ruby, having struggled throughout his life to keep his head above water, and having failed in previous nightclub ventures, was determined that this would not happen to his beloved Carousel. But Abe Weinstein, who ran Abe's Colony Club next door to the Carousel on Commerce Street, and his brother, Barney, who ran the Theatre Lounge around the corner on Jackson, started to seriously hurt Ruby in the summer and fall of 1963 by violating AGVA's ban on "striptease contests" and performances by "amateurs."[312] As conspiracy author Seth Kantor put it, "The clumsy, sometimes overly enthusiastic amateur strippers were drawing a lot of customers and, what was worse, the

---

*All of Ruby's long-distance calls from his home and from the Carousel Club between September 26, 1963, and November 22, 1963, are set forth by the Warren Commission in Commission Exhibit No. 2303 (25 H 237–245).

Weinsteins were getting by with entertainers they didn't have to pay for."[313] "Ruby," the Warren Commission concluded, "apparently believed his two competitors, the Weinstein brothers, were scheduling amateur shows in a manner calculated to destroy his business."[314] Jack himself used to have amateur nights, but when AGVA notified all the club owners in February of 1963 to stop, he immediately complied and his competitors did not.[315] And right up to within days of the assassination, Ruby was pleading everywhere for help in stopping the Weinsteins.[316]

When Ruby's personal appeals asking AGVA to force the Weinsteins to cease and desist failed, he reached out, wherever he could, to people he felt might get AGVA to do its job. And when one thinks of putting pressure on unions during this period, one automatically thinks of organized crime, which either had infiltrated or had influence over many unions throughout the country. So Ruby, with his union roots in Chicago, naturally reached out, among others, to mob figures. He told the Warren Commission, "I knew persons of notorious backgrounds years ago in Chicago, and I left the union when I found out the notorious organization [mob] had moved in there." He went on to speak of the "unfair competition" he had been facing in Dallas that "had been running certain shows that we [in the business] were [prohibited] to run by regulation of the union, but they [Weinsteins] violated all the rules of the union, and I didn't violate it, and consequently I was becoming insolvent because of it . . . Every person I called, and sometimes you may not even know a person intimately, you sort of tell them, well, you are stranded down here and you want some help—if they know of any official of the American Guild of Variety Artists to help me. Because my competitors were putting me out of business. I even flew to New York to see Joe Glazer [who headed up a large theatrical agency], and he called Bobby Faye, the national president [actually the administrative secretary of AGVA, but "the true head of AGVA in 1963" per the HSCA]. That didn't help." Ruby said that "all" of his calls in October and November "were related" to getting people to "help me with the American Guild of Variety Artists . . . That is the only reason I made those calls." None, he said, were "in anyway [related] to the underworld."[317]

The Warren Commission and FBI did not do as complete a job as they should have in investigating all of Ruby's phone calls, made from his home and the Carousel Club. But the investigation they did caused them to conclude that all his calls were related to AGVA and the Weinsteins.[318] And Ruby's sister Eva testified that she was very familiar with her brother's problem with the Weinsteins and knew "he had contacted people all over the country trying to find out who knew the bigwigs in the union [AGVA]" who could help him.[319] Ruby even called his brother Hyman in Chicago. "He wanted me to contact some people in Chicago who had connections with AGVA in New York," Hyman recalled, and he made some calls for his brother.[320] Even Larry Crafard, the drifter who worked at the Carousel, recalled that Ruby "was doing his best to get the union to force them [the Weinsteins] to stop."[321]

If the Warren Commission and FBI didn't do quite as thorough a job as they should have investigating Ruby's telephone calls, certainly the HSCA did, conducting an extensive computer analysis of all his telephone toll records during the period in question. And although the HSCA's chief counsel, G. Robert Blakey, eventually became very partial to the notion that organized crime was behind Kennedy's death, the committee, after this analysis, was compelled to conclude "that the evidence surrounding the calls was generally consistent—at least as to the time of their occurrences—with the explanation that they were for the purpose of seeking assistance in [Ruby's] labor dispute."[322]

However, the HSCA said it was "not satisfied" with the explanations given for the calls to three of the mob figures Ruby contacted. One was Irwin Weiner, a Chicago bondsman well known as a financial front man for organized crime and the insurance broker and bondsman for Jimmy Hoffa's Teamsters Union, whom Ruby called, records showed, for twelve minutes on October 26, 1963. The FBI, aware of the call, sought to question Weiner about it on November 27, 1963, but he declined to cooperate. The reason he later gave is that when the FBI called his home after Ruby killed Oswald, he was in Florida, and the agent told his daughter that he wanted to talk to her father about the assassination of the president. "She was shaking with fright," Weiner later testified before the HSCA, and "because of the way they mistreated my daughter," he refused to talk to them.[323] Although Weiner later told a reporter that Ruby's call had nothing to do with Ruby's labor problems (though not saying what the nature of the call was), he told the HSCA that he might have told any reporter who called him anything, since he was not under oath and always lied to reporters.[324]

In Weiner's testimony before the HSCA, he said he may have met Ruby "four or five times in my life," mostly in the 1930s as a result of his going to school with Ruby's brother Earl, a friend of Weiner's, and didn't remember anything about these brief occasions, and "never had anything to do with Jack Ruby at any time in my life." He assumed that Ruby called him in October because of his earlier relationship with Earl.[*]

Weiner told the HSCA, "Jack Ruby called me. Evidently he had a nightclub in Dallas, Texas." He said that Ruby said that "one night a week he had an amateur striptease. Some union that was affiliated with entertainers had stopped him . . . because the amateur entertainers were not members of the union. He stopped and another competitor of his opened up." Some lawyer had told Ruby, Weiner recalls, to get an injunction against his competitor, but he would need a bond to do this. Ruby "wanted to know if I would write a bond . . . I told him no . . . That was the extent of our conversation."[325]

The notion that Weiner, a mob bail bondsman, was involved with Ruby in the assassination of Kennedy is so far-fetched that, as indicated, when Weiner declined to talk to the FBI, the FBI never made any further effort to contact or interview him.[326] But wait. Maybe Ruby wanted to know if, after he killed Oswald for the mob (or was Oswald's handler in Oswald's killing of Kennedy), the mob would be kind enough to help him post bond for his release on bail pending trial. I say we look into the Weiner matter further.

Another telephone contact that troubled the committee was with Robert "Barney" Baker, a top aide to teamster boss Jimmy Hoffa, an avowed enemy of the Kennedys, particularly JFK's brother Bobby, who, as the attorney general, eventually succeeded in putting Hoffa behind bars. This history naturally was alarming to the HSCA, but there is little else about Ruby's two conversations with Baker to arouse suspicion. Baker, who had a background in settling labor disputes,[327] was someone whom Ruby would likely call. Baker told the FBI in 1964 that Ruby called him in November of 1963 (telephone records show it was November 7, 1963) at his home in Chicago. He wasn't in but returned the call, collect, to Ruby that day, after his wife advised him of it. Ruby, who Baker said was a complete stranger, told him, "You don't know me but we have mutual friends," whom

---

[*]Indeed, Earl Ruby told author Gerald Posner, "I gave Irwin Weiner's number to my brother. I had gone to school with Weiner . . . He was a big bondsman for everyone, and he handled the Mafia . . . I thought he might be able to help Jack with the union. Jack didn't even know Weiner, for God's sake" (Posner, *Case Closed*, p.363). However, in Earl Ruby's testimony before the HSCA years earlier, in 1978, he did not mention, as one would have expected him to, that he had advised his brother to call Weiner in 1963 (9 HSCA 1043).

he did not name. Ruby proceeded to tell him of his dispute with his competitors, who were "attempting to knock me out," and that the "mutual friends" had said Baker was good at handling matters such as this, and then asked Baker if he would contact AGVA in New York for him. Baker declined, having been released in June from a federal penitentiary in Minnesota after serving time for violating the Labor-Management Relations Act (Taft-Hartley), with a condition of his parole being that he not engage in labor dispute matters for five years. Because Baker indicated he had no further contact with Ruby, whereas the HSCA claimed the records showed Ruby called him the next day (November 8) too, the committee said it was "hard to believe that Baker . . . could have forgotten it."[328] But it is the discussion itself that one is likely to remember, fifteen years later, not whether it required one phone call or two. In the absence of anything else, and the HSCA had absolutely nothing else, this is much to-do about nothing.[*]

The final telephone conversation the HSCA was troubled by was a one-minute call made by Ruby at 9:13 p.m. on October 30, 1963, to the business office of the Tropical Court Tourist Park, a trailer park in New Orleans. The owner of the park and manager of the one-man office was Nofio J. Pecora (alias Joseph Pecorano), an associate of New Orleans mob boss Carlos Marcello, suspected by many in the conspiracy community of being behind Kennedy's murder. Telephone records showed that four months earlier Marcello had called the same number at the park that Ruby had. This would, indeed, look a little suspicious were it not for the fact that a fairly good friend of Ruby's, New Orleans nightclub manager Harold Tannenbaum, happened to live at the park. Ruby had visited Tannenbaum's club, the French Opera House, in June of 1963 to scout for talent, and Tannenbaum had introduced Ruby to a marquee stripper, "Jada" (Janet Adams Conforto), who ended up working for Ruby at the Carousel. Since that time, Ruby and Tannenbaum had been in regular contact by telephone. Pecora told the HSCA that the subject phone call was probably to his office to relay a message to someone who lived at the park, though he said he did not recall talking to Ruby, whom he said he did not know, or relaying any message from Ruby to Tannenbaum. But he obviously must have, since phone records show that Tannenbaum called Ruby one hour after Ruby called Pecora's park office.[329] It is understandable, of course, that Pecora, in 1978, would not recall the Ruby phone call fifteen years earlier, and there can be no reasonable question that the call from Ruby was for Tannenbaum. If the conspiracy theorists want to believe and allege that Ruby's call was actually to talk to Pecora for one minute (or less) about the murder of JFK, I guess this is a free country and they have that right under the First Amendment.[†]

The position of the conspiracy community—that these phone calls by Ruby to mob

---

[*]Not that Baker needs any support, but anti-conspiracy author Posner says that Baker's telling the FBI in 1964 about the subject of his conversation with Ruby, independent of knowing that Ruby had also told the police that the conversation was about his labor problems, confirms that that was what the conversation was really about (Posner, *Case Closed*, p.364). But that presupposes the very point in issue—that Ruby's call to Baker had nothing to do with the assassination. I mean, if it was about the assassination, we could expect Ruby and Baker to be on the same page as to the alleged subject matter of this conversation.

[†]In *Case Closed*, Posner writes that the Warren Commission did not place those like "Weiner, Pecora, or Baker under oath. However, the telephone calls are not evidence of a conspiracy to kill JFK, since most of the calls were made before the President's trip to Dallas was even announced" (Posner, *Case Closed*, p.365 footnote). This is a little misleading in that although many phone calls fell into that category, the calls he cites, the same ones the HSCA found troubling, were made on October 26, October 30, and November 7 and 8, all *after* the president's trip to Texas was announced on September 26, 1963 (CE 1368–1369, 22 H 620–621).

figures in September, October, and November of 1963 were related to the assassination—necessarily assumes that Ruby not only silenced Oswald for the mob, but also was a party with the mob in a conspiracy to murder the president. Why would the mob have these alleged conversations with Ruby in the months leading up to Kennedy's murder if he was not? But not too many people, even in the conspiracy community, believe that Ruby was part of the conspiracy to murder Kennedy. Most simply believe that the mob contacted him to kill Oswald once Oswald survived the assassination, the implication being that after Oswald killed Kennedy for the mob, the mob immediately tried to kill him (or hoped law enforcement would) and failed. But the conspiracy theorists offer no evidence that the mob tried to kill Oswald right after he killed Kennedy, and there would be no reason for the mob to feel completely confident that law enforcement would kill Oswald, which, as we know, they did not.

So in one sense, the conspiracy community believes that Ruby's calls in the September–November period leading up to the assassination were assassination-related, and then, inconsistently, they believe the mob contacted Ruby only after Oswald survived the assassination. But as author Gerald Posner points out, if the latter is true, then we could expect Ruby's contacts with mob figures by phone (since the conspiracy community has locked itself into this alleged mode of communication by the mob with Ruby) to have increased after the assassination.[330] Yet, *all* of Ruby's contacts by phone with unsavory mob figures took place in the many weeks *before* the assassination. There is no evidence of any taking place between the assassination on November 22 and Ruby's killing of Oswald on November 24.[331]

It could not be clearer from all the direct and circumstantial evidence that the increased number of calls Ruby made in the two months preceding the assassination to those connected to the underworld were related to his effort to seek their help in solving his labor problems with the Weinsteins, and the Warren Commission and HSCA so found. When there is not a speck of evidence pointing in the opposite direction, there's really nothing more that needs to be said, except that even if we were to accept the premise that Ruby was a part of a conspiracy with organized crime to kill Kennedy and/or Oswald, we can virtually know that the mob would not have been talking to him about it from phones all over the country. Even assuming, for the sake of argument, that they didn't think of the possibility of their telephone conversations being tapped by the FBI, surely they would have to know that Ruby's phone records would automatically be obtained and would reveal the existence of his contact with them. Obviously, either the mob would summon Ruby out of town to receive instructions, or one of the mob conspirators would be dispatched to Dallas to meet privately with Ruby.

Before moving on, I should ask the rhetorical question that if Ruby was a member of the mob or was as well connected with organized crime as so very many conspiracy theorists insist, and particularly if he was involved with it in a plot to murder Kennedy and/or silence Kennedy's killer, how come he wasn't able to get the mob to help him in such a small matter as getting AGVA on his side in his dispute with the Weinsteins? Particularly when the FBI found that AGVA was frequently used by members of organized crime as a front for their criminal activities, and was described by others as having "racketeer" links and being "completely corrupt." Instead, Bobby Faye, the person who ran AGVA at the time, didn't even show Ruby the courtesy of meeting with him when Ruby flew to New York City in August of 1963 seeking the union's help.[332] Can there really be too much doubt that if the Mafia were in Ruby's corner, just one phone call to the Weinsteins would

probably have solved the problem for Ruby? And yet as late as two days before the assassination, Ruby made a long-distance call to Chicago for the purpose of getting AGVA
support.[333]

There are essentially two periods to Ruby's life, the Chicago and the Dallas years. With
respect to the Chicago years, the Warren Commission concluded that "Ruby was unquestionably familiar, if not friendly, with some Chicago criminals, but there is no evidence
that he ever participated in organized criminal activity." The Commission went on to say
that those who knew Ruby in Chicago did not connect him to organized crime.[334] As Dave
Yaras, who along with Lenny Patrick was another alleged mob hit man in Chicago who
knew Ruby well enough to refer to him by his nickname, Sparky, and by all accounts was
a leading member of the Chicago Syndicate, told the FBI in 1963, Ruby was "positively
not Outfit [the name of the mob in Chicago] connected."[335]

Well-known Chicago mobster Lenny Patrick, Ruby's neighborhood chum, said he lost
track of Ruby after grammar school, and the next time he became aware of him was when
he learned Ruby was selling items such as salt shakers with one of his brothers. He said
he was "certain" that Ruby had nothing to do with the rackets in Chicago. He told the
FBI the day after Ruby shot Oswald, "No matter how much you investigate, you'll never
learn nothing, as he [Ruby] had nothing to do with nothing."[336] And James Allegretti,
reputed to be a top organized-crime figure in Chicago at the time, told the FBI that he
had never even heard of Jack Ruby's name before he killed Oswald, having no knowledge
of him in the Chicago area.[337] Other Chicago mobsters and associates told the FBI the
same thing.[338]* In other words, although Ruby may have drifted around the edges of the
Chicago underworld, he never entered and became a part of it.

The HSCA came to the same conclusion—that Ruby was not a member of organized
crime in Chicago.[339]

Former FBI agent Bill Roemer, who investigated the mob in Chicago, told author Gerald Posner in 1992, "Ruby was absolutely nothing in terms of the Chicago mob. We had
thousands and thousands of hours of tape recordings of the top mobsters in Chicago,
including Sam Giancana, and Ruby just didn't exist as far as they were concerned. We
talked to every hoodlum in Chicago after the assassination, and some of the top guys in
the mob, my informants. I had close relationships with them—they didn't even know who
Ruby was."[340]

With respect to Dallas, the Warren Commission stated that its evaluation of the record
revealed no evidence connecting Ruby to organized crime in Dallas, and went on to say

---

*The Warren Commission said it found it "difficult to attach credence to a newspaper reporter's contrary
statement [to the FBI] that his undisclosed 'syndicate sources' revealed Ruby was connected with organized
crime and confidence games" (WR, p.790; newspaper reporter: CE 1321, 22 H 495–496). There are several
reasons for rejecting this. It is totally at odds with what others have said about Jack Ruby and with everything
we know about Ruby. Also, the reporter, a crime writer for the *Chicago Daily News*, apparently never thought
enough of the information to write about it in his *own* newspaper (apparently this reporter was the one out of
a thousand reporters who didn't like scoops), and finally, he refused to identify his sources. We know that the
information provided by the "sources" was incorrect in two instances. They told the reporter that Ruby had
been arrested in Milwaukee on bookmaking charges and in Chicago on charges of "confidence games," but
there is no evidence of either of these arrests. He was also told by his "sources" that Ruby was part of a group
of Chicago mobsters who went to Dallas in 1947 to take over gambling. This is an old charge that we have seen
has been proved false.

that both state and federal law enforcement officials came to the conclusion that Ruby "was not affiliated with organized crime activity."[341] As Dallas assistant district attorney Bill Alexander, who prosecuted Ruby, put it, "If there was any connection between Ruby and the syndicate, Mafia, or other hoodlums, it would have come to the attention of our office through various gamblers and hoodlum informants of his office, and no such information has come to our attention."[342]

The Warren Commission went on to say that not only law enforcement but also "numerous persons have reported that Ruby was not connected with [organized crime] activity."[343]* As his sister Eva said, "Jack himself never had any connection with gangsters for money, for business, for sociability. On the other hand," she said, "when we saw them we acknowledged them."[344] This observation went far beyond Ruby's family. A few examples: Reagan Turman, a longtime boxer friend of Ruby's who also worked for Ruby on many occasions, including managing Ruby's Vegas Club, said that although Ruby was "acquainted with practically all the known gamblers in the Dallas area, he had no business dealings with them at all."[345] Frank Ferraro, who worked as a handyman for Ruby at the Carousel, said that "'there were no illegal activities' that Ruby was involved in."[346] Johnnie Hayden got to know Ruby well as the business representative of the American Federation of Musicians, and said that Ruby "talked and dressed like a Chicago hoodlum, but had no known hoodlum connections."[347] And so on. In fact, even those few who did not like Ruby rejected out of hand the notion he was connected to organized crime. As mentioned earlier, Sam Lasser was a concessionaire at Ruby's Vegas Club before a business dispute ended their relationship. He said he had no use for Ruby, characterizing him as a man of high temper, a show-off, and a "real tough guy," but said he felt "certain Ruby had no connection with any hoodlum element."[348] Janet Conforto, Ruby's head stripper, "Jada," at the Carousel Club until late October of 1963 when the relationship degenerated into accusations, recriminations, and a dispute over wages and Conforto sought a restraining order against Ruby, said that although Ruby would tell people he "knew all the boys," she did not know of any association he had with the underworld.[349] The Warren Commission summarized the situation by saying that its "investigation disclosed no one in either Chicago or Dallas who had any knowledge that Ruby was associated with organized criminal activity."[350]†

---

*Author Gerald Posner agrees with the conspiracy theorists that the Warren Commission "underplayed Jack Ruby's underworld associations" (Posner, *Case Closed*, p.411). But it would have been hard for the Commission to underplay those associations when none were of any significance to underplay. If any were, what were they? Even the HSCA never came up with anything. And even assuming, for the sake of argument, that the Warren Commission underplayed Ruby's underworld associations, it couldn't have been, as many conspiracy theorists allege, intentional. To believe that, one would have to believe that the seven distinguished Commission members were trying to protect the American Mafia and cover up their possible involvement in the assassination.

Though this is a more subtle point, since a Mafia connection with Ruby in the killing of Oswald necessarily bespeaks premeditation, if the Warren Commission were trying to protect the mob (which is a thought unworthy of even being considered), anything that showed a lack of premeditation on Ruby's part would of course help them. Yet, although the Warren Report adequately shows Ruby's propensity for violence, it negligently fails (though the Commission's volumes don't) to focus in on the spontaneity of that violence and Ruby's extreme volatility, which would tend to be supportive of an unpremeditated act, and hence, away from the conclusion that Ruby was a part of any conspiracy to kill Oswald.

†Although several of Ruby's friends and acquaintances noted that he engaged in playing cards and attended the horse races, Ruby did not consider himself to be a gambler (CE 1536, 23 H 27; CE 1559, 23 H 48; CE 1742, 23 H 351; 5 H 201, WCT Jack L. Ruby). Jack's longtime girlfriend of nine years plus, Alice Nichols, stated that he gambled on occasion, but that she did not believe Jack gambled with any large amounts of money,

The Commission further concluded that its investigation of Ruby did not "produce any grounds for believing that Ruby's killing of Oswald was part of a conspiracy."[351]

The HSCA reached the same conclusion about Ruby not being a member of organized crime "in Dallas or elsewhere."[352] However, the HSCA Report went on to say that although there was no evidence available to the committee that Ruby was a member of organized crime, he "had a *significant number of associations* and *direct* and indirect *contacts* with *underworld figures*, a number of whom were *connected* to the *most powerful La Cosa Nostra leaders*. Additionally, Ruby had numerous associations with the Dallas criminal element."[353] This was either innocently sloppy language or deliberately misleading, allowing conspiracy theorists to cite this language, which unquestionably suggests that Ruby was connected to the Mafia. If this wasn't just terrible writing, then shame on the HSCA for making a statement that implies what its own thorough investigation clearly disproves. Shame on the HSCA for writing this about someone whom its own investigation showed to be no more than a buffoon, someone who had far less connection to the Mafia than Frank Sinatra, Dean Martin, and Sammy Davis Jr.* And shame on the HSCA staff, most of whom were lawyers and investigators, for not knowing that when they make an assertion like this, they have at a minimum a moral, if not a legal burden to prove it. They failed miserably in their effort to prove this allegation, unless one is naive enough to believe that Ruby's association with the likes of Joe Campisi and Joe Civello satisfied the HSCA's burden of proof, a burden so low that an ant would have difficulty crawling under it.

Also, although I believe the Warren Commission and FBI could have gone into more depth than they did on Ruby's possible connection with organized crime, I also believe that the HSCA's position that the FBI "was *seriously* delinquent in investigating the Ruby-underworld connection" was *seriously* overstated.[354]

R uby's travels outside of Dallas have proved to be fodder for conspiracy theorists, who allege the trips were probably for some clandestine purpose. But it is Ruby's trip (or, as some believe, trips) to Cuba that has garnered the most attention. Jack went to Cuba around Labor Day of 1959 as the guest of his friend, Lewis McWillie, a gambler Jack met in Dallas around 1947 or 1948. McWillie worked at the Top of the Hill Club between Dallas and Fort Worth. He and Ruby became fast friends and, according to McWillie's mother, visited with each other on an almost daily basis.[355] McWillie went to Cuba in September of 1958 and became manager of the gambling casino at the Tropicana Night Club.[356] He told the HSCA that the Fox brothers, the owners of the Tropicana, which had the premier cabaret in Latin America, were trying to stir up business for the casino, so McWillie suggested he call his friend Jack Ruby and ask if he could bring Tony Zoppi, the entertainment columnist for the *Dallas Morning News* who was a friend of Jack's, down to Havana to see the Tropicana. The idea was to have Zoppi write a great column that would induce Dallasites to visit Havana, and the Foxes thought it was a good idea. When Ruby called Zoppi, Zoppi agreed and McWillie sent two tickets, one for Zoppi and one

---

and that he confined his gambling to card games (Nichols [Alice R.] Exhibit No. 5355, 20 H 673, 679). Another acquaintance, though, remembers Jack as betting "heavily" with frequent telephone bets on horse races and basketball games (CE 1505, 22 H 924).

*Particularly Sinatra, who much evidence shows was very friendly with leading mob figures like Lucky Luciano and Sam Giancana for years (e.g., see Summers and Swan, *Sinatra*, pp. 130–133, 252–255).

for Ruby, but as Zoppi said in a 1976 letter, "Jack Ruby and I were supposed to visit [McWillie] in Havana but I got sidetracked. Jack went on ahead . . . The quick buck artists [conspiracy theorists] are saying Jack went down there to plan the assassination. He couldn't have planned a gas station holdup . . . All of a sudden he's a CIA agent, a Mafia don, etcetera, etcetera, [it's] sickening."[357]

The understanding had been that Zoppi and Ruby could stay at any hotel they wanted during their trip to Havana, all expenses paid by the Foxes, but when Ruby showed up sometime around Labor Day Weekend—September 4, 5, and 6, 1959*—alone, the Foxes, understandably upset, didn't pay for any of Ruby's expenses, and he ended up staying at a small hotel.[358]

Along the lines of the "guilt by association" thinking of most assassination conspiracy believers, since McWillie knew Florida mob boss Santo Trafficante, who had operated the Sans Souci Hotel in Havana before Castro took power in early January of 1959, it follows that Ruby, while in Cuba, must have met Trafficante, who the conspiracy theorists claim was a prisoner at the time in Trescornia, a Cuban detention camp on the outskirts of Havana. Trafficante, however, denied under oath that he ever met Ruby, telling the HSCA, when asked if he knew Ruby, "No, sir, I never remember meeting Jack Ruby."

Question: "Are you aware it has been alleged that Jack Ruby visited with you while you were at Trescornia; have you heard that?"

Answer: "I've heard that but I don't remember him visiting me . . . There was no reason for this man to visit me . . . I have never seen this man before. I have never been to Dallas. I never had no contact with him. I don't see why he was going to come and visit me."[359] Indeed, not only is there no credible evidence that Ruby ever met Trafficante in Havana (or elsewhere), but such a meeting would have been impossible since Trafficante was released from Trescornia on August 18, 1959, and left for Miami that same day.[360] So Trafficante was no longer in Havana when Ruby arrived there around Labor Day. Even if Trafficante had been there, such a meeting between Ruby and Trafficante would have been difficult since McWillie himself wasn't close to Trafficante. "He knew who I was," McWillie said about Trafficante, "and he shook hands with me when he saw me, but that was it." McWillie told the HSCA that he did not visit Trafficante in Trescornia, although he visited two other inmates there, one twice, while Trafficante was there, and may have simply said hello to Trafficante on the second visit. He said Ruby did not know Trafficante, and he did not believe (though he said it was possible) that Ruby was visiting him in Havana at the time he went to Trescornia, and accompanied him there.[361]

The HSCA, which looked very hard for a Ruby-Trafficante connection, admitted it was relying "mainly" on the fact that McWillie knew Trafficante, but this, of course, was no evidence at all, particularly with McWillie saying he was the most casual of acquaintances with Trafficante, and the HSCA failing to prove otherwise.

The only other thread the HSCA had to go on was that a British journalist, John Wilson Hudson, who was allegedly detained in the same prison in Havana as Trafficante in 1959, told the American embassy in London shortly after Kennedy's assassination that a man named "Santos" (presumably Trafficante) was "visited frequently" by a man named

---

*Three tourists from Chicago told the FBI they saw Ruby at the Tropicana during Labor Day Weekend. However, the FBI was unable to verify their story through a search of records at the hotel in Miami Beach they said they stayed at before leaving for Cuba. The airline they said they flew on from Key West to Havana was no longer in existence and the location of the airline records was unknown. (CE 1765–1774, 23 H 375–379, 381–382)

Ruby.[362] But why would Ruby visit Trafficante "frequently" or at all? To plan Kennedy's assassination, though Kennedy hadn't yet been elected? If not, for what other reason? The story is completely uncorroborated and sounds ridiculous on its face. Rather than visiting Trafficante "frequently," McWillie says that during Ruby's visit to Cuba, "he was right out there where I worked. Every morning when I got up he was there. When I left the place, he went with me to eat and went to bed . . . I don't remember a darn thing he did but bug me all week."[363] Yet during a six-day visit to Havana, Ruby, according to Hudson, visited "frequently" with Trafficante.

Having nothing at all to go on, the HSCA was far, far too tentative in merely saying that "the evidence was not sufficient to form a final conclusion as to whether or not such a meeting [between Ruby and Trafficante] took place."[364]

For years, the person the conspiracy theorists have tried to connect Ruby with the most, of course, is Lee Harvey Oswald. Both lived in the Oak Cliff area of Dallas, 1.63 miles by surface street from each other. The conspiracists are convinced that Ruby and Oswald knew each other before the events of November 22, 1963, and predictably, like people who see Elvis in supermarkets, several people thought they saw Oswald hanging out with Ruby at the Carousel Club, some even alleging that they were homosexual lovers. The Warren Commission, naturally, had no choice but to investigate each and every one of these claims, and said, "All such allegations have been investigated but the Commission has found none which merits credence," concluding that "Ruby and Oswald were not acquainted."[365] It should be noted that Ruby's prosecutors knew that getting the death penalty against Ruby would be easier if they could link Ruby to Oswald—creating the specter of their being part of a conspiracy to kill Kennedy—than if Ruby was just some enraged citizen seeking vigilante justice. But the Dallas DA's office, and Dallas police detectives assigned to work with the DA's office on the case, were unable to connect Ruby and Oswald in any way. Dallas district attorney Henry Wade said that "you can see how much it would have helped us . . . if we could prove Oswald and Ruby were together . . . Everything that indicated there might be a connection was checked out more carefully than anything else by our office," but he said they could find no connection.[366] No one would have wanted to show that Ruby knew Oswald more than author Seth Kantor, who wrote a pro-conspiracy book about Ruby, yet after thoroughly investigating all the claims, he said, "There is no evidence, . . . not a shred of proof . . . that Ruby and Oswald even knew each other, despite claims by several people over the years that the two had been seen together."[367]

Although author Gerald Posner said that "the Warren Commission and the Select Committee . . . both concluded there was no 'evidence they [Oswald and Ruby] were ever acquainted,'"[368] this is misleading. The HSCA, as opposed to the Warren Commission, never did get around to expressly saying, as Posner said, that there wasn't any evidence that Ruby had any contact or acquaintanceship with Oswald. In fact, the HSCA, in some of the most irresponsible and misleading language of its entire investigation, said its investigation revealed that "the Warren Commission was, in fact, incorrect in concluding that Oswald and Ruby had no significant associations." The HSCA said it found "associations of both Ruby and Oswald that were unknown to the Warren Commission."[369] (Actually, the Warren Commission only said Ruby and Oswald "were not acquainted." By the use of the nebulous word *associations*, the HSCA was giving itself much more latitude, expanding the situation, clearly, to include people Ruby and Oswald each knew, though they may not have known each other.) But what were these "significant associations"? If the HSCA found them, it certainly kept them an enormous secret. In a blatant violation of research and scholarship principles, remarkably, the HSCA didn't give one single citation in its report for its highly inflammatory, misleading, and almost assuredly erroneous assertion about the alleged Ruby-Oswald associations. And there's nothing in its volumes specifically addressing this question, and answering it affirmatively with solid, credible citations and support.

We should not forget that in addition to the Warren Commission and FBI trying to find any connection between Oswald and Ruby (as well as Tippit), there was the media. As *Dallas Morning News* reporter Jim Ewell would later say, "If there'd ever been any connection between Oswald, Tippit, and Jack Ruby, we would be talking about it [now] as if it happened." He pointed out, "There was an all out intensive effort on the part of the press [in Dallas] to be the first to find these connections, and there were some very good reporters in those days looking into that." Ewell and fellow *Morning News* reporter Hugh Aynesworth were a part of that effort. He said they all wanted to "break the 'story of the century'" that there was a "conspiracy behind the assassination of Kennedy." Also in Dallas, he adds, were "some of the best newspapermen" from around the country "trying to find those angles. You also had the best from the television networks." But Ewell said no one found anything. "It was never established."[370]

Much has been made in the biographies of Ruby about his sexuality. It would appear that for many of the FBI agents who interviewed acquaintances of Ruby starting immediately after Ruby shot Oswald and continuing for many months afterward, part of the standard list of questions included one that asked, either directly or indirectly, whether or not Jack Ruby was homosexual. The responses ran the gamut of opinion from "definitely not homosexual"[371] to "Ruby attempted to get . . . an ex-prize fighter, . . . a bouncer at the Vegas Club, to go to bed with him."[372]

One thing is clear: there is plenty of evidence that Ruby availed himself of the company of women and did engage in sexual relationships with them.[373] In fact, Larry Crafard, the handyman at the club, said that Ruby had once told him he had had a sexual relationship "with every one of the girls who worked for him."[374] One acquaintance noted though that Ruby "was peculiar in that after he had gone to bed with a woman, he was scornful of her and would not go out with her again."[375] Indeed, one girl at the Carousel said that the girls at the club who had sex with Jack usually lasted "no more than a week . . . All you had to do was hold out against him to stay with him."[376] Two of Jack's former employees stated that he went to bed with various girls at the Carousel, usually those who were applying for jobs, but his affairs were brief and seldom deep.[377]

But then there was Tawny Angel, the raven-haired Carousel stripper with a stunning figure, even for a stripper, whom Jack fell head over heels for from almost the first moment he laid eyes on her. It was obvious to all the other girls that Jack heard violins whenever Tawny approached. He got downright nasty with Tawny's boyfriend when he came to the club, and soon told him he'd have to wait outside for her. Tawny had one big problem that temporarily worked to Jack's advantage. She couldn't stay away from the bottle, so much so that her boyfriend left her because of it, and Jack was there to catch her, nursing her wounds and giving her whatever she wanted. Tawny eventually moved in with Jack, and he was never happier. He told her he loved her and proposed marriage, but Tawny had no feelings for Jack and walked out on him in the middle of the night. Jack carried a real torch for Tawny for some time. "I loved that miserable little broad," Jack told Alice (not Ruby's girlfriend, Alice Nichols), a stripper who was kind of a mother hen to the other girls, "and now it hurts. I wanted to marry her. She had a lot of class. I miss her." In due time, Jack got over Tawny, Alice convincing him that she was just a selfish lush who had used him.[378]

Evidence does indicate that Jack gave the impression he had homosexual tendencies. And apparently Jack himself thought that people thought he was homosexual. Karen "Little Lynn" Carlin, one of Jack's strippers, said that although Ruby never said he was homosexual and, indeed, had once propositioned her, "he was always asking the question, 'Do you think I am a queer? Do you think I look like a queer?' Or 'have you ever known a queer to look like me?'"[379] And according to Earl Norman, one of Jack's emcees, one time Jack remarked to Earl, after putting a cigar in his mouth and lighting it, "I don't look gay now, do I?"[380]

Here, from various FBI reports, are references to some of the statements acquaintances made with regard to Ruby's sexuality: "did not have homosexual tendencies to his knowledge but did have some slightly effeminate characteristics";[381] "heard . . . that Ruby dated both men and women";[382] "Ruby was a very aggressive 'wolf'" with women;[383] "heard . . . 'gossip' . . . that Ruby was a homosexual";[384] "was sure he went out with quite a number [of girls]";[385] "of the opinion that Ruby preferred 'gay company'";[386] "a normal male . . . with no effeminate actions";[387] "his main pastime was 'chasing the girls'";[388] "the man might be somewhat queer . . . Just the way he talked and mostly the way he walked."[389]

Jack actually did have a slight speech impediment, "sort of a lisp," and was conscious of it.[390] Under a U.S. Treasury Department letterhead there was this from an assistant regional commissioner: "There is a strong indication that Jack Ruby is either a homosexual or a bisexual, although there is no concrete evidence to support this contention."[391] Jack's good friend and Carousel emcee Wally Weston chuckled when he recalled being asked by people about whether or not Jack was homosexual. He said he would simply say, "Go ask Jack. I'm sure he'll tell you."[392]

The Warren Commission concluded, "There is no evidence of homosexuality on [Ruby's] part," pointing out that many reports to the contrary were "inherently suspect" and "all the allegations were based on hearsay or derive from Ruby's lisp or a 'feeling' that Ruby was a 'sissy' . . . and sometimes spoke in a high-pitched voice when angry."[393]

Apart from any sexual encounters, one longtime acquaintance, both professional and social, stated that in all the years he had known Jack, he could only recall one instance where Jack had gone out on a date with a woman. He felt Jack's sole interests were his clubs and his dogs. One wonders how well this person really knew Jack in view of Jack's relationship with Tawny Angel and the ten-year relationship he had with a dignified and intelligent Dallas secretary and divorcee named Alice Nichols. She told the Warren Commission they'd see each other once a week, sometimes twice, and Jack had even brought up the possibility of getting married and having a family at one point, but the two never wed, and they parted in 1959. Ruby himself said he at one time considered marrying Nichols, and he passed a lie detector test on this point.[394] Nichols, who was four years Ruby's junior, was close enough to Jack that he confided quite a bit in her, as her testimony before the Commission revealed. Ruby thought enough of Nichols to introduce her to Jack's dad when he came to Dallas on one occasion.[395]

Much has also been said of Ruby's almost fanatical attachment to his dogs, whom he referred to as "my children" or "babies" or "kids." A friend of Jack's who knew him for years said, "I never saw anybody so crazy" about his dogs.[396] Ruby owned as many as nine or ten at a time and frequently took a bunch of them with him in his car and to the club. A friend of Jack's who said something about the "dogs" once got an immediate angry response from Ruby: "I told you not to call these children of mine dogs any more. These are my children, and I respect them just like you respect your kids." And Jack defended their conduct. A friend visiting Jack's apartment was stunned to see his couch eaten up, and the backboard all eaten out, and asked, "Jack, what in the world happened?" Jack's irritated response was, "My children. Anything wrong with that? My children ate it up." Another said Ruby "cried like a baby when one of his dogs got hurt." One employee feared Ruby was going to hit her when he became enraged that she had fed some pizza to one of his dogs. Rabbi Silverman, from Ruby's synagogue, recalled that one time Ruby had seven dachshunds in his car with him. At Ruby's trial, Silverman related an incident when Ruby came to visit him at his home one day with several of his dogs. "Suddenly, he began to cry," Silverman told the jury. "He said, 'I'm unmarried.' Then, pointing to Sheba, he added, 'This is my wife, these are my children.'" Sheba was Jack's favorite and always with him. As roommate George Senator put it, "Jack goes to the club, Sheba goes with him."[397] Jack had just murdered Oswald in front of millions of people, and with the world's attention on him and while being interrogated by the police, he asked a detective to take care of Sheba, who was still waiting patiently for Jack in the car parked outside.[398]

Surprisingly, Jack's love affair with his "children" only started around 1958 or 1959, when Alice Nichols said Jack received his first dog, a dachshund, as a gift, having never owned a dog before then. That dog was killed shortly thereafter and Jack quickly got another dachshund.[399] He was so concerned for the welfare of his dogs that even when he gave a close friend a dachshund as a gift for his children, Jack came by once every six months to see how the dog was getting along.[400]

The dogs probably never minded, but Jack Ruby was a man possessed of some strange and often contradictory traits. He was a health faddist and regularly exercised and lifted weights in his apartment and at the YMCA, where he also swam regularly. He was proud of his physical condition and extremely sensitive about his personal appearance, watching his diet to make sure his sturdy frame (five feet eight inches, 175 pounds) would not get out of hand. One acquaintance stated that Ruby would frequently ask him if he, Ruby, looked all right, if his suit fit, and if he had any offensive body odors.[401]*

Though fastidious in his personal appearance, he apparently lived like a slob. George Senator said, "Jack didn't live too clean." The roommate went on to tell investigators, "Though he was very clean about himself, he wasn't clean around the apartment."[402] Another acquaintance noted that Jack would take two or three showers a day but his car was a dirty "rattletrap."[403]

There was no greater contradiction, though, in Ruby's life than in his own temperament. Nearly everyone who knew Ruby for some time had stories of his many physical

---

*"Was Jack concerned about baldness?" Warren Commission counsel asked George Senator, Ruby's roommate. "Oh, you should only know. He used to drive me crazy." Senator went on to tell of Ruby's going somewhere for "treatments" for his growing baldness and "the stuff" Ruby would "rub into his head." (14 H 288)

altercations, as well as his acts of kindness and generosity. The same man who treated his employees well and would do anything for someone he liked would also "belt someone at the drop of a hat."[404] Breck Wall, a friend of Ruby's, said that Ruby "was a wonderful man. He was a lot of fun and had a great personality . . . but he had a violent temper. He hit my partner, Joe Peterson, and knocked him down the stairs and knocked out a tooth . . . We had no idea it was even coming."[405] The many brawls Ruby was involved in resulted from the most salient trait in Ruby's makeup, one that people like Breck mentioned more than any other: his hot and explosive temper. FBI agents may have interviewed close to one hundred people who *knew Ruby well*, and in their published reports in the Warren Commission volumes the reader would be hard-pressed to find one interviewee who did not mention Ruby's temper, or at least how "very emotional" he was, if the question of Ruby's temperament was discussed. It is noteworthy that not one said he was *not* hot tempered. The following types of comments about Ruby were mentioned over and over again in the FBI reports and elsewhere: "He is hot-tempered";[406] Ruby had an "uncontrollable temper";[407] "an extremely emotional and excitable individual";[408] "I'm impressed that Ruby has lived as long as he has due to his extremely short and high temper";[409] "impulsive, violent . . . erratic";[410] he "is a man with a violent temper";[411] Ruby was "totally unpredictable. One minute he is nice, and the next minute he goes berserk";[412] he had a "peculiar personality and violent temper";[413] "highly emotional person who has no control over his emotions";[414] "could explode in a moment's notice . . . without provocation";[415] "very high-strung, very excitable person";[416] "had a very bad temper";[417] was "a very emotional man";[418] had "a very nasty temper";[419] "erratic and hot-headed . . . sometimes he would get so mad he would just shake";[420] and on and on and on.

But Ruby's anger was about as permanent as a breath upon a mirror. A comedian who worked for him said Ruby was remarkable in that he could "change moods in an instant."[421] His friend for years, William Serur, said Ruby "explodes and gets mad . . . quicker than any person I ever saw, but he can cool off quicker than any person I ever saw,"[422] an extreme volatility that would certainly be ideal, would it not, for a cold and experienced mob hit man. Almost laughably, after flying into a rage over something and just as quickly cooling down, Ruby would often completely forget what he had been so angry about.[423]

The fights (mostly beatings Ruby administered) that resulted from Ruby's uncontrollable temper were legendary at his clubs. A waitress from the B & B Restaurant, visiting the Carousel Club, saw Ruby approach a couple in their fifties who were arguing, grab the woman by the arm, lead her to the flight of approximately twenty stairs, and then give her a shove down. He then knocked the short, slender, gray-haired male companion of hers to the floor and repeatedly kicked him.[424] Once Ruby struck a cabdriver who came into the club looking to collect a fare.[425] Another time he knocked a man down inside the club, then threw him down the flight of stairs and did not even attempt to determine if the man had been injured.[426] One patron watched Ruby and another individual he believed to be an off-duty policeman throw a customer down the stairs who had gotten into an argument at the bar.[427] But one time Ruby had to retreat behind the bar, grab his gun, and fire a warning shot into the ceiling to stop a fight he was unsuccessful in breaking up.[428] Another time, when a patron who was about six foot three and 230 pounds slapped a woman during an argument, Ruby beat him to the floor, threw him out the Vegas Club door, and then forced him to crawl down the street. "If you are that type of man, crawl away," Ruby ordered.[429]

Ruby's choice of weapons in beating people who angered him was eclectic and included his feet,[430] knees,[431] brass knuckles,[432] and pistol, as in "pistol whipping."[433] But since he liked to fight, his fists were definitely his favorite. Indeed, one night at the Vegas Club, when an unidentified man pulled his pistol on Ruby, who was behind the bar, Ruby, though his own pistol was within easy reach beneath the bar, chose to jump over the bar, slap the pistol from the man's hand, and almost beat him to death with his fists, after which he put the man's pistol in the man's pocket and threw him out.[434] "Sherri Linn," one of Ruby's strippers, said that Ruby "liked to use his fists" and would fight "for no reason at all."[435] Using fists not only is validating, but gives a man bragging rights, something feet, knees, brass knuckles, and pistols don't do. And Ruby would claim to people that he had once beaten up a prize fighter in his club,[436] though this was never attested to by a third party.

But certainly Jack couldn't be proud of the time when he sucker punched a patron from behind, and after knocking him down proceeded to kick him in the face. And this was the brother of one of Ruby's exotic dancers. She feared Ruby would kill her brother before someone stopped the "fight."[437]

A frequent patron noted, in what is certainly a classic understatement, that Ruby would in some cases "take more severe action than the situation seemed to warrant."[438]

Ejection down the stairs seemed to be Ruby's preferred method of disposing of unruly patrons, but he didn't save that solely for his customers. He threatened to throw one of his female employees, a cigarette girl, down the stairs during an argument over forty-five to fifty dollars in wages.[439]

Jack simply couldn't help himself when it came to being physical. Despite their recurring arguments, of all his siblings he was the closest to his sister Eva.* When she went to the hospital for a week in November of 1963, he visited her two or three times a day, and he spent more time grieving with her over the assassination weekend than anyone else. But when the two of them would get into it over money or the operation of the Vegas Club, Jack couldn't even resist giving Eva a slap across the kisser now and then.[440]

Because Ruby had been a very good street fighter going back to his days in Chicago, kept in good physical shape, and was always a strong man, no one can recall Ruby, no matter whom he took on, getting beat up himself. But that doesn't mean he always won. It seems that one fellow Ruby pummeled not only had never heard of the Marquis of Queensbury rules, but also, unfortunately for Jack, had Mike Tyson genes in him before Iron Mike was even born. Willis "Dub" Dickerson, a musician who had worked for Jack at one of his clubs in the early 1950s, dropped by the Carousel one night and pulled up a chair at a table of four, partially blocking the aisle. When Ruby told him to move his chair and Dub told Jack to "go to hell," they naturally ended up out on the street. After Jack knocked Dickerson down with a blow to the head and Dickerson got up, Jack pushed him against a wall and, with his left hand in Dickerson's face holding him to the wall, began kneeing him in the groin. Dub didn't like this, of course, and proceeded to bite down hard on Jack's very available left forefinger, partially severing it at the first joint. Jack later had to have the tip of the finger amputated. Dickerson saw Jack a few times thereafter and Jack wasn't angry at all with him, knowing that all is fair in love and street fighting.[441]

---

*Ruby's brother Sam was the only other sibling who lived in Dallas, but except for seeing him on Jewish holidays and speaking over the phone occasionally, he was not close to him. All his other siblings lived in Chicago or Detroit. (WR, p.803)

Jack was the consummate glad-hander, but one employee noted, as had others, that although he was an extrovert and friendly with everybody, he appeared to have very few close friends.[442] Wally Weston, Jack's emcee at the Carousel, had a simple explanation: Ruby never had close friends because of his violent temper and peculiar personality.[443] Yet this was a man who minutes after striking up a conversation with a total stranger and learning of his problems gave him his apartment key and insisted he go there and stay with him. The man ended up living with Jack for a little over a year.[444]

That generosity was one of the traits, among others, fondly remembered by former Ruby employees. In a book about Ruby, Diana Hunter and Alice Anderson, two of Jack's Carousel "girls," wrote,

> Jack Ruby was our boss, but that was all we were ever sure of. We never knew exactly what to expect of him. He raged at us. He praised us. He browbeat us. He helped us. He was tight-fisted with us. He was generous. Often in the crush of busy evenings at the Carousel, when the music was loud, we reviled Jack Ruby. But we also loved that guy . . . He grumbled about the salaries he had to pay us. Yet he was generous to a fault. He loaned money to friends without seeming to care if he was ever paid back. He opened his apartment to acquaintances who needed a place to sleep. He offered a job to anyone who needed one, whether or not the person was qualified . . . That toughness which Jack Ruby displayed on occasion was mostly for show. He was crude in his language and his manners, true. But the girls who worked at the Carousel saw in him a nature that was kind and generous. We knew him best as a man with a longing to make friends and keep them. And he had a kind of honesty that transcended everything. When he disliked something, he was quick to admit it. When he loved something, it was all the way.[445]

Many of the sentiments of Hunter and Anderson were undoubtedly summed up in their book's dedication, which read, "In Loving Memory of Jack Ruby, Our Raging Boss, Our Faithful Friend, the Kindest-Hearted Sonuvabitch We Ever Knew."

Ruby's generosity wasn't limited, as indicated, to his employees, as he could be compassionate and bighearted toward anyone down on their luck, often giving destitute or poor people out on the street more than just small change without their even soliciting it from him. Dallas police officer T. M. Hansen Jr. said he had personally seen Ruby doing this several times, adding, "I have heard a lot of people say that he helped a lot of people."[446] "Jack is a very compassionate person," his sister Eileen would tell the Warren Commission. "He always feels sorry for the underdog."[447] Tammi True, one of Jack's favorite strippers, said that "Jack was always picking people up off the street . . . that didn't have a place to stay or any money . . . We had three or four guys sleeping in the club every night because they didn't have a place to stay."[448]

There was another side to Ruby's generosity and compassion that, unlike his help to the poor, was perhaps not quite as altruistic. Ruby would always pick up a dinner check and was always giving people presents, some felt because he wanted to be liked.[449] And Joyce Gordon, a stripper at the Carousel, said, "Jack did a lot of things because he thought he'd get a pat on the back, a medal, be praised for what he was doing."[450]

And the overall positive view of Ruby by those on the inside was also often tempered by the unkind realities seen by those same people. The girls alluded to it when they stated, "Jack was a paradox, a lot of contradictions."[451]

One comedian, who had a routine that poked fun at President Kennedy and his wife, told the FBI that Ruby told him that his jokes were funny but only an idiot would laugh at them. Ruby then went on to prohibit his entertainers from using any material that would reflect adversely against "Negroes, Jews or the Kennedys," adding he didn't appreciate comedians "knocking the president or his wife." Another comedian at the club had told what he felt were completely "inoffensive" Jewish jokes one night, but Ruby took offense at them and told the comic, "My people have suffered enough." Yet, with respect to blacks, a musician who hung out frequently at the Carousel said that while he never heard Ruby express hatred or make inflammatory remarks about them, he nevertheless referred to them in the vulgar vernacular, and on one occasion he observed Ruby refuse admittance to the club to a mixed group of black and white businessmen.[452]

Billy Joe Willis, a Carousel Club drummer for two years, characterized his boss as a highly emotional person who had no control over his emotions, someone who was prone to argue with his employees over trivial matters and fire them with the slightest provocation.[453] And Ruby beat the handyman at the Carousel Club so badly over a disagreement that the man had to be taken to Parkland Hospital for emergency treatment.[454]

Although Ruby appeared decisive in the ironhanded running of his club, he apparently had trouble making even the smallest decisions. Either that or he had an inordinate need to have contact with others. One friend told the FBI that he was in stores with Jack on two occasions, once to buy toothpaste and the other time to buy batteries. Both times Jack solicited the opinions of the employees and several customers in the store before making his purchase.[455] If Ruby wasn't neurotic, no one is.

Ruby seemed to be a lightning rod for opinions. Everyone who knew him had a rather strong one about him. When one reads all of the FBI reports on Ruby in the Warren Commission volumes, a somewhat paradoxically consistent picture of contradictions emerges—difficult to fully understand yet making Ruby almost predictable in his behavior. As mentioned earlier, there was perhaps no group of individuals, including his family, who knew Ruby better than his employees at the Carousel. For the most part they loved him, mood swings and all. As former employees Hunter and Anderson perceived Ruby's way of thinking, "Every score had to be evened, every wrong, real or imagined, had to be righted. He couldn't stand to see anyone 'get away' with something. And he saw no reason to wait for the proper authorities to take action. Invariably, he plunged right in and tried to do it himself,"[456] all completely compatible with what he did to Oswald in the basement of Dallas City Hall.

For those who logically believe that Ruby was not involved in any conspiracy to silence Oswald, there are, in these observations of Ruby's makeup, keys to the puzzle as to why he shot Oswald. But the observation of Ruby that explains not the "why he shot Oswald," but the "why he was there" question, was provided by several people who knew Ruby well. William Howard, who knew Jack for more than ten years, said simply, "He liked to be in the middle of things no matter what it was."[457] Newspaperman Tony Zoppi seconded that, saying, "If there was one Ruby trait that stands out it is that he had to be where the action was. He was . . . all over the place, wherever anything exciting was happening. That's why the President's assassination and all the follow-up activity at the jail with Oswald and the press attracted Jack like a magnet. It was a natural for him."[458] Wes Wise, of KRLD TV-radio in Dallas, said that as a sports broadcaster for the station he saw Ruby "at almost every boxing match I ever attended. He would be at every football game . . . He'd be at fires, he'd be at major accidents."[459] This quality of Ruby's long predated Dallas. Ben Epstein, who grew up with Ruby, chumming around with him at neighborhood hangouts like the barbershop and pool hall, said that Ruby had a strong affinity for being "where the action was."[460]*

The fact was that Jack Ruby never saw a crowd that he didn't want to be a part of. On that fateful Sunday morning, what he saw at City Hall motivated him to take himself, with his hair-trigger temper, with his desire to right any wrong, with his penchant for taking the law into his own hands, into that basement. Though the evidence lends itself to the inference that Ruby probably intended to kill Oswald the first chance he had when he left his apartment that Sunday morning, it was Ruby's need to be in the middle of things that proved to be the catalyst, the one necessary ingredient in his makeup that made the shooting of Oswald when and where it happened a reality.

And so it was that on Thursday, November 21, 1963, the eve of President John F. Kennedy's visit to Dallas, Jack Ruby had the last "normal" day of his life. When he went to bed that night, or actually in the wee hours of Friday morning as was his normal custom, he had no idea, like millions of Americans, what was about to happen to his country and most certainly to himself.† The next day would see the assassination of the president of his beloved country and the subsequent unfolding of events that would culminate in his shooting Oswald, a seemingly unpredictable event, which was not all that unpredictable if you really knew Jack Ruby. But Thursday was normal and for Jack that meant a day filled with activities, most if not all of which reflected one of the myriad facets of his personality.

Thursday began as it usually did with the locking up of the club around 2:00 a.m. after the previous evening's patrons had left. One of Jack's dancers, Karen Carlin ("Little Lynn"), had had too much of Jack's rotgut champagne and had gotten sick and passed out in a nearby parking garage. Jack stayed with her until 4:00 or 5:00 a.m. and then joined Larry Crafard, the Carousel Club handyman, for breakfast at the Lucas B & B Restaurant next door to the Vegas Club before going home to bed. Later that morning, around 10:30 or 11:00, he received a call from Connie Trammel, a girl he had met previously at the Carousel Club. She asked him for a ride downtown for a job interview with Lamar Hunt, son of Texas oilman H. L. Hunt. Jack agreed to pick her up and drive her to her appointment. On the way there, Jack made one stop at the Merchants State Bank to purchase a five-hundred-dollar cashier's check to pay the monthly rent for his Vegas Club, and then later, after they arrived, he stopped in to see one of his lawyers in the same building.[461]

---

*Barney Weinstein, one of Ruby's competitors with his nearby Theatre Lounge, nonetheless had a soft spot for Jack and knew him well. He would later say, "Jack had to *be* there, even when he wasn't wanted." Weinstein said he once put on a benefit for a performer of his who died and Jack offered to sell ten tickets. "But he never let well enough alone. He met people as they came in that night and tried to get them to buy *more* tickets. I said, 'Jack, leave them alone. They already bought their tickets.' So then he wanted to sell *special* tickets for the best seats; he wanted to be my usher; he wanted to help, and he only got in the way. Once he dropped by when my houseman had not come in. He said, 'Don't worry, I'll stay and take care of any trouble.' I told him, 'I don't *want* you to, Jack.' You know, he doesn't stop trouble, he starts it . . . Jack had seven fights a week. I've had three fights in thirty years . . . But he stayed anyway. He had a wonderful heart. When he hardly knew me, he read about my mother's funeral in the newspapers and came to it. He just had to get into everything, including the excitement of that weekend Kennedy died." (Wills and Demaris, *Jack Ruby*, pp.13–14)

†Just the previous day, Ruby approached Joseph P. Rossi, who was engaged in the real estate business and had known Jack for eleven years. Shortly after Oswald's murder Rossi told the FBI that Ruby had discussed opening a new club and wanted Rossi to invest money in the club and perhaps help in management of the venture. Ruby talked of future plans in a manner that indicated he did not anticipate getting into any kind of trouble. (FBI Record 124-10062-10290, January 13, 1964, pp.1–2; see also 15 H 237, WCT Joseph Rossi)

Probably sometime that morning, Jack called Graham Koch, the lawyer handling his problem with delinquent income and excise taxes, for advice.[462]

Around noon, Dallas police lieutenant W. F. Dyson and three fellow officers were in the office of Assistant District Attorney Ben Ellis on the sixth floor of the Dallas County Records Building when Ruby walked in and passed out some advertisement cards on his stripper "Jada." Either just before or after Ruby passed out his Jada cards to Dyson and his fellow officers, Ruby stopped in to see a longtime acquaintance of his, Assistant District Attorney Bill Alexander, whose office was in the adjacent Dallas County Criminal Courts Building, and who within months would help get a sentence of death for Jack for killing Oswald. There he inquired about a friend, Robert Craven, and Craven's arrest for passing four bad checks.[463] Right after he left the Criminal Courts Building, Ruby visited Max Rudberg of AAA Bonding Service to discuss a peace bond hearing coming up on the charge filed against him by his employee, the stripper Jada, whose cards, as we've seen, he was still nonetheless passing out.[464]

During the noon hour, Ruby called John Newnam, the advertising salesman for the *Dallas Morning News*, to arrange ads for the Vegas and Carousel clubs,[465] and sometime during the day Jack gave a pass to the Carousel to an acquaintance he met on the street.[466]

It is not known for sure when Ruby went to the Carousel Club that Thursday afternoon. He thought it was in the early afternoon hours.[467] The Carousel utility worker, Larry Crafard, could only say Ruby arrived "sometime between 12:00 and 3:00" and left the club later in the afternoon.[468] Chances are he left somewhere between 3:00 and 3:30 p.m. because around that time he tried to make a dinner date with a woman waiting for a bus on Commerce Street (the street the Carousel Club was on) whom he had met two or three months earlier at the club when she showed up there with the doctor she worked for. Ruby's pitch to her this Thursday afternoon, "With your looks, you should be in show business," never got him his date, but she did give him her phone number.[469]

Ruby called Crafard at the club later in the afternoon, telling him he wanted him to bartend that night at the Vegas Club, and about 7:30 p.m. Ruby picked Crafard up at the Carousel and drove him to the Vegas Club.[470] Jack was overseeing the Vegas Club as well as the Carousel because his sister Eva was at home and in quite a bit of pain while she was recuperating from surgery (hysterectomy and the removal of a large abdominal tumor) performed earlier that month.[471] Ruby returned to the Carousel at around 9:00 p.m. and talked with Lawrence Meyers, a sales manager for a Chicago-based automobile accessory company who had met Ruby several years earlier during one of his trips to Dallas. Meyers and his lady friend from Chicago, Jean Aase, visited with Ruby for a while, and Meyers invited Ruby to join him and his brother and his brother's wife later that evening for drinks at the Bon Vivant Room, the club at the Cabana Motel where Meyers and Aase were staying.[472] Jack said he would try to stop by, and then left shortly after to have dinner with his good friend Ralph Paul at the Egyptian Lounge, arriving around 9:45 or 10:00 p.m. and staying for about forty-five minutes.[473] Joe Campisi, owner and operator of the Egyptian Lounge, apparently was not there that night.

Ruby returned to the Carousel after dinner and had a normal evening—interacting with the crowd as emcee, and getting into a verbal argument with a foul-mouthed drunk in the crowd who wanted Ruby, who was giving away prizes, to get off the stage and bring on the girls, Ruby eventually forcing him to leave without incident.[474] Another incident happened while Ruby was on the stage giving a brief demonstration of his twistboard to stimulate sales. "Even President Kennedy tells us to get more exercise," Ruby said, inducing a heckler to shout, "That bum." Jack responded immediately, "Don't ever talk that way about the President."[475]

Around 11:30 Jack took Lawrence Meyers up on his invitation and joined him and his brother and wife at the Bon Vivant Room at the Cabana Motel. Jack, ever the entrepreneur, tried to interest Lawrence's brother Eddie, a Pepsi distributor, in the twist-board as a tie-in with the Pepsi operation. Eddie wasn't interested and Jack left after twenty to thirty minutes to go back to the Carousel.[476] Jack got back to the club, closed up around 2:00 a.m.,[477] and picked up Crafard at the Vegas Club around 2:30 a.m. They had breakfast next door at the Lucas B & B, after which he dropped Crafard off at the Carousel, where he was staying, around 3:30 or 4:00 a.m.[478] Ruby then went directly home.

As indicated, it had been a typical day for Jack—caring about his friends, caring about his club, working on his personal problems, handing out club cards, trying to pick up a woman, socializing with friends, trying to make a buck, schmoozing with customers, ejecting customers—before he went to bed in the early hours of Friday, November 22, 1963.[479]

Dr. Renatus Hartogs, the New York City psychiatrist who examined Oswald when Oswald was thirteen, and went on to write a book about Oswald and Ruby, *The Two Assassins*, found many similarities between the two. A few he mentioned are that both, at a young age, "were poverty-stricken emotionally as well as sometimes economically . . . Violence threaded through the life of each . . . [Psychiatric] help was suggested for each," Oswald at the Bronx Children's Court, Ruby at Chicago's Institute for Juvenile Research. "Both were truants" in school, "both were educationally deprived. Oswald went only as far as the tenth grade, Ruby . . . only finished the eighth grade." Both "were impulsive men driven by their fantasies," and "Oswald acted as though he believed he had the right and the calling to kill the President of the United States . . . Ruby appears to have felt he had the right to avenge the murder . . . Neither could accept the slightest degree of frustration without throwing a temper tantrum," et cetera.[480] Hartogs could have added, among a few other things, that both Ruby and Oswald had uncommonly neurotic mothers whose own families found them impossible to get along with, and who the authorities concluded were incapable of properly rearing their sons. It is interesting to note that, as we saw earlier, the primary influence on Lee Harvey Oswald's young life was his mother, his father having passed away before his birth. Though Joseph Rubenstein was alive throughout Jack's youth, most of young Jack's adolescent years were spent without the presence of his father, and Ruby, like Oswald, was reared during this period by his mother. The similarities in their backgrounds go beyond this. As author David Lubin points out, "Oswald and Ruby were classic losers. Violent, undereducated, raised in broken homes by neurotic, paranoid, and . . . emotionally unstable mothers, unable to hold a steady job (Oswald) or stay out of debt (Ruby) . . . [Each was] puffed up with compensatory delusions of self-importance."[481]

The two men, of course, differed in many ways, among which was that Oswald was extremely political, unpatriotic, and tended toward intellectualism, Ruby the exact opposite on all three counts. In any event, the rage and psychic chaos in both men, unharnessed by any emotional stability, ultimately exploded in a way that not only was self-destructive but, particularly in the case of Oswald, changed the world.

As can be seen from the biography of Jack Ruby, two things are very clear. One, he was not a member of organized crime, and two, even if he had wanted to be, they could never have afforded to let him in. In addition to having a volatile, unstable personality, Jack Ruby was not mentally sound. Indeed, as we learned from his trial, he was suffering from organic brain damage. Even Marina Oswald, whose husband Ruby killed, remarked pitifully that just from seeing "his [Ruby's] picture in the paper now, it is an abnormal face."[482] Even a prosecution witness at Ruby's trial, the general manager at the parking lot where Ruby parked his car, said that he "sometimes wondered about Jack's sanity."[483] And a close friend of Ruby's testified at the trial he "was sure" Ruby was "suffering from some form of . . . mental disturbance."[484] The mob might want its members to be vicious killers, but not looney birds.

Ruby's mental infirmity seemed to deteriorate quickly into a pathological paranoia following his arrest and incarceration for Oswald's murder. Being "deprived of the Preludin and Benzedrine that he had come to know so well" added to the decline of his mental state.[485] The close-to-child-like mentality and paranoia, interspersed with periods of normality and lucidity, led to the following type of words and speech by Ruby in his testimony before the Warren Commission on June 7, 1964, in Dallas. To remind the reader, Ruby has by now been convicted of Oswald's murder and sentenced to death. The setting is formal, he is on the witness stand, and his questioner is Earl Warren, the chief justice of the U.S. Supreme Court. Among the hundreds of people who gave testimony before the Commission or its staff, not one sounded even remotely similar to Ruby. Apart from the casualness and adolescent innocence in Ruby's remarks, in which he converses with Warren as if he is talking to a male buddy of his at his club, Ruby, unlike any other Commission witness, all of whom were only on the stand to answer questions, asked most of the questions and did nearly all the talking. Here are some nonsequential excerpts, a small sampling—some of which, in view of the circumstances, approach skit-like humor—to give you a further sense of the man who conspiracy theorists say was closely associated with the Mafia and killed Oswald for them:

Ruby to Chief Justice Warren: "Is there any way to get me to Washington?"
Warren: "I beg your pardon."
Ruby, not wanting to tell his "story" in Dallas, repeats himself: "Is there any way of you getting me to Washington? . . . I would like to . . . go to Washington and . . . take all the tests that I have to take."
Ruby, upon seeing Gerald Ford in the room: "What state are you from, Congressman?"
Ford: "Michigan, Grand Rapids, Michigan."
Later, Ruby: "Unless you get me to Washington, you can't get a fair shake out of me . . . Unless you get me to Washington immediately, I am afraid after what Mr. Tonahill [Ruby's lawyer who is with him] has written there, which is unfair to me regarding my testimony here—you want to hear what he wrote?"
Ruby, after reading some words: "It is too bad, Chief Warren, that you didn't get me to your headquarters six months ago."
Later, Ruby to Warren: "Is there any way of getting a polygraph here? . . . I wish the president were right here now. It is a terrible ordeal. I tell you that."
After Ruby attempted to relate what happened chronologically, Warren says to Ruby: "You have told us most of what happened up to the time of the incident."
Ruby: "This is still only Friday night, Chief."

Warren: "Yes, that is true."

Ruby: "Well, I will go to a certain point, and if I stop, you will have to understand if I stop to get my bearings together."

Ruby, returning with his entreaty to go to Washington: "Gentlemen, if you want to hear any further testimony, you will have to get me to Washington soon, because it has something to do with you, Chief Warren. Do I sound sober enough to tell you this?"

Warren: "Yes, go right ahead."

Ruby: "I want to tell the truth, but I can't tell it here. Does that make sense to you?"

Warren replies that he really couldn't see why Ruby couldn't tell his story now, but before Ruby responds, Ruby, seeing an unfamiliar face in the room, asks: "What is your name?"

Warren Commission assistant counsel Joe Ball: "Joe Ball."

Warren: "Mr. Joe Ball. He is an attorney from Los Angeles who has been working for me."

Ruby to Ball: "Do you know Belli [Ruby's former lawyer who is not in the room]?"

Ball: "I know of him."

Ruby proceeds to refer to Warren, Congressman Ford, Sheriff Bill Decker, and several Warren Commission assistant counsels as "boys": "Boys, I am in a tough spot. I tell you that."

Ruby to Warren: "Chief Warren, your life is in danger in this city, do you know that?"

Warren: "No, I don't know that."

Ruby: "I would like to talk to you in private."

Warren: "You may do that when you finish your story."

Ruby: "I bet you haven't had a witness like me in your whole investigation, is that correct? . . . When are you going back to Washington?"

Warren: "Very shortly after we finish this hearing."

Ruby: "If you request me to go back to Washington with you right now, that couldn't be done, could it?"

Warren: "No, it could not be done. There are a good many things involved in that, Mr. Ruby."

Ruby, on the stand but cross-examining his questioner: "What are they?"

After Warren fails to satisfy Ruby with his answer, Ruby performs some excellent cross-examination of Warren, who as a former prosecutor undoubtedly had never been cross-examined by a witness before.

Ruby: "You said you have the power to do what you want to do, is that correct?"

Warren: "Exactly."

Ruby: "Without any limitations?"

Warren: "Within the purview of the executive order which established the Commission."

Ruby: "But you don't have a right to take a prisoner back with you when you want to?"

Warren, on the ropes: "No. We have the power to subpoena witnesses to Washington if we want to do it, but we have taken the testimony of 200 or 300 people here in Dallas without going to Washington."

Ruby, keeping Warren on the ropes: "Yes, but those people aren't Jack Ruby."

Warren, beat down by his witness and conceding defeat: "No, they weren't."

Ruby finally levels with Warren in a rambling, at times incoherent story as to why he wanted to say what he had to say only if he were taken to Washington. He starts out by stating, "Gentlemen, my life is in danger here . . . I may not live tomorrow to give any further testimony," implying that if he told the truth in Dallas he might be killed, but then in a disconnect, he fizzles out by saying that the reason he wanted to go to Washington is that his story has to be said "amongst people of the highest authority [he indicates later, President Johnson] that would give me the benefit of [the] doubt. And following that, immediately give me the lie detector test." He later returns to his paranoia and broadens the number of those in danger. "I tell you, gentlemen, my whole family is in jeopardy [though he suggests all three of his sisters are already "lost"] . . . Naturally, I am a foregone conclusion . . . My brothers Sam, Earl, Hyman . . . my in-laws . . . they are in jeopardy of loss of their lives . . . Does that sound serious enough to you, Chief Justice Warren?"

He maligns his lawyers for not letting him (presumably at his trial before the jury) tell "the truth about Jack Ruby and his emotional breakdown. Of why that Sunday morning—that thought never entered my mind prior to that Sunday morning when I took it upon myself to try to be a martyr . . . you might say. But I felt very emotional and very carried away for Mrs. Kennedy, that with all the strife she had gone through, . . . that someone owed it to our beloved president that she shouldn't be expected to come back to face trial of this heinous crime. And I have never had the chance to tell that, to back it up, to prove it. Consequently, right at the moment I am being victimized as a part of a plot . . . At this moment, Lee Harvey Oswald isn't guilty of committing the crime of assassinating President Kennedy. Jack Ruby is . . . There is an organization here [in Dallas], Chief Justice Warren, if it takes my life at this moment to say it, and Bill Decker said be a man and say it, there is a John Birch Society right now in activity . . . Take it for what it is worth, Chief Justice Warren. Unfortunately for me, for me giving the people the opportunity to get in power, because of the act I committed, has put a lot of people in jeopardy with their lives. Don't register with you, does it?"

Warren: "No, I don't understand that."

Ruby: "Would you rather I just delete what I said and just pretend that nothing is going on? . . . I won't be living long now. I know that. My family's lives will be gone . . . Saturday I watched Rabbi Seligman. Any of you watch it that Saturday morning? He . . . eulogized that here is a man that fought in every battle, went to every country, and had to come back to his own country to be shot in the back." Ruby starts to cry. "I must be a great actor. I tell you that. That created a tremendous emotional feeling for me, the way [Seligman] said that . . .

"Sunday morning [I] saw a letter to Caroline, two columns . . . The most heartbreaking letter . . . Alongside that letter . . . was a small comment in the newspaper . . . that Mrs. Kennedy may have to come back for the trial of Lee Harvey Oswald. That caused me to go like I did . . . I don't know, Chief Justice, but I got so carried away. And I remember prior to that thought, there has never been another thought in my mind. I was never malicious toward this person.* No one requested me to do anything. I never spoke to anyone about attempting to do anything. No subversive organization gave me any idea.

---

*In his torrent of words, Ruby obviously misspoke here, from the context probably meaning that prior to this thought of killing Oswald on Sunday morning he had no previous thought to kill him. This likelihood is further increased by Ruby's being notorious for misusing words. *Malicious* doesn't mean an intent to kill, but *malice aforethought*, a term most lay people have heard, does, and this could have been the source of Ruby's incorrect selection of the word *malicious*. Of course, there is also the possibility that Ruby wasn't confused at all, and in his mind, the further back in time his hatred for Oswald and decision to kill him commenced (i.e., Friday afternoon), the more likely he'd get the death penalty because of the longer premeditation.

No underworld person made any effort to contact me. It all happened that Sunday morning."[*]

Ruby speaks about driving downtown to send the money order to the stripper in his club, but first stopping in Dealey Plaza to see the wreaths "and I saw them and started to cry again." He then "walked . . . from the Western Union to the ramp. I didn't sneak in . . . There was an officer . . . talking to a Sam Pease in a car parked up on the curb . . . There was no one near me when I walked down that ramp . . . and there was the person that—I wouldn't say I saw red—it was a feeling I had for our beloved President and Mrs. Kennedy, that he was insignificant to what my purpose was." He says that since he had just left the Western Union a few minutes earlier, "you wouldn't have time enough to have any conspiracy . . . as it was told about me. I realize it is a terrible thing I have done, and it was a stupid thing, but I was just carried away emotionally. Do you follow that?"

Warren: "Yes, I do indeed, every word."

Ruby: "I had the gun in my right hip pocket, and impulsively, if that is the correct word here, I saw him, and that is all I can say. And I didn't care what happened to me."

Addressing himself to the allegation that he called mob figures in the days before he killed Oswald, he says, "I knew persons of notorious backgrounds years ago in Chicago. I was with the union back in Chicago, and I left the union when I found out the notorious organization had moved in there . . . Then recently, I had to make so many numerous calls that I am sure you know of . . . because of trying to survive in my business. My unfair competition had been running certain shows [in violation of] all the rules of the union . . . and consequently I was becoming insolvent because of it. All those calls were made . . . in relation to seeing if they can help out with the American Guild of Variety Artists . . . Every person I . . . called, and sometimes you may not even know a person intimately, you sort of tell them, well, you are stranded down here and you want some help—if they know of any official of the American Guild of Variety Artists to help me. Because my competitors were putting me out of business. I even flew to New York to see Joe Glazer, and he called Bobby Faye. He was the national president. That didn't help . . . All these phone calls were related not in any way . . . with the underworld because I have been away from Chicago 17 years down in Dallas. As a matter of fact I even called a Mr.—hold it before I say it—[He] . . . headed the American Federation of Labor . . . in the state of Texas . . . Miller. Is there a Deutsch I. Maylor? I called a Mr. Maylor here in Texas to see if he could help me out."

After Ruby denies knowing Oswald, he speaks of his close friend "Mr. McWillie," a gambler. "He is a pretty nice boy, and I happened to be idolizing him." McWillie, he says, was a "key man" at the Tropicana nightclub and casino in Havana that was owned by "the Fox brothers" from "Miami, Florida." He says McWillie was always asking him to visit him in Havana. He says McWillie finally sent him some tickets and he visited McWillie in Havana but Ruby says he "was bored with the gambling because I don't gamble." He speaks of McWillie calling him from Havana once to try to get "four little cobra guns" from a local gun seller, Ray Brantley, who owned Ray's Hardware, and who knew McWillie, because he felt uneasy with Castro's new regime and wanted protection. Ruby

[*]This was not the first time Ruby said he acted alone in killing Oswald. He told the FBI on the very day he killed Oswald that he was not involved in any conspiracy with anyone, that no one asked him or suggested to him that he shoot Oswald (Hall [C. Ray] Exhibit No. 2, 20 H 44). On December 21, 1963, he told the FBI, "I told no one I was going to kill him. No one knew I was going to shoot him. I didn't discuss anything with anyone about shooting him" (Hall [C. Ray] Exhibit No. 3, 20 H 57).

says he called Brantley and asked him to send the guns to McWillie, saying he didn't know if this was illegal (Warren said he didn't either), and says Brantley later denied that Ruby called him, Ruby believing he did this because perhaps it was illegal.

Ruby again returns in his virtual monologue, without transition, to the John Birch Society, saying it was trying to make people believe he was in on the plot to kill Kennedy, and when Warren asks him "what basis" he has for saying this, Ruby says, "Just a feeling of it." Later, he says, "I am as innocent regarding any conspiracy as any of you gentlemen in the room," and returning to his past association in Chicago with criminal types, he says he was "in the livelihood of selling tickets to sporting events," and in doing this, "your lucrative patrons are some of these people, but you don't mean anything to those people. You may know them as you get acquainted with them at the sporting events or the ballpark . . . the prizefights . . . So when I say I know them . . . personalities that are notorious, that is the extent of my involvement in any criminal activity. I have never been a bookmaker. I have never stolen for a living. I am not a gangster . . . I don't know any subversive people that are against my beloved country."

When Warren asks Congressman Ford, "Congressman, do you have anything further?" Ruby pipes in, "You can get more out of me. Let's not break up too soon."

Ruby once again returns to the "very powerful" John Birch Society, saying that "through certain falsehoods said about me to other people, the John Birch Society, I am as good as guilty as the accused assassin of President Kennedy," suggesting the Birch Society was doing this because he was of the "Jewish faith." He says he wished "President Lyndon Johnson would . . . hear me, not accept just circumstantial facts about my guilt or innocence . . . before he relinquished certain powers to these certain people." When Warren says he has no idea what Ruby is talking about, Ruby says, "I want to say this to you. The Jewish people are being exterminated at this moment. Consequently, a whole new form of government is going to take over our country, and I know I won't live to see you another time . . . I am used as a scapegoat and there is no greater weapon that you can use to create some falsehood about some[one] of the Jewish faith, especially at the terrible heinous crime such as the killing of President Kennedy . . . It may not be too late . . . if our president, Lyndon Johnson, knew the truth from me. But if I am eliminated, there won't be any way of knowing . . . I am the only one that can bring out the truth to our president . . . But he has been told, I am certain, that I was a part of a plot to assassinate the president." Ruby says that if the president and his people learn the truth from him, "maybe my people won't be tortured and mutilated." The president had to learn, Ruby says, "why I was down in that basement Sunday morning, and maybe some sense of decency will come out . . . without my people going through torture and mutilation."

Warren: "The president will know everything you have said."

Ruby: "But I won't be around, Chief Justice, . . . to verify these things."

Ruby's attorney, Joe Tonahill: "Who do you think is going to eliminate you, Jack?"

Ruby: "I have been used for a purpose, and there will be a certain tragic occurrence happening if you don't take my testimony and somehow vindicate me so my people don't suffer because of what I have done."

Warren: "But we *have* taken your testimony. We have it here. It will be in permanent form for the president of the United States . . . and for the people of the entire world. It will be recorded for all to see. That is the purpose of our coming here today."

Ruby: "All I want is a lie detector test and you refuse to give it to me . . . And then I want to leave this world. But I don't want my people to be blamed for something that is untrue." Ruby asks Warren, "When are you going to see the president?"

Warren answers that he has no appointment scheduled but he'll tell the president what Ruby said when he sees him.

Ruby: "How do you know if the facts I stated about everything I said . . . are the truth or not?"

Warren responds that the polygraph test might answer that question.

Ruby says that when Warren leaves town, "I am finished. My family is finished," later repeating, "There was no conspiracy" and "All I want to do is tell the truth, and the only way you can know it is by the polygraph."

Warren: "That we will do for you."[486]

Warren would later say that Ruby was "clearly delusional" and refer to him as "the poor fellow," adding, "I really felt sorry for him, very sorry for him."[487]

The next month, July 18, 1964, in Dallas, Ruby was administered the polygraph test he so fervently wanted by the polygraph expert from the FBI lab in Washington, Bell P. Herndon.*

Completely apart from the issue of how accurate a polygraph test is, most lay people, as I imagine was the case with Ruby, believe it can detect a liar. No one asked Ruby to take a polygraph test, so the argument cannot be made that he went along with it because he felt he would look guilty if he refused. It was Ruby who insisted he be given the test, and although this is not conclusive, it very definitely is circumstantial evidence of his innocence on the issue of whether he knew Oswald and whether he acted alone. The following are among the questions Ruby was asked, in no discernible pattern, each of which concerns an issue one or more conspiracy theorists have raised: "Did you shoot Oswald because of any influence of the underworld?" (Ruby's answer: "No"); "Did any long-distance calls which you made before the assassination of the president have anything to do with the assassination?" ("No"); "Did you know the Officer Tippit who was killed?" ("No"); "Did you ever meet with Oswald and Officer Tippit at your club?" ("No"); "Were you at the Parkland Hospital at any time on Friday?" ("No"); "Did you know Oswald before November 22, 1963?" ("No"); "Did you assist Oswald in the assassination?" ("No"); "Did you shoot Oswald to silence him?" ("No"); "Did you talk with any Dallas police officers on Sunday, November 24, prior to the shooting of Oswald?" ("No"); "Did you walk past the guard at the time Lieutenant Pierce's car was parked on the ramp exit?" ("Yes"); "Were you on the sidewalk at the time Lieutenant Pierce's car stopped on the ramp exit?" ("Yes"); "To your knowledge, did any of your friends or did you telephone the FBI in Dallas between 2 or 3 a.m. Sunday morning?" ("No"); "Is everything you told the Warren Commission the entire truth?" ("Yes"); "Was your trip to Cuba solely for pleasure?" ("Yes"); "Did you shoot Oswald in order to

---

*Before the test was administered to Ruby, his lawyer, Joe Tonahill, said on the record that "when I entered the defense of Jack Ruby back in December of 1963 with Mr. Belli, at that time we insisted before undertaking his defense that he agree to a polygraph test and truth serum test or any other scientific test that would reflect whether or not there was a connection between him and Lee Harvey Oswald or in any respect a conspiracy. He agreed and insisted at that time that there was no such conspiracy . . . [and] he did not know Lee Harvey Oswald and there was no connection between them and that he would undertake any type of a scientific test that we could have made available for him. Jack Ruby has insisted on those tests ever since. We have from time to time proposed to the FBI . . . that a lie detector test be given Mr. Ruby. We have filed motions to obtain scientific tests" (14 H 507, WCT Jack L. Ruby).

save Mrs. Kennedy the ordeal of a trial?" ("Yes"); "Did you first decide to kill Oswald on Sunday morning?" ("Yes").[488]

Herndon concluded that "based on the hypothesis that Ruby was mentally competent and sound, the charts could be interpreted . . . to indicate that there was no area of deception present with regard to his response to the relevant questions during the polygraph examination."[489]

Of course, the hypothesis of mental competence on Ruby's part is a problematic one. Dr. William Beavers, who attended the polygraph session, later testified that he saw Ruby nine or ten times up to a month before the session, and concluded that Ruby was suffering from "psychotic depression" with evidence of "auditory hallucinations" and a "definite delusional system." At the time of the polygraph test, he felt Ruby's depression had diminished but he had become more delusional. Despite this, the psychiatrist said, "in the greater proportion of the time that he answered questions, I felt he was aware of the questions and that he understood them, and that he was giving answers based on an appreciation of reality." However, he felt there was little question on the part of himself and three other psychiatrists who examined Ruby that Ruby was "mentally ill" and should be in a mental hospital, not a prison.[490]

During the polygraph examination, as was always the situation with Ruby, there were the sadly humorous incidents. In one, Ruby asks his polygrapher (Herndon), "Do I sound like a man with an unsound mind to you?" and Herndon, instead of responding with the almost obligatory and civil "no," says, "I'm not qualified to answer that question." At another point Ruby asks Herndon, "Have I been evading any of your questions?" After Herndon says he's been most cooperative, Ruby says, "But you can't tell how I stand, can you?" When Herndon says it will take him time to analyze the charts back in Washington, Ruby asks if he "will still be around when the answers come back," and he is assured he will.

And in a situation that could rise to the dignity of a sick skit or cartoon, Dallas assistant district attorney Bill Alexander, the prosecutor who had asked for and gotten a sentence of death against Ruby so he could "fry" Ruby at Huntsville, Texas, was one of ten people in the room, and the one whom Ruby was the friendliest with. Ruby actually asked Alexander's assistance in helping to frame the questions, and at one point had a private three-minute conference with him, the two of them referring to each other throughout the several-hour session as "Jack" and "Bill." At another point, Ruby says to his own lawyer, Joe Tonahill, "Joe, I'd appreciate it if you weren't in the room. Can I ask you to leave, Joe? . . . I prefer Bill to you."

Tonahill responds, "Let the record show that Mr. Ruby says he prefers Bill Alexander being here, . . . who is the assistant district attorney who asked that a jury give him the death sentence, to myself, who asked the jury to acquit him, his attorney."[491]

The pitiable Jack Ruby depicted on these pages is the same Jack Ruby whom conspiracy theorists throughout the years have consistently referred to as an important criminal associate of the national syndicate, the Mafia, and someone whom the Mafia ultimately chose to silence Oswald and extricate it from its biggest problem ever. Just a few examples from the conspiracy community: "Ruby was a pivotal contact man for criminal activity in Dallas" and was "closely connected to the mob."[492] "Ruby had known all along what he had to do: silence Lee Harvey Oswald forever . . . In the Mafia, if you are ordered to kill someone, and you refuse to carry out the order, you pay for your refusal with your life."[493] "Jack Ruby was a Mafia operative . . . Oswald was shot [by Ruby] to silence him."[494] "Jack Ruby . . . handled syndicate interests in Dallas."[495] "The murder of Lee Harvey Oswald by Jack Ruby had all of the earmarks of a gangland slaying."[496] "Ruby had been Chicago's 'man in Dallas' for years, running strip joints, gambling rackets, and narcotics for the Outfit . . . As the person representing the Outfit in Dallas, the task had quite naturally fallen to Ruby to silence Oswald."[497] Alleging that the Mafia was behind Kennedy's murder, author David Scheim says that "the star of Oswald's murder contract was the long-time Dallas mobster and police fixer, Jack Ruby."[498]

It is very noteworthy that without exception, *not one of these conspiracy theorists knew or had ever met Jack Ruby*. Without our even resorting to his family and roommate, all of whom think the suggestion of Ruby being connected to the mob is ridiculous, *those who knew him*, unanimously and without exception, think the notion of his being connected to the Mafia, and then killing Oswald for them, is nothing short of laughable.

As we have seen, Ruby wasn't a member or even an associate of organized crime. To supplement what has already been written in the biography of Ruby, Ruby's roots were in Chicago, and few knew more about the mob in Chicago than Lenny Patrick, the "Jewish capo" of the Chicago mob suspected of being behind many of the "Outfit's" murders in Chicago. Right after Ruby killed Oswald, the late William Roemer, the senior FBI agent assigned to investigate organized crime in Chicago, contacted Patrick, whom he had hounded for years. Patrick, Roemer said, "was a very personable guy, except that he had killed six people." Roemer said that Patrick was not a mob informant for the FBI, but Roemer added, "I had done a big favor for Lenny, so I could talk to him." Patrick told Roemer that he knew Ruby and that Ruby wasn't a part of organized crime in Chicago, going on to call Ruby unstable and unreliable. Of course, if the mob had Ruby kill Kennedy, Patrick couldn't be expected to tell Roemer the truth. But Roemer knew Patrick well and said that what Patrick told him "was convincing" to him.[499]

Jack Clark, an investigative consultant for the Chicago Police Department, told ABC in 2003, "I knew Sparky in the 40s and 50s. He was in all the gymnasiums with all the boxers. It was *well* known that Jack Ruby was *meshuga*—that Jack wasn't playing with a full deck. He was a nice guy, but he just wasn't playing with a full deck." As to whether he had ties with organized crime in Chicago, Clark said, "The Chicago mob had nothing to do with Jack Ruby. Jack Ruby was working with the rag-tag guys, on the street, downtown Chicago. Some of them were bookmakers. They were just guys who made a buck through their wit or charm. But they were not gangsters."[500]

Luis Kutner, a Chicago lawyer who knew Ruby from Ruby's Chicago days, before Ruby moved to Dallas, told investigators for the HSCA that Ruby was "the type of person who was always seeking out someone who was in the limelight" and that "Jack Ruby had no connection with organized crime other than his mouth."[501]

Janet Conforto ("Jada"), Ruby's headline stripper at the Carousel, had all types of problems with Ruby over the high wages she was supposed to receive, but, as noted earlier, acknowledged that she was unaware of any association he had with members of the underworld, though she said he'd like to say, "I know all the boys," an apparent reference to racketeers.[502] If you were trying to prove Ruby's connection to organized crime, how much could you deposit in the bank with that type of remark, particularly from a braggart like Ruby, who, after one short conversation with DA Henry Wade at police headquarters on the night of the assassination, was telling people later in the evening that

Wade was his "friend." But of course Ruby, particularly because he came from the wrong side of the tracks in Chicago and operated a strip joint in Dallas, did know members of the mob, like Dallas mob boss Joe Civello. But again, so did Frank Sinatra, Dean Martin, and Sammy Davis. It means nothing at all. The only thing that means anything is whether he was a mobster himself. And Ruby was not. In fact, former Ruby prosecutor Bill Alexander says Ruby "wasn't even a common criminal. He didn't steal. He didn't pimp. He wasn't a drunk. Jack wasn't a lawbreaker."[503]

During the HSCA testimony of Jack Revill, a detective in charge of the criminal intelligence section of the Dallas Police Department at the time of the assassination, counsel asked, "Did you have any knowledge of Jack Ruby's associations with any gamblers or anyone else involved with illegal activity?"

Revill: "Jack Ruby was the type of person who would have been *acquainted* with persons involved in gambling activities and other criminal activities, but as far as Jack Ruby being actively engaged or a member of any groups, no, nothing to indicate this."

Question: "What was your personal impression of Jack Ruby?"

Revill: "Jack Ruby was a buffoon. He liked the limelight. He was highly volatile. He liked to be recognized with people, and I would say this to this committee: if Jack Ruby was a member of organized crime, then the personnel director of organized crime should be replaced."[504]

Bert Shipp, the assistant news director for Dallas's WFAA-TV (Channel 8) around the time of the assassination, knew Ruby well and had a similar assessment: "The Mafia wouldn't have trusted Jack Ruby to take change to the bank . . . I've talked to two guys that were pretty high up in [local organized crime], and they laugh when you talk to them about Jack Ruby . . . being part of the mob, the Mafia."[505] In other words, the mob didn't get to be as successful as it was by trusting someone like Jack Ruby.*

Hugh Aynesworth, a *Dallas Morning News* reporter at the time of the assassination who had more firsthand knowledge about the participants in the assassination drama than any other reporter, and writes about them well in his book, *JFK: Breaking the News*, knew Ruby because he'd see him around town whenever anything was happening. "My goodness," Aynesworth said, "I even saw him at a restaurant fire, a police raid. How he'd find out about these things, I don't know, but he'd be there." At the suggestion that Ruby was a member of organized crime, Aynesworth laughs. "Mafia guys aren't talkers," he says. "Ruby, if he found out anything he thought was important, he'd tell someone else about it within one block. Jack was the type of guy, if he was at a fire, he'd run two or three blocks to tell people there was a fire."[506] Aynesworth sums up Ruby this way: "Jack Ruby was the quintessential wannabe but never-was." He was "full of big stories, bigger dreams and lusty braggadocio."[507]

If Ruby's sieve-like mouth made him someone the mob wouldn't conspire to birdwatch with, he "made up for it," as the expression goes, by being so volatile and emotional. As a friend of Ruby's, one who had known him for over fifteen years, said, he couldn't "plan anything in advance" because he "couldn't concentrate on one topic for more than five minutes."[508]

---

*Though he did not personally know Ruby, Ralph Salerno, the chief consultant to the HSCA on organized crime who spent twenty years with the New York Police Department investigating the Mafia, told the HSCA, "Jack Ruby cannot be characterized as an organized crime figure in any way in my estimation. Jack Ruby would not have made a pimple on the back of the neck of a real organized crime figure" (5 HSCA 464).

Rabbi Hillel E. Silverman, who knew Ruby and his sister Eva for about ten years prior to the assassination and visited him two or three times a week when Ruby was in custody, described Ruby as a "simple and shallow, yet eccentric and unbalanced man" of little intelligence and education. "I think I know Jack Ruby well enough to say," Silverman said, "that he was not a member of any organized criminal element, and I find it inconceivable that he conspired with anyone to kill Oswald," adding that he felt confident that Ruby's decision to kill Oswald was a "spur-of-the-moment act."[509]

Elmer Gertz, one of Ruby's main appellate lawyers who succeeded in securing a reversal of Ruby's death sentence for murdering Oswald, and later wrote a book, *Moment of Madness: The People vs. Jack Ruby*, referred to Ruby as "an undisciplined man-child," and says, "Ruby was a compulsive talker," and "if he were involved in a conspiracy, in five minutes the whole world would know it."[510]

Emmett Colvin, another of Ruby's criminal appellate lawyers, said the notion that Ruby was a hit man for organized crime when he killed Oswald was "ludicrous. Jack Ruby was a pitiful man. Having practiced law since 1942, I am well aware of the characteristics of a hit man. These are cold, calculating people. This cannot be equated to Jack Ruby."[511]

Bill Alexander, who we know prosecuted Ruby for Oswald's murder, had known Jack for years, though he had never socialized with him. He said, "It's funny that I'd be in a position of defending Ruby, but Ruby has been maligned and besmirched for years with these mob allegations by people who are just not in possession of the facts." He told me that in all his years as a part of Dallas law enforcement, "I never heard anyone say that Ruby had any association with organized crime, or was involved in any kind of organized criminal activity. I can tell you that with all the scrutiny he was under because of the clubs he was operating, if he'd have been involved with the mob or doing anything bad, Dallas police intelligence would have picked up on it." When I asked Alexander about the age-old assertion that the mob got Ruby to silence Oswald for them, Alexander, who rarely laughs, couldn't resist laughing. "The mob," he said, "would not have let Ruby within five miles of one of their meetings because he was an extroverted blabbermouth."[512]

Tony Zoppi, for years the entertainment columnist for the *Dallas Morning News*, who knew Ruby very well and said, "We were really good friends," also laughs at the notion that Ruby was connected to organized crime. "It is so ludicrous to believe that Ruby was part of the mob. The conspiracy theorists want to believe everybody but those who really knew him."[513]

As indicated earlier, who could have possibly known Jack Ruby, warts and all, as much as the cocktail waitresses and strippers at his club who worked with him and were exposed to his personality seven nights a week? "Jack's girls" both loved and hated him, with a lot more love than hate. Two of his strippers, Diana Hunter and Alice Anderson, speaking for themselves as well as, they knew, for the others, wrote, "We believe we knew Jack Ruby better than anybody else, including all those experts who tried so hard to analyze him from the day he committed his notorious crime until the day he died more than three years afterward . . . And we're as sure as we can be that Jack Ruby . . . was not part of any conspiracy."[514]

In addition, those on the wrong side of the law in Dallas referred to Jack as a "fink"[515] because he gave information to the Dallas Police Department on criminal activity he learned about. Dallas police detective Joe Cody, who used to ice-skate with Ruby from time to time, said that Ruby was "very cooperative" with the Dallas Police Department, and on "several cases" passed on information "that resulted in arrests."[516] "People in Dallas . . . knew Ruby was a snitch," Zoppi says. "The word was on the street that you couldn't trust him because he was telling the cops everything. You have to be crazy to think any-body would have trusted Ruby to be part of the mob."[517]

Seth Kantor, author of *The Ruby Cover-Up*, writes, "Ruby was an informer on every different police level there was. He fed tips to . . . the Dallas police force regularly. He met in Dallas with two Chicago detectives to provide them information less than three months before the Kennedy assassination."[518]

Indeed, and please get this, during the Kefauver Committee hearings (named after its chairman, U.S. Senator Estes Kefauver from Tennessee) investigating organized crime in 1950, Ruby actually contacted his lawyer friend from Chicago, Luis Kutner, who had become a staff attorney for the Kefauver Committee, and volunteered to testify as a wit-ness *against* the mob. And although he was unable to furnish the Senate committee with any information of real value, he traveled to Chicago from Dallas when the committee was there and met with Rudolph Halley, who was the chief counsel for the committee, and George Robinson, one of his investigators.[519] With Ruby's background of wanting to testify against the mob, to think it would come to him after Oswald killed Kennedy and say, "Jack, we got a little job for you," is high humor.

In addition to Ruby's being close to law enforcement, emotionally volatile and erratic in his behavior, and someone who couldn't keep a secret, all of which would automati-cally disqualify him as a Mafia hit man, we know that whomever the mob employed would be someone it knew was not virtually crazy, which Ruby was close to being. These are just a few of the observations about Ruby's mental condition from those who knew him. Stripper Janet Conforto said that "I don't think he is sane."[520] Ruby's prosecutor, Henry Wade, said, "No question Ruby had some loose cells in his brain."[521] At his trial Ruby was shown to have organic brain damage, and lay witnesses told the jury about their impressions of Ruby: The general manager of the parking lot next to the Carousel said he "sometimes" wondered "about Jack's sanity."[522] A close friend of Ruby's said he "was sure" that Ruby was "suffering from some form of . . . mental disturbance."[523] Edward Pullman, whose wife was employed by Ruby at the Carousel, said, "I realized that he was a very erratic person . . . I have seen him just haul off and lambast or hit someone without thinking twice . . . He was psycho . . . I mean, he was not right."[524] Just the type of hit man the mob would hire to commit the second biggest murder in its history, a man it could have total confidence in.

To repeat, to think that organized crime would come to someone of Ruby's background and ask him to murder Oswald for them is worse than a bad joke, particularly when there's not the tiniest speck of evidence that they did so.

If Ruby didn't kill Oswald for the mob, just why did he kill Oswald? Rabbi Silverman summed it up this way: "He [Ruby] did this in a fit of anger and passion. He was a great patriot and he thought he was doing a great favor for the people of the United States. He was doing justice, Texas justice, to a terrible man who had shot his beloved president."[525]

Two of Ruby's brothers also mentioned the "patriotic" motivation. "Our brother did this for only one reason—he's a good, patriotic American, and he got carried away," said Hyman Rubenstein.[526] Ruby's brother Earl said his brother was "almost aggressively patri-otic."[527] "Jack was the most patriotic member of the family," Earl said, and he "was tremen-dously in favor of President Kennedy. He was a great admirer of the president. He thought he was a great guy."[528] Ruby's sister Eva, who knew Ruby the best, testified that her brother "didn't have" any attitude toward politics, but "if you said anything against" America or its leaders, "he would knock the hell out of you."

Question: "In other words, what you are saying to me is that if he has any kind of 'ism' at all, it would be Americanism?"

"That's right—he has that—he does have that—that's his greatest."[529]

Though there probably was a patriotic component to Ruby's act, most others who knew him put a little more of the emphasis on a more selfish motivation.

From his impression of Ruby, Dallas detective Jim Leavelle said he doubted that Ruby "had given what he did much thought, but I believe what thought he did give to it was that he would be a hero for what he did, and when his case was taken to the grand jury, he'd only get a slap on the wrist and told not to do it again. In his mind I think he saw himself standing at the front door of the Carousel Club and people would come from far and wide to shake the hand of the man who killed the president's assassin." Leavelle said the first time he met Ruby, at the Silver Spur in 1950, Ruby told him he had always wanted to see two police officers in a death struggle with someone "and I could jump in to the fight and save the officer's lives and be a hero."[530]

Not only did the chief prosecutor, Bill Alexander, believe that Ruby killed Oswald thinking he would become a hero, and argued this to the jury that convicted Ruby, but several members of the jury believed that was Ruby's chief motivation for the killing. (See Ruby trial section later in the book.) Dallas attorney Jim Martin, believed to be the first lawyer who saw Ruby when Ruby was taken into custody, said, "He never expected to spend a night in jail."[531] And Ruby's first lawyer, Tom Howard, told Captain Will Fritz he believed that Ruby probably felt that he would be a hero "and would be carried out on the shoulders of those present."[532] Among many others, Ruby's Dallas and Havana friend Lewis McWillie also believed Ruby thought he would become a national hero.[533] "I'm sure when he shot Oswald he thought this would make him a hero," said Carousel stripper Janet Conforto.[534] When Ruby's friend Breck Wall visited Ruby in jail, he said, "The first thing out of Jack's mouth was 'I'm a hero.' And that's what really floored me, because everyone was still in shock over what happened. And I told him, 'No, you're not.'"[535]

But of course Ruby's fabled temper (he was "completely uncontrollable when he was angry," said Conforto),[536] together with the deep love and respect he had for the president and his family, were more than contributing factors in Ruby's killing of Oswald. Without them, it is doubtful the motivation to be a hero would have been enough. When we tie all of these factors together (Ruby's sense of patriotism and deep affection for Kennedy, his desire to be a hero, his anger at Oswald for what he had done, etc.), "Ruby's killing of Oswald," I argued to the London jury, "has all the earmarks of a *very personal* killing completely devoid of any outside influence."[537] Looking at all the components making Jack Ruby who he was, Tammi True, one of Jack's strippers who knew him very well, said, "My first reaction [upon learning that Ruby had shot Oswald] was, if *anyone* in the world could have done that, it was Jack."[538]

I said earlier that the *only* people who believe Ruby was connected to organized crime and killed Oswald for the mob are those who didn't know Ruby. That is a true statement with one exception, which isn't strong at all, and it's from someone who probably hardly knew Ruby. Seth Kantor was a reporter for the *Dallas Times Herald* for a few years in the early 1960s and later wrote a book called *The Ruby Cover-Up*. When Kantor wrote in an article datelined Dallas, November 25, 1963, "In disbelief, I watched *a friend of mine*, Jack Ruby, gun to death the man charged with killing President Kennedy," his former *Times Herald* colleagues scoffed at his claim that Ruby had been a friend.[539] In the 450 pages of Kantor's book, the only thing he could say to establish his bona fides as someone who knew Ruby was "Ruby was someone I had known at the start of the Kennedy administration when I had been a reporter on a Dallas newspaper."[540] Per his testimony before the Warren Commission, that period of time was less than two years, "between September 1960 until May 1962."[541] So not only his brief time in Dallas but also his failure, in his book, to refer to any meaningful association with Ruby indicate that he was not really someone who "knew Jack Ruby." He probably saw Ruby a few times around town, as almost everyone did, and exchanged greetings with him. Moreover, Kantor doesn't expressly say in his book, as nearly all conspiracists who believe the mob was behind Kennedy's murder do, that Ruby *definitely* killed Oswald for the mob, although he comes very close: "the mob would have had no problem finding itself a Jack Ruby to silence Oswald. Ruby had been preparing most of his life for the job," and "the mob was Ruby's 'friend.' Ruby *could well have been* paying off an IOU the day he was used to kill Lee Harvey Oswald."[542]

The only example Kantor gives to show that Ruby had affirmatively done something *for* the mob and on its behalf is to say that Ruby had been "running errands for the mob one way or another since he was the 16 year old Chicago street fighter who delivered sealed envelopes for the Capone people and kept his mouth shut about it."[543] (What? He "kept his mouth shut about it"? This is clearly very loose writing.) So in Kantor's mind, if Ruby delivered a few sealed envelopes for the mob when he was a Chicago teenager, and kept his mouth shut about it, this one piece of "evidence" is enough to meet the burden of proof that Ruby may have murdered Oswald for the mob as just a normal progression? That, of course, is ridiculous, even if the sealed-envelope story is true. But we can't be sure of that either. How the story got started was when the former world boxing champion Barney Ross told the FBI in 1964 that in the mid-1920s he associated with a group of around twelve youths, among whom was Ruby, at the Kit Howard Gymnasium in Chicago. At the time, Ross said, Capone hadn't become famous and the kids didn't know he was a racketeer. Before they learned he was, which was around 1927, Capone, who would come by the gymnasium on occasion, would sometimes give one of the youths "a dollar to deliver an envelope to someone in the downtown section of Chicago." He said he believed Capone did this to make the youths think they were earning a dollar "in order to keep them from hanging around the streets." Ross said that whenever he ran such an errand for Capone, the envelope he carried "did not appear to contain anything"—that is, Capone had them delivering empty envelopes—and this stopped when the group learned that Capone was a big mobster. Moreover, he said that Ruby "might" have seen Capone at the gym and "might" have run, like him, errands for Capone, but he didn't know.[544]

And *this* is the support, the *only* support, Kantor gives for saying Ruby may have killed Oswald for the mob because he "had been preparing most of his life for the job."

But even if we consider Kantor to be an exception to the assertion that only those who did not know Ruby think he killed Oswald for the mob, let's look at how Kantor stood up on cross-examination at the London trial. Called by Gerry Spence as a defense witness who was supposedly the leading expert on Ruby, one who would connect Ruby to organized crime, Kantor gave testimony regurgitating all the old assertions about Ruby's mob contacts, phone calls to them on the days before the assassination, and so on. Because of time constraints, my questions to Kantor were necessarily abbreviated and rapid-fire. But by the end of it, most trial observers were asking whether Kantor was really a *defense* witness. A good portion of my cross-examination, omitting most transitional as well as preliminary questions, follows:

Q: Jack Ruby died January 3, 1967, from natural causes while in custody?

A: That's correct.

Q: You agree there was no evidence Jack Ruby and Lee Oswald knew each other?

A: I'm aware of that.

Q: [Assuming Kantor did, in fact, see Ruby at Parkland Hospital after the assassination, which Kantor maintained but the Warren Commission disputed, I asked this question.] At the hospital Ruby was in a state of emotional shock, is that correct?

A: That's correct.

Q: And did you learn that after the assassination Ruby was going from place to place, as his lawyer said, like a wild man?

A: Absolutely, sir.

Q: And when you saw Ruby at Parkland Hospital you thought it was perfectly normal to see him there because you described him as a goer to events, a man about town?[*]

A: Yes.

Q: And you wrote this about Ruby in your book, did you not: "When he liked you, he wanted to do anything and everything he could to help you. If he didn't like someone, he could curse them and fight them. He had a few arrests because of the passionate way he had expressed his feelings of dislike for people?"

A: Yes, I did.

Q: You also wrote Ruby was a very emotional man.

A: That's correct.

Q: Dr. Beavers, a psychiatrist appointed by the trial judge at Ruby's trial to examine Ruby, reported back to the judge that he found Ruby to be "acutely mentally ill," is that correct?

A: Yes.

Q: You are also aware that at Ruby's trial there was medical testimony that his electroencephalograms, to measure the electric activity of the brain, showed that he had organic brain damage?

A: Yes, I remember that.

Q: So you would agree, would you not, that Mr. Ruby was not a well man?

A: He might not fall within the pattern of the norm.

Q: You're aware of the three suicide attempts he made while in custody for the Oswald slaying?

A: Well, two come to mind.

Q: In one attempt he stood back about twenty feet, ran as hard as he could and rammed his head against the wall. Also, he tried to hang himself, and then electrocute himself?

A: I remember those.[†]

---

[*]At the trial, I had no time to go into the issue of whether Kantor was confusing seeing Ruby at Parkland with his seeing him elsewhere. Moreover, I was in no position to prove Kantor was wrong, so my questions assumed that Kantor had seen Ruby at Parkland.

[†]The ramming of his head against the wall on April 26, 1964, was not a little game Ruby was playing. He was knocked unconscious and had to be hospitalized. (HSCA Record 180-10113-10493, May 29, 1964) Ruby's

Q: Mr. Kantor, you would agree that Jack Ruby had a very deep affection for President Kennedy. There was all types of evidence for that?

A: Yes.

Q: In fact, Dr. Guttmacher, one of Ruby's psychiatrists, said that Ruby told him, quote, "I fell for that man," referring to the president?

A: That's correct.

Q: And Dr. Bromberg said that in talking to Ruby about the president, "Essentially it was the speech of a man in love with another man; it was love that passed beyond a rational appreciation of a great man." Wasn't that true?

A: That was the quote, yes.

Q: Ruby also told Bromberg he felt like—"This was the end of my life when the president died," is that correct?

A: That's correct.

Q: He also told Bromberg, "When the president died I felt like a nothing person. I was afraid I would crack up. Such a great man, and then to be snuffed out." Is that correct?

A: That's correct.

Q: And when you saw Jack Ruby at Parkland Hospital, he had tears in his eyes, is that correct?

A: Yes. He was obviously under emotional strain, yes.

Q: And he asked you at Parkland, "Should I close my clubs?" Is that correct?

A: Yes, he did.

Q: And that Saturday night, you actually went by one of his two clubs, the Carousel, and it was closed. Is that correct?

A: It was closed.

---

conviction for Oswald's murder thrust him into great despair, triggering a hastening of the mental degenerative process and causing him to lose all hope for a successful appeal and to not cooperate with his lawyers, who were seeking to reverse his conviction on appeal. To protect Ruby from himself, Sheriff Decker assigned two round-the-clock guards to watch over Ruby, who slept on a mattress on the bare floor, lights always shining directly on him. When his sister Eva would visit him, he would urge her to do away with herself because he said his whole family was in jeopardy. His visions of his brother Earl and his children being dismembered were so clear that Eva said that since she wasn't in daily contact with the rest of the family, she had "to sort of tell real lies, that I just got through talking" with them "and everything was okay." He also told her that "25 million Jews have been slaughtered" and sometimes he could hear planes overhead bombing the Jews, and also saw Jews being boiled in oil. (Belli with Carroll, *Dallas Justice*, pp.261–264; 14 H 471, WCT Eva Grant; Kantor, *Ruby Cover-Up*, pp.316–319)

Not everyone was convinced of the sincerity of Ruby's delusions. When he'd sometimes put his ear to the wall and say to his guards, "Shhh. Do you hear the screams? They are torturing the Jews again down in the basement," they would tell him, "O.K., Jack, cut the crap or we won't play cards with you anymore." (Wills and Demaris, *Jack Ruby*, pp. 255–256)

After Ruby's sentence of death, Ruby's lawyers had a psychiatrist, Dr. Louis Jolyon West, examine Ruby for them, and the judge, Judge Brown, assigned another psychiatrist (R. L. Stubblefield) to examine Ruby for the court. West's conclusion was that Ruby was "obviously psychotic" and "completely preoccupied with his delusions of persecution of the Jews," believing that "all the Jews in America were now being slaughtered" because "the president's assassination and its aftermath were now being blamed on him," a Jew. West was convinced Ruby was not feigning psychosis, giving several reasons, among which were that West doubted "that someone unfamiliar with technical psychiatry could play the part of a paranoid delusional psychotic person with such accuracy, consistency, and typical detail." Also, he said Ruby doesn't want "to go to a mental hospital . . . and violently rejects the idea that he is mentally ill," whereas "the true malingerer usually grasps eagerly" at such a diagnosis. Stubblefield agreed that Ruby had "an acute psychiatric illness" and also did not believe that he was feigning mental illness. (HSCA Record 180-10113-10493, May 29, 1964)

Q: You interviewed George Senator, who lived with Jack Ruby, shortly after the assassination and he told you that Ruby had been grieving over the president's death and had been crying and wept quite a bit, is that not true?

A: Yes.

Q: An employee of Ruby's, Andy Armstrong, told you Ruby cried heavily over the president's death, did he not?

A: That's what he said.

Q: And Ruby's sister Eva said that on the night of the assassination Ruby cried, and after he ate he went to the bathroom and threw up, is that correct?

A: That's right. He ate a lot of food.

Q: And then he later said he even felt worse than when his mother and father died?

A: He did.

Q: Jack Ruby was the type of man who liked to ingratiate himself with other people, is that right? Particularly those in authority, like the police?

A: Yes.

Q: He often used the term *love* to describe his feelings for the Dallas police?

A: That's what I understand.

Q: And many of them would stop by his club for free drinks?

A: They did.

Q: Are you aware that during the days after the assassination he brought sandwiches to the police, to the press, and to people at KLIF radio station in Dallas?

A: Yes, I am. That's correct.

Q: With respect to the Friday-night press conference that he was at, during which he stood on the table, he described his feelings to Dr. Bromberg this way: "I am above everybody. They can not move me," and Bromberg said Ruby "felt like a big guy and had a strong feeling of being in with the police, of being a right guy," do you recall that?

A: Yes, I do.

Q: So in summary you describe Ruby as kind of a town character whom most of the police and townspeople knew?

A: Yes, I described that.

Q: On the night of the assassination, at the police department, Ruby, of all things, was even setting up radio interviews for the district attorney, Henry Wade. Is that not true?

A: He did do that.

Q: He was also a publicity hound. Is that correct?

A: He was.

Q: He also had a bizarre relationship with his dogs, did he not?

A: I would say so, yes.

Q: Well, he had as many as ten dogs, one of whom he called Sheba, and Sheba was his wife, and the other nine were his children?

A: That's correct.

Q: And would he take them, particularly Sheba, wherever he went?

A: Yes, she traveled with him continually.

Q: In fact, Sheba waited patiently in his car while he went inside the police station and shot Oswald?

A: That's correct.

Q: Rabbi Silverman, who was Ruby's rabbi, and who knew him well, tells the story—and it's in your book—of Ruby suddenly crying over his dogs in the rabbi's presence and saying he was unmarried and all he had was his dogs, referring to Sheba as his wife and the other dogs as his children? Is that correct?

A: That is correct.

Q: Mr. Kantor, you agree, do you not—again I'm citing your book—that the general consensus of those like yourself who have studied Ruby was that Ruby thought he would be a hero to the world for having killed Oswald, a presidential assassin?

A: I'm certain of it, yes.

Q: In fact, at least at the beginning there was an outpouring of telegrams to him all praising him for what he had done and all praising him as a hero?

A: His attorney received many of those.

Q: In fact, he hired an agent to handle book and show business offers he anticipated would come his way?

A: He made inquiries.

Q: And he tried to get the operator of radio station KLIF in Dallas to publicize what he had done as the act of a national patriot, is that correct?

A: That is correct.

Q: Around the time of the assassination, Ruby was having a lot of trouble with two of his competitors, Abe and Barney Weinstein, who were staging amateur nights and cutting into Ruby's attendance at his club; and he was trying to get the union, the American Guild of Variety Artists, to stop the Weinsteins, and AGVA—that's the union—was not complying?

A: That's correct.

Q: So Ruby was making calls to people to help him, is that correct?

A: Well, I understand he was making those calls, yes.

Q: Well, his call to Barney Baker was to ask Baker for help with AGVA?

A: That's what Barney Baker said.

Q: Are you aware that the House Select Committee on Assassination investigated these same phone calls that you testified to on direct examination and concluded, "Testimony to the committee supported the conclusion that Ruby's phone calls were by and large related to his labor troubles." Is that correct?

A: Yes, that's correct.

Q: You're also aware that after a very comprehensive examination of Ruby's financial records, the House Select Committee uncovered no evidence that Ruby or members of his family profited from the killing of Oswald in any way, are you not?

A: I'm aware of that, yes.

On direct examination, Spence had established through Kantor that "Ruby was in bad trouble with the IRS and had been for some time, and his debt had come to a little more than $39,000." Spence then asked, "And do you know what money Ruby had just before the shooting?" Kantor said, "Well, on the afternoon of the shooting of President Kennedy, he turned up at his bank, the Merchants State Bank in Dallas, and a vice president of the bank, a William Cox, noted that Ruby was holding $7,000 in cash in his hands while he was standing in the line at the teller's cage. However, Mr. Ruby put none of this in his account." Spence dropped the matter at this point and went on to other questions.

Continuing my cross-examination of Kantor:

Q: Now, about Ruby having a lot of cash on him on the day of the assassination—Seth, you've been honest with me over the phone—do you feel you painted an accurate picture for the jury on the significance of the money he had that day?

A: Well, I interviewed the vice president of the bank, and that's what he told me.

Q: To save time, because I don't think you painted quite the picture that you wanted to, on page 62 of your book you say, "'Jack always carried a large roll of cash,' remembers Bill Cox, then the loan officer of the bank. 'He would just come into the bank to make change for the club,' said Cox, who vividly remembers Ruby standing in line at a teller's cage on the afternoon of November 22, after Kennedy was slain. 'Jack was standing there crying and he had about $7,000 in cash on him on the day of the assassination. He and I talked and I warned him that he'd be knocked in the head one day carrying all that cash on him. I was concerned because *it was common for Ruby to walk in and out of the bank with large amounts of money on him.* Armed bandits watch patterns like that.'"*

Q: Do you think you conveyed that picture to the jury on direct examination?

A: Well, if you're helping me, I appreciate it.

Q: Mr. Kantor, are you implying to this jury that by Ruby saying in his testimony before the Warren Commission that he had something to say and wanted to go to Washington, that he was referring to a conspiracy? Are you implying that to this jury?

A: I hope that I'm implying that Jack Ruby was maintaining that he had more information to reveal, yes.

Q: How could you possibly say that, Mr. Kantor, when in the same identical testimony of Mr. Ruby before the Warren Commission, he specifically and expressly said that no one else was involved with him. Let me read you his testimony on this point, Mr. Kantor. Pages 198 to 199, volume 5: "I never spoke to anyone about attempting to do anything. No subversive organization gave me any idea. No underworld person made any effort to contact me. It all happened that Sunday morning." Correct?

A: Those are his words. Yes. I understand, yes.

Q: All right. Page 204 of his testimony: "I am as innocent regarding any conspiracy as any of you gentlemen in the room." Page 212: "There was no conspiracy." So we know, Mr. Kantor, that when Jack Ruby was talking to the chief justice about going to Washington, he had to have been talking about something other than a conspiracy?

A: I don't agree with that, sir.

Q: So, in other words, you think he's telling the chief justice, "Chief Justice, I acted

---

*It is not 100 percent certain that the incident described by Cox took place on the afternoon of the assassination, although a situation similar to the one Cox describes (absent Ruby's crying) may have taken place at some previous time. The citation Kantor gives for this incident is an interview he had with Cox in Dallas on August 3, 1976, thirteen years after the assassination. But a very detailed chronology and reconstruction by the HSCA of all of Ruby's known movements on the afternoon of the assassination, anchored by many witnesses and phone records, does not show any visit by Ruby to any bank on that afternoon (9 HSCA 1099–1100, 1102–1105).

Indeed, it's not certain that this incident (like countless other incidents in the case) ever took place. To me, it doesn't have a ring of truth to it. For starters, since Cox apparently never told Kantor that he asked Ruby, or that Ruby volunteered the information, how would Cox know the exact or even approximate amount of currency Ruby was holding in his hands? And why would Ruby be holding all this currency in his hands in the first place, particularly since he didn't deposit any of it? Moreover, what was Ruby doing in line in the first place? Merchants State Bank records showed that the only activity on the Carousel Club's account that day was a $31.87 withdrawal by check to pay a city water bill. (*Dallas Morning News*, October 12, 1978, p.16A)

alone. No one was involved with me. Please take my word. But I want to go to Washington to tell you that someone else was involved?"

A: Well, I believe that that is quite possible. For one thing, one of his early attorneys, a man named Joe Tonahill, from Jasper, Texas, told me that he was positive that the room was bugged, that Ruby's words were being carried elsewhere, and that it was not a safe place for Ruby to be.

Q: Tonahill didn't know that, but he suspected the room was bugged?

A: That's correct.

Q: But if by Ruby saying he wanted to go to Washington he meant he was going to implicate some conspirators, and the conspirators would obviously know what he meant, then Ruby would not have been safe in Dallas either, is that correct?

A: I'm not sure that he felt safe in Dallas as it was.

Q: Yet he died of natural causes over two years later. Is that correct?

A: Yes, sir.

Q: Did Mr. Ruby ever say or imply why he wanted to go to Washington and see the president? Did he ever say why to anyone?

A: No, *he didn't say he wanted to see the president.*

I proceeded to read Ruby's testimony about the John Birch Society. I then read this from his testimony: "And I wish that our president, Lyndon Johnson, would have delved deeper into the situation, *hear me*, not to accept just circumstantial facts about my guilt or innocence. I want to say this to you. The Jewish people are being exterminated at this moment. Consequently, a whole new form of government is going to take over our country, and I know I won't live to see you another time. It may not be too late, whatever happens, *if our President Lyndon Johnson knew the truth from me.* But if I am eliminated, there won't be any way of knowing."

Q: Isn't it clear, Mr. Kantor, that in Mr. Ruby's scrambled and deteriorating mind, he felt the John Birch Society was accusing him of being involved in the murder of President Kennedy, and because of it, the Jewish people were being exterminated, and he wanted to go to Washington and tell the president himself to stop this genocide. Isn't that kind of obvious from this?

A: That comes across, yes.

Q: But you forgot about that?

A: My own question is no. [*sic*]

Q: I want to read a quote from your book, Mr. Kantor, and then ask you if you meant these words. "Ruby was, as his mother had been, an incessant talker. He was brash and mercurial and never would have been trusted with knowledge of any plot to silence Oswald that would cause him to wind up in the arms of the police." I take it you meant those words?

A: I meant them.

Kantor went on to say that if the mob had approached Ruby to kill Oswald, Ruby "would have bragged about it" to others.

My allotted time had run out, but there was no need to ask any further questions anyway.[545]

Since I couldn't have gotten more out of Kantor than if I had called him as a prosecution witness,[*] Spence, to mitigate the damage done by his own witness's answers on cross, started his redirect examination of Kantor:

> Q: Well, you are probably the politest witness we've had, and I give you that. And I appreciate that. But the jury may have been misled by your answers, because what you were being read was a series of questions, a series of statements out of your book that weren't in context, isn't that true?
> A: That's correct.[546]

But how can you take out of context, for just one example, Kantor saying that Ruby "never would have been trusted" by the mob to kill Oswald for them?

You know, if we knew only one thing about Jack Ruby—that on the night of the assassination and into the early morning hours of the next day, Saturday, he was tied up for hours trying to deliver sandwiches to the police and employees of a radio station who were working into the night—we would know that he was not planning, at the behest of the mob, to kill Oswald the following day.[†] But since the majority of Americans do not know this fact, as well as a great number of other facts that make the notion of Ruby killing Oswald for the mob too silly for words, many will continue to think that "Ruby silenced Oswald for the mob."

If the reader will be forbearing and indulge me my use of facetiousness about a serious subject to illuminate some very substantive points *all supported by the known evidence*, what follows is the type of conversation, with one variation or another, that would have *had* to have taken place if organized crime had actually sent a representative to ask Ruby to silence Oswald for them.

Vito: Jack, I've got a little job for you. The boys want you to whack Oswald. You know, silence him.

Jack: Vito, to tell you the truth, I've been thinking that someone should kill that scum. But geez, Vito, you want me to do it?

Vito: Yeah, Jack. That's what the guys want.

Jack: Okay, Vito, okay, . . . Vito?

Vito: Yeah, Jack?

Jack: I was just thinking . . .

Vito: Jack, you know you've never been too good at that, but what are you thinking, Jack?

---

[*]I had Rabbi Hillel Silverman waiting in the wings in London to call as a rebuttal witness, if needed. But he wasn't, and I wanted to save time so we'd have more time for our final summations. The rabbi took his not being called to the stand graciously.

[†]The "Four Days in November" section covered in a fair amount of detail Ruby's conduct and activities on the three days leading up to his killing of Oswald, on the premise that, as the Warren Commission said, "if Jack Ruby were involved in a conspiracy, his activities and associations during this period would, in some way, have reflected the conspiratorial relationship" (WR, p.333). Not just with his sandwiches, but with everything else he said and did, it couldn't be more clear that Ruby wasn't involved with organized crime or anyone else in his killing of Oswald. Indeed, as previously indicated, on the afternoon of the assassination he was so distraught that he wanted to fly back to Chicago that night to be with his sister, Eileen Kaminsky, but she talked him out of it, telling him that their infirm sister, Eva, needed him in Dallas (15 H 283, WCT Eileen Kaminsky).

Jack: Well, I really hate that no-good creep Oswald, and he deserves to die, but why do the guys want to whack him? Aren't they happy about what he did? I mean, with JFK's kid brother going after them big-time, I don't know, but it seems to me all of you should love him, because with JFK gone, you might get Bobby off your back.

Vito: Jack, you're even more stupid than you look. Why in the hell would we want you to whack Oswald and silence him if Oswald hadn't whacked Kennedy for us? If he had nothing to tell the feds about us, what would there be to silence? Oswald's a nut, and the guys are terrified he'll crack or something and point the finger at them, so we have to silence him.

Jack: *Vito, the mob had President Kennedy killed*? . . . That's terrible. Just, just terrible. I, I don't want to say it because I've always looked way up to you guys, but that's the most terrible thing I could ever imagine. Just awful. I, I can't say I appreciate it. I tell you that.

Vito: Jack, we had no choice. At one time we liked the guy, but after he let that little bastard brother of his run wild against us, we ended up hating him.

Jack: You may have hated him, but I loved President Kennedy. He was a big hero to me. I've been crying like a baby over it.

Vito: Jack, I don't want to hear your damn sob stories. The boys want you to do the job, okay?

Jack: Vito, I'd love to kill that little worm. I mean, somebody's gotta do it. But the fact it's in my mind that I'm doing it for the people who had JFK killed, someone I loved, I don't know, it's kinda like a different story.

Vito: Jack, I got the solution to the problem.

Jack: What, Vito?

Vito: Just put it out of your mind . . . er, head, that we had JFK rubbed out. That way you won't be bothered by it. You can kill that fruitcake Oswald for yourself, not for us.

Jack: Geez, Vito, that's really a good idea. How does a guy come up with clever thinking like that? Thanks, Vito.

Vito: Fuhgedaboudit, Jack. Anything for an old pal.

Jack: When do you want me to do it, Vito?

Vito: The sooner the better. The nutcase could talk at any time.

Jack: Okay, Vito, okay . . . Vito, one last question.

Vito: What is it, Jack?

Jack: I hate to sound selfish, but what's in it for me? I mean, the Dallas police will arrest me for murder, probably even kill me on the spot.

Vito: Jack, you *are* being selfish. Think of the boys, Jack, think of the boys, not yourself.

Jack: I'm trying, Vito, but it's hard to do. I tell you that. They might kill me, Vito.

Vito: Jack, they're not going to kill you. The first thing they'll do is be all over you like flies on manure. By the time they draw their guns, there'll be ten cops already on top of you, and if they shot you then, they might accidentally shoot one of their own.

Jack: Yeah, I can see what you mean, Vito. But even if they don't kill me, I don't want to spend the rest of my life behind bars.

Vito: Jack, c'mon. After a few months, the guys will spring you.

Jack: Is that a promise, Vito?

Vito: Jack, you have my word.

Jack: Okay, Vito, okay.

Vito: Jack?

Jack: Yeah, Vito?

Vito: One last thing before I go. We have to make sure, real, real sure, that Oswald is killed, in fact, right on the spot. We can't afford to have him last for even a minute. So make sure you don't aim at his head. In fact, don't even aim at his heart. Shoot him in the belly, Jack. That's the quickest way by far to kill him right on the spot.

Jack: Okay, Vito, anything you say.

Vito: Thanks, Jack. We'll owe you one . . . Oh, Jack?

Jack: Yeah, Vito?

Vito: I forgot to ask. You ever fire a pistol at anyone before?

Jack: No, Vito, but I've always packed one just in case.

Vito: Just to help you out, Jack, you pull the trigger with your middle finger.

Jack: Gee thanks, Vito. I didn't know that.

Jack Duffy, a longtime student of the assassination and a Fort Worth attorney, immediately spotted the absurdity of the notion that a hit man for the mob would not shoot Oswald in the head, or at least his heart, when he was right next to Oswald and it would have been so easy for him to do so. Because Ruby actually shot Oswald in the stomach (see photo section), Oswald's dying wasn't a sure thing. In fact, he survived for almost two hours after the shooting. Indeed, Dr. Malcolm Perry, who worked on Oswald, told the Warren Commission that despite the severity of Oswald's injuries, he and his assistants "were very close, I think, to winning the battle . . . At one point, once we controlled the hemorrhage and once I had control of the aorta and was able to stop the bleeding [in] that area, I actually felt we had a very good chance."[547]

And unbelievably, a close-up enlargement of Ruby's right hand at the time of the shooting shows that Ruby, the big mob hit man, pulled the trigger with his middle finger, not the more natural, and reliable right index finger. His lawyer, Melvin Belli, was convinced this was a sure symptom of a psychiatric problem.[548]

The above conversation between Ruby and Vito, the reader might say, is silly. But it's not nearly as silly and far-out as Mafia chieftains deciding to get Jack Ruby, of all people, to commit the second most important murder in their history for them, the most important being, if you're a conspiracy theorist, their murder of Kennedy.

Organized Crime

One of the two principal groups (the other being the CIA)[*] whom conspiracy theorists have accused of being behind the assassination is organized crime, popularly referred to as the Mafia or Cosa Nostra, loosely translated as "Our Thing." Most organized-crime scholars considered the word *Mafia*[†] as referring to Italian members of major organized-crime "families" in America whose ancestors came from Italy. In the beginning, having only one Italian parent was not enough for membership in the Mafia. Also, it has been written that if a person (or his parents) didn't come from the specific Italian island or region of Sicily, he could do business and break bread with the Mafia, but he couldn't become a member, and the ancestry of all Mafia members in the early years was Sicilian. Mafia don Joseph Masseria, himself from Sicily, first opened the doors of the American Mafia to non–Sicilian Italians in 1919, though only at the lower level. Thereafter, many came from other regions, particularly the adjacent southern region of Calabria. And years later, even the Masseria limitation was erased, perhaps the most prominent examples being Vito Genovese, who in the 1950s was the boss of one of New York's biggest Mafia families and who came from a village near Naples in the southern region of Campania, where the Mafia is called Camorra, and Frank Costello (Francesco Castiglia), one of the most powerful mafioso ever, and a rival of Genovese's, who came from a small village in Calabria.[1]

---

[*]The latest Gallup Poll (November 10–12, 2003) showed that 37 percent of Americans believed the Mafia was involved in Kennedy's assassination, and 34 percent believed the CIA was. Among other leading people or entities believed to be involved in the assassination were Lyndon Johnson, 18 percent; Castro's Cuba, 15 percent; and the Soviet Union, 15 percent. The reason these numbers add up to more than 100 percent is that many people believed that more than one of these persons or groups were involved in the assassination. As noted earlier in the book, the Gallup Poll showed that 75 percent of all Americans believed there was a conspiracy in the assassination, only 19 percent believed that the assassin acted alone, and 6 percent had no opinion.

[†]The letters refer to an old Sicilian death slogan, *Morte Alla Francia Italia Anala*—"Death to the French Is Italy's Cry"—which arose out of the French invasion of Sicily in 1282, although the word *Mafia* would later come to mean "manly" in Sicily.

But in the early years, no Mafia don could have roots anywhere other than Sicily. Indeed, the biggest and most powerful Italian mobster of all, even exceeding Charles "Lucky" Luciano, was Chicago's Al (short for Alphonse) Capone, who ruled Chicago in the 1920s like no other gangster ever ruled any American city. Capone was helped by the estimated $15 million in payoffs he made annually to city and state officials, including the Chicago Police Department, for protection. "Scarface Al," who once noted, "You can go further with a kind word and a gun than with a kind word alone," was born in Brooklyn of parents who immigrated from Naples, not the island of Sicily, and he always wanted to be a Mafia boss. But as mob historian Frederic Sondern has written, "He couldn't because he was a Neapolitan." The irony is that Capone was so big he could designate who the Mafia boss would be in Chicago (e.g., Antonio Lombardo), but couldn't (at least in those days) be that person himself.[2]*

Today, the only requirement is that a Mafia member be Italian.[3] However, many non-Italians throughout the years, mostly Jewish (e.g., Meyer Lansky, Jacob "Greasy Thumb" Guzik, Louis "Lepke" Buchalter, Arthur "Dutch Shultz" Flegenheimer, Moe Dalitz, Jake Shapiro, Longy Zwillman, and Benjamin "Bugsy" Siegel), became very close "criminal associates" of Mafia families with considerable power. Writing in 1969, mob authority Ralph Salerno said that "a man like Meyer Lansky [the mob's financial wizard, true name Maier Suchowljansky] is the equal of any family boss, and the superior of some."[4]

The FBI refers to the Mafia as La Cosa Nostra.[5] "It's not Mafia," mob informant Joe Valachi told FBI agent James J. Flynn, who had gained Valachi's confidence by friendly visits with him behind bars, in September of 1962. "That's the expression the outsider uses . . . It's Cosa Nostra."[6] Chicago mob members, however, refer to themselves as the Outfit or Syndicate,[7] and Lucky Luciano's biographer, writing in 1975, said Valachi was only referring to what the "Italian-American syndicate in the New York area" called itself. And even within the New York mob families, Sciacca quotes Luciano in the late 1950s telling a federal narcotics undercover agent, "I'll tell you something, kid. There's always been a Mafia, but it's not like those sons-a-bitches tell it in the newspapers . . . The Mafia's like any other organization, except we don't go in for advertising. We're big business, is all."[8] In any event, because *Mafia*, not *Cosa Nostra*, is the much more well-known term, I shall refer mostly to organized crime in this book as the Mafia, organized crime, or the mob.

We also learned from Valachi, for the first time, the initiation rites for the Mafia. With a gun and a knife on top of a table at which are seated many Mafia members, the initiate is told, "This represents that you live by the gun and the knife and you die by the gun and the knife." The initiate extends the finger he shoots with, and the end of it is pricked with a pin and squeezed until the blood comes out. He is told that "this blood means that we are now one Family." The initiate is instructed to cup his hands. A piece of paper is put inside and lit with a match, the initiate being told to say, all in Italian, "This is the way I will burn if I betray the secret of this Cosa Nostra." Referring to *omerta*, the vow of silence—never to "rat on" any member or any of the brotherhood's activities—Valachi, who went through the rite when he joined the Mafia in 1930, said the initiate is told, "Here are the two most important things you have to remember. Drill them into your head. The first is that to betray the secret of Cosa Nostra means death without trial. Sec-

---

*Capone rose to power in Chicago through gang wars with his rivals, during which upwards of five hundred murders took place in the last half of the 1920s, the most famous being the Saint Valentine's Day massacre in 1929, when Capone's killers, dressed as policemen, lined seven members of rival Bugsy Moran's North Side gang up against a garage wall and machine-gunned them down.

ond, to violate any member's wife means death without trial."[9]* It was believed that in the early years of the Mafia, an aspiring member of a mob family had to take part in at least one murder before he was accepted. But as long ago as 1967, one graying mafioso complained to a reporter for *Life* magazine, "Today, you got a thousand guys in here that never broke an egg."[10]

Today, because of endless federal prosecutions and members who found it to their clear advantage to break the vow of silence, organized crime is a shell of its former self. But in its heyday, in the 1920s through most of the 1960s, there were twenty-four, semi-independent "families" in charge of certain criminal activity in their respective geographical areas in the United States,[†] and the collective families were reported, in 1967, to be grossing around $40 billion a year from their illegal activities, far more than any major American corporation such as General Motors or U.S. Steel.[11] Lansky himself acknowledged that the vast conglomerate of criminal enterprises he oversaw financially was "bigger than U.S. Steel."[12] In New York, the mob, among its many other activities, controlled the port (the nation's largest) as well as the city's garment industry (which produced most of America's clothing).[13] Indeed, for years the mob had a grip on Las Vegas gambling casinos, and in the 1930s made substantial but ultimately unsuccessful inroads into taking over Detroit's auto industry and the big screen in Hollywood.

The American Mafia's power and wealth has always been hidden, peripheral, and surreptitious. Not so with its Sicilian ancestors. "By the beginning of the nineteenth century," Italian author Michele Pantaleone writes, the Sicilian Mafia "was already a criminal organization interwoven into the country's political and economic life . . . More efficient than the police, [it] penetrated deeply into all aspects of the town's life." Indeed, the Mafia's reach was so extensive that in many Sicilian villages even disputes involving crimes among nonmembers would be mediated, for a fee from both parties, by a mafioso, and "no one dared to call in the police when there was Mafia intervention." When Don Calogero Vizzini, the leader of the Sicilian Mafia, died of natural causes in 1954, "his funeral was . . . attended by many local and provincial authorities and politicians . . . For eight days the municipal and Christian Democrat offices were closed, and black crepe banners hung from the windows."[14]

The only American mobster who even remotely approached this type of acceptance in the community was, of course, Capone in Chicago. During Prohibition, when he was providing alcoholic beverages to a citizenry with unhappily parched palates, he was cheered at Wrigley Field and Comiskey Park, and for at least one local election, the city fathers sent an emissary to Capone at his fortress-like headquarters on the top three floors of Chicago's downtown Lexington Hotel to ask him if they could have a free elec-

---

*Other cardinal commandments of the Mafia have come to light through the years, two of which are that "a mafioso must obey implicitly the orders of a council of brothers senior to him," and "a mafioso may never, under any circumstances, appeal to the police, the courts, or any other governmental authority for redress" (Sondern, *Brotherhood of Evil*, p.54).

†Once nationwide, it is believed that today only one "Outfit" in Chicago and New York City's five organized-crime families remain. They are "about all that's left," says mob historian Selwyn Raab. However, as recently as 2002, federal court records show that the Bonanno family in New York City, still with about one hundred members (about half their traditional strength), was considering whether to induct ten new mob wannabes. Joseph Coffee, who pursued the mob as a New York City police detective for over thirty years, believes the aura and lifestyle of the Mafia will continue to attract new members irrespective of how many mob leaders are convicted and imprisoned. "It's the high life, the nightclubs, the bimbos, the easy money," he says. "It's always been that." (Richard Willing, "The Sopranos, the Mafia," *USA Today*, March 10–12, 2006, pp.1A–2A)

tion without the corrupting influence and muscle of his organization. Mob historian Frederic Sondern writes that when Capone returned to Chicago in March of 1930 after serving ten months in Pennsylvania for carrying a concealed weapon, "he was welcomed home like returning royalty by cheering crowds and many of Chicago's principal officials."[15]

Although the American Mafia continues to decline, the Sicilian Mafia, though not as violent as it once was, is flourishing and has literally been accepted by the Italian authorities as a fact of life. This was no more demonstrated than when Pietro Lunardi, the minister of infrastructure for Italy's prime minister, Silvio Berlusconi, said in 2001 that the Mafia was a reality that "we have to live with." As indicated, the Sicilian Mafia, from its origins, had always been a part of the social and economic fabric of Sicily. But what caused it to temper its violence in recent years was the rage by all of Italy against it when it blew up the car driving the crusading anti-Mafia judge Giovanni Falcone from a Palermo airport in 1992, killing Falcone, his wife, and three police bodyguards. Two months later, Falcone's associate and the chief prosecutor in Palermo, Paolo Borsellino, was murdered by a car bomb, along with five bodyguards, as he arrived for a visit with his mother outside her apartment building. The crackdown by an enraged nation culminated in the arrest the following year of Salvatore "The Beast" Riina, the Sicilian boss of bosses. His successor, Bernardo "The Tractor" Provenzano, made a wise decision to cut down on the violence against non-mafioso citizens and public figures, but after more than forty years on the run, thirteen of which he was the boss of bosses, in 2006 Provenzano finally ran out of luck. On April 11, he was arrested in his then hideout, a dilapidated farmhouse in the countryside outside the Sicilian town of Corleone. Law enforcement and Mafia experts believe that Provenzano's arrest was not a crippling blow to the still powerful and well-organized Sicilian mob.[16]

Speaking of Corleone, no Mafia clan was more violent than the one in Corleone, the mountain town south of Palermo that was immortalized in the 1969 *Godfather* movie when writer Mario Puzo gave the town's name to his "godfather"* (Don Vito Corleone, played by Marlon Brando), where judges, police officers, recalcitrant politicians, and fellow mafiosi were routinely murdered. But today, though the Mafia's grip on Sicilian economic life is still strong, fear of the Mafia by non-mafiosi is nowhere near what it once was, including in Corleone, per Antonio Iannago, the town's deputy mayor.

According to Eurispes, an Italian think tank in Rome, the Italian Mafia, mostly concentrated in Sicily but existing throughout the country, took in profits of about $123 billion in 2004, approximately 10 percent of Italy's gross domestic product, mostly from drug trafficking, protection money, and corruption payoffs in big business, construction deals, and public works projects. With respect to protection money, it is estimated that 80 percent of Palermo's merchants pay protection money, known as the *pizzo*, more than ever before, but in smaller amounts. The slogan is *Pagare tutti, pagare meno*, meaning "everyone pays less, but everyone pays." And no merchant reports the payoffs to the

---

*According to an obituary on Mario Puzo, the term *godfather*, the title of his book, which became one of the biggest-selling novels of all time, is not a Mafia term. "In fact, the term 'godfather' as a synonym for a Mafia don did not exist before Puzo made it up." (Obituary of Puzo, *Newsday*, July 3, 1999, p.A3) However, it apparently was a Mafia term but not a synonym for a Mafia don. Rather, new Mafia members were assigned to someone who was designated as their "godfather," a person who was "responsible" for the new member and was his "*gombah*." (*New York Times*, October 2, 1963, p.28; Maas, *Valachi Papers*, p.96) *Goombah* or *compare* is also a term for a mobster's buddy, who isn't necessarily a mob member (*USA Today*, March 10, 2006, p.4A).

police. "The Mafia doesn't even need to threaten anymore. People look to the Mafia and seek it out for favors," says Enrico Bellavia, a Sicilian journalist and author. Bellavia says the situation has evolved to the point where people in Sicily don't even ask themselves whether the Mafia is a bad organization. They just see it as a staple in their lives—indeed, "a force that can [often] resolve their individual needs."[17]

The first Mafia family in America was founded in 1875 in New Orleans by a group of Sicilian immigrants. Mafia author Thomas Reppetto writes that "the largest city in the South was a natural destination for Italians. New Orleans had been a terminus for Italian fruit ships since before the Civil War, and descriptions of the city had been carried back to the mother country by sailors and merchants who, by and large, preferred its climate to the colder and less predictable weather of Boston or New York."[18] In the early years in America, most mafiosi committed small crimes against each other. As one, perhaps apocryphal, story tells it, when the son of one such immigrant was told that his father had victimized his own fellow Italian immigrants, his response is said to have been, "Well, of course, it had to have been that way. My father didn't know how to say stick 'em up in English. Who else could he rob?" But soon the Mafia, or "Black Hand," as it was sometimes called in the early years because Mafia extortionists would leave the imprint of a black hand on their warnings, branched out from small crimes in the "Little Italy" sections of cities like New York and Chicago into major crime—mostly gambling, extortion, bootlegging, labor racketeering, and narcotics*—all over the nation. That has been its business since then. This business has only been successful, however, because of murder and the threat of it.

Ironically, it was the religious and social conservatives, helped by fire-and-brimstone preachers like the colorful evangelist Billy Sunday, who launched organized crime in America and its biggest local gangster ever, Capone, into the really big time and filled its coffers as never before.† Their temperance movement led to the passage of the Eighteenth Amendment in 1919 (it went into effect in 1920), which prohibited "the manu-

---

*The boss of bosses, Luciano, got his start in major crime by importing narcotics under Arnold ("A. R.") Rothstein, the most influential figure in the New York underworld before his murder in 1928. Rothstein was famous for fixing the 1919 World Series between the Chicago White Sox and the Cincinnati Reds. Indeed, Luciano's first criminal arrest was for selling opium to an undercover agent in 1916. (Sciacca, *Luciano*, pp.7–8, 23, 45)

†The Bureau of Internal Revenue (later, Internal Revenue Service) estimated Capone's annual income in the late 1920s, mostly from the sale of alcohol, as being close to $100 million—$50 million from bootlegging, $25 million from gambling, $10 million from organized prostitution, and about the same from narcotics distribution (Sondern, *Brotherhood of Evil*, pp.76–77). While many Americans know that the still-legendary mob figure (whose name to this day is identified with the Windy City probably more than even Michael Jordan's) was convicted of federal income tax evasion, effectively ending his criminal career, what most don't know is that the man who is credited with his downfall, Elliot Ness, had very little to do with it, not even participating in Capone's trial. Ness, whose greatly exaggerated exploits were chronicled in *The Untouchables*, a book and TV series based thereon, was a federal Prohibition agent in the Department of Justice, and he did, indeed, lead successful (though not debilitating) raids on Capone's breweries. He was also, by all accounts, honest and incorruptible. But it was the accountants of the Bureau of Internal Revenue of the Treasury Department, led by Frank J. Wilson, an agent in the intelligence unit of the bureau, whose investigation of Capone for not paying taxes on the income derived from his sale of alcohol, who finally brought Capone down. Capone was convicted in 1931 and sentenced to eleven years in the federal penitentiary. He served eight years and was paroled in 1939, suffering from syphilis. Al Capone died from a brain hemorrhage at his Palm Island, Florida, home in 1947 at the age of forty-eight after suffering a stroke followed by a bout of pneumonia. (Bergreen, *Capone*, pp.44, 272, 484, 486, 571, 604–605)

facture, sale, or transportation of intoxicating liquors" in the United States. Prohibition, the effort to dry up America, was wildly unpopular, and the imbibing of alcohol,
which knew (and still knows) no sociological or economic boundaries, demanded a solution. The Mafia came to the rescue by its illicit and highly priced sale of alcohol to
thirsty Americans throughout the land. An inevitable concomitant to the circumven-
tion of the Volstead Act (which implemented the Eighteenth Amendment and extended
Prohibition by making it unlawful to "possess or use" alcohol) was the corruption of
those who were supposed to enforce the ill-advised law. With payoffs to the police, West
Fifty-second Street in New York, for instance, "was an almost unbroken row of
speakeasies" that openly sold alcohol.[19] The abysmal failure of the social experiment
was memorialized by the passage of the Twenty-first Amendment in 1933, which repealed
the Eighteenth Amendment.

Throughout the years, New York City alone has been the home of five of the twenty-
four Mafia families in the United States (currently the Bonanno, Colombo, Gambino, Genovese, and Lucchese families), and New Jersey one. Each "family" (or *borgata*) is headed
by a *capo* or boss or don, the second in command being the *sotto-capo* or underboss. A *con-
siglieri* or counselor is typically an elder member who serves as an adviser. A "crew" or
"regime" of ten or so foot soldiers of the "family" is controlled by a midlevel boss referred
to as a *caporegima* or lieutenant, whose job is to carry out the orders of the capo within the
family. The Mafia members who perform the everyday business are called *soldati*, the soldiers or "button men" who are taking the initial step necessary to rise in the family.

Before organized crime's substantial disintegration in the 1980s and 1990s, the Mafia
in the United States was controlled by a group resembling a board of directors, as it were,
known as "the commission." The commission established policy and settled all important disputes. Though not every boss of a mob family was on the commission, every member of the commission was a Mafia family boss.[20] In Mafia leader Joseph Bonanno's 1983
autobiography, *A Man of Honor*, he said that although Mafia leaders from around the
country could sit on the commission, its most important members, and the only permanent ones, were the heads of the five New York City mob families.[21] The commission is
no longer believed to exist.[22]

"The commission" and the "national crime syndicate" (in which organized crime went
national under a corporate-like umbrella) were created by Mafia *capo de tutti capi* (boss
of all bosses) Charles "Lucky" Luciano (true name, Salvatore Lucania). Mob historians
give different years for the birth of the commission and crime syndicate, most saying they
took place at a meeting of mob leaders in Chicago in 1931. But Luciano's biographer says
the year was 1933 and it was at a mob meeting at a Park Avenue hotel in New York City.
The distinguishing feature about the national syndicate is that it included racketeers and
gangs who were not Italian, and hence, not a part of the Mafia. Luciano felt there was
strength in diversity and cooperation, and the Italian mob families, he proposed, would
be willing to recognize a criminal organization in a city or area of the country in which
they were not operating, and give them autonomy. However, disputes and territorial problems would inevitably develop and they would be resolved by the syndicate's board of
directors, which came to be known as the aforementioned national commission,[23] and
whose members were and remained exclusively Italian.

Luciano emerged as the Mafia's top leader in 1931 following the three-year Castel-
lammarese War (so-named because most of the participants came from the region of
northwestern Sicily near Castellammare del Golfo) between two New York City mob

families, a deadly conflict in which many were killed, including the heads of both families, Salvatore Maranzano and Joseph Masseria.[*] Luciano ran his loosely knit but vast criminal empire from his luxurious suite at the top-of-the-line Waldorf-Astoria hotel in New York City, where he lived under the alias "Charles Rose."[24]

The commission, Luciano thought and others came to agree, could help avoid such bloody conflicts in the future.

Luciano was born in 1897 near Palermo, Sicily, and grew up in the toughest section of New York City at the time, the Lower East Side near the Brooklyn Bridge. It was during this period that Luciano aligned himself with Meyer Lansky to form one of the most powerful and long-standing relationships in mob history.[†] Legend has it that, for a penny or two a day, "Luciano offered younger and smaller Jewish kids his personal protection against beatings on the way to school. If they didn't pay, he'd beat them up. One runty kid refused to pay, a thin little youngster from Poland, Meyer Lansky. Luciano fought

---

[*]Though never confirmed, it is believed by many that Luciano (together, some say, with Vito Genovese, Luciano's underling at the time) had a hand in both Maranzano's and Masseria's deaths, guiding his then boss, Masseria (whom he was unable to stop fighting with Maranzano), to an Italian restaurant on Coney Island on April 15, 1931, where he was ambushed and murdered by men believed to be from his own gang. Luciano had excused himself to go to the restroom just before the murder took place. When Maranzano, who viewed himself as the new "boss of bosses," felt that he also could not coexist with Luciano, who had taken over Masseria's gang, or Vito Genovese, on September 10, 1931, he lured Luciano and Genovese to his office to be murdered by Vincent "Mad Dog" Coll, who at age twenty-two was already a notorious executioner, but Luciano learned what was in store for him, and instead Maranzano was met by four of Meyer Lansky's gunmen, who shot him to death. (*New York Times*, October 3, 1963, p.24; Nelli, *Business of Crime*, pp.203–206) Whether or not Luciano was behind the murders of Masseria and Maranzano, mob historians believe that their deaths marked the end of the dominance of the Mafia by old-time, tradition-beholden mafiosi, to whom the town one came from in Sicily was just as important, or more, than making money, which was the *only* concern of Luciano and Lansky.

[†]If it was Luciano, credited by mob historian Frederic Sondern as being "second only to Al Capone in organizational genius," who created the corporate-like structure of the Mafia with rules and by-laws, it was, by common consensus, his boyhood friend Meyer Lansky who, as mob writer Nicholas Gage said, "developed the worldwide network of couriers, middlemen, bankers, and frontmen that [allowed] the underworld to take profits from illegal enterprises, send them halfway around the world, and then have the money come back laundered clean to be invested in legitimate businesses" (Gage, "Little Big Man Who Laughs at the Law," p.65). Lansky was called the "Little Man," and Luciano would always tell his followers to "listen to him." Luciano once said, "I learned . . . that Meyer Lansky understood the Italian brain almost better than I did . . . I used to tell Meyer that he may've had a Jewish mother, but someplace he must've been wet-nursed by a Sicilian." An FBI agent who pursued Lansky said, "He would have been chairman of the board of General Motors if he'd gone into legitimate business." (Court TV Crime Library, *Criminal Minds and Methods*, http://www.crimelibrary.com/gangsters_outlaws/mob_bosses/index.html; *New York Times*, January 16, 1983, p.29) The five-foot four-inch Lansky, who led a very quiet, unpretentious family life in Miami, sent one of his sons to West Point, made contributions to charitable causes, and never had bodyguards—relying for protection instead on the FBI agents who followed him everywhere, even slowing his car down when they fell too far behind—had a personal net worth estimated between $100 and $300 million in the early 1970s. Unlike most of his mob friends, who were either murdered, deported, or deposed, Lansky died in 1983 of natural causes at the age of eighty-one in Miami Beach, Florida. (Gage, "Little Big Man Who Laughs at the Law," pp.62–65; death of Lansky: *New York Times*, January 16, 1983, p.29)

Lansky's earlier counterpart was Jacob "Greasy Thumb" Guzik, who was Al Capone's minister of finance for his Chicago mob in the 1920s. Though Jews were common mob associates in the early years, by the 1960s and 1970s there were few Jews (or any non-Italians) high up in organized crime. New Jersey mobster Angelo DeCarlo, in an FBI wired phone conversation in the 1960s, referred to Lansky as the most respected non-Italian in the underworld. "There's only two Jews recognized in the whole country today," he said. "That's Meyer and . . . Moe Dalitz [the head of the so-called Cleveland syndicate], but Dalitz ain't got much recognition." (Gage, "Little Big Man Who Laughs at the Law," p.65)

As big as Lansky was in the underworld, he was, after all, not Italian, and mob historian Selwyn Raab puts Lansky's stature in perspective when he notes that although "Lansky accompanied Luciano to Mafia conventions, [he] was never allowed to sit in on discussions" (Raab, *Five Families*, p.40).

him one day and was amazed how hard Lansky fought back. They became bosom buddies after that."[25]

In addition to creating a national crime syndicate, Luciano made other changes among
the six New York and New Jersey families, one of which endeared him to Mafia foot soldiers like no one before or since. Previously, a Mafia don could order the death of a low-
level Mafia member for any reason at all, and no one could object, creating a state of fear
and anxiety in the men. Luciano decreed that hereafter, the ultimate penalty could not
be imposed unless the charges by the boss against the Mafia member were presented to
a special judicial council consisting of a representative from each of the six families, and
only the "court," by a majority vote, could approve of the man's death. (In the event of
a tie, the boss of the family seeking the member's death would have the deciding vote.)

And then there was the old tradition of Mafia members greeting each other with a
kiss. Loathed by most new members, Luciano changed the greeting to a handshake, satisfying the old-country "Mustache Petes" that this was a bad practice. "We stick out,"
he said, "kissing each other in restaurants and places like that."[26] But there was one tradition Luciano was in no mood to tamper with in the least. Once becoming a member,
one could not leave the Mafia. "The only way out is in a box," he said.[27] *Arrivederci Roma*,
yes. *Arrivederci borgata*, no.

The mob, whose lifestyle has been romanticized with great commercial success in
novels and on the big screen, and whose mythological culture of honor among thieves
("Code of the Underworld") and genuine loyalty to family and respect for women and
children have unquestionably forged a psychological connection to the American public
(witness the enormous popularity of *The Sopranos* and mob films like the *Godfather*
series, *Goodfellas*, *Donnie Brasco*, and many more),[*] saw its mostly uncontested salad days
in America come to an end when Robert F. Kennedy was appointed attorney general by
his brother, President John F. Kennedy, in January of 1961. Prior to that, the Department of Justice, which the attorney general heads, did not focus heavily on organized
crime in America, although after the discovery of the mob summit meeting in the
obscure New York town of Apalachin in 1957, RFK's predecessor, William P. Rogers, did
increase the size of the organized-crime section and attempted to instill some life into it.
But little was being done. William Hundley, who took over the organized-crime section
at the Department of Justice in 1958, was shocked to find "there was absolutely nothing

---

[*]Although the power and influence of the American Mafia has been in steady decline, the nation's fascination with the Mafia continues. As Joanne Weintraub of the *Milwaukee Journal* writes, "Unlike many of our
cultural preoccupations which come and go, America's interest in the Mafia seems to be as constant and nearly
as voracious as our appetite for lasagna, linguine, and biscotti." Mario Puzo, whose book *The Godfather* sold
an incredible 21 million copies, observed, "Just because a guy's a murderer, he can't have endearing traits?" I
guess I'd have to agree. I mean, while the furnaces were blazing in places like Auschwitz, Treblinka, and
Chelmno, the smell of burning human flesh permeating the countryside, Adolf Hitler, in the rarefied atmosphere of Berchtesgaden high in the Bavarian Alps, was, historians tell us, very concerned about the health of
his dog Blondi. All sarcasm aside, the interesting and arguably revealing thing is that Americans are apparently not even turned off by the non-endearing traits of the Mafia, like killing people who don't want to die.
I haven't seen *The Sopranos*, but I assume the killings are for the most part internecine (killing other mafiosi,
and never killing innocent people outside the Mafia, which would never go over well) and probably always
have an element of revenge, which at its core is a raw form of justice, not a pejorative notion. So it's all fun
and games. As *USA Today* reported on viewers' enthrallment with the show, making murder fun, "Who gets
whacked in *Sopranos*? Is Adriana really dead? Will Christopher get whacked? Or is crazy Tony B. next? Fans
have been debating possible murders and floating plot lines for HBO's hit Mob show, *The Sopranos*" (*USA
Today*, June 4, 2004, p.9E).

going on in the Justice Department . . . There was only a couple of guys in the OC section clipping newspapers."[28]

Actually, it was more than that. Since leading mob figures from around the country were able to leave their respective cities to attend the meeting without the FBI having any knowledge of their movements (the FBI would never have even known of the meeting if a New York State Police sergeant hadn't discovered it), Rogers set up a special group on organized crime in his office under the supervision of his assistant, Milton R. Wessel. The purpose of this group was to serve as a clearinghouse to coordinate the activities of mob figures, but it received no support from J. Edgar Hoover's FBI, on which the group was necessarily dependent for its raw data. In fact, at the annual convention of the International Association of Police Chiefs in Los Angeles on October 3, 1960, when the proposal for a national nerve center to coordinate the fight against organized crime was formally presented, Hoover, greatly respected by police chiefs around the country, took the podium to tell the chiefs that "the persons who endorse these grandiose schemes have lost sight of some basic facts. America's compact network of state and local law enforcement agencies traditionally has been the nation's first line of defense against crime. Nothing could be more dangerous to our democratic ideals than the establishment of an all-powerful police agency on the federal scene. The truth of these words is clearly demonstrated in the experience of nations ruled by ruthless tyrants both here in the Western Hemisphere and abroad." The proposal was not adopted and Wessel's nascent group was abolished.[29] It was clear that as late as 1960, Hoover was resisting the notion of his FBI vigorously pursuing organized crime in America.

Henry Peterson, a career prosecutor in the attorney general's office who served under RFK's predecessors (including Rogers) as well as RFK, and eventually headed the organized-crime section under Attorney General Ramsey Clark, said that before Robert Kennedy, "When you talked about organized crime, people would ask you to define what you meant. Robert Kennedy came in and said, 'Don't define it, do something about it.' His instructions were: 'Don't let anything get in your way. If you have problems, come see me. Get the job done, and if you can't get the job done, get out.'"[30] Author William Shannon wrote that RFK's "zeal to break up the syndicates was reminiscent of a sixteenth century Jesuit on the hunt for heresy."[31]

One big reason for the Department of Justice not focusing heavily on organized crime before RFK's tenure is that the department's investigative arm, Hoover's FBI, was using most of its resources during this period to combat Communism domestically—a mission with which virtually everyone agrees Hoover was obsessed. Although some have said the reason for the FBI's inattention to organized crime was that the mob (specifically Meyer Lansky) possessed compromising photographs of Hoover in homosexual situations and blackmailed him into calling off his dogs, no credible evidence has ever surfaced to substantiate this allegation.*

The chief peddler of this argument is conspiracy theorist Anthony Summers. But the "evidence" Summers cites is so sleazy and so transparently unworthy of belief (e.g., that

---

*The first published rumor about Hoover's sexual orientation was a *Collier's* magazine article of August 19, 1933, that only vaguely alluded to his sexuality: "In appearance," the article read, "Mr. Hoover looks utterly unlike the story-book sleuth . . . He dresses fastidiously, with Eleanor blue as the favored color for the matched shades of his tie, handkerchief and socks . . . He is short, fat, businesslike, and walks with a mincing step" (Gentry, *J. Edgar Hoover*, pp. 158–159). For years the rumor was rampant in Washington, D.C., social circles.

Hoover, who we know was more concerned about his reputation and legacy than perhaps any other public figure in America, would go out in public to famous nightclubs and racetracks and hold hands with his alleged lover, Clyde Tolson; dress up like a woman and engage in sex orgies with several participants at leading New York hotels; have homosexual sex parties at his home with men, including some of the top officials at the FBI; and permit mobsters to point to him at racetracks and shout out loud, so everyone could hear, that he was a "fucking, degenerate queer") that I'm not going to dignify Summers's charges by a serious discussion of them. I don't know what Hoover's sexual orientation was.[*] What I do know is that Summers failed miserably in trying to prove his allegation. How he got a book published in 1993 with scurrilous trash like this in it, I don't know.[32]

Summers picked on an awfully difficult guy for his preposterous allegations. Even if Hoover had the sexual orientation Summers asserts he did, by all accounts he was exceptionally proper, even stiff in his demeanor. Compare the following description of Hoover with Summers's Hoover: When recalling her going to Washington to testify before the Warren Commission, Marina Oswald said, "Seven or more men met me; apparently they were all FBI. But when I shook hands with Mr. Hoover, who was with them, I was chilled from top to bottom. It was as if you met a dead person. He had a coldness like someone from the grave."[33] Though Hoover was no prude, taking an occasional drink and dining regularly at night spots like Toots Shor's, 21, and the Stork Club in New York, friends said they never heard him tell an off-color story in his life.[34]

Hoover's counterpart in the federal intelligence community for several years was CIA Director Richard Helms. He was quite familiar with Hoover's lifestyle, describing it as extremely routine, even banal. He goes on to say that "in the Washington fish bowl . . . I find it impossible to believe that anyone as well known and as easily identified as Hoover might have managed a clandestine sex life. Was Hoover eccentric? Yes. Very eccentric? Yes, indeed. An active homosexual? No way."[35]

Here's what Cartha D. "Deke" DeLoach, the deputy director, the number-three man in the FBI hierarchy, who worked alongside Hoover and Tolson for many years, has to say:

> When Anthony Summers' *Official and Confidential* was first published, I read it with disbelief . . . Summers charges in his book that Hoover and [Clyde] Tolson [Hoover's number-one assistant in the FBI] were homosexual lovers . . . It so disgusted me that I simply put it out of my mind. Even when it was repeated in newspapers and echoed on TV talk shows, I concluded that the fair-minded people of America would reject so ridiculous an accusation based on such flimsy evidence, that their good sense would see through the fraud. But . . . I discovered that in the wake of Summers' book, Hoover's homosexuality was widely accepted as undeniable truth . . . Neither man [Hoover and Tolson] was a homosexual . . . No one who knew Hoover and Tolson well in the FBI has ever even hinted at such a charge. *You can't work side by side with two men for the better part of twenty years and fail to recognize signs of such affections.* Contrary to what Summers would have

---

[*]Many of Hoover's defenders say that his life was so consumed by the FBI that he was asexual. Even someone like William Turner, a ten-year veteran of the FBI who definitely was not a Hoover apologist, wrote, "My impression is that Hoover was a misanthrope devoid of erotic impulses, that he was frigid, and that he felt no passion either way" (Turner, *Rearview Mirror*, p.8).

you believe, neither Hoover nor Tolson was the least bit effeminate. Both were tough and manly.[36]

As indicated, there is no credible evidence that Hoover's not going after organized crime was connected to his sexual orientation. So what was his reason? According to DeLoach, it was much more simple. Although organized crime was a national organization run by the commission of mob leaders since the early 1930s, as late as 1957 "Hoover had insisted there was no such thing as La Cosa Nostra . . . He believed the gangs were local, and he expected local authorities to take care of the problem* . . . His enormous faith in the agency he had created persuaded him that no such complex *national* criminal organization could exist without him knowing about it. He didn't know about it; ergo, it did not exist."[37]

Additionally, Hoover always maintained that prior to the antiracketeering laws in a crime bill passed in 1961, the FBI never had enough federal laws to use to go after the mob. But this rings hollow. Why would Hoover have gone after something he himself did not think existed? Hundley, of the Department of Justice, said that the FBI should have "at least been aware of what the hell was going on. I mean, how can you have the top investigative agency in the world [FBI] and have all these top hoods meeting up in Apalachin and they didn't even know about it?"[38]

Writer Nick Pileggi, who has followed and written about organized crime for years (his nonfiction book *Wiseguys* was the basis for the movie *Goodfellas*), said, "They [organized crime] owned politicians. They owned unions . . . The FBI said they didn't exist. It was unbelievable. Glorious."[39] Following the startling discovery by New York State Police of the summit meeting of fifty-nine mob leaders in Apalachin, New York, on November 14, 1957, which generated front-page stories around America for days, Hoover, at the suggestion of Clyde Tolson, did at least commission his FBI research unit to prepare two in-depth papers, one on the Mafia in Sicily, the second on the Mafia in the United States. Shortly thereafter, a "Top Hoodlum" program was established at the FBI, and the first targets for investigation were supposed to be the Mafia leaders at the Apalachin meeting. By 1959, the FBI had opened up a "La Cosa Nostra" file and commenced some limited electronic surveillance of a few mob figures, including Chicago's Sam Giancana. But everyone agrees that the FBI effort against organized crime did not increase and intensify very substantially until the appointment of RFK as attorney general in 1961.[40]

However, until Joseph Valachi came forward as a federal informant in September of 1962, a year before he went public before the cameras, Hoover wasn't nearly as helpful as Kennedy wanted him to be, still preoccupied with fighting the American Communist Party, which exasperated RFK to no end. Kennedy told a reporter for the *London Sunday Times* in December of 1961, "It is such nonsense to have to waste time prosecuting the [American] Communist Party. It [American Communist Party] couldn't be more feeble and less of a threat, and besides, its membership consists largely of [undercover] FBI

---

*And, indeed, in New York, local prosecutor Thomas Dewey had temporarily broken up Lucky Luciano's Mafia family in 1936. But Hoover had to know that in Chicago it took a federal counterpart of his, the Treasury Department, to end Al Capone's career in 1931.

That DeLoach was correct about Hoover's state of mind is supported by Hoover's testimony under oath before the House Appropriations Subcommittee in 1961. Addressing himself to the issue of his bureau's not giving as much assistance to fighting organized crime as some people would like, Hoover criticized those who sought "fantastic panaceas as to how to solve *local crimes*." (Schlesinger, *Robert Kennedy and His Times*, p.264)

agents."[41] In a 1971 letter to Hoover from Assistant FBI Director William Sullivan shortly after Hoover forced him to resign, Sullivan wrote that even when the membership of the Communist Party was down to around 80,000 in the mid-1940s, "you caused a Communist scare in this nation when it was entirely unwarranted . . . What happened when the Communist party went into rapid decline? You kept the scare campaign going just the same for some years. However, when the membership figures kept dropping lower and lower you instructed us not to give them out to the public . . . At the time of my leaving the Bureau this week, the membership figures . . . are down to an amazing 2800 in a nation of 200 million people and you still conceal this from the people. Of the 2800 only about half are active and wholly ineffective. I think it is a terrible injustice to the citizens and an unethical thing for you to do to conceal this important truth from the public."[42] What few knew was that Hoover's fear and passion against Communism started way back in 1919, five years before he became FBI director, when he thoroughly researched the origin and philosophy of the worldwide Communist movement.[43]

Since federal law enforcement, before the Kennedy administration, hadn't quite come out of its anesthesia over the threat that organized crime posed to the nation, it was left mostly up to congressional committees to conduct inquiries from time to time. The first was the Senate Select Committee to Investigate Organized Crime in Interstate Commerce (named after its chairman, Senator Estes Kefauver). The Kefauver Committee held widely publicized hearings in thirteen major cities throughout the country (as well as Saratoga, New York) in 1950 and 1951, a time when Mafia leader Frank Costello was considered to be the most powerful mobster in the land. But Kefauver's committee, which took testimony from mob experts, politicians, and mobsters, including Costello, did not make much of a dent in the mob. This was primarily because most of its inquiry was directed to the mob's control of professional gambling, particularly casino gambling and its effect on interstate commerce, although its ultimate conclusions on the power and deleterious influence of organized crime were never better stated:

1. There is a nationwide crime syndicate known as the Mafia, whose tentacles are found in many large cities. It has international ramifications which appear most clearly in connection with the narcotics traffic.
2. Its leaders are usually found in control of the most lucrative rackets in their cities.
3. There are indications of a centralized direction and control of these rackets, but leadership appears to be in a group rather than a single individual.
4. The Mafia is the cement that helps to bind the . . . syndicate of New York and the . . . syndicate of Chicago as well as smaller criminal gangs and individual criminals throughout the country.
5. The domination of the Mafia is based fundamentally on "muscle" and "murder." The Mafia is a secret conspiracy against law and order which will ruthlessly eliminate anyone who stands in the way of its success in any criminal enterprise in which it is interested. It will destroy anyone who betrays its secrets. It will use any means available—political influence, bribery, intimidation, et cetera, to defeat any attempt on the part of law enforcement to touch its top figures.[44]

Starting in January of 1957, the Senate Select Committee on Improper Activities in the Labor or Management Field (popularly referred to as the McClellan Committee after its chairman, Senator John L. McClellan, or the "Rackets Committee") foreshadowed, for the first time, the real war that would eventually be waged against the mob by the Kennedy brothers from Massachusetts. Then-Senator John F. Kennedy and his brother Robert, appointed chief counsel of the committee, took the lead in investigating the mob's corrupt influence in labor unions[*] and management throughout the country. For three years as chief counsel of the committee, RFK "grilled, taunted, and derided many of the most vicious and vengeful men in America." For instance, when RFK asked Chicago mob boss Sam "Momo" Giancana whether he disposed of his enemies by stuffing their bodies in trunks, and Giancana coupled his invoking the Fifth Amendment with a chuckle, RFK sneeringly remarked, "I thought only little girls giggled, Mr. Giancana."[45]

The hearings before the McClellan Committee in the wake of the mob's Apalachin meeting determined that twenty-three out of the fifty-nine organized crime figures who attended "were directly connected with labor unions or with labor-management bargaining groups." JFK called the mob a "nationwide, highly organized, and highly effective internal enemy."[46] Still, the Department of Justice wasn't entirely convinced. As indicated, things changed overnight with JFK's appointment of RFK to head the Justice Department in 1961. Immediately, RFK used his authority to get Director Hoover to shift his primary emphasis away from fighting internal Communism to organized crime.[47] In *Kennedy Justice*, author Victor S. Navasky writes that "Robert Kennedy's organized-crime drive ranked at the top of the nation's domestic priorities."[48]

In September and October of 1963, RFK's Justice Department coordinated the nationally televised hearings of McClellan's Senate Permanent Investigations Subcommittee looking into organized crime in America. The highlight, by far, was the testimony of Joseph Valachi, starting on September 27, 1963, and continuing through October 8. Valachi (a defector from the Vito Genovese Mafia family in New York, who, while awaiting trial for murder, communicated to the authorities that he was willing to "talk" if he could get a deal) put on the record, for the first time ever, the existence throughout the country of the mob "families," their inner structure and workings, the names of leaders of the families and the murders they ordered, as well as the names of the actual hit men and victims. With the help of large, detailed charts prepared by the subcommittee staff, Valachi, a member of the mob for more than thirty of his sixty years, chronicled the evolution of the Mafia from the reigns of mob leaders Joe Masseria and Salvatore Maranzano in 1930 up to the present. Valachi's testimony, which law enforcement was able to confirm as being truthful, "made it possible for police intelligence men to begin to see the dimensions of syndicated crime and stop looking at it as a series of unconnected cases."[49]

---

[*]In particular, RFK led the assault on Jimmy Hoffa, the International Brotherhood of Teamsters' president since 1957, and his union, the nation's largest and most powerful union at the time, establishing that organized crime had helped Hoffa control and dominate the Teamsters, being complicit in the beatings and perhaps murders of Hoffa's opponents in the union. RFK's Justice Department ultimately convicted Hoffa in 1964 of jury tampering and defrauding the union's pension fund out of almost $2 million. His thirteen-year prison sentence, which he started to serve in 1967, ended four years later when President Nixon signed an Executive Grant of Clemency. Actually, the Teamsters had been the subject of scrutiny by the Senate's Permanent Investigations Subcommittee as early as December of 1956, when the committee's chief accountant, Carmine Bellino, and chief counsel, Robert F. Kennedy, looked into the misuse of Teamster funds by Hoffa's predecessor, Dave Beck, resulting in Beck's conviction and removal from office. (McClellan, *Crime without Punishment*, pp.3, 13, 14; Kennedy, *Enemy Within*, pp.3–4, 24; Sheridan, *Fall and Rise of Jimmy Hoffa*, pp.3, 7, 32–33, 210)

The mob, still very much alive and kicking, had nonetheless been dealt a solar plexus blow. In late 1966, a survey conducted by the New York City Police Department found that more members of organized crime "had been sent to jail in the New York–New Jersey–Connecticut metropolitan area during the three years since Valachi talked than in the previous thirty years."[50] Although Valachi's credibility has been challenged by some, RFK called Valachi's testimony "the greatest intelligence breakthrough" in the history of the federal fight against organized crime, adding that "for the first time the FBI changed their whole concept of crime in the United States."[51] Also, RFK said, "For the first time an insider, a knowledgeable member of the racketeering hierarchy, has broken the underworld's code of silence."[52] Coupled with RFK's tenacity, Valachi's testimony initiated the diminution of the Mafia's power, from which, to this moment, it has never recovered.

The HSCA observed that "the Kennedy administration brought about the strongest effort against organized crime that had ever been coordinated by the Federal Government."[53] Robert M. Morgenthau, U.S. attorney for the Southern District of New York, who was one of the local prosecutors carrying out RFK's agenda, said that "for pretty close to 25 years, organized crime had a free run. I mean, from the end of Prohibition down to 1960. And I think it kind of had woven its way into at least a part of the fabric of society . . . It really wasn't until Robert F. Kennedy became Attorney General that an organized program was developed."[54] As a statistical measure of the increased emphasis the Kennedy administration put on fighting organized crime, between 1960 (prior to the Kennedy administration) and 1963, there was a 250 percent increase in the number of attorneys assigned to combat organized crime, from 17 to 60; more than a 900 percent increase in the number of days in the field, from 660 to 6,172; a 1,250 percent increase in the number of days before the grand jury, from 100 to 1,353; and a 1,700 percent increase in the number of days in court, from 61 to 1,081. From 1961 to 1963 there was a 500 percent increase in the number of defendants indicted, from 121 to 615, and a 400 percent increase in the number of defendants convicted, from 73 to 288.[55]

Because RFK knew how much he and his brother's administration had hurt the mob, one of his first thoughts after his brother's death was that maybe the mob had his brother killed. Within days he asked his office to check into any possible Mafia (or Hoffa) links to the assassination.[56] He also personally called Julius Draznin, a Chicago lawyer for the National Labor Relations Board who had excellent sources in the underworld and whom he had sought out before to secure sensitive information on people like Frank Sinatra and Judith Exner (see later text). "Do you have any angles on this [Jack's death]?" he asked Draznin. "Can you tap in on this?" Draznin called RFK back in a few days. "There's nothing," he told RFK.[57]

Conspiracy theorists have alleged for years that the mob made substantial monetary contributions to Kennedy's presidential campaign against Nixon in 1960 in the hope or understanding that if he were elected, he'd go easy on them, and when he didn't, the "betrayal" caused his death. If, indeed, Kennedy had made such a promise to induce campaign contributions, it was *some* betrayal. I mean, almost immediately after being sworn in, he directed or allowed his attorney general brother, RFK, to go after organized crime with far more vigor than any prior presidential administration. But before one even gets to the issue of betrayal, it is difficult to see why, with JFK's father, Joseph

Kennedy, being a bottomless pit for campaign funds,* JFK would even want to take the chance of accepting mob money? He'd have to know that if it were discovered, it would automatically kill his run for the presidency. One could say, "The same argument could be made about JFK's extramarital relationships with women. If JFK was reckless there, why not with the mob?" The difference, of course, is that not only wouldn't the public disclosure of womanizing be anywhere near as devastating as would the revelation that Kennedy was in bed with organized crime, but JFK, we have since learned, literally *needed* these other women. He did not need the mob.

This moldy *theory of retribution* against Kennedy by the mob is so devoid of evidence that although conspiracy theorists and millions of Americans continue to spout it unthinkingly, the HSCA, which conducted an intensive investigation of organized crime's possible involvement in the assassination, *never even bothered to mention it once in its report.*

But is the allegation of organized crime contributing substantial money to Kennedy's campaign true? There is some evidence that of all the leaders of organized crime, Chicago's Sam Giancana, alone, may have made a contribution to JFK's 1960 campaign. In 1997, singer Frank Sinatra's daughter, Tina, confirmed that Joe Kennedy, JFK's father, had personally asked her father at Hyannis Port to ask Giancana, not for money, but to help get out the union vote (mostly Democratic) in Chicago, and her father had done so.[58] Since it is well known that Sinatra supported JFK in his campaign, financially and in other ways, and that Sinatra and Giancana were friends, it makes sense that the singer might have suggested to Giancana it would be a good move to contribute to the campaign. And in G. Robert Blakey and Richard Billings's *Plot to Kill the President*, they quote a December 21, 1961, conversation between Johnny Roselli and Giancana (which Blakey told me was "in a transcript of an FBI surveillance tape given to the Committee [HSCA] by the FBI") in which Roselli says that Sinatra had been in touch with Joe Kennedy. "He's [Sinatra's] got it in his head," Roselli said, as if Sinatra's belief was not justified, "that they're [the Kennedys] going to be faithful to him." When Giancana says, "In other words, then, the *donation* that was made . . .," Roselli interrupts, "That's what I was talking about."

"In other words," Giancana says, "if I ever get a speeding ticket, none of these f____s would know me."

"You told that right, buddy," Roselli replied.[59] And in a January 1962 FBI wiretap of Giancana talking to John D'Arco, a Giancana associate, about the fact that Chicago mayor Richard Daley wanted to put a former FBI agent named Spencer in as a candidate for sheriff of Cook County, Giancana, talking about Spencer, made this remark: "He's like Kennedy. He'll get what he wants out of you, but you won't get anything out of him."[60] Even assuming a Giancana contribution to Kennedy's campaign, from the context of this wiretap and Giancana's remark to Roselli about a "donation," it hardly sounds like a multimillion dollar contribution from the leaders of organized crime, for which JFK's lack of appreciation would cause them to want to kill him.

Although it is possible the mob hedged its bets in the 1960 election, the theory that it

---

*It was common knowledge that Joseph Kennedy was spending whatever was necessary out of his fortune to get his son into 1600 Pennsylvania Avenue, and JFK would facetiously deflect criticism about this. For instance, during his campaign for the presidency in 1960, he told the press at the annual Gridiron Club dinner in Washington, D.C., that "I have just received the following wire from my generous daddy: 'Dear Jack—Don't buy a single vote more than is necessary. I'll be damned if I'm going to pay for a landslide.'" (Parmet, *Jack*, p.439)

heavily supported Kennedy financially seems extremely improbable. As stated earlier, during the Eisenhower and Nixon administrations the Justice Department under Attorney General William P. Rogers did not aggressively pursue the mob. Why would the mob leaders think things would get better with JFK in the Oval Office when they knew of his highly hostile feelings toward them, as demonstrated by his performance on the McClellan Committee a few years earlier? And although they would have no way of knowing that JFK would appoint RFK as attorney general, they certainly would have every reason to believe (particularly since RFK had been chief counsel to the McClellan Committee) that RFK would be helping his brother, in some way, fight organized crime.

At bottom, the story that the mob financially supported Kennedy's run for president is nothing more than a rumor, an unconfirmed allegation. And if we're going to descend to rumors and unconfirmed allegations, Ed Partin, a Teamster official in Louisiana, said that in late September of 1960, he was with Jimmy Hoffa in New Orleans when New Orleans mob boss Carlos Marcello gave Hoffa "a suitcase filled with $500,000 cash which was going to Nixon. It was a half-million-dollar contribution. The other half [of the million promised] was coming from the mob boys in New Jersey and Florida."[61] At least this allegation makes sense, since the mob knew, from JFK and RFK's McClellan Committee days, how determined and passionate the two brothers were about destroying organized crime in America, and Hoffa was supporting Nixon for the presidency. Announcing the endorsement of Nixon by the general executive board of the International Brotherhood of Teamsters on September 7, 1960, Hoffa said that Nixon's opponent, Kennedy, "presents a very real danger to our nation if he is successful in buying our country's highest office."[62]

So there is no credible evidence that the mob made substantial contributions to JFK's 1960 campaign for the presidency, nor has any evidence ever surfaced to substantiate the allegation that after the mob financially backed JFK's bid for the presidency, it became infuriated with him when he never treated it well in return, and ordered his death because of it.

In any event, no one would question that the mob was being hurt big-time by the Kennedy administration, and the conventional belief among many conspiracy theorists is not the retribution theory of some of their colleagues, but that the mob killed Kennedy simply to get RFK "off their back." For example, former *Life* magazine editor Richard Billings, who wrote the HSCA Report with Robert Blakey, and coauthored with Blakey the book *The Plot to Kill the President*, says, "We know the motive" for the mob's killing JFK. "The motive was that Bob Kennedy was determined to wipe them out."[63] But this is an anemic argument since organized crime would have no assurance that Robert Kennedy would not continue to be attorney general under LBJ, which he in fact did for almost a year, resigning on September 2, 1964, to run for the U.S. Senate from the state of New York. And if RFK concluded that the mob had killed his brother, it could expect a vendetta by him against them of unprecedented proportions. Moreover, even if one were to concede that organized crime had a motive to kill Kennedy, as I discussed earlier, motive is only a starting point in any investigation, not the solution to the murder that conspiracy theorists want people to believe. Contrary to the allegation by conspiracy theorists that after Kennedy's assassination the fight against organized crime virtually stopped, the number of indictments against organized-crime figures (though not convictions) actually continued to rise dramatically. But there can be no question that once RFK left office in 1964, the Department of Justice's effort against organized crime, without the engine of RFK's passion, suffered measurably. One telling barometer: in fiscal year 1964, the number of "man days" in the field by members of the organized-crime section was 6,699; by fiscal year 1966 it had dropped to 3,480.[64]

In any criminal case, if you're going to accuse someone of a crime, you have to come up with some evidence that he committed it. There is no credible evidence of any kind that organized crime was involved in the assassination of President Kennedy.

From early 1961 through the assassination in 1963, the FBI conducted extensive electronic surveillance (i.e., "bugging" by hidden microphones to pick up all conversations in a given area) of the nine members of organized crime's national commission, the group, as indicated, that made decisions of national importance for the mob and gave approval or disapproval to other mafiosi wanting to engage in important acts. The HSCA said,

> The committee's review of the surveillance transcripts and logs, detailing the private conversations of the commission members and their associates, revealed that there were extensive and heated discussions about the serious difficulties the Kennedy administration's crackdown on organized crime was causing. The bitterness and anger with which organized crime leaders viewed the Kennedy administration are readily apparent in the electronic surveillance transcripts, with such remarks being repeatedly made by commission members Genovese, Giancana, Bruno, Zerilli, Patriarca and Magaddino . . . While the committee's examination of the electronic surveillance program revealed no shortage of such conversations during that period, the committee *found no evidence* in the conversations of the formulation of any specific plan to assassinate the President . . . The committee concluded that had the national crime syndicate, as a group, been involved in a conspiracy to kill the President, some trace of the plot would have been picked up by the FBI surveillance of the commission . . . Given the far-reaching possible consequences of an assassination plot by the commission, the committee found that such a conspiracy would have been the subject of serious discussion by members of the commission, and that no matter how guarded such discussions might have been, some trace of them would have emerged from the surveillance coverage.[65]*

---

*The HSCA added, however, that "an individual organized crime leader who was planning an assassination conspiracy against President Kennedy *might well have* avoided making the plan known to the commission or seeking approval for it from commission members. Such a course of unilateral action seemed to the committee to have been particularly *possible* in the case of powerful organized crime leaders who were well established, with firm control over their jurisdictions" (HSCA Report, p.167). But all of this is not only pure speculation, but extremely unreasonable speculation at that. The HSCA came up with only one leader in the history of organized crime subsequent to the establishment of the national commission in the early 1930s who acted in matters of murder without first seeking commission approval. In 1957, New York mob leader Vito Genovese engineered the assassination of fellow mafioso Albert Anastasia while he was seated in a barber's chair near Central Park, and six months earlier a Genovese hit man had shot at and attempted to murder Mafia leader Frank Costello without the knowledge or consent of the commission. (Genovese did seek and obtain commission approval for the murder and attempted murder after the fact.) (HSCA Report, pp.167–168) But this clearly was highly exceptional behavior—by just one leader in one year. More importantly, one can't begin to compare (as the HSCA did without appropriate comment) killing a fellow mafioso without commission approval, an act that would not bring any retribution by the U.S. government against organized crime, with killing the president of the United States, which, as previously indicated, would bring a retaliation against them by the federal government of an unprecedented magnitude.

In any event, the only two mob leaders the HSCA could think of who might possibly act unilaterally were Carlos Marcello and Santo Trafficante, and the committee proceeded to say that it was unlikely that either had done so in this case (see later discussion).

As an example of FBI surveillance of the mob on a local level, William Roemer of the Chicago office of the FBI and his men had succeeded in installing two "bugs" in the Armory Lounge, mobster Sam Giancana's favorite watering hole in the Windy City, and at "Little Al's" (named after Al Capone), the Chicago mob's headquarters in a custom tailoring shop at 620 North Michigan. Having listened for hours to the two bugs in the FBI's "tech room" on the weekend after the assassination, Roemer described the mobsters' reaction to Kennedy's death as "gleeful." Indeed, an associate of Philadelphia mob boss Angelo Bruno was heard saying, "It's too bad his brother Bobby wasn't in that car, too." But Roemer heard not the slightest suggestion that the mob was complicit in Kennedy's murder. In fact, one of Giancana's closest henchmen, Chuckie English, opines that Kennedy was killed by "a Marxist." Giancana responded, "He was a marksman who knew how to shoot." But Giancana said nothing that even vaguely implied mob participation.[66]

Roemer said that his people had started bugging the same two mob hangouts in July of 1959, and it continued until 1965. ("We did not wiretap the phone. They wouldn't talk on the phone.") Roemer said the FBI heard the mobsters "talking about every crime you could imagine. [But] in all that time [1959–1965] there was not an inkling that the JFK assassination was connected to any part of the mob."[67*]

Moreover, as indicated earlier, not only would the mob's killing of Kennedy bring no assurance that RFK wouldn't continue to go after it as attorney general under Lyndon Johnson, but unless the mob had LBJ in its hip pocket—and there's no evidence of that— what assurance could it possibly have that LBJ, as president, would be any more congenial to its interests than JFK was? Indeed, for all the mob would know, he might be worse. Organized-crime figures might be criminals, but no one has ever accused them of being simple-minded. They can think as logically as anyone else. During a meeting of several local mobsters on February 9, 1962, in Philadelphia that the FBI had bugged, mob associate Willie Weisburg expressed such a hatred for Kennedy that he exclaimed, "Honest to God . . . I hope I get a week's notice. I'll kill. Right in the [obscenity] White House. Somebody's got to get rid of this [obscenity]." Here's how Angelo Bruno, the Philadelphia mob chieftain who was a member of the national commission, responded:

> Look, Willie, . . . there was a king, do you understand? And he found out that everybody was saying that he was a bad king. This is an old Italian story. So, there was an old wise woman about 140 years old. So, he figured, let me go talk to the old wise woman. She knows everything. So he went to the old wise woman. So he says to her, I came here because I want your opinion. He says, do you think I'm a bad king? She says, no, I think you are a good king. He says, well how come every-

---

[*]Not that there weren't loose and meaningless ventings before the assassination by individual mafiosi— the type you could expect to hear from thousands of everyday Americans who have a deep hostility for a particular president. On October 31, 1963, an FBI bug picked up the following conversation between Peter Magaddino and his brother Stefano, the mob boss in upstate New York. Peter: "President Kennedy, he should drop dead." Stefano: "They should kill the whole family, the mother and father, too." And on May 2, 1962, an FBI bug picked up Michelino Clemente, a member of the Vito Genovese family in New York City, saying, "Bob Kennedy won't stop today until he puts us all in jail all over the country. Until the commission meets and puts its foot down, things will be at a standstill." Around this same time, an unidentified Genovese family member is heard saying, "I want the President indicted because I know he was whacking all those broads. Sinatra brought them out. I'd like to hit Kennedy. I would gladly go to the penitentiary for the rest of my life, believe me." (Davis, *Mafia Kingfish*, pp. 315–316)

body says I'm a bad king? She says because they are stupid. They don't know. He says, well, how come, why do you say I'm a good king? Well, she said, I knew your great grandfather. He was a bad king. I knew your grandfather. He was worse. I knew your father. He was worse than them. You, you are worse than all of them, but your son, if you die, your son is going to be worse than you. So it's better to be with you. (All laugh)[68]

The mob was using common sense. Something the conspiracy theorists wouldn't dream of doing.

To me, the thought that organized crime would actually decide to kill the president of the United States is completely far-fetched and preposterous. Yet none other than leading anti-conspiracy author Gerald Posner thinks the mob may have been on the brink of murdering Kennedy. Posner wrote in *Penthouse* magazine, "Mafia kingpins may, indeed, have plotted to murder JFK, but Oswald beat them to it."[69] In a 1993 radio debate with conspiracy theorist Peter Dale Scott, he said, "I wouldn't be surprised if Marcello and Trafficante sat around the table and said, 'Let's kill Kennedy.'" When television host Charlie Rose asked Posner in a September 15, 1993, interview whether he thought the Mafia was out to kill Kennedy, Posner replied, "*No question.* They could have had Kennedy on a hit list." And in *Case Closed*, he writes, "Mobsters may have discussed killing JFK . . . but [Oswald] beat the mafia to Kennedy."[70]

Posner has also said that although Ruby's conduct on the weekend of the assassination rules out Ruby having killed Oswald for organized crime, there is otherwise "the odor of a Mafia hit all around Ruby's murder of Lee Harvey Oswald."[71] But since when does the mob employ a blabbermouth and virtual idiot like Ruby to carry out an important contract for it? When does it have its hit man shoot the victim not in the head or even the heart but in the stomach, the least vulnerable part of the upper body? And when does the mob have its hit man carry out the hit right before the eyes of law enforcement, thereby guaranteeing he would be apprehended and grilled, and hence, possibly talk? Show me a precedent for any of these things.

It is nothing short of remarkable that Robert Blakey, a respected authority on organized crime who worked in the organized-crime section of the U.S. attorney general's office under Robert Kennedy, and later became chief counsel for the HSCA, also says in his book *The Plot to Kill the President* that "the murder of Lee Harvey Oswald by Jack Ruby had all the earmarks of a gangland slaying." (And, of course, if the mob had Oswald silenced, that means they had Oswald kill Kennedy.) Why? Because, Blakey says, "a key witness [was] shot down by a shadowy figure at close range in public."[72] But Blakey doesn't go on to cite any examples of similar mob murders, for the simple reason that none exist. Yes, mob figures have been murdered in public, but the killings don't take place right in front of law enforcement, and the unknown killers (though only one may kill, he is always accompanied by at least one or more associates) always escape. About the only similarity between Ruby's killing of Oswald and a mob hit is that mob killings are nearly always accomplished by use of a handgun.[73] But of course, most homicides, period, are committed with a handgun.

Indeed, I can't think of one mob execution that was carried out by one killer, acting alone, nor can I think of one mob execution where the killers were *immediately appre-*

hended by law enforcement. Rather than Ruby's killing of Oswald having the "earmarks" of a mob killing, the reality is that it unquestionably has the earmarks of a non-mob killing. Mafia historian Frederic Sondern describes the almost ritualistic procedure (there are, of course, exceptions and variations) of a mob killing. After a "sentence of death is agreed upon" by ranking members of the Mafia, "a small committee is designated to implement the decision. One of these writes to a cousin or uncle, perhaps in Chicago, Detroit or elsewhere in the almost indecipherable Sicilian-Italian dialect for 'two good men' to do 'some heavy work.' No such letter, even if found, would ever prove anything in court. Before long the two 'good men' arrive, for example, in New York. Their preparation for the task is always meticulous, which is the reason that Mafia killers are so seldom caught [never at the scene]. For days, sometimes for weeks, they study the habits and schedule of the condemned."[74] Really sounds like Ruby's killing of Oswald, doesn't it? Sondern also points out that the execution is virtually always by handgun. Even the location on the victim's body in which he is shot follows tradition, the killers "aiming for the head and neck." The reason for the neck is that if, perchance, the victim survives the shots to the head, "the victim can rarely articulate the name or description of his assailant before he dies."[75] As we know, Ruby shot Oswald in the stomach, which, unlike the head, can never be as reliably fatal.

After serving for the HSCA, Blakey said he was convinced that organized crime, specifically Carlos Marcello and Santo Trafficante, had killed Kennedy. But Frank Salerno, Blakey's chief organized-crime investigator on the HSCA, and a former New York Police Department detective who had headed up the force's fight against organized crime for twenty years, said, "I have the greatest respect for Robert Blakey, but I cannot join him in this hypothesis." Salerno said that in all his years investigating organized crime, "there was no indication of their involvement [in Kennedy's murder]. Since that time up to the current day, you have had a large number of high-level members of organized crime who have made a deal with the government and testified against their fellows. None of them have ever suggested that they knew of or even heard of involvement by organized crime in the death of President Kennedy."[76] Blakey responds to Salerno's observation by saying that he agrees with Salerno "that it wasn't the national commission" of organized crime who ordered Kennedy's murder, alleging that Kennedy's murder resulted from "a local operation of two [Mafia] families at most: Marcello in New Orleans and Trafficante in Florida."[77] But that's not what Salerno said. Salerno is very well aware of Blakey's position, set forth in his book and elsewhere, that Marcello and Trafficante were behind Kennedy's murder. In other words, he knows Blakey's "hypothesis," and *this* is what Salerno disagrees with. His statement clearly shows that not only doesn't he agree that organized crime (the national commission or what have you) killed Kennedy, but also he doesn't agree with Blakey's hypothesis that the two individual organized-crime families of Marcello and Trafficante did.

To believe the conspiracy theorists who contend that organized crime was behind Kennedy's murder, we'd have to completely overlook the fact that, as opposed to its counterparts in Sicily,* the mob in America has absolutely no history of going after public offi-

---

*The author of a book on the Sicilian Mafia said that the list of political figures mobsters have killed "is staggering" (Pantaleone, *Mafia and Politics*, p.202).

cials. The mob not only has religiously avoided doing so, but has taken severe, affirmative steps to prevent it. For example, in 1935, when Bronx racketeer Arthur "Dutch Schultz" Flegenheimer became a target of racket-busting New York State special prosecutor Thomas Dewey in New York City, he went to Lucky Luciano and Albert Anastasia (the head of Murder, Inc., the death enforcement arm of the national crime syndicate) demanding Dewey's death. When Luciano refused and Schultz decided he was going to do it on his own, Luciano ordered his murder on October 23, 1935, in a Newark, New Jersey, bar and grill. "[Luciano] found almost universal agreement among underworld chieftains," mob writer Peter Maas notes, "that if Schultz were allowed to murder Dewey, it could trigger exactly the kind of all-out drive against organized crime that they were anxious to avoid. Thus, Schultz himself had to be liquidated."[78]

Likewise, no one in organized crime made a move against Prohibition agent Elliot Ness when he was trying to put Al Capone and his gang out of business in Chicago in the late 1920s. The mob has never gone after law enforcement officers in this country. One would literally have to go all the way back to 1890 to find anyone who even *accused* the Mafia of killing a member of law enforcement or, for that matter, any public official. In that year, nineteen members of the New Orleans Mafia were indicted for murdering the first superintendent of the New Orleans Police Department, one David Hennessy, as he was walking home on the drizzly night of October 15, 1890. His friend Bill O'Connor, a captain of the Boylan Protection League who had been walking with him, had just split off to walk to his own nearby residence when five men ambushed Hennessy with a fusillade of more than fifteen bullets, six of which hit Hennessy, who fired back at the fleeing men. O'Connor, hearing the shots, ran back to Hennessy, and kneeling down beside him, asked, "Who gave it to you, Dave?" "Dagoes [a slur for Italians]," Hennessy whispered back. Hennessy lapsed into unconsciousness and died the following day.[79]

But the following year on March 13, 1891, after a highly publicized two-week trial against nine of the defendants (the DA decided to try the remaining ten separately at a later date), the jury acquitted six and couldn't reach a verdict on three. The jury foreman said that "the state made out a poor case." Another juror said, "I'm sorry I couldn't please the whole community, but I had to do what I thought was right." Thousands in New Orleans were aghast at the verdicts and a local firebrand lawyer, W. S. Parkerson, declared at a huge rally the next day that "when courts fail, the people must act. Our chief of police is assassinated in our very midst by the Mafia society, and its assassins again turned loose on the community. Are you going to let it continue?" "No, no," the crowd roared back, "Hang the dagoes," and proceeded to form a lynching mob of over twelve thousand that stormed and broke through the barricaded Parish Prison and ended up riddling with bullets and murdering eleven of the nineteen Mafia members, the largest recorded lynching in U.S. history. Eight of the nineteen had escaped by hiding well within the jail, one in the women's section. Of the ten defendants who hadn't yet been tried, five were murdered. All charges were dropped against the remaining five following the March 14 massacre. Although President Benjamin Harrison publicly expressed his regrets and took $25,000 out of a special White House fund to be distributed among the families of the victims, no member of the lynch mob was ever prosecuted, the consensus being that vigilante justice had been called for. Even a *New York Times* editorial on March 18, 1891, said that although the lynching "is to be deplored, it would be difficult to find any one individual who . . . deplored it very much." Indeed, the New Orleans incident ignited strong anti-Italian sentiments throughout the entire country. Were the murdered Italians, in fact, guilty? A subsequent investigation by the "Federal District Attorney" of Louisiana found that the evidence was "not conclusive one way or the other," and his office was "unable to obtain any direct evidence connecting these persons with the Mafia or any other association of a similar character in the city."[80] A 1999 movie, *Vendetta*, starring Christopher Walken, was about the Hennessy murder and its aftermath.

In any event, a precedent dating back to the 1890s when the Mafia was in its infancy, particularly one that was not confirmed by any convictions, hardly supports the proposition that the modern-day American Mafia goes after public figures.

In their book *The Plot to Kill the President*, the authors, Robert Blakey and Richard Billings, in addition to relying on the Hennessy case, and trying hard to show that the mob going after law enforcement or public officials was not unprecedented, mention a 1926 murder of the mayor of little Culp, Illinois, but they can only speculate that he was killed "*probably* because he had been corrupted by a bootlegging syndicate," the authors not even alleging that the syndicate was the Mafia; the murder of an assistant state attorney in Chicago, also in 1926, "who was *believed* [the authors give no source for this "belief" of theirs] to have been looking into the activities of Al Capone"; and the murder of an Illinois state legislator in 1936 who was killed "*in all likelihood* [the authors are again speculating, and offer no source] by the Capone gang." When the pickin's are this slim and speculative, the authors would have done themselves a favor by not even mentioning the above killings. To go from what they have dredged out of the past to help support their belief that the Mafia murdered Kennedy (particularly when they do not present one stitch of credible evidence to support this conclusion) is, to be charitable, wholly unjustified. Even the authors are forced to concede that "office holders who were victims of organized crime [the authors offered no evidence that *any* office holder was murdered by organized crime] violence generally served at a low level of government. They each had been in close contact with the underworld—either as conscientious opponents or as corrupt collaborators."[81]

When the HSCA asked Chicago mobster Lenny Patrick if he thought organized crime was behind Kennedy's assassination, he responded dismissively, "In my opinion, I don't think they are crazy . . . It is silly. They know that. They wouldn't do that."[82]

"Mafia boss Joseph Bonanno articulated the principles of the game," writes author Anthony Summers. "It was a strict underground rule, he said, never to use violent means against a law enforcement officer."[83] All the more so, of course, the president of the United States.

With this long history, are we to believe that organized crime decided not only to completely change course, but to start, of all places, at the very top of the hill by murdering the most powerful public official and man on earth? Are we really to believe that the Mafia, which considered it too risky to kill a police officer, found the risk acceptable if the victim was the president of the United States? One whose brother was the chief law enforcement officer in the country? As mafioso Johnny Roselli told Los Angeles mob boss Jimmy "The Weasel" Fratiano, "It's against the fucking rules [of the mob] to kill a cop, so now we're going to kill the President?"[84] And instead of employing reliable and close-lipped professional killers to do the job, which the mob almost invariably does, getting the likes of Lee Harvey Oswald and Jack Ruby to carry out its mission? It would have been the most insane, unwise, senseless, and self-destructive thing the mob could have ever done. And we know that, despite its criminality, as the House Select Committee on Assassinations put it, "Mafia figures are rational, pragmatic businessmen."[85] As I told the jury at the London trial, when the Mafia came to America from Sicily, "they didn't leave their brains behind in Palermo."[86]

Out of the literally thousands of mob murders throughout the years, the HSCA could only come up with two examples in mob history where the mob had someone *outside* its organization commit murder for it, and both of these murders took place *after* JFK's assassination: the murder of a Kansas City businessman in 1970 by four young black men, and that of a fellow mafioso, Joseph Colombo, in New York City in 1971 by a young black man with a petty criminal record.[87] And with respect to the second murder, of Colombo, this was one mobster being killed on the orders of one or more other mobsters. And the mob and everyone else knows that finding who was behind this type of killing (which the authorities never did) has never had a high priority in law enforcement—the thinking being that one less mobster is one less crime figure law enforcement has to worry about.

The only other example where the Mafia broke with its almost invariable rule of not going outside the mob to get someone to commit a serious crime for it involved Victor Riesel, a nationally syndicated labor columnist who, in 1956, had been writing unfavorably about six or seven New York City locals of the United Auto Workers, which had close ties to the Thomas Lucchese crime family, one of the Mafia's five families in New York City. On the evening of April 5, 1956, a drug addict unconnected to the mob approached Riesel on Broadway and threw sulfuric acid in his face, blinding Riesel. A subsequent investigation revealed that the mob had paid the addict five hundred dollars to do the deed.[88]

That's it. Two murders and one aggravated assault in the long history of the mob among literally thousands of killings and assaults.

The HSCA stated, "A person like Oswald—young, active in controversial political causes, apparently not subject to the internal discipline of a criminal organization—would appear to be the least likely candidate for the role of Mafia hit man, especially in such an important murder. Gunmen used in organized crime killings have traditionally been selected with utmost deliberation and care, the most important considerations being loyalty and a willingness to remain silent if apprehended. These are qualities best guaranteed by past participation in criminal activities."[89] To believe the mob (supposedly "*wise*guys") would employ an unknown quantity like Oswald to carry out its most important murder ever turns logic completely on its head. Indeed, the only thing the mob would know about him was that he was terribly strange and unstable, and additionally seemed to love Fidel Castro, someone the mob hated for taking away its multibillion-dollar gambling empire in Havana.

Quite apart from the extreme improbability that the mob, which already felt enormous governmental heat from RFK's Justice Department, would do something that could increase that heat—I told the London jury, to a degree akin "to the surface of the sun"—even if the mob were crazy enough to do so, it would never in a million years get the markedly unhinged and unreliable Lee Harvey Oswald and almost childlike Jack Ruby to do its bidding. Oswald and Ruby. Two nuts.

Interestingly enough, Carlos Marcello, the portly, five-foot six-inch head of the Mafia in New Orleans (believed to be the smallest Mafia "family" in the country at the time, with only about twelve members), who always insisted to the media that he was only a tomato salesman who dabbled in real estate investments, allegedly made a threat to kill Kennedy in September of 1962 and to do it with a "nut," no less. And when conspiracy theorists get down to their most serious discourse, such as lengthy books alleging the mob's being behind Kennedy's murder, it's not generally the national leadership they accuse, but one of two mob leaders, Marcello *or* Florida mob leader Santo Trafficante. (As we saw, G. Robert Blakey believes *both* were likely involved.) And of the two, Marcello has been the principal suspect.[*]

The individual to whom Marcello allegedly made the threat was one Edward Becker. Becker, at the time a licensed private investigator in California working for a corporate client on the Billie Sol Estes financial scam, is presently living in retirement in Las Vegas, Nevada. He's had a multifaceted career, including coauthoring a book about mobster Johnny Roselli, being an investigative reporter for the *Oakland Tribune*, and producing and writing a local Los Angeles television show.

In a series of five lengthy telephone conversations[†] between August 13 and September 26, 1999, Becker (eighty-two at the time) told me he was "friendly" with the mob "to this very day." On the September 1962 day in question, Becker said he was at Marcello's Churchill Farms, his 6,500-acre estate in Jefferson Parish outside New Orleans, through the auspices of Carl Roppolo, a close family friend of Marcello's whom Marcello affectionately referred to as his "nephew." (And Roppolo referred to Marcello as his "uncle.") In addition to Roppolo, Jack Liberto (Marcello's barber and a close friend) was at Churchill Farms. Earlier in the day, Roppolo and Becker had pitched a legitimate business deal (ultimately, never agreed on) to Marcello at his office in the Town and Country Motel in the city, and after the meeting Marcello drove the group in his black Cadillac to his sprawling farmhouse to relax.

Becker, by most accounts a colorful character whom people opened up to, had worked as the director of public relations for the Riviera Hotel in Las Vegas from 1955 to 1958 when it was controlled by the Chicago mob, finally leaving after his boss, Gus Greenbaum, and Greenbaum's wife, Bess, were the victims of an underworld killing in Phoenix. Because Marcello knew of Becker's background in Las Vegas ("Greenbaum was dead and I was still alive, so I must have been okay"), and also knew that Becker had been friendly with Johnny Roselli, as well as Becker's having had entree to him through his "nephew," Becker believes that Marcello felt "comfortable" with him. As was second nature to him as a private eye, and because he says he has always been "fascinated" by the mob and its culture (as are millions of Americans), Becker said he didn't want to pass up the opportunity to hear the legendary mobster emote. The way he puts it, it "was fun" to him, saying he found big-time mobsters "interesting people. It's not easy to crack that world, and when you do, you take advantage of the situation." With Roppolo and Marcello's barber

---

[*]One conspiracy theorist is not satisfied having Marcello merely being "behind" the assassination. In his book *The Elite Serial Killers of Lincoln, JFK, RFK, and MLK*, author Robert Gaylon Ross writes that there were eleven members of the "death squad" at Dealey Plaza, but the "control point" was on the second floor of the Book Depository Building, where he says Carlos Marcello was one of three gunmen firing at Kennedy (Ross, *Elite Serial Killers*, p.103).

[†]As just one example of the help I received from so many people in the writing of this book, I knew I couldn't write intelligently about Becker without talking to him personally. But how would I go about locating someone like him? If anyone knew how, I knew who it would be—Chicago's Jim Agnew, the former publisher of *Real Crime Book Digest* who had helped me many times in the past. Jim is almost a character out of fiction who looks exactly like you would expect an Irish cop walking the beat on a New York street in an old Bing Crosby movie to look. Whatever is going on in this country that's being written about, particularly in the area of crime, Jim somehow knows about it. And he has many contacts who can get him all types of information. I called Jim and asked him if he could locate Becker for me. A half hour later, Jim called back with Becker's unlisted home phone number, no less, in Las Vegas.

not in the room at the time, having "decided to wander around the farmhouse and grounds," Becker says he "intentionally provoked" Marcello (known to friend and foe in Louisiana as the "Little Man" because of his height) into talking about what was going on in his life by saying, "These SOB's [the Kennedys], they're really going after everybody," and "Bobby Kennedy is really giving you a rough time,"[*] whereupon Marcello, per Becker, exploded in anger that he intended to kill not only Robert Kennedy but also JFK, explaining that "the dog [JFK] will keep biting you if you only cut off its tail [RFK]," but if the dog's head were cut off, it would die. Marcello also uttered what Becker (whose mother is half Italian and who grew up in an Italian neighborhood in New Haven, Connecticut, but spoke few words of Italian) construed from Marcello's voice and demeanor to be a "Sicilian curse," the essence of which Becker remembered phonetically: "*Livarsi na petra di la scarpa*" ("Take the stone out of my shoe," a translation he said he got not long after the incident from an Italian friend of his in Las Vegas).

When Becker told Marcello that if Marcello did this he would immediately become a suspect (because of the well-publicized effort the Kennedy administration was making to re-deport him), Marcello responded, "You [referring to himself] get a nut to do it."

Assuming for the sake of argument that this conversation took place, this sequence, of course, is very important. If Marcello had, without prompting, brought up the "nut" reference, it could possibly mean he had already given some thought to the matter. But Becker was very, very clear with me that Marcello's "nut" remark was a spontaneous response to Becker's warning to him.[†]

But, of course, *if* Marcello had given the matter some prior thought, and *if* he or any other mob leader did actually intend to kill the president, not more than a few moments' reflection would be necessary to yield the obvious course of action he'd have to take.[‡] The inevitable question that presents itself is this: If any person or group of

---

[*] The U.S. government had been seeking to deport Marcello (true name, Calogero Minacore), who was born in Tunis, North Africa, to Sicilian-born parents and had never become a naturalized American citizen, since 1953. But a 1953 order to deport Marcello as an "undesirable alien" wasn't implemented until Attorney General Robert Kennedy did so on April 4, 1961, the INS arresting Marcello when he walked into an INS office in New Orleans on a regular visit to report as an alien, and flying him in an INS airplane to Guatemala, from which he illegally reentered the United States less than two weeks later. (9 HSCA 62, 71–72; 1953 deportation order: Davis, *Mafia Kingfish*, p. 176)

[†] Inasmuch as the sequence is so critical here, it was reassuring to me when I later played an old *Frontline* documentary in which Becker was one of several people interviewed by host Jack Newfield. Newfield: "Did he [Marcello] actually say that he was going to get a nut to do the assassination so it can't be traced to him?" Becker: "Yeah, yeah. Well, I said to him [that if Kennedy were killed] 'right away they know it's you. I mean, you've got everything going for you. The one that hates him. Everybody knows it.' He said 'Don't worry, you get a nut to do this thing and nobody's looking at you.'" ("JFK, Hoffa and the Mob," *Frontline*, PBS, November 17, 1992)

[‡] One step conspiracy theorists say Marcello would not have had to take is to get permission from the national commission of the Mafia to kill the president. As indicated earlier, the first "family" of the Mafia came from Sicily and settled in New Orleans in 1875. A "highly reliable source" told the FBI in 1972 that "inasmuch as this 'family' was the predecessor of all subsequent 'families,' it has been afforded the highest respect and esteem, and because of its exalted position, the New Orleans 'family' could make decisions on its own without going to the 'Commission'" (FBI report, October 24, 1972, La Cosa Nostra file, Bureau No. 92-6054-3176; HSCA Report, p. 172). Patrick Collins, an FBI agent who investigated Marcello and his organization in the 1960s, formed the same view, telling the HSCA that the New Orleans Mafia family "was unique among all the mobs" in that it "didn't have to consult the commission in the same way as the other families did. There was a unique independence of sorts" (9 HSCA 66; HSCA staff interview of Patrick J. Collins on November 15, 1978). However, on a crime of the monumental magnitude of murdering the president, I think we can assume that Marcello, if he had had such thoughts, would know that his privileged exemption from reporting to the commission would not apply.

people had the resources (which organized-crime figures surely do) to employ a third party to kill the president of the United States, what would that person or group then do? Would they hire someone who is an expert gunman with a track record of successful murders, a reliable, professional hit man with a proven history of being closed-mouthed, thereby greatly reducing the likelihood that any finger of suspicion would ever be pointed back at them? Or would they get a nut to do it, increasing the likelihood immeasurably that something would go wrong and the trail would lead back to them, or the nut would simply point the finger at them, and their only defense would be that they could say to the authorities, "Why would I get a nut to do something like this?" When the choice is between *no* finger of suspicion against you at all, and a finger of suspicion against you whose only limited benefit allows you to say, "Why would I hire a nut like this?" the choice can *only* be the former. And this isn't just abstract, esoteric logic. This is the very, very simplest of common sense. Show me any precedent at all for the mob taking the opposite option.

The HSCA investigated Becker's allegation and questioned whether Marcello had ever made the remark to Becker, concluding that it was "unlikely that an organized-crime leader personally involved in an assassination plot would discuss it with anyone other than his closest lieutenants."[90] But this is surprisingly flabby and self-contradictory reasoning because it is necessarily based on the assumption that Marcello did, in fact, plan to murder Kennedy, when at the same time the HSCA concluded it had no evidence of this and it was "unlikely" that Marcello was in fact involved in the assassination.[91] While it is undoubtedly true that if Marcello were engaged in a plot to murder Kennedy he would never have confided in Becker, if he wasn't, and had no such intent, it wouldn't be particularly shocking to me that someone like Marcello—particularly since he'd have no way of knowing that a little over a year later a real nut named Lee Harvey Oswald would actually kill the president—might make a threat to kill Kennedy even to a stranger sitting next to him in a corner bar.

Becker told me that after his allegation was published for the first time in Ed Reid's 1969 book *The Grim Reapers*, he continued to associate with mobsters in Las Vegas, none of whom treated him any differently. "There was no hostility at all," which he felt confident there would have been if Marcello or the mob had been behind the assassination. "There were no threats, nothing at all." He said, "Even Marcello's man in Las Vegas, Mario, at the Sands," continued to treat him well. It should be pointed out that in *The Grim Reapers*, in which the entire incident is capsulized in a few paragraphs, the author, Reid, doesn't mention his source, Becker, by name.[92] However, since the only other two people at Churchill Farms that day (whose identity Reid also does not give) were Carl Roppolo and Marcello's barber, Becker said Marcello had to know the author's source.

In concluding that it was unlikely Marcello would have confided in Becker, the HSCA also questioned Becker's reliability for truth but failed to adequately set forth the basis for its position. To me, Becker comes across as a sensible, candid person who at least "sounds" very believable and matter-of-fact when telling his story, and he points out that he never sought to exploit or capitalize on the story in any way. "People came to me. I never went to them." He said he never tried to sell the story to the tabloids or anyone else, that he had been interviewed about it perhaps twenty times, yet "I never took or asked for a dime for any of the interviews." He said, "I wish he [Marcello] had never said it and I wish I had never heard it."

The owner of the private investigative agency in Los Angeles that Becker worked for, Julian Blodgett, was an FBI agent for fourteen years, leaving in 1957 to head up, between 1957 and 1961, the Los Angeles County DA office's Bureau of Investigation, a group I worked closely with on many of my murder cases. Blodgett told me that he has known Becker for thirty years and Becker had "always been truthful and honest with me," saying he was "99.9 percent" sure Becker was telling the truth about the Marcello incident. "I have no reason to doubt Ed," he said, adding that Becker was the type of person whom everyone liked, and that he had a way of ingratiating himself "into situations that other people could only dream about."[93]

I personally give the incident no less than a 50 percent probability of its happening just the way Becker said it did.

It should be noted that apart from what may or may not have been said, it appears from all the circumstantial evidence that Becker *did* at least meet with Marcello in September 1962. The HSCA said, "The Bureau's [FBI's] files from November 1962 noted that Becker had in fact traveled through Louisiana during that period . . . The Bureau's own November 26, 1962, interview report on Becker noted that he had informed the Bureau of two business meetings with Marcello that he had attended with Carl Roppolo in recent weeks."[94] Becker told me that when FBI agents interviewed him in Beverly Hills, California, on November 26, 1962, it was his investigation of the Billie Sol Estes case that they were working on, although the first thing they asked him was, "What were you doing with Marcello?" He said that very question indicated that they knew he had met with Marcello, most likely as a result of their surveillance of Marcello. He said he responded, "If you were that close to me, you must have known." He went on to tell them about the business proposition he and Roppolo had made to Marcello—to have Marcello be the distributor in the New Orleans area for an oil additive that Roppolo had come up with called "Mustang."[*]

The main issue, then, seems to be not whether Becker met with Marcello (a strong probability), but whether Marcello said what Becker claims he said. To the FBI's discredit, the bureau never, at any time, investigated Becker's allegations, instead making an effort to discredit him. Even though the HSCA was aware of this, it nonetheless embraced the FBI's view vis-à-vis Becker by concluding, "*As a consequence of his [Becker's] underworld involvement*, the informant had a questionable reputation for honesty and may not be a credible source of information,"[95] suggesting there is a presumption that anyone who has ever had any association with mob figures is most likely a liar. With that curious attitude, one wonders why the U.S. attorney's office, in prosecutions of mob figures, routinely offers to juries the testimony of former mobsters who turn state's evidence and are frequently believed by the juries. And that's where the snitch has something to gain by lying—immunity from prosecution or a reduced sentence. Here, it would seem that Becker had nothing to gain.

---

[*]Even assuming Becker is telling the truth, he has made contradictory statements—probably out of confusion or lack of memory—about one point. He told HSCA investigators that he never told the FBI about Marcello's Kennedy threats because he was "afraid" Marcello or his associates might learn he had done so (9 HSCA 83). This makes sense. And in my first conversation with him on August 13, 1999, he told me the first time he had ever told the authorities about Marcello's threats was to the HSCA in 1978. But in a later conversation he said he *did* start to tell the FBI about the threats, "but they weren't interested. They were agents who were only working on the Billie Sol Estes case." In any event, none of the FBI reports of interviews with or about Becker make any reference to Marcello's threats against Kennedy, and all deal with the Billie Sol Estes case.

Becker, by the way, has no criminal record except a misdemeanor conviction in his early twenties for stealing two hundred dollars from a photographer friend of his who, he told me, owed him the money. When an HSCA investigator interviewed Becker on October 24, 1978, about his Marcello allegation, he said, "I am willing to take a polygraph and always have been. I will take a polygraph, stress exam, or any other type of test."[96]

When I asked Becker if he believed, at the time, what Marcello said to him about intending to kill Kennedy, he chuckled and said, "No. If the mobsters killed everyone they threatened to kill, we'd be depopulated." He then proceeded to tell me that he spent a lot of time at the Riviera in Las Vegas, and in Los Angeles, with Johnny Roselli (about whom he later coauthored the book *All-American Mafioso*) when the New York mob (Roselli's affiliation) was in the process of building the Tropicana and Roselli and his people would "hang out at the Riviera." And every time Roselli would get angry with someone, "He'd threaten to kill him. That's the way the mobsters talked."* However, Becker said that when he heard Kennedy had been killed, which was fourteen months after Marcello's threat, his first thought was that Marcello was behind it and had meant what he said. But today, after much reflection and study, he feels very confident that Marcello was not involved in the assassination. As indicated, one reason among many he has for this belief is the way he was treated by the mob once his revelation of what Marcello told him became public. In fact, he said, in 1970 he and his wife were flying to Washington, D.C., on business and they stopped off in Shreveport, Louisiana (where he first met Carl Roppolo, Marcello's "nephew"), and "had a nice dinner and evening with Roppolo and his wife."

On the issue of the mob not going after public officials in America, Becker said that "on no less than a half-dozen occasions" throughout the years when a mobster would be complaining bitterly about, and reviling, a public official, "I'd ask them, tongue in cheek, and using their language, 'Geez, why don't you whack him?' and they'd always say, with little variation, 'No, no, we don't kill cops or politicians.'" Becker said, "It's like it's a part of their constitution." The exceptions, if any, are so very few and far between, and so insignificant, as to be irrelevant—as Dean Jennings's 1967 book on Bugsy Siegel and the mob is titled, *We Only Kill Each Other*.[97] This reality is known among students of organized crime as "internecine warfare."

Carlos Marcello was *not* one of the nine national commission members in 1963, and he was also the lone Mafia leader whom the FBI was unable to eavesdrop on for many years. A former FBI official knowledgeable about the FBI's surveillance program told the HSCA, "That was our biggest gap. With Marcello, you've got the one big exception in our work back then. There was just no way of penetrating that area. He was too smart."[98]†

---

*An example of "mob talk," from a federal wiretap of a telephone conversation between gangster Johnny Formosa and Chicago mob boss Sam Giancana over the failure of Giancana's friend Frank Sinatra to have President Kennedy stop the authorities from prosecuting Giancana: Formosa: "Let's show 'em. Let's show those [obscenity] Hollywood fruitcakes that they can't get away with it as if nothing's happened. Let's hit Sinatra. Or I could whack out a couple of those other guys. [Peter] Lawford and that [Dean] Martin, and I could take the nigger [Sammy Davis Jr.] and put his other eye out." Giancana: "No . . . I've got other plans for them." (Kelley, *His Way*, pp. 296, 531)

†The other mob boss the FBI found difficult to penetrate was Santo Trafficante, but the bureau was able to conduct some electronic eavesdropping on him (HSCA Report, p. 175). A Cuban exile, José Aleman, claimed that Trafficante (who admitted, in his testimony before the HSCA, to participating in the unsuccessful CIA conspiracy to assassinate Fidel Castro) told him that Kennedy was "going to be hit." The HSCA investigated the claim and concluded that "the relationship between Trafficante and Aleman, a business acquaintance, does not seem to have been close enough for Trafficante to have mentioned or alluded to such a murder plot." In addition to there being no evidence that Trafficante, or Marcello, or any other mob figure, had actually had

One reason was probably that Marcello's New Orleans Mafia family was very small and most of its operations were controlled by his loyal younger brothers, Joseph, Peter, Pascal, Vincent, Sammy, and Anthony.[99]

But for over a year and a half starting in February of 1979, the FBI was finally able to conduct electronic surveillance on Marcello at his office in New Orleans and wiretap his phone as part of its BRILAB (code name for "bribery of organized labor") operation. On July 19, 1998, the Assassination Records Review Board released the transcript of thirteen conversations of Marcello that related to the Kennedy assassination. Most took place in the summer of 1979, when the HSCA released its report on the assassination. John Volz, the U.S. attorney in New Orleans at the time who got the court order for the electronic surveillance and wiretapping, told me, "There were nineteen months of BRILAB surveillance, and hundreds of hours. I didn't listen to all the tapes, but the prosecutors I assigned to the case did. I can tell you, there was nothing on those tapes indicating any complicity by Marcello in the assassination."[100]

The transcripts are revealing on several levels, one of the most important of which is that although the HSCA's report suggested that it was "unlikely" that Marcello was involved in the assassination, reporters at the time like Jack Anderson strongly implied his involvement, and the articles on his possible involvement were on the front page of Marcello's local paper, the New Orleans *Times-Picayune*. Yet Marcello and his intimates, though angry at the negative publicity, treated the suggestion of his involvement in the assassination as absurd and, indeed, would bring it up in their conversations *after* more important discussions about business and, in one instance, women they were sharing. The following are some excerpts:

In a July 13, 1979, phone conversation between Isaac Irving Davidson and Marcello, Davidson, a close friend of Marcello's who was a Washington lobbyist for organized labor (as well as the Dominican Republic), comments about an Anderson article in the *Washington Post* the previous day that erroneously reported that the imminent HSCA report would name Marcello as the "chief suspect" in the assassination.

Davidson: "You had as much to do with Kennedy as I have."

Marcello: "Yeah, well, I ain't worried about that."

Marcello then proceeds to talk about something that is more real to him, a proposed civil lawsuit against a New Orleans figure named "Cronvich [phonetic spelling]."

On July 18, 1979, Marcello calls his office and speaks to his secretary, Loretta, to tell her to set up an appointment with someone for the next day.

Then, Marcello: "Let's see what else I want . . . You've got the [*Times-Picayune*] newspaper there?"

Loretta: "Yeah, I got it."

Marcello: "Okay, cut that uh."

Loretta: "Yeah, I know."

Marcello: "That Kennedy deal, that whole thing . . . And put it in the mail."

---

the president killed—as opposed to uncorroborated allegations that they talked about doing it—the HSCA said that "as with Marcello, the committee noted that Trafficante's cautious character is inconsistent with his taking the risk of being involved in an assassination plot against the President." (HSCA Report, p.175) For a more in-depth discussion of the Aleman-Trafficante issue, see the FBI conspiracy section.

(The HSCA Report came out the previous day and was all over the news. Knowing the HSCA at least considered the possibility of his involvement in the assassination, he apparently wasn't even going to bother going out immediately to get the paper, content to have Loretta send it to him in the mail. He obviously was very worried.)

Later that day (July 18), Joe Campisi, the owner of the restaurant in Dallas (the Egyptian Lounge) where Jack Ruby dined frequently, and a friend of Marcello's and other underworld figures throughout the country, calls Marcello. *After* a conversation about business and women, he tells Marcello about an article on the HSCA Report in the *Dallas Morning News.*

Campisi: "They had a big write-up here yesterday morning about all that shit, you know."

Marcello: "That Kennedy deal?"

Campisi: "Oh yeah. And uh they said that Jack Ruby had all the connections. You wouldn't know Jack Ruby if the mother fucker was uh crawl in your room."

Marcello: "Shit, he never talked to me in his li . . . I don't even know him."

Later on that same day (July 18), an unknown male (UM) calls Marcello. After talking about business and contract matters for most of the conversation, the man talks about President Carter asking his cabinet to resign, then about Ted Kennedy being on television that morning talking about Mary Jo Kopechne. This incites Marcello. "Yeah, that mother fucker [Ted Kennedy] . . . If we'd uh done that we'd go in the penitentiary." He then segues into newspapers talking about his alleged hatred for JFK and RFK, and he tells the man about his testimony before the HSCA.

Marcello: "They asked me that . . . I say I ain't never hate nobody. I say I have a argument with people . . . You know what I mean? I can have argument with you . . . but I make up, maybe tomorrow, next week or next month."

UM: "Yeah."

Marcello: "But ain't hatin' ya to kill ya. I'm a kill somebody? Shit. President or (laugh) [It's only a laugh to you, Carlos. Conspiracy theorists don't know enough to laugh about something as silly as this] Attorney General? . . . I say I used to love John Kennedy President . . . I say he would a made the best President if he'd a lived."

UM: "Ya."

Marcello: "I uh I say I was really hurt when they, when they killed him . . . Far as Bobby Kennedy, I didn't hate him either . . . [but] I never did like him. How could I like a man that throwed me out to the dogs?"

(Marcello, the Tunisian-born immigrant, spoke broken English all his life.)

On August 1, 1979, another unknown man calls Marcello's office. Apparently Marcello is not in and he speaks to Loretta about a recent Jack Anderson article about her boss. He reminds her that he has been a close friend of Marcello's for "almost well, thirty-five years." What is instructive about his remarks is that intimates of Marcello's would obviously have a much, much better sense of whether Marcello had been involved in the assassination than anyone else. And if they knew, or thought, or even wondered about whether he did, it is rather unlikely they'd be talking like this in an unguarded and private (to them) conversation. The man complains bitterly that the Anderson article was "absolutely vicious . . . They got Carlos mixed up in this . . . And I wanta tell you something. Uh, Uh, it's all I can do [to] restrain myself."

Loretta: "Well, that's right . . . It's ridiculous, it really is."

UM: "It is, but you see, at the same time, how is he gonna fight it, cause the minute he opens his mouth, he's gonna lose."

Loretta: "You just don't pay any attention to him [Anderson]. Period."

UM: "Well, but you see, a lot of people do."

Loretta: "Well, that's the sad part about it. People believe everything they read."

With respect to this issue of how intimates of Marcello's viewed the charges against him, in an earlier July 17, 1979, phone conversation between Marcello's lobbyist friend Isaac Irving Davidson, calling from Marcello's office at the Town and Country Motel in New Orleans, and a Jim Draykel, Davidson tells Draykel that he's been close to Marcello for twenty-five years, that the HSCA Report scheduled to come out that day was "all bullshit" and that he had talked to Walter Sheridan (a top aide to RFK) "and he says it's all bullshit too . . . The only reason it makes [Carlos] feel badly is because of his grandchildren, [they] all hear that bullshit."

It *is* all bull . . . and will always be bull . . . to anyone who is using the gray matter between their ears. That, of course, automatically excludes virtually all of the resident habitues of the conspiracy community.

After reviewing several hundred hours of conversations recorded by telephonic wiretapping and bugs on the premises, the FBI concluded that "nothing developed in the Brilab investigation . . . could be considered evidence in the Kennedy assassination."[101]

It has to be repeated that even if we accept Becker's allegation, *no evidence has ever surfaced that Marcello had Kennedy killed by Oswald or anyone else.* The HSCA, in its investigation of Marcello, said that although it could not positively conclude that "Marcello and his associates were not involved" in the assassination (i.e., the committee couldn't prove a negative), it pointed out that "Marcello's uniquely successful career in organized crime has been based to a large extent on a policy of prudence; he is not reckless. As with the case of the Soviet and Cuban Governments, a risk analysis indicated that he would be unlikely to undertake so dangerous a course of action as a Presidential assassination."[102] Speaking not just of Marcello, but also Trafficante, *Newsweek* pointed out that one of the big problems with "fingering them as the culprit" was "their own prudence. The two men lasted as dons for decades in part by being cagey, not by trying to kill the president of the United States."[103]

It is noteworthy that Marcello, who died in New Orleans on March 2, 1993, at the age of eighty-three, was never charged with any murder during his storied career in organized crime. It is perhaps even more noteworthy that other than some early assault and robbery charges brought against him in his late teens and early twenties, over the almost sixty-year period between 1935 and his death in 1993, with one exception being a charge of assault in 1966 for taking a wild swing at someone he thought was impeding his way as he walked through a crowd at New Orleans International Airport, he was never charged with any crime involving physical violence of any kind.[104] All of the charges against him were nonviolent in nature. In 1938, Marcello was convicted of selling marijuana to an FBI undercover officer. For the next forty-two years, other than the assault charge in 1966, there were no prosecutions of any kind against him. In 1981, he was convicted of mail fraud and conspiracy to violate federal racketeering laws in his effort to win a multimillion-dollar state group insurance contract (later reversed by a U.S. Supreme Court decision that changed what constituted fraud under federal law), and in 1983, for conspiracy to bribe a federal judge in California presiding over the trial of underworld friends of his. After serving six and a half years in prison on these charges, and in very poor health, he was paroled in 1989.

However, Marcello's chief nemesis, Aaron Kohn, the former FBI agent out of Chicago who took over the privately financed New Orleans Metropolitan Crime Commission in 1953 and was its managing director for twenty-four years, doggedly investigated Marcello for years and became convinced, though he could not prove, that Marcello was behind three and possibly four murders in New Orleans.[105] Even if true, this would be very small potatoes next to the murder-drenched Mafia families in cities like New York, Chicago, and Philadelphia.

No one was ever more respected in New Orleans law enforcement than John Volz. His outstanding resumé bespeaks enormous experience and stature. From 1963 to 1968 he was an assistant district attorney under Jim Garrison, heading up the section on narcotics enforcement. After a year as a special agent for the federal Bureau of Narcotics and Dangerous Drugs (the predecessor to today's Drug Enforcement Administration), he returned to the DA's office as Garrison's chief assistant district attorney between 1970 and 1974. From 1974 to 1978 he was New Orleans's first federal public defender and was the U.S. attorney in New Orleans from 1978 to 1991. From 1991 to 1993 he served as special counsel to the Department of Justice. No one has more of a background in New Orleans law enforcement than he, and no one knows the "players" any better than he. When I asked him about the notion that Marcello may have been behind Kennedy's assassination, he had a one-word reply: "Absurd." Marcello (whom Volz personally prosecuted in 1981 on the charge of conspiring to obtain an insurance contract by bribery), he acknowledged, was the head of organized crime in New Orleans, but he hastened to add that New Orleans organized crime wasn't anything like "the Eastern Mafia families." For instance, he said, "Marcello, almost exclusively, was into gambling,* not extortion, narcotics, or murder."[106]

Extortion, of course, has been a staple of organized crime almost from its inception. The essence of Mafia extortion during the mob's heyday was simple: either you paid for "protection" or you'd be murdered or maimed for life. Yet *Life* magazine, in an in-depth three-part series on organized crime in America in 1967, which was decidedly negative about Marcello, nonetheless reported, "[Marcello's] Jefferson Music Company almost monopolizes vending machines and pinball games in Jefferson Parish. Each year he *lends* thousands of dollars to restaurant or tavern owners *if they agree to accept* his jukeboxes, cigarette machines or pinball games."[107] Some extortion. The thrust of *Life*'s investigation of Marcello was that through payoffs and favors extending all the way up to the governor's office, Marcello's gambling empire was permitted to flourish unimpeded.

When I mentioned Aaron Kohn's allegation about murder, Volz said, "Aaron [now deceased] was a good man and his office and mine worked together on many cases, but many times he kind of went off half-cocked, basing conclusions on hearsay and unsubstantiated rumor." Volz added that the federal authorities "investigated Marcello for thirty

---

Life magazine reported in 1967 that Marcello controlled "illegal but wide-open gambling casinos in Jennings, Lafayette, Bossier City, West Baton Rouge and Morgan City, Louisiana" (Smith, "Carlos Marcello," p.94). None of these, by the way, were within New Orleans DA Jim Garrison's jurisdiction. Marcello was believed to be worth in excess of $25 million from his gambling enterprises. Like so many on the wrong side of the law have demonstrated, they can possess some traits that more on the right side should have. For instance, among Marcello's charities, *Life* reported that he contributed $100,000 to agencies helping victims of Hurricane Betsy in 1965 and gave $10,000 to the Girl Scouts. When New Orleans was looking for a site to build a domed stadium for its new NFL team, the Saints, Marcello offered to give the city (in return for the parking concession) two hundred acres of his Churchill Farms estate to build the arena. The city declined.

years, and let me tell you this, if they—and I was a part of that effort—had come up with any credible evidence that Marcello was responsible for any murders, or was involved in narcotics, I can guarantee you, we would have come down hard on him and there would have been prosecution."

When I said I had heard that people feared Marcello, he confirmed that this was so, explaining that "Marcello was more a myth. His reputation was much worse than he was, and he enjoyed this and profited from it. He had a reputation for being violent, which he wasn't, and he loved it because he scared a lot of people."[108]*

Since Marcello had no history of violence, the suggestion that he would start committing violent crimes by committing the most violent crime of all, murder, and do so against the most powerful man on earth, makes no sense at all.

One important addendum to all of this: In their desperation to connect Oswald with organized crime (necessary because why would Ruby silence Oswald for the mob, as they claim, if Oswald hadn't killed Kennedy for the mob?), the conspiracy theorists who allege in their books that Marcello had Kennedy killed, and that Oswald was his hit man, try to connect Oswald with Marcello through Oswald's uncle, Charles "Dutz" Murret. Since there is no evidence that Marcello had Kennedy killed, and the whole notion that he did makes no sense at all, what follows necessarily is a meaningless discussion. Nevertheless, let's look at what the conspiracy theorists say. We know from the biography of Oswald in this book that Oswald had a moderately close relationship with his mother's sister, Lillian Murret (his aunt), and her husband, Dutz, even staying at their home in New Orleans for two weeks in April of 1963 while he looked for a job and waited for Marina and their daughter, June, to join him from Dallas.

According to a 1944 FBI report, Dutz Murret was the operator of two illegal handbook (bookmaking) clubs in the French Quarter at the time. In these early years he also managed a few pro fighters, having been a boxer himself when he was younger.[109] But that was almost two decades before the assassination. Was he still involved in gambling and bookmaking in the 1960s? Everyone seems to concede that point, but there doesn't seem to be any hard evidence to support it. Indeed, the HSCA Report refers to Murret as a "minor" gambling figure in the 1940s and 1950s and "possibly" until his death in 1964.[110] But even "possibly" is too strong a word because the HSCA cites no evidence to support it for the 1960s. In fact, as far as I can tell, the report doesn't offer any support for Murret being involved in gambling in the 1950s, only the 1940s. Citing Marguerite Oswald's statement that Murret had been a bookmaker "for many, many years"[111] doesn't address itself to the issue since Marguerite only knew the goings on of her sister and husband in the 1930s and 1940s, not later.

And of course if Dutz Murret was just a bookmaker, at *some* time in his life, that

---

*If Marcello liked to scare people in the absence of being actually violent, he also wanted people to believe he had more power than he did. There's no evidence to support the degree of power and influence he suggested in several of the aforementioned BRILAB tapes while talking to undercover FBI agents and his friend and attorney Vincent Marinello: "It takes time to get where I'm at. To know all these people—governors, business, the [state] attorney general, they know me"; "Yeah, I got 'em all where I want 'em"; "I had [Louisiana] Governor McKeithen for eight years"; "Maybe I can make a phone call to the attorney general. Now I'm not saying I can do it. I gotta man can do it"; "We own de teamsters"; "I got the only man in the United States can tell 'em [the Teamsters leadership] what the fuck to do"; "No matter who gets in there, you know I'm a find a way to get to 'em." (Davis, *Mafia Kingfish*, pp.577–578)

wouldn't help the conspiracy theorists. Their main argument is their claim that around the time of the assassination, Dutz was working for Sam Saia, a prominent New Orleans gambling figure who, per Aaron Kohn, was "very close to Carlos Marcello," and *that* is how they try to connect Oswald (through Murret) with Marcello, who they claim was behind the assassination.[112]

But there is no evidence that Murret was associated with Saia at any time near the assassination. Indeed, the only evidence on this point, from Murret's wife, Lillian, suggests he wasn't. In her deposition before the HSCA, the always candid Mrs. Murret testified that "in the thirties and forties" her husband worked for Sam Saia, a man she said was "in the gambling business," at Saia's club, the Lomalinda, in the French Quarter. When HSCA counsel asked her if her husband continued to work for Saia in the 1950s and 1960s, she replied, "Maybe he did."

"Up until his death?"

"Oh, no. He was working on the riverfront when he died."

"Are you pretty sure that Dutz was not involved in any gambling activities during 1963?"

"I am sure he was not," Mrs. Murret answered. "He worked pretty hard up there on the riverfront." And she made it very clear that when her husband did work for Saia he did not work at the riverfront at the same time (i.e., the riverfront being the day job and the gambling business at night and/or over weekends).

"Did he have both jobs at the same time?" HSCA counsel asked.

"No," Mrs. Murret answered without equivocation, clearly adding that he went to work at the riverfront *after* he quit the gambling business. So when Mrs. Murret testified that her husband had been working at the riverfront (checking boxcars coming in for the T. Smith and Company steamship line) "for quite a few years," that means that, if true, Murret would have long been out of his association with Saia or with gambling and other gamblers around the time of the assassination.[113] And, as indicated, that's bad for the conspiracy theorists.

The 1978 testimony of Dutz Murret's son, Eugene, before the HSCA was even worse for the conspiracy theorists, since it was a little more precise. Eugene Murret, a lawyer working as the judicial administrator of the Supreme Court of Louisiana at the time of his testimony, was very clear that although his father had been a bookie for years, at some point "*before* 1959," his father "was a self-employed bookie." When asked if he worked before 1959 for Sam Saia, he answered, "Well, that would have been *way back*, I think," the implication being before the 1950s. He said his father "mainly ran his own operation most of the time and maybe with one or two other people as time went along," adding that although his father at some point in time worked with Saia, whenever he worked with anyone else it was usually with a man named Larry Rue, not Saia. He said his father's bookie operation "was solely and exclusively to support his family and that is about what it made," and believed he quit bookmaking around 1959 or slightly earlier because "business might have been bad, it might have been off" and "not producing the kind of income he needed to support his family," suggesting his father wanted a job that "was eight hours a day and steady income."[114]

But let's assume, for the sake of argument, that Murret, unbeknownst to Lillian or his family, kept his hand in the gambling business during the last years of his life by working evenings and weekends. It is certainly highly improbable that he'd be able to do this without their knowledge, but it's possible. It's also very unlikely that if he was moonlighting as a bookie, he would try to conceal it from his family since, in his family, it was never something to hide, his son Eugene even telling the HSCA that in high school he used to visit his father at his bookie establishments. It's also possible that Mrs. Murret and Eugene lied under oath, though it is unclear why they would do this when they readily admitted Dutz worked as a gambler at one time. It really was nothing to be that ashamed of in New Orleans. As Mrs. Murret said, "Gambling at that time was wide open," though it is not clear whether it remained that way in later years. Murret was apparently never perceived as a "real criminal" when he was involved in the gambling business, law enforcement apparently looking the other way at such activity in those years, one indication of which is that Murret doesn't appear to have had any criminal record. Indeed, Lillian referred to him as being "very square," and at the time in the summer of 1963 when Oswald was arrested for his confrontation on the streets and needed bail money, Dutz was away at Manresa, a "Catholic retreat house" where he went more than once a year.[115]

But again, to please the conspiracy theorists, and without any evidence to support it, let's assume that Dutz Murret was working with Sam Saia around the time of the assassination at Saia's Lomalinda club, where gambling activity took place, and Saia was connected to Marcello. So what? Marcello, of course, had gambling and other enterprises throughout the Gulf States region, so Dutz working for someone who in turn was close to Marcello is of no consequence. And the HSCA learned that bookmakers throughout the New Orleans area subscribed, for a fee, to a Marcello-controlled wire service, which enabled them to get race results.[116] However, the HSCA was unable to find any evidence that Murret knew or even met Marcello, his only known connection being that he worked for Saia at one time, who apparently would have been paying Marcello for the use of the latter's wire service.[117]

But if we were to believe the conspiracy theorists, Murret worked for Marcello himself. One example among many: In his book *Contract on America*, author David E. Scheim writes that Murret was "associated with Marcello's criminal organization." Well, "associated" implies a lot more than merely working for someone who subscribes to Marcello's wire service, even if we were to assume for the sake of argument that Murret himself, not Saia, paid the subscriber's fee. Elsewhere, Scheim writes that Murret was a "criminal operative in the empire" of Marcello and "Murret worked as a bookie in Marcello's criminal organization." In other words, without any evidence to support his assertion, Scheim says that Murret worked not for himself or even Saia, but directly for Marcello.[118] Emile Bruneau, himself a gambler and a close friend of Murret's for years, didn't hesitate to tell authorities that Murret worked for Saia at one time and "assumed," without knowing, that he knew New Orleans crime figure Nofio Pecora. But he said that though he couldn't be sure, "I don't think" Murret knew Marcello.[119] And Murret's wife, Lillian, told the HSCA that although her husband probably knew of Marcello (who didn't?) she was "sure he didn't know him personally."[120]

But even if we make the further assumption that Marcello wanted to kill Kennedy, and Murret worked directly for Marcello, isn't there still a big piece of the puzzle missing? Why does Marcello get in touch with Oswald, of all people, to kill Kennedy for him? I mean, did he interview all the many underlings in his "empire" to find out if any of them, or anyone they knew, was willing to kill Kennedy for him, and one of his many interviewees, Murret, suggested his nephew Oswald (thereby now bringing Murret in as yet another co-conspirator in the assassination of Kennedy)? This is the line of reasoning of former HSCA chief counsel Robert Blakey in his book *The Plot to Kill the President*:

> We [he has to be referring to his coauthor here, not the HSCA, which did not subscribe to any of what follows] considered it unlikely that [Oswald] would have bragged openly, least of all to his own relatives, of having tried to assassinate [General] Walker, but Marina knew, and she *might not have been* so loath to tell about it. [No evidence has ever surfaced that Marina told anyone back then about Oswald's attempt on Walker's life. All of the evidence is that she told absolutely no one, and only acknowledged it when Oswald's letter of instructions to her, written before his attempt on Walker's life, surfaced in the cookbook after the assassination.] She had, after all, confided to Ruth Paine about the beatings she got from Oswald. [As if telling someone with whom you are living that your husband had beaten you is the same as telling your husband's aunt and uncle that he tried to murder someone.] We, therefore, believed it was *quite possible* that the Murrets learned of the Walker incident, and Dutz Murret was in an ideal position to connect his nephew with organized crime, since he himself was an underworld figure. We did not have reason to believe that Murret was a co-conspirator in the assassination, but we did regard him a likely conduit of information about Oswald—his conduct, his political beliefs, his violent bent (specifically, the assault on Walker)—to people who had the motive and the capability to plot the assassination.[121]

So *maybe* Marina told the Murrets about Oswald trying to kill Walker, and *maybe* Dutz Murret told people close to Marcello about it, and *maybe* Marcello decided Oswald was his man. And *maybe* if I had wings I could fly. It's okay to ruminate and daydream, but to use these reveries as the basis for the conclusion that Marcello had Oswald kill Kennedy is astonishing, particularly when there is no evidence at all that Marcello had anyone, much less Oswald, kill Kennedy. One would not expect such reasoning from someone of the considerable intelligence and stature of Blakey, who currently is a professor of law at Notre Dame Law School. Blakey continues to surprise when he concedes that "other than Murret, we were unable to identify [any] underworld associates of Oswald, though we *theorized* they would have been unlikely to be seen with him in public."[122] And based only on Oswald's being a nephew of Murret, Blakey concludes that Oswald killed Kennedy for the mob?

I find it remarkable that Blakey, who is a leading authority on organized crime, actually believes that the mob would decide to kill Kennedy. Remarkable in the sense that, unlike virtually all students of the mob, he apparently, at least with respect to the Kennedy assassination, has very little respect for the mob's intelligence and pragmatism. I mean, for the Mafia to murder Kennedy they'd have to be crazy. And for them to get Oswald, of all people, to do it for them, they'd have to be, in a legal sense, *not guilty by reason of insanity*.

Blakey's position is additionally remarkable because other than the fourth-bullet conspiracy conclusion of the HSCA, which he embraces, Blakey demonstrated much common sense and competence as chief counsel for the committee.*

---

*When I say "other than," is this analogous to "other than that, Mrs Lincoln, how was the play?" No. Booth ruined everything, whereas as sophomoric and irresponsible (because it was essentially foundationless) as the fourth-bullet conspiracy conclusion of the HSCA was, the HSCA still did a commendable job overall under Blakey's counsel.

Years after all their deaths, Carlos Marcello, Santo Trafficante, and Jimmy Hoffa were accused of having Kennedy murdered by the late Frank Ragano, a mob attorney who represented not only Trafficante but also Hoffa when he was president of the largest union in the country, the International Brotherhood of Teamsters. Since trial lawyers, as Ragano was, live in a world of lies, either by their client or by their opposition, one would think Ragano would be capable of a better lie than the one he told in his 1994 book, *Mob Lawyer*.

Many who have implicated themselves or others in the assassination either are within the grasp of, or flirting very heavily with, psychosis, or have such a passion for the notion of a conspiracy that they're willing to believe virtually anything. We've already seen both of these types on these pages. But Ragano, being a completely rational person who obviously just made up his story for his own self-aggrandizing reasons (to be discussed later), clearly doesn't fit into either category.

If we're to believe Ragano, around 2:30 p.m. on July 23, 1963, in the executive dining room of the Marble Palace Hotel in Washington, D.C. (so far, Ragano is not too bad—the details smack of the truth, right?), Hoffa, under constant investigation and indictment at the hands of RFK's Justice Department (the most recent incident being his indictment the previous month, along with seven associates, for looting $25 million from the Teamsters pension fund), said to him, "Something has to be done. The time has come for your friend [Trafficante] and Carlos [Marcello, Trafficante's close mob friend] to get rid of him, kill that son-of-a-bitch John Kennedy."* The theory, Ragano carefully explains to his readers, is that Hoffa felt that Kennedy's successor, LBJ, hated Robert Kennedy so much he'd never keep him on as attorney general, and LBJ wouldn't pursue Hoffa because Hoffa had made large cash contributions to LBJ's political campaigns. "This has got to be done," he quotes Hoffa as telling him. "Be sure to tell them what I said. No more fucking around. We're running out of time—something has to be done."[123]†

Now mind you, by Ragano's own admission, he says he couldn't believe what Hoffa had told him, but the very next day at the Royal Orleans Hotel in New Orleans, he dutifully says he passed on the message to the two mobsters. "Marteduzzo [Little Hammer, Hoffa's Sicilian nickname] wants you to do a little favor for him. You won't believe this, but he wants you to kill John Kennedy. He wants you to get rid of the President right away." Ragano says he thought that Hoffa's wish would be met with laughter from the two mobsters, but, he tells his readers, there was "silence. Santo and Carlos exchanged glances. Their facial expressions were icy. Their reticence was a signal that this was an uncomfortable subject, one they were unwilling to discuss."[124] (In a *Frontline* documentary, Ragano said that when he told Marcello and Trafficante that Hoffa wanted them to kill Kennedy, "they looked at one another and I got the distinct impression that it was as

---

*In November of 1992, Ragano told essentially the same story to a national audience in a *Frontline* TV special, but he said the conversation took place not at the Marble Palace Hotel but in Hoffa's office at the Teamsters headquarters in Washington, D.C. Marble Palace Hotel? Jimmy's office? Better make up your mind, Frankie. ("JFK, Hoffa and the Mob," *Frontline*, PBS, November 17, 1992)

†Ragano also writes in his book that in 1972, when Jimmy Hoffa, who had been released after serving four years of a thirteen-year sentence for labor racketeering and jury tampering, was unsuccessful in wresting control of the Teamsters back from his handpicked successor, Frank Fitzsimmons, who he felt had "double-crossed" him, he asked Ragano to ask Trafficante "to get rid of that fucking Fitz" for him. Ragano writes that when he passed the request on to Trafficante, Trafficante said impassively, "'Just tell him that it will be done.' Santo was obviously annoyed at Jimmy's demands and had no intention of getting entangled with him." (Ragano and Raab, *Mob Lawyer*, pp.267–268)

if, well, that's what we were going to do anyhow."[125] This is what Ragano also told *New York Post* reporter Jack Newfield in an earlier 1992 interview.[126])

Two weeks after the assassination, Ragano says in his 1994 book, he was in the passenger seat of a car in New Orleans driven by Marcello's brother, Joe. Carlos and Trafficante were in the backseat. When a news item on the car radio questioned whether Oswald acted alone in the assassination, Ragano reports that Trafficante said, "Carlos, you mark my words. Before this thing is over with, they're going to blame you and me for the killing."[127] But twenty-seven years earlier, in an interview with the FBI in Tampa, Florida, on April 10, 1967, Ragano said the above incident (this later version had Carlos Marcello driving, Trafficante in the front seat, and Ragano in the backseat alone) took place not two weeks after the assassination but *four years later*, in 1967, and what prompted Trafficante's remark was the car radio's news about New Orleans DA Jim Garrison's investigation of the assassination. Ragano told the FBI that the allegations about Trafficante being involved in Kennedy's death "were ridiculous," and illustrated Trafficante's attitude about the assassination by telling the agents about Trafficante's alleged remarks in the car and his belief that he would be "framed" by law enforcement to put him behind bars.[128] So, according to Ragano, up until 1967, Trafficante was innocent.

But in the aforementioned 1992 *Frontline* documentary, Ragano said that before dying, Trafficante confided to Ragano that he and Marcello had Kennedy murdered. In his book, he elaborated on the incident. According to Ragano, on March 13, 1987, in Tampa, Florida, just four days before Trafficante's death, Trafficante called him. In an extremely enfeebled voice ("between gasps I could hear him wheezing") Trafficante said, "Frank, please come and see me today . . . I want to talk to you. It's very important." Trafficante was figuratively on his deathbed, per Ragano. During a drive in Ragano's car, the Mafia leader, per Ragano, told him in Italian, "*Carlos é futtutu. Non duvevamu ammazzari a Giovanni. Duvevamu ammazzari a Bobby*" ("We shouldn't have killed Giovanni [John in Italian]. We should have killed Bobby").[129] Ragano doesn't say in his book why Trafficante, who, like the HSCA said, was always "discreet,"[130] would confess to the biggest murder ever.

Conspiracy theorist Anthony Summers, who *smells* a rat almost everywhere in the assassination of President Kennedy, but unlike most of his brethren in the conspiracy community is rational, responsible, and intelligent enough to never say he thinks he actually *found* the rat (i.e., "The mob killed JFK," etc.), checked this last story out. He learned that on March 13, 1987, Trafficante was no longer living in Tampa, having taken up permanent residence at his home in North Miami Beach, and hadn't been to Tampa since the previous Christmas holidays. Trafficante's widow (who Ragano says he saw in the Tampa home when he picked up her husband for the ride), his two daughters, and several friends and neighbors told Summers the meeting between Ragano and Trafficante not only didn't take place but couldn't have, since he was in North Miami Beach the entire day. Summers also learned from hospital records that Trafficante was treated in the dialysis unit of Miami's Mercy Hospital the previous evening, March 12, until 7:15 p.m., and was back in the unit by the afternoon of March 14, leaving a one-day window for him to fly to his father confessor, Ragano, for his mea culpa. But there is no evidence, other than Ragano's word, that Trafficante, near death, did so. Oh yes. Ragano told Summers he had three witnesses who could corroborate his story, but he declined to tell Summers who they were.[131]

But quite apart from Summers's good investigative work exposing Ragano's story, the story from start to finish does not make one iota of sense. Ragano writes in his book, after revealing Trafficante's alleged confession, that "Carlos [and] Santo . . . undoubtedly had roles in Kennedy's death,"[132] but had he forgotten that earlier in his book he wrote that Trafficante and Marcello were "two ultra-cautious men . . . two prudent godfathers," and the thought that they would "dare to get involved in a plot against the President . . . was too absurd for credibility . . . It was absurd to contemplate that these Mafia dons or any Mafia boss had the audacity to pull off the biggest hit the world—the murder of the President of the United States"?[133] Of course, that's what I have said more than once in this book—that the thought that Trafficante, Marcello, or any of the mob leaders would plot to murder the president is too ridiculous to even mention. If that's an absurd thought, multiply by one thousand the unlikelihood that Trafficante and Marcello would murder the president of the United States *simply as a favor for Jimmy Hoffa*, a union leader, and someone whom Trafficante, Ragano says, *had never even met.*[134] No sensible person would believe a story like that.

There's perhaps an even bigger reason why we know that Ragano's entire story is a giant fabrication. Were it true, he'd never in a million years talk about it since he'd automatically be exposing himself to the high probability of being killed twice over. First, if he had conveyed the message from Hoffa to Trafficante that he believes resulted in Kennedy's murder, as a criminal lawyer for several years Ragano would have to know that he'd also be guilty of the assassination under the law of aiding and abetting. Indeed, he writes, after the alleged confession from Trafficante, about his "possible complicity in the assassination."[135] Since there's no statute of limitations for murder, he could be prosecuted for the president's murder and sentenced to death. Second, no one knows better than he that, as the flap on the dust jacket of his own book says, "A bullet in the head is the customary penalty for violation of *omerta*, the Mafia's code of silence." But you see, Ragano never had any of these fears, since he knew he hadn't aided and abetted any crime, nor squealed on those who he said did, so knowing neither the authorities nor the Mafia would pay any attention to his blather, he felt perfectly safe to say what he did.

Why did Ragano make up his tale? Some have suggested that Ragano may have been seeking revenge for the fact that Trafficante refused to loan him money at an earlier time when he needed it. After Ragano was disbarred from the practice of law in 1976 following his conviction for income tax evasion, he was near bankruptcy, and when he asked Trafficante for a loan he was devastated by the response: "Ask me for anything—except money."[136] But although bitter for a long time about the rejection, Ragano, whose license to practice law had been reinstated, defended Trafficante in a subsequent 1986 federal racketeering case in Tampa (which ended in a mistrial when the judge ruled there wasn't enough evidence for the case to proceed), and attended his funeral the next year. In any event, I find it hard to believe that Ragano would try to implicate not only Trafficante in Kennedy's murder, but also himself (even if he knew the mob and authorities would know his story was a fraud) just to get revenge against someone he couldn't even hurt (since Trafficante was already dead), all because his request for a loan was turned down fifteen years earlier. I would think the likelier reasons for Ragano's fable were more self-aggrandizing in nature. At the time he first told it in 1992, he was in the process of writing his book, and the allegation, per the dust jacket and promotional material, was the most sensational and explosive part of the book. So the hope of stimulating book sales probably was at the heart of the story. Also, as a concomitant thereof, the opportunity to be a media celebrity and tell his story, as he did on several national TV shows, may have held its appeal to him. Another possibility is that when he first came forward with his story in 1992, he was fighting to stay out of prison for a second conviction in 1990 for income tax evasion (he was unsuccessful), and by some manner of thinking he may have thought the story, and the prospect of telling more, would give him some leverage with the authorities. Fighting to stay out of prison and promoting his book may have been the combination that caused Ragano, close to thirty years after the assassination, to come up with his whopper.

Ragano had no credibility left to squander, but if anyone thought he did, his testimony before the ARRB should disabuse them of this notion. Let's let the ARRB tell it: "Ragano . . . stated in his book that he possessed original, *contemporaneous* notes of meetings with organized crime figures. To determine whether Ragano's notes were relevant to the assassination, the Review Board subpoenaed the notes and deposed Ragano. He produced several handwritten notes regarding the assassination, but he could not definitely state whether he took them during the meetings [with mob figures] in the 1960's or later when he was working on his book in the 1990's."[137] Really believable, isn't it?

Before going on, I should note that although the Hoffa plan to kill President Kennedy is clearly a fabrication of Frank Ragano's, it is pretty well accepted that Hoffa, though never ordering, at least discussed the possibility of murdering his chief nemesis, the president's brother, RFK. The main confirmation for this came from one of Hoffa's close confidants, Edward Partin, a Baton Rouge teamsters official with a criminal record who informed the authorities in September of 1962 that he had participated in such a discussion with Hoffa. In October of 1962, the FBI gave Partin a polygraph test and he passed. In an interview with the HSCA in 1978, Partin reaffirmed the account of Hoffa's discussion with him about having RFK killed, Hoffa suggesting a lone gunman with a rifle equipped with a telescopic sight shooting RFK as he rode in a convertible. While there are the similarities to the president's death, the HSCA observed that they "were not so unusual as to point ineluctably in a particular direction." Hoffa also discussed the alternative possibility of killing RFK with plastic explosives, but Partin said Hoffa never pursued the matter of killing RFK.[138]

The HSCA also confirmed that in early 1967, Frank Chavez, another Teamsters official, spoke to Hoffa about murdering Robert Kennedy, even suggesting ways to get the job done, but Hoffa "sharply rebuked his aide, telling him that such a course of action was dangerous and should not be considered."[139]

The HSCA noted that, unlike the various organized-crime figures with whom he associated, "Hoffa was not a confirmed murderer,"* his association with them having derived from the nature of his union activities. Further, the only credible evidence pertained to Hoffa's discussion about killing RFK, not President Kennedy, and even with RFK it never went beyond mere talking with Partin, and Hoffa sternly rejected the proposal set forth by Chavez. The committee also said it was doubtful Hoffa would have risked something as extremely dangerous as a plot to murder President Kennedy at the very time he was under active investigation by RFK's Justice Department. Accordingly, the HSCA concluded it was "improbable that Hoffa had anything to do with the death of the President."[140]

The HSCA could have added the most important point of all—that there was *no evidence* of any kind that Hoffa was involved in the president's death.

---

*Though he probably had, as many people who never kill do, murderous instincts. The bantam Hoffa, at a dinner he had with RFK at his lawyer's home in Washington, D.C., before they became bitter enemies, told RFK, "I do to others what they do to me, only worse" (Kennedy, *Enemy Within*, p.41).

Other than a virtual madman (as Oswald was), no person or group in America would ever seriously consider murdering the president of the United States. For well over a century this has been so, and will continue to be so indefinitely if our culture and democratic form of government remain in existence. The president is simply someone you don't mess with. That is why, as I have said, the very thought of groups like organized crime, the CIA, military-industrial complex, and so on, sitting around and actually planning to murder the president of the United States is inherently crazy on its face, and except for the necessities of this book, I reject the proposition out of hand.

But if, for instance, the mob did intend to "mess with" the president because it wanted to get his brother, Robert Kennedy, off its back, what it would do is something like this (and I maintain the mob wouldn't even try to do this against the president): It is well known, and too well chronicled to require documentation, that President Kennedy was a hound dog when it came to women, continuing his indiscriminate liaisons with many women through his one thousand days in office. As *Time* magazine observed in 1975, "Even after he entered the White House, the handsome and fun-loving Kennedy never stopped pursuing attractive women—nor they him . . . Once, he startled two proper Britons, Prime Minister Harold MacMillan and Foreign Minister R.A.B. Butler, during a 1962 conference in Nassau by casually confiding that if he went too long without a woman, he suffered severe headaches."[141] The story was just a rumor, but because of the continuing revelations through the years of Kennedy's girlfriends, *Time* magazine's Hugh Sidey wrote in 2003, "This story has been largely discounted, but now it has new currency."[142]

It is also well known that one of Kennedy's lovers was Judith Campbell Exner, an attractive, blue-eyed Las Vegas and Palm Springs party girl and one-time starlet who was introduced to Kennedy in 1960 by Frank Sinatra in Sinatra's "presidential suite" at the Sands Hotel in Las Vegas.[143] During a two-year period, she saw Kennedy as well as Chicago mobster Sam Giancana, although, per Exner, she did not share her bed with Giancana until after she broke up with Kennedy.

And where did these interludes with the president take place? Not only at the White House (the White House telephone logs showed some seventy calls from Exner to the president during a fifty-four-week period in 1961 and early 1962),[144] but at various hotels around the country, even at her apartment below the Sunset Strip near Doheny Drive in West Los Angeles,[145]* which was probably provided for by Giancana since Exner had no

---

*Even former Florida senator George Smathers, a close friend of JFK's who, during JFK's Senate years, flew off to places like the Riviera and Havana with the married JFK for "bachelor holidays" of easy living, acknowledged to author Michael Beschloss that he personally saw Judith Campbell Exner being taken into the president's private quarters at the White House by William Thompson, a railroad lobbyist who had gone with Kennedy and Smathers on their 1958 pleasure trip to Havana (Beschloss, *Crisis Years*, p.141). With respect to Kennedy's women, Beschloss writes that "Kennedy's Choate School friend Le Moyne Billings felt that in the late 1940's after Kennedy's beloved sister Kathleen [with whom, among all his siblings, he was the closest] was killed in an air crash and he was told that he too might soon die of Addison's disease, 'he just figured there was no sense in planning ahead anymore. The only thing that made sense . . . was to live for the moment, treating each day as if it were his last, demanding of life constant intensity, adventure, and pleasure.' [Of course, several years before Kathleen's death, and with avoidance of war being a simple matter given the power and influence of his father, Joe, John Kennedy enlisted in the navy and risked his life, becoming a war hero.] Even as President, Kennedy's tomorrow-we-die streak remained, evinced by his promiscuity with women and his indifference to physical risk. Secret Service men complained that he was 'a notoriously poor driver who drove through red lights and took many unnecessary chances.' Sometimes he dismissed the agents, saying, 'Whoever wants to get me, will get me'" (Beschloss, *Crisis Years*, p.10).

other visible means of support during this period. It would seem that if the mob were going to do anything at all to the president, it could have—particularly when it had, through Giancana, a handle on Exner and her whereabouts—gotten a compromising photo of Kennedy and her together, or even film or audio of their lovemaking in one of the hotel suites or Exner's apartment.* Then the mob could have delivered a copy of what they had to the president or one of his people with the explicit or implied threat that if RFK didn't stop vigorously pursuing organized crime, the world would see or hear what the mob had. But *murder* the president? Please, okay? Just please. And select the completely unstable and unreliable Lee Harvey Oswald to get the job done? And then have the almost childlike Jack Ruby, after Oswald had already been in police custody for three days and grilled for *twelve* hours, kill Oswald to silence him? Again, please.

As set forth earlier, the Warren Commission examined, in considerable depth, Jack Ruby's connection with organized crime and concluded that Ruby's "denial" of being associated with organized crime was "confirmed" by law enforcement agencies. It also concluded that its own investigation produced no grounds for believing that Ruby's killing of Oswald "was part of a conspiracy."[146] However, assistant Warren Commission counsel Burt W. Griffin testified before the HSCA that other than Ruby's possible involvement with the mob, "the possibility that someone associated with the underworld would have wanted to assassinate the President . . . [was] not seriously explored" by the Warren Commission.[147] The HSCA, more conspiracy-oriented than the Warren Commission, criticized the Commission for this narrow focus and did conduct a more expansive investigation of organized crime's possible involvement in the assassination. Ultimately, the committee concluded that "the national syndicate of organized crime . . . was not involved in the assassination of President Kennedy." It went on to say it could "not preclude the possibility [who could preclude such a possibility?] that individual members may have been involved."[148]

With respect to the possibility of organized crime, or individual members, being involved in the assassination, it's not as if the mob's oath of *omerta* still permanently zippers the lips of all mafiosi. Following Joseph Valachi's lead in 1963, there has been a string of Mafia members who, as part of a plea bargain, have sung like canaries to law enforcement about the mob's misdeeds, including murder. But as indicated earlier, not once in close to forty-five years has any mob member told law enforcement he knew (or had even heard within the mob) of any mob involvement in the assassination. And the electronic surveillance and wiretapping of mob figures by the FBI has continued through the years, yet not the slightest hint of the mob being behind the assassination has been picked up.

Speaking of Valachi, even if we assume for the sake of argument and against all evi-

---

But at least as to JFK's legendary womanizing, his latest biographer, Robert Dallek, points out that long before the diagnosis of Addison's disease and the death of his sister Kathleen in 1948, and the death of his brother Joe Jr. in 1944 when his plane exploded in midair crossing the English Channel, JFK was unable to exercise any restraint when it came to women, and started accumulating an impressive list of conquests by his late teens. "He had so many women, he could not remember their names," Dallek writes. While it is easy enough for a man to be a womanizer on his own, with JFK it was an accepted family tradition, an "entitlement" of his privileged background, if you will. His father, a natural role model for a young man, took licentiousness to new levels, the former ambassador to Great Britain trying to get in bed one night with one of his daughter's friends who was staying over. (Dallek, *Unfinished Life*, pp.47–49)

*I mean, it's not as if the mob did not have access to electronic surveillance equipment. It did. Indeed, in October 1960 Giancana himself arranged for the bugging of the Las Vegas apartment of comedian Dan Rowan to find out if his then girlfriend, singer Phyllis McGuire, was being unfaithful to him with Rowan (Blakey and Billings, *Plot to Kill the President*, p.381; Gentry, *J. Edgar Hoover*, p.486; see also 10 HSCA 174).

dence and logic, that the Mafia decided to kill Kennedy, it never would have set the date for November 22, 1963. *Just the previous month*, Valachi's sensational testimony before the Senate Permanent Investigations Subcommittee had placed a far, far bigger spotlight on the Mafia than ever before in its history. Indeed, nothing remotely like it had ever occurred. Yes, mobsters had been called before congressional committees before, but after being sworn in, they'd take the Fifth. But Valachi, as *Newsweek* pointed out, was "the first good singing voice in the history of Senatorial crime investigations . . ., spill[ing] out the terror, the atrocities, the inside-out moralities of life in the underworld society that he called Costa Nostra."[149] Under hot television lights in a Senate caucus room crowded with more than five hundred spectators, including twenty U.S. marshals to ensure his protection, Valachi exposed the Mafia to an enthralled, national audience. Even in the caucus room full of professionals, Valachi's "sinister story held his listeners in its grip."[150] After the first day of his testimony, *Newsweek* said "millions of viewers looked forward" to his next appearance before the subcommittee. How big was Valachi's story? Big enough to be the main, front-page headline in the *New York Times* the first two days of his testimony, with two other front-page stories on the third day. Similar headlines appeared in papers across America, and Valachi, overnight, became so well known that national comedians told jokes about his canary role. And the Grand Council of Columbus Associations, an Italian-American organization, publicly expressed its resentment over the national spotlight being given Valachi's testimony and story. Mario Biaggi, a New York City police lieutenant who was the president of the council, called the Valachi hearings "a grim circus" and charged that the effect of it was to attribute the nation's crimes to Italians.[151]

With this backdrop of the national spotlight being on the Mafia as never before, with Bobby Kennedy's Justice Department putting unprecedented heat on organized crime, and with Kennedy and Senator McClellan, the senate subcommittee chairman, calling for new and tougher legislation to combat the Mafia, I can just picture Vito Genovese, the "boss of bosses," per Valachi, in his hospital bed with a heart condition at the federal penitentiary in Leavenworth, Kansas,[152] telling a mob courier in a raspy voice, "Tell the boys that it's always good to strike when the iron's hot. We're hot now. We've been waiting for the spotlight like this for a long time. Now's the best time to whack Kennedy."

Even if one *wanted* to believe that Genovese or any other Mafia leader would order Kennedy's death around the time of the Valachi hearings, how could one do it without tying up and gagging one's intellect first?

No other reasoning is needed or has to be adduced to show that organized crime was not behind the assassination of John F. Kennedy, but I should add one more point: although organized crime had considerable power in the world of crime at the time of the assassination, what power could it possibly have had over others to get them to go along with its plot to murder Kennedy?

Quite apart from the absence of any evidence, as well as the illogic, that organized crime killed Kennedy, we know that this theory by conspiracy theorists is absolutely negated by many other theories they cherish and hold close to their bosoms. For instance, the conspiracy theorists believe that the route of the president's motorcade in front of the Book Depository Building was set up by the conspirators who killed the president. But even Jim Garrison, the New Orleans DA who prosecuted an innocent man for conspiracy to murder Kennedy (see later text) asks, How in the world would the Mafia be able to control the parade route?[153] The theorists believe that the Zapruder film was tampered with, that the wounds on Kennedy's body were altered, and the autopsy surgeons distorted their findings. But again, how could organized crime have exercised any influence or control over such matters and people? And so on. To pull off the monstrous conspiracy that conspiracy theorists have crafted in their minds, many agencies of government, like the FBI, even the Secret Service, would have had to have cooperated. But how in the world could organized crime have control over such agencies?

Equally importantly, it is conspiracy dogma that the Warren Commission suppressed the truth about the assassination from the American people. But it covered it up for whom? Organized crime? Please. If the Warren Commission were to cover up the truth, which is a notion ludicrous on its face, it would be to protect a person, agency, or group that was a part of its establishment world. The CIA, Secret Service, FBI, military-industrial complex, or LBJ would qualify. But the mob? Again, please. (For the same reason, the Warren Commission covering up for Castro, anti-Castro Cuban exiles, or the KGB is silly on its face. And by extension, the chief investigative arm for the Warren Commission, the FBI, covering up for Castro, the KGB, or organized crime is also ludicrous on its face.)

That the Warren Commission would not be covering up for organized crime is a verity that no reasonable person can dispute. Yet conspiracy theorists (Jim Garrison was a rare exception), even very intelligent ones like David E. Scheim, who has a doctorate in mathematics from MIT, apparently haven't thought about this. In his book *Contract on America*, Scheim, clearly without cognizance of this verity, has no trouble writing things like this: "Glaring clues to Mafia assassination culpability [for Kennedy's murder] were buried, distorted and disingenuously deflected in the Warren Commission's final report"; "Telephone records and other documents showed extensive contacts between Ruby [whom Scheim describes as the most important source of information on the Kennedy assassination then alive] and underworld figures from across the country in the months before the assassination . . . That evidence establishing these criminal ties had been repeatedly suppressed or distorted by the Warren Commission."[154] Another verity is at play here: there is virtually no correlation between intelligence and common sense.

To put it mildly, it is almost insane to believe that organized crime would decide to murder the president of the United States, then take this insanity to an even higher level by getting Oswald, of all people, to do the job, then take the insanity to previously unimaginable heights by getting Ruby to silence Oswald. What fool could possibly believe this?

CIA

For years, conspiracy theorists have written books about the Central Intelligence Agency's involvement in the assassination of JFK. And as conspiracy theorist E. Martin Schotz, a mathematician and practicing psychiatrist, puts it, "I and other ordinary citizens know, *know for a fact*, that there was a conspiracy [to murder Kennedy] and that it was organized at the highest levels of the CIA."[1] The fact that Schotz and his fellow conspiracy theorists haven't been able to come up with *any* evidence connecting the CIA to the assassination or Oswald has not troubled them in the least. In their opinion, they *have* been able to come up with *motive* (JFK's refusal to give air support to the CIA-sponsored Bay of Pigs invasion, his allegedly being soft, in the eyes of some, on Communism, his aim to cut the CIA budget by 20 percent by 1966,[2] etc.), *means*, and *opportunity*, which, as mentioned earlier, is not coming up with any hard evidence at all.

Whatever the CIA's short laundry list of dissatisfactions (some merely illusory, some real) with Kennedy, as I discuss later in the anti-Castro Cuban exile section of this book, Kennedy was highly disturbed with the CIA for its incompetence and its having misled him on the probable success of the Bay of Pigs invasion in 1961. Perhaps the most famous alleged quote from Kennedy about his animus toward the CIA after the Bay of Pigs debacle was that he wanted "to splinter the CIA into a thousand pieces and scatter it to the winds." But in the two and a half years after the attempted invasion he never did anything remotely close to this, and it is not known to whom he supposedly said these words. The *New York Times* only said that Kennedy made this statement "to one of the highest officials of his administration."[3]

The reality is that the relationship between Kennedy and the CIA, though strained by the Bay of Pigs debacle, was not nearly as bad and combustible as conspiracy theorists would want people to believe. And as we shall see, and most important on the issue of motive, the period of difficult relations was apparently short-lived.[*]

[*]It is true, however, that in the immediate wake of the assassination, Kennedy's brother Robert had under-

We know that no one has ever come up with any evidence of any kind that the CIA decided to kill Kennedy, and got Oswald or anyone else to do the job for it. Indeed, despite the admitted problems Kennedy had with the CIA over the Bay of Pigs invasion, William Colby, who was a ranking official in the CIA during the period of the assassination and went on to become CIA director, would later write, "The fact of the matter is that the CIA could not have had a better friend in a President than John F. Kennedy. He understood the Agency and used it effectively, exploiting its intellectual abilities to help him analyze a complex world, and its paramilitary and covert political talents to react to it in a low key way."[4]

And in 1996, the CIA released a study titled "Getting to Know the President, CIA Briefings of Presidential Candidates, 1952–1992," by the CIA deputy director for intelligence, John L. Helgerson. On a one-year assignment, Helgerson interviewed "former presidents, CIA directors, and numerous others involved" in the nine presidencies covered by the subject period to ascertain the CIA's relationship with the various presidents. On the issue so dear to conspiracy theorists—the CIA's alleged animosity for Kennedy, and hence, its motive to kill him—it is very noteworthy that Helgerson's study reported that "the [CIA's] relationship with Kennedy was not only a distinct improvement over the more formal relationship with Eisenhower, *but would only rarely be matched in future administrations.*" And alluding, by implication, to the strained period with Kennedy following the Bay of Pigs invasion in April of 1961, the report goes on to say that "in November 1961, Allen Dulles had been replaced by John McCone, who served Kennedy as DCI [Director of Central Intelligence] for almost two years. In the *early part* of this period, McCone *succeeded in rebuilding the Agency's relationship with Kennedy.* McCone saw Kennedy frequently, and the President—more than any other before or since—would telephone even lower level Agency officers for information or assistance."[5]

One reason why it's been so easy for the conspiracy theorists to focus on the CIA is that since it officially started operations on September 18, 1947 (after being created under the National Security Act passed in July of that year to help fight the cold war against Communism and give the president centralized and coordinated foreign intelligence, which the country lacked prior to the Japanese attack on Pearl Harbor), it has been a shadowy, somewhat autonomous governmental agency whose mantra seems to be secrecy (its motto in a clandestine operation is that if the participants say nothing at all they're talking too much), Machiavellian intrigue, and operating outside the constraints of the law. As former CIA director Richard Helms once said about the culture of the CIA, "The only sin in espionage is getting caught."

If the CIA could actually have begun a study, code-named "Artichoke," in 1954 (later abandoned as not being feasible) to find out whether a person, through mind control, could be induced to commit an assassination against his will;[6] get in bed with organized crime in a plot to murder Castro;* sponsor the coup (its first attempt to topple a foreign

---

standable suspicions about CIA involvement in his brother's death, as he did about Castro and organized crime. RFK's aide, Walter Sheridan, said that RFK had told him, "You know, at the time I asked [CIA Director John] McCone . . . if they [CIA] had killed my brother, and I asked him in a way that he couldn't lie to me. And they hadn't" (Interview of Walter Sheridan by Roberta Greene on June 12, 1970, for RFK Oral History Program, John F. Kennedy library).

*On June 23, 1976, the U.S. Senate's Select Committee to Study Governmental Operations with Respect to Intelligence Activities (popularly known as the Church Committee after its chairman, Senator Frank Church of Idaho) released its report dated April 23, 1976, in which it stated that "between 1960 and early 1963 the

government) against Iran's prime minister, Mohammed Mossadegh, in 1953, which actually aborted a move toward democracy in that country; engineer, by funding and directing a rebel force, the frightened resignation of Jacobo Arbenz Guzmán, the leftist Guatemalan president, in 1954; plot to assassinate the left-leaning premier of the Republic of the Congo, Patrice Lumumba, in 1960; be heavily supportive (to the extent of supplying arms) to dissidents who eventually assassinated Dominican Republic strongman Rafael Trujillo in 1961; encourage a coup of South Vietnam's president, Ngo Dinh Diem, that resulted in his assassination in early November of 1963; promote the military coup against Chile's Salvador Allende in 1973; and so on—how much of a stretch is it to believe the agency had the type of mentality to murder its own president? Almost as much of a stretch as to believe that American soldiers who kill their counterparts in wars to defeat a foreign dictator like Hitler or Mussolini are just as likely to commit treason by trying to forcibly overthrow the government of the United States. But not to the buffs. They see no difference at all between the CIA, an American federal agency, trying to kill Castro and killing their own president.

In its early years more than now, the CIA was composed mostly of men who, though not necessarily born to the manor, were tweedy, often intellectual, Ivy League alumni (authors Warren Hinckle and William Turner observed that Yale's secretive Skull and Bones Society had "more CIA men than the Vatican has cardinals")[7] who shared a deeply patriotic love for this country and its always rim-full plates and cocktail glasses, and a pulsating fear that global Communism might end the party.[*] Though they were "gentlemen" warriors, they procured ring-around-the-collar men much more coarse than they to implement their plans. And they were committed and passionate enough to not be above whatever it took—including assassination of foreign leaders, even breaking bread with organized crime—to carry out their mission "in the national interest."[8][†]

These men (e.g., Harvard-trained lawyers like Tracy Barnes and Desmond FitzGerald, Yale economics professor Richard Bissell, Wall Street lawyer Frank Wisner, etc.), author Evan Thomas writes, "were not a secret cabal. Their views on the need for covert action against the Soviet Union and communist insurgencies around the world were widely shared

---

CIA attempted to use underworld figures for [Castro's] assassination," but found no connection between these attempts and Kennedy's assassination. Although the committee reached no final conclusion and recommended further investigation, it said it could find no CIA complicity in the assassination (Church Committee Report, pp.2–3, 6). The moving force behind investigating whether the CIA was involved in Kennedy's assassination was Senator Richard Schweiker of Pennsylvania, and the chairman of the committee assigned Schweiker and Senator Gary Hart of Colorado to head up, as a subcommittee, the investigation of this issue. This is why this particular report (the Church Committee had a broader mandate) is often referred to as the Schweiker or Schweiker-Hart Subcommittee Report. This book refers to it as the Church Committee Report.

[*]The fear was deeper than that. Only those who lived through it can accurately recall it. Michael Burke, the chief of covert operations for the CIA in Germany for part of the cold war (he went on to head the New York Yankees), says, "The Cold War in those days was a very real thing with hundreds of thousands of Soviet troops, tanks and planes poised on the East German border, capable of moving to the English Channel in forty-eight hours." Another CIA official at the time, Hugh Cunningham, perhaps expressed it the best. Survival itself was at stake, he remembers. "What you were made to feel was that the country was in desperate peril and we had to do whatever it took to save it." (Marks, *Search for the "Manchurian Candidate"*, p.28)

[†]To those who find humor in incongruity, as I can, the image of highly educated and urbane Ivy League types dressed in Brooks Brothers suits and speaking ferociously grammatical English (down to the forms of the verb "to be"), sitting around a table sipping martinis and casually musing about the best way to do in, say, Fidel Castro, might induce a smile.

at the upper levels of government . . . If their masters in Congress and the executive branch did not know precisely what [they] were up to in this era, it is in part because they did not wish to know." Thomas said that these men "found in their [previous] wartime experiences a sense of drama and meaning that could not be matched back at their law firms or lecture halls in peacetime. They saw the opportunity of American predominance [in world affairs] and reached out to seize it." Thomas quotes a former deputy inspector of the CIA, Ed Applewhite, who worked alongside the elitist pioneers of the CIA, as saying, "They arrogated to themselves total power, with no inhibiting precedent. They could do what they wanted, just as long as 'higher authority,' as we called the president, did not expressly forbid it. They were extremely aristocratic in their assumptions . . . , very romantic and arrogant. They had a heaven-sent obligation and, God knows, what opportunity. They ate it up."[9] The freewheeling life they were leading was so intoxicating that the independently wealthy FitzGerald would let "his paychecks pile up on the front-hall table" of his Georgetown home.[10]

But at the bottom of it all, and hence, the historical context in which all of the CIA's "homicidal tendencies" in the 1950s through the mid-1970s have to be viewed, but not condoned, is this country's—some now say—hysterical fear of the spread of Communism.* Let's not forget that the early years of the CIA were contemporaneous with a culture in Washington and elsewhere in which loyalty oaths and blacklists were looked on as acceptable means to combat Communism here at home.

Internationally, many nations in Eastern Europe and elsewhere did indeed fall under Communist (i.e., Soviet) influence or control following the end of the Second World War. The war had no sooner ended than a new struggle began. The Communist threat, emanating from what came to be called the "Sino-Soviet bloc," led to a U.S. policy of containment intended to prevent further encroachment into the "Free World." And this policy enjoyed widespread popular support in America. Castro's assumption of power in Cuba was viewed as particularly ominous since it was the first significant penetration by the Communists into the Western Hemisphere, a Soviet outpost at America's doorstep.[11]

With the Soviet leaders making no effort to conceal their objective of a world Communistic state, America's leaders were willing to commit U.S. combat troops abroad (e.g., Korea and Vietnam) to abort the "domino effect" of Soviet imperialism. And in some cases, assassination was deemed to be the most appropriate means to prevent the metastasizing of Communism. Though clearly contrary to American ideals, the Church Committee said that "the [assassination] plots occurred in a Cold War atmosphere perceived to be of crisis proportions" and concluded that "those involved [at the CIA] . . . appeared to believe they were advancing the best interests of their country." Despite all the plotting and all the efforts, the Church Committee found that "no foreign leaders were killed as a result of assassination plots initiated by officials of the United States."[12]

We all know, of course, that today's CIA has reached a nadir in the public's perception of its competence and effectiveness, mostly because of its catastrophic failure to learn of

---

*It wasn't the Karl Marx, Friedrich Engels brand of Communism that America feared so much, but the Russian, totalitarian kind, symbolized by the erection of the Berlin Wall in the summer of 1961. The wall, built by the Communists not to keep people from getting in but to keep them from getting out (those who tried were often shot on the spot by armed guards atop the concrete and barbed-wire structure), spoke more eloquently, all by itself, than the millions of words being written at the time on both sides of the Iron Curtain trying to sell the virtues of democracy vis-à-vis Communism, and vice versa. Capitalism, with all its inevitable sins, was a saint next to Russia among all freedom-loving people.

Osama bin Laden's plan to attack the United States on September 11, 2001, and its terribly clumsy and incorrect assessment of Iraq's alleged weapons of mass destruction. But it wasn't always this way. As Philip Taubman writes, in the early years CIA Director Allen W. Dulles was able to build "a first class intelligence agency, a pioneer in espionage science and technology." The CIA took the lead "in developing exotic hardware that revolutionized the spy business, including highflying spy planes and satellites. Eisenhower's decision to turn the project over to the CIA instead of the Air Force—he thought the agency was more nimble and better at keeping secrets—gave it an important new role that produced some prized accomplishments, including the first photo reconnaissance satellite in 1960."[13]

The five paragraphs that created the CIA in the National Security Act of July 26, 1947, do not specifically authorize the conduct of *covert* political activity nor, apparently, was that the original intent—its main function being the "correlation, evaluation and dissemination" of "intelligence as [it] relates to the national security."[14] So how did the CIA, our government's principal *foreign* intelligence spy organization,* get involved in foreign assassination plots and become the paramilitary force it was in the 1960s? One could argue that it was in its genes. The CIA's genetic predecessor, the Office of Strategic Services (OSS), was formed in December of 1942 at the height of the Second World War[†] and headed by William "Wild Bill" Donovan, a prominent Wall Street lawyer and World War I hero (Congressional Medal of Honor). Donovan was "an incurable romantic" who "molded the OSS into his own image: dashing, slightly madcap, and highly effective." He set the tone for the later CIA by recruiting men from the nation's upper class such as the son of Andrew Mellon and both sons of J. P. Morgan Jr., and including scholars such as Arthur Schlesinger Jr., Walt Rostow, and William Langer. "This led to sniffing [by some] that OSS stood for 'Oh So Social.'" But no one claimed the OSS didn't get the job done.[15]

However, anyone concluding that Donovan only recruited from the elite would be wrong. It just so happened that the elite had much to offer. But the main imperative that drove Donovan was to find whoever could do the job, resulting, for instance, in his arranging for the release of a few master forgers from prison to work for the OSS. Shunning bureaucracy and convention, the free-wheeling Donovan was able to do things like this not only because it was his nature but also because he had the confidence of Franklin D. Roosevelt, the man who created the OSS by presidential order and appointed him to head it and to whom Donovan reported directly. They tell the story of Donovan, a Republican, bringing a silent pistol invented by his OSS into the Oval Office and firing it, and Roosevelt responding by telling Donovan he was the only Republican he would allow in the Oval Office with a gun.[16]

Operating mainly in the European theater, with headquarters in London, the OSS was the nation's first foreign spy agency. President Truman disbanded it on October 1, 1945,

---

*Under 61 Stat. 495 Chapter 343 (The National Security Act of 1947), Section 102 created the Central Intelligence Agency. Section 102 (d) (3) provided "that the Agency shall have *no . . . internal* [domestic] *security functions.*" Prior to the creation of the CIA, in 1940 the FBI started conducting foreign intelligence operations in Central and South America to gather information on the Nazis during the Second World War. This was terminated with the creation of the CIA as the lead federal agency in the gathering of foreign intelligence. (Whitehead, *FBI Story*, pp.15, 211–212; HSCA Report, p.241)

†Often referred to as "the first genuine foreign intelligence agency in U.S. history" (Powers, *Man Who Kept the Secrets*, p.25), it was not. The Special Intelligence Service, a branch of the FBI formed in 1940, apparently was. (See endnote discussion.)

just two years before the CIA was created, and as writer William Bleuer points out, "Most of the early leaders and members of the CIA, like Allen Dulles and Richard Helms [even a much later leader, William Casey], cut their covert teeth with the OSS in World War II." An integral part of the OSS's mission of sabotage, espionage, and covert action in enemy territory was to aid in bringing about the death of America's adversaries. Indeed, the pipe-smoking patrician Dulles, from his headquarters in Bern, Switzerland, became famous for his covert work with German military officers plotting the assassination of Hitler. To OSS veterans in the CIA, the "Cold War was [merely] a corollary of the shooting war from the beginning."[17]*

After the first four paragraphs of the aforementioned National Security Act of 1947, which enumerate the functions of coordinating, evaluating, and disseminating intelligence, paragraph five allows the CIA to perform such "other functions" relating to intelligence and affecting the national security "as the National Security Council† may from time to time direct." (See expanded discussion on this issue with respect to the Special Group, a National Security Council creation, in the section dealing with whether President Kennedy knew of the CIA's plan to kill Castro.) And at its first meeting in December of 1947, the National Security Council issued a top-secret directive granting the CIA authority to conduct *covert* psychological operations, primarily to counter, reduce, and discredit "International Communism" throughout the world in a manner consistent with U.S. foreign and military policies.[18]

In December of 1963, President Truman, deeply dismayed over the direction in which the CIA had gone, wrote from his home in Independence, Missouri,

> I think it has become necessary to take another look at the purpose and operations of our Central Intelligence Agency—CIA. At least I would like to submit here the original reason why I thought it necessary to organize this agency during my administration . . . A President's performance in office is as effective as the . . . information he gets . . . The Departments of State, Defense, Commerce, Interior and others are constantly engaged in extensive information gathering . . . But their collective information reached the President all too frequently in conflicting conclusions. At times, the intelligence reports tended to be slanted to conform to established positions of a given department . . . Therefore, I decided to set up a special organization charged with the collection of all intelligence reports from every available source, and to have those reports reach me as President without departmental "treatment" or interpretations. I wanted and needed the information in its "natural raw" state . . . The most important thing about this move was to guard

---

*Partnerships and relationships formed by the OSS with allies *before* the war ended (e.g., future CIA counterintelligence head James Angleton with British counterintelligence chief Kim Philby), and with prior enemies immediately afterward (e.g., Nazi General Reinhard Gehlen, who, knowing Germany was about to fall and planning to reinvent himself as anti-Nazi, moved fifty steel containers of his intelligence files on Russia from the Russian front back to a secure location underground in the German state of Bavaria and offered them to the OSS and his American captors), would carry far into the cold war struggle between the United States and the Soviet Union. Some were helpful (Gehlen, through his National German Intelligence Service [BND], which worked closely with U.S. intelligence) and others not (Philby). (Helms with Hood, *Look over My Shoulder*, pp.83–85; Trento, *Secret History of the CIA*, pp.22–23; Powers, *Man Who Kept the Secrets*, pp.28, 85–86; Ashley, *CIA Spy Master*, p.61)

†The National Security Council was also created by the National Security Act. Its members are the president, vice president, and secretaries of state and defense, with advisory members being the director of the CIA and chairman of the Joint Chiefs of Staff.

against the chance of intelligence being used to influence or lead the President into unwise decisions . . . For some time I have been disturbed by the way the CIA has been diverted from its original assignment. It has become an operational and at times a policy-making arm of the government . . . I never had any thought that when I set up the CIA it would be injected into peacetime cloak-and-dagger operations . . . This quiet, intelligence arm of the President has been so removed from its intended role that it is being integrated as a symbol of sinister and mysterious foreign intrigue.[19]

Since it has been established beyond all doubt that Oswald killed Kennedy, the conspiracy theorists who propound the idea of the CIA being behind Oswald's act are necessarily starting out in a very deep hole before they even take their first breath of air. This is so because Oswald was a Marxist, and a Marxist being in league with U.S. intelligence just doesn't ring true. More specifically, why would a passionate pro-Castro follower like Oswald want to join forces with the very U.S. intelligence agency—the CIA—that Oswald knew was behind the Bay of Pigs invasion to overthrow Castro, his hero? The conspiracy theorists realize, of course, the difficulty of knitting these conflicting threads together, and try to get around the problem by saying that Oswald was only "posing as a pro-Castro sympathizer." In other words, Oswald was really a rightist who was only *acting* like a leftist. "Oswald's actual political orientation was extreme right wing," said New Orleans DA Jim Garrison. "Oswald would have been more at home with *Mein Kampf* than *Das Kapital*."[20] "Oswald was an American agent *posing* as a Marxist," says conspiracy theorist James DiEugenio.[21] But this contention cannot seriously and rationally be made. To believe it, one would have to disbelieve not only all of Oswald's words, including those uttered when he was only a teenager, but all of his conduct, as well as the impressions (many given under oath) of the considerable number of people who knew Oswald personally and spoke of his being a confirmed and passionate Marxist. In other words, one would have to believe that year in and year out for almost a decade, Oswald was putting on an Academy Award–winning performance, fooling everyone, including his family and wife, by the virtuosity of his acting skills.

In its final report, the HSCA took the Warren Commission to task for what it characterized as a virtual lack of investigation of the CIA, which itself was one of the federal agencies investigating the assassination. "Testifying before the Commission," the HSCA Report says, "CIA Director John A. McCone indicated that 'Oswald was not an agent, employee, or informant of the Central Intelligence Agency. The Agency never contacted him, interviewed him, talked with him, or solicited any reports or information from him, or communicated with him directly or in any other manner . . . Oswald was never associated or connected directly or indirectly in any way whatsoever with the Agency.' McCone's testimony was corroborated by Deputy Director Richard M. Helms."[22] Helms had told the Warren Commission, "I had all of our records searched to see if there had been any contacts at any time prior to President Kennedy's assassination by anyone in the Central Intelligence Agency with Lee Harvey Oswald. We checked our card files and our personnel files and all our records. Now, this check turned out to be negative."[23]

The HSCA Report then goes on to say, "The record reflects that once these assurances had been received, no further efforts were made by the Warren Commission to pursue the matter."[24] But this simply is not true. Although the HSCA can take justifiable credit in investigating the CIA more than the Warren Commission did, the starting point for any investigation of the CIA, and the principal way to investigate it, would be to look at its entire internal file. If the people responsible for preparing the HSCA Report had bothered to read the very next page in the above-quoted joint testimony by McCone and Helms before the Warren Commission, they would have learned that the Warren Commission did, in fact, do this precise thing. Lee Rankin, Warren Commission chief counsel, asked Helms, "Can you tell the Commission as to whether or not you have supplied us all the information the agency has, at least in substance, in regard to Lee Harvey Oswald?"

Mr. Helms: "We have; all."

Representative Ford: "Has a member of the Commission staff had full access to your files on Lee Harvey Oswald?"

Mr. Helms: "He has, sir."

Representative Ford: "They have had the opportunity to personally look at the entire file?"

Mr. Helms: "We invited them to come out to our building in Langley and actually put the file on the table so that they could examine it."

Chairman Warren: "I was personally out there, too, and was offered the same opportunity. I did not avail myself of it because of the time element, but I was offered the same opportunity."

Mr. Rankin: "Mr. Helms, can you explain, according to the limitations of security, the reasons why we examined materials but did not always take them, in a general way?"

Mr. Helms: "Yes, I can. In our communications between individuals working overseas and in Washington, we for security reasons have a method of hiding the identities of individuals in telegrams and dispatches by the use of pseudonyms and cryptonyms. For this reason, we never allow the original documents to leave our premises. However, on the occasion when the representatives of the Commission staff looked at these files, we sat there and identified these pseudonyms and cryptonyms and related them to the proper names of the individuals concerned, so that they would know exactly what the correspondence said."

Mr. Rankin: "By that you mean the representatives of the Commission were able to satisfy themselves that they had all the information for the benefit of the Commission without disclosing matters that would be a threat to security; is that right?"

Mr. Helms: "It is my understanding that they were satisfied."[25]

When I asked Warren Commission assistant counsel W. David Slawson (whose area of inquiry for the Warren Commission was the possibility of a conspiracy) about the HSCA's remark that the Warren Commission never went beyond McCone's and Helms's assurances, he said, "That's wrong. Rankin, [William] Coleman, I, and a few other members of the staff went over to CIA Headquarters at Langley, and to the best of my recollection—this was over thirty-five years ago—we looked at the entire CIA file." (Warren Commission assistant counsel William Coleman told me that he and other members of the Commission staff went over to CIA headquarters "several times" to look at the Oswald file.) He added that although the Warren Commission staff ended up leaving most of the documents pertaining to Oswald in the CIA files, "We did get copies of a substantial number of them." Slawson said that CIA agent Raymond Rocca, chief of research and analysis for counterintelligence, was assigned as the liaison between the Warren Commission and the CIA, and "whenever we needed anything, he got us what we needed. Rocca was not passive. For instance, he suggested lines of inquiry to us and helped us interpret and contextualize whatever KGB or other foreign intelligence documents came into our possession."[26]

It was Slawson's belief that the CIA was very cooperative with the Warren Commission. The HSCA, after having said in its report that the Warren Commission did not investigate whether the CIA had any association with Oswald, went on later to say, in seeming contradiction, that it "contacted both members of the Warren Commission staff and those representatives of the CIA who played significant roles in providing CIA-generated information to the Commission. The general consensus of these people was that the Commission and the CIA enjoyed a successful working relationship during the course of the Commission's investigation."[27] Slawson said that an example of CIA cooperation was when he, Coleman, and another assistant counsel, Howard P. Willens, flew to Mexico City to investigate Oswald's contact with the Cuban consulate and Soviet embassy in April of 1964. He said that David Atlee Phillips, an official at the CIA station in Mexico City, and his number-one assistant (Slawson could not recall his name) took them into their operations room and "showed us everything, how they wiretapped all calls coming into the Soviet Embassy, where they had hidden cameras and listening devices, et cetera. They didn't hold back anything."

Slawson said, "I can assure you that if, at any time, we came into possession of any evidence at all that showed any kind of relationship between Oswald and the CIA, or in any way pointed toward CIA complicity in the assassination, we would have vigorously pursued it. But nothing like this ever surfaced."[28] Coleman told me, "We looked at every conspiracy theory out there. We could find nothing to support any of these various theories."[29]

It's curious the HSCA Report would state that the Commission never pursued the Oswald-CIA association further when, as indicated, the fact that the Commission did is on the very next page of the volume of Warren Commission testimony the HSCA cited, and is also in one of the volumes of the HSCA itself. HSCA volume 11, page 493 speaks of another visit to CIA headquarters, this time by Warren Commission counsel Samuel Stern, on March 25, 1964. "Stern's memorandum of his visit reveals that he reviewed Oswald's file with [Raymond] Rocca." Stern also noted in his memorandum, the HSCA said, that in addition to reviewing Oswald's entire file, "Rocca provided him for his review a computer printout of the references to Oswald-related documents located in the Agency's electronic data storage system. [Stern] stated 'there is no item listed . . . which we [the Warren Commission] have not been given in either full text or paraphrase.'"

With respect to its own investigation, the HSCA said that "recognizing the special difficulty in investigating a clandestine agency, the committee sought to resolve the issue of Oswald's alleged association with the CIA by conducting an inquiry that went beyond taking statements from two of the Agency's most senior officials." Accordingly, the committee made an effort "to identify circumstances in Oswald's life or in the way his case was handled by the CIA that possibly suggested an intelligence association." It also "undertook an intensive review of the pertinent files, including the CIA's . . . Oswald file and hundreds of others from the CIA, FBI, Department of State, Department of Defense and other agencies. Based on these file reviews, a series of interviews, depositions and executive session hearings was conducted with both Agency and non-Agency witnesses. The contacts with present and former CIA personnel covered a broad range of individuals, including staff and division chiefs, clandestine case officers, area desk officers, research analysts, secretaries and clerical assistants." The HSCA also pointed out that "each of the present and former Agency employees contacted by the committee was released from his secrecy oath by the CIA."

Quite impressive, right? The conclusion formed from all of this? The HSCA said, "The results of this investigation *confirmed* the Warren Commission testimony of McCone and Helms . . . *The committee found no evidence of any relationship between Oswald and the CIA.*"* The HSCA added that "taken in their entirety, the items of circumstantial evidence that the committee had selected for investigation as possibly indicative of an intelligence association [CIA *or other*] did not support the allegation that Oswald had an intelligence agency relationship."[30]

Also, contrary to allegations by conspiracy theorists, the HSCA could find no evidence that Oswald "ever received any intelligence training or performed any intelligence assignments during his term of service."[31] Although Kerry Wendell Thornley, a member of Oswald's unit at El Toro Marine base near Santa Ana, California, testified before the Warren Commission, "Oswald, *I believe*, had a higher clearance" than confidential, "probably a secret clearance,"[32] the HSCA learned that Oswald only had a security clearance of confidential (the lowest) and "never received a higher classification."[33] Oswald's Marine Corps records show that he was "granted final clearance up to and including CONFIDENTIAL."[34] While it is true that John Donovan, the officer in charge of Oswald's radar crew in Santa Ana, testified before the Warren Commission that Oswald "must have had secret [above confidential, but below top secret] clearance to work in the Radar Center,"[35] the HSCA concluded that Donovan's assumption was incorrect. A review by the HSCA of the U.S. Marine Corps personnel files of four enlisted men who had worked with Oswald in either Japan or California (Richard Call, Zack Stout, Robert Augg, and Nelson Delgado) revealed that all only had, like Oswald, a security clearance of confidential.[36]

The CIA (specifically, the Special Investigations Group [SIG] of the CIA's counterintelligence unit) did not open a 201 file (a file kept on an individual, including CIA employees, that brings him into the agency's records system) on Oswald until December 9, 1960, *after* he had defected to the Soviet Union, and then only after the agency had received a request from the State Department for information on American defectors.[37] However, the agency, before December 9, was already receiving information on Oswald from other agencies of the government.[38] It had four written communications in 1959 from the State Department pertaining to Oswald's defection to the Soviet Union, the first one dated October 31, 1959, from Moscow, and a fifth communication dated May 25, 1960.[39]

The CIA told the HSCA that there were "no specified criteria for automatically opening a 201 file on an American."[40] And when the HSCA reviewed the 201 files of twenty-nine other defectors, eight of whom had 201 files opened *before* their defection, they found

---

*The reader should realize that many in the conspiracy community would give their right arm if they could prove that Oswald was a CIA agent. If they could do this, it would be the answer to their most wondrous dreams, the solution, at last, to the Kennedy assassination. This is because they are too blind when it comes to the assassination to realize that even if Oswald were a CIA agent, it would only be one step in their quest for the Holy Grail. They'd still have to prove that the reason why the CIA lied about Oswald's relationship with the agency was not because it didn't want the world to know that one of its agents murdered the president (as, on a lesser scale, a religious order would not want it to be known that one of its priests was a child molester), but because number one, the CIA decided to murder Kennedy, and number two, the agency got Oswald to murder Kennedy for it.

that for only four of the remaining twenty-one the files were opened *because* of the defection. The files on the seventeen other defectors were opened from four months to several years after the defection. The HSCA said that "at the very least, the committee's review indicated that during 1958–1963, the opening of a [201] file years after a defection was not uncommon. [Oswald's defection to the Soviet Union first came to the attention of American officials in Moscow on October 31, 1959. So his 201 file was opened more than thirteen months later.] In many cases, the event was triggered by some event, independent of the defection, that had drawn attention to the individual involved."[41]

The HSCA went on to say that "the existence of a 201 file does not necessarily connote any actual relationship or contact with the CIA." Though not automatic, such a file is normally opened by the CIA when "a person is considered to be of potential intelligence or counterintelligence significance." Oswald's 201 file, the HSCA said, "contained no indication that he had ever had a relationship with the CIA."[42]

The CIA dossier or 201 file on Oswald after December 9, 1960, and up to November 22, 1963, consisted of twenty-nine documents: seven documents received from the FBI, ten from the Department of State, two from the Department of Navy, one from the Immigration and Naturalization Service, four newspaper clippings, and five internal CIA notes, all of which the CIA turned over to the Warren Commission on March 6, 1964.[43] In fact, prior to October 9, 1963, when the Mexico City office of the CIA sent a memorandum to CIA headquarters in Washington, D.C., that an American male identifying himself as Lee Oswald contacted the Soviet embassy in Mexico City, "the Oswald file held by CIA [headquarters] consisted *entirely* of press materials and disseminations received from the Department of State, the Federal Bureau of Investigation, and the Navy Department."[44]

As indicated, and to the great dismay of the conspiracy community, the HSCA said that from its entire investigation, it found "no evidence" of any relationship that Oswald ever had with the CIA. The committee went on to say, "Moreover, the Agency's investigative efforts prior to the assassination regarding Oswald's presence in Mexico City served to confirm the absence of any relationship with him. Specifically, when apprised of his possible presence in Mexico City, the Agency both initiated internal inquiries concerning his background and, once informed of his Soviet experience, notified other potentially interested Federal agencies of his possible contact with the Soviet Embassy in Mexico City."[45]

Not only is there no evidence that Oswald had any relationship with the CIA (i.e., no relationship that CIA headquarters was aware of and sanctioning), but as we've seen elsewhere in this book, Oswald clearly was not CIA agent or operative material. As John Scelso, chief of clandestine operations for the CIA in the Western Hemisphere at the time of the assassination, put it in sworn testimony before the HSCA,

> Oswald was a person of a type who would never have been recruited by the Agency . . . His personality and background completely disqualified him for clandestine work or for work as an agent to carry out the instructions of the Agency . . . When the Agency hires an agent, engages someone to do our work and gives him a certain amount of training and places him under our guidance, whether we pay him or not, or whether he signs an agreement or not, he has to meet certain standards. He has to go through a security check, a file check. And the Counter-intelligence Staff has to examine his personality and background and evaluate his reliability . . . Oswald, by virtue of his background and so on, would miserably fail to meet

our minimum qualifications. Oswald would have been debriefed had he walked in and volunteered information, you see. However, he would not have been given any mission to perform. He might have been given instructions, you see, which would tend to neutralize him and make him less of a nuisance and danger than he otherwise would be, like go away and do not contact us any more . . . Oswald's whole pattern of life was that of a very badly, emotionally unbalanced young man.[46]

And author Peter Grose points out that in addition to Oswald's "loose and undisciplined" life, "he stood out from his environment. His strange odyssey [to Russia] only invited questions from all around him. This is not the sort of person that those who build intelligence networks seek for their agents."[47]

But if the CIA, as an agency, wasn't involved with Oswald in the assassination, what about the argument by many conspiracy theorists that "rogue elements" or agents within the CIA may have been, and it was they who were behind Oswald and the assassination? The conspiracy community has made this argument ad nauseam, but after well over forty years of investigation, isn't it fair to ask the conspiracy theorists what evidence they have to support this contention? Of course, not only don't they have any evidence, but with very few exceptions (e.g., David Atlee Phillips, see later text), they never even tell us just who they believe these rogue agents were. Instead, they can be no more specific than to resort to vague allusions such as "fairly senior or even highly placed . . . renegade CIA agents,"[48] or "lower echelons" at the agency,[49] or "angry . . . more fanatical rogue agents" at the CIA,[50] or "a number of aberrant agents" in the CIA.[51] I say this to the conspiracy community: Is that all you people have? *After over forty years of investigation?*[*]

With respect to the argument that rogue agents within the CIA were behind Kennedy's murder, the HSCA said it "attempted to identify [any such] CIA employees" but was unable to do so.[52] The committee said that in that regard, "an effort was also made to locate a man identified as Maurice Bishop who was said to have been a CIA Officer who had been seen in the company of Lee Harvey Oswald. The effort to find 'Bishop' was likewise unsuccessful."[53]

The source of the Bishop-Oswald sighting was one Antonio Veciana Blanch, one of the founders of Alpha 66, a militant, anti-Castro exile group. In March of 1976, Veciana told a staff investigator for U.S. Senator Richard S. Schweiker, a member of the Church Committee, that between 1960 and 1973 he had a working relationship in the anti-Castro effort with someone known to him as Maurice Bishop, whom he believed to be a CIA agent. Veciana said that in 1973 Bishop had given him a suitcase containing $253,000 in cash for his services over the years in attempting to assassinate Castro. Two hundred and fifty-three thousand dollars? A quarter of a million dollars? In some kind of balloon payment delivered only at the end of thirteen years of work? Surely a believ-

---

[*]Many conspiracy theorists take their theory about rogue or maverick agents even further and allege, without having the courtesy of providing an iota of evidence, that the CIA leadership found out what the rogue agents did and covered up for them to protect the CIA from extinction. But this is ludicrous. If the nation found out that some rogue CIA agents had murdered the president, there would be extreme shock, but the CIA itself would very likely survive. But if the CIA leadership covered up the awful deed and the nation found out, not only would this most certainly sound the death knell for the CIA, but the CIA leaders would have their reputations and careers destroyed and they'd be prosecuted for being accessories after the fact to Kennedy's murder.

able story. (What's particularly laughable about this is that Veciana was Alpha 66's secretary of finance.) Veciana said that at one of his meetings with Bishop—in Dallas in August or early September of 1963—Lee Harvey Oswald was present. Veciana repeated these claims in testimony before the HSCA in April of 1978.[54]

We know (see Oswald biography) that Veciana could not have met with Oswald and Bishop in Dallas in late August or early September of 1963, because we know Oswald was in New Orleans during this entire period. Moreover, though Veciana claims to have met with Bishop more than a hundred times, he could not point to a single witness to corroborate his association with Bishop, or help HSCA investigators locate Bishop, which they made an intense and unsuccessful effort to do. Coupled with the additional fact that the HSCA felt Veciana "had been less than candid" and waited more than ten years after the assassination to reveal his information, the committee concluded it "could not . . . credit Veciana's story of having met with Lee Harvey Oswald."[55]

HSCA investigator Gaeton Fonzi had been convinced that Bishop was David Atlee Phillips, the head of the Cuba section at the CIA station in Mexico City at the time of the assassination, but when Fonzi arranged for Veciana to see Phillips at the HSCA hearings in Washington, D.C., Veciana said that although there was a "physical similarity," Phillips was not Bishop. "No. It is not him," he stated unequivocally.[56] However, Fonzi remained convinced that "Maurice Bishop was David Atlee Phillips" and that Phillips "played a key role in the conspiracy to assassinate President Kennedy,"[57] but never provided any evidence to support his accusation.

An investigative journalist and former senior editor of *Greater Philadelphia Magazine*, Fonzi had long been a conspiracy theorist. Brought in as an HSCA investigator by Richard Sprague, the prominent Philadelphia prosecutor who was the HSCA's first chief counsel, Fonzi believed that the CIA was complicit in the assassination, and the heart of his belief was that Phillips, using the pseudonym Maurice Bishop, was Oswald's CIA case officer whom Veciana saw in Dallas in Oswald's presence. It became a canard that many embraced, often to their considerable detriment. In their 1980 book, *Death in Washington*, authors Donald Freed and Fred Landis asserted not only that Phillips played a role in the cover-up of the assassination of former Chilean foreign minister Orlando Letelier (along with his aide, Ronni Moffit) in Washington, D.C., in 1976, but also that he used the alias Maurice Bishop in serving as Oswald's CIA case officer.[58] Phillips's 1982 libel lawsuit against the two authors and their publisher was settled in February 1986 with a retraction and an unspecified (but "suitable," per Phillips) sum of money.[59]

I spent a goodly amount of time preparing Phillips for his testimony in the London docu-trial as a rebuttal witness to Edwin Lopez, the former HSCA investigator who, like Fonzi, suggested CIA complicity in the assassination, and he said the entire Maurice Bishop allegation was "false and crazy."[60] But Phillips eventually decided not to testify. The main reason was that he had another libel lawsuit pending against the *London Observer* for publishing the same Maurice Bishop allegation, and his lawyer felt it would not be advisable for him to get into the same issue, if it came up, at our London trial because opposing counsel in the libel lawsuit might be able to derive some advantage from it. Additionally, though he had told me in an earlier letter, "I am going to depend on you to make it easier for me to avoid . . . violating my secrecy agreement" with the CIA, he wrote that as a former CIA officer, "I would probably be a lousy witness anyway, because I would have to avoid confirming or denying information" contained in still-classified reports, and "a jury would probably believe I was stonewalling."[61] On October 7, 1986, attorneys for the *London Observer* "unreservedly apologized" to Phillips in Britain's High Court for suggesting he was in any way involved in Kennedy's assassination, and agreed to pay all his legal expenses and a "substantial" sum in settlement.[62] On October 12, 1986, the *Observer* printed its retraction in which it said that "there was never any evidence to support the suggestion" that Phillips knew Oswald.

HSCA officials regretted not only parroting Fonzi's Maurice Bishop allegation, but also having him as one of their investigators. In the November 1980 issue of the *Washingtonian*, Fonzi wrote a blistering, inordinately long article (virtually book size at eighty thousand words) about the HSCA, suggesting it was a farce that played "political games." He continued to allege that Phillips might be Bishop and said that "what the Kennedy assassination still needs is an investigation guided simply, unswervingly, by the priority of truth," describing Chief Counsel G. Robert Blakey as a mere hired hand whose main objective was to shield government institutions from effective scrutiny and criticism.[63]

The *Washingtonian* being a prestigious publication, Blakey and Gary Cornwell, deputy chief counsel to the HSCA, felt it advisable to respond in the *Congressional Record*. Blakey rued the day he departed from his policy of hiring impartial investigators, saying he kept Fonzi on the staff after Sprague left because "I felt that his obsession [over the CIA's complicity in the assassination] would help assure that this aspect of the committee's investigation would receive its due," adding that committee staff members "derisively referred to [Fonzi] as an 'Ahab' and to his quest as a search for 'Moby Dick.'" Cornwell was no more kind in his denunciation of Fonzi, referring to his "bad faith" and "lost credibility."[64] Michael Ewing, a member of the HSCA staff, was so put off by Fonzi's article in the *Washingtonian* that he felt obliged to send a personal letter to Phillips himself, saying, "I wouldn't want you to think that there are many of us who think like Gaeton Fonzi . . . I would like you to know that Fonzi's writing does not reflect the views of responsible former members of the Select Committee."[65] In an eight-page letter to the editor of the *Washingtonian*, Ewing said that Fonzi "worked exclusively out of Miami, locating and interviewing Cubans," and that he "never worked on the Committee in Washington" other than for a short period "during the editing process at the very end of the investigation. I think Fonzi's nearly total absence from Washington—where, of course, the investigation was planned, directed and concluded—was probably a primary factor behind his embarrassingly misinformed perceptions of how the investigation was conducted."[66]

Congressman Richardson Preyer of North Carolina, the chairman of the HSCA subcommittee on the JFK assassination, also saw fit to write Phillips on November 19, 1980, to say, "I can understand your concern over the Fonzi article. Mr. Fonzi's views are not shared by me nor, I think, by the Committee. I believed your testimony and did not find the testimony of Veciana credible."[67]

One of the main leads on a CIA-Oswald relationship that the HSCA pursued was the allegation of one James B. Wilcott, a finance officer for the CIA from 1957 until 1966. At the time of the assassination, Wilcott was assigned to the CIA station in Tokyo. (Oswald was assigned to the First Marine Air Wing at Atsugi Naval Air Station, about thirty-five miles southwest of Tokyo, in 1957–1958.) Wilcott testified before the committee that the day after the assassination, "there was at least six or seven people, specifically, who said that they either knew or believed Oswald to be an agent of the CIA," but could only recall the name of one, Jerry Fox, who "at least made some mention of it." He did name several other fellow workers who made references to Oswald being an agent, but they did so only "in a speculative manner." Wilcott said, "I didn't really believe this when I heard it, and I thought it was absurd. Then, as time went on, I began to hear more things in that line." The main thing, he testified, was an incident "two or three months after the assassination . . . when a [CIA] case officer came up to my window to draw money and he specifically said . . . 'Well, Jim, the money that I drew the last couple of weeks ago or so was money' either for the Oswald project or for Oswald," he could not remember which. If we're to believe Wilcott's story, the CIA case officer had been drawing money for Oswald or the Oswald project even though Oswald had already been dead for at least a month and a half. Since the CIA is notorious for secrecy, why would a CIA officer share the information that the presidential assassin had been a CIA agent with someone like Wilcott, who merely worked in the finance section? When asked that very question, Wilcott could only say lamely, "I don't know how to answer that question."

Wilcott's story started to quickly unravel when he was unable to identify the case officer who allegedly told him this, and could not recall what the officer told him Oswald's cryptonym was. Nonetheless, though he had no evidence to support his position, he told the HSCA it was "my belief that [Oswald] was a regular agent and this was a regular project of the Agency to send Oswald to the Soviet Union." He also believed Marina Oswald was a CIA agent who had been recruited before Oswald's "phony defection" to the Soviet Union "and was waiting there in Tokyo for Lee Harvey Oswald."[*]

When Wilcott was asked, "Were you ever able to find any indication in any of the Tokyo station's records that Oswald was, in fact, a CIA agent?" he responded, "Well, I never really looked," even, he said, at his own disbursement records. Wilcott had a ready answer for why he never furnished his allegedly valuable information to the Warren Commission. "I really didn't think that the Warren Commission was out to really get at the facts," but he did bother to write an unpublished article on the matter, which he gave to the HSCA.[68] Wilcott's credibility suffered even further when an intelligence analyst whom Wilcott said he discussed the Oswald allegation with at the post told the committee he wasn't in Tokyo at the time of the assassination, the committee verifying that he had been transferred back to the United States in 1962, the previous year. Finally, the committee interviewed many CIA personnel who had been stationed in Tokyo at the time, including the chief of the post and other personnel who surely would have known if Oswald had had any association with the agency in Tokyo, and all had no knowledge of such an association. The HSCA concluded that based on all the evidence, "Wilcott's allegation was not worthy of belief."[69]

Another alleged Oswald-CIA link emerged when Gerald Patrick Hemming Jr. told conspiracy author Anthony Summers in 1978 that he was a former Marine sergeant who had been stationed at Atsugi air base in Japan working as a radar control operator shortly before Oswald did. He told Summers that he had been recruited by naval intelligence while there, and that he had met Oswald once at the Cuban consulate in Los Angeles. (At the time, Hemming was reportedly pro-Castro, but later switched sides when he and fellow former marine Frank Sturgis went to Cuba to help Castro in his revolution, and became

[*]The ARRB "examined extensive CIA records concerning the history and operations of the CIA in or against the Soviet Union in the late 1950s and early to mid 1960s. The Review Board found no records that suggested that Oswald had ever worked for the CIA in any capacity, nor did any records suggest that Oswald's trip and defection to the Soviet Union served any intelligence purpose" (Final Report of the ARRB, p.85).

disenchanted with Castro.) From the questions Oswald asked, Hemming said he got the impression that Oswald was "an informant or some type of agent working for somebody," and that at Atsugi, Oswald would have been "a prime candidate for recruitment" by some U.S. intelligence agency. Apart from the fact that Hemming doesn't make the allegation that Oswald was a CIA agent, only that he sensed he was "some type of agent," Summers acknowledges that "Hemming's reliability as a source has on occasion been called into question."[70]

Although it is an article of faith among most conspiracy theorists that the CIA was directly behind or at least somehow involved in the assassination, other than fanciful daydreaming on their part, the likes of Wilcott and Hemming are the only basis for their allegation.

One relationship Oswald had which conspiracy theorists find particularly suspicious and incriminating is his friendship in Dallas with the Russian emigré of purportedly noble pedigree, George de Mohrenschildt. This relationship is discussed in depth earlier in this book, but it should be noted here that virtually all conspiracy theorists postulate that de Mohrenschildt had a very close relationship with the CIA, either as an agent or as some other type of operative, and many suspect he had a hand in the assassination.* But the HSCA thoroughly checked de Mohrenschildt's background and concluded that there was "no evidence that de Mohrenschildt had ever been an American intelligence agent." His contact with the agency seemed to be limited to being debriefed several times in Dallas between 1957 and 1961 by J. Walton Moore of the CIA's Domestic Contact Service. For instance, Moore interviewed de Mohrenschildt following his return from a trip to Yugoslavia in 1957. (De Mohrenschildt went there, under salary with the International Cooperation Administration [ICA] in Washington, D.C., to "help [the ICA] develop oil resources" in Yugoslavia. The HSCA said that Moore "was an *overt* CIA employee . . . He was not part of a *covert* or clandestine operation.")

Around this time, as the HSCA pointed out, "upon returning from trips abroad, as many as 25,000 Americans annually provided information [about countries they had visited] to the CIA's Domestic Contacts Division [actually, Domestic Contact Service] on a nonclandestine basis. Such acts of cooperation should not be confused with an actual Agency relationship."[71] But since a great many conspiracy theorists believe the CIA was behind the assassination, they feel it simply cannot be a benign coincidence that Oswald had a friend who was connected in any way with the CIA.

Speaking of coincidences, as mentioned in the Oswald biography section, what a remarkable coincidence that de Mohrenschildt knew Jackie Kennedy and her mother, Janet Auchincloss. Additionally, as alluded to earlier, de Mohrenschildt, quite a writer of letters, wrote a letter to President Kennedy on February 16, 1963, congratulating Kennedy on his recent goal to try to make the average sedentary American more physically fit. De Mohrenschildt told Kennedy of the long and physically rigorous journey, by foot, that he and his wife had taken in 1961 throughout Latin America, and said that if the "typescript and many photographs" of the journey he offered to send Kennedy

---

*If he did, he certainly would have had a difficult time doing so, he and his wife having left Dallas to live in Haiti (where he had a contract with the Haitian government) at the end of May in 1963, almost a half year before the assassination (9 H 167, 276, WCT George S. de Mohrenschildt). And as I understand it, communication facilities (which would have been needed to stay in touch with Oswald) in Papa Doc Duvalier's dump of an island were not noted for their efficiency.

impressed him, "I would ask you, Mr. President, for a foreword to my book." He closed by saying, "By the way, I am an old friend of the Bouvier family and of Mrs. Janet Auchincloss, but I prefer to write to you directly, as 'getting fit' seems to be a personal concern of yours. Please accept my sincere wishes of success in all your endeavors. Sincerely yours, George De Mohrenschildt."*

A man of George de Mohrenschildt's innate theatricality just had to exit this planet with a bang. His Haitian adventure, intended to put him on easy street like all of his others, had failed, his Haitian Holding Company folding in 1967. George and Jeanne returned to Dallas, where George seemed to be resigned, for the first time in his life, to living a more mundane existence, and took a position as an assistant professor of foreign languages, teaching French at Bishop College, a small black school in South Dallas.[72] In the early 1970s he started slipping into dementia, Jeanne later saying that he began acting in an "insane manner," having delusions of persecution. He also attempted suicide and beat her, breaking several of her ribs and damaging several teeth. In November of 1976, she finally got him committed to a state mental institution. But he was released after around three months.[73]

If George was limiting himself to an ordinary life of teaching with an occasional attempted suicide, someone else wanted to bring him back on stage for one last chance at a prize. NOS Television (a small group of TV and radio stations in the Netherlands) journalist Willem Oltmans, who attended Yale University in 1950, met Marguerite Oswald on an American Airlines flight from New York to Dallas in 1964, and Marguerite succeeded in convincing Oltmans that her son may not have acted alone in the assassination. Back in the Netherlands, when he told a clairvoyant, Gerard Croiset, Marguerite's story, Croiset said that Oswald had a Dallas friend with the letters *sch* and *de* in his name. This man was of noble descent and was a geologist, Croiset said, and it was he, backed by big Texas oil interests, who had been the architect behind Kennedy's assassination, Oswald being the fall guy. Oltmans returned to Texas, and Marguerite pointed to de Mohrenschildt as Croiset's mysterious Mr. X. Oltmans eventually hooked up with de Mohrenschildt, and per de Mohrenschildt, they became personal friends and de Mohrenschildt believed he had "convinced" Oltmans that he "had nothing to do whatsoever with the JFK assassination." Indeed, de Mohrenschildt thought about suing Croiset but said he was probably "broke" anyway. Despite de Mohrenschildt's denials, Oltmans persisted in trying to get de Mohrenschildt to confess, visiting him and Jeanne every year and hoping for a breakthrough.

According to Oltmans, but not de Mohrenschildt, he got what he wanted in February of 1977 in Dallas. On April 12, 1977, after an appearance on the *Good Morning America* show that morning where he said Oswald and de Mohrenschildt were involved

---

*On December 12, 1963, de Mohrenschildt wrote a letter from Port-au-Prince, Haiti, to "Mrs. Janet Lee Auchincloss, 3044 O Street N.W., Washington D.C.," the salutation of "Dear Janet" certainly indicating familiarity. "I ask you," he wrote, "to express my deepest sympathy to your daughter and tell her that both my brother and I will always remember her as a charming little girl from East Hampton." He alludes to "the strange fate which made me know Jackie when she was a little girl" and adds, in an indelicate aside, that this fate "made me also know the assassin (or *presumbable* [sic] assassin), his wife and child. And your daughter has been of such help to the Cystic Fibrosis Research Foundation which we had started in Texas several years ago. [De Mohrenschildt's only son died in 1960 of cystic fibrosis.] She was an honorary chairman of this Foundation." De Mohrenschildt proceeded to become even more indelicate, no, insensitive, by saying, "I still have a lingering doubt, notwithstanding all the evidence, of Oswald's guilt." (De Mohrenschildt Exhibit Nos. 13 and 14, 19 H 556–557) Mrs. Auchincloss turned the letter over to the Warren Commission (9 H 275, WCT George S. de Mohrenschildt).

in a conspiracy to kill Kennedy, Oltmans told the HSCA in executive session all he knew about the de Mohrenschildt story. He testified that when he would visit de Mohrenschildt every year or so in Dallas, the latter was always "a man who wins tennis matches, who is always suntanned, who jogs every morning, who is as healthy as a bull." But Jeanne de Mohrenschildt told him during one visit in late 1976 that George was in a mental hospital and receiving electric shock treatments, and when Oltmans saw him on February 23, 1977, though he was out of the mental hospital, there was a "total transformation" in him. He was "shaking" and "trembling." Oltmans said, "I couldn't believe my eyes. The man had changed drastically." Oltmans said that de Mohrenschildt took him out to Bishop College. Per Oltmans, de Mohrenschildt proceeded to confide in him that he was "responsible" for what Oswald had done "because I guided him. I instructed him, to set it up." De Mohrenschildt begged Oltmans to "take me out of the country because they are after me," *they* being Jews, the CIA, and FBI. Because of feeling "responsible" for Oswald's conduct, de Mohrenschildt spoke many times to Oltmans of wanting to kill himself, not wanting to be around when his children learned of his responsibility, and said he had tried to commit suicide several times but had failed.

When Oltmans excitedly called collect from a pay phone in the library at Bishop College to his home office in the Netherlands to report that he had gotten a "confession" in the Kennedy assassination from de Mohrenschildt, he was instructed "to get him at any cost . . . to the Netherlands." But de Mohrenschildt suddenly started to waver and it wasn't until March 1 that the two flew, at NOS's expense, to New York, stayed overnight at the Waldorf hotel (NOS's "at any cost"), and then traveled on to London and the Netherlands the next day. In Amsterdam on March 3 and 4, de Mohrenschildt negotiated with the head of Dutch National Television himself, Karl Enklraar, as well as the representative of a book publishing house, on the sale of TV, film, and book rights to his story, all of which, he said, was contained within a manuscript he had left behind in Dallas. The understanding was that NOS would put de Mohrenschildt up in a hotel for a month and be given a staff to help him get the story out quickly.

Just what was that story? What, specifically, were the instructions on the assassination de Mohrenschildt had given Oswald? HSCA counsel Robert Tanenbaum kept pressing Oltmans, who assured Tanenbaum he had nine hours of tape, some on film, of his conversations with de Mohrenschildt, tapes he had somehow neglected to bring with him to the hearing. But he said he had some of his notes of the taped interviews with him. Fine, said Tanenbaum, who wanted to know what his notes said. "What were his instructions?"

"I think that—I don't know. I guess it was the cross-fire, to round up, you see. He also said that Oswald had many friends among the Cubans."

Oltmans was full of it. And he was full of it largely because de Mohrenschildt—if he, indeed, told anything at all to Oltmans—was full of it. A can't give B something that A doesn't have. But when Tanenbaum kept pressuring him for concrete information, Oltmans reluctantly said de Mohrenschildt had indicated there was more than one gunman, and H. L. Hunt, the Dallas oil man, was apparently somehow involved.

The exasperated HSCA counsel asked Oltmans, "Mr. Oltmans, did he tell you what his instructions were to Oswald?"

"No."

"Did he tell you what his instructions were from H. L. Hunt, or anyone else?"

"No." Oltmans, trying to defend himself, said that de Mohrenschildt "talked in question marks—like, 'Why do you think Oswald wrote to Hunt?'— . . . and in circles.* He wasn't on record yet. He was negotiating to go on record" (i.e., apparently de Mohrenschildt was devilishly exploring how much money he could get for selling nothing, or whatever he decided to pull out of his hat). And, Oltmans said, before he could press him for the details (nine hours wasn't enough?), de Mohrenschildt, no contract yet being signed, "walked out" on him, disappearing right from "under my own nose. So I hadn't [yet] asked everything I planned to."

How and when had George disappeared? Oltmans said that George "was a nervous wreck," and to get a breath of fresh air away from the intense negotiations, George and he drove to Brussels for several days. Early on the afternoon of March 5 at their hotel, the Metropole, George said he wanted to take a walk and would be back "in an hour." He left with his attaché case and never returned, leaving all of his belongings, even his pipe and keys, behind. In late March, George's Dallas lawyer called Oltmans to inform him George had returned to America and was in South Florida.[74]†

De Mohrenschildt had flown to New York City and taken a Greyhound bus from there to Florida to visit his daughter Alexandra, who was staying at the seaside mansion of Mrs. Nancy Tilton. Mrs. Tilton was the cousin of de Mohrenschildt's first wife, and when the latter abandoned Alexandra shortly after she was born, Mrs. Tilton raised her. Alexandra had lived with Mrs. Tilton off and on all her life and they referred to one another as mother and daughter. De Mohrenschildt had told Oltmans that when he called Alexandra from the Waldorf hotel and told her he was going to the Netherlands, Alexandra had told him, "Papa, come back to Palm Beach. I will save you."[75]

De Mohrenschildt arrived in West Palm Beach on the evening of March 16, 1977, and was picked up by Mrs. Tilton and a friend of Alexandra's, Katherine Loomis. His only baggage was a green attaché case‡ and a few articles of clothing. He was taken to Mrs. Tilton's home in Manalapan, a town of a few hundred people just south of Palm Beach,

---

*When de Mohrenschildt wasn't asking questions instead of giving answers, and was not talking in circles, he was refreshingly informational. For instance, Oltmans said de Mohrenschildt told him a group of people killed Kennedy, but he didn't know if Oswald was one of the shooters. "I am still not sure," he said, "whether Oswald shot himself or not. I have never been able to ascertain that." And he said governmental agencies were involved in the assassination. "I think he said it was the CIA and FBI," Oltmans told the HSCA, adding that George had told him "the proof of that is in my manuscript." That disjointed manuscript of de Mohrenschildt's relationship with Oswald did not have, of course, any such proof. What it did have was more of George's haziness. For instance, at one point he says, "I never, never worked for CIA . . . I cannot say that I never was a CIA agent, I cannot prove it. I cannot prove either that I ever was. Nobody can." George de Mohrenschildt, his inherited sense of *noblesse oblige* still intact, was just trying to be helpful. (12 HSCA 314)

Before HSCA counsel Tanenbaum's questions exposed Oltmans as having nothing to say, Oltmans, because he was a journalist, received a lot of national exposure, giving "various morning press and television interviews," including on the aforementioned *Good Morning America* show and an NBC show, as well as a front-page story in the *New York Times* (*New York Times*, April 2, 1977, pp.1, 12; see also *New York Times*, April 4, 1977, p.50). The *Times*, wondering about the "flurry of publicity created by Oltmans" with his oblique hearsay charges, decided to call the Netherlands to find out just who Oltmans was. "He is half journalist, half showman. Nobody takes him very seriously," said Peter d'Hamacourt, whom the *Times* described as being "widely regarded as one of the best investigative reporters in the Netherlands." D'Hamacourt said that Oltmans's work consisted of "a lot of guessing stories," adding, "You don't know where his facts end and his imagination begins." The news director of a large daily in Rotterdam described Oltmans to the *Times* as "the stuntman of Dutch journalism. He has great skill in moving in on a small story and working on it until he builds it up into an exclusive big deal. He pumps up all his stories, and we think him not to be very reliable." (*New York Times*, April 12, 1977, p.18)

†De Mohrenschildt's daughter, Alexandra, would later tell a reporter for the *New York Times* that her father was "mentally and physically afraid" of Oltmans, and "he felt he had been drugged in Amsterdam" (*New York Times*, April 4, 1977, p.50).

‡Among the papers later found in de Mohrenschildt's attaché case was a two-page personal affidavit written by him in Brussels, Belgium, dated March 11, 1977, attesting to his friendship with Lee Harvey Oswald (Palm Beach County Sheriff's Office Death Investigation Report on George de Mohrenschildt, April 4, 1977, p.4).

where Alexandra was waiting. Between March 16 and March 28, 1969, though having bouts of depression during which he spoke of suicide, he otherwise seemed to enjoy his leisure at the sun-splashed villa facing the sea. He had agreed to be interviewed by writer Edward Epstein in four sessions for a fee of four thousand dollars paid by *Reader's Digest*. The first session was a short one at the Breakers hotel in Palm Beach on March 28 that basically covered de Mohrenschildt's early life and did not get very much into his relationship with Oswald.[76]

On March 29, after an early-morning breakfast prepared by the cook, a Miss Romanie, de Mohrenschildt took a short walk on the beach, then drove to the Breakers for his second session with Epstein in a car Epstein rented for him. Meanwhile, HSCA investigator Gaeton Fonzi, in Miami, had been apprised by his office in Washington (which had been alerted by Oltmans, who had been in touch with Tanenbaum since February about the story) as to where de Mohrenschildt was staying, so he went to the Tilton residence around 10:00 a.m. to interview de Mohrenschildt. When Alexandra told Fonzi her father was in Palm Beach, he left his card and said he'd call back later in the day. When de Mohrenschildt returned home for lunch and Alexandra told him of the HSCA investigator's visit, he seemed upset by the news but did not appear to be overly fearful. Around 1:30 p.m., after bidding good-bye to his daughter and her friend, Katherine Loomis, who were going shopping, de Mohrenschildt went upstairs to his room, presumably to rest for awhile before returning to the Breakers for the next scheduled session at 4:00 that afternoon. But at roughly 2:15 p.m., he apparently left his room and walked the short distance down the hallway to Mrs. Tilton's room. He removed a double-barrel 20-gauge shotgun from its resting place beside her bed, along with two live 20-gauge shotgun shells from a nightstand beside the bed. He then walked out of the bedroom, entered a small hallway off the main hallway, sat in a chair, placed the barrel of the shotgun in his mouth, and fired it at an upward angle through the roof of his mouth and into his brain.[77]

In the conspiracy community, de Mohrenschildt's suicide shortly after he learned an HSCA investigator was seeking to interview him immediately elevated de Mohrenschildt to a higher position than he already had as a probable conspirator in the assassination of Kennedy, book after book implying a possible connection between the suicide, Oswald, and the CIA's role in Kennedy's murder, suggesting he was murdered.[78]*

Indeed, if we're to believe HSCA investigator Gaeton Fonzi, the committee's investigation of Kennedy's murder only survived as long as it did "because de Mohrenschildt committed suicide. That basically is why the committee survived."[79]

Immediately, de Mohrenschildt's last interview with Epstein assumed major importance to conspiracy theorists. But on the issue of de Mohrenschildt's contact with Oswald for the CIA, Epstein writes vaguely that de Mohrenschildt said that in late 1961 at a lunchtime meeting with J. Walter Moore to discuss a trip to Central America from which de Mohrenschildt had just returned, "although no specific requests were made by Moore, de Mohrenschildt gathered that he would be appreciative to learn more about this

---

*If what the conspiracy theorists say is true, almost by definition the CIA would have had to put de Mohrenschildt on to Oswald. But if we're to believe de Mohrenschildt's widow, Jeanne, that's not what happened. "We had been hearing for months that some American Marine idiot that defected to Russia had come back with a Russian wife . . . The Russian Colony, as we called it, was talking about him. Somehow they didn't like him at all. He was poor. I told George to go to Fort Worth and bring him over here. He was reluctant because he was tired . . . But he went . . . That's how we met them [the Oswalds]." (Jim Marrs, "Widow Disputes Suicide," *Fort Worth Star-Telegram*, May 11, 1978)

unusual ex-Marine's activities in Minsk." He quotes de Mohrenschildt as telling him, "I would never have contacted Oswald in a million years if Moore had not sanctioned it."[80] Assuming de Mohrenschildt told Epstein precisely what Epstein said he did, if anything it goes in the exact opposite direction of what the conspiracy theorists believe—that Oswald was a secret CIA operative, and when he killed Kennedy, he was acting at the agency's behest. Because if Oswald were a CIA operative whom the agency thought so highly of that it had entrusted the assassination to him, why would it ask (and, apparently, vaguely at that) de Mohrenschildt, who wasn't even a CIA operative, to keep tabs on Oswald?

By far the most reasonable inference is that either de Mohrenschildt, who was delusional and approaching dementia at the time he killed himself, made up or imagined the purported CIA-implied instruction to him,[*] or even if everything de Mohrenschildt told Epstein was true, it doesn't connote anything sinister at all. As the HSCA said, Moore's duties in the Dallas office of the CIA were to gather information from people in the Dallas area who had information on foreign matters.[81] Since de Mohrenschildt was a friend of Oswald's, and Oswald was a defector to the Soviet Union who had returned to America, Moore would obviously be interested in learning, through de Mohrenschildt, what Oswald had to say about Minsk and Russia. But when de Mohrenschildt testified before the Warren Commission, not only didn't he suggest that Moore was interested in learning about Oswald's activities in Minsk, but he thinks he may have asked Moore about Oswald. De Mohrenschildt told the Warren Commission that because Oswald was a defector, he tended to believe that he "asked point-blank [Max] Clark [whose wife was a part of the Russian emigré community in Dallas with de Mohrenschildt] or Walter Moore about Oswald. I probably spoke to both of them about him. My recollection is . . . that either of them said he is a harmless lunatic."[82] However, although Moore said he had interviewed de Mohrenschildt, he told the HSCA that he never spoke to de Mohrenschildt about Oswald.[83]

When HSCA staff investigator Harold Leap asked Moore if he knew Oswald, Moore replied, "I never met or talked to Lee Harvey Oswald. In fact, I never heard of the name until the day of the assassination."

Question: "Are you aware that allegations have been made that de Mohrenschildt asked permission of you to contact Lee Harvey Oswald?"

Answer: "Yes, the allegation is not true."[84]

The Palm Beach County sheriff's office, which investigated de Mohrenschildt's death, concluded he died "by his own hand."[85] As indicated, the conspiracy theorists find de Mohrenschildt's suicide highly suspicious (many suspect he was actually murdered), but they don't go on to say why—they can't because no conspiratorial inference can be drawn. Neither the Warren Commission nor the HSCA ever considered de Mohrenschildt a suspect in the assassination. Even if they did, why wouldn't simply telling the truth and denying guilt to an HSCA investigator be preferable to killing oneself? Indeed, even if de Mohrenschildt were guilty, again, why wouldn't lying under oath and denying guilt, which thousands of defendants in criminal cases do every day throughout the land, be preferable to killing oneself? It makes absolutely no sense at all that de Mohrenschildt would "rather die than lie" to an HSCA investigator, even if he was eventually asked to

---

[*]Another possibility is that he was simply giving Epstein something for his money. Epstein had already paid de Mohrenschildt two thousand of his four-thousand-dollar fee (Epstein, *Assassination Chronicles*, p.557).

testify under oath. In fact, de Mohrenschildt had already testified under oath about his relationship with Oswald before the Warren Commission in 1964. Even if he were involved in the assassination, which there's absolutely no evidence of, why wouldn't he, in 1977, be willing to simply tell the same story under oath again?

What does make sense (and the conspiracy books don't usually tell their readers this) is that George de Mohrenschildt, age sixty-five at the time of his death, had in recent years, as indicated, become a deeply depressed and mentally unstable individual who *wanted* to die. The Palm Beach County sheriff's office conducted a fairly thorough investigation of de Mohrenschildt's death, and everyone whom chief investigating officer Thomas Neighbors (a detective for the Palm Beach County sheriff's office) spoke to confirmed that de Mohrenschildt was mentally ill. His investigative report said that Mrs. Tilton recounted that during de Mohrenschildt's stay, "he discussed previous attempts at suicide . . . [and] expressed feelings of persecution from unspecified Jewish elements, the federal government, and [being] blackmailed by an attorney in Dallas, but she knew that he was suffering from mental illness and depression and she did not lend credence to his fears." His daughter Alexandra told Neighbors that her father had been shadowed with the suspicion among conspiracy theorists that he had been involved in the assassination and that this, along with other personal problems, disturbed him to the point where he had made several previous attempts on his life, was committed briefly to a mental institution, and since his stay in Florida had expressed a desire to commit suicide.

When Neighbors reached de Mohrenschildt's wife, Jeanne, by phone in Los Angeles, she elaborated on his mental condition. He wrote, "She stated that . . . over the past several years he has been acting in an 'insane manner.' He constantly was in fear of what he termed the 'Jewish Mafia' and the FBI, but she felt his fears were groundless . . . On November 9, 1976, Mrs. de Mohrenschildt signed commitment papers in Dallas . . . to have her husband placed in a mental home for treatment [actually, the psychiatric unit at Parkland Memorial Hospital] . . . In the affidavit she stated that the victim suffered from depression, heard voices, saw visions, and believed that the FBI and 'The Jewish Mafia' were persecuting him." Also, that he "had attempted suicide four times in 1976 by slashing his wrists, trying to drown himself in a bathtub, and twice taking overdoses of medicine." De Mohrenschildt was confined for eight weeks in Parkland, during which time, per his lawyer Pat Russell, he received heavy shock treatment.[86]*

Neighbors said in his report that shortly before de Mohrenschildt shot himself with Mrs. Tilton's shotgun, "he questioned Mrs. Viisola (the maid) about a scratching sound which apparently annoyed him. He speculated that it was a cat, which there are none in the Tilton residence, and he began to pace up and down the long main hallway, calling for a cat . . . Mrs. Viisola felt that the visitor was not behaving normally and was, in her own words, slightly mad."[87]

The Palm Beach County sheriff's office was able to determine the precise time of death on March 29, 1977, at 2:21 (and 3 seconds) p.m. because Mrs. Tilton, who was out, was recording a television program and the "gunshot is audible" (per the sheriff's office

---

*On October 29, 1976, just a week and a half before his commitment at Parkland, de Mohrenschildt went to a Dallas psychiatrist, telling him, "I am depressed. I am killing myself," and asked that he be committed as a mental patient to Terrell State Hospital in Terrell, Texas, near Dallas. Four days later, after the psychiatrist had made arrangements for admitting him voluntarily, de Mohrenschildt changed his mind and decided not to go to Terrell. (Earl Golz, "Oswald Friend Vowed Suicide, Psychiatrist Claimed," *Dallas Morning News*, April 1, 1977, p.20A)

report) on the tape recorder. There were no "non-television-related sounds on the tape cassette," the report said, to indicate anything other than a suicide.*

Oh yes, in the left pocket of de Mohrenschildt's pants when his body was found was a clipping of a front-page headline about him from the *Dallas Morning News* dated March 20, 1977 (nine days earlier), captioned "Mental Ills of Oswald Confidant Told."[88] Apparently de Mohrenschildt's mental problems went way back. For instance, as noted earlier, Mrs. Igor Vladimir Voshinin, a member of the Russian emigré community in Dallas who knew de Mohrenschildt well, told the Warren Commission back in 1964 that "he was a neurotic person. He had some sort of headaches and sometimes he would flare into a rage absolutely for no reason at all practically . . . He complained to me several times that he could not concentrate very well."[89]

Along with all his other demons, according to one of his friends, Samuel B. Ballen, who had dinner in Dallas with de Mohrenschildt shortly before he died, de Mohrenschildt was "beating himself pretty hard" with guilt over the assassination. He knew Oswald had liked and looked up to him, and wondered whether something he had done or said, something "childish" and "sophomoric" on his part, might have nudged Oswald over the edge in the direction he ultimately took. Ballen felt depressed over his meeting with de Mohrenschildt, later recalling that for all of his friend's frailties, the greatest of which was his "utter irresponsibility," George, he believed, was "one of the world's great people," and looking back, felt he had been dining with "Hemingway before the suicide."[90]

Both the HSCA and the Warren Commission took a more than casual interest in de Mohrenschildt to determine if he was an intelligence agent with a possible connection to the assassination, the latter question being the whole point of the exercise. The HSCA never got around to addressing itself to this ultimate point of its inquiry, but it did so indirectly by concluding it had found "no evidence that de Mohrenschildt had ever been an American intelligence agent."[91] And nothing in its report or volumes suggests he was acting at the behest of any foreign country in his association with Oswald. The Warren Commission said its investigation had not produced "any evidence linking [de Mohrenschildt] in any way with the assassination of President Kennedy."[92]

The effort by the conspiracy theorists to connect Oswald to the CIA is so intense that one conspiracy author, John Newman, actually managed to devote 612 pages to the task. In *Oswald and the CIA*, Newman, a former military intelligence officer, reads between the

---

*The inimitable Mark Lane, however, perpetually up to his conspiratorial patter, found sounds indicating, to him, foul play. He wrote in the November 1977 edition of *Gallery* magazine that he attended de Mohrenschildt's coroner's inquest (which ruled that de Mohrenschildt's death was a suicide, the medical examiner who conducted the autopsy, Dr. Gabino Cuevas, testifying to his belief that the gunshot was self-inflicted) and that "the various servants testified that an alarm system installed by the owner of the house caused a *bell to ring* . . . whenever an outside door or window was opened. The courtroom became silent as the tape recording was played. Just after a commercial . . . a gentle bell was heard, and then the shotgun blast." (Mark Lane, *Gallery*, November 1977) Detective Neighbors (now a lieutenant) told me that he too was at the inquest. He said that when any door or window at the Tilton mansion was opened, a "beeping sound," not a bell, was heard, that a beeping sound was heard on the tape just before the shotgun blast, but he had determined it was caused by the live-in maintenance man, Coley Wimbley, walking out the backdoor of the home. "The next beeping sound on the tape was at least ten minutes later. An assassin would be expected to get out of there long before that." Neighbors said he meticulously went over the movements of everyone coming in and out of the house and "no beeps were unaccounted for." Neighbors said he had no doubt de Mohrenschildt had committed suicide. "He was a very disturbed individual at the end. He was hiding from the world, thinking the world was against him." (Telephone interview of Thomas Neighbors by author on November 6, 2000)

lines and the grammatical contours of hundreds of documents (CIA, FBI, Department of State, etc.) and finds "peculiar," "strange," "unusual," and "intriguing" entries and omissions everywhere concerning Oswald, from which he constructs one anemic inference upon another. His book reminds me of the story about two psychiatrists who pass each other on the street one day and when one says, "Good morning," the other mutters to himself, "I wonder what he meant by that?" After taking his readers on a guided "journey through the labyrinth" of intelligence documents and files on Oswald, Newman, despite the presumptuous title of his book, comes up completely empty-handed.[93] If any reader can find in Newman's book any evidence that Oswald was a CIA agent or operative, or even that he, at any time, talked to or communicated with a member of the CIA, on the street, over the phone, by carrier pigeon, or in any other way, please let me know.

I have a very important suggested area of research for Mr. Newman and other members of the conspiracy community. If Oswald was a CIA operative—indeed, if he killed Kennedy for the CIA—I would imagine he would have been paid handsomely by his employers. Even if he wasn't, we certainly can assume he was not working for free. Yet we know that Oswald always was very low on money, leaving behind for his wife and two children the grand total of $183.87. We also know from his 1962 federal income tax returns (Oswald was in Russia in 1960 and 1961) that his declared income was $1,354.06.[94] Granted, he would not declare money given to him from the CIA to kill Kennedy, but the question for researchers is, What did Oswald do with his CIA (or FBI, KGB, mob, etc.) money? Although he didn't have to draw attention to himself by flaunting it on luxuries, wouldn't he have at least used it to pay for a normal, regular room for himself instead of living in a virtual closet on North Beckley? So what did Oswald do with his CIA money? Where is there one tiny piece of evidence that Oswald lived, in any way at all, above his means?

Though if Oswald had been a CIA agent or operative, we could probably expect the CIA to deny this fact, what follows are brief excerpts from the CIA's 1963 report on its awareness of Oswald prior to the assassination. It should be noted that after almost *forty-four years* of investigation and searching by conspiracy theorists for contrary evidence, nothing has ever surfaced to rebut these assertions by the CIA:

Lee Oswald defected to the Soviet Union in October 1959 . . . Since Oswald was a former Marine and a U.S. citizen, his defection was of primary interest to the State Department, the FBI, and the Navy Department. CIA does not investigate U.S. citizens abroad unless we are specifically requested to do so by some other Government Security agency. No such request was made in this case . . . During the 2½ year period that Oswald was in the Soviet Union, CIA had no sources in a position to report on his activities or what the KGB might be doing with him. The good Soviet sources we had were engaged in reporting on other important matters, and they were not directed to check on U.S. defectors like Oswald . . . It was suspected that Oswald and all other similar defectors were in the hands of the KGB and carefully watched by them, so any casual operation to learn their whereabouts or activities would have been highly dangerous and probably unsuccessful . . . To sum up our interest in Lee Oswald before he visited Mexico, we knew he was a U.S. defector to the Soviet Union, we read the FBI reports on him, we watched as the State Department did its job of screening him for repatriation, and we knew the FBI was keeping track of him in the U.S.A. As a footnote, it should be added that we were not even aware of the existence of Jack Ruby, the Dallas nightclub owner who later shot Oswald. We had a few Rubys in our files, but none were Jack Ruby. On 9 October 1963, our Mexico City Station received information from a very sensitive source indicating that Lee Oswald had been in contact with the Soviet Embassy there on 1 October . . . It appeared that he had visited the Embassy as early as 28 September 1963 . . . The name Lee Oswald meant nothing to our Mexico City Station, but our Headquarters in Washington checked its files and when we disseminated the report on 10 October 1963 to the FBI, the State Department, the Immigration and Naturalization Service, and the Navy Department, we commented in the report that he might be identical with the former Marine who had defected to the Soviet Union in 1959.[95]

To repeat, because it warrants being repeated, after over four decades of painstaking scrutiny by literally thousands of conspiracy-minded researchers in this country as well as around the world, no one has come up with any evidence to contravene anything set forth in this simple CIA report of December 20, 1963, a little less than one month after the assassination.

Vladimir Semichastny was the director of the KGB during Oswald's time in Russia. The KGB surveilled Oswald and quickly learned, Semichastny said, that he was a "mediocre, uninteresting, useless man." He said it best about Oswald's alleged connection to the CIA: "I had always respected the CIA and FBI, and we knew their work and what they were capable of. It was clear that Oswald was not an agent, *couldn't* be an agent, for the CIA or FBI."[96]

In addition to conspiracy theorists being unable to find any evidence of Oswald killing Kennedy for the CIA, four national investigative commissions or committees found no CIA involvement in Kennedy's death. The Warren Commission concluded that Oswald acted alone and he was not an agent of the CIA.[97] The HSCA also searched and searched and could find "no evidence of any relationship between Oswald and the CIA."[98] Apart from finding no connection between the CIA and Oswald, the committee likewise (even assuming for the sake of argument that Oswald was not the assassin) could find no connection between the CIA and the assassination itself.* And it should not be forgotten that the HSCA had every reason to want to uncover such a CIA conspiracy. Not only would it be doing its job, it would also receive a great deal of praise, even adulation, from the American people. And the HSCA was particularly predisposed to wanting to find evidence of CIA (or FBI, Secret Service, etc.) complicity since it desperately needed (but never got) any proof to support its ultimate conclusion of a conspiracy. All the committee had was the eventually discredited "fourth bullet" from the acoustic analysis, *nothing else*. But after a very intensive investigation of the CIA, the HSCA concluded that the CIA was "not involved in the assassination."[99]

---

*If the CIA were in any way involved, one could reasonably expect the agency to try to divert the Warren Commission's investigation from certain potentially incriminating areas by invoking the "national security" argument. But when the HSCA asked J. Lee Rankin, general counsel for the Warren Commission, "To your recollection did the CIA ever indicate to you, to the Chief Justice, or to the Commission in general that you should not pursue a line of investigation because of national security reasons?" Rankin answered, "They never did to me and they never did to any member of the Commission that I know of." Question: "Did you ever have a feeling that the CIA was trying to encourage you to go in a particular direction in your investigation?" Answer: "No." (HSCA Record 180-10105-10332, HSCA deposition of J. Lee Rankin on August 17, 1978, p.66)

Two other national bodies investigated possible CIA involvement in the assassination of President Kennedy. Going beyond the mandate of the executive order signed by President Gerald Ford on January 4, 1975, to "determine whether any domestic CIA activities exceeded the Agency's statutory authority," the so-called Rockefeller Commission (formally, "Commission on CIA Activities within the United States'), named after its chairman, Vice President Nelson A. Rockefeller, investigated whether the CIA was involved in the assassination of JFK. In addition to Rockefeller himself, the members of the Commission included distinguished Americans such as C. Douglas Dillon, former secretary of the Treasury; Lane Kirkland, secretary-treasurer of the AFL-CIO; former California governor Ronald Reagan; Erwin N. Griswold, former U.S. solicitor general and former dean of Harvard Law School; and Lyman L. Lemnitzer, former chairman of the Joint Chiefs of Staff. David W. Belin, a former assistant Warren Commission counsel, was the executive director, and a staff of nine attorneys with substantial investigative experience was recruited. President Ford directed the CIA and other federal agencies to cooperate with the commission. The commission wrote that "much of the evidence [it] examined has come from CIA files and personnel. But the Commission has sought wherever possible to verify the evidence independently." After five months of investigation, in its June 6, 1975, report to President Ford, the commission said that "numerous allegations have been made that the CIA participated in the assassination of President John F. Kennedy. The Commission staff investigated these allegations. On the basis of the staff's investigation, the Commission concluded there was no credible evidence of any CIA involvement" in the assassination of President Kennedy.[100]

Finally, the U.S. Senate's 1975–1976 Church Committee, though highly critical of the CIA's plots to assassinate Castro and the CIA's concealing this information from the Warren Commission, said its investigation had not "uncovered evidence" of CIA complicity in Kennedy's assassination.[101]

It is very noteworthy that the *only* books written that suggest the CIA was behind the assassination are those by conspiracy theorists, who are convinced that a conspiracy was behind the assassination *whether or not the CIA was involved*. On the other hand, a considerable number of books have been written about the CIA and its history, warts and all, and not one of their authors, even though they had every ethical, professional (Pulitzer Prize, esteem of peers, etc.), and commercial reason to expose the CIA, or rogue elements thereof, as being behind the assassination, found the need to devote more than a paragraph or two in their long books to Lee Harvey Oswald and the assassination. (Where there are more than a few paragraphs, the discussion usually concerns Yuriy Nosenko's information about Oswald that divided the CIA over Nosenko's bona fides—see KGB conspiracy section later in text.) What does that tell you? It can only tell you one thing. They never wrote anything about the CIA's alleged connection to the assassination because in their minds there simply was nothing substantive and credible to write about. And this dismissal, by omission, of the allegation of CIA complicity in the assassination (which, if true, would be far and away the most important part of their book) reflects their obviously considered assessment that such an allegation is so groundless it deserved none of their ink.

Indeed, as I have alluded to elsewhere in this book, the very thought of CIA officials (or rogue elements) sitting around the table at CIA headquarters or elsewhere actually plotting to murder the president of the United States belongs, if anywhere, in a Robert Ludlum novel. For those who may not know—people oftentimes refer to a particular true-crime book as a novel—novels are fiction, not nonfiction.

FBI

The other federal intelligence agency that many conspiracy theorists have sought to implicate in the assassination is the FBI, the main villain being J. Edgar Hoover, its longtime director. Born in Washington, D.C., on New Year's Day in 1895 of American, British, German, and Swiss stock, Hoover graduated from George Washington University's nighttime school of law in 1916, passed the bar, and was admitted to practice before the Supreme Court of the District of Columbia in 1917. In July of that same year, he started working for the Department of Justice as a clerk in the files division, earning an annual salary of $990. The Department of Justice remained his only employer for fifty-five years, Hoover dying while still in office in 1972. Today, FBI headquarters in Washington, D.C., are in the J. Edgar Hoover Building, which was dedicated on September 30, 1979.

It is often said that Hoover, in 1924, became the first director of the FBI. This is not completely accurate. The first criminal investigative division in the Department of Justice was created on July 1, 1908, and informally called the Special Agent Force. It consisted of thirty-five investigators under the command of a "chief examiner," Stanley W. Finch. The head of the Justice Department, Charles J. Bonaparte (a grandnephew of Napoleon Bonaparte), formalized this arrangement by issuing an order on July 26, 1908, and the FBI considers that day as the date of its birth. So technically, Finch was the first director of what eventually became known as the Federal Bureau of Investigation. The Special Agent Force was named the Bureau of Investigation on March 16, 1909. Finch was succeeded by A. Bruce Bielaski in 1912, William J. Flynn in 1919, and William J. Burns in 1921. Hoover, who had become an assistant director of the Bureau of Investigation, was appointed director, at the age of only twenty-nine, on May 10, 1924. The Bureau of Investigation was renamed the Federal Bureau of Investigation (FBI) on March 22, 1935.[1]

Though, on the operational charts, it is under the jurisdiction of the attorney general

in the Department of Justice, through practice and tradition the FBI, particularly during the Hoover years, has had "a very large measure of autonomy in their operations."[2]

The conspiracy theorists who maintain that the FBI was behind the assassination say
that the bureau "could not do its job [investigating the assassination] because its leader at
the time of the assassination, J. Edgar Hoover, participated in the conspiracy."[3] In other
words, how can you possibly trust members of the conspiracy to investigate their own
conspiracy? Unfortunately, there is not a shred of evidence to support this wild allegation.

The suspicion that the FBI may have been involved in the assassination stemmed in
part from the early revelation that the FBI had interviewed Oswald in New Orleans and
Dallas before the assassination, and the finding of Agent Hosty's name, contact information, and license plate number in Oswald's address book. Both of these matters are
discussed elsewhere in this book and provide no basis whatsoever for the inference of FBI
complicity. But what immediately caused concern and anxiety, particularly with the Warren Commission, was the rumor that Oswald had been a paid FBI informant. This rumor
started, tentatively, just two weeks after Kennedy's death, in a December 8, 1963, article
in the *Philadelphia Inquirer* by reporter Joseph Goulden in which he referred to "the FBI
attempt to recruit Oswald as an informant." Goulden said his unnamed source "did not
know if the FBI succeeded in hiring Oswald." But two articles appearing shortly thereafter stated that the bureau had succeeded, officially starting the rumor. The first was a
January 1, 1964, article in the *Houston Post* by Alonzo (Lonnie) Hudkins in which Hudkins said his (again) unnamed source told him that Oswald had been assigned informant
number S179 and was on the FBI payroll receiving $200 per month at the time of the
assassination.* Hudkins's article created such a storm that at 5:30 p.m. on January 22, just
two days after the Warren Commission first met with its staff, Chairman Warren hurriedly called the members of the Commission into emergency session to inform them
that General Counsel Rankin had received a telephone call earlier in the day from Waggoner Carr, the attorney general of Texas, in which he informed Rankin of the rumor circulating in Dallas and seemingly embraced the rumor as possibly being true.[4]

Who was Hudkins's unnamed source who started the rumor? What follows here is a
series of denials and contradictions (unavoidably difficult reading) that make the answer
to this question impossible at this time. When Secret Service agent Lane Bertram interviewed Hudkins on December 17, 1963 (pursuant to a phone call by Hudkins to the Dallas office of the Secret Service the previous day), Hudkins said that his source was Allan
Sweatt, chief of the Criminal Division of the Dallas sheriff's office. Sweatt, he said, had
told him it was his "opinion" that Oswald was a paid FBI informant,[5] though Sweatt's saying it was only his opinion is inconsistent with the details he allegedly gave Hudkins of
Oswald receiving $200 per month and having an informant number of "S172" (not 179).

On February 8, 1964, Hudkins elaborated on his story to the FBI, telling Agents Vincent Drain and James Wood that his original belief that Oswald was an FBI informant
started when Dallas assistant district attorney William Alexander told him that in
Oswald's notebook, taken from his apartment on the afternoon of the assassination, there
appeared the name of FBI agent James Hosty, Hosty's office and home telephone numbers, and the license plate number on Hosty's car. He coupled this information with what
Oswald's mother, Marguerite, had told him in an interview, that she believed her son had
been doing important subversive work for the government. He said that subsequently a

*A January 27, 1964, article in the *Nation* by Harold Feldman repeated the charges.

Dallas official not working for the federal government had told him Oswald was on the payroll of either the FBI or the CIA, with "voucher number 179" (not 172), and received no less than $150 nor more than $225 per month. The Dallas official presumably was Sweatt, though the details given to the FBI were slightly different from what Hudkins told the Secret Service. Hudkins refused to disclose the identity of the Dallas official to the FBI or to furnish a signed statement.[6]

Earlier (January 25, 1964), however, Alexander told the FBI that Hudkins had come to him sometime in December saying he was working on a really good story trying to prove Oswald was a paid informant for the FBI or CIA, Hudkins saying he had received information that Oswald's address book had Hosty's name and telephone number in it as well as possibly the license plate number of his car. Alexander, who already knew this, told Hudkins, "It looks like you have the story there," suggesting to Hudkins that his information was correct. Alexander also said that after a bond hearing for Ruby on January 21, while reporters were standing around outside the courtroom waiting for a ruling from the judge, he heard a number of them talking about the possibility that Oswald was a counterspy for the FBI or CIA and also remembered hearing one reporter—he didn't know who—talking about Oswald receiving $200 a month from one of these federal agencies beginning in September of 1962 and his payroll voucher number being 179.[7] When the FBI reinterviewed Alexander on February 13, he reiterated his story and vigorously denied he was the source of the rumor when the special agents told him that their investigation "strongly implied that he was."[8]

It would have been nice if Allan Sweatt, whom Hudkins originally said he received his information from, had cleared up the matter, but he simply muddied it further. On the evening of January 24, 1964, the Secret Service informed a member of the Warren Commission staff that Sweatt had been interviewed and stated he received his information about the allegation and details of Oswald's paid informant status from Alexander *and* Hudkins. And Secret Service inspector Thomas J. Kelley expressed his view that Hudkins "was not very reliable," based on previous unfounded reports which he had furnished to the Secret Service.[9]

In Hudkins's testimony before the Church Committee in 1975, his vague and incoherent answers were only exceeded by the inept questioning of a Church Committee staff member. In bits and pieces, Hudkins claimed that he did not receive information from Sweatt about Oswald receiving $200 a month from the FBI and having an informant number of S172. In one of the very few good questions asked, staff counsel queried Hudkins as to why Secret Service agent Lane Bertram would state, in his report, that Hudkins had told him this if Hudkins hadn't? Hudkins responded, "I would like to ask Lane [Bertram] that myself . . . All of his [Bertram's] stuff was obviously to my mind routed through the FBI . . . It had to come from the FBI." So according to Hudkins, FBI agents made up the story that Oswald, the accused presidential assassin, had been a paid FBI informant. Well, they'd certainly have a great motive to make up such a story—to implicate themselves in Kennedy's murder.

Hudkins also denied telling the FBI on February 8 or any other time about believing Oswald was an FBI or CIA informant with voucher number 179 who received between $150 and $225 per month. So apparently the FBI report by Special Agents Drain and Wood was also a fabricated, untruthful report. The true story, Hudkins said, is that he admitted to Drain the previous month that he, *Dallas Morning News* reporter Hugh Aynesworth, and Assistant DA Bill Alexander, during a conference call, presumably on another matter, decided to concoct the story that Oswald was a paid informant for the FBI with a payroll number of S172 or S179 (he said they never discussed the amount of money Oswald was paid each month) so they could test whether their phones were being tapped by the FBI. When Church Committee staff member William Wallach mentioned that Alexander hadn't told Chief Justice Warren and General Counsel Rankin this when he, DA Henry Wade, and Texas attorney general Waggoner Carr met with them in Washington on January 24, 1964, Hudkins said, "Knowing Bill Alexander, he wasn't lying to them. He just wasn't telling them all the information [he knew]."[10]

When the HSCA interviewed Hudkins in 1978, he said that he and Aynesworth (he never mentioned Alexander this time) decided to test their suspicion that they were under FBI surveillance by discussing over the telephone a fabricated FBI payroll number for Oswald. He said they discussed the numbers S172 and S179. According to Hudkins he was soon contacted by the FBI to find out what he knew about Oswald's alleged informant status. He said that in his January 1, 1964, article for the *Houston Post* on the Oswald informant allegation, he merely quoted what others had said. It consisted of "wondering aloud" rather than having any evidence, adding that he did not know whether Oswald was an FBI informant.[11]*

When I called Aynesworth about all of this, he chuckled and said, "Lonnie made up the whole story," though he said there was a kernel of truth to it. Aynesworth, who later became a *Newsweek* correspondent, told me, "Lonnie was a nice, friendly, likable guy, but he had a habit of making up stories." That's why, Aynesworth said, Hudkins had ended up losing jobs at papers. (He had been with the *Dallas Morning News*, then *Houston Post*, the *Baltimore News-American*, then some paper up in Buffalo, all before Aynesworth lost track of him in the late 1970s. In his testimony before the Church Committee in November of 1975, Hudkins listed eleven media employers in his career to that point.) Aynesworth said that since he was the lead reporter on the Kennedy assassination for the paper of record on the case, the *Dallas Morning News*, "All leads on the case came across my desk. During the week following the assassination, I was working very hard on my account of Oswald's escape route, and Lonnie was calling me constantly for leads. On one of his calls, he said he had a hunch that Oswald was a paid informant for the FBI. He asked me to check and see what I could find. The next time Lonnie called I got a number, S172, off my desk—with all the papers and reports on my desk there were always a lot of numbers and I can't remember at all where I got the number—and gave Lonnie the number just to get rid of him more than anything else. So I made up this number, and the next thing you know Lonnie wrote his big story in the *Houston Post* saying the number was S179, and Oswald was paid $200 a month. There's nothing to this Oswald FBI informant story. And as far as Lonnie and I testing our suspicions that we were under FBI surveillance by the two of us making up the number and talking about it over the phone, that's not true at all, although there was a period, when I later got a hold of Oswald's diary before anyone else, that I believe the FBI was tapping my number."[12]

Since Aynesworth has acknowledged that he was the source of the FBI informant number (which Hudkins changed by seven digits), the allegation that Bill Alexander, DA Henry

---

*Hudkins wrote in his *Post* article, "Was Lee Harvey Oswald a stool pigeon for a federal government agency? . . . If the answer is 'yes,' then the 24-year-old accused . . . slayer of President Kennedy pulled one of the biggest and certainly the most embarrassing double-crosses in the nation's history. And if the answer is 'no,' it will go down as just another one of the fantastic rumors floating around in official and unofficial circles in Dallas" (Lonnie Hudkins, "Oswald Rumored as Informant for U.S.," *Houston Post*, January 1, 1964).

Wade's chief assistant, was a party to making the informant story up, falls. When I called Alexander anyway for his comments on the allegation, his recollection of the incident was that "Lonnie [Hudkins] and one or two of his fellow reporters covering the assassination got the idea—I don't know from where—that maybe Oswald was an FBI informant. Hudkins told me, or maybe it was one of the other reporters involved, I forget, that to flush out the FBI, they made up a bogus FBI informant number for Oswald, and one of them called the FBI and asked whether this number belonged to Oswald, hoping that in the process they might find out if, in fact, Oswald was an informant. They got nowhere. I heard it said that I was one of the ones who had dreamed up this whole Oswald FBI informant story, but that's not true. I was told about it. I didn't do anything." Alexander said he was never party to any telephone conference call with Hudkins and Aynesworth in which it was decided to come up with the phony informant story.

When I asked Alexander if he called the FBI to let the bureau know it was a phony story, Alexander, no fan of the FBI because of what he believes is its lack of cooperation with local law enforcement, said no. "I thought it was a funny story, but I decided to let them [FBI] find out on their own it was all bull——." However, the Warren Commission took the rumor very seriously, and Alexander said that on January 23, 1964, he, Henry Wade, and Texas attorney general Waggoner Carr were summoned back to Washington, where they met the following day with Warren, Rankin, and another person whom Alexander can't recall. Alexander said Wade knew nothing about the matter and all Carr knew was someone calling him on the phone and telling him about the rumor. Alexander said he didn't want to hurt Hudkins and his fellow reporters, who were "nice guys and hadn't really hurt anyone by their prank," but he also "didn't want to mislead the Warren Commission," so he told them it was common knowledge among the media covering the case in Dallas that the story about Oswald's informant number and wages of $200 per month from the FBI was false and trumped up by some reporters to flush the FBI out, but he doesn't think he mentioned Hudkins's name.[13]

There is no transcript or recording of the informal January 24, 1964, meeting in Washington, but Rankin, who was present at the meeting, never said in his memorandum to the files subsequent to the meeting that anyone in the Texas contingent (which included Carr's assistants, Leon Jaworski and Dean Storey) had said the rumor was false and trumped up. However, Rankin did say that Alexander and Wade "both indicated that they would not vouch for the integrity or accuracy" of the reporters who were promulgating the story.[14]

District Attorney Henry Wade, in his testimony before the Warren Commission, said he had heard the rumor that Oswald was an FBI informant but had no knowledge of its veracity, and added that "Alexander mentioned it some, but Alexander is not a great lover of the FBI. They fuss all the time openly."[15]

Whatever the illegitimate birth of the rumor, it has led a robust life among conspiracy theorists, despite the fact that there is no evidence to support it. The Warren Commission took the testimony of FBI Director J. Edgar Hoover, Assistant to the Director Alan H. Belmont, FBI agents John W. Fain and John L. Quigley (who interviewed Oswald in Fort Worth upon his return from Russia), and FBI agent James P. Hosty, people who would have knowledge of Oswald's informant status if it were true. "All declared, in substance," the Commission said, "that Oswald was not an informant or agent of the FBI, that he did not act in any other capacity for the FBI, and no attempt was made to recruit him in any capacity . . . This [position was] corroborated by the Commission's independent review of the Bureau files dealing with the Oswald investigation."[16]* Among other evidence under penalty of perjury, on February 6, 1964, Hoover gave a sworn affidavit to the Warren Commission that he "caused a search to be made of the records of the Federal Bureau of Investigation, United States Department of Justice, by employees of the said Bureau of Investigation acting under his direction, and that said search discloses that Lee Harvey Oswald was never an informant of the FBI, was never assigned a symbol number in that capacity, and was never paid any amount of money by the FBI in any regard. Such a statement can be made authoritatively and without equivocation because of the close supervision FBI Headquarters affords its security informant program and because of the safeguards established to ensure against any abuse or misuse of the program."[17] And on February 12, 1964, Hoover sent to Rankin nine additional affidavits from each FBI agent who had any direct contact with Oswald (e.g., Hosty, Fain) or would have had any indirect contact with him if he had been a paid informant (e.g., J. Gordon Shanklin, special agent in charge of the Dallas FBI office, who would have had to "authorize and approve of any payment to confidential informants"), all attesting under penalty of perjury that Oswald was not an FBI informant.[18] The HSCA likewise conducted an investigation of the issue and "found no credible evidence that Oswald was an FBI informant."[19]

When, in analyzing an allegation (here, the Oswald FBI informant story), you find that you're spending most of your time not in trying to determine if it's the truth, since you know it's a lie, but who (here, Hudkins, Alexander, Sweatt, Aynesworth, etc.) is telling the truth about the lie, then it's time to move on to another subject.

Apart from the rumor that Oswald was a paid informant for the FBI, the belief has persisted among some conspiracy theorists that Oswald worked for the FBI in some never-disclosed capacity, and eventually killed Kennedy as a hit man for the FBI. But no one has ever offered any evidence to support this allegation, and the reason, obviously, is that none exists. The notion of Oswald working for the FBI produced a rather humorous exchange between Warren Commission members Allen Dulles and John McCloy at an executive session of the Commission on January 27, 1964:

Dulles, to the Commission at large: "This fellow [Oswald] was so incompetent that he was not the kind of fellow that Hoover would hire . . . Hoover didn't hire this kind of stupid fellow."

McCloy: "I wouldn't put much confidence in the intelligence of all the agents I have run into. I have run into some awfully stupid agents."

Dulles: "Not *this* irresponsible."

McCloy: "Well, I can't say I have run into a fellow comparable to Oswald but I have run into some very limited mentalities both in the CIA and the FBI. (Laughter)"[20]

Besides the informant allegation, other alleged specific associations between Oswald and the FBI have surfaced throughout the years. One that has received some attention is the allegation of one Orest Pena, a member of an anti-Castro group, the Cuban Revolutionary Council, who operated a New Orleans bar, the Habana Bar and Lounge. On national television (CBS) in 1975, Pena claimed for the first time that he had seen Oswald with FBI agent Warren de Brueys "numerous times" in New Orleans, and that before he, Pena,

---

*The FBI first opened a file on Oswald on October 31, 1959, when a United Press International release reported that Oswald had defected to the Soviet Union (CE 833, 17 H 787–789; CE 834, 17 H 804).

testified before the Warren Commission in 1964, de Brueys threatened him physically not to reveal this information.[21] Pena repeated the allegation of de Brueys's threat in his 1978 deposition before the HSCA, saying de Brueys told him "that if I talk about him [before the Warren Commission] he will get rid of my ass." Pena added that the Warren Commission counsel who took his testimony in 1964, Wesley J. Liebeler, did not let him talk freely, so he decided to "keep my mouth shut." So if we're to believe Pena, not only de Brueys, but also Liebeler was an accessory after the fact to the murder of Kennedy, trying to suppress the truth. No one has insulted Liebeler by asking him if he prevented Pena from talking freely (his Warren Commission testimony consumed seventeen pages in the volumes, about thirty pages of transcript, in which Pena gives many long and free-flowing answers), but de Brueys, in his deposition before the HSCA, categorically denied ever threatening Pena to not tell the truth in his Warren Commission testimony.[22]

How did Pena know de Brueys? Pena told the HSCA that he had been an FBI informant and "Warren C. de Brueys was the FBI agent assigned to me." Although de Brueys also denied this, it's more a matter of semantics than disagreement in that de Brueys acknowledged that since Pena was a bar owner, he was an occasional source of information for him, but there was no systematic reporting relationship. The HSCA found that FBI records confirmed that Pena was not an FBI informant for de Brueys or any other agent.[23]

On the matter of seeing de Brueys with Oswald "numerous times" in New Orleans, Pena backed down in his HSCA testimony. Pena testified that he used to see Oswald "go to the restaurant [Greek restaurant on Decatur Street in New Orleans] in the morning with other federal agents from the Customs House Building," that he saw de Brueys at the restaurant "at the same time," and that he saw Oswald, de Brueys, and several other federal agents leaving the restaurant together and going back to the Customs House Building. When he was specifically asked if he ever observed "Oswald and de Brueys speaking to each other," Pena responded, "I cannot answer that question. If I cannot prove myself what de Brueys did to me, how am I going to prove other things?"

Question: "My question is, Mr. Pena, do you recall ever seeing Oswald and de Brueys speaking together or acting in such a way that you would think that they knew each other?"

Answer: "I believe they knew each other very, very well."

Question: "Can you explain why you believe Oswald and de Brueys knew each other very well?"

Pena answered unresponsively and unintelligibly that "my belief, I would have to report in as informant to Mr. de Brueys. I have to report myself to Mr. de Brueys and that is my point of view on that question." He then immediately added what appeared to be the main reason for his belief that Oswald and de Brueys knew each other: "When Oswald was transferred to Dallas, Mr. Warren de Brueys was transferred to Dallas, Texas, at the same time." He said he was "very, very, very sure" this was "before the assassination."[24]

De Brueys testified that it was "an unmitigated lie" that he knew Oswald or that Oswald was an FBI informant for him. "It has no basis whatsoever in fact." He added he never even met Oswald, and never "knowingly" spoke to him over the phone, explaining that people can call "under pretension." And the HSCA confirmed that de Brueys was sent to Dallas on temporary assignment to aid in the investigation the day *after* the assassination, and remained there until January 24, 1964.[25] Further, Dallas FBI agent Jim Hosty, who was de Brueys's partner in Dallas in the post-assassination investigation, told me de Brueys "arrived in Dallas from New Orleans the day after the assassination."

Pena's bartender at his place, Evaristo Rodriguez, had testified before the Warren Commission that a few days before or after Oswald's August 9, 1963, confrontation on the street with Carlos Bringuier, whom Rodriguez knew, Oswald came into his bar in the early morning hours with a Latin man ("He could have been a Mexican; he could have been a Cuban"), that Oswald "was drunk" (a very unlikely condition for Oswald), and although Oswald's companion had ordered a tequila, Oswald asked for a lemonade—a drink, Rodriguez said, they didn't serve in the bar. Rodriguez asked Pena what to do and Pena said to take a little of the lemon flavoring and squirt in some water.[26] Even assuming Rodriguez's identification of Oswald was accurate (the time, "between 2:30 and 3:00 o'clock in the morning," and the man being "drunk" do not sound like Oswald, but the man protesting the price of the lemonade, twenty-five cents, as being too high and accusing the owner of the bar, therefore, of being a "capitalist" does), and that he did not make it up, or that he was not one of the great many people after the assassination who were convinced they had seen Oswald somewhere when we know they could not have, the point is that when Orest Pena was called to the stand after Rodriguez and asked if he, Pena, ever saw Oswald at any time other than that alleged night in Pena's bar when Oswald ordered a lemonade, he answered, "No, I didn't . . . I saw him once," the time at his bar.[27] This, of course, flatly contradicts his statement on CBS eleven years later and his HSCA testimony fourteen years later that he had seen Oswald many times with de Brueys.

Indeed, Pena has made contradictory statements as to whether he even saw Oswald that one night at his bar. His bartender, Rodriguez, testified Pena was in the back part of the bar that night and said, "I don't believe that Orest saw Oswald."[28] Although Pena did tell the FBI in a December 5, 1963, interview that he had seen Oswald at the bar that night, in a June 9, 1964, FBI interview he said he had never told anyone he had seen Oswald in the bar, then proceeded to tell the Warren Commission he didn't think he had told the FBI this on June 9.[29] In view of Pena's waiting so many years before he came up with his allegation, his "frequently evasive" testimony before committee, and the many conflicts and contradictions in his story, the HSCA concluded the obvious, that Pena "was not a credible witness."[30]

One naturally wonders what the origins are for apparent fabrications like Pena's. But in his case, we may not have to look any further than the peerless Mark Lane. The mere exposure to Lane and his blandishments and suggestions has caused witness after witness in the Kennedy case to experience a remarkable improvement in their memory and suddenly come up with, for the first time, very pro-conspiracy observations. And Mark Lane's footprints, fingerprints, and palm prints may be all over Pena's story. It seems that Orest was serving more than booze at his place at 117 Decatur Street in the French Quarter. Rooms at his Habana club were also being used for prostitution, and when he was arrested for it, whom did he seek out? Not a New Orleans attorney, but Mark Lane. Lane, in his book *Plausible Denial*, doesn't say when this was, but it clearly was *before* Pena's public accusations were aired on CBS in 1975, since Lane suggests to his readers that Pena told him things he did not already know. There is a suggestion that Lane never got paid any fee by Pena for his representation. The quid pro quo? "He [Pena] told me that if I did so [represented him] he would tell me all that he knew about Oswald." Since everyone already knows the only information—pro-conspiracy—Lane has any interest in, Pena would have known what Lane wanted to hear. Lane writes that "Pena told me that Oswald had worked for the FBI. He showed me the buildings in New Orleans where de Brueys and Oswald had met." Not only, per Lane, was Pena privy to all this information, but remarkably he even knew that "the CIA was aware of the relationship [between Oswald and de Brueys]."[31]

One other New Orleans person has come forward with an allegation of a connection between Oswald and the FBI. This one, if true, goes beyond Pena's story in its conspiratorial implications. Adrian Alba, the part owner and operator of the Crescent City Garage in New Orleans who became acquainted with Oswald when the latter worked next door at the Reily coffee company in May, June, and July of 1963 (see Oswald biography), told the HSCA in a 1978 deposition that one day during the subject period, an FBI agent from out of town entered his garage, showed his credentials, and requested to use one of the Secret Service cars garaged there, a dark green Studebaker. (In an earlier interview, he told HSCA investigators it was a "light green Plymouth.")[32] That same day or the next, Alba, about a quarter of a block away, claims he observed this agent, inside the Studebaker, hand a white envelope to Oswald (who was standing outside the car) in front of the Reily coffee company. There was no exchange of words between Oswald and the agent, and Oswald, having been in a bent-over position to receive the envelope, turned away from the car window and held the envelope close to his chest as he walked back to the Reily building "in a crouched position." Alba said he believes he saw a similar transaction a day or so later, but he was farther away and did not see what was handed to Oswald. He did not recall when the Secret Service car was returned to his garage or by whom.[33]*

One of the big problems with Alba's story is that he waited so many years (fifteen) to tell it. In two interviews with the FBI in New Orleans, one on November 23, 1963, the very day after the assassination, and one two days later, Alba made no reference to the suspicious incident he recalled so vividly fifteen years later.[34] In his lengthy testimony before the Warren Commission on April 16, 1964, he again never mentioned the incident. And it must be noted that by April 1964, conspiracy theories that Oswald may have been, among many other charges, a paid agent of the CIA or FBI were already rampant and publicized in America. Indeed, though Alba did not address himself directly to this fact in his testimony, he did say, "Things I have seen on television, of course, and read in the newspapers, and so forth, has laid out some suggestive pattern that Lee Oswald was a subversive, et cetera, toward the country, and maybe even the President, or something; but prior to that assassination he gave me no indication at any time he was burdened with such a charge, or that he was concerned or involved with anything of that nature." And at the end of his testimony, when Warren Commission counsel asked him, "If you can't think of anything else, anything else you would like to add at this point, I have no further questions," Alba said, "I would feel free if there was, but I don't think there's anything further that I would like to add that can be of any help to you."[35]

What perhaps destroys Alba's credibility about the incident even more than the fifteen-year delay in telling the authorities is the reason he has given for the delay. Although he told Summers that in 1963 he was fearful of telling his story[36] (even though when Alba was interviewed by the FBI back then, Penn Jones and his ridiculous "mysterious deaths" allegation hadn't yet surfaced, that silliness not starting until 1966), he told the HSCA that the very first time he even remembered these two incidents was in 1970, seven years later, when his memory was triggered by a television commercial of the

---

*It is not clear whether this was the first time Alba told this story. In Anthony Summers's book *Conspiracy*, he says Alba related this incident to him when he interviewed Alba in 1978, the same year as Alba's HSCA deposition, but Summers gives no month or day. Summers says Alba thought the FBI agent was "visiting New Orleans from Washington," and said Alba told him the agent returned the car to the garage in a few days. (Summers, *Conspiracy*, pp.282–283)

Rosenberg furniture store in New Orleans, which urged people to shop at the store by cab. The commercial showed, Alba said, a "Jewish merchant, in a bent-with-age posture running out to the cab" to pay the fare for the customer.[37]

The HSCA investigated Alba's story. Among other things, the committee found that in 1963, "several Secret Service Agents had signed out two Studebakers, a Ford and a Chevrolet [from Alba's garage] at various times, but the records do not indicate that any FBI agents had signed out any of these cars."* The HSCA rejected Alba's story as being of "doubtful reliability."[38] Further indication of Alba's lack of reliability is that he told *Case Closed* author Gerald Posner that "it was a fact" that Robert Kennedy had personally selected Lee Harvey Oswald to kill Castro, and when Oswald instead killed his brother, RFK went around crying out, at the Justice Department, "Oh God, I killed my brother, I killed my brother."[39]

The HSCA thoroughly investigated every alleged association between Oswald and the FBI and found nothing at all. Since the committee concluded that Oswald killed Kennedy, it also logically concluded that "absent a relationship between Oswald and the FBI, grounds for suspicions of FBI complicity in the assassination become remote."[40]

When the conspiracy theorists accuse the FBI of being behind the Kennedy assassination, the object of their scrutiny is always J. Edgar Hoover. But they virtually never bother to present a motive other than that Hoover "hated" Kennedy.[41] Actually, though no one disputes that Hoover intensely disliked RFK, his nominal superior at the Department of Justice who did not treat him with the respect he required of others, the evidence is at best ambiguous as to whether he harbored the same animosity for JFK, though no one says affirmatively that he liked JFK. Former assistant FBI director William Sullivan, whom Hoover forced to retire in 1971 after Sullivan had asked him to resign (telling Hoover he ruled the bureau by fear and he did not intend to be intimidated), is one of the few who has publicly said that Hoover did not like JFK. But he does not offer anything substantive in his book to support this, limiting himself to assertions such as "the director never disguised his true feelings for Jack Kennedy . . . when he was among his close aides," without favoring us with even one quote or paraphrase of just what Hoover said.[42] What we do know is that in addition to the Kennedy glamour being inimical to his starched-collar notion of public office, the sanctimonious Hoover was apparently offended by Kennedy's sexual hijinks, particularly with married women.

Conspiracy theorists who make an extra effort to come up with a motive claim that Hoover had Kennedy killed to keep his job. You see, Hoover was coming up for mandatory retirement under federal law on January 1, 1965, when he would be seventy years old, and unless there was a presidential waiver,† which was much more likely under Pres-

---

*Former New Orleans FBI agent Warren de Brueys said that Alba's story that an FBI agent was driving a Secret Service car "sounds sort of asinine" because the FBI in New Orleans had its "own garage, separate and apart from the Secret Service. I don't know if that's ever happened where an FBI agent would be driving a Secret Service car. I am not saying it couldn't happen, but the odds were a million to one against those sort of facts existing" (Earl Golz, "Oswald Allegedly Given Envelope," *Dallas Morning News*, August 7, 1978, p.4D).

†It was the conventional wisdom in Washington (RFK had mentioned it to too many people) that President Kennedy did not intend to waive Hoover's compulsory retirement date (Gentry, *J. Edgar Hoover*, p.536). William Hundley, the chief of the Justice Department's organized-crime section under William Rogers, told author Ovid Demaris, "We all got the message that they were going to retire him after Jack got re-elected and Hoover hit seventy. And it got back to him [Hoover]" (Demaris, *Director*, p.143). William Sullivan, Hoover's number-three

ident Johnson (whom he was very friendly with, being neighbors in Washington for nineteen years, and with whom he shared a dislike for Ivy League patricians in Washington) than under Kennedy, he'd be out of a job in a little over a year.[43] Apart from the preposterous notion that Hoover would be behind Kennedy's murder to keep his job or for any other reason, conspiracy theorists, when they excitedly posit their theory, never stop to realize that even if a particular person or group had some motive to kill Kennedy, that person or group would have an even more compelling motive not to do it—if they did it and got caught, they could be arrested, prosecuted, convicted, and sentenced to death. It should be added that Hoover was a man who was so concerned about his image and reputation that the head of the Dallas FBI field office ordered that Oswald's note to FBI agent James P. Hosty be destroyed because he knew that if Hoover found out about it, he would go orbital with anger over exposing him and his agency to the charge of *negligence* in not alerting the Secret Service to Oswald. And this same fellow, Hoover, apparently had no fear of his possibly being exposed to the charge of *murder?* Former attorney general Nicholas Katzenbach, nominally Hoover's boss at the Department of Justice when Katzenbach was attorney general, told the HSCA that "Mr. Hoover resented criticism to a degree greater than any other person that I have ever known."[44]

One of the few conspiracy theorists who has added a touch of substance to the heretofore very simplistic thinking about Hoover's alleged connection with the assassination does not conclude that Hoover was behind the assassination or that he was a co-conspirator. Instead, he stitches a series of facts and assumptions (presented as facts to his readers) together to support the scenario that the mob killed Kennedy, and that Hoover learned of its plans through the report of two Miami FBI agents and elsewhere and, wanting to keep his job, never did anything to prevent the murder from happening. In *Act of Treason: The Role of J. Edgar Hoover in the Assassination of President Kennedy*, author Mark North builds his case around Florida Mafia chieftain Santo (referred to by some as Santos) Trafficante allegedly telling Cuban exile José Aleman in September of 1962 that President Kennedy was "going to be hit." North's book is perhaps the only one in the entire library of conspiracy books that postulates a theory that, though almost assuredly not true, has some commonsense inferences on its side (other than that some group had a motive to kill Kennedy, so therefore it must have), which, if true, though not establishing a crime, would forever mark Hoover as one of history's greatest villains. It is therefore surprising that his book and theory have received all the attention of a new fly in the forest from his peers in the conspiracy community.

A note about Trafficante: Though Trafficante has frequently been referred to, as here, as the head of the Florida Mafia, and though he was certainly the most powerful Mafia figure in Florida (attending the infamous November 14, 1957, meeting of the

---

man, told author Curt Gentry that when Hoover learned he was going to be retired, "he was very, very unhappy about it" (Gentry, *J. Edgar Hoover*, p.536). On May 8, 1964, President Johnson signed Executive Order 11154 waiving Hoover's mandatory retirement. In a Rose Garden ceremony attended by leaders of both parties, Johnson told the assembled guests and media that Hoover was a "hero to millions of decent citizens, and an anathema to evil men." Saying Hoover was a "quiet, humble and magnificent public servant," he told Hoover the nation needed him, and hence, exempted him from compulsory retirement for an "indefinite period of time," tantamount to a lifetime appointment (*New York Times*, May 9, 1964, p.12). Hoover remained FBI director for eight more years, until his death from a heart attack on May 2, 1972, at the age of seventy-seven.

mob's leadership in Apalachin, New York), the Trafficante family's principal sphere of influence, according to the McClellan Committee, was in Tampa and central Florida, not Miami and Florida's east coast. Trafficante's father, Santo Trafficante Sr., a Sicilian immigrant, was one of the pioneers and overseers, along with Meyer Lansky (the mob's moneyman, who first opened up Havana to the mob—with the blessing of his new friend, military strongman Colonel Fulgencio Batista—way back in 1933), of mob gaming interests in wide-open Havana. Grooming his son, one of six, to be a mobster, Santo Sr. sent Santo Jr., while in his twenties, to New York to serve his apprenticeship under Mafia boss Carlos Gambino. Unlike nearly all other Mafia leaders, Santo Jr. became well read and gave the appearance of being moderately cultured and sophisticated.[*] His lawyer, Frank Ragano, described him as wise and very clever. Santo Jr., who lived in Havana for several years, took over the Havana operations from his father in the early 1950s (and the Tampa operations in 1954 when his father died). But in Havana, Santo Jr. was always just under Lansky, who himself took up residence in Havana during periods in the 1950s as well as earlier, between 1937 and 1940, when he was operating the gambling casino at the Hotel Nacional and the local racetrack, which he had leased from the National City Bank of New York. Havana was Lansky's empire, and at the time it was a virtual playground for wealthy Americans with sybaritic appetites.

Trafficante's primary base was Havana's Sans Souci Hotel and Casino. From 1952 through 1958, Cuban dictator Fulgencio Batista's last of two reigns (the first being from 1940 to 1944, though the general was the most powerful man in Cuba for years before then), the San Souci (along with eleven other casinos or hotels the mob either owned or controlled, including the Deauville, which Trafficante also ran, and Lansky's two main hotels, the Hotel Nacional and the spectacular Havana Riviera) shared its proceeds with Batista. The mob, and reportedly U.S. intelligence, had helped return Batista to power in an almost bloodless military coup on March 10, 1952. He remained in power for six years until he was overthrown by Castro's revolution, fleeing from the island by plane on January 1, 1959.[45] When Castro assumed power in 1959, he ordered all the casinos closed. For all practical purposes, this had already been done. Mobs of Cubans, angry at the rule of Batista, had taken over the city. They had stormed the casinos, overturned card tables and roulette wheels, and thrown slot machines into the street. Lansky fled back to the states, but Castro detained Trafficante in a small jail for several months, though he eventually agreed to release him.[46†]

Like his New Orleans intimate, Carlos Marcello, in 1963 Trafficante was not a member of the "national commission," the nine-member group that made decisions of national importance to the Mafia.[47]

José Aleman's story first appeared in a long article about Trafficante in the May 16, 1976, edition of the *Washington Post*. Aleman was a young, rich revolutionary in Batista's Cuba whose father, José Aleman Sr., had been the minister of education under Ramón Grau San Martin, a previous president. Aleman Jr. was involved in a March 13, 1957,

---

[*]Not all Mafia bosses were coarse and uneducated. Perhaps the biggest exception was Johnny Torrio, Al Capone's mentor (whose own mentor was Chicago's first big crime boss, "Diamond Jim" Colosimo), who, even during Capone's heyday in Chicago, some believed was in control of Capone. Torrio's enormous influence was not limited to the Chicago mob; he was also very influential with Lucky Luciano and the New York families. Torrio, a soft-spoken family man, spoke five languages, "actually read most of the books in his extensive library," loved the opera, and was a friend of the great Enrico Caruso. (Sciacca, *Luciano*, p.20)

†Castro would soon allow the casinos to reopen, but not under mob control. Eventually, the Cuban government took over all the hotels (5 HSCA 26) and gambling was prohibited.

failed attack on the presidential palace to overthrow Batista. At the time, Aleman was the leader of Directorio Revolucionario Estudiantil, a group of militant Cuban students who were supportive of Castro. "Our main trouble is Batista," Aleman was quoted as saying around that time. "Kill him or get him out of the country and Cuba could return to a democracy."[48] But Castro turned out to be worse, in Aleman's eyes, than Batista, and Aleman was forced into exile as a counterrevolutionary. His wealthy father had left Cuba for Florida before the revolution, becoming very big in Miami real estate with his ownership of beachfront hotels, Miami Stadium, and other interests worth around $20 million.[49]

When Aleman's father died in 1950, the inheritance taxes were so high that Aleman's family had to sell Miami Stadium to pay them. Coupled with other business reverses and poor management, by 1962 Aleman was almost in debt, only owning the run-down Scott Bryan Hotel in Miami Beach. In the late 1950s Aleman had become friendly with agents in the FBI office in Miami when he convinced them, early on, that Castro was actually a Communist (not advertised by the "Bearded One" initially), and particularly when they found him to be "reliable" and a valuable source of information by alerting them to exiles he suspected as being agents of Castro. He told the *Washington Post*'s George Crile III that in September of 1962 a revolutionary colleague of his (George Nobregas) told him that Trafficante, whom he had never met and only knew by reputation as a casino operator in Havana, wanted to meet him. Trafficante, his colleague said, felt indebted to Aleman's cousin, Garcia Bango, an attorney who represented Trafficante in Cuba and had succeeded in getting him out of a Cuban detention center and returned to the United States. Trafficante wanted to express his gratitude by helping Aleman out of his current financial difficulties. Aleman said that when they met at the Scott Bryan, the Tampa-based mob chief told him that a $1.5 million Teamster loan to replace his ramshackle hotel with a twelve-story condominium, and a penthouse apartment for Aleman, had already been cleared by Jimmy Hoffa. During an evening of talk that followed, Trafficante, Aleman said, started speaking out against Kennedy's treatment of Hoffa, who he felt was a friend of blue-collar people. "Mark my words, this man Kennedy is in trouble, and he will get what is coming to him," Aleman quoted Trafficante as saying. When Aleman responded that he felt Kennedy would be reelected, he said Trafficante responded, "No, José, he is going to be hit." Though he had several meetings with Trafficante thereafter, the loan never came through. Aleman told the *Post* that he informed his FBI contacts of Trafficante's statement that Kennedy was going to be hit.[50]

On March 12, 1977, Aleman was interviewed by HSCA staff investigator Gaeton Fonzi, and Fonzi's report of the interview said that "Aleman . . . got the impression that Trafficante was hinting that *Hoffa* was going to make the hit, *not him*, and that Kennedy would never make it to the election because of Hoffa."[51]

When Aleman, wearing an expensive pin-striped suit, testified before the HSCA on September 27, 1978, the heart of his story to the *Washington Post* remained the same, but the details and interpretation differed. The meetings with Trafficante were in June and July of 1963, not September of 1962, Aleman now said. Also, the reason for the original meeting with Trafficante was entirely different from what he told the *Post*.

Aleman: "Mr. George Nobregas came to me and said that J. J. Vila, director of public relations in the city of Miami, wanted to see me because he had a message from President Bosch of the Dominican Republic, and President Bosch was a man that was very grateful to my father and that he wanted to talk to me about bringing to the Dominican Republic a lot of businessmen and whoever wanted to invest there."

HSCA counsel Gary Cornwell: "So you understood that it was a request from people with business interests?"

Aleman: "Yes . . . At the same time, he said that one of the possible individuals who was interested in going was Santos Trafficante, going to the Dominican Republic."

Moreover, although Aleman testified that Trafficante did mention a Teamster loan to him, Trafficante added that "Hoffa could not secure the loan so far."

When HSCA counsel asked Aleman what he took the words "he is going to be hit" to mean, the bespectacled, distinguished-looking Aleman, speaking slightly broken English, said that Trafficante may only have meant that Kennedy was "going to be hit with a lot of votes from the Republicans or anything . . . The way he said that word, I interpreted with a lot of votes from the Republican Party or something like that." But clearly, Aleman, for reasons of his own, probably his fear of retaliation by organized crime (it didn't help that he knew Trafficante was in the next room, listening to his testimony),* was not testifying truthfully here. If Trafficante said what Aleman said he did, Aleman could not possibly have construed the words to mean what he told the HSCA. Additionally, HSCA investigator Fonzi, in his 1977 interview of Aleman, clearly got the impression that he was talking about murder, not Republican votes. I mean, since when is "Jimmy Hoffa" a synonym for "Republican votes"? Aleman added in his testimony before the HSCA, "This happened fifteen years ago and to the best of my recollection I think that is the word ["hit"] he put. I am not saying positively that. I mean, the wording he put was something he [Kennedy] is not going to make it . . . He is not going to be re-elected. In a long conversation like that I didn't pay too much attention on it."[52]

From this very shaky foundation, North, in *Act of Treason*, assumes as fact that Trafficante definitely *did* tell Aleman that Kennedy was going to be hit, and that the hit he was referring to was not by Hoffa but by his close associate, Carlos Marcello, who, North assumes as fact, had told Trafficante of it, and that Marcello and organized crime *did* in fact thereafter have Kennedy murdered (for which there is no evidence). To tie Hoover into it all, North accepts without question Aleman's statement to the *Post* that he *did* tell his FBI contacts at the time about Trafficante's threatening words. North then asserts that the agents wrote up a report of the incident, which he says included Trafficante's threat, and that Hoover eventually saw it. Though he offers no support for this assertion, his assumption is a reasonable one.

Additionally, North has a compelling point on his side. In the 1976 *Washington Post* article, the author, George Crile III, says that when he asked Aleman's two FBI contacts, George Davis and Paul Scranton, "to comment on Aleman's conversations with Trafficante," though they acknowledged frequent contacts with Aleman, "both declined to comment," explaining they "would have to have clearance." This is common, and hence, not troubling. But then Scranton added, per Crile, "I wouldn't want to do anything to embarrass the Bureau." One very strong inference from this is that Aleman had, indeed, told the agents of Trafficante's alleged threat. However, the FBI could be embarrassed not only if the agents did put the threats in their report and their superiors did nothing about it, but also if they didn't bother to put the threats in their report—that is, bureau offi-

---

*As author Curt Gentry puts it, "The switch from bullets to ballots" by Aleman undoubtedly came because Aleman "feared possible reprisal from the Trafficante organization" (Gentry, *J. Edgar Hoover*, p.496 footnote). Aleman told the HSCA that since the *Washington Post* story, "I have been very much worried. I am very much concerned about my safety . . . I [have] been in my house because I mean Santos Trafficante can try to do anything at any moment" (5 HSCA 322–323).

cials would be embarrassed by their own blunders as well as by those of their men in the field, as with the Hosty and Shanklin situation. Assuming Aleman did tell the agents what Trafficante allegedly told him, my guess is that they did not put it in their reports, though I in no way feel serene about this conclusion. I conclude this for several reasons. Crile writes, "Aleman says that he reported this conversation to his FBI contacts, who expressed interest *only* in Trafficante's business proposals. Aleman assumed that they dismissed the Kennedy warnings as gangland braggadocio." However, Aleman told Crile that on the day of the assassination the agents came out to see him and suddenly had a lot of interest in what Trafficante said. "They wanted to know more and more," Aleman said, adding that they stayed until they had explored every possible angle and then told him to keep the conversation confidential.[53]

The main reason I don't believe the agents put Trafficante's alleged threat in their reports is that the HSCA reviewed all FBI reports submitted in 1962 and 1963 by the agents dealing with Aleman, and the reports "did not reveal a record of any such disclosure or comments at the time."[54] North, in his book, makes a fairly good argument, but only at the cost of not telling his readers the absolutely critical fact that the FBI reports from the Miami agents contained no reference to Trafficante's alleged threat.

The HSCA also said (again, not mentioned by North in his book) that "the FBI agent who served as Aleman's contact during that period denied ever being told any such information by Aleman."[55] But the HSCA gives no citation of authority for that assertion so we don't know, for sure, whether the committee was talking about Davis or Scranton. However, almost for sure, it was Davis. Through a retired FBI agent contact, I wrote to Davis's last known address in West End, North Carolina, seeking his comments on the Aleman matter, and received a letter back from his widow on July 1, 2000, that he had died the previous August. I had no address for Scranton, but she forwarded my letter to a retired FBI agent, Bill Kelly, who worked with both of them in 1963 in Miami.

Kelly told me that he and George Davis were assigned to the Internal Security-Cuba section of the Miami field office, and the section was broken down into an anti-Castro squad (working with anti-Castro Cuban exiles), which Davis headed, and a pro-Castro squad (investigating Cuban exiles and Americans who were pro-Castro), of which he, Kelly, was a member. Unofficially, they were called the "Tamale Squads." Though he did not know Aleman, Kelly said that Davis, not Scranton, would have been Aleman's FBI contact because his recollection (which he later confirmed with two other retired agents from the Miami field office) was that Scranton did not work Internal Security. His principal job was "police training coordinator," and he was also assigned to the organized-crime squad. Since even in 1978, in his appearance before the HSCA, Aleman spoke broken English, I assume he spoke much worse English in 1963, and since there may have been a communication problem, I asked Kelly if Davis spoke Spanish. "George didn't speak a word of Spanish. We used to kid him about it." Before Castro ascended to power in 1959, Kelly said, no one in the Miami FBI office spoke Spanish. "There wasn't any need for it. Davis had been working Internal Security since 1956, and he just stayed on even after Castro took over. There was no better or more respected agent in the entire FBI than George Davis. As early as 1956, when no one would listen, he told the State Department that Castro was a Communist." Kelly said that although Davis didn't speak Spanish, Scranton did. "My guess is that George took Scranton along when he spoke to Aleman."[56]

I asked Kelly to try to locate Scranton for me so I could interview him. Kelly finally reached Scranton by phone several days later. Scranton, in his eighties, had just had a massive stroke and was not inclined to speak to me, so I gave Kelly some questions to ask Scranton for me. In a July 31, 2000, telephone conversation with Kelly, Scranton, though speaking slowly, Kelly said, because of his stroke, said very clearly and deliberately, "I have absolutely no recollection of Aleman ever having said that Trafficante told Aleman before the assassination, or any other time, that Kennedy was to be hit. If Aleman had made that statement to us, I guarantee I would have written it up, even if George [Davis] hadn't, for transmission to [FBI] headquarters."

Scranton also confirmed that he did not work Internal Security, but Kelly, feeling he already knew the answer (that Scranton could speak Spanish), did not ask Scranton why he went along with Davis on the Aleman interview. Kelly also did not ask Scranton why he told the *Post*'s Crile, "I wouldn't want to do anything to embarrass the Bureau," and when I asked Kelly, who was very helpful, to call Scranton back on this point a few days later, Scranton was in the hospital with another stroke. When Kelly called Scranton back on August 9, after Scranton had been released from the hospital, and asked him if he had made the subject remark to the *Post*'s Crile, he told Kelly he did not recall telling Crile this, but that it was a quarter of a century ago and in any event his memory had been affected by his recent strokes.

As circumstantial evidence as to what happened in this case, I asked Kelly how many people in the FBI chain of command would have seen a memo from Davis or Scranton quoting Trafficante as saying Kennedy was going to be hit. "I may leave out someone along the way," Kelly said, "but at a minimum, Davis's memo would go to Howard Albaugh, the supervisor of the Internal Security section of the [Miami FBI field] office, then to Wesley Grapp, the agent in charge of the [Miami field] office, then, because of its extreme importance, it would be teletyped [not airtelled, he said, which was priority mail] to the Internal Security-Cuba section at headquarters in [Washington, D.C.], and, because of Trafficante, to the organized-crime division, then it would go to either the assistant director of internal security or domestic intelligence, or both, as well as to the assistant director back then who had responsibility for organized crime, then to Clyde Tolson, the assistant director, then to the old man [Hoover]." Kelly added that even if, for some strange reason, the memo had been sent by Airtel, before it was placed in an envelope the same people in Miami would have seen it, and when it arrived at FBI headquarters in Washington, D.C., it would have been opened by a clerk at the bureau and the same people at headquarters would have seen it. When I told Kelly about the charge in North's book, he said, "That's just ridiculous. Hoover would never suppress something like this. Even if he wanted to, he couldn't because he'd know too many other people had already seen the report." Conceding that Hoover was a "dictator," Kelly said Hoover was "a good man, a benevolent dictator."[57]

Now let's look at what Mark North gives his readers as support for his assertion that there was an FBI report of the Trafficante-Aleman incident and it did reach Hoover's desk. "Pursuant to standard FBI procedure, the two agents [George Davis and Paul Scranton] report the assassination plan to their superior, Miami SAC Wesley Grapp."* North

---

*North gives no citation of authority for this that makes any sense. He first lists the "*Washington Post*, 2-13-62," which is seven months *before* the alleged conversation between Aleman and Trafficante ever took place, then spends the rest of the note he cites as authority for the Trafficante-Aleman incident talking not about Trafficante and Aleman, but Carlos Marcello and Ed Becker, alleging, without proof, that Hoover also had knowledge of Marcello's plan to murder Kennedy (North, *Act of Treason*, pp.604–605 note 3). When an assertion like the one North makes is the key point of your book, you obviously have to have a lot of support for what you are saying. North has *nothing*.

then writes that "the information is then sent by [FBI] AIRTEL to Hoover." North gives no source or citation of authority at all for this assertion, which goes to the heart of his book. He simply states an assumption on his part as fact. What does Hoover do with this information he now has (courtesy of Mark North), that the mob is going to murder Kennedy? North speculates that "Hoover shifts his efforts from attempting to gain political leverage over the President to ensuring the success of the contract [to kill Kennedy]. Word of the plot is withheld from the Secret Service."[58]

It should be pointed out that in addition to Scranton's denial and the absence of an FBI report confirming that Aleman told the agents what he said he did, Aleman's testimony before the HSCA itself isn't perfectly clear on this matter. Indeed, although at one place in his testimony he said he did tell the agents this, at another point he implies he may not have. He said, "If, in any way, I would have thought the context at that time was that something was going to happen in that respect, *I would have immediately advised the proper authorities about it.*" Whereupon HSCA counsel asked Aleman this leading question: "And didn't you do so?" And Aleman said he did, although not as expressly as HSCA counsel clearly wanted. Aleman said, "I talked in some way to members of the FBI about what was going on in the conversation [with Trafficante], and I told them that something wrong was in some way." When HSCA counsel pressed and said to Aleman, "I believe you previously told me . . . that you did specifically tell the FBI about the comments of Trafficante on this occasion," instead of simply saying yes, Aleman only responded, "We talked in some way," suggesting the difficulty of "trying to recollect things that happened 15 years ago."[59]

As to the more seminal question of whether Trafficante ever made the remark to Aleman in the first place, in testimony before the HSCA on September 28, 1978,* Trafficante said, "I want to tell you something now, Mr. Stokes [chairman of the HSCA]. I am sure as I am sitting here that [in] all the discussion I had with Mr. Aleman, that I never made the statement that Kennedy was going to get hit." Trafficante's vehement denial, of course, by itself means nothing. But he did add something noteworthy concerning Aleman's implication in his testimony that Trafficante made his threat in English.[60] "I spoke to [Aleman] in Spanish. No reason for me to talk to him in English because I can speak Spanish fluently and he speaks Spanish. That is his language. There was no reason for me to tell him in English that Kennedy is going to get hit."[61]

But far more importantly, for those who believe that Trafficante was behind Kennedy's murder, and cite his alleged statement to Aleman as support, why in the world would Trafficante confide such a monstrous murder plot to Aleman, who not only wasn't a fellow mafioso, but also was someone he had never met before? It makes no sense at all. The HSCA said it "found it difficult to comprehend why Trafficante, if he was planning or had personal knowledge of an assassination plot, would have revealed or hinted at such a sensitive

---

*Like a typical mobster, Trafficante took the Fifth Amendment as to all questions (including "Did you ever discuss with any individuals plans to assassinate President Kennedy prior to his assassination?") when he was first called to the stand (HSCA Record 180-10114-10180, Testimony of Santos Trafficante before HSCA on March 16, 1977, pp.7–15), but the HSCA subsequently compelled his testimony by an order it got from the U.S. District Court for the District of Columbia conferring immunity on Trafficante from having anything he said under oath being used against him. The immunity order did not extend to perjury by Trafficante. (5 HSCA 346–348) Though conspiracy theorists like to cite Trafficante's refusal to answer the question of whether he had ever discussed plans to murder Kennedy (e.g., Davis, *Mafia Kingfish*, pp.427–428), not too much should be read into this. The conspiracists don't point out that before Trafficante was granted immunity, he also took the Fifth when asked, "Will you tell us when and where you were born?" (5 HSCA 346, Testimony of Santos Trafficante before HSCA on September 28, 1978)

matter to Aleman,"* particularly, it said, when Trafficante had a reputation for being cautious and discreet. (FBI agent Jim Kenney, who investigated Trafficante for fifteen years, said in a November 17, 1992, *Frontline* documentary on the mob that "our investigation of Santo Trafficante throughout the years proved to be frustrating in that he maintained a low profile and he was very, very circumspect about whom he would talk with and meet with.")[62] The HSCA ended up rejecting Aleman's story, concluding that "there were substantial factors that called into question the validity of Aleman's account."[63]

On the one hand, if Trafficante were actually behind the assassination, his confiding such a murder plot to Aleman is, as indicated, nonsensical and not worthy of belief. But this doesn't mean he didn't say what Aleman said he did. By George Davis's own admission to George Crile in the *Washington Post*, "José's a real nice fellow. He's a reliable individual." Even the HSCA, which did not accept Aleman's story, said he was a "reputable person who did not seek to publicize his allegations." Moreover, what would Aleman possibly have to gain by making up such a story? It seems like he could only hurt himself. And FBI agent Paul Scranton's telling the *Post*'s George Crile III that he did not want to comment on Aleman's allegation without clearance because "I wouldn't want to do anything to embarrass the Bureau" certainly sounds, as least to a layman unfamiliar with the practice of FBI agents, as if Aleman *did* tell them what he claims Trafficante told him, and they either didn't put it in their report, or they did and no action was taken. However, Kelly, a thirty-year veteran of the bureau, told me, "Don't read too much into those words of Scranton's. It's a standard response by agents, even when there's nothing that could embarrass the bureau. I've used almost those exact words myself many times in my career. Don't forget that FBI policy back then, and I believe even today, is that only three people in a field office are authorized to say anything of substance to the media: the agent in charge of the field office [special agent-in-charge], the assistant agent-in-charge, and the press liaison guy."[64]

The situation seems irreconcilable unless, taking into account the problems of communication between Aleman and Trafficante (if, in fact, Trafficante spoke to Aleman, as Aleman suggests, in English) as well as between Aleman and the two agents, one of whom spoke no Spanish, one concludes that, as the HSCA said, "it is possible that Trafficante may have been expressing a personal opinion, 'The President ought to be hit.'"[65]

There are several parenthetical observations to be made about the Trafficante-Aleman incident. One is that even if Trafficante said precisely what Aleman said he did, as discussed elsewhere in this book, there is absolutely no credible evidence that Trafficante was connected in any way with the assassination, so his utterance to Aleman wouldn't have any relevance to this case. Furthermore, although FBI electronic surveillance of Trafficante was limited, its on-site surveillance of him was very extensive. In a letter to J. Edgar Hoover in 1967, Frank Ragano, Trafficante's lawyer, complained of the absolutely suffocating surveillance of "Mr. Trafficante and members of his family [that] has been going on since 1961," and beseeched Hoover to order a stop to it. Ragano wasn't just talking. Not only did he give Hoover physical descriptions of the agents, but he also provided the license plate numbers of four of their cars.[66] To believe that someone under this type of "surveillance," as Ragano put it, would nonetheless decide to order the murder of the president of the United States is simply ridiculous.

---

*Of course, as with the alleged Marcello-Becker conversation, if Trafficante had nothing to do with the assassination, such loose talk by him to Aleman would be unremarkable and of no significance.

Additionally, as alluded to earlier, when HSCA staff investigator Gaeton Fonzi interviewed Aleman on March 12, 1977, a year and a half before his HSCA testimony on September 27, 1978, he wrote, "[Aleman] also said that Trafficante brought up Jimmy Hoffa's name and said that Hoffa would never forgive the Kennedys for what they did to him. Aleman said he got the impression that Trafficante was hinting that Hoffa was going to make the hit, not him, and that Kennedy would never make it to the election because of Hoffa. This, says Aleman, was the one aspect of the conversation with Trafficante that [*Washington Post* reporter George] Crile did not properly put into perspective in his piece; otherwise, the piece was very accurate."[67]*

Finally, as indicated earlier, the HSCA reviewed all the reports that Davis and Scranton prepared on their contacts with Aleman and found no mention of the Trafficante threat. Therefore, if Hoover had received information in a report from Davis and Scranton about the threat, this necessarily means he had to order the destruction of these reports and the preparation of new ones, thus automatically bringing into the cover-up not only the earlier mentioned chain of command, but Davis and Scranton as well. The extremely high improbability of all of this happening is one of the reasons why I believe that if Aleman told Davis and Scranton about the Trafficante threat, they did not put it in their report or reports.

But *if* Aleman told FBI agents Davis and Scranton what Trafficante allegedly told him, and *if* they put this in their report, and *if* the report reached Hoover, and *if* Hoover, believing the mob would in fact kill Kennedy, did not furnish this information to the Secret Service or do anything else about it because he was hoping the mob would kill Kennedy, thereby avoiding his impending compulsory retirement, Hoover, even though the mob did not, in fact, end up killing Kennedy, would, as indicated, be an incredible villain. I am very, very confident that this scenario did not happen. However, based on the existing record, there is no way that one can dismiss the notion completely out of hand. I mean, to retain power, men have done much worse things than stand by and let someone else commit a murder that redounds to their benefit.

One footnote to the Trafficante-Aleman issue: Contrary to Mark North's conclusion that if the assumed facts set forth in his scenario were true, they would make Hoover guilty of treason,[68] they would not. Treason is the only crime defined in the U.S. Constitution: "Treason against the United States shall consist only in levying War against them, or adhering to their Enemies, giving them Aid and Comfort."[69] Neither clause would apply to Hoover's alleged conduct, the courts defining "enemy" as a "foreign power," and ruling that aid to the foreign country has to take place while the United States is "in a state of open hostility" with the other country (i.e., while we're at war).[70]

The main contention by the fringe element of the conspiracy community is that Hoover actually conspired to have Kennedy murdered (unlike Mark North's allegation of passivity on Hoover's part). But they present not the tiniest sliver of evidence to support

---

*In 1983 in Miami, Aleman, who had become convinced that his 1978 HSCA testimony against Trafficante had prevented his financial recovery and adversely marked him and his family for the rest of their lives, was penniless and despondent. For no apparent reason, he went berserk, shooting and killing his sixty-nine-year-old aunt and seriously wounding three cousins. Police were called to the scene, and in the ensuing shootout where four Miami Police Department SWAT team members were wounded, Aleman committed suicide by shooting himself in the temple. (Davis, *Mafia Kingfish*, p.446; Benson, *Who's Who in the JFK Assassination*, p.6)

their wild allegation. However, because Hoover is such a central figure in the assassination saga, a very brief profile of who J. Edgar Hoover was, and how he ran his empire, is called for.

J. Edgar Hoover, since his appointment as FBI director in 1924, at once formed and effectively ran perhaps the finest, most incorruptible law enforcement agency in the world, while being personally beset by obsessions, paranoia, and insecurities that would run off the edge of the paper of any psychiatric report analyzing him. Just one illustrative example: In 1959 in California, Hoover's chauffeur-driven car was struck from behind while in the process of making a left turn, and he was shaken up. Thereafter, on instructions from Hoover, his drivers had to take him to his destination without making a left turn.[71]

Hoover, it seemed, believed he was incapable of error as the FBI's director, something akin to the doctrine of papal infallibility in the Catholic Church. As former FBI agent Joseph L. Schlott wrote, "In the FBI under Mr. Hoover, you had to work on the premise that the Director was infallible." Indeed, Hoover himself would only admit to having been conned twice in his life (not in FBI business, naturally), "once by a door to door salesman who sold him black sawdust for his flower bed as pure manure, and once by the Birdman of Alcatraz, who sold him a sparrow dyed yellow as a canary."[72]*

Above all, Hoover was a megalomaniac—he had to be the only person in the FBI who received the acclamation of the public. When the most famous G-man ever (other than Hoover), Melvin Purvis, who most believed to be the key agent in the tracking down and killing of John Dillinger (the bureau's "Public Enemy Number One") in the alley behind the Biograph Theater in Chicago in 1934, received national attention and fame, Hoover could not tolerate it. Purvis, who at one time was a big favorite of Hoover's, and was the recipient of several personal letters from him, suddenly became persona non grata at the bureau. Hoover had told Purvis in one letter, "Well, son, keep a stiff upper lip and get Dillinger for me and the world is yours." But after Purvis became widely known as "the man who got Dillinger," he was demoted to a desk job in the Chicago office and forced to resign the following year.[†] In Hoover's 1938 book, *Persons in Hiding*, he devotes much space to Dillinger (more than the likes of notorious outlaws like Ma Barker, Baby Face Nelson, and Charles "Pretty Boy" Floyd, all FBI prey),[‡] the most famous "person in hid-

---

*The number-one G-man (the name coined by gangster George "Machine Gun" Kelly for government men) loved the ponies, and at one time or another visited and bet at virtually every major racetrack in the country, even having a number of horses named after him, but didn't cash that many winning tickets. "Edgar is a sucker at the track," a friend said. "He'll let somebody tout him a horse with information he would throw out the window back at the FBI." (Knebel, "J. Edgar Hoover," p.30; G-men coined by Kelly: Whitehead, *FBI Story*, p.15)

†Purvis, still enormously popular with the American public, wrote a memoir, *American Agent*, lent his name to product endorsements, and became "the voice of an unofficial radio adventure, *Top Secrets of the FBI*." Author Richard Powers writes, "For the rest of Purvis' life, the Bureau quietly sabotaged his efforts to build a second career either in entertainment or in the security field . . . When Purvis committed suicide in 1960 with his Bureau revolver, Hoover's executive council debated and then rejected the idea of sending a letter to the widow. [She] telegraphed Hoover, 'We are honored that you ignored Melvin's death. Your jealousy hurt him very much, but until the end I think he loved you.'" (Powers, *Broken*, pp.154–155)

‡Remarkably, or coincidentally, Dillinger, Floyd, Barker, and Nelson were all hunted down and killed by the FBI within a mere six-month period, making heroes in the public eye of Hoover and his G-men almost overnight, and marking the year, 1934, as the biggest one in the bureau's fabled history. FBI chronicler Richard Powers writes that Hollywood also helped turn the FBI "into American legend through movies about the Bureau's gangbusting cases, beginning with James Cagney's *G-Men*, in 1935. [Later films included *The FBI Story* starring Jimmy Stewart in 1959 and television's *The FBI* from 1965 to 1974.] There was FBI entertainment in every media: radio shows, pulp magazines, and even bubble gum cards." The overall effect was to persuade the public "that all crime was local and the Bureau's job was to take over cases that were too difficult for the local police." (Powers, *Broken*, photo section; Theoharis with Poveda, Rosenfeld, and Powers, *FBI*,

ing" the FBI has ever brought to ground, and the one about whose celebrated capture the bureau has always taken the greatest pride. Yet remarkably, in his telling of the Dillinger capture, Hoover does not even mention Melvin Purvis. In fact, the name Melvin Purvis doesn't appear anywhere in the book, even though Purvis was also very instrumental in bringing to an end the career in crime of Baby Face Nelson and Pretty Boy Floyd.[73]

It is common in nonfiction for authors to ignore the accomplishments of competitors or people they don't like (for whatever reason). When they do this, their books, in which they have an obligation to rise above their pettiness for the historical record, lose credibility. Because of Hoover's pettiness, I read his book, not just the part on Dillinger, with a jaundiced eye.

Hoover not only easily controlled, in a dictatorial fashion, his entire agency, but also induced enormous fear in (and hence, largely controlled) every major public figure—including President John F. Kennedy—who ever strayed in his personal life. His gunpowder? The very well-known secret dossiers ("Hoover's files" they were known as) he kept in two file cabinets behind the desk of his secretary, Helen Gandy, on wayward congressmen, diplomats, celebrities, and so on.[74] William Sullivan, a former assistant director of the FBI under Hoover, said that the dossiers or files did not necessarily include references to "sex alone, but financial irregularities or political chicanery. He gathered all the dirt that was present on people in high-ranking positions . . . Knowledge is powerful, and he had knowledge of the most damaging kind, knowledge of people's misbehavior."[75] Emanuel Celler, for years chairman of the House Judiciary Committee, liked and respected Hoover, but said Hoover "had a dossier on every member of Congress and every member of the Senate." Though he could not speak for the Senate, he said, "The members of the House were aware of this" and many "had a lot of skeletons in their closet . . . That's what made him so feared." Celler said, "There's no question in my mind" that Hoover tapped the telephones of congressmen.[76] Author Victor S. Navasky wrote that "the Director, with the FBI files as his private library, [was the] *de facto* caretaker to the nation's reputations."[77]

The brimming contents of these files were gathered by Hoover's agents through the wiretapping of telephones (which was unlawful but routinely authorized for years by the U.S. attorney general in national security cases) or "bugging" (installing, usually by criminal trespass, hidden microphones in people's homes, apartments, etc., to pick up nontelephonic verbal communications), called "black bag jobs" in the FBI. Even where national security wasn't involved, as was frequently the case, it was widely reported that Hoover regularly ordered telephone taps (wiretaps) and bugging without the approval of the attorney general,[78] who had no legal authority to allow them anyway.

Hoover's abuse of the national security exception was notorious, perhaps the most prominent example being his secret Counterintelligence Program (COINTELPRO), a program that took Hoover's FBI far beyond its sole mandate to enforce federal law. Deciding he knew what was best for America, its values, and its culture, Hoover's COINTELPRO was a series of covert missions starting in 1956 (to 1971) to identify, penetrate, and neutralize what Hoover decided were subversive elements in the United States, including, Hoover believed, civil rights groups, black liberation and antiwar groups, and the political Left, mostly American Communists. However, the first group COINTELPRO

---

pp.176–177) Though still admired as a competent and clean law enforcement agency, because of an accumulation of events, including the revelations in the 1970s and 1980s of Hoover's abuse of power, today's FBI no longer enjoys the mythical status it once did in the nation's eyes, and being the nation's lead agency against terrorism within our shores, the bureau took a serious blow after the destruction of the twin towers of the World Trade Center in New York City on September 11, 2001.

operated against, ironically, was a group on the Far Right, the Ku Klux Klan. A favorite tool of COINTELPRO was to fabricate and spread pernicious rumors and write anonymous letters with false accusations about individual members of these groups. A report from the House Select Committee on Intelligence ("Pike Committee Report") in 1976 said that in the process, "careers were ruined, friendships severed, reputations sullied, businesses bankrupted and, in some cases, lives endangered."[79] A typical example of COINTELPRO: The bureau learned, through electronic surveillance, of a civil rights leader's plan in 1964 to attend a reception at the Soviet mission to the United Nations honoring a Soviet author. The FBI arranged to have news photographers at the scene to photograph him entering the Soviet mission.[80]

One of the very worst examples of COINTELPRO abuse occurred in the late 1960s and involved prominent Hollywood actress Jean Seberg, a known supporter and financial contributor to the Black Panthers, a militant black nationalist group. When she became pregnant in 1970, the FBI became aware of it through the wiretap of a telephone conversation from Black Panther headquarters to Seberg, and the special agent in charge of the Los Angeles FBI office sent an Airtel to Hoover on April 27, 1970, stating that "permission is requested to publicize the pregnancy of Jean Seberg, well-known movie actress, by Ray Hewitt of the Black Panthers Party . . . by advising Hollywood gossip columnists in the Los Angeles area of the situation. It is felt that the possible publication of Seberg's plight could cause her embarrassment and serve to cheapen her image with the general public. It is proposed that the following letter from a fictitious person be sent to local columnists." Permission was granted and on May 19, 1970, *Los Angeles Times* gossip columnist Joyce Haber published the story, which was syndicated to about a hundred papers around the country. On August 23, Seberg, who was married to French diplomat and novelist Romain Gary, prematurely delivered a baby daughter, who died two days later. At the infant's funeral, Seberg opened the casket to prove the child was white and the story about her a lie. According to the *Los Angeles Times*, the story "triggered the actress' downward spiral across a decade, her husband and others close to her said. For nine years, Seberg tried to take her life around the baby's birthday. On September 8, 1979, her body was found naked in the back of a Renault parked on a Paris side street, the death credited to an overdose of barbiturates."[81]*

Hoover's illegal wiretaps to gain compromising information on anyone he perceived to be a threat to his power, and oftentimes on political opponents of the president then in the White House (sometimes at the request of the president himself), started in the 1930s under FDR, reaching their zenith in the 1960s under the Machiavellian LBJ, Hoover's personal friend. Only one president, Truman, had virtually no relationship with Hoover, to the extent of not even allowing Hoover to deal directly with him, forcing Hoover to deal with Truman's chief military aide, Brigadier General Harry Vaughn.[82]

Hoover's power was such that President Kennedy was fond of telling people when they asked why he never fired Hoover, "You don't fire God."[83] LBJ had a more earthy way of

---

*It was one thing for the FBI, acting within its jurisdiction to investigate domestic subversion, to use illegal means to do so. But prior to investigative reporter Seymour Hersh's front-page article in the December 23 and 24, 1974, editions of the *New York Times*, it was not publicly known that the CIA, with no jurisdiction domestically, had been illegally spying on American citizens since the Nixon administration. Hersh's articles caused President Gerald Ford to order CIA Director William Colby to report to him "within a matter of days" on the published allegations. (*New York Times*, December 23, 1974, pp.1, 19; *New York Times*, December 24, 1974, pp.1, 4) Hersh's explosive revelations are widely credited with Ford's creation of the Rockefeller Commission on January 4, 1975, to determine whether the CIA was exceeding its statutory authority.

putting it: "In the long run, I'd rather have Edgar on the inside pissing out, than on the outside hosing me down."[84]

After Hoover died, *New York Times* reporter Tom Wicker wrote that Hoover had "wielded more power, longer, than any man in American history."[85] And Hoover was never shy about letting everyone know just how powerful he was, referring to his FBI headquarters office as "SOG" or "Seat of Government."[86] In fact, the term "Seat of Government" was even used routinely in official FBI documents, for example, "All of the supervisors and officials who came into contact with this case at the *seat of government*, as well as agents in the field . . ."[87] It seemed that Hoover didn't know his place in the executive branch of government, and during his lifetime no one was about to remind him.

Virtually every Hoover biography, from Curt Gentry's best-selling *J. Edgar Hoover: The Man and the Secrets* on down, has confirmed not only that Hoover had a bulging, six-hundred-page file on JFK's dalliances,* but also that Kennedy was well aware of what Hoover had on him.[88] And Hoover made sure his targets knew, directly or indirectly, that he had the goods on them.

The most blatant, outrageous, and vile example of this was the fifteen FBI bugging tapes of Martin Luther King, containing words and physical sounds of King with other women in hotel rooms around the country. These tapes were sent to King (whom Hoover despised and viewed as a Communist pawn dangerous to America, which resulted in King's telephone also being tapped under authorization from RFK on national security grounds) at King's Southern Christian Leadership Conference office in Atlanta in mid-November of 1964. FBI coverage of King had revealed that King's wife, Coretta, "opened his mail for him when he was on the road." A letter accompanying the tapes was from an anonymous writer, who told King that he was "a complete fraud . . . and an evil, vicious one at that . . . You are done." One note is believed to have actually encouraged King to commit suicide, reading, "King, there is one thing left for you to do. You know what it is."[89] DeLoach confirmed that the FBI's wiretaps of King's phone, which RFK approved, were at the request of the FBI, not RFK. However, in May of 1968, columnist Drew Pearson said that RFK ordered the wiretaps on King's phone, and that he would soon release the documentation he had to support this, which he never did.[90] Hoover showed his personal distaste for King and his firsthand involvement in the effort to destroy him in a handwritten note at the bottom of an internal FBI memo discussing the "microphone surveillance" of King in his room at the Shroeder Hotel in Milwaukee. "King is a tomcat," Hoover scribbled, "with obsessive degenerate sexual urges."[91] Hoover even went so far as to try to peddle a dossier on King, which included a taped composite of King's sexual activities in various hotel rooms, to key members of the Washington, D.C., press corps, but they declined to accept his offer.[92]

By all accounts, though there is no record of what was said, Hoover's lunch with Kennedy at the White House on March 22, 1962 (at which he brought along an FBI memo on Judith Campbell Exner, prepared for him two days earlier, that set forth the dates of her calls to the White House and the fact that she had "associated with prominent underworld figures Sam Giancana of Chicago and John Roselli of Los Angeles"), was to inform

---

*These dalliances started before his presidency, with his affair in 1941 with the married (separated) and beautiful, honey-blonde Inga Arvad (former Miss Denmark and Miss Europe), who for a time was erroneously suspected of being a Nazi spy, and continued into 1962 with Judith Campbell Exner, and 1963 with a stunning, Elizabeth Taylor–resembling call girl, Ellen Rometsch, whom Bobby Kennedy quietly deported back to Germany.

the president that he must cease seeing Exner. It is no coincidence that White House records show the last of seventy telephone calls put through the White House switchboard to Exner's number occurred that afternoon after the luncheon.[93]

Just as those who wear their patriotism on their sleeves usually have very little left inside—in a similar vein one is reminded of Ralph Waldo Emerson's remark that "the louder he talked of his honor, the faster we counted our spoons"—many law-and-order extremists like Hoover very often have no compunction about violating the law themselves. In addition to the well-chronicled fact that Hoover often used FBI personnel to make repairs to his home, there is at least one clear case of a prosecutable felony (grand theft) committed by Hoover; many people have gone to jail for less. "As you know," former assistant FBI director William Sullivan wrote to Hoover in 1971, a few days after he left the FBI, "I had a number of men working for many months writing your book, *Masters of Deceit*, for you. Contrary to what you have said it was not done on private time. It was done on public time, during the day at taxpayers' expense [we're obviously talking here about well over $100,000] . . . Do you realize the amount of agent time that was spent not only in writing the book but on advertising and publicizing it all around the country? All our field offices were told to push it . . . We even wrote reviews here at the Headquarters which were sent to the field to have printed by different papers."[94] Louis Nichols, the FBI's first publicist and lobbyist, and a Hoover partisan who was more responsible for the lionization of Hoover in the public's eye than anyone else, confirmed Sullivan's story about *Masters of Deceit*, which sold 250,000 copies in hardcover and 2 million in paperback.[95]

Returning to the central issue, as previously stated, no one, ever, has produced one piece of evidence connecting J. Edgar Hoover with Kennedy's death, and your more responsible conspiracy theorists don't devote any space to the charge. Indeed, the very thought that J. Edgar Hoover decided to murder President John F. Kennedy is too far-fetched for any but the most suspicious and irrational minds. Hoover had already proved (the March 22, 1962, luncheon with JFK over Judith Campbell Exner) the power he had to blackmail the president, and it is therefore ridiculous to say that he would try to kill Kennedy—and thus expose himself to a sentence of death—in order to keep his job. When we couple all of this with the fact that, as author Curt Gentry writes, "Hoover's concern with preserving his good name became an obsession" and "the fear that his carefully constructed image would come tumbling down obsessed him most of his life" (the "hundreds of hours" he spent "fussing over the blueprints" to the building in Washington, D.C., that currently bears his name is a metaphor for his all-consuming concern over his image and reputation),[96] the thought becomes too crazed to put to paper, and I apologize to his surviving relatives, if he has any, for even discussing this issue.

The Warren Commission found no evidence of FBI involvement in the assassination.[97] And the HSCA, having examined the allegation of FBI complicity in the assassination, concluded that the FBI was "not involved in the assassination of President Kennedy."[98] (Both the Warren Commission and the HSCA had the good taste not to even ask the question of whether J. Edgar Hoover, individually, was involved.) And the earlier Church Committee, in 1975, after investigating the possibility of U.S. intelligence (specifically the FBI and CIA) being involved in the assassination, said it did not uncover "any evidence" of such involvement.[99]

Secret Service

One other U.S. intelligence agency has had the suggestion of complicity in the assassination leveled against it by the conspiracy theorists, the Secret Service, but nowhere near as much as the CIA and FBI.

The U.S. Secret Service, a bureau of the Department of the Treasury, dates back to 1865, the last year of the Civil War, when it was created primarily to combat the widespread counterfeiting of U.S. currency. Nearly one-third of all currency in circulation at the time was counterfeit, and the country's financial stability was in jeopardy. In 1894, since the Secret Service was the only federal investigative agency at the time, it began to provide informal and part-time protection to the president. In 1902, following the assassination of President William McKinley the previous year, the Service, without statutory authority, and in addition to its anticounterfeiting mandate, assumed full-time responsibility for the protection of the president. Following the election of William Howard Taft in 1908, the Secret Service started protecting the president-elect. In 1913, Congress enacted legislation expressly providing for full-time Secret Service protection of the president. Although the Secret Service began protecting the vice president in 1945, it wasn't until 1951 that Congress enacted legislation authorizing such protection, but only upon the vice president's request. Legislation in 1962 required protection of the vice president, with or without his request.

During fiscal year 1963, the Secret Service had an average strength of 513 personnel, 351 of whom were special agents (weapon-carrying personnel, whether members of the Presidential Protection Division or some other division), with sixty-five field offices throughout the country. The core of the presidential security arm of the Secret Service is the White House detail, which in 1963 consisted of 36 special agents and 6 special agent-drivers.[1]

With respect to the Secret Service, for all intents and purposes the inquiry about complicity in the assassination begins and ends with the motorcade route. This is so because if the Service or any of its agents were involved in the assassination, they necessarily would have had a determinative or at least important hand in helping to make sure the limousine proceeded beneath Oswald's window on Elm Street. But all the evidence shows they did not have such a hand; in fact, the Secret Service let it be known that it favored, for security reasons, a different destination for the motorcade, which would have meant a different route altogether, and no assassination.

On November 4, 1963, Gerald Behn, the special agent in charge of the White House's Secret Service detail, called Forrest Sorrels, the special agent in charge of the Dallas field office of the Secret Service, to inform him of the president's intent to visit Dallas "around November 21st." He said that two buildings had been suggested for a luncheon site following the presidential motorcade—the Trade Mart, a new and attractive convention hall off the Stemmons Freeway to the northwest of Dealey Plaza, and the old Women's Building located on the fairgrounds in the southern part of Dallas— and asked Sorrels to survey both sites. Sorrels immediately did and reported back to Behn that same day that "security-wise the Women's Building appeared to be preferable" (because there were only two entrances to the building, whereas the Trade Mart had many entrances as well as suspension bridges on the second and third floors) but that, as opposed to the Trade Mart, the one-story building "wasn't a very nice place to take the president" because the ceiling was low and the "air-conditioning equipment and everything was all exposed."[2] So Sorrels made no choice. However, Behn, who was in charge of trip security, did, announcing on November 5 that he favored the Women's Building.[3] But selection of the luncheon site was out of the hands of the Secret Service. It was to be decided by politicians.

Today, there are two main parties in Texas, the dominant Republican Party and the Democratic Party. However, in 1963 Texas was essentially a one-party state (Democratic) and the party was clearly divided along liberal and conservative lines. The relationship between the two wings of the party was so bitter and combustible that, for instance, they even engaged in fistfights on the floor of the 1960 Democratic national convention in Los Angeles. The liberals, led by Senator Ralph Yarborough, lobbied the White House hard for the Women's Building, which not only had a larger seating capacity, permitting more of the president's supporters to attend, but also had an atmosphere more compatible with that of the common man, the so-called working class. But the conservative wing of the party, led by Governor Connally, was fiercely opposed to the Women's Building site, demanding that the luncheon be held at the Trade Mart, the headquarters in Dallas for the city's predominantly conservative business community.[4]*

The White House ultimately deferred to the governor, and Kenneth O'Donnell, special assistant to the president, notified the Secret Service of its position on November 14, 1963.[5] A presidential advance man, Jerry Bruno, wrote in his November 15, 1963, diary entry, "The White House announced that the Trade Mart had been approved.† I met with

---

*If the truth be told, many in Dallas, the most conservative large city in Texas, viewed Kennedy as a "pinko" (colloquial for Communist) and didn't even want him to come. (But as long as he was coming, they, the conservatives, wanted to be in charge.) How could Kennedy possibly be viewed as a Communist? In these circles, said Dallas Democratic political organizer Elizabeth Forsling Harris, "anybody who had any interest in what might be called social equality," or thought the government should serve "the needs of all the people, was, ipso facto, a Commie" (HSCA Record 180-10078-10272, Deposition of Elizabeth Forsling Harris before HSCA on August 16, 1978, pp.8, 49).

†The decision may have been helped by a report from Winston G. Lawson, the Secret Service White House advance agent for the trip, to Gerald Behn. Although he did not make a recommendation for the Trade Mart

O'Donnell and [Press Secretary Bill] Moyers who said that Connally was unbearable and on the verge of canceling the trip. They decided they had to let the Governor have his way." As the HSCA concluded, "The Secret Service was, in fact, a bystander in the process; its protective functions were subordinated to political considerations."[6]

However, just because the Trade Mart was chosen didn't mean there was going to be a motorcade to get to it. Indeed, both Governor Connally and Frank Erwin, the executive secretary of the Texas State Democratic Committee, objected to the motorcade, fearing that because Dallas was so conservative, there might be some incident or sign along the parade route that would be embarrassing to the president. Connally also felt that the motorcade, requiring the president's interaction with the crowd along the motorcade route, would put an excessive strain on the president, especially in view of his tight schedule.[7] In the end, the White House wishes for a motorcade prevailed. Kenneth P. O'Donnell told the Warren Commisssion, "We had a motorcade wherever we went. Particularly when we went to a large city, the purpose of going there was to give the president as much exposure to the people . . . as possible. The speaking engagement was a luncheon which was rather limited. And the president would not want to leave Dallas feeling that the only ones that were able to see him were a rather select group."[8]

The fateful decision to send the motorcade along Main Street and then in front of the Book Depository Building was somewhat preordained by the prior decision to make the Trade Mart the luncheon site. (If the Women's Building, in a different part of the city, had been selected, the motorcade would not have passed by the Depository Building.) Sorrels and Winston G. Lawson, a member of the White House Secret Service detail in Washington who acted as an advance agent for the Dallas trip, obviously could have come up with a different route from Love Field to the Trade Mart without passing by the Book Depository Building. But Main Street had always been the traditional parade route in Dallas (including for the only previous presidential visit, by President Roosevelt in 1936, which Sorrels, who joined the Service in 1923, had worked), and to reach the Trade Mart from Main Street, the most direct route is the Stemmons Freeway. And contrary to the allegations by conspiracy theorists, the only practical way for westbound traffic on Main Street to reach the northbound lanes of the Stemmons Freeway is by way of Elm Street past the Book Depository Building. Continuing on Main *past* Houston (instead of turning right on Houston to Elm) does not enable one to get on the Stemmons Freeway. An island separates Main from Elm at the Stemmons Freeway, and it extends beyond the freeway for the specific purpose of preventing drivers on Main Street from trying to get on the Stemmons Freeway by changing lanes across Elm Street (on the right) to do so. Dallas police officials were briefed on the parade route on November 15, and they agreed it was a proper one, not expressing a belief that any route might be better.[9]

But even if it could be shown that the Secret Service was responsible for the selection of the luncheon site and the motorcade route, the notion that the Secret Service was behind the assassination is, like virtually all the conspiracy theories, ridiculous on its face. What conceivable motive would the Secret Service have had? None. In fact, even if Secret

---

over the Women's Building, after visiting both buildings on the morning of November 13 Lawson told Behn that the Trade Mart had two security advantages over the Women's Building. Number one, the internal security system at the Mart barred entry to everyone other than lessees of commercial space at the building and their customers. Number two, there was no kitchen at the Women's Building, so the food would have to be brought in from the outside. (4 H 336–338, WCT Winston G. Lawson; 11 HSCA 517)

Service agents got away with it, it would only hurt their individual careers in the Secret Service that the president had been killed on their watch.*

Why, indeed, would an agency (or any member thereof) whose agents are literally trained to take a bullet themselves to protect the president want to murder him? As former Secret Service agent Dennis McCarthy writes in his book, *Protecting the President*, "Every minute of every day, agents are on duty protecting the President, both as an individual and as a symbol of the government that he leads." And part of their duty is to give their very life to save his, if necessary. All agents are trained, McCarthy says, "to put themselves between the President and the source of the shots," making themselves "as large a target as possible." A celebrated example was when John Hinckley attempted to assassinate President Ronald Reagan just after Reagan had exited the Hilton Hotel in Washington, D.C., on March 30, 1981. McCarthy writes, "The first shot was fired when Reagan was just three feet from the limousine door that Agent Tim McCarthy was holding open. Immediately, Tim turned in the direction of the shots, spread his arms and legs to protect the President, and took a bullet in the abdomen."[10]

In response to a series of questions submitted to him by J. Lee Rankin, general counsel for the Warren Commission, the then chief of the Secret Service, James J. Rowley, wrote that one of the "two general principles in emergencies involving the President" that the Secret Service has "consistently followed" is for agents "to place themselves between the President and any source of danger."[11]

Though it defies logic that the Secret Service was involved in the assassination, many conspiracy theorists don't agree. For instance, although he responsibly concludes that the Service was not involved, Walt Brown, in his book *Treachery in Dallas*, can't resist asking rhetorical questions like, "Why was a fifty-four year old Secret Service Agent the driver of the car? Why, since it was Dallas, did the head of the [Secret Service] White House Detail stay in Washington?"[12] (Hmm. Maybe the Secret Service was behind the assassination after all.) Conspiracy theorist Harrison Edward Livingstone, in his book *Killing the Truth*, has it all figured out. He writes that "Secret Service Agents close to the President who knew of some of his feminine liaisons resented it, sat in judgment of him, and cooperated with the plotters to kill him."[13] Livingstone, of course, does not, cannot, cite any source for his speculation other than his own very fertile imagination. It should be noted that Warren Commission assistant counsel Arlen Specter, who conducted the questioning of the Secret Service agents before the Commission and interviewed them beforehand, said that only Roy Kellerman (who he did not say showed any dislike for the president, only appeared "blasé") "did not seem to share the other agents' attachment to Kennedy," adding that William Greer "clearly felt deep affection for Kennedy, which I sensed had been reciprocal."[14] As Greer would later say, "He [the president] and I were pretty close friends. He treated me just wonderful."[15]

Only one book I'm aware of, Vincent Palamara's *Third Alternative—Survivor's Guilt: The Secret Service and the JFK Murder*, is devoted solely to the Secret Service's role in the case. From his exhaustive investigation, Palamara ends up finding the Secret Service guilty of incompetence, not complicity in the murder. Although Palamara seems honest and intel-

---

*The murder of Kennedy remains the only murder ever of a president who was under Secret Service protection.

ligent, and his 1993 book is reasonably well researched, I found it very difficult to read. It virtually has no discernible structure or organization, being a rambling and discursive, almost stream-of-consciousness exploration of the Secret Service's protection—or lack thereof—of the president, with no index or even page numbers. Yes, you heard me right. No page numbers. Although Palamara is "suspicious" of the conduct of three agents (Bill Greer, Emory Roberts, and mostly Floyd Boring—"Boring is interesting," Palamara writes), he seems to conclude, with no concrete evidence to support his conclusion, that his *Third Alternative* for the Secret Service's role in the assassination is not the guilt or innocence of the Service, but an "innocent" but intentional "security stripping test" by the Service to "test the President's security" that "unknowingly backfired into a full-blown assassination," for which, apparently, the Secret Service was defenseless. Among the many examples, he says, of the deliberate "security stripping": the railroad overpass was not cleared of people (Palamara does not say why the overpass should have been cleared of people as opposed to other areas, and ignores the fact that two Dallas police officers were assigned to be on top of the overpass); buildings along the motorcade route were not checked out;[*] there was no bubbletop on the limousine;[†] the Service went along with a route that necessitated a 120-degree turn at Houston and Elm that slowed the limousine down to a dangerous speed; and so on.[16]

Palamara, moving almost exclusively in the world of conspiracy theorists, resisted forfeiting his common sense for as long as he could as he proceeded reasonably well in his assassination research. But somewhere along the way he got off the bus and in 1997 declared, "It is now my strong belief, after shaking off years of equivocation, that several [Secret Service] agents *had* to have been involved in the actual assassination by getting wind of the impending threat and letting it happen."[17]

Palamara, naturally, welcomes whatever company he can get. And in an interview with the HSCA in 1978, John Marshall, the retired former special agent in charge of the Miami

---

[*]In 1963 it was not the practice of the Secret Service to check out, in advance, buildings along the routes a presidential motorcade took (HSCA Record 180-10074-10392, HSCA interview of Dallas SAC Forrest Sorrels on March 15, 1978, p.4; WR, p.664). James Rowley, the chief of the Service, told the Warren Commission, "Except for [an] inauguration or other parades involving foreign dignitaries accompanied by the president in Washington, it has not been the practice of the Secret Service to make surveys or checks of buildings along the route of a presidential motorcade . . . With the number of men available to the Secret Service and the time available, surveys of hundreds of buildings and thousands of windows is not practical . . . In accordance with its regular procedure, no survey or other check was made by the Secret Service, or by any other law enforcement agency at its request, of the Texas School Book Depository Building . . . prior to the time the president was shot." Rowley went on to say that since the assassination, "there has been a change in this regard." (5 H 467)

Interestingly, Forrest Sorrels recalls that while driving the motorcade route with Winston Lawson prior to the actual motorcade, when they turned from Main Street to Houston, Lawson "was startled to see the building facing us. He asked me what building it was and I told him it was the book warehouse" (HSCA Record 180-10074-10392, HSCA interview of Forrest Sorrels on March 15, 1978, p.4).

[†]Contrary to the suggestion of Palamara, and the belief of many, even if the bubbletop had been on the limousine it would not have prevented the assassination because, as noted earlier in the book, it was only a plastic shield at that time, furnishing protection only against inclement weather (WR, p.2; HSCA Report, p.183 note 2). The decision not to use the bubbletop was made at Love Field right after Air Force One landed there from Fort Worth. Secret Service agents wanted the bubbletop to be used because they were expecting rain, but Kennedy didn't want the bubbletop, and presidential assistant Bill Moyers, on the phone from Austin, Texas, told the Secret Service, "Get that God-damned bubble [top] off unless it's pouring rain." (HSCA Record 180-10078-10272, Deposition of Elizabeth Forsling Harris before HSCA on August 16, 1978, p.28)

Remarkably, although the FBI had a bulletproof car for its director in 1963, the Secret Service did not have the foresight or common sense to have one for the president of the United States (LBJ Record 177-10001-10237, Telephone conversation between LBJ and J. Edgar Hoover, November 29, 1963, pp.7–8).

Secret Service, told his interviewers that the Secret Service "could possibly have been involved in the assassination," though he had nothing specific to support his speculation. The HSCA interviewer wrote that "it is the first time that an agent has acknowledged the possibility that the Secret Service could have been involved."[18] Of course, as they say, "could have, schmood have."

And then, there's the inimitable Colonel L. Fletcher Prouty, whom you will meet later as an adviser to Oliver Stone on Stone's movie *JFK*. In the December 1999 edition of the magazine *Prevailing Winds*, Prouty asserts nakedly that on the day of the assassination "what happened to the Secret Service was not that the Secret Service didn't do their job. They were told: 'Your unit isn't needed, you can go home.'" But as conspiracy theorist Walt Brown responds, "Colonel Prouty, who are these Secret Service agents? Who was 'sent home' from Dallas before the motorcade? Are you suggesting that the White House detail was *not* there?"[19]

With respect to the argument made by Prouty and some other conspiracy theorists that the president's protection was so bad it must have been intentional, I have a question. If that reasoning has merit, why don't these same theorists allege that the Secret Service must have been complicit in the two attempted murders of Gerald Ford in 1975? In one of them, on September 5, 1975, former Charles Manson follower Lynette "Squeaky" Fromme, attired in a bright red robe and matching turban, no less,[*] was able to walk up to within two feet of Ford in a public park in Sacramento and pull out and point her .45 caliber Army Colt pistol at him before being thrown to the ground.

What makes the Secret Service's conduct even more egregiously incompetent in the Fromme-attempted assassination is that the Manson "Family" hated former president Nixon for declaring, in the middle of Manson's trial for the Tate-LaBianca murders, that Manson was guilty. Also, for his continuation of the Vietnam War. And they had taken to calling President Ford, "the new face of Nixon." After Manson was convicted of the murders he was incarcerated at San Quentin, but in October of 1974 was transferred to Folsom State Prison, fifteen miles west of Sacramento. Fromme moved to Sacramento to be near Manson and headed up the last remnants of the Family not behind bars. A few weeks before Ford came to Sacramento, Fromme and Sandra Good, a Family member, issued a communiqué to the media in Sacramento that "if Nixon's reality wearing a new face [i.e, Ford] continues to run this country against the law, your homes will be bloodier than the Tate-LaBianca homes and My Lai put together." I don't know how many other potential likely assassins of Ford there could have possibly been in Sacramento, but even without the Manson Family's feelings against him, I would think that Fromme and Good, being Manson Family members, would have been on the list of people in Sacramento that the Secret Service would be watching when Ford came to town, but they were not.[20]

Talk about being given a heads-up. On September 20, 1975, forty-five-year-old Sarah Jane Moore, a former FBI paid informant turned radical, called Inspector Jack O'Shea of the San Francisco Police Department and told him she was part of the protest movement in the city and was thinking of driving from San Francisco to Stanford University the following day to "test" the security system around President Ford when he spoke

[*]In his 1973 book, *20 Years in the Secret Service: My Life with Five Presidents*, Rufus W. Youngblood, one of sixteen Secret Service agents in the Dallas motorcade, writes that "as a Secret Service agent you are constantly on the alert for the individual who somehow does not fit" (Youngblood, *20 Years in the Secret Service*, p.12).

there. Moore implied, without expressly saying, that because of her state of mind, maybe O'Shea should put her in custody. O'Shea dispatched two officers to Moore's residence, where they arrested her on a misdemeanor charge of being in possession of an unloaded .44 caliber revolver. (Moore had many bullets in her residence.) The police confiscated the revolver and released Moore from custody, but O'Shea called the local office of the Secret Service that night to alert them to Moore's implied threat against President Ford and the fact she was found in possession of the revolver. The following day, September 21, the Secret Service interviewed Moore, ran a background check on her (which probably showed that she was, in fact, a former FBI informant) and, unbelievably, released her from custody, later saying that Moore was "not of sufficient protective interest to warrant surveillance during the President's visit," referring to Ford's visit the next day in San Francisco. This gross negligence is magnified by the fact that Fromme's attempt on Ford's life had taken place just sixteen days earlier. The following morning at eleven, Moore bought a .38 caliber Smith & Wesson revolver from a private seller, and four and a half hours later took a shot at Ford as he walked to his limousine after leaving the St. Francis Hotel. A former marine standing near her was able to push her arm down almost at the instant she pulled the trigger, causing the bullet to miss Ford.[21]

And then there was the attempted murder of President Reagan by John Hinckley, the son of a Denver oil executive, on March 30, 1981, behind the Hilton Hotel in Washington, D.C. The incompetence of the Secret Service enabled Hinckley, carrying a loaded .22 caliber gun, to position himself just ten feet from the president among TV camera crews and reporters assembled outside the back door of the hotel. Hinckley fired six shots at Reagan, one hitting the president in the chest. In emergency surgery, doctors removed the bullet from Reagan's left lung. Again, making the incompetence worse, three civilians in the crowd behind the hotel, including an AP reporter and Pinkerton detective, said they (but apparently not the Secret Service) had noticed Hinckley looking "fidgety, agitated," acting even "hostile" toward the reporters, and at times walking rapidly back and forth.[22]

The Fromme, Moore, and Hinkley cases are far more egregious examples of a lack of adequate Secret Service protection than the Kennedy assassination, yet the conspiracy theorists remain silent about them.

Although there is absolutely no evidence that the Secret Service was involved in the assassination, its performance left something to be desired, the HSCA concluding that "the Secret Service was deficient in the performance of its duties."[23] Warren Commission assistant counsel Arlen Specter put it better: "The Secret Service had the responsibility to protect the president and they did not protect the president."[24]* Among other things—although these failures almost assuredly did not contribute to what ultimately happened—the Protective Research Section (PRS) of the Secret Service, whose job it is to gather and evaluate information on people and groups who are thought to present some potential danger to the president and make sure it is usefully disseminated, did not forward on to the agents responsible for Kennedy's Dallas trip information it had on threats to the president's life for his November 2, 1963, trip to Chicago (which had been can-

---

*Fourteen months later, Gerald Behn, the special agent in charge of the White House's Secret Service detail at the time of the assassination, was demoted by Rowley. It is not known whether the demotion was related to the assassination, but a demotion right after the assassination would have been more likely to be construed that way, and if, indeed, Behn was demoted because of the assassination, this may have been the reason why Rowley waited over a year.

celed, but apparently for other reasons) or his November 18, 1963, trip to Miami (the Joseph Milteer threat [see later text], which the Secret Service learned of on November 12), actions the HSCA said should obviously have been taken.[25] Indeed, not only didn't the name Lee Harvey Oswald appear in any Secret Service file prior to November 22, 1963—there being no record that it even knew of his existence—but the PRS never gave the Secret Service detail traveling with the president the name of even one individual in its "trip file" for the entire Dallas area who might be considered dangerous![26] According to Secret Service agent Rufus Youngblood, that was because a search of PRS files "revealed that there were no *known* individuals in the Dallas area [which had a population of around 700,000] who posed a direct threat to the President."[27]

In a secret internal memo dated December 10, 1963, from FBI special agent J. H. Gale to Clyde Tolson, the number-two man at the bureau, in which he signed off on disciplinary action against thirteen FBI agents for their negligent pre-assassination handling of the case, Gale says that the FBI also never had Oswald's name on any list of people to check out and watch when Kennedy came to Dallas. He writes, "It is definitely felt that subject Oswald should have been on the Security Index (SI) based on the following facts." Gale sets forth eight facts, among which were Oswald's defection to Russia and his contact with the Soviet embassy in Mexico that September and October.[28] It is not the direct responsibility of the FBI to protect the president, but if Oswald had been on such an FBI Security Index, it would have been the responsibility of the FBI to furnish the information on Oswald to the PRS. The head of the PRS told the Warren Commission that the Secret Service had a standing request to all federal agencies to provide "any and all information that they may come in contact with that would indicate danger to the president."[29] And Sorrels said that if the FBI had informed him "that a defector to Russia was working along the motorcade route, I would have picked him up as part of the presidential protection."[30]

Then there was the now famous incident of nine Secret Service agents, four of whom were assigned to the motorcade route, having had beer and mixed drinks at the Fort Worth Press Club the night before the motorcade, the last one leaving at 2:00 a.m. Seven agents then proceeded to the Cellar Coffee House in Fort Worth, which served no intoxicating beverages. Most left by 3:00 a.m., but one remained until 5:00 a.m. In a later investigation, their supervisor advised that each of the agents reported for duty on time the next day, with full possession of his mental and physical capabilities.[31] Though "the use of intoxicating liquor of any kind, including beer and wine," by Secret Service agents "while they are in a travel status [with the president] is prohibited,"[32] Chief Rowley elected not to discipline the agents because it might give rise to the inference by others that this violation had contributed to the assassination, and he was convinced that this was not the case.[33]

Those who believe the Secret Service was involved in the assassination should almost be put in the same zany category as those who believe that maybe Jackie Kennedy or RFK was involved. The mainstream conspiracy community has never made the allegation of Secret Service complicity. For example, in perhaps the principal book propounding the conspiracy theory of the assassination, Anthony Summers's *Conspiracy*, the author doesn't devote one page, not even one paragraph or one sentence, to the possibility of the Secret Service being involved. (As to whether there were "Secret Service" agents on the grassy knoll, he says that they were not "authentic" agents.)[34] The idea is so outlandish that the Warren Commission couldn't force itself to ask the question of Secret Service complicity, but the HSCA did, and concluded that it found "no evidence of Secret Service complicity in the assassination."[35]

With respect to the issue of Oswald being a hit man for any U.S. intelligence agency such as the CIA, FBI, and Secret Service, there is, of course, no evidence of this whatsoever. One would think the conspiracy theorists, having failed abysmally to connect Oswald in any way to these intelligence agencies, would have their energy and enthusiasm drained. But they have remained undeterred and undaunted. Suggesting that the roots behind the assassination may have been in New Orleans, author Anthony Summers writes, "It may be that Oswald was at least—in the months before the assassination—one remove away from the formal structures of the intelligence community. In the world of intelligence, many operations are run through 'cut-outs,' buffer organizations or individuals whose sins can never formally be laid at the door of any agency or government. Thus, it *may* have been with Oswald in New Orleans."[36] And it also *may* be that since, after more than forty years of relentless searching, no one has ever come up with one iota of evidence connecting Oswald to any federal intelligence agency or even to any such "cut-out" buffer organization, the best course of action for those in the conspiracy community would be to just give up and find a new passion.

KGB

As the reader may have already inferred from the pages of this book and from simple common sense, none of the conspiracy theories make any sense. And among them, the theory that Oswald was acting at the behest of the KGB when he killed Kennedy, fueled in large part because Oswald was a Marxist who defected to the Soviet Union, is one of the very worst. As *Newsweek* pointed out in 1993, "Why risk nuclear war to replace a young hardliner with an old one?" And, "Khrushchev was trying to make peace with Kennedy in 1963, not kill him."[1]

Indeed, on the very day before the assassination, the National Council of Soviet-American Friendship was meeting in Washington, D.C., and a message from Khrushchev, written on November 19, was read to the council. Khrushchev observed "the 30th anniversary of the establishment of diplomatic relations between the United States and the U.S.S.R. Normalization of relations between our countries, associated with the name of a great American, President Franklin D. Roosevelt, was an historical landmark in developing relations between the Soviet and American people." He recalled "the grim years of World War Two when we fought together side by side against the common enemy, Hitler's Germany. The experience of the war years . . . shows that, despite the difference in our social systems, businesslike cooperation and friendly relations between the U.S.S.R. and United States are quite possible. Development of such cooperation on the basis of the principles of peaceful co-existence would meet the interests of people of our countries and would affect the entire international situation."[2]

And for his part, Kennedy gave no indication to Khrushchev by deed or word that he wanted to extend American hegemony throughout the world, and would therefore pose a threat to the Soviet Union. Kennedy's foreign policy was always containment, not military expansionism. He had a pluralistic view of the world that, Arthur Schlesinger Jr. writes, was a central thesis set forth by Kennedy to Khrushchev at their Vienna summit in June of 1961, a thesis "which implied that nations should be free to seek their own roads to salvation without upsetting the balance between the superpowers." The previous November, Schlesinger writes, Kennedy told an audience at the University of Washington "that the United States is neither omnipotent nor omniscient—that we are only 6 percent of the world's population—that we cannot impose our will upon the other 94 percent of mankind—that we cannot right every wrong or reverse each adversity—and that therefore there cannot be an American solution to every world problem."[3] So even if Khrushchev were irrational enough to want to murder any adversary he perceived as constituting a threat to the Soviet Union, why would he feel Kennedy was such a threat? He didn't. As Khrushchev said in a 1967 Moscow interview, "Although President Kennedy was young, he was obviously interested in finding ways to avoid conflict with the Soviet Union and somehow to solve those problems which might lead to war."[4]

There could be little question that after taking each other's measure when they met as leaders for the first time at the Vienna summit in 1961, Kennedy and Khrushchev, despite the bluster and veiled threats at the summit by both sides, had started to forge a special tie that eased cold war tensions. By the summer of 1963 the two leaders even established a "hot line" for instantaneous communication between them.[5]

Indeed, Khrushchev's main adversary at the time of Kennedy's death was not the United States, but China. Though both Communist nations wanted to turn the world Communistic, competition between them for leadership of the international Communist movement as well as disagreement on how to achieve world dominion (Khrushchev advocated a strategy that emphasized economic, diplomatic, and ideological means; Mao Tse-tung, the Chinese leader, was inclined to more violent revolutionary tactics and subversion) led to increasing and public acrimony between the two nations, Khrushchev fearing the Chinese position would heighten the risk of nuclear war with America.[*] While the Sino-Soviet split widened, it appeared that Kennedy was moving cautiously toward a possible detente with Russia, which Khrushchev welcomed. For instance, to the consternation of conservatives, on October 9, 1963, just a month and a half before the assassination, Kennedy approved the sale of $250 million worth of wheat to the Soviet Union when Khrushchev turned to America for help in feeding millions behind the Iron Curtain.[6]

If the Soviet Union were, in fact, behind the assassination, the mission would undoubtedly have been assigned to the KGB, its Secret Service. And as set forth earlier in this book, while Oswald was in the Soviet Union between 1959 and 1962, the KGB, rather than conspiring with Oswald, initially thought he might be an American intelligence agent, and even when that appeared unlikely, its agents followed him everywhere, including opening his mail and bugging his apartment in Minsk. Such conduct by the KGB really sounds as if it were in a conspiracy with Oswald to murder Kennedy, doesn't it?

The contents of the five-foot-long KGB file on Oswald, naturally, have been hard to come by. But on February 4, 1964, Yuriy (frequently spelled "Yuri") Ivanovich Nosenko, a thirty-six-year-old KGB agent, walked out of his room at the Hotel Rex in Geneva,

---

[*]In fact, at the time Khrushchev was ousted as Soviet premier on October 15, 1964, informed sources said that his constant rift with Peking (now Beijing), which gave every indication of heading toward a showdown, was the pivotal issue in his downfall. Not that the Soviet hierarchy wanted to get muscular with the West, but clearly China did not like Khrushchev, subjecting him to vitriolic personal attacks, and his successor, Leonid I. Brezhnev, a protégé of Khrushchev's, said even before he became premier that the Soviet-Sino split had to end. (*New York Times*, October 16, 1964, p.14; *New York Times*, October 17, 1964, p.1)

Switzerland, and, leaving a wife and two children behind in Russia and his suitcase in his hotel room, defected to the West by going to a CIA safehouse in Geneva. Nosenko had been listed as an "expert" on the Soviet delegation to the seventeen-nation disarmament conference in Geneva, but his actual function was to act as the KGB's watchdog over the rest of the Soviet delegation.[7] He had first approached American intelligence officers in Geneva when he was last there in June of 1962. Nosenko would eventually tell his CIA and FBI debriefers that as an agent in charge of KGB investigations of diplomats, journalists, tourists, and defectors from the United States (the American department of the internal counterintelligence service of the KGB), he was fully cognizant of the Oswald case. He said that he was one of the agents who had been assigned to Oswald and that he had looked at the KGB's entire five-volume file on Oswald. He assured his American inquisitors that Oswald was never a KGB operative and that the KGB believed Oswald to be "mentally unstable" and had no use for him.[8]

Nosenko ran into immediate credibility problems because Anatoliy Golitsyn, a KGB agent who had defected to the West in early 1962, got the ear of James Jesus Angleton, the CIA's legendary chief of counterintelligence whom David Atlee Phillips referred to as the "CIA's answer to the Delphic Oracle: seldom seen, but with an awesome reputation nurtured over the years by word of mouth and intermediaries padding out his office with pronouncements which we seldom professed to understand fully but accepted on faith anyway."[9]* KGB files would later reveal that Golitsyn, whom the KGB tried to discredit by falsely implicating him in contraband operations across the Finnish border, had betrayed a wide range of intelligence to the CIA, particularly on KGB methods of operation. However, he also fed Angleton and the CIA some unintentional misinformation that sprang from his paranoid tendencies—for example, that as part of the KGB's effort at global deception, the Sino-Soviet split and the Prague Spring in Czechoslovakia were merely charades to deceive the United States.[10]

Golitsyn convinced Angleton that Nosenko was a double agent and false defector who was part of a KGB disinformation effort to neutralize the CIA,† and that the KGB had already planted one of its agents "within the highest echelons of U.S. intelligence."[11] Golitsyn told Angleton that any subsequent KGB defector who vouched for Nosenko would also be a false defector, and indeed, Golitsyn said, any CIA officers who claimed to believe Nosenko's alleged bona fides could possibly be moles for the KGB.

Angleton, already a congenitally suspicious person who was notorious for believing the KGB was behind every tree, was particularly amenable to accepting the mole possibility. Harold "Kim" Philby, Angleton's counterpart as head of counterintelligence for the British SIS (Secret Intelligence Service), was a brilliant spy, someone whom a young Angleton, along with other OSS (Office of Strategic Services) agents during the Second World War, greatly admired, looked up to, and learned from. Angleton became a close friend of Philby's, but Philby turned out to be a double agent who had worked with a

---

*In what has to be one of the most interesting and, at least to me, funny lines ever to come out of the CIA's storied history, *the CIA director himself*, William Colby, after calling Angleton "supersensitive," had to confess that although he did not suspect Angleton and his staff of engaging in improper activities, he "just could not figure out what they were doing at all" (Colby and Forbath, *Honorable Men*, pp.334, 364). Colby would eventually fire Angleton, after the latter's thirty years with the agency. Author David Martin would say of Angleton that he fulfilled public fantasies of the master spy, looking and sounding like a character out of a Graham Greene or John le Carré novel. (Martin, *Wilderness of Mirrors*, photo section, pp.211–214).

†However, Angleton did not believe—nor is there any evidence that Golitsyn tried to convince him—that Oswald was acting under the control of the KGB when he killed Kennedy.

KGB case officer for years. The Cambridge-educated Philby was actually recruited as a Soviet spy in 1934, six years before he joined the SIS. Angleton would later say, "Looking back on it, Kim taught me a great deal. He taught me never to assume anything . . . Once I met Philby, the world of intelligence that had once interested me, consumed me." Philby's double-agent status was an intelligence disaster not only for London but also, though to a much lesser extent, for Washington, since at the time his duplicity was discovered in 1951, he was the SIS's liaison with the CIA in Washington (since 1949) and on the best of terms with intelligence officers, from CIA Director Allen Dulles on down, many of whom told him things over drinks they "regretted ever since." Remarkably, Philby was so iconic and politically connected in Britain that he was allowed to resign from the SIS and was not publicly denounced as a Russian spy until after he defected, in 1963, to the Soviet Union, where the Soviets eventually put his image on a stamp.[12] Philby, living a reasonably pleasant life in Russia with his American-born wife, Eleanor, was well protected by the KGB, who believed that the CIA might try to assassinate him if it could find him.[13]

In a book about Angleton, *Cold Warrior*, Tom Mangold writes, "For twelve years, from 1962 until 1974, the CIA conducted a civil war within its own corridors over Nosenko's bona fides. An issue that would normally have been settled within weeks by mature men became a decade of destructive battles which left Nosenko . . . abused to the point of torture,[*] the operations of the CIA's most important division effectively paralyzed, and the reputation of some of the agency's most senior officers destroyed . . . The CIA's entire top management was sucked into the battle. Neutrality was regarded with contempt."[14]

The internal conflict virtually tore the CIA in half, one side being led by Angleton, the other side, which accepted Nosenko's bona fides, by eventual CIA director William Colby. The latter group ultimately prevailed. In a September 1, 1978, letter to the HSCA, written on behalf of the director of Central Intelligence, Scott Breckenridge of the CIA's Office of Legislative Counsel wrote that "the final conclusion [of the CIA] was that [Nosenko] is a bona fide defector, a judgment that has been reinforced convincingly by 14 years of accumulated evidence." Breckenridge said that the CIA was "unable to resolve satisfactorily the question of his bona fides until well after the Warren Commission had completed its work."[15]

Indeed, if the old expression "put your money where your mouth is" applies to the CIA, it seems very clear that the prevailing powers that be at the CIA came to the conclusion that Nosenko was bona fide a lot earlier than 1978, when they merely reported their conclusion. Apparently, when Nosenko defected on February 4, 1964, he was promised $25,000 a year in compensation by the CIA for future services. But "no effort was made to fulfill the promise until 5 years after Nosenko's defection." The CIA told the HSCA that "*following acceptance of Nosenko's bona fides in late 1968*, an arrangement was

---

[*]Among other things, the CIA has acknowledged that Nosenko was confined (at one time, in a ten-by-ten-foot cell) at secure CIA locations from April 1964 through October 1967, during which time he was intermittently interrogated, was under "constant visual observation," and "did not have access to TV, radio or newspapers." Nosenko was in "solitary confinement" during this three-and-a-half-year period. (*Los Angeles Times*, March 8, 1976, p.1; ten-by-ten-foot cell: Gest, Shapiro, Bowermaster, and Geier, "JFK: The Untold Story of the Warren Commission," p.37). His contact with other people "was limited to Agency personnel from April 1964–December 1968" (12 HSCA 544–545). Richard Helms, the CIA deputy director of plans and CIA director during this period, wrote that "despite what has been reported in some of the literature, [Nosenko] was never drugged or subjected to any form of physical abuse, and was regularly examined by an Agency doctor" (Helms with Hood, *Look over My Shoulder*, p.243).

worked out whereby Nosenko was employed as an independent contractor for the CIA, effective March 1, 1969. His first contract called for him to be compensated at a rate of $16,500 a year. As of 1978 he is receiving $35,325 a year. In addition to regular, yearly compensation, in 1972 Nosenko was paid for the years 1964–1969 in the amount of $25,000 a year . . . He also received . . . for March 1964 through July 1973 amounts totaling $50,000 to aid in his resettlement in the private [sector]."[16]

Nosenko is not mentioned in the Warren Commission volumes. However, inasmuch as he defected in February of 1964, when the FBI was right in the middle of its assassination investigation, he naturally did not escape the attention of the bureau, which interviewed Nosenko twice in February and three times in March of 1964.[17] The FBI told the HSCA it had "no direct access to Nosenko from April 3, 1964, until April 3, 1969" (nearly all of which time Nosenko was in CIA custody), and that on October 1, 1968, four years after the Warren Commission concluded its investigation, it had advised the CIA that it "found no substantial basis to conclude that Nosenko was not a bona fide defector." The FBI further told the HSCA that "effective May 11, 1977, the FBI *and* CIA concurred that Nosenko was a bona fide defector" and it did not "perceive any credible evidence that Nosenko's defection was a Soviet ploy to mask Soviet governmental involvement in the assassination."[18]

Unlike the Warren Commission, which did not feel it had the capacity back in 1964 to determine Nosenko's bona fides (see endnote discussion), and despite the aforementioned CIA and FBI assurances, the HSCA made every effort to determine whether or not Nosenko was a bona fide defector, but eventually the committee threw up its arms and conceded it was "unable to resolve" this issue. The HSCA did conclude, however, that Nosenko was "an unreliable source of information about the assassination, or, more specifically, as to whether Oswald was ever contacted, or placed under surveillance, by the KGB."[19] But the matter of surveillance was conclusively put to rest by Norman Mailer's book, *Oswald's Tale*, published in 1995, in which Mailer was able to procure actual tapes and transcripts from the KGB's surveillance of Oswald. (See Oswald biography section.)

The reason why the HSCA concluded Nosenko was unreliable was that it caught him in too many inconsistencies. For example, Nosenko told the HSCA in 1978 that Oswald had been under extensive KGB surveillance, including mail interception, wiretapping, and physical observation. But in 1964 he told the CIA there had been no such surveillance. Nosenko also told the CIA in 1964 that Oswald never received any psychiatric examination in Moscow after his suicide attempt, but he told the HSCA in 1978 he had. The HSCA also tended to disbelieve Nosenko's claim that the KGB never had any direct contact with Oswald because it was not interested in him and never even bothered to interview him. Nosenko said that although the KGB was interested in the U-2 plane, the spy agency did not know that Oswald might have knowledge about the plane.[20] One clear piece of misinformation Nosenko gave the HSCA was that Oswald's phone in Minsk was "tapped,"[21] but Marina said they had no phone in their apartment in Minsk.[22]

Nosenko, when confronted by the HSCA with contradictions between what he had told the CIA and what he told the committee, said that the transcripts he was shown of the CIA interrogations were inaccurate (the tapes showed they were not) and that nothing he told the CIA prior to 1967 could be relied on because he had been drugged by the CIA.[23]

In any event, whatever dispute there is about the accuracy of several of Nosenko's statements about Oswald, and although there is a residue of disbelief among some to this day about his bona fides, subsequent events have strongly enhanced his credibility on his two main points, that he was not a KGB mole but a bona fide defector, and that Oswald was never a KGB operative.

In the wake of the failed, hard-line coup against Gorbachev in the late summer of 1991, when there was euphoria over the fall of Communism, there was a brief interlude of increased openness by the KGB, and ABC News *Nightline* correspondent Forrest Sawyer and senior producer Bob Haverill, after much lobbying on their part in Moscow, were allowed to look and take notes from, but not make copies of, Oswald's KGB file (No. 31451) for several hours one day in mid-September.

Valentin Kandurian, lieutenant colonel, KGB: "We are opening the door."

Sawyer: "The original material."

Kandurian: "The original, exactly, this is the original material."

Sawyer: "Is this everything?"

Kandurian: "Yes. This is it."

Of course, to an agency whose highest virtue is deception, Kandurian's assurances cannot be automatically accepted. However, Sawyer, for several reasons, was under the impression he was viewing the original file. "The reformers who are running the KGB have it not at all in their interest to protect the past. The file was voluminous. It was quite old. It was quite detailed and it was not self-contradictory, so if it was falsified, it had to be falsified, I think, sometime long ago, and the KGB never dreamed then that they would release their files. Finally, there is corroboration." Sawyer said that Nosenko, back in 1964, "claims to have seen the file" and Nosenko said "virtually the same things" he, Sawyer, had found in it.

One report in the file read, "Taking into account that the personality of the applicant [Oswald] is absolutely unclear to us and the fact that the first directorate of the KGB and counter-intelligence have no interest in Lee Harvey Oswald . . . he [was] refused citizenship." But because there was some suspicion that Oswald was an American intelligence agent, the KGB monitored his movements throughout Russia, code-naming its target, in a play on Lee Harvey, "Likhoi."[24]

The issue of Nosenko's credibility as a bona fide defector was virtually laid to rest by the publication, in 1999, of the book *The Sword and the Shield: The Mitrokhin Archive and the Secret History of the KGB* by British author Christopher Andrew and his coauthor Vasili Mitrokhin, who had worked for years in the foreign intelligence archives of the KGB. Before defecting to Britain through the British SIS in 1992, Mitrokhin spent over a decade making notes and transcripts of these highly classified files, which he smuggled out of the archives and kept beneath the floor in his dacha. Andrew had exclusive access to both Mitrokhin and his archive. Internal KGB documents provided by Mitrokhin showed that the KGB viewed Nosenko's defection as a serious setback, made every effort to discredit him after he defected, and added him to its list of "particularly dangerous traitors" to be assassinated abroad if the effort would not carry an unacceptable risk. In 1975, the KGB actually found a gangster willing to kill Nosenko for $100,000, but before the contract killer could earn his fee, he was arrested for other crimes.[25]

Vladimir Semichastny, the head of the KGB at the time of Oswald's defection to the Soviet Union, told NBC through an interpreter in 1993 that when Oswald first defected to the Soviet Union, the KGB took an interest in him. But "Oswald turned out to be a mediocre, uninteresting man. We had had high expectations of him as an informant, but nothing ever came of it. We soon learned we couldn't put any hopes on him. We realized that Oswald was a useless man. I was told at some point in time that he didn't like this country and was considering leaving. I told my workers immediately, 'Let him go. Try to keep him from changing his mind.'"[26] And Semichastny wasn't just saying this to an American audience thirty years after the assassination. In an internal 1963 KGB memo from Semichastny to the Central Committee of the Communist Party of the Soviet Union, he writes, "During the time of Oswald's stay in the USSR, and after he left our country, the Committee for State Security exhibited no interest in him."[27]

This impression of Oswald as useless, and the notion of the KGB using him in any way being a bad joke, was widespread. UPI correspondent Aline Mosby, who interviewed Oswald in Moscow in 1959, says that she had a strong impression that Oswald was "emotionally unbalanced, and wanted to be a 'big shot.' I quickly sized him up as a little nobody that the Russians would not be interested in. My impression was confirmed when they shipped him off to Minsk."[28] That Mosby was not engaging in post-assassination revisionism is established by the fact that in her *pre*-assassination book about her Moscow experience, *The View from No. 13 People's Street*, she was so unimpressed with Oswald she made no reference to him at all.[29]

Former FBI assistant director Cartha DeLoach told CNN on November 21, 1993, "The Russians have an excellent intelligence operation. And they wouldn't have dealt with Oswald. They wouldn't deal with someone who was mentally unbalanced. They just wouldn't do that." When Paul Roderick Gregory, a member of the Russian community in Dallas who got to know Oswald and Marina well, was asked whether Oswald might have been an agent of the Soviet Union, he responded, "If the Soviets wanted to get someone, they could get someone a lot more reliable. They would have a lot more sense than to get him."[30]

One of the most prevalent beliefs among conspiracy theorists is that the KGB may have recruited Oswald as an agent for the Soviets as far back as when he was a radar specialist at Atsugi air base in Japan.[31] But obviously, if the Soviets had, the very last thing they would have had him do is defect to their country. As a Marine radar specialist in Japan he may have eventually reached the point where he could have provided them with valuable classified information. By defecting to Russia and publicly speaking out against the United States, he would lose all possibility of ever being in a position to gain access to U.S. military information helpful to the Soviets.

The most recent revelations about Oswald in the Soviet Union occurred on August 5, 1999, when the National Archives released more than eighty pages of long-secret documents that Russia's president, Boris Yeltsin, gave to President Clinton as a gesture of friendship when the two met at the "Big 8" summit in Cologne, Germany, in June of 1999. (Clinton had requested the file from Yeltsin back in 1993, the thirtieth anniversary of JFK's death.) Among them was a November 26, 1963, internal memorandum stamped "Top Secret" and "Highest Priority" from the Soviet ambassador to the United States, Anatoly Dobrynin, dealing with the November 9, 1963, letter Oswald had sent to the Soviet embassy in Washington, D.C., the one he typed when he was at Ruth Paine's house visiting his wife and daughters. Dobrynin thought the letter was a fake. "This letter was clearly a provocation," Dobrynin says in the memo. "It gives the impression we had close ties with Oswald [in the letter, Oswald mentioned his visit with a KGB official at the Russian embassy in Mexico City when he was seeking a Russian visa] and were using him for some purposes of our own . . . The suspicion that the letter is a forgery is heightened by the fact it was typed, whereas the other letters the embassy had received from Oswald before were handwritten. One gets the definite impression that the letter was concocted by those who, judging from everything, are involved in the President's assassination. It is possible Oswald himself wrote the letter as it was dictated to him, in return for some promises, and then, as we know, he was simply bumped off after his usefulness had ended."

That same day, November 26, another one of the Yeltsin documents shows that the Soviet foreign minister, Andrei Gromyko, and KGB chairman, Vladimir Semichastny, sent a letter classified "Secret" to the Soviet Central Committee stating that

> the American Press is spreading various slanderous allegations about "connections" between Oswald and the Soviet Union and Cuba. Oswald, accused of assassinating the President of the USA J. Kennedy, was later killed under mysterious circumstances. Some representatives of the American press are trying to justify their insinuations [by] referring to the fact that Oswald had been in the Soviet Union from October, 1959 till June 1962 . . . After Oswald has been killed himself, the real face of those circles who are responsible for the killing of President Kennedy, and who are now trying to cover their tracks, is more evident . . . If American authorities contact the Soviet Embassy in Washington with a request to supply them with some information regarding Oswald's stay in the Soviet Union, they can be provided with a relevant document relating to it.

News of the death of Kennedy, who was widely hailed in the Russian media as an "outstanding American statesman" who was "striving for peace," was greeted by great shock and consternation. Grief was felt throughout the Russian leadership and people, including the satellite nations, with tributes and commentaries about the fallen president dominating the news and airways for days.[32] Church bells were tolled throughout the Soviet Union in memory of the fallen president. Even the KGB showed its respect, providing approximately twenty men who spoke English to handle duties in the immediate vicinity of the American embassy in Moscow to ensure that no disrespect was shown during this period.[33] Moscow Radio had interrupted a concert of classical music at 10:55 p.m. to report Kennedy's death, and played funeral music until it signed off at midnight.[34]

Since, in a dictatorship like the Soviet Union, there is strictly enforced censorship and the people can hardly form any opinion opposite of what they are allowed to hear, what is the likelihood that the Soviet Union would permit its people to have a favorable view of someone whom they did not like and intended to assassinate? This is why it is instructive that, as the *New York Times* reported, "in death Mr. Kennedy was praised and mourned in Moscow as no Western statesman before him had been . . . There could be no doubt about the depth of the feeling that the death had evoked among plain Soviet citizens." The *Times*'s Moscow bureau provided some representative quotes: "Here was a man who tried to do good, and they would not let him live." "What will U.S.-Soviet relations be in the future? Will the hope of peace be diminished?"[35] "Those wretches [referring to Kennedy's killer or killers]. In his own country! Wasn't he protected?"[36] The outpouring of emotion appeared second only to that in the United States. Premier and Mrs. Khrushchev sent personal messages of condolence to Mrs. Kennedy, and when Khrushchev and Foreign Minister Gromyko went to the residence of the U.S. ambassador in Moscow, Foy D. Kohler, on the morning after the assassination to pay their tribute and sign the condolence book, Gromyko "had tears in his eyes."[37] In a November 25 letter to President Johnson, Khrushchev said, "J.F. Kennedy's death is a grievous blow to all people for whom the cause of peace and Soviet-American cooperation is dear."[38]

TASS, the official Soviet press agency, in its first announcement about the assassination on November 23, was of the firm view that Kennedy had been killed by "extreme rightwing elements" in the United States.[39] On November 25, Moscow Radio stated its belief that the assassination "was a provocation by the Fascist forces and the reactionary circles who are madly resisting all steps leading to international relaxation. These are the elements that not only killed the U.S. President but strike at the interests of the U.S. people."

That this wasn't just for public consumption is the fact that documents in several internal KGB files enunciated the same belief. For instance, a December 1963 report from the deputy chairman of the KGB to the Central Committee reads, in part, "A reliable source . . . reported in late November that the real instigators of this criminal deed [assassination of Kennedy] were three leading oil magnates from the South of the USA—Richardson, Murchison and Hunt, all owners of major petroleum reserves in the southern states who have long been connected to pro-fascist and racist organizations in the South."[40]

The internal KGB documents further reflect the belief that Oswald was chosen as the assassin by the right wing because of his Russian-Marxist background so as to divert public attention away from the right wing and make the assassination appear to be the result of a Communist plot.[41]

According to a top-secret FBI document (because of the importance of this document, I'm excerpting substantial portions of it) declassified in 1996, a "source who has furnished reliable information in the past and who was *in Russia* on the date of the assassination" gave the FBI the following information on December 4, 1963: Officials of the Communist Party of the Soviet Union, the informant said, believed that the assassination was the result of

> some well-organized conspiracy on the part of the "ultraright" in the United States to effect a "coup." They seemed convinced that the assassination was not the deed of one man, but that it arose out of a carefully planned campaign in which several people played a part. They felt that those elements interested in utilizing the assassination and playing on anti-communist sentiments in the United States would then utilize this act to stop negotiations with the Soviet Union, attack Cuba and thereafter spread the war. As a result of these feelings, the Soviet Union immediately went into a state of national alert.

The document also says that "Soviet officials were fearful that without leadership, some irresponsible general in the United States might launch a missile at the Soviet Union." The declassified FBI document goes on to say that Soviet officials said that "Lee Harvey Oswald had no connection whatsoever with the Soviet Union. They described him as a neurotic maniac who was disloyal to his own country and everything else." The document quotes a second "reliable" source as saying that

> Nikolai T. Fedorenko, the Permanent Representative to the Soviet Mission to the United Nations, held a brief meeting with all diplomatic personnel employed at the Soviet Mission on November 23, 1963 [in New York City]. During this meeting, Fedorenko . . . stated that Kennedy's death was very much regretted by the Soviet Union and had caused considerable shock in Soviet Government circles. Fedorenko stated that the Soviet Union would have preferred to have had President Kennedy at the helm of the American Government. He added that President Kennedy had, to some degree, a mutual understanding with the Soviet Union, and had tried seri-

ously to improve relations between the United States and Russia. Fedorenko also added that little or nothing was known by the Soviet Government concerning President Lyndon Johnson and, as a result, the Soviet Government did not know what policies President Johnson would follow in the future regarding the Soviet Union.[*]

Since the Soviets didn't know what they could expect of Johnson, do those conspiracy theorists who actually believe the Soviet Union was behind Kennedy's assassination want us to believe that, in effect, the Soviets said, "Let's kill Kennedy so we can find out"? I'm being facetious, but only to demonstrate how inconceivable it would be for the Soviets to murder Kennedy when they would have no way of knowing if his successor would be worse than Kennedy, particularly when U.S.–Soviet relations under Kennedy were relatively good.

Perhaps more tellingly (since, as indicated, any Soviet plot to kill Kennedy would have to involve the KGB), this second source said that Colonel Boris Ivanov, "chief of the Soviet Committee for State Security (KGB) Residency in New York City" (presumably the Soviet embassy in New York City, most of whose officials could be expected to be KGB),

> held a meeting of KGB personnel on the morning of November 25, 1963. Ivanov informed those present that President Kennedy's death had posed a problem for the KGB and stated that it was necessary for all KGB employees to lend their efforts to solving the problem. Ivanov stated that it was his personal feeling that the assassination . . . had been planned by an organized group . . . [and] that it was therefore necessary *that the KGB ascertain* with the greatest possible speed *the true story surrounding President Kennedy's assassination.* Ivanov stated that the KGB was interested in knowing all the factors and all of the possible groups which might have worked behind the scenes to organize and plan this assassination.[42]

It really sounds as if the KGB and Khrushchev and the Soviet Union were behind the assassination after all, doesn't it? Along these same lines, we all know that before Gorbachev, the Soviet media, most prominently the Soviet newspapers *Pravda* and *Izvestia*, were simply a propaganda arm of the Communist Party and never published anything harmful to its interests. Indeed, *before* anything but routine, benign news was published, the Communist Party had to first clear it. Yet the September 28, 1964, edition of *Pravda* and the September 21, 1965, edition of *Izvestia* had large articles criticizing the Warren Commission's conclusion that there was no conspiracy in the Kennedy assassination.[43] Why would agents *(Pravda, Izvestia)* of the conspirators

---

[*]That this "reliable" informant seemed to have good information was corroborated by Thomas Hughes, the director of intelligence and research at the State Department, who sent a memo to Secretary of State Dean Rusk the day after the assassination setting forth what his office had picked up from its international sources. In addition to saying that "the Soviet Union and the Eastern European countries displayed the same sense of shock as the rest of the world at the assassination of President Kennedy" and that "Soviet media gave considerable and sympathetic coverage to the tragedy, including for the first time a Telstar transmission," he said that "at the same time there were signs of uncertainty about the course which President Johnson will follow" (WC Record 179-40005-10409, November 23, 1963).

What little the Soviets could have known of Johnson from his few public pronouncements could not have sounded, to them, too congenial to their interests. For instance, on June 2, 1960, in Washington, D.C., Johnson said, "Mr. Khrushchev does not understand that Americans of whatever their political creed—Republican or Democrat—will stand united against him in his effort to divide the country and weaken the hopes of freedom." And in Berlin, on August 19, 1961, he said, "The Communist dictatorship has the power temporarily to seal a border, but no tyranny can survive beyond the shadow of its own evil strength." (*New York Times*, November 24, 1963, p.7)

(Soviet Union, KGB) behind Kennedy's assassination want to criticize a report that concluded there was no evidence of a conspiracy? Wouldn't you think they'd want to remain as quiet as a painting on a wall?

Quite apart from the fact that no evidence has ever surfaced connecting the Soviet Union or KGB in any way with Kennedy's murder—and indeed, all the evidence points to the exact opposite—simple common sense, that rarest of attributes among conspiracy theorists, tells us the Soviets never would have sponsored Kennedy's assassination. And no one articulated this common sense better than Secretary of State Dean Rusk in his testimony before the Warren Commission.

Rusk: "I have not seen or heard of any scrap of evidence indicating that the Soviet Union had any desire to eliminate President Kennedy nor in any way participated in any such event. Standing back and trying to look at that question objectively despite the ideological differences between our two great systems, I can't see how it could be to the interest of the Soviet Union to make any such effort. Since I have become secretary of state I have seen no evidence of any policy of assassination of leaders of the free world on the part of the Soviets, and our intelligence community has not been able to furnish any evidence pointing in that direction. I am sure that I would have known about such bits of evidence had they existed but I also made inquiry myself to see whether there was such evidence, and received a negative reply. I do think that the Soviet Union, again objectively considered, has an interest in the correctness of state relations. This would be particularly true among the great powers, with which the major interests of the Soviet Union are directly engaged."

Warren Commission counsel: "Could you expand on that a little bit so that others than those who deal in that area might understand fully what you mean?"

Rusk: "Yes. I think that although there are grave differences between the Communist world and the free world, between the Soviet Union and other major powers, that even from their point of view there needs to be some shape and form to international relations, that it is not in their interest to have this world structure dissolve into complete anarchy, that great states and particularly nuclear powers have to be in a position to deal with each other, to transact business with each other, to try to meet problems with each other, and that requires the maintenance of correct relations and access to the leadership on all sides. I think also that although there had been grave differences between Chairman Khrushchev and President Kennedy, I think there were evidences of a certain mutual respect that had developed over some of the experiences, both good and bad, through which these two men had lived. I think both of them were aware of the fact that any chairman of the Soviet Union and any president of the United States necessarily bear somewhat special responsibility for the general peace of the world; indeed, without exaggeration, one could almost say the existence of the Northern Hemisphere in this nuclear age. So that it would be an act of rashness and madness for Soviet leaders to undertake such an action as an act of policy.* Because everything would have been put in jeopardy or at stake in connection with such an act. It has not been our impression that madness

---

*As Soviet premier Nikita Khrushchev said in a Teletyped letter to Washington at the height of the Cuban missile crisis in 1962, "Only lunatics or suicides, who themselves want to perish," would risk a nuclear war (Thomas, "Bobby at the Brink," p.56).

Few knew the character of the Russian bear as well as George Kennan, the American diplomat who studied the Soviet Union and its leadership for years. In his famous "Long Telegram" from the American embassy in Moscow in 1946 to his superiors at the State Department in Washington, D.C., he said, "Soviet power, unlike that of Hitlerite Germany is . . . not adventuristic . . . *It does not take unnecessary risks*" (Kennan, *Memoirs, 1925–1950*, p.557).

has characterized the actions of the Soviet leadership in recent years. I think also that it is relevant that people behind the Iron Curtain, including people in the Soviet Union and including officials in the Soviet Union, seem to be deeply affected by the death of President Kennedy. Their reactions were prompt, and I think genuine, of regret and sorrow. Mr. Khrushchev was the first to come to the embassy to sign the book of condolences. There were tears in the streets of Moscow. Moscow Radio spent a great deal of attention to these matters."[44]

In short, Russia had absolutely nothing to gain but much to lose in killing Kennedy.

Though Rusk's reasoning is impeccable and cannot be controverted, the Warren Commission did not rely alone on such common sense. As it stated (and the volumes of the Commission demonstrate), the Commission "examined all the known facts regarding Oswald's defection, residence in the Soviet Union, and return to the United States. At each step the Commission sought to determine whether there was any evidence which supported a conclusion that Soviet authorities may have directly or indirectly influenced Oswald's actions in assassinating the President,"[45] but it could not find any such evidence.[46] The HSCA, after its own thorough investigation, stated its belief that on the basis of the evidence it had seen, "the Soviet Government was not involved in the assassination of President Kennedy."[47]

Even were we to imagine the unimaginable, that the Soviets wanted to murder Kennedy, they obviously would have employed someone who was stable, not completely unstable like Oswald. Also, to distance themselves from the vile deed as much as possible, they would have chosen someone with no known previous contact or association with them, not a Marxist who had defected to their country just a few years earlier. With respect to this same issue of distancing, a foreigner in the Soviet Union, as Oswald was, cannot marry a Soviet citizen without the permission of the Soviet government.[48] If the KGB had any intention of using Oswald as its agent to kill Kennedy, it makes little sense that it would have allowed him to marry Marina *and* take her with him back to America. The KGB would know that having a Russian wife would most likely increase the probability of surveillance or interest in him by U.S. intelligence during the height of the cold war, which would not be beneficial to its plans. A Russian wife would even, necessarily, make Oswald more conspicuous to his neighbors (again, incompatible with its interests), and would even decrease his freedom of movement and mobility.[49]

Indeed, if the KGB did send Oswald, as a secret agent, to America in June of 1962 for the apparent purpose, as some conspiracy theorists would want us to believe, of assassinating Kennedy, would it have allowed him, right up through the summer of 1963, to draw attention to himself and continue to be openly Marxist (passing out pro-Castro leaflets on the streets of New Orleans and proclaiming his Marxism on New Orleans radio, etc.)? Such a proposition is too absurd to even comment on.

Right Wing

The initial belief, exemplified by an FBI Teletype, that the right wing in America, scalding angry at Kennedy for his pro–civil rights stance, was responsible for Kennedy's death
didn't last very long—the seventy-five minutes between the time of the assassination at
12:30 p.m. on November 22, 1963, and the arrest of Oswald, an avowed Marxist as the
only suspect, at 1:45 p.m. that day.[1]

Actually, at the beginning Kennedy was not a particularly aggressive advocate of
expanding civil rights in America. In fact, during the better part of his short presidency,
civil rights leaders like Martin Luther King frequently expressed their dissatisfaction with
the insufficient vigor with which they felt Kennedy was legislatively promoting their
agenda. He was, for example, completely silent on civil rights in his January 20, 1961,
inaugural speech.[2]* But civil rights have never been the sole concern of the nation's black

*Kennedy's brother RFK, the nation's attorney general, was always more outspoken and passionate about
civil rights than the president, turning the power of his office to the vigorous enforcement of civil rights laws
in the South after his original emphasis on organized crime.

From all I have read, it seems that JFK was much more easy-going and less intense than his younger brother,
Bobby, for whom the adjective "ruthless" was frequently used, and who had his severe detractors as well as
his even more dedicated followers. On the matter of RFK's being intense and passionate, syndicated columnist David Broder wrote, "His distinguished quality was his capacity for what can only be called moral outrage. 'That is unacceptable,' he said of many conditions that most of us accepted as inevitable—so long as we
and ours were spared their damage. Poverty, illiteracy, malnutrition, prejudice, crookedness, conniving—all
such accepted evils were a personal affront to him . . . He cared passionately about his family, his country, and
this world, and he was prepared to play his part in the drama of his times, no matter what it might be or what
it might cost" (David Broder, "The Legacy of Robert Kennedy," *Dallas Times Herald*, May 31, 1978). Tom
Billings, JFK's close friend, recalled that when RFK gave a stirring civil rights speech in May of 1961 at the
University of Georgia at Athens, JFK "wasn't too happy . . . He said it wouldn't do him any good to bring
that kind of civil rights talk directly into the heart of the South" (Beschloss, *Crisis Years*, p.304). On the other
hand, *Look* senior editor Laura Berquist wrote, "I first began trailing [Kennedy] in 1956, just after he'd
lost the nomination for Vice-President. Democratic insiders pooh-poohed his quest for the presidency as
impossible—he was too rich, too glamorous, had too much father . . . But in Columbia, South Carolina,

population. Certainly, for most of the disproportionate number of blacks living in poverty, their lowly economic condition is of perhaps even more immediate concern to them. And Kennedy had said eloquently in his speech that "if a free society cannot help the many who are poor, it cannot save the few who are rich." How much of a jump was it for a black man to conclude that someone who wanted to help the poor would also be mindful and protective of his civil rights? A 1962 national poll among blacks showed that next to Martin Luther King, John Kennedy was their favorite public figure,[3] and they took his death particularly hard. "When my father died," a black New York City cab-driver told the *New York Times* right after the assassination, "I didn't shed a tear until the funeral was almost over. When Mr. Kennedy died, I cried so much I couldn't drive this cab. I didn't know I could love a white man that much."[4]

One Kennedy biographer, Richard Reeves, attributed his lassitude about civil rights not to his being unsympathetic to the plight of blacks in America, but more to his being, at bottom, a politician, and polls showed that the majority of Americans wanted to proceed slowly in the area of civil rights, the nation's temperature for civil rights change being lukewarm at best. "For Kennedy, civil rights, Negro demands, were just politics, a volatile issue to be defused." Reeves also notes that Kennedy's blue-blood roots had not given him the knowledge and feelings about the deep suffering of many blacks in America that one with a more proletarian background might have. ("The only Negro he spent time with" for fourteen years prior to his becoming president, per Reeves, was his valet, George Thomas.)[5] As author Victor S. Navasky wrote, "The civil rights program of the new Administration was more limited than John Kennedy's campaign rhetoric would have suggested or than civil rights activists hoped."[6]

However, the aristocratic president, whose penchant for philosophy, poetry, and the arts made him beloved by the eastern intellectual cognoscenti, had an instinctual concern for the less fortunate, the natural extension of his patrician sense of *noblesse oblige*. In other words, Kennedy's heart was in the right place, and he did, finally, in a televised speech to the nation on the evening of June 11, 1963—two and a half years into his presidency—speak forcefully for the first time of the "moral crisis" in America of blacks not having the same rights as whites. He stated, "One hundred years of delay have passed since President Lincoln freed the slaves, yet their heirs, their grandsons, are not fully free. They are not yet freed from the bonds of injustice. They are not yet freed from social and economic oppression. And this nation, for all its hopes and all its boasts, will not be fully free until all its citizens are free." He said, "I am, therefore, asking the Congress to enact legislation giving all Americans the right to be served in facilities which are open to the public—hotels, restaurants, theaters, retail stores and similar establishments . . . I am also asking Congress to authorize the Federal Government to participate more fully in lawsuits designed to end segregation in public education."[7] "Kennedy was the first president," civil rights leader John Lewis observed, "to say the issue of race was a *moral* issue. That tied him to the black community forever."[8] Indeed, *Look* magazine observed, Kennedy "was the first President since Lincoln to marshal all his authority for the cause of the Negro."[9] Although Kennedy's speech was cobbled together almost at the last moment and contained repetition, even some ad lib by JFK, it was one of his very finest moments,

---

a conservative bastion, I heard him [Berquist doesn't give the year] speak out on civil rights with a ferocious, startling candor. I knew then he was better than the glamour image that dogged and often irked him" (Berquist, "John Fitzgerald Kennedy," p.35).

one of the most powerful and important (yet surprisingly unheralded) civil rights speeches ever given by a public figure.[*]

Even before June 11, 1963, however, as we saw earlier in this book, on September 30, 1962, Kennedy and his brother Robert, the attorney general, had dispatched U.S. marshals and troops to "Ole Miss," the University of Mississippi at Oxford, to escort a black, James Meredith, into the administration building to enroll (his fourth attempt) over the opposition of the segregationist governor, Ross Barnett, and rioters shouting, "Two-four-one-three, we hate Kennedy."

Although an interracial group of 230,000 Americans marched in Washington, D.C., on August 28, 1963,[†] to urge Congress to enact Kennedy's comprehensive civil rights legislation (the march was culminated by King's "I have a dream . . ." oration), the proposed legislation, which would be the most sweeping civil rights legislation since Reconstruction, was never enacted during the Kennedy presidency. That would have to wait until Kennedy's successor, ironically a southerner, shepherded through Congress the landmark Civil Rights Act of 1964 and the Voting Rights Act of 1965. But certainly, the seeds of racial equality and justice, brought to fruition during LBJ's presidency, had been planted very firmly during the Kennedy years, and it was said by many that the Civil Rights Act of 1964 was a "memorial" to the slain president.[‡]

---

[*]Because of the speech's importance, for those who are interested, most of its text appears in an endnote. What made the speech particularly remarkable is that, as indicated, it was prepared within just hours of its delivery, 8:00 p.m. EST. Earlier in the day, JFK had been watching television reruns of U.S. Deputy Attorney General Nicholas Katzenbach's encounter in 100-degree heat with the Alabama segregationist Governor George Wallace "at the schoolhouse door" of the University of Alabama at Tuscaloosa. Katzenbach was seeking the peaceful admission, pursuant to a court order, of two black students to the all-white university, and Wallace, who had campaigned for governor on the slogan of "segregation now, segregation tomorrow, segregation forever," refused to step aside. (Kennedy federalized the Alabama National Guard in the late morning and Wallace stepped aside only when an Alabama National Guard brigadier general, Henry Graham, confronted Wallace at the door in midafternoon and said, "Governor Wallace, it is my sad duty to inform you that the National Guard has been federalized. Please stand aside so that the order of the court may be accomplished.") Kennedy decided, "I want to go on television tonight." As late as one hour before the speech, Kennedy was asking his aides to help him with ideas and articulations for his address. (Reeves, *President Kennedy*, pp. 518–521; HSCA Report, p. 32)

Kennedy had already let the good folks of Alabama know that its segregationist philosophy did not sit well with him. Nothing is more important to Alabamians, even today, than the fortunes of their college football team at Tuscaloosa. And before the 1963 Orange Bowl in Miami, President Kennedy visited the locker room of the integrated Oklahoma Sooners. He did not visit Coach Bear Bryant's Crimson Tide, which was still all-white. (Will, "Eleven Men and Sic 'Em," p. 88)

[†]Kennedy tried to discourage Martin Luther King from holding the march, "fearing that it would lead to violence, looting and—more important—a mark against his Administration." Despite the entreaties of King and other civil rights leaders, Kennedy did not participate in the march. However, when the march, which was peaceful and did not ignite any violence, was over, he invited King and others to the White House "where he congratulated them—in private" (*Los Angeles Times*, November 22, 1993, p. A11).

[‡]Indeed, it went further than that. One of the biggest apparent misconceptions that has developed about the passage of these two acts is that they were pushed through Congress only by the strength of Johnson's personality and the deepness of his commitment. Neither Johnson's congressional magic nor his strong support for civil rights can be denied, but according to those who should know—the congressional leaders of both parties—this simply was not true. Though unquestionably the assassination speeded up the passage of Kennedy's legislative program (not just the civil rights bill, but the proposed tax cut to stimulate the economy, both of which were being delayed—the civil rights bill by the House Judiciary Committee, the tax-cut bill by the Senate Finance Committee), they say Kennedy's bill would have passed, with or without Johnson.

Among a plethora of Kennedy initiatives in the areas of mental illness, trade, mass transportation, juvenile delinquency, antipoverty (Kennedy started the movement to eradicate poverty in America three days before his assassination, calling it an "attack on poverty," Johnson changing the name to the "war on poverty"), the biggest ones at the moment of his death were his civil rights bill and tax reduction bill. Speaking primarily of these two bills, Senator Mike Mansfield (D-Mont.), the leader of the Senate majority, said in November of 1964, "The assassination made no real difference. Adoption of [Kennedy's] tax bill and the civil rights bill

Despite Kennedy's efforts to fog up their view, it was very clear to the nation's racists, primarily in the Ku Klux Klan–infested South, whose side he was on, and they of course developed a strong hatred for him. It wasn't just the conviction among racists and reactionaries that blacks were still chattels to be owned and used by the white man, but the abiding belief that any social measures to improve their lot would take this country in the inevitable direction of socialism and hence, in their mind, Communism. ("Integration is Communism inspired," Mississippi's Governor Ross Barnett charged.) In the middle of the cold war with Communist Russia, this was another reason for the Far Right's hatred of Kennedy. As if that were not enough, there was the fear among the radical Right that a progressive administration like Kennedy's would ultimately turn this nation over to the United Nations, a one-world government controlled, they believed, by international Jews.

The most powerful group in the Far Right during this period, claiming a membership of 100,000, was the John Birch Society. Headed by Robert Welch, the society advocated segregation, an invasion to liberate Cuba, and the abolition of foreign aid. The society's principal *bête noire* was Communism, and it kept files on "Comsymps," all those they suspected were Communists or Communist sympathizers. The Minutemen was a smaller paramilitary group of around 25,000 members who were training in camps around the country, preparing to provide armed resistance to what they predicted was an imminent Communist invasion. They had recently declared Dallas an "impregnable" city, vowing to trap the Reds in the desert surrounding Dallas with their "guerilleros."[10] The yet smaller Ku Klux Klan, with its murderous antipathy for blacks, only accepted into its ranks "loyal citizens born in the United States, Christian, white, with high morals, of the Protestant faith, believing in Americanism and the supremacy of the white race." All three of these groups, as well as religious groups like the Christian Anti-Communist Crusade, viewed Kennedy as a threat to America and its values, and actively fomented opposition and venom against him and his administration. This is why many of them rejoiced in his death. "Kennedy died a tyrant's death," Richard Ely, president of the ultraconservative Memphis Citizens Council, said after the assassination. "He encouraged integration, which has the support of Communism. He was a tyrant."[11]

With the heavy migration of southern blacks—who felt there had to be more to life than cotton, spirituals, and the Ku Klux Klan—to large northern cities disrupting the calcified social structure of these cities (with resultant riots), and the South continuing to resist integration in each and every public facility, the 1960s was a period of almost unparalleled civil strife between blacks and whites in America. Blacks, particularly in the South under the leadership of Martin Luther King, were demanding their share of the American dream, and white supremacists were not only resisting, but resorting to mur-

---

might have taken a little longer, but they would have been adopted." His counterpart in the Senate, Everett M. Dirksen (R-Ill.), said, "This program was on the way before November 22, 1963. Its time had come." In the House, Representative Carl Albert (D-Okla.), the leader of the House majority said, "The pressure behind this program had become so great that it would have been adopted in essentially the same form whether Kennedy lived or died." His counterpart, Representative Charles A. Hallek (R-Ind.), said, "The assassination made no difference. The program was already made."

The head of Kennedy's legislative team, Lawrence F. O'Brien, who carried on in the same capacity for Johnson, said, "If we were ever sure of anything, it was that the tax bill and the civil rights bill would be passed." (Wilson, "What Happened to the Kennedy Program?" pp.117–121; delay by House Judiciary Committee and Senate Finance Committee: Reeves, *President Kennedy*, p.658) Without slighting LBJ's considerable contributions in the least, it is hard to ignore the reality that LBJ was carrying out the vision and reform agenda of JFK.

der to prevent it, much of the violence occurring right in the months preceding Kennedy's assassination. On April 23, 1963, William L. Moore, a thirty-five-year-old white mailman and World War II veteran from Binghamton, New York, bearing a sign on his back urging equality for blacks, was shot to death along a remote stretch of highway near Colbran, Alabama. Moore, known for his "one-man marches," was on his way from Chattanooga, Tennessee, to Jackson, Mississippi, to deliver a letter (found on his body) to Governor Barnett, which said, "The white man cannot truly free himself until all men have their rights." On June 12, 1963, the descendant of a southern shareholding family, Byron De La Beckwith, shot and killed Medgar W. Evers, the secretary of the Mississippi NAACP, as he was walking in his driveway to the front door of his home in Jackson. And on September 15, 1963, in Birmingham, Alabama, four KKK members detonated a bomb at a black Baptist church, killing four young girls and injuring twenty parishioners. (The killings continued after Kennedy's death. For instance, on June 21, 1964, near Philadelphia, Mississippi, a deputy sheriff delivered three civil rights workers, two northern whites and a black Mississippian, to a squad of Ku Klux Klansmen, who gunned them to death.)

Though there had not yet been any murders in Dallas directly traceable to the civil rights movement, the city was widely perceived as being a hub of right-wing fanaticism. Among other things, it was the home of oil magnate H. L. Hunt, a Kennedy critic who funded conservative causes, and Major General Edwin A. Walker, a leader of the John Birch Society in Dallas whom Kennedy, as we saw earlier in this book, had relieved of his command in West Germany for distributing right-wing literature to his troops, prompting Walker to resign from the military.* Byron Skelton, a national Democratic committeeman from Texas concerned about the president's safety, wrote Attorney General Robert Kennedy seeking to dissuade his brother from coming to Texas. Indeed, as noted earlier, a month before the assassination, Adlai Stevenson had spoken in Dallas at a United Nations Day celebration, and leaving the auditorium was confronted by an angry mob of hecklers, one of whom crashed her sign down on top of his head, another expectorating on him. The next day, Stevenson spoke to Kennedy assistant Arthur Schlesinger about the "very ugly and frightening" atmosphere in Dallas and wondered whether the president should travel there.† But political considerations outweighed the fears. As previously indicated,

---

*Emblematic of right-wing extremism in parts of Dallas and the South prior to the assassination, Walker gave a speech to the Annual Leadership Conference of the White Citizens' Council of America in Jackson, Mississippi, a little less than a month before the tragedy in Dealey Plaza. A few excerpts: "The Kennedys have liquidated the government of the United States. It no longer exists. The nation has no government. The Constitution is well on the way to destruction . . . Ladies and gentlemen, your State Department is . . . well infiltrated with Communists . . . and it has been for a long time, Republican or Democrat, Eisenhower or Kennedy . . . The best definition I can find today for Communism is 'Kennedy liberalism,' or 'Kennedy socialism' . . . [Kennedy] is the greatest leader of the anti-Christ movement that we have had as a president of the United States . . . I have seen this country being sold out, lock, stock, and barrel by a bunch of sophisticated, professor, Harvard liberals . . . It's interesting that the Communists killed first the people that helped them in their revolution . . . So we've got something to look forward to, ladies and gentlemen [i.e., the Communists taking over and killing the Kennedys] . . . Now, I'm not a fanatic, but I do get mad and angry when the truth can't be told in this country. And I'm not an extremist either." Walker said that when people ask him why he went to Mississippi, his response is, "I'll go to Kalamazoo next or Alaska, if that's where the Russians and Communists want to enter next. It just happened that they entered Mississippi and then they entered Alabama." (Transcript of Walker's speech in Jackson, Mississippi, on October 25 or 26, 1963, published in the *Fourth Decade*, January 2001, pp.17–19, 21, 26–27)

†"Messages were crisscrossing this town [Dallas] that something was going to happen and the right wing was going to be blamed for it," General Walker would later recall to a Texas reporter. "I made sure I was out

in October, *Newsweek* reported that Kennedy's position on civil rights had cost him 3.5 million votes, and that no Democratic president had been so disliked in the South.[12]

It was amidst this highly charged and combustible atmosphere that Kennedy, trying to shore up his image in the South, came to Dallas on November 22, 1963, and the Far Right predictably greeted him with its vitriol. It started the previous day and continued throughout the morning of the assassination when five thousand throwaway handbills captioned "Wanted for Treason" were distributed on the streets of Dallas. As set forth in seven numbered paragraphs, among the many "treasonous activities against the United States" that Kennedy was wanted for was "turning the sovereignty of the U.S. over to the communist controlled United Nations," giving "support and encouragement to the Communist inspired racial riots," and appointing "Anti-Christians to Federal office."[13] The author of the handbill was one Robert A. Surrey, a business and political associate of retired General Walker.[14] Naturally, when Kennedy was shot, the instinctive reaction of a great many was that it must have been at the hands of his political enemy, the radical Right. Leftist Thomas G. Buchanan, perhaps hyperbolizing a bit, wrote that before Oswald's arrest, Kennedy's death "had been universally attributed to southern white-supremacy fanatics."[15]

And the immediate response of the FBI clearly illustrates its belief (before Oswald was arrested) that the Far Right was behind the assassination: agents called H. L. Hunt and told him that his and his family's lives would probably be threatened "as a result of the president's death," and urged him to leave town (Dallas) at once. Although the headstrong Hunt "objected strenuously," his chief of security, former FBI agent Paul Rothermel, ordered plane tickets for Hunt and his wife and they departed for Washington, D.C., Hunt saying that rather than go into hiding somewhere, "I believe I can do better going to Washington to help Lyndon. He's gonna need some help."[16] A Teletype from FBI headquarters in Washington, D.C., to all FBI field offices just over an hour after the shooting assumed that the right wing was responsible for Kennedy's murder, directing all field offices to "immediately establish whereabouts of . . . all known Klan and hate group members, known racial extremists . . . [who] may possibly have been involved."[17] And the Atlanta FBI office immediately "ascertained the whereabouts" of Joseph Milteer (see later text), J. B. Stoner, and Melvin Bruce, all prominent members of the militant Far Right.[18]

But today, even among conspiracy theorists, the belief that the Far Right was behind Kennedy's murder has not had, to use an entertainment term, legs. It has taken a backseat to the more popular theories about the mob, CIA, and military-industrial complex. In fact, some conspiracy books don't even bother to mention the right wing. But there continue to be conspiracy books that do mention it as a possible suspect in the assassination, and they usually focus their attention on Dallas multimillionaire H. L. Hunt or Georgia right-wing extremist Joseph Milteer.

Hunt, the founder and president of the Hunt Oil Company headquartered in Dallas, was the wealthiest and most powerful of all the big Texas oil barons. He was also eccentric, someone who, it was said, brought his lunch to work every day in a brown paper bag so he wouldn't have to buy it. He was so close with his money that he never left tips for waitresses, even when twelve people were at his table.[19] But like most people, he had pas-

---

of Dallas that day. It drove them [the authorities] crazy that I was in New Orleans, Oswald's old stomping ground. I was on a plane flying from New Orleans to Shreveport when the pilot announced that Kennedy had been killed. I've got the plane and everyone who was on it, if you want to check." Walker added, "They asked me if I wanted to cancel my speech that night, and I said 'Hell, no.'" (Cartwright, "Old Soldier," p.59)

sions, among which were having more than one wife (at one time), gambling, writing a torrent of letters to the editors of newspapers large and small throughout the country, and supporting conservative causes.

Terrified of the Communist threat, Hunt funded his pet, "LIFE LINE," a right-wing organization whose fifteen-minute radio broadcasts of Christian fundamentalism and political conservatism went out six days a week (the Sabbath broadcast was all religion) to 354 stations in the country. Though very conservative, "Hunt remained an independent" throughout the years,[20] and there's no evidence that he ever belonged to radical Right groups like the John Birch Society. His principal attack on Kennedy came during the presidential campaign of 1960 when Hunt, hoping LBJ would get the Democratic nomination, secretly funded the dissemination of two hundred thousand copies of a sermon by the Reverend W. A. Criswell of Dallas's First Baptist Church in which Criswell said that "the election of a Catholic as president would mean the end of religious freedom in America."

There being no evidence that Hunt had anything to do with the assassination,[*] the fringe conspiracy theorists postulate he had a motive, and to their way of thinking, if he had a motive this alone means he's guilty of the murder.

Hunt's motive, per the conspiracy theorists? In addition to Kennedy's pro–civil rights stance,[†] mainly his alleged desire to reduce the oil-depletion allowance.[21]

The oil-depletion allowance, dating in this country to the Revenue Act of 1916, was a recognition by Congress of the uniqueness of "extractive" industries, whose business literally requires the sale of its primary asset (in this case, oil). Other businesses, like manufacturing, obviously don't require this. Because their capital asset is depleted with every sale, Congress gave the oil and gas industries a substantial tax break. Since 1926, and through Kennedy's term of office, the tax break (oil-depletion allowance) exempted from taxation the first 27.5 percent of the gross income of oil and gas producers, with a limit of 50 percent of net income. Originally being at 5 percent, it was increased to 12.5, then 25, and finally, in 1926, to 27.5 percent. Indicative of the power of the oil and gas lobby, in 1963 the depletion allowance was 23 percent for sulfur and 15 percent for metal.[22]

What was Kennedy's position on the oil-depletion allowance? In response to an inquiry by Gerald C. Mann, the director of the Kennedy-Johnson 1960 Texas Democratic Campaign, on Kennedy's position vis-à-vis the allowance, Kennedy wrote in an October 13, 1960, letter to Mann that "I have consistently . . . made clear my recognition of the value and importance of the oil-depletion allowance. [It] has served us well . . . A healthy domestic oil industry is essential to national security."

---

[*]In desperation, the conspiracy theorists have tried (e.g., Shaw with Harris, *Cover-Up*, p.167) to connect Hunt to Kennedy's murder by pointing out that one of his sons, Nelson "Bunker" Hunt, admitted to the FBI that he contributed between two and three hundred dollars toward payment of the negative "Welcome Mr. Kennedy" advertisement in the *Dallas Morning News* on the morning of the assassination, which asked Kennedy twelve "why" questions (see earlier text) (CE 1885, 23 H 690, FBI interview of Nelson Bunker Hunt on May 15, 1964; CE 1031, 18 H 835). You see, Bunker was probably in on the conspiracy himself, and being so, he wanted to advertise his complicity by helping to pay for the advertisement. By the way, the advertisement was a reasonably dignified criticism of Kennedy's policies, which the ad suggested gave aid and comfort to international Communism. The ad was signed by one Bernard Weissman, "chairman" of the "American Fact-Finding Committee." Weissman had recently been discharged from the U.S. Army in Germany, where he and two men who served with him agreed to form a politically conservative organization when they returned to the states. (WR, p.295; 5 H 489–497, WCT Bernard Weissman)

[†]Although Hunt was a "social Darwinist" who believed minorities, like blacks, did not do well because they were innately less advantaged, he had no reputation for racial hatred, and certainly was no fanatic about keeping the black man down (Hurt, *Texas Rich*, pp.30–31).

Although there were unsuccessful congressional efforts to reduce the oil-depletion allowance in 1950, 1951, 1954, 1957, 1958, and 1960, at no time during Kennedy's term of office was there any publicized proposal or legislative effort to repeal or reduce the allowance. In the January 24, 1963, tax reduction ($13.6 billion) and reform package Kennedy presented to Congress, as the *New York Times* said, Kennedy "avoided a head-on fight over the controversial 27½ per cent depletion allowance for oil and gas producers." However, Kennedy, who had come to believe that the oil and gas titans had become too greedy, proposed changes in the capital gains tax as a part of his reform package that would generate an additional $300 million a year from the oil and gas people.[23] But by September 1963, seeing how the reform features of his tax bill were being diluted and eviscerated in the House Ways and Means Committee by congressmen beholden to big oil and other corporate interests that contributed to their campaigns, Kennedy told his secretary of the Treasury, C. Douglas Dillon, that he was dropping his reforms.[24]

But even if Kennedy had reduced or even eliminated the oil-depletion allowance, the notion that Hunt (and, per the conspiracy theorists, other big oilmen like Clint Murchison) would hire someone to kill Kennedy because of it is really too ridiculous to talk about—unless, of course, there is some evidence, which there is not.

Interestingly, in 1975 a copy of a handwritten letter dated November 8, 1963, and presumably signed by Oswald, was mailed anonymously from Mexico City to Texas conspiracy theorist Penn Jones.* The letter, to "Mr. Hunt," read as follows:

> I would like information concerding [*sic*] my position.
>
> I am asking only for information. I am suggesting that we discussed the matter fully before any steps are taken by me or anyone else.
>
> Thank you.
Lee Harvey Oswald[25]

If legitimate, which it was not, the letter would indeed be some evidence connecting Hunt to the assassination. In March of 1977, Jones turned a copy of the letter over to the *Dallas Morning News* for analysis. Three handwriting experts employed by the *News* concluded that the writing belonged to Oswald.[26] In 1978, the first hint of forgery emerged when handwriting experts from the HSCA said that although the "writing pattern" was "consistent" with other documents known to have been written by Oswald, the writing in this letter was suspicious because it was "much more precisely and much more carefully written." Also, the "H" in Harvey differed "significantly" from Oswald's handwriting. In other words, if it were a forgery, the forgers weren't real pros. The HSCA concluded that "we were unable to come to any firm conclusion regarding this particu-

---

*Accompanying the letter was a typed note in Spanish saying that the sender, who signed his name as "P.S.," had sent a copy of the letter to the FBI in late 1974 but had not heard back from the bureau. "Señor P.S.," as the sender became known, said that fearing what might happen to him, he intended to go into hiding for awhile, but left a return address of "Insurgentes Sud, No. 309, Mexico, Df, Mexico." Number 309 South Insurgentes in Mexico City at the time was a four-story white stone apartment building containing a number of lower-middle-class flats. On the first floor of the building were low-quality clothing stores and a shop that sold lottery tickets. Two other assassination researchers, Harold Weisberg and Howard Roffman, also received copies of the handwritten letter to Hunt in the mail. Each wrote letters to the Mexico City return address on the envelope, but received no answer, though their letters were not returned as undelivered. (*New York Times*, April 4, 1977, p.50)

lar document. It is suspicion [sic], although we are not able to accurately determine that it is specifically a forgery."[27]

For years no one knew for sure whether the letter was a forgery or not, and who "Mr. Hunt" was, although most of the conspiracy community assumed he was the Texas oil magnate. Both mysteries were cleared up in 1999 with the publication of the book *The Sword and the Shield* by Christopher Andrew and Vasili Mitrokhin. As indicated earlier, Mitrokhin was the former KGB agent who worked in the foreign intelligence archives of the KGB for almost thirty years and defected to Britain in 1992, taking a decade's accumulation of notes and transcripts with him. It turns out that the KGB, naturally eager to deflect the continuing suspicion of some that it was behind the assassination, and to promote the more popular theory that the CIA was responsible for Kennedy's murder, forged the letter, its addressee referring to E. Howard Hunt, the shadowy CIA officer who seemed to be part of so many CIA intrigues and whose name, in conspiracy literature, is sometimes confused with H. L. Hunt. Mitrokhin said that before the letter was sent to "three of the most active conspiracy buffs, . . . the forgery was twice checked for authenticity by the Third Department of the KGB's OTU (Operational Technical) Directorate."[28]

The allegation of right-wing responsibility for the assassination that has always carried the most serious implications is that involving Joseph Milteer, a sixty-one-year-old right-wing extremist. Having inherited enough money to make him independent, Milteer lived in a rundown mansion in Quitman, Georgia. He belonged to militantly conservative groups like the National States Rights Party, the White Citizens' Council, and the Dixie Klan. In October of 1963 he formed his own party, the obscure Constitutional American Parties of the U.S. in Valdosta, Georgia.

On November 9, 1963, William Somersett, a union organizer and former Ku Klux Klansman who had become a paid informant for the Intelligence Division of the Miami Police Department in 1962, but still retained close ties to the right-wing community, allowed the Miami police to set up a recorder in the broom closet of his Miami apartment and secretly tape a conversation with his old friend Milteer. If one selectively excerpts from the transcript of the conversation, as most conspiracy theorists have done,[*] it reads as if Milteer was definitely part of the conspiracy to kill Kennedy or had intimate knowledge of it, right down to the details. Here's an example, from Henry Hurt's *Reasonable Doubt*: "Milteer informed a 'friend' that the assassination of JFK was in the works. Milteer explained that Kennedy *would* be killed 'from an office building with a high-powered rifle.' He stated that 'they will pick up somebody within hours afterwards . . . just to throw the public off.'"[29] Sounds pretty cut and dried, right? But when we look at the entire portion of the transcript dealing with Kennedy, it's clear that Milteer really had no advance knowledge of any plot at all and was merely engaging in loose talk.

Somersett: "I don't know. I think Kennedy is coming here [Miami] on the 18th [November 18, 1963], or something like that, to make some kind of speech. I don't know what it is, but I imagine it will be on the TV and you can be on the look[out] for that. I think it is the 18th that he is supposed to be here for a speech. I don't know [what] it's supposed to be about."

[*]To their credit, Gary Shaw and Larry Harris, in *Cover-Up*, did not.

Milteer: "You can bet your bottom dollar he is going to have a lot to say about the Cubans. There are so many of them here."

Somersett: "Yes. Well, he will have a thousand bodyguards. Don't worry about that."

Milteer: "The more bodyguards he has, the more easier it is to get him."

(It should be noted that when anyone, in conversation, makes a reference to bodyguards, this frequently causes the person to whom he or she is talking to speculate about how effective the bodyguards can be in protecting the subject person. Indeed, the idea for the tape-recording session originated with an assistant to the local Florida state attorney, and as indicated, Miami police set the tape-recording up. So it seems clear that Somersett brought up the subject of bodyguards confident it would elicit a response from Milteer similar to what Milteer ended up saying. But that doesn't necessarily make Milteer's response incriminating.)

Somersett: "What?"

Milteer: "The more bodyguards he has, the easier it is to get him."

Somersett: "Well, *how* in the hell do you figure would be the best way to get him?"

Milteer: "From an office building with a high-powered rifle."

(So we see that Somersett has asked Milteer *how* Kennedy *could* be killed, and Milteer is simply answering how it could be done. Yet Henry Hurt, who read the same words you have just read, told his readers that Milteer informed Somersett "that Kennedy *would* be killed from an office building with a high-powered rifle."[30] It should be further noted that Milteer's observation as to how Kennedy could easily be killed by a high-powered rifle from an office building is one that many people had made, including the president himself. "[Kennedy] often talked about how easy it would be for somebody to shoot at him with a rifle from a high building."[31] Indeed, Forest Sorrels, head of the Dallas Secret Service office, said that when he was discussing with local authorities the route the president's motorcade should take through Dallas, he made the remark "that if someone wanted to get the president of the United States, he could do it with a high-powered rifle . . . from some building."[32])

Milteer: "How many people does he have going around looking just like him? Do you know about that?"

Somersett: "No, I never heard he had anybody."

Milteer: "He sure has got them."

Somersett: "He has?"

Milteer: "He has about fifteen. Whenever he goes anyplace . . . he knows he is a marked man."

(No one has ever said that as part of Kennedy's security there were Kennedy doubles wherever he went, much less fifteen of them. The fact that Milteer said this indicates that even if there were a conspiracy to kill Kennedy, Milteer was not an integral part of it.)

Somersett: "You think he knows he's a marked man?"

Milteer: "Sure he does. Sure does—yeah."

Somersett: "They are really going to try to kill him?"

Milteer: "Oh yeah, it is in the working. Brown, himself. *Brown is just as likely to get him as anybody*. He didn't say so, but he tried to get Martin Luther King."

(Although Milteer says that killing Kennedy "is in the working," he says this in response to a very leading question that Milteer buys into. Moreover, it is clear from the context that this is absolutely loose talk on Milteer's part. Milteer certainly is not saying that he is a party to any conspiracy to kill Kennedy, and Brown is going to be the hit man. He's merely speculating here that Brown would be a likely hit man. By the way, "Brown" is believed to be Jack Brown, at that time the Imperial Wizard of the Dixie Klan in Chattanooga, Tennessee.)[33]

Somersett: "He did?"
Milteer: "Oh yes. He followed him for miles and miles, and couldn't get close enough to him."
Somersett: "I never asked Brown about his business or anything, you know just what he told me, told us, you know. But after the conversation, and the way he talked to us, there is no question in my mind who knocked the church off in Birmingham, you can believe that, that is the way I figured it."
Milteer: "That is right, it is the only way you can figure it."
Somersett: "That is right."
Milteer: "Not being there, not knowing anything."

(Brown obviously fed Somersett and Milteer a line of hooey about Birmingham. Within days of the church bombing there, the FBI arrested four suspects, all members of the Ku Klux Klan, and these four, to this day, are the only ones believed to have been involved. None are named Brown. Their names are Robert E. "Dynamite Bob" Chambliss, Bobby Frank Cherry, Thomas Blanton Jr., and Herman Frank Cash.)[34]

Somersett: "But from his conversation, as you and me know him, but if they did, it is their business, like you say."
Milteer: "It is up to the individual."
Somersett: "That is right. They are individual operators, we don't want that within the party. Hitting this Kennedy is going to be a hard proposition, I tell you, I believe, you may have figured out a way to get him. You may have figured out the office building, and all that. I don't know how them Secret Service agents cover all them office buildings, or anywhere he is going. Do you know if they do that or not?"
Milteer: "Well, if they have any suspicions, they do that, of course. But without suspicion, chances are that they wouldn't. You take there in Washington, of course. It is the wrong time of year, but you take pleasant weather, he comes out on the veranda, there, and somebody could be in a hotel room across the way there, and pick him off just like—(fades out)."

(Since Kennedy was scheduled to come to Miami in nine days, and the tape-recorded conversation took place in Miami, it appears that Somersett's speculation was probably about Kennedy being killed in Miami, not Dallas. Yet Milteer responds about Washington, D.C., not Dallas. In any event, it's clearly just speculative, loose talk by Milteer.)

Somersett: "Is that right?"
Milteer: "Sure, disassemble a gun, get on out. You don't have to take a gun up there.

You can take it up in pieces, all those guns come knock[ed] down. You can take them apart . . ."

Somersett: "Boy, if that Kennedy gets shot, we have got to know where we are at. Because, you know, that will be a real shake, if they do that."

Milteer: "They wouldn't leave any stone unturned there, no way. They will pick up some-body within hours afterwards, if anything like that would happen, just to throw the public off."

(Henry Hurt didn't tell his readers that immediately after Milteer said, "They will pick up somebody within hours afterwards," his very next words were "*if* anything like that would happen," words clearly showing that Milteer was not saying Kennedy was about to be murdered, but rather, what would happen *if* he were.)[35]

Somersett: "Oh, somebody's going to have to go to jail, if he gets killed."
Milteer: "Just like that Bruno Hauptman in the Lindbergh case, you know."[36]

Such is the lifeblood of the conspiracy theorists' movement—deliberate (or terribly incompetent) distortion of the official record, the precise thing they all accuse the War-ren Commission of.

Miami police turned the transcript of the Somersett–Milteer conversation over to the Secret Service on November 12, and it was furnished to the Service's advance agents for the president's upcoming trip to Miami Beach on November 18. There is no indication that the Secret Service took Milteer's words seriously, although Special Agent Robert Jamison of the Miami Secret Service had Somersett call Milteer in Valdosta on Novem-ber 18, before Kennedy arrived in Miami that day, to verify Milteer was there, not in Miami. When Somersett verified he was and further advised the Secret Service that he did not know of any violence-prone associates of Milteer's in the Miami area, the Pro-tective Research Section of the Secret Service closed the case and didn't notify the Wash-ington, D.C., Secret Service detail in charge of the upcoming Dallas trip or the Secret Service in Dallas of Milteer's remarks.

In the late afternoon on the day after the assassination, Somersett met Milteer at the Union train station in Jacksonville, Florida, and journeyed with him to Columbia, South Carolina, to meet with four members of the Ku Klux Klan. With all of Milteer's clear speculation turning out to have actually occurred, it was easy for him to *now* sound as if he really knew. "Everything ran true to form," he said (not on tape) to Somersett during the train trip. "I guess you thought I was kidding you when I said he *would* be killed [as we have seen, this was not what Milteer had said] from a window with a high-powered rifle." When Somersett asked Milteer whether he had originally been guessing, Milteer replied, "I don't do any guessing."[37]

The HSCA investigated an allegation that two Dealey Plaza photographs, one by James Altgens, the other by Mark Bell, showed Milteer in the motorcade crowd, but three foren-sic anthropologists for the HSCA concluded the man was not Milteer. Among other things, the man in the photo was "substantially taller" (almost six inches) than Milteer, who was five feet four inches.[38] To the allegation that Milteer called a friend *from* Dallas on the morning of the assassination, the HSCA said it "could find no evidence that Mil-teer was *in* Dallas on the day of the assassination."[39]

The FBI interviewed Milteer[*] and investigated the entire Milteer story, concluding he was not a suspect in the assassination.[40] And the HSCA, conducting its own investigation, was unable to find any connection between Milteer's statements and the assassination. Indeed, a thorough HSCA investigation found no connection between any of Milteer's associates and Oswald or Ruby, or with any of the latters' associates.[41]

The Milteer tape story first surfaced publicly in an article by reporter Bill Barry in the *Miami News* on February 2, 1967. Milteer died in February of 1974.

The argument that the right wing was behind Kennedy's assassination suffers, like all other conspiracy theories, from the inconvenient and stubborn reality that there is no evidence of its involvement. Moreover, since we know Oswald killed Kennedy, the only way for right wingers to have been involved in the assassination would be if they had gotten Oswald to kill Kennedy for them. But why would the Far Right even think that an avowed Marxist (someone, by the way, who just five months earlier had attempted to murder one of its own, right-wing icon Major General Edwin Walker) would be willing to murder someone whom the right wing viewed as very liberal? Indeed, why would Oswald, who detested the Far Right, even think of doing its bidding?

Parenthetically, if the Far Right had decided to kill Kennedy, it is hard to believe they would have picked Dallas, a roiling center of ultraconservative activity, as the locus for the assassination, for they would have to know that such a locus would immediately attract suspicion to them, which is precisely what happened prior to Oswald's arrest. It is also very hard to believe that liberals on the Warren Commission and its staff, like Chief Justice Warren and Assistant Counsel Norman Redlich, would cover up the assassination (as almost all conspiracy theorists believe they did) for the Far Right.

---

[*]The FBI report of the interview on November 27, 1963, says that "Milteer emphatically denies ever making threats to assassinate President Kennedy or participating in any such assassination. He stated he has never heard anyone make such threats . . . He stated he does not know, nor has he ever been in the presence of Lee Harvey Oswald or Jack Ruby" (CD 20, p.1, December 1, 1963).

LBJ

Because LBJ, above all others, profited the most from the assassination of Kennedy, a death that enabled him to achieve his lifetime goal, many in the conspiracy community have always suspected his involvement in the alleged plot. And according to a 2003 Gallup Poll, an astonishing 18 percent of Americans, nearly one out of every five people, also suspect him of being involved.[1] The rumor that Kennedy was going to replace Johnson—weakened by the burgeoning bribery and influence-peddling scandal involving his Senate aide and friend Bobby Baker—on the 1964 ticket has served to fortify these suspicions. Indeed, an article in the *Dallas Morning News* on the day of the assassination was captioned "Nixon Predicts JFK May Drop Johnson."

It is curious how this rumor gained traction when just a little over three weeks earlier, Kennedy had said he wanted LBJ to run with him again. At an October 31 news conference, a reporter, referring to "talk that Lyndon B. Johnson would be dumped next year," asked the president if he wanted Mr. Johnson on the ticket and if he expected that he would be on the ticket. "Yes to both those questions," the president said, "That's correct."[2]

Arthur Schlesinger, a member of Kennedy's inner circle and later a chronicler of the Kennedy presidency, called the belief that Kennedy would jettison Johnson "wholly fanciful. Kennedy . . . considered [Johnson] able and loyal. In addition, if Goldwater was to be the Republican candidate, the Democrats needed every possible asset in the South." Within the Kennedy administration at the time of the assassination, "Johnson's renomination" was "assumed."[3] The president told a confidant in October of 1963 that the idea of dumping Johnson was "preposterous on the face of it. We've got to carry Texas in '64 and maybe Georgia."[4] And in April of 1964, Robert F. Kennedy said that there had been no intention of dropping Johnson from the ticket.[5]

It has also been alleged (certainly true) that Johnson, the Texas hillbilly with the boorish manners and pedestrian education (who also happened to be extraordinarily complex and talented), was never comfortable in a presidential administration dominated by Ivy

League intellectuals, many with bluish blood coursing through them. He deeply resented their poorly veiled condescension toward him and being the butt of their jokes,[*] cementing the view, in the eyes of conspiracy theorists, that Johnson just *had* to be, in some way, complicit in the tragedy of Dealey Plaza.

It cannot be disputed that Johnson achieved much enduring good during his presidency and had some good and honorable qualities to his makeup. I find it difficult to believe that men of substance and unquestionable character like Bill Moyers would have devoted their energies so wholeheartedly to his service if he did not. But he was also a carnivorous political animal who crossed moral and ethical lines from time to time in his ascent to power. Acclaimed biographies of LBJ, such as Robert A. Caro's three volumes (*Path to Power* in 1982, *Means of Ascent* in 1990, and *Master of the Senate* in 2002), eliminate all doubt as to this point. Robert Dallek captured the essence of Johnson well in the two-word title to his LBJ biography: *Flawed Giant*. In 1978, when Tom Snyder on the *Tomorrow Show* asked LBJ friend and respected confidant Jack Valenti, "Was Lyndon Johnson an honest man?" Valenti smiled and answered wryly, "He was an honest man except when honesty didn't suit the situation."[6]

I guess it all started with LBJ's highly controversial runoff win over Texas governor Coke Stevenson in the 1948 Democratic primary for the U.S. Senate. Johnson had supposedly lost by 113 votes until a "corrected" vote came in from the now infamous Precinct 13 ballot box in Alice, Texas, giving Johnson 202 additional votes and Stevenson only 1. "Landslide Lyndon" defeated Stevenson by 87 votes statewide, and the suspicion of fraud, and LBJ's complicity or knowledge therein, was immediate.[7] Indeed, the subtitle of J. Evetts Haley's 1964 book, *A Texan Looks at Lyndon*, is *A Study in Illegitimate Power*. However, the notion that LBJ would actually decide to have Kennedy murdered (or be a

---

[*]JFK biographer Richard Reeves writes that "more than once the President had chewed out his own people for making fun of Johnson" (Reeves, *President Kennedy*, p.118). Sam Houston Johnson, LBJ's brother, wrote in his book that the Kennedy people made his brother's stay in the vice presidency "the most miserable three years of his life. He wasn't the number two man in the administration; he was the lowest man on the totem pole . . . I know him well enough to know he felt humiliated time and time again, that he was openly snubbed by second-echelon White House staffers who snickered at him behind his back and called him 'Uncle Cornpone'" (Johnson, *My Brother Lyndon*, p.108). And at the center of it all, LBJ believed, was RFK, whom he disliked not just for Bobby's notorious brusqueness (LBJ, coarse in his own right, was nonetheless a highly sensitive soul), but for his lack of respect for him. Bobby rarely invited Johnson to the frequent social gatherings of the Kennedy clan and administration at his Hickory Hill estate in McLean, Virginia. Johnson was particularly resentful of Bobby's access to the president. "Every time they have a conference," LBJ complained to a reporter for the Associated Press, "don't tell me about who is the top adviser. It isn't McNamara, the chief of staff, or anybody like that. Bobby is first in, last out. And Bobby is the boy he [JFK] listens to." (Shesol, *Mutual Contempt*, pp.107–110)

On the other hand, though LBJ's and RFK's animus for each other was mutual and well known ("[Robert] Kennedy's hatred of LBJ was . . . primitive and unreasoning" [Thomas, *Robert Kennedy*, p.292]), it is not clear that there was hostility between Johnson and the president himself, as opposed to the president's staff. Indeed, JFK assistant and historian Arthur Schlesinger Jr., who should know, says, "John Kennedy always had a certain fondness for Lyndon Johnson. He saw his Vice President, with perhaps the merest touch of condescension, as an American original, a figure out of Mark Twain . . . The President, Ben Bradlee observed in 1963, 'really likes his roguish qualities, respects him enormously as a political operator.'" And a prominent political analyst at the time, William S. White, said that LBJ "had a cordial relationship with President Kennedy." How did LBJ feel about Kennedy? Schlesinger says Johnson told Dean Rusk, "He's done much better by me than I would have done by him under the same circumstances. Kennedy always treated me fairly and considerately." (Schlesinger, *Robert Kennedy and His Times*, pp.621–622; William White observation: NBC News, *Seventy Hours and Thirty Minutes*, p.107) And LBJ was under the impression that JFK "likes me," but knew that RFK did not (Thomas, *Robert Kennedy*, p.278).

party to such a plot by others) is not one that, to my knowledge, any rational and sensible student of the assassination has ever entertained for a moment.

But conspiracy theorists are not rational and sensible when it comes to the Kennedy assassination. The first conspiracy author to accuse Johnson of complicity in a book was the German-born American Communist Joachim Joesten, who wrote in his 1968 *Dark Side of Lyndon Baines Johnson* that there was a "grand conspiracy to kill the President of the United States . . . It was an all-American plot in which Lyndon B. Johnson, acting in cahoots with the Dallas oligarchy and with the local branches of the CIA, the FBI, and the Secret Service, played the leading part."[8]

Joesten spawned many successors. "Students of the assassination cannot discount the idea that Johnson, in some way, played a role in the Dallas tragedy," writes conspiracy theorist Jim Marrs in *Crossfire.*[9] "Lyndon Johnson" is one of the "prime suspects in the JFK assassination," Ralph D. Thomas says in his book *Missing Links in the JFK Assassination Conspiracy.*[10] The evidence suggests, conspiracy theorists J. Gary Shaw and Larry Harris write in their book *Cover-Up*, that Johnson "might have had prior knowledge of the assassination" or that "he might have made an agreement to protect Kennedy's killers."[11] "It is now very easy to suspect that a mutuality of purpose between LBJ and powerful sources in Texas . . . had much to do with the behind-the-scenes doings that led to the gunfire in Dealey Plaza," says Walt Brown in his book *Treachery in Dallas*. Johnson knew, Brown says, that his political life "depended on John Kennedy's political death."[12] Conspiracy author Noel Twyman writes in *Bloody Treason*, "Recognizing that Lyndon Johnson was part of the conspiracy to assassinate John F. Kennedy is something that I have come to reluctantly."[13] The outrageous lawyer-author Barr McClellan says, "Stated simply, LBJ killed JFK."[14] New Orleans DA Jim Garrison also weighed in on this point. In a speech on November 14, 1967, before the Radio and Television News Association of Southern California in Los Angeles, he accused LBJ of exerting pressure on state officials not to extradite witnesses in Garrison's investigation and of concealing evidence from the American people. The fact, Garrison said, that Johnson "has profited from the assassination more than any other man makes it imperative that he see that the evidence is released so that we can know that he is not involved."[15]

A contention of some conspiracy theorists is that Johnson "lured" Kennedy into coming to Texas, the implication being that he was part of a conspiracy to kill Kennedy. But *U.S. News & World Report*, whose comprehensive coverage of the assassination through the years has stood out, investigated this issue by interviewing several witnesses who would know, and found that actually Johnson was "against" JFK's trip to Texas.[16]

Although conspiracy theorists never require any evidence as a condition precedent to their imputing guilt to some person or group in Kennedy's murder—motive or *cui bono* (who gained?) is always enough—they obviously are overjoyed when they actually come up with evidence that supports their theory. But as is the situation with every other conspiracy theory, the LBJ-did-it devotees are hard-pressed to come up with anything. However, they do have some arrows in their quiver. How about Jean Hill (the witness, the reader will recall from earlier in the book, who, after twenty-three years, suddenly remembered seeing a gunman behind the picket fence firing at Kennedy) telling conspiracy researchers, "Isn't it odd that the Vice President crouched down before the first shot?"[17] Not only is there no evidence that Johnson had crouched down, but if Johnson had, he must not have had too much confidence in the hit man he and his group allegedly hired to kill Kennedy, since Johnson's limousine was two cars behind the president's car.

Then we have in many conspiracy books a statement like the following from Craig Zirbel's *Texas Connection*: "Before Kennedy was buried, Johnson ordered the assassination limousine . . . to be shipped to Detroit for complete refurbishing." Zirbel, an Arizona lawyer, says that this is "the deliberate destruction of evidence" by the "prime suspect."[18] What citation of authority does Zirbel give for Johnson's alleged order? As is perhaps the favorite tradition of the conspiracy community, he simply cites another conspiracy theorist as his authority, in this case, Jim Marrs and his book *Crossfire*. Marrs says, "Within seventy-two hours of Kennedy's death—at Johnson's order—the Presidential limousine . . . was shipped to Detroit where the body was replaced and the interior completely refurbished."[19] Of course, Marrs doesn't bother to cite any authority for this information either. Penn Jones Jr., the conspiracy theorist who started the "mysterious deaths" allegation that survives, even though it is pure nonsense, to this very day, was perhaps the first theorist to allege (again, without any citation of authority) that right after the assassination, Johnson ordered that the car be completely refurbished, a "blatant act of destruction of evidence," he cried.[20]

This argument by the critics has no demonstrable merit. Not only couldn't I find any documentation that Johnson personally ordered that the limousine be rebuilt, but before the limousine was sent back to Detroit, where it was manufactured, FBI and Secret Service agents examined and photographed the car in great detail at the White House garage in Washington, D.C., on the evening of November 22 through the early morning hours of November 23, and removed every piece of conceivable evidence from it.[21] More important, the limousine was not, as the buffs allege without any supporting authority, immediately rebuilt. The rebuilding of the car did not commence until over a year later in Detroit, and it wasn't complete until May 11, 1964, a year and a half after the assassination.[22]

But don't despair. The theorists have more evidence against LBJ. According to Craig Zirbel in his *Texas Connection*, Texas senator Ralph Yarborough, who was in LBJ's car in the motorcade, told someone (Zirbel doesn't say whom) that at the exact time of the assassination Johnson had his ear up against a small walkie-talkie, listening to the device, which was "turned down real low." Yarborough had a reputation for sometimes being a little flaky in his observations and positions, but I have been unable to find his saying this in any of the statements he has made about the assassination. And, as before, Zirbel neither quotes a source nor cites a document.[23]* Nor did Johnson or any of the other occupants of the car ever say this in their testimony or affidavits to the Warren Commission. But if Johnson were, indeed, listening to a walkie-talkie "turned down real low" moments before the assassination, it wouldn't surprise me. He obviously had to be in last-minute radio

---

*Conspiracy researcher Vincent Palamara makes the same allegation as Zirbel, stating that Yarborough said that Secret Service agent Rufus W. Youngblood "and LBJ were listening to a walkie-talkie with the volume set too low for the Senator to hear what they were picking up" and that presidential assistant Dave Powers "agreed with Yarborough" (Vince Palamara, "The 'Breakdown' of the Infrastructure of the Secret Service on November 22, 1963," *Fourth Decade*, September 1997, p.20). And Palamara, as opposed to Zirbel, does give a source, but the source he gives doesn't support what he says. Palamara's source, page 166 of *The Death of a President* by William Manchester, reads, "According to Johnson, Rufus Youngblood hurled him to the floor before the fatal shot. Youngblood himself doubts that he moved that quickly. Ralph Yarborough goes further: he insists that Youngblood never left the front seat. It is the Senator's recollection that the agent merely leaned over the seat and talked to Johnson in an undertone. He contends that there was insufficient space in the rear for Youngblood. Dave Powers, who glanced back, confirms the Senator." Where Palamara gets his "listening to a walkie-talkie" from this quote, I don't know.

contact with his man in the sixth-floor window and the other shooters who were about to get Kennedy in a triangulation of fire. If any reader thinks it's silly for me to be writing about such silliness, I must remind him or her that this silliness is what *all of* the conspiracy allegations are about, the same silliness that has caused most of the American people to believe Kennedy was killed as a result of a high-level conspiracy, and the same silliness that has prompted the writing of this book.

Perhaps the crown jewel in the tiara of allegations by conspiracy theorists that LBJ was behind Kennedy's murder is the statement of his alleged mistress, Madeleine Brown, that the night before the assassination, Johnson, in so many words, admitted his guilt. In her 1997 book, *Texas in the Morning: The Love Story of Madeleine Brown and President Lyndon Baines Johnson*, the attractive redhead, an advertising account executive who associated with a crowd in Austin and Dallas of easy circumstances, and clearly knew most of the political players in the Democratic Party, describes her passionate romance with the then congressman, commencing in 1948 while she was separated from her husband, and continuing on into his presidency. She said she had a son, Steven (who died of lymphatic cancer in 1990), by LBJ, and the son does bear a resemblance to the former president.[*] Yet she is unable to offer any letter or document to substantiate her claim of a relationship with LBJ, and the one photo she submits in her book as evidence of being in LBJ's presence shows her and her son seated at a party and a man standing nearby with his back to the camera. She claims the man is Johnson, but he does not appear to be, at least to me. In any event, to say that the story Miss Brown comes up with strains credulity is to be much too magnanimous.

Brown says that on the evening before the assassination, she attended a social event at the Dallas home of Texas oil magnate Clint Murchison. "It was my understanding," she said, "that the event was scheduled as a tribute honoring his long time friend, J. Edgar Hoover, whom Murchison had first met decades earlier through President William Howard Taft." Hoover, she says, was at the party, as was John McCloy (who ended up on the Warren Commission), Richard Nixon (who *was* in town that night, leaving Dallas from Love Field at 10:05 a.m. on American Airlines Flight 82 on the morning of the assassination), H. L. Hunt (the right-wing oil baron), and a host of other Dallas luminaries. Because of his hectic schedule, Johnson, she says, wasn't supposed to be at the party, but he made an unscheduled appearance as the party was breaking up. "I knew how secretively Lyndon operated. Therefore, I said nothing . . . not even that I was happy to see him. Squeezing my hand so hard it felt crushed from the pressure, he spoke with a grating whisper—a quiet growl into my ear, not a love message, but one I'll always remember: 'After tomorrow those goddamn Kennedys will never embarrass me again—that's no threat—that's a promise.'" The following morning around 11:00 a.m., she says, Jesse Kellam, LBJ's close friend and political operative in Austin who was organizing an Austin fund-raiser for Kennedy that night, which Brown was assisting with, called her to confirm her schedule. He told her, she says, that she probably would not be able to see Lyndon that night for more than fifteen minutes. Recalling that flashes of wild lovemaking

---

[*]On June 18, 1987, the son, Steven Mark Brown, filed a $10.5 million lawsuit against Lady Bird Johnson, claiming, "My legal birthrights have been violated and a conspiracy was formed to deprive me of my legal heirship." The suit was dismissed in 1989 when Steven, then a naval operations specialist, "failed to appear in court." (Dave Perry, "Texas in the Imagination," self-published article, October 26, 2002, pp.10–11; *Dallas Morning News*, June 19, 1987, p.34A; *Dallas Morning News*, October 3, 1990, p.A33, obituary of Steven Mark Brown)

danced in her head, she said she responded, "Jesse, for any time I have with Lyndon, I am grateful." But Jesse warned, "Lyndon is in a terrible mood, screaming about the Kennedys. All he can say is, 'Those goddamn Kennedys will never embarrass me again after today.'"[24]

So if we're to believe Miss Brown, Lyndon Baines Johnson, who by common consensus was one of the most shrewd men ever to ponderously grace (an oxymoron?) this nation's political stage, decided not only to murder President Kennedy, but also to tell others about it. The man whose photograph could be alongside words like *sly*, *wily*, and *clever* in the dictionary was intent on advertising his part in the conspiracy to his girlfriend, to Jesse Kellam, and to God knows how many other people. I wouldn't believe a story like that if you shouted it in my ears for one hundred years. Yet, as one example among many, Craig Zirbel writes in the *Texas Connection* that it's "crystal clear that Johnson was aware that Kennedy was going to be murdered . . . He told his girlfriend it was going to happen."[25] In his 1992 book, *The Man Who Knew Too Much*, which came out five years before Brown's book, Dick Russell quotes Brown telling him about LBJ's threat vis-à-vis Kennedy before the assassination, and does not question her veracity at all.[26]

Brown hardly deserves this rebuttal, but she says that LBJ was at the Murchison party in Dallas the evening before the assassination, but he couldn't have been if he had wanted to because he was in Houston that night, about 225 miles away. "I was chairman of a huge dinner in Houston honoring Albert Thomas that Thursday night," LBJ aide Jack Valenti says, and "the two speakers were the vice president and the president. I rode in a car with LBJ to the [Houston] airport and we flew on Air Force Two to Fort Worth, where we talked at the Texas hotel until one in the morning [1 a.m., November 22, 1963]."[27]

What about Hoover? Hoover would have had a difficult time making it to the party. His daily log shows that he was at his office starting at 8:57 in the morning of November 21, 1963, and left the office at 5:14 p.m. On Friday morning, he was back in his office at 9:00 a.m., leaving at 6:01 p.m.[28] If someone wants to believe that on Thursday evening, after leaving his office at 5:14 p.m., Hoover raced to the airport to catch a flight to Dallas for the alleged party with Murchison, Nixon, and others, then took a red-eye (did they have red-eyes back then?) back to Washington, D.C., that night or caught a 4:00 or 5:00 a.m. flight the next morning, I guess there's nothing I can do to stop him.

And as far as Nixon was concerned (Nixon was a partner in a New York City law firm that represented Pepsi and he was in town attending a soft drink bottler's convention), if he came to the party he had to be a very late show because on the night before the assassination, he had a "ringside" seat with a group from Pepsi that included actress Joan Crawford, the wife of Pepsi's CEO, listening to a performance by French singer Robert Clary in the Empire Room of Dallas's Statler Hilton.[29] Tony Zoppi, the entertainment writer for the *Dallas Morning News*, was there that night, and told Gary Mack, the Sixth Floor Museum's curator, that when he left the Empire Room around a quarter to eleven to file his story before deadline for the next morning's edition, Nixon was still there with this group.[30]

Indeed, Dallas assassination researcher David Perry has conducted a very extensive investigation into all of Brown's allegations, and there is no question in his mind that not only weren't LBJ and Hoover at the party, but there was no such party. Perry gathered several pieces of evidence debunking Brown's "party" story. For one, he learned that Clint Murchison Sr., at whose home the party allegedly took place, was in ill health at the time, dating from a stroke in 1958, and had moved out of his Dallas home four years earlier, turning over the ownership of the home to one of his three sons, John, and John's wife Lupe. In 2002, Perry interviewed Mrs. Eula Tilley, the wife of Clint Sr.'s chauffeur, Warren Tilly, who could not speak at the time because of throat cancer. She told Perry, "Both Warren and I worked for Mr. Murchison for a long time. He had seven houses, you know . . . I know he wasn't at any party when Kennedy was shot. He did not have a home in the Dallas area. He was at his Glad Oaks Ranch between Athens and Palestine [Texas, about 120 miles southeast of Dallas]. I'm not sure how long before the assassination we were at the ranch but it was more than a few days. I remember because I was serving lunch to Mr. Murchison and his neighbor Woffard Cain. One of them said Kennedy had been shot."[31]

Additionally, a party the likes of which Brown spoke of, with luminaries such as Nixon, LBJ, and Hoover attending, would have automatically made the next morning's newspapers—at least the entertainment and society sections if not the daily news. Perry therefore scoured the papers (*Dallas Morning News* and *Dallas Times Herald*) but found no reference to any such party.[32] Perry makes the telling point that after all of his investigation, "The only person I know of who claimed [he or] she was actually at the [alleged] party was the late Madeleine Brown."[33]

Perry, in fact, questions whether Brown even had an affair with Johnson, finding her story of the alleged relationship riddled with fabrications, inconsistencies, and unconfirmed allegations. For instance, the first time Brown went public with her story was nearly twenty years after the assassination, at a Dallas news conference on November 5, 1982, saying she "was the mistress of Lyndon Baines Johnson" and had decided to "clear the record." And she never said anything about having a child by him.[34] That extremely important embellishment would come much later.

Perry also notes that in Brown's book, she said she first met Johnson at a grand party attended by Dallas's high and mighty at Dallas's Adolphus hotel "three weeks" before LBJ's Senate victory party in Austin on October 29, 1948.[35]* But Perry checked all the local newspapers for several days on both sides of October 8–9, 1948 (three weeks earlier), and there was no reference to any such high-powered and high-society party. Indeed, Perry confirmed that LBJ was in Washington, D.C., around this time, the first time that LBJ came to Dallas that October being on October 22 to give a luncheon speech to the Dallas Reserve Officers' Association.[36]

Apparently, Brown has so little credibility that in the three volumes historian Robert A. Caro has written thus far on LBJ (only the volume on his presidency remains unpublished), Brown wasn't entitled to a single word of mention. And it's not because Caro refrained from discussing LBJ's alleged extramarital affairs—for example, his relationship with Alice Glass.[37] It appears Caro found Brown simply too ludicrous and her claims too unfounded to dignify with even one word.

Brown, by the way, has gone far beyond her absurd allegation about LBJ's supposed admission to being behind Kennedy's murder, proving beyond all doubt that she is not a person worthy of any belief. Among her incredible pronouncements, she told conspiracy author Harrison Livingstone in 1992 that "Lyndon Johnson did not die naturally." His

---

*Brown says LBJ invited her to attend the victory party at the Driskill Hotel in Austin, which she did. "He had an apartment in the Driskill," she said, "and we routinely started having an affair." (Brown, *Texas in the Morning*, pp.9, 14; affair at Driskill: Affidavit by Madeleine Brown in lawsuit filed by her son against Mrs. Johnson, *Dallas Morning News*, June 19, 1987, p.34A) She said the affair continued until 1969 (*Dallas Morning News*, October 3, 1990, p.A33).

own Secret Service killed him, she alleged. "They hated him." Also, "There were three plots to kill Kennedy, and the other two were backup plots. One of them was LBJ's plot, which took JFK out with the KGB's help"; "Billie Sol [Estes] knows all three shooters" who killed Kennedy; "Why do you think that John J. McCloy and Richard Nixon were there when Kennedy died? . . . They put aside their warfare and came together to kill Kennedy"; "[H. L.] Hunt called Ruby and ordered him to kill Lee Harvey Oswald."[38]

Madeleine Brown, naturally, has been publicly embraced by the conspiracy community, and prior to her death often attended its conventions, such as the November 19–23, 1998, one in Dallas. On November 6, 1992, Brown was convicted of forging a relative's will back on September 2, 1988. The conviction was reversed on appeal in 1994 on a procedural error. Brown died in 2002.

One question about LBJ for the conspiracy theorists: If he was part of a plot to kill Kennedy, and the Warren Commission thereafter officially concluded there was no plot, wouldn't he be very happy and likely to keep quiet? Would he be likely to say more than once that, as he told the *Atlantic* in 1973, "I never believed that Oswald acted alone although I can accept he pulled the trigger"? Indeed, if LBJ were complicit in the assassination, why would he appoint a blue-ribbon commission to investigate the assassination (the Warren Commission)* consisting of seven men of impeccable reputation and unquestioned probity, *five of whom were Republicans*? Wouldn't he know that the likelihood he could get such a group to protect him and cover up for him would be substantially diminished? I mean, even as to Chief Justice Warren alone, are we to believe that Johnson established the Warren Commission by executive order to "ascertain all the facts relating to the assassination," but then, as I told the jury in London, "took Warren aside and said, 'However, Chief, if you really do find out the facts, you keep those facts under your robe. Okay, Chief?'"

And a final question for Miss Brown, wherever her soul is today: You dedicated your book "in loving memory" of your son and Lyndon Johnson. If accusing Johnson of having Kennedy murdered is a part of your "loving" memory of him, what in the world would you be saying about him if you hated him? That it was he, not Hitler, who was responsible for the Holocaust?

If it is possible to write a sillier book than Madeleine Brown's alleging that LBJ was behind Kennedy's murder, it is Barr McClellan's 2003 book, *Blood, Money and Power: How LBJ Killed JFK*. After taking us through more than two hundred pages of his dreamy fairy tale, as we saw earlier, the author has LBJ confessing to the murder when he was about to die, thinking that his honesty in admitting to having murdered Kennedy would actually improve (?!!?) his poor reputation with the American people.

---

*"I was there," says Jack Valenti, a former top aide to LBJ, "when President Johnson ruminated about the assassination, and the urgency to enlist the most prestigious citizens within the Republic to inspect this murder carefully, objectively, swiftly" (Bernard Weinraub, "Valenti Calls [movie] 'J.F.K.' 'Hoax' and 'Smear,'" *New York Times*, April 2, 1992, pp.C15, C24).

Cuba

Just as present-day Cuba and Fidel Castro are synonymous with each other, the thinking that Cuba was behind JFK's murder is synonymous with saying that Castro was behind it. And the theory that the Cuban government had Kennedy killed always focuses exclusively on Castro.

Suspicion of Cuban complicity in the assassination reached its high-water mark shortly after the assassination, when the American people learned that Oswald revered Castro and had sought to go to Cuba just two months earlier. Also, there was known hostility between the U.S. and the Cuban leadership, starting with the Cuban cabinet's authorization on July 6, 1960, of the expropriation of all U.S.-owned property in Cuba. President Eisenhower responded that same day by ordering a reduction in the amount of sugar to be imported from Cuba, and then ended diplomatic relations with Cuba on January 2, 1961. Our support of the Bay of Pigs invasion on April 17, 1961, and the Cuban missile crisis in the fall of 1962 contributed to the belief among many that Castro somehow had a hand in the president's murder. Indeed, as an internal memorandum of the supersecret National Security Agency (NSA), the federal intelligence agency charged with the electronic eavesdropping and deciphering of messages to and from foreign adversaries, says, "Immediately after the assassination, NSA initiated a large-scale manual and machine *review* of SIGINT [Signals Intelligence], including all U.S./Cuba traffic [around the time of the assassination]. A computer search was initiated using Oswald's name as the minimum for research criteria. Additionally, all traffic between Cuba/New Orleans and Cuba/Dallas was manually reviewed." The electronic eavesdropping disclosed that "Cuban military forces went on alert immediately after the assassination." The NSA concluded that "a thorough review has revealed no intelligence material revealing or suggesting Cuban involvement in the assassination of President Kennedy."[1]

This conclusion by the NSA is in keeping with the conclusion of every other investigative body that has evaluated the issue. And today, although the belief still persists among some, the overwhelming majority of Americans as well as most conspiracy theorists have discarded the theory that Cuba was behind the assassination. It should be noted, however, that as late as 1978, fifteen years after the assassination, the question of Cuban complicity in Kennedy's murder was apparently of sufficient concern for three members of the HSCA and three staff members to make two trips to Cuba to investigate the issue, which included a four-hour, tape-recorded interview with Castro on April 3, 1978, in Havana.

The few conspiracy theorists who still cling to the theory of Cuban complicity in the assassination always cite as one of their principal authorities former president Lyndon Johnson, who told many people that he believed Castro had Kennedy murdered. Joseph Califano Jr., an LBJ aide from 1965 to 1969, told the *Wall Street Journal*, "Johnson believed, as he said to me, that Fidel Castro was responsible for Kennedy's assassination. In a reference to attempts by the Kennedy brothers to assassinate Castro, Johnson told me, 'Kennedy tried to kill Castro, but Castro got Kennedy first.'"[2] But unless a president, because of his position, was privy to information about Castro's having Kennedy killed—which Johnson never claimed or intimated he was—his reasoning and opinion on the matter are no more apt to be authoritative than anyone else's. And Johnson's belief is bereft not only of evidence but of common sense.[*]

One of the chief proponents of LBJ's reasoning was Italian-born mobster Johnny Roselli (real name, Filippo Sacco). When the CIA first decided to assassinate Castro in August of 1960, it gave the assignment to former FBI agent Robert Maheu, at the time a top aide in Las Vegas to Howard Hughes. Maheu, in turn, passed the contract on to Roselli, who in turn enlisted Mafia kingpins Santo Trafficante Jr. and Sam Giancana to carry it out.[3][†]

The HSCA noted that it was significant that public revelations by Roselli (through his

---

[*]Though LBJ blamed Castro for Kennedy's murder, if the Kennedy family ever entertained such thoughts, the sentiment was never picked up by JFK Jr., an extreme unlikelihood if the family had such beliefs. JFK Jr. sought out and had a social dinner with Castro at the Council of Ministers in Havana on the evening of October 27, 1997. And at the end of the very long evening, during which the Bearded One delivered one of his rambling but eloquent multi-hour performances, for which he is famous, JFK Jr. thanked Castro for the evening and said, "I'll bring my wife the next time I come." Does one have such a dinner and conversation with someone he suspects of having had his father murdered? The only reference to the assassination Castro made to JFK Jr. came at the end, when they were leaving the dining room. "You know, Lee Harvey Oswald was trying to come here," Castro said, half a question, half declaration. (As we know, in late September 1963 Oswald had applied for a visa at the Cuban consulate in Mexico City, but his request had been denied.) "Yes, I did know that," JFK Jr. replied. Castro paused, then said, "It was a difficult time, and you know we didn't let many Americans into Cuba." "Yes," JFK Jr. said quietly. It would clearly appear that Castro was offering a veiled apology. He knew that if Oswald had been allowed into Cuba when he applied for the visa, almost assuredly he would not have been in Dallas less than two months later. (*George Magazine*, October 1999, p.158 et seq.)

[†]"What was your reaction to [being asked to kill] President Castro?" Trafficante was asked in his testimony before the HSCA. Trafficante: "Well, at that time I think it was a good thing because he had established a Communist base ninety miles from the United States, and being that the government of the United States wanted it done, I'd go along with it, the same thing as a war. I figure it was like war." (5 HSCA 358)

There are many, like Johnny Roselli, who believe that Trafficante never made any attempt to kill Castro. Another who held this belief was Trafficante's lawyer, Frank Ragano. Ragano says that when the CIA asked Trafficante to kill Castro, he just played along, believing it would be impossible to kill Castro without the killer or killers getting killed themselves. Even though Castro had caused Trafficante and the mob to lose millions of dollars when he closed down the mob-run casinos in Havana, and the mob had every desire to regain control and ownership of its very profitable gambling empire, Trafficante, Ragano said, was "realistic and philosophical," viewing it as a "lost cause, especially after the Bay of Pigs," and had no intention of going after Castro for the CIA. "It was just a big scam. There was no intention, no effort whatsoever to assassinate Fidel Castro." Ragano said Trafficante told him he lied to the HSCA in 1978 when he testified he had tried to kill Castro. (Interview of Frank Ragano, "JFK, Hoffa and the Mob," *Frontline*, PBS, November 17, 1992; see also a long endnote to the section "Cover-Up by the CIA and FBI in the Warren Commission's Investigation of the Assassination," on whether JFK authorized the CIA plots to kill Castro)

Washington lawyer, Edward P. Morgan, contacting syndicated columnists Drew Pearson and Jack Anderson) about the plots to kill Castro "corresponded with his efforts to avoid deportation in 1966 and 1971 and to escape prosecution for illegal gambling activities in 1967. It was Roselli who managed the release of information about the plots and who proposed the so-called turnaround theory of the Kennedy assassination (Cuban exiles hired by the Mafia as hit men, captured by Castro, were forced to 'turnaround' and murder President Kennedy). The committee found it quite plausible that Roselli would have manipulated public perception of the facts of the plots, then tried to get the CIA to intervene in his legal problems as the price for his agreeing to make no further disclosures."[4]

The first two articles alluding to the turnaround theory, a syndicated column by Jack Anderson on March 3, 1967, and one by Drew Pearson on March 7, 1967, did not mention Roselli by name and did not attract too much attention. But an article by Anderson and Les Whitten on September 7, 1976, in the *Washington Post* did attract attention because of the recent Church Committee revelations of the CIA-mob plot to kill Castro and because of the discovery of Roselli's dismembered body on August 7, just one month before the article was printed. And it did mention Roselli by name, saying that "before he died, Roselli hinted to associates that he knew who had arranged President Kennedy's murder. It was the same conspirators, he suggested, whom he had recruited earlier to kill Cuban Premier Fidel Castro. By Roselli's cryptic account, Castro learned the identity of the underworld contacts in Havana who had been trying to knock him off. He [Castro] believed, not altogether without basis, that President Kennedy was behind the plot." Castro then "enlisted the same underworld elements" to kill Kennedy.[5]

In addition to the fact that there is no evidence that Castro ever learned the identity of the Cubans supposedly enlisted by the mob between 1961 and 1963 to kill him, Roselli's turnaround theory is irrational on its face. Even if Castro had decided to kill Kennedy, how could Castro, from his base in Cuba, *force* hit men for the mob to come back to this country (where he'd immediately lose physical control of them) to kill Kennedy? And even if Castro, an intelligent person by all accounts, had the irrational thought he could do this, he would still have to know that they would never be as dependable to carry out such an assignment as his own agents would be. Needless to say, the HSCA did not find Roselli's turnaround theory credible.[6]

Also, there is a predicate for the turnaround theory that has never been proved. There's no evidence that hit men for the mob were ever captured by Castro. Further, Jimmy "The Weasel" Fratiano, a West Coast organized-crime figure, said that Roselli told him there was no truth to his theory, and Roselli acknowledged in his testimony before the Church Committee on April 23, 1976, that he had "no facts" to support it.[7]

On July 28, 1976, Roselli disappeared in Miami. On August 7, three fishermen found his butchered body, with his legs sawed off, inside an oil drum on the edge of a sandbar in Dumfoundling Bay, Key Biscayne, Florida. The drum had been weighted down by chains but gases created by the decomposition of Roselli's body gave the drum enough buoyancy for it to rise to the surface. An unnamed Mafia figure told the *New York Times* that two men, one an old friend, the other a visitor from Chicago, had lured Roselli aboard a private boat at a nearby marina. Out on the water, while Roselli sipped a vodka, the man from Chicago grabbed him from behind and held his hand tightly over Roselli's nose and mouth until he was asphyxiated, not a difficult feat since the seventy-year-old Roselli had emphysema.[8] Though conspiracy theorists claim he was silenced because of his knowledge of a conspiracy to assassinate President Kennedy, there simply is no evidence, anywhere, that he was a part of or had any knowledge of any such conspiracy, and the Justice

Department concluded that Roselli's murder and the murder of Sam Giancana[*] were unrelated to the CIA-mob plots to kill Castro.[9] Such a conclusion makes sense. If Roselli's or Giancana's killers were trying to silence them because of their knowledge of the CIA-mob plots to kill Castro, why not also kill Florida mob boss Santo Trafficante, to whom both went to actually carry out the job? And why not kill Roselli *before* he testified before the Church Committee, which he first did on June 24, 1975 (the first of three times, the last time being on April 23, 1976, a little over three months before his murder), at which time he spilled all the beans there were to spill about the CIA-mob plot to kill Castro?

Purported support for the belief that Castro was of a mind to kill Kennedy was an informal discussion Castro had with two American reporters following a reception at the Brazilian embassy in Havana on the evening of September 7, 1963. Castro spoke, per usual for him, on a wide range of subjects, one of which was Kennedy. The UPI reporter, whose article was published in the *New York Times*, quoted Castro as saying that "Kennedy is a cretin," the "Batista of his time and the most opportunistic American president of all time. Kennedy is thinking more about re-election than the American people."[10] The AP reporter, Daniel Harker, took something far more explosive away from the three-hour meeting. He wrote, "Bitterly denouncing what he called recent U.S.-prompted raids on Cuban territory, Castro said: 'United States leaders should think that if they are aiding terrorist plans to eliminate Cuban leaders, they themselves will not be safe.'"[11] Did Castro thereby suggest, as Harker says, that if there were such plots, he would retaliate in kind? Even if he did, it would most likely be only loose swagger on his part, in no way negating the fact that there's no evidence he had Kennedy killed, and that he was well aware that such an act would be the most reckless, unwise, and suicidal action he could ever take. (See later text.)

But I personally doubt that Castro said specifically what Harker quotes him as saying. I learned many years ago the truth of the observation that "quotation marks don't make a quote," as most lay people assume they do. I myself have often been quoted incorrectly, several times substantially so. In the first place, if Castro had threatened a retaliatory assassination, it is very hard to believe that the UPI reporter who was present would not have found such a statement sufficiently important to include in his fourteen-paragraph story on the meeting, which he did not do. Just as important was Castro's response when the

---

[*]Giancana, age sixty-six, was shot twice in the head, once in the region of the mouth, and six times in the neck on June 19, 1975, while he was preparing a late-night snack of his favorite dish, Italian sausage and escarole, in the basement kitchen of his home in the Oak Park area of Chicago. A June 21, 1975, headline story in the *Chicago Tribune* reported that the Oak Park Police Department had been "watching" Giancana's home at the time of the murder and "the killer who shot Giancana may have passed directly under the gaze of lawmen." Earlier on the day of the murder, staff members of the Church Committee had arrived in Chicago to make arrangements with Giancana for his scheduled appearance before the committee in Washington, D.C., on June 24, five days away. That morning's *Chicago Tribune* captioned an article "Report CIA Scheme to Poison Castro" that said "the assassination plot . . . was directed by Sam Giancana and John Roselli."

At the time of Giancana's execution-style murder, he no longer controlled the Chicago mob, having lived in exile in Mexico from 1966 to July 18, 1974, when Mexico deported him, and the Chicago "Outfit" had excluded him from all its activities, "believing that the investigations he had inspired had crimped mob business in Chicago." However, a federal grand jury in Chicago had recently questioned Giancana about mob activities there, and although he hadn't yet told the grand jury anything of value, the Chicago mob may have feared he eventually would. *Time* magazine said that "the gang-slaying theory was lent credence by a shadowy report that on hearing of the shooting, the Mafia's boss of bosses, Carlo Gambino, promptly passed word that Giancana's killer was to be executed . . . a frequent Mafia precaution after a major 'hit.'" ("Demise of a Don," p.26; *Washington Post*, June 21, 1975, p.1; Giancana, Hughes, and Jobe, *JFK and Sam*, pp.65–66; Blakey and Billings, *Plot to Kill the President*, pp.390–391)

HSCA interviewed him in Havana on April 3, 1978. If Castro had been involved in the assassination and had told Harker what Harker quoted him as saying, the likelihood that Castro would have admitted telling Harker anything remotely close to what Harker wrote would obviously have been nil. We could have expected Castro to say that Harker either was a liar or had grossly misquoted him. The fact he said neither at least goes in the direction of his recollection of the incident having credibility. Castro said, "I don't remember literally what I said, but I remember my intention in saying what I said and it was to . . . let the United States government know that we knew about the existence of . . . plots against our lives . . . I said something like those plots start to set a very bad precedent, a very serious one . . . that could become a boomerang against the authors of those actions. That to set those precedents of plotting the assassination of leaders of other countries would be . . . very negative" (i.e., it could result in one or more of the victim nations retaliating in kind). Castro added that "I didn't say it as a threat. I did not mean by that that we were going to take measures, similar measures, like a retaliation for that." Castro said he would say the same thing today as he said back then "because I didn't mean a threat by that."[12] I, for one, believe Castro.

Another related story that Castro flatly denies, and with good reason, was the one told by British tabloid journalist Comer Clark. In an October 1967 edition of the *National Enquirer*, he wrote that on July 15, 1967, he had an exclusive interview with Castro late one night in a Havana pizzeria. He quotes Castro as saying, "Lee Oswald came to the Cuban Embassy in Mexico City twice. The first time, I was told, he wanted to work for us. He was asked to explain, but he wouldn't. He wouldn't go into details. The second time he said something like: 'Someone ought to shoot that President Kennedy.' Then Oswald said—and this was exactly how it was reported to me—'Maybe I'll try to do it.' This was less than two months before the U.S. President was assassinated . . . Yes, I heard of Lee Harvey Oswald's plan to kill President Kennedy. It's possible I could have saved him. I might have been able to, but I didn't. I never believed the plan would be put into effect."[13] The HSCA learned that Clark, who died in 1972, "wrote extensively for the sensationalist press in England. His articles include such items as 'British Girls as Nazi Sex Slaves' [and] 'I Was Hitler's Secret Love.'"[14] When the HSCA asked Castro on April 3, 1978, about Clark's allegation, he responded in a blizzard of denunciatory words. Among them: "This is absurd. I didn't say that . . . It has been invented from the beginning until the end . . . It's a lie from head to toe. If this man [Oswald] would have done something like that, it would have been our moral duty to inform the United States." Denying that he had ever met Clark or been interviewed by him, he said, "How could [this man] interview me in a pizzeria? I never go to public restaurants . . . I would never have given a journalist an interview in a pizzeria . . . What is the job of that journalist? What is he engaged in? . . . You should . . . find [out] who he is and why he wrote it."[15]

In yet another example of good investigative journalism on his part, conspiracy theorist Anthony Summers interviewed Clark's widow and assistant. The widow told Summers that Clark had never mentioned interviewing Castro. Most importantly, Summers writes that the assistant, Nina Gadd, said that "*she* generated the story, without even going to Havana, on the basis of allegations made to her" by an unnamed Latin American foreign minister.[16]

As it turns out, though Clark's story was a fabrication in that he had never spoken to Castro, an earlier source told the FBI essentially the same story. In a June 17, 1964, letter to Warren Commission general counsel J. Lee Rankin, J. Edgar Hoover said a "confidential source" who had "furnished reliable information in the past" reported that Castro had "recently said" that "our people in Mexico gave us the details" of Oswald's visit to the Mexican consulate, and when his request for a visa "was refused him, he headed out saying 'I'm going to kill Kennedy for this.'"[17] The story doesn't make sense. *Why would Oswald threaten to kill Kennedy because the Cuban consulate turned down his request for a visa?* What's the connection? Silvia Duran, the secretary at the consulate who dealt with Oswald and was present at the time of Oswald's outburst when his request for a visa was denied, said she heard no such threat by Oswald against Kennedy.[18] And the Cuban consul, Eusebio Azcue, who was also present, also said no such threat by Oswald was made, adding that if it had, he would "have passed this information on to Fidel."[19] It should be noted that the Warren Commission should have included in its report Oswald's alleged threat to kill Kennedy at the Cuban consulate in Mexico City, but it did not, and I have not been able to find Hoover's letter to Rankin in any of the Commission's volumes of exhibits.

The story was given a fillip by a secretary at the Cuban consulate whose office was on the second floor, Luisa Calderon Carralero. In a CIA-intercepted telephone call several hours after the assassination, when a male called Calderon at the consulate and asked her if she had heard the news of the president's death, she replied, in a joking manner, "Yes, of course, I knew it almost before Kennedy . . . Imagine, one, two, three and now, that makes three [she laughs], what barbarians!"[20] The HSCA construed Calderon's remark, if true, as indicating either "foreknowledge or mere braggadocio. The preponderance of the evidence led the committee to find that it was braggadocio." When the committee sought to interview Calderon in Cuba, she declined based on illness. However, she did respond to the HSCA's written interrogatories, denying any foreknowledge of the assassination. Because the HSCA sensed from the demeanor of many other employees at the Cuban consulate that they were telling the truth when they denied having any foreknowledge of the assassination, the committee concluded that Oswald had not "voiced a threat [to kill Kennedy] to Cuban officials." With respect to the "confidential, reliable source" who said he did, the HSCA said, "However reliable the confidential source may be, the committee found it to be in error in this instance."[21]

How did this story, which arguably connected Castro with Kennedy's assassination, get started? A few days after the assassination (November 26), Gilberto Alvarado Ugarte, a twenty-three-year-old Nicaraguan secret agent purporting to be working against the Cuban Communists for his country's security service, went to the American embassy in Mexico City and claimed that on September 18, 1963, he was at the Cuban consulate seeking to get to Cuba with the intent to infiltrate Castro's forces. While standing by the bathroom door, he said he saw three men conversing on an adjacent patio. One was a black man, tall and thin, with reddish hair. The second was a Canadian with blonde hair, and the third man was Lee Harvey Oswald. A tall Cuban joined the group only long enough to pass some currency to the black man. Alvarado said he then overheard the black man say to Oswald, "I want to kill the man," whereupon Oswald replied, "You're not man enough, I can do it." The black man then said, "I can't go with you, I have a lot to do." He then gave Oswald $6,500 in large-denomination American bills (he doesn't say how he knew it was $6,500—did he see and bother to count the denominations adding up to $6,500?), $5,000 as compensation to kill Kennedy and $1,500 as expense money, saying, "This isn't much."[22] Could anyone with an IQ above 50 possibly believe that this was Oswald's recruitment into the conspiracy to kill Kennedy, and his payment for being the triggerman? Well, Thomas Mann, the U.S. ambassador to Mexico at the time, did believe it. He cabled his superiors at the State Department in Washington that "Castro is the kind of person who would avenge himself in this way. He is the Latin type of extremist who reacts viscerally rather than intellectually." Mann added that "the unprofessional, almost lackadaisical way in which the money is alleged by Alvarado to have been passed to Oswald fits the way Cubans would be expected to act if the Russians were not guiding them." Mann requested, in his cable, that the aforementioned Luisa Calderon be arrested because she may have been present when Oswald was given the money.[23] Mann didn't have his fill. Though only the ambassador to Mexico, not a member of U.S. intelligence, he requested through the State Department that the FBI send a knowledgeable agent from Washington down to Mexico City to investigate Alvarado's claim,[24] and he himself wanted to get actively involved in investigating whether Oswald killed Kennedy for Castro. Hoover, who referred to Mann as "one of the pseudo-investigators, a Sherlock Holmes," was opposed to sending anyone to Mexico City, feeling the FBI agent assigned to the American embassy in Mexico City, Clark Anderson, could do whatever was necessary, and besides, this was a matter for the CIA in Mexico City to handle. Mann was so persistent, however, that Hoover, mostly to pacify Mann, ultimately did send an agent to Mexico City for a few days, but the agent didn't even get to interrogate Alvarado and was sent home.[25]

Apart from the fact that Oswald was in New Orleans, not Mexico City, on September 18, 1963 (the day Alvarado said the incident took place), when Mexico police interrogated Alvarado, he admitted, in writing, that he had made up the whole matter. His motive, he said, was that he hated Castro and hoped his story would cause the United States to "take action" against him. When reinterrogated by the CIA, he first claimed the Mexico police had pressured him into retracting his story, and that his retraction, not his first statement, was false. He was then given a polygraph test by a CIA polygraph expert assisted by an FBI agent. The test indicated he was probably lying, prompting Alvarado to say, "I know such machines are accurate, and therefore, I suppose I must be mistaken."[26]

On December 1, 1963, less than a week after Alvarado's claim, another Mexican, Pedro Gutierrez Valencia, a credit investigator for a large Mexico City department store, wrote a letter to President Johnson, making a claim analogous to but not corroborative of Alvarado's: The date (September 30 or October 1, 1963) was different from Alvarado's; there were two men, not three; and the location was in front of the Cuban embassy, not on a patio to the rear of the consulate. Gutierrez, leaving the embassy after conducting a credit investigation of one of its employees, claims he heard a heated discussion, in English, between a Cuban and an American in which he could understand only the words "Castro," "Cuba," and "Kennedy." The Cuban counted out American dollars and gave them to the American, at which time they got into the Cuban's car and drove off. Gutierrez said the American was Oswald.[27]

Again, the extreme improbability that any agreement and payment for Kennedy's murder would take place not in private, but literally out in the open in view of others, and under the other circumstances Gutierrez described, is alone enough to discount the story. But other facts that undermine Gutierrez's credibility emerged. It turns out that Gutierrez, like Alvarado, was a zealous anti-Castro activist and thus had a motive similar to Alvarado's for lying: to convince the United States that Castro was behind the assassination, thus inducing this nation to remove Castro from power. But even if Gutierrez did see two men and heard the three words, Gutierrez conceded he saw "Oswald" face-to-face for only a "split second," at all other times during the incident only seeing the backs of "Oswald" and the other man.[28]

On June 5, 1978, HSCA staff member Edwin Lopez interviewed Gutierrez on tape, and all Gutierrez would say is that he bumped into Oswald at the Cuban consulate but "I don't remember him [Oswald] being accompanied by another person." When Lopez pressed Gutierrez about the fact that he told President Johnson that he saw Oswald with, Lopez incorrectly says, a Cuban-American (Gutierrez had only said the man was Cuban, not Cuban-American), Gutierrez replied, "That is an enigma to me. I do not remember him being accompanied by a Cuban-American." When Lopez asked Gutierrez about his assertion that the Cuban handed money to Oswald, Gutierrez said, "I do not ever remember that occurring."[29] So much for Pedro Gutierrez.

So there is no credible evidence connecting Castro, by way of the alleged incidents outside the Cuban embassy, with the assassination. It should be added that even if Castro were able to kill Kennedy without being discovered, he was aware, as he said, "that the death of the leader does not change the system. It has never done that."[30] In other words, what reason would Castro have had to believe that the U.S. posture toward him would be better under LBJ? None. He apparently knew very little about LBJ. According to French journalist Jean Daniel, who was with Castro on the day of the assassination, Castro had a series of questions for him after Kennedy's death was finally confirmed: "What is [Johnson's] reputation? What were his relations with Kennedy? With Khrushchev? What was his position at the time of the attempted invasion of Cuba?"[31]

In a two-hour radio and television address to his people on the evening following the assassination, the Cuban leader said that the assassination of Kennedy was "grave and bad news . . . from the political point of view" because it could change U.S. foreign policy "from bad to worse."[32] And it wasn't just Castro who felt this way. An NSA intercept picked up a message on November 27, 1963 (just four days after the assassination), from the Brazilian ambassador to Cuba to his foreign office, stating that Cuban officials "were unanimous in believing that any other president would be even worse" than Kennedy.[33]

Perhaps the most direct accusation that Castro was behind Kennedy's death came from someone whose story was so lacking in credibility that a member of the HSCA, during open proceedings, accused the accuser of blatant perjury.

On May 1, 1961, Antulio Ramirez Ortiz, a U.S. citizen of Puerto Rican origin, boarded a National Airlines flight out of Miami destined for Key West and, using a knife and a gun, hijacked the plane to Cuba. In testimony before the HSCA, Ramirez said that once the plane landed in Havana, Cuba's secret service police took him to their headquarters but didn't bother to question him for three or four months. (He claimed that in 1959 he had delivered a phony message for the Cuban secret service to the Dominican Republican consulate in New York City, so Havana knew him.) During that period, he lived at the headquarters and worked in the kitchen. He said a female coworker told him one day that in the room where the secret service stored its files, she had seen a file on him with photos in it. Why she would be looking through those secret files and have access to them he did not know. Out of curiosity, one day he walked into the room (apparently the Cuban secret police had no security and even kitchen employees could peruse their files) and while looking for his file he noticed one labeled "Oswald-Kennedy." Looking inside, he saw a photo of Oswald and a report written in Russian, in which, he testified, Oswald's wife was described as "belonging to the Soviet secret police," and he told the HSCA that "the Russian secret police were recommending this person [Oswald] to the Cuban government." One big problem is that when HSCA counsel asked Ramirez if he was able to "read Russian," Ramirez answered, "No," adding he could recognize some of the Russian characters, however.

But Ramirez's story gets, as Lewis Carroll said, "curiouser and curiouser," or, more aptly, sillier and sillier. Ramirez said that from the moment he landed in Havana, the Cuban secret service "thought I was working for the CIA." Yet not only did the secret service police apparently allow him free run of their headquarters in 1961, but after they arrested him for espionage in September of 1963, instead of imprisoning him, they merely "detained" him for a month. The following month they freed him on condition that he would start working for them. Though he was drawing a "full salary" and they were paying his hotel expenses, when HSCA counsel asked what he was doing in return for this, he replied, "Absolutely nothing." But wait. The Cuban secret service at least had something important they wanted to share with him. One of the Cuban secret service agents named Martin (Ramirez didn't know his last name) confided in him over drinks at the Hotel Saratoga in Havana in early November of 1963 that the Cubans intended to kill Kennedy "in this very month of November. Read the papers."

With the exception of a brief period when he was hospitalized in a mental institution and received psychiatric care, Ramirez continued to float around Havana, leaving in 1975 for the United States. When asked by HSCA counsel how the Cuban government allowed him to leave knowing he possessed information that it had Kennedy killed, Ramirez responded, "Because I had something more valuable than all that. If I were dead, they would have a problem," though he didn't elaborate on this. In other words, the Cubans didn't think they'd have much of a problem if they killed the president of the United States, but thought they'd have real problems killing Ramirez. You don't say.

When Ramirez arrived in Miami in 1975, the FBI arrested him. He said he never told the FBI what he knew because he was saving the material for a book he intended to write about his experiences. (The five-hundred-page manuscript he eventually wrote, titled "Castro's Red Hot Hell," was never published.) After being convicted of hijacking the National Airlines plane, Ramirez was sentenced to twenty years and sent to the federal penitentiary at McNeil Island in Washington State. In April of 1978, he contacted the HSCA with a plan to capture Kennedy's killers. What Ramirez wanted was to be let out of prison and "set up in a nice cozy place, easy to watch from a distance. If possible, in a not too populated area of California, close to the beach." From there, he said, he could lure Cuban agent Martin and other fellow agents to where he was for the purpose of killing him (you see, they couldn't kill him in Cuba, they had to sneak into this country to do so) at which time they could be arrested by the FBI.

Needless to say, the HSCA did not go along with the ludicrous Ramirez. The acting HSCA chairman, Congressman Floyd Fithian, told Ramirez, "I believe you have been lying to me. I believe you have not told the truth . . . Frankly, I have lost patience with you . . . and I do not want a continuation of [your] cock and bull story before this committee of the Congress."[34]

The HSCA found that some of Ramirez's allegations, such as the identities of Cuban officials he named, could be corroborated, but said that "the essential aspects of his allegations were incredible," and hence, rejected his story.[35]

Yet another preposterous allegation that Castro ordered Kennedy's death came from one Pascual Enrique Ruedolo Gongora, a fifty-year-old Cuban living in New York City who wanted to be deported back to Cuba. Shortly after the assassination, he told Gregory Banon, the Spanish consul in New York City, that he was in one of five or six groups that Castro sent to the United States to assassinate President Kennedy. There was one problem with Gongora's story, in addition to the complete implausibility of it. Gongora, who had been living in a twelve-dollar-per-week apartment paid by New York City's Department of Welfare from October 4 to November 28, 1963, when he was deported back to Cuba via Madrid, happened to be crazy, severely so. In an October 18, 1963, letter to Robert Kennedy from New York City, Gongora wrote, "I feel very ill," and added that he needed to be deported because a particular heroin trafficker who was being protected by the U.S. government was out to harm him, and in Cuba he (the trafficker) "even set set dogs on women . . . Eighteen thousand women [were] killed by dogs for the pleasure of sadistic neurotics, scoundrels and vice addicts." After Gongora returned to Cuba in late November of 1963, he somehow managed to return to the United States (Castro apparently wasn't interested in silencing one of the "talking" killers he sent to assassinate Kennedy), where he was admitted to Bellevue Psychiatric Hospital in New York City and diagnosed as a paranoid schizophrenic. Gongora, who had been arrested on two narcotic charges in the United States, admitted to past psychiatric care in Cuba.[36]

The search for any thread or whisper of a conspiracy in the Kennedy assassination has been endless. One such whisper, which, if true, conspiracy theorists thought connected Castro with the events in Dealey Plaza, was an allegation that first surfaced in the 1976 Church Committee Report. The CIA received information from some unidentified source that on the night of the assassination a Cubana Airlines flight from Mexico City (not Dallas, mind you) to Cuba was delayed some five hours, from 6:00 to 11:00 p.m. EST, awaiting an unidentified passenger. This passenger reportedly arrived at the airport in a twin-engine aircraft at 10:30 p.m. and boarded the Cubana Airlines plane without passing through customs, where he would have needed to show his passport. He traveled in the cockpit, the source said, thereby avoiding identification by the passengers.[37] The HSCA investigated the matter and found that the Cubana flight departed for Havana at 8:30 p.m., two hours *before* the arrival of the private aircraft carrying the mysterious passenger, so he could not have taken the subject flight.[38] So much for the Cubana Airlines mysterious passenger rumor, or so one would think.

Author Henry Hurt asserts that "the mystery passenger is believed to have been one Miguel Casas Saez." He quotes CIA documents released under the Freedom of Information Act which say that Casas's aunt in Remedios, Las Villas, Cuba, told a source (her dentist) that Casas was in Dallas on the day of the assassination and returned to Cuba that day on "a . . . plane" from "Mexico," that he was one of Raul Castro's men, and "very brave." Another Cuban source said Casas had left Remedios for the United States on a "sabotage and espionage mission," and two other sources said that Casas was a "poor person" and "poorly dressed" before he disappeared from Remedios for several weeks (though not stated, supposedly in the fall of 1963), but upon returning had "much money," and owned "large amounts of T-shirts, jackets and shoes, all American made." (Hurt doesn't tell his readers that another source from the same CIA documents he quotes from said that Casas, who left Cuba for the United States on September 26, 1963, on a small boat, was caught in a hurricane and ended up in Puerto Rico temporarily, came back from the states, and was seen in Remedios on November 18, 1963, four days before the assassination.) None of the sources in the CIA documents connect Casas in any way with the assassination, or even allege such a connection. But from this, Hurt, trying to establish a Castro connection to the assassination, remarkably and amusingly concludes that Casas was the Cubana Airlines mystery passenger—that is, the passenger who we know could not have existed, or the passenger who really did exist and had the supernatural power to be in two places at the same time, taking off from Mexico City to Havana at 8:30 p.m. on November 22, 1963, even though he did not *arrive* at the Mexico City airport until 10:30 p.m.[39]

Fidel Castro told several members of the HSCA during their visit with him in Havana on April 3, 1978, something that is almost too obvious (to rational people, that is) to state:

> Who here could have operated and planned something so delicate as the death of the United States president? That [is] insane. From the ideological point of view, it [would be] insane. And from the political point of view, it [would be] a tremendous insanity. I am going to tell you here that nobody, nobody ever had the idea of such things . . . Anyone who subscribed to that idea would have been judged insane, absolutely sick. Never, in twenty years of revolution, I never heard anyone suggest nor even speculate about a measure of that sort, because who could think about the idea of organizing the death of the president of the United States? *That would have been the most perfect pretext for the United States to invade our country, which is what I have tried to prevent for all these years, in every possible sense.* Since the United States is much more powerful than we are, what could we gain by a war with the United States? The United States would lose nothing. The destruction would have been here.[40]

Former CIA director Richard Helms said that if the United States had learned that Castro had Kennedy killed, "We would have bombed Cuba back into the Middle Ages."[41]

Along these lines, and as indicated earlier, NSA documents of eavesdropping intercepts released by the ARRB on August 19, 1997, revealed that immediately after the assassination, an "emotional and uneasy" Fidel Castro mobilized his armed forces out of fear the United States would blame him for Kennedy's murder and launch an invasion in retaliation.[42] One intercept of a cable sent from a foreign ambassador in Havana back home contained these words: "I got the immediate impression that Castro was frightened, if not terrified."[43]

In Castro's statement to the HSCA, he could have added that even if he had been insane enough to try and kill Kennedy, since there's normally an "internal logic" *within* the realm of insanity, why would he select as his triggerman someone like Oswald who was a known Castro sympathizer? This would only increase the suspicion that it was he who was behind the assassination. Say what you want about Castro's politics, but no one has ever accused him of being simpleminded. To the contrary, he is regarded by virtually everyone to be a highly intelligent and pragmatic person.

With respect to Castro's intelligence and pragmatism, Frank Mankiewicz, who was RFK's press secretary, and spent many hours in Havana interviewing Castro for a book he coauthored in 1975, *With Fidel*, said he was "very impressed" with Castro, that he was "smart as hell, enormously well-read and very eloquent." Indeed, Mankiewicz, who has met several world leaders, said, "It's unfortunate Castro grew up in Cuba, where the highest office he could achieve was the head of Cuba. Wherever he was, like a nation in Europe, he absolutely would have been a leader." Mankiewicz laughed off the notion that Castro would have tried to kill Kennedy. "He is an ultimate survivor, and when it comes to anything that would jeopardize his security, he was quite conservative and careful." About Castro's legendary charisma, he said Castro "would suck up all the oxygen in the room" when he entered. Mankiewicz gave an example of Castro's well-honed sense of humor (which itself requires intelligence). "When I asked him why he was so popular with the Cuban people, Castro [who is well over six feet tall] said, 'It helps if you are 6 inches taller than anyone else in the country.'"[44]

Before we go on, there is another source whom some conspiracy theorists rely on for the idea that Castro had JFK killed, and it is none other than JFK's brother RFK. As previously noted, Bobby Kennedy believed that if there had been a conspiracy to murder JFK, he, Bobby, may have been responsible because the murder may have been in retaliation for the aggressive and unrelenting war he waged against organized crime and Castro. In one of his heavily quoted post-assassination remarks, he told Bill Moyers in the spring of 1968, "I have . . . wondered at times if we did not pay a very great price for being more energetic than wise about a lot of things, *especially Cuba*."[45] This, of course, was just speculative rumination on RFK's part, and all the available credible evidence shows that neither Cuba (Castro) nor organized crime was behind JFK's death. But in a sense (a sense that he probably was not alluding to in his remark), his speculation was probably accurate. Though we can rest assured Castro did not have Oswald kill Kennedy, we have seen in considerable detail in the Oswald biography in this book that JFK and RFK's war against Castro's Cuba almost for certain played some role in Oswald's decision to kill the president.

One argument used by anti-conspiracy people against Castro's complicity, the merit of which is unclear, is based on the fact that in the fall of 1963, as Richard Goodwin, White House assistant to Kennedy, wrote, "Kennedy dispatched an emissary [William Attwood, a special adviser to the American delegation to the United Nations] to talk with the Cuban delegate to the United Nations in hopes of laying the groundwork for some rapprochement."[46] Though the HSCA, in 1978, confirmed this,[47] there is no question that right up to the day of the assassination, Cuban-American relations were raw, bitter, and volatile. Indeed, on November 18, 1963, just days before the assassination, Kennedy, in a major foreign policy speech before the Inter-American Press Association in Miami Beach, Florida, all but invited the Cuban people to overthrow Castro's Communist regime and promised prompt U.S. aid if they did.[48]

But that very same day, November 18, Attwood called Havana and spoke by phone with a member of Castro's staff, believed to be Major Rene Vallejo. Pursuant to White House instructions, Attwood informed Castro's staff member what he had previously told Carlos Lechuga, Cuba's ambassador to the United Nations, on September 23, 1963, in New York City—that the United States favored preliminary negotiations with Cuba on the issue of accommodation between the two countries at the United Nations (rather than Cuba, as the Cubans wanted), and that the United States desired to work out an agenda for these talks.[49]

In addition, the French journalist who had a series of interviews with Castro during the week leading up to and including the assassination, Jean Daniel, said that at his meeting with Castro in Havana the following day, November 19, Castro, right after a relentless indictment of U.S. policy toward Cuba for the CIA's training, equipping, and organizing of Cuban exiles for a counterrevolution, suddenly took a less hostile position. He quotes Castro as saying, "Kennedy could still be the man" who could perhaps understand the explosive realities of Cuba and meet them halfway. "He [Kennedy] still has the possibility of becoming in the eyes of history the greatest President of the United States, the leader who may at last understand that there can be co-existence between capitalists and socialists . . . I know, for example, that for Khrushchev, Kennedy is a man you can talk with. I have gotten this impression from all my conversations with Khrushchev. Other leaders have assured me that to attain this goal, we must first await his re-election. Personally, I consider him responsible for everything, but I will say this: He has come to understand many things over the past few months; and then too, in the last analysis, I'm convinced that anyone else would be worse . . . If you see him again [Daniel had interviewed the president on October 24], you can tell him that I'm willing to declare Goldwater my friend if that will guarantee [his] re-election."[50]*

Castro, it appears, had (as is so common in human relations) ambivalent, schizophrenic feelings about Kennedy. Journalist Frank Mankiewicz and the coauthor of his book on Castro, Kirby Jones, had several recorded conversations with Castro during three visits to Cuba in 1974 and 1975. In one conversation, while Castro spoke of Kennedy's responsibility for approving (though, Castro believed, not enthusiastically) the already existing plans to invade Cuba (which Castro said originated with Vice President Nixon during the Eisenhower administration), and saying he was already responsible for other acts "of aggression" toward Cuba which prevented him from being called a friend of Cuba, he nonetheless had some good things to say about Kennedy. Referring to Kennedy as an "intelligent" and "brilliant man," he felt his most affirmative virtue was that "he was a courageous man," a man (unlike Lyndon Johnson, he said) who was "capable of revising a policy because he had the courage to do so," and Castro had "interpreted" the Jean Daniel visit "as a definite gesture on Kennedy's part" toward detente. "I have no doubts," Castro said, "that Kennedy would someday have reconsidered his policy towards Cuba." Castro went on to say that although he and his people "must take into consideration [Kennedy's] responsibility for measures that were taken against us, we did not hold personal grudges against him, nor did we have reason to wish for his death, and least of all the tragic death he suffered. I say this in all honesty, in all sincerity, that we were grieved, it was very unpleasant to learn of his death, and we would have preferred that he continue in the presidency of the United States."[51]

And Daniel was having lunch with Castro at Castro's modest summer home in the resort town of Varadero Beach at one-thirty (Cuban time) on the afternoon of the assassination. When the telephone rang thereafter and a secretary in guerrilla garb informed Castro that Mr. Dortico, president of the Cuban Republic, had an urgent communication for him, "Fidel picked up the phone," Daniel writes, "and I heard him say: 'Como? Um a tentado?' ('What's that? An attempted assassination?') He then turned to us to say that Kennedy had just been struck down in Dallas. Then he went back to the telephone and exclaimed in a loud voice 'Herido? Muy gravemente?' ('Wounded? Very seriously?')

---

*What a terrible irony that the person (Castro) whom Oswald *may* have killed Kennedy for (see discussion under "Motive") was at that moment in time, unbeknownst to Oswald, wanting to establish a rapprochement with Kennedy, not murder him.

He came back, sat down and repeated three times the words: 'Es uno mala noticia.' ('This is bad news.')" When the news finally came in of Kennedy's death, Castro lamented to Daniel, "At least Kennedy was an enemy to whom we had become accustomed. This is a serious matter, an extremely serious matter."[52]

In his televised speech to the Cuban people on the evening of November 23, the night following the assassination, Castro suggested that "ultra-conservative circles" were behind the assassination, and that these circles were responsible for seeking to put the blame on him. "The information about Lee H. Oswald is a Machiavellian plan against Cuba. Oswald never had contacts with us. We have never heard of him. [He would later learn about Oswald coming to the Cuban consulate in Mexico City.] But in the dispatches he's always presented as a Castro Communist."[53]

Three separate, independent bodies investigated the possibility of Cuban complicity in Kennedy's murder. In 1964, the Warren Commission concluded it could find "no evidence" that Cuba was "involved in the assassination of President Kennedy."[54] In 1976, the Church Committee said it had "seen no evidence that Fidel Castro or others in the Cuban Government plotted Kennedy's assassination in retaliation for U.S. operations against Cuba."[55] And in 1979, the HSCA concluded that "the Cuban Government was not involved in the assassination of President Kennedy."[56] Wherever President Johnson is today, he should defer to this collective judgment.

The Odio Incident and
Anti-Castro Cuban Exiles

It has been my experience in the prosecution of criminal cases that in virtually every complex murder case, there is at least one event or the testimony of one witness that does not fit comfortably into the mosaic of the known facts. Such is the case with the Sylvia Odio incident in the Kennedy assassination, in which Miss Odio said Oswald and two Cubans visited her at her apartment in Dallas in late September of 1963, and one of the Cubans told her the following day of Oswald's reference to the desirability of Kennedy being assassinated. Conspiracy theorists have long pointed to the Odio incident as powerful evidence of a conspiracy in the assassination. Indeed, Warren Commission assistant counsel Wesley Liebeler said that at the time the Warren Commission submitted its final report in September of 1964, "I did not have any other . . . line of investigation that I wanted to pursue and I don't know that anyone else on the staff did either" except for the Sylvia Odio incident.

HSCA deputy chief counsel Gary Cornwell: "The Sylvia Odio incident was never resolved to your satisfaction, was it?"

Liebeler: "No, not really."[1]

I had learned that before defense attorney Gerry Spence and I got involved in the London docu-trial, Mark Redhead had visited Odio, who was living in Washington, D.C., seeking to have her testify at the trial, and she was disinclined to do so. However, he intended to make a further effort. I knew, of course, that even if she eventually agreed (which she did not), as with all witnesses the final determination of whether she would be called to the stand would be made by Spence or me.

When I first read about the Odio incident during my preparation for trial, I was deeply troubled. As previously pointed out, whether Oswald was or was not a part of a conspiracy would not be an issue for the jury to resolve at the trial, and Spence would be presenting evidence against his own client to suggest that Oswald was. Judge Lucius Bunton had agreed to give my offered instruction that if the jurors, though it was not their burden, nonetheless concluded that Oswald was part of a conspiracy, under the law they must (even if they believed he was not the actual killer) return a verdict of guilty. This is so because of the vicarious liability theory of conspiracy, which holds that each member of a conspiracy is criminally responsible for all crimes committed by his co-conspirators in pursuance of the objective of the conspiracy. However, any belief by the jury in the existence of a conspiracy could only spell problems for me, because all the evidence I intended to present to prove Oswald's guilt, without exception, showed Oswald always acting alone in his deadly mission. Therefore, if, for whatever reason, the jury smelled a conspiracy, this could only serve to diminish my credibility in their eyes. More importantly, the complicity of others was incompatible with the thrust of my case, and could reasonably cause the jury to question the validity of all or at least some of the evidence I was presenting against Oswald. In other words, if the jurors ultimately came to conclude that there was a conspiracy, it might raise a reasonable doubt in their mind as to whether Oswald had, in fact, killed Kennedy, since it may have been another member of the conspiracy who had pulled the trigger. So the Odio incident took on great importance in my eyes. And despite the countless claims of conspiracy by the conspiracy theorists throughout the years, it remains a fact that the Odio incident, if true, was, and continues to be, the only event where Oswald is put allegedly in the company of a mysterious companion (here, two) shortly before the assassination, and where he allegedly uttered the desirability of Kennedy's murder in the presence of at least one other person.

The Cuban regime that preceded Fidel Castro was that of Cuban dictator Fulgencio Batista, which the United States had supported for years. It was widely reviled for its corruption, enabling Castro to rise to power with the support of not only the poor[*] and the nation's youth but also most of the middle class and even many of the rich, including Sylvia Odio's family. Perhaps no one has captured, in a few words, the essence of why Castro was so popular better than President Dwight D. Eisenhower. In his book *Waging Peace*, after noting that during Castro's revolution against Batista, "sentimental support for Castro was widespread" in the United States, he writes,

> Castro's struggle had been going on for years. On the 26th of July 1953, a date which gave his movement its name, he and a little band of followers had unsuccessfully attacked the Moncada Barracks in Santiago de Cuba. After a tempestuous 3½ years of fighting, imprisonment, and exile in Mexico [where he met and joined hands with Argentinian revolutionary Ernesto "Che" Guevara], Castro returned to Cuba, where he hid out in the Sierra Maestra mountains, conducting intermittent guerrilla forays. Herbert L. Matthews of the *New York Times*, having held exclusive talks with Castro in his mountain hideout, proclaimed him "the most remarkable and romantic figure to arise in Cuban history since José Martí

[*]Castro himself, who took a law degree from the University of Havana in 1950 and briefly practiced law in Havana, almost exclusively representing the poor, often without fee, in cases with social and political implications, did not come from the poor of Cuba he sought to help. Born in 1926 in the eastern Cuban province of Oriente, his Spanish-born father fought in Cuba for the Spanish army during the War of Independence in 1898, and stayed on to become a sugar plantation owner of some means, leaving an estate of more than $500,000 when he died in 1956. (NARA Record 176-10011-100189, "Psychiatric Personality Study of Fidel Castro," Central Intelligence Agency, December 1, 1961, pp.7, 9, 12, 34; Meneses, *Fidel Castro*, pp.32–33, 37)

[1853–1895, Cuban patriot and writer], the hero of the Wars of Independence."
And in the absence of reports to the contrary, and the universal revulsion against
the Batista government, it is not surprising that large numbers of his readers should
have echoed Matthews' views. Castro promised free elections, social reform,
schools, housing, and an end to corruption. Though some individuals, in and out
of government, voiced suspicions that the Castro movement was Communist
inspired and supported, these rumblings were drowned out by the chorus of plau-
dits encouraging the "liberator."[2]

Castro's overthrow of Batista in early January of 1959 was initially heralded in the
United States by a majority of Americans.[3] Indeed, Senator John F. Kennedy himself,
just a year and a half before he tried to depose him, sang Castro's praise. In his 1960 book,
The Strategy of Peace, he writes that "we should now reread the life of Simón Bolivar, the
great 'Liberator' . . . of South America in order to comprehend the new contagion for
liberty and reform now spreading south of our borders . . . Fidel Castro is part of the
legacy of Bolivar,* who led his men over the Andes Mountains vowing 'war to the death'
against Spanish rule." (Kennedy's editor writes in a footnote that "the regime of Batista
and his army had been highly repressive; it had arrested many thousands of people, jailed
them, tortured and executed them. Since he had ousted President Carlos Prio Socarras
in 1952, civil liberty had been without a home in Cuba.")[4] The telling point is that
Kennedy wrote these words *after* he had been fully aware, as his editor writes in another
footnote, that Castro had "ruthlessly executed many of his enemies, publicly asserted that
Cuba would not align itself with the West in the Cold War, and placed Communists in
some key posts of government." Kennedy writes that "whether Castro would have taken
a more rational course after his victory had the United States Government not backed
the dictator Batista so long† and so uncritically, and had it given the fiery young rebel
[Castro] a warmer welcome in his hour of triumph, especially on his trip to this country
[Eisenhower didn't meet with Castro, palming him off on Nixon, who reportedly was
chilly toward the bearded Fidel], we cannot be sure."[5]

The Batista regime was known mostly for its corruption, but he was also a brutal dictator, his intelligence arm BRAC (Buro para Repressión de las Actividades Communistas,
"Bureau for Repression of the Communist Activities") visiting torture and often murder
on his political opposition.[6] Indeed, the denunciation of Castro's firing squads, in which
150 ex-Batista officials were publicly executed within two weeks of Castro's assuming
power in early January 1959, and at least 506 within three months,[7] has to be tempered
with the acknowledgment that at least some (and perhaps many) of those killed had themselves committed murder, and hence, their execution was no different from a death penalty
being carried out against a convicted murderer here in the states—absent due process, of
course. For instance, one of Batista's henchmen, Ramón Calvinio, who worked under
Colonel Esteban Ventura, a top police chief in Batista's regime, got away but resurfaced

---

*Bolivar was the Venezuelan revolutionary leader of the early nineteenth century (1783–1830) who led sev-
eral Spanish colonies in South America in their fight for independence from Spain. The region of northern
South America in which he fought now comprises the countries of Bolivia (named in honor of Bolivar),
Venezuela, Ecuador, Peru, and Colombia.

†That the U.S. government supported Batista and had a friendly relationship with him right up to (but
not during or beyond) the point where Batista's government was about to fall to Castro's rebels in late 1958
cannot be disputed. See, for instance, Smith (U.S. ambassador to Batista's Cuba), *Fourth Floor*, pp.168–176.

allegedly as part of the rebel invasion at the Bay of Pigs in 1961. In nationally televised interrogations of some of the captured rebels, Calvinio was confronted by a woman who screamed that he had killed her husband before her eyes. Weeping, the woman shouted at Calvinio, "Do you remember me, Calvinio, do you remember my husband? I hope I can be on the firing squad that will shoot you." Another accuser was a man who charged Calvinio with having assassinated his friends in the Castro underground movement.[8*]

For months after Castro took over the reign of power, there were "mutual expressions of friendship and cooperation" between the United States and Castro's revolutionary government. Additionally, President Eisenhower's appointment of Philip Bonsal as U.S. ambassador to Cuba to replace Ambassador Earl E. T. Smith, "who was known to be personally suspicious of Castro, was a clear signal to the new Cuban leader that the United States was interested in amicable relations" with his new government.[9]

In any event, to the great dismay of the United States and many in Cuba, Castro soon drifted more and more toward repression, and under the influence of his brother Raul and Che Guevara, who were more ideological Communists than the pragmatic Fidel,[10] toward a Communistic society. But the "outing" was not as swift and clear as many now believe. The strongest message didn't occur until May 17, 1959, over four and a half months after Castro came to power, with the passage of the Agrarian Reform Law, which limited private ownership of land to one thousand acres, the government confiscating and distributing the remaining land to peasants. At the time, approximately 75 percent of Cuba's arable land was owned by foreign interests.[11†] And actually, it wasn't until October 19 that an incident occurred which precipitated the formation of the first organized anti-Castro opposition *within* Cuba. Major Huber Matos, one of the principal heroes of Castro's revolution and one of Castro's highest-ranking officers, resigned from Castro's army in declared protest against Castro's increasingly demonstrated favoritism toward known Communists. Matos was arrested two days later, tried and convicted of treason, and sentenced to twenty years in prison.

The cat almost out of the bag, Castro met secretly shortly thereafter with his National Agrarian Reform Institute (INRA) managers from the various provinces of Cuba and outlined a plan to communize Cuba within three years. Manuel Artime Buesa, a first lieutenant in Castro's "Red Army," and Castro's manager in Oriente province who would later be one of the leaders of the Bay of Pigs invasion, was present at the meeting and would later say, "I realized that I was a democratic infiltrator in a Communist govern-

---

*Che Guevara's biographer, Jorge G. Castañeda, writes that the firing squad executions (mostly at Havana's La Cabaña fortress) have to be seen "within the context of the time. There was no bloodbath . . . After the excesses of Batista, and the unleashing of passions during those winter months, it is surprising that there were so few abuses and executions" (Castañeda, *Compañero*, pp.143–144). The chief person in charge of the executions was Castro's younger brother, Raul, described in a 1961 CIA psychiatric study on his brother, Fidel, as "sadistic" ("Cuba: Raul Castro Directly Responsible for 550 Executions," Truth Recovery Archive on Cuba, undated; NARA Record 176-10011-10189, "Psychiatric Personality Study of Fidel Castro," Central Intelligence Agency, December 1, 1961, p.5). The United States publicly deplored the mass executions of Batista's lieutenants, and Castro charged back that the United States had never voiced objections to killing and torture by Batista (HSCA Report, p.104).

†Remarkably, the United States did not object to the confiscation of property, per se, U.S. Ambassador Bonsal telling the Cuban minister of state on June 1, 1959, that the United States supported the Agrarian Reform Law "provided just and prompt compensation" was made. On June 11, the U.S. government told the Cuban government that the Reform Law "gives serious concern to the Government of the United States with regard to the adequacy of provision for compensation" to those whose property was expropriated. (HSCA Record 180-10075-10138, Sklar, *U.S. Cuban Relations, 1959–1964*, p.CRS-9)

ment." Artime went back to his province and on October 29, 1959, penned what would become a famous letter to "Dr. Fidel Castro Ruz, Sierra Maestra," in which he resigned his post in the Red Army and his INRA command and defended Huber Matos as a "patriot." The letter was a strong indictment of Castro's Cuban government on the ground that it was heavily infiltrated with Communists, and it accused Castro of, in effect, outlining a plan at the INRA meeting to communize Cuba. Artime immediately went into hiding and started to organize students and peasants to fight against Castro and Communism. By early November, the counterrevolutionary Artime had cells of his underground movement in each province in Cuba, and had published his manifesto, *Comunismo, para qué?* (Communism, What For?). His movement was called Movimiento de Recuperacion Revolucionaria (MRR), the first anti-Castro group inside Cuba and one originating from within Castro's own ranks.[12]

On the same day that Matos came out against Castro, October 19, 1959, the U.S. government began its embargo on U.S. goods to Cuba. Five days later, in response to the embargo, Castro nationalized all remaining[*] U.S. properties in Cuba.[13] This was extremely significant since the United States virtually "owned" Cuba before this. As Senator John F. Kennedy said, "At the beginning of 1959, U.S. companies owned about 40 percent of the Cuban sugar lands, almost all of the cattle ranches, 90 percent of the mines and mineral concessions, 80 percent of the utilities and practically all the oil industry, and supplied two-thirds of Cuba's imports."[14]

But it wasn't until January 2, 1961, that the U.S. government broke off all diplomatic relations with Cuba. By April of 1961, more than a hundred thousand Cubans had fled Castro's revolution, nearly all to the United States, where, to this very day, they and most of their progeny have been living in anticipation of Castro's overthrow.[15]

Sylvia Odio was born in Havana, Cuba, in 1937, one of ten children and the oldest daughter of Amador and Sarah Odio. In Batista's Cuba, the Odios were members of the wealthy aristocracy, Amador being the owner of the country's largest trucking company. *Time* magazine described him as the "transport tycoon" of Latin America.

Sylvia's parents, from their youth, had been idealistic and active opponents of a succession of tyrants who ruled Cuba, going back to the reign of General Gerardo Machado in the 1930s. In fact, twice during the dictatorship of Batista, the Odios were forced into exile for their dissident activity. Their nationalistic fervor and desire for democracy caused them to be early supporters of Castro (despite the fact that Castro's whole 26th of July Movement was to bring about land reform and secure a bigger share of the country's wealth for the working class), and the trucks of Amador Odio's company, bearing arms and medical supplies, helped sustain Castro's insurgency movement in the Sierra Maestra mountains, the mountain range in Cuba's Oriente province from which Castro launched his guerilla revolution against Batista.

But when the Odios subsequently learned, as did most Cubans, that the promise of the revolution to restore democracy in Cuba was illusory—that it had merely replaced

---

[*]In March of 1959, the Cuban government took over the United States–owned Cuban Telephone Company. In May, in the first large-scale nationalization of foreign-owned companies and industries, the Cuban government began appropriating U.S. companies. By the summer of 1960, Castro had seized more than $700 million in U.S. property. (HSCA Report, p.104)

one dictator (Batista) with another (Castro) and that Castro had betrayed the revolution and was in fact a Marxist who apparently had concealed this fact to further his revolutionary goals—they became founding members, with Manuel "Manolo" Ray and others, of Movimiento Revolucionario del Pueblo (MRP), an anti-Castro organization. Members of the MRP frequently utilized the Odios' home in Havana and their small farm near Havana to conduct MRP activities. This led to the arrest and imprisonment of Amador and Sarah by the Castro regime in 1961, the two receiving long prison terms.[16]

As a teenager, Sylvia had been sent to the Eden Hall Convent of the Sacred Heart in Philadelphia for high school and graduated in 1954. She returned to Cuba to enter the University of Villanova, where she studied law. On the side she wrote stories published in Latin American literary magazines. She abandoned her studies after three years in 1957 to marry Guillermo Herrera, son of a Havana family that other Cuban exiles described as "cultured, old, extremely wealthy, and socially well-known." Soon after the wedding, the young couple lived for nine months in New Orleans.[17] At the time of her parents' arrest, Sylvia was twenty-four and living in Ponce, Puerto Rico, with her husband and four children. The following year, her husband deserted her and the children. The imprisonment of her parents and the sudden transformation of her life from one of privilege and wealth to that of deprivation, causing her to be left alone to fend for herself and her children, induced emotional problems.[18] Mrs. Lucille Connell, a close friend of Sylvia's, said that Sylvia had a condition much more common in Latin than in American women—when "conscious reality" got "too painful to bear" for Sylvia, she sometimes would go "completely unconscious."[19]

Annie and Sarita, Sylvia's younger sisters, had settled in Dallas before Sylvia. Sarita, a student at the University of Dallas, had become friendly with Connell, a Dallas society matron who provided financial and social assistance to the Dallas Cuban Refugee Center. Connell was also active in the Mental Health Association of Dallas, and her son was a psychiatrist. Talking about Dallas's conservatism, she said that in Dallas, being active in mental health activities "would [alone] make you a part of the Communist plot." When she learned of Sylvia's plight from Sarita, Connell sent Sylvia part of her airfare to come to Dallas for a visit with her sister in March 1963. She also made efforts to find an appropriate psychiatrist for Sylvia, and they eventually settled on Dr. Burton C. Einspruch at the Southwestern Medical School, who started treating her in April with some success. Connell, with whom Sylvia was staying, noticed that the fainting tapered off and eventually ended.[20] At the end of June, Sylvia went back to Puerto Rico to collect her four young children and settle them in her new apartment at 1084 Magellan Circle in Dallas.[21]

Bright and pretty, well educated, charming, and imbued with the social graces imparted to her by the sisters of the Sacred Heart, whose mission was to provide superior education for "the daughters of gentlefolk," Sylvia, through Connell's introductions, became acquainted with and accepted by the highest strata of Dallas society, including the family of John Rogers, who owned Texas Industries (she stayed with the Rogers family for a period after her hospitalization following JFK's death). For a time she dated Lawrence Marcus, one of the owners of the exclusive department store Neiman Marcus, where she worked for a while. In fact, her psychiatrist, Dr. Einspruch, who got to know Sylvia well, said that Miss Odio had unquestionably passed Mrs. Connell on the social ladder and was "at the very top" in Dallas.[22] By September, when she was working at the National Chemsearch Company in Irving, her emotional problems had subsided, and she was planning to move to a better apartment closer to her work. The last week of September, her seventeen-year-old sister, Annie, came to the Magellan Circle apartment to help Sylvia pack for the move on October 1, and to tend to Sylvia's children.[23]

As alluded to briefly in the Oswald biography in this book, Sylvia Odio testified before the Warren Commission that the week prior to the October 1 moving date, as she was getting dressed to go out to a friend's house just before 9:00 p.m., the doorbell rang and her sister Annie went to the door. When Annie came back and said, "Sylvia, there are three men at the door," Sylvia put on her housecoat and went to the door. With October 1, 1963, as a reference date, she said the visit was either the previous Thursday (September 26) or Friday (September 27) evening.

Two of the men at the door, she testified, appeared to be Cubans. The third was an American. The Cubans, she said, told her they were very good friends of Sylvia's father (about whom, she testified, they knew "almost incredible details," including where he was imprisoned on the Isle of Pines, Fidel Castro's Devil's Island in Cuba) and members of JURE (the Cuban Revolutionary Junta), the anti-Castro organization that succeeded MRP and of which Sylvia herself was a member in Dallas. JURE was headed by Manolo Ray, who in the earlier MRP years had often hidden from Castro in the Odios' Havana residence. She testified that the two Cubans identified themselves only by their fictitious underground "war names." She recalls one of the Cubans' names as being "Leopoldo." He was the taller of the two Cubans and did most of the talking. The other one's name was "something like Angelo." She said "they both looked very greasy, like the kind of low Cubans, not educated at all." Leopoldo said, "We wanted you to meet this American. His name is Leon Oswald," mentioning his name twice. For the most part, the American kept quiet, saying "just a few little words in Spanish, trying to be cute . . . like 'Hola.'" When Sylvia asked him if he had ever been to Cuba, he said he had not.[24]

She described the American as being around five feet ten inches tall and "kind of a skinny man, a description that generally fits Oswald." For those who believe Odio might have fabricated her whole story from media accounts, she apparently wasn't aware of something that had been widely published—Oswald's age of twenty-four. In her testimony to the Warren Commission, nearly a year after the assassination, she said she guessed that "Leon" was about thirty-four or thirty-five at the time she met him.

"Have you," Warren Commission counsel asked, "read the newspapers and watched television since the assassination and observed Oswald?"

"I read some of it," Sylvia answered.

"Did you read how old he was?"

"I don't even know what age he is."[25]

If this was fabrication, it was clever indeed.

Odio testified that Leopoldo told her they had just come from New Orleans. One of the Cubans took out a letter written in Spanish asking for donations to help fund JURE activities. The Cubans wanted Sylvia to translate the petition into English and to send it out seeking funds. Not only had other small groups of Cubans come to her door asking her to help with JURE, but Antonio Alentado, the head of JURE in Dallas, had earlier shown her the same petition and made the same request. Because she was very busy with her job and four children, she had declined to become that actively involved in the Dallas chapter of JURE. When she asked the Cubans if they had been sent by Alentado and they said no, that they were trying to organize the Dallas area on their own, she told them she would be unable to help them. (Odio told FBI agent James Hosty in her first interview with the authorities on December 18, 1963, that she declined to help because her parents were still in prison in Cuba and she feared they would possibly be harmed.) Watching the three men drive off through the window of her apartment, she noticed that Leopoldo was driving. The next day, Odio testified, Leopoldo called her after she got home from work. She felt he was trying to get "fresh" with her, "trying to be too nice, telling me that I was pretty." He then asked her what she thought of the American. When she replied she "didn't think anything," he proceeded to tell her they wanted to introduce Leon (over the telephone Leopoldo never mentioned the name Oswald) to the underground because "he is great, he is kind of nuts. He told us we don't have any guts . . . because President Kennedy should have been assassinated after the Bay of Pigs and some Cubans should have done that because he was the one that was holding the freedom of Cuba, actually." Killing the president, the American had said, would be "so easy to do." Leopoldo said that Leon was a former marine and an "expert shotman," and told Odio the American was the type who might be able to go underground in Cuba and kill Castro.[26]

Three days after the three men visited her, Sylvia said she wrote to her father at the Nueva Gerona prison on the Isle of Pines in Cuba asking him if he knew the two Cuban visitors who came to her door purporting to be his friends. She recalls giving him the war names of one or two of the Cubans, but said she probably only referred to the third man as an "American."[27] It was Christmas Day 1963 before Amador was allowed to write back. In his letter to "My children" (his ten sons and daughters, all of whom he and Sarah had removed from Cuba to safety and who now lived in Miami and Dallas, the younger ones in orphanages), the words were meticulously printed in very tiny letters on one sheet with no margins, making the most of the single page he was allowed to write on. It is a letter of a man struggling hard to keep his family together spiritually in spite of the circumstances that had scattered them in exile, and it is full of praise, exhortations, admonitions, and hope for the future. Eventually he speaks directly to Sylvia about her mysterious visitors, and underlines his words. "Tell me *who this is who says he is my friend*," he writes. "*Be careful. I do not have any friend who might be here, through Dallas, so reject his friendship until you give me his name.*"[28]*

It was no doubt good advice. Refugees whose friends and relatives were held prisoner in Cuba were preyed on by scam artists who claimed they could help secure release of prisoners in much the way people with incurable diseases are preyed on by quacks. Moreover, the security problems of the anti-Castro underground in America were great. No one knew which of their friends and colleagues might be spies for the Castro regime.

Although Odio testified she may have told Lucille Connell about the visit from the three men, the only other person she is certain she told before the assassination was her psychiatrist, Dr. Einspruch.[29] Einspruch confirmed in a deposition given to the HSCA on July 11, 1978, that Odio had told him, prior to the assassination, of the visit from the three men. He said she told him two of the men were "Cubans or Latins" and the third man was an "Anglo," though he did not recall whether or not she mentioned his name was Leon at that time. He said she did, however, after the assassination, when she identified Leon as Oswald to him. Einspruch did not recall Odio ever telling him that Leopoldo had called her a day later and told her about Leon saying that Kennedy should be assassinated.[30]

At the time of the assassination, Sylvia was still working at National Chemsearch. The company manufactured and sold products like soap and cleanser to large companies and

---

*The letter contains fatherly asides to each one of his beloved children. To Sylvia he writes, "Do not abandon your literature. Persevere. Write a good book even though it takes you years."

institutions, not retail stores, and because she was bilingual, she worked in its International Department taking orders from Latin countries.[31]

When Sylvia returned to work from lunch on November 22, 1963, and learned the president had been assassinated, she passed out and was taken by ambulance to a hospital in Irving. Though there had been no mention of Oswald on the news yet, she "established a connection" in her mind between the assassination and the visit of the three men, particularly the reference to the fact that "the Cubans should have killed President Kennedy . . . I was so upset about it. So probably the lunch had something to do with it, too, and I was so upset, that that is why I probably passed out."[32]* Because the two non-Anglos at her door were anti-Castro Cubans, Odio would later say that her immediate fear that Cuban exiles might be accused of the president's death may have contributed to her fainting.[33]

Odio said that when she saw Oswald on television later that day from her hospital room, she immediately recognized him as the Anglo Leon. "I kept saying it can't be to myself; it just can't be. I mean it couldn't be, but when my sister walked into the hospital [room] and she said, 'Sylvia, have you seen the man?' . . . I said, yes, and she said, 'That was the man that was at the door' . . . so I had no doubts then." When asked by Warren Commission counsel if she had any doubts that Leon was Oswald, she replied, "I don't have any doubt."[34]

Odio did not contact the authorities about the visit from the two Cubans and the man she was now certain was Oswald. She told an HSCA investigator in 1976 that she and her sister were extremely frightened and worried about the welfare of their parents in Cuba and of their brothers and sisters, not knowing if others were involved in the assassination and what the consequences to them and their family would be if they came forward. "I never wanted to go to the [authorities]. I was afraid. I was young at the time, I was recently divorced, I had young children, I was going through hell. Besides, it was such a responsibility to get involved because who is going to believe you? Who is going to believe that I had Oswald in my house? I was scared and my sister Annie was very scared at the time."[35]†

On August 28, 1964, the Warren Commission's chief counsel, J. Lee Rankin, wrote to FBI Director J. Edgar Hoover, stating that "it is a matter of some importance to the Commission that Mrs. Odio's allegations either be proved or disproved."[36]

T he two questions, of course, that bedeviled and concerned the Warren Commission (as well as the HSCA) were whether or not two Cubans and an American did in fact visit Odio in September of 1963, and much more importantly, if they did, whether the American was Oswald. Although not explicitly stating it, the Warren Report implies that the Commission did believe there was such a visit,[37] never once seeming to question her story about the two Latin men and one American man coming to her door. However, the Commission concluded that Oswald was not the American man because he could not have been

---

*Jeannine Ewing was the secretary to Harry Lane, the executive vice president of sales at National Chemsearch at the time of the assassination. She thinks that Sylvia Odio worked at the company, which had close to 150 employees, for "less than a year." She went out to lunch several times with Odio and described her as "pleasant and very intelligent." "Was there anything about her that you would say was goofy or unusual, either in her mannerisms or mentally?" I asked. "Oh, no," Ewing answered. "But she did say several times that she hated President Kennedy." Ewing did not personally see Odio faint at work that day, but she knew she did, and heard from others in the office that Odio had said, "I know who did it" just before she fainted. (Telephone interview of Jeannine Ewing by author on February 13, 2006)

†The FBI learned about the Odio incident through Odio's friend Lucille Connell (HSCA Record 180-10101-10283, April 5, 1976, pp.1–2), who had learned of the incident from Sylvia's sister Sarita (10 HSCA 28).

in Dallas on the dates and time given by Miss Odio, around 9:00 p.m. on September 26 or 27, 1963, and, indeed, "Oswald was not at Miss Odio's apartment in September of 1963."[38]

If, indeed, as Odio testified before the Warren Commission, the visit from the two Cubans and one American took place around 9:00 p.m. on the evening of September 26 or 27, 1963,[39]* it would clearly appear that Oswald could not have been present. The Warren Commission, as a result of a very thorough and meticulous investigation by the FBI as well as the Secret Service, replete with extensive documentary evidence in addition to eyewitness testimony, proved that he was in Mexico on the evenings of both of these days (see later text).

The FBI investigation concluded that Oswald was in New Orleans from April 24, 1963, when he left Dallas for New Orleans, until at least 8:00 a.m. on September 25, 1963. Ruth Paine and Marina Oswald left Oswald behind when they departed New Orleans for Dallas on September 23.[40] On September 24, Oswald went to the office of the Louisiana Division of Employment Security in New Orleans to sign for his Texas unemployment compensation for that week.[41] He received $33 per week in unemployment compensation.[42] That week's check, dated September 23, 1963, was picked up by the U.S. Postal Department from the Texas Employment Commission in Austin, Texas, at 5:15 that evening.[43] The Warren Commission concluded that the earliest time Oswald could have obtained the Texas check from his post office box in New Orleans was 5:00 a.m. on September 25, 1963.[44] Although the date Oswald cashed this check at the Winn-Dixie Store in New Orleans is not indicated on the check, it is believed he must have cashed it sometime between 8:00 a.m. (when the store opened for the day) and 1:00 p.m. on September 25. Store records show that the cashier who cashed the check, Mrs. Thelma Fisher, left work at 1:00 p.m. on September 25.[45] So Oswald's presence in New Orleans until at least the morning (8:00 a.m.) of September 25 seems to have been firmly established by the Warren Commission. The Commission noted, however, that "between the morning of September 25th and 2:35 a.m. on September 26th" Oswald's whereabouts were "not strictly accounted for."[46]

The FBI and Secret Service established that the following day, September 26, Oswald, whose ultimate destination was Mexico City, was traveling on Continental Trailways bus number 5133, which left Houston at 2:35 a.m. for Laredo, Texas. The 5133 passengers, en route to Laredo, were transferred to bus number 304 at Corpus Christi, which arrived in Laredo about 1:20 p.m. that day.[47]†

As indicated previously, a young couple from Liverpool, England, Mr. and Mrs. John

---

*In the FBI's first interview of Odio on December 18, 1963, she said the incident took place in "late September or early October, 1963" (CD 205, p.1).

†Checking bus, train, and airline schedules and records, the Secret Service and FBI were unable to firmly establish how Oswald got to Houston from New Orleans on the first day of his Mexico City trip, and whether he visited Dallas in between (WR, p.323; CE 2131, 24 H 717; CE 3086, 26 H 694–698; CE 3075, 26 H 675–678). A statement in the Warren Report that Oswald had told passengers on the bus to Laredo that "he had traveled from New Orleans *by bus*, and made no mention of an intervening trip to Dallas" (WR, p.324), is an overstatement. The main citation given for this is the affidavit of passengers Mr. and Mrs. John McFarland. Question: "Did he [Oswald] mention any names or places either in the United States or Mexico, in any connection whatsoever?" Answer: "Only New Orleans, whence he said he had come. In the course of conversation, we worked out he must have left New Orleans at about the same time we had left Jackson, Mississippi, i.e., 2:00 p.m. on Wednesday, September 25, 1963." (11 H 214–215, WC affidavit of Mr. and Mrs. John McFarland) The FBI checked with Greyhound and Continental Trailways bus drivers of all trips out of New Orleans on September 25, 1963 (the date it is believed Oswald left New Orleans), whose destination could have taken Oswald to Laredo, Texas, and none of them were able to recall any passenger resembling Oswald on their trips (CE 2192, 25 H 8).

McFarland, gave an affidavit to the American consulate in Liverpool that they first became aware of Oswald, whom they thereafter recognized from pictures in the newspapers at the time of the assassination, on the Houston-to-Laredo bus "probably about 6:00 a.m., after it became light."[48]

After he departed Laredo, Texas, on bus number 516 of the Flecha Roja bus line for Mexico City at 1:45 p.m. on September 26, 1963, witnesses and Mexican immigration records reflect that Oswald crossed the border to Nuevo Laredo, Mexico, sometime before 2:00 p.m. on September 26.[49]

The reason the exact time of day is not known is that Helio Tuexi Maydon, the Mexican immigration inspector (Maydon worked on September 26 from 6:00 a.m. to 2:00 p.m.) who stamped Oswald's tourist card, FM-8 No. 240085, failed to record the precise time of day.[50]

Since the evidence is overwhelming that Oswald could not, as Sylvia Odio alleges, have been at her apartment in Dallas on the evenings of either September 26 or 27 (since on the evening of September 26 he was on a bus in Mexico traveling to Mexico City, and on the evening of September 27 he was in Mexico City), can we therefore discard her story as being unfactual? In an infrequently cited second interview with the FBI on September 10, 1964, a month and a half after her Warren Commission testimony, Odio acknowledged that the visit by the three men could possibly have been on Wednesday night, September 25, 1963.[51] Although the FBI agents had made every effort possible to confirm Oswald's whereabouts during the day and evening of September 25, they were unable to do so.[52]

However, the premise that Oswald visited Odio on the evening of the twenty-fifth creates its own set of problems, though not, as we have seen with the twenty-sixth and twenty-seventh, of a prohibitory nature. The Warren Commission established that the only bus out of Dallas on the evening of September 25 after 9:00 p.m. (the time of the visit, per Odio) that Oswald could have taken and would have enabled him to connect with the Houston bus to Laredo was a Continental Trailways bus departing Dallas at 11:00 p.m. However, that bus, traveling through San Antonio, did not connect with the Houston-to-Laredo bus until 10:35 (in Alice, Texas) on the morning of the twenty-sixth, more than four hours *after* the McFarlands first reported seeing Oswald on their bus.[53] Moreover, no tickets were sold during the period September 23–26, 1963, for travel between Dallas and Laredo by the Dallas office of Continental Trailways.[54]

There is a further problem that circumstantially militates against Oswald being at Odio's door with his two Cuban friends at around 9:00 on the evening of September 25. Mrs. Estelle Twiford of Houston, Texas, said that one evening "during the week prior to the weekend that my husband flew home to visit me from New Orleans," she received a telephone call sometime between seven and ten o'clock from Oswald requesting to speak to her husband, Horace. (Estelle and Horace distributed literature in Texas for the Socialist Labor Party, and Horace had routinely mailed Oswald literature in Dallas, and Oswald's address book contained the name Horace Twiford with Twiford's address and phone number.)[55] As discussed earlier in this book, when Oswald was told that Twiford's husband, a merchant seaman, was at sea, Oswald said he had hoped to discuss ideas with him for a few hours before he left for Mexico. Horace Twiford was able to fix the week of the Oswald call because he said he had flown home from New Orleans to visit his wife on September 27 (a Friday) and was told by his wife that Oswald had called "during the week preceding my visit home. I had been home on the previous weekend, and neither at that time nor prior thereto had my wife said anything about a call from Oswald." Since we know Oswald was in New Orleans on September 23 and 24 (see earlier text), and Mexico on September 26 and 27, it appears the call was on the evening of the twenty-fifth. Mrs. Twiford assumed the call from Oswald was a local (Houston) one because, she said, no operator was involved and because of Oswald's remark that he wanted to "discuss ideas" with her husband "for a few hours." However, Oswald did not specifically tell her he was in Houston at the time of the call.[56] If Oswald, in fact, was in Houston sometime between 7:00 and 10:00 p.m. on the evening of September 25, wanting to meet with Horace Twiford for a few hours, this would essentially rule out his being at Sylvia Odio's residence at nine o'clock that same evening.

If Oswald was not the American who visited Odio on the evening of September 25, 26, or 27, 1963, who was? And who were the two Cubans? Based on the description of the three men given by Miss Odio, and the two war names of Leopoldo and possibly Angelo, the Warren Commission had the FBI conduct a far-reaching canvass of the anti-Castro community in the United States to locate them. On September 16, 1964, the FBI located one Loran Eugene Hall in Johnsandale, California. Loran Hall (whose name bears a phonetic resemblance to Odio's "Leon Oswald") had been involved in anti-Castro paramilitary activities in Florida. He told the bureau that he, a Mexican-American from East Los Angeles named Lawrence Howard, and William Seymour from Arizona (who, Hall said, resembled Oswald) had visited Odio in Dallas in September of 1963 to solicit funds for the anti-Castro movement.[57] The FBI had not completed its investigation of this matter by the time the Warren Report, published on September 24, 1964, was submitted for publication, and the Report informed its readers of this fact.[58] Within a week of Hall's statement, and with the Warren Commission no longer in existence, Howard and Seymour were interviewed by the FBI and denied ever having met Odio. Howard said Hall was a "scatter-brain, unreliable, emotionally disturbed, and an egotistical liar." On September 20, 1964, Hall himself recanted his story.[59] Nonetheless, on October 1, 1964, in Miami, Florida (where Odio had just moved to from Dallas), the FBI showed photos of Hall, Howard, and Seymour to Odio, who said none of them were among the men who had visited her. Her sister Annie was also shown the three photos and she too failed to recognize any of the men.[60] Additionally, an examination of the payroll records of the Beach Welding Supplies Company of Miami Beach, Florida, revealed that Seymour, the one who allegedly looked like Oswald, was employed with the company and worked forty-hour weeks during the period September 5 to October 10, 1963.[61]

The HSCA reinterviewed Hall, Howard, and Seymour, and again searched the anti-Castro community for the three men who had visited Odio, extending their search to even include pro-Castro activists. The search produced three men who may have been in Dallas in September 1963. Photographs of the men were shown to Odio, who could not identify them as the men who had visited her.[62]

Assuming Sylvia Odio is telling the truth, the identity of Leopoldo and Angelo remains unknown to this day. From their appearance, the things they said, their detailed knowledge of Odio's father, the fact they had the identical petition in their possession that Dallas JURE leader Antonio Alentado had—indeed, from the fact they had Sylvia Odio's home address—one can reasonably conclude they were, in fact, anti-Castro Cuban exiles.

Certainly, no one has suggested they were pro-Castro Cubans, nor is there any evidence to warrant this conclusion.

It's not even known where they were from. The assumption has always been New Orleans, simply because Leopoldo told Odio, "We have just come from New Orleans." But they could have been from Miami, the headquarters for all of the anti-Castro groups[63] and the city where the overwhelming majority of anti-Castro Cubans have always lived. New Orleans may simply have been a city where they had been for awhile, and the city from which they departed on their trip to Dallas. Indeed, although they never expressly said so, Sylvia Odio got the impression from the two Cubans at her door that after Dallas "they were leaving for Puerto Rico *or Miami*."[64]

Even if they were from New Orleans, however, we cannot automatically assume that they would have been aware of Oswald's confrontation with *anti*-Castro Cubans the very previous month, and hence, have known of Oswald's real identity as being *pro*-Castro and most likely anti-Kennedy. Although there was mention of the confrontation in the media,[65] it was a very minor story, and therefore the two Cubans may not have heard the news account. And since the anti-Castro movement was disorganized and fractured, we also cannot assume that word of the minor confrontation would have spread quickly in New Orleans's anti-Castro community. For instance, Bringuier, who was very active in the anti-Castro movement in New Orleans, didn't even know that there was an anti-Castro training camp in New Orleans across from Lake Pontchartrain.[66]

Whether Leopoldo and Angelo were from New Orleans, Miami, or elsewhere, if Leon was in fact Oswald, and they in fact knew he was actually pro-Castro, then the visit to Odio's house makes little sense. Neither would Leopoldo's words to Odio the following day. He would know that Castro was the last person in the world Oswald would want to harm.

Although we have seen that the evidence of time and place compels the conclusion that Oswald could not have visited Odio on September 26 or 27, 1963, and most probably did not do so on September 25, there nevertheless are countervailing reasons why we cannot automatically dismiss Odio's allegations—namely, her credibility and corroborating evidence. As stated, we can infer from the Warren Report (and the fact that the Commission had the FBI conduct an extremely detailed and comprehensive investigation of Odio's story) that the Warren Commission staff did not write Odio's story off and believed her to be truthful, though mistaken, in her relation of the events to which she testified. Among others, Wesley Liebeler, who examined her for the Warren Commission, said, "I think [Odio] believes that Oswald was there. I do not think she would lie about something like that."[67] Assistant Counsel W. David Slawson, whose area of investigation for the Warren Commission was the possibility of a conspiracy in the assassination, wrote in his report to the Commission that "Mrs. Odio has been checked out thoroughly through her psychiatrist and friends, and, with one exception—a layman [not identified] who speculates that she may have subconscious tendencies to over-dramatize or exaggerate—the evidence is unanimously favorable, both as to her character and reliability and as to her intelligence."[68] Moreover, the problems that caused Odio to seek psychiatric assistance were not those that could affect her perception or credibility, and Odio was not hallucinatory.[69] A Warren Commission staff report noted that "Doctor [Burton] Einspruch [Odio's psychiatrist] stated that he had great faith in Miss Odio's story of having met Lee Harvey Oswald," believing the story to be "completely true." Einspruch, who had been seeing Odio on the average of once a week since April of 1963, said that while Odio was "given to exaggeration, all the basic facts which she provides are true." He stated her tendency to exaggerate is that of an emotional type, characteristic of many Latin-American people, and being one of degree rather than basic fact.[70] Manolo Ray, who had known Sylvia Odio and her family for years, told the FBI that Odio was an intelligent person of good character who would not have fabricated or been delusional about the incident at her door.[71]

Dr. Einspruch told the HSCA he felt Odio's emotional problems were "situational." In addition to the obvious problem of her husband leaving her to fend for herself and four children, Einspruch said Odio was not doing well economically, "she was an immigrant, her parents were imprisoned . . . she had all the difficulties one might anticipate a displaced person would have."[72]

The HSCA, after a thorough evaluation of all the evidence, stated that "the committee was inclined to believe Sylvia Odio" to the extent that "three men did visit her apartment in Dallas prior to the Kennedy assassination and identified themselves as members of an anti-Castro organization," and that "one of these men at least looked like Lee Harvey Oswald and was introduced to Mrs. Odio as Leon Oswald."[73] As is normally not the case with those who are lying, the HSCA noted that Odio was consistent with her story over a period of many years, with only minor details changing.[74]

The most important question, of course, is the following: Even if we make the assumption that Odio is being truthful, as the HSCA concluded and the Warren Commission implied, did she mistakenly believe the Anglo among the three men was Oswald? As discussed earlier in this book, there is something phenomenally distinctive about each human's physiognomy. So much so that, as mentioned earlier, no two people (other than identical twins) look almost exactly like each other. So much so that even animals recognize people they've seen before. Though there are factors that militate against identification, such as poor vision, distance, darkness and shadows, obstructions, oblique views, and so on, after you see and talk to someone close-up for several minutes, when you see that person again, particularly within a short period of time, a bell of recognition immediately goes off. This is why, if Odio is being truthful, it is extremely difficult to disregard her identification of Oswald.

The Warren Commission showed Odio several photos of Oswald. With two, she pointed out differences between the photo and Oswald. In one, Oswald looked shaven, she said, and on the night at her apartment, Oswald had a "little mustache" and he "did not look shaved." In another, she said that although everything else was the same, the lips "did not look like the same man." Also, "I am not too sure of that picture. He didn't look like this . . . he was more smiling than in this picture." *Yet, even with these two photos of Oswald*, she identified him as being the one in her apartment that night. And with other photos of Oswald, she made an unqualified identification. Asked whether one photograph of Oswald "was the man who was in your apartment," she jocularly stated that "if it is not [Oswald], it is his twin." Also, when shown New Orleans television (WDSU) footage of street scenes of Oswald in August of 1963, she identified Oswald, and added that "he had the same mustache." When asked, "When did you first become aware of the fact that this man who had been at your apartment was the man who had been arrested in connection with the assassination?" she replied, "It was immediately." "As soon as you saw his picture?" "Immediately, I was so sure." When asked once again by Warren Commission counsel, "Do you have any doubts in your mind after looking at these pictures that the man that was in your apartment was . . . Lee Harvey Oswald?" she again replied, "I don't have any doubts."[75]*

No one examining the evidence in the Odio matter can feel too sanguine about the conclusion he reaches, yet I feel that the slight preponderance of evidence is that Oswald was, in fact, the American among the three men who visited Odio. I say that for several reasons. One is that there is, as trial lawyers like to say, that unmistakable "ring of truth" to Odio's testimony. An imperfect analogy is a U.S. Supreme Court justice's observation about obscenity, that he couldn't define it but he knew it when he saw it. Most of all, of course, is her positive identification of Oswald from photos and film. Moreover, her physical description of height and weight matches Oswald. The men telling her that they had "just come from New Orleans" and Leopoldo telling Odio that the American had been a marine, and that he was "kind of nuts," all fit Oswald precisely. And the name Leon Oswald is clearly too close to be a coincidence. Unless Odio had fabricated this entire story, and had gotten these identifying details on Oswald through media accounts, these details speak loudly for the fact that the American was indeed Oswald.

The hypothesis of fabrication is difficult to square with the facts here. Odio certainly can't be accused, for instance, of wanting to attach herself, for publicity purposes—as so many people do—to a high-visibility public event. To the contrary, she contacted neither the authorities nor the media about her belief that Oswald had visited her. Rather, she deeply feared her being associated with the incident. The only person she is sure she told, when he called her on the day after the assassination, was her psychiatrist.[76] In this vein, when CBS's Martin Phillips contacted her to be on a Dan Rather CBS television special on the assassination, she refused.[77] It should be further noted parenthetically that Odio subsequently declined Mark Redhead's further entreaties that she testify at the London trial, even though she was aware that the trial would be shown on national television in the United States and in many foreign countries, including England, France, Germany, and Australia. It simply stands to reason that if Odio had fabricated the aforementioned details about her visits that evening, this would be the work of someone who was intent on getting the story out. But, as we have seen, Odio did not do this. Nor has she ever attempted to profit, in any way, from her story, the first time she even granted a television interview being for a PBS *Frontline* special *thirty years later*.

Also, and perhaps most importantly, if Odio had fabricated her story, it is almost inconceivable that she would have said that before the assassination that Oswald was in the presence of two Cuban members of JURE, the anti-Castro group formed in Miami whose founder, Manolo Ray, had very close ties to Odio's parents. In fact, as indicated earlier, the parents cofounded, with Ray, the MRP, some of whose members became the original nucleus for JURE.[78] Indeed, Odio, herself a member of JURE, was actively involved in the anti-Castro movement and "desperate" to do anything she could to free her mother

---

*When an interviewer from the HSCA spoke to Odio on January 16, 1976, and asked her about the possibility that the man at her door merely looked very much like Oswald, she replied, "When you see someone as close as I'm seeing you now, even closer because we were standing by my door for about fifteen minutes and the light was . . . coming down upon their faces, when I saw him on television I recognized him immediately. And this guy had a special grin, a kind of funny smirk" (HSCA Record 180-10101-10280, January 16, 1976, p.1), the smirk being an identifying characteristic of Oswald so many other people had commented on.

and father from their imprisonment in Cuba under Castro. She would never have thought that putting the presidential assassin in the company of JURE members before the assassination would be helpful to any of her dreams. In fact, why would Odio be trying to implicate *any* anti-Castro group in Kennedy's assassination? Only by Odio saying that Oswald appeared at her door with *pro*-Castro Cubans would Odio or any other Cuban exile have any hope of igniting a U.S. response that would topple the Cuban dictator. The fact that the story she told could only, if at all, be prejudicial to her interests is circumstantial evidence she was telling the truth. Adding further credibility to Odio's story is her telling her father and psychiatrist, *prior* to the assassination, of the visit by the three men. The fact that she did not mention the name Leon to her father, and may or may not have to her psychiatrist, is inconsequential, since prior to the assassination the name of the American who visited her that night had no significance. When her psychiatrist, Dr. Einspruch, called her on the day of or the day after the assassination, he recalls she did mention "Leon" to him as being Oswald.[79]

Finally, there is corroboration for Sylvia Odio's story in the form of her younger sister, Annie, who answered the door when the three men came to the apartment. Annie Odio, without the emotional and psychiatric baggage that some feel corrodes the credibility of Sylvia Odio, also positively identified Oswald as being the American and one of the three men. When she first saw Oswald on television on the afternoon of the assassination, her first thought, she said, was, "My God. I know this guy, and I don't know from where! But I'm not going to tell anybody because they're going to think I'm crazy." When Annie spoke to Sylvia later that day and Sylvia reminded her of the three men at the door, Annie then remembered where she had seen Oswald.[80]

My belief in Odio's story, though I'm not prepared to take it to the bank, and though it admittedly does not rise to the status of certainty or even beyond a reasonable doubt, necessarily constitutes a rejection of the Warren Commission's conclusion that Odio's story is not believable because Oswald could not have been at her door when she said he was. The distinction between literary fiction and nonfiction comes to mind. It is said that one advantage an author of fiction has is that he can give wings to his imagination, whereas in nonfiction one is restricted to the facts. However, to be good fiction a story should be somewhat believable. But nonfiction doesn't have to be believable. If it happened, whether it is believable or not is irrelevant. The likelihood is that the event Odio described did, in fact, take place, most probably on the evening of September 24 or 25, 1963. In an April 28, 1964, letter to J. Edgar Hoover, Rankin, general counsel for the Warren Commission, wrote that "the only time [Oswald] could have been in Odio's apartment appears to be the nights of September 24 or 25, 1963, most likely the latter."[81]

With respect to September 24, the Warren Commission concluded[82] that "under normal procedures" Oswald could not have received his Texas unemployment compensation check in New Orleans, which was dated and mailed on Monday, September 23, 1963,[83] before 5:00 a.m. on September 25, 1963, a Wednesday (see earlier text). However, Marina told the FBI that Oswald received his unemployment check every Tuesday.[84] In fact, the Warren Commission itself said that Oswald cashed the previous week's check at the Winn-Dixie Store in New Orleans on Tuesday, September 17, 1963.[85] If, then, Oswald had received his next check on Tuesday, September 24, it's possible he cashed it at the Winn-Dixie Store between 8:00 a.m. and 1:00 p.m. on that day, not, as believed, the following day, Wednesday, September 25.

If that happened, Oswald and his two Cuban friends could have departed New Orleans by automobile during the daytime on September 24 and reached Sylvia Odio's door in Dallas, 530 miles away (approximately an eight-hour drive at 65 mph), by nine o'clock that evening, September 24. In fact, Marina told the Warren Commission that Oswald told her he intended to leave New Orleans the very next day after her departure on September 23, 1963, that is, September 24.[86] (There was a conflicting story, however, that Oswald was seen leaving his apartment in New Orleans on the evening of September 24 carrying two suitcases,[87] which, if true, would have made it impossible for him to have been in Dallas that evening.)

Odio testified that "they kept mentioning they had come to visit me at such a time of night . . . because they were leaving on a trip." She said they added, "We may stay until tomorrow, or we might leave tomorrow night."[88] As we know, the next day Leopoldo called Odio after she returned from work (late afternoon or early evening) and they had the conversation about Oswald, Kennedy, and Castro. If this was the late afternoon or early evening of September 25, and Oswald was still with the Cubans, this would have given Oswald adequate time to drive thereafter with the Cubans from Dallas to Houston (at 240 miles away, approximately a three-and-a-half-hour drive at 65 mph), where Oswald could have then caught Continental Trailways bus number 5133 at 2:35 a.m. on September 26 bound for Laredo, Texas. This September 24, 1963, scenario would also be compatible with Mrs. Twiford's belief that she sensed Oswald was calling her "from the Houston area," somewhere "between seven and ten o'clock" in the evening. (If Oswald and the Cubans were at Odio's door on September 25, however, since the incident took place at 9:00 p.m. in Dallas, he could not have called Twiford from the Houston area that evening.)

It's pure speculation, but since we know the purpose of Oswald's trip to Mexico was to reach Cuba, he could have easily conned the Cubans into believing that he was seeking to go to Cuba to further the Cubans' goals, which they erroneously believed were the same as his. Believing Oswald was furthering their interests, they may have agreed to drive him as far as Houston. If they did drive Oswald to Houston, almost due south from Dallas, and if they were going to return to New Orleans, New Orleans would have virtually been straight east from Houston for them. Driving Oswald from Houston to Laredo, however, would have been completely out of the Cubans' way.

The meeting at the door could also have happened on the evening of September 25. If it did, when Leopoldo called Odio after she came home from work on the day after the meeting at the door—which would be the early evening of September 26—Oswald couldn't have still been in Dallas with his two Cuban friends (we know that on the evening of September 26 Oswald was on a bus, in Mexico, traveling to Mexico City), and would have had to have gotten to Houston on the evening of September 25 without their assistance.

Since the weight of the evidence in the Odio case is that the event Odio described did, in fact, take place, the countervailing evidence prompting the inference that her story is not believable should yield. It yields in this case, in my view, by accepting the probability that the seemingly airtight case the Warren Commission fairly and effectively constructed against Odio's story is somewhere defective, be it in the documentary evidence (e.g., as to the earliest time Oswald could have received his unemployment check in New Orleans) or the recollection of witnesses as to the dates and times they saw or spoke to Oswald (e.g., the affidavit of Mr. and Mrs. McFarland and Mrs. Twiford, etc.), which would not be uncommon at all.

It bears repeating that the Warren Commission conceded that "between the morning of September 25 and 2:35 a.m. on September 26" Oswald's whereabouts were "not strictly accounted for."

If Oswald did not leave Dallas for Houston with his two Cuban friends on the evening of September 25, or get there by some other means earlier in the day, then how did he get to Houston from New Orleans in time for him to board the Houston-to-Laredo bus at 2:35 on the morning of September 26? The Warren Commission believed that on September 25, Oswald probably took the 12:30 p.m. bus out of New Orleans, arriving in Houston at 10:50 p.m.[89] However, as indicated, although the Warren Commission checked all public modes of transportation from New Orleans to Houston on September 25, it could not come up with any evidence from witnesses or records (passenger manifest, ticket reservation or sale, listing Oswald's name or any alias of his) of his being on any plane, train, or bus from New Orleans to Houston that day.[90] The relevance of this (at least with respect to buses, the most likely mode of transportation Oswald would have used given the sorry state of his finances, and the mode we know he did use from Houston to Mexico City) is that, as author Jean Davison points out in her book, *Oswald's Game*, this is "an unusual circumstance, since there were passengers who had seen [Oswald] on every other leg of his bus trip to Mexico City and back to Dallas."[91] The very *absence* of any witness or record that Oswald used commercial transportation out of New Orleans is itself at least some circumstantial evidence that he did not do so and goes in the direction of supporting the conclusion that Oswald left New Orleans with the two Latins, and was at Odio's door on the evening of September 24 or 25, 1963.

If, as I believe it appears, Oswald did visit Odio with the two Cubans, what conclusion should be drawn from the incident? The HSCA candidly stated that "it was unable to reach firm conclusions as to the meaning or significance of the Odio incident to the President's assassination."[92] A few have suggested that the American at Odio's door was an Oswald imposter. This whole question of identification gives rise to the so-called Second Oswald issue so popular among conspiracy theorists, which was discussed earlier in this book. If it was not Oswald at Odio's door, says Warren Commission critic and conspiracy theorist Mark Lane, "few alternatives present themselves save that someone impersonated him—perhaps in an effort to frame him nearly two months before the assassination."[93] There is no limit on the scenarios imagined by conspiracy theorists. The Second Oswald theory is but an example of their fecund imagination.

The theory of an Oswald imposter at Odio's door (a theory that neither the Warren Commission nor the HSCA considered) is based on the argument that it was the anti-Castro movement that was seeking to frame Oswald by the Odio incident, Leopoldo introducing the American with him as Leon Oswald and telling Odio the following day that he was an ex-marine.[94] Since Oswald's pro-Castro sentiments were out in the open and known to many, the thinking goes that if the assassination could be blamed on anyone associated with Castro, this might very well induce a U.S. invasion to overthrow him, the never-ending dream of anti-Castro Cuban exiles. This theory seems wholly implausible. If we're to ascribe such a sophisticated conspiracy to the two Cubans (and any who were behind them), since they were aware of many details about Odio's father, we can assume they made it their business to know about Odio's substantial emotional problems and her recourse to psychiatric help. Why would they choose Odio, of all people, to be the best person they could find whom the authorities would believe?

Indeed, why would they even think Odio would inform the authorities? As we have seen, she did not. Odio's friend Lucille Connell told the FBI about the incident. Not being able to foresee the action of someone like Lucille Connell, the conspirators would have to realize that if Odio didn't notify the authorities, their whole plan to frame Oswald would die, since the Odio incident is the only one that has ever surfaced where Oswald allegedly mentioned the name *Kennedy* and the word *assassination* in the same sentence. But why in the world would the conspirators put all their eggs in Sylvia Odio's flimsy basket? It doesn't make sense.[*]

Moreover, even if anti-Castro conspirators foresaw Odio coming forward with the information Leopoldo gave her,[†] as Jean Davison points out in her insightful book, although Oswald might be implicated in the president's assassination, wouldn't the Cubans automatically fear that the anti-Castro movement might also be, since two supposed representatives of the movement were *with* Oswald? Such a result, obviously, would never serve any purpose of theirs.[95]

Finally, and most conclusively, the intent to frame Oswald would presuppose that it was the framers (anti-Castro Cuban exiles) who ultimately killed Kennedy. Since we know, beyond all doubt, that it was Oswald who killed Kennedy, this eliminates the possibility of a frame-up as the motivation for the Odio incident. As stated earlier, you frame innocent people, not guilty ones.

Some have suggested it was Oswald who was seeking to do the framing for the assassination of Kennedy he himself intended to commit. But this theory also seems entirely implausible. Although Oswald may have uttered statements that Kennedy should have been assassinated for the Bay of Pigs invasion (an idle observation undoubtedly made by many), there is no compelling evidence or reason to believe that as early as September 25, 1963, he was already actually planning to kill the president. And the theory that he was seeking to frame anti-Castro Cuban exiles for the assassination at the time of the Odio incident necessarily presupposes that his decision to kill Kennedy had already been made. But if that were true, why would he be in Mexico City just a few days later desperately seeking a visa to go to Cuba? Second, Oswald never made any reference to the assassination to Odio, and would have had no way of knowing that Leopoldo would do so the following day.

Since we know Oswald's Marxist pedigree is beyond dispute, and his infiltration of anti-Communist groups had already been established by the Carlos Bringuier incident in New Orleans just the previous month, it should be noted that his association with anti-Castro Cubans in the Odio incident, if it indeed took place, would therefore not be remarkable. And there are similarities to the two incidents beyond mere infiltration. In both cases, Oswald made much of his experience in the Marines: in the Bringuier incident speaking of his training in guerrilla warfare which would enable him to train anti-

---

[*]Some have argued that it's highly unlikely the Cubans would be trying to frame Oswald on September 24, 25, 26, or 27, 1963, when Kennedy's itinerary for his Texas visit wasn't announced until November 1, 1963, more than one month later. However, word that the president would be visiting the state first appeared in the Dallas papers on September 13, 1963, and Dallas being the state's second-largest city, it could be assumed that any trip by the president to Texas would probably include his coming to Dallas. Coincidentally, the September 26 edition of the *Dallas Morning News* had a front-page story on the president's planned trip to Texas. (HSCA Report, pp.37, 132)

[†]Conspiracy author Sylvia Meagher writes that Leopoldo "took pains to plant seeds which inevitably would incriminate Oswald in the assassination . . . so that an anonymous phone call [from framers] would be enough to send the police straight after [Oswald]" (Meagher, *Accessories after the Fact*, p.379). But Meagher doesn't go on to point out that there is no evidence any such anonymous call was ever made.

Castro forces; in the Odio situation, telling Leopoldo he was an expert rifleman in the Marines and willing to kill Kennedy because of the Bay of Pigs. The similarity of the incidents even extends to the fact that Oswald was apparently not too convincing in his effort to portray himself as anti-Castro. Odio told FBI agent Hosty that Leopoldo told her Oswald did not appear sincere to him.[96] And Bringuier told the Warren Commission that after his first meeting with Oswald in the retail clothing store where Bringuier was a salesman, "I didn't know what was inside of me, but I had some feeling that I could not trust him."[97]

If Oswald, by posing as an anti-Castroite, had any motivation beyond infiltration, what it was is impossible to say. However, his motive for infiltration may not have been any more arcane than the obvious—to report to Castro or his people (whom we know he was on his way to try to meet with within a matter of days by way of Mexico City) what the anti-Castro movement was up to in this country, including, if he were lucky enough to become privy to it, the extremely important information of specific death plots against Castro, which would make his contribution to Castro immense. In fact, this pedestrian motivation to tell the political Left what the political Right was up to was demonstrated by Oswald in late October of 1963, the very next month, when he stood up at an ACLU meeting he attended with Ruth Paine's husband, Michael, and, per Michael, "reported what had happened at the meeting of the Far Right which had occurred at Convention Hall the day before, U.N. Day."[98]

As to the ostensible motivation behind the visit by the two Cubans—to solicit Odio's help, by way of a written petition, in raising funds for the anti-Castro movement—as referred to earlier, other anti-Castro Cuban exiles had previously come to her door seeking the identical help from her.[99] And as to what was said, although Leopoldo told Odio about Oswald's assertion that Kennedy should have been assassinated by anti-Castro Cubans after the Bay of Pigs debacle, Odio's recollection of the conversation contains no indication that Leopoldo was sympathetic to this thought. Indeed, when it came to the subject of assassination, Leopoldo's interest seemed to be in Castro's death, not Kennedy's. Odio testified that Leopoldo "wanted me to introduce this man [Oswald]. He thought that I had something to do with the underground . . . and I could get men into Cuba." Leopoldo went on to tell Odio that Oswald would be "the kind of man" to enter Cuba by way of the underground and kill Castro.[100]

But even if Leopoldo did in fact have an interest in murdering Kennedy (and there's no evidence of this), we still are left with his statement to Odio that "we probably won't have anything to do with him. He is kind of loco," a statement which obviously goes in a direction *away* from a conspiracy.

In addition to the allegation by some conspiracy theorists that one side was trying to frame the other in the Odio incident, many conspiracy theorists have simply asserted that the incident proves the existence of a conspiracy in the assassination between Oswald and others. Conspiracy doyenne Sylvia Meagher says that the Odio incident is "Proof of the Plot" and that it demolishes the "proposition that Oswald was a *lone* assassin." It poses, she said, "the outlines of a plot implicating Cubans of some denomination, perhaps with non-Cuban backers, joined in a conspiracy against the life of the President of the United States."[101] In *Conspiracy*, author Anthony Summers refers to the Odio affair as "the most compelling human evidence of conspiracy" in the JFK assassination.[102] While admittedly the incident does raise suspicions that go in that direction, the suspicions seem to be spontaneous and visceral in nature. A more sober analysis of what actually transpired and what was said would seem to substantially diminish the virility of the conspiracy conclusion.

However, although the Odio incident certainly is no proof, nor even significant evidence of a conspiracy to kill the president, it cannot be treated dismissively either. Leopoldo and Angelo are shadowy (never having been identified) figures whose personal agenda, if we are to believe Odio, *included murder* (of Castro). Their association with Oswald, the known killer of Kennedy, less than two months before the assassination emits a troubling aroma of possible conspiratorial intrigue. A reasonable possibility of the scope and nature of this possible intrigue was set forth by W. David Slawson and William Coleman, assistant counsels for the Warren Commission whose area of investigation was foreign conspiracy. In a June 1964 memorandum to the Commission titled "Oswald's Foreign Activities: Summary of Evidence Which Might Be Said to Show That There Was Foreign Involvement in the Assassination of President Kennedy," they postulated a scenario that might constitute a conspiracy in a law school examination, but might fall short of a chargeable conspiracy in the real world. They wrote that anti-Castro Cubans in New Orleans, aware of Oswald's pro-Castro sympathies, and realizing that if anything happened the public at large would also learn of them, and perhaps sensing Oswald's penchant for violence, "encouraged" Oswald to kill the president when he came to Dallas, perhaps even deceiving him into believing they might assist him afterward in his escape. As with those who would have framed Oswald, the motive, Slawson and Coleman point out, would be the expectation that the public "would then blame the assassination on the Castro Government, and the call for its forceful overthrow would be irresistible. A second Bay of Pigs invasion would begin; this time, hopefully, to end successfully." Slawson and Coleman acknowledged that this scenario was only "wild speculation" on their part, but one that warranted additional investigation.[103]

It is important to note that as opposed to all the other fantastic (as in fantasy) and preposterous conspiracy theories, which are irrational on their face, with anti-Castro Cuban exiles we're talking about men whose fathers, children, and brothers, members of Brigade 2506 (the invasion force), were slaughtered on the sands of the Bay of Pigs, with many of the exiles blaming Kennedy for what happened to their loved ones. The CIA-sponsored invasion of Cuba on April 17–19, 1961, was originally scheduled to take place at Trinidad on the southern coast of Cuba. The invasion site was changed to the Bay of Pigs a few weeks before April 17. Its original code name, Operation Pluto, was later changed to Operation Zapata, the Bay of Pigs being on the Zapata Peninsula. Of the 1,390 Cuban exiles who constituted the invasion force, 114 were killed, 97 escaped,[*] and 1,179 were captured, including José Miro Torra, the son of Dr. José Miro Cardona, the president of the Cuban Revolutionary Council, the main Cuban exile group. After a four-day trial in their prison courtyard in late March and early April of 1962, in which even their defense attorney denounced them as traitors and cowards, they were convicted of treason and sentenced by

---

[*]Many of those who escaped, after being repulsed on the beaches by Castro's militia, tanks, and planes, were able to get on small rowboats that drifted to one of the nearby keys, where they subsisted on coconuts, crabs, and salt water until they were picked up days later by an American destroyer (Aguilar, *Operation Zapata*, pp.309, 310). Brigade 2506 was named after the number of the last volunteer who was accepted in Miami to be part of the exile force, Carlos Rodriguez Santana. Santana died in an accident during training in Guatemala. (Rodriguez and Weisman, *Shadow Warrior*, p.54)

a Cuban tribunal to thirty years of hard labor. Castro told José (Pepe) Pérez San Román, the Brigade 2506 commander, "To prove that we are truly generous, we are not going to kill you."[104] This decision had been made by Castro a year earlier. During a long harangue against the captured brigade prisoners in Havana's Sports Palace that started at 11:30 p.m. on April 26, 1961, and continued to 3:00 the next morning, he told them he had every reason to shoot them all, but his revolution would be kind to them and would spare their lives. Some in the brigade "cheered him wildly."[105] Just three days earlier, speaking on Havana TV in his customary green fatigues, Castro had said he would not consider clemency for the captured rebels unless the United States halted aid to all anti-Cuban rebels.[106]

The historian Theodore Draper referred to the invasion as "a perfect failure." Though many Cuban defenders also lost their lives on and around the beaches known in Cuba as Playa Girón (the main beachhead) and Playa Larga, the battle was a rout. So much so that in documents declassified by Cuba commemorating the fortieth anniversary of the invasion, Castro, who barked out orders to his defenders by telephone from a position near the beach, is recorded as telling his brother, Raul, who was far from the fighting, "You have been missing the party."[107]

The members of the invading force blamed what happened on Kennedy's supposed decision (see later text) to withdraw promised air support at the last moment. With the blood of their loved ones, they believed, on Kennedy's hands, the realistic and not fantastic desire for revenge makes sense. As Warren Commission critic Harold Weisberg has put it, "If any men capable of murdering the President had a motive," it was the Cuban exiles.[108]

As indicated, Slawson and Coleman called their aforementioned theory "wild speculation," and there is no evidence to support their theory and scenario. It should be noted, however, that if the Odio incident in fact occurred, neither Oswald (pretending to be anti-Castro) nor the anti-Castro Cubans (pretending to Oswald that if he killed Kennedy they would be of assistance to him) would have to pretend about one thing—their mutual contempt for the president arising out of the botched Bay of Pigs attack, but for different reasons: for Oswald, that Kennedy had authorized the invasion; for the Cubans, that he failed to furnish the air support they believed he had promised them.

Or had he? The brigade of Cuban exiles (mostly recruited from the large Cuban population in Miami) who invaded Cuba, as well as their leaders, have said many times that the failure of the plan was, as previously indicated, a result of the lack of promised air support, and for that they directly blamed President Kennedy. Barry Sklar, a Latin American affairs specialist for the U.S. government's Foreign Affairs and National Defense Division, writes that "exile leaders believed that the United States promised air and sea cover for the invasion force and that its failure to materialize was a major reason for the invasion's defeat."[109] But Arthur M. Schlesinger Jr., who was a special assistant to the president throughout the entire period, not only participating in most of the administration's meetings on the invasion but writing a white paper for the president in which he inveighed against the invasion, disagrees. He writes in his book *A Thousand Days*, a friendly but incisive biography of JFK in the White House, that "mythologists have . . . talked about a supposed presidential decision to 'withdraw United States air cover.' There was never, of course, any plan for United States air cover, and no air cover for the landing forces was withdrawn."[110]

Indeed, on April 12, 1961, just five days before the invasion, President Kennedy was asked at a press conference, "Mr. President, has a decision been reached on how far this country would be willing to go in helping an anti-Castro uprising or invasion of Cuba?"

(It was public knowledge that an invasion of the island was imminent. What started out as a covert operation had long since become known. Only the date of the invasion—April 17—was unknown.) The president was unambiguous in his reply: "I want to say that there will not be, *under any conditions*, an intervention in Cuba by United States armed forces." He went on to say that the U.S. government would do everything possible "*to make sure that there are no Americans involved*"* in such an action, adding that "as I understand it, *this Administration's attitude is . . . understood and shared by the anti-Castro exiles from Cuba in this country.*" And it's not as if this statement by Kennedy was buried in the media's coverage of the conference. A front-page headline the following day in the *New York Times* read, "President Bars Using U.S. Force to Oust Castro." The *Times* reported that elsewhere in the press conference, "the President indicated by indirection that he would continue the Eisenhower policy of supplying aid and military training to refugee groups" seeking to overthrow Castro.[111] This, of course, was substantially misleading. More than just "aid and training" was involved. The invasion was CIA-organized, and hence U.S. government–sponsored. But Kennedy made it clear that U.S. military forces would not physically participate in the invasion.

The innocuous "Eisenhower policy" referred to by Kennedy was much more muscular than he had indicated. Indeed, the institutional stem for the eventual Bay of Pigs invasion goes back to the Eisenhower administration. What Eisenhower authorized and approved of on March 17, 1960, was a March 16, 1960, "Top Secret" CIA document drafted by CIA wunderkind Richard Bissell and titled "A Program of Covert Action against the Castro Regime." The very first words of the document read, "Objective: The purpose of the program outlined herein is to bring about the replacement of the Castro regime with one more devoted to the true interests of the Cuban people and more acceptable to the U.S. in such a manner as to avoid any appearance of U.S. intervention. Essentially, the method of accomplishing this end will be to induce, support, and so far as possible, direct action, both inside and outside of Cuba, by selected groups of Cubans," the type who could be expected to undertake such a mission "on their own initiative." Paragraph d provides that "preparations have already been made for the development of an adequate paramilitary force outside of Cuba . . . A number of paramilitary cadres will be trained at secure locations outside of the United States so as to be available for immediate deployment into Cuba."

Although invasion plans under the auspices of the CIA and the U.S. government gained speed, momentum, and force under the Kennedy administration, culminating in the Bay of Pigs invasion on April 17, 1961, there is no question that not only did it all start under Eisenhower, but Eisenhower was not just a passive signatory to the plans. Eisenhower was arguably almost as obsessed as the Kennedys with removing Castro from power.† So committed that he called a meeting in the Oval Office on January 3, 1961 (a little over two weeks before he left office), attended by, among others, the CIA chief, Allen Dulles; chair-

---

*By "involved," the president apparently meant "fighting." Certainly, we were "involved" to the extent that quite apart from the CIA having 588 personnel assigned to the project, as well as organizing and funding the invasion, five U.S. Navy destroyers and the aircraft carrier *Essex* escorted the anti-Cuban invasion force's seven vessels (carrying the invasion troops and their supplies) to the beaches of the Bay of Pigs by protecting them in the event of attempted interdiction by Castro's forces (Wyden, *Bay of Pigs*, pp.125, 210, 212, 216; 588 CIA personnel: Kornbluh, *Bay of Pigs Declassified*, p.46).

†"Cuba seems to have the same effect on American Administrations," Wayne Smith, a former U.S. State Department officer in Havana, said, "as the full moon used to have on werewolves" (McKnight, *Breach of Trust*, p.330).

man of the Joint Chiefs of Staff, Lyman Lemnitzer; and the secretary of defense, Thomas Gates. The main topic was Cuba, and when to sever diplomatic relations with Castro. Eisenhower opened the meeting by saying he was "constantly bombarded by people outside of government as to the situation in Cuba." So committed that although the record of the long meeting doesn't indicate there was any serious follow-up to his seemingly offhanded remark, Eisenhower said that he "would move against Castro before the 20th" (when he would be leaving office) if he were provided a really good excuse by Castro (note this would not appear to be referring to the upcoming Bay of Pigs invasion by *Cuban* exiles in April—since the exile force, on January 3, was in no operational position to invade in less than three weeks—but to an invasion by *U.S.* forces), and then actually adding that "failing that, perhaps we could think of *manufacturing* something that would be generally acceptable." Later in the meeting Eisenhower spoke knowledgeably about the training of the exile force and how to make it stronger, as well as whom to recognize as the new leader of Cuba if the invasion by the exiles was successful.[112]

Although Kennedy made it clear that the U.S. military would not actually participate in the invasion itself, he did authorize a preinvasion air strike on Cuba's air force. In the early morning hours of April 15, two days before the invasion, CIA-directed Cuban exile pilots flew eight U.S. planes (war surplus B-26s, light bombers) to attack three Cuban airfields (one on the outskirts of Havana, one at San Antonio de los Baños, thirty miles south of Havana, and one at Santiago de Cuba, over four hundred miles southeast of Havana). Why only eight of the twenty-two B-26s available at the brigade's Puerto Cabezas, Nicaragua, air base (code-named "Happy Valley") were used has never been satisfactorily answered. One aircraft was shot down, one lost an engine from ground fire and landed at Key West, and another, low on fuel on the return flight, was forced to land at Grand Cayman Island. The rest returned to Puerto Cabezas.[113] The returning exile pilots estimated that they had destroyed twenty-two to twenty-four of Castro's planes, believed to be over half of Castro's air force. The estimate was inflated. Based on all sources, including aerial photography, Cuba's air force prior to D-day consisted of thirty-six planes, eighteen of which were believed to be operational. During the Bay of Pigs invasion, Castro had seven aircraft in the air, the conclusion being that eleven operational aircraft had been taken out by the U.S. air strike on April 15.[114]

Kennedy originally had authorized a second air strike on Castro's planes at Cuban airfields (this is not to be confused with air support and cover for the invading forces at the time of the invasion), hoping to finish the job of neutralizing the Cuban air force, thereby greatly enhancing the invading brigade's chance of success by eliminating air assaults on the landing force. The strike was to occur at dawn on April 17, 1961, coinciding with the landing of the exile invasion force on the three beaches (denominated Red, Blue, and Green, though landing on Green was canceled at the last moment) at the Bay of Pigs.[*] Late in the day on April 16, Kennedy did, in fact, withdraw this second air strike after Secretary of State Dean Rusk advised him that a second strike would put the United States in an untenable position internationally.[115]

What makes the withdrawal of the second air strike difficult to understand is the question of how much worse could a second air strike (which might have finished off Castro's

---

[*]Actually, the first members of the brigade force (officially called the Cuban Expeditionary Force), led by Brigade Commander José Pérez San Román and two teams of six frogmen each, went ashore at Blue Beach at one hour and fifteen minutes past midnight on Monday morning, April 17 (Aguilar, *Operation Zapata*, p.21; Wyden, *Bay of Pigs*, pp.131, 217–220). Around sunup, 177 brigade paratroopers also landed, dropped from the sky by six brigade C-46s (Wyden, *Bay of Pigs*, p.232).

remaining air force) be in the eyes of the international community than the one that had already taken place?

Because of Kennedy's withdrawal of a second strike, Castro still had enough planes (T-33 jets, B-26s—given to Batista by the U.S. government—and British Sea Furies) to strafe the beachhead and offshore supply ships, raising deadly havoc with the invading brigade as well as some of its ships. One ship, the *Houston* (which had transported troops and supplies and still had 180 troops aboard), was hit and went aground on the west shore of the Bay of Pigs, five miles from Red Beach. The *Rio Escondido*, carrying ten days of ammunition and other important supplies, was sunk.[116]

Haynes Johnson, in his book *Bay of Pigs*, written with four of the brigade civilian and military leaders (Manuel Artime, the civilian exile leader, who was the CIA favorite among all the rebel leaders; José [Pepe] Pérez San Román, brigade commander; Erneido Oliva, second in command; and Enrique Ruiz-Williams, a lower brigade officer), mentions only one lone brigade B-26 (piloted by a Cuban) attempting to provide air cover for the troops landing on the beaches at daybreak on the first day of the invasion. But facing Castro's faster T-33 jets and Sea Furies, "the slower Brigade plane didn't have a chance" and was quickly shot down.[117] Without air cover from American jets, which were available on the aircraft carrier *Essex* just fifteen miles from shore, the brigade landing force was essentially at the unchallenged mercy of Castro's air force, and the fate of the invasion was sealed.

On this very key issue of whether the landing forces had air cover from their own B-26s (not U.S. jets) on D-day, there is some ambiguity. As indicated, Haynes Johnson, speaking from the authority of those who were there, says only one B-26 provided air support and was quickly shot down. Peter Wyden's very authoritative book *Bay of Pigs* only mentions two brigade B-26s providing air cover four hours *after* large numbers of troops had already started landing at sunup, both of which, after dropping bombs on an enemy column, were quickly shot down by a T-33 and a Sea Fury, and one B-26 providing cover later in the day, which was also shot down. Wyden never explicitly says how many B-26s supplied air cover during D-day, but the implication is very few, and they were not very effective.

The next day, D+1 (April 18), six brigade B-26s piloted by Cuban exiles (and two American CIA contract men known as "Peters" and "Seig," who were authorized by the CIA's Richard Bissell without knowledge or approval from the Kennedy administration) successfully bombed a column of Cuban trucks and tanks approaching the beach, destroying seven tanks and inflicting an estimated eighteen hundred casualties, an unrealistically high number. But the efforts of the slower B-26s during the three days of war were virtual suicide missions, with nine of the sixteen being shot down, most by the surprisingly effective Cuban T-33 jets. Here and there over a period of three days, the brigade, ashore and with makeshift command posts established, achieved small tactical successes. But it was clear early on that it was only a matter of time before the brigade, without American air support and outnumbered fifteen to one by Castro's twenty thousand troops, would succumb. Nonetheless, during most of the battle, the brigade leaders still felt, as Johnson wrote, "that victory was inevitable. [They felt] it was inconceivable that they would be stranded" by the American military.[118]

To save the invasion on the second day, April 18, the CIA and Joint Chiefs of Staff had beseeched Kennedy to reverse his publicly stated position and allow U.S. planes and ships to come to the rescue of the brigade on the two beaches. Kennedy wavered for a moment but refused the request. U.S. military forces would not physically participate in the invasion. In the hope that Kennedy just might change his mind, Admiral Arleigh Burke, chief of naval operations, had placed two Marine battalions on ships in his fleet of destroyers and carriers that had accompanied the brigade to the Bay of Pigs and remained offshore to lend logistical support. Later on April 18, Burke made one last plea to Kennedy, who reiterated he did not "want the United States involved in this."

"Hell, Mr. President," Burke said, "we *are* involved . . . Can we send a few planes [U.S. Navy jets aboard the carrier *Essex*]?"

"No, because they could be identified as United States," Kennedy retorted.

"Can we paint out their numbers?"

"No."

"Can we get something in there?"

"No."

"If you'll let me have two destroyers, we'll give gunfire support and we can hold the beachhead with two ships forever."

"No."

"One destroyer, Mr. President?"

"No," Kennedy said.[119] In speaking of the pilots of the U.S. jets aboard the *Essex*, Wyden writes that their "inability to help the brigade moved them to tears."[120] Robert Kennedy would later say that "D plus one" (April 18, the second day of the invasion), when "the CIA asked for air cover, Jack [JFK] was in favor of giving it. However, Dean Rusk was strongly against it. He said that we had made a commitment that no American forces would be used and the President shouldn't appear in the light of being a liar."[121]

What follows is just one of many desperate pleas for American military help before the invasion ended in defeat on April 19. At 11:52 p.m. on April 18, the Cuban exile brigade commander, Pepe San Román, radioed from the beach, "Do you people realize how desperate the situation is? Do you back us up or quit? All we want is low jet cover and jet close support. I need it badly or cannot survive. Please don't desert us. Am out of tank and bazooka ammo. Tanks will hit me at dawn. I will not be evacuated. Will fight to the end if we have to. Need medical supplies urgently."[122]

The Cuban exile community is virtually unanimous in its belief that American jets could have saved the invasion. Exile leader Dr. José Miro Cardona, in testimony on May 25, 1961, before a committee appointed by Kennedy and headed by General Maxwell Taylor to determine the cause of the invasion's failure, said that "in talking with the refugees and everyone who has come back [from the invasion], it seems apparent that but for three jets, the invasion force would have won the fight."[123] A "Mr. Betancourt," the air liaison officer for the second brigade battalion that landed at Red Beach, testified, "We know the success of the Brigade depended on the success of the air strikes. Otherwise, it's just like sending a bunch of human beings to get killed. There's no point in asking why the American jet planes didn't help us. They could have very well. They could have been our planes as far as we were concerned. We could have arranged to take all the insignia off."[124] Exile leader Manuel Antonio (Tony) de Varona told the committee on May 18, "I would just like to state that we would be in Cuba today if it was not for the lack of air support that our forces suffered. All those who've returned said that [with] three airplanes, they would have been successful in their invasion attempt."[125]*

---

*What Kennedy also did not authorize and only learned about nearly two years later is that on the morning of April 19, the third and final day of the invasion, CIA Deputy Director of Plans Richard Bissell, in a last-ditch effort to save the invasion, dispatched five American *civilian* pilots and one Cuban exile pilot, all flying B–26s, from the airfield at Puerto Cabezas, Nicaragua, to the Bay of Pigs, five hundred miles away. They

Kennedy felt enormous sorrow over the failed invasion and the fate of the captured rebels, and encouraged and authorized the formation of a group of citizens to raise millions of dollars from private Americans to pay ransom for the prisoners' release. In December of 1962 Castro was paid $2,925,000 in cash and given $53 million worth of medicine and baby food, meeting his conditions for the release of the brigade prisoners. "As a Christmas bonus," Castro also allowed one thousand Cuban relatives of the prisoners to leave Cuba by ship.[126]

Richard Bissell, who was the perspicacious brainchild behind the invasion and who, with CIA Director Allen Dulles in tow, had sold the merits of it to President Kennedy and the Departments of State and Defense, would later write sourly that Kennedy's cancellation of the second air strike was "certainly the gravest contributing factor in the operation's failure."[127]

As deputy director of plans, Bissell was in charge of all covert and clandestine operations of the CIA at the time of the invasion. There are those who maintain that Bissell, of all people, had no right to complain. The nature of the invasion was ill advised to begin with. Also, when Rusk was speaking to the president over the phone from Rusk's office close to 9:00 p.m. on Sunday evening, April 16, Charles Cabell (Dulles's deputy), Bissell, and Bissell's deputy, C. Tracy Barnes (whom Bissell, back in March of 1960, had delegated the operational responsibility of "putting together a team to overthrow Castro"), were there too. At one point in Rusk's conversation with the president, Rusk held the phone out to Bissell, giving him an opportunity to repeat his arguments in favor of a second air strike (which he and Cabell had made to Rusk to no avail) to the president himself. But after starting to reach for the phone, Bissell withdrew his hand and shook his head, apparently feeling no further argument would succeed. In a later report on the episode by the presidential committee, Bissell's failure to press his case with the president was severely criticized. If Bissell had spoken to the president, who apparently, along with everyone else, had great respect for Bissell's intellect, just maybe the president would have reversed his order canceling the second air strike, and this might have changed the outcome of the invasion.[128]

In any event, when we're talking about motive on the question of who killed President

---

were to provide air cover for the brigade already on the beach, fight Castro's pilots in the sky, and destroy any concentration of Cuban troops and equipment in the combat area. The pilots were all members of the 117th Tactical Reconnaissance Wing of the Alabama Air National Guard in Birmingham who had been enlisted by the CIA in early January of 1961. Twenty other members of a contingent from the Wing were also enlisted to train exile pilots at the Guatemalan air base at Retalhuleu near the Pacific Ocean in the southwestern part of the country and transport the Brigade 2506 invasion force from its training camps in Guatemala to Puerto Cabezas, Nicaragua, the departure point for the invasion. The five American pilots were Riley Shamburger (flying with his observer, Wade Gray—all of the observers were also from the Wing), Thomas "Pete" Ray (with observer Leo Baker), Don Gordon (with Jack Vernon), Bill Petersen (with an exile observer), and Hal McGee (with an unidentified flight engineer from the Wing). The observer for the Cuban exile pilot, Gonzalo Herrera, leaped from the aircraft onto the ground before flight at the Puerto Cabezas air base and fled into the woods, so Herrera flew alone. Though the B-26s inflicted some damage on Cuban forces and supplies on the ground, they were largely ineffective, and two of the American pilots, Shamburger and Ray, together with their observers, Gray and Baker, were shot down over the Bay of Pigs and died. (Persons, *Bay of Pigs*, pp.4–14, 17–18, 71–72, 89–95, 101, 156 [see also *CIA* on page 158 of book's index, where the author, a member of the Wing contingent, says his employment contract for the mission was with the CIA]; Thomas, *Very Best Men*, pp.261–262; on Bissell authorizing the last-minute effort without Kennedy's knowledge and Kennedy finding this out two years later: Wyden, *Bay of Pigs*, p.278) Ray's son, Thomas Ray Jr., a San Francisco attorney, told me that it wasn't until seventeen years after the invasion that his family got his father's remains back from Castro. Ray said his father and the other pilots worked "for the CIA," and that there was only one flight, but the CIA wouldn't acknowledge this lone flight by CIA pilots "for many years." (Interview of Thomas Ray Jr. by author on November 21, 1997)

Kennedy, the issue is not whether the exiles were correct in their belief that air support and cover was promised, but whether they had that belief, which they clearly did. One cannot read Schlesinger's account of the Bay of Pigs debacle as well as Haynes Johnson's without concluding that what the Kennedy administration was telling the exile leaders in the United States, and what the CIA and American military advisers were telling the brigade force of 1,390 men,[*] were two very different things. The latter—mostly in training at the main invasion training camp at Trax in the Guatemala mountains, but also in Nicaragua, Panama, Miami, New Orleans, Phoenix, Camp Peary (a CIA training base near Williamsburg, Virginia), and even Fort Knox—were told that U.S. military and air support *would* be involved in the invasion.[129] Pepe San Román, the brigade commander, said that at Camp Trax, "Frank," the American leader of the camp, told him that there would be more than air support. "He assured us," San Román said, "that we were going to have protection by sea, by air, and even from under the sea."[130] Peter Wyden, in *Bay of Pigs*, writes that "Colonel Frank and other CIA briefers" used one word to reassure the brigade leaders more than any other. There would be an "umbrella" above, they said, to guard the entire operation against Castro's planes.[131]

It may not have been intentional misrepresentation on the part of those like "Frank" who were dealing directly with the brigade. Virtually no one, including the exiled leaders, believed that an operation organized and directed by the CIA, and sponsored and almost completely funded by the U.S. government, one that had been originally approved by President Eisenhower and then by President Kennedy, would not have American military might behind it. This is why, notwithstanding Kennedy's press conference statement on April 12 that the United States would not be involved militarily, he nonetheless dispatched a contingent the very next day to meet with Miro Cardona, the president of the Cuban Revolutionary Council, to make sure he understood. But even that wasn't enough. Schlesinger writes that Cardona "displayed resistance and incredulity at the statement that no United States troops would be used. He waved the President's news conference disclaimer aside as an understandable piece of psychological warfare . . . 'Everyone knows,' Miro said, 'that the United States is behind the expedition.'"[132] The exiles were not the only ones who did not believe the president. CIA agent Howard Hunt,

---

[*]Author Haynes Johnson, in his book *The Bay of Pigs*, wrote that Castro spoke disparagingly of the brigade "as mercenaries, war criminals and sons of the jaded rich who were coming to regain their vast holdings at the expense of the workers. In reality, Brigade 2506 was a cross-section of Cuba. The men ranged in age from 16 to 61, with the average 29. There were peasants and fishermen as well as doctors, lawyers and bankers. A larger percentage of the men were married and had children, and there were a number of father-and-son pairs aboard the ships. By profession, students, with 240, were the largest group, but there were mechanics, teachers, artists, draftsmen, newspaper reporters, engineers, musicians, three Catholic priests and one Protestant minister, geologists, cattlemen and clerks. Some fifty of the men were Negroes and many more had Negro blood . . . While the vast majority were Catholics, there were also Protestants and even Jews in the Brigade. With the exception of 135 former professional soldiers—who had served both under Castro and Batista—most of the men had no previous military training or experience." There were also two Americans in the brigade landing force at the Bay of Pigs, both of whom had helped train the force back at Camp Trax in Guatemala—Grayston "Gray" Lynch and William "Rip" Robertson. Gray and Rip, in fact, were the first to land, as frogmen, in the two beachheads of the invasion, Playa Girón and Playa Larga. (Johnson with Artime et al., *Bay of Pigs*, pp.98–99, 103, 106, 221)

But there can be little question that many in the rebel invading force didn't just serve under Batista as a requirement of Cuban citizenship, but had been staunch supporters of him. Castro used this to his political advantage after the rebel invasion was repulsed. President Kennedy was aware of this liability and had ordered that Batista supporters be purged from the exile force. But according to informed rebel leaders, the CIA ignored the order, believing that these men had much needed military experience that outweighed their political background. (Tad Szulc, "Cuba Asserts U.S. Used Batista Men," *New York Times*, April 26, 1961, p.2)

who worked at the operational level of the Bay of Pigs project, spending much time with exile leaders at his safe house in Miami, and also visited the brigade at the training camps in Guatemala, said that when the president made his April 12 declaration, "my project colleagues and I did not take him seriously. The statement was, we thought, a superb effort in misdirection."[133]

In *Bay of Pigs*, Haynes Johnson writes,

> From the beginning, the Cuban counter-revolutionists viewed their new American friends with blind trust . . . Virtually all of the Cubans involved believed [so] much in the Americans—or wanted so desperately to believe—that they never questioned what was happening or expressed doubts about the plans. Looking back on it, they agree now their naivete was partly genuine and partly reluctance to turn down any offer of help in liberating their country. In fact, they had little choice; there was no other place to turn . . . To Cubans, the United States was more than the colossus of the north, for the two countries were bound closely by attitudes, by history, by geography and by economics. The United States was great and powerful, the master not only of the hemisphere but perhaps of the world, and it was Cuba's friend. One really didn't question such a belief. It was a fact; everyone knew it. And the mysterious, anonymous, ubiquitous American agents who dealt with the Cubans managed to strengthen that belief.[134]

Johnson quotes Pepe San Román, the brigade military commander, as saying that "most of the Cubans [in the brigade] were there because they knew the whole operation was going to be conducted by the Americans, not by me or anyone else. They did not trust me or anyone else. They just trusted the Americans. So they were going to fight because the United States was backing them."[135]

In *Dagger in the Heart*, Cuban attorney Mario Lazo writes, "The Bay of Pigs defeat was wholly self-inflicted in Washington. Kennedy told the truth when he publicly accepted responsibility . . . The heroism of the beleaguered Cuban Brigade had been rewarded by betrayal, defeat, death for many of them, long and cruel imprisonment for the rest. The Cuban people . . . were left with feelings of astonishment and disillusionment, and in many cases despair. They had always admired the United States as strong, rich, generous—but where was its sense of honor and the capacity of its leaders? The mistake of the Cuban fighters for liberation was that they thought too highly of the United States. They believed to the end that it would not let them down. But it did."[136]

Lest there be any doubts that the invasion brigade expected U.S. military help, the anguished cry of Pepe San Román at the Bay of Pigs to the American military, "Do you back us up or quit? . . . Please don't desert us," should dispel all of them. So the motive to kill Kennedy would seem to be there. But there is more to the story (see later text).

In a June 1, 1961, memorandum, RFK said that his brother "felt very strongly that the Cuba operation had materially affected . . . his standing as president and the standing of the United States in public opinion throughout the world . . . The United States couldn't be trusted. The United States had blundered."[137]

Though it is stated in all the books that Kennedy publicly acknowledged full responsibility for the failure of the invasion (e.g., "In the orgy of national self-recrimination that followed the Bay of Pigs operation, President Kennedy took the full blame"),[138] considered by many to be the most humiliating incident during the Kennedy presidency, the authors[139] normally give Kennedy's remark to the press on April 21 that "victory has a hundred fathers and defeat is an orphan" as their support for this. But this remark could just as well be construed as a reference to an unfortunate fact of public life than as an acknowledgment of responsibility or blame. However, on April 24, Kennedy removed all ambiguity about responsibility for the Bay of Pigs by authorizing the release of a White House statement that said, "President Kennedy has stated from the beginning that as President he bears sole responsibility . . . and he restates it now . . . The President is strongly opposed to anyone within or without the administration attempting to shift the responsibility."[140]

But privately Kennedy was incensed at the CIA for misleading him by its gross miscalculation that the invasion would succeed, even without U.S. military participation, and at himself for being naive enough to believe the spy agency. One of the elements in the CIA's calculus that was sold to Kennedy was that the invasion would trigger an insurrection by the Cuban people against Castro that would aid and coalesce with the invading force. That didn't, of course, happen. Was CIA intelligence unaware of the popularity Castro enjoyed at the time among the Cuban masses?

The defeat at the Bay of Pigs had another consequence. In August 1961, four months after the invasion, Richard Goodwin, assistant special counsel to the president, reported back to President Kennedy on his return from a meeting of the Organization of American States in Punta del Este, Uruguay, on August 17, that he had spoken to Castro's chief lieutenant, Ernesto "Che" Guevara, and the latter "wanted to thank us very much for the invasion . . . It had been a great political victory for them, enabled them to consolidate, and transformed them from an aggrieved little country to an equal."[141] Apparently unwittingly, the invasion had succeeded in transforming a revolution merely to overthrow Batista and capitalism into one now identified with Cuban nationalism.

Though Kennedy did not want to make his displeasure with the CIA a public matter, it was clear that the CIA leadership behind the disastrous invasion would have to go. Shortly after the Bay of Pigs he called CIA Director Allen Dulles, Lieutenant General Charles Cabell, the deputy director of the CIA, and Richard Bissell, the CIA deputy director for plans, into his office. (Bissell was the brainy former professor of economics at Yale who developed the U-2 spy plane, was one of the key formulators and implementers of the Marshall Plan, and, as indicated, the architect behind the Bay of Pigs invasion.) "Under the British system," he told them with a smile, "I would have to go. But under our system, I'm afraid it's got to be you."[142] After the intentional passage of a decent amount of time following the failure at the Bay of Pigs, Kennedy accepted the resignation of Dulles on September 27, 1961, the retirement of Cabell on January 31, 1962, and the resignation of Bissell on February 17, 1962.

Kennedy redeemed himself, in part, with the exiled Cuban community by eventually giving more support, in every way, to the anti-Castro movement than ever before, though again, there was no promise that U.S. forces would fight Castro. "Before the invasion when we asked for arms it was difficult to get them, but now it's easier," said Cuban exile leader Manolo Ray.[143] "Cuba must not be abandoned to the Communists," Kennedy told the American Society of Newspaper Editors on April 20, the day after the Bay of Pigs debacle, adding that with respect to his administration's policy of nonintervention, "Our restraint is not inexhaustible." He spoke of the "new and deeper struggle."[144]* The exiles, still wanting to believe that Kennedy's heart was in the right place, dug in even harder.

In the latter part of 1961, the Special Group (formally called NSC 5412, the secret, informal, National Security Council subcommittee that approved or disapproved of all proposed CIA covert activities) was augmented by two new members, Attorney General Robert Kennedy and General Maxwell Taylor, for the express purpose of overseeing Operation Mongoose, the government's plan established after the Bay of Pigs to remove Castro from power.[145] That the new group, called "Special Group (Augmented)," and Operation Mongoose were a presidential initiative was made clear by the creating document, a November 22, 1961, memorandum from presidential assistant Richard Goodwin to the secretaries of state and defense, the director of the CIA, attorney general, General Edward Lansdale, and chairman of the Joint Chiefs of Staff. Paragraph one of the memorandum stated that the object was "to help Cuba overthrow the Communist regime and establish a free Cuba. All available assets will be directed to this and as a matter of urgent national priority." The effort was to be "under the general guidance of the Attorney General [RFK], with [Air Force] General [Edward] Lansdale as his chief of operations. The NSC 5412 group will be kept informed of activities." Though the CIA would be more heavily involved in carrying out the mission than any other federal agency, JFK had shifted the primary supervision of the effort away from the CIA, which had failed him so badly in the Bay of Pigs, to the Department of Defense at the Pentagon, a clear slap in the face to the CIA.

Lansdale was a counterinsurgency specialist in the Office of Special Operations of the Defense Department who had worked in U.S. covert operations in the Philippines (where he successfully helped put down a growing Communist insurgency with what some felt were "brilliant" counterrevolutionary tactics) and Vietnam, and became the model for the hero in the best-selling novel *The Ugly American* who courageously fought against Communist guerillas in these two nations. President Kennedy once called Lansdale America's answer to James Bond. Although raids on Cuban installations by exile groups were to continue vigorously under Mongoose, the main part of Lansdale's plan to overthrow Castro, which he presented on January 18, 1962, was to organize anti-Castro Cubans (both exiles and those still living in Cuba) into "a movement *within* Cuba to the point where it could mount an insurrection" against Castro's regime. A plan, by the way, that the CIA felt was unrealistic from the beginning.[146] As Lansdale told the Church Committee, he wanted "the [Cuban] people themselves [to] overthrow the Castro regime."[147] Severely disrupting the Cuban economy (by an economic embargo, commando raids blowing up oil refineries, chemical plants, etc., and sabotaging cargo to Cuba from other countries) would supposedly incite discontent by the Cuban people with Castro.[148]†

---

*In his speech to the nation's newspaper editors in Washington, D.C., which was carried by national radio and television, Kennedy defended himself from the assaults by many that if America had intervened militarily, the invasion would have succeeded, by noting that "we made it repeatedly clear that the armed forces of this country would not intervene in any way. Any unilateral American intervention in the absence of an external attack upon ourselves or an ally would have been contrary to our traditions."

†However, at an August 10, 1962, meeting of the Special Group (Augmented) in Secretary of State Rusk's office, someone, believed to be Secretary of Defense Robert McNamara, raised the issue, for discussion only, of the assassination of Castro being included in Operation Mongoose as an acceptable alternative way of overthrowing Castro's regime. Though memories differed and the minutes of the meeting were silent as to whether the issue was even raised, the consensus is that the suggestion was quickly discarded by the Special Group members, although Lansdale himself acknowledged that thereafter, he "thought it would be a possibility someplace down the road in which there would be some possible need to take action such as that [assassination]." (*Alleged Assassination Plots*, pp. 161–167)

The next day, January 19, at a meeting of principal Mongoose participants held in Robert Kennedy's office, Kennedy said that the solution to the Cuban problem was a "top priority," and that "no time, money, effort or manpower is to be spared."[149] Robert Kennedy was, by all accounts, not just a figurehead in the administration's efforts to over-throw Castro. "Bobby Kennedy was running it, hour by hour," Alexander Haig says. "I was a part of it, as deputy to Joe Califano and military assistant to General Vance. We were conducting two raids a week at the height of that program against mainland Cuba . . . Weekly reports were rendered to Bobby Kennedy. He had a very tight hand on the oper-ation."[150] Sergio Arcacha, an anti–Castro Cuban exile heavily involved in the effort to over-throw Castro, told *Life* magazine reporter Holland McCombs, "We used to call Bobby Kennedy and he would take care of it."[151] Richard Helms, who as the CIA's deputy direc-tor of plans had overall supervision of the CIA's Mongoose effort, told the Church Com-mittee that he and RFK "were constantly in touch with each other" with respect to Mongoose, even down to details like RFK asking him if a particular land sabotage effort was organized yet and had it left. "The Attorney General was on the phone to me, he was on the phone to Mr. Harvey [operational head of Mongoose] . . . He was on the phone even to people on Harvey's staff, as I recall it."[152] An October 4, 1962, "Memorandum for Record" of the minutes of a meeting of the Special Group (Augmented) on that day starts by saying, "The Attorney General opened the meeting by saying that higher authority [presumably the president] is concerned about progress on the *Mongoose* pro-gram and feels that more priority should be given to trying to mount sabotage operations . . . He urged that 'massive activity' be mounted within the entire *Mongoose* frame-work."[153]*

Called by many the "secret war" to overthrow Castro, Mongoose, which it should be repeated commenced *after* the Bay of Pigs invasion, was the best example of the CIA becoming a paramilitary organization. Buying its own fleet of ships and boats, even planes, the CIA registered its ownership under fictitious companies, altered them for combat, and employed civilian mercenaries and Cuban exiles to operate them.[154]

The HSCA wrote that the nerve center of Operation Mongoose, the United States' new and deeper struggle against Castro,

> was established in the heartland of exile activity, Miami. There, on a secluded, heavily wooded 1,571 acre tract that was part of the University of Miami's south campus, the CIA set up a front operation, an electronics firm called Zenith Tech-nological Services. Its code name was JM/WAVE and it soon became the largest CIA installation anywhere in the world outside of its headquarters in Langley, Vir-ginia. The JM/WAVE station† had, at the height of its activities in 1962, a staff of

---

*Though RFK's total immersion in, and direction of, Operation Mongoose cannot be questioned, too many have assumed that he was likewise heavily involved in the Bay of Pigs invasion. But there is no evidence of this. The invasion took place just three months after RFK's brother was inaugurated on January 20, 1961, and although JFK gave his approval to the CIA operation, it had already been in existence for almost a year and bar-reling down the track when he did so. RFK was aware of the invasion plans, but he was first briefed on the oper-ation by the CIA on April 12, 1961, just five days before the invasion. (Thomas, *Robert Kennedy*, p.120)

†Though all important decisions came from Washington and Langley, the day-to-day operations of Mon-goose fell to the chief of the CIA's station at JM/WAVE, thirty-four-year-old Theodore Shackley, considered one of the agency's most promising young men, who was brought back from assignment in Berlin to head a team charged with preparing a "vulnerability and feasibility study" of Castro's regime and then to run JM/WAVE (Branch and Crile, "Kennedy Vendetta," pp.50–51).

more than 300 Americans, mostly case officers. Each case officer employed from four to ten Cuban "principal agents" who, in turn, would be responsible for between ten and thirty regular agents . . . It was the JM/WAVE station that monitored, more or less controlled, and in most cases funded the anti-Castro groups. It was responsible for the great upsurge in anti-Castro activity and the lifted spirits of the Cuban exiles as American arms and weapons flowed freely through the training camps and guerilla bases spotted around South Florida. Anti-Castro raiding parties that left from small secret islands in the Florida Keys were given the "green light" by agents of the JM/WAVE station. The result of it all was that there grew in the Cuban exile community a renewed confidence in the U.S. Government's sincerity and loyalty to its cause.[155]

And from February of 1962 on, JM/WAVE and the Cuban exiles it managed conducted a great number of missions against mainland Cuba with varying degrees of success.[156]*

But a second betrayal awaited the Cuban exiles. As the major U.S. concession in the agreement between Kennedy and Soviet premier Nikita Khrushchev to resolve the Cuban missile crisis (and in return for the Soviets' withdrawing from Cuban soil their missiles with nuclear warheads targeted on U.S. cities), in late October of 1962 Kennedy, in addition to secretly agreeing to withdraw fifteen Jupiter missiles of ours from Turkey, made a "no invasion" pledge regarding Cuba.[157] The missile crisis started at 9:00 a.m. on October 14, 1962, when a CIA U-2 spy plane and low-level reconnaissance flights confirmed what CIA informants in Cuba had been reporting: the existence of launching pads and Soviet nuclear missiles in Cuba, installed that summer, as well as medium-range ballistic missile (MRBM) bases under construction. (Later, two intercontinental-range ballistic missile [IRBM] bases were found to be under construction.) At the time, the CIA estimated that ten thousand Soviet troops were in Cuba. The actual number, the Soviets would later admit, was forty thousand.

The first major meeting of the Kennedy administration on the ominous missile sightings was in the Cabinet Room on the morning of October 16, when the CIA made a formal presentation, with photographs and charts, of its findings to the president and eleven key advisers, including several members of his cabinet, who would meet regularly with him or RFK throughout the crisis as an ad hoc group called "Ex Comm" (the Executive Committee of the National Security Council). The group consisted of Vice President Johnson, Secretary of State Dean Rusk, Secretary of the Treasury C. Douglas Dillon, RFK, CIA Director John McCone, Undersecretary of State George Ball, Deputy Secretary of Defense Roswell Gilpatric, Ambassador-at-Large Llewellyn Thompson, special presidential counsel Ted Sorenson, special assistant to the president for national security affairs McGeorge Bundy, and chairman of the Joint Chiefs of Staff Maxwell Taylor. The group, which lived and worked together almost around the clock during the crisis, heard the advice of others and was sometimes joined in its deliberations by people

---

*The Cuban economy did, in fact, begin to deteriorate and weaken. And the paramilitary raids by the exiles caused a fear in Cuba that they foreshadowed another invasion. Arguably, one of the main reasons why Castro turned to Russia for economic support and military assistance was to offset the effects of Operation Mongoose. (Branch and Crile, "Kennedy Vendetta," p.61)

like former secretary of state Dean Acheson and UN Ambassador Adlai Stevenson.[158] No corresponding special policy group was created by the Kremlin to deal with the crisis, Khrushchev relying on his existing foreign policy advisers.[159]

For thirteen tense days and nights thereafter, Kennedy and his top advisers deliberated on how to handle the world's closest brush with a nuclear holocaust, the group predictably breaking down into hawks and doves. Would it be a blockade, or air strikes to knock out the missile sites, or an outright invasion of Cuba—air strikes or an invasion carrying a possible risk of the Soviets retaliating militarily and triggering an eventual nuclear war? "I guess this is the week I earn my salary," JFK would say.[160]

With World War III hanging in the balance, not all of "the President's men" were urging a peaceful resolution. In an October 19, 1962, exchange with the president, General Curtis LeMay, air force chief of staff, said, "This [proposed] blockade and political action, I see leading into war . . . This is almost as bad as the appeasement at Munich . . . I just don't see any other solution except direct military action *right now*."[161] Indeed, the members of the Joint Chiefs of Staff unanimously agreed that a military invasion, not a blockade, was called for.[162]* Not only called for, but, per JFK assistant Arthur Schlesinger, desired. "Some of them [members of the Joint Chiefs of Staff] were quite disappointed when a . . . peaceful settlement came about."[163]

Bobby Kennedy told the *New York Times* in 1964 that the Ex Comm group was split 7 to 5 on whether to bomb or blockade, though he did not say which course the majority preferred. In his later book, *Thirteen Days*, he says the majority favored a blockade, and that he and McNamara were on the side of a blockade, but that Acheson joined the military in advocating bombing. RFK told the *Times* that when his brother asked his intelligence officers to estimate how many innocent civilians would be killed in Cuba by bombing the missile sites and they reported back twenty-five thousand, he ruled this military option out.[164]

In a televised speech to the nation on the evening of October 22, 1962, in which he told Americans in a fair amount of detail what had transpired to that point and his decision to initiate a "strict quarantine on all offensive military equipment under shipment to Cuba," Kennedy called on Premier Khrushchev to immediately "halt and eliminate this clandestine, reckless, and provocative threat to world peace," by "withdrawing these weapons from Cuba." Kennedy said, "It shall be the policy of this nation to regard *any* nuclear missile launched from Cuba against *any* nation in the Western Hemisphere as an attack by the Soviet Union on the United States requiring a full retaliatory response upon the Soviet Union." Kennedy signed a "proclamation of interdiction" the following day which went into effect on October 24 at 10:00 a.m., the order imposing a naval blockade halting all Soviet ships carrying weapons and warheads to Cuba. That same day, Soviet ships that were heading for Cuba altered course and avoided contact with U.S. ships blockading the island.

A flurry of diplomatic exchanges followed for several days and Khrushchev eventually backed down and acceded to Kennedy's demands, messaging Kennedy on October 28, 1962, "I regard with great understanding your concern and the concern of the United

---

*Kennedy, wanting above all to avoid, if possible, a war of any kind with Russia, wasn't too partial to the aggressive LeMay, much less his suggestion. He told his aide Kenneth O'Donnell, "Those brass hats have one great advantage in their favor. If we . . . do what they want us to do, none of us will be alive later to tell them they're wrong." (Thomas, "Bobby at the Brink," p.52)

States people in connection with the fact that the weapons you describe as 'offensive'* are formidable weapons indeed. Both you and we understand what kind of weapons these are. In order to eliminate as rapidly as possible the conflict which endangers the cause of peace . . . the Soviet Government . . . has given a new order to dismantle [these] arms . . . and to crate and return them to the Soviet Union." Kennedy messaged Khrushchev back that same day, praising the latter's "statesmanlike decision" as an "important and constructive contribution to peace."[165] The crisis was over. It had been a crisis "that historians have called the most dangerous moment in recorded time."[166] Secretary of Defense McNamara would later recall that a Saturday night during the crisis was a "beautiful fall evening," and "as I left President Kennedy's office to return to the Pentagon, I thought I might never live to see another Saturday night."[167]†

Kennedy's no-invasion pledge caused rage in the exile community. Wrote one prominent exile, "For hundreds of thousands of exiles eager to stake their lives to liberate their native land, it was a soul-shattering blow."[168] "Suddenly," the HSCA observed, "there was a crackdown on the very training camps and guerilla bases which had been originally established and funded by the United States, and the exile raids which once had the government's 'green light' were now promptly disavowed and condemned." In some cases, the Kennedy administration went beyond this, U.S. Customs and the Coast Guard, respectively, arresting members of an anti-Castro force in training in the Florida Keys and anti-Castro raiders on four exile ships off the Florida coast. The U.S. crackdown on the exiles caused Dr. José Miro Cardona, the head of the Cuban Revolutionary Council, an umbrella group that had been receiving an estimated $2.4 million annually in U.S. support, to resign. And Cardona had been looked upon by many of the exiles as a mouthpiece for the Americans. Cardona accused Kennedy of "breaking promises and agreements" to support another invasion of Cuba, and declared that Kennedy had become "the victim of a master play by the Russians." Other voices were heard in the chorus alleging betrayal. Captain Eddie Rickenbacker, the ace World War II pilot, said that "the Kennedy administration has committed the final betrayal of Cuban hopes for freedom by its order to block the activities of exile Cuban freedom fighters to liberate their nation from Communism."[169]

Although the Church Committee stated categorically that "the Mongoose Operation was disbanded following the Cuban Missile Crisis . . . and the SGA [Special Group (Augmented)] was abolished,"[170] it would be wrong to infer that Kennedy's no-invasion pledge in the missile crisis ended Mongoose, because it did not. Though the Special Group (Augmented) was, indeed, terminated, and at least protocol dictated that, as the Church Committee said, "the Special Group, chaired by McGeorge Bundy, re-assumed responsibility for reviewing and approving covert actions in Cuba," Mongoose, if not in name, contin-

---

*The word *offensive* was set forth in Kennedy's letter to Khrushchev the previous day, October 27. It was in this October 27 letter that Kennedy told Khrushchev that in return for the Soviet Union's removing offensive weapons from Cuba, he was willing to "give assurances against an invasion of Cuba."

†Though it has almost been universally accepted that in the confrontation between Kennedy and Khrushchev, Kennedy won (i.e., "Khrushchev blinked"), this depends somewhat on the perspective. In a series of taped interviews of Khrushchev at his dacha near Moscow in early 1967 (he was removed from power in October of 1964), Khrushchev said that the 1962 missile crisis had resulted in a victory for the Soviet Union, reasoning that he had sent missiles to Cuba to protect that country from American attack, and since there was no attack, his action served its purpose. "What was the American aim?" he asked. "They aimed to liquidate Socialist Cuba. The invasion by the Cuban emigres was part of the American plan. Our aim was to preserve Cuba, and Cuba still exists." (*New York Times*, June 27, 1967, p.15)

ued. And RFK, who was not a member of the Special Group, continued to ride herd on the effort to overthrow Castro. Richard Helms, the CIA deputy director of plans at the time who was heading up the CIA effort in Mongoose, says in his memoir, *A Look over My Shoulder*, that the only thing that changed with the Mongoose operation was the cessation of support, ever again, of any future effort by the exiles to *invade* Cuba. Other than that, he said, the Mongoose operation continued and "[President Kennedy] and his brother *remained* absolutely determined to trounce Castro once and forever."[171] (This makes sense since Mongoose, though never explicitly rejecting the invasion possibility, never contemplated it as its plan for overthrowing Castro anyway. So as with the Bay of Pigs, this may be another instance where the exiles were misled.) And the HSCA itself, after suggesting, in so many words, that the United States ended all exile raids on Cuba after the no-invasion pledge, goes on to say on a succeeding page that "some extremely significant Cuban exile raids and anti-Castro operations . . . took place, despite the crackdown, between the time of the missile crisis and the assassination of President Kennedy," though it was unclear, the committee said, "to what extent, if any, the military activities of the anti-Castro exile groups were sanctioned or supported by the Kennedy administration or by the CIA or both."[172]*

Indeed, on December 29, 1962, two months *after* the missile crisis ended, Kennedy and the First Lady flew to Miami to personally welcome the returning Bay of Pigs prisoners in a huge, emotional ceremony at the Orange Bowl that brought many to tears. Holding the brigade's flag (depicting a rifleman with a fixed bayonet moving forward) handed to him by Brigade Commander Pepe San Román (with brigade leaders Manuel Artime and Erneida Oliva standing nearby) "for temporary safekeeping," Kennedy proclaimed to the survivors, "I can assure you that this flag will be returned to this Brigade in a free Havana." The throng of forty thousand Cuban exiles, many shouting "*Guerra, Guerra*" ("War, War") and "*Libertad, Libertad*" ("Liberty, Liberty") erupted in tumultuous applause.[173]†

Though this was not an invasion pledge (again, Kennedy had promised Khrushchev just two months earlier that the United States would not invade Cuba), this clearly reflected the U.S. government's continued support—I would think not just as cheerleaders—of the plan to overthrow Castro. Indeed, one of the Cuban exile pilots who had flown in the Bay of Pigs invasion, Eduardo Ferrer—a Cubana Airlines pilot who hijacked his own commercial flight to Miami to join up with the brigade—told author Peter Wyden

---

*In fact, in a front-page *Miami Herald* headline story on November 10, 1963 (just twelve days before the assassination), captioned "War in Cuba: Fidel Battling an Iceberg," the reporter, Al Burt, quoting unnamed sources of his in the Cuban exile community, wrote that "recent events make it undeniable that a secret war is being waged against Fidel Castro." Saying that "the full size and scope of the war has not been revealed," he analogized it to an iceberg, "the part that shows only hints at the part that doesn't . . . What is known reveals a well-organized and equipped military operation that . . . keeps opposition alive inside the island . . . Sources point out that the war stepped up its pace in the last three months." Burt also said that on October 21, 1963, "the Cuban Armed forces captured an armed band of infiltrators" who admitted that their mission was to "prepare the people for [an] armed uprising." (*Miami Herald*, November 10, 1963, pp.A1, A16; see also Waldron with Hartmann, *Ultimate Sacrifice*, pp.231–232, 668–669, for discussion of article and its implications) If Burt's sources were correct, the operation referred to virtually had to have been with U.S. knowledge and support. See also endnote discussion on what we *do* know was going on at the time—contingency plans for a U.S. invasion of Cuba if an uprising did, in fact, materialize.

†He also told them, again to wild applause, that "I can assure you that it is the strongest wish of the people of this country . . . that Cuba shall one day be free again, and when it is, this Brigade will deserve to march at the head of the first column." Jackie Kennedy then told the throng, in nearly flawless Spanish, that the brigade members were "the bravest men in the world."

that when Kennedy made his way down to the field after his speech to shake hands with more brigade leaders, exchanging words here and there, he said to Ferrer, "You didn't get any help from us."

"No, Mr. President," Ferrer replied, "but I expect it the next time."

"You better believe there's going to be a next time," Kennedy told him, suggesting that next time would be different. Ferrer beamed and told Wyden "I believed in him again."[174]

There were over one hundred anti-Castro exile groups (some formed in Cuba, others in the United States) during the immediate years following the Cuban Revolution.

The first prominent group in the United States was the Frente Revolucionario Democratico ("Democratic Revolutionary Front," or FRD). The revolutionary *frente*, or front, consisted of five exile groups and was the first large anti-Castro group formed on American soil, one that was literally put together by the CIA (when it hosted Cuban exile leaders in New York City on May 11–12, 1960) to implement President Eisenhower's March 17, 1960, directive to the CIA to recruit and train a guerilla force of Cuban exiles to overthrow Castro. On March 18, 1961, in Miami, the CIA put pressure on the FRD and the MRP (the Cuban anti-Castro group, Movimiento Revolucionario del Pueblo, "People's Revolutionary Movement") to join forces with the FRD into a new group, the Cuban Revolutionary Council (CRC), which the United States would treat as the Cuban provisional government if Castro were overthrown. On March 22, the two groups agreed and the CRC was formed, with various anti-Castro leaders sitting on the council. However, the FRD and the CRC continued to function as separate entities until October of 1961, when the FRD was completely absorbed by the CRC in order to avoid the confusion resulting from duplication of personnel, activities, and funding. Lest there be any doubt as to the involvement of the CIA in these two anti-Castro groups, CIA documents themselves confirm this fact. "The FRD was created with Agency [CIA] assistance, guidance and financial support," and was "the front organization for recruiting the members of the Bay of Pigs invasion force."[175] "The CRC had direct access to and support from the White House as well as CIA."[176]

Among the other prominent exile groups were the following: Cuban Revolutionary Junta (JURE); Movimiento de Recuperacion Revolutionaria (the "Movement for the Recovery of the Revolution," or MRR), the group whose members were the original nucleus for Brigade 2506; Alpha 66, one of the most militant and organized of all anti-Castro groups; Second National Front of Escambray (SNFE, a group closely affiliated with Alpha 66); Directorio Revolucionario Estudiantil ("Student Revolutionary Directorate," or DRE), which was a militant as well as a psychological warfare outfit that published its own newspaper, *Trenchera* (Trenches), and was an outgrowth of an activist student group started on the campus of the University of Havana; 30th of November Movement; International Penetration Forces (InterPen); Christian Democratic Movement of Cuba (MDC); Junta of the Government of Cuba in Exile (JGCE); Movimiento Insurreccional de Recuperacion Revolucionaria (MIRR); Ejercito Invasor Cubano (EIC); United Organization for the Liberation of Cuba; Cuban Constitutional Crusade (CCC); and Commandos L-66. Many of these groups, of course, worked together, and their members frequently left one group to join another, since all had the same objective: the overthrow of Castro.

Virtually all militant anti-Castro groups were headquartered in Miami, the center of the exile community, where over one hundred thousand Cubans had arrived by small boats and planes to plot their counterrevolution against Castro so they could return to their homeland. Over their small cups of *café cubano* (a strong expresso coffee so popular among the exiles) in the many little restaurants of Little Havana (southwest Miami), thousands of exiles mapped their strategies on table napkins. As already alluded to, many of the members of the anti-Castro groups, including some of appreciable wealth, had been supportive of Castro's revolution against the corrupt Batista regime but became greatly disillusioned with and eventually violently opposed to Castro when he confiscated their property, and renounced the country's long affiliation with the United States and embraced Marxism.[177] Others were hard-core "Batistianos" who had fled Cuba around the same time their leader, Fulgencio Batista, did, on New Year's Day 1959, or stayed for awhile in Cuba working in the underground against Castro. It should be reiterated that Castro's broken pledges of free elections and a free press, and the more than five hundred public executions of ex-Batista officials within three months after he assumed power, convinced many Cubans on *both* sides of the revolution that Castro was a dictator, not the political savior he had held himself out to be.[178]

Although it is not implausible that anti-Castro Cuban exiles angry at Kennedy over the Bay of Pigs* might encourage Oswald, or some other likely candidate, to kill Kennedy as an act of revenge on their part, it is highly implausible that anyone in the anti-Castro movement, other than an uneducated, unintelligent group of street warriors, would think there was even the smallest of possibilities that the assassination would precipitate a U.S. invasion of Castro's Cuba. The leadership of the various anti-Castro groups would have to know that even if a *pro*-Castro *Cuban national* killed Kennedy, the expectation of our invading Cuba would be very remote, since how could we know Castro was behind it? Even more improbably, how could any group of conspirators with any respectable level of intelligence believe that if an *American* like Oswald—who was simply a supporter of Castro, and who had never been to Cuba, and had absolutely no connection with the Castro regime—killed Kennedy, that the American government would decide to invade Cuba? When, in fact, Oswald was arrested for Kennedy's murder and was believed by Americans to be the president's assassin, and his pro-Castro sympathies had become known, there was no cry from any segment of our society to launch a military attack on Cuba.

And the leaders of the many anti-Castro counterrevolutionary groups, almost without exception, *were* intelligent and educated. Manuel Antonio de Varona, the leader of the FRD, had been president of the Cuban Senate and then prime minister in the administration of President Carlos Prío. Manuel Artime, the nephew of a popular poet, José Angel, and the head of the MRR, had a bachelor of science degree and completed most of his studies to become a doctor in Cuba. Justo Carrillo, one of the original leaders of the FRD, was president of the Bank for Industrial and Agricultural Development under

---

*As already indicated, support for Kennedy remained strong among many in the exile community. In a 1976 interview with *Miami News* Latin community writer Hilda Inclan, Carlos Prío, the former president of Cuba, said, "When Kennedy was killed, Cuban exiles here [in Miami] who were active against Castro had not yet lost faith in the President. Cubans were still waiting for Kennedy to fulfill his promise to help free Cuba" (*Miami Daily News*, May 20, 1976).

Leopoldo, one of the two Cubans who appeared at Sylvia Odio's door, told her in the telephone conversation the next day that the Cuban people bore no malice toward President Kennedy because of the Bay of Pigs episode (CD 205, p.1, December 18, 1963). This clearly was too broad a statement, of course.

Castro. José Ignacio, head of the MDC, was a history professor in Cuba. Manuel "Manolo" Ray, head of JURE (and before that in Cuba, the MRP), had been an engineer in Cuba who became the minister of public works under Castro.[179] Miro Cardona, the head of the CRC, had been a lawyer and professor at the University of Havana and was Castro's first prime minister and then his ambassador to the United Nations.[180] And so on. Indeed, even the "delegates" (leaders in their respective communities) of the anti-Castro groups were normally intelligent and educated. For instance, Carlos Bringuier, the New Orleans delegate of the DRE who had the street confrontation with Oswald in New Orleans in the summer of 1963, had been an attorney in Cuba.

So not only were the anti-Castro leaders men of intelligence and stature, but they were not criminals or murderers, a prerequisite, I would think, for anyone deciding to murder the president of the United States out of revenge.

Moreover, at least the brigade leaders (the men who, along with the members of their brigade, risked their lives to free Cuba) were not antagonistic toward Kennedy at the time of his death.* In writing *The Bay of Pigs* with the main brigade leaders, Haynes Johnson obviously had to get to know them fairly well, and they confided in him. For instance, Pepe San Román, the brigade commander, admitted that while in prison following his capture at the Bay of Pigs, he ruminated that "I hated the United States, and I felt I had been betrayed. Every day it became worse and then I was getting madder and madder and I wanted to get a rifle and come and fight against the United States." But San Román, Artime, and Oliva, all of whom were at the Bay of Pigs and felt deep betrayal, welcomed Kennedy with open arms at the Orange Bowl. Why? It's clear that on reflection they knew that although Kennedy had not come through for them at that point in time, his heart was always in the right place.

Johnson writes, "For all of them [referring to the brigade members, most likely an overstatement by Johnson], and especially the leaders, the death of Kennedy came with shattering impact . . . They believed in President Kennedy and he gave them reason to hope for the future. They believed, no matter what mistakes he personally made during their invasion, that he had saved their lives with his strong warning to Castro immediately upon their defeat [i.e., they believed it was Kennedy's words in a speech the day after the invasion ended, that "our restraint is not inexhaustible" and the U.S. "must take an even closer and more realistic look at the menace of external Communist intervention and domination in Cuba," not Castro's humanity, that were responsible for Castro's not risking the possible consequences of executing them]; . . . that he had liberated them from prison; and that he meant what he said in the Orange Bowl—that he wanted them to return at the head of the column to a free Havana, and he wanted to be there on that day."[181]

I would imagine that virtually the entire activist anti-Castro community in Miami showed up at the Orange Bowl on December 29, 1962, less than eleven months before the assassination. And for those who weren't there, they undoubtedly knew everything about the event from Cuban-American radio and newspapers. They had to know, then, that brigade leaders San Román, Artime, and Oliva—who landed on the treacherous beaches of the Bay of Pigs, saw their comrades killed before their eyes, and were eventually captured (after hiding in the swamps for days, with little food or water) and impris-

---

*Indeed, nearly half of the brigade members who landed on the shores of the Bay of Pigs enlisted in the U.S. Army within two months after their liberation.

oned for a year and a half in Castro's prisons—had made peace with Kennedy and stood by his side as the American and Cuban national anthems were played, even giving him the brigade flag for safekeeping. Knowing this, any anti-Castro militant, or militants, thinking about killing Kennedy would have had to realize that such an act would be going against their brigade leaders, who, along with their troops, were the legendary heroes and soul of the anti-Castro movement. For the thought of assassination to have gone beyond the above realization is not a likely thing.[182]

There is a piece of significant circumstantial evidence, in addition to the common sense of it all, that no anti-Castro group, or even individual members thereof, was complicit in the assassination. It is well known that both the *anti-* and the *pro*-Castro groups were heavily infiltrated by the other side. Bill Kelly, a retired FBI agent who worked in the Internal Security-Cuba section of the Miami field office, which investigated and monitored the two groups full-time during the early 1960s, told me that "half the anti-Castro groups were pro-Castro informants." When I told him that sounded awfully high, he said, "Put it this way. A lot, a lot of pro-Castro informants infiltrated the anti-Castro groups. They were called 'G-2 Agents.' G-2 was the Cuban Intelligence Service. When we'd identify them, we'd arrest them for being in violation of the Foreign Agents Registration Act, which required them to register, which they never did, with the State Department. Because these were crimes committed on American soil, the FBI, not the CIA, had jurisdiction." Kelly noted that "if pro-Castro agents were operating in any other country against the interests of the United States, then it would be CIA jurisdiction. However, not all of these informants were actually G-2 people being paid by Castro. There also were volunteers."

I asked Kelly to estimate the likelihood that Castro, because of this infiltration, would know if any of the anti-Castro groups were behind the assassination. "With the level of infiltration he had, I can say he would have known with almost 100 percent metaphysical certitude," he responded.[183] In fact, FBI headquarters said it believed that there were "more than two hundred agents of Cuban G-2 in the Miami area, all targeted against the exile movement."[184] We know that when it was learned after the assassination that Oswald had a reverence for Castro and his revolution and even had a Fair Play for Cuba chapter in New Orleans, much suspicion focused on Castro's possible involvement in the assassination. To a much lesser degree, that suspicion continues to this very day. As the HSCA said, if Castro learned that *anti*-Castro groups had killed Kennedy, he "would have had the highest incentive to report" this to American authorities "since it would have dispelled suspicions" of his involvement in the assassination.[185] Yet no such information ever came from Castro, information he would almost undoubtedly have possessed if, indeed, anti-Castro Cuban exiles had been behind Kennedy's assassination.

Sergio Arcacha, a New Orleans Cuban exile leader, told author Gus Russo, "Castro knew everything we were doing. He had people everywhere." Russo goes on to write, "In truth, Castro didn't need 'people everywhere' because the Cuban exiles were notorious for being their own worst enemies. Justin Gleichauf, the former chief of the CIA's Miami office, has put it this way: 'To a Cuban, a secret is something you tell to only a hundred people.'"[186] Arcacha himself, just one week before the invasion, told a reporter in New Orleans that the invasion "could begin this afternoon, tomorrow, anytime. We are just waiting for the signal."[187] Cuban intelligence and infiltration of the exiles was such that, according to a January 12, 1961, report, which was among the documents declassified by the Cuban government in March of 2001, the Cubans had detailed knowledge of the CIA camps in Guatemala and Florida, where most of the anti-Castro invasion forces were being trained.[188]

As highly speculative as any possible umbilical cord was between anti-Castro Cubans and Oswald's act of murder, I would come to believe after the London trial that the very remote possibility of anti-Castro Cuban exiles being involved with Oswald in the assassination, even if in the most tangential of ways, was the *only* conspiracy possibility in the entire case that had any merit. A possibility, I might add, that would never be capable of exciting conspiracy theorists and supporting a thriving cottage industry dealing with the facts and mythology of the assassination. It is not only more "sexy" for the CIA, organized crime, or the military-industrial complex, et cetera, to be involved in the assassination, as opposed to comparatively impotent anti-Castro Cuban exiles, but it is infinitely more grave and momentous if leading agencies of our own government, or powerful groups in our society, who felt Kennedy was implementing policies antithetical to their interests, decided to alter the course of American history by a bullet rather than the ballot box.

I should underline that the aforementioned possibility is only a possibility. There is no evidence that the anti-Castro leadership, or even rogue members of any anti-Castro exile group, ever participated, in any way, in the assassination, and three separate investigations have so concluded. The Warren Commission found that the allegation of anti-Castro Cuban involvement in the assassination was "without any factual basis";[189] the HSCA, though saying it could "not preclude the possibility" (how could this *ever* be done?) that individual members of an anti-Castro group were involved, reported that "the evidence was sufficient to support the conclusion that anti-Castro groups . . . were not involved in the assassination";[190] and the Senate's Church Committee said there was "no evidence" that any anti-Castro group was involved in Kennedy's murder.[191]

Cover-Up by the CIA and FBI in the Warren Commission's Investigation of the Assassination

A refrain one constantly hears from the conspiracy theorists is that the CIA and FBI kept critical information from the Warren Commission. The unmistakable inference is that these two agencies withheld *many* things from the Commission, probably because one or both of them (particularly the CIA) were complicit in the assassination. But when the conspiracy theorists finally get around to setting forth just what was withheld, they only come up with the same, old, tired matters about the CIA not informing the Warren Commission about its plot to kill Castro, and the FBI tearing up Oswald's note allegedly threatening to blow up the FBI building. Nothing more of any substance.

With respect to the FBI tearing up the note from Oswald (discussed earlier in book), it couldn't be more obvious that this was just an attempt by the Dallas office of the FBI to protect itself from J. Edgar Hoover's wrath. If the note surfaced, Hoover would know that many in the nation would blame him and the FBI's negligence for not alerting the Secret Service or anyone else about Oswald before the president came to Dallas.[*] As J. Gordon Shanklin, the head of the Dallas FBI office who eventually had FBI agent James Hosty (to whom Oswald addressed the note) destroy the note, told Hosty when Hosty told him the note was "just your typical guff," "What do you mean, 'typical guff'? This note was written by Oswald, the probable assassin of the President, and Oswald brought this note into *this* office just ten days ago. What the hell do you think Hoover's going to do if he finds out about this note? . . . He's going to lose it." Hosty, though having been opposed to destroying the note, went along with its destruction thereafter to the extent

---

[*]Former attorney general Nicholas Katzenbach told the HSCA that "Hoover resented criticism to a degree greater than any other person that I have ever known . . . [And] if the Bureau made any mistake or anything for which the public could criticize the bureau, the bureau would do its best to conceal the information from anybody" (3 HSCA 646, 700, Testimony of Nicholas Katzenbach before the HSCA on September 21, 1978). *Time* magazine went so far as to say that Hoover "cared less about crime than about perpetuating his . . . image" ("Truth about Hoover," p.14).

that he never brought it up in his testimony before the Warren Commission, relying on the explanation that the Commission hadn't "asked me about the note."[1] As Bill Alexander, the Dallas assistant DA at the time, told author Gerald Posner, "I worked with those fellows at the FBI over many years. What they were doing with the Hosty situation is covering their asses . . . People like Shanklin were running for cover to make sure no one could point a finger and say, 'You failed to spot Oswald as a threat.' "[2]

Some have said that agents in the Dallas field office of the FBI also deleted Oswald's reference to Hosty in his address book when the Dallas Police Department turned the book over to the field office, but they did not. The Hosty reference—his name, FBI address, phone number, license plate number—remained in the address book for the Warren Commission to see.[3] However, the Dallas office, in its December 23, 1963, report to the Warren Commission, made no reference to the entry in the address book,[4] though it referred to other entries of less significance. Why? Dallas FBI special agent Robert P. Gemberling, who was the Dallas field office's "coordinator" of the investigation into the assassination of Kennedy, instructed Special Agent John T. Kesler to submit to him a list of all names and items in Oswald's address book that were "leads" requiring "investigation attention." Virtually all of the names and matters referred to in Kesler's thirty-page report to Gemberling were previously "unknown" to the FBI. Inasmuch as the identity of Special Agent Hosty was known to both Kesler and himself, Gemberling did not consider the Hosty information a "lead" and hence did not include it in his own report of December 23, 1963, to the Warren Commission.[5]

It should be noted, however, that the February 11, 1964, report from FBI headquarters to the Warren Commission that included nonleads as well as leads did specifically refer to the Hosty entry, and in an even earlier January 27, 1964, letter to the Warren Commission, the FBI notified the Commission of the Hosty reference in Oswald's address book. The HSCA "concluded that there was no plan by the FBI to withhold the Hosty entry in Oswald's address book for sinister reasons."[6]

Another alleged FBI cover-up ("The whole thing cries cover-up from the very outset," conspiracy theorist Bernard Fensterwald wrote Congressman Thomas Downing of the HSCA on March 8, 1976) turned out to be much to do about nothing when the FBI documents pertaining to the allegation were subsequently declassified. On November 26, 1963, Captain Paul Barger of the Irving Police Department told FBI special agent Robert C. Lish that an informant told him that on November 23, 1963, he had overheard a telephone conversation between telephone number BL-31628 in Irving, Texas (Ruth Paine's residence, though the phone number was still listed in the name of her husband, Michael), and CR-55211 in Arlington (Bell Helicopter, Michael Paine's workplace) in which the male voice said that he felt sure Lee Harvey Oswald had killed the president but he did not feel Oswald was responsible, adding, "We both know who is responsible." Barger said he was extremely busy at the time and could not remember who his informant had been. But the real problem is that when Lish asked Barger for his written record of the conversation he had with his informant and Barger furnished the notes, there was no reference to the words "We both know who is responsible." The only words on the notes were "Oswald wouldn't have any reason to do it, but when you get right down to it, the only guilty person it [is?] that bastard himself." So obviously, Barger had orally given Agent Lish incorrect information, and he conceded as much when he said that when he told Lish what his informant told him, he did not have his notes on hand and was speaking from memory.[7]

In any event, both Michael Paine and Ruth Paine were interviewed by the FBI, and though each acknowledged speaking over the phone about Oswald on the day after the assassination, Michael Paine said he never made the statement "We both know who is responsible" at any place, at any time, or under any circumstances. With respect to the other remark, he said he stated on numerous occasions that Oswald "wouldn't have had any reason" to do it; however, although he believed Oswald did, in fact, kill Kennedy, the words "the only guilty person [is] that bastard himself" did not sound to him like his statement.[8] Ruth Paine also told the FBI that her husband never told her, "We both know who is responsible." About the other ("bastard") remark, she said she could not recall her husband using those exact words, but the meaning of the words would be "compatible" with his feelings on November 23, 1963.[9] Regarding this alleged November 23, 1963, telephone conversation with her husband while he allegedly was *at his place of work*, Paine added to me, "Michael *never* worked on Saturdays."[10] November 23 was a Saturday.

The 1976 Church Committee Report said, "The evidence suggests that during the Warren Commission investigation, top FBI officials were continually concerned with protecting the Bureau's reputation and avoiding any criticism for not fulfilling investigative responsibilities." This paranoia primarily originated with the FBI director himself who, the Senate Select Committee said, had a "known hostility to criticism or embarrassment of the Bureau."[11] Indeed, even without Hoover knowing of Oswald's threatening note to Hosty, the day after the assassination Hoover ordered an internal investigation to determine whether the FBI had adequately investigated Oswald's potential for subversive actions or violence and whether he should have been listed on the FBI's security index.[12] On December 10, 1963, the report by the bureau's Inspection Division found numerous deficiencies in the pre-assassination investigation and recommended various forms of discipline, such as censure, probation, and transfer for seventeen members of the FBI, including four supervisors at headquarters and one assistant director.[13] A representative example of a cited deficiency: "Special Agent [name deleted] advised that New York [field office of FBI] did not report Oswald's 4-21-63 Fair Play For Cuba contact to Dallas [field office] until letter sent 6-27-63, and Dallas did not feel it necessary to report it to Bureau [headquarters] until 9-10-63. [Deleted agent's name] admits it 'possibly' would have been better to have reported on the matter earlier."[14] Hoover subsequently carried out most of the disciplinary actions recommended.[15] One could only imagine what the bureau's Inspection Division and particularly Hoover would have done to Shanklin, even Hosty, if they had learned about Oswald's note and the destruction of it.

One other alleged attempt on the part of the FBI to withhold key information from the Warren Commission comes not so much from the conspiracy theorists but from a quasi-conspiracy soul mate of theirs, former FBI agent James Hosty himself. In his book *Assignment: Oswald*, Hosty says that shortly before his testimony before the Warren Commission, someone removed "two key items" (both had been sent from FBI headquarters) from his file on Oswald in his Dallas office. One was an October 18, 1963, communiqué from the CIA to the FBI stating that while Oswald was in Mexico City he was in contact with the Russian embassy and had probably spoken to one Valeriy Kostikov at the embassy. The second document contained a reference to the November 9, 1963, letter Oswald had written to the Soviet embassy in Washington, D.C., in which he refers to speaking to a "Comrade Kostin" (believed to be Kostikov) at the Russian embassy in Mexico City. Based on these two documents, Hosty said he figured Kostikov "was just a simple administrative officer at the Embassy."

But Hosty says he later learned that Kostikov was a KGB agent in Department 13, the department of the KGB that dealt in sabotage and assassination. Hosty suggests that the reason the FBI (who he correctly presumes knew this fact)[*] kept this information from him is that the bureau, in league with the CIA, the Warren Commission, and President Johnson himself, didn't want him to introduce this information into the public record when he testified before the Warren Commission, for fear, Hosty says, that it could precipitate a nuclear war with the Soviet Union.[16]

One immediate problem with Hosty's thinking is this: Hosty said he read both documents before they disappeared from his files. Obviously, neither contained a reference to Kostikov being a KGB agent. Indeed, this is the predicate for Hosty's whole argument. Since the documents did not contain a reference to Kostikov being a KGB agent, how in the world would their removal from his file, which he felt was highly suspicious, prevent him from knowing Kostikov was a KGB agent? It obviously makes no sense at all. Moreover, if the documents had contained a reference to Kostikov's KGB status, since Hosty had already read both documents, he could have testified to their essential content before the Warren Commission even if he did not have them in his physical possession.

It is also noteworthy that unlike his published book, his earlier 1986 manuscript of the book pointed out (page 20) that right after the assassination, when he located his Oswald file, the two subject documents were "right on top" of the file. Obviously, they were important, and just as obviously, his supervising agents had a right, without his permission, to look into the file (and remove any documents they deemed important) on someone who had just been identified as the president's assassin. Indeed, one such supervising agent, Kenneth Howe, testified to this being routine procedure in *any* case.[17] Hosty goes on to say in his published book, however, that when he returned to Dallas after testifying before the Warren Commission in Washington, the two subject documents had been placed back in the file, suggesting again, he says, that his superiors didn't want him to have access to these documents prior to his testimony.[18] But this is ludicrous since his superiors would have to assume that since these two documents had been in his file, he had read them and knew the contents anyway.

Hosty asserts that when he referred to the two documents in a pre-testimony session with a Warren Commission staffer in May of 1964, Assistant FBI Director Alan Belmont muttered in Hosty's ear, "Damn it, I thought I told them not to let you see that one from the Washington field office" (he was referring to the October 18, 1963, CIA communiqué to FBI headquarters advising the FBI of Oswald's probable contact in Mexico City with Kostikov at the Soviet embassy).[19] This incident seems highly unlikely to have occurred. What could possibly have been in that document that the FBI did not want Hosty to see? Nothing. All the good stuff—about Kostikov being a KGB agent—was never, per Hosty himself, in either document.

It should be mentioned that the Warren Commission, before Hosty's testimony on May 5, 1964, *already knew* that Kostikov was a KGB agent who was a member of Department 13. In a memo to the Warren Commission on January 31, 1964, the CIA informed the Commission that "Kostikov is believed to work for Department Thirteen of the First Chief Directorate of the KGB. It is the Department responsible for executive action, including sabotage and assassination. These functions of the KGB are known within the Service itself as 'Wet Affairs' (mokryye dela)."[20]

Though not directly relevant to the Hosty issue, on December 20, 1963, before the

---

[*]An internal FBI memorandum of November 27, 1963, from W. C. Sullivan to D. J. Brennan Jr. speaks of "Kostikov's connection with the 13th Department of the KGB, which handles sabotage and assassinations." The memorandum goes on to say that this information on Kostikov was "based on data developed both by the Bureau and CIA."

CIA sent its memo to the Warren Commission, a CIA report titled "CIA Work on Lee Oswald and the Assassination of President Kennedy" said that "Kostikov is *believed* to work for Department 13 of the KGB, the department responsible for sabotage and assassination. This *belief* is based on the fact that Kostikov once was responsible for a Soviet agent whose mission was sabotage and whom Kostikov passed on to another KGB officer who was positively known to work for Department 13. *Almost* invariably, sabotage agents are handled only by Department 13 officers . . . The files of our Mexico City station were reviewed in the three or four days after the assassination to see if anything in Kostikov's past activities incriminated him. No clue was found linking him to the assassination or to anything remotely related to it." The report said that even on the day of the assassination, nothing suspicious was noted at the Russian embassy in Mexico City, with Soviet officials, including Kostikov, coming and going "as usual."[21]*

An earlier draft of the CIA report, dated December 13, 1963, noted that

> Oswald's dealing with KGB men like Obyedkov [a guard at the Soviet embassy Oswald spoke to on October 1, 1963] and Kostikov was nothing more than a grim coincidence, a coincidence due in part to the Soviet habit of placing intelligence men [KGB] in the Embassies in positions where they receive a large portion of the visitors and phone calls. All of the five Consular Officers in the Soviet Embassy [in Mexico City] are known or suspected intelligence officers. Certainly, if Oswald had been a Soviet agent in training for an assassination assignment or even for sabotage work, the Soviets would have stopped him from making open visits and phone calls to the Soviet Embassy in Mexico City after he tried it a couple of times. Our experience in Mexico, studying the Soviet intelligence service at close range, indicates that they do make some mistakes and are sometime insecure in their methods, but that they do not persist in such glaring errors.[22]

In other words, if the KGB was preparing Oswald to be its assassin of Kennedy, it is virtually inconceivable that it would have him meet its agents at the Russian embassy, a place it had to know was under CIA surveillance.

Hosty has always believed that he, along with several other agents, should not have been disciplined by Hoover for their pre-assassination investigative failures. After all, the evidence seems to support Hosty's position that he did not know of Kostikov's true identity before the assassination, and he was not aware of anything Oswald did that should have led him to believe Oswald was a possible candidate to kill the president. Most of the agents merely got letters of censure. Hosty got that along with a thirty-day suspension of pay (which the bureau paid him when he retired in 1979) and was transferred to the Kansas City field office. He feels Hoover tried to make him the scapegoat for the assassination,

---

*The December 20, 1963, report should not be construed to mean that the CIA's knowledge of and interest in Kostikov's possible role in the assassination only commenced weeks or even days after the assassination. Indeed, though a CIA report said there was "little in Headquarter's file on Kostikov," on November 23, 1963, the day after the assassination, the CIA was sufficiently interested in Kostikov to generate this directive from CIA headquarters in Washington, D.C., to its Mexico City station: "Urgently require info Valeriy Vladmirovich Kostikov travels outside Mexico, hour by hour whereabouts 22 Nov . . . any indications unusual activities involving KGB and Sovemb [Soviet embassy] personnel 17 through 30 Nov." A CIA Teletype from the Mexico City station to headquarters later that day (November 23) confirmed an earlier Teletype that Kostikov had only left Mexico once in September, and "no recent unusual KGB and Sovemb personnel activities 17 Nov to date." (CIA Record 104–10127–10207, "Mexico City Chronology," pp.6, 55)

and this is why he has an animus for his old boss, calling him an "SOB." In the process of trying to settle a score with the bureau, Hosty, a good man but perhaps a little paranoid (understandably so) because of this incident, and perhaps because he unconsciously tried to increase the marketability of his book, ended up engaging in some groundless and sometimes wild speculation. He also regurgitated rumors that were not only improbable on their face but for which there was no credible evidence or support—for instance, that Oswald, in Mexico City, had told the Cuban consulate that he was "going to kill Kennedy"; that he had a "clandestine meeting with the KGB hit man Kostikov" in Mexico City; and that Oswald had maintained contact with one Vitaliy Gerosimov, an official at the Soviet embassy in Washington who Hosty says was the contact "for deep-cover Soviet espionage agents in the United States."[23]

Although in his book Hosty made a great deal of who Kostikov allegedly was ("I find it more than disturbing that the day after Oswald offered to kill the president for the Cubans, he was seen meeting with the KGB's chief assassination expert for the Western Hemisphere"),[24] and testified for the defense at the London trial that Kostikov was in charge of assassinations for the KGB in the Western Hemisphere, he was much more subdued and realistic under my cross-examination of him. Among other things he said it was "my understanding" that Kostikov did *not* know who Oswald was when Oswald came to the Soviet embassy. In answer to my question as to whether it was "reasonably inferable" that Oswald only spoke to Kostikov about securing a visa, he answered, "Yes. It was concerning his request for he and his family to return to the Soviet Union." When I asked him, "You're certainly not suggesting to this jury that Kostikov—who at one time may or may not have been a member of any KGB assassination unit—you're not suggesting that he had anything to do with the assassination. Is that correct?" Hosty responded, "There is no evidence to that effect." Indeed, when I asked him why would the FBI or J. Edgar Hoover want to keep it "a secret from you that Kostikov was in the KGB?" he answered that "J. Edgar Hoover was not directly responsible. This was the Russian espionage section [of the FBI] who did that. We have an awful lot of special regulations . . . in counterintelligence, there are a lot of provisions that say don't say this, don't say that." When I asked Hosty, "But you don't know why FBI headquarters would not want you to know Kostikov was a member of the KGB?" he replied, "I don't know why." Ten years later, in his book, he claimed he did know why.

I tried to summarize my feeling about the entire Kostikov matter for the jury in London by asking Hosty, "The charge has been made . . . that Oswald was a dangerous enough person for you to have alerted the Secret Service about him before President Kennedy came to Dallas?"

"That charge has been made," Hosty answered.

Question: "I know this is going to be a hard question for you to answer, Mr. Hosty, but since you have been criticized for your handling of the case . . . isn't this the main reason you place so much emphasis on Kostikov and your not knowing he was a KGB agent, because the Kostikov matter enables you to make the argument that if you had known, you would have handled the Oswald matter differently?"

Hosty: "I *would* have handled it differently."[25]

With respect to the CIA, during testimony before the HSCA on September 22, 1978, House Representative Christopher J. Dodd asked former CIA director Richard Helms, "Other than the anti-Castro assassination plots, was there any other information pertaining to [the assassination of] the president that you are aware of and that the Warren Commission was not told about?*... Are there other things that you can recall that might have had relevancy—things of importance to the Warren Commission's investigation of the assassination of [Kennedy]?"

Helms: "Well, I don't know of any others. I can't think of what they might have been ... None come readily to mind."[26]

The 1976 Church Committee found that "between 1960 and early 1963 the CIA attempted to use underworld figures for [Castro's] assassination. By May 1962, the FBI knew of such plots and in June 1963 learned of their termination . . . Neither the CIA nor the FBI told the Warren Commission about the CIA attempts to assassinate Fidel Castro."[27]† The CIA itself has admitted its plot to assassinate Castro. When Helms was asked in his testimony before the Church Committee if he had been part of the CIA's "assassination plot against Castro," he responded, "I was aware that there had been efforts made to get rid of him."[28] The CIA has also acknowledged that it involved the Mafia in its goal of killing Castro. When G. Robert Blakey, the HSCA chief counsel, asked Helms during his September 22, 1978, appearance before the committee, "Let me ask you a moral question . . . Would you tell me and the members of this committee and . . . the American people what possibly could have been the moral justification for the CIA entering into an alliance with the Mafia to execute the president of a foreign country?" Helms could only respond, "There was none. I have apologized for this. I can't do any more than apologize on public television that it was an error in judgment . . . For my part in this and to the extent I had anything to do with it, I am heart sorry."[29]

During the Church Committee hearings in 1975, Helms gave several reasons for his not telling the Warren Commission about these plots. He testified, "I was instructed to reply to inquiries from the Warren Commission for information from the Agency. I was not asked to initiate any particular thing."

Question: "In other words, if you weren't asked for it, you didn't give it?"

Helms: "That's right, sir."[30] Helms also told the committee, "My recollection at the time was that it was *public knowledge* that the United States was trying to get rid of Castro."[31] Further deflecting responsibility from himself, he pointed out that "Mr. Allen Dulles was a member of the Warren Commission. And the first [CIA-mob] assassination plot happened during his time as director [Dulles was the CIA director from February 26, 1953 to November 29, 1961, when he was succeeded by John McCone] . . . He was sitting right there in [the Warren Commission's] deliberations and knew about this."[32]†

---

*There was no need for the CIA to inform the Warren Commission of the CIA's effort to overthrow Castro. Everyone already knew this. Indeed, President Kennedy even took full responsibility for the failure of the Bay of Pigs invasion back in 1961. What the CIA didn't tell the Warren Commission about was the CIA's plots to kill Castro, and as the Church Committee said, "It is unlikely that anyone in the Warren Commission knew of [the] CIA assassination efforts. Former Senator John Sherman Cooper, a member of the Commission, advised the Select Committee that the subject never came up in the Commission's deliberations. Lee Rankin, Chief Counsel for the Warren Commission, and Burt Griffin, Howard Willens, and David Belin of the Commission staff have all stated they were not aware of the CIA plots." (Church Committee Report, pp.67–68)

†The CIA-mob plot to kill Castro was separate and distinct from AMLASH, the code name for the Cuban figure close to Castro with whom the CIA conspired to overthrow Castro (HSCA Report, p.107). See endnote discussion on whether the AMLASH operation included plans for Castro's murder.

‡When Helms testified before the HSCA three years later, in 1978, he responded similarly. When HSCA staff counsel asked him "why the Warren Commission was not told by you of the anti-Castro assassination plots," Helms responded, "I [was] never asked to testify before the Warren Commission about our operations." Question: "If the Warren Commission did not know of the operation, it certainly was not in a position to ask you about it. Is that not true?" "Yes, but how do you know they did not know about it? How do you know Mr. Dulles had not told them? How was I to know that? And besides, I was not the director of the agency,

Though Helms spoke categorically of Dulles's knowledge, it is not clear whether Helms assumed this or he was speaking from personal knowledge. The pipe-smoking Dulles, who was the longest-serving CIA director ever, certainly had never acknowledged that he knew of the CIA-mob plot to kill Castro, and the available record is not entirely clear that he did, though one could draw that inference. The Church Committee and the HSCA learned that in September of 1960, Richard Bissell, CIA deputy director for plans, and Colonel Sheffield Edwards, chief of the CIA's Office of Security, briefed Dulles and his deputy, General Charles Cabell, "on the existence of a plan involving members of the syndicate. The discussion was circumspect; Edwards deliberately avoided the use of any 'bad words.' The descriptive term used was 'an intelligence operation.' Edwards is quite sure that [Dulles and Cabell] clearly understood the nature of the operation he was discussing . . . Edwards recalls that Mr. Dulles merely nodded, presumably in understanding and approval."[33] And Bissell testified before the Church Committee, "I can only say that I am quite sure I came away from that meeting . . . convinced that he knew the nature of the operation."[34] Not overly convincing at all.

More so is the December 11, 1959, memorandum by J. C. King, head of the CIA's Western Hemisphere Division, to Dulles that contained four "Recommended Actions," one of which was that "thorough consideration be given to the elimination of Fidel Castro," which Dulles approved of in writing.[35] But again, the word *elimination* is not unequivocal, nor could the HSCA uncover any evidence that Dulles became aware that steps were later taken to actually carry out (though unsuccessfully) the subject "recommended" action. And the Church Committee was equally confused, saying, "Certain . . . evidence before the Committee suggests that Dulles and Cabell did know about the assassination plots; other evidence suggests they did not."[36]

One piece of evidence indicating that Dulles did not know that an actual *decision* had been made to kill Castro, and if he did, he did not approve, is a cable sent on July 21, 1960, from CIA headquarters to its Havana station stating that "possible removal of top three [Cuban] leaders is *receiving serious consideration* at HQ'S." But the duty officer (not identified by name by the Church Committee) testified that the very next day he sent a countermanding cable to the Havana station, and that "to the best of my knowledge, my memory is that the director [Dulles], not the deputy director [Bissell] . . . had countermanded the cable and had directed that—had indicated that assassination was not to be considered."[37] Although the Church Committee said that "the evidence as to whether Allen Dulles, CIA Director during the Eisenhower Administration, was informed of the Castro assassination operation is not clear," it ultimately concluded that it was "likely" that "Dulles knew about and authorized the actual plots [to kill Castro] that occurred during his tenure."[38] The committee could not take Dulles's testimony on the matter, Dulles being deceased.

When Helms testified before the Rockefeller Commission and was asked about the possibility that Castro had retaliated against Kennedy because of CIA attempts against him, I somehow believe Helms when he answered, "I don't recall the thought ever having occurred to me at the time. The first time I ever heard such a theory . . . was in a pecu-

---

and in the CIA, you did not go traipsing around to the Warren Commission or to congressional committees or to anyplace else without the director's permission." "Did you ever discuss with the director whether the Warren Commission should be informed of the anti-Castro assassination plots?" "I did not, as far as I can recall." (JFK Document 014710, Testimony of Richard Helms before Executive Session of HSCA on August 9, 1978, pp.30–31; 11 HSCA 482–483)

liar way by President Johnson."[39] But whether the thought occurred to Helms or not, surely someone at the CIA had to know that even if there was no known connection between the Castro plots and Kennedy's assassination, they had a duty to inform the Warren Commission of these plots. This is particularly true when the CIA knew that the Commission was investigating the possible involvement of Castro in Kennedy's death. Certainly the plots against Castro would be *relevant* to the issue of Castro's motive.

As opposed to the Bay of Pigs invasion, Robert Kennedy was deeply involved in Operation Mongoose, the U.S. effort to remove Castro from power. In a June 11, 1964, letter from Chief Justice Earl Warren to RFK, Warren asked if RFK was "aware of any additional information relating to the assassination of President John F. Kennedy" that his Justice Department had not made available to the Commission, particularly in the area of a "foreign conspiracy." Although one can see why RFK would not, in response, mention the U.S. effort to *oust* Castro, since this was common knowledge and he could rightfully assume the Warren Commission already knew about it, he also had learned (see endnote discussion) of the CIA's attempt to *murder* Castro, which was not a matter of common knowledge and which, in terms of a motive by a foreign country to kill President Kennedy, would be information "relating to the assassination." Yet in RFK's August 4, 1964, response (seven weeks after Warren's request, which, in terms of protocol alone, was an improper delay), RFK, who never testified before the Warren Commission though he volunteered to do so, said his Department of Justice had furnished the Commission "all information relating in any way to the assassination of President John F. Kennedy."[40] So if Allen Dulles knew of the CIA plot to murder Castro and kept this fact from the Warren Commission, it clearly appears that RFK was also covering up this nation's effort to murder Castro.[*] Exposure of the effort would have been damaging to his and his brother's reputation and legacy (even though it has never been established that either Kennedy brother had approved of the assassination effort [see endnote discussion]), and the Kennedy family, not surprisingly, was always protective of the aura of Camelot.

Before we go any further, however, I must note that the failure of the CIA and RFK to inform the Commission of the plots against Castro did not in any way stop the Commission from investigating the possibility of Castro's involvement. The argument by Warren Commission critics goes like this: because the Commission did not know of the plots against Castro, it did not explore the possibility that Castro may have had Kennedy killed to retaliate or to preempt further attempts on his life. But that argument has wobbly legs, because even without knowledge of the plots, as indicated, the Commission certainly did have knowledge of Kennedy's attempt to remove Castro from power by his support of the Bay of Pigs invasion, and arguably this would give Castro a similar motive to retaliate. In light of this, the Commission undertook an intensive investigation of any possible connection between Oswald and Cuba (which is synonymous with Castro). "Literally dozens of allegations of a conspiratorial contact between Oswald and agents of the Cuban Government have been investigated by the Commission," the Warren Report noted, and it did not uncover any "evidence that the Cuban Government had any involvement in the assassination," or "that the Cuban Government had [any] relationship with Lee Harvey Oswald" other than his attempt to get a visa at the Cuban consulate.[41]

---

[*]I suppose it is possible that RFK *assumed* the Warren Commission already knew much more than he did. He might have *assumed* that Allen Dulles knew all about the attempts on Castro, and *assumed* that Dulles, as a part of the Commission, had informed the Commission about them.

Not only the FBI, the Warren Commission's chief investigative arm, but the Secret Service investigated every conceivable known contact Oswald had that could lead to Cuba's involvement in the assassination. Indeed, the Secret Service's investigation "dealt almost entirely with the Cuban angle."[42] And if Castro was behind Oswald's act, these investigations would very probably have discovered it. If not, how would knowledge of the CIA plots to kill Castro have helped the Warren Commission discover it? In other words, how would the Commission's investigation of Oswald's ties to Cuba have been measurably different if it *had* known of the U.S. plot to kill Castro? Warren Commission assistant counsel Burt W. Griffin says, "If we had known that the CIA wanted to assassinate Castro, then all of the Cuban motivations [to kill Kennedy] that we were exploring . . . made much, much more sense."[43] Translation: we would have suspected Castro as a possible conspirator behind the assassination *more than we did*. But again, how would the Commission's *investigation* of Castro have been significantly, if at all, different?

When HSCA counsel asked John Scelso, who originally headed up the CIA investigation of the assassination (which was far less comprehensive than the Warren Commission's and FBI's, even the Secret Service's), "Is there anything else that you would have done differently [if you had known about the CIA plots to kill Castro]?" his answer, though containing many words, came down to not much more than finding out more about the CIA plots and whether Castro knew of them. "If Helms had disclosed the Cuban assassination plots, we would have gone at that hot and heavy. We would have queried the agent [he didn't clarify whom he meant here, but presumably an agent involved in the plot] about it [the plots] in great detail. I would have had him polygraphed . . . to see if he had a double-agent informing Castro about our poison pen things . . . I would have had all our Cuban sources queried about it."[44] The assertion of Raymond Rocca, the CIA's chief of research and analysis for counterintelligence, is no more satisfying. He says that had he known of the anti-Castro plots, "a completely different procedural approach probably would and should have been taken."[45] But he didn't say what different approach he would have taken. Moreover, Rocca's superiors at the CIA *did* know of the plots on Castro. (I mean, they were behind the plots.) How did it change *their* approach to investigating the assassination?

Parenthetically, the Warren Commission shouldn't feel bad about not knowing of the CIA's attempt to murder Castro. If we're to believe Scelso, the CIA veteran whom Richard Helms originally put in charge of the CIA's investigation of the assassination, he didn't know about it either.[46]

It bears repeating that even without knowledge of the CIA's attempt on Castro's life, the Warren Commission certainly knew of the Bay of Pigs invasion of Cuba in April of 1961. And although no U.S. military personnel actually fought on Cuban soil, as the HSCA said, "U.S. sponsorship of the landing was readily apparent. President Kennedy [even] publicly acknowledged 'sole responsibility' for the U.S. role in the aborted invasion."[47] And as far as the issue of relevance to Castro's possible motive is concerned, the CIA's plot to murder him would hardly have changed his thinking vis-à-vis the United States. We can assume he knew that if the separate and distinct Bay of Pigs invasion had succeeded, the U.S. plans for him did not include expatriating him to the United States and supporting his run for Congress.

Although the CIA's failure to inform the Warren Commission of its plots against Castro's life was obviously wrong and a serious violation of responsibility and trust, it did not seem to inhibit the Warren Commission's investigation, as conspiracy theorists would want us to believe. Also, two important considerations have to have been at play here. One is too obvious to state—that the CIA, for purposes of national security and geopolitical considerations, didn't want it to be known to the outside world, or even internally in the United States, that it was involved to the sordid business of trying to murder a foreign leader. Second, the CIA and FBI, like all rational people, knew almost within hours that Oswald had killed Kennedy. And from the realization of who Oswald was as well as the surrounding circumstances (for instance, no one assisting Oswald to escape or driving him to his death), they became very confident early on that he acted alone. So concealing the collateral truth of the plot to kill Castro would not invalidate the central truth that Oswald acted alone.

No one has put the reason for the CIA's (and FBI's) failure to inform the Warren Commission of the Castro plots any better than writer and assassination researcher Max Holland. Concerning those members of the CIA (and FBI, attorney general's office, etc.) who were confronted with the issue of whether to inform the Warren Commission about the plots or not, he writes,

> Officials in the know faced a genuine dilemma only if they had information pointing [to the Cuban government's involvement with Oswald in the assassination]. The Warren Commission could not [be allowed to] deliver to the American people and the world a false conclusion—that might well affect the stability of the government or shake important institutions to their foundations. But there was every reason not to spill secrets that merely echoed the finding that Oswald acted alone. The Commission, though denied important supporting information, *would still publish the correct conclusion*, and the U.S. Government could keep its deepest secrets. It was a convenient act of denial and dismissal, but also one perceived as necessary in the midst of the cold war. Complete candor would not have changed the Report's two essential conclusions at all—though it might have done a great deal to prevent its slide into disrepute later.[48]

The bottom line is that the CIA withheld the information from the Warren Commission solely to protect its reputation, as sullied as many people believe it already was, not to conceal its involvement with Oswald in the assassination. The CIA's dirty laundry not only handcuffed it from telling the truth, but also deterred the U.S. Department of Justice from prosecuting a member of organized crime. In a May 10, 1962, memo about a meeting he had had with RFK the previous day, Hoover, talking about mobster Sam Giancana's unlawful organized-crime activities, wrote, "He [Kennedy] stated of course it would be very difficult to initiate any prosecution against [Giancana] because Giancana could immediately bring out the fact that the United States Government had approached him to arrange for the assassination of Castro."[49]

The conspiracy theorists have tried to convert the FBI's attempt (in destroying Oswald's note to Hosty) to avoid the accusation it could have prevented the assassination, and the CIA's attempt to cover up its misdeeds on another matter (plot to kill Castro), into an attempt by both agencies to cover up their participation in the assassination of President Kennedy. This is the world of non sequiturs and enormous broad jumps in which the conspiracy theorists dwell and for which they are justifiably famous.

Jim Garrison's Prosecution
of Clay Shaw and
Oliver Stone's Movie *JFK*

Oliver Stone's 1991 movie, *JFK*, was inspired by and primarily based on New Orleans district attorney Jim Garrison's 1988 book, *On the Trail of the Assassins*, which chronicles Garrison's investigation and unsuccessful 1969 prosecution of New Orleans business-man Clay Shaw for conspiring, the March 22, 1967, indictment said, "with David W. Fer-rie, Lee Harvey Oswald and others to murder John F. Kennedy." It is, to this day, the only prosecution ever arising out of Kennedy's murder.

Clay Shaw was an urbane, accomplished, cultured man and a very respected figure in New Orleans's civil and social life. Indeed, in the March 1967 issue of *New Orleans' Town and Country Magazine*, he was listed, along with Garrison, as one of the thirty-five "most important men in New Orleans." After serving in the Second World War, reaching the rank of major and being awarded the Croix de Guerre (the French military award for heroism in battle) and the Bronze Star, Shaw was one of the founders of the New Orleans International Trade Mart, where he served as managing director from 1946 to 1965. He was the moving force behind the eventual construction of a thirty-three-story head-quarters for the Mart on Canal Street. The Mart, credited with substantially increasing trade at the port of New Orleans, was a model for cities around the world.

Shaw was also an integral force in the restoration of the historic French Quarter, one of the sixteen homes he restored being the 1821 residence of the noted naturalist John James Audubon. Shaw's work was of such quality that it caught the attention of such pub-lications as *House & Garden*, *House & Home*, and *Town & Country*. The six-foot four-inch, silver-haired, distinguished-looking man was fluent in four languages, traveled widely, reportedly once dined with Churchill, read the great books of literature, regularly attended the symphony, opera, and ballet, and became an accomplished playwright (*Sub-merged*, *The Idol's Eye*, and others). He lived in a showplace home in the French Quarter with a brass-knockered red door, and his circle of friends included the likes of Tennessee Williams. It was not publicly known that he was also a homosexual. (Garrison, of course, subtly exploited this fact to give more credibility to his allegation that Shaw conspired with Ferrie, another homosexual.) Above all, Shaw was a gentleman, one who could hardly muster up more than a sense of pity for the sick man who was, without any justification, destroying his life. As someone once described Shaw, he was "the unlikeliest villain since Oscar Wilde."

Indeed, the immediate reaction to the charges against Shaw among the great many in New Orleans who knew him was of stunned disbelief. "Garrison can't be serious," "Clay Shaw? Incredible," "Impossible," "The most ridiculous thing I've ever heard," and similar responses were heard throughout the Crescent City. Many even found it humorous that the DA actually thought a man like Shaw would be involved in a plot to assassinate "anyone, let alone a President of the United States."[1] But these responses were only from those who knew him personally. Most of the people of New Orleans didn't, and like citizens of any city, they made the normal assumption that Garrison, the district attorney of their parish, wouldn't bring such serious charges against anyone unless he thought he had something substantial.

As for Shaw's politics, two New Orleans reporters at the time who were very familiar with him, said, "Those closest to him identify him as a liberal, and many say he was an ardent admirer of President Kennedy . . . Shaw described himself as a liberal of the old-fashioned Wilson-Roosevelt breed."[2] Indeed, Shaw said he voted for Kennedy in 1960 and felt Kennedy was an excellent president, "in the same tradition" of Wilson and Roosevelt.[3]

When Shaw learned from Assistant DA Andrew Sciambra on March 1, 1967, that Garrison actually intended to charge him that day with conspiracy to murder Kennedy, he exclaimed to Sciambra, "You've got to be kidding, you've *got* to be kidding." Sciambra said he wasn't and asked Shaw to take a polygraph test, which Shaw indignantly refused to do.* In his lawyer's office the next day after being charged, Shaw told a large throng of reporters that he did not know Oswald or Ferrie, had never been to Ferrie's apartment, and had not "conspired with anyone at any time or at any place to murder our late and esteemed president," adding that he had "only the highest and utmost respect and admiration" for Kennedy.[4]†

David Ferrie was a manic-depressive, cartoonish figure who wore a scruffy, red homemade wig and fake oversized eyebrows (he was hairless due to the disease alopecia praecox)—in short, someone not normally seen outside a carnival tent. The son of a Cleveland police captain, and a Roman Catholic by birth, Ferrie, in his frenetic existence, was, among other things, a seminary student in Cleveland for two years in his early twenties, a commercial pilot for Eastern Airlines, a flying instructor, high school aeronautical science teacher, private investigator, accomplished pianist, service station proprietor, psychologist without credentials, hypnotist, self-styled clergyman of the Orthodox Old Catholic Church of North America, and searcher for a cure for cancer, at

---

*While agreeing to take such a test is a good sign, if you know you're 100 percent innocent but fear the test results might be unfavorable for whatever reason (e.g., the polygrapher is part of a team out to falsely accuse you, or he is incompetent, or you are understandably anxious), refusing to take such a test is not that relevant.

†The intelligent Shaw would later observe, in his own way, what so many others have: "People believe in a conspiracy because when death comes to the figure of a prince, as it did to Kennedy, struck down in his prime, it should come under a panoply of great tragedy with all the resulting high court intrigue—almost something out of Shakespeare—not from some poor little psychotic loser crouched with a mail-order rifle behind a stack of cardboard boxes in a warehouse" (Kirkwood, *American Grotesque*, p.28).

one time sharing his book-strewn apartment in New Orleans with white mice he kept for research purposes. He was, by virtually all accounts, a "brilliant" but tormented man. Ferrie had ambivalent feelings about Kennedy in general but was highly condemnatory of the president for allegedly withdrawing air support to the anti-Castro invading force at the Bay of Pigs, and became actively involved in the anti-Castro movement in New Orleans. His anti-Communism was such that he made the irrational charge that the Roosevelt and Truman administrations had been "driving us to communism."[5] Garrison at one time believed that Ferrie, who had been fired as an Eastern Airlines pilot in 1961 because of charges pending against him that he had sexual relations with a fifteen-year-old boy, was supposed to have flown Kennedy's real killers (not Oswald) away from Dallas after the assassination.

With respect to the third member of Garrison's alleged conspiracy, Garrison believed that "not one" shot "was fired by Lee Harvey Oswald."[6] Oswald's supposed role in the conspiracy was to present himself to the world as a pro-Castro Marxist, though, per Garrison, his "political orientation was extreme right wing." Garrison maintained that Oswald was manipulated by his co-conspirators into unwittingly setting himself up as a decoy and patsy so that the real killers of Kennedy could escape. Kennedy was murdered, per Garrison, "by a precision guerrilla team of at least seven men" located at the grassy knoll, the Book Depository Building, and the Dal-Tex Building. One man fired from each location, a separate one picking up the shells. One member of the team feigned an epileptic seizure as a diversionary tactic just before the motorcade reached the ambush point.[7]

In Garrison's mind, lurking behind the scenes and pulling the strings on the three marionettes—Shaw, Ferrie, and Oswald—were rogue elements of the CIA. "The Central Intelligence Agency was deeply involved in the assassination," Garrison announced on January 31, 1968, on national television (Johnny Carson's *Tonight Show*). Three weeks later he finetuned it. "President Kennedy was killed by *elements* of the Central Intelligence Agency of the United States Government," he told TV reporter Willem L. Oltmans on February 22, 1968. Ferrie, Garrison told Oltmans, was a "CIA employee" and Oswald "worked for the CIA."[8] Indeed, in Garrison's book on the assassination he goes so far as to say that Shaw's connection with the CIA may actually have been high enough "to request that I be eliminated."[9] In a July 19, 1967, television interview with station WKBW in Buffalo, Garrison said, "The CIA knows the names of every man involved in the assassination, including the names of the individuals who pulled the triggers from the grassy knoll."

Although Garrison, before the trial, told anyone who would listen that the CIA was behind the assassination, he produced no evidence at the trial of CIA involvement and presented no evidence that Oswald, Ferrie, or Shaw was ever associated, in any way, with the CIA or any other agency of U.S. intelligence. *Remarkably, not once at the trial did Garrison or his team even mention the CIA.*

Jim Garrison,* a former pilot who flew thirty-five reconnaissance missions in France and Germany during World War II and a former FBI agent (for four months), ran successfully for New Orleans DA in 1962 as a fiercely independent "reform" candidate with the image of an honest loner taking on a corrupt and entrenched establishment. Though he had little money, he used it judiciously, hoarding it until the last moment, then satu-

---

*Garrison's given name was Earling Carothers Garrison. The Iowan legally changed his name to Jim Garrison in the early 1950s.

rating the television screens in New Orleans with commercials during the final twenty-four hours of the campaign. (He had lost two previous political races, for assessor in 1957 and criminal district judge in 1960.) Once elected, the flamboyant, bright, and articulate forty-one-year-old immediately initiated a blitzkrieg campaign against vice on Bourbon Street by personally—with the cameras clicking—padlocking or raiding honky-tonks, striptease joints, and gay bars. He also attacked the city's bail bond system as corrupt and assailed the New Orleans Police Department as being soft on crime.[10] But Garrison never went after organized crime in New Orleans, causing some to suspect he was involved with the mob. However, almost invariably in major U.S. cities, organized-crime prosecutions are brought by federal authorities (Department of Justice, FBI, and U.S. attorneys), not state or local law enforcement.

In any event, in October of 1966, when Garrison seriously commenced his investigation into the assassination of Kennedy (he had first made a preliminary inquiry immediately following the president's death into Oswald's alleged connection with Ferrie, but it went nowhere), he was a popular DA among the electorate. In a city and state where corruption among oftentimes colorful public officials was so common it was accepted with bemused tolerance by the people,* Garrison, appearing incorruptible, was to many a breath of fresh air. The six-foot six-inch (some said six-foot seven-inch) prosecutor, who carried an equally outsized ego and was called the "Jolly Green Giant," had a charismatic, populist aura, and deep mellifluous voice that even charmed some of his adversaries. As a reporter would later write, "New Orleans fell in love with him. He looked like Perry Mason and sounded like Eliot Ness,"[11] and his lovely blonde wife, Leah, the mother of his five children, was considered a political asset by the city's denizens.

When news of Garrison's investigation became known in the conspiracy community, the buffs flocked to New Orleans like swallows to San Juan Capistrano. Though they had been screaming their conspiracy blather before the Warren Commission's report even came off the presses in 1964, they were on the outside looking in, and no one in authority on the inside was paying any attention to them. Now someone on the inside—though not the federal government—with an institutional base and the power of subpoena was saying the same thing they were, and they were excited and delighted. The office of the New Orleans district attorney gave an immediate cachet to their allegations.

---

*Where else but Louisiana would a sitting governor, Huey Long, the "kingfish" of "every man is a king" fame, feel free to joke that "one of these days the people of Louisiana are going to get good government—and they aren't going to like it." Long was the Depression-era Louisiana politician who, as governor and then U.S. senator, "dominated every level of Louisiana government by bullying or buying off anyone who got in his way." He was shot to death in Baton Rouge in 1935 by a Baton Rouge doctor, the son-in-law of a judge who was a bitter enemy of Long's, and against whom Long, then a U.S. senator, had engineered a bill that would have gerrymandered the judge into a district that would not reelect him. Huey's brother, Earl, kept the Long dynasty going into the 1960s as a three-time governor, part of his last term being spent in a mental institution his wife had him committed to after he openly started romancing Blaze Starr, a stripper. Earl once said that the voters of Louisiana "don't want good government. They want good entertainment." Four-time Louisiana governor Edwin ("Fast Eddie") Edwards, though not related to the Long family, was just as colorful. Despite his open gambling and deep suspicions of his corruption, the silver-haired, smooth-talking Edwards was very popular with the people, causing him to once boast that the only way he could lose at the polls was if he were "caught in bed with a dead girl or a live boy." When he ran for reelection in 1991 against former Ku Klux Klan member David Duke, his supporters had bumper stickers that read, "Vote for the crook. It's important." After surviving twenty-two grand jury investigations and two trials, Edwards was finally convicted on corruption charges (taking bribes for riverboat gambling licenses) in 2000 and is now in federal prison. (Miguel Bustillo, "Louisiana Tires of Its Rogues," *Los Angeles Times*, January 27, 2006, p.A24; Williams, *Huey Long*, pp.861, 865–866)

Down to New Orleans came Mark Lane and Penn Jones, Richard Popkin, Tom Katen and Vincent Salandria, Edward Jay Epstein, William Turner and Jones Harris, Harold Weisberg and David Lifton, Mary Ferrell, Mae Brussel, Richard E. Sprague, Raymond Marcus, Allan Chapman and social satirist Mort Sahl, among others, to volunteer their services in aid of the investigation.

These people couldn't have been more dedicated. Sahl, to give you one illustrative example, was at the top of his game as the premier intellectual stand-up comic of his time, an intimate of Frank Sinatra and Marilyn Monroe who dined with the likes of President Nixon, shared the cover of *Time* magazine with Nixon and JFK (August 8, 1960), and made hundreds of thousands of dollars a year. Enduring the ridicule of his peers for identifying himself with someone as unpopular with the mainstream media as Garrison, he worked with Garrison off and on for four years without a cent of salary, even expense money, his yearly income dipping to as low as $13,000 during this period. But the cause (a "responsibility to America" as Sahl put it) transcended everything else for Sahl and his colleagues. Upon arriving in New Orleans, Sahl had taken a cab to Garrison's home at 4600 Owens Boulevard in the city. "I walked to the door," Sahl would later write, "and a man emerged, all six foot seven inches of him, wearing a bathrobe. I said, 'I'm Mort Sahl, and I came down here to shake your hand.' 'I hope you're available to do a lot more than that,'" Garrison replied. Sahl said he got "a desk in the DA's office, took an apartment in New Orleans, and went out to do college concerts when I needed money to buy groceries and pay the rent." Sahl would later tell Johnny Carson on his show that Garrison was "the most important man in America."[12]

Perhaps with a bit of hyperbole, William Gurvich, a private investigator who assisted Garrison's office in the initial phases of the investigation, told Edward Wegmann, Shaw's civil attorney for years who helped put together the criminal defense team that represented Shaw at his trial, that much of the early investigative work was done, not by Garrison's office, but by Warren Commission critics like Sahl who had descended on New Orleans. In fact, as with Sahl, Garrison actually gave several of them, who had come to be known as the "Dealey Plaza Irregulars," DA investigator credentials. But other than Bill Turner, a former FBI agent and perhaps the only Dealey Plaza Irregular whom Garrison called to help out, not one of them had one day of experience in investigating a crime. Thomas Bethell, a member of Garrison's regular staff, said at the time that the trouble with these conspiracy theorists "is that the only way they can make a strong impression on Garrison is by coming up with flamboyant nonsense . . . They, therefore, represent a serious threat to the sanity of the investigation."[13]

But long before a New Orleans jury, after thirty-four days of trial testimony and argument, returned a swift verdict of not guilty against Shaw on March 1, 1969, two years to the day after Garrison had charged Shaw with conspiracy to murder Kennedy, most of the conspiracy theorists had departed from New Orleans, totally disenchanted with Garrison and his investigation (Mark Lane and Mort Sahl were among the few who stayed to the bitter end). What they had found in Garrison, to their dismay, was the embodiment of an overzealous prosecutor who wanted to get a conviction at any cost, one totally devoid of all prosecutorial ethics. The buffs may believe in crazy conspiracy theories, but they do not believe in prosecuting an innocent man (which Clay Shaw unquestionably was) for murder with perjurious testimony. Garrison had crossed the line, even with the buffs, and they denounced him. Respected assassination researcher Paul Hoch, who leans toward the conspiracy theory, said that Garrison had prosecuted someone "I believe was innocent."[14] Referring to the "persecution" of Shaw by Garrison, he said that though Shaw may have had some connections to the CIA, this in no way justified Oliver Stone "ignoring what Garrison did to him."[15] Leading Warren Commission critic and conspiracy maven Sylvia Meagher wrote that "as the Garrison investigation continued to unfold, it gave cause for increasingly serious misgivings about the validity of his evidence, the credibility of his witnesses, and the scrupulousness of his methods."[16] There is no better or substantive book on the assassination attacking the findings of the Warren Commission than Josiah Thompson's *Six Seconds in Dallas*. Thompson's assessment of Garrison's investigation and prosecution of Shaw? "Completely without merit."[17] Even David Lifton, who took a solitary journey into dementia with his book *Best Evidence*, found Garrison, after only a few days' exposure to him, to be "a reckless, irrational, even paranoid demagogue" who might, he wrote, "seriously hurt innocent people."[18]

The belief among many in the conspiracy community is that Garrison's fiasco in New Orleans actually set their movement back several years. Up until the HSCA reinvestigated the assassination in the late 1970s, conspiracy theorists, trying to peddle their theories, more often than not had Garrison's misadventure thrown in their face. If Garrison turned up nothing, the thinking went, why would we believe your theory has any more merit? This was particularly true since Garrison had already incorporated so many of their theories (e.g., Kennedy was shot from the grassy knoll; Oswald was a patsy; the CIA, anti-Castro Cuban exiles, military-industrial complex, Dallas Police Department, organized crime, and just about every other major group you can think of, were involved in the assassination) into his position. "The New Orleans fiasco," wrote conspiracy author Howard Roffman, "caused the virtual destruction of whatever foundation for credibility [that] had previously been established by the critics of the Warren Report."[19] Garrison's case against Shaw was a "grotesque charade," conspiracy author Robert Sam Anson wrote. "Years would pass before anyone . . . would take the notion of conspiracy seriously again."[20] Meagher added to her earlier observation, saying that "Garrison was a dangerous charlatan." Calling Shaw "an innocent man" (but still reiterating her belief that Oswald was likewise "totally innocent" of Kennedy's murder), she said Garrison "did enormous harm not [only] to Clay Shaw and others but to the credibility and standing of all the critics of the Warren Report. It was Garrison's contemptible antics that put the whole case into cold storage for many years. That some critics still believe and defend him simply astounds me."[21]

In 1978, the HSCA, with its fourth-bullet conspiracy conclusion, gave a renewed patina of credibility to the notion of conspiracy in the assassination. But Garrison himself remained a pariah to all except those on the jagged margins of the conspiracy community—that is, until maverick Hollywood film producer and director Oliver Stone (*Platoon, Wall Street, The Doors, Born on the Fourth of July*, etc.), an eleven-time Academy Award nominee, read Garrison's book, *On The Trail of the Assassins* (three times, he says), purchased the movie rights (for $250,000), and resurrected Garrison from his legal grave.*

---

*It all started in Havana in 1988. Stone was there to accept an award for his movie *Salvador*, to be presented by Colombia's Nobel laureate Gabriel García Márquez. In a "creaky" elevator of Havana's old and ven-

In Stone's hands, the thoroughly discredited Garrison became a courageous, Capraesque, American patriot fighting for justice and to save the country from dark and sinister forces out to subvert our American way of life. That Garrison's reputation could not have been much worse before Stone is not a debatable point. Garrison himself told a New Orleans newspaper that his national image had become one of "a fool or a madman." When he saw Stone's screenplay, he commented what "a beautiful, magnificent job" it was.[22] Yes, indeed.

Stone is an unreconstructed liberal (the word *liberal* is not a pejorative term to me) who infuses his films with a moral indignation and passion for justice that many understandably find infectious. The only child of a Jewish father and French Catholic mother, Stone grew up in a traditional, conservative home in New York City, where his father did well as a Wall Street stockbroker. In his postadolescent years, Stone, who in his early years looked up to Barry Goldwater, disliked Hubert Humphrey, and disdained Democrats because he says "my father did," dropped out of Yale in 1964 after his freshman year, taught English in Saigon, and drifted down to Mexico, where he wrote an unpublished novel. He enlisted in the military in 1967 and was wounded twice in Vietnam (receiving the Purple Heart and Bronze Star). He would later say, "I began to distrust the government through my Vietnam experience, when I started to see the degree of lying and corruption that was going on."[23] So he had a predilection, going in, to believe the conspiracy theorists who have blamed the nation's power structure for Kennedy's murder. When you couple this with a hubris that knows no bounds, the mixture was bound to be combustible. And it was.

Stone's $40 million, three-hour-and-eight-minute Warner Bros. production, *JFK*, was launched by the studio with a $15 million publicity campaign that included television spots in the fifty major markets and full-page ads in the nation's major dailies. The movie,* released on December 20, 1991, was a box office success, 25 million people viewing it, with a domestic gross alone of $70,405,498. (The worldwide gross was $205.4 million.) Shot on location in Dallas, New Orleans, and Washington, D.C., the film stirred passions and interest in the assassination by the American people more than any other event since November 22, 1963. Those who saw it who already believed in a conspiracy had their myths about the case not only confirmed, but expanded and fortified. Those who knew nothing about the case and had formed no opinion (i.e., the nation's youth) overwhelmingly bought Stone's cinematic fantasy—hook, line, and sinker. At the public tennis courts where I play when I can find time, a teen who had seen *JFK* overheard me telling a third

---

erable Nacional Hotel, which once hosted a big conference of American Mafia leaders, Ellen Ray recognized Stone. She was the New York City publisher of Sheridan Square Press, a very small, now defunct house that published Garrison's book and the *Covert Action Information Bulletin*, which featured exposés on the CIA. She handed him a copy of *On the Trail of the Assassins*. Stone initially assumed Ray was "just another sandal-wearing advocate of a cause," but he took the book with him to the Philippines, where he was wrapping up filming for *Born on the Fourth of July*. The high-stakes tale woven by Garrison of a presidential assassination, with intrigue that in part reminded him of a Raymond Chandler thriller, immediately excited Stone, who thought it a great story. (Robert Scheer, "Oliver Stone Builds His Own Myths," *Los Angeles Times*, December 15, 1991, Calendar section, p.34; Lambert, *False Witness*, p.208) In its hardcover edition by Sheridan Square Press, Garrison's book made no splash at all and was mostly ignored by the critics. But the paperback edition by Warner Books, which came out in December of 1991 in virtual conjunction with the movie *JFK*, spent thirteen weeks on the *New York Times* best-seller list, several at number one, and has had twenty printings. (Lambert, *False Witness*, p.208 footnote 2)

*Stone wrote the screenplay for *JFK* with Zachary Sklar, the editor of Garrison's book, *On the Trail of the Assassins*.

party that there was no evidence of a conspiracy in the Kennedy assassination. "Mr. Bugliosi," he said, "I'm surprised you don't think there was a conspiracy. *They even made a movie about it.*"

The old aphorism that "a picture is worth a thousand words" not only manifests itself in a movie, but is magnified because of the emotional thrust (generated by the context, live motion as opposed to a still frame, and background music that subliminally "tells" the viewer how to feel) that drives a motion picture. Vincent Canby, film critic for the *New York Times*, writes that "anything shown in a movie tends to be taken as truth." In fact, the mind and heart of the viewer are so totally captured that entire audiences of law-abiding citizens routinely and tensely hope that the protagonists on the screen are able to successfully pull off major bank robberies and other heists (e.g., the 2001 movies *Ocean's Eleven* and *The Score*).*

So the visual message in most instances is certainly more powerful than the written one. With respect to the latter, as I say in the introduction to this book about the misleading books on the assassination, you only know if someone is lying to you if you know what the truth is. If you don't, and make a natural assumption that the writer is honorable and telling you the truth, you normally accept it. Obviously, that reality is even more pronounced when the purveyors of the propaganda are popular movie favorites of the audience whom they implicitly believe, like Kevin Costner (Stone's Jim Garrison in *JFK*), Jack Lemmon, and Donald Sutherland. I mean, would Kevin Costner lie to his adoring public? Rejecting the message of the clean-cut, wholesome-looking Costner (Garrison) is like rejecting motherhood, apple pie, and the American flag.

Stone, obviously, knew this, and eagerly sought Costner, believed to be a conservative Republican who would be expected to accept the establishment view of no conspiracy, as his first choice to play Garrison from the very beginning. Speaking as euphemistically as he could to veil the banality of his objective in having the audience unconsciously conclude, "I like Kevin Costner, so what he's portraying must be true," Stone said, "Kevin was the perfect choice for Jim Garrison because he reminds me of those Gary Cooper, Jimmy Stewart qualities—a moral simplicity and a quiet understatement . . . He anchors the movie in a very strong way . . . You empathize with him, and his discoveries become yours." Costner's agent was Creative Artists Agency president Michael Ovitz, and it helped, in getting Costner, that Ovitz, Stone said, "was a strong fan" of the projected movie and urged Costner to take the role.

The strong supporting cast of Sissy Spacek, Joe Pesci, Jack Lemmon, Walter Matthau, Ed Asner, Donald Sutherland, and Tommy Lee Jones, among others, served to achieve the same purpose. "Familiar, comfortable faces," Stone said, that walk the audience "through a winding path in the dark woods. Warner [Bros.] thought it was too costly to have them but those actors all waived their normal fees to help the picture."[24] As political columnist Charles Krauthammer (who nonetheless, because of the trivialization of our political culture, isn't convinced that Stone's propaganda will stick) puts it, "In one corner: a $40 million Hollywood film, featuring the nation's number one heartthrob, endowed with a publicity budget of millions, showing in 900 movie theaters. In the other

---

*The mesmerizing power to influence viewers that inheres in the movie experience is summed up in a joke comic Mort Sahl tells about a guy who went to see the late Nazi-hunter Simon Wiesenthal, and said, "The good news is that Oliver Stone wants to do a movie on your life. The bad news is that Kevin Costner is going to play Hitler" (*USA Today*, December 20, 1991).

corner: perhaps a dozen scribblers writing in various magazines and op-ed pages [attacking the movie and its message]. You don't need Marshall McLuhan to figure out who's got more clout."[25]

Garrison's prosecution of Clay Shaw had no pernicious influence in stifling the truth about the assassination. To the contrary, as indicated, it hurt the conspiracy movement. But *JFK*, the movie about Garrison's prosecution of Shaw, has caused far more damage to the truth about the case than perhaps any single event other than Ruby's killing of Oswald, which the American people widely view as an act by Ruby to "silence" Oswald. U.S. Senator Arlen Specter, an assistant counsel for the Warren Commission, says that "Stone's film has done more than any other single effort to distort history and the Commission's work."[26] This may be true for the simple reason that more people (many of whom had never, and would have never, read a conspiracy book in their life) have seen Stone's movie than have read all the conspiracy books put together. There were far more national magazine cover stories as well as editorials and articles in the nation's press following the release of *JFK* than at any time since the assassination. There were several prime-time television shows that did specials on the movie, and talk radio brimmed with comments about it. Stone's movie had such an impact and stirred such a national debate that Congress even launched hearings (at which Stone testified) resulting in the enactment of the President John F. Kennedy Assassination Records Collection Act of 1992, which mandated the release to the public of all previously sealed documents on the assassination. "In the few short months since *JFK* came out," the *Los Angeles Times* reported, "Congress, the White House, and the National Archives have been deluged with letters, calls and visitors all demanding that the documents be made public."

Today in America, no name is associated in the public mind with the position that there was a conspiracy in the assassination as much as that of Oliver Stone. An example, among many, of this fact is the statement of former president Gerald Ford, the last surviving member of the Warren Commission, on his eighty-seventh birthday, that "there has been no new evidence that could undercut" the two conclusions of the Commission that Oswald killed Kennedy and acted alone, "Oliver Stone notwithstanding."[27] The most famous conspiracy theorist before Stone was Mark Lane. But for every person who knows of Mark Lane's opposition to the Warren Commission, five know of Oliver Stone's. And surveys have shown (see later text) that the vast majority of Stone's audience accepted the movie's message as holy writ. Writing in the *Washington Post*, Senator Patrick Moynihan feared that the movie "is what citizens under thirty or forty are going to be thinking soon."[28] The *London Times* observed that "Mr. Stone is certain to ingrain his version on the fertile minds of millions."[29] *Newsweek* quickly got to the kernel of the problem, writing that "more people believe the . . . CIA-LBJ-Pentagon plot cooked up by movie producer Oliver Stone than they do the Warren Commission."[30]

Indeed, though this may be a slightly extravagant claim, Michael L. Kurtz, professor of history at Southeastern Louisiana University, writes that "with the exception of *Uncle Tom's Cabin*, Harriet Beecher Stowe's explosive novel dramatizing the horrors of the institution of slavery, *JFK* probably had a greater direct impact on public opinion than any other work of art in American history."[31] This is the precise reason why I want to spend a good deal of time on the film. In doing so, the problem I have is this: Am I elevating Oliver Stone's movie by holding it to be worthy of denigration? Only theoretically. The denigration will be so complete that to say Stone and his movie have been elevated would be a contradiction. The better question, perhaps, is whether by even bothering to denigrate Stone and his movie, am I thereby diminishing, in however small a way, what I hope to be the stature of this book? I believe so. Serious nonfiction books don't stoop to the discussion of wild fairy tales, which the movie *JFK* is. But I'm not sure I have a choice. Because of the enormous impact *JFK* has had on the views of millions of people about the assassination, on balance I'd rather descend a level in this book if the book and the contemplated television documentary based thereon can substantially, if not totally, reverse the damage *JFK* has done.

Though Stone's audience accepted *JFK*, the establishment media for the most part excoriated it. The movie created such a furor that full-blown, critical reviews came out *before* the movie was even in the theaters. That decent rascal Harold Weisberg, the dean of all assassination researchers, somehow got a pirated copy of the first draft (conspiracy theorist David Lifton is convinced Weisberg got the copy from his friend Robert Groden, who was on Stone's payroll) of the script and furnished it to George Lardner, the national security writer for the *Washington Post* who covered the Shaw trial. When Lardner learned that the movie was going to "closely follow" Garrison's investigation and book, he wrote in the *Post*, "What that means is that Oliver Stone is chasing fiction. Garrison's investigation was a fraud."[32] Looking at the script, Lardner observed that there wasn't space "to list all the errors and absurdities" in the film. Syndicated columnist George Will said, "Stone is forty-five going on eight. In his three hour lie, Stone falsifies so much he may be an intellectual sociopath."[33] Nicholas Lemann wrote in *GQ*, "I know life is supposed to be full of surprises, but . . . I never thought I'd see someone make an all-out effort to rehabilitate Jim Garrison . . . There are enough good journalists around today who covered Garrison back in his heyday to guarantee that Stone will be called on this . . . Garrison was a pernicious figure, an abuser of government power and the public trust."[34] Dan Rather, on *CBS Evening News*, rhetorically lamented, "What happens when Hollywood mixes facts, half-baked theories, and sheer fiction into a big budget film and then tries to sell it as, quote, 'truth' and 'history'?" The *Wall Street Journal*: "What Mr. Stone is basically selling is political grotesquery itself. Thus, former New Orleans D.A. Jim Garrison . . . becomes a relentless truth seeker. We have to say we admire Mr. Stone's brass." *Newsweek* magazine called Stone's movie, "twisted history."[35]

Even some former allies of Garrison's weren't kind to Stone. In the *Atlantic*, Edward Jay Epstein, a Garrison foot soldier who became very disillusioned with him, wrote that the movie was a "journey from fact to fantasy," with Garrison, to prove his point, "deliberately falsifying reality and depicting events that never happened." The caption of the article describes the movie as "a distortion that . . . threatens to become the story we accept."[36] Even the inimitable Mark Lane, while saluting Stone for putting the issue of a conspiracy before the public, commented that "it was bad that he did so by falsifying the record."[37] "It would have been better had he stuck to the facts."[38]

Though I am never elliptical and always state the obvious (since so often in life things are only obvious once they are stated), the point I am about to make may seem so obvious it doesn't have to be stated. But I'm going to state it anyway. The problem with Stone is not, really, that he egregiously fictionalized the Kennedy assassination. It's that he tried to convince everyone he was telling the truth. I believe that for the most part writers and filmmakers have an obligation to never tamper with the important facts of historical events. But if they do, they unquestionably (it's not arguable) have the obligation to let their audience know this. Stone didn't, and this is the only reason why I believe he deserves all the scalding invective he has received in his attempt to rewrite history. Don DeLillo decided to fictionalize the Kennedy assassination like Stone. But unlike Stone, he had the common decency to acknowledge that his apparently fine book (I don't read fiction), *Libra*, was fiction, and it appeared on best-seller fiction lists. That's why there are two booklists, fiction and nonfiction. Although a certain amount of dramatic license in a film or book about a historical event can be excused for narrative purposes, there is never any justification for distorting the essence of what happened. Stone, minute after minute in *JFK*, dressed up his fiction (frequently in grainy black-and-white simulated scenes shot on 8- or 16-millimeter film to project a sense of authenticity)* as historical fact, virtually the only significant accuracies in his film being actual excerpts of the Zapruder film (for which Stone reportedly paid the Zapruder family $40,000 to license) and other archival footage that he cannily and seamlessly interspersed—without the audience being able to tell which was real and which was not—with the reenactment footage.[39]

When Stone was met with an unexpected avalanche of media criticism for the distortions and inventions in his movie around the time of its release, some of which he was forced to acknowledge, he retreated by saying that the Warren Commission was a myth and *JFK* was a "counter-myth,"[40] but, obviously, he said this just to get him past the moment.

To be fair, in his interviews Stone has never *expressly* said that what is depicted in *JFK* is unquestionably the truth (although he has said exactly that in every other way), and when he said in a December 23, 1991, *Time* interview that he wanted his audience to *"consider the possibility* that there was a coup d'etat that removed President Kennedy,"[41] one could, if not vigilant, be seduced into thinking that Stone, in his movie, was just tossing out an alternative scenario of the assassination for his audience's consideration. But to do so would be to completely ignore the movie itself as well as the overall thrust of Stone's remarks and interviews. When he says, "There is a saying: 'A lie is like a snowball—the longer it is rolled, the larger it is.' The Warren Commission . . . is that lie," and therefore not entitled to be believed, and that his movie, on the other hand, is "a seamless jig-saw puzzle that will allow the audience for the first time, *to understand what happened and why*," and that he "had to take the assassination out of Dallas and the conspiracy out of New Orleans and bring it all back to Washington, where it *really* began," and that "the assassination was America's first coup d'etat, and it worked,"[42] by definition he is not saying that he is merely offering an alternative view. He is saying his view is the correct view, the only view. You can't tell one major lie about the assassination after another for three consecutive hours, and with full knowledge that, as Vincent Canby says, "anything shown in a movie tends to be taken as the truth," and escape responsibility for your monstrous hoax by suggesting you are only presenting an alternative view for the audience's consideration.

Did, indeed, Stone want his audience to believe his fiction was reality? About that there can be no dispute.† In addition to the aforementioned remarks he made, Stone told *Newsweek*, "I think people are more on my side than the government's. If they don't

---

*Stone's director of photography, Robert Richardson, said that he and Stone tried to create "a strong documentary feel" for much of the movie. In a diary entry during the filming, Richardson wrote, "Utilize the opening documentary material to establish a concrete foundation of factual reality. Let the audience move through the material, never doubting its authenticity." (Fisher, "Why and Hows of *JFK*," p.45)

†To convince his audience they were seeing the truth, Stone used every timeworn, cinematic trick in the book. Just one of many examples: As *Entertainment Weekly* pointed out, "In *JFK*'s hierarchy of good and evil, hero Jim Garrison and his staff are uniformly attractive, stalwart, earnest, and often bathed in golden light. Villains Shaw, Ferrie, Jack Ruby and Guy Banister are evasive, unsavory thugs with bad skin, often shown in shifty-eyed close-up" (Daly, "Camera Obscura," p.17).

believe me this go-round, they'll believe me when another shocking thing happens."[43] Stone lamented to *USA Today* that "instead of [the media] spending so much energy saying 'Stone's interpretation of history is fiction,' *which it is not*, why don't they devote the same energy to asking why Kennedy was killed?"[44] He told the *Dallas Morning News* before the shooting of the film commenced in Dallas that he was a "cinematic historian," his movie would be "a history lesson," and he was confident he would be remembered as "a good historian as well as a good dramatist."[45] In fact, in newspaper advertisements for the film throughout the country were these words in bold letters: "The Truth Is the Most Important Value We Have." As Edward Epstein wrote in the *Atlantic*, "From the moment [*JFK*] was released, its Director, Oliver Stone, so passionately defended its factual accuracy that he became, for all practical purposes, the new Garrison."[46] Unbelievably, Stone told *Time* magazine, "I think this movie, hopefully, if it's accepted by the public, will at least move people away from the Warren Commission."[47] He wanted his movie, he wrote with towering arrogance in the January 1992 edition of *Premiere*, to "replace the Warren Commission Report."[48] Can you imagine that? A Hollywood producer wants his movie to *replace* the official and most comprehensive investigation of a crime in history. It's a measure of Stone's sense of self that such a thought, even if a vagrant one, would even enter his head. Arrogance thought it already had a bad name. That was before it met Oliver Stone. Taking his movie very, very seriously, Stone frequently praised his twelve researchers for all the arduous work they had done. He told Richard Bernstein of the *New York Times* that "every point, every argument, every detail in the movie . . . has been researched, can be documented, and is justified."[49] (Stone hardly ever uses the word *speculate* in the film, and when he does, it is invariably lost and forgotten by the context, the torrent of "factual" words that follow, and most of all by the acting out of the thought on screen by the evil conspirators.)

Stone has compared his movie to the film *Rashômon*, the 1950 Japanese classic in which the same event is seen from several points of view as opposed to an unequivocal defense of any particular theory. Nonsense. *JFK* has one theme and one theme only that runs throughout: that Kennedy's murder was the result of a massive conspiracy emanating from the highest corridors of power in America, that all we stand for as a nation is being attacked and taken over by these sinister forces, and that his fearless prosecutor, and inferentially, Stone, who has the moral courage to tell his story, are the only ones manning the ramparts—the last angry and courageous men. Shedding all pretenses and *Rashômon* allusions, in his commentary to the book *Oliver Stone's USA*, Stone writes that his movie is "about a conspiracy to kill President Kennedy."[50]

Because Stone continuously misrepresented the facts throughout his film, is he therefore an unmitigated fraud? Yes and no. As crazy as all the nuts, rumors, and speculation are that Stone managed to shoehorn into his movie, I sense that he, like a great number of other people, honestly believes much of this nonsense.[*] But as we shall see, where we

---

[*]Harry Connick Sr., who was the New Orleans district attorney at the time the movie was made, told me that before Stone started filming in New Orleans, he and Kevin Costner paid him a courtesy visit. Near the end of the visit, Stone asked him, "What about the Clay Shaw case? How do you feel about it?" Connick replied, "I think it stinks, a terrible abuse of prosecutorial power." Stone, he says, became agitated by this, and fired back, "How do you explain someone being able to fire three rounds within . . . ?" Connick forgets the number of seconds Stone mentioned, or the degree of accuracy Stone said Oswald supposedly had. Connick retorted, "I don't know what that has to do with Mr. Garrison bringing charges against Mr. Shaw." Connick said the conversation became heated (Costner, he recalls, said very little throughout and did not join in the dispute), and he tried to explain to Stone the role of a public prosecutor to be fair and seek justice, which, he

know that Stone is a fraud is in those critical situations in his movie where he flat-out invented scenes and characters to help him prove the point he was trying to make.

Even in the areas of the film that I sense Stone believes to be true, I cannot exonerate him of willful duplicity without thereby convicting him of reckless stupidity—reckless in that instead of balancing out his advisers with reputable anti-conspiracy scholars, or even respectable conspiracy theorists, he had to know he was relying almost exclusively on the extreme fanatical fringe of the conspiracy community. As indicated, Stone primarily based his movie on Jim Garrison's *On the Trail of the Assassins*. But, as noted, this is a book whose author has been completely discredited and is even an embarrassment to the conspiracy community. The second book, per the screen credits, that Stone based his movie on is Jim Marrs's *Crossfire*. But Marrs is a conspiracy theorist who has rarely met a conspiracy theory he didn't like. In his only other book, *Alien Agenda*, Marrs tells us that we have "non-human visitors" among us, and that our government, with full knowledge of these aliens in our midst, has conspired, with a "wall of silence," to "hide away the alien presence" and keep the truth from the American people.[51] Sound familiar? Garrison and Marrs also served as advisers to Stone on his movie.

These were Stone's other principal advisers: Robert Groden, the photographic expert for the conspiracy community, served as the reenactment coordinator. As pointed out earlier in this book, few, if any, have less credibility than he. Among other things, he is the fellow who insists that the backyard photos Marina took of Oswald holding a Carcano rifle are fake, and that Oswald's head was superimposed by the authorities on someone else's body. Larry Howard was the late, gadfly cofounder of the JFK Assassination Research Center in Dallas that became a repository for assassination memorabilia and every kooky conspiracy book that had ever been written. Howard always use to boast that he had never read any book on the assassination himself, but faxed Stone that he and his people had "uncovered the real truth behind the assassination. JFK was murdered by the people who control the power base in the United States. In their minds he was a threat to national security and had to be eliminated." That's all that Stone had to hear, bringing Howard aboard with a payment of $80,000 to the latter's research center.[52] L. Fletcher Prouty, a former air force colonel who worked in the Pentagon's Office of Special Operations (which provided support for covert operations), convinced Stone, without a shred of evidence to support him, that the military-industrial complex had Kennedy killed because Kennedy wanted to withdraw American troops from Vietnam and it wanted war. Unbelievably, Prouty even flirted with the possibility that McGeorge Bundy, Kennedy's national security adviser and former Harvard dean and Ford Foundation president, was part of the conspiracy to kill Kennedy.[53]

Prouty (since deceased) was a right-wing zany who was a member of the Liberty Lobby, the middle-of-the-road, sensible group that supported neo-Nazi David Duke's 1988 candidacy for president and embraces the notion that the Holocaust is really a Jewish hoax. He also served as a consultant to Lyndon LaRouche's right-wing National Democratic Policy Committee "at a conference of which he provided a presentation comparing the U.S. Government's prosecution of LaRouche (for conspiracy and mail fraud) to the pros-

---

told Stone, Garrison did not do. When I asked Connick if Stone was interested enough in the true facts of the Shaw case to ask if he and his people could look at whatever files the DA's office had on it, he said, "No, he never asked me. It was clear he had his agenda, and his mind was already made up." (Telephone interview of Harry Connick Sr. by author on March 13, 2000)

ecution of Socrates."[54] Prouty is clearly someone with both feet planted firmly in the air. But Prouty, who served as an editorial adviser on publications of the Church of Scientology, makes up for his perverse right-wing beliefs by apparently, per author Edward Epstein, having no personal credibility. Epstein interviewed Prouty for his book *Legend*, and said that the *Reader's Digest* staff fact-checked Prouty and wouldn't publish the part of *Legend* involving Prouty's assertions because they found he had "falsified" so much of his military career. "He will say almost anything that someone wants to hear . . . He's extremely accommodating," Epstein said.[55]

With Garrison and the rest of the aforementioned motley crew,[*] Stone obviously was in good hands, and *JFK*'s audience had every reason to take everything in the movie as the equivalent of inspired scripture.

Because, to my knowledge, the well-earned vilification of Stone by the establishment media has never been supported by an in-depth analysis of his film,[†] such analysis for the most part being limited to newspaper columns and short magazine articles with only a few examples here and there of the lies in the film, and because of the film's enormous adverse effect on millions of unknowledgeable Americans who innocently drank Stone's moonshine and, inebriated, passed it on to countless others in their circle, as indicated, I decided to give the film a fairly thorough treatment in this book. My first step was to rent the video of the long movie and spend nine hours and twenty-four painful minutes watching it (three times) to enable me to set forth a goodly number of Stone's lies and fabrications. Inasmuch as the movie is virtually a continuous lie, to set forth all the lies would take a book in itself.[‡] But what follows, in numbered form, is an adequate list (a few other major lies in Stone's film appear in other sections of this book):

---

[*]Stone *did* have at least one legitimate and knowledgeable adviser during the filming in Dallas, Jim Leavelle, the Dallas police detective who headed up the Tippit investigation and to whom Oswald was handcuffed at the time he was shot by Ruby. The only problem is that Stone would never take Leavelle's advice. Leavelle said that Stone would ask him how something happened and then change the facts and film it differently. When Stone asked him one time whether he liked what Stone had done, Leavelle, who said he otherwise had a cordial relationship with Stone, told Stone, "It's okay if it's just a movie, but if you want to depict what actually happened, it's not worth a damn." Stone kept pestering Leavelle to play his own part in the movie but the respected former detective declined, telling Stone, "I don't want me or my name attached to the movie because someone might see it and think I approved of this picture." When I asked Leavelle, "I take it you didn't think very much of the movie?" he responded, "Well, they got the city right and the person killed right, but there's not much else that's correct." (Telephone interview of James Leavelle by author on April 11, 2002)

[†]Although there has been no prior in-depth analysis of Stone's movie *JFK*, which, as indicated, was built around New Orleans DA Jim Garrison's prosecution of Clay Shaw, Garrison's prosecution of Shaw has itself been the subject matter of several books in which Garrison's outrageous and foundationless pursuit of Shaw has been successfully eviscerated and exposed as a fraud. Actually, the first in-depth exposé of Garrison's case was an excellent, thirty-six-page article, "A Reporter at Large," by Edward Epstein in the July 13, 1968, edition of the *New Yorker*. The most in-depth examination of Garrison's entire fraudulent case against Shaw is Patricia Lambert's 1998 book, *False Witness*, which also has a very good section on the movie *JFK*. What follows in these pages concerning Garrison's investigation and prosecution of Shaw is a condensed history of the Garrison-Shaw affair with new material and many new inferences.

[‡]For those who wonder why I didn't make it easier on myself by simply using Stone's *JFK: The Book of the Film* to get all of the dialogue and scenes in the movie as well as Stone's alleged evidentiary support for everything, *The Book of the Film* does not, as its title might suggest, contain the actual word-for-word dialogue in the movie. On unnumbered page sixteen of the book, Stone acknowledges that it's not a book of the film but of one of the earlier drafts of the script. I found it varied in a number of places from the words in the film, so it could not be relied on. As for Stone's evidentiary support, his chief researcher for the book as well as the film (Jane Rusconi, a recent Yale graduate) for the most part simply used statements made in the past by the very same kooks and nuts Stone presents in the movie, and relied on books and articles previously written by Stone's pro-conspiracy advisers and others of like mind, virtually ignoring the wealth of credible evidence to the contrary.

1.* In the movie, Garrison is depicted as a scrupulously honest DA of unimpeachable probity and morality who is only interested in the truth and unwilling to cut any corners to get it. We know, of course, that this was not the real Garrison, who, as it was said about a later, well-known prosecutor, Ken Starr, "violated every prosecutorial rule in the book" in relentless pursuit of his quarry. Even Stone has allowed, in interviews, how there was a dark side to the garrulous Garrison, but he never even hinted at it in the movie, instead rationalizing that the movie was about the assassination, not Garrison, and he didn't want to divert the audience's attention by getting into a "biography" of Garrison.† However, Garrison and the assassination are inseparable in the movie since Stone is presenting Garrison's view of it. If Garrison is shown to be corrupt in his conduct during his investigation, this would inevitably compromise, in any audience's mind, the arguments he makes and the conclusions he reaches. I mean, for most people it's rather difficult to separate the credibility of a charge someone is making from the credibility of the person making it. Stone lied about Garrison in his movie because he had a message to give his viewers and he wouldn't give them any truth, anywhere in the movie, that might militate against that message. So right from the start, Stone deliberately misled his audience about who the hero of his movie really was.

Garrison's conduct was so egregiously bad that several important members of his staff resigned in disgust when they saw that Garrison was pursuing an innocent man by having his staff bribe, intimidate, and even hypnotize witnesses. One of them, William Gurvich, ran and owned with his two brothers the Gurvich Brothers Detective Agency in New Orleans, a very prominent and reputable firm. Garrison had asked him to lead the investigation of Clay Shaw, which Gurvich did, for "$1 a year"; his real compensation was heading up a potentially historic investigation. Though one of Garrison's strongest supporters at the start of the investigation, Gurvich became disillusioned when he saw there was no real evidence against Shaw. So troubled was he that on June 8, 1967, he flew to Washington, D.C., to meet privately with Robert Kennedy and told Kennedy that the Garrison inquiry in New Orleans had "no basis in fact" and that "we can't shed any light on the death of your brother so you should not hope for such." Gurvich said that after hearing this, RFK "appeared to be rather disgusted to think that someone was exploiting his brother's death."[56] The private meeting with RFK leaked when a Kennedy spokesman said Kennedy was "extremely grateful" that Gurvich had come to see him. When a *Newsday* reporter asked Gurvich to comment, Gurvich allowed that "I think Mr. Garrison believes in what he is doing. He is sincere."[57] Gurvich's disenchantment with Garrison's probe went downhill even further from there as he became more and more aware of the unscrupulous methods Garrison and his staff were employing to develop a nonexistent case.

At a press conference in New Orleans on June 26, 1967, Gurvich announced his resignation from Garrison's staff and said there was "no truth" to Mr. Garrison's contention that he had found a conspiracy in the assassination of Kennedy, and that there was "no case" against Mr. Shaw. He also urged the Orleans Parish grand jury to start an immediate investigation into the way Garrison was conducting his inquiry, and sent a telegram to the grand jury stating he was prepared "to give evidence of travesties of justice on the

---

*For any reader searching, item number 2 does not appear until page 1381.

†It should be noted that Stone *did* find time in his movie to bring out to his audience not just once, but twice, the biographical fact that his hero, Garrison, was a pilot in World War II.

part of the District Attorney in the case of Louisiana vs. Clay Shaw."[58] The following evening on CBS, he said, "I was very dissatisfied with the way the investigation was being conducted . . . and decided that if the job of an investigator is to find the truth, then I was to find it. I found it. And this led to my resignation."

"Well, what then is the truth?" CBS news reporter Edward Rabel asked.

"The truth, as I see it, is that Mr. Shaw should never have been arrested."[59]

Garrison, stung by Gurvich's public attacks, struck back by saying Gurvich, the long-time New Orleans resident, was linked with the "Eastern Establishment," which was trying to destroy his case. Further, he claimed that Gurvich had asked to help in the investigation, and foolishly asserted that Gurvich owned a "night-watchman service" and only played a very minor role in the investigation, mostly as a photographic expert and chauffeur. But much evidence rebuts Garrison's assertion. For instance, the *New Orleans States-Item*, whose February 17, 1967, article first brought worldwide attention to what Garrison was doing in New Orleans, could be expected to know just who was who on Garrison's staff, and it referred to Gurvich as Garrison's "chief investigator."[60] Indeed, it was Gurvich who had announced to the world at a packed press conference on March 1, 1967, that Clay Shaw had been arrested for Kennedy's murder.[61]

Gurvich went in front of the Orleans Parish grand jury on June 28, urging it not to indict Shaw (which it ultimately did), and spoke of Garrison's unconscionable investigation, which included putting pressure on a well-known New Orleans burglar to break into Shaw's home and place something there.[62] The burglar, John Cancler ("John the Baptist"), told a national NBC audience on June 19 that while incarcerated in the Parish prison, a DA investigator asked him to "do a job for us." The investigator drove him to a home in the 1300 block of Dauphine Street. "What am I supposed to take out of the house?" he asked. "Nothing," he was told. He was supposed to put something *in* the house. "What was it all about?" he asked. When he was told it had something to do with the assassination of President Kennedy, he became frightened and declined.[63]

In addition to the above (as well as hypnotizing and intimidating Perry Russo, his main witness against Shaw, into testifying that he was present when Shaw, Ferrie, and Oswald conspired to murder Kennedy—see later text and endnote), the following is one more of the many examples of the highly improper practices that Garrison and his staff engaged in to get Shaw. Al Beauboeuf was a homosexual lover of David Ferrie's. Garrison wanted him to testify to anything he knew about Ferrie's alleged involvement with Shaw and Oswald in a conspiracy to kill Kennedy. At a meeting on March 1, 1967, between Hugh Exnicios (Beauboeuf's lawyer) and Lynn Loisel, a New Orleans police officer on loan to Garrison, that took place in Exnicios's office, Exnicios secretly tape-recorded what Garrison was willing to give for Beauboeuf's testimony. Loisel is careful enough to say, "The only thing we want is the truth." But then, remarkably, he also says, "*We can change the story around,* you know . . . to positively beyond a shadow of a doubt eliminate him [Beauboeuf] from any type of conspiracy." In return for his testimony, Loisel says, "I'm, you know, fairly certain we could put $3,000 on him (sound of snapping of fingers) just like that, you know. I'm sure we'd help him financially and I'm sure we'd . . . get him a job."

Exnicios: "Is this something you have thought up yourself or that Garrison—he knows about the situation?"

Loisel: "That's right."

Exnicios: "And he's [Garrison] agreed that if we could in someway assist you, that you would be able to give . . . these things?"

Loisel: "That's correct."[64]

Exnicios was convinced the tape was clear evidence that Loisel, acting on Garrison's authority, had offered Beauboeuf a bribe to testify falsely. He proceeded to try to get the DA of nearby Jefferson Parish, where his office was located, to file criminal charges against Loisel and Garrison, but the DA (Frank Langridge) declined and told Garrison about the tape. Conspiracy theorists love to point out that on April 12, 1967, Beauboeuf signed an affidavit at Garrison's office in which he said that Loisel had not offered him a bribe to testify falsely, that all Loisel wanted was the truth. But, of course, the tape ("We can change the story around, you know") speaks for itself. And the conspiracy theorists, predictably, don't mention that Beauboeuf told many people thereafter that he was threatened by Loisel into signing the affidavit, claiming that Loisel and fellow DA investigator Lou Ivon came to his home the previous evening, April 11, and Loisel said they would circulate obscene photos of him seized from Ferrie's apartment if he didn't cooperate and sign the statement they wanted from him. Worse, he claims one of them held him while the other put a gun in his face. While the record isn't clear which one did what, Beauboeuf is very clear that it was Loisel who said to him, "I don't want to get into any s . . . , and before I do I'll put a hot load of lead up your ass."[65]

The staff at NBC in New York, which was doing an exposé on Garrison, asked Beaubouef if he'd be willing to take a polygraph test on the truthfulness of his charges. He agreed and took the test on May 9, 1967, from a polygrapher at the offices of Mutual Protective Association in New Orleans. In response to questions, he said he did not know Clay Shaw or Lee Harvey Oswald, and Ferrie never told him anything about being involved in the Kennedy assassination. Also, Loisel did attempt to bribe him (which we already know) and Loisel threatened to circulate compromising pictures of him and also threatened "to put a load of hot lead" up his ass if he accused Loisel of attempting to bribe him. The polygrapher reported to NBC that Beauboeuf had answered all questions truthfully.[66]

Remarkably, the New Orleans Police Department, after an investigation of the matter, concluded that Loisel and Ivon (both of whom denied threatening Beauboeuf) had "not violated any rules of the code of conduct of the New Orleans Police Department."[67]

Equally remarkably, perhaps unprecedented in the annals of the prosecutorial profession in America, within just four months after Garrison filed charges against Shaw for Kennedy's murder, Aaron Kohn, director of the New Orleans Metropolitan Commission, said that citizens and witnesses had made an incredible "22 criminal allegations . . . against Mr. Garrison and his staff in the course of [Garrison's] investigation of the Kennedy assassination." The charges included "attempts to intimidate and bribe witnesses, inciting such felonies as perjury [and] conspiracy to commit battery . . . and public bribery." He asked the state attorney general, Jack Gremillion, to look into the allegations.[68]

On May 27, 1968, Shaw brought a civil action against Garrison, petitioning the United States District Court in New Orleans to enjoin Garrison from proceeding with his prosecution. The forty-seven-page complaint alleged that Garrison had conducted a "reign of terror by the misuse and abuse of the powers" of his office, resulting in a denial to Shaw of his constitutional right to a fair trial, that Shaw was "not only innocent, but has no knowledge whatsoever of the alleged crime," and Garrison's prosecution of him was merely to obtain a judicial forum "to discredit the Warren Report and its findings, and not to objectively determine the involvement of plaintiff."[69] On May 28, U.S. District

Judge Frederick Heebe issued a temporary restraining order against Garrison, pending a hearing on the matter, prohibiting him from commencing the trial against Shaw, then scheduled for June 11, and said, "There is a very real likelihood that the plaintiff [Shaw] may prevail on the merits."[70] In Shaw's amended complaint of June 13, he said that Garrison and his deputies knew they had "no valid or legal evidence to support the charges" against him, and pointed out that the grand jury indictment against him "was based solely and only on . . . the hypnotically induced testimony [of Perry Russo]." On August 13, a three-judge panel of the U.S. District Court for the Eastern District of Louisiana denied Shaw's request for an injunction, holding that if his constitutional rights were violated, he could obtain relief by appealing any conviction against him. The court did, however, order Garrison to postpone the trial of Shaw, now scheduled for September 10, until the U.S. Supreme Court could rule on Shaw's appeal of the lower court's ruling.[71]

Since Garrison had always alleged that the Warren Commission had suppressed the truth from the American people and that the federal government was now doing everything to sabotage the trial (e.g., not releasing records he needed from the National Archives, allegedly putting pressure on state governments not to extradite important witnesses—see endnote for discussion on the lack of merit of this charge), the stage was set for Chief Justice Earl Warren's Supreme Court to reverse the lower court's ruling and enjoin Garrison from proceeding against Shaw. At least I would expect Warren to try to convince his brethren on the Court to do this since Warren's reputation could be destroyed if Garrison proved that others, not Oswald, were responsible for Kennedy's death and Warren had orchestrated the cover-up. But on December 9, the U.S. Supreme Court affirmed the ruling of the U.S. District Court, thereby allowing Garrison to bring Shaw to trial. The Court's judgment included the statement that "the Chief Justice [Warren] took no part in the consideration or decision of this case," having recused himself.[72]

At the heart of Garrison's prosecution of Shaw were three operating principles. One, anything that supported his conspiracy theory *du jour*—no matter how far-fetched and lacking in credibility the story was, no matter how the information was gained—is to be believed. Two, everything is fair in love, war, and a criminal prosecution. And three, "propinquity" (i.e., geographic proximity) suggests an incriminating connection. In *False Witness*, author Patricia Lambert writes that "Garrison applied this odd notion to almost any situation. He assumed a person was connected to an intelligence agency because he maintained a residence or an office near it. He imagined individuals were cohorts who rented post office boxes in the same building . . . Garrison didn't believe coincidences happened."[73] In two memorandums, dated February 10 and April 7, 1967, written for "The Smith File," the code name for his investigation of the assassination before it became known to the public, and titled "Time and Propinquity: Factors in Phase I," Garrison methodically sets forth how the lives and relationships of various people (he believed had some connection to the plot to kill Kennedy or to the plotters) intersected in New Orleans, no matter how tangentially. For instance, he writes in one of the memos that "on August 30, 1961, Layton Martens was arrested for investigation when police found him sitting in [David] Ferrie's car waiting for Ferrie . . . By May, 1963, Lee Harvey Oswald is living in the 4900 block of Magazine [Street]. One block away toward downtown is the 800 block of Lyons Street. On that block lived two uncles of Layton Martens." In other words, this would connect Oswald to Martens, and by necessary extension to Ferrie, Oswald's alleged co-conspirator in the assassination.

Former Garrison aide Tom Bethell, writing that Garrison's time and propinquity theory was completely unhinged, quotes Garrison, who was thumbing through the New Orleans city directory, as saying, "Sooner or later, because people are lazy, you catch them out on propinquity."[74]

So we see that far from the very sensible and level-headed prosecutor Stone depicted for his audience, the real Garrison was anything but.

Garrison's intemperate and irresponsible pronouncements and charges were also mind-boggling. News of his secret investigation first surfaced on February 17, 1967, in the *New Orleans States-Item* when reporter Rosemary James disclosed that Garrison had spent $8,000 in three months sending members of his staff to Texas, Washington, D.C., and elsewhere, running down leads on the assassination.[75] On February 24, one week later, Garrison, in a press conference after lunch at the Petroleum Club in New Orleans, and after the expenditure of only the aforementioned $8,000 in investigative travel expenses, announced that "my staff and I solved the case weeks ago. I wouldn't say this if I didn't have evidence beyond a shadow of a doubt. We know the key individuals, the cities involved, and how it was done . . . There were several plots . . . The only way they are going to get away from us is to kill themselves . . . It's a case we will not lose, and anybody that wants to bet against us is invited to, but they will be disappointed." Garrison said, "There is no doubt that the entire thing [alleged plot to kill Kennedy] was planned in New Orleans." For good measure, Garrison told the press, "I have no reason to believe that Lee Harvey Oswald killed anybody in Dallas on November 22, 1963."[76]* Garrison said that "the key to the whole case is through the looking glass. Black is white. White is black. I don't want to be cryptic, but that's the way it is."[77] Of course, Garrison was just bluffing. In fact, Perry Russo, Garrison's star witness and the one around whom he virtually built his entire case, hadn't even been interviewed by Garrison's staff yet. That took place the following day, February 25, when they spoke to him for the very first time. Not one scrap of evidence has ever emerged that on February 24, the day Garrison announced that he and his staff had "solved the case," he had any evidence connecting anyone, in any way, with the assassination. *If there were nothing else at all, this alone, by definition, would be enough to prove beyond all doubt that Garrison had no personal credibility with respect to this case.*

No assassination theory, many originating with the Dealey Plaza Irregulars and bought by Garrison, was too wild or far-out for Garrison's taste, and all this played particularly well locally. Garrison's legal sideshow was tailor-made for the Mardi Gras City, where phantasmal mystery, voodoo, and dark intrigue are treasured commodities. It is said that no other people love fantasy more than the people of New Orleans, and their elected DA intended to give them as much as their girths could hold. Before he finally settled in on elements of the CIA working for "war-oriented elements of the American power structure" as being behind the plot to kill Kennedy,[78] the fertile-minded Orleans Parish DA saw many other different villains behind the plot and had screwy visions of how it was pulled off.

In her book about Garrison and the Shaw trial, *False Witness*, the best book on the case, Patricia Lambert chronicles, with citations, Garrison's progression of fantastic and

---

*Because the *States-Item* disclosure on February 17 had caused Garrison to sharply curtail using DA funds to pursue his fantasy, on the very day he announced he had "solved" the case, February 24, a group of at least fifty New Orleans businessmen, calling their organization "Truth and Consequences, Inc.," each pledged $100 per month to help Garrison fund his investigation (*New York Times*, February 25, 1967, p.56; *Los Angeles Times*, February 25, 1967, p.1).

bizarre theories, all of which he shared with the media. Some additional theories of Garrison's with citations are also herein included.[*]

In late February of 1967, Garrison confided to some reporters that the conspirators behind Kennedy's murder first planned to murder Castro, with Lee Harvey Oswald as the assassin, but when Oswald was denied entry to Cuba, they switched from Castro as the victim to Kennedy.[†] (To the media at large, he was more circumspect, saying only on February 24 that there was more than one plot, and "a change of course did occur. Now that is more than I wanted to say.") When *Life* magazine's Richard Billings interviewed Garrison two days after police found pieces of leather and rope, whips, chains, and so on, in Shaw's home (on March 1, 1967), Garrison told Billings the seized articles held the key to the assassination. In Billings's contemporaneous notes of the interview he wrote that Garrison had told him, "I'm now convinced it [the assassination] was a sadist plot," that he had read the Marquis de Sade and knew that sadists escalate from whipping to killing. "Shaw is a phi beta kappa sadist," Garrison told Billings. "I'll develop expert testimony that a sadist would have motivation for a presidential assassination."

But a few days later, Garrison, wanting to be democratic, brought more groups into the assassination. Kennedy's murder, he said, "was a homosexual thrill killing" committed by four homosexuals—Ferrie, Ruby, Oswald, and Shaw. (Ferrie and Shaw were, indeed, homosexuals, and Ruby's sexual orientation was never clear. When it was pointed out to Garrison that Oswald was married with two children, Garrison responded that Oswald was "a switch-hitter.") In addition to these four homosexuals seeking thrills, Garrison said that "masochists" were also involved in the assassination, but he did not identify who they were. "If you placed a masochist in a room along with a button that would blow up the White House," Garrison said, "he probably would press that button for the thrill of it."

---

[*]In addition to all the various conspiracies to murder Kennedy that sprouted from Garrison's pregnant and paranoid mind, Garrison spoke of a massive and ever present second conspiracy by the U.S. government to suppress the truth from the American people. "It did not occur to me," he told a Dallas TV audience in December of 1967, "that the President [LBJ] would have federal agencies conceal the truth from the people. That they would frame a man, Oswald, who had never fired a shot, and that they would knowingly protect the assassins" (Interview of Jim Garrison by Murphy Martin, WFAA-TV, Dallas, Texas, on December 9, 1967). And in a May 29, 1968, press release from his office, Garrison said that "the federal government is a party with a special interest in this case. Our investigation has shown that the federal investigation was faked and the Warren Commission inquiry was faked to conceal the fact that President Kennedy was killed in a professionally executed ambush." Because Garrison's investigation and his allegation of a federal cover-up received national attention, what he was saying was affecting the views of many Americans. A national Harris Poll in early 1967, before Garrison's probe became well known, showed 44 percent of Americans believing Kennedy was murdered as a result of a conspiracy (*Washington Post*, March 6, 1967). By May of 1967, after three months of publicity about Garrison's charges, a Harris Poll showed 66 percent of Americans now believed there was a conspiracy (*Washington Post*, May 29, 1967), representing an increase of approximately 30 million Americans. (Epstein, *Assassination Chronicles*, p.276)

[†]Garrison confided in greater detail to famed investigative journalist Jack Anderson, who interviewed him for six hours at Garrison's home in New Orleans. In a long verbal report to the FBI's Cartha D. DeLoach at FBI headquarters in Washington, D.C., on his interview of Garrison, Anderson said it was Garrison's firm belief that Shaw "had been approved by the CIA to engineer a plot that would result in the assassination of Fidel Castro." Garrison said Shaw and his partner Ferrie "conceived the idea of sending Oswald to Mexico in a fake attempt to re-enter the Soviet Union" as a device to "gain ready access to Cuba," where Oswald had agreed to kill Castro. Garrison said Oswald returned to New Orleans from Mexico (Oswald went to Dallas, not New Orleans, after traveling to Mexico) and advised Ferrie and Shaw he was backing out of the Castro plot, whereupon Shaw and Ferrie, guided by several anti-Castro Cubans in their midst, then conceived the idea, mostly because of the Bay of Pigs debacle, of having Oswald go to Dallas for the purpose of being a "patsy" for their new plot to kill Kennedy. In a switch from the belief of almost all conspiracy theorists, Garrison told Anderson that Ferrie and Shaw, not organized crime, instructed Ruby to kill Oswald. (Memorandum from FBI Deputy Director C. D. DeLoach to Assistant Director Clyde Tolson, April 4, 1967, pp.1–2; *New York Times*, February 25, 1967, p.56)

In May of 1967, Garrison said in an interview that the people involved in the conspiracy to kill Kennedy "were all anti-Castro oriented and had been engaged in anti-Castro training." Also in May, Ray Marcus, one of his Dealey Plaza Irregulars, showed Garrison enlarged photographs of the trees and shadows of the grassy knoll in which Marcus claimed he saw four killers concealed in the bushes, so Garrison, not wanting to rain on anyone's parade, added four more assassins to his firing squad,[79] but with one proviso, that he add a fifth one whom Marcus had apparently missed. Garrison told CBS the photos showed "three [assassins] behind the stone wall" on the grassy knoll "and two behind [the fence on] the grassy knoll . . . before they dropped completely out of sight," but "you can make an identification from their faces."[80] On June 22, he told a Nashville paper that a fourteen-man team of anti-Castro Cubans who had trained, he said, in New Orleans had killed Kennedy.[81] In September, he said that "insanely patriotic oil millionaires" were the ones who were behind the assassination, and "the corroborating evidence is in our files." Also, "elements of the Dallas police force are clearly involved." In October 1967 he told *Playboy* magazine that his office had developed evidence that, as previously indicated, the president was assassinated by a "precision guerrilla team of at least seven men" who had fired "from three directions." He also said that "former employees" of the CIA "had conspired to assassinate the president."[82]

In early December he explained, on television, how the murder took place. There was a sewer opening in front of the president's car, and the assassin who killed Kennedy shot him with a .45 caliber bullet from there, and then fled through the sewers, evoking images of the persecuted suspect in *Les Misérables* fleeing through the sewers of Paris to escape the monstrous Ken Starr–like prosecutor.[*] By the day after Christmas, Garrison said at a press conference that there was "an infinitely larger number [of people involved in the conspiracy] than you would dream." In Dealey Plaza alone there could have been, he said, as many as fifteen people involved in the assassination.[83]

Garrison eventually added a sixteenth assassin and concluded that the sixteen were firing from several locations in Dealey Plaza.[84] With sixteen assassins, surely Oswald had to at least be one of them, right? No, Garrison assured people. "Oswald didn't shoot at the President," he declared confidently.[85]

But if Garrison couldn't find room for Oswald, along the way he did find room in his conspiracy constellation for the "Minutemen,"[86] "the paramilitary right,"[87] and elements of "the invisible Nazi substructure."[88]

With his New Year's resolution being to find additional assassins, in January of 1968 he revealed three new ones—the three tramps found in a box car near Dealey Plaza shortly

---

[*]To get a fuller impression of just how crazy Garrison was, let's look at his December 9, 1967, interview by reporter Murphy Martin on WFAA-TV in Dallas for a further description of how the assassination from the sewer took place: "Just a little bit in front of where the president was killed there is a sewer opening. Dealey Plaza used to have a bunch of houses and they were taken down to make the plaza. You have a surface drainage system with pipes through which a man can crawl. The small ones are fifteen inches wide, and the large ones are thirty inches wide. One of the assassins went . . . through the subsurface drainage system . . . [He] was the one who killed the president, [the one] who fired the .45 from right by the side of the car and tore the president's head off. Now, we went into the sewer one morning early . . . and we found a man fits in there very easily. We also found that after shooting from it, it's easy to crawl under the street through the fifteen-inch pipe, then you're in the thirty-inch sewer which leads out of Dealey Plaza to another part of town. Entrance can be gained . . . to the sewer area . . . through a manhole." Garrison said he and some members of his staff had gone to the sewer area "in the dark hours of the morning, and waited till the sun came up, and . . . you could see so clearly to the occupants inside the [presidential] car." Garrison added that the Warren Commission "refused to look at the [Zapruder] film because they knew [Kennedy] was shot from the front at least twice . . . They fooled the American people, consciously, knowingly . . . They [the U.S. government] ratified the execution, and concealed evidence wherever possible. They destroyed evidence in every possible way."

after the assassination—on Johnny Carson's *Tonight Show*.[89] But, he said in February, the assassination "operation" was "100% Central Intelligence Agency."[90]

As Rosemary James, the New Orleans reporter who covered the entire Shaw investigation and trial for the now defunct *States-Item* newspaper, said, "Every time press interest in the case would start to wane, Garrison would propound a new theory . . . He went from a highly intelligent eccentric to a lunatic in one year."[91] But while Garrison, on only one horse, tried to ride off in a great number of different directions, on one point he remained steadfast: "The evidence indicates that Lee Harvey Oswald did not fire a shot."[92]

William Gurvich, Garrison's chief investigator who resigned in disgust when he saw Garrison had no case against Shaw, said that at one point in the investigation, Garrison's proposed arrest list for the assassination, in addition to Shaw, included "one of the city's [New Orleans] leading coffee importers, one of the area's leading doctors of international reputation, an FBI agent assigned to the local office, two leaders of the local Cuban refugee organization, and the owner of one of the largest local hotels."[93]

Newsweek magazine reported that "some of [Garrison's] staff became alarmed about his behavior. He would call meetings, then disappear into the men's room for awhile, emerge with a new theory and send aides to try to prove it." Garrison found no problems with this reverse methodology. Charles Ward, who later became a judge on the Louisiana State Court of Appeals, was Garrison's chief assistant in the DA's office at the time and helped out in the Shaw case. He told the New Orleans *Times-Picayune* in 1983 that "most of the time you marshal the facts, then deduce your theories. But Garrison deduced a theory, then marshaled his facts. And if the facts didn't fit, he'd say they had been altered by the CIA."[94]

As we saw in an earlier section, at one point Garrison's aides had to literally talk him out of indicting a dead man (Garrison thought he was alive) and the three tramps on the fifth anniversary of the assassination. But on December 10, 1967, no one succeeded in stopping Garrison from filing a criminal complaint against one Edgar Eugene Bradley, alleging Bradley did "willfully and unlawfully conspire *with others**" to murder John F. Kennedy." Garrison's evidence against Bradley? A young man from Van Nuys, California, lived in the home of a woman who was involved in a lawsuit with Bradley, and when she told him that Bradley looked like one of the three tramps arrested in the railroad yards, he wrote a letter to Garrison to this effect, adding for good measure that Bradley had offered him ten thousand dollars to kill Kennedy when the latter was a U.S. senator, but he had turned Bradley down. Several years later it was determined that the man, a member of the Minutemen, was fourteen years old at the time Bradley allegedly made him the offer. When Dallas deputy sheriff Roger Craig (whose credibility, or severe lack thereof, was discussed earlier in this book) told Garrison that he saw Bradley in Dealey Plaza on November 22, 1963, posing as a Secret Service agent, and Garrison's star witness, Perry Russo, said Ferrie knew Bradley, that's all Garrison needed to charge Bradley with Kennedy's murder.

*With others? What others? Garrison had a grand jury indict Clay Shaw for conspiring with Oswald and Ferrie "and others," but he at least named Oswald and Ferrie, two human beings. Here, the out-of-control Garrison didn't even name one person Bradley had supposedly conspired with. Was he suggesting that Bradley had perhaps conspired with Shaw, Oswald, and Ferrie to murder Kennedy? If he was, why didn't he add Bradley's name to the existing indictment against Shaw? If he wasn't saying that Bradley was conspiring with these three, was he suggesting that Bradley was a part of a separate, second conspiracy to murder Kennedy in Dallas? That Bradley and his conspirators just, fortuitously, decided to kill Kennedy at the very same time and place that another group of conspirators, who they didn't even know existed, did?

Bradley (a North Hollywood, California, business representative for right-wing radio evangelist Carl McIntire), who *was* in Texas on the day of the assassination (but El Paso, not Dallas), said, "I shot who?" when the press notified him of the murder charges against him. He proceeded to say that Garrison "must be nuts. This man is either being highly paid to do this or he's off his rocker."[95] On November 8, 1968, there being no evidence presented by Garrison's office connecting Bradley to the assassination, California governor Ronald Reagan denied Garrison's extradition request. Edwin Meese, Reagan's press secretary, said that Garrison's office had been given the chance to present witnesses to substantiate the allegation but had not done so.[96]

Garrison even told conspiracy author Paris Flammonde that with respect to the assassinations of President Kennedy, Senator Robert Kennedy, and Martin Luther King, "there is enough data available in all three cases to state, as a probability, that they were all accomplished by the same force and that they were all . . . [U.S.] intelligence assassinations."[97]

This is the irrational person who Oliver Stone deliberately misled millions of Americans into believing was the solid, sober-minded, level-headed, and heroic All-American figure portrayed by Kevin Costner. Stone's Garrison was the personification of an honest and completely responsible public servant.

I personally know of no American prosecutor who has ever abused his office's power of subpoena and power to file unwarranted criminal charges against perceived adversaries to the degree that Garrison did in the Shaw case, causing fear and intimidation—undoubtedly precisely what Garrison was seeking to accomplish—in the minds of all those who might oppose what he wanted. As Shaw asserted in his May 1968 civil lawsuit against Garrison and two of his top assistants, "All who oppose the defendants or disagree with the theories expounded by them incur their wrath and displeasure, and the defendants misuse and abuse the powers of their office by filing criminal charges of one sort or another against them."[98]* Garrison's unprofessional antics were so notorious in New Orleans at the time that when David Chandler, a *Life* magazine reporter from New Orleans who wrote a series of articles in April and September of 1967 about organized crime in Louisiana containing unflattering references to Garrison (which Garrison called lies), was subpoenaed by Garrison before the Shaw grand jury to testify on what he had written, the federal district court in New Orleans, on March 11, 1968, enjoined Garrison from enforcing his subpoena. The court said that "Garrison has stated his lack of regard for the truthfulness of the very testimony being sought . . . Chandler's fear of prospective prosecution for perjury . . . is well founded." Chandler was thereby saved from an almost certain charge of perjury by Garrison.

Little of this, unfortunately, was reaching the masses. Most people were all too willing to believe that a beloved president had been murdered and the authorities were concealing the truth from them. But was Garrison really an intrepid DA who was willing to take on the government to uncover the truth for them? On June 19, 1967, a major national network, NBC, had told Americans, in so many words in its television special on the case, *The JFK Conspiracy: The Case of Jim Garrison*, that Garrison wasn't legitimate and that his charges were fraudulent. Garrison knew he had to fight back nationally. *Playboy* gave Garrison the longest interview in the history of the magazine in its October 1967 issue, thirty-seven pages, and among other radio and TV appearances, Mort Sahl got him on

---

*An endnote to this paragraph sets forth most, but perhaps not all, of the people Garrison charged with crimes if they testified to anything, or did anything, that frustrated his case.

the Johnny Carson show on January 31, 1968. "Johnny" may have been a comedian, but he had a good, solid head on his shoulders, and he could spot a phony, or at least an empty vessel, when he saw one. When Garrison kept hammering away that the truth in the Kennedy assassination was being suppressed from the American people, Carson asked Garrison, "Who's suppressing all of this information? On whose order?"

"I'll tell you who's suppressing it, the federal government is suppressing it."

"Who in the federal government?" Carson pressed.

"The administration of your government is suppressing it because they know that the Central Intelligence Agency . . ."

"On whose order?" Carson interrupted, not letting Garrison evade his question.

"On the order of the president of the United States."

"For what possible reason?"

"Why don't you ask him, John?" (laughter and applause)

"I know what he'd say. (applause) I think he would say . . . 'Mr. Garrison has come up with no credible evidence to support any of his theories.'"

Garrison went on to tell Carson, "I am trying to tell you that there is no question, as a result of our investigation, that an element of the Central Intelligence Agency of our country killed Kennedy, and that the present administration is concealing the facts. There is no question about it at all."

"That is your opinion."

"No, it is not. I know it," Garrison assured Carson.[99]

The lunacy of Garrison and his investigation of Shaw naturally carried over to Shaw's trial, which commenced with opening statements by Garrison for the prosecution and by Shaw's chief defense lawyer, Irvin Dymond, for the defense, on February 6, 1969, after fourteen court days of jury selection, which had started on January 21. Most of Garrison's witnesses were prosecutorial nightmares. For instance, one witness, Vernon Bundy, was a twenty-nine-year-old black heroin addict who in 1967 was in Orleans Parish prison on a parole violation for a theft conviction the previous year. On March 16, 1967, two days after Clay Shaw's preliminary hearing had commenced, Bundy contacted Garrison's office with an almost laughably improbable and transparently fabricated story. Indeed, in the one-hour June 19, 1967, NBC news exposé on Garrison's apparently trumped-up charges against Shaw, and which seven investigative reporters for NBC had spent several weeks working on,[100] two fellow inmates of Bundy's, Miguel Torres and John Cancler, said that Bundy had told them his story was a lie he came up with to get "cut loose" from prison. However, both thereafter pleaded their Fifth Amendment right against self-incrimination when the Orleans Parish grand jury asked them to repeat their story under oath. It is not known whether they took the Fifth because they didn't want to lie, or because they knew about Garrison's habit of prosecuting people for perjury when their truthful testimony hurt him or his agenda.*

_____

*Knowing the thrust of the NBC special, Garrison, the day before it aired, complained in a letter to the Federal Communications Commission (FCC) that NBC had the "calculated objective" of destroying his case, and asked the FCC to prevent the special from being shown, which the FCC declined to do (*New York Times*, June 19, 1967, p.27). On June 20, 1967, the day after the NBC special aired, Garrison lashed out at NBC as being a party to the "establishment" conspiracy to destroy him, and implied that the CIA had been behind and had financed the special. Garrison added, for good measure, that "all of the screaming and hollering now being heard is evidence that we have caught a very big fish . . . It is obvious that there are elements in Wash-

In any event, according to Bundy, he was preparing a heroin injection for himself next to the concrete seawall at Lake Pontchartrain on a Monday morning in June or July of 1963 when he saw Clay Shaw get out of a black sedan, pass by him, and walk fifteen to twenty feet away, where he was approached by Lee Harvey Oswald, who he said was "dirty" and "looked like a real junkie himself." Bundy said he saw Shaw and Oswald talk about "fifteen to twenty" minutes, during which time Shaw handed Oswald a roll of money and also told Oswald, with Bundy standing nearby, "I told you to shut up. You're talking too loud." Why Shaw would want to talk to and pay Oswald—presumably to be involved in the assassination of Kennedy—in public, with someone standing nearby, as opposed to inside his car or someone's home, is not known. Nor is it known why Bundy, instead of taking his fix behind closed doors somewhere, would do so in public, knowing, as he must have, that if he were caught he could be prosecuted as well as be found in violation of his parole.

Oh, yes. Bundy decided to gild the lily by telling the DA that as Oswald walked away, a pamphlet fell out of his pocket onto the ground. Bundy took time out from his heroin injection to retrieve the pamphlet, which he said had "Free Cuba" language on it.[101]

No one, of course, believed a word Bundy said, and in the more than three years since the assassination, he had never told this story before. In fact, reporter Frank McGee said on the June 19 NBC News special that NBC investigators had learned that Bundy had failed a polygraph test, and because of this, Garrison's first assistant district attorney, Charles Ward, urged Garrison not to call Bundy to the witness stand at Shaw's preliminary hearing in 1967.[102] In fact, the polygrapher, James Kruebbe, had personally told Garrison, in the presence of Ward and fellow prosecutor James Alcock, that Bundy "wasn't telling the truth."[103] But Garrison, knowing he was possibly presenting perjurious testimony, did, and had Bundy repeat his tale at Shaw's trial in 1969. At the trial, after Shaw, per Bundy's request, walked twice from the back of the courtroom toward him, Bundy testified he was sure Shaw was the man he had seen that day. "I watched his foot the way it twisted that day. This is one way I identified this man the next time I saw him[*]. . . . That is the foot [Shaw's right foot] that twisted that day. The twisting of his foot had frightened me that day on the seawall when I was about to cook my drugs."[104] Shaw did have a slightly stiff walk from a bad back,[105] but who else had ever said that his foot twisted when he walked? On cross-examination by Shaw's lawyer, Bundy denied telling Torres and Cancler that he had made the Shaw story up.[106]

And then there was the New York City accountant, Charles Spiesel, a short and dapper man with an authoritative voice and mien who told the Shaw jury that one evening in June of 1963 he was at La Fitte's Blacksmith Shop, a bar in the French Quarter, when he recognized a man (David Ferrie) he had flown in the air force with during the Second

---

ington, D.C., which are desperate because we are in the process of uncovering their hoax." (*Times-Picayune* [New Orleans], June 20 and 21, 1967; Epstein, *Assassination Chronicles*, p.245) Garrison demanded equal time (*New York Times*, July 5, 1967, p.83). He didn't get it, but NBC did give him a half hour of prime time on the evening of July 15 to rebut the allegations against him. With an audience of 20 million listening, Garrison elected to not respond directly to the various charges made in the one-hour special (saying he wouldn't "dignify" them), choosing instead to speak in general terms. "If our investigation was as haywire as they would like to have you think," he said, "then you would not see such a coordinated barrage [against me] coming from the news centers in the East . . . As long as I am alive, no one is going to stop me from seeing that you obtain the full truth . . . and no fairy tales." (Epstein, "Reporter at Large," p.64)

[*]Watching Shaw walk outside the sheriff's office in the New Orleans County Criminal Courts Building on March 16, 1967, Bundy told Assistant District Attorney John Volz, "That's him. I'm sure of it. He had the same *limp* when I saw him on the Lakefront" (Memorandum from John Volz to Jim Garrison, March 17, 1967).

World War. (There is no record of Ferrie having ever served in the air force.) Ferrie was with two women and another man, and they invited him, he said, to a party at a second-floor apartment in the French Quarter. At the party were ten or eleven men, including Shaw, who was the host, though it was not his apartment. The apartment's occupants were out of town and had given Shaw the keys. Spiesel testified that "someone brought up the name of President Kennedy and just about everybody began to criticize him. Then someone said 'somebody ought to kill the son-of-a-b!'" Ferrie expressed the opinion it could be done, and Shaw smiled and agreed. A young man with a beard and a splint said he'd like to be the one to do it "in a couple of weeks" when his splint was removed. Spiesel said the group finally agreed that the killing "would have to be done with a high-powered rifle with a telescopic sight." Shaw, per Spiesel, asked Ferrie if the assassin could be flown away from the assassination site to safety and Ferrie said it could be done.

Spiesel's testimony, naturally, had a stunning effect on the media and the rest of the spectators in the courtroom. But on cross-examination, when Irvin Dymond, Shaw's lead defense attorney, asked Spiesel if he had noticed anything unusual about Ferrie's physical appearance, Spiesel said, "No," which was the equivalent of saying he had never met Ferrie, and his whole story was poppycock. Without exception, everyone who met Ferrie was startled by his bizarre appearance, Ferrie being, as someone once said in a different context, a sight seldom seen in Christendom. What about Ferrie's hair? Spiesel was asked.

"Fairly well-groomed," he said about the grotesque, dime-store wig Ferrie had glued on his head.

"Did he have unusual eyebrows?"

"A little thinner than most men's, not unusual outside of that," Spiesel responded about the inordinately thick, pasted-on eyebrows Ferrie wore.

Spiesel was a nut of the first water, and on Dymond's cross it came out he believed that from 1948 to 1964 a New York psychiatrist, the New York Police Department, the Pinkerton detective agency, the New York Horse Racing Association, and others had conspired to torture him mentally in New York, New Jersey, Washington, D.C., and New Orleans, and that, acting as his own lawyer, he had filed a $16 million lawsuit against them. Dymond read into the record the entire text of the embarrassing complaint filed by Spiesel. The effect of the reading was apparent on Spiesel as he nervously made stroking motions above his head with his right hand, missing his scalp completely. His left hand rested firmly on the arm of the witness chair, his fingers tapping on the wood. Spiesel also said on cross-examination that he had been hypnotized "by possibly fifty or sixty" people "against my will" over the period between 1948 and 1964, including by the New York Police Department, causing him to suffer "hypnotic delusions" and lose the ability to have "normal sexual relations." Others, he said, tried to enter his home disguised as members of his family. Why would all these people and groups want to do this? Shaw's attorney asked. Spiesel said he did not know but suggested it was a Communist conspiracy to spy on him. How, Shaw's attorney asked Speisel, would he know if he was being hypnotized? "When someone tries to get your attention, catch your eye," Spiesel said, "that's a clue right off." Is it possible, Shaw's attorney asked, that he was under hypnosis at the time he supposedly heard Shaw and Ferrie conspire with others to kill Kennedy?

"I don't really know if it did happen," Spiesel acknowledged.

Spiesel admitted that he currently had fifteen lawsuits against him in New York City for nonpayment of debts and that he had filed for bankruptcy. By this time, Garrison's prosecutors would have mortgaged their homes to get Spiesel off the witness stand, but it was too late, as Spiesel inflicted further punishment on himself and the DA who called him to the stand. His self-administered coup de grace was when he testified that before his daughter had left home in New York City for Louisiana State University, he finger-printed her, and again fingerprinted her when she returned home because he wanted to make sure she was the same person who had left home, not one of his "enemies" who had taken to impersonating members of his family to destroy him.[107]

When Tom Bethell, Garrison's chief researcher, left Garrison's office out of disgust over Garrison's investigation of Shaw, he sent a memo to the defense attorneys setting forth names and addresses of all the prosecution witnesses, including a summary of their expected testimony. This was extremely helpful to the defense since at the time in Louisiana, there was no right of "discovery" of the opposition's witnesses and statements, meaning the prosecution could present surprise witnesses at the trial without the defense having had an opportunity to prepare for their testimony. Bethell told me that the prosecutor in Garrison's office who interviewed Spiesel in New York City (and whose name, out of consideration for the prosecutor, he did not want to reveal to me) had reported back to Garrison that Spiesel would make an excellent witness "if it weren't for the fact that he was crazy." The prosecutor had learned, among other things, of Spiesel's finger-printing his daughter. Although Bethell didn't furnish the defense attorneys with this information, once they learned of Spiesel's identity through Bethell, their own investi-gation uncovered all of Spiesel's quirkiness and eccentricities, including the fingerprint-ing, and the prosecution was stunned when all of this came out on cross-examination.[108]

The prosecutor whose name Bethell did not want to give me was James Alcock. He had interviewed Spiesel on July 13, 1967, at a restaurant in Greenwich Village. Alcock's three-page memorandum of the interview to Garrison on July 17 makes no reference to learning of Spiesel's fingerprinting his daughter, and closes by saying, "Mr. Spiesel is willing to testify and only requests that we attempt to get him some per diem accounting work while he is in the city."

The FBI had a file on Spiesel, dating back to 1949, that chronicled his bizarre accu-sations, including the charge that his enemies had placed people in his home disguised as his father and mother. Spiesel's father, Boris, a New York City fur merchant, told the FBI his son was mentally disturbed.[109]

The sad-sack prosecutors couldn't even put a U.S. postman on the witness stand with-out evoking smirks and ripples of laughter from the courtroom audience. Garrison was alleging that the name Shaw used as an alias when he conspired with Ferrie and Oswald to murder Kennedy was Clay Bertrand (see later discussion). In the summer of 1966, Shaw executed a change of address form so his mail would be sent to the home of his friend, one Jeff Biddison at 1414 Chartres Street, while Shaw was on vacation. The postal worker, James Hardiman, told the jury that he delivered several letters addressed to Clem (not Clay) Bertrand to Biddison's house that summer. On cross-examination, he was asked, "Did you ever deliver any mail to that address, that is, 1414 Chartres Street, addressed to a Mr. Cliff Boudreaux?"

Yes, the postal worker answered.

"Now, Mr. Hardiman, if I told you I just made that name up, would your testimony be the same?"

"Maybe you made it up," Hardiman answered, "but I have delivered Boudreaux mail there, too."[110]

One may wonder why Garrison was beset by so many goofy witnesses. But as author James Phelan pointed out, "There are certain sensational cases that have a fascination for unstable people and fetch them forth in droves . . . Celebrated cases also attract witnesses who are not psychotic, but who falsely identify key figures out of faulty memory or a desire to lift themselves out of dull anonymity into the spotlight." The difference between Garrison and most responsible prosecutors in these high-visibility cases is that the latter don't call the kooks to the witness stand. Garrison did. Phelan says, "The Garrison case had a disastrously low threshold, across which trooped a bizarre parade of people eager to bolser his conspiracy scenario."[111]And Garrison welcomed them with open arms.

Garrison's star witness at the Shaw trial, and the one around whom he virtually built his entire case, was Perry Russo (David Ferrie died before the trial—see later text), a twenty-five-year-old Baton Rouge insurance salesman who was a friend of David Ferrie's. Russo claimed that he was in Ferrie's apartment in New Orleans in mid-September of 1963 when he heard Ferrie, Shaw (using the alias Clay Bertrand), and Oswald conspire to kill Kennedy.[112] The only problem is that cross-examination revealed that the first four times Russo told everything he knew about Ferrie—including to *Baton Rouge State-Times* reporter Bill Bankston on February 24, 1967 (two days after Ferrie's death), and later in the day to Jim Kemp of TV station WAFB in Baton Rouge—he never mentioned any such thing, not even bringing up the names Oswald, Shaw, or Bertrand, much less any conspiracy by them. In fact, when Kemp asked him if Ferrie had ever mentioned "Lee Harvey Oswald's name," Russo answered, "No. I had never heard of Oswald until the television [coverage] of the assassination."[113] Russo only spoke about the Shaw-Ferrie-Oswald conspiracy meeting when he was put under sodium pentothal and hypnosis four years later in 1967, and even then, only after being asked leading questions.

But one can see why Russo needed truth serum and hypnosis to recall hearing three people plot to murder President Kennedy four years earlier. Without truth serum and hypnosis, a plot to murder the president of the United States just wasn't important enough for someone like him to remember. But what about around the time of the alleged incident? Surely he must have remembered the incident at least for a while back then, right? And if so, why, he was asked at Shaw's preliminary hearing on March 15, 1967, hadn't he gone to the authorities when, just two months after the meeting of conspirators he claimed he was privy to, the president was murdered? Again, apparently a plot to murder the president of the United States just wasn't important enough to Russo. He responded casually, "I had an involvement with school, which was *more pressing to me*."

If that wasn't unbelievable enough, when Shaw's lawyer asked, "You claim you were present at a meeting where the assassination was planned and you say you did not know whether your testimony would be valuable to the Warren Commission?" Russo answered, "Now, they ["Bertrand, Oswald, Ferrie"] did not say anything about [the specific city of] Dallas," as if their not doing so was some justification for his not coming forward. Russo, who had to know how pathetic his answers were, tried to inject some plausibility into his story by adding some other reasons why he hadn't come forward back in 1963. One was that even though the man he saw conspire to murder Kennedy was introduced to him as "Leon Oswald," and over TV the president's killer was called "Lee Harvey Oswald," the two men "did not look alike exactly." Also, he had confidence in the FBI, and "if they wanted me, [to] ask me anything, they could," not explaining how they could possibly contact him if he never told them he existed.[114]

On January 26, 1971, close to two years after Clay Shaw's not-guilty verdict on March

1, 1969, Russo told Edward Wegmann, one of Shaw's lawyers, that he never saw Clay Shaw in Ferrie's apartment ("absolutely not"), and Garrison's office had done "a complete brainwashing job" on him.[115] On April 16, 1971, Russo gave a tape-recorded interview to William Gurvich (the former Garrison investigator) and two of Shaw's attorneys, Wegmann and F. Irvin Dymond. Russo told of Garrison and his staff telling him before the trial that they had a contract with *Life* magazine for twenty-five thousand dollars, and that "after the Shaw conviction" they would "either give that to me or see somehow I got a lot of it for my trouble." Saying, "I guess I always knew [Shaw] had nothing to do with anything," Russo stated that Garrison's staff threatened him: if he went back on what he said under hypnosis, "the courthouse [would be] planted on top of me."[116]*

Jerry Cohen, a *Los Angeles Times* reporter I knew who covered the Shaw trial for the *Times*, told me when he returned to Los Angeles after the not-guilty verdict was reached, "Vince, the trial was the most unbelievable joke you could ever imagine. Though no one was confident of what the New Orleans jury would do, nearly everyone in the courtroom, including the media, knew that Shaw was innocent and Garrison had no evidence against him. The jury returned with their verdict in forty-five minutes or so [actually, fifty-four minutes]. The consensus was that they had a cup of coffee, chose their foreman, and could have returned in ten minutes, but they sat it out a few more minutes for appearance purposes.† I tell you, Garrison should be in jail for what he did. This is a sick, dangerous man." Salvatore Panzeca, Shaw's original defense attorney who remained on his team throughout the trial, told me, "Garrison knowingly prosecuted an innocent man. In my forty-one years as a criminal defense attorney, I have never had a client more cooperative, intelligent and innocent than Clay Shaw."[117] Milton Brener, who was a prosecutor in Garrison's office before the Shaw case and ended up writing a book about the case, told me, "Of course Shaw was innocent. The entire case against him was a figment of Garrison's imagination. He pulled it completely out of thin air."[118] Indeed, Garrison's case against Shaw was so outrageous and so lacking in any credible evidence against Shaw that even Garrison's own wife, as Oliver Stone himself acknowledged in an article, didn't believe in his case, and she and Garrison separated right after the trial.[119] When a prosecutor's own wife isn't on his side, that's pretty bad, isn't it? I mean, can it get any worse?

The media savaged Garrison, who didn't have the courage to show up in court throughout a good part of the trial (averaging about one day a week), not even when the all-male (nine whites, three blacks) jury returned its verdict of not guilty at one in the morning on March 1, 1969, two years to the day after Shaw had been arrested in the case. In a front-page editorial on March 1, the *New Orleans States-Item* said, "District Attorney Jim Garrison should resign. He has shown himself unfit to hold the office of District Attorney or any other office. Mr. Garrison has abused the vast powers of his office. He has perverted the law rather than prosecuted it. His persecution of Clay Shaw was a per-

---

*There simply is no space in this book to adequately cover Garrison's entire investigation of Shaw and Shaw's complete trial, although much is included in this book. As I have indicated, entire books have been written on this subject alone, and even these books can only highlight the investigation and trial. However, since the heart of Garrison's case against Shaw was Perry Russo, for those who are interested I have included an in-depth discussion of Perry Russo in an endnote that actually is longer than any discussion of Russo in any book on the case to date.

†As it was later learned, the jury actually took two ballots. On the first ballot, a high school teacher, impressed with the witnesses from Clinton, Louisiana, who said they saw Oswald and Shaw together in their town (see endnote discussion), voted to convict. On the next ballot, the not-guilty vote was unanimous.

version of the legal process such as has not been often seen. Clay Shaw has been vindicated, but the damage to his reputation caused by Mr. Garrison's witch hunt may never
be repaired. This travesty of justice is a reproach to the conscience of all good men and
must not go unanswered. Mr. Garrison himself should now be brought to the bar to answer
for his conduct."[120] The *New York Times* opined in an editorial that Garrison's prosecution of Shaw was "one of the most disgraceful chapters in the history of American
jurisprudence."[121]

The *Los Angeles Times* editorial observed that "the really frightening thing" is that
since Garrison only used Shaw to further his own ends, "Shaw could have been any man."
Saying "the processes of justice had been outrageously abused" by Garrison, the *Times*
concluded that "if there is one fact proven beyond all dispute in the Shaw case it is that
Jim Garrison is unfit to hold public office."[122]

For his part, Shaw would later say, "If a jury could convict me on such shoddy evidence as Garrison presented, I would gladly have gone to jail—it would be the safest place
in a world gone mad."[123]*

Again, Garrison is the man whom Stone presented to his audience as the most solid
and rational of men, one with impeccable ethics who was an intrepid fighter for justice.

Unbelievably, the shameless and unconscionable Garrison, after the irreparably grievous harm he had already inflicted on an innocent man, decided to inflict further harm on
Shaw, his model obviously not being common sense and decency, but again, Victor Hugo's
maliciously tenacious Inspector Javert in *Les Misérables*. On March 3, 1969, the first business day after the not-guilty verdict came down, Garrison, instead of skulking away into
the night with his tail between his legs, filed two counts of perjury against Shaw for denying on the witness stand that he knew Lee Harvey Oswald and David Ferrie. (It is
extremely rare, almost unheard of, for a defendant, after his criminal trial, to be prosecuted for committing perjury in his defense, whether or not he was convicted of the offense
for which he was on trial. It's just not done, even where there is no doubt in the DA's mind
the defendant committed perjury. It's a perjury that is almost invariably overlooked and
even expected by prosecutors. After all, if the defendant were going to admit having committed the crime, he would have pled guilty and there would not have been any trial.)†

On January 18, 1971, Shaw made a motion for a temporary restraining order to prevent Garrison from proceeding against him. Shaw contended that Garrison was acting

---

*Though he was found not guilty, the trial cost Shaw over $200,000, which he said was his life's savings,
and ruined what had been his excellent reputation in New Orleans. Financially and emotionally broken from
Garrison's fraudulent charges, Shaw died of lung cancer on August 14, 1974, before his $5 million civil action
against Garrison (filed on February 28, 1970) for malicious prosecution came to trial. Shaw, the man Garrison said had conspired to murder Kennedy, said after the trial, "I was a great admirer of Kennedy. I thought
he had given the nation a new turn after the rather drab Eisenhower years . . . I felt he was vitally concerned
about social issues, which concerned me also. I thought he had youth, imagination, style, and élan. All in all,
I considered him a splendid president." ("Clay Shaw," p.32)

Despite the overwhelmingly negative publicity, Garrison nonetheless was reelected DA later that same
year by an "only in New Orleans" laissez-faire citizenry, but he lost his bid for reelection in 1973. However,
he was elected to a ten-year term as an appellate judge on the Louisiana Fourth Circuit Court of Appeal in
1978 and was reelected in 1988. He died on October 21, 1992, at the age of seventy. The death certificate says
the cause of death was "congestive heart failure," though his attending physician, Dr. Frank Minyard, said,
"It was [the] Kennedy [case] that killed him." On his headstone at the cemetery in Metairie are the words
"Let Justice Be Done, Though the Heavens Fall." (Mellen, *Farewell to Justice*, pp.368–369)

†At a 1971 hearing, federal judge Herbert Christenberry took notice of the unusual nature of Garrison's
conduct, writing, "No witness who testified before this court, including Garrison, could give another instance
in which a defendant who took the stand and was acquitted was subsequently charged by Mr. Garrison with
perjury" (*Shaw v. Garrison*, 328 F. Supp. 390, 400 [1971]).

"in bad faith" and was abusing his prosecutorial powers. The motion was granted, and on January 25, a three-day hearing commenced on the issue of whether Garrison should be permanently enjoined from prosecuting Shaw on the perjury charges. Numerous witnesses testified, including Shaw, who again said he had never met Oswald or Ferrie. Russo was also called to the stand but invoked the Fifth Amendment against self-incrimination. U.S. federal district court judge Herbert W. Christenberry ruled on May 27, 1971, that Shaw was entitled to the relief sought, and signed a permanent injunction on June 7.

In his ruling Christenberry scathingly denounced Garrison, using words like "appalling," "outrageous," and "inexcusable" to describe Garrison's conduct in different areas of the case. He said, "Garrison undertook his baseless investigation [of Shaw] with the specific intent to deprive Shaw of his rights under the First, Fifth, and Fourteenth Amendments to the Constitution of the United States." In one part of his written opinion, he in essence accused Garrison of subornation of perjury, writing that Garrison "resorted to the use of drugs and hypnosis on Russo, purportedly to corroborate, but more likely to concoct his story."[124]

Garrison appealed, but the U.S. Supreme Court refused to hear the appeal. Garrison had succeeded, however, in torturing Shaw for two years after the not-guilty verdict on the conspiracy-to-commit-murder charge. In his diaries, Shaw referred to the "Kafkaesque horror" Garrison had put him through to further some perceived greater good.

In an address on the Bill of Rights (and its progenitor, the English Magna Carta) at Tulane Law School on October 30, 1964, Garrison had dwelled on the fact that the Bill of Rights, which he properly elevated to sacred status, was adopted "to protect the governed from the men who govern them," and that attacks on these fundamental rights can invariably be "identified by the great *superior* virtue which the attackers bear inscribed on their battle flag." The attacks are always ostensibly "for the good of the state," some "great virtue of the day." A twenty-four-hour watch is needed to protect our Bill of Rights, he said, because someone is always trying to deprive us of them "in the interest of justice, of course." I believe Jim Garrison believed those words when he spoke them, but somewhere down the line, and for whatever reason, he became the precise embodiment of the villains he feared and denounced in his 1964 speech.

Harry Connick Sr. (father of the singer), the New Orleans DA who ran against and defeated Garrison in 1973, told me that the Clay Shaw prosecution was "absolutely the most terrible, gross, abominable prosecution" he has ever encountered in his many years in law enforcement. "Garrison went to extremes to prosecute an innocent man." Connick, who was an assistant U.S. attorney at the time of the Shaw investigation and trial, said that even before the Shaw case, the legal community in New Orleans viewed Garrison "as a four flusher. He frequently made allegations and charges he couldn't back up. So there was a suspicion down here from the moment he brought charges against Shaw—and before we learned Garrison had no evidence—that it might turn out to be a phony case."[125] *Newsweek* reporter Hugh Aynesworth said that Jim Garrison was "right," there *was* a conspiracy in New Orleans, but it was his "scheme to concoct a fantastic 'solution' to the death of John F. Kennedy."[126]

Can anything positive be said about Garrison in his prosecution of Clay Shaw? Tom Bethell, Garrison's chief research assistant on the case, said, "When Ferrie died, the office staff was jubilant because we all knew there was no substance to Garrison's charges, and this gave him a wonderful opportunity to get off the hook and tell the media hordes covering the case who were questioning whether he had anything, 'Look, I tried to find out the truth, but *they* silenced my main suspect.' The public would have thought he had been on to something big, and he would have looked like a hero. Instead, he proceeds to almost immediately charge Shaw with the murder. People in the office were putting their hands to their forehead. The sense was 'How are we going to handle this now?'" Bethell offers this insight: "If this whole Garrison crusade was only political calculation on his part, he'd have taken the opportune course and ended it when Ferrie died. But there was also madness here." Bethell said he personally liked Garrison, saying he was "amusing, charming," but he was "very, very irresponsible, to an extent that was just amazing."[127] In a 1991 article, Bethell wrote, "I knew Clay Shaw was innocent; in fact I think everyone in the DA's office also knew it, except for Garrison himself, who was incapable of thinking straight on the subject."[128]

John Volz, a prosecutor in Garrison's office who was a pallbearer at Garrison's funeral, confirmed Bethell's rendition of events. "When Ferrie died, we [fellow prosecutors in the office] advised him to get out of all this. But Jim wouldn't listen. Instead, he said, 'This is just the beginning.'" Volz also agrees with Bethell that Garrison's conduct at the time of Ferrie's death led him to believe that Garrison "actually believed most of this craziness," and although he believes Garrison was completely wrong in his prosecution of Shaw, he was "well-intentioned."[129]*

Is one possibility simply that Stone's hero, Garrison, had truly gone mad? There are those who think so. Warren Commission critic Harold Weisberg was one of Garrison's strongest earliest supporters, and he went to New Orleans to help Garrison on his case. Garrison reciprocated by writing the foreword to Weisberg's 1967 book, *Oswald in New Orleans*. But months before the trial, he disavowed Garrison. Although he was not inclined to elaborate, Weisberg told me he was a witness in New Orleans to Garrison "making up" a piece of evidence against Shaw, and when he saw this he said, "I knew I had to sever my association with Garrison." Weisberg said that Garrison the man "was one of the greatest tragedies in the investigation of Kennedy's assassination. He was highly talented, intelligent, and articulate, but somewhere down the road he *lost contact with reality*. I just don't understand what he was up to. There just was no evidence of Shaw's guilt."[130] Clay Shaw, the man whose life Garrison had destroyed, and someone who must have given considerable thought to the matter, also thought Garrison suffered from a psychological illness. "Personally," Shaw said, "I think he's quite ill, mentally. He was, as you know, discharged from the Army after a diagnosis of anxiety and told to take psychotherapy.† I know he has been to a number of analysts. I think, basically, he is getting

---

*Garrison's chief investigator at the time, William Gurvich, had a slightly less flattering take on why Garrison continued on after Ferrie's death. He told *Newsweek* reporter Hugh Aynesworth that the reason Garrison didn't walk away from the case was that "he was already pumped up with the adoration of the conspiracy people and all. He was getting calls from all over the country, from Europe, even from Japan and Australia. He couldn't buy a meal in New Orleans. Or pay for a cab ride. He was exciting the whole town—and boy, was he caught up in it" (Aynesworth with Michaud, *JFK: Breaking the News*, pp.238–239).

†After the Second World War, Garrison joined the army reserve. In 1951 his reserve unit was called to active duty for the Korean War, which had started the previous year. Garrison, after being hospitalized at the U.S. Army Hospital in Fort Sill, Oklahoma, and Brooke Army Hospital at Fort Sam in Houston, Texas, from August to October 1951, was discharged from active duty with the rank of captain on October 31, 1951, effective January 9, 1952, "by reason of physical disability." Doctors at Brooke Army Hospital in Texas found that he was suffering from a chronic moderate "anxiety reaction," manifested by chronic hypochondriasis (the psychiatric term for hypochondria, the abnormal condition characterized by a depressed emotional state and imaginary ill health), exhaustion syndrome, and gastrointestinal discomfort, and that he had a "severe and disabling psychoneurosis of long duration. It has interfered with his social and professional adjustment to a marked degree. He is considered totally disabled from the standpoint of military duty and moderately incapacitated in civilian adaptability. His illness existed long before his call to active duty, July 24, 1951, and is of

worse all the time. I think there is a division of his mind. With one-half of his mind he is able to go out and fabricate evidence, and then by some osmosis, he is able to convince the other half that the fabrication is the truth."[131]

My view (for whatever it's worth, seeing that I did not know Garrison, and being aware that it conflicts with the views of some people who did know him) is that Garrison eventually came to realize that his suspicions about Shaw were unfounded, yet he persisted in prosecuting an innocent man. My sense is that Edward Wegmann, one of Shaw's attorneys, summed up the entire case and Garrison's motive for bringing it as well as anyone I've heard: "An innocent man has been the victim of a ruthless, unethical and fraudulent public prosecutor . . . who, with premeditation and full knowledge of the falsity of the charges brought against [Shaw] . . . used him for the sole purpose of obtaining a judicial forum for [his attack] upon the credibility of the . . . Warren Commission."[132] In other words, and pardon the play on words, Clay Shaw was "just a patsy."

There is strong support for the conclusion that Garrison knew Shaw was innocent (hence, the argument that he used Shaw to attack the Warren Commission becomes the most plausible explanation for Garrison's prosecution of Shaw). Although Garrison would have never admitted knowingly prosecuting an innocent man for murder, his conduct speaks quite eloquently for that proposition.

In view of the fact that Garrison had accused Shaw of conspiring to murder the president of the United States, one would expect Garrison himself to face Shaw in court and cross-examine him during his testimony on February 27, 1969. But instead, he let his assistant, James Alcock, do so. And even with Alcock, if one wasn't told that Shaw was on trial for Kennedy's murder, one would hardly have known this from Alcock's cross-examination. Not only was it extremely short (consuming exactly fifty pages of transcript)—one would automatically expect the cross-examination of someone accused of conspiring to murder the president of the United States to go on for several days and take up hundreds of pages of transcript—but it couldn't possibly have been more soft and civil. So much so that it could have been Shaw's own lawyer asking the questions. So soft, civil, and nonconfrontational, in fact, that when Shaw's lawyer was asked if he had any questions to ask on redirect examination, Dymond said no, seeing no need to explain away or mitigate any damage to his client's cause that came out during cross-examination. It couldn't have been more obvious that Alcock never had his heart in what he was doing, and knew further that there was nothing of any substance to cross-examine Shaw about. (For the record, Shaw denied on direct examination knowing or ever having met Oswald, Ferrie, or Perry Russo, ever having conspired with them or anyone else to murder President Kennedy, and ever having worked for the CIA.)[133]*

the type that will require a long-term psychotherapeutic approach, which is not feasible in a military hospital." (*New York Times*, December 30, 1967, p.28; Flammonde, *Kennedy Conspiracy*, pp.11–12; Rogers, "Persecution of Clay Shaw," p.54; Lambert, *False Witness*, pp.13–14)

The story of Garrison's psychiatric history first broke in a December 29, 1967, copyrighted article in the *Chicago Tribune*. Garrison fired back that same day through his chief assistant, Charles Ward, who said that army doctors had diagnosed his boss as having an "anxiety reaction during the Korean War. They subsequently concluded that if it was there, it's gone now. The Army would not allow a man who had a psychiatric illness to hold the rank of lieutenant colonel in the Army Reserve" (*New York Times*, December 30, 1967, p.28).

*Garrison's constant charge was that the CIA (or rogue elements thereof) was behind the assassination. Yet, with Shaw on the witness stand and the golden opportunity to cross-examine him, Alcock never asked Shaw one single question dealing with his alleged association with the CIA or any other federal agency of U.S. intelligence.

If Alcock's cross-examination of Shaw, by itself, didn't clearly demonstrate that Garrison knew Shaw had nothing to do with the assassination, and that he had committed the unpardonable sin of charging an innocent man with conspiracy to commit murder just to give him the opportunity to present evidence challenging the findings of the Warren Commission, then Garrison's final summation to the jury on February 28, 1969, would seem to eliminate all doubt. Instead of referring to Shaw (or "the defendant") a great number of times as he tried to connect him to the conspiracy and murder, as any prosecutor would do if he believed the person he was prosecuting was guilty, unbelievably Garrison only referred to Shaw *once* in his entire summation, and then not to say that the evidence showed he was guilty. *Not once* did Garrison tell the jury he had proved Shaw's guilt or that the evidence pointed toward Shaw's guilt. (Alcock, in his summation, did.)* What he told the jury was, "You are here sitting in judgment of Clay Shaw,"[134] an absolutely valueless statement since the jury, obviously, already knew why they were there.

Is there any further evidence? Yes.

As indicated earlier, the indictment only charged Shaw, Ferrie, and Oswald with *conspiracy* to murder Kennedy, not with murdering him. Garrison was thereby sending an important signal. Since under the law of conspiracy Shaw would be responsible for (and hence, guilty of) all crimes committed by his co-conspirators in furtherance of the object of the conspiracy, a charge of conspiracy to commit murder is virtually always accompanied by a separate charge of the murder itself. If Garrison was sincerely convinced Shaw had conspired to murder Kennedy, why not do what 99.9 percent of all DAs would have done—also charge him with Kennedy's murder? I don't know the answer to that question, but the only thing that makes any sense to me is that he knew Shaw was innocent or had very serious doubts about his guilt. If Shaw had been convicted of murder, Garrison knew that under Louisiana law, the punishment *had* to be either life imprisonment or the death penalty. But *conspiracy* to commit murder was only punishable in Louisiana by imprisonment "at hard labor for not less than one nor more than 20 years."[135] So perhaps Garrison, knowing he was up to no good, only wanted to use Shaw up to a certain point. He didn't want to have Shaw's death or life imprisonment on his conscience for the rest of his life.†

In his first book on the assassination, *Heritage of Stone*, published one year after Clay Shaw's 1969 trial, Garrison, incredibly, never talks about Clay Shaw once in the entire 224 pages. (He does in his book *On the Trail of the Assassins* in 1988, nineteen years later.) Nor Perry Russo. In fact, Clay Shaw's name only appears three times in the book, in three separate footnotes at the back, and then only when the source for the testimony of two witnesses at Shaw's trial is listed as "*State of Louisiana v. Clay Shaw*." Since the cover of *Heritage of Stone* says that the book is Garrison's "own version of the conspiracy behind the assassination of JFK," why wasn't Shaw, the only man Garrison prosecuted for conspiracy to murder Kennedy, mentioned?[136]‡

---

*Garrison, the man who conducted one of the most fraudulent prosecutions in the annals of crime, *did* tell the jury, however, that "the government's handling of the investigation of John Kennedy's murder was a fraud. It was the greatest fraud in the history of our country. It probably was the greatest fraud ever perpetrated in the history of humankind."

†One additional benefit to Garrison of only charging Shaw with conspiracy is that under Louisiana law, instead of the normal requirement that all twelve jurors must concur in order to convict, when conspiracy alone is alleged, only nine out of twelve jurors must concur to render a guilty verdict (*La. Stat. Ann.*, Code of Criminal Procedure, Art. 782). So Garrison only needed nine jurors to convict Shaw. He couldn't even get one.

‡Since we know Garrison's conduct was inexcusable and he brought severe discredit to the prosecutorial profession, what does that say about his assistants who did not leave the office—as some of their colleagues

So we see, from all of Garrison's conduct showing what his motivations probably were for prosecuting Shaw, that Oliver Stone's movie, at its very core, was one huge lie. Stone himself seems to have sensed what Garrison was up to, and embraced it. Though he tried, in every way he could, to convince the millions who saw his movie that Clay Shaw was an integral part of a conspiracy to kill Kennedy, he told the New Orleans *Times-Picayune* in 1961, "I have to tell you that I'm not that concerned about whether Shaw was innocent or guilty [say what?] . . . This movie is . . . about a much larger international story."[137] Stone became even bolder several months later when he told *Esquire* magazine, "Garrison was trying to force a break in the case. If he could do that, it was worth the sacrifice of one man [Shaw]. When they went onto the shores of Omaha Beach, they said, 'We're going to lose five, ten, fifteen thousand people to reach our objective.' I think Jim [Garrison, whose strengths and faults, Stone said, made him "like King Lear"] was in that kind of situation."[138]

2. Near the beginning of Oliver Stone's film, a woman named Rose Cherami is shown being thrown out of a moving car on a country road, then pleading with her attendants on her hospital bed, "They're going to kill Kennedy. Please call somebody."

To conspiracy theorists, Melba Christine Marcades, aka (along with fourteen other aliases) Rose Cherami,[*] has been, for years, almost as much a part of the lore and mythology of the assassination as the grassy knoll itself. And most conspiracy theorists have not questioned Cherami's story and have accepted what Stone depicted on the screen. But what Stone depicted was not quite what happened. The man most familiar with Cherami's story, the late Francis Fruge, was a Louisiana State Police officer when

---

did, out of disgust—but instead soldiered on to do Garrison's bidding for him? It would seem they were either remarkably simple-minded, or equally complicit with Garrison, or too weak of character to stand up to him. On October 11, 2000, I wrote the following letter to two of Garrison's principal assistants and spear-carriers against Shaw—lead trial prosecutor James Alcock, now a lawyer in private practice in Houma, Louisiana, and Andrew Sciambra, the assistant of Garrison's who was most responsible for the testimony of Garrison's principal witness against Shaw, Perry Russo. Sciambra is presently a magistrate judge of the Criminal District Court in New Orleans:

Dear Mr. Alcock (Mr. Sciambra),

I am a lawyer and author from Los Angeles who is presently in the process of writing a book about the assassination of President John F. Kennedy. Although the focus of my book will not be the Garrison investigation and prosecution of Clay Shaw, I will be writing a certain amount about it. As a former prosecutor, I can tell you in all candor that I'm finding it very difficult to come up with anything good to say about the handling of the case by the New Orleans DA's office. Since you were an integral part of that investigation and prosecution, I'd like to interview you about your involvement in the case. It seems to me that if there was any legal or moral justification for the conduct of your office in this case, you would be one of the few people who would be in possession of this information, and I would be very interested, of course, in hearing it, and incorporating your account into my book.

If you are inclined to grant me an interview, please write me at [my address] and I will then work with your secretary in setting up a time that will be convenient for you.

Sincerely,
Vincent Bugliosi

If you know that Garrison's and your investigation and prosecution of Clay Shaw are going to be critically examined in a major book, and if you know there is a good defense for your conduct, I would think you'd make sure that your defense would be presented in the book. But neither Mr. Alcock nor Mr. Sciambra responded to my letters.

[*]Although the New Orleans DA's office, and later, the HSCA, spelled her name "Cheramie," it's clear from her FBI rap sheet that when using this alias at the time of her many arrests, she invariably spelled her name without the "e" at the end (FBI Record 2 347 922).

around 10:00 p.m. on the evening of November 20, 1963 (two days before the assassination), he was called to the emergency ward of the Moosa Memorial Hospital in Eunice, Louisiana, by Mrs. Louise Guillary, the administrator of the hospital. Cherami, age thirty-nine, was under the influence of drugs and had been brought to the hospital by Frank Odom, a longtime resident of the area whom Fruge knew. Cherami had been hitchhiking when she was struck by Odom's car. It happened on Highway 190, a strip of road "extending from Opelousas, birthplace of Jim Bowie, to the Texas border where a gas station more than likely doubled as a brothel."[139] She had sustained no fractures or lacerations, only bruises and abrasions. Fruge said Cherami was "very incoherent," and after he locked her up at the Eunice jail for safekeeping until she sobered up, he returned to the Eunice Police Department's annual ball, which he had been attending.

About an hour later, he was summoned to the jail cell. Cherami "had taken all of her clothes off" and was "what we would call 'climbing the walls,' scratching herself, and I recognized it right away as withdrawals . . . from drugs," Fruge told the HSCA. Fruge had a doctor come to the jail, "and he gave her a shot to sedate her." The doctor, F. J. De Rouen, advised Fruge to bring her to a hospital. Fruge told the HSCA that during the two-hour ambulance drive to the East Louisiana State Hospital in Jackson, during which Cherami was in a straightjacket, Cherami related to Fruge that "she was coming from Florida to Dallas with two men who she said were Italians, or resembled Italians. They had stopped at this lounge [a house of prostitution called the Silver Slipper] . . . and they'd had a few drinks and had gotten into an argument or . . . something. The manager of the lounge threw her out, and she got out on the road and hitchhiked . . . and this is when she got hit by a vehicle . . . [So Cherami herself confirmed Odom's story that she was struck by a passing car, not thrown out of any car as Stone showed his audience.] I asked her what she was going to do in Dallas. She said *she* was going to pick up some money, pick up her baby, and kill Kennedy."[140] Fruge's deposition to the HSCA was on April 18, 1978. In an interview with an HSCA investigator eleven days earlier, on April 7, 1978, Fruge quoted Cherami as telling him, "*We're* [referring to herself and the men she was with] going to kill President Kennedy when he comes to Dallas in a few days."[141]

Fruge said that he checked Cherami into the hospital at three in the morning on November 21 (Thursday). A 1978 HSCA report of a staff interview of Dr. Victor Weiss said that Weiss "verified that he was employed as a resident physician at the hospital in 1963. He recalled that on Monday, November 25, 1963, he was asked by another physician, Dr. [Don] Bowers, to see a patient who had been committed November 20th or 21st. Dr. Bowers allegedly told Weiss [there's no reference to the HSCA having interviewed Bowers] that the patient, Rose Cherami, had stated before the assassination that President Kennedy was going to be killed. Weiss questioned Cherami about her statements . . . She did not have any specific details of a particular assassination plot against Kennedy, but had stated that the 'word in the underworld' was that Kennedy would be assassinated. She further stated that she had been traveling from Florida to her home in Texas when the man traveling with her threw her from the automobile in which they were riding."[142]

Note that as opposed to what Cherami told Fruge, in her new and evolving story neither she, nor she and the two men she was with, were going to kill Kennedy, but some other unidentified person or persons (the "word in the underworld") were going to do so. Also, contrary to what she told Fruge, which was verified by Frank Odom (who struck the hitchhiking Cherami and brought her to the hospital), Weiss said that Cherami told him she was thrown out of the car by the man she was traveling with.

When Fruge went back to the hospital on Monday, November 25, three days after Kennedy was murdered, Cherami now told Fruge that the two men she was with, not her, were going to Dallas to kill Kennedy. After the killing, she said, the three of them were going to go to a house in Dallas, where she was going to pick up her baby and around eight thousand dollars. From there they were going to drive to Houston, where a seaman was scheduled to arrive on a boat in nearby Galveston with eight kilos of heroin.*

So if we're to believe Cherami's last story, the conspirators who plotted to kill Kennedy apparently employed two friends of Cherami's to do the job, let her be a part of it, even though she was a disoriented drug addict, and then, after killing Kennedy, instead of trying to escape, they had more important things to do, such as pick up her baby and then drive to Houston to meet the heroin smuggler.

Fruge testified that the next day, Tuesday, November 26, on the chance that Cherami might be telling the truth about the heroin pickup, he and several other members of law enforcement flew to Houston with Cherami. On the plane there was a newspaper with the caption of an article to the effect that the authorities in Dallas had not been able to establish any relationship between Jack Ruby and Lee Harvey Oswald. Fruge said that when Cherami saw this, she started laughing and said, "Them two queer son-of-a-bitches. They've been shacking up for years." Cherami said she knew this because she used to work as a stripper for Ruby at a club of his in Dallas called The Pink Door. (There is no record of Ruby ever operating a strip club in Dallas called "The Pink Door." In fact, it is the consensus of researchers that Ruby's Carousel Club was the first strip club he had ever operated.) Fruge said that the Houston drug pickup never went down because the seaman never showed up. He said that "the Customs Agent [with whom they were working on the possible heroin pickup] put Cherami back on the street and we came back to Louisiana."[143]

The HSCA chased some of the flimsiest conspiracy allegations to the ends of the earth during its investigation of the assassination, but it did not do this with Cherami's allegation, not even bothering, apparently, to interview Dr. Bowers or anyone at the house of prostitution from which Cherami said she was ejected before she went hitchhiking and was struck on the highway. And the reason for the inattention was equally clear. Cherami was a heroin addict who was frequently disoriented. Also, the HSCA learned she had "previously furnished the FBI false information concerning her involvement in prostitution and narcotics matters and that she had been confined to a mental institution in Norman, Oklahoma, on three occasions."[144] In addition, an FBI rap sheet on her covering the period from February 13, 1941, through October 21, 1964, lists fifty-one arrests ranging from public drunkenness, vagrancy, prostitution, and driving under the influence of narcotics, to larceny, driving a stolen auto across state lines, and arson.[145] Lastly, not only was her story completely improbable, but she kept changing it every time she told it.

---

*In uncharacteristically sloppy scholarship, the HSCA wrote that Cherami reportedly told the police that she and the two men she was with were "transporting a quantity of heroin from Florida to Houston at [Jack] Ruby's insistence" (10 HSCA 199). But there is no record of her having ever said this, and the HSCA listed, as its only source for this, an article in the March 1977 edition of *Argosy* magazine. The article's author, without citing any source for his statement, wrote that "Rose Cherami and a companion were driving back from Florida with a shipment of dope that was bound for . . . Jack Ruby." (Martindale, "Bizarre Deaths following JFK's Murder," p.52) Author Gerald Posner took the erroneous HSCA statement and made it worse by writing that Cherami had said "that she had been thrown out of the car *by* Ruby" (Posner, *Case Closed*, p.446).

But Oliver Stone, naturally, did not give his audience any of this background on Cherami. He showed her being thrown out of a car when we know she was not; he never mentioned the many inconsistent stories she told; and to make her story more credible, he changed her words from "I" and "we're" to "they're" going to kill the president, and did not mention her wild allegation that Ruby and Oswald were sexual partners. All the movie audience saw was a woman being thrown out of a car and pleading with hospital attendants to "call somebody" to save the president's life.

Later in the film, Stone compounds his gross misrepresentation of the facts about Cherami when he conveys to his audience that Cherami was thereafter killed as a result of a "hit and run," the clear implication being that she was silenced. Indeed, virtually all the conspiracy books that mention Cherami use the same words.[146] But after interviewing, on April 4, 1967, the officer who investigated Cherami's death, Officer J. A. Andrews of the Texas Highway Patrol, Fruge wrote, "Officer Andrews stated that subject died of injuries received from an automobile accident on Highway No. 155, 1.7 miles east of Big Sandy, Upshur County, Texas, at 3:00 a.m., on September 4, 1965. Subject died at the hospital in Gladewater, Gregg County, Texas. The inquest was held by Justice of the Peace Ross Delay, Precinct No. 3, Gregg County, Texas. The accident was reported to Officer Andrews by the operator of the car [Jerry Don Moore], after he had taken the subject to the hospital. Andrews stated that the operator related that the victim was apparently lying on the roadway with her head and upper part of her body resting on the traffic lane, and although he had attempted to avoid running over her, he ran over the top part of her skull, causing fatal injuries. An investigation of the physical evidence at the scene of the accident was unable to contradict this statement."[147] Not your usual hit and run.*

3. Unbelievably, Stone depicts Oswald throughout the movie as a right winger posing as a Marxist. (In a scene from the movie, Garrison even tells his staff that "when Oswald went to Russia, he was not a real defector. He was an intelligence agent on some type of mission for our government, and remained one till the day he died.") But we know from all the evidence that if anyone was ever a committed Marxist—starting from when he began reading *Das Kapital* in his early teens—it was Oswald. Stone got this perversion of the truth directly from Garrison. To make his theory that the CIA (certainly, if anything, right wing, not left wing) was behind the assassination more believable, Garrison told his readers in *On the Trail of the Assassins* that Oswald was a right-wing agent provocateur for U.S. intelligence, not a Marxist. To get his readers to swallow this absurdity, he did what he did best—lie. For instance, he tells his readers that "only one man who had been at the [El Toro] Marine Base with [Oswald] testified [before the Warren Commission] that Oswald had exhibited Marxist leanings, . . . Kerry Thornley . . . This made me wonder if any member of the Warren Commission had actually read the other Marines' affidavits, which overwhelmingly contradicted Thornley's claims." Speaking of one marine, Nelson Delgado (who testified for the defense at the London trial), Garrison writes, "I headed straight for his testimony [before the Warren Commission]. I found that Delgado, who bunked next door to Oswald for the better part of eleven months, had *no recollection whatever* of Oswald's

---

*Officer Andrews closed the case as an "accidental death," though he felt it was curious that Cherami, if she was hitchhiking, would be on Highway 155 as opposed to "one of the U.S. Highways." But Andrews, probably not familiar with Cherami's background of narcotic stupors, would not have known that the disoriented Cherami may not have even known where she was.

Marxist leanings."[148] Any reader not having volume 8 of the Warren Commission volumes, and not knowing what a mountebank Garrison was, would have no reason to disbelieve him. The reality is that Delgado's testimony is peppered with references to Oswald's Marxist leanings. For example: "He [Oswald] was for, not the Communist way of life, [but] the Castro way of life." "He had one book . . . *Das Kapital.*" "Call [Richard Call, a fellow marine] used to call Oswald 'Oswaldovich' . . . We would call him 'Comrade.'"[149]

Additional marines, other than Delgado and Thornley, who give the lie to Garrison's statement that Thornley was the only marine who told the Warren Commission that Oswald exhibited Marxist leanings: James Botelho: "Oswald referred . . . to 'American capitalist warmongers' . . . My impression is that although he believed in pure Marxist theory, he did not believe in the way Communism was practiced by the Russians."[150] Donald Camarata: "I personally observed that Oswald had his name written in Russian on one of his jackets, and played records of Russian songs."[151] Paul Murphy: "While at Santa Ana [El Toro Marine Base], Oswald had a subscription to a newspaper printed in English which I believe was titled either 'The Worker' or 'The Socialist Worker.' . . . I am of the opinion that he was generally in sympathy with Castro."[152] Richard Call: "Many members of the unit kidded him about being a Russian spy."[153] Erwin Donald Lewis: "I know from personal observation that he read the 'Daily Worker.'"[154]*

Yet Garrison led his readers to believe that none of these statements existed, and Stone led his audience to believe that Oswald was a member of the right wing.

4. The reader of this book already knows the enormous amount of evidence that points irresistibly to Oswald's guilt. Everything he said, everything he did, all the physical and scientific evidence, points to him as the murderer of Kennedy. Unbelievably, *other than alluding to Oswald's connection to the murder weapon, Stone's sense of history and honesty were such that he never mentioned even one piece of this evidence to his audience.* (Evidence like Oswald carrying a large brown bag into the Book Depository Building on the morning of the assassination, his fingerprints and palm print being found at the sniper's nest, his being the only employee of the building to flee the building after the shooting, the provable lies he told during his interrogation, etc.—Stone presented none of this to his audience.) And even with this one exception of the murder weapon, Stone proceeded to make one misrepresentation after another not only to completely negate Oswald's connection to it, but to support Stone's own contention of a frame-up. Early in the film, the audience is told that the murder weapon was a Mannlicher-Carcano rifle that records showed had been mailed to Oswald's alias, A. Hidell. Garrison's assistant is shown asking Garrison why someone like Oswald would order a rifle through the mail that could be traced back to him when he could have bought it in Dallas and used a phony name. Garrison suggests, without any evidence to support him, that Oswald didn't order the weapon, that the order was made by others "to frame him, obviously."

---

*Not only was Oswald a committed Marxist to the day he died ("I'm a Marxist," he told Captain Fritz on the morning he was killed by Ruby [Kelley Exhibit A, 20 H 443; CE 2064, 24 H 490]), but even though he was disillusioned with Russia, not believing the Russians were truly following the Marxist dream and blueprint, he remained much closer to Russia than to the United States. Ruth Paine told me, "He did not encourage Marina to learn English," but because "she wanted to, she tried to read the labels on cans or read grocery ads where there were pictures to help her. He spoke to her only in Russian, and wouldn't help her with English." Indeed, she said, "If I started to talk to him in English he'd answer in Russian." (July 13, 1986, typewritten response to author by Paine to questions 18 and 19(a), among 123 questions submitted by author to her)

But Stone was just getting started. With respect to the background photograph Marina took of Oswald holding the Carcano, Stone shows Oswald telling the Dallas police it was a fake photograph, that his head had been superimposed on someone else's body. He then shows Garrison's assistant telling Garrison that two photographic experts had confirmed it was a fake photo, Oswald's head being "pasted," she tells Garrison, on someone else's body. The audience isn't told that a panel of photographic experts for the House Select Committee on Assassinations confirmed that the photograph was genuine and that "it could find no evidence of fakery,"[155] nor are they told that Marina herself acknowledged that she took the photograph, nor that a copy of the photograph was determined by handwriting experts to have Oswald's handwritten inscription on the back of it, "To my dear friend George [de Mohrenschildt], from Lee." It was dated April 1963 and signed "Lee Harvey Oswald."[156] So apparently the framers of Oswald made the fake photo of him holding the rifle, and when he saw it (those who framed Oswald not only put together the fake photo of Oswald but made sure that he, the person being framed, got a copy of it so he would know what they were up to), he liked it so much that he decided to join in the frame-up of himself by writing an inscription on the back of it.

So Stone, with one falsehood after another, eliminated the Carcano rifle as a piece of evidence that incriminated Oswald.[*] The bottom line is that although it would be hard to find any criminal defendant, anywhere, against whom there was as much evidence of guilt as there was against Oswald, Stone never presented *any* of this evidence to his audience. Because nothing else demonstrates so clearly what a prodigious lie Stone's film was, it bears repeating in italics: *Oliver Stone, in his movie* JFK, *never saw fit to present for his audience's consideration one single piece of evidence that Oswald killed Kennedy*! So a murder case (the Kennedy assassination) where there is an almost unprecedented amount of evidence of guilt against the killer (Oswald) is presented to millions of moviegoers as one where there wasn't one piece of evidence at all. There oughta be a law against things like this.

As if the above is not outrageous enough, the preternaturally audacious Stone wrote in the January 1992 edition of *Premiere* magazine that he used his movie "as a forum for presenting *all* the evidence in the JFK case across the board."[157]

5. In a similar vein to the above, several scenes in Stone's film show Dealey Plaza witnesses telling Garrison and his staff that the shots came from behind the picket fence on the grassy knoll. Not one witness is shown telling Garrison and his staff that the shots came from the Book Depository Building, where Oswald was. Stone's unenlightened audience could only assume from this that no witnesses to the assassination thought the shots came from the Book Depository Building, when in fact many witnesses did. Once again, Stone was changing reality for his unsuspecting audience.

6. With respect to the murder of Dallas police officer J. D. Tippit, *JFK*'s audience is told that "one witness constituted the totality of the witness testimony identifying Lee Oswald" as Tippit's killer.

Stone has one scene where Oswald is shooting Tippit, and another where someone else is shown murdering him.[†] This, of course, is a monstrous deception. The reality is

---

[*]As far as Oswald's palm print being found on the rifle, Stone shows a federal agent (presumably FBI) putting Oswald's palm print on the rifle when Oswald's body was at the morgue (see long endnote discussion).

[†]However, as Stone's Garrison tells the audience, even if it was Oswald who killed Tippit, it was only because he realized he was being set up as a patsy. And therefore, in the audience's mind, the killing was more in the nature of self-defense, and hence would not connect him to the assassination of Kennedy.

that a total of ten witnesses either saw Oswald kill Tippit or saw him with a gun at the Tippit murder scene or saw him running away—armed with a gun—from the vicinity of the murder scene.[158] Naturally, Stone never told his audience that four cartridge cases found near the Tippit murder scene were conclusively determined to have been fired in Oswald's .38 caliber Smith & Wesson revolver.

7. In the movie, the actor portraying Lee Bowers is shown testifying before the Warren Commission that at the time of the shooting in Dealey Plaza he saw a "flash of light and smoke" coming from behind the area of the picket fence. The audience is not told that in two statements made to the authorities on the day of the assassination, and in his Warren Commission testimony, Bowers said no such thing. Bowers, as we saw earlier in the text, made these claims for the first time more than two years later when he fell into the nimble hands of Mark Lane.

8. Julia Mercer, one of the zanies who emerged to tell their crazy stories about the assassination, is presented in the film as a perfectly believable witness who saw Jack Ruby behind the driver's seat of the truck parked on Elm before the assassination—the truck was holding up traffic—and saw another occupant of the truck take a rifle from the truck up the grassy knoll. (To clean up Mercer for his audience so she wouldn't come across as she was, goofy, Stone didn't have the actress portraying Mercer say, as Mercer did years earlier, that she thought the man with the rifle was Oswald. After all, Oswald was supposed to be inside the Book Depository Building at the time of the assassination, not the gunman behind the picket fence.)

Later in the film, the audience is told that Kennedy was killed by "professional" assassins. But what professional assassins, or any killer for that matter, would draw attention to themselves by parking halfway up on a curb on a street heavy with traffic as Elm was before the assassination? Or would such a "professional," right in front of three police officers— Stone never told his audience about the officers—and witnesses in many passing cars, take the murder rifle off the truck and carry it up to the grassy knoll in plain view of all these people an hour and a half before Kennedy was scheduled to be driving by? Since this is a story that no one, not even a ten-year-old, would believe, why, Oliver, did you put it in your film? Is it because you subscribe to H. L. Mencken's observation that no one has ever gone broke overestimating the unintelligence of the American people, and your audience was a microcosm of the American people? Or is it because you knew that your audience's mind, at that point, would be so anesthetized by the avalanche of conspiracy preachments issuing from the mouths of Costner, Lemmon, Sutherland, and Matthau, all accompanied by seductively sinister and ominous background music, that none of them would see how your *professional* assassin story and Mercer's story were absurdly inconsistent? But even if you insisted on having the loony Mercer tell her story to your audience, shouldn't you have had the decency to also tell them that Dallas police officer Joe Murphy, one of the three officers, identified the stalled truck as belonging to a nearby construction company, that Murphy said there were three construction workers in the truck and none walked up the grassy knoll with a rifle or anything else, and that the truck, with all three men inside, was pushed away by another truck from the construction company?

9. Along with Julia Mercer, the even more pathetic Jean Hill, whom everyone, even her own husband, laughed at, is presented in the film as a totally credible witness. As discussed earlier in this book, she made a statement on the day of the assassination to the Dallas sheriff's office and later gave testimony to the Warren Commission, and in neither instance did she claim to have seen anything of significance, other than thinking she

saw someone who looked like Jack Ruby running from the direction of the Texas School Book Depository Building toward the grassy knoll. Neither did she say that she saw any-one firing a gun from the grassy knoll. *Twenty-six years later* she told the story, for the first time, that she "saw a man fire from behind the wooden fence" and added that she also saw "a puff of smoke."[159] But in the movie, Stone has Hill telling all of these things just *twenty minutes* after the assassination. "I saw a flash of light in the bushes," Hill's character, played by Ellen McElduff, tells the movie audience, "and that shot just ripped his head off. I looked up and I saw smoke coming from over there on the knoll." Stone then shows a scene where Hill is in an office being grilled by an intimidating plainclothes officer, not identified. When she tells him, "I saw a man shooting from over there, behind the fence. Now, what are you going to do about that? You gotta go out there and get him," he responds loudly, hovering over her in a threatening way, "We have that taken care of." He goes on to instruct her, almost angrily, "You only heard three shots [all of which, he had told her, "came from the Book Depository Building"], and you're not to talk about this with anybody. No one. Do you understand me?"

How does Stone get around Hill's not telling the Dallas sheriff's office on the day of the assassination or the Warren Commission about seeing a man shoot Kennedy from behind the picket fence on the grassy knoll and seeing the flash of light and smoke there too? Easy. He *does not tell* the movie audience about the actual statement she made to the sheriff's office. As far as Hill's testimony before the Warren Commission is concerned, Stone has Hill tell his audience, "When I read my testimony as published by the Warren Commission, it was a fabrication from start to finish."

Stone is so bad he makes the Mark Lanes and Robert Grodens of the world look like exemplars of honesty and rectitude.

10. In Stone's movie, U.S. Senator Russell B. Long of Louisiana tells Garrison, while on a plane flight with him, that three experts tried to duplicate what Oswald did, and "not one of them could do it." This, of course, is not true. As we have seen, one of the three not only duplicated what Oswald did, but fired better than Oswald did.

11. In the movie, Garrison's assistant, at the sixth-floor window with Garrison, tells Garrison, "Try to hit a moving target at eighty-eight yards through heavy foliage? No way." But the eighty-eight-yard shot is the fatal shot that hit the president in the head at the time of Zapruder frame 313. And from the window there's absolutely no obstruction, heavy foliage or otherwise, at frame 313. In fact, even as early as frame 210 all obstruction to view is gone.[160]

12. Garrison's assistant adds, "There was a tree there blocking the first two shots." Wrong. The oak tree was not an obstruction at all for the shot at around frame 160 (only becoming an obstruction around frame 166), and the consensus of most experts who have studied the Zapruder film is that the second shot, the first shot that struck the president (in the upper right back), was fired between frames 210 and 225. By those frames, the leaves of the oak tree no longer obscured the view from the sixth-floor window.[161]

13. Garrison's assistant in the movie tells him that Oswald was "at best a medium shot." Senator Russell Long tells Garrison that Oswald was "no good" as a rifleman. Stone, of course, doesn't tell his audience that Oswald qualified as a sharpshooter with a rifle in the Marines.

14. Garrison's assistant also tells Garrison that it "takes a minimum of 2.3 seconds to recycle this thing [the Carcano]," that is, to pull the bolt back to reload, reaim, and fire. Stone does not tell his audience that the HSCA concluded that the 2.3-second minimum

was only if a shooter of the Carcano used the telescopic sight on the rifle. "The committee test-fired a Mannlicher-Carcano rifle using the open iron sights. It found that it was possible for two shots to be fired within 1.66 seconds."[162]

Clearly, judging from all of this so far, one has to be impressed with the superb work of the twelve people who Stone said diligently researched the facts and evidence for his film.

15. The audience in *JFK* is told that there were "three teams" of killers of Kennedy, all "professional riflemen" flown in from out of the country. One team, Garrison says in the movie, was in the Book Depository Building, another in the Dal-Tex Building, and the third team on the grassy knoll. He doesn't make it clear how many members there were for each team but says that there were "ten to twelve men,"* but only "three shooters." In addition, he speaks of "spotters" and men coordinating the shots by radio and by the signal of opening an umbrella. The three shooters, he says, fired six shots in a "triangulation of fire."

As the reader of this book knows, the Warren Commission concluded that the overwhelming evidence was that only three shots were fired in Dealey Plaza. And only three cartridge casings were found in Dealey Plaza. Even Warren Commission critic Josiah Thompson, in a study of 190 persons who were present at the time of the shooting and either testified before the Warren Commission or gave affidavits to the Commission on the number of shots fired, found that of the 172 who said they had an opinion, the overwhelming majority, 136, heard three shots. Do you know how many heard six shots, Oliver? Are you ready? Just one. And that was Jesse Price[163] (see endnote). But even if Price were as sober thinking as a judge, if 136 people in Dealey Plaza that day heard three shots, and only one heard six, whom is it more reasonable to believe? Everyone (except, apparently you, Oliver) would say the 136 people. How did you come up with your six shots, Oliver? What inside information did you have that no one else has?

Then Stone really outdoes himself. As indicated, Stone, in his movie, maintains that the three shooters were "professional riflemen." And we know that these shooters would have been firing at relatively short distances—the two shots that hit Kennedy from the Book Depository Building being around only 59 and 88 yards; any corresponding shots from the grassy knoll being around 57 and 35 yards; and any from the Dal-Tex Building, around 80 to 110 yards. When a soldier "qualifies" with his rifle on the range, the shortest distance is 100 yards, and the distances go up to 500 yards. So, as Garrison tells the jury in the film, with the short distances and the limousine only traveling 11 mph, it was a "turkey shoot" to hit the president. In other words, to use another bird metaphor, the president was a "sitting duck." But Oliver, did you take the time to read your own script? Remember that only the upper part of the president's body was visible in the limousine, and the shooters would obviously be aiming at the president's head, the most vulnerable part of his body. Now listen to what, in your movie, your protagonist, Garrison, tells the Clay Shaw jury about how Kennedy's "professional riflemen" did in their "turkey shoot." "The first shot misses the car completely." Not only didn't the bullet fired by one of the professional hit men hit Kennedy's head, or even his upper body or torso, *it missed the presidential limousine completely*! "The second shot hits Kennedy in the throat" (still miss-

---

*I have no idea why sophisticated conspirators like the CIA, military-industrial complex, et cetera, would want so many killers and accomplices (ten to twelve) at the assassination scene, which would mean that not just one, but all ten or twelve would have to escape, thereby immeasurably increasing the likelihood of detection and apprehension.

ing the target head). "The third shot hits Kennedy in the back" (again, missing the target head). "The fourth shot misses Kennedy and hits Connally in the back" (again, missing not only the target head, but even Kennedy's upper body). "The fifth shot misses the car completely." What? The professional hit men missed that very big car a *second* time? "The sixth shot," which Garrison says was fired from the grassy knoll, was the "fatal shot" that "hits Kennedy in the head." So Oliver, at a very short distance for any shooter, much less a professional, your "professional riflemen," firing, as you say, at a very easy target to hit, actually *missed the car completely on two out of six of their shots, missed Kennedy's body three out of six times*, and *missed the target (Kennedy's head) five out of six times!* And these, Oliver, were the professional assassins hired, you say, by the military-industrial complex and the CIA to kill Kennedy? Oliver, didn't this make you wonder if all your imaginings were silly beyond belief?[*]

16. Stone shows his audience a sketch drawn by Robert Groden of Kennedy and Connally in the presidential limousine in which Connally is seen seated directly in front of Kennedy. In the movie, Garrison then ridicules the "magic bullet" passing on a straight line through Kennedy's body and then making a right turn in midair and left turn to strike Connally. But Oliver, even though Groden probably lied to you as he lied to his readers, if your twelve researchers had bothered to open up their eyes and look at any of the great number of photos of Kennedy and Connally in the presidential limousine, they would have seen that Connally was seated to Kennedy's left front. And therefore, the "magic bullet" didn't have to do anything magical at all in midair in order to go on and hit Connally. All it had to do, Oliver, is continue traveling on a straight line.

17. Although, as we know, there is absolutely no evidence that the so-called magic or pristine bullet (Commission Exhibit No. 399) that the Warren Commission concluded struck Kennedy and Connally was planted on Connally's stretcher at Parkland Hospital, not to worry. Since conspiracy theorists firmly "believe" this, Stone validates their belief for his audience and removes all doubt by simply having a mysterious figure deposit the bullet on what appears to be Connally's stretcher at the hospital.

18. Louis Witt was standing[†] on the edge of the grass next to the sidewalk on the north side of Elm Street close to the Stemmons Freeway sign at the time of the shooting in Dealey Plaza. As the president rode by, Witt opened his black umbrella and held it up over his head.[164][‡] Even though Witt, the "umbrella man," was located by the HSCA in 1978 and identified as a supervisor for a nearby insurance company who was on a lunch break waiting to heckle the president, Stone does not disclose this to his audience. Instead, Stone depicts the umbrella man as a member of the conspiracy who was never identified and who opens his umbrella as a signal to the assassins for them to start shooting at the president. In a statement to HSCA investigators and in testimony before the HSCA Witt said that he was a "very conservative Republican" who "never liked the Kennedys," and the whole purpose of the umbrella incident was "to heckle the president's motorcade

[*]As we know, the Warren Commission and the HSCA, as well as all the many forensic pathologists who either conducted the autopsy on the president or studied the autopsy photos and X-rays of his wounds, concluded that only two shots hit the president, and both struck him from the rear. Stone, of course, doesn't tell his audience any of this.

[†]The famous photo of Witt sitting on the edge of the grass on the north side of Elm, his feet on the sidewalk and a black man to his right, was taken shortly after the shooting in Dealey Plaza (4 HSCA 432–435, 441).

[‡]Portions of the opened, black umbrella can be seen fairly clearly to the right of the Stemmons Freeway sign in the lower left part of Zapruder frames 223–228.

. . . I just knew it [umbrella] was a sore spot with the Kennedys." Witt explained that when JFK's father was the ambassador to England, he and the prime minister (Neville Chamberlain, whose position at Munich Joe Kennedy had supported) were accused of appeasing Hitler, and the umbrella the prime minister brought back to England from Germany came to be a symbol, in Britain, of that appeasement. Witt had heard that people in Tucson or Phoenix had brandished umbrellas when "some members of the Kennedy family came through."[165]*

19. The movie audience is told that while William S. Walter, an FBI security clerk at the New Orleans field office, was on duty on the evening of November 17, 1963, five days before the assassination, he received a Teletype from FBI headquarters addressed to all special agents in charge of FBI field offices around the country, warning of a possible assassination attempt against President Kennedy during his trip to Dallas, and instructing them to contact criminal, racial, and hate-group informants in order to determine whether there was any basis for the threat. But, Garrison tells his staff in the film, Walter said that "nothing was done." The audience isn't told that Walter never came forward with his story about a Teletype until five years after the assassination, or that the FBI instituted an investigation at each of its fifty-nine field offices, which yielded no evidence indicating the existence of such a Teletype. Nor is the audience told that none of the more than fifty FBI employees of the New Orleans FBI field office stated they had any knowledge of the Teletype. Nor are they told that when Walter came up with an alleged replica of the Teletype, the FBI determined it was fraudulent because it varied in format and wording from the standard Teletype used at the time. The audience also was not told that the HSCA asked Walter in a March 23, 1978, deposition if he knew of anyone who could substantiate his allegation, and he mentioned his former wife, Sharon Covert, who worked at the New Orleans office with him at the time, but when the HSCA contacted her she said that Walter had never mentioned any such allegation to her. The HSCA concluded "that Walter's allegations were unfounded."[166] Unfounded to the FBI and HSCA, but certainly not to Oliver Stone or, for that matter, to the millions in his audience, who only heard Walter's obviously fabricated and unchallenged story.

20. Students of Jim Garrison's prosecution of Clay Shaw know that one of the key elements of Garrison's case against Shaw, which was emphasized in Stone's film, was Garrison's allegation that Shaw's homosexual alias around New Orleans was Clay Bertrand,† the name Shaw used when he allegedly conspired with Oswald and David Ferrie to assas-

---

*We *can* thank Oliver Stone for some small favors. At least he didn't put on screen the accusation by conspiracy theorist Robert B. Cutler in his 1975 self-published book, *The Umbrella Man*, that Witt's umbrella actually had a sophisticated, battery-powered, rocket-launcher attachment that fired a fléchette (a small, steel dart) containing a paralyzing chemical into the president's throat at Zapruder frame 183 (in a 1976 copyrighted diagram, Cutler changed the frame to 188) to neutralize him so that his head would be a stationary target during the shooting sequence by multiple assassins almost immediately thereafter. (4 HSCA 437; Benson, *Who's Who in the JFK Assassination*, p.97) This is too much even for conspiracy author David Wrone, who writes, "How does one aim a miniature fléchette hidden in an umbrella and at right angles to the target without a sight?" (Wrone, *Zapruder Film*, p.100)

†Quite apart from the fact that there was no credible evidence that Shaw used the alias Clay Bertrand, as Shaw would later say, "For about 17 or 18 years I had been managing director of the International Trade Mart here [in New Orleans], and in that capacity I was in the public eye a great deal. I was on television quite often and my picture had been in the local papers. I attended many civic affairs, luncheons, meetings. In addition, I'm a highly recognizable fellow. I'm rather outsized—6 ft., 4 inches tall—and I have a shock of prematurely grey hair that is almost white. In a town of this size, where I had made perhaps 500 speeches and knew literally thousands of people, the idea that I would go around here trying to use an alias is utterly fantastic." ("Clay Shaw," p.31)

sinate Kennedy, and the name he used when he allegedly contacted New Orleans attorney Dean Andrews the day after the assassination to ask Andrews, who was in a hospital bed with pneumonia at the time, to represent Oswald. Garrison tried desperately to prove, during his investigation of Shaw and at Shaw's trial, that Shaw, indeed, was Bertrand, but he failed miserably, not presenting one witness other than the completely discredited Perry Russo to testify that Shaw was Bertrand.

Dean Andrews was a very colorful, rotund, New Orleans attorney with a penchant for dark glasses and jive talk whom everyone liked and no one took too seriously. Andrews's testimony before the Warren Commission was what started the entire speculation that Clay Shaw was Clay Bertrand. Andrews told the Warren Commission he represented Oswald in the summer of 1963 in Oswald's effort to get rid of his "dishonorable discharge" from the Marines, adding that Oswald discussed with him his status as a citizen (since he had renounced his citizenship in Russia), as well as his wife's status in America. He said Oswald came into his office "accompanied by some gay kids . . . Mexicanos." Andrews said he assumed that Clay Bertrand had sent Oswald to him since Bertrand regularly called him on behalf of gay kids "either to obtain bond or parole for them," adding that he had done "some legal work" for Bertrand in the past, saying that he was "bisexual, what they call a swinging cat." Andrews, who allowed he had a "pretty vivid imagination," said that he didn't think he'd be able to find Bertrand (even though Bertrand was supposedly a law client of his), that he had last seen him about six weeks earlier in a New Orleans bar (whose name he couldn't recall) where "this rascal [Bertrand] bums out. I was trying to get past him so I could . . . call the Feebees [FBI] . . . but he saw me and spooked and ran."[167]

The first law enforcement agency Andrews called about the Bertrand story was the Secret Service, on November 25, 1963, from his hospital bed. The Secret Service report of its interview of Andrews says the Andrews "seemed to feel that he had been previously contacted by Clay Bertrand with another case, but he could not place him or furnish any information to assist in identifying or locating him."[168] This was considerably different from what he told the Warren Commission eight months later, on July 21, 1964. And later in the day on November 25, he told the FBI agents who interviewed him at the hospital about Bertrand calling him to represent Oswald, but dramatically changed who Bertrand was, saying that Bertrand himself was a young man between the ages of twenty-two and twenty-three, and that the only time he had seen Bertrand was when "Clay Bertrand accompanied Oswald" to his office when Oswald was seeking Andrews's representation. There was no mention of having represented Bertrand in the past or having called him regularly on behalf of gay kids. And, oh yes, Clay Bertrand had blond hair and a crewcut and was around five feet seven inches tall.[169] A week later, Andrews told the FBI that Bertrand was "approximately six feet one inch to six feet two inches tall,"[170] having grown six or seven inches in eight days. But there were more miracles ahead. Andrews told the Warren Commission on July 21, 1964, that Bertrand was five feet eight inches tall,[171] Bertrand somehow managing to shrink five to six inches in only seven months, a not inconsiderable feat.

When the FBI and Secret Service asked Andrews for any records to confirm that Oswald or Bertrand had ever been clients of his, he was unable to locate any pertaining to either of them, later telling the Warren Commission his office had been "rifled," but by whom he did not know.[172]

No one believed Andrews's story—that is, except Jim Garrison, who was absolutely sure that there was a man in the French Quarter using the alias Clay Bertrand. Reportedly, in the fall of 1966 Garrison began to suspect that Bertrand was Shaw because from Andrews's testimony before the Warren Commission, one could infer that Bertrand was a homosexual and, of course, he had the same first name as Shaw—Clay. One of Garrison's assistants, Frank Klein, had noted that Clay Shaw lived in the French Quarter and was gay. With nothing more than this, Garrison was off and running.[173] And Garrison wouldn't even listen to his own staff. In a February 25, 1967, memorandum to Garrison, DA investigator Louis Ivon wrote, "To ascertain the location of one Clay Bertrand, I put out numerous inquiries and made contact with several sources in the French Quarter area . . . I'm almost positive from my contacts that they would have known or heard of a Clay Bertrand. The information I received was negative results. On February 22, 1967, I was approached by 'Bubbie' Pettingill in the Fountainbleau Motor Hotel . . . whom I had earlier contacted about Clay Bertrand. He stated that Dean Andrews admitted to him that Clay Bertrand never existed."

Andrews would later say that he had several meetings about the assassination with Garrison at the old Broussard's restaurant in New Orleans, the first on October 29, 1966. At a second meeting shortly before Christmas, 1966, and at subsequent ones, Andrews says that Garrison put pressure on him to admit that Clay Shaw was Clay Bertrand, but Andrews said he told Garrison he wasn't. However, Garrison continued to persist, and Andrews would later tell a national TV audience, "[Garrison] wanted to shuck me like corn, pluck me like a chicken, stew me like an oyster." Andrews said he "wanted to see if this cat [Garrison] was kosher." Andrews's plan? When Garrison wanted to know the identities of the male companions who accompanied Oswald to his office, Andrews only gave him one, a name he fabricated out of thin air—Manuel Garcia Gonzales. Surely enough, Garrison bit, and charged the fictitious Gonzales with selling narcotics so he could pick him up and interrogate him on what he, Garrison, was really concerned with. As New Orleans attorney Milton Brener writes, "Garrison was to become convinced that Manuel Garcia Gonzales was one of the assassins in Dallas and, apparently, for a time believed that he was the leader of the group and the prime culprit. Writing for *Tempo* magazine, an Italian publication, in April 1967, Garrison stated he would gladly give up Clay Shaw if he could but get hold of the true assassin—Manuel Garcia Gonzales." When a man with the name Manuel Garcia Gonzales was thereafter arrested in Miami on the narcotics charge, Andrews told Garrison that he was the wrong Gonzales, that Garrison had "the right ha-ha but the wrong ho-ho."[174]

In *On the Trail of the Assassins*, Garrison only admits to having one meeting with Andrews about the Kennedy case, a lunch "in early 1967" at Broussard's restaurant, and acknowledged that when he asked Andrews to identify Bertrand, Andrews responded, "I don't know what he looks like and I don't know where's he's at." However, when Garrison, disbelieving Andrews, told Andrews he intended to call him before the grand jury and "if you lie to the grand jury as you have been lying to me, I'm going to charge you with perjury," Andrews allegedly said, "If I answer that question . . . , if I give you that name you keep trying to get, then it's goodbye Dean Andrews. It's bon voyage, Deano. I mean like permanent. I mean like a bullet in my head."[175] One would think that such a statement (which was depicted in Stone's movie) was powerful and important enough—being an implied admission that Shaw was Bertrand and reflecting Andrews's belief that Shaw was connected to the assassination—for Garrison to memorialize in a memorandum to the file—that is, if it was actually made. But Steve Tilley, the chief archivist at the National Archives for the Kennedy assassination, said that no such record of the alleged meeting and conversation at Broussard's appears "among the records of the New Orleans District Attorney or the papers of Jim Garrison" at the archives. In fact, Tilley said, "I was unable to locate any document that pertains to any conversation between Garrison and Andrews in a New Orleans restaurant."[176]

Indeed, the only record I could find of any interview of Andrews by the New Orleans DA's office was an April 4, 1967, memorandum from DA investigator William Gurvich to Garrison about a March 2, 1967, interview of Andrews by Gurvich and Assistant DAs James Alcock, Richard Burns, and Andrew Sciambra. Andrews told his interviewers that he had seen photos of Clay Shaw but had never met him, and when he was shown several photographs of various persons, including Clay Shaw, he could not identify any of them as being Clay Bertrand. He told his interviewers that Bertrand, like Shaw, had "grey hair" (in Andrews's Warren Commission testimony, he said Bertrand's hair was "sandy") and he thought he "was bisexual" (Shaw was homosexual).[177]

Andrews told the Shaw grand jury on March 16, 1967, that "you all want me to identify Clay Shaw as Clay Bertrand . . . and I can't . . . I can't connect the two." But then he said, "I can't say he is and I can't say he ain't."[178] An angry Garrison, not believing Andrews, secured a five-count perjury indictment against Andrews that same day.[179] "Personally, I like Dean," Garrison said. "Everyone does. But I have to show him I mean business."[180] Andrews fought back, filing a $100,000 suit against Garrison for malicious prosecution, alleging that he personally told Garrison "that there was no connection between Clay Shaw and Clay Bertrand."[181]

On June 28, Andrews testified again before the Shaw grand jury, this time saying that "I have never seen this man, Shaw, never talked to him. If this case is based on the fact that Clay Shaw is Clay Bertrand, it's a joke . . . Clay Shaw is not Clay Bertrand." Still hanging by a thread to part of his obvious fabrication, however, he added that Bertrand was really a friend of his named Eugene Davis, the owner of Wanda's Seven Seas bar in the French Quarter, and it was really Davis who called him at the hospital to represent Oswald. How could Davis be Bertrand? The hipster lawyer said a woman "back in the '50s at a fag reception . . . introduced me to Davis as Clay Bertrand."[182] On July 17, that thread finally broke and the pathetic Andrews called a press conference and not only confessed again that "Clay Shaw ain't Clay Bertrand," but finally admitted that Clay Bertrand "never existed," saying he made the whole story up to get attention for himself. The next day, July 18, Garrison proceeded to file an additional perjury charge against Andrews for lying to the Shaw grand jury on June 28 that Bertrand was Eugene Davis.[183]

Not even someone of Garrison's rascality and deceit could find a way to use Andrews to his benefit at Shaw's trial. Andrews testified for the defense that Clay Shaw was not Clay Bertrand, that he had never met or known Clay Shaw, and that the first time he had ever seen Shaw was "when I saw his picture in the paper in connection with the investigation" four years after Kennedy's murder.

What about Andrews's testimony before the Warren Commission that someone whose voice he recognized as Clay Bertrand's called him on November 22 or 23, 1963 ("Friday or Saturday" he said), in a New Orleans hospital and asked him to defend Lee Harvey Oswald in Dallas? Andrews told the Shaw jury that he "never received a phone call from Clay Bertrand" when he was at the hospital. Indeed, he added, "No one called me to say that." Of course, the very notion that Bertrand, whom the conspiracy theorists believe to be Clay Shaw, and whom they further believe conspired with Oswald to kill Kennedy, would hire a joke like Andrews to defend Oswald is crazy. If Bertrand were Shaw, and

Shaw and Oswald conspired to kill Kennedy, obviously Shaw could be expected to do anything, including selling all or most of his holdings, to pay for the best possible legal representation for Oswald.

So who, if anyone, did call him at the hospital, and for what? Andrews testified that "the phone call I received was from Gene Davis [a friend] involving two people who were going to sell an automobile and they wanted the title and a bill of sale notarized." Andrews said he was "under sedation" and "under the influence of opiates" and "using oxygen" at the hospital, and "elected [to take] a course that I have never been able to get away from." He said, "I don't know whether I suggested [to Davis after the discussion about the automobile sale], 'Man, I would be famous if I could go to Dallas and defend Lee Harvey Oswald, or whoever gets that job is going to be a famous lawyer.'" He said he never told the FBI or Warren Commission about Gene Davis because he did not want "to implicate an innocent man," so he said, "I used the name Clay Bertrand as a cover to mentioning Gene Davis." He had only heard the name Clay Bertrand once before in his life at the "fag wedding reception" thirteen years earlier when he claimed that Gene Davis, whom he already knew, was introduced to him as Clay Bertrand by a woman named Big Jo. But later in his testimony he acknowledged that "Clay Bertrand is a figment of my imagination."[184]*

When Garrison's own chief trial prosecutor, James Alcock, asked Andrews on cross-examination if he remembered telling Warren Commission counsel Wesley Liebeler that he saw Clay Bertrand six weeks prior to his testimony before the Commission, Andrews responded that was just "huffing and puffing."

"Huffing and puffing under oath?"

"Bull session."

"Do you recall making that statement under oath?"

"I assume I must have made it."

"That wasn't correct, was it?"

"No."

What about Andrews telling the Warren Commission that he called a fellow lawyer, Sam "Monk" Zelden, from his hospital bed on November 24 and asked Zelden if he wanted to go to Dallas with him to defend Oswald? "No explanation," Andrews told the Shaw jury. "Don't forget I am in the hospital sick. I might have believed it myself or thought after a while [that I had been] retained there, so I called Monk. I would like to be famous, too."

Throughout Andrews's testimony, the hip-talking lawyer had the courtroom erupting

---

*At the Shaw trial, Eugene Davis testified that he had met Andrews at a gay bar in the Quarter around 1956 or 1957, and had known Andrews through the years. He testified he was never introduced to anyone as Clay Bertrand and had never used that name. Further, that he did not call nor have telephone contact with Andrews on the day of the assassination or any of the days immediately following the assassination. (FBI Record 124-10067-10035, FBI report of Eugene Davis's testimony at Clay Shaw trial on February 27, 1969, gathered from the New Orleans *Times-Picayune*, February 28, 1969, p.2) At the grand jury proceedings in the Shaw case, Davis testified that Andrews had represented him on two legal matters, that he, Davis, had never had or used an alias, had never known or met Lee Harvey Oswald, had no idea who Clay Bertrand was, if there was such a person, and had "never, never" attended any gay wedding. Davis said he had two sons and a daughter with a wife who had "run off with somebody else." At the end of his testimony, lamenting the fact that he had been dragged into the case with all the unfavorable publicity in the media, Davis said, "Whoever is using me as a black sheep, or whatever the thing is here, I sure would appreciate it, Mr. Garrison, if you would get to the bottom of this." (Transcript of testimony of Eugene Davis before Orleans Parish grand jury, June 28, 1967, pp.1, 4–6, 9, 14, 19–20, 24–25)

in laughter to the point of the bailiff saying, "Order, please." A few examples: "Do you speak Spanish?" the judge asked Andrews. "Poco poco, loco, judge," Andrews dead-panned. Claiming the attorney-client privilege in his alleged representation of Oswald, he said the answer to any question about it "might, may, might, tend, would or could" incriminate him. To his "I would like to be famous, too," answer, he added, "Other than as a perjurer." Andrews said he saw Oswald on TV in his hospital room when "he shot this guy *Ruby*." (Say what?)

And Andrews is, according to many conspiracy theorists, one of the essential keys to solving the mystery of the Kennedy assassination. Andrews is so lacking in credibility that James Alcock acknowledged before the Shaw jury that Andrews's entire story was fraudulent. Responding to Andrews's claim that the reason he lied to the March 16, 1967, grand jury that he had actually met a man named Clay Bertrand on two occasions was that he was "hemmed in with that Warren Commission Report" that the grand jurors "were reading from while they were asking me questions," and "there was no way I could get off the hook," Alcock told Andrews, "Dean, the only one that hemmed you in was yourself when you lied under oath to the Warren Commission."

But Andrews had the last word, and it stung Alcock and Garrison before the Shaw jury. "I told the DA's office," Andrews testified, "that Clay Bertrand wasn't Clay Shaw *before* I went there [grand jury], but nobody believed me."[*] Alcock never even attempted a retort to this.[185]

Oliver Stone, having to know full well that Clay Shaw was not Clay Bertrand, and that Andrews's story was a fabrication, had an easy solution for convincing his audience that Andrews's admission at the Shaw trial that Shaw wasn't Bertrand was untrue. He simply invented a scene, during Shaw's booking for Kennedy's murder, where he has Shaw say something that Shaw never said—that his alias was Clay Bertrand. "Any aliases?" Stone's movie audience hears the booking officer ask Shaw. "Clay Bertrand," Shaw, after a pause, answers resignedly.

21. Garrison, in his book, and Stone, in his movie, depict David Ferrie as a frenzied and erratic Kennedy hater and anti-Communist who worked in New Orleans with a fiercely right-wing former FBI agent named Guy Banister[†] to train anti-Castro Cuban exiles at a camp just north of Lake Pontchartrain near New Orleans. The camp allegedly operated under the aegis of the CIA. It appears that Ferrie may have done some detective work at times for Banister's detective agency. And both Ferrie and Banister were, indeed, actively involved in the anti-Castro movement, though the extent of their involve-

---

[*]Indeed, Andrews told the grand jury that he had told Garrison personally that Shaw was not Bertrand. "I told the Jolly Green Giant [Garrison's nickname] in Brennan's [Broussard's?] restaurant he wasn't that." Question: "You told Garrison that?" Answer: "Right. I told him that Clay Shaw was not Bertrand." (Transcript of testimony of Dean Andrews before the Orleans Parish grand jury, June 28, 1967, p.12)

[†]Banister had been the special agent in charge of the Chicago office of the FBI in the late 1940s and early 1950s. After his retirement from the bureau in 1954 he moved to New Orleans and in the mid-1950s became the assistant superintendent of police with the New Orleans Police Department. In 1957, New Orleans mayor De Lesseps "Chep" Morrison fired Banister after he allegedly threatened a waiter at a New Orleans restaurant with his revolver. Shortly thereafter, he set up his own private detective agency in New Orleans, where he remained until his death from a heart attack in 1964. Although by all accounts he was sympathetic to right-wing causes, and stridently anti-Communist, Jim Garrison's description of him as a "rigid exponent of law and order" probably defined who he was even better. That's why he had index cards in his office not only on 27,000 Communists in the United States but also on members of the Nazi Party and Ku Klux Klan. (Garrison, *On the Trail of the Assassins*, p.2; HSCA Record 180-10072-10214, Interview of Joseph Newbrough Jr. by HSCA on April 10, 1978, p.1; 10 HSCA 126)

ment has never been clearly quantified. However, this is just a diversion from the only matter that counts. There is no credible evidence that Oswald, Ferrie, and Shaw (Garrison's three co-conspirators, whom Stone shows his audience together on the screen plotting Kennedy's murder) ever knew each other. And no one, of course, ever asked Oswald if he knew Shaw or Ferrie, Shaw denied at his trial that he knew or ever met Ferrie or Oswald, and Ferrie denied, till the day he died, knowing Oswald or Shaw.[186]*Granted, the denials would mean nothing if there was any credible evidence to the contrary, but there has never been. A scene in *JFK* showing Ferrie and Shaw cavorting at a homosexual party dressed in wild, transvestite garb is a Stone fabrication. In *False Witness*, Patricia Lambert writes that some pictures did surface nearly two years *before* the trial in a "widely read newsletter [May 12, 1967, issue of *Councilor*, a right-wing Shreveport, Louisiana, paper] . . . published by a Garrison supporter" showing Shaw and a friend named Jeff Biddison, not Ferrie, "dressed in business suits with 'mop-strand' wigs on their heads." In one of the pictures was "a former radio announcer who resembled Ferrie named Robert Brannon . . . Both Garrison and Shaw's attorneys investigated the pictures, and Robert Brannon, who died in 1962, was positively identified by Mrs. Lawrence Fischer, who had been at the party, as well as by Robert Cahlman of radio station WYES, who knew Brannon well . . . The pictures were taken around 1949 (before David Ferrie had moved to New Orleans) by photographer Miles De Russey at a party given by a Tulane University student."[187]

The proof, of course, that Ferrie and Shaw do not appear together in the subject photograph (or any other photograph) is that if they did, surely Garrison, who feverishly tried to link Ferrie to Shaw at Shaw's trial, would have introduced it into evidence, but he did not. Nor did he make any reference to such a photo in *On the Trail of the Assassins*. Yet with Garrison himself serving as a consultant, Stone outrageously depicts Shaw and Ferrie apparently reveling in high badinage at a French Quarter party. And in Stone's appearance before the National Press Club on January 15, 1992, he told the assembled media, "After the [Shaw] trial we came into possession of a picture that shows that Clay Shaw and David Ferrie were at a party together."[188]

When Garrison assistant John Volz asked Ferrie in a December 15, 1966, interview whether Ferrie would "be willing to submit to a polygraph" on all of his denials, Ferrie responded, "Certainly." He said he would also "be willing to submit to truth serum. I have no hesitation at all."[189] But Garrison's office elected not to give Ferrie a lie detector test or any other kind of test. Not only, as indicated, did Ferrie deny ever having any contact with Oswald or Shaw, but Garrison's own book, *On the Trail of the Assassins*, never

---

*In 1993, a photograph surfaced of a Civil Air Patrol (CAP) cookout in New Orleans, showing Ferrie and Oswald in it, though not anywhere near each other. At the time the photo was taken, sometime in 1955, Oswald, who joined the CAP briefly on July 27, 1955, was clearly a member of the group, but Ferrie, a pilot who had previously commanded the group, was not, having been expelled from it on December 31, 1954. However, he apparently continued to be associated with the group in an unofficial capacity, and the HSCA was unable to determine if Ferrie and Oswald actually knew each other in the CAP. (9 HSCA 103–115) With respect to Ferrie having no recollection of ever having met Oswald, even if Ferrie had met Oswald at a CAP meeting, as the owner of the photo, John Ciravolo, told author Patricia Lambert in a July 9, 1997, interview, "I'm in the picture [too], and I'm sure David Ferrie wouldn't remember me, either" (Lambert, *False Witness*, p.61). Prior to the emergence of the photograph, the person most cited as putting Oswald and Ferrie together at the CAP in New Orleans was Edward Voebel, a high school friend of Oswald's in New Orleans who got Oswald interested in the CAP unit. Voebel testified before the Warren Commission that Oswald only attended "two or three meetings" and then "lost interest." Voebel said, "I think [Captain Ferrie] was there when Lee attended one of those meetings, but I'm not sure of that." (8 H 14)

makes any reference to Ferrie's telling him or any member of his staff that he was involved in the assassination, had any knowledge of it, or even knew Shaw and Oswald. (That was for Garrison's witness, Perry Russo, to do.) Yet, unbelievably again, Stone, who says he read *On the Trail of the Assassins* three times, paid a quarter of a million dollars for it, and based his movie primarily on it, invents a scene in a hotel room where Ferrie, in a highly agitated state, makes—by implication—a confession to Garrison and his assistants that he was a co-conspirator in Kennedy's assassination. "I knew Oswald. I taught him everything," Ferrie says. Ferrie goes on that he, Shaw, and Oswald were all members of the CIA, and that Shaw had him "by the balls" because of compromising photos Shaw had of him. Ruby, he says, was "a bagman for the Dallas mob." Garrison asks Ferrie who killed Kennedy. Ferrie, apparently angry at the naivete of the question, yells out the very incriminating words, indicating he had personal knowledge of a conspiracy to kill Kennedy, "*The shooters don't even know*. Don't you get it?"

Ferrie's contact at the DA's office was Louis Ivon, one of Garrison's investigators. Ivon worked hard to get Ferrie to cooperate with Garrison's investigation and turn state's evidence against Shaw. When Ferrie, within days of his death, called Ivon to complain about the media hounding him relentlessly since publication of a front-page article in the February 18, 1967, *New Orleans States-Item* with a photograph of Ferrie and captioned "Eyed as Pilot of 'Getaway' Craft-Flier," Ivon put Ferrie up for two nights at a New Orleans motor hotel. The only reference to this in Garrison's book was his writing that Ivon had rented a room for Ferrie at the "Fountainbleau Motel" under an assumed name on two separate nights, and Ivon had told Ferrie, "You call us anytime you need us, and we'll give you a hand," and suggested that Ferrie order whatever room service he wanted and that he try to relax. And the only reference in Garrison's book to Ivon or anyone else in his office talking to Ferrie during this precise period about the assassination is Garrison's saying that Ivon told Ferrie, "I only wish you were on our side. I can guarantee you that the boss would give his right arm to have your mind working with us." No response from Ferrie is indicated, obviously meaning that nothing Ferrie said was of any significance.[190] In *JFK: The Book of the Film* by Stone and coauthor Zachary Sklar, the source for the conversation wherein Ferrie allegedly indicated he had personal knowledge of a conspiracy to kill Kennedy is listed as Louis Ivon. "At times, however, *we had to put words in Ferrie's mouth*," *The Book of the Film* concedes on page 88 to its very small number of readers. How nice. But Stone, of course, did not acknowledge this to the millions of people who saw his film.

Garrison's book is close to four hundred pages of fluff and nonsense in which he desperately tries to convince his readers of a conspiracy to murder Kennedy. An implied confession from Ferrie to him and his assistants would have been the very centerpiece of his book. The highly incriminating words of Ferrie in Stone's movie ("*The shooters don't even know*. Don't you get it?") are not to be found anywhere in Garrison's book because apparently even Garrison was unwilling to say that a man admitted complicity in a murder when he did not. But Oliver Stone had no such reservation. As indicated, Stone fabricated, for his audience, this dramatic admission by Ferrie of a conspiracy to kill Kennedy. Since I'm not a student of Hollywood films, I don't know if *JFK* is a reflection on Oliver Stone's other works, some of which, I'm told, are excellent. But if it is, the question has to be asked, Has there ever been a filmmaker who has taken more liberties with the truth? And does Stone have any qualms about what he did? Here's what he told *Newsweek*: "Is Clay Shaw violated by my work? Is he going to come haunt me at night, drive me to the edge of madness? I have to live with my conscience and if I have done wrong, it's going to come back on me. But John Kennedy might be in my dreams, too, saying, 'Do it, go out there, find my assassins, bring them to justice.'"[191]

22. David Ferrie was found dead in his second-floor New Orleans apartment on the morning of February 22, 1967. In the movie, Ferrie, shortly after his "confession" to Garrison and his assistants, is shown being murdered by two Latin men who are forcing something down his throat. Suspicious, right? But that's only if you've already forgotten that Ferrie didn't confess to Garrison. Moreover, the coroner's report on the autopsy of Ferrie, conducted by Dr. Ronald A. Welsh, a pathologist for Orleans Parish, at 3:00 p.m. on February 22, 1967, listed the "Classification of Death" as "Natural"—that is, Ferrie had died from natural causes. The cause of death was a "rupture of berry aneurysm of Circle of Willis [a circle of blood vessels located along the undersurface of the brain between the brain and the skull base] with massive hemorrhage." Of course, aneurysms have been known to rupture from severe, blunt trauma, but the report said, "There are no external marks of violence on the body at any point" and "there are no evidences of trauma or contusions to the scalp at any point." Walsh found evidence of "hypertensive cardiovascular disease," indicating high blood pressure.[192]*

As to Oliver Stone's showing his audience two men forcing something down Ferrie's throat, a sample of Ferrie's blood was taken on February 22 to determine the presence or absence of "alcohol, barbiturates, cyanide, heavy metals," or "caustic agents." The toxicology report dated February 24 from the Orleans Parish toxicologist, Dr. Monroe S. Samuels, and chemist, Angela P. Comstock, said the blood specimen "was negative" as to the presence of these substances.[193] Oliver Stone, naturally, did not furnish his audience with this information.

Ferrie had been under enormous stress from Garrison's investigation of him, and was angry about Garrison's harassment, which included staking out his apartment. "The DA's men established a 24-hour surveillance in the basement of a house across the street from Ferrie's apartment building where they set up motion picture cameras to record the movements in and out of Ferrie's building."[194] On February 17, Ferrie told Dave Snyder, an investigative reporter for the *New Orleans States-Item*, in a long interview that he was giving serious thought to filing a lawsuit against Garrison. Snyder noticed that Ferrie's "steps were feeble" and Ferrie said he had encephalitis (inflammation of the brain causing abnormal sleepiness). Ferrie told Snyder of his fear of arrest and his anger and bitterness over Garrison's accusations against him.[195]

The following day, four days before Ferrie's death, Andrew Sciambra and Louis Ivon of the New Orleans DA's office went to Ferrie's apartment pursuant to Ferrie's telephone

---

*For many at the time, the sudden and untimely death of Ferrie, just four days after he had been identified in the media as a target of Garrison's investigation, seemed to confirm Garrison's allegation that powerful, unknown forces were behind the assassination, forces that would never permit Garrison to peel away the layers to the truth. "He sure took a bad time to die," Attorney General Ramsey Clark told President Johnson on the evening of Ferrie's death (Tape-recorded conversation between Clark and LBJ at 6:40 p.m., February 22, 1967, in Holland, *Kennedy Assassination Tapes*, p.402). To a media that was becoming impatient with Garrison for his failure to provide substantive evidence of his startling charges, Ferrie's death caused a heightened interest in the case. Maybe, the journalists thought, Garrison was on to something after all. The problem for Garrison was that, if we're to believe him, with Ferrie's death he had lost his main suspect in the Kennedy assassination. But Garrison was not about to let a little thing like death derail his determination to solve the assassination. Within three short days, he had a new chief suspect, Clay Shaw, and four days later, March 1, introduced Shaw to the world when he placed him under arrest for having conspired to murder Kennedy.

request that they do. Per their memorandum to Garrison of their interview of Ferrie, Ferrie said "that the reason he had called us was that he was getting concerned over our investigation. He had heard all kinds of rumors that he was going to be arrested and that he wanted to find out if these rumors were true." But the memo is silent as to what, if anything, Sciambra and Ivon told Ferrie in response to his question about whether the rumors were true. Sciambra, the writer of the memo, said that Ferrie had greeted him and Ivon at the bottom of the stairs to his apartment and told them he would follow them up the stairs because "it would take him some time to climb up the stairs as he was sick and weak and had not been able to keep anything in his stomach for a couple of days. He moaned and groaned with each step he took up the stairs." Once inside his apartment, Ferrie "laid down on the sofa . . . with two pillows under him" as they spoke to him. Sciambra went on to say he did not believe Ferrie was "as sick as he pretended to be," but did not spell out why he formed this opinion. During the interview, Ferrie complained that the media was "hounding him to death" and, indeed, a reporter from the New Orleans *Times-Picayune* called him shortly thereafter while they were there.

Ferrie cursed Jack Martin (true name, Edward Stewart Suggs), a part-time private detective and former friend of his (see later discussion), during the interview, saying Martin started the investigation of him because Martin was jealous of his relationship with attorney G. Wray Gill.* Martin, he said, was trying to ruin him and was "a screwball who should be locked up." When Sciambra asked Ferrie, "Dave, who shot the President?" Ferrie answered, "Well, that's an interesting question and I've got my own thoughts about it." Ferrie then proceeded to sit up and draw a sketch of Dealey Plaza and the Texas School Book Depository Building and "went into a long spiel about the trajectory of bullets in relation to the height and distance." He then gave a "lecture on anatomy and pathology [and] named every bone in the human body and every hard and soft muscle area" and concluded that one bullet could not have caused all the damage the Warren Commission claimed it did. To the question of whether he knew Clay Shaw, Ferrie responded, "Who's Clay Shaw?"

"How about Clay Bertrand?"

"Who's Clay Bertrand?"

"Clay Bertrand and Clay Shaw are the same person," Sciambra said.

"Who said that?"

"Dean Andrews told us," Sciambra answered.

"Dean Andrews might tell you guys anything. You know how Dean Andrews is."[196]

Some time that same day, February 18, Ferrie went down to the FBI's field office in New Orleans and told them he was a sick man, was disgusted with Garrison, intended to sue him for slander, and wanted to know what the bureau could do to help him "with this nut" Garrison.[197] Around that time, Ferrie was also suffering from severe headaches.[198] Carlos Bringuier, the anti-Castro activist with whom Oswald had the street confrontation in August of 1963, told author Gerald Posner he saw Ferrie two days before he died and "he looked real sick. He told me, 'I feel very sick. I should be in bed. My

---

*Ferrie elaborated on the problem in an earlier interview with the FBI. He said he had been working as an investigator and law clerk for Gill since March of 1962. Martin began visiting him at Gill's office, and because Gill didn't want Martin "hanging around" his office, Ferrie admits he put Martin out of Gill's office in an undiplomatic manner. Since that time, Ferrie said, Martin had been out to hurt him "in every manner possible," including, finally, trying to connect him with the assassination. (CD 75, pp.287, 293, FBI interview of David Ferrie by SAs Ernest C. Wall Jr. and L. M. Shearer Jr. on November 25, 1963)

physician told me to stay in bed. I have a big headache. Garrison is trying to frame me.'"[199] All of this tension—being a suspect in the murder of the president of the United States, particularly when you know the charge is spurious—may very well have contributed to his death. Dr. Ronald A. Welsh, who conducted the autopsy on Ferrie, told author Patricia Lambert that there was "scar tissue indicating that Ferrie had had another bleed, a small one, previously, . . . one or two of them at least two weeks before he died. This is a common occurrence with berry aneurysms. People have one or two before they blow out completely . . . His headaches were from the . . . early bleeds."[200]

The last known person who spoke to Ferrie before he died was *Washington Post* reporter George Lardner Jr., who arrived at Ferrie's apartment around midnight and stayed until almost 4:00 a.m. on the day Ferrie died. Ferrie told Lardner that he "didn't know [Oswald] and had no recollection of ever meeting him," and that Garrison's investigation was a "witch hunt."[201] The forty-eight-year-old Ferrie was found dead in bed around 11:40 a.m. later that morning, lying on his back under a sheet, nude, with two unsigned and undated typewritten notes nearby, one that began, "To leave this life is, for me, a sweet prospect," and closed, "If this is justice, then justice be damned." The other was addressed to "Dear Al" and read in part, "When you receive this I will be quite dead . . . I wonder how you are going to justify and rationalize things . . . All I can say is that I offered you love and the best I could. All I got in return, in the end, was a kick in the teeth. Hence, I die alone and unloved . . . I wonder what your last days and hours are going to be like. As you sow, so shall you also reap. Goodby, Dave." "Al" is believed to be Al Beauboeuf, a homosexual companion of Ferrie's to whom Ferrie left all his personal property in his will.[202]

On the day of Ferrie's death, February 22, Garrison, calling Ferrie "one of history's most important individuals," told the media, "There is no reason to suppose there was anything but suicide involved."[203] Why, in Garrison's mind, had Ferrie committed suicide? Garrison told reporters that Ferrie "knew we had the goods on him and he couldn't take the pressure . . . A decision had been made earlier today to arrest Ferrie early next week" for being part of the conspiracy to murder Kennedy. "Apparently, we waited too long."[204] But this almost assuredly was not true, just loose talk on Garrison's part. In his own book, where he discusses the circumstances of Ferrie's death, he makes not the slightest allusion to having decided to arrest Ferrie. Indeed, he suggests the exact opposite. "With David Ferrie around to lead us, however unconsciously, to Clay Shaw . . . I knew we could have continued to develop an ever stronger case against Shaw. With Ferrie gone, it would be a lot harder."[205] Garrison's lead prosecutor against Shaw, James Alcock, told author Patricia Lambert that "to my knowledge, there was no intent to arrest David Ferrie."[206]

This is hardly surprising since, although Garrison suspected Ferrie of being somehow involved in the assassination, there was no evidence against Ferrie to base an arrest on. (Perry Russo's allegation against Ferrie wasn't made to Garrison's office until February 25, *three days after Ferrie's death.*) Former assistant Warren Commission counsel Wesley Liebeler, who helped conduct the New Orleans phase of the investigation into Kennedy's death, told the *New York Times* on the day of Ferrie's death in 1967 that Edward Voebel, a high school classmate of Oswald's, told local and federal investigators on the day of the assassination back in 1963 that he thought Oswald had served briefly in a New Orleans Civil Air Patrol unit commanded by Ferrie, and three days later they received reports that Ferrie had made a trip to Texas on the day of the assassination. "We checked all of this out, and it just did not lead anywhere," among other things learning that Ferrie had gone to Houston rather than Dallas on November 22, 1963. "The FBI did a very substantial piece of work on Ferrie. It was so clear that he was not involved that we didn't mention it in the Report. Garrison has a responsibility to indicate just why he thinks Ferrie might have been involved, and so far as I can determine he has given no reason."[207] But Garrison did not do this because he could not do this. All he could say to the media in a formal statement he issued to the press later on the day of Ferrie's death was that "evidence developed by our office had long since confirmed that he was involved in events culminating in the assassination of President Kennedy."[208] But what could that evidence have been, particularly since, as indicated, Perry Russo had not yet surfaced with his totally discredited story about Ferrie conspiring with Shaw and Oswald?

Tom Bethell, the researcher and keeper of the files at the New Orleans DA's office during this period, tells the story about Mark Lane coming into his office one day having been authorized by Garrison to look at Ferrie's file. "You know, Mark," Bethell told Lane, "the Ferrie file is embarrassing. There's absolutely nothing in it of any importance"—by that, he told me, he meant that the DA's office had "nothing at all connecting Ferrie to the assassination." Lane responded that if anyone else looked at the file and couldn't find anything of any value, "just tell them the important stuff is kept in a different file." Bethell told me that this "convinced me that Lane wasn't troubled at all by the fact that Garrison was proceeding against Ferrie without any evidence."[209]

In fairness to Oliver Stone, just as the New Orleans coroner's medical conclusion that Ferrie died from a ruptured blood vessel in the brain virtually forecloses his having been murdered, if, indeed, the two notes found in his room were suicide notes, they would likewise virtually* foreclose his having died, as the coroner said, from a ruptured aneurysm in the brain. Whether the notes were, in fact, suicide notes is not completely clear, though the "To leave this life" one obviously goes in that direction. Of course, Ferrie was in very ill health at the time of his death, and he may very well have written the subject notes at some earlier time in possible contemplation of impending death. In any event, there is absolutely no evidence that David Ferrie was murdered. But in Oliver Stone's fine hands, there is no question that he was. Stone shows Ferrie being murdered (which, as we've seen, even Stone's hero, Garrison, didn't believe), obviously to silence him before he elaborated on his incriminating statements to Garrison, statements we know he never made.

23. In the movie, Jack Martin (played by Jack Lemmon), a down-and-out alcoholic private eye sidekick to Guy Banister, 'fesses up to Garrison at a racetrack (and why would any moviegoer disbelieve Jack Lemmon?) that at one time or another he had seen Oswald, Ferrie (whom, as indicated, he actually did know), and Shaw together in Banister's office. Garrison, in *On the Trail of the Assassins*, says that in late 1966 Martin told him about seeing Ferrie and Oswald in Banister's office in the summer of 1963.[210] Martin didn't say anything about seeing Clay Shaw there, but no problem. In his movie, Oliver Stone decided to gratuitously toss in Shaw for good measure.

Naturally, Stone doesn't tell his audience that Martin's credibility was so bad that as desperate as Garrison was to show the Shaw jury that his three alleged co-conspirators

---

*I say "virtually" as opposed to "positively" because at a press conference on February 22, 1967, the coroner, Dr. Chetta, theorized the possibility of a link between Ferrie's aneurysm and suicide if Ferrie ingested pills to kill himself and the pills induced such violent retching that it burst a blood vessel (*Los Angeles Times*, February 24, 1967, p.6). But this was before the negative toxicology report came out on February 24. On February 25, Chetta announced to the media that there was "no indication whatsoever of suicide or murder" in Ferrie's death. (*Times-Picayune* [New Orleans], February 26, 1967; see also *Los Angeles Times*, February 24, 1967, pp.1, 6)

knew each other, *he never called Martin to the stand during Shaw's trial to tell the jury what Stone had Martin (Lemmon) tell his audience.* That tells you more than anything just how total Martin's lack of credibility was. In the previously mentioned, secretly taped conversation in the law office of Hugh Exnicios (the lawyer representing Ferrie's friend, Al Beauboeuf, a potential witness at the time in Garrison's investigation of Clay Shaw) with Garrison investigator Lynn Loisel on March 10, 1967, when Loisel mentions an "informer," Exnicios asks, "You're talking about Jack Martin?"

Loisel: "No, no, no. Phew . . . that sack of roaches . . . believe you me, anything that he said, 99 percent of it was checked out to be *false*, you know, made-up, lies, jealousy, everything else. Oh, boy."

Exnicios: "I'm glad to hear that it's not Jack Martin."

Loisel: "Man, we will be torn to pieces, but not like that."[211]

So Oliver Stone's own protagonists, Garrison and his staff, didn't believe a word that Martin said, yet Stone presented Martin to his audience, unchallenged, as a highly believable witness who had seen Oswald, Ferrie, and Shaw together. And of course Stone doesn't tell his audience that Martin had been in mental wards in two states, including the psychiatric ward of Charity Hospital in New Orleans in 1957.[212] When FBI agents went to the hospital on January 17, 1957, to speak to him about his claim he was an FBI agent, his psychiatrist informed them that Martin was suffering from a "character disorder," and that an interview of him by the agents might prolong his hospitalization. Indeed, people like Aaron Kohn, managing director of the Metropolitan Crime Commission in New Orleans, as well as others routinely described Martin as a "mental case."[213] Yet Garrison himself implicitly acknowledges that Martin is the person whose information started his aborted investigation of the assassination in November of 1963, and his full-scale investigation in December of 1966.[214]*

Naturally, Stone also didn't tell his audience that the HSCA thoroughly investigated Martin's allegations and concluded that "in light of Martin's previous contradictory statements to authorities shortly after the assassination in which Martin made no such allegation about having seen Oswald [in Banister's office], it may be argued that credence should not be placed in Martin's statements to the committee."[215]

24. Without having any evidence to support their suspicions, for years conspiracy theorists have believed that the militantly anti-Communist and anti-Castro Guy Banister, who retained his connections to the intelligence community when he retired from the FBI in 1954, played some type of undefined role in the assassination, the various players in the assassination (Oswald, Ferrie, Shaw) being connected to each other through him. Stone

---

*But the person who Garrison says reignited his *interest* in investigating the assassination in the autumn of 1966 (and before he called Martin into his office) was the U.S. senator from Louisiana, Russell Long, whom he knew and whose father was Huey "Kingfish" Long, the most colorful and powerful politician in Louisiana history. In November of 1966, Garrison found himself, as noted earlier, seated on a plane next to Long on a flight from New Orleans to Washington, and when the subject turned to the Kennedy assassination, the senator expressed his doubts about the Warren Commission finding that Oswald had acted alone. He just didn't believe that Oswald, using a cheap, bolt-action rifle with a defective scope, could have fired two out of three shots with deadly accuracy at a moving target. Someone else was also involved, Long told Garrison, who at that time had put the Kennedy assassination behind him. When Garrison asked Long who would have had a motive to kill Kennedy, Long replied, "I wouldn't worry about motive until I find out if there appeared to be more than one gunman." After returning to New Orleans, Garrison, who respected Long's intelligence and stature, immediately ordered the entire set of Warren Commission volumes to study, and he was on his way. (Garrison, *On the Trail of the Assassins*, pp.13–15; Mann, *Legacy to Power*, pp.254–256; *Morning Advocate* [Baton Rouge], February 21, 1967)

tried his best to link Oswald to Banister and hence prove that Oswald was really right wing, not Marxist, and Oswald to the CIA, which undoubtedly had a hand in the paramilitary anti-Castro activities being partly coordinated out of Banister's office. Garrison is shown in the movie taking two of his assistants to the corner of Camp and Lafayette streets one Sunday morning and pointing out that the office address Oswald used on his Fair Play for Cuba leaflets was 544 Camp Street in New Orleans. (Actually, Oswald only used this office address on some of the leaflets. Other addresses he used were his home address and his post office box number. Number 544 Camp Street was a block away from where he worked at the Reily coffee company.) Garrison (Kevin Costner) then notes that 531 Lafayette Street, the address for Banister's office, is around the corner in the same building (Newman Building), and "both addresses go to the same place, Banister's office upstairs." But they didn't. As Joe Newbrough, a private detective in Banister's office, told *Frontline* in 1993, 544 Camp Street and 531 Lafayette had "totally separate entrances, and [were] probably 60 steps apart." He said that once you entered 544 Camp Street, you could not, from there, get to Banister's office. The Camp Street entrance, he said, "went strictly to the second floor of the building . . . You had to exit the second floor to the sidewalk, walk around the corner, and go into Banister's office."[216]

The three-story Newman Building on the corner of Camp and Lafayette has long since been replaced by the Federal Courthouse, which takes up the whole block, but in 1996 author Patricia Lambert asked New Orleans *Times-Picayune* assistant metro editor David Snyder, who covered the Shaw trial and was very familiar with the old Newman Building, if Newbrough was correct, and he verified for her that Banister's Lafayette Street offices were not linked interiorly with those of 544 Camp Street.[217]

Stone's twelve researchers, of course, couldn't find out this information for their audience, even though much of *JFK* was filmed in New Orleans. In fact, when Garrison, in the film, tells the two members of his staff that both addresses led directly to Banister's office, it is presented as a very important revelation. In any event, the Secret Service interviewed three tenants of 544 Camp Street who were there during the summer of 1963. None had ever seen Oswald at 544 Camp. Also, Sam Newman, the owner of the building, told the FBI that he had never rented an office in his building to Oswald or the Fair Play for Cuba Committee, and never recalled seeing Oswald in his building.[218] Newman likewise told the Secret Service that not only had he never rented an office in his building to Oswald and had never seen Oswald in the building, but he hadn't even rented space in the building to anyone new since around September 1962, which is before Oswald returned to New Orleans.[219]* The Warren Commission concluded there was no evidence that either "the Fair Play for Cuba Committee [or] Lee Harvey Oswald ever maintained an office" at 544 Camp Street.[220]

25. In a scene from *JFK*, one Beverly Oliver, who sang in a strip club (the Colony Club) located next to Jack Ruby's Carousel Club in Dallas at the time of the assassination, tells Garrison that she used to go to Ruby's club a lot, and one time at the club Ruby introduced her to Oswald and Ferrie. Very predictably, the Warren Commission heard allegations and rumors that Oswald was seen with Ruby at one or the other of Ruby's two clubs in Dallas, but we have already seen that after a very thorough investigation, which

*Assassination researcher Gus Russo believes that when the national office of the Fair Play for Cuba Committee denied Oswald's request to set up a local chapter in New Orleans, he simply appropriated this address near where he worked to give the appearance of substance to his one-man operation (Russo, *Live by the Sword*, p.550 note 23).

included interviewing employees of Ruby's and going to the sources of the allegations and rumors, the Commission found no merit to any of them and concluded that there was no credible evidence Ruby and Oswald knew each other or had ever had any contact with each other.[221] Stone didn't bother, of course, to tell his audience any of this. Nor did he tell them that no one, other than Beverly Oliver, had ever put Ruby and Oswald together at one of Ruby's clubs, never mind in the presence of Ferrie too.

Perhaps more importantly, Stone didn't tell his audience just who Beverly Oliver (portrayed in the movie by actress Lolita Davidovich) is. She is not one of the people the Warren Commission spoke to for the simple reason that she never surfaced in the assassination conspiracy miasma until 1970, when she claimed to be the "Babushka Lady." Around frame 55 of the film taken by Dealey Plaza spectator Mary Muchmore is seen a woman (with her back to Muchmore's camera) standing near the curb on the south side of Elm Street right around the time of the president's fatal head shot. Her arms are raised toward the front of her face, and the impression is that she is holding something in her hands, such as a camera or, more unlikely (since she is so close to the presidential limousine), binoculars.[222] What tantalized conspiracy theorists for years was the possibility that the unidentified lady had additional motion-picture footage of the assassination. Because she was wearing a brown coat and a triangular scarf, the type of scarf popular with Russian women and known as a babushka, she became known as the Babushka Lady. Beverly Oliver met conspiracy theorist Gary Shaw at a church revival in Joshua, Texas, in 1970 and told him she was the Babushka Lady, though she has never proved to most people's satisfaction that she was even in Dealey Plaza that day. Her story was that she was using a new, Super-8 Yashica movie camera that day, and that after the assassination two men who identified themselves as FBI agents came over to the Colony Club and asked for her undeveloped film, which they said they would return to her in ten days. She turned her film over to them without getting a receipt or their names. She said she never saw the film again nor did she make any inquiries about it.[223] Among other problems with her story, such as her coming forward seven years later, assassination researcher Jerry Ruffner contacted Yashica and learned it "did not put a Super-8 camera on the [U.S.] market until 1969," six years after the assassination.[224]

When confronted with this fact, Oliver, who apparently is as elusive as mercury, responded with a written article in 1993 to those who questioned her veracity, by saying the camera "might not have even had a manufacturer's model name on it . . . Yashica, Fushika, who really cares what kind of camera it was . . . I had a new camera a friend gave me, saying it was 'experimental,' a camera which no one else in Dallas had at the time." She went on to say that she was seventeen years old at the time, and then proceeded to bury the Babushka Lady controversy by contradicting what she first told Gary Shaw and what she said, as late as 1988, in the British television production *The Men Who Killed Kennedy*. Oliver said the woman identified by Shaw in his book *Cover-Up* as the Babushka Lady "is not me."* However, she maintained that she was in Dealey Plaza at the time of the assassination, though conveniently neglecting to say where she was located on Elm Street, and "filmed the entire motorcade sequence in graphic horror as it drove through Dealey Plaza down Elm Street."[225]

*Even without Beverly Oliver's admission, it appears obvious from the Babushka Lady photo that Oliver was not she. Photos of Oliver at the time show her to be a teenager of average weight. But even though one can't see her face, the Babushka Lady gives every appearance of being heavier and much older, almost matronly.

About the Ruby, Oswald, and Ferrie sighting, Oliver told conspiracy researchers in 1971 that several weeks before the assassination, an acquaintance of hers, a stripper known as Jada (Janet Adams Conforto), was seated at a booth of the Carousel Club with Ruby and another man. When Oliver sat down with them to have a drink, Oliver says Ruby introduced the man as "Lee Harvey Oswald of the CIA."[226] But Jada told the FBI in 1963 that she had never seen Oswald with Ruby at the Carousel Club or anywhere else.[227] Oliver later embellished her story to the conspiracy researchers by saying that David Ferrie, who we know lived in New Orleans, was so frequently at Ruby's club in Dallas in 1962 and 1963 that she took him to be the "Assistant Manager." To my knowledge no one else has ever put Ferrie in Ruby's club.[*]

Since emerging in 1970, Oliver has been a permanent fixture with the fringe element of the conspiracy community, and when not traveling with her preacher-husband on the itinerant, Southern Baptist revival circuit, she has been a drawing attraction at some buff conventions. Among other things, she claims that she and her first husband, a well-known Texas gangster named George McGann ("a man who earned his living in the mob, killing people," she says) who was gunned down in a gangland killing in Lubbock, Texas, in 1970, had a two-hour private meeting with Richard Nixon in a Miami hotel right in the midst of his 1968 campaign for president.[228] When, on August 6, 1990, a twenty-nine-year-old unemployed Texas salesman named Ricky White called a press conference at the JFK Assassination Information Center in Dallas claiming his father, Roscoe White, a deceased Dallas police officer, was the grassy knoll gunman who had killed Kennedy, the obliging Beverly Oliver stepped forward to claim that, indeed, she had seen Roscoe White, in his uniform, walking away from the grassy knoll after the shooting that day.

Only the lunatic fringe of the conspiracy movement listens to a word Beverly Oliver has to say. Respected and meticulous conspiracy theorist Paul Hoch referred to her as having "very low inherent credibility" in an April 3, 1977, letter he wrote to U.S. Representative Christopher Dodd of the HSCA. The HSCA, which interviewed a considerable number of nuts and kooks in its investigation of the assassination and mentioned them in its volumes, felt that Oliver's credibility was so bad that an interview of her by a staff attorney on March 17, 1977, wasn't worthy of mention.

As indicated, no one had ever put Ruby, Oswald, and Ferrie together. But Beverly Oliver did. The woman who filmed the assassination with a camera that did not exist at the time, who had a two-hour tête-à-tête with Richard Nixon in the middle of his 1968 presidential campaign, who saw a fictitious assassin leaving the grassy knoll after the president was shot, whose credibility is so low that even most mainstream conspiracy theorists totally disregard her, was presented by Oliver Stone to his audience as an unchallenged, unimpeachable witness who had drinks with Ruby, Oswald, and Ferrie in Ruby's club before the assassination. Again, there oughta be a law against this type of thing.

---

[*]Beverly Oliver is so outrageous that in 1997 she contacted James Earl Ray's lawyers with some explosive information. Ray, in Memphis, Tennessee, had been arguing that a mysterious and long-sought figure he had met by the name of "Raoul" was the mastermind behind the assassination of Reverend Martin Luther King Jr., and it was Raoul, not he, who had shot and killed King on April 4, 1968, in Memphis. (Ray pled guilty in 1969 and was sentenced to ninety-nine years in prison, but in later years tried to set aside his conviction on the ground that he was innocent and had been coerced into pleading guilty.) Oliver told Ray's lawyers that at the time she met Oswald and Ferrie at Ruby's nightclub, Raoul was with them. (Michael Dorman, "Prosecutors Probe Claims by Ray's Lawyers about King Assassin," *Newsday*, December 10, 1997, p.A24)

By the way, Beverly Oliver co-wrote, with Coke Buchanan, her autobiography, *Night-mare in Dallas*, in 1994. Seeing the obvious benefit of being the Babushka Lady, she changed her story, once again maintaining that she was.[229] Though Ms. Oliver is confused as to who she is, I am not. She is someone without one ounce of credibility in the Kennedy case. But not to Oliver Stone. In her book she points out that she was a paid "technical consultant" to Stone in *JFK*, and proudly displays a smiling Stone warmly embracing her on the Dallas set of the movie.

26. In a *JFK* movie scene, Jack Ruby tells Chief Justice Earl Warren, "Mr. Chief Justice, do you understand that I cannot tell the truth here, in Dallas? That there are people here who do not want me to tell the truth. My life is in danger. If I am eliminated, there won't be any way of knowing any bit of the truth . . . And consequently, a whole new form of government is going to take over the country." Ruby begs Warren to take him to Washington, D.C., where he can tell the truth. What is the truth Ruby wants to tell? Well, if you're watching the movie, there can be no doubt what it is. That Ruby was a part of a conspiracy, and that he silenced Oswald for those who got him to do it. And that he can identify these people and expose the conspiracy only if he is taken to Washington. But as we have seen, in his actual testimony before the Warren Commission Ruby clearly and unequivocally told Warren "there was no conspiracy," and "I am as innocent regarding any conspiracy as any of you gentlemen in this room," and "no one else requested me to do anything. I never spoke to anyone about attempting to do anything. No subversive organization gave me any idea. No underworld person made any effort to contact me. It all happened that Sunday morning." Stone, naturally, didn't show his audience Ruby telling Warren any of this, deliberately and inexcusably misleading them to further the thrust of his movie. Stone also doesn't tell his audience, of course, about all of Ruby's psychotic ramblings in his testimony before the Warren Commission.

If the reader is not already completely disgusted by, and revolted with, Oliver Stone and his movie, I can't imagine why not. But read on.

27. Stone was confronted with a real dilemma on how to handle Perry Russo, Jim Garrison's star witness at Clay Shaw's trial. He very much wanted to include Russo's testimony that he was present in David Ferrie's apartment in mid-September of 1963 and heard Ferrie, Shaw (using the alias Clay Bertrand), and Oswald conspire to kill Kennedy. But even as outrageously dishonest about the facts as he was willing to be, Stone knew that he couldn't present Russo's testimony without some mention of the fact that, as previously noted, Russo only said this (and then only after leading questions) after he was put under the influence of sodium pentothal and then hypnosis. Even if Stone thought he could get by with not mentioning Russo's first four interviews, Stone would have to at least mention the sodium pentothal and hypnosis. It just was too well known for even him to ignore. What to do? Not to worry. Stone simply eliminated Perry Russo as a character in his movie and substituted in his place a fictitious homosexual prostitute (which Russo was not) named Willie O'Keefe, who in the movie tells Garrison that Shaw had paid him for sex on several occasions. Through Stone's device of substituting a fictitious character for Perry Russo, he thereby succeeded in putting on screen his and Garrison's three co-conspirators together in Ferrie's apartment in New Orleans talking about killing Kennedy, and with O'Keefe witnessing it all, without having any of the considerable baggage that Perry Russo, who has been completely discredited, would have brought to the movie.

After excoriating the Warren Commission for its fraudulent investigation, Walt

Brown, a leading conspiracy theorist, writes, "By the time of [Oliver] Stone's December 20, 1991, release of 'JFK,' the public was ready for a dose of reality, and they got it." What?! How, one may ask, could an intelligent person like Walt Brown, who has a PhD in American history from the University of Notre Dame, who has written books on the assassination, and who, I believe, does want to know the truth, write something like this? I do not have the answer to that question, except to say that, as a songwriter lyricized about people in love (and Brown and his fellow travelers are hopelessly in love with the notion of a conspiracy in the Kennedy assassination), "Smoke Gets in Your Eyes."

28. If there is a high-water mark in Stone's tapestry of lies about the case, it is perhaps when Garrison goes to Washington, D.C. (Stone probably had in mind Jimmy Stewart's character in Frank Capra's *Mr. Smith Goes to Washington*). There's a scene on a bench near the Lincoln Memorial in which Garrison has a meeting (with a character who only refers to himself as "X") that Stone admittedly invented virtually out of whole cloth. "Garrison's meeting with X did not happen," Stone acknowledged on *Nightline* on December 19, 1991. The idea of X and the military-industrial complex's involvement in the assassination came from one of Stone's movie advisers, former Air Force Colonel Fletcher Prouty, who is referred to earlier in this book and who never met Garrison in real life. "X is primarily Fletcher Prouty," Stone told the National Press Club on January 15, 1992. Prouty, indeed, has always claimed to have the same military background that X told Garrison he, X, had. But as we saw earlier in the book, Prouty's credibility about his background is highly suspect.

In the movie, X (played by Donald Sutherland) presents himself as a former member of U.S. military intelligence who tells Garrison he was "one of the secret guys in the Pentagon who supplied military hardware" for, he says, "Black Operations, Black Ops—assassinations, coup d'etats, rigged elections" in foreign countries, and tells Garrison, in a fourteen-minute monologue that may be the longest peroration in motion picture history, the "why" of the assassination. X starts by telling Garrison that because of the Bay of Pigs fiasco (the CIA-sponsored invasion of Cuba in 1961 to oust Castro), Kennedy was very upset with the CIA, and shortly thereafter (June 28, 1961) National Security Action Memorandums (NSAMs) numbered 55, 56, and 57 were signed by McGeorge Bundy, Kennedy's foreign affairs adviser. X said the memos provided that from that point on "the Joint Chiefs of Staff would be wholly responsible for all *covert*, paramilitary action in peacetime. This basically ended the reign of the CIA," he adds, and the agency was outraged and therefore wanted Kennedy eliminated. Apart from X's irrational non sequitur, X's statement in the film is a lie. NSAM 55 doesn't even deal with the issue, and NSAM 56 suggests no such thing, merely saying that "it is important that we anticipate now our possible future requirements in the field of unconventional warfare and paramilitary operations . . . The President requests that the Secretary of Defense, in coordination with the Department of State, *and the CIA*, make such an estimate of requirements." Only NSAM 57 specifically deals with the issue, but it says the precise opposite of what Stone has X tell Garrison in the film. It provides in paragraph 2(a) that "the Department of Defense will normally receive responsibility for *overt* paramilitary operations. Where such an operation is to be wholly *covert* or disavowable, *it may be assigned to CIA*, provided it is within the normal capabilities of the agency."

Additionally, though Kennedy was very upset with the CIA over its bungling of the Bay of Pigs invasion, and "allowed" its leaders, including the director himself, Allen Dulles, to resign in the aftermath of the debacle, his animus toward the agency was not long-lived, and his overall relationship with the CIA was good. (See discussion on this issue in the "CIA" section.)[*]

Then X, with the slight, confident smile of a lunatic, tells Garrison that "the Warren Commission is fiction," and proceeds to go beyond the CIA and lay out the principal reason for the assassination. It coalesces with the opening scene of the movie where President Dwight D. Eisenhower, in his farewell address to the nation on January 17, 1961, warns of the "acquisition of unwarranted influence, whether sought or unsought, by *the military-industrial complex*" in our society. X tells Garrison that the "power structure" was behind Kennedy's assassination and it was a "coup d'etat . . . President Kennedy was murdered by the highest levels of our government." "Who benefitted?" X asks Garrison, the only message being that whoever did must have killed Kennedy. X lectures that "the organizing principle of any society is war. War is the biggest business in America, and Kennedy wanted to end the cold war . . . He signed a treaty with the Soviets to ban nuclear testing, he refused to invade Cuba in 1962 [Cuban missile crisis], and he set out to withdraw from Vietnam. All of that ended on November 22, 1963."

There's a fictitious scene in the movie of the Joint Chiefs of Staff, in the presence of white-collared business executives, angrily denouncing Kennedy's policies. It is clear, X tells Garrison, that they hate him, as do the captains of industry—"defense contractors, big oil, bankers"—because without war, they'll lose "big money, a hundred billion dollars." In short, the military-industrial complex wanted, needed war, and Kennedy wanted to end the Vietnam War, so they decided to kill him.[†] Just like that. As I said earlier in this

---

[*]Also historians agree that JFK and his brother RFK were of the same mind about virtually every issue pursued by the Kennedy administration. Indeed, as one author wrote, RFK was "his brother's troubleshooter, lightning rod, spokesman, adviser, no-man [as in yes and no], eyes and ears ('Little Brother Is Watching'), whiphand overseer of the FBI and CIA and [all of the] presidential wishes and thoughts that the President would not let himself be heard to speak" (Beschloss, *Crisis Years*, p.303). No one (except, perhaps, Oliver Stone's X, who did not exist) was more aware of JFK's disenchantment with the CIA over the Bay of Pigs than former CIA director Richard Helms, who was the CIA's chief of operations at the time. In his memoirs, he writes that in the wake of the Bay of Pigs, "at the Agency [CIA] the impression was that Robert Kennedy . . . would serve as his brother's vengeful hatchet man." But Helms goes on to say that "whether it was the result of General [Maxwell] Taylor's perceptive and levelheaded approach, the influence of Admiral Burke and Allen Dulles [JFK had appointed General Taylor to head the aforementioned executive inquiry as to why the Bay of Pigs invasion had failed, and Burke, chief of naval operations, and CIA Director Allen Dulles were on the committee], or his own findings, [Robert] Kennedy was to develop a more balanced view of the Agency than he had in the days after the collapse of the ZAPATA [code name for invasion] operation. In the weeks that followed, we were relieved to learn that he was a quick study. The two months of back-to-back interviews and briefings with the committee left Kennedy with an abiding interest in covert action and a measure of respect for the Agency." Elsewhere, Helms, who worked very closely with RFK for over a year on Operation Mongoose, the administration's effort to overthrow Castro, said about RFK, "*as always* speaking for his brother." (Helms with Hood, *Look over My Shoulder*, pp.182, 205)

[†]That the majority of the Joint Chiefs of Staff (one of whose members, Air Force Chief of Staff Curtis LeMay, Kennedy almost outwardly detested because of his crude bravado and hard-line, saber-rattling rhetoric) wanted our nation to militarily intervene in Vietnam has been established and is almost a given. That's usually, though not always, the military's mind-set. As General George S. Patton Jr. wrote in a letter to his hero, General John J. (Black Jack) Pershing, at the time of the First World War, "War is the only place where a man really lives." Indeed, as far back as October of 1961, the Joint Chiefs of Staff took the position on Vietnam that "the time is now past when actions short of intervention by outside forces could reverse the rapidly worsening situation" (Joint Chiefs of Staff memorandum to Secretary of Defense Robert McNamara on October 5, 1961). It also is well known that Kennedy's relationship with the nation's military leaders was only lukewarm. Basically, he did not trust their judgment, particularly after the Bay of Pigs, where they had endorsed the CIA operation, and they weren't enamored with his overly cautious military instincts. But where is there any evidence in American history that when our military leaders wanted a war and their commander in chief wouldn't give it to them, they even thought about murdering him, much less actually doing it?

book, that's what we do in America. If the president is pursuing policies that members of a certain segment of our society, like Wall Street, the unions, or the military, don't like, why they simply kill him. Of course.

And of course, not one member of the Joint Chiefs of Staff or one corporate leader would ever think of not going along with this plan to murder the president and instead alert the president or call the authorities. After all, what's the big deal about joining in a conspiracy to murder the president of the United States? If any reader of this book were on the Joint Chiefs of Staff or a corporate leader and the president's policies were going to interfere with your objectives or cut into your profits, you wouldn't think twice about conspiring to murder him, would you? More seriously, even if we imagine the unimaginable, that the Joint Chiefs of Staff and leaders of American industry were crazy enough to be willing to murder Kennedy because of his plan to end the cold war, would they be so crazy as to not at least first try to beat him at the ballot box by putting all their money, power, and influence behind his opponent when he came up for reelection in just one year? Or if not that, where is there any evidence that the Joint Chiefs of Staff and the titans of industry first demanded an audience with the president and tried to talk him out of his expected (in their minds, if we accept Stone's thesis) withdrawal from Vietnam? Instead, Stone simply shows his audience several bemedaled generals in a smoke-hazed room profaning Kennedy and boozing it up as they set in motion the murder of their commander in chief. Stone adopts the military-industrial-complex theory of the assassination as the principal theme of his film, ostensibly superseding the Shaw-Ferrie-Oswald troika, unless there was a connection between the two groups, which Stone never indicates to his audience.

Since we know that the conversation between X and Garrison never took place and was invented by Stone for his movie, and inasmuch as no one has ever produced one single particle of evidence that the military-industrial complex was behind Kennedy's assassination, no further discussion of the issue is really necessary. However, even though the military-industrial-complex-killing-Kennedy theory is offensive to one's intelligence, because of Stone's movie ("What makes Stone so dangerous," a Hollywood producer acquaintance of mine told me, "is that he's a great filmmaker. He makes his films believable"), millions of otherwise intelligent Americans now subscribe to it. A representative example: In a November 1999 *Playboy* interview, the savvy governor of Minnesota, Jesse Ventura, was asked, "Who do you think killed President Kennedy?" He replied, "The military-industrial complex. I believe Kennedy was going to withdraw us from Vietnam and there were factions that didn't want that."[230] So even though Stone invented the conversation on the bench, and there's no evidence the military-industrial complex had anything to do with the assassination, because the theory has taken hold in the conspiracy community and among many Americans, let's examine the allegation as it was presented in the movie.

X tells Garrison that the objectives of the military-industrial complex in murdering Kennedy worked. He tells Garrison that Kennedy had a "plan for getting all U.S. personnel out of Vietnam by the end of 1965" and that NSAM 263, signed on October 11, 1963, "ordered home the first 1,000 troops" of the 16,500 military advisers then in Vietnam* by the end of 1963. X says that four days after the assassination, "Lyndon Johnson

---

*Our military presence in Vietnam (opposing Communism), in the form of military advisers, arms, and equipment, dated back to the administration of President Eisenhower during the Indochina War between France and the Vietminh, the Communist-led Vietnamese nationalists. The war, which started in 1946, ended

signs National Security [Action] Memo 273, which essentially reverses [Kennedy's] withdrawal policy."

So Stone wanted his audience to believe that the issue was very clear-cut: Kennedy *wanted* to withdraw from Vietnam (NSAM 263 spelled out his intentions), he was murdered because of it,* and shortly after his murder, LBJ, by NSAM 273, set aside Kennedy's plans. But that doesn't begin to tell the story of what really happened. If Stone had told it, his whole thesis would have crumbled. In the first place, even though NSAM 273 was issued under President Johnson on November 26, 1963, four days after Kennedy's death, the draft, containing the identical language in its relevant clauses, was prepared by McGeorge Bundy, Kennedy's special assistant for national security affairs, on November 21, 1963, *while Kennedy was still president.*[231]† So no inference can be drawn that after Kennedy died, Johnson, by NSAM 273, changed course.

Few question that Kennedy did not want to employ combat troops in Vietnam. "Kennedy had no intention of dispatching ground forces to save Vietnam," says historian and JFK special assistant Arthur Schlesinger Jr. "Having watched the French Army fail in Vietnam . . ., he had no desire to send the American Army into the same quagmire."[232] General James M. Gavin wrote in the *Saturday Evening Post* that "having discussed military affairs with [Kennedy] often and in detail for fifteen years, I know he was totally opposed to the introduction of combat troops in Southeast Asia."[233] Roger Hilsman, Kennedy's assistant secretary of state for Far Eastern affairs, says that "on numerous occasions President Kennedy told me that he was determined not to let Vietnam become an American war. He agreed to have Americans serve as advisers . . . but he refused every suggestion to send American combat forces."[234] And the National Security Action Memorandums, all of which had to express his will, clearly show he wanted to withdraw from Vietnam. Indeed, Kennedy's intent to withdraw from Vietnam can be traced as far back as May 8, 1962, when his secretary of defense, Robert McNamara, in Saigon attending the fifth of eight SECDEF (Secretary of Defense) conferences held on the Vietnam War during the Kennedy presidency, ordered General Paul D. Harkins, commander of the Military Advisory Command in Vietnam, to start working on a plan to remove all American military advisers from Vietnam.

None of this, however, is synonymous with saying that irrespective of circumstances, Kennedy *would* have withdrawn and would never have employed American combat troops

---

with the Geneva Accords of 1954 (which the United States refused to endorse) calling for the withdrawal of all French troops from Indochina (which included Vietnam [divided by the Accords at the 17th parallel into North and South Vietnam], Cambodia, Laos, Thailand, Malaya, and Burma), which the French had dominated and colonized since the mid-nineteenth century. By the end of the war, the United States had 342 military advisers in Indochina, mainly in Saigon, assisting the French Expeditionary Corps.

*Stone told the National Press Club that his movie *JFK* "suggests it was Vietnam that led to the assassination of John Kennedy, that he became too dangerous, too strong an advocate of changing the course of the Cold War, too clear a proponent of troop withdrawal for those who supported the idea of a war in Vietnam" (C-Span transcript of appearance by Oliver Stone before National Press Club on January 15, 1992, p.5).

†NSAM 273 came out of the now famous "Honolulu Conference" of November 20, 1963, at CINCPAC (Commander in Chief of the Pacific) headquarters in Hawaii. There, President Kennedy's top national security people, including Secretary of Defense Robert McNamara, Secretary of State Dean Rusk, CIA Director John McCone, and McGeorge Bundy met to formulate a post-Diem (South Vietnamese President Ngo Dinh Diem was assassinated on November 2) American foreign policy vis-à-vis Vietnam, the withdrawal plans for the 1,000 troops, and the increase in U.S. *covert* actions against the North Vietnamese. (Newman, *JFK and Vietnam*, pp.429–435; O'Leary and Seymour, *Triangle of Death*, p.49) Author Craig Roberts erroneously writes that the draft of NSAM 273 was "prepared for LBJ" (Roberts, *Kill Zone*, p.98). But not only was the draft prepared while Kennedy was still alive, but its language can only be interpreted as referring to President Kennedy, not LBJ.

as his successor eventually did. Presidents, like all humans, often do things they had hoped they'd never have to do. Lawrence Freedman, professor of war studies at King's College, London, says in his book, *Kennedy's Wars*, that "to get out of Vietnam was less of a decision" for JFK "than a working assumption" that the South Vietnamese government, whose side we supported, would be able to repel the Vietcong (South Vietnam Communist guerrilla rebels) with U.S. military assistance. But he goes on to say that "it requires something of a leap of faith to assume that Kennedy would have stuck to a predetermined policy come what may. This was, after all, a man who prized flexibility and keeping open all options."[235]

It would be nice, one could say, if Kennedy himself had told us if he'd ever be willing to employ American combat troops in Vietnam. Well, he did, on the last day of his life. In the already prepared text of the speech Kennedy was scheduled to give at the Dallas Trade Mart after the motorcade through Dealey Plaza, Kennedy suggests he *would* have used American combat troops *if the situation called for it*. In addressing the issue of the wisdom of assisting 3.5 million allied forces in Southeast Asia to repel the advance of Communism, the text reads, "Our assistance . . . can be painful, risky, and costly . . . But we dare not weary of the task . . . We in this country, in this generation, are—by destiny rather than by choice—the watchman on the walls of world freedom . . . A successful Communist breakthrough in these areas [which he said included "Vietnam, free China, Korea, India, Pakistan, Thailand, Greece, Turkey, and Iran"], *necessitating direct United States intervention*, would cost us several times as much as our entire foreign aid program—and might cost us heavily in American lives as well . . . Reducing our efforts to train, equip and assist [the allied] armies can only encourage Communist penetration and *require in time the increased overseas deployment of American combat forces*."[236]

Does any reader of this book think that Oliver Stone would have ever dreamed of quoting the above in his travesty of a movie?[*]

Moreover, NSAM 273 (November 26, 1963) does not, as Stone's audience was told,

---

[*]One thing that militates against Kennedy ever sending combat troops to Vietnam and, even if he decided he wanted to, to his not ordering U.S. soldiers to engage in armed conflict in Vietnam without an actual congressional declaration of war (as opposed to the mere congressional resolution in 1964 flowing from the Gulf of Tonkin incident, which was cited as support for our further military involvement in Vietnam) is that Kennedy, unlike so many of his predecessors and successors, understood that as president he did not have the constitutional *right* to engage the nation in war.

Although Article II, Section 2 (1) does provide that "the President shall be Commander-in-Chief of the Army and Navy of the United States," technically this only places the president at the head of this nation's armed forces. It clearly envisions, as a predicate to his conducting war as the head of the nation's armed forces, that war has been *declared*. And Article I, Section 8 (11) ("The Congress shall have power . . . to declare war") exclusively and unambiguously gives that power to Congress, not the president. So much for the apparent intent of the framers of the Constitution. The reality is that throughout this nation's history, presidents, with-*out* the approval of Congress, have time and again committed American military forces abroad. In fact, only five times in the nation's history has Congress declared war: the War of 1812; the Mexican War, 1846; the Spanish-American War, 1898; World War I, 1917; and World War II, 1941. Political commentator Russell Baker has wryly observed that "presidents now say, sure, the Constitution gives Congress the right to declare war, but it doesn't forbid presidents to *make* war, so long as they don't *declare* it. As a result, the declared war has become obsolete. Its successor is the undeclared war."

In a March 1962 press conference, Kennedy said that if combat troops "in the generally understood sense of the word" (i.e., fighting soldiers, not advisers) were required in Vietnam, that would call for a "*constitutional* decision, [and] of course, I would go to Congress" (Schlesinger, *Robert Kennedy and His Times*, pp.708–709). Kennedy's realization that a congressional declaration of war was truly necessary may have had at least some deterrent effect on him, if only in the sense that he knew that if he were going to follow the Constitution he could not commence war at his whim, but would have to negotiate a major, heavily publicized hurdle in Congress.

reverse NSAM 263 (October 11, 1963). In fact, it specifically *reaffirms* Kennedy's decision to withdraw 1,000 troops by the end of 1963, providing in its second numbered paragraph that "the objectives of the United States *with respect to the withdrawal of U.S. military personnel remain as stated in the White House statement of October 2, 1963.*"* The White House statement of October 2, 1963, became the basis and precursor for NSAM 263, which provided for "the implementation of plans to withdraw 1,000 U.S. military personnel [from Vietnam] by the end of 1963." The October 2 statement was read to the media by Press Secretary Pierre Salinger following a National Security Council meeting convened by Kennedy earlier in the evening. At that meeting the recommendations set forth in a ten-page memorandum of that same date (October 2) from General Maxwell D. Taylor (chairman of the Joint Chiefs of Staff) and Robert S. McNamara (secretary of defense), based on their one-week fact-finding mission for Kennedy in Vietnam, were discussed. The resulting statement, in part, said that Taylor and McNamara "reported that by the end of this year [1963] the United States program for training Vietnamese should have progressed to the point *where one thousand United States military personnel assigned to South Vietnam can be withdrawn,*" and that "the U.S. military task [in Vietnam] can be completed by the end of 1965."[237]

Not only didn't Stone tell his movie audience that NSAM 273, under President Johnson, actually reaffirmed NSAM 263† issued under Kennedy, but also Stone couldn't find thirty seconds in his three-hour-and-eight-minute movie, and Stone's two Vietnam advisers, L. Fletcher Prouty and John M. Newman, couldn't find one paragraph of space in their respective 366- and 506-page books (Prouty's *JFK: The CIA, Vietnam, and the Plot to Assassinate John F. Kennedy* and Newman's *JFK and Vietnam*), to point out that there was much more to Taylor and McNamara's memo to the president of October 2, 1963, than withdrawing 1,000 military advisers from Vietnam by the end of 1963 and enunciating the objective of removing the remainder of the U.S. military task force from Vietnam by the end of 1965. But since the main motive for the assassination of Kennedy in Stone's movie was Kennedy's intent to withdraw from Vietnam, this apparently is all that he wanted his audience to know. Other than a single, one-sentence paragraph in Newman's book that had nothing to do with the heart of the October 2 memo, the only two paragraphs of the memo he quotes in his book (on page 402) are the withdrawal paragraphs. That's also all that Prouty talks about (on page 279) in his comments about the memo.

However, the October 2 memo goes on for ten pages, and the main thrust of it is not withdrawal, which is secondary, but how to deal with the very repressive policies of Ngo Dinh Diem (the president of the Republic of Vietnam whose ascension to power in 1955 was largely engineered by our country to promote democracy in Vietnam, but who himself became dictatorial, repressing by imprisonment, torture, and death, dissident members of the Buddhist majority, though we continued to support his regime) and his terrorist brother and political adviser, Ngo Dinh Nhu. The concern was not only

---

*"As is stated in the Pentagon Papers, NSAM 273, . . . only three days after [Johnson] assumed the Presidency, was intended primarily to *endorse* the policies pursued by President Kennedy and to ratify provisional decisions reached in Honolulu just before the assassination" (*Pentagon Papers*, vol.3, p.2).

†As George Lardner, national security reporter for the *Washington Post*, said, "There was no abrupt change in Vietnam policy after JFK's death" (George Lardner Jr., "On the Set: Dallas in Wonderland—How Oliver Stone's Version of the Kennedy Assassination Exploits the Edge of Paranoia," *Washington Post*, May 19, 1991, p.D5).

humanitarian. "Our policy is to seek to bring about the abandonment of repression *because of its effect on the popular will to resist [the Vietcong]*." The memo agonizes over whether or not it would "be wise to promote a coup" against Diem by his generals (who eventually murdered Diem and his brother on November 2), but decides against it. Indeed, the paragraph of the memo (number 3) dealing with the withdrawal of 1,000 military advisers is followed by a paragraph (number 4) which reads that *the specific purpose for the withdrawal* action is "to impress upon Diem our disapproval of his political program [of repression]." Elsewhere the memo refers to "numerous possibilities of applying pressure to Diem in order to incline him to the direction of our policies." If one reads not only Taylor and McNamara's October 2, 1963, memo to Kennedy, but McNamara's book *In Retrospect*, the main issue being discussed by the president and his advisers during the period of the October 2 memo and the October 11 NSAM 263 was not the withdrawal of troops from Vietnam, but whether to support a coup of Diem.[238] But we learned years later from a Hollywood producer and his daffy adviser, Colonel Prouty, that the real coup being contemplated at the time, and eventually carried out, was not against Diem but against the president of the United States.

This is not to suggest that Kennedy didn't hope he'd be able to withdraw all U.S. troops by 1965, as recommended in the October 2 McNamara-Taylor memorandum and repeated in the October 2 White House statement that followed. Other than right-wing extremists in our society, any sensible president would have wanted, as Kennedy did, to prevent the flower of America's youth from shedding its blood on foreign soil.* But the October 2 memo, in conjunction with other statements by the president, made it very clear that Kennedy's backing out of Vietnam was *contingent upon* the Vietnamese government being able to successfully resist the Vietcong. For instance, the minutes of the National Security Council meeting on October 11 show that the withdrawal of the 1,000 men "should be carried out routinely as part of our general posture of withdrawing people *when they are no longer needed*." And the October 2 Taylor-McNamara memo speaks of the "present favorable military trends"—that is, at the time of the ordered withdrawal of 1,000 troops on October 11, the United States had cause to believe that the South Vietnamese would repel the Vietcong *on their own*. Indeed, the *New York Times* headline of October 3, 1963, following the White House statement the previous night about the withdrawal of U.S. forces, read, "Vietnam *Victory* by the End of '65 Envisaged by U.S." Reporting from Saigon on October 2, 1963, *New York Times* reporter David Halberstam said that "the military [including General Paul D. Harkins, head of the U.S. military mission in Vietnam] believe the war is being won."[239]

Most important, the October 2 memo, like the White House statement later that evening, says (not, of course, mentioned in the film or the two books) that "the security of South Vietnam remains vital to United States security. For this reason, *we adhere to*

---

*Ken O'Donnell, Kennedy's appointments secretary and political right hand, says that actually, Kennedy would have wanted to withdraw American troops before 1965, but, as he told Senator Mike Mansfield (who recommended to JFK that we withdraw from Vietnam after JFK sent him there in 1962 to assess the situation) during a meeting in the Oval Office in the spring of 1963, "I can't do it until 1965—after I'm reelected." O'Donnell quotes the president as telling him after Mansfield left the office, "In 1965, I'll become one of the most unpopular presidents in history. I'll be damned everywhere as a Communist appeaser. But I don't care. If I tried to pull out completely now from Vietnam, we would have another Joe McCarthy red scare on our hands, but I can do it after I'm reelected. So we had better make damned sure that I *am* reelected." (O'Donnell and Powers with McCarthy, *Johnny, We Hardly Knew Ye*, pp.16, 472)

the overriding objective of denying this country to Communism and of suppressing the Viet-cong insurgency as promptly as possible . . . Any long-term reduction of aid cannot but have an eventual adverse affect on the military campaign . . . Hence, immediate reductions must be selected carefully and be left in effect for short periods."[240] And it was clear that the "overriding objective" set forth by Taylor and McNamara was accepted by Kennedy. The White House statement was almost a carbon copy of the memo. The statement said, in part, that "the security of South Vietnam is a major interest of the United States . . . *We will adhere* to our policy of working with the people and government of South Vietnam to deny this country to Communism and to suppress the externally stimulated and supported* insurgency of the Viet Cong as promptly as possible. Effective performance in this undertaking *is the central object of our policy in South Vietnam.*"[241] Quite a difference, right, between the above and X telling Garrison in the movie that in effect Kennedy was abandoning South Vietnam to the Communists.

Apart from the fact that NSAM 273, after Kennedy's murder, specifically ratified, by its very language, the 1,000-troop withdrawal of NSAM 263, and that the draft of 273 was written *before* Kennedy's assassination, there's nothing in 273 that represents a clear departure from 263 and U.S. commitment to help the South Vietnamese repel the Vietcong if the situation demanded it. Kennedy's secretary of defense, Robert McNamara, who remained in his post under LBJ after Kennedy's murder, wrote in his book *In Retrospect*, "[NSAM] 273 made clear that Johnson's policy *remained the same as Kennedy's*: 'to assist the people and government of South Vietnam to win their contest against the externally directed and supported Communist conspiracy' through training support and *without* the application of *overt* U.S. military force."[242]

Much has been made, by the conspiracy theorists who believe Kennedy was murdered by members of the military-industrial complex, of President Johnson's letter of January 1, 1964, to Diem's successor, Major General Duong Van Minh, chairman of South Vietnam's Revolutionary Council, in which he stated that "the United States will continue to furnish you and your people with the fullest measure of support in this bitter fight. We shall maintain in Vietnam American personnel and material as needed to assist you in achieving victory."[243] The fact that Johnson didn't append to his pledge of support that the military advisers aspect of it would terminate at the end of 1965 (something that, diplomatically, Kennedy may not have added either) has been interpreted, in a stretch by the conspiracy theorists, to mean that as early as January 1, 1964, Johnson intended to change Kennedy's 1965 withdrawal plans for his military advisers, those who trained the Vietnamese military, and indeed intended to introduce U.S. combat troops into the Southeast Asian conflict. The theorists maintain that this "fact" about Johnson's intent was somehow known *before* the assassination by those who ordered Kennedy's death, and indeed was the reason for it. But no one has ever offered any evidence to support this allegation. Moreover, on January 27 and 29, almost a full month after Johnson's letter to Duong Van Minh, Secretary of Defense McNamara all but decimated the inference drawn by conspiracy theorists from the letter when he testified before the House Armed Services Committee that "it is a Vietnamese war. They are going to have to assume the primary responsibility for winning it. Our policy is to *limit* our support to logistical and training

---

*A reference to the North Vietnamese Communist government (Democratic Republic of Vietnam) of President Ho Chi Minh in Hanoi, which supported militarily and manipulated the Vietcong in their joint effort to overthrow the South Vietnamese government (Republic of Vietnam) of President Ngo Dinh Diem in Saigon.

support."[244] (This from a man who would later become an advocate of escalation, the Vietnam War becoming known to many as "McNamara's War," a war he would later acknowledge was wrong.) In other words, the policy of nonintervention by combat troops was still extant in the Johnson administration at the time of Johnson's letter to Duong Van Minh.

Some other very relevant points about the October 2 memo: Taylor and McNamara went to Vietnam to assess the military situation accompanied by representatives, per the memo, "of the State Department [and the] *CIA*," and said that the recommendations in the memo (including the 1,000-troop withdrawal) were "concurred" upon by these representatives, "subject to the exceptions noted," one of which was by William E. Colby, chief of the CIA's Far East division at the time, who really had no objection to the memo's recommendations but added that our relation with Diem "should be supplemented by selected and restricted unofficial and personal relationships with individuals" in Diem's government where "persuasion could be *fruitful without derogation of the official U.S. posture*."[245] But wait. I thought the CIA was a part of this conspiracy to murder Kennedy. And as far as the Joint Chiefs of Staff being behind Kennedy's murder because he wanted to withdraw from Vietnam, although most of them undoubtedly wanted to escalate our involvement in Vietnam, let's not forget that the *chairman of the Joint Chiefs of Staff*, Maxwell Taylor, is the person who made the recommendation for withdrawal along with Kennedy's secretary of defense, Robert McNamara. The very language of NSAM 263 couldn't be any clearer: "The President considered the recommendations contained in the report of Secretary McNamara and General Taylor on their mission to South Vietnam. The President approved the military recommendations contained in Section IB (1-3) of the report . . . to withdraw one-thousand U.S. military personnel by the end of 1963."

In an October 21, 1996, article he wrote for *Newsweek*, Oliver Stone says, "[Robert] McNamara explains in his book [*In Retrospect*] that at a 'very important' National Security Council meeting on October 2, 1963, *President Kennedy* made three decisions: 1) To completely withdraw all U.S. forces from Vietnam by December 31, 1965; 2) To withdraw 1,000 U.S. troops by the end of 1963 to begin the process; and 3) To make a public announcement, in order to put this decision 'in concrete.'"[246] There is only one inference to draw from this. That it was all Kennedy's idea to withdraw, and that he was so forceful about it that he wanted to make a public announcement to put his decision "in concrete." But when we turn to pages 79 and 80 of McNamara's book, we learn that it was he who told Kennedy before the meeting, "I think, Mr. President, we must have a means of disengaging from this area." He goes on to say that at the National Security Council meeting that followed, "the President *finally* agreed . . . [and] endorsed *our* recommendation to withdraw 1,000 men by December 31, 1963 . . . Because I suspected others might try to get him to reverse the decision, I urged him to announce it publicly. That would set it *in concrete*." So although we know that Kennedy did not want to send U.S. troops to Vietnam, it appears he was not enthusiastic at all about withdrawing military advisers.

By the way, if the need for the billions of dollars of profits by the military-industrial complex was so great that its members felt compelled to kill Kennedy when he was merely *about* to withdraw *one-sixteenth* of our *military advisers* in Vietnam, and it could not be known for sure whether he would withdraw all forces, why didn't they kill President Nixon a few years later when he not only wasn't ambiguous about his determination to withdraw from Vietnam, but actually did end our involvement in the war? Didn't they need the money anymore?

Another fatal flaw in the theory that the military-industrial complex was behind the assassination is this: Are the conspirators going to murder Kennedy not even knowing if his successor, Lyndon Johnson, is going to be any better? What assurance, one may ask, would the conspirators have had that LBJ would be more of a hawk on Vietnam? Was their position, "Let's murder Kennedy, and hope for the best with Johnson"? If so, they must have had some very anxious moments, and wondered whether their murder of Kennedy was a big mistake. In fact, although there had been U.S. air attacks on North Vietnam in 1964 and 1965, it wasn't until March 6, 1965, *almost a full year and a half after the assassination*, that Johnson finally decided to send the first U.S. ground combat troops to Vietnam, and then only Marines to provide security for the Da Nang air base, thereby freeing South Vietnamese troops for other tasks. (The 3,500-man 9th Marine Expeditionary Brigade landed at Da Nang, South Vietnam, on March 8, 1965, the first American combat troops to be deployed in the country.) And even then, Johnson was so hesitant, and did it so gingerly, that he asked his secretary of defense, Robert McNamara, if their identity could be disguised by calling them "security battalions similar to MP's," and McNamara said the media would see through it.[247*]

In a February 20, 1964, telephone conversation with McNamara, Johnson had virtually parroted a remark JFK made to Walter Cronkite on September 2, 1963, telling McNamara about the Vietnamese, "It's their war and it's their men. And we're willing to train them . . . Our purpose is to train these people."[248] And in a telephone conversation Johnson had with his national security adviser, McGeorge Bundy, on May 27, 1964 (over half a year *after* the assassination), LBJ refers to the Vietnam War as "the biggest damn mess that I ever saw," and added, "I don't think it's worth fighting for." Earlier that same day in a phone conversation with Senator Richard Russell of Georgia, LBJ speaks about the "little old sergeant that works for me . . . and he's got six children, and I just put him up as the United States Army, Air Force and Navy every time I think about making this decision, and think about sending that father of those six kids in there. And what the hell are we going to get out of his doing it? And it just makes the chills run up my back." "It does me, [too]," Russell says.[249]

Former U.S. senator George McGovern writes that even *before* the assassination, "I knew that both Johnson and Russell opposed American involvement in Vietnam when it was proposed to them as senators by the Eisenhower administration . . . If it had been up to Lyndon Johnson, we would not have gone into Vietnam in the first place."[250] And when, as vice president, Johnson went on a fact-finding mission to Vietnam in May of

---

[*]As we know, the number of American combat troops in Vietnam would eventually swell to over 500,000, of whom 58,000 would die. The Vietnam War (called the American War by the Vietnamese) would claim an estimated 3.6 million Vietnamese lives. (David Shipler, "Robert McNamara and the Ghosts of Vietnam," *New York Times Magazine*, August 10, 1997, pp.30, 50; the highest troop deployment was 529,000 in 1968: *New York Times*, January 28, 1973, p.1) Although the number of troops deployed and casualties were vastly greater in the Second World War (as well as the First World War), remarkably, by December of 1967, "the United States had dropped more tons of explosives—1,630,500—on North and South Vietnam than it did on all World War II targets (1,544,463) and twice as many tons as were dropped during the Korean War" (Wicker, *JFK and LBJ*, p.286).

America's military involvement in Vietnam ended with the cease-fire agreement signed in Paris on January 27, 1973, by representatives of the United States, North Vietnam, South Vietnam, and the Vietcong (*New York Times*, January 28, 1973, pp.1, 24). On March 29, the last U.S. combat troops in Vietnam were withdrawn. However, the war continued between North and South Vietnam until Saigon, South Vietnam's capital, fell to the Communists on April 30, 1975. Today, of course, there is no North and South Vietnam, just the one Communist nation of Vietnam, whose capital is Hanoi. Saigon was renamed Ho Chi Minh City.

1961 for Kennedy, his May 23, 1961, written report to JFK upon his return counseled JFK to make it clear to President Diem that "barring an unmistakable and massive invasion of South Vietnam from without, that we have no intention of employing combat U.S. forces in Vietnam or using even naval or air-support, which is but the first step in that direction." France's enormous misadventure in Vietnam, he told JFK, conjured up the terrible specter of American soldiers "bogged down chasing irregulars and guerrillas over the rice fields and jungles of Southeast Asia while our principal enemies China and the Soviet Union stand outside the fray and husband their strength."[251]

In a 1973 interview, former president Johnson said, "All the time, in 1964, I really hoped we could negotiate our way out of a major war in Vietnam."[252]* Indeed, during his 1964 campaign for the presidency, when his Republican opponent, Senator Barry Goldwater, criticized Johnson for not being more militarily aggressive in Vietnam, Johnson told a campaign audience in Manchester, New Hampshire, that while "others are eager to enlarge the conflict by supplying American boys to do the job that Asian boys should do, [that] action would offer no solution at all to the real problems in Vietnam."[253] And in a September 25, 1964, speech in Texas responding to Goldwater's charge that he was falling down on the job in repelling the growth of global Communism, LBJ said, "It's easy to tell the other fellow, 'Here is our ultimatum and you do as we say or else,' but that will never be the policy of this country under my leadership . . . We are not about to start another war." Johnson said he did not want a "land war" in Asia, adding, however, that "we are not about to run away from where we are."[254]

When McGeorge Bundy, a military hawk in his administration, sent a memo to LBJ on January 27, 1965, on behalf of himself and another hawk, Secretary of Defense McNamara, recommending military intervention in Vietnam ("the time has come for harder choices," Bundy put it), LBJ turned elsewhere for help, asking his secretary of state, Dean Rusk, "to instruct [your] experts once again to consider all possible ways for finding a peaceful solution."[255] Johnson, in an August 19, 1969, tape recording of himself and two aides helping him write his memoir, *The Vantage Point*, said it about as succinctly as possible: "Until July 1965, I tried to keep from going into Vietnam."[256]†

None of this, naturally, is in *JFK*. The *Los Angeles Times*, in a review of the January 14, 2002, History Channel special *LBJ and Vietnam: In the Eye of the Storm* (which was

---

*See endnote for a discussion of the allegation that the Gulf of Tonkin incident was staged and used as a pretext by LBJ to go to war.

†A classic day during this period wherein Johnson must have felt like he was the rope in a tug-of-war, being pulled from both sides, was July 1, 1965, which was after the war had begun but before the big buildup. Undersecretary of State George Ball, a lone dove among the Vietnam principals in the Johnson administration, sent LBJ a memo forcefully and presciently arguing that a massive intervention in Vietnam would inflict a terrible toll on this country. "The decision you face now, therefore, is crucial," Ball said. "Once large numbers of U.S. troops are committed to direct combat they will begin to take heavy casualties in a war they are ill-equipped to fight in a non-cooperative if not downright hostile countryside. Once we suffer large casualties we will have started a well-nigh irreversible process. Our involvement will be so great that we cannot—without national humiliation—stop short of achieving our complete objectives. Of the two possibilities, I think humiliation would be more likely than the achievement of our objectives—even after we have paid terrible costs." Ball recommended "cutting our losses" and withdrawing from Vietnam before it was too late, or making U.S. deployment there very limited. That same day Johnson received a memo from Ball's superior, Dean Rusk, who had come over to the side of the hawks, arguing that South Vietnam had to be defended from Communist aggression with U.S. troops. "The integrity of the U.S. commitment is the principal pillar of peace throughout the world," Rusk argued to LBJ. "If that commitment becomes unreliable, the communist world would draw conclusions that would lead to our ruin." Rusk predicted that if the Communists in Vietnam were not stopped, it would "almost certainly" end in a "catastrophic war" for America. (*Pentagon Papers*, vol.4, pp.22–23; vol.3, p.415)

based in large part on the White House tapes of Johnson set forth in Michael Beschloss's two books, *Taking Charge: The Johnson White House Tapes, 1963–1964*, and *Reaching for Glory: Lyndon Johnson's Secret White House Tapes, 1964–1965*), concluded what was so obvious from the tapes, that rather than "the hawkish brute" eager to escalate our involvement in Vietnam, Johnson was "the most reluctant of warriors.* In recording after recording of late-night phone calls with military and political advisers, Johnson can be heard trying with growing desperation to find a way out of the murky conflict. When he does agree to dramatically ramp up the American troop commitment, he appears to do so after exhausting all other possibilities, and [then] only with the belief it will bring a quick end to the war."[257] And Johnson's own words on the tapes aren't the only evidence of his agonizing over what to do. For instance, a March 7, 1965, tape-recorded diary entry by the president's wife, Lady Bird Johnson, says, "In talking about the Vietnam situation [during dinner] Lyndon summed it up quite simply—'I can't get out, and I can't finish it with what I have got. And I don't know what the hell to do.'"[258] Writing in the *New York Times*, Michiko Kakutani observes that "the tapes underscore [Johnson's] own early doubts about the war" and reflect "his agonized decision-making over Vietnam."[259]

Yet all that Oliver Stone showed his audience was that LBJ was gung ho for a war in Vietnam,† one scene showing him forcefully telling military leaders on November 26, 1963, the day after they buried Kennedy, "Just get me elected. I'll give you the damn

---

*Two other contravening dynamics were at play here, however, both of which involved pride and human weakness. Johnson knew that his cherished "Great Society," the label given to his administration's effort to eliminate poverty in America—the one, he thought, that would be "his passport to historical immortality"—would necessarily be compromised by the budget demands of a war in Vietnam. But he told his biographer, Doris Kearns, "Losing the Great Society was a terrible thought, but not so terrible as the thought of being responsible for America's losing a war to the Communists. Nothing could possibly be worse than that." (Kearns, *Lyndon Johnson and the American Dream*, pp.210–211, 259–260; see also Dallek, *Flawed Giant*, p.400, for Johnson pestering the director of the Bureau of the Budget, Charles Schultz, to cut back on reform programs) What Johnson wanted, of course, was to have it both ways, which he could do if he could find a peaceful resolution to the mushrooming conflict in Vietnam.

The other dynamic was a quite ironic one, particularly in the fact that, though it was coming from his political Left, it may possibly have been more influential on his ultimate decision to go to war than that which was coming from the war hawks on his Right, and that was "the almost obsessive intensity of Johnson's feelings about Robert Kennedy," which had been reciprocated by Kennedy, even more so, since the Democratic convention in 1960. Kearns writes that "Kennedy's mere existence intensified Johnson's terror of withdrawing from Vietnam. And when Kennedy became an open opponent of the war [this] only helped to stiffen his [Johnson's] unwillingness" to yield in Vietnam. (Kearns, *Lyndon Johnson and the American Dream*, p.259)

†Not only was LBJ depicted in the film as wanting war, but Stone makes it very clear in the film that he believes LBJ was part of the conspiracy to murder Kennedy. At the moment in the movie when X tells Garrison about "the perpetrators" of Kennedy's assassination, Stone spotlights LBJ and the Joint Chiefs of Staff with real television footage. Indeed, he has Garrison tell his staff in the movie, "This was a military-style ambush from start to finish, a coup d'etat, with Lyndon Johnson waiting in the wings."

If the old injunction "Put your money where your mouth is" has merit, and assuming, as some conspiracy theorists like Oliver Stone suggest, that the military-industrial complex conspired with the CIA and with LBJ to murder Kennedy, a 1965 CIA document titled "Cost Reduction Program" is not helpful to them on the CIA and LBJ part of the conspiracy. As indicated previously in an endnote to the "CIA" section, according to the document, the last CIA budget under Kennedy, in 1963, was $550 million. The very next year, under LBJ, it dropped to $517 million, and was $525 million in 1965. It dropped again to $505 million in 1966, an amount supplemented by $40 million for "Southeast Asia escalation." Some thanks from LBJ to a group (CIA) that along with the military-industrial complex supposedly murdered Kennedy to make him president. Although the CIA would later tell Steven Aftergood, a senior research analyst at the Federation of American Scientists, that the 1964–1965 figures were "not accurate," one wonders if the agency said that only because it was not ordered to disclose the budget for these years to Aftergood, as it was for 1963. After all, the 1964–1966 figures appear in an official CIA document titled "Cost Reduction Program, FY 1966, FY 1967, Central Intelligence Agency" dated September 1, 1965, that was declassified from Top Secret on March 10, 1998.

war." (He was already president, of course, but would be coming up for election in one year.) The source? Stanley Karnow, in his 1983 book, *Vietnam: A History*, claims that at a White House reception on Christmas Eve, 1963, a month after Kennedy's assassination, Johnson told the Joint Chiefs of Staff this.[260] That's what Stone offers against all the evidence and the historical record to the contrary cited above. And even if we were to accept, at full value, this highly suspect entry in Karnow's book for which Karnow cites no source, but which Stone completely subscribes to, it still poses a big problem for Stone. LBJ's remark, if indeed it was ever made, was made *after*, not before, the conspirators supposedly murdered Kennedy. What evidence does Stone offer in his movie that *before* Kennedy's murder Johnson told or indicated to the conspirators he wanted war? Nothing. Nothing at all. And, as indicated, he doesn't present to his audience any of the overwhelming and conclusive evidence that once LBJ became president, he did everything possible to avoid war. If Stone had done so (i.e., if he had told the truth), it would have completely contradicted and refuted the main theme of his movie—that Kennedy did not want to go to war in Vietnam and LBJ did, and that's why Kennedy was murdered.

Right to the very end, the Vietnam War weighed more heavily on Johnson than any other chapter in his presidency. Indeed, although he eventually committed himself to the war, because of doubts about the conflict that never left him he was unwilling to commit the United States to an all-out war, prompting General William C. Westmoreland, Johnson's chief of military operations in Vietnam, to later write, "A major problem [in the U.S. prosecution of the war] was that Washington policy decisions forced us to fight with but one hand."[261] In April of 1967, Westmoreland said in a New York City speech that "in effect, we are fighting a war of attrition." He proceeded to fly to Washington, where he asked the president to increase the number of ground troops from the existing 470,000 to 550,500, the "minimal essential force," or 670,000, the "optimum." Johnson, shocked, asked, "Where does it all end?" When Secretary of Defense McNamara queried Westmoreland as to how long it would take to win the war, the jut-jawed general responded, "With the optimum force about three years; with the minimum force, at least five."[262] He got neither.

With the war escalating out of control in 1965–1968, and the Communists' Tet offensive in early 1968 into more than a hundred South Vietnamese towns and villages (elements even fighting their way onto the grounds of the American embassy in Saigon) demonstrating (though the Vietcong sustained tremendous losses) beyond all doubt the resiliency of the Communist forces and that the war was far from over, Johnson lost his stomach for the conflict and elected to not run for reelection.[263]* But there were con-

---

*Surely, one of the catalysts for Johnson's decision was the run for the Democratic nomination for president by Minnesota senator Eugene J. McCarthy. Although McCarthy's candidacy was at first thought to be quixotic, he inspired thousands of young people throughout the country with his strong anti–Vietnam War position and rhetoric, and they mobilized their support for him in the 1968 New Hampshire primary, "hordes of them" traveling there to knock on doors, stuff envelopes, and do whatever they could to help his cause. At the time, it was assumed that Johnson would seek reelection, though he had not formally declared and was not on the primary ballot. Alarmed by the increasingly popular campaign of McCarthy, New Hampshire Democratic leaders organized a major write-in campaign for Johnson and they were confident of victory. Johnson won, but not handily, getting 49 percent of the vote to McCarthy's 42 percent, a result that shocked the political world. The president's vulnerability suddenly becoming evident, just four days later Senator Robert F. Kennedy, who had decided earlier not to run, announced his candidacy. As with McCarthy, he tethered it to the antiwar movement. Just two weeks later, Johnson announced he would not seek reelection. (Art Pine, "Eugene McCarthy; Candidacy Inspired Antiwar Movement," *Los Angeles Times*, December 11, 2005, pp. A1, A34)

tributing factors. "I felt that I was being chased on all sides by a giant stampede coming at me from all directions," he told his biographer, Doris Kearns.

> On one side, the American people were stampeding me to do something about Vietnam. On another side, the inflationary economy was booming out of control. Up ahead were dozens of danger signs pointing to another summer of riots in the cities. I was being forced over the edge by rioting blacks, demonstrating [over Vietnam] students, marching welfare mothers, squawking professors, and hysterical reporters. And then the final straw. The thing I feared from the first day of my Presidency was actually coming true. Robert Kennedy had openly announced his intention to reclaim the throne in the memory of his brother. And the American public, swayed by the magic of the name, were dancing in the streets. The whole situation was unbearable to me. After thirty-seven years of public service, I deserved something more than being left alone in the middle of the plain, chased by stampedes on every side.

In a televised address to the nation on the evening of March 31, 1968 (a little over two months before RFK was assassinated in Los Angeles), Johnson began his speech by announcing his decision to stop air and naval attacks on North Vietnam, except in the area of the Demilitarized Zone, in the hope, he said, that "President Ho Chi Minh [will] respond positively and favorably to this new step of peace." He then shocked the nation's viewers by saying, "With America's sons in the fields far away, with America's future under challenge right here at home . . . I do not believe that I should devote an hour or a day of my time to any personal partisan [political] causes . . . Accordingly, I shall not seek, and will not accept, the nomination of my party for another term as your President."[264]

As seen earlier, the evidence is very conflicting and ambiguous, at best, as to whether or not Kennedy, if he had lived, would have eventually withdrawn from Vietnam.

As previously alluded to, on September 2, 1963, less than three months before his death, he told Walter Cronkite of CBS, "In the final analysis, it is their [South Vietnamese] war. They are the ones who have to win or lose it." Stone, naturally, put that segment of the Cronkite interview on the screen for his audience. But Stone didn't show his audience Kennedy thereafter telling Cronkite, "*But I don't agree with those who say we should withdraw. That would be a great mistake* . . . This is a very important struggle even though it is far away. We took all this—made this effort to defend Europe. Now Europe is quite secure. We also have to participate—we may not like it, in the defense of Asia." Since these additional words by Kennedy would have been in direct opposition to the main point of Stone's movie, that Kennedy was murdered because he intended to withdraw from Vietnam, Stone, in the finest traditions of the conspiracy profession, simply eliminated these words for his audience.* And a week later, in an interview with David Brinkley on NBC, Kennedy

---

*But I understand. Stone simply didn't have room in his three-hour-and-eight-minute film for the additional seventeen words italicized above. Just like Ken Starr, in his September 9, 1998, report to Congress on the President Clinton–Monica Lewinsky scandal, couldn't find the space in his 452-page, 119,000-word report—one that was overflowing with one sexually explicit reference after another, many of which Starr found the space to repeat—to include these seventeen words of Ms. Lewinsky's testimony before a federal grand

affirmed his belief in the "domino theory," suggesting that if South Vietnam fell to the Communists, it would have a domino effect, harming American interests throughout Southeast Asia (and, elliptically, the world). Speaking of China, he added, "China is so large, looms so high . . . that if South Vietnam went, it would . . . give the impression that the wave of the future in Southeast Asia was China and the Communists."[265] Naturally, these words of Kennedy also are not heard in Stone's film.

Just like the conflicting evidence, there are, of course, conflicting views on whether or not Kennedy would have withdrawn from Vietnam. McNamara wrote in 1995 that he believed it "highly probable that, had Kennedy lived, he would have pulled us out of Vietnam."[266] And Kennedy biographer Robert Dallek writes that "it was hardly conceivable that Kennedy would have sent tens of thousands more Americans to fight in so inhospitable a place as Vietnam. Reduced commitments, especially of military personnel, during a second Kennedy term were a more likely development."[267] But Nicholas Lemann wrote in *GQ* magazine, in 1992, "Robert Kennedy, who was probably in a better position than anyone else to know what his brother's intentions in Vietnam were, had this to say on the subject in an in-depth interview conducted for the historical record in 1964 [by John Barlow Martin for the John F. Kennedy library], the year after his brother's death: Interviewer: 'Did the President feel that we would have to go into Vietnam in a big way?' Kennedy: 'We certainly considered what would be the result if you abandoned Vietnam, even Southeast Asia, and whether it was worthwhile trying to keep and hold on to.' Interviewer: 'What did he say? What did he think?' Kennedy: 'He reached the conclusion that probably it was worthwhile."[268]*

McGeorge Bundy, Kennedy's special assistant for national security matters who signed NSAMs 263 and 273, told *Newsweek*, "I don't think we know what he would have done if he'd lived. I don't know, and I don't know anyone who does know."[269] Indeed, as *Time* magazine observed, "Even [Kennedy] may not have known what he really planned to do in Vietnam after the election."[270]

Since we are attempting to know the unknowable, those of us who are further handicapped by not knowing Kennedy personally are in no position to weigh in meaningfully on the issue. But based merely on what I have read about John F. Kennedy, I sense that he was a rationalist, even more, in fact, than an intellectual, which he surely was too.† Because he was a rationalist who had personally experienced the horrors of war,‡ I feel

---

jury: "The president never asked me to lie, and no one promised me a job for my silence," words that severely undercut Starr's obstruction-of-justice charge against Clinton. But again, I understand. There was a space problem. But I wonder if Starr would have managed to find room in his extensive report if Lewinsky had testified, "The president asked me to lie, and I was promised a job for my silence."

*On the issue of what Kennedy would have done, if any politician at the time was more aware of the consequences of inaction when action was called for it was Kennedy. Indeed, in his senior year at Harvard, he wrote a thesis on the British and French appeasement of Hitler at Munich that was so well received by the faculty it enabled him to graduate cum laude even though he had previously been a mediocre student. He decided to expand the thesis into a book, *Why England Slept*, that became a best seller in the summer of 1940. So Kennedy could have been expected to have all tentacles out assessing the danger to America, if it existed, of withdrawing from Vietnam.

†Someone who did know Kennedy fairly well, and whose job included studying Kennedy closely, was Sander Vanocur, the White House correspondent for NBC during the Kennedy administration. Vanocur said Kennedy "was, by temperament . . . a man governed at all times by a sense of restraint and proportion." (Vanocur, "Kennedy's Voyage of Discovery," p.42)

‡The late army colonel David H. Hackworth, who received seventy-eight combat awards during the Korean and Vietnam wars and was often referred to during his lifetime as "America's most decorated living solider,"

Kennedy would have only sent combat troops to Vietnam if he strongly believed that the Communist (Hanoi and the Vietcong) aggression was a part of Soviet Communism's plan to ultimately conquer the world—that is, if he strongly believed that his failure to fight in Vietnam would imperil this nation's security. Since we know, not just from hindsight *but from the absence of evidence to the contrary at the time* that the Communist aggression was nothing more than a civil war between North Vietnam (and the Vietcong) and South Vietnam,[*] my guess is that his rationalism, coupled with his firsthand knowledge that war was hell, would have prevailed. This is why I am inclined to agree with this assessment by Kenneth P. O'Donnell and David F. Powers, next to Bobby Kennedy the president's closest advisers: "All of us who listened to President Kennedy's repeated expressions of his determination to avoid further involvement in Vietnam are sure that if he had lived to serve a second term, the members of American military advisers and technicians in the country would have steadily decreased. He *never* would have committed U.S. Army combat units and draftees to action against the Viet Cong."[271] In other words, there would never have been a Vietnam War with its enormous loss of lives and cataclysmic consequences for decades to come.

There is also no question in the minds of two others of his closest aides, Theodore C. Sorensen and Arthur Schlesinger Jr., that Kennedy would not have sent combat troops to Vietnam. In a 2005 op-ed piece in the *New York Times*, they wrote of their being witnesses to seeing Kennedy, leaning back in his Oval Office rocking chair, "tick off all his options [in Vietnam] and then critique them." They said he concluded "that withdrawal was the viable option," and they point out that his clear predilection was set forth in a November 14, 1963, press conference, just eight days before his death, in which he stated, "That is our object, to bring Americans home."[272]

But what Kennedy would have done is a question whose answer is lost to history. No one knows—that is, except Oliver Stone, who knew for sure, proceeded to present it as a fact to his audience, and built a central part of his movie around the proposition that because Kennedy was going to withdraw, he was murdered.

Parenthetically, the larger notion Stone propounded in his film (of which the Vietnam withdrawal, he suggested, was the most important manifestation, the straw that broke the camel's back) was that Kennedy's being "soft on Communism" triggered a deadly response from members of the military-industrial complex. Hating Communism as they did, they were greatly angered by any move by Kennedy toward detente with the Soviet Union (which Kennedy obviously preferred over a nuclear war). As support for Kennedy being soft on Communism, Stone showed an excerpt of Kennedy's speech at American University in Washington, D.C., on June 10, 1963: "*We must reexamine our own attitudes*

---

said that "most combat vets pick their fights carefully. They look at their scars, remember the madness, and are always mindful of the fallout" (*Los Angeles Times*, May 6, 2005, p.B12).

[*]Although as early as 1950, the Soviet Union and Communist China recognized Ho Chi Minh's revolutionary and Communist-controlled "Democratic Republic of Vietnam" as the sovereign government of Vietnam (Butwell, *Southeast Asia*, pp.23, 28), this doesn't alter the fact that the United States intervened in an essentially internal civil war between North and South Vietnam, not a war intended by North Vietnam to help spread global Communism. In fact, Ho Chi Minh, though a Communist, rose to power as the leader of a nationalist (not Communist) movement to resist France's continued rule in the country. (Butwell, *Southeast Asia*, p.23) And, as Leslie Gelb, a senior official in LBJ's administration, writes, with the defeat of South Vietnam "no dominoes fell." He goes on to say that three years after the fall of Saigon in 1975, "the standing and the power of the U.S. in Asia were greater than at any time since the end of World War II." (Gelb, "Would Defeat in Iraq Be So Bad?" p.40)

toward the Soviet Union . . . Our most basic, common link is that we all inhabit this small planet. We all breathe the same air. We all cherish our children's future. And we are all mortal." Stone's audience didn't hear the prelude to this statement—the reality that we live "in an age when a single nuclear weapon contains almost ten times the explosive force delivered by all of the allied air forces in the Second World War," where "the deadly poisons produced by a nuclear exchange would be carried by wind and water and soil and seed to the far corners of the globe and to generations yet unborn . . . I speak of peace, therefore, as the necessary rational end of rational men." The president's remarks, obviously, did not betray any softness toward Communism, only a concern for survival of the human race. Since when is *detente* and a desire for peace the equivalent of capitulation to the enemy? In a memorandum to Robert Manning, assistant secretary of state, on June 11, 1963, McGeorge Bundy said, "This speech should not be misunderstood as indicating any weakening in the American resolution to resist the pressures for Soviet expansion." It was "designed to emphasize the positive opportunities for a more constructive and less hostile Soviet policy."[273]

Contrary to Kennedy's being soft on Communism, the generally accepted view of historians has been that Kennedy, with a nod here and a nod there to political doves, was a moderate. Some even felt he was a cold warrior at heart. We know, for instance, that during his less than three years in office at the height of the cold war, and despite the Nuclear Test-Ban Treaty (between the United States, Soviet Union, and Great Britain) that was agreed on in July of 1963 but not formally ratified until October 7, 1963,[*] he substantially increased our military capability against Russia as well as the nation's defense budget. In the president's speech in Fort Worth on the morning of the assassination, he pointed out that "in the past three years we have increased the defense budget of the United States by over 20 percent, increased the program of acquisition of Polaris submarines from 24 to 41, increased our Minuteman missile-purchase program by more than 75 percent, doubled [i.e., increased by 100 percent] the number of strategic bombers and missiles on alert, doubled the number of nuclear weapons available in the strategic alert forces, increased the tactical nuclear forces deployed in Western Europe by over 60 percent, added five combat-ready divisions to the Armies of the United States and five tactical fighter wings to the Air Force of the United States, increased our strategic airlift capability by 75 percent and increased our special counterinsurgency forces which are engaged now in South Vietnam by 600 percent."[274] Since our sworn enemy at the time was Soviet Communism, and therefore this military buildup was, indeed, against the Communist threat, not the Bolivian civilian militia, certainly the American military couldn't be too unhappy with the above numbers, could it? Nor could the defense industry (the "industrial" part of Stone's military-industrial complex), which made billions off building these weapons, have been.

And after all, it was Kennedy who campaigned for president in 1960 arguing that there was a "missile gap" between the Soviet Union and us (citing the launching of the Soviet

---

[*]"This treaty is not the millennium," Kennedy would say about the treaty that banned nuclear testing "in the atmosphere, in outer space, and under water." He said, "It will not resolve all conflicts, or cause the Communists to forgo their ambitions, or eliminate the dangers of war. It will not reduce our need for arms . . . But it is an important step—a step toward peace—a step toward reason—a step away from war." The treaty, very reluctantly agreed to by Kennedy's own Joint Chiefs of Staff, culminated five years of negotiation. It did not ban nuclear testing underground because of Soviet opposition to on-site inspection. (Joint Chiefs of Staff reluctantly agree: Schlesinger, *Thousand Days*, pp.896, 912–913) Kennedy viewed the test ban "the touchstone of his entire foreign policy," and once told an aide who was very close to him that if he had to lose the 1964 election because of it, then he was "willing to pay the price." (Vanocur, "Kennedy's Voyage of Discovery," p.45)

Sputnik on October 4, 1957, and by a powerful rocket, the Soviet SS-6, that was capable of reaching U.S. soil from Russia) that America had to close and then overcome;[*] who challenged Russia to an arms race in 1961; and who made Nikita Khrushchev blink during the Cuban missile crisis in 1962. And it was Kennedy who wrote these words to Khrushchev on April 18, 1961: "Mr. Chairman . . . You should recognize that free people in all parts of the world do not accept the claim of historical inevitability for Communist revolution. What your government believes is its own business; what it does in the world is the world's business." In a letter to Khrushchev on October 22, 1962, Kennedy wrote that "the United States could not tolerate any action on your part which in a major way disturbed the existing over-all balance of power in the world." As Pierre Salinger has written, "If the strength and stridency of Kennedy's anti-communism have ever been in doubt, they should be dispelled . . . The theme of anti-communism [was] recurrent" in his administration. In NSAM 132, a memo to Fowler Hamilton, administrator of the Agency for International Development, signed by Kennedy on February 19, 1962, Kennedy said, "As you know, I desire the appropriate agencies of this Government to give utmost attention and emphasis to programs designed to counter Communist indirect aggression, which I regard as a grave threat during the 1960's. I have already written the Secretary of Defense 'to move to a new level of increased activity across the board' in the counter-insurgency field."[275]

Conscious, as all presidents are, of their place in history, one can reasonably assume that Kennedy would have made every effort to prevent a geopolitical tilt toward Communism in the world from taking place "on his watch."

But all of this is really beside the point. Since X categorically tells Garrison in the film about the military-industrial plot to kill Kennedy, and there are scenes in *JFK* actually depicting the Joint Chiefs of Staff setting in motion this conspiracy to murder Kennedy, what evidence does Stone have that such a conspiracy actually took place? For starters, as previously indicated, Stone has admitted that he made up the scene in Washington between X and Garrison. Moreover, Stone has no *evidence* that such a conspiracy ever took place. He simply manufactured the entire conspiracy out of whole cloth for his gullible audience. But he *did* have a source for the naked *allegation* that such a conspiracy took place: the redoubtable, aforementioned Fletcher Prouty—you know, the fellow who was an active member of the group that believes the Holocaust is a Jewish hoax. Just who, specifically, did the late Mr. Prouty allege were the members of the military-industrial complex who actually conspired to murder Kennedy? Prouty didn't mention one single name, falling back, instead, on the always available, guilty, and universally maligned "they."

But let's listen to Prouty tell, in his own words in Lyndon LaRouche's publication, *Executive Intelligence Review*, what he believed happened. Prouty said that after NSAM 263 was published on October 11, 1963, ordering the withdrawal of 1,000 military advisers from Vietnam,

> to those working close to the scene in the Pentagon, and to those people who had the prospect of building helicopters and fighter aircraft and guns and tanks and all the rest of it, this was terrible. This was anathema. *They* had had plenty of orders through

---

[*]It is by no means certain that there was any missile gap at all. Indeed, there are those who believe that if there were such a gap, it was in America's favor, and Kennedy knew it, his political campaign allegation being disingenuous. However, this has not been proved.

World War II. There was a big build-up for the Korean War, and now, for ten years, *they* had been building up on the prospect that there would be even a bigger war, a consumers' war, for them in Vietnam. Amid all these pressures, *it's not too unrealistic* [certainly not for someone like you, Mr. Prouty] to see that some of them sat somewhere and said, "Look, we've got to do some planning. We've got to get this guy Kennedy out of office." And the more *they* thought about it, and the more *they* talked about it, *they* realized that legitimate, honest-to-God . . . political planning was not going to get him out. Kennedy was going to win. At that point, somewhere, *a small voice* said, "We're going to get that bastard out right now," and there are ways to do it. As Lyndon Johnson said, "We have a Murder, Incorporated,"* a professional group—no Lee Harvey Oswald, or other goons like that—a professional group, trained, equipped, salaried, and everything, to do assassinations. *They* were given a job. *They* did their job. *They* killed the President. There was a coup d'etat in this country, and following it, the biggest residual job people have had within that group has been to run this cover story.[276]

This "small voice" Prouty imagined and speculated that "they," the conspirators, heard, was heard only by Prouty. And when people start to hear small voices in their head . . . well, I think you know what I'm about to say.

So this small-voice reverie and naked theorizing of Fletcher Prouty's was converted by Oliver Stone, with full knowledge that he had absolutely nothing to support it, into the motive for Kennedy's murder in his fantasy movie. Stone presented to his audience Prouty's fantasizing about the Joint Chiefs of Staff and the defense industry plotting Kennedy's murder as though it actually happened. Prouty's small voice, then, became the principal foundation and spin for the whole movie.

Two footnotes to all of this: First, when Robert Kennedy is shown in Stone's movie being murdered in Los Angeles in 1968, Garrison tells his assistants, "They [the same power structure that murdered JFK] killed Robert Kennedy." And it's very clear that Stone wants his audience to believe that "they" also killed Martin Luther King Jr., whose murder is also shown. "And now King," Garrison tells his wife in exasperation over her less-than-total acceptance of his conspiracy theories. "Don't you think this [referring to the Kennedy case by looking at the Warren Commission volume in his hand] has something to do with that [referring to the story on the television screen about King's murder]?" Stone removed all ambiguity as to what he was trying to convey in *JFK* in a December 23, 1991, *Time* interview:

Question: "Is it accurate to say that you think the assassinations of John Kennedy, Martin Luther King and Bobby Kennedy are linked?"

Stone: "These three leaders were pulling out of the war in Vietnam and shaking up the country. Civil rights, the cold war itself, everything was in question. There's no doubt that these three killings are linked, and it worked. That's what's amazing. They [the conspirators] pulled it off."[277]

And when asked by a reporter in his appearance before the National Press Club on January 15, 1992, "Did you mean to imply in *JFK* that the U.S. government might be

---

*LBJ's reference in an interview with Leo Janos to the CIA-backed attempted assassination of Fidel Castro (Janos, "Last Days of the President," p.39).

implicated in the assassination of both Martin Luther King Jr. and Bobby Kennedy?" Stone answered "Yes."[278]

Second, as we've seen, Stone has occupants of the highest corridors of power in our national government conspiring with the nation's most powerful business and industrial titans to murder President Kennedy. But as we've also seen, another major part of Stone's *JFK* depicts the plot to kill the president being hatched by Clay Shaw, David Ferrie, and Lee Harvey Oswald in the presence of a homosexual prostitute. How did each of these two completely disparate groups happen to decide on killing Kennedy at the very same place and time? Did either get in the other's way at Dealey Plaza? Or were they working together? But if so, how in the world would the Joint Chiefs of Staff and presidents of our nation's largest corporations have known of the existence of the shabby, New Orleans conspirators? And how would the latter have possibly known that the former were planning to murder Kennedy? When the Joint Chiefs of Staff, et cetera, decided to kill Kennedy, even if they somehow found out about their soul mates in New Orleans, would they have been likely to entrust the mission to kill the president to such a motley group of losers? Stone isn't troubled by any of these questions and none are dealt with in the movie, Stone not providing his audience with any scene connecting the two groups.

29. Stone used X to dispense other goodies to his audience. X tells Garrison that he was in New Zealand at the time the president was shot and "Oswald was charged at 7:00 p.m. Dallas time with Tippit's murder. That was two in the afternoon the next day, New Zealand time [nineteen-hour time difference between Dallas and New Zealand], but already their papers had the entire history of the unknown, twenty-four-year-old . . . Oswald—studio pictures, biographical data, Russian information—and were pretty sure he killed the president." This was proof to X that the conspirators had determined before the assassination that Oswald was to be the patsy and they already had information to send out on him before he was even charged. But number one, was X, who supposedly was in Christchurch, New Zealand, at the time (Prouty, allegedly, actually was), the only person in a foreign country who felt the information about Oswald reached him or her (such as an employee at a newspaper, or radio or TV station) earlier than it should have? The information on Oswald went out from Dallas throughout the entire civilized world and there's nothing in the vast literature I have seen on the assassination indicating that anyone in Paris, Rome, Brussels, Berlin, London, or anywhere else, felt they received information on Oswald earlier than they should have. Or was X suggesting that for some unfathomable reason the conspirators were interested in getting out a quick story on Oswald only in Christchurch, New Zealand? What was so important about Christchurch?

In any event, Stone doesn't tell his audience that there was nothing unusual about the New Zealand paper having an "Extra" edition (headlined "Kennedy Shot Dead") out on Oswald and the Tippit killing by 2:00 p.m. on November 23. Without even hearing what the Christchurch newspaper's explanation for all of this is (see later), if the first information on Oswald went out over the wires in Dallas at 7:00 p.m., when Oswald was charged with Tippit's murder, then obviously this would not have given the New Zealand paper enough time to have already published details about Oswald's life at that moment in New Zealand, which would be 2:00 p.m. the next day. But information on Oswald's background started going out over the wires several hours *before* he was formally charged with Tippit's murder. Though he was charged at 7:00 (actually 7:05) p.m. Dallas time, he was arrested five hours and ten minutes earlier, at 1:50 p.m. Dallas time (8:50 a.m. the next day, New Zealand time), and Captain Glen King, Dallas police chief Jesse Curry's administrative assistant, testified that he had heard that an hour after Oswald's arrest (2:50 p.m. Dallas time, 9:50 a.m. New Zealand time) a member of the media already had a photo of Oswald.[279] All indications are that from the moment Oswald arrived, in custody, at the Dallas Police Department around 2:00 p.m. forward, it was the policy of the Dallas Police Department to be very cooperative with the press and to make them privy to the main things happening on the case.[280] However, I have been unable to find a record of which media outlet first got the news out about Oswald's arrest and the time it did so. But under no circumstances was it later than 3:54 p.m. Dallas time when Bill Regan of NBC News announced on national television that "Lee Oswald seems to be the prime suspect in the assassination of John F. Kennedy." So wire stories about Oswald's background would have started going out all over the world no later than 3:54 p.m. Dallas time (10:54 a.m. New Zealand time), giving any newspaper in New Zealand over three hours, more than ample time, to publish a brief sketch of Oswald's background before 2:00 p.m.

After Stone's movie was released, the *Christchurch Star*, responding to conspiracy theorists, reported that the *Star* "knew of Oswald's being in custody by 10 a.m." and immediately "began gathering information about him." The paper said that

> Bob Cotton, Chief Reporter of the *Christchurch Star* . . . at the time, can recall clearly the events of November 1963. He says that even in 1963, global communication was fast and effective everywhere and an assassination of a U.S. President meant that everything and everyone on the *Star* worked doubly quick. News [at that time] came by . . . various wire services . . . Photographs were usually wired to Australia, then to Auckland and thence to Christchurch. This time, to get the photographs early, some of the geographical links were by-passed through technical ingenuity at the *Star*. Even so, the paper would not have been published until 1:30 p.m. or 2:15–2:30 p.m., depending on the edition. Bob Cotton says that the *Star* was *never* published in the morning during his time on the newspaper (from 1958). Bob Cotton also . . . says that Lee Harvey Oswald was not a stranger to the media. Information on him would have been readily available in U.S. newspapers . . . and would have been sent out quickly. In 1959 there had been much coverage in newspapers about young men defecting to the Soviet Union, and Oswald's defection had been covered in detail in *The Washington Post*, *The Washington Evening Star* and *The New York Times*. Again, it was widely reported when Oswald, now with a Russian wife and child, returned to the United States in 1962.[281]

The particular article in the *Christchurch Star* that Prouty referred to was an AP wire story that contained absolutely no information about Oswald that wasn't already known *before* the assassination, such as that he "had defected to the Soviet Union in 1959," that "while in the Soviet Union he worked in a factory in Minsk," that he "returned to the United States in 1962," had a "[Russian] wife and child," that he was the "chairman of the 'Fair Play for Cuba Committee,'" and so on. In fact, the photo of Oswald shown in the *Christchurch Star* was the photo taken of him at the Hotel Berlin in Moscow on October 16, 1959. It has come to be known as the "Moscow defection photo," and was shown in several American newspapers in 1959, including page two of the *Fort Worth Star-Telegram* on November 16, 1959.

30. X tells Garrison in *JFK*, "Many strange things were happening on November 22nd. At 12:34 p.m., the *entire* telephone system went dead in Washington [D.C.] for a solid

hour . . . to keep the wrong stories from spreading if anything went wrong with the [assassination] plan." But the entire telephone system did not go out for an entire hour in Washington, D.C. As author William Manchester writes in *The Death of a President*, there was such a mass of phone calls being made in Washington (and, of course, elsewhere) immediately after the assassination that the phone circuits were overloaded. "Lines would go dead, return to normal when a sufficient number of people had hung up, and go dead again and return to life, over and over. The pattern was repeated throughout the country."[282]* But this wasn't true with *all* lines in the D.C. area. In a January 1992 interview of Oliver Stone by Sam Donaldson on ABC's *Prime Time*, Donaldson told Stone, "I made a dozen calls during that time from the Capitol to the White House and elsewhere in Washington. The telephone system wasn't out." Whereupon Stone replied, "I'll have to look into that." So contrary to what Stone told his audience, there was no blackout for an hour in the nation's capital, and no one, other than Oliver Stone and some conspiracy theorists, has ever said that there was.

But telephone lines in New York City did go out for awhile. Per the *New York Times*, news of the president's murder "spread quickly" and so many "hundreds of thousands [of people] reached for so many telephones that the system blacked out and operators had to refuse calls."[283] Likewise in Boston. Per the *Boston Globe*, "Boston's telephone communications were virtually paralyzed. Switchboards at newspapers, radio and television stations were clogged . . . Many waited 20 minutes to get a dial tone because of the overload."[284]

31. In *JFK*, Garrison tells his staff that "when Oswald went to Russia, he was not a real defector. He was an intelligence agent on some kind of mission for our government, and remained one until the day he died." As further evidence for his audience that Oswald was a U.S. intelligence agent, one of Garrison's assistants tells him that when Oswald wanted to return to the United States, "the State Department issued Oswald a passport within forty-eight hours." Garrison: "Did Marina have any trouble getting out of Russia?" "No, none, either," she says. We know that both of these statements are absolutely untrue, Oswald and Marina struggling with bureaucratic red tape for several months before their applications were approved by the Soviets.[285]

But Stone wasn't satisfied with these falsehoods. He wanted more groups involved in the assassination. Remarkably, to show Oswald's connection with the KGB, Garrison's assistant tells him in the movie that when Oswald first arrived in Russia, he "disappears for six weeks, presumably with the KGB," and when he reappears in Minsk, he is given "royal treatment," living "high-on-the-hog" with a good apartment and five thousand rubles per month. Garrison responds that this had to be because he gave the Soviets radar secrets that they used to shoot down U-2 pilot Gary Powers.

So now we have the pathetically disoriented Oswald, just out of his teens, being an agent for the CIA (the principal agency of U.S. intelligence) *and* the KGB. But Oliver, you don't have any evidence that Oswald was an agent for either the CIA or the KGB, only wild speculation that you passed on to your audience as reality. Not only is your speculation wild, but it's also wildly inconsistent. You say the CIA (and the military-industrial complex) wanted to (and did) kill Kennedy because he was "soft on Communism."

---

*Manchester writes that at Parkland Hospital in Dallas, Steve Landregan, the hospital administrator who was asked to call O'Neal's mortuary for a casket for the president, couldn't get an outside line because "Dallas' Southwestern Bell . . . was crippled by overloaded exchanges and circuits." He "ran from office to office, picking up receivers" until he finally got "a dial tone." (Manchester, *Death of a President*, p.291)

But if Kennedy were, indeed, "soft on Communism," wouldn't he be the exact type of president the KGB and Soviets would want to keep? Have you no respect at all for your viewers, who have made you a very rich man? I know you wanted your audience to believe that everyone and their grandmother was involved in the assassination, but didn't you go a little too far in leading your audience to believe that both the CIA *and* the KGB were behind Oswald's killing Kennedy?

32. Throughout the movie, Stone makes it clear that President Kennedy was a political martyr who was doing wonderful and noble things for this country. He is described as "the slain young king." Garrison says, "John Kennedy was the godfather of my generation," and Kennedy's murder was "one of the most terrible moments in the history of this country." With Stone's and Garrison's reverence for JFK, what more loathsome and reprehensible way is there to honor his memory than to deliberately distort the history of his assassination and attempt to make a kind of hero out of the person who murdered him? Under what conceivable theory would Kennedy have wanted that? Yet that's precisely what the outrageous Stone, in contradiction of all facts and evidence, did in his picture. Throughout *JFK*, Garrison accepts the notion that Oswald is innocent, someone who was just, as Oswald himself proclaimed, "a patsy." With the exception of when Oswald was resisting arrest and one time when he was physically aggressive with Marina, Stone depicts Oswald in the movie—by his words, body language, and context—as being quiet, passive, meek, never conspiratorial or menacing. (It goes without saying that Stone never showed his audience Oswald's attempted assassination of retired Major General Edwin Walker.) Stone has Garrison saying in the movie that on the day of the assassination Oswald had "handlers" who were manipulating him, but that Oswald's nonchalant conduct in the lunchroom, when he wasn't even out of breath, indicated that he himself never fired a shot at Kennedy. So Oswald, per Stone, was completely innocent.

But Stone had to go even further. He wanted his audience to have sympathy for Oswald, the audience being told that after Oswald's arrest, "false statements about Oswald circulated the globe." Then, to a background of sad music, and with Marina, holding her newborn daughter in her arms, crying at her husband's grave site, Garrison laments to the Shaw jury, "Who grieves for Lee Harvey Oswald, buried in a cheap grave under the name Oswald? Nobody." Worse still, Stone had to try to make Oswald an American patriot and hero risking his own life (if discovered by his "handlers") to save Kennedy's life. Ignoring the evidence of what the essence of the note actually said (see earlier in book), Garrison says in the movie that the note Oswald left for Agent James Hosty at Dallas FBI headquarters about ten days before the assassination probably was "describing the [forthcoming] assassination attempt on JFK" to alert the authorities.

Continuing in his quest to have Oswald be an imperfect hero, Stone has Garrison saying in the movie, "I think we can raise the possibility that Oswald may have been the original source of the [FBI] telex dated November 17th warning of the assassination in Dallas on November 22nd." In other words, Stone wanted his audience to believe that not only didn't Oswald murder Kennedy, *he tried to prevent his murder*.

Stone's disdain for history led him to cast the real Jim Garrison as Earl Warren, the U.S. chief justice who chaired the Commission named after him, a person whom Garrison vilified in life for his role as the head of the Warren Commission. *New York Times* columnist Anthony Lewis wrote, "The best insight into Oliver Stone's character, for me, was his treatment of Chief Justice Warren. Earl Warren no doubt had his faults. But he loved this country with all his heart, and the assassination tore him apart. The notion that he would cover up that assassination is contemptible, a contempt well expressed by Stone's choice of the real Jim Garrison to play Earl Warren in the film."[286]

If one were to conclude that the above is a total recitation of all the lies, distortions, and fabrications in the movie *JFK*, it is not. There are many others, some of which, as previously indicated, I discuss in other parts of this book. As I said earlier, the movie is virtually one continuous lie in which Stone couldn't find any level of deception and invention beyond which he was unwilling to go. And yet, the whole thrust of the movie is that what was being depicted on the screen was the truth, and everyone *else* was lying. In fact, the audience is expressly told this. Garrison tells reporters in one scene, "Is the Government worth preserving when it lies to the people?" In another scene, Garrison says, "The truth is the most important value we have." Indeed, at the end of the movie these words appear on the screen: "Dedicated to the Young in Whose Spirit the Truth Marches On." And in his June 1993 foreword to Robert Groden's book, *The Killing of a President*, Stone thanks Groden for "ensuring the . . . accuracy of key scenes in Dealey Plaza" (right—like six shots being fired instead of three; three shooters instead of one; placing Connally directly in front of Kennedy instead of to his left front; etc.),[*] and closes by saying, "May all the truth be known . . . soon." But Oliver, how can the truth be known when you did everything within your power to make sure that your audience never knew what the evidence showed the truth to be? How are you helping the truth to be known when you asked millions of people watching your film (and watching it to this very day on video or DVD) to accept your blatant inventions and falsehoods? In your topsy-turvy, *Alice in Wonderland* world, how are you spelling your word *truth*? *LIE*? You say you want the truth to be known soon. But as former president Gerald Ford put it so well, if it's the truth that there was a conspiracy in the assassination, and the evidence of it is as strong as Stone and his colleagues say it is, "why would Oliver Stone [have to] resort to ignoring, distorting, and even inventing facts?"[287]

Without knowing Oliver Stone personally, my sense is that he is a person with humanitarian instincts who identifies with the disadvantaged and aggrieved in our society and has a yearning for justice for all, both very admirable traits. In achieving what he perceives to be, as he says, a "higher truth" in the Kennedy assassination, he was willing to take enormous liberties with the truth, making him a classic example of one who believes that the end justifies the means. But that is only half of it. The invariable suggestion he has made when confronted with the accusation that his film was not a strictly factual rendition of the assassination is that he never invented anything that would alter the essence of what happened—that is, they were only trivializations that always become necessary when a filmmaker utilizes a narrative to present a historical event.[†] But this is just continuing the lie. Stone's lies and fabrications were so serious, so gross, so outrageous, that they *did* totally change the essence of what happened. Moreover, since all of the evidence

---

[*]This is what Stone's chief advisers on the movie have said about *JFK*: "The most accurate and influential depiction of the evidence in the Kennedy assassination since the Zapruder film was shown on 'Goodnight America'" (Groden, *Killing of a President*, p.210); "What the movie has done is to annihilate the Warren Commission" (Prouty, "President Kennedy Was Killed by a Murder, Inc.," p.37).

[†]In many interviews he has gone further. He told *Time* magazine in 1991, "We did a lot of homework." He said his technical advisers went over the script with a "fine tooth-comb. *Everything* that we have in there we stand behind." (Morrow and Smilgis, "Plunging into the Labyrinth," p.76)

shows that Oswald killed Kennedy, and there's no credible evidence that there was any conspiracy in the assassination, what possible "higher truth" was Stone attempting to serve by his deliberate lies?[*]

In the process, Stone defamed the character and reputation of completely innocent people and groups by suggesting they were involved in either the conspiracy to murder Kennedy or the cover-up of the murder. I probably missed a few, but at one time or another in his film, Stone has the following people and groups (some of whose interests were the exact opposite of other conspirators' interests) acting (or being referred to) conspiratorially in the assassination of Kennedy: CIA and KGB (bitter enemies, but they got together on this one), FBI, Secret Service, Castro, anti-Castro Cuban exiles, the Dallas Police Department, the mayor of Dallas (per Stone, the mayor, who was the brother of a CIA official Kennedy had once fired over the Bay of Pigs fiasco, was instrumental [untrue] in changing the parade route to Elm Street so the professional assassins would have a better shot at Kennedy), LBJ, military defense contractors, oilmen, bankers, the Joint Chiefs of Staff, Clay Shaw, David Ferrie, Guy Banister, organized crime, the Office of Naval Intelligence, army intelligence, and the right wing of America.[†]

But as preposterous and full of lies as Stone's *JFK* was, surveys showed that the vast majority of the audience believed the movie, implicitly accepting it as the literal truth. The *Los Angeles Times* conducted a survey of theatergoers in Los Angeles and San Diego after they viewed the film. Some representative responses: "I think it should be required viewing for every person in America." "In the past, I always felt that it would be a waste of taxpayers' money—it's over, leave the family alone. But I no longer feel that way. You see something like this and it makes you think anything is possible." "Much of it was startling information I just hadn't known before. To hear that maybe the Dallas Police were involved, the Mafia, the FBI, the CIA . . . Did the Government think we just wouldn't care what was happening and that they, above all, were the higher power? I thought, more than anything, the movie was very disturbing." "It's certainly changed my opinion. I assumed the Warren Commission was accurate. You come away from a film like this feeling very ignorant, because you assume you knew everything there was from reading all the news accounts, and it turns out you really knew very little."

The *Times* said that the foregoing reactions "were repeated in theaters across the coun-

---

[*]There was one good fallout from the movie *JFK*. As noted earlier, it provoked an outcry by many of those who had seen the movie that all the files on the assassination be opened up and all documents be released to the American public, documents that otherwise were not scheduled to be released until the year 2039. Not just Congress, but the White House and the National Archives were inundated by phone calls and letters demanding that all assassination documents be released to the public. In fact, every Warren Commission assistant counsel still alive (twelve), as well as past presidents Richard M. Nixon and Gerald R. Ford, joined the chorus demanding the opening of the files, and Congress responded with "The President John F. Kennedy Assassination Records Collection Act of 1992," which ordered the release of all assassination-related documents. (See long endnote discussion.)

If Stone's movie had been discredited by those who were knowledgeable about the assassination, it had achieved a measure of legitimacy, thanks to Congress. To the point, in fact, that even some who recognize Stone's movie as being a cinematic fraud wonder aloud if, in the last analysis, the movie should be looked on positively. But using the same reasoning, perhaps we should give the Third Reich credit for the creation of the state of Israel.

[†]At bottom, what caused Stone to believe all these groups and people were involved in Kennedy's assassination? As I've said earlier in this book, he embraces the non sequitur that if someone has a motive to commit a crime, he must have done it. "If you understand 'why' [we believe] Kennedy was killed," he said while filming *JFK*, "then you begin to understand 'who' [killed him]" (Interview of Stone in *Dallas Morning News*, April 14, 1991, p.8C).

try during the weekend" of the film's release. "Only a few questioned its conclusions." At AMC's large Century 14 Theater in Century City (Los Angeles), reporter Deborah Starr Seibel said that "despite the film's startling premise that some of our highest government officials had decided to eliminate their own Commander-In-Chief, not one person said they were shocked by the conspiracy theory set forth in *JFK* by co-writer and director Oliver Stone."[288]

New York Newsday arranged for a large group of college students to see *JFK* and then be interviewed. Reporter John Hane wrote that they agreed the government and military "were involved in a massive cover-up." The only student quoted who had any reservations said, "I believe that there were definitely . . . shots coming from the grassy knoll. But [Oliver Stone] went a bit overboard. He didn't have the proof to incriminate everybody up to LBJ. The only proof Stone gives us is some guy coming out of the Lincoln Memorial and spilling the beans." So even this student bought Stone's shots from the grassy knoll (and hence, a conspiracy) and accepted Stone's X as really existing and meeting with Garrison. This viewer merely thought that X wasn't enough to implicate everybody.

Some representative remarks from the other students: "I knew nothing about this. I was dumbfounded by the movie. It was mind-blowing." "I was just so taken by this movie. I'm sick of this government. Like, we elect these people?" "Why should I have to wait until 2039 to find out the truth? Why can't something be done?" "There were too many people involved in the assassination and so they'll continue to teach it in a way that doesn't offend. It's like how they teach the history of the Third Reich to students in Germany." "I believe what I saw. I totally believe it." "I always thought Oswald shot him. But now I'm convinced it was a plot." "If Oswald was a patsy, why not Hinckley [referring to John Hinckley Jr., the man who shot President Reagan]?"[289]

Reporter Robert O'Harrow Jr. wrote in the *Washington Post*, "In some two dozen interviews at three sets of theaters [in the Washington, D.C. area] yesterday and on New Year's Eve, people coming out of the movie made it clear they believe the film's elaborate theories."[290] And so on around the country. As the *New York Times*'s Tom Wicker said, the danger of *JFK* is that for those "too young to remember November 22, 1963, *JFK* is all too likely to be taken as the final, unquestioned explanation."[291] David Ansen at *Newsweek* went further, saying that "an entire generation of filmgoers is hereafter going to look at these events through Stone's prism."[292]

Although, as previously indicated, the mainstream media, for the most part, excoriated Stone's film, how did Hollywood itself treat this abomination? It thought it was just fine. Stone won the 1991 Golden Globe Award for Best Director, and the film was nominated for an Academy Award for Best Picture, Best Director, and Best Screenplay. Writing a historical-drama review in which he gave *JFK* four stars out of a four-star rating, film critic Roger Ebert gushed that the movie was "a masterpiece . . . If Garrison's investigation was so pitiful . . . then where are the better investigations by Stone's attackers? . . . It's impossible to believe the Warren Report because the physical evidence makes its key conclusion impossible: one man with one rifle could not physically have caused what happened on November 22, 1963, in Dallas."[293] If you say so, Roger.

Since film critics aren't necessarily historians, perhaps Ebert's review shouldn't be considered shocking. But what about Marcus Raskin, writing in the *American Historical Review*, the prestigious publication of the American Historical Association, an organization founded in 1884 and chartered by Congress in 1889? The *Review* is so brainy and upper crust it doesn't even have advertisements. Raskin wrote in an issue with erudite

companion articles (such as those dealing with the Afroasiatic roots of classical civiliza-
tion, three middle-class women's organizations in Boston and their evolution from the
nineteenth into the twentieth century, and recent rethinking of intellectual history) that
"the film JFK . . . has had an extraordinary effect on the public consciousness." (I agree
so far. Indeed, as stated earlier, that's the reason for this very long section on the movie
in this book; absent this effect, the film would not be entitled to more than one sentence
or two.) But then Raskin goes on to say that "contrary to what some would like to believe,
[*JFK*] is surprisingly accurate. On the complex question of the Kennedy Assassination
itself, the film holds its own against the Warren Commission."[294]

There are few groups, if any, in America who are more elitist than the Eastern literati—
that is, except in the presence of Hollywood royalty, where many are as obsequious before
Hollywood's luminaries as the rest of America. This was never more clearly on display
than at a town hall debate on *JFK* in New York City on the evening of March 3, 1992,
sponsored by the Nation Institute and the Center for American Culture Studies at
Columbia University. The moderator was Victor Navasky, the distinguished, longtime
editor of the *Nation* (who, to his credit, did not exalt Stone), and among the participants
were Stone and authors Norman Mailer, Nora Ephron, and Edward Epstein. Stone gave
no inch or compliments to the other three authors, but they (even Epstein, the only one
with the temerity to offer a mild criticism of *JFK* in Stone's presence, pointing out there
is a difference between fiction and nonfiction, and *JFK* "mixed" the two) couldn't help
weaving into their comments a fawning praise for Stone and his film. The sellout audience of fifteen hundred like-minded people gave Stone a thunderous applause when he
was introduced and by far the biggest hand after his remarks, whistles and all. Epstein's
tepid attack drew little support, whereas Stone's rebuttal to it was met with very robust
applause.

But perhaps the highlight of the evening was when Ms. Ephron, defending Stone
against attacks by his critics, said that when the press criticizes directors for "trivial inaccuracies" in their films about historical events, such as "breakfast that was actually dinner, a silver fork that was actually stainless steel, . . . this is all nonsense . . . There are
people, however, who say that maybe there's a special obligation in this area. That, for
instance, young people will see *JFK* and think the Joint Chiefs of Staff killed President
Kennedy. *But I don't know why they're going to think this way more than I do.*" What?!!
When no one in the audience caught what she had obviously intended to be a serious
laugh line—that she also believed the Joint Chiefs of Staff had murdered Kennedy—she
paused, waiting for the audience to finally get it before she continued. And when they did
and she got the laugh she wanted, she went on to say, "Eventually, they'll grow up and
figure it out for themselves. And if they don't, it's not the filmmaker's responsibility." I
thought Ms. Ephron, an otherwise gifted intellectual, had already said quite enough, but
she had more to say. She added, "The real danger is not that we'll have an inaccurate
movie, *which never hurt anyone.* The real danger is that the wholesale, knee-jerk objection" to these movies "might result in something far worse, which is a chilling effect on
works of art." But in view of the reality that people believe and are influenced by what
they see on the screen, it's too obvious to state that bad art presented as history can indeed
do damage. Consider the hypothetical example of a major, important film that denies the
existence of the Holocaust.

One of the people on the panel of questioners at the town hall "debate" that night,
Max Holland, said it well: "I cannot accept that facts don't matter and that all facts are

equally important. And when a filmmaker invents or ignores facts to support a thesis, he crosses the line."[295]

It's not enough that Oliver Stone's movie poisoned the minds of millions of Americans about the assassination. Warner Bros., which produced the film, most likely did not know what an enormous falsehood the movie was,[*] and therefore unwittingly compounded the damage the movie had done by funding a 1991 study guide to the movie for American high school students that was prepared by Learning Enrichment Inc. of New York City. Appallingly, the study guides were sent to thirteen thousand teachers throughout the land to be used in their social studies and history classes.

The guide contains a synopsis of *JFK* (which the teachers are encouraged to have their students see), including a denigration of the Warren Commission's "magic bullet" by a ridiculous drawing that has the bullet making a right turn in midair, an allegation that four days after the assassination, NSAM 263, calling for the withdrawal of 1,000 troops from Vietnam, was canceled, and so on. "You might want to tell students," the study guide urges teachers, "about the intensive research Oliver Stone undertook before making the film." The teachers are told that the guide was assembled to help them "provide both background and context for student viewing [of the film] and discussion." The guide says, "After viewing *JFK* . . . invite students to begin the discussion by saying whatever comes to mind. What did they feel while viewing the movie? What questions did it raise?"

The cover of the guide includes this quote from Stone: "I hope they [the viewers of his movie] become more aware of how politics are played out *and how our kings are killed.*" The message in Stone's movie and the study guide is that when the nation's power structure doesn't like the policies of an American president, it simply murders him. What a poisonous thought to put into the minds of our nation's youth about the country they live in.

I could go on condemning the relentless perversion of reality known as *JFK*. But enough. The reason, as indicated, for all the time I have already devoted to the subject is, as the *Chicago Tribune* noted, because of "the danger that Stone's film and the pseudo-history it so effectively portrays" will end up being the "popularly accepted version. After all, what can scholarship avail against Kevin Costner, Sissy Spacek (Garrison's wife in the movie), Donald Sutherland, et al., on the big screen with Dolby stereo?"

I believe that history is sacred and should not knowingly be tampered with. In imposing a narrative on a historical event, obviously a certain amount of dramatic license and embellishment is unavoidable, but even this device should be used with great caution and economy. Outright fabrications of important matters that necessarily cause viewers or readers to reach a different conclusion is a cultural crime. We can only ensure the past's future if we respect its truths.

Someone once described history as the thinnest thread of what's remembered, stretch-

---

[*]A major Hollywood studio doesn't normally fork over $40 million blindly to fund a picture, but that appears to be what happened here. Stone got a handshake deal for a $20 million budgeted movie (later increased to $40 million) before cappuccino was even served at a 1989 dinner at The Grill restaurant in Beverly Hills. Stone, accompanied by his CAA agent, Paula Wagner, made his "pitch" to Terry Semel, president and chief operating officer at Warner Bros., Bob Daly, chairman of the board and chief executive officer at the studio, and Bill Gerber, a studio production executive. Semel did read Garrison's book, at Stone's suggestion, and said he was "blown away by the fact that clearly something else happened" than what the Warren Commission had concluded. (*Los Angeles Times*, December 15, 1991, Calendar section, pp.5, 28, 33)

ing across an ocean of what's been forgotten. But the history of the assassination has not
been forgotten by Oliver Stone. Except for those instances where ignorance is his only
defense, it's been deliberately ignored or invented. That's fine. But he had a moral, if not
a legal obligation, to tell his audience what he was up to. Pulitzer Prize–winning historian Arthur Schlesinger Jr., writing in the *Wall Street Journal*, has a more charitable view
of Stone and a less menacing view of *JFK* than I. He writes that Stone "is an artist, and
artists are often hopelessly loyal to their fantasies, and their fantasies often hopelessly
abuse the truth. History will survive."[296] The eminent historian is most assuredly correct
if we define history in the narrow sense of being an exact synonym for the facts—what
actually happened. Facts don't and can't change. Not even God can change the past. However, if we define history in the broader sense of that which succeeding generations believe
and accept as the truth, then Stone, more than any other *single* American, is responsible
for 75 percent of Americans currently believing that a dark and wide-ranging conspiracy
involving the highest reaches of our government was responsible for the death of President Kennedy, which is only pseudo-history.

Indeed, it is in this latter sense of *perceived* history that Stone himself defines history.
On the set of *JFK*, he said, "I'm *shaping* history, to a degree."[297] And in his introduction
to his friend Fletcher Prouty's book, Stone, alluding to the fact that the victor writes the
history of an event, asks, "Who owns reality? Who owns our history? He who makes it up
so that most everyone believes it. That person wins." For once, I agree with Oliver Stone.
That is, unless the fabricator is exposed, as I trust I have done in this book.

Conclusion of No Conspiracy

By now it has to be more than obvious to the reader of this book that Oswald acted alone in killing the president. Not only does all of his conduct speak unerringly only to this conclusion, but also, as I believe I have demonstrated, the various conspiracy theories are utterly vapid and bankrupt. Does what you have read prove beyond *all* doubt that there was no conspiracy in Kennedy's assassination? Probably not, if only because such a degree of proof will perhaps always be unattainable. Why? Because, first, Oswald is dead (and absent a confession from a conspirator, only Oswald could tell us if he acted in concert with anyone), and second, it's normally much more difficult to prove a negative than a positive. However, there is sufficient evidence to satisfy, beyond a *reasonable* doubt, the world's leading skeptic that Oswald acted alone—that there was no conspiracy. That Oswald, a lone nut, killed Kennedy and was thereafter killed by another lone nut, Ruby. Two small men who wanted to become big, and succeeded. Or, to ennoble their ignoble deeds, as author David Lubin says, "the lethal tussle in the basement of city hall was a fight between two would-be paladins. Each regarded himself as a knight on a mission to avenge wrong and restore right."[1]

If, as is the situation with the conspiracy theorists, there is no evidence to support your allegation, from a legal standpoint you're out of court. But even if you're out of court, if you can at least argue that "well, there's no evidence of this, but logic and common sense tell you it is so," you still have talking rights and you can still play the game, as it were. But when you not only have no evidence, but logic and common sense tell you it isn't so, it's time to fold your tent. No evidence plus no common sense equals go home, zipper your mouth up, take a walk, forget about it, get a life. Of course, the hard-core conspiracy theorists, who desperately want to cling to their illusions, are not going to do any of these things. If they were to accept the evidence of no conspiracy, those whose lives have been heavily immersed in the assassination for years would also have to accept that they have "wasted" the last twenty or thirty (or however many) years of their lives on something that has no merit. And consciously or subconsciously, it is difficult for anyone to do this. So they are prime candidates for being "in denial" and impervious to the points being made. It should be added that if these conspiracy theorists were to accept the truth, not only would they be invalidating a major part of their past, but many would be forfeiting their future. That's why talking to them about logic and common sense is like talking to a man without ears. The bottom line is that they *want* there to be a conspiracy and are constitutionally allergic to anything that points away from it. In fact, if Oswald himself appeared in front of them and said, "Hey, guys, knock off all this silliness. I killed Kennedy and acted alone," they'd probably tell him, "Look, we know a heck of a lot more about this case than you do, so go back to wherever you came from."

It's essentially become a religious belief with the theorists that there was a conspiracy behind Kennedy's death, and with religious beliefs, the believer knows the truth, so there has to be an explanation for everything that seems to contradict that truth. Their reasoning, then, is to start the debate assuming the very point that has to be proved (Kennedy was killed as a result of a conspiracy), and anything that is at odds with this belief has to have an explanation, no matter how ridiculous and far-out it may be. Nothing you tell the conspiracy theorists can shake their belief in a conspiracy. In situations where even they can't come up with an explanation, they shield themselves from the evidence by either distorting or ignoring it. This type of intellectual carpentry by the buffs allows them to proceed forward with their fantasy, unfazed by the inconvenient interposition of reality.

The example I am about to give illustrates the religious obsession and startling illogic of conspiracy theorists. A very prominent and well-respected medical doctor who is a sincere and eloquent member of the new wave in the conspiracy community wrote me (on August 30, 2001) that "for nearly ten years now, I have slept, jogged, eaten, gone to the bathroom, and dreamed about this case." This doctor went on to tell me, unbelievably, that it was terribly illogical of me to say that one shouldn't reject the findings of the Warren Commission without bothering to first read the Warren Report. Such a reading was unnecessary, he said. The profound passion and equally profound irrationality reflected in that way of thinking are the norm, not the exception, in the ethos of the hard-core conspiracy community. The arguments that follow are not just for the conspiracy community, but mostly for the millions of Americans who, not knowing the facts, have been duped by the conspiracy theorists into buying their drivel, misinformation, and flat-out fabrications.[*]

---

[*]Apart from the fact that most people instinctively want to believe there was a conspiracy in the assassination, perhaps the biggest reason why the JFK conspiracy phenomenon will continue indefinitely is that nutty or huckster authors and television documentarians will keep it alive by seizing on one (or more) of the literally hundreds of erroneous and mostly ridiculous allegations that swarms of people have made in the past. The author or documentarian only has to negotiate three hurdles, two of which are disposed of in less than a second. First, the fact that the allegation is silly on its face, though it should be a problem, is no problem at all since most of the author's or documentarian's audience is predisposed to believing in the conspiracy theory of the assassination, and hence isn't likely to find the allegation ridiculous. The second problem—that the person making the allegation and the allegation itself have already been completely and thoroughly discredited—is easily handled simply by not mentioning this fact to the reading or viewing audience. The third and final problem the author or documentarian has to deal with is the one that takes all his time and energy. But if he is persistent, as most are, he invariably succeeds. He tries to find the original person (or persons) who made the allegation (or, if he or she has died, their children, spouse, and other surviving relatives) as well as other people who lend support to the allegation. In this latter regard there always are more than enough people out there who are either kooky themselves (like the original alleger) or not kooky but willing to make sufficiently irresponsible remarks that in some way support the allegation and therefore warrant their being mentioned in a book or scene in a TV documentary.

The above is the basic template for the continuing life of the conspiracy movement by way of new books and television documentaries. As with much of the past, it is my belief that almost every book, movie, or television documentary on the assassination in the future will be very likely to follow, in one form or another, this template.

As with the evidence of Oswald's guilt, which has already been presented in very abbreviated, summary form, here's the evidence of *no* conspiracy. As you are reading this list, I would ask you to take a moment to ask yourself whether the individual point you are reading, *all alone and by itself*, clearly shows there was no conspiracy. I believe you will find this to be the case with many of the points.

1. Perhaps the most powerful single piece of evidence that there was no conspiracy in the murder of President Kennedy is simply the fact that after all these years there is *no credible evidence*, direct or circumstantial, that any of the persons or groups suspected by conspiracy theorists (e.g., organized crime, CIA, KGB, FBI, military-industrial complex, Castro, LBJ, etc.) or anyone else conspired with Oswald to kill Kennedy. And when there is *no evidence* of something, although not conclusive, this itself is very, very persuasive evidence that the alleged "something" does not exist. Particularly here where the search for the "something" (conspiracy) has been the greatest and most comprehensive search for anything in American, perhaps world, history.

I mean, way back in 1965, *before* over forty additional years of microscopic investigation of the case by governmental groups and thousands of researchers, Dwight Macdonald wrote, "I can't believe that among the many hundreds of detectives, Federal Bureau of Investigation and Secret Service agents, and [counsel] for the Warren Commission . . . not one would be bright or lucky enough to discover or stumble across some clue [of a conspiracy] if there were any there."[2] But not one clue of a conspiracy has ever surfaced. And this is so despite the fact that the two people the conspirators would have had to rely on the most not to leave a clue, Lee Harvey Oswald and Jack Ruby, were notoriously unreliable.

A conspiracy is nothing more than a criminal partnership. And although conspiracies obviously aren't proved by the transcript of a stenographer who typed up a conversation between the partners agreeing to commit the crime, there has to be some substantive evidence of the conspiracy or partnership's existence. And in the conspiracy prosecutions I have conducted, I have always been able to present direct evidence of the co-conspirators acting in concert before, during, or after the crime, and/or circumstantial evidence from which a reasonable inference of concert or meeting of the minds could be made. In the Oswald case, if, for instance, Oswald had disappeared for a few days before the assassination without adequate explanation, or within these few days he was seen in the company of a stranger, or there was evidence he had come into some serious money, or he had made any statement to anyone, such as Marina, suggesting, even vaguely, a conspiratorial relationship, or someone had called him at the Paine residence and he left the room and took the call in another room, or he was seen getting in a car after the shooting in Dealey Plaza, or any of a hundred other possible events or circumstances had occurred, that would be one thing. But here, there is *nothing, nothing*. Just completely foundationless speculation and conjecture.

Traditionally, the way to reach a conclusion in a criminal case is to draw reasonable inferences from solid evidence. So the evidence is the foundation on which all inferences and conclusions are based. Conspiracy theorists, in contrast, make completely baseless assumptions and then proceed to make further assumptions based on these assumptions. As an example, they assume, without any evidence, that there was a conspiracy in the assassination and that Oswald was an unwitting participant. They then proceed to assume, again without any evidence, that Oswald became aware of this conspiracy at the time of the shooting in Dealey Plaza, and believe that he was being set up to take the fall for the assassination, and *this* is why he fled the Book Depository Building. *But where is there any evidence to support either of these two assumptions?**

This is particularly startling and noteworthy when one stops to realize that those making the allegation of conspiracy necessarily have the burden of proof. I mean, it makes no sense for A to say to B, "I allege that there is a conspiracy here. Now you prove there isn't." The alleger always, by definition, has the burden of proof. To say that those alleging a conspiracy in the Kennedy assassination have not met their burden of proof would be the understatement of the millennium. Here, the absence of any credible evidence of a conspiracy is bad enough for the conspiracy theorists, but, as demonstrated on these pages, there is much, much evidence pointing irresistibly in the direction of *no* conspiracy.

2. *Not only is there no credible evidence* that organized crime, the CIA, Castro, LBJ, and so on, conspired with Oswald to murder the president, but such a plan would be incredibly reckless, irrational, and dangerous for any of these persons or groups to even entertain, and hence, unlikely and far-fetched.

3. And if there's *no credible evidence* that any of the aforementioned persons or groups were behind the assassination, what other person or group in our society would possibly be behind Oswald's act? The Des Moines Rotary Club? The Boston Symphony? Some U.S. senators? The Miami City Council? The United States Department of Indian Affairs? The Southern Baptist Christian Conference? I hope the reader isn't thinking how silly I am. The buffs are silly. I'm a rather serious person.

4. As mentioned in the introduction of this book, we all know from our own experiences in life that it is almost impossible to keep a secret. And that's when only a few people, even two, are involved, and even if the matter that one wishes to remain undisclosed isn't terribly important. Somehow or other the information gets out, and it does so rather quickly, whether induced by one's conscience, as in a death-bed confession, or through a former wife or mistress, or inadvertently, or simply because people can't keep their mouths shut.[†] As I told the jury in London, "I'll stipulate that three people can keep a

---

*Here's a very small sampling of what *all* conspiracy theorists do—*have* to do—since they are unable to offer any *evidence* of a conspiracy. "I *believe* the CIA . . . role in the Kennedy assassination was this: they presented members of organized crime, who had a major bone to pick with the Kennedy administration, with the opportunity and plan. All the Mafia had to do was carry it out. And that's exactly what happened" (Wecht, *Cause of Death*, p.71). "Angry talk in the corporate boardrooms *may* have grown into deadly plots on golf courses . . . But oilmen . . . could not have moved against Kennedy on their own. They needed allies within government and within the intelligence community. Such allies were there—among the anti-Castro Cubans, in the CIA, organized crime, and within the federal government. All were most receptive to the idea of a change of leadership" (Marrs, *Crossfire*, p.278). "*My personal inclination is* . . . that Lee Harvey Oswald fired no shots at President Kennedy or Governor Connally and that he was . . . a patsy, set up to take the blame while the real assassins escaped" (Kurtz, *Crime of the Century*, p.xxvii). "*My opinion* . . . [is that] the Mafia joined forces with a few Kennedy haters from the CIA, radical anti-Castro Cuban exiles, and others in the extreme right wing, both civilian and military. A plan was formulated to assassinate the president . . . Hoover and Johnson were brought into the plot. Their role was to prevent a serious investigation of the crime" (Twyman, *Bloody Treason*, pp.832–833).

Not one of the above conspiracy "theorists," and the thousands of others exactly like them, produced for their readers one speck of evidence to support their naked conjecture.

†Note that peripheral figures in any conspiracy would be more likely to come forward because their limited role would not result in serious punishment—in fact, most likely no punishment at all because of a plea bargain in which they'd have to name higher-ups. And their inducement would be considerable financial rewards (books, TV movies based on their disclosures, etc.). And mere informants, who wouldn't be exposed to any legally adverse consequences, would only have financial rewards for coming forward.

secret, but only if two are dead." On a national scale we see this phenomenon at work with one presidential administration after another being unable to control, frequently for even a few days, "leaks" to the media on matters they did not want known. (One example among thousands: *USA Today* reported on July 19, 2002, that "recent news leaks [of classified information from a congressional probe of 9-11 intelligence failures] have infuriated the White House and prompted Defense Secretary Donald Rumsfeld to issue a memo warning that staffers who spill secrets are jeopardizing American lives.")[3] In the Kennedy case itself, we saw that although only a few members of the FBI's Dallas office were involved, they were unable to keep secret their effort to suppress Oswald's leaving a threatening note at the Dallas office about ten days or so before the assassination.

When we apply this literal rule of life to the alleged massive conspiracy the conspiracy theorists claim existed in the murder of the president of the United States—massive not only in the considerable number of people who would have had to be involved[*] but also in the great number of details and matters that would have had to be suppressed, any one of which could have exposed the plot or given rise to an inference of its existence, and which allegedly included the doctoring of many photographs and X-rays, even the Zapruder film itself, and the murder of over a hundred people to silence them, and *then* the cover-up of each of *these* murders—we can be certain that if such a conspiracy took place, its existence would have broken out of its original shell in a thousand different ways, and relatively quickly. Yet after forty-four long years, not one *credible* word, not one syllable has ever surfaced about any conspiracy to kill Kennedy. (There *have* been noncredible confessions of guilt in the Kennedy case, nearly all of which have been discussed in depth in this book—for example, Chicago mobster Sam Giancana allegedly telling his brother Chuck that he was behind the murders of JFK, RFK, and Marilyn Monroe, that he met with LBJ and Richard Nixon in Dallas before the assassination and told them he and the CIA were planning to murder JFK, and that Jack Ruby coordinated the whole assassination for Sam. Because none of these confessions are even remotely credible— indeed, many are downright amusing—no serious person has ever paid any attention to them.) The reason why not the slightest trace of a conspiracy has ever been uncovered, of course, is that no such conspiracy ever existed.

When we add to the above the allegation by conspiracy theorists that a *second* massive

---

[*]In addition to the representatives of the group or groups (CIA, military-industrial complex, mob, etc.) the conspiracy theorists claim were behind the assassination, these original conspirators would be forced to enlist the cooperation and services of an ever-expanding group of conspirators to help them conceal and cover up their guilt, and what had actually happened, an expansion that would necessarily become bigger and bigger with the passage of time to the point of farce, the number of people required to be a part of the conspiracy ending up in the thousands, with only Yankee Stadium being able to accommodate one of their reunions.

For instance, if the conspiracy involved the framing of Oswald (as most conspiracy theorists believe), almost every individual piece of evidence against Oswald would itself require the complicity of several people in the conspiracy. Just one example: Firearms experts for the Warren Commission (four experts) and HSCA (five experts) concluded that the two bullets that struck and killed Kennedy were fired from Oswald's rifle. But if, in fact, Oswald's rifle wasn't the murder weapon, this means that the conspirators would have had to approach these nine experts and get them to lie, to say that it was the weapon. Now multiply this additional number of nine people many times over for many other pieces of evidence against Oswald (e.g., fingerprint experts, handwriting experts, witnesses who said they saw Oswald at the Tippit murder scene, the three autopsy surgeons and all the other pathologists who later concurred in their essential findings). Indeed, did the conspirators get Howard Brennan to say he saw Oswald firing a rifle in the sniper's nest, Dallas police officers to say Oswald pulled his gun on them when they approached him in the Texas Theater, even his wife, Marina, to say she felt positive he had killed Kennedy, and that he had confessed to her his attempted murder of General Walker? Et cetera, et cetera.

conspiracy existed—by the Warren Commission[*] and its leading assistant counsels to suppress the truth about the assassination from the American people—and not one word has ever leaked in over forty years of the existence of *that* conspiracy either, the only reasonable conclusion is that only people who subscribe to rules of absurdity, not rules of life, could possibly believe that a conspiracy to kill Kennedy ever existed. The conspiracy argument in the Kennedy assassination requires the belief that for over forty years a great number of people have been able to keep silent about the plot behind the most important and investigated murder of the twentieth century. In other words, it requires a belief in the impossible. Political columnist Charles Krauthammer, writing in 1992, pointed out the absurdity of the cover-up premise: "That in a country where the fixing of a handful of game shows could not be held secret, a near-universal assassination conspiracy has remained airtight for 28 years."[4] How, sensible people ask, could such a vast conspiracy remain leakproof for almost four and a half decades, or even four and a half days? British writer D. M. Thomas marvels at the absurdity of the notion that "a network of conspirators killed Kennedy, corrupted the medical and legal investigations, and buried the truth, all without a hitch."

In his book, *Loving God*, former presidential assistant Charles Colson, in writing about Watergate, said, "With the most powerful office in the world at stake, a small band of hand-picked loyalists [of President Richard Nixon] . . . could not hold a conspiracy together for more than two weeks."[5]

5. Obviously, the more complicated a plot is, the greater the likelihood that something will go wrong and it won't work. Everyone intuitively knows this, and hence we can assume that if there had been a plot to kill Kennedy, the plotters would have made it as uncomplicated as possible. But the massive conspiracy envisioned by most conspiracy theorists necessarily would be extremely complex, and this fact is greatly exacerbated by the ineptitude of human beings.

I'm talking about the staggering incompetence at every level of our society, one that normally prevents any group, large or small, including the U.S. government and its agencies, from performing at anywhere near optimum capacity? Indeed, on a scale of one to ten, they normally operate below five. Incompetence is so widely prevalent that I expect it, and when I find competence I am always pleasantly surprised. Let's look at just one example among a great many, this one at the CIA, the main federal agency conspiracy theorists suspect of being behind the assassination. In 1994, Aldrich Ames, chief of the CIA's Soviet counterintelligence branch, pleaded guilty to the biggest espionage case in U.S. history. Ames furnished the Soviets U.S. secrets in return for more than $2 million. His perfidy led to the deaths of several Russian undercover agents working for the United States in the Soviet Union. Ames told his interrogators it was "really easy" to obtain the top-secret information even after he was transferred to anti-narcotics work in the early 1990s.

In noting that it took an incredible nine years for Ames's colleagues and superiors at CIA headquarters to catch him, syndicated columnist Mary McGrory wrote that "Ames

---

[*] "Here we were, seven men, I think five of us were Republicans," Commission member John McCloy said. "We weren't beholden to [the Johnson] Administration. Besides that, we had our own integrity to think of. You can rely on common sense. And you know that seven men aren't going to get together, of that character, and concoct a conspiracy, with all the members of the staff we had [one general counsel, fourteen assistant counsels, eleven staff members], with all of the investigative agencies [working under us]. It would have been a conspiracy of a character so mammoth and so vast" (Transcript of *CBS News Inquiry: The Warren Report*, part IV, June 28, 1967, p.13, CBS Television Archives).

and his wife did everything they could to arouse suspicion, living it up in the most provocative manner. What G5-14, on a salary of $69,000-plus, pays half a million in cash [$540,000] for a house in Arlington, Virginia, buys a bright red Jaguar [which he drove to work] and runs up Trumplike charges on his credit card?"[6] A November 1994 report on the Ames case from the Senate Intelligence Committee found "gross negligence" ("negligence" being a euphemism here for incompetence) at CIA headquarters in Langley, Virginia, and reports from both the Senate Intelligence Committee and the House Select Committee on Intelligence "agreed that the agency [CIA] is in deep disarray," a condition, they said, that long predated the Ames case.[7]

I mean, in 1986 the National Aeronautics and Space Administration (NASA), with billions of dollars spent, and the finest scientific minds available, and with the space shuttle *Challenger* right in front of their noses for inspection, and with a defective pressure seal wrongly designed *and about which they had been advised and warned on numerous occasions*, sent seven astronauts to their death because of their dreadful incompetence. Speaking of NASA, on the first day of the *Apollo 8* flight that circumnavigated the moon, when Colonel Frank Borman, the commander of the flight, was sending transmissions back to Cape Kennedy, he referred to the *Apollo 8* flight as the *Gemini 8* flight, a flight he had participated in three years earlier. That's life in the real world.

While we're talking about incompetence, let's look at an extreme example of it in the Kennedy case itself. Established procedure in the Secret Service during a presidential motorcade is to scan not only the crowds but also the roofs and windows of buildings as the motorcade goes along.[8] But apparently, and unbelievably, not one of the sixteen Secret Service agents in the motorcade through Dealey Plaza was looking anywhere near the upper floors of the Book Depository Building. If they had, they would have seen (as several Dealey Plaza witnesses who never had any obligation to look for such things did) a figure or a rifle in the window where Oswald was. But there's no evidence, from any of the reports of the agents, that they saw anything in Oswald's window, or even saw the three black Book Depository employees in the two windows beneath Oswald's window. Pardon my pique, but where in the hell were their heads when the president's limousine passed by the Book Depository Building, other than up the proverbial place? Special Agent Roy Kellerman told the Warren Commission that in the Secret Service detail protecting the president, "when you are driving down [the] street . . . and you have buildings on either side of you, you are going to scan your eyes up and down" the buildings.[9] Can you imagine that? Thirty-two trained eyes belonging to sixteen men whose duty and responsibility was to protect the president, and not one of these thirty-two eyes saw Oswald, or a rifle, or anything worthy of their attention in the sniper's nest window. But several lay people did, and they were only there to watch the motorcade, not watch over the president's security.

The question is, How could the vast number of conspirators contemplated by the theorists have pulled off this incredibly complex conspiracy to such a degree of skill— never bumbling or slipping in any way that would reveal or even suggest their existence to one outside their group—that eternal secrecy would be guaranteed? Easy. You see, we know human beings are unable to keep their mouths shut and routinely incompetent, frequently stumbling over their own feet. But the conspirators envisioned by the theorists have their mouths permanently zippered and are extraordinarily competent, even prescient, being able to predict faultlessly all of the many uncontrollable variables in their mission to the point where everything worked perfectly, and with mathematical precision.

As Richard White, professor of history at the University of Washington, and speaking in a generic sense, says, "You can't trust the government to do anything right—except, of course, to conspire and cover up. Then it becomes diabolically efficient. The very people who are wildest for government conspiracies are often the same people who believe the government is incapable of delivering the mail efficiently."[10] In other words, the conspiracists believe that Murphy's law (whatever can go wrong will go wrong) doesn't apply to the alleged conspiracy in the assassination and cover-up.

The above deals with the murder and cover-up. But with the many groups supposedly involved in the conspiracy, like the CIA, mob, anti-Castro Cubans, and military-industrial complex, how could they handle all the logistical complexities and inevitable disagreements among themselves over details during the planning phase *leading up* to November 22, without anything they did out of the ordinary (and by definition, they would have had to do things out of the ordinary) coming to the attention of just one person outside their group?

6. If Oswald conspired with anyone, they waited quite awhile to bring him aboard. The conspiracy couldn't have been hatched before October 1, 1963, when we know Oswald was still in Mexico City desperately trying to get to Cuba. If he had succeeded in getting to Cuba, who believes he would have ended up killing Kennedy? No one I've ever heard of. And how believable is it that a plot to kill the president of the United States, the most powerful man on earth, would be born after October 1, just seven weeks before Kennedy's death? To believe something like that is to be addicted to silliness. The absurdity of the notion that Oswald conspired with others to kill Kennedy can be spotlighted by the fact that on the very day, September 26, 1963, that it was announced in both Dallas newspapers that Kennedy was going to come to Texas on November 21 and 22 and that Dallas would likely be one of the cities he would visit,[11] Oswald was on a bus traveling to Mexico City determined to get to Cuba.

Indeed, since Kennedy's motorcade route past the Book Depository Building wasn't selected until November 18,[12] and announced in a paper for the first time on the morning of November 19 in the *Dallas Morning News*,[13] we not only thereby know that Oswald getting a job at the Book Depository Building on October 15 was unrelated to President Kennedy's trip to Dallas and the assassination, but it would seem that *any conspiracy involving Oswald as the hit man would have had to be hatched no earlier than November 19, just three days before Kennedy's death* (i.e., unless the argument is made—which I have yet to hear even the daffy conspiracy buffs make—that *wherever* Kennedy went when he came to Dallas, it was Oswald's job to track him down and kill him). Surely no person with an ounce of sense could possibly believe that the CIA, mob, and so on, recruited Oswald to kill Kennedy just three days before the assassination.

7. In the same vein, during the five-week period leading up to the assassination, we know Oswald was taking driving lessons from Ruth Paine and was about to apply for a learner's permit. In fact, we know that as late as November 16, just six days before the assassination, Oswald went to the state's license examination bureau in Dallas to get his driver's permit, only leaving because the line was very long.[14] How likely is it that Oswald would be taking driving lessons and going down to get a learner's permit on November 16 if he was planning on murdering the president six days later? As mentioned earlier in this book, his leaving nearly all his money and his wedding ring behind on the morning of the assassination clearly demonstrated his awareness of what he could expect his life to be like after he pulled the trigger. The mundane exercise of learning to drive and look-

ing forward to one day having a driving license speaks loudly *for* the proposition that Oswald's intent to murder the president was formed somewhat on the spur of the moment not long before the day of the assassination, and as a necessary corollary and concomitant to this, *against* the proposition that a group like the CIA or organized crime conspired with Oswald to have him kill Kennedy for them.

Other things Oswald did during the month leading up to the assassination clearly represented a person in the normal, humdrum rhythm of life, not someone preparing, with others, to murder the president of the United States. For example, we already know that on November 1, three weeks before the assassination, he rented a mail box at the Terminal Annex near the Book Depository Building. At $1.50 per month, he paid $3.00 for two months, the rental expiring on December 31, five weeks after the assassination.[15] The relevance of this is clear since we know that Oswald was very tightfisted with his money, what precious little of it he had. And although to you and me $1.50 is nothing, everything in life is relative, and to Oswald it *was* something. Here's someone who is paying $8.00 a week in rent, can't live with his wife and daughters because he can't afford an apartment for the three of them, and has a net worth of little over $200.00. He never would have just thrown away that extra $1.50 for the second month if he didn't intend to use the mail box for that month of December, particularly, as I say, when he was notorious for literally watching every penny.

Also, on November 1 he sent a letter to Arnold Johnson, the director of information for the American Communist Party in New York City, in which he told Johnson of his being introduced, by a friend, to the local chapter of the ACLU, and asked Johnson to advise him "to what degree, if any" should he "attempt to heighten [the group's] progressive tendencies?"[16] Around that same time, Oswald sent a $2.00 registration fee to the ACLU in New York City to become a new member, the ACLU receiving the $2.00 on November 4.[17] On November 9, Oswald wrote a letter to the Soviet embassy in Washington, D.C., asking it to "please inform us [him and Marina] of the arrival of our Soviet entrance visas as soon as they come [in]," mailing the letter on November 12.[18]

Indeed, in the late evening of November 20, just two days before the assassination, Oswald took a load of his clothing to a "washateria" (laundromat) near his home.[19] Though the thought of killing the president had probably already entered his mind, the act of washing a load of his clothing clearly reflects that no final decision (if one at all) had yet been made, and of course it automatically *would* have been made by this time if he had been the hit man in a conspiracy to murder the president. If by Wednesday evening he had already committed himself to killing Kennedy, his state of mind would have had to be that if he got caught, Dallas County would be doing his laundry at least for awhile, and if he was able to flee to Mexico or where have you, like the title of Billie Holiday's song, he would be "traveling light" while getting there, not carrying a bundle of laundry in his arms.

For all intents and purposes, Oswald's conduct during the month before the assassination alone precludes the notion of a conspiracy.

8. Again in the same vein, if you're the triggerman for the mob, CIA, Castro, or anyone else in the biggest murder case in American history, what's more likely? That on the night before the murder, you're at your home, apartment, or "safe house" preparing for the following day, and are either meeting with or at least available to your "handlers" for last-minute instructions or consultation? Or that you're going to be visiting your wife, who is staying at someone else's home, and begging her to come back home

to you?* Common sense, which Voltaire tells us is *not* that common, dictates that it's the former, not the latter.

It is reasonably clear that when Oswald went to visit his wife and two children the night before Kennedy came to Dallas, it was his intention to get his rifle and assassinate the president the next day—as indicated, what other reason would he have had to go there, for the first time, on a Thursday night? It is equally reasonably clear that this intention of his was not irrevocable but conditional. If Marina was willing to come back to him, a possibility he already knew was faint, he was prepared to forego his plans concerning Kennedy. If Marina, then, had agreed to come back to Oswald on the night before the president came to Dallas, it is almost a certainty the assassination would never have taken place.†

It is interesting to note that as we saw in the Oswald biography section, Marina herself feels this way. In a narrative written in Russian by Marina at the request of the Warren Commission, and translated by the Commission, she said about the night before the assassination, when her husband virtually begged her to come back to him and she refused to do so, "Of course, if I had known what was going to happen, I would have agreed without further thought. Perhaps, if Lee was planning anything, he staked everything on a card. That is, if I agreed to his proposal to go with him to Dallas, he would not do what he had planned, and, if I did not, then he would."[20]

Oswald's entreaty to Marina to come back to him on the night before the assassination virtually precludes, all by itself, the existence of a conspiracy.

9. This book has proved beyond *all* doubt that Oswald was a highly unreliable, highly disturbed, and emotionally unhinged political fanatic. His own wife, Marina, described him as "not a very trustworthy [trusting?] person."[21] At the London trial, when I asked Ruth Paine, who knew Oswald very well, "Do you feel he [Oswald] was the type one would employ to accomplish a serious mission?" she answered, "No. I would not have employed him for *any* job. I didn't see him as stable enough."

"He was unstable and flighty?"

"Yes . . . He acted from his emotions primarily . . . rather than working from a set of logical ideas."[22]

To believe that a group of conspirators like the CIA or mob would entrust the biggest murder in American history to Oswald, of all people, is too preposterous a notion for any rational person to harbor in his or her mind for more than a millisecond. How could they possibly have confidence in someone like Oswald to take care of their monumental mission in a way that would involve no problems for them, when he couldn't even adequately take care of himself (he was living in a virtual closet on November 22, 1963), much less his wife and two children?

10. Not only wouldn't any group of conspirators ever dream of putting its entire future into the hands of Oswald, but the evidence is very clear that Oswald himself, being such a loner and someone with a mind of his own who disliked taking orders from anyone, would be highly unlikely to work with anyone else on such a mission.[23] As author Jean Davison points out, the ultimate weakness of the conspiracy theorists' contention that Lee Harvey Oswald was framed is their erroneous conception of Oswald.

---

*Recall that Oswald told his wife he was "tired of living alone," that he didn't want her to remain with Ruth Paine any longer, and that if she were willing he would "rent an apartment in Dallas tomorrow" for the two of them and their children (1 H 65–66, WCT Marina N. Oswald).

†Of course, using this type of "but for" causation, we could say that if someone had bought Hitler's paintings in Vienna in 1913, perhaps the Second World War would not have taken place.

"In every conspiracy book, Oswald is a piece of chaff blown about by powerful, unseen forces—he's a dumb and compliant puppet with no volition of his own."[24] But we know from all the evidence that Oswald was the exact opposite of this, in the extreme, that he was anything but meek and malleable. Here's someone who described himself as having a "mean streak of independence"; someone who for awhile in grade school even refused to salute the flag in the morning with his fellow students;[25] someone who, during high school, when ordered to jog around the field with the other players during tryouts for the football team, told the coach, "This is a free country, and I don't have to do it";[26] someone who, as a fellow marine who was stationed with Oswald in Japan said, "was often in trouble for failure to adhere to rules and regulations and gave the impression of disliking any kind of authority";[27] and someone who, as another marine who was stationed with Oswald in San Diego said, "was an argumentative type of person [who] would frequently take the opposite side of an argument just for the sake of a debate."[28]

There were no exceptions to this perception of Oswald's independence from those who knew him. A member of the Russian emigré community in Dallas said that Oswald wasn't "responsible enough to have . . . anybody above him really telling him what to do."[29]* "He resented any type of authority," another said.[30] Still another said, "I just thought he was a person that couldn't get along with anybody or anyone."[31]

Yet the conspiracy theorists want us to believe that the man who couldn't get along in school, couldn't get along in the Marines, someone we know couldn't even get along with his own wife, was supposedly selected by a group of conspirators to get along with them in committing the biggest murder in American history.

No one knew Oswald better than Marina, and when she was asked, under oath, by the HSCA, "Can you visualize him working with an accomplice?" she answered, "Personally, I can't," basing this on the fact, she said, that "living with a person for a few years you . . . have some kind of intuition about what he might do or might not."[32] Earlier, before the Warren Commission, when she was asked whether she felt that her husband "acted in concert with someone else," she responded, "No, only alone."

"You are convinced that his action was his action alone, that he was influenced by no one else?"

"Yes, I am convinced."[33]

Marina's biographer, Priscilla McMillan, who spent a great number of hours interviewing Marina, writes, "I have often asked Marina whether Lee might have been capable of joining with an accomplice to kill the President. Never, she says. Lee was too secretive ever to have told anyone his plans. Nor could he have acted in concert, accepted orders, or obeyed any plan by anybody else. The reason Marina gives is that Lee had no use for the opinions of anybody but himself. He had only contempt for other people. 'He was a lonely person,' she says. 'He trusted no one. He was too sick. It [killing Kennedy] was the fantasy of a sick person, to get attention only for himself.'" McMillan says that Marina believed that with respect to the assassination, Lee acted on impulse and first thought seriously about killing the President only a day or two before he did it.[34]

---

*This, in fact, is why he found the repressive Soviet system intolerable. Oswald's ability to hold down some menial jobs there and here in the United States, where the instructions were minimal and based not on the caprices of his supervisors but on the requirements of the job itself, and where his very survival (food and shelter), as well as that of his wife and children, depended on his employment, cannot be cited as an exception to the aforementioned character trait of independence that Oswald had.

Not that by itself it would carry great weight, but it should be noted that no evidence has ever surfaced that Oswald, either around the time of the assassination or at any prior time, ever hinted, even accidentally, to anyone, including his wife, that he was working for or associated with any agency or group of people, and the Warren Commission, after an exhaustive inquiry, was unable to find any such evidence. And as to Oswald's connection to any other individual, such as Jack Ruby, Warren Commission assistant counsel Arlen Specter said, "The Commission left no stone unturned to track down Oswald's background to the maximum extent possible, to see if he had dealings with anyone else who might have been a co-conspirator," and nothing was found.[35]

11. As we've seen in this book, at the time of the assassination and Ruby's killing of Oswald, *those who knew Oswald and Ruby well*, including family members, rejected the likelihood or notion that either had acted in concert with others to carry out their respective deeds. Yet years later, thousands of conspiracy theorists, *not one of whom knew or had ever met either Oswald or Ruby*, are convinced Oswald (in those cases where they don't go further and say he was just a patsy) and Ruby were members of a conspiracy. On this one point alone of familiarity with the subject, who is more likely to be correct—those who knew the two men or those who did not?

12. In a similar vein, we know from common sense and the experience of our lives, that more than anything else, survivors of a murder victim want the person or persons who killed their loved one to be brought to justice. What reason do we have for believing that the Kennedy family is any different? (As President Kennedy's brother Robert said, "Nobody is more interested than I in knowing who is responsible for the death of President Kennedy.")[36] Yet conspiracy theorists, without any evidence to support their position, are apparently convinced that John F. Kennedy's survivors are an exception. (Indeed, several are so crazy as to believe that RFK actually knew who killed his brother and joined in the conspiracy to cover it up.)[37]

It is noteworthy, then, that the Kennedy family has been supportive of the Warren Commission's conclusion that Oswald acted alone. Because of Bobby Kennedy's fierce opposition to organized crime, which his brother the president supported, and because of JFK's efforts, with RFK's help, to remove Castro from power in Cuba, and with the concomitant dissatisfaction with JFK by the CIA and anti-Castro Cuban exiles over the administration's failure to provide air support during the Bay of Pigs invasion, RFK's first instinct—there have been too many reports from various sources to deny this—immediately after the assassination was to suspect a possible retaliatory killing by one of the people or groups he went after. However, after the coffee cooled and the FBI and Warren Commission investigated the assassination, he issued the following statement to the media on September 27, 1964: "I am convinced [Lee Harvey] Oswald was solely responsible for what happened and that he did not have any outside help or assistance. I have not read the report, nor do I intend to. But I have been briefed on it and I am completely satisfied that the Commission investigated every lead and examined every piece of evidence. The [Warren] Commission's inquiry was thorough and conscientious."[38] RFK, who undoubtedly knew every one of the seven Commission members personally, had no doubt about their integrity in this case, while thousands of conspiracy theorists down through the years, 99.9 percent of whom never knew even one, much less all seven, deeply distrust them.

Perhaps one thing speaks louder than any words, however, with respect to RFK's feelings. During the entire Warren Commission period, he was the nation's attorney general, the chief law enforcement officer in the land with jurisdiction over the FBI, the main investigative arm for the Commission. If at any time he had sensed that the Warren Commission and the FBI weren't doing enough or the right things, wouldn't he have automatically put pressure on them to do so? I would think he would do this even if the victim were not his brother—all the more so when it was. But he never did. Does that not speak volumes? Not only did he not do anything, but in a letter to the Warren Commission on August 4, 1964, he affirmatively told the commissioners he could "state definitely that I know of no credible evidence to support the allegations that the assassination of President Kennedy was caused by a domestic or foreign conspiracy," adding that "I have no suggestions to make at this time regarding an additional investigation which should be undertaken by the Commission prior to the publication of its report."

The president's youngest brother, Senator Edward Kennedy, told *Time* magazine in 1975, "There were things that should have been done differently. There were mistakes made. But I know of no facts that have been brought to light which would call for a reassessment of the conclusion. I'm fundamentally satisfied with the findings of the Warren Commission."[39]

What about JFK Jr., the slain president's son? Since he literally grew up at the feet of his elders in the Kennedy family, if the sense throughout the years was that his father had been murdered as a result of a conspiracy, surely JFK Jr. would have known about it. And just as surely, the late son of the president would look favorably on someone like Oliver Stone, who ostensibly was trying to do everything he could to uncover that conspiracy. But when JFK Jr.'s staff at his magazine, *George*, asked him to interview Stone to help get the fledgling magazine off the ground in its second issue in November of 1995, thinking it would be a blockbuster commercial success, JFK Jr. balked. When his aides persisted, he agreed to have dinner with Stone at Rockenwagner, a Santa Monica, California, restaurant, and when Stone asked John Jr. rhetorically whether he *really* believed Oswald alone had killed his father, adding that there had to be a conspiracy, John excused himself and walked away. After he returned, the dinner was politely brought to a close as soon as possible. John later told his aides, "I just couldn't sit across a table from that man for two hours. I just couldn't," and Stone was not interviewed for the magazine. John's biographer, Richard Blow, who worked with him at the magazine, said that Stone "made John feel like Captain Kirk being stalked by the world's looniest Trekkie."[40]

It's instructive, is it not, that the Warren Commission's conclusion of no conspiracy in the assassination is accepted by the brothers and son of the murdered president, but categorically rejected by thousands of conspiracy theorists who were strangers to the president?

13. If a group like the CIA or organized crime was behind Oswald's murder of Kennedy, is it likely that Oswald was so strapped for money at the time he murdered Kennedy that he never had a pot to grow flowers in, having, per the Warren Report, only $183 to his name at the time of his arrest?[41]* In addition to the $170 he had left for

---

*The Warren Commission, to check on the possibility of a conspiracy in the assassination, ordered an extremely thorough investigation of Oswald's finances by the IRS and the FBI, covering the period June 13, 1962, when he returned from the Soviet Union, up through the date of his arrest on November 22, 1963. Inquiries were made at banks in New Orleans, Fort Worth, Dallas, Houston, and Laredo for any record of a checking, savings, or loan account or a safe-deposit box in the name of Oswald, any of his aliases, or members of his immediate family. No such account or safe-deposit box was located. The FBI did find one bank account

Marina, at the time of his arrest Oswald had a $5 bill, eight $1 bills, a fifty-cent piece, three dimes, a nickel, and two pennies on his person.[42] A total of $183.87—a big hit man for the mob or CIA. Right. We know that contract killers get thousands of dollars to eliminate people no one has ever heard of, but to kill the president of the United States the mob or CIA is not going to pay its hit man anything, not even any money up front?

When, on June 22, 1996, I went to the rooming house where Oswald lived at the time of the assassination, Kaye Puckett, who currently runs the place her family has owned since 1939, and was married with three children and living at the rooming house in 1963, showed me where Oswald's room was, right off the living room to the left when you enter the home. I was astonished at how small it was. When I said to Mrs. Puckett, "This looks more like a large closet to me than a room," she responded that at one time it had been used as a telephone room for all the tenants (it had also, at another time, been used as a small library) and was never intended to be a regular room to rent, but it was all that was available to Oswald when he came to the rooming house in October of 1963, the other regular rooms being rented out, and he settled for it. So the CIA or mob or military-industrial-complex conspirators were really taking good care of their hit man, weren't they?

Surely no one believes that Oswald would have agreed to commit the biggest murder in American history as a paid hit man for someone else without getting some real money up front.

Quite apart from Oswald's not receiving any large sum of money around the time of the assassination as a down payment to kill Kennedy, virtually all conspiracy theorists have alleged that Oswald was an agent of U.S. intelligence during the years leading up to the assassination, many claiming he was even a double agent, helping the KGB. But if this is so, unless the theorists want us to believe he was working free for these agencies (completely unrealistic), where is there any evidence that Oswald, at any point in his adult life, was spending more money than he was earning from his various jobs? To the contrary, all the evidence is that Oswald was always very poor. Poor to the point where he had

---

of Oswald's prior to the subject period. Before he left for the Soviet Union, and while he was stationed at the U.S. Marine Corps Air Station at El Toro, Oswald opened up a savings account at the West Side State Bank in Fort Worth with a deposit of $200.00 on December 8, 1958. Interest of $3.00 was credited to the account on June 3, 1959, and the account was closed on September 14, 1959, with the amount on deposit at the time being $203.00. Telegraph companies were also checked for the possibility of his having received money orders. Also, personnel at all locations where Oswald was known to have cashed payroll and unemployment checks were queried as to the possibility of his having cashed other checks. Further inquiries were made at Oswald's places of employment, at his residences, and with local credit associations, hospitals, utility companies, state and local government offices, post offices, employment agencies, et cetera, for any evidence of Oswald being in possession of extra money. Nothing turned up. And Marina testified she knew of no sources of income her husband had other than wages and unemployment compensation during this period. The Commission's investigation of Oswald's income and expenditures during this period was so comprehensive and precise that, remarkably, the amount its investigators and accountants estimated Oswald had on November 22, 1963, turned out to be within $19.00 of what he actually had. They found that Oswald received a total of $3,665.89 in cash during this period from wages, unemployment compensation, loans, and gifts from friends, and they estimated his expenditures to be $3,501.79, leaving a balance of $164.10. At the time of Oswald's arrest, he had, we know, $13.87 on his person and had left $170.00 behind for Marina at the Paine residence. (WR, pp.328, 745; 1 H 82–83, WCT Marina N. Oswald; see also, for example of inquiries into Oswald's finances, CE 1135, 22 H 114–115; CE 1141, 22 H 126–151; CE 1164, 22 H 215–222; Oswald's Fort Worth bank account: CE 1150, 22 H 180)

One amusing incident in the Commission's effort to find out where every penny came and went with Oswald was when staff member Richard Mosk called *Time* magazine to double-check on his $3.87 yearly subscription. A subscription employee asked Mosk, "Where is Mr. Oswald now?" (Gest, Shapiro, Bowermaster, and Geier, "JFK: The Untold Story of the Warren Commission," p.38)

to borrow money to pay for his and Marina's transportation to the United States from Russia. To the point where Oswald owned one suit to his name, a Russian-made, poorly fitting garment of heavy fabric that was unsuitable for the warm climate of Texas and Louisiana.[43] To the point where Ruth Paine described the Oswalds as "very poor,"[44] and Oswald's aunt, Lillian Murret, said the Oswalds "were practically starving" in the summer of 1963 in New Orleans.[45] To the point where, as indicated, their friend in Dallas, Paul Gregory, told the Warren Commission that he would often take them shopping for groceries and he was "amazed at how little they bought,"[46] and their friends would bring food and groceries to their apartment.[47] To the point where Jeanne de Mohrenschildt didn't feel she could really judge whether Marina was the type to make a home out of where they lived because "they had so few things," and you can't "make a home out of nothing . . . They were so poor."[48] To the point where near the end Oswald was living in a very tiny $5 \times 13\frac{1}{2}$ foot room at a rooming house for which he paid eight dollars a week.

As mentioned in the introduction to this book, no one has studied the assassination more than the late Warren Commission critic Harold Weisberg. And as Weisberg confided to me in a letter three years before his death, he had "not found a shred of evidence" to support the position that Oswald was a paid agent for anyone, adding that Oswald "never had an extra penny, so he had no loot from being an agent."[49]*

14. The very rifle that Oswald owned and used to murder the president points away from a conspiracy. One thought that almost immediately occurred to me at the beginning of my research for the London trial was this: Why would whatever group (mob, CIA, KGB, etc.) that was allegedly behind Oswald furnish its hit man with a used, surplus, nineteen-dollar mail-order rifle (one that—get this—had a homemade sling)?[50] Not that Oswald's rifle wasn't able to get the job done. Safely assuming that Kennedy's head was the target of whoever pulled the Carcano trigger, one in three shots from the rifle did directly hit the target. But is it sense or nonsense to believe that members of a group like the CIA or mob or military-industrial complex, needing to make sure that Kennedy was killed, would let their hit man try to carry out the biggest murder ever with anything other than a very high-quality rifle? The fact that Oswald used the type of rifle he did is almost, by itself, prima facie evidence that he acted alone and there was no conspiracy. Oh, by the way, the clip on Oswald's Carcano could hold six live rounds.[51] But we know Oswald fired three rounds, and only one cartridge was found in the chamber,[52] and the clip was empty.[53] So the big group behind the assassination had its assassin set out on the morning of November 22 to kill the president of the United States with a clip that was missing two rounds.

15. Additionally, if some group was behind Oswald's killing of Kennedy, it obviously wouldn't have had him use any rifle that was so easily traceable to him, as the Mannlicher-Carcano was, since he would be a link to the group.

16. If, indeed, groups like the CIA, mob, military-industrial complex, or whatever, were behind the assassination, not only would they have made sure their hit man had the

---

*Oswald's 1962 federal income tax return listed a total income of $1,354.06, $727.81 in wages from Jaggers-Chiles-Stovall and $626.25 from Leslie Welding Company; $57.40 in withholding tax was deducted from his wages. But even this $57.40 represented a significant amount of money to Oswald. He attached to his return a letter in which he said that in view of his having two dependents in 1962, "I believe if you check your records . . . you will find I should get a substantial refund from the taxes taken from my wages for fiscal 1962." (CD 107, pp.38–39, January 13, 1964) Though it wasn't much, Oswald did receive a 1962 income tax refund check from the federal government for $57.40 on April 2, 1963 (CE 1165, 22 H 224).

best firearm available, but since they wouldn't want him to be apprehended and questioned, they almost assuredly would have equipped the firearm with a sound suppressor, most commonly known as a silencer. Silencers go all the way back to the turn of the twentieth century, and a firearms expert for the Los Angeles Police Department told me that as of 1963 they were already sophisticated enough to "substantially diminish the report" of the weapon and to "alter or disguise the sound," such as to make it sound like "the hitting of a pile of wood with a hammer" or "the operation of machinery." He said silencers are effective, and shots at Kennedy from a weapon with the best silencer then available "probably wouldn't have even been heard above the background noise of the motorcade and crowd" in Dealey Plaza.[54]

17. A related reality presents itself, which will take a bit more time to explain. The mere fact that Oswald's rifle was a *military* rifle (the Carcano was the rifle of the Italian military, the Second World War equivalent of our M-1 rifle) also speaks against a conspiracy for the simple reason that only 6.5-millimeter, full metal-jacketed (FMJ), military-type bullets were ever made for that rifle, not soft-point bullets, the most destructive and deadly bullets by far. Soft-point bullets, a term used by firearms people to refer to partially metal-jacketed bullets with an exposed (unjacketed) lead nose, expand or mushroom upon contact with a human body, thereby causing greater destruction to the victim's internal organs. (The FMJ-type bullets that Oswald fired have a "closed" nose of metal.) Having unexposed soft lead, they also are much more likely than FMJ bullets to break up into many fragments when they hit bone inside the body, additionally increasing their killing power. With the objectives of making war as civilized and humane as possible, and wounding and immobilizing the adversary rather than killing him,[*] the July 29, 1899, Hague Convention's "Declaration Concerning Expanding Bullets" (still adhered to by all armies of the world) specifically prohibited the use in international armed conflict "of bullets which expand or flatten easily in the human body," since they cause much more pain, suffering, and internal hemorrhaging. (And Article 23 [e] of the "Annex to Hague Convention IV Respecting the Laws and Customs of War on Land" of October 18, 1907, prohibits the employment of "arms, projectiles, or material of a nature to cause *superfluous injury*.") Only FMJ military bullets are permitted. These bullets (the type Oswald fired) can obviously also kill, but if they encounter only soft tissue, they can be expected, unlike soft-point bullets, to travel right through the body (as the bullet that struck the president in the upper-right back did) and frequently are not fatal.[†] Indeed, Dr. Malcolm Perry, one of the two principal doctors who attempted to resuscitate the president at Parkland Hospital, thought the president could have survived this wound,[55] but the head wound was fatal.

What all of this means is that if a group of conspirators, like the CIA, mob, or KGB, sophisticated in the killing of humans, was behind the assassination—as conspiracy theorists postulate as a certitude—they had their triggerman use the least deadly type of bullet, one that was specifically designed to injure, *not* kill. How nonsensical is that?

It should be noted that, like Oswald, James Earl Ray, the assassin of Martin Luther King Jr. on April 4, 1968, in Memphis, Tennessee, didn't have two nickels to rub together. Yet, unlike the very cheap, old, mail-order rifle Oswald used, the large-bore deer rifle Ray

---

[*]Wounding rather than killing one's adversary is also militarily advantageous in that the wounded soldier requires, at an absolute minimum, at least one other soldier to take care of him, thus removing two of one's enemy from the battlefield.

[†]Most police departments use soft-point bullets, principally because they don't want their bullets to pass through the body of the intended target and kill innocent people nearby (1 HSCA 378).

used to kill King, a brand new .30–06 caliber Remington, cost over seven hundred dollars,[56] the equivalent of about a two-thousand-dollar rifle today, and the bullet that killed King was a *soft-point* bullet.[57] It may be interesting to the reader to know that the "front-line" people from the HSCA (firearms, photographic, medical, etc., experts who analyzed the evidence, as opposed to the U.S. congressmen on the House Select Committee) whom I worked very closely with on the London trial were not at all confident there was no conspiracy in the assassination of Martin Luther King, whose murder, along with JFK's, the HSCA also reinvestigated. (The HSCA concluded, "There is a likelihood that James Earl Ray assassinated Doctor Martin Luther King as a result of a conspiracy.")[58] All of them, however, felt there was no conspiracy in the assassination of JFK, that the allegations were all foundationless.

18. Another point is that Oswald, though a good shot, qualified as a sharpshooter and a marksman in the Marines, but never as an expert. He certainly was not the professional shooter with sniper-like accuracy any group of conspirators would have automatically employed to kill the president of the United States. The CIA or mob or military-industrial complex would have chosen someone not only from the expert category, but from among the very best within that special category.

19. If, for instance, organized crime (or the CIA, military-industrial complex, etc.) decided to commit the biggest murder in American history, which would result in a retaliation against them of unprecedented proportions if they were discovered to be behind it, they would select a hit man who not only was exceptionally professional and tight-lipped but also had a very successful track record with them. *Oswald had no track record with them.* Yet they're going to use and rely on someone like him to kill the president of the United States? Really?

20. Without exception, all the pro-conspiracy books arguing that Oswald was a hit man for some powerful group (as we know, most contend he wasn't involved in the assassination at all but was framed) promote the notion that Oswald's relationship with the group went back some time, and for groups like U.S. intelligence and the KGB, at least four to five years. Further, they claim he was being groomed by them as a presidential assassin or for some other very serious mission. But how likely is it that with the biggest murder ever coming up on his plate, Oswald (on his own or with the group's knowledge and consent) would try to murder some *other* public figure first? (As we know, Oswald attempted to murder Major General Edwin Walker just months earlier, on April 10, 1963.) Would the rationale be that he needed live target practice for the main event? As the expression goes, *please*.

One footnote to this: Whatever group was allegedly behind Oswald, Walker, a virulent right winger who was one of the leaders of the John Birch Society in Dallas, would represent to their interests the exact opposite of what the moderately liberal JFK would. So there wouldn't have been any commonality between the intended victims.

21. In a similar vein, if Oswald, as part of a conspiracy, was scheduled to murder the president of the United States, how likely is it that his physical, mental, and emotional immersion in, and preparation for, such an extremely important and dangerous mission was so minimal, and his concern about it so little, that just two or so weeks before the scheduled murder, the main thing on his mind was to go into the local office of the FBI in Dallas and threaten to blow up the building if one of the agents didn't stop bothering his wife?

22. Moreover, if Oswald were about to murder the president in two or so weeks, would

he do anything at all that had the potential of drawing anyone's attention to him, particularly the attention of the FBI?

23. On October 4, 1963, Oswald applied for a job as a "typesetter trainee" at the Padgett Printing Company in Dallas and was turned down because (the bottom of the application reads) "Bob Stovall [the president of Jaggers-Chiles-Stovall, where Oswald previously worked] does not recommend this man. He was released [there] because of his record as a troublemaker." Stovall also informed Padgett that Oswald had "communistic tendencies."[59]

If Oswald was the scheduled hit man in a conspiracy to murder Kennedy, why would those behind him (CIA, mob, FBI, etc.) have him apply for a job just seven weeks before the assassination that wasn't on the presidential motorcade route and would never be? Padgett Printing is located today where it was back in 1963, at 1313 North Industrial Boulevard in Dallas, a boulevard of light industry and no tall office buildings, where large crowds of people would be nonexistent. After the presidential limousine was scheduled to get off Elm Street onto the Stemmons Freeway en route to the Trade Mart, North Industrial Boulevard, to the west of the freeway, would be running roughly parallel to it, including the location at 1313 North Industrial Boulevard. However, per Dave Torok, president of Padgett Printing, the company's building has always been only one story, and the Stemmons Freeway, he said, "is a good half mile away, and you can't see it from our building, even from the roof."[60]

The point, of course, is that if Padgett Printing Company had hired Oswald on October 4, Kennedy would not have been a target for Oswald to shoot and kill on November 22. And if Oswald were scheduled to be the hit man for the conspiracy to murder Kennedy, why would his employers (CIA, mob, etc.) have him apply for a job that, if he were hired, would eliminate him as their chosen assassin?

But there's more bad news for the poor, hapless conspiracy theorists, who would gladly settle for anything real, no matter how small, to keep their hopes alive, instead of getting hit with one haymaker after another to their dreams. On October 8, the Texas Employment Commission (TEC) sent Oswald out for a job interview at the Solid State Electronics Company of Texas. He didn't get the job because the company was looking for a sales clerk, and he had no experience that qualified him for that position. "I sure would like to have the job," he told James Hunter of Solid State, who interviewed him. "Every place I go they want experience."[61] And again, the problem for the theorists is that Solid State was located at 2647 Myrtle Springs in Dallas, out beyond Parkland Hospital and nowhere near the motorcade route.

The next day, October 9, the TEC sent Oswald to the Burton-Dixie Corporation for a job as a clerk trainee. Emmett Hobson at Burton-Dixie knows that the company didn't hire Oswald, but told the FBI he didn't recall why, and could not recall the background information Oswald had given him. Burton-Dixie was located at 817 Corinth in Dallas, an industrial area near Oak Cliff, which again, unfortunately for the buffs, was nowhere near the motorcade route.[62]

On October 14, Oswald applied for a job at the Wiener Lumber Company in Dallas. The proprietor, Sam Wiener, was impressed with Oswald as a prospective employee until Oswald was asked to show his Honorable Discharge Card, which Oswald, of course, was unable to do. In the "Remarks" section of Oswald's application, Wiener typed, "Although this man makes an excellent appearance and seems quite intelligent he seemed unable to understand when I continually and clearly asked him for his honorable discharge card or papers for the latest (just ended) hitch. I believe he does not have [it] and will not get such a card or paper. Do not consider for this reason only."

The lumber company was at the corner of Inwood Road and Maple Avenue, near Love Field, so was close to the motorcade route, but again, not on it. The closest that the president's motorcade came to this location was at the intersection of Lemmon Avenue and Inwood Road, a little more than three-quarters of a mile from Wiener Lumber.[63]

Again, the fact, alone, that Oswald was applying for jobs up through October 14 at locations not on the motorcade route virtually precludes the notion of conspiracy among rational people.

24. In the same vein, although Oswald applied for his job at the Book Depository Building with Roy Truly on October 15, the Depository had two buildings, the one at Houston and Elm that everyone knows about, and another building called the "Warehouse," located at 1917 Houston, a building that was larger than the one at Houston and Elm but with two fewer stories.* The Warehouse was not on the parade route, being about four blocks north of the Book Depository Building. (Indeed, at that time in 1963, Houston Street became unpaved one block north of Elm.) Truly just as well could have assigned Oswald to work in the building at 1917 Houston as at the building at Houston and Elm. "I might have sent Oswald to work in a warehouse two blocks away," Truly said. "Oswald and another fellow reported for work on the same day [October 15] and I needed one of them for the depository building. I picked Oswald." Truly said he "hired" the other "boy" for the Warehouse.[64] Neither Oswald nor the supposed conspirators behind him could have possibly known or foreseen which building Truly would have assigned Oswald to. And if Truly had sent Oswald to 1917 Houston, Kennedy would not have passed under Oswald's window and there wouldn't have been an assassination. What type of massive conspiracy by the CIA, mob, et cetera, to murder Kennedy would be completely dependent on what building Truly assigned the assassin to? I mean, would any group of conspirators choose a location for killing Kennedy that depended on an arbitrary decision such as this one that was wholly beyond its control? Of course, we could make Roy Truly part of the conspiracy to kill Kennedy, something that would be perfectly all right with the conspiracy theorists.

It should be noted further that, as we saw in this book, there is absolutely no evidence that any group such as the CIA or mob had anything to do with Oswald getting a job at the Book Depository Building, the building that literally enabled Oswald to successfully kill Kennedy.

25. Oswald told Marina he didn't care for his job at the Book Depository Building, and as late as November 9 (Ruth Paine thinks it may have been November 2),[65] just thirteen days before the assassination, he applied for a job, per Marina, at "some photographic" company but did not get it.[66] So up to thirteen days before the assassination, or twenty at the most, Oswald sought a job that would have taken him away from his sniper's nest right above the president's limousine. Some conspiracy.

26. We know why Oswald shot Kennedy from the Book Depository Building. He worked there. Besides, no better opportunity to kill Kennedy would probably ever come to him. But if a powerful organization like the CIA, KGB, or organized crime, with vast

---

*Per Gary Mack, curator at the Sixth Floor Museum at Dealey Plaza in Dallas, the building is no longer there, the Woodhall Rogers Freeway going right through the old location (Interview of Gary Mack by author on March 14, 2002).

resources at its disposal, decided to kill the president of the United States, obviously it would reconnoiter assassination sites around the country where the president was scheduled to be, searching for the very best one it could find. With this in mind, why in the world would any of these groups have chosen a location for their hit man that had a giant and heavily foliaged oak tree obstructing his view of the president during several of the critical seconds in which he would want to be tracking and shooting the president? And why would they choose to shoot the president at a time when at least 80 percent of his body was concealed and protected by the body of his limousine?

27. If a group like the mob or the CIA was behind Oswald's assassination of Kennedy, in the period of time leading up to the assassination they (his "handlers," per conspiracy lore) would obviously have to be in touch with him. But in a telephone conversation, Mrs. Puckett told me that none of the seventeen tenants of the rooming house in 1963 had their own phone. She said they all shared "one communal pay phone on the wall in the hall back near the kitchen, and with all of them having only this one phone, it was in use a lot."[67]

Also, Oswald spent every weekend, except one, with his wife and children at the Paine residence in Irving, and missed no days of work at the Book Depository Building. In the evenings we know he went to the nearby washateria on occasion, and went out on the evenings of October 23, a Wednesday, when he attended a speech by General Walker, and October 25, a Friday night when he was in Irving and attended a meeting of the American Civil Liberties Union. But other than this, according to Mrs. Puckett's mother (Mrs. Johnson) and the housekeeper, Earlene Roberts, in the five weeks prior to the assassination Oswald simply never went out. Mrs. Johnson said that except for watching TV with the other renters sometimes (during which, she said, if they talked to him, he wouldn't answer), "I just really never did see that man leave [his] room . . . 95 percent of the time he would sit in his room."[68] Earlene Roberts said, "He was always home at night—he never went out."[69] And Ruth Paine testified at the trial in London that Oswald was a loner who never had a relationship with anyone other than Marina, and never received or made any calls at her house phone while he was in her home. When I asked her, "So you're not aware of any contacts he had with anyone?" she answered, "No."[70]

So it would seem that the biggest murder plot in American history, with the inevitable follow-up conversations, could only have taken place under the following circumstances: Oswald called his mob or CIA contacts from his job at the Book Depository Building, or they called and asked for him. But Roy Truly, the superintendent at the Book Depository, testified before the Warren Commission that there was only one phone (on the first floor) for the employees to use during their lunch hour "for a minute" and they were "supposed to ask permission to use the phone." And Truly said, "I never remember ever seeing him [Oswald] on the telephone" during work hours.[71] Or on the way home from work Oswald got off the bus to call his co-conspirators from a pay phone. Or they called him at the rooming house (Earlene Roberts, the housekeeper, said that Oswald never received any telephone calls),[72] or he called them with a bunch of change from the busy communal pay phone on the wall in the hall back near the kitchen of the rooming house.[73] Just how likely is any of this?

Moreover, Arthur Johnson, the landlord at Oswald's rooming house, told *Dallas Morning News* reporter Hugh Aynesworth on the afternoon of the assassination that Oswald "*always* talked in that foreign language when he talked on the phone." Whom was he talking to? Roberts, the housekeeper, told Aynesworth that Oswald "dialed that BL number [Irving, Texas, where Marina was living] a lot."[74] As far as receiving phone calls, the landlady, Mrs. Johnson, like Earlene Roberts, said she didn't recall Oswald ever receiving a call at the rooming house.[75]

28. Part of a criminal's invariable preparation for any premeditated crime is to contemplate how to pull it off *without being caught*. Although Oswald may have been disoriented enough not to have considered this part of the venture, we can be more than 100 percent certain that a group like the CIA, mob, or military-industrial complex would have. Since we know this to be true, if a group was behind Oswald's act, it is absolutely inconceivable that it wouldn't have done everything possible to avoid having its hit man captured and interrogated by the authorities, which carried the enormous danger of his cracking and implicating the group. No matter how far removed the group personally may have been from his act, he would have to have sufficient knowledge to incriminate whoever approached him to do the job, that person could in turn put the hat on the person or persons above him, and so on up to the architects of the assassination themselves. Since they would know this, at a very minimum they would have tried to provide for Oswald's escape. But much more probably, a car would have been waiting for him at a prearranged place after he left the Depository Building, not to help him escape, but to drive him to his death.[*] Yet here we have Oswald, right after the assassination, leaving the Depository Building, completely alone and wandering out on the streets, trying to get back to his home by catching a bus, then deciding to get off and find a cab. *This fact alone, and all by itself, tells any sensible person that Oswald acted alone, that there was no conspiracy in the assassination to kill Kennedy.*

And as indicated, when Oswald was arrested he only had $13.87 on his person,[76] not enough to get him far away from Dallas, which, in the unlikely event the mob or CIA didn't arrange for his immediate death, they would have wanted him to be.

Even if we make the completely unreasonable assumption that a group behind Oswald's killing Kennedy would not have made every effort to help Oswald escape or kill him after he left the Book Depository Building to ensure he wasn't captured and interrogated (i.e., apparently the group wanted him to be grilled for hours on end *before* it killed him), and accept the assumption made by so very many that it decided, instead, to have Ruby silence Oswald for it, let's see where that takes us. There are two realities to consider. First, by the time Ruby shot Oswald, Oswald had already been interrogated for twelve hours over a three-day period (Friday, Saturday, and Sunday) by investigators from the Dallas Police Department, FBI, and Secret Service, as well as by the U.S. Post Office inspector and U.S. marshall in Dallas.[77] Second, if it was the group's plan to get someone to silence Oswald after Oswald killed Kennedy, all rational minds have to agree that the group surely would not have waited until *after* Oswald killed Kennedy before it started looking for someone to silence Oswald. This would all be worked out, of course, well in advance.

In view of these two realities, the evidence that Ruby did not silence Oswald for any group such as the mob is that if he had been chosen to kill Oswald, he would have done so the first opportunity he had, rather than give the authorities two more days to interrogate Oswald, and that was on Friday evening at the Dallas Police Department. That

---

[*]Silencing Oswald by driving him to his execution after he left the Book Depository Building would have made infinitely more sense to the conspirators than waiting until he was in police custody to do so. With Oswald heavily guarded, they'd have to know it would be much more difficult and problematic that they'd be able to get close enough to Oswald to kill him, and even if they did, they'd know this second hit man of theirs would himself be immediately apprehended and grilled by the authorities.

evening, while Oswald was being grilled in the Homicide and Robbery office by Captain Fritz and others, Ruby, we know, was right outside Fritz's office talking to reporters. At one point, Fritz brought Oswald out of the office and Oswald walked right past Ruby, coming within two to three feet of him.[78] And Ruby admitted to the FBI that he had his revolver, the one he used to kill Oswald two days later, in his right front trouser pocket because he had a lot of money from his nightclub on his person.[79] Ruby's own attorney, Tom Howard, said Ruby was armed with his revolver that Friday night.[80]* Presumably at the request of his lawyers, Ruby wrote his version of the events that led up to his shooting of Oswald on 3 × 5 inch cards, and the cards were given to his lawyers. Some were prepared before his trial, others in advance of a motion for a new trial. On one of the cards, he wrote in his handwriting, "Had I wanted to get him [Oswald] I could have reached in and shot [him] when either Fritz [or] Curry brought him out in the hall, when they told the press that they would bring him down in the basement."[81]

In addition to the fact that if Ruby killed Oswald for the mob (or any other group) he would have done so on Friday night to prevent further interrogation of Oswald, there is another reason why Ruby would have killed Oswald Friday night. The mob and Ruby would necessarily have to believe that Oswald would be extremely well protected by Dallas law enforcement, so Ruby would have no choice but to kill him the first opportunity he had since he would have had no way of knowing that he would ever have another opportunity to do so.

The fact that Ruby did not kill Oswald on Friday night, when it would have been so easy for him to have done so, is virtually conclusive evidence, *all by itself*, that he didn't kill Oswald on Sunday for anyone but himself, which in turn is just further evidence that there was nothing inside of Oswald to silence because he too acted alone.

29. One other indication that Oswald's decision to kill the president was essentially spontaneous (and therefore, devoid of any conspiracy with others) and formed sometime after the route of the president's motorcade in front of Oswald's workplace first became public only three days before the assassination, is his lack of planning to ensure his survival. Although Oswald wanted to survive—he tried to escape, and also physically resisted arrest, striking the arresting officer and drawing his revolver before it was wrenched away from him—he apparently never thought out his escape, even to the obvious point of bringing his revolver to work with him so that he would have it to defend and extricate himself from any possible confrontation with the authorities after his attempt on the president's life the next day. Instead, he admitted during his interrogation by Captain Fritz of the Dallas Police Department that after he left the Book Depository Building following the assassination, he went back to his room at 1026 North Beckley in Dallas and got his revolver.[82]

30. If Oswald had conspired with others to murder Kennedy, why would he not have explored the possibility with the authorities of saving his own life by implicating them? This would be particularly true if, as the conspiracy theorists allege, he was "set up" by co-conspirators to take the blame, that he was "the designated fall guy." In fact, they cite his statement in custody that he was just a "patsy" as support for this proposition. But

*The argument that Ruby later told the Warren Commission he did not have his revolver that night, that he had lied when he said he did to save his life (how?) (5 H 205, 14 H 553), is unavailing. Not only is it likely he did, since this was his first story, but even if he didn't, if he had been given the assignment by the mob to kill Oswald (obviously as soon as possible before further interrogation of Oswald continued) he *would* have been armed that Friday night.

if, indeed, Oswald's co-conspirators set him up, he'd have all the more reason to implicate them, having no reason at that point to feel any loyalty toward those who had betrayed him. Yet Oswald, throughout his twelve hours of interrogation, never suggested in any way that he was part of any conspiracy to kill Kennedy. Because Oswald knew that there was so much evidence against him, including his ownership of the murder weapon, and that a sentence of death was going to be automatic, to save his life he most likely would have implicated others if there were any to implicate (an extremely common occurrence in criminal cases, i.e., "turning state's evidence"), yet he said nothing. This fact is circumstantial evidence that there simply were no co-conspirators for him to implicate.[*]

And what about Ruby? As we have seen, it is scripture among conspiracy theorists that "Jack Ruby silenced Oswald for the mob." But they don't ask themselves, "Who was supposed to silence Jack Ruby?" Ruby, we know, lived more than three long years (1,154 days) after killing Oswald before passing away on January 3, 1967, and never once suggested that he killed Oswald for someone else. But if mobsters were behind Ruby's act, they could never know if Ruby would talk someday. Yet there is no evidence that the mob or anyone else tried to silence Ruby. We've observed that the emotionally erratic and unreliable Oswald would have been one of the last people in the world the mob (or any other group of alleged conspirators) would have relied on to carry out its biggest murder ever. But Ruby was equally unreliable. Why would the mob choose someone to silence Oswald who was a notorious blabbermouth, had a volcanic temper, and was so emotionally unstable? The notion that the mob (or anyone else) got the goofy Oswald, of all people, to kill Kennedy and then got the even goofier Jack Ruby, of all people, to silence Oswald is downright laughable. I told the jury in London that the mob could just as well have "gone down to Disneyland and gotten Mickey Mouse and Donald Duck to do their bidding for them."[83]

Several years after I made that remark in London, I read *The Last Mafioso*, Ovid Demaris's biography of Los Angeles mob boss Jimmy "The Weasel" Fratiano, the highest-ranking mafioso ever to "turn" on the mob, his testimony for the federal government in the early 1980s sending many of them to prison for life. Fratiano was particularly close to fellow mafioso Johnny Roselli, and Fratiano quotes Roselli as telling him one day while they were driving through the Santa Monica mountains shortly after Roselli's testimony before the HSCA in Washington, D.C., in 1976, "[They're] all hot,

---

[*]Ruby's killing of Oswald not only is no evidence that Ruby silenced Oswald for the mob as so many people believe, but actually is further evidence of no conspiracy in the assassination. Such an act by Ruby would have been extremely unwise for any group of conspirators, and this fact would have been very obvious to them. As I argued to the jury in London, "By having Ruby kill Oswald, they would be increasing the peril of their own apprehension" (Transcript of *On Trial*, July 25, 1986, p.1049). Since the killing took place right in front of over seventy Dallas law enforcement officers, the conspirators could be 100 percent certain that Ruby would be arrested immediately and grilled thereafter. Secondly, the conspirators would also know that if Ruby was unsuccessful in his effort to shoot Oswald (or even if he did succeed but Oswald managed to survive because of immediate medical attention), then they'd have to worry not just about one, but two people talking. And at that point, what possible reason would Oswald have for continuing to protect those who were behind his act once he learned they had tried to murder him? Even if we were to assume the optimum, that the conspirators somehow *knew* that Ruby would succeed in killing Oswald immediately, what would they gain by eliminating one conspirator (Oswald) when in the process they would automatically be turning over a new conspirator (Ruby) to the authorities? And let's not forget that the conspirators had to know (the thought would have had to have entered at least one of their minds) that by having someone kill Oswald, a great many people who were not even thinking of a conspiracy in the assassination would be now, thinking that a group of conspirators may have been behind Oswald's act and they decided to silence him. How could any conspirators possibly believe that drawing attention to the possibility of a conspiracy would have helped them?

you know, about who killed Kennedy. Sometimes I'd like to tell them the mob did it, just to see the expression on their stupid faces. You know, we're supposed to be idiots, right? We hire a psycho like Oswald to kill the President and then we get a blabbermouth, two-bit punk like Ruby to shut him up. We wouldn't trust those jerks to hit a fucking dog."[84] I don't know if Roselli told Fratiano this, or Fratiano, for some reason, made it up, but either way, it clearly reflects a mafioso's view of the preposterous theory that organized crime, even if it made the even more preposterous decision to murder the president of the United States, would hire Oswald and Ruby to do its bidding for them.

31. I spoke earlier of the virtual impossibility of all the people involved in any conspiracy to kill the president keeping it a secret for even a few days, much less over forty years. But there's a perhaps even more difficult, and related, reality that the original conspirators would have to overcome. Let's assume, for example, that the CIA was behind the assassination. *After* the assassination, how could the CIA have gotten the FBI, Secret Service, Dallas Police Department, the autopsy doctors, indeed, the Warren Commission itself, to go along with the horrendous crime the agency had committed and do the great number of things the conspiracy theorists say these various groups and people did to cover up the CIA's complicity in Kennedy's murder? Wouldn't that be an impossible task?* The only way (there is no other way) that agencies and people like the FBI, autopsy doctors, et cetera, would all agree to cover up the murder of the president of the United States for the CIA (or mob, FBI, military-industrial complex, etc.) would be if they themselves were part of the original conspiracy to kill Kennedy. And again, no rational person can possibly believe that these groups and people all got together to murder the president. The bottom line is that conspiracy musings of the conspiracy theorists are outrageously hallucinatory and bear no relation to reality.

32. Even though there's not a lick of evidence that the CIA, mob, FBI, or any other group conspired with Oswald to kill Kennedy, if the conspiracy theorists could at least show that he had an association or connection with any of these groups, they would then have something to talk about. But here, other than explainable contacts (e.g., the FBI interviewing Oswald when he returned to the United States from Russia, and his very limited attempt to infiltrate anti-Castro Cuban exiles), after the most extensive investigation of a single individual ever conducted, no one has ever come up with any evidence of an association, relationship, or contact that Oswald had with any of these groups. The reason there's no evidence is that no such evidence exists. As I have said before in this book, it's all just sublime silliness.

Since we know that Oswald killed Kennedy, and since there is no evidence that Oswald had any relationship with groups like organized crime, the CIA, the military-industrial complex, or any other group, this fact alone removes these groups from any suspicion of being complicit in the assassination.

---

*Not according to New Orleans DA Jim Garrison, who believed that elements of "the intelligence community" (primarily, he says, "individuals in the CIA's covert operations apparatus") were behind Kennedy's murder. "As soon as the *non*-participating elements in the intelligence community saw that a coup d'etat had occurred, they moved quickly to support the official story. Motivated in some instances by self-preservation and in others by a belief that Kennedy had brought the assassination on himself by compromising too often with the Soviets, *the remainder of the government*—from high elected officials to heads of departments and agencies—lined up to add their solemn voices to the growing chorus chanting the great lie." (Garrison, *On the Trail of the Assassins*, pp.324, 331) Can you imagine that, folks, "the remainder of the government"? If most conspiracy theorists had just one tiny speck of common sense about the assassination inside their brain, it would be extremely lonely.

After over forty years of the most prodigiously intensive investigation and examination of a murder case in world history, certain powerful facts exist which cannot be challenged: Not one weapon other than Oswald's Mannlicher-Carcano rifle has ever been found and linked in any way to the assassination. Not one bullet other than the three fired from Oswald's rifle has ever been found and linked to the assassination. No person other than Oswald has ever been connected by evidence, in any way, to the assassination. No evidence has ever surfaced linking Oswald to any of the major groups suggested by conspiracy theorists of being behind the assassination. And no evidence has ever been found showing that any person or group framed Oswald for the murder they committed. One would think that faced with these stubborn and immutable realities, the critics of the Warren Commission, unable to pay the piper, would finally fold their tent and go home. But instead, undaunted and unfazed, they continue to disgorge even more of what we have had from them for over forty years—wild speculation, theorizing, and shameless dissembling about the facts of the case.

The purpose of this book has been twofold. One, to educate everyday Americans that Oswald killed Kennedy and acted alone, paying for his own bullets. And two, to expose, as never before, the conspiracy theorists and the abject worthlessness of all their allegations. I believe this book has achieved both of these goals.

BOOKENDS

The Murder Trial of Jack Ruby

On November 26, 1963, a Dallas County grand jury indicted Jack Ruby ("Jack Rubenstein, alias Jack Ruby") for the murder of Lee Harvey Oswald. Trial judge Joe B. Brown would be presiding over the case. The affable, bespectacled, fifty-six-year-old was known for running a very loose courtroom and for having modest legal talent—so modest, in fact, that his friend, Dallas district attorney Henry Wade, urged him not to handle the case, telling Brown, "This case is too big for you."[1] Brown, who didn't make it through high school and graduated from a small Dallas law school that went out of business after a few years, was taken by celebrity and was greatly impressed by the size and composition of the media covering the trial. "Just think," he told his bailiff, "we've got newsmen from all over the world here, and Pulitzer Prize winners and famous columnists and TV commentators right here in my courtroom."[2]

Wade's office was seeking the death penalty against Ruby, the electric chair at Huntsville state prison, and Wade himself, whose cornball manner concealed a good legal mind, would prosecute the case, make the important decisions, and be the nominal head of the prosecution team,[*] although the actual lead trial prosecutor would be Wade's assistant, William Alexander, who conducted "the bulk of the prosecution's" case.[3][†] Having

---

[*]Although having nothing to do with the Kennedy assassination or his prosecution of Ruby or even his long career as a criminal prosecutor, ironically another case, and a civil one at that, has been more responsible for the fame of Wade's name, the 1973 U.S. Supreme Court abortion case of *Roe v. Wade*. In 1969, a Texas woman, unmarried and pregnant and using the pseudonym Jane Roe, filed a class-action suit in a federal court against Wade, seeking an injunction prohibiting Wade's office from enforcing the Texas law that made abortion a crime. Wade resisted and the case finally reached the U.S. Supreme Court, which, in a 7-2 ruling, struck down the abortion laws of Texas and Georgia (a companion case to *Roe* was also heard by the court) and legalized abortion throughout the land.

[†]Alexander referred to himself as the "chief prosecutor since ... I put the prosecution's case together. Henry Wade, of course, being the district attorney, sat in on it" (Sneed, *No More Silence*, p.542, interview of Bill Alexander).

anticipated prosecuting and devouring Oswald, until Ruby stopped that dream, Alexander had joked to reporters that "you can't have rabbit stew without a rabbit."[4]

Ruby's first lawyer was Tom Howard, a veteran criminal defense attorney in Dallas. Howard, though never having handled a big publicity case before, and operating without a secretary or law library out of a small storefront office across the street from the Dallas Police Department, had a reasonably successful record as a criminal defense attorney.[*]

Howard had successfully represented Jack a couple of years back on a liquor license dispute over a half bottle of beer found on a table at the Carousel after hours. He had gotten that charge dismissed. It wasn't going to be as easy getting this one tossed out, but Howard's plan was to try to convince the jury to convict Ruby of "murder without malice" on the rationale that the killing was in the heat of passion with adequate provocation (Oswald had killed Kennedy), thus negating malice and shielding Ruby from a possible death sentence.

To elaborate, there were two types of murder in Texas that Ruby could be found guilty of: murder with malice aforethought and murder without malice aforethought. As in all states, the word *aforethought* is a useless appendage since it does not mean what it sounds like, premeditation. In most states, there is first-degree and second-degree murder, first degree requiring a showing of premeditation and deliberation along with malice. Texas, to this day, has no degrees of murder, and premeditation and deliberation are not elements of murder that have to be proved. So unlike in most states, the Dallas prosecutors did not have to show that Ruby premeditated and deliberated his killing of Oswald. All they had to prove is that he killed with malice. In Texas, "malice" in a murder case is proved when it can be shown that the killer intended to kill, where there was no legal justification or excuse for his act, and where he was not "under the immediate influence of a *sudden passion* arising from an adequate cause, by which is meant such cause as would commonly produce a degree of anger, rage, resentment or terror in a person of ordinary temper, sufficient to render the mind incapable of cool reflection." If it is shown that he *was* under such influence, the crime is murder *without* malice. (In most states, it would be voluntary manslaughter.) Even though the prosecution had no legal burden in the Ruby case to show premeditation, premeditation was very relevant since the presence or absence of premeditation could help to prove or disprove malice. If, for instance, Ruby had premeditated the killing of Oswald, it was not the result of a "sudden passion."

Murder with malice in Texas carries a punishment of death or imprisonment for more than two years (in Texas, the "more than two years" is usually life). Murder without malice is punishable by a maximum of five years' imprisonment. That's what Howard was shooting for.

To make the jury more comfortable returning a verdict of murder without malice, although Howard had no intention of ultimately trying to convince the jury that Ruby was insane (he didn't believe he was), he did intend to show, through a psychiatrist or two, as well as Ruby's friends and associates, that Jack, shall we say, was not quite right, that he was emotionally unstable, something that no one who knew Ruby could possibly

[*]Howard told the media he had handled at least thirty-five capital cases "and I've never had a client executed" (*New York Times*, November 26, 1963, p.15). But the trial lawyer hasn't been born who can get thirty-five life sentences (or aquittals) in thirty-five cases where the DA was seeking the death penalty—at least not in Texas. Indeed, it's very unlikely that the coarse-tongued Howard, who was married to a woman who had shot and killed her lover, had even tried anywhere near thirty-five capital cases. Dallas prosecutor Jim Bowie said, "Tom Howard defends whores and pimps [and] does it damn well." (Wills and Demaris, *Jack Ruby*, pp.83, 85)

quarrel with. As a device to get Ruby's mental infirmity into the official record, on December 2 Howard requested a pretrial competency (sanity to stand trial) hearing.

Howard believed that such a simple approach coupled with an expressed plea by Ruby for mercy from the witness stand, as well as the unstated sense of many to "pin a medal on Jack" for killing Oswald, might result in a favorable verdict and light sentence, as opposed to the death penalty. There was some logic behind this thinking. After all, newspaper polls in Dallas taken after Ruby killed Oswald showed, remarkably, that nearly half of the people questioned felt that Ruby should receive no punishment at all.[5] It's an old joke about Texas murder trials that the first matter to be settled is whether the varmint who got himself killed damn well deserved what he got. Legend has it that the first question sheriffs investigating a homicide in rural Texas ask is, "Did he *need* killing?" Indeed, Ruby received hundreds of supportive letters and telegrams (and very few critical of him) from people not just in Texas but all over the world. A sampling from some of the telegrams: "Congratulations. You have done what every loyal American citizen would like to have done. God bless you." "Heartiest congratulations, but [Oswald] died too fast." "Thank you for doing what every freedom-loving citizen of the world wanted to do." "Congratulations. May God bless you." "Thank you. May the Lord and Texas justice have mercy on you. May you live to be a thousand." "Our family cannot find in our hearts to censure you. We send you our love and support." "Had I the guts I'd have done it.[*] Thanks for trying to vindicate Dallas." "To a job well done. You are a great man, Jack Ruby." "Congratulations, you deserve a medal, all the world is in back of you." "Thank you sir. God bless you." "I kiss your feet."[6] In other words, Howard's reasoning apparently went, how bad could the jury consider Ruby's act to be when he had simply done to Oswald what a great number of other Americans wanted to do and which the state of Texas would have eventually done anyway? Indeed, even the wife of U.S. Supreme Court Justice William O. Douglas acknowledged to an interviewer that she had shouted, "Good! Give it to him again!" when she saw Ruby shoot Oswald on her television screen.[7]

So Howard wasn't overly worried about the case, even if Jack was hardly the ideal defendant—a Jewish striptease joint operator in a very conservative, overwhelmingly Anglo-Saxon Protestant city who had also made the Dallas police, and Dallas, a city noted for its civic pride, look bad. But again, Jack shot down the most loathed man in America, and that had to count for something in court, Howard reasoned.

This strategy changed when Ruby's family, not feeling Howard had enough stature and legal talent for a case this big, brought famed San Francisco lawyer Melvin Belli into the case on December 10, 1963.[†] Though he was often described as "flamboyant,"[‡] there

---

[*]When Wally Weston, a comedian who worked at Ruby's Carousel Club as the master of ceremonies, went to visit Ruby in jail, he said the first thing Ruby said, and with a smile, was, "I got balls, ain't I, baby?" Weston responded, "Yeah, Jack, and they're going to hang you by them, too." (Transcript of "Who Was Lee Harvey Oswald?" *Frontline*, PBS, November 16, 1993, p.42)

[†]Reportedly, the first big-name lawyer the Ruby family sought before Belli was the legendary Houston criminal defense attorney Percy Foreman. But Foreman wanted a guarantee of $75,000, which the Rubys were unwilling to pay, and additionally, he rubbed Earl Ruby the wrong way. (Aynesworth with Michaud, *JFK: Breaking the News*, p.171; "Good-by Belli," p.19) I'll never forget an appearance I had on *The Merv Griffin Show* years ago with Foreman, when Foreman told an open-mouthed Griffin, "Merv, all my clients are poor. They're either poor when they walk in the door, or poor when they walk out. I take everything they have," whereupon he proceeded to enumerate what he took. I don't remember exactly what that included but I vaguely recall his saying their home, paintings on the wall, motorcycle, and so on.

[‡]Everything about Belli, his clothing, his words, his lifestyle (he was married six times), even his law office, fell into this category. About the last he said, "Some say my office at 722 Montgomery Street looks like a gold-rush whorehouse, but actually it's a museum of my life and travels. San Franciscans love to gawk

was considerable substance behind the sheen. Known as the "king of torts" (torts are civil not criminal wrongs), Belli[*] had actually sown new ground in the area of tort law with his skill at using "demonstrative evidence" (evidence that addresses the physical senses of the jury, such as a model of a human skeleton, scale mock-ups of an accident scene, greatly enlarged photographs, live experiments, and so on)[†] as a plaintiff's lawyer in personal injury cases, and for the record-breaking monetary awards juries were returning for his clients. The problem is that he was primarily a civil not a criminal lawyer, although he had tried, and continued to try after the Ruby case, a criminal case now and then that caught his fancy. Belli, then, was a legal heavyweight, but not in criminal law, and he demonstrated this in several ways, which are chronicled in the major books on the trial. As the trial judge, Joe Brown, would later write, "Belli undoubtedly was, as the newspapers called him, the king of torts, but at trying a criminal case in Texas, he wasn't even royalty."[8] Lead Ruby prosecutor Bill Alexander, who had an acerbic relationship with Belli during the trial, acknowledged to me that "Belli was probably a better lawyer in his field than we were in ours, but he was in the wrong ballpark."[9]

Wanting a Texas lawyer at his side, Belli brought in Joe Tonahill, a colorful and towering trial lawyer from Jasper in East Texas whose homespun style had proved effective with country juries, along with a Los Angeles associate of Belli's, Sam Brody. Phil Burleson, a young Dallas lawyer with appellate experience, was hired to primarily handle legal briefs and research. Howard was consigned to the bleachers, looking on, and shortly thereafter resigned from the defense team.

Surprisingly, for a lawyer of Belli's intelligence and experience, he did nothing to endear himself to the Dallas citizenry, a microcosm of which he would eventually have to rely on for a fair trial for his client. Noted for his flashy but expensive sartorial splendor, he declined to change his attire one lick, including his customary vested suits with silk linings, his rich pastel shirts and ties, and a gold watch chain, items just not seen among Dallas men with their off-the-rack attire. Indeed, his fur-collared Chesterfield overcoat and red velvet briefcase may have been unique among lawyers anywhere in the Panhandle State. And his pronouncements to the local and national media, who followed him like faithful puppies wherever he took himself in Dallas, including restaurants, was confrontational. "He repeatedly criticized the state of Texas. He lectured about Dallas' need to make Ruby a sacrificial goat . . . 'The people of Dallas,' he told the press, 'perhaps unconsciously have to have a sacrifice in order to cleanse themselves.'"[10] But if Belli intended to put the city of Dallas itself on trial, he had to expect its citizens not to like this, with whatever way that feeling played out.

One might think that Belli would at least have tried to get Dallas's legal community on his side, but he alienated it too when he arrived in Dallas by characterizing members of the district attorney's staff as "yokels."[11] If someone wanted to hide anything from Alexander and Wade, he joked, put it in a law book and they'd never find it.[12]

---

in the windows. And the Gray Line has the office on one of its tours" (Belli with Kaiser, *Melvin Belli*, photo section).

[*]Pronounced "Bell-eye" "not Belli" as in one's belly, he would lecture any members of the media who, perchance, were among the few who hadn't heard his name pronounced before.

[†]Belli, often called the "Father of Demonstrative Evidence," started to popularize this method of presenting evidence to a jury in the early 1940s in San Francisco. His theory, undoubtedly true, was that in addition to *telling* a jury what the evidence was, if you could let them see and feel the evidence, even taste or smell it, your chances of favorably reaching the jury were enhanced.

At a change-of-venue hearing on February 10–13, 1964, during which Belli presented forty-one witnesses in support of his motion to move the trial out of Dallas because Ruby could not get "a fair trial" there, he argued that because many blamed the city for the assassination taking place there, and for negligently allowing the shooting of Oswald to occur, Dallas itself was on trial, and in effect, the jury might have to convict Ruby to acquit the city. There can be little question that Belli's concern was not a frivolous one. There was a collective sense of guilt among the citizenry, mostly about Kennedy being killed there, that continued for years thereafter. Just a day after the assassination, remarks like this were being made by Dallas citizens: "Dallas can't hold its head up this morning." "I think Dallas died right with [the president]. We're the ones that are going to suffer. History will never erase it." A cabby, when learning that his passengers were from New York, said, "New York? Are you here to take pictures of our black-eye?" Ruby himself told his sister, Eileen Kaminsky, on the afternoon of the assassination, "What a black mark for Dallas."

The feeling was so prevalent that Dallas's mayor, Earle Cabell, felt moved to say in defense, "There are maniacs all over the world, and in every city of the world. This was a maniac. It could have happened in Podunk as well as Dallas."[13] But apart from Oswald's action severely damaging Dallas, Cabell testified for the defense at the venue hearing that Ruby couldn't get a fair trial in Dallas because what Ruby did had further hurt the city very badly. Ruby's lawyer Joe Tonahill said that prior to Cabell's statement on the witness stand, Ruby was upbeat about his chances, but what Cabell said affected Ruby deeply. "Why, I love this city, Joe," he said to Tonahill. Cabell told the Warren Commission that he had known Ruby "for several years." Jack had a habit of taking people up to Cabell at public functions and introducing them to him as "my friend, the Mayor." Now, for the first time, Jack was hearing from his "friend," the head of the city, the essentially official word that he was no hero, but someone who had disgraced Dallas, and Tonahill said Cabell's words hit Ruby "like a ton of bricks."[14]

In the venue hearing, the prosecution never called one opposing witness to the stand, instead filing with the court thirty-eight affidavits from Dallas citizens swearing under oath that Ruby could get a fair trial in the city. On February 14, Judge Brown did not grant the defense motion, but he did not deny it either, postponing his decision until a jury was selected, at which time he'd decide whether *that* jury could give Ruby a fair trial.[15]

Under Belli's direction, the defense team decided to come up with an "imaginative" defense. Almost out of hand, Belli rejected Howard's "murder without malice" strategy and decided on a scientific and sophisticated medical defense of temporary insanity, with psychiatric experts testifying for the defense. In other words, he didn't want to settle for anything less than an acquittal, a verdict of not guilty based on Ruby's insanity at the time of the shooting. Ruby entered a plea of "not guilty" to the murder indictment against him, not "not guilty by reason of insanity,"[16] for the simple reason that there was no such plea in Texas, as there is in most states, and there still isn't to this very day. However, even in Texas the defense can put on an affirmative insanity defense to the charges against the accused, and the Texas Penal Code provides that "no act done in a state of insanity can be punished as an offense." The question would not be whether Ruby unlawfully killed Oswald—there were eighty million eyewitnesses[*] to affirm that proposition—but what

---

[*]In fact, the *New York Times* had observed that Ruby's shooting of Oswald "marked the first time in 15 years around the globe that a real-life homicide had occurred in front of live cameras . . . The Dallas shooting [was] easily the most extraordinary moments of TV that a set owner ever watched" (*New York Times*, November 25, 1963, pp. 1, 10).

was on Ruby's mind, if anything, at the time he did so. Bob Huffaker, who covered the Ruby trial for Dallas's CBS affiliate, KRLD, wrote that Ruby "had failed to envision actually being charged with murder for what he had conceived as an act of patriotism. Ruby had fancied himself a hero, and he was deflated when the King of Torts hired specialists to sully his righteousness with hints of mental problems."[17]

Texas utilizes the main rule for insanity in the nation, the M'Naughten "right-wrong" test (stemming from the 1843 English case of the *Queen v. Daniel M'Naughten*), which provides that a defendant is not criminally responsible for his act and is legally insane if at the time of the act he was laboring "under such a defect of reason from a disease of the mind as not to know the nature and quality [interpreted as meaning "consequences"] of the act he was doing, or if he did know it, that he did not know that what he was doing was wrong." The seminal question for Belli was, what "disease of the mind" did Ruby have that caused him not to know that what he did was wrong? Belli had Ruby examined by psychiatrists, psychologists, and neurologists in late December at the Dallas county jail. The psychologist, Dr. Roy Schafer from Yale University, told Belli in his January 7, 1964, report that a battery of tests on Ruby indicated "the presence of brain dysfunction on a *physical* basis [i.e., Ruby had *organic* brain damage, satisfying the "disease of the mind" requirement of M'Naughten *if* it could be connected up with his act of killing Oswald] . . . His test responses are very similar . . . to those obtained from patients who have psychomotor seizures . . . [and] could also be those of a person with a history of traumatic head injuries or encephalitis." Schafer recommended an electroencephalographic (EEG) test, which measures fluctuations in the electrical activity of the brain, and a neurological examination.[18]

The EEG and neurological findings of Dr. Martin Towler of Dallas were that Ruby was "suffering from a seizure disorder [that] most accurately falls into the category of a Psychomotor Variant." Dr. Frederic Gibbs, a Chicago neurologist who was considered to be the leading pioneer in the science of electroencephalography, reviewed Towler's EEG recordings, agreed with Towler, and said that Ruby's brain waves were "common in epileptics." When a psychiatrist, Dr. Walter Bromberg, concluded that at the time Ruby shot Oswald he was acting in a "fugue" state or temporary blackout triggered by depression and rage, Belli had all the elements (or so he thought) of a successful medical defense virtually unheard of at the time—that when Ruby shot Oswald he was in the throes of a psychomotor epileptic seizure, a condition manifested by periods, usually transitory, in which a person, functioning only on learned reflexes, does not act like himself, sometimes engaging in agressive aberrational behavior, and thereafter cannot remember what he did.[*]

---

[*]Before Belli's doctors examined Ruby, Dallas assistant DA Bill Alexander, who had known Ruby on a friendly basis for many years, took Dallas psychiatrist Dr. John Holbrook into Ruby's cell the day after he shot Oswald to examine Ruby. At a later bail hearing for Ruby, Alexander testified that when Ruby asked him, "Shall I talk to him, Bill? What would you do?" he said, "Jack, all we want is a fair, square psychiatric evaluation of you. If you're nuts, you ought to go to the state insane asylum, and if you're all right, we are going to have to prosecute you. I would talk to the man." In response to Ruby wondering if he was "getting into some kind of trap," Alexander testified he said, "No, Jack. I wouldn't let any friendship go down the drain just to mess you around." (Belli with Carroll, *Dallas Justice*, pp.58–59) (Alexander told me that on the stand he had "cleaned up a little" what he told Ruby. He said he actually told Ruby, "Jack, if you're crazy you need to go to the insane asylum. And if you're not crazy, we're going to try to burn your ass." Alexander also denied telling Ruby of their friendship. "I knew Ruby for ten or twelve years," he told me, "but we weren't friends. Never had a cup of coffee with him. Never went to his club. I used to bump into him at sporting events and around town. What I told Jack was 'I've known you too long to fuck you.'" [Telephone interview of William Alexander by author on December 11, 2001]) When Alexander was asked on the stand if, in fact, the very next day, after confer-

It should be noted that in the vast majority of M'Naughten insanity defenses, defense attorneys do not contend that their client didn't know what he was doing, only that he didn't know it was wrong. Here, Belli was going to contend that Ruby was unaware of what he was doing (did not know "the nature and quality" of his act), which of course delivers one to the same destination—that is, you can't know what you did was wrong when you don't even know you did it.

Jury selection commenced on February 17, 1964, and after fourteen days in which 162 prospective jurors out of a potential jury pool of 900 were questioned, both sides finally agreed on 12. The all-white jury consisted of eight men and four women. Eleven of the twelve had seen the television footage of Ruby shooting Oswald. The jury was sequestered throughout the trial, each living in a small, windowless room above the county jail. Like all sequestered juries, they were insulated from outside news about the case. The only things on TV they could watch were movies and situation comedies. They could read newspapers and magazines only after they had been heavily censored. "Bo [the court bailiff] really cut up our newspapers tonight," one juror complained in his diary. "I told him if he starts cutting out Ann Landers, I'll go home."[19]

After Judge Brown denied the defense motion for a change of venue, the trial of the man who killed the man who killed Kennedy, started on March 4, 1964, with 370 reporters from fourteen countries, representing 111 news organizations, in attendance. The trial had been transferred from Judge Brown's regular forty-eight-seat courtroom to the much larger (ninety-four-seat) courtroom of a fellow judge, Frank Wilson, to help accommodate the press. Only a few seats were left for the general public.[20] The three networks asked Brown to let them televise the trial, and the publicity-loving Brown was all in favor of it. But the opposition came from many sources, including fellow judges, Dallas civic leaders, and the prosecutors. Still, Brown was inclined to let the cameras in. When a strongly worded statement released by the Board of Governors of the American Bar Association, which opposed and "deplored" the proposal to televise the trial, arrived on his desk,[21] Brown, who had hired Sam Bloom, the head of a Dallas advertising firm, to be his press adviser, reportedly said to Bloom, who had joined in the opposition, "But Sam, couldn't you give me just one camera?" Bloom shook his head no, and the trial wasn't televised—to everyone's relief except Belli, who, like Brown, wanted the trial televised.[22]*

Though Brown was pressured out of televising the trial ("We had a terrible time talking him out of that," a member of the Dallas power structure would recall), that didn't

---

ring with Holbrook and being assured that Ruby was not insane, he told the press that he intended to prosecute Ruby for murder and ask for the death penalty, Alexander answered, "I sure did." (Belli with Carroll, *Dallas Justice*, p.59; after conferring with Holbrook: Kaplan and Waltz, *Trial of Jack Ruby*, p.60)

Was it duplicitous of Alexander to encourage Ruby to talk to Holbrook? Not if you know Alexander the way I think I've gotten to know him. He's just a straight shooter who would prosecute his . . . well, you know whom I mean, if she ran afoul of the law. At the trial, Alexander, who once said that impeachment was too good for Earl Warren—he needed hanging—told reporters, "They want to examine Ruby's brain? We'll be glad to deliver it to them from Huntsville after we fry him." (Gertz, *Moment of Madness*, p.6) Frontier lore and legend have invariably focused on the marshals and sheriffs of the lawless West, not the prosecutors, but the tall, rawboned Alexander, with his gallows humor told with a slight grin, would have fit the mold precisely.

*In another appearance on *The Merv Griffin Show* I won't forget, this time with Belli, Griffin would ask Mel a question, he'd answer, then he'd ask me a question, and Mel would try to answer that question too. I'm pretty aggressive in a courtroom, but since this was not a trial or even a debate, I was more amused than anything else. I chuckled to Griffin during a break, "Merv, Mel loves the camera and I'm not going to compete with him for it. If you want me to be more involved you'll have to be more insistent that you want to hear from me." I forget just what happened during the next segment or two but my recollection is that I participated more.

stop the limelight-seeking judge from allowing TV cameras into his home to film him on his sickbed when the flu kept him off the bench one day during the trial.[23]

The heart of the trial was the legitimacy, or lack thereof, of Belli's defense for Ruby that he didn't really know what he was doing when he shot Oswald. Ruby, of course, knew exactly what he was doing, and it had nothing to do with any hocus-pocus psychomotor epileptic seizure. But Ruby had long since become a pathetic,[*] bewildered, humiliated (by courtroom allegations he was crazy, had hurt Dallas and the nation, was possibly a latent homosexual, etc.), almost anonymous bystander to the trial proceedings, having turned over his defense to his high-powered attorneys. It was becoming obvious to many early on that just as his hero, JFK, was "dead in the center of his parade," and Oswald "dead in the center of his custodians," Ruby, chewing gum at the defense table in as serious a concentration as he was capable of, was "dead in the center" of his trial.[24] And Ruby seemed to know, even before the trial started, how the little "class" he had always sought, but never achieved, in his dealings with the outside world would be irrevocably shorn away by his lawyers, who would portray him as someone who belonged in a mental institution. A Dallas artist sketching his courtroom portrait during pretrial hearings was asked by Ruby to not make the sketch "too rough" on him. "Leave me a little dignity," he importuned the artist.[25] Ruby's prosecutor, Bill Alexander, would later say, "You could see Jack go down day by day during the trial. Belli was doing exactly the opposite of what he wanted. Jack knew that he was going to be found guilty of something. He didn't mind being found guilty of killing Oswald because Oswald killed the President, but he didn't want anybody to think that he was retarded, or mentally handicapped, or an insane person. Whatever else you can say about him, Jack had a lot of pride."[26]

The Ruby trial took place on the second floor of the Dallas Criminal Courts Building in an old-fashioned courtroom with high ceiling fans, wooden benches, and spittoons next to each of the two counsel tables as well as the judge's chair. During the prosecution's case, it put on police witnesses who had spoken to Ruby after the shooting and who testified, in refutation of the defense theory, that Ruby had said things like "I hope I killed the son-of-a-bitch," "I intended to shoot him three times," and "Someone had to do it, you guys [Dallas police] couldn't."[27] Most damaging of all was the testimony of one officer, Sergeant Patrick Dean, that in response to questioning commencing around ten minutes after the shooting of Oswald, Ruby said he "first thought" he'd kill Oswald "if he got a chance" when he saw him two nights earlier in the show-up room and he "noticed the sarcastic sneer on Oswald's face." Ruby added that he "wanted the world to know that Jews do have guts."[28]

All of Ruby's remarks were irreconcilable with the "fugue" state, temporary insanity defense Belli was propounding. And Ruby's statement that he first thought of killing Oswald on Friday, two days earlier, showed premeditation and conflicted with the defense position that the shooting was a spur-of-the-moment act. Even though the defense, at the moment, was seeking a not-guilty verdict under the insanity defense, it still had available, as a fallback position, a verdict of murder *without* malice. Dean's testimony, if believed, showed that Ruby premeditated the murder, helping to preclude any defense

---

[*]Indeed, in his daily diary, one of the jurors, J. Waymon Rose, wrote that Ruby "looks pitiful and alone, as though he is a head of cabbage." Elsewhere, he referred to "the pitiful, lost look" Ruby had in his eyes. (*Dallas Morning News*, August 3, 2002, p.30A)

argument that the killing was without malice, which required that the killing result from a "sudden passion." District Attorney Wade would later say that Dean's testimony about premeditation "was probably the most harmful" testimony of all to Ruby's defense at the murder trial.[29]*

But it was hard for the prosecution to get around what was obvious to virtually everyone—that there was a screw loose somewhere in Ruby, that he was mentally unsound. Even a prosecution witness, Garnett Claud Hallmark, the general manager of Allright Auto Parks where Ruby had parked his car for three years, testified that he "sometimes wondered about Jack's sanity."[30] And William Serur, who had known Ruby well as a friend for over ten years, testified for the defense that he "was sure" that Ruby was "suffering from some form of mental disturbance."[31] After another witness at Ruby's trial (who had testified to Ruby's bizarre behavior, such as sometimes getting up from their dinner together and leaving for no reason whatsoever) was asked if he had "formed any type of opinion as to Jack's mental state?" he answered, "Well, with apologies to Jack, I've always considered him . . .," at which time a prosecution objection to the witness's continuing his obvious answer was sustained by the judge.[32] No matter. The message was clear. Jack's needle wasn't quite pointing north. And another witness at the trial who was a close friend of Jack's said, during cross-examination by the prosecution, that Ruby's "crazy" behavior the past several years caused him to believe he was "a sick man of some type."[33]†

The defense case, as expected, was primarily medical. Belli had his psychologist, Dr. Roy Schafer, testify at the trial that Ruby's tests showed he had "organic brain damage" and that Ruby had psychomotor epileptic seizures where he acted in a fugue state. However, on cross-examination, he only speculated that Ruby "might have been" (not was) *in* such a fugue state at the time he shot Oswald, and said he had no opinion as to whether Ruby knew right from wrong at the time he shot Oswald.[34] The defense's EEG expert, Dr. Martin Towler, testified that from his reading of Ruby's abnormal EEG he concluded that Ruby was subject to a "type of seizure disorder that we refer to as a psychomotor variant epilepsy," but, again, he formed no conclusion as to the heart of the defense case, that Ruby was *in* such a state at the time of the shooting.[35] So the defense presented testimony that Ruby had organic brain damage and psychomotor epilepsy. But that wasn't enough to carry the day.

Belli's intended star psychiatric witness was supposed to be Dr. Manfred Guttmacher, a prominent psychiatrist and leading expert on criminal psychology from Baltimore. Belli

*Despite this critical testimony by Dean against Ruby (whose truthfulness was challenged by a Warren Commission assistant counsel—see endnote discussion), Dean, who admitted being a friend of Ruby's and the recipient of a bottle of whiskey from him every Christmas, said that after the trial Ruby sent word he wanted to see him in his jail cell. "He hugged me and was glad to see me," Dean recalled. "I saw he had a pair of broken glasses, so I got the prescription and bought him a new pair." Eight months later Ruby gave Dean his copy of the Warren Commission Report with the inscription, "Your Buddy, Jack Ruby." (Earl Golz, "Ex-Officer Fears 'Set-up,'" *Dallas Morning News*, March 25, 1979, p.34A)

†In fact, although prosecutor Bill Alexander told me he did not believe that Ruby was insane or even mentally ill, he acknowledged to me that Ruby was "wired up different." Of course, for even a straight shooter like Alexander, it would be mighty difficult for him, as Ruby's prosecutor, to acknowledge that Ruby was mentally ill. (Telephone interview of William Alexander by author on December 11, 2001)

As part of Ruby's insanity defense, Belli attempted to introduce at the trial certified copies of the hospital commitments for mental illness of Ruby's mother, Fanny, one of his brothers, Earl, and one of his sisters, Eileen, on the ground that mental illness ran in his client's family and was hereditary, but Judge Brown ruled the documents were "not admissible . . . under Texas law." However, in his direct examination of Dr. Martin Towler, Belli did sneak into the record that Ruby's mother had been hospitalized for mental illness. (Kaplan and Waltz, *Trial of Jack Ruby*, pp.214, 225, 242; Earl Ruby's hospitalization in a psychopathic ward: 14 H 372, WCT Earl Ruby)

would later write that Guttmacher was supposed "to crown our medical testimony . . . pull it all together"[36] by testifying that Ruby was *in* a psychomotor epileptic seizure *at the time* of the shooting, thereby qualifying him as not knowing right from wrong or the nature and consequences of his act under the M'Naughten test for insanity. Guttmacher, in fact, told the Dallas jury that at the time of the shooting, Ruby was under "tremendous emotional impact" from the assassination, and the "deep, heavy, hostile, aggressive part of his makeup . . . became focused on [Oswald]." Guttmacher concluded that "I don't think that he was capable of distinguishing right from wrong and realizing the nature and consequences of his act at the time of the alleged homicide . . . I think there was a temporary, very short-lived psychotic episode."

There was only one thing missing: no reference to the heart of Belli's defense—that Ruby was *in* a psychomotor epileptic seizure *at the time of the killing*. Ruby's "disease of the mind" under M'Naughten was *not connected to* his act of killing Oswald. Indeed, on cross-examination by Bill Alexander, Guttmacher testified, "I think he has psychomotor epilepsy . . . I [have] not maintained he was *in* a state of psychomotor epilepsy [at the time of the shooting]." Guttmacher had presented Belli with a memorandum on March 3, the eve of the trial, that said it was his belief "that it is scientifically unsound . . . to assert with absolute assurance that Oswald's murder took place *while* Ruby was in an epileptic attack of some sort . . . What we have to develop is that Jack has a definitely abnormal and damaged brain [as evidenced by] the psychological tests of Dr. Schafer . . . and the definitely abnormal brain waves . . . There is abundant evidence in the medical literature that people with brain waves like Jack's . . . are given to psychopathic-like behavior, particularly to irrational outbursts of aggression, often when under stress, which can or cannot be actual seizure attacks."[37] (Reportedly, Guttmacher went further, expressing the view that Ruby had exhibited too many indications of uninterrupted consciousness, that the shooting had been carried off too efficiently, with too little fumbling, for an epileptic seizure to be a real possibility.)

That Guttmacher could be so professional and objective in his assessment of Ruby makes his conclusion on the witness stand—that Ruby didn't know that killing Oswald was wrong and didn't even know the nature and consequences of his act (that he was firing a bullet into Oswald's body that could cause Oswald's death)—all the more incomprehensible. On cross-examination, Guttmacher said his "best diagnosis" of Ruby's condition at the time of the shooting was that Ruby was "a mental cripple and was carrying on his shoulders an insufferable emotional load and, to use the vernacular, he cracked under it momentarily." Belli would later say that he had hoped Guttmacher's testimony would be the "highpoint of the trial."[38] One could say ironically that Guttmacher's testimony was exactly that. But he delivered it in a big way not for the defense but for the prosecution. The inevitable question that presents itself, of course, is why would Belli base his entire defense on psychomotor epilepsy when he never had one single medical expert to testify that Ruby was *in* such a state at the time of the shooting?* (Dr. Walter Bromberg, the psychiatrist who had interviewed Ruby for eighteen hours prior to the trial, only testified that Ruby was "mentally ill" and had killed Oswald during an episode

---

*The closest Belli came to establishing his point was not from the testimony by his psychiatrists and medical witnesses but from the testimony of one of Ruby's strippers at the Carousel Club, Penny Dollar (true name, Patricia Ann Kohs). Kohs said that one of Jack's fights at the Carousel Club was with a taxi driver. "Jack knocked him down the stairs," she told the jury. "Then we came down . . . Jack was beating his head on the sidewalk. Then he stopped all of a sudden and said, 'Did I do this?'" (Belli with Carroll, *Dallas Justice*, p. 171)

he called an "epileptic equivalent," but studiously refused to say that Ruby had psychomotor epilepsy or that he was in an epileptic seizure at the time he shot Oswald.)[39]

The defense decided not to put Ruby on the stand, a very common defense strategy to avoid cross-examination of the defendant by the prosecution. But what was the fear here? As Belli tells it, Ruby not only told him he didn't want to testify because "I'll go all to pieces," but also said the opposite to him: "I just went in and shot him . . . Maybe I ought to . . . get on the stand and tell the truth." But Belli believed that Ruby's blunt assertion about his state of mind ("I just went in and shot him") was actually not the truth, that Ruby had merely made it up *after* he came out of his unconscious, psychomotor epileptic seizure at the time of the shooting to fill in the blanks of his amnesia (in psychiatry, called "confabulation"), had come to believe it himself, and on the witness stand would blurt out enough incriminating statements to bury himself.[40]

When Belli rested his case, he had put on an extremely anemic defense, particularly in view of the fact that in Texas the defense had the burden of proving that Ruby was insane by a preponderance of the evidence.[41]* Virtually everyone in our society knows that in a criminal case in America, the prosecution, not the defendant, has the burden of proof. But because of the almost unique circumstances of this case in which Ruby's killing of Oswald was televised, coupled with the fact that the defense, by its apparent sole reliance on the insanity defense, was not forcing the prosecution to prove that the killing did not result from a "sudden passion," for all intents and purposes it was the defendant, Ruby, who had the *only* legal burden of proof at the trial. True, the prosecution had to prove beyond a reasonable doubt that Ruby intentionally killed Oswald without any justification in law, but an estimated eighty million people saw Ruby kill Oswald, and it was an intentional act without any legal justification. The only real legal burden, then, was the defense's burden to prove, by a preponderance of the evidence (substantially lower than beyond a reasonable doubt, but still a burden), that Ruby was insane at the time he shot Oswald. *Only* if Ruby met that burden was he entitled to a not-guilty verdict. Because of the defense put on by Belli, in this case there couldn't possibly be any failure of proof by the prosecution that would entitle Ruby to the same not-guilty verdict.

In rebuttal, among other medical experts, the prosecution called Dr. Sheff Olinger, a Dallas neurologist, to testify that although Ruby's EEG brain waves were "unusual," they did not show organic brain damage, the "disease of the mind" required under the M'Naughten test of insanity, nor was he subject to psychomotor epileptic seizures.[42] The noted neurologist Dr. Frederic Gibbs, who had taught Olinger's teacher, disagreed with Olinger, testifying on surrebuttal for the defense that "it was clear" from Ruby's EEG tracings that Ruby "had a particular, very rare type of epilepsy" that "occurs in only one-half percent of epileptics" and frequently results in a "lack of emotional control, convulsive and excessive types of behavior."[43]†

Welcome to the world of forensic experts. They can't agree on the time of day, and

---

*In the federal courts, as opposed to most states, when a defendant pleads not guilty by reason of insanity, the prosecution has the burden of proving, beyond a reasonable doubt, that the defendant was *sane* at the time of his act. Most legal observers agree that this very high burden of proof in the federal courts was largely responsible for the not-guilty-by-reason-of-insanity verdict in the trial of William Hinckley for the attempted assassination of President Ronald Reagan in 1981.

†However, on cross-examination by prosecutor Alexander, Gibbs conceded he had "no opinion" as to whether Ruby was in the throes of an epileptic seizure at the time he shot Oswald that prevented him from knowing right from wrong or from understanding the nature and consequences of his act (Kaplan and Waltz, *Trial of Jack Ruby*, p.300).

almost invariably (there are refreshing exceptions) testify during their career as either defense or prosecution experts, but not both. For this reason, when I prosecuted cases I always searched for forensic witnesses with a more balanced history. I didn't want the opposing attorney, during cross-examination of my experts, to ask the question I asked of his experts to destroy their credibility:

"Doctor, how many times have you testified as an expert in your specialty of forensic psychiatry?"

"Oh, maybe 100, 125 times."

"Doctor, in those 100 or 125 times, did you ever once testify for the prosecution? [long pause] I don't believe so, counselor."

The final arguments to the jury were very brief for a murder case of this importance, but the four prosecutors and three defense attorneys agreed on two and a half hours for each side. Curiously, instead of doing what was logical and normal, particularly in a big case—having the arguments start in the morning, or early afternoon, with everyone fresh—Judge Brown overruled Belli's objections and ordered that they commence after the regular court day on Friday evening, March 13, 1964. They didn't conclude until 1:05 Saturday morning, the jury stifling yawns throughout the five hours.[44]

Alexander opened for the prosecution. Treating the defense's medical case dismissively (e.g., Dr. Schafer, the defense psychologist, "thinks he can diagnose anything with ink spots," and referring to Ruby's defense as "this epilepsy business"), he made the telling point that if Ruby, indeed, was an epileptic, then why didn't the defense present any evidence during the trial through testimony of his family and people close to Ruby of prior epileptic spells? He told the jury that what was involved here was nothing more than that "Jack Ruby misjudged public temperament. He thought that he could kill Oswald, that perhaps he would be a hero by doing it* . . . [He] wanted to become famous and make money out of the act . . . I tell you that he is nothing but a thrill killer seeking notoriety." In other words, Ruby was just a nobody trying to become a somebody. Alexander asked the jury to return a verdict of death against Ruby not just because he murdered Oswald "but because he has mocked American justice while the spotlight of the world is on us." Alexander argued that Oswald "was entitled to the protection of the law until the law chose no longer to protect him and punish him."[45]

Though Belli's psychomotor epilepsy defense had imploded through the testimony of his *own* expert witnesses, in his summation he refused to retreat, literally becoming his own expert for the proposition that Ruby should be found not guilty by reason of insanity because Ruby's EEG tracings proved it. The king of torts was forced to rely on his pet—demonstrative evidence—but not, as in most of his civil cases, to fortify his case. It now was his whole case. Ruby would live or die on it. "Ladies and gentlemen of the jury," Belli argued, "finally we showed you the actual tracings themselves . . . and you your-

---

*Many on the Ruby jury, after hearing all the evidence, came to the same conclusion. For instance, the wife of jury foreman Max Causey (deceased) said, "[My husband] really thought that Ruby thought he was going to be a hero because he was going to kill the guy who shot the president." Juror Douglas Sowell said that "Ruby thought he'd be a hero in the public eye if he did it. I believe he thought that, I really do. I think that motivated him, that he thought that rather than being a murderer, he'd be a hero." Juror R. J. "Bob" Flechtner said, "I think he just went down there and shot Oswald and thought he was going to be a hero. And he thought he was doing the right thing, and our society says he didn't do the right thing." (Dempsey, *Jack Ruby Trial Revisited*, pp.3–4, 159, 171) In a later, May 24, 1965, hearing in Dallas over Ruby's legal representation, Ruby admitted as much, voluntarily taking the witness stand and saying, "I should have never tried to be heroic" (*Dallas Morning News*, May 25, 1965, p.1).

selves saw those five-to-a-second waves and notched tracings," and he said his esteemed experts had concluded that the tracings clearly showed "organic brain damage" and "the psychomotor variant type of epilepsy." But Belli did not go on to say, because he could not, that his experts said Ruby was *in* an epileptic state when he shot Oswald.

From this focused but fatally defective argument, Belli went on to ramble discursively on a range of different, disconnected arguments that had no basis in law. An eloquent orator, he was reduced to actually arguing to the jury that since under Texas law (as opposed to any other state) it was excusable homicide (not, as in other states, manslaughter) to kill your wife or her paramour if you caught them in flagrante delicto, "then is there not [such an] excuse for the shooting of the assassin of my President?" He went on to analogize Ruby to the "village clown, the village idiot," an indirect way, apparently, of seeking sympathy and mercy for his client.[46] That's really all Belli had left in his arsenal, and when DA Henry Wade, in the prosecution's final summation, said, "I ask you, ladies and gentlemen of the jury, to show Jack Ruby the same mercy and the same compassion and the same sympathy that he showed Lee Harvey Oswald, [and] if you do that you can vote only one verdict, that of guilty of murder *with* malice and of death,"[47]* on March 14, the jury, after only two hours and nineteen minutes of deliberation, agreed, rejecting Belli's insanity defense and finding Ruby "guilty of murder with malice" and assessing "his punishment at death."[48]

Though the trial was not televised, millions of Americans viewed the reading of the jury's verdict on live national television. As soon as Judge Brown read the verdict, Belli jumped to his feet and began a denunciation of the twelve members of the jury, all white Protestants, who had condemned Ruby to the electric chair. Pointing to the jury box he cried out, "May I thank this jury for a verdict that is a victory for bigotry." As the jurors began filing out of the courtroom, he shouted at them, "I want to assure you we will appeal this to a court where there is justice and impartiality." Surrounded by the media in the courtroom, Belli first unloaded on the jury, saying it had made Dallas "a city of shame forevermore" by a verdict that was "the biggest disgrace in the history of American law." He also had a few kind words for Judge Brown, saying, "This was a kangaroo railroading court . . . and everyone knew it. Judge Brown went down the line for every motion the District Attorney made. He committed 30 errors."[49] Bursting out of the courtroom, Belli delivered perhaps an even more serious tirade to the media. "This jury wasn't concerned even with listening to us in arguments. They had their minds made up," he said. When a reporter asked Belli to repeat his accusation, Belli said, "Repeat this? I'll repeat this with

---

*Remarkably, Belli had neglected, in his summation, to do something that criminal defense attorneys do automatically (999 out of 1,000 times)—urge the jury, if they were disposed against Ruby on the facts and the law, to at least spare his life, which they had the power to do. In his summation, Belli did not have to put all his eggs in one basket and be imprisoned by his psychomotor epileptic defense. Not only didn't Belli ask the jury to give Ruby life imprisonment instead of death if they found him guilty of murder with malice, but since Judge Brown gave the jury an instruction on "murder without malice," where the punishment for a conviction thereunder was "no longer than five years" in prison, Belli had a fallback, alternative argument if the jury decided to reject the insanity defense. That he should have done so has been reflected upon by many, including the judge. "By [Belli's] dependence on his single, daring defense, Belli neglected other legal avenues he might have followed to save Jack Ruby from the electric chair" (Holloway, *Dallas and the Jack Ruby Trial*, p. 8). Instead, Belli asked the jury to exonerate Ruby completely. "If you put a felony brand of *any* kind on Jack Ruby, he won't be eligible for Veteran's Administration [benefits]. He *is* now, being an ex-serviceman," he argued (Belli with Carroll, *Dallas Justice*, p. 242). "Belli gave it to us by going for broke—all or nothing . . .," Bill Alexander said. "He told the jury it was acquittal or nothing. You can't give a jury that kind of dare. And all he had going for him was some fancy doctors' talk and a few mildly abnormal squiggles on a piece of paper" (Wills and Demaris, *Jack Ruby*, p. 123).

every breath I have in me for as long as I live. And I'll stop practicing law if we don't reverse this [verdict on appeal] and make these people of Dallas ashamed of themselves."[50]*
Shortly thereafter, Belli told a reporter for ABC radio, "I've reassessed my feelings about Dallas. I think that it's sicker than I originally felt when I came here—those horrible, bigoted, little, narrow, nasty people that sat in judgment of this 'Jew boy.' I hope to get back to New York and stand in Times Square and see some free Jews, niggers, if you will [Belli was not racist in the least], and some Puerto Ricans, and some dagos, and Chinese, some free Americans walk by and take 'em by the hand and say 'Thank God, I'm back in America and out of Dallas.' "[51]

The trial, excluding the selection of the jury, had only lasted a little over eight court days! The sentence of death stunned the national and international press corps. Several polls of reporters showed them predicting a long prison sentence.[52] Even the judge was "shocked" by the sentence of death.[53] "After all," Judge Brown said, "we are talking about a man who killed the man who assassinated President Kennedy."[54] In fact, if there is one thing that stands out in people's minds more than anything else about the Ruby trial, it's that he was sentenced to death. *New York Times* reporter Jack Langguth was in Dallas at the time of the verdict and felt he knew the pulse of the city enough to say that "the people of Dallas did not want Jack Ruby back among them boasting of his crime and acquittal. Neither did they want him sentenced to death." The editor of the *Dallas Times Herald*, A. C. Greene, told Langguth, "This verdict [of death] was almost as shocking to everyone as Ruby's own shooting had been." Upstairs in the courthouse after the verdict, one sheriff's deputy turned to another and remarked, "Too strong." The other deputy raised an eyebrow. "Prison would have been better. This won't stand up."[55]

Most students of the Ruby case are likewise troubled by the sentence, wondering why the jury gave Ruby the ultimate punishment. Even without Belli arguing murder without malice to them, and even with their finding that Ruby killed Oswald *with* malice, the jury still could have given Ruby a sentence of life or any number of years more than two. In the perceptive book *Jack Ruby*, the coauthors write, "Men hesitate when asked to put a human being to death. But this jury had seen Ruby gradually exanimated [become lifeless] before their eyes, turned into a thing; and things are easily disposed of."[56]

For his part, Belli says that the jury, by their verdict, fulfilled their duty by making Ruby "the scapegoat for the unpunishable guilt of a community." But how and why did the jury feel this was their duty? Belli, in so many words, blamed the Dallas "oligarchy," embodied in the Dallas Citizens Council, for the jury verdict. According to *U.S. News & World Report*, the Dallas Citizens Council consisted at the time of about 250 men who

---

*And Ruby would launch an appeal, but not with Belli as his lawyer. Within a week after the verdict, a letter signed by Ruby, but with his two sisters and three brothers behind it, was on its way to Belli's San Francisco law office firing him from the case. ("Good-by, Belli," p.19) On June 7, 1964, near the beginning of his testimony before the Warren Commission, Ruby told Chief Justice Warren, "Mr. Belli evidently did not go into my case thoroughly, circumstantially. If he had gone into it, he wouldn't have tried to vindicate me on an insanity plea to relieve me of all responsibility, because circumstantially everything looked so bad for me. It can happen—it happens to many people who happen to be at the wrong place at the right time. Had Mr. Belli spent more time with me, he would have realized not to try to get me out completely free" (5 H 182).

Mel Belli, according to his former law partner, Seymour Ellison, took his loss in the Ruby case, and then being fired by Ruby, "harder than anything else in his legal career. He literally went into a shell for about a month, very rarely even showing up at the office. He even turned down a big publicity case at the time involving an ax murderess named Jean Toman who insisted she would only be represented by Mel. It was the type of high-visibility case Mel would normally have a relish for trying" (Telephone interview of Seymour Ellison by author on October 7, 2006).

were chief executive officers of important companies in Dallas. "Membership is by invitation only," the magazine said, and it's "the group that really runs Dallas." Author William Manchester, who spent much time in Dallas doing research for his book, *The Death of a President*, wrote, "I had never seen a city so tightly held by so few. Boston, Baltimore and Philadelphia have their courtly establishments. Power there, however, is largely sham power. In Dallas, it is disquietingly real, naked, arrogant. There is something almost Teutonic about Big D's materialism, its deference to the men of sinew."

Formed in 1937 by Dallas banker Bob Thornton (after whom a Dallas expressway is named), the Dallas Citizens Council is largely credited with making Dallas a booming metropolis of gleaming skyscrapers and a center of commerce that, in 1963, added more office space than any other American city except New York. Most Dallasites are proud of their business-like, cosmopolitan image. The "Big D" (as Texans call Dallas) is markedly different from smaller and unhurried Fort Worth, "the old cow town" just thirty miles down the road to its west, where cowboy boots and Stetson hats are still very common attire for men, and the presence of stockyards contributes to the feeling of frontier days. Belli argued that on any issue affecting the modern image of Dallas as a civilized, though admittedly right-wing conservative community, the Citizens Council went to work manipulating community opinion to its liking—not an irrational accusation, and one that probably holds true to this very day in a few cities around the country. Belli maintained that since the assassination had seriously blackened the image of Dallas, "prompt execution of Ruby would serve somehow to restore that image and show what a law-abiding place the city was . . . The Dallas oligarchy had its own orders for the get-Ruby campaign," Belli says, adding they "desperately wanted to convict Ruby." Although Belli's allegation may or may not be true, where he falls down is failing to come up with any evidence, direct or circumstantial, to show *what specifically* the Dallas civic leaders in this case did to help ensure that the jury (which Belli referred to as the "establishment" jury and "an entirely WASP jury eager to do its Dallas duty") returned the verdict they wanted. He maintains that the coverage of the Ruby case by the *Dallas Morning News*, the paper of record in Dallas, reflected "the attitude of the Dallas oligarchy," but again he doesn't show in what way.[57]

I, of course, am not in a position to pass judgment on the merits of Belli's charge, but one thing is clear. As Belli points out, in the early 1960s Dallas was a "city noted for aggressive, white, Protestant narrow-mindedness," a city not known "for its racial tolerance."[58] Anti-Semitism was not uncommon, and although this probably is a complete coincidence, my research showed that for the first two days after Ruby shot Oswald, all of the many captioned articles on the case in the *Dallas Morning News*, the main establishment paper, referred to Ruby as "Rubenstein" (e.g., "Rubenstein at [*Dallas Morning*] *News* at Time of Shooting," "Any Oswald-Rubenstein Tie in Dallas Sought by Police"), whereas the evening paper, the now-defunct *Dallas Times Herald*, continued to refer to Ruby as everyone else always has, "Jack Ruby." Since Ruby legally changed his name in 1947 from his birth name of Rubenstein to Ruby, this throws into question the motivation behind the prosecution's decision to resurrect the name Rubenstein for the Dallas jury by having the grand jury indict "Jack Rubenstein, alias Jack Ruby," which, since Ruby had changed his name, was legally incorrect.

Bill Alexander has his own view on how Ruby could have avoided a sentence of death (and as the lead trial prosecutor, Alexander has a better handle on the issue than perhaps anyone else). "A local lawyer," Alexander told me, "would have said, 'Judge, this will be short. I only have one witness, the defendant.' After calling Ruby to the stand, the questions would have gone something like this: 'Your name?' 'Jack Ruby.' 'You are the defendant in this case?' 'Yes.' 'Jack, you've heard all the police testify in this case. Is what they said substantially true and correct?' 'Yeah, pretty much.' 'You did really kill that feller?' 'Yes.' 'This gun here, state's exhibit 1, is that your gun?' 'Yes.' 'Is that the gun you killed him with?' 'Yes.' 'Whatcha do it for, Jack?' 'He killed my president and was smirking at us.' 'Well, Jack, whataya think this jury oughta do with you?' 'I don't know, but please don't give me death. Whatever they think is right, I'll take.'"

Alexander asks, "Now how in the hell do you cross-examine someone like that?" I asked Alexander, "If, in fact, Ruby had presented such a defense, would you and Wade still have sought the death penalty against him?" I realized the moment I asked the question, that I really had no right putting him on the spot like this. Alexander paused for a few moments, then said, "Yeah, we would have done it, but in a left-handed sort of way. We would have told them, 'Death is an option, but we're not demanding it.'"[*]

I asked Alexander the obvious question—why did the jury come back with a verdict of death? Just because Ruby's lawyers used the wrong defense, why hold it against Ruby? The facts were the same—Ruby killed Oswald in a state of rage over Oswald's having killed Kennedy, and certainly, Ruby did not want death. "Belli just dared that jury to give Ruby the death penalty," Alexander replied, "and they didn't like that, and they didn't like Belli either." Alexander said that from the moment Belli arrived in Dallas, he had displayed a condescending attitude with "nasty little remarks" about the city and its people,[†] and there was "no doubt about it" that Belli's demeanor, flashy dress, and attitude "turned the jury off."

"Are you saying," I asked Alexander, "that the jury took out their contempt for Belli, and the defense he presented, on Ruby?"

"Yes, to a certain unconscious extent I think they did."[59] "The jury wasn't sentencing Jack Ruby, they were sentencing Melvin Belli," Alexander told an earlier interviewer.[60]

The acclaimed journalist Murray Kempton covered the Ruby trial for the *New Republic* and the *London Spectator*. He wrote about the verdict: "In point of fact, Ruby received no defense at all. The impression is inescapable that Mr. Belli made himself the defendant almost at once, that District Attorney Wade and his assistants happily accepted him as such, and that, in the end, when the jury ordered Ruby to the block, Belli was more an object of its disfavor than his client."[61]

No juror, of course, would ever admit taking his or her adverse feelings against Belli

---

[*]In one of my capital cases, the defendant had left the military service and learned that his wife, a woman of rare beauty whom people came to court just to ogle, had had an affair. He stalked the man for two weeks and finally, after waiting in the backseat of the man's car, shot him to death. It was a circumstantial-evidence case and after the verdict of guilty of first-degree murder, although my office wanted me to seek the death penalty, in my summation in the penalty trial (in contrast to Texas, the penalty trial, with the same judge and jury, is separate from the guilt trial in California) I went against my office—at least to the extent that I never pushed for or even affirmatively asked for death, instead telling the jury there were good arguments for life imprisonment as well as death. I learned later from a law student of mine whose spouse was on the jury that despite this, on the first ballot the majority of jurors voted for death, but because of the position I had taken, one by one they eventually came over to life imprisonment. For years thereafter, the defendant's mother would write me a Christmas card always thanking me for saving, she felt, her son's life.

[†]"You know what really made them [Dallasites] mad at me?" the fun-loving barrister, who traveled the world and stayed at its finest hotels with friends like actor Errol Flynn, would later ask. "My saying that they do not even know what to use a bidet [a low basin, used especially in France, for bathing one's private parts] for—the one I saw in Dallas had flowers planted in it" (Wills and Demaris, *Jack Ruby*, p.82).

out on Ruby. However, one juror (who might not be representative at all, since a few jurors spoke of how impressed they were with Belli) did almost say this. Juror Douglas Sowell said, "Belli antagonized everybody. I mean he was just very blunt on his letting us know that we were just country bumpkins down here in Dallas. He didn't make any friends."

Question by interviewer: "Do you think that had a negative influence?"

Answer: "Oh, I think it had a negative influence . . . Belli hurt his case."[62]

Ruby's family agreed. In the aforementioned letter sent by Ruby and his family to Belli in which Belli was fired, one of the reasons given was Belli's "constant bitter criticism of Dallas and the people of Texas" that the family felt was harmful to Ruby's cause.[63]

Only a few of the jurors have spoken out, for attribution, as to why they returned a verdict of death, and their answers have been far less than satisfying. Juror J. Waymon Rose could only say, "Well, I'm for the death penalty. I'm for it to deter serious crime. And I don't think it's used enough." Hardly a justification for the death penalty in *this* case, unless Rose was in favor of it for *all* murder cases, in which case he shouldn't have been seated on the Ruby jury. Juror Douglas Sowell said that the jury returned a rather swift verdict of death because "we had already told [the judge and lawyers] that we *could* give the death penalty." Yes, but merely being *capable* of returning a verdict of death doesn't mean you intend to do so in every murder case. Juror J. G. Holton Jr. said, "I just have my beliefs—that if you kill somebody, the state needs to take your life." This jury obviously was a hanging one and a prosecutor's dream. It seems the defense should have asked them during jury selection if they were *capable* of returning a sentence of life imprisonment.

Perhaps the most troubling observation came from jury foreman Max Causey. We learn from Causey that on the first ballot, three of the jurors, including himself, did vote for life imprisonment but were quickly turned around by the other nine. He then goes on to say, "I personally feel that Mr. Belli and his team selected a nearly impossible defense for Ruby," the psychomotor epileptic seizure argument being "very difficult to sell to the jury."* He adds, in agreement with Bill Alexander, "Any good lawyer could have gotten Ruby off with something less than a death sentence if he had thrown Ruby on the mercy of the court and pleaded plain old 'temporary insanity' brought on by emotional stress over the loss of his beloved president."[64] So was this some type of a game with the Ruby jury? If Belli lost on his psychomotor epilepsy gamble, then Ruby had to pay the ultimate price? But again, irrespective of Belli's strategic error, the jury still had, in front of them, the same defendant and the same act by that defendant. Belli's error logically should not have stripped the jury of the discretion it had to come back with a sentence of life.

Going in, Belli said he knew that it was "impossible" to get "a good jury" from the highly conservative Dallas jury panel. "Rather, it was our task to head off the dedicated hangmen, those whose minds were completely closed to us." Searching for any ray of sunlight he could find, one of the reasons why he accepted, without challenging, his first juror was, per his contemporaneous trial notes, that he "smiles at me."[65] (The most famous defense attorney of all, Clarence Darrow, often said he would never willingly accept a juror whom he could not elicit a smile from during jury selection.) That first juror, Max

---

*"We didn't buy" the psychomotor epilepsy defense from the "so-called expert witnesses," Ruby juror J. Waymon Rose said. "It was ridiculous . . . It just didn't impress us at all," said another juror, Douglas Sowell. "That [psycho]motor epilepsy stuff didn't make much sense," added juror J. G. Holton Jr. (Dempey, *Jack Ruby Trial Revisited*, pp.139, 157, 183)

Causey, became the jury foreman who guided the jury to a conviction of murder and sentence of death for Belli's client.

As discussed in depth in the conspiracy section of this book, after the trial Ruby insisted that the Warren Commission give him a polygraph, which it did, on July 18, 1964. But just before he took it, incredibly, he asked that one of his attorneys, Joe Tonahill, leave the room and that Bill Alexander stay, saying, "I prefer Bill Alexander." Ruby even asked "Bill" to frame some of the questions, which Alexander did, and Alexander, always referring to Ruby as "Jack," had off-the-record conferences with Ruby during the test.[66] Alexander told me that after the polygraph test, an FBI agent asked Ruby why he would want Alexander, who prosecuted him and asked for the death penalty against him, to help with the questions, not one of his own lawyers. Ruby responded that "after all this legal business is over with, Alexander or Wade will call the governor and tell him to spare my life and he will. My lawyers can't do this." I asked Alexander if he would have, as Ruby said, intervened with the governor if Ruby were scheduled to die. Very interestingly, after a short pause, Alexander answered, "I don't know."[67]

Had I been the prosecutor, I would not have sought the death penalty in the Ruby case. In California and in most states, except for killings that take place during the perpetration or attempted perpetration of an inherently dangerous felony, like robbery, without premeditation one can't even be convicted of first-degree murder, only second degree, and without such a conviction, the prosecution can't even ask for the death penalty. But apart from the fact that this was not a clear case of premeditated murder, as a basic rule I never sought the death penalty where there were "substantial mitigating circumstances," in which case I would only seek life imprisonment. In this case, in addition to the fact that Ruby unquestionably had considerable mental problems, which by itself, if severe enough, is a mitigating circumstance in some cases, the overwhelming bulk of Americans had an enormous and justifiable animus against Oswald for killing the president. Ruby, by *all* the evidence, was one of them. Killing Oswald in a state of rage ("I hope I killed the son-of-bitch," Ruby said) to avenge, in his inflamed mind, the most serious murder in American history certainly would have constituted "substantial mitigating circumstances." (In an even more personal example, although I never had such a case, I would never have sought the death penalty against, let's say, a parent who murdered the killer of his or her child.)

In the many cases where I sought the death penalty, I would say to the jury, "If this is not a proper case for the imposition of the death penalty, what would be?" I could not, in good conscience, have made that argument in the Ruby case. Indeed, even Marina Oswald said she was opposed to Ruby being executed.[68] While it is true she opposed capital punishment anyway, it is well known that many others who are opposed to it are in favor of it for those who kill their loved ones. A prominent example is movie director Roman Polanski, an opponent of capital punishment who wanted the death penalty for the Manson family killers of his eight-and-a-half-month pregnant wife, Sharon Tate.

In a remarkable vignette in their book, *The Trial of Jack Ruby*, authors John Kaplan and Jon Waltz tell the story of a judge who had the right idea but went too far with it.

Shortly after Jack Ruby shot and killed Lee Harvey Oswald in the basement of the Dallas Police and Courts Building, another act of violence occurred in Sioux City, Iowa. There, on the afternoon of Sunday, November 24, 1963, Vaschia

Michael Bohan, a 47 year-old dental technician, and his mother were seated in the living room of their home watching a television program about the funeral arrangements for President Kennedy. Suddenly, Bohan's 68 year-old stepfather entered the room and loudly cursed the assassinated president. Bohan rose, picked up a pair of sewing scissors, and stabbed his stepfather six times, once in the mouth and five times in the chest. The older man fell to the floor dead, and at 2:52 P.M.— one hour and thirty-two minutes after the shooting of Oswald—Bohan called the Sioux City Police Department to report his crime. Two police officers arrived shortly thereafter and he surrendered without resistance. On Monday, November 25, 1963, Bohan, like Ruby, was arraigned on a charge of murder. He pleaded not guilty and demanded a preliminary hearing . . . In December, Bohan changed his plea to guilty. On the day before Christmas he appeared in the courtroom of District Judge George M. Paradise for sentencing. The judge had pondered the accused's crime and the atmosphere in which it had taken place. Referring to the assassination of President Kennedy, Judge Paradise stated that "the entire nation was under stress and strain from the tragedy." He continued: "But that is not a reason for a citizen of the nation to release his emotions to the extent of causing another tragedy." The defendant's deed, he concluded, would weigh forever on his conscience. He sentenced Bohan to eight years in prison and a one thousand dollar fine. The judge suspended the prison sentence and ended the hearing by wishing the defendant a Merry Christmas and a Happy New Year. Bohan paid his fine and went home.[69]

Any discussion about Ruby being sentenced to death turned out to be moot and academic. On October 5, 1966, the Texas Court of Criminal Appeals reversed Ruby's murder conviction and sentence of death on two grounds. First, Ruby's statement to Sergeant Dean about deciding to kill Oswald when he saw him at the police lineup on Friday night "constituted an oral confession of premeditation" made by Ruby while in police custody, and therefore it should not have been heard by the jury because the law in Texas expressly provides that a defendant's oral statements while in custody are inadmissible unless committed to writing and signed by the accused, which was not done here. The exception for "spontaneous" admissions was rejected here because Ruby's question to the police *before* the interrogation as to whether his answers would be made available to the news media was held to have negated any suggestion of spontaneity. Second, the appellate court said that the trial court erred in refusing to grant the defense's motion for a change of venue out of the charged atmosphere existing in Dallas at the time, which, they said, prevented Ruby from getting a fair trial there. A concurring opinion said that "the citizenry of Dallas" most likely "consciously and subconsciously felt that Dallas was on trial."

The case was remanded back to the trial court for a new trial, with instructions to transfer it "to some county other than Dallas."[70] On December 5, 1966, the new trial judge, Louis Holland, transferred the retrial to Wichita Falls, Texas, approximately 150 miles northwest of Dallas. Although one of Ruby's lawyers, Elmer Gertz, would later write that Wade and Alexander again said they would seek the death penalty against Ruby,[71] this was so only, apparently, because Ruby intended to plead not guilty again and go to trial. District Attorney Wade told the media after the reversal of Ruby's conviction that he might go along with a sentence of life imprisonment for Ruby if Ruby would be willing to plead guilty to murder.[72]

Looking back, Phil Burleson said, "I had been court appointed as lead counsel for the retrial in Wichita Falls, and my argument was going to be murder without malice, which under the law at that time meant . . . that he acted in the heat of sudden passion. And the maximum sentence at that time . . . was five years, and Jack had already . . . served three and a half, four years."[73] In other words, Burleson intended to present the same defense that Ruby's first lawyer, Tom Howard, wanted to use, one that even the lead prosecutor, Bill Alexander, believes would have worked. Why didn't Mel Belli do what would appear to be the obvious, and instead seek an outright acquittal, walking Ruby out of court a free man? Seymour Ellison, a longtime law partner of Belli's, told me that "Mel was obsessed with the thought of walking Ruby out the door when millions of people had seen his client kill Oswald. He told me, 'Sy, if I can do that I'll be right up there with Clarence Darrow.'"[74]*

While some would say that if this was really the main motivation behind Belli's legal strategy at Ruby's trial, then Belli had committed the ultimate sin of a trial lawyer, putting his interest before that of his client, particularly serious when Belli was playing with Ruby's life (not just a routine sentence in prison, the result in 99 percent of criminal cases). But that would presuppose that Belli believed he had very little chance of securing a not-guilty verdict. And we don't know that. Two points have to be noted in this regard. Mel Belli had a great passion for the law and fought hard for hundreds of clients through the years, particularly the poor and unpowerful against major corporations. Perhaps more importantly on this issue, most of Belli's civil cases involved medical evidence, and it was often said that he knew as much about medicine, even autopsies, as did the doctors he called to the witness stand, people sometimes lightly calling him "Dr. Belli." And although Belli's defense of Ruby was in a criminal trial, he was using a medical defense, albeit a novel one at the time in the criminal law. What I am saying is that Belli, now deceased, may have sincerely thought he would be able to secure a not-guilty verdict for Ruby, in which case illusions of being the equal of Darrow would be irrelevant.

Before a new trial date could be set, Ruby died at Parkland Hospital in Dallas on January 3, 1967, the same hospital in which Kennedy and Oswald had died, and his autopsy was conducted that same day by Dr. Earl Rose. Under "Cause of Death," the autopsy report reads, "Pulmonary emboli immediate cause of death secondary to bronchiolar carcinoma of the lungs."[75] Dr. Rose said the "embolism had come from Ruby's legs."[76]

Ruby was buried January 9, 1967, in his hometown of Chicago. Two of Ruby's appellate lawyers who got his conviction reversed, Elmer Gertz and William Kunstler, served as pallbearers.[77] That same day in Dallas, four doctors, including Dr. Rose, sectioned Ruby's brain and concluded he had "multiple metastatic neoplastic lesions."[78] "Ruby had cancer of the brain," Dr. Rose said, "and it was the same cancer that was in his lungs. It had spread."[79]

---

*Although Belli was the most famous trial lawyer in America at the time, he had achieved his fame in the practice of civil law, while Darrow had achieved his in criminal law.

A Conversation with Marina

My friend David Phinney, a longtime student of the assassination, and someone with a keen sense of history, had been urging me for some time to interview Marina Oswald. I told him I had Marina on my list of people to talk to but I was in no rush to do so since she had already been interviewed countless times in great depth and I knew there was nothing new I could learn from her. I also knew that although in the early years her credibility was good, in recent years she has hitched her wagon to all the goofy conspiracy theories that have proliferated. But since she is, after all, the widow of Kennedy's assassin, and derivatively a historic figure in her own right, I took Phinney's advice and paid Marina a visit earlier than I had intended during a trip to Dallas on November 30, 2000.[*]

When I walked, midafternoon, into the Army-Navy Surplus Store in Dallas where she was working full-time as a clerk, my Fort Worth friend, lawyer Jack Duffy, who had made several calls to locate the low-profile Marina for me, introduced me to her. Marina, unsmiling, said to Duffy crisply, "I know who he is. I've seen him many times on TV." I interjected lightly, "I've been on a few times." "Are you proud of it?" Marina asked in a challenging way. I won't say that my meeting with Marina went downhill from that point, but it never got too much better either. Pulling up chairs outside the back of the store, and accompanied by her friend and store manager Linda Wilson, who drove Marina to and from work each day, Marina proceeded to tell me that she had already heard I was writing a book about the assassination and asked me not to write it. When I asked her why, she told me, "Because I know you won't be fair. You're not interested in the truth. I've already been told what you're going to say—that Lee is guilty." I told her I would be scrupulously fair and would include opposing views in my book, including hers. She brushed this off, saying that "people listen to you. No one cares what I say." She said that

---

[*]See endnote discussion for possibility that if I had waited to interview Marina, as I was going to do, I may not have gotten to interview her.

any book by me saying her late husband killed Kennedy would cause further harm to her, her two daughters by Lee, and her son by the man she divorced but still lives with on a seventeen-acre farm in a small town just east of Dallas. I told her that she and her children were all innocent victims, but in writing my book I had no choice but to discuss the facts as I knew them to be. She told me I didn't know all the facts, that there were "many documents" I've never seen. When I asked the chain-smoking woman with the blue, intelligent eyes what those documents were, she just dismissed my question with a wave of her hands.

Marina, wearing very light makeup, was dressed in the most inexpensive of slacks and a pullover sweater. There was no sense of the modern woman about her, and her clothing and demeanor still spoke of the old country to me. She told me she feels "very strongly" that her former husband did not kill Kennedy. When I reminded her that she told the Warren Commission that she believed he had killed Kennedy, the essence of her long, rambling explanation was that "all that they showed me against him led me to believe it." I asked her if the authorities ever told her what to say or threatened her in any way. She said they never told her what to say, but "they kept talking to me over and over again. I was exhausted, and had a four-week-old child, and at one point I didn't want to answer—the word, I think, is *tattle on*—my friends and relatives in Russia. And I felt their questions about them were not relevant, but they told me if I wanted to stay here in this country, I'd have to answer all their questions."

At what point in time, I asked her, did she come around to the belief that her husband was innocent? "About fifteen to twenty years later," she said,[*] when she started to see things more clearly and do more reading on the subject. She said she realized she had been "lied to." What lies? I asked. She answered curiously, "You're catching me off guard," and she could not tell me. But she was sure of one thing—"Lee was set up as a patsy." She doesn't specifically know by whom, but they were connected, she said, to the U.S. government. Who then, I asked, did kill Kennedy? "Cubans," she replied. "Pro-Castro or anti-Castro Cubans?" I asked. "Anti-Castro Cubans," she assured me. Who covered

[*]On September 9, 1964, Marina told the Warren Commission, "I have no doubt that he did kill the president" (5 H 608). As late as November 23, 1980, she told Dan Carmichael of United Press International that her husband was "not innocent" of Kennedy's murder. But I knew Marina had come a long way since she told *Dallas Morning News* reporter Hugh Aynesworth a few months after the assassination how "ashamed and sorry" she was for what her husband had done (*Dallas Morning News*, March 7, 1964, sect.4, p.1).

The first time Marina publicly asserted a change in her position was in a November 1988 interview in *Ladies' Home Journal*, and she had only come three-quarters of the way to where she is today. "It was a very complicated plot, brilliantly executed," she told the *Journal*. "Could any intelligent person believe that that kind of thing was organized by one man? When Lee was arrested, I remember he said, 'I'm a patsy.' I strongly believe that with all the evidence that has come to light, he probably was telling the truth . . . I don't think that all this was about John F. Kennedy. It was more about Robert, who was going after organized crime, and who would not be attorney general anymore if his brother was killed. When I was questioned by the Warren Commission, I was a blind kitten. Their questioning left me only one way to go; guilty. I made Lee guilty. He never had a fair chance . . . I buried all his chances by my statements . . . But I was only twenty-two then, and I've matured since. I think differently. [I'm sure you do, Marina, but I didn't know that all the things you told the Warren Commission and FBI you saw with your own eyes and heard with your own ears actually never happened. Your eyes and ears hadn't "matured" yet at the tender age of twenty-two? In any event, and this is a critical point that has to be noted, other than her belief in her husband's guilt, *Marina has never retracted any of the testimony she gave to the Warren Commission and later to the HSCA*.] Only half the truth has been told. I want to find out the whole truth. It may be a bitter truth at the end for me. But I want the truth. In America, a wonderful country, you should get the truth." (Blythe and Farrell, "Marina Oswald, Twenty-five Years Later," pp.183, 237) By 1992, Marina told *Time* that "Lee simply did not shoot anybody," adding, "I do believe it was a conspiracy, carefully orchestrated and covered up" ("Marina's Turn," p.71).

this fact up? I asked. "The CIA covered it up," she said, because the anti-Castro Cubans had been working for the CIA, and the CIA was afraid that if they didn't cover up the assassination for the anti-Castro Cubans, the latter would let it be known that they had tried to kill Castro for the CIA.

"Lee," she said, worked "undercover for someone in the American government," but when I asked her whom, she said she did not know. She believes he knew the assassination was going to take place and told the FBI about it, but doesn't know why the FBI didn't stop the assassination. She also believes that LBJ and the CIA, along with the FBI, knew the assassination was going to take place, and later, the Mafia "ordered Ruby" to kill her husband. When I told her she was implicating quite a few groups, she replied that "they all work together."

When I asked her why, if her husband knew the assassination was going to take place, yet was innocent himself, he didn't tell the authorities after his apprehension about what he knew, she said, "Lee didn't want to come forward. He didn't want to betray the people he was loyal to." But why, I asked, would he feel any loyalty to those who had betrayed him by setting him up as a patsy? She said she didn't know the answer to that question, and could only repeat "that Lee was very loyal to these people." Who were these people? I once again asked Marina, and Marina, who till this day still speaks slightly broken English, again said she did not know.

Although, as indicated, I did not come to interrogate Marina about the facts of the case, since this had already been done ad nauseam, a few references to factual matters were made. When she insisted on Oswald's innocence, suggesting he would never do such a murderous act, I reminded her that he had, in fact, attempted to murder Major General Edwin Walker, and she readily admitted he had, telling me she knew this because "Lee told me he did." But she hastened to add that the president was different because "Lee liked Kennedy." And Jack Duffy, who has studied the assassination for many years and leans toward the conspiracy theory, asked Marina if she had taken "the backyard photos" of Oswald holding the Carcano rifle. "Yes," she answered evenly, "I did." "That settles that issue," Duffy said.

My sense of Marina after meeting her is essentially the same as it was before, with the exception that she was a little more feisty and intense than I had anticipated. Although her mind has clearly become addled by the impregnation of all the conspiracy theories she has heard and read about, I feel that as to matters about which she has personal knowledge, she is a truthful person—easily as truthful as the average person, perhaps more so.

In parting, she said that the previous thirty-seven years had been terrible, but told me she had "a favorite motto" that applies to her life: "Tragedy does not always come to harm you." By that she meant that my assessment of her as being a victim was wrong. "I have been victimized, but I have not become a victim," she told me. The experience, she said, had caused her to learn about herself. And what had she learned? I asked. For the first time in our forty- to forty-five-minute conversation, a very slight smile crossed her face. "There are certain things for only me to know," she said. I bid her good-bye and told her I would be kind to her in my book and I had one bit of very good advice to give her. "What?" she asked eagerly. "You should stop smoking," I said with a smile to soften my injunctive words, whereupon she proceeded to point to the cigarette in her hand and say that at the time she started smoking years ago, "They [the tobacco manufacturers] didn't tell us about all the bad ingredients in their cigarettes." I told her that that was one conspiracy to cover up the truth that I agreed with her on.

In a follow-up telephone conversation on December 5, 2000, Marina, expressing concern about the privacy of her children, said her daughter June had been the valedictorian at the University of Texas with a straight-A average and now has an excellent job with a business corporation in Texas that takes her around the world. Her other daughter, Rachel, also has a college degree and is a registered nurse married to a prominent Austin physician. When I told her that her children doing well was a testament to the job she had done in raising them, she said she did not need my compliments,[*] and refusing to take any credit, said that sometimes children do well because of what's inside of them, not because of their rearing. The father of her son, Mark, is Dallas carpenter Kenneth Porter, whom she married in 1965 and divorced in 1974. The two worked out their differences and have continued to live under the same roof, Marina keeping his last name. Mark, she says, is the only child of hers who does not have a college degree. She said he has a blue-collar job, but "he's not a garbage collector." When I asked Marina, who became a U.S. citizen in 1991, what she enjoyed doing in her leisure moments, she said she reads a lot, all nonfiction, and is interested in philosophy. We finished our conversation by her telling me that "although I've been polite to you today [I hadn't sensed any difference in our two conversations] doesn't mean I like you." I chuckled, telling her that I felt she had a good sense of humor.

When I placed the December phone call, Linda Wilson, Marina's supervisor, answered. Before turning the phone over to Marina, she told me, "Marina is one of the sweetest, most kind and generous persons you could ever be around. She's a very, very fine person." As an example of Marina's generous ways, she said, "Anyone at the store who comes up short for a purchase, like the kids, or needs a dollar for the bus, or whatever, Marina is always the first one to reach into her purse."

---

[*]Indeed, the only compliment that Marina would accept from me in our two conversations was when I told her she was "a down-to-earth person." "Thank you," she said.

The People and Groups Involved in the Plot to Kill Kennedy

The reader has learned by now that according to the conspiracy community, much of the world was out to get President Kennedy, and that the people and groups out to kill him were apparently literally fighting among themselves over who got to fire the first shot. And, of course, ever since the murder, virtually the whole world, even those who weren't involved in the murder, has eagerly participated in the cover-up for those who did conspire to murder Kennedy.

When longtime conspiracy theorist Penn Jones Jr. passed away in 1998, there were several tributes to him in a conspiracy theorist publication. One read, "The research community has lost one of its best-loved and most influential figures. But at least we know that Penn Jones Jr. is now in a better place, a place where he can *at least learn the truth* about what happened in Dealey Plaza all those years ago."[1] A joke told in the comparatively small anti-conspiracy community about the conspiracy buffs' belief that just about everyone was involved in the cover-up of the assassination has them lined up in front of God at the end of time asking him, "Tell us, God, who really killed President Kennedy?" When God replies, "Listen, I'm just going to tell you one time and one time only, and then I want you to forget about this matter—Lee Harvey Oswald killed Kennedy and he acted alone," the buffs, in terrible angst, nudge each other nervously and say, "This is a lot bigger than we thought."

As we've seen, the heart of a criminal conspiracy is two *or more* people getting together and agreeing to commit a crime. But with conspiracy theorists, "or more" is never enough. What follows are three lists (not complete ones, I must add) of groups, countries, and people allegedly involved in the murder of JFK. The first list is of groups and countries believed by one or more conspiracy theorists to be behind the assassination (sources for the accusation are given only for the most obscure and far-out groups).

1. CIA
2. Organized crime

3. FBI

4. Secret Service

5. Office of Naval Intelligence

6. KGB (Soviet Union)

7. American Communists

8. Cuba

9. Anti–Castro Cuban exiles

10. Germany

11. U.S. Army

12. Military–industrial complex (the Joint Chiefs of Staff and leaders of American business, particularly the defense industry)

13. Dallas Police Department

14. Dallas County Sheriff's Department

15. *Dallas Morning News*

16. Texas oilmen

17. International banking cabal

18. Illuminati

19. Majesty Twelve (MJ-12), the secret, shadow government of the United States[2]

20. Minutemen

21. Dallas oligarchy (wealthy civic leaders in Dallas who are believed to rule the city)

22. Right wing in America

23. Mossad (Israeli intelligence agency)[3]

24. Government of South Vietnam[4]

25. Red China

26. Nationalist China

27. Poland

28. Anti-Defamation League[5]

29. French OAS[6]

30. Renegade members of Hitler's elite staff who fled Germany after World War II[7]

31. Republican Party of Omaha[8]

32. Mayor Daley machine in Chicago[9]

33. Catholic Church[10]

34. U.S. Department of Agriculture[11]

35. Forces that were behind the 1964 U.S.-Belgian rescue operation in the Congo[12]

36. Martians and Venusians[13]*

37. American Council of Christian Churches[14]

38. Exiled czarist Russians[15]

39. Eastern establishment

40. National Aeronautics and Space Administration

41. Defense Industrial Security Command

42. U.S. Defense Intelligence Agency

---

*The late Mary Ferrell, a conspiracy researcher from Dallas, said she had books in her collection saying that the Martians and Venusians were responsible for the assassination (*Dallas Morning News*, November 20, 1983). Ferrell is believed to have had the largest private collection of JFK assassination–related documents ever, but sold it to an individual named Oliver Curme from California for a sum in excess of $1.5 million (*JFK/Deep Politics Quarterly*, January 2003, p.35).

43. International Brotherhood of Teamsters
44. Ku Klux Klan

    Although the number of co-conspirators who would have had to participate in the conspiracy as members of the groups allegedly behind the assassination—such as the CIA, organized crime, and military-industrial complex—would necessarily be very high, the following is a partial list of those co-conspirators who have been specifically named and identified by one or more conspiracy theorists as being members of the conspiracy to murder Kennedy. (The reader should not conclude that every person on this list is believed by all or even most conspiracy theorists to have been a member of the conspiracy to murder Kennedy. If just one conspiracy theorist, at any time, accused this person of complicity, the person's name appears on this list.)

1. Tony Accardo
2. Dean Acheson
3. Joseph Alsop
4. James Jesus Angleton
5. Bobby Baker
6. Robert "Barney" Baker
7. Guy Banister
8. W. O. Bankston
9. Bernard Barker
10. Charles Batchelor
11. Benjamin Bauman
12. Thomas Beckham
13. Jerry Belknap
14. Paul Bethel
15. Louis M. Bloomfield
16. Hale Boggs
17. Martin Bormann
18. Orlando Bosch
19. George Bouhe
20. Jack Bowen
21. Eugene Hale Brading
22. Edgar Eugene Bradley
23. Leslie Norman Bradley
24. "Brother-in-law"
25. McGeorge Bundy
26. George Bush (Senior)
27. George Butler
28. Harold Byrd
29. General Charles Cabell
30. Earle Cabell
31. Claude Barnes Capehart
32. Carlos (last name unknown)
33. Alex Carlson

34. Dan Carswell
35. Cliff Carter
36. Lieutenant Colonel Bevin Cass
37. Luis Castillo
38. Fidel Castro
39. Max Cherry
40. Joe Civello
41. Edward Clark
42. Thomas Clines
43. Joseph R. Cody
44. Roy M. Cohn
45. Lucien Conein
46. John Connally
47. Ramon Cortes
48. Kent Courtney
49. William Craver
50. John Crawford
51. Robert Crowley
52. Kenneth Hudson Croy
53. Jesse Curry
54. William Dalzell
55. I. Irving Davidson
56. Harry Dean (aka Harry Fallon)
57. Patrick Dean
58. Bill Decker
59. Louise Deckert
60. Eladio del Valle
61. John De Menil
62. George de Mohrenschildt
63. Herminio Diaz
64. Joe DiMaggio
65. Walter Dornberger
66. Robert Easterling
67. Jack Faulkner
68. Fernandez Feito
69. David Ferrie
70. Abe Fortas
71. Will Fritz
72. Maurice Gatlin
73. William Gaudet
74. Sam Giancana
75. G. Wray Gill
76. Manuel García Gonzales
77. T. Gonzales
78. William Greer
79. Peter Gregory
80. Antoine Guerini

81. Billy James Hargis
82. Roy Hargraves
83. William "Blackie" Harrison
84. William Harvey
85. Richard Helms
86. Gerald Patrick Hemming
87. Jim Hicks
88. Jimmy Hoffa
89. Chauncey Holt
90. J. Edgar Hoover
91. Lawrence Howard
92. David Hoy
93. Patrick Hoy
94. Howard Hughes
95. E. Howard Hunt
96. H. L. Hunt
97. Morris Jaffe
98. Walter Jenkins
99. Lyndon Johnson
100. Mr. Jones (fictitious name)
101. Clarence Jones
102. Clifford Jones
103. Sam Kail
104. Roy Kellerman
105. Nikita Khrushchev
106. Jules Ricco Kimble
107. Pat Kirkwood
108. Fred Korth
109. Jake Kosloff
110. Valeriy Kostikov
111. Larry LaBorde
112. Edward Lansdale
113. Meyer Lansky
114. Richard Lauchli
115. Jack Lawrence
116. Yves Leandez
117. James Melvin Liggett
118. Gilberto Policarpo Lopez
119. Grayston Lynch
120. Quinton Pino Machado
121. General John Magruder
122. Robert Maheu
123. George Mandel (aka Giorgio Mantello)
124. Amos Manor
125. Carlos Marcello
126. Layton Martens
127. Jack Martin

128. John Martino
129. Rolando Masferrer
130. John McCloy
131. John McCone
132. Carl McIntire
133. Robert McKeown
134. Mike McLaney
135. Gordon McLendon
136. Jim McMahon
137. L. J. McWillie
138. Major General John B. Medaris
139. L. D. Miller
140. Joseph Milteer
141. William Monteleone
142. David Sanchez Morales
143. Clint Murchison
144. Ferenc Nagy
145. Madame Nhu
146. Richard Nixon
147. Gordon Novel
148. Dr. Alton Ochsner
149. Ken O'Donnell
150. Harry Olsen
151. Aristotle Onassis
152. Marina Oswald
153. Michael Paine
154. Ruth Paine
155. Kim Philby
156. David Atlee Phillips
157. Robert "Tosh" Plumlee
158. Luis Posada
159. James W. Powell
160. Jack Puterbaugh
161. Carlos Quiroga
162. Paul Raigorodsky
163. William Reily
164. Sid Richardson
165. William Robertson
166. Charles Rogers
167. Alexander Rorke
168. Johnny Roselli
169. Eugene Rostow
170. John Rousselot
171. James Rowley
172. Jack Ruby
173. Ruth Ann (last name unknown)
174. Mike Ryan

175. Emilio Santana
176. Felipe Vidal Santiago
177. Saul (last name unknown)
178. Aldo Vera Seraphine
179. Theodore Shackley
180. Clay Shaw
181. Walter Sheridan
182. Charles Siragusa
183. "Slim"
184. Mr. Smith (fictitious name)
185. Sergio Arcacha Smith
186. Carlos Prío Socarrás
187. Jean René Souetre
188. Arlen Specter
189. Lew Sterrett
190. Adlai Stevenson
191. Frank Sturgis (Frank Fiorini)
192. William Sullivan
193. Kerry Thornley
194. J. D. Tippit
195. Santo Trafficante
196. "Troit"
197. Tammi True
198. Igor Vagonov
199. Adolf Vermont Jr.
200. Wernher Von Braun
201. Igor Voshinin
202. Henry Wade
203. General Edwin Walker
204. Brock Wall
205. George Wallace
206. Harry Weatherford
207. Ed Weisl
208. Mitch WerBell
209. Lieutenant Colonel George Whitmeyer
210. General Charles Willoughby
211. Edwin Wilson
212. Louie Witt
213. Mr. X (fictitious name)
214. Abraham Zapruder

The following is a partial list of assassins—that is, those whom one or more conspiracy theorists have actually named and identified as having fired a weapon at Kennedy in Dealey Plaza (or as being part of the assassination group) from locations including the second and sixth floors of the Book Depository Building, the Dal-Tex Building, the County Records Building, the grassy knoll, the railroad overpass, the area around the pergola, the presidential limousine itself, a manhole on Elm Street, and a storm drain near the north

end of the Triple Underpass.* Other conspiracy theorists have named some of these people as only being a member of the conspiracy to kill Kennedy, not an assassin. Apparently,
so many people wanted to kill Kennedy that they had to draw straws to get the best firing
positions, and from the main assassination location they must have been standing shoulder to shoulder. At least we haven't reached the situation, *yet*, where they are perched on
top of each other's shoulders. But the century is still young.

1. Gus Abrams
2. Felix Alderisio
3. Black Dog Man
4. Roger Bocognani
5. Orlando Bosch
6. Eugene Hale Brading
7. Edgar Eugene Bradley
8. T. Casey Brennan
9. Morgan Brown
10. Richard Cain (Ricardo Scalzetti)
11. "Carlos"
12. Daniel Carswell
13. Cliff Carter
14. Fred Lee Chrisman
15. Patrick T. Dean
16. Eladio del Valle
17. Harold Doyle
18. John Ernst
19. Loy Factor
20. David Ferrie
21. James Files
22. Desmond FitzGerald
23. Franklin Folley (Frank Sinatra's drummer)
24. Clyde Foust
25. Richard Gaines
26. Herminio Diaz Garcia
27. John Gedney
28. Charles Givens
29. Manuel García Gonzales
30. William Greer
31. Jack Grimson
32. Al Groat
33. Loran Hall

---

*At least one writer (not even a confirmed conspiracy theorist, but obviously eager to join in the confirmed
silliness) posits the possibility that two assassins fired from virtually the same spot. "Even if it were determined," Edward Jay Epstein says, "that all the bullets fired came from the same rifle—and microballistic analyses of the fragments recovered indicated they were fired from Oswald's weapon—it would still be at least
theoretically conceivable that the rifle was passed from the hands of one sniper to another between shots"
(Epstein, *Legend*, p.334). Yes, and it is also *theoretically* possible that the assassin was a robed nun whose eyes
were closed and who used her Catholic prayer book as a gun rest.

34. Charles Harrelson
35. Jim Hart
36. Gerald Patrick Hemming
37. George Hickey (accidentally shot Kennedy)
38. Jim Hicks
39. Chauncey Holt
40. E. Howard Hunt
41. Harold Isaacs
42. Lyndon Johnson*
43. "Junior"
44. Roy Kellerman
45. Klu Klux Klan (two unidentified members)
46. Pedro Luis Diaz Lanz
47. Jack Lawrence
48. "Lebanon"
49. John Mertz
50. Michael Victor Mertz
51. Joseph Milteer
52. David Sanchez Morales
53. Charles Nicolleti
54. Lee Harvey Oswald
55. Lenny Patrick
56. Robert Lee Perrin
57. Sauveur Pironti
58. James Powell
59. "Raul"
60. George Reese
61. Manuel Rivera
62. Charles Rogers
63. Alexander Rorke
64. Johnny Roselli
65. Jack Ruby
66. Miguel Saez
67. Guillermo Novo Sampol
68. Ignacio Novo Sampol
69. Emilio Santana
70. Lucien Sarti
71. Saul (#1) (Accuser: Hugh McDonald)
72. Saul (#2) (Accuser: Ricky White)
73. William Seymour
74. Jean René Souetre
75. Frank Sturgis
76. J. D. Tippit

---

*No, really. Per *Newsweek*, someone at the November 1991 Assassination Symposium in Dallas argued that "Kennedy was shot by LBJ himself, who concealed his six-guns under a cape" (Gates with Manly, Foote, and Washington, "Bottom Line: How Crazy Is It?" p.52).

77. Malcolm Wallace
78. Harry Weatherford
79. Roscoe White
80. Louie Witt
81. Dave Yaras
82. "Zed" (code name)

With at least eighty-two gunmen shooting at Kennedy in Dealey Plaza that day, it's remarkable that Kennedy's body was sufficiently intact to make it to the autopsy table.

To reemphasize, the above three lists are only partial. And they don't even include those involved in the cover-up of the conspiracy to kill Kennedy, which virtually all buffs say the entire Warren Commission was guilty of. The alleged cover-up participants also include, *among a great many others*, the HSCA staff, Marina Oswald, the three autopsy surgeons, and "the remainder of the [federal] government" that was not behind the assassination (per New Orleans DA Jim Garrison). Indeed, conspiracy theorist E. Martin Schotz says the president's own brother, Robert F. Kennedy, knowingly participated in the cover-up.

One would think that at least five people (Jackie Kennedy, Governor Connally and his wife, Nellie, William Greer, the Secret Service driver of the presidential limousine, and Roy Kellerman, the Secret Service passenger in the front seat) might forever be immune from being accused, by the terminally wacky buffs, of being involved in the conspiracy to murder Kennedy, if for no other reason than that they themselves were in the line of fire. But not so fast say the conspiracy buffs, unwilling to concede by exemption any *Homo sapiens* who were alive and breathing on November 22, 1963. Conspiracy theorist James H. Fetzer has removed Greer, who was directly within the line of fire for both shots that hit Kennedy, from the line-of-fire defense, claiming that Greer, as a part of the conspiracy, deliberately stopped the limousine after the first shot to make Kennedy an easier target for the remaining shots. So apparently Greer, per Fetzer, decided to place his own life on the line to see that Kennedy was killed. And two young buffs from Canada also removed Greer as well as his partner, Kellerman, from the line-of-fire defense by actually contending that Greer himself turned around and shot Kennedy, Kellerman holding the steering wheel while his partner did the deed. In fact, a Tulsa citizen, serving as his own lawyer, went so far as to file a lawsuit on September 30, 1996, asking the court to find Greer and Kellerman guilty of murdering Kennedy.[16]

That leaves three other passengers in the presidential limousine. Surely at least they have to be immune from the pointed finger, right? Well, not all of them. A few weeks after the assassination, Governor Connally's wife, Nellie, wrote an account of the assassination on a yellow pad. Thirty years later, *Newsweek* published excerpts from the account. One excerpt refers to Nellie's visit to her husband's bedside in the recovery room at Parkland Hospital. "He asked me about the President," she wrote, and when she told him the president was dead, his reply was, "I knew."[17] Conspiracy theorist and author Walt Brown writes, "Those two words ["I knew"] will probably—*and perhaps should*—generate two conspiracy books."[18] In other words, there's at least a chance that Connally was so intent on joining in the conspiracy to murder Kennedy that, like Greer, he was even willing to risk his own life. In fact, conspiracy theorist Harrison E. Livingstone, in his book *The Radical Right and the Murder of John F. Kennedy*, informs his readers that "those in the know in Texas believe that Connally was part of the planning for the assassination."[19]

I don't know about Nellie, but it's probably just a matter of time before some nutty buff removes Jackie's Oleg Cassini pillbox hat and tries to put the conspiracy hat on her. I mean, she wasn't quite as much in the line of fire as Connally and Greer were. And God knows, with JFK's flagrant womanizing, she certainly had a motive. Indeed, how long do we have to wait for some deranged conspiracy theorist to write an article or book stating that President Kennedy was in very ill health, that he had been told he didn't have too long to live,* and that he, yes *he*, was a party to the conspiracy to have himself murdered?† The motive? Polls showed his popularity was in decline and he viewed his murder as a good career move. And we know that Kennedy's popularity did, in fact, rise dramatically as a result of his death on November 22, 1963.

But all of the above assumes that John F. Kennedy was actually killed on November 22, 1963. And we don't know this. Indeed, conspiracy theorist George Thomson, a swimming-pool engineer, is convinced that twenty-two shots were fired in Dealey Plaza, and five people were killed, but not JFK. Officer Tippit was impersonating JFK in the presidential limousine and it was he who was killed. Kennedy escaped and was seen a year later in New York reveling at a private birthday party for author Truman Capote.[20] Who am I to say that George Thomson is wrong?

A verbal exchange on September 17, 1977, at a "Critics Conference" in Washington, D.C., in which G. Robert Blakey, chief counsel for the HSCA, met with nine prominent Warren Commission critics and conspiracy theorists from around the country, captured the essence of the conspiracy movement. When Blakey noted that "nobody has ever suggested that the U.S. Fish and Wildlife Service" was involved in the assassination, conspiracy theorist Kathy Kinsella spoke up. "Give us time," she said.[21]

---

*After all, as early as 1947, an English physician diagnosed JFK's Addison's disease during his trip to Ireland, and when Kennedy returned to the states from London in September of 1947, "he was so ill that a priest came aboard the *Queen Mary* to give him extreme unction [the "last rites" of the Catholic Church] before he was carried off the ship on a stretcher" (Dallek, *Unfinished Life*, p.153).

†A variation of this notion is that spun by Oswald's mother, Marguerite, to author Jean Stafford. Although she told Stafford her son had been "framed" for Kennedy's murder, she allowed, "Now maybe Lee Harvey Oswald was the assassin. But does that make him a louse? No. No! Killing does not necessarily mean badness. You find killing in some very fine homes for one reason or another. And as we know, President Kennedy was a dying man. So I say it is possible that my son was chosen to shoot him in a mercy killing for the security of the country. And if this is true, it was a fine thing to do and my son is a hero." (Stafford, *Mother in History*, pp.12, 18)

Lincoln-Kennedy Coincidences

I am including this brief section in my book for two reasons. One, the coincidences between Lincoln's and Kennedy's lives and deaths are so incredible that one can't help but shake one's head in wonderment and fascination. But that alone would not justify their inclusion in the book. What does is the fact that in the world of the conspiracy theorists, there is no such thing as a coincidence. Events and circumstances never fortuitously happen and by mere chance relate to each other. They are actually manifestations and evidence of two or more people acting in concert toward a mutual, sinister goal.

The remarkable Lincoln-Kennedy coincidences, several of them first noticed and published three days after Kennedy's death by Dayton, Ohio, artist and Lincoln scholar Lloyd Ostendorf, follow:

1. Lincoln was elected president in 1860, Kennedy in 1960.

2. Both Lincoln and Kennedy were elected president after each had unsuccessfully sought to get the vice presidential nomination of their party—Lincoln in 1856, Kennedy in 1956.

3. Both Lincoln and Kennedy had served in the U.S. House of Representatives—Lincoln elected in 1846, Kennedy in 1946.

4. The man Lincoln defeated to become president, Stephen Douglas, was born in 1813. The man Kennedy defeated to become president, Richard Nixon, was born in 1913.

5. Both Lincoln and Kennedy, while in their thirties, married a pretty, sophisticated twenty-four-year-old brunette who spoke French fluently.

6. Both Lincoln and Kennedy had sons who died during their presidency—Lincoln's son William dying at the age of eleven, Kennedy's son Patrick dying two days after his birth.

7. Both Lincoln and Kennedy, far more than any presidents before them, sought equality for blacks as an inalienable right required by a decent and just nation. And both of their dramatic efforts failed during their lives, the seeds only bearing fruit shortly after their deaths, in Lincoln's case with the abolition of slavery by the Thirteenth Amendment to the U.S. Constitution on December 18, 1865,[*] in Kennedy's case with the Civil Rights Act of 1964 and the Voting Rights Act of 1965.

8. Kennedy's secretary was named Lincoln.[†]

9. Both Lincoln and Kennedy were murdered on a Friday.

10. Both were shot once in the head.

11. Both were seated at the time they were shot.

12. Both were shot from behind, in the back of their head.

13. Both were shot by assassins who were to their right rear.[‡]

14. Both Lincoln's and Kennedy's wives were seated next to them at the time they were shot.[§]

15. Each wife, after her husband was shot in the head, cradled his head in her lap.

16. Both Lincoln and Kennedy were in the presence of another couple, and in each case the man was also wounded by the assassin (Connally by gunshot, Major Henry R. Rathbone when Booth stabbed him as Rathbone lunged at Booth after Booth shot Lincoln).

17. *Lincoln* was shot in *Ford*'s theater. Kennedy was shot in a *Lincoln* limousine (manufactured by *Ford* Motor Company).

18. Though both Lincoln and Kennedy were shot in the head, which normally causes immediate death, neither died instantly, and feverish efforts to resuscitate them were

---

[*]Lincoln's Emancipation Proclamation on January 1, 1863, did not free a single slave since *almost all* the slaves at that time, close to four million, were in the South (all were below the Mason-Dixon line), which was then under the control of the Confederate Army.

[†]Though it is frequently stated in the many lists of Lincoln-Kennedy coincidences that Lincoln's secretary was named Kennedy, his main secretary was John G. Nicolay. Lincoln's only other secretary was John Hay.

[‡]Nearly all Lincoln-Kennedy coincidence lists say that "Lincoln's assassin, John Wilkes Booth, shot Lincoln in a theater, then fled to a warehouse. Kennedy's assassin, Lee Harvey Oswald, shot Kennedy from a warehouse and fled to a theater." But Booth fled on horseback to the Maryland home of Dr. Samuel A. Mudd, who treated Booth's broken left leg. Booth was shot to death by a Union sergeant while hiding in a burning barn in Virginia twelve days after he shot Lincoln.

[§]Contrary to what some lists say, Mrs. Lincoln was seated to Lincoln's right, while we know Mrs. Kennedy was seated to Kennedy's left.

made by several physicians, both presidents responding with an increased though weak pulse before expiring.

19. On the day Lincoln was killed, he told an aide that he knew there were those who wanted him dead. "If it is to be done," he said, "it is impossible to prevent it." On the day of Kennedy's murder, he said in his Fort Worth hotel room to Jackie and an aide how easy it would be for someone to shoot him from a "high building with a high powered rifle, and there's nothing anybody could do."

20. Unlike 99 percent of the population, both presidential assassins, John Wilkes Booth and Lee Harvey Oswald, were known by their three names.*

21. Both Booth and Oswald were shot and killed before they were brought to trial.

22. Both Booth and Oswald were killed by one shot from a revolver.

23. Both Lincoln's and Kennedy's successors were named Johnson.

24. Lincoln's successor, Andrew Johnson, was born in 1808, and Kennedy's successor, Lyndon Johnson, in 1908.

25. Both Andrew Johnson and Lyndon Johnson were southern Democrats.

26. Both Andrew Johnson and Lyndon Johnson had served as United States senators.

27. The names Lincoln and Kennedy each contain seven letters.

28. The names John Wilkes Booth and Lee Harvey Oswald each contain fifteen letters.

29. The names Andrew Johnson and Lyndon Johnson each contain thirteen letters.

I can only hope the above list will help conspiracy theorists realize that coincidences that seem to defy mathematical probabilities do happen in life. That's why there is a name for them, why they are called *co*incidences. In fact, they are so common that we sometimes loosely suggest the phenomenon when no real coincidence exists. "Of all the gin joints, in all the towns, in all the world, she walks into mine," Humphrey Bogart says in the movie *Casablanca* about his lover, Ingrid Bergman.

---

*Though it is frequently stated in the lists of Lincoln-Kennedy coincidences that Booth was born in 1839 and Oswald in 1939, Booth was born in 1838. Also, it is frequently stated that Booth and Oswald were southerners. But though Booth clearly was on the side of the South during the Civil War, he was born in Maryland, the northernmost of the slave states that was nevertheless a part of the Union during the Civil War. Indeed, one of the biggest defeats suffered by the Confederate forces of General Robert E. Lee in Lee's move north was the battle of Antietam in Maryland in 1862, when the Union Army repulsed the Confederate advance in what may have been the bloodiest single day (September 17) of the entire Civil War, with 23,000 Union and Confederate soldiers being killed or wounded. Although Maryland is below the Mason-Dixon line, causing some people to consider Maryland a southern state, the famous line separated the free states from the slave states, not the North from the South. Maryland was and is a "border state" between the North and the South, but I don't believe it is considered a southern state in the public consciousness.

Epilogue

For most Americans, interest in the Kennedy assassination has held firm for going on half a century, our nation unwilling to bury Kennedy or his legacy of inspiring a generation—his youthful image, vigor, and promise seemingly frozen in time.[1] This is why the pain of his loss lives on. Most believe that interest in the assassination and its perceived mysteries will endure for centuries to come.

Come rain or come shine, in cold or hot weather, people from all over the nation and the world (about two million annually) make their pilgrimage to Dealey Plaza, designated a National Historical Landmark district in October of 1993. Alone, or in twos or threes or more, they whisper and point and stand at or near the two Xs on Elm Street that mark the spots where Kennedy was struck down by two bullets. Repaving the street has only momentarily obliterated the Xs. Within days, assassination buffs or hawkers (who peddle pamphlets, CDs, books, and various other items on the assassination, usually on weekends) have repainted them.[2]*

The site where Kennedy's assassin was himself gunned down by Ruby, the underground garage in City Hall, is presently closed to the public. But the city fathers, in an effort to revitalize what is now a declining part of downtown Dallas, are expected to open it to the public as a tourist attraction, along with Oswald's jail cell on the fifth floor of the

---

*At 6:45 on the morning of December 12, 2003, a fifty-year-old Dallas man, Richard E. Clem, fired a bullet into his head while standing on the white X on Elm that marks where Kennedy was fatally wounded in the head forty years earlier. Clem, a twenty-seven-year postal employee, was found by the police lying in a pool of blood, his feet, perhaps unintentionally on his part, pointing toward the grassy knoll. Clem left no suicide note and his son was reluctant to say that his father's decision to kill himself was due to the president's assassination. He did say his father often went to Dealey Plaza to think, had read many books about the assassination, and was "greatly interested how our president could be murdered in broad daylight, in front of hundreds of people, police officers, secret service officers, etc., and still leave behind so many questions." Clem was not known to be part of the conspiracy community. (Michael Grabell, "Man Found Shot Where JFK Slain," *Dallas Morning News*, December 13, 2003, p.1B)

old Police and Courts Building (part of City Hall) in 2007. The Dallas Police Department moved out of the now mostly vacant building to new headquarters in 2003. The city administration had moved out of City Hall in 1978.[3]

With respect to President Kennedy's grave site, in 1962, the year before Kennedy was assassinated, one million people visited Arlington National Cemetery. During the six months following the assassination, *nine* million came. Today, approximately four and a half to five million people visit the cemetery each year. When I asked Tom Sherlock, the cemetery's historian, "Approximately how many of these visitors visit President Kennedy's grave site?" he replied, "99.9 percent. Unless they're coming here specifically to visit a loved one's grave, they're coming to see JFK's grave and the Tomb of the Unknown Solider."[4]

The John F. Kennedy Presidential Library and Museum in Boston, Massachusetts, opened on October 21, 1979, with David Powers, who was in the presidential motorcade in Dallas and was one of JFK's very closest aides and confidants, as curator, a position he maintained up to his death in 1998. The museum and library contain no assassination-related materials other than several hundred selected books on the assassination, an archivist telling me in 2004 that "we celebrate the president's life, not his death." The museum and library have been averaging about 225,000 visitors per year, with 210,594 in 2004.[5]

As with no other case in American history, network and cable TV, as well as the nation's print media, unfailingly continue to mark the anniversaries of Kennedy's death with feature stories and presentations. And of course conspiracy authors continue to write books on their pet theories of the assassination, eighty-four new books coming out since 2003 alone. (Telephone interview of James Sawa on November 26, 2006)

But the only day-in-and-day-out operation or memorial to the assassination of any significance is the Sixth Floor Museum at Dealey Plaza in Dallas. In 1977, Dallas County purchased the turn-of-the-century building at Elm and Houston, which had been leased to the Texas School Book Depository Company between 1962 and 1970, for the dual purpose of saving a historical site and using the office space. The building reopened in 1981 as the Dallas County Administration Building and eventually the first five floors were occupied by offices, the sixth and seventh floors remaining vacant, with very few visitors allowed to go to the sixth floor. In 1983, the nonprofit Dallas County Historical Foundation was created to raise funds for and to operate a $3.5 million museum on the sixth floor, and the museum opened to much fanfare on February 20, 1989. The museum is meant to be a permanent historical and educational display of photographs, films, graphics, charts, and other related interpretive materials pertaining to the assassination. Under the direction of the museum's curator, Gary Mack, and its executive director, Jeff West, as of 2005 the museum had collected over twenty-five thousand items pertaining to the assassination, including oral history audiotapes and videotapes of witnesses and others associated in some way with the participants or events of November 22 to 24, 1963. Artifacts include Abraham Zapruder's camera, one of the three first-generation copies of the out-of-camera original film made on the afternoon of the assassination (the other two, with the out-of-camera film, are at the National Archives), and the FBI model of Dealey Plaza used by the Warren Commission. Everyone, naturally, wants to go to the "corner window," the sniper's nest window where Oswald fired at Kennedy below, but the area is now enclosed by Plexiglas. However, one can clearly see the window and study the area from close quarters. Gerry Spence and I went to the window in 1986, before it was enclosed.

The Sixth Floor Museum attracts an average of 450,000 visitors annually, and well over 4 million people have gone to the museum since it opened in 1989. The museum, which also operates a bookstore on the premises selling books and miscellaneous items related to the assassination and the Kennedy family, is managed by a staff of over forty full- and part-time employees and is open seven days a week (except Christmas) from 9:00 a.m. to 6:00 p.m. at an admission cost of ten dollars. In 2002, the museum renovated and opened the seventh floor, renting it out for special events, such as an exhibit in March of 2003 of silk-screen portraits of Jacqueline Kennedy created by Andy Warhol in the months following the assassination.

In 1970, the city of Dallas erected the JFK Memorial. Located on a block of land owned by Dallas County and bordered by Main, Record, Elm, and Market streets, the memorial, just one block east of Dealey Plaza, is a cenotaph, an empty tomb erected in memory of a deceased person whose body is buried elsewhere. The inscription on a plaque near the cenotaph reads, "An open tomb that symbolizes the freedom of Kennedy's spirit." The very large, white structure (2,500 square feet and thirty feet high), consisting of seventy-two white, precast concrete columns, was designed by Philip Johnson, a prominent architect and friend of the Kennedy family. The simple inscription "John Fitzgerald Kennedy" is in gold leaf on two sides of a low, black granite block in the center of the tomb. Bleak, and with no apparent attempt to be aesthetically pleasing to the eye, there were suggestions a few years ago that the tomb be torn down.[6]

Directly across the street from the JFK Memorial at 110 South Market is the Conspiracy Museum, a two-story structure that has a bookstore, gift shop, documentary theater, and exhibits such as "The Three Hobos," "Mystery Death List," and a wall chart display of "Who Killed JFK?" The museum is open seven days a week and has smaller exhibits dealing with the assassinations of Lincoln and RFK as well as JFK. The president of the museum, Tom Bowden, advertises it as "the only place in Dallas to learn about the conspiracy" surrounding the assassination of Kennedy. The museum's predecessor at the same location was the Assassination Information Center, which was founded in 1989 by the late Larry Howard. Shortly after he died in 1994, and under the new ownership of R. B. Cutler, the Conspiracy Museum started up.

The Rose Hill Cemetery where Oswald was buried is now known as Shannon Rose Hill Memorial Park, located in a low-income area of Fort Worth at 7301 East Lancaster. During a visit there on November 30, 2000, a Memorial Park official told me that around four or five people a week visit Oswald's grave. Originally, Oswald's headstone had his first name on it as well as the years of his life, but after the exhumation in 1981, a new, flat, red headstone simply says, "OSWALD," with no first name or years on it. Facing Oswald's grave from a nearby road inside the cemetery, one can see where Oswald's mother, Marguerite, who died of cancer in 1981, is buried, without any headstone or marker, to Oswald's left. To his right is a headstone with the name "Nick Beef" on it. No one is buried there. The official said she had been told that several years ago some person had paid for the small plot and requested that the fictitious name be placed on the headstone. She did not know why.[7]

Though an entire nation grieved over the death of President Kennedy, his assassin's mother grieved hard for her son in the years before she died. Her sole purpose in life seemed to be to convince the world of her son's innocence. "Lee Harvey Oswald died an innocent man," she would say. Persuaded that he "was framed," she would point out that "he was neither tried nor convicted for his alleged crime." At times she would go beyond this, as when she told the media, in support of her petition to have her son reburied in Arlington National Cemetery, that her son had "done more for his country than any other living human being." Or when, claiming to have "a very unusual ESP," she said, "so doesn't it stand to reason that if my boy shot the President, I would have *known* at the time it happened?" Living in isolation from her family, she never saw her two grandchildren by Lee after November of 1963, and she spent her final years trying to ward off poverty by selling his letters from Russia and other memorabilia to pay the rent.

In May of 1964, during a television program about President Kennedy's grave, the scene shifted to her son's grave and the announcer's words cut to the bottom of her heart. "The assassin's grave has on it a dead tree," she recalled his saying. "And a picture was shown of a tree. The leaves had fallen off and it certainly looked dead. Alone in my house I broke down and wept. I soon learned that the tree had been planted a few days earlier, since my last visit to the cemetery. I did not know who put it there, but it had not been watered. I was determined that by the next Sunday my son's grave would be the nicest-looking in that section of the Rose Hill Burial Park. I pruned the tree, and I felt sure that there was life left in the roots. So I went back every day for a week, morning and evening, to water the tree. And in five days, the 'dead' tree in which the television announcer found so much ironic symbolism, started to bloom. Some may wonder why I take such an interest in the grave. First of all, my son is buried there. Regardless of what the world says or thinks, he is still my son. I keep the grave nice, too, because of the many people who come to visit. I, as a mother, want these people to go back home knowing a mother's love for a son is everlasting."[8]

In Memoriam

John F. Kennedy Library

Everyone remembers where they were and what they were doing the moment they heard Kennedy had died.

—Common observation about Kennedy's murder

It was a transforming moment for America because we lost hope. Every president who succeeded Kennedy—they all had good points and bad points—but the legacy of hope died with him. You never had that sense again that we were moving forward, that we could do things.

—Helen Thomas, White House correspondent, United Press International

My really first conscious thoughts were just "My God, what a . . . great tragedy . . . What a horrible, horrible tragedy," and how, in the space of a fleeting moment, things can change. Here we were, two relatively young men—we were almost the identical age, riding with what I would like to believe were two of the most beautiful wives in this country. The President and Jackie were happy. We were proud to be their hosts in Texas, and had a tremendous welcome in San Antonio, Houston, Fort Worth and Dallas . . . There was just joy, anticipation, wonderful throngs of people . . . And then in the space of a few seconds . . . it is unbelievable how an incident can happen that changed all of our lives, changed the course of history for many people in so many different ways you will never know.

> —Governor John Connally to CBS correspondent Martin Agronsky at Connally's
> Parkland Hospital bedside a few days after the assassination

People have to realize that that was a very innocent time, and the very idea that a president could be shot down in the streets of America was absolutely unthinkable.

> —Sixty-six-year-old Ventura County, California, resident

I think that for young people, of which I was one at the time, he spoke to the best of our instincts. He brought people together. He didn't drive them apart. His spirit, elan, and charisma were uniquely American. For those of us who remember, it is undying.

> —U.S. Senator Dianne Feinstein

It is more satisfying to believe that Kennedy died as a victim of a cause rather than at the hands of a deranged gunman.

> —Thomas Reed Turner, Abraham Lincoln scholar

In 1963, I lived in the small mountain village of Miraflores, Colombia, with several other Peace Corp volunteers. One of our compadres returned home that evening by horseback. He told of meeting a *campesino* [farmer] on the trail who called out to him "*Han matado a nuestro presidente*" (They have killed our president). He assumed that the president of Colombia had been killed.

> —C. J. Lemonds of Plano, Texas, in a letter to the editor of *Dallas Morning News*

I don't get why anyone wanted to shoot him. What did he do wrong?

> —Dallas high school student in 2003

The first thing about him was his driving intelligence. His mind was always on fire. His reading was prodigious, his memory almost total recall of facts and quotations. A friend of mine once crossed the Atlantic on a liner with the Kennedy family years ago. She remembered the day 12-year-old Jack was ill in his stateroom. There lay the thin, freckled little boy reading Churchill's early life, other books scattered about his bed. John Kennedy's intellectuality was perhaps the hallmark of his nature, even more than his youth . . . He was that rare and precious combination, the man of contemplation as well as the man of action. He had a sharp sense of history from his immense reading, and was acutely conscious of what his own place in history might be.

> —CBS commentator Eric Sevareid

For the millions who mourned Kennedy, the grief and disbelief that followed his killing left a mark that is indelible to this day. Many likened the event to the death of a family member.

—*Dallas Morning News*, November 17, 2003

At the time Kennedy was killed I was 8 years old and in the third grade of my school in a small, rural village in northern Honduras called La Veinte y Ocho. Everyone there considered Kennedy to be the president of the people, not just the president of the United States, because he was concerned about the poor. For instance, under a program called CARITAS, the Kennedy administration started providing milk for the first time ever for school children in Honduras and throughout Central America. The people of my village took Kennedy's death very hard and I clearly remember there was a lot of mourning and crying.

—Carlos Pena, now an American citizen living in Los Angeles

To show you the way that the minds of people were poisoned against the community [Dallas], I went to Detroit about two months after the assassination for a meeting with the automotive people. I got in a cab and I said, "Take me to the Detroit Athletic Club, please." The cab driver said, "You must be from the South." And I said, "I am." He said, "Where are you from?" I said, "Texas." He said, "Where in Texas?" I said, "Dallas." He stopped the cab and said, "Get out. I ain't taking you anywhere."

—James Chambers Jr., president of the *Dallas Times Herald*

He appealed to and elicited a sense of idealism instead of cynicism.

—Peace Corps volunteer Tina Martin

What John F. Kennedy left us with most of all was an attitude. To put it in the simplest terms, he looked ahead. He knew no more than anyone else what the future was going to be like, but he did know that that was where we ought to be looking.

—Bruce Catton, senior editor of the *American Heritage* magazine

His life was such—the radiance he shed—that if we live to be a hundred, we will remember how he graced this earth, and how he left it.

—Melville Bell Grosvenor, president and editor of National Geographic Society

He brought gaiety, glamour, and grace to the American political scene in a measure never known before. That lightsome tread, that debonair touch, that shock of chestnut hair, that beguiling grin, that shattering understatement—these are what we shall remember. He walked like a prince and he talked like a scholar. His humor brightened the life of the Republic. Shown his latest nephew in August, he commented, "He looks like a fine baby—we'll know more later . . ." When the ugliness of yesterday has been forgotten, we shall remember him, smiling.

—*Washington Evening Star* editorial

He was the most civilized President we have had since Jefferson, and his wife made the White House the most civilized house in America [alluding undoubtedly to the famous dinners the president and his wife hosted whose attendance was heavily sprinkled with cultural icons from the world of theater, art, literature, music, the sciences, and academe].

—Historian and author Arthur M. Schlesinger Jr.

Kennedy brought more than courage and energy to the White House. Like Sir Winston Churchill, he had a style of his own. And, like Churchill, he had that indefinable thing called grace. Churchill always had style but he developed grace late. Kennedy always had it, and showed it in his quiet humor, even at his own expense, and in his avoidance of political brawling. Grace helped him enormously in American foreign relations: his good nature, his warmth, his good will, and generally his good judgment. It helped him with American voters, too. Kennedy fitted into the presidency almost elegantly.

—James Marlowe, Associated Press

John Fitzgerald Kennedy was struck down in his prime, as he was still striding buoyantly through the halls of Camelot. He had served his thousand days as America's leader with wit and charm and courage and grace. That is the way most Americans choose to remember him and the brief, shining moments of his presidency.

—Bob Clark, Washington correspondent, ABC News

When Jack quoted something, it was usually classical, but I'm so ashamed of myself—all I keep thinking of is this line from a musical comedy. At night, before we'd go to sleep, Jack liked to play some records; and the song he loved most came at the very end of this record. The lines he loved to hear were: *Don't let it be forgot, that once there was a spot, for one brief shining moment that was known as Camelot.* There'll be great Presidents again, but there'll never be another Camelot again . . . it will never be that way again.

  —Jacqueline Kennedy, giving birth to the Camelot appellation as it applied to JFK's
      thousand days in office, in an interview with historian Theodore H. White for the
      December 6, 1963, *Life* magazine memorial edition on President Kennedy

I should have known that he was magic all along. I did know it—but I should have guessed it could not last. I should have known that it was asking too much to dream that I might have grown old with him and see our children grow up together.

—Jacqueline Kennedy

I've never covered anything like it [President Kennedy's assassination]. Not before, not since, and I don't expect to in this lifetime, nor any lifetime beyond, to infinity and beyond.

—Dan Rather, CBS News

Forever young in our collective minds, if John F. Kennedy, at forty-three the youngest man to be elected president in American history, were alive today, he would be ninety years old.

Abbreviations Used for Citations

Because of space constraints in this book, all of the source notes (citations) for the material in the main text are in the CD-ROM attached to the book.

AFIP, Armed Forces Institute of Pathology
ARRB, Assassination Records Review Board
ARRB MD, Assassination Records Review Board, Medical Deposition
ASAIC, assistant special agent-in-charge (Secret Service)
CD, Warren Commission document
CE, Warren Commission exhibit
DA, district attorney
DMA, Dallas Municipal Archives (formerly the Dallas Municipal Archives and
    Records Center)
DOJ, Department of Justice
DOJCD, Department of Justice, Criminal Division
DPD, Dallas Police Department
FOIA, Freedom of Information Act
H, Warren Commission hearings and exhibits (volumes 1–15 are testimony; volumes
    16–26 are exhibits)
HPSCI, House Permanent Subcommittee on Intelligence
HSCA, House Select Committee on Assassinations (12 volumes)
JCS, Joint Chiefs of Staff
KISS-SCOW, Kissinger-Scowcroft
LBJ, Lyndon Baines Johnson
NARA, National Archives and Records Administration
NAS-CBA, National Academy of Science's Committee on Ballistic Acoustics

NSA, National Security Agency
ONI, Office of Naval Intelligence
SA, special agent
SAC, special agent-in-charge (FBI)
SAIC, special agent-in-charge (Secret Service)
SSCIA, Senate Select Committee on the CIA
WC, Warren Commission
WCT, Warren Commission testimony
WR, Warren Report
Z, Zapruder film

Note: For further information about the format of the citations in this book, as well as a discussion about Warren Commission documents (CDs) and exhibits (CEs), the breakdown of the Warren Commission volumes, and the National Archives' assignment of their numbers to documents in the Archives, see endnote.

Acknowledgments

There are very few people who manage to complete a long and difficult journey without having a lot of help along the way, and I am no exception. But the list of names of those who have helped me in some way, if only to answer one question among the thousands I have asked since I first started work on this book in 1986, is unmanageably long for an acknowledgments section. So to those of you whom I do not mention in this section, and you know who you are, I say thank you so very much.

I can tell those who have not seriously studied the assassination of President John F. Kennedy that it is a bottomless pit. With every project that we take on in our lives, we intuitively know, without even giving it a thought, that if we work long and hard enough we will reach the bottom of the pile. But I found, as others also have, that there is no bottom to the pile in the Kennedy case. It is endless, and I say this not as a casual turn of phrase. At the very moment I am writing these words on my yellow pad, I'm aware that there are at least a hundred people in the United States alone who are dedicating their lives to this case, examining every word and paragraph in every document they can find (the millions of pages on the case at the National Archives alone would take a lifetime to read) to come up with some inconsistency, discrepancy, or hint of a conspiracy in the assassination. And when there are a hundred or more intelligent minds working almost full-time on something (and, in the Kennedy case, thousands of others working part-time), they can create a lot of mischief. For many years during the writing of this book, I've been responding to their findings. But alas, most things, good and bad, come to an end in life, and at least for me, this book will be the end of my immersion in the Kennedy case, as I must go on to other endeavors. For me to continue to address the mostly imaginary issues of this case would be to sacrifice the rest of my life inasmuch as the allegations are, and will continue to be, without end.

The following people have helped me the most in this terribly long journey I am now bringing to an end. I must start with my erudite editor—by my lights, the best in the business—Starling Lawrence. Star's limitless patience and unconditional support, always saying yes, never no, to whatever I needed, coupled with the sagacious advice and guidance he gave me through the many years, elevates him to a very special position on my list. No one has a better ear, if you will, for the right or wrong word in a sentence. And the times were very numerous when Star immediately caught that word, or told me I was going over the top on some point. And when someone as highly critical as I am (I'd find fault with a beautiful morning sunrise) accepts the advice of someone over 90 percent of the time, that person has to be special. And Star is. I've been so blessed to have him as my editor on this monumental odyssey of mine.

And I want to thank Mary Babcock, a hardworking and meticulous copy editor who helped me so very much in rounding my manuscript into its final form.

And then there is Rosemary Newton, who has been like my secretary for this book. Though Rosemary works freelance, typing this book has been her main job, occupying most of her working day for many years. (And in the last several years the times have been many when I have also asked Rosemary to search for something on the Internet for me.) I wrote and dictated at my home and then made literally hundreds of trips to Rosemary's home in the hills, picking up drafts of sections she had typed and dropping off new work for her. Rosemary has had a very tough job working with me on this book, yet she was always competent and extraordinarily reliable. In a way, she worked more closely with me than anyone else and became the person on whom I relied the most.

In addition to transcribing, from my audio dictation, the contents of 72 sixty-minute and 8 ninety-minute tapes, during which she had to listen to my less-than-dulcet voice and my speaking a mile a minute, Rosemary had to decipher and type at least a thousand (maybe many more) inserts of mine handwritten in pencil on yellow legal paper. Though resulting from much dictation, the book you have read is, much more than dictation, a book of inserts. By that I mean the first drafts of sections I wrote (e.g., Zapruder film, wounds to the president, CIA, Oliver Stone, etc.), which I then dictated, were not overly long. But they all increased far beyond their original size in the many subsequent drafts with the addition of yellow-page inserts (as well as inserts on the top, sides, bottom, and between the lines of the pages). If you could read some of these inserts you would have great compassion for Rosemary. While still within an insert on the handwritten yellow or typewritten white page, she would be very apt to get directions like this: "Now to Insert 36 [arbitrary number] on the seventh yellow page following page 67." Fine. But when she gets there she sees I've inserted a five-page handwritten endnote which has three footnote inserts in it, any one of which could itself contain an endnote or direct her to one or more other places. And then back to where she left off on the original insert perhaps an hour earlier. Often the pages and flow of the point I was trying to make got so garbled with inserts, deletions, arrows, et cetera, that it was impossible for me, the architect of the madness, to follow. Yet Rosemary never complained and more than once figured out my own labyrinth for me. As if the above were not enough, a great number of times I would write so small on a page (to squeeze in what I wanted in the only space available) that without a magnifying glass only the world's most myopic person could read what I had written. I don't have to tell Rosemary how very grateful I am to her. She deserves some type of medal.

This book, as you know, is itself broken down into two books, Book One being on *what happened*, the non-conspiracy part, and Book Two, on *what did not happen*, the conspiracy allegation part of this sweeping story. For Book One, I was fortunate to have two people who made noteworthy writing contributions. Even though he worked with me for a relatively short part of my long journey, no one helped me as much as Dale Myers, the Emmy Award–winning computer animation specialist and superb student of the assassination from Detroit, Michigan. Dale helped me in the writing of several sections of Book One, most notably on acoustics, "Four Days in November" (particularly in the Oswald interrogations), and all matters dealing with still photography. I am deeply grateful to Dale for lending his time, energy, and considerable expertise to this literary project.

The other person who played a writing role, though a smaller one, was Fred Haines, a soft-spoken and extremely well-read intellectual. Fred's fine hand has survived in several places of the "Lee Harvey Oswald" and "Four Days in November" sections. And it was Fred's suggestion, a great one, I feel, and one for which I am indebted to him, to have the latter section, and to a lesser extent the Oswald biography (as opposed to every other part of the book), written in a narrative style normally reserved for fiction, giving this part of this nonfiction book a literary quality it would not have had without it. Very few nonfiction books can be written in such a narrative style without resorting to invention, but the unprecedented richness of the historical record on every single incident in this case has permitted it. Thus, as opposed to "Rimma accompanied Oswald to the train station, where he departed for Minsk," this: "Always faithful Rimma saw him off at the station. He was depressed and wanted her to accompany him on the overnight train trip, but by now he understands that such things were not as simple in the Soviet Union as they might have been in the states. It was snowing as they said their good-byes. Both of them were crying."

I also want to thank Patrick Martin for all the work he put into the graphics in the photo section of the book to help make them what they are, and Douglas Martin, Fred Kuentz, and Michael McDermott for the similar contributions they made with their respective graphics.

Other individuals who stand out among the many who have helped me along the way include Dr. Michael Baden, the great pathologist who headed up the forensic pathology panel of the House Select Committee on Assassinations. With his many duties (he's still a pathologist, he lectures, serves as a consultant on important criminal cases, even appears as a regular on a television reality series) he still always got back to me when I called, and took the time to answer my many questions dealing with the medical aspects of the assassination. Though I did not rely on him quite as much, whenever I did call on Dr. Baden's friend and counterpart in this case, Dr. Cyril Wecht, the famed pathologist and coroner (up to January of 2006) of Allegheny County in Pittsburgh, he unfailingly found time in his very busy day, or in the evenings or on weekends, to answer my questions.

And then there were two people in Dallas, both of whom I could invariably count on to make me laugh in response to their dry, homespun Texas humor, but more importantly, to help me get to the bottom of several problem areas in the case I was exploring. I'm speaking of Bill Alexander, the former top prosecutor in the Dallas DA's office who was the lead prosecutor in the trial of Jack Ruby for killing Lee Harvey Oswald, and was scheduled to prosecute and put Oswald away if Ruby hadn't gotten to him first, and former Dallas County sheriff James C. Bowles, who probably was a member of Dallas law enforcement (fifty-three years) longer than anyone else in Dallas history. Alexander, in his mid-eighties, is still practicing law, and Bowles just retired in 2005. Though both were always busy—especially Bowles when he was still sheriff—they always found time in their day to answer my many questions. Together, the two of them were part of Dallas law enforcement for a great number of years and know it as well or better than any two other people alive. They graciously shared their accumulated knowledge and wisdom with me, and even helped me to the extent of putting me in contact with former members of Dallas law enforcement I had been unable to locate.

The main source for this book on the assassination is, of course, as it must be, the twenty-seven volumes of the Warren Commission, the granddaddy of all literature on the assassination. Not too far behind are the thirteen volumes of the HSCA. The next great source, among so many others, is the collection of countless documents on the assassination stored at the National Archives, the temple to America's past, in College Park, Maryland. There simply is no way that this book ended up being the book I think it is without the wonderful cooperation I received from Steven D. Tilley, up until April of 2004 (he has since been elevated) the chief person in charge of these documents (the JFK Assassination Records Collection) at the archives, and his staff, particularly his able assistant James R. Mathis. Tilley and his staff, more than once, went above and beyond the call of duty to locate obscure but important documents for me. My requests for specific documents, several of which alone contained over a hundred pages each (e.g., the testimony of a witness before the HSCA), were continuous. I kept wondering whether I'd soon be getting a letter from Steve or one of his assistants saying, "Vince, please. Enough is enough," but I never did. What I always got, never accompanied by a complaint, was a very large envelope in the mail containing everything I had requested that they could find. I of course am very grateful to Steve and his staff for all the tremendous assistance they gave me.

Although I am proud to say that I have done 99.9 percent of my own research for everything I wrote in this book (which is typical for me, not feeling comfortable relying on others to do research for me), I want to give very special thanks to four individuals, three of whom are avid students of the assassination, who have helped me in so many diverse ways. Having no official connection to the case like a Bill Alexander, Dr. Michael Baden, or Steven Tilley, just their friendship and their desire to help me, they were always there for me, without hesitation, whenever I needed them—whether it was to take a photo of an angle at Dealey Plaza I needed, secure someone's phone number for me, loan me one of their many books on the assassination, in some cases get a document for me they had ready access to, or whatever. They are Jack Duffy of Fort Worth (who has been with me on this book the longest), David Phinney of Los Angeles, Jim Agnew of Chicago, and Bill Drenas of Lowell, Massachusetts. I'll never forget the help these four gave me and will always be especially grateful to them.

And then there is Gary Mack, the curator of the Sixth Floor Museum at Dealey Plaza in Dallas since 1994 and a student of the assassination since 1975. Gary carries in his head an enormous wealth of knowledge about the case—much of it not the type one would find in the Warren Report or the report of the HSCA—which he is generous to share with whoever asks. If I called Gary once in the past years, I called him thirty times, always for his input on some arcane issue, and nearly always he was able to help me, for which I am, of course, very appreciative and indebted. I also want to thank Gary's research colleague, fellow Texan David Perry, a former insurance investigator from Grapevine, Texas, who was also very helpful to me on the many occasions I called him for assistance. Dave has made a specialty out of debunking (sometimes in league with Mack) people like Ricky White and Madeleine Brown who come out of the woodwork with their phony assassination-related tales. The story I like to tell about David is the time I found a reference to a nut in a conspiracy book, one I had never heard of before and about whom there was no reference in any other book on the assassination that I was aware of. I called Dave to find out what he knew about the kook and his allegation, but a small part of me was hoping that Dave, too, had never heard of him, enabling me to say to him, "I finally found a nut you've never heard of." But before I could even get the second syllable of the man's name out of my mouth, Dave started bombarding me with a blizzard of information on him. He knew all about this guy and his allegation and had already debunked the man's story.

Thanks are also in order to John H. Slate, the very diligent chief of the Dallas Municipal Archives who was invariably helpful to me whenever I needed his assistance, and the many members of the reference staff at the Dallas Public Library. I must not forget the staff of the Pasadena Public Library, where I spent literally hundreds of hours on their machines looking at microfilm and to a lesser extent microfiche. Since up to last year, when they got new machines, the machines were in terrible condition from overuse, and I'm not proficient with mechanical things, I would frequently need their help to fix or adjust a malfunctioning unit, and not once were the staff members anything but helpful and pleasant. And then there were the virtually hundreds of books the library staff got for me that were not at their library but at one of their branches, and the considerable number they got for me through their interlibrary loan service—most out of print and several very obscure—from libraries not only throughout California, but in other states, like one published in 1798, a copy of which they located for me at Brigham Young University in Provo, Utah.

I also want to express my appreciation, ironically, to three people who, unlike those already mentioned, had no conscious intent to help me but nevertheless did. I'm referring to the publishers of the three main conspiracy community publications, which I subscribed to and carefully read through the years. They are Jerry Rose's monthly *Decade* series, Jim DiEugenio's bimonthly *Probe*, and Walt Brown's *JFK / Deep Politics Quarterly*. (The *Decade* series, ending in the fourth decade after the assassination, and *Probe* are no longer in existence.) Although I usually didn't agree with the conclusions set forth in the articles in these publications, I found all three to be scholarly and informative, and here and there I picked up valuable points from Rose, DiEugenio, and Brown (as well as from the many private assassination researchers who contributed to their publications) that I hadn't come across in my own research and that had been overlooked by the Warren Commission and HSCA. Also, I learned from these publications the principal areas of interest in the mainstream conspiracy community, which I knew I would have to address in my book if it was going to be the book I wanted it to be.

Although I have done far, far more work on this book than any other book I've ever written, I can honestly say I enjoyed my labor, because apart from the terrible tragedy of Kennedy's death (other than that, Mrs. Lincoln, how was the play?), the case, as any long-time assassination researcher will tell you, is endlessly intriguing and fascinating. Only one section, Oswald's biography, was pure pain for me to write. One reason is that I am a nonfiction, true-crime writer normally working with trial transcripts, police and autopsy reports, witness statements, et cetera, and writing someone's biography is not my cup of tea. Secondly, I was dealing with a subject (Oswald) who moved no fewer than seventeen times in a sixteen-year period before joining the Marines, and had been in the military and in Russia. Nearly every day while writing this section I spent a good part of it with a magnifying glass looking at sketchy, faint, and often difficult-to-decipher grade school, military, and other records, and trying to reconcile conflicting memories of chronological events with documentary evidence that just didn't seem to fit. So it was an unpleasant task, but I had no choice but to "bite the bullet" and do it. I questioned when it would ever end, at one point envisioning a large, empty tub that I knew would one day be full of water, but only because of my putting one drop of water into it at a time. I took to telling people I was on a "lead diet" (biting the bullet) and working "eight days a week," because it was the only section of the book I wrote in which almost without exception, I worked on the case throughout the night in my dreams. I thought the "eight days a week" line was original and clever and so did those I used it on until one day someone reminded me, "Hey, that's a Beatles song," and it rang a distant bell to me. It was a great relief to finally finish this section and return to the luxury of working only seven days a week.

I've always been able to work seven days a week for months on end, sometimes, when required, a hundred or more hours a week, without manifesting any physical problems. In other words, I find work easy. When I was a prosecutor, trying a two- or three-month murder case before a jury wasn't fatiguing at all, although I knew some trial lawyers who, after a two- or three-day drunk driving case, would say they had to go to Palm Springs to recuperate. For whatever reason, I always seemed to be immune to the deprivations of hard work. But I had never encountered the Kennedy assassination before. Although I feel I can still get up and run around the block without any problem, for the first time in my life I feel (I'm not sure and certainly hope it's not true) that the research and writing of this book may have taken a toll on me. And one reason is that, as I've indicated, there simply is no end to the case, and more than once I wondered if I had bitten off more than I could chew.

What I can say with a lot more confidence is that without all the help I got from so many people along the way in this long journey of mine, not only wouldn't this book be the book it is, but I would have had a much more difficult time reaching the finish line to write these acknowledgments.

Bibliography

BOOKS

Adamson, Bruce Campbell. *Oswald's Closest Friend: The George de Mohrenschildt Story.* Santa Cruz, Calif.: Self-published, 2001.

Adelson, Alan. *The Ruby Oswald Affair.* Seattle: Romar Books, 1988.

Adler, Bill. *The Eloquent Jacqueline Kennedy Onassis: A Portrait in Her Own Words.* New York: William Morrow, 2004.

Agee, Philip. *Inside the Company: CIA Diary.* New York: Stonehill, 1975.

Aguilar, Luis. *Operation Zapata: The "Ultrasensitive" Report and Testimony of the Board of Inquiry on the Bay of Pigs.* Frederick, Md.: Aletheia Books, 1981.

Alsop, Stewart. *The Center: People and Power in Political Washington.* New York: Harper & Row, 1968.

Andrew, Christopher, and Vasili Mitrokhin. *The Sword and the Shield: The Mitrokhin Archive and the Secret History of the KGB.* New York: Basic Books, 1999.

Anslinger, Harry J., and Will Oursler. *The Murderers: The Story of the Narcotic Gangs.* New York: Farrar, Straus & Cudahy, 1961.

Anson, Robert Sam. *"They've Killed the President!" The Search for the Murderers of John F. Kennedy.* New York: Bantam Books, 1975.

Arévalo, Juan José. *The Shark and the Sardines.* New York: Lyle Stuart, 1961.

Armstrong, John. *Harvey and Lee: How the CIA Framed Oswald.* Arlington, Texas: Quasar, 2003.

Ashley, Clarence. *CIA Spy Master.* Gretna, La.: Pelican, 2004.

Associated Press. *The Torch Is Passed: The Associated Press Story of the Death of a President.* New York: Associated Press, 1963.

Austin, Anthony. *The President's War: The Story of the Tonkin Gulf Resolution and How the Nation Was Trapped in Vietnam.* Philadelphia: Lippincott, 1971.

Aynesworth, Hugh, with Stephen G. Michaud. *JFK: Breaking the News: A Reporter's Eyewitness Account of the Kennedy Assassination and Its Aftermath.* Richardson, Texas: International Focus Press, 2003.

Ayton, Mel. *The JFK Assassination: Dispelling the Myths.* Bognor Regis, West Sussex, United Kingdom: Woodfield Publishing, 2002.

Baden, Michael M., with Judith Adler Hennessee. *Unnatural Death: Confessions of a Medical Examiner.* New York: Ivy Books, 1989.

Baker, Judyth Vary. *Lee Harvey Oswald: The True Story of the Accused Assassin of President John F. Kennedy by His Lover.* Victoria, British Columbia, Canada: Trafford, 2006.

Bamford, James. *Body of Secrets: Anatomy of the Ultra-Secret National Security Agency.* New York: Doubleday, 2001.

Bane, Bernard M. *Is President John F. Kennedy Alive—and Well?* Boston: BMB Publishing, 1997.

Barron, John. *Operation Solo: The FBI's Man in the Kremlin.* Washington, D.C.: Regnery, 1996.

Belin, David W. *Final Disclosure: The Full Truth about the Assassination of President Kennedy.* New York: Scribner's, 1988.

Belin, David W. *November 22, 1963: You Are the Jury.* New York: Quadrangle, 1973.

Belli, Melvin M., with Maurice C. Carroll. *Dallas Justice: The Real Story of Jack Ruby and His Trial.* New York: McKay, 1964.

Belli, Melvin M., with Robert Blair Kaiser. *Melvin Belli: My Life on Trial; An Autobiography.* New York: Popular Library, 1977.

Benson, Michael. *Encyclopedia of the JFK Assassination.* New York: Facts on File, 2002.

Benson, Michael. *Who's Who in the JFK Assassination: An A-to-Z Encyclopedia.* Secaucus, N.J.: Carol Publishing Group, 1993.

Bergreen, Laurence. *Capone: The Man and the Era.* New York: Simon & Schuster, 1994.

Beschloss, Michael R. *The Crisis Years: Kennedy and Khrushchev, 1960–1963.* New York: Edward Burlingame, 1991.

Beschloss, Michael R. *Reaching for Glory: Lyndon Johnson's Secret White House Tapes, 1964–1965.* New York: Simon & Schuster, 2001.

Beschloss, Michael R., ed. *Taking Charge: The Johnson White House Tapes, 1963–1964.* New York: Simon & Schuster, 1997.

Bethell, Tom. *The Electric Windmill: An Inadvertent Autobiography.* Washington, D.C.: Regnery Gateway, 1988.

Bickman, Leonard, and Thomas Henchy. *Beyond the Laboratory: Field Research and Social Psychology.* New York: McGraw-Hill, 1972.

Biles, Joe G. *In History's Shadow: Lee Harvey Oswald, Kerry Thornley and the Garrison Investigation.* San Jose, Calif.: Writers Club Press, 2002.

Bird, Kai. *The Chairman: John J. McCloy and the Making of the American Establishment.* New York: Simon & Schuster, 1992.

Bishop, Jim. *The Day Kennedy Was Shot.* New York: Funk & Wagnalls, 1968.

Bissell, Richard. *Recollections of a Cold Warrior.* New Haven: Yale University Press, 1996.

Blair, Joan, and Clay Blair Jr. *The Search for JFK.* New York: Berkley, 1976.

Blakey, G. Robert, and Richard N. Billings. *Fatal Hour: The Assassination of President Kennedy by Organized Crime.* New York: Berkley Books, 1992.

Blakey, G. Robert, and Richard N. Billings. *The Plot to Kill the President.* New York: Times Books, 1981.

Blinkov, Samuil, and Il'ya I. Glezer. *The Human Brain in Figures and Tables.* Translated from Russian by Basil Haigh. New York: Basic Books, 1968.

Block, Alan A. *Perspective on Organizing Crime: Essays in Opposition.* Dordrecht, The Netherlands: Kluwer Academic, 1991.

Block, Lawrence, ed. *Gangsters, Swindlers, Killers, and Thieves: The Lives and Crimes of Fifty American Villains.* New York: Oxford University Press, 2004.

Blow, Richard. *American Son: A Portrait of John F. Kennedy Jr.* New York: Henry Holt, 2002.

Bonavolonta, Jules, and Brian Duffy. *The Good Guys: How We Turned the FBI 'round —and Finally Broke the Mob.* New York: Simon & Schuster, 1996.

Bonner, Judy Whitson. *Investigation of a Homicide: The Murder of John F. Kennedy.* Anderson, S.C.: Droke House, 1969.

Brandt, Charles. *"I Heard You Paint Houses": Frank "the Irishman" Sheeran and the Inside Story of the Mafia, the Teamsters, and the Last Ride of Jimmy Hoffa.* Hanover, N.H.: Steerforth Press, 2004.

Brener, Milton. *The Garrison Case: A Study in the Abuse of Power.* New York: Clarkson N. Potter, 1969.

Brennan, Howard L., with J. Edward Cherryholmes. *Eyewitness to History: The Kennedy Assassination as Seen by Howard L. Brennan.* Waco, Texas: Texian Press, 1987.

Breuer, William B. *Vendetta! Fidel Castro and the Kennedy Brothers.* New York: Wiley, 1997.

Brown, Anthony Cave. *Treason in the Blood.* Boston: Houghton Mifflin, 1994.

Brown, Madeleine. *Texas in the Morning: The Love Story of Madeleine Brown and President Lyndon Baines Johnson.* Baltimore: Conservatory Press, 1997.

Brown, Thomas. *JFK: History of an Image.* Bloomington: Indiana University Press, 1988.

Brown, Walt. *The Guns of Texas Are Upon Us.* Williamsport, Penn.: Last Hurrah Press, 2005.

Brown, Walt. *The People v. Lee Harvey Oswald.* New York: Carroll & Graf, 1992.

Brown, Walt. *Treachery in Dallas.* New York: Carroll & Graf, 1995.

Brown, Walt. *The Warren Omission: A Micro Study of the Methods and Failures of the Warren Commission.* Wilmington, Del.: Delmax, 1996.

Buchanan, Thomas G. *Who Killed Kennedy?* New York: G. P. Putnam, 1964.

Bugliosi, Vincent, with Curt Gentry. *Helter Skelter: The True Story of the Manson Murders.* New York: W. W. Norton, 1994.

Burleigh, Nina. *A Very Private Woman: The Life and Unsolved Murder of Presidential Mistress Mary Meyer.* New York: Bantam, 1998.

Butwell, Richard. *Southeast Asia: A Political Introduction.* New York: Praeger, 1975.

Califano, Joseph A., Jr. *Inside: A Public and Private Life.* New York: Public Affairs, 2004.

Callahan, Bob. *Who Shot JFK? A Guide to the Major Conspiracy Theories.* New York: Simon & Schuster, 1993.

Campbell, Rodney. *The Luciano Project: The Secret Wartime Collaboration of the Mafia and the U.S. Navy.* New York: McGraw-Hill, 1977.

Canal, John A. *Silencing the Lone Assassin.* St. Paul, Minn.: Paragon House, 2005.

Caro, Robert A. *The Path to Power.* New York: Alfred A. Knopf, 1982.

Carter, Lauren. *The Most Evil Mobsters in History.* New York: Barnes & Noble Books, 2004.

Castañeda, Jorge G. *Compañero: The Life and Death of Che Guevara.* New York: Vintage, 1998.

Castro, Fidel. *Che: A Memoir.* New York: Ocean Press, 1994.

Chandler, David Leon. *Brothers in Blood: The Rise of the Criminal Brotherhoods.* New York: Dutton, 1975.

Chang, Laurence, and Peter Kornbluh, eds. *The Cuban Missile Crisis, 1962: A National Security Archive Documents Reader.* New York: New Press, 1992.

Chapman, Gil, and Ann Chapman. *Was Oswald Alone?* San Diego: Publishers Export, 1967.

Cirules, Enrique. *The Mafia in Havana: A Caribbean Mob Story.* Melbourne, Australia: Ocean Press, 2004.

Claflin, Edward B., ed. *JFK Wants to Know: Memos from the President's Office, 1961–1963.* New York: Morrow, 1991.

Clarke, James W. *American Assassins: The Darker Side of Politics.* Princeton, N.J.: Princeton University Press, 1990.

Clemente, Carmine D. *Anatomy: A Regional Atlas of the Human Body.* 3rd ed. Baltimore: Urban & Schwarzenberg, 1987.

Colby, William, and Peter Forbath. *Honorable Men: My Life in the CIA.* New York: Simon & Schuster, 1978.

Collier, Peter, and David Horowitz. *The Kennedys: An American Drama.* New York: Summit Books, 1984.

Colson, Charles W. *Loving God*. Grand Rapids, Mich.: Zondervan, 1983.

Committee to Investigate Assassinations, under the direction of Bernard Fensterwald Jr. and compiled by Michael Ewing. *Assassination of JFK by Coincidence or Conspiracy?* New York: Zebra Books, 1977.

Connally, Nellie, and Mickey Herskowitz. *From Love Field: Our Final Hours with President John F. Kennedy*. New York: Rugged Land, 2003.

Cook, Fred J. *The FBI Nobody Knows*. New York: Macmillan, 1964.

Cooper, Milton William. *Behold a Pale Horse*. Sedona, Ariz.: Light Technology, 1991.

Cormack, A. J. R. *The World Encyclopedia of Modern Guns*. London: Octopus Books, 1979.

Corry, John. *The Manchester Affair*. New York: Putnam, 1967.

Corson, William R. *The Armies of Ignorance: The Rise of the American Intelligence Empire*. New York: Dial Press, 1977.

Corson, William R., and Robert T. Crowley. *The New KGB: Engine of Soviet Power*. New York: Morrow, 1985.

Craig, John R., and Philip A. Rogers. *The Man on the Grassy Knoll*. New York: Avon, 1992.

Crenshaw, Charles A., with Jens Hansen and J. Gary Shaw. *JFK: Conspiracy of Silence*. New York: Signet, 1992.

Crenshaw, Charles A., with J. Gary Shaw, Gary Aguilar, and Brad Kizzia. *Trauma Room One: The JFK Medical Coverup Exposed*. New York: Paraview Press, 2001.

Curry, Jesse E. *Retired Dallas Police Chief Jesse Curry Reveals His Personal JFK Assassination File*. Dallas: Self-published, printed by American Poster and Printing Company, 1969.

Cutler, Robert B. *The Umbrella Man*. Beverly Farms, Mass.: Self-published, 1975.

Dallek, Robert. *Flawed Giant: Lyndon Johnson and His Times, 1961–1973*. New York: Oxford University Press, 1998.

Dallek, Robert. *An Unfinished Life: John F. Kennedy, 1917–1963*. Boston: Little, Brown, 2003.

Dankbaar, Wim, ed. *Files on JFK: Interviews with Confessed Assassin James E. Files and More New Evidence of the Conspiracy That Killed JFK*. The Netherlands: Self-published, 2005.

Davis, John H. *The Kennedys: Dynasty and Disaster, 1848–1983*. New York: McGraw-Hill, 1984.

Davis, John H. *Mafia Kingfish: Carlos Marcello and the Assassination of John F. Kennedy*. New York: McGraw-Hill, 1989.

Davison, Jean. *Oswald's Game*. New York: W. W. Norton, 1983.

Davy, William. *Let Justice Be Done: New Light on the Jim Garrison Investigation*. Reston, Va.: Jordan, 1999.

DeLoach, Cartha. *Hoover's FBI: The Inside Story by Hoover's Trusted Lieutenant*. Washington, D.C.: Regnery, 1995.

Demaris, Ovid. *Director: An Oral Biography of J. Edgar Hoover*. New York: Harper's Magazine Press, 1975.

Demaris, Ovid. *J. Edgar Hoover, as They Knew Him*. New York: Carroll & Graf, 1975.

Demaris, Ovid. *The Last Mafioso: The Treacherous World of Jimmy Fratianno*. New York: Times Books, 1981.

Dempsey, John Mark, ed. *The Jack Ruby Trial Revisited: The Diary of Jury Foreman Max Causey*. Denton: University of North Texas Press, 2000.

Denton, Sally, and Roger Morris. *The Money and the Power: The Making of Las Vegas and Its Hold on America, 1947–2000*. New York: Alfred A. Knopf, 2001.

De Stefano, George. *An Offer We Can't Refuse: The Mafia in the Mind of America*. New York: Faber & Faber, 2006.

DiEugenio, James. *Destiny Betrayed: JFK, Cuba, and the Garrison Case*. New York: Sheridan Square Press, 1992.

DiEugenio, James, and Lisa Pease, eds. *The Assassinations: Probe Magazine on JFK, RFK, MLK and Malcolm X*. Los Angeles: Feral House, 2003.

Donovan, James. *Strangers on a Bridge: The Case of Colonel Abel*. New York: Atheneum House, 1964.

Douglas, Gregory. *Regicide: The Official Assassination of John F. Kennedy*. Huntsville, Ala.: Monte Sano Media, 2002.

Duffy, James R. *Who Killed JFK? The Kennedy Assassination Cover-Up, the Web*. New York: Shapolsky Publishers, 1988.

Dulles, Allen. *The Craft of Intelligence*. New York: Harper & Row, 1963.

Eddowes, Michael. *The Oswald File*. New York: Clarkson N. Potter, 1977.

Eisenberg, Dennis, Uri Dan, and Eli Landau. *Meyer Lansky: Mogul of the Mob*. New York: Paddington Press, 1979.

Eisenhower, Dwight D. *The White House Years*. Vol. 2: *Waging Peace, 1956–1961*. Garden City, N.Y.: Doubleday, 1965.

Epstein, Edward Jay. *The Assassination Chronicles*. New York: Carroll & Graf, 1992.

Epstein, Edward Jay. *Inquest: The Warren Commission and the Establishment of Truth*. New York: Viking, 1966.

Epstein, Edward Jay. *Legend: The Secret World of Lee Harvey Oswald*. New York: Reader's Digest Press, 1978.

Escalante, Fabian. *The Cuba Project: CIA Covert Operations 1959–1962*. Melbourne, Australia: Ocean Press, 2004.

Estes, Billie Sol. *Billie Sol Estes: A Texas Legend*. Granbury, Texas: BS Productions, 2005.

Evans, Monte. *The Rather Narrative: Is Dan Rather the JFK Conspiracy's San Andreas Fault?* Barrington, R.I.: Barbara Books, 1990.

Evica, George Michael. *And We Are All Mortal: New Evidence and Analysis in the John F. Kennedy Assassination*. West Hartford, Conn.: Self-published, printed by the University of Hartford, 1978.

Exner, Judith, as told to Ovid Demaris. *My Story*. New York: Grove Press, 1977.

Fairclough, Adam. *Race and Democracy: The Civil Rights Struggle in Louisiana, 1915–1972*. Athens: University of Georgia Press, 1995.

Feldman, Harold. *Fifty-one Witnesses: The Grassy Knoll*. San Francisco: Idlewild, 1965.

Fenster, Mark. *Conspiracy Theories: Secrecy and Power in American Culture*. Minneapolis: University of Minnesota Press, 1999.

Fetzer, James H., ed. *Assassination Science: Experts Speak Out on the Death of JFK*. Chicago: Catfeet Press, 1998.

Fetzer, James H., ed. *The Great Zapruder Film Hoax: Deceit and Deception in the Death of JFK*. Chicago: Catfeet Press, 2003.

Fetzer, James H., ed. *Murder in Dealey Plaza: What We Know Now That We Didn't Know Then about the Death of JFK*. Chicago: Catfeet Press, 2000.

Fite, Gilbert C. *Richard B. Russell, Jr., Senator from Georgia*. Chapel Hill: University of North Carolina Press, 1991.

Flammonde, Paris. *The Kennedy Conspiracy: An Uncommissioned Report on the Jim Garrison Investigation*. New York: Meredith Press, 1969.

Fonzi, Gaeton. *The Last Investigation*. New York: Thunder's Mouth Press, 1993.

Ford, Gerald R., and John R. Stiles. *Portrait of the Assassin*. New York: Simon & Schuster, 1965.

Fox, Sylvan. *The Unanswered Questions about President Kennedy's Assassination*. New York: Award Books, 1965.

Franqui, Carlos. *Family Portrait with Fidel: A Memoir*. New York: Random House, 1984.

Freed, Donald, with Fred Simon Landis. *Death in Washington: The Murder of Orlando Letelier*. Westport, Conn.: Lawrence Hill, 1980.

Freedman, Lawrence. *Kennedy's Wars: Berlin, Cuba, Laos, and Vietnam*. New York: Oxford University Press, 2000.

Fritz, Will. *The Kennedy Mutiny*. Akron, Ohio: Self-published, 2002.

Fuhrman, Mark. *A Simple Act of Murder: November 22, 1963*. New York: William Morrow, 2006.

Furiati, Claudia. *ZR Rifle: The Plot to Kill Kennedy and Castro; Cuba Opens Secret Files*. Melbourne, Australia: Ocean Press, 1994.

Fursenko, Aleksandr, and Timothy Naftali. *"One Hell of a Gamble": The Secret History of the Cuban Missile Crisis.* New York: W. W. Norton, 1997.

Galanor, Stewart. *Cover-Up.* New York: Kestrel Books, 1998.

Gambino, Richard. *Vendetta: The True Story of the Largest Lynching in U.S. History.* Toronto: Guernica, 2000.

Garrison, Jim. *A Heritage of Stone.* New York: Berkley, 1972.

Garrison, Jim. *On the Trail of the Assassins: My Investigation and Prosecution of the Murder of President Kennedy.* New York: Warner Books, 1988.

Gates, Gary Paul. *Air Time: The Inside Story of CBS News.* New York: Harper & Row, 1978.

Gedney, John Forrester. *The Making of a Bum: From Notoriety to Sobriety.* Melbourne, Fla.: Gami Publishing, 2001.

Gellman, Barton. *Contending with Kennan: Toward a Philosophy of American Power.* New York: Praeger, 1984.

Gentry, Curt. *J. Edgar Hoover: The Man and the Secrets.* New York: W. W. Norton, 1991.

Gertz, Elmer. *Moment of Madness: The People vs. Jack Ruby.* Chicago: Follett, 1968.

Giancana, Antoinette, John R. Hughes, and Thomas H. Jobe. *JFK and Sam: The Connection between the Giancana and Kennedy Assassinations.* Nashville: Cumberland House, 2005.

Giancana, Sam, and Chuck Giancana. *Double Cross: The Explosive, Inside Story of the Mobster Who Controlled America.* New York: Warner Books, 1992.

Gibson, Donald. *The Kennedy Assassination Cover-Up.* New York: Nova Science Publishers, 2005.

Goldberg, Robert Alan. *Enemies Within: The Culture of Conspiracy in Modern America.* New Haven: Yale University Press, 2001.

Goldman, Albert. *Ladies and Gentlemen—Lenny Bruce!!* New York: Random House, 1974.

Goldsmith, John A. *Colleagues: Richard B. Russell and His Apprentice, Lyndon B. Johnson.* Macon, Ga.: Mercer University Press, 1998.

Gosch, Martin A., and Richard Hammer. *The Last Testament of Lucky Luciano.* New York: Dell, 1976.

Greene, A. C. *Chance Encounters: True Stories of Unforeseen Meetings, with Unanticipated Results.* Albany, Texas: Bright Sky Press, 2002.

Griffin, Joe, with Don DeNevi. *Mob Nemesis: How the FBI Crippled Organized Crime.* Amherst, N.Y.: Prometheus Books, 2002.

Groden, Robert J. *The Killing of a President: The Complete Photographic Record of the JFK Assassination, the Conspiracy and the Cover-Up.* New York: Viking Studio Books, 1993.

Groden, Robert J. *The Search for Lee Harvey Oswald: The Comprehensive Photographic Record.* New York: Penguin Studio Books, 1995.

Groden, Robert J., and Livingstone, Harrison Edward. *High Treason: The Assassination of President John F. Kennedy; What Really Happened.* New York: Conservatory Press, 1989.

Grolier's Encyclopedia. Danbury, Conn.: Grolier, 1993.

Grose, Peter. *Gentleman Spy: The Life of Allen Dulles.* Amherst: University of Massachusetts Press, 1996.

Gun, Nerin E. *Red Roses from Texas.* London: Frederick Muller, 1964.

Guth, DeLloyd J., and David Wrone. *The Assassination of John F. Kennedy: A Comprehensive and Legal Bibliography, 1963–1979.* Westport, Conn.: Greenwood Press, 1980.

Haig, Alexander M., Jr., with Charles McCarry. *Inner Circles: How America Changed the World; A Memoir.* New York: Warner Books, 1992.

Haldeman, H. R., with Joseph DiMona. *The Ends of Power.* New York: Times Books, 1978.

Haley, J. Evetts. *A Texan Looks at Lyndon: A Study in Illegitimate Power.* Canyon, Texas: Palo Duro Press, 1964.

Hampton, Wilborn. *Kennedy Assassinated! The World Mourns; A Reporter's Story.* Cambridge, Mass.: Candlewick Press, 1997.

Hanson, William H. *The Shooting of John F. Kennedy: One Assassin, Three Shots, Three Hits—No Misses.* San Antonio, Texas: Naylor, 1969.

Hartogs, Renatus, and Lucy Freeman. *The Two Assassins.* New York: Thomas Y. Crowell, 1965.

Hatcher, Julian S., Frank Jury, and Jac Weller. *Firearms Investigation, Identification, and Evidence.* Harrisburg, Penn.: Stackpole, 1957.

Heiner, Kent. *Without Smoking Gun: Was the Death of Lt. Cmdr. William B. Pitzer Part of the JFK Assassination Cover-Up Conspiracy?* Walterville, Ore.: TrineDay, 2004.

Helms, Richard, with William Hood. *A Look over My Shoulder: A Life in the Central Intelligence Agency.* New York: Random House, 2003.

Hemingway, Mary Welsh. *How It Was.* New York: Alfred A. Knopf, 1976.

Hepburn, James. *Farewell America: The Plot to Kill JFK.* Roseville, Calif.: Penmarin Books, 2002.

Hersh, Seymour M. *The Dark Side of Camelot.* Boston: Little, Brown, 1997.

Heymann, C. David. *A Woman Named Jackie.* New York: Carol Communications, 1989.

Higgins, Trumbull. *The Perfect Failure: Kennedy, Eisenhower, and the CIA at the Bay of Pigs.* New York: W. W. Norton, 1987.

Highlights: The History of Parkland Hospital. Dallas: Parkland Memorial Hospital, March 2000.

Hinckle, Warren, and William W. Turner. *Deadly Secrets: The CIA-Mafia War against Castro and the Assassination of J.F.K.* New York: Thunder's Mouth Press, 1992.

Hlavach, Laura, and Darwin Payne, eds. *Reporting the Kennedy Assassination: Journalists Who Were There Recall Their Experiences.* Dallas: Three Forks Press, 1996.

Hoensch, Jörg K. *A History of Modern Hungary, 1867–1986.* London: Longman Group, 1988.

Hofstadter, Richard. *The Paranoid Style in American Politics and Other Essays.* New York: Alfred A. Knopf, 1965.

Holland, Max, ed. *The Kennedy Assassination Tapes.* New York: Alfred A. Knopf, 2004.

Holloway, Diane, ed. *Dallas and the Jack Ruby Trial: Memoir of Judge Joe B. Brown, Sr.* San Jose, Calif.: Author's Choice Press, 2001.

Holloway, Diane, ed. *The Mind of Oswald: Accused Assassin of John F. Kennedy.* Victoria, British Columbia, Canada: Trafford, 2000.

Hoover, J. Edgar. *Persons in Hiding.* Boston: Little, Brown, 1938.

Hope, Bob, with Melville Shavelson. *Don't Shoot, It's Only Me: Bob Hope's Comedy History of the United States.* New York: Putnam, 1990.

Hosty, James P., Jr., with Thomas Hosty. *Assignment: Oswald.* New York: Arcade Publishing, 1996.

Houts, Marshall. *Where Death Delights: The Story of Dr. Milton Helpern and Forensic Medicine.* New York: Coward-McCann, 1967.

Huffaker, Bob, Bill Mercer, George Phenix, and Wes Wise. *When the News Went Live: Dallas 1963.* Lanham, Md.: Taylor Trade Publishing, 2004.

Hughes, J. W. *Square Peg for a Round Hole.* Concord, Calif.: Self-published, 1993.

Hunt, Howard. *Give Us This Day.* New Rochelle, N.Y.: Arlington House, 1973.

Hunter, Diane, and Alice Anderson. *Jack Ruby's Girls.* Atlanta: Hallux, 1970.

Hunt-Jones, Conover. *JFK: For a New Generation.* Dallas: The Sixth Floor Museum and Southern Methodist University Press, 1996.

Hurt, Harry, III. *Texas Rich: The Hunt Dynasty, from the Early Oil Days through the Silver Crash.* New York: W. W. Norton, 1981.

Hurt, Henry. *Reasonable Doubt: An Investigation into the Assassination of John F. Kennedy.* New York: Holt, Rinehart & Winston, 1985.

Israel, Lee. *A Biography of Dorothy Kilgallen.* New York: Delacorte, 1979.

James, Rosemary, and Jack Wardlaw. *Plot or Politics: The Garrison Case and Its Cost.* New Orleans: Pelican Publishing, 1967.

Jennings, Dean. *We Only Kill Each Other: The True Story of Mobster Bugsy Siegel, the Man Who Invented Las Vegas.* New York: Pocket, 1967.

Joesten, Joachim. *The Dark Side of Lyndon Baines Johnson*. London: Dawnay, 1968.

Joesten, Joachim. *Oswald: Assassin or Fall Guy?* New York: Marzani & Munsell, 1964.

Johnson, Haynes, with Manuel Artime and others. *The Bay of Pigs: The Leaders' Story of Brigade 2506*. New York: W. W. Norton, 1964.

Johnson, Sam Houston. *My Brother Lyndon*. New York: Cowles, 1969.

Jones, Penn, Jr. *Forgive My Grief: A Critical Review of the Warren Commission Report on the Assassination of President John F. Kennedy*. Vol. 1. Midlothian, Texas: Midlothian Mirror, 1966.

Jones, Penn, Jr. *Forgive My Grief: A Critical Review of the Warren Commission Report on the Assassination of President John F. Kennedy*. Vol. 2. Midlothian, Texas: Midlothian Mirror, 1967.

Jones, Penn, Jr. *Forgive My Grief: A Critical Review of the Warren Commission Report on the Assassination of President John F. Kennedy*. Vol. 3. Midlothian, Texas: Midlothian Mirror, 1969.

Kantor, Seth. *The Ruby Cover-Up*. New York: Kensington Publishing, 1978.

Kantor, Seth. *Who Was Jack Ruby?* New York: Everest House, 1978.

Kaplan, John, and Jon R. Waltz. *The Trial of Jack Ruby*. New York: Macmillan, 1965.

Karnow, Stanley. *Vietnam: A History*. New York: Viking, 1983.

Kearns, Doris. *Lyndon Johnson and the American Dream*. New York: Harper & Row, 1976.

Kelley, Kitty. *His Way: The Unauthorized Biography of Frank Sinatra*. New York: Bantam Books, 1986.

Kennan, George. *Memoirs, 1925–1950*. Boston: Atlantic Monthly Press, 1967.

Kennedy, John F. *The Strategy of Peace*. Edited by Allan Nevins. New York: Harper & Brothers, 1960.

Kennedy, Robert F. *The Enemy Within*. New York: Harper & Brothers, 1960.

Kennedy, Robert F. *Thirteen Days*. New York: W. W. Norton, 1969.

Kirkpatrick, Lyman B., Jr. *The Real CIA*. New York: Macmillan, 1968.

Kirkwood, James. *American Grotesque: An Account of the Clay Shaw–Jim Garrison Kennedy Assassination Trial in the City of New Orleans*. New York: Simon & Schuster, 1970.

Knight, Peter Z., ed. *Conspiracy Theories in American History: An Encyclopedia*. Santa Barbara, Calif.: ABC-CLIO, 2003.

Koepke, Jim. *Chasing Ghosts: The Remarkable Story of One Man's Investigation into the Assassination of President John F. Kennedy*. Baltimore: PublishAmerica, 2004.

Kornbluh, Peter, ed. *Bay of Pigs Declassified: The Secret CIA Report on the Invasion of Cuba*. New York: New Press, 1998.

Kornbluh, Peter, ed. *The Pinochet File: A Declassified Dossier on Atrocity and Accountability*. New York: New Press, 2003.

Kroth, Jerome. *Conspiracy in Camelot: The Complete History of the Assassination of John Fitzgerald Kennedy*. New York: Algora, 2003.

Kuntz, Tom, and Phil Kuntz, eds. *The Sinatra Files: The Secret FBI Dossier*. New York: Three Rivers Press, 2000.

Kurtz, Michael L. *Crime of the Century: The Kennedy Assassination from a Historian's Perspective*. Knoxville: University of Tennessee Press, 1982.

Lacey, Robert. *Little Man: Meyer Lansky and the Gangster Life*. Boston: Little, Brown, 1991.

La Fontaine, Ray, and Mary La Fontaine. *Oswald Talked: The New Evidence in the JFK Assassination*. Gretna, La.: Pelican Publishing, 1996.

Lambert, Patricia. *False Witness: The Real Story of Jim Garrison's Investigation and Oliver Stone's Film JFK*. New York: M. Evans, 1998.

Landis, C., and W. Hunt. *The Startle Reaction*. New York: Holt, Rinehart, 1939.

Lane, Mark. *Plausible Denial: Was the CIA Involved in the Assassination of JFK?* New York: Thunder's Mouth Press, 1991.

Lane, Mark. *Rush to Judgment*. New York: Dell, 1966.

Lane, Mark. *Rush to Judgment*. New York: Dell, 1992.

Lattimer, John K. *Kennedy and Lincoln: Medical and Ballistic Comparisons of Their Assassinations*. New York: Harcourt Brace Jovanovich, 1980.

Law, William Matson, with Allan Eaglesham. *In the Eye of History: Disclosures in the JFK Assassination Medical Evidence*. Southlake, Texas: JFK Lancer Publications, 2005.

Lawrence, Lincoln. *Were We Controlled?* New Hyde Park, N.Y.: University Books, 1967.

Lazo, Mario. *Dagger in the Heart: American Policy Failures in Cuba*. New York: Funk & Wagnalls, 1968.

Leaming, Barbara. *Jack Kennedy: The Education of a Statesman*. New York: W. W. Norton, 2006.

Leonard, Jerry. *The Perfect Assassin: Lee Harvey Oswald, the CIA and Mind Control*. Bloomington, Ind.: 1st Books Library, 2002.

Lewis, Richard Warren. *The Scavengers and Critics of the Warren Report: The Endless Paradox. Based on an Investigation by Lawrence Schiller*. New York: Delacorte Press, 1967.

Lifton, David S. *Best Evidence: Disguise and Deception in the Assassination of John F. Kennedy*. New York: Macmillan, 1980.

Livingstone, Harrison Edward. *High Treason 2: The Great Cover-Up; The Assassination of President John F. Kennedy*. New York: Carroll & Graf, 1992.

Livingstone, Harrison Edward. *Killing Kennedy and the Hoax of the Century*. New York: Carroll & Graf, 1995.

Livingstone, Harrison Edward. *Killing the Truth: Deceit and Deception in the JFK Case*. New York: Carroll & Graf, 1993.

Livingstone, Harrison Edward. *The Radical Right and the Murder of John F. Kennedy: Stunning Evidence in the Assassination of the President*. Baltimore: Conservatory Press, 2004.

Loftus, Elizabeth F. *Eyewitness Testimony*. Cambridge, Mass.: Harvard University Press, 1996.

Loken, John. *Oswald's Trigger Films: The Manchurian Candidate, We Were Strangers, Suddenly*. Ann Arbor, Mich.: Falcon Books, 2000.

Lorenz, Marita, with Ted Schwarz. *Marita: One Woman's Extraordinary Tale of Love and Espionage from Castro to Kennedy*. New York: Thunder's Mouth Press, 1993.

Lubin, David M. *Shooting Kennedy: JFK and the Culture of Images*. Berkeley: University of California Press, 2003.

Ludwig, Jurgen. *Current Methods of Autopsy Practice*. Philadelphia: W. B. Saunders, 1979.

Luttwak, Edward. *Coup d'Etat: A Practical Handbook*. New York: Alfred A. Knopf, 1969.

Maas, Peter. *The Valachi Papers: The First Inside Account of Life in the Cosa Nostra*. New York: G. P. Putnam's Sons, 1968.

MacNeil, Robert. *The Right Place at the Right Time*. Boston: Little, Brown, 1982.

Mahoney, Richard D. *Sons and Brothers: The Days of Jack and Bobby Kennedy*. New York: Arcade, 1999.

Mailer, Norman. *Oswald's Tale: An American Mystery*. New York: Random House, 1995.

Mallon, Thomas. *Mrs. Paine's Garage and the Murder of John F. Kennedy*. New York: Pantheon, 2002.

Manchester, William. *The Death of a President*. New York: Harper & Row, 1967.

Mangold, Tom. *Cold Warrior: James Jesus Angleton: The CIA's Master Spy Hunter*. New York: Simon & Schuster, 1991.

Mankiewicz, Frank, and Kirby Jones. *With Fidel: A Portrait of Castro and Cuba*. Chicago: Playboy Press, 1975.

Mann, Robert. *Legacy to Power: Senator Russell Long of Louisiana*. New York: Paragon House, 1992.

Marchetti, Victor, and John D. Marks. *The CIA and the Cult of Intelligence*. New York: Alfred A. Knopf, 1974.

Marcus, Raymond. *The Bastard Bullet: A Search for Legitimacy for Commission Exhibit 399*. Los Angeles: Self-published, 1966.

Marks, John. *The Search for the "Manchurian Candidate": The CIA and Mind Control*. New York: Times Books, 1979.

Marrs, Jim. *Alien Agenda: Investigating the Extraterrestrial Presence among Us*. New York: HarperCollins, 1997.

Marrs, Jim. *Crossfire: The Plot That Killed Kennedy.* New York: Carroll & Graf, 1989.

Martin, David C. *Wilderness of Mirrors: How the Byzantine Intrigues of the Secret War between the CIA and the KGB Seduced and Devoured Key Agents James Jesus Angleton and William King Harvey.* New York: Harper & Row, 1980.

Matthews, James P. *Four Dark Days in History.* Los Angeles: Special Publications, 1963.

May, Ernest R., and Philip D. Zelikow, eds. *The Kennedy Tapes: Inside the White House during the Cuban Missile Crisis.* Cambridge, Mass.: Harvard University Press, 1997.

McCarthy, Dennis V. N., with Philip W. Smith. *Protecting the President: The Inside Story of a Secret Service Agent.* New York: William Morrow, 1985.

McClellan, Barr. *Blood, Money and Power: How LBJ Killed JFK.* New York: Hanover House, 2003.

McClellan, John L. *Crime without Punishment.* New York: Duell, Sloan & Pearce, 1962.

McConnell, Brian. *The History of Assassination.* Nashville: Aurora Publishers, 1970.

McCoy, Alfred W. *The Politics of Heroin in Southeast Asia: CIA Complicity in the Global Drug Trade.* New York: Harper & Row, 1972.

McDonald, Hugh C. *Appointment in Dallas: The Final Solution to the Assassination of JFK.* New York: Zebra Books, 1992.

McKeever, Porter. *Adlai Stevenson: His Life and Legacy.* New York: William Morrow, 1989.

McKnight, Gerald. *Breach of Trust: How the Warren Commission Failed the Nation and Why.* Lawrence: University of Kansas Press, 2005.

McMillan, Priscilla Johnson. *Marina and Lee.* New York: Harper & Row, 1977.

McNamara, Robert S., with Brian VanDeMark. *In Retrospect: The Tragedy and Lessons of Vietnam.* New York: Times Books, 1995.

Meagher, Sylvia. *Accessories after the Fact: The Warren Commission, the Authorities, and the Report.* New York: Vintage, 1976.

Meagher, Sylvia. *Subject Index to the Warren Report and Hearings and Exhibits.* New York: Scarecrow Press, 1966.

Meagher, Sylvia, in collaboration with Gary Owens. *Master Index to the J. F. K. Assassination Investigation: The Reports and Supporting Volumes of the House Select Committee on Assassinations and the Warren Commission.* Metuchen, N.J.: Scarecrow Press, 1980.

Mellen, Joan. *Farewell to Justice: Jim Garrison, JFK's Assassination, and the Case That Should Have Changed History.* Dulles, Va.: Potomac Books, 2005.

Meneses, Enrique. *Fidel Castro.* New York: Taplinger Publishing, 1966.

Menninger, Bonar. *Mortal Error: The Shot That Killed JFK.* New York: St. Martin's Press, 1992.

Méray, Tibor. *Thirteen Days That Shook the Kremlin: Imre Nagy and the Hungarian Revolution.* New York: Praeger, 1959.

Messick, Hank. *Lansky.* New York: Berkley, 1971.

Miller, Merle. *Lyndon: An Oral Biography.* New York: Putnam, 1980.

Model, F. Peter, and Robert J. Groden. *JFK: The Case for Conspiracy.* New York: Manor Books, 1976.

Moenssens, Andre A., and Fred E. Inbau. *Scientific Evidence in Criminal Cases.* Mineola, N.Y.: Foundation Press, 1978.

Moldea, Dan E. *Dark Victory: Ronald Reagan, MCA, and the Mob.* New York: Viking, 1986.

Moldea, Dan E. *The Hoffa Wars: Teamsters, Rebels, Politicians, and the Mob.* New York: Paddington Press, 1978.

Moldea, Dan E. *The Killing of Robert F. Kennedy: An Investigation of Motive, Means and Opportunity.* New York: W. W. Norton, 1997.

Moore, Jim. *Conspiracy of One: The Definitive Book on the Kennedy Assassination.* Fort Worth, Texas: Summit Group, 1991.

Morin, Relman. *Assassination: The Death of President John F. Kennedy.* New York: Signet, 1968.

Morrow, Robert D. *First Hand Knowledge: How I Participated in the CIA-Mafia Murder of President Kennedy.* New York: S.P.I. Books, 1992.

Mosby, Aline. *The View from No. 13 People's Street.* New York: Random House, 1962.

Moss, Armand. *Disinformation, Misinformation, and the "Conspiracy" to Kill JFK Exposed.* Hamden, Conn.: Archon Books, 1987.

Myers, Dale K. *With Malice: Lee Harvey Oswald and the Murder of Officer J. D. Tippit.* Milford, Mich.: Oak Cliff Press, 1998.

Nagle, John M. *A Guide to the Sites of November 22, 1963: Facts, Questions, Pictures, and History.* Dallas: Self-published, 2005.

NASA, Nazis, and JFK: The Torbitt Document and the Kennedy Assassination. With a foreword by David Hatcher Childress and an introduction by Kenn Thomas. Kempton, Ill.: Adventures Unlimited Press, 1996.

Navasky, Victor S. *Kennedy Justice.* New York: Atheneum, 1971.

NBC News. *Seventy Hours and Thirty Minutes, as Broadcast on the NBC Television Network by NBC News.* New York: Random House, 1966.

Nechiporenko, Oleg. *Passport to Assassination: The Never-Before-Told Story of Lee Harvey Oswald by the KGB Colonel Who Knew Him.* New York: Carol Publishing, 1993.

Nelli, Humbert S. *The Business of Crime: Italians and Syndicate Crime in the United States.* New York: Oxford University Press, 1976.

Newcombe, Fred T., and Perry Adams. *Murder from Within.* Santa Barbara, Calif.: Probe, 1974.

Newman, Albert H. *The Assassination of John F. Kennedy: The Reasons Why.* New York: Clarkson Potter, 1970.

Newman, John M. *JFK and Vietnam: Deception, Intrigue, and the Struggle for Power.* New York: Warner Books, 1992.

Newman, John M. *Oswald and the CIA.* New York: Carroll & Graf, 1995.

Newseum, with Cathy Trost and Susan Bennett. *President Kennedy Has Been Shot: Experience the Moment-to-Moment Account of the Four Days That Changed America.* Narrated by Dan Rather. Naperville, Ill.: Sourcebooks, 2003.

Nixon, Richard. *Six Crises.* New York: Doubleday, 1962.

Norris, W. R., and R. B. Cutler. *Alek James Hidell, Alias Oswald.* Manchester, Mass.: GKG Partners, 1985.

North, Mark. *Act of Treason: The Role of J. Edgar Hoover in the Assassination of President Kennedy.* New York: Carroll & Graf, 1991.

Noyes, Peter. *Legacy of Doubt.* New York: Pinnacle, 1973.

O'Brien, Michael. *John F. Kennedy: A Biography.* New York: Thomas Dunne Books, 2005.

O'Donnell, Kenneth P., and David F. Powers with Joseph McCarthy. *Johnny, We Hardly Knew Ye: Memories of John Fitzgerald Kennedy.* Boston: Little, Brown, 1972.

Oglesby, Carl. *The Yankee and the Cowboy War: Conspiracies from Dallas to Watergate.* Mission, Kansas: Sheed Andrews & McMeel, 1976.

O'Leary, Brad, and L. E. Seymour. *Triangle of Death: The Shocking Truth about the Role of South Vietnam and the French Mafia in the Assassination of JFK.* Nashville: WND Books, 2003.

Oliver, Beverly, with Coke Buchanan. *Nightmare in Dallas.* Lancaster, Penn.: Starburst Publisher, 1994.

O'Neill, Tip, with William Novak. *Man of the House: The Life and Political Memoirs of Speaker Tip O'Neill.* Boston: G. K. Hall, 1988.

Oswald, Robert L., with Myrick Land and Barbara Land. *Lee: A Portrait of Lee Harvey Oswald by His Brother.* New York: Coward McCann, 1967.

O'Toole, George J. A. *The Assassination Tapes: An Electronic Probe into the Murder of John F. Kennedy and the Dallas Coverup.* New York: Penthouse, 1975.

Palamara, Vince. *The Third Alternative—Survivor's Guilt: The Secret Service and the JFK Murder.* Pittsburgh: Self-published, 1993.

Pantaleone, Michele. *The Mafia and Politics.* London: Chatto & Windus, 1966.

Parmet, Herbert S. *Jack: The Struggles of John F. Kennedy.* New York: Dial Press, 1980.

Parmet, Herbert S. *JFK: The Presidency of John F. Kennedy.* New York: Penguin Books, 1984.

The Pentagon Papers: The Defense Department History of United States Decisionmaking on Vietnam. Senator Gravel edition. Boston: Beacon Press, 1971–1972.

Persons, Albert C. *Bay of Pigs.* Jefferson, N.C.: McFarland, 1990.

Phelan, James. *Scandals, Scamps, and Scoundrels: The Casebook of an Investigative Reporter.* New York: Random House, 1982.

Phillips, David Atlee. *The Night Watch.* New York: Atheneum, 1977.

Piper, Michael Collins. *Final Judgment: The Missing Link in the JFK Assassination Conspiracy.* Liberty Lobby, 1998.

Popkin, Richard H. *The Second Oswald.* New York: Avon, 1966.

Posner, Gerald. *Case Closed: Lee Harvey Oswald and the Assassination of JFK.* New York: Random House, 1993.

Powers, Francis Gary, with Curt Gentry. *Operation Overflight: The U-2 Spy Pilot Tells His Story for the First Time.* New York: Holt, Rinehart & Winston, 1970.

Powers, Richard G. *Broken: The Troubled Past and Uncertain Future of the FBI.* New York: Free Press, 2004.

Powers, Richard G. *Secrecy and Power: The Life of J. Edgar Hoover.* New York: Free Press, 1986.

Powers, Thomas. *The Man Who Kept the Secrets: Richard Helms and the CIA.* New York: Pocket Books, 1979.

President John F. Kennedy: Assassination Report of the Warren Commission. FlatSigned Rare Books, FlatSigned.Com, 2004.

Prouty, L. Fletcher. *JFK: The CIA, Vietnam, and the Plot to Assassinate John F. Kennedy.* New York: Birch Lane Press, 1992.

Raab, Selwyn. *Five Families: The Rise, Decline, and Resurgence of America's Most Powerful Mafia Empires.* New York: Thomas Dunne Books, 2005.

Ragano, Frank, and Selwyn Raab. *Mob Lawyer.* New York: Scribner's, 1994.

Ramsay, Robin. *Who Shot JFK?* London: Pocket Essentials, 2002.

Ranelagh, John. *The Agency: The Rise and Decline of the CIA.* New York: Simon & Schuster, 1986.

Rather, Dan, with Mickey Herskowitz. *The Camera Never Blinks: Adventures of a TV Journalist.* New York: William Morrow, 1977.

Reeves, Richard. *President Kennedy: Profile of Power.* New York: Simon & Schuster, 1993.

Reid, Ed. *The Grim Reapers: The Anatomy of Organized Crime in America.* Chicago: Henry Regnery, 1969.

Reppetto, Thomas. *American Mafia: A History of Its Rise to Power.* New York: Henry Holt, 2004.

Reston, James. *Deadline: A Memoir.* New York: Random House, 1991.

Reynolds, Quentin James. *Courtroom: The Story of Samuel S. Leibowitz.* New York: Farrar, Straus, 1950.

Richards, David. *Played Out: The Jean Seberg Story.* New York: Random House, 1981.

Roberts, Charles. *The Truth about the Assassination.* New York: Grosset & Dunlap, 1967.

Roberts, Craig. *Kill Zone: A Sniper Looks at Dealey Plaza.* Tulsa, Okla.: Consolidated Press International, 1997.

Roberts, Craig, and John Armstrong. *JFK: The Dead Witnesses.* Tulsa, Okla.: Consolidated Press International, 1995.

Robertson, Jerry. *Documents and Photos for John Armstrong's Book Harvey and Lee.* Lafayette, Ind.: Self-published, 2004.

Robison, John. *Proofs of a Conspiracy against All the Religions and Governments of Europe, Carried on in the Secret Meetings of Free Masons, Illuminati, and Reading Societies.* New York: George Forman, 1789.

Rodriguez, Felix I., and John Weisman. *Shadow Warrior: The CIA Hero of a Hundred Battles.* New York: Simon & Schuster, 1989.

Rodríguez Cruz, Juan Carlos. *The Bay of Pigs and the CIA.* New York: Ocean Press, 1999.

Roffman, Howard. *Presumed Guilty.* London: Associated University Presses, 1975.

Ross, Robert Gaylon, Sr. *The Elite Serial Killers of Lincoln, JFK, RFK, and MLK.* Spicewood, Texas: RIE, 2001.

Rupp, Rebecca. *Committed to Memory: How We Remember and Why We Forget.* New York: Crown, 1998.

Russell, Dick. *The Man Who Knew Too Much: Hired to Kill Oswald and Prevent the Assassination of JFK.* New York: Carroll & Graf/Richard Gallen, 1992.

Russo, Gus. *Live by the Sword: The Secret War against Castro and the Death of JFK.* Baltimore: Bancroft Press, 1998.

Russo, Gus. *The Outfit: The Role of Chicago's Underworld in the Shaping of Modern America.* New York: Bloomsbury, 2001.

Sahl, Mort. *Heartland.* New York: Harcourt Brace Jovanovich, 1976.

Salandria, Vincent J. *False Mystery: Essays on the Assassination of JFK.* Louisville, Colo.: Square Deal Press, 2004.

Salerno, Ralph, and John S. Tompkins. *The Crime Confederation: Cosa Nostra and Allied Operations in Organized Crime.* New York: Doubleday, 1969.

Sample, Glen, and Mark Collom. *The Men on the Sixth Floor.* Garden Grove, Calif.: Sample Graphics, 2001.

Sauvage, Léo. *The Oswald Affair: An Examination of the Contradictions and Omissions of the Warren Report.* Cleveland: World Publishing, 1966.

Savage, Gary. *JFK First Day Evidence.* Monroe, La.: Shoppe Press, 1993.

Schacter, Daniel L. *The Seven Sins of Memory: How the Mind Forgets and Remembers.* Boston: Houghton Mifflin, 2001.

Scheim, David E. *Contract on America: The Mafia Murders of John and Robert Kennedy.* Silver Spring, Md.: Argyle Press, 1983.

Schieffer, Bob. *This Just In: What I Couldn't Tell You on TV.* New York: Putnam, 2003.

Schlesinger, Arthur M., Jr. *Robert Kennedy and His Times.* Boston: Houghton Mifflin, 1978.

Schlesinger, Arthur M., Jr. *A Thousand Days: John F. Kennedy in the White House.* Boston: Houghton Mifflin, 1965.

Schlesinger, Stephen, and Stephen Kinzer. *Bitter Fruit: The Untold Story of the American Coup in Guatemala.* Garden City, N.Y.: Doubleday, 1982.

Schlott, Joseph L. *No Left Turns.* New York: Praeger, 1975.

Schotz, E. Marlin. *History Will Not Absolve Us: Orwellian Control, Public Denial and the Murder of President Kennedy.* Brookline, Mass.: Kurtz, Ulmer & Delucia Book Publishers, 1996.

Sciacca, Tony. *Luciano: The Man Who Modernized the American Mafia.* New York: Pinnacle Books, 1975.

Scott, Peter Dale. *Crime and Cover-Up: The CIA, the Mafia, and the Dallas-Watergate Connection.* Santa Barbara, Calif.: Open Archives Press, 1993.

Scott, Peter Dale. *Deep Politics and the Death of JFK.* Berkeley: University of California Press, 1993.

Seigenthaler, John. *A Search for Justice.* Nashville: Aurora Publishers, 1971.

Semple, Robert B., Jr., ed. *Four Days in November: The Original Coverage of the John F. Kennedy Assassination by the Staff of the* New York Times. New York: St. Martin's Press, 2003.

Shannon, William V. *The Heir Apparent: Robert Kennedy and the Struggle for Power.* New York: Macmillan, 1967.

Shaw, J. Gary, with Larry R. Harris. *Cover-Up: The Governmental Conspiracy to Conceal the Facts about the Public Execution of John Kennedy.* Cleburne, Texas: Self-published, 1976.

Shaw, Maud. *White House Nannie: My Years with Caroline and John Kennedy, Jr.* New York: New American Library, 1966.

Sheridan, Walter. *The Fall and Rise of Jimmy Hoffa.* New York: Saturday Review Press, 1973.

Shesol, Jeff. *Mutual Contempt: Lyndon Johnson, Robert Kennedy, and the Feud That Defined a Decade.* New York: W. W. Norton, 1997.

Sirica, John J. *To Set the Record Straight: The Break-in, the Tapes, the Conspirators, the Pardon.* New York: W. W. Norton, 1979.

Sloan, Bill. *JFK: Breaking the Silence.* Dallas: Taylor Publishing, 1993.

Sloan, Bill, with Jean Hill. *JFK: The Last Dissenting Witness.* Gretna, La.: Pelican, 1992.

Smith, Earl E. T. *The Fourth Floor: An Account of the Castro Communist Revolution.* Washington, D.C.: Selores Foundation Press, 1987.

Smith, Matthew. *Conspiracy: The Plot to Stop the Kennedys.* New York: Citadel Press, 2005.

Smith, Matthew. *JFK: The Second Plot.* Edinburgh: Mainstream, 1992.

Smith, Matthew. *Say Goodbye to America: The Sensational and Untold Story behind the Assassination of John F. Kennedy.* Edinburgh: Mainstream, 2001.

Smith, R. Harris. *OSS: The Secret History of America's First Central Intelligence Agency.* New York: Delta Books, 1973.

Smith, W. H. B. *Small Arms of the World: The Basic Manual of Military Small Arms, American, Soviet, British, Czech, German, French, Belgian, Italian, Swiss, Japanese, and All Other Important Nations.* 10th ed. Harrisburg, Penn.: Stackpole Books, 1973.

Sneed, Larry A. *No More Silence: An Oral History of the Assassination of President Kennedy.* Dallas: Three Forks Press, 1997.

Sondern, Frederic. *Brotherhood of Evil: The Mafia.* New York: Farrar, Straus, & Cudahy, 1959.

Sparrow, John. *After the Assassination: A Positive Appraisal of the Warren Report.* New York: Chilmark Press, 1967.

Specter, Arlen, with Charles Robbins. *Passion for Truth: From Finding JFK's Single Bullet to Questioning Anita Hill to Impeaching Clinton.* New York: William Morrow, 2000.

The Speeches of Senator John F. Kennedy's Presidential Campaign of 1960. Washington, D.C.: Government Printing Office, 1961.

Sprague, Richard E. *The Taking of America 1-2-3.* Rev. ed. Self-published, 1979.

Stafford, Jean. *A Mother in History.* New York: Farrar, Straus & Giroux, 1966.

Steinberg, Alfred. *Sam Johnson's Boy: A Close-up of the President from Texas.* New York: Macmillan, 1968.

Stone, Oliver, and Zachary Sklar. *JFK: The Book of the Film.* New York: Applause, 1992.

Sturdivan, Larry M. *The JFK Myths: A Scientific Investigation of the Kennedy Assassination.* St. Paul, Minn.: Paragon House, 2005.

Sullivan, William C., with Bill Brown. *The Bureau: My Thirty Years in Hoover's FBI.* New York: W. W. Norton, 1979.

Summers, Anthony. *Conspiracy.* New York: McGraw-Hill, 1980.

Summers, Anthony. *Goddess: The Secret Lives of Marilyn Monroe.* New York: Macmillan, 1985.

Summers, Anthony. *Not in Your Lifetime.* New York: Marlowe, 1998.

Summers, Anthony. *Official and Confidential: The Secret Life of J. Edgar Hoover.* New York: Putnam, 1993.

Summers, Anthony, with Robbyn Swan. *The Arrogance of Power: The Secret World of Richard Nixon.* New York: Viking, 2000.

Summers, Anthony, and Robbyn Swan. *Sinatra: The Life.* New York: Alfred A. Knopf, 2005.

Tagg, Eric R. *Brush with History: A Day in the Life of Deputy E. R. Walthers.* Garland, Texas: Shot in the Light Publishing, 1998.

Tague, James T. *Truth Withheld: A Survivor's Story.* Dallas: Excel Digital Press, 2003.

Taylor, Maxwell D. *Swords and Plowshares.* New York: W. W. Norton, 1972.

TerHorst, Jerald F., and Ralph Albertazzie. *The Flying White House: The Story of Air Force One.* New York: Coward, McCann & Geoghegan, 1979.

Theoharis, Athan G., ed. *Culture of Secrecy: The Government versus the People's Right to Know.* Lawrence: University Press of Kansas, 1998.

Theoharis, Athan G., with Tony G. Poveda, Susan Rosenfeld, and Richard Gid Powers, eds. *The FBI: A Comprehensive Reference Guide.* Phoenix: Oryx Press, 1999.

Thomas, Evan. *Robert Kennedy: His Life.* New York: Simon & Schuster, 2000.

Thomas, Evan. *The Very Best Men: Four Who Dared: The Early Years of the CIA.* New York: Simon & Schuster, 1995.

Thomas, Hugh. *Cuba; or, Pursuit of Freedom.* London: Eyre & Spottiswoode, 1971.

Thomas, Ralph D. *Missing Links in the JFK Assassination Conspiracy.* Austin, Texas: Thomas Investigative Publications, 1992.

Thomas, Ralph D. *Photo Computer Image Processing and the Crime of the Century.* Austin, Texas: Thomas Investigative Publications, 1992.

Thompson, Josiah. *Six Seconds in Dallas: A Micro-study of the Kennedy Assassination.* New York: Bernard Geis Associates, 1967.

Thornley, Kerry W. *The Idle Warriors.* Avondale Estates, Ga.: IllumiNet Press, 1991.

Thornley, Kerry W. *Oswald.* Chicago: New Classics House, 1965.

Toplin, Robert Brent. *Oliver Stone's USA: Film, History, and Controversy.* Lawrence: University Press of Kansas, 2000.

Torcia, Charles E. *Wharton's Criminal Law.* 15th ed. Deerfield, Ill.: Clark Boardman Callaghan, 1993–1996.

Trask, Richard B. *National Nightmare on Six Feet of Film: Mr. Zapruder's Home Movie and the Murder of President Kennedy.* Danvers, Mass.: Yeoman Press, 2005.

Trask, Richard B. *Photographic Memory: The Kennedy Assassination, November 22, 1963.* Dallas: Sixth Floor Museum, 1996.

Trask, Richard B. *Pictures of the Pain: Photography and the Assassination of President Kennedy.* Danvers, Mass.: Yeoman Press, 1994.

Trask, Richard B. *That Day in Dallas: Three Photographers Capture on Film the Day President Kennedy Died.* Danvers, Mass.: Yeoman Press, 1998.

Trento, Joseph J. *The Secret History of the CIA.* Roseville, Calif.: Prima, 2001.

Tully, Andrew. *CIA, the Inside Story.* New York: William Morrow, 1962.

Turner, William W. *Rearview Mirror: Looking Back at the FBI, the CIA, and Other Tails.* Granite Bay, Calif.: Penmarin Books, 2001.

Turner, William W., and Jonn G. Christian. *The Assassination of Robert F. Kennedy: A Searching Look at the Conspiracy and Cover-Up, 1968–1978.* New York: Random House, 1978.

Twyman, Noel. *Bloody Treason: The Assassination of John F. Kennedy, on Solving History's Greatest Murder Mystery.* Rancho Santa Fe, Calif.: Laurel, 1997.

Unger, Irwin, and Debi Unger. *LBJ: A Life.* New York: John Wiley, 1999.

United Press International. *Four Days: The Historical Record of the Death of President Kennedy.* New York: American Heritage, 1964.

Valentine, Douglas. *The Strength of the Wolf: The Secret History of America's War on Drugs.* New York: Verso, 2004.

Voltaire. *Dissertation sur la mort de Henri IV.* Vol. 2. Ed. Furne, 1835.

Waldron, Lamar, with Thom Hartmann. *Ultimate Sacrifice: John and Robert Kennedy, the Plan for a Coup in Cuba, and the Murder of JFK.* New York: Carroll & Graf, 2005.

Warren, Earl. *The Memoirs of Earl Warren.* Garden City, N.Y.: Doubleday, 1977.

Weberman, Alan J., and Michael Canfield. *Coup d'État in America: The CIA and the Assassination of John F. Kennedy.* San Francisco: Quick American Archives, 1992.

Wecht, Cyril H. *Cause of Death.* New York: Penguin, 1994.

Weisberg, Harold. *Case Open.* New York: Carroll & Graf, 1994.

Weisberg, Harold. *Never Again! The Government Conspiracy in the JFK Assassination.* New York: Carroll & Graf, 1995.

Weisberg, Harold. *Oswald in New Orleans: Case of Conspiracy with the CIA.* New York: Canyon Books, 1967.

Weisberg, Harold. *Photographic Whitewash: Suppressed Kennedy Assassination Pictures.* Hyattstown, Md.: Self-published, 1967.

Weisberg, Harold. *Post Mortem: JFK Assassination Cover-Up Smashed!* Frederick, Md.: Self-published, 1975.

Weisberg, Harold. *Whitewash: The Report on the Warren Commission.* Hyattstown, Md.: Self-published, 1965.

Weisberg, Harold. *Whitewash II: The FBI-Secret Service Cover-Up.* Hyattstown, Md.: Self-published, 1966.

Weisberg, Harold. *Whitewash IV: Post Assassination Transcript.* Hyattstown, Md.: Self-published, 1966.

White, Stephen. *Should We Now Believe the Warren Report?* New York: Macmillan, 1968.

White, Theodore H. *In Search of History: A Personal Expedition.* New York: Harper & Row, 1978.

White, Theodore H. *The Making of the President, 1964.* New York: Atheneum, 1965.

Whitehead, Don. *The FBI Story: A Report to the People.* New York: Random House, 1956.

Wicker, Tom. *JFK and LBJ: The Influence of Personality upon Politics.* New York: William Morrow, 1968.

Williams, James Doyle. *The Dolphus Starling, Minnie Lee Williams Family, An Autobiography, Family-Careers.* Self-published, October 1990.

Williams, T. Harry. *Huey Long.* New York: Alfred A. Knopf, 1969.

Wills, Garry, and Ovid Demaris. *Jack Ruby.* New York: Da Capo Press, 1994.

Wilson, Kirk. *Unsolved Crimes: The Top Ten Unsolved Murders of the 20th Century.* New York: Carroll & Graf, 2002.

Windchy, Eugene G. *Tonkin Gulf.* Garden City, N.Y.: Doubleday, 1971.

Wise, David. *The American Police State: The Government against the People.* New York: Random House, 1976.

Wise, David, and Thomas B. Ross. *The Invisible Government.* New York: Random House, 1964.

Wofford, Harris. *Of Kennedys and Kings: Making Sense of the Sixties.* New York: Farrar, Straus & Giroux, 1980.

Wrone, David R. *The Zapruder Film: Reframing JFK's Assassination.* Lawrence: University Press of Kansas, 2003.

Wyden, Peter. *Bay of Pigs: The Untold Story.* New York: Simon & Schuster, 1979.

Yeltsin, Boris. *The View from the Kremlin.* London: HarperCollins, 1994.

Youngblood, Rufus W. *20 Years in the Secret Service: My Life with Five Presidents.* New York: Simon & Schuster, 1973.

Zelizer, Barbie. *Covering the Body: The Kennedy Assassination, the Media, and the Shaping of Collective Memory.* Chicago: Chicago University Press, 1992.

Zirbel, Craig. *The Texas Connection: The Assassination of President John F. Kennedy.* Scottsdale, Ariz.: Texas Connection, 1991.

Zubin, David M. *Shooting Kennedy: JFK and the Culture of Images.* Berkeley: University of California Press, 2003.

ARTICLES IN MAGAZINES AND JOURNALS

Aguilar, Gary L. Letter to editor. *Federal Bar News & Journal,* June 9, 1994.

Aguilar, Gary L., Cyril H. Wecht, and Rex Bradford. "A Neuroforensic Analysis of the Wounds of President John F. Kennedy: Part 2—A Study of the Available Evidence, Eyewitness Correlations, Analysis, and Conclusions." *Neurosurgery-Online.com,* vol. 57, no. 3, September 2005.

Alvarez, Luis W. "A Physicist Examines the Kennedy Assassination Film." *American Journal of Physics,* vol. 44, no. 9, September 1976.

"America's Long Vigil." *TV Guide,* issue 565, vol. 12, no. 4, January 25, 1964.

Ansen, David. "A Troublemaker for Our Times." *Newsweek,* December 23, 1991.

Anson, Robert Sam. "The Shooting of *JFK.*" *Esquire,* November 1991.

Armstrong, Ken. "Dallas Puzzle—By a Canadian Eyewitness." *Liberty,* July 15, 1964.

"As the Book Appears: A Close Look at the Facts." *U.S. News & World Report,* January 23, 1967.

"The Assassination: History's Jury." *Newsweek,* December 16, 1963.

Attwood, William. "In Memory of John F. Kennedy." *Look,* December 31, 1963.

Auchincloss, Kenneth, with Ginny Carroll and Maggie Malone. "Twisted History." *Newsweek*, December 23, 1991.

Aynesworth, Hugh. "The JFK 'Conspiracy'." *Newsweek*, May 15, 1967.

Bardach, Ann Louise. "The Spy Who Loved Castro." *Vanity Fair*, November 1993.

Beck, Melinda, and Anne Underwood. "I Wanted to Be a Hero." *Newsweek*, November 22, 1993.

Berendt, John. "Name: Igor 'Turk' Vaganov." *Esquire*, August 1967.

Berquist, Laura. "John Fitzgerald Kennedy, 35th President of the United States." *Look*, November 17, 1964.

Beschloss, Michael. "An Assassination Diary." *Newsweek*, November 23, 1998.

Beschloss, Michael. "The Day That Changed America." *Newsweek*, November 22, 1995.

"Best of '86." *Time*, January 5, 1987.

Bethell, Tom. "Conspiracy to End Conspiracies." *National Review*, December 16, 1991.

Bethell, Tom. "Jim Garrison's Great Escape." *American Spectator*, December 1998.

Bethell, Tom. "Was Sirhan Sirhan on the Grassy Knoll?" *Washington Monthly*, March 1975.

"Birch View of JFK." *Newsweek*, February 24, 1964.

Blythe, Myrna, and Jane Farrell. "Marina Oswald, Twenty-five Years Later." *Ladies' Home Journal*, November 1988.

"The Bold and the Beautiful." *U.S. News & World Report*, December 26, 1966.

"The Book That Has Backfired." *U.S. News & World Report*, December 26, 1966.

Branch, Taylor, and George Crile III. "The Kennedy Vendetta: How the CIA Waged a Silent War against Cuba." *Harper's Magazine*, August 1975.

Breo, Dennis L. "JFK's Death—The Plain Truth from the MDs Who Did the Autopsy." *Journal of the American Medical Association*, vol. 267, no. 20, May 27, 1992.

Breo, Dennis L. "JFK's Death, Part II—Dallas MDs Recall Their Memories." *Journal of the American Medical Association*, vol. 267, no. 20, May 27, 1992.

Breo, Dennis L. "JFK's Death, Part III—Dr Finck Speaks Out: 'Two Bullets, from the Rear'." *Journal of the American Medical Association*, vol. 268, no. 13, October 7, 1992.

Breslin, Jimmy. "A Death in Emergency Room No. One." *Saturday Evening Post*, December 14, 1963.

Bunton, Judge Lucius. "Texas Judge Offers Perspectives on Presiding at Oswald's Trial." *Texas Bar Journal*, November 1988.

Cartwright, Gary. "I Was Mandarin." *Texas Monthly*, December 1990.

Cartwright, Gary. "The Old Soldier." *Texas Monthly*, February 1991.

Cartwright, Gary. "Who Was Jack Ruby?" *Texas Monthly*, November 1975.

Chandler, David. "The 'Little Man' Is Bigger Than Ever." *Life*, April 10, 1970.

Chevigny, Bell Gale. "Surviving Revolution and Obscurity." *Ms.*, April 1987.

Chomsky, Noam. "Vain Hopes, False Dreams." *Z Magazine*, September 1992.

Christensen, Dan. "JFK, King, the Dade County Links." *Miami Magazine*, December 1976.

"Clay Shaw: An Exclusive Penthouse Interview." *Penthouse*, September 1969.

Connally, John. "Why Kennedy Went to Texas." *Life*, November 24, 1967.

Corliss, Richard. "Who Killed JFK?" *Time*, December 23, 1991.

Corn, David, and Gus Russo. "The Old Man and the CIA: A Kennedy Plot to Kill Castro?" *Nation*, March 26, 2001.

Crenshaw, Charles A., and J. Gary Shaw. "Commentary on JFK Autopsy Articles." *Journal of the American Medical Association*, vol. 273, no. 20, May 24, 1995–May 31, 1995.

Cushman, Robert F. "Why the Warren Commission?" *New York University Law Review*, vol. 40, May 1965.

Daly, Steve. "Camera Obscura." *Entertainment Weekly*, January 17, 1992.

Daniel, Jean. "When Castro Heard the News." *New Republic*, December 7, 1963.

Davidson, Bill. "A Profile in Family Courage." *Saturday Evening Post*, December 14, 1963.

"The De-briefing Process for the U.S.S.R's Defectors." *Newsweek*, February 24, 1964.

"The Demise of a Don." *Time*, June 30, 1975.

Devlin, Lord. "Death of a President, the Established Facts." *Atlantic*, March 1965.

"Did This Man Happen upon Kennedy's Assassins?" *Maclean's Reports*, November 1967.

"A Different Look at Dallas, Texas." *U.S. News & World Report*, February 3, 1964.

"Discovering History with a Car Collector: Feature Car: The Kennedy Lincoln." *Car Collector*, April 2005.

Dudman, Richard. "Commentary of an Eyewitness." *New Republic*, December 21, 1963.

Epstein, Edward. "Reporter at Large." *New Yorker*, July 13, 1968.

Epstein, Edward. "The Second Coming of Jim Garrison." *Atlantic*, March 1993.

"Fateful Two Hours without a President." *U.S. News & World Report*, November 14, 1966.

"FBI: Shaken by a Cover-Up That Failed." *Time*, November 3, 1975.

Fisher, Bob. "The Why and Hows of JFK." *American Cinematographer*, February 1992.

Fonzi, Gaeton. "Seduced by the Web-Weavers." *Pennsylvania Gazette*, November 1993.

Fonzi, Gaeton. "Who Killed JFK?" *Washingtonian*, November 1980.

Freese, Paul L. "The Warren Commission and the Fourth Shot: A Reflection on the Fundamentals of Forensic Fact-Finding." *New York University Law Review*, vol. 40, May 1965.

Gage, Nicholas. "The Little Big Man Who Laughs at the Law." *Atlantic*, July 1970.

Gates, David, with Howard Manly, Donna Foote, and Frank Washington. "Bottom Line: How Crazy Is It?" *Newsweek*, December 23, 1991.

Gavin, James M. "We Can Get Out of Vietnam." *Saturday Evening Post*, February 24, 1968.

Gelb, Leslie. "Would Defeat in Iraq Be So Bad?" *Time*, October 23, 2006.

Gertz, Elmer. Review of "My Life as a Radical Lawyer." *Real Crime Digest*, August 30, 1993.

Gertz, Elmer. "The 30th Anniversary of the Kennedy Assassination." *Real Crime Book Digest*, October–November 1995.

Gest, Ted, and Joseph Shapiro with David Bowermaster and Thom Geier. "JFK: The Untold Story of the Warren Report." *U.S. News & World Report*, August 17, 1992.

Goldman, Peter, with John J. Lindsay. "Dallas: New Questions and Answers." *Newsweek*, April 28, 1975.

Goldman, Peter, with Elaine Shannon, Diane Camper, and Lee Donosky. "Rush to Judgment." *Newsweek*, January 15, 1979.

Golz, Earl. "Confidential: The FBI's File on JFK." *Gallery*, November 1982.

Golz, Earl. "Confidential: The FBI's File on JFK—Part Two." *Gallery*, December 1982.

"Good-by Belli." *Newsweek*, March 30, 1964.

Goodhart, Arthur. "The Mysteries of the Kennedy Assassination and the English Press." *Law Quarterly Review*, vol. 83, January 1967.

Goodhart, Arthur. "The Warren Commission from the Procedural Standpoint." *New York University Law Review*, vol. 40, May 1965.

Goodman, Craig G. "History of the U.S. Petroleum Depletion Allowance, Part III." *Oil and Gas Quarterly*, vol. 39, March 1991.

Greenstein, Fred I. "Diffusion of News of the Kennedy Assassination." *Public Opinion Quarterly*, Summer 1965.

Groden, Robert. "A New Look at the Zapruder Film." *Rolling Stone*, April 24, 1975.

Grosvenor, Melville Bell. "The Last Full Measure." *National Geographic*, March 9, 1964.

"Growing Rift of LBJ and Kennedy." *U.S. News & World Report*, January 2, 1967.

Guinn, Vincent. "JFK Assassination: Bullet Analysis." *Analytical Chemistry*, vol. 51, no. 4, April 1979.

Hall, Kermit. "The Virulence of the National Appetite for Bogus Revelation." *Maryland Law Review*, vol. 56, no. 1, 1997.

Hansen, Mark. "Truth Sleuth or Faulty Detector." *American Bar Association Journal*, May 1999.

"Historic Photo Report." *U.S. News & World Report*, December 9, 1963.

Holland, Max. "The Demon in Jim Garrison." *Wilson Quarterly*, Spring 2001.

Holland, Max. "The JFK Lawyers' Conspiracy." *Nation*, February 20, 2006.

Holland, Max. "The Key to the Warren Report." *American Heritage*, vol. 46, no. 7, November 1995.

Holmes, John Clellon. "The Silence of Oswald." *Playboy*, November 1965.

"In the Works: Tighter Laws on Gun Sales." *U.S. News & World Report*, December 9, 1963.

"Investigations." *Time*, December 13, 1963.

Isaacson, Walter. "If Kennedy Had Lived." *Time*, April 13, 1992.

"Jack Kennedy's Other Women." *Time*, December 29, 1975.

Jackson, Donald. "The Evolution of an Assassin." *Life*, February 21, 1964.

Janos, Leo. "The Last Days of the President: LBJ in Retirement." *Atlantic*, January 1973.

"JFK: The Death and the Doubts." *Newsweek*, December 5, 1966.

Johnson, Priscilla. "Oswald in Moscow." *Harper's Magazine*, April 1964.

Kaiser, Robert Blair. "The Mystery Tramps in Disguise?" *Rolling Stone*, April 24, 1975.

Kaplan, David A. "The JFK Probe—25 Years Later." *National Law Journal*, November 28, 1988.

Katz, Bob. "Mark Lane, the Left's Leading Hearse Chaser." *Mother Jones*, August 1979.

Kelley, Kitty. "The Dark Side of Camelot." *People*, February 29, 1988.

Kempton, Murray. "Jack Ruby on Trial." *New Republic*, March 7, 1964.

Kempton, Murray, and James Ridgeway. "Romans." *New Republic*, December 7, 1963.

"Kiss of Death." *Newsweek*, October 7, 1963.

Knebel, Fletcher. "J. Edgar Hoover, the Cop and the Man." *Look*, May 31, 1955.

Knebel, Fletcher. "A New Wave of Doubt." *Look*, July 12, 1966.

Kornbluh, Peter. "JFK & Castro: The Secret Quest for Accommodation." *Cigar Aficionado*, October 1999.

Lacayo, Richard. "How Sick Was J.F.K.?" *Time*, December 2, 2002.

Lattimer, J. K. "Additional Data on the Shooting of President Kennedy." *Journal of the American Medical Association*, vol. 269, no. 12, March 24, 1993.

Lattimer, J. K., J. Lattimer, and G. Lattimer. "An Experimental Study of the Backward Movement of President Kennedy's Head." *Surgery, Gynecology, and Obstetrics*, February 1976.

Lattimer, John K. "Observations Based on a Review of the Autopsy Photographs, X-rays and Related Materials of the Late President John F. Kennedy." *Resident and Staff Physician*, May 1972.

Lattimer, John K., Angus Laidlaw, Paul Heneghan, and Eric J. Haubner. "Experimental Duplication of the Important Physical Evidence of the Lapel Bulge of the Jacket Worn by Governor Connally When Bullet 399 Went through Him." *Journal of the American College of Surgeons*, vol. 178, May 1994.

Lattimer, John K., and Jon Lattimer. "The Kennedy-Connally Single Bullet Theory." *International Surgery*, vol. 50, no. 6, December 1968.

Lattimer, John K., Edward B. Schlesinger, and H. Houston Merritt. "President Kennedy's Spine Hit by First Bullet." *Bulletin of the New York Academy of Medicine*, Second Series, vol. 53, no. 3, April 1977.

Lemann, Nicholas. "The Case against Jim Garrison." *GQ*, January 1992.

Levine, Jack. "Hoover and the Red Square." *Nation*, October 20, 1962.

Levy, Michael L., Daniel Sullivan, Rodrick Faccio, and Robert Grossman. "A Neuroforensic Analysis of the Wounds of President John F. Kennedy: Part 2—A Study of the Available Evidence, Eyewitness Correlations, Analysis, and Conclusions." *Neurosurgery*, vol. 54, no. 6, June 2004.

Lewis, Flora. "The Tragedy of Bertrand Russell." *Look*, April 4, 1967.

Lundberg, George D. "Closing the Case in JAMA on the John F. Kennedy Autopsy." Editorial. *Journal of the American Medical Association*, vol. 268, no. 13, October 7, 1992.

Macdonald, Dwight. "A Critique of the Warren Report." *Esquire*, March 1965.

Magnusen, Ed, edited by Ronald Krise. "The Truth about Hoover." *Time*, December 22, 1975.

Mailer, Norman. "The Amateur Hit Man." *New York Review of Books*, May 11, 1995.

Mailer, Norman. "Oswald in the U.S.S.R." *New Yorker*, April 10, 1995.

Manchester, William. "The Death of a President." *Look*, January 24, 1967.

Manchester, William. "William Manchester's Own Story." *Look*, April 4, 1967.

Mandel, Paul. "End to Nagging Rumors: The Six Critical Seconds." *Life*, December 6, 1963.

Marchetti, Victor. "CIA to Admit Hunt Involvement in Kennedy Slaying." *Spotlight*, August 14, 1978.

"Marina's Turn." *Time*, September 21, 1992.

Martin, Harold H. " 'Help Us Fight!' Cry the Angry Exiles." *Saturday Evening Post*, June 8, 1963.

Martindale, David. "The Bizarre Deaths following JFK's Murder." *Argosy,* March 1977.

"A Matter of Reasonable Doubt." *Life*, November 25, 1966.

McGill, Ralph Emerson. "Hate Knows No Direction." *Saturday Evening Post*, December 14, 1963.

McKinley, James. "Cries of Conspiracy." Part V of "Playboy's History of Assassination in America." *Playboy*, May 1976.

McKinley, James. "The End of Camelot." Part IV of "Playboy's History of Assassination in America." *Playboy*, April 1976.

McNamara, Robert. "The Lessons of October." *Newsweek*, February 13, 1989.

Morgenthau, Tom, with Elaine Shannon. "Tales of Conspiracy." *Newsweek*, July 30, 1979.

Morley, Jefferson. "The Good Spy: How the Quashing of an Honest C.I.A. Investigator Helped Launch 40 Years of JFK Conspiracy Theories and Cynicism about the Feds." *Washington Monthly*, December 2003.

Morrow, Lance, and Martha Smilgis. "Plunging into the Labyrinth." *Time*, December 23, 1991.

Mosk, Richard M. "Conspiracy Theories and the JFK Assassination: Cashing in on Political Paranoia." *Los Angeles Lawyer*, November 1992.

"Murder of Innocence." *Reporter*, October 1992.

Nash, George, and Patricia Nash. "The Other Witnesses." *New Leader*, October 12, 1964.

Nichols, John. "President Kennedy's Adrenals." *Journal of the American Medical Association*, vol. 201, no. 2, July 10, 1967.

Nichols, John. "The Wounding of Governor Connally of Texas." *Maryland State Medical Journal*, October 1977.

Norton, Linda, James A. Cottone, Irvin M. Sopher, and Vincent J. M. DiMaio. "The Exhumation and Identification of Lee Harvey Oswald." *Journal of Forensic Science*, January 1984.

"A Note from Jack Ruby." *Newsweek*, March 27, 1967.

Oliver, Revilo P. "Marksmanship in Dallas." *American Opinion*, February 1964.

Olson, Don, and Ralph F. Turner. "Photographic Evidence and the Assassination of President John F. Kennedy." *Journal of Forensic Sciences*, vol. 16, no. 4, October 1971.

O'Toole, George, and Paul Hoch. "Dallas: The Cuban Connection." *Saturday Evening Post*, March 1976.

"Pages from a Family Album." *Look*, November 17, 1964.

Petty, Charles. "JFK—An Allonge." *Journal of the American Medical Association*, vol. 269, no. 12, March 24, 1993.

Phelan, James. "Rush to Judgment in New Orleans." *Saturday Evening Post*, May 6, 1967.

Phelan, James. "The Vice Man Cometh." *Saturday Evening Post*, June 8, 1963.

Phillips, Kevin. "Fat City." *Time*, September 26, 1994.

"Pike Committee Report." *Village Voice*, February 16 and 23, 1976.

"Playboy Interview: Jesse Ventura." *Playboy*, November 1999.

"Playboy Interview: Jim Garrison." *Playboy*, October 1967.

"Playboy Interview: Mark Lane." *Playboy*, February 1967.

Posner, Gerald. "Cracks in the Wall of Silence." *Newsweek*, October 12, 1998.

Prouty, Fletcher. "President Kennedy Was Killed by a Murder, Inc." *Executive Intelligence Review*, February 7, 1992.

Rahn, K. A., and L. M. Sturdivan. "Neutron Activation and the JFK Assassination, Part I, Data and Interpretation." *Journal of Radioanalytical and Nuclear Chemistry*, vol. 262, no. 1, October 2004.

Randall, Teri. "Clinicians' Forensic Interpretations of Fatal Gunshot Wounds Often Miss the Mark." *Journal of the American Medical Association,* vol. 269, no. 16, April 28, 1993.

Randich, Eric, Wayne Duerfeldt, Wade McLendon, and William Tobin. "A Metallurgical Review of the Interpretation of Bullet Lead Compositional Analysis." *Forensic Science International*, April 2002.

Randich, Eric, and Patrick M. Grant. "Proper Assessment of the JFK Assassination Bullet Lead Evidence from Metallurgical and Statistical Perspective." *Journal of Forensic Sciences*, vol. 51, no. 4, July 2006.

Raskin, Marcus. "JFK and the Culture of Violence." *American Historical Review*, April 1992.

Reeves, Richard. "JFK: Secrets & Lies." *Reader's Digest*, April 2003.

"The Right to Be Wrong." *Newsweek*, March 30, 1964.

Rogers, Warren. "The Persecution of Clay Shaw." *Look*, August 26, 1969.

Saunders, Charles J., and Mark S. Zaid. "The Declassification of Dealey Plaza: After Thirty Years, a New Disclosure Law at Last May Help to Clarify the Facts of the Kennedy Assassination." *South Texas Law Review*, vol. 34, October 1993.

Schonfeld, Maurice W. "The Shadow of a Gunman." *Columbia Journalism Review*, July–August 1975.

Schwartz, Sorrell L. Letter to editor. *Time*, February 16, 1981.

"Seventy-five Year Secrecy for Exhibits in JFK Killing." *U.S. News & World Report*, January 4, 1965.

Sidey, Hugh. "All the Way with JFK." *Time*, May 26, 2003.

Sidey, Hugh. "When It Counted, He Never Faltered." *Time*, December 2, 2002.

"$650,000 for Family of Man Killed by Oswald." *U.S. News & World Report*, November 2, 1964.

Smith, Sandy. "Carlos Marcello, King Thug of Louisiana." *Life*, September 8, 1967.

Smith, Sandy. "The Crime Cartel." *Life*, September 1, 1967.

Smith, Wayne. "JAMA Knows Best: The Medical Journal Called the JFK Case Closed—and the Verdict Went Unchallenged." *Columbia Journalism Review*, September–October 1993.

Solomon, Jolie. "True Disbelievers." *Newsweek*, November 22, 1993.

"Sorrow Rings a World." *Life*, December 6, 1963.

Sprague, Richard E. "The Assassination of President John F. Kennedy: The Application of Computers to the Photographic Evidence." *Computers and Animation*, vol. 19, May, June, and July 1970; vol. 20, March and May 1971.

Stetler, Russell. "Can Congress Crack the Kennedy Assassination?" *Inquiry*, March 16, 1978.

"Still Secret: The KGB's Oswald File." *Newsweek*, July 5, 1999.

Stolley, Richard. "Shots Seen Round the World: A Journalist's Behind-the-Scenes Story of the Most Historic Home Movie Ever." *Entertainment Weekly*, January 17, 1992.

Stolley, Richard. "What Happened Next . . ." *Esquire*, November 1973.

Stone, Oliver. "Oliver Stone Talks Back." *Premiere*, January 1992.

Stone, Oliver. "Was Vietnam JFK's War?" *Newsweek*, October 21, 1996.

Sturdivan, Larry M., and K. A. Rahn, "Neutron Activation and the JFK Assassination, Part II, Extended Benefits." *Journal of Radioanalytical and Nuclear Chemistry*, vol. 262, no. 1, October 2004.

Sullivan, Daniel, Rodrick Faccio, Michael L. Levy, and Robert Grossman. "The Assassination of President John F. Kennedy: A Neuroforensic Analysis—Part 1: A Neurosurgeon's Previously Undocumented Eyewitness Account from Trauma Room 1." *Neurosurgery*, vol. 53, no. 5, November 2003.

Summers, Anthony. "Hidden Hoover." *Vanity Fair*, March 1993.

Summers, Anthony, and Robbyn Summers. "The Ghosts of November." *Vanity Fair*, December 1994.

Szulc, Tad. "Cuba on Our Mind." *Esquire*, February 1974.

Talbot, David. "Fatal Flaw." *Image*, March 29, 1992.

Thomas, D. B. "Echo Correlation Analysis and the Acoustic Evidence in the Kennedy Assassination Revisited." *Science & Justice*, vol. 41, no. 1, 2001.

Thomas, Evan. "At War over a Tragic Film." *Newsweek*, January 17, 1992.

Thomas, Evan. "Bobby at the Brink." *Newsweek*, August 14, 2000.

Thomas, Evan. "The Real Cover-Up." *Newsweek*, November 22, 1993.

Thompson, Thomas. "In Texas a Policeman and an Assassin Are Laid to Rest Too." *Life*, December 6, 1963.

Thomson, J. Anderson, Jr., Joy Boissevain, and Clare Aukofer. "Lee Harvey Oswald—Another Look." *Mind and Human Interaction*, vol. 8, no. 2, Spring/Summer 1997.

Thorburn, William. "Cases of Injury to the Cervical Region of the Spinal Cord." *Brain, a Journal of Neurology*, vol. IX, 1887.

"Three Patients at Parkland." *Texas State Journal of Medicine*, vol. 60, January 1964.

"To Help You Keep the Record Straight about That Book." *U.S. News & World Report*, February 6, 1967.

Trillin, Calvin. "The Buffs." *New Yorker*, June 10, 1967.

"The Truth about Hoover." *Time*, December 22, 1975.

"Truth about Kennedy Assassination." *U.S. News & World Report*, October 10, 1966.

Vanocur, Sander. "Kennedy's Voyage of Discovery." *Harper's Magazine*, April 1964.

Viorst, Milton. "The Mafia, the CIA, and the Kennedy Assassination." *Washingtonian*, November 1975.

"The Warren Commission Report." *Time*, October 2, 1964.

Wecht, Cyril. "The Medical Evidence in the Assassination of President John F. Kennedy." *Forensic Science Gazette*, vol. 4, no. 4, September 1973.

Wecht, Cyril, and Robert P. Smith. "The Medical Evidence in the Assassination of President John F. Kennedy." *Forensic Science*, vol. 3, fig. 2, 1974.

Welsh, David. "The Legacy of Penn Jones." *Ramparts*, November 1966.

West, Jessemyn. "Prelude to Tragedy: The Woman Who Sheltered Lee Oswald's Family Tells Her Story." *Redbook*, July 1966.

Whalen, Richard J. "The Kennedy Assassination." *Saturday Evening Post*, January 14, 1967.

"What Does Oliver Stone Owe History?" *Newsweek*, December 23, 1991.

Wheeler, Keith. "Cursed Gun—The Track of C2766." *Life*, August 27, 1965.

"Who Killed JFK? Just One Assassin." *Time*, November 24, 1975.

"Who Knew about 'Bugging' . . . RFK's Story—and the FBI's." *U.S. News & World Report*, December 26, 1966.

Will, George F. "Eleven Men and Sic 'Em." *Newsweek*, November 7, 2005.

Wilson, Richard. "What Happened to the Kennedy Program?" *Look*, November 17, 1964.

Wrone, David R. "Review of Gerald Posner, *Case Closed*." *Journal of Southern History*, vol. 6, February 1995.

Zoglin, Richard. "What If Oswald Stood Trial?" *Time*, December 1, 1986.

GOVERNMENT REPORTS

Alleged Assassination Plots Involving Foreign Leaders, An Interim Report of the Select Committee to Study Governmental Operations with Respect to Intelligence Activities, United States Senate, Together with Additional, Supplemental, and Separate Views. 94th Congress, 1st session, Senate Report No. 94-465. Washington, D.C.: Government Printing Office, 1975. (*Alleged Assassination Plots*)

Covert Action in Chile 1963–73. Church Committee Staff Report. Washington, D.C.: Government Printing Office, 1975.

Drugs, Law Enforcement and Foreign Policy: A Report Prepared by the Subcommittee on Terrorism,

Narcotics and International Operations of the Committee on Foreign Relations. 100th Congress, 2d session, Senate. December 1988. Washington, D.C.: Government Printing Office, 1989.

Final Report of the Assassination Records Review Board. Washington, D.C.: Government Printing Office, 1998. (Final Report of the ARRB)

Final Report of the Select Committee on Assassinations, U.S. House of Representatives, Ninety-fifth Congress, Second Session, Summary of Findings and Recommendations. House Report 95-1828. Washington, D.C.: Government Printing Office, 1979. (HSCA Report)

Foreign Relations of the United States, 1961–1963. Vol. 2: *Vietnam, 1962.* Washington, D.C.: Government Printing Office, 1990.

Foreign Relations of the United States, 1961–1963. Vol. 4: *Vietnam, August–December 1963.* Washington, D.C.: Government Printing Office, 1991.

Foreign Relations of the United States, 1961–1963. Vol. 11: *Cuban Missile Crisis and Aftermath.* Washington, D.C.: Government Printing Office, 1996.

Forensic Analysis: Weighing Bullet Lead Evidence. Committee on Scientific Assessment of Bullet Lead Elemental Composition Comparison, Board on Chemical Sciences and Technology, National Research Council. Washington, D.C.: National Academies Press, 2004.

Hearings before the Legislative and National Security Subcommittee of the Committee on Government Operations, House of Representatives. 103rd Congress, 1st session, November 17, 1993. Washington, D.C.: Government Printing Office, 1994. (Conyers Committee Hearing)

Hearings before the Subcommittee on Civil and Constitutional Rights of the Committee on the Judiciary, House of Representatives, on FBI Oversight. 94th Congress, 1st and 2nd sessions, 1973–1974. Washington, D.C.: Government Printing Office, 1976. (*FBI Oversight*)

The Investigation of the Assassination of President John F. Kennedy: Performance of the Intelligence Agencies. Book V. *Final Report of the Select Committee to Study Governmental Operations with Respect to Intelligence Activities.* 94th Congress, 2nd session, Senate Report No. 94-755. Washington, D.C.: Government Printing Office, 1976. (Church Committee Report)

"1968 Panel Review of Photographs, X-Ray Films, Documents, and Other Evidence Pertaining to the Fatal Wounding of President John F. Kennedy on November 22, 1963, in Dallas, Texas." (Clark Panel Report)

Report of the Committee on Ballistic Acoustics. Commission on Physical Sciences, Mathematics, and Resources, National Research Council. Washington, D.C.: National Academies Press, 1982. (CBA Report)

Report of the President's Commission on the Assassination of President Kennedy. Warren Commission. Washington, D.C.: Government Printing Office, 1964. (Warren Report)

Report to Accompany S. 3006, The President John F. Kennedy Assassination Records Collection Act of 1992. 102nd Congress, 2nd session, Senate Report No. 102-328. Washington, D.C.: Government Printing Office, 1992. (1992 Senate Report)

Report to the President by the Commission on CIA Activities within the United States. New York: Manor Books, June 1975. (Rockefeller Commission Report)

"Review Requested by the Department of Justice of the Acoustical Reports Published by the House Select Committee on Assassinations." Technical Services Division, Federal Bureau of Investigation, November 19, 1980. (TSD Report)

Sklar, Barry. *U.S. Cuban Relations, 1959–1964: An Analysis.* Washington, D.C.: Library of Congress, Congressional Research Service, 1978.

Supplementary Detailed Staff Reports on Intelligence Activities and the Rights of Americans. Book III. *Final Report of the Select Committee to Study Governmental Operations with Respect to Intelligence Activities.* 94th Congress, 2nd session, Senate Report No. 94-755. Washington, D.C.: Government Printing Office, 1976. (*Supplementary Detailed Staff Reports*)

Texas Supplemental Report on the Assassination of President John F. Kennedy and the Serious Wounding of Governor John B. Connally, November 22, 1963 [by Attorney General Waggoner Carr]. Austin, Texas: Attorney General's Office, 1964. (*Texas Supplemental Report*)

Index

Numbers in italic type in this index refer to the endnote section on the compact disc. Thus, *614n* refers to an endnote found on page 614 of the *Endnotes* section of the CD. Numbers in ordinary type (e.g.: 241, or 665n) refer to the main text, and the "*n*" in such cases indicates a footnote rather than an endnote.